Hornbook Series and Basic Legal Texts
Nutshell Series

and

Black Letter Series

of

WEST PUBLISHING COMPANY
P.O. Box 64526
St. Paul, Minnesota 55164–0526

Accounting

FARIS' ACCOUNTING AND LAW IN A NUTSHELL, 377 pages, 1984. Softcover. (Text)

Administrative Law

AMAN AND MAYTON'S HORNBOOK ON ADMINISTRATIVE LAW, Approximately 750 pages, 1993. (Text)

GELLHORN AND LEVIN'S ADMINISTRATIVE LAW AND PROCESS IN A NUTSHELL, Third Edition, 479 pages, 1990. Softcover. (Text)

Admiralty

MARAIST'S ADMIRALTY IN A NUTSHELL, Second Edition, 379 pages, 1988. Softcover. (Text)

SCHOENBAUM'S HORNBOOK ON ADMIRALTY AND MARITIME LAW, Student Edition, 692 pages, 1987 with 1992 pocket part. (Text)

Agency—Partnership

REUSCHLEIN AND GREGORY'S HORNBOOK ON THE LAW OF AGENCY AND PARTNERSHIP, Second Edition, 683 pages, 1990. (Text)

STEFFEN'S AGENCY-PARTNERSHIP IN A NUTSHELL, 364 pages, 1977. Softcover. (Text)

NOLAN–HALEY'S ALTERNATIVE DISPUTE RESOLUTION IN A NUTSHELL, 298 pages, 1992. Softcover. (Text)

RISKIN'S DISPUTE RESOLUTION FOR LAWYERS VIDEO TAPES, 1992. (Available for purchase by schools and libraries.)

American Indian Law

CANBY'S AMERICAN INDIAN LAW IN A NUTSHELL, Second Edition, 336 pages, 1988. Softcover. (Text)

Antitrust—see also Regulated Industries, Trade Regulation

GELLHORN'S ANTITRUST LAW AND ECONOMICS IN A NUTSHELL, Third Edition, 472 pages, 1986. Softcover. (Text)

HOVENKAMP'S BLACK LETTER ON ANTITRUST, Second Edition approximately 325 pages, April 1993 Pub. Softcover. (Review)

HOVENKAMP'S HORNBOOK ON ECONOMICS AND FEDERAL ANTITRUST LAW, Student Edition, 414 pages, 1985. (Text)

SULLIVAN'S HORNBOOK OF THE LAW OF ANTITRUST, 886 pages, 1977. (Text)

Appellate Advocacy—see Trial and Appellate Advocacy

Art Law

DUBOFF'S ART LAW IN A NUTSHELL, Second Edition, approximately 325 pages, 1993. Softcover. (Text)

Banking Law

LOVETT'S BANKING AND FINANCIAL INSTI-

List current as of January, 1993

Banking Law—Cont'd

TUTIONS LAW IN A NUTSHELL, Third Edition, 470 pages, 1992. Softcover. (Text)

Civil Procedure—see also Federal Jurisdiction and Procedure

CLERMONT'S BLACK LETTER ON CIVIL PROCEDURE, Third Edition, approximately 350 pages, May, 1993 Pub. Softcover. (Review)

FRIEDENTHAL, KANE AND MILLER'S HORNBOOK ON CIVIL PROCEDURE, Second Edition, approximately 1000 pages, May 1993 Pub. (Text)

KANE'S CIVIL PROCEDURE IN A NUTSHELL, Third Edition, 303 pages, 1991. Softcover. (Text)

KOFFLER AND REPPY'S HORNBOOK ON COMMON LAW PLEADING, 663 pages, 1969. (Text)

SIEGEL'S HORNBOOK ON NEW YORK PRACTICE, Second Edition, Student Edition, 1068 pages, 1991. Softcover. (Text) 1992 Supplemental Pamphlet.

SLOMANSON AND WINGATE'S CALIFORNIA CIVIL PROCEDURE IN A NUTSHELL, 230 pages, 1992. Softcover. (Text)

Commercial Law

BAILEY AND HAGEDORN'S SECURED TRANSACTIONS IN A NUTSHELL, Third Edition, 390 pages, 1988. Softcover. (Text)

HENSON'S HORNBOOK ON SECURED TRANSACTIONS UNDER THE U.C.C., Second Edition, 504 pages, 1979, with 1979 pocket part. (Text)

MEYER AND SPEIDEL'S BLACK LETTER ON SALES AND LEASES OF GOODS, Approximately 300 pages, 1993. Softcover. (Review)

NICKLES' BLACK LETTER ON COMMERCIAL PAPER, 450 pages, 1988. Softcover. (Review)

STOCKTON AND MILLER'S SALES AND LEASES OF GOODS IN A NUTSHELL, Third Edition, 441 pages, 1992. Softcover. (Text)

STONE'S UNIFORM COMMERCIAL CODE IN A NUTSHELL, Third Edition, 580 pages, 1989. Softcover. (Text)

WEBER AND SPEIDEL'S COMMERCIAL PAPER IN A NUTSHELL, Third Edition, 404 pages, 1982. Softcover. (Text)

WHITE AND SUMMERS' HORNBOOK ON THE UNIFORM COMMERCIAL CODE, Third Edition, Student Edition, 1386 pages, 1988. (Text)

Community Property

MENNELL AND BOYKOFF'S COMMUNITY PROPERTY IN A NUTSHELL, Second Edition, 432 pages, 1988. Softcover. (Text)

Comparative Law

FOLSOM, MINAN AND OTTO'S LAW AND POLITICS IN THE PEOPLE'S REPUBLIC OF CHINA IN A NUTSHELL, 451 pages, 1992. Softcover. (Text)

GLENDON, GORDON AND OSAKWE'S COMPARATIVE LEGAL TRADITIONS IN A NUTSHELL. 402 pages, 1982. Softcover. (Text)

Conflict of Laws

HAY'S BLACK LETTER ON CONFLICT OF LAWS, 330 pages, 1989. Softcover. (Review)

SCOLES AND HAY'S HORNBOOK ON CONFLICT OF LAWS, Student Edition, 1160 pages, 1992. (Text)

SIEGEL'S CONFLICTS IN A NUTSHELL, 470 pages, 1982. Softcover. (Text)

Constitutional Law—Civil Rights

BARRON AND DIENES' BLACK LETTER ON CONSTITUTIONAL LAW, Third Edition, 440 pages, 1991. Softcover. (Review)

BARRON AND DIENES' CONSTITUTIONAL LAW IN A NUTSHELL, Second Edition, 483 pages, 1991. Softcover. (Text)

ENGDAHL'S CONSTITUTIONAL FEDERALISM IN A NUTSHELL, Second Edition, 411 pages, 1987. Softcover. (Text)

MARKS AND COOPER'S STATE CONSTITUTIONAL LAW IN A NUTSHELL, 329 pages, 1988. Softcover. (Text)

Constitutional Law—Civil Rights—Cont'd

NOWAK AND ROTUNDA'S HORNBOOK ON CONSTITUTIONAL LAW, Fourth Edition, 1357 pages, 1991. (Text)

VIEIRA'S CONSTITUTIONAL CIVIL RIGHTS IN A NUTSHELL, Second Edition, 322 pages, 1990. Softcover. (Text)

WILLIAMS' CONSTITUTIONAL ANALYSIS IN A NUTSHELL, 388 pages, 1979. Softcover. (Text)

Consumer Law—see also Commercial Law

EPSTEIN AND NICKLES' CONSUMER LAW IN A NUTSHELL, Second Edition, 418 pages, 1981. Softcover. (Text)

Contracts

CALAMARI AND PERILLO'S BLACK LETTER ON CONTRACTS, Second Edition, 462 pages, 1990. Softcover. (Review)

CALAMARI AND PERILLO'S HORNBOOK ON CONTRACTS, Third Edition, 1049 pages, 1987. (Text)

CORBIN'S TEXT ON CONTRACTS, One Volume Student Edition, 1224 pages, 1952. (Text)

FRIEDMAN'S CONTRACT REMEDIES IN A NUTSHELL, 323 pages, 1981. Softcover. (Text)

KEYES' GOVERNMENT CONTRACTS IN A NUTSHELL, Second Edition, 557 pages, 1990. Softcover. (Text)

SCHABER AND ROHWER'S CONTRACTS IN A NUTSHELL, Third Edition, 457 pages, 1990. Softcover. (Text)

Copyright—see Patent and Copyright Law

Corporations

HAMILTON'S BLACK LETTER ON CORPORATIONS, Third Edition, 732 pages, 1992. Softcover. (Review)

HAMILTON'S THE LAW OF CORPORATIONS IN A NUTSHELL, Third Edition, 518 pages, 1991. Softcover. (Text)

HENN AND ALEXANDER'S HORNBOOK ON LAWS OF CORPORATIONS, Third Edition, Student Edition, 1371 pages, 1983, with 1986 pocket part. (Text)

Corrections

KRANTZ' THE LAW OF CORRECTIONS AND PRISONERS' RIGHTS IN A NUTSHELL, Third Edition, 407 pages, 1988. Softcover. (Text)

Creditors' Rights

EPSTEIN'S DEBTOR-CREDITOR LAW IN A NUTSHELL, Fourth Edition, 401 pages, 1991. Softcover. (Text)

EPSTEIN, NICKLES AND WHITE'S HORNBOOK ON BANKRUPTCY, Approximately 1000 pages, January, 1992 Pub. (Text)

NICKLES AND EPSTEIN'S BLACK LETTER ON CREDITORS' RIGHTS AND BANKRUPTCY, 576 pages, 1989. (Review)

Criminal Law and Criminal Procedure—see also Corrections, Juvenile Justice

ISRAEL AND LAFAVE'S CRIMINAL PROCEDURE—CONSTITUTIONAL LIMITATIONS IN A NUTSHELL, Fourth Edition, 461 pages, 1988. Softcover. (Text)

LAFAVE AND ISRAEL'S HORNBOOK ON CRIMINAL PROCEDURE, Second Edition, 1309 pages, 1992 with 1992 pocket part. (Text)

LAFAVE AND SCOTT'S HORNBOOK ON CRIMINAL LAW, Second Edition, 918 pages, 1986. (Text)

LOEWY'S CRIMINAL LAW IN A NUTSHELL, Second Edition, 321 pages, 1987. Softcover. (Text)

LOW'S BLACK LETTER ON CRIMINAL LAW, Revised First Edition, 443 pages, 1990. Softcover. (Review)

SUBIN, MIRSKY AND WEINSTEIN'S THE CRIMINAL PROCESS: PROSECUTION AND DEFENSE FUNCTIONS, Approximately 450 pages, February, 1993 Pub. Softcover. Teacher's Manual available. (Text)

Domestic Relations

CLARK'S HORNBOOK ON DOMESTIC RELA-

Domestic Relations—Cont'd

TIONS, Second Edition, Student Edition, 1050 pages, 1988. (Text)

KRAUSE'S BLACK LETTER ON FAMILY LAW, 314 pages, 1988. Softcover. (Review)

KRAUSE'S FAMILY LAW IN A NUTSHELL, Second Edition, 444 pages, 1986. Softcover. (Text)

MALLOY'S LAW AND ECONOMICS: A COMPARATIVE APPROACH TO THEORY AND PRACTICE, 166 pages, 1990. Softcover. (Text)

Education Law

ALEXANDER AND ALEXANDER'S THE LAW OF SCHOOLS, STUDENTS AND TEACHERS IN A NUTSHELL, 409 pages, 1984. Softcover. (Text)

Employment Discrimination—see also Gender Discrimination

PLAYER'S FEDERAL LAW OF EMPLOYMENT DISCRIMINATION IN A NUTSHELL, Third Edition, 338 pages, 1992. Softcover. (Text)

PLAYER'S HORNBOOK ON EMPLOYMENT DISCRIMINATION LAW, Student Edition, 708 pages, 1988. (Text)

Energy and Natural Resources Law—see also Oil and Gas

LAITOS AND TOMAIN'S ENERGY AND NATURAL RESOURCES LAW IN A NUTSHELL, 554 pages, 1992. Softcover. (Text)

Environmental Law—see also Energy and Natural Resources Law; Sea, Law of

FINDLEY AND FARBER'S ENVIRONMENTAL LAW IN A NUTSHELL, Third Edition, 355 pages, 1992. Softcover. (Text)

RODGERS' HORNBOOK ON ENVIRONMENTAL LAW, 956 pages, 1977, with 1984 pocket part. (Text)

Equity—see Remedies

Estate Planning—see also Trusts and Estates; Taxation—Estate and Gift

LYNN'S INTRODUCTION TO ESTATE PLANNING IN A NUTSHELL, Fourth Edition, 352 pages, 1992. Softcover. (Text)

Evidence

BROUN AND BLAKEY'S BLACK LETTER ON EVIDENCE, 269 pages, 1984. Softcover. (Review)

GRAHAM'S FEDERAL RULES OF EVIDENCE IN A NUTSHELL, Third Edition, 486 pages, 1992. Softcover. (Text)

LILLY'S AN INTRODUCTION TO THE LAW OF EVIDENCE, Second Edition, 585 pages, 1987. (Text)

MCCORMICK'S HORNBOOK ON EVIDENCE, Fourth Edition, Student Edition, 672 pages, 1992. (Text)

ROTHSTEIN'S EVIDENCE IN A NUTSHELL: STATE AND FEDERAL RULES, Second Edition, 514 pages, 1981. Softcover. (Text)

Federal Jurisdiction and Procedure

CURRIE'S FEDERAL JURISDICTION IN A NUTSHELL, Third Edition, 242 pages, 1990. Softcover. (Text)

REDISH'S BLACK LETTER ON FEDERAL JURISDICTION, Second Edition, 234 pages, 1991. Softcover. (Review)

WRIGHT'S HORNBOOK ON FEDERAL COURTS, Fourth Edition, Student Edition, 870 pages, 1983. (Text)

First Amendment

GARVEY AND SCHAUER'S THE FIRST AMENDMENT: A READER, 527 pages, 1992. Softcover. (Reader)

Future Interests—see Trusts and Estates

Gender Discrimination—see also Employment Discrimination

THOMAS' SEX DISCRIMINATION IN A NUTSHELL, Second Edition, 395 pages, 1991. Softcover. (Text)

Health Law—see Medicine, Law and

Human Rights—see International Law

Immigration Law

WEISSBRODT'S IMMIGRATION LAW AND

Immigration Law—Cont'd

PROCEDURE IN A NUTSHELL, Third Edition, 497 pages, 1992. Softcover. (Text)

Indian Law—see American Indian Law

Insurance Law

DOBBYN'S INSURANCE LAW IN A NUTSHELL, Second Edition, 316 pages, 1989. Softcover. (Text)

KEETON AND WIDISS' INSURANCE LAW, Student Edition, 1359 pages, 1988. (Text)

International Law—see also Sea, Law of

BUERGENTHAL'S INTERNATIONAL HUMAN RIGHTS IN A NUTSHELL, 283 pages, 1988. Softcover. (Text)

BUERGENTHAL AND MAIER'S PUBLIC INTERNATIONAL LAW IN A NUTSHELL, Second Edition, 275 pages, 1990. Softcover. (Text)

FOLSOM'S EUROPEAN COMMUNITY LAW IN A NUTSHELL, 423 pages, 1992. Softcover. (Text)

FOLSOM, GORDON AND SPANOGLE'S INTERNATIONAL BUSINESS TRANSACTIONS IN A NUTSHELL, Fourth Edition, 548 pages, 1992. Softcover. (Text)

Interviewing and Counseling

SHAFFER AND ELKINS' LEGAL INTERVIEWING AND COUNSELING IN A NUTSHELL, Second Edition, 487 pages, 1987. Softcover. (Text)

Introduction to Law—see Legal Method and Legal System

Introduction to Law Study

HEGLAND'S INTRODUCTION TO THE STUDY AND PRACTICE OF LAW IN A NUTSHELL, 418 pages, 1983. Softcover. (Text)

KINYON'S INTRODUCTION TO LAW STUDY AND LAW EXAMINATIONS IN A NUTSHELL, 389 pages, 1971. Softcover. (Text)

Judicial Process—see Legal Method and Legal System

SINHA'S JURISPRUDENCE (LEGAL PHILOSOPHY) IN A NUTSHELL. Approximately 350 pages, 1993. Softcover. (Text)

Juvenile Justice

FOX'S JUVENILE COURTS IN A NUTSHELL, Third Edition, 291 pages, 1984. Softcover. (Text)

Labor and Employment Law—see also Employment Discrimination, Workers' Compensation

LESLIE'S LABOR LAW IN A NUTSHELL, Third Edition, 388 pages, 1992. Softcover. (Text)

NOLAN'S LABOR ARBITRATION LAW AND PRACTICE IN A NUTSHELL, 358 pages, 1979. Softcover. (Text)

Land Finance—Property Security—see Real Estate Transactions

Land Use

HAGMAN AND JUERGENSMEYER'S HORNBOOK ON URBAN PLANNING AND LAND DEVELOPMENT CONTROL LAW, Second Edition, Student Edition, 680 pages, 1986. (Text)

WRIGHT AND WRIGHT'S LAND USE IN A NUTSHELL, Second Edition, 356 pages, 1985. Softcover. (Text)

Legal Method and Legal System—see also Legal Research, Legal Writing

KEMPIN'S HISTORICAL INTRODUCTION TO ANGLO-AMERICAN LAW IN A NUTSHELL, Third Edition, 323 pages, 1990. Softcover. (Text)

REYNOLDS' JUDICIAL PROCESS IN A NUTSHELL, Second Edition, 308 pages, 1991. Softcover. (Text)

Legal Research

COHEN AND OLSON'S LEGAL RESEARCH IN A NUTSHELL, Fifth Edition, 370 pages, 1992. Softcover. (Text)

COHEN, BERRING AND OLSON'S HOW TO FIND THE LAW, Ninth Edition, 716 pages, 1989. (Text)

Legal Writing and Drafting

MELLINKOFF'S DICTIONARY OF AMERICAN

Legal Writing and Drafting—Cont'd

LEGAL USAGE, 703 pages, 1992. Softcover. (Text)

SQUIRES AND ROMBAUER'S LEGAL WRITING IN A NUTSHELL, 294 pages, 1982. Softcover. (Text)

Legislation—see also Legal Writing and Drafting

DAVIES' LEGISLATIVE LAW AND PROCESS IN A NUTSHELL, Second Edition, 346 pages, 1986. Softcover. (Text)

Local Government

MCCARTHY'S LOCAL GOVERNMENT LAW IN A NUTSHELL, Third Edition, 435 pages, 1990. Softcover. (Text)

REYNOLDS' HORNBOOK ON LOCAL GOVERNMENT LAW, 860 pages, 1982 with 1990 pocket part. (Text)

Mass Communication Law

ZUCKMAN, GAYNES, CARTER AND DEE'S MASS COMMUNICATIONS LAW IN A NUTSHELL, Third Edition, 538 pages, 1988. Softcover. (Text)

Medicine, Law and

HALL AND ELLMAN'S HEALTH CARE LAW AND ETHICS IN A NUTSHELL, 401 pages, 1990. Softcover (Text)

JARVIS, CLOSEN, HERMANN AND LEONARD'S AIDS LAW IN A NUTSHELL, 349 pages, 1991. Softcover. (Text)

KING'S THE LAW OF MEDICAL MALPRACTICE IN A NUTSHELL, Second Edition, 342 pages, 1986. Softcover. (Text)

Military Law

SHANOR AND TERRELL'S MILITARY LAW IN A NUTSHELL, 378 pages, 1980. Softcover. (Text)

Mining Law—see Energy and Natural Resources Law

Mortgages—see Real Estate Transactions

Natural Resources Law—see Energy and Natural Resources Law, Environmental Law

TEPLY'S LEGAL NEGOTIATION IN A NUTSHELL, 282 pages, 1992. Softcover. (Text)

Office Practice—see also Computers and Law, Interviewing and Counseling, Negotiation

HEGLAND'S TRIAL AND PRACTICE SKILLS IN A NUTSHELL, 346 pages, 1978. Softcover (Text)

Oil and Gas—see also Energy and Natural Resources Law

HEMINGWAY'S HORNBOOK ON THE LAW OF OIL AND GAS, Third Edition, Student Edition, 711 pages, 1992. (Text)

LOWE'S OIL AND GAS LAW IN A NUTSHELL, Second Edition, 465 pages, 1988. Softcover. (Text)

Partnership—see Agency—Partnership

Patent and Copyright Law

MILLER AND DAVIS' INTELLECTUAL PROPERTY—PATENTS, TRADEMARKS AND COPYRIGHT IN A NUTSHELL, Second Edition, 437 pages, 1990. Softcover. (Text)

Products Liability

PHILLIPS' PRODUCTS LIABILITY IN A NUTSHELL, Third Edition, 307 pages, 1988. Softcover. (Text)

Professional Responsibility

ARONSON AND WECKSTEIN'S PROFESSIONAL RESPONSIBILITY IN A NUTSHELL, Second Edition, 514 pages, 1991. Softcover. (Text)

LESNICK'S BEING A LAWYER: INDIVIDUAL CHOICE AND RESPONSIBILITY IN THE PRACTICE OF LAW, 422 pages, 1992. Softcover. Teacher's Manual available. (Coursebook)

ROTUNDA'S BLACK LETTER ON PROFESSIONAL RESPONSIBILITY, Third Edition, 492 pages, 1992. Softcover. (Review)

WOLFRAM'S HORNBOOK ON MODERN LEGAL ETHICS, Student Edition, 1120

Professional Responsibility—Cont'd

pages, 1986. (Text)

WYDICK AND PERSCHBACHER'S CALIFORNIA LEGAL ETHICS, 439 pages, 1992. Softcover. (Coursebook)

Property—see also Real Estate Transactions, Land Use, Trusts and Estates

BERNHARDT'S BLACK LETTER ON PROPERTY, Second Edition, 388 pages, 1991. Softcover. (Review)

BERNHARDT'S REAL PROPERTY IN A NUTSHELL, Second Edition, 448 pages, 1981. Softcover. (Text)

BOYER, HOVENKAMP AND KURTZ' THE LAW OF PROPERTY, AN INTRODUCTORY SURVEY, Fourth Edition, 696 pages, 1991. (Text)

BURKE'S PERSONAL PROPERTY IN A NUTSHELL, Second Edition, approximately 400 pages, May, 1993 Pub. Softcover. (Text)

CUNNINGHAM, STOEBUCK AND WHITMAN'S HORNBOOK ON THE LAW OF PROPERTY, Second Edition, approximately 900 pages, May, 1993 Pub. (Text)

HILL'S LANDLORD AND TENANT LAW IN A NUTSHELL, Second Edition, 311 pages, 1986. Softcover. (Text)

Real Estate Transactions

BRUCE'S REAL ESTATE FINANCE IN A NUTSHELL, Third Edition, 287 pages, 1991. Softcover. (Text)

NELSON AND WHITMAN'S BLACK LETTER ON LAND TRANSACTIONS AND FINANCE, Second Edition, 466 pages, 1988. Softcover. (Review)

NELSON AND WHITMAN'S HORNBOOK ON REAL ESTATE FINANCE LAW, Second Edition, 941 pages, 1985 with 1989 pocket part. (Text)

Regulated Industries—see also Mass Communication Law, Banking Law

GELLHORN AND PIERCE'S REGULATED INDUSTRIES IN A NUTSHELL, Second Edition, 389 pages, 1987. Softcover. (Text)

Remedies

DOBBS' HORNBOOK ON REMEDIES, Second Edition, approximately 1000 pages, April, 1993 Pub. (Text)

DOBBYN'S INJUNCTIONS IN A NUTSHELL, 264 pages, 1974. Softcover. (Text)

FRIEDMAN'S CONTRACT REMEDIES IN A NUTSHELL, 323 pages, 1981. Softcover. (Text)

O'CONNELL'S REMEDIES IN A NUTSHELL, Second Edition, 320 pages, 1985. Softcover. (Text)

Sea, Law of

SOHN AND GUSTAFSON'S THE LAW OF THE SEA IN A NUTSHELL, 264 pages, 1984. Softcover. (Text)

Securities Regulation

HAZEN'S HORNBOOK ON THE LAW OF SECURITIES REGULATION, Second Edition, Student Edition, 1082 pages, 1990. (Text)

RATNER'S SECURITIES REGULATION IN A NUTSHELL, Fourth Edition, 320 pages, 1992. Softcover. (Text)

Sports Law

CHAMPION'S SPORTS LAW IN A NUTSHELL,. Approximately 300 pages, January, 1993 Pub. Softcover. (Text)

SCHUBERT, SMITH AND TRENTADUE'S SPORTS LAW, 395 pages, 1986. (Text)

Tax Practice and Procedure

MORGAN'S TAX PROCEDURE AND TAX FRAUD IN A NUTSHELL, 400 pages, 1990. Softcover. (Text)

Taxation—Corporate

SCHWARZ AND LATHROPE'S BLACK LETTER ON CORPORATE AND PARTNERSHIP TAXATION, 537 pages, 1991. Softcover. (Review)

WEIDENBRUCH AND BURKE'S FEDERAL INCOME TAXATION OF CORPORATIONS AND STOCKHOLDERS IN A NUTSHELL, Third Edition, 309 pages, 1989. Softcover. (Text)

Taxation—Estate & Gift—see also Estate Planning, Trusts and Estates

McNulty's Federal Estate and Gift Taxation in a Nutshell, Fourth Edition, 496 pages, 1989. Softcover. (Text)

Peat and Willbanks' Federal Estate and Gift Taxation: An Analysis and Critique, 265 pages, 1991. Softcover. (Text)

Taxation—Individual

Dodge's The Logic of Tax, 343 pages, 1989. Softcover. (Text)

Hudson and Lind's Black Letter on Federal Income Taxation, Fourth Edition, 410 pages, 1992. Softcover. (Review)

McNulty's Federal Income Taxation of Individuals in a Nutshell, Fourth Edition, 503 pages, 1988. Softcover. (Text)

Posin's Federal Income Taxation, Second Edition, approximately 650 pages, May, 1993 Pub. Softcover. (Text)

Rose and Chommie's Hornbook on Federal Income Taxation, Third Edition, 923 pages, 1988, with 1991 pocket part. (Text)

Taxation—International

Doernberg's International Taxation in a Nutshell, 325 pages, 1989. Softcover. (Text)

Bishop and Brooks' Federal Partnership Taxation: A Guide to the Leading Cases, Statutes, and Regulations, 545 pages, 1990. Softcover. (Text)

Burke's Federal Income Taxation of Partnerships in a Nutshell, 356 pages, 1992. Softcover. (Text)

Schwarz and Lathrope's Black Letter on Corporate and Partnership Taxation, 537 pages, 1991. Softcover. (Review)

Taxation—State & Local

Gelfand and Salsich's State and Local Taxation and Finance in a Nutshell, 309 pages, 1986. Softcover. (Text)

Torts—see also Products Liability

Kionka's Black Letter on Torts, 339 pages, 1988. Softcover. (Review)

Kionka's Torts in a Nutshell, Second Edition, 449 pages, 1992. Softcover. (Text)

Prosser and Keeton's Hornbook on Torts, Fifth Edition, Student Edition, 1286 pages, 1984 with 1988 pocket part. (Text)

Trade Regulation—see also Antitrust, Regulated Industries

McManis' Unfair Trade Practices in a Nutshell, Third Edition, approximately 450 pages, 1993. Softcover. (Text)

Schechter's Black Letter on Unfair Trade Practices, 272 pages, 1986. Softcover. (Review)

Trial and Appellate Advocacy—see also Civil Procedure

Bergman's Trial Advocacy in a Nutshell, Second Edition, 354 pages, 1989. Softcover. (Text)

Clary's Primer on the Analysis and Presentation of Legal Argument, 106 pages, 1992. Softcover. (Text)

Dessem's Pretrial Litigation in a Nutshell, 382 pages, 1992. Softcover. (Text)

Goldberg's The First Trial (Where Do I Sit? What Do I Say?) in a Nutshell, 396 pages, 1982. Softcover. (Text)

Hegland's Trial and Practice Skills in a Nutshell, 346 pages, 1978. Softcover. (Text)

Hornstein's Appellate Advocacy in a Nutshell, 325 pages, 1984. Softcover. (Text)

Jeans' Handbook on Trial Advocacy, Student Edition, 473 pages, 1975. Softcover. (Text)

Trusts and Estates

ATKINSON'S HORNBOOK ON WILLS, Second Edition, 975 pages, 1953. (Text)

AVERILL'S UNIFORM PROBATE CODE IN A NUTSHELL, Second Edition, 454 pages, 1987. Softcover. (Text)

BOGERT'S HORNBOOK ON TRUSTS, Sixth Edition, Student Edition, 794 pages, 1987. (Text)

MCGOVERN, KURTZ AND REIN'S HORNBOOK ON WILLS, TRUSTS AND ESTATES–INCLUDING TAXATION AND FUTURE INTERESTS, 996 pages, 1988. (Text)

MENNELL'S WILLS AND TRUSTS IN A NUTSHELL, 392 pages, 1979. Softcover. (Text)

SIMES' HORNBOOK ON FUTURE INTERESTS, Second Edition, 355 pages, 1966. (Text)

TURANO AND RADIGAN'S HORNBOOK ON NEW YORK ESTATE ADMINISTRATION, 676 pages, 1986 with 1991 pocket part. (Text)

WAGGONER'S FUTURE INTERESTS IN A NUTSHELL, 361 pages, 1981. Softcover. (Text)

Water Law—see also Environmental Law

GETCHES' WATER LAW IN A NUTSHELL, Second Edition, 459 pages, 1990. Softcover. (Text)

Wills—see Trusts and Estates

Workers' Compensation

HOOD, HARDY AND LEWIS' WORKERS' COMPENSATION AND EMPLOYEE PROTECTION LAWS IN A NUTSHELL, Second Edition, 361 pages, 1990. Softcover. (Text)

*

CRIMINAL PROCEDURE

Second Edition

By

Wayne R. LaFave
David C. Baum Professor of Law and
Center for Advanced Study Professor of Law,
University of Illinois

Jerold H. Israel
Alene and Allan F. Smith Professor of Law,
University of Michigan

HORNBOOK SERIES

This book is an abridgement of LaFave and Israel's forthcoming second edition of the multi-volume "Criminal Procedure" in West's Criminal Practice Series.

WEST PUBLISHING CO.
ST. PAUL, MINN., 1992

This is an abridgement of a forthcoming second edition of LaFave & Israel's multi-volume *Criminal Procedure*, Criminal Practice Series, West Publishing Co., 1992.

Library of Congress Cataloging-in-Publication Data

LaFave, Wayne R.
Criminal Procedure / by Wayne R. LaFave and Jerold H. Israel -- 2nd ed.
p. cm. -- (Hornbook series)
Includes index.
ISBN 0–314–79327–5
1. Criminal procedure—United States. I. Israel, Jerold H., 1934– . II. Title. III. Series.
KF9619.L34 1992
345.73'05—dc20
[347.3055]
91–25618
CIP

ISBN 0–314–79327–5

PRINTED ON 10% POST CONSUMER RECYCLED PAPER

LaFave & Israel, Crim.Pro. 2d Ed. HB
1st Reprint—1993

Preface

This text is intended primarily for use by law students during their study of criminal procedure. There is, to be sure, no substitute for careful examination of the basic sources—the appellate opinions, statutes, and critical commentary which are to be found in the modern casebooks dealing with this subject. It is neither intended nor expected that this Hornbook on criminal procedure will be of particular use to the student who has not grappled with those materials. Rather, this book has been prepared on the assumption that the diligent student may find a textual treatment of the subject useful as he or she[1] undertakes the necessary process of reviewing and synthesizing the regularly assigned materials.

We have sought to analyze the law governing all of the major steps in the criminal justice process, starting with investigation and ending with post-appeal collateral attacks. Of course, a complete review of all the fine points relating to each and every step in the process would require more than one volume. Accordingly, we have varied the depth of our coverage, taking into consideration both the significance of the particular procedure and the attention typically given to it in a law school criminal procedure course. For every step in the process, however, we have covered, at a minimum, the major themes underlying the governing legal standards and those basic issues that the case law and literature suggest to be the most pressing. We have also sought to go beyond describing "the law" as it currently stands, exploring as well its historical roots and underlying policies. We believe this approach will prove useful to law students.

This book is abridged from the forthcoming second edition of our multi-volume *Criminal Procedure* treatise. We have retained most of the analysis from that larger work, but not much of the supporting documentation. Our supposition in this regard is that a law student who uses a collateral text in connection with course preparation or review is primarily interested in explanation rather than citations to authority. In general, descriptions of lower court rulings and statutory provisions are not followed by illustrative citations, although a specific case or statute noted in the text often will be cited. Supporting citations for descriptions of positions taken by commentators are treated in largely the same manner. So too, brief quotations that are largely illustrative of a line of cases usually are not footnoted. In all

1. To make our sentence structure as short and direct as possible, we generally have not used the phrases "he or she" or "his and her." Consistent with traditional rules of construction in statutes and legal texts, masculine pronouns (which is what we usually use) should be read to refer to both male and female actors unless the context clearly indicates otherwise.

instances, students desiring the full documentation can turn to the corresponding section in the treatise.[2]

We have treated the opinions of the Supreme Court of the United States somewhat differently, both because of their special significance and because these are the opinions most frequently included in assigned course materials. We have always made reference to the leading Supreme Court opinions which deal with the topic at hand, although we have not included string-citations of Supreme Court rulings on settled points. Our cut-off date for Supreme Court opinions was the end of the October 1990 term (i.e., July 1991). The cut-off date for other material was a few months earlier.

Both authors come away from this project impressed, as always, with the richness of literature in the field. We remain indebted not only to the authors of the articles cited both in the Hornbook and the treatise, but also to many others whose work we could not include without overloading the footnotes. A project of this type also necessarily builds on past endeavors and necessarily reflects the assistance of those who have worked with us on those endeavors. We are especially indebted in this regard to Yale Kamisar, our co-author on *Modern Criminal Procedure, Basic Criminal Procedure* and *Criminal Procedure and the Constitution.*

Over the years, on this project and others, we have received the benefit of the excellent work of many student research assistants. Their number has grown far too long to mention them all, but the size of the group makes us no less appreciative of the individual contribution of each of these students. We also are deeply indebted to our secretaries, Carol Haley and Carolyn Lloyd, who have seen this project through from start to finish.

While we both stand responsible for the work as a whole, Wayne LaFave had the initial responsibility for chapters 3–7, 9–10, 12–13, 17–18 and 21–22, and Jerold Israel had initial responsibility for the remaining chapters. Each of us would appreciate hearing from readers who have criticisms or suggestions relating to the chapters for which we have initial responsibility.

2. By matching the Hornbook text to the text of the similarly titled subsection in the treatise, the reader should have no difficulty in finding in the treatise footnote references to all cases, commentary, and statutes described in the Hornbook. The second edition of the treatise will cite over a thousand lower court cases. While the treatise does not seek to present a jurisdiction-by-jurisdiction laundry list of citations on any issue, those citations, along with Westlaw references, should quite readily take the reader to similar opinions in other jurisdictions. Indeed, many of the cases cited were selected because they were fairly recent and collected earlier opinions or because they contained extensive discussions likely to be cited in future cases. The citation of articles in the treatise follows a similar pattern. Many are the most recent in a long line of commentary, helpful in part because they collect prior authority.

Finally, we would like to recognize the support of our families. Labor of love though it may be, preparation of a text such as this can be terribly demanding, and we appreciate greatly the patience of our families in this regard.

JEROLD H. ISRAEL
WAYNE R. LAFAVE

December 1, 1991
Ann Arbor, Michigan
Champaign, Illinois

*

WESTLAW® Overview

LaFave & Israel's *Criminal Procedure* provides a comprehensive and detailed discussion of the law of criminal procedure. To supplement the information supplied in this hornbook, you can access WESTLAW, a computer-assisted legal research service of West Publishing Company. WESTLAW contains a broad library of criminal procedure resources, including case law, statutes, rules and regulations, commentary and current legal developments.

To help you coordinate WESTLAW research with this book, a WESTLAW appendix is included in this edition. This appendix provides information on databases, search techniques and sample research problems.

THE PUBLISHER

*

Summary of Contents

Table of Contents

PART TWO. DETECTION AND INVESTIGATION OF CRIME

PART FIVE. POST–CONVICTION REVIEW; APPEALS AND COLLATERAL REMEDIES

*

CRIMINAL PROCEDURE

*

Part One

INTRODUCTION AND OVERVIEW

Chapter 1

AN OVERVIEW OF THE CRIMINAL JUSTICE PROCESS

Table of Sections

§ 1.1 Analyzing the Process

The subject of this treatise is the law of criminal procedure—i.e., the law governing that series of procedures through which the substantive criminal law is enforced. Part One of the treatise discusses some general features of the criminal justice process and of the law governing that process; Parts Two to Five then consider the particular legal standards governing each of the major steps (save one) in the process. The discussion in Parts Two to Five largely follows the chronological sequence of the process, moving from the detection and investigation of crime, to the institution of formal charges against accused persons, to the adjudication of those charges, to the sentencing of the convicted defendant, and, finally, to the appellate and collateral review of judicial decisions rendered throughout the process. The one major step omitted from our coverage is the administration of those restraints imposed upon the convicted defendant pursuant to his sentence. The law governing corrections has grown so extensively, and has so many features that set it apart from the remainder of the criminal justice process, that it is most appropriately treated as a separate subject matter.

In this, our first chapter, we provide an overview of the criminal justice process that hopefully will serve as a useful backdrop for our later discussions of the laws governing particular procedures. Tremendous variations exist in the process as applied in different jurisdictions, so any overview must inevitably overgeneralize. We have sought to minimize this deficiency by briefly noting in §§ 1.2–1.3 those factors responsible for most of the process variations. The basic overview itself is presented in §§ 1.4–1.6. It is divided into three segments, each looking at the process from a different perspective. Section 1.4 describes each step as a case is carried from the point of investigation to the final review of a conviction. Section 1.5 then considers the primary sources of the laws that govern the overall process. Finally, in § 1.6, we examine some of the basic goals that underlie these laws and shape the process.

§ 1.2 Process Variations and Structural Elements

A useful description of the American criminal justice process must begin by acknowledging that there is no single set of criminal justice procedures applied uniformly throughout this country. Initially, the law that governs the process will vary from one jurisdiction to another. Indeed, the content of that law often will vary within the individual jurisdiction according to the nature and the level of the offense involved. Secondly, even where the governing law is identical, there is likely to be considerable variation, from one community to another, in the process as it exists in practice, due to differences in the manner in which that law is applied. At least with respect to certain aspects of the process, differences in the mode and spirit of administering the law may prove more significant in analyzing the process than differences in the content of the law being applied.

In our § 1.4 overview, we take note of a few of the more significant variations in the governing law and the manner of its administration, but our primary focus is upon the general characteristics of the procedural pattern found for most felony cases in most jurisdictions. Many other variations are noted in later chapters, and still others are too numerous and not sufficiently significant to merit discussion in a single-volume text. This section and the next briefly examine some of the factors that contribute to the presence of so many variations in the process. In this section, consideration is given to four structural elements that account for process variations, while § 1.3 considers differences in the administrative environment that also contribute to those variations.

(a) Allocation of State and Federal Authority. Within our federated system of government, it is the states that have borne the primary responsibility for defining criminal behavior and enforcing the law against those who engage in such behavior. While the federal government has the authority to adopt its own criminal code (an authority it has exercised from the outset), the reach of that authority does not extend to declaring behavior criminal simply because it is contrary to the public welfare. Unlike the state governments, which can legislate on the basis of their general police power, the federal government's regulatory authority in the field of criminal law, as in other fields, is limited to those subjects as to which the federal constitution grants Congress legislative authority, such as interstate and foreign commerce and the operation of the federal government. With the Supreme Court's recognition of the broad reach of those enumerated powers, particularly through the commerce clause, Congress could conceivably extend the federal criminal code to encompass a substantial portion of the more serious offenses traditionally proscribed by state criminal codes. Traditionally, however, the federal criminal code has been far more limited in scope, extending to garden variety criminal acts, such as assaults, only where the victim has some connection to the national government. While Congress in recent years has been inclined to expand the reach of the federal code, both as to white collar and street crime, it has done so without dramatically expanding the federal apparatus for enforcement of the federal criminal code. Thus, the vast majority of all prosecutions in this country continue to be brought in state courts under state law. Of the roughly 1.5 million felony prosecutions initiated each year, over 97% are state prosecutions, and the dominance of state prosecutions is even greater when one adds misdemeanor prosecutions, which outnumber felony prosecutions by a ration of 8–10 to 1 and are over 99% state prosecutions.

The primary role of the states in defining and enforcing the criminal law carries with it central responsibility for shaping of the criminal justice process through which that law is enforced. Just as each state can shape its substantive criminal code to fit the value judgments and traditions shared by its people, it can also shape the procedures that will be used in administering that code. As a result, in many respects, we have fifty-one different criminal justice processes, one for each of the states and one for the federal government.[1] Each jurisdiction's process must comply with federal constitutional requirements, but those requirements, notwithstanding broad interpretation by the Supreme Court, still reach only the most basic elements of the process. Individual jurisdictions retain considerable autonomy in formulating their own procedural systems within the framework of the constitutional prerequisites.

Of course, the allocation to each jurisdiction of primary responsibility for shaping its own criminal justice process does not necessarily have to result in substantial variations from one jurisdiction to another, at least in the laws regulating the process. Though given considerable autonomy, the states could seek on their own initiative to achieve uniformity. In many other fields, the states have done exactly that, usually by adopting model acts or by modeling their individual state laws after a dominant federal provision. In the criminal justice field, however, the states have largely avoided that path. Looking to the fifty-one different processes, one finds a common basic structure provided by the common heritage of the English common law and preserved in part by the commands of the federal constitution. Within that structure, however, many common law procedures have

§ 1.2

1. In many respects, the District of Columbia, the Commonwealth of Puerto Rico, and the Virgin Islands could be added as separate jurisdictions for this counting. Although Congress retains legislative authority in each of these jurisdictions, each has its own criminal code and own criminal justice process separate from that governing the enforcement of federal crimes of general applicability.

been modified and many new procedures have added, with limited efforts to achieve any significant degree of uniformity. The end result is fifty-one procedural systems that reflect a common core, but also reveal, at each step in the process, anywhere from a few to great many variations. Of course, the extent to which those variations matter depends upon the breadth of the inquiry. For example, if one is concerned only with the general question of the responsibility for the determination of guilt, then the systems appear similar as they all utilize a jury trial. If one probes deeper and looks to the general system of selecting jurors, then variations exist, but they can be placed fairly neatly into two or three patterns. However, if one goes deeper still, and looks to the precise authority of the defense, the prosecution, and the trial court in the process of selecting jurors (i.e., the law governing voir dire, challenges for cause, and peremptory challenges), then one finds multiple variations extending over a broad continuum.

Why have the states failed to gather around a single model to produce a more substantial degree of uniformity, as is found in many other fields in which state law plays a dominant role? There certainly has not been a shortage of proposed models, as the same groups that proposed the models adopted in other fields have also been at work (with little success) in the field of criminal procedure. The states also have had available the federal models provided by the Federal Rules of Criminal Procedure and various extensive federal statutory provisions dealing with particular aspects of the process, but these models also have been utilized only to a limited extent. While many states have adopted court rules that follow the basic format of the Federal Rules, no more than a half-dozen are sufficiently similar in content to be characterized as true federal replicas. Also, while certain federal statutes (most notably, the Federal Bail Reform Act of 1966) have served as a model for numerous state statutes, those statutes commonly depart from one or more of the basic provisions of the federal statute.

Several factors undoubtedly have contributed to the diverse approaches adopted by the different states in dealing with different aspects of the criminal justice process. Initially, criminal procedure is not a subject as to which there is a natural pressure to achieve uniformity. Unlike fields such as commercial law, the lack of uniformity here is not likely to be a deterrent to the free flow of goods, services, or persons between states or to create conflicts in the treatment of individuals wth respect to the same transaction or relationship. Second, certain aspects of criminal procedure raise basic issues of public policy on which jurisdictions are likely to be divided in accordance with the prevailing political philosophy of its electorate. There are few areas, if any, of legislative choice in which the role of symbolic politics is more pervasive than criminal justice reform. Decisionmakers here are most unlikely to conclude that it is more important to achieve uniformity than to adopt the position most consistent with the prevailing ideological assumptions of the relevant constituency (or the individual decisionmaker). Moreover, since the process is integrated, with one procedure building upon another, once two jurisdictions have diverged on a basic procedure, they are likely to be divided again in regulating other, related procedures.

The administrative environment in the particular jurisdiction, as discussed in § 1.3, also is a factor that contributes to the shaping of the jurisdiction's law governing the process. No two states will be precisely the same in this regard, and each will certainly be substantially different from a fair number of other states. Indeed, even where states are similar in demography and share a regional social philosophy, local traditions are likely to have produced somewhat administrative cultures. Perhaps even more significant than the differences among the states is the substantial difference between the administrative environment of the states in general and of the federal system, for it is the federal system that so often provides the model for uniformity in other fields. The federal system differs in the nature of the crimes to which its resources are devoted, with its primary concentration upon white collar and organized criminal activity as opposed to the usual street crimes. In addition, there are numerous factors that separate federal participants in the administration of the process from the typical state participants. Thus, federal law enforcement officers ordinarily have different qualifications, different training and different responsibilities (which do not include the general peacekeeping, traffic control, and social service functions performed by local police); federal prosecutors exercise considerably more control over the investigative process, are not elected officials, and are subject to a central authority, the Attorney General; and federal trial judges are totally insulated from the electorate and have a criminal caseload which is substantial, but still considerably less than that carried by state trial judges in most urban areas.

Finally, over the last several decades, still another factor arguably has contributed to the extent of the divergence among the laws of the different states, and that is the accelerated pace of legal reforms in the criminal justice process. Over that period, perhaps no other institution of government has been the target of more widespread, persistent, and vociferous criticism. That criticism has come from almost every possible source, including the public, the academics, the politicians, and those charged with the administration of the process. It has challenged the process from almost every possible perspective, although in recent years the primary line of criticism has been the ineffectiveness of the process in gaining the conviction and the appropriate punishment of those who commit crimes. Faced with such widespread criticism, which commonly has characterized the criminal justice process as on the brink of collapse, and with a public mood that places crime among the top domestic concerns, legislatures and courts have rushed to reform the process. In large part, such reforms have occurred on a piecemeal basis, looking first to one aspect of the process and then to another, and then often returning to that first considered as the previous reform turns out to be a failure or an incomplete success or a new philosophy moves to the forefront. The end result has been different jurisdictions making different choices at different times among different areas of reform and different alternatives, all of which has produced greater variation in the law from one jurisdiction to another. Thus, as discussed in Chapter 26, the traditional sentencing structure utilizing largely discretionary, indeterminate sentences of incarceration in felony cases has been replaced or modified in different ways in different jurisdictions. Unlike the situation found as recently as thirty years ago, we no longer have a single common structure used in almost all states, but instead have a variety of sentencing structures, including traditional indeterminate sentencing, guideline regulated indeterminate sentencing, discretionary determinate sentencing, guideline regulated determinate sentencing, and presumptive-determinate sentencing.

(b) The Role of Discretion. Variations in the administration of the criminal justice process exist not only between jurisdictions, but also within individual jurisdictions. Perhaps the most significant factor leading to such intra-jurisdiction variations is the broad allocation of discretion to the officials administering the process. At almost every step in the process, the law of any jurisdiction will leave to one or another official some discretionary authority—that is, grant to that official the authority to act upon personal judgment. Such authority is rarely absolute, but it is often subject to only the most minimal legal restraints. Discretionary authority tends to be at its broadest where the decision is one not to exercise governmental power adversely to an individual—as where the police decide not to investigate a complaint even though they have a basis for investigating or not to arrest even though the grounds for an arrest exist, or where the prosecutor decides not to charge even though a charge could be sustained at trial. But considerable discretionary latitude often exists, as well in choosing between procedures when a particular official decides to go forward with the criminal justice process.

Having decided to investigate, the police often have broad discretion in choosing between one investigative procedure or another. Where a search is needed, as to many types of searches, police have discretion as to whether they will seek warrant authorization or proceed without a warrant. When identification evidence must be obtained, the police often will have discretion as to whether to utilize photo-identification, a lineup, or a single person "showup." When a person is to be charged and present before a court, the police often have a choice between arresting that person or utilizing a summons. Similar breadth is found in the prosecution's use of the process. Having decided to charge, the prosecutor often has considerable room for choice in the framing of that charge. In some instances, the prosecutor has available the option of prosecuting under different statutes that may be applicable to the same basic conduct. Where more than one offense has been committed, the prosecutor must decide whether all of the offenses will be charged, and if so, whether they will be brought together for presentation in a single proceeding. In many states, the prosecution can determine through its mode of proceeding whether its decision to charge will be reviewed by a grand jury or by a magistrate at a preliminary hearing. The prosecution also has extremely broad latitude in deciding whether it will offer concessions to a defendant in return for his entry of a guilty plea or the giving of testimony against another defendant.

Judges also are given considerable discretion, often through legal standards phrased in terms that invite personal evaluation of ambiguous concepts. In many jurisdictions, pretrial release provisions grant the magistrate considerable leeway in determining what conditions will be required for releasing the defendant pending trial. Subject only to the prohibition against arbitrary misuse of authority, the trial judge may be guided by personal preference in shaping various aspects of the pretrial and trial process. Thus, in many jurisdictions, such issues as whether defense counsel can personally question prospective jurors on voir dire or can inspect police reports lies largely within the trial judge's discretionary authority. Once the trial starts, more of the judge's decisions tend to be controlled by fairly specific legal standards, but even here, open-ended standards will provide a fairly loose rein as to at least a few decisions. In sentencing, while many states in recent years have taken steps to limit, or at least channel, the judge's discretion, considerable leeway remains as to most sentencing decisions in many jurisdictions and to at least some sentencing decisions in all jurisdictions.

The heavy reliance upon broad grants of discretion in the criminal justice process has long been a source of controversy. The authorization of discretionary decisionmaking has been defended on several grounds, varying with type of decision and the official involved. Many forms of discretion are justified as a necessary tool in responding to heavy caseloads with limited resources. The flexibility provided by discretion permits enforcement officials to engage in the ranking and prioritizing that ensures the most effective use of the resources available to them. Discretion also allows decisions to be made without being subject to the ponderous process of judicial review and thereby conserves resources. Certain areas of discretion are defended on the ground that they involve the exercise of authority that simply is too inconsequential to justify the expenditure of additional resources through judicial review. So too, in some instances, the particular authority is granted primarily to serve the interests of the enforcement agency, and proponents of discretion argue that agency officials therefore should be allowed to utilize or forego utilizing that authority without judicial review.

Various aspects of discretion are justified by reference to the limitations of legal regulation. Where appropriate decisionmaking requires consideration of numerous factors that vary with each case, an attempt to regulate that decision as to all of the situations likely to arise (assuming that they all could be envisioned) would require an elaborate statute, containing many detailed provisos, exceptions, and qualifications. Such a statute would often be cumbersome, especially where it governs a decision that must be made instantaneously and under the pressure of exigent circumstances. At that point, it is argued, the system is better served by allowing for discretion and permitting informal norms to regulate the use of that authority. So too, other types of decisions are thought to require judgments of a type that cannot readily be regulated by the law because they depend upon professional expertise or the weighing of conflicting policies to achieve substantive justice in the individual case. Such decisions, it is argued, also are best left to the discretion of the professional involved, especially when they involve "human values" or an element of prediction. Finally, even where the law can appropriately regulate by reference to a few factually-based circumstances, it must be recognized that other circumstances generally deemed irrelevant may nonetheless have a just bearing on the exercise of authority in the exceptional case. Thus, it is argued, some degree of discretion is needed to supplement the law if it is to achieve its true objectives in application. That need is exacerbated by the legislative tendency in the area of crime control to frame legislation with an eye to its political symbolism, to focus on the worse scenario, and to overgeneralize for fear that a serious offender would slip through a legal loophole provided by a narrower prohibition.

Discretionary authority also is justified as a desirable means of providing for local community control over the process, and thereby supplementing a primary objective of the structure of agency fragmentation as discussed in subsection (d). Discretion, it is argued, allows for community influence over the process, in contrast to norms set forth on a statewide basis under state law. It permits the community to control through its political structure various aspects of the process that need to be adjusted to take account of local community values and an administrative environment likely to differ significantly from one community to another.

Critics of discretion acknowledge that a certain degree of discretionary authority is needed in the criminal justice process, but they see far fewer instances in which broad discretion is justified. For most areas, they conclude that the value of such discretion is outweighed by its costs. They argue that in a country that prides itself on being a "nation of law and not men," discretionary authority should be limited to instances of absolute necessity. They question whether discretion facilitates the efficient allocation of resources, noting that the relevant agencies and individuals often are prone to make judgments based on self-interest rather than the overall objectives of the process. They note that local control, where desirable, does not necessarily mandate discretion, as local governments may use their lawmaking authority to regulate in accordance with local values and needs. They see the law in general as having far more capacity to regulate a wide variety of decisions, noting that where absolute standards are inappropriate, discretion can nonetheless be channeled through appropriate legislative guidelines. Most significantly, they give greater weight to the costs of discretion. They see discretion as detracting from the educational function of the law and invariably undercutting the basic principle of equal justice—that similar cases be treated in a similar fashion. Discretion, they note, at its best results in random capriciousness in the treatment of similarly situated subjects of the process, and at its worst results in invidious discrimination tied to such factors as race and socio-economic status. In the criminal justice process, this potential for misuse is magnified both by the immense number of agencies and individual actors who are given discretionary authority and the fact that the exercise of discretion, at least in the routine case, commonly is hidden from public view.

Broad grants of discretionary authority are well established in the American criminal justice process. Over the years, however, there has been a constant movement back and forth, between increased discretionary authority and increased regulation by legal standard, in an effort to achieve a satisfactory balance between the two. In recent years, as noted in our discussions of various aspects of the process, the movement has been toward eliminating or channeling the exercise of discretionary authority.[2] Nonetheless, as suggested above, there remains a considerable range of discretionary authority, which invariably leads to considerable diversity in the administration of the process.

The extent of the variations resulting from the grant of discretionary authority will depend upon a variety of factors. Those factors include the number of different actors making discretionary decisions, the extent to which those actors share the same personal value judgments, and the restraints imposed by the institutional framework within which they operate. Institutional restraints can be especially significant where a particular agency (e.g., a prosecutor's office) seeks to obtain uniformity in the decisions of individual officials by prescribing standards for their exercise of discretionary authority and carefully monitoring their use of such authority.

Even should discretionary authority be exercised in a fairly consistent manner as to individual communities within a state, there is likely to be substantial variation on a statewide level between different communities. For at that level, the number of different officials exercising discretionary authority is greater, differences in communities are more likely to produce a divergence in personal value judgments, and as discussed in § 1.3, the various agencies, even as they attempt to obtain uniformity within their ranks, are likely to be quite different from one another. Indeed, the variations in the exercise of discretionary authority among different communities within a single state can be so great that the criminal justice process in two such communities, through operating under the legal standards of the same state, can appear as different from each other as from the criminal justice process in another state having quite different laws.

(c) The Range of Offenses. The substantive law which is enforced through the criminal justice process encompasses a tremendously broad range of offenses. Consider, for example, the harms that give rise to substantive law violations. Included in any criminal code are crimes of violence against the person, property crimes, public-order crimes, regulatory offenses, vice offenses, and misuses of positions of trust. Similar variety is found in the range of objectives and mental elements that may lead to criminal liability. Offenders include persons who act out of passion, persons acting under influence of alcohol or drugs, persons who act in a cold and calculated attempt to gain profit, and persons who simply are negligent. Significant differences in behavior and motivation will exist not only between different crimes, but within the coverage of a single crime. The crime of burglary, for example, will encompass various modes of entry into different types of buildings by persons intending different ulterior crimes. Robbery may be the work of the unemployed youth who suddenly spots a particularly vulnerable victim walking alone on a dark street, a seasoned expert who executes a carefully planned hold-up of an establishment that will yield a "high score" (e.g., a bank), or a drug addict who seeks a "quick buck" by holding-up the sole attendant in the nearest all-night establishment.

A criminal justice process that will be applied to such a broad range of offenses (and offenders) necessarily requires a certain degree of flexibility, and that flexibility, in turn, will lead to variations in the process as applied. To accommodate differences in crimes, the process, at various stages, must provide a range of alternative procedures geared to those differences. This element of flexibility is most notable at the investigatory stage. Investigatory procedures that are more than adequate in dealing with most crimes will be of little value as to others. Accordingly, additional procedures will be authorized with those other offenses in mind. Indeed, many of the investigative practices that have proven most controversial (e.g., the use of agents provocateur and electronic surveillance) have been introduced into the process because they were thought to be essential to the successful

2. See e.g., our discussions as to discretion and the use of statutory or administrative guidelines with respect to pretrial release (§ 12.1), the prosecution and police decision to proceed (§ 13.2), the authorization of pretrial discovery (§ 20.2), plea negotiation (§ 21.2), and sentencing (§ 26.3).

investigation of particular types of offenses. In other aspects of the process as well, such as sentencing and the timing and scope of the trial, procedures have been shaped to allow for variations among offenses.

Most often, as in the instances described above, the law governing the process simply authorizes a range of process options designed to accommodate differences in offenses and leaves to the police, prosecutor, or judge the discretion to select the option that best suits the particular type of offense. In other instances, however, legal requirements will tie the use of a procedure to particular offenses. Thus, statutory provisions governing electronic eavesdropping and preventive detention limit those procedures to particular offenses. So too, various special procedures apply to prosecutions in which the state seeks the imposition of capital punishment.

The most substantial legal differentiation based on offense category is found in the separate treatment of minor and major crimes. The categorization of offenses as minor or major for procedural purposes typically follows the distinction drawn in the substantive law between misdemeanors and felonies.[3] In some jurisdictions, however, that line is used to distinguish between minor and major offenses at some stages of the process, but not others. Thus, at the investigatory stage, the jurisdiction may distinguish between misdemeanors and felonies, and at the trial stage, it may distinguish between lower level misdemeanors (e.g., those punishable by no more than 90 days imprisonment) and higher level misdemeanors and felonies, which are grouped together. For the sake of brevity, our discussion of the separate treatment of minor offenses here and in § 1.4 assumes a single dividing line under which all misdemeanors are treated as minor crimes.[4]

The overview presented in § 1.4 focuses on the procedures applicable to felonies and mentions only the most basic variations from those procedures in the application of the process to misdemeanors. In every jurisdiction, one will find many additional differences in the procedures that apply to misdemeanors, extending to every stage in the process. For example, at the investigatory stage, a special warrant requirement may apply to arrests for misdemeanors; at the pretrial stage, the law governing discovery may not be applicable to misdemeanors; at the trial stage, the jury trial right for misdemeanor prosecutions may exist only through a trial *de novo*; and at the sentencing stage, determinate sentences of incarceration will be utilized for misdemeanors even in jurisdictions that have indeterminate sentencing for felonies. The end product of these differences is a legal process for misdemeanors that, while similar in its basic principles to the process applicable to felonies, nonetheless varies in both major and minor respects at numerous points in the progression of the process.

Our § 1.4 overview also does not take account of the differences in the procedures that may be applied to different minor crimes within the same state as a result of differ-

3. American jurisdictions commonly use one of two different standards in distinguishing between felonies and misdemeanors. Some classify as felonies all offenses punishable by a maximum term of imprisonment of more than one year; offenses punishable by imprisonment for one year or less are then misdemeanors. Others look to the location of the possible imprisonment. If the offense is punishable by imprisonment in a penitentiary, it is a felony; if punishable only by a jail term, it is a misdemeanor. As a matter of practice, both dividing lines frequently produce the same result since state correction codes commonly provide for imprisonment in the penitentiary if a sentence exceeds one year and for imprisonment in jail if the sentence is for one year or less.

4. Our discussion of the treatment of misdemeanors excludes the ordinary traffic violation. In many jurisdictions, all but the most serious traffic violations (e.g., driving while intoxicated) have been decriminalized. Indeed, even in those jurisdictions in which all traffic violations are technically misdemeanors, the less serious traffic offenses often are governed by somewhat different procedures than are applicable generally to other lower level misdemeanors. On the other hand, our discussion does encompass city ordinance violations in those jurisdictions in which ordinances largely duplicate in substance and penalty state misdemeanor provisions governing such offenses as assault, petty theft, etc. Such ordinances commonly are used as a basis for prosecution in lieu of the state misdemeanor provisions (often because the fines collected for ordinance violations go to the city), with the prosecution brought by the city attorney rather than the local prosecutor. In jurisdictions of this type, the procedure applied to ordinance violations is basically the same as that applied to lower level misdemeanors generally.

ences in the courts dealing with those crimes. The trial of minor offenses traditionally has been the function of the courts of limited jurisdiction, which are known in different jurisdictions as magistrate courts, justice of the peace courts, municipal courts, police courts, or recorder's courts. We refer to all of these courts as "magistrate courts" because judges of such courts commonly are described in judicial opinions as "magistrates" (presumably because they perform a role similar to the original English magistrate). In many states, there will at least be two different types of magistrate courts, each operating in different geographical districts. Very often there will be significant differences in the procedures applied in each type of court. This is especially likely where, as in the vast majority of states, there exists a type of magistrate court in which the judges do not have to be lawyers. Magistrate courts with lay judges typically are treated as courts "not-of-record." Misdemeanor procedures in such courts often differ substantially from those utilized in magistrate courts with lawyer-judges. For example, trials in courts-not-of-record may be limited to bench trials and the rules of evidence may be applied in a rather loose fashion. However, a misdemeanor defendant convicted in a court not-of-record is entitled to a retrial of the charges (a trial *de novo*) before the next highest court rather than simply to the usual appellate review on the record available to defendants convicted in magistrate courts "of record." [5]

(d) Agency Fragmentation. While the responsibility for prescribing the laws governing the process is divided among the federal system and the individual states, the greatest degree of fragmentation of authority is found in the assignment of responsibility for administration of the process. Though that fragmentation exists as well in the administrative components of defense counsel and judiciary, it is most prominent in the organization of the state agencies that bear the primary responsibility for the enforcement of the substantive criminal law—that is, the police and prosecutorial agencies.[6] Indeed, the decentralization or "balkanization" of state law enforcement agencies is probably the most prominent feature of the administrative structure of the criminal justice process.

Initially, there exists a division between police and prosecutorial agencies. Although prosecutors commonly are described as the "chief law enforcement officer" of the jurisdiction, the prosecutor has no direct regulatory authority over the police. Prosecutorial and police agencies are not only legally separate, but most often they are parts of different units of local governments. The federal system, in which most of the major police agencies (most notably, the F.B.I.) and the United States Attorneys are part of a single agency (the Department of Justice), is atypical in this regard. At the state level, there will be no single executive official, such as the United States Attorney General, with supervisory control over both police and prosecutors.

5. Historically, courts not-of-record lacked the capacity to prepare a transcript of their trials. Without that record, their convictions could not be subjected to the traditional form of appellate review. Accordingly, when the conviction was appealed, the higher court simply gave the case *de novo* consideration through a new trial. Today, magistrate courts not-of-record often have the facilities to provide a verbatim transcript of their proceedings, but convictions in those courts remain subject to review by a trial *de novo*. That procedure has been retained, in large part, due to concern that a person convicted of a misdemeanor should be entitled to a more formal and thorough trial than is provided in courts not-of-record.

6. There are, of course, many more autonomous organizations that provide defense services (including both public defenders and private legal practices), but fragmentation here is viewed as far less significant because of the role of counsel. Counsel's responsibility to the individual client necessarily demands that counsel operate as an autonomous unit even if a part of a larger organization (although certain institutional pressures may work against that objective).

Fragmentation in the structure of the judiciary is less pronounced than in other components of the administrative structure. Most states and the federal government have a single unified court system under which the highest court has substantial administrative authority over all lower courts. That authority will be exercised through the use of court rules applicable throughout the judicial system (and in some jurisdictions, through the use of administrative orders). There are, however, some states in which unification is not complete, and certain lower courts can be regulated by the highest state court only through appellate review of individual decisions by those courts.

Within the state systems, there is not only division between prosecutor and police, but also substantial fragmentation in the allocation of authority for each of these functions. Throughout the United States, there are over 17,000 agencies at the state level that can be characterized as police agencies. While a small percentage of these agencies are statewide agencies, most are units of local governments (counties, cities, and townships). Indeed, over 90% of all municipalities with a population of 2,500 or more have their own police departments. As a result, no state has less than 10 different police agencies and only five have fewer than a 100 different police agencies.

Prosecutorial authority at the state level also tends to be fragmentized, although usually not as heavily as police authority. A few states make the attorney general responsible for all prosecutions under state law. Typically, however, the officials with primary responsibility for prosecutions under state law are local prosecuting attorneys (sometimes called the "district attorney," "county attorney," or "state attorney"). Local prosecutors are selected either from a single county or from a group of counties combined to form a single prosecutorial district in sparsely populated areas. In many states, the state attorney general has some supervisory authority over local prosecutors, but that authority tends to be limited. Quite often the attorney general is still another autonomous prosecutor with the independent authority to initiate prosecutions under some or all state laws. Where state law permits municipalities to enact ordinances that largely duplicate state misdemeanor offenses, city attorneys will also be a autonomous prosecutorial authority as to prosecutions under those ordinances.

While the fragmentation of police and prosecutorial authority is designed to serve other goals as well, one major function of fragmentation is to provide some degree of local community control over the exercise of law enforcement authority and to thereby accommodate a pluralist society.[7] This opens the door to another layer of laws bearing upon the process. Local communities may adopt ordinances bearing upon police enforcement activities or may, through various political controls, mandate the adoption of internal agency regulations that guide officers in the exercise of certain controversial aspects of their authority. Most often, however, as discussed in § 1.3(b), the influence of local communities will be exerted informally in a fashion that provides a more pervasive yet less confining directive to local officials. Thus, the values reflected in the statements and actions of local political leaders often find their way into the general message that the local police agency conveys to its officers regarding such matters as the exercise of discretion, the interpretation of ambiguous legal standards, and the tolerance of departures from certain legal standards. Since local communities often differ in the values they support, those differences will invariably produce some degree of variation in the administration of the same laws from one community to another in the same state.

Even apart from the influence of local community values, the sheer number of different prosecutorial and police agencies will, in itself, produce variations in the administration of the law by those agencies. With the level of fragmentation as high as it is, differences in agency perspectives will surely exist even apart from any direction supplied by the local community. Indeed, complete likemindedness among so many agencies dealing with often controversial subjects would be contrary to human nature. Thus, fragmentation and administrative variations go hand in hand even in those jurisdictions in which individual

7. Fragmentation as to police authority is seen as a further protection against the authoritarianism that might flow from the misuse of an all-powerful national police force. As to both prosecutor and police, fragmentation also is thought to better ensure accountability to the public and thereby to encourage the cooperation of the public. Fragmentation is seen too as facilitating change and experimentation since, with so many independent agencies, it is more likely that at least one will be willing to depart from the traditional. Fragmentation also is praised as facilitating administrative variation to meet special problems that may be presented by unique local conditions.

agencies are fairly well insulated from the electorate.

§ 1.3 Variations in Institutional Settings

As Roscoe Pound noted in the seminal empirical study of the criminal justice process, to accurately describe the operation of that process, one must take into account not only the applicable law, but also (i) the people who administer the process, (ii) the organizations of which they are a part, and (iii) the administrative environment in which they operate.[1] These are certainly the most important factors influencing the manner in which all laws are administered. They are especially important to an understanding of the criminal justice process because of the substantial grants of discretionary authority that are made by the law governing the process. Any proposal to transpose the law of one jurisdiction to another must take into consideration the three factors cited by Pound, as differences relating to those factors could affect dramatically the application of that law in the jurisdiction to which it is transposed. Indeed, the law in a particular jurisdiction is likely to be shaped in various aspects to meet the bureaucratic needs of the various agencies charged with the administration of the process, with those needs largely being the product of Pound's three factors.[2]

Our focus in this section will be upon variations found in the second and third factors noted by Pound. Taken together, those two factors may be characterized as providing the "institutional setting" for the process as it is applied in a particular community. In focusing on that institutional setting, we do not mean to downplay the first factor cited by Pound—the people administering the process—and its potential for producing significant differences in the application of the process. That there will be variations in the attitudes and abilities of individual administrators, and that those differences will influence their performance, is a point so obvious as not to require further discussion. Moreover, to some extent, such differences will be subordinated to the influence of the institutional setting. The standards for selection of personnel, an aspect of the institutional setting, will help determine the range of differences among individual administrators. In addition, elements of the institutional setting will work to shape performance in a particular manner, notwithstanding differences among individuals. Studies show, for example, that even police officers on the beat—operating in a position traditionally characterized by extensive autonomy—are substantially influenced in their performance by the specific demands and general policies of the particular police department in which they serve.

Differences in institutional setting may produce variations in practice in several ways. Initially, such differences often have a substantial bearing on the exercise of discretionary authority. Indeed, in some instances, although the law leaves decisionmaking to the personal judgment of the individual actor, the institutional setting clearly dominates that decisionmaking process and leaves the actor little room for personal variation. Differences in institutional setting may also play a significant role where the law seeks to regulate decisionmaking by specifying standards to which the actor must adhere. Where those standards are ambiguous, the institutional setting is likely to have a bearing on how they are interpreted. Where the standards are clear, the institutional setting may determine how consistently and carefully they are implemented. For in the criminal justice field, as in other legal fields, the standards prescribed

§ 1.3

1. Criminal Justice in Cleveland (R. Pound and F. Frankfurter, eds. 1922).

2. Consider, for example, the frequent reference to caseload pressures in the shaping of various aspects of the law. The Supreme Court has noted the influence of such pressures in its discussion of the law governing several aspects of the process, including plea bargaining, the joinder of parties, and collateral review of convictions. So too, on occasion, in fashioning certain bright line rules, the Court has referred to institutional pressures that might lead officials to manipulate more flexible standards so as to undercut the basic objective of the law.

by the law are not always the standards followed in practice.

In any particular community, one is likely to find at least a few unwritten rules, shaped by the institutional setting, that effectively modify the standards set forth in the governing law, with the end result being the frequently mentioned distinction between the "law on the books" and the "law in the real world." In some instances, those unwritten rules exist because all of the affected participants have agreed to pay no attention to the inconsistent legal standard, at least in certain situations. In others, those unwritten rules will prevail, notwithstanding the opposition of certain participants that they adversely affect. That most often occurs where the judicial process has limited capacity to ensure adherence to the written law and the institutional setting conveys to the officials involved the message that the value of the practice promoted by the unwritten rule outweighs the costs of occasional judicial action responding to their disregard of the law.

The precise bearing of the institutional setting upon the criminal justice practice will vary, of course, from one community to another. It is probably true that, at least in certain communities, the characteristics of the organizations involved in administering the process, and the practical pressures under which they must operate, have as much to do with shaping the everyday administration of the process as the applicable legal principles. In contrast, in many other communities, the law is likely to be the dominant force in shaping the process, with differences in institutional setting operating only interstitially.

(a) Organizational Variations. As noted in § 1.2(d), for at least three of the major components in the administration of the criminal justice process (police, prosecutor, and defense counsel), administrative authority is divided among a substantial number of completely autonomous units. The administrative structure of the judiciary tends to be far less fragmented, but it still treats individual judges as at least partially autonomous. With so many separate organizational units in each administrative component, some degree of variation is certain to be found in almost every aspect of organizational structure. Among the more significant variations are those that relate to organizational role, selection of personnel, size, allocation of responsibilities within the organization, and caseload pressures. Differences in each of these qualities are thought to produce, in turn, at least some differences in organizational practice in administrating the process.

Perhaps the most important differences in organizational role are found among police agencies. All police agencies, by definition, are given the task of enforcing the substantive criminal law (i.e., investigating possible violations of that law and apprehending possible offenders). Some very significant agencies, such as the F.B.I. and certain state police agencies, have responsibilities largely limited to law enforcement (sometimes further limited to particular laws). In contrast, the vast majority of police agencies, including all of those that are part of local governments, are "general agencies" that have numerous additional responsibilities. Those responsibilities include the provision of basic social services (e.g., providing emergency aid), the maintenance of public order (e.g., traffic control), and the prevention of crime (e.g., by providing a physical presence through patrol activities). The more diverse responsibilities of the general agencies may affect in several ways their law enforcement performance as compared to that of agencies focused primarily on that task. First, with the general agency's limited resources spread over a broad range of activities, many of its personnel will be relatively inexperienced in the investigation of serious crimes. Typically, patrol officers, who represent the vast bulk of the local police force, will devote less than 20% of their time to significant violations of the criminal law. While the more experienced detectives are also engaged in the investigation of those violations, their work commonly builds upon that of the patrol officers who provide the first line of inquiry. Second, the diverse responsibilities of the general agency can lead it to adopt a broader perspective in the selection of its officers, as the qualities needed in criminal investigation and related enforcement activities often are not the same that assist the officer in performing other police roles, such as social service functions. Third, the diverse responsibilities of the general agency may lead it to adopt administrative policies that detract from investigative success, as where officers are encouraged to adopt a flexible and informal style that will serve them well in various community interactions but make more difficult adherence to the formalistic legal requirements governing police investigation.

Differences in personnel selection are found among organizations within each of the components engaged in administering the criminal justice process. Among police agencies, the primary selection distinctions are in educational requirements (e.g., whether officers must have more than a high school diploma), the strength and scope of affirmative action programs for the hiring of minorities, and the rate of new hiring due to officer turnover. Among prosecutor's offices, a critical distinction is whether the selection of assistants will be highly political (with assistants expected at the least to be of the same political party as the elected prosecutor, if not active campaign supporters) or will be based on non-partisan, merit oriented standards. Although high turnover is common to all prosecutors' offices, those offices do vary dramatically in their ability to retain a substantial corp of career professionals.

In the area of defense representation, a major selection distinction is found in the systems used to appoint counsel to represent indigents. In many jurisdictions, counsel will be provided through an assigned counsel system that relies heavily on "courthouse regulars" in the private bar. In others, indigents will be represented almost exclusively by counsel furnished by public defender agencies. Still others use a mixed system with the defender agency and appointed private counsel each representing a substantial portion of the indigent defendants. Among retained counsel, even greater diversity will be found, with counsel including general practitioners, corporate practitioners who handle white collar cases, highly skilled trial lawyers who concentrate on "big cases," and the previously mentioned "courthouse regulars" who handle a high volume of criminal cases.

Judicial selection methods ordinarily will be uniform within a state, but may differ with the level of the court. Selection methods employed by the different states include: (1) partisan elections; (2) non-partisan elections; (3) appointment by the chief executive, with the consent of the legislature; (4) election by the legislature; and (5) some variation of the Missouri Plan, under which nominees are proposed by an independent commission, selection is made by the governor, and the appointees subsequently run unopposed in retention elections.

How do all these differences in selecting personnel affect performance? That is a matter of debate as to each, although it is clear that some have a more direct and immediate impact upon administration of the criminal justice process than others. There is little evidence, for example, that officers with only a high school diploma perform less effectively in direct law enforcement activities than officers with more education. Different type of defense counsel, on the other hand, clearly do present, as a group, different styles of representation. The broadest differences in the method of selecting judges would appear to have a bearing on the types of persons selected, and that in turn, should bear upon judicial performance. The end result is that it is often difficult to pinpoint a particular administrative consequence of a difference in the selection process, but it can safely be assumed that such difference will affect the process somewhere along the line.

The most striking contrasts in organizational size are found in police and prosecutorial agencies. Close to two-thirds of all local police agencies have less than 20 sworn officers and over one-third have less than 5 officers. In the largest cities, on the other hand, local departments commonly have several thousand officers. The range among prosecutors' offices is not quite so dramatic. Over three-fourths have 4 or fewer assistants, with many having only a single prosecutor (sometimes employed on a part-time basis). In metropolitan districts, on the other hand, the office may have 100 or more assistants. Such differences in size can have a bearing on various aspects of the performance of the police and prosecutorial functions. Small police agencies cannot utilize specialized units that may be more effective in dealing with particular types of crimes, make use of sophisticated criminal investigation techniques that require costly equipment, or provide extensive training programs (although combined efforts with other departments may overcome these limitations). Small prosecutor offices similarly have difficulty in developing expertise outside the area of the most common offenses and motions, and certain cases (e.g., extensive conspiracies) may require more manpower than they can readily muster. On the other hand, larger police and prosecutor offices will face greater obstacles in ensuring uniform adherence to agency policies. Such offices are far more likely to have a complicated bureaucratic structure that will include detailed written guidelines, internal reporting requirements, and a variety of specialized units and highly structured programs aimed at particular types of offenses or offenders.

Significant differences in the allocation of authority within an organization are more likely to be found among larger units, as the range of alternatives available to smaller units tends to be limited. Among large prosecutor offices, for example, some will utilize a hierarchial structure with different prosecutors assigned to each major stage in the process, while others will assign cases to individual prosecutors who will carry a case from the point at which it first enters the office to final disposition. Offices using the latter structure often give the individual prosecutor far more autonomy on charging, plea bargaining, and other discretionary decisions. A somewhat similar division is found in the allocation of cases in multi-judge courts. Some such courts utilize individual dockets while others rely upon a central docket. That difference can have a bearing on the extent of judicial participation in plea bargaining and the efforts exerted to obtain a speedy disposition of cases. Among large police offices, differences in the internal division of responsibility for investigation between detectives, special squads, and patrol officers may influence the degree to which particular investigative procedures are utilized.

The criminal justice system in all of its components commonly is pictured as lacking the resources to deal adequately with the quantitative demands imposed upon it. There are more offenses than the police can possibly investigate, more persons arrested and charged than can possibly be tried, and more convicted than can be handled with appropriate care by the corrections system. The precise impace of caseload pressures upon the administration of the process is open to debate. Many see such pressures as the primary contributor to prosecutorial charging decisions based on less than complete information, the assembly line processing of cases by magistrates, the emphasis upon disposition of cases through plea bargaining, and routinized decisionmaking in sentencing.

While the criminal justice system in the vast majority of communities is undermanned and underfinanced to some extent, the weight of the resulting caseload pressures varies substantially from one community to another. Such pressures undoubtedly impose a great burden upon police, prosecutors, public defenders, and courts in large cities. There are other communities, however, particularly in rural areas, where the pressure of numbers is not nearly as significant. Here, the process as applied often will be quite different, particularly in style of administration, although those differences may be attributable to a combination of factors of which lighter caseloads is only one.

(b) Community Values. With an administrative system in which most components are purposely fragmented in order to preserve some degree of local control, it would be surprising if the criminal justice process as applied were not influenced by variations in the dominant values of different local communities, at least as those values are reflected in the political climate of the particular community. Nonetheless, some would contend that those variations have an impact only in a fairly limited range of situations. Differences in community values, they argue, have a bearing primarily in individual cases that gain some special notoriety because of the particular participants or other special circumstances that attract media attention and in certain classes of cases (e.g., spouse abuse and drunk driving fatalities) that touch a special nerve in the community as a whole or in a special segment of the community. In the run-of-the-mill case involving the run-of-the-mill offense, those differences are seen as having little impact. Here, it is argued, those administrating the process are sufficiently shielded from political pressures to act largely upon their own institutional interests without regard to community values that may lead in another direction.

While differences in community values may be so confined in their influence in certain communities, there undoubtedly are other communities in which those differences have had an impact upon across-the-board administrative policies. Thus, one study pointed to a significant diversity in the focus of police patrols that was tied in large part to differences in community priorities.[3] Some departments followed a "watchman" style of patrol (emphasizing order maintenance through informal police procedures), others a "legalistic" patrol style (emphasizing full use of the patrol officer's arrest power), and still others a "service" style (giving priority to officer responsiveness to the full range of citizen requests for assistance). The choice among patrol styles was seen as heavily influenced by the local political culture, including such factors as whether the community was heterogeneous or homogeneous, or whether it had a highly charged political atmosphere or an apolitical approach that emphasized professionalism and "good government." Moreover, even where officials operate in relative obscurity and can adopt policies without concern as to any community reaction, the influence of community values may be felt indirectly. Community values often play a role in the initial selection of elected prosecutors, judges, and sheriffs, at least limiting the persons selected to those with predispositions not sharply inconsistent with local political culture, and the policies subsequently adopted by those officials will commonly be guided by those same predispositions that allowed their initial selection.

(c) **System Culture.** In each local community, one is likely to find certain practices that simply exist as a part of the local culture developed within the criminal justice system. These are practices of long and settled use, now followed as a matter of tradition rather than as a product of any overt decision by current policy makers. Very often, these traditions relate to the interactions of different participants in the process, and not infrequently they would be difficult to explain as a rational compromise of the current interests of those participants. Indeed, they may lead the participants to accept positions contrary to conventional wisdom, but which can be challenged only at the risk of upsetting an essential working relationship.

Characteristics that distinguish local cultures are sometimes widespread and sometimes fairly unique. Local culture has produced the unusual use of procedural options in a fashion that is distinctive to a particular community. It also explains, however, some fairly common contrasts in the administration of the process. That is true, for example, of differences that stem from variations in the extent to which the local system culture promotes the spirit of cooperative venture.

Studies of the trial court "work group" have found in some jurisdictions an overriding cooperative relationship between defense attorneys, prosecutors, and judges, reflected in such behavior as informal mutual discovery of information, pro forma granting of continuances, and cooperative negotiation leading to non-trial dispositions. In other jurisdictions, particularly where the same prosecutor and defense counsel are not regularly before the same judge, the relationship between the participants is much more formal,

3. J. Wilson, Varieties of Police Behavior (1968).

controlled largely by the letter of the law, and often reflecting continuous adversarial challenge. A similar variation is found in the ongoing working relationship between police and prosecutors. In some communities, the tradition is one of close cooperation. The police will adjust the use of their arrest authority to the charging policies of the prosecutor's office, and the prosecutors, in turn, will rely heavily on the wishes of the police in striking plea-bargains. In other communities, the police and prosecutor will lean toward a position of strict independence from each other, accepting the possibility that their different viewpoints will lead to antagonistic positions and, occasionally, a form of guerrilla warfare.

Local culture has also been cited as the dominant factor in producing in many communities allocations of administrative authority that are far different from what one might expect simply from looking at the law governing the process. Sentencing authority has been, in effect, shifted from the court to the prosecutor by a tradition of almost automatic judicial acceptance of prosecutorial sentencing recommendations, at least in the vast majority of cases resolved by plea bargaining. The charging decision has been shifted effectively to the magistrate where it is the practice at preliminary hearings to reject a higher charge, notwithstanding a showing of probable cause, because the magistrate believes the case simply is "not worth" that higher charge. The investigative process has come under the control of the prosecutor where the local tradition grants the prosecutor the option to "take over" the criminal investigation in cases of significant public interest.

§ 1.4 The Steps in the Process

In this section, we will describe briefly the major steps taken in the processing of a criminal case. Our focus, as noted previously, is on the processing of a "typical case" in a "typical jurisdiction." [1] This means that our description basically is limited to those procedures employed by most states in processing most of their felony and misdemeanor cases. Where no single procedural pattern is followed by a substantial majority of the states, we will note the major alternatives followed by significant groups of states. However, variations adopted by only a few states, or variations applied only to a limited class of cases, are largely ignored.

While our primary objective in this section is to provide an overview of the interrelated procedural steps that constitute the total process, we have also sought to provide some indication of the significance of the different steps as measured in quantitative terms. This hopefully will assist the reader in gauging the practical significance of the various legal standards discussed in the subsequent chapters. While some of these standards relate to procedures employed in the vast majority of criminal prosecutions, others concern procedures utilized in fewer than even one percent of all instances of process use.

(a) Step 1: The Reported Crime. Although many official actions are taken in a

§ 1.4

1. The overview also follows what might be described as the "typical" sequence of procedural steps in such a case. Certain types of cases, however, are not likely to follow that chronology. For example, there are cases in which the prosecutor will want to approve the police decision to proceed before the arrest is made. As a result, both the prosecutor's screening and the magistrate's screening (through the magistrate's issuance of an arrest warrant) will have come before rather than after the arrest. Similarly, where the grand jury's investigative authority is utilized, grand jury review occurs at the outset and defendant usually will have been indicted before he is arrested. Such differences in chronology means that the arrest will play a more limited role than in the typical case, where the police officer's warrantless arrest, made on his own initiative, constitutes the first step in the decision to charge. This, in turn, has a bearing on the review procedure that follows the arrest, and may also affect other elements of the subsequent procedure (e.g., the setting of bail).

In addition to ignoring variations in chronology for exceptional cases, a step-by-step overview, such as that presented here, also suffers from its treatment of each step as if it were started and completed at a single point in the process. While some steps have definite starting and ending points, others are ongoing procedures. Investigatory procedures, for example, do not always stop with the filing of charges, but may continue on through to the time of trial. Similarly, the prosecutor's decision to go forward with the charges, though made initially at a particular point in the proceeding, is ongoing in the sense that it is subject to reconsideration at various subsequent stages in the proceedings.

general effort to prevent crime (e.g., police patrols), the criminal justice process is usually viewed as starting with official action that focuses on a particular crime. The most common starting point, from this perspective, is the episode that leads to the police recording of an offense as a "reported crime" or a "known offense." That episode usually will be the police observation of what appears to be criminal activity or the report of an interested citizen (usually the victim) that a crime has occurred. Our overview will proceed, assuming such an episode, but there are atypical cases in which the initial official action focusing on a particular crime stems from a different source. In some instances, the process may start with information concerning possible criminal activity coming to the attention of the prosecutor and serving as a springboard for an investigation conducted through the grand jury. In other instances, the process may not be initiated in a reactive mode to the possible commission of a crime, but in a proactive mode to a potential future offense. Thus, recognizing that potential, the police may set traps through decoys and sting operations to ferret out persons inclined to engage in a particular type of criminal activity (e.g., vice offenses).

(b) Step 2: Pre-arrest Investigation. Once the police become aware of the possible commission of a crime, they must determine (1) whether the crime actually was committed and (2) if it was, whether there is sufficient information pointing to the guilt of a particular person to justify arresting and charging him. Pre-arrest investigative procedures are designed to answer these questions and to collect evidence that may be helpful in establishing guilt at trial. The particular procedures used will vary with the circumstances of the crime. In some instances, a police officer will observe a crime being committed in his presence and will make an arrest "on the spot." In such cases, the pre-arrest investigation consists of no more than the officer's initial observation. In other cases, the officer will observe activity that is suspicious, though not necessarily criminal, and will seek further information to determine whether to make an arrest. Where an alleged offense has been called to the officer's attention by an interested citizen, the officer also is likely to seek further information.

Where additional information is sought, the officer may utilize a variety of investigatory techniques to gather that information. Perhaps the most common is to question the suspect. Pre-arrest questioning may be accompanied by the temporary detention of the suspect on the street or at home, but does not involve taking him into custody, as occurs with an arrest. The scope of the officer's questioning may range from merely asking the suspect to identify himself to asking him to respond to an accusation made by others. Where the crime investigated involved violence, or there is some other reason to believe the suspect could be armed, the officer may undertake some sort of search of the temporarily detained suspect (usually a pat-down or "frisk" of the suspect's outer clothing). In a small percentage of these police-suspect encounters, the officer also may search the car of a suspect who was stopped while driving.

Along with the police-suspect encounter, the other common pre-arrest investigatory techniques are the interviewing of witnesses (including the victim) and the examination of the scene of the crime. In certain types of cases (e.g., homicides and burglaries), that examination may include the collection of physical evidence (e.g., fingerprints) that will be subjected to scientific analysis. For other offenses, commonly those committed by specialized professional criminals, police informants may be contacted for information concerning possible offenders. Thorough searches of homes and offices, and electronic eavesdropping through wiretaps and similar devices, are also used in certain types of investigations. These procedures, however, commonly require prior judicial authorization through the issuance of a search warrant, and are employed in only a small portion of all criminal investigations.

(c) Step 3: The Arrest. Once the officer has acquired sufficient information to justify arresting a suspect, the arrest ordinarily is the next step in the criminal justice process.

An arrest generally occurs when the officer takes the suspect into custody for the purpose of transporting him to the station and there charging him with a crime.[2] Although an arrest may be authorized in advance by a judicially issued warrant, the vast majority of all arrests are made on the officer's own initiative, without a warrant.

Arrests will be distributed over a variety of offenses, with the vast majority of arrests (70–80%) being for misdemeanor offenses. The number of arrests will be substantially smaller than the number of reported crimes; for those crimes on which the F.B.I. collects data, there is approximately one arrest for every five offenses reported to the police.[3] A substantial percentage of the persons arrested (typically 10–20%) will be under the age limit for juvenile court jurisdiction. Ordinarily, those arrestees will be separated from the adult arrestees shortly after being taken into custody, although some will later be returned to regular criminal justice process and be prosecuted as adults. We will follow, from this point on, only those arrestees who are adults or treated like adults.

(d) Step 4: Booking. Immediately after making an arrest, the arresting officer usually will search the arrestee's person and remove any weapons, contraband, or evidence relating to a crime. He then will arrange for the transportation of the arrestee to the police station, a centrally located jail, or some similar "holding" facility. It is at this facility that the arrestee will be taken through a process known as "booking." Initially, the arrestee's name, the time of his arrival, and the offense for which he was arrested are noted in the police "blotter" or "log." The arrestee then will be photographed and fingerprinted. Typically, he also will be informed of the charge on which he has been booked and will be allowed to make at least one telephone call. When booked on a minor offense, he may be able to obtain his release on "stationhouse bail," i.e., by posting cash as a security payment and promising to appear before a magistrate at a specified date. Persons arrested on serious offenses, and those arrested on minor offenses but unable to gain their release, will remain at the holding facility until ready to be presented before a magistrate (see step 8). Ordinarily, they will be placed in a "lockup," which usually is some kind of cell. Before entering the lockup, they will be subjected to another search, more thorough than that conducted at the point of arrest. This search is designed primarily to inventory the arrestee's personal belonging and to prevent the introduction of contraband into the lockup.

(e) Step 5: Post-arrest Investigation. The extent of the post-arrest investigation will vary with the fact situation. In some situations, such as where the arrestee was caught "red-handed," there will be little left to be done. In other situations, police will utilize many of the same kinds of investigative procedures as are used before arrest (e.g., interviewing witnesses, searching the suspect's home, and viewing the scene of the crime). Post-arrest investigation does offer one important investigative source, however, that ordinarily is not available prior to the arrest—the person of the arrestee. Thus, the arrestee may be placed in a lineup or simply taken to a place where a witness can view him individually (a "showup"). He may be required to provide handwriting or hair samples that can be compared with evidence the police have found at the scene of the crime.

2. As an alternative to the traditional "custodial arrest," many jurisdictions grant the officer discretion to briefly detain a person subject to arrest and to then release him upon issuance of a citation (sometimes called an "appearance ticket"). This alternative is most commonly authorized for misdemeanor offenses, and sometimes is limited to particular types of misdemeanors.

3. The "arrest-clearance" rate for reported crimes (which is basically the percentage of reported offenses resulting in the arrest of a suspected offender) varies from over 90% for some offenses to less than 15% for others. Those crimes that tend to come to the attention of the police only through an officer's personal observation of the crime (usually followed by an immediate arrest) have the highest arrest-clearance rates. Substantially lower rates are found for offenses that become known to the police primarily through victim reports. Here, the most significant factor will be the victim's ability to identify the offender. Thus, the arrest-clearance rate for burglary (15%) is far less than that for aggravated assault (over 60%).

He also may be questioned at length about the crime for which he was arrested and any other crime thought to be related. Although we do not have precise data on these post-arrest procedures involving the arrestee, the best available estimates indicate they are not applied to the vast majority of arrestees. In most communities, they are used almost exclusively in the investigation of felony cases and even then not in most of those investigations.

(f) Step 6: The Decision to Charge. Sometime between the booking of the arrestee and his presentation before a magistrate, there will be a review of the decision to file charges. Initially, the police officer making the arrest fills out an arrest report, which is reviewed by a higher ranking police officer. That officer may conclude either that charges should not be brought or that they should be based on a lower level offense than that for which the arrestee was booked. The decision not to charge may be based upon the officer's conclusion that there is insufficient evidence or that the particular offense can more appropriately be handled by a "stationhouse adjustment" (e.g., in the case of a fight among acquaintances, a warning and lecture may be deemed sufficient). If the officer decides against prosecution, the arrestee may be released from the lockup on the officer's direction (although some departments follow the practice of seeking prosecutor approval before releasing felony arrestees). In some jurisdictions, the police will drop as many as 10–15% of their arrests (predominantly misdemeanor arrests) at this point. In others, the police will do little screening themselves, leaving that task almost exclusively to the prosecutor.

The second review of the decision to charge is usually the review by the prosecuting attorney. Prosecutor offices vary considerably, however, both as to the timing and extent of their review. In some jurisdictions, prosecutors regularly screen all felony and misdemeanor cases before charges are filed with the court. In other jurisdictions, pre-charge prosecutorial review is limited to exceptional cases, primarily those in which the police seek the prosecutor's advice. Here, the primary prosecutorial screening occurs sometime after charges have been filed. For felonies, that point usually will be just before the prosecutor is required to present the case at a preliminary hearing or grand jury screening. For misdemeanors, there may not be review until the case is ready to go to trial (and thus the prosecutor may never review those misdemeanor charges to which the defendant pleads guilty). Still other jurisdictions prefer a midway position, with prosecutors undertaking a pre-charge screening of all felony cases, but utilizing a post-charge review for all but the most serious misdemeanors.

The timing of the screening is likely to have an impact upon the scope of the screening, as prosecutors tend to have less information available to them the earlier their review is undertaken. However, even among prosecutors utilizing the most prompt post-arrest screening, there is considerable variation in the sources considered in deciding whether to charge. The practice ranges from prosecutors who read only the police reports to those who regularly interview the police officer and often the victim of the crime as well. By far the most common grounds for deciding not to proceed are the insufficiency of the evidence and witness reluctance to testify.

Though we can hardly characterize any particular pre-charge screening program as common to most jurisdictions, a fairly common pattern is found in the eventual results of the overall screening carried on through the entire criminal justice process. In the end, at least as to felonies, the cases against 30–50% of all arrestees are likely to be rejected, dismissed, or diverted as a result of such screening.[4] If only a small percentage of the

4. The "diverted" prosecution refers to the disposition of the case under a pre-charge or post-charge diversion program operating through the prosecutor's office or the trial court's probation office. Under such a program, charges are held in reserve and not filed, or dismissed if previously filed, upon the arrestee's compliance with an agreed upon "rehabilitative program" that may include such conditions as maintaining regular employment and making restitution to the victim. The percentage of felony cases disposed of by initial rejection of charges or a

felony cases are rejected at pre-charge screening, then there will be a much higher percentage dismissed at subsequent stages when the prosecutor engages in more thorough screening. Those dismissals will come on a prosecution motion to terminate the prosecution (a *nolle prosequi* motion), which will be granted automatically by the trial court.

Statistics on charge reductions reflect a less consistent pattern than that characterizing dismissals. The percentage of reductions attributable to the screening process varies considerably, but prosecutors have been known to reduce the offense from that designated in the police booking in as many as half of the felony cases subjected to pre-charge screening. In many jurisdictions, certain types of felony arrests, most notably those involving non-professional thefts, are almost automatically reduced to misdemeanors (e.g., first-offense shoplifting reduced to petty theft). While most reductions occur before the initial charge is filed, a substantial number of reductions often occur later in the proceedings on the prosecutor's motion. Where plea bargaining takes the form of a charge bargain rather than a sentence bargain (see step 12), most of the later reductions are likely to be attributable to plea bargaining rather than post-charge prosecutorial screening.

(g) Step 7: Filing the Complaint. Assuming that the pre-charge screening results in a decision to prosecute, the next step in the criminal justice process is the filing of charges with the magistrate court. Typically, the initial charging instrument will be called a "complaint." In misdemeanor cases, which may be tried before the magistrate court, the complaint will serve as the charging instrument throughout the proceedings. In felony cases, on the other hand, the complaint serves to set forth the charges only before the magistrate court; an information or indictment will replace the complaint as the charging instrument when the case reaches the general trial court. The complaint ordinarily includes a brief description of the offense and is sworn to by a complainant. The complainant usually will be either the victim or the investigating officer. When an officer-complainant did not observe the offense being committed, but relied on information received from the victim or other witnesses, he will note that the facts alleged in the complaint are based on "information and belief."

Following the filing of the complaint and prior to or at the start of the first appearance (see step 8), the magistrate will conduct an *ex parte* review of the detention of the accused. This review is limited to ensuring that the arrest and complaint are supported by sufficient incriminating information to establish probable cause to believe the defendant committed the crime charged in the complaint. The magistrate's review may be based on the complaint itself where the complaint alleges the facts establishing probable cause (e.g., that the complainant observed the offense). In other cases, it may be based on a police officer's affidavit setting forth available information establishing probable cause. In some jurisdictions, the magistrate also may base his determination upon a brief oral statement presented by the complainant. If the magistrate finds that probable cause has not been established, he will direct the prosecution to promptly produce more information or release the arrested person. Such instances tend to be quite rare, however.[5]

subsequent dismissal usually is much greater than the percentage disposed of under diversion programs (typically, no more than 5%).

Diversion programs are more commonly utilized for misdemeanor arrestees, and play a much more significant role in the attrition of misdemeanor arrests through dispositions other than trial or guilty plea. However, available statistics on the attrition of misdemeanor arrests as a result of rejection, diversion, and dismissal are quite sparse, making it difficult to assess the overall rate for misdemeanor arrests as compared to felony arrests.

5. In many states, if the defendant was arrested without a warrant (as is usually the case), the magistrate will issue an arrest warrant after finding probable cause. Since the defendant has already been arrested, the warrant is not being used here for its traditional function of obtaining prior judicial approval for the arrest. Instead, the post-arrest warrant serves simply to provide judicial authorization for continuing to hold the arrestee in custody. In most jurisdictions, the post-arrest issuance of a warrant is viewed as an unnecessary formality, and the magistrate's finding of probable cause will combine with the complaint to authorize continuing custody.

(h) Step 8: The First Appearance. With the complaint having been filed, the case is now before the magistrate, and the arrestee (who is now formally a defendant) must be presented before the court. This appearance before the magistrate usually is described as the "first appearance," although some jurisdictions call it the "initial presentment" or the "arraignment on the warrant." Where the arrested person was released by police on a citation or stationhouse bail, the first appearance will not be scheduled until several days after the arrest. In most instances, however, the arrestee will still be in custody, and state law will require that he be brought before the magistrate without unnecessary delay. Ordinarily, the time consumed in booking, transportation, reviewing the decision to charge, and limited post-arrest investigation makes it unlikely that the arrestee will be presented before the magistrate until at least several hours after his arrest. Thus, if the magistrate court does not have an evening session, a person arrested in the afternoon or evening will not be presented before the magistrate until the next day. Many jurisdictions do not allow much longer detention than this, as they impose a 24 hour limit on pre-appearance detention, requiring both the filing of the complaint and the presentation of the detained arrestee within that period. Others, desiring to limit weekend sessions of the court, allow up to 48 hours of pre-appearance detention.

The first appearance often is a quite brief proceeding. Initially, the magistrate will make certain that the person before him is the person named in the complaint. The magistrate then will inform the defendant of the charge in the complaint and will note various rights that the defendant may have in further proceedings. The range of rights mentioned will vary from one jurisdiction to another. Commonly, the magistrate will inform the defendant of his right to remain silent and warn him that anything he says in court or to the police may be used against him at trial. The magistrate also will inform the defendant of his right to be represented by counsel and his right to appointed counsel if he is indigent. Although the timing varies, most jurisdictions at least initiate the process of providing counsel for the indigent defendant at the first appearance. The magistrate first will determine that the defendant is indigent and desires the assistance of appointed counsel. The magistrate then will either himself arrange for representation by the public defender or appointed private counsel or notify the judge in charge of appointments.

Other aspects of the first appearance are likely to depend upon whether the defendant is charged with a felony or misdemeanor. In the felony case, the magistrate will advise the defendant of the next step in the process, the preliminary hearing, and will set a date for that hearing unless the defendant desires to waive it. If the defendant is charged with a misdemeanor, he will not be entitled to a preliminary hearing (or a subsequent grand jury review). The misdemeanor charge is triable to the magistrate, and the magistrate therefore can proceed with a misdemeanor case in the same fashion as a general trial court receiving a felony case. For the misdemeanor, the first appearance becomes an arraignment on the complaint, equivalent to the arraignment on the information or indictment in a felony case (see step 12).[6]

The final function of the magistrate at the first appearance is to set bail (i.e., set the conditions under which the defendant can obtain his release from custody pending the

6. The initial step in the magistrate's arraignment of the misdemeanor defendant involves an explanation of available pleas to the charge stated in the complaint and an entry of a plea to that charge. While most misdemeanor defendants eventually plead guilty, many will not do so at the first appearance since they have not yet had the opportunity to consult with counsel or others (e.g., relatives) whose advice might be sought. They will plead not guilty or will be allowed to defer entry of their plea to a later date. In a jurisdiction relying primarily on post-charge screening, a significant percentage of the misdemeanor cases may be dismissed as a result of such screening at or before the defendant's next scheduled court appearance. For the cases that survive this screening, the rate of guilty pleas is likely to be between 80–95%. For these defendants, the next step in the process is sentencing (see step 15). For the defendants who go to trial, the next step will be the filing of pretrial motions (see step 13).

final disposition of his case). If the defendant obtained his release previously by posting stationhouse bail, the magistrate will merely review that bail. In felony cases, the defendant ordinarily will still be in custody and the magistrate will be making the initial decision on bail. At one time, bail was limited almost entirely to the posting of cash or a secured bond, purchased from a professional bondsman. Today, the defendant may also be able to obtain his release by depositing with the court cash equal to ten percent of the amount of the bond set by the magistrate. Indeed, several states make such extensive use of the ten percent alternative that they have effectively eliminated the role of the professional bondsman. In addition, courts today frequently authorize release upon the defendant's unsecured promise to appear (commonly called "release on personal recognizance" on an unsecured "personal bond.") In some jurisdictions, a preventive detention procedure will allow the magistrate to order that the defendant be detained because the available conditions for release will not provide satisfactory assurance against his potential flight or potential commission of an offense posing danger to the community. A significant percentage of defendants will fail to gain their release either because of preventive detention or an inability to meet financial conditions set by the court. In felony cases, that percentage may well reach one-third, with a much higher percentage for some felonies (e.g., murder) than for others (e.g., tax evasion). In misdemeanor cases, the percentage remaining in custody will be much lower, very often less than 10%.

(i) Step 9: Preliminary Hearing. Following the first appearance, the next scheduled step in a felony case ordinarily is the preliminary hearing. In many jurisdictions, however, a substantial portion of the felony caseload will be disposed of during the period (usually one or two weeks) between the first appearance and the scheduled preliminary examination. As mentioned previously, where the primary screening by the prosecutor occurs after charges are filed, a substantial number of felony charges are likely to be dismissed or reduced to a misdemeanor during this period. Even for those felony charges that remain, a preliminary hearing will not necessarily be held. The defendant ordinarily may waive his right to a preliminary hearing, and it is not unusual for a substantial percentage (e.g., 20–30%) to waive, usually because they intend to plead guilty. Also, even if the defendant desires a preliminary hearing, state law allows the prosecutor to bypass the hearing in a significant number of states. Indeed, prosecutors use this bypass authority so frequently in some jurisdictions that preliminary hearings are a rarity.

Where the preliminary hearing is held, it will provide, like grand jury review, a screening of the decision to charge by a neutral body. In the preliminary hearing, that neutral body is the magistrate, who must determine whether, on the evidence presented, there is probable cause to believe that defendant committed the crime charged. Ordinarily, the magistrate will already have determined that probable cause exists as part of the *ex parte* screening of the complaint (see step 7). The preliminary hearing, however, provides screening in an adversary proceeding in which both sides are represented by counsel. Jurisdictions vary in the evidentiary rules applicable to the preliminary hearing, but most require that the parties rely primarily on live witnesses rather than affidavits. Typically, the prosecution will present its key witnesses and the defense will limit its response to the cross-examination of those witnesses. The defendant has the right to present his own evidence at the hearing, but traditional defense strategy advises against subjecting defense witnesses to prosecution cross-examination in any pretrial proceeding.

If the magistrate concludes that the evidence presented establishes probable cause, he will "bind the case over" to the next stage in the proceedings. In an indictment jurisdiction (see step 10), the case is boundover to the grand jury, and in a jurisdiction that permits the direct filing of an information (see step 11), the case is boundover directly to the general trial court. If the magistrate finds that the probable cause supports only a misdemeanor charge, he will reject the felony charge and allow the prosecutor to substitute the lower charge, which will then be set for trial in the magistrate court. If the magistrate finds that the prosecution's evidence does not support any charge, he will order that the defendant be released. The rate of dismissals at the preliminary hearing quite naturally varies with the degree of previous screening exercised by the prosecutor. In a jurisdiction with fairly extensive screening, the percentage of dismissals is likely to fall in the range of 5–15% of the cases heard.

(j) Step 10: Grand Jury Review. Although all American jurisdictions still have provisions authorizing grand jury screening of felony charges, such screening is mandated only in those states requiring felony prosecutions to be instituted by an indictment, a charging instrument issued by the grand jury. In other states, the prosecution may proceed either by grand jury indictment or by information at its option. Slightly under half of the states currently require grand jury indictments for at least some classes of felony prosecutions. In several of these "indictment states," prosecution by indictment is required only for felonies subject to the most severe punishment (life imprisonment and capital punishment). In the remaining indictment jurisdictions, including the federal system, a grand jury indictment is required in all felony prosecutions (unless waived by the defendant). If there has been a preliminary hearing, the magistrate's decision at that hearing is not binding on the grand jury. It can reject prosecution notwithstanding a preliminary hearing bindover, or reinstitute prosecution even though the magistrate concluded that the prosecution's evidence was inadequate.

The grand jury is composed of a group of private citizens who are selected to review cases presented over a term that may range from one to several months. Traditionally the grand jury consisted of 23 persons with the favorable vote of a majority needed to indict. Today, many states use a somewhat smaller grand jury (e.g., 12) and some require more than a simple majority to indict. As in the case of the magistrate at the preliminary hearing, the primary function of the grand jury is to determine whether there is sufficient evidence to justify a trial on the charge sought by the prosecution. The grand jury, however, participates in a screening process quite different from the preliminary hearing. It meets in a closed session and hears only the evidence presented by the prosecution. The defendant has no right to offer his own evidence or to be present during grand jury proceedings. If a majority of the grand jurors conclude that the prosecution's evidence is sufficient, the grand jury will issue the indictment requested by the prosecutor. The indictment will set forth a brief description of the offense charged, and the grand jury's approval of that charge will be indicated by its designation of the indictment as a "true bill." If the grand jury majority refuses to approve a proposed indictment, the charges against the defendant will be dismissed. In most indictment jurisdictions, grand juries refuse to indict in only a small percentage (e.g., 3 to 8%) of the cases presented before them.

(k) Step 11: The Filing of the Indictment or Information. If an indictment is issued, it will be filed with the general trial court and will replace the complaint as the accusatory instrument in the case. Where grand jury review either is not required or has been waived in the particular case, an information may be filed with the trial court. Like the indictment, the information is a charging instrument which replaces the complaint, but it is issued by the prosecutor rather than the grand jury. Where state law does not require prosecution by indictment, the common practice of prosecutors is to choose the option of proceeding by information in the vast majority of their prosecutions. In most of these "information states," the charge in the information must be supported by a preliminary hearing bindover (unless the preliminary hearing was waived).

(*l*) Step 12: Arraignment on the Information or Indictment. After the indictment or information has been filed, the defendant is arraigned—i.e., he is brought before the trial court, informed of the charges against him, and asked to enter a plea of guilty, not guilty, or, as is permitted under some circumstances, *nolo contendere.* Most of the cases that reach the arraignment stage will not go to trial. Depending upon the quality of prearraignment screening, anywhere from 10–25% of the cases will be dismissed as a result of a *nolle prosequi* or a successful defense motion. A more substantial portion of the felony charges, typically 60–80%, will result in guilty pleas either to the offense charged or to a lesser charge. Thus, for those charges resolved on the merits (i.e., excluding dismissals), guilty pleas often account for 75–90% of the dispositions. There are a fair number of communities in which the ratio of guilty pleas to trials is somewhat lower (although a ratio below 2 to 1 is quite unusual). One factor that may have a substantial influence on plea rates is the extent to which the prosecutor is willing to plea bargain—i.e., grant concessions in return for a guilty plea. While the vast majority of prosecutors make substantial use of plea bargaining, they vary markedly both as to the type of cases in which they will grant major concessions and as to the nature of those concessions.

(m) Step 13: Pretrial Motions. In most jurisdictions, a broad range of objections must be raised by a pretrial motion. Those motions commonly present challenges to the institution of the prosecution (e.g., claims regarding the grand jury), attacks upon the sufficiency of the charging instrument, requests for discovery of the prosecution's evidence, and requests for the suppression of evidence allegedly obtained through a constitutional violation. While some pretrial motions are made only by defendants who intend to go to trial, other motions are advanced almost as frequently by defendants expecting to plead guilty even if the motion succeeds. Nevertheless, pretrial motions are likely to be made in no more than 10% of all felony cases that reach the trial court. In misdemeanor cases, pretrial motions may be made in less than one percent of the cases before the magistrate court. The use of pretrial motions varies, of course, with the nature of the case. In narcotics cases, for example, motions to suppress are quite common. In the typical forgery case, on the other hand, pretrial motions of any type are quite rare.

As a group, pretrial motions are likely to result in the dismissal of not more than 5% of all of the felony cases before the trial judge (and they are likely to have even less impact on the misdemeanor docket). The pretrial motion most likely to produce a dismissal is the motion to suppress. Quite frequently, if the defendant gains suppression of unconstitutionally obtained evidence, there will be insufficient remaining evidence to continue with the prosecution.

(n) Step 14: The Trial. As noted previously, most felony and misdemeanor cases are likely to be disposed of either by a guilty plea or by a dismissal. Quite commonly, only 5–15% of the felony cases that reach the trial court actually will go to trial. Misdemeanor cases tend to have an even lower trial rate. Magistrate courts often have trials in well under 5% of the cases presented before them. Most trials will not be lengthy affairs. Misdemeanor trials typically last less than one day. Felony trials may take somewhat more time, particularly when tried to a jury, but most will be completed within two full days.

In all jurisdictions, the defendant will have a right to a jury trial for all felony offenses and for misdemeanors punishable by more than 6 months imprisonment (although the jury trial right in the misdemeanor cases may exist only through a trial de novo). Most states also provide a jury trial for lesser misdemeanors as well. Juries traditionally were composed of 12 persons, but many states now utilize 6 person juries in misdemeanor cases and several use the smaller juries in noncapital felony cases as well. Of course, the right to a jury trial can be waived, and in most jurisdictions, a significant number of defendants will waive the jury in favor of a bench trial. Over the country as a whole, however, roughly 70% of all felony trials are tried to a jury. In misdemeanor cases, in contrast, bench trials often are in the majority even in jurisdictions that extend the defendant's jury trial right to all misdemeanors. In all but a few jurisdictions, the jury verdict in misdemeanor and felony cases, whether for acquittal or conviction, must be unanimous. Where the jurors cannot agree, no verdict is entered and the case may be retried. Such "hung juries" occur in a small percentage of cases (e.g., 3–6%).

The criminal trial resembles the civil trial in many respects. There are, however, several distinguishing features that are either unique to criminal trials or of special importance in such trials. These include (1) the presumption of defendant's innocence, (2) the requirement of proof beyond a reasonable doubt, (3) the right of the defendant not to take the stand, (4) the exclusion of evidence obtained by the state in an illegal manner, and (5) the more frequent use of incriminating statements of defendants. In most jurisdictions, the misdemeanor trial will be almost indistinguishable from a felony trial. In some jurisdictions, however, misdemeanor trials tend to be less formal, with rules of evidence applied in a rather loose fashion.

Whether a criminal case is tried to the bench or to a jury, the odds favor conviction over acquittal. The acquittal rate for felonies generally does not exceed one-third. At the misdemeanor level, the rate of acquittals often is somewhat lower. A substantial variation exists, however, among the different types of crimes. Acquittal rates for rape and robbery tend to be considerably higher, for example, than acquittal rates for forgery or assault. Where the offense is one that is not likely to produce either an offender caught "red-handed," more than one eyewitness, or contraband discovered in the defendant's possession, the acquittal rate for the offense is likely to be higher than the average for offenses generally.

***(o)* Step 15: Sentencing.** Following conviction, the next step in the process is the imposition of a sentence by the judge. Basically three different types of sentences may be used: financial sanctions (e.g., fines, restitution orders); some form of release into the community (e.g., probation, unsupervised release, house arrest); and incarceration in a jail (for lesser sentences) or prison (for longer sentences). The process applied in determining the sentence is shaped in considerable part by the sentencing options made available to the judge by the legislature. For a particular offense, the judge may have no choice. The legislature may have prescribed that conviction automatically carries with it a certain sentence and there is nothing left for the judge to do except impose that sentence. Most frequently, however, legislative narrowing of options on a particular offense does not go beyond eliminating the community release option (by requiring incarceration) and setting some limits on the use of those sanctions that remain available.

The sentence of incarceration for a felony offense probably presents the widest diversity of approach to judicial sentencing authority. In states utilizing indeterminate sentences, the sentencing structure calls for a maximum and minimum term of imprisonment, with the parole board determining the actual release date within the span set by those two terms. The legislature always sets the outer limit for the maximum term, but beyond that point, division of sentencing authority between the judge and the legislature varies with the jurisdiction and the offense. Possibilities include judicial authority to set both terms, judicial authority to set only the minimum (with the maximum and sometimes a mandatory minimum prescribed by law), and judicial authority to set only a maximum within the prescribed outer-limit (with the minimum then set by law as certain percentage of the judicially set maximum). In some jurisdictions, the judge has complete discretion in setting the term or terms within his control. In others, however, guidelines direct the judge in exercising his authority, although departures from the guidelines are allowed upon a judicial finding of specific justification. Where jurisdictions utilize determinate sentencing, the sentencing structure calls for a single fixed term of imprisonment and there is no earlier release through parole. Here too, the judge may be given broad discretion in setting the term or may be subject to a guideline system. Still other jurisdictions utilize a presumptive-determinate sentencing scheme under which the determinate sentence is to be set within a narrow range prescribed by the legislature for the particular crime unless the judge finds present certain aggravating or mitigating factors that carry with them additions to or deductions from the presumed range.

The process utilized in felony sentencing varies to some extent according to whether judicial discretion is broad or is channeled or limited by guideline or legislative reference to specific sentencing circumstances. In all jurisdictions, the process is designed to obtain for the court information beyond that which will have come to its attention in the course of trial or in the acceptance of a guilty plea. The primary vehicle here is the presentence report prepared by the probation department, although the prosecution and defense commonly will be allowed to present additional information and to challenge the information contained in the presentence report. The presentation of this information is not subject to the rules governing the presentation of information at trial. The rules of evidence do not apply, and neither the prosecution nor the defense has a right to call witnesses or to cross-examine the sources of adverse information presented in the presentence report or in any additional documentation presented by the opposing side. However, where the sentencing authority of the judge is restricted by guidelines or presumptive sentencing provisions that require findings of fact as to specific factors, the sentencing process tends to be more formal. Here, the court often will find it necessary to hold an evidentiary hearing and utilize trial-type procedures if the presence of a critical factor is controverted.

Sentences that are not automatically mandated, at least as to felony convictions and the misdemeanor convictions that started out as felony charges, will be geared to a wide range of factors in addition to the basic elements of the crime of conviction. In choosing among allowable alternatives, the judge may consider, and often under guidelines will be required to consider, such factors as aggravating and mitigating circumstances relating to the particular offense, past criminal convictions, criminal behavior that did not result in a conviction, and the defendant's acceptance of responsibility. The end result is that it became very difficult without close analysis of individual cases to compare sentences even where convictions were for the same offense. Nonetheless, some general patterns emerge by reference to the level of the offense for which the sentence is imposed. As to misdemeanor convictions, at least where they do not reflect a negotiated plea reduction from a felony charge, the vast majority of sentenced defendants will be sentenced to a fine and/or some form of community release. Lower level felony convictions and plea-reduced misdemeanor convictions more commonly result in a sentence of incarceration (often to a short jail term), although a substantial proportion of such offenders (e.g., 40%) are likely to be sentenced only to probation. Convictions for higher level felonies typically produce sentences of incarceration in prison. While the terms will vary by offense and sentence structure, an illustrative mean for the offenses of robbery and aggravated assault, measured by time actually served, would be in the neighborhood of 30–40 months. Substantially longer terms will be imposed, however, where the defendant is proceeded against as a recidivist. On the other side, even for offenses such as robbery and aggravated assault, alternatives to lengthy terms of imprisonment, such as short jail terms or probation, will be used in a substantial percentage of cases (e.g., 20%).[7]

(p) Step 16: Appeals. In felony cases, initial appeals will be taken to the intermediate appellate court or to the state supreme court if there is no intermediate appellate court. Initial appeals in misdemeanor cases will be taken to the general trial court, and in some

7. The decrease in numbers, even at this level of offense, between those convicted and those incarcerated, further reflects what has been described as the "funnel shape" or "sieve effect" of the criminal justice process: as the process moves through each of its stages, and as to the burden imposed upon the individual increases, the process is used more sparingly. At each stage an increased justification is needed for imposing the additional burden, and fewer persons are brought to that stage and subjected to its burdens. Thus, fewer persons are arrested than subjected to investigation, fewer charged than arrested, fewer brought to adjudication than initially charged, fewer convicted than adjudicated, and fewer incarcerated than convicted.

jurisdictions will consist of a trial *de novo*. Although all convicted defendants are entitled to appeal their convictions, appeals are taken predominantly by those defendants who were sentenced to imprisonment. Imprisoned defendants convicted pursuant to a guilty plea may challenge their pleas on appeal, but such challenges are made in only a very small portion of all plea cases and account for just a narrow slice of all appeals. The vast majority of the appeals will come from imprisoned defendants who are seeking review of a trial conviction. In some jurisdictions, as many as 90% of the defendants who were convicted after trial and sentenced to prison will appeal their convictions. Even with almost automatic appeal by this group, however, the total number of appeals still is not likely to exceed 15% of all felony convictions. Where the jurisdiction provides for appellate review of sentencing (as where a sentencing judge departs from a sentencing guideline), that percentage may be slightly higher. At the misdemeanor level, on the other hand, the appeals rate will be substantially lower.

The rate of reversals on appeal varies with the particular appellate court, but tends to fall within the range of 10–20% of the cases heard. In many jurisdictions, the most common objection raised on appeal is the trial court's admission of evidence obtained through an allegedly unconstitutional search. That objection also provides the most common basis for reversal. Other grounds raised quite frequently (but with much less success) are the insufficiency of the evidence, the incompetency of counsel, constitutional violations in identification procedures, and challenges to the admission of defendant's incriminating statements made to the police.

(q) Step 17: Postconviction Remedies. After the appellate process is exhausted, imprisoned defendants may be able to use postconviction remedies to challenge their convictions on limited grounds. In particular, federal postconviction remedies allow state as well as federal prisoners to challenge their convictions in the federal courts on certain constitutional grounds. The federal district courts receive roughly 9,000 such postconviction applications each year. Relief is granted on less than 4 percent of these petitions, however, and the relief often is limited to requiring a further hearing. In the state systems, postconviction remedies are used far less frequently.

§ 1.5 The Laws Regulating the Process

A diverse body of laws governs the various procedures noted in the previous section. Specific legal requirements will be discussed in later chapters. Our objective here is merely to provide an introduction to the different regulatory roles played by the different types of laws that establish those requirements.

(a) Varied Sources. The legal standards governing the criminal justice process ordinarily are provided by several different sources. In a state criminal prosecution, for example, the applicable legal standards are provided by (1) the United States Constitution, (2) the state constitution, (3) state statutes, (4) state court rules, and (5) common law decisions adopted by state courts.[1] Of course, not every step in the process is regulated by standards contained in each of these sources. For some steps, the applicable standards come primarily from one or two sources. The filing of the information or indictment, for example, tends to be governed primarily by state court rules and state statutes. Nevertheless in researching the law applicable to a particular procedure, all sources must be checked, since it is entirely possible that, in the particular

§ 1.5

1. Federal legislation also controls certain limited aspects of state proceedings, primarily through congressional regulation of state and federal investigative practices that have a direct bearing on certain agencies of interstate commerce. See, e.g., the electronic surveillance provisions of the Omnibus Crime Control and Safe Streets Act of 1968, discussed in § 4.2.

jurisdiction, all may contribute to the overall regulation of that procedure.[2]

(b) Interplay of the Federal Constitution and State Law. The natural starting point in examining the law governing a particular procedure is the federal constitution. Under Article VI, the mandates of the federal constitution are the "Supreme Law of the Land" and prevail over any contrary state law. The overall range of federal constitutional regulation of state criminal procedure is discussed in Chapter 2. For the purpose of this overview, it is sufficient to note that the degree of constitutional regulation varies considerably with the particular procedure. For some procedures, such as searches and seizures, federal constitutional regulation is quite extensive. For others, however, most of the major legal controls come from local law. The state grand jury's screening of the decision to charge in felony cases is illustrative. The federal constitution is concerned primarily with the selection of the grand jurors, requiring that the state not discriminate on racial or other arbitrary grounds. Whether a defendant may insist upon grand jury screening, the type of evidence the grand jury may consider, the scope of judicial review of grand jury proceedings, and various other matters relating to grand jury procedures are all governed by state law.

Though state law tends to play its most substantial role in areas lightly regulated by the federal constitution, it also has a quite significant role in many areas extensively regulated by the federal constitution. Even where most extensive, constitutional regulation is likely to leave significant gaps to be filled by state laws that build upon constitutional standards. For example, constitutional rulings provide the basic requirements for the issuance of search warrants, but they do not treat such subjects as the display of the warrant and the issuance of receipts for items seized by the police. Such matters commonly are governed by state law, usually either by state statute or court rule. More significantly, state law also may regulate precisely the same procedures as the federal constitution and impose more rigorous regulations. While Article VI bars a state from authorizing a practice prohibited by the federal constitution, a state may add its own prohibitions above and beyond those found in the federal constitution. Indeed, in almost every area of constitutional regulation, at least one state has imposed a limitation upon governmental action somewhat more restrictive than that imposed by the federal constitution, and in some areas, most states have followed that path. The federal constitutional right to a jury trial, for example, applies only to non-petty offenses, but most states grant defendants a right to a jury trial for petty as well as non-petty offenses.

(c) Sources of State Law. Among the several sources of state law, the state constitutions have tended to play the least significant role in the regulation of the criminal justice process. State courts generally have held that the state guarantees do not impose more rigorous limitations, but are simply identical in scope to similar federal provisions. On occasion, however, state courts, finding fault with what they view as unduly narrow interpretations of the federal constitution by the United States Supreme Court, have adopted a broader interpretation of a similar state guarantee. As discussed in § 2.10, in recent years, there has been a decided trend in this direction, resulting in an expanded role of state constitutional guarantees.

In most states, for most subjects, statutory provisions are the dominant source of state law regulating the criminal justice process. Most relevant statutory provisions are found in a state's Code of Criminal Procedure, although certain subjects having a bearing on both civil and criminal cases (e.g., jury selection) are likely to be covered elsewhere in the state's statutes and in limited areas local ordi-

2. While this section focuses primarily on state prosecutions, the discussion is also applicable, with slight variations, to federal prosecutions. For most of the discussion of the different types of state laws regulating state prosecutions, one can readily substitute their federal counterparts in describing the regulation of federal prosecutions—i.e., federal statutes, court rules, and common law decisions of federal courts.

nances may apply interstitially. Prior to the 1960's, many of the state criminal procedure codes consisted merely of an accumulation of separately adopted provisions, with many of those provisions dating back to the turn of the century. As a result, the codes were spotty in coverage, and their provisions occasionally were inconsistent in approach, if not directly in conflict. Over the last few decades, however, more than one-third of the states have adopted new codes that are carefully integrated and comprehensive in coverage. The new codes commonly contain provisions relating to almost every stage of the criminal justice process, starting with arrest and ending with postconviction review.

In over two-thirds of the states, the codes are supplemented by Rules of Criminal Procedure, adopted by the highest state court. Court rules commonly deal with such subjects as the timing of motions, the form of pleadings, the scope of pretrial discovery, and the entry of guilty pleas. In those states where codes were old and not very comprehensive, court rules often were expanded to cover subjects treated by statute in other jurisdictions, such as prompt trial requirements, the granting of bail, and the structure of the grand jury. Today, court rules may continue to treat such subjects notwithstanding the adoption of new codes. Where state constitutions recognize the independent authority of the state's highest court to adopt court rules, those rules will prevail over contrary state legislation provided they fall within the scope of the constitutional delegation of authority (typically, to make rules governing "practice and procedure"). In many jurisdictions, however, the state constitution limits court rules to subjects not governed by statute or expressly provides that the legislature can repeal or change court rules. Also, in other states, the rule-making power of the courts is based upon legislative authorization rather than a state constitutional provision.

Prior to the adoption of extensive codes and court rules, a substantial portion of the state law governing criminal procedure came directly from the common law rulings of state courts. Today, most state judicial decisions are likely to involve interpretations of state constitutions, statutes, or court rules, but common law rulings still have considerable significance. Earlier common law rulings often must be considered in determining the meaning of subsequently adopted statutes or court rules, since many of the code provisions and court rules are based on those rulings. Also, in certain areas of criminal procedure, state law continues to be developed primarily through rulings based on the common law authority of the courts. Thus, the admissibility of evidence still is governed largely by common law rulings in most states, notwithstanding the recent codification movement spurred by the Federal Rules of Evidence.[3]

3. Appellate courts also may impose procedural requirements in the exercise of their supervisory power over the administration of criminal justice in the lower courts. Although such standards are issued as part of the judicial decisionmaking process, they may be viewed as distinct from common law rulings because they are not based on precedent, but on the court's authority to provide for "sound judicial administration."

Perhaps the most extensive use of this supervisory authority is found in the federal court system, where the authority is exercised not only by appellate courts but also by district courts. Federal courts have adopted a wide variety of standards governing federal criminal procedure in the exercise of what the Supreme Court has described as their "supervisory authority over the administration of criminal justice in the federal courts." McNabb v. United States, 318 U.S. 332, 63 S.Ct. 608, 87 L.Ed. 819 (1943). Leading Supreme Court decisions governing the scope of that authority include McNabb v. United States (discussed in § 6.3 at note 1); Mallory v. United States (discussed in § 6.3 at note 3); United States v. Payner (discussed at § 9.2 at note 9); United States v. Hasting (discussed in § 15.6 at note 14); and Bank of Nova Scotia v. United States (discussed in § 15.6 at note 3).

A case describing a clearly permissible use of that authority is Thomas v. Arn, 474 U.S. 140, 106 S.Ct. 466, 89 L.Ed.2d 435 (1985) (supervisory authority permits a federal court of appeals to adopt a rule conditioning appeal from a district court decision adopting a magistrate's recommendation upon the timely filing of objections to the magistrate's report prior to the district court ruling). However, as evidenced by the rulings in *Payner, Hasting,* and *Bank of Nova Scotia,* not all uses of the supervisory authority are so readily sustainable. The most controversial uses of the supervisory authority involve either (1) the adoption of standards that go beyond constitutional minimums in an effort to provide clear-cut and easily administered prohibitions applicable to federal trial courts or prosecutors or (2) the adoption of broader remedies than are constitutionally or statutorily mandated in order to more effectively deter violations of constitutional or statutory prohibitions by federal officials.

The discussion above deals only with state law that specifies standards for the process as such. Other sources add standards directed at the performance of those who administer the process. Thus, police agencies may adopt internal regulations directing officers to follow certain procedures in making an arrest, structuring an identification procedure, or conducting a particular type of search. Similarly, a prosecutor's office may adopt guidelines specifying the standards to be applied by assistant prosecutors in making a variety of prosecutorial decisions. Also, both prosecutors and defense attorneys will be subject to a code of ethics adopted by the particular jurisdiction in regulating the legal profession, and the judiciary will be subject to a similar code applicable to judges.[4] Such regulatory standards are designed only as guidelines for evaluating performance within the internal operations of the particular agency or the internal regulation of the profession. Violation of the standards may result in sanctions such as reprimand, discharge, or loss of a professional license, but they do not give to the defendant any rights that can be enforced in the course of the criminal proceeding against him. Thus, the preamble to what is certainly the most extensive set of regulatory standards for prosecutors, the United States Attorneys' Manual, notes that the standards set forth there provide "only internal Department of Justice guidance" and "[do] not create any rights, substantive or procedural, enforceable at law by any party in any manner civil or criminal." Courts traditionally have accepted such disclaimers and have rejected the contention that a defendant is entitled to relief solely because such an internal standard of performance has been violated. At the same time, however, they often have been influenced by those internal standards in fashioning the content of common law and even constitutional rules that regulate the process. For that reason, as well as the influence of internal guidelines in shaping performance, an examination of the laws bearing on a particular step in the process should always go beyond the usual sources of state law and consider also the content of any relevant internal regulatory standards.

§ 1.6 Basic Goals of the Process

Notwithstanding variations among jurisdictions in their laws regulating the criminal justice process, basic similarities are found in the structure of the process as to all jurisdictions. Those similarities result from a common theoretical framework, derived in large part from the English common law, that established the primary tenets of the American criminal justice process. The starting point for the construction of that theoretical framework is the central mission of the process, but that mission serves only to set the stage for the choices that reveal the varied goals of the process.

Although a system of legal process may serve other ends as well, its basic reason for being is to promote the objectives of the substantive law by providing the procedures necessary to achieve the effective application of that law. The criminal justice process is no exception in this regard, as it provides the procedures through which the substantive

The use of the supervisory power in such cases often raises significant issues (i) as to the invasion of executive branch powers (in regulating prosecutors) and (ii) as to the relationship between federal statutory standards or court rules and the discretion vested in the trial and appellate courts. The Supreme Court has stressed that a federal court may not invoke its supervisory power to circumvent statutory standards, see e.g., *Bank of Nova Scotia,* supra, but it is not always clear when the imposition of a broader restriction or the adoption of a broader remedy operates to "circumvent" a statutory command rather than to "supplement" such command.

4. With the single exception of California, the state regulatory provisions governing the professional conduct of lawyers are modeled on one or the other of two products of the American Bar Association—the Model Code of Professional Responsibility (1969) and the Model Rules of Professional Conduct (1983). While the Rules were designed to supersede the Code, a substantial minority of the states have so far stayed with the Code. Variations also exist among different states using the same model. Among the group of roughly 35 states that have adopted the Rules, close to half have made substantial modifications, often retaining certain standards found in the Code. Also, with respect to both the Code and the Rules, subsequent amendments adopted by the A.B.A. have not always been added by the states that adopted the original version. State regulatory codes governing the judiciary tend to be modeled in large part on the A.B.A. Code of Judicial Conduct (1972).

criminal law can be enforced—that is, the procedures through which the government can detect, apprehend, convict, and sentence those who have committed crimes. However, as illustrated by the variety of criminal justice systems throughout the world, a process may be shaped in various ways to achieve that degree of enforcement necessary to serve the ends of the substantive law.[1] Precisely how the process is to be shaped will depend upon a selection among diverse structural goals that can be seen as furthering effective enforcement. It also will depend upon whether and to what extent the system seeks to serve other goals that are inconsistent with the full enforcement of the criminal law.[2]

In the subsections that follow, we briefly describe those goals of both types that have come to have the most significance in shaping the process in American jurisdictions.[3] While the fundamental tenets of such goals are widely shared, disagreement exists both as to the precise scope of particular goals and as to how the goals should be balanced against one another. Such disagreements explain in part the differences among state laws as well as divisions within the Supreme Court over the meaning of federal constitutional provisions that relate to criminal procedure. Those differences and divisions will be discussed in later chapters. At this point, we will focus only on the general character of the goals, leaving for later discussion their precise reach and their precise relationship to each other.

(a) Discovery of the Truth. The discovery of the truth is an essential goal of any criminal justice process that is to serve the ends of the substantive criminal law through the effective enforcement of that law. From the perspective of a criminal law aimed at ensuring that offenders receive their "just deserts," the process ideally should identify all of those who are guilty while, at the same time, avoid the mistaken imposition of punishment upon any who are innocent. From a perspective that focuses on crime prevention, less than complete accuracy is more readily accepted, but a reliable system for discovery of the truth is still essential. If that system is so unreliable as to frequently allow the guilty to escape liability, it will lose much of its potential for crime control through deterrence, incapacitation, and rehabilitation. If it has a tendency to be over-inclusive, holding

§ 1.6

1. How effective that enforcement must be depends, in part, upon how one views the aims of the substantive criminal law. If the criminal law is viewed as directed primarily at ensuring that offenders receive their "just deserts," then the process ideally should ensure that all offenders are subjected to the sanctions provided by the criminal law. If the substantive criminal law is viewed as directed primarily at crime control, then the process arguably need not be quite as efficient. Preventing crime may be seen as dependent initially upon factors extending beyond the enforcement of the criminal law in itself, and insofar as criminal law enforcement supplements those factors, through deterrence, incapacitation, and rehabilitation, it arguably can have a sufficient impact without gaining the conviction of all offenders. Yet, a substantive criminal law aimed at crime control still requires a substantial degree of successful enforcement, both to achieve that measure of crime control that comes from the impact of enforcement upon those offenders who are convicted and to ensure that enforcement will have an educational and deterrent impact upon others.

2. Such goals, as discussed in subsection (a), deflect or make more difficult the discovery of the truth, and therefore more difficult the task of detecting, apprehending, and convicting offenders. Indeed, in individual cases, they may effectively preclude the punishment of the guilty. Accordingly, they commonly are characterized as reflecting process objectives that exist independent of, and that often take priority over, the achievement of the ends of the substantive law through its enforcement. Others contend, however, that a long range instrumentalist perspective of such goals shows their consistency with those ends. They see such goals as giving to the process a sense of dignity and decency that reinforces the moral content of the substantive criminal law and thereby encourages citizen cooperation in its enforcement. That consequence, in turn, is thought to be far more important in the achieving of the ends of the criminal law than the immediate impact of frustrating the enforcement of the criminal law in particular cases.

3. The initial starting point for the structuring of the process was the English common law system, which was brought over to the American colonies and adopted in the original states and in the federal system. However, the particulars of the English process were then reshaped to fit the needs of the particular jurisdiction (although the basic goals reflected in the English common law were largely retained). In some instances, procedures were introduced that appeared to borrow from the legal systems of the other countries that also produced early settlers. More frequently, some strictly American inventions were added. The end result is a structure that is similar in some respects to that found in England and other common law countries, but is unique in its combination of procedures.

liable also people who are actually innocent, it will be weakened in its deterrent impact and wasteful in its utilization of incapacitation and rehabilitation.

Effective discovery of the truth requires a process that can both uncover wrongdoing and determine with reliability the identity of the offender. Initially, the investigatory elements of the process must be capable of allowing police to readily identify possible sources of relevant information and evidence and must give the police the authority to obtain such information and evidence when these sources are not cooperative. The law governing the investigatory process authorizes a broad range of procedures that serve these ends. These include the allowable use, subject to certain limitations, of the authority to search persons and property, to require suspects to participate in identification procedures, to utilize informers and undercover agents, and to ask questions of witnesses and suspects. It also grants even broader investigative authority to the grand jury, operating with the prosecutor as its legal advisor.

Discovery of the truth also requires an adjudicatory process that is reliable both in the conviction of the guilty defendant and the exoneration of the defendant who is erroneously accused. Many aspects of the legal regulation of the trial look to ensuring such reliability in adjudication. Included here are the adversary structure of the trial, prohibitions against certain actions of the adversaries that would deceive fact-finders, evidentiary rules that promote the production of reliable evidence, legal standards designed to eliminate jurors and judges who are likely to be biased either in favor of the state or the defendant, and restrictions upon the scope of a single trial so as to preclude a mixing of issues that could confuse the factfinder. Various pretrial procedures, such as the allowable discovery of the opponent's evidence, are aimed at supplementing the capacity of the trial to produce a reliable verdict. Certain legal restrictions imposed upon adjudication through guilty plea also serve, in part, to ensure the reliability of convictions produced by the process.

While the discovery of the truth is a major goal of the criminal justice process, there exists other goals that clearly are truth-deflecting. Here we have such goals as respecting the value of human dignity, discussed infra in subsection (g). Legal standards seeking to further these truth-deflecting goals both restrict the state's ability to uncover the truth through the investigatory process and render the adjudicatory process less reliable (usually detracting from its capacity to ensure the conviction of the guilty rather than its capacity to ensure the acquittal of the innocent). At the investigatory stage, legal standards implementing such goals restrict the government's ability to obtain reliable incriminatory evidence. At the trial stage, they both preclude the prosecution's use of certain reliable incriminatory evidence that it has obtained and place upon the prosecution greater obligations in establishing guilt.

Precisely where the balance should lie between the truth-deflecting goals of the process and the truth-seeking objective of the process is a matter of continuing debate. That issue underlies much of the current controversy relating to the appropriate scope of various legal rights granted the defendant. It also lies at the core of the debate over the desirability of incorporating within the process new legal standards that would either grant to the state additional investigative authority or place further limitations upon its existing authority. Very often, as indicated in many of our descriptions of leading cases, the courts speak directly to this issue; but even where there is no overt recognition of the need to discover the truth or to further goals that clearly restrict the truth-finding capacity of the process, the question of balance remains as the critical consideration in explaining the current shaping of the law.

Still another factor sometimes balanced against the truth-seeking goal of the process, although usually not with such open recognition, is the limitations of available administrative resources. As noted in § 1.3(a), in most jurisdictions, those charged with administering the process operate under the pressures of heavy caseloads. In part those pressures are accommodated by broad grants of discretion that allow law enforcement officials to focus their efforts on offenders and offenses whose prosecution will most readily serve the ends of the substantive criminal law. However, the structure of the adjudicating process may also be shaped by the need to respond to caseload pressures. Thus, some courts have recognized that those pressures have played a significant role in shaping the law governing such subjects as plea bargaining, the joint trial of offenders, and the provision of appointed counsel for indigent offenders—arguably at some cost to the reliability of the adjudicatory process.

(b) Establishing an Adversary System of Adjudication. The advancement of an adversary system of adjudication clearly ranks among the most significant goals of the American criminal justice process. Though this goal relates primarily to the trial, it also shapes many pretrial proceedings, particularly those that are aimed at trial preparation (e.g., discovery) or themselves involve adjudication (e.g., the preliminary hearing). An adversary system of adjudication vests decision-making authority, both as to law and fact, in a neutral decisionmaker who is to render a decision in light of the materials presented by the adversary parties. In an adversary criminal proceeding, there often will be two such neutral decisionmakers, the jury (as to factual issues) and the judge (as to legal issues); the adversary parties, of course, are the prosecution and the defense.[4] The decisionmaker in a pure adversary system operates as a generally silent referee, determining the case as it is presented, and leaving it very much to the parties to choose the battleground. The adversary model gives to the parties the responsibility of investigating the facts, interviewing possible witnesses, consulting possible experts, and determining what will or will not be told. Each party is expected to present the facts and interpret the law in the light most favorable to its side, and through a searching counter-argument and cross-examination, to challenge the soundness of the presentations made by the other side. The judge and jury are then to adjudicate impartially the issues posed by the conflicting presentations of the parties.

The American criminal justice process actually seeks a "modified" or "regulated" adversary system as opposed to the "pure" adversary model described above. It does not provide for a totally silent or inactive judge, and it does not allow the parties to shape the case entirely on their own. These restrictions stem, in part, from other goals of the process that would be substantially undercut by an adversary system in its purest form. Even with these restrictions, however, the American criminal justice process remains sufficiently adversarial in its overall character to stand in sharp contrast to the largely inquisitorial system of adjudication found in continental Europe.[5] Under the European system,

4. Although the English used a system of private prosecution, with the complainant bringing the prosecution through his privately retained counsel, by the advent of the American Revolution, the concept of crime as a wrong committed against the state (rather than simply an action injurious to the individual victim) was firmly established in this county, and the state was well on its way to achieving complete control over the prosecution of crime. Although some vestiges of the colonial system of private prosecution remained (and, indeed, continue to exist today in certain jurisdictions, see § 13.3(b)), the state, through the prosecutor, had a monopoly over the presentation of case against the accused. The victim's role was simply that of a potential witness, and his or her participation was dependent upon the decision of the prosecutor. In recent years, however, although the prosecution remains the sole advocate for the state, legislation has been adopted in many jurisdictions to ensure that the defendant has some input at certain points in the process. See §§ 13.3, 26.5(d). That movement has not been carried so far, however, as to significantly alter the status of the prosecutor as the basic adversary opposing the defense.

5. The term "inquisitorial" is used rather loosely in American legal commentary. Some commentators use it to describe a procedure founded on producing forced confessions, often through torture, as illustrated by the Star Chamber and the Spanish Inquisition. See Watts v. Indiana, 338 U.S. 49, 69 S.Ct. 1347, 93 L.Ed. 1801 (1949) (Frankfurter, J., concurring). Others use it to describe a system that shifts the burden of proof to the defendant and forces him to establish his innocence, or that allows the state through judicial process to obtain evidence from the accused. Cf. Note 10 infra. More commonly, the term "inquisitorial" is used, as we use it here, to denote a system in which a judicial authority, rather than the parties, has the basic responsibility for eliciting the relevant facts. The characterization of modern continental systems as "inquisitorial" rests largely on the presence of that judicial responsibility.

the primary responsibility for development of all relevant facts lies first with a magistrate, and then with the trial judge. Although the prosecutor and defense counsel are given an opportunity to contribute, particularly at trial, their role is far more limited than the role of counsel in the American process.

The adversary system was received in this country as part of the English common law. Why the English developed an adversary system of adjudication, as opposed to an inquisitorial system, remains a matter of considerable speculation. Some commentators suggest that the adversary system was an outgrowth of theological concepts, previously reflected in the practices of compurgation and trial by battle, that have long since been rejected. Whether or not that is the case,[6] the adversary system has today come to be supported on quite different grounds. It is thought to constitute, from a utilitarian viewpoint, the system of adjudication most likely to produce accurate verdicts. It also is favored as a system that respects individual autonomy and reflects the proper relationship between the individual and the state.

The superiority of the adversary process in producing accurate verdicts rests on two premises. First, it is argued that the adversaries will uncover more facts and transmit more useful information to the decisionmaker than would be developed by the judicial officer bearing that responsibility in an inquisitorial system. The self-interests of the parties will ensure that all relevant evidence is produced and that the strengths and weaknesses of the evidence are fully explored. Second, it is argued that the adversary system avoids the kind of decisionmaker bias likely to be found in inquisitorial proceedings. Because the decisionmaker in the adversary system is not himself involved in the development of the facts, he is more likely to approach the evidence at trial in an uncommitted fashion and delay reaching a decision until the case is fully explored.

Critics of the adversary system are especially dubious of the proposition that partisan advocacy by prosecution and defense will best assure the discovery of all relevant information. Many contend that, left to serve their own interests, the adversaries often will resort to tactics of gamesmanship that debase the truth-finding function. They will suppress and distort evidence, utilize surprise to ambush their opponent, and cajole and intimidate witnesses. The end result, the critics claim, is a battle of wits and guile, designed to mislead the decisionmaker rather than to lead him to the truth. Still other critics claim that the adversary system rests on the unrealistic proposition that the advocates will be roughly equal in ability. They note, in particular, that the prosecution has, in the police, an investigative agency far superior to anything which even the wealthiest defendant can employ.

Though it has strongly supported the adversary system, the American criminal justice process has not ignored these criticisms. In response to the first criticism, it has fashioned various rules designed to prohibit those partisan tactics that are aimed at misleading the decisionmakers, particularly the more vulnerable jury. In response to the second criticism, it has granted the defense various rights designed to ensure that it is as able as the prosecution to present its best case.[7] Indeed,

6. The development of the adversary system also has been attributed to other aspects of English procedure, particularly trial by jury and the practice of private prosecution. Other commentators suggest that the English adversary process was shaped in large part by the same philosophy of competition and individualism that was reflected in the free enterprise system. Much as fierce individualistic economic competition was thought to produce better and cheaper goods, the presentation of conflicting viewpoints by partisan advocates was thought the most effective means for ascertaining the truth.

7. As the adversary system is seen as a superior method of discovering the truth, the focus of this effort should be on ensuring that the defense has the tools necessary to produce the truth, and not on seeking to give the defense an equal chance of "winning" without regard to the truth. As commentators and courts have noted, the adversary process should not be viewed as promoting essentially a "sporting contest" in which the two sides are to be evenly matched and "forensic skills," rather than the truth, are to determine the outcome. Insofar as the defense is given certain procedural rights that go beyond what is necessary to allow it to present all favorable evidence and to challenge the reliability of the prosecution's evidence, those procedural advantages must be justified by goals that exist independent of the adver-

the system has been taken beyond that point to cast the prosecutor in a role that "differs from that of the usual advocate; his duty is to seek justice, not merely to convict." Whether such efforts have been successful in meeting the criticisms of the adversary system or, indeed, whether the efforts have gone too far and undermined the strength of the adversary system, remain issues of continuing debate. As will be seen, this debate underlies many of the most controversial legal questions considered in subsequent chapters.

Apart from its alleged superiority in producing accurate decisions, the adversary process also is valued for what it says about the status of the defendant as an individual. Consistent with the premise that the individual is the source of the government's sovereignty, the adversary system treats the defendant as an equal to the prosecution. As Thurmond Arnold has noted: "When a great government treats the lowliest of criminals as an equal antagonist, strips itself of the executive power which it possesses, and submits the case to 12 ordinary men, allowing the judge only the authority of an umpire, we have a gesture of recognition to the dignity of the individual which has an extraordinary dramatic appeal." [8] The adversary system also is said to reflect a commitment to the individual's self-control over the "basic mode of his participation in the adjudicatory process." The defendant plays an active role in his own defense. Indeed, if he so desires, he may decide to forego his defense and plead guilty.

The importance of achieving an adversary system of adjudication is reflected in a wide range of legal standards governing the criminal justice process. The structuring of an adversary system underlies many of the guarantees of the Bill of Rights, such as the Sixth Amendment rights of the defendant to the assistance of counsel, to confront opposing witnesses, and to compulsory process for obtaining witnesses in his favor. Statutory provisions dealing with such subjects as the notice function of charging instruments and the impartiality of factfinders also are concerned with the implementation of the adversary system. So too are many restrictions imposed under common law judicial precedents, such as limitations upon counsels' closing arguments and upon the court's comments in charging the jury. Most of the laws relating to the adversary system deal with trial procedures, as the trial is the centerpiece of the system. However, the needs of an adversary system also are reflected in laws governing pretrial preparation, adversary screening procedures, and even in laws governing police acquisition of evidence.[9]

(c) Establishing an Accusatorial System. The American criminal justice process is designed to be accusatorial as well as adversary. The concepts of adversary adjudication and accusatorial procedure complement each other, but they are not virtual equivalents. The

sary process, such as those discussed infra in subsections (c) and (g).

8. T. Arnold, Symbols of Government 145 (1935). Some argue that the adversary process similarly responds to a basic distrust of public officials by limiting the role of the judge.

9. Thus, Francis Allen, examining several Supreme Court decisions granting the assistance of counsel to defendants subjected to various police investigative procedures, concluded that those decisions were reflections of the Court's "enthusiasm for adversary proceedings." What the Court had sought to do here, Professor Allen noted, was "to extend * * * the adversary process into areas of the system in which, theretofore, adversary proceedings were unknown." Allen, The Judicial Quest for Penal Justice: The Warren Court and Criminal Cases, 1975 Ill.L.F. 518, 530. Characterizing the state's authority to obtain evidence from a suspect who is not assisted by counsel, the Supreme Court has noted: "Our system of justice is, and always has been, an inquisitorial one at the investigative stage (even the grand jury is an inquisitorial body) * * *." McNeil v. Wisconsin, ___ U.S. ___, 111 S.Ct. 2204, 115 L.Ed.2d 158 (1991).

In recent years, commentators have spoken of a "decline" in the adversary system resulting from the disposition of the vast majority of all cases by guilty pleas and by prosecutor dismissals, rather than by trials. Whether or not these alternative dispositions are more common today than in earlier periods is debatable. There is considerable evidence suggesting that trials have been the exception, rather than the general rule, for at least the major part of this century. In any event, less frequent use of the trial does not detract from the significance of the adversary system as it bears upon various aspects of pretrial proceedings, including the negotiation of guilty pleas. See also Arnold, supra note 5, at 128–48 (noting the symbolic significance of the trial, notwithstanding the more common use of alternative modes of disposition).

adversary element of the criminal process assigns to the participants the responsibility for developing the legal and factual issues of the case, while the accusatorial element assigns responsibility as between the parties with respect to the persuasion of the decisionmaker on the ultimate issue of guilt. An accusatorial procedure requires the government to bear the burden of establishing the guilt of the accused, rather than the accused to bear the burden of establishing his innocence. As the Supreme Court has noted, an accusatorial system requires the "government in its contest with the individual to shoulder the entire load." The prosecution must produce sufficient evidence to convince the trier of fact of the accused's guilt, and it must do so "by evidence independently and freely secured," without compelling the accused to assist in this prosecution responsibility.[10]

England's adoption of an accusatorial system probably grew out of the early English view of the criminal prosecution as a means of providing personal redress, with the person claiming to be the injured party having to personally establish his right to redress. The accusatorial system is justified today, however, on grounds consistent with the subsequent recognition of crimes as public wrongs, with prosecutions brought by the state on behalf of the community as a whole. Foremost among these is the view that criminal sanctions are so severe that special care must be taken to ensure they are not imposed upon innocent persons. Also involved is a distrust of governmental authority, based on a recognition that public officials may seek to invoke the criminal justice machinery to serve their own ends, rather than to protect the public. Some argue that the accusatory process also seeks to respond to a governmental capacity to gather and preserve evidence that far exceeds the capacity of the defendant. Under this view, the requirement that the government bear the burden of proof, utilizing its own resources, is designed to redress the "advantage" that inheres in a governmental prosecution due to the government's superior investigative resources and greater public support.

The accusatorial nature of the criminal justice process is seen in various elements of the process. It is reflected not only in the allocation of the burden of persuasion, but also in such concepts as the presumption of innocence and the privilege against self-incrimination. The allocation of the ultimate burden of persuasion to the prosecution is, of course, the primary ingredient of an accusatorial system. It gives the accused the right to remain inactive and secure until the prosecution has taken up its burden and produced a case sufficient to carry the case to the jury. If the prosecution fails in its case-in-chief to establish a prima facie case for conviction, the defense is entitled to a directed acquittal without the necessity of ever producing its own evidence. The presumption of innocence, while often characterized as a mere restatement of the allocation of the burden of persuasion, conveys a special admonition that also strengthens the accusatorial nature of the process. When the jury is informed of the presumption, it is told, in effect, to judge an accused's guilt or innocence solely on the evidence adduced at trial and not on the basis of suspicions that may arise from the fact of his arrest, indictment, or custody. Finally, the privilege against self-incrimination serves that prong of the accusatory process that forces the government not only to establish its case, but to do so by its own resources. It prohibits the state from easing its burden of proof by simply calling the defendant as its

10. Murphy v. Waterfront Commission, 378 U.S. 52, 84 S.Ct. 1594, 12 L.Ed.2d 678 (1964); Tehan v. United States ex rel. Shott, 382 U.S. 406, 86 S.Ct. 459, 15 L.Ed.2d 453 (1966). The prohibition here, it should be noted, is against compelling the accused to assist, not against using the accused as a source of evidence. Thus, an accusatorial system will prohibit the state from forcing the defendant to make incriminatory statements, but will not bar the government from granting the defendant an opportunity voluntarily to make such statements or even from encouraging him to do so in certain ways. Nor will it bar taking physical evidence from him by search and seizure. This authority has been characterized by some commentators as similar to that possessed by the judge in an inquisitorial system and therefore reflecting an inquisitorial aspect of the American process that has coexisted with its accusatorial tradition.

witness and forcing him to make the prosecution's case.

(d) Minimizing Erroneous Convictions. While the accusatory and adversary elements of the criminal justice process are designed in part to minimize the likelihood of erroneous convictions, protection of the innocent accused against an erroneous conviction is an important independent goal of the process. Indeed, many would argue that it is the goal of highest priority. Where a conflict exists between protecting the innocent and other goals, it is the protection of the innocent that almost always prevails.

Although the goal of minimizing erroneous convictions is closely tied to the truthfinding function of the process, it extends substantially beyond that function. Reliable factfinding, as a goal in itself, would seek to ensure equally the accuracy of both guilty verdicts and acquittals. Protection of the innocent, however, places greater priority on the accuracy of the guilty verdict. It reflects a desire to minimize the chance of convicting an innocent person even at the price of increasing the chance that a guilty person may escape conviction. Thus, while the Supreme Court has stated that "the basic purpose of the trial is the determination of the truth," it also has noted that impairment of the trial's "truthfinding function" is of primary concern where "serious questions [are raised] about the accuracy of guilty verdicts." [11] For, as the Court also has observed, it is "a fundamental value determination of our system that it is far worse to convict an innocent person than let a guilty man go free." [12]

The goal of minimizing the risk of an erroneous conviction is served by two somewhat different sets of legal standards. Initially, it is advanced, in part, by the various rules designed to ensure factfinding accuracy. While most such standards apply with equal force to preclude an erroneous finding of guilt or innocence, others are more extensive in their protection against an erroneous conviction of the innocent. Thus, though the law seeks generally to preclude delay in adjudication that might result in the loss of evidence (as witnesses become unavailable or their memories fade), the defendant is given the special benefit of a constitutional right to a speedy trial.

Protection against erroneous convictions also is provided by legal standards that accord to the defendant the benefit of all factual doubts. The most substantial protection of this type is provided by requirements relating to the burden of proof. The prosecution is not only required to bear the burden of proof, but to do so in accordance with the high evidentiary standard of establishing guilt beyond a reasonable doubt. The requirement of a unanimous jury verdict, imposed in most jurisdictions, reinforces the protection of these proof standards. The defendant is given the benefit of factual doubts in a somewhat less direct fashion by other legal standards, such as those affording absolute finality to acquittals while allowing for subsequent challenges to convictions.

(e) Minimizing the Burdens of Accusation and Litigation. Even though eventually acquitted, an innocent person charged with a crime suffers substantial burdens. The accusation casts a doubt on the person's reputation that is not easily erased. Frequently, the public remembers the accusation and still suspects guilt even after an acquittal. Moreover, even where an acquittal is accepted by the public as fully vindicating the accused, that does not remedy other costs suffered in the course of gaining that verdict. The period spent by the accused awaiting trial commonly is filled with a substantial degree of anxiety and insecurity that disrupts the daily flow of his life. That disruption is, of course, even greater if he is incarcerated pending trial. The accused also must bear the expense and ordeal of the litigation process itself.

In light of these substantial burdens, a criminal justice process concerned with the protection of the innocent cannot limit itself

11. Tehan v. United States ex rel. Shott, supra note 10; Williams v. United States, 401 U.S. 646, 91 S.Ct. 1148, 28 L.Ed.2d 388 (1971).

12. In re Winship, 397 U.S. 358, 90 S.Ct. 1068, 25 L.Ed.2d 368 (1970).

to avoiding erroneous convictions. It must seek also to reduce to an acceptable level the risk of accusations being brought against innocent persons. Since the burdens of an accusation are not as great as the burdens of a conviction, the acceptable degree of risk of an erroneous accusation can be somewhat greater than the risk of an erroneous conviction. It is not necessary to limit the bringing of accusations to cases in which conviction is almost certain, and thereby to forego many cases in which valid convictions might eventually be obtained. Adequate protection against erroneous accusations does require, however, that accusations at least be supported by sufficient evidence to produce a substantial likelihood of conviction.

Of course, in limiting the number of erroneous accusations, the system does not solve the problem of the accused who is appropriately charged, based on substantial evidence, but is eventually acquitted at trial (and therefore must be viewed as quite possibly innocent). Some defendants will inevitably fall in this category. No matter how careful the screening, predicting the outcome of litigation is too uncertain to avoid mistakes. While the system cannot avoid imposing some litigation burdens on properly accused defendants who will eventually be acquitted, it can seek to minimize their burdens, insofar as that is consistent with preserving a practicable system of adjudication. However, since the defendants who will fall in this category cannot be identified at the outset, to assist these defendants, the system must minimize litigation burdens for all defendants, including the many who will eventually be found guilty.

The goal of minimizing the risk of erroneous accusations is achieved primarily through the various screening procedures of the criminal justice process. Initially, the police officer is prohibited from taking a person into custody for the purpose of charging him with a crime (i.e., arresting the person) without probable cause to believe he is guilty. Moreover, the officer's probable cause determination is subject to ex parte screening by a magistrate, either in the issuance of a warrant prior to arrest or in the subsequent review of a warrantless arrest. In most jurisdictions, felony charges are subject to further review by the magistrate at a preliminary hearing, an adversary screening procedure. In many jurisdictions, as an alternative or additional felony screening procedure, the grand jury will review the prosecution's evidence to determine whether it is sufficient to justify the proposed indictment.

The additional goal of eliminating unnecessary litigation burdens is reflected in various other rights of the accused. Provisions for pretrial release on bail seek to avoid pretrial incarceration where there is an alternative means of reasonably assuring defendant's presence at trial. The defendant's right to a speedy trial is designed, in part, to limit the length of pretrial incarceration (where bail is not available) and to minimize the anxiety and concern of the accused pending trial. Venue requirements seek, in part, to ensure that the defendant will be tried in a convenient forum. The double jeopardy prohibition, supplemented by joinder requirements, also seeks to reduce the burdens of litigation by restricting the use of multiple trials for closely related offenses.

(f) Providing Lay Participation. Another basic goal of the criminal justice process is to provide for the participation of laymen as decisionmakers in the process. Traditionally, lay participation was provided through the trial jury, the grand jury, and the use of lay magistrates. Today, the trial jury stands alone as the only generally available source of lay participation in many jurisdictions. While approximately 40 states have some non-lawyer magistrates, the vast majority of cases in those states are processed by magistrates who are lawyers. Also, over one-half of the states no longer make regular use of the grand jury even in felony cases.

Lay participation in the criminal justice process is designed to serve several different functions, but those functions all rest, to some extent, on a single value judgment—that the administration of the criminal justice process is too important a matter to be left exclusively in the hands of government officials. Lay jurors have an independence from the government bureaucracy not found in judges or prosecutors. Along with this independence, lay petit jurors and grand jurors offer further advantages as factfinders simply because they are selected from a cross-section of the community. Their participation as community representatives is viewed as lending a special sense of "legitimacy" to the criminal justice process, making unpopular decisions more readily acceptable to the public. Indeed, as community representatives, the jurors may refuse to convict (or charge, in the case of the grand jury) where they conclude that, notwithstanding an obvious violation, enforcement of the letter of the law would result in a clear miscarriage of justice. The cross-section selection process is also credited with giving lay jurors certain advantages over professional decisionmakers in making more accurate factfinding decisions.

(g) Respecting the Dignity of the Individual. The criminal justice process also is designed to provide a system of administration that is consistent with respect for the dignity of the individual. The concept of human dignity, as used in this context, is far from precise, but it may be described roughly as encompassing the basic needs of the human personality, including privacy, autonomy, and freedom from humiliation and abuse. Requiring that criminal justice practices respect human dignity is justified on several grounds. First, it is argued that all persons in a democratic society, including criminals, are entitled to their personal dignity. Second, it is contended that the methods used in crime control reflect the basic political ideology of the society, and the failure to respect the dignity of the individual in the criminal justice process will soon carry over to other aspects of government regulation. Finally, ensuring respect for individual dignity is viewed as essential in obtaining public acceptance of the process and in promoting respect for the law it enforces. "Misuse of the machinery of criminal justice," Justice Frankfurter once noted, "may undermine the safety of the State" itself.[13]

The insistence of the criminal justice process upon respect for individual dignity is reflected in various legal requirements of the process. Many of the legal standards that implement other goals serve this goal as well. Thus, requirements designed to promote an adversary system of adjudication recognize the dignity of the individual by giving the defendant an element of control over his own defense. Similarly, the privilege against self-incrimination, while an essential element of an accusatorial system, also has been described as based on "our respect for the inviolability of the human personality." Still other legal requirements focus entirely on ensuring respect for human dignity. Thus, the prohibition against cruel and unusual punishment bars punishments which lower the honor and dignity of the individual. The Fourth Amendment prohibition against unreasonable searches and seizures guarantees respect for the privacy of the individual, although it does permit government officials to invade that privacy upon a showing of probable cause. Numerous common law standards, such as that bestowing privileged status upon marital communications, also recognize the essential needs of the human personality.

Perhaps more so than with any other goal, the goal of respecting human dignity often comes into conflict with the truth-finding goal of the process. In large part, that conflict arises where application of human dignity principles will result in denying the factfinder probative evidence pointing towards guilt, although potentially exculpatory evidence also will be kept from the factfinder in rare instances. Probative evidence may be kept from the factfinder through restrictions that relate to both the acquisition and the use of evidence. As a result of prohibitions designed to ensure respect for human dignity, such as the Fourth Amendment prohibition against searches without probable cause, the govern-

13. Pennekamp v. Florida, 328 U.S. 331, 66 S.Ct. 1029, 90 L.Ed. 1295 (1946) (concurring opinion). See also Jackson, J., dissenting in Shaughnessy v. United States ex rel. Mezei, 345 U.S. 206, 73 S.Ct. 625, 97 L.Ed. 956 (1953): "Due process of law is not for the sole benefit of an accused. It is the best insurance for the Government itself against those blunders which leave lasting stains on a system of justice."

ment is kept from engaging in practices that might well produce reliable, incriminatory evidence. Moreover, when those prohibitions are violated and otherwise valid evidence is obtained through such violations, that evidence ordinarily will be excluded from the trial because of the illegality involved in its acquisition. The end result may be that a guilty person will go free, but the process accepts that sacrifice in efficiency as a cost of preserving respect for human dignity. It recognizes that preservation of social order and domestic tranquility require not only freedom from crime, but also freedom from an overreaching government.

(h) Maintaining the Appearance of Fairness. The criminal justice process seeks not only to provide fair procedures, but also to maintain the appearance of fairness in the application of those procedures. As the Supreme Court once noted, "justice must satisfy the appearance of justice."[14] That the criminal justice procedures are fair, in fact, is not sufficient; the procedures also must be perceived as fair (and as fairly administered) by both the public and the participants.

The appearance of fairness is essential to the effectiveness of the process. Initially, it is a vital element in maintaining public confidence in the process. Because three of the primary administrators of the process—judge, prosecutor, and defense counsel—are all members of the same profession, there may be a tendency on the part of those outside the profession to view the process with some suspicion. That suspicion can be offset by ensuring that the application of the process is open to public view and the bases for its decisions are part of the public record. These same factors also may be helpful in reconciling the losing defendant to his fate. Even though he may disagree with the result, he knows who made the decision and how it was achieved. Finally, the appearance of fairness, as it relates to the trial stage in particular, is necessary to fulfill what commentators have characterized as the "symbolic function" of the trial. That function is described as providing a "series of object lessons and examples" through which "society is trained in right ways of thought and action, not by compulsion, but by parables which it interprets and follows voluntarily."

Legal standards aimed primarily at maintaining a positive perception of the criminal justice process include those guaranteeing the openness of the process and those prohibiting practices that suggest possible bias. In the former category are the constitutional and statutory standards that guarantee public access to the trial and to such pretrial proceedings as the preliminary hearing. Openness is also provided by statutes allowing public inspection of documents and records relating to an even broader range of proceedings. Legal standards aimed at eliminating any suggestion of bias include several that rely on the mere possibility of prejudice (rather than proof of actual prejudice) to grant relief. One such standard, for example, requires automatic reversal of a conviction where a judge had a possible financial or personal interest in his rulings, without inquiry as to whether that interest actually produced a biased decision. At times, the process' interest in ensuring an appearance of fairness will prevail even over the defendant's desire to forego a particular procedural right. Thus, some jurisdictions insist that the defendant be present at trial even though he would prefer to be tried in absentia, with only his lawyer present.

(i) Achieving Equality in the Application of the Process. In a society dedicated to achieving "equal justice under law," it is only natural that another goal of the criminal justice process is to achieve equality in the administration of the process. The concern here is primarily that each jurisdiction be evenhanded in its treatment of defendants. This does not mean that procedures must be applied in the same way to all defendants, but simply that like defendants must be treated alike. In other words, distinctions drawn between defendants must be based on grounds that are properly related to the functions of the process.

14. Offutt v. United States, 348 U.S. 11, 75 S.Ct. 11, 99 L.Ed. 11 (1954).

What constitutes a proper basis for disparate treatment of defendants will vary with what is being decided. In determining whether to press charges, for example, a prosecutor could rationally draw distinctions based on a variety of factors (such as differences in the defendants' past records) that would have no rational bearing in a determination as to which defendants will receive six-person rather than twelve-person juries. As a result, there are some areas (primarily those relating to discretionary authority) in which considerable discrimination among defendants is to be expected, and others in which discrimination will rarely be tolerated. In addition, there are certain factors, such as race and religion, that are viewed as improper grounds for discrimination in every aspect of the process. To a large extent, indigency falls in this category, although the state's obligation to the indigent falls short of providing him with precisely the same assistance that might be available to a non-indigent defendant.

A wide range of laws serve to prohibit improper discrimination, with most limited in scope to discrimination in a specific problem area. The primary general provision barring discrimination is the Fourteenth Amendment's equal protection clause. Other constitutional guarantees, such as the Sixth Amendment's counsel and jury provisions, have been read to bar certain types of discrimination in that aspect of the process covered by the particular guarantee. Statutory provisions often extend beyond these constitutional guarantees in seeking to reduce the discriminatory impact of the process. Thus statutory provisions reduce the discriminatory impact upon indigent defendants both by providing them with assistance beyond that constitutionally required and by reducing reliance upon procedures (e.g., money bail) less likely to be available to the poor. The recent movement to limit judicial discretion in sentencing similarly reflects, in part, an interest in reducing a type of discrimination (that based upon differences in the sentencing philosophies of individual judges) that is not barred by the Fourteenth Amendment.

(j) The Coalescence of Goals. While some of the legal standards that shape the criminal justice process serve to implement only one particular process goal, many serve two or more goals. The privilege against self-incrimination provides an apt illustration of the coalescence of several goals within a single procedural right. In describing the values served by the privilege, the Supreme Court, in *Murphy v. Waterfront Commission,*[15] referred to values relating to the advancement of an accusatorial process, the minimization of erroneous convictions, the minimization of erroneous accusations, and the protection of the dignity of the individual. Cases interpreting the privilege against self-incrimination have continuously referred to this combination of interests in determining the scope of the privilege. As these cases illustrate, the identification of the full range of goals served by a particular right is often crucial, since the combination of goals often may require that the right be given much broader scope than any single goal.

15. Supra note 10.

Chapter 2

THE CONSTITUTIONALIZATION OF CRIMINAL PROCEDURE

Table of Sections

---

§ 2.1 The Elements of Constitutionalization

During the 1960's, when Supreme Court rulings were rapidly extending the reach of the Bill of Rights' provisions applicable to the criminal justice process, some commentators predicted that constitutional regulation of the process eventually would become so extensive as to produce, in effect, a constitutional code of criminal procedure. That prediction has not materialized, and from today's perspective, seems unlikely to do so in the future. The development of a body of constitutional standards as comprehensive in its coverage and as detailed in its requirements as the typical statutory code of criminal procedure would require substantial modification of current doctrines, especially as to areas of coverage. For, while many steps in the process have indeed become subject to constitutional standards so extensive and intricate that they rival even the Internal Revenue Code, many other steps are barely touched by constitutional controls. Here, the law of the particular jurisdiction provides such regulation (sometimes extensive and sometimes quite sparse) as is applicable.

The failure of constitutional regulation to completely dominate the criminal justice process should not lead one to depreciate the significance and uniqueness of that regulation. Looking at the process as a whole, constitutional standards combine to constitute what is surely the most important single body of law governing the process. It also is undisputed that in no other nation has so large and intricate a corpus of law relating to criminal justice emerged from constitutional interpretation.

One need only survey the various provisions of the Constitution to recognize the potential significance of constitutional law in the regulation of the criminal justice process. No aspect of the federal government, apart from its basic organization, receives more attention in the Constitution than the administration of the criminal law. As originally proposed, without the Bill of Rights, the Constitution had only a few provisions that related to the criminal process. However, ratification was made contingent on the adoption of the Bill of Rights, a series of ten Amendments designed to ensure that the federal government did not overstep its authority and deny the rights of individuals. Of the 24 separate rights specified in the first eight of those amendments, thirteen are aimed specifically at the criminal justice process. The Fourth Amendment guarantees the right of the people to be secure against unreasonable searches and seizures, and prohibits the issuance of warrants unless certain conditions are met. The Fifth Amendment requires prosecution by grand jury indictment for all infamous crimes (except certain military prosecutions), and prohibits placing a person "twice in jeopardy" or compelling him to be a "witness against himself." The Sixth Amendment lists several rights applicable "in all criminal prosecutions"—the rights to a speedy and public trial, to a trial by an impartial jury of the state and district in which the crime was committed, to notice of the "nature and cause of the accusation," to confrontation of opposing witnesses, to compulsory process for obtaining favorable witnesses, and to the assistance of counsel. The Eighth Amendment adds prohibitions against excessive bail or fines and against cruel and unusual punishment. Finally, aside from these guarantees directed specifically to the enforcement of the criminal law, the Fifth Amendment subjects the criminal justice process, along with other legal processes, to its general prohibition against the deprivation of "life, liberty, or property" without "due process of law."

While the inclusion of these guarantees in the Bill of Rights created a potential for extensive constitutional regulation of the nation's criminal justice processes, two important doctrinal developments were required before that potential could be realized. First, those guarantees had to be made applicable in large part to state proceedings. Although federal criminal jurisdiction has been expanding over the years, roughly 99% of all criminal prosecutions still are brought in the state systems. For the Constitution to have a major impact, its major provisions had to be held applicable to state as well as federal proceedings. This occurred through the Court's rulings under the Fourteenth Amendment—although it was not until the 1960's, almost 100 years after that Amendment's adoption, that the Court finally concluded that the Amendment made applicable to the states most of those Bill of Rights guarantees relating to criminal procedure.

Extensive constitutional regulation of the criminal justice process was also dependent upon the Supreme Court's adoption of expansive interpretations of the individual guarantees. The Bill of Rights guarantees are not, of course, self-defining. Their impact depends in large part upon choices that must be made in determining their reach. Interpreted narrowly, the guarantees would have a minimal effect on the process; they would govern only a small portion of the total process and impose restrictions of limited significance even as to those areas. Interpreted broadly, and supplemented by requirements designed to secure their implementation, the guarantees would have a significant impact on almost every aspect of the process. Over the past several decades, the Supreme Court has favored expansive interpretations of the Bill of Rights guarantees. This is not to say that the Court's rulings have necessarily adopted the broadest conceivable readings of individual guarantees, but the readings adopted clearly have been sufficiently broad to give substantial scope to the constitutional regulation of the process.

In this chapter, we will examine in some depth these two crucial developments in the constitutionalization of criminal procedure—the extension of the constitutional guarantees to state proceedings and the adoption of a preference for expansive interpretations of individual guarantees. The first development, discussed in §§ 2.2–2.6, is fairly well completed, but the echoes of the battles that led to its adoption are still heard in disagreements over the role that the "interests of federalism" should play in the formulation of constitutional standards. The second development, discussed in §§ 2.7–2.8, remains the subject of an ongoing debate among the justices, at least as what weight should be carried by a presumption favoring expansive interpretations. A third development that bears on the second, the limitation of the retroactive application of new, expansive rulings, is considered in § 2.9. Section 2.10 discusses still another related development—the "new federalism" movement that has produced numerous state court rulings adopting more expansive interpretations of state constitutional provisions than the Supreme Court has adopted of analogous federal constitutional provisions.

§ 2.2 The Fourteenth Amendment and the Extension of the Bill of Rights Guarantees to the States

Prior to adoption of the Fourteenth Amendment in 1868, *Barron v. Baltimore*[1] had firmly established that the Bill of Rights was intended to constrain only the newly established federal government. Since the language of only a few of the Amendments explicitly refer to branches of the federal government, it was not altogether surprising that the plaintiff in *Barron* maintained that the Fifth Amendment prohibition against the taking of property without just compensation applied to state as well as federal action. Rejecting that contention, Chief Justice Marshall noted that the Constitution had been established by the people of the United States "for their own government, and not for the government of the individual State. Each State established a constitution for itself and in that constitution, provided such limitations and restrictions in the powers of its particular

§ 2.2

1. 32 U.S. (7 Pet.) 243, 8 L.Ed. 672 (1833).

government, as its judgment dictated." In the few instances in which federal constitutional intervention in a state's treatment of its citizens was thought to be necessary, the Constitution had clearly indicated that purpose by explicitly stating that the particular provision applied to the states. Thus, Article I, Section 10 provided that "[n]o State shall * * * pass any Bill of Attainder, ex post facto law, or law impairing the Obligation of Contracts." Marshall reasoned: "Had Congress [which proposed the Amendments] engaged in the extraordinary occupation of improving the constitutions of the several states by affording the people additional protection from the exercise of power by their own governments in matters which concerned themselves alone, they would have declared this purpose in plain and intelligible language."

The framers of the Fourteenth Amendment, the 39th Congress, clearly sought to engage in that "extraordinary occupation" described by Marshall in *Barron.* As in Article I, Section 10, the language of the Amendment clearly evidenced a goal of "affording the people additional protection from the exercise of power by their own governments." What was not so clear was exactly how far Congress intended to go in this regard, particularly in section one of the Amendment. That section provided:

> All persons born or naturalized in the United States, and subject to the jurisdiction thereof, are citizens of the United States and of the State wherein they reside. No State shall make or enforce any law which shall abridge the privileges or immunities of citizens of the United States; nor shall any State deprive any person of life, liberty, or property, without due process of law; nor deny to any person within its jurisdiction the equal protection of the laws.

The first sentence of section one obviously was designed to override the ruling in *Dred Scott v. Sanford.*[2] That infamous decision had held that a Negro, because his "ancestors were imported into this country, and sold as slaves," could not become a "citizen" within the meaning of the Constitution. In granting both national and state citizenship to all persons born in the United States, the first sentence of section one nullified *Dred Scott* and ensured that both the recently freed and previously freed blacks would thereafter be "citizens" under the Constitution.

Once section one moved beyond the granting of citizenship, its precise objectives became less clear. The second sentence evidenced a purpose of protecting the freed blacks—and other persons who might be the subject of discrimination—from abuses of state power; but the limitations the second sentence sought to impose upon state action were couched in terms—such as "equal protection" and "due process"—that were open to varying interpretations. In the years since the adoption of the Fourteenth Amendment, a substantial part of the Supreme Court's workload has been devoted to defining and redefining those terms. One of the more troublesome issues has been determining the extent to which the prohibitions of section one encompass the guarantees found in the Bill of Rights—that is, the extent to which the Fourteenth Amendment imposes upon the states the same prohibitions that are imposed upon the federal government by the Bill of Rights. Over the years, essentially three different positions have been advanced within the Court on this issue: (1) the "total incorporation" position, advanced in numerous dissents, but never adopted by the Court majority; (2) the "fundamental fairness" position, consistently supported by a majority prior to 1960; and (3) the selective incorporation doctrine that has prevailed as the majority view since the mid–1960's. Not all of the justices supporting a particular position agreed on the precise scope of that position, and some commentators have suggested that four to six different positions actually were advanced.[3] For our

2. 60 U.S. (19 How.) 393, 15 L.Ed. 691 (1857).

3. The division between Justice Black and other supporters of total incorporation as to the scope of the due process clause led to the characterization of Justice Black's position as "total incorporation" and the position of the other supporters as "total incorporation plus." See § 2.3, at note 4. The position taken by those justices who would selectively incorporate most fundamental guaran-

purposes, however, it is best to focus on most basic divisions which create three major positions, with less substantial differences treated as variants of those positions.

Since the selective incorporation doctrine has clearly won the day, one might ask why we devote two full sections to the "defeated" positions of total incorporation and fundamental fairness. Initially, an understanding of each is needed to fully appreciate the selective incorporation position. The judicial debate between the supporters of the total incorporation and fundamental fairness positions undoubtedly had substantial influence on the much later articulation and eventual adoption of the selective incorporation doctrine. But more significantly, strains of that debate have current vitality. The concerns that were expressed by the judicial proponents of the fundamental fairness position are advanced today, in only slightly altered form, in discussions relating to the need to give consideration to system variations among different jurisdictions in fashioning a national standard under an incorporated Bill of Rights guarantee. So too, the criticism of the totality-of-the-circumstances approach of the fundamental fairness reappears today in discussions both of the standards to be adopted under particular guarantees and the use of the due process clause to bar state action apart from the application of an incorporated guarantee. Indeed, as will be seen in § 2.6(e), a basic strand of the fundamental fairness concept remains a viable and frequently used measure for regulating constitutionally both state and federal criminal procedure. Finally, an understanding of the historic pattern of the Court's decisions interpreting the Fourteenth Amendment as it relates to the Bill of Rights lends perspective to the developments discussed in § 2.7—the Court's adoption of a preference for expansive interpretations of those guarantees and the shifts in the emphasis given to that preference.

§ 2.3 Total Incorporation

The total incorporation doctrine holds that the Fourteenth Amendment incorporates all of the Bill of Rights guarantees and thereby applies those guarantees to the states in the same manner in which they are applied to the federal government. Although it never received majority support, this doctrine was the subject of significant debate in both Supreme Court opinions and legal commentaries. As a result, it was an exceptionally influential minority position, particularly in its contributions to the Court's eventual acceptance of the selective incorporation doctrine.

(a) The Rationale of Total Incorporation. The debate over the validity of the total incorporation doctrine has focused primarily on three issues: (1) whether the doctrine finds textual support in the language of the Fourteenth Amendment; (2) whether the legislative history of the Fourteenth Amendment suggests that one of its purposes was to make applicable to the states all of the guarantees found in the Bill of Rights; and (3) whether the practical impact of the doctrine works in favor or in opposition to adopting such an interpretation of the Amendment.

Critics of the total incorporation doctrine contend that the doctrine is negated by the very wording of the Fourteenth Amendment. Certainly, they argue, no support for the doctrine is found in the due process clause. As Justice Frankfurter noted in *Adamson v. California*,[1] if the 39th Congress intended to make applicable to the states all of the first eight amendments, it would hardly have done so by simply including a prohibition against the denial of due process. The guarantee of due process is itself only one of many guarantees found in the Bill of Rights, and therefore a most unlikely shorthand reference to all of the other guarantees as well. "It would be

tees, but only partially encompass others, see e.g., the description of Justice Fortas' position in § 2.6(a), has sometimes been described as "neo-incorporationist." The difference in the approach of the pre–1930's and post–1930's fundamental fairness rulings, particularly as to values protected by the Bill of Rights' specifics [see § 2.4(b), (c)], has led some commentators to also characterize those earlier and later rulings as establishing two different positions.

§ 2.3

1. 332 U.S. 46, 67 S.Ct. 1672, 91 L.Ed. 1903 (1947).

extraordinarily strange," Justice Frankfurter noted, "for a Constitution to convey such specific commands in such a round-about and inexplicit way."

Perhaps recognizing the deficiencies of relying upon the due process clause, Justice Black, a leading supporter of total incorporation, suggested that the doctrine looked to the historic purpose of the Fourteenth Amendment "as a whole," and to the language of the privileges and immunities clause in particular.[2] "What more precious 'privilege' of American citizenship could there be," he asked, "than the privilege to claim the protection of our great Bill of Rights?" "[W]ouldn't a prohibition against state abridgment of the 'privileges and immunities of citizens of the United States' " therefore be an "eminently reasonable way of expressing the idea that henceforth the Bill of Rights shall apply to the States?"

Critics of total incorporation respond that the privileges and immunities clause can be read to support total incorporation only if it is torn from its historical roots and read apart from the total language of the Fourteenth Amendment. They note that the "privileges and immunities of national citizenship" were understood at the time to include only those rights that arose out of the citizen's relationship to the federal government, such as his right to vote in a federal election. The privileges and immunities clause in Article IV (requiring that citizens of each state receive all of the "privileges and immunities" of other states) had been given a somewhat broader interpretation, but clearly not so broad as to include all of the guarantees included in the Bill of Rights. Moreover, the critics argue, even apart from the limited historical content of the privileges and immunities concept, the Fourteenth Amendment's inclusion of a due process clause suggests on its face that the privileges and immunities clause was hardly intended to incorporate the Bill of Rights. If the privileges and immunities clause had that purpose, why would the framers also have added a due process prohibition that itself was included within the incorporated first eight amendments? Finally, the critics ask, why incorporate the Bill of Rights in a provision that refers to the protection of citizens, as compared to a provision like the due process clause, which refers to "any person," and therefore protects aliens as well as citizens? Certainly, they argue, the framers would not have desired to grant such privileges as jury trial and grand jury indictment, as applied to state proceedings, only to citizens. If the framers intended to make the Bill of Rights applicable to the states, wouldn't they have done so in a way that extended those guarantees to all persons, just as they applied to all persons in federal proceedings?

Supporters of total incorporation contend that any such difficulties in the textual support for their position are more than offset by an historical record that clearly establishes that the framers did intend to make the Bill of Rights applicable to the states. As they read that record, the major congressional supporters of the Fourteenth Amendment were dissatisfied with state protection of individual liberties and intended through that Amendment "to nationalize civil liberties in the United States." Relying especially on the comments of Representative Bingham, a key draftsman of section one, and of Senator Howard, who presented the Amendment before the Senate, Justice Black argued that, "with full knowledge of the import of the *Barron* decision, the framers and backers of the Fourteenth Amendment proclaimed its purpose to be to overturn the constitutional rule that decision had announced."

Critics of this historical analysis contend that it gives far too much weight to the statements of only a few members of Congress. They note that section one of the Amendment was presented to both the Congress and the ratifying states as a measure designed basically to provide a constitutional foundation for the Civil Rights Act of 1866.[3] That Act ini-

2. Duncan v. Louisiana, 391 U.S. 145, 88 S.Ct. 1444, 20 L.Ed.2d 491 (1968) (Black, J., dissenting).

3. Act of April 19, 1966, C 31, § 1, 14 Stat. 27. See generally Jones v. Alfred H. Mayer Co., 392 U.S. 409, 88 S.Ct. 2186, 20 L.Ed.2d 1189 (1968). That this was viewed

tially declared all persons born in the United States to be citizens, and then provided that such citizens, without regard to race, would have the "same rights in every State" to contract, sue, hold and inherit property, and to enjoy the "full and equal benefits of all laws and proceedings for the security of person and property," as were "enjoyed by white citizens." In seeking to constitutionalize this prohibition against discrimination, the critics note, the framers had no need to make the Bill of Rights applicable to the states.

The primary discussion of the practical impact of the total incorporation doctrine, and its bearing on the adoption of the doctrine, is found in the opinions of Justices Black and Frankfurter in *Adamson.* Although relying primarily on his historical analysis, Justice Black also argued that adoption of the total incorporation position would remove the Court from the pitfalls of the fundamental fairness standard that the Court then employed in determining what rights of the individual were protected against state invasion by the due process clause of the Fourteenth Amendment. Justice Black viewed that due process standard as unacceptably vague and open-ended. He characterized it as a "natural law" concept that invited decisions based on the subjective, idiosyncratic views of individual justices. Total incorporation, he argued, would lead the Court back to the "clearly marked constitutional boundaries * * * of policies written into the Constitution." [4]

Responding to Justice Black, Justice Frankfurter took a quite different view of the practical consequences of total incorporation. Those "sensitive to the relation of the states to the central government as well as the relation of some of the Bill of Rights to the process of justice," could hardly insist upon state compliance with every aspect of the procedure constitutionally imposed upon the federal government. Some of the Bill of Rights requirements, he noted, "are enduring reflections of experience with human nature," but others simply "express the restricted views of Eighteenth Century England regarding the best methods for ascertainment of facts." Surely, he argued, "[t]o suggest that it is inconsistent with a truly free society to begin prosecution without an indictment, to try petty civil cases without the paraphernalia of a common law jury, to take into consideration that one who has full opportunity to make a defense remains silent, is, in de Tocqueville's phrase, 'to confound the familiar with the necessary.' "

Without doubt, Justice Frankfurter's illumination of the practical consequences of total incorporation—particularly the imposition of requirements that the states prosecute by

as the sole purpose of the second sentence of the Amendment—and not the incorporation of the Bill of Rights—is evident, the critics contend, from the ratification process. Thus, the states did not express concern that they might be providing to citizens through the second sentence rights which were not currently provided to any person—white or black—under state law. While state constitutions or statutes matched various Bill of Rights guarantees, they fell short of others. In particular, a substantial number of states fell below the requirements of either the Fifth Amendment as to prosecution by grand jury indictment or the Seventh Amendment as to the availability of jury trials in civil cases. Yet, those same states ratified the Amendment without any indication that they believed that their state procedures would have to be changed.

4. Justice Black's assumption that total incorporation would foreclose continued reliance on a fundamental fairness standard of due process obviously rested on more than a mere incorporation of the Bill of Rights under the Fourteenth Amendment. The Bill of Rights, after all, included a due process clause and that clause was repeated in the Fourteenth Amendment itself. While total incorporation would permit reliance upon the various other Bill of Rights provisions, it would still leave open the use of the due process clause for those cases that did not fit within those other provisions, and it would not, in itself, bar continued application of a fundamental fairness standard in such cases. To completely foreclose reliance upon this "natural law" concept, a different definition of due process also was needed. Justice Black had previously urged adoption of such a position, arguing that due process essentially required only an even-handed application of pre-existing law. See § 2.4, at note 1. It was this position that led Justice Murphy to write his separate *Adamson* dissent in which he expressed agreement with total incorporation, but noted that he was "not prepared to say" that the Fourteenth Amendment was "entirely and necessarily limited by the Bill of Rights." "Occasions may arise," he noted, "where a proceeding falls so far short of conforming to fundamental standards of procedure as to warrant constitutional condemnation in terms of a lack of due process despite the absence of a specific provision in the Bill of Rights." Justice Murphy's position is sometimes described as "total incorporation plus" to distinguish it from Justice Black's "total incorporation" position. See § 2.2, note 3.

indictment and provide jury trials in civil cases involving claims above twenty dollars—raised problems for the supporters of total incorporation. Justice Black responded that the Bill of Rights was not an "outworn 18th Century 'straight jacket,'" that the federal government had not been "harmfully burdened" by application of its guarantees and neither would the states be so burdened. Others, however, though favoring Justice Black's position, recognized that the practical difficulties might be greater than he suggested. For example, the federal government had avoided granting jury trials in minor civil cases by limiting the jurisdiction of federal courts to cases involving substantial monetary claims, but the states could not realistically follow the same approach. To provide jury trials in all cases involving more than twenty dollars might impose an intolerable strain on the already overburdened state courts. When the Court moved to selective incorporation in the 1960's, commentators immediately noted that the selective incorporation doctrine would enable the Court to impose upon the states most of the Bill of Rights guarantees without also including the troublesome grand jury and civil jury trial requirements.

(b) Rejection by the Court. Although the total incorporation doctrine was not squarely considered by the Supreme Court until the 1890's, it had already been foredoomed by the earlier ruling in the *Slaughter–House Cases,*[5] the Court's first decision interpreting the Fourteenth Amendment. *Slaughter–House* involved a challenge by a group of butchers to a Louisiana statute granting monopoly rights to a New Orleans slaughter-house. The butchers argued that the statute violated their right to carry on a trade, recognized in *Corfield v. Coryell*[6] as a privilege and immunity of state citizenship, and therefore was contrary to the privileges and immunities clause of the recently enacted Fourteenth Amendment. In a 5–4 decision, the Court rejected that claim. The majority relied substantially on the phrasing of the Fourteenth Amendment's two references to citizenship. In the first sentence, it was noted, the Amendment referred to both national and state citizenship. The second sentence, on the other hand, referred only to abridgment of the privileges and immunities of United States citizenship. The privileges and immunities of state citizenship, recognized in *Corfield,* were obviously intended to remain within the protection of Article IV and the states themselves. The Fourteenth Amendment sought to protect only the privileges and immunities of national citizenship. This interpretation, the Court noted, was consistent with "the whole theory of the relations of the state and federal governments to each other." To adopt the position urged by the plaintiffs would make the Court "a perpetual censor upon all legislation of the States."

Once the *Slaughter–House* majority limited the protected privileges to those of national citizenship, it followed that the Fourteenth Amendment would not be construed to require the states to recognize the guarantees found in the Bill of Rights. The *Slaughter–House* opinion cited as examples of privileges of national citizenship the right to travel from state to state, the claim of protection on the high seas, and the "privilege of the writ of habeas corpus." The privileges and immunities of national citizenship were confined, the Court noted, to that class of rights which "owe their existence to the federal government, its National character, its Constitution, or its laws." While the privileges of national citizenship encompassed rights created by the Constitution, those rights, including the rights found in the first eight Amendments, applied only to the citizen's dealings with the federal government. A state's refusal to provide similar rights in its own proceedings had no bearing upon national citizenship since it did not interfere with the citizen's relationship to the federal government. It was only when the state interfered with that relationship that it violated the privileges and immunities clause.

5. 83 U.S. (16 Wall.) 36, 21 L.Ed. 394 (1873).

6. 6 F.Cas. (No. 3230) 546 (C.C.E.D.Pa.1823).

During the early 1890's, three cases involving claims that the state had imposed cruel and unusual punishment squarely presented the total incorporation interpretation of the Fourteenth Amendment.[7] As might be expected, the Court rejected that interpretation as inconsistent with *Slaughter-House.* It reasoned that the privileges and immunities of national citizenship arose out of "the nature and essential character of the national government," and therefore could not encompass an immunity from state imposition of a punishment alleged to be cruel and unusual. In one of the cases, however, three justices dissented, advancing a total incorporation rationale. Without seeking to distinguish *Slaughter-House,* they argued that, since the Bill of Rights established privileges and immunities of citizens as to the federal government, "the Fourteenth Amendment, as to all such rights, place[d] a [similar] limit upon state power by ordaining that no State shall make or enforce any law which shall abridge them."[8]

Although the cruel and unusual punishment cases might have been thought to have settled the issue, total incorporation was debated again in the early 1900's. Over the dissents of the first Justice Harlan, the Court again reaffirmed the *Slaughter-House* view of the privileges of national citizenship and held that the Fourteenth Amendment did not require state adherence to the Bill of Rights guarantees. In the last of those cases, *Twining v. New Jersey,*[9] the majority recognized that the total incorporation position had "undoubtedly * * * [been] entertained by some of those who framed the Amendment," but concluded that it was "not profitable to examine the weighty arguments in its favor, for the question is no longer open in this court."

Following *Twining,* the total incorporation doctrine was not given serious attention in a Supreme Court opinion for almost forty years. Then, in 1947, four dissenting justices in *Adamson v. California*[10] suddenly resurrected the doctrine. Justice Black, in a lengthy dissent joined by Justice Douglas, argued that the Court should reexamine the history of the Fourteenth Amendment and adopt the selective incorporation doctrine. Justice Murphy, in a much shorter dissent, joined by Justice Rutledge, noted his agreement that "the specific guarantees of the Bill of Rights should be carried over intact into the first section of the Fourteenth Amendment." The majority, however, flatly rejected that view, noting that it was inconsistent with the long line of cases that had prevailed since *Slaughter-House.* Thus, almost eighty years after the adoption of the Fourteenth Amendment, the Court came within one vote of dramatically reshaping the Amendment's scope. In the years since, *Adamson* has been viewed by the justices as settling the total incorporation issue, notwithstanding the close vote in that case. Of course, there can be no guarantee that the question will not be reopened in the future, but that seems most unlikely, as the current application of the selective incorporation doctrine has achieved much the same result as total incorporation without disturbing either *Slaughter-House* or its derivative rulings.

§ 2.4 Fundamental Fairness

Unlike the total incorporation doctrine, the fundamental fairness doctrine rests solely on the due process clause. The doctrine has basically two prongs. First, it reads the due process clause as prohibiting state action that violates those rights of the individual that are deemed to be "fundamental." Over the years, the Court variously described the standard for determining whether a right is fundamental. Due process was said to require adherence to those rights that are "implicit in the concept of ordered liberty," that are "so rooted in the traditions and conscience of our people as to be ranked fundamental," and that "lie at the base of all our civil and political institutions." Due process also was described as prohibiting

7. In re Kemmler, 136 U.S. 436, 10 S.Ct. 930, 34 L.Ed. 519 (1890); McElvaine v. Brush, 142 U.S. 155, 12 S.Ct. 156, 35 L.Ed. 971 (1891); O'Neil v. Vermont, 144 U.S. 323, 12 S.Ct. 693, 36 L.Ed. 450 (1892).

8. Field, J., dissenting in O'Neil v. Vermont, supra note 7.

9. 211 U.S. 78, 29 S.Ct. 14, 53 L.Ed. 97 (1908).

10. Supra note 1.

those state actions that "offend those canons of decency and fairness which express the notions of justice of English-speaking peoples even toward those charged with the most heinous offenses," that are "repugnant to the conscience of mankind," or that deprive the defendant of "that fundamental fairness essential to the very concept of justice." Although these different phrasings arguably suggest some subtle variations in content, they generally were viewed as expressing a single standard, frequently described in shorthand form as the "ordered liberty" or "fundamental rights" standard.

The second prong of the fundamental fairness doctrine concerns the relationship between the ordered liberty standard and the guarantees found in the Bill of Rights. Simply put, it maintains that there is no necessary correlation between the protection afforded by the Bill of Rights and due process protection of fundamental rights. The concept of due process has "an independent potency" which exists apart from the Bill of Rights, although in a particular case it may afford protection that parallels a Bill of Rights guarantee. It was this second element of the fundamental fairness doctrine that led to the doctrine's eventual rejection. Accepted by the Supreme Court majority for almost one hundred years, the fundamental fairness doctrine was discarded in the 1960's, when the Court adopted, through selective incorporation, a quite different view of the relationship between the Bill of Rights guarantees and the ordered liberty standard of due process.

(a) The Rationale of Fundamental Fairness. The fundamental fairness doctrine proceeds from the premise that the Fourteenth Amendment's due process clause was designed to make applicable to the states the same basic limitation that had been imposed upon the federal government under the Fifth Amendment's due process clause. At the time of the adoption of the Fourteenth Amendment, there had been only a few Supreme Court decisions interpreting the Fifth Amendment's due process clause, but the basic nature of the clause was well established. The concept of due process dated back to the Magna Charta, and it had been discussed at length by both English and American commentators. These authorities were seen as having established in due process a flexible concept of justice that concentrated on the essence of fairness rather than the familiarity of form. Due process was "a concept less rigid and more fluid than those envisaged in other specific and particular provisions of the Bill of Rights." Justice Frankfurter described it as "perhaps, the least frozen concept in our law—the least confined to history and the most absorptive of powerful social standards of a progressive society." Its basic objective was to provide "respect enforced by law for that feeling of just treatment which has evolved through centuries of Anglo–American constitutional history and civilization." As such, it had a "natural law" background which extended beyond procedural fairness and imposed limits as well on the substance of state regulation.

Whether the due process clauses of the Fourteenth and Fifth Amendments actually were intended to have either the flexibility or the breadth provided by this "basic justice" concept of due process is open to debate. The use of due process to impose substantive limits upon legislation has been widely criticized as beyond the purpose of the two clauses. A few commentators have also argued that the procedural protections of due process were aimed largely at rights recognized by historical usage. The Supreme Court, however, has persistently and almost unanimously accepted that flexibility and breadth which is embodied in the ordered liberty standard, particularly as applied to procedural limitations. While there has been disagreement as to exactly how the ordered liberty standard should be applied, only Justice Black clearly rejected the use of that standard in determining procedural protections. Justice Black maintained that due process required only an even-handed application of those procedures previously established by law in the particular jurisdiction. Looking to the language of the Magna Charta, which required adherence to the "law of the land," Justice Black read the due process clause as recognizing only a "right to be tried by independent and unprejudiced courts using established procedures and applying valid pre-existing laws." [1] Although the Court recognized that even-handed administration of pre-existing procedures was an element of ordered liberty, it also consistently rejected Justice Black's contention that due process should require no more than regular adherence to the "law of the land."

Proponents of the fundamental fairness position contend that, once one accepts the flexible concept of due process embodied in the ordered liberty standard, it logically follows that the content of due process will have no necessary ties to the Bill of Rights guarantees. Clearly, as a "standard for judgment in the progressive evolution of the institutions of a free society," due process may impose limits beyond those found in the specifics of the Bill of Rights. Even though a particular practice was historically accepted as consistent with a particular Bill of Rights guarantee, changes in technology or "refinement[s] in our sense of justice" may render it contrary to the ordered liberty standard in its current setting. The extension of due process beyond the specifics of the Bill of Rights guarantees was implicitly recognized, it is argued, by the very inclusion of a due process clause in the Fifth Amendment.

The capacity of Fourteenth Amendment due process to provide protection overlapping with that granted under the specific guarantees of the Bill of Rights (i.e., the guarantees other than the Fifth Amendment due process clause) is, perhaps, a more troublesome issue. In one of the earlier Fourteenth Amendment cases, *Hurtado v. California,*[2] the Court suggested that due process might encompass only safeguards other than those found in the specific Bill of Rights guarantees. Fourteenth Amendment due process paralleled Fifth Amendment due process, the Court argued, and if the Fifth Amendment clause encompassed any of the rights found in the specific guarantees, there would have been no reason to include those other guarantees in the Bill of Rights. Thus, to read the due process clause as encompassing rights protected by the remaining guarantees, would be contrary to a "recognized canon of interpretation" that one of several interrelated provisions should not be read to render the other provisions "superfluous." The *Hurtado* suggestion was short-lived, however, and the Court eventually found within Fourteenth Amendment due process various rights also protected by specific Bill of Rights guarantees.[3] The canon of interpretation cited in *Hurtado,* the Court later noted, was simply an "aid to construction," which must yield to the traditional ordered liberty standard of due process. Due process was understood historically as encompassing all truly fundamental rights, whether or not those rights also happened to be recognized in a particular Bill of Rights guarantee. Because due process was such a vague guarantee, the framers of the Bill of Rights could well have thought it desirable to add the more specific provisions, even though the rights encompassed might also be protected by the Fifth Amendment's due process clause.

Once it was acknowledged that the "ordered liberty" standard could encompass rights that were also protected by the Bill of Rights guarantees, the question arose as to how the Court was to determine which of those rights were safeguarded by due process. The fundamental fairness doctrine rejected the contention that a particular right was "implicit in the concept of ordered liberty"

§ 2.4

1. Duncan v. Louisiana, 391 U.S. 145, 88 S.Ct. 1444, 20 L.Ed.2d 491 (1968) (Black, J., concurring). When Justice Black spoke of the state's obligation to adhere to pre-existing law—i.e., not to create new law for the particular case—he assumed that the pre-existing law, consistent with his position on total incorporation, included the Bill of Rights guarantees. If a state practice did not violate a specific Bill of Rights guarantee, and the state had applied that practice in an even-handed manner, the practice could not be held unconstitutional, under Justice Black's view, even though it was contrary to basic traditions of American criminal procedure. See, e.g., In re Winship, 397 U.S. 358, 90 S.Ct. 1068, 25 L.Ed.2d 368 (1970), in which Justice Black argued (in dissent) that the Constitution could not be interpreted to require that proof of guilt be established beyond a reasonable doubt.

2. 110 U.S. 516, 4 S.Ct. 111, 28 L.Ed. 232 (1884).

3. See Chicago, Burlington & Quincy R.R. v. Chicago, discussed at note 5 infra.

simply because it was recognized in the Bill of Rights. Not all of the Bill of Rights guarantees could be deemed basic to a free society. Some, for example, simply reflected "the restricted views of Eighteenth Century England regarding the best method for the ascertainment of facts." States might readily adopt different procedures, in light of current knowledge, and equally provide for fundamental fairness. In the case of still other guarantees, the core element of the guarantee might be fundamental while its other aspects might constitute only details of implementation that had come to be a part of the guarantee merely by force of custom. Analyzed from the independent perspective of the ordered liberty standard, only the core element of the guarantee would then be a requisite of due process. In sum, under the fundamental fairness position, some rights protected by the first eight amendments might be found totally encompassed by due process, others partially encompassed, and still others completely outside the requirements of due process.

At least as it later developed, a key element of the fundamental fairness doctrine was its focus on the factual setting of the individual case. Where a defendant contended that a state had denied him due process by failing to recognize a right that would have been protected by the Bill of Rights, the issue presented was not whether that right, viewed in the abstract, was "implicit in the concept of ordered liberty." Rather, it was whether the state's action had resulted in a denial of fundamental fairness in the context of the particular case. An asserted denial of due process was to be tested "by an appraisal of the totality of facts in a given case." For "that which may, in one setting, constitute a denial of fundamental fairness, shocking to the universal sense of justice, may, in other circumstances, and in the light of other considerations, fall short of such denial." Consistent with this approach, due process would be defined on a case-by-case basis, with "its full meaning * * * gradually ascertained by the process of inclusion and exclusion in the course of the decisions of cases as they arise."

(b) Application of Fundamental Fairness: The Pre–1930's Cases. The Supreme Court's application of the fundamental fairness doctrine can be divided roughly into two periods. During the first period, that extending from the adoption of the Fourteenth Amendment to the early 1930's, the Supreme Court reviewed comparatively few state criminal cases. In the overwhelming majority of those cases, the Court ruled against the defendant's due process claim. Moreover, where the claim was based on state action contrary to a particular aspect of a Bill of Rights guarantee, the Court did not always limit its rejection to that narrow element of the guarantee. There was a tendency to speak broadly, and to suggest that fundamental fairness did not require adherence to the guarantee as a whole.

The first major due process ruling of this period was *Hurtado v. California*.[4] The defendant there had been prosecuted for murder on a prosecutor's information, following a magistrate's finding of probable cause at a preliminary hearing. The defendant claimed that Fourteenth Amendment due process required the state to initiate prosecution only by grand jury indictment, just as the Fifth Amendment required grand jury indictment for federal prosecutions. With only Justice Harlan dissenting, the Court flatly rejected that claim. As noted previously, the *Hurtado* majority initially suggested that the due process clause would not be read as encompassing the same rights as a specific Bill of Rights provision (here, the Fifth Amendment's indictment provision) as that would render the specific guarantee superfluous. However, the Court then went on to consider the need for prosecution by indictment under a traditional fundamental fairness analysis. Due process, the Court noted, encompasses only those "fundamental principles of liberty and justice which lie at the base of all our civil and political institutions," and therefore must look to "the very substance of individual rights" rather than "particular forms of procedure." Looking to the underlying function

4. Supra note 2.

of grand jury review, the Court found that California had adopted a substitute procedure that "carefully considers and guards the substantial interest of the prisoners." Accordingly, the California procedure did not violate due process even though it departed from traditional common law procedure.

Though the *Hurtado* opinion rejected defendant's grand jury claim, it had developed a fundamental fairness analysis that could readily mandate at least some aspects of other Bill of Rights guarantees. That could only occur, however, if the Court first rejected *Hurtado's* initial suggestion that the due process clause could not be read as overlapping any of the specific guarantees. The *Chicago Railroad Case,*[5] decided in 1897, performed that function with a ruling that found such an overlapped right within due process protection. The Court there held that due process encompassed a prohibition also found in the Fifth Amendment—the prohibition against the government taking property without providing just compensation. Following *Chicago Railroad,* Supreme Court opinions considered various due process claims based upon procedural safeguards found in specific guarantees of the Bill of Rights. While the Court rejected these claims in all of the pre–1930 cases, it did so solely on the ground that the particular safeguards were not sufficiently fundamental.

The ruling and opinion in *Twining v. New Jersey*[6] is illustrative of the Court's application of the fundamental fairness doctrine in the pre–1930's to claims based on procedural safeguards specified in the Bill of Rights. The defendant there contended that due process had been violated by a jury instruction that allowed an unfavorable inference to be drawn from his failure to testify. The Court assumed for the purposes of argument that this instruction would have violated the Fifth Amendment privilege against self-incrimination in a federal prosecution. It also acknowledged that the Fourteenth Amendment could encompass rights safeguarded in the Bill of Rights, though this was so "not because those rights are enumerated in the first eight amendments, but because they are of such a nature that they are included in the conception of due process of law." The Court concluded, however, that defendant's claim here did not rest on such a right. Moreover, its reasoning was not limited to defendant's contention that his exercise of the self-incrimination privilege should be free from adverse comment. Rather, looking to the substantial exceptions to the self-incrimination privilege traditionally recognized in "English law," to the rejection of the privilege in civilized countries "outside the domain of the common law," and to the fact that "four only of the thirteen original states insisted upon incorporating the privilege in the Constitution," the Court concluded that the privilege as a whole simply was "not an unchangeable principle of universal justice."

Although the pre–1930's rulings consistently rejected procedural due process claims tied to safeguards specified in the Bill of Rights, the Court did recognize a few due process claims based upon other types of procedural defects. In each instance the defense stressed the basic unfairness of the state practice rather than any parallel protection in the Bill of Rights. In *Moore v. Dempsey,*[7] a case involving alleged mob domination of a trial, the Court reasoned that due process was not met where the "whole proceeding is a mask—[where] * * * counsel, jury and judge were swept to the fatal end by an unresistible wave of public passion, and * * * the state courts failed to correct the wrong." The emphasis in *Moore* was on the totality of the circumstances rather than the deprivation of specific safeguards such as an impartial jury or effective assistance of counsel. In *Tumey v. Ohio,*[8] the Court held that due process was violated where the trial judge was compensated by fees received only when the defendant was found guilty. The Court had no difficulty in concluding that a disinterested judge was an

5. Chicago, Burlington & Quincy R.R. v. Chicago, 166 U.S. 226, 17 S.Ct. 581, 41 L.Ed. 979 (1897).

6. 211 U.S. 78, 29 S.Ct. 14, 53 L.Ed. 97 (1908).

7. 261 U.S. 86, 43 S.Ct. 265, 67 L.Ed. 543 (1923).

8. 273 U.S. 510, 47 S.Ct. 437, 71 L.Ed. 749 (1927).

essential element of due process, though that safeguard was not mentioned in any of the specific guarantees of the Bill of Rights.

Tumey and *Moore* reflected a willingness of the Court to find due process violations, without regard to the specifics of the Bill of Rights, where state practices directly threatened the accuracy of the fact-finding process. This position was carried forward in the post–1930's period of fundamental fairness analysis. Thus, in *Mooney v. Holohan,*[9] the Court held that a prosecutor's knowing reliance on perjured testimony violates due process. And in *Thompson v. Louisville,*[10] a conviction totally devoid of evidentiary support was held to violate due process. The significant change during the post–1930 period was in the Court's approach to claims based on safeguards specified in the Bill of Rights, many of which did not relate directly to the reliability of the fact-finding process.

(c) Application of Fundamental Fairness: The Post–1930's Cases. In applying the fundamental fairness doctrine from the early 1930's through the early 1960's, the Court was far more willing to find within due process certain aspects of the specific guarantees of the Bill of Rights. Due process was viewed as encompassing many of the same basic principles as the Bill of Rights guarantees, but the due process limitations flowing from those principles generally were assumed to be narrower in scope than those imposed under the individual guarantees. *Powell v. Alabama,*[11] decided in 1932, was the first case to apply the fundamental fairness doctrine in this fashion.

Powell involved a capital charge in which the trial judge "appointed" all members of the local bar to represent nine young and illiterate defendants. The end result was representation that was insufficient by any standard. The Supreme Court held that the state's failure to provide adequate legal representation for the defendants resulted in a denial of due process. In reaching that conclusion, the Court did not rely upon the Sixth Amendment provision granting defendants the right to the assistance of counsel, but upon the due process requirement of a fair hearing. Where defendants, as here, were incapable of representing themselves, effective appointed counsel was a prerequisite for a fair hearing.

The *Powell* ruling had been limited to the special circumstances suggested by that case—"a capital case * * * where the defendant * * * is incapable of adequately making his own defense because of ignorance, feeble mindedness, illiteracy or the like." Six years later, in *Johnson v. Zerbst,*[12] the Court held that the Sixth Amendment right to counsel required federal courts to appoint lawyers for indigent defendants in all felony cases. Defendants in state cases immediately argued that the due process right to counsel should extend as far as the Sixth Amendment right. Relying on a fundamental fairness analysis, the Court rejected that contention in *Betts v. Brady.*[13] The due process clause was "less rigid and more fluid" than the Sixth Amendment. It focused on the facts of the particular case, and therefore required appointed counsel only when the special circumstances of the case indicated that the assistance of counsel was needed to ensure a fair trial.

In the years following *Powell,* due process cases considering various Bill of Rights safeguards adopted the general approach taken in the right-to-counsel cases. In *Wolf v. Colorado,*[14] for example, the Court held that due process encompassed the basic privacy interest safeguarded by the Fourth Amendment, but not the full scope of the Amendment's protection of that interest. The *Wolf* opinion initially concluded that the "security of one's privacy against arbitrary intrusions by the police—which is at the core of the Fourth Amendment—is basic to a free society * * * [and] therefore implicit in the 'concept of ordered liberty.'" The Court then held, how-

9. 294 U.S. 103, 55 S.Ct. 340, 79 L.Ed. 791 (1935).

10. 362 U.S. 199, 80 S.Ct. 624, 4 L.Ed.2d 654 (1960).

11. 287 U.S. 45, 53 S.Ct. 55, 77 L.Ed. 158 (1932).

12. 304 U.S. 458, 58 S.Ct. 1019, 82 L.Ed. 1461 (1938).

13. 316 U.S. 455, 62 S.Ct. 1252, 86 L.Ed. 1595 (1942).

14. 338 U.S. 25, 69 S.Ct. 1359, 93 L.Ed. 1782 (1949).

ever, that the Fourth Amendment remedy of excluding illegally seized evidence was not required by due process. A review of contemporary practices in the American states and the ten jurisdictions of the United Kingdom convinced the Court that the exclusionary rule was not so essential to the implementation of the protected right of privacy as to be imposed upon the states through the Fourteenth Amendment.

In several other cases decided during the post–1930 period, the Court rejected due process claims based upon a particular aspect of a Bill of Rights guarantee, yet suggested that other aspects of the guarantee might well be encompassed by due process. *Palko v. Connecticut* [15] is illustrative. In that case, defendant challenged a Connecticut statute which permitted the state to appeal defendant's initial acquittal, gain reversal on the basis of a trial court error, and then retry the defendant on the same charge. The Court assumed that a similar federal practice would violate the double jeopardy prohibition of the Fifth Amendment. It noted, however, that the decisive issue under the due process clause was more narrowly framed. The question to be asked was: "Is that kind of double jeopardy to which the statute has subjected * * * [defendant] a hardship so acute and shocking that our policy will not ensure it?" The answer here was "No," but the Court added that the answer might be otherwise "if the state were permitted after a trial free from error to try the accused over again." The state here, it noted, was not "attempting to wear the accused out by a multitude of cases with accumulated trials," but simply seeking to obtain a single trial "free from the corrosion of substantial legal error."

By the late 1950's the Court had indicated, either by holding, dictum, or implication, that due process included elements of most of the criminal process guarantees found in the Bill of Rights. The ordered liberty standard could be said to encompass at least one aspect of each of the following guarantees: the Fourth Amendment prohibition against unreasonable searches, the Fifth Amendment double jeopardy bar, the Fifth Amendment privilege against self-incrimination, the Sixth Amendment right to a public trial, the Sixth Amendment right to notice, the Sixth Amendment right to confrontation of opposing witnesses, the Sixth Amendment right to the assistance of counsel, and the Eighth Amendment prohibition against cruel and unusual punishment. The Court had also held, however, that ordered liberty did not encompass various other aspects of these same guarantees, and it did not require prosecution by indictment, as mandated by the Fifth Amendment, under any circumstances.

(d) Subjectivity and Fundamental Fairness. In *Adamson v. California,* [16] Justice Black, in the course of urging adoption of total incorporation, launched a vigorous attack against the alleged subjectivity of the fundamental fairness doctrine. Although Justice Black could not convince a majority of the Court to adopt his position on total incorporation, his criticism of the fundamental fairness doctrine contributed substantially to the development and eventual adoption of the selective incorporation position. A major argument advanced in favor of selective incorporation was that it would offer far less potential for a subjective application of the ordered liberty standard than did the fundamental fairness doctrine. Justice Black's criticism may also have contributed, in part, to the departure from a "circumstances-of-the-case" analysis in some of the 1950's decisions applying the fundamental fairness doctrine.

Justice Black contended that the fundamental fairness doctrine permitted the Court to "substitut[e] its own concepts of decency and fundamental justice for the language of the Bill of Rights." Application of the fundamental fairness concept, he noted, "depended entirely on the particular judge's idea of ethics and morals" rather than upon "boundaries fixed by the written words of the Constitution." Although Justice Black thought that many fundamental fairness rulings reflected

15. 302 U.S. 319, 58 S.Ct. 149, 82 L.Ed. 288 (1937).

16. 332 U.S. 46, 67 S.Ct. 1672, 91 L.Ed. 1903 (1947).

this basically idiosyncratic approach to adjudication, perhaps his prime examples were the decisions in *Rochin v. California*[17] and *Irvine v. California.*[18]

In *Rochin,* the police, having "some information" that defendant was selling narcotics, entered his home without a warrant and forced open the door to his bedroom. When the surprised defendant immediately shoved into his mouth two capsules believed to be narcotics, the police grabbed him and attempted to extract the capsules, which defendant then swallowed. The police then took the protesting defendant to a doctor, who forced an emetic solution into defendant's stomach, causing him to vomit up the capsules. Describing the total course of police action as "conduct that shocks the conscience," the Court held that due process no more permitted the use of the capsules in evidence than it would a coerced confession. "Due process," the Court added, was a principle that "precludes defining * * * more precisely than to say that convictions cannot be brought about by methods that 'offend a sense of justice.' "

In *Irvine,* the plurality described the police action as flagrant and deliberate misconduct, but held that it was not so offensive as to violate due process. The police in *Irvine* had made repeated illegal entries into defendant's home for the purpose of installing secret microphones, including one in his bedroom, from which they listened to his conversations for over a month. The plurality distinguished *Rochin* as a case involving "coercion, violence * * * [and] brutality to the person" rather than, as here, a "trespass to property, plus eavesdropping." However, Justice Frankfurter, who had written for the Court in *Rochin,* concluded that the two cases were not distinguishable. Though "there was lacking [in *Irvine*] physical violence, even to the restricted extent employed in *Rochin,*" the police had engaged in a "more powerful and offensive control over Irvine's life than a single limited physical trespass." For Justice Black, the division of the Court in *Irvine,* and the contrasting results reached in *Rochin* and *Irvine,* clearly revealed an "ad hoc approach" that consisted of no more than determining whether "five justices are sufficiently revolted by local police action" to "shock [the victim of that action] into the protective arms of the Constitution." [19]

In both *Rochin* and *Irvine,* Justice Frankfurter took sharp exception to Justice Black's characterization of the Court's fundamental fairness analysis as largely subjective. Admittedly, the case-by-case application of the "ordered liberty" standard required the exercise of judicial judgment in an "empiric process" for which there was no "mechanical yardstick." That did not mean, however, that judges were "at large" to draw upon their "merely personal and private notions" of justice. In each case, the Court was required to undertake a "disinterested inquiry pursued in the spirit of science." It looked not to personal preferences, but to external evidence of permanent and pervasive notions of fairness, such as the positions taken in the federal constitution and early state constitutions, the standards currently applied in the various states, and viewpoints of other countries with similar jurisprudential traditions.[20] More-

17. 342 U.S. 165, 72 S.Ct. 205, 96 L.Ed. 183 (1952).

18. 347 U.S. 128, 74 S.Ct. 381, 98 L.Ed. 561 (1954).

19. Mapp v. Ohio, 367 U.S. 643, 81 S.Ct. 1684, 6 L.Ed.2d 1081 (1961) (Black, J., concurring, quoting from Justice Clark's concurring opinion in *Irvine*). Another case often cited along with *Rochin* and *Irvine* as illustrating the subjectivity of fundamental fairness analysis is Breithaupt v. Abram, 352 U.S. 432, 77 S.Ct. 408, 1 L.Ed.2d 448 (1957). The Court there held that the taking of a blood sample from an unconscious driver (who had been involved in a fatal accident and was believed to be intoxicated) did not violate due process. The majority stressed that the taking of a blood sample had become "routine in our everyday life," and the interests of society in gaining scientific evidence of intoxication, to help deter "the increasing slaughter on our highways," outweighed "so slight an intrusion" of a person's body. In dissent, Chief Justice Warren, joined by Justices Black and Douglas, argued that reversal was required if *Rochin* "is to retain its vitality and stand as more than an instance of personal revulsion against particular police methods."

20. In the leading article on due process methodology, Kadish, Methodology and Criteria in Due Process Adjudication—A Survey and Criticism, 66 Yale L.J. 319 (1957), the author noted four different sources frequently considered by the Court in seeking to establish prevailing moral judgments: (1) "the opinions of the progenitors of

over, in evaluating that evidence and reaching its conclusion, the Court was limited by the traditional standards of judicial review, requiring reasoned results that build upon prior decisions. Thus, while the fundamental fairness standard might require a more finely tuned analysis than other areas of constitutional adjudication, it rested on a process of rational inquiry entirely consistent with the "nature of our judicial process."

Justice Black's criticism of the fundamental fairness doctrine also rested in part on his assumption that the alternative of relying upon the "clearly marked boundaries" of specific Bill of Rights guarantees offered far less room for subjective judgments. This assumption also was challenged by justices favoring the fundamental fairness doctrine. Justice Harlan, for example, argued that Justice Black's formula for achieving judicial restraint was "more hollow than real." He suggested that the specific provisions of the Bill of Rights often were no less amenable to a subjective interpretation than the fundamental fairness standard of due process. Under Justice Black's position, the focus of judicial inquiry would be shifted from the flexible concept of "ordered liberty" to equally flexible terms found in most of the Amendments. Terms like "probable cause," "unreasonable search" and "speedy and public trial" it was noted, are hardly self-defining. Justice Harlan acknowledged that reliance upon the specifics of the Bill of Rights might produce different results, but the analysis involved would be no less subjective.[21]

§ 2.5 Selective Incorporation

(a) Fundamental Fairness and Selective Incorporation: Similarities and Differences. During the 1960's, the prevailing due process position shifted from the fundamental fairness doctrine to the selective incorporation doctrine. In several respects, the two doctrines are much alike. Both read the due process clause as encompassing only those rights deemed fundamental under an ordered liberty standard. Both recognize that the ordered liberty standard includes substantive as well as procedural rights, and that it is an expansive concept, not limited to rights established by historical usage at the time of the Constitution's adoption. Both agree also that the ordered liberty standard may encompass rights found in the specific Bill of Rights guarantees, as well as rights that extend beyond those guarantees. There is crucial disagreement, however, as to how the ordered liberty standard should be used in identifying fundamental rights.

Initially, the two doctrines differ in the scope of the right assessed under the ordered liberty standard when that right is found in a Bill of Rights guarantee. The fundamental fairness doctrine focuses on that aspect of the guarantee that was denied by the state in the

American institutions" (e.g., colonial history, early state constitutions, and federal constitutions); (2) the "implicit opinions of the policy-making organs of state governments"; (3) the "explicit opinions of other American courts"; and (4) the opinions of other countries in the Anglo–Saxon tradition. The author concluded that due process determinations did lend themselves to rational inquiry, although the Court's institutional limitations posed difficulties in pursuing an appropriate inquiry.

21. See e.g., Duncan v. Louisiana, 391 U.S. 145, 88 S.Ct. 1444, 20 L.Ed.2d 491 (1968) (Harlan, J., dissenting). Justice Black's own position in *Rochin* is commonly cited in support of Justice Harlan's argument. Justice Black agreed that there had been a constitutional violation in *Rochin,* but he based that conclusion on the Fifth Amendment privilege against self-incrimination rather than any "evanescent" standard of fundamental fairness. To find that the privilege had been violated, however, Justice Black arguably had to make value judgments very much like those considered under a fundamental fairness analysis. To treat the stomach pumping as compulsory self-incrimination, Justice Black had to conclude (1) that the privilege went beyond the compulsion of testimonial evidence and included the production of nontestimonial evidence, and (2) that the privilege reached beyond the legal compulsion flowing from a court directive threatening contempt and also prohibited the compulsion resulting from the application of physical force by the police. The highly debatable nature of the first proposition, in particular, is evinced by later cases indicating that a majority of the Court, unlike Justice Black, would not have accepted that proposition. See the cases discussed in § 7.2 and § 8.12(d). Moreover, as Justice Black's own dissent in one of those later cases indicates, to justify applying the Fifth Amendment to the compulsion of nontestimonial evidence, one must turn to basically the same kind of analysis of the nature of society's "respect for the dignity of the individual" as was employed in Justice Frankfurter's opinion for the Court in *Rochin.* See the discussion of Schmerber v. California, in § 7.2 at note 5. Consider also § 8.14. As to the issues raised by the second proposition, see §§ 6.2, 6.5.

particular case. Moreover, it often assesses the significance of that element of the guarantee in light of the special circumstances of the individual case. The selective incorporation doctrine, on the other hand, focuses on the total guarantee rather than on the particular aspect presented in an individual case. It assesses the fundamental nature of the guarantee as a whole, rather than the fundamental nature of any one requirement of the guarantee. Consider, for example, the situation presented in *Palko v. Connecticut.*[1] Applying the fundamental fairness doctrine, the Court there asked whether the ordered liberty standard required protection against "that kind of double jeopardy"—a retrial following an appellate reversal of an initial acquittal—that had been imposed upon the defendant there. Applying the selective incorporation doctrine, the Court instead would ask whether the ordered liberty standard encompasses the basic concept underlying the Fifth Amendment's overall prohibition against double jeopardy.

The difference in the scope of the right assessed carries over to the scope of the rulings under the two doctrines. A fundamental fairness ruling theoretically should go no farther than to establish due process protection parallel to the one aspect of the Bill of Rights guarantee presented in the particular case. Selective incorporation, however, judging the guarantee as a whole, produces a ruling that encompasses the full scope of the guarantee. When a guarantee is found to be fundamental, due process, in effect, "incorporates" that guarantee, and carries over to the states precisely the same prohibitions as apply to the federal government under that guarantee. Under selective incorporation, a ruling that a particular guarantee is within the ordered liberty concept makes applicable to the states all of the standards previously developed in applying that guarantee to federal criminal prosecutions. This has led some commentators to describe the incorporation element of selective incorporation as having a "wholesale character."

The selective incorporation doctrine also departs from the fundamental fairness doctrine in its analysis of the ordered liberty concept. Whereas the fundamental fairness cases often asked whether a "fair and enlightened system of justice" would be "impossible" without a particular safeguard, selective incorporation "proceed[s] upon the * * * assumption that state criminal processes are not imaginary and theoretical schemes but actual systems bearing virtually every characteristic of the common law system that has been developing contemporaneously in England and in this country."[2] Accordingly, it directs a court to test the fundamental nature of a right within the context of that common law system of justice, rather than against some hypothesized "civilized system" or some foreign system growing out of different traditions. The question to be asked, the Court has noted, is whether a procedure "is necessary to an Anglo-American regime of ordered liberty." Consistent with this approach, considerable weight is given to the very presence of a right within the Bill of Rights, since that presence in itself establishes that a substantial body of opinion viewed the right as essential to a fair common law system.

(b) The Rationale of Selective Incorporation. There are those who argue that the selective incorporation doctrine has no coherent constitutional rationale. They contend that it constitutes no more than a result-oriented modification of the total incorporation theory—a doctrine devised to achieve total incorporation, minus the civil jury trial and grand jury guarantees. The Court wanted to expand Fourteenth Amendment protection to encompass all but those few guarantees that would cause the greatest disruption if applied to the states, and selective incorporation was created and accepted because it could eventually lead to exactly that result. Selective incorporation, these critics argue, is a doctrine that lacks the textual and historical support of either total incorporation or

§ 2.5

1. See § 2.4 at note 15.

2. Duncan v. Louisiana, 391 U.S. 145, 88 S.Ct. 1444, 20 L.Ed.2d 491 (1968).

fundamental fairness, a doctrine justified only by its end product.

While the Supreme Court majority has not responded to such criticism, individual justices have done so in separate opinions justifying the shift from fundamental fairness to selective incorporation. Together, they offer four reasons why selective incorporation provides a truer application of the ordered liberty standard than a fundamental fairness analysis: (1) selective incorporation adheres more closely to the earlier due process decisions which recognized that the ordered liberty looked to the "absorption" of individual guarantees; (2) selective incorporation reduces the potential for "impermissible subjective judgments" in defining due process; (3) selective incorporation promotes certainty in the law and thereby facilitates state court enforcement of due process standards; and (4) selective incorporation places in more appropriate perspective the "legitimate interests of federalism." While it is unlikely that every justice supporting selective incorporation accepted all four of these interrelated justifications, they all apparently relied upon at least one of the four.

(c) Prior Precedent and the "Absorption" of Individual Guarantees. It may seem strange that a doctrine that resulted in the overruling of so many decisions has been justified by reference to prior precedent, but several justices have offered precisely that justification for the selective incorporation doctrine. They point to statements in various earlier opinions describing due process as having "absorbed" or "made applicable" to the states particular Bill of Rights guarantees. However, as several commentators have noted, the most that can be derived from the earlier due process cases is two lines of precedent, one applying the classic case-by-case analysis of fundamental fairness, and the other fully absorbing a few selected guarantees. The process of "absorption" in *Powell v. Alabama* [3] was typical of the first grouping, which contained all of the criminal procedure rulings. While *Powell* was sometimes described as having absorbed the right to counsel, the Court there clearly limited any such absorption, at least with respect to appointed counsel, to the special circumstances of that case. On the other side, however, another series of cases, applying to the states those "freedom[s] * * * which the First Amendment safeguards," reflected a much broader process of absorption. Those decisions appeared to apply to the states, whole and intact, the several First Amendment guarantees. The Court's opinions here commonly began by noting that a First Amendment guarantee had "been made applicable" to the states by the Fourteenth Amendment, and then proceeded to discuss the issue presented solely in terms of the history and policy of the First Amendment. A broad range of different principles relating to various First Amendment guarantees were invoked in these cases, but the Court majority never once stopped to consider whether a particular principle might not be essential to ordered liberty. Moreover, while the First Amendment cases were the clearest instances of complete absorption, opinions treating state takings of property without providing full compensation suggested that the Fifth Amendment's just compensation clause also may have been applied whole and intact in state cases.

If the due process clause could, in effect, "incorporate" the First Amendment, and perhaps the just compensation guarantee of the Fifth Amendment, did that not provide adequate precedent for selectively incorporating other guarantees as well? Admittedly, *Palko, Powell* and other fundamental fairness rulings had adopted a quite different approach, but what was to distinguish one line of cases from the other? Were these simply two lines of inconsistent precedent, with the Court free to choose one over the other, or was there some rational basis for distinguishing those cases that totally absorbed particular guarantees? Justices supporting the traditional fundamental fairness approach argued that a reasoned distinction was found in the nature

3. See § 2.4, at note 11.

of the rights involved.[4] The supporters of selective incorporation rejected this distinction, however, and concluded that the logic of the fundamental fairness standard, as recognized in the First Amendment cases, required application to the states of "the full sweep of the specific [guarantee] being absorbed."

(d) Selective Incorporation as a Means of Avoiding Subjectivity. Taking a page from Justice Black's argument favoring total incorporation, justices supporting selective incorporation maintained that selective incorporation would avoid much of the subjectivity inherent in the fundamental fairness doctrine. They noted initially that the selective incorporation doctrine, in contrast to the fundamental fairness doctrine, did not look to the "totality of the circumstances" of the particular case in determining whether a right was necessary to "ordered liberty." To permit evaluation of a right in light of "the factual circumstances surrounding each individual case" led, in their view, to judgments that were "extremely subjective and excessively discretionary." Selective incorporation was also said to reduce subjectivity by focusing on the fundamental nature of the Bill of Rights guarantee as a whole, rather than on a particular aspect of the guarantee. "[O]nly impermissible subjective judgments," it was argued, "can explain stopping short of the full sweep of the specific guarantee being absorbed." Under selective incorporation, once a guarantee was held fundamental, discretion would be reduced because the Court's analysis thereafter would rest on the language and history of the guarantee. There would be no need to return, in case after case, to the standard of "ordered liberty." Selective incorporation therefore also had the advantage of "avoid[ing] the impression of personal, ad hoc adjudication by every Court which attempts to apply the vague contents and contours of 'ordered liberty' to every different case that comes before it."

Justices opposing selective incorporation rejected the assumption that a fundamental fairness analysis was substantially more subjective than the interpretation of a specific guarantee. Moreover, they noted, even if that assumption were accepted, it did not necessarily follow that selective incorporation was to be preferred over the fundamental fairness doctrine. A judgment still had to be made as to whether the additional potential for subjectivity in the fundamental fairness doctrine was offset by other attributes of the doctrine. The proponents of selective incorporation, it was argued, themselves implicitly acknowledged that elimination of subjectivity should not be the controlling factor in the choice of Fourteenth Amendment doctrine. They had chosen selective incorporation over total incorporation even though the former doctrine utilizes the supposedly subjective ordered liberty standard in determining whether a particular guarantee was "incorporated" in due process. Moreover, aside from Justice Black, justices supporting selective incorporation would not fully eliminate the use of a fundamental fairness analysis tied to circumstances of the particular case. They accepted the view that due process protection extends beyond the specifics of the Bill of Rights, though such additional protection commonly rests on precisely that type of fundamental fairness analysis.

(e) Facilitating State Enforcement of Due Process Standards. The shift from fundamental fairness to selective incorpo-

4. In the course of distinguishing between those guarantees that had been "brought within the Fourteenth Amendment by a process of absorption" and those that had not, the Court in *Palko* pointed to the unique role of freedom of speech and thought. That freedom, the Court noted, "is the matrix, the indispensable condition, of nearly every other form of freedom." In subsequent cases, the Court spoke of the "preferred position" of all First Amendment rights, including freedom of religion. These statements suggested that First Amendment guarantees were viewed as so important that each and every aspect of those guarantees was automatically deemed essential to ordered liberty. Of course, this "preferred position" analysis did not explain the just compensation cases, but the departure from a traditional fundamental fairness analysis in those cases was clouded, as the selective incorporationists acknowledged. See Israel, Selected Incorporation Revisited, 71 Geo.L.J. 253 (1982) (also discussing Professor Henkin's theory that the distinction between the full absorption in the First Amendment and just compensation cases and the more traditional fundamental fairness analysis in cases like *Palko* and *Powell* rested on the different characteristics of "substantive" and "procedural" guarantees).

ration was also justified as necessary to ensure effective state court enforcement of due process limitations. The traditional fundamental fairness doctrine, it was argued, produced due process standards too uncertain to be applied consistently by state courts. Supreme Court decisions tied to the totality of the circumstances of the individual case were viewed as leaving the state courts without a dependable gauge for resolving cases that were not directly on point. The end product of the fundamental fairness approach, Justice Goldberg suggested, was to "require * * * [the] Supreme Court to intervene in the state judicial process with a considerable lack of predictability and with a consequent likelihood of considerable friction." [5] Moreover, at a time when the criminal side of the Court's docket was growing more and more active, it was doubtful that the Court had the capacity to develop both a general body of principles interpreting specific guarantees for federal criminal cases and a second-level, "shadow" group of principles for all of the issues posed in state cases.

Compared to the fundamental fairness doctrine, the "practical utility" of selective incorporation was undeniable. Once a particular guarantee was held to be fundamental, state courts were directed to the specific language of that guarantee and to the various decisions interpreting that language in the context of federal prosecutions. That precedent clearly resolved numerous issues, and offered basic guidelines for the resolution of others. Critics of selective incorporation responded, however, that it was inappropriate to extend the state's obligation beyond what due process required under a fundamental fairness analysis simply to promote convenience of administration. They believed that the fundamental fairness cases were not as uncertain, nor the federal precedent as certain, as the supporters of selective incorporation maintained. Moreover, administrative convenience could not prevail over concerns of federalism. The key to the Constitution's recognition of state autonomy, they argued, lay in allowing the states to develop their own rules for obtaining fundamental fairness, "not in achieving procedural symmetry or * * * serving administrative convenience."

(f) The Legitimate Interests of Federalism. Reviewing the Supreme Court's fundamental fairness decisions for a twenty-five year period immediately following *Powell v. Alabama,* Professor Francis Allen noted that "the first and most striking fact to emerge from a survey of the Court's opinions * * * is the obvious importance of the Court's interpretation of the obligation of federalism in the development of the applicable constitutional doctrine." [6] Although those opinions rested primarily on the historical development of the concept of due process, they rarely failed to note the need to respect the "sovereign character of the several states" by giving the states the widest latitude consistent with assuring fundamental fairness. Those earlier opinions generally did not break down the interests at stake in limiting intrusions upon state authority, but Justices Frankfurter and Harlan did so in several separate opinions responding to the possible adoption of a total or selective incorporation doctrine.[7] First, rulings that went beyond the minimum requirements of fundamental fairness would undermine the values of local control of the criminal justice process. Second, application of the same constitutional standards to the federal and state governments would ignore major differences between the federal and state criminal justice systems. Third, incorporation of Bill of Rights guarantees would fail to leave adequate room for the diversity and experimentation needed for the states to eventually devise wiser and fairer criminal justice systems. Opinions supporting selective incorporation recognized all three of

5. Pointer v. Texas, 380 U.S. 400, 85 S.Ct. 1065, 13 L.Ed.2d 923 (1965) (Goldberg, J., concurring).

6. Allen, The Supreme Court, Federalism, and State Systems of Criminal Justice, 8 DePaul L.Rev. 213, 251 (1959).

7. See e.g., Adamson v. California, 332 U.S. 46, 67 S.Ct. 1672, 91 L.Ed. 1903 (1947) (Frankfurter, J., concurring); Malloy v. Hogan, 378 U.S. 1, 84 S.Ct. 1489, 12 L.Ed.2d 653 (1964) (Harlan, J., dissenting).

these concerns, but either rejected their relevancy or downgraded their significance.

The justices supporting selective incorporation did not see that doctrine as imposing limitations that would substantially interfere with the true interests of local control. What was occurring here was quite different from the usual transfer of state authority to the federal government. The Court's rulings did not take enforcement responsibility from local police agencies and place it in the hands of a national police agency. Nor did the rulings take the responsibility for defining crime from local legislatures and place it in the hands of Congress. The Court was acting only to protect the individual, and the justices saw in that purpose a crucial distinction. Thus, Justice Goldberg reasoned:

> [T]o deny to the States the power to impair a fundamental constitutional right is not to increase federal power, but rather to limit the power of both federal and state governments in favor of safeguarding the fundamental rights and liberties of the individual. In my view this promotes rather than undermines the basic policy of avoiding excess concentration of power in government, federal or state, which underlies our concepts of federalism.[8]

Supporters of selective incorporation also recognized that the state criminal justice systems bore responsibilities (as reflected in the wider spectrum of laws enforced) and faced difficulties (as reflected in the greater diversity of enforcement officials) that differed somewhat from the responsibilities borne and difficulties faced by the federal criminal justice system. They viewed these differences as largely irrelevant, however, to the application of the selective incorporation doctrine. Where the circumstances faced by the states were substantially different, the various guarantees were sufficiently flexible to give consideration to those differences, even if that required reexamining past precedent developed in the narrower context of the federal system.[9] Critics of selective incorporation responded that, to "avoid unduly fettering the states," the Court would frequently be forced to relax the constitutional standards that were now being applied to both the federal and state governments. The end result, they argued, would be a "watering down [of] protections against the Federal government," thereby "discarding * * * the possibility of federal leadership by example." The supporters of selective incorporation apparently assumed, however, that the need for more flexible standards to accommodate special problems of the states would be rare, and that those standards would be carefully tied to the particular setting so as to limit their applicability.

In *New State Ice Co. v. Liebman,*[10] Justice Brandeis admonished the Court against undue interference with state experimentation:

> To stay experimentation in things social and economic is a grave responsibility. Denial of the right to experiment may be fraught with serious consequences to the Nation. It is one of the happy incidents of the federal system that a single courageous State may, if its citizens choose, serve as a laboratory; and try novel social and economic experiments without risk to the rest of the country.

One of the major justifications advanced for the fundamental fairness doctrine had been that it attended to Justice Brandeis' admonition by providing ample room for diversity (and thus experimentation) in state procedure. When the Court shifted to selective incorporation, justices critical of the new doctrine argued that the majority had failed to heed Justice Brandeis' admonition, as selective incorporation gave no weight whatsoever to the value of experimentation. Justices Goldberg and Black responded that the Bran-

8. Pointer v. Texas, supra note 5 (concurring opinion).

9. The majority opinion in *Duncan v. Louisiana,* supra note 2, selectively incorporating the Sixth Amendment right to jury trial, illustrates this viewpoint. The state there argued that the Sixth Amendment jury trial guarantee was unsuited to state proceedings, particularly in its requirements of twelve person juries and unanimous verdicts. The Court acknowledged that those requirements had been developed in the somewhat different context of federal judicial proceedings. It noted, however, that the pre-incorporation Sixth Amendment rulings were "always subject to reconsideration." See also § 2.6(b).

10. 285 U.S. 262, 52 S.Ct. 371, 76 L.Ed. 747 (1932) (dissenting opinion).

deis admonition had relevance only to the application of the discredited doctrine of substantive due process. Recognition of the state's capacity to experiment, they noted, did not extend to "experiment[s] with the fundamental liberties of citizens safeguarded by the Bill of Rights." [11]

§ 2.6 Application of the Selective Incorporation Doctrine

(a) The Decisions of the Sixties. The shift from fundamental fairness to selective incorporation occurred during the 1960's. It began with a series of cases in which the majority opinions were sufficiently ambiguous so that it could not be said with certainty that the Court had adopted selective incorporation. Those cases, *Mapp v. Ohio,*[1] *Robinson v. California,*[2] *Ker v. California,*[3] and *Gideon v. Wainwright,*[4] apparently made fully applicable to the states the Fourth Amendment prohibition against unreasonable searches, the Eighth Amendment prohibition against cruel and unusual punishment, and the Sixth Amendment right to counsel, but they failed to clearly base their rulings on a selective incorporation analysis. However, in *Malloy v. Hogan,*[5] decided in 1964, the Court undisputably established that selective incorporation had become the majority view. *Malloy* held that the privilege against self-incrimination was a fundamental right and therefore safeguarded against state action under the "applicable federal standard of the Fifth Amendment." Rejecting the prosecution's contention that due process protection might be "less stringent" than that provided by the Fifth Amendment itself, the Court noted that cases such as *Ker v. California* and *Gideon v. Wainwright* had "rejected the notion that the Fourteenth Amendment applies to the States only a 'watered-down,' subjective version of the individual guarantees of the Bill of Rights." Once the Court has determined, upon analysis of the whole of a guarantee, that the guarantee protects a fundamental right, that guarantee "would be enforced against the States under the Fourteenth Amendment according to the same standards that * * * [apply] against federal encroachment."

A series of cases decided during the remainder of the decade reaffirmed the position taken in *Malloy.* Those cases held applicable to the states, under the same standards applied to the federal government, the Sixth Amendment rights to speedy trial,[6] to a trial by jury,[7] to confront opposing witnesses,[8] and to compulsory process for obtaining witnesses,[9] and the Fifth Amendment prohibition against double jeopardy.[10] In each case, the Court relied squarely upon a selective incorporation analysis. Moreover, in *Duncan v. Louisiana* [11] the Court noted that it had narrowed the focus of the inquiry under the "ordered liberty" standard; the crucial issue was not whether a particular guarantee was fundamental to every "fair and equitable" criminal system "that might be imagined," but whether it was fundamental "in the context of the criminal processes maintained by the American states." The *Duncan* Court recognized

11. Pointer v. Texas, supra note 5 (Goldberg, J., concurring).

§ 2.6

1. 367 U.S. 643, 81 S.Ct. 1684, 6 L.Ed.2d 1081 (1961). Overruling Wolf v. Colorado, see § 2.4(c), *Mapp* held that due process required a state to exclude from a trial all unconstitutionally seized evidence. Two years later, Ker v. California, 374 U.S. 23, 83 S.Ct. 1623, 10 L.Ed.2d 726 (1963), held that the constitutionality of state searches would be judged under precisely the same standards applied to federal searches under the Fourth Amendment.

2. 370 U.S. 660, 82 S.Ct. 1417, 8 L.Ed.2d 758 (1962) (applying the Eighth Amendment prohibition against cruel and unusual punishments).

3. See note 1 supra, describing *Ker.*

4. 372 U.S. 335, 83 S.Ct. 792, 9 L.Ed.2d 799 (1963) (applying the Sixth Amendment right to counsel).

5. 378 U.S. 1, 84 S.Ct. 1489, 12 L.Ed.2d 653 (1964).

6. Klopfer v. North Carolina, 386 U.S. 213, 87 S.Ct. 988, 18 L.Ed.2d 1 (1967).

7. Duncan v. Louisiana, 391 U.S. 145, 88 S.Ct. 1444, 20 L.Ed.2d 491 (1968).

8. Pointer v. Texas, 380 U.S. 400, 85 S.Ct. 1065, 13 L.Ed.2d 923 (1965).

9. Washington v. Texas, 388 U.S. 14, 87 S.Ct. 1920, 18 L.Ed.2d 1019 (1967).

10. Benton v. Maryland, 395 U.S. 784, 89 S.Ct. 2056, 23 L.Ed.2d 707 (1969).

11. Supra note 7.

further that this approach, along with selective incorporation's focus on the nature of the right as a whole, would be far more likely to produce a finding that a particular guarantee was implicit in the concept of "ordered liberty." [12]

By the end of the decade, the Court had, as Justice Brennan later noted, changed the "face of the law." The decisions of the 1960's had selectively incorporated all but four of the Bill of Rights guarantees relating to the criminal justice process. Moreover, of those four remaining guarantees, it seemed likely that three would be held to be fundamental once that issue was squarely presented for decision. *In re Oliver,*[13] a 1948 ruling finding a due process violation in a denial of a public trial, had been described in dictum as having selectively incorporated that Sixth Amendment guarantee (and the Court later so held).[14] Since *Oliver* also spoke of due process protection of "[a] person's right to a reasonable notice of a charge against him," a similar reading seemed likely as to the notice provision of the Sixth Amendment (and the Court subsequently so stated).[15] Possible incorporation of the Eighth Amendment's prohibition of excessive bail was perhaps more questionable, but shortly into the 1970's, the Court indicated that that provision also was likely to be deemed fundamental.[16] The only criminal procedure guarantee that continued to be treated as not fundamental and therefore not incorporated was the Fifth Amendment requirement of prosecution by indictment; *Hurtado v. California* [17] stood alone among the pre–1960's rulings rejecting incorporation as a precedent with continuing vitality.

(b) Selective Incorporation in the Post–1960's. In the years since the 1960's, the selective incorporation doctrine has been firmly embedded in Fourteenth Amendment jurisprudence as case after case has applied the incorporated guarantees to state criminal proceedings. Initially, a few justices supporting the fundamental fairness position wrote separate opinions continuing to question the selective incorporation rationale, but that practice soon stopped as those justices left the Court and weight of precedent increased. There was, however, one brief but significant challenge to the doctrine, presented in a series of cases decided during the 1970's. Although rejected, that challenge did require modification of one of the major arguments that had been advanced in favor of the selective incorporation doctrine—the contention that the doctrine would add predictability to the constitutional regulation of state criminal procedure by its incorporation of the considerable body of Supreme Court precedent that had been developed in applying the various criminal procedure guarantees to the federal criminal justice process.

The rationale of the 1970's challenge to the doctrine was first articulated in a concurring opinion by Justice Fortas in *Duncan v. Louisiana,* one of the landmark incorporation cases of the 1960's. While accepting selective incorporation as the general rule, Justice Fortas argued that a modification of that doctrine was required for guarantees like that involved in *Duncan,* the Sixth Amendment right to jury trial. Here, he noted, the Court was concerned with "more than a principle of justice applicable to individual cases." The

12. The *Duncan* majority noted, as an example, that while "a criminal process which was fair and equitable but used no juries is easy to imagine," analysis of the jury trial guarantee in light of the structure of the "Anglo–American regime of ordered liberty" produced a "quite different" view of significance of the Sixth Amendment guarantee.

13. 333 U.S. 257, 68 S.Ct. 499, 92 L.Ed. 682 (1948).

14. See Washington v. Texas, supra note 9; Duncan v. Louisiana, supra note 7. The public trial right was held applicable to state cases in Gannett Co. v. DePasquale, 443 U.S. 368, 99 S.Ct. 2898, 61 L.Ed.2d 608 (1979).

15. See Gannett Co. v. DePasquale, supra note 14 (noting that all guarantees of the Sixth Amendment, including the "right of notice," are "applicable to the states"). The Court has not had occasion in the post-incorporation era to apply this Sixth Amendment guarantee in a state case.

16. In Schilb v. Kuebel, 404 U.S. 357, 92 S.Ct. 479, 39 L.Ed.2d 502 (1971), the Court found it unnecessary to reach that issue, but noted: "Bail, of course is basic to our system of law, * * * and the Eighth Amendment's prescription of excessive bail has been assumed to have application to the states through the Fourteenth Amendment." Here again, the Court has not had occasion to apply the guarantee in a state case.

17. See § 2.4, at note 4.

Sixth Amendment, as interpreted in cases involving federal jury trials, also imposed a "system of administration"; it prescribed, for example, the size of the jury (twelve) and the form of their verdict (unanimous). Such requirements, he suggested, might very well not be fundamental, and therefore should not be applied to the states (although remaining binding in federal cases). It was not necessary to adhere so "slavishly" to selective incorporation as to impose upon the states the total Sixth Amendment guarantee, including "all its bag and baggage, however securely or insecurely affixed they may be by law or precedent."

The Court had no need to decide in *Duncan* itself whether absolute parallelism (disparagingly characterized by Justice Harlan as "jot for jot" and "case-by-case" incorporation) would be mandated for every aspect of the jury trial guarantee. Nonetheless, Justice White's opinion for the Court strongly indicated that such parallelism would be required. At the same time, however, Justice White acknowledged that previous interpretations of the Sixth Amendment, relating to such matters as jury size, may have been influenced by the fact that the requirements there imposed would apply only in the "limited environment" of the federal courts where "uniformity is a more obvious and immediate consideration." But those decisions, he added, were "always subject to reconsideration."

The "reconsideration route" suggested by Justice White was presented to the Court in *Williams v. Florida,*[18] where the state sought to utilize a six-person jury in a non-capital felony case. Although a long line of Supreme Court precedent had assumed that the Sixth Amendment demanded a twelve-person jury, the Court majority sustained the Florida procedure. *Duncan* was characterized as granting to state defendants a right to precisely the same type of jury trial as the Sixth Amendment would demand "were [defendants] tried in federal courts." However, upon examination of the history and purpose of the jury trial guarantee, the Court concluded that the earlier cases had erred in assuming that a twelve-person jury was a "*sine qua non* of the jury trial guarantee." The twelve-person jury was simply an incidental feature of common law practice and not constitutionally required as to either federal or state cases.

Two years later, in a similar situation, all but one justice agreed that complete parallelism was required, but the one justice rejecting that position determined the outcome of the case. *Apodaca v. Oregon*[19] presented the question of whether a state could allow a less than unanimous jury verdict. Eight justices agreed that the critical issue was whether earlier Supreme Court opinions in cases involving federal juries had been correct in assuming that unanimity was a mandate of the Sixth Amendment. The eight split evenly on that issue, with four reasoning that unanimity was essential to the function of the jury and four reasoning that it was not. Relying on Justice Fortas' reasoning in his *Duncan* concurrence, the remaining member of the *Apodaca* Court, Justice Powell, concluded that on this type of issue the Fourteenth Amendment and the Sixth Amendment could produce different results. He would therefore uphold the state's right to utilize a non-unanimous jury verdict, although he would rule otherwise as to a federal jury, where the Sixth Amendment would directly apply. Because Justice Powell contributed the deciding vote, the Court in *Apodaca* reached a result that was anomalous in light of the majority's commitment to parallelism—the state's use of non-unanimous verdicts was upheld, though the same Court would have reached a different constitutional result in a federal case.

Justice Powell gained the support of two other justices in arguing for a separate constitutional standard for state proceedings in *Crist v. Bretz,*[20] but the Court majority again rejected that view. At issue in *Crist* was the definition of the starting point for the attachment of jeopardy under the double jeopardy clause. While the Court's earlier rulings had assumed that jeopardy attached with the im-

18. 399 U.S. 78, 90 S.Ct. 1893, 26 L.Ed.2d 446 (1970).

19. 406 U.S. 404, 92 S.Ct. 1628, 32 L.Ed.2d 184 (1972).

20. 437 U.S. 28, 98 S.Ct. 2156, 57 L.Ed.2d 24 (1978).

panelment of the jury, the state argued that it should be given the leeway to view jeopardy as not attaching until the first witness was sworn. The Court majority was not receptive to that contention insofar as it might suggest a separate constitutional standard for state proceedings. Once again, the proper approach was to reexamine the validity of the assumption made in earlier cases. Here, however, the Court concluded that the earlier cases had not adopted some "arbitrarily chosen rule of convenience" based on traditional federal practice (as the state argued), but a standard tied to a major function of the double jeopardy bar and therefore constitutionally mandated.

In the years since *Crist,* the Court has considered various constitutional claims that Justice Fortas might have characterized as dealing primarily with a "system of administration." No member of the Court has suggested, however, that the particular requirement might not be constitutionally demanded for state proceedings while constitutionally mandated in federal proceedings. The focus in each instance—consistent with the view of selective incorporation advanced by the Court majority in the cases discussed above—was on whether the particular standard was indeed a basic element of the constitutional guarantee in question. Thus, it now appears to be a settled principle, unlikely to be reexamined, that selective incorporation requires full application of all aspects of an incorporated guarantee to the states.

(c) Selective Incorporation and the Concerns of Federalism. Although the "pendulum of federalism" in the Supreme Court arguably has swung back to greater sensitivity to the prerogatives of the states, that shift has not led to either the restructuring or rejection of the selective incorporation doctrine, as it has with some other doctrines initiated in the 1960's. As suggested by the cases discussed in the previous section, the Court has been able to accommodate the renewed concern for the values of federalism within the framework of the doctrine. In particular, it has been able to take into consideration both the diversity of settings presented by state criminal procedure and the potential for instituting improvements in the process through innovative state experimentation.

When the selective incorporation doctrine was first adopted, some commentators argued that it would bar consideration of the diverse settings in which state criminal justice systems operated. Application of a single constitutional standard supposedly would undercut important local administrative adjustments, particularly those relating to judicial proceedings. Post-incorporation rulings established, however, that states could justify many local variations that were based on special administrative needs. In *North v. Russell,*[21] for example, a two-tier system for the trial of misdemeanors, with non-lawyer magistrates operating at the first level, was sustained as an appropriate balance of the limited resources of rural communities and the procedural rights of defendants. Similarly, in *Shadwick v. Tampa,*[22] recognizing the "stiff and unrelenting caseloads" borne by many municipal courts, the Court held that the Fourth Amendment was not violated by the issuance of arrest warrants for municipal ordinance violations by non-lawyer clerks of municipal courts. Justice Powell's opinion for a unanimous Court initially noted that the issuance of warrants by judges or lawyers was to be preferred, but then, in language reminiscent of earlier fundamental fairness opinions, added that "our federal system" requires recognition of the "national innovation and vitality" provided by "plural and diverse state activities." Accordingly, the states were "entitled to some flexibility and leeway in their designation of magistrates, so long as all are neutral and detached and capable of the probable-cause determination required of them."

North, Shadwick, and various search and seizure opinions recognizing the special problems of local law enforcement,[23] evidence a

21. 427 U.S. 328, 96 S.Ct. 2709, 49 L.Ed.2d 534 (1976).

22. 407 U.S. 345, 92 S.Ct. 2119, 32 L.Ed.2d 783 (1972).

23. See e.g., South Dakota v. Opperman, 428 U.S. 364, 96 S.Ct. 3092, 49 L.Ed.2d 1000 (1976) (recognizing the difficulties of securing impounded automobiles against

substantial potential for accommodation to community diversity within a framework of selective incorporation. Admittedly, not all such claims for accommodation have been successful.[24] Also, selective incorporation arguably provides less room for accommodation than would be available under a fundamental fairness standard. Nevertheless, there remains sufficient opportunity for recognition of substantial local concerns to convince several justices who would give significant weight to such concerns that there is no need to turn away from the selective incorporation doctrine.

Critics of selective incorporation also argued that that doctrine would preclude innovative experiments that might otherwise improve the criminal justice process. Here again, however, the adverse impact has not been nearly as substantial as the critics suggested. Not all innovations presented to the Courts have been upheld,[25] but the justices have had no difficulty in giving weight to the value of experimentation. In *Chandler v. Florida*,[26] for example, the Court looked to that value in holding that, subject to certain safeguards, a state could permit the televising of a trial over defendant's objection. The Court noted that Florida had adopted its guidelines for televising trials only after a carefully reviewed pilot program had proven successful, that eighteen other states had experimented with such guidelines, and that the issue was under study in yet another dozen states. This strong display of state interest, supported by its generally careful and cautious approach, worked in Florida's favor. The Court concluded that where, as here, it could not say that the state activity automatically violated due process, it would be guided by Justice Brandeis' admonition in *New State Ice Co. v. Liebman* to respect state experimentation. In restoring the relevance of Justice Brandeis' admonition, *Chandler* may have put to rest the concerns created by the earlier rejection of that admonition by Justices Goldberg and Black in their support of the selective incorporation doctrine.[27]

(d) The Retention of Due Process Methodology. The traditional due process analysis under the fundamental fairness standard focused upon the totality of the circumstances of the individual case. Consideration was given to variety of factors relating to a challenged state practice, including administrative justifications, the extent to which the practice might be inconsistent with a basic goal of the criminal justice process, and the prejudicial impact upon the outcome of the particular case. The end result was a methodology that Justice Black characterized as inherently subjective but Justice Frankfurter viewed as both inherent in the concept of due process and a necessary attribute of constitutional adjudication of complex issues. Not all practices, he noted, could be readily categorized constitutionally as clearly prohibited or permitted; in many instances, reference had to be made to how they were used, and what impact they had in the setting of the particular case. Some proponents of the fundamental fairness position apparently assumed that the Court's ability to continue to use this traditional methodology would be sharply restricted by adoption of an incorporationist

theft and therefore upholding routine inventory searches); Cady v. Dombrowski, 413 U.S. 433, 93 S.Ct. 2523, 37 L.Ed.2d 706 (1973) (upholding a warrantless search of an impounded automobile believed to contain a weapon; earlier automobile search cases involving federal officers were distinguishable because local police had additional responsibilities relating to vehicle operations and public safety).

24. See e.g., Crist v. Bretz, supra note 20 (state could not utilize traditional local rule that jeopardy did not attach until first witness sworn); Smith v. Hooey, 393 U.S. 374, 89 S.Ct. 575, 21 L.Ed.2d 607 (1969) (where an accused person imprisoned in another jurisdiction demanded a speedy trial, the state's failure to comply could not be justified by the transportation costs or administrative problems involved in seeking his temporary release from the other jurisdiction for purposes of trial).

25. See e.g., Coy v. Iowa, 487 U.S. 1012, 108 S.Ct. 2798, 101 L.Ed.2d 857 (1988) (holding unconstitutional a state practice which allowed child victims of sex abuse to testify from behind a screen blocking defendant from their sight); Brooks v. Tennessee, 406 U.S. 605, 92 S.Ct. 1891, 32 L.Ed.2d 358 (1972) (holding unconstitutional a state law—designed to extend to the defendant the policy underlying the sequestration of prospective witnesses—that required a defendant desiring to testify to do so before any other defense witnesses were heard).

26. 449 U.S. 560, 101 S.Ct. 802, 66 L.Ed.2d 740 (1981).

27. See the text following note 10 of § 2.4.

position. Reliance upon the specific guarantees, rather than the more flexible concept of due process, would lead to constitutional standards that were more categorical in nature. Admittedly, clauses like the "reasonableness" clause of the Fourth Amendment would still allow a circumstance-specific analysis, but other guarantees, using less flexible terms, would not.

Undoubtedly, the constitutional standards applied to the states in the post-incorporationist era do tend to be less circumstance-specific than the standards applied under the fundamental fairness standard. But many rulings under a variety of incorporated guarantees have taken a form very similar to that traditionally applied under due process. The announced standards have incorporated a balancing process, an element of prejudicial impact, or a consideration of governmental motive that necessarily requires an examination of the particular circumstances of the individual case. Among the standards that can be so characterized are the *Strickland v. Washington* test for determining when counsel's performance was so inadequate as to deny the defendant the effective assistance of counsel guaranteed by the Sixth Amendment,[28] the *Wheat v. United States* standard for determining when a disqualification of defense counsel resulted in a denial of defendant's Sixth Amendment right to counsel of choice,[29] the *Barker v. Wingo* balancing test for determining when defendant has been denied his Sixth Amendment right to a speedy trial,[30] and the "manifest necessity" test applied in determining when a mistrial ordered without a defense request can produce a double jeopardy violation.[31] Indeed, on occasion, the standard applied under an incorporated guarantee may largely parallel that utilized under due process in dealing with a related practice.[32]

(e) The Independent Force of Due Process. In its application of the fundamental fairness standard, the Supreme Court occasionally utilized the due process clause to impose constitutional restrictions upon criminal justice practices that arguably would not fall within the reach of any of the other Bill of Rights guarantees.[33] That practice remained permissible under the selective incorporation doctrine, as that doctrine viewed due process as continuing to have an independent force apart from its incorporation of those guarantees held to be fundamental. It might have been anticipated, however, that the Court in the post-incorporation era would seek to develop its rulings out of the incorporated guarantees, utilizing due process as a last resort for regulating practices patently beyond the reach of those guarantees. That has not proven to be the case. The Court has continued to be comfortable with due process based rulings, and it has relied on the due process clause in regulating a variety of practices that arguably could have been reached under the incorporated guarantees. Thus, preindictment delay has been held to be subject to a standard of due process rather than the Sixth Amendment's speedy trial guarantee [34]; rulings relating to the seating of prospective jurors aware of prejudicial pretrial publicity have been based on the due process clause rather than defendant's Sixth Amendment right to an impartial jury [35]; government action denying defendant access to a potential defense witness or discouraging a called witness from testifying has been judged under a standard of due process as well as the Sixth Amendment right to compulsory process [36]; and in one notable case, the Court looked to the fundamental fairness test of due process rather than the Sixth Amendment

28. See § 11.10(a).

29. See § 11.9(d).

30. See § 18.2(a).

31. See § 25.2(c).

32. Compare, for example, the *Wheat* standard as to disqualification of counsel [see § 11.9(c)] and the due process standard governing a denial of a continuance that may preclude defendant's representation by counsel of choice [see § 11.4(c)]. See also note 36 infra.

33. See § 2.4 at notes 7–10.

34. See § 18.5

35. See § 23.2.

36. See Webb v. Texas and United States v. Valenzuela–Bernal, discussed in § 24.3(e).

rights of confrontation and compulsory process in finding that the combined impact of restricting defendant's cross-examination of a hostile defense witness and precluding testimony of other defense witnesses so limited his ability to present his defense as to invalidate his conviction.[37]

As the above cases indicate, the Court's reliance upon the independent force of due process in the post-incorporation era has been more than sporadic. Indeed, rulings based on due process have been so frequent and so varied in coverage that once the criminal justice process moves beyond the investigative stage, that body of rulings arguably plays as significant a role in the regulation of the process as the rulings under the incorporated guarantees. Due process serves as a primary grounding for the constitutional restraints imposed upon the prosecutor; the prohibition against vindictive charging, the obligation to disclose material exculpatory evidence, and the bar against improper and prejudicial closing arguments all flow from due process.[38] Constitutional limitations relating to various aspects of the guilty plea, including plea bargaining and plea acceptance, are based upon the due process clause.[39] Due process limitations also plays a significant role at trial. The basic constitutional restrictions relating to proof responsibilities at trial—the government's obligation to establish guilt beyond a reasonable doubt, the limitations on classifying defenses as affirmative, and the restrictions on the use of presumptions—all stem from due process rulings.[40] The defendant's right of presence and right to testify are both based, in part, on due process.[41] The due process clause also serves as the source of prohibitions designed to ensure judicial impartiality and mandated judicial action to preclude or respond to outside influences that might affect the impartiality of the jury.[42] When the process moves to the sentencing stage, constitutional procedural protections diminish, but most of those that do exist are due process based.[43] Beyond that point, at probation and parole revocation proceedings, the Sixth Amendment guarantees do not apply, and due process clearly is the key source of constitutional safeguards.[44]

Another feature of the post-incorporation use of due process has been the frequency with which due process has been held to impose categorical prohibitions rather than prohibitions dependent upon the more traditional totality-of-the-circumstances analysis. Categorical prohibitions are also to be found in the pre-incorporation due process rulings,[45] but they are more common in the post-incorporation rulings. Illustrative are due process rulings requiring prosecution proof of guilt beyond a reasonable doubt,[46] the appointment of counsel in juvenile delinquency proceedings,[47] and the provision of dual hearings in parole revocation cases.[48] Each ruling imposed a fixed requirement applicable to a general category of cases. Such due process rulings, however, still remain in the minority. Due process rulings more often have followed the traditional mode, requiring ad hoc weighing of the circumstances to determine whether the ultimate standard of "fairness" has been violated. That is the situation, for example, in determining whether a prosecutor's closing argument violated due process,[49] whether an eyewitness identification procedure was so conducive to irreparable mistaken identification that use of its fruits violated

37. Chambers v. Mississippi, 410 U.S. 284, 93 S.Ct. 1038, 35 L.Ed.2d 297 (1973).

38. See §§ 13.5, 20.7, 24.5.

39. See §§ 21.2, 21.4.

40. See In re Winship, 397 U.S. 358, 90 S.Ct. 1068, 25 L.Ed.2d 368 (1970); Carella v. California, 491 U.S. 263, 109 S.Ct. 2419, 105 L.Ed.2d 218 (1989).

41. See §§ 24.2(a), 24.4(d).

42. See §§ 22.4(a), 23.2–3, 24.6.

43. See § 26.4.

44. See §§ 11.1(b), 26.2(c).

45. See e.g., Tumey v. Ohio, § 2.4 at note 8, establishing an absolute bar against compensation of judges geared to fees paid upon conviction.

46. See note 40 supra.

47. In re Gault, § 11.1, note 10.

48. Morrissey v. Brewer, § 26.2 at note 4.

49. See § 24.6(h).

due process,[50] and whether the failure to appoint counsel to assist an indigent in a parole revocation proceeding violates due process.[51] In other instances, due process violations have turned upon the presence of an improper motive,[52] a standard that ordinarily narrows the focus of the inquiry but still requires an examination of the special circumstances of the individual case. Thus, due process rulings can still be characterized as more likely to impose circumstance-specific standards than rulings based on the incorporated guarantees. Yet, with various categorical standards adopted under the due process clause and various circumstance-specific standards adopted under even the most specific incorporated guarantees, whether a particular standard is grounded on a incorporated guarantee or due process may well have no influence on the type of standard adopted.[53]

§ 2.7 The Preference for Expansive Interpretations

(a) The Nature of the Preference. As noted in § 2.1, the constitutionalization of criminal procedure has been a product of both the extension of various Bill of Rights guarantees to the states and the adoption of expansive interpretations of those guarantees. Of course, whether a particular interpretation is appropriately characterized as "expansive" depends largely upon one's perspective. Some see as expansive any interpretation that goes beyond the narrowest reading that could be derived from the language or history of the guarantee being applied. From this perspective, almost all of the Supreme Court's interpretations have been expansive. For example, the Fifth Amendment's self-incrimination prohibition has been held to go beyond merely protecting the defendant from being compelled to give incriminating testimony at his own trial. Similarly, the prohibition against double jeopardy has been extended beyond merely barring a retrial on the same offense following an acquittal.

Some would view an interpretation as truly expansive only if it gives the guarantee the broadest reading that could conceivably be developed from its language, history, or overall policy. From this perspective, very few of the Court's interpretations have been truly expansive. The right to jury trial, for example, does not extend to all cases that might be deemed "criminal" in nature. The self-incrimination clause does not prohibit compelling a person to produce all types of evidence that might be incriminating. The double jeopardy prohibition does not bar all retrials of defendants for the same offense.

For most commentators, to characterize an interpretation as expansive, it must do more than barely exceed the narrowest possible reading, but it need not necessarily adopt the broadest conceivable reading. The emphasis is as much upon how the Court approaches the provision as upon the scope of its reading. Expansive interpretations start from a presumption of liberal construction. They treat a constitutional guarantee not as narrow and technical, but as reflecting an important policy that must be safeguarded against circumvention and even minor encroachments. An expansive approach reflects, in particular, a willingness to expand the scope of the guarantee to meet changed conditions, especially growth in governmental authority. Judged by this standard, the Supreme Court's construction of the criminal procedure guarantees, as a general matter, clearly reflects a preference for expansive interpretation. The Court's treatment of those guarantees stands in sharp contrast, for example, to its treatment of the constitutional prohibition against state impairment of the obligation of contracts. The much closer analogy is its approach to the First Amendment, where the Court speaks of applying "more exacting judicial scrutiny" in judging the constitutionality of governmental action.

To say that the overall trend of the Court's constitutional criminal procedure rulings has

50. See § 7.4.

51. Gagnon v. Scarpelli, § 11.1 at note 9.

52. See §§ 13.5, 24.3(d), 26.8.

53. See also § 2.8(c) discussing the division among the justices relating to the appropriate breadth of constitutional rulings.

favored expansive interpretation does not, of course, suggest that the Court has uniformly favored that position throughout its history. As discussed in subsection (b), the degree of support for expansive interpretation has varied from one period in the Court's history to another.[1] Moreover, the preference has always existed as no more than a principle that guides interpretation in a general fashion. Even when given great weight, it does not invariably require the adoption of the most expansive of all possible interpretations. Indeed, the special setting of the individual case may lead the Court to adopt a fairly narrow construction of a particular guarantee. The preference was at its strongest during the decade of the 1960's; yet during that period, the same Court that adopted numerous expansive interpretations of constitutional safeguards also issued several major rulings that fell far short of what one might expect from a strong expansionist philosophy.[2]

(b) The Shifting Strength of the Preference. While there were occasional rulings prior to *Boyd v. United States* that adopted expansive interpretation of criminal procedure guarantees, the *Boyd* decision,[3] in 1886, clearly set forth and applied a preference for what it described as a "liberal" construction of those guarantees.[4] Indeed, few rulings of the Court, if any, have adopted a more expansive interpretation of a particular guarantee than did the *Boyd* Court in applying the Fourth Amendment and the self-incrimination privilege of the Fifth Amendment. During the period between *Boyd* and the start of the 1920's, the Court decided relatively few criminal procedure cases as compared to later periods. Yet several of its rulings reflected landmark expansionist interpretations of particular Bill of Rights guarantees as applied to the federal criminal justice process.[5] At the same time, as discussed in § 2.4(b), federalism concerns led the Court to narrowly construe the Fourteenth Amendment's due process clause as applied to state cases.

During the 1920's, federal criminal cases presenting constitutional issues, particularly Fourth Amendment claims, reached the Court more frequently. The results were mixed. Several significant decisions carried forward the philosophy of *Boyd,* but others adopted what might be characterized as a narrow and technical view of the Fourth Amendment in particular.[6] As noted in § 2.4(c), during the 1930's, the Court initiated a gradual movement toward a more expansive reading of the fundamental fairness doctrine of due process as applied to the states. At the same time, its rulings in federal cases frequently reflected an expansionist approach, as in the extension of the Sixth Amendment right to counsel to require appointed counsel for the indigent.[7] That philosophy arguably lost some force in the 1940's, particularly as to the Fourth Amendment, but then regained strength in the 1950's.

During the 1960's, covering the latter half of Chief Justice Warren's tenure, the Court undoubtedly showed a consistently stronger preference for expansionist rulings than in any other period of the Court's history. The end result was what commentators came to describe as the Warren Court's criminal procedure "revolution." The Court not only adopted the selective incorporation doctrine, as described in § 2.6, but it also rendered various interpretations of the incorporated

§ 2.7

1. Commentators disagree as to why the Court has been more receptive to expansive interpretations in one period than another. Some look primarily to the Court's composition, stressing differences in the philosophical outlook of the majority of justices sitting in a particular period. Others stress the social and political setting of the period.

2. While these rulings are sometimes attributed to a "late retreat" toward the end of the Warren Court period, several came during the same terms in which the Warren Court rendered some of its most expansive rulings. See e.g., Chapman v. California (1967), § 27.6(c), and the decisions subsequently overruled in the cases cited in note 12 infra.

3. 116 U.S. 616, 6 S.Ct. 524, 29 L.Ed. 746 (1886).

4. See §§ 8.7(a), 8.12(a).

5. See e.g., Bram v. United States, § 6.2(a); Counselman v. Hitchcock, § 8.10(a); Weeks v. United States, § 3.1(a).

6. Compare e.g., Silverthorne Lumber Co. v. United States, § 9.3(a) and Marion v. United States, § 3.4(f), with Olmstead v. United States, § 4.1(a).

7. See Johnson v. Zerbst, § 11.1(a).

guarantees that went far beyond their previous application in federal cases. Guarantees were extended into new areas previously viewed as beyond the scope of constitutional regulation,[8] and constitutional standards in areas subject to regulation were made more rigorous.[9] Indeed, the pace of expansion was so rapid, and the range of expansion so broad, that the Warren Court rulings, in less than a decade, outstripped all of the expansionist rulings over the Court's prior history in the degree of additional regulation imposed upon the combined state and federal criminal justice processes.

Commentators have divided in their overall characterization of the Supreme Court's rulings for the period since the Warren Court revolution. Some have seen the decisions first of the Burger Court and then of the Rehnquist Court as merely slowing down the expansionist momentum. There was some retreat, they argue, but not the true counterrevolution that had been anticipated in light of the new composition of the Court. They cite rulings of the post-Warren era that have extended constitutional guarantees to areas not considered by the Warren Court,[10] have carried forward the logic of various rulings of the Warren Court,[11] and even have rejected some narrow Warren Court decisions to impose rigorous restraints that the Warren Court declined to adopt.[12] Other commentators, however characterize such decisions as reflecting the exception rather than the general rule, and claim that the Court's rulings reflect a fundamental shift in position. Under either of these characterizations, the post-Warren Court rulings still fit readily within the framework of a general preference for expansive interpretations of criminal procedure guarantees, at least if that concept is defined along the lines set forth in subsection (a). To say that the justices have not carried their interpretations as far as their predecessors would have done, or even that they have retreated substantially from prior rulings, is to establish only that the preference has diminished in strength. That the preference remains viable is evidenced by the Court's continued willingness, in general, to look to the functions of the guarantees as a grounding for interpretation, to recognize the need to extend the guarantees to meet changed circumstances, and to reject readings that treat the guarantees as technical requirements. The presumption favoring liberal construction today may be more readily outweighed by other considerations, at least in some areas, but it hardly has disappeared.

(c) The Reasons for the Preference. The Court has only infrequently commented upon the premises that underly its adoption of a preference for expansive interpretations of criminal procedure guarantees. Moreover, those comments have identified only in very general terms the reasons why the Court believes it can justifiably play a more "activist" role in interpreting those guarantees than in interpreting other constitutional provisions. Commentators, in contrast, have offered a series of well developed rationales that provide a grounding for adoption of especially expansive interpretations of the criminal procedure guarantees. One can only speculate as to whether the justices actually have had those rationales in mind as they shaped their criminal procedure rulings. However, several of the rationales cited do find support in occasional comments of the justices. These ratio-

8. See e.g., Katz v. United States, § 4.1(c); Camara v. Municipal Court, § 3.9(a); In re Gault, 387 U.S. 1, 87 S.Ct. 1428, 18 L.Ed.2d 527 (1967) (due process held to require adequate written notice of charges and availability of appointed counsel, and self-incrimination privilege held applicable, in juvenile delinquency proceedings that may lead to commitment in state institution).

9. See e.g., Chimel v. California, § 3.6(c); Miranda v. Arizona, § 6.5; Bruton v. United States, § 17.2(b).

10. See e.g., Tennessee v. Garner, § 3.5(a); Faretta v. California, § 11.5(a); Burks v. United States, § 25.4(b). Perhaps the most frequently cited illustration here is the Court's effort to impose constitutional regulations in the substantive standards and procedures utilized in imposing capital punishment. See § 26.1(b).

11. See e.g., Edwards v. Arizona and Minnick v. Mississippi, § 6.9(g); Payton v. New York, § 3.6(a); Ake v. Oklahoma, § 11.2(d).

12. See Taylor v. Louisiana, § 22.2(d) (adopting under the Sixth Amendment a position that the Warren Court had rejected in a due process ruling); Batson v. Kentucky, § 22.3(d) (overruling the Warren Court's *Swain* decision).

nales look primarily to three factors, each discussed below: (1) the relationship of criminal procedure to the general protection of civil liberties; (2) the relationship of criminal procedure to the protection of minorities; and (3) the presence of various structural elements that enhance the Court's authority in exercising constitutional review of the criminal process. It seems likely that all three of these factors contributed to some extent in the development of the preference for expansionist interpretations, with the contribution of each varying with the individual justice and the particular period in the Court's history.

At least since the end of World War I, the Court has made the protection of civil liberties one of its primary concerns. It has shifted its focus from the protection of property rights to the protection of liberties deemed more fundamental to the preservation of individual freedom. The Court has left no doubt that it considers the procedural rights of the accused to be among those more fundamental freedoms. It has accepted the premise that procedural fairness and regularity in the enforcement of the criminal law are essential to a free society. "In the end," it has explained, "life and liberty can be as much endangered from illegal methods used to convict those thought to be criminals as from actual criminals themselves." Indeed, it has added, the "quality of a nation's civilization can be largely measured by the methods it uses in the enforcement of its criminal law." [13]

The Court also has suggested, starting with its famous footnote in the *Carolene Products* [14] case, that one of its major functions is to protect against discrimination those "discrete and insular minorities" who could not count on the protection of the political process. Safeguarding the rights of the accused has been viewed in two respects as an element of this role of the Court. First, accused persons are themselves viewed as a highly unpopular minority. As Justice Frankfurter noted, it is precisely because appeals based on criminal process guarantees are so often made by "dubious characters" that infringement of those guarantees calls for "alert and strenuous resistance"; other constitutional protections, such as the First Amendment guarantees, "easily summon powerful support against encroachment," but criminal process guarantees are "normally invoked by those accused of crime, and criminals have few friends." [15] Second, the criminal process is seen as having a special bearing upon various disadvantaged minority groups. Thus, Professor Pye has noted:

> It is hard to conceive of a Court that would accept the challenge of guaranteeing the rights of Negroes and other disadvantaged groups to equality before the law and at the same time do nothing to ameliorate the invidious discrimination between rich and poor which existed in the criminal process. It would have been equally anomalous for such a Court to ignore the clear evidence that members of disadvantaged groups generally bore the brunt of unlawful police activity.[16]

The Court's willingness to adopt expansive interpretations also has been attributed to several factors that make the exercise of judicial review more readily supportable in the criminal justice area than in other areas of constitutional adjudication. It is argued that the Court, having less concern about challenges to its basic authority, has felt freer to play an activist role in developing criminal procedure standards. Foremost among the factors cited as giving the Court this freedom is the structure of the applicable constitutional guarantees. The specificity of most of the guarantees found in the Fourth, Fifth, and Sixth Amendments arguably permits criminal procedure rulings to be more firmly rooted in

13. Miranda v. Arizona, 384 U.S. 436, 86 S.Ct. 1602, 16 L.Ed.2d 694 (1966); Spano v. New York, 360 U.S. 315, 79 S.Ct. 1202, 3 L.Ed.2d 1265 (1959).

14. United States v. Carolene Products Co., 304 U.S. 144, 152, fn. 4, 58 S.Ct. 778, 783, fn. 4, 82 L.Ed. 1234 (1938). See also Lusky, Footnote Redux: A Carolene Products Reminiscence, 82 Colum.L.Rev. 1093 (1982).

15. Harris v. United States, 331 U.S. 145, 67 S.Ct. 1098, 91 L.Ed. 1399 (1947) (dissenting opinion).

16. Pye, The Warren Court and Criminal Procedure, 67 Mich.L.Rev. 249, 256 (1968).

the text and history of constitutional provisions than constitutional rulings in other areas. Even when the criminal procedure rulings are based upon the more open-ended provisions of the Bill of Rights, such as the due process clause, no doubt exists that the particular clause was designed to apply to the criminal process, though the precise scope of that application may be debatable.

The Court's criminal procedure rulings are also said to rest on a firmer constitutional foundation because they so infrequently produce the kind of direct conflict with representative institutions that gives rise to criticisms of its rulings as anti-majoritarian. Unlike constitutional rulings in various other areas, the Court's criminal procedure rulings rarely place it in immediate conflict with the legislature. Rulings on police investigative techniques generally deal with practices that have been instituted by the police without any formal approval of local or state legislative bodies. Rulings relating to trial and pretrial practices generally are concerned with procedures instituted by lower courts. Although the judges of these courts may be elected, they are not viewed as politically responsible representatives of the electorate comparable to legislators.

Another factor cited as contributing to the preference for expansive interpretations is the Court's confidence in its expertise in dealing with at least those procedural issues that relate to the process of adjudication. The Supreme Court has not described its competence in this area in quite the same way as commentators, who claim that lawyers (and judges) have unique expertise in deciding "what procedures are needed fairly to make what decisions." Yet, the Court has clearly indicated that it views itself as exercising a special responsibility in reviewing procedures of adjudication. Those procedures, it is noted, relate directly to the integrity of the judicial process. Moreover, while the Court's rulings on adjudicatory procedure undoubtedly have a bearing on the achievement of substantive policies, they do not prohibit the legislature from setting substantive standards, but merely require that proof of violation of these standards be established in a certain way. Accordingly, as Justice Jackson noted, the determination of "procedural fairness" is treated as "a specialized responsibility within the competence of the judiciary on which they do not bend before political branches of Government, as they should on matters of policy which comprise substantive law." [17]

§ 2.8 Factors Influencing the Extent of the Preference

As noted in § 2.7(a), the application of a presumption favoring liberal construction of criminal procedure guarantees has not invariably produced interpretations that are uniformly expansive. Numerous factors may affect the Court's willingness to adopt an expansive interpretation in an individual case. Some of those factors relate to the setting of the case and the particular guarantee being applied, but others are more general in nature. Among these are (1) the relationship of a proposed expansive interpretation to the reliability of the factfinding process, (2) a long-established historical acceptance of the practice that would be invalidated under that interpretation, (3) the desirability of fashioning a broad constitutional standard that extends beyond the particular facts of the individual case, and (4) the impact of a proposed ruling on the efficient enforcement of the criminal law. Each of these factors has been viewed by at least some justices as having a substantial bearing on how far the Court should carry its preference for expansive interpretations. The Court's determination of the weight to be given to one or another of these factors often has been crucial in the adoption or rejection of a particular expansive interpretation. That determination has varied, however, with the composition of the Court, as the justices have persistently divided over the significance of each of the factors.

17. Shaughnessy v. United States ex rel. Mezei, 345 U.S. 206, 73 S.Ct. 625, 97 L.Ed. 956 (1953) (dissenting opinion).

(a) The Priority of Reliability Guarantees. Over the years, various justices have maintained that a higher priority should be given to those constitutional rights that serve basically to ensure that the process arrives at the truth and thereby avoids the conviction of the innocent. They argue that the Court should give somewhat broader protection, particularly in the construction of remedies, to those guarantees that seek to achieve factfinding accuracy, as opposed to those that serve other interests, such as respecting the dignity of the individual. They would, for example, permit a collateral attack upon a conviction rendered by a biased jury, but would not make that remedy available to challenge a conviction based upon unconstitutionally seized evidence (the Fourth Amendment violation having no bearing upon the reliability of that evidence).[1] Similarly, in determining whether a newly imposed constitutional requirement should be applied retroactively, they would give primary weight to whether convictions that had been obtained without that requirement might well be inaccurate.[2]

Of course, as noted in § 1.6, constitutional guarantees frequently serve both to protect the innocent and to implement other goals as well. In such cases, justices arguing that factfinding reliability should receive higher priority may be willing to extend the scope of the guarantee only insofar as it achieves the reliability objective. Thus, they would refuse to apply the self-incrimination privilege to bar most police interrogation, but would apply the policies of the privilege to the extent necessary to exclude potentially unreliable confessions obtained through such interrogation.[3] Similarly, the double jeopardy protection against reprosecution following an acquittal would be given a more expansive interpretation than the double jeopardy protection against multiple punishment for the commission of a single offense.[4]

Various other justices have flatly rejected the contention that priority should be given to those guarantees that seek to ensure factfinding integrity. They argue that all constitutional guarantees should be treated alike and extensive relief should be available for any constitutional violation. They acknowledge that some remedies afforded for violations of guarantees protecting individual dignity (such as the exclusion of evidence obtained through a Fourth Amendment violation) often operate to protect the "guilty," but they note that those remedies also serve the interests of society as a whole. They also contend that attempts to separate the different interests protected by a single guarantee produce uneven interpretations of the guarantee that only serve to undermine the Court's authority. Expansive protection of all guarantees is essential, in their view, to ensure respect for the place of the Constitution in regulating the criminal justice process.

(b) The Significance of Historical Acceptance. The justices also have been divided, though far less sharply, as to the significance to be attached to the historical acceptance of a challenged practice, particularly where that acceptance dates back to the time of the adoption of the Constitution. The justices generally have agreed that historical acceptance has less significance in interpreting "open-ended" guarantees, such as the due process clause, which arguably were intended to be "molded to the views of contemporary society." Their disagreement has arisen primarily as to the more specific guarantees, such as the self-incrimination privilege, which are said to have a more clearly defined historical content. The issue here, as some justices see it, is whether in the interpretation of these guarantees it can truly be said that "a page of history is worth a volume of logic."

§ 2.8

1. See §§ 28.3(b), (c). Consider also § 28.4(g).

2. See §§ 2.9(e), 28.36(c).

3. See Miranda v. Arizona, 384 U.S. 436, 86 S.Ct. 1602, 16 L.Ed.2d 694 (1966) (Harlan, J., dissenting).

4. See §§ 25.3, 26.7. See also § 25.4. Of course, even under this view, it does not follow that guarantees aimed at avoiding erroneous convictions will necessarily be given the broadest possible interpretation. Other concerns may lead the Court to a narrower interpretation. See e.g., §§ 7.4(b), 20.6(b), 24.3(d), (g).

In various cases interpreting the more specific guarantees, the Court has stated that a substantial record of historical acceptance will create a strong presumption of constitutionality.[5] This position does not arise out of a concept that constitutional interpretation must invariably be tied to the "original intent" of framers, for even if that concept were otherwise acceptable, original intent can hardly be ascertained solely by reference to the framer's view of a particular practice. Rather, the presumption rests on the premise that constitutional interpretation should be strongly guided by the wisdom and experience reflected in the earlier understanding of the particular guarantee. Accordingly, a practice may be sustained by an historical record of acceptance even though that practice might otherwise be viewed as inconsistent with the general thrust of the guarantee. "Logic," it is said, "must defer to history and experience."

In contrast to the above rulings, in still other cases, often dealing with the same guarantees, a differently composed majority has given little weight, if any, to historical acceptance. Indeed, in several instances, cases that relied on historical acceptance in upholding a certain practice were later overruled (and the practice held unconstitutional) with little or no mention of that history.[6] While such opinions do not go so far as to hold historical acceptance to be irrelevant, they do reflect a willingness to look for, and readily find, reasons for discounting that acceptance. In particular, because of various fundamental changes that have occurred in the criminal justice process since the adoption of the Bill of Rights (such as the creation of the modern police department), a Court that is looking for such a reason often will have no difficulty in citing changed circumstances that arguably place the challenged practice in a different light than existed at the time of its initial acceptance. Moreover, some justices will reason, even without regard to changed circumstances, that the overarching purpose of the guarantee must take precedence and require rejection of historically accepted practices if they are nonetheless logically inconsistent with that purpose.

In sum, the influence of historical acceptance upon the adoption of expansive interpretations has varied with the nature of the clause applied and the judicial philosophy of the individual justice. For some justices, at least as to the more specific clauses, historical acceptance has been a significant restraining factor. For others, it has been no more than a makeweight, relied upon or pushed aside according to whether the justice would otherwise view the practice as constitutional or unconstitutional.

(c) The Desirability of Per Se Rules. The scope of an expansive interpretation will be controlled in part by general principles governing the appropriate breadth of constitutional rulings resolving individual cases. Here again, however, the Court often has been divided. Some justices have favored rulings that are geared to the special circumstances of the decided case, while others have been inclined to adopt more generalized rulings, imposing what are commonly described as "flat" or "per se" prohibitions. Although an expansive interpretation may be incorporated in either type of ruling, adoption of a per se prohibition ordinarily provides for broader implementation by extending the reach of the interpretation.

All of the justices recognize that, in a particular setting, the language or history of a guarantee may require an absolute prohibition that operates without regard to case-by-

5. See e.g., United States v. Watson, 423 U.S. 411, 96 S.Ct. 820, 46 L.Ed.2d 598 (1976) (historical acceptance of warrantless arrests); Costello v. United States, 350 U.S. 359, 76 S.Ct. 406, 100 L.Ed. 397 (1956) (tradition that grand jury may consider evidence that would be inadmissible at trial); Green v. United States, 356 U.S. 165, 78 S.Ct. 632, 2 L.Ed.2d 672 (1958) (historical acceptance of the power of federal courts to punish for criminal contempt without prosecution by indictment or jury trial), overruled in Bloom v. Illinois, infra note 6.

6. See e.g., Gideon v. Wainwright, 372 U.S. 335, 83 S.Ct. 792, 9 L.Ed.2d 799 (1963), overruling Betts v. Brady, 316 U.S. 455, 62 S.Ct. 1252, 86 L.Ed. 1595 (1942); Bloom v. Illinois, 391 U.S. 194, 88 S.Ct. 1477, 20 L.Ed.2d 522 (1968), overruling Green v. United States, supra note 5; Camara v. Municipal Court, 387 U.S. 523, 87 S.Ct. 1727, 18 L.Ed.2d 1930 (1967), overruling Frank v. Maryland, 359 U.S. 360, 79 S.Ct. 804, 3 L.Ed.2d 877 (1959).

case balancing. The privilege against self-incrimination, for example, absolutely prohibits compelling a defendant to testify, without regard to the circumstances of the case. Disagreements as to the appropriate scope of the Court's rulings tend to arise primarily in the application of open-ended guarantees (which traditionally have fostered flexible standards) and in the extension of the more specific guarantees to new settings (as in the application of the self-incrimination clause to police interrogation). Here, the justices often see themselves as having leeway to choose between a broad categorical ruling and a ruling that is tied to the various circumstances of the individual case.[7]

Supporters of per se rules commonly argue that the Court is forced to adopt such rules, where the choice is reasonably available, by the "exigencies of its effort to provide supervision of state and federal systems of criminal justice through the use of judicial power." They stress that the Court establishes constitutional guidelines within the restrictive framework of an extremely limited docket. Gradual development of constitutional standards, with each decision tied to the individual case, is viewed as incompatible with the limited number of lower court cases that can be reviewed each year.

Supporters of flat rules also argue that per se standards are needed to ensure that the Court's rulings are consistently applied, and fully implemented, by the lower courts. Highly particularized standards that rely upon a case-by-case analysis tend to be opaque and intricate, resulting in confusion and inconsistent application among lower courts. Moreover, such standards are too readily evaded. While few majority opinions have openly acknowledged a concern that local judges will be insensitive to constitutional claims (especially where the defendant's guilt is clear), commentators maintain that such concern is implicit in numerous Supreme Court opinions. Flat rules, it is claimed, respond to that concern as well as to the administrative burdens carried by the lower courts. They are readily understood, applied without extensive factfinding, and provide less room for manipulation by the judge disposed to frustrate federal standards.

Flat or "bright line" rules are viewed in this regard as especially appropriate in regulating police practices. Commentators contend that the Court has come to recognize that police administration, like any large, overworked, and amorphous bureaucracy, will not respond automatically and with enthusiasm to pronouncements from on high imposing upon it additional burdensome requirements. Accordingly, the Court must turn to bright line rulings producing high visibility benchmarks that capture the attention of both police and public. Because of their certainty and notoriety, such rulings are seen as less likely to be ignored, misunderstood, or purposely misconstrued by police agencies.[8]

On the other side, justices opposing the adoption of generalized rules argue that such rules ignore the intricacy of the criminal justice process. The factual settings presented are said to be too varied to permit a single case to serve as a jumping-off point for the creation of a per se rule. These justices argue that the Court should adhere to the common law tradition, with the new standards developed interstitially. Eventually, the Court may reach a point where it is familiar enough with the variety of situations presented to fashion a more general standard; that will be appropriate, however, only where "the factual premises for [the] rule are so generally prevalent that little would be lost and much would be gained by abandoning case-by-case analy-

7. See § 2.6(d), (e).

8. The special setting of police operations has sometimes been "turned around" to favor bright line rules that arguably give the police greater authority than would be allowed under an examination of the circumstances of a particular case. Some justices have argued, for example, that there is special need in interpreting the Fourth Amendment to provide police with clear guidelines, permitting their adoption of standardized investigative procedures. Accordingly, they have been willing to carve out generalized areas of acceptable police authority even though, in some instances, the exercise of that authority may not be justified by the exigency which in general supports its constitutionality. See §§ 3.5(b), 3.7(a) (discussing the allowable scope of a search incident to arrest).

sis" because "the per se rule will achieve the correct result in almost all cases." In most areas, they note, the diversity of the interests that must be balanced will require a perpetually flexible standard.

Opponents of per se rules warn also that such rules are less readily modified to meet changed or unforeseen circumstances. Flat rules make it difficult for the Court to shift its position without directly overruling prior precedent. By promoting the adoption of new standards at a rapid pace, flat rules also restrict the opportunity for intervention by legislative bodies that may have a far superior capacity to remedy the underlying problem.

Justices favoring standards that focus on the individual case acknowledge that such standards may be more difficult for lower courts to administer. Ease of administration is not accepted, however, as a legitimate justification for imposing upon the state restrictions broader than needed to fulfill the purposes of the constitutional guarantee. The possibility of evasion by courts, police, or prosecutor also is viewed as an inadequate justification for imposing broad standards or prophylactic safeguards. Responding to the evasion argument, Justice White once noted that he simply "[did] not share this pervasive distrust of all official investigations," and Justice Harlan suggested that those who wanted to evade would not be effectively deterred by more generalized requirements.[9]

(d) The Appropriateness of Prophylactic Rules. An additional element is added to the debate over generalized rules where the rule in question is one that the Court would characterize as "prophylactic." Although there is some division over exactly where that characterization applies, most of the justices would utilize it only where the rule in question imposes a preventive safeguard that may reach beyond the presence of an actual constitutional violation. A prophylactic rule exists where the Court sets forth a certain standard while acknowledging that some instances falling within its proscription would not actually present a violation of the functions served by the constitutional guarantee at issue. The broader safeguard is imposed either because (i) the propensity for a constitutional violation is so great in the particular setting as to justify a broader measure as an administrative matter, (ii) the difficulty of ascertaining whether a violation actually occurred administratively justifies the broader measure, or (iii) there is a special need for the extra deterrence provided by the broader measure.

A prophylactic rule can take any of several different forms. Initially, it may be stated as an absolute prohibition of certain action. The bright line standard of *Michigan v. Jackson*[10] fits in this category. *Jackson* holds that where an accused requests the assistance of counsel, a subsequent police initiated discussion with the accused will render any resulting statement inadmissible, notwithstanding the accused's alleged waiver at that point of his right to consult with counsel. Although it is possible that an accused could change his mind and execute a waiver that would be acceptable under traditional Sixth Amendment standards, *Jackson* eschews a case-by-case inquiry into that possibility. It adopts, instead, a prophylactic prohibition against police-initiated discussions following an initial assertion of the right to counsel, treating such police action as presumptively rendering involuntary any responsive waiver.[11]

A prophylactic rule can also be imposed in the form of a remedial measure, as was done in *Maine v. Moulton.*[12] The Court there dealt with the use of an informant to elicit information from an indicted defendant. The Sixth Amendment barred the deliberate elicitation of information relating to the charged offense, but it did not bar the elicitation of information relating to other possible criminal activities, as defendant had not been placed in the status of an "accused" as to such uncharged

9. United States v. Wade, 388 U.S. 218, 87 S.Ct. 1926, 18 L.Ed.2d 1149 (1967) (White, J., dissenting); Miranda v. Arizona, supra note 3 (Harlan, J., dissenting).

10. Discussed at § 6.4(f).

11. See Michigan v. Harvey, 494 U.S. 344, 110 S.Ct. 1176, 108 L.Ed.2d 293 (1990) (so describing the *Jackson* rule).

12. See § 6.4(e).

offenses. Because the Court was concerned that law enforcement personnel might too readily cite the investigation of uncharged offenses where the undercover agent's elicitation actually was designed to obtain information relating to the charged offense, it imposed a general prohibition against prosecution use in evidence of statements made to the undercover agent relating to charged offense. Thus, as a deterrent measure, the remedy of exclusion was applied even though it might encompass some statements volunteered in response to an elicitation that truly had been directed exclusively to the uncharged offense (and therefore had not violated the Sixth Amendment).

Prophylactic rules may also take the form of requirements that certain affirmative procedures be followed to preclude constitutional violations. That structure was utilized in the two rulings most commonly characterized as paradigmatic of prophylactic requirements—*Miranda v. Arizona*[13] and *North Carolina v. Pearce*.[14] *Miranda* required the police to give various warnings to an interrogated suspect in order to ensure that custodial interrogation did not result in compulsion contrary to the suspect's privilege against self-incrimination. Absent such warnings, custodial interrogation, no matter what the circumstances, was presumed to have produced a compelled statement.[15] *Pearce* concluded that there was a substantial likelihood that a judge who imposes a higher sentence on a defendant following his successful appeal (and subsequent retrial and conviction) might be acting vindictively, which would violate due process. Because it would be most difficult for the defendant to establish actual vindictiveness, the Court required, as a prophylactic safeguard, that the judge set forth the reasons for the sentence and limit those reasons to factors that were not readily utilized to mask a vindictive purpose.

Prophylactic rulings often come very close to per se rulings that are based on an instrumental reading of a particular guarantee. *Gideon v. Wainwright* is illustrative.[16] The Court there held that an indigent felony defendant was entitled under the Sixth Amendment to the assistance of appointed counsel. This ruling appeared to be based on the view that the Sixth Amendment establishes the assistance of counsel as an essential prerequisite for a fair proceeding. While there conceivably could be cases in which a felony defendant has no need for counsel, the Sixth Amendment deems such exceptions too rare to allow anyone other than defendant to place his case in that category (which he can do by waiving counsel). Under this view of *Gideon,* the flat requirement that counsel be made available in all felony cases was a constitutionally mandated standard, flowing from the directive of the Sixth Amendment, rather than a prophylactic standard. Justice Powell, however, later argued that *Gideon* had adopted a prophylactic standard.[17] This conclusion apparently followed from his view of the Sixth Amendment as requiring that counsel be provided at state expense only where the defendant would be prejudiced by the lack of counsel. While that might be so difficult to determine as to permit the *Gideon* Court to insist that counsel be available in all felony cases, such a requirement was "prophylactic" as it extended beyond the precise function of the Sixth Amendment guarantee.

As the two different characterizations of *Gideon* suggest, the distinction between a prophylactic rule and a traditional bright line requirement will often depend upon whether the Court is willing to view a particular guarantee as having an instrumental reach, serving itself as a safeguard against certain unfairness rather than simply prohibiting the actual unfairness. Thus, the conclusion of *Tumey v. Ohio* that due process requires the appearance of fairness, as well as actual fairness, led to a bright line bar against judicial compensation through fines that the Court

13. See § 6.5.

14. See § 26.8.

15. See Oregon v. Elstad, 470 U.S. 298, 105 S.Ct. 1285, 84 L.Ed.2d 222 (1985) (so explaining *Miranda*).

16. See § 11.1(a).

17. Argersinger v. Hamlin, 407 U.S. 25, 92 S.Ct. 2006, 32 L.Ed.2d 530 (1972) (concurring opinion of Powell, J.).

has never deemed "prophylactic."[18] For some justices, this distinction is little more than a matter of phrasing and has no bearing on the advisability or consequence of a rule that operates as a preventive device. Such a rule, from their viewpoint, presents no greater difficulty than any other "flat" rule, no matter how it is characterized. Other justices, however, see the distinction as quite important.

Justice Black, for one, viewed prophylactic rules as judicial "legislation," going beyond the authority of the Court. In general, however, legitimacy has not been the critical issue. The Court is seen as having authority to "tailor judicially-created rules to implement constitutional guarantees" just as it has authority to fashion rules of administration to facilitate other areas of adjudication. But because those rules are judicially-created, at least as seen by the Court majority, they occupy a lesser status than constitutional requirements. As suggested in *Miranda,* they presumably can be replaced by equally protective administrative safeguards imposed by Congress.[19] Also, their reach may be confined to provide precisely the degree of safeguard thought to be necessary by the current Court majority. Thus, statements obtained in violation of the prophylactic prohibition of *Jackson v. Michigan* have been held to be available to the prosecution for impeachment use though not admissible in the prosecution's case-in-chief.[20] So too, a previously announced prophylactic rule may be withdrawn or modified in light of pragmatic considerations thought not to have been adequately developed in its original promulgation.[21]

When the concept of prophylactic rulings was first suggested in the 1960's, such rulings were seen as offering the potential for a dramatic extension of Supreme Court regulation of criminal procedure. Prophylactic standards remained the exception, however, rather than the general rule. Moreover, with the current Court majority viewing prophylactic rules as more malleable due to their judge-made status, the rigor of the continued implementation of those prophylactic rules previously adopted necessarily remains in doubt. Nonetheless, with the legitimacy of the prophylactic standard now firmly established, the prophylactic rule, by virtue of its very malleability, offers a unique potential for extending regulatory authority. It may provide for certain justices an enticing vehicle for imposing a general standard that those justices might otherwise hesitate to adopt as a constitutional mandate.

(e) Weighing the Impact Upon Efficiency. Adoption of an expansive ruling often will impose a substantial burden upon the administration of the criminal justice process. That burden can take various forms, including increased expenses for an already underfunded system, additional hearings for already congested court dockets, and perhaps even insurmountable obstacles to the solution of some crimes. The extent to which such "practical costs" should be considered by the Court has been a matter of continuing debate among the justices.[22] As with the division over the desirability of per se rules, the disagreement here arises primarily in the appli-

18. See § 2.4 at note 8. See also § 1.6(g).

19. See § 6.6(e).

20. See Michigan v. Harvey, supra note 10. See also § 9.6(a).

21. See New York v. Quarles, § 6.7(a); Texas v. McCullough, § 26.8(b).

22. Some commentators argue that, insofar as the justices claim that such factors will not be considered, or will not be given significant weight, they are simply seeking to preserve a mechanistic image of the judicial process that hides the value judgments actually involved in that process. Others would distinguish in this regard between burdens imposed upon those interests that stand in direct conflict with the application of a guarantee (such as the state's interest in introducing all relevant evidence) and burdens imposed upon an incidental interest (such as avoiding delay and reducing financial costs). Consideration of the former burdens, it is argued, is inherent in evaluating the function of the guarantee and the need for its extension, while the same is not true of the latter burdens because of their incidental nature.

Commentators notwithstanding, the justices profess, at least in some situations, that they have not weighed the potential impact of their ruling upon the efficient administration of the process. Indeed, Justice Black claimed that consideration of practical costs was always improper. See e.g., his opinions in Williams v. Florida, 399 U.S. 78, 90 S.Ct. 1893, 26 L.Ed.2d 446 (1970) and Baldwin v. New York, 399 U.S. 66, 90 S.Ct. 1886, 26 L.Ed.2d 437 (1970).

cation of open-ended clauses [23] and in the application of the more concrete clauses to new settings.[24] Thus, the Court has noted that where the text or history of a particular provision produces a "constitutional command that * * * is unequivocal," the practical costs incurred in applying that command become irrelevant. The command itself strikes a balance between the rights of the accused and society's need for effective enforcement of the criminal law, and the Court is bound to accept that balance.[25]

Where the application of a guarantee is acknowledged to be less than clear, the justices tend to divide roughly along the following lines in weighing practical costs. For some, if the burden imposed would be great, the Court should hesitate to extend the guarantee unless its extension is essential to fulfilling the function of the guarantee. For others, practical costs are a subordinate concern. They are to be given weight only where the burden is substantial and clear, relates to an important state interest, and cannot be offset by other measures; and even then, they need not be controlling. Occasionally this difference in philosophy will produce a disagreement as to whether a particular burden should be given any weight whatsoever. More frequently, it is reflected in the justices' evaluation of the likely scope of the burden. Thus, in *Miranda,* though looking at the same data, the majority concluded that its decision would "not in any way preclude police from carrying out their traditional investigatory role" and thus "should not constitute an undue interference with a proper system of law enforcement," while one dissent found that the Court was taking "a real risk with society's welfare" and another concluded that the Court's ruling would "measurably weaken" the enforcement of the criminal law and result in an inability to prosecute successfully a "good many criminal defendants."

§ 2.9 The Non-retroactivity Doctrine

(a) The Significance of Retroactive Application. In *Linkletter v. Walker,*[1] decided in June 1965, the Court for the first time held that a newly adopted constitutional ruling need not be given full retroactive application. Prior to *Linkletter,* each new constitutional ruling, civil or criminal, had been applied not only to all cases initiated thereafter, but also to all previously initiated cases that were still subject to judicial review. On the civil side, retroactive application generally extended only to cases that were still pending in the ordinary course of the appellate process. Where the opportunity for appellate review had been exhausted, the civil judgment was viewed as "final" and it would stand even though based on procedures that the Supreme Court had later held invalid. In criminal cases, however, a conviction remained subject to attack, even after the exhaustion of direct appellate review, through the collateral remedy of habeas corpus.[2] The habeas writ was available to a convicted defendant so long as he remained in "custody" (thus including at least the imprisoned defendant), and the issues cognizable under the writ encompassed all constitutional challenges to a conviction. Utilizing the writ, a prisoner could challenge his conviction, no matter how old, as constitutionally invalid under the standards prescribed in the Supreme Court's most recent constitutional rulings. The habeas court was required to grant the writ if the petitioner's conviction was obtained through practices now deemed unconstitutional; that those practices were commonly accepted as constitutional at the time of trial was irrelevant. While the habeas court, in ordering the pris-

23. Thus, opinions in Fourth Amendment cases frequently discuss practical costs in determining whether a particular type of search should be barred as unreasonable. See e.g., Marshall v. Barlow's, Inc., 436 U.S. 307, 98 S.Ct. 1816, 56 L.Ed.2d 305 (1978); Steagald v. United States, 451 U.S. 204, 101 S.Ct. 1642, 68 L.Ed.2d 38 (1981).

24. See e.g., the opinions in Miranda v. Arizona, § 6.5; Braswell v. United States, § 8.13(d); Richardson v. Marsh, § 17.2(b).

25. Payton v. New York, 445 U.S. 573, 100 S.Ct. 1371, 63 L.Ed.2d 639 (1980).

§ 2.9

1. 381 U.S. 618, 85 S.Ct. 1731, 14 L.Ed.2d 601 (1965).

2. See Ch. 28.

oner's release, typically would also grant the state the opportunity to retry the petitioner, retrial often would be impractical due to the lapse in time since the original trial.

As the Supreme Court itself noted, this combination of automatic retroactive application and the remedy of habeas corpus raised the specter that a dramatically expansionist new constitutional ruling might "open * * * wide the prison doors of the land." Thus, when the Warren Court in the early 1960's announced a series of new rulings that could affect the conviction of a substantial portion of the prison populace in various states, it was not surprising that Court soon found occasion to reexamine the previous practice of complete retroactive application of new rulings. That reexamination came in *Linkletter,* where the Court concluded that at least some new constitutional rulings need not be given full retroactive effect. Utilizing the *Linkletter* doctrine of non-retroactivity, the Court in subsequent years held non-retroactive many of its most precedent-shattering criminal procedural rulings of the 1960's and 1970's. Several commentators have suggested that the *Linkletter* doctrine, by providing a means of ensuring that overrulings would not result in massive jail deliveries, "liberated the Court to remold the criminal process still more freely." The Court itself has acknowledged "the impetus that the [non-retroactivity] technique provides for the implementation of long overdue reforms, which otherwise could not be practicably effected."

In *United States v. Johnson,*[3] decided in 1982, the Court majority declared that "retroactivity must be rethought" and began a gradual departure from the doctrine developed in *Linkletter* and its progeny. Today, the non-retroactivity doctrine of *Linkletter* has been largely, if not entirely, replaced by a quite differently structured doctrine of non-retroactivity, developed in series of post-*Johnson* rulings. The *Linkletter* doctrine and the standards developed under that doctrine cannot be ignored, however. They explain the pre-*Johnson* precedents on the retroactivity of various Warren Court landmark rulings, and those precedents, the Court has said, are to be left "undisturbed" as to their precise holdings. More significantly, the developments under *Linkletter* provide a backdrop essential to understanding fully the new, post-*Johnson* standards. Finally, *Linkletter* and its progeny remain important historical markings in the Court's ongoing attempt to place within the conceptual framework of constitutional interpretation the dramatic doctrinal shifts that so often have accompanied changes in the Court's composition.

(b) The *Linkletter* Rationale of Non-retroactive Application. In holding that new constitutional rulings need not always be given full retroactive application, *Linkletter* rejected what it described as the Blackstonian theory that a new ruling merely sets forth the law as it always existed. Modern jurisprudential theory, *Linkletter* noted, acknowledges that judges do not simply "discover" law, but actually "make [law] interstitially." Consistent with this view, lower courts frequently had recognized that an earlier precedent was an "existing judicial fact until overruled," and that consideration must therefore be given to the hardship that retroactive application of an overruling decision would impose upon those who relied upon the earlier precedent. In many instances, that hardship had led lower courts to limit their new rulings to non-retroactive application, and the Supreme Court had consistently held that this practice did not violate due process. While the lower court cases had dealt largely with common law rulings, there was "no impediment—constitutional or philosophical—to the use of the same [practice] in the constitutional area." Although the Court's new constitutional rulings had been applied retroactively in the past, that precedent hardly established an "absolute rule of retroaction." Each case required a weighing of the merits and demerits of retroactive application, and the fact that Court had struck a particular balance for certain past overrulings did not necessarily mean that the same balance must be struck as to all others.

3. 457 U.S. 537, 102 S.Ct. 2579, 73 L.Ed.2d 202 (1982).

Turning to the overruling decision relied upon in the case before it—the *Mapp v. Ohio* overruling of *Wolf v. Colorado*[4]—the *Linkletter* Court held that the *Mapp* ruling, requiring exclusion of evidence obtained in violation of the Fourth Amendment, should not apply to a habeas corpus challenge to a pre–*Mapp* conviction.[5] In determining whether an overruling decision should be applied retroactively, the Court noted, it would look to "the prior history of the rule in question, its purpose and effect, and whether retrospective operation will further retard its operation." In the case of *Mapp,* the purpose of the new rule was a particularly significant factor. Referring to three recent law-changing decisions that had been given full retroactive effect, the *Linkletter* Court noted that each dealt with a right that "went to the fairness of the trial—the very integrity of the factfinding process." The *Mapp* exclusionary rule not only was not aimed at factfinding accuracy, but was designed specifically to deter illegal police action in the future. This purpose, the Court reasoned, "would [not] be advanced by making the rule retrospective"; the "misconduct of the police prior to *Mapp* had already occurred and will not be corrected by releasing the prisoners involved."

(c) Application of the *Linkletter* Doctrine. Application of the *Linkletter* doctrine of non-retroactivity presented three issues: (1) what constituted a "new ruling" for the purposes of that doctrine; (2) what standards would be utilized in determining whether a new ruling should be given retroactive or non-retroactive application; (3) where the ruling would not be given full retroactive application, what was its starting point for application of the ruling to subsequently decided cases.

Although *Linkletter* dealt with a previously unanticipated overruling decision, the pre-*Johnson* decisions made clear that the *Linkletter* rationale was not limited to such decisions, but applied to all "newly adopted constitutional doctrines." The key was whether the particular decision "announced a 'new' rule at all, or whether it simply applied a well-established constitutional principle to govern a case which is closely analogous to those which have been previously considered in the prior caselaw." Where the Court overruled a prior precedent, that automatically constituted a new ruling even when that overruling had been foreshadowed by earlier Supreme Court decisions. An overruling necessarily involved more than simply applying a settled precedent to another fact situation. Similarly, a true case of first impression in the Supreme Court was likely to establish a new rule, especially where the lower court rulings had generally sustained the practice now being rejected by the Court. Beyond this, there was no set pattern as to what constituted a new ruling; the characterization was dependent in large part on whether the Court majority believed that the particular ruling in question rested upon an expansion of doctrine.

Once the Court found that a particular decision had indeed established a new rule, its analysis turned to the three factors cited in *Linkletter*'s discussion of the equity of retroactive application. Those factors were commonly described as the "*Linkletter–Stovall* criteria" as a result of their restatement in *Stovall v. Denno*.[6] The "criteria guiding the resolution of the [retroactivity] question," *Stovall* noted, "implicate (a) the purpose to be served by the new standards, (b) the extent of the reliance by law enforcement authorities on the old standards, and (c) the effect on the administration of justice of a retroactive application of the new standards." Foremost among those factors, the Court added, was the "purpose to be served by the new constitutional rule." In particular, where the new rule's "major purpose" was to "overcome an aspect of the criminal trial that substantially impairs its truth-finding function" and the new rule thereby "raise[d] serious questions about

4. See § 2.6, note 1.

5. At the time *Linkletter* was decided, Fourth Amendment challenges to convictions were generally cognizable on habeas corpus. This position was later changed. See Stone v. Powell, discussed in § 2.3(b).

6. 388 U.S. 293, 87 S.Ct. 1967, 18 L.Ed.2d 1199 (1967).

the accuracy of guilty verdicts," that rule was to be given "complete retroactive effect" without regard to the other *Stovall* criteria.

Of the three *Stovall* criteria, the first—the purpose served by the new rule—proved most difficult to apply. Certain new rulings, such as the extension of the indigent's right to appointed counsel to misdemeanor cases, were readily accepted as necessary to ensure factfinding reliability and therefore requiring fully retroactive application.[7] On the other side, rulings expanding Fourth Amendment protection clearly did not touch upon the reliability of the factfinding process and therefore were held non-retroactive.[8] Easily placed in the same category was a ruling that established a prophylactic safeguard to prevent judicial vindictiveness in sentencing.[9] Difficulties arose, however, where the new constitutional standard had been fashioned to serve multiple ends, including accurate factfinding. Here, the Court sought to distinguish between standards that tended "incidentally" to ensure factfinding accuracy and those directed primarily to that end. Consideration also was given to the presence of additional factfinding safeguards that would have been applicable without regard to the new rule. In the end, the Court noted, the "extent to which a condemned practice infects the integrity of the truth-determining process at trial is a 'question of probabilities,'" and retroactivity would be required only when "an assessment of those probabilities indicates that the condemned practice casts doubt upon the reliability of the determination of guilt."

Illustrative of a case making such an evaluation of the probabilities was *Stovall v. Denno* itself. The Court there rejected retroactive application of *United States v. Wade*,[10] a case establishing a right to counsel at post-indictment lineups. The Court conceded that the *Wade* requirement sought in part to enhance the reliability of the factfinding process by prohibiting unfair identification procedures. However, the *Wade* rule did so only be establishing a prophylactic safeguard, a right to counsel, that would apply without regard to the fairness of the lineup in the particular case. If *Wade* were not applied retroactively, the use of unfair lineups in past cases could still be challenged on due process grounds. Here, the Court concluded, the impact upon the accuracy of the factfinding process was not so substantial as to ignore the other two *Stovall* criteria. The *Wade* ruling had not been foreshadowed in earlier cases; law enforcement officers had "fairly relied" on the "virtually unanimous weight of [prior] authority" allowing lineups without counsel. Since that practice extended throughout the country, to void the conviction of every defendant identified in a lineup without counsel would have an impact upon the administration of criminal justice "so devastating as to need no elaboration." The burden of hearings to determine whether the *Wade* violation tainted other identification evidence or constituted harmless error would be significant, and the inquiry undoubtedly would be "handicapped by the unavailability of witnesses and dim memories." Upon examination of all three *Stovall* factors, the Court viewed the balance as clearly falling on the side of non-retroactivity.

Although the *Linkletter–Stovall* standards provided the usual guidelines for determining the retroactivity of new constitutional rulings, there was one area in which they were held to have no bearing. A new ruling that denied the state's basic authority to try and convict a defendant automatically had retroactive application. Where a new ruling established that the state lacked the power to act, no matter what procedure it applied, that ruling raised a jurisdictional defect always open to challenge. Thus, where the Court had held that the substantive law creating an offense violated the self-incrimination privi-

7. See Berry v. City of Cincinnati, 414 U.S. 29, 94 S.Ct. 193, 38 L.Ed.2d 187 (1973) holding retroactive the ruling in Argersinger v. Hamlin, discussed in § 11.2(a).

8. See e.g., Desist v. United States, 394 U.S. 244, 89 S.Ct. 1030, 22 L.Ed.2d 248 (1969), holding non-retroactive Katz v. United States, discussed in § 3.2(a).

9. See Michigan v. Payne, 412 U.S. 47, 93 S.Ct.1966, 36 L.Ed.2d 736 (1973) holding non-retroactive North Carolina v. Pearce, discussed in §§ 2.8(d), 26.8.

10. See § 7.3.

lege, all defendants convicted of that offense were entitled to the new ruling.[11] Similarly, full retroactive force was given, without consideration of the *Stovall* criteria, to the double jeopardy ruling in *Waller v. Florida,* which prohibited the state from prosecuting the defendant for the same acts that had served as the basis for a previous municipal ordinance prosecution.[12]

The law-changing decision in the *Linkletter* case, *Mapp v. Ohio,* had already been applied to cases pending on direct review, so the only issue considered by the *Linkletter* Court was whether *Mapp* should be applied on a habeas corpus challenge. Subsequent cases noted, however, that the *Linkletter* rationale did not logically justify drawing a distinction between final convictions challenged in a habeas action and convictions challenged "at various stages of trial and direct review." A finding that a new ruling should not be applied retroactively necessarily recognizes that there has been justifiable reliance on the previously accepted constitutional standard. That reliance, the Court noted, does not lose its validity merely because it occurred shortly before the new ruling was announced and defendant's conviction happens not to be final. If non-retroactive application is to be geared to reliance, the critical point for application of the new ruling must be the operative event regulated by that ruling, rather than the finality of the conviction. Where the non-retroactive new ruling was directed at a police practice, it would be applied only to police action occurring after the date of the new ruling. Thus, *Stovall* held the *Wade* ruling on counsel at a lineup inapplicable to lineups conducted before the *Wade* decision was announced.[13] Similarly, where the new ruling related to a trial or other judicial proceeding, it would be applied only to cases in which that proceeding was held after the date of the new ruling.[14]

Of course, the Court's policy of tying the application of a non-retroactive ruling to the date of the operative event recognized one exception; the defendant in the case in which the new ruling was announced received the benefit of that ruling even though the operative event in his case obviously occurred before the new ruling. The Court recognized that this produced a lack of uniformity in the treatment of similarly situated persons. It was even possible, the Court acknowledged, that "different standards for the protection of constitutional rights could be applied to two defendants simultaneously tried in the same courthouse for similar offenses," with one gaining the advantage of additional protection simply because his case was chosen for Supreme Court review. The Court responded, however, that this seeming anomaly was "an unavoidable consequence of the necessity that constitutional adjudications not stand as mere dictum." The defendant in the case announcing the new rule admittedly was a "chance beneficiary" of that rule, but a standard that followed the civil distinction between final and non-final judgments, thereby allowing the benefit of the rule to all cases pending on direct review, would simply create a larger group of fortuitous beneficiaries. Inherent in any form of prospective decisionmaking was

11. See United States v. United States Coin and Currency, 401 U.S. 715, 91 S.Ct. 1041, 28 L.Ed.2d 434 (1971) (retroactive application of Fifth Amendment rulings that invalidated a forfeiture proceeding for money possessed by one who failed to comply with the wagering tax law).

12. Robinson v. Neil, 409 U.S. 505, 93 S.Ct. 876, 35 L.Ed.2d 29 (1973). The Waller v. Florida rulings discussed in § 25.5(c).

13. One exception to this approach was the application of the *Miranda* ruling to all cases tried after the date of that decision. See Johnson v. New Jersey, 384 U.S. 719, 86 S.Ct. 1772, 16 L.Ed.2d 882 (1966). This ruling was later explained as based on the assumption that the interrogation "would be sufficiently proximate to the commencement of the defendant's trial that no undue burden would be imposed upon prosecuting authorities by requiring them to find evidentiary substitutes for statements obtained in violation of the constitutional protections afforded by *Miranda.*" See Jenkins v. Delaware, 395 U.S. 213, 89 S.Ct. 1677, 23 L.Ed.2d 253 (1969) (holding *Miranda* inapplicable where defendant's original trial was before *Miranda* decision and defendant was subsequently retried after that decision). Subsequent cases, as in *Stovall* refused to make a similar assumption as to other police practices.

14. See e.g., Adams v. Illinois, 405 U.S. 278, 92 S.Ct. 916, 31 L.Ed.2d 202 (1972) (Coleman v. Alabama [see § 14.4] holding that an indigent accused had a constitutional right to counsel at a preliminary hearing held non-retroactive and therefore applicable only to preliminary hearings held after the date of the *Coleman* decision).

the possibility that "some defendants benefit from the new rule while others do not, solely because of the fortuities that determine the progress of their cases." [15]

(d) Restricting *Linkletter*: Retroactive Application to Convictions Not Yet Final. At issue in *United States v. Johnson* was the retroactive application of the Court's ruling in *Payton v. New York*.[16] *Payton* had held that, where exigent circumstances did not exist, the Fourth Amendment barred a warrantless entry into a suspect's home for the purpose of arresting him. Although the warrantless entry in the *Johnson* case had occurred before the Supreme Court's *Payton* decision, the defendant's conviction was still pending on direct review when *Payton* was announced. That conviction therefore was not yet "final" on the date of new ruling. As the Court later noted, a conviction will be categorized as final on the date of a new ruling only if the "conviction had [previously] been rendered, the availability of appeal exhausted, and the time for a petition for certiorari elapsed or a petition denied." [17]

Justice Blackmun's opinion for the Court in *Johnson* held that the *Linkletter–Stovall* criteria should not govern the applicability of *Payton* to a conviction not yet final when *Payton* was decided. As to such a conviction, it found persuasive Justice Harlan's criticism of the earlier decisions that had utilized the *Linkletter–Stovall* criteria to limit the future application of new, non-retroactive rulings to the date of the operative event.[18] That criticism had recognized the inequities produced by applying a new ruling to the benefit of the defendant in the case in which the new rule was announced and then refusing to apply that new rule subsequently to cases pending on direct appellate review. Such a result, Justice Blackmun argued, was inconsistent with sound principles of judicial decisionmaking. It "tended to cut the Court loose from the force of precedent" in deciding in favor of the new rule, violated an appellate court's responsibility "to resolve all cases before us on direct review in light of our best understanding of governing constitutional principles," and presented a realistic possibility that the Court would be forced to "mete out different constitutional protection to defendants simultaneously subjected to identical police conduct." There was no satisfactory basis, the *Johnson* Court concluded, for granting the benefit of the new rule announced in *Payton* to the defendant Payton and not to defendants, like Johnson, whose convictions were not yet final on the date of the *Payton* decision. Accordingly, without regard to the *Linkletter–Stovall* criteria, the *Payton* ruling would be applied to all such non-final convictions.

While the reasoning in *Johnson* could easily sustain the conclusion that all new constitutional rulings should thereafter be applied to all convictions not yet final, the holding of the case was much narrower. The *Johnson* Court stressed that it was dealing only with a new ruling involving the application of the Fourth Amendment and its exclusionary rule. Moreover, the Court distinguished those new rulings that reflected "clear breaks with the

15. Jenkins v. Delaware, supra note 13. Justice Harlan, in particular, found this reasoning unpersuasive. He urged a reassessment of retroactivity doctrine that would focus on the distinction between direct appellate review and habeas corpus review. See his separate opinions in Desist v. United States, 394 U.S. 244, 89 S.Ct. 1030, 22 L.Ed.2d 248 (1969), and Mackey v. United States, 401 U.S. 667, 91 S.Ct. 1160, 28 L.Ed.2d 404 (1971). Justice Harlan challenged the *Linkletter*-Stovall retroactivity analysis on several interrelated grounds: it was an instrumentalist product "of the Court's disquietude with the impact of its fast-moving pace of constitutional innovation in the criminal field," adopted as "a technique that provided an impetus" for what some justices viewed as "long overdue reforms, which otherwise could not practically be effected"; it rested on a premise of judicial lawmaking that failed to adequately distinguish changes produced by judicial analysis from those imposed by a legislative body; it created an unacceptable distinction between defendants raising the same issue on appeal, with the outcome dependent on whether the particular defendant was fortunate enough to have his appeal chosen as the vehicle for announcing the new rule; and it failed to recognize the quite distinct functions of judicial review on a direct appeal and judicial review in applying the extraordinary remedy of habeas corpus. Consider also subsections (d) and (e) infra, noting the Court's later adoption of Justice Harlan's position.

16. See § 3.6(a).

17. See Griffith v. Kentucky, discussed at note 23 infra.

18. See note 15 supra.

past." These were described as new rulings that either (1) explicitly overruled a past decision, (2) "disapproved a practice this Court arguably has sanctioned in prior cases," or (3) "overturn[ed] a longstanding and widespread practice to which this Court ha[d] not spoken, but which a near-unanimous body of lower court ha[d] expressly approved." Such "clear-break" cases, the Court noted, had "almost invariably" been denied retroactive application, but there was no need to reexamine the correctness of that position here. *Payton,* while it announced a new rule, did not fall in the clear-break category. It had dealt with an open issue on which the lower courts had been split.

The Court had divided 5–4 in *Johnson* and it had included in its majority the author of the *Stovall* opinion (Justice Brennan). It thus was far from clear whether the *Johnson* ruling would be restricted to new rulings that both involved the Fourth Amendment and were not clear-break cases, or would be extended beyond one or both of these limitations. Although it remained sharply divided on the retroactivity issue, the Court eventually rejected both limitations, holding that all new rulings will automatically be applied to any conviction not yet final at the time of the new ruling.

Shea v. Louisiana [19] was the critical case in extending the *Johnson* ruling beyond Fourth Amendment cases. *Shea* involved a challenge to a state appellate court's refusal to apply on direct appellate review a Supreme Court ruling that had been rendered after defendant's conviction at trial but prior to the resolution of his appeal. Accordingly, although the case reached the Supreme Court on a subsequent habeas application, the question presented was the lack of retroactive application of a new ruling to a conviction not final at the time of new ruling, rather than the initial application of the new ruling to a final conviction on habeas review. The new ruling in question was *Edwards v. California,*[20] a case establishing a per se rule proscribing police-initiated questioning of an arrested suspect after he had responded to *Miranda* warnings by requesting counsel. Although based on language found in the *Miranda* opinion itself, the Court had characterized *Edwards* as a new ruling, although not a new ruling in the "clear-break" category. The Court had already held, under the *Linkletter–Stovall* criteria, that *Edwards* would not be applied retroactively to a habeas petitioner whose conviction had been final when *Edwards* was decided.[21] Petitioner argued, however, that as *Johnson* had suggested, different considerations should apply to a non-final conviction. In another 5–4 decision, the Court agreed.

Justice Blackmun's opinion for the Court in *Shea* concluded that the *Johnson* reasoning supporting automatic retroactive application of new rulings to non-final convictions was equally applicable to the *Edwards* ruling. Though the *Johnson* holding was limited to Fourth Amendment claims, there was "nothing about a Fourth Amendment rule that suggests that in this context it should be given greater retroactive effect than a Fifth Amendment rule." "Indeed," Justice Blackmun noted, "a Fifth Amendment violation may be more likely to affect the truthfinding process than a Fourth Amendment violation." Justice Blackmun's reasoning clearly indicated that, with the possible exception of clear-break cases, new constitutional rulings in all areas would thereafter be applied retroactively to all non-final convictions.[22]

19. 470 U.S. 51, 105 S.Ct. 1065, 84 L.Ed.2d 38 (1985).

20. See § 6.9(g).

21. See Solem v. Stumes, 465 U.S. 638, 104 S.Ct. 1338, 79 L.Ed.2d 579 (1984).

22. Dissenting in *Shea,* Justice White criticized the majority for failing to recognize that the retroactivity issue raises concerns that go beyond insuring that "like defendants are treated alike." Indeed, the majority position, Justice White argued, did not afford such equal treatment. It was true that the Court had avoided the situation in which the benefit of a new rule would be given to the defendant in whose case it was announced while being denied to others whose convictions also were not yet final. But the majority's position would allow that benefit to be denied to prisoners who sought on habeas review to attack previously finalized convictions. Thus, even under the majority's position, "otherwise identically situated defendants may be subject to different constitutional rules, depending on just how long ago now-unconstitutional conduct occurred and how quickly cases proceed through the criminal justice system." Once it is recognized that full retroactive effect will not

In *Griffith v. Kentucky,*[23] another 5–4 decision, the Court answered the second question left open in *Johnson,* holding that even clear-break rulings would be applied retroactively to convictions not yet final at the time of the ruling. With Justice Blackmun again writing for the Court, the majority agreed that, "for the same reasons that persuaded us in *United States v. Johnson* to adopt different conclusions as to convictions on direct review from those that already had become final," it was "inappropriate" to "engraft * * * [an] exception based solely upon the particular characteristics of the new rules." The adoption of a clear-break exception for non-final convictions would create "the same problem of not treating similarly situated defendants the same" and would be contrary to "the principle that this Court does not disregard current law when it adjudicates a case pending before it on direct review."

Although *Johnson, Shea,* and *Griffith* had all been 5–4 decisions, the subsequent ruling in *Teague v. Lane*[24] found the Court unanimous in its acceptance of the position announced in those cases (although some justices agreed to that position only because the Court was willing in *Teague* also to hold, as discussed infra, that new rulings generally would not applied retroactively to final convictions). Thus, as to convictions not yet final on the date of a new ruling, that ruling, even if a clear-break ruling, will govern. Pre–*Johnson* rulings reaching a contrary result have not been overruled as to the specific new rules they considered, but the basic approach to non-retroactivity taken there has been discarded.

(e) Rejecting *Linkletter:* Finalized Convictions and the *Teague* Standards. Justice Harlan had criticized the *Linkletter–Stovall* rationale not only because it refused to apply new rulings to defendants whose convictions were currently pending on direct appeal, but also because it often did result in applying new rulings on collateral attack to convictions that had been finalized before the new ruling was issued.[25] It was Justice Harlan's position that, subject to two exceptions, the law applicable on collateral attack should be that "prevailing at the time [the prisoner's] conviction became final." The *Linkletter–Stovall* analysis, he argued, was flawed in its focus solely upon the function and impact of the new ruling. The proper frame of reference should not be a balancing process based upon the respective merits of retrospective and non-retrospective application of the particular ruling, as required under *Linkletter–Stovall,* but the function of federal habeas review of prior convictions. Federal habeas review was designed, in large part, to provide "a necessary incentive for trial and appellate judges throughout the land to conduct their proceedings in a manner consistent with established constitutional principles." That review served a "deterrent function," as those courts knew that they could not fail conscientiously to apply previously announced constitutional principles and escape federal court reversal because of the docket limitations of the Supreme Court; such rulings would be subject to review by lower federal courts through the writ of habeas corpus. This deterrent function, Justice Harlan had noted, is adequately fulfilled by applying the law that prevailed when the original trial and appellate proceedings took place.

In *Teague v. Lane,*[26] although there was no opinion for the Court on the retroactivity issue, a majority expressed agreement with Justice Harlan's viewpoint. Justice O'Connor, speaking also for Chief Justice Rehnquist, Justice Scalia, and Justice Kennedy, expressed full agreement with Justice Harlan's general position in her plurality opinion. Justice Stevens, joined by Justice Blackmun, did likewise in a concurring opinion. Justice White, although noting that he still remained

be given to all defendants, Justice White argued, it makes more sense to turn to the *Linkletter–Stovall* criteria to assess retroactivity as to both final and non-final convictions rather than to draw an absolute distinction between "direct review and collateral attack."

23. 479 U.S. 314, 107 S.Ct. 708, 93 L.Ed.2d 649 (1987).

24. 489 U.S. 288, 109 S.Ct. 1060, 103 L.Ed.2d 334 (1989).

25. See note 15 supra.

26. See note 24 supra.

convinced of the soundness of the *Linkletter–Stovall* analysis, concluded that, in light of *Johnson, Shea,* and *Griffith,* that approach had now been firmly rejected as to non-final convictions. Accordingly, he concurred in the result reached by the plurality as "an acceptable application in collateral proceedings of the theories embraced by the Court in cases dealing with direct review." Thus, seven justices expressed agreement with the principle that, subject to certain exceptions, a new ruling should not be applied on a habeas review of a conviction that had been final at the date of that new ruling.

Justice O'Connor's plurality opinion in *Teague* initially set forth the standards that would thereafter limit a federal habeas court, as a general rule, to applying the constitutional standards that prevailed at the time that the prisoner's conviction became final. That restriction would bar a habeas court from either relying upon a subsequent Supreme Court precedent that established a new rule or itself adopting an interpretation of an earlier Supreme Court precedent that produced a new rule. What constituted a "new rule" for this purpose was left for development in future cases, but as a general proposition, Justice O'Connor noted, "a case announces a new rule if the result was not *dictated* by precedent existing at the time the defendant's conviction became final." Justice O'Connor then turned to two exceptions under which the function of habeas review did justify retroactive application of a new rule. These dealt basically with two types of new rulings that Justice Harlan had viewed as necessarily cognizable on habeas review in light of habeas functions that went beyond its general deterrent function with respect to state courts. The first was the new rule that places "certain kinds of primary, private individual conduct beyond the power of the criminal law-making authority to proscribe"—i.e. rulings finding a constitutional bar to the substantive offense for which the defendant was convicted (which had also been given automatic retroactive application under *Linkletter–Stovall* standard [27]). As for the second exception, Justice Harlan had described it as encompassing a new ruling that requires observance of procedures "implicit in the concept of ordered liberty," but Justice O'Connor concluded that a somewhat narrower phrasing was necessary to limit this exception to the "watershed rules of criminal procedure" that Justice Harlan had in mind. The second exception, Justice O'Connor stated, should be limited to those new rulings mandating procedures "central to an accurate determination of innocence or guilt."

Justice O'Connor in *Teague* spoke only for a plurality. While Justices Stevens and Blackmun also agreed with the central premise of Justice Harlan's position, they did not necessarily accept the plurality's concept of a new rule and they clearly rejected its modification of Justice Harlan's second exception. They also disagreed with the plurality's position that a habeas court must initially ask whether the constitutional interpretation urged by the habeas petitioner would constitute a new rule, and if that is the case (and neither of the two exceptions apply), never reach the merits of that interpretation.[28] Justice White's cryp-

27. See note 11 supra.

28. Justices Stevens and Blackmun argued that the newness of the proposed ruling need not be the threshold issue, as the determination of newness might itself lead the habeas court to first assess the merits of the proposed ruling. Justice O'Connor rejected that approach, arguing that to find first that the requested ruling had merit and then to conclude that it could not be applied retroactively would be to render an advisory opinion on the merits of the claim. Statements in later cases accept Justice O'Connor's position and treat the question of newness as a mandatory threshold issue. See e.g., Sawyer v. Smith and Penry v. Lynaugh, discussed in § 28.6(b). The end result is to sharply limit the Supreme Court's opportunities for establishing new constitutional rulings that expand constitutional protections. As noted in Justice Brennan's dissent in *Teague,* many of the Court's most significant extensions of constitutional protections have come in the past in habeas cases, with the Court first announcing the rule and then concluding in a later case that the new rule would not be applied retroactively to other prisoners under the *Linkletter–Stovall* criteria. With the Court now precluded from establishing new rulings in habeas cases (except where one of the two *Teague* exceptions apply), its opportunity to create new law will be limited largely to those cases that come

tic concurring opinion spoke to none of these issues that divided the other justices constituting the majority. Thus, it remained to be seen exactly how the divisions noted in *Teague* would be resolved. As discussed in § 28.6, the Court majority in later rulings has followed the principles announced in Justice O'Connor's plurality opinion.

While the Court's post-*Teague* rulings provide important contributions to both the concept of a new ruling and the scope of the second *Teague* exception, their focus has been on the nature of the habeas remedy rather than upon the nature of judicial lawmaking and its relation to the retroactive application of constitutional rulings.[29] On the latter issue, the post-*Johnson* rulings, including *Teague*, basically have taken the Court back to that view of the lawmaking function in constitutional jurisprudence that existed prior to *Linkletter*. Of course, *Teague* imposes limits on the retroactive application of new constitutional rulings that did not exist prior to *Linkletter*, but those limits stem from the Court's reexamination of the role of the habeas remedy rather than the concerns that prevailed in *Linkletter*. Although *Teague* and the *Linkletter–Stovall* criteria both look to the purpose to be served by the new constitutional ruling, they do so from different perspectives. *Linkletter–Stovall* approached the ruling's purpose from the perspective of a Court which recognized the reliance interest of law enforcement agencies that had not anticipated new rulings and sought to accommodate that interest where doing so was consistent with the function of the newly announced rule. *Teague*, on the other hand, evaluates purpose in light solely of the special functions of the habeas remedy. It is not concerned as such with either the unpredictability of the new ruling or the severity of the impact that its retroactive application would have upon the administration of justice. Under the post-*Johnson* rulings, the most novel and unpredictable new ruling will be applied retroactively to a conviction not yet final, without regard to either its purpose, the nature of the reliance on the law now overturned, or the widespread impact of the retroactive application of the new ruling. On the other hand, under *Teague*, even where the prior law pointed in a direction that would have led any official competently advised by counsel to recognize the likelihood of the ruling eventually imposed, that ruling will not be applied retroactively on habeas review if it was not dictated by prior precedent and does not fall within either of the *Teague* exceptions.

§ 2.10 The Emergence of State Constitutional Law

(a) The "New Federalism" Movement. Every state constitution has either a separate bill of rights or a series of internal provisions protecting certain rights of the individual. Those provisions relating to criminal procedure typically cover much the same ground as the Fourth, Fifth, Sixth, and Eighth Amendments, although state constitutions often also include certain procedural guarantees that do not have a federal counterpart (e.g., a defense right of appeal). Until roughly 1940–50, when the Supreme Court intensified its application of the Fourteenth Amendment to the states through a broader reading of the fundamental fairness standard,[1] the state constitutional provisions provided the only significant constitutional regulation of state criminal procedure. That regulation, however, consisted primarily of the basic structuring of the process through the obvious commands of the state constitutional guarantees; additional content provided by state court interpretation of those guarantees tended to be only marginally significant. The criminal procedure rulings of state courts usually were based upon common law requirements or statutory interpretations, and the interpretations of state constitutional guarantees were not, in general, especially rigorous. One could find in many states occasional expansive interpreta-

before it upon the grant of certiorari to review the direct appeal of a conviction.

29. See § 28.6(b) as to the Court's adoption of a concept of a new ruling having a somewhat broader sweep than the concept discussed in subsection (c) supra. See § 28.6(c) as to the limited scope given to the second *Teague* exception.

§ 2.10

1. See § 2.4(c).

tions of such guarantees,[2] but much smaller was the number in which the pattern of state constitutional decisions approached the reach of the regulation that the Supreme Court had imposed upon the federal criminal justice process in its constitutional rulings.[3] From an expansionist perspective, state constitutional law was largely a "sleeping and inactive body of jurisprudence."

During the period that immediately preceded the Warren Court revolution of the 1960's, state courts became more accustomed to the concept of constitutional regulation of the criminal justice process as they were required to respond to the increasing federal court review under the fundamental fairness doctrine. Several state courts adopted expansive interpretations of state constitutional guarantees that went beyond what the Supreme Court majority was willing to require of the states under the Fourteenth Amendment. Then, during the Warren Court period, with the adoption of the selective incorporation doctrine, there was a dramatic increase in federal constitutional regulation, and state courts were increasingly concerned with the interpretation and application of the Supreme Court's new rulings. For the most part, the state courts during this period did very little with their state constitutional provisions. It generally was assumed that those provisions went no farther than the incorporated federal guarantees as interpreted by the Supreme Court (and, in light of past state court precedent, very often did not go nearly as far).

In the mid-1970's, the state constitutional provisions took on a new role in several states. The rulings of the Burger Court reflected at least a slackening of the pace of the Court's expansionist interpretations, and in the eyes of Justices Brennan and Marshall (and various state court justices), a full scale retreat from the direction marked out by the Warren Court revolution.[4] State courts vigorously applying and extending Warren Court precedent, particularly in the area of police practices, on various occasions had their interpretations of the Fourth and Fifth Amendments overturned by the Supreme Court. Dissents by Justices Marshall and Brennan, and majority opinions as well, noted that the states remained free to impose through their own constitutions limitations beyond those demanded by the federal guarantees. In *State v. Opperman,*[5] the South Dakota Supreme Court responded affirmatively to that suggestion. The South Dakota Supreme Court originally had held that warrantless automobile inventory searches violated the Fourth Amendment, but a divided Supreme Court had reversed that ruling on a different reading of its precedent.[6] On remand, the state court turned to its own constitution and held that the inventory search violated that constitution's guarantee governing searches and seizures. The South Dakota court acknowledged that the language of the state guarantee was "almost identical to that found in the Fourth Amendment," but stressed that it had "always assumed the independent nature of our state constitution regardless of any similarity between the language of that document and the federal constitution."

Initially, only a handful of state courts regularly turned to their state constitutions to impose restrictions that the Supreme Court had held not to be demanded under an incorporated guarantee. However, this practice soon received considerable promotion from several different sources. Organizations within the defense bar urged its members to seek state court rulings based on both state and federal constitutions so that favorable rulings

2. The two most often cited illustrations are Carpenter v. County of Dane, 9 Wis. 249 (1859) (relying on the state constitution, as well as a state statute, to require the appointment of counsel for indigent defendants in felony cases—a requirement not imposed in federal cases until 1938, see § 11.1, note 2), and State v. Slamon, 73 Vt. 212, 50 A. 1097 (1901) (exclusion of evidence obtained through illegal searches required more than a decade before the Supreme Court imposed a similar requirement in federal cases in Weeks v. United States, § 3.1, note 3).

3. This stood in contrast to the role of state constitutional law in other fields, in particular that of economic regulation. See Note, 53 Colum.L.Rev. 829 (1953) (noting state views on substantive due process).

4. See § 2.8(b).

5. 247 N.W.2d 673 (S.D.1976).

6. See South Dakota v. Opperman, § 3.7(e).

would not be subject to review by a Supreme Court of uncertain (or unfriendly) disposition.[7] Prominent state supreme court justices called attention in legal commentary to the theoretical justifications for a more expansive interpretation of state constitutional guarantees. Academic writers devoted numerous articles to that practice, which they dubbed "the new federalism movement" and characterized as a potentially momentous development. Justice Brennan, in a widely cited article, urged the state courts, in the interest of a "healthy federalism," to respond to the weakened federal protection of individual liberties by forging ahead of the Supreme Court in the protection of those liberties.[8]

By 1988, one commentator counted more than 450 post–1970 opinions of state courts that took state constitutions beyond Supreme Court interpretations of analogous federal guarantees. More than one-third of those rulings concerned the criminal justice process. While a substantial portion of the rulings came from slightly over a dozen state courts, an even larger number of state courts had made an occasional contribution to the new federalism movement. The lion's share of the rulings were reacting to specific Supreme Court holdings (rather than to the anticipated application of current federal precedent to new situations). Indeed, for almost every ruling of the Burger or Rehnquist Courts that could be characterized as retracting from the thrust of Warren Court precedent, at least one state court (and in some instances, more than a half-dozen state courts) has reached a contrary ruling under its state constitution.[9] In addition, state courts have rejected several of the narrower constitutional interpretations accepted by the Warren Court, fashioning more protective state constitutional standards. In many instances, the state courts have adopted the reasoning urged by dissenting opinions in the Supreme Court. In others, state courts have adopted a quite different analytical mode for a particular guarantee, which has produced greater protection than the analytical framework accepted by all members of the Supreme Court. Overall, while the new federalism movement has yet to receive wholehearted support from a majority of the state courts, it has gained sufficient support to lead commentators to suggest that a defense lawyer "who claims some constitutional protection and who does not argue that the state constitution provides that protection is skating on the edge of malpractice."

(b) The Appropriateness of a Mirroring Presumption. Although generally praised by commentators, the new federalism movement has sparked a heated debate among judges of the highest state courts. The movement was fueled initially by an ideological opposition to what were viewed as Burger Court departures from the thrust of the Warren Court revolution, and to some extent, the early debate focused on the merits of this "conservative drift" of the Supreme Court. However, much of the current debate has focused on the appropriate role of state courts in interpreting state constitutional provisions where those provisions parallel incorporated federal guarantees. Thus, one finds the new federalism movement being opposed by state

7. Michigan v. Long, 463 U.S. 1032, 103 S.Ct. 3469, 77 L.Ed.2d 1201 (1983), held that Supreme Court review would not be precluded where state constitutional analysis was interwoven with federal analysis so as to leave doubt as to whether the state court ruling was "alternatively based on a bona fide, separate, adequate, and independent [state law] ground." However, a ruling would meet the adequate state ground standard where the state court indicated "clearly and expressly" that the state constitution furnishes a separate grounding for its decision and federal constitutional precedent was looked to only as analogous precedent rather than incorporated as the sole content of the state provision. See also § 28.4(b).

8. Brennan, State Constitutions and the Protection of Individual Rights, 90 Harv.L.Rev. 489 (1977). See also Brennan, The Bill of Rights and the States: The Revival of State Constitutions as Guardians of Individual Rights, 61 N.Y.U.L.Rev. 535 (1986) (praising the state courts for having "responded with marvelous enthusiasm to many not-so-subtle invitations to fill the gaps left by decisions of the Supreme Court majority").

9. Space limitations preclude discussion of most of those state court rulings in this volume. A more extensive discussion of state court constitutional rulings will be found in our treatise. Where reference is made to significant dissents in Supreme Court rulings, particularly where the dissent concluded that the majority was departing from a previously suggested bright-line standard, one can anticipate a likely adoption of that bright-line standard under an analogous constitutional provision in one or more states.

court judges who are equally skeptical of the wisdom of the constricted Supreme Court rulings that their brethren would refuse to incorporate as a state constitutional standard. So too, one finds it supported by state court judges who have no difficulty with those Supreme Court rulings but insist that state courts have an obligation to develop an independent analysis in interpreting state constitutions. The critical issue dividing these opponents and proponents of the new federalism movement has not been the merits of the Supreme Court's rulings, but the general validity of adopting a "mirroring presumption" that would ordinarily incorporate analogous Supreme Court precedent.

A mirroring presumption initially assumes that a state constitutional guarantee will mirror in content the corresponding federal guarantee and then accepts the latest Supreme Court precedent as setting forth that content. It directs the state court to follow the interpretation of the federal analog adopted by Supreme Court even though the judges of the state court may disagree with the Supreme Court's reasoning and conclusion. Under such a presumption, a state court divergence from the Supreme Court's current precedent is justified only where the language of the state guarantee or the historical purpose of that guarantee clearly calls for such divergence. As discussed in subsection (c), a number of state courts, adopting a "lockstep" interpretation of state guarantees, rely heavily upon such a presumption. Still other courts adhere to a fairly loose version of a mirroring presumption. The courts most actively participating in the new federalism movement, however, flatly reject any form of the presumption. They view Supreme Court precedent, even where the state and federal provisions are identical in text and historical background, as entitled to no greater weight than the rulings of any court of a sister jurisdiction. Supreme Court precedent, from this viewpoint, should have a bearing on the interpretation of a state constitutional guarantee only insofar as the reasoning of the Supreme Court is found to be intellectually persuasive by the state court.

Proponents of a mirroring presumption acknowledge that a state court has the authority to disregard analogous Supreme Court rulings in interpreting its own state's constitution. The issue, as they see it, is the desirable exercise of judicial restraint to forego independent analysis and almost blindly incorporate Supreme Court precedent. They acknowledge that such deference to the opinions of the Supreme Court would not be expected in the treatment of a state common law doctrine or even in the interpretation of a broadly phrased state statute that has a federal analog (e.g., a state antitrust provision similar to the Sherman Act). State constitutional guarantees that parallel incorporated federal guarantees are seen as presenting unique concerns that call for a special element of judicial statesmanship.

Initially, supporters of a mirroring presumption stress the adverse image of the judicial role that attends a state court divergence from the Supreme Court's interpretation of a similar guarantee. Constitutional guarantees should reflect fundamental values, they note, but those values will hardly be viewed as such when their content appears to be as fluid as the whims of the particular judges ruling on an issue. State court divergence, particularly where based on no more than a policy disagreement, conveys a public image of result-oriented jurisprudence consisting of "all sail and no anchor." Second, proponents note that, in practical impact, state constitutional interpretation necessarily is skewed by the federal supremacy clause. State court rulings effectively serve only to expand individual rights; rulings reading state constitutions as affording less protection than Supreme Court precedents are meaningless because federal constitution requirements must be met in any event. While state courts rejecting a mirroring presumption sometimes have concluded that state guarantees offer only the same protection as the federal guarantees, the new federalism movement has gained attention and praise primarily because of the many state court rulings that have rejected Supreme Court precedent and imposed greater state constitutional safeguards. Such "lopsided jurisprudence" is seen as creating the image of a state constitutional jurisprudence strategically used by liberal state courts to serve the cause of rights-maximization while insulating such rulings decisions from otherwise adverse Supreme Court review.

Finally, a failure to adopt a mirroring presumption is characterized as especially pernicious with respect to guarantees that regulate police practices. Here, it is argued, uniformity and predictability are especially important features of constitutional governance. Law enforcement officers should be "entitled to rely upon the decisions of [the Supreme Court] and should not have to anticipate that a federally guaranteed constitutional right will be given a broader interpretation under an all but identical provision in a state constitution." When state and federal officers work together, their task should not be made more complex by the uncertainty as to whether an eventual prosecution will be brought in a federal court (applying only Supreme Court precedent) or a state court (applying additional limitations under a state constitution).

Critics of the mirroring presumption find all of the above arguments unpersuasive. They note that state constitutional interpretation can actually bring greater certainty to the law governing police practices through the application of bright line prohibitions where the current Supreme Court precedent has produced only ambiguity and hairline distinctions. Moreover, simply following the latest Supreme Court precedent hardly brings stability to the law where that precedent itself is so frequently the product of directional shifts. The answer to the image of result-oriented jurisprudence, the critics argue, is reasoned decisionmaking, with the state court explaining precisely why it views the Supreme Court's ruling as unpersuasive. The presence of a divergence between federal and state law hardly suggests in itself that the state law should be treated as less principled. If Supreme Court dissents can be more cogent than majority opinions, the same can be true of state court opinions disagreeing with those majority opinions (or, in some instances, disagreeing with both the majority and dissenting opinions and offering a fresh analysis).

Several responses are offered to the contention that a mirroring presumption is needed to respond to the skewed impact of state constitutional interpretation. First, the description of state jurisprudence as skewed in favor of rights-maximization is criticized as the product of a false starting point. Thus, Justice Linde of Oregon has noted: "The right question is not whether a state's guarantee is the same as or broader than its federal counterpart as interpreted by the Supreme Court. The right question is what the state's guarantee means and how it applies in the case at hand." [10] No difficulty arises if the state constitution is treated as a separate body of law to be examined before turning to the federal constitutional issue, rather than a supplemental font of safeguards to be considered only when the state court believes "the Supreme Court Justices are dead wrong."

Many supporters of the new federalism movement see the skewed impact of state constitutional interpretation as the positive and logical product of state constitutional guarantees. Inherent in a federalist system, they argue, is a "double security" for the rights of the individual. The framers of the federal constitution looked first to the state constitutions and then, with the adoption of the Fourteenth Amendment, to the combination of the state and the federal constitutions, to prohibit state invasions of individual liberty. A mirroring presumption alters this division of responsibility by looking to the Supreme Court as the sole guardian of individual rights and thereby undercuts a basic premise underlying both state and federal constitutions. It abrogates the obligation that the state judiciary owes to the framers of the state constitution and to the people of the state, making the state no more than a "judi-

10. Linde, E. Pluribus—Constitutional Theory and State Courts, 18 Ga.L.Rev. 165 (1984). One of the leading proponents of an independent state jurisprudence for its own sake, Justice Linde has criticized those approaches to the new federalism movement that focus basically upon its potential for expanding individual rights. Compare Brennan, note 8 supra.

cial colony by decision." The mirroring presumption is criticized as resting on the false premise that similarly worded state and federal constitutional guarantees have the same core purpose and therefore should be similarly interpreted. That premise ignores the fact that the state and federal constitutional provisions often were adopted at different times, with respective framers having in mind different social and economic conditions. Also, it fails to take into account that constitutional interpretation commonly rests on considerations that go far beyond historical analysis, and that the people of the state selected the members of their own high court, and not the Justices of the Supreme Court, to weigh those considerations in light of the values and needs of their particular state.

A skewed impact is also justified by reference to the institutional position of state courts that frees it from restraints imposed upon the Supreme Court. Supreme Court rulings, it is argued, are subject to restraints flowing from the national scope of the Court's pronouncements. As the Court itself has acknowledged, notwithstanding its adoption of selective incorporation, federalism concerns remain as a constraint upon its development of the incorporated guarantees.[11] A state court, on the other hand, need not dilute safeguards in the interest of preserving state autonomy as it is an agency of the state itself. So too, the Court must shape its rulings to what is realistically achievable within the varied criminal justice settings found throughout the nation as a whole. The state court operates within a smaller and often more homogeneous jurisdiction, allowing the development of constitutional principles more closely attuned to local circumstances. Judicial review in the Supreme Court may be further restrained by its antidemocratic nature. State courts, in contrast, may have less concern in taking activist positions as their decisions "are dramatically more accountable to democratic influences." State judges in the vast majority of states may be voted out of office. The amendment of the state constitution is far easier to achieve than the amendment of the federal constitution. Indeed, in several instances, state rulings that went beyond Supreme Court precedents were overturned by subsequent state amendments. Such amendments have even gone so far as to specifically prohibit state courts from adopting interpretations of particular state guarantees that extend beyond what is required by the federal constitution.[12]

Critics of the new federalism, in response, find especially unpersuasive that line of argument which favors state courts taking a more activist stance than the Supreme Court. They reject the contention that a "pure independent approach is a necessary corollary of the theory that each state is a sovereign entity." Principles of state autonomy, they note, guarantee to each state court only the right to adopt legal requirements not inconsistent with federal constitutional requirements; such principles no more mandate that state courts adopt a more activist stance than they mandate more protective state legislation. Federalism ensures that the states have a shared authority to safeguard individual rights, but it does not prescribe that such protection reach a higher level.

Similarly, state court decisionmaking is not seen as substantially different from Supreme Court decisionmaking because of the special institutional position of state courts. At issue is the meaning of basic principles, and that should not vary depending upon the ease with which the electorate can remove a judge or overturn a decision through constitutional

11. See § 2.6(c).

12. See Cal.Const.Art. 1, § 28 (California's Victims' Bill of Rights, which provides in its truth-in-evidence provision that, with certain exceptions, all relevant evidence shall be admissible, and thereby precludes use of an exclusionary remedy except where required by federal law); Fla.Const.Art. 1, § 12 (requiring that the Florida search and seizure guarantee be "construed in conformity with the Fourth Amendment of the United States Constitution"). In Florida v. Casal, 462 U.S. 637, 103 S.Ct. 3100, 77 L.Ed.2d 277 (1983), Chief Justice Burger, concurring in a dismissal, noted that "the people of Florida" through this provision had "shown acute awareness" of the "means to prevent" state court interpretations of state law that "require *more* than the Federal Constitution," and expressed the view that state citizens should keep in mind that they have this power "to amend state law to ensure rational law enforcement."

amendment. Distinctions as to both judicial tenure and the amendment process also exist among different state courts, and just as they have not been cited there to gauge permissible degrees of judicial activism, nether should they be used to distinguish between state and federal courts. So too, those federalism restraints that may continue to influence the Supreme Court in the post-incorporation era are characterized by the critics as minimal and irrelevant. Moreover, they are viewed as tending to relate to concerns—such as the administrative flexibility needed to respond to diverse community settings and the value of local experimentation—that are fully applicable in all but, perhaps, the smallest of states.

Alleged distinctions in the historical traditions or shared values of particular states also are rejected as a proper grounding for a general policy of judicial activism that carries state rulings beyond those of the Supreme Court. The distinctions between the various states, it is argued, are not so great as to require different interpretations of immutable principles. State and federal constitutional guarantees reflect basic elements of fairness that should not change when state lines are crossed.

Critics of the new federalism do not claim that the Supreme Court is in any sense infallible in its definition and application of the common national values that underly constitutional guarantees, although they sometimes note that it is the most practiced court in those tasks. Their basic contention is that the Court occupies a special position entitling its rulings to considerable deference, as reflected in a mirroring presumption. The Supreme Court is viewed as the one court with the distinct and elevated status necessary to ensure the public acceptance essential to the retention of those constitutional values. Those in opposition argue that there is no evidence that independence in state court interpretations detracts from the role of the Supreme Court. Indeed, it may encourage acceptance of the Court's expansionist rulings, particularly in the controversial criminal justice field, by casting them in a more moderate light. In any event, they note, the issue is not of public acceptability, but of basic judicial obligation.

(c) Diverse State Court Approaches. State courts have varied in their weighing of the above arguments. Some have adopted a strong mirroring presumption applied on a guarantee-by-guarantee basis. Once the court determines that a particular guarantee is basically similar to the corresponding guarantee in the federal constitution, the state guarantee thereafter is interpreted "in harmony with the Supreme Court's opinions." Applying this approach to a state search and seizure guarantee, for example, the state court will look to federal precedent on all Fourth Amendment issues. Commonly described as a "lockstep" approach to state constitutional interpretation, this mode of analysis has lost ground among state courts in recent years but is still followed in several states. Other state courts also apply a mirroring presumption, but on an issue-by-issue basis. Thus, the state court may conclude that the state search and seizure guarantee will be interpreted in harmony with the Supreme Court's Fourth Amendment rulings on the warrant requirement, but not as to the question of what constitutes a search. On the latter issue, some ground for divergence, such as a difference in the texts of the two provisions, may lead to a more protective ruling under the state provision.

Consistent with the underlying function of a mirroring presumption, courts applying such a presumption will not reject a Supreme Court interpretation of a counterpart federal provision simply because they disagree with the Supreme Court's reasoning. A different state court interpretation will be followed only where supported by "neutral criteria." Even where the neutral criteria is limited to textual and historical differences, the opportunity for divergence may be substantial. Slight textual differences are commonplace. For example, while the Fourth Amendment refers to the right of the people to be secure in their "effects," the constitutions of many states use instead the term "possessions." A court inclined to go its own way could find a basis for divergence in that textual distinction. As supported by the common usage of the term "possessions" when it first was adopted in the state constitutions, that term could be held to encompass examinations of certain areas that are not within the protected zones of privacy under current Fourth Amendment jurisprudence. Even when the constitutional language is identical, because state constitutions were adopted at different times and discussions of their provisions were often tied to contemporary interpretations, grounds for divergence might be found in the legislative history of the state provision. The critical question, as one commentator put it, is whether the state court dissatisfied with Supreme Court precedent is going to approach such factors in the fashion of a person "standing on tiptoes at a parade looking for one's friends in the crowd."[13]

In several states, the neutral criteria that may support a divergence include a broad range of factors. The most frequently cited list is that set forth by New Jersey's Justice Handler in *State v. Hunt.*[14] Justice Handler cited seven "standards or criteria for determining when to invoke our State Constitution as an independent source for protecting individual rights": (1) textual differences in the federal and state constitutions; (2) "legislative history" of the state provision indicating a broader meaning than the federal provision; (3) preexisting state law; (4) differences in federal and state constitutional structure; (5) subject matter of particular state or local interest; (6) particular state history or traditions; and (7) "distinctive attitudes of a state's citizenry." Utilizing such criteria, the New Jersey Supreme Court was able to conclude that the state constitution rejected the Supreme Court's "good faith" exception to the exclusionary rule even though the framers of the state constitution had specifically rejected a proposal that would have added an exclusionary rule provision to the state constitution and the state courts had refused to adopt an exclusionary rule prior to the selective incorporation of the Fourth Amendment.[15]

Although a broad neutral criteria approach affords considerable leeway for divergence, that approach has been rejected by numerous courts that favor a totally independent role of the state court in interpreting its constitution. Those courts reject the starting point assumption that state guarantees should be interpreted in harmony with Supreme Court rulings absent some state specific consideration justifying a divergent interpretation. They also reject the suggestion that it is inappropriate to adopt a differing interpretation of a state constitution guarantee simply because the state court views the Supreme Court's reasoning as faulty. State courts taking this "pure independent" approach treat Supreme Court opinions as no more persuasive than the strength of their reasoning, but they differ as to the need to even look to those Supreme Court opinions. Some courts will look initially to the federal constitutional standard and reach the state constitutional issue only if defendant's claim fails under that standard. Moreover, where the court has no difficulty with the federal constitutional standard, it may not even comment on the state law question or rapidly put it aside. This "interstitial" approach to state constitutional issues has been criticized because it results in extended discussion of the state claim only where the state court goes beyond Supreme Court precedent and because it hinders the development of an independent state jurispru-

13. Teachout, Against the Stream, 14 Vt.L.Rev. 13 (1988).

14. 91 N.J. 338, 450 A.2d 952 (1982) (concurring opinion).

15. State v. Novembrino, 105 N.J. 95, 519 A.2d 820 (1987). The Court majority noted that during the post-incorporation era the "exclusionary rule" had become "embedded in our jurisprudence," state law-enforcement agencies had bolstered the quality of the warrant application process (which would be diluted by a "good faith exception), and current experience in New Jersey showed no need for a good faith exception as defective warrants were "relatively uncommon" and posed "no significant obstacles to law enforcement efforts." Justice Handler, concurring in the result, argued that the exclusionary rule (without a good faith exception) should be adopted as a "common law principle" rather than incorporated in a state constitution that had been adopted without an exclusionary rule and had not previously been interpreted as incorporating such a rule. Justice Garibaldi, in dissent, concluded that there were no historical or policy reasons that would distinguish New Jersey from the national experience that led to the Supreme Court's adoption of the good faith exception.

dence by limiting the instances in which state law issues are considered.

Adopting what has been described as a "state law primacy" approach, other courts support a totally independent reading of the state constitution that looks first to the state issue. The focus here, moreover, is on examination of basic state sources. Analogous Supreme Court precedent may be mentioned only in passing. Indeed, counsel have been warned by one state court against relying too heavily on federal precedent and producing "legal argument [that] consists of a litany of federal buzz words memorized like baseball cards."[16] If the court should find that the state constitution does not support the defendant's claim, it will then turn to the federal constitution. Otherwise there will be no consideration of federal constitutional law except as it might cast light on the text, history, or other aspects of the state constitution.

Still other state courts, adopting what they call a "dual sovereignty" approach, looking to both federal and state constitutions in every case. Each, however, is analyzed separately and independently. Where the same conclusion is reached under both constitutions, the uniformity of result may be seen as bolstering the state law holding. Also, where the court sustains a claim under both constitutions, it discourages any attempt to reverse its state law ruling through a constitutional amendment, as the same result would be required in any event under federal law. This end is furthered by the fact that such a two-pronged ruling cuts off Supreme Court review of the state court's conclusions on the federal constitutional question, as its ruling rests independently on a state court ground. That result may suggest to critics, however, that the state court has merely engaged in a tactical use of state constitutional law.

16. State v. Jewett, 146 Vt. 221, 500 A.2d 233 (1985).

Part Two

DETECTION AND INVESTIGATION OF CRIME

Chapter 3

ARREST, SEARCH AND SEIZURE

Table of Sections

§ 3.1 The Exclusionary Rule and Other Remedies

(a) Origins of the Exclusionary Rule. The Fourth Amendment remained largely unexplored until 1886 when, in *Boyd v. United States,*[1] the Court held that the forced disclosure of papers amounting to evidence of crime violated the Fourth Amendment *and* that such items therefore were inadmissible in the proceedings against Boyd. Though the Fourth Amendment unlike the Fifth contains no express exclusionary rule, the Court reached this result by linking the two amendments together, noting it had "been unable to perceive that the seizure of a man's private books and papers to be used in evidence against him is substantially different from compelling him to be a witness against himself." Yet in *Adams v. New York*[2] the Court declared that "the weight of authority as well as reason" supported the common-law rule that courts will not inquire into the means by which evidence otherwise admissible was acquired.

In 1914 the Court decided *Weeks v. United States,*[3] where the defendant questioned the use in a federal trial of evidence seized from his home by local police and later by federal officers. The Court held that to admit evidence illegally seized by federal officers would, in effect, put a stamp of approval on their unconstitutional conduct: "To sustain [unlawful invasion of the sanctity of his home by officers of the law] would be to affirm by judicial decision a manifest neglect, if not an open defiance, of the prohibitions of the Constitution, intended for the protection of the people against such unauthorized action." But while that evidence thus had to be excluded, the Court went on to say that the same result was not required as to the fruits of the first search, "as the 4th Amendment is not directed to individual misconduct of such officials." (In two 1927 cases, the Supreme Court concluded otherwise as to state searches with either federal participation[4] or a federal purpose.[5])

Because the Bill of Rights was designed as a limitation on the federal government only, it was settled very early that the Fourth Amendment "has no application to state process."[6] With the adoption of the Fourteenth Amendment, however, forbidding the states to "deprive any person of life, liberty, or property, without due process of law," there arose the question of the relation of that limitation upon the states to the limitations upon federal action in the first eight Amendments. Over the years, many of those guarantees were "incorporated" into the Fourteenth Amendment and applied to the states, and thus the stage was set for consideration of the issue which reached the Court in *Wolf v. Colorado*[7]: whether a state court conviction violates due process because based upon evidence which, in federal court, would have been excluded on Fourth Amendment grounds. The Court in *Wolf,* while not hesitating to say that the "security of one's privacy against arbitrary intrusion * * * which is at the core of the Fourth Amendment * * * is * * * enforceable against the States," concluded the *Weeks* exclusionary rule was another matter. Because it was "not derived from the explicit requirements of the Fourth

§ 3.1

1. 116 U.S. 616, 6 S.Ct. 524, 29 L.Ed. 746 (1886).

2. 192 U.S. 585, 24 S.Ct. 372, 48 L.Ed. 575 (1904).

3. 232 U.S. 383, 34 S.Ct. 341, 58 L.Ed. 652 (1914).

4. Byars v. United States, 273 U.S. 28, 47 S.Ct. 248, 71 L.Ed. 520 (1927) (evidence admissible in federal court because "the search in substance and effect was a joint operation of the local and federal officers").

5. Gambino v. United States, 275 U.S. 310, 48 S.Ct. 137, 72 L.Ed. 293 (1927).

6. Smith v. Maryland, 59 U.S. (18 How.) 71, 15 L.Ed. 269 (1855).

7. 338 U.S. 25, 69 S.Ct. 1359, 93 L.Ed. 1782 (1949).

Amendment," was not followed in "most of the English-speaking world," and had been expressly rejected in 30 states, the Court concluded it was not "a departure from basic standards" to leave the victims of illegal state searches "to the remedies of private action and such protection as the internal discipline of the police, under the eyes of an alert public opinion, may afford."

Any thought that *Wolf* meant state courts were permitted to admit all unconstitutional evidence was dispelled three years later in *Rochin v. California,*[8] where police engaged in a series of unlawful acts which culminated in the defendant being given an emetic by force to retrieve drugs he had swallowed. The Court held that the Fourteenth Amendment required exclusion of evidence obtained by "conduct that shocks the conscience." But it soon became apparent that *Rochin* did not require exclusion with respect to all serious Fourth Amendment violations, for it was held not to apply to illegal month-long electronic eavesdropping [9] or to extraction of blood from an unconscious person.[10] Another post-*Wolf* development of significance was the demise of the "silver platter" doctrine, whereby illegally obtained evidence was admitted in federal courts when obtained by state officers. In rejecting that doctrine in *Elkins v. United States,*[11] the Court emphasized that the determination in *Wolf* that Fourteenth Amendment due process prohibited illegal searches and seizures by state officers marked the "removal of the doctrinal underpinning" for the admissibility of state-seized evidence in federal prosecutions. (As for somewhat the reverse of *Elkins,* the Court had earlier held that a federal official could be enjoined from turning over such evidence and from giving testimony concerning the evidence in a state prosecution.[12]

In *Mapp v. Ohio,*[13] overruling *Wolf* and holding "that all evidence obtained by searches and seizures in violation of the Constitution is, by that same authority, inadmissible in a state court," the Court reasoned:

> Since the Fourth Amendment's right of privacy has been declared enforceable against the States through the Due Process Clause of the Fourteenth, it is enforceable against them by the same sanction of exclusion as is used against the Federal Government. Were it otherwise then just as without the *Weeks* rule the assurance against unreasonable federal searches and seizures would be "a form of words," valueless and undeserving of mention in a perpetual charter of inestimable human liberties, so too, without that rule the freedom from state invasions of privacy would be so ephemeral and so neatly severed from its conceptual nexus with the freedom from all brutish means of coercing evidence as not to merit this Court's high regard as a freedom "implicit in the concept of ordered liberty."

Wolf was pushed aside as "bottomed on factual considerations" lacking "current validity," in that during the intervening years more and more states had opted for the exclusionary rule, and experience had shown that the other remedies alluded to in *Wolf* were "worthless and futile." In an oft-quoted passage the Court in *Mapp* went on to say:

> Moreover, our holding * * * is not only the logical dictate of prior cases but it also makes very good sense. There is no war between the Constitution and common sense. Presently, a federal prosecutor may make no use of evidence illegally seized, but a State's attorney across the street may, although he supposedly is operating under the enforceable prohibitions of the same Amendment. Thus the State, by admitting evidence unlawfully seized, serves to encourage disobedience to the Federal Constitution which it is bound to uphold.

8. 342 U.S. 165, 72 S.Ct. 205, 96 L.Ed. 183 (1952).

9. Irvine v. California, 347 U.S. 128, 74 S.Ct. 381, 98 L.Ed. 561 (1954).

10. Breithaupt v. Abram, 352 U.S. 432, 77 S.Ct. 408, 1 L.Ed.2d 448 (1957).

11. 364 U.S. 206, 80 S.Ct. 1437, 4 L.Ed.2d 1669 (1960).

12. Rea v. United States, 350 U.S. 214, 76 S.Ct. 292, 100 L.Ed. 233 (1956), where the Court stressed it was "not asked to enjoin state officials nor in any way to interfere with state agencies in enforcement of state law," and that the case raised "not a constitutional question but one concerning our supervisory powers over federal law enforcement agencies."

13. 367 U.S. 643, 81 S.Ct. 1684, 6 L.Ed.2d 1081 (1961).

(b) Purposes of the Exclusionary Rule. The deterrence of unreasonable searches and seizures is a major purpose of the exclusionary rule. This was acknowledged by the Court in *Wolf* ("the exclusion of evidence may be an effective way of deterring unreasonable searches"), *Elkins* ("Its purpose is to deter—to compel respect for the constitutional guaranty in the only effectively available way—by removing the incentive to disregard it"), and *Mapp* (rule a "deterrent safeguard without insistence upon which the Fourth Amendment would have been reduced to 'a form of words'"). Later, in *Linkletter v. Walker,*[14] the rule was characterized as "an effective deterrent to illegal police action," while in *Terry v. Ohio*[15] the Court stressed that the rule's "major thrust is a deterrent one." But the rule serves other purposes as well. There is, for example, what the *Elkins* Court referred to as "the imperative of judicial integrity," namely, that the courts not become "accomplices in the willful disobedience of a Constitution they are sworn to uphold." This language was later relied upon in *Mapp* and *Terry*. A third purpose of the exclusionary rule, as more recently stated most clearly by some members of the Court, is that "of assuring the people—all potential victims of unlawful government conduct that the government would not profit from its lawless behavior, thus minimizing the risk of seriously undermining popular trust in government."[16] This is not merely another statement of the deterrence objective, for the emphasis is on the effect of exclusion upon the public rather than the police.

The purposes of the exclusionary rule are of more than academic concern, for the Court's perception of them will determine the scope and, ultimately, the fate of the exclusionary rule. It is clear the Court has never taken the latter two purposes to be so important that the rule must be unqualified, as is illustrated by the fact that the government may "profit" from wrongdoing and the court may be an "accomplice" thereto whenever the defendant lacks standing.[17] But it is nonetheless true that the reach of the exclusionary rule may be affected by what are seen as its purposes, as is illustrated by *United States v. Calandra.*[18] The majority took into account only the deterrence function in holding that a grand jury witness may not refuse to answer questions on the ground they are based upon illegally seized evidence, reasoning that any "incremental deterrent effect which might be achieved by extending the rule to grand jury proceedings is uncertain at best." The dissenters, in reaching the contrary conclusion, stressed the other two functions and relegated deterrence to "at best only a hoped for effect of the exclusionary rule."

Calandra is noteworthy in another respect. While in *Mapp* the exclusionary rule was said to be "part and parcel of the Fourth Amendment's limitation upon [governmental] encroachment of individual privacy," the *Calandra* majority characterized the rule as "a judicially-created remedy designed to safeguard Fourth Amendment rights generally through its deterrent effect, rather than a personal constitutional right of the party aggrieved." That language has been viewed with dismay as a "signal" that the Court may "reopen the door still further and abandon altogether the exclusionary rule."[19]

(c) The Exclusionary Rule Under Attack. The validity and efficacy of this exclusionary rule have been vigorously debated over the years. Much of this debate is more remarkable for its volume than its cogency. There is, for example, the oft-heard complaint that the exclusionary rule "handcuffs" the police, which is nonsense because the objection goes not to this particular remedy but to the Fourth Amendment restrictions upon police authority. That argument was rejected when the Fourth Amendment was adopted. The objection that Fourth Amendment standards are often lacking in clarity is of the same order. The concern is legitimate, but to

14. 381 U.S. 618, 85 S.Ct. 1731, 14 L.Ed.2d 601 (1965).

15. 392 U.S. 1, 88 S.Ct. 1868, 20 L.Ed.2d 889 (1968).

16. United States v. Calandra, 414 U.S. 338, 94 S.Ct. 613, 38 L.Ed.2d 561 (1974) (dissent).

17. See §§ 9.1, 9.2.

18. 414 U.S. 338, 94 S.Ct. 613, 38 L.Ed.2d 561 (1974).

19. Brennan, J., dissenting in *Calandra.*

suggest that it would vanish if the exclusionary rule were abandoned is to concede the warning in *Weeks* that without the suppression doctrine the Fourth Amendment would be no more than "a form of words." As for the complaint that the rule only comes to the aid of the guilty, it rests upon a gross misperception. The exclusionary rule, as noted in *Elkins v. United States,*[20] "is calculated to prevent, not to repair"; suppression in a particular case is intended to influence police conduct in the future, and thus the innocent and society are the principal beneficiaries.

Chief Justice Burger, in *Bivens v. Six Unknown Named Agents,*[21] asserted in dissent that the hope the Fourth Amendment could be enforced "by the exclusion of reliable evidence from criminal trials was hardly more than a wistful dream," and that "there is no empirical evidence to support the claim that the rule actually deters illegal conduct of law enforcement officials." A more accurate characterization is that the available data fall short of an empirical substantiation *or* refutation of the deterrent effect of the exclusionary rule, and thus the Chief Justice's allocation of the burden of proof is merely a way of announcing a predetermined conclusion. The exclusionary rule is like capital punishment in that it is easy to see when the deterrent effect has failed but not when it has succeeded. That the suppression doctrine has had a deterrent effect is nonetheless suggested by various post-exclusionary rule events, such as the dramatic increase in use of search warrants where nearly none were used before, stepped up efforts to educate police on Fourth Amendment law where such training had before been virtually nonexistent, and creation and development of working relationships between police and prosecutors. A majority of the Supreme Court has indicated its willingness to assume "that the immediate effect of exclusion will be to discourage law enforcement officials from violating the Fourth Amendment by removing the incentive to disregard it."[22]

In *Bivens* the Chief Justice suggested the exclusionary rule should be "replaced" by a statute permitting victims of Fourth Amendment violations to go before a special tribunal and collect damages from the government. But it is to be doubted that this would be a suitable substitute for a number of reasons: (1) most such victims lack the aura of respectability needed to collect enough damages to make the action worth the effort; (2) for that reason and others these victims will have difficulty securing effective legal representation; (3) requiring government payment of damages will not deter the police, in that the compartmentalization of government will prevent the taxing authorities from putting effective pressure on the police; (4) the violate now and pay later character of the remedy makes it ineffective both as a deterrent and a means of giving credibility to Fourth Amendment rights; and (5) shunting the issues off to a special tribunal would withdraw from the Supreme Court and other appellate courts the important function of spelling out police authority under the Fourth Amendment.

Various suggestions have been made for limiting the exclusionary rule in one way or another. For example, Justice White, dissenting in *Stone v. Powell,*[23] expressed the view that the exclusionary rule "should be substantially modified so as to prevent its application in those many circumstances where the evidence at issue was seized by an officer acting in the good-faith belief that his conduct comported with existing law and having reasonable grounds for this belief," for the simple reason that in such circumstances "the exclusion can have no deterrent effect." This proposal has been questioned on the ground that because of the difficulty of determining what is a reasonable mistake of law, it would put a premium on the ignorance of the police officer and the department which trains him and would unduly complicate the factfinding process in that evidence of the officer's state of mind would be generally difficult to come

20. 364 U.S. 206, 80 S.Ct. 1437, 4 L.Ed.2d 1669 (1960).

21. 403 U.S. 388, 91 S.Ct. 1999, 29 L.Ed.2d 619 (1971).

22. Stone v. Powell, 428 U.S. 465, 96 S.Ct. 3037, 49 L.Ed.2d 1067 (1976).

23. 428 U.S. 465, 96 S.Ct. 3037, 49 L.Ed.2d 1067 (1976).

by apart from his self-serving testimony. Moreover, it could stop judicial development of Fourth Amendment rights, as suppression would always be denied absent a clear precedent declaring the search unconstitutional.

In *United States v. Leon,*[24] the Supreme Court, 6–3, adopted part of the "good faith" exception, holding that "the Fourth Amendment exclusionary rule should be modified so as not to bar the use in the prosecution's case-in-chief of evidence obtained by officers acting in reasonable reliance on a search warrant issued by a detached and neutral magistrate but ultimately found to be unsupported by probable cause." The majority reasoned: (i) that the exclusionary rule is a "judicially created remedy designed to safeguard Fourth Amendment rights generally through its deterrent effect," the applicability of which "must be resolved by weighing the costs and benefits of preventing the use" in evidence of illegally seized evidence; (ii) exclusion to deter magistrates is inappropriate, as "the exclusionary rule is designed to deter police misconduct rather than to punish the errors of judges," "there exists no evidence suggesting that judges and magistrates are inclined to ignore or subvert the Fourth Amendment," and there is no basis "for believing that exclusion of evidence seized pursuant to a warrant will have a significant deterrent effect on the issuing judge or magistrate"; (iii) in a with-warrant case, exclusion to deter the policeman is ordinarily inappropriate, for usually "there is no police illegality" because the officer justifiably relied upon the prior judgment of the magistrate; and thus (iv) "the marginal or nonexistent benefits produced by suppressing evidence obtained in objectively reasonable reliance on a subsequently invalidated search warrant cannot justify the substantial costs of exclusion."

The soundness of *Leon* is certainly open to question. The dissenters seriously questioned whether the exclusionary rule is merely a "judicially created remedy" for Fourth Amendment violations, subject to being narrowed "through guesswork about deterrence," rather than (as indicated in *Weeks*) "a right grounded in that Amendment to prevent the government from subsequently making use of any evidence so obtained." As for the majority's concern about the "costs" of the exclusionary rule, the dissenters noted that available statistics indicate "that federal and state prosecutors very rarely drop cases because of potential search and seizure problems," and that to the extent there is a cost "it is not the exclusionary rule, but the Amendment itself that has imposed this cost" by preferring freedom and privacy over more efficient law enforcement processes. As for the "benefits" of the exclusionary rule in deterrence terms, the dissenters observed that the goal of institutional deterrence is served even when the actors in a particular case did not know they were acting illegally. Under *Leon,* by comparison, magistrates know "that they need not take much care in reviewing warrant applications, since their mistakes will from now on have virtually no consequence," and police will know "that if a warrant has simply been signed, it is reasonable, without more, to rely on it."

Whether *Leon* is a stepping-stone to adoption of a more general "good faith" exception remains to be seen. Certainly much of the majority's reasoning—especially that in with-warrant cases there is no need to deter the magistrate and usually no need to discourage the officer from relying upon the magistrate's judgment and actions—does not carry over to the without-warrant situation, where there would also exist more difficult (if not imponderable) issues of what kinds or degrees of ignorance of Fourth Amendment law are objectively reasonable. But some of the majority's language in *Leon,* particularly the assertion that the exclusionary rule "cannot be expected, and should not be applied, to deter objectively reasonable law enforcement activity," will doubtless be relied upon by those seeking an expansion of the *Leon* holding.

Expansion in a different direction occurred in *Illinois v. Krull,*[25] holding 5–4 that "a sim-

24. 468 U.S. 897, 104 S.Ct. 3405, 82 L.Ed.2d 677 (1984).

25. 480 U.S. 340, 107 S.Ct. 1160, 94 L.Ed.2d 364 (1987).

ilar exception to the exclusionary rule should be recognized when officers act in objectively reasonable reliance upon a *statute* authorizing [the search in question], but where the statute is ultimately found to violate the Fourth Amendment." Despite many pre-*Leon* decisions by the Court to the contrary, the *Krull* majority concluded "[t]he approach used in *Leon* is equally applicable to the present case" because (i) application of the exclusionary rule when the police reasonably relied on a statute would "have as little deterrent effect on the officers' actions" as in the *Leon* situation, and (ii) "legislators, like judicial officers, are not the focus of the rule," as there "is nothing to indicate that applying the exclusionary rule to evidence seized pursuant to the statute prior to the declaration of its invalidity will act as a significant, additional deterrent" to the occasional enactment of a statute later determined to confer unconstitutional search authority. The dissenters, though conceding the good faith of the police who relied on the statute, stressed that statutes "authorizing unreasonable searches were the core concern of the Framers of the Fourth Amendment," and rightly so, as a "judicial officer's unreasonable authorization of a search affects one person at a time; a legislature's unreasonable authorization of searches may affect thousands or millions." Moreover, they persuasively noted, "[l]egislators by virtue of their political role are more often subjected to the political pressures that may threaten Fourth Amendment values than are judicial officers."

It is important to understand that *Leon* does not hold that the exclusionary rule is totally inapplicable whenever a warrant had been obtained. *Leon* has to do with a presumptively invalid warrant, such as one issued on less than probable cause (assumed to be so in *Leon*) or one issued with an insufficient particularity in description (assumed to be so in the companion case of *Massachusetts v. Sheppard* [26]). Fourth Amendment violations relating to execution of the warrant are untouched by *Leon,* as is reflected by the majority's caution that its discussion "assumes, of course, that the officers properly executed the warrant and searched only those places for those objects that it was reasonable to believe were covered by the warrant." The Court also emphasized it was not suggesting "that exclusion is always inappropriate in cases where an officer has obtained a warrant and abided by its terms," and that exclusion is still called for whenever the officer lacks "reasonable grounds for believing that the warrant was properly issued."

This encompasses at least four situations. Firstly, the Court expressly left untouched the *Franks* doctrine,[27] whereunder a warrant facially sufficient is invalid if based upon knowingly or recklessly made falsehoods in the affidavit. Secondly, there is the situation in which the officer knows that the magistrate has "wholly abandoned his judicial role." This would include the circumstances in the case cited by the Court,[28] where the magistrate "allowed himself to become a member, if not the leader of the search party," and presumably also the situation earlier referred to in *Leon,* where the magistrate serves "merely as a rubber stamp for the police." (This may result in inquiry at suppression hearings into whether the magistrate examined the affidavit before signing the warrant and, if so, how intense his scrutiny was.) Thirdly, the Court said "a warrant may be so facially deficient—i.e., in failing to particularize the place to be searched or the things to be seized—that the executing officers cannot reasonably presume it to be valid." (This will doubtless result in considerable litigation of the question of how far off the mark of extant particular description requirements [29] a description must be before an officer should know it is deficient.[30]) Lastly, *Leon* is inappli-

26. 468 U.S. 981, 104 S.Ct. 3424, 82 L.Ed.2d 737 (1984).

27. See § 3.4(d).

28. Lo–Ji Sales, Inc. v. New York, 442 U.S. 319, 99 S.Ct. 2319, 60 L.Ed.2d 920 (1979).

29. See § 3.4(e), (f).

30. In this regard, it should be noted that in *Sheppard* the search warrant authorized search for "controlled substances" and related paraphernalia, though the affidavit in support showed probable cause to search for certain specified evidence of a homicide. In holding this came within the *Leon* rule, the Court stressed that the detec-

cable when the affidavit was "so lacking in indicia of probable cause as to render official belief in its existence entirely unreasonable." It is on this language that most of the post-*Leon* suppression motions in with-warrant cases have focused. Given the fact that the Court had adopted a relaxed standard of assessing probable cause just a year earlier in *Illinois v. Gates*,[31] whereunder it suffices if a reviewing court finds the magistrate had a "substantial basis" for concluding there was a "fair probability" evidence would be found, how if at all has *Leon* departed from existing requirements? As the *Leon* dissenters put it, is it not "virtually inconceivable that a reviewing court, when faced with a defendant's motion to suppress, could first find that a warrant was invalid under the new *Gates* standard, but then, at the same time, find that a police officer's reliance on such an invalid warrant was nevertheless 'objectively reasonable' under the test announced today"?

A partial answer to that question may be that *Gates* and *Leon* can produce different results because of their different focus: the former is concerned with the *magistrate's* decision, to be given deference in all "doubtful or marginal cases," while the latter involves the decision to seek and execute a warrant by the *police*, who ordinarily are entitled to assume the magistrate is acting properly. This important difference is highlighted in the assertion in *Leon* that the question to be resolved is "whether a reasonably well-trained officer would have known that the search was illegal despite the magistrate's authorization." But this seemingly hindsight perspective was thereafter rejected by the Court in another context where, purporting to follow "the same standard" as in *Leon*, it was concluded that the fact the magistrate acted favorably on the warrant request was irrelevant. This is because, the Court explained, the question "is whether a reasonably well-trained officer * * * would have known that his affidavit failed to establish probable cause and that he should not have applied for the warrant." [32]

As for the suggestion that the exclusionary rule not apply in the most serious cases, where there is a substantial disproportion between the magnitude of the policeman's constitutional violation and the defendant's crime, such a limitation would withdraw the exclusionary rule from those cases in which it is most effective and other restraints are least effective, and would likely result in the police concluding that the Fourth Amendment could be ignored in such cases. And the proposal that the exclusionary rule be limited to institutional failures by permitting the police to make a showing of the police department's regulations, training programs, and disciplinary history as to the practice at issue, though directed at the desirable objective of prompting law enforcement agencies to engage in meaningful rulemaking, also would add another especially subjective factual determination to suppression hearings.

(d) The Significance of Underlying Motivation: More on the Deterrence Objective and Inquiry Into Subjective Matters. The question of whether a "bad" intent or motivation by the searching police officer is to be taken into account in deciding whether evidence should be suppressed was presented in *Scott v. United States*,[33] where federal agents operating a judicially authorized wiretap failed to attempt any compliance with the Fourth Amendment requirement of minimization of interception. In rejecting the petitioners' claim that this "lack of good faith efforts" required suppression even if no minimization would have been feasible in this case, the Court elected to evaluate the Fourth Amend-

tive who directed the search apparently never noticed the discrepancy, that he was also the affiant and thus "knew what items were listed in the affidavit presented to the judge," and that "he had good reason to believe that the warrant authorized the seizure of those items." The Court cautioned it was not deciding what the result would be as to "an officer who is less familiar with the warrant application."

31. 462 U.S. 213, 103 S.Ct. 2317, 76 L.Ed.2d 527 (1983), discussed in § 3.3(c).

32. Malley v. Briggs, 475 U.S. 335, 106 S.Ct. 1092, 89 L.Ed.2d 271 (1986), thus concluding that a rule of absolute immunity would be inappropriate in a § 1983 action against an officer based on his conduct in *applying for* a warrant.

33. 436 U.S. 128, 98 S.Ct. 1717, 56 L.Ed.2d 168 (1978).

ment claim by "an objective assessment of an officer's actions in light of the facts and circumstances then known to him" and "without regard to the underlying intent or motivation of the officers involved." Generally, this is a sound rule and is fully consistent with the purposes of the Fourth Amendment and its exclusionary rule,[34] as may be seen by examination of some of the situations in which problems of this kind arise.

One kind of case is that in which the police, though lacking the grounds required by the Fourth Amendment, decide to make an arrest or search, but before they can so act upon that decision they are confronted with additional facts supplying the requisite grounds. Most courts refuse to suppress the evidence in such circumstances, and rightly so. "We might wish that policemen would not act with impure plots in mind," but that is hardly "a sufficient basis for excluding, in the supposed service of the Fourth Amendment, probative evidence obtained by actions—if not thoughts—entirely in accord with the Fourth Amendment," especially since a contrary rule would require courts to undertake "an expedition into the minds of police officers." [35] In other words, the deterrence objective would not be served by exclusion in such circumstances.

What if the officer *does* act on his "bad" state of mind in the sense that he engages in Fourth Amendment activity despite a *mistaken* belief he lacks the grounds for such action? Though it might be argued that in such a case the deterrence objective calls for exclusion so as to impress upon the officer that he should not arrest when he believes probable cause is lacking (in which case often it will in fact be lacking), the prevailing view is that an officer is no more the judge of the insufficiency of his facts than of their sufficiency. On balance, that is a correct result; here again, the evidence was "obtained by actions—if not thoughts—entirely in accord with the Fourth Amendment," and thus what is to be communicated to the officer is that the information he had *did* amount to probable cause, a message which hardly would be conveyed by suppression of evidence.

Then there are cases in which it might be said that the officer's "underlying intent or motivation" reflects that he was operating under the wrong legal theory, such as where an officer arrests a robbery suspect for vagrancy, but the facts at hand constitute grounds to arrest for robbery but not for vagrancy. The prevailing view is to uphold the arrest, which is correct. Exclusion in the interest of deterrence is unjustified here, especially because such situations are often attributable to complicated legal distinctions between offenses or an officer's failure to record all the bases or the strongest basis upon which the arrest was made. Sometimes the gap between the relied upon but unavailing theory and the availing but unrelied upon theory is greater, as where a warrantless search of a vehicle is undertaken by the police as an inventory of an impounded car, not justified on the facts, but in actuality the car was subject to warrantless search on probable cause. It has been held that upholding the police action on a court-devised theory of justification would be improper because it would not deter future unconstitutional impoundments or inventories, but the prevailing view is again to the contrary. The *Scott* rule produces the better result even here. Suppression for police reliance upon the wrong theory even when there exists a valid theory would deter unconstitutional searches only if, absent such extension of the exclusionary rule, it may be assumed police will conduct searches on grounds they know or suspect to be insufficient in the hope that their actions will later be upheld on some other grounds of which they are presently unaware. That assumption seems fanciful.

34. And thus has been relied upon by the Court in other circumstances. *See, e.g.,* Horton v. California, ___ U.S. ___, 110 S.Ct. 2301, 110 L.Ed.2d 112 (1990) (rejecting inadvertent discovery limitation on plain view doctrine because "evenhanded law enforcement is best achieved by the application of objective standards of conduct, rather than standards that depend upon the subjective state of mind of the officer").

35. White, J., dissenting from dismissal of writ as improvidently granted in Massachusetts v. Painten, 389 U.S. 560, 88 S.Ct. 660, 19 L.Ed.2d 770 (1968).

Scott has been objected to on the ground that it undermines the long established rule that an arrest may not be used as a pretext to search, which prompts consideration of *Abel v. United States.*[36] There immigration agents, acting pursuant to an administrative warrant for deportation, arrested Russian spy Colonel Abel, but he later claimed this was an illegal subterfuge because those agents were working hand-in-glove with FBI agents whose underlying objective was to acquire evidence of Abel's espionage. The Supreme Court held that a "finding of bad faith" could not be made on the record, which, as stated by the district court, was that the immigration agents' conduct "differed in no respect from what would have been done in the case of an individual concerning whom no such information was known to exist." Thus, the "underlying intent or motivation of the officers involved" (to use the *Scott* phrase again) does not require suppression where, even assuming that intent or motivation was the dominant one in the particular case, the Fourth Amendment activity undertaken is precisely the same as would have occurred had that intent or motivation been absent. This is a correct result; because the action would have been taken in any event, there is no *conduct* which ought to have been deterred and thus no reason to bring the Fourth Amendment exclusionary rule into play.

That highlights the remaining situation in which the Fourth Amendment activity would not have been undertaken *but for* the "underlying intent or motivation" which, standing alone, could not supply a lawful basis for the police conduct. Illustrative is a case in which the driver of an automobile suspected of unlawful drug activity is placed under custodial arrest for a traffic violation and then searched, though the arrest was not one which would have been made by a traffic officer on routine patrol against any citizen driving in the same manner. Such situations involve what the Supreme Court in *Abel* characterized as "serious conduct by law-enforcing officers," and have resulted in suppression of evidence so acquired. Here at last, it would seem, is a case in which the *Scott* rule does not apply, for courts ordering suppression in such circumstances typically emphasize the underlying "bad" motive of the arresting-searching officers. But that is hardly the most desirable way to go at the problem, if for no other reason than that determining the existence of such a motive on a case-by-case basis is very difficult. Such a determination would be unnecessary if courts, by applying the line of Supreme Court cases teaching that arbitrary action is unreasonable under the Fourth Amendment,[37] were to require a showing that the Fourth Amendment activity challenged on pretext grounds "was carried out in accordance with *standard procedures* in the local department." [38] It is the departure from those procedures, and not the reason for it, which amounts to a Fourth Amendment violation, and in that sense the *Scott* rule applies even here. That is, in the illustration put above, the driver's Fourth Amendment rights were violated by his custodial arrest, but this would have been equally true had the officer deviated from the established practice merely by inadvertence, so that it is again correct to say that the outcome does not turn upon the officer's "underlying intent or motivation."

(e) Constitutional vs. Other Violations. *Mapp v. Ohio* [39] declared that state and federal officers were obligated to respect "the same fundamental criteria," and in *Ker v. California,*[40] the Court held that "the standard of reasonableness is the same under the Fourth and Fourteenth Amendments." This means that close attention must be paid to the basis of Supreme Court decisions dealing with searches and seizures by federal officers, as a declared standard based upon the Fourth Amendment would be equally applicable to the states, but this would not be so as to a

36. 362 U.S. 217, 80 S.Ct. 683, 4 L.Ed.2d 668 (1960).

37. See the cases discussed in § 3.9 permitting searches even without traditional probable cause where undertaken pursuant to an established plan.

38. South Dakota v. Opperman, 428 U.S. 364, 96 S.Ct. 3092, 49 L.Ed.2d 1000 (1976).

39. 367 U.S. 643, 81 S.Ct. 1684, 6 L.Ed.2d 1081 (1961).

40. 374 U.S. 23, 83 S.Ct. 1623, 10 L.Ed.2d 726 (1963).

standard based only upon the Court's supervisory power over federal courts.

When a state court finds that a certain arrest or search passes muster under the Fourth Amendment but that it violates the comparable provision of the state constitution, there appears to be no dissent from the conclusion that the fruits thereof must be suppressed in proceedings in the courts of that state. Where, however, the police conduct is merely in violation of a statutory provision, a rule of court, or an administrative regulation, the same result does not inevitably follow. If the provision in question actually says that the sanction is exclusion of evidence, as is true of some federal and state statutory provisions, then that settles the matter. Absent such a declaration, courts are more likely to utilize the exclusionary rule when the provision in question confers a substantial right, especially if it is one which can be said to relate rather closely to Fourth Amendment protections. In the search warrant area, for example, courts are not inclined to require exclusion of evidence for failure to follow statutes dealing with such matters as prompt return of the warrant to the court, but are likely to rule otherwise as to statutes requiring very prompt execution. Somewhat the same approach is generally taken as to administrative regulations, though there is greater reluctance to utilize an exclusionary rule in this setting and possibly influence the administrative agency involved to reduce its efforts at self-regulation.[41]

In *Elkins v. United States,*[42] the Court abolished the so-called "silver platter" doctrine under which federal courts could receive the fruits of unconstitutional searches by state officers. Thus, it is now clear that if the Fourth Amendment has been violated the evidence must be suppressed: (i) when offered in federal court, though the search was by state officers; (ii) when offered in state court, though the search was by federal officers; and (iii) when offered in one state, though the search was by officers of another state. What then is the result when the violation in question is not of Fourth Amendment dimensions, as in *Burge v. State*[43] where evidence offered in a Texas court was constitutionally obtained in Oklahoma but yet was acquired in violation of the Oklahoma rule that a wife cannot give a consent to search which will be effective against her husband? Courts do not utilize the exclusionary rule in such circumstances, and rightly so; the prospect of deterrence is remote, as is the judicial taint from acceptance of the evidence, and there has been no profit from wrongdoing attributable to the prosecuting jurisdiction. Sometimes that result is explained upon the conflict-of-laws principle that the law of the forum governs on the lawfulness-of-the-search issue, but that surely is not the reason. If the situation in *Burge* had been reversed, so that consent-by-spouse was illegal in Texas (the prosecuting state) but not in Oklahoma (the state where the search occurred), it would be ridiculous to suppress the evidence.

(f) Application of Exclusionary Rule in Criminal Proceedings. Questions sometimes arise as to the applicability of the exclusionary rule at stages of the criminal process other than the trial, as illustrated by *United States v. Calandra.*[44] A grand jury witness objected that he should not have to answer questions based upon information purportedly acquired by an earlier illegal search of his premises, but the Supreme Court disagreed. The Court reasoned that such "extension of the exclusionary rule would seriously impede the grand jury" by requiring suppression hearings on "issues only tangentially related to the grand jury's primary objective," dam-

41. In United States v. Caceres, 440 U.S. 741, 99 S.Ct. 1465, 59 L.Ed.2d 733 (1979), the Court declined to utilize the exclusionary sanction as to evidence obtained in violation of IRS regulations prohibiting "consensual electronic surveillance" between taxpayers and IRS agents unless certain prior authorization is obtained, reasoning: "In the long run, it is far better to have rules like those contained in the IRS Manual, and to tolerate occasional erroneous administration of the kind displayed by this record, than either to have no rules except those mandated by statute, or to have them framed in a mere precatory form."

42. 364 U.S. 206, 80 S.Ct. 1437, 4 L.Ed.2d 1669 (1960).

43. 443 S.W.2d 720 (Tex.Crim.App.1969).

44. 414 U.S. 338, 94 S.Ct. 613, 38 L.Ed.2d 561 (1974).

age that would not be offset by substantial benefits in terms of "incremental deterrent effect." This is because illegally seized evidence is already excludable at trial, and thus additional exclusion at the grand jury stage, the Court explained, "would deter only police investigation consciously directed toward the discovery of evidence solely for use in a grand jury investigation." This overlooks the fact that the prior search had been directed at witness Calandra and that thus under the law of standing only Calandra and not the person later indicted could call the police to task for their conduct.

In *Costello v. United States* [45] the Court concluded that "neither the Fifth Amendment nor any other constitutional provision prescribes the kind of evidence upon which grand juries must act," and in that case and subsequent decisions [46] the Court rejected self-incrimination challenges to grand jury indictments. Relying upon those cases, federal courts and most state courts have refused to permit defendants to attack indictments on the ground that evidence before the grand jury was obtained in violation of the Fourth Amendment, which is a sound result. Because the objection would be made by the same person who could object at trial, the standing problem noted above does not exist here. Moreover, there is no feasible way to determine these issues in an adversary setting *before* the evidence is received by the grand jury, and post-indictment challenges on Fourth Amendment grounds would necessitate an elaborate assessment of all the evidence tendered to the grand jury in that case, a burden which is hardly worth whatever deterrent effect would be achieved by nullifying indictments grounded in illegally acquired evidence. That reasoning obviously does not carry over to the issue of whether the exclusionary rule should be applied to the probable cause determination at a preliminary hearing, but there as well the rule in the federal system [47] and most but not all states is that suppression of evidence is not possible at the preliminary hearing. That result is typically explained on the ground that it thus avoids the necessity for multiple determinations of admissibility and for lesser judicial officers to pass upon complex constitutional issues. If those reasons are convincing, they would also support the conclusion that a Fourth Amendment suppression motion may not be utilized to keep evidence out of a pretrial bail hearing, an issue which has seldom reached the courts.

If a defendant manages to have certain evidence suppressed from his trial on Fourth Amendment grounds but is convicted nonetheless, may the excluded evidence be taken into account at his sentencing hearing? Utilizing a *Calandra*–style balancing approach, it has been held that the answer is yes, because there is a need for unfettered access to information by the sentencing judge, and no appreciable increment in deterrence would result from excluding a second time at sentencing. But this is not inevitably true, and thus it is necessary to recognize two exceptions: (1) where the police are assembling a dossier to be offered to a sentencing judge should the subject ever be convicted of an offense, and (2) where police have accumulated sufficient evidence to convict and then seize additional evidence unlawfully solely to affect the sentence. By a somewhat similar balancing process courts have held that the exclusionary rule generally need not be applied in proceedings to revoke a suspended sentence, probation or parole. Here again, an exception must be recognized when suppression *would* further the objective of deterrence, as when the search was conducted by someone who knew of the conditional release status of the individual and who thus should have appreciated the possibility of revocation proceedings. Indeed, it may be argued that revocation of such conditional release is such a common consequence of police search activity that exclusion in the name of deterrence is needed in *all* cases.

45. 350 U.S. 359, 76 S.Ct. 406, 100 L.Ed. 397 (1956).

46. Lawn v. United States, 355 U.S. 339, 78 S.Ct. 311, 2 L.Ed.2d 321 (1958); United States v. Blue, 384 U.S. 251, 86 S.Ct. 1416, 16 L.Ed.2d 510 (1966).

47. Giordenello v. United States, 357 U.S. 480, 78 S.Ct. 1245, 2 L.Ed.2d 1503 (1958).

(g) Application of Exclusionary Rule in Non-criminal Proceedings. In *One 1958 Plymouth Sedan v. Pennsylvania,*[48] the Court held that in proceedings for the forfeiture of an automobile to the state because it had been used in the illegal transportation of liquor, such use could not be proved by liquor taken from that car in an unconstitutional search. As for earlier cases holding that the government was not required to return unlawfully seized narcotics [49] or an unregistered still, alcohol and mash,[50] the Court noted that they "concerned objects the possession of which, without more, constitutes a crime," so that repossession would have subjected the owners to criminal penalties and "would clearly have frustrated the express public policy against the possession of such objects." By comparison, in the instant case there "is nothing even remotely criminal in possessing an automobile," and return of it "to the owner would not subject him to any possible criminal penalties for possession or frustrate any public policy concerning automobiles, as automobiles." The Court added that it would be "anomalous" to apply the exclusionary rule in a criminal proceeding for the crime in question, for which a $500 fine could be imposed, but not in proceedings intended to penalize the criminal by depriving him of a $1,000 automobile.

Under the *Plymouth Sedan* analysis, the exclusionary rule does not apply in proceedings to forfeit such per se contraband as gambling devices and obscene literature. When the object is the fruits of crime, such as gambling profits, the application of *Plymouth Sedan* is unclear; it could be argued, on the one hand, that permitting the criminal to keep his ill-gotten gains frustrates public policy, and on the other that absent exclusion police will be encouraged to make lawless searches for the very purpose of depriving criminals of their profits. The latter concern is legitimate, and explains why most courts do apply the exclusionary rule in that type of forfeiture action. Somewhat similar analysis supports the conclusion that police should not be free of Fourth Amendment restraints when dealing with juveniles or drug addicts, so that the exclusionary rule applies in juvenile delinquency proceedings and addict commitment proceedings.

In *United States v. Janis,*[51] a city police officer seized certain records and funds in a gambling raid and then turned them over to the Internal Revenue Service, where they served as the basis of an IRS assessment satisfied in part by levying upon the seized funds. Janis then sued in federal court for return of the money, and the government counterclaimed for the unpaid balance. The Supreme Court held that the exclusionary rule did not apply in those proceedings in such circumstances, reasoning that no appreciable gain in terms of deterrence would be realized by suppression in a proceeding "to enforce only the civil law of the other sovereign," as it "falls outside the offending officer's zone of primary interest." The trouble with *Janis* is that the facts of the case do not support the result, for it was shown that there was an established pattern of cooperation whereby that officer routinely notified the IRS whenever he uncovered a gambling operation involving a substantial amount of cash. Thus, as the *Janis* dissenters noted, "the deterrent purpose of the exclusionary rule is wholly frustrated" by the decision. Absent the special facts relied upon in *Janis,* the exclusionary rule is applied in civil tax proceedings, a conclusion supported by the *Plymouth Sedan* case in that here as well the penalties can far exceed those from criminal prosecution.

Courts have held or assumed that the exclusionary rule applies in a wide range of administrative proceedings, all the way from FTC hearings to uncover discriminatory pricing practices to hearings to suspend or expel a student from school. Many of these decisions are supported by the *Plymouth Sedan* reasoning that the exclusionary rule applies to pro-

48. 380 U.S. 693, 85 S.Ct. 1246, 14 L.Ed.2d 170 (1965).

49. United States v. Jeffers, 342 U.S. 48, 72 S.Ct. 93, 96 L.Ed. 59 (1951).

50. Trupiano v. United States, 334 U.S. 699, 68 S.Ct. 1229, 92 L.Ed. 1663 (1948).

51. 428 U.S. 433, 96 S.Ct. 3021, 49 L.Ed.2d 1046 (1976).

ceedings which are "quasi-criminal in character," in that their object "is to penalize for the commission of an offense against the law" and could "result in even greater punishment than the criminal prosecution." Under the *Calandra* balancing approach, it may be said that the exclusion-for-deterrence point is quite strong when the search was undertaken for the specific purpose of obtaining information to offer in such administrative proceedings and relatively weak when the search was not directed at a person known to be amenable to such proceedings. As for the cost side of the *Calandra* equation, it may vary from situation to situation. Similar analysis is called for as to the seldom-litigated-question of whether the exclusionary rule applies to legislative hearings.

An extreme and fundamentally unsound cost-benefit analysis was utilized by the majority in *I.N.S. v. Lopez–Mendoza,*[52] where the Court held 5–4 that the exclusionary rule is inapplicable in a civil deportation hearing. The deterrent value of the exclusionary rule in this context was deemed to be reduced because (i) "deportation will still be possible when evidence not derived directly from the arrest is sufficient to support deportation," (ii) INS agents know "that it is highly unlikely that any particular arrestee will end up challenging the lawfulness of his arrest," (iii) "the INS has its own comprehensive scheme for deterring Fourth Amendment violations" by training and discipline, and (iv) "alternative remedies" including the "possibility of declaratory relief" are available for institutional practices violating the Fourth Amendment. On the cost side, the Court continued, are these factors: (i) that application of the exclusionary rule "in proceedings that are intended not to punish past transgressions but to prevent their continuance or renewal would require courts to close their eyes to ongoing violations of the law," (ii) that invocation of the exclusionary rule at deportation hearings, where "neither the hearing officers nor the attorneys * * * are likely to be well versed in the intricacies of Fourth Amendment law," "might significantly change and complicate the character of these proceedings," and (iii) that because many INS arrests "occur in crowded and confused circumstances," application of the exclusionary rule "might well result in the suppression of large amounts of information that had been obtained entirely lawfully." White, J., dissenting, correctly noted that "unlike the situation in *Janis,* the conduct challenged here falls within 'the offending officer's zone of primary interest,'" and that "the costs and benefits of applying the exclusionary rule in civil deportation proceedings do not differ in any significant way from the costs and benefits of applying the rule in ordinary criminal proceedings."

Finally, it must be asked whether the Fourth Amendment exclusionary rule applies in purely private litigation, that is, a civil action in which a governmental unit or representative is not a party. Some authority is to be found to the effect that the fruits of an illegal police search may not be used in a private lawsuit, but it is to be doubted that this conclusion is compelled under the *Calandra* approach. The *Janis* reasoning that there is no gain in deterrence when the proceeding in which the evidence is offered "falls outside the offending officer's zone of primary interest" is more persuasive here than in *Janis.*

(h) The Exclusionary Rule and "Private" Searches. In *Burdeau v. McDowell,*[53] the Court concluded that because the Fourth Amendment's "origin and history clearly show that it was intended as a restraint upon the activities of sovereign authority, and was not intended to be a limitation upon other than governmental agencies," it did not call for exclusion in the instant case, where "no official of the federal government had anything to do with the wrongful seizure * * * or any knowledge thereof until several months after the property had been taken." The *Burdeau* rule squares with the modern emphasis upon the deterrence function of the exclusionary rule, as the private searcher is

52. 468 U.S. 1032, 104 S.Ct. 3479, 82 L.Ed.2d 778 (1984).

53. 256 U.S. 465, 41 S.Ct. 574, 65 L.Ed. 1048 (1921).

often motivated by reasons independent of a desire to secure a criminal conviction and seldom engages in searches upon a sufficiently regular basis to be affected by the exclusionary sanction.

It should not be assumed that a search is private whenever the physical act is done by a private person. This quite clearly is not the case when the search has been ordered or requested by a government official, when it is a joint endeavor of a private person and government official, or when the government official was standing by giving tacit approval. It is otherwise if the private person acted in direct contravention of police instructions. One recurring situation is that in which a private person examines an object and then turns it over to the police for further examination, where close attention is needed to exactly what was done on both occasions. In *Walter v. United States,*[54] for example, private persons to whom a shipment of boxes was misdelivered opened them and found packages of film with suggestive drawings and explicit descriptions of the contents on the outsides, so they turned the boxes over to FBI agents, who screened the films and determined they were obscene. The Court held the screening was a governmental search because it exceeded the scope of the prior private search, and distinguished the case from one in which "the results of the private search are in plain view when materials are turned over to the Government," in which case mere observation of what remained exposed by the private search would not amount to a governmental search. (The Court later held, in *United States v. Jacobsen,*[55] that "field testing" of a white powder first uncovered by a private search did not itself constitute a search because the test would only reveal whether or not the powder was an illegal substance and thus would not "compromise any legitimate interest in privacy."[56]) This leaves the hardest case, namely, where a private party opens a package and finds something incriminating and then repackages it and delivers it to the police, who examine the contents of the package in no greater detail than did the private party. *Walter* does not resolve this situation, but in *Jacobsen* the Court held that so long as the police conduct enabled them "to learn nothing that had not previously been learned during the private search" it "infringed no legitimate expectation of privacy and hence was not a 'search' within the meaning of the Fourth Amendment."

Courts have not hesitated to admit into evidence under the *Burdeau* rule the fruits of searches conducted by persons who, while not employed by the government, have as their responsibility the prevention and detection of criminal conduct, such as store detectives and insurance investigators. Some have argued for a contrary result, contending that the reasoning of *Marsh v. Alabama,*[57] holding that when a private company owned and operated a town it was performing a "public function" and thus was subject to constitutional restraints in the same fashion as any other town, applies here. The *Marsh* analogy is especially appealing where private police actually supplant the public police or deal regularly with the general public, particularly if it may be said they are not disinterested in criminal convictions as an aid to the private objectives of their employer, for in such instances there is both a need for and an opportunity for deterrence by application of the Fourth Amendment exclusionary rule.

Somewhat the reverse of the above problem is whether the exclusionary rule applies when the search was by a public employee not assigned to law enforcement responsibilities, such as a teacher. The cases go both ways, but the better view is that searches by such persons are not "private." This is consistent with the teaching of *Burdeau,* which says the Fourth Amendment "applies to governmental

54. 447 U.S. 649, 100 S.Ct. 2395, 65 L.Ed.2d 410 (1980).

55. 466 U.S. 109, 104 S.Ct. 1652, 80 L.Ed.2d 85 (1984).

56. The Court applied the reasoning from United States v. Place, 462 U.S. 696, 103 S.Ct. 2637, 77 L.Ed.2d 110 (1983), holding that the sniffing of a suitcase by a narcotics detection dog was no search because it "discloses only the presence or absence of narcotics, a contraband item."

57. 326 U.S. 501, 66 S.Ct. 276, 90 L.Ed. 265 (1946).

action" and is a "restraint upon the activities of sovereign authority." [58] It also furthers the deterrence objective of the exclusionary rule in those cases in which the public employee has a duty to investigate unlawful activity. As for searches by police officers during their off duty hours, they are "private" only if the officer was clearly acting for some personal and private purpose at the time.

In *Knoll Associates, Inc. v. Federal Trade Commission,*[59] the court adopted a "ratified intent" theory, reasoning that if a private person made a search for the purpose of aiding the government and the government then uses that evidence later, the taint of the illegal action is thereby transferred to the government so as to make the use unlawful. The theory is in error because it wrongly assumes that the Government has some control over the taker's intent, and it has not been adopted by other courts. One step beyond that theory is the position taken in the dissent in *Sackler v. Sackler,*[60] namely, that the action of the judicial branch in receiving the fruits of the search into evidence is alone sufficient government involvement to bring the Fourth Amendment into play. But, while some have suggested that position is supported by *Shelley v. Kraemer,*[61] holding that judicial enforcement of private restrictive covenants constitutes "state action" subject to constitutional restraints, this is not the case. In *Shelley* the lower court was asked to compel a private citizen to do an act which would be unconstitutional for the state to perform, whereas in *Sackler* the court was merely asked to give evidentiary status to illegally seized information. Moreover, in *Shelley* the challenged racial discrimination could not have occurred unless the court enforced the discriminatory restrictive covenant, while in *Sackler* the invasion of privacy took place before the court was called on to admit the evidence.

(i) The Exclusionary Rule and Searches by Foreign Police. If the police of a foreign country, acting to enforce their own law and without instigation by American officials, conduct a search which would not meet the requirements of the Fourth Amendment if conducted in this country, and the fruits are later offered into evidence here, the evidence is not subject to suppression on constitutional grounds. The Fourth Amendment is not directed at foreign police, and no purpose would be served by applying the exclusionary rule in such a case, as it would not alter the search and seizure policies of the foreign nation. If the foreign official acted with the purpose, at least in part, of finding evidence which could be turned over to American authorities, the result is no different. There is no reason why the foreign official in such circumstances should be expected to discover and apply a rather complicated body of law from another country. This is so even if the foreign official may have been prompted to so act because information was supplied to him about the suspect by American authorities.

If the American authorities have actually requested or participated in the foreign search, it has been suggested that the case should be dealt with just as were state police searches in response to a federal request in the silver platter era, which means that the exclusionary rule would be applicable because

58. It must be emphasized, however, that the question of whether the Fourth Amendment applies and that of whether that Amendment's exclusionary rule applies need not inevitably be answered in the same way. In New Jersey v. T.L.O., 469 U.S. 325, 105 S.Ct. 733, 83 L.Ed.2d 720 (1985), the Court noted the split of authority as to whether the exclusionary rule is applicable to searches by teachers, but found it unnecessary to resolve that issue. But the Court unhesitantly applied to teachers the established doctrine that the Fourth Amendment is "applicable to the activities of civil as well as criminal authorities." The Court concluded: "In carrying out searches and other disciplinary functions pursuant to such policies, school officials act as representatives of the State, not merely as surrogates for the parents, and they cannot claim the parents' immunity from the strictures of the Fourth Amendment." See also O'Connor v. Ortega, 480 U.S. 709, 107 S.Ct. 1492, 94 L.Ed.2d 714 (1987), relying on *T.L.O.* in concluding that "[s]earches and seizures by government employers or supervisors of the private property of their employees, therefore, are subject to the restraints of the Fourth Amendment." Again, the Court had no occasion to decide whether the exclusionary rule would also apply in such circumstances.

59. 397 F.2d 530 (7th Cir.1968).

60. 15 N.Y.2d 40, 255 N.Y.S.2d 83, 203 N.E.2d 481 (1964).

61. 334 U.S. 1, 68 S.Ct. 836, 92 L.Ed. 1161 (1948).

of such request or participation.[62] But this is not the law, and rightly so, as the dynamics here are quite different. The state-federal silver platter problem was one of preventing federal authorities from circumventing the Fourth Amendment by getting state officials to do what they would otherwise do themselves, while the foreign-American relationship is legitimate because investigations extending to other countries naturally depend on cooperation from the local authorities. Thus, it may generally be said that noncompliance with Fourth Amendment standards by the foreign police does not require exclusion in this situation either, as there is no reason why foreign officers need or could be expected to be deterred from their failure to know and follow the law of another country. There doubtless are a few special situations in which it may fairly be concluded that the exclusionary rule should apply because the circumstances indicate the American authorities are rather directly accountable for the excesses which have occurred.

Even if there has been direct U.S. involvement in the foreign search, the Fourth Amendment may be inapplicable for yet another reason. In *United States v. Verdugo–Urquidez*,[63] the Court apparently ruled that the phrase "the people" in the Fourth Amendment (and the First, Second, Ninth and Tenth Amendments) "refers to a class of persons who are part of a national community or who have otherwise developed sufficient connection with this community to be considered part of that community." The defendant in the instant case was deemed not to be such a person; he was a Mexican citizen and resident who, to be sure, just two days earlier had been turned over to U.S. authorities by Mexican police, but "this sort of presence—lawful but involuntary—is not the sort to indicate any substantial connection with our country." [64] But, because the three dissenters agreed that the Fourth Amendment applies whenever "a foreign national is held accountable for purported violations of the U.S. criminal laws," while two concurring Justices placed great emphasis upon the inapplicability of the Fourth Amendment's warrant clause to the search in the instant case,[65] the application of *Verdugo–Urquidez* to a foreign search of an alien's property made even without probable cause is less than clear.

(j) Challenge of Jurisdiction. In *Ker v. Illinois*,[66] the Court indicated that the mere fact the defendant had been arrested in violation of the Fourth Amendment did not affect the jurisdiction or power of the court to subject that individual to trial.[67] The result is the same even when the illegality amounted to total avoidance of established extradition procedures in acquiring the presence of the defendant from another country [68] or another state.[69] As the Court explained in *Frisbie v. Collins* [70]: "There is nothing in the Constitution that requires a court to permit a guilty person rightfully convicted to escape justice because he was brought to trial against his will." That now appears to be somewhat of an overstatement, for there is developing the view that if defendant's presence is acquired by government conduct of a most shocking

62. See Lustig v. United States, 338 U.S. 74, 69 S.Ct. 1372, 93 L.Ed. 1819 (1949), a leading case on the state-federal silver platter.

63. 494 U.S. 259, 110 S.Ct. 1056, 108 L.Ed.2d 222 (1990).

64. The Court added it was an open question whether even the illegal aliens seized in the United States in I.N.S. v. Lopez–Mendoza, 468 U.S. 1032, 104 S.Ct. 3479, 82 L.Ed.2d 778 (1984), were such persons, though their situation was different from the defendant's here because they "were in the United States voluntarily and presumably had accepted some societal obligations."

65. Kennedy, J., stressed this was not a case in which "the full protections of the Fourth Amendment would apply" because of the "absence of local judges or magistrates available to issue warrants"; Stevens, J., emphasized that "American magistrates have no power to authorize such searches."

66. 119 U.S. 436, 7 S.Ct. 225, 30 L.Ed. 421 (1886).

67. The Court has often reaffirmed *Ker.* See, e.g., I.N.S. v. Lopez–Mendoza, 468 U.S. 1032, 104 S.Ct. 3479, 82 L.Ed.2d 778 (1984) (mere fact person summoned to a deportation hearing following an unlawful arrest has no bearing on the deportation proceedings).

68. Ker v. Illinois, 119 U.S. 436, 7 S.Ct. 225, 30 L.Ed. 421 (1886).

69. Frisbie v. Collins, 342 U.S. 519, 72 S.Ct. 509, 96 L.Ed. 541 (1952).

70. 342 U.S. 519, 72 S.Ct. 509, 96 L.Ed. 541 (1952).

and outrageous character, then due process would bar conviction.

A somewhat different question is whether, when extradition processes are utilized to acquire the presence of the defendant, he is entitled to a determination in the asylum state of probable cause. In *Michigan v. Doran,*[71] where the state court had refused extradition because papers submitted by the demanding state were in conclusory form and did not set out facts showing probable cause, the Supreme Court reversed. Because the Extradition Clause[72] contemplates "a summary and mandatory executive proceeding," said the Court, "once the governor had granted extradition,[73] a court considering release on habeas corpus can do no more than decide (a) whether the extradition documents on their face are in order; (b) whether the petitioner has been charged with a crime in the demanding state; (c) whether the petitioner is the person named in the request for extradition; and (d) whether the petitioner is a fugitive."[74] This means that "once the governor of the asylum state has acted on a requisition for extradition based on the demanding state's judicial determination that probable cause existed, no further judicial inquiry may be had on that issue in the asylum state." The Michigan court had thus taken a step not open to it under the Extradition Clause in holding the arrest warrant asserting a probable cause finding deficient merely because the factual basis of that finding was not revealed.

The concurring opinion in *Doran* correctly noted that the majority had ignored the "presence and significance of the Fourth Amendment in the extradition context," and went on to conclude that *Gerstein v. Pugh*[75] means "that, even in the extradition context, where the demanding State's 'charge' rests upon something less than an indictment, there must be a determination of probable cause by a detached and neutral magistrate, and that the asylum State need not grant extradition unless that determination has been made." Nothing said by the *Doran* majority refutes this, and thus it may be said that at a minimum a person facing extradition is protected by the Fourth Amendment from the "significant restraint on liberty" inevitably involved in forced interstate transportation, when the papers sent to the asylum state by the demanding state include neither a copy of an indictment nor a copy of an arrest warrant which asserts that a judicial finding of probable cause has occurred. The major weakness in the *Doran* majority opinion is the willingness to assume that such a self-serving declaration in the warrant is inevitably correct, which empirical studies have shown is not the case. Perhaps *Doran* does not foreclose all forms of attack upon such a warrant; the concurring opinion, noting the majority says the governor's grant of extradition "is prima facie evidence that the constitutional and statutory requirements have been met," construes this as "a suggestion that the governor's review and determination

71. 439 U.S. 282, 99 S.Ct. 530, 58 L.Ed.2d 521 (1978).

72. U.S. Const. art. IV, § 2: "A Person charged in any State with Treason, felony, or other Crime, who shall flee from Justice, and be found in another State, shall on Demand of the executive Authority of the State from which he fled, be delivered up, to be removed to the State having Jurisdiction of the Crime."

73. In Puerto Rico v. Branstad, 483 U.S. 219, 107 S.Ct. 2802, 97 L.Ed.2d 187 (1987), the Court stated and then examined the two propositions of Kentucky v. Dennison, 65 U.S. (24 How.) 66, 16 L.Ed. 717 (1860): "first, that the Extradition Clause creates a mandatory duty to deliver up fugitives upon proper demand; and second, that the federal courts have no authority under the Constitution to compel performance of this ministerial duty of delivery." The Court reaffirmed the first, concluding that the Extradition Clause "afford[s] no discretion to the executive officers or courts of the asylum State." But the Court rejected the second because "there is no justification for distinguishing the duty to deliver fugitives from the many other species of constitutional duty enforceable in the federal courts."

74. Relying on this language, the Court held in California v. Superior Court, 482 U.S. 400, 107 S.Ct. 2433, 96 L.Ed.2d 332 (1987), that when Smolin was charged with kidnapping under a Louisiana statute covering taking one's own child from a person to whom custody had been granted, the California court erred in barring extradition upon the basis of an earlier California custody decree awarding Smolin sole custody of his children. Because the Louisiana information and related documents "set forth the facts that clearly satisfy each element of the crime of kidnapping as it is defined" by statute, the court in the asylum state may not even inquire into whether the charge would withstand a motion to dismiss in the demanding state.

75. 420 U.S. 103, 95 S.Ct. 854, 43 L.Ed.2d 54 (1975).

effects only a rebuttable presumption that there has been a judicial determination in the demanding State."

(k) The "Constitutional Tort." 42 U.S.C.A. § 1983 provides: "Every person who, under color of any statute, ordinance, regulation, custom, or usage, of any State or Territory, subjects, or causes to be subjected, any citizen of the United States or other person within the jurisdiction thereof to the deprivation of any rights, privileges, or immunities secured by the Constitution and laws, shall be liable to the party injured in an action at law, suit in equity, or other proper proceeding for redress." Pursuant to this statute, an action for damages may be brought in a federal court against municipal and state officers by a plaintiff alleging a violation of his Fourth Amendment rights. It is a defense that a reasonable person in the officer's position would have a good faith belief that his conduct was lawful.[76]

In *Monell v. New York City Dep't of Social Services,*[77] the Court overturned its earlier ruling that governments were "wholly immune" from § 1983 suits, concluding that Congress had intended municipalities to be included "among the persons to whom § 1983 applies." [78] The municipality may not be held liable on a respondeat superior theory, that is, simply because it employed the offending officer. "Instead," the Court said in *Monell,* "it is when execution of a government's policy or custom, whether made by its lawmakers or by those whose edicts or acts may fairly be said to represent official policy, inflicts the injury that the government as an entity is responsible under § 1983." [79] Thus, when the question is whether a Fourth Amendment violation by an officer may be said to amount to "execution of a government's policy or custom," there can arise such issues as whether a directive in a police manual can be said to be "official policy," whether inadequate training of police can constitute the requisite "official policy," [80] and whether a "custom" may be established by a pattern of nondiscipline for certain Fourth Amendment violations. A municipality has no immunity from liability under section 1983 flowing from its constitutional violations and may not assert the good faith of its officers as a defense to such liability.[81]

Though § 1983 is not applicable to federal officials, the gap was filled, at least with respect to Fourth Amendment violations, in *Bivens v. Six Unknown Named Agents,*[82] where plaintiff's complaint seeking damages for an alleged illegal arrest and search by federal officers was held to state "a cause of action under the Fourth Amendment." If the officer invokes his qualified immunity, the "relevant question * * * is the objective (albeit fact-specific) question whether a reasonable officer

76. Harlow v. Fitzgerald, 457 U.S. 800, 102 S.Ct. 2727, 73 L.Ed.2d 396 (1982).

This is so even when the action is brought against the officer for his conduct in applying for a warrant. The argument that absolute immunity should be the rule here, given the fact that a magistrate found the officer's request proper and issued the warrant, was rejected in Malley v. Briggs, 475 U.S. 335, 106 S.Ct. 1092, 89 L.Ed.2d 271 (1986), reasoning that the proper question in such circumstances "is whether a reasonably well-trained officer * * * would have known that his affidavit failed to establish probable cause and that he should not have applied for the warrant."

77. 436 U.S. 658, 98 S.Ct. 2018, 56 L.Ed.2d 611 (1978).

78. But, the Court later held, "a State is not a person within the meaning of § 1983." Will v. Michigan Dep't of State Police, 491 U.S. 58, 109 S.Ct. 2304, 105 L.Ed.2d 45 (1989).

79. Where "action is directed by those who establish government policy, the municipality is equally responsible whether the action is to be taken only once or to be taken repeatedly," so dismissal of the county was improper where the prosecutor directed deputies on one occasion forcibly to enter a clinic to serve capiases on employees there. Pembaur v. City of Cincinnati, 475 U.S. 469, 106 S.Ct. 1292, 89 L.Ed.2d 452 (1986).

80. In City of Canton, Ohio v. Harris, 489 U.S. 378, 109 S.Ct. 1197, 103 L.Ed.2d 412 (1989), the Court held "that the inadequacy of police training may serve as the basis for § 1983 liability only where the failure to train amounts to deliberate indifference to the rights of persons with whom the police come into contact."

81. Owen v. City of Independence, 445 U.S. 622, 100 S.Ct. 1398, 63 L.Ed.2d 673 (1980). But where the officer asserted no such defense and the jury verdict was in his favor, this finding removes any basis for liability against the city, and this is so even if department regulations might have authorized the kind of unconstitutional action alleged to have occurred. City of Los Angeles v. Heller, 475 U.S. 796, 106 S.Ct. 1571, 89 L.Ed.2d 806 (1986).

82. 403 U.S. 388, 91 S.Ct. 1999, 29 L.Ed.2d 619 (1971).

could have believed" the action taken "to be lawful, in light of clearly established law and the information [the officer] possessed." [83] Though *Bivens* was not read as also imposing liability upon the employer-government, in 1974 Congress amended the Federal Tort Claims Act to permit recovery against the government, "with regard to acts or omissions of investigative or law enforcement officers of the United States Government," for any claim arising "out of assault, battery, false imprisonment, false arrest, abuse of process, or malicious prosecution." [84] In such an FTCA action, the government may not assert the same good-faith reasonable belief defense which is available to individual officers. This FTCA amendment was not intended by Congress to provide an exclusive remedy, and thus a *Bivens* action against the offending officer is still permissible.[85]

(*l*) Criminal Prosecution; Disciplinary Proceedings. 18 U.S.C.A. § 242 provides: "Whoever, under color of any law, statute, ordinance, regulation, or custom, willfully subjects any inhabitant of any State, Territory, or District to the deprivation of any rights, privileges, or immunities secured or protected by the Constitution or laws of the United States, * * * shall be fined not more than $1,000 or imprisoned not more than one year, or both; and if death results shall be subject to imprisonment for any term of years or for life." One who "acts under 'color' of law" within the meaning of that statute "may be a federal officer or a state officer," [86] and it makes no difference that state or federal law does not affirmatively authorize the deprivation which has occurred.[87] The "willfully" requirement has been construed by the Supreme Court to avoid vagueness objections, and as interpreted means "a purpose to deprive a person of a specific constitutional right." [88]

In light of the concern which has been expressed about the sufficiency of existing machinery for disciplining police who have violated the constitutional rights of citizens, it is appropriate to ask to what extent federal courts may remedy such deficiencies. In *Rizzo v. Goode,*[89] where the district court had directed police administrators in Philadelphia to make revisions in police manuals spelling out for police their powers and to upgrade the disciplinary system, the Supreme Court reversed. The Court concluded that equitable relief against the administrators was not available where they "had played no affirmative part" in the constitutional violations objected to, and that "principles of federalism" did not permit the federal district court to inject itself "by injunctive decree into the internal disciplinary affairs of this state agency."

(m) Expungement of Arrest Records. Though some legislatures have adopted statutes dealing with the use, dissemination and expungement of arrest records, the question here is whether there is a constitutional right to such expungement when the arrest violated the Fourth Amendment. Some cases have held that there is as part of the constitutional right to privacy, but the more recent cases have ruled otherwise on the strength of *Paul v. Davis,*[90] holding that this penumbral right has to do only with "matters relating to marriage, procreation, contraception, family relationships, and child rearing and education." Some authority is to be found to the effect

83. Anderson v. Creighton, 483 U.S. 635, 107 S.Ct. 3034, 97 L.Ed.2d 523 (1987). The Court went on to reject the Creightons' contentions that such qualified immunity was inappropriate as to any warrantless searches or to any search in violation of the Fourth Amendment (because, they claimed, it "is not possible * * * to say that one 'reasonably' acted unreasonably"), explaining: "Law enforcement officers whose judgments in making these difficult determinations are objectively legally reasonable should no more be held personally liable in damages than should officials making analogous determinations in other areas of law."

84. 28 U.S.C.A. § 2680(h).

85. Carlson v. Green, 446 U.S. 14, 100 S.Ct. 1468, 64 L.Ed.2d 15 (1980).

86. Screws v. United States, 325 U.S. 91, 65 S.Ct. 1031, 89 L.Ed. 1495 (1945).

87. United States v. Classic, 313 U.S. 299, 61 S.Ct. 1031, 85 L.Ed. 1368 (1941).

88. Screws v. United States, 325 U.S. 91, 65 S.Ct. 1031, 89 L.Ed. 1495 (1945).

89. 423 U.S. 362, 96 S.Ct. 598, 46 L.Ed.2d 561 (1976).

90. 424 U.S. 693, 96 S.Ct. 1155, 47 L.Ed.2d 405 (1976).

that the expungement remedy can be grounded on the Fourth Amendment, but while dictum in some cases would suggest that an arrest without probable cause is per se a basis for expungement, the decisions do not support that proposition. Typically, expungement has occurred or been recognized as potential relief where there was a Fourth Amendment violation of an egregious nature. In any event, a balancing process is called for, which suggests that total expungement (as contrasted to limits on use) will be inappropriate when some legitimate future use could be made of the record.

(n) Injunction. The longstanding principle that equity will not grant relief to a petitioner who has an adequate remedy at law has proved to be no barrier to plaintiffs seeking in federal court to enjoin repeated or continuing Fourth Amendment violations, for in such circumstances neither the exclusionary rule nor an action for money damages will suffice. There must also be a threat of imminent harm, which means injunctive relief will not be available absent a clear pattern or stated policy of continuing police action of the kind challenged. In *Rizzo v. Goode,*[91] the Court ruled that repeated unconstitutional conduct by only a few officers would justify injunctive relief only against them, not against the department at large or the officers in charge of the department. This is unfortunate, for the approach utilized by the district court in *Rizzo,* directing those in charge of the department to revise police manuals and complaint procedures, avoided the major practical limitations upon federal injunctive relief: the virtual impossibility of formulating an injunction against police violations which clearly expressed what was prohibited and what was permitted, and the impracticality of involving the court in the day-to-day operations of the police department.

(*o*) Self-Help. The common law right to resist an unlawful arrest has given way in many jurisdictions to the modern view that the use of force is not justifiable to resist an arrest which the actor knows is being made by a peace officer, even though the arrest is unlawful. It has sometimes been asserted that this view cannot be squared with the Fourth Amendment, but as a general proposition this is not so. The state in removing the right to resist has merely withdrawn a remedy which not infrequently causes far graver consequences for both the officer and the suspect than does the unlawful arrest itself, and has required the arrestee to submit peacefully and pursue his remedies through the judicial process. But if an arrest was so flagrant an intrusion on a citizen's rights that his resistance would be virtually inevitable, it well may be that conviction for the resistance would violate due process.

The same reasoning applies to other forms of self-help undertaken in active resistance to a Fourth Amendment violation, such as forcible opposition to the execution of an invalid search warrant. But it does not follow that criminal punishment may be imposed for a mere failure to surrender rights under the Amendment. For example, one may not be convicted of assisting a federal offender to avoid apprehension where the charge is based upon a passive refusal to submit to an illegal search.

§ 3.2 Protected Areas and Interests

(a) The *Katz* Expectation of Privacy Test. For some years the Supreme Court was of the view that for there to be a Fourth Amendment search there must have been a physical intrusion into "a constitutionally protected area."[1] These areas were those enumerated in the Fourth Amendment itself: "persons," including the bodies[2] and attire[3] of individuals; "houses," including apart-

91. 423 U.S. 362, 96 S.Ct. 598, 46 L.Ed.2d 561 (1976).

§ 3.2

1. Silverman v. United States, 365 U.S. 505, 81 S.Ct. 679, 5 L.Ed.2d 734 (1961).

2. Schmerber v. California, 384 U.S. 757, 86 S.Ct. 1826, 16 L.Ed.2d 908 (1966).

3. Beck v. Ohio, 379 U.S. 89, 85 S.Ct. 223, 13 L.Ed.2d 142 (1964).

ments,[4] hotel rooms[5] garages,[6] business offices,[7] stores,[8] and warehouses;[9] "papers," such as letters;[10] and "effects," such as automobiles.[11] Then came *Katz v. United States,*[12] where FBI agents overheard defendant's end of telephone conversations by attaching an electronic listening and recording device to the exterior of the public telephone booth from which he was calling. The Court rejected a characterization of the issue as whether a public telephone booth is a constitutionally protected area within which a person has a right of privacy. Though the Fourth Amendment "protects individual privacy against certain kinds of governmental intrusion, * * * its protections go further, and often have nothing to do with privacy at all," while other aspects of privacy are protected by other provisions of the Constitution or left to state law. As for determining whether a particular area is "constitutionally protected," it "deflects attention" from the problem: "For the Fourth Amendment protects people, not places. What a person knowingly exposes to the public, even in his own home or office, is not a subject of Fourth Amendment protection. * * * But what he seeks to preserve as private, even in an area accessible to the public, may be constitutionally protected." It was thus deemed "clear that the reach of that Amendment cannot turn upon the presence or absence of a physical intrusion into any given enclosure," and that instead the critical point, justifying the conclusion that this activity amounted to a search, was that "a person in a telephone booth * * * who occupies it, shuts the door behind him, and pays the toll that permits him to place a call is surely entitled to assume that the words he utters into the mouthpiece will not be broadcast to the world."

Justice Harlan, concurring, elaborated the point in language which has often been relied upon by lower courts in interpreting and applying *Katz:*

> As the Court's opinion states, "the Fourth Amendment protects people, not places." The question, however, is what protection it affords to those people. Generally, as here, the answer to that question requires reference to a "place." My understanding of the rule that has emerged from prior decisions is that there is a twofold requirement, first that a person have exhibited an actual (subjective) expectation of privacy and, second, that the expectation be one that society is prepared to recognize as "reasonable." Thus, a man's home is, for most purposes, a place where he expects privacy, but objects, activities, or statements that he exposes to the "plain view" of outsiders are not "protected" because no intention to keep them to himself has been exhibited. On the other hand, conversations in the open would not be protected against being overheard, for the expectation of privacy under the circumstances would be unreasonable.

Katz is an extremely important case even outside of electronic eavesdropping settings because it marks a movement toward a redefinition of the scope of the Fourth Amendment. This is not to say that it produced clarity where before there had been uncertainty, as the Court substituted for a workable tool that often proved unjust a new test which was difficult to apply. The full potential of the *Katz* approach (which certainly has not in all respects been realized) can thus be seen only by consideration of various police investigative practices in light of *Katz,* as is done herein. But a few general observations are called for first.

Justice Harlan said that the defendant must "have exhibited an actual (subjective) expectation of privacy," while the majority in *Katz* likewise introduced a subjective element by saying that the government's conduct di-

4. Clinton v. Virginia, 377 U.S. 158, 84 S.Ct. 1186, 12 L.Ed.2d 213 (1964).

5. Stoner v. California, 376 U.S. 483, 84 S.Ct. 889, 11 L.Ed.2d 856 (1964).

6. Taylor v. United States, 286 U.S. 1, 52 S.Ct. 466, 76 L.Ed. 951 (1932).

7. United States v. Lefkowitz, 285 U.S. 452, 52 S.Ct. 420, 76 L.Ed. 877 (1932).

8. Amos v. United States, 255 U.S. 313, 41 S.Ct. 266, 65 L.Ed. 654 (1921).

9. See v. City of Seattle, 387 U.S. 541, 87 S.Ct. 1737, 18 L.Ed.2d 943 (1967).

10. Ex parte Jackson, 96 U.S. (6 OTTO) 727, 24 L.Ed. 877 (1877).

11. Preston v. United States, 376 U.S. 364, 84 S.Ct. 881, 11 L.Ed.2d 777 (1964).

12. 389 U.S. 347, 88 S.Ct. 507, 19 L.Ed.2d 576 (1967).

rected at Katz "violated the privacy upon which he justifiably relied." But while it is often rather easy to say that the police made no search because the defendant surely did not actually expect privacy, as where a person openly engaged in criminal conduct in Times Square at high noon, a subjective expectation does not add to, nor can its absence detract from, an individual's claim to Fourth Amendment protection, for otherwise the government could diminish that protection by announcing in advance an intention to do so. Justice Harlan later came around to this position, counseling that analysis under *Katz* "must * * * transcend the search for subjective expectations," for "our expectations, and the risks we assume, are in large part reflections of laws that translate into rules the customs and values of the past and present." [13]

Consider next Justice Harlan's second requirement, that the expectation be one "that society is prepared to recognize as 'reasonable,'" which was apparently intended to give content to the word "justifiably" in the majority statement that the eavesdropping "violated the privacy upon which he justifiably relied while using the telephone booth." Though the Court has since, at least on occasion, referred to this as the "reasonable 'expectation of privacy' test," [14] suggesting that a justified expectation is one which a reasonable man would have depending upon the statistical probability of being discovered in the circumstances, this is not really what *Katz* is all about.[15]

> If two narcotics peddlers were to rely on the privacy of a desolate corner of Central Park in the middle of the night to carry out an illegal transaction, this would be a reasonable expectation of privacy; there would be virtually no risk of discovery. Yet if by extraordinary good luck a patrolman were to illuminate the desolate spot with his flashlight, the criminals would be unable to suppress the officer's testimony as a violation of their rights under the fourth amendment.[16]

Thus, for an expectation to be considered justified it is not sufficient that it be merely reasonable; something in addition is required. As for what this something is, Justice Harlan later suggested it must "be answered by assessing the nature of a particular practice and the likely extent of its impact on the individual's sense of security balanced against the utility of the conduct as a technique of law enforcement." [17] That is, the ultimate question under *Katz* "is a value judgment," namely, whether, if the particular form of surveillance practiced by the police is permitted to go unregulated by constitutional restraints, the amount of privacy and freedom remaining to citizens would be diminished to a compass inconsistent with the aims of a free and open society." [18]

Putting the issue in that way raises yet another very fundamental question: whether the *Katz* expansion of Fourth Amendment protections is an all-or-nothing proposition. Take, for example, the use of specially-trained dogs who can detect by smell the presence of drugs inside of luggage, cars or premises. In making the "value judgment" called for above, one might understandably conclude that such a law enforcement practice should not be totally unregulated, that is, that unrestrained use of such dogs in a dragnet fashion would be intolerable in a free society. But if the matter were put differently, and it were asked whether every such use of a dog, certainly a relatively minor intrusion compared

13. United States v. White, 401 U.S. 745, 91 S.Ct. 1122, 28 L.Ed.2d 453 (1971) (dissent).

14. Terry v. Ohio, 392 U.S. 1, 88 S.Ct. 1868, 20 L.Ed.2d 889 (1968).

15. Probability is occasionally important in making a judgment as to whether the place of police surveillance was a "public vantage point," but a place which is on other grounds clearly such a point does not have to be frequently used. Thus in Florida v. Riley, 488 U.S. 445, 109 S.Ct. 693, 102 L.Ed.2d 835 (1989), all members of the Court agreed that whether aerial surveillance at 400 ft. was a search depended upon whether such use of helicopters was sufficiently "rare," but several Justices emphasized that as for any surveillance of defendant's residence from an adjacent public road, it would make *no* difference how often travelers used the road.

16. Note, 43 N.Y.U.L.Rev. 968, 983 (1968).

17. United States v. White, 401 U.S. 745, 91 S.Ct. 1122, 28 L.Ed.2d 453 (1971) (dissent).

18. Amsterdam, Perspectives on the Fourth Amendment, 58 Minn.L.Rev. 349, 403 (1974).

to entry and ransacking of a house to find narcotics, requires full probable cause and a warrant in hand, then the "value judgment" might well come out differently. Some movement away from the traditional all-or-nothing position has occurred. As for the probable cause requirement, *Terry v. Ohio*[19] is significant because it permitted a certain lesser intrusion (a brief stopping for investigation) upon a lesser quantum of evidence, and thus might well be relied upon in support of the conclusion that certain other lesser intrusions should be brought within the Fourth Amendment's protections under *Katz* and then judged by the *Terry* standard. As for the warrant requirement, *United States v. Chadwick*[20] is significant because it recognizes that sometimes a search warrant is not required when the Fourth Amendment intrusion is not substantial, and thus it lends support to the notion that certain police practices should be protected under the *Katz* formula but yet not to the extent that a warrant would be required. It is fair to say, however, that courts have not done enough by way of playing the *Katz* formula against the "reduced" Fourth Amendment protections possible under the *Terry* and *Chadwick* approaches, with the result that *Katz* has not received the expansive interpretation which might otherwise have occurred.

(b) Plain View, Smell and Hearing; Aiding the Senses. In *Coolidge v. New Hampshire*[21] the Court discussed at some length the notion that "under certain circumstances the police may seize evidence in plain view without a warrant." The fact there has been a plain view in the *Coolidge* sense does not mean there has been no search; indeed, the Court's discussion was of cases of searches by warrant, during hot pursuit, incident to arrest, and the like in which objects other than those which justified the search were discovered. That is, the concern in *Coolidge* was with when a *seizure* of those objects would be permissible, as to which the requirements of (i) a valid prior intrusion; (ii) inadvertent discovery of the objects;[22] and (iii) it being immediately apparent the objects are evidence, were discussed. By comparison, the concern here is with plain view in the sense of there being no Fourth Amendment *search* at all, as where an officer without making any intrusion sees an object on the person of an individual, in premises, or in a vehicle, in which case the three *Coolidge* requirements are simply irrelevant.

It is equally important to understand that while the characterization of an observation as a nonsearch plain view situation settles the lawfulness of the observation itself, it does not inevitably follow that a warrantless seizure of the observed object would be lawful. As the Supreme Court has explained, the plain view doctrine "authorizes seizure of illegal or evidentiary items visible to a police officer" only if the officer's "access to the object" itself has a "Fourth Amendment justification."[23] If an officer standing on the public way is able to look through the window of a private residence and see contraband, he must except in extraordinary circumstances obtain a warrant before entering those premises to seize the contraband.[24] If he had been looking into a vehicle, the warrant issue must again be resolved, though in most instances a warrant is

19. 392 U.S. 1, 88 S.Ct. 1868, 20 L.Ed.2d 889 (1968).

20. 433 U.S. 1, 97 S.Ct. 2476, 53 L.Ed.2d 538 (1977).

21. 403 U.S. 443, 91 S.Ct. 2022, 29 L.Ed.2d 564 (1971).

22. This dictum in *Coolidge* was later rejected in Horton v. California, ___ U.S. ___, 110 S.Ct. 2301, 110 L.Ed.2d 112 (1990).

23. Illinois v. Andreas, 463 U.S. 765, 103 S.Ct. 3319, 77 L.Ed.2d 1003 (1983).

See also Horton v. California, ___ U.S. ___, 110 S.Ct. 2301, 110 L.Ed.2d 112 (1990) ("not only must the officer be lawfully located in a place from which the object can be plainly seen, but he or she must also have a lawful right of access to the object itself").

24. Compare Taylor v. United States, 286 U.S. 1, 52 S.Ct. 466, 76 L.Ed. 951 (1932) (though police, standing where they had a right to be, saw contraband in open view in a garage by looking through a small opening, their warrantless entry to seize the contraband was unconstitutional); with Steele v. United States, 267 U.S. 498, 45 S.Ct. 414, 69 L.Ed. 757 (1925) (police, standing where they had a right to be, looked into garage and saw contraband in open view through doorway; this furnished probable cause for obtaining warrant by which they lawfully entered and seized the contraband).

not required in such circumstances.[25] If the object had been seen on an individual, it is still necessary that the seizure of that object occur pursuant to a warrant, incident to arrest, or without warrant but under exigent circumstances.[26] But if the object is in plain view within an accessible container, then there is apparently no constitutional barrier to the seizure and opening of that container.[27] Because in at least some other circumstances a search warrant is needed to open even an accessible container,[28] this means that what can be properly characterized as a plain view situation in such circumstances—a matter which has caused the Court considerable difficulty [29]—is especially important.

Just as what an officer sees where he is lawfully present is a nonsearch plain view, what he learns by reliance upon his other senses while so located is likewise no search. Thus, when surveilling officers in one motel room are able to hear with the naked ear conversations occurring in the adjoining room, this is not a search because there has been no intrusion upon a justified expectation of privacy. By like reasoning it has been held that it is no search for a lawfully positioned officer to smell incriminating odors.

Over fifty years ago, in *United States v. Lee,*[30] the Supreme Court held that use of a Coast Guard cutter searchlight at night to see aboard a schooner was no search. *Lee* was cited with approval in *Katz* for the proposition that "what a person knowingly exposes to the public * * * is not a subject of Fourth Amendment protection," and that reference has been stressed in post-*Katz* cases holding that use of artificial illumination by a lawfully positioned officer does not constitute a search.[31] *Lee* likened the use of the searchlight "to the use of a marine glass or a field glass," and thus it is not surprising that the cases after *Katz* agree that the use of binoculars does not, per se, constitute a search. But, while it is certainly sensible to conclude that ordinary use of such common devices for aiding the senses does not intrude upon any justified expectation of privacy (as compared to use of a magnetometer or X-ray machine or radiographic scanner to see inside an object, or use of electronic eavesdropping or wiretapping equipment to overhear conversations, all of which are Fourth Amendment searches), there may be particular situations in which the nature of the equipment or the manner of its use dictates a contrary conclusion. Illustrative would be use of a very high-powered telescope to observe from a considerable distance what was occurring inside premises (including the content of documents being read), where these premises were so situated that it was impossible to see inside from any closer vantage point. By like reasoning, the better

25. See § 3.7(b).

26. See, e.g., Cupp v. Murphy, 412 U.S. 291, 93 S.Ct. 2000, 36 L.Ed.2d 900 (1973), finding exigent circumstances to be present.

27. Cf. Illinois v. Andreas, 463 U.S. 765, 103 S.Ct. 3319, 77 L.Ed.2d 1003 (1983), relying upon the plain view doctrine in concluding that a container may be opened without a warrant if the contents were previously lawfully exposed to police view and were then determined to be illegal or evidentiary items and the surveillance of the container in the interim, while not perfect, did not give rise to "a substantial likelihood that the contents have been changed."

28. See, e.g., United States v. Chadwick, 433 U.S. 1, 97 S.Ct. 2476, 53 L.Ed.2d 538 (1977).

29. In Texas v. Brown, 460 U.S. 730, 103 S.Ct. 1535, 75 L.Ed.2d 502 (1983), the plurality took the position that when an officer saw in a car a tied balloon with a powdery substance within it, the warrantless seizure and search of that container was justified under the plain view doctrine. Two concurring Justices said that reasoning accorded "less significance to the Warrant Clause of the Fourth Amendment than is justified," while three other concurring Justices said that under the since-repudiated *Ross* rule (see § 3.7(c)) the container could be seized without a warrant but could not be searched without a warrant unless there was probable cause as to the vehicle generally or there was "virtual certainty" as to the contents of the balloon. See also United States v. Jacobsen, 466 U.S. 109, 104 S.Ct. 1652, 80 L.Ed.2d 85 (1984), utilizing a sort of plain-view-once-removed doctrine in holding that where a private person had searched a package and then partially closed it, a federal agent at the invitation of such person could expose to view what had previously been seen by the private person without this constituting a search.

30. 274 U.S. 559, 47 S.Ct. 746, 71 L.Ed. 1202 (1927).

31. Citing *Lee,* the Court in United States v. Dunn, 480 U.S. 294, 107 S.Ct. 1134, 94 L.Ed.2d 326 (1987), held that "the officers' use of the beam of a flashlight, directed through the essentially open front of respondent's barn, did not transform their observations into an unreasonable search within the meaning of the Fourth Amendment."

view is that if a flashlight is used not simply to illuminate at night what would be readily visible in the daytime, but rather to see what is inside a secured building through a minute opening, this constitutes a search.

Many uses of photo surveillance, though they enhance the naked-eye perception, do not constitute a search. This is true where a telescopic lens of a type generally in use is employed and where pictures taken with standard equipment are then enlarged in the development process, but not necessarily where more sophisticated equipment is used. In *Dow Chemical Co. v. United States,*[32] the majority held it was no search to engage in aerial photography of the outdoor areas of a large industrial complex even though as a result it was possible to detect pipes as small as half an inch in diameter. But *Dow* was limited in several ways: (1) the Court grounded the decision in the character of the place being surveilled, and intimated the result would be different as to "an area immediately adjacent to a private home, where privacy expectations are most heightened"; (2) the Court also deemed significant what was revealed, noting that "no objects as small as ½-inch diameter such as a class ring, for example, are recognizable, nor are there any identifiable human faces or secret documents captured in such a fashion as to implicate more serious privacy concerns"; and (3) the Court indicated that, in any event, the result might be different if the surveillance involved "highly sophisticated surveillance not generally available to the public, such as satellite technology." (The four dissenters in *Dow* objected that "satellite photography hardly could have been more informative" than the $22,000 camera used here, which members of the public are not "likely to purchase.")

In recent years police have made extensive use of specially trained dogs to detect the presence of explosives or, more commonly, narcotics. A few courts have held that such reliance upon the trained canine nose to detect that which the officer could not discover by his own sense of smell constitutes a search, but most courts have held or assumed otherwise. The latter view was adopted in *United States v. Place,*[33] where the Court emphasized that "the canine sniff is *sui generis*" because, unlike any other investigative procedure, it "discloses only the presence or absence of * * * a contraband item" and "does not expose noncontraband items that otherwise would remain hidden from public view." Though the sniffing in *Place* was done upon reasonable suspicion, which seemingly would suffice even if the sniffing were characterized as a limited search, the Court's analysis apparently means that the conduct there, exposure of luggage in a public place to a trained canine, is constitutionally permissible even if done without any suspicion or in a wholesale or at random fashion. Arguably the same is not true as to use of these dogs against people, even if this can be accomplished without first detaining the person. Use of such dogs to ascertain what is inside a dwelling has been held to be a search.

(c) **Residential Premises.** If a person has abandoned the place where he formerly resided, this terminates any justified expectation of privacy which he had with respect to those premises. The question of abandonment for Fourth Amendment purposes does not turn on strict property concepts, and thus it is possible for there to be abandonment even if a tenant retained the lawful right to possession. The question in such circumstances is whether the defendant abandoned the premises in the sense of having no apparent intention to return and make further use of them. If the tenant has not left but the rental period has expired, this does not inevitably terminate the justified privacy expectation, for it may generally be said that the tenant would be justified in expecting the landlord to resort to the eviction procedures required by law rather than self-help. Because of the transitory nature of most motel and hotel rental arrangements, a guest would not be justified in assuming that the manager, at the termination of the rental period, would not immedi-

32. 476 U.S. 227, 106 S.Ct. 1819, 90 L.Ed.2d 226 (1986).

33. 462 U.S. 696, 103 S.Ct. 2637, 77 L.Ed.2d 110 (1983).

ately clear the room for occupation by another guest.

An unconsented police entry into a residential unit, be it a house, apartment, or hotel or motel room, constitutes a search under *Katz.* The mere presence of a hallway in the interior of a single family dwelling, without more, is not in itself an invitation to the public to enter, so that entry of even such a place is a search, but there is no invasion of privacy when a policeman without force enters the common hallway of a multiple-family residence. The result is otherwise when the apartment building hallway is accessible only by key or a buzzer system, for such safeguards give rise to a justified privacy expectation in the hallway. As for merely looking into the residence, it may generally be said that it is no search for an officer to obtain such a view from the public way, a neighbor's property, or that part of the curtilage which constitutes the normal means of access to and egress from the house, while on the other hand it *is* a search for an officer to stray from that path to engage in window-peeping. But it would not be consistent with *Katz* to say there is *never* a search when the observation is from outside the building and curtilage, for there certainly is a justified expectation of privacy in not being seen or heard from vantage points not ordinarily utilized by the public or other residents. By like reasoning, the better view is that even when the officer is lawfully present in a place used by the public (e.g., the hallway of an apartment building), it is a search to engage in conduct which is offensive in its intrusiveness in the sense that it uncovers that which the resident may fairly be said to have sufficiently protected from scrutiny. Certainly *Katz* should not be read as permitting unrestrained peeping through keyholes and transoms.[34]

Under the traditional pre–*Katz* view, the protections of the Fourth Amendment also extended to other structures within the curtilage, that is, all buildings in close proximity to a dwelling and used in connection therewith. Under this approach, it has been held that police entry of such buildings as a garage or barn is a search, which is also the result dictated by *Katz.* By contrast, the other aspect of the pre–*Katz* rule, which was that a garage or barn outside the curtilage was not protected by the Fourth Amendment, has no current vitality; now it is necessary to inquire whether the nature of the structure and other circumstances are indicative of a justified privacy expectation. Thus, in *United States v. Dunn*[35] the Court assumed without deciding that a barn *outside* the curtilage "enjoyed Fourth Amendment protection and could not be entered and its contents seized without a warrant," but yet held that merely peering into the barn's open front from an open fields vantage point was no search.

Lands adjoining the dwelling also fell within the pre–*Katz* curtilage concept and are clearly protected by *Katz* under some circumstances. In expectation of privacy terms, quite clearly it is not objectionable that an officer has come upon the land in the same way that any member of the public could be expected to do, as by taking the normal route of access along a walkway or driveway or onto a porch. The nature of the premises must be taken into account, for as a general matter lands adjacent to a multiple-occupancy dwelling are more likely to be viewed as public areas. Consideration must also be given to the degree of scrutiny involved; casual observation of what any visitor could have seen may be no search, while a detailed examination even in an area frequently used by the public may well constitute a search under *Katz.* Looking into protected adjoining lands from other locations is governed by considerations like those previously discussed. It is no search to observe on that land what a neigh-

34. In the pre-Katz decision of McDonald v. United States, 335 U.S. 451, 69 S.Ct. 191, 93 L.Ed. 153 (1948), where an officer climbed through a window into a rooming house and then stood on a chair so as to look through the transom into defendant's room, the government argued that the entry of the house only trespassed on the landlady's rights and that looking through the transom was no search, so that the viewing of gambling paraphernalia was lawfully obtained. The Court did not "stop to examine that syllogism for flaws," but merely proceeded to "reject the result."

35. 480 U.S. 294, 107 S.Ct. 1134, 94 L.Ed.2d 326 (1987).

bor could readily see, but resort to extraordinary efforts to overcome the defendant's reasonable attempts to maintain the privacy of his curtilage is a search.

As for viewing by overflight, the Supreme Court took a permissive stance in *California v. Ciraolo,*[36] where police flew over defendant's fenced curtilage and saw marijuana plants growing there. Because the observations "took place within public navigable airspace" and were of "plants readily discernible to the naked eye as marijuana," the majority reasoned this was no search because "any member of the public flying in this airspace who glanced down could have seen everything that these officers observed." The four dissenters cogently reasoned that "the actual risk to privacy from commercial or pleasure aircraft is virtually nonexistent," as persons in them "normally obtain at most a fleeting, anonymous, and nondiscriminating glimpse of the landscape and buildings over which they pass." (*Ciraolo,* involving surveillance from a fixed wing aircraft at 1,000 feet, was relied upon in *Florida v. Riley,*[37] holding surveillance from a helicopter at 400 feet was likewise no search but denying "that an inspection of the curtilage of a house from an aircraft will always pass muster under the Fourth Amendment simply because the plane is within the navigable airspace specified by law." [38]) *Ciraolo* does not settle what the result would be if the police in the aircraft had used some sense-enhancing equipment; in the companion case of *Dow Chemical Co. v. United States,*[39] holding use of rather sophisticated camera equipment from an airplane was no search, the decision was grounded in the nature of the premises surveilled, a large industrial plant, and the Court cautioned that the result might be different if the surveillance had been of "an area immediately adjacent to a private home, where privacy expectations are most heightened."

(d) "Open Fields." In *Hester v. United States,*[40] where agents retrieved evidence which had been thrown into a field, the Court held that "the special protection accorded by the Fourth Amendment * * * is not extended to the open fields." Courts applied *Hester* to virtually any land not within the curtilage, even if fenced or posted with no trespassing signs, such as wooded areas, desert, vacant lots in urban areas, open beaches, reservoirs, and open waters. Although the vitality of this *Hester* "open fields" rule was uncertain after *Katz,* it was ultimately reaffirmed by the Supreme Court in *Oliver v. United States.*[41] One reason for this result given by the *Oliver* majority, that the "persons, houses, papers, and effects" language of the Fourth Amendment means its protections cannot be extended to open fields, constitutes a literal-minded interpretation totally inconsistent with the Court's prior decisions such as *Katz.* A second reason given in *Oliver,* "that an individual may not legitimately demand privacy for activities conducted out of doors in fields, except in the area immediately surrounding the home," makes sense only if there is some good reason to proceed upon the basis of such a generalization in lieu of assessing the facts of the particular case (e.g., in *Oliver,* that the police had bypassed a locked gate and a "No Trespassing" sign in order to get to the so-called "open fields").[42] The *Oliver* majority concluded there was: an ad hoc approach would make it too "difficult for the policeman to discern the scope of his authori-

36. 476 U.S. 207, 106 S.Ct. 1809, 90 L.Ed.2d 210 (1986).

37. 488 U.S. 445, 109 S.Ct. 693, 102 L.Ed.2d 835 (1989).

38. Somewhat curiously, the Riley plurality noted there was no "intimation here that the helicopter interfered with respondent's normal use of the greenhouse or of other parts of the curtilage. As far as this record reveals, no intimate details connected with the use of the home or curtilage were observed, and there was no undue noise, no wind, dust, or threat of injury." All members of the Court seemed to agree that flights at some particular altitude would be sufficiently "rare" to make a householder's expectation of privacy reasonable, but there was not agreement on just what degree of rarity is required or on whom the burden falls on the degree-of-rarity issue.

39. 476 U.S. 227, 106 S.Ct. 1819, 90 L.Ed.2d 226 (1986).

40. 265 U.S. 57, 44 S.Ct. 445, 68 L.Ed. 898 (1924).

41. 466 U.S. 170, 104 S.Ct. 1735, 80 L.Ed.2d 214 (1984).

42. The Court apparently accepted the traditional, broad view of what comes within the "open fields" rule, stating it was clear "that the term 'open fields' may include any unoccupied or undeveloped area outside of the curtilage," including an area which is "neither 'open' nor a 'field' as those terms are used in common speech."

ty" in a particular instance. But the dissenters argued with some force that it would not be an unfair imposition upon the police to expect them to make precisely the same kinds of judgments that the rest of us must make to avoid violating the criminal trespass laws.[43]

But somewhat similar case-by-case assessments are sometimes necessary to ascertain where the curtilage ends and "open fields" begins. In *United States v. Dunn,*[44] the Court asserted "that curtilage questions should be resolved with particular reference to four factors: the proximity of the area claimed to be curtilage to the home, whether the area is included within an enclosure surrounding the home, the nature of the uses to which the area is put, and the steps taken by the resident to protect the area from observation by people passing by." Thus the Court in that case concluded that a barn and immediately adjoining lands were outside the curtilage, as they were (i) 60 yards from the house, (ii) outside a fence surrounding the house, (iii) "not being used for intimate activities of the home," and (iv) not protected from observation from nearby open fields.

(e) Business and Commercial Premises. Offices and stores and other business and commercial premises are also entitled to protection against unreasonable searches and seizures,[45] though the nature of these premises is such that much police investigative activity directed at them will not constitute a search. Law enforcement officials may enter commercial premises at the times they are open to the public and may explore those portions of the premises to which the public has ready access,[46] including the examination of articles available for inspection by potential customers. On the other hand, it is a search for police to enter without consent premises to which the public at large does not have access, such as the work area of a factory or a private club open only to members. Surveillance from outside business premises is governed by the same considerations discussed earlier concerning looking into dwellings. As for surveillance of the outdoor areas of businesses, such as the space between buildings within a large, fenced-in industrial complex, the Supreme Court in *Dow Chemical Co. v. United States*[47] declared that such places "can perhaps be seen as falling somewhere between 'open fields' and curtilage, but lacking some of the critical characteristics of both." The Court intimated that with regard to physical entry of such lands the curtilage analogy would prevail, but then held that as to aerial surveillance the place was "more comparable to an open filed," meaning such surveillance was no search. The four dissenters in *Dow* understandably complained about the majority's failure to "explain how its result squares with *Katz* and its progeny."

Police sometimes engage in clandestine surveillance of public rest rooms in an attempt to detect criminal activity—typically use of drugs or homosexual conduct—occurring therein. When this is done by looking through a hole or vent into a closed stall, it is

43. They thus concluded: "A clear, easily administrable rule emerges * * *: Private land marked in a fashion sufficient to render entry thereon a criminal trespass under the law of the state in which the land lies is protected by the Fourth Amendment's proscription of unreasonable searches and seizures."

44. 480 U.S. 294, 107 S.Ct. 1134, 94 L.Ed.2d 326 (1987).

45. Mancusi v. DeForte, 392 U.S. 364, 88 S.Ct. 2120, 20 L.Ed.2d 1154 (1968). In United States v. Dunn, 480 U.S. 294, 107 S.Ct. 1134, 94 L.Ed.2d 326 (1987), the Court assumed without deciding that a barn outside the curtilage would be protected against physical entry; respondent argued "that he possessed an expectation of privacy, independent from his home's curtilage, in the barn and its contents, because the barn is an essential part of his business."

46. In Donovan v. Lone Steer, Inc., 464 U.S. 408, 104 S.Ct. 769, 78 L.Ed.2d 567 (1984), the Court concluded that an "entry into the public lobby of a motel and restaurant for the purpose of serving an administrative subpoena" did not constitute a Fourth Amendment intrusion.

And in Maryland v. Macon, 472 U.S. 463, 105 S.Ct. 2778, 86 L.Ed.2d 370 (1985), the Court held that the "officer's action in entering the bookstore and examining the wares that were intentionally exposed to all who frequent the place of business did not infringe a legitimate expectation of privacy and hence did not constitute a search within the meaning of the Fourth Amendment." (The Court in *Macon* also concluded that purchase of some magazines for sale in the store was not a Fourth Amendment "seizure," as "respondent voluntarily transferred any possessory interest he may have had in the magazines to the purchaser upon the receipt of the funds.")

47. 476 U.S. 227, 106 S.Ct. 1819, 90 L.Ed.2d 226 (1986).

clear that under *Katz* this amounts to a search. It has been held that such surveillance into a stall without doors is no search, on the theory that there is no right to expect privacy given this design. But some cases recognize that even in such circumstances there is still a justified expectation of privacy against being observed from hidden vantage points. On the other hand, if police merely enter a rest room and see conduct occurring within a stall which is readily visible to any one who so enters, this is not a search. By like reasoning, it has correctly been held that surveillance into fitting rooms in clothing stores to detect shoplifting is a search.

(f) Vehicles. There is no justified expectation of privacy in a vehicle which one has abandoned. Abandonment in this context is not a question of whether or not someone had a proprietary or possessory interest in the automobile under common law property concepts, but rather whether the defendant was entitled to have a reasonable expectation that the automobile would be free from governmental intrusion. Thus, abandonment may occur not only by intending to relinquish any claim to the vehicle but by dealing with it in such a way that privacy could hardly be justifiably expected, as where a car is left behind in escaping from pursuit by the police or is left unclaimed for some time on another's property. When a car is parked by the side of the road, it is necessary to consider such factors as the condition of the vehicle, its location, and the length of time it has remained there.

Assuming lawful presence of the officer by the vehicle, generally it is no search for the officer to see or smell what is inside the car without physical intrusion into it, or for him to photograph or examine the exterior of the vehicle or perhaps even to do some "testing" of the exterior.[48] There will occasionally be instances, however, in which the scrutiny is so intense, resulting in discovery of what had been concealed by reasonable means, that under the *Katz* rationale the police conduct must be designated a search. As for examination of vehicle identification numbers, obviously no search is involved when the number can be seen through the window of the vehicle.[49] The cases holding that it is no search to intrude physically into the car in order to ascertain a hidden number are short on analysis and conflict with *Katz,* as the Supreme Court more recently concluded in *New York v. Class.*[50] More appealing is the contention that these numbers are quasi-public information and that consequently a search of that part of the car displaying the number is a minimal invasion of a person's privacy which may be undertaken on reasonable suspicion and without a warrant. But in *Class* the Court accepted a somewhat different proposition, namely, that inspection of the VIN "is within the scope of police authority pursuant to a traffic stop" prompted by an observed traffic violation, and that "concern for the officer's safety" justifies the officer's entry of the car to uncover the VIN on the door jamb or dashboard instead of having the driver reenter to do so.

(g) Personal Characteristics. In *United States v. Dionisio,*[51] the Court held that requiring the person to give voice exemplars is no search because "the physical characteristics of a person's voice, its tone and manner, as opposed to the content of a specific conversation, are constantly exposed to the public," so that "no person can have a reasonable expectation that others will not know the sound of his voice." By the same reasoning the Court ruled in the companion case of *United States v. Mara* [52] that it is no search to

48. In Cardwell v. Lewis, 417 U.S. 583, 94 S.Ct. 2464, 41 L.Ed.2d 325 (1974), where the police conduct was the taking of paint scrapings from the exterior of the car and the matching of the tread of a tire with a cast of a tire impression left at the crime scene, the plurality said it failed "to comprehend what expectation of privacy was infringed. Stated simply, the invasion of privacy, 'if it can be said to exist, is abstract and theoretical.'" The four dissenters deemed it unnecessary to reach that issue, as they concluded the car had earlier been illegally seized.

49. New York v. Class, 475 U.S. 106, 106 S.Ct. 960, 89 L.Ed.2d 81 (1986).

50. 475 U.S. 106, 106 S.Ct. 960, 89 L.Ed.2d 81 (1986).

51. 410 U.S. 1, 93 S.Ct. 764, 35 L.Ed.2d 67 (1973).

52. 410 U.S. 19, 93 S.Ct. 774, 35 L.Ed.2d 99 (1973).

require a person to give handwriting exemplars. *Dionisio* likened the sound of a person's voice to his "facial characteristics," and thus it is clear that it is not a search simply to observe those characteristics or to photograph them. The Court has also referred to fingerprinting as nothing more than obtaining "physical characteristics * * * constantly exposed to the public." [53] At the other extreme, seizing evidence from within the body by taking a blood sample or using a breathalyzer quite clearly is a search. Hard situations exist in between, such as the taking of a sample of hair. It may be said that hair is also a characteristic "constantly exposed to public view" and that consequently the taking of it is no search, but *Cupp v. Murphy* [54] (holding it was a search to scrape visible dried blood from defendant's finger and subject it to microscopic analysis) suggests that in such cases it may make a difference whether the hair is being kept merely to preserve a readily observable characteristic or to enable much closer scrutiny than "public view" allows.

(h) Abandoned Effects. The Supreme Court has upheld the examination of certain effects on the ground that they had been abandoned, such as glass containers thrown into a field [55] and objects put into a hotel room waste basket before checking out.[56] Abandonment in this context may be based upon an intent to relinquish all claim to the object, as in these cases, or by simply relinquishing control of the object to such an extent and in such circumstances that examination of it by others would not be unlikely.[57] Property is not considered abandoned when a person throws away incriminating articles due to the unlawful activities of police officers, as where the disposal was prompted by police efforts to make an illegal arrest or search.[58] Mere denial of ownership is not proof of an intent to abandon, but at least in some circumstances courts are inclined to hold that the denial deprived the person disclaiming ownership of any justified expectation in the object.

Even inspection of one's garbage left for collection outside the curtilage of a home is no search, the Supreme Court held in *California v. Greenwood.*[59] In that case, police obtained evidence of the defendants' narcotics use by having the trash collector pick up the plastic garbage bags the defendants had left on the curb in front of their house, and then give the bags to the police without first mixing the contents with refuse from other houses. The Court reasoned this was no search because the defendants had no "subjective expectation of privacy in their garbage that society accepts as objectively reasonable," as "plastic garbage bags left on or at the side of a public street are readily accessible to animals, children, scavengers, snoops, and other members of the public. * * * Moreover, respondents placed their refuse at the curb for the express purpose of conveying it to a third party, the trash collector, who might himself have sorted through respondents' trash or permitted others, such as the police, to do so." This is, as the two dissenters pointed out,[60] an unduly narrow interpretation of the kind of police activity which is subject to Fourth Amendment limitations under the *Katz* test. Because *Greenwood* is limited to "trash left for collection in an area accessible to the public," it should not be construed as permit-

53. Cupp v. Murphy, 412 U.S. 291, 93 S.Ct. 2000, 36 L.Ed.2d 900 (1973).

54. 412 U.S. 291, 93 S.Ct. 2000, 36 L.Ed.2d 900 (1973).

55. Hester v. United States, 265 U.S. 57, 44 S.Ct. 445, 68 L.Ed. 898 (1924).

56. Abel v. United States, 362 U.S. 217, 80 S.Ct. 683, 4 L.Ed.2d 668 (1960).

57. Under this approach, a person "clearly has not abandoned that property" when, in response to a police inquiry, he tossed the grocery bag he was carrying onto the hood of his car and then attempted to protect it from inspection by the officer. Smith v. Ohio, 494 U.S. 541, 110 S.Ct. 1288, 108 L.Ed.2d 464 (1990).

58. When the disposal is as a result of a police chase, the question then is whether the chase is itself Fourth Amendment activity which, absent a factual basis, makes the abandonment an illegal fruit. No, the Court concluded in California v. Hodari D., ___ U.S. ___, 111 S.Ct. 1547, 113 L.Ed.2d 690 (1991), discussed in § 3.8(c).

59. 486 U.S. 35, 108 S.Ct. 1625, 100 L.Ed.2d 30 (1988).

60. They emphasized that the defendants had only exposed to the public the exterior of opaque containers, that the "mere *possibility* that unwelcome meddlers *might* open and rummage through containers does not negate the expectation of privacy," and that the defendants placed their refuse at the curb only because a county ordinance commanded them to do so.

ting police to enter the curtilage and seize garbage kept there. It is unclear what the result should be if the police have the garbage collector make his usual pickup from within the curtilage but then turn the refuse over to them unmixed with neighbors' garbage, though that part of the *Greenwood* reasoning about defendant "conveying * * * to a third party" is seemingly applicable even there.

(i) "Mere Evidence" in General and Private Papers in Particular. In *Gouled v. United States* [61] the Court held that a search warrant could not always be utilized "to secure evidence to be used against [a person] in a criminal or penal proceeding" because such action is permissible only "when a primary right to such search and seizure may be found in the interest which the public or the complainant may have in the property to be seized, or in the right to the possession of it." This "mere evidence" rule, whereby items were subject to lawful seizure only if they were the fruits or instrumentalities of crime, was later extended by the Court to warrantless searches as well [62] but was finally abandoned in *Warden v. Hayden.*[63] The Court reasoned that

> nothing in the nature of property seized as evidence renders it more private than property seized, for example, as an instrumentality; quite the opposite may be true. Indeed, the distinction is wholly irrational, since, depending on the circumstances, the same "papers and effects" may be "mere evidence" in one case and "instrumentalities" in another. * * *
>
> * * * The requirement that the Government assert in addition some property interest in material it seizes has long been a fiction, obscuring the reality that government has an interest in solving crime.

Hayden did not mark the end of uncertainty as to whether certain effects were immune from seizure, for the Court cautioned that "the items of clothing involved in this case are not 'testimonial' or 'communicative' in nature, and their introduction therefore did not compel respondent to become a witness against himself in violation of the Fifth Amendment." The Court finally addressed the Fifth Amendment issue squarely in *Andresen v. Maryland,*[64] involving seizure pursuant to warrant of specified documents relating to a fraudulent sale of land. Noting that the "historic function" of the privilege against self-incrimination has been to protect a "natural individual from compulsory incrimination through his own testimony or personal records," [65] the Court concluded there had been no Fifth Amendment violation in this case because there was no compulsion, that is, the "petitioner was not asked to say or to do anything." In particular, the Court stressed that (i) the creation of the documents by petitioner had been voluntary; (ii) he was not required to play a part in handing them over to the police; and (iii) he was not required to authenticate them at trial. This situation, the Court added, is quite different from that in which the evidence is acquired by subpoena, where "the Fifth Amendment may protect an individual * * * because the very act of production may constitute a compulsory authentication of incriminating information."

Though the Court in *Andresen* repeatedly stressed that the papers seized were "business records," it seems clear that the Court's Fifth Amendment analysis would compel the very same result were the documents much more private in nature, such as a diary. This leaves the question which was neither raised nor resolved in *Andresen:* whether, because diaries and personal letters that record only their author's personal thoughts lie at the heart of our sense of privacy, such private papers are entitled to special Fourth Amendment protection. It has sometimes been argued that the Fourth Amendment should be read as barring seizure of such very private papers, or that, even if not constitutionally required, it is sound policy to bar seizure of

61. 255 U.S. 298, 41 S.Ct. 261, 65 L.Ed. 647 (1920).

62. United States v. Lefkowitz, 285 U.S. 452, 52 S.Ct. 420, 76 L.Ed. 877 (1932).

63. 387 U.S. 294, 87 S.Ct. 1642, 18 L.Ed.2d 782 (1967).

64. 427 U.S. 463, 96 S.Ct. 2737, 49 L.Ed.2d 627 (1976).

65. For more on the history of the privilege, see § 8.14.

such papers unless they have served or are serving a substantial purpose in furtherance of a criminal enterprise.

(j) Surveillance of Relationships and Movements. One way in which law enforcement agents obtain information concerning a person's associations and activities is by examination of the detailed records kept by those agencies with which that person has had occasion to do business. Such activity is unlikely to be characterized as a search after *United States v. Miller,*[66] involving subpoenas directed at two banks for all records they had concerning defendant and his company. Defendant's contention that the subpoenas were defective was brushed aside because the Court concluded "that there was no intrusion into any area of which respondent had a protected Fourth Amendment interest." In support, the Court reasoned that (1) because the records in question were "the business records of the banks," respondent "can assert neither ownership nor possession"; (2) there was no "legitimate expectation of privacy concerning the information kept in bank records," as "the documents obtained, including financial statements and deposit slips, contain only information voluntarily conveyed to the banks and exposed to their employees in the ordinary course of business"; and (3) a "depositor takes the risk, in revealing his affairs to another, that the information will be conveyed by that person to the government."

The *Miller* result and reasoning are highly questionable. Certainly the assertion that there is no protected Fourth Amendment interest when there is "neither ownership nor possession" is contrary to *Katz,* which teaches that such property concepts cannot "serve as a talismanic solution to every Fourth Amendment problem." As for the Court's expectation of privacy point, the fact of the matter is that the customer of a bank expects that the documents, such as checks, which he transmits to the bank in the course of his business operations will remain private, and rightly so given banks' legal obligation to maintain the secrecy of their depositors' transactions. Finally, the Court in *Miller* is in error in saying that its result is supported by the "false friend" cases of *United States v. White,*[67] *Hoffa v. United States,*[68] and *Lopez v. United States.*[69] The proposition (as it was put in *Hoffa*) that the Fourth Amendment will not come to the rescue of one who "voluntarily confides his wrongdoing" to another is not applicable here, as disclosure of one's financial affairs to a bank is not entirely volitional, since it is impossible to participate in the economic life of contemporary society without a bank account. Moreover, in cases like *Hoffa* the police obtained nothing more than was known by the intermediary, which is not true in a *Miller* type of case because the authorities are able to piece together all of the banking records so as to obtain a virtual current biography of the individual, while the bank and its employees see the customer's checks briefly and individually and thus have no direct, significant contact with the underlying transactional information which would reveal conclusions about the customer's lifestyle.

Miller was relied upon in *Smith v. Maryland,*[70] holding that it is no search for the police to utilize a "pen register," a device which records all telephone numbers dialed from a particular phone. The Court concluded Smith could claim no legitimate expectation of privacy because when he used his phone he "voluntarily conveyed numerical information to the telephone company and 'exposed' that information to its equipment in the ordinary course of business," and thereby "assumed the risk that the company would reveal to police the numbers he dialed." This reasoning is just as unsound as that in *Miller.* Even if it may be said that subscribers know phone companies monitor calls for internal reasons, it hardly follows that they expect this information to be made available to the general public or the government. By like reasoning, a mail cover (a form of surveillance in which law enforcement authorities have

66. 425 U.S. 435, 96 S.Ct. 1619, 48 L.Ed.2d 71 (1976).

67. 401 U.S. 745, 91 S.Ct. 1122, 28 L.Ed.2d 453 (1971).

68. 385 U.S. 293, 87 S.Ct. 408, 17 L.Ed.2d 374 (1966).

69. 373 U.S. 427, 83 S.Ct. 1381, 10 L.Ed.2d 462 (1963).

70. 442 U.S. 735, 99 S.Ct. 2577, 61 L.Ed.2d 220 (1979).

postal authorities record all external markings, including return addresses, on all mail to a particular addressee) should be considered a search, but the contrary result has been reached by resort to the all-or-nothing approach to privacy reflected in *Miller* and *Smith.*

Another surveillance technique which is becoming increasingly common involves the use of an electronic tracking device, as where a beacon or "beeper" is attached to a car, airplane or container and the movements of that object are then tracked by picking up the signals emitted periodically. Some courts focused upon the act whereby the beeper was attached to the underbody of a vehicle parked in a public place or was attached to a vehicle or inserted into a container before delivery of same to the suspect, with varying results. But the Supreme Court in *United States v. Karo*[71] concluded that the mere installation of a beeper or transfer to another of a beeper-laden object is no "search," because that act alone "infringed no privacy interest" in that it "conveyed no information at all," and is no "seizure" because "it cannot be said that anyone's possessory interest was interfered with in a meaningful way." It is thus necessary to consider the more significant event of the beeper's subsequent monitoring.

In *United States v. Knotts,*[72] the Supreme Court was confronted with a situation in which police first arranged with the seller of chloroform to place a beeper inside a chloroform container thereafter sold to a suspect and then traced the chloroform by beeper monitoring alone to a secluded cabin, resulting in the issuance and execution of a warrant to search that cabin for an illegal drug laboratory. In response to a challenge of the monitoring of the beeper, the Court held that no Fourth Amendment search had occurred. The Court reasoned that the surveillance objected to "amounted principally to the following of an automobile on public streets and highways," which if accomplished merely by visual surveillance would be no search because one "travelling in an automobile on public thoroughfares has no reasonable expectation of privacy in his movements from one place to another," and that "scientific enhancement of this sort raises no constitutional issues which visual surveillance would not also raise."

But the practice of beeper monitoring cannot be dismissed on the notion that it merely permits the police to learn what they could otherwise have discovered by direct observation, as the value of the device lies in its ability to convey information not otherwise available to the government. Nor is it correct to say, as the Court assumed in *Knotts,* that use of a beeper is essentially the same as use of binoculars. It involves something more than magnification of the observer's senses, for it transforms the vehicle into a messenger in the service of those watching it and thus conveys information as useful as any obtained from a wiretap. Precisely because the unrestrained utilization of electronic tracking devices to monitor the movements of anyone who travels from one place to another would be intolerable, the practice should be characterized as a search under the *Katz* formula and subjected to at least some Fourth Amendment restraints.

In *Karo* the Court answered in the affirmative the question reserved in *Knotts,* "whether monitoring of a beeper falls within the ambit of the Fourth Amendment when it reveals information that could not have been obtained through visual surveillance." Noting first that unquestionably it would be an unreasonable search to surreptitiously enter a residence without a warrant to verify that the container was there, the Court reasoned that "the result is the same where, without a warrant, the Government surreptitiously employs an electronic device to obtain information that it could not have obtained by observation from outside the curtilage of the home. * * * Even if visual surveillance has revealed that the article to which the beeper is attached has entered the house, the later monitoring not only verifies the officers' observations but also

71. 468 U.S. 705, 104 S.Ct. 3296, 82 L.Ed.2d 530 (1984).

72. 460 U.S. 276, 103 S.Ct. 1081, 75 L.Ed.2d 55 (1983).

establishes that the article remains on the premises." The Court next concluded that absent "truly exigent circumstances" such use of the beeper was governed by "the general rule that a search of a house should be conducted pursuant to a warrant." [73] Such monitoring was characterized by the Court as "less intrusive than a full-scale search," but the Court did not have occasion to decide whether as a consequence such a warrant could issue upon reasonable suspicion rather than probable cause.

§ 3.3 Probable Cause

(a) General Considerations. Because the warrant clause of the Fourth Amendment provides that "no Warrants shall issue, but upon probable cause," it is apparent that a valid arrest warrant [1] or a valid search warrant [2] may issue only upon a showing of probable cause to the issuing authority. In the many instances in which police may arrest and search without first obtaining a warrant,[3] their conduct is governed by the other half of the Fourth Amendment, which declares the right of the people to be secure "against unreasonable searches and seizures." But it is clear that such an arrest [4] or search [5] is unreasonable if not based upon probable cause; as the Supreme Court explained in *Wong Sun v. United States,*[6] were the requirements less stringent than when a warrant is obtained, then "a principal incentive now existing for the procurement of * * * warrants would be destroyed."

It is generally assumed that the same quantum of evidence is required whether one is concerned with probable cause to arrest or probable cause to search. But each requires a showing of probabilities as to somewhat different facts and circumstances, and thus one can exist without the other. In search cases, two conclusions must be supported by substantial evidence: that the items sought are in fact seizable by virtue of being connected with criminal activity, and that the items will be found in the place to be searched. It is *not* also necessary that a particular person be implicated. By comparison, in arrest cases there must be probable cause that a crime has been committed and that the person to be arrested committed it, which of course can exist without any showing that evidence of the crime will be found at premises under that person's control.

The Supreme Court has long expressed a strong preference for the use of arrest warrants and search warrants. Resort to the warrant process, the Court has declared, is preferred because it "interposes an orderly procedure" [7] involving "judicial impartiality" [8] whereby "a neutral and detached magistrate" [9] can make "informed and deliberate determinations" [10] on the issue of probable cause. To leave such decisions to the police would allow "hurried actions" [11] by those "engaged in the often competitive enterprise of ferreting out crime." [12] This preference has resulted in a subtle difference between the probable cause required when there is no warrant and that required when there is. As the

73. In response to the government's claim that a warrant should not be required because of the difficulty in satisfying the particularity requirement of the Fourth Amendment, in that it is usually not known in advance to what place the container with the beeper in it will be taken, the Court concluded that it would suffice if the warrant were "to describe the object to which the beeper is to be placed, the circumstances that led agents to wish to install the beeper, and the length of time for which beeper surveillance is requested."

§ 3.3

1. Henry v. United States, 361 U.S. 98, 80 S.Ct. 168, 4 L.Ed.2d 134 (1959).

2. United States v. Harris, 403 U.S. 573, 91 S.Ct. 2075, 29 L.Ed.2d 723 (1971).

3. See §§ 3.5, 3.6, 3.7.

4. Henry v. United States, 361 U.S. 98, 80 S.Ct. 168, 4 L.Ed.2d 134 (1959).

5. Chambers v. Maroney, 399 U.S. 42, 90 S.Ct. 1975, 26 L.Ed.2d 419 (1970).

6. 371 U.S. 471, 83 S.Ct. 407, 9 L.Ed.2d 441 (1963).

7. United States v. Jeffers, 342 U.S. 48, 72 S.Ct. 93, 96 L.Ed. 59 (1951).

8. Ibid.

9. Johnson v. United States, 333 U.S. 10, 68 S.Ct. 367, 92 L.Ed. 436 (1948).

10. Aguilar v. Texas, 378 U.S. 108, 84 S.Ct. 1509, 12 L.Ed.2d 723 (1964).

11. Ibid.

12. Johnson v. United States, 333 U.S. 10, 68 S.Ct. 367, 92 L.Ed. 436 (1948).

Court put it in *United States v. Ventresca,*[13] "in a doubtful or marginal case a search under a warrant may be sustainable where without one it would fail." This "deference to the decision of the magistrate to issue a warrant" means that a reviewing court is not to conduct "a de novo probable cause determination" but instead is merely to decide "whether the evidence viewed as a whole provided a 'substantial basis' for the magistrate's finding of probable cause." [14]

When the police make an arrest or search without a warrant, they initially make the probable cause decision themselves. The "on-the-scene assessment of probable cause provides a legal justification for arresting a person suspected of crime, and for a brief period of detention to take the administrative steps incident to arrest," but an ex parte "judicial determination of probable cause [is] a prerequisite to extended restraint on liberty following arrest." [15] This means that judicial review of probable cause for the arrest need occur only if the arrestee fails to obtain his prompt release unaccompanied "by burdensome conditions that effect a significant restraint on liberty." [16] Otherwise, a subsequent judicial determination of whether there was probable cause for the warrantless police action will ordinarily occur only if initiated by the defendant upon a motion to suppress evidence claimed to be a fruit of an illegal arrest or search.

When police arrest or search with a warrant, the probable cause determination is made by a magistrate in the first instance. Under the traditional approach his decision was not final; it was still open to the defendant upon a motion to suppress to argue that evidence obtained by execution of the warrant should be suppressed because the warrant was not in fact issued upon probable cause. However, in *United States v. Leon,*[17] the Supreme Court adopted a "good faith" exception to the exclusionary rule in with-warrant cases. This means that upon the motion to suppress evidence obtained pursuant to a warrant, the evidence will be admissible (without regard to whether there was in fact probable cause) if the officer could have reasonably believed the warrant was valid.[18]

(b) Nature of Probable Cause. In *Brinegar v. United States,*[19] the Court characterized the probable cause requirement as "the best compromise that has been found for accommodating" the often opposing interests of privacy and effective law enforcement. This raises the question of whether this "compromise" must always be struck in precisely the same way, or whether instead probable cause may require a greater or a lesser quantum of evidence, depending upon the facts and circumstances of the individual case.

It is now clear that certain unique investigative techniques are governed by a special, less demanding probable cause test. In *Camara v. Municipal Court,*[20] for example, the Court engaged in a "balancing" of "the need to search against the invasion which the search entails" in approving such a probable cause test for housing inspection warrants; thus " 'probable cause' to issue a warrant to inspect must exist if reasonable legislative or administrative standards for conducting an area inspection are satisfied with respect to a particular building." This *Camara* balancing approach was thereafter employed in upholding other kinds of so-called administrative or regulatory searches,[21] and was later used by the Court in *Terry v. Ohio* [22] to support the conclusion that a brief stopping for investigation and a frisk incident thereto are permissible upon grounds falling short of probable cause to make a full-fledged arrest and a full

13. 380 U.S. 102, 85 S.Ct. 741, 13 L.Ed.2d 684 (1965).

14. Massachusetts v. Upton, 466 U.S. 727, 104 S.Ct. 2085, 80 L.Ed.2d 721 (1984), applying the holding in Illinois v. Gates, 462 U.S. 213, 103 S.Ct. 2317, 76 L.Ed.2d 527 (1983).

15. Gerstein v. Pugh, 420 U.S. 103, 95 S.Ct. 854, 43 L.Ed.2d 54 (1975).

16. Ibid. For more on this, see § 3.5(a).

17. 468 U.S. 897, 104 S.Ct. 3405, 82 L.Ed.2d 677 (1984).

18. See § 3.1(c).

19. 338 U.S. 160, 69 S.Ct. 1302, 93 L.Ed. 1879 (1949).

20. 387 U.S. 523, 87 S.Ct. 1727, 18 L.Ed.2d 930 (1967).

21. See § 3.9.

22. 392 U.S. 1, 88 S.Ct. 1868, 20 L.Ed.2d 889 (1968), discussed in § 3.8.

search of the person incident thereto. In both instances, the Court deemed it most significant that the practices at issue were clearly distinguishable from the typical arrest or search in that they involved a significantly lesser intrusion into freedom and privacy.

Some have argued for a more extended use of this balancing process, whereby in each case the probable cause for the investigative technique used would be determined by weighing the degree of intrusion and the law enforcement need in that particular case. But the Supreme Court has declined the invitation to adopt a proposed "multifactor balancing test" along those lines. As the Court put it in *Dunaway v. New York,*[23]

> the protections intended by the Framers could all too easily disappear in the consideration and balancing of the multifarious circumstances presented by different cases, especially when the balancing may be done in the first instance by police officers engaged in the "often competitive enterprise of ferreting out crime." * * * A single, familiar standard is essential to guide police officers, who have only limited time and expertise to reflect on and balance the social and individual interests involved in the specific circumstances they confront.

Notwithstanding this language, it might still be argued that there are a few search practices (such as eavesdropping and wiretapping,[24] search of a private home during the nighttime,[25] or intrusions into the human body [26]) which, because of their unusual degree of intrusiveness, require more than the usual quantum of probable cause.[27]

Probable cause may not be established simply by showing that the officer who made the challenged arrest or search subjectively believed he had grounds for his action. As emphasized in *Beck v. Ohio* [28]: "If subjective good faith alone were the test, the protections of the Fourth Amendment would evaporate, and the people would be 'secure in their persons, houses, papers, and effects,' only in the discretion of the police." The probable cause test, then, is an objective one; for there to be probable cause, the facts must be such as would warrant a belief by a reasonable man. (If the objective probable cause test is met, it is not also necessary to establish that the particular officer making the arrest or search subjectively believed probable cause was present.) Notwithstanding this objective test, the Supreme Court has made it clear that the expertise [29] and experience [30] of the officer are to be taken into account, which is as it should be. This usually means that a trained and experienced officer will have probable cause in circumstances when the layman would not, as when an officer is able to identify an illegal substance by smell or sight because of his training and experience. But sometimes an experienced officer will be held *not* to have had probable cause if a man with his special skills, though perhaps not a layman, should

23. 442 U.S. 200, 99 S.Ct. 2248, 60 L.Ed.2d 824 (1979), discussed in § 3.8(g).

24. See Berger v. New York, 388 U.S. 41, 87 S.Ct. 1873, 18 L.Ed.2d 1040 (1967), where Stewart, J., concurring, observed that "electronic eavesdropping for a 60-day period * * * involves a broad invasion of a constitutionally protected area. Only a most precise and rigorous standard of probable cause should justify an intrusion of this sort."

25. See Gooding v. United States, 416 U.S. 430, 94 S.Ct. 1780, 40 L.Ed.2d 250 (1974), where three members of the Court argued that such searches "involve a greater intrusion than ordinary searches and therefore require a greater justification."

26. See Schmerber v. California, 384 U.S. 757, 86 S.Ct. 1826, 16 L.Ed.2d 908 (1966), stressing that "intrusions into the human body" are particularly offensive and thus may be undertaken only upon "a clear indication that in fact such evidence will be found," seemingly a higher test than that usually required to show probable cause.

27. However, the Supreme Court has rejected the notion that a higher probable cause standard should apply "when First Amendment interests would be endangered by the search," as when search warrants for allegedly obscene materials are involved. New York v. P.J. Video, Inc., 475 U.S. 868, 106 S.Ct. 1610, 89 L.Ed.2d 871 (1986). The Court reasoned that "the longstanding special protections" of other kinds which apply in such cases, see, e.g., § 3.4(a), (f), were sufficient.

28. 379 U.S. 89, 85 S.Ct. 223, 13 L.Ed.2d 142 (1964).

29. United States v. Ortiz, 422 U.S. 891, 95 S.Ct. 2585, 45 L.Ed.2d 623 (1975) ("officers are entitled to draw reasonable inferences from these facts in light of their knowledge of the area and their prior experience with aliens and smugglers").

30. Johnson v. United States, 333 U.S. 10, 68 S.Ct. 367, 92 L.Ed. 436 (1948) (probable cause may be based upon a distinctive odor where the officer is "qualified to know the odor").

have recognized that no criminal conduct was involved.

Though the Supreme Court once held that a "search warrant may issue only upon evidence which would be competent in the trial of an offense before a jury," [31] this is no longer the law. In *Brinegar v. United States*,[32] the Court noted:

> For a variety of reasons relating not only to probative value and trustworthiness, but also to possible prejudicial effect upon a trial jury and the absence of opportunity for cross-examination, the generally accepted rules of evidence throw many exclusionary protections about one who is charged with standing trial for crime. Much evidence of real and substantial probative value goes out on considerations irrelevant to its probative weight but relevant to possible misunderstanding or misuse by the jury. * * *
>
> In dealing with probable cause, however, as the very name implies, we deal with probabilities. These are not technical; they are the factual and practical considerations of everyday life on which reasonable and prudent men, not legal technicians, act. The standard of proof is accordingly correlative to what must be proved.

Information which would be inadmissible at trial on hearsay grounds may be used to show probable cause,[33] as may a person's criminal record.[34] But in *Spinelli v. United States* [35] the Court characterized a general assertion of criminal reputation (i.e., that defendant was "known" as a gambler) as "a bald and unilluminating assertion of suspicion that is entitled to no weight" in determining probable cause. That conclusion is solidly grounded in the fundamental Fourth Amendment principle that probable cause must be shown on the basis of facts rather than mere conclusions,[36] which means that *facts* which would contribute to a bad reputation may be taken into account.[37]

The Court in *Brinegar* declared that "in dealing with probable cause * * * we deal with probabilities," but did not identify the degree of probability needed other than to say that "more than bare suspicion" and "less than evidence which would justify * * * conviction" was required. Some of the Supreme Court's decisions may be read as adopting a more-probable-than-not test, so that, for example, there would not be grounds to arrest unless the information at hand provided a basis for singling out but one person.[38] But the lower court cases generally do not go this far, and instead merely require that the facts permit a fairly narrow focus, so that descriptions fitting large numbers of people or a large segment of the community will not suffice. This latter position has been defended on the ground that it strikes a fair balance between the interests of privacy and effective law enforcement, in that arrests for investigative purposes sometimes must be permitted upon somewhat general descriptions provided by crime victims and witnesses. If that is so, then it may be necessary to distinguish those

31. Grau v. United States, 287 U.S. 124, 53 S.Ct. 38, 77 L.Ed. 212 (1932).

32. 338 U.S. 160, 69 S.Ct. 1302, 93 L.Ed. 1879 (1949).

33. Draper v. United States, 358 U.S. 307, 79 S.Ct. 329, 3 L.Ed.2d 327 (1959).

34. Brinegar v. United States, 338 U.S. 160, 69 S.Ct. 1302, 93 L.Ed. 1879 (1949).

35. 393 U.S. 410, 89 S.Ct. 584, 21 L.Ed.2d 637 (1969).

36. Aguilar v. Texas, 378 U.S. 108, 84 S.Ct. 1509, 12 L.Ed.2d 723 (1964).

37. E.g., Jones v. United States, 362 U.S. 257, 80 S.Ct. 725, 4 L.Ed.2d 697 (1960) (relevant that suspects "are familiar to the undersigned and other members of the Narcotics Squad" and "had admitted to the use of narcotic drugs and displayed needle marks as evidence of same").

38. Wong Sun v. United States, 371 U.S. 471, 83 S.Ct. 407, 9 L.Ed.2d 441 (1963) (where informant said Toy, operator of laundry on certain street, had heroin, but several laundries on that street operated by persons named Toy, probable cause lacking because there was no showing the officers "had some information of some kind which had narrowed the scope of their search to this particular Toy"); Mallory v. United States, 354 U.S. 449, 77 S.Ct. 1356, 1 L.Ed.2d 1479 (1957) (arrest of three blacks with access to basement where rape by masked black man occurred was illegal; police may not "arrest, as it were, at large * * * in order to determine whom they should charge before a committing magistrate on 'probable cause' "); Johnson v. United States, 333 U.S. 10, 68 S.Ct. 367, 92 L.Ed. 436 (1948) (where officers smelled burning opium outside hotel room, entry could not be justified as a step toward a lawful arrest because "the arresting officer did not have probable cause to arrest petitioner until he had entered her room and found her to be the sole occupant").

cases in which the uncertainty goes not to who the perpetrator of the crime is but rather to whether any crime has occurred, as when the police observe a person engaging in suspicious activity. As to this latter situation, it is commonly said that an arrest and search based on events as consistent with innocent as with criminal activity are unlawful, so that if the observed pattern of events occurs just as frequently or even more than frequently in innocent transactions, then it is too equivocal to constitute probable cause. Utilizing the more-probable-than-not test here but not in the first situation is defensible on two grounds: (1) permitting arrests for equivocal conduct would result in more frequent interference with innocent persons than would permitting arrests upon a just-received somewhat general description from a crime victim or witness, as the latter is anchored in a time-space sense to known criminal activity; and (2) the law enforcement need is greater in the victim/witness description situation, as these cases often involve much more serious criminal activity as to which experience has shown that the likelihood of apprehending the offender is slight unless he is promptly arrested in the vicinity of the crime.

Probable cause is not defeated by an after-the-fact showing that the relevant provision in the substantive criminal law is unconstitutional. In reaching that conclusion in *Michigan v. DeFillippo,*[39] the Court reasoned:

> Police are charged to enforce laws until and unless they are declared unconstitutional. The enactment of a law forecloses speculation by enforcement officers concerning its constitutionality—with the possible exception of a law so grossly and flagrantly unconstitutional that any person of reasonable prudence would be bound to see its flaws. Society would be ill served if its police officers took it upon themselves to determine which laws are and which are not constitutionally entitled to enforcement.[40]

(c) Information From an Informant. The term "informant" is used here to describe an individual who learns of criminal conduct by being a part of the criminal milieu; it does not refer to the average citizen who by happenstance finds himself in the position of a victim of or a witness to a crime. The Supreme Court and other courts have with considerable frequency confronted the question of when probable cause may be said to exist exclusively or primarily upon the basis of information from such a person.

At issue in *Aguilar v. Texas*[41] was a search warrant affidavit stating: "Affiants have received reliable information from a credible person and do believe that heroin, marijuana, barbiturates, and other narcotics and narcotic paraphernalia are being kept at the above described premises for the purpose of sale and use contrary to the provisions of the law." The Court concluded it did not meet the requirements of the Fourth Amendment:

> Although an affidavit may be based on hearsay information and need not reflect the direct personal observations of the affiant, * * * the magistrate must be informed of some of the underlying circumstances from which the informant concluded that the narcotics were where he claimed they were, and some of the underlying circumstances from which the officer concluded that the informant, whose identity need not be disclosed, * * * was "credible" or his information "reliable." Otherwise, "the inferences from the facts which lead to the complaint" will be drawn not "by a neutral and detached magistrate," as the Constitution requires, but instead, by a police officer "engaged in the often competitive enterprise of ferreting out crime," * * * or, as in this case, by an unidentified informant.

This two-pronged test was also applied by the Court to police claims of probable cause to

39. 443 U.S. 31, 99 S.Ct. 2627, 61 L.Ed.2d 343 (1979).

40. Though the Court in *DeFillippo* distinguished the instant case from prior cases in which exclusion of evidence was required because the unconstitutional provisions, "by their own terms, authorized searches under circumstances which did not satisfy the traditional warrant and probable cause requirements of the Fourth Amendment," this substantive-procedural line was later obliterated entirely in Illinois v. Krull, 480 U.S. 340, 107 S.Ct. 1160, 94 L.Ed.2d 364 (1987), discussed in § 3.1(c).

41. 378 U.S. 108, 84 S.Ct. 1509, 12 L.Ed.2d 723 (1964).

make an arrest or search without a warrant.[42] Under the first or "basis of knowledge" prong, facts had to be revealed which permitted the judicial officer making the probable cause determination to reach a judgment as to whether the informant had a basis for his allegations that a certain person had been, was or would be involved in criminal conduct or that evidence of crime would be found at a certain place. By contrast, under the second or "veracity" prong, sufficient facts had to be brought before the judicial officer so that he could determine either the inherent credibility of the informant or the reliability of his information on this particular occasion. But in *Illinois v. Gates,*[43] the Supreme Court, though casting not the slightest doubt upon the correctness of the result in *Aguilar,* decided

> to abandon the "two-pronged test" established by our decisions in *Aguilar* and *Spinelli.*[44] In its place we reaffirm the totality of the circumstances analysis that traditionally has informed probable cause determinations. * * * The task of the issuing magistrate is simply to make a practical, common-sense decision whether, given all the circumstances set forth in the affidavit before him, including the "veracity" and "basis of knowledge" of persons supplying hearsay information, there is a fair probability that contraband or evidence of a crime will be found in a particular place. And the duty of a reviewing court is simply to ensure that the magistrate had a "substantial basis for . . . conclud[ing]" that probable cause existed. * * * We are convinced that this flexible, easily applied standard will better achieve the accommodation of public and private interests that the Fourth Amendment requires than does the approach that has developed from *Aguilar* and *Spinelli.*

The majority in *Gates* felt that the two-pronged test was too rigid and that it improperly accorded "these two elements * * * independent status," when in fact "a deficiency in one may be compensated for * * * by a strong showing as to the other."

This abandonment of the *Aguilar* test in *Gates* is most unfortunate. As Justice White (concurring because he found probable cause to exist by applying the *Aguilar* factors) wisely noted, "the question whether a particular anonymous tip provides the basis for issuance of a warrant will often be a difficult one." This being the case, he continued, the Supreme Court should "attempt to provide more precise guidance by clarifying *Aguilar–Spinelli,*" instead of opting for the direct opposite course by which "it appears that the question whether the probable cause standard is to be diluted is left to the common-sense judgments of issuing magistrates" without meaningful review. Moreover, as Justice White also cogently noted, the *Gates* majority's claim that a deficiency as to one of the *Aguilar* prongs can be compensated for by a strong showing as to the other cannot be taken literally. Were it so interpreted, it would lead to the bizarre result, repeatedly rejected by the Court in the past[45] in cases reaffirmed by the *Gates* majority, that the unsupported assertion or belief of an honest person satisfies the probable cause requirement.

It is not entirely clear to exactly what extent *Gates* constitutes a significant "watering-down" of the probable cause standard as it had developed under the *Aguilar* two-pronged formula. But it does seem safe to say that *Gates* does *not* mean that lower courts are writing on a completely clean slate when they now confront the question of when an informant's information amounts to probable cause. Even the *Gates* majority agreed "that an informant's 'veracity,' 'reliability' and 'basis of knowledge' are all highly relevant in determining the value of his report." Because this is so, courts continue to rely upon

42. McCray v. Illinois, 386 U.S. 300, 87 S.Ct. 1056, 18 L.Ed.2d 62 (1967).

43. 462 U.S. 213, 103 S.Ct. 2317, 76 L.Ed.2d 527 (1983).

44. The reference is to Spinelli v. United States, 393 U.S. 410, 89 S.Ct. 584, 21 L.Ed.2d 637 (1969), an oft-cited case applying the *Aguilar* formula and elaborating upon it.

45. E.g., Whiteley v. Warden, 401 U.S. 560, 91 S.Ct. 1031, 28 L.Ed.2d 306 (1971); Jones v. United States, 362 U.S. 257, 80 S.Ct. 725, 4 L.Ed.2d 697 (1960); Nathanson v. United States, 290 U.S. 41, 54 S.Ct. 11, 78 L.Ed. 159 (1933).

the elaboration of these factors in earlier cases decided under the now-discarded *Aguilar* formula. (But it must be remembered, as the Court later emphasized,[46] that *Gates* "did not merely refine or qualify the 'two-pronged test' " but instead abandoned it in favor of a "totality of the circumstances analysis.") Thus, while the discussion which follows examines decisions predating *Gates,* it is nonetheless relevant on the question of what constitutes probable cause in the post-*Gates* era.

Police often attempt to establish the credibility of the informant on the basis of his past performance, as in *McCray v. Illinois.*[47] There, the officer testified the informant had given him information about narcotics activities 15 or 16 times in the past, resulting in numerous arrests and convictions, and on cross-examination even named some of the persons convicted. Because this testimony "informed the court * * * of the underlying circumstances from which the officer concluded that the informant * * * was 'credible,' " the Supreme Court unhesitatingly concluded there was "no doubt * * * that there was probable cause to sustain the arrest and incidental search in this case."

Lower courts have consistently held that a declaration the informant's past information led to convictions is a sufficient showing of the informer's credibility, even when information on a single past occasion produced a single conviction and even without any specific identification of the prior convictions. It will also suffice that on a prior occasion the informant said a certain object, such as narcotics, would be found at a certain place and that this information was verified by a search uncovering the object. It has frequently been held sufficient that the informant's prior information led to arrests, but the better view is that such an allegation is inadequate, as a mere statement that police decided to arrest on the prior occasion indicates nothing about the lawfulness of that arrest or whether anything learned incident to or following the arrest verified what the informant had said. And while cases may be found approving of assertions which merely say the informant's prior information proved to be "correct," "true and correct," "reliable" or "valid," other decisions view such characterizations as conclusory and thus insufficient. Although the *Gates* case has occasionally been interpreted as approving such general assertions, that is incorrect. To view such allegations as alone establishing veracity would violate a cardinal principle reaffirmed by the *Gates* majority: "Sufficient information must be presented to the magistrate to allow *that official* to determine probable cause; his action cannot be a mere ratification of the bare conclusion of others."[48] In any event, past performance relates only to the matter of veracity; as Justice White put it in *Spinelli v. United States*[49]: "The past reliability of the informant can no more furnish probable cause for believing his current report than can previous experience with the officer himself."

If no such showing is made as to the informant's credibility, then it is necessary to consider whether it has been established that the informant's information is reliable on this particular occasion. One means of showing this was recognized in *United States v. Harris,*[50] where the search warrant affidavit recited that the informant said he had purchased illicit whiskey from a named person for two years, most recently in the past two weeks, in the course of which he saw that person obtain the whiskey from a specified building. What appeared to be a majority of the Court concluded that the information given was shown to be reliable because it "was plainly a declaration against interest since it could readily warrant a prosecution and could sustain a conviction against the informant himself." The Court reasoned:

> Common sense in the important daily affairs of life would induce a prudent and disinterested observer to credit these statements.

46. Massachusetts v. Upton, 466 U.S. 727, 104 S.Ct. 2085, 80 L.Ed.2d 721 (1984).

47. 386 U.S. 300, 87 S.Ct. 1056, 18 L.Ed.2d 62 (1967).

48. Emphasis added.

49. 393 U.S. 410, 89 S.Ct. 584, 21 L.Ed.2d 637 (1969).

50. 403 U.S. 573, 91 S.Ct. 2075, 29 L.Ed.2d 723 (1971).

People do not lightly admit a crime and place critical evidence in the hands of the police in the form of their own admissions. Admissions of crime, like admissions against proprietary interests, carry their own indicia of credibility—sufficient at least to support finding of probable cause to search. That the informant may be paid or promised a "break" does not eliminate the residual risk and opprobrium of having admitted criminal conduct. Concededly admissions of crime do not always lend credibility to contemporaneous or later accusations of another. But here the informant's admission that over a long period and currently he had been buying illicit liquor on a certain premises, itself and without more, implicated that property and furnished probable cause to search.

The four dissenters in *Harris* objected that "where the declarant is also a police informant it seems at least as plausible to assume, without further enlightenment either as to the Government's general practice or as to the particular facts of this case, that the declarant-confidant at least believed he would receive absolution from prosecution for his confessed crime in return for his statement." That criticism does not compel the conclusion that the admission-against-interest approach should never be used, but rather that it should be used with caution; as the Supreme Court said in a related context, a person's statement "against his penal interest" carries with it an "indicia of reliability" if it may also be said that the statement was made "under circumstances when he would have no reason to lie." [51] Certainly the admission-against-interest rationale is inappropriate when not even the police know the identity of the informant, for if the informant is not known to the police he stands no real risk of prosecution. It does not follow, as the *Harris* dissenters argued, that this is also the case if the informant's identity is known to the police but not disclosed to others. But such a case does call for particular caution, for if the informant's name is not disclosed then it is more likely (at least as a general proposition) that he is a person whose indiscretions are tolerated by the police on a continuing basis in exchange for information and who thus will perceive little risk in admitting such indiscretions. By comparison, there is much more reason to conclude that veracity is shown when the informant comes forward as an affiant or when his identity is disclosed in the affidavit or upon the motion to suppress.

For a declaration against penal interest to establish reliability, the declaration must have a sufficient nexus to the information critical to the probable cause determination. To take an obvious and unlikely case, if a person were to walk into a police station and give a full confession to a robbery and then announce that a named person was guilty of an unrelated rape, the admission with respect to the robbery could hardly be taken as showing that the information about the rape was reliable. What is needed is a showing that the informant's statements against his own penal interest were closely related to the criminal activity for which probable cause to arrest or search is being established; it is *not* necessary that the admissions incriminate the informant in the *same* crimes as the ones then under investigation. Moreover, for the rationale of *Harris* to apply the admission must be unequivocal; it will not suffice that the informant admits to being present during another's crime or describes the crime in such detail as to suggest his possible involvement in it.

Just how important it remains after *Gates* to show veracity in one of these ways is less than clear. The *Gates* majority says that the informant's veracity is still "highly relevant," but then asserts that a deficiency in that respect could be compensated for by a "strong showing" of basis of knowledge. Thus, "even if we entertain some doubt as to an informant's motives, his explicit and detailed description of alleged wrongdoing, along with a statement that the event was observed first-hand, entitled his tip to greater weight than might otherwise be the case." But surely the mere act of reciting a detailed account does not show veracity, nor does an informant's claim of first-hand knowledge. To conclude

51. Dutton v. Evans, 400 U.S. 74, 91 S.Ct. 210, 27 L.Ed.2d 213 (1970).

otherwise would be to put informants on the same footing as police and the victims of and witnesses to crime when, as Justice Brennan noted in his *Gates* dissent, "there certainly is no basis for treating anonymous informants as presumptively reliable."

The other prong of the now-abandoned *Aguilar* test concerned "basis of knowledge," which *Gates* teaches also remains a "highly relevant" consideration in determining the value of an informant's report. The most obvious and direct way of showing such a basis is by setting out for the benefit of the judicial officer who must make the probable cause decision an explanation as to exactly how the informant claims to have come by the information he gave to the officer. As Justice White explained in his very helpful concurring opinion in *Spinelli v. United States* [52].

> If the affidavit rests on hearsay—an informant's report—what is necessary under *Aguilar* is one of two things: the informant must declare either (1) that he has himself seen or perceived the fact or facts asserted; or (2) that his information is hearsay, but there is good reason for believing it—perhaps one of the usual grounds for crediting hearsay information. * * * [I]f, for example, the informer's hearsay comes from one of the actors in the crime in the nature of admission against interest, the affidavit giving this information should be held sufficient.

But this does not mean that a basis of knowledge may be shown only in such a direct fashion. If there is not such a direct showing, said the Court in *Spinelli,* it may nonetheless be possible to assume a sufficient basis of knowledge from the wealth of detail which has been provided:

> The detail provided by the informant in *Draper v. United States* [53] * * * provides a suitable benchmark. While Hereford, the Government's informer in that case, did not state the way in which he obtained his information, he reported that Draper had gone to Chicago the day before by train and that he would return to Denver by train with three ounces of heroin on one of two specified mornings. Moreover, Hereford went on to describe, with minute particularity, the clothes that Draper would be wearing upon his arrival at the Denver station. A magistrate, when confronted with such detail, could reasonably infer that the informant had gained his information in a reliable way. Such an inference cannot be made in the present case. Here, the only facts supplied were that Spinelli was using two specified telephones and that these phones were being used in gambling operations. This meager report could easily have been obtained from an offhand remark heard at a neighborhood bar.

If self-verifying detail can establish a basis of knowledge (clearly, it cannot show the informant's veracity), then exactly what kind of detail will suffice? What is needed, to put the proposition in the language of the *Gates* case, are details about matters sufficiently related to the criminal activity reported that it may be fairly concluded the informant "had access to reliable information of the * * * illegal activities." Such was the case in *Draper* because, as Justice White later explained in his *Gates* concurring opinion, the fact the informer could predict two days in advance what clothing Draper would be wearing suggested Draper "had planned in advance to wear these specific clothes so that an accomplice could identify him," and this gave rise to a "clear inference * * * that the informant was either involved in the criminal scheme himself or that he otherwise had access to reliable, inside information." By contrast, if in the *Aguilar* case the informant had been able to describe the furnishings inside the house (instead of, say, a particular furnishing in which it was indicated the drugs were stored), that would not give rise to such a "clear inference." It would only show that the informant or someone with whom he communicated had been in that house, and a direct assertion to that effect would not suffice to show basis of knowledge re the presence of drugs there.

52. 393 U.S. 410, 89 S.Ct. 584, 21 L.Ed.2d 637 (1969).

53. 358 U.S. 307, 79 S.Ct. 329, 3 L.Ed.2d 327 (1959).

Just how important it remains after *Gates* to show a basis of knowledge in one of these ways is not entirely clear. Though it is at least arguable that a basis of knowledge was established in that case, some of the majority's comments on this point are none too reassuring. As noted earlier, in abandoning the *Aguilar* two-pronged test the Court in *Gates* said that "a deficiency in one may be compensated for * * * by a strong showing as to the other." By way of example, the Court then declared that if "a particular informant is known for the unusual reliability of his prediction of certain types of criminal activities in a locality, his failure, in a particular case, to thoroughly set forth the basis of his knowledge surely should not serve as an absolute bar to a finding of probable cause based on his tip." But this assertion does not deserve to be taken too seriously. For one thing, the case cited in support of this proposition, *United States v. Sellers,*[54] is in fact a very striking example of the self-verifying-detail principle. For another, as Justice White noted in his concurrence regarding that statement by the majority:

> If this is so, then it must follow *a fortiori* that "the affidavit of an officer, known by the magistrate to be honest and experienced, stating that [contraband] is located in a certain building" must be acceptable. * * * It would be "quixotic" if a similar statement from an honest informant, but not one from an honest officer, could furnish probable cause. * * * But we have repeatedly held that the unsupported assertion or belief of an officer does not satisfy the probable cause requirement, and the majority "expressly reaffirms" these holdings.

Although the *Spinelli* Court utilized the earlier *Draper* case to illustrate the self-verifying detail situation, *Draper* was not decided upon such a basis. Rather, *Draper* was based upon yet another device for rehabilitating what would otherwise be an insufficient or incomplete report of an informant: partial corroboration. Federal narcotics agent Marsh had been told by an informant who had given him reliable information in the past that Draper would return from Chicago by train on one of two specified days; in addition, the informer gave a detailed physical description of Draper and of the clothing he would be wearing, and said that he would be carrying a tan zipper bag and that he habitually walked real fast. These details were not put before a magistrate. Rather, the agent maintained a surveillance at the train station and when the described person appeared as predicted he was arrested, resulting in the discovery of the heroin. In upholding the arrest and search, the majority in *Draper* emphasized that

> Marsh had personally verified every facet of the information given him by Hereford except whether petitioner had accomplished his mission and had the three ounces of heroin on his person or in his bag. And surely, with every other bit of Hereford's information being thus personally verified, Marsh had "reasonable grounds" to believe that the remaining unverified bit of Hereford's information—that Draper would have the heroin with him—was likewise true.

Corroboration of part of the informant's tale is another way in which the concern with veracity may be met, as the informant's present good performance shows him to be probably credible just as does past good performance. But in *Draper* the informant's credibility was otherwise established, and thus the corroboration of which the Court spoke was apparently deemed relevant on the matter of basis of knowledge. Courts have commonly used corroboration in this way. Any lingering doubts about the propriety of utilizing corroboration for this latter purpose have been dispelled by *Gates*. There the majority found probable cause because of the partial corroboration even though, as Justice Stevens lamented in his dissent, *neither* veracity *nor* basis of knowledge was otherwise established.

As for what kind or amount of corroboration is needed, *Gates* rejects the notion that corroboration of innocent activity will not suffice. "In making a determination of probable

54. 483 F.2d 37 (5th Cir.1973).

cause the relevant inquiry is not whether particular conduct is 'innocent' or 'guilty,' but the degree of suspicion that attaches to particular types of non-criminal acts." In that case, an anonymous letter said that a named couple made their living selling drugs, that the wife drives the car to Florida and flies back, after which the husband flies to Florida and drives back with a car full of drugs, and that another such trip was about to occur. A few days later the police determined that the husband had flown to Florida, and surveillance of him there established that upon arrival he took a taxi to a motel where his wife had rented a room and that the next day they left in his car and drove north on an interstate highway. On those facts a warrant to search the car and their residence was obtained. In concluding this amounted to probable cause, the *Gates* majority none too convincingly reasoned as follows: (1) the facts obtained by independent investigation were alone quite suspicious, as "Florida is well-known as a source of narcotics and other illegal drugs," and Gates' observed conduct "is as suggestive of a pre-arranged drug run, as it is of an ordinary vacation trip"; (2) the anonymous letter was then deserving of some weight, as the "corroboration of the letter's predictions that the Gates' car would be in Florida, that Lance Gates would fly to Florida in the next day or so, and that he would drive the car north toward Bloomingdale all indicated, albeit not with certainty, that the informant's other assertions also were true"; and (3) the details in the letter concerned "future actions of third parties ordinarily not easily predicted," thus suggesting the writer of the letter "also had access to reliable information of the Gates' alleged illegal activities." But, as the Stevens dissent quite properly notes, the corroboration in this case actually counts for very little. For one thing, the limited investigation established neither when the wife had gone to Florida nor whether the husband was making an immediate return trip to Illinois, and thus there was nothing inherently suspicious in what had been observed. For another, both the husband and wife had been seen together in Florida, thus disproving the assertion in the letter that they were never gone at the same time, a rather critical allegation because it squared with the further assertion that they already had "over $100,000 worth of drugs in their basement."

Upon a motion to suppress in a case where the prosecution claims information from an informant supplies probable cause, the defendant may seek the identity of the informant in an effort to learn whether the informant actually exists, whether he actually gave fruitful information in the past, and whether the informant actually gave the information alleged in this instance. Counsel will usually be thwarted in these efforts because of what is commonly referred to as the informer's privilege. In *McCray v. Illinois,*[55] the Court rejected the claim that defendants are *always* entitled upon demand to learn of the informant's name, and instead concluded "that it should rest entirely with the judge who hears the motion to suppress to decide whether he needs such disclosure as to the informant in order to decide whether the officer is a believable witness." This means that disclosure should be required on occasion, as when some aspect of the police conduct appears inexplicable if an informant actually reported what it is claimed he said. But, because it is difficult if not impossible to articulate a standard which sufficiently honors the informer's privilege and yet sufficiently guards again undetectable police perjury, a growing number of courts are utilizing the device of an in camera hearing, whereby the informant is produced privately for examination by the judge only.

(d) Information From a Victim or Witness. The Supreme Court has seldom had occasion to speak to the matter of victim-witness veracity. However, in *Jaben v. United States,*[56] involving a complaint filed by an IRS agent which was based in part upon interviews with persons who had knowledge of the defendant's financial condition, the Court made it clear that these persons were not to

55. 386 U.S. 300, 87 S.Ct. 1056, 18 L.Ed.2d 62 (1967).

56. 381 U.S. 214, 85 S.Ct. 1365, 14 L.Ed.2d 345 (1965).

be viewed in the same light as the typical police informant:

> [U]nlike narcotics informants, for example, whose credibility may often be suspect, the sources in this tax evasion case are much less likely to produce false or untrustworthy information. Thus, whereas some supporting information concerning the credibility of informants in narcotics cases or other common garden varieties of crime may be required, such information is not so necessary in the context of the case before us.

The Court has since proceeded as if veracity may be assumed when information comes from the victim of or a witness to criminal activity,[57] a position rather consistently taken by lower courts. But circumstances may make that presumption inoperative in a particular case; the cases holding veracity was properly presumed frequently emphasize that the police were unaware of any apparent motive to falsify. If the person who purports to have witnessed criminal activity is unwilling to identify himself to the police, then it would ordinarily be improper to presume reliability.

As for "basis of knowledge," one prong of the since-abandoned *Aguilar* test but now a "highly relevant" consideration under the *Illinois v. Gates*[58] "totality of the circumstances" formula, it is generally not a major problem as to the so-called citizen-informer. Eyewitnesses by definition are not passing along idle rumor, for they have been the victims of the crime or have otherwise seen some portion of it. Great detail as to why the person was in a position to observe what was reported is not required, though some explanation regarding the basis of knowledge of the victim or witness is clearly called for when it appears the purported knowledge could have been obtained only by the utilization of some expertise beyond that of the typical layman. As for the somewhat unusual case in which the victim or witness also conveys to the police information from others, this hearsay-upon-hearsay may also be considered if it is specially shown or fairly inferable from the circumstances that both the veracity and basis of knowledge requirements are met by the source of the information related.

In a victim-witness type of case there is seldom any serious problem presented concerning either veracity or basis of knowledge; rather, the major difficulty usually encountered is whether the information obtained from direct observation by a presumptively reliable person is complete and specific enough to constitute probable cause to search a particular place or (as is much more frequently in issue) to arrest a particular person. Sometimes the victim or witness can identify the perpetrator by name or by identifying his picture in police files, but more typically the police must act quickly on the basis of a description of the perpetrator. Even assuming that the Fourth Amendment probable cause test does not mean more-probable-than-not in this context,[59] the description will not suffice if it is equally applicable to a great many individuals in the area. In determining what kind of description in what circumstances will suffice, courts have considered these factors:

(1) Particularity of description. A victim or witness will typically describe the perpetrator in terms of some of the following characteristics: race, sex, age, height, weight, build, complexion, hair, and clothing. Generally, the more of these identifying characteristics which are available, the more likely it is there will be grounds to arrest a person found with most or all of those characteristics. But there is more to it than counting the number of points of comparison; consideration must be given to the uniqueness of the points of identification—the extent to which they aid in singling out a person from the general public.

(2) Size of the area. The time which has elapsed between the crime and the arrest is an important consideration, for it shows what distance the perpetrator of the crime could have traveled—the radius of the area within which the perpetrator might then be. If the

57. Chambers v. Maroney, 399 U.S. 42, 90 S.Ct. 1975, 26 L.Ed.2d 419 (1970).

58. 462 U.S. 213, 103 S.Ct. 2317, 76 L.Ed.2d 527 (1983).

59. See § 3.3(b).

elapsed time is short, such as five or ten minutes, then this area is fairly small, and a matching up of a person in the area with a rather general description which might not otherwise suffice will be adequate for probable cause.

(3) Number of persons in the area. The fewer persons about, the less chance there is that a description of a given particularity would fit persons other than the individual at hand. Thus, rather general descriptions have been found sufficient in the early morning hours when few persons were on the street.

(4) Direction of flight. Courts frequently take note of the fact that the police had been advised of the direction in which the offender was fleeing on foot or by vehicle. This is appropriate, for it shows that of the total relevant area (measured by a radius the length of possible flight since the time of the crime), a particular slice is more likely than the rest to contain the individual or vehicle sought.

(5) Actions by or condition of person arrested. Illustrative of such additional facts are that the suspect was running in a direction away from the crime scene, that he was furtively looking back, or that upon a lawful stopping for investigation he gave an implausible explanation for his presence.

(6) Knowledge that the person or vehicle was involved in other similar criminality on a prior occasion. Thus the arrest of the occupants of a car for bank robbery finds added support in the fact that the car was recognized as having been used to transport the fruits of an earlier robbery and one of the occupants was recognized as a person involved in that prior robbery.

(e) Information From or Held by Other Police. In *United States v. Ventresca,*[60] involving a search warrant affidavit reciting that certain events had been observed by the affiant's fellow officers, the Court in upholding the warrant stated: "Observations of fellow officers of the Government engaged in a common investigation are plainly a reliable basis for a warrant applied for by one of their number." Following the lead of *Ventresca,* lower courts have consistently held that another law enforcement officer is a reliable source and that consequently no special showing of reliability need be made as a part of the probable cause determination.

In *Ventresca,* the other officers passed on to the affiant the facts they had uncovered in their investigation, and thus that case is unlike the common situation in which a directive or request for action is circulated within or between law enforcement agencies unaccompanied by any recitation of the underlying facts and circumstances, resulting in an arrest being made by an officer unaware of the facts constituting probable cause. Such was the case in *Whiteley v. Warden,*[61] where a policeman arrested two men in response to a bulletin stating an arrest warrant for them had issued in another part of the state. After finding the warrant invalid, the Court turned to the contention that the arrest was lawful because the policeman was entitled to assume that whoever authorized the bulletin had probable cause:

> We do not, of course, question that the Laramie police were entitled to act on the strength of the radio bulletin. Certainly police officers called upon to aid other officers in executing arrest warrants are entitled to assume that the officers requesting aid offered the magistrate the information requisite to support an independent judicial assessment of probable cause. Where, however, the contrary turns out to be true, an otherwise illegal arrest cannot be insulated from challenge by the decision of the instigating officer to rely on fellow officers to make the arrest.

Thus, under the *Whiteley* rule police are in a limited sense "entitled to act" upon a communication through official channels. Although the Court did not elaborate upon that observation, it apparently means the arresting officer is himself not at fault and thus should not be held personally responsible in a civil action or disciplinary proceedings if it turns out that there was no probable cause at

60. 380 U.S. 102, 85 S.Ct. 741, 13 L.Ed.2d 684 (1965).

61. 401 U.S. 560, 91 S.Ct. 1031, 28 L.Ed.2d 306 (1971).

the source. But when the question arises in the context of an effort to exclude evidence obtained as a consequence of action taken pursuant to the communication, then it must be determined whether the law enforcement system as a whole has complied with the requirements of the Fourth Amendment. This means that the evidence must be excluded if facts adding up to probable cause were not in the hands of the officer or agency which gave the order or made the request, for were it otherwise an officer or agency possessed of insufficient facts could circumvent the Fourth Amendment by the simple device of directing or asking some other officer or agency to make the arrest and search.

Whiteley must in turn be distinguished from the case in which there has been no directive or request but the arresting or searching officer attempts to justify his action on the ground that other officers were at that time in possession of the necessary underlying facts. In such circumstances, the knowledge of other police cannot ordinarily be imputed to the arresting or searching officer, for to hold otherwise would encourage police officers to search on the hope that the total knowledge of all those officers involved in a case will later be found to constitute probable cause. A contrary result has been reached when there was a close working relationship between the officer who acted and the officer who had the requisite information, and in addition the circumstances indicated that had not the former officer acted the latter most certainly would have conducted the arrest or search himself.

When police come into contact with an individual for some reason, it is not uncommon for them to run a radio check on him and his vehicle to see if either is wanted, and a lawful arrest may result if the requirements of *Whiteley* are met. Problems arise when the records do not accurately reflect the current situation, as where a person is arrested for driving a car listed in police files as stolen notwithstanding its earlier recovery by the police. This arrest is illegal, for the police may not rely upon incorrect or incomplete information when they are at fault in permitting the records to remain uncorrected.

(f) First-Hand Information. Although the kinds of suspicious events and circumstances which police on patrol confront are virtually infinite in their variety, there are a few recurring situations worth noting, such as where a person is arrested because of his association with a known offender, as in *United States v. Di Re.*[62] There, an OPA investigator was told by one Reed that he was to buy counterfeit ration coupons from one Buttitta at a certain place, so the investigator and a detective trailed Buttitta's car to the designated place. There they found Reed in the rear seat holding counterfeit coupons, and upon being asked he said he received them from Buttitta, the driver. Di Re, a passenger in the front seat, was also arrested on the theory that his presence indicated he was implicated in a conspiracy to knowingly possess counterfeit coupons, but the Supreme Court concluded that probable cause for his arrest was lacking:

> The argument that one who "accompanies a criminal to a crime rendezvous" cannot be assumed to be a bystander, forceful enough in some circumstances, is farfetched when the meeting is not secretive or in a suspicious hideout but in broad daylight, in plain sight of passers-by, in a public street of a large city, and where the alleged substantive crime is one which does not necessarily involve any act visibly criminal. If Di Re had witnessed the passing of papers from hand to hand, it would not follow that he knew they were ration coupons, and if he saw that they were ration coupons, it would not follow that he would know them to be counterfeit. Indeed it appeared at the trial to require an expert to establish that fact. Presumptions of guilt are not lightly to be indulged from mere meetings.

Di Re intimates that when the offense *does* involve an "act visibly criminal," then the chances are substantially greater that a companion is more than a mere bystander. As a general matter this is so, but yet it cannot be said that probable cause is always present

62. 332 U.S. 581, 68 S.Ct. 222, 92 L.Ed. 210 (1948).

upon those facts. If, for example, *A* and *B* are standing on a corner and *C* walks up to *B* and makes a purchase of narcotics from *B*, it is by no means apparent that *A* is an accomplice in this transaction.[63] When as in *Di Re* the ongoing criminal activity is not evident to the associate, it is then clearly necessary also to consider such aspects of the nature and extent of the association as may indicate the associate is an accomplice.

Observation of furtive gestures may properly be taken into account in determining whether probable cause exists. As concluded in *Sibron v. New York*,[64] "deliberately furtive actions * * * at the approach of strangers or law officers are strong indicia of mens rea, and when coupled with specific knowledge on the part of the officer relating the suspect to the evidence of crime, they are proper factors to be considered in the decision to make an arrest." Thus, if the police see a person in possession of a highly suspicious object and then observe that person make an apparent attempt to conceal that object from police view, probable cause is then present. But when no such object is seen and the officer merely observes a movement which could be an attempt to hide something, this does not amount to probable cause.

Flight of a person from the presence of police does not alone amount to probable cause. But, as the Court recognized in *Peters*, flight is a "strong indicia of mens rea." Thus, a person's flight upon approach [65] of the police may be taken into account and may well elevate the pre-existing suspicion up to probable cause. But in some circumstances the flight will be so ambiguous that it cannot be considered even to that limited extent.[66]

Officers on patrol frequently utilize interrogation as a means to obtain more information about suspicious persons and circumstances, and the suspect's response will sometimes elevate the prior suspicions up to probable cause. Responses known to be false or which are implausible, conflicting, evasive or unresponsive may well constitute probable cause when considered together with the prior suspicions. Justice White, concurring in *Terry v. Ohio*,[67] asserted that "refusal to answer furnishes no basis for arrest," which may well be correct if construed to mean that such refusal does not alone constitute grounds for arrest.[68] But, though it has occasionally been held that no adverse inference may be drawn from such a refusal, the better view is that refusal to answer is one of "the factual and practical considerations of everyday life" [69] which an officer may consider, together with the evidence that gave rise to his prior suspicion, in determining whether there are grounds for an arrest.

(g) Special Problems in Search Cases. Probable cause in arrest cases usually involves historical facts (i.e., is it probable that a certain person did at some *prior* time commit an offense?), while in search cases the concern is always with facts relating to a

63. By comparison, it does seem clear that there is probable cause to arrest a person who on a continuing basis is present at a place where criminal activity is openly and repeatedly conducted. Ker v. California, 374 U.S. 23, 83 S.Ct. 1623, 10 L.Ed.2d 726 (1963).

64. 392 U.S. 40, 88 S.Ct. 1889, 20 L.Ed.2d 917 (1968).

65. The approach itself is no Fourth Amendment seizure, and thus even if no reasonable suspicion then exists the flight cannot be characterized as a fruit of an illegal seizure. See the discussion of California v. Hodari D., ___ U.S. ___, 111 S.Ct. 1547, 113 L.Ed.2d 690 (1991), in § 3.8(c).

66. Wong Sun v. United States, 371 U.S. 471, 83 S.Ct. 407, 9 L.Ed.2d 441 (1963) (where federal agent knocked on door of laundry at 6 a.m. and used ruse that he seeking his laundry and then said he an agent when suspect was closing door, suspect's flight into the house was ambiguous, as "the officer never adequately dispelled the misimpression engendered by his own ruse").

67. 392 U.S. 1, 88 S.Ct. 1868, 20 L.Ed.2d 889 (1968).

68. In Brown v. Texas, 443 U.S. 47, 99 S.Ct. 2637, 61 L.Ed.2d 357 (1979), the Court noted it did not have to decide "whether an individual may be punished for refusing to identify himself in the context of a lawful investigatory stop which satisfies Fourth Amendment requirements." And in Kolender v. Lawson, 461 U.S. 352, 103 S.Ct. 1855, 75 L.Ed.2d 903 (1983), the Court held unconstitutional on void for vagueness grounds a statute making it a crime for a person lawfully stopped under *Terry* not to provide "credible and reliable" identification, but did not have occasion to decide whether a more certain substantive offense of this type would be constitutional.

69. Brinegar v. United States, 338 U.S. 160, 69 S.Ct. 1302, 93 L.Ed. 1879 (1949).

current situation (i.e., it is probable that evidence of crime is *presently* to be found in a certain place?). This is why search cases often present the unique problem of whether the information relied upon to establish probable cause has grown "stale." Illustrative is *Sgro v. United States,*[70] holding that there was not probable cause to search a hotel for illegal intoxicants where the affidavit alleged a purchase of beer there over three weeks earlier.

Probable cause is not determined by merely counting the number of days between the time of the facts relied upon and the warrant's issuance, and thus, as stated in *Sgro,* the matter "must be determined by the circumstances of each case." One important factor is the character of the criminal activity under investigation. When the affidavit recites an isolated violation probable cause ordinarily dwindles rather quickly with the passage of time, but when it recites facts indicating activity of a protracted and continuous nature the passage of time becomes less significant. Especially when the crime under investigation is not a continuing one, the nature of the property sought is an important factor. Illustrative is *United States v. Steeves,*[71] involving a warrant to search for various items relating to a bank robbery which had occurred three months earlier, where the court concluded there was no longer probable cause that the robber still had at his residence the "highly incriminating" money bag taken from the bank, though there was probable cause he still had the clothing he had worn during the robbery. Yet another factor is the opportunity which those involved in the crime would have had to remove or destroy the items sought during the time which has elapsed. Some cases assert it is relevant that the police acted with dispatch as soon as the facts were made known to them, but this obviously has *no* bearing on the probable cause issue.

Because the time the facts relied upon occurred is critical in determining whether there is probable cause to search, failure to state when they occurred is fatally defective. But where undated information is factually interrelated with other, dated information in the affidavit, then the inference that the events took place in close proximity to the dates actually given may be permissible. Similarly, when the affidavit says that the events occurred "within" a specified period of time, it must be tested by considering whether the information would be stale if the events occurred at the earliest possible time in that period. Use of the word "recently" is permissible when the reported facts clearly show a continuing course of conduct which would support a finding of present probable cause even if those facts had occurred a few months ago, but under the better view is insufficient when the fact in question is a one-time purchase or viewing of drugs.

Some cases present the converse issue of whether the officer's information was too "fresh." This issue arises when the police have obtained an "anticipatory search warrant," one based upon an affidavit showing probable cause that at some future time (but not presently) certain evidence of crime will be located at a specific place. Despite some contrary authority, the better and prevailing view is that such warrants are constitutional and indeed are to be preferred over forcing the police to go to the scene without a warrant and there make a decision at the risk of being second-guessed by the judiciary if they are successful in recovering evidence. Moreover, the typical anticipatory warrant is more likely to establish that probable cause will exist at the time of the search than the typical warrant based solely upon the known prior location of the items to be seized. It is important, of course, that the issuing judge be satisfied that there is no likelihood that an anticipatory warrant will be executed before the events critical to the ripening of probable cause.

The more complicated probable cause determination which must be made in search cases may be said to include four ingredients: time; crime; objects; and place. Assuming no

70. 287 U.S. 206, 53 S.Ct. 138, 77 L.Ed. 260 (1932).

71. 525 F.2d 33 (8th Cir.1975).

problem with respect to time (as discussed above), it is still necessary that there be established a sufficient nexus between (1) criminal activity, (2) the things to be seized, and (3) the place to be searched. Difficulties concerning whether the necessary relationships have been established can arise in an infinite variety of ways, but only a few illustrations will be given here.

Even if the connection between things and place is clear beyond question, probable cause may still be lacking because it is not also shown to be probable that those items constitute the fruits, instrumentalities, or evidence of crime. Thus an affidavit stating a truckload of lumber had been unloaded at defendant's residence at night makes it sufficiently probable that the lumber would be found there, but yet is defective because it fails to connect the lumber with any criminal offense. A second type of situation is that in which it is clear that certain identifiable items are connected with criminal activity, but the difficult question is whether it is probable that those items are to be found at the specified place. For example, if a warrant to search a person's apartment for drugs was based upon an affidavit disclosing only that he had made an isolated street sale of drugs at a distant location, it might be doubted whether there had been a sufficient showing that he probably keeps his stash of drugs at the apartment.

§ 3.4 Search Warrants

(a) When Warrant May Be Utilized. Later sections of this Chapter define the various situations—such as search incident to arrest, search in response to exigent circumstances, and search by consent—in which the police may conduct a search without first obtaining a search warrant. By examination of the boundaries of those warrantless search categories, it may be determined when a search warrant *must* be obtained in order to conduct a lawful search under the Fourth Amendment. By comparison, the concern here is with whether there are some situations in which, because of what is sought, from whom it is sought, or how it would be obtained, not even the usual protections of the search warrant process will permit the search to be made.

At one time, under what came to be known as the "mere evidence" rule, search warrants could only be used to find certain objects.[1] But this rule was rejected in *Warden v. Hayden*;[2] the Court noted that nothing in the Fourth Amendment supported such a rule and that nothing in the nature of the property seized as evidence renders it more private than other property, particularly since the same object could be "mere evidence" in one case and an instrumentality in another. The evidence seized in *Hayden* was items of clothing, and the Court cautioned that they "are not 'testimonial' or 'communicative' in nature, and their introduction therefore did not compel respondent to become a witness against himself in violation of the Fifth Amendment." The self-incrimination issue was finally resolved in *Andresen v. Maryland*,[3] upholding the seizure of business records pursuant to a search warrant. Though the records were incriminating and some contained statements made by the petitioner, the Court concluded that when a search warrant rather than a subpoena is used there is no Fifth Amendment violation because "the individual against whom the search is directed is not required to aid in the discovery, production, or authentication of incriminating evidence."

Whenever the seizure of large quantities of books or films or similar materials is contemplated for the purpose of bringing about their destruction as contraband, the protections afforded by the search warrant process will not suffice. Rather, under such circumstances there must be a prior judicial determination of obscenity in an *adversary* proceeding in order to avoid "danger of abridgement of the

§ 3.4

1. Gouled v. United States, 255 U.S. 298, 41 S.Ct. 261, 65 L.Ed. 647 (1921).

2. 387 U.S. 294, 87 S.Ct. 1642, 18 L.Ed.2d 782 (1967).

3. 427 U.S. 463, 96 S.Ct. 2737, 49 L.Ed.2d 627 (1976). For more on the history on policies of the privilege, see § 8.14.

right of the public in a free society to unobstructed circulation of nonobscene books." [4] That rule does not bar use of the usual search warrant procedures in order to obtain a limited number of copies of an allegedly obscene publication for evidentiary purposes. The usual warrant procedures will also suffice for seizure of a single copy of an allegedly obscene film, provided (i) that "a prompt judicial determination of the obscenity issue in an adversary proceeding is available at the request of any interested party," and (ii) that copying of the film is permitted "on a showing to the trial court that other copies of the film are not available" to the exhibitor pending that determination.[5]

Some intrusions into the body are so extreme that they cannot be permitted at all, and some require more than the usual search warrant safeguards. In *Rochin v. California,*[6] the police made a forcible entry into Rochin's room and, upon observing him put two capsules in his mouth, unsuccessfully attempted to extract them by force, after which they took him to a hospital where a doctor forced an emetic solution through a tube into Rochin's stomach, resulting in vomiting by which the two capsules were retrieved. Characterizing this series of events as "conduct that shocks the conscience," the Court concluded the evidence had to be suppressed because the police actions violated Fourteenth Amendment due process.[7] But in *Schmerber v. California,*[8] where a physician took a blood sample at police direction from an injured arrestee over his objection, the majority ruled that the extraction of blood violated neither the due process clause nor the Fourth Amendment. The Court identified three factors which were critical to that holding: (i) there had been a "clear indication" that the extraction would produce evidence of crime, i.e., that defendant was intoxicated while driving; (ii) the test was "a reasonable one" in the sense that such tests are "commonplace" and involve "virtually no risk, trauma, or pain"; and (iii) the test "was performed in a reasonable manner," in that the blood was "taken by a physician in a hospital environment according to accepted medical practices."

Similarly, even court-ordered surgery has been allowed where (1) the evidence sought was relevant, could have been obtained in no other way, and there was probable cause to believe that the operation would produce it; (2) the operation was minor, was performed by a skilled surgeon, and every possible precaution was taken to guard against any surgical complications, so that the risk of permanent injury was minimal; (3) before the operation was performed the court held an adversary hearing at which the defendant appeared with counsel; and (4) thereafter and before the operation was performed the defendant was afforded an opportunity for appellate review. In *Winston v. Lee,*[9] the Supreme Court applied the *Schmerber* balancing test to the surgery issue by focusing "on the extent of the intrusion on respondent's privacy interests and on the State's need for the evidence," and concluded that in the case before it the lower court had properly declined to authorize surgery to remove a bullet. The Court placed particular emphasis upon two facts: (i) "the proposed surgery, which for purely medical reasons required the use of a general anesthetic, would be an 'extensive' intrusion on respondent's personal privacy and bodily integrity"; and (ii) the state's need for the bullet to establish that defendant was the robber shot by the victim was not high, as the state had "substantial additional evidence" that defendant was the robber.

Zurcher v. Stanford Daily [10] concerned execution of a warrant at a newspaper's offices for photographs of demonstrators who had

4. A Quantity of Copies of Books v. Kansas, 378 U.S. 205, 84 S.Ct. 1723, 12 L.Ed.2d 809 (1964).

5. Heller v. New York, 413 U.S. 483, 93 S.Ct. 2789, 37 L.Ed.2d 745 (1973).

6. 342 U.S. 165, 72 S.Ct. 205, 96 L.Ed. 183 (1952).

7. The police conduct was not assessed in Fourth Amendment terms, for at that time the Fourth Amendment exclusionary rule had not yet been held applicable to the states.

8. 384 U.S. 757, 86 S.Ct. 1826, 16 L.Ed.2d 908 (1966).

9. 470 U.S. 753, 105 S.Ct. 1611, 84 L.Ed.2d 662 (1985).

10. 436 U.S. 547, 98 S.Ct. 1970, 56 L.Ed.2d 525 (1978).

injured several policemen. The lower court had reasoned that the much less intrusive subpoena duces tecum should ordinarily be utilized against nonsuspects, and concluded "that unless the Magistrate has before him a sworn affidavit establishing proper cause to believe that the materials in question will be destroyed, or that a subpoena duces tecum is otherwise 'impractical,' a search of a third party for materials in his possession is unreasonable *per se,* and therefore violative of the Fourth Amendment." The Supreme Court disagreed, observing that there was nothing in the language or history of the Fourth Amendment to support such a distinction, and that the Amendment "has itself struck the balance between privacy and public need" by permitting issuance of warrants to search property in *all* cases upon a showing of probable cause. Dissenting Justice Stevens cogently responded that this history should not be controlling because the risk to third parties perceived by the lower court was virtually nonexistent prior to the recent abandonment of the "mere evidence" rule. But he provided no answer to the other point made by the majority: "that search warrants are often employed early in an investigation, perhaps before the identity of any likely criminal and certainly before all the perpetrators are or could be known," so that as a practical matter it would seldom be possible for the police to show which seemingly blameless third parties were in fact involved in the criminal activity or sufficiently sympathetic to those who were involved to destroy or remove evidence implicating them. The Court in *Zurcher* went on to reject the contention that the First Amendment ordinarily bars execution of a search warrant on the premises of a newsgathering organization, but did stress the need for courts to "apply the warrant requirements with particular exactitude when First Amendment interests would be endangered by the search."

(b) The "Neutral and Detached Magistrate" Requirement. The search warrant process is preferred because it involves a "neutral and detached magistrate"[11] in the critical decision of whether to permit the search, and thus it is necessary to ask what kinds of persons under what circumstances may be allowed to issue warrants. In *Coolidge v. New Hampshire,*[12] for example, the warrant was issued by the state attorney general, acting as a justice of the peace, although he had personally taken charge of the murder investigation to which the warrant related and was later to serve as chief prosecutor at trial. To the state's argument that the attorney general had in fact acted as a "neutral and detached magistrate," the Court responded "that there could hardly be a more appropriate setting than this for a *per se* rule of disqualification rather than a case-by-case evaluation of all the circumstances," as "prosecutors and policemen simply cannot be asked to maintain the requisite neutrality with regard to their own investigations." The courts are not in agreement as to whether this *per se* rule also applies when the person issuing the warrant had law enforcement responsibilities which did not or could not extend to the case for which the warrant was sought, but there is much to be said for the proposition that any effort to assess the neutrality of a law enforcement official in such instances on a case-by-case basis would involve the lower courts in a complicated fact-finding process which is better avoided by a prophylactic rule.

At issue in *Connally v. Georgia*[13] was a warrant issued by an unsalaried justice of the peace who received five dollars for each warrant issued but nothing for reviewing and denying a warrant application. A unanimous Court held that a warrant issued under such circumstances violated the protections of the Fourth Amendment:

> His financial welfare * * * is enhanced by positive action and is not enhanced by a negative action. The situation, again, is one which offers "a possible temptation to the average man as a judge * * * or it might lead him not to hold the balance nice, clear and true be-

11. Johnson v. United States, 333 U.S. 10, 68 S.Ct. 367, 92 L.Ed. 436 (1948).

12. 403 U.S. 443, 91 S.Ct. 2022, 29 L.Ed.2d 564 (1971).

13. 429 U.S. 245, 97 S.Ct. 546, 50 L.Ed.2d 444 (1977).

tween the State and the accused." It is, in other words, another situation where the defendant is subjected to what surely is judicial action by an officer of a court who "has a direct, personal, substantial, pecuniary interest" in his conclusion to issue or deny the warrant.

The Court held in *Shadwick v. City of Tampa* [14] that municipal court clerks could constitutionally issue *arrest* warrants for breach of municipal ordinances. A unanimous Court concluded that a "magistrate," in the Fourth Amendment sense, need not necessarily be a lawyer or judge, but "must meet two tests. He must be neutral and detached, and he must be capable of determining whether probable cause exists for the requested arrest or search." These tests were found to be met because the clerk worked within the judicial branch and, by virtue of his position, would be able to determine if there was probable cause as to "common offenses covered by a municipal code." *Shadwick* has been relied upon in holding that *search* warrants may be issued by nonlawyer commissioners or judges, but there is something to be said for the conclusion that search warrant cases are different because the probable cause issues are much more complex and likely to be beyond the ken of a layman.

The conduct of the magistrate in a particular case may show that he was not then "neutral and detached," as is illustrated by *Lo–Ji Sales, Inc. v. New York* [15] where a town justice issued an open-ended search warrant for obscene materials and then accompanied the police during its execution and made probable cause determinations at that time as to particular articles. In rejecting the claim that the on-the-scene determinations saved the warrant, the Court stated that there had been "an erosion of whatever neutral and detached posture existed at the outset" because the justice "allowed himself to become a member, if not the leader of the search party which was essentially a police operation."

(c) Oath or Affirmation; Record. The Fourth Amendment command that "no Warrants shall issue but upon probable cause, supported by Oath or affirmation," has prompted litigation concerning what information, transmitted in what fashion and under what circumstances, may be taken into account later in deciding whether a warrant was issued on probable cause. In *Whiteley v. Warden* [16] the Court ruled that "an otherwise insufficient affidavit cannot be rehabilitated by testimony concerning information possessed by the affiant when he sought the warrant but not disclosed to the issuing magistrate," reasoning that a contrary rule would "render the warrant requirement of the Fourth Amendment meaningless." Where by statute or court rule a search warrant may issue only upon affidavit, a defective affidavit may not be saved by oral statements to the magistrate, even if they were given under oath. Such reliance on oral testimony does not violate the Fourth Amendment, and while it has been held that this is so even when no contemporaneous record was made, it has been persuasively argued that reliance upon oral testimony should not be allowed in such a case because there is too much leeway for after-the-fact rehabilitation of insufficient testimony. Such utilization of oral testimony must be distinguished from the so-called oral or telephonic search warrant procedure authorized in some jurisdictions, whereby the affiant gives his sworn statement to the magistrate via telephone or other means of communication, after which if the magistrate approves issuance of the warrant he causes an original warrant to be prepared and orally authorizes the officer to prepare a duplicate warrant for use in execution. It has been held that this procedure complies with the "Oath or affirmation" requirement and is not otherwise constitutionally defective.

Whether the information is transmitted orally or in writing, the "Oath or affirmation" requirement means the information must be sworn to. No particular ceremony is necessary to constitute the act of swearing; it is only necessary that something be done which

14. 407 U.S. 345, 92 S.Ct. 2119, 32 L.Ed.2d 783 (1972).

15. 442 U.S. 319, 99 S.Ct. 2319, 60 L.Ed.2d 920 (1979).

16. 401 U.S. 560, 91 S.Ct. 1031, 28 L.Ed.2d 306 (1971).

is understood by both the issuing magistrate and the affiant to constitute the act of swearing. The true test is whether the procedures followed were such that perjury could be charged if any material allegation contained therein is false. There is a split of authority as to whether a false-name affidavit, utilized to conceal the identity of an informer-affiant, meets that test.

(d) Probable Cause: The Facially–Sufficient Affidavit. Until *Franks v. Delaware,*[17] courts were split on whether a defendant could ever introduce additional evidence at a suppression hearing for the purpose of proving that some of the allegations in a facially-sufficient search warrant affidavit were false. The Supreme Court in *Franks,* rejecting the lower court's absolute ban upon such evidence, stressed several "pressing considerations": (i) "a flat ban on impeachment of veracity could denude the probable cause requirement of all meaning," as an officer could resort to false allegations and "remain confident that the ploy was worthwhile"; (ii) the hearing before the magistrate, because "necessarily ex parte" and "frequently * * * marked by haste," "not always will suffice to discourage lawless or reckless misconduct"; (iii) *Mapp* rejected the claim that alternative sanctions are likely "to fill the gap"; (iv) given the fact the magistrate's determination of the sufficiency of the evidence is now open to challenge at the suppression hearing, also allowing veracity challenges "would not diminish the importance and solemnity of the warrant-issuing process"; (v) probable cause is already at issue at the suppression hearing, and thus the claim that this added challenge "will confuse the issue of the defendant's guilt with the issue of the State's possible misbehavior is footless"; and (vi) allowing a veracity challenge does not extend the exclusionary rule to a new area, as there is "no principled basis for distinguishing between the question of the sufficiency of an affidavit, which also is subject to a post-search re-examination, and the question of its integrity."

As for what inaccuracies jeopardize the warrant, the Court in *Franks* held it must be established "that a false statement knowingly and intentionally, or with reckless disregard for the truth, was included by the affiant in the warrant affidavit." This means, as the Court emphasized, that "allegations of negligence or innocent mistake are insufficient." Some have argued that even innocent mistakes should be covered, but surely this is not so, as the Fourth Amendment only requires that the affiant act reasonably. But because that is the case, one might logically argue that negligent (i.e., unreasonable) mistakes should be covered. The Court in *Franks* did not explain its failure to draw the line in that way, but may have been influenced by doubts as to whether negligent misrepresentations could be effectively deterred and by the difficulty in determining whether an officer was negligent or completely innocent in not checking his facts further.

Franks emphasizes that the deliberate falsity or reckless disregard must be "that of the affiant, not of any nongovernmental informant." This means that if a private informer gives information to an officer who as the affiant reports what he was told and why he considers the informer reliable (e.g., past experience with him), the defendant could challenge the accuracy of the officer's recitation of what he was told or why he believed the infomer reliable, but may not raise the issue of whether in fact the informer was lying. This is as it should be, for the Fourth Amendment "probable cause" test requires not absolute certainty but only that the government have good reason for believing in the existence of the necessary facts. *Franks* strongly intimates that the result would be otherwise if the officer-affiant received his information from another policeman, as the Court took note of its declaration on a prior occasion "that police could not insulate one officer's deliberate misstatement merely by relaying it through an officer-affiant personally ignorant of its falsity." As for the unusual situation in which a private person is himself the affiant and makes a deliberately or recklessly false

17. 438 U.S. 154, 98 S.Ct. 2674, 57 L.Ed.2d 667 (1978).

statement, there has been no government wrongdoing in such a case, and thus it would seem that the warrant should be upheld if the cooperating police and the magistrate had reasonable grounds to believe the affiant.

Franks leaves no doubt as to what consequences are to follow from the requisite inaccuracies. No hearing is needed unless "the alleged false statement is necessary to the finding of probable cause," and suppression is to occur only if the defendant proves perjury or reckless disregard *and* it then appears that "with the affidavit's false material set to one side, the affidavit's remaining content is insufficient to establish probable cause." This is a sound result in the case of reckless misrepresentation, but the Court in *Franks* never explained why it rejected the position which a number of other courts had previously adopted, namely, that intentional falsehoods always render the warrant invalid because the fullest deterrent sanctions of the exclusionary rule should be applied to such serious and deliberate wrongdoing.

To obtain a *Franks* hearing, the defendant must "point out specifically the portion of the warrant affidavit that is claimed to be false" and give "a statement of supporting reasons. Affidavits or sworn or otherwise reliable statements of witnesses should be furnished, or their absence satisfactorily explained." If that threshold showing is made, then a hearing is held at which the defendant has the burden to prove "by a preponderance of the evidence" that the challenged statements are false and that their inclusion in the affidavit amounted to perjury or reckless disregard for the truth. The *Franks* allocation of the burden is unjust; it should suffice that the defendant proves the statements false, after which the affiant should have to show that the false statement was not intentionally or deliberately made, for he alone is in a position to justify his errors. Indeed, without access to the informant it may be impossible for the defendant even to prove that the affiant (rather than the informant) lied, and thus it is to be doubted that this burden may constitutionally be imposed on defendant if at the same time the informer privilege is used to deny defendant the identity of the informant.[18]

(e) Particular Description of Place to Be Searched. The Fourth Amendment provides that no warrants shall issue except those "particularly describing the place to be searched." Absolute perfection in description is not required; it "is enough if the description is such that the officer with a search warrant can, with reasonable effort ascertain and identify the place intended."[19] As for urban premises, the common practice is to identify the place by street address. This is sufficient, but a street address is not essential when other descriptive facts identify the premises to be searched. Rural property is often described by giving the owner's name and general directions for reaching it, which will suffice.

Problems arise when a facially-sufficient description is determined to be less precise than was assumed, as where the warrant refers to apartment 3 in a certain building but there are apartments with that number on each floor, or where identifying numbers and other descriptive facts do not all fit the same premises. In these circumstances, courts are inclined to permit officers to resolve the matter on the basis of other facts (e.g., owner's name) not in the warrant description but known to them from the affidavit or otherwise, or by making common-sense judgments as to which of the several descriptive facts was most likely mistaken.

A search warrant for an apartment house or hotel or other multiple-occupancy building will usually be held invalid if it fails to describe the particular subunit to be searched with sufficient definiteness to preclude a search of one or more subunits indiscriminately. This is because the basic requirement of the Fourth Amendment is that the officers who are commanded to search be able from

18. Cf. Lego v. Twomey, 404 U.S. 477, 92 S.Ct. 619, 30 L.Ed.2d 618 (1972), declaring that suppression hearing procedures must be such as to allow "a reliable and clearcut determination" of the defendant's claim.

19. Steele v. United States, 267 U.S. 498, 45 S.Ct. 414, 69 L.Ed. 757 (1925).

the particular description of the search warrant to identify the specific place for which there is probable cause. This means that, in the absence of a probable cause showing as to all the living units so as to justify a search of them all, a search warrant directed at a multiple-occupancy structure will ordinarily be held invalid if it describes the premises only by street number or other identification common to all the subunits located within the structure. A significant exception to that rule is: if the building in question from its outward appearance would be taken to be a single-occupancy structure and neither the affiant nor other investigating officers nor the executing officers knew or had reason to know of the structure's actual multiple-occupancy character until execution of the warrant was under way, then the warrant is not defective for failure to specify a subunit within the named building. This exception is sensible if narrowly construed so as to apply only when: (i) the multiple-occupancy character of the building was not known and could not have been discovered by reasonable investigation; (ii) the discovery of the multiple occupancy occurred only after the police had proceeded so far that withdrawal would jeopardize the search; and (iii) upon discovery of the multiple-occupancy, reasonable efforts were made to determine which subunit is most likely connected with the criminality under investigation and to confine the search accordingly.

A similar situation was involved in *Maryland v. Garrison,*[20] where police obtained and executed a search warrant for "the premises known as 2036 Park Avenue third floor apartment," only to discover thereafter that the third floor was divided into two apartments and that the contraband they had discovered was in the apartment of a person not theretofore suspected. The Court held the warrant itself was valid, though "we now know that the description of that place was broader than appropriate"; such a warrant is invalid, the Court explained, only if when obtained "the officers had known, or even if they should have known, that there were two separate dwelling units on the third floor." Similarly, the execution of the warrant was lawful as well, as "the officers' failure to realize the overbreadth of the warrant was objectively understandable and reasonable."[21]

As for a warrant to search a vehicle, there are many descriptive facts which can be given: owner's or operator's name, make, model, year, color, license number, location, etc. A few of these, such as make-plus-license or make-plus-operator, are sufficient to meet the Fourth Amendment particularity requirement. Assuming an otherwise sufficient description, it is not necessary that the warrant indicate the location of the car or the name of the owner. When a warrant is issued for search of certain premises and "all automobiles thereon," it is likely to be vulnerable to attack because of insufficiency of description and lack of probable cause extending also to such vehicles. As for a facially-sufficient vehicle description which turns out to be partially erroneous because not all of the facts fit, the rule is the same as noted above as to premises: the warrant will still be upheld if other facts known by the executing officer or reasonable inferences by him as to where the mistake lies make it possible to identify a particular vehicle.

As for the infrequent cases in which a warrant is obtained to *search* a person, the individual must be described with such particularity that he may be identified with reasonable certainty. The person's name will suffice, but a name is not essential if certain other facts, such as location and physical description, are given. Sometimes a search war-

20. 480 U.S. 79, 107 S.Ct. 1013, 94 L.Ed.2d 72 (1987).

21. Alluding to the line of lower court authority summarized in the preceding paragraph, the three dissenters in *Garrison* distinguished the instant case, where the building *was* known to be of a multiple-occupancy character, as one which imposed an obligation on the police to "make an investigation adequate to draw the warrant with sufficient specificity." They reasoned that neither the warrant nor its execution were valid, as the police should have known when obtaining the warrant and did know when executing it that there were seven units in the 3-story building, and thus "should have been aware that further investigation was necessary to eliminate the possibility of more than one unit's being located on the third floor."

rant will authorize the search of a specified premises or vehicle and in addition "any and all persons found therein;" such a warrant is not lacking particularity in the sense that the officer will be unable to ascertain to whom the warrant applies, but may well be defective because the probable cause showing is insufficient in that it does not establish that anyone present at the time of warrant execution probably is involved in the criminal activity in such a way as to have evidence thereof on his person.

(f) Particular Description of Things to Be Seized. Another specific command of the Fourth Amendment is that no warrants shall issue except those "particularly describing the * * * things to be seized." Speaking of that limitation, the Supreme Court said in *Marron v. United States:* [22] "The requirement that warrants shall particularly describe the things to be seized makes general searches under them impossible and prevents the seizure of one thing under a warrant describing another." A particular description of the objects to be seized does aid in preventing general searches, as that description determines the permissible intensity and length of the search which may be undertaken in executing the warrant. As for the second objective of preventing the seizure of objects on the mistaken assumption that they fall within the magistrate's authorization, *Marron* goes on to say that "nothing is left to the discretion of the officer executing the warrant," but few warrants could pass such a strict test, and thus it is more accurate to say that the warrant must be sufficiently definite so that the officer executing it can identify the property sought with reasonable certainty. A third purpose underlying the particularity requirement, not mentioned in *Marron,* is to prevent the issuance of warrants on loose, vague or doubtful bases of fact. [23] That is, the requirement of particularity is closely tied to the requirement of probable cause to search, under which it must be probable (i) that the described items are connected with criminal activity, and (ii) that they are to be found in the place searched. The less precise the description of the things to be seized, the more likely it will be that either or both of those probabilities has not been established. (By the same token, a clear statement of the objects to be seized will be defective if it is broader than can be justified by the probable cause showing.)

Consistent with these three purposes are certain general principles which may be distilled from the decided cases in this area. They are: (1) A greater degree of ambiguity will be tolerated when the police have done the best that could be expected under the circumstances, by acquiring all the descriptive facts which reasonable investigation of this type of crime could be expected to uncover and by ensuring that all of those facts were included in the warrant. (2) A more general type of description will be sufficient when the nature of the objects to be seized are such that they could not be expected to have more specific characteristics. (3) A less precise description is required of property which is, because of its particular character, contraband. (4) Failure to provide all of the available descriptive facts is not a basis for questioning the adequacy of the description when the omitted facts could not have been expected to be of assistance to the executing officer. (5) An error in the statement of certain descriptive facts is not a basis for questioning the adequacy of the description if the executing officer was nonetheless able to determine, from the other facts provided, that the object seized was that intended by the description. (6) Greater care in description is ordinarily called for when the type of property sought is generally in lawful use in substantial quantities. (7) A more particular description than otherwise might be necessary is required when other objects of the same general classification are likely to be found at the particular place to be searched. (8) The greatest care in description is required when the consequences of a seizure of innocent articles by mistake is most substantial, as when

22. 275 U.S. 192, 48 S.Ct. 74, 72 L.Ed. 231 (1927).

23. Go–Bart Importing Co. v. United States, 282 U.S. 344, 51 S.Ct. 153, 75 L.Ed. 374 (1931).

the objects to be seized are books or films [24] or the papers of a newsgathering organization.[25]

A defective description in the warrant sometimes may be saved by an adequate description in the affidavit. At a minimum it must appear that the executing officer also had the affidavit with him and made reference to it, but some courts require that the two documents be physically connected and that the warrant expressly refer to the affidavit. However, a warrant with an insufficient description may not be rehabilitated by showing that the executing officer was aware of other facts which enabled him to know exactly what things were intended to be covered, or that the officer for that reason or by luck only seized the items which an adequate description would have covered.

If a search warrant is issued to search a place for several items, but it is later determined that not all of those items are described with sufficient particularity or that probable cause does not exist as to all of the items described, it is often possible to sever the tainted portion of the warrant from the valid portion so that evidence found in execution of the latter will be admissible. Assume, for example, a warrant for a gun used in and money taken in a bank robbery, and assume also that there is probable cause to search for the gun and that it is particularly described but that there is either no probable cause or no adequate description of the money. If the police, while looking in a desk drawer for the gun, were to find money which by its wrappings clearly came from that robbery, the money would be admissible because found in plain view in execution of the valid part of the warrant. But if the money was found after the gun was located or by looking where the gun could not be (e.g., an envelope), the money would not be admissible.

(g) Time of Execution. Some jurisdictions provide by statute or court rule that a search warrant must be executed within a certain time after issuance, such as ten days, in which case execution after the specified time will result in exclusion of the evidence.[26] Sometimes a delay in execution will amount to a Fourth Amendment violation, for such delay is constitutionally permissible only where the probable cause recited in the affidavit continues until the time of execution. It is possible, therefore, that an unconstitutional delay may have occurred notwithstanding execution within the time set by rule or statute, and, of course, notwithstanding the fact that the jurisdiction has set no fixed time within which warrants must be executed.

About half of the states restrict the execution of search warrants to daytime hours absent some special showing and authorization. One common restriction is that the affidavit must be "positive" the property sought is on the premises, which has not been read literally but has been construed to require a much stronger probability showing than otherwise would be necessary. A second, more sensible approach is to require a special showing of a need to execute the warrant in the nighttime. Relatively little attention has been given to the question of whether special limitations upon nighttime searches flow from the Fourth Amendment, but in *Gooding v. United States* [27] three members of the Court took the view that a special showing of need for such a search was constitutionally required under the Fourth Amendment principle "that increasingly severe standards of probable cause are necessary to justify increasingly intrusive searches."

No special showing is needed to execute a search warrant for premises in the absence of the occupant, as such execution is not significantly different from that which would otherwise occur. An inventory is required in any event; the occupant if present could not necessarily detect or prevent a broader search; and the fact that such execution will likely require forcible entry is not a sufficient detriment to make a search unreasonable where a

24. Stanford v. Texas, 379 U.S. 476, 85 S.Ct. 506, 13 L.Ed.2d 431 (1965).

25. Zurcher v. Stanford Daily, 436 U.S. 547, 98 S.Ct. 1970, 56 L.Ed.2d 525 (1978).

26. Sgro v. United States, 287 U.S. 206, 53 S.Ct. 138, 77 L.Ed. 260 (1932).

27. 416 U.S. 430, 94 S.Ct. 1780, 40 L.Ed.2d 250 (1974).

warrant based on probable cause has been obtained. As for when the execution of the warrant is deliberately timed to occur without being known to those living at or using the premises (e.g., entry to install wiretapping devices), which appeared to concern the Supreme Court in *Berger v. New York*,[28] the cases upholding the federal wiretapping law have stressed that normal investigative procedures were tried and failed or appear unlikely to succeed. It has been intimated that some such showing might also be necessary for a so-called "surreptitious entry" warrant, authorizing police to enter and merely scrutinize an ongoing criminal operation (e.g., an illegal drug lab) within.

(h) Entry Without Notice. It is generally required, often by statute, that police give notice of their authority and purpose prior to making entry in the execution of a search warrant. This requirement, grounded in the Fourth Amendment,[29] serves several worthwhile purposes: (i) it decreases the potential for violence, as an unannounced entry could lead an individual to believe his safety was in peril and cause him to take defensive measures; (ii) it protects privacy by minimizing the chance of entry of the wrong premises, and even when there is no mistake allows those within a brief time to prepare for the police entry; and (iii) it prevents the physical destruction of property by giving the occupant an opportunity to admit the officer.

Such notice is ordinarily required as a prerequisite to entry by force, by use of a pass key, or by merely opening a closed door. Whether passage through an open door is the kind of entry which ordinarily requires prior announcement is a matter which continues to divide the courts, though it would appear that the need for notice in such a case may depend upon other circumstances. Notice is not required when there is entry by ruse, as when an undercover agent gains access to premises, for in such circumstances the concerns underlying the notice requirement are not present. To comply with the notice requirement, police must identify themselves as police and indicate that they are present for the purpose of executing a search warrant, after which they may enter when admitted by an occupant or upon being refused admittance (either affirmative refusal or failure to respond to the announcement will suffice).

Police are excused from the usual notice requirement when reasonably acting to prevent destruction or disposal of the items named in the warrant. As for the kind of showing of this risk which is required, some courts deem it sufficient that the items named in the warrant are by their nature amenable to ready disposal or destruction, such as narcotics or gambling records. But an increasing number of courts have rejected that "blanket rule" in favor of a requirement that some special facts in the individual case, such as information that the defendant has the evidence in a place where it could be readily disposed of, establish the danger. Another exception is where compliance with the usual notice requirement would increase the peril of the officers or others, which ordinarily requires a showing beyond the fact that the defendant is known to own a weapon. There is also what is commonly called the "useless gesture" exception, which simply means that notice is not required when it is evident from the circumstances that the authority and purpose of the police is already known to those within the premises.

A small number of jurisdictions have adopted legislation permitting magistrates to issue search warrants specifically authorizing entry without prior notice upon a sufficient showing to the magistrate of a need to thereby prevent destruction of evidence or harm to the executing officers. It has sometimes been held that these so-called no-knock search warrants are unconstitutional because the existence of the requisite emergency can be judged only in light of circumstances of which the

28. 388 U.S. 41, 87 S.Ct. 1873, 18 L.Ed.2d 1040 (1967).

29. The Supreme Court has not dealt with this precise question, but in Ker v. California, 374 U.S. 23, 83 S.Ct. 1623, 10 L.Ed.2d 726 (1963), did deal, albeit somewhat ambiguously, with the closely analogous question of notice prior to entry for purposes of making an arrest, and it has generally been assumed that *Ker* (discussed in § 3.6(b)) is also applicable to search warrants.

officer is aware at the moment of execution, but this is somewhat of an overstatement. As for whether the Fourth Amendment *requires* the magistrate to pass on the no-knock issue if the facts are then available, the answer would appear to be no, as the Court in another context has rejected the contention that "search warrants also must include a specification of the precise manner in which they are to be executed."[30]

(i) Detention and Search of Persons. Police executing a search warrant sometimes search individuals found in the described place at the commencement of the warrant execution or who arrive there during the execution. On occasion this occurs because the warrant describes certain premises and also a certain person. There is no inherent defect in a single warrant which authorizes search of a place and a person, and thus the search in such a case will be a valid execution of the warrant, subject of course to the possibility that upon a subsequent motion to suppress it will be found that the information supporting the warrant did not show probable cause as to the named person. A second kind of situation is that in which a person at the scene is arrested and then searched. This will constitute a valid search incident to arrest *if* the arrest was lawful, but it must be remembered that mere presence at a place for which the police have a search warrant does not alone constitute grounds to arrest.[31]

If the person is not named in the warrant and cannot be lawfully arrested, the police may still desire to search him for the objects named in the search warrant. In *Ybarra v. Illinois,*[32] the state claimed that in such a situation the police should be entitled to search if there was only a reasonable suspicion, under the *Terry v. Ohio*[33] standard, that this person had the named objects on his person. But the Court, following the "governing principle" of *United States v. Di Re,*[34] concluded that the interest in productive warrant execution was not so strong as to justify a departure from the usual probable cause standard, and thus the police may lawfully search the person on the premises only upon probable cause that he has the named objects on his person. That probable cause was not present in *Ybarra,* where the person searched was merely a customer in a bar being searched for drugs.

Yet another possibility is that the police will want to search persons present for their own protection, that is, to ensure they will not be attacked with weapons while they proceed with execution of the warrant. The Court in *Ybarra* also spoke to this issue, and concluded that the *Terry* frisk standard was applicable in this context, so that an officer may conduct such a limited search of persons present "to find weapons that he reasonably believes or suspects are then in the possession of the person he has accosted."

As for whether a person on the premises where a search warrant is being executed sometimes may be detained incident to that execution absent grounds for arrest, the Court answered in the affirmative in *Michigan v. Summers.*[35] Using the balancing test of the *Terry* case, the Court reasoned that such a detention was "substantially less intrusive" than a full-fledged arrest and served three important government interests: (i) "the legitimate law enforcement interest in preventing flight in the event that incriminating evidence is found"; (ii) "minimizing the risk of harm to the officers"; and (iii) "the orderly completion of the search," which may be facilitated if the occupants of the premises are present. Although the *Summers* Court thus concluded that such a detention was permissible absent full probable cause, it is important to note that the Court did not merely extend *Terry* to this situation and require a case-by-

30. Dalia v. United States, 441 U.S. 238, 99 S.Ct. 1682, 60 L.Ed.2d 177 (1979) (court order authorizing interception of conversations need not specify covert entry as the manner of execution).

31. See § 3.3(f).

32. 444 U.S. 85, 100 S.Ct. 338, 62 L.Ed.2d 238 (1979).

33. 392 U.S. 1, 88 S.Ct. 1868, 20 L.Ed.2d 889 (1968).

34. 332 U.S. 581, 68 S.Ct. 222, 92 L.Ed. 210 (1948) (holding that an occupant of a vehicle may not be subjected to a search merely because there are grounds to search the car).

35. 452 U.S. 692, 101 S.Ct. 2587, 69 L.Ed.2d 340 (1981).

case determination of whether there was reasonable suspicion sufficient to justify the detention. Rather, the Court opted to relieve police and lower courts of the necessity to engage in case-by-case balancing by announcing a general rule: detention of persons at the scene of a search warrant execution is permissible incident to that execution if (1) those persons are "occupants" (apparently meaning "residents," another term used by the Court), and (2) the warrant authorizes a "search for contraband" rather than a "search for evidence." This is a sensible rule, for it is in such circumstances that all three of the government interests mentioned above are likely to come into play.

(j) Scope and Intensity of the Search. A search made under authority of a search warrant may extend to the entire area covered by the warrant's description. For example, if the warrant authorizes a search of "premises" at a certain described geographical location, buildings standing on that land may be searched. If the place is identified by street number, the search may extend to those buildings within the curtilage and the yard within the curtilage. If the warrant specifies only a certain portion of a building, such as the first floor, only that portion may be searched, but if the warrant also refers to the curtilage the search may extend to such areas as courtyards, driveways and parking areas. Police may pass through areas adjacent to the described premises (so that what they see while doing so is a lawful "plain view") when such action is necessary to gain access to the described area.

In order to search containers in the described premises which might contain the items named in the warrant, it is not necessary that the warrant also describe those containers.[36] But where the container is a personal item, caution is required, for the warrant will not inevitably extend to that item. In *United States v. Micheli,*[37] on the one hand, upholding search of a briefcase found in an office and known to belong to a co-owner of the business, the court reasoned that because he thus "had a special relation to the place, which meant that it could reasonably be expected that some of his personal belongings would be there," it was reasonable for the police to conclude that the warrant "comprehended within its scope those personal articles, such as his briefcase, which might be lying about the office." But in *Commonwealth v. Platou,*[38] concerning search of suitcases known to belong to the tenant's overnight guest, the court concluded the warrant authority did not extend to those containers because the probable cause showing did not cover them. Had there been some reason to believe that the tenant could have concealed the objects named in the warrant in his guest's suitcases, the result in *Platou* would have been different. (*Platou* was recently overruled on the ground that "it would be ineffective and unworkable to require police officers to make the distinction between which articles of clothing and personal property belong to the resident and which belong to the visitor before beginning the search." [39])

A single search warrant may be issued for certain premises and also for a described vehicle, in which case search of both will be lawful if the supporting affidavit establishes probable cause as to both. It has often been held that a warrant describing only premises authorizes search of vehicles found on those premises. This is a dubious proposition in any event, but certainly is not applicable as a matter of course to vehicles known to belong to a visitor.

The permissible intensity of the search within the described premises is determined by the description of the things to be seized. As the Supreme Court has put it, "the same meticulous investigation which would be appropriate in a search for two small canceled checks could not be considered reasonable where agents are seeking a stolen automobile

36. United States v. Ross, 456 U.S. 798, 102 S.Ct. 2157, 72 L.Ed.2d 572 (1982).

37. 487 F.2d 429 (1st Cir.1973).

38. 455 Pa. 258, 312 A.2d 29 (1973).

39. Commonwealth v. Reese, 520 Pa. 29, 549 A.2d 909 (1988).

or an illegal still." [40] This means that a search into closets, desks, boxes and other containers will exceed the authority of the warrant unless some item described in the warrant could be concealed therein.[41] When the purposes of the warrant have been carried out, the authority to search is at an end. Thus, if the warrant describes only a particular package and it is found, any evidence discovered in a continuation of the search of the premises beyond that time must be suppressed. But under some circumstances, such as where the warrant authorizes search for "an unknown quantity of narcotics," the police apparently have a free hand—notwithstanding the quantity of the described item already found—to continue with the search until the entire described place has been covered.

(k) What May Be Seized. At one time it was the rule, per *Marron v. United States,*[42] that the "requirement that warrants shall particularly describe the things to be seized * * * prevents the seizure of one thing under a warrant describing another." But in *Coolidge v. New Hampshire* [43] the Court held that unnamed objects "of incriminating character" could be seized under the "plain view" doctrine:

> As against the minor peril to Fourth Amendment protections, there is a major gain in effective law enforcement. Where, once an otherwise lawful search is in progress, the police inadvertently come upon a piece of evidence, it would often be a needless inconvenience, and sometimes dangerous—to the evidence or to the police themselves—to require them to ignore it until they have obtained a warrant particularly describing it.

Though the Court in *Coolidge* did not elaborate upon the proposition that the object found in plain view may be seized only if it is an "article of incriminating character," it has been properly interpreted to mean that there must exist probable cause that the object is a fruit, instrumentality or evidence of a crime.[44] In determining whether there is probable cause, it is necessary to consider what the executing officers knew concerning the nature of the crime under investigation, its elements, and possible means of proving those elements, as is illustrated by *Andresen v. Maryland.*[45] The warrant was for documents relating to defendant's crime of false pretenses in the sale and conveyance of a certain Lot 13T, but the executing officers also seized documents pertaining to another lot in the same subdivision. In upholding the seizure, the Court stressed the perceived relevance of those documents in proving the intent-to-defraud element of the Lot 13T charge because the defendant had dealt with this other lot in essentially the same way and thus could not claim "his failure to deliver title to Lot 13T free of all encumbrances was mere inadvertence."

The Court in *Coolidge* cautioned that a seizure based upon the plain view doctrine "is legitimate only where it is immediately apparent to the police that they have evidence before them; the 'plain view' doctrine may not be used to extend a general exploratory search from one object to another until something incriminating at last emerges."[46] The Court referred to the concurring opinion in

40. Harris v. United States, 331 U.S. 145, 67 S.Ct. 1098, 91 L.Ed. 1399 (1947), dealing with the analogous situation of search of premises incident to arrest at a time when it was deemed permissible to search defendant's premises if he was arrested there.

41. United States v. Ross, 456 U.S. 798, 102 S.Ct. 2157, 72 L.Ed.2d 572 (1982).

42. 275 U.S. 192, 48 S.Ct. 74, 72 L.Ed. 231 (1927).

43. 403 U.S. 443, 91 S.Ct. 2022, 29 L.Ed.2d 564 (1971).

44. In Texas v. Brown, 460 U.S. 730, 103 S.Ct. 1535, 75 L.Ed.2d 502 (1983), the plurality opinion asserted that "the phrase 'immediate apparent' [in *Coolidge*] was very likely an unhappy choice of words, since it can be taken to imply that an unduly high degree of certainty as to the incriminating character of evidence is necessary for an application of the 'plain view' doctrine," and then concluded it was intended to be merely a "statement of the rule * * * requiring probable cause for seizure in the ordinary case."

45. 427 U.S. 463, 96 S.Ct. 2737, 49 L.Ed.2d 627 (1976).

46. Later, in construing *Coolidge,* the Court stated that the incriminating character must *itself* be in plain view. In Horton v. California, ___ U.S. ___, 110 S.Ct. 2301, 110 L.Ed.2d 112 (1990), the Court gave, as one reason the seizure of vehicles *as* evidence in *Coolidge* did not meet the requirements for a plain view warrantless seizure, the failure to meet the "immediately apparent" requirement: "the cars were obviously in plain view, but their probative value remained uncertain until after the interiors were swept and examined microscopically."

Stanley v. Georgia,[47] where police executing a warrant for gambling paraphernalia found reels of film which they viewed with a projector found in another room and then seized as obscene. The concurring opinion in *Stanley,* endorsed in *Coolidge,* said it was "not a case where agents in the course of a lawful search came upon contraband, criminal activity, or criminal evidence in plain view" because "the contents of the films could not be determined by mere inspection." If interpreted literally, the "immediately apparent" requirement might be viewed as barring any examination at all of an article beyond that necessary to determine it is not one of the items named in the warrant. For many years, most lower courts were not that strict; a limited inspection of an object, such as picking it up to note a brand name or serial number, was permitted as to objects not named in the search warrant *provided* there was a reasonable suspicion the inspected items were the fruits, evidence or instrumentalities of crime. But that approach was rejected in *Arizona v. Hicks,*[48] holding full probable cause was needed to pick up an item of stereo equipment to ascertain its serial number (which revealed it was stolen property). The majority deemed it unwise "to send police and judges into a new thicket of Fourth Amendment law" by recognizing a third category of police conduct between "a plain-view inspection" requiring no suspicion and "a 'full-blown search' " requiring probable cause.

The most controversial aspect of the exploration of the plain view doctrine in *Coolidge* is the conclusion that "the discovery of evidence in plain view must be inadvertent" because, while "the inconvenience of procuring a warrant to cover an inadvertent discovery is great," "the situation is altogether different" when "the police know in advance the location of the evidence," for in such a case they could have easily had the object in question included in their warrant authorization. Though less than a majority of the Court subscribed to this limitation,[49] most lower courts embraced the inadvertence requirement. As for its meaning, if it is to make any sense at all it must at least mean that a discovery of objects not named in the warrant is *always* inadvertent, without regard to the personal hopes or expectations of the executing officers, if there were not sufficient grounds to justify the issuance of a warrant which also named those objects as among the things to be seized. Because the Court is not prepared to require the police to return for a second warrant when the discovery was "inadvertent," the only plausible explanation for requiring such action in the remaining cases (without regard to the risk that the evidence might be lost in the interim) is because the police could have (and thus should have) included the discovered object in the first warrant.

Even so interpreted, the "inadvertent discovery" limitation is unsound. As the Court admitted, it does nothing to prevent illegal entries or to limit the scope of searches under a warrant, but only protects the possessory interest of a defendant in his effects, an interest hardly worth protecting by a difficult-to-administer rule whereunder the police turn out to have greater power if it is *not* shown at the suppression hearing that they had probable cause. Moreover, if it is still true, as the Court held some years ago, that "the police are not required to guess at their peril the precise moment at which they have probable cause,"[50] exclusion of evidence should not re-

47. 394 U.S. 557, 89 S.Ct. 1243, 22 L.Ed.2d 542 (1969).

48. 480 U.S. 321, 107 S.Ct. 1149, 94 L.Ed.2d 347 (1987).

49. Four members of the Court vociferously dissented from any such qualification of the plain view doctrine, while Justice Harlan concurred in a part of the Stewart opinion other than that in which the "inadvertent discovery" limitation is set out. In Texas v. Brown, 460 U.S. 730, 103 S.Ct. 1535, 75 L.Ed.2d 502 (1983), four members of the Court stated that because "the *Coolidge* plurality's discussion of 'plain view' * * * has never been expressly adopted by a majority of this Court," it was "not a binding precedent" but "should obviously be the point of reference for further discussion of the issue." Two other members of the Court saw "no reason at this late date to imply criticism of [*Coolidge*'s] articulation of this exception" because it "has been accepted generally for over a decade." The remaining three Justices, without addressing this point, cited *Coolidge* as a precedent on the plain view doctrine.

50. Hoffa v. United States, 385 U.S. 293, 87 S.Ct. 408, 17 L.Ed.2d 374 (1966).

sult from the fact that the police, from an abundance of caution or out of a misapprehension of what it takes to obtain a warrant covering certain evidence, failed to demonstrate to the magistrate the maximum intrusion which they were then constitutionally entitled to make. Such considerations doubtless influenced the Court to hold in *Horton v. California*[51] that inadvertence "is not a necessary condition" to a plain view seizure. In *Horton,* the Court indicated its disapproval of Fourth Amendment "standards that depend upon the subjective state of mind of the officer,"[52] and added that adherence to the Fourth Amendment's particularity-of-description requirements "serves the interest in limiting the area and duration of the search that the inadvertence requirement inadequately protects."

(*l*) Miscellaneous Requirements. By statute or court rule, many jurisdictions have imposed requirements upon the execution of search warrants which go beyond those already discussed. One common provision is that an officer executing a warrant must exhibit or deliver a copy of the warrant at the place searched, so that the aggrieved party will know there is color of authority for the search. Another is that the officer must provide a receipt for the things seized in execution of the warrant. Yet another is that a prompt return of an executed warrant, accompanied by an inventory of the things seized, be made to the issuing authority. Under the prevailing view, these provisions are deemed to be ministerial only, so that failure to comply with them does not void an otherwise valid search.

When a failure to leave an inventory serves to conceal from the absent occupant the fact that a search warrant execution occurred there, then the problem is more serious. In striking down a state wiretapping law, the Supreme Court in *Berger v. New York*[53] objected it "has no requirement for notice as do conventional warrants, nor does it overcome this defect by requiring some showing of special facts." (The problem is solved in the federal wiretapping law by the provision that an inventory must be served within 90 days.[54]) The issue has arisen as to the so-called "surreptitious entry" warrant authorizing police to enter and look around during the occupant's absence, as to which the warrant must provide explicitly for notice within a reasonable time subsequent to that entry.

§ 3.5 Seizure and Search of Persons and Personal Effects

(a) Arrest. "To deprive a person of his liberty by legal authority" is the traditional definition of arrest, and for many years courts tended to accept such a definition, so that a mere stopping of a vehicle constituted an illegal arrest if probable cause could be established only by consideration of facts obtained subsequent to the stopping. But this is no longer true in light of *Terry v. Ohio,*[1] which established (i) that a seizure need not be called an arrest in order to subject it to the requirements of the Fourth Amendment; and (ii) that a seizure which is limited in its intrusiveness may be reasonable under the Fourth Amendment even in the absence of the probable cause traditionally required for arrest.

If a person is stopped upon less than probable cause, after which the officer sees incriminating evidence, it must be determined whether this amounts to an illegal arrest at the moment of stopping, as the defendant will claim, or a lawful arrest after observation of the evidence, as the prosecution will contend. Though the fact the officer did not make a formal announcement of arrest is not controlling, it is sometimes said that for police restraint to be an arrest it must have been performed with the intent to effect an arrest and must have been so understood by the party arrested. But, while the prosecution can hardly deny the existence of an arrest in

51. ___ U.S. ___, 110 S.Ct. 2301, 110 L.Ed.2d 112 (1990).

52. As it has on other occasions. See § 3.1(d).

53. 388 U.S. 41, 87 S.Ct. 1873, 18 L.Ed.2d 1040 (1967).

54. 18 U.S.C.A. § 2518(8)(d).

§ 3.5

1. 392 U.S. 1, 88 S.Ct. 1868, 20 L.Ed.2d 889 (1968).

the face of both of these elements, this is not to say that the absence of one or the other always necessitates the conclusion there was yet no arrest. Because making the issue turn upon either the subjective intent of the police officer or the subjective perception of the suspect would mean that the matter would be decided by swearing contests, courts are now inclined to use an objective test. The question is said to be what a reasonable man, innocent of any crime, would have thought had he been in the defendant's shoes. Essentially the same approach is taken when the issue is not whether there was an arrest or some lesser seizure, but instead whether there was an arrest or merely a nonseizure voluntary presence by the defendant.

The question of when an arrest occurred cannot be answered in the abstract, that is, without consideration of why the question is being asked. Courts properly take a somewhat different approach when it is the prosecution which is contending that an arrest was made at a particular time so as to justify a search as incident to that arrest. In this context, "the prosecution must be able to date the arrest as *early* as it chooses following the obtaining of probable cause,"[2] for given grounds for arrest and some degree of seizure which ripened into an arrest thereafter, the search should not be brought into question by speculation about the precise point at which the arrest occurred.

At common law, a peace officer was authorized to arrest a person for a felony without first obtaining an arrest warrant whenever he had "reasonable grounds to believe" that a felony had been committed and that the person to be arrested had committed it (i.e., what now constitutes Fourth Amendment probable cause). Under this approach, followed today by most jurisdictions, an arrest warrant is not required in a felony case even if it was feasible to obtain one. But it was not until *United States v. Watson,*[3] "the first square holding that the Fourth Amendment permits a duly authorized law enforcement officer to make a warrantless arrest in a public place[4] even though he had adequate opportunity to procure a warrant after developing probable cause for arrest,"[5] that the constitutionality of this rule was settled. The Court in *Watson* commenced with the proposition that a "strong presumption of constitutionality" was due the statute authorizing such arrests, and then concluded the presumption was not overcome in light of the fact that the statute was consistent with "the Court's prior cases," "the ancient common-law rule," and "the prevailing rule under state constitutions and statutes." The Court declined to transform its oft-stated preference for arrest warrants "into a constitutional rule" and thereby "encumber litigation with respect to the existence of exigent circumstances, whether it was practicable to get a warrant, whether the suspect was about to flee, and the like." The *Watson* majority failed to examine the issue stated by the dissenters, "whether the privacy of our citizens will be better protected by ordinarily requiring a warrant to be issued before they may be arrested." Had they done so, they could have responded that a greatly expanded warrant system might well turn the warrant process into a mechanical routine without meaningful protection.

The common law rule with respect to misdemeanors was quite different; a warrant was required except when a breach of the peace occurred in the presence of the arresting officer. Most jurisdictions now follow a broader rule, usually that arrest without warrant is proper for *any* misdemeanor occurring in the officer's presence, sometimes that the felony arrest rule applies also to misdemeanors, and sometimes the middle position that warrantless misdemeanor arrests are permitted on probable cause if certain exigent circumstances are believed to be present. It appears that the Fourth Amendment presents no barrier to abolition of the felony-misdemeanor

2. Sibron v. New York, 392 U.S. 40, 88 S.Ct. 1889, 20 L.Ed.2d 917 (1968) (Harlan, J., concurring).

3. 423 U.S. 411, 96 S.Ct. 820, 46 L.Ed.2d 598 (1976).

4. A warrant is ordinarily required to enter private premises to arrest; see § 3.6(a).

5. As correctly characterized by Powell, J., concurring.

distinction so as to permit warrantless arrests on probable cause in all cases.

As for the meaning of the "in presence" test, it certainly includes those instances in which the officer views the offense, even when done with binoculars or when instruments (e.g., a radar speed measuring device) must be utilized to make a judgment about what has been seen. An officer may utilize all of his senses in determining whether a misdemeanor is occurring, and thus he will sometimes detect the crime by hearing, smell or touch. But it is not enough that the officer relied only upon his own senses in determining that the misdemeanor occurred; the offense must occur in the officer's presence. Thus, an in presence arrest may not be made for the misdemeanor of driving under the influence when a policeman comes upon the scene of an accident and is told by an obviously intoxicated person that he had been driving the vehicle. (This illustrates why the "in presence" requirement is an unsatisfactory limitation upon the power of the police to make warrantless arrests.) Though the "in presence" rule might be construed as requiring that the misdemeanor *in fact* have occurred in the officer's presence, the modern view is that the officer may arrest if he has probable cause to believe the offense is being committed in his presence. This is sound, for it provides a workable standard (based on how the situation is reasonably perceived at the time, rather than how it turned out) for judging police conduct, and makes it apparent that the officer's senses need not directly detect the misdemeanor so long as they reveal facts providing the reasonable belief that the offense is *now* occurring.

On the question of whether the lawfulness of a warrantless arrest is affected by the way it is characterized by the police at the time of arrest or subsequent booking, it has sometimes been held that an arrest "for investigation" or "on suspicion" of a certain crime is unlawful. Those cases are in error; especially because such designations are often utilized to indicate that the situation requires special attention, such as evaluation by detectives or by the prosecutor's office, the lawfulness of the arrests should be determined upon the basis of the facts at hand when they were made and not because of the characterization employed. What then if the arrest was made for one offense but the prosecution later, conceding grounds to arrest for that crime were lacking, tries to justify the arrest as being for another offense? Because of concern about post hoc manipulation of the facts by the police in order to give an unlawful arrest the appearance of legality, some contend that the arrest should be judged exclusively in terms of the offense entered at the time of booking. That view has not prevailed. Some courts take the position that the booking entry is irrelevant to the determination of the lawfulness of the arrest, some that booking for another offense will not invalidate the arrest if there was no bad faith on the part of the police, and some others that there must be a nexus between the crime specified at booking and the offense now relied upon to uphold the arrest.

Though under *Watson* an officer may arrest without first obtaining a warrant, the Court in *Gerstein v. Pugh*[6] decided that the officer's probable cause assessment justified only the arrest and "a brief period of detention to take the administrative steps incident to arrest." At that point, "the reasons that justify dispensing with the magistrate's neutral judgment evaporate," as there is "no longer any danger that the suspect will escape or commit further crimes while the police submit their evidence to a magistrate." Consequently, the Court held in *Gerstein,* "the Fourth Amendment requires a judicial determination of probable cause as a prerequisite to extended restraint on liberty following arrest." This post-arrest probable cause showing, the Court added, may be made "without an adversary hearing" because the standard "is the same as that for arrest," which "traditionally has been decided by a magistrate in a nonadversary proceeding on hearsay and written testimony." This means the required procedure here is essentially like that utilized to obtain an

6. 420 U.S. 103, 95 S.Ct. 854, 43 L.Ed.2d 54 (1975).

arrest warrant; the magistrate must be given the underlying facts rather than mere conclusions, and a complaint merely reciting the charge in the language of the statute will not suffice. *Gerstein* says the determination is to be made "promptly after arrest," but left the states with the "flexibility" to incorporate the requisite post-arrest probable cause determination into other pretrial procedures (e.g., defendant's first appearance in court). Taking both interests into account, the Court later concluded in *County of Riverside v. McLaughlin* [7]: (1) that a probable cause determination within 48 hours of arrest is presumptively reasonable, though a particular defendant may show such a delay was unreasonable because "for the purpose of gathering additional evidence to justify the arrest, a delay motivated by ill will against the arrested individual, or delay for delay's sake"; and (2) that a later probable cause determination is presumptively unreasonable, meaning "the burden shifts to the government to demonstrate the existence of a bona fide emergency or other extraordinary circumstance" (i.e., something more than an intervening weekend or a desire to consolidate the probable cause determination with other pretrial proceedings). As for which defendants arrested without a warrant are entitled to a post-arrest probable cause determination, *Gerstein* clearly applies to a defendant held in jail because of an inability to obtain his release on bail. The Court stressed that "pretrial release may be accompanied by burdensome conditions that effect a significant restraint on liberty," citing statutory provisions permitting imposition of restrictions on travel and place of abode and release only during the daytime, justifying the conclusion that a probable cause determination is required when release is accompanied by restraints of that magnitude. The Court did not refer to other bail provisions concerning release on financial conditions, and thus it appears the protections of *Gerstein* do not extend to a defendant who has been able to gain release by posting bail. But it would often seem unfair and impractical (and, indeed, presumptively unreasonable under *McLaughlin*) to defer the probable cause determination until after it is learned whether the defendant was able to "pay his way" out of jail.

The requirement of the Fourth Amendment that no warrant shall issue, but upon probable cause, supported by oath or affirmation and particularly describing the person or things to be seized, applies to arrest warrants as well as search warrants, and thus much of what has been said earlier with respect to the issuance of search warrants [8] applies to the obtaining of arrest warrants. For one thing, the warrant must be issued by a "neutral and detached magistrate." [9] This is not to say that the authority to issue arrest warrants must "reside exclusively in a lawyer or judge, for a court clerk may constitutionally be given that power if he works within the judicial branch under the supervision of a judge and, though not law-trained, is capable of making the kinds of probable cause judgments needed in the category of cases which may come before him.[10] For another, the warrant may issue only upon probable cause, and this requires a sworn complaint or testimony setting out the underlying facts and circumstances.[11] A conclusory information sworn to by the prosecutor will not suffice,[12] but an indictment "fair on its face" returned by a "properly constituted grand jury" conclusively determines the existence of probable cause and requires issuance of an arrest warrant without further inquiry.[13] Also, to meet the Fourth Amendment particularity requirement an arrest warrant must name the person to be arrested or give other facts which permit his identification with reasonable certainty. An arrest made pursuant to a war-

7. ___ U.S. ___, 111 S.Ct. 1661, 114 L.Ed.2d 49 (1991).

8. See § 3.4.

9. Giordenello v. United States, 357 U.S. 480, 78 S.Ct. 1245, 2 L.Ed.2d 1503 (1958).

10. Shadwick v. City of Tampa, 407 U.S. 345, 92 S.Ct. 2119, 32 L.Ed.2d 783 (1972).

11. Whiteley v. Warden, 401 U.S. 560, 91 S.Ct. 1031, 28 L.Ed.2d 306 (1971).

12. Albrecht v. United States, 273 U.S. 1, 47 S.Ct. 250, 71 L.Ed. 505 (1927).

13. Ex parte United States, 287 U.S. 241, 287 S.Ct. 129, 77 L.Ed. 283 (1932), which the Court in *Gerstein* emphasized was still valid.

rant is not inevitably valid. As the Supreme Court has explained, while an officer is "entitled to assume" that the warrant was issued upon "the information requisite to support an independent judicial assessment of probable cause," if it turns out that this was not the case or that the arrest warrant was invalid in some other respect, the arrest cannot be upheld on the basis of the warrant.[14] Arrest of the wrong person under the warrant does not render the arrest unlawful if the officer acted in good faith and had reasonable, articulable grounds to believe that the suspect is the intended arrestee.

Over the years, the prevailing assumption in most jurisdictions has been that, except for minor traffic violations, arrest is the normal way by which to invoke the criminal process. This state of affairs has rightly been criticized, and various recent law reform efforts have stressed the need for broader use of the citation alternative. As for the notion that the Fourth Amendment's reasonableness requirement is met only when probable cause is present *and* an actual need for custody exists, some holdings to this effect are to be found outside the criminal procedure field and a few criminal procedure cases may be read as lending some support to that proposition. Yet, the current view is that where grounds exist to believe a person has committed a crime, the public interest in law enforcement is assumed to outweigh the individual's interest in liberty and to justify an arrest of that person.

But *Watson,* the Court later cautioned in *Tennessee v. Garner,*[15] should not be read as meaning that if the probable cause "requirement is satisfied the Fourth Amendment has nothing to say about *how* that seizure is made." Thus, the Court in *Garner* held that "use of deadly force to prevent the escape of all felony suspects, whatever the circumstances, is constitutionally unreasonable," and then explained:

> Where the officer has probable cause to believe that the suspect poses a threat of serious physical harm, either to the officer or to others, it is not constitutionally unreasonable to prevent escape by using deadly force. Thus, if the suspect threatens the officer with a weapon or there is probable cause to believe that he has committed a crime involving the infliction or threatened infliction of serious physical harm, deadly force may be used if necessary to prevent escape, and if, where feasible, some warning has been given.[16]

The Fourth Amendment reasonableness standard, the Court later elaborated, (1) applies to "*all* claims that law enforcement officers have used excessive force—deadly or not—in the course of an arrest, investigatory stop, or other 'seizure' of a free citizen"; (2) "requires careful attention to the facts and circumstances of each particular case, including the severity of the crime at issue, whether the suspect poses an immediate threat to the safety of the officers or others, and whether he is actively resisting arrest or attempting to evade arrest by flight"; (3) "must embody allowance for the fact that police officers are often forced to make split-second judgments—in circumstances that are tense, uncertain, and rapidly evolving—about the amount of force that is necessary in a particular situation"; and (4) asks "whether the officers' actions are 'objectively reasonable' in light of the facts and circumstances confronting them, without regard to their underlying intent or motivation." [17]

(b) Search of the Person at Scene of Prior Arrest. In *Chimel v. California* [18] the Court declared that when an arrest is made "it is reasonable for the arresting officer to search the person arrested in order to remove any weapons that the latter might seek to use

14. Whiteley v. Warden, 401 U.S. 560, 91 S.Ct. 1031, 28 L.Ed.2d 306 (1971).

However, an officer's belief in the validity of the warrant will ordinarily suffice under the *Leon* "good faith" exception to the exclusionary rule, discussed in § 3.1(c).

15. 471 U.S. 1, 105 S.Ct. 1694, 85 L.Ed.2d 1 (1985).

16. The three dissenters objected: "A proper balancing of the interests involved suggests that use of deadly force as a last resort to apprehend a criminal suspect fleeing from the scene of a nighttime burglary is not unreasonable within the meaning of the Fourth Amendment."

17. Graham v. Connor, 490 U.S. 386, 109 S.Ct. 1865, 104 L.Ed.2d 443 (1989).

18. 395 U.S. 752, 89 S.Ct. 2034, 23 L.Ed.2d 685 (1969).

in order to resist arrest or effect his escape" and also "to search for and seize any evidence on the arrestee's person in order to prevent its concealment or destruction." This language highlighted a very significant issue which the Court did not have to resolve on that occasion: whether, on the one hand, the right to make such searches of the person flows automatically from the fact a lawful arrest was made, or whether, on the other, such searches may be undertaken only when the facts of the individual case indicate some likelihood that either evidence or weapons will be found. Lower courts were divided on the issue until the Supreme Court, in *United States v. Robinson* [19] and the companion case of *Gustafson v. Florida,*[20] held that the broader view was consistent with the protections of the Fourth Amendment. In *Robinson,* where heroin had been found in a cigarette package in defendant's pocket following his arrest for driving after revocation of his license, the court of appeals held the search to be unreasonable because there was no evidence to search for, given the nature of the offense, and because the officer's interest in self-protection could have been met by only a frisk of the arrestee. But the Supreme Court, noting its "fundamental disagreement" with the court of appeals' "suggestion that there must be litigated in each case the issue of whether or not there was present one of the reasons supporting the authority for a search of the person incident to a lawful arrest," concluded:

> A police officer's determination as to how and where to search the person of a suspect whom he has arrested is necessarily a quick ad hoc judgment which the Fourth Amendment does not require to be broken down in each instance into an analysis of each step in the search. The authority to search the person incident to a lawful custodial arrest, while based upon the need to disarm and to discover evidence, does not depend on what a court may later decide was the probability in a particular arrest situation that weapons or evidence would in fact be found upon the person of the suspect. A custodial arrest of a suspect based on probable cause is a reasonable intrusion under the Fourth Amendment; that intrusion being lawful, a search incident to the arrest requires no additional justification. It is the fact of the lawful arrest which establishes the authority to search, and we hold that in the case of a lawful custodial arrest a full search of the person is not only an exception to the warrant requirement of the Fourth Amendment, but is also a "reasonable" search under that Amendment.

The majority in *Robinson* justified this result by claiming that the prior decisions of the Court and also the "original understanding" of the Fourth Amendment established that the "general authority" to search a person incident to arrest is "unqualified." Though a close examination of those sources justifies the conclusion that they are hardly unequivocal in this respect, there is much to be said for the *Robinson* holding. Standardized procedures to be applied in all cases regardless of particular factual variations are sometimes to be preferred over a case-by-case determination approach, especially as to those forms of police action which involve relatively minor intrusions into privacy, occur with great frequency, and virtually defy on-the-spot rationalization on the basis of the unique facts of the individual case. Search of an arrested person is precisely that kind of police activity, for: (1) search incident to arrest is the most common variety of police search practice and occurs under an infinite variety of circumstances; (2) though the police would have already determined there was probable cause to arrest, it does not necessarily follow that there is also probable cause the arrestee *presently* has evidence of that crime with him or *presently* is armed, and the latter are much more complex and difficult determinations; (3) the decision to search an arrestee's person cannot be made with the degree of forethought and reflection possible for most other search decisions, as the circumstances arise from the arrest itself, which is often unanticipated, and the fact of arrest produces an immediate need to search if the self-protective and evidence-saving functions are to be real-

19. 414 U.S. 218, 94 S.Ct. 467, 38 L.Ed.2d 427 (1973).

20. 414 U.S. 260, 94 S.Ct. 488, 38 L.Ed.2d 456 (1973).

ized; (4) search of a person is a relatively minor intrusion upon a person who, by hypothesis, has already been subjected to the more serious step of arrest. Finally, the frisk alternative put forward by the court of appeals would not suffice to accomplish the self-protection objective. It is sufficient in a *Terry v. Ohio* [21] type of situation in which there is a brief on-the-street face-to-face encounter in which the officer can observe the suspect's every move, but would not be certain to uncover more carefully concealed weapons to which the arrestee would have access during his subsequent transportation to the station and further detention thereafter.

Yet, there is reason for concern about the application of this "general authority" to search in cases involving traffic violations. "There is," as the *Robinson* dissenters put it, "always the possibility that a police officer, lacking probable cause to obtain a search warrant, will use a traffic arrest as a pretext to conduct a search." What avenues are open to deal with the pretext arrest problem, which the *Robinson* majority preferred to "leave for another day"? The most obvious is to meet it head on by excluding evidence obtained in a search incident to a traffic arrest upon a showing that the arrest was nothing more than a pretext to search for evidence. But, while some defendants have prevailed on this basis, this is not an adequate remedy for the simple reason that trial courts cannot be expected to determine with any fair rate of accuracy the uncommunicated intentions or expectations of the police. In *Robinson,* for example, it appears that the arresting officer was aware of defendant's prior narcotics convictions, but in face of the officer's expected denial that the traffic arrest was a pretext to search for narcotics, it is impossible to reach any firm conclusion on the pretext issue. Another way of dealing with the problem might be to remove the temptation to engage in pretext arrests by broadening the exclusionary rule so as to exclude from evidence anything but a weapon found in a search incident to an arrest for a crime, such as a traffic violation, for which there existed no justification to search for anything but a weapon. However, the Supreme Court has not indicated it is receptive to such an extension of the exclusionary rule. Yet another possibility, inasmuch as *Robinson* declares what may be done incident to a "custodial arrest," (i.e., a seizure of the person with the intention of thereafter having him transported to the police station or other place to be dealt with according to law), would be to require that there be established by legislation or police regulation some rational scheme for determining when a noncustodial alternative (i.e., a citation) should be utilized as the means for invoking the criminal process.[22] Unfortunately, the Court failed to take note of this possibility, by which it could have distinguished *Robinson,* where the officer was acting pursuant to detailed police regulations which required him to arrest for that kind of traffic offense and required a mere violation notice for most others, and *Gustafson,* where there was no such regulation and the officer was apparently free to arrest or ticket at his complete discretion. Perhaps this is attributable, as Justice Stewart suggests in his *Gustafson* concurring opinion, to the fact that the petitioner there "fully conceded the constitutional validity of his custodial arrest," so that there remains to be resolved what Stewart characterized as the "persuasive claim * * * that the custodial arrest of the petitioner for a minor traffic violation violated his rights under the Fourth and Fourteenth Amendments."

Though the Supreme Court in *Robinson* stated it was not reaching the other issue considered by the court of appeals, which was what the officer could do in the absence of a "custodial arrest," the Court's emphasis upon the fact "that the danger to an officer is far greater in the case of the extended exposure which follows the taking of a suspect into custody and transporting him to the police station than in the case of the relatively fleet-

21. 392 U.S. 1, 88 S.Ct. 1868, 20 L.Ed.2d 889 (1968).

22. For more on whether the Fourth Amendment reasonableness requirement should be interpreted to require attention to the need-for-custody issue, see § 12.5.

ing contact resulting from the typical *Terry*-type stop" strongly suggests agreement with the court of appeals disposition. That is, in such a case only a patdown for weapons is permissible, provided the officer has reasonable grounds to believe that the person with whom he is dealing may be armed and presently dangerous. This is not to say, however, that the officer may do nothing else in the interest of his own protection. In *Pennsylvania v. Mimms,*[23] the Court held that a driver stopped for ticketing may be ordered out of his car without the officer showing any particular grounds for believing he was in danger, as "this additional intrusion can only be described as de minimus."

Police sometimes find it necessary to employ force in conducting a search of a person at the arrest scene. Such force cannot be used as a matter of course as a part of the previously discussed "standardized procedures," and thus it is necessary at the outset that the officer act on probable cause to believe that specific evidence is being disposed of. If that is the case, then the police may use reasonable force to prevent loss of the evidence. The problem usually arises when the arrestee attempts to swallow evidence, as to which the police may properly respond by forcing open his mouth or choking him to the extent necessary to prevent swallowing of the evidence.

Finally, it is important to distinguish a *search* of the person from *seizure* of the objects found. Even though under *Robinson* the search may be undertaken following a lawful custodial arrest as a matter of routine and without particular grounds, what is found may be seized and retained by the police only if they have probable cause that the object is a fruit, instrumentality or evidence of crime. If the rule were otherwise, an officer who desired to inculpate an arrested person in another crime could seize everything in that person's immediate possession upon the prospect that on further investigation some of it might prove to have been stolen or to be contraband.

(c) Search of the Person During Post-Arrest Detention. When an arrested person has been delivered to the place of his forthcoming detention, he may be subjected to a rather complete search of his person. One ground upon which such searches are commonly upheld is as a search incident to arrest under the previously discussed *Robinson* case. In *United States v. Edwards*[24] the Court held "that searches and seizures that could be made on the spot at the time of arrest may legally be conducted later when the accused arrives at the place of detention." If the search is based upon *Robinson,* then, as already noted, no probable cause is needed to justify the search except that which establishes grounds for the preceding arrest.

A second theoretical justification for search of an arrestee's person upon his arrival at the station is that of inventory incident to his booking into jail. This inventory, which is a search for Fourth Amendment purposes, has been rather consistently upheld by the courts as meeting these legitimate objectives: (1) protecting the arrestee's property while he is in jail; (2) protecting the police from groundless claims that they have not adequately safeguarded the defendant's property; (3) safeguarding the detention facility by preventing introduction therein of weapons or contraband; and (4) ascertaining or verifying the identity of the person arrested. That view has been taken by the Supreme Court where "standardized inventory procedures" have been followed, even if the contents of containers such as a purse are examined in the process.[25] In those few jurisdictions

23. 434 U.S. 106, 98 S.Ct. 330, 54 L.Ed.2d 331 (1977).

24. 415 U.S. 800, 94 S.Ct. 1234, 39 L.Ed.2d 771 (1974).

25. Illinois v. Lafayette, 462 U.S. 640, 103 S.Ct. 2605, 77 L.Ed.2d 65 (1983), where a unanimous Court rejected the claim that the interests stated above could be sufficiently served by merely sealing the purse within a bag or box and putting it in a secured locker. The Court declared it was "hardly in a position to second-guess police departments as to what practical administrative method will best deter theft by and false claims against its employees and preserve the security of the stationhouse. It is evident that a stationhouse search of every item carried on or by a person who has lawfully been taken into custody by the police will amply serve the important and legitimate governmental interests involved.

which have adopted a search-incident-to-arrest rule narrower than *Robinson,* the extent of legitimate inventory activity is likely to be litigated and on occasion results in a decision imposing limits grounded in state law upon that conduct, such as that the inventory may not extend to closed containers.

Assuming a lawful search upon defendant's arrival at the station, there remains the question of what may be seized. There is authority that here as with search at the arrest scene, objects may be seized only upon probable cause that they constitute evidence, instrumentalities or fruits of crime, while another view is that after a person has been deprived of the possession of his property upon being incarcerated, he may not thereafter complain if police have his property examined. The latter position makes sense only if an arrestee has no privacy interest in the effects being held for him, an issue which is raised more directly by considering whether the arrestee and his effects remain legitimate targets of search during the entire period of custody.

An issue of that kind reached the Supreme Court in *United States v. Edwards,*[26] where defendant was arrested and jailed for attempting to break into a post office and then, a day later, his clothing was taken from him to determine whether it contained paint chips from the window the burglar had tried to pry open. The Court upheld this warrantless search, reasoning "that Edwards was no more imposed upon than he could have been at the time and place of the arrest or immediately upon arrival at the place of detention," and that "it is difficult to perceive what is unreasonable about the police examining and holding as evidence those personal effects of the accused that they already have in their lawful custody as the result of a lawful arrest." In trying to identify the scope of the *Edwards* holding, it is useful to note at the outset that the broad issue of whether an arrestee's person and effects remain "fair game" for search during his incarceration can be broken down into two inquiries: whether a warrant is required; and whether probable cause the search will produce evidence is required. In *Edwards* the Court focused on the warrant issue and concluded no warrant was needed, hardly a surprising result because, though there were no exigent circumstances, the clothing was clearly evidence of the crime and was in plain view at the time of seizure. But the Court says that the result would be the same had the police seized evidence then "held under the defendant's name in the 'property room' of the jail," and thus it may fairly be concluded that *Edwards* means at least that no warrant is needed when (i) an object lawfully came into police view at the time of a search upon the arrestee's arrival at the place of detention, (ii) later investigation established that this item is of evidentiary value, and (iii) the item remains in police custody as a part of the arrestee's inventoried property.

In contrast to that situation, which might be characterized as a second look-probable cause type of case, is that in which what is involved is a search into the arrestee's effects to discover that which was not found in the booking inventory. Illustrative is *Brett v. United States,*[27] where defendant's clothes, then stored in the property room of the police department, were searched three days after booking and found to contain heroin. The court concluded this was an illegal search because even if there was probable cause there was no basis for proceeding without a warrant; this was not a "plain view" case, there was "ample opportunity" to get a warrant, and the fact "the police have custody of a prisoner's property for the purpose of protecting it while he is incarcerated does not alone constitute a basis for an exception to the requirement of a search warrant." The contrary and prevailing view is that no warrant is required in such a case because the

"Even if less intrusive means existed of protecting some particular types of property, it would be unreasonable to expect police officers in the everyday course of business to make fine and subtle distinctions in deciding which containers or items may be searched and which must be sealed as a unit."

26. 415 U.S. 800, 94 S.Ct. 1234, 39 L.Ed.2d 771 (1974).

27. 412 F.2d 401 (5th Cir.1969).

warrant process is intended to determine whether probable cause exists, and thus is unnecessary because these searches may be made without probable cause. In the language of the *Edwards* majority, the police may do during the entire period of incarceration what "they were entitled to do incident to the usual custodial arrest and incarceration." It is not correct to say, however, that *Edwards* has settled this point, for the Court there cautioned that such warrantless searches must still be reasonable and that in the instant case "probable cause existed for the search and seizure of respondent's clothing." Thus, it may still be argued that a "second look," especially for evidence unrelated to the crime for which the arrest was made, which involves a greater degree of scrutiny than was undertaken at the time of arrest or booking, should be permitted only upon probable cause, for to allow police the unlimited authority to scrutinize an arrestee's effects to see if he can be linked with some offense bestows upon the police an undeserved windfall and provides them with a temptation to make subterfuge arrests.

Whatever *Robinson* and *Edwards* mean in other contexts, they have no effect upon the *Schmerber v. California* [28] limits upon the taking of a blood sample or a comparable intrusion into the body. A warrantless search of that kind will be upheld only if (i) the process is "a reasonable one" which is "performed in a reasonable manner," such as that the "blood was taken by a physician in a hospital environment according to accepted medical practices"; (ii) there was in advance "a clear indication that in fact [the evidence sought] will be found"; and (iii) there were exigent circumstances, such as "a need to take the test before the percentage of alcohol in the blood diminishes." Also, some authority is to be found to the effect that so-called "routine" strip searches may not be employed against all classes of arrestees, as the extreme intrusion on one's personal dignity occasioned by such searches requires that some justifiable basis exists.

In assessing any search occurring during post-arrest detention, it is essential to determine not only that the initial arrest was lawful, but also that the custody at the very time of the search was lawful. One possibility is that the evidence found must be suppressed because the custody at that time was unlawful in that, in the interim since the lawful arrest, the police have come upon additional facts now indicating there is *not* probable cause the defendant has committed an offense. Another possibility is that suppression will be ordered because, though the original probable cause persists, the police failed to afford this defendant the usual opportunities for stationhouse release.

(d) Other Search of the Person. Sometimes the police will conduct a warrantless search of a person and find evidence of crime and then place that individual under arrest. Although a search may not both precede an arrest and serve as part of its justification, sometimes a broader rule is asserted, namely, that a warrantless search of the person is unlawful whenever made prior to arrest. But that is not the case; as the Supreme Court concluded in *Rawlings v. Kentucky,*[29] "where the formal arrest followed quickly on the heels of the challenged search of petitioner's person, we do not believe it particularly important that the search preceded the arrest rather than vice versa," so long as the fruits of the search were "not necessary to support probable cause to arrest."

As for searching a person for evidence without any arrest at all, the Court confronted this issue in *Cupp v. Murphy,*[30] where defendant voluntarily appeared at the station in connection with the strangulation murder of his wife, police asked him to submit scrapings from under his fingernails when they saw what appeared to be dried blood on his finger, and when he refused the police proceeded to take the scrapings without a warrant. The

28. 384 U.S. 757, 86 S.Ct. 1826, 16 L.Ed.2d 908 (1966). On the Fifth Amendment aspects of *Schmerber,* see § 8.12(d).

29. 448 U.S. 98, 100 S.Ct. 2556, 65 L.Ed.2d 633 (1980).

30. 412 U.S. 291, 93 S.Ct. 2000, 36 L.Ed.2d 900 (1973).

Court, though stressing it was not holding "that a full *Chimel* search would have been justified in this case," concluded that in light of the circumstances (including that Murphy began rubbing his fingers together when he ascertained the police believed there was evidence on them), the police were justified "in subjecting him to the very limited search necessary to preserve the highly evanescent evidence they found under his fingernails." At a minimum, therefore, *Cupp* establishes that (i) if there is probable cause for arrest but no arrest, and (ii) if the suspect is reasonably believed to be in the actual process of destroying "highly evanescent evidence," then (iii) that evidence may be preserved if this can be accomplished by a search which is "very limited" as compared to a full search of the person. Many lower court cases, however, support a broader but sound rule: a warrantless search is proper if the officer had probable cause to believe that a crime had been committed and probable cause to believe that evidence of the crime would be found and that an immediate, warrantless search was necessary in order to prevent the destruction or loss of evidence. This means, for example, that when a person reasonably believed to have been driving under the influence is taken to a hospital for treatment instead of arrested, a warrantless taking of a blood sample to determine alcohol content would be proper in the same way as if that person had been arrested.

(e) Seizure and Search of Containers and Other Personal Effects. If the police lawfully arrest a person, may they then [31] search containers and other personal effects belonging to that individual on the ground that this is a legitimate search incident to arrest? The teaching of *Chimel v. California* [32] is that, at a minimum, the arrestee's effects may be examined on a search-incident-to-arrest theory only if they can be said to be " 'within his immediate control'—construing that phrase to mean the area from within which he might gain possession of a weapon or destructible evidence." At least until recently, courts were inclined to uphold searches of effects as searches incident to arrest without close attention to whether in the particular case the police restraints upon the arrestee or the nature of the fastening devices on the container were such that there was no realistic opportunity for the arrestee to gain access to the *interior* of that container, which would seem to be the issue posed by *Chimel.* It was as if the carried container was an extension of the person and thus subject to search under *United States v. Robinson* [33] without any showing of justification based upon the facts of the individual case, and likewise subject to search under *United States v. Edwards* [34] even after it had been taken from the arrestee.

But the Court's later decision in *United States v. Chadwick* [35] indicated the search-incident-to-arrest theory was much more limited than customarily assumed. There, the defendants were arrested while standing next to an open auto trunk into which they had just placed a double-locked footlocker the agents believed contained marijuana; the defendants, the car and the footlocker were all taken to the federal building, where the agents unlocked and searched the locker without a warrant. The Court held this was not a lawful search incident to arrest, as "once law enforcement officers have reduced luggage or other personal property not immediately associated with the person of the arrestee to their exclusive control, and there is no longer any danger that the arrestee might gain access to the property to seize a weapon or destroy evidence, a search of that property is no longer an incident of the arrest." Though the reach of *Chadwick* was somewhat unclear because the Court did not say whether the result would be different had the police *immediately* searched the footlocker, the case ap-

31. A search of a container cannot be justified as incident to arrest if the probable cause for the contemporaneous arrest was provided by the fruits of that search. Smith v. Ohio, 494 U.S. 541, 110 S.Ct. 1288, 108 L.Ed.2d 464 (1990).

32. 395 U.S. 752, 89 S.Ct. 2034, 23 L.Ed.2d 685 (1969).

33. 414 U.S. 218, 94 S.Ct. 467, 38 L.Ed.2d 427 (1973).

34. 415 U.S. 800, 94 S.Ct. 1234, 39 L.Ed.2d 771 (1974).

35. 433 U.S. 1, 97 S.Ct. 2476, 53 L.Ed.2d 538 (1977).

peared to have this effect: (i) the right to routinely search incident to arrest without showing any need in the particular case, recognized as to search of the person in *United States v. Robinson,*[36] also extends to containers on the person such as a wallet and containers such as a purse which are "immediately associated" with the person; (ii) in all other instances probable cause and (absent true exigent circumstances) a search warrant are needed whenever the police have—or, could have—taken exclusive control of the container, even if the container was in the arrestee's control at the moment of arrest.

But the vitality of the second half of that equation is to be doubted in light of the Court's more recent analysis in *New York v. Belton.*[37] The Court there adopted the general rule that incident to the arrest of a passenger in a car the passenger compartment of the vehicle (including containers found therein) may be searched as a matter of routine. Because the Court had earlier held that the Fourth Amendment protection of a container is the same whether it is within or without a vehicle,[38] and because the assertion in *Belton* of a need for a "bright line" on what constitutes "immediate control" seems equally applicable to containers not found in cars, the likely consequence of *Belton* is a comparably broad search-of-container-incident-to-arrest rule. This would mean that a container in the arrestee's possession may be searched incident to arrest if the search is contemporaneous with the arrest, without regard to any of the following: (i) whether on the facts of the particular case there was a likelihood the arrestee could get into the container; (ii) whether the police had already subjected the container to their exclusive control; and (iii) whether there was a likelihood that a weapon or evidence of the crime for which the arrest was made would be found. The criticisms which may be directed to the *Belton* rule[39] are equally applicable to the above rule.

A second possible basis upon which to justify a search into containers possessed by an arrestee is the need to inventory them incident to the arrestee's booking and post-arrest detention. There is authority that whenever the defendant's suitcase or some similar container was properly impounded by the police at the time of his arrest (or otherwise lawfully came into the custody of the police), an item-by-item inventory of its contents at the station is permissible both to preserve the property of the accused and to forestall the possibility that the accused may later claim that some item has not been returned to him. That view was adopted by the Supreme Court unanimously in *Illinois v. Lafayette,*[40] permitting "a stationhouse search of every item carried on or by a person who has lawfully been taken into custody by the police" if done pursuant to "standardized inventory procedures," because it "will amply serve the important and legitimate governmental interests involved." As for the position theretofore taken by a minority of courts that it would suffice if the container was merely sealed and secured without examination of the contents, the Court rejected this on the grounds that it could not "second-guess police departments as to what practical administrative method will best deter theft by and false claims against its employees and preserve the security of the stationhouse," and that "it would be unreasonable to expect police officers in the everyday course of business to make fine and subtle distinctions in deciding which containers or items may be searched and which must be sealed as a unit."

Another potential basis for upholding warrantless search of personal effects is that the search in question was made (i) upon probable cause to believe that the effects contained evidence of crime and (ii) when it would not have been practicable to obtain a search warrant first because of certain exigent circumstances. The significant issue here is precisely what constitutes exigent circumstances in

36. 414 U.S. 218, 94 S.Ct. 467, 38 L.Ed.2d 427 (1973).

37. 453 U.S. 454, 101 S.Ct. 2860, 69 L.Ed.2d 768 (1981).

38. Arkansas v. Sanders, 442 U.S. 753, 99 S.Ct. 2586, 61 L.Ed.2d 235 (1979).

39. See § 3.7(a).

40. 462 U.S. 640, 103 S.Ct. 2605, 77 L.Ed.2d 65 (1983).

this context. At one time, courts were inclined to permit warrantless searches of containers by analogy to the rules governing vehicle searches,[41] especially the ruling in *Chambers v. Maroney*[42] that "for constitutional purposes" there was no difference between seizing the item to be searched and holding it while a warrant is obtained, and simply proceeding to make an immediate warrantless search. This meant that if the circumstances were sufficiently exigent as to justify a warrantless seizure of a container, it somehow followed that an immediate warrantless search was also permissible. But that conclusion was rejected by the Supreme Court in the previously described *Chadwick* case, where it was reasoned that because "a person's expectations of privacy in personal luggage are substantially greater than in an automobile," the rule for automobiles could not be extended to such containers; rather, when the circumstances are sufficiently exigent to allow the police to make a warrantless seizure of the luggage, this does not permit the "far greater intrusion" of examining the contents thereof but only the continued possession of the container while a warrant is sought. Any thought that these "substantially greater" expectations derived from the special steps taken by the defendant in *Chadwick,* who was transporting a double-locked footlocker, was dissipated by *Arkansas v. Sanders,*[43] holding that *Chadwick* also applied to a "small, unlocked suitcase" because "respondent's failure to lock his suitcase [did not] alter its fundamental character as a repository for personal, private effects." This means a search warrant is needed to search containers absent true exigent circumstances, such as that the object contained evidence which would lose its value unless the container were opened at once or that immediate search would facilitate the apprehension of confederates or the termination of continuing criminal activity. To this must be added the following caveat from *Sanders:*

> Not all containers and packages found by police * * * will deserve the full protection of the Fourth Amendment. Thus, some containers (for example a kit of burglar tools or a gun case) by their very nature cannot support any reasonable expectation of privacy because their contents can be inferred from their outward appearance. Similarly, in some cases the contents of a package will be open to "plain view," thereby obviating the need for a warrant.[44]

The holding in *Sanders,* that a search warrant is needed even when the container is located within a vehicle, was later overruled in *California v. Acevedo.*[45] But because *Acevedo* is grounded primarily in a perceived need for "one clear-cut rule to govern automobile searches," whether the requisite probable cause extends to the automobile generally or only to a specific container therein,[46] that decision does not eliminate the warrant requirement for search of containers *not* found in vehicles. However, it will doubtless be argued by some that *Acevedo* should be extended to the latter situation as well, for (as the concurring opinion in that case put it) "it is anomalous for a briefcase to be protected by the 'general requirement' of a prior warrant when it is being carried along the street, but

41. See § 3.7(b).

42. 399 U.S. 42, 90 S.Ct. 1975, 26 L.Ed.2d 419 (1970).

43. 442 U.S. 753, 99 S.Ct. 2586, 61 L.Ed.2d 235 (1979).

44. In Texas v. Brown, 460 U.S. 730, 103 S.Ct. 1535, 75 L.Ed.2d 502 (1983), involving the warrantless seizure and search of a tied-up balloon seen in a car under circumstances strongly suggesting it contained drugs, three concurring Justices said the warrantless search of the balloon might well be justified on the ground that its contents could be so inferred: "Whereas a suitcase or a paper bag may contain an almost infinite variety of items, a balloon of this kind might be used only to transport drugs. Viewing it where he did could have given the officer a degree of certainty that is equivalent to the plain view of the heroin itself." They later said, as to this exception to *Ross,* that " 'virtual certainty' " is a more meaningful indicator than visibility, as one "might actually see a white powder without realizing that it is heroin, but be virtually certain a balloon contains such a substance in a particular context."

45. ___ U.S. ___, 111 S.Ct. 1982, 114 L.Ed.2d 619 (1991), discussed in § 3.7(c).

46. When there is probable cause as to the vehicle generally, the Court earlier held in United States v. Ross, 456 U.S. 798, 102 S.Ct. 2157, 72 L.Ed.2d 572 (1982), *Sanders* does not govern and thus a valid warrantless automobile search may extend to containers found in the car. See § 3.7(c).

for that same briefcase to become unprotected as soon as it is carried into an automobile."

A variation of sorts on the plain view situation referred to in *Sanders* is the so-called "controlled delivery." When police lawfully see the contents of a container in transit (most likely because it was lawfully opened by customs officials upon its entry into the country or by the suspicious agents of a private domestic courier), they often arrange for it to be delivered under surveillance, after which the recipient is arrested and the container seized and opened. No warrant is needed to justify the opening of the container, the Supreme Court explained in *Illinois v. Andreas*,[47] because this does not amount to a Fourth Amendment search. "No protected privacy interest remains in contraband in a container once government officers lawfully have opened that container and identified its contents as illegal. The simple act of resealing the container to enable the police to make a controlled delivery does not operate to revive or restore the lawfully invaded privacy rights."[48] In *Andreas,* the container (a metal container with a wooden table inside, within which a customs inspector found marijuana) had been out of police view inside defendant's apartment 30 to 45 minutes before he reemerged with it, but the Court concluded that did not require a different result absent "a substantial likelihood that the contents of the container have been changed during the gap in surveillance." Because of the "unusual size of the container, its specialized purpose, and the relatively short break in surveillance," the Court deemed it "substantially unlikely that the respondent removed the table or placed new items inside the container while it was in his apartment."

§ 3.6 Entry and Search of Premises

(a) Basis for Entry to Arrest. *Payton v. New York*[1] holds "that the Fourth Amendment * * * prohibits the police from making a warrantless and non-consensual entry into a suspect's home in order to make a routine felony arrest." The Court first noted it was "a 'basic principle of Fourth Amendment law' that searches and seizures inside a home without a warrant are presumptively unreasonable," while "objects * * * found in a public place may be seized by the police without a warrant." The *Payton* majority then concluded that "this distinction has equal force when the seizure of a person is involved" because "an entry to arrest and an entry to search for and to seize property implicate the same interest in preserving the privacy and the sanctity of the home, and justify the same level of constitutional protection." The Court reasoned that

> any differences in the intrusiveness of entries to search and entries to arrest are merely ones of degree rather than kind. The two intrusions share this fundamental characteristic: the breach of the entrance to an individual's home. The Fourth Amendment protects the individual's privacy in a variety of settings. In none is the zone of privacy more clearly defined than when bounded by the unambiguous physical dimensions of an individual's home—a zone that finds its roots in clear and specific constitutional terms: "The right of the people to be secure in their * * * houses * * * shall not be violated." * * * In terms that apply equally to seizures of property and to seizures of persons, the Fourth Amendment has drawn a firm line at the entrance to the house. Absent exigent circumstances, that threshold may not reasonably be crossed without a warrant.

In response to the contention that "only a search warrant based on probable cause to believe the suspect is at home at a given time can adequately protect the privacy interests at stake," the Court in *Payton* declared:

47. 463 U.S. 765, 103 S.Ct. 3319, 77 L.Ed.2d 1003 (1983).

48. This language was relied upon in United States v. Jacobsen, 466 U.S. 109, 104 S.Ct. 1652, 80 L.Ed.2d 85 (1984), where employees of a shipping company opened a suspicious package and found a white powder and then summoned a federal drug agent, who upon arrival was invited to reopen the then unsealed package and examine the powder. The Court deemed that limited reopening, because it "enabled the agent to learn nothing that had not previously been learned during the private search" and thus "infringed no legitimate expectation of privacy," to constitute no search at all.

§ 3.6

1. 445 U.S. 573, 100 S.Ct. 1371, 63 L.Ed.2d 639 (1980).

> It is true that an arrest warrant requirement may afford less protection than a search warrant requirement, but it will suffice to interpose the magistrate's determination of probable cause between the zealous officer and the citizen. If there is sufficient evidence of a citizen's participation in a felony to persuade a judicial officer that his arrest is justified, it is constitutionally responsible to require him to open his doors to the officers of the law. Thus, for Fourth Amendment purposes, an arrest warrant founded on probable cause implicitly carries with it the limited authority to enter a dwelling in which the suspect lives when there is reason to believe the suspect is within.

This makes sense if there is some reason why it is unnecessary to have a judicial determination of "probable cause to believe the suspect is at home," which would seem to be the case. Though it appears that such probable cause is needed, this requirement would often be an insurmountable barrier if it could be met only by specific facts in the individual case instead of by inference. Because rudimentary police procedure dictates that a suspect's residence be eliminated as a possible hiding place before a search is conducted elsewhere, it is permissible for the police to infer that the defendant is home except when they have "special knowledge" indicating otherwise. That being so, the Court in *Payton* was quite correct in concluding there was no need to involve the magistrate in simply applying that inference.

When the police wish to enter the premises of a third party to make an arrest, it is clear that they must have probable cause to believe that the named suspect is present within at the time. Quite obviously this probable cause can be established only by facts of the particular case rather than by inference, and quite obviously as well this probable cause determination is central to protection of the privacy rights of the third party. This explains why the Supreme Court in *Steagald v. United States*[2] held that a search warrant, based upon a magistrate's determination that it is probable the person to be arrested is now in those premises, is the kind of warrant needed in those circumstances.

In *Payton,* the Court noted it had "no occasion to consider the sort of emergency or dangerous situation, described in our cases as 'exigent circumstances,' that would justify a warrantless entry into a home" to make an arrest. The Court's prior cases have only declared that any possible warrant requirement was obviated when the police were in "hot pursuit" of the offender.[3] Many lower courts utilize the list of "considerations" set out in *Dorman v. United States*[4]: (1) whether "a grave offense is involved"; (2) whether "the suspect is reasonably believed to be armed"; (3) whether there is "a clear showing of probable cause" of the person's guilt; (4) whether there is "strong reason to believe that the suspect is in the premises"; (5) whether there is a "likelihood that the suspect will escape if not swiftly apprehended"; (6) whether the entry is "made peaceably"; and (7) whether the entry is "made at night," which on the one hand is more intrusive and on the other may show the impracticality of getting a warrant.[5] It is to be doubted, however, that an on-the-spot balancing of these factors makes for a workable test, and thus it may be that warrants should be required for "planned" arrests but not for those in which the occasion for arrest arose while the police were in the field investigating the conduct which provides the basis for the arrest.

Though declining to express approval of "all of the factors included in" the *Dorman*

2. 451 U.S. 204, 101 S.Ct. 1642, 68 L.Ed.2d 38 (1981).

3. United States v. Santana, 427 U.S. 38, 96 S.Ct. 2406, 49 L.Ed.2d 300 (1976); Warden v. Hayden, 387 U.S. 294, 87 S.Ct. 1642, 18 L.Ed.2d 782 (1967). But in Welsh v. Wisconsin, 466 U.S. 740, 104 S.Ct. 2091, 80 L.Ed.2d 732 (1984), the Court declined to uphold the police entry on a hot pursuit theory, as the police entered on the basis of a witness' information of defendant's nearby activity of driving while intoxicated minutes earlier, and thus "there was no immediate or continuous pursuit of the petitioner from the scene of a crime."

4. 435 F.2d 385 (D.C.Cir.1970).

5. In Minnesota v. Olson, 495 U.S. 91, 110 S.Ct. 1684, 109 L.Ed.2d 85 (1990), where the grave crime of murder was involved but the murder weapon had been recovered, and 3 or 4 police squads had the house surrounded, the Court did "not disturb the state court's judgment that these facts do not add up to exigent circumstances."

standard, the Court in *Welsh v. Wisconsin*[6] placed great emphasis (too much, it would seem) on the first of these factors in concluding that "it is difficult to conceive of a warrantless home arrest that would not be unreasonable under the Fourth Amendment when the underlying offense is extremely minor." In *Welsh* police had entered defendant's home without a warrant to arrest him for the offense of driving while intoxicated, in which he had been engaged in the immediate vicinity just minutes before. The state claimed exigent circumstances, namely, a need to obtain evidence of the defendant's blood alcohol level, which the Supreme Court had previously found compelling in other circumstances.[7] But the Court concluded "the best indication of the state's interest in precipitating an arrest" was the fact that the state had "chosen to classify the first offense for driving while intoxicated as a noncriminal, civil forfeiture offense for which no imprisonment is possible," and thus held that in such circumstances "a warrantless home arrest cannot be upheld simply because evidence of the petitioner's blood-alcohol level might have dissipated while the police obtained a warrant." As the two dissenters correctly observed, the statutory scheme was doubtless adopted "to increase the ease of conviction and the overall deterrent effect of the enforcement effort" and thus hardly manifested an expression that the defendant's conduct was so insignificant as to be undeserving of effective enforcement.[8]

The *Payton–Steagald* warrant requirement is inapplicable when the police are otherwise lawfully present within the premises, such as to execute a search warrant or by virtue of consent. There is likewise no need for a warrant, the Court concluded in *United States v. Santana*,[9] if the arrested defendant was standing directly in the doorway, but *Payton* teaches it is not enough that the door is open and the person to be arrested is clearly visible within. The lower courts are not in agreement as to whether *Santana* may be extended to cases in which the defendant was "at" but not "in" the door, but the better view is that such de minimus physical intrusions as reaching in to seize the person do not invoke the warrant requirement. Such a warrantless arrest is not rendered illegal by the fact that the police summoned the defendant to the door without revealing their intention to arrest him or by resort to noncoercive subterfuge, but the result is otherwise when the police utilize coercion or a false claim of authority to gain the defendant's presence at (or even outside) the door.

(b) Entry Without Notice to Arrest. The proposition that police must ordinarily give notice of their authority and purpose prior to making an entry of premises to arrest a person therein, which has common law credentials and is often found expressed by statute, seems to have been viewed by the Supreme Court in *Ker v. California*[10] as a Fourth Amendment requirement. It reduces the potential for violence to both the police officers and the occupants of the house into which entry is sought, guards against the needless destruction of private property, and symbolizes the respect for individual privacy summarized in the adage that "a man's house is his castle." The requirement applies to entry by force, by use of a pass key, by merely opening an unlocked door, and at least in some circumstances to passage through an already open door, but it does not extend to entry by ruse because such activity does not intrude upon the aforementioned interests.

What is required is that the officer, upon identifying himself as such, demand that he

6. 466 U.S. 740, 104 S.Ct. 2091, 80 L.Ed.2d 732 (1984).

7. Schmerber v. California, 384 U.S. 757, 86 S.Ct. 1826, 16 L.Ed.2d 908 (1966) (warrantless extraction of blood).

8. They also correctly observed that "the Court's approach will necessitate a case-by-case evaluation of the seriousness of particular crimes, a difficult task for which officers and courts are poorly equipped."

9. 427 U.S. 38, 96 S.Ct. 2406, 49 L.Ed.2d 300 (1976).

10. 374 U.S. 23, 83 S.Ct. 1623, 10 L.Ed.2d 726 (1963). *Ker* is a less than definitive treatment of the issue, however, for Justice Harlan concurred on the limited ground that state searches should only be judged by "concepts of fundamental fairness," four members of the Court concluded there were grounds to enter without notice, and the four dissenters concluded otherwise.

be admitted for the purpose of making the arrest. He may then enter upon submission by the occupant or if his demand is not promptly complied with, which means he must give the occupant a reasonable opportunity to come to the door. Entry without such notice is permissible in an emergency, that is, when the officer acts on a reasonable belief that compliance would increase his peril, frustrate the arrest, or permit the destruction of evidence. Some jurisdictions follow the so-called "blanket rule" under which an emergency can be grounded upon the general category of the case involved, but the better view, supported by *Ker,*[11] is that the emergency must be shown to exist upon the facts of the particular case. Thus, it is not enough that the person to be arrested is known to own a weapon or is involved in criminal activity typically necessitating use of easily disposable evidence. (A few jurisdictions authorize the issuance of so-called no-knock warrants, whereunder the magistrate would authorize entry without prior notice because of a sufficient showing to him of a need to do so.) Announcement is also unnecessary when it would be a "useless gesture," that is, when the authority and purpose of the police is already known to those inside.

(c) Search Before and Incident to Arrest. In *Warden v. Hayden,*[12] the Supreme Court made clear the unquestioned authority of police lawfully within premises for the purpose of making an arrest to search those premises to the extent necessary to find the individual to be arrested. Such a search is ordinarily limited to examining places where a fugitive could conceal himself, but *Hayden* also establishes that sometimes the police may do more. There one officer found weapons in a bathroom flush tank and another found clothing of the type described by the victim in the washing machine, and the Court upheld the search into those places because it was necessary for the police to ensure that they "had control of all weapons which could be used against them or to effect an escape." Because the Court stressed that these searches occurred "as part of an effort to find a suspected felon, armed, within the house into which he had run only minutes before," it is to be doubted that a weapons search is permissible as a matter of course in every case in which the police enter to arrest.

The longstanding rule that if the defendant was arrested in his own premises this automatically justified a warrantless search of the entire premises incident to that arrest was rejected in *Chimel v. California.*[13] After noting that it is reasonable to search the *person* of the arrestee to prevent him from concealing or destroying evidence and to prevent resistance or escape, the Court continued:

> And the area into which an arrestee might reach in order to grab a weapon or evidentiary items must, of course, be governed by a like rule. A gun on a table or in a drawer in front of one who is arrested can be as dangerous to the arresting officer as one concealed in the clothing of the person arrested. There is ample justification, therefore, for a search of the arrestee's person and the area "within his immediate control"—construing that phrase to mean the area from within which he might gain possession of a weapon or destructible evidence.
>
> There is no comparable justification, however, for routinely searching any room other than that in which an arrest occurs—or, for that matter, for searching through all the desk drawers or other closed or concealed areas in that room itself. Such searches, in the absence of well-recognized exceptions, may be made only under the authority of a search warrant. The "adherence to judicial processes" mandated by the Fourth Amendment requires no less.

The Court thus wisely limited the authority to search without warrant incident to arrest by circumscribing that authority in terms of the rationale for making such a search.

11. The plurality opinion, in approving the failure to give notice in that case, placed considerable emphasis on the fact that in addition to the officers' knowledge that narcotics "could be quickly and easily destroyed," there also existed "ground for the belief that [Ker] might well have been expecting the police" because of his earlier furtive conduct.

12. 387 U.S. 294, 87 S.Ct. 1642, 18 L.Ed.2d 782 (1967).

13. 395 U.S. 752, 89 S.Ct. 2034, 23 L.Ed.2d 685 (1969).

Especially in the years which immediately followed *Chimel,* courts applied the rule loosely by finding unhesitantly that the arrestee had a substantial area "within his immediate control" notwithstanding his arrest. The correct approach is to inquire what places it would be *possible* for the arrestee presently to reach, which necessitates consideration of such factors as (1) whether the arrestee was placed in some form of restraints, such as handcuffs; (2) the position of the officer vis-a-vis the defendant in relation to the place searched; (3) the ease or difficulty of gaining access within the container or enclosure searched; and (4) the number of officers present in relation to the number of arrestees or other persons. (More recently, in *New York v. Belton,*[14] the Court adopted a more generous search-incident-arrest rule for search of vehicles after arrest of passengers,[15] but gave no indication that *Chimel* itself was being expanded.) Courts generally have not considered whether *Chimel* obligates the police to take measures to narrow the range of the arrestee's control, but when the police rely upon their purported knowledge of the arrestee's dangerous propensities in support of a search somewhat broader than might otherwise be permissible, their claim may be rejected because of their failure to take appropriate steps to restrain the arrestee.

(d) Search and Exploration After Arrest. If the defendant is arrested at a particular place in the premises, even at the front door, the circumstances may be such that he will be allowed to move about the premises prior to departure, as where it is necessary for him to change his clothes or put on additional clothing. In such a situation, it is proper for the police in the interest of self-protection to accompany the defendant to the other part of the residence where the clothes are to be obtained and inspect the interior of a closet or drawer where the defendant says he wants to obtain clothing.

After a defendant is arrested within premises, the police sometimes make a cursory inspection of other parts of those premises for the purpose of determining whether there are possible accomplices present. Such a search has been upheld when the police had *some* reason to anticipate finding accomplices, but is not justified if police enter to arrest defendant for a past offense it is known he committed alone or for which all confederates are known to have been apprehended. But at least when the criminal activity is rather serious, exploration for potential accomplices is reasonable even absent concrete information indicating the accomplices are now present.

Yet another reason why police sometimes make a cursory inspection of the balance of the premises is to ensure their own safety while departing with the arrestee. The question of when such a "protective sweep"[16] is permissible reached the Supreme Court in *Maryland v. Buie,*[17] where the state court had required full probable cause of a dangerous situation. By analogy to *Terry v. Ohio*[18] and *Michigan v. Long,*[19] the Court opted for a less demanding reasonable suspicion test. The state had argued for a "bright-line rule" to the effect that "police should be permitted to conduct a protective sweep whenever they make an in-home arrest for a violent crime"; the Court responded that individualized suspicion is required under *Terry,* but then without explanation adopted a two-part sweep rule which included another kind of bright line. Specifically, the Court in *Buie* held (1) "that as an incident to the arrest the officers could, as a precautionary matter and without probable cause or reasonable suspicion, look in closets and other spaces immediately adjoining

14. 453 U.S. 454, 101 S.Ct. 2860, 69 L.Ed.2d 768 (1981).

15. See § 3.7(a).

16. Defined by the Court in *Buie,* infra, as "a quick and limited search of a premises, incident to an arrest and conducted to protect the safety of police officers or others," which "is narrowly confined to a cursory visual inspection of those places in which a person might be hiding."

17. 494 U.S. 325, 110 S.Ct. 1093, 108 L.Ed.2d 276 (1990).

18. 392 U.S. 1, 88 S.Ct. 1868, 20 L.Ed.2d 889 (1968).

19. 463 U.S. 1032, 103 S.Ct. 3469, 77 L.Ed.2d 1201 (1983).

the place of arrest from which an attack could be immediately launched"; and (2) that for a more extensive sweep "there must be articulable facts which, taken together with the rational inferences from those facts, would warrant a reasonably prudent officer in believing that the area to be swept harbors an individual posing a danger to those on the arrest scene." No effort was made to define either the "immediately adjoining" category or the factors bearing on this variety of reasonable suspicion. As to the latter, earlier lower court decisions have said this is a matter which requires consideration of the seriousness of the offense, the likelihood that the crime for which the arrest was made involved confederates, the likelihood that other persons are now present in the premises, and the extent to which the circumstances and surroundings make difficult a safe withdrawal from the premises with the arrestee.

As for whether the police may accompany the defendant into the home following his arrest outside so that the defendant may obtain identification, get his effects, or change clothes, the Supreme Court answered in the affirmative in *Washington v. Chrisman.*[20] Such action was deemed permissible without regard to the likelihood that the arrestee would attempt to escape; as the Court put it in *Chrisman,* "it is not 'unreasonable' under the Fourth Amendment for a police officer, as a matter of routine, to monitor the movements of an arrested person, as his judgment dictates, following the arrest."

(e) Warrantless Entry and Search for Evidence. In earlier days, the Supreme Court sometimes intimated that a warrantless search of premises for evidence could *never* be justified under the Fourth Amendment,[21] and sometimes alluded to the possibility that such a search would be upheld upon a showing of genuine exigent circumstances.[22] No case concerning this issue reached the Court in the pre-*Chimel* era, for then the police could usually avoid the issue by the simple expedient of arresting the defendant there and then searching the entire premises incident to that arrest. But after *Chimel* a case seemingly raising this issue, *Vale v. Louisiana,*[23] reached the Court. Police set up a surveillance of a house in which Vale was thought to be residing, as they had a warrant to arrest him because of a bond increase on his previous narcotics charge. They saw him come out of the house and apparently make a drug sale to a person who drove up and sounded his horn, so the police moved in and arrested Vale just as he was about to reenter the house. The police then took him inside and made a cursory inspection of the house, during which time Vale's brother and mother entered the premises, and the officers then proceeded to search the house and discovered Vale's stash of narcotics. Though the state claimed that the search was lawful because made on probable cause narcotics would be found and in response to a risk the narcotics would be disposed of if the police were to delay for a search warrant, the Court in *Vale* disagreed.

One response by the Court was that the state's rationale "could not apply to the present case, since by their own account the arresting officers satisfied themselves that no one else was in the house when they first entered the premises." This observation does not square with the facts, which again were that when the detailed search uncovering the drugs was undertaken two close relatives of the defendant were on the premises. Equally baffling is the assertion that because the officers "were able to procure two warrants for the appellant's arrest" and "had information that he was residing at the address where they found him," there was "no reason * * * to suppose that it was impracticable for them to obtain a search warrant as well." The facts support precisely the opposite conclusion; a search warrant for drugs could hardly have issued merely because Vale's bond was being raised, as the probable cause for the warrant came into being only minutes before

20. 455 U.S. 1, 102 S.Ct. 812, 70 L.Ed.2d 778 (1982).

21. Agnello v. United States, 269 U.S. 20, 46 S.Ct. 4, 70 L.Ed. 145 (1925).

22. Johnson v. United States, 333 U.S. 10, 68 S.Ct. 367, 92 L.Ed. 436 (1948).

23. 399 U.S. 30, 90 S.Ct. 1969, 26 L.Ed.2d 409 (1970).

the search was conducted. But putting those two points aside, *Vale* is significant because it appears to recognize that a warrantless search of a dwelling for evidence may be undertaken in "an exceptional situation," and also because it seemingly asserts that the risk-of-evidence-loss "emergency" is to be very narrowly circumscribed. In concluding no such emergency existed in the instant case, the Court emphasized that the "goods ultimately seized were not in the process of destruction" nor "about to be removed from the jurisdiction."

Although some courts have resisted a broader formulation on the ground that the police can too easily conjure up reasons why evidence within premises might be subject to future destruction or disposal, the lower courts have generally not accepted the *Vale* formulation as controlling. They have been inclined to state the exception in broader terms, covering instances in which the police reasonably conclude that the evidence would be destroyed or removed if they delayed the search while a warrant was obtained. The most careful treatment of this point appears in *United States v. Rubin,*[24] where the court, after noting the broader dictum in other Supreme Court cases,[25] concluded the *Vale* language should not be taken too seriously in light of the Court's assumption that not even a threat of destruction was present. The court in *Rubin* then formulated this test:

> When Government agents, however, have probable cause to believe contraband is present and, in addition, based on the surrounding circumstances of the information at hand, they reasonably conclude that the evidence will be destroyed or removed before they can secure a search warrant, a warrantless search is justified. The emergency circumstances will vary from case to case, and the inherent necessities of the situation at the time must be scrutinized. Circumstances which have seemed relevant to courts include (1) the degree of urgency involved and the amount of time necessary to obtain a warrant * * *; (2) reasonable belief that the contraband is about to be removed * * *; (3) the possibility of danger to police officers guarding the site of the contraband while a search warrant is sought * * *; (4) information indicating the possessors of the contraband are aware that the police are on their trail * * *; and (5) the ready destructibility of the contraband and the knowledge "that efforts to dispose of narcotics and to escape are characteristic behavior of persons engaged in the narcotics traffic."

What one thinks of the *Rubin* formulation is likely to depend upon one's assumptions as to whether the police could resolve their dilemma by some less intrusive alternative, which naturally leads to the so-called impoundment alternative. It has sometimes been suggested that it would be preferable for officers to impound the dwelling until they can obtain a search warrant, during which time those occupants who could not lawfully be arrested would be forced to leave the building or else remain therein subject to immediate police surveillance. In recent years more and more courts have expressed their approval of the impoundment alternative. For impoundment to be reasonable, these decisions indicate, the persons present when the police enter should be permitted to leave if they choose that option, and in any event the period of impoundment should be relatively short.

The Supreme Court addressed this important practice, albeit in a somewhat obscure manner, in *Segura v. United States.*[26] There police made a warrantless entry of an apartment, arrested all the occupants (who were promptly removed from the scene), and then remained within 19 hours until a search warrant was obtained and executed. The Court held, 5–4, "that where officers, having probable cause, enter premises, and with probable

24. 474 F.2d 262 (3d Cir.1973).

25. United States v. Jeffers, 342 U.S. 48, 72 S.Ct. 93, 96 L.Ed. 59 (1951) (warrant needed as "no question of * * * imminent destruction, removal, or concealment of the property"); McDonald v. United States, 335 U.S. 451, 69 S.Ct. 191, 93 L.Ed. 153 (1948) (warrant needed, as no "property in the process of destruction" or "likely to be destroyed"); Johnson v. United States, 333 U.S. 10, 68 S.Ct. 367, 92 L.Ed. 436 (1948) (warrant needed as "no evidence or contraband was threatened with removal or destruction").

26. 468 U.S. 796, 104 S.Ct. 3380, 82 L.Ed.2d 599 (1984).

cause, arrest the occupants who have legitimate possessory interests in its contents and take them into custody and, for no more than the period here involved, secure the premises from within to preserve the status quo while others, in good faith, are in the process of obtaining a warrant, they do not violate the Fourth Amendment's proscription against unreasonable seizures." The Court went on to hold that in any event any illegality in the initial entry would not require suppression of the evidence first discovered in the later execution of the search warrant.[27]

Curiously, the first holding in *Segura* was elaborated and explained in a part of the opinion joined in by only two members of the Court. It was there noted that the Court had in other contexts approved warrantless seizures in circumstances where a warrantless search would have been impermissible,[28] and the two could see "no reason * * * why the same principle should not apply when a dwelling is involved." Those two Justices next concluded that the entry could be disregarded; absent exigent circumstances, the entry might constitute an illegal *search* (as the lower court had held), but it had nothing to do with the *seizure* because the interference with possessory interests was no greater than had the officers guarded the premises without entry. This would make the 19 hours of occupation irrelevant, but presumably only because those persons with a possessory interest in the premises were in custody during that time.[29]

Of a quite different order from the situations previously discussed are those in which an immediate search of premises is necessary because of a risk of bodily harm or even death. Such a warrantless search may be undertaken upon reasonable cause to believe that those premises contain (1) individuals in imminent danger of death or serious bodily harm; or (2) things imminently likely to burn, explode, or otherwise cause death, serious bodily harm, or substantial destruction of property; or (3) things subject to seizure which will cause or be used to cause death or serious bodily harm if their seizure is delayed.

Some courts for years recognized an exception to the general rule that a search warrant is needed to search premises for evidence, namely, that police could enter without a warrant to conduct an investigation at the scene of a possible homicide. But in *Mincey v. Arizona*,[30] after noting that no "emergency threatening life or limb" had been established, the Court "decline[d] to hold that the seriousness of the offense under investigation itself creates exigent circumstances of the kind that under the Fourth Amendment justify a warrantless search," and thus concluded "that the 'murder scene exception' created by the Arizona Supreme Court is inconsistent with the Fourth and Fourteenth Amendments." It is important to note that *Mincey* lacks *all* of the characteristics which lower courts traditionally relied upon in recognizing such an exception: this was not an investigation into a then unknown cause of death, as the police knew it was murder and knew who the perpetrator was; this was not a case in which an occupant of the premises had summoned police and tacitly approved of the investigation; and this was not an investigation which was kept within narrow temporal and spatial dimensions. This makes it more understandable why the Court failed to permit some degree of warrantless investigation, as it had done just a few weeks before in the analogous case of *Michigan v. Tyler*,[31] concerning investigation within premises of the cause of

27. On this branch of *Segura*, see § 9.4(b).

28. E.g., Arkansas v. Sanders, 442 U.S. 753, 99 S.Ct. 2586, 61 L.Ed.2d 235 (1979); United States v. Chadwick, 433 U.S. 1, 97 S.Ct. 2476, 53 L.Ed.2d 538 (1977), discussed in § 3.7(c)1.

29. The two Justices emphasized that those persons "were under arrest and in the custody of the police throughout the entire period the agents occupied the apartment," so that the "actual interference with their possessory interests in the apartment and its contents was, thus, virtually nonexistent." The dissenters declared that "what is even more strange about the Chief Justice's conclusion is that it permits the authorities to benefit from the fact that they had unlawfully arrested" an occupant of the apartment.

30. 437 U.S. 385, 98 S.Ct. 2408, 57 L.Ed.2d 290 (1978).

31. 436 U.S. 499, 98 S.Ct. 1942, 56 L.Ed.2d 486 (1978).

a fire.[32] (But in the more recent case of *Thompson v. Louisiana*,[33] lacking the various extreme circumstances present in *Mincey*, the Court again declined to recognize a murder scene exception to the warrant requirement. Absent a warrant, the Court declared, evidence would be admissible only if discovered in plain view while police were assisting the injured party or were checking the premises for other victims or the killer.) Yet another consequence of *Mincey* is that courts are inclined to uphold search warrants issued in such situations even though they are not at all specific as to what is being sought, the reason being that *Mincey* has deprived the police of an opportunity to make sufficient observations to enable the officers to identify the specific instruments or other evidence of the crimes to which a warrant would be directed.

(f) Warrantless Entry and Search for Other Purposes. Police may enter a dwelling without a warrant to render emergency aid and assistance to a person they reasonably believe to be in distress and in need of that assistance. If they entered because of a purported emergency and find evidence of crime, that evidence will be admissible only if the state shows that the warrantless entry fell within this exception, using an objective standard as to the reasonableness of the officer's belief. But that standard is to be applied by reference to the circumstances then confronting the officer, including the need for a prompt assessment of sometimes ambiguous information concerning potentially serious consequences. As it has sometimes been put, the question is whether the officers would have been derelict in their duty had they acted otherwise.

Police may also enter private property for the purpose of protecting the property of the owner or occupant or some other person. The most common case is that in which the police have reason to believe that the premises in question have been burglarized or vandalized. If the police are lawfully on the premises for this purpose, they may look to see if the burglar or vandal is still present, and may also take necessary steps to identify the occupant so that he may be notified.

The other reasons for which police or other public officials might enter private premises are so varied that generalization is virtually impossible, though it is useful to ask in all such cases whether there was a "compelling urgency" for the action taken. Thus in *G.M. Leasing Corp. v. United States*,[34] where IRS agents made a warrantless entry of corporate offices to levy on property subject to seizure, the Court rejected the government's contention "that the warrant protections of the Fourth Amendment do not apply to invasion of privacy in furtherance of tax collection," and thus held the agents' entry unreasonable because there had been no showing of exigent circumstances.

(g) What May Be Seized. Assuming now a lawful warrantless entry or search of private premises on one of the bases heretofore discussed, there remains the separate question of what may be seized. The Court in *Coolidge v. New Hampshire*[35] indicated "plain view" seizures would often be proper in such circumstances, and then referred to *Warden v. Hayden*,[36] which teaches that to justify such a seizure there must be "a nexus—automatically provided in the case of fruits, instrumentalities or contraband—between the item to be seized and criminal behavior," that is, probable cause "to believe that the evidence sought will aid in a particular apprehension or conviction."

Except when there is some established justification for more closely examining an object (e.g., where it is within the "immediate control" of the arrestee for *Chimel* purposes), this probable cause, the Court also said in *Coolidge*, must be "immediately apparent," as "the 'plain view' doctrine may not be used to extend a general exploratory search from one object to another until something incrimina-

32. See § 3.9(e).

33. 469 U.S. 17, 105 S.Ct. 409, 83 L.Ed.2d 246 (1984).

34. 429 U.S. 338, 97 S.Ct. 619, 50 L.Ed.2d 530 (1977).

35. 403 U.S. 443, 91 S.Ct. 2022, 29 L.Ed.2d 564 (1971).

36. 387 U.S. 294, 87 S.Ct. 1642, 18 L.Ed.2d 782 (1967).

ting at last emerges."[37] For a time, many lower courts held it was nonetheless proper for police to pick up an item and take closer note of its character or identifying characteristics, *provided* there was a preexisting reasonable suspicion the object was subject to seizure. But that approach was rejected in *Arizona v. Hicks*,[38] holding full probable cause was needed to pick up an item of stereo equipment to ascertain its serial number (which revealed it was stolen property). The majority deemed it unwise "to send police and judges into a new thicket of Fourth Amendment law" by recognizing a third category of police conduct between "a plain-view inspection" requiring no suspicion and "a 'full-blown search'" requiring probable cause.

Yet another requirement set out in *Coolidge* is "that the discovery of evidence in plain view must be inadvertent." This requirement, though not endorsed by a majority of the Court,[39] was readily accepted by most lower courts. However, the doctrine is by no means sound,[40] and was ultimately rejected by the Court in *Horton v. California.*[41] In *Horton,* the Court indicated its disapproval of Fourth Amendment "standards that depend upon the subjective state of mind of the officer," and added that adherence to the Fourth Amendment's particularity-of-description requirements "serves the interest in limiting the area and duration of the search that the inadvertence requirement inadequately protects."

Somewhat different than the "inadvertent discovery" doctrine is the notion that evidence found within premises will be suppressed if the entry was a subterfuge.[42] Few cases of this kind are to be found, probably because proof of such a subterfuge is a difficult matter. One type of situation is that in which the police passed up a prior opportunity to arrest defendant on the street and followed him home and then entered the premises to arrest, though there was absolutely no reason for foregoing the earlier arrest opportunity. Another is where the entry is to arrest for a minor offense so insignificant that no such action would have been taken but for the fact the police desired to look around the premises in the hope of finding evidence of another, more serious offense.

Finally, it is important to note that whatever rules may exist with respect to the seizure of other objects in plain view within premises, they do not automatically carry over to instances in which the seizure is of allegedly obscene materials. As pointed out in *Roaden v. Kentucky*,[43] involving the warrantless seizure of a film from a projection booth incident to arrest of the theatre owner there, the First Amendment is also involved in such a situation, necessitating examination of "what is 'unreasonable' in the light of the values of freedom of expression." This being so, a war-

37. Later, in construing *Coolidge,* the Court stated that the incriminating character must *itself* be in plain view. In Horton v. California, ___ U.S. ___, 110 S.Ct. 2301, 110 L.Ed.2d 112 (1990), the Court gave, as one reason the seizure of vehicles *as* evidence in *Coolidge* did not meet the requirements for a plain view warrantless seizure, the failure to meet the "immediately apparent" requirement: "the cars were obviously in plain view, but their probative value remained uncertain until after the interiors were swept and examined microscopically."

38. 480 U.S. 321, 107 S.Ct. 1149, 94 L.Ed.2d 347 (1987).

39. Four members of the Court dissented, and Harlan, J., concurred in a part of the opinion other than that in which the inadvertent discovery limitation is stated. In Texas v. Brown, 460 U.S. 730, 103 S.Ct. 1535, 75 L.Ed.2d 502 (1983), four members of the Court stated that because "the *Coolidge* plurality's discussion of 'plain view' * * * has never been expressly adopted by a majority of this Court," it was "not a binding precedent" but "should obviously be the point of reference for further discussion of the issue." Two other members of the Court saw "no reason at this late date to imply criticism of [*Coolidge*'s] articulation of this exception" because it "has been accepted generally for over a decade." The remaining three Justices, without addressing this point, cited *Coolidge* as a precedent on the plain view doctrine.

40. See § 3.4(k).

41. ___ U.S. ___, 110 S.Ct. 2301, 110 L.Ed.2d 112 (1990).

42. In Horton v. California, ___ U.S. ___, 110 S.Ct. 2301, 110 L.Ed.2d 112 (1990), rejecting the inadvertence requirement, the two dissenters opined the decision "should have only a limited impact" because there remained untouched the pretextual search doctrine. However, the majority in *Horton* expressed a distaste for Fourth Amendment rules "that depend upon the subjective state of mind of the officer," which lends support to the conclusion that any pretext doctrine must be grounded instead upon departure from standard practice rather than motivation. See § 3.1(d).

43. 413 U.S. 496, 93 S.Ct. 2796, 37 L.Ed.2d 757 (1973).

rantless seizure is permissible in that kind of case only where "there are exigent circumstances in which police action literally must be 'now or never' to preserve the evidence of the crime."

§ 3.7 Search and Seizure of Vehicles

(a) Search Incident to Arrest. Back when courts generally permitted a full warrantless search of the defendant's premises merely because of his arrest there, a comparable unrestrained search was permitted of vehicles in the possession or general control of the arrestee at the time of his arrest. But then came *Chimel v. California*,[1] in which the Court held that because the rationale underlying search incident to arrest is the need to prevent the arrestee from obtaining a weapon or destroying evidence, such a search could extend only to "the arrestee's person and the area 'within his immediate control'—construing that phrase to mean the area from within which he might gain possession of a weapon or destructible evidence." Though it was sometimes held that the *Chimel* rule did not carry over to vehicles, the prevailing view was otherwise. Courts thus deemed the proper inquiry to be whether and to what extent it was *possible* for the arrestee to reach the particular place in the car notwithstanding his arrest, necessitating consideration of such factors as whether the arrestee had been handcuffed, the position of the defendant and the arresting officer in relation to the vehicle, and the ease or difficulty of gaining entry to the vehicle or to a particular container or enclosure therein.

The need for such a case-by-case assessment was largely obviated by *New York v. Belton*.[2] In that 5–4 decision, the majority reasoned: (1) Fourth Amendment protections "can only be realized if the police are acting under a set of rules which, in most instances, make it possible to reach a correct determination beforehand as to whether an invasion of privacy is justified in the interest of law enforcement"; (2) "no straightforward rule has emerged from the litigated cases respecting the question involved here"; (3) this has caused the courts "difficulty" and has put the appellate cases into "disarray"; (4) the cases suggest "the generalization that articles inside the relatively narrow compass of the passenger compartment of an automobile are in fact generally, even if not inevitably, within 'the area into which an arrestee might reach in order to grab a weapon or evidentiary item' "; and thus (5) "the workable rule this category of cases requires" is best achieved by holding "that when a policeman has made a lawful custodial arrest of the occupant of an automobile, he may, as a contemporaneous incident of that arrest, search the passenger compartment of that automobile," inclusive of "the contents of any containers found within the passenger compartment."

Despite the fact that it is often advantageous to both privacy interests and law enforcement interests if rules of police conduct are stated in terms of easily understood standardized procedures which may be routinely followed, the wisdom of the *Belton* rule is open to question. The Court is unconvincing in its claim that a case-by-case application of the *Chimel* principle in vehicle cases had proved unworkable. Moreover, the results produced under the *Belton* "bright line" well exceed those which usually would be reached by a case-by-case application of *Chimel*. This is particularly troubling when it is considered that *Belton* permits broad searches of vehicles without any probable cause that evidence will be found therein, provided only that there is probable cause to arrest an occupant. This is no less than an invitation to subterfuge, for police wishing to search a car but lacking grounds to do so need only await the commission of some minor offense by the driver or other occupant and then arrest before the search.

Belton applies only when there has been a "custodial arrest," and therefore it does not change the pre-existing rule that a search of an automobile incident to arrest is not per-

§ 3.7

1. 395 U.S. 752, 89 S.Ct. 2034, 23 L.Ed.2d 685 (1969).

2. 453 U.S. 454, 101 S.Ct. 2860, 69 L.Ed.2d 768 (1981).

missible when the person merely receives a citation at the scene, even though he will be allowed to reenter his car and go his way. *Belton* requires that the arrest and search be "contemporaneous," and thus it appears that the search of the vehicle must occur at the place of arrest and not later at the station. There is disagreement as to whether *Belton* also means the search must be made before the arrestee is taken from the scene, but clearly it is unnecessary that he have continuing access to the car. Thus, a search of a vehicle under *Belton* is permissible even after the defendant has been removed from the car, handcuffed and placed in a squad car, and even if he is in the custody of several officers. The term "passenger compartment" in *Belton* has been construed to mean all areas reachable without exiting the vehicle, without regard to the likelihood that such reaching actually occurred in the particular case. It would seem, notwithstanding the fears of the *Belton* dissenters of a contrary interpretation, that the *Belton* "bright line" rule does not permit the dismantling of the vehicle to get inside door panels, the opening of sealed containers, or other searches into particular places to which the arrestee unquestionably had no access immediately preceding his apprehension.

(b) Search and Seizure to Search for Evidence. The Supreme Court considered the question of whether a warrantless automobile search for evidence was lawful in the prohibition-era case of *Carroll v. United States*.[3] Federal agents stopped a car they had probable cause to believe contained illegal liquor and immediately subjected it to a warrantless search. In upholding that action, the Court recognized "a necessary difference between a search of a store, dwelling house, or other structure in respect of which a proper official warrant readily may be obtained and a search of a ship, motor boat, wagon, or automobile for contraband goods, where it is not practicable to secure a warrant, because the vehicle can be quickly moved out of the locality or jurisdiction in which the warrant must be sought." On the facts of *Carroll*, the point was well taken, for the officers lacked a basis for "in presence" misdemeanor arrests of the occupants and thus could not have prevented them from moving the vehicle while a warrant was being sought.

Some courts concluded *Carroll* could not be extended to cases in which the vehicle occupants were arrested, for the simple reason that exigencies do not exist when the vehicle and the suspect are both in police custody. But the Supreme Court, in *Chambers v. Maroney*,[4] did not agree. In upholding the warrantless search at the police station of a station wagon seized upon arrest of the occupants for a just-committed armed robbery, the Court stated:

> Neither *Carroll*, nor other cases in this Court require or suggest that in every conceivable circumstance the search of an auto even with probable cause may be made without the extra protection for privacy that a warrant affords. But the circumstances that furnish probable cause to search a particular auto for particular articles are most often unforeseeable; moreover, the opportunity to search is fleeting since a car is readily movable. Where this is true, as in *Carroll* and the case before us now, if an effective search is to be made at any time, either the search must be made immediately without a warrant or the car itself must be seized and held without a warrant for whatever period is necessary to obtain a warrant for the search. * * *
>
> Arguably, because of the preference for a magistrate's judgment, only the immobilization of the car should be permitted until a search warrant is obtained; arguably, only the "lesser" intrusion is permissible until the magistrate authorizes the "greater." But which is the "greater" and which the "lesser" intrusion is itself a debatable question and the answer may depend on a variety of circumstances. For constitutional purposes, we see no difference between on the one hand seizing and holding a car before presenting the probable cause issue to a magistrate and on the other hand carrying out an immediate search without a warrant. Given probable cause to

3. 267 U.S. 132, 45 S.Ct. 280, 69 L.Ed. 453 (1925).

4. 399 U.S. 42, 90 S.Ct. 1975, 26 L.Ed.2d 419 (1970).

search, either course is reasonable under the Fourth Amendment.

On the facts before us, the blue station wagon could have been searched on the spot when it was stopped since there was probable cause to search and it was a fleeting target for a search. The probable-cause factor still obtained at the station house and so did the mobility of the car unless the Fourth Amendment permits a warrantless seizure of the car and the denial of its use to anyone until a warrant is secured. In that event there is little to choose in terms of practical consequences between an immediate search without a warrant and the car's immobilization until a warrant is obtained.[5]

This passage from *Chambers* is truly remarkable. There is no explanation as to why it is a "debatable question" whether the seizure of a car is a lesser intrusion than a search of its interior, when the Court just months before had found not at all debatable a similar issue.[6] Secondly, the choices are characterized as "immediate search" and "holding a car before presenting the probable cause issue to a magistrate," thus ignoring the fact that the case involved neither of these but instead a holding of a car which was followed by a warrantless search. Thirdly, the Court jumped to the conclusion that "the mobility of the car" "still obtained at the station house," though the owner of the car was among those arrested for a serious crime; he clearly would be in no position to claim the car in the interval needed to get a warrant, and there is no indication that the owner asked that the car be turned over to some third party. That is, resort to the warrant process in order to protect the owner's privacy interest would not have involved any greater intrusion upon the owner's possessory interest in the car. Because *Chambers* cannot be rationalized in terms of the oft-stated principle that a search warrant is required except in exigent circumstances, it was perhaps inevitable that members of the Court would later disagree frequently as to its application.

In *Coolidge v. New Hampshire*,[7] the police after months of investigation arrested defendant for murder and contemporaneously seized his car from his driveway and later searched it because it was believed to have been used in commission of the crime. Though the car was seized pursuant to a warrant, the warrant was invalid, and thus an effort was made to justify it as a lawful warrantless seizure and search. Four members of the Court noted that "the police had known for some time of the probable role of the Pontiac car in the crime" and that the defendant "had already ample opportunity to destroy any evidence he thought incriminating," which might well distinguish *Coolidge* from *Chambers* and *Carroll* if the notion were that a warrant is needed when there is neither a need for an immediate search nor a need for an immediate seizure. But in concluding the warrantless seizure and search were unlawful, they emphasized other purported distinguishing characteristics: that the objects sought "were neither stolen nor contraband nor dangerous"; that this was not a car "stopped on the open highway" but "an unoccupied vehicle, on private property"; and that the police had taken steps so that neither Coolidge nor his wife could gain access to the car. But, as other members of the Court correctly noted, none of those three facts distinguishes the case from *Chambers*. *Coolidge* was limited to its facts in a series of subsequent decisions all upholding warrantless

5. The warrantless search need not occur immediately upon arrival of the vehicle at the place where it is to be held. As the Court noted in United States v. Johns, 469 U.S. 478, 105 S.Ct. 881, 83 L.Ed.2d 890 (1985), there "is no requirement that the warrantless search of a vehicle occur contemporaneously with its lawful seizure." But the Court cautioned that police could not "indefinitely retain possession of a vehicle and its contents before they complete a vehicle search," for in some circumstances "the owner of a vehicle or its contents might attempt to prove that delay in the completion of a vehicle search was unreasonable because it adversely affected a privacy or possessory interest."

6. United States v. Van Leeuwen, 397 U.S. 249, 90 S.Ct. 1029, 25 L.Ed.2d 282 (1970) (holding that the proper course of action, given probable cause to search packages placed in the mails, was to withhold routing and delivery of the packages for the period necessary to obtain a search warrant).

7. 403 U.S. 443, 91 S.Ct. 2022, 29 L.Ed.2d 564 (1971).

searches of vehicles.[8] Though in some of the cases the Court pretended that exigent circumstances were necessary, it became apparent (as the Court finally acknowledged in *United States v. Chadwick* [9]) that warrantless vehicle searches were being permitted "in cases in which the possibilities of the vehicle's being removed or evidence in it destroyed were remote, if not non-existent." On what basis? Because, as the majority said in *Chadwick,* quoting the *Cardwell* plurality: "One has a lesser expectation of privacy in a motor vehicle because its function is transportation and it seldom serves as one's residence or as the repository of personal effects * * *. It travels public thoroughfares where both its occupants and its contents are in plain view." Putting aside the fact that this characterization is certainly not beyond dispute, it would appear to provide the only possible basis for explaining *Chambers* and the post-*Coolidge* cases.

In *California v. Carney,*[10] the *Chambers* vehicle exception was held applicable to a motor home which "is being used on the highways, or if it is readily capable of such use and is found stationary in a place not regularly used for residential purposes." [11] The majority emphasized both justifications for the vehicle exception, noting that a motor home in such circumstances is "readily mobile" and has "a reduced expectation of privacy stemming from its use as a licensed motor vehicle subject to a range of police regulation inapplicable to a fixed dwelling." The three dissenters objected that the Court's prior cases (especially the container-in-a-vehicle cases discussed in the next subsection) "teach us that inherent mobility is not a sufficient justification for the fashioning of an exception to the warrant requirement * * * in the face of heightened expectations of privacy in the location searched," and that motor homes, "by their common use and construction, afford their owners a substantial and legitimate expectation of privacy when they dwell within." [12]

(c) Search of Containers and Persons Within. In *United States v. Chadwick,*[13] three persons were arrested for transportation of marijuana, following which the police seized and later searched without a warrant a double-locked footlocker which had just been put into the open trunk of a car belonging to one of the defendants. The Court declined to uphold the search by analogy to the previously-discussed vehicle cases, reasoning that ve-

8. See Florida v. Meyers, 466 U.S. 380, 104 S.Ct. 1852, 80 L.Ed.2d 381 (1984) (holding on authority of *Thomas,* following, that lower court erred in concluding warrantless search of car improper where, as here, car had been impounded 8 hours earlier and was presently stored in a secure area); Michigan v. Thomas, 458 U.S. 259, 102 S.Ct. 3079, 73 L.Ed.2d 750 (1982) (stressing that "the justification to conduct such a warrantless search does not vanish once the car has been immobilized; nor does it depend upon a reviewing court's assessment of the likelihood in each particular case that the car would have been driven away, or that its contents would have been tampered with, during the period required for the police to obtain a warrant"); Colorado v. Bannister, 449 U.S. 1, 101 S.Ct. 42, 66 L.Ed.2d 1 (1980) (unanimous Court concludes that where probable cause to search developed after car stopped for traffic violation, "it would be especially unreasonable to require a detour to a magistrate before the unanticipated evidence could be lawfully seized"); Texas v. White, 423 U.S. 67, 96 S.Ct. 304, 46 L.Ed.2d 209 (1975) (defendant arrested while attempting to pass fraudulent checks at drive-in window of bank; warrantless search "later at the station house" upheld despite dissenters objection instant case different from *Chambers* because here "there is no indication that an immediate search would have been either impractical or unsafe for the arresting officers"); Cardwell v. Lewis, 417 U.S. 583, 94 S.Ct. 2464, 41 L.Ed.2d 325 (1974) (after defendant's arrest, his car towed from public lot and examined; four Justices concluded there were exigent circumstances though "the police might have obtained a warrant earlier," while four others deemed this an illegal seizure because the police could have gotten a warrant in advance).

9. 433 U.S. 1, 97 S.Ct. 2476, 53 L.Ed.2d 538 (1977).

10. 471 U.S. 386, 105 S.Ct. 2066, 85 L.Ed.2d 406 (1985).

11. The Court declined to "pass on the application of the vehicle exception to a motor home that is situated in a way or place that objectively indicates that it is being used as a residence," but suggested: "Among the factors that might be relevant in determining whether a warrant would be required in such a circumstance is its location, whether the vehicle is readily mobile or instead, for instance, elevated on blocks, whether the vehicle is licensed, whether it is connected to utilities, and whether it has convenient access to a public road."

12. The dissenters then concluded a warrantless search would be permissible only "when the motor home is traveling on the public streets or highways, or when exigent circumstances otherwise require an immediate search without the expenditure of time necessary to obtain a warrant."

13. 433 U.S. 1, 97 S.Ct. 2476, 53 L.Ed.2d 538 (1977).

hicles have a "diminished expectation of privacy" but that the footlocker did not because it was "not open to public view" or "subject to regular inspections and official scrutiny on a continuing basis" and because it "is intended as a repository of personal effects." But because "the Government does not contend that the footlocker's brief contact with Chadwick's car makes this an automobile search," *Chadwick* did not settle the question of whether containers in a vehicle may be searched without a warrant in an otherwise lawful warrantless search of the vehicle.

That issue seemingly was reached in *Arkansas v. Sanders,*[14] involving a warrantless search of an unlocked suitcase found in the trunk of a cab in which the arrestee had been riding at the time of his arrest. Thus confronted with "the task of determining whether the warrantless search of respondent's suitcase falls on the *Chadwick* or the *Chambers/Carroll* side of the Fourth Amendment line," the Court ruled "that the warrant requirement of the Fourth Amendment applies to personal luggage taken from an automobile to the same degree it applies to such luggage in other locations." This is because the container's location within a vehicle affected neither the defendant's expectation of privacy as to the container's contents nor the true exigencies of the situation; the use of a suitcase "as a repository for personal items" is especially evident in such circumstances, and once the police have taken the case from the car its mobility is no longer affected by its prior location. Thus, said the Court in *Sanders,* the police should have seized the suitcase and then held it while a search warrant was sought, as there were no truly exigent circumstances mandating an immediate search.

Sanders was later limited to the special situation present in that case, where there was probable cause to search a particular container but not probable cause to search the vehicle generally. When the latter, broader form of probable cause exists, the Court held in *United States v. Ross,*[15] "the scope of the warrantless search authorized by [the automobile] exception is no broader and no narrower than a magistrate could legitimately authorize by warrant," so that if "probable cause justifies the search of a lawfully stopped vehicle, it justifies the search of every part of the vehicle and its contents that may conceal the object of the search." Thus in *Ross,* where (unlike *Chadwick* and *Sanders*) there was probable cause to search the entire vehicle for drugs, the police lawfully searched a brown paper bag and a zippered pouch found in the trunk.[16] The *Ross* Court explained that this conclusion was consistent with its earlier application of the *Carroll* rule on search of vehicles, and that it was justified by the practical consideration that "prohibiting police from opening immediately a container

14. 442 U.S. 753, 99 S.Ct. 2586, 61 L.Ed.2d 235 (1979).

15. 456 U.S. 798, 102 S.Ct. 2157, 72 L.Ed.2d 572 (1982).

16. The necessity under *Ross* for probable cause to search the entire vehicle and not simply a single container therein apparently refers to the situation which exists when the search activity is commenced, so that it does not matter that by the time the container is searched the police by search have eliminated other locations in the car as places where the sought items might be found.

In Texas v. Brown, 460 U.S. 730, 103 S.Ct. 1535, 75 L.Ed.2d 502 (1983), involving the warrantless seizure and search of a tied-up balloon seen in a car under circumstances strongly suggesting it contained drugs, the four-Justice plurality mistakenly approved the police action under the plain view doctrine. As three of the concurring Justices noted, the situation could be squared with *Ross* because the officer had also seen plastic vials and loose white powder in the glove compartment, which apparently "provided probable cause to believe that contraband was located somewhere in the car—and not merely in the one balloon at issue."

In United States v. Johns, 469 U.S. 478, 105 S.Ct. 881, 83 L.Ed.2d 890 (1985), agents saw two pickup trucks make contact with airplanes at a remote airstrip, approached the vehicles and smelled the odor of marijuana, and saw in the back of the trucks many packages wrapped in plastic and sealed with tape, which based on their experience they knew was how marijuana was commonly packaged. The defendants claimed this was a *Sanders* rather than a *Ross* type of case, but the Court disagreed: "Given their experience with drug smuggling cases, the officers no doubt suspected that the scent was emanating from the packages that they observed in the back of the pickup trucks. The officers, however, were unaware of the packages until they approached the trucks, and contraband might well have been hidden elsewhere in the vehicles. We agree with the Court of Appeals * * * that the Customs officers had probable cause to believe that not only the packages but also the vehicles themselves contained contraband."

in which the object of the search is most likely to be found and instead forcing them first to comb the entire vehicle would actually exacerbate the intrusion on privacy interests."[17] *Ross* was correctly decided within the framework of existing Fourth Amendment law, as it is more akin to *Chambers* than to *Chadwick,* but is for that reason subject to the same criticisms which have been directed at *Chambers.*

The distinction drawn in *Ross* is now irrelevant, however, for in *California v. Acevedo,*[18] involving search of a paper bag in a car on probable cause limited to the bag, the Court concluded "that it is better to adopt one clear-cut rule to govern automobile searches and eliminate the warrant requirement for closed containers set forth in *Sanders.*" The Court could see "no principled distinction in terms of either the privacy expectation or the exigent circumstances between the paper bag found by the police in *Ross* and the paper bag found by the police here," for in each case the container was "equally easy for the police to store and for the suspect to hide or destroy." Also, the Court reasoned, the distinction drawn in *Ross* (i) "provided only minimal protection for privacy," given the search-incident-to-arrest rule of *Belton* and also the fact that a search warrant would be "routinely forthcoming" whenever the container was lawfully seized; and (ii) "impeded effective law enforcement," because police had experienced difficulty in determining whether *Carroll* or instead *Sanders* was applicable in particular cases. The *Acevedo* dissenters cogently noted that the majority failed to explain why privacy in the contents of a container dissipated upon placement of the container into a vehicle, and that the majority's assertion *Sanders* had burdened law enforcement was "unsupported, inaccurate, and, in any event, an insufficient reason for creating a new exception to the warrant requirement."

Assuming a lawful warrantless search of a vehicle, may it automatically extend to the person of an occupant? No, the Supreme Court held in *United States v. Di Re,*[19] for the need to do so is no greater than the necessity "for searching guests of a house for which a search warrant had issued," which the government conceded would not be lawful. However, it has been argued that if the objects sought are not found in the car and they are of a size that they could be concealed on the person, then the occupants of the vehicle should be subject to search if the officer has reason to suspect one of them has the objects concealed on his person. In support, it is said that the *DiRe* analogy is unsound and that it is absurd to say that the occupants can take the narcotics out of the glove compartment and stuff them in their pockets, and drive happily away after the vehicle has been fruitlessly searched.

(d) Seizure for Other Purposes. If a vehicle is itself evidence of crime, may it be seized without a warrant as evidence in plain view? Not necessarily, concluded at least four members of the Court in *Coolidge v. New Hampshire,*[20] as a warrantless seizure on a plain view theory is permissible only upon "inadvertent discovery" of the item seized, because the "requirement of a warrant to seize imposes no inconvenience whatever" when "the police know in advance the location of the evidence and intend to seize it." But in *Cardwell v. Lewis,*[21] involving the war-

17. This is not to suggest that the search of the package must occur immediately. In United States v. Johns, 469 U.S. 478, 105 S.Ct. 881, 83 L.Ed.2d 890 (1985), two pickup trucks smelling of marijuana and containing many packages wrapped in the manner marijuana was commonly packaged were seized by agents. The packages were placed in a warehouse and opened without a warrant three days later. Applying *Ross,* the Court declined to hold "that searches of containers discovered in the course of a vehicle search are subject to temporal restrictions not applicable to the vehicle search itself." Thus the packages—as with the vehicle in which they were found—could be searched well after seizure of the vehicles, provided only that the delay was not "unreasonable because it adversely affected a privacy and possessory interest." There was no unreasonable delay here, as a warrantless search of the packages would have been lawful earlier, and in the interim the defendants had not sought return of the property.

18. ___ U.S. ___, 111 S.Ct. 1982, 114 L.Ed.2d 619 (1991).

19. 332 U.S. 581, 68 S.Ct. 222, 92 L.Ed. 210 (1948).

20. 403 U.S. 443, 91 S.Ct. 2022, 29 L.Ed.2d 564 (1971).

21. 417 U.S. 583, 94 S.Ct. 2464, 41 L.Ed.2d 325 (1974).

rantless seizure of defendant's car from a public parking lot some time following his arrest elsewhere, four members of the Court deemed this lawful; no mention was made of the "inadvertent discovery" limitation, though it was claimed the instant case differed from *Coolidge* "in the circumstances of the seizure," apparently a reference to the possibility that the defendant's wife might have gained access to the car had it not been immediately seized. In *Horton v. California*,[22] the Court rejected the *Coolidge* "inadvertent discovery" requirement but then seemingly endorsed the *result* in *Coolidge* as grounded in noncompliance with two other conditions of a plain view warrantless seizure: (i) the seized objects' incriminating character "must also be 'immediately apparent,'" which was not the case in *Coolidge* because "the cars were obviously in plain view, but their probative value remained uncertain until after the interiors were swept and examined microscopically"; and (ii) "not only must the officer be lawfully located in a place from which the object can be plainly seen, but he or she must also have a lawful right of access to the object itself," which was not the case in *Coolidge* because "the seizure of the cars was accomplished by means of a warrantless trespass on the defendant's property."

It is common at both the federal and state level to find statutes authorizing the seizure and subsequent forfeiture of a vehicle because it was used in certain criminal activity. The courts were once in disagreement as to whether such seizures could be made without a warrant, but here as well courts are now inclined to uphold the warrantless seizures for forfeiture by analogy to the *Chambers–Carney* line of cases. In *G.M. Leasing Corp. v. United States*,[23] involving a warrantless seizure of automobiles from public streets and lots as part of a levy on a corporation's assets for tax deficiencies. A unanimous Court upheld the seizures with the brief comment that the seizures "did not involve any invasion of privacy." But the Court went on to hold that the rule was otherwise as to warrantless searches, and thus unanimously held the agents had violated the Fourth Amendment when they entered the premises of the corporation and seized its books. The Court explained this was because under the *Camara* principle[24] the where-to-search issue could not be left to the discretion of an agent in the field, which highlights the fact that the Court never satisfactorily explained why the what-to-seize issue (i.e., was the corporation the alter ego of the taxpayer, subjecting its cars to levy) should be left to the agents in the field.

Police impound vehicles for a variety of reasons. This occurs when a vehicle is found abandoned, illegally parked or in unsafe mechanical condition, and, most frequently, when the owner or operator of the vehicle has been arrested in or near the car. Generally, courts are of the view that when a person is arrested away from home, the police may impound the personal effects that are with him at the time to ensure the safety of those effects. But the better view, consistent with *Dyke v. Taylor Implement Mfg. Co.*,[25] is that immediate impoundment of a car after the driver has been arrested for a minor traffic violation is improper because the police are obligated to give the defendant a reasonable opportunity to post his bail and obtain his prompt release. Moreover, if the driver is not afforded the usual opportunity to post bond, as provided by statute, rule of court or perhaps even police custom, then his improper continued detention contaminates the impoundment of the vehicle which results therefrom, so that whatever is found in the course of an inventory during impoundment must be suppressed.

22. ___ U.S. ___, 110 S.Ct. 2301, 110 L.Ed.2d 112 (1990).

23. 429 U.S. 338, 97 S.Ct. 619, 50 L.Ed.2d 530 (1977).

24. See § 3.9(a).

25. 391 U.S. 216, 88 S.Ct. 1472, 20 L.Ed.2d 538 (1968), where the driver, arrested for reckless driving, was at the courthouse to make bail at the time of the search, and the Court noted that the search of the vehicle could not be deemed incident to impoundment because "the police seem to have parked the car near the courthouse merely as a convenience to the owner, and to have been willing for some friend or relative to McKinney (or McKinney himself if he were soon released from custody) to drive it away."

A broader question, relevant whatever the cause of the vehicle operator's arrest, is whether impoundment should be considered the only feasible disposition of the car or whether, instead, the police should consider other possible alternatives or even consult the arrestee concerning them. Some courts took the latter positions, but in *Colorado v. Bertine*,[26] the Court rejected, as a Fourth Amendment matter, the argument that the impoundment of the car was improper because the arrested driver was not "offered the opportunity to make other arrangements." Rejecting an "alternative 'less intrusive' means" approach,[27] the Court concluded impoundment was lawful "even though courts might as a matter of hindsight be able to devise equally reasonable rules requiring a different procedure." But the Court cautioned that the individual officer's impound-or-lock-and-leave decision must be made "according to standard criteria," which was deemed to be met in the instant case because a police "directive establishes several conditions that must be met before an officer may pursue the park and lock alternative." This latter conclusion seems erroneous, for the applicable police regulation placed *no* restrictions upon resort to the impoundment alternative.

(e) **Search for Other Purposes.** It is common practice for the police to conduct an inventory of the contents of vehicles they have taken into their custody in order to protect the vehicle and the property in it, and to safeguard the police or other officers from claims of lost possessions. This practice received little attention from the Supreme Court [28] until *South Dakota v. Opperman*,[29] in which defendant's illegally parked car was towed to the city impound lot where an officer, observing articles of personal property in the car, proceeded to inventory it, finding a bag of marijuana in the unlocked glove compartment. The Court concluded:

> The Vermillion police were indisputably engaged in a caretaking search of a lawfully impounded automobile. * * * The inventory was conducted only after the car had been impounded for multiple parking violations. The owner, having left his car illegally parked for an extended period, and thus subject to impoundment, was not present to make other arrangements for the safekeeping of his belongings. The inventory itself was prompted by the presence in plain view of a number of valuables inside the car. * * * [T]here is no suggestion whatever that this standard procedure, essentially like that followed throughout the country, was a pretext concealing an investigatory police motive.
>
> On this record, we conclude that in following standard police procedures, prevailing throughout the country and approved by the overwhelming majority of courts, the conduct of the police was not "unreasonable" under the Fourth Amendment.

Although some jurisdictions have as a matter of local law taken a narrower view, such as that noninvestigative police inventory searches of automobiles without a warrant must be restricted to safeguarding those articles which are within plain view of the officer's vision, most courts follow what they perceive to be the implications of the *Opperman* holding.

The Court in *Opperman* was unwilling to impose upon the police, in the case where they have impounded a car without contemporaneous contact with the owner or possessor, the burden of complying with the procedure proposed by the four dissenters: "reasonable efforts under the circumstances to identify

26. 479 U.S. 367, 107 S.Ct. 738, 93 L.Ed.2d 739 (1987).

27. Relying upon the earlier rejection as to an arrestee's carried effects in Illinois v. Lafayette, 462 U.S. 640, 103 S.Ct. 2605, 77 L.Ed.2d 65 (1983).

28. The practice in its most common form failed to reach the Court. See Cady v. Dombrowski, 413 U.S. 433, 93 S.Ct. 2523, 37 L.Ed.2d 706 (1973) (atypical in that police had probable cause car contained gun, search upheld as part of "community caretaking functions"); Dyke v. Taylor Implement Mfg. Co., 391 U.S. 216, 88 S.Ct. 1472, 20 L.Ed.2d 538 (1968) (inventory improper because car parked temporarily while driver arranging for bail); Harris v. United States, 390 U.S. 234, 88 S.Ct. 992, 19 L.Ed.2d 1067 (1968) (evidence lawfully found while officer doing no more than securing the doors and windows); Cooper v. California, 386 U.S. 58, 87 S.Ct. 788, 17 L.Ed.2d 730 (1967) (car being held for forfeiture action several months away, inventory proper where police to have "car in their custody for such a length of time").

29. 428 U.S. 364, 96 S.Ct. 3092, 49 L.Ed.2d 1000 (1976).

and reach the owner of the property in order to facilitate alternative means of security or to obtain his consent to the search." What then of the more common situation in which the car was impounded incident to arrest of the operator? The four *Opperman* dissenters concluded that in such a case "his consent to the inventory is prerequisite to an inventory search." But in *Colorado v. Bertine*,[30] the Court rejected the notion that resort to such "alternative 'less intrusive' means"[31] is ever necessary. (However, the Court indicated that if such alternatives are sometimes utilized, then this must occur pursuant to "standardized criteria" set out in police regulations.)

In *Opperman* the vehicle was kept at "the old county highway yard," only partially fenced and a situs of past vandalism. The Court was unwilling to impose the burden or providing secure impoundment facilities as an alternative to inventory. There remained the claim, however, that if a particular jurisdiction does have secure facilities, then it has no need for inventory. But in *Bertine* the Court rejected such a claim, reasoning that "the security of the storage facility does not completely eliminate the need for inventorying; the police may still wish to protect themselves or the owners of the lot against false claims of theft or dangerous instrumentalities." Yet another issue is whether some special need vis-a-vis the particular car is necessary to trigger the authority to inventory. Because the *Opperman* opinion notes that the "inventory was prompted by the presence in plain view of a number of valuables inside the car," the case may be read as permitting inventory only upon such an observation. But that would be an unsound limitation; whatever right of inventory otherwise exists need not be "triggered" by the observation of such articles, for their absence does not reduce the likelihood of personal effects being present elsewhere in the car. To put the matter another way, the right to inventory is not limited by a probable cause requirement in the sense that there must be a case-by-case determination of the likelihood of valuables being in the vehicle.[32] Rather, it is sufficient that a particular inventory is not arbitrary, that is (as it was put in *Opperman*), that it "was carried out in accordance with *standard procedures* in the local police department."[33] Courts have rightly suppressed evidence found in an inventory where no such procedures existed or the existing procedures were not followed.

Finally, assuming that a particular inventory is otherwise lawful, *Opperman* does not foreclose challenge regarding the permissible scope of a vehicle inventory. The Court approved of examination within the unlocked glove compartment, "since it is a customary place for documents of ownership and registration, * * * as well as a place for the temporary storage of valuables." This would indicate that inventories may routinely extend to unlocked glove compartments, and also supports the conclusion that there is *no* right to "inventory" those parts of a vehicle in which one would not expect to find valuables stored. The inventory in *Opperman* did not extend to the locked trunk, and thus the case (as the dissenters noted) does not settle "whether the police might search a locked trunk or other compartment." But *Colorado v. Bertine*,[34] although not involving inventory into a trunk, rather clearly indicates such an inventory would be approved by the Court, as the Court upheld inventory within a vehicle kept in a secure storage facility on the ground the police are entitled "to protect themselves * * * against false claims of theft or dangerous instrumentalities."

30. 479 U.S. 367, 107 S.Ct. 738, 93 L.Ed.2d 739 (1987).

31. Relying upon the earlier rejection as to an arrestee's carried effects in Illinois v. Lafayette, 462 U.S. 640, 103 S.Ct. 2605, 77 L.Ed.2d 65 (1983).

32. In Colorado v. Bertine, 479 U.S. 367, 107 S.Ct. 738, 93 L.Ed.2d 739 (1987), the Court rejected the notion that the inventorying police must weigh the defendant's privacy interest against "the possibility" in the individual case that "dangerous or valuable items" would be found during the inventory.

33. In Colorado v. Bertine, 479 U.S. 367, 107 S.Ct. 738, 93 L.Ed.2d 739 (1987), the Court reemphasized that "[o]ur decisions have always adhered to the requirement that inventories be conducted according to standardized criteria."

34. 479 U.S. 367, 107 S.Ct. 738, 93 L.Ed.2d 739 (1987).

The *Opperman* inventory did not involve an opening of containers in the vehicle, and the dissenters were thus prompted to stress that "the Court's opinion does not authorize the inspection of suitcases, boxes, or other containers which might themselves be sealed, removed and secured without further intrusion." However, the Supreme Court more recently held "that it is not 'unreasonable' for police, as part of the routine procedure incident to incarcerating an arrested person, to search any container or article in his possession, in accordance with established inventory procedures." [35] Relying on that case, the Court in *Colorado v. Bertine* [36] upheld an inventory which extended to a backpack within the vehicle, and held that extending a vehicle inventory to containers therein did not depend upon the likelihood "that the containers might serve as a repository for dangerous or valuable items."

Bertine indicated a majority of the Court would deem it "permissible for police officers to open closed containers in an inventory search only if they are following standard police procedures that mandate the opening of such containers in every impounded vehicle." [37] However, the Court's later decision in *Florida v. Wells* [38] suggests that something short of this will likely suffice. The holding in *Wells,* agreed to by the entire Court, is only that the inventory there was unlawful because the police agency "had no policy whatever with respect to the opening of closed containers encountered during an inventory search." But dictum in *Wells,* justifiably objected to by four members of the Court,[39] goes on to say that "a police officer may be allowed sufficient latitude to determine whether a particular container should or should not be opened in light of the nature of the search and characteristics of the container itself."

In *Opperman,* the police, when they looked in the glove compartment, also found "miscellaneous papers" (a checkbook, an installment loan book, and a social security status card), which, so far as the record indicates, they removed without examination. *Opperman* thus should not be read as authorizing examination of such documents. Justice Powell, in his separate opinion, emphasized that approval of the inventory in the instant case "provides no general license for the police to examine all the contents of such automobiles," and correctly noted in this connection that "the police may discover materials such as letters or checkbooks that 'touch upon intimate areas of an individual's personal affairs,' and 'reveal much about a person's activities, associations and beliefs.' "

Courts have also upheld warrantless searches into vehicles for a variety of other purposes. If an arrestee's car is not impounded but is to be left at the scene of the arrest, some limited police activity to secure the car and its contents is reasonable. If a person's car, because of an accident or other circumstances, is to remain in a location where it is vulnerable to intrusion by vandals, then the police, if they have probable cause that the vehicle contains a weapon or similar device which would constitute a danger if it fell into the wrong hands, may conduct a warrantless search for that item.[40] A limited search of an automobile in an effort to ascertain ownership is permissible in some circumstances, such as where the car has apparently been abandoned or where the arrested driver is

35. Illinois v. Lafayette, 462 U.S. 640, 103 S.Ct. 2605, 77 L.Ed.2d 65 (1983).

36. 479 U.S. 367, 107 S.Ct. 738, 93 L.Ed.2d 739 (1987).

37. This language is from the opinion of three concurring Justices. The four-Justice plurality opinion seems less demanding, requiring only that the opening of closed containers be "according to standardized criteria." The two dissenters would not permit a vehicle inventory to extend to closed containers within the car.

38. 495 U.S. 1, 110 S.Ct. 1632, 109 L.Ed.2d 1 (1990).

39. Brennan and Marshall, JJ., interpreted *Bertine* as "premised on the city's inventory policy that left no discretion to individual officers as to the opening of containers"; Blackmun and Stevens, JJ., opined a state "probably could adopt a policy which requires the opening of all containers that are not locked, or a policy which requires the opening of all containers over or under a certain size, even though these policies do not call for the opening of all or no containers," but objected to the "entirely different" proposition of the majority "that an individual policeman may be afforded discretion in conducting an inventory search."

40. Cady v. Dombrowski, 413 U.S. 433, 93 S.Ct. 2523, 37 L.Ed.2d 706 (1973).

possibly not the owner and does not otherwise establish the matter of ownership. Also, if an officer has probable cause to believe that a vehicle has been the subject of burglary, tampering, or theft, he may make a limited warrantless entry and investigation of those areas he reasonably believes might contain evidence of ownership. And if the police find a person unconscious or disoriented and incoherent in a vehicle, it is reasonable for them to enter the vehicle for the purpose of giving aid to the person in distress and of finding information bearing upon the cause of his condition.

(f) Plain View, Subterfuge and Related Matters. Police may ordinarily seize evidence in plain view without a warrant, provided the initial intrusion which brings the police within plain view of such an article is itself lawful,[41] and thus when police seize evidence from a vehicle pursuant to any of the activities heretofore discussed, it is necessary at the outset to ascertain the lawfulness of the activity by which the police obtained the car and entered it. An object may not be seized from a car merely because the police plain view of it was lawfully acquired; there must be probable cause that the object is a fruit, instrumentality or evidence of crime. And under the "immediately apparent" requirement of *Coolidge v. New Hampshire*,[42] this probable cause must be determined without examination of the object other than is justified by the purpose underlying police entry of the vehicle.

Somewhat related is the question of under what circumstances the police may conduct an examination of some object (a car or personalty found therein) subsequent to the time they have taken custody of it. If the basis of the initial seizure of the item is that it constitutes evidence, it is plainly within the realm of police investigation to subject that object to scientific testing and examination for the purpose of determining its evidentiary value. If a vehicle is seized because it is reasonably believed to contain evidence, we have seen in *Chambers v. Maroney*[43] that the search may be undertaken later at the station instead of at the scene, and this is so even though it was feasible to conduct the search at the scene.[44] It would seem, however, that *Chambers* "contemplated some expedition in completing the searches so that automobiles could be released and returned to their owners."[45] In *United States v. Johns*,[46] where packages in a truck were opened three days after the vehicle was seized on probable cause the packages contained marijuana, the Court in upholding the search cautioned that possession of the vehicle "indefinitely" was not being approved and noted that in the instant case the defendants "never sought return of the property." A third situation is that in which a vehicle is in police custody for some other reason (e.g., an impoundment), and there then develops for the first time probable cause to search the car. Warrantless searches have been upheld in such circumstances, a result which might be defended on the ground that the vehicle was no less mobile than the vehicle in *Chambers* at the time of the search. Finally, it must be asked whether a lawfully impounded vehicle or items removed therefrom for safekeeping may later be searched or examined without probable cause that evidence will be discovered. *United States v. Edwards*,[47] discussed earlier,[48] seems to permit doing later what could have been done earlier, and thus may support the argument that when items have been exposed to police view under unobjectionable circumstances, then no reasonable expectation of privacy is breached by an officer taking a second look at such items. But *Edwards* cannot be extended to permit either (1) observation of items which need not be observed in the first instance for purposes of safekeeping, or (2) reexamination of items earlier inventoried to a significantly greater

41. Coolidge v. New Hampshire, 403 U.S. 443, 91 S.Ct. 2022, 29 L.Ed.2d 564 (1971).

42. 403 U.S. 443, 91 S.Ct. 2022, 29 L.Ed.2d 564 (1971).

43. 399 U.S. 42, 90 S.Ct. 1975, 26 L.Ed.2d 419 (1970).

44. Texas v. White, 423 U.S. 67, 96 S.Ct. 304, 46 L.Ed.2d 209 (1975).

45. White, J., dissenting in *Coolidge.*

46. 469 U.S. 478, 105 S.Ct. 881, 83 L.Ed.2d 890 (1985).

47. 415 U.S. 800, 94 S.Ct. 1234, 39 L.Ed.2d 771 (1974).

48. See § 3.5(c).

extent than was first necessary for purposes of completing the inventory.

The assertion by some members of the Court in *Coolidge* that a seizure on a plain view theory is permissible only upon "inadvertent discovery" of that object was later repudiated by a majority of the Court in *Horton v. California*.[49] This is an especially desirable turn of events in this context, for the previously stated criticisms [50] of the "inadvertent discovery" limitation are particularly compelling as to vehicle inventories. Though it had occasionally been held that evidence found in such an inventory must be suppressed if the police had suspected they might find such an item, this makes no sense whatsoever. What makes an inventory search reasonable under the requirements of the Fourth Amendment is not that the subjective motives of the police were simplistically pure, but rather that the facts of the situation indicate the inventory search was reasonable under the circumstances, i.e., that per *Opperman* and *Bertine* it was conducted pursuant to "standard police procedures." Departure from such procedures (or, indeed, a departure from the usual practice motivated by ulterior motives, a matter much more difficult for the defendant to establish) requires suppression of the evidence as come by through a pretext. Illustrative are instances in which the vehicle was searched incident to or inventoried following an arrest which would not have occurred but for the desire to search for evidence of some other crime, in which the vehicle was examined after defendant was denied an opportunity for release ordinarily afforded in such cases, or in which the vehicle was impounded when the usual practice is to leave the car at the scene or inventoried when the usual practice is merely to secure the vehicle.

§ 3.8 Stop and Frisk and Similar Lesser Intrusions

(a) Stop and Frisk: Fourth Amendment Theory. The issue of whether the police have the right to stop and question a suspect, without his consent, in the absence of grounds for an arrest was confronted by the Supreme Court for the first time in *Terry v. Ohio*.[1] A Cleveland police officer, after seeing three men repeatedly look into a store as if they were "casing" it for a stickup, approached the men and asked them to identify themselves and, when they only mumbled something, patted them down and found weapons on two of them. After stating the issue in the narrowest possible terms, "whether it is always unreasonable for a policeman to seize a person and subject him to a limited search for weapons unless there is probable cause for an arrest," the Court concluded:

> Each case of this sort will, of course, have to be decided on its own facts. We merely hold today that where a police officer observes unusual conduct which leads him reasonably to conclude in light of his experience that criminal activity may be afoot and that the persons with whom he is dealing may be armed and dangerous, where in the course of investigating this behavior he identifies himself as a policeman and makes reasonable inquiries, and nothing in the initial stages of the encounter serves to dispel his reasonable fear for his own or others' safety, he is entitled for the protection of himself and others in the area to conduct a carefully limited search of the outer clothing of such persons in an attempt to discover weapons which might be used to assault him.
>
> Such a search is a reasonable search under the Fourth Amendment, and any weapons seized may properly be introduced in evidence against the person from whom they were taken.

It soon became clear that *Terry* was not limited to cases based upon direct observations by the investigating officer, as in *Adams v. Williams* [2] the Court concluded that "reasonable cause for a stop and frisk" had been provided when an informant who had given

49. ___ U.S. ___, 110 S.Ct. 2301, 110 L.Ed.2d 112 (1990).

50. See § 3.4(k).

§ 3.8

1. 392 U.S. 1, 88 S.Ct. 1868, 20 L.Ed.2d 889 (1968).
2. 407 U.S. 143, 92 S.Ct. 1921, 32 L.Ed.2d 612 (1972).

reliable information in the past said a man seated in a nearby car was carrying narcotics and had a gun at his waist.

One important contribution of the *Terry* case to Fourth Amendment theory was the Court's conclusion that restraining a person on the street is a "seizure" and an exploration of the outer surfaces of his clothing is a "search," without regard to the labels which police or others choose to put on those activities. Another was the Court's further development of its recently-adopted balancing test as a means for judging the constitutionality of unique practices. Just the year before, in *Camara v. Municipal Court,*[3] the Court, by "balancing the need to search against the invasion which the search entails," held that warrants for housing inspections could be issued without the traditional quantum of case-by-case probable cause if appropriate legislative or administrative standards for area or periodic inspections were met. The *Camara* balancing test was quoted and relied upon in *Terry,* but it was now applied in a slightly different way: the police conduct had to be justified upon the facts of the individual case, but a lesser quantum of evidence was required.

Some have suggested that use of the balancing test in the manner contemplated by *Terry,* necessitating application on a case-by-case basis of some sort of probability standard different in some degree from the traditional probable cause standard, involves such subtle considerations that police would have great difficulty applying the test and courts would be most reluctant to second-guess the police. This would be a legitimate concern if the *Terry* balancing test somehow required striking the balance anew in each and every case, instead of merely calling for somewhat different treatment of street encounters generally and custodial arrests generally. That *Terry* involves only the latter was made clear in *Dunaway v. New York,*[4] where the Court rejected a proposed "multifactor balancing test of 'reasonable police conduct under the circumstances' to cover all seizures that do not amount to technical arrests" because it would provide insufficient guidance to police.

A third contribution to Fourth Amendment theory in *Terry* lies in the Court's response to the argument that a police power to stop and frisk should not receive express recognition because police have often utilized such street encounters for improper purposes, such as the wholesale harassment of minority groups. To this, the Court noted that the exclusionary rule "is powerless to deter invasions of constitutionally guaranteed rights where the police either have no interest in prosecuting or are willing to forego successful prosecution in the interest of serving some other goal." That language has been criticized in some quarters as saying that the police can set the limits of the exclusionary rule by ignoring it under some circumstances. But it must be read with another comment by the Court, namely, that the "exclusionary rule * * * cannot properly be invoked to exclude the products of legitimate police investigative techniques on the ground that much conduct which is closely similar involves unwarranted intrusions upon constitutional protections." Thus, the Court's quite valid point is really this: If exclusion of the fruits of *all* street encounters by declaring them all to be in violation of the Fourth Amendment would somehow put a stop to those engaged in for harassment and other improper purposes, it could at least be argued that the benefits derived would be worth the cost, but no such argument can be made here because the illegal encounters are usually motivated by objectives other than conviction and thus cannot be influenced by the exclusionary rule.

(b) Dimensions of a Permissible "Stop." If, as *Terry* teaches, there is a certain kind of police conduct, typically called a "stop," which may be undertaken upon less evidence than is needed for arrest because it is a lesser intrusion than an arrest, then it is obviously important to know just what kind of a seizure, undertaken for what purpose and made in what manner, can qualify as that lesser intru-

3. 387 U.S. 523, 87 S.Ct. 1727, 18 L.Ed.2d 930 (1967), discussed further in § 3.9(a).

4. 442 U.S. 200, 99 S.Ct. 2248, 60 L.Ed.2d 824 (1979).

sion. For example, because in *Terry* the officer acted in the interest of crime *prevention,* which was stressed by the Court, and because all members of the Court agreed some added power was necessary for that purpose, it might be asked if *Terry* stops may also be made for the purpose of crime *detection.* The proper answer is yes. When immediately after the perpetration of a crime the police may have no more than a vague description of the possible perpetrator, it would be irrational to deprive the officer of the opportunity to "freeze" the situation for a short time, so that he may make inquiry and arrive at a considered judgment about further action to be taken.

This conclusion is supported by *United States v. Hensley,*[5] where the Court concluded that a *Terry* stop on less than full probable cause would sometimes be permissible for the purpose of investigating criminal activity which had occurred on some prior occasion. But the Court cautioned that the "factors in the balance may be somewhat different" in such a case,[6] so that the reasons for permitting a seizure merely upon reasonable suspicion might not always be compelling. Thus, the Court cautiously limited its holding, expressly authorizing the stopping of "a person suspected of involvement in a past crime" only as to "felonies or crimes involving a threat to public safety," where "it is in the public interest that the crime be solved and the suspect detained as promptly as possible."

Similar reasoning supports the conclusion that a *Terry* stop may be made of a nonsuspect who might be able to supply information, though it may well be that the Fourth Amendment does not permit the stopping of potential witnesses to the same extent as those suspected of crime.

As for whether a *Terry* stop may be made for investigation of all types of crimes or only those of a relatively serious nature, the *Adams* decision is sufficiently ambiguous that this may fairly be said to be an open question outside the *Hensley* type of situation. Though admittedly articulation of offense-category limits as a matter of Fourth Amendment interpretation (as opposed to a policy reflected in a statute) would be most difficult, in support of such limits it may be said (i) that the need factor of the *Camara* balancing test cannot be sufficiently assessed without consideration of the seriousness of the crime under investigation, (ii) that meaningful review of police action is most difficult as to minor offenses such as loitering or disorderly conduct because these crimes are so diverse and diffuse, and (iii) that permitting stops for such minor crimes as marijuana possession presents the most obvious temptation to abuse the frisk as an occasion for searching for contraband.

Another important issue is whether the police conduct may still qualify as a lesser intrusion and thus a *Terry* stop if it includes force or a threat of force. Though it has occasionally been held that such action as surrounding the suspect or drawing weapons converts the police conduct into an arrest because the restriction of liberty of movement was complete, this is in error, for a stopping differs from an arrest not in the incompleteness of the seizure but in the brevity of it. The better view, therefore, is that surrounding the suspect will sometimes be an appropriate way of making the stop and maintaining the status quo, just as the drawing of weapons will sometimes be a reasonable precaution for the protection of officers and bystanders.[7] Hand-

5. 469 U.S. 221, 105 S.Ct. 675, 83 L.Ed.2d 604 (1985).

6. As the Court explained: "A stop to investigate an already completed crime does not necessarily promote the interest of crime prevention as directly as a stop to investigate suspected ongoing criminal activity. Similarly, the exigent circumstances which require a police officer to step in before a crime is committed or completed are not necessarily as pressing long afterwards. Public safety may be less threatened by a suspect in a past crime who now appears to be going about his lawful business than it is by a suspect who is currently in the process of violating the law. Finally, officers making a stop to investigate past crimes may have a wider range of opportunity to choose the time and circumstances of the stop."

7. As the Supreme Court recognized in United States v. Hensley, 469 U.S. 221, 105 S.Ct. 675, 83 L.Ed.2d 604 (1985). Responding to a flyer that the driver of a car was wanted for investigation of robbery and that the suspect should be considered armed and dangerous, the officer approached the car "with his service revolver drawn and pointed in the air." The Court declared that this "con-

cuffing ordinarily is improper, but may be resorted to when necessary to thwart the suspect's attempt to frustrate further inquiry. Although as a general matter it is not proper to place the detainee in a police car, such a step is permissible when dictated by special circumstances (e.g., inclement weather). There may occasionally be instances in which the use of physical force to make the stop will be justified, and also instances in which entry of private premises will be necessary to seize a fleeing suspect.

The police conduct should be judged in terms of what was done rather than what the officer involved may have called it at the time. If an officer tells the suspect he is under arrest but then conducts only a frisk and finds a weapon, a later determination that grounds for arrest were lacking should not render inadmissible the discovered weapon if there were in fact grounds for a stop and the frisk. Obviously the result would be otherwise if the search exceeded that permissible under *Terry*. In *Sibron v. New York* [8] the Court approved the reverse of the above proposition, so that if an officer perceives his conduct as a stop only but he makes a full search of the person rather than a mere frisk, the evidence found is admissible if in fact the officer had grounds to arrest.

Though the Court in *Terry* had little to say about the stopping part of the stop-and-frisk phenomenon, it did stress that an arrest "is a wholly different kind of intrusion upon individual freedom" which "is inevitably accompanied by future interference with the individual's freedom of movement," thus intimating that there were time and place limits upon a lawful stop. The permissible length depends upon the circumstances of the particular case. The results of the initial stop may arouse further suspicion or may dispel the questions in the officer's mind. If the latter is the case, the stop may go no further and the detained individual must be freed. But if the officer's suspicions are confirmed or are further aroused, the stop may be prolonged and the scope enlarged as required by the circumstances. This is not to say that the detention may continue as long as the reasonable suspicion persists; rather, it must be asked whether the police are diligently pursuing a means of investigation likely to resolve the matter one way or another very soon and whether it is essential to that investigation that the suspect's presence be continued during that interval.[9]

In pre-*Terry* days courts were inclined to hold that any movement of the suspect, even to a police call box a block away, converted the detention into an arrest for which full probable cause was required, but today courts are inclined to permit some movement of the suspect in the immediate area of the stop. It has been held that it is improper to transport the suspect to the crime scene, even if it is relatively close, for possible identification by the victim or witnesses when there exist less intrusive and more reasonable alternatives, such as bringing the victim and witnesses to the detention scene or arranging for such a confrontation on some future occasion. The prevailing view is to the contrary, and rightly so; usually the matter can be resolved most expeditiously by transporting the suspect, and if the identification is delayed the risks of error are substantially increased. However, a taking of the suspect to the police station in lieu of conducting the investigation at the scene will ordinarily take the police conduct outside the *Terry* rule.[10]

duct was well within the permissible range in the context of suspects who are reported to be armed and dangerous."

8. 392 U.S. 40, 88 S.Ct. 1889, 20 L.Ed.2d 917 (1968).

9. This approach was taken by the Court in United States v. Sharpe, 470 U.S. 675, 105 S.Ct. 1568, 84 L.Ed.2d 605 (1985), rejecting the court of appeals' approach because it "would effectively establish a *per se* rule that a 20-minute detention is too long to be justified under the *Terry* doctrine."

10. Dunaway v. New York, 442 U.S. 200, 99 S.Ct. 2248, 60 L.Ed.2d 824 (1979), discussed further in § 3.8(g).

As the Court reiterated in Hayes v. Florida, 470 U.S. 811, 105 S.Ct. 1643, 84 L.Ed.2d 705 (1985), "our view continues to be that the line is crossed when the police, without probable cause or a warrant, forcibly remove a person from his home or other place in which he is entitled to be and transport him to the police station, where he is detained, although briefly, for investigative purposes." But the Court went on to intimate that the investigative procedure used in *Hayes,* fingerprinting, would have been permissible without a warrant and on

Florida v. Royer[11] illustrates that a wrong choice of investigative techniques by the police can escalate a valid *Terry* stop into an illegal arrest. There a suspected drug courier was lawfully questioned in an airport concourse and then required to accompany the police about 40 feet to a small police office, where the suspect consented to a search of his suitcases after they were obtained from the airline and also brought to the room. Although the total elapsed time was 15 minutes, the four-Justice plurality in *Royer* concluded that the consent was the fruit of an illegal arrest. Some of the plurality's language suggests these Justices viewed the situation as equivalent to a taking to a police station, for it was stressed that Royer was held in "a police interrogation room." But they placed greater emphasis upon the asserted requirements that a *Terry* stop "last no longer than is necessary to effectuate the purpose of the stop" and that "the investigative methods employed should be the least intrusive means reasonably available to verify or dispel the officer's suspicion in a short period of time." These requirements were not met here, the plurality reasoned, as "the primary interest of the officers was * * * in the contents of his luggage," and thus the officers could have more expeditiously sought consent on the spot or could have used a narcotics detection dog, available at the airport, to check out the suitcases. Justice Brennan, concurring, though not "certain that the use of trained narcotics dogs constitutes a less intrusive means," asserted that a *Terry* stop "must be so strictly limited that it is difficult to conceive of a less intrusive means that would be effective to accomplish the purpose of the stop." The four dissenting Justices in *Royer*, though prepared to require that the police act reasonably in investigating a *Terry* detainee, rejected the more demanding "least intrusive means" principle, for which they found no support in prior cases. More recently, the Court has cautioned against "unrealistic second-guessing," and has declared that the "question is not simply whether some other alternative was available, but whether the police acted unreasonably in failing to recognize or to pursue it."[12]

(c) Action Short of a Stop. Not all police-citizen contacts constitute Fourth Amendment "seizures" which must be justified by showing grounds for the detention. "Only when the officer, by means of physical force or show of authority, has in some way restrained the liberty of a citizen," said the Court in *Terry*, "may we conclude that a 'seizure' has occurred." The Court then proceeded to "assume" that no seizure had occurred in that case until the frisk because it was unnecessary to pinpoint the precise earlier time at which the seizure commenced. The issue of what constitutes an encounter short of a *Terry* stop appeared to be presented more directly in *United States v. Mendenhall*,[13] where federal drug agents approached the defendant as she was walking through an airport concourse, identified themselves and asked to see her identification and airline ticket, which she produced for their inspection. Justice Stewart, in a part of his opinion joined by only one other member of the Court, concluded there had been no seizure, explaining:

> We conclude that a person has been "seized" within the meaning of the Fourth Amendment only if, in view of all of the circumstances surrounding the incident,[14] a reasonable person[15] would have believed that he was not free to leave. Examples of circum-

reasonable suspicion were it achieved by "a brief detention in the field."

11. 460 U.S. 491, 103 S.Ct. 1319, 75 L.Ed.2d 229 (1983).

12. United States v. Sharpe, 470 U.S. 675, 105 S.Ct. 1568, 84 L.Ed.2d 605 (1985).

13. 446 U.S. 544, 100 S.Ct. 1870, 64 L.Ed.2d 497 (1980).

14. In Florida v. Bostick, ___ U.S. ___, 111 S.Ct. 2382, 115 L.Ed.2d 389 (1991), the Court reversed a state court finding of seizure because the state court purportedly "adopted a *per se* rule prohibiting the police from randomly boarding buses as a means of drug interdiction." The Court remanded so that the state court could apply "the correct legal standard," which requires evaluation of "the totality of the circumstances."

15. In Florida v. Bostick, ___ U.S. ___, 111 S.Ct. 2382, 115 L.Ed.2d 389 (1991), the Court concluded that "the 'reasonable person' test presupposes an *innocent* person," and thus rejected the claim that the entire encounter (including a consent to search luggage the defendant knew contained drugs) was of necessity not voluntary.

stances that might indicate a seizure, even where the person did not attempt to leave, would be the threatening presence of several officers, the display of a weapon by an officer,[16] some physical touching of the person of the citizen, or the use of language or tone of voice indicating that compliance with the officer's request might be compelled. * * * In the absence of some such evidence, other inoffensive contact between a member of the public and the police cannot, as a matter of law, amount to a seizure of that person.

On the facts of this case, no "seizure" of the respondent occurred. The events took place in the public concourse.[17] The agents wore no uniforms and displayed no weapons. They did not summon the respondent to their presence, but instead approached her and identified themselves as federal agents. They requested, but did not demand to see the respondent's identification and ticket. Such conduct without more, did not amount to an intrusion upon any constitutionally protected interest. The respondent was not seized simply by reason of the fact that the agents approached her, asked her if she would show them her ticket and identification, and posed to her a few questions. Nor was it enough to establish a seizure that the person asking the questions was a law enforcement official.

By way of footnote, it was added that "the subjective intentions of the DEA agent in this case to detain the respondent, had she attempted to leave, is irrelevant except insofar as they may have been conveyed to the respondent." [18] More recently, a majority of the Supreme Court has endorsed the Stewart "reasonable person" standard.[19] However, in *Florida v. Bostick* [20] the Court recognized that literal application of the "free to leave" test would be inappropriate in some circumstances (e.g., in the present case, where defendant was questioned on a bus he did not want to leave in any event), and thus said that in such circumstances "the appropriate inquiry is whether a reasonable person would feel free to decline the officers' requests or otherwise terminate the encounter."

The lower court cases tend to find that it is not a seizure to approach a stationary pedestrian and ask him a question, or even to overtake a walking pedestrian and ask him to halt or to summon him to where the officer is, but that more dramatic steps, such as stopping a vehicle,[21] do bring the Fourth Amendment into play. Though the proposition is seldom articulated in precisely this form, the lower court decisions for the most part can be reconciled by this proposition: there is no Fourth Amendment seizure when the policeman, although perhaps making inquiries which a private citizen would not be expected to make, has otherwise conducted himself in a manner consistent with what would be viewed as a nonoffensive contact if it occurred between two ordinary citizens.

In *California v. Hodari D.*,[22] after a group of youths fled upon approach of a police car, one officer pursued Hodari on foot, prompting Hodari to throw to the ground what upon inspec-

16. In Florida v. Bostick, ___ U.S. ___, 111 S.Ct. 2382, 115 L.Ed.2d 389 (1991), the majority expressed "doubt" as to whether a seizure had occurred (but remanded for a determination of that issue), noting "the officers did not point guns at Bostick." The three dissenters, who argued there was a seizure, emphasized, inter alia, that one officer "held a gun in a recognizable weapons pouch."

17. In Florida v. Bostick, ___ U.S. ___, 111 S.Ct. 2382, 115 L.Ed.2d 389 (1991), the Court reversed a state finding of a seizure where that court purportedly "rested its decision on a single fact—that the encounter took place on a bus." But the Court acknowledged that "the cramped confines of a bus are one relevant factor that should be considered" when a court considers "all the circumstances surrounding the encounter."

18. That must be distinguished from the quite different point made in Brower v. County of Inyo, 489 U.S. 593, 109 S.Ct. 1378, 103 L.Ed.2d 628 (1989), namely, that for a seizure to have occurred there must have been "a governmental termination of freedom of movement *through means intentionally applied*," as the Fourth Amendment does not address "the accidental effects of otherwise lawful government conduct."

19. Florida v. Royer, 460 U.S. 491, 103 S.Ct. 1319, 75 L.Ed.2d 229 (1983) (4–Justice plurality and Blackmun, J., dissenting, apply that standard; no express rejection of that standard by other members of the Court).

20. ___ U.S. ___, 111 S.Ct. 2382, 115 L.Ed.2d 389 (1991).

21. Indeed, the Supreme Court has asserted without qualification that "stopping a car and detaining its occupants constitutes a seizure within the meaning of the Fourth Amendment." United States v. Hensley, 469 U.S. 221, 105 S.Ct. 675, 83 L.Ed.2d 604 (1985).

22. ___ U.S. ___, 111 S.Ct. 1547, 113 L.Ed.2d 690 (1991).

tion proved to be cocaine. The state court concluded that Hodari had been "seized" when he saw the officer pursuing him, and that consequently the cocaine was the fruit of that illegal (because without reasonable suspicion) seizure, but the Supreme Court disagreed. The word "seizure" in the Fourth Amendment, the Court declared, means "a laying on of hands or application of physical force to restrain movement, even when it is ultimately unsuccessful," [23] and also "*submission* to the assertion of authority," but not a "show of authority" as to which "the subject does not yield." As for Hodari's reliance on the *Mendenhall* test, the Court responded that the requirement "a reasonable person would have believed that he was not free to leave" "states a necessary, but not a *sufficient* condition for seizure * * * effected through a 'show of authority.'" The *Hodari D.* dissenters cogently argued that "the character of the citizen's response should not govern the constitutionality of the officer's conduct," and noted that the majority's holding could well "encourage unlawful displays of force that will frighten countless innocent citizens into surrendering whatever privacy rights they may still have."

The Supreme Court utilized the *Mendenhall* "reasonable person" test in *I.N.S. v. Delgado*,[24] upholding resort to "factory surveys," where with the employer's consent or pursuant to a warrant issued on a showing of probable cause that numerous illegal aliens were employed at a particular factory, numerous INS agents would survey the work force. In concluding that no seizure had occurred, the Court stressed (i) that "when people are at work their freedom to move about has been meaningfully restricted, not by the actions of law enforcement officials, but by the workers' voluntary obligations to their employers"; (ii) that stationing agents at the doors "posed no reasonable threat of detention to these workers while they walked through the factories on job assignments"; and (iii) that the individual respondents had not been seized because they had been subjected to "nothing more than a brief encounter" while at their work station or while moving about the factory, and "it was obvious from the beginning of the surveys that the INS agents were only questioning people."

(d) Grounds for a Permissible "Stop." Although the Court in *Terry* claimed it was "decid[ing] nothing today concerning the constitutional propriety of an investigative 'seizure' upon less than probable cause," a lesser standard was suggested when the Court related the holding to a situation "where a police officer observes unusual conduct which leads him reasonably to conclude in light of his experience that criminal activity may be afoot." The Court later indicated in *Adams v. Williams* [25] that a stopping for investigation could be made even when "there is no probable cause to make an arrest," but made no effort to articulate exactly what the standard was. More recently, in *United States v. Cortez*,[26] the Court noted that the various phrases used by the lower courts, such as "founded suspicion," were "not self-defining" but that the essence of the standard was that "the detaining officers must have a particularized and objective basis for suspecting the particular person stopped of criminal activity." Assuming a sufficient degree of suspicion, it is *not* also necessary that there be unavailable a less intrusive investigative technique.[27]

But the precise words used are less important than an understanding of the manner in which the standard differs from that for arrest. The *Terry* reference to when "criminal activity *may be* afoot" strongly suggests that

23. But, the majority went on to say that if it was unsuccessful the seizure would terminate, for it is incorrect "to say that for Fourth Amendment purposes there is a *continuing* arrest during the period of fugitivity." This means, the Court added, that if the officer had grabbed Hodari "but Hodari had broken away and had *then* cast away the cocaine, it would hardly be realistic to say that the disclosure had been made during the course of an arrest."

24. 466 U.S. 210, 104 S.Ct. 1758, 80 L.Ed.2d 247 (1984).

25. 407 U.S. 143, 92 S.Ct. 1921, 32 L.Ed.2d 612 (1972).

26. 449 U.S. 411, 101 S.Ct. 690, 66 L.Ed.2d 621 (1981).

27. United States v. Sokolow, 490 U.S. 1, 109 S.Ct. 1581, 104 L.Ed.2d 1 (1989) (concluding "such a rule would unduly hamper the police's ability to make sufficient on-the-spot decisions" and "would require courts to 'indulge in "unrealistic second-guessing"'").

even though the arrest standard may sometimes require that guilt be more probable than not, this is never the case as to a stopping for investigation,[28] where the very purpose is to clarify an ambiguous situation. Thus, if police saw men moving from one residence to another via car several boxes seen to contain large commercial-type electric typewriters, this would not be grounds for arrest, but these actions, though consistent with innocent activity, are suspicious enough to justify a temporary detention for the purpose of inquiry. Sometimes it is certain that a crime has occurred but quite uncertain as to who the perpetrator is, in which case again a stop may be permissible though an arrest would not be. *Luckett v. State,*[29] where a police officer stopped a green car with a license prefix 82J on the basis of a radio broadcast that such a car had been used by persons fleeing from a recent burglary, provides an excellent illustration of this point. The court quite properly concluded that while the officer "did not have probable cause to stop every green automobile with an 82J license prefix and formally arrest its occupants," there was a basis for a *Terry* stop.

The most common type of investigative stop situation is when, as in *Terry,* a patrolman observes suspicious conduct. The protean variety of observed circumstances which might lead to a stop makes generalization virtually impossible, but a few comments are in order: (1) Most such stops are for investigation of property crimes, and thus often are based upon the fact that the suspect is carrying some object in suspicious circumstances or is in a suspicious relationship to a car or building. (2) Because "deliberate furtive actions and flight at the approach of strangers or law officers are strong indicia of *mens rea,*"[30] efforts to avoid the police or avoid being seen by them can contribute to grounds for a stop and, if the means of avoidance are sufficiently extreme, may themselves justify the stop. (3) It is proper to consider the surrounding circumstances and the suspect's relationship to them, such as whether he "fits" the area in which he is found, whether it is a high crime area, whether he is about at a time of day when the suspected criminality is most likely to occur, and whether he is in the company of one who can be arrested for a present or recent crime. (4) It is proper to take account of the suspect's past criminal record, though such a record standing alone is never a basis for a stop. (5) The officer, based upon his training and experience, is allowed to make "inferences and deductions that might well elude an untrained person," but if his actions are later challenged he must be able to explain those inferences and deductions so as to show that there was "a particularized and objective basis" for the stop.[31] (6) If during an earlier nonseizure contact the person made contradictory or otherwise suspicious remarks, those comments may be taken into account.[32]

Another common situation is that in which a stop is made because a person is found near the scene of a recent crime and the police wish to determine if that person was the perpetrator. Though a "dragnet approach" is impermissible, detentions greater in number than the number of known perpetrators are proper if selective investigative procedures are utilized which provide a reasonable possibility that any person stopped is a perpetrator. In making that judgment, officers may properly consider: (1) the particularity of the description of the offender or the vehicle in which he fled; (2) the size of the area in which the offender might be found, as indicated by such facts as the elapsed time since the crime occurred; (3) the number of persons about in that area; (4) the known or probable direction of the offender's flight; (5) observed activity by the particular person stopped; and

28. As the Supreme Court has more recently put it, the requisite "level of suspicion is considerably less than proof of wrongdoing by a preponderance of the evidence." United States v. Sokolow, 490 U.S. 1, 109 S.Ct. 1581, 104 L.Ed.2d 1 (1989).

29. 259 Ind. 174, 284 N.E.2d 738 (1972).

30. Sibron v. New York, 392 U.S. 40, 88 S.Ct. 1889, 20 L.Ed.2d 917 (1968).

31. United States v. Cortez, 449 U.S. 411, 101 S.Ct. 690, 66 L.Ed.2d 621 (1981).

32. Florida v. Rodriguez, 469 U.S. 1, 105 S.Ct. 308, 83 L.Ed.2d 165 (1984).

(6) knowledge or suspicion that the person or vehicle stopped has been involved in other criminality of the type presently under investigation.

A third kind of situation, that in which the stopping is made on the basis of information received from an informant, occurs with much less frequency, but reached the Supreme Court in *Adams v. Williams*,[33] where an informant told the officer a man in a nearby car was carrying narcotics and had a gun at his waist. The Court concluded this "information carried enough indicia of reliability to justify the officer's forcible stop of Williams," as the "informant was known to him personally and had provided him with information in the past," the "informant here came forward personally to give information that was immediately verifiable at the scene," and under state law the informant was "subject to immediate arrest for making a false complaint had Sgt. Connolly's investigation proven the tip incorrect." The question raised by *Adams* is to what extent there is a lesser standard here than when a full arrest or search is made on an informant's tale, in which case probable cause is ordinarily lacking unless (i) the underlying circumstances show reason to believe that the informant is a credible person, and (ii) the underlying circumstances show the basis of the conclusions reached by the informant. As to the first or credibility aspect, the points relied upon in *Adams* are extremely weak; merely saying the informant had given information in the past without even indicating whether it proved to be accurate does not show credibility, and in the absence of any suggestion that the informer was aware of the seldom-used false complaint statute it cannot be said that credibility has been shown by the fact the informer was in the area and could have been arrested if his story proved to be false. As for the second or basis-of-knowledge prong, the Court in *Adams* offers nothing; the informer never said how she knew what she claimed to know, and certainly she did not give so many details as to permit an inference that she had a reliable source. Because of this failure of the Court in *Adams* to explain what departure from the then extant *Aguilar v. Texas*[34] formula, if any, was permissible, the post-*Adams* lower court cases were in disarray and not infrequently permitted stops based upon an informant's story though there was *absolutely no indication* of that informant's credibility or basis of knowledge.

There is much to be said for the proposition that just as strong a showing of both credibility and basis of knowledge should be required here as for arrest, though here the facts would not need to show as high a probability of criminal conduct. But when the Court revisited this area in *Alabama v. White*,[35] it decided otherwise: "Reasonable suspicion is a less demanding standard than probable cause not only in the sense that reasonable suspicion can be established with information that is different in quantity or content than that required to establish probable cause, but also in the sense that reasonable suspicion can arise from information that is less reliable than that required to show probable cause." In *White*, police received an anonymous call that the defendant, Ms. White, would leave a certain apartment in a certain vehicle, would be going to a certain motel, and would be in possession of an ounce of cocaine inside a brown attache case. A woman was then seen to leave the building where that apartment was, get in the described vehicle and drive in the direction of the motel, at which point she was stopped. The Court declared: (i) that it was not prepared to say that an anonymous call by itself "could never provide the reasonable suspicion necessary for a *Terry* stop"; (ii) that nonetheless the call in this case was standing alone insufficient, for like the call in *Illinois v. Gates*[36] it gave absolutely no indication of reliability or basis of knowledge; (iii) that some corroboration of the anonymous informant's story is clearly insufficient, such as the discovery of the described vehicle out-

33. 407 U.S. 143, 92 S.Ct. 1921, 32 L.Ed.2d 612 (1972).

34. 378 U.S. 108, 84 S.Ct. 1509, 12 L.Ed.2d 723 (1964).

35. ___ U.S. ___, 110 S.Ct. 2412, 110 L.Ed.2d 301 (1990).

36. 462 U.S. 213, 103 S.Ct. 2317, 76 L.Ed.2d 527 (1983).

side the specified apartment, for "anyone could have 'predicted' that fact because it was a condition presumably existing at the time of the call"; and (iv) that the total corroboration in the instant "close case" was sufficient, as "the caller's ability to predict respondent's *future behavior*, because it demonstrated inside information—a special familiarity with respondent's affairs," meant it was "reasonable for police to believe that a person with access to such information is likely to also have access to reliable information about that individual's illegal activities." But that is a questionable conclusion; as the three dissenters in *White* noted, "anybody with enough knowledge about a given person to make her the target of a prank, or to harbor a grudge against her, will certainly be able to formulate a tip about her like the one predicting Vanessa White's excursion."

A similar problem can arise when the stop is made on the basis of information received via police channels, as illustrated by *United States v. Hernandez.*[37] There, an officer stopped a van on the basis of a radio message that it contained several illegal aliens, and *after* the stop observed circumstances providing grounds for an arrest which when made resulted in the discovery of certain evidence. The defendant relied upon *Whiteley v. Warden,*[38] holding that an arrest made in response to a police bulletin may be upheld only upon a subsequent showing of probable cause at the source (which had not been done here), but the court responded that no such showing was needed to support an investigatory stop instead of an arrest. Such a conclusion is in error and has been properly rejected by other courts, for to accept all police bulletins at face value is to abandon any requirement of an "indicia of reliability" (to use the *Adams* language). By the same token, there is no reason to be more demanding than *Whiteley* in this context, and thus (as the Supreme Court held in *United States v. Hensley*[39]) a stopping in reliance upon a conclusory flyer issued by another department indicating the person is wanted for investigation of a felony is lawful, *provided* the flyer "has been issued on the basis of articulable facts supporting a reasonable suspicion." In other words, with a *Terry* stop as with a full-fledged arrest, it suffices that the facts justifying the seizure were then in the hands of the directing or requesting agency.

In *Brown v. Texas,*[40] in the course of holding that police did not have grounds to stop a man who was seen walking away from another man in an alley in an area with a high incidence of drug traffic, a unanimous Court emphasized that under the Fourth Amendment a seizure must either "be based on specific, objective facts" or "be carried out pursuant to a plan embodying explicit, neutral limitations on the conduct of individual officers." In support of the latter part of this statement, the Court cited *Delaware v. Prouse*[41] and *United States v. Martinez-Fuerte,*[42] which state that stopping of all cars at a checkpoint to examine drivers' licenses or to question occupants about their alienage would be lawful because the intrusion is not "subject to the discretion of the official in the field." This raises the question of whether this standardized procedures approach, which originated in *Camara v. Municipal Court*[43] and has been utilized generally in assessing so-called inspections or administrative searches,[44] has any application to stop-and-frisk cases. That is, if in *Brown* it had been established that the officers stopped the defendant pursuant to a police department "plan" to question all pedestrians found in the "high drug problem area," would the outcome have been different? Though certainly there is good reason to favor such law enforcement planning by police agencies, it is rather doubtful that resort to that kind of plan in lieu of continued reliance upon an individualized suspicion approach, would be permitted. This is because,

37. 486 F.2d 614 (7th Cir.1973).

38. 401 U.S. 560, 91 S.Ct. 1031, 28 L.Ed.2d 306 (1971).

39. 469 U.S. 221, 105 S.Ct. 675, 83 L.Ed.2d 604 (1985).

40. 443 U.S. 47, 99 S.Ct. 2637, 61 L.Ed.2d 357 (1979).

41. 440 U.S. 648, 99 S.Ct. 1391, 59 L.Ed.2d 660 (1979).

42. 428 U.S. 543, 96 S.Ct. 3074, 49 L.Ed.2d 1116 (1976).

43. 387 U.S. 523, 87 S.Ct. 1727, 18 L.Ed.2d 930 (1967).

44. See § 3.9.

as the Supreme Court has intimated, the neutral plan approach is for use in those situations "in which the balance of interests precludes insistence upon 'some quantum of individualized suspicion.' "[45] If a plan dealing generally with a certain constant law enforcement concern, such as drug trafficking, could somehow be more carefully and tightly formulated than suggested above, it is of course possible that it would be deemed to pass muster under *Camara.* More likely, however, is the possibility that a plan addressing a "special" problem existing at a certain time and place would be upheld.

(e) "Frisk" for Weapons. In determining the lawfulness of a frisk, two matters are to be considered: (i) whether the officer was rightly in the presence of the party frisked so as to be endangered if that person was armed; and (ii) whether the officer had a sufficient degree of suspicion that the party frisked was armed and dangerous. As to the first, Justice Harlan helpfully commented in his separate *Terry* opinion that if "a policeman has a right * * * to disarm a person for his own protection, he must first have a right not to avoid him but to be in his presence." Thus a mere bulge in a pedestrian's pocket, insufficient to justify a stopping for investigation, would not be a basis for a frisk by a passing officer, though quite clearly the same bulge would entitle the officer to frisk a person he had already lawfully stopped for investigation. And while some language in *Terry* could be read as saying a frisk would be in order incident to a lawful stop only if a preliminary inquiry were made and did not clear up the matter, such a limitation would be unsound and has not been followed by the Supreme Court [46] or the lower courts.

As for the second factor, *Terry* says that what is required is that the officer's observations lead him "reasonably to conclude * * * that the persons with whom he is dealing may be armed and presently dangerous." The use of the phrase "may be" makes it apparent that it will suffice that there is a substantial possibility the person is armed, and that there need not be the quantum of evidence which would justify an arrest for the crime of carrying a concealed weapon. Sometimes this possibility may be said to exist merely because of the nature of the crime under investigation, while on other occasions something in addition will be required, such as a bulge in the suspect's clothing, a sudden movement by the suspect toward a pocket or other place where a weapon could be hidden, or awareness that the suspect was armed on a previous occasion. The test is an objective one, and thus the officer need not later demonstrate that he was in actual fear. If the *Terry* test for a frisk cannot be met, this does not mean that the officer is powerless to do anything in the interest of self-protection. The teaching of *Pennsylvania v. Mimms* [47] is that without any showing the particular suspect may be armed, an officer may require a person lawfully stopped to alight from his car in order to diminish "the possibility, otherwise substantial, that the driver can make unobserved movements." [48]

The Court in *Terry* emphasized that what is here referred to as a "frisk" must "be confined in scope to an intrusion reasonably designed to discover guns, knives, clubs, or other hidden instruments for the assault of the police officer," and found the officer had so limited his actions by patting down the clothing first and reaching inside only upon feeling a weapon. In the companion case of *Sibron v. New York,*[49] the officer was deemed to have exceeded the permissible scope of such a search in that he made "no attempt at an initial limited exploration for arms" but instead "thrust his hand into Sibron's pocket."

45. United States v. Martinez–Fuerte, 428 U.S. 543, 96 S.Ct. 3074, 49 L.Ed.2d 1116 (1976).

46. In Adams v. Williams, 407 U.S. 143, 92 S.Ct. 1921, 32 L.Ed.2d 612 (1972), the protective search was upheld though the officer asked no questions of the suspect.

47. 434 U.S. 106, 98 S.Ct. 330, 54 L.Ed.2d 331 (1977).

48. In United States v. Hensley, 469 U.S. 221, 105 S.Ct. 675, 83 L.Ed.2d 604 (1985), where there was reasonable suspicion the driver was armed and dangerous, the Court held the officer's conduct was "well within the permissible range" when he had both the driver and the passenger step out of the car, resulting in the observation of a gun through the passenger door.

49. 392 U.S. 40, 88 S.Ct. 1889, 20 L.Ed.2d 917 (1968).

Though this means that usually a frisk must commence with a pat-down, *Adams v. Williams*[50] indicates there are exceptions, for there the officer's conduct was upheld though he immediately reached into the suspect's clothing. Because the informant in that case had indicated the exact location of the weapon, some courts have taken that to be the basis of the *Adams* exception, but a more reasonable interpretation is that the immediate search was upheld because the suspect's failure to comply with the officer's request that he get out of the car made the possible weapon, as the Court put it, "an even greater threat." As for the permissible extent of the pat-down, the Court in *Terry* unfortunately quoted a rather distressing description,[51] in fact intended to describe what may be done after arrest and before transportation to the station. The need is only to find implements which could be reached by the suspect during the brief face-to-face encounter, not to uncover items cleverly concealed and to which access could be gained only with considerable delay and difficulty, and thus the pat-down should be limited accordingly.

In *Terry,* the Court stressed that the officer "did not place his hands in [the suspects'] pockets or under the outer surface of their garments until he had felt weapons." But the officer need not be absolutely certain that the individual is armed and thus the question is whether there was anything in the officer's perception to indicate it was not a weapon because of its size or density. This would, for example, bar a search when only a soft object was felt in the pat-down. Assuming grounds for a search because of the pat-down, that search must be limited to retrieving and inspecting the suspect object; as the Court stressed in *Terry,* the officer there, once he felt what appeared to be weapons, "merely reached for and removed the guns."

As for whether such a protective search may ever extend beyond the person of the suspect, one way in which this question arises is when an officer searches within a vehicle in which the stopped suspect was riding. In *Michigan v. Long*[52] the Supreme Court held "that the search of the passenger compartment of an automobile, limited to those areas in which a weapon may be placed or hidden, is permissible if the police officer possesses a reasonable belief based on 'specific and articulable facts which, taken together with the rational inferences from those facts, reasonably warrant' the officers in believing that the suspect is dangerous and the suspect may gain immediate control of weapons." In *Long,* an officer actually saw a knife in the car before the search and the person under investigation for erratic driving was being allowed to reenter the car to get the vehicle registration. But the Court unfortunately took an expansive view of what constitutes danger in the context of a *Terry* stop of a person in an automobile, understandably prompting the dissenters to declare that "the implications of the Court's decision are frightening." For one thing, the Court in *Long* asserted that if the investigation did not result in an arrest, then the suspect "will be permitted to reenter his automobile, and he will then have access to any weapons inside." Just why the suspect would want to attack the officer who had told him he was free to go was not explained. For another, the Court stressed the risk that a *Terry* suspect might "break away from police control and retrieve a weapon from his automobile." One might think that in any case where such a danger was perceived by the officer, who is entitled to order the suspect out of the car,[53] he would move him a sufficient distance away or take other steps to overcome the danger. But the Court in *Long* declared that officers are not required to "adopt alternate means to ensure

50. 407 U.S. 143, 92 S.Ct. 1921, 32 L.Ed.2d 612 (1972).

51. "[T]he officer must feel with sensitive fingers every portion of the prisoner's body. A thorough search must be made of the prisoner's arms and armpits, waistline and back, the groin and the area about the testicles, and entire surface of the legs down to the feet."

52. 463 U.S. 1032, 103 S.Ct. 3469, 77 L.Ed.2d 1201 (1983).

53. Pennsylvania v. Mimms, 434 U.S. 106, 98 S.Ct. 330, 54 L.Ed.2d 331 (1977).

their safety in order to avoid the intrusion involved in a *Terry* encounter."

Another circumstance in which the question arises whether a protective search may extend beyond the person of the suspect is when the officer examines the contents of items carried by the suspect, such as a purse, shopping bag, or briefcase. Though case authority upholding such conduct is to be found, there is much to be said for the notion that the officer should simply put the object out of the suspect's reach for the duration of the encounter. But given the Supreme Court's approach in *Long,* it may be argued that even this alternative means can be disregarded.

Because a frisk, unlike a search incident to an arrest, has but a single purpose, that of finding weapons which could be used to harm the officer, it has sometimes been suggested that the best way to ensure that officers act for that purpose alone and do not use the frisk as a pretext to search for evidence is by adopting a special exclusionary rule for frisk situations to the effect that only weapons are admissible. The Supreme Court has declined to adopt such a rule,[54] and lower courts readily admit other objects deemed to have been lawfully uncovered by the frisk. Others object to the proposal because it would introduce difficult fact issues (e.g., if a gun was found, was it found before the narcotics were found so that the narcotics may be said to have been found incident to an arrest rather than incident to a stop only) and would often confront the officer with the "repellent" obligation to turn loose an obviously guilty person.

(f) Roadblocks. The use of checkpoints to uncover violations of a certain type by persons passing by is one kind of regulatory search discussed later.[55] By contrast, the concern here is with utilization of a roadblock for much the same purpose as in many stop-and-frisk situations: discovery and apprehension of a person who recently has committed a particular crime in the area. Illustrative would be a case in which, following a bank robbery and information the robber had left town in a vehicle via a certain road, all cars travelling that road were stopped at a checkpoint so that each of them could be checked for the robber. It has been suggested that if an officer has reasonable cause to believe that a felony has been committed and that stopping all or most vehicles moving in a particular direction or directions is reasonably necessary to permit a search for the perpetrator or victim of such felony in view of the seriousness and special circumstances of such felony, then he may order the drivers of such vehicles to stop, and may search such vehicles to the extent necessary to accomplish such purpose.

The Supreme Court has never dealt with the issue, and the lower court cases are not particularly helpful, for in the main they merely assume the legality of the roadblock in the course of holding admissible items seen in plain view when a car stopped or thrown from the car as it was being required to stop, or in holding there were grounds to arrest by matching an occupant in the stopped car with a description of the wanted person. It would seem, however, that the Fourth Amendment limits on use of roadblocks should be somewhat different than those upon an ordinary *Terry* stop: (1) a roadblock should be permitted only upon a reliable report of a crime, and not upon suspicion of criminal conduct; (2) a roadblock should be permitted only for a rather serious crime carrying with it a strong public interest in prompt apprehension of the perpetrator; (3) a roadblock should be permitted only if reasonably located, that is, there must be some reasonable relation between the commission of the crime and the establishment and location of the roadblock, which necessitates consideration of police knowledge concerning the number of alternative paths of escape or the particular direction in which the perpetrator is reasonably believed to be headed.

54. Michigan v. Long, 463 U.S. 1032, 103 S.Ct. 3469, 77 L.Ed.2d 1201 (1983).

55. See § 3.9(f), (g).

(g) Detention at the Police Station for Investigation. In *Davis v. Mississippi*,[56] petitioner and 24 other black youths were detained for questioning and fingerprinting in connection with a rape for which the only leads were a general description and a set of fingerprints. The Court held that petitioner's prints should have been excluded as the fruits of a seizure in violation of the Fourth Amendment, but intimated that a detention at the station might sometimes be permissible on evidence insufficient for arrest:

> Detentions for the sole purpose of obtaining fingerprints are no less subject to the constraints of the Fourth Amendment. It is arguable, however, that because of the unique nature of the fingerprinting process, such detentions might, under narrowly defined circumstances, be found to comply with the Fourth Amendment even though there is no probable cause in the traditional sense. * * * Detention for fingerprinting may constitute a much less serious intrusion upon personal security than other types of police searches and detentions. Fingerprinting involves none of the probing into an individual's private life and thoughts that marks an interrogation or search. Nor can fingerprint detention be employed repeatedly to harass any individual, since the police need only one set of each person's prints. Furthermore, fingerprinting is an inherently more reliable and effective crime-solving tool than eyewitness identifications or confessions and is not subject to such abuses as the improper lineup and the "third degree." Finally, because there is no danger of destruction of fingerprints, the limited detention need not come unexpectedly or at an inconvenient time. For this same reason, the general requirement that the authorization of a judicial officer be obtained in advance of detention would seem not to admit of any exception in the fingerprinting context.

The *Davis* dictum has had considerable impact. Statutes or court rules authorizing brief detention at the station by court order on less than the grounds needed for arrest, where the purpose of the detention is to conduct various identification procedures, were adopted in several jurisdictions. These provisions have been upheld by the courts, and other cases have upheld such procedures even in the absence of a specific statute or rule.

The matter was cast into some doubt by *Dunaway v. New York*,[57] where defendant confessed after being picked up and brought to the station for a brief period of questioning. Though he had not been told that he was under arrest and had not been booked, the Court rejected the state's claim that such a seizure did not require probable cause for arrest but only a lesser quantum of evidence under the *Terry* balancing test. The Court reasoned that "the detention of petitioner was in important respects indistinguishable from a traditional arrest," as he "was not questioned briefly where he was found" but instead was "transported to a police station" and "would have been physically restrained if he had refused to accompany the officers or had tried to escape their custody." Though this language might be viewed as a repudiation of the *Davis* dictum, a more careful assessment of *Dunaway* shows that it is fully compatible with *Davis*.

This conclusion is supported by the following: (1) The issue in *Dunaway* is narrowly stated as concerning only "the legality of custodial questioning on less than probable cause for a full-fledged arrest." (2) The holding is likewise limited to seizure "for interrogation." (3) The only reference back to *Davis* by the Court was to show that the detention there did not come within the dictum because the suspect was "also subjected to interrogation." (4) The *Davis* dictum contemplated a limited detention which "need not come unexpectedly or at an inconvenient time," while in *Dunaway* the Court was dealing with defendant's abrupt seizure from a neighbor's home. (5) The *Davis* dictum also contemplated that without exception "the authorization of a judicial officer be obtained in advance of detention," while in *Dunaway* the Court was confronted with a warrantless seizure under circumstances which were unquestionably not exigent. (6) A major concern voiced in *Dunaway*, that a separate balancing test for sta-

56. 394 U.S. 721, 89 S.Ct. 1394, 22 L.Ed.2d 676 (1969).

57. 442 U.S. 200, 99 S.Ct. 2248, 60 L.Ed.2d 824 (1979).

tionhouse detentions could cause Fourth Amendment protections to "all too easily disappear * * * when that balancing may be done in the first instance by police officers," is inapplicable to the warrant procedure contemplated by *Davis.* (7) Especially because both decisions were authored by Justice Brennan, one would expect any repudiation of the *Davis* dictum to be stated forthrightly. (8) The *Dunaway* Court makes absolutely no mention of the statutes, court rules or appellate decisions which have *Davis* as their foundation. It is thus not at all surprising that the Court has more recently opined again that "the Fourth Amendment might permit the judiciary to authorize the seizure of a person on less than probable cause and his removal to the police station for the purpose of fingerprinting," and has taken specific note of the adoption of procedures in several states in reliance upon the *Davis* dictum.[58]

(h) Brief Seizure of Objects. A detention for investigation of a somewhat different kind, involving objects rather than a person, was involved in *United States v. Van Leeuwen.*[59] A postal clerk advised a policeman that he was suspicious of two packages of coins just mailed, and the packages were then held at the post office while an investigation was conducted which culminated in the issuance of a warrant and search of the packages there 29 hours after they were mailed. Citing *Terry,* a unanimous Court declared that the suspicious circumstances "certainly justified detention, without a warrant, while an investigation was made." But the Court then disposed of the case with a broader pronouncement:

> No interest protected by the Fourth Amendment was invaded by forwarding the packages the following day rather than the day when they were deposited. The significant Fourth Amendment interest was in the privacy of this first class mail; and that privacy was not disturbed or invaded until the approval of the magistrate was obtained.

Van Leeuwen was an easy case because the defendant was unable to show that the invasion intruded upon either a privacy interest in the contents of the packages or a possessory interest in the packages themselves. It thus did not resolve the constitutionality of the practice of detaining the luggage possessed by suspected drug couriers at airports while further investigation (typically, exposure of the suitcases to a drug-detection dog) was conducted, later confronted by the Court in *United States v. Place.*[60] Using the *Terry* balancing of interests approach, the Court there concluded that "the governmental interest in seizing the luggage briefly to pursue further investigation is substantial," and that because "seizures of property can vary in intrusiveness, some brief detentions of personal effects may be so minimally intrusive of Fourth Amendment interests that strong countervailing governmental interests will justify a seizure based only on specific articulable facts that the property contains contraband or evidence of a crime." But the Court then cautioned that "in the case of detention of luggage within the traveler's immediate possession, the police conduct intrudes on both the suspect's possessory interest in his luggage as well as his liberty interest in proceeding with his itinerary," in that "such a seizure can effectively restrain the person since he is subjected to the possible disruption of his travel plans in order to remain with his luggage or to arrange for its return." For this reason, said the Court in *Place,* "the limitations applicable to investigative detentions of the person * * * define the permissible scope of an investigative detention of the person's luggage on less than probable cause." This would appear to mean that in such circumstances the container may be detained without full probable cause only so long as could the suspect from whose possession it was taken, so that the suspect at his option may also remain at the place of the seizure for that length of time and then reclaim the container unless in the interim the suspicion has grown into probable cause.

58. Hayes v. Florida, 470 U.S. 811, 105 S.Ct. 1643, 84 L.Ed.2d 705 (1985).

59. 397 U.S. 249, 90 S.Ct. 1029, 25 L.Ed.2d 282 (1970).

60. 462 U.S. 696, 103 S.Ct. 2637, 77 L.Ed.2d 110 (1983).

§ 3.9 Inspections and Regulatory Searches

(a) General Considerations. In the discussion which follows, the concern is with a variety of rather special search practices which are commonly described either as "inspections" or as "regulatory searches." These practices are directed toward certain unique problems unlike those ordinarily confronted by police officers in their day-to-day investigative and enforcement activities. Some of the practices, such as the examination of the effects of persons entering the country from abroad, have been followed for many years and have rather strong historical credentials, while others, such as the airport hijacker detection screening process, are rather recent innovations undertaken in an effort to respond to new problems. However, they all have this in common: it is generally assumed that the problems to which they are addressed could not be adequately dealt with under the usual Fourth Amendment restraints and that consequently the practices must be judged by somewhat different standards.

A theoretical basis for doing precisely this did not clearly emerge until the Supreme Court's decision in *Camara v. Municipal Court*.[1] In the course of holding that unconsented safety inspections of housing could be conducted pursuant to a warrant issued upon less than the usual quantum of probable cause, the Court declared that "there can be no ready test for determining reasonableness other than by balancing the need to search against the invasion which the search entails." Under this balancing theory, the Court continued, it is necessary to consider (i) whether the practice at issue has "a long history of judicial and public acceptance," (ii) whether the practice is essential to achieve "acceptable results," and (iii) whether the practice involves "a relatively limited invasion of * * * privacy." Assessing those factors, the Court in *Camara* held that inspection warrants could issue pursuant to "reasonable legislative or administrative standards" even without case-by-case probable cause. That is, searches of the kind at issue could occur so long as procedures were followed to ensure against the arbitrary selection of those to be subjected to them. The *Camara* balancing test was later used in *Terry v. Ohio*[2] to permit brief seizures for investigation upon evidence less than that required for a full-fledged arrest. There a case-by-case determination was required, but the special circumstances justified the practice on what one might call a "watered-down" version of probable cause. Use of the *Camara–Terry* balancing test in assessing the various practices discussed herein has frequently resulted in the conclusion that these practices may constitutionally be undertaken on one or both of the bases just described, that is, upon a showing in the individual case of reasonable suspicion short of traditional probable cause, or upon a showing that the individual case arose by application of standardized procedures involving neutral criteria.

(b) Inspection of Housing. In *Camara v. Municipal Court*,[3] concerning the constitutionality of the San Francisco housing inspection scheme whereunder "routine" inspections for violations of the city housing code could be made without a warrant, the Court had occasion to resolve two important issues: (i) whether such inspections must be conducted pursuant to a warrant; and (ii) what grounds are needed to undertake such inspections. On the warrant issue, the majority reasoned that because no showing had been made "that fire, health, and housing code inspection programs could not achieve their goals within the confines of a reasonable search warrant requirement," and because also the searches at issue "are significant intrusions" which "when authorized and conducted without a warrant procedure lack the traditional safeguards which the Fourth Amendment guarantees," unconsented housing inspections could ordinarily be conducted only pursuant to a search warrant. But then,

§ 3.9

1. 387 U.S. 523, 87 S.Ct. 1727, 18 L.Ed.2d 930 (1967).

2. 392 U.S. 1, 88 S.Ct. 1868, 20 L.Ed.2d 889 (1968).

3. 387 U.S. 523, 87 S.Ct. 1727, 18 L.Ed.2d 930 (1967).

utilizing the balancing test described above, the Court rejected appellant's claim that such a warrant requires "probable cause to believe that a particular dwelling contains violations of * * * the code being enforced," and instead held that reasonable standards based upon such factors as the passage of time, the nature of the building, or the condition of the entire area would suffice:

> First, such programs have a long history of judicial and public acceptance. * * * Second, the public interest demands that all dangerous conditions be prevented or abated, yet it is doubtful that any other canvassing technique would achieve acceptable results. Many such conditions—faulty wiring is an obvious example—are not observable from outside the building and indeed may not be apparent to the inexpert occupant himself. Finally, because the inspections are neither personal in nature nor aimed at the discovery of evidence of crime, they involve a relatively limited invasion of the urban citizen's privacy.

This branch of *Camara* is exceedingly important because of the fact that the Court gave express recognition to the balancing theory, which permitted the Court on that and later occasions to view the Fourth Amendment as something other than a rigid standard, requiring precisely the same quantum of evidence in all cases. But it is unfortunate that the Court in *Camara* did not apply this balancing approach with more precision and care. For one thing, the Court's reliance upon a "long history of judicial and public acceptance" is vulnerable from the point of view of both accuracy and cogency. As to the longstanding judicial acceptance, the fact is that housing inspection cases reached the courts only in recent years and in small numbers, and that these cases typically focused upon the warrant issue rather than the question of what grounds were needed to conduct an inspection. As for the longstanding public acceptance, the continued operation of these inspection programs may show only a "history of acquiescence."[4] Because that is so and also because similar or greater evidence of judicial and public acceptance of long-used procedures has not deterred the Court from finding those procedures constitutionally defective, the first factor listed in *Camara* is deserving of little if any weight.

As for the second factor, the Court unfortunately begins with the assertion that "the public interest demands that all dangerous conditions be prevented or abated," which ties in with the Court's earlier emphasis upon the need for "universal compliance" with housing code standards. But one might just as logically contend that there is a need for universal compliance with the criminal law and that the public interest demands that all dangerous offenders be convicted and punished, so that *Camara*-style warrants would also be permissible for that purpose as well. The fact of the matter is, as four members of the *Camara* majority had earlier stated: "Health inspections are important. But they are hardly more important than the search for narcotics peddlers, rapists, kidnappers, murderers, and other criminal elements."[5] Thus, the Court should have instead elaborated upon its statement that "acceptable results" cannot be achieved under the traditional probable cause requirement. The essential point is that criminal law enforcement typically is directed toward aggressive conduct, most often occurring in public places, which usually leaves a trail of discernible facts, so that the traditional probable cause test has not prevented an acceptable level of criminal law enforcement. By comparison, most housing code violations occur within private premises and cannot be detected from the outside and are not often the subject of a complaint which could serve as the basis for a warrant if the traditional probable cause requirement were applicable.

In describing the third factor, the Court in *Camara* says the invasion of privacy from these inspections is "limited" because they are "neither personal in nature nor aimed at the discovery of evidence of crime." This language is unfortunate, for it lends itself to

4. Frank v. Maryland, 359 U.S. 360, 79 S.Ct. 804, 3 L.Ed.2d 877 (1959) (dissent).

5. Ibid.

the interpretation that a lesser quantum of evidence is required when the object of the search is not criminal prosecution. That interpretation would be unsound; the Fourth Amendment is intended to protect personal privacy rather than to prevent the conviction of criminals. The meaningful distinction here is that these inspections involve a lesser intrusion than that which ordinarily occurs in the course of a criminal investigation. Inspection for the accumulation of debris and of plumbing, heating, ventilation, gas and electrical systems takes less time than the usual search for evidence of crime and does not involve rummaging through private papers and effects. A police search for evidence brings with it damage to reputation resulting from an overt manifestation of official suspicion of crime, while a routine inspection which is part of a periodic or area inspection plan does not single out any one individual. A search in a criminal investigation is made by armed officers, whose presence may lead to violence, it may be conducted at any time of the day or night, and must usually be conducted by surprise. By contrast, the housing inspection is conducted by an inspector whose presence is perceived by the public as less offensive, is performed during regular business hours, and need not involve inspection without advance notice.

The overstated necessity of 100 per cent code enforcement, the reliance upon assumed judicial and public acceptance of current enforcement programs, and the failure to be more precise about the significance of the fact that evidence of crime was not sought, all make *Camara* an imperfect model of this new Fourth Amendment calculus. The result would have carried more force had the Court set forth with more precision and detail the two factors that support it: (1) the inability to accomplish an acceptable level of code enforcement under the traditional probable cause test; and (2) the relatively minor invasion of personal privacy and dignity that attends periodic and area inspection programs.

As for the extent of the *Camara* warrant requirement, the Court stressed its holding was not "intended to foreclose prompt inspections, even without a warrant, that the law has traditionally upheld in emergency situations." Such an emergency is unlikely to arise in this context. Most housing code violations cannot readily be concealed without being corrected; to the extent that householders take advantage of notice to correct deficiencies, the purpose of the housing code are advanced rather than thwarted. Warrantless entry is permissible in the face of "an imminent and substantial threat to life, health, or property," but such a danger is unlikely as to an inspection which is merely part of an area or periodic inspection plan. *Camara* also indicates that "warrants should normally be sought only after entry is refused," and thus the consent alternative has been given preferred status.

(c) Inspection of Businesses. In *See v. City of Seattle*,[6] concerning defendant's conviction for not permitting a warrantless fire inspection of his locked commercial warehouse, the Court concluded that a "businessman, like the occupant of a residence, has a constitutional right to go about his business free from unreasonable official entries upon his private commercial property" and that consequently the *Camara* holding extended to the instant case. But the Court cautioned it was not implying "that business premises may not reasonably be inspected in many more situations than private homes, nor do we question such accepted regulatory techniques as licensing programs which require inspections prior to operating a business or marketing a product." Just a few years later, in *Colonnade Catering Corp. v. United States*,[7] the Court ruled the *See* warrant requirement was inapplicable to inspection of the business premises of a liquor licensee. This conclusion was based upon "the long history of the regulation of the liquor industry during pre-Fourth Amendment days" rather than any close analysis of the benefits or burdens of requiring a warrant in this context. Then

6. 387 U.S. 541, 87 S.Ct. 1737, 18 L.Ed.2d 943 (1967).

7. 397 U.S. 72, 90 S.Ct. 774, 25 L.Ed.2d 60 (1970).

came *United States v. Biswell*,[8] upholding a warrantless inspection pursuant to a statute authorizing such inspections during business hours of the premises of any firearms or ammunition dealer for the purpose of examining required records and the firearms or ammunition stored there. The Court reasoned that (1) such inspections are a "crucial part of the regulatory scheme" for controlling the firearms traffic; (2) that the negligible protections of a warrant were offset by the fact that a warrant requirement "could easily frustrate inspection" here, as under this inspection scheme (unlike that in *Camara*) "unannounced, even frequent, inspections are essential," and the "necessary flexibility as to time, scope and frequency is to be preserved"; and (3) that these inspections "pose only limited threats to the dealer's justifiable expectations of privacy," as when he "chooses to engage in this pervasively regulated business and to accept a federal license, he does so with the knowledge that his business records, firearms and ammunition will be subject to effective inspection."

Colonnade and *Biswell* were distinguished in *Marshall v. Barlow's, Inc.*,[9] because each concerned a "closely regulated industry," while the statutory provision held unconstitutional in the instant case permitted warrantless OSHA inspections of "any factory, plant, establishment, construction site, or other area, workplace or environment where work is performed by an employee." Though it was acknowledged that the act in question "regulates a myriad of safety details that may be amenable to speedy alteration or disguise," the Court in *Barlow's* deemed this an insufficient reason to permit warrantless inspections, for "the great majority of businessmen can be expected in normal course to consent to inspection without a warrant." *Barlow's* was in turn distinguished in *Donovan v. Dewey*,[10] upholding a statute authorizing warrantless inspections of underground and surface mines. While in *Barlow's* the statutory scheme was so loose as to leave matters in the "unbridled discretion" of administrative officers, that was not true in the instant case because "the statute's inspection program * * * provides a constitutionally adequate substitute for a warrant." The *Dewey* Court stressed that (1) "the Act requires inspection of *all* mines and specifically defines the frequency of inspection"; (2) a mine operator could know the inspector's purpose and the limits of the inspection because "the standards with which a mine operator is required to comply are all specifically set forth" in the statute and published administrative regulations; and (3) "the Act provides a specific mechanism for accommodating any special privacy concerns that a specific mine operator might have," as if entry is refused the government may only seek to enjoin future refusals, a proceeding which "provides an adequate forum for the mine owner to show that a specific search is outside the federal regulatory authority, or to seek from the District Court an order accommodating any unusual privacy interests that the mine owner might have."

Similarly, in *New York v. Burger*,[11] upholding a warrantless inspection of an auto junkyard, the Court stressed the presence of these factors: (1) the business was "closely regulated," considering the duration and extensive nature of the regulatory scheme; (2) "a 'substantial' government interest," combatting auto theft, supported the regulatory scheme; (3) warrantless inspections are "necessary to further [the] regulatory scheme," as frequent and unannounced inspections are necessary to detect stolen cars and parts; (4) the statutory inspection scheme "provides a 'constitutionally adequate substitute for a warrant' " by informing the businessman that inspections will occur regularly, of their permissible scope, and who may conduct them; and (5) the permitted inspection is "carefully limited in time, place, and scope" (business hours only, auto dismantling business only, and of records, cars and parts only).

8. 406 U.S. 311, 92 S.Ct. 1593, 32 L.Ed.2d 87 (1972).

9. 436 U.S. 307, 98 S.Ct. 1816, 56 L.Ed.2d 305 (1978).

10. 452 U.S. 594, 101 S.Ct. 2534, 69 L.Ed.2d 262 (1981).

11. 482 U.S. 691, 107 S.Ct. 2636, 96 L.Ed.2d 601 (1987).

Generally, it may be said that courts have tended not to give close scrutiny to business inspection schemes, largely because of two erroneous assumptions. One, to be found in the earlier Supreme Court case of *Zap v. United States* [12] and still occasionally relied upon by lower courts, is that certain privileges, such as doing business with the government or obtaining a license from the government, may be conditioned upon the surrender of Fourth Amendment rights. But the Supreme Court has more recently rejected that kind of theory,[13] and has done so in cases where the so-called privilege was a license issued by the state [14] or a contractual relationship with the state.[15] The second assumption is that the decision to enter into a business subject to regulation by the government, including inspection, amounts to "implied consent" to such inspections. Though utilized in *Barlow's* to support the conclusion that the businessmen in *Colonnade* and *Biswell* had "in effect" consented by engaging in a "closely regulated industry," the theory is unsound; as the *Barlow's* dissenters correctly note, the "consent is fictional" and thus is no substitute for analysis of the particular regulatory scheme under the *Camara* balancing test (during which another form of "implied consent," that businessmen consent to entry by the general public to public parts of their business during regular business hours, is properly taken into account). This latter view was accepted by the Court in *Dewey*.

Precisely when a warrantless business inspection scheme is constitutional remains unclear. For one thing, the Court seems to have adopted the dubious assumption that if the inspection is of a "closely regulated industry," then (at least if, as the Court put it in *Biswell*, the inspection is in "the context of a regulatory inspection system of business premises which is carefully limited in time, place, and scope") this alone is enough to justify proceeding without a warrant, and there is no need to show that a warrant system would actually be impracticable in that context. But *Burger* may mark a departure from that unwise assumption, for the Court there listed as a separate important consideration the need for frequent and unannounced inspections which would make the warrant requirement impractical. For another, by saying that warrants for OSHA inspections would not impose a "serious burden" because "the great majority of businessmen can be expected in normal course to consent to inspection," the *Barlow's* majority appears to have overlooked the fact that there is no way to tell in advance which businessmen will not consent. Thus, it is either necessary for the inspector to be armed with a warrant in advance in every case or else to get a warrant after being turned away, thereby making possible the "speedy alteration or disguise" of safety violations the Court acknowledged could readily occur. The former is certainly undesirable, and the latter practice makes sense only if it may be said that correction of violations before the inspector reappears with a warrant is not objectionable, which appears to be what the majority assumed in *Barlow's*. But in any event, *Dewey* suggests that a warrantless inspection scheme is most likely to pass muster if the businessman is free to turn the inspector away and then is afforded an opportunity to challenge the authority to inspect in an adversary setting (there, an action by the government to enjoin further refusal), a procedure which would seem to afford even greater protection than the administrative warrant process.

As for the grounds needed to conduct a business inspection, the Court in *Barlow's* followed the *Camara* standard, stating:

> A warrant showing that a specific business has been chosen for an OSHA search on the basis of a general administrative plan for the enforcement of the Act derived from neutral sources such as, for example, dispersion of employees in various types of industries across a given area, and the desired frequency of

12. 328 U.S. 624, 66 S.Ct. 1277, 90 L.Ed. 1477 (1946).

13. Sherbert v. Verner, 374 U.S. 398, 83 S.Ct. 1790, 10 L.Ed.2d 965 (1963).

14. Spevack v. Klein, 385 U.S. 511, 87 S.Ct. 625, 17 L.Ed.2d 574 (1967).

15. Slochower v. Board of Higher Education, 350 U.S. 551, 76 S.Ct. 637, 100 L.Ed. 692 (1956).

searches in any of the lesser divisions of the area, would protect an employer's Fourth Amendment rights.

Thus, the magistrate is to determine that there are reasonable legislative or administrative standards in existence and that the proposed inspection would conform to those standards, especially in terms of selection of the place to be inspected. As for the grounds needed when no warrant is required, the lower court cases are silent on the question, and the Supreme Court has not been particularly helpful. The Court's observations in *Biswell* concerning the need for "unannounced, even frequent, inspections" and "flexibility as to time, scope, and frequency" might be read as meaning the authorities never need show why they selected a particular business in a no-warrant situation, or as meaning only that the standards in such a case are somewhat different (e.g., re-inspection permitted with greater frequency).

In *Burger* the Court asserted that "the warrant and probable-cause requirements * * * have lessened application" to a closely regulated business, but then gave no indication that any grounds were required to justify a particular warrantless inspection. This understandably prompted the three dissenters to object that "the State could not explain why Burger's operation was selected for inspection," highlighting that the inspection here had the same defect as in *Barlow's:* failure "to provide any standards to guide inspectors either in their selection of establishments to be searched or in the exercise of their authority to search." The essential point is that even a closely regulated businessman should not be singled out for more intensive attention than is the norm for those in that business.

(d) Welfare Inspections. The question in *Wyman v. James* [16] was whether a recipient of welfare benefits may be required to submit to a warrantless home visit by a caseworker as a condition to the continued receipt of those benefits. The Court answered in the affirmative, but relied primarily upon two erroneous notions (that a home visit is not a "search * * * in the Fourth Amendment meaning of that term"; and that the Fourth Amendment limits of *Camara* have no application when criminal prosecution is not threatened) which made it unnecessary to confront directly the basic questions of whether either the warrant requirement or the usual probable cause requirement should apply in such circumstances.

As for the grounds needed to justify such an inspection, the *Camara* reasoning would seem to be equally applicable here, for the primary concern in this context is that the search be related to a coherent policy followed by the agency and not merely an excuse for harassing a particular unpopular welfare recipient. Thus it would suffice that a particular home visit was in accordance with an established schedule to make such visits at designated intervals or was undertaken upon a "watered-down" probable cause showing that the child's welfare was in danger. As for the warrant requirement, no reason is apparent why it would be impractical in this context, provided of course it is recognized that warrantless action may be undertaken upon a suspicion the child is in some immediate jeopardy.

(e) Inspections at Fire Scenes. As the Supreme Court put it in *Michigan v. Tyler,*[17] a "burning building clearly presents an exigency of sufficient proportions to render a warrantless entry 'reasonable'," as "it would defy reason to suppose that firemen must secure a warrant or consent before entering a burning structure to put out the blaze." But the question here is whether, when the occupant's justified expectation of privacy remains notwithstanding the fire,[18] it is permissible for the authorities to conduct an inspection of

16. 400 U.S. 309, 91 S.Ct. 381, 27 L.Ed.2d 408 (1971).

17. 436 U.S. 499, 98 S.Ct. 1942, 56 L.Ed.2d 486 (1978).

18. In Michigan v. Clifford, 464 U.S. 287, 104 S.Ct. 641, 78 L.Ed.2d 477 (1984), the plurality stated: "Some fires may be so devastating that no reasonable privacy interests remain in the ash and ruins, regardless of the owner's subjective expectations." However, in that case, where defendant's home was rendered uninhabitable by the fire but personal belongings remained therein and defendant had arranged to have the house secured against intrusion in their absence, they concluded he "retained reasonable privacy interests" in the premises.

those premises for the purpose of determining the cause of the fire. *Camara* suggests an affirmative answer; applying the balancing test to this situation, it may be reasoned that the "need to search" is in part a need to ascertain if the cause is one which could result in a renewal of the fire, hardly a matter which can be determined by external observation of the premises, and that there is here as in *Camara* a "limited invasion" because once again the inspection does not require rummaging through personal effects but instead is directed toward such facilities as the heating, ventilation, gas and electrical systems and the possible accumulation of combustibles. The Court in *Tyler* did not engage in such an assessment, but reached a result consistent with it, namely, that the mere fact a fire has occurred on the premises justifies officials "to remain in a building for a reasonable time to investigate the cause of a blaze after it has been extinguished," and that if later entries "detached from the initial exigency and warrantless entry" are made, then a warrant is required.

It is to be doubted that requiring a warrant here after the "initial exigency" has passed makes sense, provided that the authorities give "fair notice of an inspection." [19] So the argument goes, a warrant is unnecessary to prevent arbitrariness in this context, for the places subject to such an inspection are limited and determined by a prior event which is beyond dispute—that the fire department recently extinguished a fire there. The majority in *Tyler* felt a warrant was nonetheless useful as a means of reassuring the property owner of the legality of the entry and "preventing harassment by keeping that invasion to a minimum," but more recently a majority of the Court indicated it would not require a warrant for a with-notice post-fire inspection into the cause of the fire.[20] Unaffected by this development is the other *Tyler* holding, namely, that "if the investigating officials find probable cause to believe that arson has occurred and require further access to gather evidence for a possible prosecution, they may obtain a warrant only upon a traditional showing of probable cause applicable to searches for evidence of crime." Such a warrant can confer greater search authority than an administrative warrant obtained to ascertain the cause of the fire.[21]

(f) Border Searches and Related Activities. In *United States v. Ramsey,*[22] the Court declared that "searches made at the border, pursuant to the long-standing right of the sovereign to protect itself by stopping and examining persons and property crossing into this country, are reasonable simply by virtue of the fact that they occur at the border." Thus, routine searches of persons and things may be made upon their entry into the country without first obtaining a search warrant and without establishing probable cause or any suspicion at all in the individual case. *Ramsey* held that the same was true of incoming international mail, at least if that mail could contain more than correspondence and the inspection does not include the reading of correspondence. These routine border searches may be made at the border when entry is by land from Canada or Mexico, at a place where a ship finally docks after coming from foreign waters, or a place where aircraft land at the end of an international flight, and there is also authority that they may be conducted inland at a "functional equivalent" of

19. As Justice Stevens, concurring, proposed.

20. In Michigan v. Clifford, 464 U.S. 287, 104 S.Ct. 641, 78 L.Ed.2d 477 (1984), four members of the Court followed the *Tyler* rule. Stevens, J., concurring, "would require the fire investigator to obtain a traditional criminal search warrant in order to make an unannounced entry, but would characterize a warrantless entry as reasonable whenever the inspector had either given the owner sufficient advance notice to enable him or an agent to be present or had made a reasonable effort to do so." The four dissenters argued that "the utility of requiring a magistrate to evaluate the grounds for a search following a fire is so limited that the incidental protection of an individual's privacy interests simply does not justify imposing a warrant requirement."

21. In Michigan v. Clifford, 464 U.S. 287, 104 S.Ct. 641, 78 L.Ed.2d 477 (1984), the plurality emphasized that the scope of an administrative search "is limited to that reasonably necessary to determine the cause and origin of a fire and to ensure against rekindling," and thus concluded the officers were not authorized to go from the basement area where the fire originated to upper rooms in the house to seek evidence incriminating the owners.

22. 431 U.S. 606, 97 S.Ct. 1972, 52 L.Ed.2d 617 (1977).

the border or if there has been virtual constant surveillance since the time of the border crossing, thus ensuring that whatever is found in the search can be said to be an object which crossed the border. In the main, these routine searches can be justified by resort to the *Camara* balancing analysis, as there is a vital national interest in preventing illegal entry and smuggling and the searches are a limited invasion in the sense that they are directed at a morally neutral class of persons who have it within their power to determine the time and place of the search.

Certain kinds of border searches are deemed to be more than routine and to require some kind of case-by-case justification. Thus a strip search, where the person is forced to disrobe to a state which would be offensive to the average person, may be undertaken only upon a "real suspicion" supported by objective, articulable facts that would reasonably lead an experienced, prudent customs official to suspect that the individual is concealing something on his person contrary to law. This standard lies somewhere in the nebulous region between mere suspicion and probable cause. As for a border search involving examination of the rectum, examination of the vagina, or the use of laxatives or emetics to determine what is in the stomach, it may be conducted only upon a "clear indication" of smuggling, which is also a standard which falls below the usual probable cause requirement. No search warrant is required even as to these non-routine and highly intrusive searches, a state of affairs which has frequently been questioned. But intrusions into the body are unreasonable if not done by medical personnel in medical surroundings utilizing customary medical techniques.

Because of the increasing utilization of alimentary canal smuggling, customs agents sometimes detain suspects at the border to await the "call of nature." The Court addressed this practice in *United States v. Montoya de Hernandez*,[23] holding: (i) "that the detention of a traveler at the border, beyond the scope of a routine customs search and inspection, is justified at its inception if customs agents, considering all the facts surrounding the traveler and her trip, reasonably suspect that the traveler is smuggling contraband in her alimentary canal"; and (ii) that such a detention is "reasonably related in scope to the circumstances which justified it initially" if the suspect is held so long as is "necessary to either verify or dispel the suspicion." This means that if, as in *de Hernandez,* the suspect declines to submit to an x-ray, then the detention on reasonable suspicion may continue until a bowel movement occurs.

To be distinguished from these border searches are a variety of activities conducted in the interior in an effort to identify and apprehend illegal aliens. One, the use of roving patrols to stop and search vehicles on the highways for illegal aliens, came before the Supreme Court in *Almeida–Sanchez v. United States*.[24] The Court held that such a search, made without a warrant and without probable cause, violated the Fourth Amendment; it could not be upheld under the *Carroll–Chambers* rule[25] because that rule applies only when there is probable cause, and it could not be upheld as a *Camara* administrative search because that case condemned searches "at the discretion of the official in the field." Two years later, in *United States v. Brignoni–Ponce*,[26] the Court was confronted with the related question of "whether a roving patrol may stop a vehicle in an area near the border and question its occupants when the only ground for suspicion is that the occupants appear to be of Mexican ancestry," and again answered in the negative. Because the "broad and unlimited discretion" claimed by the government could result in the stopping of many innocent people, this practice likewise could not be brought within the reasoning of *Camara*. Rather, the stop-and-frisk rule of *Terry v. Ohio*[27] was deemed to strike the proper balance in this context, which

23. 473 U.S. 531, 105 S.Ct. 3304, 87 L.Ed.2d 381 (1985).
24. 413 U.S. 266, 93 S.Ct. 2535, 37 L.Ed.2d 596 (1973).
25. See § 3.7(b).
26. 422 U.S. 873, 95 S.Ct. 2574, 45 L.Ed.2d 607 (1975).
27. 392 U.S. 1, 88 S.Ct. 1868, 20 L.Ed.2d 889 (1968).

means that roving patrols may stop vehicles for the purpose of questioning only upon facts "that reasonably warrant suspicion that the vehicles contain aliens who may be illegally in the country." Factors which may be taken into account, the Court helpfully added in *Brignoni,* include: (i) the "characteristics of the area," including its "proximity to the border, the usual patterns of traffic on the particular road, and previous experience with alien traffic"; (ii) "information about recent illegal border crossings in the area"; (iii) the "driver's behavior," such as "erratic driving or obvious attempts to evade officers"; (iv) the type of vehicle, such as a station wagon with large compartments, which "are frequently used for transporting concealed aliens"; (v) that the vehicle seems "heavily loaded" or has "an extraordinary number of passengers"; (vi) that persons are observed "trying to hide"; (vii) "the characteristic appearance of persons who live in Mexico, relying on such factors as the mode of dress and haircut"; and (viii) such other facts as are meaningful to the officer "in light of his experience detecting illegal entry and smuggling."

Two other decisions of the Court are concerned with the use of fixed checkpoints to discover illegal aliens. In *United States v. Ortiz,*[28] involving use of a checkpoint at which all cars travelling on a certain road were required to stop for investigation and were sometimes searched as a part of that investigation, the government claimed that use of the checkpoint sufficiently limited the officers' discretion and made the circumstances of the search less intrusive. The Court disagreed on both counts. For one thing, the record indicated that only a small percentage of the vehicles passing the checkpoint were stopped to the extent that questioning or search was undertaken, making it apparent that "checkpoint officers exercise a substantial degree of discretion in deciding which cars to search." For another, the "greater regularity attending the stop does not mitigate the invasion of privacy that a search entails," especially when "only a few are singled out for a search." The Court in *Ortiz* thus held "that at traffic checkpoints removed from the border and its functional equivalents, officers may not search private vehicles without consent or probable cause."

This then leaves the possibility of utilizing a fixed checkpoint merely to stop vehicles and question the occupants, as to which the government prevailed in *United States v. Martinez–Fuerte.*[29] The *Camara* balancing test produced a different result here than in the three other cases, the Court reasoned, as "the potential interference with legitimate traffic is minimal," and the "checkpoint operations both appear to and actually involve less discretionary enforcement activity." Though it is true that the practices at issue in *Martinez–Fuerte* are certainly less intrusive than those held unconstitutional in the three earlier cases, this is not to say that the reasoning or result in *Martinez–Fuerte* is unassailable. One major weakness in the Court's analysis is the conclusion it need not consider the "less-restrictive-alternative arguments" of the defendants, that is, the defendants' contention that the government could check the flow of illegal aliens by other means which did not so intrude upon Fourth Amendment values. This seems inconsistent with *Camara,* where one critical factor was that "acceptable results" could not be achieved in any other way. The second weakness concerns the Court's conclusion that "no particularized reason need exist to justify" the selective referral of some motorists to a secondary inspection area. Given the opportunity for arbitrariness in this screening process, it may be argued (as did the *Martinez–Fuerte* dissenters) that these referrals should be tested by the *Terry* reasonable suspicion standard.

(g) Vehicle Use Regulation. Although the practice of stopping vehicles at random to check drivers' licenses and vehicle registrations and determine that the vehicles are in proper mechanical condition had often been upheld by the lower courts, the Supreme Court decided otherwise in *Delaware v.*

28. 422 U.S. 891, 95 S.Ct. 2585, 45 L.Ed.2d 623 (1975).

29. 428 U.S. 543, 96 S.Ct. 3074, 49 L.Ed.2d 1116 (1976).

Prouse[30] "by balancing its intrusion on the individual's Fourth Amendment interests against its promotion of legitimate governmental interests." On the need side of the scales, the Court agreed "that the States have a vital interest in ensuring that only those qualified to do so are permitted to operate motor vehicles, that these vehicles are fit for safe operation, and hence that licensing, registration, and vehicle inspection requirements are being observed." But the Court then pointed out that discretionary spot checks would not greatly advance those interests. On the matter of drivers' licenses, "the percentage of all drivers on the road who are driving without a license is very small and * * * the number of licensed drivers who will be stopped in order to find one unlicensed operator will be large indeed," while by comparison checking those drivers who have committed a traffic violation is "much more likely" to uncover an unlicensed driver. As for vehicle registration, this can be determined by simply noting "license plates indicating current registration," which does not require stopping of the vehicle. Likewise, random stopping of vehicles for safety inspections would make little "incremental contribution to highway safety," as many violations of safety requirements "are observable" without stopping the car, and others can be detected by an "annual safety inspection" scheme. On the intrusion side of the scale, the Court in *Prouse* correctly concluded that such a random stop is not "of any less moment than that occasioned by a stop by border agents on roving patrol" in terms of creating anxiety, interfering with freedom of movement, causing inconvenience, and consuming time. The Court thus held

> that except in those situations in which there is at least articulable and reasonable suspicion that a motorist is unlicensed or that an automobile is not registered, or that either the vehicle or an occupant is otherwise subject to seizure for violation of law,[31] stopping an automobile and detaining the driver in order to check his driver's license and the registration of the automobile are unreasonable under the Fourth Amendment. This holding does not preclude the State of Delaware or other States from developing methods for spot checks that involve less intrusion or that do not involve the unconstrained exercise of discretion. Questioning of all oncoming traffic at roadblock-type stops is one possible alternative.

It thus appears that the Court would uphold the use of a checkpoint, as have the lower courts, when used to check drivers' licenses and vehicle registrations or to conduct safety inspections of vehicles. And while the *Prouse* majority describes the practice in terms of dealing with "all oncoming traffic," it would seem that Justice Blackmun is correct in saying in his concurring opinion "that the Court's reservation also includes other not purely random stops (such as every 10th car to pass a given point) that equate with, but are less intrusive than, a 100% roadblock stop." It is not necessary for a checkpoint to stop every car in order to be systematic, but only for officers to be following some pattern that will minimize their discretion in choosing whether to stop a particular auto. Also, it should be noted that the Court in *Prouse* explained its ruling was not intended to "cast doubt on the permissibility of roadblock truck weigh stations and inspection checkpoints, at which some vehicles may be subject to further detention for safety and regulatory inspection than are others," another procedure which has been upheld by the lower courts.

Yet another practice which is being more frequently relied upon by the police is the sobriety checkpoint, at which traffic is stopped at a temporary location so that each driver may be observed to see if he is under the influence and, if signs of intoxication are detected, may be directed out of the traffic flow for further scrutiny and perhaps sobriety tests. In *Michigan Dept. of State Police v.*

30. 440 U.S. 648, 99 S.Ct. 1391, 59 L.Ed.2d 660 (1979).

31. In New York v. Class, 475 U.S. 106, 106 S.Ct. 960, 89 L.Ed.2d 81 (1986), the Court concluded "that a demand to inspect the VIN, like a demand to see license and registration papers, is within the scope of police authority pursuant to a traffic stop" prompted by an observed traffic violation.

Sitz,[32] an injunctive action in which only the initial stopping was at issue, the Court upheld the use of such checkpoints. Utilizing a balancing test similar to that employed in *Prouse*, the majority in *Sitz* stressed these factors: (1) the states' strong interest in eradicating the serious drunken driving problem; (2) the slight "intrusion on motorists subjected to a brief stop at a highway checkpoint," where (as in the instant case) "checkpoints are selected pursuant to [established] guidelines, and uniformed police officers stop every approaching vehicle"; and (3) that it is for "politically accountable officials" to decide "as to which among reasonable alternative law enforcement techniques should be employed," and that this checkpoint was such an alternative because it produced results superior to those in *Martinez-Fuerte*.[33] Lower courts, in upholding the operation of such checkpoints when proper procedures have been followed, typically stress the necessity (i) that the decision of where and when the roadblock is to be operated not be left to officers in the field; (ii) that the checkpoint be conducted in a regularized manner so as not to alarm those approaching and stopping at it; (iii) that all vehicles be stopped at the roadblock or at least that those which are stopped be selected by neutral criteria; (iv) that selective referral for continued investigation (and thus more than momentary detention) of some of those stopped be pursuant to the *Terry* reasonable suspicion test; and (v) that advance publicity be given to the forthcoming use of this enforcement technique.

The Coast Guard is authorized by statute [34] to stop vessels upon the high seas and waters of the United States to conduct inspections. These special inspection powers do not extend to search into private books, papers or personal belongings, but it is permissible to examine safety equipment, inspect documentation papers, check the identification number on the beam or frame to ensure it matches the number in those papers, and otherwise identify the ship when no documentation is supplied. The *Prouse* decision does not bar or limit exercise of that statutory authority. As explained in *United States v. Villamonte–Marquez* [35]:

> The nature of waterborne commerce in waters providing ready access to the open sea is sufficiently different from the nature of vehicular traffic on highways as to make possible alternatives to the sort of "stop" made in this case less likely to accomplish the obviously essential governmental purposes involved. The system of prescribed outward markings used by States for vehicle registration is also significantly different than the system of external markings on vessels, and the extent and type of documentation required by federal law is a good deal more variable and more complex than are the state vehicle registration laws. The nature of the governmental interest in assuring compliance with documentation requirements, particularly in waters where the need to deter or apprehend smugglers is great, are substantial; the type of intrusion made in this case, while not minimal, is limited.

(h) Airport Searches. When airplane hijacking became a major problem in the late 1960's, the government first attempted to deal with it by establishing procedures for identifying a relatively select group of air passengers who should be subjected to close preboarding screening. When a passenger checked in for a flight, the agent would apply a behavioral profile, based upon a detailed study of all then known hijackers, to determine if he was a potential hijacker. In the boarding area, a person so identified would have to pass through a magnetometer set to detect the amount of metal in a small handgun. A person who both fit the profile and triggered the magnetometer would be interviewed, and if he failed to supply adequate identification he would be frisked and his carry-on luggage searched. Consequently, these more intrusive actions were undertaken against a very small percentage of passengers. Utilizing the bal-

32. ___ U.S. ___, 110 S.Ct. 2481, 110 L.Ed.2d 412 (1990).

33. In *Sitz*, 1.5% of the drivers passing the checkpoint were arrested for being under the influence; in *Martinez–Fuerte* illegal aliens were found in 0.12% of the vehicles.

34. 14 U.S.C.A. § 89(a).

35. 462 U.S. 579, 103 S.Ct. 2573, 77 L.Ed.2d 22 (1983).

ancing test, courts upheld these searches on the ground that they were based upon the reasonable suspicion required by *Terry v. Ohio*.[36] On the need side of the equation there was the fact that air piracy presented extreme dangers to the traveling public and could be effectively dealt with only if the potential hijacker was intercepted on the ground. On the intrusion side, it was relevant that the searches were of a morally neutral class who must voluntarily come to and enter the search area and were under the supervision of airlines who have a substantial interest in assuring that their passengers are not unnecessarily harassed. Those considerations made it reasonable to conduct the searches upon the degree of suspicion provided by the profile-plus-magnetometer-plus-questioning selection process, which experience had shown produced a person carrying a weapon six per cent of the time.

In 1973 this selective process was abandoned in favor of a program whereunder *all* passengers were checked before boarding. Every passenger was required to pass through the magnetometer, and his carry-on luggage was inspected either by hand or by passing it through an x-ray device. If the magnetometer sounded, the passenger had to remove items from his person until he was able to pass through the device without triggering it, and if the x-ray detected a suspicious object the passenger was not allowed to proceed unless he permitted an examination of the contents of the luggage. Especially because use of the magnetometer and x-ray both qualify as searches, the question arose as to whether subjecting all passengers to these searches was constitutionally permissible. Employing the balancing test once again, the courts decided this procedure also passed Fourth Amendment muster, not because there was a reasonable suspicion of those searched, but rather because (as in *Camara*) it involved a general regulatory scheme without the potential for arbitrariness. But, because an administrative screening search must be as limited in its intrusiveness as is consistent with satisfaction of the administrative need that justifies it, it is critical that each person be able to avoid search by electing not to board the aircraft. The point is not that one has consented or impliedly consented to the search by virtue of deciding to be an airline passenger; rather, it is a matter of narrowing the search to the need, plus the notion that advance notice of the risks and how to avoid them is an ingredient which may make an inspection system reasonable. Even under the new system, *Terry* reasonable suspicion will sometimes come into play, as where a person has "passed" the inspection in the literal sense but it has produced facts of a highly suspicious nature.

Analysis similar to that used in the airport screening cases has been used to uphold other inspection schemes which contemplate examining all persons who wish to enter a particular place where there are special security needs. Illustrative are checkpoint inspections of visitors to a penal institution, to a military installation, or to government buildings which have been the targets of violence or threats of violence.

(i) Searches Directed at Prisoners. In keeping with the Supreme Court's declaration that "a prisoner is not wholly stripped of constitutional protections when he is imprisoned for crime,"[37] many courts held that prisoners have a Fourth Amendment expectation of privacy "of a diminished scope." Under that approach, a "shakedown" search of the cells and personal effects of the prisoners, undertaken either pursuant to an established routine of making such searches periodically or in response to an incident at the prison or jail, is constitutionally permissible under the *Camara* standardized procedures principle, and even a search directed at only one or a few prisoners is proper if undertaken upon reasonable suspicion. But that approach was rejected by the Supreme Court in the 5–4 decision of *Hudson v. Palmer*,[38] involving a section 1983 action brought by a state prison

36. 392 U.S. 1, 88 S.Ct. 1868, 20 L.Ed.2d 889 (1968).

37. Wolff v. McDonnell, 418 U.S. 539, 94 S.Ct. 2963, 41 L.Ed.2d 935 (1974).

38. 468 U.S. 517, 104 S.Ct. 3194, 82 L.Ed.2d 393 (1984).

inmate who alleged a prison guard had conducted a "shakedown" search of his cell and had destroyed his noncontraband property for purposes of harassment. The majority, per the Chief Justice, in holding "that the Fourth Amendment has no applicability to a prison cell," reasoned:

> The two interests here are the interest of society in the security of its penal institutions and the interest of the prisoner in privacy within his cell. The latter interest, of course, is already limited by the exigencies of the circumstances: A prison "shares none of the attributes of privacy of a home, an automobile, an office, or a hotel room." * * * We strike the balance in favor of institutional security, which we have noted is "central to all other correctional goals" * * *. A right of privacy in traditional Fourth Amendment terms is fundamentally incompatible with the close and continual surveillance of inmates and their cells required to ensure institutional security and internal order. We are satisfied that society would insist that the prisoner's expectation of privacy always yield to what must be considered the paramount interest in institutional security. We believe that it is accepted by our society that "[l]oss of freedom of choice and privacy are inherent incidents of confinement."

The Court added that for "the same reasons" the seizure and destruction of a prisoner's effects did not fall within the protections of the Fourth Amendment.[39] (The four dissenters in *Hudson* seriously questioned this latter conclusion [40] and also disputed whether it was inevitably the case that a prisoner had no privacy expectation in his effects.[41]) *Hudson* is not unquestionably applicable to pretrial detention facilities.[42]

As for a search of the person of a prisoner, it may be lawfully undertaken as part of a general routine inspection without any showing of individualized suspicion, and a particular prisoner may be searched upon reasonable suspicion that he is in possession of the fruits, instrumentalities or evidence of either criminal behavior or conduct in violation of prison regulations. Also permissible as falling under the general routine theory is the standardized practice of searching prisoners whenever they have come into contact with others, such as visitors, who could have passed them contraband. Even strip searches are allowed in such circumstances; in *Bell v. Wolfish*,[43] the Supreme Court used the balancing test to uphold a practice whereby pretrial detainees were required to expose their body cavities for visual inspection as a part of a strip search conducted after every visit with a person from outside the institution, but the Court's assertion that there was a security risk which could be met in no other way is not particularly convincing. *Hudson* apparently is not controlling here; as the dissent noted, the majority "appears to limit its holding to a prisoner's 'papers and effects' located in his cell" and apparently "believes that at least a prisoner's 'person' is secure from unreasonable search and seizure."

The Supreme Court in *Procunier v. Mar-*

39. But the Court did indicate that if a prisoner was subjected to "calculated harassment unrelated to prison needs," then this would violate the Eighth Amendment proscription upon cruel and unusual punishment.

40. They reasoned (i) that the majority's assumption that a prisoner was without any legal possessory interests whatsoever to which the Fourth Amendment's unreasonable seizures prohibition could attach did not "comport with any civilized standard of decency"; (ii) that the majority's claim society would not recognize any such expectation as reasonable was wrong, as reflected by the contrary view reflected with virtual unanimity in the recent commentary and federal decisions; and (iii) that the seizure here, assuming plaintiff's allegations to be true, was most certainly "unreasonable" under the Fourth Amendment because undertaken without any "penological justification."

41. "I cannot see any justification for applying this rule to minimum security facilities in which inmates who pose no realistic threat to security are housed. I also see no justification for reading the mail of a prisoner once it has cleared whatever censorship mechanism is employed by the prison and has been received by the prisoner."

42. The Court's holding is stated in terms of "a prison cell," and much (but certainly not all) of the Court's analysis concerns circumstances existing in facilities housing those convicted of crime. But O'Connor, J., concurring, stated the broader proposition that the "fact of arrest and incarceration abates all legitimate Fourth Amendment privacy and possessory interests in personal effects."

43. 441 U.S. 520, 99 S.Ct. 1861, 60 L.Ed.2d 447 (1979).

tinez,[44] concerning censorship of prison mail, declared that an "obvious example of justifiable censorship of prisoner mail would be refusal to send or deliver letters concerning escape plans or containing other information concerning proposed criminal activity, whether within or without the prison," and lower courts have reasoned that by implication this permits the inspection of all mail for such contents. The same reasoning has been used to justify eavesdropping upon conversations of prisoners and visitors. It has been questioned, however, whether the risk of escape or further criminal conduct is sufficiently great as to *all* types of detainees to justify those practices across the board.

(j) Searches Directed at Probationers and Parolees. Although there is some authority to the effect that the Fourth Amendment rights of probationers and parolees are of precisely the same scope and dimension as those of the public at large, the weight of authority is to the contrary. As to parolees, it has often been held that their residences may be searched without a warrant or even without probable cause, that their vehicles may be searched without either a warrant or a probable cause showing, and that they may be arrested without probable cause. And while there is some disagreement as to whether a probationer's Fourth Amendment rights are diminished to the same extent and degree as those of a parolee, there is considerable authority supporting the proposition that probationers may also be lawfully subjected to searches which, absent their probation status, would be deemed unlawful because of the absence of probable cause or a search warrant or both.

A variety of theories have been articulated by the courts in purported justification for these holdings. With respect to parolees, the notion most commonly relied upon is that such persons are in the "constructive custody" of the government while on parole and thus are in essentially the same position, in terms of their Fourth Amendment rights, as persons who are still serving time in prison. But this is more of a conclusion than a theory, resting upon a fiction which tends to divert attention from the underlying issues, and has been rejected by the Supreme Court in other contexts.[45] Some courts instead stress that parole or probation is an "act of grace," from which it is concluded that such beneficence may be attended by whatever restrictions upon privacy the government may deem appropriate. Other courts have wisely rejected that notion, and the Supreme Court has declared in a related context that it "is hardly useful any longer to try to deal with this problem in terms of whether the parolee's liberty is valuable and must be seen as within the protection of the Fourteenth Amendment."[46] A third theory, most likely to be relied upon when such a "waiver" is expressly set out and agreed to by the probationer or parolee at the time of his conditional release, is that searches of such persons are proper because consented to as part of the "contract" of release. But this simply is not so under the *Schneckloth v. Bustamonte*[47] voluntariness test for consent searches; the probationer who purportedly waives his rights by accepting such a condition has little genuine option to refuse, and the waiver cannot be said to be voluntary in any generally-accepted sense of the term.

There is yet another theory which *does* make sense, and that is that some "special" Fourth Amendment rules apply in this area by application of the *Camara* balancing test. On the need side of the equation, the basic point is that the very existence of these forms of conditional release for convicted criminals reflects a legislative judgment that these men can achieve effective rehabilitation only with the aid of supervision and guidance from governmental officials, and that in certain types of cases, close surveillance reduces the rate of recidivism. Such was the approach taken in

44. 416 U.S. 396, 94 S.Ct. 1800, 40 L.Ed.2d 224 (1974).

45. Morrissey v. Brewer, 408 U.S. 471, 92 S.Ct. 2593, 33 L.Ed.2d 484 (1972).

46. Morrissey v. Brewer, 408 U.S. 471, 92 S.Ct. 2593, 33 L.Ed.2d 484 (1972).

47. 412 U.S. 218, 93 S.Ct. 2041, 36 L.Ed.2d 854 (1973), on remand 479 F.2d 1047 (9th Cir.1973).

Griffin v. Wisconsin,[48] upholding search of a probationer's home without a warrant or full probable cause because of the "special needs" of the probation system. The warrant requirement was deemed inappropriate for probation officers, who "have in mind the welfare of the probationer" and must "respond quickly to evidence of misconduct." The usual probable cause standard was deemed inapplicable because it "would reduce the deterrent effect of the supervisory arrangement" and because "the probation agency must be able to act based upon a lesser degree of certainty than the Fourth Amendment would otherwise require in order to intervene before a probationer does damage to himself or society."

Because the degree of risk is not the same as to all probationers and parolees, it would seem that under the *Camara* approach the restrictions should not be identical in all cases, but instead should result from a case-by-case assessment at the time of release of what degree of surveillance is necessary in the particular case. But *Griffin* is to the contrary.[49] As for that part of the *Camara* balancing test which requires that the special search authority be limited to the unique problem giving rise to the need for it, it may fairly be concluded that the rehabilitation objective is best served by giving the special authority only to parole and probation officers and not to the police.[50] It follows that if a probation or parole officer used his special power as nothing more than the agent of the police, then the search is unlawful.

(k) Searches Directed at Students. Searches directed at the persons or effects of students while on the premises of an educational institution have on occasion been upheld even when they could not pass the Fourth Amendment requirements applicable in the typical criminal investigation. This is sometimes done under the doctrine of *in loco parentis* (literally, in place of a parent). But that doctrine can hardly be applied at the college level, where the overwhelming majority of the students have reached adulthood, and at the high school and grade school levels is so often used merely as a slogan that is much more forthright simply to assess all such searches under the *Camara* balancing test. Likewise, exaggerated doctrines of consent and implied consent have no place here either.

At the pre-college level, the lower court cases indicate that the person and locker of a student may be searched upon reasonable suspicion of a violation of the criminal law or reasonable regulation of the educational institution. Part of the *Camara*-type reasoning used to justify such a rule is that schools are confronted with serious discipline problems, especially concerning the use of drugs, and have a unique responsibility to deal with those problems effectively. The state, so the argument goes, having compelled students to attend school and thus associate with the immature and unwise closely and daily, thereby owes those students a safe and secure environment. It is less apparent, however, that "acceptable results" (to use the *Camara* terminology) can be achieved only by watered-down Fourth Amendment standards, as many of the appellate cases indicate that the search was undertaken on the basis of information from another student sufficient to meet the traditional probable cause test. As far as the "limited intrusion" factor of *Camara* goes, it is very difficult to make a judgment on that factor in this context, but it is noteworthy that most of the reported cases that have

48. 483 U.S. 868, 107 S.Ct. 3164, 97 L.Ed.2d 709 (1987).

49. The Court in *Griffin* upheld an administrative regulation which permitted warrantless searches without full probable cause of *all* probationers' homes. The four dissenters objected: "There are many probationers in this country and they have committed crimes that range widely in seriousness. The Court has determined that all of them may be subjected to such searches in the absence of a warrant."

50. Griffin v. Wisconsin, 483 U.S. 868, 107 S.Ct. 3164, 97 L.Ed.2d 709 (1987), supports such a limitation, for (1) in allowing a search without a warrant the Court stressed the search would not be by a "police officer who normally conducts searches against the ordinary citizen" but rather by a probation officer who is "supposed to have in mind the welfare of his probationer"; and (2) in allowing search without full probable cause, the Court stressed the need to take into account special facts from "an ongoing supervisory relationship" which are not "the usual elements that a police officer or magistrate would consider."

approved searches of the student's person have involved relatively mild intrusions. As for locker searches, it is certainly relevant whether the school has made it clear that possession of the locker is nonexclusive as against the school, not because this shows consent, but rather because it is a factor bearing upon the reasonableness of the inspection system. The point is that such advance notice provides the student with an opportunity to limit the effect of the intrusion by not keeping highly personal materials in the locker provided by the school.

The Supreme Court has dealt with this general problem but once, in *New Jersey v. T.L.O.*,[51] involving search of a high school student's purse. The Court held that "the Fourth Amendment applies to searches conducted by school authorities," but that under the *Camara* balancing test such a search could be conducted without a warrant and without full probable cause. What is required is that the search of the student be justified at its inception (i.e., that there be "reasonable grounds for suspecting that the search will turn up evidence that the student has violated or is violating either the law or the rules of the school") and that it be reasonable in scope (i.e., that "the measures adopted are reasonably related to the objectives of the search and not excessively intrusive in light of the age and sex of the student and the nature of the infraction"). The Court also cautioned that there were several issues regarding searches directed at students which it had not resolved, such as "whether individualized suspicion is an essential element of the reasonableness standard," "whether a schoolchild has a legitimate expectation of privacy in lockers, desks, or other school property provided for the storage of school supplies," and whether a higher standard would be needed in "assessing the legality of searches conducted by school officials in conjunction with or at the behest of law enforcement agencies."

At the college level, the cases in the main have concerned searches of rooms in dormitories maintained by the educational institution and rented to students matriculating there. One view is that here as well the reasonable suspicion test applies, and the emphasis once again is upon the special need to maintain a proper educational atmosphere. The contrary view is that traditional Fourth Amendment standards apply to such searches, a conclusion which is supported by the fact that application of the *Camara* balancing test here does not produce a convincing showing that broader authority is needed. For one thing, the searches at issue cannot be characterized as a limited intrusion; a student's dormitory room is his home for all practical purposes, and he has the same interest in the privacy of his room as any adult has in the privacy of his home. Nor is the need as strong as at the high school level. College students are more mature and less in need of general supervision, their presence is not compelled by attendance laws, they are not in day-long close contact with one another in a single location, and their dorm rooms are not concerned with the academic affairs of the university community.

***(l)* Searches Directed at Public Employees.** *O'Connor v. Ortega*,[52] a § 1983 action challenging search by a doctor's supervisors of his desk and filing cabinets at the state hospital where he was employed, focused attention upon the somewhat limited Fourth Amendment rights of public employees. Though the Court was firmly of the view that "[s]earches and seizures by government employers or supervisors of the private property of their employees * * * are subject to the restraints of the Fourth Amendment," the protections of the Amendment were deemed to be somewhat different in this context. Even assuming that the facts of the particular case show that the employee had a justified expectation of privacy in the particular area searched,[53] it is nec-

51. 469 U.S. 325, 105 S.Ct. 733, 83 L.Ed.2d 720 (1985).

52. 480 U.S. 709, 107 S.Ct. 1492, 94 L.Ed.2d 714 (1987).

53. Though finding the record in the instant case inconclusive on the point, the four-Justice plurality opinion asserted that "some government offices may be so open to fellow employees or the public that no expectation of privacy is reasonable." That conclusion was rejected by a majority of the Court—the four dissenters, and also Scalia, J., concurring, who would accept as a

essary in this context to "balance the invasion of the employee's legitimate expectations of privacy against the government's need for supervision, control and the efficient operation of the workplace." One consequence of this balancing is that no search warrant is needed for intrusions "for legitimate work-related reasons wholly unrelated to illegal conduct." Moreover, intrusions "for noninvestigatory, work-related purposes, as well as for investigation of work-related misconduct, should be judged by the standard of reasonableness under all the circumstances" rather than the traditional quantum of probable cause.[54]

Drug testing of government employees (or, of private employees pursuant to government regulation) has been addressed by several courts recently. Upon a weighing of the competing public and private interests, most lower courts have concluded that such testing is constitutional at least in those instances in which there was reasonable individualized suspicion. These cases reflect the judgment that the individualized suspicion test fairly accommodates the legitimate interest in employee privacy without unduly restricting the employer's opportunity to monitor and control drug use by employees. Whether random or more generalized testing is also permissible upon some special showing is a more difficult question, though the Supreme Court has upheld two such inspection schemes where testing was triggered by a specific event and where, in addition, it was concluded a special need existed for testing in such circumstances. In *Skinner v. Railway Labor Executives' Ass'n*,[55] concerning blood and urine tests required of railroad employees following major train accidents or incidents and breath and urine samples authorized to be taken from railroad employees who violate certain safety rules, the Court stressed the need "to prevent or deter that hazardous conduct" by "those engaged in safety-sensitive tasks" and also the "limited discretion exercised" by the testing employers. In *National Treasury Employees v. Von Raab*,[56] concerning urinalysis tests required of Customs Service employees upon their transfer or promotion to positions having a direct involvement in drug interdiction or requiring the carrying of firearms, the Court emphasized the "Government's compelling interests in preventing the promotion of drug users to positions where they might endanger the integrity of our Nation's borders or the life of the citizenry." [57]

§ 3.10 Consent Searches

(a) Nature of Consent. Consent searches are sometimes relied upon by police when probable cause is present but they feel either that they do not have time to get a warrant or that they would simply like to avoid that time-consuming process, but more often an effort is made to obtain consent where proba-

governing general rule that "the offices of government employees * * * are covered by Fourth Amendment protections." Even the plurality opinion accepted the conclusion that the doctor had a justified expectation of privacy as to the interior of the desk and filing cabinets in his office, as he "did not share his desk or filing cabinets with any other employees," he kept personal effects therein, and the hospital had no regulation or policy discouraging such practice.

54. The four dissenters objected that the warrant and probable cause requirements had been abandoned in favor of a more lenient balancing approach by assertion of a "special need" which was never demonstrated. "There was no special practical need that might have justified dispensing with the warrant and probable-cause requirements. Without sacrificing their ultimate goal of maintaining an effective institution devoted to training and healing, to which the disciplining of Hospital employees contributed, petitioners could have taken any evidence of Dr. Ortega's alleged improprieties to a magistrate in order to obtain a warrant."

55. 489 U.S. 602, 109 S.Ct. 1402, 103 L.Ed.2d 639 (1989).

56. 489 U.S. 656, 109 S.Ct. 1384, 103 L.Ed.2d 685 (1989).

57. Two Justices dissented in both cases, reiterating their opposition to any "special needs" exception to the probable cause requirement, protesting widening of that exception to include search of the person without even reasonable suspicion, and questioning the majority's weighing of the factors in the balancing-of-interests process. Two other Justices dissented in *Von Raab*, contending that while the result in *Skinner* was supported by "the demonstrated frequency of drug and alcohol use by the targeted class of employees, and the demonstrated connection between such use and grave harm," in *Von Raab* the government had not noted a single instance "in which the cause of bribe-taking, or of poor aim, or of unsympathetic law enforcement, or of compromise of classified information, was drug use."

ble cause is lacking and no warrant could be obtained. The issue of whether a consent search is simply a matter of the consenting party having acted voluntarily or whether instead the waiver of a constitutional right is involved, necessitating a showing of "an intentional relinquishment or abandonment of a known right," was finally resolved in *Schneckloth v. Bustamonte.*[1] The Court there upheld a consent to search a car given during a street encounter in which no Fourth Amendment warnings were given. Noting that the voluntariness standard was the traditional means for balancing the interests in the police interrogation area, the Court observed that in the consent search area there are also "two competing concerns [which] must be accommodated * * *—the legitimate need for such searches and the equally important requirement of assuring the absence of coercion." A "fair accommodation" of those competing interests, the majority concluded in *Schneckloth,* lies in "the traditional definition of 'voluntariness,'" as a need to show the consenting party was aware of his rights would "create serious doubt whether consent searches could continue to be conducted" in light of the prosecution's difficulty in proving such awareness.

As for the suggestion that this would not be so if the police advised a person of his rights before eliciting his consent, the Court responded:

> [I]t would be thoroughly impractical to impose on the normal consent search the detailed requirements of an effective warning. Consent searches are part of the standard investigatory techniques of law enforcement agencies. They normally occur on the highway, or in a person's home or office, and under informal and unstructured conditions. The circumstances that prompt the initial request to search may develop quickly or be a logical extension of investigative police questioning. The police may seek to investigate further suspicious circumstances or to follow up leads developed in questioning persons at the scene of a crime. These situations are a far cry from the structured atmosphere of a trial where, assisted by counsel if he chooses, a defendant is informed of his trial rights. * * * And, while surely a closer question, these situations are still immeasurably, far removed from "custodial interrogation" where, in *Miranda v. Arizona,* we found that the Constitution required certain now familiar warnings as a prerequisite to police interrogation.

Thus, while a "strict standard of waiver" applies "to those rights guaranteed to a criminal defendant to insure * * * a fair criminal trial," it need not extend to the "protections of the Fourth Amendment," which "are of a wholly different order, and have nothing whatever to do with promoting the fair ascertainment of truth at a criminal trial."

The most common criticisms of *Schneckloth* are: (1) the Court at the very outset asserted that the "precise question in this case * * * is what must the state prove to demonstrate that a consent was 'voluntarily' given," thus overlooking the critical fact that coercion (did the police use undue pressure) and unknowing surrender (did defendant know he had a right not to surrender his privacy) are two quite different matters; (2) the Court assumed without question that "guidance" on the issue at hand could be gleaned from the decisions on the voluntariness of confessions, when in fact the nature of the competing interests in the two areas is quite different, as police can obtain information verbally from a suspect only if he chooses to give it, while much physical evidence can be acquired without the cooperation of the suspect; and (3) the Court never satisfactorily explained why the intentional-relinquishment-of-a-known-right waiver concept should apply to trial rights but not to the right to privacy, and overlooked its prior teaching that "no system of criminal justice can, or should, survive if it comes to depend for its continued effectiveness on the citizens' abdication through unawareness of their constitutional rights."[2]

§ 3.10

1. 412 U.S. 218, 93 S.Ct. 2041, 36 L.Ed.2d 854 (1973).

2. Escobedo v. Illinois, 378 U.S. 478, 84 S.Ct. 1758, 12 L.Ed.2d 977 (1964).

A somewhat different issue concerning the meaning of consent in this context is illustrated by *United States v. Elrod*,[3] where Wright consented to a search of a room occupied by him and Elrod, revealing the fruits of a bank robbery, but that evidence was suppressed because of later-acquired information showing "that Wright was mentally incompetent at the time that he signed the consent form." As for the government's claim the matter should not be controlled by that evidence, the court said of that objection:

> Presumably it is a lamentation that to the burdens which now almost make a constitution seer out of a policeman on the beat will be added the esoteric function of an amateur psychiatrist. No matter how genuine the belief of the officers is that the consenter is apparently of sound mind and deliberately acting, the search depending on his consent fails if it is judicially determined that he lacked mental capacity. It is not that the actions of the officers were imprudent or unfounded. It is that the key to validity—consent—is lacking for want of mental capacity, no matter how much concealed.

Some courts, however, have articulated the consent search standard in a way which would produce a different result on the *Elrod* facts; the issue is said to be whether the officers, as reasonable men, could conclude that defendant's consent was given.

At the time *Schneckloth* was decided, the Court's "voluntariness" test from the confession cases would have supported the *Elrod* result, for it was then accepted that a confession could be "coerced" by innocent conduct of the police when a condition of the suspect was unknown to them.[4] But the rule is now otherwise as to confessions,[5] and presumably this means the *Schneckloth* rule will not produce the result reached in *Elrod*. Other aspects of *Schneckloth* also lend support to the conclusion. The Court emphasized both the value of searches made by consent, and the fact that the Fourth Amendment is unique because it does not protect against police action undertaken upon "reasonably, though mistakenly, believed" facts. Both of those considerations underlie the appealing notion that because the Fourth Amendment is only concerned with discouraging unreasonable activity on the part of law enforcement officers, it is not violated when a search is conducted upon a reasonable (albeit mistaken) belief that voluntary consent has been granted.

(b) Factors Bearing on Validity of Consent. The Court held in *Schneckloth* that "the question whether a consent to a search was in fact 'voluntary' or was the product of duress or coercion, express or implied, is a question of fact to be determined from the totality of the circumstances." One factor likely to produce a finding of no consent under this test is a claim by the police that they can make the search in any event. Thus, if the police claim that they have a search warrant and the person then submits to a search because of that claim, but it later turns out that the police actually had no warrant[6] or the prosecution later declines to rely upon the warrant as the basis for the search,[7] the evidence must be suppressed because it was obtained by a submission to a claim of lawful authority. The same is true when the police have incorrectly asserted that they have a right to make a warrantless search under the then existing circumstances or have intimated as much by merely declaring that they have come to search[8] or are going to search.[9] A threat by the police to *obtain* a search warrant is not materially different from a claim that a warrant has already issued, and thus such a threat is likely to invalidate a subsequent consent if there were not then grounds upon which a warrant could issue. But if there were grounds for issuance of a

3. 441 F.2d 353 (5th Cir.1971).

4. Blackburn v. Alabama, 361 U.S. 199, 80 S.Ct. 274, 4 L.Ed.2d 242 (1960).

5. See Colorado v. Connelly, 479 U.S. 157, 107 S.Ct. 515, 93 L.Ed.2d 473 (1986), discussed in § 6.2(b), (c).

6. Go–Bart Importing Co. v. United States, 282 U.S. 344, 51 S.Ct. 153, 75 L.Ed. 374 (1931).

7. Bumper v. North Carolina, 391 U.S. 543, 88 S.Ct. 1788, 20 L.Ed.2d 797 (1968).

8. Amos v. United States, 255 U.S. 313, 41 S.Ct. 266, 65 L.Ed. 654 (1921).

9. Johnson v. United States, 333 U.S. 10, 68 S.Ct. 367, 92 L.Ed. 436 (1948).

search warrant, then the advice of a law enforcement agent that, absent a consent to search, a warrant can be obtained does not constitute coercion, as in such a case the person has been correctly advised of his legal situation. In the eyes of some courts, a police threat to *seek* a search warrant is not coercive because the officer was merely telling the defendant what he had a legal right to do. But it is to be doubted whether the ordinary person, when confronted with a request by an officer to consent to a search, would discriminate between the statement that otherwise the officer would *get* a search warrant, as compared with a statement that otherwise he would *apply for* a warrant. Absent such claims, consideration must be given to whether the circumstances were coercive, which necessitates attention to whether the person was confronted with many officers or a display of weapons, whether he was in custody and if so whether the circumstances of the custody were coercive, and whether the alleged consent was obtained in the course of stationhouse interrogation.

In *Schneckloth,* the majority, in responding to the argument that the failure to require the prosecution to establish knowledge as prerequisite to a valid consent would relegate the Fourth Amendment to the special province of "the sophisticated, the knowledgeable, and the privileged," observed that the "traditional definition of voluntariness we accept today has always taken into account evidence of minimal schooling [and] low intelligence." Consistent with this position, courts determining the voluntariness of a consent must assess whether the individual was immature and impressionable or experienced and well-educated, and whether that person was in an excited emotional state, mentally incompetent, or under the influence of drugs or alcohol at the time the purported consent was given. (But, by virtue of the significant change in the "voluntariness" test which has occurred in the law on confessions as a result of *Colorado v. Connelly,*[10] involuntariness cannot be grounded solely in the defendant's mental condition, for "the crucial element of police overreaching"—that is, "coercive" police conduct, such as exploiting defendant's deficient mental condition—must be present.) A consent is suspect if given by one who earlier refused to consent, unless some reason appears to explain the change in position. By like reasoning, if the consent is preceded by a valid confession or by cooperation in the investigation generally, this enhances the chances that the consent was voluntary, and the same may be said of cooperation in the search itself. What then if the consent was by a person suspected of the crime under investigation but who denied his guilt? One view, taken in *Higgins v. United States,*[11] is that if such a denial preceded an alleged consent which led to the discovery of incriminating evidence, then the consent must be held invalid, as "no sane man who denies his guilt would actually be willing that policemen search his room for contraband which is certain to be discovered." But *Higgins* has not received general acceptance. Sometimes it is simply distinguished away, which is certainly correct in cases where it appears the defendant thought the incriminating evidence had been removed or was cleverly concealed and thus not likely to be discovered, or where the objects found were not obviously incriminating in character. On other occasions the *Higgins* test has been rejected as an unworkable test based upon hindsight which, in any event, is grounded in the erroneous assumption that the pressure exerted on a criminal by the realization that "the jig is up" amounts to coercion. The Supreme Court has summarily rejected a *Higgins*-type argument by asserting the question is what a reasonable *innocent* person would have done.[12]

The Supreme Court in *Schneckloth,* as a consequence of adopting the voluntariness test for consent searches, concluded that "while the subject's knowledge of a right to refuse is a factor to be taken into account, the prosecution is not required to demonstrate

10. 479 U.S. 157, 107 S.Ct. 515, 92 L.Ed.2d 473 (1986).

11. 209 F.2d 819 (D.C.Cir.1954).

12. Florida v. Bostick, ___ U.S. ___, 111 S.Ct. 2382, 115 L.Ed.2d 389 (1991).

such knowledge as a prerequisite to establishing a voluntary consent." That is, consent may be established without a showing that the police warned the consenting party of his Fourth Amendment rights or that he was otherwise aware of those rights. Though the Court there emphasized that the decision was "a narrow one," extending only to the situation in which "the subject of the search is not in custody," a few years later the Court extended the *Schneckloth* rule to a case in which the consent was obtained from a person in police custody. In that case, *United States v. Watson*,[13] it was stressed that the "consent was given while on a public street, not in the confines of the police station," but lower courts have in the main utilized the "totality of the circumstances" approach without regard to the nature of the custody. Such an extension of *Schneckloth,* it may be argued, ignores the teaching of *Miranda v. Arizona* [14] that there is "compulsion inherent in custodial surroundings" and overlooks the fact that the concern in *Schneckloth* about warnings being "impractical" under the "informal and unstructured conditions" of a roadside search does not extend to situations in which the person has been taken into custody. In any event, proof by the prosecution that the consenting party was warned of his rights or that he was aware of his rights is often a significant factor leading to a finding of voluntary consent, and sometimes will be essential if prior coercion is to be overcome.

Some courts have held that a consent to search given during custodial interrogation must be preceded by *Miranda* warnings, because the request to search is a request that defendant be a witness against himself, which he is privileged to refuse under the Fifth Amendment. But the prevailing and better view is to the contrary, for a consent to search, as such, is neither testimonial nor communicative in the Fifth Amendment sense. Although the giving of *Miranda* warnings may contribute to a finding of voluntariness, these warnings are not equivalent to Fourth Amendment warnings in terms of overcoming prior coercion, for a defendant might well not understand that the "silence" referred to covers not allowing a search. There may be circumstances in which a consent to search will be invalidated because made without counsel or waiver of the right to counsel. The Supreme Court has held that "a person's Sixth and Fourteenth Amendment right to counsel attaches only at or after the time that adversary judicial proceedings have been initiated against him," [15] and then only as to a "critical stage," which means when "the accused required aid in coping with legal problems or assistance in meeting his adversary." [16] A post-charge solicitation of the defendant to consent to a search would appear to be such a situation. And in any event, a pre-consent refusal of a person's request to consult counsel would weigh heavily against finding that consent to be voluntary.

(c) Consent by Deception. A rather special type of consent case, involving considerations different from those discussed above, is that in which the police have obtained consent to intrude into a certain private area by resort to deceit. One situation, which the Supreme Court has confronted with some frequency, is that in which the person conceals the fact that he is a policeman or that he has already agreed to act on behalf of the police. In *On Lee v. United States*,[17] where an informant wired for sound entered defendant's laundry and engaged him in incriminating conversations, the Court rather summarily concluded that "Chin Poy entered a place of business with the consent, if not by the implied invitation, of the petitioner," and that "the claim that Chin Poy's entrance was a trespass because consent to his entry was obtained by fraud must be rejected." Similarly, in *Hoffa v. United States*,[18] where an old friend of the defendant gave incriminating

13. 423 U.S. 411, 96 S.Ct. 820, 46 L.Ed.2d 598 (1976).

14. 384 U.S. 436, 86 S.Ct. 1602, 16 L.Ed.2d 694 (1966).

15. Kirby v. Illinois, 406 U.S. 682, 92 S.Ct. 1877, 32 L.Ed.2d 411 (1972).

16. United States v. Ash, 413 U.S. 300, 93 S.Ct. 2568, 37 L.Ed.2d 619 (1973).

17. 343 U.S. 747, 72 S.Ct. 967, 96 L.Ed. 1270 (1952).

18. 385 U.S. 293, 87 S.Ct. 408, 17 L.Ed.2d 374 (1966).

testimony based upon his visits to defendant's hotel room as an agent of the government, the Court characterized the situation as one of "misplaced confidence" and concluded that it was *not* true that "the Fourth Amendment protects a wrongdoer's misplaced belief that a person to whom he voluntarily confides his wrongdoing will not reveal it." *Lewis v. United States,*[19] decided the same day, involved a situation in which a federal drug agent gained access to defendant's home by misrepresenting his identity and expressing a willingness to purchase narcotics. Stressing that "the petitioner invited the undercover agent to his home for the specific purpose of executing a felonious sale of narcotics," the Court concluded that

> when, as here, the home is converted into a commercial center to which outsiders are invited for purposes of transacting unlawful business, that business is entitled to no greater sanctity than if it were carried on in a store, a garage, a car, or on the street. A government agent, in the same manner as a private person, may accept an invitation to do business and may enter upon the premises for the very purposes contemplated by the occupant.

These decisions, then, appear to support the following proposition: when an individual gives consent to another to intrude into an area or activity otherwise protected by the Fourth Amendment, aware that he will thereby reveal to this other person either criminal conduct or evidence of such conduct, the consent is not vitiated merely because it would not have been given but for the nondisclosure or affirmative misrepresentation which made the consenting party unaware of the other person's identity as a police officer or police agent.

Though some consider even *Lewis* as objectionable on the ground that deliberate deception about an obviously material fact should be regarded as inconsistent with voluntariness, a more appropriate concern is that of keeping the above-stated principle within reasonable bounds. One attractive proposal is that permissible deception by a stranger *must* include a stated intention on his part to join the consenting party in criminal activity, for in that way innocent persons will be spared from intrusions upon their privacy by deception. But lower courts in the main have not recognized such a limitation, and have instead relied upon the broader proposition that the Fourth Amendment affords no protection to one who voluntarily reveals incriminating evidence to another in the mistaken belief that the latter will not disclose it. Even that formulation should often bar some of the more extreme forms of deception, such as police entry of a private home in the guise of an employee of the gas company.

A somewhat different kind of case is that in which the consenting party knows he is dealing with a law enforcement officer or agent, but there is some deception as to the latter's objective or purpose. Certainly it is not objectionable that the agent has manifested a willingness to be bribed.[20] But what of a misrepresentation as to the reason a consent to search was being sought, as in *Alexander v. United States,*[21] where officers seeking stolen marked money obtained consent to search by claiming they were looking for stolen jewelry? Though the court there concluded the "fraudulent warning" deprived the consent of its validity, it is by no means clear that this is so. The fact remains that the police did not "see * * * anything that was not contemplated," an important factor in *Lewis*; that such deception has been tolerated in the voluntariness-of-confession cases; and that this kind of deception does not pose a risk to innocent persons because it will likely produce a consent which would otherwise have been withheld only from a person guilty of the undisclosed crime. By comparison, when the police misrepresentation of purpose is so extreme that it deprives the individual of the ability to make a fair assessment of the need to surren-

19. 385 U.S. 206, 87 S.Ct. 424, 17 L.Ed.2d 312 (1966).

20. Lopez v. United States, 373 U.S. 427, 83 S.Ct. 1381, 10 L.Ed.2d 462 (1963).

21. 390 F.2d 101 (5th Cir.1968).

der his privacy, as in *People v. Jefferson*,[22] where police gained entry to defendant's apartment on the false claim they were investigating a gas leak, the consent should not be considered valid.

(d) Third Party Consent: General Considerations. Although in *Schneckloth* it was noted that under some circumstances a person's privacy may be lawfully invaded by virtue of consent obtained from a third party, the Court has experienced some difficulty over the years in identifying just what it takes to give a certain third party this power. In *Stoner v. California*,[23] holding a hotel clerk could not consent to search of a guest's room, the Court reasoned that the guest could surrender his rights only "directly or through an agent" and found no evidence that the "clerk had been authorized by the petitioner" to permit the police to enter his room. In *Bumper v. North Carolina*,[24] holding the consent by defendant's grandmother had been coerced, the Court left little doubt that but for the coercion the evidence would have been admitted because she "owned both the house and the rifle," that is, the place searched and the thing seized. Then, in *Frazier v. Cupp*,[25] holding defendant's cousin could consent to a search of a duffel bag which he held and in which both he and his cousin kept some of their personal effects, the Court appeared to abandon the agency and property theories in favor of an "assumption of risk" formulation: "Petitioner, in allowing [his cousin] Rawls to use the bag and in leaving it in his house, must be taken to have assumed the risk that Rawls would allow someone else to look inside."

Then came *United States v. Matlock*,[26] where, following defendant's arrest in the yard of the house in which he lived, a Mrs. Graff consented to search of the bedroom she shared with defendant. The Court deemed it clear that the prosecution "may show that permission to search was obtained from a third party who possessed common authority over or other sufficient relationship to the premises or effects sought to be inspected." The Court then dropped this explanatory footnote:

> Common authority is, of course, not to be implied from the mere property interest a third party has in the property. The authority which justifies the third-party consent does not rest upon the law of property, with its attendant historical and legal refinements, * * * but rests rather on mutual use of the property by persons generally having joint access or control for most purposes, so that it is reasonable to recognize that any of the co-inhabitants has the right to permit the inspection in his own right and that the others have assumed the risk that one of their number might permit the common area to be searched.

The Court thus identified two bases for its "common authority" rule: (i) that the consenting party could permit the search "in his own right"; and (ii) that the defendant had "assumed the risk" that a co-occupant might permit a search. It is important to keep both of them in mind in assessing the issues which commonly arise about the circumstances which will validate or invalidate a search by third party consent:

(1) Does the validity of third party consent depend upon the existence of amicable relations between that party and the defendant? In *Kelley v. State*,[27] where defendant's wife summoned police to their home to have him arrested on a charge of beating her and then showed them where he kept his supply of illegal liquor, the court answered in the affirmative, suppressing the evidence because "her actions were hostile to her husband and obviously to his interests." But the prevailing and better view is to the contrary, for the antagonism does not bear upon the two considerations stressed in *Matlock*. By remaining in the marital household the wife has maintained her "equal authority" over those premises, and the defendant's expectations of

22. 43 A.D.2d 112, 350 N.Y.S.2d 3 (1973).

23. 376 U.S. 483, 84 S.Ct. 889, 11 L.Ed.2d 856 (1964).

24. 391 U.S. 543, 88 S.Ct. 1788, 20 L.Ed.2d 797 (1968).

25. 394 U.S. 731, 89 S.Ct. 1420, 22 L.Ed.2d 684 (1969).

26. 415 U.S. 164, 94 S.Ct. 988, 39 L.Ed.2d 242 (1974).

27. 184 Tenn. 143, 197 S.W.2d 545 (1946).

privacy are, if anything, diminished as a consequence of his assault upon another occupant of those premises.

(2) Can a third party give effective consent after being instructed by defendant not to do so? In *People v. Fry*,[28] police obtained the consent of defendant's wife to search the family home, but the evidence obtained thereby was suppressed because the police "knew her husband had instructed her not to consent and, under these circumstances, were not entitled to rely upon her consent as justification for their conduct." If the *Stoner* agency theory were the sole basis upon which a third party consent could be upheld, there would be little reason to question the *Fry* result. But it cannot be squared with the two *Matlock* bases. In light of the third party's ability to permit the search "in his own right," it may be said that defendant's instructions cannot invalidate consent that did not depend on his authority in the first place. As for the "assumption of risk" aspect, certainly there is a risk, stronger in some cases than in others, that the other occupant will not comply with such a request.

(3) Is a third party's consent invalidated by the defendant's prior or contemporaneous refusal to consent to such a search? Yes, it has sometimes been held, because constitutional rights may not be defeated by the expedient of soliciting several persons successively until the sought-after consent is obtained. But the cases holding to the contrary may be more readily squared with *Matlock,* for here again the other occupant retains his "own right" to allow a search and the defendant has participated in a living situation in which there inheres the risk that in defendant's absence another occupant might admit the police. What then if defendant was *present* and objecting at the time? *Matlock* cautiously puts this situation to one side, for the Court there said that "the consent of one who possesses common authority over premises or effects is valid as against the *absent,* nonconsenting person with whom that authority is shared."[29] One view is that even here *Matlock* permits the third party to act in his own or the public interest, while the contrary position is that the consent of both is required when both are present because persons with equal rights in a place would ordinarily accommodate each other by not admitting persons over another's objection while he was present. So the argument would proceed, using *Matlock* terminology, a person's authority to consent in his "own right" does not go so far as to outweigh an equal privacy claim by another occupant who is actually present asserting his right, and the defendant by his joint occupancy or use has only "assumed the risk" as to what will happen when he is not present to protect his own interests. Even if this is so, there will be cases in which some other circumstance justifies giving one of these "equal" rights greater recognition than the other, and of course there are also cases in which the rights of the two occupants are not equal and the matter can thus be resolved by giving recognition to the superior interest.

(4) Is a third party's consent ineffective when the police bypassed an opportunity to seek consent from the defendant? The cases answer no, and they appear to be supported by both the facts and the rationale of *Matlock.* This is generally a sound result, perhaps even when the bypassed opportunity was at the time of the defendant's arrest while present at the place later searched. But when the positions of the two persons are not equal, so that it may be said the police passed up an obvious opportunity to seek consent from a defendant with a clearly superior interest in the place, this has been held to invalidate the consent obtained from the third party with a lesser interest.

(5) Is a third party's consent affected by the fact that the defendant maintained exclusive control as to certain areas or effects? *Matlock* is rather ambiguous on this point, for the Court said the question was whether Ms. Graff had "common authority" over the premises, which was deemed to rest on "mutual use of the property" by one "having joint

28. 271 Cal.App.2d 350, 76 Cal.Rptr. 718 (1969).

29. Emphasis added.

access or control for most purposes." Perhaps it is of no significance that the Court failed to allude specifically to the principle, recognized in prior lower court decisions, that persons sharing premises may nonetheless retain areas of exclusive control. But it is well to remember that the Court has taken a firm stand against extreme or strained applications of the exclusive control concept. In *Frazier v. Cupp*,[30] in response to defendant's argument that his cousin (who possessed and consented to search of defendant's duffel bag) only had permission to use one compartment in the bag, the Court declined to "engage in such metaphysical subtleties in judging the efficacy of Rawls' consent" and concluded defendant had assumed the risk by allowing Rawls to use the bag and in leaving it in his house. Thus, while it has sometimes been suggested that under *Matlock* police are obligated to ascertain the possibly unique pattern of living arrangements between defendant and the third party so as to determine the extent of the "common authority," courts generally are not inclined to be that demanding.

(6) May a third party consent be upheld when the police had a reasonable but mistaken belief that the third party had authority over the place searched? In *Stoner v. California*,[31] in response to the argument that the police "had a reasonable basis for the belief that the [hotel] clerk had authority to consent to the search" of a guest's room, the Court properly asserted that "the rights protected by the Fourth Amendment are not to be eroded * * * by unrealistic doctrines of 'apparent authority.'" The police in *Stoner* were fully aware of the relevant facts (i.e., that the person consenting was a clerk and that defendant was currently renting the room in question), and thus the mistake was as to the clerk's *legal* authority, which if it were to prevail would in effect allow the police to expand the law of third party consent by their misperceptions of what the Fourth Amendment allows. But what if the error was as to a *factual* matter and the reasonably assumed fact, if true, would put the consenting party in a position to give a valid consent; that is, what if in *Stoner* the police had acted upon the clerk's consent in the reasonable but mistaken belief that no one was renting the room in question? In such a case, the Supreme Court concluded in *Illinois v. Rodriguez*,[32] the search is lawful, for what the defendant "is assured by the Fourth Amendment itself * * * is not that no government search * * * will occur unless he consents; but that no such search will occur that is 'unreasonable.'" In this and many other Fourth Amendment contexts, a police officer's actions can be reasonable even when grounded in factual assumptions which turn out to be incorrect. But the Court in *Rodriguez* cautioned it was *not* suggesting "that law enforcement officers may always accept a person's invitation to enter premises. Even when the invitation is accompanied by an explicit assertion that the person lives there, the surrounding circumstances could conceivably be such that a reasonable person would doubt its truth and not act upon it without further inquiry," in which case "warrantless entry without further inquiry is unlawful unless authority actually exists."

(7) May a third party consent be upheld when the defendant had a reasonable but mistaken belief as to the extent of the risk involved? This interesting question is prompted by *Commonwealth v. Latshaw*,[33] where defendant *A* stored containers of marijuana in a barn with the consent of *B*, who *A* was led to believe had exclusive possession and control of that barn, but in fact the barn belonged to and was under the control of *C*, who consented to a police search of the barn. In upholding the consent, the court in *Latshaw* concluded that *C*'s "independent right * * * to authorize the search of her property" could not be affected by *B*'s conduct in misleading *A*. In other words, when the two bases of the *Matlock* "common authority" rule come into conflict, the consenting per-

30. 394 U.S. 731, 89 S.Ct. 1420, 22 L.Ed.2d 684 (1969).

31. 376 U.S. 483, 84 S.Ct. 889, 11 L.Ed.2d 856 (1964).

32. ___ U.S. ___, 110 S.Ct. 2793, 111 L.Ed.2d 148 (1990).

33. 481 Pa. 298, 392 A.2d 1301 (1978).

son's authority to permit the search "in his own right" is to prevail over a showing that the defendant had not "assumed the risk" of consent by the person who gave it. This is a sound result, as (a) it is still important in such circumstances to recognize the owner's "legitimate interest in exculpating himself or herself from possible criminal involvement with the suspected contraband," as the court put it in *Latshaw;* (b) *A* was ignorant as to the true identity of the person in possession, but in a more general sense "assumed the risk" that whoever was in possession might for some reason admit others; and (c) permitting the police to proceed on the situation as it appears to the person who summoned them and consented to the search is to be preferred over a rule which nullifies the search by an after-the-fact assessment of defendant's reasonably mistaken impressions of the situation.

(e) **Common Relationships in Third Party Consent.** It may generally be said that one spouse may give consent to a search of the family residence which will be effective against the other spouse. At one time there was a tendency to view consent by the wife with greater suspicion on the ground that the husband is the head of the household, but the modern view is that the wife has no less authority than the husband because she normally exercises as much control over the property in the home as the husband. It is possible in a particular case that the consent will be held ineffective because the area searched was within the "exclusive control" of the defendant, but this is much less likely in husband-wife cases than in other shared occupancy situations. There is somewhat greater reluctance to uphold a wife's consent to search of her husband's car, but it is not inconsistent with *Matlock* to suggest that the wife's consent should suffice if the vehicle is the family car, without regard to whether the wife is a registered co-owner or uses it as a driver instead of only as a passenger.

If a son or daughter, whether or not still a minor, is residing in the home of the parents, generally it is within the authority of the father or mother to consent to a police search of that home which will be effective against the offspring. This is unquestionably so as to areas of common usage, and is also true of the bedroom of the son or daughter when a parent has ready access for purposes of cleaning it or when because of the minority of the offspring the parent is still exercising parental authority. Because in the latter circumstances the parent's rights are superior to the rights of children who live in [the] house, a parent's consent would prevail even if the child were present and objecting and even if the child had taken special measures in an effort to ensure he had exclusive use of the area searched. When the tables are turned and it is the offspring who has consented and a parent is the defendant, the effectiveness of the consent depends upon: (1) the age of the child, because as children grow older they gradually acquire discretion to admit whom they will on their own authority; and (2) the scope of the consent given, in that a teenager could admit police to look about generally but a child of eight could merely admit police to that part of the house which any caller would be allowed to enter.

Turning to property relationships, it may generally be said that a lessor who has granted the lessee exclusive possession over a certain area may not, during the period of the tenancy, consent to a police search of that area. This is so whether the arrangement involves the rental of a house, an apartment, a room in a rooming house, hotel or motel, or even a locker. The rule is not otherwise merely because the lessor has by express agreement or by implication reserved the right to enter for some special and limited purpose.[34] The landlord may consent to search of common areas, such as a hallway in an apartment building. It logically follows that the tenant may consent to a search of the area he has leased, but not a portion of the premises the landlord has retained as his own. Where two or more persons occupy a dwelling place jointly, the general rule is that a joint tenant can consent to police entry and search of the entire house or apartment, even

34. Chapman v. United States, 365 U.S. 610, 81 S.Ct. 776, 5 L.Ed.2d 828 (1961).

though they occupy separate bedrooms. This is certainly true of common areas such as a kitchen or bathroom, but not as to places under the "exclusive control" of another tenant, a matter the police are obligated to make some inquiry about in ambiguous situations. Similarly, while a host can consent to a search of his premises occupied by a guest, this does not inevitably extend to a suitcase or like object in which a person has a high expectation of privacy even when a guest in another's home. Generally, a guest cannot give consent to a search of the premises which will be effective against his host. In bailment cases, the bailee may give effective consent if the nature of the bailment is such, as it was in *Frazier v. Cupp*,[35] where defendant left his duffel bag with his cousin, that defendant has "assumed the risk" the bailee would do so. The bailor does not have authority to consent to an intrusion into the bailee's possessory interest, but in some circumstances may have the power to terminate the bailment for violation of its terms by the bailee and to then allow the search.

In employment relationships, where the question arises whether an employee's consent was effective, courts are inclined to assess the responsibilities of the particular employee, which makes sense from both an agency and an assumption of risk point of view. Thus, a caretaker left in charge of a farm for a few weeks has greater authority to consent to a search there than a farm hand working at a particular location on the farm while his employer is occupied elsewhere on the property. Courts are understandably influenced by the "status" of the employee (e.g., office manager vs. clerk) and the character of the place searched (e.g., warehouse vs. private office). When the consent is by the employer and the objecting defendant is an employee, courts consider (1) the extent to which the particular area searched had been set aside for the personal use of the employee, and (2) the extent to which the search was prompted by a unique or special need of the employer to maintain close scrutiny of employees. Finally, there are the third party consent cases involving what might be called the educational relationship, in which a student objects to a search allowed by a school official. Generally, it may be said that the courts have upheld such searches when made of lockers in a high school, but not when made of a college dorm room. These cases reflect both that such consent is more likely to be upheld in order to maintain discipline over young students and that it is less likely to be upheld when the place in question is a residential area having only a tangential relationship to the educational enterprise.

(f) Scope of Consent. Even if it is determined that the consent of the defendant or another authorized person was "voluntary" within the meaning of *Schneckloth,* it does not inevitably follow that evidence found in the ensuing search will be admissible. This is because it is also necessary to take account of any express or implied limitations on the consent which mark the permissible scope of that search in terms of its time, duration, area or intensity. This matter of scope, the Supreme Court has decided, is determined by neither the subjective intentions of the suspect nor the subjective interpretation of the officer; rather, the standard "is that of 'objective' reasonableness—what would the typical reasonable person have understood by the exchange between the officer and the suspect?"[36] Police customarily ask for consent not in the abstract but in terms of a particular place, such as a certain residence or vehicle, and if the person responds with a consent which is general and unqualified, then ordinarily the police may conduct a general search of that place. This means that when the object the police indicated they are looking for could be concealed therein,[37] they may even search un-

35. 394 U.S. 731, 89 S.Ct. 1420, 22 L.Ed.2d 684 (1969).

36. Florida v. Jimeno, ___ U.S. ___, 111 S.Ct. 1801, 114 L.Ed.2d 297 (1991).

37. In Florida v. Jimeno, ___ U.S. ___, 111 S.Ct. 1801, 114 L.Ed.2d 297 (1991), the Court noted that "the scope of a search is generally defined by its expressed object," meaning that when the officer told defendant "that he would be looking for narcotics in the car," it was "objectively reasonable for the police to conclude that the general consent to search respondent's car included consent to search containers within that car which might bear drugs."

locked containers found in that place, but not that they may break into locked containers or otherwise do physical damage in carrying out the search.[38] The scope of the search must be more narrowly confined when expressly stated to cover only a portion of a certain place, when the thing the police say they are looking for quite obviously necessitates looking only in a particular place, or when the person giving the consent makes it apparent that he does not expect that the police can gain access to a certain part of the designated place.

The most common limitation on the scope of a search by consent is that upon the intensity of the police activity permitted. This limitation is not ordinarily expressly stated by the consenting party, but arises from the fact that the police have indicated that the consent is being sought for a particular purpose. Illustrative is *United States v. Dichiarinte,*[39] where defendant consented to a search of his home in response to a police inquiry whether he had any narcotics, but the police opened and read incriminating documents. The court quite correctly concluded that this conduct extended beyond that authorized by the defendant, and asserted: "Government agents may not obtain consent to search on the representation that they intend to look only for certain specified items and subsequently use that consent as a license to conduct a general exploratory search." But if the police search only where the items they purport to be looking for could be concealed, under the "plain view" doctrine they may seize other items if they have probable cause they are the fruits, instrumentalities or evidence of some crime.

As a general rule, a consent to search may be said to have been given on the understanding that the search will be conducted forthwith and that only a single search will be made. Though there is some authority that consent once given may not be withdrawn, the better view is that though a consent to search is not terminated merely by a worsening of the consenting party's position, a consent may be withdrawn or limited at any time prior to the completion of the search. A revocation of consent does not operate retroactively to render unreasonable a search conducted prior to the time of revocation, any more than the giving of consent may be said to retroactively validate a search conducted prior to the time the consent was given.

38. "It is very likely unreasonable to think that a suspect, by consenting to the search of his trunk, has agreed to the breaking open of a locked briefcase within the trunk, but it is otherwise with respect to a closed paper bag." Florida v. Jimeno, ___ U.S. ___, 111 S.Ct. 1801, 114 L.Ed.2d 297 (1991).

39. 445 F.2d 126 (7th Cir.1971).

Chapter 4

WIRETAPPING AND ELECTRONIC SURVEILLANCE

Table of Sections

§ 4.1 Historical Background

(a) The *Olmstead* Case. The first wiretapping case to reach the United States Supreme Court was *Olmstead v. United States,*[1] involving the interception by federal agents of messages passing over telephone wires. In a 5–4 decision, the Court held that such activity did not amount to a Fourth Amendment search or seizure because (1) the agents obtained access to the telephone wires without any "entry of the houses or offices of the defendants," meaning that no "place" had been searched within the meaning of the Amendment; and (2) the agents obtained the content of the conversations which passed over the wires but did not acquire any physical objects, and thus no "things" had been seized within the meaning of the Amendment. It made no difference that the conduct was in violation of a state law making it a misdemeanor to "intercept" telegraphic or telephonic messages, as that statute did not declare evidence so obtained was inadmissible and, in any event, a state statute "can not affect the rules of evidence applicable in courts of the United States."

As discussed later, both reasons given in *Olmstead* for holding the Fourth Amendment inapplicable have since been rejected by the Supreme Court. It is not surprising, therefore, that in recent years the forceful dissents in *Olmstead* have received the greatest attention. In an exhaustive dissenting opinion, Justice Brandeis argued that "every unjustifiable intrusion by the Government upon the privacy of the individual, whatever the means employed, must be deemed a violation of the Fourth Amendment." In addition, he contended that the government, as "the omnipresent teacher," should not be upheld in its admitted violation of a state wiretapping law. Justice Holmes, in a brief separate dissent on the latter ground only, characterized wiretapping in violation of state law as "dirty business" which a judge should not "allow * * * to succeed." In an oft-quoted passage, Holmes reasoned that it is "a less evil that some criminals should escape than that the Government should play an ignoble part."

(b) Section 605. The majority in *Olmstead* noted that "Congress may of course protect the secrecy of telephone messages by making them, when intercepted, inadmissible in evidence in federal criminal trials." The Federal Communications Act of 1934 was later enacted, and it provided in part in § 605 that "no person not being authorized by the sender shall intercept any communication and divulge or publish the existence, contents, substance, purport, effect, or meaning of such intercepted communication to any person."[2] Though this legislation did not contain an express declaration of an exclusionary rule as apparently contemplated by *Olmstead,* it was interpreted to have this effect. In *Nardone v. United States,*[3] the Supreme Court held that under § 605 a federal officer could not testify in federal court concerning the contents of wiretapped conversations because to "recite the contents of the message in testimony before a court is to divulge the message." This case reached the Court a second time after the defendants were retried on evidence discovered as a result of information acquired by the wiretapping, and this time it was held that this exclusionary rule extended to derivative evidence as well.[4] In other cases also having to do only with the admissibility of the fruits of wiretapping in federal courts, the Court held that the prohibitions of § 605 extended to intrastate communications[5] and to actions of state officers.[6]

The protections of § 605 were not absolute. For one thing, traditional notions of standing were applied to this exclusionary rule, meaning that one who was not a party to the tapped conversation could not object to the use against him of evidence obtained by wire-

§ 4.1

1. 277 U.S. 438, 48 S.Ct. 564, 72 L.Ed. 944 (1928).

2. Former 47 U.S.C.A. § 605.

3. 302 U.S. 379, 58 S.Ct. 275, 82 L.Ed. 314 (1937).

4. Nardone v. United States, 308 U.S. 338, 60 S.Ct. 266, 84 L.Ed. 307 (1939).

5. Weiss v. United States, 308 U.S. 321, 60 S.Ct. 269, 84 L.Ed. 298 (1939).

6. Benanti v. United States, 355 U.S. 96, 78 S.Ct. 155, 2 L.Ed.2d 126 (1957).

tapping.[7] For another, § 605 did not cover tapping by consent. "Each party to a telephone conversation takes the risk that the other party * * * may allow another to overhear the conversation." [8] Moreover, federal investigative agencies continued to engage in a considerable amount of wiretapping notwithstanding the prohibitions of § 605. Some occurred pursuant to the generally accepted notion that the statute did not entirely prohibit foreign intelligence wiretapping undertaken in the interest of national security. Much more was attributable to the fact that the Department of Justice and the FBI took the position that § 605 did not prohibit wiretapping alone, but only tapping followed by "divulgence," and that it was not "divulgence" when one member of the government communicated to another, but only when he communicated outside the government (e.g., by revealing the wiretap information in court).

Since it involved the use of state-gathered wiretap evidence in a prosecution in a state court, the case of *Schwartz v. Texas* [9] posed the wiretapping counterpart of *Wolf v. Colorado.*[10] Relying upon *Wolf,* the Court held the evidence admissible. Though it was recognized that "[t]he problem under § 605 is somewhat different [than *Wolf*] because the introduction of the intercepted communication would itself be a violation of the statute," i.e., a prohibited "divulgence," the Court nonetheless concluded that "in the absence of an expression by Congress, this is simply an additional factor for a state to consider in formulating a rule of evidence for use in its own courts." But, in *Benanti v. United States* [11] the Court ignored the search and seizure precedents (later overruled in *Elkins v. United States* [12]) and proceeded to exclude state-gathered wiretap evidence proffered in a federal prosecution, reasoning that the statute "contains an express, absolute prohibition against the divulgence of intercepted communications."

This last observation, especially when coupled with the later overruling of *Wolf* by *Mapp v. Ohio,*[13] made it apparent that *Schwartz* could not survive. But it was not actually overruled until *Lee v. Florida,*[14] decided just two days before the electronic surveillance provisions of the Crime Control Act of 1968 [15] were signed into law. The Court in *Lee* emphasized that its ruling was "counseled by experience," especially that "[r]esearch has failed to uncover a single reported prosecution of a law enforcement officer for violation of § 605 since the statute was enacted." Thus the Court concluded that here as in *Mapp* "nothing short of mandatory exclusion of the illegal evidence will compel respect for the federal law 'in the only effectively available way—by removing the incentive to disregard it.' " *Lee* was held to be nonretroactive,[16] and thus it had a limited impact because later wiretapping was covered by Title III of the 1968 Act.

(c) Non-telephonic Electronic Eavesdropping. As time passed it became apparent that the fears expressed by Justice Brandeis in *Olmstead*—that the "progress of science in furnishing the Government with means of espionage is not likely to stop with wire-tapping"—were justified. Highly sophisticated means of electronic eavesdropping were developed and put into use, largely uncontrolled by the law. They were not within the prohibitions of § 605, for it applied only when telephone, telegraph or radiotelegraph conversations were overheard. Moreover, the protections of the Fourth Amendment applied only if there was a physical invasion or "trespass" into a constitutionally protected area. No such trespass was deemed to exist in *Olm-*

7. Goldstein v. United States, 316 U.S. 114, 62 S.Ct. 1000, 86 L.Ed. 1312 (1942).

8. Rathbun v. United States, 355 U.S. 107, 78 S.Ct. 161, 2 L.Ed.2d 134 (1957).

9. 344 U.S. 199, 73 S.Ct. 232, 97 L.Ed. 231 (1952).

10. 338 U.S. 25, 69 S.Ct. 1359, 93 L.Ed. 1782 (1949).

11. 355 U.S. 96, 78 S.Ct. 155, 2 L.Ed.2d 126 (1957).

12. 364 U.S. 206, 80 S.Ct. 1437, 4 L.Ed.2d 1669 (1960).

13. 367 U.S. 643, 81 S.Ct. 1684, 6 L.Ed.2d 1081 (1961).

14. 392 U.S. 378, 88 S.Ct. 2096, 20 L.Ed.2d 1166 (1968).

15. 18 U.S.C.A. §§ 2510–2520.

16. Fuller v. Alaska, 393 U.S. 80, 89 S.Ct. 61, 21 L.Ed.2d 212 (1968).

stead, where the taps from house lines were made in the streets near the house; in *Goldman v. United States,*[17] where federal officers merely placed a detectaphone against the wall of an adjoining office where they were lawfully present; or in *On Lee v. United States,*[18] where incriminating statements were picked up via a "wired for sound" former acquaintance of petitioner who entered his premises with consent.

That the Constitution furnished some protection against the electronic seizure of conversations was finally established in *Silverman v. United States.*[19] There, a unanimous Court held that listening to incriminating conversations within a house by inserting an electronic device (a so-called "spike mike") into a party wall and making contact with a heating duct serving the house occupied by petitioners, "thus converting their entire heating system into a conductor of sound," amounted to an illegal search and seizure. The Court declared that in such circumstances "we need not pause to consider whether or not there was a technical trespass under the local property law relating to party walls," thus suggesting that *Silverman* established not only that conversations can be seized within the meaning of the Fourth Amendment but also that a Fourth Amendment search for them might occur without a trespass. This seemed even more certain when a few years later the Court, in *Clinton v. Virginia,*[20] summarily rejected the state court's holding that *Silverman* did not apply where the spike mike "was not driven into the wall but was 'stuck in' it."[21]

Any lingering doubts were dispelled by *Katz v. United States.*[22] The issue in *Katz* was whether recordings of defendant's end of telephone conversations, obtained by attaching an electronic listening and recording device to the outside of a public telephone booth, had been obtained in violation of the Fourth Amendment. Expressly rejecting the "trespass" doctrine of *Olmstead* and *Goldman,* the Court held that the government action constituted a search and seizure within the meaning of the Fourth Amendment. This was because that conduct "violated the privacy upon which [the defendant] justifiably relied while using the telephone booth." *Katz* thus made it clear that, with the possible exception of the case in which a conversation is overheard or recorded with the consent of a party to the conversation, wiretapping and electronic eavesdropping are subject to the limitations of the Fourth Amendment.

17. 316 U.S. 129, 62 S.Ct. 993, 86 L.Ed. 1322 (1942).

18. 343 U.S. 747, 72 S.Ct. 967, 96 L.Ed. 1270 (1952).

19. 365 U.S. 505, 81 S.Ct. 679, 5 L.Ed.2d 734 (1961).

20. 377 U.S. 158, 84 S.Ct. 1186, 12 L.Ed.2d 213 (1964).

21. Clinton v. Commonwealth, 204 Va. 275, 130 S.E.2d 437 (1963).

22. 389 U.S. 347, 88 S.Ct. 507, 19 L.Ed.2d 576 (1967).

§ 4.2 Title III and the Fourth Amendment

(a) Summary of Title III. About a year after the Supreme Court in *Berger v. New York*[1] held that a certain state eavesdropping statute violated the Fourth Amendment, the Congress adopted comprehensive legislation on the subject of wiretapping and electronic surveillance. This legislation is commonly referred to simply as Title III (as it will be hereinafter), as it makes up that part of the Omnibus Crime Control and Safe Streets Act of 1968.[2] Title III was adopted because there was common agreement that its predecessor, § 605, was the worst of all possible solutions. Private citizens and public officials could ignore the prohibition against wiretapping without fear of prosecution, while law enforcement officers could not use electronic surveillance to investigate and prosecute even the most serious crimes.

Under Title III, the Attorney General, Deputy Attorney General, Associate Attorney General, any Assistant Attorney General, any

§ 4.2

1. 388 U.S. 41, 87 S.Ct. 1873, 18 L.Ed.2d 1040 (1967).

2. 18 U.S.C.A. §§ 2510–2520. In 1986 there was added 18 U.S.C.A. §§ 2701–2710, having to do with stored wire and electronic communications and transactional records access, including the requirements for government access. But, per § 2708 there is no statutory exclusionary rule for violation of these provisions, and thus they are not discussed further herein.

acting Assistant Attorney General, or any Deputy Assistant Attorney General in the Criminal Division specially designated by the Attorney General may authorize application * * * to a federal judge for an order permitting interception of wire or oral communications (i.e., wiretapping or electronic eavesdropping) by a federal agency having responsibility for investigation of the offense as to which application is made, when such interception may provide evidence of certain enumerated federal crimes. A comparable provision permits, when authorized by state law, application by a state or county prosecutor to a state judge when the interception may provide evidence of "murder, kidnapping, gambling, robbery, bribery, extortion, or dealing in narcotic drugs, marijuana or other dangerous drugs, or other crime dangerous to life, limb, or property, and punishable by imprisonment for more than one year." The judge may only grant an interception order as provided in § 2518 of the Act, and evidence obtained in the lawful execution of such order is admissible in court.

An interception order may be issued only if the judge determines on the basis of facts submitted that there is probable cause for belief that an individual is committing, has committed, or is about to commit one of the enumerated offenses; probable cause for belief that particular communications concerning that offense will be obtained through such interception; that normal investigative procedures have been tried and have failed or reasonably appear to be unlikely to succeed if tried or to be too dangerous; and probable cause for belief that the facilities from which, or the place where, the communications are to be intercepted are being used, or are about to be used, in connection with the commission of such offense, or are leased to, listed in the name of, or commonly used by such person. Each interception order must specify the identity of the person, if known, whose communications are to be intercepted; the nature and location of the communications facilities as to which, or the place where, authority to intercept is granted; a particular description of the type of communication sought to be intercepted, and a statement of the particular offense to which it relates; the identity of the agency authorized to intercept the communications and of the person authorizing the application; and the period of time during which such interception is authorized, including a statement as to whether or not the interception shall automatically terminate when the described communication has been first obtained. No order may permit interception "for any period longer than is necessary to achieve the objective of the authorization, nor in any event longer than thirty days." Extensions of an order may be granted for like periods, but only by resort to the procedures required in obtaining the initial order.

Interception without prior judicial authorization is permitted whenever a specifically designated enforcement officer reasonably determines that "(a) an emergency situation that involves (i) immediate danger of death or serious physical injury to any person, (ii) conspiratorial activities threatening the national security interest, or (iii) conspiratorial activities characteristic of organized crime that requires a wire, oral or electronic[3] communication to be intercepted before an order authorizing such interception can with due diligence be obtained, and (b) there are grounds upon which an order could be entered." In such a case, application for an order must be made within 48 hours after the interception commences, and, in the absence of an order, the interception must terminate when the communication sought is obtained or when the application for the order is denied, whichever is earlier. Title III does not limit the constitutional power of the President to act for various purposes, such as to obtain foreign intelligence information deemed essential to the security of the United States.

Within a reasonable time but not later than 90 days after the filing of an application which is denied or the termination of an authorized period of interception, the judge must cause to be served on the persons named

3. Defined in § 4.3(a).

in the order or application and other parties to the intercepted communications, an inventory which shall include notice of (1) the fact of the entry of the order or application; (2) the date of the entry and the period of authorized interception, or the denial of the application; and (3) the fact that during the period communications were or were not intercepted. A similar inventory is required as to interceptions terminated without an order having been issued.

Where the disclosure would be in violation of Title III, "no part of the contents of [an intercepted wire or oral] communication and no evidence derived therefrom may be received in evidence in any trial, hearing, or other proceeding in or before any court, grand jury, department, officer, agency, regulatory body, legislative committee, or other authority of the United States, a State, or a political subdivision thereof." Any intentional interception or disclosure of any wire, oral or electronic communication without the prior consent of a party thereto, except as authorized under Title III, is a criminal offense punishable by a fine or imprisonment for not more than five years or both. Any person whose wire, oral or electronic communications are intercepted, disclosed or used may bring a civil action against the offending party and may recover the actual damages suffered or statutory damages (the greater of $10,000 or $100 a day for each day of violation), plus punitive damages and a reasonable attorney's fee and other reasonable litigation costs. A good faith reliance on a court order or legislative authorization constitutes a complete defense to any civil or criminal action brought.

(b) Continued Surveillance. The most obvious difference between a search for tangible items and the search for wire, oral or electronic communications allowed under Title III is the time dimension of the latter kind of search. A search warrant for some physical object permits a single entry and prompt search of the described premises,[4] while Title III permits continuing surveillance up to 30 days, with extensions possible. During the authorized time, all conversations over the tapped line or within the bugged room may be overheard and recorded without regard to their relevance.

As reflected in *Berger v. New York,*[5] this striking difference accounts for the major constitutional obstacle to legalized electronic surveillance. In holding a New York law unconstitutional, the Court emphasized that it (1) permitted installation and operation of surveillance equipment for 60 days, "the equivalent of a series of intrusions, searches, and seizures pursuant to a single showing of probable cause"; (2) permitted renewal of the order "without a showing of present probable cause for the continuance of the eavesdrop"; and (3) placed "no termination date on the eavesdrop once the conversation sought is seized." While Title III permits extensions only upon a new showing of probable cause and requires that interception cease once "the objective of the authorization" is achieved, it does permit continued surveillance for up to 30 days upon a single showing of probable cause, and thus goes well beyond the kind of with-warrant electronic surveillance the Supreme Court has approved or indicated would be permitted.

As stated in *Berger,* the bugging of a secret agent earlier upheld in *Osborn v. United States*[6] was pursuant to an order which "authorized one limited intrusion rather than a series or a continuous surveillance. And, we note that a new order was issued when the officer sought to resume the search and probable cause was shown for the succeeding one. Moreover, the order was executed by the officer with dispatch, not over a prolonged and extended period." Similarly, in *Katz v. United States*[7] the Court noted that the "surveillance was so narrowly circumscribed that a duly authorized magistrate * * * clearly apprised of the precise intrusion * * * could constitutionally have authorized * * * the very limited search and seizure that the

4. See § 3.4(j).

5. 388 U.S. 41, 87 S.Ct. 1873, 18 L.Ed.2d 1040 (1967).

6. 385 U.S. 323, 87 S.Ct. 429, 17 L.Ed.2d 394 (1966).

7. 389 U.S. 347, 88 S.Ct. 507, 19 L.Ed.2d 576 (1967).

Government asserts in fact took place." The surveillance in *Katz* was limited in that the agents had probable cause to believe defendant was using certain public telephones for gambling purposes about the same time almost every day and thus activated the surveillance equipment attached to the outside of the phone booth only when defendant entered the booth.

Decisions holding that continued surveillance may also be squared with the Fourth Amendment rely upon the analysis of Justices Harlan and White, who dissented in *Berger*. Their contention was that an electronic surveillance which is continued over a span of time is no more a general search than the typical execution of a search warrant over a described area. As Justice White argued:

> Petitioner suggests that the search is inherently overbroad because the eavesdropper will overhear conversations which do not relate to criminal activity. But the same is true of almost all searches of private property which the Fourth Amendment permits. In searching for seizable matters, the police must necessarily see or hear, and comprehend, items which do not relate to the purpose of the search. That this occurs, however, does not render the search invalid, so long as it is authorized by a suitable search warrant and so long as the police, in executing that warrant, limit themselves to searching for items which may constitutionally be seized.

This analogy by Justice White is less than perfect unless it may be concluded that the overhearing or recording of a series of conversations is merely a search, from which certain particularly described conversations will thereafter be seized. This was the position of Justice Harlan, who contended: "Just as some exercise of dominion, beyond mere perception, is necessary for the seizure of tangibles, so some use of the conversation beyond the initial listening process is required for the seizures of the spoken word." A majority of the Supreme Court has never addressed this particular point, although language in the opinions seemingly contrary to Justice Harlan's theory is to be found. In *Katz*, for example, there is language characterizing "electronically listening to and recording" of defendant's words as a "search and seizure." But this has not deterred the lower courts from consistently holding that Title III is not rendered unconstitutional solely because it authorizes wiretaps which may last several days and encompass multiple conversations.

(c) Lack of Notice. The Supreme Court in *Berger v. New York* [8] also found the New York eavesdropping law "offensive" because it "has no requirement for notice, as do conventional warrants, nor does it overcome this defect by requiring some showing of special facts. On the contrary, it permits uncontested entry without any showing of exigent circumstances. Such a showing of exigency, in order to avoid notice would appear more important in eavesdropping, with its inherent dangers, than that required when conventional procedures of search and seizure are utilized." This criticism goes to the very heart of all eavesdropping practices because, as the Court observed, success inevitably depends upon secrecy.

The *Berger* Court did not explore this matter in greater detail, and thus it is not entirely clear whether Title III is somewhat vulnerable on this basis. However, the lower courts have consistently rejected constitutional challenges to the legislation on such grounds with the following arguments: (1) One reason for advance notice, as emphasized by four members of the Court in *Ker v. California*,[9] is to guard the entering officer from attack on the mistaken belief he is making a criminal entry, and this danger is generally not present in eavesdropping cases. Either the eavesdropping is accomplished without any trespass or else a covert entry to plant an eavesdropping device is made at a time when it is known no one is present within. (2) Another reason for notice is so that the individual will be aware that a search was conducted, but in the more typical search case this notice may come only after the event by discovery of the warrant and a receipt at the place searched.

8. 388 U.S. 41, 87 S.Ct. 1873, 18 L.Ed.2d 1040 (1967).

9. 374 U.S. 23, 83 S.Ct. 1623, 10 L.Ed.2d 726 (1963).

That notice is comparable to the Title III requirement of service of an inventory within 90 days. (3) In executing search warrants for physical evidence, prior notice is not required when there is reason to believe such notice would result in the destruction or removal of the evidence sought. Though the Court in *Berger* was unwilling to uphold all eavesdropping without notice on this ground, this "exigency" does exist in some circumstances. One of these circumstances, so the argument goes, is that which must exist under Title III by virtue of the requirement of a showing that "normal investigative procedures have been tried and have failed or reasonably appear to be unlikely to succeed if tried or to be too dangerous." [10]

The Supreme Court apparently finds these arguments compelling, for in *Katz v. United States,*[11] after noting it had upheld court-ordered electronic recording of particular conversations in *Osborn v. United States,*[12] the Court stated:

> Although the protections afforded the petitioner in *Osborn* were "*similar* * * * to those * * * of conventional warrants," they were not identical. A conventional warrant ordinarily serves to notify the suspect of an intended search. But if Osborn had been told in advance that federal officers intended to record his conversations, the point of making such recordings would obviously have been lost; the evidence in question could not have been obtained. In omitting any requirement of advance notice, the federal court that authorized electronic surveillance in *Osborn* simply recognized, as has this Court, that officers need not announce their purpose before conducting an otherwise authorized search if such an announcement would provoke the escape of the suspect or the destruction of critical evidence.

(d) Probable Cause. One aspect of the more general Fourth Amendment issue of whether the "probable cause" requirement is a fixed or a variable test,[13] is the question of whether the probable cause needed to conduct a Title III surveillance is in some respects greater than the probable cause ordinarily required to obtain a search warrant. Justice Stewart spoke to this question in his concurring opinion in *Berger v. New York* [14]:

> I would hold that the affidavits on which the judicial order issued in this case did not constitute a showing of probable cause adequate to justify the authorizing order. The need for particularity and evidence of reliability in the showing required when judicial authorization is sought for the kind of electronic eavesdropping involved in this case is especially great. The standard of reasonableness embodied in the Fourth Amendment demands that the showing of justification match the degree of intrusion. By its very nature electronic eavesdropping for a 60–day period, even of a specified office, involves a broad invasion of a constitutionally protected area. Only the most precise and rigorous standard of probable cause should justify an intrusion of this sort.

Justice Stewart thus concluded that though the evidence in the instant case "might be enough to satisfy the standards of the Fourth Amendment for a conventional search or arrest," it "was constitutionally insufficient to constitute probable cause to justify an intrusion of the scope and duration that was permitted in this case." However, defendants who have made this type of argument in the lower courts have not prevailed.

(e) Particular Description. The eavesdropping statute struck down in *Berger* required very little by way of particularizing the conversations to be seized; it merely required the naming of "the person or persons whose communications * * * are to be overheard or recorded." The Court held this did not meet the Fourth Amendment requirement that the things to be seized be particularly described, and declared that the "need for particularity * * * is especially great in the case of eavesdropping [because it] involves an intrusion on privacy that is broad in scope." Yet, as Justice Harlan noted in his

10. 18 U.S.C.A. § 2518(3).

11. 389 U.S. 347, 88 S.Ct. 507, 19 L.Ed.2d 576 (1967).

12. 385 U.S. 323, 87 S.Ct. 429, 17 L.Ed.2d 394 (1966).

13. See § 3.3(b).

14. 388 U.S. 41, 87 S.Ct. 1873, 18 L.Ed.2d 1040 (1967).

dissent, the cases on search for tangible items make it clear that the particularity requirement of the Amendment is a flexible one, depending upon the nature of the described things and whether the description readily permits identification by the executing officer.

Title III requires a particular description of the "type of communication sought to be intercepted, and a statement of the particular offense to which it relates." [15] Just what was intended by this language is unclear, as the legislative history fails to define the phrase "type of communication." These are among the most important words in the entire statute because the particularization requirement serves two very important functions here as in other contexts: it helps indicate to the officers where they are to look for the evidence sought; and it tells the officers when the search must cease because the described items have been found. It is now generally accepted that this particularization requirement can be fulfilled by indicating the offense under investigation, without further details about the anticipated conversations. Despite that development, the lower courts have rather consistently held that the statutory formula in Title III is sufficient to meet the Fourth Amendment particularity requirement as explicated in *Berger.* The reasoning underlying these decisions is not unlike that in the Harlan dissent in the *Berger* case; it is said that it would be virtually impossible to predict in advance the exact language of a conversation which has not yet occurred, and that to demand more would render Title III totally ineffective.

(f) Covert Entry. In *Dalia v. United States,*[16] FBI agents entered an office to install a bug and reentered to remove it, all pursuant to a court order which allowed the interception of all oral communications at that office concerning a certain conspiracy but which did not explicitly authorize entry of those premises. In upholding the surveillance, the Court first concluded that the "Fourth Amendment does not prohibit *per se* a covert entry performed for the purpose of installing otherwise legal electronic bugging equipment." This naturally led to the question whether Congress had intended to authorize such an entry pursuant to the Title III procedures, which the Court answered in the affirmative. In light of the legislative history of Title III, "one simply cannot assume that Congress, aware that most bugging requires covert entry, nonetheless wished to except surveillance requiring such entries from the broad authorization of Title III, and that it resolved to do so by remaining silent on the subject."

The most controversial part of *Dalia,* however, involves the third branch of the decision, where the majority rejected the contention that because the authorizing court did not explicitly set forth its approval of the covert entries, they violated petitioner's Fourth Amendment privacy rights. Noting that the Warrant Clause of the Fourth Amendment imposes requirements that warrants issue on "probable cause" by "neutral, disinterested magistrates" and that they "particularly describe" the place to be searched and things to be seized, the Court found nothing in the Amendment or prior decisions under it suggesting that "search warrants also must include a specification of the precise manner in which they are to be executed. On the contrary, it is generally left to the discretion of the executing officers to determine the details of how best to proceed with the performance of a search authorized by warrant—subject of course to the general Fourth Amendment protection 'against unreasonable searches and seizures.'" The Court in *Dalia* added that it "would promote empty formalism * * * to require magistrates to make explicit what unquestionably is implicit in bugging authorizations: that a covert entry, with its attendant interference with Fourth Amendment interests, may be necessary for the installation of the surveillance equipment." Three of the four dissenters in *Dalia* disagreed with the majority's interpretation of Title III, while two said that interpretation

15. 18 U.S.C.A. § 2518(4).

16. 441 U.S. 238, 99 S.Ct. 1682, 60 L.Ed.2d 177 (1979).

could not be squared with the Fourth Amendment because covert entry "entails an invasion of privacy of constitutional significance distinct from that which attends non-trespassory surveillance; indeed, it is tantamount to an independent search and seizure."

(g) Emergency Interception Without a Warrant. There has been virtually no use of the provision in Title III which permits interception without prior judicial approval when there are grounds for an interception order but an emergency exists involving "(i) immediate danger of death or serious physical injury to any person, (ii) conspiratorial activities threatening the national security interest, or (iii) conspiratorial activities characteristic of organized crime that requires a wire, oral or electronic communication to be intercepted before an order authorizing such interception can with due diligence be obtained." [17] As a consequence the courts have not been called upon to assess its constitutionality.

In *Katz v. United States* [18] the Supreme Court condemned the warrantless eavesdropping challenged in that case, but the facts made it perfectly clear that there was ample time to secure a warrant. *Katz* therefore cannot be read as prohibiting all warrantless electronic surveillance. The Fourth Amendment doubtless would permit such surveillance under at least some circumstances, but it is unclear whether that may be said of all of the cases which might be fit within the statutory language just quoted. This is attributable in part to the fact that the relevant statutory terms are ambiguous and are not clarified by legislative history, and in part to the uncertainty which generally exists as to when a warrantless search is permissible to prevent the destruction or loss of evidence. It does seem, however, that the case in which the strongest showing of need could be made falls within the more recently added item (i) of the statutory exception.[19]

(h) Use of Secret Agents. Because Title III declares interception to be lawful where "one of the parties to the communication has given prior consent to such interception," [20] it does not forbid the use of eavesdropping equipment to record or transmit what a suspect says to a secret agent. Whether this practice can be squared with the Fourth Amendment is an issue the Supreme Court has had before it on several occasions. In *On Lee v. United States,*[21] an undercover agent "wired for sound" entered defendant's laundry and engaged him in an incriminating conversation, which an agent outside the laundry was able to hear on a receiving set. In a 5–4 decision, the Court rejected the claim that the undercover agent had committed a trespass because consent to his entry was obtained by fraud, and dismissed as "verging on the frivolous" the further contention that the agent outside "was a trespasser because by these aids he overheard what went on inside." Similarly, in *Lopez v. United States,*[22] where the secret agent had a recording device concealed on his person, the majority, relying upon *On Lee,* concluded that

> this case involves no "eavesdropping" whatever in any proper sense of that term. The Government did not use an electronic device to listen in on conversations it could not otherwise have heard. Instead, the device was used only to obtain the most reliable evidence possible of a conversation in which the Government's own agent was a participant and which that agent was fully entitled to disclose. And the device was not planted by means of an unlawful physical invasion of petitioner's premises under circumstances which would violate the Fourth Amendment. It was carried in and out by an agent who was there with petitioner's assent, and it neither saw nor heard more than the agent himself.

When the Court in *Katz v. United States* [23] rejected the "constitutionally protected area" approach in favor of a justified expectation of

17. 18 U.S.C.A. § 2518(7).

18. 389 U.S. 347, 88 S.Ct. 507, 19 L.Ed.2d 576 (1967).

19. National Comm'n for the Review of Federal and State Laws Relating to Wiretapping and Electronic Surveillance, Electronic Surveillance Report 16 (1976).

20. 18 U.S.C.A. § 2511(2)(c).

21. 343 U.S. 747, 72 S.Ct. 967, 96 L.Ed. 1270 (1952).

22. 373 U.S. 427, 83 S.Ct. 1381, 10 L.Ed.2d 462 (1963).

23. 389 U.S. 347, 88 S.Ct. 507, 19 L.Ed.2d 576 (1967).

privacy analysis of the what-is-a-search issue, the continuing vitality of *On Lee* and *Lopez* was in doubt. Then came *United States v. White,*[24] where a government informer engaged defendant in conversations in a restaurant, defendant's home, and the informer's car while the informer was carrying a concealed radio transmitter. The court of appeals held that this electronic eavesdropping constituted a search, but the Supreme Court did not agree. Asserting that *Katz* "left undisturbed" the notion "that however strongly a defendant may trust an apparent colleague, his expectations in this respect are not protected by the Fourth Amendment when it turns out that the colleague is a government agent regularly communicating with the authorities," the Court concluded:

> If the law gives no protection to the wrongdoer whose trusted accomplice is or becomes a police agent, neither should it protect him when that same agent has recorded or transmitted the conversations which are later offered in evidence to prove the State's case.
>
> Inescapably, one contemplating illegal activities must realize and risk that his companions may be reporting to the police. If he sufficiently doubts their trustworthiness, the association will very probably end or never materialize. But if he has no doubts, or allays them, or risks what doubt he has, the risk is his. In terms of what his course will be, what he will or will not do or say, we are unpersuaded that he would distinguish between probable informers on the one hand and probable informers with transmitters on the other. Given the possibility or probability that one of his colleagues is cooperating with the police, it is only speculation to assert that the defendant's utterances would be substantially different or his sense of security any less if he also thought it possible that the suspected colleague is wired for sound.

The Court added that this result was bolstered by the fact that a recording will often produce a "more reliable rendition of what a defendant has said than will the unaided memory of a police agent," and that "with the recording in existence it is less likely that the informant will change his mind," and there is "less chance that threat or injury will suppress unfavorable evidence and less chance that cross-examination will confound the testimony."

Although the way in which the Court split in *White*[25] has prompted some dispute as to whether there were five votes for the above position, the lower courts have consistently read *White* to mean that there is no Fourth Amendment barrier to participant monitoring of conversations. But there is much to be said for the position taken in Justice Harlan's forceful dissent in *White:*

> Authority is hardly required to support the proposition that words would be measured a good deal more carefully and communication inhibited if one suspected his conversations were being transmitted and transcribed. Were third-party bugging a prevalent practice, it might well smother that spontaneity—reflected in frivolous, impetuous, sacrilegious, and defiant discourse—that liberates daily life. Much offhand exchange is easily forgotten and one may count on the obscurity of his remarks, protected by the very fact of a limited audience, and the likelihood that the listener will either overlook or forget what is said, as well as the listener's inability to reformulate a conversation without having to contend with a documented record. All of these values are sacrificed by a rule of law that permits official monitoring of private discourse limited only by the need to locate a willing assistant.

He thus concluded a contrary result was needed "to protect * * * the expectation of the ordinary citizen, who has never engaged in illegal conduct in his life, that he may carry on his private discourse freely, openly, and spontaneously without measuring his every word against the connotations it might carry when instantaneously heard by others unknown to him and unfamiliar with his situation or analyzed in a cold, formal record

24. 401 U.S. 745, 91 S.Ct. 1122, 28 L.Ed.2d 453 (1971).

25. Four members of the Court joined in the opinion quoted above. Brennan, J., concurred in the result on the ground that *Katz* was not retroactive, but opined that both *On Lee* and *Lopez* were "no longer sound law." Black, J., concurred with the result for the reasons stated in his *Katz* dissent.

played days, months, or years after the conversation."

§ 4.3 Title III: What Surveillance Covered

(a) Meaning of "Interception." Title III prohibits, except in the manner provided therein, any "interception" of communications. The critical word "intercept" is defined by the statute as meaning "the aural or other acquisition of the contents of any wire, electronic, or oral communication through the use of any electronic, mechanical, or other device,"[1] which requires consideration of three important questions: (1) What communications are protected—that is, what is the meaning of the phrase "any wire, electronic, or oral communication"? (2) What means of interception are covered—that is, what is "any electronic, mechanical, or other device"? (3) What kind of activity is covered—that is, what constitutes "the aural or other acquisition of the contents"?

As for the first question, Title III itself provides a definition for each of the three types of communications covered. As for "wire communication," it "means any aural transfer[2] made in whole or in part through the use of facilities for the transmission of communications by the aid of wire, cable, or other like connection between the point of origin and the point of reception (including the use of such connection in a switching station) furnished or operated by any person engaged in providing or operating such facilities for the transmission of interstate or foreign communications or communications affecting interstate or foreign commerce and such term includes any electronic storage of such communication, but such term does not include the radio portion of a cordless telephone communication that is transmitted between the cordless telephone handset and the base unit."[3] As explained in the legislative history, the reference to a switching station makes it clear that cellular communications, whether between two cellular phones or between such a phone and a land line phone, are included. Wire communications includes transmission by fiber optic cable or radio of voice and even conversion of a voice signal to digital form. Wire communication in storage, like voice mail, is protected as well. A reference to common carriers in the pre–1986 law was stricken because after deregulation many non-common carriers offer communications services. Even private networks and intra-company systems are within the protection of the statute. The cordless phone exception is based on the fact they are so readily intercepted even by AM radio.

Title III defines "oral communication" as "any oral communication uttered by a person exhibiting an expectation that such communication is not subject to interception under circumstances justifying such expectation, but such term does not include any electronic communication."[4] The legislative history indicates that this definition is intended to reflect existing law, especially the approach taken by the Supreme Court in *Katz v. United States.*[5] This being so, it would seem that the decisions interpreting *Katz* for Fourth Amendment purposes[6] have relevance here. The exception at the end of the definition, added in 1986, expresses disapproval of those cases treating radio communication as falling within this category.

The third type of communication, "electronic communication," added to the statute in 1986, means "any transfer of signs, signals, writing, images, sounds, data, or intelligence of any nature transmitted in whole or in part by a wire, radio, electromagnetic, photoelectronic or photooptical system that affects interstate or foreign commerce."[7] As the legislative history explains, a communication is an electronic communication if it is not carried

§ 4.3

1. 18 U.S.C.A. § 2510(4).
2. Defined in 18 U.S.C.A. § 2510(18) as "a transfer containing the human voice at any point between and including the point of origin and the point of reception."
3. 18 U.S.C.A. § 2510(1).
4. 18 U.S.C.A. § 2510(2).
5. 389 U.S. 347, 88 S.Ct. 507, 19 L.Ed.2d 576 (1967).
6. See § 3.2.
7. 18 U.S.C.A. § 2510(12).

by sound waves and cannot fairly be characterized as containing the human voice. Communications consisting solely of data, for example, and all communications transmitted only by radio are electronic communications, as are electronic mail, digitized transmissions, and video teleconferences. The statutory definition goes on to explicitly exclude the radio portion of a cordless telephone communication that is transmitted between the cordless telephone handset and the base unit, any wire or oral communication, any communication made through a tone-only paging device, and any communication from a tracking device. (It must be emphasized at this point that it is not enough to understand what is collectively covered by the phrase "any wire, electronic, or oral communication"; though Title III sets out procedures for lawfully intercepting all three types of communication, the statutory exclusionary rule[8] was deliberately *not* amended correspondingly, meaning that violation of these procedures may result in suppression under the statute only if they involve wire or oral communications.)

Turning now to the second question, the meaning of "electronic, mechanical, or other device," it is defined by statute as meaning "any device or apparatus which can be used to intercept a wire, oral or electronic communication."[9] This provision goes on to state two exceptions. One is "any telephone or telegraph instrument, equipment or facility, or any component thereof, (i) furnished to the subscriber or user by a provider of wire or electronic communication service in the ordinary course of its business and being used by the subscriber or user in the ordinary course of its business or furnished by such subscriber or user for connection to the facilities of such service and used in the ordinary course of its business; or (ii) being used by a communications common carrier in the ordinary course of its business, or by an investigative or law enforcement officer in the ordinary course of his duties." The other is "a hearing aid or similar device being used to correct sub-normal hearing to not better than normal." Because there is no interception unless such a device is used, this means, for example, that Title III does not apply to an instance in which a police officer standing near a person using a telephone can hear the conversation without using any sort of artificial aid. As for the first of the two exceptions, it has been interpreted to cover the normal use of an extension telephone, the listening in by a telephone operator just long enough to verify that the call has been connected, and the answering of a phone by a police officer who is lawfully present.

Finally, there is the question of what activity is covered by the phrase "aural or other acquisition of the contents," that is, of "any information concerning the substance, purport, or meaning of that communication."[10] The critical phrase "aural acquisition" is not defined in the Act, and the legislative history gives no clue as to its intended meaning. Read literally, it could be taken to mean that the unattended use of a tape recorder or similar device to record conversations which are not simultaneously heard by a human monitor is not an interception. But, while at least one court has reached that conclusion, other courts have construed the statute as covering unmonitored recording. That is a desirable result, as from the perspective of the speakers, their interests—which are paramount under Title III—are as adversely affected by a postponed listening as by a present overhearing. However, in a case in which a person is lawfully overhearing a conversation, it is not an interception to record what is heard. The "or other" language, added in 1986, clarifies that it is illegal to intercept the non-voice portion of a wire communication.

In *United States v. New York Telephone Co.*,[11] the Court held that "the language of the statute and its legislative history establish beyond any doubt that pen registers," devices which do not record phone conversations but merely make a record of the numbers dialed from a given phone and the time of dialing,

8. 18 U.S.C.A. § 2518(10)(a).

9. 18 U.S.C.A. § 2510(5).

10. 18 U.S.C.A. § 2510(8).

11. 434 U.S. 159, 98 S.Ct. 364, 54 L.Ed.2d 376 (1977).

"are not governed by Title III." The Court reasoned:

> Pen registers do not "intercept" because they do not acquire the "contents" of communications, as that term is defined by 18 U.S.C. § 2510(8). Indeed, a law enforcement official could not even determine from the use of a pen register whether a communication existed. These devices do not hear sound [and thus] do not accomplish the "aural acquisition" of anything. They decode outgoing numbers by responding to changes in electrical voltage caused by the turning of the telephone dial (or the pressing of buttons on push button telephones) and present the information in a form to be interpreted by sight rather than by hearing.[12]

By like reasoning, it may be concluded that it is not an interception within the meaning of Title III to use a diode device to determine the origin of an incoming call, to examine telephone company toll records, or to trace a signal given out by a transmitting device ("beeper") concealed in a vehicle or object to facilitate surveillance of it. Such results may be more readily reached under the 1986 amendment to the statute which deleted from the definition of "contents" reference to information concerning "the identity of the parties to such communication or [its] existence."

(b) Phone Company Activities. By virtue of the limitations upon the meaning of "interception" in the context of Title III, discussed above, it is clear that certain activities engaged in by telephone companies are not at all proscribed by the Act. This includes the making and keeping of toll records, the use of pen registers or other call-tracing devices to see if a particular person is making harassing phone calls or is otherwise misusing the telephone service, and the use of a diode trap whereby annoying phone calls can be traced by preventing disconnection when a call is made to a phone to which the device is attached. But sometimes investigations conducted by telephone companies go beyond this. Especially when the company is investigating the fraudulent use of company lines by the use of a "blue box" or other equipment which permits the bypassing of long distance automatic billing mechanisms, investigators will actually monitor and record calls to determine the speakers' identities and the extent of illegal use.

Because such activity *does* fall within the statutory definition of what constitutes an interception, it must be assessed under a special provision which declares that it is not unlawful "for an operator of a switchboard, or an officer, employee, or agent of a provider of wire or electronic communication services, whose facilities are used in the transmission of a wire communication, to intercept, disclose, or use that communication in the normal course of his employment while engaged in any activity which is a necessary incident to the rendition of his service or to the protection of the rights or property of the carrier of such communication." [13] (This statute goes on to say that these providers may "not utilize service observing or random monitoring except for mechanical or service quality control checks.") Monitoring by the company to obtain evidence for a wire fraud prosecution falls within the "protection of the rights or property" part of the statute. Such monitoring has been upheld where it continued for several weeks, where it continued after the identity of one perpetrator was learned but it was known unidentified others were involved, and even where entire conversations were recorded. As for the "rendition of his service" part of the statute, it has been held to permit, for example, a long distance operator to remain on the line to verify that the call has been connected.

(c) Consent. An important exception to the usual Title III requirement that an interception occur only pursuant to a court order has to do with interceptions made by prior consent. The Act specifically provides that it "shall not be unlawful under this chapter for

12. Later, in Smith v. Maryland, 442 U.S. 735, 99 S.Ct. 2577, 61 L.Ed.2d 220 (1979), the Court held that use of a pen register is not governed by the Fourth Amendment. See § 3.2(j).

13. 18 U.S.C.A. § 2511(2)(a)(i).

a person acting under color of law to intercept a wire, oral or electronic communication, where such person is a party to the communication or one of the parties to the communication has given prior consent to such interception." [14] A similar provision covers persons not acting under color of law.[15] The legislative history indicates that the consent exception was intended to reflect existing law in such cases as *Lopez v. United States* [16] and *On Lee v. United States,*[17] which has since been followed by the Court in *United States v. White.*[18] It is thus clear that law enforcement authorities are free to make consensual interceptions in a variety of ways: (1) by having the consenting party wear or carry a tape recorder with which he records his face-to-face conversations with another; (2) by having the consenting party wear a transmitter which broadcasts his conversations to agents equipped with a receiver; or (3) by having the consenting party to a telephone conversation record it or permit another to listen in on an extension.

The legislative history sheds some light upon the scope of this consent exception. For one thing, the "prior consent" language of the statute means that retroactive authorization would not be possible. Secondly, the requisite consent may be express or implied. Surveillance devices in banks or apartment houses for institutional or personal protection would be impliedly consented to. And finally, "party" would mean the person actually participating in the communication, so that interception by impersonation is permissible under the consent provision. For example, if police officers executing a search warrant for gambling paraphernalia answer the phone while there, impersonate the gambler and record the ensuing conversation, this is lawful under Title III.

(d) National Security Surveillance. When Title III was enacted, there was included in it an express declaration that nothing therein "shall limit the constitutional power of the President to take such measures as he deems necessary to protect the Nation against actual or potential attack or other hostile acts of a foreign power, to obtain foreign intelligence information deemed essential to the security of the United States, or to protect national security information against foreign intelligence activities," or "to protect the United States against the overthrow of the Government by force or other unlawful means, or against any other clear and present danger to the structure or existence of the Government." [19] Since at least 1940, there had been presidential sanction for warrantless electronic surveillance in furtherance of national security, and the apparent purpose of the above language was not to disturb whatever powers in this regard the President actually has under the Constitution.

The scope of those powers was at issue in *United States v. United States District Court,*[20] where the government claimed that its warrantless surveillance of a purely domestic radical group engaged in a conspiracy to destroy federal government property was authorized under that statutory provision. But the Court without dissent concluded "that the Government's concerns do not justify departure in this case from the customary Fourth Amendment requirement of judicial approval prior to initiation of a search or surveillance." That conclusion was rested upon the following four considerations: (1) Though in a case such as this the investigative duty of the executive may be stronger, it is equally true that "Fourth Amendment protections become the more necessary when the targets of official

14. 18 U.S.C.A. § 2511(2)(c).

15. 18 U.S.C.A. § 2511(2)(d), which is however qualified so as to not cover the situation in which "such communication is intercepted for the purpose of committing any criminal or tortious act in violation of the Constitution or laws of the United States or of any State or for the purpose of committing any other injurious act."

16. 373 U.S. 427, 83 S.Ct. 1381, 10 L.Ed.2d 462 (1963) (bribe offer recorded by use of concealed recorder).

17. 343 U.S. 747, 72 S.Ct. 967, 96 L.Ed. 1270 (1952) (incriminating remarks made to undercover agent wired for sound).

18. 401 U.S. 745, 91 S.Ct. 1122, 28 L.Ed.2d 453 (1971).

19. Former 18 U.S.C.A. § 2511(3), repealed upon enactment of the Foreign Intelligence Surveillance Act of 1978, discussed herein.

20. 407 U.S. 297, 92 S.Ct. 2125, 32 L.Ed.2d 752 (1972).

surveillance may be those suspected of unorthodoxy in their political beliefs." (2) Executive officers of government do not qualify under the Fourth Amendment as neutral magistrates, as "unreviewed executive discretion may yield too readily to pressures to obtain incriminating evidence and overlook potential invasions of privacy and protected speech." (3) It is not true "that internal security matters are too subtle and complex for judicial evaluation." (4) Prior judicial approval will not "fracture the secrecy essential to official intelligence gathering," as judges "may be counted upon to be especially conscious of security requirements in national security cases." The Court added that it recognized "that domestic security surveillance may involve different policy and practical considerations from the surveillance of 'ordinary crime,'" and that consequently "Congress may wish to consider protective standards for [domestic security surveillance] which differ from those already prescribed for specified crimes in Title III."

In the *United States District Court* case, the Supreme Court emphasized that it was dealing with a situation in which the warrantless surveillance had been directed at a "domestic organization," said "to mean a group or organization (whether formally or informally constituted) composed of citizens of the United States and which has no significant connection with a foreign power, its agents or agencies." Though this certainly implied that a case arising under the foreign affairs part of the statute might come out differently, the Court did not have occasion to pursue that point or to elaborate just what kind of connection with a foreign government would be necessary to put a case into that category. The question seldom reached the lower courts, though *Zweibon v. Mitchell*[21] deserves mention. Damages were sought by members of the Jewish Defense League from the Attorney General and several FBI agents because of warrantless wiretapping purportedly undertaken to obtain foreign intelligence information. The theory was that JDL activities were putting a severe strain on Soviet–American relations and had created the threat of retaliation by Soviet citizens against American Embassy personnel in Moscow. Relying individually upon either the Fourth Amendment or the language in Title III, the eight members of the court concluded that the mere fact the actions of the domestic organization might provoke action abroad harmful to the United States was not enough to put the case into the foreign affairs category. It was thus concluded "that a warrant must be obtained before a wiretap is installed on a domestic organization that is neither the agent of nor acting in collaboration with a foreign power."

The matter is now dealt with by another statute, the Foreign Intelligence Surveillance Act of 1978.[22] This Act provides that the Chief Justice of the United States is to publicly designate seven district judges from seven of the federal judicial circuits "who shall constitute a court which shall have jurisdiction to hear applications for and grant orders approving electronic surveillance anywhere within the United States under the procedures set forth in this Act," and that he is also to publicly designate three judges from the federal district courts or courts of appeals who shall "comprise a court of review which shall have jurisdiction to review the denial of any application made under this Act." Upon a proper application, a judge of this court is to enter an ex parte order approving electronic surveillance for 90 days or until its purpose is achieved, whichever is less, if he finds, inter alia, that "there is probable cause to believe" that "the target of the electronic surveillance is a foreign power[23] or an agent of a foreign power" and that "each of the facilities or

21. 516 F.2d 594 (D.C.Cir.1975).

22. 50 U.S.C.A. §§ 1801–1811.

23. Defined as meaning "a foreign government or any component thereof," "a faction of a foreign nation or nations, not substantially, composed of United States persons," "an entity that is openly acknowledged by a foreign government or governments to be directed and controlled by such foreign government or governments," "a group engaged in international terrorism or activities in preparation therefore," "a foreign-based political organization, not substantially composed of United States persons," or "an entity that is directed and controlled by a foreign government or governments."

places at which the electronic surveillance is directed is being used, or is about to be used, by a foreign power or an agent of a foreign power." But, it is further provided that "no United States person[24] may be considered a foreign power or an agent of a foreign power solely upon the basis of activities protected by the first amendment to the Constitution of the United States."

The FISA also deals with warrantless surveillance. It provides that "the President, through the Attorney General, may authorize electronic surveillance without a court order under this title to acquire foreign intelligence information for periods of up to one year" if, inter alia, the Attorney General certifies in writing under oath (with a copy of that certification transmitted under seal to the special court) that the surveillance is "solely directed at" the acquisition of the contents of communications "transmitted by means of communications used exclusively between or among foreign powers" and that "there is no substantial likelihood that the surveillance will acquire the contents of any communication to which a United States person is a party."

Evidence acquired in noncompliance with FISA is subject to suppression by "an aggrieved person" in "any trial, hearing, or other proceeding in or before any court, department, officer, agency, regulatory body, or other authority of the United States, a State, or a political subdivision thereof." However, "if the Attorney General files an affidavit under oath that disclosure or an adversary hearing would harm the national security of the United States," then the appropriate federal district court must "review in camera and ex parte the application, order and such other materials relating to the surveillance as may be necessary to determine whether the surveillance of the aggrieved person was lawfully authorized and conducted. In making the determination, the court may disclose to the aggrieved person under appropriate security procedures and protective orders, portions of the application, order, or other materials relating to the surveillance only where such disclosure is necessary to make an accurate determination of the legality of the surveillance."

§ 4.4 Title III: Application for and Issuance of Court Order

(a) Application Procedure. In contrast to the situation which generally obtains as to conventional search warrants, which may be sought by any law enforcement officer, application for a Title III order must be authorized by a high-level official. In the federal system, only the "Attorney General, Deputy Attorney General, Associate Attorney General, any Assistant Attorney General, any acting Assistant Attorney General, or any Deputy Assistant Attorney General in the Criminal Division specially designated by the Attorney General, may authorize an application."[1] This provision is intended to centralize in a publicly responsible official subject to the political process the formulation of law enforcement policy on the use of electronic surveillance techniques.

In United States v. Giordano,[2] the Court was confronted with a violation of this authorization requirement, for the Attorney General's executive assistant, not an official designated by the statute, had in fact been the person who placed the Attorney General's initials on an authorizing memo which the Attorney General had not seen. The Court held "that the provision for pre-application control was intended to play a central role in the statutory scheme and that suppression must follow when it is shown that this statutory requirement has been ignored." Similarly, if at the state level the authorization is by a person other than enumerated in Title III, the "principal prosecuting attorney of any State,

24. Defined as meaning "a citizen of the United States, an alien lawfully admitted for permanent residence * * *, an unincorporated association a substantial number of members of which are citizens of the United States or aliens lawfully admitted for permanent residence, or a corporation which is incorporated in the United States, but does not include a corporation or an association which is a foreign power."

§ 4.4

1. 18 U.S.C.A. § 2516(1).

2. 416 U.S. 505, 94 S.Ct. 1820, 40 L.Ed.2d 341 (1974).

or the principal prosecuting attorney of any political subdivision thereof, if such attorney is authorized by a statute of that State to make application," [3] then once again the application is invalid and the evidence must be suppressed. But, the authority at the state level may be delegated.

In *Giordano,* the Court noted that under the statute "the mature judgment of a particular, responsible Department of Justice official is interposed as a critical precondition to any judicial order." Though this might suggest that an authorization could be brought into question because of the limited extent of the review by the authorizing official, that is not the case. While it has been held that the authorizing official's personal judgment is certainly necessary, courts have not been inclined to permit any challenge of the quality of the review undertaken by him. That view has sometimes been criticized on the ground that the authorization requirement is meaningless if some semblance of meaningful review is not required.

Under Title III, applications for surveillance orders in both the federal and state systems may be made only to a "judge of competent jurisdiction." [4] In the federal system, this means only "a judge of a United States district court or a United States court of appeals." [5] On the state level it means "a judge of any court of general criminal jurisdiction of a State who is authorized by a statute of that State to enter orders authorizing interceptions of wire, oral or electronic communications." [6]

(b) Contents of Application.[7] Each Title III application must "be made in writing upon oath or affirmation" and must include a considerable amount of information specified in the statute. It must "state the applicant's authority to make such application," which presumably can be met merely by identifying that person as holding the office specified in the statute, and it must also disclose "the identity of the investigative or law enforcement officer making the application, and the officer authorizing the application." In *United States v. Chavez,*[8] the Supreme Court was confronted with a situation in which the latter requirement was not met in that the application erroneously asserted that a certain assistant Attorney General was the authorizing official when in fact the Attorney General had authorized the application. Noting that the application would have been in order if the Attorney General had been identified, the Court concluded this identification requirement was not so central to the protections of Title III as to require suppression of the evidence obtained as a consequence of that application.

Next, the statute requires that the application set out "a full and complete statement of the facts and circumstances relied upon by the applicant to justify his belief that an order should be issued." Certain particulars are then specified in the statute, beginning with "details as to the particular offense that has been, is being, or is about to be committed," which has been interpreted to require only an indication of the general nature of the criminal conduct under investigation rather than a specification of a particular statute. Another requisite particular is "a particular description of the nature and location of the facilities from which or the place where the communication is to be intercepted," which in the case of a wiretap can be met by giving the particular phone number or (if the probable cause showing permits) by referring to all phones at a certain address. Under the so-called "roving tap" provision added in 1986, specification of the facilities or place may be excused upon a particularized showing of need.[9] Still another particular is "a

3. 18 U.S.C.A. § 2516(2).

4. 18 U.S.C.A. § 2516(1) & (2).

5. 18 U.S.C.A. § 2510(9)(a).

6. 18 U.S.C.A. § 2510(9)(b).

7. Unless otherwise indicated, the statutory references in this subsection are to 18 U.S.C.A. § 2518(1).

8. 416 U.S. 562, 94 S.Ct. 1849, 40 L.Ed.2d 380 (1974).

9. 18 U.S.C.A. § 2518(11) says noncompliance is permitted in the case of oral communications when there is in the application "a full and complete statement as to why such specification is not practical and identifies the person committing the offense and whose communications are to be intercepted" and when also the judge "finds that such specification is not practical"; and in the case of wire communications when the application "iden-

particular description of the type of communications sought to be intercepted," which courts have generally read as requiring no more than an indication of the offense under investigation. In justification, it is said that the actual content cannot be stated because the conversations have not yet taken place and it is virtually impossible for an applicant to predict exactly what will be said.

The fourth particular, "the identity of the person, if known, committing the offense and whose communications are to be intercepted," has proved a source of difficulty and has twice been considered by the Supreme Court. One question, dealt with in *United States v. Kahn,*[10] concerns just what the obligation of the government is to discover and name the persons to be heard. *Kahn* involved a wiretap to intercept book-making-related conversations "of Irving Kahn and others as yet unknown," pursuant to which agents heard calls by Kahn from Arizona to his wife at his Chicago home in which he discussed his gambling wins and losses, and calls by his wife to another gambler in which she discussed betting information. The court of appeals held that all of these conversations had to be suppressed—those by the wife because Irving Kahn was not a party, and those by him because the government should have discovered his wife's involvement (meaning she was not an "other, as yet unknown"). The Supreme Court reversed. After concluding that conversations not involving Irving Kahn were covered by the order because it authorized interception of conversations "of" (not "between") him "and others," the Court turned to the question of what persons must be identified in the application. Rejecting the lower court's "known or discoverable" test, the Court held "that Title III requires the naming of a person in the application or interception order only when the law enforcement authorities have probable cause to believe that the individual is 'committing the offense' for which the wiretap is sought." Nothing in the statute, the Court concluded, supports "an additional requirement that the Government investigate all persons who may be using the subject telephone in order to determine their possible complicity." The probable cause referred to in *Kahn* goes to the person's name, his involvement in the criminal activity under investigation, and also his use of the phones or facilities to be tapped or bugged. *Kahn* has been read as meaning the authorities need not make even a minimal effort to learn the identity of a person as to whom probable cause regarding complicity and use already exists. Some have criticized *Kahn,* arguing that a better approach would be to impose a standard of reasonable diligence in the attempt to learn each of the elements necessary to the naming of an individual in an application.

The question in *United States v. Donovan*[11] was what the consequences of noncompliance with this part of the statute, as construed in *Kahn,* must be. There, government agents lawfully executing a wiretap learned the named individuals were discussing gambling with several other persons, but in obtaining an extension they failed to name these other persons. Though there was probable cause as to these others, so that this was a violation of the statute, the Court held that suppression was nonetheless not required. This was because the "naming" requirement was deemed not to play a "substantive role" in the regulatory scheme, in that even with the omissions "the application provided sufficient information to enable the issuing judge to determine that the statutory preconditions were satisfied." The reasoning was brought into seri-

tifies the person believed to be committing the offense and whose communications are to be intercepted, and the applicant makes a showing of a purpose, on the part of that person, to thwart interception by changing facilities" and in addition the judge finds "that such purpose has been adequately shown." Illustrative of an oral communication would be a case in which the suspect moves from room to room in a hotel; illustrative of a wire communication would be where a terrorist went from phone booth to phone booth numerous times to avoid interception. Only a limited number of federal officials are authorized to seek this special kind of order. 18 U.S.C.A. § 2518(12) says that if such an order is issued interception is not to begin "until the facilities from which, or the place where, the communication is to be intercepted is ascertained by the person implementing the interception order."

10. 415 U.S. 143, 94 S.Ct. 977, 39 L.Ed.2d 225 (1974).

11. 429 U.S. 413, 97 S.Ct. 658, 50 L.Ed.2d 652 (1977).

ous question by the three *Donovan* dissenters.[12]

The statute also requires that the application contain "a full and complete statement as to whether or not other investigative procedures have been tried and failed or why they reasonably appear to be unlikely to succeed if tried or to be too dangerous." This is an important part of the legislative scheme. As the Supreme Court has explained, it is designed to assure that electronic eavesdropping is not "routinely employed as the initial step in criminal investigation," [13] or "resorted to in situations where traditional investigative techniques would suffice to expose the crime." [14] Yet, the requisite showing is not great and is to be tested in a practical and commonsense fashion, and in practice the standard has been watered down to one of investigatory utility, rather than necessity. The showing can be made in any one of three ways. One is by showing the failure of other methods, which need not go so far as to indicate that every conceivable investigatory alternative has been unsuccessfully attempted. The second is by showing other methods are unlikely to succeed, which can be accomplished, for example, by indicating the difficulty in penetrating a particular conspiracy or by asserting that a conventional search warrant would not likely produce incriminating evidence. The third alternative is showing other methods would be too dangerous, either in terms of disclosing the investigation or placing an officer or informant in physical danger.

Title III also requires that the application contain "a statement of the period of time for which the interception is required to be maintained." Moreover, if "the nature of the investigation is such that the authorization for interception should not automatically terminate when the described type of communication has been first obtained," then "a particular description of facts establishing probable cause to believe that additional communications of the same type will occur thereafter" is also required. When the objective is to intercept a particular conversation, it is usually not difficult to state the time period,[15] but most cases are not of that kind. The statute contemplates that where a course of conduct embracing multiple parties and extending over a period of time is involved, the order may properly authorize proportionally longer surveillance. In such circumstances, making the requisite showing has not proved difficult; where there is probable cause of a continuing offense, almost inevitably there is probable cause to believe that there will be more than one relevant conversation.

The application must also include "a full and complete statement of the facts concerning all previous applications known to the individual authorizing and making the application, made to any judge for authorization to intercept, or for approval of interceptions of, wire, oral or electronic communications involving any of the same persons, facilities or places specified in the application, and the action taken by the judge on each such application." This provision serves to prevent "judge shopping" and also provides the judge with a basis upon which to assess the statements of probable cause and investigative necessity in the applications. If the earlier request was granted, the judge is alerted to inquire why there is a need for further surveillance; if it was denied, the judge is alerted to determine whether its deficiencies carry over to the present application. The "previous applications" provision is central to the statutory scheme, so that a deliberate omission of that information requires suppression of evidence obtained by a warrant issued pur-

12. They noted that "what is at issue here is more than a simple list of names," in that there is another requirement in the statute that the government disclose the history of all prior applications as to the named persons, which "would at the least cause a judge to consider whether the application before him was an attempt to circumvent the restrictive rulings of another judge or to continue an unjustified invasion of privacy."

13. United States v. Giordano, 416 U.S. 505, 94 S.Ct. 1820, 40 L.Ed.2d 341 (1974).

14. United States v. Kahn, 415 U.S. 143, 94 S.Ct. 977, 39 L.Ed.2d 225 (1974).

15. See Osborn v. United States, 385 U.S. 323, 87 S.Ct. 429, 17 L.Ed.2d 394 (1966), a pre-Title III case which nonetheless illustrates the point very well.

suant to the defective application. It must be emphasized, however, that the provision only requires disclosure of what is "known" by the person authorizing and making the application, and also that it does not cover prior interceptions of the same person pursuant to an application in which that person was not named or required to be named.

The final requirement, applicable only "where the application is for the extension of an order,"[16] is that the application contain "a statement setting forth the results thus far obtained from the interception, or a reasonable explanation of the failure to obtain such results." It is designed to provide the issuing judge with an opportunity to evaluate the actual investigative need for continued electronic surveillance at the time the extension application is presented.

(c) **Review of Application.** In reviewing a Title III application, the judge "may require the applicant to furnish additional testimony or documentary evidence in support of the application."[17] Though such inquiry is discretionary, resort to it may sometimes be critical, for it provides an informal and expeditious means of curing minor, technical defects, or supplying even a major element omitted by oversight, such as an informant's "track record." Use of the word "testimony" highlights the fact that information in support of any search warrant must be given under oath. A suitable record should be made of it, and the best practice in this regard is to use a court reporter.

Before a Title III eavesdropping order may be entered by the judge, he must determine on the basis of the facts submitted that

> (a) there is probable cause for belief that an individual is committing, has committed, or is about to commit a particular offense enumerated in section 2516 of this chapter;
>
> (b) there is probable cause for belief that particular communications concerning that offense will be obtained through such interception;
>
> (c) normal investigative procedures have been tried and have failed or reasonably appear to be unlikely to succeed if tried or to be too dangerous;
>
> (d) except as provided in subsection (11),[18] there is probable cause for belief that the facilities from which, or the place where, the wire or oral communications are to be intercepted are being used, or are about to be used, in connection with the commission of such offense, or are leased to, listed in the name of, or commonly used by such person.[19]

There is nothing in the statute which requires that particular words be used in the requisite finding or indeed that the finding be actually expressed in words rather than by the act of the judge.

Absent a finding of each of the four matters listed in the statute, the judge may not issue the order. But by the statute's use of the word "may," it would appear that the judge has discretion not to issue the order even if such findings can be made. There is not complete agreement, however, as to whether this is so. In any event, denial of an application is appealable[20] but should be overturned on appeal only if it is clearly erroneous.

(d) Contents of Order. A Title III interception order must specify certain matters which go to satisfying the particularity of description requirement of the Fourth Amendment. These are: "(a) the identity of the person, if known, whose communications are to be intercepted; (b) the nature and location of the communications facilities as to which, or the place where, authority to intercept is granted; (c) a particular description of the type of communication sought to be intercepted, and a statement of the particular offense to which it relates."[21] These requirements are comparable to those which exist as to the application, and what was said about

16. Under 18 U.S.C.A. § 2518(5), extensions may be granted, but only upon an application which meets all the usual requirements under § 2518(1) and only if the judge makes all the usual findings under § 2518(3).

17. 18 U.S.C.A. § 2518(2).

18. This is a reference to the "roving tap" provision discussed in note 9 supra.

19. 18 U.S.C.A. § 2518(3).

20. 18 U.S.C.A. § 2518(10)(b).

21. 18 U.S.C.A. § 2518(4).

them in that context earlier is equally applicable here. The order must also identify the person authorizing the application, as to which the same may be said, and in addition must identify the agency authorized to intercept the communications.[22]

The order must also contain several directives concerning its execution, most of which go to the time of the permitted surveillance. There must be "a provision that the authorization to intercept shall be executed as soon as practicable," [23] which reflects not only the need for prompt execution before the probable cause information becomes stale [24] but also the fact that eavesdropping devices often cannot be installed as promptly as a conventional warrant may be executed. The order must also specify "the period of time during which such interception is authorized," [25] which may not be "for any period longer than is necessary to achieve the objective of the authorization, nor in any event longer than thirty days." [26] That specification must include "a statement as to whether or not the interception shall automatically terminate when the described communication has been first obtained." [27] In addition, the order must contain a provision that it "must terminate upon attainment of the authorized objective, or in any event in thirty days." [28] Apart from these limits, the order must also contain a directive that the interception "be conducted in such a way as to minimize the interception of communications not otherwise subject to interception," [29] and, at the discretion of the court, "may require reports to be made to the judge who issued the order showing what progress has been made toward achievement of the authorized objective and the need for continued interception." [30] These reports constitute an extremely important safeguard when the authorized surveillance is lengthy.

Finally, in a case in which the applicant has so requested, the order is to "direct that a provider of wire or electronic communication service, landlord, custodian, or other person shall furnish the applicant forthwith all information, facilities, and technical assistance necessary to accomplish the interception unobtrusively and with a minimum of interference with the services that such service provider, landlord, custodian, or person is according the person whose communications are to be intercepted." [31] This language was added in 1970 in response to a decision holding that in the absence of such a provision the phone company could not be compelled to cooperate.

§ 4.5 Title III: Executing the Order

(a) Recording. Execution of a Title III order has no functional or theoretical equivalent in traditional search warrant law. The traditional warrant typically is served very promptly, is executed in a brief period of time, results in the seizure of a few objects, and by its observed execution or receipt of an inventory assures that the subject of the search is promptly made aware of the search and what was seized. By contrast, a Title III order often cannot be executed very promptly, is likely to be executed over a considerable span of time, usually results in the interception of many communications, and is executed secretly and thus without the subject of the search being aware of it or of what had been seized. For this reason, certain special requirements have understandably been imposed by statute with respect to execution of Title III orders.

22. 18 U.S.C.A. § 2518(4)(d).

23. 18 U.S.C.A. § 2518(5).

24. See § 3.3(g).

25. 18 U.S.C.A. § 2518(4)(e).

26. 18 U.S.C.A. § 2518(5). By 1986 amendment to this provision, the 30 days "begins on the earlier of the day on which the investigator or law enforcement officer first begins to conduct an interception under the order or ten days after the order is entered."

27. 18 U.S.C.A. § 2518(4)(e).

28. 18 U.S.C.A. § 2518(5).

29. 18 U.S.C.A. § 2518(5).

30. 18 U.S.C.A. § 2518(6), also stating these reports "shall be made at such intervals as the judge may require."

31. 18 U.S.C.A. § 2518(4), also providing: "Any provider of wire or electronic communication service, landlord, custodian or other person furnishing such facilities or technical assistance shall be compensated therefor by the applicant at the prevailing rates."

One such requirement is that the contents of any intercepted communication "shall, if possible, be recorded on tape or wire or other comparable device * * * in such way as will protect the recording from editing or other alterations."[1] The purpose of this requirement is to ensure that an accurate record of the conversation is made in the first instance and not altered in the interim before its use. This means that monitoring agents should record everything which is overheard by them, whether or not it is deemed pertinent.

(b) Minimization. One very important provision in Title III requires that an interception order be executed "in such a way as to minimize the interception of communications not otherwise subject to interception under this chapter."[2] This minimization duty implements a constitutional prerequisite to the validity of all court-ordered electronic surveillance, for the Supreme Court, in striking down the New York eavesdropping statute in *Berger v. New York,*[3] deemed that statute to permit unconstitutional general searches because it allowed seizure of "the conversations of any and all persons coming into the area covered by the device * * * indiscriminately and without regard to their connection to the crime under investigation."

What is to be minimized is the interception of "communications not otherwise subject to interception" under Title III, which appears to mean communications other than those "concerning" the offense which was the basis of the order. This suggests that a communication is pertinent and thus not subject to the minimization limitation if it in some respect provides information helpful to the investigation, without regard to whether it includes an incriminating remark directly implicating the speaker in criminal activity. As for the other, nonpertinent communications, it must be emphasized that the statute does not absolutely forbid their interception, but merely requires that measures be adopted to reduce the extent of such interception to a practical minimum.

In determining whether the surveilling agents sufficiently complied with the minimization requirement, it is necessary to assess the facts of the particular case. The Supreme Court has had one occasion to make such an assessment, in *Scott v. United States.*[4] There, government agents intercepted for a one-month period virtually all conversations over a particular telephone suspected of being used in furtherance of a conspiracy to import and distribute narcotics, though only forty percent of those conversations were shown to be narcotics related. In the course of concluding that the minimization requirement had not been violated, the Court enumerated a number of factors which are to be taken into account in deciding the minimization issue:

> [B]lind reliance on the percentage of nonpertinent calls intercepted is not a sure guide to the correct answer. Such percentages may provide assistance, but there are surely cases, such as the one at bar, where the percentage of nonpertinent calls is relatively high and yet their interception was still reasonable. The reasons for this may be many. Many of the nonpertinent calls may have been very short. Others may have been one-time only calls. Still other calls may have been ambiguous in nature or apparently involved guarded, or coded language. In all these circumstances agents can hardly be expected to know that the calls are not pertinent prior to their termination.

§ 4.5

1. 18 U.S.C.A. § 2518(8)(a).

2. 18 U.S.C.A. § 2518(5). A 1986 amendment to this section adds: "In the event the intercepted communication is in a code or foreign language, and an expert in that foreign language or code is not reasonably available during the interception period, minimization may be accomplished as soon as practicable after such interception. An interception under this chapter may be conducted in whole or part by Government personnel, or by an individual operating under a contract with the Government, acting under the supervision of an investigative or law enforcement officer authorized to conduct the interception." Under the first sentence, says the legislative history, the translator or decoder will listen to tapes and make available to investigators the minimized portions and preserve the rest for possible court perusal later. The last sentence added is intended to free FBI agents from the routine activity of monitoring.

3. 388 U.S. 41, 87 S.Ct. 1873, 18 L.Ed.2d 1040 (1967).

4. 436 U.S. 128, 98 S.Ct. 1717, 56 L.Ed.2d 168 (1978).

In determining whether the agents properly minimized, it is also important to consider the circumstances of the wiretap. For example, when the investigation is focusing on what is thought to be a widespread conspiracy more extensive surveillance may be justified in an attempt to determine the precise scope of the enterprise. And it is possible that many more of the conversations will be permissibly interceptable because they will involve one or more of the co-conspirators. The type of use to which the telephone is normally put may also have some bearing on the extent of minimization required. For example, if the agents are permitted to tap a public telephone because one individual is thought to be placing bets over the phone, substantial doubts as to minimization may arise if the agents listen to every call which goes out over that phone regardless of who places the call. On the other hand, if the phone is located in the residence of a person who is thought to be the head of a major drug ring, a contrary conclusion may be indicated.

Other factors may also play a significant part in a particular case. For example, it may be important to determine at exactly what point during the authorized period the interception was made. During the early stages of surveillance the agents may be forced to intercept all calls to establish categories of nonpertinent calls which will not be intercepted thereafter. Interception of those same types of calls might be unreasonable later on, however, once the nonpertinent categories have been established and it is clear that this particular conversation is of that type. Other situations may arise where patterns of nonpertinent calls do not appear. In these circumstances it may not be unreasonable to intercept almost every short conversation because the determination of relevancy cannot be made before the call is completed.

In the instant case, the Court reasoned, most of the 60% of the calls which turned out not to be material to the narcotics investigation were either "very short," "ambiguous in nature," or "one-time conversations" which fit into no previously established category, and thus there had been no minimization violation.

A more controversial aspect of the *Scott* case concerns the fact that the district court had found the surveilling agents "made no attempt to comply" with the minimization requirement and had concluded that this standing alone was a basis for suppression. The Supreme Court rejected that position in favor of the notion that "[s]ubjective intent alone * * * does not make otherwise lawful conduct illegal or unconstitutional," meaning that the officers' presumed failure to make even a good-faith effort to comply with the minimization requirement was not itself a reason for excluding the evidence obtained. The Court asserted this was sound Fourth Amendment doctrine and also good Title III law.

(c) Amendment and Extension. It is necessary to distinguish the Title III procedures for extension of an eavesdropping order from those dealing with what amounts to a retroactive amendment of a prior order. As for extension, this is possible only upon an application which meets the usual requirements and only after the court makes the findings usually required before an interception order may issue.[5] "The period of extension shall be no longer than the authorizing judge deems necessary to achieve the purposes for which it was granted and in no event for longer than thirty days," [6] but there is no prohibition on obtaining successive extensions of the same original order. The statute does not require by its own terms a fresh showing of probable cause in the extension application, but it has been suggested that such a showing is essential in light of the *Berger v. New York* [7] prohibition upon protracted electronic searches upon a single showing of probable cause.

When officers are conducting a court-ordered surveillance under Title III with respect to one particular crime, it sometimes happens that they will intercept conversations which refer to or are evidence of some other type of crime. The contents of such communications

5. 18 U.S.C.A. § 2818(5).

6. Ibid.

7. 388 U.S. 41, 87 S.Ct. 1873, 18 L.Ed.2d 1040 (1967).

are for some purposes treated just like the contents of communications of the type named in the order [8], that is, an officer with authorized knowledge of them may use them "to the extent such use is appropriate to the proper duties" [9] and also "may disclose such contents to another investigative or law enforcement officer to the extent that such disclosure is appropriate to the proper performance of the official duties of the officer making or receiving the disclosure." [10] But, the contents of these communications concerning other crimes may be testified to in a federal or state proceeding only if a judge finds upon subsequent application, "made as soon as practicable," that "the contents were otherwise intercepted in accordance with the provisions of this chapter." [11] This latter situation does not include instances in which these contents are merely set out and sworn to in an application for another Title III order or in a complaint for an arrest warrant.

Though the statute does not state what is to appear in the amendment application, the legislative history indicates it should include a showing that the original order was lawfully obtained, that it was sought in good faith and not as a subterfuge search, and that the communication was in fact incidentally intercepted during the course of a lawfully executed order. It has been suggested that this situation is the eavesdropping equivalent of the plain view doctrine, so that the requirements applicable to it [12] must also be shown to have been met here. The courts have not been very demanding with respect to the "as soon as practicable" timing limitation on an amendment application, but these cases may be criticized on the ground they disregard the principle of ongoing judicial supervision embodied in that part of the Act.

(d) Post-surveillance Notice. Title III also provides that certain persons are to receive post-surveillance notice that the surveillance occurred. The judge is required to serve this notice "[w]ithin a reasonable time but not later than ninety days after the filing of an application for an order of approval * * * which is denied or the termination of the period of an order or extensions thereof," except that upon "an ex parte showing of good cause to a judge of competent jurisdiction the serving of the inventory required by this subsection may be postponed." [13] The "reasonable time" requirement has been broadly construed. As for the "good cause" for postponement, it has been held to include such reasons as protecting the integrity of an ongoing investigation or ensuring that persons would not flee to avoid arrest.

By statute, this notice is to include "(1) the fact of the entry of the order or the application; (2) the date of the entry and the period of authorized, approved or disapproved interception, or the denial of the application; and (3) the fact that during the period wire, oral, or electronic communications were or were not intercepted." [14] The notice is to be served "on the persons named in the order or the application, and such other parties to intercepted communications as the judge may determine in his discretion that is in the interest of justice." [15] This in no event covers a person who is merely identified in the communications of another, and as to parties to communications not named in the order or application appellate courts have been disinclined to question the discretion exercised by the judge in deciding which of them should receive notice. Because "a judge is likely to require information and assistance beyond that contained in the application papers and the recordings of intercepted conversations made available by law enforcement authorities" in order to exercise his discretion intelligently, the Supreme Court concluded in *United States v. Donovan* [16] that those authorities have a "routine duty to supply the judge with relevant information." Specifically,

8. 18 U.S.C.A. § 2517(5).
9. 18 U.S.C.A. § 2517(2).
10. 18 U.S.C.A. § 2517(1).
11. 18 U.S.C.A. § 2517(5).
12. See § 3.4(k).
13. 18 U.S.C.A. § 2518(8)(d).
14. 18 U.S.C.A. § 2518(8)(d).
15. Ibid.
16. 429 U.S. 413, 97 S.Ct. 658, 50 L.Ed.2d 652 (1977).

the judicial officer must have, at a minimum, knowledge of the particular categories into which fall all the individuals whose conversations have been intercepted. Thus, while precise identification of each party to an intercepted conversation is not required, a description of the general class, or classes, which they comprise is essential to enable the judge to determine whether additional information is necessary for a proper evaluation of the interests of the various parties. Furthermore, although the judicial officer has the duty to cause the filing of the inventory [notice], it is abundantly clear that the prosecution has greater access to and familiarity with the intercepted communications. Therefore we feel justified in imposing upon the latter the duty to classify all those whose conversations have been intercepted, and to transmit this information to the judge. Should the judge desire more information regarding these classes in order to exercise his [statutory] * * * discretion, * * * the government is [also] required to furnish such information as is available to it.

In *Donovan,* where two names had been omitted from the list and those individuals thus did not receive notice until they were indicted eight months later,[17] the Court held this did not require suppression because Congress did not mean for "post-intercept notice * * * to serve as an independent restraint on resort to the wiretap procedure." The *Donovan* Court emphasized that the omission was inadvertent and had not prejudiced the defendants, which has been taken to mean that suppression is required if names are deliberately withheld or if prejudice resulted from lack of timely notice. Courts are generally disinclined to find that a defendant has established prejudice, but it would seem prejudice exists when the conversation is not inherently incriminating but is subject to explanation and interpretation and the delay in notice has diminished the speaker's opportunity to marshal his explanations.

(e) Sealing. Title III also requires that "the contents of any wire, oral, or electronic communication intercepted by any means authorized by this chapter shall, if possible, be recorded on tape or wire or other comparable device" and that such recording "be done in such way as will protect the recording from editing or other alterations." [18] It further provides that "immediately upon the expiration of the period of the order, or extension thereof, such recordings shall be made available to the judge issuing such order and sealed under his direction." [19] This sealing requirement, the Supreme Court has noted, "is to ensure the reliability and integrity of evidence obtained by means of electronic surveillance"; "the seal is a means of ensuring that subsequent to its placement on tape, the Government has no opportunity to tamper with, alter, or edit the conversations that have been recorded." [20]

The Title III sealing requirement has an explicit exclusionary remedy for noncompliance. It provides that "the presence of the seal provided for by this subsection, or a satisfactory explanation for the absence thereof, shall be a prerequisite for the use or disclosure of the contents of any wire, oral, or electronic communication or evidence derived therefrom." [21] This provision was construed in *United States v. Ojeda Rios,*[22] where the Court held: (1) that the requirement is not that of "just any seal but a seal that has been obtained *immediately* upon expiration of the underlying surveillance order"; (2) that consequently the "absence" the Government must explain "encompasses not only the total absence of a seal but also the absence of a timely applied seal"; (3) that the required "satisfactory explanation" requires "that the Government explain not only why such a delay occurred but also why it is excusable"; and (4) that the Government may establish a reasonable excuse for delay by showing reliance upon an erroneous interpretation of

17. Notice was then given to them as a party to the forthcoming trial, as provided in 18 U.S.C.A. § 2518(9).

18. 18 U.S.C.A. § 2518(8)(a).

19. 18 U.S.C.A. § 2518(8)(a).

20. United States v. Ojeda Rios, ___ U.S. ___, 110 S.Ct. 1845, 109 L.Ed.2d 224 (1990).

21. 18 U.S.C.A. § 2518(8)(a).

22. ___ U.S. ___, 110 S.Ct. 1845, 109 L.Ed.2d 224 (1990).

Title III which "was objectively reasonable at the time."

§ 4.6 Title III: Remedies

(a) Violations Requiring Exclusion. If a particular instance of electronic eavesdropping does not meet the requirements of the Fourth Amendment, then of course the judicially-created exclusionary rule for that Amendment comes into play,[1] in which case what is said elsewhere herein about the dimensions of that rule is applicable. Of concern here, by contrast, is the statutory exclusionary rule of Title III. The statute at one point declares that no information derived from eavesdropping "may be received in evidence in any trial, hearing, or other proceeding * * * if the disclosure of that information would be in violation of this chapter."[2] This language is somewhat misleading, and it has been properly suggested that it should be read as requiring the exclusion of evidence the *seizure* of which was in violation of the chapter. In any event, more attention has been focused upon the wording of another provision to the effect that a suppression motion may be made on "the grounds that (i) the communication was unlawfully intercepted; (ii) the order of authorization or approval under which it was intercepted is insufficient on its face; or (iii) the interception was not made in conformity with the order of authorization or approval."[3]

In 1986, Title III was substantially amended so as to also cover the interception of any "electronic communication," defined as "any transfer of signs, signals, writing, images, sounds, data, or intelligence of any nature transmitted in whole or in part by a wire, radio, electromagnetic, photoelectronic or photooptical system that affects interstate or foreign commerce."[4] However, neither of the two exclusionary rule provisions quoted above was amended, so that both continue to be limited only to violations having to do with wire or oral communications.[5] This was no oversight. A new provision states that the "remedies and sanctions described in this chapter with respect to the interception of electronic communications are the only judicial remedies and sanctions for nonconstitutional violations of this chapter involving such communications."[6] The legislative history expressly declares that the Title III statutory exclusionary rule has no application to the interception of electronic communications, but no rationale for this curious distinction is given.

In *United States v. Giordano,*[7] the government argued that the phrase "unlawfully intercepted" in that provision meant only an interception obtained in violation of the Constitution. The Supreme Court rejected that contention and concluded from the legislative history that "Congress intended to require suppression where there is failure to satisfy any of those statutory requirements that directly and substantially implement the congressional intention to limit the use of intercept procedures to those situations clearly calling for the employment of this extraordinary investigative device." As the Court put it later in *Giordano,* suppression under this statutory exclusionary rule is required whenever the particular statutory provision violated "was intended to play a central role in the statutory scheme." This obviously means, as the Court noted in the companion case of *United States v. Chavez,*[8] "that paragraph (i) was not intended to reach every failure to follow statutory procedures."

Giordano supplies a useful illustration of how the "central role" test is to be applied. At issue there was a failure to comply with the statutory requirement that the "Attorney General, or any Assistant Attorney General

§ 4.6

1. Berger v. New York, 388 U.S. 41, 87 S.Ct. 1873, 18 L.Ed.2d 1040 (1967).

2. 18 U.S.C.A. § 2515. Such seemingly absolute language has not been deemed to bar admission of such information for impeachment purposes.

3. 18 U.S.C.A. § 2518(10)(a).

4. 18 U.S.C.A. § 2510(12).

5. For definition of these terms, see § 4.3(a).

6. 18 U.S.C.A. § 2518(10)(c).

7. 416 U.S. 505, 94 S.Ct. 1820, 40 L.Ed.2d 341 (1974).

8. 416 U.S. 562, 94 S.Ct. 1849, 40 L.Ed.2d 380 (1974).

specially designated by the Attorney General" must authorize application for a federal surveillance order.[9] That requirement, the Court concluded, did play a "central role" because the statute reflected a congressional intent to limit eavesdropping not merely by a probable cause requirement and a nature-of-offense limitation but also by having "a senior official in the Department of Justice" decide that the situation was one warranting resort to such surveillance. Because it was "reasonable to believe that such a precondition would inevitably foreclose resort to wiretapping in various situations where investigative personnel would otherwise seek intercept authority from the court and the court would very likely authorize its use," this precondition was unquestionably central to the statutory scheme.

By comparison, in *Chavez* the Court concluded that the misidentification of the authorizing official in the application and order "did not affect the fulfillment of any of the reviewing or approval functions required by Congress" because the statutory provisions thereby violated do "not establish a substantive role to be played in the regulatory system." (Four members of the Court, dissenting in *Chavez,* persuasively argued that these identification requirements were central to the intention of Congress to attach "personal responsibility and political accountability" to the person actually giving the approval.) And in *United States v. Donovan,*[10] where the violation was the failure to include in the application the names of all persons as to whom there was probable cause and who were likely to be overheard, the Court concluded *Chavez* rather than *Giordano* was controlling. This was because the missing information would not "have precluded judicial authorization of the intercept" and even without that information "the application provided sufficient information to enable the issuing judge to determine that the statutory preconditions were satisfied." (There were three dissenters in *Donovan,* who cogently noted that the requirement of naming all such persons was very important in the statutory scheme and could affect whether the judge issued the warrant, for the government would also have to disclose the history of prior applications as to the named persons, which would "at the least cause a judge to consider whether the application before him was an attempt to circumvent the restrictive rulings of another judge or to continue an unjustified invasion of privacy.")

As for the "insufficient on its face" test of paragraph (ii), it was also addressed in *Chavez.* The Court concluded, in effect, that it applies only when the order can be determined to be insufficient without resort to other facts. Thus, because in that case the order did identify a person as having authorized the application who had the authority to give such authorization, the fact it was subsequently shown he actually did not give the requisite approval "does not detract from the facial sufficiency of the order." By like reasoning, it was concluded in *Donovan* that the failure to have a complete list of persons in the order did not make the order "insufficient on its face," for again this was not apparent from the order itself. As for the paragraph (iii) "not made in conformity" test, the Court in *Giordano* observed it concerns only "the manner of conducting the court-approved interceptions" and thus was not in issue there.

One final problem, addressed in another branch of the *Donovan* case, needs to be specially noted. The government in that case also failed to inform the judge of all identifiable persons whose conversations were intercepted, thus making it impossible for the judge to exercise fully his discretionary authority to decide what parties should receive notice. In concluding that violation did not require suppression, the Court reasoned:

> Nothing in the structure of the Act or this legislative history suggests that incriminating

9. 18 U.S.C.A. § 2516(1). In 1984 this provision was amended so that it now also includes the Deputy Attorney General and Associate Attorney General. In 1986 this provision was amended to include any Assistant Attorney General and any acting Assistant Attorney General, plus any Deputy Assistant Attorney General in the Criminal Division designated by the Attorney General.

10. 429 U.S. 413, 97 S.Ct. 658, 50 L.Ed.2d 652 (1977).

conversations are "unlawfully intercepted" whenever parties to those conversations do not receive discretionary inventory notice as a result of the Government's failure to inform the District Court of their identities. At the time inventory notice was served on the other identifiable persons, the intercept had been completed and the conversations had been "seized" under a valid intercept order. The fact that discretionary notice reached 39 rather than 41 identifiable persons does not in itself mean that the conversations were unlawfully intercepted.

One way to read that paragraph is as just another illustration of the "central role" test being used to admit evidence notwithstanding the statutory violation. But another plausible reading, especially in light of the Court's recognition that there remained open the question whether "suppression might be required if the agents knew before the interception that no inventory would be served," is that any noncompliance subsequent to a lawful interception, no matter how serious, cannot operate to retroactively invalidate the prior interception. This would mean, for example, that if the government *deliberately* withheld names from the judge or if the withholding actually prejudiced a person who thereby was deprived of timely notice, there would still be no suppression under the statute. Though this result is arguably supported by a literal reading of the statute, it is well to note that the legislation does not even cover the post-interception violation which *is* prejudicial. It thus may be that courts are empowered to exclude evidence, even beyond what is provided for in the Title III exclusionary rule, when they do so for the purpose of overcoming prejudice. Whether it follows that courts may also do so for the purpose of deterring deliberate statutory violations is another matter. The Court in *Donovan* appears to have left these issues open by carefully noting that the defendants made no claim of prejudice and also that the violation was unintentional, so that it was "not called upon to decide whether suppression would be an available remedy if the Government knowingly sought to prevent the District Court from serving inventory notice on particular parties."

(b) Who May Exclude When. The subject of Fourth Amendment standing, including the ruling in *Alderman v. United States* [11] that in an eavesdropping case the parties to the conversation and the persons with a possessory interest in the place where the conversation occurs all have standing, is discussed elsewhere herein.[12] Of concern here is Title III standing. The statute says that any "aggrieved person" may move for suppression,[13] and that term is defined as meaning "a person who was a party to any intercepted wire, oral, or electronic communication or a person against whom the interception was directed." [14] Read literally, this definition would seem to be narrower in some respects and broader in some respects than Fourth Amendment standing; it seems to leave out the person with the possessory interest in the place surveilled and to include the target of the surveillance who was neither that person nor one of the speakers. But, as the Court noted in *Alderman,* the legislative history shows this definition was intended "to reflect existing law," and thus the Court there concluded Congress had not extended the exclusionary rule. Thus, courts are inclined to define Title III standing as being exactly the same as Fourth Amendment standing, even to the point of taking into account Fourth Amendment developments postdating enactment of Title III. This is not to suggest that the Title III exclusionary rule has exactly the same dimensions as the Fourth Amendment exclusionary rule; for example, because Title III proscribes private wiretapping its exclusionary rule also extends to evidence falling into the government's hands after a private search.

There is another way, however, in which the Fourth Amendment exclusionary rule and the Title III exclusionary rule are unquestionably different. The former, as a creature of

11. 394 U.S. 165, 89 S.Ct. 961, 22 L.Ed.2d 176 (1969).

12. See § 9.1(b).

13. 18 U.S.C.A. § 2518(10)(a).

14. 18 U.S.C.A. § 2510(11).

the Supreme Court, can be applied in such circumstances as the Court believes will further its objectives.[15] Thus, while it applies at a criminal trial, it does not inevitably apply in other proceedings, as is best illustrated by *United States v. Calandra.*[16] There, the Court refused to allow a grand jury witness to invoke the exclusionary rule, reasoning that a contrary result "would achieve a speculative and undoubtedly minimal advance in the deterrence of police misconduct at the expense of substantially impeding the role of the grand jury." But the Title III exclusionary rule, by virtue of the statute, applies "in any trial, hearing, or proceeding in or before any court, department, officer, agency, regulatory body, or other authority of the United States, a State, or a political subdivision." [17] This means, for example, that the Title III exclusionary rule may be invoked by a party in a bail hearing, a parole proceeding, or a police department disciplinary proceeding.

The legislative history of the language quoted above unequivocally states that "[b]ecause no person is a party as such to a grand jury proceeding, the provision does not envision the making of a motion to suppress on the context of such a proceeding itself, but only that if a motion to suppress is granted in another context "its scope may include use in a future grand jury proceeding." [18] This means, for example, that a prospective defendant cannot merely by virtue of that status invoke the Title III exclusionary rule before the grand jury considering his case. But in *Gelbard v. United States* [19] the Court held that a grand jury witness may refuse to testify where his testimony is sought on the basis of illegal electronic surveillance. This is because, the Court explained, that testimony would constitute "evidence derived" from violation of Title III, and another part of the Act expressly provides that such evidence may not "be received in evidence in any trial, hearing, or other proceeding in or before any court, *grand jury,* department, officer, agency, regulatory body, legislative committee, or other authority of the United States, or a political subdivision thereof." [20] The Court reasoned that if that prohibition was "not available as a defense to the contempt charge, disclosure through compelled testimony makes the witness the victim, once again, of a federal crime."

It is important to note that *Gelbard* was a 5–4 decision and that a majority was achieved only with the concurring opinion of Justice White. He agreed that "at least where the United States has intercepted communications without a warrant in circumstances where court approval was required, it is appropriate * * * not to require the grand jury witness to answer and hence further the plain policy of the wiretap statute." But he suggested a different result would obtain "where the Government produces a court order for the interception" but "the witness nevertheless demands a full-blown suppression hearing to determine the legality of the order":

> Suppression hearings in these circumstances would result in protracted interruption of grand jury proceedings. At the same time prosecutors and other officers who have been granted and relied on a court order for the interception would be subject to no liability under the statute, whether the order is valid or not; and, in any event, the deterrent value of excluding the evidence will be marginal at best.

This position has been adopted by the lower courts.

(c) Disclosure of Illegal Electronic Surveillance. After enacting Title III, Congress recognized that victims of illegal wiretapping might have grounds to suspect, but yet have difficulty proving, that wiretapping had occurred. It thus enacted a provision [21] that in "any trial, hearing, or other proceeding in or before any court, grand jury, department, officer, the agency, regulatory body, or other authority of the United States," upon a claim

15. See § 3.2(f), (g).
16. 414 U.S. 338, 94 S.Ct. 613, 38 L.Ed.2d 561 (1974).
17. 18 U.S.C.A. § 2518(10)(a).
18. S.Rep. No. 1097, 90th Cong., 2d Sess. 106 (1968).
19. 408 U.S. 41, 92 S.Ct. 2357, 33 L.Ed.2d 179 (1972).
20. 18 U.S.C.A. § 2515 (emphasis added).
21. 18 U.S.C.A. § 3504(a)(1).

by "a party aggrieved" that the evidence is inadmissible as the fruit of an "unlawful act," "the opponent of the claim shall affirm or deny the occurrence of the alleged unlawful act."

In order to put the government to the task of responding, the aggrieved party must articulate a colorable basis for his claim of surveillance. Once that burden has been met, the government must make a "factual, unambiguous, and unequivocal" response. Something more than a purely conclusory denial of surveillance is required, but precisely what will suffice may vary from case to case. This is because the more specific the defendant's claim of surveillance, the more detailed and extensive must be the government's response.

The response by the government must normally be in the form of sworn testimony or an affidavit. This response, which ordinarily will come from the prosecutor, must indicate the results of his inquiry of all appropriate investigative agencies to determine if any of them have conducted surveillance of the complaining party. The cases require that the prosecutor or the primary investigating agency submit an affidavit, but impose no affidavit requirement upon the various agencies responding to a request to check their records. The assumption is that responses to such requests, signed by responsible officials with obvious awareness that their replies are to be submitted in court proceedings, suffice to permit the court to determine compliance with the statute.

(d) Disclosure of Electronic Surveillance Records. Under Title III, suppression is provided for not only as to the contents of an illegally intercepted wire or oral communication, but also as to "evidence derived therefrom." [22] This naturally raises the question of what procedures are required to facilitate a determination whether other evidence is the fruit of such a surveillance. The statute merely provides that if a suppression motion is made, then the judge "may in his discretion make available to the aggrieved person or his counsel for inspection such portions of the intercepted communication or evidence derived therefrom as the judge determines to be in the interests of justice."

The issue reached the Supreme Court in 1969 in a series of cases not involving Title III: *Alderman v. United States, Ivanov v. United States,* and *Butenko v. United States.*[23] *Alderman* concerned convictions for conspiring to transmit murderous threats in interstate commerce, while the other cases involved convictions for transmitting national defense information to the Soviet Union. The defendants sought disclosure of all surveillance records so that they might show that some of the evidence admitted against them grew out of illegally overheard conversations. The government urged that in order to protect innocent third parties participating or referred to in irrelevant conversations overheard by the government, surveillance records should first be subjected to in camera inspection by the trial judge. He would then turn over to defendants and their counsel only those materials "arguably relevant" to defendants' convictions, in the sense that the overheard conversations arguably underlay some items of evidence offered at trial.

The Court, in a 5–3 decision, held that a defendant should receive *all* surveillance records as to which he has standing. The government's proposal was rejected on the ground that the trial judge often would not be in a position to determine what conversations were relevant:

> An apparently innocent phrase, a chance remark, a reference to what appears to be a neutral person, the identity of a caller or the individual on the other end of a telephone, or even the manner of speaking or using words may have special significance to one who knows the more intimate facts of an accused's life. And yet that information may be wholly colorless and devoid of meaning to one less well acquainted with all relevant circumstances. Unavoidably, this is a matter of judgment, but in our view the task is too complex, and the margin for error too great, to rely wholly on the in camera judgment of

22. 18 U.S.C.A. § 2518(10)(a).

23. 394 U.S. 165, 89 S.Ct. 961, 22 L.Ed.2d 176 (1969).

the trial court to identify those records which might have contributed to the Government's case.

To protect innocent third parties, the Court added, the trial court could place defendants and counsel under enforceable orders against unwarranted disclosure of the materials they would be entitled to inspect.

Justice Fortas, dissenting in part in *Alderman,* argued that the in camera screening procedure should be followed when the trial judge makes written and sealed findings "that disclosure would substantially injure national security interests." In his dissent, Justice Harlan subscribed to a narrower view that such screening would be appropriate whenever the defendant is charged with spying for a foreign power, in which case protective orders would not deter disclosure to others and the location of listening devices crucial to espionage work would otherwise be needlessly disclosed. In an unsuccessful petition for rehearing, the Attorney General argued against disclosure of records of surveillance activities to gather "foreign intelligence information" on the ground that such activity was practiced by all nations and thus not unreasonable.

Giordano v. United States [24] emphasized that disclosure under *Alderman* was available only to one who "has standing to assert the illegality of the surveillance" and that "a finding by the District Court that the surveillance was lawful would make disclosure and further proceedings unnecessary." And in *Taglianetti v. United States,*[25] the Court rejected defendant's contention that he was entitled to examine additional surveillance records to establish that he might be a party to some other conversations. Distinguishing *Alderman,* the Court concluded that the trial judge could be expected to identify defendant's voice without the defendant's assistance.

By statute, Congress has attempted to limit the impact of *Alderman* in the federal courts.[26] For one thing, records of an unlawful surveillance which occurred prior to the enactment of Title III need not be disclosed "unless such information may be relevant to a pending claim of * * * inadmissibility," which presumably is to be determined by the judge in camera. For another, on the legislative finding that "there is virtually no likelihood" that evidence offered to prove an event would have been obtained by exploitation of an unlawful surveillance occurring more than five years prior to that event, no such claim is to be considered. The constitutionality of these provisions is open to some doubt, as the *Alderman* decision was cast in terms of "the scrutiny which the Fourth Amendment exclusionary rule demands."

(e) Civil Remedies. Title III expressly provides that "any person whose wire, oral, or electronic communication is intercepted, disclosed, or intentionally used in violation of this chapter may in a civil action recover from the person or entity which engaged in that violation" appropriate relief, including: appropriate equitable or declaratory relief; damages and punitive damages in appropriate cases; and a reasonable attorney's fee and other reasonable litigation costs.[27] The damages may be the greater of the sum of the plaintiff's actual damages and the violator's resulting profits, or statutory damages of the greater of $100 a day or $10,000. Good faith reliance on a court warrant or order, grand jury subpoena, legislative authorization, or request of a law enforcement officer is a defense.

(f) Criminal Penalties. Title III makes it a crime for a person, except as permitted by the statute, to "intentionally" intercept, endeavor to intercept, or procure another to intercept or endeavor to intercept a communication; to "intentionally" disclose or endeavor to disclose to another the contents of a communication "knowing or having reason to know" that it was obtained by an illegal interception; or to "intentionally" use or endeavor to use the contents of a communication

24. 394 U.S. 310, 89 S.Ct. 1163, 22 L.Ed.2d 297 (1969).

25. 394 U.S. 316, 89 S.Ct. 1099, 22 L.Ed.2d 302 (1969).

26. 18 U.S.C.A. § 3504.

27. 18 U.S.C.A. § 2520.

"knowing or having reason to know" that it was obtained by an illegal interception.[28] The "intentionally" mental state was substituted for "willfully" in 1986 to emphasize that inadvertent interception is not criminal. Under this provision, a person acts intentionally if his conduct or the result thereof was his conscious objective. The previously mentioned "good faith reliance" defense [29] is also available in a criminal prosecution. With limited exceptions, a person convicted of this offense may be fined or imprisoned not more than five years or both.[30] Another provision with like penalties makes it a crime to possess, manufacture, distribute, advertise or mail "any electronic, mechanical, or other device, knowing or having reason to know that the design of such device renders it primarily useful for the purpose of the surreptitious interception of wire, oral, or electronic communication." [31] Exceptions are provided for law enforcement agents and their suppliers and for providers of wire or electronic communication service and their agents.[32]

28. 18 U.S.C.A. § 2511(1).

29. 18 U.S.C.A. § 2518(10)(a).

30. 18 U.S.C.A. § 2511(4)(a).

31. 18 U.S.C.A. § 2512(1).

32. 18 U.S.C.A. § 2512(2).

Chapter 5

POLICE "ENCOURAGEMENT" AND THE ENTRAPMENT DEFENSE

Table of Sections

Sec.

§ 5.1 Encouragement of Crime and the Defense of Entrapment

(a) Encouragement of Criminal Activity. Certain criminal offenses present the police with unique and difficult detection problems because they are committed privately between individuals who are willing participants. Consequently, in addition to employing search and seizure techniques, routine and electronic surveillance, and informants to expose such consensual crime, law enforcement officers actually encourage commission of these offenses. At the heart of this encouragement practice is the need to simulate reality. An environment is created in which the suspect is presented with an opportunity to commit a crime. The simulation of reality must be accurate enough to induce the criminal activity at the point in time when the agents are in a position to gather evidence of the crime.

The tactics used vary from case to case. Some solicitations are innocuous, but since persons engaged in criminal activity are generally suspicious of strangers, government agents typically do more than simply approach a target and request the commission of a crime. Multiple requests or the formation of personal relationships with a subject may be necessary to overcome that suspicion. In addition, appeals to personal considerations, representations of benefits to be derived from the offense, and actual assistance in obtaining contraband or planning the details of the crime are frequently employed.

(b) Entrapment Defense as a Limit. The more extreme forms of encouragement activity are a matter of legitimate concern for a variety of reasons. Of central concern is the possibility that the encouragement might induce a person who otherwise would be law-abiding to engage in criminal conduct. Yet, as a historical matter, the traditional response of the law was that there were no limits upon the degree of temptation to which law enforcement officers and their agents could subject those under investigation. The attitude was that the courts would "not look to see who held out the bait, but [rather] who took it."[1]

Even today, neither courts nor legislatures have affirmatively developed detailed guidelines for police and their agents to follow when engaging in encouragement activity. However, there did ultimately develop, originally in the state courts, a defense called "entrapment" which may be interposed in a criminal prosecution. Beginning with the decision in *Sorrells v. United States*[2] in 1932, the development of the law of entrapment became largely an activity of the federal courts, with the states then adopting the doctrine thereby created. The classic definition of entrapment is that articulated by Justice Roberts in *Sorrells:* "Entrapment is the conception and planning of an offense by an officer, and his procurement of its commission by one who would not have perpetrated it except for the trickery, persuasion, or fraud of the officer."

(c) Scope of the Defense. The defense of entrapment has been asserted in the context of a wide variety of criminal activity, including prostitution, alcohol offenses, counterfeiting, price controlling, and, probably most spectacularly, bribery of public officials. However, the great majority of the cases in which an entrapment defense is interposed involve a charge of some drug offense. There is a dearth of case authority on the question of whether the entrapment defense is available no matter what the nature of the charge brought against the defendant. But in *Sorrells* there appears a caution that the defense might be unavailable where the defendant is charged with a "heinous" or "revolting" crime, and the Model Penal Code formulation of the defense expressly makes it "unavailable when causing or threatening bodily injury is an element of the offense charged and the prosecution is based on conduct causing or threatening such injury to a person other than the person perpetrating the entrapment."[3] In support of this latter limitation, it is explained that one "who can be persuaded to cause such injury presents a danger that the public cannot safely disregard," and that the impropriety of the inducement will likely be dealt with by other means because the public will, "in all probability, demand the punishment of the conniving or cooperating officers."[4]

The defense of entrapment is only available when the encouragement was conducted by either personnel of law enforcement agencies or persons cooperating with law enforcement agencies, including paid informants and persons charged with crime who are cooperating in the hope of obtaining leniency. As it was put in *Sherman v. United States,*[5] the government cannot make use of an informer and then "claim disassociation through ignorance." The doctrine of entrapment does not extend to acts of inducement on the part of a private citizen who is not acting in cooperation with, or as an agent of, a law enforcement official. If the entrapment defense was based upon the notion that a person is not culpable whenever he engages in what would otherwise be criminal conduct because of the strong inducement of another person, this limitation would be open to serious question. What this limitation reflects, then, is that the

§ 5.1

1. People v. Mills, 178 N.Y. 274, 70 N.E. 786 (1904).
2. 287 U.S. 435, 53 S.Ct. 210, 77 L.Ed. 413 (1932).
3. ALI Model Penal Code § 2.13 (1962).
4. ALI Model Penal Code 24 (Tent. Draft No. 9, 1959).
5. 356 U.S. 369, 78 S.Ct. 819, 2 L.Ed.2d 848 (1958).

purpose of the defense is to deter misconduct in enforcing the law.

Though the defense of entrapment is ordinarily interposed in the context of criminal prosecution, a number of states have recognized entrapment as a defense to an administrative proceeding involving revocation or suspension of a license to practice a profession, trade, or business. Few courts have considered the issue, and the cases in which the matter is alluded to at all usually reflect nothing but the tacit assumption that the defense is available in administrative proceedings but inapplicable to the case at bar. Nevertheless, extension of the entrapment defense to administrative disciplinary proceedings seems to be warranted by the policies underlying its application in criminal cases.

§ 5.2 Subjective Versus Objective Test for Entrapment

(a) The Subjective Approach. There are currently two major approaches to the defense of entrapment, each involving a distinct test and rationale and each with somewhat different procedural consequences. This division is reflected in the Supreme Court's decisions dealing directly with the subject of entrapment. The majority view is usually referred to as the "subjective approach," although it is also called the federal approach or the *Sherman–Sorrells* doctrine, a reference to the fact that this test was adopted by a majority of the Supreme Court in the cases of *Sherman v. United States*[1] and *Sorrells v. United States.*[2]

A two-step test is used under the subjective approach: the first inquiry is whether or not the offense was induced by a government agent; and the second is whether or not the defendant was predisposed to commit the type of offense charged. A defendant is considered predisposed if he is ready and willing to commit the crimes such as are charged in the indictment, whenever opportunity was afforded. If the accused is found to be predisposed, the defense of entrapment may not prevail. The predisposition test reflects an attempt to draw a line between "a trap for the unwary innocent and the trap for the unwary criminal."[3] The emphasis under the subjective approach is clearly upon the defendant's propensity to commit the offense rather than on the officer's misconduct.

The underlying rationale of the subjective approach is grounded in the substantive criminal law. The defense is explained in terms of the defendant's conduct not being criminal because the legislature intended acts instigated by the government to be excepted from the purview of the general statutory prohibition. As stated by the majority in *Sorrells:* "We are unable to conclude that it was the intention of the Congress in enacting this statute that its processes of detection and enforcement be abused by the instigation by government officials of an act on the part of persons otherwise innocent in order to lure them to its commission and to punish them."

(b) The Objective Approach. The subjective approach to entrapment has been consistently affirmed by a majority of the Supreme Court, and is adhered to by the federal courts as well as a majority of the state courts. However, there is growing support for the objective approach, variously described as the "hypothetical person" approach or the Roberts–Frankfurter approach (after the writers of the concurring opinions in *Sorrells* and *Sherman*). The objective approach is favored by a majority of the commentators, and is reflected in the formulation of the entrapment defense appearing in the American Law Institute's Model Penal Code. At least eleven states have adopted it either by statute or judicial decision. A few other jurisdictions have adopted a combination of the objective and subjective tests.

The objective approach focuses upon the inducements used by the government agents. This means that entrapment has been established if the offense was induced or encour-

§ 5.2

1. 356 U.S. 369, 78 S.Ct. 819, 2 L.Ed.2d 848 (1958).
2. 287 U.S. 435, 53 S.Ct. 210, 77 L.Ed. 413 (1932).
3. Sherman v. United States, 356 U.S. 369, 78 S.Ct. 819, 2 L.Ed.2d 848 (1958).

aged by "employing methods of persuasion or inducement which create a substantial risk that such an offense will be committed by persons other than those who are ready to commit it." [4] In applying this test, it is necessary to consider the surrounding circumstances, such as evidence of the manner in which the particular criminal business is usually carried on. Though such practices as appeals to sympathy or friendship, offers of inordinate gain, or persistent offers to overcome hesitancy are suspect, courts in jurisdictions using the objective test have been reluctant to lay down absolutes. Though such temptations may be impermissible in some instances, each case must be judged on its own facts. Thus, it would seem that this "objective" focus upon the propriety of the police conduct leaves as much room for value judgments to be made as does the "subjective" focus upon the defendant's state of mind.

The rationale behind the objective approach is grounded in public policy considerations. Proponents of this approach reject the legislative intent argument. They believe that courts must refuse to convict an entrapped defendant not because his conduct falls outside the proscription of the statute, but rather because, even if his guilt has been established, the methods employed on behalf of the government to bring about the crime "cannot be countenanced." [5] To some extent, this reflects the notion that the courts should not become tainted by condoning law enforcement improprieties. If government agents have instigated the commission of a crime, then the courts should not in effect approve that "abhorrent transaction" [6] by permitting the induced individual to be convicted. But the primary consideration is that an affirmative duty resides in the courts to control police excesses in inducing criminal behavior, and that this duty should not be limited to instances in which the defendant is otherwise "innocent." So viewed, the entrapment defense appears to be a procedural device (somewhat like the Fourth Amendment and *Miranda* exclusionary rules) for deterring undesirable governmental intrusions into the lives of citizens.

As currently applied, the two approaches differ more than merely at the theoretical level. True, in *Sorrells* and *Sherman* the majority (subjective approach) and minority (objective approach) opinions agreed as to the result on the facts there presented.[7] But the concurring justices in *Sherman* were the dissenters in *Masciale v. United States,*[8] decided the same day. And in *United States v. Russell,*[9] the result would certainly have been different had the objective test been utilized. However, neither of the two approaches is

4. ALI Model Penal Code § 2.13 (1962).

5. Sherman v. United States, 356 U.S. 369, 78 S.Ct. 819, 2 L.Ed.2d 848 (1958) (Frankfurter, J., concurring).

6. Sorrells v. United States, 287 U.S. 435, 53 S.Ct. 210, 77 L.Ed. 413 (1932) (Roberts, J., concurring).

7. In *Sherman,* a government informer met defendant at a doctor's office where he was being treated to cure his narcotics addiction, and the informer induced defendant to sell his drugs after making repeated requests and saying that he was not responding to treatment and was suffering as a consequence. The majority, applying the subjective approach, concluded that a 9-year-old sale of narcotics conviction and a 5-year-old possession conviction did not show predisposition, "particularly when we must assume from the record he was trying to overcome the narcotics habit at the time." The four concurring Justices concluded that such appeals to sympathy "can no more be tolerated when directed against a past offender than against an ordinary law-abiding citizen."

In *Sorrells,* the majority held the lower court had erred in ruling as a matter of law that there could be no entrapment, where it was shown "that the act for which defendant was prosecuted was instigated by the prohibition agent, that it was the creature of his purpose, that defendant was an industrious, law-abiding citizen, and that the agent lured defendant, otherwise innocent, to its commission by repeated and persistent solicitation in which he succeeded by taking advantage of the sentiment aroused by reminiscences of their experiences as companions in arms in the World War." Three members of the Court concurred, but relied upon the objective approach.

8. 356 U.S. 386, 78 S.Ct. 827, 2 L.Ed.2d 859 (1958). The majority, using the subjective approach, concluded the "trial court properly submitted the case to the jury"; the four dissenters, using the objective approach, concluded that the lower court "should itself have ruled on the issue of entrapment and not left it to determination by the jury."

9. 411 U.S. 423, 93 S.Ct. 1637, 36 L.Ed.2d 366 (1973). There, an undercover agent supplied an essential but difficult to obtain ingredient for defendants' operation of a "speed" laboratory. The majority ruled that "the jury finding as to predisposition was supported by the evidence" and was "fatal to his claim of entrapment." Three dissenters urged adoption of the objective test.

uniformly more favorable to defendants, as is reflected by this brief comparison:

> Under the [subjective approach], if A, an informer, makes overreaching appeals to compassion and friendship and thus moves D to sell narcotics, D has no defense if he is predisposed to narcotics peddling. Under the [objective approach] a defense would be established because the police conduct, not D's predisposition, determines the issue. Under the [subjective approach], A's mere offer to purchase narcotics from D may give rise to the defense provided D is not predisposed to sell. A contrary result is reached under the [objective approach]. A mere offer to buy hardly creates a serious risk of offending by the innocent.[10]

(c) Objections to the Subjective Approach. Proponents of the objective approach raise three main arguments against the subjective approach. First of all, the "legislative intent" theory is attacked as sheer fiction. It is argued that the Congress or state legislature intended to proscribe precisely the conduct in which the defendant engaged, as is reflected by the fact that the conduct is unquestionably criminal if the temptor was a private person rather than a government agent. Because the prior innocence of the defendant will not sustain the defense of entrapment, then, so the argument proceeds, the public policies of deterring unlawful police conduct and preserving the purity of the courts must be controlling. Those policies, it is concluded, are not effectuated by looking to the defendant's predisposition.

A second criticism of the subjective approach is that it creates, in effect, an "anything goes" rule for use against persons who can be shown by their prior convictions or otherwise to have been predisposed to engage in criminal behavior. This is because if the trier of fact determines that a defendant was predisposed to commit the type of crime charged, then no level of police deceit, badgering or other unsavory practices will be deemed impermissible. Such a result is unsound, it is argued, because it ignores "the possibility that no matter what his past crimes and general disposition the defendant might not have committed the particular crime unless confronted with inordinate inducements."[11] Moreover, so this reasoning proceeds, this notion that the permissible police conduct may vary according to the particular defendant is inconsistent with the objective of equality under the law.

Yet a third objection to the subjective approach is that delving into the defendant's character and predisposition not only "has often obscured the important task of judging the quality of police behavior,"[12] but also has prejudiced the defendant more generally. This is because once the entrapment defense is raised, certain usual evidentiary rules are discarded, and the defendant will be subjected to an "appropriate and searching inquiry into his own conduct and predisposition as bearing upon that issue."[13] This means a prosecutor may admit evidence of a prior criminal record, reputation evidence, acts of prior misconduct, and other information generally barred as hearsay or as being more prejudicial than probative.

(d) Objections to the Objective Approach. Proponents of the subjective approach have likewise raised various criticisms concerning the objective approach. One of them is that defendant's predisposition, at least if known by the police when the investigation in question was conducted, has an important bearing upon the question of whether the conduct of the police and their agents was proper. For example, if it is known that a particular suspect has sold drugs in the past, then it is proper to subject that person to more persuasive inducements than would be permissible as to an individual about whose predisposition the authorities know nothing. By like token, knowledge that a target has a weakness for a vice crime but is currently abstaining is also a fact that merits consideration when assessing an agent's conduct.

10. ALI Model Penal Code 19 (Tent.Draft No. 9, 1959).

11. Sherman v. United States, 356 U.S. 369, 78 S.Ct. 819, 2 L.Ed.2d 848 (1958) (Frankfurter, J., concurring).

12. ALI Model Penal Code 20 (Tent.Draft No. 9, 1959).

13. Sorrells v. United States, 287 U.S. 435, 53 S.Ct. 210, 77 L.Ed. 413 (1932).

Thus, the objective approach is said to be inherently defective because it eliminates entirely the need for considering a particular defendant's criminal predisposition.

A second major criticism of the objective approach is that the "wrong" people end up in jail if a dangerous, chronic offender may only be offered those inducements which might have tempted a hypothetical, law-abiding person. This is because, for example, the fact that the defendant in a particular case has been a shrewd, active member of a narcotics ring prior to and continuing through the incident in question is irrelevant under the objective test to a determination of the propriety of the inducements used. So the argument continues, to avoid this acquittal of wary criminals, courts are likely to allow agents substantial leeway in determining the limits of permissible inducement, with the result that this same freedom will allow the police to lead astray the unwary innocent.

Still another criticism directed at the objective approach to entrapment is that it will foster inaccuracy in the factfinding process. It is argued that the nature of the inducement offered in secret is a factual issue less susceptible to reliable proof than the issue of predisposition. This is because if a defendant claims that an inducement was improper, the agent can take the stand and rebut the allegations, resulting in a swearing match. Especially because the defense of entrapment ordinarily assumes an admission of guilt (unless inconsistent defenses are permitted), this means the factfinder will often have to make the imponderable choice between the testimony of an informer, often with a criminal record, and that of a defendant who has admittedly committed the criminal act.

A fourth objection relates to the public policy justifications of the objective approach. It is questioned whether the "purity" of the courts is itself a sufficient justification, and whether the objective approach can be expected to serve the deterrence objective in a meaningful way. Because courts are disinclined to adopt per se rules regarding what are impermissible police inducements, it is doubted whether there will actually result significant restrictions upon the types of inducements which police are entitled to utilize. Moreover, so the argument continues, even if such limitations are developed the police will still be left with the discretion to decide upon the context or target of encouragement activity. To this are added the familiar arguments against other attempts to deter the police, such as that they can be thwarted by police perjury or that they will be totally ineffective when the police are acting for objectives other than conviction. For all these reasons, this line of argument concludes, the deterrence objective should be dismissed in favor of an effort to do justice to the individual defendant in the particular case.

§ 5.3 Procedural Considerations

(a) Admissibility of Evidence of Defendant's Past Conduct. Entrapment, it has been said, is a "dangerous and judicially unpopular defense that should only be used in a few cases with ideal fact situations or in desperate circumstances where no other defense is possible." [1] This perceived danger is largely attributable to various procedural consequences which attend interposition of an entrapment defense where the majority, subjective approach is followed. And of the procedures which are relevant in this respect, certainly of primary importance is the readiness with which evidence of defendant's past conduct is received as bearing upon defendant's predisposition.

As the Supreme Court put it in *Sherman v. United States,*[2] under the subjective approach the prosecution may engage in a "'searching inquiry into [defendant's] own conduct and predisposition' as bearing on his claim of innocence." In most jurisdictions this means that once entrapment has been raised as a defense, the usual evidentiary rules are no longer followed. For the purported purpose

§ 5.3

1. Hardy, The Traps of Entrapment, 3 Am.J.Crim.L. 165 (1974).

2. 356 U.S. 369, 78 S.Ct. 819, 2 L.Ed.2d 848 (1958).

of allowing the factfinder access to all information bearing upon the "predisposition" issue, courts have allowed the receipt into evidence of defendant's prior convictions, prior arrests, and information about his "reputation" and even concerning "suspicious conduct" on his part. The result is that otherwise inadmissible hearsay, suspicion and rumor is brought into the case and the defendant, in effect, is put on trial for his past offenses and character.

This indiscriminate attitude toward predisposition evidence is by no means a necessary feature of the subjective test. This is because less prejudicial means of determining the readiness and willingness of a defendant to engage in the criminal conduct will often be available. The most promising alternative is testimony about the defendant's actions during the negotiations leading to the charged offense, such as his ready acquiescence, his expert knowledge about such criminal activity, his admissions of past deeds or future plans, and his ready access to the contraband. Another possibility is evidence obtained in a subsequent search or otherwise which shows that the defendant was involved in a course of ongoing criminal activity.

(b) Triable by Court or Jury. Traditionally, the entrapment defense has been regarded as a matter for the jury rather than for determination by the judge. (Even where this is unquestionably the case, the judge may rule on the sufficiency of the proof to raise the issue in the first place, and where uncontradicted evidence supports the conclusion that the defendant was entrapped the issue may of course be decided as a matter of law by the court.) Under the majority, subjective approach to entrapment, grounded upon the implied exception theory, it is apparent that "the issue of whether a defendant has been entrapped is for the jury as part of its function of determining the guilt or innocence of the accused."[3] In support of this state of affairs, it has been argued that determining matters of credibility and assessing the subjective response to the stimulus of police encouragement are peculiarly within the ken of the jury. Also, it has been observed that if the matter is placed in the hands of the jury there is an opportunity for jury nullification, meaning that "the jury, if it wishes, can acquit because of the moral revulsion which the police conduct evokes in them, notwithstanding any amount of convincing evidence of the defendant's predisposition."[4] On the other hand, the argument has been made that the case for putting the matter in the hands of the court is especially strong under the subjective approach. This is because where the rules of evidence on proving predisposition are very loose, which is usually the case, the defense can be raised only at great price to the defendant if that evidence becomes known to the jury.

Under the objective approach to entrapment, the judge-versus-jury issue is more evenly balanced. In favor of having the matter decided by the judge is the notion that it is the function of the court to preserve the purity of the court. Similarly, it may be said that to the extent the objective approach rests upon a deterrence-of-police rationale this function also is the proper responsibility of the court, just as it is when the court rules on suppression motions. And there is the added point made by Justice Frankfurter in *Sherman,* namely,

> that a jury verdict, although it may settle the issue of entrapment in the particular case, cannot give significant guidance for official conduct for the future. Only the court, through the gradual evolution of explicit standards in accumulated precedents, can do this with the degree of certainty that the wise administration of criminal justice demands.

Also, there is a sense in which trial of the issue before the judge would be to the state's advantage; the defendant would not be able to divert the jury's attention from his crime by attacking the police.

However, not all of the states which have adopted the objective approach submit the issue to the judge instead of the jury. In light

3. Sherman v. United States, 356 U.S. 369, 78 S.Ct. 819, 2 L.Ed.2d 848 (1958).

4. 1 National Comm'n on Reform of Federal Criminal Laws, Working Papers 324 (1970).

of the above considerations, it is not entirely clear why this is so. Perhaps the explanation is that the issue is deemed an appropriate one for the jury because the jury has particular competence on the question of what temptations would be too great for an ordinary law-abiding citizen.

(c) Inconsistent Defenses. The traditional view has been that the defense of entrapment is not available to one who denies commission of the criminal act with which he is charged, for the reason that the denial is inconsistent with the assertion of such a defense. However, a trend in the opposite direction appears to be developing, and there is much to be said in favor of this latter position. For one thing, it avoids serious constitutional questions concerning whether a defendant may be required, in effect, to surrender his presumption of innocence and his privilege against self-incrimination in order to plead entrapment. Also, it would seem that the adversary process is itself a sufficient restraint upon resort to positions which are truly inconsistent. In a case where two positions are unquestionably logically inconsistent, a defendant who pursued both positions would certainly be found to be lacking credibility.

The matter was settled in the federal courts by *Mathews v. United States,*[5] where the Supreme Court held that even if a defendant denies one or more elements of the crime, he is entitled to an entrapment instruction whenever there is sufficient evidence from which a reasonable jury could find entrapment. Such a result, the Court noted, squared with the fact that federal defendants were allowed to raise inconsistent defenses in other contexts. The Court found unpersuasive the government's claims "that allowing a defendant to rely on inconsistent defenses will encourage perjury, lead to jury confusion, and subvert the truthfinding function of the trial."

Even in jurisdictions where the traditional view persists, the defendant must be allowed to raise the defense of entrapment without admitting the crime whenever the circumstances are such that there is no inherent inconsistency between claiming entrapment and yet not admitting commission of the criminal acts. Thus, the inconsistency rule does not apply when the government in its own case in chief has interjected the issue of entrapment into the case. And if a defendant testifies that a government agent encouraged him to commit a crime which he had never contemplated before that time and that he resisted the temptation nonetheless, there is nothing internally inconsistent in thereby claiming entrapment and that the crime did not occur. Asserting the entrapment defense is not necessarily inconsistent with denial of the crime even when it is admitted that the requisite acts occurred, for the defendant might nonetheless claim that he lacked the requisite bad state of mind.

(d) Burden of Proof. In those jurisdictions which follow the majority, subjective approach to entrapment, it is generally accepted that the defendant has the burden of establishing the fact of inducement by a government agent. The extent of this burden is less than clear. Some courts require a defendant to sustain a burden of persuasion by proving government inducement by a preponderance of the evidence. Many courts, however, indicate that the defendant only has the burden of production, which can be met by coming forward with "some evidence" of government conduct which created a risk of persuading a nondisposed person to commit a crime. In any event, once the defendant's threshold responsibility is satisfied, the burden is then on the government to negate the defense by showing beyond a reasonable doubt defendant's predisposition.

In states where the objective approach is followed, the entire burden of production and persuasion is on the defendant, who must establish the impropriety of the police conduct by a preponderance of the evidence. This is a consequence of the entrapment defense under this approach being an "affirmative defense" rather than something which

5. 485 U.S. 58, 108 S.Ct. 883, 99 L.Ed.2d 54 (1988).

negatives the existence of an element of the crime charged. Such an allocation of the burden of proof might be questioned on the ground that as a general matter the government is in a much better position than the defendant to obtain and preserve evidence on the question of what kinds of government inducements were utilized in the particular case. This has led to the suggestion that perhaps the real basis for placing the burden of persuasion on the defendant is that entrapment is a disfavored defense, so that factual doubts should be resolved against it.

§ 5.4 Other Challenges to Encouragement Practices

(a) Contingent Fee Arrangements. From time to time the courts have given consideration to whether additional restraints upon encouragement practices by police and their agents are needed. The restraints considered in some respects resemble the entrapment defense, for they are also concerned with situations in which a government agent has induced a crime. But they are clearly different than the majority, subjective approach to entrapment, for these three restraints (if imposed) would protect even those defendants predisposed to commit the crime charged. They are also different in some respects from the objective approach to entrapment, though they share with it the purpose of deterring the police from improper practices.

One practice which has occasionally been a cause of concern is that of entering into a contingent fee arrangement with a person acting on behalf of the police to bring about commission of a crime by some other person. The compensation may be monetary, but frequently it takes the form of offers of leniency regarding charges pending against the informant. Depending upon the particular arrangement, contingent fee arrangements may provide the informant with an incentive to engage in unfair tactics and then misrepresent the nature of those tactics subsequently. If the contingency only involves providing a controlled opportunity to another person to engage in criminal conduct, then the incentive to employ unfair tactics may not be great. But if the compensation is contingent upon the subject's commission of a controlled offense, the informer's testimony about that commission in court, or the conviction of the subject for commission of that offense, then the risks of misrepresentation and unfair tactics substantially increase.

The landmark case on this subject is *Williamson v. United States,*[1] where federal agents told one Moye that they would give him $200 and $100, respectively, for legally admissible evidence that two specified persons were engaged in illicit liquor dealings. Moye made a purchase from one of them and produced evidence against both, for which he was paid the promised amount. Exercising its supervisory power over the administration of criminal justice in the federal courts, the court of appeals reversed the resulting conviction. The court explained:

> Without some * * * justification or explanation, we cannot sanction a contingent fee agreement to produce evidence against particular named defendants as to crimes not yet committed. Such an arrangement might tend to a "frame up," or to cause an informer to induce or persuade innocent persons to commit crimes which they had no previous intent or purpose to commit. The opportunities for abuse are too obvious to require elaboration.

While *Williamson* had broad potential, the case has actually had relatively little impact. Courts confronted with a *Williamson* claim have almost invariably been able to distinguish that case in some way. *Williamson* itself contains language supporting one such distinction, for it is indicated therein that a contingent fee would be permissible if the informant was carefully instructed about the distinction between permissible encouragement opportunities and impermissible entrapment. Moreover, *Williamson* has been deemed not controlling where there existed a special need for contingent fees due to the difficulty of the investigation or where the

§ 5.4

1. 311 F.2d 441 (5th Cir.1962).

informant was directed to a person as to whom the police already had a reasonable suspicion.

The *Williamson* case was, in effect, disapproved in *United States v. Grimes.*[2] The court there reasoned that a contingent fee informer is "no more likely to [lie and manufacture crimes] than witnesses acting for other, more common reasons," such as a codefendant hoping for leniency or an informant who feels that his future employment may depend upon his success on this occasion. Thus, it was held in *Grimes* that in all such circumstances the better rule is one which leaves "the entire matter to the jury to consider in weighing the credibility of the witness-informant." It may be questioned, however, whether that is a sufficient response to cases where the contingencies are likely to provide a strong incentive for overreaching and falsification, as where the fee is paid only upon conviction of the target of the investigation. But *Grimes* finds support in the Supreme Court's expressed unwillingness in *United States v. Russell*[3] to establish "fixed rules" of due process in the entrapment area or to give the federal judiciary "a 'chancellor's foot' veto" over law enforcement practices of which it disapproves.

(b) Inducements to Those Not Reasonably Suspected. It has sometimes been suggested that a government agent should not be permitted to solicit an offense absent at least "reasonable suspicion" that his target is engaged in such criminal activity. Thus, one commentator argues:

> To hold that government agents need no reasonable basis for selecting an individual as a target for inducement to commit a crime would be intolerable. The effect would be to give police officers untrammelled discretion to test the criminal propensities of any citizen.
>
> An imperfect analogy may be drawn to the Supreme Court's recent decision[4] that discretionary spot stops to check motorists' licenses and automobile registrations violate the fourth amendment unless the police officer has an articulable and reasonable suspicion that the law is being violated.[5]

Such a requirement would to some degree lend support to the entrapment doctrine's objective of ensuring that the police detect but not create crime. Its main thrust, however, would be to protect the interests of privacy and freedom from unreasonable intrusions.

Some authority is to be found that reasonable suspicion is an encouragement prerequisite, but most of the decisions on this issue have rejected this theory. *Russell* seems to have sapped it of any remaining vitality by indicating that the entrapment defense is intended to protect nondisposed defendants rather than to control police conduct. However, Operation Abscam has prompted renewed interest in this issue, for there a convicted swindler and other middlemen who were themselves under investigation decided which politicians would be offered bribes. It has been said that "Abscam shows [that the] central evil of entrapment is discriminatory law enforcement, whether the police zero in on a 'politician' or a 'drug dealer.'"[6] Thus the argument that the law should require that officers employing such temptations first obtain a warrant.

(c) Government "Overinvolvement" in a Criminal Enterprise. In *Sorrells v. United States*[7] and *Sherman v. United States,*[8] the entrapment doctrine was explained in terms of the presumed intention of Congress rather than as a matter of constitutional law. This means, of course, that Congress may depart from the *Sorrells–Sherman* test if it wishes, and that state courts and legislatures may do likewise. In short, the law of entrapment is not itself of constitutional dimension. But there remains for consideration the question

2. 438 F.2d 391 (6th Cir.1971).

3. 411 U.S. 423, 93 S.Ct. 1637, 36 L.Ed.2d 366 (1973).

4. The reference is to Delaware v. Prouse, 440 U.S. 648, 99 S.Ct. 1391, 59 L.Ed.2d 660 (1979).

5. Note, 67 Geo.L.J. 1455, 1471 (1979).

6. Chevigny, A Rejoinder, The Nation, Feb. 23, 1980, p. 205. But this contention has been rejected in the Abscam appeals. See, e.g., United States v. Myers, 692 F.2d 823 (2d Cir.1982); United States v. Jannotti, 673 F.2d 578 (3d Cir.1982).

7. 287 U.S. 435, 53 S.Ct. 210, 77 L.Ed. 413 (1932).

8. 356 U.S. 369, 78 S.Ct. 819, 2 L.Ed.2d 848 (1958).

of whether certain kinds of government involvement in a criminal enterprise would warrant the conclusion that the due process rights of the person induced had been violated.

In *United States v. Russell,*[9] an undercover agent supplied the defendant and his associates with 100 grams of propanone, an essential but difficult to obtain ingredient in the manufacture of methamphetamine ("speed"); the defendants used it to produce two batches of "speed," which pursuant to agreement the agent received half of in return. The defendant, convicted of unlawfully manufacturing and selling the substance, conceded on appeal that the jury could have found him predisposed, but claimed that the agent's involvement in the enterprise was so substantial that the prosecution violated due process. In particular, he contended that prosecution should be precluded when it is shown that the criminal conduct would not have been possible had not the agent "supplied an indispensable means to the commission of the crime that could not have been obtained otherwise, through legal or illegal channels." The Court in *Russell* found it unnecessary to pass on that contention because the record showed that propanone "was by no means impossible" to obtain by other sources. Though acknowledging that "we may some day be presented with a situation in which the conduct of law enforcement agents is so outrageous that due process principles would absolutely bar the government from invoking judicial processes to obtain a conviction," the majority concluded "the instant case is distinctly not of that breed" because the agent had simply supplied a legal and harmless substance to a person who had theretofore been "an active participant in an illegal drug manufacturing enterprise." Three dissenters urged adoption of the objective approach to entrapment and asserted that if propanone "had been wholly unobtainable from other sources" the agent's actions would be "conduct that constitutes entrapment under any definition."[10]

Then came *Hampton v. United States,*[11] where petitioner, convicted of distributing heroin, objected to the denial of his requested jury instruction that he must be acquitted if the narcotics he sold to government agents had earlier been supplied to him by a government informant. Three members of the Court concluded that the difference between the instant case and *Russell* was "one of degree, not of kind," in that here the government supplied an illegal substance which was the corpus delicti of petitioner's crime and thus "played a more significant role" in enabling the crime to occur. But such conduct as to a predisposed defendant was deemed not to violate due process. Significantly, two concurring Justices, while agreeing that "this case is controlled completely by *Russell,*" expressed their unwillingness "to join the plurality in concluding that, no matter what the circumstances, neither due process principles nor our supervisory power could support a bar to conviction in any case where the Government is able to prove disposition." The three dissenters[12] in *Hampton* urged that conviction be "barred as a matter of law where the subject of the criminal charge is the sale of contraband provided to the defendant by a Government agent." The instant case, they contended, was different from *Russell* because (i) here the supplied substance was contraband, and (ii) here the "beginning and end of this crime" coincided with the government's involvement. "The Government," they protested, "is doing nothing less than buying contraband from itself through an intermediary and jailing the intermediary."

Russell and *Hampton,* then, indicate that a majority of the Court accepts the notion that there may well be *some* circumstances in which a due process defense would be avail-

9. 411 U.S. 423, 93 S.Ct. 1637, 36 L.Ed.2d 366 (1973).

10. One of those dissenters also joined in another dissent by another member of the Court in which it was argued that whether the ingredient could be obtained from other sources was "quite irrelevant" and concluding: "Federal agents play a debased role when they become the instigators of the crime, or partners in its commission, or the creative brain behind the illegal scheme."

11. 425 U.S. 484, 96 S.Ct. 1646, 48 L.Ed.2d 113 (1976).

12. The ninth member of the Court, Stevens, J., took no part in the case.

able even to a defendant found to be predisposed. However, those two cases do not provide clear guidance as to how the police conduct is to be assessed in making this judgment, though they do justify the conclusion that instances of government conduct outrageous enough to violate due process will be exceedingly rare. Special note must thus be taken of *United States v. Twigg,*[13] apparently the first case since *Hampton* in which a defendant prevailed on a due process defense. Neville and Twigg were convicted of conspiracy to manufacture "speed." A government informer proposed to Neville that the laboratory be established, and Neville assumed responsibility for raising the capital and arranging for distribution, while the informer supplied the equipment, raw materials and laboratory site and was in complete charge of the lab because he alone had the expertise to manufacture the drug. Distinguishing *Russell* as a case in which the defendant was an active participant before the government agent appeared on the scene, and *Hampton* as concerned with "a much more fleeting and elusive crime to detect," the majority in *Twigg* concluded that the government involvement had reached "a demonstrable level of outrageousness." In reaching that conclusion, the court stressed (i) that "the illicit plan did not originate with the criminal defendants": (ii) that the informer's expertise was "an indispensable requisite to this criminal enterprise"; and (iii) that, "as far as the record reveals, [Neville] was lawfully and peaceably minding his own affairs" until approached by the informant.

Twigg thus suggests that the previously discussed "reasonable suspicion" prerequisite may on occasion emerge as an aspect of the due process limits upon encouragement activity. The point seems to be that over-involvement by the government to the extent reflected in *Twigg* is permissible, if at all, only against a person who is reasonably suspected of criminal conduct or design. The other important principle recognized in *Twigg* is that "the practicalities of combating" a certain type of criminal activity must be taken into account in determining whether "more extreme methods of investigation" are constitutionally permissible. However, there is reason to question the application of that sound principle in the *Twigg* case to conclude that more extreme methods are needed to detect drug distribution than drug manufacture.

13. 588 F.2d 373 (3d Cir.1978).

Chapter 6

INTERROGATION AND CONFESSIONS

Table of Sections

§ 6.1 Introduction and Overview

(a) The Need for Confessions. No area of constitutional criminal procedure has provoked more debate over the years than that dealing with police interrogation. In large measure, the debate has centered upon two fundamental questions: (1) how important are confessions in the process of solving crimes and convicting the perpetrators? and (2) what is the extent and nature of police abuse in seeking to obtain confessions from those suspected of crimes? Conclusive evidence on these two points is lacking, and thus it is not surprising that this debate continues.

An oft-quoted statement supporting the proposition that confessions are necessary in criminal investigation and prosecution is that of Justice Frankfurter in *Culombe v. Connecticut:* [1]

> Despite modern advances in the technology of crime detection, offenses frequently occur about which things cannot be made to speak. And where there cannot be found innocent human witnesses to such offenses, nothing remains—if police investigation is not to be balked before it has fairly begun—but to seek out possibly guilty witnesses and ask them questions, witnesses, that is, who are suspected of knowing something about the offense precisely because they are suspected of implication in it.

In elaboration of this position, a leading proponent of police interrogation as an investigative technique has presented forceful argument in support of these three points:

> 1. Many criminal cases, even when investigated by the best qualified police departments, are capable of solution only by means of an admission or confession from the guilty individual or upon the basis of information obtained from the questioning of other criminal suspects. * * *
>
> 2. Criminal offenders, except, of course, those caught in the commission of their crimes, ordinarily will not admit their guilt unless questioned under conditions of privacy, and for a period of perhaps several hours. * * *
>
> 3. In dealing with criminal offenders, and consequently also with criminal suspects who may actually be innocent, the interrogator must of necessity employ less refined methods than are considered appropriate for the transaction of ordinary, everyday affairs by and between law-abiding citizens.[2]

§ 6.1

1. 367 U.S. 568, 81 S.Ct. 1860, 6 L.Ed.2d 1037 (1961).

2. Inbau, Police Interrogation—A Practical Necessity, 52 J.Crim.L.C. & P.S. 16, 17, 19 (1961).

The major difficulty, however, is that of trying to quantify the first of these propositions. Statistics have occasionally been offered on one side of the argument or the other, but they are inconclusive. Those tending to show that confessions are offered into evidence in only a small fraction of criminal prosecutions for serious crimes hardly demonstrate that confessions are unimportant, for they do not show how many of the considerable number of cases disposed of by guilty plea were not contested precisely because the defendant had given a confession. As for statistics offered to show that confessions are frequently relied upon in criminal prosecutions, they also prove something other than the matter at issue; the fact a confession was obtained in a particular case and was tendered by the prosecutor at trial does not, standing alone, establish there existed a need in that instance to resort to interrogation. But even if we could fairly assess the availability of alternatives, there remains the question of whether interrogation is necessarily the most undesirable of the lot. Justice Goldberg answered this in the affirmative in *Escobedo v. Illinois* [3] when he declared "that a system of criminal law enforcement which comes to depend on the 'confession' will, in the long run, be less reliable and more subject to abuses than a system which depends on extrinsic evidence independently secured through skillful investigation." But this is not a proposition which is beyond dispute. Some forms of "extrinsic evidence," such as eyewitness identification, are also attended by serious risks of unreliability.

(b) The Extent of Police Abuse. As the Supreme Court noted in *Miranda v. Arizona*,[4] police interrogation "still takes place in privacy," which "results in secrecy and this in turn results in a gap in our knowledge as to what in fact goes on in the interrogation rooms." Because of this secrecy (for some a sufficient indication in itself of abuse), there is lacking sufficient empirical evidence to assert with confidence what always, usually, or often occurs in the course of police interrogation. This being so, attention has often turned to celebrated cases of confessions later proved false or to judicial opinions (including many Supreme Court decisions) revealing outrageous police tactics. Those favoring restrictions upon interrogation rely heavily upon these cases, while their opponents claim such incidents are extraordinary, having no relation to the ordinary day-to-day operations of the police.

Because complete factual data is lacking, it is not surprising that the participants in the confessions controversy have different perceptions of what occurs in interrogation rooms. But there does seem to be general agreement that the forms of illegality have become less extreme, in that the use of overt physical violence has largely given way to the employment of more subtle kinds of pressure. But to say, as was conceded in *Miranda*, that "the modern practice of in-custody interrogation is psychologically rather than physically oriented," is not to conclude that police abuse is nonexistent. It does complicate the assessment, however, because it thus becomes somewhat more difficult to determine exactly what ought to be encompassed within the term "abuse."

(c) The Supreme Court's Response. From 1936 to nearly thirty years later, the Supreme Court dealt with confessions admitted in state criminal proceedings in terms of the fundamental fairness required by the Fourteenth Amendment due process clause. A so-called "voluntariness" test, which depended upon the "totality of the circumstances," was used to determine whether the Constitution required exclusion of a confession. The dimensions of this test changed over the years as the Supreme Court's concerns about the interrogation process broadened. At first, the question was simply one of whether the methods used had produced an unreliable confession; then the Court undertook to deter unfair police interrogation practices even if they produced reliable statements; and still later the Court's decisions reflected concern with whether the interroga-

3. 378 U.S. 478, 84 S.Ct. 1758, 12 L.Ed.2d 977 (1964).

4. 384 U.S. 436, 86 S.Ct. 1602, 16 L.Ed.2d 694 (1966).

ted defendant had been substantially deprived of the choice whether or not to talk to the police. As the years passed, it became increasingly apparent that this test was most difficult to administer because it required a finding and appraisal of all relevant facts surrounding each challenged confession.

Essentially the same approach was used by the Supreme Court during this period on the infrequent occasions when confessions admitted in federal prosecutions were reviewed. In such instances, it might logically be thought that the Court was then relying upon the due process clause of the Fifth Amendment. However, the tendency was to refer to earlier holdings in which the basis of exclusion was the Fifth Amendment privilege against self-incrimination or a common law rule of evidence. Beginning in 1943, a confession obtained by federal officers and offered in a federal prosecution could also be excluded on the ground that it was received during a period of "unnecessary delay" in taking the arrested person before a judicial officer. Although these decisions were grounded upon the Court's supervisory power over the federal courts, most commentators viewed them as attempts by the Court to avoid the tremendous problems inherent in the due process voluntariness test, and there was some expectation that this so-called *McNabb–Mallory* rule would ultimately be rested upon a constitutional foundation and applied to the states. This did not come to pass; indeed, Congress enacted legislation which appears to have repealed this rule even on the federal level.

Perhaps the reason this did not come to pass was because subsequent decisions holding that there was a constitutional right to counsel at certain pretrial "critical stages" provided a better stepping stone. The anticipated move away from sole reliance upon the voluntariness test occurred in *Escobedo v. Illinois*,[5] suppressing the defendant's confession because it was obtained in violation of his right to counsel at the time of interrogation. *Escobedo* was a cautious step, for the holding was carefully limited to the unique facts of the case. It was generally assumed, however, that this newly established right to counsel in the police station would thereafter be expanded on a case-by-case basis. That did not occur, for in the now famous case of *Miranda v. Arizona*[6] the Court moved off in a different direction by relying instead upon the Fifth Amendment privilege against self-incrimination. But in recent years the Court has returned to the right-to-counsel theory as a means of deciding certain cases not amenable to easy resolution under *Miranda.*

In *Miranda,* the Court held that a person "deprived of his freedom of action in any significant way" could not be questioned unless he waived his rights after being advised (i) "that he has the right to remain silent"; (ii) "that anything said can and will be used against the individual in court"; (iii) "that he has the right to consult with a lawyer and to have the lawyer with him during interrogation"; and (iv) "that if he is indigent a lawyer will be appointed to represent him." Today *Miranda* is most often invoked in confession suppression hearings, and thus the emphasis in this Chapter is upon the basis and meaning of that decision.

This is not to suggest, however, that today the admissibility of an incriminating statement is determined only by application of the *Miranda* rules, for this most certainly is not the case. For one thing, there will be times when *Miranda* will not even be applicable, either because the defendant was not in custody or otherwise "deprived of his freedom of action in any significant way" or because the police did not engage in interrogation or its "functional equivalent." As for the right to counsel, it will be applicable only to those cases in which the statement was obtained after that right has attached, but in such cases it may be extremely important because, for example, police conduct can violate that right even if it does not constitute interrogation under *Miranda.* As for the "voluntariness" due process test, it is always worthy of consideration; it is possible that there has

5. 378 U.S. 478, 84 S.Ct. 1758, 12 L.Ed.2d 977 (1964).

6. 384 U.S. 436, 86 S.Ct. 1602, 16 L.Ed.2d 694 (1966).

been an effective waiver of *Miranda* rights followed by police conduct which made the subsequently given confession involuntary.

§ 6.2 The "Voluntariness" Test

(a) The Common Law Rule. Under the early common law, confessions were admissible at trial without any restrictions whatsoever, so that even an incriminating statement which had been obtained by torture was not excluded. But, some time prior to the middle of the eighteenth century English trial judges began placing restrictions on the admissibility of confessions. Sometimes the question was put in terms of whether the defendant's confession had been induced by a promise of benefit or threat of harm, while on other occasions the inquiry was more directly put in terms of whether the circumstances under which the defendant had spoken impaired the reliability of the confession. But it became more common for the courts simply to ask whether the confession had been made "voluntarily," that is, without certain improper inducements. These included actual or threatened physical harm, a promise not to prosecute, a promise to provide lenient treatment upon conviction, and deceptive practices so extreme that they might have produced a false confession (not merely using a fellow prisoner as an undercover agent or misleading the defendant as to the strength of the case against him). There was no attempt to assess the effect of an inducement on a particular suspect.

The Supreme Court's early decisions on the admissibility of confessions in federal courts relied upon the common law rule. The rule was stated by the Court in terms of whether there had been such an inducement that "the presumption upon which weight is given to such evidence, namely, that one who is innocent will not imperil his safety or prejudice his interests by an untrue statement, ceases." [1] In the 1897 case of *Bram v. United States*,[2] the Court appeared to base exclusion upon violation of the Fifth Amendment privilege against self-incrimination, but the Court later pulled back from that position.[3] Nonetheless, *Bram* influenced the Court to state the rule of exclusion more broadly, so that it was not merely a matter of whether the confession was reliable or whether a forbidden inducement had been used, but rather whether the confession "was, in fact, voluntarily made." [4] So expanded, the common law standard merged into the definition of due process voluntariness developed in the state court cases subsequently decided by the Court.

(b) Due Process and the "Complex of Values." It was not until *Brown v. Mississippi* [5] that the Court barred the use of a confession in the state courts. It could not, of course, dispose of the state confession on the same grounds as were resorted to in the earlier cases. Under our federal system, the Supreme Court may not proscribe mere rules of evidence for the states, and the Fifth Amendment privilege was then not deemed applicable to the states.[6] Thus the confessions in *Brown*, obtained by brutally beating the suspects, were struck down on the notion that interrogation is part of the process by which a state procures a conviction and thus is subject to the requirements of the Fourteenth Amendment due process clause. Though *Brown* declared that due process was violated when a conviction was rested "solely" upon a confession so obtained, later cases made it clear that the mere use at trial of such a confession was unconstitutional.[7]

§ 6.2

1. Hopt v. Utah, 110 U.S. 574, 4 S.Ct. 202, 28 L.Ed. 262 (1884).

2. 168 U.S. 532, 18 S.Ct. 183, 42 L.Ed. 568 (1897).

3. Thus in United States v. Carignan, 342 U.S. 36, 72 S.Ct. 97, 96 L.Ed. 48 (1951), the Court expressed doubt about "[w]hether involuntary confessions are excluded from federal criminal trials on the ground of a violation of the Fifth Amendment's protection against self-incrimination, or from a rule that forced confessions are untrustworthy."

4. Ziang Sung Wan v. United States, 266 U.S. 1, 45 S.Ct. 1, 69 L.Ed. 131 (1924).

5. 297 U.S. 278, 56 S.Ct. 461, 80 L.Ed. 682 (1936).

6. Twining v. New Jersey, 211 U.S. 78, 29 S.Ct. 14, 53 L.Ed. 97 (1908), overruled by Malloy v. Hogan, 378 U.S. 1, 84 S.Ct. 1489, 12 L.Ed.2d 653 (1964).

7. Payne v. Arkansas, 356 U.S. 560, 78 S.Ct. 844, 2 L.Ed.2d 975 (1958). On whether admission of such a confession can ever qualify as harmless error, see § 26.-6(d).

This due process test is customarily referred to as the "voluntariness" requirement, the term frequently used by the Court in enunciating the due process requisites for admissibility.[8] But that term is not at all helpful in determining the policies which underlie this particular constitutional limitation. As the Court candidly put it in *Blackburn v. Alabama,*[9] "a complex of values underlies the stricture against use by the state of confessions which, by way of convenient shorthand, this Court terms involuntary." A closer examination of the Court's decisions in this area over the years reflects three important values deserving specific mention.

In *Brown,* the confessions clearly were of doubtful reliability, and thus that case might be read as announcing a due process test for excluding confessions obtained under circumstances presenting a fair risk that the statements are false. Concern with this risk was emphasized in several subsequent cases, and this led many state courts to the conclusion that unfairness in violation of due process exists when a confession is obtained under circumstances affecting its testimonial trustworthiness. But, while ensuring the reliability of confessions is a goal under the due process voluntariness standard, it is incorrect to define the standard in terms of that one objective. In *Rogers v. Richmond,*[10] defendant's confession was obtained after the police pretended to order his ailing wife arrested for questioning, and the state court had ruled that the statement need not be excluded "if the artifice or deception was not calculated to procure an untrue statement." The Supreme Court disagreed, emphasizing that convictions based upon coerced confessions must be overturned "not because such confessions are unlikely to be true but because the methods used to extract them offend an underlying principle in the enforcement of our criminal law: that ours is an accusatorial and not an inquisitorial system." *Rogers* thus made certain what had been strongly intimated in several earlier cases, namely, that the due process exclusionary rule for confessions (in much the same way as the Fourth Amendment exclusionary rule for physical evidence) is also intended to deter improper police conduct.

In *Townsend v. Sain,*[11] the ailing defendant had been given a drug with the properties of a truth serum, after which he gave a confession in response to questioning by police who were unaware of the drug's effect. Although the confession was not obtained by conscious police wrongdoing and apparently was reliable, the Court nonetheless held its use impermissible: "Any questioning by police officers which *in fact* produces a confession which is not the product of free intellect renders that confession inadmissible." *Townsend* thus highlights another theme which runs through many of the earlier cases: the confession must be a product of the defendant's "free and rational choice." This phrase, however, was not used in an absolute sense, but rather in conjunction with a recognized need to exert some pressure to obtain confessions. As the Court seems to have acknowledged in *Miranda v. Arizona,*[12] the question of whether a confession was "voluntary" had theretofore been determined by a lesser standard than, say, the question of whether a testator's will was his voluntary act.

Viewing the voluntariness test in terms of its underlying values, then, it may be said that the objective of the test is to bar admission of those confessions (i) which are of doubtful reliability because of the practices used to obtain them; (ii) which were obtained by offensive police practices even if reliability is not in question (for example, where there is strong corroborating evidence); or (iii) which were obtained under circumstances in which the defendant's free choice was significantly impaired, even if the police did not resort to offensive practices.

8. E.g., Watts v. Indiana, 338 U.S. 49, 69 S.Ct. 1347, 93 L.Ed. 1801 (1949).

9. 361 U.S. 199, 80 S.Ct. 274, 4 L.Ed.2d 242 (1960).

10. 365 U.S. 534, 81 S.Ct. 735, 5 L.Ed.2d 760 (1961).

11. 372 U.S. 293, 83 S.Ct. 745, 9 L.Ed.2d 770 (1963).

12. 384 U.S. 436, 86 S.Ct. 1602, 16 L.Ed.2d 694 (1966).

But in *Colorado v. Connelly*[13] the Court in effect denied the existence of the third category listed above, holding that the state court had erred in excluding a confession volunteered to police by a defendant who suffered from a psychosis that interfered with his ability to make free and rational choices. Absent "the crucial element of police overreaching," the Court reasoned, "there is simply no basis for concluding that any state actor has deprived a criminal defendant of due process." *Townsend* was distinguished as a case involving "police wrongdoing" in questioning a person who had been given a truth serum, though in fact the Supreme Court in that earlier case proceeded on the assumption that neither the police doctor who administered the drug nor the police who did the questioning were aware of the drug's truth serum character. *Connelly* is grounded in the notion that "state action" beyond merely receiving defendant's confession into evidence is necessary, that at a minimum there must be "police conduct causally related to the confession," and that this conduct must be "coercive" (such as exploiting defendant's deficient mental condition).

(c) Relevant Factors in the "Totality of Circumstances." The Fourteenth Amendment due process voluntariness test requires examination of the "totality of circumstances"[14] surrounding each confession. As a general matter, this means that it is necessary to assess the characteristics and status of the person who gave the confession and also the conduct of the police in obtaining it. But if the conduct of the police was "inherently coercive,"[15] then suppression in the interest of deterring such conduct in future cases is appropriate without first making any judgment about the impact of that conduct upon the particular defendant. On the other hand, when the question comes down to whether *this* defendant's free choice was substantially impaired, then any facts which tend to show that he is more or less susceptible to pressures than the average person are particularly relevant.

A significant number of the confession cases which have reached the Supreme Court have involved actual or threatened physical brutality or deprivation, such as whipping or slapping the suspect, depriving him of food or water or sleep, keeping him in a naked state or in a small cell, holding a gun to his head or threatening him with mob violence. When such outrageous conduct is present "there is no need to weigh or measure its effects on the will of the individual victim." Another very important consideration is whether the defendant was subjected to extended periods of incommunicado interrogation. Of particular significance in this regard is whether the suspect was subjected to lengthy and uninterrupted interrogation, whether he was kept in confinement an extended period of time even though subjected only to intermittent questioning, whether he was moved from place to place and questioned by different persons so as to be disoriented, whether he was questioned in solitary confinement or at some isolated place away from the jail, and whether he was held incommunicado up until the time of the confession (especially if family, friends or counsel were turned away). Under the more extreme of these circumstances, such as where there have been a couple of weeks of uninterrupted detention or virtual nonstop interrogation for 36 hours, the situation is "inherently coercive" and suppression of the confession is mandated.

In *Bram v. United States*,[16] the Court declared that a confession "obtained by any direct or implied promises, however slight," is not voluntary. Illustrative are *Rogers v. Richmond*,[17] holding defendant's confession was coerced where it was obtained in response to a police threat to take defendant's wife into

13. 479 U.S. 157, 107 S.Ct. 515, 93 L.Ed.2d 473 (1986).

14. Haynes v. Washington, 373 U.S. 503, 83 S.Ct. 1336, 10 L.Ed.2d 513 (1963).

15. Ashcraft v. Tennessee, 322 U.S. 143, 64 S.Ct. 921, 88 L.Ed. 1192 (1944).

16. 168 U.S. 532, 18 S.Ct. 183, 42 L.Ed. 568 (1897).

17. 365 U.S. 534, 81 S.Ct. 735, 5 L.Ed.2d 760 (1961).

custody, and *Lynumn v. Illinois*,[18] deciding that the confession was coerced where defendant was told she could lose her welfare payments and the custody of her children but that if she cooperated the police would help her and recommend leniency. Similarly, lower courts have often held that a confession is involuntary if made in response to a promise that the result will be nonprosecution, the dropping of some charges, or a certain reduction in the punishment defendant may receive. However, merely promising to bring defendant's cooperation to the attention of the prosecutor is not objectionable, nor is a promise that if defendant confesses the prosecutor would discuss leniency. Also, more generalized assurances that assistance will be sought, or that certain facilities are available are not inherently coercive. There is also authority that promises of leniency are not objectionable when made in response to solicitation by the accused. The cases go both ways on the question of what the result should be when a confession has been obtained in response to a police assertion that cooperation would facilitate prompt release on bail or would mean that the defendant would fare better in subsequent proceedings. In the latter situation, the difficulty is in attempting to reconcile the voluntariness requirement with the plea bargaining process and especially the role of the police in that practice. A mere threat to take action which would be lawful and necessary absent cooperation (e.g., to obtain a warrant) is not objectionable.

The Court in *Bram* also stated that a confession was involuntary if obtained by any other "improper influence," but the courts have not had an easy time in trying to resolve what other police conduct deserves to be so characterized. This is particularly true with respect to police trickery and deception. Although dictum in *Miranda v. Arizona*[19] was highly critical of such activity, as a general matter it may be said that the courts have not deemed such conduct sufficient by itself to make a confession involuntary. One type of trickery involves misrepresenting to the suspect the strength of the existing case against him, as in *Frazier v. Cupp*.[20] During the interrogation of Frazier concerning a homicide, the police told him that his cousin Rawls, with whom he had been on the evening in question, had been brought in and had already confessed. The Court concluded that the "fact that the police misrepresented the statements that Rawls made is, while relevant, insufficient in our view to make this otherwise voluntary confession inadmissible." Similarly, lower courts have held confessions admissible when they were prompted by such misrepresentations as that the murder victim was still alive, that nonexistent witnesses have been found, that the murder weapon had been uncovered, that defendant's prints were found at the crime scene, and that an accomplice had confessed and implicated the defendant. Courts are much less likely to tolerate misrepresentations of law, such as that defendant's confession could not be used against him at trial or that the previously obtained confession of an accomplice could be so used.

Another type of deceit is the so-called "false friend" technique, whereby the interrogator represents that he is a friend acting in the suspect's best interest. Extreme versions of this technique have been condemned by the Supreme Court. In *Leyra v. Denno*[21] a confession was held involuntary where obtained by a police psychiatrist who was represented as a general practitioner brought in to relieve defendant's acutely painful sinus attack, and in *Spano v. New York*[22] a confession was ruled involuntary where obtained by a policeman who was a close friend of the defendant and who told defendant he would be in trouble unless defendant confessed. Dictum in the *Miranda* case was critical of the "Mutt and Jeff" routine, whereby the defendant is questioned by a hostile interrogator and then a supposedly sympathetic one. But the courts have not generally disapproved of the police

18. 372 U.S. 528, 83 S.Ct. 917, 9 L.Ed.2d 922 (1963).

19. 384 U.S. 436, 86 S.Ct. 1602, 16 L.Ed.2d 694 (1966).

20. 394 U.S. 731, 89 S.Ct. 1420, 22 L.Ed.2d 684 (1969).

21. 347 U.S. 556, 74 S.Ct. 716, 98 L.Ed. 948 (1954).

22. 360 U.S. 315, 79 S.Ct. 1202, 3 L.Ed.2d 1265 (1959).

giving "friendly" advice to the defendant or expressing sympathy for him. A quite different kind of "false friend" situation, that in which by deception the defendant is made unaware that the person with whom he is conversing is a police officer or police agent, clearly does not make the defendant's statement involuntary even though he acted in the mistaken impression that this person could be trusted not to reveal it. Police appeals to the defendant's sympathies, such as by the now-famous "Christian burial speech" ploy, do not automatically render a confession involuntary, and the same is true of exhortations to tell the truth or assertions that the suspect had been lying.

Under the *Miranda* case, certain warnings must precede custodial interrogation, and this means a failure to give those warnings will result in exclusion of the confession under that decision. Nonetheless, on occasion the question may arise as to the relevance of the absence of such warnings to the voluntariness issue. This can occur when the confession at issue (i) was obtained prior to the *Miranda* decision,[23] (ii) was obtained from a suspect not in custody and thus not covered by *Miranda,* or (iii) is admissible for a special purpose if voluntary notwithstanding the *Miranda* violation.[24] As the Court put it in *Procunier v. Atchley,*[25] failure to give the warnings is not inherently coercive, but is "relevant only in establishing a setting in which actual coercion might have been exerted." On the other hand, the fact the warnings were given is an important factor tending in the direction of a voluntariness finding. This fact is important in two respects. It bears on the coerciveness of the circumstances, for it reveals that the police were aware of the suspect's rights and presumably prepared to honor them. And, as with the factors discussed below, it bears upon the defendant's susceptibility, for it shows that the defendant was aware he had a right not to talk to the police.

Especially in an otherwise close case, it is appropriate also to take account of the particular characteristics of the person who was subjected to interrogation, in order to judge the extent of his ability to resist the external pressures brought to bear upon him. The Supreme Court has taken into consideration the suspect's age, sex, and race whenever those factors have tended to indicate less than average ability to resist. Likewise relevant is the fact that the defendant might have been more willing to confess because he was suffering from a physical injury, physical illness, physical fatigue, mental illness, mental deficiency, or an abnormality caused by drugs or alcohol. Courts have also taken into account the suspect's education level, and his prior experience with the police. But *Connelly,* discussed above, makes it clear that such characteristics of the defendant, in isolation, cannot alone "ever dispose of the inquiry into constitutional 'voluntariness.'" Thus, as the Court in *Connelly* elaborated, "while mental condition is surely relevant to an individual's susceptibility to police coercion, mere examination of the confessant's state of mind can never conclude the due process inquiry."

Connelly says there must also exist "the crucial element of police overreaching," which was not present in that case because the police merely received the confession of a person who approached them and volunteered it. *Connelly* thus leaves uncertain how the "overreaching" judgment is to be made in the more typical interrogation situation. There is a split of authority as to whether the very act of interrogating one known to be under a substantial mental disability supplies the requisite coercion. It would seem, however, that the propriety of the investigative and interrogation techniques used must be judged in light of what the police knew or should have known about defendant's ability to comprehend the events and circumstances.

(d) Critique of the "Voluntariness" Test. One major defect in the due process "volun-

23. *Miranda* applies only to cases in which the trial began after the date of that decision. Johnson v. New Jersey, 384 U.S. 719, 86 S.Ct. 1772, 16 L.Ed.2d 882 (1966).

24. As when the confession is offered for impeachment purposes. See § 9.6(a).

25. 400 U.S. 446, 91 S.Ct. 485, 27 L.Ed.2d 524 (1971).

tariness" test is that it leaves the police without needed guidance. This is in part attributable to the fact that the term itself is imprecise. Virtually all incriminating statements—even those made under brutal treatment—are "voluntary" in the sense of representing a choice of alternatives, yet very few are "voluntary" in the sense that they would have been given even absent official pressure of some kind. Moreover, a standard which varies from case to case depending upon how dull or alert or how soft or tough the particular suspect happened to be was not likely to have much of an impact upon the police.

Secondly, the due process standard impaired the effectiveness and the legitimacy of judicial review. Because of the aforementioned ambiguity, even conscientious trial judges were left without guidance for resolving confession claims. Moreover, the nature of the voluntariness test virtually invited judges to give weight to their subjective preferences. The "totality of circumstances" approach of the Supreme Court both facilitated pro-police rulings at suppression hearings and diminished the chances that the defendant would obtain relief at the appellate level. And the Supreme Court, which took only about one confession case a year during the heyday of the voluntariness test, was able to deal only with the tip of the iceberg. Perhaps the strongest evidence of the ineffectiveness and the unworkability of the voluntariness test is *Davis v. North Carolina.*[26] No one other than the police had spoken to the defendant during the sixteen days of detention and interrogation which preceded his confessions, and in holding the confessions involuntary the Court noted it had "never sustained the use of a confession obtained after such a lengthy period of detention and interrogation as was involved in this case." Yet two state courts and two federal courts had previously held that these confessions were lawfully admitted into evidence against Davis.

Davis was an unusual confession case in that the relevant facts clearly appeared on the record and were uncontested. The more typical case is one in which there is a "swearing contest" over what happened behind closed doors, and thus a third major defect in the due process voluntariness test is that its application is fatally dependent upon resolution of that swearing contest. In the usual case, it is impossible to determine whether the "facts" asserted by the police or those put forward by the defendant more closely correspond to the events that actually occurred in the interrogation room.

These circumstances explain why the Supreme Court undertook the search, discussed in the balance of this Chapter, for alternative means to deal with the confessions problem.

§ 6.3 The Prompt Appearance Requirement

(a) The *McNabb–Mallory* Rule. The previously discussed voluntariness test was, of course, equally applicable to confessions utilized in federal prosecutions, for any confession inadmissible because obtained in violation of the Fourteenth Amendment due process clause would likewise be subject to suppression under the Fifth Amendment due process clause. Beginning in 1943, however, the Supreme Court developed another line of authority, not expressly grounded in the Constitution, which was frequently utilized in federal criminal prosecutions. Under what became known as the *McNabb–Mallory* rule, the Court required the suppression of any confession obtained during custody which was illegal by virtue of a failure to honor a defendant's right to be brought promptly before a judicial officer following his arrest. This rule provided a basis for suppressing many confessions which, upon closer examination of the circumstances, might have been found to be excludable as a matter of due process, but it clearly extended to other confessions as well.

The rule had an uncertain beginning in McNabb v. United States,[1] a case involving the murder of a federal revenue agent during a raid on an illegal still. Several uneducated

26. 384 U.S. 737, 86 S.Ct. 1761, 16 L.Ed.2d 895 (1966).

§ 6.3

1. 318 U.S. 332, 63 S.Ct. 608, 87 L.Ed. 819 (1943).

mountaineers were arrested late at night and were subjected intermittently to prolonged questioning over the next several days, resulting in confessions by three of them. The confessions were admitted as voluntary and the defendants were convicted. But the Supreme Court found it "unnecessary to reach the Constitutional issue pressed upon us" because the case could be resolved by the Court's "exercise of its supervisory authority over the administration of criminal justice in the federal courts." Specifically, because the record did not show that the confessing defendants had been taken before a judicial officer in a timely fashion as required by federal law, the Court concluded the convictions

> cannot be allowed to stand without making the courts themselves accomplices in wilful disobedience of law. Congress has not explicitly forbidden the use of evidence so procured. But to permit such evidence to be made the basis of a conviction in the federal courts would stultify the policy which Congress has enacted into law.

Because the Court in *McNabb* repeatedly stressed the "circumstances disclosed here," such as that the defendants were uneducated, and at another point asserted that a conviction could not stand when based on evidence obtained in "flagrant disregard of the procedure which Congress has commanded," it was by no means clear that the decision required suppression of any confession obtained in violation of the prompt appearance statute. But in the later case of *Upshaw v. United States*[2] the Court flatly stated that "a confession is inadmissible if made during illegal detention due to failure promptly to carry a prisoner before a committing magistrate." Then, finally, came *Mallory v. United States*,[3] in which a unanimous Court held that a confession was inadmissible because procured in violation of a provision in the federal rules[4] (not extant when *McNabb* was decided) to the effect that an arrested person must be taken before a committing magistrate "without unnecessary delay."

Mallory is also important because it contains the Court's most detailed discussion of what constitutes "unnecessary delay":

> The police may not arrest upon mere suspicion but only on "probable cause." The next step in the proceeding is to arraign the arrested person before a judicial officer as quickly as possible so that he may be advised of his rights and so that the issue of probable cause may be promptly determined. The arrested person may, of course, be "booked" by the police. But he is not to be taken to police headquarters in order to carry out a process of inquiry that lends itself, even if not so designed, to eliciting damaging statements to support the arrest and ultimately his guilt.
>
> The duty enjoined upon arresting officers to arraign "without unnecessary delay" indicates that the command does not call for mechanical or automatic obedience. Circumstances may justify a brief delay between arrest and arraignment, as for instance, where the story volunteered by the accused is susceptible of quick verification through third parties. But the delay must not be of a nature to give opportunity for the extraction of a confession. * * *
>
> In every case where the police resort to interrogation of an arrested person and secure a confession, they may well claim, and quite sincerely, that they were merely trying to check on the information given by him.

Lower courts have ordinarily treated the *McNabb–Mallory* rule as less than an absolute prohibition upon pre-appearance interrogation or upon delays in bringing an arrestee before a magistrate. Questioning has been allowed in "threshold" situations (i.e., shortly after arrest at the arrest scene, in the squad car, or at the station), in circumstances where it was intended to clarify or verify a story given earlier by the defendant, and even in other circumstances in which the interrogation was characterized as "investigatory." Delays in taking the defendant before a magistrate have been deemed not "unnecessary" where attributable to the unavailability of a magistrate outside of normal hours, the book-

2. 335 U.S. 410, 69 S.Ct. 170, 93 L.Ed. 100 (1948).

3. 354 U.S. 449, 77 S.Ct. 1356, 1 L.Ed.2d 1479 (1957).

4. Fed.R.Crim.P. 5(a).

ing process, efforts to apprehend defendant's confederates, efforts to confirm information through independent sources, cooperation of the defendant with the police, or efforts by the police to reduce an oral confession to written form.

Early Supreme Court decisions marked other important limits upon this particular exclusionary rule, namely: a confession obtained during a period of lawful detention is not subject to suppression merely because of a subsequent failure promptly to take the confessing defendant before a magistrate;[5] at least absent a showing that a subterfuge was involved, a confession for one crime is not subject to suppression where it was obtained upon remand of defendant to the police following his prompt appearance before a magistrate on a different (even lesser) charge;[6] and a confession obtained by federal agents from a defendant in state custody is not subject to suppression even where exclusion would have been required if the custody had been federal, unless it appears there was a "working arrangement" between state and federal officials.[7] And in the post-*Mallory* case of *Cleary v. Bolger*[8] the Court, stressing the traditional reluctance of federal courts to interfere with state proceedings, held it was improper for a federal court to enjoin a state official from testifying at a state criminal trial about his witnessing of a confession which would have been inadmissible in federal court under *McNabb–Mallory*.

(b) Reactions to the Rule. Reactions to the *McNabb–Mallory* rule over the years have been mixed. On the one hand, some see the prompt appearance requirement coupled with an exclusionary sanction as serving several worthwhile functions: it prevents wholesale or dragnet arrests on suspicion, gives force to the notion that an arrest (even on probable cause) is not properly a vehicle for the investigation of crime, and ensures that the substance of the accusatorial system is preserved. But of greatest significance here is the notion that this rule is intimately related to the problem of eliminating the third degree, in that use of coercion to obtain confessions most frequently occurs while the defendant is being held in violation of a prompt appearance statute. The *McNabb–Mallory* rule was thus seen as an outgrowth of the Court's awareness of the tremendous problems of proof raised by the "coerced confession" issue, which meant to some that there was a need for something like it to govern state confession cases.

Those generally opposed to the exclusion of evidence as a means of deterring the police saw *McNabb–Mallory* as another instance of an unsound judicial policy which turns criminals loose as a means of punishing the police. Others objected to the rule on the ground that it unwisely tended to "collapse" the arrest and charging decisions and to prevent even fair questioning intended to determine whether a person lawfully arrested should be charged. Such views prompted repeated efforts to have Congress either repeal or revise the *McNabb–Mallory* rule. This was finally accomplished as a part of the Omnibus Crime Control and Safe Streets Act of 1968. One provision states that a voluntary confession "shall not be inadmissible solely because of delay" in bringing the person before a magistrate "if such confession was made or given by such person within six hours immediately following his arrest or other detention," to which there is added the proviso that this time limitation "shall not apply in any case in which the delay in bringing such person before such magistrate or other officer beyond such six-hour period is found by the trial judge to be reasonable considering the means of transportation and the distance to be traveled to the nearest available such magistrate or other officer."[9] Though that language would seem to restrict the *McNabb–Mallory* rule to confessions obtained after the six-hour period and reasonable extensions thereof, yet

5. United States v. Mitchell, 322 U.S. 65, 64 S.Ct. 896, 88 L.Ed. 1140 (1944).

6. United States v. Carignan, 342 U.S. 36, 72 S.Ct. 97, 96 L.Ed. 48 (1951).

7. Anderson v. United States, 318 U.S. 350, 63 S.Ct. 599, 87 L.Ed. 829 (1943).

8. 371 U.S. 392, 83 S.Ct. 385, 9 L.Ed.2d 390 (1963).

9. 18 U.S.C.A. § 3501(c).

another provision declares that any confession shall be admissible in a federal prosecution "if it is voluntarily given" [10] and that delay in appearance before a magistrate is but one of several factors "to be taken into consideration by the judge" but which "need not be conclusive on the issue of voluntariness." [11] This provision has been construed to mean that there is no per se rule of exclusion merely because of impermissible delay.

(c) Prompt Appearance in the States. Early on in the development of the *McNabb–Mallory* rule, the Supreme Court held that it was not constitutionally mandated and that consequently it was not applicable to trials in the state courts.[12] Although, as noted above, some have praised the rule as a means of dealing with an issue of constitutional magnitude—the coerced confession problem, it does not now seem at all likely that the Court will impose such a rule upon the states. But prompt appearance is a common if not universal requirement under state law, and thus there remains the possibility that a state might adopt an exclusionary rule as a means of enforcing that requirement.

The vast majority of state courts passing on the question have rejected the *McNabb–Mallory* approach outright, opting instead for the traditional due process voluntariness test. But there are now at least half a dozen states which follow the *McNabb–Mallory* approach in some respect. Some states utilize a per se rule of exclusion, while others require a showing of a causal connection between the illegal delay and the challenged confession. The wisdom of this development at the state level is a matter of dispute, and involves much the same considerations noted above regarding the *McNabb–Mallory* debate. It has been argued, however, that the case for this approach is now less substantial than it once was because the Supreme Court has in the interim provided other effective means for safeguarding the vital Fourth and Fifth Amendment interests which the *McNabb–Mallory* rule was intended to protect.

§ 6.4 The Right to Counsel

(a) Pre–*Massiah* Developments. Under the "totality of circumstances" approach to the due process voluntariness test, the Court began making special note of the fact that the confessing defendant had been denied access to counsel,[1] and thus this deprivation plus other circumstances could mean that the defendant's confession was involuntary. By the late 1950's, however, a minority of the Court was actually asserting that a suspect had a constitutional right to have counsel present during police interrogation.

In *Crooker v. California*,[2] the petitioner claimed his voluntary confession should be suppressed because obtained after the police denied his specific request to contact his lawyer. The majority rejected this contention, asserting that such a rule "would effectively preclude police questioning—*fair as well as unfair*—until the accused was afforded opportunity to call his attorney," and found support in the *Betts v. Brady* [3] rule that due process did not impose a flat requirement of appointed counsel in all serious state trials. But the four dissenters declared that as a matter of due process "the accused who wants a counsel should have one at any time after the moment of arrest."

A year later came *Spano v. New York*,[4] where, after an indicted defendant surrendered with his retained attorney, police questioned him and obtained a confession. The opinion of the Court by the Chief Justice concluding the confession was not voluntary emphasized numerous factors, including that the police "ignored his reasonable requests to

10. 18 U.S.C.A. § 3501(a).

11. 18 U.S.C.A. § 3501(b).

12. Gallegos v. Nebraska, 342 U.S. 55, 72 S.Ct. 141, 96 L.Ed. 86 (1951).

§ 6.4

1. Harris v. South Carolina, 338 U.S. 68, 69 S.Ct. 1354, 93 L.Ed. 1815 (1949); Haley v. Ohio, 332 U.S. 596, 68 S.Ct. 302, 92 L.Ed. 224 (1948); Malinski v. New York, 324 U.S. 401, 65 S.Ct. 781, 89 L.Ed. 1029 (1945).

2. 357 U.S. 433, 78 S.Ct. 1287, 2 L.Ed.2d 1448 (1958).

3. 316 U.S. 455, 62 S.Ct. 1252, 86 L.Ed. 1595 (1942).

4. 360 U.S. 315, 79 S.Ct. 1202, 3 L.Ed.2d 1265 (1959).

contact the local attorney whom he had already retained." However, four concurring Justices accepted the defendant's contention that his absolute right to counsel (defendant had been indicted on a capital charge and thus did not fall under the *Betts* rule) had attached prior to his interrogation, as he had already been indicted for murder and the police had thus not been involved in the questioning of a suspect in the course of investigating an unsolved crime. Because a year earlier the Chief Justice had taken the position that the right to counsel should begin even earlier, it appeared that the position taken by the *Spano* concurring Justices commanded a majority of the Court.

Several cases decided in 1963 strengthened the assumption that there was now a right to counsel at post-indictment interrogation. One was *White v. Maryland,*[5] holding that the absolute right to counsel in a capital case was applicable at defendant's preliminary arraignment where he entered a guilty plea which, though subsequently withdrawn, was later introduced into evidence against him. Because *White* concerned the evidentiary use of White's uncounseled plea of guilty, a problem not greatly different from the use of an uncounseled confession, and because it recognized a pretrial right to a lawyer who would have helped only to avoid making incriminating evidence available, the decision seemed quite relevant. *White* took on even greater significance when *Betts* was overruled in *Gideon v. Wainwright,*[6] holding that the absolute right to counsel for indigent state defendants extended to all serious cases. Also noteworthy was *Haynes v. Washington,*[7] which appeared to recognize a closer relationship than had theretofore been acknowledged between the due process voluntariness requirement and a suspect's right to contact his attorney during the interrogation process.

(b) The *Massiah* Case. The argument that the right to counsel attaches when the defendant is indicted and his status thereby changes from "suspect" to "accused" was finally accepted by the Court in a case which did not even involve custodial interrogation. In *Massiah v. United States,*[8] Massiah, indicted for federal narcotics violations, retained counsel, pled not guilty and was released on bail. Codefendant Colson, who unknown to Massiah was cooperating with the authorities and had a radio transmitter in his car, invited Massiah to discuss the pending case, and during their conversations in the car Massiah's damaging admissions were overheard by a federal agent, who testified as to them at Massiah's trial. Perhaps to avoid a difficult eavesdropping issue, the Supreme Court decided *Massiah* on Sixth Amendment grounds, holding

> that the petitioner was denied the basic protections of that guarantee when there was used against him at his trial evidence of his own incriminating words, which federal agents had deliberately elicited from him after he had been indicted and in the absence of his counsel. It is true that in the *Spano* case the defendant was interrogated in a police station, while here the damaging testimony was elicited from the defendant without his knowledge while he was free on bail. But, as Judge Hays pointed out in his dissent in the Court of Appeals, "if such a rule is to have any efficacy it must apply to indirect and surreptitious interrogations as well as those conducted in the jailhouse. In this case, Massiah was more seriously imposed upon * * * because he did not even know that he was under interrogation by a government agent."

The three dissenters objected that in the instant case there was neither any "inherent danger of police coercion justifying the prophylactic effect of another exclusionary rule," nor any "unconstitutional interference with Massiah's right to counsel" in the sense of preventing or spying upon his consultations with counsel.

Although *Massiah* was also applied in state proceedings,[9] it had a rather limited impact

5. 373 U.S. 59, 83 S.Ct. 1050, 10 L.Ed.2d 193 (1963).
6. 372 U.S. 335, 83 S.Ct. 792, 9 L.Ed.2d 799 (1963).
7. 373 U.S. 503, 83 S.Ct. 1336, 10 L.Ed.2d 513 (1963).
8. 377 U.S. 201, 84 S.Ct. 1199, 12 L.Ed.2d 246 (1964).
9. McLeod v. Ohio, 381 U.S. 356, 85 S.Ct. 1556, 14 L.Ed.2d 682 (1965).

until finally, in 1977, it was revitalized and expanded in *Brewer v. Williams.*[10] In the confessions area, it was overshadowed by *Escobedo v. Illinois,*[11] decided just a few weeks later, and by *Miranda v. Arizona,*[12] which came two years later. Lower courts were inclined to give *Massiah* as narrow an interpretation as possible.

(c) The *Escobedo* Case. Just five weeks after *Massiah,* the Court decided *Escobedo v. Illinois.*[13] Escobedo was taken into custody and questioned concerning a fatal shooting, but his retained counsel obtained his release. About ten days later one DiGerlando told police that Escobedo had fired the fatal shots, so Escobedo was again arrested and then informed of that allegation. He repeatedly asked to see his retained attorney, who came to the police station but was barred from seeing his client. After the police arranged a confrontation between DiGerlando and Escobedo, Escobedo incriminated himself in the killing, and this enabled an assistant prosecutor to obtain a more elaborate written confession, which was admitted at Escobedo's trial. He was convicted of murder.

The Supreme Court, in a 5–4 decision, reversed the conviction. The majority opinion was highly critical of reliance upon confessions in general and interrogation of those without counsel in particular, asserting "that a system of criminal law enforcement which comes to depend on the 'confession' will, in the long run, be less reliable and more subject to abuses than a system which depends on extrinsic evidence independently secured through skillful investigation." It seemed that the Court was about to announce a broad right-to-counsel-at-the-station rule, for it was said that preindictment interrogation was just as much a "critical stage" as the preliminary hearing in *White v. Maryland,*[14] and that *Massiah* was apposite because "no meaningful distinction can be drawn between interrogation of an accused before and after formal indictment." But the *Escobedo* holding was cautiously limited to the facts of the case:

> We hold, therefore, that where, as here, [1] the investigation is no longer a general inquiry into an unsolved crime but has begun to focus on a particular suspect, [2] the suspect has been taken into police custody, [3] the police carry out a process of interrogations that lends itself to eliciting incriminating statements, [4] the suspect has requested and been denied an opportunity to consult with his lawyer, and [5] the police have not effectively warned him of his absolute constitutional right to remain silent, the accused has been denied "the Assistance of Counsel" in violation of the Sixth Amendment to the Constitution as "made obligatory upon the States by the Fourteenth Amendment," * * * and that no statement elicited by the police during the interrogation may be used against him at a criminal trial.

The combination of sweeping language at some points and the above limited holding engendered conflicting views about the implications of the case. But *Escobedo* appeared to be a landmark decision which could only expand as the Court further considered the Sixth Amendment's application at the police station. This did not happen because just two years later the Court instead, in Miranda v. Arizona,[15] adopted a much broader rule based upon the Fifth Amendment privilege against self-incrimination. But in the interim, and thereafter as to trials which predated *Miranda* and thus were not governed by that decision,[16] the lower courts had to determine the meaning of *Escobedo.* Most attributed significance to each of the five "elements" in the *Escobedo* holding: (1) While the Court later and rather unconvincingly said in *Miranda* that the focus requirement of *Escobedo* was intended to mean deprivation of freedom in a significant way, this requirement was utilized to find *Escobedo* inapplicable where the suspect was in custody on another charge and the interrogation was undertaken while

10. 430 U.S. 387, 97 S.Ct. 1232, 51 L.Ed.2d 424 (1977).
11. 378 U.S. 478, 84 S.Ct. 1758, 12 L.Ed.2d 977 (1964).
12. 384 U.S. 436, 86 S.Ct. 1602, 16 L.Ed.2d 694 (1966).
13. 378 U.S. 478, 84 S.Ct. 1758, 12 L.Ed.2d 977 (1964).
14. 373 U.S. 59, 83 S.Ct. 1050, 10 L.Ed.2d 193 (1963).
15. 384 U.S. 436, 86 S.Ct. 1602, 16 L.Ed.2d 694 (1966).
16. Johnson v. New Jersey, 384 U.S. 719, 86 S.Ct. 1772, 16 L.Ed.2d 882 (1966).

the case was in the investigatory rather than accusatory stage. (2) *Escobedo* was deemed not to apply when the suspect was not in police custody, though it was acknowledged that custody could exist without there being a formal arrest. (3) *Escobedo* was read as not governing volunteered statements, or even interrogation undertaken primarily for another purpose, such as to locate a kidnapping victim. (4) *Escobedo* was considered not to require a warning of the right to counsel, and to be applicable only if the suspect made a clear and unambiguous request for counsel. (5) *Escobedo* was held not to apply if the police had warned the suspect of his right to remain silent.

Indeed, the Supreme Court itself ultimately came to treat *Escobedo* as nothing more than a "false start" toward the new approach to the confessions problem undertaken later in *Miranda*. In *Kirby v. Illinois*,[17] the Court held that the Sixth Amendment right to counsel at a police lineup attached "only at or after the time that adversary judicial proceedings have been initiated." Noting that *Escobedo* was the "only seeming deviation" from a long line of cases accepting that starting point, the Court in retrospect concluded that the " 'prime purpose' of *Escobedo* was not to vindicate the constitutional right to counsel as such, but, like *Miranda*, 'to guarantee full effectuation of the privilege against self-incrimination.' " Moreover, added the *Kirby* Court, *Escobedo* is now limited in its "holding * * * to its own facts."

(d) The *Williams* Case. When in 1966 the Supreme Court decided *Miranda v. Arizona*,[18] grounded in the Fifth Amendment privilege against self-incrimination, it remained unclear at best whether the "pure" Sixth Amendment right to counsel approach[19] continued to have any vitality or significance in the confession area. It seemed clear that *Miranda* had displaced *Escobedo*,[20] but just what it had done to the *Massiah* rule was quite uncertain—*Massiah* was not even mentioned in *Miranda*. So matters stood until 1977, when in *Brewer v. Williams*[21] the Supreme Court breathed new life into *Massiah*.

Williams was arraigned in Davenport, Iowa, on an outstanding arrest warrant prior to his transportation to Des Moines on a murder charge. Though the police had assured Williams' lawyer that he would not be interrogated during the trip, a detective made a "Christian burial speech," to the effect that because of the worsening weather it would be necessary to find the body now to ensure the victim a Christian burial. Williams then directed the police to the body. On Williams' motion to suppress all evidence relating to or resulting from the statements he made to the police, the trial judge found that "an agreement was made between defense counsel and the police officials to the effect that the Defendant was not to be questioned on the return trip to Des Moines" and that the evidence had been elicited from Williams during "a critical stage in the proceedings requiring the presence of counsel on his request," but ruled that Williams had "waived his right to have an attorney present during the giving of such information." There was no mention of *Massiah* by either the bare majority or the dissenters when the state supreme court affirmed. On federal habeas corpus, the district court concluded that Williams had not waived any of his constitutional protections, and ruled for him on three alternative and independent grounds: (1) that he had been denied his constitutional right to the assistance of counsel; (2) that he had been denied his rights under *Escobedo* and *Miranda*; and (3) that in any event his self-incriminatory statement had been involuntarily made. The federal court of appeals affirmed on the first two grounds.

17. 406 U.S. 682, 92 S.Ct. 1877, 32 L.Ed.2d 411 (1972).

18. 384 U.S. 436, 86 S.Ct. 1602, 16 L.Ed.2d 694 (1966).

19. To be contrasted with the "right" to counsel under the *Miranda* case, which is not derived directly from the Sixth Amendment but which the Court deemed a necessary safeguard of the Fifth Amendment privilege against self-incrimination.

20. Y. Kamisar, supra note 15, at 163.

21. 430 U.S. 387, 97 S.Ct. 1232, 51 L.Ed.2d 424 (1977).

The Supreme Court, in yet another 5–4 decision, affirmed the judgment of the court of appeals. The majority concluded there was "no need" either to assay the district court's ruling the statements were involuntary or the district and appellate courts' application of the *Miranda* rule to these facts, because "it is clear that the judgment before us must in any event be affirmed upon the ground that Williams was deprived of a different constitutional right—the right to the assistance of counsel." One theory as to why the Court opted for the long-dormant *Massiah* rule is that the Court thereby avoided for the moment the question of whether *Miranda* claims, like Fourth Amendment claims under *Stone v. Powell*,[22] could not be raised by state prisoners on federal habeas corpus. Another is that *Massiah* afforded an easier route to reversal than *Miranda* because it was unnecessary under the former decision to determine whether the Christian burial speech was "interrogation," and because a waiver of *Massiah* rights is not as readily found as a waiver of *Miranda* rights. But the *Williams* majority made no mention of any of these points.

Rather, the Court proceeded immediately to the conclusion that "[t]he circumstances of this case are * * * constitutionally indistinguishable from those presented in *Massiah.*" Though *Massiah* was a post-indictment case, it was now clear under *Kirby v. Illinois*[23] that the right to counsel arises "at or after the time that judicial proceedings have been initiated," which was the case here because Williams had been arraigned on the warrant in Davenport. It was also clear that the detective had "designedly set out to elicit information from Williams." Moreover, the fact that

> the incriminating statements were elicited surreptitiously in [*Massiah*], and otherwise here, is constitutionally irrelevant. Rather, the clear rule of *Massiah* is that once adversary proceedings have commenced against an individual, he has a right to legal representation when the government interrogates him. It thus requires no wooden or technical application of the *Massiah* doctrine to conclude that Williams was entitled to the assistance of counsel guaranteed to him by the Sixth and Fourteenth Amendments.

The *Williams* majority then rejected the state court's conclusion that waiver had occurred here merely because during the trip Williams did not assert that right or a desire not to talk in the absence of counsel. The four dissenters, on the other hand, contended that Williams had "relinquished his right not to talk to the police about his crime," and also claimed that the instant case was unlike *Massiah* because the police had not deliberately sought to isolate Williams from his counsel, had not acted solely for the purpose of obtaining incriminating evidence, and had not engaged in conduct which was "tantamount to interrogation."

(e) When the Right to Counsel Begins. Although the *Massiah* right to counsel had generally been interpreted as arising only upon indictment, in *Brewer v. Williams*[24] the Court declared that "the right to counsel granted by the Sixth and Fourteenth Amendments means at least that a person is entitled to the help of a lawyer at or after the time that judicial proceedings have been initiated against him—'whether by way of formal charge, preliminary hearing, indictment, information, or arraignment.' " Noting that a warrant had been issued for Williams' arrest and that he had been arraigned on that warrant before a judge and that he had been committed by the court to confinement in jail, the Court concluded there "can be no doubt in the present case that judicial proceedings had been initiated."[25]

22. 428 U.S. 465, 96 S.Ct. 3037, 49 L.Ed.2d 1067 (1976).

23. 406 U.S. 682, 92 S.Ct. 1877, 32 L.Ed.2d 411 (1972).

24. 430 U.S. 387, 97 S.Ct. 1232, 51 L.Ed.2d 424 (1977).

25. In Michigan v. Jackson, 475 U.S. 625, 106 S.Ct. 1404, 89 L.Ed.2d 631 (1986), the Court deemed "untenable" in light of *Brewer* the state's argument that the arraignment (in the sense of the defendant's initial appearance, not the pleading stage; see § 1.4(h)) did not represent the initiation of formal legal proceedings. The Court added that "arraignment signals the initiation of adversary judicial proceedings" without regard to whether it has the particular characteristics which would make "the arraignment itself * * * a critical stage requiring the presence of counsel." See § 11.2(b).

Clearly this test is not met merely because the defendant has been arrested without a warrant, nor is it met merely because the investigation has focused upon the defendant. Though "focus" was one of the several elements in *Escobedo,* that case has been limited to its own facts,[26] and the Supreme Court later held in *Hoffa v. United States*[27] that focus alone did not ripen the Sixth Amendment right to counsel. Even against the contention that indictment was delayed for the specific purpose of allowing the government to "beef up" its case with admissions obtained by stealth and trickery, it has been held that the government is under no obligation to cease an ongoing investigation when probable cause to obtain an indictment comes into existence.

There is an apparent split of authority on the question of whether the filing of a complaint is alone enough to give rise to a Sixth Amendment right to counsel, though the difference probably is explainable by the fact that this document is used for multiple purposes. Cases holding that filing the complaint constitutes the initiation of judicial proceedings for Sixth Amendment purposes under *Williams* typically stress express recognition in that jurisdiction of the complaint as one type of charging document. On the other hand, decisions holding that filing the complaint (or, indeed, filing the complaint and issuance of an arrest warrant thereon) does not have this effect emphasize use of the complaint simply as a means of obtaining a warrant. In support of the latter position, it is noteworthy that the *Williams* test quoted above was taken from *Kirby v. Illinois,*[28] where the Supreme Court explained that a person is entitled to counsel once the government has "committed itself to prosecute, and * * * the adverse positions of government and defendant have solidified." Thus, so the argument proceeds, the mere fact the police obtained an arrest warrant for some purpose, such as to comply with *Payton v. New York,*[29] should hardly be determinative. But this issue, which the Supreme Court seems to have recognized remains open for decision by that Court,[30] is complicated by the fact that in many jurisdictions a complaint might be utilized for either of the two purposes mentioned above. At no point in *Williams* does the Court discuss the circumstances behind issuance of the complaint and warrant, that is, whether the government really had "committed itself to prosecute." Perhaps the assumption is that whatever the reasons underlying the complaint-warrant process, at least from the time defendant is brought into court and arraigned on the warrant (at which point it or the complaint underlying it becomes a tentative charging document) the Sixth Amendment right to counsel applies.

Assuming that "judicial proceedings have been initiated," is it in addition essential to recognition of the Sixth Amendment right that counsel actually have been retained by or appointed for the defendant? While in both *Massiah* and *Williams* the defendant was already represented by an attorney, this is not necessary. As the Court has noted, "in *McLeod v. Ohio*[31] * * * we summarily affirmed a decision that the police could not elicit information after indictment even though counsel had not yet been appointed."[32] What then if judicial proceedings have not been initiated but the defendant in fact has counsel appointed for or (more likely)

26. Kirby v. Illinois, 406 U.S. 682, 92 S.Ct. 1877, 32 L.Ed.2d 411 (1972).

27. 385 U.S. 293, 87 S.Ct. 408, 17 L.Ed.2d 374 (1966).

28. 406 U.S. 682, 92 S.Ct. 1877, 32 L.Ed.2d 411 (1972).

29. 445 U.S. 573, 100 S.Ct. 1371, 63 L.Ed.2d 639 (1980), holding that a warrant is ordinarily needed to enter defendant's premises to arrest him.

30. In Edwards v. Arizona, 451 U.S. 477, 101 S.Ct. 1880, 68 L.Ed.2d 378 (1981), the Court decided the case on *Miranda* grounds and thus found it unnecessary to respond to the state's argument that *Massiah–Williams* was not applicable where only a criminal complaint had been filed, which under the state constitution was not a sufficient charging document.

31. 381 U.S. 356, 85 S.Ct. 1556, 14 L.Ed.2d 682 (1965).

32. Edwards v. Arizona, 451 U.S. 477, 101 S.Ct. 1880, 68 L.Ed.2d 378 (1981). Consider also that in United States v. Henry, 447 U.S. 264, 100 S.Ct. 2183, 65 L.Ed.2d 115 (1980), the Court applied *Massiah–Williams* to use of an undercover agent where the use was arranged for on Nov. 21 but counsel was not appointed until Nov. 27.

retained by him? In *Miranda v. Arizona,*[33] the Court dropped a footnote commenting that in *Escobedo* the police also prevented his attorney from seeing him and that this action by itself "constitutes a violation of the Sixth Amendment right to the assistance of counsel and excludes any statement obtained in its wake." But when the court later discredited *Escobedo* to the extent that it purported to mark the beginnings of the Sixth Amendment right to counsel,[34] it was apparent this footnote did not settle the matter. In *Moran v. Burbine,*[35] the Court rejected such an interpretation of the Sixth Amendment, noting "it makes little sense to say that the Sixth Amendment right to counsel attaches at different times depending on the fortuity of whether the suspect or his family happens to have retained counsel," especially since the Sixth Amendment, "by its very terms, * * * becomes applicable only when the government's role shifts from investigation to accusation."

If judicial proceedings have been initiated and the *Massiah–Williams* right to counsel has thus attached, does it attach for all purposes or only with respect to matters related to those proceedings? This issue reached the Supreme Court in *Maine v. Moulton,*[36] where, after Colton and Moulton were indicted for theft, Colton told police of Moulton's suggestion a state witness be killed and agreed to record later conversations with Moulton, and the recorded statements thereafter obtained in which Moulton discussed the thefts were admitted in his trial on those and other charges. The Court in *Moulton* agreed that the fact a defendant had been charged with one offense was no reason to give him special protection in the investigation of other, uncharged crimes, and thus concluded that "to exclude evidence pertaining to charges as to which the Sixth Amendment right to counsel had not attached at the time the evidence was obtained, simply because other charges were pending at that time, would unnecessarily frustrate the public's interest in the investigation of criminal activities." From this, the four dissenters reasoned there was no basis for exclusion in the instant case, as the simple fact was that the *Massiah–Brewer* Sixth Amendment right did not apply where, as here, "the police undertook an investigation of separate crimes." Though there is some logic to that position, the *Moulton* majority rejected it on essentially pragmatic grounds in favor of the conclusion that any statements obtained in such circumstances are admissible at trial of the new crime but not at trial of crimes theretofore charged. The majority saw this as "a sensible solution to a difficult problem" because the dissenters' approach "invites abuse by law enforcement personnel in the form of fabricated investigations."

(f) Waiver of Counsel. The Court in *Brewer v. Williams*[37] acknowledged that the right to counsel there recognized could be waived and that such waiver would not inevitably necessitate participation by defendant's lawyer. The majority declared it was *not* holding "that under the circumstances of this case," namely, where an attorney had actually advised defendant not to talk to the police and had extracted an agreement from the police not to question defendant, "Williams *could not,* without notice to counsel, have waived his rights under the Sixth and Fourteenth Amendments." *Williams* is thus consistent with prior authority that the Sixth Amendment right to counsel is the right of the client rather than the attorney, so that it may be waived by the client without counsel's participation.

Seemingly inconsistent with this conclusion is the previously quoted statement in *Miranda* about *Escobedo,* namely, that the conduct of the police in turning away the lawyer was by itself "a violation of the Sixth Amendment." If, as noted above, the right is that of the defendant, then it might be asked why there is any violation here if the defendant on his own waives the right. As to such tactics,

33. 384 U.S. 436, 86 S.Ct. 1602, 16 L.Ed.2d 694 (1966).

34. Kirby v. Illinois, 406 U.S. 682, 92 S.Ct. 1877, 32 L.Ed.2d 411 (1972).

35. 475 U.S. 412, 106 S.Ct. 1135, 89 L.Ed.2d 410 (1986).

36. 474 U.S. 159, 106 S.Ct. 477, 88 L.Ed.2d 481 (1985).

37. 430 U.S. 387, 97 S.Ct. 1232, 51 L.Ed.2d 424 (1977).

perhaps the point is that they bear upon the effectiveness of any waiver of the right to counsel by the defendant. If, as in *Escobedo,* the defendant was aware that his lawyer was being prevented from seeing him, this certainly should cast doubt upon any waiver of counsel subsequently obtained from the defendant, for defendant's realization may well have underscored the police dominance of the situation. Even absent such awareness, it has sometimes been held that if police failed to admit counsel to see a person in custody or to inform the person of the attorney's efforts to reach him, then they cannot thereafter rely on defendant's "waiver" of counsel because, having been denied facts critical to his decision, he cannot be said to have made a knowing choice. The Supreme Court rejected this latter conclusion in a *Miranda* context,[38] but has thereafter asserted that "in the Sixth Amendment context, this waiver would not be valid." [39]

The Court in *Williams* emphasized in various ways that courts should be reluctant to find a waiver of the right to counsel. It was noted that the burden of showing waiver is on the prosecution, that what must be shown is "an intentional relinquishment or abandonment of a known right," [40] that the right is not lost merely by a lack of request by the defendant, that "every reasonable presumption" must be indulged against waiver, and that a "strict standard" equal to that concerning waiver of counsel at trial applies. Whether this means that waiver of the "pure" right to counsel under *Williams* calls for something more than the waiver of counsel under *Miranda* is a matter on which lower courts were divided until the issue was resolved by the 5–4 decision in *Patterson v. Illinois.*[41] Taking the "pragmatic approach" that the warnings and waiver procedure required depend largely upon "the scope of the Sixth Amendment right to counsel" at the particular stage of the criminal process at issue, the *Patterson* majority concluded the requirements of *Miranda* would suffice because the "State's decision to take an additional step and commence formal adversarial proceedings against the accused does not substantially increase the value of counsel to the accused at questioning, or expand the limited purpose that an attorney serves when the accused is questioned by authorities." That is, "because the role of counsel at questioning is relatively simple and limited," as compared to counsel's responsibilities at trial, there is "no problem in having a waiver procedure at that stage which is likewise simple and limited," as compared to the more complicated waiver procedures which obtain with respect to counsel at trial.[42]

In *Williams* the Supreme Court stressed that "waiver requires not merely comprehension but relinquishment." Thus, while it there appeared that the defendant "had been informed of and appeared to understand his right to counsel," any claim of relinquishment was refuted by his "consistent reliance upon the advice of counsel in dealing with the authorities," his statements "that he desired the presence of an attorney before any interrogation took place," his awareness of the agreement between the police and his counsel "that no interrogation was to occur during the journey," and the fact that the police "made no effort at all to ascertain whether Williams wished to relinquish that right." Lower courts take into account such factors as whether there was a police agreement with counsel not to interrogate, whether defendant asserted his right to counsel, whether the police tried to talk defendant out of consulting with counsel, and whether defendant's statement was volunteered.

Waiver is a possibility only when the defendant makes a statement to one known to be in a position adverse to him, such as a police

38. Moran v. Burbine, 475 U.S. 412, 106 S.Ct. 1135, 89 L.Ed.2d 410 (1986), discussed in § 6.9(c).

39. Patterson v. Illinois, 487 U.S. 285, 108 S.Ct. 2389, 101 L.Ed.2d 261 (1988).

40. Johnson v. Zerbst, 304 U.S. 458, 58 S.Ct. 1019, 82 L.Ed. 1461 (1938).

41. 487 U.S. 285, 108 S.Ct. 2389, 101 L.Ed.2d 261 (1988).

42. The dissenters contended that a formal charge "substantially alters the relationship between the state and the accused," so that from that time forward "warnings offered by an opposing party, whether detailed or cursory, simply cannot satisfy this high standard."

officer, police agent, or examining psychiatrist.[43] As the Supreme Court ruled in *United States v. Henry*,[44] "the concept of a knowing and voluntary waiver of Sixth Amendment rights does not apply in the context of communications with an undisclosed undercover informant acting for the government." This is because in such an instance the defendant, being unaware the other person "was a government agent expressly commissioned to secure evidence, cannot be held to have waived his right to the assistance of counsel" by freely communicating with him.

The special waiver-after-assertion-of-rights rules which govern in the *Miranda* area as to a case in which the defendant, upon receiving the *Miranda* warnings from police, invoked his right to counsel [45] also apply to the Sixth Amendment right. Thus the Court held in *Michigan v. Jackson* [46] that when the Sixth Amendment right has attached, "if police initiate interrogation after a defendant's assertion, at an arraignment or similar proceeding, of his right to counsel, any waiver of the defendant's right to counsel for that police-initiated interrogation is invalid." The Court in *Jackson* explained (i) that "the reasons for prohibiting the interrogation of an uncounseled prisoner who has asked for the help of a lawyer are even stronger after he has been formally charged"; (ii) that even though the request for counsel at arraignment is not specifically tied to the matter of police questioning, it is proper to "presume that the defendant requests the lawyer's service at every critical stage of the prosecution"; and (iii) that police ignorance of that at-arraignment invocation of the right is irrelevant, for "one set of state actors (the police) may not claim ignorance of defendant's unequivocal request for counsel to another state actor (the court)." "Preserving the integrity of an accused's choice to communicate with police only through counsel is the essence" of *Jackson*, and thus the bar on police-initiated interrogation does not arise merely because of indictment.[47] And in any event, because the Sixth Amendment right is "offense-specific" and "cannot be invoked once for all future prosecutions," it follows that "its *Michigan v. Jackson* effect of invalidating subsequent waivers in police-initiated interviews is offense-specific."[48] This means, for example, that if a defendant exercises his Sixth Amendment right when brought into court on an armed robbery charge, that is no bar to subsequent police-initiated questioning about an unrelated murder.[49]

(g) Infringement of the Right. Assuming now a situation in which judicial proceedings have been initiated and consequently the Sixth Amendment right to counsel has attached, and assuming also that this right has not been waived by the defendant, there remains the question of what activity constitutes an infringement of that right so as to require suppression of any statement obtained thereby. In *Massiah v. United States*,[50] the police arranged for a codefendant to discuss their pending trial with the defendant while they were in the codefendant's car, which had a radio transmitter concealed in it. The Court declared that defendant's right to counsel was violated "when there was used against him at his trial evidence of his own incriminating words, which federal agents had deliberately elicited from him." And in *Brewer v.*

43. See Estelle v. Smith, 451 U.S. 454, 101 S.Ct. 1866, 68 L.Ed.2d 359 (1981) (*Massiah–Williams* covers examination by psychiatrist to determine defendant's competency to stand trial, and thus fruits thereof may not be used at penalty phase of capital case).

Compare Buchanan v. Kentucky, 483 U.S. 402, 107 S.Ct. 2906, 97 L.Ed.2d 336 (1987) (because defendant's counsel himself requested the examination and presumably discussed it with his client, and *Smith* put counsel on notice that if he invoked an extreme emotional disturbance defense the report of examination might be used by the prosecution in rebuttal, such use did not infringe upon defendant's right to counsel).

44. 447 U.S. 264, 100 S.Ct. 2183, 65 L.Ed.2d 115 (1980).

45. See § 6.9(g).

46. 475 U.S. 625, 106 S.Ct. 1404, 89 L.Ed.2d 631 (1986).

47. Patterson v. Illinois, 487 U.S. 285, 108 S.Ct. 2389, 101 L.Ed.2d 261 (1988).

48. McNeil v. Wisconsin, ___ U.S. ___, 111 S.Ct. 2204, 115 L.Ed.2d 158 (1991).

49. McNeil v. Wisconsin, ___ U.S. ___, 111 S.Ct. 2204, 115 L.Ed.2d 158 (1991).

50. 377 U.S. 201, 84 S.Ct. 1199, 12 L.Ed.2d 246 (1964).

Williams,[51] where the activity objected to was the "Christian burial speech" on the ride from Davenport to Des Moines, the Court deemed *Massiah* applicable because the detective "deliberately and designedly set out to elicit information from Williams just as surely as—and perhaps more effectively than—if he had formally interrogated him." Both *Massiah* and *Williams* at some point refer to the police conduct as "interrogation," but the facts of those cases make it clear that this does not mean interrogation in the narrow sense of the word.

The claim that the "decisive fact in *Massiah* * * * was that the police set up the confrontation between the accused and a police agent" was rejected in *Maine v. Moulton*,[52] finding an infringement of the right to counsel even when it was the defendant who initiated the meeting with his codefendant, who by the time of the meeting was a police agent. As the Court explained, while "the Sixth Amendment is not violated whenever—by luck or happenstance—the State obtains incriminating statements from the accused," a "knowing exploitation by the State of an opportunity to confront the accused without counsel being present is as much a breach of the State's obligation not to circumvent the right to assistance of counsel as is the intentional creation of such an opportunity."

Though the language used in the *Massiah* and *Brewer* cases would seem to require "action undertaken with the specific intent to evoke an inculpatory disclosure," [53] whether that is still the case remains somewhat unclear because of the confusing case of *United States v. Henry*.[54] Henry is a "jail plant" case; government agents contacted a federal informant serving a term in a city jail and "told him to be alert to any statements made by the federal prisoners, but not to initiate any conversation with or question Henry regarding the bank robbery." The informant later reported "that he and Henry had engaged in conversation and that Henry had told him about the robbery of the Janaf bank," and he so testified at Henry's trial. Though the government argued before the Supreme Court that the incriminating statements were "not the result of any affirmative conduct on the part of government agents to elicit evidence," the 6–3 majority in *Henry* held that the incriminating statements had been "deliberately elicited." This was so, the Court stated later on in the opinion, by virtue of the government "intentionally creating a situation likely to induce Henry to make incriminating statements." That language was understandably criticized by the dissenters, who noted that it removed the word "deliberately" from the *Massiah–Williams* test and "would cover even a 'negligent' triggering of events resulting in reception of disclosures." But despite the unfortunate "likely to induce" phrase, *Henry* appears to be viewed by the majority as a genuine "deliberately elicited" type of case. Though the majority's analysis lacks precision, the Court seems to conclude that the government's instructions not to question Henry about the robbery (i) are not to be taken too seriously given the fact that the government was using an informer who would be paid only if he produced incriminating information, (ii) did not bar all affirmative action by the informer, who admittedly had "some conversations" with Henry on the topic of the robbery, and (iii) consequently disproved neither that the government intended to obtain incriminating statements nor that the government contemplated some affirmative action by its agent to achieve that result. In other words, after *Henry* it is still true that *Massiah* turns solely on the underlying intent of the government's agents. This means there is no *Massiah–Williams* violation if the person acting with the intention of eliciting an incriminating statement is not a government agent, or if the government agent who elicits an incriminating response does so exclusively for some other legitimate purpose.

A slightly different question which may be asked about *Henry* is whether it extends *Mas-*

51. 430 U.S. 387, 97 S.Ct. 1232, 51 L.Ed.2d 424 (1977).

52. 474 U.S. 159, 106 S.Ct. 477, 88 L.Ed.2d 481 (1985).

53. United States v. Henry, 447 U.S. 264, 100 S.Ct. 2183, 65 L.Ed.2d 115 (1980) (Blackmun, J., dissenting).

54. 447 U.S. 264, 100 S.Ct. 2183, 65 L.Ed.2d 115 (1980).

siah so as to include both "active" and "passive" efforts to obtain incriminating evidence from a defendant. For the reasons stated above, the majority did not believe it was dealing with a "passive" type of case. Moreover, the majority cautioned it was not "called upon to pass on the situation where an informant is placed in close proximity but makes no effort to stimulate conversations about the crime charged." Later, in *Kuhlman v. Wilson*,[55] the Court ruled that because "the primary concern of the *Massiah* line of decisions is secret interrogation by investigatory techniques that are the equivalent of direct police interrogation," "a defendant does not make out a violation of that right simply by showing that an informant, either through prior arrangement or voluntarily, reported his incriminating statements to the police." *Kuhlman* illustrates, however, the difficulty in drawing the line between "active" and "passive" efforts. Defendant first gave his cellmate the same story of noninvolvement he had earlier given the police, to which the cellmate, placed there by police with instructions not to question defendant but to listen for information, responded that the explanation "didn't sound too good." The defendant did not alter his story until a few days later, after his brother visited him and expressed the family's concern with his apparent involvement in a murder. The majority concluded this meant defendant's confession had not been "deliberately elicited" by his cellmate, but three dissenting Justices thought otherwise because, though "the *coup de grace* was delivered by respondent's brother," the "informant, while avoiding direct questions, nonetheless developed a relationship of cellmate camaraderie with respondent and encouraged him to talk about his crime."

To be distinguished from the "jail plant" cases, the *Henry* majority noted, is the "situation where the 'listening post' is an inanimate electronic device," for "such a device has no capability of leading the conversation into any particular subject or prompting any particular replies." Especially after *Kuhlman,* it seems clear that mere use of the device does not infringe upon the right to counsel, for it cannot be said that the bugging in any sense increases the defendant's predisposition toward making an incriminating response. Thus the existing authority, noted in *Henry,* to the effect that the mere use of an electronic device to record a prisoner's conversations with a visitor does not violate the Sixth Amendment, is correct.

(h) Critique of the Right to Counsel Approach. Whether the *Massiah* rule, as elaborated and extended in such cases as *Williams* and *Henry,* is a sensible and desirable doctrine is a matter on which opinions differ. In criticism, it is asserted that the *Massiah* rule is unnecessary because *Miranda* protects against the coercive pressures of custodial interrogations while the due process voluntariness test affords sufficient protection in noncustodial situations. In much the same vein, it is objected that if *Massiah* is perceived of as providing some sort of protection against improper police practices, then it is fundamentally unsound because those practices do not somehow become improper only upon the initiation of judicial proceedings. On the other hand, some do find offensive certain police practices likely to be reached only by the *Massiah* rule, such as use of an undercover agent to elicit incriminating remarks, and for them the problem with the rule is that it is too narrow because not extended to similar conduct that occurs after formal arrest.

In answer to such criticisms, it might be observed that *Massiah,* after all, is grounded in the Sixth Amendment right to counsel and thus should be assessed in terms of its protection of that right instead of as an alternative to or extension of either *Miranda* or the voluntariness test. But there is disagreement even when *Massiah* is so viewed. One position, as reflected by Justice Rehnquist's dissent in *Henry,* is that the *Massiah* rule cannot be explained even on this basis because it does not protect legitimate Sixth Amendment interests: "the confidentiality of communications between the accused and his attorney," and the "role of counsel * * * to offer advice

55. 477 U.S. 436, 106 S.Ct. 2616, 91 L.Ed.2d 364 (1986).

and assistance in the preparation of a defense and to serve as a spokesman for the accused in technical legal proceedings." In response, it is contended that this overlooks the fact that from at least the time of *White v. Maryland*[56] the Sixth Amendment has also functioned as a shield, enabling the defendant to frustrate the state's efforts to obtain evidence directly from him.

Even assuming the latter position is correct, so that there properly comes a point after which the Sixth Amendment right to counsel protects against all self-incrimination, compelled or not, there is room for dispute as to whether that point has been correctly defined in the *Massiah* line of cases. One question is whether the right to counsel rule turns on distinctions which are unresponsive to the government's need for evidence. It thus might be asked whether *Massiah,* which erected a Sixth Amendment shield around a defendant who had been arrested and indicted many months earlier, is more understandable than *Williams,* where such a shield was erected around a defendant shortly after his arrest and apparently before even the magnitude of the crime had been ascertained by the proper prosecuting authority. A second question is whether these distinctions are objectionable because often, albeit not in *Williams,* they are conducive to manipulation by the police.

(i) The "Repeal" of the *Massiah* Rule. In the Crime Control Act of 1968, Congress purported to "repeal" the *Massiah* rule for federal prosecutions. This was done by providing that in the federal courts a confession "shall be admissible in evidence if it is voluntarily given,"[57] and that various enumerated factors to be taken into account on the voluntariness issue, including "whether or not such defendant was without the assistance of counsel when questioned and when giving such confession," "need not be conclusive on the issue of voluntariness."[58] This legislation has been largely ignored, and properly so, for to the extent it purports to nullify the Sixth Amendment right to counsel as recognized in *Massiah* and subsequent Supreme Court decisions it is most certainly unconstitutional.

§ 6.5 The Privilege Against Self–Incrimination: *Miranda*

(a) The Privilege in the Police Station. The Fifth Amendment provides that no person "shall be compelled in any criminal case to be a witness against himself." A literal reading of that language certainly suggests that the privilege against self-incrimination has no application to unsworn statements obtained by station-house interrogation, and for a good many years this was the common assumption. The notion was that compulsion to testify meant *legal* compulsion, which is not present in the police questioning context because the interrogated suspect is threatened neither with perjury for testifying falsely nor with contempt for refusing to testify at all. However, the Supreme Court in *Bram v. United States*[1] seemed quite clearly to conclude otherwise, for it was there asserted that "[i]n criminal trials, in the courts of the United States, wherever a question arises whether a confession is incompetent because not voluntary, the issue is controlled by that portion of the fifth amendment * * * commanding that no person 'shall be compelled in any criminal case to be a witness against himself.'" But this assertion was not relied upon by the Court in subsequent confession cases, and the Court later expressed doubt that the privilege was relevant in confession cases.[2]

Then came *Malloy v. Hogan,*[3] which did not involve a confession but nonetheless was important in two significant respects to the ultimate acceptance of the privilege against self-incrimination as a constitutional restraint

56. 373 U.S. 59, 83 S.Ct. 1050, 10 L.Ed.2d 193 (1963), holding on Sixth Amendment grounds that defendant's withdrawn guilty plea, obtained at a hearing at which he was not represented by counsel, could not be admitted against him.

57. 18 U.S.C.A. § 3501(a).

58. 18 U.S.C.A. § 3501(b).

§ 6.5

1. 168 U.S. 532, 18 S.Ct. 183, 42 L.Ed. 568 (1897).

2. United States v. Carignan, 342 U.S. 36, 72 S.Ct. 97, 96 L.Ed. 48 (1951).

3. 378 U.S. 1, 84 S.Ct. 1489, 12 L.Ed.2d 653 (1964).

upon police interrogation practices. *Malloy* held that the privilege was applicable to the states, and then supported that conclusion by declaring that "today the admissibility of a confession in a state criminal prosecution is tested by the same standard applied in federal prosecutions since 1897" in *Bram.* This made it appear that the privilege was the established basis for assaying federal confessions. Promptly thereafter came *Escobedo v. Illinois,*[4] which, while grounded upon the Sixth Amendment right to counsel, spoke unhesitantly of "the right of the accused to be advised by his lawyer of his privilege against self-incrimination." Any lingering doubts were dispelled two years later by *Miranda v. Arizona,*[5] holding that the privilege "is fully applicable during a period of custodial interrogation."[6]

(b) The *Miranda* Rules. In *Miranda,* yet another 5–4 decision, the majority began by examining "various police manuals and texts," a "valuable source of information about present police practices." From the several psychological ploys and strategems outlined therein, the Court concluded that even without resort to brutality "the very fact of custodial interrogation exacts a heavy toll on individual liberty and trades on the weaknesses of individuals." Next examining the facts of the four cases under collective consideration, the Court concluded that even though it "might not find the defendants' statements to have been involuntary in traditional terms," those statements were obtained under circumstances in which the "potentiality for compulsion is forcefully apparent." In each case the defendant was interrogated by police who had custody of him and who did not advise him that he could remain silent or otherwise "insure that the statements were truly the product of free choice." The Court thus concluded that "[u]nless adequate protective devices are employed to dispel the compulsion inherent in custodial surroundings, no statement obtained from the defendant can truly be the product of his free choice."

The necessary "protective devices" were then described in some detail in what the *Miranda* dissenters disparagingly called a "constitutional code of rules for confessions." *Miranda* thus represents a striking contrast to both *Escobedo v. Illinois,*[7] decided two years earlier, and the Court's usual "totality of circumstances" approach to the due process voluntariness issue. While the holding in *Escobedo* had been cautiously limited to the facts of the particular case before the Court, the *Miranda* holding most certainly was not, for it contained a set of rules to be followed by police in all future custodial interrogations. And while "totality of circumstances" holdings were not easily applied to other cases with somewhat different pressures or defendants of somewhat different susceptibilities, the nature of the *Miranda* rules was such that this was not true of this landmark decision. These rules, which are discussed further in the remaining sections of this Chapter, may be summarized as follows:

(1) These rules are required to safeguard the privilege against self-incrimination, and thus must be followed in the absence of "other procedures which are at least as effective in apprising accused persons of their right of silence and in assuring a continuous opportunity to exercise it."

(2) These rules apply "when the individual is first subjected to police interrogation while in custody at the station or otherwise deprived of his freedom of action in any significant way," and not to "[g]eneral on-the-scene questioning as to facts surrounding a crime or other general questioning of citizens in the fact-finding process" or to "[v]olunteered statements of any kind."

(3) Without regard to his prior awareness of his rights, if a person in custody is to be subjected to questioning, "he must first be informed in clear and unequivocal terms that he has the right to remain silent," so that the ignorant may learn of this right and so that

4. 378 U.S. 478, 84 S.Ct. 1758, 12 L.Ed.2d 977 (1964).

5. 384 U.S. 436, 86 S.Ct. 1602, 16 L.Ed.2d 694 (1966).

6. On the history and policies of the privilege, see § 8.14.

7. 378 U.S. 478, 84 S.Ct. 1758, 12 L.Ed.2d 977 (1964).

the pressures of the interrogation atmosphere will be overcome for those previously aware of the right.

(4) The above warning "must be accompanied by the explanation that anything said can and will be used against the individual in court," so as to ensure that the suspect fully understands the consequences of foregoing the privilege.

(5) Because this is indispensable to protection of the privilege, the individual also "must be clearly informed that he has the right to consult with a lawyer and to have the lawyer with him during interrogation," without regard to whether it appears that he is already aware of this right.

(6) The individual must also be warned "that if he is indigent a lawyer will be appointed to represent him," for otherwise the above warning would be understood as meaning only that an individual may consult a lawyer if he has the funds to obtain one.

(7) The individual is always free to exercise the privilege, and thus if he "indicates in any manner, at anytime prior to or during questioning, that he wishes to remain silent, the interrogation must cease"; and likewise, if he "states that he wants an attorney, the interrogation must cease until an attorney is present."

(8) If a statement is obtained without the presence of an attorney, "a heavy burden rests on the Government to demonstrate that the defendant knowingly and intelligently waived his privilege against self-incrimination and his right to retained or appointed counsel," and such waiver may not be presumed from the individual's silence after warnings or from the fact that a confession was eventually obtained.

(9) Any statement obtained in violation of these rules may not be admitted into evidence, without regard to whether it is a confession or only an admission of part of an offense or whether it is inculpatory or allegedly exculpatory.

(10) Likewise, exercise of the privilege may not be penalized, and thus the prosecution may not "use at trial the fact that [the defendant] stood mute or claimed his privilege in the face of accusation."

Although these rules sound inflexible and unbending, neither the Supreme Court nor the lower courts have generally taken a rigid approach in the application of *Miranda.* Indeed, the Supreme Court asserted in *Michigan v. Tucker*[8] that the *Miranda* decision

> recognized that these procedural safeguards were not themselves rights protected by the Constitution but were instead measures to insure that the right against compulsory self-incrimination was protected. * * * The suggested safeguards were not intended to "create a constitutional straitjacket," * * * but rather to provide practical reinforcement for the right against compulsory self-incrimination.

This curious characterization of *Miranda,* which ignores much of the language in that case, seems to have deprived *Miranda* of its constitutional basis without explaining what other basis it might have. But it is most likely explainable by the fact that in *Tucker* the Court was trying to avoid exclusion of a pre-*Miranda* confession obtained by a policeman who failed to foresee the necessity to give all of the warnings outlined in *Miranda.*[9]

(c) The Experience Under *Miranda.* Various surveys and empirical studies have been undertaken in an effort to gauge the impact of the *Miranda* decision upon police interrogation practices. As for police compliance with *Miranda,* in the months immediately following the decision it was determined that police did not regularly or completely give the warnings before interrogation. This was largely attributable to delays in police training about the new requirements, and later studies found that police were regularly advising suspects of their rights before at-

8. 417 U.S. 433, 94 S.Ct. 2357, 41 L.Ed.2d 182 (1974).

9. A consequence of the fact that the Court held in Johnson v. New Jersey, 384 U.S. 719, 86 S.Ct. 1772, 16 L.Ed.2d 882 (1966), that *Miranda* was not retroactive but that nonetheless it would apply to trials begun after the date of that decision even though the interrogation predated *Miranda.*

tempting to question them. However, this implementation of *Miranda* has been on a limited, formalistic basis. The practice is to read the suspect the warnings printed on "*Miranda* cards" carried by the police, often intoned in a manner designed to minimize or negate their importance and effectiveness.

Giving the warnings, at least in that fashion, has not seemed to reduce the amount of talking by suspects. Various studies have indicated that defendants given the warnings seldom request counsel and that about as many confessions are obtained by giving the *Miranda* rights as were gotten before the *Miranda* decision. It also appears that *Miranda* has had little effect upon clearance and conviction rates. This apparently is because most suspects do not grasp the significance of the warnings and seem unable really to understand that the object of the policeman's questions is to gather evidence which could be used to put them in jail.

(d) Critique of the *Miranda* Approach. There exists a considerable difference of opinion concerning the extent to which *Miranda* has "solved" pre-existing problems concerning police interrogation practices in this country. Nonetheless, it is possible to identify some of the strengths and weaknesses of *Miranda.* On the plus side, it may be said—even in the face of the experience reported above—that *Miranda* serves important symbolic functions, such as correcting the appearance that the poor and unsophisticated are particularly vulnerable to police exploitation. *Miranda* has also served an educational purpose in the sense of ensuring that police are frequently reminded of the rights of the people with whom they deal. Moreover, *Miranda* provided much needed guidance for the police by prescribing a series of set procedures to be followed in every instance of custodial interrogation. It was thus not difficult for the well-intentioned police officer to perceive exactly what was expected of him—a distinct improvement over the ambiguous due process voluntariness test. *Miranda* also simplified to some extent judicial review of police interrogation practices.

Yet, as the experience reported above seems to confirm, there appears to be a very fundamental inconsistency in the *Miranda* majority's analysis. The Court places heavy emphasis on the notion that the decision of one in custody whether or not to incriminate himself cannot be truly voluntary, but yet concludes that the choice to dispense with counsel can be voluntary in the same circumstances. This inconsistency has been noted both by those who believe that *Miranda* did not go far enough—that the Court should have insisted on the presence of an attorney during interrogation, required initial consultation with an attorney or friend, or even mandated that warnings and waivers occur before a neutral magistrate—and by those, such as the dissenters in *Miranda,* who believe the Court went too far.

A cogent criticism of the old "voluntariness" test, namely, that because the critical events occur in secrecy the admissibility of the confession will be determined by the outcome of a "swearing contest" in court, applies to *Miranda* as well. This is because the heralded warnings need not be given by a disinterested person, and the defendant's decision to waive his rights need not be made before a disinterested party or recorded in any fashion. The warnings waiver may and often does occur while the suspect is isolated, in the privacy of the interrogation room, with only the police as observers, and this raises doubts not only about the validity of the waiver but about the propriety of post-waiver actions as well.

(e) The "Repeal" of *Miranda.* In the Crime Control Act of 1968, Congress purported to "repeal" *Miranda* in federal prosecutions. This was done by providing that in the federal courts a confession "shall be admissible in evidence if it is voluntarily given," [10] and that various enumerated factors to be taken into account on the voluntariness issue, such as "whether or not such defendant was advised or knew that he was not required to

10. 18 U.S.C.A. § 3501(a).

make any statement and that any such statement could be used against him," "whether or not such defendant had been advised prior to questioning of his right to the assistance of counsel," and "whether or not such defendant was without the assistance of counsel when questioned and when giving such confession," "need not be conclusive on the issue of voluntariness." [11] This legislation is unconstitutional to the extent that it purports to repeal *Miranda.*

An argument to the contrary might be grounded in the Court's later assertion in *Michigan v. Tucker* [12] that *Miranda* "recognized that these procedural safeguards were not themselves rights protected by the Constitution but were instead measures to insure that the right against compulsory self-incrimination was protected." But even putting aside the special circumstances in which those comments were made [13] and even accepting the proposition that the *Miranda* rules are judge-made regulations for implementing constitutional commands, it hardly follows that the rules themselves have no constitutional status. The *Miranda* rules apply to the states, and thus they must have at least some constitutional sanction in the eyes of the Court. But it still may be argued that under such cases as *Katzenbach v. Morgan* [14] the Court must defer to the superior factfinding processes of the Congress. Starting with the notion that in *Miranda* the Court made a factual finding that custodial interrogations are inherently coercive, it may be contended that the statutory provision quoted above is grounded in a congressional finding of fact to the contrary. But, even putting aside the fact that the legislative history of this provision is devoid of any such factfinding, this argument rests upon a misconstruction of *Miranda,* for the opinion does not assert that every instance of custodial interrogation is coercive. Rather, *Miranda* is grounded in the notion that unless prophylactic measures are employed there will be inadequate assurance that any confession obtained in secret is not procured by compulsion violating the privilege against self-incrimination.

Finally, there is the argument that the legislation is constitutional because Congress has done nothing more than respond to the invitation it received in *Miranda:*

> It is impossible for us to foresee the potential alternatives for protecting the privilege which might be devised by Congress or the States in the exercise of their creative rule-making capacities. Therefore we cannot say that the Constitution necessarily requires adherence to any particular solution for the inherent compulsions of the interrogation process as it is presently conducted. Our decision in no way creates a constitutional straitjacket which will handicap sound efforts at reform nor is it intended to have this effect. We encourage Congress and the States to continue their laudable search for increasingly effective ways of protecting the rights of the individual while promoting efficient enforcement of our criminal laws. However, unless we are shown other procedures which are at least as effective in apprising accused persons of their right of silence and in assuring a continuous opportunity to exercise it, the following safeguards must be observed.

But a careful reading of this language shows that the invitation to Congress and the states is merely to come up with other ways of "apprising accused persons of their right of silence." This legislation hardly does that, for it merely turns the clock back to the voluntariness doctrine, and thus does not represent a constitutional alternative for dealing with the central problem before the Court in *Miranda.*

§ 6.6 *Miranda:* When Interrogation Is "Custodial"

(a) "Custody" vs. "Focus." Because these *Miranda* safeguards were deemed necessary to counteract the combined effects of interrogation and custody, the meaning of the Court's "custodial interrogation" phrase is a matter of considerable importance. By way

11. 18 U.S.C.A. § 3501(b).

12. 417 U.S. 433, 94 S.Ct. 2357, 41 L.Ed.2d 182 (1974).

13. See text at note 9 supra.

14. 384 U.S. 641, 86 S.Ct. 1717, 16 L.Ed.2d 828 (1966).

of explanation, the Court said this meant "questioning initiated by law enforcement officers after a person has been taken into custody or otherwise deprived of his freedom of action in any significant way."

Some of the difficulty which arose concerning the exact meaning of that language was prompted by a footnote appended thereto: "This is what we meant in *Escobedo* when we spoke of an investigation which had focused on an accused." This made it appear that custody and focus were alternative grounds for requiring the warnings, though there was certainly reason to question such a conclusion. For one thing, *Escobedo v. Illinois* [1] had held that the Sixth Amendment right to counsel attached when a series of events coincided, but "focus" was one of the events and "custody" was another, thus making it quite plain that the Court had *not* then viewed the two terms as synonymous. Moreover, any notion that this footnote meant that *Miranda* rights came into being upon arrest *or* the accumulation of facts which would justify arrest appeared to be dispelled shortly thereafter in *Hoffa v. United States.*[2] There the Court emphatically declared, albeit not in a *Miranda* context, that there "is no constitutional right to be arrested" and that police "are under no constitutional duty to call a halt to a criminal investigation the moment they have the minimum evidence to establish probable cause."

The "focus" approach was expressly rejected in *Beckwith v. United States.*[3] There the petitioner claimed he was entitled to the full *Miranda* warnings when he was interviewed at home by IRS agents because he was at that time the focus of a criminal investigation. The Court responded:

> An interview with government agents in a situation such as [this one] simply does not present the elements which the *Miranda* Court found so inherently coercive as to require its holding. Although the "focus" of an investigation may indeed have been on [petitioner] at the time of the interview in the sense that it was his tax liability which was under scrutiny, he hardly found himself in the custodial situation described by the *Miranda* Court as the basis for its holding. *Miranda* implicitly defined "focus," for its purposes, as "questioning initiated by law enforcement officers *after* a person has been taken into custody or otherwise deprived of his freedom of action in any significant way."

On like reasoning, a plurality in *United States v. Mandujano* [4] rejected the argument that a "putative" or "virtual" defendant called before a grand jury is entitled to the *Miranda* warnings, which "were aimed at the evils seen by the Court as endemic to police interrogation of a person in custody."

(b) Purpose of Custody. *Mathis v. United States* [5] posed the question of whether *Miranda* applies when the purpose of the custody is unrelated to the purpose of the interrogation. There an IRS agent failed to give petitioner the *Miranda* warnings when questioning him about his prior income tax returns while petitioner was incarcerated in a state jail serving a state sentence. The government argued *Miranda* was inapplicable because the petitioner had not been jailed by the interrogating federal officers but was there for an entirely different offense, but the Court rejected that distinction as "too minor and shadowy to justify a departure from the well-considered conclusion of *Miranda* with reference to warnings to be given to a person held in custody." The significance of *Mathis* is best highlighted by setting out the position of the three dissenters, rejected by the majority: "*Miranda* rested not on the mere fact of physical restriction but on a conclusion that coercion—pressure to answer questions—usually flows from a certain type of custody, police station interrogation of someone charged with or suspected of a crime. Although petitioner was confined, he was at the time of interrogation in familiar surroundings. * * * The rationale of *Miranda* has no

§ 6.6

1. 378 U.S. 478, 84 S.Ct. 1758, 12 L.Ed.2d 977 (1964).
2. 385 U.S. 293, 87 S.Ct. 408, 17 L.Ed.2d 374 (1966).
3. 425 U.S. 341, 96 S.Ct. 1612, 48 L.Ed.2d 1 (1976).
4. 425 U.S. 564, 96 S.Ct. 1768, 48 L.Ed.2d 212 (1976).
5. 391 U.S. 1, 88 S.Ct. 1503, 20 L.Ed.2d 381 (1968).

relevance to inquiries conducted outside the allegedly hostile and forbidding atmosphere surrounding police station interrogation of a criminal suspect." Thus, it is now clear that *Miranda* applies to interrogation of one in custody for another purpose or with respect to another offense.

(c) Subjective vs. Objective Approach. A most fundamental question concerning the *Miranda* "custody" element is whether it is to be determined by some subjective factor, either that the suspect in fact believed he was in custody or that the police officer intended to take custody, or whether instead an objective test of the "reasonable man" type governs. Under the first subjective approach, which focuses upon the state of mind of the suspect, a defendant would be in custody for *Miranda* purposes if he believed he was in custody. In defense of this approach, it may be said that it relates directly to the "potentiality for compulsion" with which the Court was concerned in *Miranda*: if the combination of custody and questioning is sufficiently coercive to call for warnings, then certainly the situation is no less coercive as to the defendant who actually but erroneously believes he is in custody. The trouble with this approach, however, is that it would place upon the police the burden of anticipating the frailties or idiosyncracies of every person whom they question.

The second subjective approach would make the outcome depend upon the intentions of the police officer, without regard to whether they were communicated to the suspect. This test, once followed by some courts and rejected by others, was at one time utilized by the Supreme Court. This first occurred in *Orozco v. Texas*,[6] where four policemen entered defendant's bedroom at 4 a.m. and questioned him without the *Miranda* warnings. The Court held that *Miranda* applied, not on the plausible ground that these unique facts established a "potentiality for compulsion" equivalent to stationhouse interrogation, but rather on the narrower point that one of the officers later testified as to his uncommunicated intentions, namely, that "petitioner was under arrest and not free to leave when he was questioned in his bedroom in the early hours of the morning." In the later case of *Oregon v. Mathiason*,[7] a majority of the Court appears to have persisted in this approach. Defendant, a parolee, was "invited" to the police station for an interview, and when he arrived he was questioned about a burglary after the officer told him falsely that his fingerprints had been found at the crime scene. In holding this was a "noncustodial situation," the *Mathiason* Court declared that the officer's false statement had "nothing to do with whether respondent was in custody for purposes of the *Miranda* rule." Such an assertion would be absurd if either a subjective understanding-of-the-suspect test or an objective test were used, and thus seems to indicate adherence to the *Orozco* intent-of-the-officer approach. Unlike the other subjective test, this approach is easy for the officer to understand, but it hardly makes sense in terms of the "potentiality for compulsion," as the uncommunicated intentions of the officer do not change the situation from the suspect's point of view.

However, both of these subjective approaches have a common defect, which is that the governing test would involve matters exceedingly difficult for courts to determine after the fact. As the point was put in *United States v. Hall*,[8] it makes no sense to have the *Miranda* "custody" factor "decided by swearing contests in which officers would regularly maintain their lack of intention to assert power over a suspect save when the circumstances would make such a claim absurd, and defendants would assert with equal regularity that they considered themselves to be significantly deprived of their liberty the minute officers began to inquire of them." Doubtless this is why a majority of the lower courts came to adopt an objective standard. The Supreme Court expressly adopted this posi-

6. 394 U.S. 324, 89 S.Ct. 1095, 22 L.Ed.2d 311 (1969).

7. 429 U.S. 492, 97 S.Ct. 711, 50 L.Ed.2d 714 (1977).

8. 421 F.2d 540 (2d Cir.1969).

tion in *Berkemer v. McCarty,*[9] involving roadside interrogation of a motorist stopped for a traffic violation. The Court, after holding *Miranda* is inapplicable in that context,[10] confronted the fact that apparently the trooper who made the stop "decided as soon as respondent stepped out of his car that respondent would be taken into custody and charged with a traffic offense," though he "never communicated his intention to respondent." This did not require a different result, the Court concluded without dissent, for a "policeman's unarticulated plan has no bearing on the question whether a suspect was 'in custody' at a particular time; the only relevant inquiry is how a reasonable man in the suspect's position would have understood his situation."

This objective approach will often require a careful examination of all the circumstances of the particular case. Account must be taken of those facts intrinsic to the interrogation: when and where it occurred, how long it lasted, how many police were present, what the officers and the defendant said and did, the presence of physical restraint or the equivalent (e.g., drawn weapons, a guard stationed at the door), and whether the defendant was being questioned as a suspect or as a witness. Events before the interrogation are also relevant, especially how the defendant got to the place of questioning—whether he came completely on his own, in response to a police request, or escorted by police officers. The Supreme Court [11] and the lower courts have also looked to what happened after the interrogation, relying upon the fact that the suspect was allowed to leave following the interrogation as strong evidence that the interrogation was not custodial. But as a matter of logic it is unsound to say that what happens later has some bearing on how a reasonable person would have perceived the situation at some earlier time. The same objection may be made as to the reliance by some courts on whether there was "focus." As a matter of logic, neither "focus" nor its absence (when not communicated to the suspect) has any direct bearing upon how a reasonable man would perceive the situation. Perhaps these cases reflect only the fact that courts are more willing to accept police representations of a noncustodial environment when it appears they lacked a basis for arrest and even after the questioning elected not to arrest.

(d) Presence at Station. One situation given specific mention in *Miranda* as being custodial is where the individual is "in custody at the station." This is obviously so when, as in the four cases involved in *Miranda,* the defendant is being held at the police station following his arrest. It does not follow, however, that all presence at the station is custodial in nature. To take the most obvious case, there is no custody if the person came to the station on his own initiative.

It has also been held that there is no custody when the person is present at the station in response to an "invitation" from the police, although in such cases a close look at all the surrounding circumstances is necessary. In *Oregon v. Mathiason,*[12] a police officer left a note at the apartment of defendant, a parolee, stating he wanted "to discuss something with you," so defendant called the officer and arranged to meet him at the state patrol office a few blocks from the apartment. When defendant appeared, he was told he was not under arrest and that the officer wanted to talk to him about a burglary. Later the officer falsely told defendant that his fingerprints had been found at the burglary scene, and defendant then confessed, after which he left the station. The Supreme Court's conclusion that defendant "came voluntarily to the police station" and thus was not initially in custody is unobjectionable. However, the Court's added conclusion that the circumstances never became custodial is open to serious question. It is true, as the Court put it in *Mathiason,* that the requirement of warnings is not imposed "simply because the questioning takes place

9. 468 U.S. 420, 104 S.Ct. 3138, 82 L.Ed.2d 317 (1984).

10. See § 6.6(e).

11. Oregon v. Mathiason, 429 U.S. 492, 97 S.Ct. 711, 50 L.Ed.2d 714 (1977), stressing that after the questioning defendant departed "the police station without hindrance."

12. 429 U.S. 492, 97 S.Ct. 711, 50 L.Ed.2d 714 (1977).

in the station house, or because the questioned person is one who the police suspect." But it is rather difficult to accept the conclusion that a parolee who is told his fingerprints had been found at a burglary scene would believe he was still free to leave.

If the so-called "invitation" involves the person going to the station in the company of the police, then a finding of custody is much more likely. *Dunaway v. New York,*[13] though not involving a *Miranda* issue, is illustrative. Acting on instructions to "pick up" petitioner and "bring him in," officers found him at a friend's house and drove him to the station. He was not told he was under arrest, no weapons were displayed, no handcuffs or any touching of petitioner was resorted to, and he was not booked, but he was then subjected to interrogation and was not told that he was free to go. The Court concluded there was "little doubt that petitioner was 'seized' in the Fourth Amendment sense when he was taken involuntarily to the police station," as "the detention of petitioner was in important respects indistinguishable from a traditional arrest." On the facts of *Dunaway,* it would seem that it also could be concluded that the situation was "custodial" for *Miranda* purposes. The result would be different if the suspect had been clearly and unequivocally advised that he was not under arrest and was free to leave at any time, or if it was made to appear that the person's presence was sought only as a witness.

(e) Presence Elsewhere. The *Miranda* Court stated that interrogation is custodial if it occurs while the individual is "in custody at the station or otherwise deprived of his freedom of action in any significant way." One reason for the latter part of this disjunctive definition is obvious: if *Miranda* governed only station-house interrogations, the police could easily circumvent the warning requirements by conducting interrogations in such places as hotel rooms or squad cars. Thus, it has been held that *Miranda* applies where, for example, a person has been apprehended and is in a police car at the time of his interrogation.

On the other hand, courts are much less likely to find the circumstances custodial when the interrogation occurs in familiar or at least neutral surroundings. Thus the Supreme Court in *Beckwith v. United States*[14] held, as have many lower court decisions, that interrogation in the suspect's home was noncustodial. Generally, the notion is that the suspect was in familiar surroundings and thus did not face the same pressures as in the police-dominated atmosphere of the station house. But the circumstances of each case must be carefully examined. The view that at-home questioning is noncustodial is strengthened when the suspect's friends or family members were present at the time. By contrast, in *Orozco v. Texas*[15] the Supreme Court concluded *Miranda* applied where four police officers entered defendant's bedroom at 4 a.m. to question him about a shooting, a proper result in that the circumstances produced a "potentiality for compulsion" equivalent to station house interrogation. Similarly, questioning has been held to be noncustodial where it occurred at the home of a friend or relative, a place of employment, a place of public accommodation, or a hospital. Once again, however, it must be emphasized that the circumstances of the particular case need to be carefully assessed. Thus, the situation might well be different as to an employee who was marched off to a security office of his employer, or as to a hospital patient who was taken to the hospital by the police or who was put into a police-dominated situation. But a person is not in custody for *Miranda* purposes merely because of his compelled appearance at a judicial proceeding to give testimony.

In *Minnesota v. Murphy,*[16] a probationer met with his probation officer at her office pursuant to her order and admitted in response to her questioning that he had committed a rape and murder some years ago. The

13. 442 U.S. 200, 99 S.Ct. 2248, 60 L.Ed.2d 824 (1979).

14. 425 U.S. 341, 96 S.Ct. 1612, 48 L.Ed.2d 1 (1976).

15. 394 U.S. 324, 89 S.Ct. 1095, 22 L.Ed.2d 311 (1969).

16. 465 U.S. 420, 104 S.Ct. 1136, 79 L.Ed.2d 409 (1984).

Court held *Miranda* was inapplicable because there was not custody:

> Custodial arrest is said to convey to the suspect a message that he has no choice but to submit to the officers' will and to confess. * * * It is unlikely that a probation interview, arranged by appointment at a mutually convenient time, would give rise to a similar impression. * * * Many of the psychological ploys discussed in *Miranda* capitalize on the suspect's unfamiliarity with the officers and the environment. Murphy's regular meetings with his probation officer should have served to familiarize him with her and her office and to insulate him from psychological intimidation that might overbear his desire to claim the privilege. Finally, the coercion inherent in custodial interrogation derives in large measure from an interrogator's insinuations that the interrogation will continue until a confession is obtained. * * * Since Murphy was not physically restrained and could have left the office, any compulsion he might have felt from the possibility that terminating the meeting would have led to revocation of probation was not comparable to the pressure on a suspect who is painfully aware that he literally cannot escape a persistent custodial interrogator.

In *Miranda,* the Court declared: "General on-the-scene questioning as to facts surrounding a crime or other general questioning of citizens in the factfinding process is not affected by our holding. * * * In such situations the compelling atmosphere inherent in the process of in-custody interrogation is not necessarily present." This is not to suggest, however, that all "on-the-scene" questioning falls outside *Miranda,* even if the person questioned is under arrest. As stated in *New York v. Quarles,*[17] "the ultimate inquiry is simply whether there is a 'formal arrest or restraint on freedom of movement' of the degree associated with a formal arrest." Such was the case in *Quarles,* where the questioning occurred in a supermarket minutes after defendant's arrest by four police officers with guns drawn and after defendant had been handcuffed. By contrast, the Court in *Berkemer v. McCarty*[18] concluded without dissent that *Miranda* warnings are not required in the circumstances present there, where defendant was subjected to roadside questioning during a routine traffic stop. The Court acknowledged that the defendant had been "seized" for Fourth Amendment purposes, but noted the seizure was a limited one, much like a *Terry* stop for investigation, and then concluded as to both that the "comparatively nonthreatening character" of the detentions justified the holding "that persons temporarily detained pursuant to such stops are not 'in custody' for the purposes of *Miranda.*" Specifically, the Court deemed it significant that such detentions are "presumptively temporary and brief" and are so perceived by the detainees, and that the circumstances of the stops are not such that a detainee "feels completely at the mercy of the police," as the stops occur in public and involve only one or two officers.

(f) Other Considerations. While the place of the interrogation is a very significant factor, it must be considered together with the other surrounding circumstances. In ascertaining, as called for by *Miranda,* whether the deprivation of freedom of action was "significant" (i.e., whether the circumstances were "likely to affect substantially the individual's 'will to resist and compel him to speak where he would not otherwise do so freely' "[19]), it is particularly important whether some indicia of arrest are present.[20] A court is not likely to find custody for *Miranda* purposes if the police were not even in a position to physically seize the suspect, but is likely to find custody if there was physical restraint such as handcuffing, drawing a gun, holding by the arm, or placing into a police car. Merely having the suspect move a short distance to facilitate conversation does not itself consti-

17. 467 U.S. 649, 104 S.Ct. 2626, 81 L.Ed.2d 550 (1984).

18. 468 U.S. 420, 104 S.Ct. 3138, 82 L.Ed.2d 317 (1984), first holding there is no general traffic violation exception to *Miranda* even when there is custody. See § 6.10(a).

19. People v. P. (Anonymous), 21 N.Y.2d 1, 286 N.Y.S.2d 225, 233 N.E.2d 255 (1967).

20. See text at note 17 supra.

tute custody. Also relevant are whether or not the suspect was told that he was free to leave and, if the events occur at the station, whether or not booking procedures were employed.

Because the Court in *Miranda* expressed concern with the coerciveness of situations in which the suspect was "cut off from the outside world" and "surrounded by antagonistic forces" in a "police dominated atmosphere" and interrogated "without relent," circumstances relating to those kinds of concerns are also relevant on the custody issue. Thus, custody is less likely to be deemed present when the questioning occurred in the presence of the suspect's friends or other third parties, and more likely to be found when the police have removed the suspect from such individuals. A court is more likely to find the situation custodial when the suspect was confronted by several officers instead of just one, when the demeanor of the officer was antagonistic rather than friendly, and when the questioning was lengthy rather than brief and routine. And surely a reasonable person would conclude he was in custody if the interrogation is close and persistent, involving leading questions and the discounting of the suspect's denials of involvement. The argument that the giving of some of the *Miranda* warnings itself establishes that the situation was custodial has been rightly rejected, for it would be bizarre if such solicitude for a suspect not actually in custody were deemed to make the suspect's statement subject to suppression under *Miranda*.

§ 6.7 *Miranda:* "Interrogation"

(a) The "Functional Equivalent" Test. Just what is encompassed within the "interrogation" part of *Miranda's* "custodial interrogation" term has caused the courts considerable difficulty. One view often taken, which finds support in the *Miranda* Court's explanation that "we mean questioning initiated by law enforcement officers," is that nothing but the asking of questions will bring a case within the constraints of *Miranda*. Another view, consistent with the observation in *Miranda* that it is the placing of an individual "into police custody" and then subjecting him "to techniques of persuasion" which together produce the "compulsion to speak," is that the word "interrogation" should not be given a narrow or literal interpretation. So matters stood until the Supreme Court finally resolved this fundamental dispute in *Rhode Island v. Innis.*[1]

In *Innis,* defendant was arrested for robbery with a sawed-off shotgun and promptly given his *Miranda* warnings, at which he said he wished to speak with a lawyer. The arresting officers then began their journey to the station with the prisoner, and during this time the officers conversed among themselves about the desirability of finding the shotgun because there was a school for handicapped children in the vicinity. At this, defendant said he would show the officers where the gun was located, which he did. His murder conviction was overturned by the state supreme court, which held the gun and testimony about its discovery were improperly admitted because defendant had been subjected to "subtle coercion" equivalent to *Miranda* "interrogation." A majority of the Supreme Court, though ultimately concluding that "respondent was not 'interrogated' within the meaning of *Miranda,*" nonetheless opted for a rather broad definition of what constitutes "interrogation."

The *Innis* majority first rejected the two extreme positions. The notion "that the *Miranda* rules were to apply only to those police interrogation practices that involve express questioning" was found to be inconsistent with the *Miranda* Court's discussion of the use of various "psychological ploys" which, "no less than express questioning, were thought, in a custodial setting, to amount to interrogation." But this did not mean "that all statements obtained by the police after a person has been taken into custody are to be considered the product of interrogation," for interrogation, "as conceptualized in the *Miranda* opinion, must reflect a measure of com-

§ 6.7

1. 446 U.S. 291, 100 S.Ct. 1682, 64 L.Ed.2d 297 (1980).

pulsion above and beyond that inherent in custody itself." The *Innis* Court then concluded

> that the *Miranda* safeguards come into play whenever a person in custody is subjected to either express questioning or its functional equivalent. That is to say, the term "interrogation" under *Miranda* refers not only to express questioning, but also to any words or actions on the part of the police (other than those normally attendant to arrest and custody) that the police should know are reasonably likely to elicit an incriminating response from the suspect. The latter portion of this definition focuses primarily upon the perceptions of the suspect, rather than the intent of the police. This focus reflects the fact that the *Miranda* safeguards were designed to vest a suspect in custody with an added measure of protection against coercive police practices, without regard to objective proof of the underlying intent of the police. A practice that the police should know is reasonably likely to evoke an incriminating response from a suspect thus amounts to interrogation. But, since the police surely cannot be held accountable for the unforeseeable results of their words or actions, the definition of interrogation can extend only to words or actions on the part of police officers that they *should have known* were reasonably likely to elicit an incriminating response.

The *Innis* definition of "interrogation" was expressly noted to be "not necessarily interchangeable" with the *Brewer v. Williams*[2] and *Massiah v. United States*[3] definition of what constitutes a violation of the Sixth Amendment right to counsel once that right has attached. For one thing, the *Williams-Massiah* "deliberately elicited" test focuses upon the intent of the police, while the *Innis* test does not. Only Justice Stevens, dissenting in *Innis,* felt that " 'interrogation' must include any police statement or conduct that has the same purpose or effect as a direct question," that is, both those "that appear to call for a response from the suspect" and "those that are designed to do so." But one of the ambiguities of *Innis* is just how far apart these two positions actually are. In an apparent attempt to bridge the gap, the majority dropped a footnote saying that the intent of the police is not irrelevant, "for it may well have a bearing on whether the police should have known that their words or actions were reasonably likely to evoke an incriminating response." This footnote goes on to say that "where a police practice is designed to elicit an incriminating response from the accused, it is unlikely that the practice will not also be one which the police should have known was reasonably likely to have that effect," which drew the following footnote rejoinder by Justice Stevens: "This factual assumption is extremely dubious. I would assume that police often interrogate suspects without any reason to believe that their efforts are likely to be successful in the hope that a statement will nevertheless be forthcoming."

This exchange is indicative of more fundamental problems with both the majority opinion and the Stevens dissent. To take the latter first of all, it surely does not make sense to conclude that under *Miranda* the existence of "interrogation" (any more than the existence of "custody"[4]) depends upon the undisclosed intentions of the officer. *Miranda* is grounded in the notion that custody plus interrogation produces a coercive atmosphere, which makes sense only when the suspect is aware of both the custody and the interrogation. The Court noted in *Innis* that it would not constitute "interrogation" for the police merely to drive past the site of the concealed weapon while taking the most direct route to the police station, and surely the result should be no different even if the police admitted their "purpose" in driving by was to elicit an incriminating response. To take a phrase from *Miranda,* the "potentiality for compulsion" would be no different in the latter situation than in the former.

Justice Stevens was apparently attracted to his intention-of-the-officer alternative because it would largely overcome what he saw as a glaring weakness in the *Innis* majority's ap-

2. 430 U.S. 387, 97 S.Ct. 1232, 51 L.Ed.2d 424 (1977).

3. 377 U.S. 201, 84 S.Ct. 1199, 12 L.Ed.2d 246 (1964).

4. See § 6.6(c).

proach. His reading of the majority's (perhaps unfortunate) "reasonably likely to elicit" language is that it necessitates a determination of the apparent probability that police speech or conduct will elicit an incriminating response. This interpretation cannot be dismissed out of hand; for one thing, it would explain the otherwise questionable *Innis* result. But so interpreted the *Innis* test would not provide adequate guidance to police and lower courts. However, that does not appear to be what the *Innis* majority really meant, for such a view of the case is inconsistent with the majority's professed aim of defining "interrogation" in a manner consistent with *Miranda's* underlying policy of prohibiting all speech or conduct which is the "functional equivalent" of direct questioning.

Just what *Innis* does mean is a matter of some uncertainty, although it would seem to turn upon the objective purpose manifested by the police. If an objective observer (with the same knowledge of the suspect as the police officer) would, on the sole basis of hearing the officer's remarks, infer that the remarks were designed to elicit an incriminating response, then the remarks should constitute "interrogation." This interpretation is consistent with the result reached in *Innis,* would not be difficult to apply because it is an objective test which does not require a determination of the actual perception of the suspect, but yet is fully responsive to the concerns in *Miranda* because it identifies the situations in which the suspect will experience the "functional equivalent" of direct questioning by concluding that the police are trying to get him to make an incriminating response. Moreover, it has the added advantage that it would put to rest a concern expressed by one member of the Court in *Innis:* that the police were expected to "evaluate the suggestibility and susceptibility of an accused." [5]

Consistent in some respects with the preceding interpretation is *Arizona v. Mauro,*[6] where, after defendant invoked his right to counsel, the police acceded to a request of his wife, also a suspect in the investigation of their son's death, to speak with defendant, but had a police officer and tape recorder conspicuously present at the meeting. The Court, in a 5–4 decision, held this did not constitute "interrogation" under the *Innis* formulation. *Mauro* apparently reflects an unwillingness of a majority of the Court to ground the "interrogation" determination in the subjective intentions of the police. The state supreme court had concluded that the proper focus was upon the intent of the police and that this intent was "so clear" that it was unnecessary to "address appellant's perceptions," and this approach was accepted by the four dissenters in *Mauro.* The *Mauro* majority, on the other hand, asserted that there was no such intent shown and added, even more unconvincingly, that the police were not even aware of "a sufficient likelihood of incrimination" under the legal standard articulated in *Innis.*

But what seems to lie at the heart of the majority position in *Mauro* is that neither the subjective intentions of the police nor their perception of a significant likelihood that a certain scenario will prompt incriminating statements by the defendant is determinative. This is reflected in the majority's statement that "the weakness of Mauro's claim that he was interrogated is underscored by examining the situation from his perspective. * * * We doubt that a suspect, told by officers that his wife will be allowed to speak to him, would feel that he was being coerced to incriminate himself in any way." That is, the bottom line in *Mauro,* as the majority sees it, is that "Mauro was not subjected to compelling influences, psychological ploys, or direct questioning."

There is much to be said for the proposition, which *seems* to underlie the majority's position in *Mauro* notwithstanding all the disclaimers, that neither the officers' intentions

5. Burger, C.J., concurring but responding to a footnote by the majority asserting the relevance of "[a]ny knowledge the police may have had concerning the unusual susceptibility of a defendant to a particular form of persuasion."

6. 481 U.S. 520, 107 S.Ct. 1931, 95 L.Ed.2d 458 (1987).

nor their strong expectations should be decisive. Rather, as suggested earlier, it makes more sense to consider the objective purpose manifested by the police—that is, what an objective observer with the same knowledge as the suspect would conclude the police were up to. *If* that is the proper approach,[7] then it is by no means clear that the majority in *Mauro* reached the correct result. When the defendant was suddenly confronted with what must have appeared to him as a police-arranged meeting with his wife at which the police maintained a presence with a tape recorder operating, it would seem that he was subjected to the "functional equivalent" of interrogation. This is because Mauro had learned that those having custody of him had produced a scenario which (in the language of Justice Stevens in *Innis*) "appear[ed] to call for a response."

(b) Questioning. The Court in *Innis* set out to determine what "words or actions on the part of the police" other than "express questioning" constitute "interrogation" within the meaning of *Miranda.* Putting the matter this way would certainly suggest that *any* time a person in custody is asked a question, surely the *Miranda* requirements apply. But no such absolute rule had been recognized by the lower courts prior to *Innis,* and it does not seem that all of those decisions are cast in doubt by the *Innis* decision. If other "words or actions" fall within *Miranda* only if "the police should know [they] are likely to elicit an incriminating response," then it is not fanciful to suggest that certain types of questioning also do not come within *Miranda* because they are unlikely to produce that kind of response. Or if, as suggested above, the unfortunate "likely to elicit" language is ignored in favor of an inquiry whether an objective observer would infer that the remarks were designed to elicit an incriminating response, it still does not follow that *all* questioning of those in custody is governed by *Miranda.*

Miranda requirements are inapplicable to questioning which produces an incriminating response which is other than "testimonial" in nature. Illustrative is *Pennsylvania v. Muniz,*[8] where the defendant, under arrest for driving under the influence, was asked a series of questions about his name, address, birthday, age, etc. The Court concluded that though defendant's videotaped responses incriminated him because his slurred speech manifested his drunkenness, the lack of *Miranda* warnings did not require suppression. Relying upon the established distinction between "testimonial" and "real or physical evidence" for purposes of the privilege against self-incrimination,[9] the Court concluded

> that any slurring of speech and other evidence of lack of muscular coordination revealed by Muniz's responses to [the officer's] direct questions constitute nontestimonial components of those responses. Requiring a suspect to reveal the physical manner in which he articulates words, like requiring him to reveal the physical properties of the sound produced by his voice,[10] * * * does not, without more, compel him to provide a 'testimonial' response for purposes of the privilege.

The *content* of one of the defendant's answer in *Muniz,* that he did not know the date of his sixth birthday, was incriminating because it would allow the inference that his mental state was confused. Four members of the Court believed this also fell into the "real or physical evidence" category,[11] but the majority disagreed. They explained that even if the matter inferred had to do with physical condition, the critical issue "is whether the inference is drawn from a testimonial act or

7. In Pennsylvania v. Muniz, ___ U.S. ___, 110 S.Ct. 2638, 110 L.Ed.2d 528 (1990), certain words were deemed not to constitute interrogation because they "were not likely to be perceived as calling for any incriminating response." Significantly, the Court did *not* say "perceived by the suspect."

8. ___ U.S. ___, 110 S.Ct. 2638, 110 L.Ed.2d 528 (1990).

9. Schmerber v. California, 384 U.S. 757, 86 S.Ct. 1826, 16 L.Ed.2d 908 (1966), discussed in § 7.2(a).

10. See United States v. Wade, 388 U.S. 218, 87 S.Ct. 1926, 18 L.Ed.2d 1149 (1967), discussed in § 7.2(b).

11. They stated: "If the police may require Muniz to use his body in order to demonstrate the level of his physical coordination, there is no reason why they should not be able to require him to speak or write in order to determine his mental coordination."

from physical evidence.[12] * * * Whenever a suspect is asked for a response requiring him to communicate an express or implied assertion of fact or belief, the suspect confronts the 'trilemma' of truth, falsity, or silence and hence the response (whether based on truth or falsity) contains a testimonial component." Under this test, the sixth birthday question "required a testimonial response": the coercive environment precluded the option of remaining silent, and the truth (that he did not know the date) was incriminating, as would have been a false statement (an incorrect guess).

Prior to *Muniz,* lower courts—usually relying upon the *Innis* assertion that "interrogation" does not include those words and actions "normally attendant to arrest and custody"—held that routine inquiries during the booking process are lawful even absent *Miranda* warnings. *Muniz,* in holding admissible the answers given to a series of booking questions, supports this conclusion. Four members of the Court concluded the answers were admissible "because the questions fall within a 'routine booking question' exception which exempts from *Miranda*'s coverage questions to secure the 'biographical data necessary to complete booking or pretrial services.' " [13] Four others deemed it "unnecessary to determine whether the questions fall within the 'routine booking question' exception to *Miranda*" because they believed the defendant's responses "were not testimonial."

A related but more difficult issue concerns questions asked for purposes of identification (e.g., "what is your name?", "where do you live?") other than as part of the booking process. For example, in the unlikely event that an on-the-street interrogation were deemed custodial, may the police make inquiries limited to the purpose of identifying a person found under suspicious circumstances or near the scene of a recent crime? An affirmative answer is suggested by *California v. Byers,*[14] holding that a statute requiring the driver of a car involved in an accident to stop and give the driver of the other car his name and address does not violate the privilege against self-incrimination, even without a restriction on the use of the required disclosures. The *Byers* Court, indicating that the required conduct was not "testimonial" in the Fifth Amendment sense and did not entail a "substantial risk of self-incrimination," noted:

> A name, linked with a motor vehicle, is no more incriminating than the tax return, linked with the disclosure of income * * *. It identifies but does not by itself implicate anyone in criminal conduct.
>
> Although identity, when made known, may lead to inquiry that in turn leads to arrest and charge, those developments depend on different factors and independent evidence. Here the compelled disclosure of identity could have led to a charge that might not have been made had the driver fled the scene; but this is true only in the same sense that a taxpayer can be charged on the basis of the contents of a tax return or failure to file an income tax return. There is no constitutional right to refuse to file an income tax return or to flee the scene of an accident in order to avoid the possibility of legal involvement.

Application of *Byers* to the situation here under discussion (which finds support in the many holdings that the privilege presents no bar to various other identification techniques [15]) would not seem inconsistent with the *Innis* definition of "interrogation."

An innocuous question which results in an incriminating response does not fall within *Miranda;* as the Court put it in *Innis,* "the police surely cannot be held accountable for the unforeseeable results of their words or actions." As for questions not quite so innocuous but not accusatory either (e.g., "what

12. They explained that therefore, while drawing a blood sample to prove intoxication was "outside of the Fifth Amendment's protection," the same would not be true "had the police instead asked the suspect directly whether his blood contained a high concentration of alcohol."

13. They also concluded that because *Innis* focuses primarily upon "the perspective of the suspect," the booking questions could not be placed outside the *Innis* definition "merely because the questions were not intended to elicit information for investigative purposes."

14. 402 U.S. 424, 91 S.Ct. 1535, 29 L.Ed.2d 9 (1971).

15. See § 7.2(b).

happened?", "what's going on here?"), the issue has been infrequently litigated because those situations usually arise in the context of a brief noncustodial encounter between an officer and citizen. However, there is authority that such situations are likewise not covered by *Miranda.* This is often explained by reliance upon the *Miranda* Court's statement that "[g]eneral on-the-scene questioning as to facts surrounding a crime or other general questioning of citizens in the fact-finding process is not affected by our holding," though sometimes that language has been deemed inapplicable whenever the situation has become custodial. In any event, it would seem that at least some such inquiries are not interrogation under the suggested interpretation of *Innis*: whether an objective observer would infer the remarks were designed to elicit an incriminating response. Such an inference might well not be drawn when the question is very general in nature, not directed at one particular person, obviously asked before there has been any sorting of suspects from witnesses, apparently asked about a seemingly innocuous matter not directly related to the police intervention, obviously spontaneous in nature, or seemingly a natural question anyone would ask given defendant's condition or other unusual circumstances.

Still another type of case is that in which the authorities claim that they were questioning for the purpose of protecting themselves or others from weapons by asking the defendant whether he had a gun or where a gun was located. Illustrative is *New York v. Quarles,*[16] where police chased a rape suspect, who was reportedly armed, inside a supermarket and then arrested him there; a frisk uncovered an empty shoulder holster, so one officer asked him, "Where is the gun?"; the suspect gestured toward a stack of soap cartons and said, "The gun is over there," and police then found a revolver behind the cartons. A majority of the Supreme Court concluded that "on these facts there is a 'public safety' exception to the requirement that *Miranda* warnings be given." The Court characterized *Miranda* as representing a willingness by the Court to impose procedural safeguards "when the primary social cost of those added protections is the possibility of fewer convictions," to be distinguished from the instant situation in which the cost would be an inability "to insure that further danger to the public did not result from the concealment of the gun." It was thus concluded "that the need for answers to questions in a situation posing a threat to the public safety outweighs the need for the prophylactic rule protecting the Fifth Amendment's privilege against self-incrimination." Otherwise, the *Quarles* majority reasoned, police would be "in the untenable position of having to consider, often in a matter of seconds, whether it best serves society for them to give the warnings in order to preserve the admissibility of evidence they might uncover but possibly damage or destroy their ability to obtain that evidence and neutralize the volatile situation confronting them."

The four dissenters in *Quarles* understandably objected that the majority's "public safety exception destroys forever the clarity of *Miranda* for both law enforcement officers and members of the judiciary," and also that the majority's cost-benefit analysis was irrelevant under the reasoning in *Miranda* and in any event failed to take account of the fact that police could lawfully question for public safety purposes provided the defendant's statements and the fruits thereof were not later used against him. But perhaps the most troublesome aspect of *Quarles* is the apparent breadth of the exception which has been created. Though the record below did not indicate that the police questioning was prompted by an actual concern for public safety, the majority disposed of that problem by declaring that the public safety exception "does not depend upon the motivation of the individual officers involved." That is, it suffices that the facts of the case, objectively viewed, show that the police,

> in the very act of apprehending a suspect, were confronted with the immediate necessity of ascertaining the whereabouts of a gun

16. 467 U.S. 649, 104 S.Ct. 2626, 81 L.Ed.2d 550 (1984).

which they had every reason to believe the suspect had just removed from his empty holster and discarded in the supermarket. So long as the gun was concealed somewhere in the supermarket, with its actual whereabouts unknown, it obviously posed more than one danger to the public safety; an accomplice might make use of it, a customer or employee might later come upon it.

But the facts in *Quarles* show no such thing. At the time of the questioning, Quarles was handcuffed and in the custody of four armed officers, and thus there was no danger whatsoever that he could get at the gun. Nor was there the slightest suggestion that he had been aided by an accomplice in the rape. As for the possibility that some other person might come onto the gun before the police could locate it, this seems equally fanciful in light of the facts that the events occurred after midnight when the store was apparently deserted and that the police knew the gun had been discarded in the immediate vicinity. But at least we know that the *Quarles* exception is not broad enough to encompass any questioning about the location of a weapon. The majority asserted *Quarles* was not inconsistent with *Orozco v. Texas,*[17] where police entered the sleeping defendant's room and then questioned him about a gun used in a murder at a restaurant several hours earlier, as there "the questions about the gun were clearly investigatory" because "they did not in any way relate to an objectively reasonable need to protect the police or the public from any immediate danger associated with the weapon."

Somewhat similar is the so-called "rescue doctrine," under which it has been held that *Miranda* warnings are unnecessary before custodial questioning undertaken to save life (e.g., in an effort to locate a kidnap victim). The issue is a difficult one. On the one hand, it may be said that such a result properly takes account of interests superior to those of the suspect. But it may be argued that such reasoning misstates the issue because the balance is not between the victim's life and defendant's Fifth Amendment rights but rather between prosecution interests and the defendant's rights. The police are of course free to acquire the life-saving information so long as they do not attempt to use it to prosecute the defendant. One court considered and rejected that reasoning on the ground that the fruit of the poisonous tree doctrine could well free the accused. Perhaps the solution lies in more careful thought about how the fruits doctrine should apply in this context, as to which "the purpose and flagrancy of the official misconduct" is relevant.[18] *Innis* puts to rest another explanation sometimes given for the rule—that *Miranda* is inapplicable because the police motive was rescue rather than obtaining an incriminating statement.

One other special purpose type of questioning has been considered by the Supreme Court. In *Estelle v. Smith,*[19] defendant was indicted for murder and the state announced its intention to seek the death penalty. Though defense counsel had not interposed an insanity defense or questioned his client's competency to stand trial, defendant was subjected to a psychiatric examination and the psychiatrist testified at the penalty phase of the trial concerning defendant's "future dangerousness," after which defendant was sentenced to death. The state claimed that a psychiatric examination did not infringe upon Fifth Amendment interests because an inquiry into defendant's state of mind was like obtaining a blood sample or voice and handwriting exemplars, but the Court rejected this contention. Because the doctor's testimony "was not based simply on his observation of respondent" but came "largely from respondent's account of the crime during their interview," the "Fifth Amendment privilege * * * is directly involved here because the State used as evidence against respondent the substance of his disclosures during the pretrial psychiatric examination." The Court added

17. 394 U.S. 324, 89 S.Ct. 1095, 22 L.Ed.2d 311 (1969).

18. Brown v. Illinois, 422 U.S. 590, 95 S.Ct. 2254, 45 L.Ed.2d 416 (1975), where the "poisonous tree" was an illegal arrest. But see § 9.5(a) concerning the added uncertainties where the "poisonous tree" is a *Miranda* violation.

19. 451 U.S. 454, 101 S.Ct. 1866, 68 L.Ed.2d 359 (1981).

that the result would have been otherwise had the doctor testified at a hearing on defendant's competency to stand trial, for "no Fifth Amendment issue would have arisen" in that context. The Court also emphasized that the instant case was not analogous

> to a sanity examination occasioned by a defendant's plea of not guilty by reason of insanity at the time of his offense. When a defendant asserts the insanity defense and introduces supporting psychiatric testimony, his silence may deprive the State of the only effective means it has of controverting his proof on an issue that he interjected into the case. Accordingly, several courts of appeals have held that, under such circumstances, a defendant can be required to submit to a sanity examination conducted by the prosecution's psychiatrist.

The Court did not have occasion to rule on such a situation in *Smith,* and in the later case of *Buchanan v. Kentucky*[20] found it necessary only to hold that "if a defendant requests [a psychiatric] evaluation or presents psychiatric evidence, then, at the very least, the prosecution may rebut this presentation with evidence from the reports of the examination that the defendant requested."

(c) Other "Words or Actions." The major impact of *Innis* is with respect to conduct other than express questioning. Prior to that decision there was a split of authority as to what the outcome should be when the police engaged in such tactics as confronting the defendant with physical evidence, with an accusing accomplice, or with the confession of an accomplice. One explanation given for admitting incriminating statements obtained in these ways was that questioning does not exist absent verbal conduct by the police, a notion which *Innis* clearly repudiates. Indeed, under *Innis* such tactics will usually be characterized as "interrogation." This may seem less likely after *Mauro,* discussed earlier,[21] rejecting the conclusion of the four dissenters "that a police decision to place two suspects in the same room and then to listen to or record their conversation may constitute a form of interrogation even if no questions are asked by any police officers." Perhaps that is so, though the majority distinguished the situation before it from those in which the police resorted to " 'psychological ploys, such as to "posi[t]" "the guilt of the subject" * * *.' "

Another line of reasoning in the pre-*Innis* cases was that it is not unfair to communicate to the defendant information about the strength of the case against him, for such information is relevant to an intelligent decision by him as to whether he should cooperate or remain silent. To the extent that this view persists, there will doubtless be pressure not to apply *Innis* to every instance in which such information has been made available to a defendant. And in any event, *Innis* is not so broad; as noted earlier, it should be interpreted as covering those instances in which the officer's words or actions would be viewed by an objective observer as designed to elicit an incriminating response, which is preferable to asking (to take some of the language in *Innis*) whether the police should have known the activity was "reasonably likely to elicit an incriminating response." This point is best illustrated by two situations which have been viewed as not within *Miranda*'s constraints and as to which *Innis* is not likely to produce a different result: where the defendant made a confession after being identified in a lineup or after witnessing police discovery of physical evidence. In terms of the probability of a defendant making an incriminating remark, these two situations probably are not significantly different from many of the others described above. But the important fact about these two situations is that the police were engaged in activity calculated to produce evidence against the defendant by other means, and thus objectively viewed they would not appear to be designed to get an incriminating response from the defendant.

Another kind of case which requires closer analysis after *Innis* is that in which the police

20. 483 U.S. 402, 107 S.Ct. 2906, 97 L.Ed.2d 336 (1987), involving not an insanity defense but rather a mental state defense of extreme emotional disturbance.

21. See § 6.7(a).

within the hearing of defendant engage in comments or conversation short of questions put to the defendant. *Innis* itself was this kind of case, for it involved a conversation among the officers about the desirability of finding the shotgun so that it would not fall into the hands of a handicapped child. The majority concluded this was not *Miranda* interrogation because the comments were just "a few off-hand remarks" rather than a "lengthy harangue," were not "peculiarly 'evocative,'" and were not made to one the police knew "was peculiarly susceptible to an appeal to his conscience concerning the safety of handicapped children." Though *Innis* is a close case, surely there are other instances in which the comments or conversations of the police will be deemed interrogation. Illustrative is the "Christian burial" speech in *Brewer v. Williams.*[22] Though the Court decided that case on other grounds, prompting concern that it was not prepared to extend the concept of interrogation as it later did in *Innis,* certainly the conduct of the police in *Williams,* where the remarks were directed at the defendant by police who knew of and were taking advantage of the fact he was deeply religious, amounts to interrogation.

But there are other instances in which the police activity will not amount to "interrogation" or a functional equivalent, though it is clear beyond dispute that an officer directed words to the suspect. Illustrative is *Pennsylvania v. Muniz,*[23] where the defendant, arrested for driving under the influence, made incriminating remarks when asked by officers to perform physical sobriety tests and to submit to a breathalyzer examination. The Court concluded there was no "interrogation within the meaning of *Miranda*" because the "limited and focused inquiries were necessarily 'attendant to' the legitimate police procedure * * * and were not likely to be perceived as calling for any incriminating response." The Court earlier reached the same conclusion as to a police request that a suspect take a blood alcohol test,[24] while lower courts have so ruled as to police statements to the suspect by way of warning him of his rights or explaining why he was arrested.

Finally, it must be asked what the significance of *Innis* is in the so-called "jail plant" case, where an undercover agent is placed with the defendant while he is in custody and listens to defendant's remarks or even encourages the defendant to make remarks about the crime. In *Hoffa v. United States,*[25] involving a "plant" of a government agent with an unincarcerated defendant, the Court summarily dismissed the claim that Hoffa's incriminating statement had been obtained in violation of the Fifth Amendment. The Court there noted that "a necessary element of compulsory self-incrimination is some kind of compulsion," and that Hoffa's choice to make incriminating remarks in the agent's presence was "wholly voluntary" and not "the product of any sort of coercion, legal or factual." It has sometimes been questioned, however, whether the same result should obtain when the defendant is in jail. So the argument goes, the confinement increases the suspect's anxiety and makes him more likely to seek discourse with others to relieve this anxiety, meaning he will be more susceptible to an undercover investigator seeking information. Moreover, though *Hoffa* was fooled he at least had the choice of his companions, but when the suspect's ability to select people with whom he can confide is completely within police control, they have a unique opportunity to exploit the suspect's vulnerability.

While the Supreme Court has applied the *Massiah* rule (available only after the right to counsel has attached) to the "jail plant" situation, at least when the plant has taken some affirmative steps to bring about the defendant's statements,[26] the Court more recently

22. 430 U.S. 387, 97 S.Ct. 1232, 51 L.Ed.2d 424 (1977).

23. ___ U.S. ___, 110 S.Ct. 2638, 110 L.Ed.2d 528 (1990).

24. South Dakota v. Neville, 459 U.S. 553, 103 S.Ct. 916, 74 L.Ed.2d 748 (1983).

25. 385 U.S. 293, 87 S.Ct. 408, 17 L.Ed.2d 374 (1966).

26. United States v. Henry, 447 U.S. 264, 100 S.Ct. 2183, 65 L.Ed.2d 115 (1980), discussed in § 6.4(g).

held in *Illinois v. Perkins* [27] "that an undercover law enforcement officer posing as a fellow inmate need not give *Miranda* warnings to an incarcerated suspect before asking questions that may elicit an incriminating response." The Court in *Perkins* reasoned:

> Conversations between suspects and undercover agents do not implicate the concerns underlying *Miranda.* The essential ingredients of a "police-dominated atmosphere" and compulsion are not present when an incarcerated person speaks freely to someone that he believes to be a fellow inmate. Coercion is determined from the perspective of the suspect. * * * When a suspect considers himself in the company of cellmates and not officers, the coercive atmosphere is lacking. * * *
>
> It is the premise of *Miranda* that the danger of coercion results from the interaction of custody and official interrogation. We reject the argument that *Miranda* warnings are required whenever a suspect is in custody in a technical sense and converses with someone who happens to be a government agent. Questioning by captors, who appear to control the suspect's fate, may create mutually reinforcing pressures that the Court has assumed will weaken the suspect's will, but where a suspect does not know that he is conversing with a government agent, these pressures do not exist.

(d) "Volunteered" Statements and Follow–Up Questioning. The *Miranda* Court emphasized that "[t]here is no requirement that police stop a person who enters a police station and states that he wishes to confess to a crime, or a person who calls the police to offer a confession or any other statement he desires to make. Volunteered statements of any kind are not barred by the Fifth Amendment and their admissibility is not affected by our holding today." It is thus clear that a statement not preceded by the *Miranda* warnings will be admissible when, for example, the defendant walks into a police station and confesses or blurts out an admission when approached by an officer near a crime scene. More important, because *Miranda* found only custody-plus-interrogation coercive, a statement may qualify as "volunteered" even though made by one in custody, one who had previously asserted his right to silence, or one who had previously requested counsel.

Assuming a truly volunteered statement, may the police follow up that statement with some questions? *Miranda* is not entirely clear on this issue; at one point custodial interrogation is defined as "questioning initiated by law enforcement officers," suggesting that police questioning designed to clarify or amplify a volunteered statement is permissible, but elsewhere it is said that the suspect must be warned "prior to any questioning." Except in extreme circumstances, courts have generally been quite willing to admit the answers to follow-up questions on the ground that these answers are a continuation of the volunteered statement. The better view, however, is that the part of defendant's statement given after the follow-up questions is volunteered only if the questions are neutral efforts to clarify what has already been said rather than apparent attempts to expand the scope of the statement previously made. This means that a question which would clarify a prior ambiguous statement (e.g., "did what?" in response to "I did it") would not constitute *Miranda* interrogation, but a question which would enhance the defendant's guilt or raise the offense to a higher degree would.

Innis should not be read as a prohibition upon all follow-up questions. While the Court there made an unqualified reference to "express questioning" as falling within *Miranda,* it was not confronted with a follow-up questioning situation. The underlying rationale of *Innis* is that *Miranda* covers only police conduct likely to be coercive when coupled with defendant's custody, which cannot be said of a question that does nothing more than seek clarification of what the defendant has already volunteered. Here again, however, the *Innis* Court's unfortunate "likely to elicit an incriminating response" language may prove a source of difficulty. If applied

27. ___ U.S. ___, 110 S.Ct. 2394, 110 L.Ed.2d 243 (1990).

literally, it would seem to foreclose even a clarifying question.

§ 6.8 *Miranda:* Required Warnings

(a) Content. The Supreme Court in *Miranda* held that before a person in custody may be subjected to interrogation he "must be adequately and effectively apprised of his rights." In particular,

> he must first be informed in clear and unequivocal terms that he has the right to remain silent. * * *
>
> The warning of the right to remain silent must be accompanied by the explanation that anything said can and will be used against the individual in court.
>
> * * * [A]n individual held for interrogation must be clearly informed that he has the right to consult with a lawyer and to have the lawyer with him during interrogation * * *.
>
> * * * [I]t is necessary to warn him not only that he has the right to consult with an attorney, but also that if he is indigent a lawyer will be appointed to represent him.

Whether the warnings must be given in precisely that language reached the Court in *California v. Prysock,*[1] on review of a lower court decision asserting that the "rigidity of the *Miranda* rules and the way in which they are to be applied was conceived of and continues to be recognized as the decision's greatest strength." The Supreme Court noted that it "has never indicated that the 'rigidity' of *Miranda* extends to the precise formulation of the warnings given" and that, "[q]uite the contrary, *Miranda* itself indicates that no talismanic incantation was required to satisfy its strictures." The Court in *Prysock* thus concluded that what is required is not "a verbatim recital of the words of the *Miranda* opinion" but rather words which in substance will have "fully conveyed to [defendant] his rights as required by *Miranda.*" Just when that has been accomplished, of course, is sometimes a difficult question.

The warning "that he has the right to remain silent" has been the source of little difficulty, as police apparently do not often deviate from this language. One variation which has surfaced, telling the suspect that he "need not make any statement," has usually been held acceptable. As for the second warning, concerning possible use of anything said by the suspect, in the excerpt quoted above the Court employed the overstatement "can and will be used." But at an earlier point the Court described the warning as being that what is said "may be used," and this alternative has been consistently approved by the lower courts. The courts have also upheld other formulations, including use of "can" alone, of "might," and of "could." The part of the second warning which cautions about use of the statement "against" the suspect has sometimes been changed so that he is told what he says may be used "for or against you." Some courts have disapproved of this variation, while others have criticized it but yet held it not an impermissible deviation from the *Miranda* formula. The former is the better view, for such a variation is not only misleading but is likely to undercut the effect of the warning by offering an inducement to speak.

Under *Miranda,* it is necessary that the right to counsel warnings cover the right to appointed counsel and the immediacy of the right in the sense that it exists both before and during interrogation. This has given rise to the question of whether the statement about appointment of counsel must particularize that appointment will precede questioning. No such language appears in the warnings quoted above, but at another point the *Miranda* Court said the defendant must be warned "that if he cannot afford an attorney one will be appointed for him prior to any questioning if he so desires." However, in *California v. Prysock*[2] the Court held that where defendant "was told of his right to have a lawyer present prior to and during interrogation" and also of "his right to have a lawyer appointed at no cost if he could not afford one," these warnings collectively "con-

§ 6.8

1. 453 U.S. 355, 101 S.Ct. 2806, 69 L.Ed.2d 696 (1981).

2. 453 U.S. 355, 101 S.Ct. 2806, 69 L.Ed.2d 696 (1981).

veyed to respondent his right to have a lawyer appointed if he could not afford one prior to and during interrogation." The three *Prysock* dissenters objected rather convincingly that under the circumstances the juvenile defendant might have understood the right to "appointed" counsel to refer only to the trial and that his right to counsel at the police station was dependent upon his or his parents' ability to hire one.

Somewhat different from *Prysock* is the case in which the police warnings convey the message that appointed counsel cannot be made available until some future time. Such a case reached the Court in *Duckworth v. Eagan,*[3] where the defendant was given the full *Miranda* warnings (including: "You have a right to talk to a lawyer for advice before we ask you any questions, and to have him with you during questioning"), but was also told: "We have no way of giving you a lawyer, but one will be appointed for you, if you wish, if and when you go to court." In holding these warnings sufficient, the majority stressed that the "if and when" statement "accurately described the procedure for the appointment of counsel in Indiana" and squared with *Miranda,* which "does not require that attorneys be producible on call. * * * If the police cannot provide appointed counsel, *Miranda* requires only that the police not question a suspect unless he waives his right to counsel." The four dissenters cogently objected that the "if and when" qualification "leads the suspect to believe that a lawyer will not be provided until some indeterminate time in the future *after questioning.*"

Assuming incomplete or inadequate *Miranda* warnings are given, may the prosecution overcome this by showing the suspect was in fact knowledgeable concerning the rights the warnings did not cover? The *Miranda* Court answered no, explaining that

> we will not pause to inquire in individual cases whether the defendant was aware of his rights without a warning being given. Assessments of the knowledge the defendant possessed, based on information as to his age, education, intelligence, or prior contact with authorities, can never be more than speculation; a warning is a clearcut fact. More important, whatever the background of the person interrogated, a warning at the time of the interrogation is indispensable to overcome its pressures and to insure that the individual knows he is free to exercise the privilege at that point in time.

As the Court put it at another point, giving warnings to the knowledgeable suspect "will show the individual that his interrogators are prepared to recognize his privilege should he choose to exercise it." Most courts have thus properly concluded that the warnings must be given even to lawyers and other suspects knowledgeable as to their *Miranda* rights.

Sometimes the police have commenced giving the *Miranda* warnings only to be interrupted by the suspect, in which circumstances the courts are somewhat more sympathetic to the prosecution's position. When the interruption in effect stated what the police omitted (e.g., "I know I don't have to make a statement"), courts are inclined to conclude that *Miranda* has been complied with. Some courts reach the same result when the interruption is a more general declaration, such as "I know my rights," though the better view is that such an ambiguous assertion does not foreclose the need for specification of those rights by the police. But even when there is the latter type of interruption or one which includes no reference to *Miranda* rights, the subsequent statement will be admissible in any event if it was volunteered.

A somewhat similar issue is whether omission of that part of the *Miranda* warnings concerning appointment of counsel can later be excused by a showing that the defendant was not indigent and thus would not have qualified for appointed counsel. The *Miranda* Court recognized some leeway was permissible here by the following footnote:

> While a warning that the indigent may have counsel appointed need not be given to the person who is known to have an attorney or is known to have ample funds to secure

3. 492 U.S. 195, 109 S.Ct. 2875, 106 L.Ed.2d 166 (1989).

> one, the expedient of giving a warning is too simple and the rights involved too important to engage in ex post facto inquiries into financial ability when there is any doubt at all on that score.

Some courts have read this as meaning that it must be shown the police were actually aware of defendant's ability to retain counsel, while others have deemed it sufficient if the prosecution later established that the defendant did have that ability at the time of the interrogation. The latter view is unobjectionable, but the same cannot be said of those decisions holding that a defendant has the burden of showing he was indigent and thus entitled to warnings about appointment of counsel.

If the defendant is actually represented by counsel at the time of his interrogation, this may have some bearing on the need for *Miranda* warnings. It is generally accepted that if the attorney was actually present during the interrogation, then this obviates the need for the warnings. As for those instances in which the attorney was not present but had arranged for the contact, there is a split of authority. One view is that it may not be assumed the defendant knew of his rights because, for example, he came to the station with his lawyer; the other is that such an assumption is justified in such circumstances. In these cases, it may make some difference whether the defendant merely surrendered himself to police custody on advice of counsel or whether he and his counsel actually arranged for an interrogation session to occur.

The characteristics of the particular suspect are relevant when the issue is whether the police did enough in giving the warnings in the language set out in *Miranda.* To take the most obvious case, if the suspect does not comprehend English then the warnings must be given in a language he understands. If the suspect is illiterate or of low intelligence, then great care must be taken to ensure that he understands his rights.

(b) Time and Frequency. With respect to the timing of the *Miranda* warnings, one question which arises is whether the warnings were given soon enough. Though it has been held that, with respect to post-warnings statements, the warnings need not have preceded any and all questioning, a careful assessment of the events preceding the warnings is necessary. It is one thing if the warnings followed mere casual conversation or limited and brief inquiries. But the warnings come too late if they were preceded by extended interrogation or conversations regarding waiver of rights. Assuming the warnings were given in a timely fashion, the question then may be whether they became "stale" after the passage of time. It is generally accepted that fresh warnings are not required after the passage of just a few hours. Authority is also to be found to the effect that this is also true even after the passage of several days where the custody has been continuous, but the contrary view has much to commend it. Clearly the passage of weeks or months is too long.

Even when the passage of time has been fairly brief, consideration must be given to changes in the circumstances in the interim. However, the courts have generally taken the position that new warnings are not required just because there has been a change in the locale of the interrogation, in the officers doing the questioning, or in the subject matter of the investigation. Even a combination of these circumstances is not deemed to call for new warnings. The rationale of these cases appears to be that to require repetition of the warnings would merely add a perfunctory ritual which would not afford meaningful additional protection to the defendant. But that is a questionable conclusion in many circumstances, and is not in keeping with the *Miranda* Court's teachings that a defendant's "opportunity to exercise these rights must be afforded to him throughout the interrogation" and that the warnings when given to one already aware of his rights serve to "show the individual that his interrogators are prepared to recognize his privilege should he choose to exercise it." In any event, repetition of the *Miranda* warnings will be necessary if the authorities are to "undo" the effects of coercive conduct following the initial warnings.

(c) Manner; Proof. In *Miranda,* the Court declared that "[s]ince the State is responsible for establishing the isolated circumstances under which the interrogation takes place and has the only means of making available corroborated evidence of warnings given during incommunicado interrogation, the burden is rightly on its shoulders." Though this would suggest that it is desirable to tape record the warnings or have them stenographically reported, the courts have not imposed such a requirement. Indeed, the uncorroborated testimony of a police officer that the warnings were given (if sufficiently detailed) will suffice even in the face of contradictory testimony by the defendant.

The warnings may be given either orally or in writing, though it has been noted that the better practice is to do both. Though giving the warnings in writing alone will suffice, it must be shown that the defendant could and did read the warnings and that he acknowledged an understanding of them. More commonly the warnings are given orally by the officer reciting the provisions from a "*Miranda* card." This alone is sufficient, provided of course that the reading is not done in a hurried or mechanical fashion.

If both oral and written warnings were given but one version was defective or incomplete, courts have held it suffices that the one set of warnings was complete and correct. This may be a sensible result when the difference between them is merely that something was omitted from one, but a contrary result is necessary if the conflict between the two is such that the suspect would be confused by the discrepancy. Two sets of warnings, *each* of which is deficient, may not be read together to create one valid set of warnings.

(d) Additional Admonitions. Defendants have sometimes contended that still other warnings are generally or in particular circumstances required by *Miranda.* For example, because the Court in *Miranda* noted that many suspects will assume that "silence in the face of accusation is itself damning and will bode ill when presented to a jury," it might be claimed that suspects are entitled to be explicitly warned of another important part of the *Miranda* holding—that the "prosecution may not * * * use at trial the fact that he stood mute or claimed his privilege in the face of accusation." But neither the Supreme Court nor the lower courts have mandated the giving of such a warning. Similarly, while the *Miranda* Court recognized that a defendant has a right to stop answering questions at any time, this right was not included within the mandated warnings and thus lower courts have concluded that such a warning is not necessary.

Defendants have also claimed that under *Miranda* they are entitled to be told of the nature of the crime about which the police wish to interrogate them. The lower courts have rather consistently held that such advice is not required. The Supreme Court concluded in *Colorado v. Spring*[4] that there is no affirmative obligation on the police to advise the defendant about the crime concerning which they wish to interrogate—even when the circumstances rather strongly suggest the desired questioning will be about a matter quite different from that later encompassed by the interrogation. Although in *Spring* the arrest had been by federal ATF agents but the post-arrest questioning after a *Miranda* waiver was about an unreported homicide in another state, defendant's statements were held to be admissible even absent any prewaiver warning that questions about the homicide would be asked. The Court reasoned that since the defendant had been told he had a right to remain silent and that *anything* he said could be used against him, he had all the information necessary for a knowing and intelligent waiver of his Fifth Amendment rights; "the additional information could affect only the wisdom of a *Miranda* waiver, not its essentially voluntary and knowing nature." As for the statement in *Miranda* that "any evidence that the accused was threatened, tricked, or cajoled into a waiver will * * * show that the defendant did not voluntarily waive his privilege," the Court responded that mere "official silence" about the desire to question concerning the

4. 479 U.S. 564, 107 S.Ct. 851, 93 L.Ed.2d 954 (1987).

murder did not constitute trickery, and cautiously left unresolved whether a waiver of *Miranda* rights would be valid had there been "an affirmative misrepresentation by law enforcement officials as to the scope of the interrogation."

§ 6.9 *Miranda*: Waiver of Rights

(a) Express or Implied. Although the Court in *Miranda* ruled that interrogation accompanied by custody is so likely to be coercive that the defendant must be warned of his right not to talk to the police and to have the assistance of counsel before and during any questioning, this does not mean the police are free to interrogate whenever they have given the requisite warnings. The Court in *Miranda* went on to hold that if thereafter the defendant is interrogated and a statement is obtained, it will be admissible only if the government meets its "heavy burden"[1] of demonstrating "that the defendant knowingly and intelligently waived his privilege against self-incrimination and his right to retained or appointed counsel." Moreover, if "the individual indicates in any manner, at any time prior to or during questioning, that he wishes to remain silent, the interrogation must cease," for he has thus "shown that he intends to exercise his Fifth Amendment privilege."

The tone and language of the majority opinion in *Miranda* seemed to indicate that the Court would be receptive to nothing short of an express waiver of the rights involved. The Court declared:

> An express statement that the individual is willing to make a statement and does not want an attorney followed closely by a statement could constitute a waiver. But a valid waiver will not be presumed simply from the silence of the accused after warnings are given or simply from the fact that a confession was in fact eventually obtained. A statement we made in *Carnley v. Cochran*[2] * * * is applicable here:
>
> "Presuming waiver from a silent record is impermissible. The record must show, or there must be an allegation and evidence which show, that an accused was offered counsel but intelligently and understandingly rejected the offer. Anything less is not waiver."
>
> * * * Moreover, where in-custody interrogation is involved, there is no room for the contention that the privilege is waived if the individual answers some questions or gives some information on his own prior to invoking his right to remain silent when interrogated.

Most lower courts nonetheless took the position that the *Miranda* waiver of rights did not have to be express, and this view was ultimately adopted by the Supreme Court in *North Carolina v. Butler.*[3] There defendant was given his *Miranda* rights orally at the time of arrest and later at the FBI office he read an "Advice of Rights" form which he said he understood, after which he said he would talk to the agents but would not sign the waiver on the form. The state supreme court excluded defendant's incriminating statement on the ground that a waiver of *Miranda* rights "will not be recognized unless such waiver is 'specifically made' after the *Miranda* warnings have been given," but the Supreme Court, in a 5–3 decision, disagreed:

> An express written or oral statement of waiver of the right to remain silent or of the right to counsel is usually strong proof of the validity of that waiver, but is not inevitably either necessary or sufficient to establish waiver. The question is not one of form, but rather whether the defendant in fact knowingly and voluntarily waived the rights delineated in the *Miranda* case. As was unequivocally said in *Miranda,* mere silence is not enough. That does not mean that the defendant's silence, coupled with an understanding of his rights and a course of conduct indicating waiver, may never support a conclusion that a defendant has waived his rights. The courts must presume that a defendant did not waive his rights; the prosecution's burden is great; but in at least some cases waiver can

§ 6.9

1. On what this means in burden-of-proof terms, see § 10.3(c).

2. 369 U.S. 506, 82 S.Ct. 884, 8 L.Ed.2d 70 (1962).

3. 441 U.S. 369, 99 S.Ct. 1755, 60 L.Ed.2d 286 (1979).

be clearly inferred from the actions and words of the person interrogated.

The *Butler* dissenters objected that by not adopting the "simple prophylactic rule requiring the police to obtain an express waiver of the right to counsel before proceeding with interrogation," the Court had resurrected the problems which had haunted it under the pre-*Miranda* voluntariness approach.

(b) Competence of the Defendant. The Court in *Butler* indicated that the waiver issue must be decided on "the particular facts and circumstances surrounding that case, including the background, experience, and conduct of the accused." This highlights the fact that whether the defendant has (as the *Miranda* Court put it) "knowingly and intelligently waived" his rights depends in part upon the competency of the defendant—that is, upon his ability to understand and act upon the warnings which *Miranda* requires the defendant have received. *Tague v. Louisiana,*[4] stresses that this showing of competency is part of the "heavy burden" to be carried by the government. The arresting officer there said he "could not recall whether he asked petitioner whether he understood the rights as read to him, and * * * 'couldn't say yes or no' whether he rendered any tests to determine whether petitioner was literate or otherwise capable of understanding his rights," but the state court held that "it can be presumed that a person has capacity to understand, and the burden is on the one claiming a lack of capacity to show that lack." The Supreme Court summarily reversed, noting that the lower court's position was clearly contrary to the previously quoted language from *Miranda* and *Butler.*

In assessing the personal characteristics of the defendant, one factor which obviously must be considered is his youthfulness. Especially when a youth has had no prior experience with the police or has a low IQ, his waiver may be found ineffective. This is not to suggest, however, that a valid waiver cannot be given by an underage defendant, for courts have frequently found waivers by juveniles to be valid. In *Fare v. Michael C.*[5] the Supreme Court held that the "totality of the circumstances approach is adequate to determine whether there has been a waiver even where interrogation of juveniles is involved." Thus, the Court continued, what is mandated is an "evaluation of the juvenile's age, experience, education, background, and intelligence, and into whether he has the capacity to understand the warnings given him, the nature of his Fifth Amendment rights, and the consequences of waiving those rights." Most states follow this approach, while the others have opted for the "interested adult" rule, under which a juvenile's waiver is not effective unless he was allowed to consult and have with him an adult interested in his welfare.

If the defendant is seriously mentally retarded, this reduces the chances that his waiver will be found valid. Either limited schooling or a low IQ can contribute to a finding of an ineffective waiver, but waivers have not infrequently been upheld notwithstanding such circumstances. A waiver can be effective even though the defendant was emotionally upset at having been apprehended or by other circumstances, though again this condition can contribute to a contrary determination. Obviously, the fact a defendant is well-educated and mature enhances the likelihood of a finding that his waiver was effective. If at the time of the alleged waiver the defendant was in considerable pain from a serious injury, this can also contribute to a finding that the waiver was not effective. But defendants have generally been unsuccessful in claiming that their *Miranda* waivers should be held invalid because they were either intoxicated or under the influence of drugs or medication at that time.

It must be emphasized, however, that such personal characteristics of the defendant existing at the time of the purported waiver are relevant only as they relate to police overreaching. Such is the teaching of *Colorado v. Connelly,*[6] rejecting a state court ruling that a

4. 444 U.S. 469, 100 S.Ct. 652, 62 L.Ed.2d 622 (1980).

5. 442 U.S. 707, 99 S.Ct. 2560, 61 L.Ed.2d 197 (1979).

6. 479 U.S. 157, 107 S.Ct. 515, 93 L.Ed.2d 473 (1986).

defendant's *Miranda* waiver was not voluntary because he suffered from a psychosis that interfered with his ability to make free and rational choices. Noting that the "voluntariness of a waiver * * * has always depended on the absence of police overreaching, not on 'free choice' in any broader sense of the word," the Court in *Connelly* concluded that "*Miranda* protects defendants against government coercion" but "goes no further than that."

A great many defendants who give *Miranda* waivers are not "competent" to do so in a certain sense, for the tactical error of that decision was not perceived by them. But this is no bar to an effective waiver for *Miranda* purposes, for a waiver need not be wise to be "intelligent" within the meaning of that case. This result is consistent with *Miranda's* emphasis upon the need to overcome the coerciveness of in-custody interrogation, and also may be explained in part by the impracticality of inquiring into defendant's awareness of all possible tactical considerations.

(c) Conduct of the Police. *Miranda* also says it must be shown that the defendant did "voluntarily waive his privilege," and as to this the conduct of the police will be particularly relevant. In *Fare v. Michael C.,*[7] the Court declared that the "totality of the circumstances approach is adequate to determine whether there has been a waiver," which indicates that the two categories of inducement which were considered sufficiently compelling to render a resulting confession inadmissible under longstanding and traditional confessions law—promises and threats—have a like adverse effect upon *Miranda* waivers. Lower courts have held waivers involuntary where obtained by a promise of some benefit or a threat of some adverse consequence.

The Court in *Miranda* indicated that even absent such threats or promises a waiver would not be upheld if obtained under coercive circumstances:

> Whatever the testimony of the authorities as to waiver of rights by an accused, the fact of lengthy interrogation or incommunicado incarceration before a statement is made is strong evidence that the accused did not validly waive his rights. In these circumstances the fact that the individual eventually made a statement is consistent with the conclusion that the compelling influence of the interrogation finally forced him to do so. It is inconsistent with any notion of a voluntary relinquishment of the privilege.

Lower courts have held waivers invalid where the defendant had been held in custody an extended period of time before being given the warnings, or where the defendant had first been subjected to persistent questioning.

The *Miranda* Court also asserted that "any evidence that the accused was threatened, tricked, or cajoled into a waiver will, of course, show that the defendant did not voluntarily waive his privilege." This condemnation of the use of trickery suggests that using interrogation techniques which create either false confidence or resignation in a defendant will per se make the defendant's subsequent waiver ineffective. As we have seen, trickery has no such per se effect under the voluntariness approach to confessions, and thus the language from *Miranda* just quoted would suggest that a waiver-of-rights analysis is, at least in this respect, more demanding than the old voluntariness inquiry. But the lower courts have not reached this conclusion; rather, they have taken an approach which, if anything, is strengthened by the Supreme Court's more recent use of "totality of the circumstances" language in this context, namely, that trickery bears on the waiver issues in essentially the same way that it does on the due process voluntariness-of-confession issue. Under this approach, *Miranda* waivers have been upheld even when obtained after the police had misrepresented the strength of the case against the defendant or the seriousness of the matter under investigation. Even assuming that these cases can be squared with *Miranda* because the trickery concerned only the wisdom of exercising the rights of which the defendant had been

7. 442 U.S. 707, 99 S.Ct. 2560, 61 L.Ed.2d 197 (1979).

warned, it still follows that there is an absolute prohibition upon any trickery which misleads the suspect as to the existence or dimensions of any of the applicable rights or as to whether the waiver really is a waiver of those rights.

Though some lower courts had held that a defendant's waiver of counsel is not sufficiently "knowing and intelligent" if police withheld from him information that an attorney had sought to consult him, the Supreme Court ruled otherwise in *Moran v. Burbine.*[8] The Court reasoned that under the *Johnson v. Zerbst*[9] waiver standard "events occurring outside of the presence of the suspect and entirely unknown to him," as compared to defendant's knowledge an attorney had been barred access, "can have no bearing on the capacity to comprehend and knowingly relinquish a constitutional right." This is so even if the withheld information "might have affected his decision to confess," as a valid waiver only requires that the defendant "understand the nature of his rights and the consequences of abandoning them." As for the defendant's other argument, that such deception should be constitutionally proscribed because it was "inimical to the Fifth Amendment values *Miranda* seeks to protect," the Court declined to disturb *Miranda's* clarity by introducing new questions about just what events would require the police to give a defendant additional information. The three dissenters in *Burbine* agreed with the majority's statement of the waiver standard, but concluded information about the ready availability of a particular attorney had a direct bearing on the waiver. As to the dissenters' fears that the doors had been opened to all sorts of deception by the police, the majority responded that on unspecified "facts more egregious than those presented here police deception might rise to a level of a due process violation."

(d) Conduct of the Defendant: Implied Waiver. While inquiry into the defendant's competency may indicate whether he *could* knowingly and intelligently waive his rights, and assessment of the police conduct may show whether such a waiver *would* be voluntary, it is still necessary to scrutinize the defendant's words and actions to see if he did *in fact* waive his *Miranda* rights. Assuming the other two inquiries present no bar to finding a waiver, the relatively easy cases are those in which the defendant makes an "express written or oral statement of waiver" which then is "strong proof of the validity of that waiver,"[10] or in which at the other extreme the defendant explicitly asserts his right to remain silent or his right to counsel. But courts are frequently confronted with fact situations which lie at neither of these extremes.

As noted earlier, the Supreme Court in *North Carolina v. Butler*[11] held that "an explicit statement of waiver is not invariably necessary to support a finding that the defendant waived the right to remain silent or the right to counsel guaranteed by the *Miranda* case." But if this is so, then even in cases not complicated by conduct of the defendant which arguably constituted a feeble attempt to assert his rights, there remains the difficult question of what facts will justify a finding of waiver by implication. On this issue, *Butler* instructs that "mere silence is not enough" but that this "does not mean that the defendant's silence, coupled with an understanding of his rights and a course of conduct indicating waiver, may never support a conclusion that a defendant has waived his rights." This certainly means, as the lower courts and the Supreme Court itself[12] have held, that a waiver is not established merely by showing that a defendant was given the complete *Miranda* warnings and thereafter gave an incriminating statement.

But what if the defendant expresses an understanding of the *Miranda* warnings he has received and thereafter an incriminating

8. 475 U.S. 412, 106 S.Ct. 1135, 89 L.Ed.2d 410 (1986).

9. 304 U.S. 458, 58 S.Ct. 1019, 82 L.Ed. 1461 (1938).

10. North Carolina v. Butler, 441 U.S. 369, 99 S.Ct. 1755, 60 L.Ed.2d 286 (1979).

11. 441 U.S. 369, 99 S.Ct. 1755, 60 L.Ed.2d 286 (1979).

12. Tague v. Louisiana, 444 U.S. 469, 100 S.Ct. 652, 62 L.Ed.2d 622 (1980).

statement is obtained from him? In the language of *Butler,* does this amount to a showing of "an understanding of his rights and a course of conduct indicating waiver"? Several courts have answered this question in the affirmative. There is, however, authority to the contrary, and it has been argued with some force that his acknowledgement of understanding adds nothing more to the circumstances beyond mere silence. The point, quite simply, is that an understanding of rights and an intention to waive them are two different things, and the latter should not be inferred merely because the former is now clearly established. That is true, yet when it is clear the defendant does understand his rights it is somewhat easier to make some judgments about the significance of his subsequent conduct in terms of whether or not those rights are being invoked. Thus, while an acknowledgement of understanding should not inevitably carry the day, it is especially significant when defendant's incriminating statement follows immediately thereafter. On the matter of waiver by implication, courts have also taken into account the fact that the defendant initiated the conversation which occurred after the warnings were given and that the defendant's contact with the police was attributable to his cooperation.

(e) Conduct of the Defendant: Implied Assertion of Rights. Another group of cases involves what might be called an assertion of rights by implication. Whatever reservations there might be about finding waiver by implication do not carry over to these cases, for the Court in *Miranda* emphatically declared that if "the individual indicates in any manner at any time prior to or during questioning, that he wishes to remain silent, the interrogation must cease" and that if he "states that he wants an attorney, the interrogation must cease until an attorney is present." Whether there has been such an assertion of rights is of considerable importance; obviously, if there has been an assertion there is no waiver, and in addition the assertion puts the defendant into a somewhat "special" situation in terms of the subsequent dealings of the police with him.[13]

As for assertion of the right to remain silent, any declaration of a desire to terminate the contact or inquiry (e.g., "Don't bother me") should suffice. On the other hand, a statement which is much more limited in the sense that it expresses an unwillingness or inability to respond to a particular inquiry (e.g., "You have asked me a question I can't answer") is not a general claim of the privilege. Depending upon the surrounding circumstances, even a statement which itself appears to amount to an assertion of the right to remain silent (e.g., "I ain't saying nothing") may be held not to have that effect. Some courts have wisely concluded that in the event of an equivocal invocation of the right to silence, the only permissible course of action for the police is to attempt to clarify the defendant's intentions.

As for assertion of the right to counsel, here as well something short of a formal or direct request will suffice, such as an unsuccessful attempt to reach an attorney or an inquiry whether the police officer could recommend an attorney. A different result has been reached where the defendant's statement was more ambiguous, such as that he did not know if he should speak to an attorney. Some courts have held that if the assertion of the right to counsel is equivocal, the police may only question to clarify the matter. An indication by the defendant that he will only want counsel at some future time is not an assertion of the right to counsel for *Miranda* purposes. Similarly, a defendant's assertion of a desire to speak with counsel about this matter on a past occasion, when the defendant was not in custody and thus no *Miranda* rights then existed, does not carry forward to become an invocation of the right to counsel with respect to a significantly later custodial interrogation.

In *Michigan v. Jackson,*[14] the Court held that when the Sixth Amendment right to counsel has attached, "if police initiate inter-

13. See § 6.9(g).

14. 475 U.S. 625, 106 S.Ct. 1404, 89 L.Ed.2d 631 (1986).

rogation after a defendant's assertion, at an arraignment or similar proceeding, of his right to counsel, any waiver of the defendant's right to counsel for that police-initiated interrogation is invalid." Does it follow that such an assertion is an invocation of the *Miranda* right to counsel as to any uncharged offenses? No, the Court later held in *McNeil v. Wisconsin,*[15] reasoning that invocation of the Sixth Amendment interest does not also constitute invocation of *Miranda* as to other, uncharged offenses, for a defendant "might be quite willing to speak to the police without counsel present concerning many matters, but not the matter under prosecution." Moreover, the Court added, a contrary rule would not be wise policy, for it would mean that "most persons in pretrial custody for serious offenses would be *unapproachable* by police officers suspecting them of involvement in other crimes, *even though they have never expressed any unwillingness to be questioned.*"

In *Fare v. Michael C.,*[16] the Supreme Court confronted the question of whether a request for someone other than an attorney constitutes an invocation of *Miranda* rights. There, a juvenile in custody on suspicion of murder was given his warnings and he then asked to have his probation officer present; this request was denied, a waiver of rights was obtained, and the juvenile then made incriminating statements. The Court held, 5–4, that the request to see the probation officer was not a per se invocation of *Miranda* rights (that is, not the equivalent of asking for a lawyer), but rather was merely a factor to be considered in the "totality of circumstances" determination of the voluntariness of the subsequent waiver. The majority explained that the per se aspect of *Miranda* was

> based on the unique role the lawyer plays in the adversary system of criminal justice in this country. Whether it is a minor or an adult who stands accused, the lawyer is the one person to whom society as a whole looks as the protector of the legal rights of that person in his dealing with the police and the courts. For this reason the Court fashioned in *Miranda* the rigid rule that an accused's request for an attorney is *per se* an invocation of his Fifth Amendment rights, requiring that all interrogation cease.

A probation officer, on the other hand, the Court continued, "is not trained in the law, and so is not in a position to advise the accused as to his legal rights," and is actually an adversary of the juvenile because "the probation officer is duty bound to report wrongdoing by the juvenile when it comes to his attention, even if by communication from the juvenile himself."

Three of the dissenters in *Fare* questioned that characterization of the probation officer's responsibilities and persuasively argued that *Miranda* requires that interrogation cease whenever a juvenile requests an adult who is obligated to represent his interests because such a request "constitutes both an attempt to obtain advice and a general invocation of the right to silence." This reasoning would appear to be especially compelling when the juvenile requests the presence of a parent, but the *Fare* rule has sometimes been applied even to such facts. But certainly a different result is called for if the juvenile manifests a desire to see his parent in order to obtain an attorney.

(f) Conduct of the Defendant: "Qualified" or Limited Waiver. Yet a third group of cases in which the focus is primarily upon the conduct of the defendant presents an added complication, as there is conduct which in isolation seems to amount to a waiver, but it is accompanied by other conduct which can be interpreted as a refusal to waive or even as an assertion of rights. Illustrative are the facts of *North Carolina v. Butler,*[17] where the defendant read a written "Advice of Rights" form, stated he understood his rights, and then refused to sign the form but nonetheless indicated he would talk. (The Court in *Butler* did not hold that this constituted a waiver, but only rejected the state court's view that nothing short of an express waiver would

15. ___ U.S. ___, 111 S.Ct. 2204, 115 L.Ed.2d 158 (1991).

16. 442 U.S. 707, 99 S.Ct. 2560, 61 L.Ed.2d 197 (1979).

17. 441 U.S. 369, 99 S.Ct. 1755, 60 L.Ed.2d 286 (1979).

suffice under *Miranda.*) Another illustration would be where the suspect indicates he is willing to talk but is unwilling to have his remarks reduced to writing, as in *United States v. Frazier.*[18]

The court in *Frazier* held that the waiver was effective notwithstanding the defendant's unwillingness to permit note taking, and some other courts have similarly ruled that an oral waiver is effective in the face of defendant's refusal to sign a written waiver. As the court put it in *Frazier,* since the suspect there had the capacity to comprehend the warnings, the police officer questioning him was not required to "place a legal interpretation on the language of *Miranda* warnings he was directed to give." But this approach conflicts with *Miranda's* policy of trying to place the accused on a more equal footing with the police at the interrogation stage and gives the accused minimal protection against a misunderstanding of the warnings. It overlooks the fundamental point noted by the *Frazier* dissenters: "capacity to understand the warnings does not by any means guarantee that they will actually be understood."

An objective view of the facts of the *Frazier* case strongly suggests that the defendant acted as he did because of a mistaken impression that an oral confession which was not contemporaneously recorded could not be used against him. Similarly, the *Butler* facts certainly suggest that the defendant misperceived the effect of a waiver which was oral rather than written. Under such circumstances, there is much to be said for the view that the police are under an obligation to clear up misunderstandings of this nature which are apparent to any reasonable observer. Short of this, it certainly makes sense in such cases to conclude that the defendant's conduct should significantly increase the prosecution's burden to overcome the presumption against waiver of *Miranda* rights.

Somewhat similar to *Frazier* is *Connecticut v. Barrett,*[19] where after receiving his *Miranda* warnings the defendant repeatedly asserted his willingness to talk about the incident and his unwillingness to give a written statement unless his attorney was present. Though the state court had ruled this amounted to an invocation of the right to counsel for all purposes, the Supreme Court concluded otherwise: "Barrett's limited requests for counsel * * * were accompanied by affirmative announcements of his willingness to speak with the authorities. The fact that officials took the opportunity provided by Barrett to obtain an oral confession is quite consistent with the Fifth Amendment. *Miranda* gives the defendant a right to choose between speech and silence, and Barrett chose to speak." Significantly, the Court in *Barrett* emphasized that the defendant's distinction between oral and written statements might have been "illogical," but that this alone would not make the waiver ineffective. But the Court also emphasized the defendant had testified to a full understanding of his *Miranda* warnings, and thus *Barrett* was not a case in which the partial or limited character of the waiver demonstrated an insufficient understanding by the defendant of the warnings he had received. *Barrett* was further limited by a cautionary footnote that the instant case did not involve "an ambiguous or equivocal response to the *Miranda* warnings" and thus did not raise the "open" question of what the police must do in such circumstances.

In other instances the question is the scope of the waiver, as is illustrated by *Wyrick v. Fields.*[20] Fields, charged with rape, after release on bail and consultation with privately retained counsel, agreed to a polygraph examination. Prior to the examination, he executed a waiver of *Miranda* rights both in writing and orally. At the conclusion of the examination, an agent told him there had been some deceit and asked him if he would explain why his answers were bothering him. Fields then admitted the intercourse but claimed it was with consent, and that statement was admitted against him at trial. A

18. 476 F.2d 891 (D.C.Cir.1973).

19. 479 U.S. 523, 107 S.Ct. 828, 93 L.Ed.2d 920 (1987).

20. 459 U.S. 42, 103 S.Ct. 394, 74 L.Ed.2d 214 (1982).

federal court held this waiver covered only the polygraph examination and that a new set of warnings was required once the polygraph examination had been discontinued and Fields was asked if he could explain the test's unfavorable results. The Supreme Court disagreed, stressing that discontinuing the polygraph "effectuated no significant change in the character of the interrogation" and that neither Fields nor his attorney could have reasonably assumed "that Fields would not be informed of the polygraph readings and asked to explain any unfavorable result."

(g) Waiver After Assertion of Rights. The discussion up to this point has been concerned with the question of what the prosecution must do in order to carry its "heavy burden" of showing a waiver of *Miranda* rights. A somewhat special problem, reserved to this point, is whether the situation is different once the defendant has actually asserted his rights. Are the police then foreclosed from thereafter seeking a waiver from that defendant? If not, is the burden in such circumstances even heavier?

The significance of the defendant's invocation of the right to remain silent reached the Supreme Court in *Michigan v. Mosley.*[21] There, defendant was arrested for several robberies and at the station was given his *Miranda* warnings; he declined to discuss the robberies and no effort was made to have him reconsider his position. Two hours later another detective in another part of the building sought to question defendant about an unrelated murder; he was given the *Miranda* warnings again and thereafter gave an incriminating statement. The *Mosley* Court concluded that the propriety of this action depended upon the interpretation to be given the following passage in *Miranda:*

> Once warnings have been given, the subsequent procedure is clear. If the individual indicates in any manner, at any time prior to or during questioning, that he wishes to remain silent, the interrogation must cease. At this point he has shown that he intends to exercise his Fifth Amendment privilege; any statement taken after the person invokes his privilege cannot be other than the product of compulsion, subtle or otherwise. Without the right to cut off questioning, the setting of in-custody interrogation operates on the individual to overcome free choice in producing a statement after the privilege has been once invoked.

After rejecting the "possible literal interpretations" that this language permits "the continuation of custodial interrogation after a momentary cessation" or, at the other extreme, that it provides permanent immunity from further interrogation." The *Mosley* Court continued:

> The critical safeguard identified in the passage at issue is a person's "right to cut off questioning." Through the exercise of his option to terminate questioning he can control the time at which questioning occurs, the subjects discussed, and the duration of the interrogation. The requirement that law enforcement authorities must respect a person's exercise of that option counteracts the coercive pressures of the custodial setting. We therefore conclude that the admissibility of statements obtained after the person in custody has decided to remain silent depends under *Miranda* on whether his "right to cut off questioning" was "scrupulously honored."

As for application of the *Mosley* "scrupulously honored" test, the majority concluded it was met on the facts of that case because "the police here immediately ceased the interrogation, resumed questioning only after the passage of a significant period of time and the provision of a fresh set of warnings, and restricted the second interrogation to a crime that had not been a subject of the earlier interrogation." Some courts have viewed the latter fact an essential one to a finding that defendant's rights were "scrupulously honored," and there is much to be said for this position. Other courts have not deemed a change in the subject matter of the inquiry to be essential. Perhaps that is unobjectionable when it is the defendant who initiated the subsequent conversation, but in other circumstances it is a highly questionable position.

21. 423 U.S. 96, 96 S.Ct. 321, 46 L.Ed.2d 313 (1975).

In any event, the "scrupulously honored" test is not met where the police did not honor the original assertion of the right to remain silent, ignored that assertion and expressed sympathy for defendant's plight, resumed questioning after a short interval, or made repeated attempts to obtain a waiver.

Justice White, concurring in *Mosley,* expressed the view that it is proper for the police to reapproach a defendant who has invoked his right to remain silent when they have new information bearing upon that decision. He put illustrations where the police undertake to tell a defendant "that his ability to explain a particular incriminating fact or to supply an alibi for a particular time period would result in his immediate release" or where on the other hand they would tell him that "the case against him was unusually strong and * * * that his immediate cooperation with the authorities in the apprehension and conviction of others or in the recovery of property would redound to his benefit in the form of a reduced charge." It is open to question whether this plea-bargaining-at-the-police-station scenario is consistent with the concerns expressed in *Miranda* and *Mosley,* though at least one court has held that it is proper to present the defendant with an objective, undistorted presentation of the extensive evidence against him. However, it is well to note that under some circumstances the confrontation of the defendant with incriminating evidence will itself constitute "interrogation" within the meaning of *Miranda,*[22] clearly prohibited as to one who has asserted and not yet waived his rights.

The defendant in *Mosley* had not invoked his *Miranda* right to counsel, and Justice White suggested that had he done so the result might well be different. He later made that point for a majority of the Court in *Edwards v. Arizona,*[23] which held "that an accused, * * * having expressed his desire to deal with the police only through counsel, is not subject to further interrogation by the authorities until counsel has been made available to him, unless the accused himself initiates further communication, exchanges or conversations with the police." This result, the Court noted, is consistent with the language in *Miranda* that "[i]f the individual states that he wants an attorney, the interrogation must cease until an attorney is present." (Consequently, the Court clarified in a later case,[24] the "available to him" language in *Edwards* means "that when counsel is requested, interrogation must cease, and officials may not reinitiate interrogation without counsel present, whether or not the accused has consulted with his attorney.[25]) Thus the defendant's confession in *Edwards* was inadmissible, for the police had visited the defendant in his cell and obtained a waiver of *Miranda* rights the morning after defendant had declared he wanted an attorney. *Edwards,* best viewed as creating a per se rule proscribing any interrogation of an accused who has invoked his right to counsel,[26] thus limits the application of *Mosley's* "scrupulously honored" test to those cases where only the right to silence was invoked.

This is evidenced by *Arizona v. Roberson,*[27] holding that *Edwards* rather than *Mosley* governs even when the later interrogation concerns a wholly unrelated crime. The majority in *Roberson* emphasized the desirability of maintaining *Edwards* as "a bright-line rule" without qualifications or exceptions in attor-

22. See § 6.7(c).

23. 451 U.S. 477, 101 S.Ct. 1880, 68 L.Ed.2d 378 (1981).

24. Minnick v. Mississippi, ___ U.S. ___, 111 S.Ct. 486, 112 L.Ed.2d 489 (1990).

25. In rejecting the state court's conclusion that the special protections of *Edwards* ceased once the defendant had consulted with an attorney, the Court in *Minnick* noted: "A single consultation with an attorney does not remove the suspect from persistent attempts by officials to persuade him to waive his rights, or from the coercive pressures that accompany custody and that may increase as custody is prolonged."

26. *Edwards* has to do with the *Miranda* Fifth Amendment right to counsel. But in Michigan v. Jackson, 475 U.S. 625, 106 S.Ct. 1404, 89 L.Ed.2d 631 (1986), the Court held that the *Edwards* limitations, as elaborated in *Bradshaw,* are also applicable when a defendant invoked his Sixth Amendment right to counsel in court at the time of his arraignment. See § 6.4(f).

27. 486 U.S. 675, 108 S.Ct. 2093, 100 L.Ed.2d 704 (1988).

ney-request cases,[28] and also that defendant's manifestation "that he did not feel sufficiently comfortable with the presence of custodial interrogation to answer questions without an attorney" is no more limited to a particular offense than is a waiver of *Miranda* rights.[29]

Sometimes, the Court noted in *Smith v. Illinois,*[30] the issue is whether defendant had invoked his right to counsel so as to come within the *Edwards* doctrine. This occurs when the defendant's actions or statements preceding or contemporaneous with the purported request for counsel make that request ambiguous or equivocal. Courts have dealt with such situations in various ways: requiring that all questioning cease notwithstanding the equivocal or ambiguous nature of the request; requiring a specified degree of clarity to trigger the right to counsel; or permitting only that interrogation designed to clarify the earlier statement. The Court had no occasion to consider such circumstances in *Smith,* but did hold that a defendant's "*post-request* responses to further interrogation may not be used to cast retrospective doubt on the clarity of the initial request itself." This is as it should be, for otherwise police could disregard a defendant's invocation of the right to counsel in the hope that subsequent interrogation would cast retrospective doubt upon it.

In *Connecticut v. Barrett,*[31] the Court concluded that a defendant's invocation of his right to counsel could be limited in some way, in which instance the *Edwards* doctrine would apply in a correspondingly limited fashion. The record reflected a clear understanding by defendant of his *Miranda* warnings, and thus his assertion of a desire to have counsel present before making a written statement meant only that "[h]ad the police obtained such a statement without meeting the waiver standards of *Edwards,* it would clearly be inadmissible"; defendant's oral statements were not likewise barred by *Edwards.* (The Court in *Barrett* emphasized that defendant's response to the *Miranda* warnings was not "ambiguous or equivocal," so that there was "no need * * * to address the question left open in *Smith v. Illinois.* ")

Eight members of the Court agreed in *Oregon v. Bradshaw*[32] that the admissibility of a confession given by a defendant who earlier invoked his *Miranda* right to counsel is to be determined by a two-step analysis. It first must be asked whether defendant "initiated" further conversation. This means that the impetus must come from the accused, not from the officers. However, if there has been some kind of police conduct preceding and allegedly contributing to the defendant's supposed "initiation," the question then becomes how that conduct is to be judged in determining where the "impetus" lies. One view, certainly subject to dispute, is that the prior police conduct is not relevant unless it actually amounted to interrogation or its functional equivalent under *Innis.* But in any event, the first prong of the initiation test requires that any previous police-initiated interrogation have ended prior to the suspect's alleged initiatory remark, for one cannot "initiate" an on-

28. *Roberson* does not mean that if defendant's Sixth Amendment right had attached as to one offense, this fact alone brings the *Edwards* rule into play as to the *Miranda* right to counsel vis-a-vis other uncharged offenses. McNeil v. Wisconsin, ___ U.S. ___, 111 S.Ct. 2204, 115 L.Ed.2d 158 (1991) (while *Edwards* rule per *Roberson* is "*not* offense-specific," Sixth Amendment right to counsel "is offense-specific" and does not focus exclusively upon custodial interrogation, so invocation of Sixth Amendment right is not also invocation of *Miranda,* which is broader "because it relates to interrogation regarding *any* suspected crime and attaches whether or not the 'adversarial relationship' produced by a pending prosecution has yet arisen").

The two dissenters in *Roberson* objected the majority's rule "will bar law enforcement officials, even those from some other city or other jurisdiction, from questioning a suspect about an unrelated matter if he is in custody and has requested counsel to assist in answering questions put to him about the crime for which he was arrested," and asserted a "more realistic view of human nature suggests that a suspect will want the opportunity, when he learns of the separate investigations, to decide whether he wishes to speak to the authorities in a particular investigation with or without representation."

29. Referring to Colorado v. Spring, discussed in § 6.8(d), upholding a *Miranda* waiver notwithstanding defendant's ignorance at that time of the subject matter of the questioning which followed.

30. 469 U.S. 91, 105 S.Ct. 490, 83 L.Ed.2d 488 (1984).

31. 479 U.S. 523, 107 S.Ct. 828, 93 L.Ed.2d 920 (1987).

32. 462 U.S. 1039, 103 S.Ct. 2830, 77 L.Ed.2d 405 (1983).

going interrogation. *Bradshaw* goes on to say that if it is found the defendant "initiated" further conversation, it must then be inquired whether defendant waived his right to counsel and to silence, "that is, whether the purported waiver was knowing and intelligent * * * under the totality of the circumstances, including the necessary fact that the accused, not the police, reopened the dialogue with the authorities."

As for what constitutes "initiation," those eight Justices in *Bradshaw* could not agree. The four-Justice plurality concluded that "inquiries or statements * * * relating to routine incidents of the custodial relationship" would not suffice but that questions which "evinced a willingness and a desire for a generalized discussion about the investigation" would. The four dissenters defined "initiation" more narrowly as "communication or dialogue *about the subject matter of the criminal investigation.*" As for the defendant's statement in *Bradshaw,* "Well, what is going to happen to me now?", the plurality concluded this was initiation under their test, while the dissenters asserted it was not under theirs. But an objective assessment of the circumstances in that case would seem to justify only one conclusion—as the dissenters put it, the defendant was merely trying "to find out where the police were going to take him." That would not amount to "initiation" under either of the tests, and is quite different from the conduct which lower courts have quite properly found sufficient to establish that the defendant had reopened the dialogue about the criminal investigation. Uncertainty about the applicable test persists after *Bradshaw,* as the other member of the Court, Justice Powell, rejected the two-step approach and deemed the confession admissible merely because there had later occurred a knowing and intelligent waiver by defendant of his rights.

§ 6.10 *Miranda:* Nature of Offense, Interrogator, and Proceedings

(a) Questioning About Minor Offense. Although the Supreme Court in *Miranda* gave no indication that its holding regarding warning and waiver of rights prior to custodial interrogation was somehow limited to serious cases, a number of lower courts concluded that such a limitation exists. Several jurisdictions held that *Miranda* has no application to misdemeanors or at least to traffic offenses. In support of this result general references were often made to the large number of these minor offenses, the lack of a need for the full panoply of constitutional protections regarding such offenses, the "practical" and "historical" differences between minor offenses and more serious crimes, and the *Miranda* Court's admonition that this decision was "not intended to hamper the traditional function of police officers in investigating crime."

This issue reached the Supreme Court in *Berkemer v. McCarty,*[1] where a unanimous Court rejected any such exception to *Miranda.* The Court first noted that the exception for misdemeanor traffic offenses proposed there "would substantially undermine" a "crucial advantage" of the *Miranda* doctrine—its clarity. Police would often be uncertain in a particular instance what the magnitude of the crime was and consequently whether warnings were required, and courts would become involved in "doctrinal complexities" concerning, for example, when a misdemeanor investigation escalates into or is a pretext for a felony investigation. The Court then concluded that the purposes of *Miranda*—relieving the inherent compelling pressures of custodial interrogation, and freeing courts from the necessity of making frequent case-by-case voluntariness determinations—are also served in the context of police interrogation related to minor traffic offenses.

(b) Questioning by Private Citizen. In the *Miranda* case the Court defined interrogation as "questioning initiated by law enforcement officers." Because of this and also because of the general doctrine that state action is a prerequisite to application of constitutional protections, it is clear that *Miranda* does not govern interrogation by private citizens acting on their own. This covers such in-

§ 6.10

1. 468 U.S. 420, 104 S.Ct. 3138, 82 L.Ed.2d 317 (1984).

stances as where the defendant was questioned by the victim, an arresting private citizen, a friend, a relative, or a newspaper reporter. Even if the private citizen falsely held himself out to the defendant as a police officer, so that it may be said the defendant was under just as much pressure as if his interrogator had been an actual officer, *Miranda* still does not apply because of the absence of state action.

That situation must be distinguished from one in which the defendant is questioned by a person who is not a government employee but who has employment responsibilities of a law enforcement nature, such as a department store security guard. In such circumstances, it might be argued that the protections of *Miranda* would be appropriate, for such security personnel also utilize detention, privacy, the appearance of authority, and psychologically coercive methods to facilitate fruitful interrogation. Moreover, it could well be contended that in such cases the "state action" hurdle may be overcome by a public function analysis, i.e., that persons performing functions essentially like those ordinarily left to governmental agencies are also subject to constitutional restraints. However, the courts have rather consistently held that such persons as security officers, railroad detectives, insurance investigators, and private investigators are not required to comply with the *Miranda* procedures. A contrary result has sometimes been reached if the interrogator, though then serving private security functions, has been given police powers by a governmental unit.

Some courts have concluded that the private person exception does not apply when the person is at the time acting as an agent of the police. Thus, *Miranda* has been held to govern where such persons as the victim, a private security officer, the defendant's parents or the victim's attorney questioned the defendant at the behest of the police. But, more compelling is the view that unless a person realizes he is dealing with a police agent, their efforts to elicit incriminating statements from him do not constitute "police interrogation" within the meaning of *Miranda.* It is the impact on the suspect's mind of the interplay between police interrogation and police custody which creates "custodial interrogation" within the meaning of *Miranda.* That, of course, is precisely the theory which was adopted by the Supreme Court in the very similar "jail plant" situation.[2]

(c) Questioning by Non-police Official. In cases where the interrogator is a public employee and thus not outside the "state action" requirement, but yet is someone other than a police officer, the *Miranda* definition of interrogation as "questioning initiated by law enforcement officers" takes on added significance. Though the extent to which the decisions rest upon this particular point is often clouded by uncertainty as to whether the defendant was even in a "custodial" situation, the courts have generally held that government agents not primarily charged with enforcement of the criminal law are under no obligation to comply with *Miranda.* Thus, at least where the official has not been given police powers, *Miranda* has been held inapplicable to questioning by school officials, welfare investigators, medical personnel, and parole or probation officers.

The notion that *Miranda* does not inevitably apply whenever questions are asked in a custodial setting by a government employee is an appealing one, for not all such interrogations would seem to have a coercive impact comparable to the police questioning which concerned the Court in *Miranda.* This is not to say, however, that the decisions referred to above are beyond dispute, for the Supreme Court in *Mathis v. United States*[3] seems to have rejected the notion that *Miranda* applies only to criminal law enforcers. *Mathis* is a case which is not clouded by uncertainties about custody, for the interrogation at issue occurred while the defendant was serving a jail sentence on an unrelated matter. The questioning was by an IRS agent and—more importantly for present purposes—one who

2. Illinois v. Perkins, ___ U.S. ___, 110 S.Ct. 2394, 110 L.Ed.2d 243 (1990).

3. 391 U.S. 1, 88 S.Ct. 1503, 20 L.Ed.2d 381 (1968).

was a "civil investigator * * * required, whenever and as soon as he finds 'definite indications of fraud or criminal potential,' to refer a case to the Intelligence Division for investigation by a different agent who works regularly on criminal matters." Such a referral occurred eight days *after* the questioning in issue, and there was no suggestion that it was improperly delayed, but yet the Court held that *Miranda* applied. The *Mathis* majority acknowledged that "tax investigations differ from investigations of murder, robbery, and other crimes" because they "may be initiated for the purpose of a civil action rather than criminal prosecution," but then concluded this was not a controlling difference because, "as the investigating revenue agent was compelled to admit, there was always the possibility during his investigation that his work would end up in a criminal prosecution." Additional proof that the Court does not view *Miranda* as limited to interrogation by police officers is provided by the recent case of *Estelle v. Smith,*[4] holding *Miranda* applicable to a psychiatric examination. The Court declared: "That respondent was questioned by a psychiatrist designated by the trial court to conduct a neutral competency examination, rather than by a police officer, government informant, or prosecuting attorney is immaterial."

Viewed in terms of the theory underlying *Miranda,* neither *Mathis* nor *Smith* is particularly objectionable. Mathis was doubtless under just as much pressure to talk to the "civil investigator" who visited him in jail as the criminal investigator who called on him later, and certainly Smith would feel compelled to converse with a psychiatrist appointed by the court to examine him. Because that is so and because the Court in these two cases did not explore the issue in greater depth, those decisions cannot be read as settling that *all* public-official interrogation of those in custody is governed by *Miranda.* They do, however, lend support to the conclusion some courts have reached that custodial interrogation (other than routine interviews) by a probation or parole officer is governed by *Miranda* because the probationer or parolee is under heavy psychological pressure to cooperate with one who can recommend his imprisonment.[5]

(d) Questioning by Foreign Police. Foreign police, even when investigating an American citizen, can hardly be expected to know and follow all of the procedures which would be required if that individual were under investigation in his own country. Thus, though a defendant may be entitled to keep out of a prosecution in this country a confession by him which was involuntarily given to a foreign policeman, he may not obtain the suppression of a confession obtained by such an official merely because the *Miranda* warnings were not given. This result is ordinarily explained on the same grounds customarily given for not suppressing evidence obtained in a foreign search: the exclusion would have little if any deterrent effect upon foreign officials.

This is not to say that *Miranda* has no extraterritorial effect. Law enforcement officers of this country are bound by *Miranda* even when interrogating on foreign soil. Moreover, it has been recognized that foreign police are governed by *Miranda* when they are acting as the agents of United States law enforcement authorities. But in this context it will take a bit more to establish the requisite agency than when police obtain the assistance of private citizens in this country. This is because cooperative efforts among police agencies of different countries is a natural and desirable arrangement, and thus should not be inherently suspect as a likely effort to accomplish indirectly that which

4. 451 U.S. 454, 101 S.Ct. 1866, 68 L.Ed.2d 359 (1981).

5. This pressure is not so great, however, that there is no need for there also to exist "custody" in the *Miranda* sense. Minnesota v. Murphy, 465 U.S. 420, 104 S.Ct. 1136, 79 L.Ed.2d 409 (1984). *Murphy,* though holding *Miranda* inapplicable because the probationer was not in custody while reporting to his probation officer's office, see § 6.6(e), intimates that had there been custody then *Miranda* would have governed because, as the probationer presumably knows, his probation officer "is a peace officer, and as such is allied, to a greater or lesser extent, with his fellow peace officers," quoting from Fare v. Michael C., 442 U.S. 707, 99 S.Ct. 2560, 61 L.Ed.2d 197 (1979).

could not be done directly. At least where the foreign police were also serving law enforcement interests of their own country, it is not enough that American officers played a substantial role in events leading up to the arrest or that the cooperation has the character of a joint venture.

(e) **Proceedings at Which Confession Offered.** Finally, there is the question of the kinds of proceedings at which a person may object to receipt of his incriminating statements because they were obtained in violation of the *Miranda* procedures. Because *Miranda* is grounded in the Fifth Amendment privilege against self-incrimination, this presents a question of exactly what constitutes incrimination within the meaning of the Amendment. As a general matter, this constitutional provision itself supplies the answer, for it declares that no person "shall be compelled in any criminal case to be a witness against himself." This most certainly means, as occurred in *Miranda,* that an improperly obtained confession is subject to suppression when offered in a criminal trial as evidence of defendant's guilt of the crime charged.[6] Some of the cases discussed earlier holding *Miranda* inapplicable to certain minor offenses, though ordinarily explained in terms of the subject matter of the interrogation, might be read as meaning *Miranda* rights cannot be invoked in a criminal trial of a minor offense. If so viewed, they are even more clearly in error.

What if the confession is tendered only at the sentencing stage of the trial? This issue confronted the Court in *Estelle v. Smith,*[7] for there defendant's statements to an examining psychiatrist were received at the penalty phase of a capital case on the crucial issue of his future dangerousness. The state argued that this raised no Fifth Amendment issue because "incrimination is complete once guilt has been adjudicated," but the Court did not agree:

> Just as the Fifth Amendment prevents a criminal defendant from being made " 'the deluded instrument of his own conviction,' " * * * it protects him as well from being made the "deluded instrument" of his own execution.
>
> We can discern no basis to distinguish between the guilt and penalty phases of respondent's capital murder trial so far as the protection of the Fifth Amendment privilege is concerned. * * * Any effort by the State to compel respondent to testify against his will at the sentencing hearing clearly would contravene the Fifth Amendment. Yet the State's attempt to establish respondent's future dangerousness by relying on the unwarned statements he made to Dr. Grigson similarly infringes Fifth Amendment values.

This latter point, that defendant may invoke *Miranda* at this proceeding because he could not be compelled to testify first-hand at such a proceeding, is fully consistent with the Court's analysis in *Miranda.* And it indicates that *Smith* is not limited to capital case penalty phase hearings, for it is more generally true that the privilege protects against use of compelled testimony in setting sentence.

Smith also teaches that *Miranda* cannot be invoked at every proceeding which is somehow connected to a criminal case. The state attempted to exempt the case from the reach of *Miranda* by pointing out that the psychiatrist's examination of defendant had been undertaken in the first instance for the beneficial purpose of determining if defendant was competent to stand trial. The Court quite properly responded that this made no differ-

6. However, it is suggested in Estelle v. Smith, 451 U.S. 454, 101 S.Ct. 1866, 68 L.Ed.2d 359 (1981), that under some circumstances a defendant may be required to waive his Fifth Amendment protections as a condition to submitting his own evidence on a certain issue. In particular, the Court noted: "When a defendant asserts the insanity defense and introduces supporting psychiatric testimony, his silence may deprive the State of the only effective means it has of controverting his proof on an issue that he interjected into the case. Accordingly, several courts of appeals have held that, under such circumstances, a defendant can be required to submit to a sanity examination conducted by the prosecution's psychiatrist."

In the later case of Buchanan v. Kentucky, 483 U.S. 402, 107 S.Ct. 2906, 97 L.Ed.2d 336 (1987), the Court held that "if a defendant requests [a psychiatric] evaluation or presents psychiatric evidence, then, at the very least, the prosecution may rebut this presentation with evidence from the report of the examination that the defendant requested."

7. 451 U.S. 454, 101 S.Ct. 1866, 68 L.Ed.2d 359 (1981).

ence given the use actually made of defendant's statements. But the Court then added that "if the application of Dr. Grigson's findings had been confined to serving" the function of "ensuring that respondent understood the charges against him and was capable of assisting in his defense," then "no Fifth Amendment issue would have arisen." In other words, *Miranda* could not be invoked at a competency-to-stand-trial hearing. Similarly, it appears that *Miranda* has no application at a parole or probation revocation proceeding, though by virtue of *Smith* the result would be otherwise at a probation revocation proceeding involving deferred sentencing. And in *Baxter v. Palmigiano*,[8] holding that "prison disciplinary hearings are not criminal proceedings" for Fifth Amendment purposes, the Court asserted in passing that *Miranda* had no relevance in that context.

On the other hand, the *Smith* approach would appear to make it certain that *Miranda* applies in juvenile delinquency proceedings. This is because the Supreme Court earlier held in *In re Gault*[9] that the Fifth Amendment privilege is otherwise applicable in juvenile court proceedings. The Court explained this result in *Gault* by saying that

> juvenile proceedings to determine "delinquency," which may lead to commitment to a state institution, must be regarded as "criminal" for purposes of the privilege against self incrimination. To hold otherwise would be to disregard substance because of the feeble enticement of the "civil" label-of-convenience which has been attached to juvenile proceedings. * * * [O]ur Constitution guarantees that no person shall be "compelled" to be a witness against himself when he is threatened with a deprivation of his liberty.

Though this last statement might be read as saying that the Fifth Amendment privilege (and thus *Miranda*) is applicable in any proceeding which could result in a deprivation of liberty, *Gault* apparently does not go this far. For example, neither the Fifth Amendment privilege generally nor *Miranda* in particular has been deemed applicable in a civil commitment proceeding. Rather, the *Gault* Court appears to have regarded juvenile incarceration as sufficiently similar to a criminal penalty to justify application of the privilege.

In *Allen v. Illinois*,[10] the 5–4 majority characterized "*Gault's* sweeping statement" as "plainly not good law," and went on to hold that admissions obtained in violation of *Miranda* requirements were thus properly received in a sexually dangerous persons proceeding against the petitioner. This conclusion was grounded in the fact that the applicable statute had a "civil label" and in addition was not "punitive either in purpose or effect" because "the State has disavowed any interest in punishment, provided for the treatment of those it commits, and established a system under which committed persons may be released after the briefest time in confinement. The Act thus does not appear to promote either of 'the traditional aims of punishment—retribution and deterrence.' " Neither the fact that the statute applied only to those charged with crime nor the fact that it required many of the safeguards applicable to criminal trials made such proceedings "criminal" within the meaning of the Fifth Amendment. (The dissenters, on the other hand, believed the proceedings *were* criminal because they required proof of a crime beyond a reasonable doubt, were initiated by a prosecutor, and resulted in incarceration in the state's prison system.) As to the latter point, the *Allen* majority cautioned: "Had petitioner shown, for example, that the confinement of such persons imposes on them a regimen which is essentially identical to that imposed upon felons with no need for psychiatric care, this might well be a different case."

8. 425 U.S. 308, 96 S.Ct. 1551, 47 L.Ed.2d 810 (1976).

9. 387 U.S. 1, 87 S.Ct. 1428, 18 L.Ed.2d 527 (1967).

10. 478 U.S. 364, 106 S.Ct. 2988, 92 L.Ed.2d 296 (1986).

Chapter 7

IDENTIFICATION PROCEDURES

Table of Sections

---

§ 7.1 Introduction

(a) The Problem of Misidentification. Eyewitness identification can be a powerful piece of evidence in a criminal prosecution. It is frequently an essential piece of evidence as well, as more scientific forms of identification evidence, such as fingerprint and handwriting analyses, are not always available. Yet it is well known that eyewitness evidence is inherently suspect and that suggestive procedures may prejudicially affect the ultimate identification. A pretrial identification proceeding may increase the risk of mistaken identification, as it occurs outside the courtroom and therefore is beyond the immediate supervision of the court.

A dramatic example of the dangers inherent in accepting the identification testimony even of several eyewitnesses in the absence of corroborative evidence is the case of Adolph Beck. Mistakenly identified by twenty-two witnesses, Beck served seven years in prison for crimes he did not commit. Subsequently, a committee formed to investigate the case concluded that "evidence as to identity based on personal impressions, however *bona fide*, is perhaps of all classes of evidence the least to be relied upon, and therefore, unless supported by other facts, an unsafe basis for the verdict of a jury." [1] More recently, seven eyewitnesses swore that Bernard T. Pagano was the man who politely pointed a small, chrome-plated pistol at them and demanded their money. Fortunately, midway through the trial of the Roman Catholic priest, Ronald Clouser admitted that he, not Father Pagano, had committed the six armed robberies.[2] These and many other examples recorded in the annals of criminal law indicate that the identification problem is a serious one and has long existed.

(b) The Causes of Misidentification. Identification testimony has at least three components. First, witnessing a crime, whether as a victim or a bystander, involves perception of an event actually occurring. Second, the witness must memorize details of the event. Third, the witness must be able to recall and communicate accurately. Dangers of unreliability in eyewitness testimony arise at each of these three stages, for whenever people attempt to acquire, retain and retrieve information accurately they are limited by normal human fallibilities and suggestive influences. Some of these potential limitations can be regulated by law, but others are unavoidable.

At one time, it was assumed by some psychological theorists that the brain operates more or less as a mechanical recording device: a person sees everything in front of himself and simultaneously records the information on a memory tape. Later, when the person wants to describe the event, he simply selects the appropriate tape and plays it back, producing a faithful account of the original event. Psychological research has clearly demonstrated, however, that this "videotape recorder" analogy is misleading. In the first place, perception is not a mere passive recording of an event but instead is a constructive process by which people consciously or unconsciously use decisional strategies to attend selectively to only a minimal number of environmental stimuli. Selective perceptual processes result in a failure to observe the details of an event, especially those that are first unimportant but later assume great significance. People have difficulty perceiving time accurately, either the duration of an event or the interval between successive events. In addition to perceptual inaccuracies caused by the brain's inherent limitations, many identification errors are due to circumstances of the observation such as a brief observation period, poor lighting conditions or a stress-inducing situation. Psychological research has demonstrated that anxiety and fear produce significant perceptual distortion. Furthermore, personal expectations, needs and biases may distort perception. Evidence indicates that people are poorer at identifying members of another race than of their own. Perception is both incomplete and inaccurate.

Furthermore, memories are not indelibly preserved on tape. The representation of an event stored in memory undergoes constant change. Some details may be altered to resolve the cognitive dissonance that arises when new information about the event differs from the original memory representation. Other details are simply forgotten. Considerable memory loss occurs during the many days—and often months—that typically elapse between the offense and an eyewitness identification of the suspect. Memory is a constructive process to which details may be added which were not present in the initial representation or in the event itself. The mere wording of a question put to an eyewitness during a deposition, interview or trial

§ 7.1

1. E. Watson, The Trial of Adolph Beck 250 (1924).

2. See Winer, Pagano Case Points Finger at Lineups, Nat'l L.J., Sept. 10, 1979, at 1, col. 4.

may affect not only the immediate answer, but also the witness' memory of the original event and thus any answers to subsequent questions about the event. Interestingly, a witness' feeling of confidence in the details of memory generally do not validly measure the accuracy of that recollection. Witnesses, in fact, frequently become more confident of the correctness of their memory over time while the actual memory trace is probably decaying. Furthermore, individual witnesses may vary in reliability and completeness of memory. Factors such as age, sex or intelligence seem to correlate significantly with reliability of memory.

Another source of errors in identification is the process by which information is retrieved from memory for purposes of making an identification. The recall process suffers from the inadequacy of the eyewitness' vocabulary. Verbal recall—a narrative description unprompted by questions—results in incomplete information retrieval. On the other hand, as the questions become more structured in order to achieve completeness, the resulting responses become more inaccurate because the witness may feel compelled to complete answers in spite of incomplete knowledge. Lineups and photo arrays are structured recognition tests. Witnesses are likely to perceive them as multiple-choice tests that lack a "none of the above" option. Thus, the witness may view the task as one of identifying the individual who best matches the witness' recollection of the culprit, even if that match is not perfect. The reliability of a lineup identification, therefore, depends upon the similarity between the suspect and the other members of the lineup. Various social psychological factors increase the danger of suggestibility, and exertion of suggestive influences by authority figures, such as policemen, tends to magnify them.

(c) The Supreme Court's Response. Traditionally, eyewitness identification testimony has been readily accepted in American criminal trials. The witness will be asked if he sees in the courtroom the person who committed the crime, and he will almost invariably answer in the affirmative and identify the defendant. Moreover, it is now generally accepted that the hearsay doctrine does not bar receipt as substantive evidence of the fact that this witness on a prior occasion, such as at a police lineup, identified the defendant as the perpetrator of the crime charged. Indeed, this earlier identification is likely to be treated as the most important of the two.

Except in the unusual case in which the identification testimony would be the fruit of an illegal arrest of the person identified,[3] there was for many years no solid constitutional basis upon which an objection to the receipt of eyewitness identification testimony could be grounded. In contrast to the situation which obtains as to the defendant's confession, the Fifth Amendment privilege against self-incrimination does not afford a criminal suspect a right of nonparticipation in identification procedures. But in 1967 the Supreme Court recognized two constitutional grounds upon which such testimony could sometimes be successfully challenged. In *United States v. Wade,*[4] the absence of counsel at a post-indictment lineup was held to make inadmissible at trial testimony about the lineup identification and also identification testimony at trial which was the fruit of the earlier identification. But the Court has since given *Wade* a narrow reading, and consequently it has had a limited impact. In *Stovall v. Denno,*[5] the Court held that identification testimony must be suppressed if the confrontation "was so unnecessarily suggestive and conducive to irreparable mistaken identification" as to constitute a denial of due process of law. *Stovall* has likewise been given a limited application, and consequently some commentators believe that a need exists for additional safeguards regarding potentially unreliable eyewitness testimony.

§ 7.2 The Privilege Against Self-Incrimination

(a) The *Schmerber* Rule. In the case of

3. See § 9.4(d).
4. 388 U.S. 218, 87 S.Ct. 1926, 18 L.Ed.2d 1149 (1967).
5. 388 U.S. 293, 87 S.Ct. 1967, 18 L.Ed.2d 1199 (1967).

Schmerber v. California,[1] the Supreme Court upheld the taking of a blood sample by a physician at police direction from the defendant over his objection after his arrest for drunken driving. Among the grounds upon which the defendant challenged the admission of the blood sample into evidence against him was that it violated his Fifth Amendment privilege not to be "compelled in any criminal case to be a witness against himself." The Court, in a 5–4 decision, rejected this contention, holding that "the privilege protects an accused only from being compelled to testify against himself, or otherwise provide the State with evidence of a testimonial or communicative nature, and that the withdrawal of blood and use of the analysis in question in this case did not involve compulsion to these ends."

In the earlier decision in *Miranda v. Arizona,*[2] the Court had described the policies underlying the privilege, there said to include such notions as that the government must "respect the inviolability of the human personality" and that the government must produce evidence against a defendant "by its own independent labors." To some extent, the taking of the blood sample had infringed those two interests, but this alone was not deemed sufficient to bring the Fifth Amendment into play. As the Court put it in *Schmerber,* "the privilege has never been given the full scope which the values it helps to protect suggest," but instead is limited to those situations in which the state seeks to submerge those values by obtaining evidence from the defendant "by the cruel, simple expedient of compelling it from his own mouth." In reaching that conclusion, the Court noted that many identification procedures were not protected by the Fifth Amendment; *Holt v. United States,*[3] holding that a defendant could be compelled to model a blouse, was cited as the "leading case."

The majority in *Schmerber* then declared:

> It is clear that the protection of the privilege reaches an accused's communications, whatever form they might take, and the compulsion of responses which are also communications, for example, compliance with a subpoena to produce one's papers. * * * On the other hand, both federal and state courts have usually held that it offers no protection against compulsion to submit to fingerprinting, photographing, or measurements, to write or speak for identification, to appear in court, to stand, to assume a stance, to walk, or to make a particular gesture. The distinction which has emerged, often expressed in different ways, is that the privilege is a bar against compelling "communications" or "testimony," but that compulsion which makes a suspect or accused the source of "real or physical evidence" does not violate it.[4]

The dissenting Justices in *Schmerber* took a less restrictive view of the Fifth Amendment's privilege. Justice Black observed that the purpose of the extraction was to obtain "testimony" from some person that the defendant was intoxicated. Furthermore, he argued, the blood sample was "communicative" in the sense of supplying information to enable a witness to communicate to the court and jury about the defendant's guilt.[5] But it is the *Schmerber* majority position which has pre-

§ 7.2

1. 384 U.S. 757, 86 S.Ct. 1826, 16 L.Ed.2d 908 (1966), also discussed in § 8.12(d). For more on the policies of the privilege, see § 8.14.

2. 384 U.S. 436, 86 S.Ct. 1602, 16 L.Ed.2d 694 (1966).

3. 218 U.S. 245, 31 S.Ct. 2, 54 L.Ed. 1021 (1910).

4. But the Court then cautioned: "Although we agree that this distinction is a helpful framework for analysis, we are not to be understood to agree with past applications in all instances. There will be many cases in which such a distinction is not readily drawn. Some tests seemingly directed to obtain 'physical evidence,' for example, lie detector tests measuring changes in body function during interrogation, may actually be directed to eliciting responses which are essentially testimonial. To compel a person to submit to testing in which an effort will be made to determine his guilt or innocence on the basis of physiological responses, whether willed or not, is to evoke the spirit and history of the Fifth Amendment."

5. Dissenting Justice Fortas agreed that the defendant's privilege against self-incrimination was applicable, and then added a due process objection: "As prosecutor, the State has no right to commit any kind of violence upon the person, or to utilize the results of such a tort, and the extractions of blood, over protest, is an act of violence."

vailed[6] and has subsequently been relied upon in holding that a great variety of identification practices are not in conflict with the privilege.

(b) Application to Identification Procedures. Once again splitting 5–4 on this issue, the Supreme Court held in *United States v. Wade*[7] that requiring a defendant to appear in a lineup and to say "put the money in the bag" did not violate his privilege against self-incrimination. The *Wade* majority reasoned:

> We have no doubt that compelling the accused merely to exhibit his person for observation by a prosecution witness prior to trial involves no compulsion of the accused to give evidence having testimonial significance. * * * Similarly, compelling Wade to speak within hearing distance of the witnesses, even to utter words purportedly uttered by the robber, was not compulsion to utter statements of a "testimonial" nature; he was required to use his voice as an identifying physical characteristic, not to speak his guilt.

On like reasoning the Court held in the companion case of *Gilbert v. California*[8] that the taking of handwriting exemplars did not violate the defendant's rights.

The dissenters in *Wade* and *Gilbert* argued that *Schmerber* was wrongly decided, in that the privilege was designed to bar the government from forcing a person to supply proof of his own crime. Alternatively, assuming *Schmerber* was controlling, the dissenters claimed the instant cases were distinguishable in that in each of them the defendant had been compelled "actively to cooperate—to accuse himself by a volitional act." But the majority's conclusion that the privilege does not necessarily apply even when the defendant is put into an active rather than a passive posture still prevails, as is indicated by the fact that the Supreme Court has since reaffirmed that there is no Fifth Amendment privilege not to give handwriting exemplars[9] or voice exemplars.[10] The lower courts have followed the *Schmerber–Wade–Gilbert* view and have thus held the Fifth Amendment privilege inapplicable to a great variety of identification procedures. Included are fingerprinting, physical examination, examination of the defendant by X-rays or ultraviolet light, taking casts of defendant's teeth or requiring him to show his teeth, requiring the defendant to remove his glasses or to put on a hat, shoe, jacket, mask or wig and beard, or requiring him to display a limp or a tattoo.

(c) Refusal to Cooperate. What happens if a defendant refuses to cooperate in an identification procedure which requires his active participation? One possibility is that the prosecutor may be permitted to comment on the refusal to cooperate. If the identification procedure in which the defendant has refused to participate or cooperate, such as a lineup or taking of exemplars, is not protected by the Fifth Amendment, then of course there is no right to refuse and thus the act of refusal is not itself a compelled communication.[11] Rather, that refusal is considered circumstan-

6. *Schmerber* was relied upon in South Dakota v. Neville, 459 U.S. 553, 103 S.Ct. 916, 74 L.Ed.2d 748 (1983), holding that the admission into evidence of a defendant's refusal to submit to a blood-alcohol test does not offend his Fifth Amendment privilege against self-incrimination. The Court reasoned that because "the state could legitimately compel the suspect, against his will, to accede to the test," the action of the state "becomes no *less* legitimate when the State offers a second option of refusing the test, with the attendant penalties, for making that choice."

7. 388 U.S. 218, 87 S.Ct. 1926, 18 L.Ed. 1149 (1967).

8. 388 U.S. 263, 87 S.Ct. 1951, 18 L.Ed.2d 1178 (1967).

9. United States v. Euge, 444 U.S. 707, 100 S.Ct. 874, 63 L.Ed.2d 141 (1980); United States v. Mara, 410 U.S. 19, 93 S.Ct. 774, 35 L.Ed.2d 99 (1973).

10. United States v. Dionisio, 410 U.S. 1, 93 S.Ct. 764, 35 L.Ed.2d 67 (1973).

11. Cf. South Dakota v. Neville, 459 U.S. 553, 103 S.Ct. 916, 74 L.Ed.2d 748 (1983) (refusal to give blood sample admissible at criminal trial, as refusal "is not an act coerced by the officer," and it makes no difference that the state did not warn the defendant of this possible consequence, as "such a failure to warn was not the sort of implicit promise to forego use of evidence that would unfairly 'trick' [him] if the evidence were later offered against him at trial"). However, in Schmerber v. California, 384 U.S. 757, 86 S.Ct. 1826, 16 L.Ed.2d 908 (1966), the Court cautioned that in some cases the administration of tests might result in "testimonial products" proscribed by the privilege. For example, the fear of pain or danger resulting from a particular test may provide a coercive device to elicit incriminating statements. Such compelled testimonial product would, of course, be inadmissible.

tial evidence of consciousness of guilt just as is escape from custody, a false alibi, or flight. But if the refusal to speak follows the giving of the *Miranda* right-to-silence warning to the defendant, and that warning did not clearly distinguish between speech in terms of communications and speech for voice identification, then the "silence is insolubly ambiguous" [12] and thus cannot be treated as some evidence of defendant's guilt.

Another possible consequence of a failure to cooperate in identification procedures is imprisonment. On occasion, courts have utilized civil contempt and criminal contempt as a means to coerce or punish the suspect who failed to comply with a court order to participate in some identification proceeding. Some, however, have objected to the use of such a sanction where the defendant has done no more than refuse to participate in a procedure which might identify him as the perpetrator of a crime.

Yet another possibility is that the police will proceed to conduct the identification procedure over the defendant's objection. It has been suggested, however, that the use of force to compel the accused to mount the stage and remain there would make the proceeding unduly suggestive and thus a violation of due process under *Stovall v. Denno.*[13] But since the *Stovall* rule extends only to identifications which are "unnecessarily suggestive," it may be argued in response that the suggestiveness has been made necessary by the defendant's resistance. Indeed, it has been reasoned that a refusal to participate in a lineup would justify the use by the police of a showup procedure in which defendant is alone viewed by the witness and, if *United States v. Wade* [14] applies, in which substitute counsel is provided. Although it has also been suggested that the use of force by the police in carrying out the identification procedure may be sufficiently shocking to the conscience of the Court to require exclusion of the real evidence so obtained under the due process rule of *Rochin v. California,*[15] it is not objectionable that the authorities have used only so much force as is necessary to overcome the defendant's resistance.

(d) Change in Appearance. A related question is what may be done in response to a suspect's drastic alteration of his appearance between the time of arrest (or the occurrence of the crime) and his appearance in a lineup. One possibility is that this alteration will be brought to the attention of the jury. Courts have concluded that evidence of defendant's alteration in appearance may be received, and even that it is appropriate to give an instruction to the jury that the evidence may be considered an indication of consciousness of guilt.

A second possibility is that the identification procedure will be conducted in such a way as to simulate the defendant's prior appearance. Illustrative is *People v. Cwikla,*[16] where defendant appeared at a pretrial identification hearing with his head and face newly shaved, allegedly for medical reasons. On application of the prosecutor, the defendant was required to don a wig and false beard for purposes of the identification hearing. Though the defendant claimed this violated his privilege against self-incrimination, the court ruled "it was not error to compel defendant to conform his appearance at the lineup to his appearance at the time of the crime." On like reasoning, other courts have held it lawful to require the defendant to wear a wig, to wear an artificial goatee, and even to submit to extensive work by makeup experts who changed his appearance to conform to an earlier photograph of him.

In *United States v. Lamb* [17] the court upheld, against a Fifth Amendment challenge, a

12. As the Supreme Court put it in the somewhat analogous situation in Doyle v. Ohio, 426 U.S. 610, 96 S.Ct. 2240, 49 L.Ed.2d 91 (1976).

13. 388 U.S. 293, 87 S.Ct. 1967, 18 L.Ed.2d 1199 (1967).

14. 388 U.S. 218, 87 S.Ct. 1926, 18 L.Ed.2d 1149 (1967).

15. 342 U.S. 165, 72 S.Ct. 205, 96 L.Ed. 183 (1952).

16. 46 N.Y.2d 434, 414 N.Y.S.2d 102, 386 N.E.2d 1070 (1979).

17. 575 F.2d 1310 (10th Cir.1978). See also Andrews v. State, 291 Md. 622, 436 A.2d 1315 (1981) (court order that defendant refrain from shaving his head and facial hair until conclusion of trial, thus requiring him to maintain appearance which most nearly corresponded

court order requiring defendant to shave his beard "where testimony indicated that Lamb had been clean-shaven at the time of the robbery, and that, therefore, Lamb's beard was an attempt to disguise his appearance to prevent trial identification." But, forcing a person to change his appearance in this way is obviously a more serious matter than simply requiring a suspect to don a wig or false beard, and thus due process considerations come into play. As concluded in *People v. Vega,*[18] when "dealing with a procedure which would deprive the defendant of his constitutionally protected right to determine his personal appearance," the state "bears the burden of establishing substantive justification for any action it may impose which limits that right." That burden was not met, the court concluded in *Vega,* where the prosecutor had not even established probable cause that the suspect had committed the crime for which the identification procedure was sought.

Finally, it is well to note that there exists a difficult question concerning whether it is ethical for a defense attorney to encourage his client to change his appearance, such as by shaving his beard, prior to a lineup or prior to a trial at which identification testimony is to be received. It has been suggested that such conduct "raises serious ethical questions" which ought to be addressed by "improvement in the definition of standards for lawyers' conduct and more effective discipline."[19] However, such conduct does not obviously fall within existing disciplinary rules.

§ 7.3 The Right to Counsel and to Confrontation

(a) Procedures Required. In *United States v. Wade,*[1] the Supreme Court confronted the question of "whether courtroom identifications of an accused at trial are to be excluded from evidence because the accused was exhibited to the witnesses before trial at a post-indictment lineup conducted for identification purposes without notice to and in the absence of the accused's appointed counsel." The defendant had been placed in a lineup made up of himself and five or six other prisoners, and each person had been required to wear strips of tape on each side of his face and to say "put the money in the bag," the words used by the perpetrator of a recent bank robbery. This lineup was conducted over a month after defendant had been indicted for the robbery and fifteen days after defense counsel had been appointed, but counsel was not notified of and was not present at the identification proceeding. At defendant's trial, two bank employees identified defendant as the robber and testified that they had earlier identified him in the lineup. In a 6–3 decision, the Court ruled that those procedures had been constitutionally inadequate, and thus concluded

> that for Wade the post-indictment lineup was a critical stage of the prosecution at which he was "as much entitled to such aid [of counsel] * * * as at the trial itself." * * * Thus both Wade and his counsel should have been notified of the impending lineup, and counsel's presence should have been a requisite to conduct of the lineup, absent an "intelligent waiver."

Earlier, in *Schmerber v. California,*[2] the Court had rejected the claim that there was a right to counsel at the taking of a blood sample because "[n]o issue of counsel's ability to assist petitioner in respect of any rights he did possess is presented." The government in *Wade* argued this was equally true of a lineup, also characterized "as a mere preparatory step in the gathering of the prosecution's evidence," but the Court did not agree. Unlike scientific techniques, such as the taking and assessment of a blood sample, "the confronta-

with what witness testified had been his appearance for preceding year, did not violate due process or privilege against self-incrimination).

18. 51 A.D.2d 33, 379 N.Y.S.2d 419 (1976).

19. Grano, *Kirby, Biggers,* and *Ash*: Do Any Constitutional Safeguards Remain Against the Danger of Convicting the Innocent?, 72 Mich.L.Rev. 717, 751 (1973).

§ 7.3

1. 388 U.S. 218, 87 S.Ct. 1926, 18 L.Ed.2d 1149 (1967).

2. 384 U.S. 757, 86 S.Ct. 1826, 16 L.Ed.2d 908 (1966).

tion compelled by the State between the accused and the victim or witnesses to a crime to elicit identification evidence is peculiarly riddled with innumerable dangers and variable factors which might seriously, even crucially, derogate from a fair trial." The Court in *Wade* explained that under past lineup practices, the defense was often unable "meaningfully to attack the credibility of the witness' courtroom identification" because of several factors which militate against developing fully the circumstances of a prior lineup identification by that witness. In particular: (1) other participants in the lineup are often police officers, or, if not, their names are rarely recorded or divulged at trial; (2) neither witnesses nor lineup participants are apt to be alert for or schooled in the detection of prejudicial conditions; (3) the suspect (often staring into bright lights) may not be in a position to observe prejudicial conditions, and, in any event, might not detect them because of his emotional tension; (4) even if the suspect observes abuse, he may nonetheless be reluctant to take the stand and open up the admission of prior convictions; and (5) even if he takes the stand, his version of what transpired at the lineup is unlikely to be accepted if it conflicts with police testimony. Moreover, the Court pointed out, the need to learn what occurred at the lineup is great; the risk of improper suggestion is substantial, and once the witness has picked out the accused in a lineup, he is unlikely to go back on his word in court.

The intended constitutional foundation of the *Wade* decision was not entirely clear from the Court's decision. The Court talked about the lineup being "a critical stage" at which defendant was as much entitled to counsel as at trial, which would seem to indicate that *Wade* is grounded in the Sixth Amendment right to counsel. But in explaining why this was so, the *Wade* majority referred to the fact that "presence of counsel itself can often * * * assure a meaningful confrontation at trial." Indeed, the Court repeatedly referred to the Sixth Amendment right to confrontation and cross-examination in *Wade*, suggesting that the decision was grounded in the Sixth Amendment right of confrontation and cross-examination, with counsel being required simply to give sufficient protection to that other right. But when the choice between these two theories later became important in determining the scope of *Wade*, the Supreme Court opted for the narrower right to counsel theory.[3]

The *Wade* majority emphasized that lineups as they were customarily conducted constituted a "critical stage" for right to counsel purposes, but that it might be otherwise if appropriate reforms were adopted:

> Legislative or other regulations, such as those of local police departments, which eliminate the risks of abuse and unintentional suggestion at lineup proceedings and the impediments to meaningful confrontation at trial may also remove the basis for regarding the stage as "critical." But neither Congress nor the federal authorities have seen fit to provide a solution. What we hold today "in no way creates a constitutional straitjacket which will handicap sound efforts at reform, nor is it intended to have this effect."

Just what substitute procedures would suffice, so that the lineup could be constitutionally conducted without counsel, is not entirely clear. The answer may depend to some extent upon precisely what the function of counsel at the lineup is thought to be, about which there is less than complete agreement.[4] But in any event it seems clear that an adequate substitute must at least provide for a means whereby the defendant can have an opportunity at trial effectively to reconstruct the procedure by which he was identified in a pretrial lineup.

(b) Time of Identification. Because both *Wade* and the companion case of *Gilbert v. California*[5] involved lineups held after indictment and appointment of counsel, lower courts were in disagreement as to whether counsel was required at any pre-indictment identifications. The issue was finally re-

3. See § 7.3(b).
4. See § 7.3(e).
5. 388 U.S. 263, 87 S.Ct. 1951, 18 L.Ed.2d 1178 (1967).

solved by the Supreme Court in the case of *Kirby v. Illinois,*[6] which involved a police station identification of the defendant shortly after his warrantless arrest and before he had been formally charged in any way. The Court held that the *Wade–Gilbert* rule applies only to identifications occurring "at or after the initiation of adversary judicial criminal proceedings—whether by way of formal charge, preliminary hearing, indictment, information, or arraignment." The rationale was that the constitutional right to counsel has traditionally been so limited, and with good reason, in that only after such initiation is a defendant "faced with the prosecutorial forces of organized society, and immersed in the intricacies of substantive and procedural criminal law."[7]

In the main, the commentators have been critical of the *Kirby* decision and have sided with the four dissenters, who pointed out that the decision did not square with the rationale of *Wade.* As one commentator put it:

> The plurality's justification for refusing to apply—or, in its words, "extend"—*Wade* and *Gilbert* is not persuasive. Although both cases involved postindictment lineups, *Wade's* rationale leaves little doubt that the postindictment language was merely descriptive. Pointing to the vagaries of eyewitness identification and to the suggestion inherent in identification procedures, *Wade* found lineups in the absence of counsel to be a serious threat to the fairness of the subsequent trial. *Wade* also concluded that such lineups undermine the right of confrontation at trial, since they are difficult to reconstruct either with direct evidence or on cross-examination. The first reason has nothing to do with the defendant's immersion in legal intricacies. From the defendant's viewpoint, the lineup is virtually devoid of legal issues; at the police officer's discretion, the defendant can be required to participate, walk, talk, and wear certain clothing. Of course, the proceeding must be fairly conducted, but this has little to do with the accused since his opinion or advice is rarely solicited or heeded. Even if the fairness requirement did confront the accused with legal intricacies, those intricacies are obviously the same whenever the lineup is conducted.
>
> *Wade's* second reason for requiring counsel—to protect the right of confrontation—does relate to the intricacies of procedural criminal law, at least to some extent. Acute perception of all lineup conditions, including the reaction of witnesses, is necessary for effective cross-examination at trial. Yet, the Court recognized in *Wade* that the perception of lineup conditions by most defendants is adversely affected by lack of training and emotional tension. These difficulties are not at all dependent upon the lineup's sequential location in the criminal process. The defendant's inability to protect his constitutional right of confrontation remains constant throughout the proceedings against him.[8]

In short, the Court in *Kirby* managed to limit *Wade* by treating it as a "pure" right to counsel case, necessitating a determination of when that right begins, instead of, as it seemed to be, a case grounded in the Sixth Amendment right to confrontation at trial, which is threatened no matter when the pretrial identification occurs. As a result, so the argument goes, the right to counsel is afforded the defendant where he least needs it, namely, for post-arraignment lineups typically conducted to refresh uncertain identifications previously made.

On the other hand, if one accepts the *Kirby* right to counsel characterization, then the ruling there is certainly an understandable one. Even "accepting the premise that the need for counsel is often equivalent in the post-indictment and pre-indictment lineup, it does not necessarily follow that appointment of counsel is constitutionally required in both situations," for the Sixth Amendment "does

6. 406 U.S. 682, 92 S.Ct. 1877, 32 L.Ed.2d 411 (1972).

7. This language in *Kirby* was relied upon in United States v. Gouveia, 467 U.S. 180, 104 S.Ct. 2292, 81 L.Ed.2d 146 (1984), holding that the Sixth Amendment does not require the appointment of counsel prior to the initiation of adversary judicial proceedings against indigent inmates who are confined in administrative detention for lengthy periods while being investigated for crimes committed in prison.

8. Grano, *Kirby, Biggers* and *Ash:* Do Any Constitutional Safeguards Remain Against the Danger of Convicting the Innocent?, 72 Mich.L.Rev. 717, 726 (1974).

not provide for counsel at every stage in which counsel's assistance is helpful."[9] Moreover, that characterization of *Wade* perhaps can best be explained on the ground that the Court deemed it impractical to impose a counsel requirement on *all* police-conducted identification proceedings, especially on-the-scene confrontations occurring just after the commission of the crime. By treating the issue solely in right to counsel terms, it was possible to exclude the earlier stages of the criminal process from the strictures of the *Wade* procedures, a limitation which would be much more difficult to rationalize under the right of confrontation theory.

Except for the language quoted earlier, the Court in *Kirby* did not explore exactly what it takes to "initiate" adversary judicial criminal proceedings and thus bring the *Wade–Gilbert* rule into play. But that language was later relied upon by the Court in *Moore v. Illinois,*[10] where it was held that an identification at a preliminary hearing was governed by *Wade.* The Court in *Moore* emphasized that it was "plain that 'the government ha[d] committed itself to prosecute' " by that time and that defendant "faced counsel for the State" at that time. By this reasoning, it seems clear that the *Wade* right to counsel comes into existence even before the preliminary hearing. Certainly

> a convincing argument can be made that a criminal prosecution commences at least with the preliminary arraignment when a formal complaint is filed in court against the accused. * * * It would defy common sense to say that a criminal prosecution has not commenced against a defendant who, perhaps incarcerated and unable to afford judicially imposed bail, awaits preliminary examination on the authority of a charging document filed by the prosecutor, less typically by the police, and approved by a court of law.[11]

On the other hand, it seems clear under the *Kirby–Moore* test that the *Wade* right to counsel does not ripen merely because the defendant has first been subjected to a warrantless custodial arrest. This means that a person so arrested may be viewed in a lineup without the presence of counsel if that occurs prior to the time of his appearance before a magistrate, except in those jurisdictions which as a matter of state law provide for a broader right to counsel at identification proceedings. And if a person is summoned to appear before a grand jury for purposes of being identified, there is again no *Wade–Gilbert* right to counsel, as the government is still in the process of investigation. There is a split of authority on the question of whether the issuance of an arrest warrant marks the initiation of adversary judicial proceedings within the meaning of *Kirby.* This may be attributable in part to the fact that a document called a "complaint" is sometimes used as a basis for issuance of an arrest warrant and on other occasions is utilized to manifest the prosecutor's preindictment charging decision. But where the complaint simply serves to provide the probable cause to issue an arrest warrant, which may be needed for reasons having nothing to do with charging,[12] it makes no sense under the *Kirby–Moore* formula to view either the issuance of the warrant or the arrest of the defendant pursuant to the warrant as invoking the *Wade* right to counsel.

(c) Nature of Identification Procedure. Regardless of when they occur, certain types of identification procedures will not trigger the right to counsel. For example, as held in *United States v. Ash,*[13] there is no right to have counsel present when the police show photographs of the defendant and others to witnesses, and this is so even if the defendant has already been indicted. Throughout the expansion of the constitutional right to counsel to certain pretrial proceedings, said the majority in *Ash,* "the function of the lawyer has remained essentially the same as his function at trial," which is to give the accused "aid in coping with legal problems or assist-

9. Israel, Criminal Procedure, the Burger Court, and the Legacy of the Warren Court, 75 Mich.L.Rev. 1320, 1368 n. 224 (1977).

10. 434 U.S. 220, 98 S.Ct. 458, 54 L.Ed.2d 424 (1977).

11. Grano, supra note 8, at 788–79.

12. See § 3.6(a).

13. 413 U.S. 300, 93 S.Ct. 2568, 37 L.Ed.2d 619 (1973).

ance in meeting his adversary." This being so, the Court reasoned that there is no such right at photo-identification, as unlike a line-up there is no "trial-like confrontation" involving the "presence of the accused." Although the defendant in *Wade* had not been confronted with legal questions, the lineup offered opportunities for the authorities to take advantage of the accused, a problem which the Court in *Ash* concluded did not exist with respect to identification by use of a photo display. Moreover, the *Ash* majority emphasized that absence of counsel from the photo-identification would not impair effective cross-examination at trial as would absence from a lineup, for photographic identifications are relatively easy to reconstruct. Justice Stewart, concurring in *Ash,* objected to the majority's distinction of *Wade* as a situation in which the lawyer is giving advice or assistance to the defendant at the lineup. He construed the lawyer's role to be that of "an observer," but then concluded that such a role need not be performed with respect to photo-identification, as in that context "there are few possibilities for unfair suggestiveness."

To the extent that *Ash* is grounded in the notion that the function of counsel in a pretrial setting is "the same as his function at trial," it cannot be squared with *Wade.*

> In post-indictment line-ups, it is not readily apparent what immediate assistance an attorney can provide. He cannot stop the line-up or see that it be conducted in a certain manner. He can give no legal advice, proffer no defenses, advance no arguments. The defendant is not in need of legal advice and the lawyer is not in a position to provide on the spot assistance against the skills of the prosecutor. In fact, his own recognized function is as a trained observer.[14]

The critical question in *Ash,* therefore, was really whether such a "trained observer" was needed at identifications made by examination of photographs. Justice Stewart did perceive this as the issue but, as noted, answered in the negative; the three dissenters, however, presented a most forceful argument to the contrary. They noted that the risk of impermissible suggestiveness is equally present in photo-identifications as it is in line-ups, and that in the former situation there is even less likelihood any irregularities will ever come to light because even the accused is not present to observe them. Moreover, photographic identifications lack scientific precision and are difficult to fully reconstruct at trial.

The majority in *Ash* also argued that even if a broader view were taken of the right to counsel, it need not extend "to a portion of the prosecutor's trial-preparation interviews with witnesses," especially in light of "the equal ability of defense counsel to seek and interview witnesses himself." The implication is that granting a right to counsel at photographic displays might lead to the extension of the right to counsel to all pretrial interviews of prospective witnesses. But this is not so.

> The fact that photographic identifications were found to be "critical" would not necessarily lead to a finding that other interviews between the prosecutor and his witnesses were "critical." * * * The basis for extending the right to counsel to the identification context was that identifications by eyewitnesses—like confessions—are such damning evidence that they may completely decide the guilt or innocence of the accused. Photographic identifications can be just as critical to the future outcome of a trial as can corporeal identifications. Routine interviews between the prosecutor and his witnesses, on the other hand, do not have the potential for such damaging results, at least assuming good faith on the part of the prosecutor.[15]

One unfortunate consequence of the *Ash* case may be that police will be encouraged to resort to photo-identification in lieu of lineups in order to obviate the necessity to have defense counsel present at the identification. This would be a most unfortunate development, as a photographic identification, even when properly obtained, is clearly inferior to

14. Note, 64 J.Crim.L.C. & P.S. 428, 433 (1973).

15. Note, 26 Stan.L.Rev. 399, 417 (1974).

a properly obtained corporeal identification. Some state courts have appreciated this problem and thus, as a matter of local law, have gone beyond *Ash* in some way. One view is that photo-identification is an improper identification procedure when the suspect is in custody and could be placed in a lineup, while another is that in such circumstances a photo-identification must be conducted in the presence of defense counsel.

Whether the lawyer is viewed as an advisor and advocate or as merely a trained observer, it is clear that the right to counsel does not attach to more scientific identification procedures, such as the taking of a blood sample. As the Court explained in *United States v. Wade* [16]:

> Knowledge of the techniques of science and technology is sufficiently available, and the variables in techniques few enough, that the accused has the opportunity for a meaningful confrontation of the Government's case at trial through the ordinary processes of cross-examination of the Government's expert witnesses and the presentation of the evidence of his own experts.

The procedures for taking and analyzing blood samples, fingerprints, clothing, hair and the like are distinguishable from lineups and photographic arrays in that they do not depend for their reliability on the recollection of a witness. Rather, their reliability depends on the scientific validity of the techniques and the skill and precision with which they are administered. The risk of suggestiveness present in eyewitness identification simply does not extend to such procedures.

On similar reasoning, the Supreme Court by a 5–4 majority held in *Gilbert v. California* [17] that the taking of handwriting exemplars is not a critical stage entitling the defendant to the assistance of counsel. The majority explained that

> there is minimal risk that the absence of counsel might derogate from his right to a fair trial. * * * If, for some reason, an unrepresentative exemplar is taken, this can be brought out and corrected through the adversary process at trial since the accused can make an unlimited number of additional exemplars for analysis and comparison by government and defense handwriting experts.

Thus, while the suspect might benefit from counsel's advice as to whether to give the exemplars or refuse and suffer the consequences, this does not involve a constitutional right to which the right to counsel might be linked.[18]

Although the *Wade* holding is stated in terms of a right to counsel at a "lineup," unquestionably it extends beyond that. In *Moore v. Illinois,*[19] the holding in *Wade* was more expansively stated as being "that a corporeal identification is a critical stage of a criminal prosecution for Sixth Amendment purposes," and thus the Court concluded that there was a right to counsel at a one-on-one showup. Indeed, as the Court observed, such a procedure is so highly suggestive that the need for counsel is especially great. The identification in *Moore* occurred at a preliminary hearing when the prosecutor asked a rape victim to point out her assailant in the courtroom, but the Court rejected the contention that there is no right to counsel at an identification procedure conducted in the course of a judicial proceeding. Though the more formal proceeding involved in *Moore* may have reduced substantially the chances of undetectable suggestiveness as compared with the typical police lineup, this was offset in the eyes of the Court by the fact that in the judicial setting the lawyer could more readily have caused something to be done to avoid the suggestiveness.

16. 388 U.S. 218, 87 S.Ct. 1926, 18 L.Ed.2d 1149 (1967).

17. 388 U.S. 263, 87 S.Ct. 1951, 18 L.Ed.2d 1178 (1967).

18. Black, J., one of the four dissenters in *Gilbert,* objected: "But just as nothing said in our previous opinions 'links the right to counsel only to protection of Fifth Amendment rights,' * * * nothing has been said which justifies linking the right to counsel only to the protection of other Sixth Amendment rights. And there is nothing in the Constitution to justify considering the right to counsel as a second-class, subsidiary right which attaches only when the Court deems other specific rights in jeopardy."

19. 434 U.S. 220, 98 S.Ct. 458, 54 L.Ed.2d 424 (1977).

Finally, in the case of corporeal identification there is the question of whether the *Wade* right to counsel applies only to the time of the viewing of the defendant by the witness or whether it extends as well to the time at which the witness communicates to the police the fact of identification. There is much to be said for the broader view, which some courts have adopted, as otherwise the defendant has no way of knowing whether the witness was improperly led or whether the witness was hesitant or unsure in his identification. There is, however, authority to the contrary, and it seems more consistent with the approach taken by the Supreme Court in *Ash.*

(d) Waiver or Substitution of Counsel. In *United States v. Wade,*[20] the Supreme Court indicated that there could be an "intelligent waiver" of counsel, in which case presence of an attorney at the identification procedures would not be required. Although this may seem consistent with the waiver permitted in *Miranda v. Arizona,*[21] it might be questioned whether the right to counsel at an identification should be subject to waiver. The argument is that while waiver of counsel under *Miranda* serves the legitimate objective of permitting the suspect to bear witness to the truth, no comparable value is served by waiver under *Wade.* However, the lower courts have consistently held that the right to counsel at identification procedures can be waived, provided of course the waiver is both intelligent and voluntary.

The *Wade* opinion does not dwell upon the question of what is required to show an effective waiver, although it seems likely that an approach similar to that dictated by *Miranda* is to be followed here. This means that a "heavy burden" rests upon the government to show an express waiver following the requisite warnings, which at least must include notice to the defendant that he has a right to counsel for this particular purpose and that counsel will be provided for him if he is indigent. While there is language in *Wade* which, if read literally, would seem to support the result that waiver of counsel must occur in the presence of counsel,[22] it is fully consistent with other waiver of counsel developments[23] to conclude that the right is that of the defendant rather than the lawyer and that consequently it may be waived by the defendant alone. Indeed, there is a sense in which a broader variety of waiver must be recognized here than in the confession context. The police have no right to require a suspect to converse with them, but surely there is a police-prosecution-public interest in a prompt lineup of a person who has been lawfully arrested. This being so, a defendant who is not indigent and thus could hire a lawyer but unreasonably delays in doing so may be deemed to have waived his right to counsel at the identification proceeding.

The Court in *Wade,* in response to the argument that a counsel requirement would "forestall prompt identifications," deliberately opted to "leave open the question whether the presence of substitute counsel might not suffice where notification and presence of the suspect's own counsel would result in prejudicial delay." Given the state's interest in a prompt lineup, it would seem that substitute counsel would suffice where he was sufficiently apprised of the circumstances so as to be able effectively to represent the defendant. On the other hand, it is not sufficient that there was a lawyer present at the lineup for some other purpose, such as to represent another individual, for that attorney could not be expected to be alert to any problems which existed as to the defendant. Moreover, police claims that they had somehow provided substitute counsel are not likely to be favorably received by the courts where it appears the police had taken their good time in arranging the lineup, so that no prejudicial delay could have resulted from permitting defendant to engage his own attorney.

20. 388 U.S. 218, 87 S.Ct. 1926, 18 L.Ed.2d 1149 (1967).

21. 384 U.S. 436, 86 S.Ct. 1602, 16 L.Ed.2d 694 (1966).

22. "Thus both Wade *and his counsel should have been notified* of the impending lineup, and counsel's presence should have been a requisite to conduct of the lineup, absent an 'intelligent waiver.'" (Emphasis added.).

23. See §§ 6.4(f), 6.9.

(e) Role of Counsel. *Wade* stresses the need to protect the defendant's "right meaningfully to cross-examine the witnesses against him and to have effective assistance of counsel at the trial itself," while in *Ash* the *Wade* rule was explained on the basis that "[c]ounsel was seen by the Court as being more sensitive to, and aware of, suggestive influences than the accused himself, and better able to reconstruct the events at trial." This suggests that defense counsel is to be only an observer at the lineup so that, at the trial, he would then be in a position to decide on the basis of his earlier observations whether it is tactically wise to bring out the lineup identification in order to cast doubt upon an in-court identification. And, if he decides to do so, he will better know what questions to ask the witness about the circumstances of the lineup.

If the lawyer is to serve as an observer because, as the Court indicated in *Wade* and *Ash,* he is better able than the defendant and others present to recognize suggestive influences, then this would suggest that it may well be necessary for him to take the stand himself to testify as to what went on at the lineup. This places the defense attorney in a dilemma. Under the Model Rules of Professional Conduct, if a lawyer learns he will be required to be a witness at trial for his client, except as to an uncontested issue, he should withdraw from the case unless doing so "would work a substantial hardship on the client." [24] At least some courts have taken even a stronger stance. In *State v. Caldwell,*[25] holding that defense counsel may not testify regarding events at the lineup unless he withdraws from the case, the court explained: "An advocate who becomes a witness is in the unseemly and ineffective position of arguing his own credibility. The roles of an advocate and of a witness are inconsistent; the function of an advocate is to advance or argue the cause of another, while that of a witness is to state facts objectively."

A second position with respect to defense counsel's function is that the identification procedure "is to be a fully adversary proceeding in which the counsel for the suspect may make objections and proposals, which if they are proper or even reasonable must be respected." [26] Support for this position can also be found in the Supreme Court cases. *Wade* says that "presence of counsel itself can often avert prejudice" and assist law enforcement "by preventing the infiltration of taint in the prosecution's identification evidence," and this prompted the dissenters to find in *Wade* "an implicit invitation to counsel to suggest rules for the lineup and to manage and produce it as best he can." Similarly, in *Ash* the Court asserts that "[c]ounsel present at lineup would be able to remove disabilities of the accused."

If the defense lawyer is to have an active role then, as a matter of tactics, he will have to decide in each case whether to try to prevent and remedy the suggestive aspects of the identification process or whether instead simply to allow them to occur so that he can bring them out at trial to the possible advantage of his client. But, it is by no means clear that he would or ought to have these choices. As one court put it, if defense counsel is allowed to take an active role in setting up the lineup, then "it might well be that, absent plain error or circumstances unknown to counsel at the time of the lineup, no challenges to the physical staging of the lineup could successfully be raised beyond objections raised at the time of the lineup." [27] Such a waiver rule seems undesirable, and this suggests that the notion of defense counsel playing an active role at the identification proceeding is unsound if this is to be the consequence. If the possibility of such waiver exists, then defense counsel would be obliged to raise every conceivable objection unless there was a sound tactical reason for not doing so, a hard choice for an attorney at a very early

24. ABA Model Rules of Professional Conduct, rule 3.7.

25. 117 Ariz. 464, 573 P.2d 864 (1977).

26. ALI Model Code of Pre-Arraignment Procedure 429 (1975).

27. United States v. Allen, 408 F.2d 1287 (D.C.Cir. 1969).

stage of his contact with the case. Moreover, it would result in courts frequently being confronted with incompetency of counsel claims because of the defense attorney's inaction at the identification proceeding.

The situation is quite different when the identification procedure in question occurs in court rather than at the police station. With respect to an in-court identification, made on the record and in the presence of a judicial officer and other observers, it is difficult to make a convincing argument that presence of a lawyer is essential to reveal otherwise undiscoverable suggestiveness. Yet the Court in *Moore v. Illinois* [28] unhesitantly extended the *Wade* rule to in-court identifications, and in doing so emphasized that the identification in that case had been done in a "suggestive manner" and that "[h]ad petitioner been represented by counsel, some or all of this suggestiveness could have been avoided." In this context, then, in contrast to the police station identification, the defense attorney is properly considered to have an active role to play. The reasons militating against that role at the police station do not obtain here; defense counsel's proposals as to how the identification should be conducted can be countered by the prosecutor and ruled on by the judge, and the case is now sufficiently far along that it is not unfair to expect defense counsel to make binding tactical choices.

(f) Consequences of Violation. If the procedures mandated by the *Wade* case are not followed and consequently a pretrial identification occurs without counsel, what are the consequences of this violation of defendant's Sixth Amendment rights? One is that testimony as to the fact of that pretrial identification is inadmissible at trial. As the Court explained in *Gilbert v. California,*[29] such testimony

> is the direct result of the illegal lineup "come at by exploitation of [the primary] illegality." * * * The State is therefore not entitled to an opportunity to show that that testimony had an independent source. Only a *per se* exclusionary rule as to such testimony can be an effective sanction to assure that law enforcement authorities will respect the accused's constitutional right to the presence of his counsel at the critical lineup. * * * That conclusion is buttressed by the consideration that the witness' testimony of his lineup identification will enhance the impact of his in-court identification on the jury and seriously aggravate whatever derogation exists of the accused's right to a fair trial.

Under this *per se* exclusionary rule, the Court explained in *Gilbert,* if evidence of the pretrial identification was received at trial, then any resulting conviction must be reversed unless the appellate court is "able to declare a belief that it was harmless beyond a reasonable doubt." Three Justices objected that such a severe sanction was unnecessary and inappropriate.[30]

What then of a subsequent in-court identification by a witness who earlier identified the defendant at an improperly conducted pretrial identification proceeding? This, the Court declared in *Wade,* presents a "fruit of the poisonous tree" problem which, consistent with the approach generally taken as to that kind of issue,[31] necessitates a determination of "[w]hether, granting establishment of the primary illegality, the evidence to which instant objection is made has been come at by exploitation of that illegality or instead by means sufficiently distinguishable to be purged of the primary taint." And this means, the Court added, that the prosecution must "establish by clear and convincing evidence that the in-court identifications were based upon observations of the suspect other than the lineup identification." The relevant factors, the Court explained in *Wade,* include

> the prior opportunity to observe the alleged criminal act, the existence of any discrepancy between any pre-lineup description and the

28. 434 U.S. 220, 98 S.Ct. 458, 54 L.Ed.2d 424 (1977).

29. 388 U.S. 263, 87 S.Ct. 1951, 18 L.Ed.2d 1178 (1967).

30. They objected in *Wade* that under the harsh per se rule it "matters not how well the witness knows the suspect, whether the witness is the suspect's mother, brother, or long-time associate, and no matter how long or well the witness observed the perpetrator at the scene of the crime."

31. See § 9.3.

defendant's actual description, any identification prior to lineup of another person, the identification by picture of the defendant prior to the lineup, failure to identify the defendant on a prior occasion, and the lapse of time between the alleged act and the lineup identification. It is also relevant to consider those facts which, despite the absence of counsel, are disclosed concerning the conduct of the lineup.

The lower court cases reflect reliance upon these and related factors. In favor of a determination that the in-court identification was not tainted, it is emphasized that the witness had a clear or lengthy opportunity to observe the perpetrator of the crime, that the witness was previously acquainted with the defendant, or that the witness gave an accurate and specific description prior to the identification. Some courts also take into account certain external factors, such as defendant's possession of fruits of the crime, which is improper because such factors have nothing to do with whether the in-court identification is independent of the earlier improperly conducted identification. As for factors tending to show that the taint is not dissipated, the lower courts consider the witness' limited opportunity for observation, any discrepancy in the description given, and any failure of the witness to identify the defendant on an earlier occasion.

The taint approach of the Court in *Wade* does not accord with psychological theory concerning identification, discussed earlier.[32] It is none too surprising, therefore, that when confronted with illegal pretrial identifications the lower courts have easily found an "independent source" for an in-court identification and have readily avoided reversing convictions by stretching, often beyond reason and logic, the doctrines of independent source and harmless error. As a practical matter, the burden is on the defense to show the presence of taint. This being so, it may well be asked whether it would be preferable, as Justice Black contended in *Wade,* that all in-court identifications be admissible so long as not supplemented or corroborated by admission of the earlier illegal identification, or whether instead the per se exclusionary rule should be extended to in-court identifications by witnesses who participated in earlier illegal identifications.

(g) The "Repeal" of the Right. In the Omnibus Crime Control and Safe Streets Act of 1968, the Congress purported to "repeal" the *Wade–Gilbert* rule in federal prosecutions. The Act provides: "The testimony of a witness that he saw the accused commit or participate in the commission of the crime for which the accused is being tried shall be admissible in evidence in a criminal prosecution in any trial court ordained and established under article III of the Constitution of the United States." [33] Though the Court in *Wade* said that the need for counsel could be removed by "[l]egislative * * * regulations * * * which eliminate the risks of abuse and unintentional suggestion at lineup proceedings and the impediments to meaningful confrontation at trial," this statute hardly does that and thus cannot be treated as having nullified the *Wade* decision.

§ 7.4 Due Process: "The Totality of the Circumstances"

(a) Generally. A companion case to *United States v. Wade*[1] and *Gilbert v. California,*[2] both recognizing a right to counsel at postindictment lineups, was *Stovall v. Denno.*[3] There, a victim of a stabbing was hospitalized for major surgery, and defendant, arrested for the offense, was brought to the victim's hospital room for a confrontation. The defendant was handcuffed to one of the seven law enforcement officials who brought him to the hospital room, and he was the only black person in the room. After being asked by an officer whether the defendant "was the man,"

32. See § 7.1(b).

33. 18 U.S.C.A. § 3502.

§ 7.4

1. 388 U.S. 218, 87 S.Ct. 1926, 18 L.Ed.2d 1149 (1967).

2. 388 U.S. 263, 87 S.Ct. 1951, 18 L.Ed.2d 1178 (1967).

3. 388 U.S. 293, 87 S.Ct. 1967, 18 L.Ed.2d 1199 (1967).

the victim identified him. At his trial, both the victim and the police who were present in the hospital room testified to that identification.

Although the defendant in *Stovall* had not been accompanied by counsel, the Court declined to decide the case under the *Wade–Gilbert* rule, holding instead that the principles in those cases would not be applied retroactively but would affect only those identification procedures conducted after the date those decisions were handed down.[4] But the Court then went on to recognize another basis upon which identification testimony could be challenged on constitutional grounds. It must be determined, said the Court in *Stovall,* by a consideration of "the totality of the circumstances," whether the confrontation "was so unnecessarily suggestive and conducive to irreparable mistaken identification" that the defendant was denied due process of law. As the Court later explained, when the issue is whether a witness at the earlier identification may now identify the defendant at trial, then it must be determined whether the identification procedure "was so impermissibly suggestive as to give rise to a very substantial likelihood of irreparable misidentification."[5] "While the phrase was coined as a standard for determining whether an in-court identification would be admissible in the wake of a suggestive out-of-court identification, with the deletion of 'irreparable' it serves equally well as a standard for the admissibility of testimony concerning the out-of-court identification itself."[6]

(b) The "Unnecessarily Suggestive" Element. Under the two-pronged *Stovall* due process test, the first question to be asked is whether the initial identification procedure was "unnecessarily" or "impermissibly" suggestive. This first inquiry can in turn be broken down into two constituent parts: that concerning the suggestiveness of the identification, and that concerning whether there was some good reason for the failure to resort to less suggestive procedures. As for what is sufficiently suggestive to prompt a *Stovall* inquiry, the Court in that case found itself confronted with one such situation, noting that the "practice of showing suspects singly to persons for the purpose of identification, and not as part of a lineup has been widely condemned." This should not be taken to mean that resort to a lineup procedure inevitably means there is an absence of suggestiveness. As the Court later concluded in *Foster v. California,*[7] the manner in which a particular lineup is conducted may make it suggestive in the *Stovall* sense. Similarly, as the Court concluded in *Simmons v. United States,*[8] in some circumstances a photographic array may be suggestive.

Assuming suggestive circumstances, the question then is whether they were impermissible or unnecessary. The Court gave a negative answer in *Stovall,* quoting the following language from the lower court's decision in support of the conclusion that "an immediate hospital confrontation was imperative":

> Here was the only person in the world who could possibly exonerate Stovall. Her words, and only her words, "He is not the man" could have resulted in freedom for Stovall. The hospital was not far distant from the courthouse and jail. No one knew how long Mrs. Behrendt might live. Faced with the responsibility of identifying the attacker, with the need for immediate action and with the knowledge that Mrs. Behrendt could not visit the jail, the police followed the only feasible procedure and took Stovall to the hospital room. Under these circumstances, the usual police station line-up, which Stovall now argues he should have had, was out of the question.

Although the *Stovall* Court's conclusion that the law enforcement authorities in that case were confronted with an emergency is open to

4. On retroactivity, see § 2.9.

5. Simmons v. United States, 390 U.S. 377, 88 S.Ct. 967, 19 L.Ed.2d 1247 (1968).

6. Neil v. Biggers, 409 U.S. 188, 93 S.Ct. 375, 34 L.Ed.2d 401 (1972).

7. 394 U.S. 440, 89 S.Ct. 1127, 22 L.Ed.2d 402 (1969).

8. 390 U.S. 377, 88 S.Ct. 967, 19 L.Ed.2d 1247 (1968).

question,[9] as is the Court's assumption that less suggestive identification procedures could not have been resorted to at the hospital, the lower courts have usually applied the *Stovall* necessity analysis broadly. Many cases have upheld hospital room showups where there has been a serious injury to the victim or witness or to the defendant; even when it appears that the hospitalized person will recover, such a procedure has been justified merely because a period of extended hospitalization lies ahead. Some courts, however, have been more demanding and thus find hospital showups unnecessary if no immediate danger of death to the suspect or witness exists.

A somewhat different kind of emergency was recognized by the Court in the *Simmons* case. The court noted that

> it is not suggested that it was unnecessary for the FBI to resort to photographic identification in this instance. A serious felony had been committed. The perpetrators were still at large. The inconclusive clues which law enforcement officials possessed led to Andrews and Simmons. It was essential for the FBI agents swiftly to determine whether they were on the right track, so that they could properly deploy their forces in Chicago and, if necessary, alert officials in other cities. The justification for this method of procedure was hardly less compelling than that which we found to justify the "one-man lineup" in *Stovall v. Denno,* supra.

The *Simmons* notion that suggestive procedures may be necessary when there is a need for law enforcement officials "to determine whether they were on the right track" has most often been applied by lower courts to justify identification procedures conducted within several hours of the crime. Perhaps because the Supreme Court in *Simmons* went on to discuss the fact that in the circumstances there present the chances of misidentification were slight, these lower court cases typically emphasize the reliability of the identification as well. These cases often give the impression, though the point is not articulated, that the finding of a need for immediate identification is balanced against the unreliability factor, in the sense that a higher risk of error will be tolerated when there was a strong need to conduct the identification procedure at that time.

Another type of case involves the so-called "accidental" showup, not planned by the police, as where a witness just happens to see the defendant in custody in the corridors of the courthouse or at the police station. Some courts seem to take the view that no due process issue exists in such circumstances, apparently because the confrontation was not due to the fault of the police or prosecutor. But this appears to be an unwarranted broadening of the *Stovall–Simmons* exception, for the mere fact that the confrontation was not deliberate does not mean that it was necessary. Perhaps because of doubts about the legitimacy of this extension, the courts frequently proceed to the next step of assessing these "accidental" showups in terms of their unreliability.

In *Neil v. Biggers,*[10] the Court found it unnecessary to decide "whether, as intimated by the District Court, unnecessary suggestiveness alone requires the exclusion of evidence." But the Court recognized that such a result might be explained on grounds similar to the Fourth Amendment and *Miranda* exclusionary rules, namely, to induce the police to follow proper procedures in the future. Such a per se rule was later rejected in *Manson v.*

9. As the dissenters in the court of appeals decision, 355 F.2d 731 (2d Cir.1966), noted, the argument that law enforcement officials were confronted with an emergency "ignores the huge amount of circumstantial identification the excellent police investigation had produced; moreover, if the state officials were motivated [by] solicitude [for Stovall], the natural course would have been to ask Stovall whether he wanted to go. The emergency argument fails both on the facts and on the law. * * * If Mrs. Behrendt's condition had been as serious as my brothers suppose, nothing prevented the prosecutor from informing the state district judge at the preliminary hearing that Stovall had to be taken immediately before her, and suggesting that counsel be assigned forthwith for the limited purpose of advising him in that regard—rather than standing silent when Stovall told the judge of his desire to have counsel and then carting him off to a confrontation by the victim which counsel might have done something to mitigate."

10. 409 U.S. 188, 93 S.Ct. 375, 34 L.Ed.2d 401 (1972).

Brathwaite[11] in favor of a "more lenient" test based on the "totality of the circumstances":

> The *per se* rule * * * goes too far [in furnishing protection against the use of unreliable eyewitness testimony] since its application automatically and peremptorily, and without consideration of alleviating factors, keeps evidence from the jury that is reliable and relevant.
>
> * * * Although the *per se* approach has the more significant deterrent effect, the totality approach also has an influence on police behavior. The police will guard against unnecessarily suggestive procedures under the totality rule, as well as the per se one, for fear that their actions will lead to the exclusion of identifications as unreliable.
>
> The third factor is the effect on the administration of justice. Here the per se approach suffers serious drawbacks. [I]n those cases in which the admission of identification evidence is error under the *per se* approach but not under the totality approach—cases in which the identification is reliable despite an unnecessarily suggestive identification procedure—reversal is a Draconian sanction. Certainly, inflexible rules of exclusion, that may frustrate rather than promote justice, have not been viewed recently by this Court with unlimited enthusiasm.

The two dissenters in *Manson* objected that there were "two significant distinctions" between the per se rule being advocated and other exclusionary rules: (1) the evidence suppressed is not "forever lost," as "when a prosecuting attorney learns that there has been a suggestive confrontation, he can easily arrange another lineup conducted under scrupulously fair conditions"; and (2) the exclusion is not of "relevant and usually reliable evidence," as exclusion "both protects the integrity of the truth-seeking function of the trial and discourages police use of needlessly inaccurate and ineffective investigatory methods." This reasoning takes on added appeal when it is considered, as noted below, that lower courts have applied the risk of misidentification element of the *Stovall* rule in such a way that due process violations are seldom found to exist.

(c) The Risk of Misidentification Element. If, as the Court has made clear, unnecessary suggestiveness "without more does not violate due process,"[12] then it might be thought that the unreliability of the pretrial identification or the trial identification, whichever is being challenged, must be established by the defendant as part of his burden to show that his constitutional rights have been violated. However, the courts, though seldom speaking to the issue, have been inclined to allocate the burden of showing reliability to the prosecution. As one court explained: "Having utilized an unfair means to establish the defendant's guilt, the State must show that the defendant was not harmed by its own transgression."[13]

When the question is the reliability of the in-court identification, the issue is phrased in terms of whether the earlier suggestive procedure created "a very substantial likelihood of irreparable misidentification."[14] When, on the other hand, the question is the reliability of the earlier identification occurring in the context of the unnecessarily suggestive procedure, the standard is quite similar; the same language, "with the deletion of 'irreparable,' "[15] is utilized. It is unlikely but theoretically possible that there could be a risk of misidentification which was substantial but not irreparable, meaning that in a particular case applying the *Stovall* rule the pretrial identification would be suppressed but not the at-trial identification by the same person. Both issues necessitate evaluation of "the totality of the circumstances," and the factors to be considered, the Court explained in *Manson,*

> include the opportunity of the witness to view the criminal at the time of the crime, the witness' degree of attention, the accuracy of

11. 432 U.S. 98, 97 S.Ct. 2243, 53 L.Ed.2d 140 (1977).

12. Neil v. Biggers, 409 U.S. 188, 93 S.Ct. 375, 34 L.Ed.2d 401 (1972).

13. State v. Cefalo, 396 A.2d 233 (Me.1979).

14. Simmons v. United States, 390 U.S. 377, 88 S.Ct. 967, 19 L.Ed.2d 1247 (1968).

15. Neil v. Biggers, 409 U.S. 188, 93 S.Ct. 375, 34 L.Ed.2d 401 (1972).

his prior description of the criminal, the level of certainty demonstrated at the confrontation, and the time between the crime and the confrontation. Against these factors is to be weighed the corrupting effects of the suggestive evidence itself.

These and similar factors have been utilized by the lower courts. Tending to support a finding of reliability is the fact that the witness had a clear or extended opportunity to view the perpetrator of the crime, that the witness had prior knowledge of the perpetrator's identity, that the witness had previously given an accurate description, or that the circumstances prompted a high degree of attention by the witness at the time of the crime. On the other hand, a finding of unreliability is somewhat more likely if the witness had a limited opportunity for observation, gave an earlier conflicting description, failed to identify the defendant on a prior occasion, or was under such stress at the time of the crime as to have his perceptions distorted. Generally, however, these lower court cases show that a *Stovall* due process violation will not be found except in outrageous situations and that a variety of very suggestive lineup procedures are being upheld. This is particularly worrisome when it is considered that the *Manson* reliability test is not very demanding in the first place and is not in all respects in accord with established psychological knowledge [16] of the phenomenon of eyewitness identification. The "level of certainty demonstrated at the confrontation" by the witness, for example, is not a valid indicator of the accuracy of the recollection.

(d) Lineups. It may generally be said that lineups are the most useful and least questionable witness identification procedure. They are obviously less suggestive than one-man showups, and are also more reliable than photographic identifications. Yet not every lineup is free from the danger of suggestive procedures. An apt illustration of a due process violation in a lineup identification is provided by *Foster v. California*.[17] In that case, the defendant was convicted of robbing a Western Union office. The manager viewed a police station lineup in which the defendant was placed with two other men who were half a foot shorter and was the only one wearing a leather jacket similar to that worn by the robber. When this did not lead to positive identification, the police permitted a one-on-one confrontation, but the witness' identification was still tentative. Ten days later another lineup was arranged at which defendant was the only person who had also appeared in the first lineup, and at last the manager was "convinced" that defendant was the man. The Supreme Court quite properly concluded [t]hat "the suggestive elements in this identification procedure made it all but inevitable" that the suspect would be identified "whether or not he was in fact 'the man.' In effect, the police repeatedly said to the witness, '*This* is the man.' "

Unfortunately, most courts have not applied the due process test this vigorously and thus have often held suggestive lineups not violative of due process under the ambiguous "totality of the circumstances" approach. For example, while commentators agree that lineups should contain about six similar participants, lower courts have upheld lineups of as few as three people. And while it seems obvious that similarity of race, physical features, size, age and dress of lineup participants is a prerequisite to avoidance of suggestion, courts have been reluctant to find due process violations even where there were significant dissimilarities of appearance or dress. Courts have also held that multiple lineup confrontations as in *Foster* do not necessarily violate due process.

(e) Use of Pictures. Several factors bear upon the suggestiveness of photographic identification procedures. Certainly a photographic array should so far as practicable include a reasonable number of persons similar to any person then suspected whose likeness is included in the array. As the number of photographs displayed decreases the suggestivity increases, and obviously displaying a single photograph to a witness is very sugges-

16. See § 7.1(b).

17. 394 U.S. 440, 89 S.Ct. 1127, 22 L.Ed.2d 402 (1969).

tive. Still, courts have been reluctant to hold that display of a single photograph violates due process, frequently relying on the witness' prior opportunity to view the defendant. Though certainly the array should not be arranged so that a particular individual stands out, courts have generally not found violations of due process simply because the contents of an array point to a particular suspect. Even if the size, color, or repetitious nature of photographs of suspects are not suggestive by themselves, the manner of presentation by the police may indicate to the witness exactly which person is suspected by the police. Yet an improper remark by a police officer will not necessarily be viewed as a due process violation, nor will the use of successive photo arrays in which only the defendant's picture reappears. In short, while photographic identifications are generally less reliable than lineup identifications and thus deserving of greater precautions to ensure maximum reliability, the courts have generally been unsympathetic to defendants attacking the suggestiveness of photographic identification procedures.

(f) One–Man Showups. As the Supreme Court acknowledged in *Stovall,* "[t]he practice of showing suspects singly to persons for the purpose of identification, and not as part of a lineup, has been widely condemned." This would suggest that showups should be deemed to violate due process absent the most imperative circumstances, but courts generally are not this demanding. Showups are commonly permitted when they occur within several hours of the crime; the two justifications given are the need for quick solution of the crime and the desirability of fresh, accurate identification by eye-witnesses. This may be convincing in the case of an on-the-scene identification, but courts have been inclined also to uphold the showup procedure when it does not take place at the scene of the crime and when it occurs many hours after the occurrence of the crime. Similarly, courts have been reluctant to hold that a showup violates due process when the confrontation is accidental, when some sort of emergency exists, when the suspect is unknown or at large, or when external factors "prove" the accuracy of the identification. Here as well, therefore, courts have relied upon the vagueness of the "totality of the circumstances" test to brush over substantial due process claims.

(g) In–Court Identifications. If a one-on-one confrontation at the police station is highly suggestive, then surely such a confrontation in court is the most suggestive situation of all, for the witness is given an even stronger impression that the authorities are already satisfied that they have the right man. As the Supreme Court declared in *Moore v. Illinois,*[18] where after defendant was led to the bench for his preliminary hearing the rape victim was called upon to make her first corporeal identification of him, it "is difficult to imagine a more suggestive manner in which to present a suspect to a witness for their critical first confrontation than was employed in this case." The due process issue was not before the Court in *Moore,* and thus the Court declined to state exactly what must be done to avoid such a situation.

The Court did, however, mention some ways in which the suggestiveness might have been prevented had defendant been represented by counsel. "For example, counsel could have requested that the hearing be postponed until a lineup could be arranged at which the victim would view petitioner in a less suggestive setting." A leading case on this point is *Evans v. Superior Court,*[19] where the court held that due process requires the prosecution to honor a defense request for a lineup where "eyewitness identification is shown to be in material issue and there exists a reasonable likelihood of a mistaken identification which a lineup would tend to resolve." The court in *Evans* reasoned that "[b]ecause the People are in a position to compel a lineup and utilize what favorable evidence is derived therefrom, fairness requires that the accused be given a reciprocal right to discover and utilize contrary evidence." Other decisions are also to

18. 434 U.S. 220, 98 S.Ct. 458, 54 L.Ed.2d 424 (1977).

19. 11 Cal.3d 617, 114 Cal.Rptr. 121, 522 P.2d 681 (1974).

be found holding that a defense request for a lineup should have been granted, although generally courts are inclined to say merely that whether such relief is called for is left to the trial court's discretion.

The Court in *Moore* also noted that "counsel could have asked that the victim be excused from the courtroom while the charges were read and the evidence against petitioner was recited, and that petitioner be seated with other people in the audience when the victim attempted an identification." Here as well, the prevailing view is to leave the matter largely within the trial judge's discretion. This is surprising, as an identification more unreliable than the witness's familiar selection of the conspicuous defendant is difficult to imagine.

Perhaps because of the fact that it is within the judge's discretion whether to grant such requests, defense counsel have on occasion resorted to self-help, sometimes with unfortunate consequences. In a case in which the defense attorney used a decoy without the trial judge's knowledge or approval, the decoy was convicted and temporarily jailed. Defense counsel's act of substituting another person for the defendant at counsel table without the court's permission or knowledge has been viewed as a violation of ethical standards and an obstruction of justice punishable by criminal contempt.

(h) The "Repeal" of the Right. As a part of the Omnibus Crime Control and Safe Streets Act of 1968, Congress adopted this provision: "The testimony of a witness that he saw the accused commit or participate in the commission of the crime for which the accused is being tried shall be admissible in evidence in a criminal prosecution in any trial court ordained and established under article III of the Constitution of the United States."[20] Just as Congress cannot by such an act destroy the constitutional right to counsel under the *Wade–Gilbert* rule,[21] it surely cannot do away with a defendant's right under *Stovall* not to be convicted on the basis of an identification so unreliable as to violate due process.

§ 7.5 Additional Possible Safeguards

(a) Jury Instructions. Because the *Wade* and *Stovall* rules have not resulted in the substantial elimination of the danger of unreliable eyewitness identification, it is appropriate to consider other possible safeguards such as jury instructions. Instructions cannot make the identifications any more reliable, but hopefully they can alert the jury to the necessity for a most careful assessment of identification evidence. In *United States v. Telfaire,*[1] the court set out an instruction for use in future identification cases:

> Identification testimony is an expression of belief or impression by the witness. Its value depends on the opportunity the witness had to observe the offender at the time of the offense and to make a reliable identification later.
>
> In appraising the identification testimony of a witness, you should consider the following:
>
> (1) Are you convinced that the witness had the capacity and an adequate opportunity to observe the offender?
>
> Whether the witness had an adequate opportunity to observe the offender at the time of the offense will be affected by such matters as how long or short a time was available, how far or close the witness was, how good were lighting conditions, whether the witness had had occasion to see or know the person in the past. * * *
>
> (2) Are you satisfied that the identification made by the witness subsequent to the offense was the product of his own recollection? You may take into account both the strength of the identification, and the circumstances under which the identification was made.
>
> If the identification by the witness may have been influenced by the circumstances under which the defendant was presented to him for identification, you should scrutinize the identification with great care. You may also consider the length of time that lapsed

20. 18 U.S.C.A. § 3502.

21. See § 7.3(g).

§ 7.5

1. 469 F.2d 552 (D.C.Cir.1972).

between the occurrence of the crime and the next opportunity of the witness to see defendant, as a factor bearing on the reliability of the identification. * * *

(3) You may take into account any occasions in which the witness failed to make an identification of defendant, or made an identification that was inconsistent with his identification at trial.

(4) Finally, you must consider the credibility of each identification witness in the same way as any other witness, consider whether he is truthful, and consider whether he had the capacity and opportunity to make a reliable observation on the matter covered in his testimony.

I again emphasize that the burden of proof on the prosecutor extends to every element of the crime charged, and this specifically includes the burden of proving beyond a reasonable doubt the identity of the defendant as the perpetrator of the crime with which he stands charged. If after examining the testimony, you have a reasonable doubt as to the accuracy of the identification, you must find the defendant not guilty.

A few other federal circuits have likewise strongly recommended that such an instruction be given when identification is a key issue in the case, while others have recommended such a special instruction in those circumstances but leave the trial judge with considerable discretion in deciding whether to use the instruction. Some state courts also utilize an instruction like that in *Telfaire,* while some others take the view that such an instruction is inappropriate because the matter is best left to final argument by the parties.

(b) Expert Testimony. Some have argued that in a case in which eyewitness testimony is of central importance, the defendant should be entitled to have a psychologist testify in his behalf on such circumstances as may be present in the particular case (e.g., presence of stress or passage of time, cross-racial or cross-ethnic identification) which psychological research has shown may cast doubt upon an eyewitness identification. But the appellate cases typically say that whether to receive such expert testimony lies within the sound discretion of the trial court. In holding that the trial judge acted within the scope of his discretion in not permitting such testimony, these cases make such assertions as that work in the field is not sufficiently developed, that the testimony would invade the province of the jury or have undue influence upon the jury, that the undue consumption of time would substantially outweigh its probative value, and that what the expert has to offer can be effectively communicated to the jury by probing questioning of the identification witnesses. In recent years, however, there has been somewhat greater willingness by trial courts to receive such evidence.

(c) Improved Police Procedures. *Wade* and *Stovall* mark only the constitutional minimum of what must be done rather than the maximum of what should be done to enhance the reliability of eyewitness identifications. As some police agencies have discovered, this is an area in which the existence of clear regulations, in the formulation of which law enforcement agencies have themselves participated, are especially beneficial. Setting clear and reasonable standards for each type of identification procedure can be of great benefit to those suspected of crime and also those charged with the responsibility of enforcing the law. "There are, thus, real benefits to be realized by the prosecution, and the public it represents, in presenting evidence of a pretrial identification made under conditions which vouch for its fairness, and hence, its probable accuracy." [2]

2. McGowan, Constitutional Interpretation and Criminal Identification, 12 Wm. & Mary L.Rev. 235, 241 (1970).

Chapter 8

GRAND JURY INVESTIGATION

Table of Sections

---

§ 8.1 Dual Functions of the Grand Jury

The grand jury is said to serve as both "the shield and the sword" of the criminal justice process. It is likened to a shield in its operation as a screening agency interposed between the government and the individual. In deciding whether to issue an indictment, the grand jury reviews the government's evidence and, in effect, screens the prosecutor's decision to charge. By refusing to indict when the evidence is insufficient or prosecution otherwise appears unjust, the grand jury is said to "function as a shield, standing between the accuser and the accused, protecting the individual citizen against oppressive and unfounded government prosecution." The grand jury is likened to a sword in its performance as an investigative agency. Here the grand jury is not reviewing cases that the prosecutor believes to be ready for prosecution, but rather examining situations that are still at the inquiry stage. Utilizing its investigative authority, the grand jury uncovers evidence not previously available to the prosecution, and thereby provides the sword that enables the government to secure convictions that might otherwise not be obtained.

In this chapter, we will concentrate upon the investigative role of the grand jury; the screening function of the grand jury will be discussed in Chapter 15. While this division facilitates treatment of the full range of the government's investigative powers in this second segment of the treatise, it has the drawback of presenting at this point only a partial picture of the grand jury. Accordingly, in reading this chapter, one should keep in mind that the two roles of the grand jury often combine in shaping the law governing grand jury practices. Various aspects of grand jury structure and authority discussed here in connection with the grand jury's investigative role also have a bearing on its screening function. Grand jury secrecy, for example, strengthens the investigation function by safeguarding witnesses against possible reprisals from those against whom they testify, but it may be even more significant in implementing the screening function by protecting the innocent person whom the grand jury refuses to charge.

It should also be kept in mind that the two roles of the grand jury commonly are performed by the same jury. In those states requiring that felony prosecutions be brought by grand jury indictment, the typical grand jury will be involved primarily in screening fully prepared cases, but that same grand jury may be called upon at any time to use its investigating authority to develop evidence not currently available to the prosecution. In jurisdictions permitting prosecution by information, grand juries ordinarily are summoned primarily for use in investigations.[1] Though such grand juries often are referred to as "investigative grand juries," they also engage in a screening function; once the investigation is complete, the grand jury then determines whether the evidence produced is sufficient to indict. Thus, the "investigative grand jury" will eventually be involved in screening, and the "screening grand jury" will not infrequently be used for investigations as well as screening.

§ 8.2 Historical Development

The law governing the grand jury has been strongly influenced by the historical development of that institution initially in England and later in this country. What follows is a brief summary of the highlights of that history as they relate to the dual functions of the grand jury. These highlights have contributed substantially to the image of the grand jury as an independent body that serves the concerns of the community both in precluding prosecutions the community views as unjust and in uncovering crimes suspected by the community but unsuccessfully investigated by the police. This perception of the grand jury as the "people's panel" has provided, in turn, the foundation for much of the grand jury's common law authority. Thus, it is not surprising that both legislative and judicial efforts to limit that authority invariably have included challenges to that image based, in part, upon a different interpretation of these same historical highlights.

(a) English Origins. The grand jury commonly is traced back to the Assize of Clarendon, issued in 1166, although some historians find earlier antecedents in institutions utilized by the Anglo-Saxons, Normans, and even the Athenians. The assize was a crucial element in the efforts of Henry II to wrest the administration of justice away from the courts of the feudal barons. It provided for "an inquiry" to be made in each community

§ 8.1

1. Many indictment and information jurisdictions also provide for grand juries of special composition or special jurisdictional authority to fulfill part of this investigatory function. The primary illustration at the state level is the "statewide grand jury," empaneled at the request of the Attorney General to investigate possible criminality that extends over several judicial districts. In the federal system, although the standard Rule 6 grand juries are utilized in the investigation of the full gamut of federal offenses, the Organized Crime Control Act authorizes the summoning of special grand juries to be utilized in extensive investigations in certain judicial districts. See 18 U.S.C.A. §§ 3332–3334. Several states also provide for an alternative investigative body in the form of a "one-man grand jury" or a "John Doe" proceeding, which basically vest in a judicial officer the investigative responsibility and authority of a grand jury.

by twelve of its "good and lawful" men. Those jurors were to be put under oath and questioned by the itinerant justices of the peace or the sheriff. It was the obligation of the jurors to accuse all they suspected, and those accused were then to be subjected to trial by ordeal. The assize clearly was designed not to provide protection for those suspected of crime, but rather to lend assistance to government officials in the apprehension of criminals. The jurors were familiar with the local scene and could present charges that otherwise might not be known by the Crown's representatives. Any hesitancy the jurors might have in bringing accusations against their neighbors would be overcome by the substantial fines the jurors faced for failing to bring forward any known offender.

By the end of the fourteenth century the English had turned to trial by jury rather than by ordeal and the original jury had been divided into two separate juries. The trial of guilt was before a twelve-person petit jury, and the accusatory jury was expanded to twenty-four persons, chosen from the entire county. The accusatory jury became known as "*le graunde inquest,*" which probably explains its eventual title of grand jury. At this point, the grand jury remained essentially a body designed to assist the Crown in ferreting out criminals. Accusations were either initiated by the jurors themselves, acting on the basis of their own knowledge, or were initiated by a representative of the Crown, typically a justice of the peace, who produced witnesses to testify before the grand jury in support of a particular charge. When the accusation was initiated by the jury itself, the formal charge filed with the court was called a "presentment." When the accusation stemmed from a case placed before the jury by the Crown's representative, the grand jury's charging document was called an "indictment." The Crown's representative ordinarily would place a proposed indictment before the grand jury, and if the grand jury found the Crown's evidence sufficient to proceed, it issued the indictment, declaring it to be a "true bill." If the jury concluded that the evidence was insufficient, it returned a finding of ignoramus ("we ignore it"), or, in later years, "no bill."

Over the next few centuries, the grand jury began to assume a significant degree of independence. Grand juries developed the custom of hearing witnesses privately in their chambers and the courts no longer required the grand jurors to explain their reasons for refusing to indict. The secrecy of the grand jury's hearings and deliberations was said to provide both jurors and witnesses protection against retribution from displeased royal officials. In the late seventeenth century, a period of great upheaval in Britain, the grand jury's new found independence was put to its severest test. The Crown brought considerable pressure upon grand juries to indict noted supporters of the Protestant cause. Grand juries resisted that pressure in several cases, including two that attracted widespread attention. Grand juries refused to indict Stephen Colledge and the Earl of Shaftesbury, both accused of high treason, notwithstanding the Crown's insistence that its evidence be presented in open court in contravention of the established custom. Although the Crown later obtained an indictment against Colledge from a different grand jury, the *Shaftesbury* and *Colledge* cases led to the grand jury being widely celebrated as a "bulwark against the oppression and despotism of the Crown." During the same period, grand juries also achieved some prominence in fighting governmental corruption, as they issued presentments based upon their inquiries into the misconduct of minor officials in matters of local administration. Thus, by the end of the century, the English grand jury had emerged, as one article put it, as "a virtual Janus who, one moment acted as the vigilant prosecutor, and the next as the defender of those who were unjustly accused."

(b) Developments in the United States. Along with other elements of the English law, the grand jury was adopted as part of the criminal justice process in the American colonies. The grand jury soon developed, however, into an important vehicle of colonial government that extended beyond the enforcement of the criminal law. The English grand jury had occasionally used its power of presentment to criticize action or inaction of government officials that fell short of criminal misconduct. The American grand juries made extensive use of that authority, and their presentment "reports" became the primary vehicle for the expression of the complaints of the citizenry on a wide range of matters. As community dissatisfaction with England's colonial policies grew stronger, these reports were most frequently critical of the Crown's officials in America. At the same time, colonial grand juries were often also at odds with royal officials as to appropriate cases for criminal prosecution. Thus, the infamous prosecution of John Peter Zenger for seditious libel was brought by a prosecutor's information because colonial grand juries twice refused to issue requested indictments. On the other side, grand juries issued criminal presentments against various royal officials, including British soldiers, on which the Crown frequently refused to prosecute.

As a result of its opposition to the British, the grand jury emerged from the American Revolution with increased prestige. State constitutions commonly required that all felony prosecutions be brought by grand jury indictment or presentment, and once it was decided to add a Bill of Rights to the federal constitution, the inclusion of a similar provision in the Fifth Amendment was accepted without controversy. In the post-revolutionary period, there were several notable instances in which grand juries rejected highly partisan indictments (as in the initial attempts to prosecute Aaron Burr), although there were others in which grand juries readily supported such indictments (as in various Sedition Act prosecutions brought against Republican publishers). At the same time, grand juries also continued to pursue on their own initiative a "public watchdog" function, especially in the western territories. Grand juries actively reviewed a wide range of grievances presented by citizens, often conducting searching investigations of corruption in government and widespread evasion of particular laws.

During the 1820's, Jeremy Bentham vigorously criticized the English grand jury, claiming that it was both unrepresentative and inefficient. The latter criticism caught hold in the United States, particularly in the sparsely populated states. The requirement that all felony prosecutions be instituted by indictment was criticized as cumbersome, costly, and unnecessary to protect the innocent. In 1859, Michigan became the first state to grant prosecutors the option of proceeding either by grand jury indictment or by a prosecutor's information. Several states followed Michigan's lead, and in 1884, the constitutionality of this shift from indictment to information was upheld in *Hurtado v. California.*[1] Over the years since, there has been a gradual movement of the states to prosecution by information, so that today only nineteen states continue to grant the defendant a right to grand jury screening in all felony cases (although several others still require an indictment for capital offenses).[2] No state, however, has gone as far as England, which finally heeded Bentham's advice and abolished the grand jury. Those states which allow prosecution by information still authorize the optional use of the grand jury. That option was retained in large part to permit continued use of the investigative grand jury.

During the same period in which a majority of the states moved to prosecution by information, grand juries were active in both information and indictment states in the investigation of corruption in local government. In several instances, the resulting indictments were so widespread as to unseat entire municipal administrations. As might be expected, local prosecutors were sometimes less than enthusiastic in cooperating with such investigations. Grand juries responded by seeking outside help (usually through court appointment of a special prosecutor) or by simply pushing forward against the wishes of a reluc-

§ 8.2

1. 110 U.S. 516, 4 S.Ct. 111, 28 L.Ed. 232 (1884), also discussed at § 2.4(b).

2. See § 15.1(b).

tant prosecutor. The most famous of these "runaway" grand jury investigations was the mid–1930's New York investigation of "racketeering" offenses, which led to the appointment of special prosecutor Thomas E. Dewey. The exploits of Dewey and his "racket busters" inspired a series of runaway grand jury investigations throughout the country and established the reputation of the grand jury as the nation's number one investigatory tool in combatting organized crime. In later years, federal grand jury investigations of a variety of white collar crimes helped the grand jury establish a similar reputation in that field and investigations of government corruption at every level further enhanced its image as the community's "watchdog over government." At the same time, the grand jury's reputation was sullied by investigations that suggested partisan political use of the grand jury's investigative authority—such as highly publicized investigations of public figures that led to damaging accusations that could not be supported at trial and investigations of alleged criminal activity of "radicals" that seemed to be directed more toward harassment than producing supportable indictments.

(c) Relevance of History. As might be expected, the critics and supporters of the investigative grand jury are divided over the lessons to be drawn from the history of that institution. They disagree in particular on two issues: (1) whether that history establishes an accommodation, particularly at the time of the adoption of the federal constitution, between the broad investigatory authority of the grand jury and the accusatory framework of American criminal procedure, and (2) whether that broad investigatory authority, if granted to the early American grand juries, was tied to a capacity for its independent exercise that has been lost with the expansion of the role of police and prosecutor in criminal investigations.

The grand jury investigation is frequently described as introducing an "inquisitorial element" into a criminal justice system that is basically accusatorial. Critics argue that the grand jury's investigative authority should therefore be viewed as an anomaly and kept within narrow confines by close judicial supervision. They recognize that this position faces difficulties if history reveals that the grand jury inquest was accepted from the outset as an institution that coexisted with the accusatorial elements of the Anglo–American criminal justice process. The critics argue, however, that a careful reading of the history of the grand jury reveals no such accommodation. First, they note, the early grand juries did not frequently exercise the basic element of its modern investigative authority—its power to compel testimony—but instead relied primarily upon information known to the jurors or the voluntary testimony of aggrieved persons. Secondly, they argue, the investigative role of the grand jury was not critical to the grand jury's initial acceptance in this country. It was the shielding role of the grand jury that earned it a place in the Bill of Rights and the early state constitutions. The grand jury's investigatory role was then viewed as entirely secondary and not necessarily distinct from its screening role. Today, it is argued, the significance of the two roles has been reversed.

Supporters of the grand jury respond that the early history of the grand jury clearly establishes the legitimacy of its extensive investigative authority. The power of the grand jury to compel testimony was recognized well before the adoption of the Constitution and was used in some of the most notable grand jury inquests. At the time of the Constitution's adoption, the grand jury was a revered institution not simply because it served as a buffer between the state and the individual, but equally for its service as a watchdog against public corruption and its capacity to ferret out criminal activity that local officials either chose to ignore or were unable to investigate. The importance of this investigative authority was implicitly recognized, it is argued, in constitutional and statutory provisions authorizing the institution of prosecution by presentment as well as indictment.

With few exceptions, American courts have accepted the position that the history of the grand jury provides a solid foundation for its broad investigative authority. The Supreme Court's discussion of that authority in *Blair v. United States*[3] is typical. The Court there noted that the grand jury's authority to resort to compulsory process had been recognized in England as early as 1612, and the inquisitorial function of the grand jury was well established at the time of the Constitution's adoption. Both the Fifth Amendment and the earliest federal statutes recognized an investigative authority of the grand jury that included the "same powers that pertained to its British prototype." The Supreme Court would not view that authority with suspicion and subject it to new limitations. The grand jury, the Court concluded, "is a grand inquest, a body with powers of investigation and inquisition, the scope of whose inquiries is not to be limited narrowly by questions of propriety or forecasts of the probable result of the investigation."

Critics of the grand jury also contend that even if a broad investigative authority is sanctioned by history, the same historical sources also indicate that that authority was tied to an assumption of substantial grand jury independence. That assumption, they continue, is contrary to current practice, and the eighteenth century prototype of the grand jury therefore is no longer relevant. The grand jury's investigative authority was designed for a rural setting. It was based on the premise that grand jurors, knowing the community, could uncover crime and corruption with very little help from government officials. However, with the increased complexity and anonymity of an urban society, the grand jury was gradually forced to relinquish its independence and turn to the prosecutor for direction.

Today, the critics argue, the sweeping powers of the grand jury are exercised in reality by the prosecutor alone. Working with the police, the prosecutor determines what witnesses will be called and when they will appear. He examines the witnesses and advises the grand jury on the validity of any legal objections the witnesses might present. If a witness refuses to comply with a subpoena, it is the prosecutor who seeks a contempt citation. If a witness refuses to testify on grounds of self-incrimination, it is the prosecutor who determines whether an immunity grant will be obtained. The grand jury must, almost of necessity, rely upon the prosecutor's resources and leadership. Few investigations can succeed without the investigative work, skillful interrogation, legal advice, and even the secretarial assistance, provided by the prosecutorial agency. So, too, grand jurors are neophytes in the field of criminal investigation and are participating only on a part-time basis; it is only natural that they are disposed to rely upon the prosecutor—the "professional" who commands the expertise necessary to their venture.

Critics argue that this change in the nature of the investigative grand jury, which has converted it into the "prosecutor's puppet," requires a corresponding change in judicial attitudes. The courts should not, they argue, feel bound by precedent that was developed during an era when grand juries were independent bodies. Instead, they should "pull back the veil of history" and view the investigating grand jury as one would view any other investigatory instrument of government. The power of the grand jury should be subject to the same kinds of limitations as are imposed upon other weapons in the government's investigative arsenal.

Supporters of the grand jury readily acknowledge that the prosecutor plays a substantial role in directing today's grand jury investigations. They suggest that this is a beneficial development that makes the investigatory authority more effective and helps to ensure that it is not misused. Moreover, it is noted, this development dates back over one hundred years, preceding many of the decisions that speak most eloquently of the necessary breadth of the grand jury's investigative authority. The key to the historical grant of that authority, they argue, was a legal structure that rendered the government's use of the grand jury's investigative powers subject

3. 250 U.S. 273, 39 S.Ct. 468, 63 L.Ed. 979 (1919), discussed in § 8.8(a).

to the veto of the jurors, who sat as community representatives. That structure has not been substantially altered, and its very presence, the argument continues, serves to hold the prosecutor in check and to distinguish grand jury investigations from investigatory tools granted directly to the prosecutor or the police. The fact that the grand jury only occasionally exercises its power to override the prosecutor does not detract from the significance of that power. The prosecutor must respect the existence of that power and act in a way that he knows, from past experience, will be acceptable to the jurors.

In recent years, courts have been divided as to whether the larger role played by prosecutors in the typical grand jury investigation requires a reexamination of the historical precedents establishing the grand jury's broad investigative authority. The Supreme Court, over some dissents, has continued to accept those precedents.[4] Other courts, however, have argued that a lesser degree of grand jury independence requires a greater degree of judicial supervision. These courts have urged that the grand jury be treated as being "for all practical purposes" no more than "an investigative and procedural arm of the executive branch of government." [5]

§ 8.3 Investigative Advantages

Compared to police investigations, grand jury investigations are expensive, time consuming, and logistically cumbersome. However, the grand jury also offers certain investigative advantages over the police. Those advantages stem mainly from five elements of the grand jury process—(1) subpoena authority backed up by potential contempt sanctions, (2) lay participation, (3) closed proceedings, (4) immunity grants, and (5) grand jury secrecy requirements. For the investigation of most crimes, the advantages provided by these aspects of the grand jury process are superfluous. Police investigations work as well and do so at far less cost. There are certain types of cases, however, in which prosecutors are likely to view the grand jury's investigatory assistance as either essential or highly desirable, and therefore worth the extra costs of the grand jury process. These are primarily cases in which investigators face one or more of the following tasks: unraveling a complex criminal structure, dealing with victims reluctant to cooperate, obtaining information contained in extensive business records, keeping a continuing investigative effort from the public gaze, or counteracting public suspicion of political manipulation of the investigation. Criminal activities likely to present such investigative problems include governmental corruption (e.g., bribery), misuse of economic power (e.g., price-fixing), and wide-spread distribution of illegal services and goods (e.g., gambling or narcotics).

(a) Subpoena Authority and the Contempt Sanction. The basic investigative advantage of the grand jury stems from its ability to use the subpoena authority of the court that impaneled it. The grand jury may utilize the subpoena duces tecum to obtain tangible evidence and the subpoena ad testificandum to obtain testimony. Both subpoenas are supported by the court's authority to hold in contempt any person who willfully refuses, without legal justification, to comply with a subpoena's directive. That authority encompasses both civil and criminal contempt, although use of the former is far more common than use of the latter. In rare cases, a recalcitrant witness may be subject to both forms of contempt.

Civil contempt is used to coerce the recalcitrant witness into complying with the subpoena. The witness is sentenced to imprisonment or to a fine (which may increase daily), but he may purge himself by complying with the subpoena. It is said that he "carries the keys of the prison in his own pockets." The civil contemnor who refuses to purge himself will remain under sentence until the grand jury completes its term and is discharged.[1]

4. See e.g., the Supreme Court rulings cases discussed in §§ 8.6, 8.7, 8.8.

5. In re Grand Jury Proceedings (Schofield), 486 F.2d 85 (3d Cir.1973), discussed in § 8.8(b).

§ 8.3

1. Some jurisdictions restrict imprisonment for civil contempt to a maximum term that is shorter than the full term of the grand jury. See e.g., 28 U.S.C.A. § 1826

Moreover, if the information that the contemnor possesses is still needed, he may be subpoenaed by a successor grand jury and again held in contempt if he continues to refuse to supply that information.

Assuming there is a continuing need for the information sought by subpoena, most jurisdictions require that the court first utilize civil contempt unless it clearly will not be successful. If civil contempt fails, or appears very likely to fail, the court may then utilize criminal contempt. Here the court simply seeks to impose punishment for violation of its order in the same manner in which punishment is imposed for a violation of the penal code.[2] The contemnor is sentenced to a fine or imprisonment for refusing to obey the subpoena and has no opportunity to purge himself. While many jurisdictions do not prescribe a specific maximum sentence for criminal contempt, the sentences imposed commonly fall in the range of several months to a few years imprisonment.

(b) Subpoena Ad Testificandum. The grand jury is especially useful in obtaining statements from persons who will not voluntarily furnish information to the police. While an individual has the right to refuse to cooperate with the police, his refusal to comply with a subpoena ad testificandum (commanding him to appear and testify before the grand jury) subjects him to a possible jail sentence for contempt. Faced with that threat, a recalcitrant witness often will have a change of heart and will give the grand jury information that he has refused to give to the police. Of course, if the information sought could be incriminating, the witness (unless granted immunity) may still refuse to cooperate by relying on his privilege against self-incrimination. Many persons, however, are unwilling to furnish information to the police, yet will testify before the grand jury without regard to the availability of the privilege. Thus, the victim of a fraudulent gambling operation or a loansharking operation may be either too embarrassed or too fearful to voluntarily furnish information to the police, yet be willing to testify before the grand jury when faced with the threat of contempt. Similarly, an employee may wish to avoid the appearance of voluntarily assisting police investigating his employer, yet testify freely under the compulsion of a subpoena.

The grand jury subpoena ad testificandum also has the advantage of requiring witnesses to give information under oath. If a witness fails to tell the truth, he may be prosecuted for perjury. Ordinarily, a person who gives false information to a police officer will not have committed a crime.[3] Accordingly, where a witness might be willing to talk to the police, but also is likely to "shade his story," requiring him to testify before a grand jury may produce more complete and truthful statements.[4]

(c) Subpoena Duces Tecum. The grand jury subpoena duces tecum offers several advantages over the primary device available to the police for obtaining records and physical evidence—the search pursuant to a warrant.

(maximum of 18 months, although term of special grand jury may be extended to 36 months maximum).

2. Criminal contempt procedures may vary somewhat from the procedures applicable to ordinary criminal prosecutions. The constitutional right to jury trial applies where the criminal contempt sentence exceeds six months imprisonment, see § 22.1(b), but charging and hearing requirements for criminal contempt cases commonly are governed by separate provisions. See e.g., Fed.R.Crim.P. 42(b). The Supreme Court has held that contempt by a grand jury witness does not fall within the Rule 42(a) provision authorizing summary criminal contempt proceedings. Harris v. United States, 382 U.S. 162, 86 S.Ct. 352, 15 L.Ed.2d 240 (1965).

3. State provisions commonly make it criminal to give false information to a police officer only when the individual makes a false report of a crime. However 18 U.S.C.A. § 1001, governing false statements to federal officials, is much broader. See ALI, Model Penal Code and Commentaries §§ 341.3–341.5 (Rev. ed. 1980).

4. Even where a witness is willing to give an entirely truthful statement to the police, there may be value in requiring him to testify before the grand jury. Once a person has testified under oath, he is likely to think twice about changing his testimony at trial and thereby providing the grounds for a perjury prosecution based on inconsistent sworn statements. Also, if the witness does change his testimony at trial, his grand jury testimony may be used to impeach him, and the petit jurors may give greater weight to an inconsistency in sworn statements than they would to an inconsistency with an unsworn statement given to the police. Finally, in some jurisdictions, the grand jury testimony may also be used as substantive evidence under exceptional circumstances.

Unlike the search warrant, the subpoena duces tecum can issue without a showing of probable cause. Moreover, even where probable cause could be established, there are times when the subpoena will have administrative advantages. For example, there may be a need to seize so many records from various locations that a search would be impractical. With a subpoena duces tecum, the party served may be required to undertake the extensive task of bringing together records from several different locations and sorting through them to collect those covered by the subpoena. At other times, there may be a need to obtain records from uninvolved third parties (e.g., a bank) and a subpoena will be preferred because it will be far less disruptive to the third party's operations.

(d) Psychological Pressure. The psychological pressure exerted by the grand jury setting also is cited as a factor that frequently enables the grand jury to obtain information from witnesses unwilling to cooperate with the police. Proponents of grand jury investigations claim that this pressure stems from the moral force exerted by the lay group of jurors. Most witnesses, it is argued, feel a compulsion to be honest and forthright in discharging their duty to testify, because their peers, the grand jurors, are persons with whom they identify. Critics of grand jury investigations claim, however, that the psychological pressure felt by the witness stems from what they describe as the "star chamber setting" of grand jury interrogation. No person stands more alone, they argue, than a witness before a grand jury; "in a secret hearing, he faces an often hostile prosecutor and 23 strangers, with no judge present to guard his rights, no lawyer by his side, and often no indication of why he is being questioned."

(e) Immunity Grants. An immunity grant is a court order granting a witness sufficient immunity from future prosecution to supplant the witness' self-incrimination privilege. Once the recalcitrant witness has been granted immunity, he may no longer rely upon the privilege. Since immunity grants are tied initially to the exercise of the privilege by a person under a legal obligation to testify, they are not available to persons who simply refuse to give a statement to the police. At the investigatory stage, almost the only way the prosecution can make use of an immunity grant is in conjunction with a subpoena directing the uncooperative witness to testify before the grand jury. The immunity grant may be used to gain information from various types of recalcitrant witnesses. For example, immunity quite frequently is given to a lower-level participant in organized crime in order to obtain testimony against higher-level participants. It also often is used to force testimony from witnesses who are not themselves involved in criminal activities, but desire not to give testimony that may hurt others. Although the privilege is not available simply to protect others, witnesses who do not actually fear personal incrimination have been known to falsely claim that they do so in order to avoid testifying against their friends. Since such claims are difficult to dispute, the prosecutor may simply prefer to grant the witness immunity.

(f) Secrecy. Grand jury secrecy requirements are commonly cited as another investigative advantage of the grand jury. Initially, those requirements are said to facilitate keeping the target of the investigation "in the dark" as to the nature of the inquiry. A person may be investigated without even knowing that he is the subject of an investigation or, if he is aware of his "target" status, without knowing which of his activities are being examined or who is providing information on those activities. Keeping these matters from the target may be essential where there is a likelihood that he might flee to avoid possible indictment or might attempt to destroy evidence or tamper with possible grand jury witnesses.

Secondly, grand jury secrecy requirements are said to have the independent value of keeping the investigation from coming to the attention of the public. When the target of a possible investigation occupies a position of prominence, public disclosure of the investigation may cause irreparable harm to his reputation even though the investigation eventually reveals no basis for prosecution. Accordingly, if an investigation were likely to become public, the prosecutor might hesitate to initiate the investigation unless he was fairly certain that it would lead to a prosecution. However, with the grand jury process keeping the investigation secret, the prosecutor may be willing to undertake an investigation on the basis of suspicions that have far less grounding. If the suspicions prove erroneous, the suspect's reputation will not have been harmed; but if the suspicions prove well founded, the prosecution will have the basis for a prosecution that otherwise might never have been brought.

Where grand jury secrecy requirements succeed in keeping targets "in the dark" and in keeping investigations from the public gaze, they clearly do offer a significant investigative advantage for certain types of cases. In practice, however, those objectives are difficult to achieve. The legal requirements as to grand jury secrecy are discussed at length in § 8.5. As noted there, secrecy requirements are far from absolute even during the pendency of an investigation. In most jurisdictions, the grand jurors, prosecutors, and grand jury personnel are sworn to secrecy, but witnesses testifying before the grand jury may disclose what they want to whomever they want. A witness friendly to the target may discuss his appearance with the target, and by recounting the prosecutor's questions, give the target a fairly complete picture of the scope of the investigation. A witness not so friendly to the target may disclose the nature of the investigation, including the specific accusations suggested by the prosecutor's questions, to those who will give that information wide circulation within the community. Thus, for an investigation to be kept secret, all of the witnesses must want to keep it secret and all must avoid confidants who might disclose their secret. Moreover, even if the witnesses desire to keep the investigation secret, other exceptions in coverage may result in a limited degree of disclosure without violation of the secrecy requirements. So too, disclosures in violation of those requirements have been known to occur in cases of high public interest, notwithstanding the threat of contempt, as it is often difficult to identify the source of an illegal disclosure. Critics of the grand jury accordingly argue that secrecy requirements have limited effectiveness, and where effective, may also serve to keep from the public abusive grand jury practices.

(g) Maintaining Public Confidence. Assuming that the investigation will become known to the public sooner or later, grand jury participation often helps in maintaining community confidence in the integrity of the investigatory process, a particularly valuable asset when the person under investigation is a public official. The community tends to be suspicious of partisan influences in such investigations, especially where the investigation results in a decision not to prosecute. The prosecutor may also look to the grand jury to help allay other public concerns, as in cases in which investigated parties are almost certain to claim police and prosecutor harassment. Critics, of course, contend that this public confidence is largely undeserved, for the grand jury is most likely to have merely "rubber stamped" the prosecutor's conclusions.

(h) Grand Jury Reports. Another investigative advantage of the grand jury is its ability to issue reports in those situations in which an investigation reveals transactions that are of questionable propriety, though not criminal.[5] A substantial number of states permit a grand jury to issue a report summarizing the evidence found on non-indictable activities thought to merit public attention. Such reports have been issued on a variety of topics ranging from improper (but not criminal) conflicts of interst to clearly fraudulent business schemes that escaped criminal liability only because of the inadequate coverage of state law. Though obviously of less significance to the prosecutor than those grand jury powers that facilitate development of a suc-

5. Grand jury reports are described as "presentments" in some jurisdictions, although a report does not fit the common law definition of a "presentment." See § 8.2(a).

cessful prosecution, the alternative of issuing a report, if a crime is not found, may be helpful in maintaining the image of the prosecutor's office as an effective "public watchdog."

State courts have divided as to whether the grand jury has a "common law authority" to issue reports in the absence of specific legislative authorization. The courts holding that such authority exists argue that the power to report is inherent in the power to investigate. They also note that the reporting power follows from the grand jury's role as the citizenry's "guardian of all that is comprehended in the police power of the state." Courts rejecting the existence of a common law reporting authority claim that grand jury reports violate the requirements of grand jury secrecy. They also argue that the issuance of a report is inconsistent with the establishment of the grand jury as an arm of the court. A judicial agency, they note, should be concerned only with determining whether a person did or did not violate the law.

Some courts have taken a middle position, accepting certain reports as within the grand jury's common law authority, but not others. Thus, it has been suggested that reports may be issued provided they do not contain derogatory information concerning identifiable individuals. Reports criticizing individuals are viewed as inflicting a "foul blow" since persons named in a report, unlike those charged in an indictment, have no trial at which they may respond. Other courts suggest that reports criticizing individuals are permissible only when those persons are government officials, noting that such reports fall within the tradition of the grand jury keeping the community informed of mismanagement in government.

Rather than rely upon the court's common law authority, a substantial number of jurisdictions have adopted legislation authorizing grand jury reports on specified subjects. Those statutes typically have sought both to limit the scope of reports critical of specific individuals and to provide certain safeguards for those individuals. The New York provision is illustrative. It authorizes reports as to the "misconduct, non-feasance or neglect" of public officials, but requires that: (1) the report be supported by the preponderance of "credible and legally admissible evidence," as determined by the court; (2) the public official be allowed to testify before the grand jury; and (3) the public official be given an opportunity to prepare an answer, which is to be appended to the report.[6]

§ 8.4 The Legal Structure of the Grand Jury

The legal structure of the grand jury plays a large role in shaping the standards that govern grand jury investigations. Many of those standards are based, in particular, on three premises that flow from that structure: (1) that the grand jurors will be representative of the community; (2) that grand jurors will possess sufficient authority to override the prosecutor and exercise control over the direction of an investigation, if they so choose; and (3) that the grand jury will be subject to the supervisory authority of the court. This section will focus upon the various elements of the grand jury structure that provide the grounding for these three premises. Another element of the grand jury structure that has a substantial influence upon investigatory standards—the secrecy requirements for grand jury proceedings—will be treated in the section that follows.[1]

6. N.Y.—McKinney's Crim.P.Law §§ 190.85–90. Congress adopted a reporting provision based substantially on the New York statute in the Organized Crime Control Act of 1972. 18 U.S.C.A. § 3333. As to reports issued by federal grand juries impaneled under Federal Rule 6, the governing standards have been aptly described as "unsettled." While many cases have stated that federal grand juries lack authority to issue reports in the absence of specific legislative authorization, other cases have permitted the issuance of reports under the special circumstances.

§ 8.4

1. See also Chapter 15, discussing elements of the grand jury structure that relate primarily to its screening role, but may also have a bearing upon certain investigatory standards.

(a) Grand Jury Selection and Size. When the grand jury first became a body separate and distinct from the trial jury, there was a tendency to select as grand jurors persons of "a higher social class" than their trial jury counterparts. That tradition was carried over to the United States. For many years, most states utilized selection procedures that were sufficiently flexible to permit the impanelment of what were commonly described as "blue ribbon" grand juries. Especially where the grand jury was to be engaged in a significant investigation, judges or jury commissioners selected juries composed largely of well-educated, middle aged or older, professionals and businessmen—the same people who were most often excused on "hardship grounds" from petit jury service. While blue ribbon grand juries were subject to challenge where the selection process was racially discriminatory,[2] claims based simply upon the failure to draw the grand jury from a cross-section of the community were commonly rejected. Starting in the 1960's, however, as petit jury selection procedures were altered to provide more representative trial juries, and lower court decisions began to suggest that a "fair cross-section" requirement was equally applicable to grand juries, a strong movement developed to apply to grand jury selection the same procedures used in selecting the petit jury.

Today, in all but a few jurisdictions, the grand jury panel is drawn from the same constituency, and selected in the same manner, as the array for the petit jury. In most jurisdictions, prospective grand jurors are selected at random from a standard list (usually a voter registration list) representative of a cross-section of the community. A substantial minority, however, still use a "key-man" or "discretionary" system.[3] While there is less assurance that the persons nominated under such a system will reflect a cross-section of the community, the nominators commonly are directed to make recommendations from all segments of the community. Of course, even where the grand jury panel is selected from a standard list, the grand jurors actually seated still may be less representative than the typical petit jury. Because grand jurors sit for much longer terms, there often is a tendency to be more lenient in excusing persons who claim that jury service will impose a severe hardship. As a result, in many jurisdictions, the grand jury is likely to have a heavier concentration of dependent spouses, retirees, and persons whose employers will continue their compensation during jury service.

Changes in the grand jury selection procedure often have been accompanied by a reduction in its size. At English common law, the grand jury was twice the size of the petit jury (although one member typically was dropped to preclude a tie, thereby reducing the number to twenty-three). Although there were some who argued that the larger size of the grand jury was a product of the jury's special investigative function, which relied in large part upon the jurors' personal knowledge of the community, the common law's use of a 23 person grand jury is more commonly seen as intended primarily to relieve the Crown of the need to gain the support of more than a bare jury majority in acquiring the twelve votes then thought necessary for indictment as well as conviction. Most American jurisdictions have gradually moved toward smaller grand juries while continuing to allow a less than unanimous vote for indictment. Today, with smaller juries, approximately half of the states permit indictment on less than twelve votes.

Many jurisdictions permit a grand jury of variable size with a majority of the maximum size required for indictment. Thus, the federal system requires 16 to 23 grand jurors with 12 votes necessary for indictment. Allowing the grand jury to drop below the maximum size accommodates the likely need to excuse one or more jurors over the long grand jury

2. See § 15.3(b).

3. See § 22.2. The discretionary or "key-man" system may have one or two layers of discretion. In some jurisdictions, the "key-man" will provide a list of nominees and the grand jurors are randomly selected from that list. In others, the jury commissioners or judge also exercise discretion in selecting persons from that list.

term. Other jurisdictions require a grand jury of a set size, but accept as a working quorum two-thirds or three-fourths of the jurors. Many of these jurisdictions, however, also require the same two-thirds or three-fourths to indict. The smaller size of the grand jury arguably may have reduced its capacity to be representative of the community, but any such reduction would appear to be more than offset by the movement to random selection of jurors from a standard list. Moreover, the adoption in many of these jurisdictions of an indictment requirement of more than a majority vote means that this most crucial decision of the grand jury must be accepted by a larger portion of those cross-section representatives.

(b) The Legal Authority of the Prosecutor. It is undisputed that the typical grand jury investigation is dominated by the prosecutor, but courts generally consider that dominance less significant if it is attributable to the grand jury's voluntary deference, rather than to the prosecutor's legal authority over the proceedings. At one time, the prosecution's dominance clearly depended upon its ability to persuade the grand jurors to accept its leadership, as the prosecutor appeared before the grand jury largely at its sufferance. To some extent that situation has changed. In most jurisdictions, the prosecutor has obtained by statute the right to make various presentations before the grand jury. In the end, however, the grand jury still retains the ultimate authority to control the direction of the investigation if it so chooses.

In all but a few jurisdictions, the prosecutor serves as the primary "legal advisor" to the grand jury. In many jurisdictions, the prosecutor is so designated by statute, while others simply view the prosecutor's role of legal advisor as inherent in the grand jury structure. In most jurisdictions the prosecutor has a right to go before the grand jury and advise it on the law even over the jurors' opposition, though a few jurisdictions apparently permit the jurors to refuse to hear the prosecutor if they so choose. Even if they cannot bar the prosecutor, grand jurors dissatisfied with the prosecutor's advice have other options. The grand jury may seek further advice from the judge, and grand jurors commonly are informed of this right either through the judge's charge or the juror's handbook. Moreover, the legal advice of prosecutor or judge is binding only in the sense that it defines the limits of the grand jury's power. The grand jury remains free to exercise its discretion and not utilize its full power, and often is informed specifically of that authority as well.

Jurisdictions vary as to the prosecutor's authority to subpoena witnesses to appear before the grand jury. In some, the prosecutor's subpoena authority is derived from the grand jury, and that body can, if it so chooses, negate a subpoena issued on its behalf by the prosecutor. In most jurisdictions, however, the prosecutor has an independent right to subpoena witnesses, and the grand jury apparently has a corresponding duty to hear those witnesses. The grand jury is not limited, however, to the witnesses subpoenaed by the prosecutor. It may insist that additional witnesses be called. This authority, moreover, is not limited to the subject under investigation. In all but a few jurisdictions, the grand jury may utilize its subpoena authority to undertake entirely new investigations. In this connection, jurisdictions commonly recognize a right of a private citizen to petition the grand jury (usually by letter or a request to testify) to undertake investigation of any matter within its jurisdiction. Indeed, *Wood v. Georgia* suggests that citizens may have a First Amendment right to send to the grand jury communications requesting investigation of specific complaints.[4]

4. 370 U.S. 375, 82 S.Ct. 1364, 8 L.Ed.2d 569 (1962) (holding unconstitutional a contempt order against a sheriff who had issued a public statement critical of a recently initiated grand jury investigation). However, statutes making it a crime to influence a grand juror or petit juror "upon an issue or matter pending before such juror" (e.g., 18 U.S.C.A. § 1504) have been viewed as restricting such a right, at least where the communication is not approved by the prosecuting attorney or the supervising court. Also, where the grand jury is limited by state law to considering sworn testimony, such a communication cannot be considered in the decision to indict.

Once a subpoenaed witness appears before the grand jury, all but a few jurisdictions allow the prosecutor to be present and examine the witness. In several states the prosecutor may do so only at the pleasure of the grand jury, but most jurisdictions give the prosecutor a right to be present and examine even where the witness was subpoenaed over the prosecutor's objection. The jurors in all jurisdictions have a right to ask their own questions, although the prosecutor may request that he be allowed to screen the questions to ensure that they are proper as to form and content. If the prosecutor and grand juror disagree on the propriety of a question, the foreman may resolve the issue or the grand juror may take the dispute to the judge.

The grand jury's authority to subpoena additional witnesses and pursue its own questions is supplemented in various jurisdictions by the grand jury's authority to obtain the appointment of special investigators, usually with the permission of the court. The grand jury may also take the more drastic step of requesting appointment of a special prosecutor. Although such appointments are rarely made, most states have statutory provisions authorizing appointment of a special prosecutor when the grand jury investigation relates to the operation of the prosecutor's office, and several states have provisions permitting the appointment for any investigation upon a showing that the prosecutor has not furnished the grand jury with sufficient legal or investigative assistance. Moreover, courts have indicated that they have inherent authority to make such appointments when necessary to preserve "the integrity of the grand jury function."

(c) Judicial Supervision. Although opinions occasionally describe the grand jury as an "independent body" that draws its authority from the "people themselves," it is more frequently characterized as "an arm of the court by which it is appointed." As the Supreme Court noted in *Brown v. United States*: "A grand jury is clothed with great independence in many areas, but it remains an appendage of the court, powerless to perform its investigative function without the court's aid, because powerless itself to compel the testimony of witnesses." [5] At one time, the grand jury's reliance upon the authority of the court was thought to give the court supervisory power over all aspects of grand jury operations except the decision to indict. Over the years, however, judicial control over certain structural elements of the grand jury has come to be limited by statute or judicial decision. For example, while the decision to impanel an investigatory grand jury traditionally rested within the discretion of the court, many jurisdictions now require automatic impanelment upon request of the prosecutor. Similarly, while it was formerly said that a court could discharge a grand jury "at any time, for any reason or no reason," many jurisdictions now permit an early discharge only where justified by "cause." Notwithstanding these restrictions, the court retains considerable supervisory authority over the grand jury's operations.

Initially, the court in its jury charge can stress the grand jury's independence, remind the jurors that prosecutors are "advocates," and caution them against imposing undue burdens on witnesses. The court may direct the jurors to investigate a particular matter, although it may not limit their investigation to that matter. Where necessary to prevent a "miscarriage of justice," the court may insist that the grand jury consider certain evidence before it decides to indict. If it finds that a prosecutor has exercised "undue influence" over the grand jury's decision to indict, through, for example, inflammatory speeches, the intimidation of witnesses, or refusing to leave while the jury votes, the court may quash the indictment. Similarly, and of special significance to the investigative grand jury, the court may quash a subpoena where the prosecution or grand jury is misusing its subpoena authority. Of course, the supervisory judge (usually the judge who impaneled the grand jury) is not present during grand jury proceedings, and therefore ordinarily is

5. 359 U.S. 41, 79 S.Ct. 539, 3 L.Ed.2d 609 (1959).

in a position to respond to abuses only when they are called to the judge's attention. That most often occurs through the motion of an indicted defendant, subpoenaed witness, or target of an investigation,[6] although, in the rare cases, the grand jurors themselves may seek judicial intervention.

Courts vary in their approach to the use of their supervisory power. Some have used that power to impose prophylactic requirements designed to prevent the mere possibility of abuse. They view grand jury procedures as reflecting upon the integrity of the judicial process and are as willing to prescribe preferred procedures in this area as they are, for example, in the area of pretrial discovery. Other courts stress the independence of the grand jurors and the prerogatives of the prosecutor that come with the responsibility of the executive branch for investigation and prosecution. They adhere to a standard of limited intervention, as suggested in the following, widely-quoted formulation: "[T]here should be no curtailment of the inquisitorial power of the grand jury except in the clearest case of abuse, and mere inconvenience not amounting to harassment does not justify judicial interference with the functions of the grand jury." Among the federal courts, this position still reflects the majority view, but there has been a growing trend to make more liberal use of the supervisory power. This movement appears to reflect, in large part, the skepticism of many courts as to whether the presence of the grand jurors does in fact restrain overzealous prosecutors in their use of grand jury powers. However, the Supreme Court has not been receptive to the use of supervisory power as either a prophylactic tool or a means of mandating prosecutorial practices not statutorily or constitutionally required, particularly where the remedy imposed is the dismissal of an indictment.[7]

§ 8.5 Grand Jury Secrecy

(a) Underlying Considerations. Following the development of grand jury independence noted in § 8.2(a), particularly in the *Colledge* and *Shaftesbury* cases,[1] the secrecy of grand jury proceedings came to be recognized as an essential element of the grand jury process. However, grand jury secrecy requirements, at least to the evidence received by the grand jury,[2] were never absolute. Grand jurors were always allowed, for example, to disclose the testimony of a witness for the purpose of charging that witness with having perjured himself before the grand jury. The courts recognized at a very early point that grand jury secrecy was not an end in itself. It was to be imposed only insofar as it might contribute to the grand jury's effectiveness in performing its investigative and screening functions.

Courts today see grand jury secrecy as contributing in several ways to the grand jury's dual roles. Thus, in *United States v. Procter & Gamble Co.,* the Supreme Court listed five different objectives of secrecy requirements:

> (1) to prevent the escape of those whose indictment may be contemplated; (2) to insure the utmost freedom to the grand jury in its deliberations, and to prevent persons subject to indictment or their friends from importuning the grand jurors; (3) to prevent subornation of perjury or tampering with the witnesses who may testify before [the] grand jury and later appear at the trial of those indicted by it; (4) to encourage free and untrammeled disclosures by persons who have information with respect to the commission of crimes; (5) to

6. The target of the investigation has standing to object only to abuses that affect his rights as opposed to the rights of the subpoenaed witness. Thus, target objections may be directed at such abuses as secrecy violations injurious to the target's reputation, or misuse of process to obtain discovery in a criminal case already brought against the target, see United States v. Doe (Ellsberg), 455 F.2d 1270 (1st Cir.1972), but not to an oppressive subpoena directed at a third party witness.

7. See Bank of Nova Scotia v. United States, discussed in § 15.6 following note 4; Costello v. United States, discussed in § 15.4 following note 1. See also note 3 of § 1.5.

§ 8.5

1. See § 8.2(a).

2. Disclosure of grand juror voting and deliberations is treated in much the same manner as disclosure of petit juror voting and deliberations, discussed in § 24.9(g). The discussion in this section will be limited to disclosure of grand jury matter other than deliberations and voting.

protect the innocent accused who is exonerated from disclosure of the fact that he has been under investigation, and from the expense of standing trial where there was no probability of guilt.[3]

Notwithstanding the breadth of this statement of objectives, courts and legislatures have clearly been moving in the direction of relaxing the rigid rules of secrecy. This development may be attributed to several factors. The widespread availability of transcripts of grand jury proceedings permits disclosure without imposing a substantial burden on the grand jurors. Formerly, when a court ordered disclosure, grand jurors had to appear in court and testify (often from skimpy minutes) as to what the witness had said in his testimony. A substantial majority of jurisdictions now require recordation of grand jury proceedings, and in those jurisdictions in which recordation remains discretionary, it commonly is utilized at least for the investigative grand juries.

Perhaps even more influential was the widespread criticism of blanket secrecy standards, which led courts to adopt a more finely tuned approach in determining the need for secrecy. Distinctions have been drawn, for example, between disclosures relating to investigations in which indictments have been returned and the jury discharged and disclosures in other settings where pending or future investigations might be directly affected. Similarly, consideration has been given to such factors as the breadth of the disclosure requested and the extent to which the underlying information has already been made public. Finally, courts and legislatures very often have struck a new balance in weighing the justifications for grand jury secrecy against the various interests served by disclosure. They have given greater weight, in particular, to the criminal defendant's interest in having available all information that will be helpful in challenging the prosecution's case.

While secrecy requirements have become less absolute, violations of those requirements continue to be viewed as a serious matter. Persons who are sworn to secrecy and violate that obligation are subject to contempt. Many jurisdictions have statutory provisions making the unauthorized disclosure of grand jury material a crime. Courts may issue equitable relief where necessary to preclude further secrecy violations. Some courts also have indicated that an exclusionary remedy will be employed to preclude civil litigants who have obtained grand jury matter without authorization from using that matter as evidence at trial. Where the violations are the responsibility of the prosecutor and involve misconduct, internal discipline may be imposed (as provided for in the Department of Justice through its Office of Professional Responsibility).

(b) Statutory Structure. Although originally developed in common law rulings, grand jury secrecy requirements today are imposed in almost all jurisdictions by statute or court rule. Secrecy provisions typically state that the grand jurors and specified persons appearing before the grand jury (usually prosecuting attorneys, clerks, and stenographers) are bound by oath not to disclose any matter occurring before the grand jury except upon court order or other stated exception. It is disclosure by these specified persons only that is subject to punishment as contempt or as a special criminal offense. States vary in their description of the exceptions under which these persons may lawfully make disclosure. Some, like Federal Rule 6(e), list several specific exceptions; others simply note that disclosure may be made by such persons in "the lawful discharge of [their] duties or upon written order of the court." Under either type of provision, the exceptions ordinarily encompass five situations: (1) disclosure by a wit-

3. United States v. Procter & Gamble Co., 356 U.S. 677, 78 S.Ct. 983, 2 L.Ed.2d 1077 (1958) quoting United States v. Rose, 215 F.2d 617 (3d Cir.1954). Still another value of a prosecutorial secrecy obligation is that it removes any prosecutorial incentive to utilize the grand jury's investigatory power for the purpose of developing information that would be useful to favored litigants (including the government itself) in civil or administrative proceedings, but which might not be available to those litigants under the discovery limits applicable to such proceedings. See subsections (g) and (h) infra and § 8.8(c).

ness of his own testimony; (2) disclosure by a prosecutor attending the grand jury to other prosecution personnel; (3) disclosure upon court order in connection with a challenge to grand jury proceedings; (4) disclosure to a defendant as a matter of discovery; (5) disclosure to third parties for use in other proceedings.[4]

Questions concerning the scope of secrecy requirements arise in a variety of procedural contexts. In some, the court is asked to rule on the validity of an already completed disclosure. The court's initial task here is to determine how the disclosure was made. That may prove a difficult, if not impossible, task where the primary evidence of the disclosure is the publication of grand jury matter by the media. While reporters responsible for such publications can be required in most jurisdictions to reveal their sources (including some jurisdictions that otherwise recognize a "newsperson's privilege"),[5] they often will refuse to do so, notwithstanding contempt sanctions. A court also may find it unnecessary to reach the issue as to whether a particular disclosure was illegal because, even if was illegal, the requested relief would be inappropriate. This is likely to be the case where a defendant seeks dismissal of an indictment, or a target seeks termination of a grand jury investigation, based on alleged violations of secrecy requirements. Such requests for what constitute, in effect, prophylactic remedies are almost always disfavored, and in some jurisdictions, such remedies simply are not allowed.[6]

Questions concerning the scope of secrecy requirements tend to be more cleanly put to the court where the challenge is brought before any disclosure is made. Such a procedural setting is presented when a party desiring disclosure petitions for release of grand jury matter, as where a defendant seeks disclosure in the course of challenging an indictment or a third party seeks disclosure in connection with another judicial proceeding. It also is presented where the prosecution requests a court order allowing it to make disclosure to another governmental entity or where the prosecution objects to a defense discovery demand on the ground that grand jury secrecy requirements bar discovery.

(c) Disclosure by a Witness. Approximately a dozen jurisdictions clearly impose an obligation of secrecy on a witness, barring his disclosure of his testimony to any person other than his counsel during the life of the grand jury.[7] The majority of jurisdictions, however, do not include the witness in the list of persons sworn to secrecy; they leave the witness free to disclose either publicly or privately both his own testimony and whatever information was revealed to him by the grand jurors or prosecutor in the process of examination. Although this exception has been criticized as creating a gigantic loophole in grand jury secrecy, it has been justified on grounds of practical necessity and the need to prevent grand jury abuses. Imposition of a

4. Secrecy requirements also may be so framed as to permit a certain degree of disclosure apart from these exceptions. For example, in many jurisdictions, judicial hearings relating to grand jury proceedings may be held in public and thereby reveal to interested spectators the subject of an ongoing investigation. But see Fed. R.Crim.P. 6(e)(5) (hearings to be closed, to the extent necessary to prevent disclosure of grand jury matters, subject to "any right to an open hearing in contempt proceedings"). In some jurisdictions, the element of the grand jury proceeding subject to secrecy obligations is so narrowly defined (e.g., limited to the "content of the grand jury proceeding") that an assistant prosecutor or court clerk would not be prohibited from disclosing to reporters the fact that a particular person has been subpoenaed to testify before the grand jury. Also, secrecy requirements, even where extensive in scope and narrow in exceptions, do not preclude the enterprising reporter or possible target from piecing together what can be learned without speaking to any persons subject to a secrecy obligation. Thus, targets and newspapers have been known to utilize a "grand jury watch"—posting employees in corridors where they can observe all persons (including possible witnesses) who enter offices leading to the grand jury's chambers.

5. See Branzburg v. Hayes, discussed in § 8.8 at note 9.

6. See Bank of Nova Scotia v. United States, discussed in § 15.6(d).

7. Those statutes by their terms tend to go beyond the life of the grand jury, but the Supreme Court held in Butterworth v. Smith, 494 U.S. 624, 110 S.Ct. 1376, 108 L.Ed.2d 572 (1990), that a law "prohibiting a grand jury witness from disclosing [the 'content, gist, or import' of] his own testimony after the term of the grand jury has ended * * * violates the First Amendment."

witness secrecy requirement has been characterized as "impractical and unreal—a partner, an employee, a relative, a friend called on to testify will come back and tell the person concerning whom he testified, and it should be so." The key to encouraging "free and untrammeled disclosures" by witnesses, it is argued, is to afford secrecy to the witness who wants that protection,[8] not to require secrecy from those who feel duty bound to disclose. Some commentators add that the ability of a witness to "go public" stands as a deterrent against grand jury harassment of witnesses. If the witness-exception were based on this ground, it might make sense to give the witness a transcript of his testimony so the public would have an accurate record of exactly what had occurred before the grand jury. The federal courts have held, however, that the witness has no right to a transcript of his testimony,[9] though transcript requests have been granted by a few district courts in the exercise of their supervisory power.

(d) Disclosure to Prosecution Personnel. Since no more than one or two prosecutors will ordinarily be present before the grand jury, provision must be made, as a matter of practical necessity, for disclosure by those attorneys to other members of the prosecution's team. Most secrecy provisions include a specific exception automatically authorizing such disclosures without court approval. The scope of those exceptions varies considerably, however. Some provisions apparently permit disclosure to any law enforcement personnel provided disclosure is made by the prosecutor "solely in the performance of his duties." Other provisions authorize automatic disclosure only to a "prosecuting attorney" for use in the performance of his duties.

Federal Rule 6(e) contains what is undoubtedly the most elaborate provision on disclosure to personnel not in attendance. It's basic thrust, however, is fairly simple. Disclosures may be made to limited personnel—other federal prosecutors and agents from various agencies (e.g., I.R.S.) assisting in the grand jury investigation—for the purpose of carrying out the duties of the prosecutor in enforcing the federal criminal law.[10] More-

8. Many witnesses, it is argued, will hesitate to testify freely if they know that their testimony will be disclosed to the target of the investigation. The prohibition against disclosure by the prosecution or jurors is seen as affording substantial protection for the witness desiring secrecy, although there remains the possibility that revelations from other witnesses may lead the target to that witness. If no indictment is issued, the witness' protection remains fairly firm, although court-ordered disclosure is possible, as noted in subsections (g) and (h) infra. The likelihood of disclosure increases substantially, however, if an indictment is issued. Disclosure may be available through a broad defense discovery provision or a broad construction of provisions allowing court-ordered disclosure in connection with a challenge to the indictment. See subsections (e) and (f) infra. Even in a jurisdiction that sharply limits those avenues for disclosure (as in the federal system), the witness' grand jury testimony will be disclosed if the witness should testify at trial, as it will then be made available to the defense for impeachment purposes. See subsection (f) infra. However, not all grand jury witnesses will necessarily be called to testify at trial; some grand jury witnesses are subpoenaed simply to obtain leads to more crucial evidence. Moreover, if the witness can be assured that his identity will be revealed only if an indictment is issued, he may have less concern about cooperating. He may be less wary of criticism of his role as an "informer" if he knows that his role will be revealed only after a grand jury has supported his judgment and veracity by issuing an indictment.

9. Some courts have expressed concern that an automatic right to a transcript may lead to intimidation of witnesses. See e.g., In re Alvarez, 351 F.Supp. 1089 (S.D.Cal.1972) (involving a narcotics investigation in which the witnesses were couriers, and noting that a cooperative witness might want to tell his associates that he gave no useful testimony, but that claim could be refuted if a transcript were available).

10. Rule 6(e) initially provides that "matters occurring before the grand jury" may be disclosed to "an attorney for the government for use in the performance of such attorney's duty." Under Rule 54(c), the phrase "attorney for government" includes basically the entire legal staffs of the United States Attorneys and Department of Justice. However, United States v. Sells Engineering, infra note 17, held that the Rule 6(e) reference to such attorney's "duty" referred solely to the performance of "prosecutorial duties." The policy of Rule 6(e), as read by *Sells,* is to allow disclosure without judicial supervision only to attorneys who are members of the "prosecution team" and thereby carrying forward the responsibilities of the grand jury. Whether this encompasses prosecuting attorneys engaged in other investigations is unclear, but another provision in Rule 6(e) allows for the transfer of information to assist other investigations by authorizing disclosures to "another grand jury."

Rule 6(e) also authorizes disclosure to "such government personnel as are deemed necessary by the attorney for the government to assist * * * in the performance of such attorney's duty to enforce federal criminal law," subject to adds a specific prohibition against such personnel utilizing grand jury material "for any purpose other than * * * enforcing federal criminal law." The Rule

over, such disclosures may be made automatically without court approval. However, to make disclosures to Justice Department attorneys engaged in civil practice, or to other federal agencies (including those employing the agents assisting the grand jury), the remaining provisions of Rule 6(e), requiring court approval, must be utilized. As for disclosure to state prosecutors, that requires court authorization, but such authorization will be granted simply upon "a showing that * * * [the grand jury matter] may disclose a violation of state law."

(e) **Disclosure Pursuant to a Challenge to Grand Jury Proceedings.** Most jurisdictions have provisions, like Federal Rule 6(e), authorizing court ordered disclosure in connection with "a motion to dismiss an indictment because of matters occurring before the grand jury." However, court ordered disclosure may also be granted in connection with other challenges to a grand jury proceeding, such as a target's request that court action be taken to stop leaks to the press. Ordinarily, disclosure will not be granted in connection with a challenge to the grand jury proceedings unless the party presenting the challenge makes some showing that there is a valid basis for the challenge. In the federal courts, the requisite showing must be substantial. On a challenge to an indictment, that showing often requires either the affidavit of a witness who was present when the alleged misconduct before the grand jury occurred or a strong suggestion of impropriety in that portion of the transcript released to the defendant for some other purpose (e.g., for pretrial discovery). This requirement of a substantial initial showing stems, in part, from the very limited grounds available for challenging indictments in the federal courts and the concern that challenges may be made for the purposes of delay and discovery. For the same reasons, most state courts apply an equally if not more restrictive standard. On the other hand, in those states which permit challenges to the sufficiency of the evidence before the grand jury, the indicted defendant commonly has a right to a complete transcript to permit him to present such a challenge.[11]

(f) **Disclosure to Defendant Pursuant to Discovery Rules.** Approximately a dozen states grant defendant a complete transcript of the grand jury proceedings that produced his indictment. In many others, the testimony of most (if not all) grand jury witnesses will be disclosed to the defendant as part of his right to pretrial discovery of all recorded statements of persons the prosecution intends to call as witnesses at trial. In the remaining jurisdictions (including the federal courts), the defendant also may obtain the recorded testimony of grand jury witnesses who testify at trial, but must wait until the trial, when that testimony is made available for impeachment use. In most of these jurisdictions, disclosure is automatic upon a showing that the trial witness testified before the grand jury (although the prosecutor may insist that the trial court, upon an in camera inspection, delete any portion of the grand jury testimony not related to the subject of the witness' current testimony). Some jurisdictions, however, require a special showing of need to obtain disclosure even at trial.

In large part, the current discovery standards noted above treat grand jury testimony in the same fashion as other prior recorded statements (e.g., those made to the police).[12] This stands in sharp contrast to the earlier discovery provisions which treated grand jury testimony separately and provided for far narrower disclosure of such testimony. Two de-

requires further that prosecutor list such personnel with the court and certify that they have been informed of this "obligation of secrecy." Since the prohibition as to prosecuting attorneys runs to further "disclosure," rather than "utilization," for purposes other than assisting the grand jury, a prosecuting attorney was held not to have violated Rule 6(e) when he reviewed grand jury materials in the privacy of his office for the purpose of preparing a civil suit, but did not disclose such matter in the subsequent civil complaint or in his conversations with associates on the civil action. United States v. John Doe, Inc. I, infra note 18.

11. See § 15.4(c).

12. See § 20.3(g). Consider, e.g., 18 U.S.C.A. § 3500(e) (including grand jury testimony within the Jencks Act provisions governing disclosure of prior recorded statements in general).

velopments explain the virtual elimination of the impact of grand jury secrecy upon pretrial and trial disclosure to the defense. First, courts have come to view the "traditional reasons for grand jury secrecy" as "largely inapplicable" to post-indictment disclosure of a trial witness' grand jury testimony, particularly where disclosure is delayed until the witness testifies at trial. Second, the interest of the defendant and the judicial system in ensuring that "a criminal conviction not be based on the testimony of untruthful or inaccurate witnesses" is generally recognized as having substantially higher priority than the interests supporting grand jury secrecy.[13]

(g) Disclosure to Private Civil Litigants. Courts and legislatures tend to view secrecy exceptions serving private civil litigants as requiring substantially greater justification than exceptions facilitating criminal prosecutions or a defendant's preparation of his case. Private civil litigants requesting disclosure of grand jury matter include both parties suing the target of a grand jury investigation and the target itself. Such requests are most likely to be presented where the activities investigated by the grand jury relate directly to a civil cause of action (as in an antitrust investigation) and the investigation was resolved without indictment or by a guilty or nolo contendere plea (and therefore there was no trial resulting in the disclosure of much of the evidence presented before the grand jury). The requests usually will relate to testimony before the grand jury, documents prepared especially for the grand jury, or documents that cannot otherwise be identified. Where a civil litigant is aware of preexisting documents that may have been presented to the grand jury, those documents ordinarily can be subpoenaed directly from the source without requiring disclosure of proceedings before the grand jury.

In jurisdictions with provisions similar to Federal Rule 6(e), requests for disclosure by private civil litigants are governed by the provision authorizing court ordered disclosure "preliminary to or in connection with a judicial proceeding." In jurisdictions with less detailed provisions, such requests will be reviewed under general provisions simply authorizing disclosures "upon written order of the court." Under either type of provision, the applicable guidelines tend to be those set forth by the Supreme Court in *Douglas Oil Co. of California v. Petrol Stops Northwest:*[14]

> Parties seeking grand jury transcripts under Rule 6(e) must show that the material they seek is needed to avoid a possible injustice in another judicial proceeding, that the need for disclosure is greater than the need for continued secrecy, and that their request is structured to cover only material so needed. Such a showing must be made even when the grand jury whose transcripts are sought has concluded its operations as it had in *Dennis [v. United States].*[15] * * * It is clear from *Procter & Gamble*[16] and *Dennis* that disclosure is appropriate only in those cases where the need for it outweighs the public interest in secrecy, and that the burden of demonstrating this balance rests upon the private party seeking disclosure. It is equally clear that as the considerations justifying secrecy become less relevant, a party asserting a need for grand jury transcripts will have a lesser burden in showing justification. * * * In sum, as so often is the situation in our jurisprudence, the court's duty in a case of this kind is to weigh carefully the competing interests in light of the rele-

13. See Dennis v. United States, 384 U.S. 855, 86 S.Ct. 1840, 16 L.Ed.2d 973 (1966) (speaking to the disclosure to the defendant of the grand jury testimony of trial witnesses): "In our adversary system for determining guilt or innocence, it is rarely justifiable for the prosecution to have exclusive access to a storehouse of relevant fact. Exceptions to this are justifiable only by the clearest and most compelling considerations."

14. 441 U.S. 211, 99 S.Ct. 1667, 60 L.Ed.2d 156 (1979).

15. See note 13 supra. *Dennis* involved a defendant's request at trial for disclosure of grand jury testimony of four key witnesses for the prosecution.

16. See note 3 supra. *Procter & Gamble* involved a civil antitrust suit brought by the government following a grand jury investigation that had terminated without issuance of an indictment. The defendants in the civil suit, who were the same parties investigated by the grand jury, sought disclosure of the grand jury transcript, arguing that the government had used the transcript in preparing its case. The Court reversed the district court order granting disclosure because defendants had not shown "with particularity" that "without the transcript a defense would be greatly prejudiced."

vant circumstances and the standards announced by this Court.

Supreme Court and lower federal court decisions point to a variety of factors that are weighed in the balancing process prescribed by *Douglas Oil.* As to most, little more can be said than that they are factors to be considered though not conclusive in themselves. The nature of the balancing test and what *Douglas Oil* described as the "substantial discretion" vested in the lower courts makes a certain degree of inconsistency in court rulings almost inevitable. Still, it also is apparent that the various lower courts are giving quite different weights to the same elements in substantially similar factual settings.

Initially, the court will look to the status of the investigation that produced the requested grand jury material. The need for secrecy clearly is greatest while the jury is still gathering evidence and considering whether to indict. As a result, third party disclosure during the pendency of an investigation will rarely, if ever, be granted. On the other hand, once the grand jury is finished with the matter, the need for secrecy declines and the petitioner's burden in establishing a particularized need declines. As the Supreme Court noted in *Douglas Oil,* however, the value of grand jury secrecy is only "reduced," not "eliminated," by the termination of the investigation. The courts must consider "not only the immediate effects [of disclosure] upon a particular grand jury, but also the possible effect upon * * * future grand juries; [p]ersons called upon to testify will consider the likelihood that their testimony may one day be disclosed to outside parties."

Another factor weighed in determining the need for secrecy is whether the third party seeks disclosure that might subject grand jury witnesses to "retribution or social stigma." One of the considerations that weighed against disclosure in *Procter & Gamble* was that witnesses in an antitrust investigation often are employees of the target companies, or their customers, competitors or suppliers, and might face discharge or other forms of retaliation if their testimony were disclosed to those companies. On the other hand, if there already has been substantial disclosure of the grand jury materials to the investigated companies, disclosure to other parties in a related civil suit is less likely to cause concern.

As stressed in *Douglas Oil,* the party seeking disclosure must establish a "particularized need." Under this standard, a request for broad disclosure is likely to work against the petitioner, as it did in *Procter & Gamble* where the Court characterized the rejected request as seeking "*wholesale* discovery." As the Supreme Court noted in *Douglas Oil,* the "typical showing of particularized need arises when a litigant seeks to use the grand jury transcript at the trial to impeach a witness, to refresh his recollection, to test his credibility and the like." The disclosure there "can be limited to those portions of a particular witness' testimony that bear upon his * * * direct testimony at trial." Moreover, such requests are less likely to be based on a speculative judgment as to need, while the use involved serves the important interest of ensuring that the factfinder is not misled. In assessing the petitioner's showing of need, even as to a fairly limited disclosure, the court also may take into consideration alternative means (such as civil discovery) that might produce the same information. The fact that disclosure will avoid the significant expense and delay of alternative measures is not in itself sufficient to establish the requisite need.

(h) Disclosure to Governmental Units. In the course of a grand jury investigation, prosecutors may uncover information that would be helpful to other government attorneys in preparing a civil suit against the target or to administrative agencies charged with regulating the activities of the target. Disclosure to such governmental units, whether they are of the same jurisdiction as the prosecutor or of a different jurisdiction, generally is controlled by the same provisions applicable to disclosures to private civil litigants. However, the standards imposed for court-ordered disclosure to governmental units tends to be more lenient than those applied to private civil litigants.

In *United States v. Sells Engineering,*[17] involving a disclosure by federal prosecutors to attorneys in the Justice Department's Civil Division, the Court rejected the contention that such intra-governmental disclosures should be allowed without regard to the standards set forth in *Douglas Oil.* It also noted, however, that the required balancing process, as set forth in *Douglas Oil,* might be applied somewhat differently for disclosures to governmental units. The Court characterized as "overstated," but nonetheless having "some validity," the government's contention that "disclosure of grand jury materials to government attorneys typically implicates few, if any, of the concerns that underlie the policy of grand jury secrecy." Prosecutors ordinarily will initiate such disclosures only after the "criminal aspect of the matter is closed." Where, as here, such disclosure was to be made to another unit of the Justice Department, a district court "might reasonably consider" that the disclosure "poses less risk of further leakage or improper use than would disclosure to private parties or the general public." However, even though these factors weighed in favor of disclosure, they did not justify dispensing with the prerequisite of a showing of particularized need, as specified in *Douglas Oil.*

The *Sells Engineering* Court also noted that, "under the particularized-need standard, the district court may weigh the public interest, if any, served by the disclosure to a government body," and "take into account any alternative discovery tools available by statute or regulation to the agency seeking disclosure." *United States v. John Doe, Inc. I,*[18] spoke further to how such factors should be evaluated. Where, as in that case, the disclosure was to help other government attorneys determine whether a contemplated civil suit should be brought, the district court could properly take into account the likelihood that the disclosure would "sav[e] the Government, the potential defendants, and witnesses, the pains of costly and time consuming depositions and interrogatories which might later have turned out to be wasted if the Government decided not to file a civil action after all." Accordingly too, while the governmental agency's capacity to obtain the same information through its own investigative authority is a consideration weighing against the need for disclosure, that factor could not be treated as a per se bar against authorizing disclosure. Indeed, that authority may strengthen the case for disclosure with respect to another concern noted by the Court—that the use of grand jury materials by other government agencies not "threaten to subvert the limitations applied outside the grand jury context on the Government's powers of discovery and investigation."

A special difficulty presented by governmental agency requests stems from the requirement under Federal Rule 6(e) that disclosure be "preliminary to or in connection with a judicial proceeding." As the Supreme Court noted in *United States v. Baggot,*[19] this requirement "reflects a judgment that not every beneficial purpose, or even every valid government purpose, is an appropriate reason for breaching grand jury secrecy." The Rule "contemplates only uses related fairly directly to some identifiable litigation, pending or anticipated," as measured by the "primary purpose of the disclosure." *Baggot* held that disclosure for use in an IRS audit of civil tax liability did not fall within the Rule since the agency's determination of tax liability and its collection of any amount determined to be due did not require judicial intervention. The mere possibility that the taxpayer might challenge the agency's non-judicial means of enforcing its determination would not make the agency proceeding "preliminary to a judicial proceeding." On the other side, where the administrative proceeding requires a judicial determination for enforcement (as in attorney disbarment), disclosure to assist the agency in the proceeding ordinarily would be within the Rule. Even here, however, the agency investigation may be at such a preliminary stage, far removed from a substantial

17. 463 U.S. 418, 103 S.Ct. 3133, 77 L.Ed.2d 743 (1983).

18. 481 U.S. 102, 107 S.Ct. 1656, 95 L.Ed.2d 94 (1987).

19. 463 U.S. 476, 103 S.Ct. 3164, 77 L.Ed.2d 785 (1983).

likelihood of a finding that would require judicial enforcement, that disclosure could not yet be viewed as preliminary to a judicial proceeding.

§ 8.6 The Right to Every Man's Evidence

The grand jury's investigative authority is commonly said to rest largely on "the long standing principle that 'the public has a right to every man's evidence.'"[1] Indeed, no aspect of grand jury power is more frequently extolled by the courts, particularly in cases rejecting challenges to subpoenas, than its right to compel the testimony of any person, subject only to "constitutional, common law or statutory privilege." The Supreme Court has described the grand jury's authority to compel testimony as "[a]mong the necessary and most important of the powers * * * [that] assure the effective functioning of government in an ordered society." While the Court has never stated precisely why it views this authority as so essential to the "welfare of society," it presumably shares the belief of many others that effective law enforcement requires the cooperation of the public, and that there are many instances in which such cooperation would not be forthcoming if it could not be compelled.

The modern tradition has been to relieve citizens of any legal responsibility to assist the police or prosecutor in the investigation of crime. Misprision is no longer a crime in most jurisdictions, and the individual has no obligation (even when there is absolutely no possibility of personal incrimination) to respond to police inquiries. At the same time, increased urbanization may have produced a setting in which fewer people feel a responsibility to the community and hence a responsibility to assist law enforcement officials. The grand jury's authority to compel testimony therefore takes on added importance. That authority is accepted, the Court has noted, not simply because it is "historically grounded," but because the "obligation of every person to appear and give testimony" is "indispensible to the administration of justice." Without it, criminal activity could be hidden behind a "wall of silence" that finds no justification in legal privilege, but is based simply on an individual's desire not to get "involved," fear of retaliation, dislike for the substantive law, or private code against "snitching."

Assuming that the authority to compel cooperation must of necessity be lodged somewhere, the courts find wisdom in the traditional delegation of that authority to the grand jury—an independent body, composed of laymen and having a membership that shifts from one term to the next. The structure of the grand jury provides assurance that investigations will be carried out free from political pressures. The capacity of a grand jury to take an investigation wherever it may lead serves to counteract suspicions of corruption and partisanship in criminal law enforcement. The grand jury therefore has the capacity not only to ferret out hidden crimes, but to relieve public concern generated by false rumors. The courts stress, however, that to serve these purposes, the grand jury must be free to carry forward wide ranging investigations.

Two points in particular have been stressed with respect to the necessary breadth of grand jury investigations. First, the grand jury must be "free from any restraint comparable to * * * [a] specific charge and showing of probable cause." It must be able to investigate "merely on suspicion that the law is being violated, or even just because it wants assurance that it is not." The jurors must be able to "act on tips, rumors, evidence offered by the prosecutor, or their own personal knowledge." They must have the capacity to "run down every available clue" and to exam-

§ 8.6

1. Branzburg v. Hayes, 408 U.S. 665, 92 S.Ct. 2646, 33 L.Ed.2d 626 (1972). Other major discussions of this principle including many of the statements quoted in the paragraphs that follow, can be found in Blair v. United States, 250 U.S. 273, 39 S.Ct. 468, 63 L.Ed. 979 (1919); Kastigar v. United States, 406 U.S. 441, 92 S.Ct. 1653, 32 L.Ed.2d 212 (1972); United States v. Dionisio, 410 U.S. 1, 93 S.Ct. 764, 35 L.Ed.2d 67 (1973); and United States v. Calandra, 414 U.S. 338, 94 S.Ct. 613, 38 L.Ed.2d 561 (1974).

ine "all witnesses * * * in every proper way." It is recognized, in this connection, that "if the investigation is to be meaningful, some exploration or fishing necessarily is inherent and entitled to exist."

Second, courts frequently note that the grand jury must be free of technical rules that would cause grand jury proceedings to be punctuated by litigation and delay. Judicial rulings must not provide the recalcitrant witness with a long list of challenges that can be used "to tie the grand jury into knots—to drag out the proceedings with technicalities instead of matters of substance." In determining whether a particular objection should be recognized, a court must consider whether its holding "would saddle a grand jury with minitrials and preliminary showings [that] would assuredly impede its investigation and frustrate the public's interest in the fair and expeditious administration of the criminal laws."

The Supreme Court has acknowledged that the obligation of the citizen to appear and testify before the grand jury is not without its burdens. Appearance may be "onerous at times" and required answers "may prove embarrassing or result in an unwelcome disclosure of * * * personal affairs"; but such personal sacrifices, the Court has noted, are "part of the necessary contribution of the individual to the welfare of the public." In this regard, the duty to testify before the grand jury is sometimes compared to the duty to testify at trial, which is imposed simply upon a determination of one of the parties that a particular person should be subpoenaed. There are, of course, certain distinctions in the two situations. The witness summoned to testify at trial knows the subject to be considered, and is not himself the target of inquiry. In the grand jury setting, the subject under inquiry may not be revealed, and the person summoned may well be a prospective defendant. The witness at trial testifies in public while the witness before the grand jury testifies in a closed proceeding. Justice Marshall has suggested that a grand jury appearance may carry with it a substantial stigma, not attached to a trial appearance, since "the public often treats an appearance before a grand jury as tantamount to a visit to the stationhouse." [2] Courts have recognized that these distinctions may require somewhat different treatment of the grand jury witness in a few situations, but they also have concluded that the protection afforded the grand jury witness is sufficient to impose a general duty to appear similar to that imposed upon the trial witness. That protection is said to stem from four sources. First, the grand jury witness retains the same constitutional, statutory and common law privileges as the trial witness. Second, the secrecy of the grand jury proceeding affords the witness protection against damage to his reputation and mitigates any element of embarrassment in his testimony. Third, the witness has the protection afforded by the presence of the grand jurors. Justice Black, in particular, gave considerable weight to this factor:

> They [the grand jurors] have no axes to grind and are not charged personally with the administration of the law. No one of them is a prosecuting attorney or law-enforcement officer ferreting out crime. It would be very difficult for officers of the state seriously to abuse or deceive a witness in the presence of the grand jury.[3]

Finally, grand juries remain subject to the supervisory authority of the court, which is available to protect witnesses against prosecutorial misuse of grand jury powers.

In recent years, these protections have been viewed by many as inadequate. Commentators, legislators, and lawyer associations have called for reform. Some have gone so far as to suggest that the grand jury's right to compel testimony either be eliminated or restricted to limited situations. They contend that a humane society need not, and should not, rely on compelled cooperation to ensure effective enforcement of its laws. Others contend that what is needed is legislative reform of the grand jury structure. Arguing that the grand

2. United States v. Mara, 410 U.S. 19, 93 S.Ct. 774, 35 L.Ed.2d 99 (1973) (dissenting opinion).

3. In re Groban, 352 U.S. 330, 77 S.Ct. 510, 1 L.Ed.2d 376 (1957) (dissenting opinion).

jurors must be more directly involved in the process, they have proposed that no subpoena, grant of immunity, or contempt citation be issued except upon approval of the jurors. Other reformers would directly prohibit various prosecutorial practices thought to be abusive, and grant the witness a variety of procedural rights. Some of these reforms have been rather warmly received. A substantial number of states, for example, now allow the witness to be accompanied by a lawyer. However, in general, legislatures and courts have been reluctant to adopt those reforms that would dramatically alter the grand jury's powers or recognize procedural objections that might lead to substantial delay in grand jury proceedings.

§ 8.7 Fourth Amendment Challenges to Subpoenas

(a) Application of Fourth Amendment: Earlier Cases. The application of the Fourth Amendment to court orders requiring production of documentary evidence began with *Boyd v. United States,*[1] a widely celebrated case that in most respects has little current vitality. *Boyd* involved a customs forfeiture proceeding in which the government sought to utilize an 1847 statutory provision allowing it to gain documentary evidence from the importer of the property to be forfeited. The provision authorized the trial judge, on motion of the government describing a particular document and indicating what it might prove, to issue a notice directing the importer to produce that document. The petitioners in *Boyd* challenged such a notice that directed them to produce the invoice for thirty-five cases of plate glass allegedly imported without payment of customs duties. The Supreme Court sustained their challenge, holding that the notice and the statute authorizing it violated both the Fourth Amendment and the self-incrimination clause of the Fifth Amendment.

Speaking to the Fourth Amendment, the *Boyd* Court acknowledged that the notice procedure "lacked certain aggravating incidents of actual search and seizure, such as forcible entry into a man's house and searching among his papers," but stressed that it nonetheless "accomplish[ed] the substantial object of those acts in forcing from a party evidence against himself." Accordingly, a "compulsory production of a man's private papers" would be treated as "within the scope of the Fourth Amendment to the constitution, in all cases in which a search and seizure would be." Having found the Fourth Amendment applicable, the *Boyd* opinion turned to the question as to whether this particular "search and seizure, or what is equivalent thereto," was unreasonable within the meaning of that Amendment. It concluded that Fourth Amendment standards had been violated since the notice sought to compel the defendants to give what was, in effect, testimony against themselves. The Fourth Amendment's reasonableness requirement, read in light of the Fifth Amendment, barred seizure of private papers constituting no more than evidence of the crime (as compared to contraband or implements of criminality).

Boyd spoke stirringly of the Court's obligation to "liberally construe" those constitutional provisions designed to safeguard "the security of person and property." Admittedly, the Court might have before it "the obnoxious thing in its mildest and least repulsive form; but illegitimate and unconstitutional practices get their first footing in that way, namely, by silent approaches and slight deviations from legal modes of procedures." In part because of such comments, the *Boyd* opinion came to be widely celebrated among civil libertarians. Justice Brandeis once described *Boyd* as a "case that will be remembered as long as civil liberties live in the United States." Nonetheless, while *Boyd* has never been directly overruled and continues to be cited and discussed by the Court,[2] very

§ 8.7

1. 116 U.S. 616, 6 S.Ct. 524, 29 L.Ed. 746 (1886).

2. That discussion looks basically to the general implications of *Boyd,* as its precise holding is contrary to two major elements of subsequently developed doctrine. Since only a single document was to be produced under the court order held invalid in *Boyd,* a Fourth Amendment challenge there would clearly fail under the current

little, if anything, remains of its analysis of the Fourth and Fifth Amendments and the relationship between the two. *Boyd* today can be viewed as a case that largely produced a "false start"—a case which serves more to explain the historical development of the law governing subpoenas duces tecum than the doctrines currently applicable.[3]

Only twenty years after *Boyd* was decided, in *Hale v. Henkel,*[4] the Court dramatically modified Boyd's Fourth Amendment analysis. *Hale* basically rejected *Boyd*'s interpretation of that Amendment's reasonableness requirement, although it reaffirmed the applicability of the Fourth Amendment to a "compulsory production of a man's private papers." The *Hale* majority initially noted that *Boyd* had erred in reading together the Fourth and Fifth Amendment protections. Any absolute prohibition against production of documentary items lay in the self-incrimination clause alone, and that clause had no application in the case before it; the challenged grand jury subpoena was directed to corporate documents and corporations did not have the benefit of the privilege. However, the Court continued, the corporation was entitled to the protection of the Fourth Amendment, and "an order for the production of books and papers" could still constitute "an unreasonable search and seizure." While it was true that "a search ordinarily implies a quest of an officer of the law, and a seizure contemplates a forcible dispossession of property, still, as was held in *Boyd,* the substance of the offense is * * * [unreasonable] compulsory production, whether under a search warrant or a subpoena duces tecum." Here, Fourth Amendment protection was violated by a subpoena duces tecum "far too sweeping in its terms to be regarded as reasonable." The subpoena had required production of corporate papers relating to transactions with various different companies, and such a broad request was capable of preventing the corporation from carrying on its business. While the government might have need for many of these documents, it would have to make some showing of that need before it could "justify an order for the production of such a mass of papers."

As Judge Friendly later noted:

> *Hale v. Henkel* left the applicability of the Fourth Amendment to subpoenas duces tecum in a most confusing state. None of the Justices seemed to think that such a subpoena could be issued only "upon probable cause, supported by oath or affirmation," as would be required for a search warrant. Nevertheless, except for Mr. Justice McKenna, all were of the view that an overbroad subpoena duces tecum against an individual would be an unreasonable search and seizure.[5]

Exactly why the Fourth Amendment applied in one respect, but not in another, was never fully explained. Justice McKenna, concurring separately, could find no basis for applying the Fourth Amendment in any respect. The majority had acknowledged that the subpoena did not involve a "quest" by the officer or a "forcible dispossession of the owner." Did not that distinction in itself establish the inapplicability of the Fourth Amendment? The service of the subpoena involved "no element of trespass or force," nor was it "secret and intrusive." The subpoena could not be "finally enforced except after challenge, and a judgment of the court upon the challenge." These safeguards and limitations, from Justice McKenna's perspective, clearly distin-

standard that prohibits only overbreadth. See Hale v. Henkel, discussed infra and in subsection (c). Since the order to produce was directed to Boyd and Sons, a partnership, the self-incrimination objection today would be precluded by the entity doctrine. See § 8.12(b) at note 13.

3. *Boyd* also had significant bearing upon the development of Fourth Amendment principles apart from the subpoena duces tecum, but here too its significance is largely historical. *Boyd* became the fountainhead for the development of the prohibition against searches for "mere evidence," a prohibition subsequently rejected in Warden v. Hayden. See § 3.2(i). *Boyd*'s suggestion of a Fifth Amendment prohibition against the seizure of personal business records also failed to survive. See Andresen v. Maryland, discussed at § 3.2(i). While *Boyd* is sometimes seen as the starting point for the development of a constitutionally mandated exclusionary remedy for Fourth Amendment violations, that concept as it evolved did not find grounding in *Boyd*'s Fifth Amendment analysis. See § 3.1(a).

4. 201 U.S. 43, 26 S.Ct. 370, 50 L.Ed. 652 (1906).

5. In re Horowitz, 482 F.2d 72 (2d Cir.1973).

guished the subpoena from the search. Justice McKenna also considered the possibility that the majority was saying that a subpoena did not involve a search except where it was "too sweeping," but he could not understand how that quality alone, improper though it may be, could transform the subpoena into a search.

The failure of the *Hale* majority to respond directly to Justice McKenna's criticism left the rationale of the majority open to two interpretations. On the one hand, the Court might be saying that the Fourth Amendment applied to all subpoenas duces tecum, but the requirements of its warrant clause were supplanted by the long history of subpoenas issued without regard to probable cause, leaving only the Fourth Amendment's general mandate of reasonableness. In this respect, *Hale* would have been a forerunner of the basic analytical position later taken in many regulatory search cases.[6] On the other hand, the Court may have viewed a subpoena as falling within the Fourth Amendment only when it was clearly overbroad and thereby had the effect of a physical search in allowing the government to sift through a mass of documents while looking for the few that might be relevant. In *Oklahoma Press Publishing Co. v. Walling,*[7] the Court suggested still a third explanation that the Fourth Amendment had no direct application but was looked to only by analogy to protect against a different form of "officious intermeddling by government officials." In that case, which involved an administrative agency subpoena duces tecum, the Court acknowledged that certain misconceptions had arisen due to the failure of lower courts to distinguish between "so-called 'figurative' or 'constructive'" searches by subpoena and "cases of actual search and seizure." The Court noted that "only in * * * [an] analogical sense can any question related to search and seizure be thought to arise" in subpoena cases. It stressed that the Fourth Amendment, "if applicable," did no more than "guard against abuse only by way of too much indefiniteness or breadth" in the subpoena. The interests to be protected were "not identical with those protected against invasion by actual search and seizure" but arose out of the right of persons to be free from "officious examination [that] can be expensive, so much so that it eats up men's substance," and thereby "become[s] persecution when carried beyond reason."

(b) Application of Fourth Amendment: *Dionisio* and *Mara*. In the latest Supreme Court opinions on the applicability of the Fourth Amendment to grand jury subpoenas, *United States v. Dionisio*[8] and *United States v. Mara,*[9] the Court left no doubt that the Fourth Amendment does not apply to subpoenas in general, although it does bar a subpoena duces tecum "too sweeping" to be regarded as reasonable. *Dionisio* and *Mara* were companion cases arising from separate grand jury investigations. In *Dionisio,* the grand jury had subpoenaed approximately 20 persons, including Dionisio, to give voice exemplars for comparison with recorded conversations that had been received in evidence. In *Mara,* the witness was directed to produce handwriting exemplars for the purpose of determining whether he was the author of certain writings. Both witnesses claimed that the subpoenas constituted unreasonable searches and seizures because they had not been supported by any showing of reasonableness. The Court of Appeals agreed. It compared the dragnet effect of the subpoena in *Dionisio* to the mass police roundup of possible suspects for fingerprinting that was condemned in *Davis v. Mississippi.*[10] The *Davis* opinion had suggested that a court order detaining a suspect for the purpose of obtaining identification evidence might be possible on a showing of less than probable cause, but the subpoena here had not been supported by anything other than a prosecutor's claim that the exemplars were "essential and necessary." The "interposition of the grand jury between the witnesses and

6. See § 3.9.

7. 327 U.S. 186, 66 S.Ct. 494, 90 L.Ed. 614 (1946).

8. 410 U.S. 1, 93 S.Ct. 764, 35 L.Ed.2d 67 (1973).

9. 410 U.S. 19, 93 S.Ct. 774, 35 L.Ed.2d 99 (1973).

10. See § 3.8(g).

the government" would not be allowed to "eliminate the Fourth Amendment protection that would [otherwise] bar the government's obtaining the evidence." *Mara* did not involve the same "dragnet procedure," but the Court of Appeals held that here too a showing of reasonableness was necessary. It was incumbent upon the government to establish that grand jury investigation was properly authorized, that the information sought was relevant to that inquiry, and that the request for exemplars was adequate but not excessive for the purposes of the relevant inquiry. These requirements, the Court of Appeals reasoned, were a logical extension of the prohibition of excessively broad subpoenas duces tecum.

The Supreme Court rejected the lower court rulings in both *Dionisio* and *Mara.* The majority opinion noted that the Fourth Amendment did prohibit the "sweeping subpoena duces tecum," as noted in *Hale,* but there was no such extreme breadth of production required in either subpoena here. The Court of Appeals had erred in analogizing the subpoena in *Dionisio* to the action of police in detaining or arresting a person for the purpose of obtaining identification exemplars. "It is clear," the Court noted, "that a subpoena to appear before a grand jury is not a 'seizure' in the Fourth Amendment sense." There was a dramatic difference in the "compulsion exerted" by a subpoena as opposed to an "arrest or even an investigative stop":

> The latter is abrupt, is effected with force or the threat of it and often in demeaning circumstances, and, in the case of arrest, results in a record involving social stigma. A subpoena is served in the same manner as other legal process; it involves no stigma whatever; if the time for appearance is inconvenient, this can generally be altered; and it remains at all times under the control and supervision of a court.

The majority acknowledged that a grand jury subpoena, though differing from the arrest or investigative stop, could be both "inconvenient" and "burdensome." Any "personal sacrifices" required, however, were merely incidental to the "historically grounded obligation of every person to appear and give his evidence before the grand jury." The addition here of directives to give identification evidence did not alter the nature of the burden imposed. Neither the voice exemplar nor the handwriting sample invaded a privacy interest protected under the Fourth Amendment. Both related to physical characteristics "constantly exposed to the public" and were to be distinguished, for example, from the taking of a blood sample.

Having found that the Fourth Amendment had no application to either the summons to appear or the directive to provide identification exemplars, the Court concluded that there was "no justification for requiring the grand jury to satisfy even the minimal requirement of 'reasonableness' imposed by the Court of Appeals." The grand jury "could exercise its 'broad investigative powers' on the basis of 'tips, rumors, evidence offered by the prosecutor, or [the jurors'] own personal knowledge,' " and it should not be required to explain the basis for each of its subpoenas. To "saddle a grand jury with minitrials and preliminary showings would assuredly impede its investigation and frustrate the public's interest in the fair and expeditious administration of the criminal laws." [11]

11. Justice Marshall, dissenting, argued that the Court had treated too lightly the "interfer[ence] with * * * personal liberty" that follows from a subpoena compelling appearance before a grand jury. He argued that the resulting stigma and restraint on the individual did not "differ meaningfully" from that "imposed on a suspect compelled to visit the police station." Justice Marshall rejected the majority's contention that such burdens followed from the individual's obligation to appear and give evidence (see § 8.6). That obligation, he argued, had been applied "only in the context of testimonial evidence, either oral or documentary," where the witness had the protection of the privilege against self-incrimination. The majority responded that it could see no basis for distinguishing between the subpoena to testify, which Justice Marshall acknowledged not to require a preliminary showing of reasonableness, and the subpoena seeking production of identification exemplars. It also rejected the contention, advanced in the dissents of both Justices Marshall and Douglas, that the Court was permitting "law enforcement officers" to "accomplish indirectly through the grand jury process" what they "could not accomplish directly themselves." The Court noted that the restrictions imposed upon the police were tied to elements of seizure that simply were not present in the grand jury subpoena.

While the *Dionisio* opinion did explain, in reasoning similar to that of Justice McKenna's concurrence in *Hale,* why the Fourth Amendment does not apply generally to subpoenas ad testificandum or duces tecum, it merely noted, without explanation beyond a citation to *Hale,* that the Fourth Amendment does "provide protection against a grand jury subpoena duces tecum too sweeping in its terms 'to be regarded as reasonable.'" Arguably, the rationale advanced by the *Dionisio* majority in distinguishing between a Fourth Amendment seizure and the directive of a subpoena lends support to the *Oklahoma Press* suggestion that the overbreadth prohibition is based only by analogy on the Fourth Amendment, but the *Dionisio* opinion does not explicitly advance that theory. Indeed, *Dionisio* specifically referred to the overbreadth prohibition as a Fourth Amendment doctrine and subsequent cases in the administrative agency setting have done the same. Thus, the Fourth Amendment grounding for the prohibition against "too sweeping" subpoenas duces tecum remains without a settled Supreme Court explanation, although the continued acceptance of the prohibition is not open to doubt.

(c) The Prohibition Against Overbreadth. Courts applying the constitutional prohibition against overly broad subpoenas duces tecum frequently start out by noting that the stated standard proscribing breadth "far too sweeping * * * to be regarded as reasonable" necessarily requires a fact-specific judgment, with each ruling tied to the circumstances of the individual case. At the same time, the courts have sought, with limited success, to develop some general criteria to guide that judgment. Initially, the subpoena poses difficulties only if it has sufficient breadth to suggest either that compliance will be burdensome or that the subpoena's scope may not have been shaped to the purposes of the inquiry.[12] If it has that breadth, the court then will turn to the three "components" of reasonableness initially developed by the lower federal courts:

> (1) the subpoena may command only the production of things relevant to the investigation being pursued; (2) specification of things to be produced must be made with reasonable particularity; and (3) production of records covering only a reasonable period of time may be required.[13]

The second element of the above formulation is commonly described as having "two prongs": first, "particularity of description" so that the subpoenaed party "know[s] what he is being asked to produce"; and second, "particularity of breadth" so that the subpoenaed party "is not harassed or oppressed to the point that he experiences an unreasonable business detriment." The requirement of adequate notice rarely poses significant difficulty, so courts looking to the second component tend to focus on the second factor, the degree of burden imposed by production.

While many courts have treated the elements of relevancy, sufficient particularity to avoid an undue burden of production, and reasonableness of time period as separate requirements of reasonableness, with a deficiency as to any one invalidating the subpoena, it is clear that the three elements are interrelated. Greater particularity, by narrowing the range of documents to be produced, will extend the time period into which the subpoena may reach. On the other hand, as a subpoena reaches farther into the past, a court is more likely to require a stronger showing of rele-

12. Various lower court opinions suggest that the overbreadth prohibition applies to a request for indiscriminate production of uncategorized documents, reflecting a needless fishing expedition, even when the production may not be particularly burdensome. Subpoenas have been quashed where the court acknowledged that production would not be "unreasonable or oppressive in the physical sense," but nevertheless viewed the grand jury request as too "sweeping and all-inclusive." See e.g., In re Certain Chinese Family Benevolent and District Associations, 19 F.R.D. 97 (N.D.Cal.1956) (rejecting subpoenas requiring various Chinese family associations to produce available membership lists, income records, and membership photographs, dating back to the association's origin, for use in an investigation of fraud by various persons claiming derivative citizenship as offspring of American citizen fathers). In many of these cases, the court's concern as to overbreadth may have been heightened by the potentially sensitive nature of the records.

13. United States v. Gurule, 437 F.2d 239 (10th Cir. 1970). This formulation, developed initially by Judge Herlands in In re Grand Jury Subpoena Duces Tecum (Provision Salesmen), 203 F.Supp. 575 (S.D.N.Y.1961), has been adopted by state as well as federal courts.

vancy. So too, the significance of the burden of production will be weighed against the strength of the showing as to relevancy and the reasonableness of the time period. Thus, courts have noted that a subpoena that clearly meets the relevancy and time period requirements will be rejected on the basis of a substantial burden of production only in the most extreme cases.[14]

While the subpoenaed party bears the ultimate burden of establishing that a challenged subpoena is unreasonable, many courts insist that the government make an initial showing of relevancy since it alone knows the precise nature of the grand jury inquiry. Ordinarily, this showing requires no more than a general description of the relationship of the material sought to the subject matter of the investigation. Moreover, the government generally is thought to be entitled to considerable leeway on the issue of relevancy. Courts recognize that "some exploration or fishing necessarily is inherent" since the grand jury will not ordinarily have a "catalog of what books and papers exist" nor "any basis for knowing what their character or contents immediately are." They note also that certain types of investigations, such as antitrust, necessarily demand a broader range of documents since the violation may be reflected in many different aspects of a company's business. Where the time period clearly is reasonable and the burden of production is limited, some courts have accepted as sufficient showings of "some possible relationship, however indirect."

§ 8.8 Challenges to Misuse of the Subpoena Authority

(a) Improper Subject of Investigation. It is generally conceded that a subpoenaed grand jury witness has no legal right to be informed of the subject matter of the grand jury's inquiry. Ordinarily, however, the witness will become aware of at least the general area of inquiry through a designation of the subject matter in the subpoena, the questions asked, or the documents requested. In rare instances, this information may suggest that the grand jury is investigating an activity for which it cannot indict. Although such an investigation would ordinarily be beyond the grand jury's investigative authority,[1] a witness' objection on that ground generally will be unavailing. *Blair v. United States,*[2] though it involved a rather convoluted subject matter objection, is generally viewed as barring all witness challenges to the grand jury's "jurisdiction" to investigate.

In *Blair,* the witness claimed that the transaction under investigation was beyond the grand jury's investigative authority because the applicable federal criminal statute was unconstitutional. The Supreme Court initially noted that consideration of the constitutionality of the statute at this point, prior to any indictment, would be contrary to the long-established practice of "refrain[ing] from passing upon the constitutionality of an act of Congress unless obliged to do so." It then proceeded, however, to speak in quite general terms of a witness' lack of capacity to challenge the "authority * * * of the grand jury," provided the jury had "de facto existence and organization." The Court treated the position of the grand jury witness as analogous to that of the trial witness. Neither could raise objections of "incompetency or irrelevancy," for those matters were of "no concern" to a wit-

14. With the advent of photocopying, the possibility that the subpoenaed party will be unable to carry on its business without the relinquished records—a major concern in *Hale*—is largely mooted. Courts commonly have viewed the expense of assembling and duplicating the materials as simply another cost of doing business, particularly where the subpoenaed party is a large corporation. Moreover, in cases where that expense imposes a true financial hardship, the government may respond by offering reimbursement of all costs. The end result is that the burden of production is given weight primarily where the court has substantial doubts as to the relevancy of the documents or the reasonableness of the time span.

§ 8.8

1. The grand jury ordinarily is limited to investigating indictable offenses "committed or otherwise triable" within the jurisdiction of the court that impanelled it. See e.g., Tenn.R.Crim.P. 6(d). An offense committed outside the jurisdiction would not be within its investigative authority unless that offense had some bearing on crimes committed within the jurisdiction. Similarly, a transaction that could not constitute a crime and was not related to possible criminal activity also would be beyond its investigative authority.

2. 250 U.S. 273, 39 S.Ct. 468, 63 L.Ed. 979 (1919).

ness, as opposed to a party. For the same reasons, witnesses also should not be allowed "to take exception to the jurisdiction of the grand jury or the court over the particular subject matter that is under investigation." The grand jury operates as a "grand inquest," which requires broad investigative powers. It must have authority, in particular, "to investigate the facts in order to determine the question of whether the facts show a case within [its] jurisdiction." The witness could not be allowed "to set limits to the investigation that the grand jury may conduct."

Relying upon *Blair,* federal courts have refused to recognize witness challenges alleging that the grand jury inquiry concerned offenses as to which prosecution would be barred by the statute of limitations, offenses that occurred outside the grand jury's judicial district, or offenses immunized from prosecution.[3] A few state courts have indicated that, contrary to *Blair,* they will allow witness objections to the subject matter of a grand jury inquiry. However, those jurisdictions also adhere to a presumption of regularity that places on the witness a substantial burden of establishing that the inquiry was directed solely at activities beyond the grand jury's reach.

(b) Relevancy Objections. In commenting upon the objections of a witness, either at trial or before the grand jury, *Blair* noted that "[h]e is not entitled to urge objections of incompetency or irrelevancy, such as a party might raise, for this is no concern of his." In light of this statement, the standard position of federal lower courts was that a grand jury witness could not object to the questions put to him on the ground that they dealt with matters having no bearing upon the subject of the grand jury inquiry. As to the subpoena duces tecum, however, the availability of a relevancy objection was somewhat more complicated. Relevancy was properly considered in assessing a Fourth Amendment claim that a subpoena duces tecum was "too sweeping to be reasonable," but where the subpoena duces tecum was so narrow in scope as to clearly rebut any Fourth Amendment challenge, most lower courts suggested that an independent objection to relevancy would not be heard. Support for this position was found in the Supreme Court's ruling of *United States v. Mara,*[4] as well as *Blair.* The lower court in *Mara* had held that a subpoena duces tecum requiring production of a handwriting exemplar would not be enforced without an initial showing that the grand jury was investigating a matter within its jurisdiction and that the information sought by subpoena was relevant to its inquiry. The prosecution had made such a showing by affidavit filed in camera, but the Court of Appeals ruled that the affidavit had to be disclosed in open court so as to permit challenge by the witness. The Supreme Court reversed. The Court held, as previously discussed in § 8.7(b), that the Fourth Amendment had no application to a subpoena duces tecum, absent a *Hale* claim of overbreadth. It then added that, with the Fourth Amendment inapplicable, no preliminary showing of reasonableness was required.

Notwithstanding *Mara,* prior to the Supreme Court's recent ruling in *United States v. R. Enterprises, Inc.,*[5] several lower federal courts had begun to depart from the position that relevancy was at issue only in connection with a Fourth Amendment objection to a subpoena duces tecum. *Mara* was read as a case rejecting only a requirement that the prosecution make a preliminary showing of reasonableness. That did not preclude the possibility of a successful relevancy objection where a witness carried the burden of showing that the subpoena duces tecum sought material

3. *Blair* has not been viewed as precluding challenges alleging prosecutorial utilization of the grand jury for improper purposes, though the subject of the inquiry is cited as a factor indicating such improper purpose. See subsections (d) and (e) infra. Consider also Morrison v. Olson, 487 U.S. 654, 108 S.Ct. 2597, 101 L.Ed.2d 569 (1988), where the Court found it unnecessary to rule upon the government's contention that *Blair* barred a witness challenge based on the alleged unconstitutionality of the authority of the independent counsel who had "caused the grand jury" to issue the subpoena (see § 13.3 at note 6), as that contention had not been properly raised before the district court and was not "jurisdictional" in nature.

4. See § 8.7 at note 9.

5. ___ U.S. ___, 111 S.Ct. 722, 112 L.Ed.2d 795 (1990).

having "no conceivable relevance to any legitimate objective of investigation by the grand jury." Moreover, one court, the Court of Appeals for the Third Circuit, went considerably beyond recognizing such a limited relevancy objection. In its widely noted opinion in the *Schofield* case,[6] that court distinguished *Mara* as concerned only with Fourth Amendment requirements, and relied on its supervisory authority to mandate for its circuit a required preliminary showing by the government not unlike that rejected in *Mara.* To obtain contempt enforcement of a subpoena against a recalcitrant witness, the "government [would] be required to make some preliminary showing by affidavit that each item [sought] is at least relevant to an investigation being conducted by the grand jury and properly within its jurisdiction, and is not sought primarily for another purpose." In subsequent rulings, the Third Circuit held this preliminary showing requirement applicable to witness refusals to testify as well as to witness refusals to produce physical evidence in response to a subpoena duces tecum. Here, however, the government's affidavit of relevancy need refer only to the general subject covered in the overall grouping of questions, rather than the information sought in an individual question. The Third Circuit also stated that the government's affidavit ordinarily should be disclosed to the witness so he could challenge its sufficiency, although in "extraordinary circumstances" an in camera presentation would be justified.

The Supreme Court in *R. Enterprises* did not comment directly upon either *Schofield* or the lower court rulings that had refused to go as far as *Schofield,* but it did speak at length to the issues raised in those rulings. The *R. Enterprises* Court flatly rejected a lower court ruling that sought to move even beyond *Schofield,* and in the course of doing so, cast considerable doubt upon a district court's authority to always insist upon a government affidavit of relevancy as *Schofield* demanded. At the same time, however, the Court recognized that a relevancy objection could be presented under Federal Rule 17(c), which deals with challenges to a subpoena duces tecum. Since the Court referred only to the requirements of that Rule and challenges to a subpoena duces tecum, it did not cast doubt upon the statement in *Blair* which suggested that a person testifying before a grand jury cannot object to relevancy of the questions put to him.

At issue in *R. Enterprises* was the interpretation of the Rule 17(c) provision that authorizes a federal district court to quash or modify a subpoena duces tecum "if compliance would be unreasonable or oppressive." In *United States v. Nixon,*[7] which dealt with a subpoena duces tecum directing production of items for use at trial, the Supreme Court had held that the moving party must show that the documents subpoenaed are relevant, admissible in evidence, and adequately specified. The lower court in *R. Enterprises* had held that these three requirements also applied to a subpoena duces tecum in a grand jury proceeding. There was no issue here as to specificity, but the government had failed to make a showing as to relevancy and admissibility. The Supreme Court unanimously ruled that the lower court had erred, as the *Nixon* standard clearly did not apply in the grand jury context.

Justice O'Connor's opinion for the Court in *R. Enterprises* cited several reasons for refusing to extend the *Nixon* standard to grand jury proceedings. Insofar as that standard looked to the evidentiary admissibility of the items subpoenaed, it contradicted a line of earlier Supreme Court rulings holding that the grand jury could consider, and issue an indictment based upon, evidence that would be inadmissible at trial.[8] The "teaching of the Court's decision[s]," Justice O'Connor noted, "is clear: A grand jury 'may compel the production of evidence or the testimony of witnesses as it considers appropriate, and its operation generally is unrestrained by the

6. In re Grand Jury Proceedings (Schofield I), 486 F.2d 85 (3d Cir.1973).

7. 418 U.S. 683, 94 S.Ct. 3090, 41 L.Ed.2d 1039 (1974). See also § 20.2(d).

8. See §§ 8.9(a), 15.5(a).

technical procedural and evidentiary rules governing the conduct of criminal trials.' " Applying the *Nixon* standard to grand juries also would present unacceptable administrative difficulties. It "would invite procedural delays and detours while courts evaluate the relevancy and admissibility of documents sought by a particular subpoena." In *Dionisio,* the Court had "expressly stated that grand jury proceedings should be free of such delays." So too, application of the *Nixon* standard would be inconsistent with the "strict secrecy requirements" of grand jury proceedings. "Requiring the Government to explain in too much detail the particular reasons underlying a subpoena" would "compromise 'the indispensable secrecy of grand jury proceedings,' " and it would "afford the targets of the investigation far more information about the grand jury's internal workings * * * than the Federal Rules of Criminal Procedure appear to contemplate."

Having rejected the application of the *Nixon* standard, Justice O'Connor then turned to the more difficult task of "fashion[ing] an appropriate standard of reasonableness" in the application of Rule 17. It was well established that "the investigatory powers of the grand jury are * * * not unlimited." The grand jury could not, for example, "engage in arbitrary fishing expeditions" or "select targets of investigation out of malice or an intent to harass." Applying such limits, however, required consideration of conflicting elements in the grand jury process. On the one hand, the decision as to the appropriate charge "is routinely not made until after the grand jury has concluded its investigation," and "one simply cannot know in advance whether information sought during the investigation will be relevant and admissible in the prosecution for a particular offense." On the other hand, the party to whom the subpoena is directed "faces a difficult situation" in challenging the improper use of a subpoena. Grand juries ordinarily "do not announce publicly the subjects of their investigations," and the subpoenaed party therefore "may have no conception of the Government's purpose in seeking production of the requested information." Thus, what was needed was a standard of reasonableness that "gives due weight to the difficult position of subpoena recipients but does not impair the strong governmental interests in affording grand juries wide latitude, avoiding minitrials on peripheral matters, and preserving a necessary level of secrecy."

Turning to the specific guidelines that give substance to such a standard, Justice O'Connor noted initially that "the law presumes, absent a strong showing to the contrary, that a grand jury acts within the legitimate scope of its authority." Consequently, "a grand jury subpoena issued through normal channels is presumed to be reasonable, and the burden of showing unreasonableness must be on the recipient who seeks to avoid compliance." In this case, that party "did not challenge the subpoena as being too indefinite, nor did [it] claim that compliance would be overly burdensome." The challenge was strictly on relevancy grounds and for such a challenge, the presumption of regularity produced the following standard: "[T]he motion to quash must be denied unless the district court determines that there is no reasonable possibility that the category of materials the Government seeks will produce information relevant to the general subject of the grand jury's investigation."

Recognizing that the above standard imposed an "unenviable task" upon the party raising a relevancy challenge, Justice O'Connor suggested that the district court had authority to ease that task through appropriate procedures. Her opinion noted in this regard:

> "It seems unlikely, of course, that a challenging party who does not know the general subject matter of the grand jury's investigation, no matter how valid that party's claim, will be able to make the necessary showing that compliance would be unreasonable. After all, a subpoena recipient 'cannot put his whole life before the court in order to show that there is no crime to be investigated.' Consequently, a court may be justified in a case where unreasonableness is alleged in requiring the Government to reveal the general subject of the grand jury's investigation before

requiring the challenging party to carry its burden of persuasion. We need not resolve this question in the present case, however, as there is no doubt that respondents knew the subject of the grand jury investigation pursuant to which the business records subpoenas were issued. In cases where the recipient of the subpoena does not know the nature of the investigation, we are confident that district courts will be able to craft appropriate procedures that balance the interests of the subpoena recipient against the strong governmental interests in maintaining secrecy, preserving investigatory flexibility, and avoiding procedural delays. For example, to ensure that subpoenas are not routinely challenged as a form of discovery, a district court may require that the Government reveal the subject of the investigation to the trial court *in camera,* so that the court may determine whether the motion to quash has a reasonable prospect for success before it discloses the subject matter to the challenging party."

Although the Court in *R. Enterprises* was unanimous in rejecting application of the *Nixon* standard, there was division as to the specific guidelines advanced in Justice O'Connor's opinion. Justice Scalia did not join the paragraph discussing the district court's possible authority to require the prosecution to set forth the general subject of the investigation. Three justices, in a separate opinion by Justice Stevens, rejected in its entirety what was described as "the Court['s] * * * attemp[t] to define the term reasonableness in the abstract, looking only at the relevance side of the balance." Justice Stevens argued that the burden imposed upon the challenging party will vary with the nature of the subpoena. A less rigorous showing of lack of relevancy would be needed where other significant interests are involved. This would be true, for example, where responding to the subpoena would be especially burdensome due to the volume and location of the documents requested, where the "subpoena would intrude significantly on * * * privacy interests, or call for the disclosure of trade secrets or other confidential material," or where "the movant might demonstrate that compliance would have First Amendment implications." Of course, Justice O'Connor's opinion did not propose a standard for such special circumstances, but Justice Stevens expressed concern that the Court's opinion "not be read to suggest that the deferential relevance standard the Court has formulated will govern decision in every case, no matter how intrusive or burdensome the request." Justice Stevens noted that relevancy is treated differently where the subpoena is so broad as to present a Fourth Amendment problem, and suggested that the relevancy assessment will often involve a similar balancing process under Rule 17(c). Thus, there would be, in effect, a varying standard of relevancy, with Justice O'Connor's "no-reasonable-possibility" standard limited to subpoenas that are in no significant way either burdensome or intrusive. Even this position, however, appears to fall short of justifying the *Schofield* requirement that the government be required to file an affidavit of relevancy in all cases as a prerequisite to gaining enforcement of a subpoena.

(c) "Chilling Effect" Objections. Grand jury witnesses have argued in various contexts that even though the testimony or documents demanded of them clearly would be relevant, the grand jury should be required to show a compelling need for that information where the impact of its inquiry is to chill the exercise of a constitutionally protected right. The Supreme Court's ruling in *Branzburg v. Hayes* [9] commonly is viewed as rejecting such a requirement, at least with respect to a chilling impact upon First Amendment rights. *Branzburg* rejected the contention that newspaper reporters could not be compelled to reveal to state grand juries the identity of their confidential sources (who were apparent participants in drug offenses) unless the prosecution first established a compelling need for that information. The Court majority questioned the potential adverse impact of such disclosures upon the reporter's ability to obtain confidential sources, and concluded that any resulting impact upon the capacity of the

9. 408 U.S. 665, 92 S.Ct. 2646, 33 L.Ed.2d 626 (1972).

press to gather and report news was more than offset by the interest of the public in criminal investigation, as reflected in the traditional investigative authority of the grand jury. How far *Branzburg* should be taken is unclear. As the Ninth Circuit has noted,[10] *Branzburg* was concerned with the press function of news gathering, which had never been placed at the core of First Amendment rights. In a series of cases involving required disclosures in other contexts (e.g., legislative hearings), the Court had required a showing of a compelling need where the disclosure had a potential chilling impact upon the exercise of basic First Amendment interests (e.g., political association).[11] The Ninth Circuit concluded that those precedents should control where a grand jury inquiry requires disclosure of information concerning clearly protected First Amendment activities. It held that where the grand jury inquiry "collides with First Amendment rights," the government must establish that "[its] interest in the subject matter of the investigation is immediate, substantial and subordinating, that there is a 'substantial connection' between the information it seeks to have the witness compelled to supply and the overriding government interest in the subject matter of the investigation, and that the means of obtaining the information is not more drastic than necessary to forward the asserted government interest." Other courts have disagreed, rejecting application of such a rigorous standard where the grand jury inquiry in no way suggests an attempt to harass a political organization and the information sought is obviously relevant to the crimes under investigation. *Branzburg,* it is noted, found a "compelling" state interest in the grand jury's role in securing the safety of the community through its investigatory power, and the grand jury therefore need not establish more than relevancy to possible criminal activity to sustain its inquiry.

A "chilling effect" argument also has been raised where the grand jury requires the testimony of an attorney, asking questions concerning client identity or the source of fee payments (matters generally not within the attorney client privilege). Finding that the attorney-client privilege provides adequate protection of the lawyer-client relationship, the lower courts generally have refused to require a special governmental showing of need to compel the attorney to testify as to matters not within the privilege. Indeed, the Second Circuit has held that no such showing was needed even where the attorney was currently representing the target of the grand jury investigation on a related criminal charge and the act of testifying before the grand jury could conceivably lead to his disqualification at trial on that charge.[12] The First Circuit has noted, however, that the district court has sufficient discretionary authority to quash such a subpoena where it concludes that compliance could have an overly chilling impact upon the defendant's right to counsel on the pending criminal charge.[13]

(d) Use for Civil Discovery. In *United States v. Procter & Gamble,*[14] the lower court granted broad disclosure of grand jury testimony to defendants in a civil antitrust action, with its ruling apparently influenced by the belief that the government had been using the grand jury process "to elicit evidence" for that civil action. The Supreme Court rejected the disclosure order as not supported by a

10. Bursey v. United States, 466 F.2d 1059 (1972), rehearing denied 466 F.2d 1090 (9th Cir. 1972).

11. See e.g., DeGregory v. Attorney General of New Hampshire, 383 U.S. 825, 86 S.Ct. 1148, 16 L.Ed.2d 292 (1966) (demand during attorney general's subversive activities inquiry for information relating to individual's earlier association with Communist Party); Gibson v. Florida Legislative Investigation Committee, 372 U.S. 539, 83 S.Ct. 889, 9 L.Ed.2d 929 (1963) (legislative committee subpoena to require production of N.A.A.C.P. membership records); Bates v. Little Rock, 361 U.S. 516, 80 S.Ct. 412, 4 L.Ed.2d 480 (1960) (municipality demand for N.A.A.C.P. membership list based on its authority to impose occupational license taxes).

12. In re Grand Jury Subpoena Served Upon Doe, 781 F.2d 238 (2d Cir.1985).

13. In re Grand Jury Matters, 751 F.2d 13 (1st Cir. 1984). Of course, the use of attorney subpoenas can also be restricted by internal guidelines or state rules of professional conduct. See U.S. Attorneys' Manual § 9–2.16(a); Mass.S.J.C.Rule 3:08.

14. 356 U.S. 677, 78 S.Ct. 983, 2 L.Ed.2d 1077 (1958). See § 8.5(g), note 16.

showing of particularized need, but it also acknowledged that the alleged government misuse of the grand jury process could constitute "good cause" warranting such extensive disclosure. There had been no finding, however, that the grand jury proceeding had in fact "been used as a short cut to [civil discovery] goals otherwise barred or more difficult to reach." If the grand jury had been employed in that fashion, the Court noted, the government clearly would have been guilty of "flouting the policy of the law," both as to the grand jury's proper function and the prescribed procedures for civil discovery. On the other hand, if the grand jury investigation were legitimate, there was no need to deny the government the incidental benefit of civil use of properly acquired evidence.

Lower courts applying the civil misuse standard of *Procter & Gamble* agree that whether or not an abuse exists depends upon the government's purpose in using the grand jury process, rather than the relevancy of the requested information to possible civil litigation. They recognize that a proper criminal investigation may readily encompass elements that also relate to civil cases, and that in some areas of the law (e.g., antitrust), the overlap between the criminal and civil investigation will be substantial. Some disagreement appears to exist, however, as to exactly how "pure" the government's purpose must be.

Several courts have suggested that the *Procter & Gamble* standard is violated only when the investigation was aimed "primarily" at civil discovery. The issue, as they see it, is whether the grand jury proceedings were a "cover" or "subterfuge" for a civil investigation. Under this view, an investigation directed at concurrent criminal and civil uses would be acceptable, at least where the criminal use was at least equal in significance. Other courts suggest that the grand jury can be used only to conduct investigations that are aimed primarily at criminal prosecution. This standard arguably would bar an investigation that is initiated with "a completely open mind as to what the appropriate remedy should be, criminal, civil, or both." If so, it probably goes beyond what the Supreme Court had in mind in *Procter & Gamble.* Read in light of the lower court rulings in that case, the language of *Procter & Gamble* suggests that the Court there was considering only that situation in which the prosecutor fully anticipated bringing a civil suit and viewed an indictment "as merely an unexpected bare possibility."

Claims of civil misuse of grand jury proceedings are most commonly raised in connection with: (1) Rule 6(e) motions for disclosure of the grand jury testimony in a completed investigation (where former targets often claim civil misuse either to bar disclosure to a government agency intending to bring a civil suit, or to gain disclosure for itself to respond to that civil suit); or (2) motions by targets of a continuing investigation to quash subpoenas or terminate the investigation. In either context the party raising the claim must overcome a "presumption of regularity," but the burden of overcoming that presumption clearly is greater in the second situation. Courts hesitate to project the purpose of an investigation while it is still ongoing. Even when the surrounding circumstances strongly suggest misuse (e.g., where the grand jury investigation was instituted shortly after the target's legal challenges stymied a civil investigation), courts have been willing on a motion to terminate to accept a prosecution affidavit of good faith as a sufficient response. A more appropriate assessment, it is argued, can be made after the investigation is ended, with adequate relief still available to the target. If the grand jury should return an indictment, that act will constitute strong evidence that there has been no perversion of the grand jury processes. If an indictment has not been returned, the target retains the opportunity to challenge the proceeding when and if a civil agency requests disclosure for use in connection with a civil suit.

(e) Use for Post-Indictment Criminal Discovery. The grand jury is given its broad investigative powers to determine whether a crime has been committed and an indictment should issue, not to gather evidence for use in cases in which indictments have already issued. Accordingly, both state and federal courts hold that it is an abuse of the grand jury process to use grand jury subpoenas "for the sole or dominating purpose of preparing an already pending indictment for trial." Those courts also hold, however, that where the primary purpose of the investigation is to determine whether others not indicted were involved in the same criminal activity, or whether the indicted party committed still other crimes, the government may go forward with the inquiry even though one result may be the production of evidence that could then be used at the trial of the pending indictment.

A claim of a dominant purpose of post-indictment discovery may be raised in various procedural settings, including a witness' motion to quash a subpoena, an indicted target's motion for a protective order restricting the scope of an investigation, and a defense objection at trial to the admission of evidence arguably derived from such grand jury misuse. In evaluating such claims, the general approach of the courts has paralleled that applied to claims of the misuse of a grand jury to obtain civil discovery. Courts have commonly noted that a "presumption of regularity" attaches to the grand jury proceeding and that the objecting party bears the burden of overcoming that presumption. Courts have also noted their reluctance to interfere with an ongoing investigation, suggesting that the true purpose of the investigation can best be assessed after it is completed. Where the objecting party can point to surrounding circumstances highly suggestive of improper use, the court may require a governmental affidavit explaining the purpose of the investigation or it may examine the grand jury transcript in camera to determine that purpose. Successful challenges are rare, but they do occur.

(f) Prosecution or Police Usurpation of the Subpoena Power. The subpoena power of the grand jury is designed for the grand jury's use, not to further independent investigations of the prosecutor or police. In most jurisdictions, the prosecutor may have subpoenas issued without advance authorization of the grand jury, but the purpose of the subpoena must be to produce evidence for use by the grand jury. This does not bar the prosecutor from screening the requested information before it is formally presented to the grand jury. Documents produced pursuant to a grand jury subpoena duces tecum commonly are first viewed and summarized by the prosecution staff, and in some instances, only the summaries are actually presented to the jurors. For similar reasons, prosecutors also often seek to use the occasion of the witness' grand jury appearance to conduct a preliminary interview. The prosecutor may not, however, have the grand jury subpoena issued as a ploy to secure the witness' attendance at the prosecutor's office for the purpose of interrogation. So too, while the prosecutor may utilize the grand jury subpoena to compel testimony from a witness who has previously refused to provide information to the police, this may be done only if the information sought truly is needed for the grand jury inquiry rather than simply to assist the police investigation.

Courts have divided as to whether special safeguards are needed to ensure that subpoenas for identification exemplars are really directed at a grand jury inquiry rather than at assisting an independent police investigation. Some courts have treated such subpoenas no differently than any other subpoena duces tecum. The subpoena can be issued without any advance grand juror authorization (indeed, even before a grand jury case has been opened), provided the prosecutor expects to present the resulting evidence before the grand jury. Moreover, the witness may be offered the opportunity to provide the exemplars voluntarily, in the offices of the prosecutor or an assisting law enforcement agency, rather than through the more cumbersome procedures specified in the subpoena—provided he is also informed of his right to contest the subpoena.

Other courts have concluded that a subpoena for production of identification exemplars requires special treatment. They have held, for example, that such subpoenas should not issue unless first approved by the grand jury. In justifying such a requirement, one court turned to the rationale of *Dionisio.* While that case had allowed the issuance of a voice exemplar subpoena without requiring a preliminary showing even as to reasonable suspicion, it had done so only because of the grand jury's "unique investigative power." If the element of juror participation which justified that power was to be "meaningful," the use of grand jury authority to impose a "major intrusion upon personal liberty" (here participation in a lineup) could not be assumed to have been automatically delegated by the jurors to the prosecutor. It is also noted, in this regard, that the person ordered to produce an identification exemplar, unlike the subject of a subpoena ad testificandum, ordinarily does not appear before the grand jury. The identification procedure is commonly conducted outside the grand jury's presence, in much the same fashion as the police investigation employing the same practice.[15]

(g) Harassment. Opinions upholding broad investigatory powers of the grand jury frequently add that, "of course," any use of those powers for the purpose of "harassment" will be subject to judicial remedy. Such statements usually do not indicate precisely what is meant by "harassment," but the reference apparently is to something more than simply using the grand jury process for some unauthorized purpose, such as civil discovery. Courts that have offered illustrations of harassment tend to stress a vindictive element in the use of the grand jury, usually a use designed to intimidate the witness. Thus, one case cited the "bad faith harassment of a political dissident" by imposing the burdens (political and otherwise) of a grand jury appearance with "no expectation that any testimony concerning a crime would be forthcoming." Similarly, repeated subpoenas to appear before one grand jury after another, without any additional investigative need, would constitute harassment, as would purposeful leaks to the press designed to create adverse publicity. It has also been argued that calling a witness before the grand jury solely to trap him into committing perjury constitutes a form of harassment.

There is no doubt that such instances of harassment are subject to judicial remedy. A subpoena issued to "punish" a witness may be quashed; purposeful leaks to the press may result in contempt sanctions; and a perjury indictment obtained by ambush may be dismissed, at least where the witness has been misled. However, none of these abuses is easily established, and the moving party bears the burden of showing they exist. The fact that the witness was called before a third grand jury, after having twice previously refused to testify, may reflect no more than a continuing need for the information and a hope that he may have changed his mind. Similarly, successive appearances required of a testifying witness may evidence no more than an investigation that has moved from one subject to another, all of which relate to the witness. The publication of matters occurring before the grand jury does not necessarily indicate that there have been leaks by government personnel, and the refusal of newspaper reporters to reveal their sources makes it difficult to pinpoint the responsibility even for patently unlawful disclosures. That a witness was called by the prosecutor with the anticipation that he might commit perjury does not necessarily suggest an "ambush"; the prosecutor's intent may have been to "flush out the truth," by confronting the witness with his own lies. In sum, harassment objections are likely to succeed only in the most outrageous cases, especially where a court starts with the premise that counsel most frequently raise such objections as a delaying tactic.

§ 8.9 Grand Jury Inquiries Based on Illegally Obtained Evidence

(a) The *Calandra* Rule. In *United States v. Calandra,*[1] grand jury witness Calandra was asked questions about certain records that had been seized previously in a search of his office. He then requested and received a postponement of the grand jury proceedings so that he could present a precharge motion

15. See In re Melvin, 546 F.2d 1 (1st Cir.1976).

§ 8.9

1. 414 U.S. 338, 94 S.Ct. 613, 38 L.Ed.2d 561 (1974).

for return and suppression of the seized records under Federal Rule 41(e). The district court granted the motion, holding that the search had been unconstitutional, and further ordered that "Calandra need not answer any of the grand jury's questions based on the suppressed evidence." A divided Supreme Court reversed, holding that the exclusionary rule could not be invoked by a grand jury witness to bar questions based on unconstitutionally seized evidence.

Viewing the exclusionary rule as basically a prophylactic remedy, the *Calandra* majority concluded that its applicability in the grand jury setting should be determined by weighing "the potential injury [in the rule's application] to the historic role and functions of the grand jury" against the potential for increased deterrence of illegal searches. On the one side, allowing grand jury witnesses to invoke the exclusionary rule "would delay and disrupt grand jury proceedings," as suppression hearings "would halt the orderly progress of an investigation and might necessitate extended litigation of issues only tangentially related to the grand jury's primary objective." On the other side, the incremental deterrent effect that might be achieved by applying the exclusionary rule in grand jury proceedings was "uncertain at best." That application would provide additional deterrence, beyond that provided by exclusion at trial, only in the unlikely case in which a police investigation was directed "toward the discovery of evidence solely for use in a grand jury investigation." Any "incentive to disregard the requirements of the Fourth Amendment" otherwise "is substantially negated by the inadmissibility of the illegally-seized evidence in a subsequent criminal prosecution of the search victim." [2] On balance, the Court would not "embrace a view that would achieve a speculative and undoubtedly minimal advance in the deterrence of police misconduct at the expense of substantially impeding the role of the grand jury."

Lower courts have viewed the balance struck in *Calandra* as going beyond Fourth Amendment violations. They have also rejected witness objections to grand jury use of evidence obtained illegally through violations of other constitutional provisions and statutory prohibitions. However, two exceptions are recognized. The *Calandra* majority distinguished *Silverthorne Lumber Co. v. United States,*[3] which upheld the right of already indicted recipients of a grand jury subpoena duces tecum to refuse to produce the same documents which had been returned to them following a successful suppression challenge to an illegal search. In that case, the *Calandra* Court noted, there had been no disruption of an ongoing grand jury proceeding, but simply an attempt by defendants to ensure that the prosecution did not circumvent the previously issued suppression order and obtain use of the documents for the pending trial. The *Silverthorne* exception, if limited to previously indicted parties, would simply permit a Fourth Amendment objection to be raised in a situation where the subpoena would probably be subject to challenge in any event as directed at post-indictment discovery.[4] The second exception to the *Calandra* rule, relating to grand jury use of information derived from illegal electronic surveillance, is discussed in the subsection that follows.

(b) Illegal Electronic Surveillance. In

2. The *Calandra* majority focused upon the deterrence achieved through application of the exclusionary rule at trial under its existing limitations, including the rules governing standing. See § 3.1(f). Its reference accordingly was to the search victim who was targeted for indictment and therefore able to object to the search as a defendant at trial. The dissenters responded that Calandra was a non-target witness, having been immunized, and that the only effective remedy for him would be prohibiting grand jury use of the illegally seized evidence. The dissenters also chastized the majority for its failure to consider other goals of the exclusionary rule beyond deterrence of illegal searches. See § 3.1(b).

3. 251 U.S. 385, 40 S.Ct. 182, 64 L.Ed. 319 (1920).

4. See § 8.8(e). Some would argue that *Silverthorne* deserves a broad reading, that it should permit a witness to refuse to respond where he had previously been successful in obtaining a pre-charge order for the return of seized property (now sought by grand jury subpoena) and that order also constituted a suppression ruling. See Fed.R.Crim.P. 41(e). Even if accepted, this reading would have limited practical effect as such pre-charge rulings are not readily obtainable. See § 10.2(c).

Gelbard v. United States,[5] grand jury witnesses refused to answer questions put to them by the prosecutor, asserting that the questions were derived from electronic surveillance that violated Title III of the Omnibus Crime Control and Safe Streets Act.[6] The issue before the Supreme Court was whether, assuming that the witnesses' assertions were correct, such use of illegally intercepted communications constituted "just cause" for a refusal to answer (and therefore relieved the witnesses of contempt liability). The Court in a 5–4 decision held that: (1) § 2515 of Title III prohibited interrogation of grand jury witnesses based on illegally intercepted communications, and (2) the witness could advance this prohibition as "just cause" for refusing to testify. The Court had little difficulty on the first point since § 2515 specifically refers to grand jury proceedings as among those proceedings in which "no evidence derived [from an illegal interception] may be received." On the second point, some difficulty was presented by § 2518(10)'s failure to include grand jury proceedings among the specified proceedings in which a motion to suppress might be brought. This omission was viewed as not inconsistent with simply allowing a grand jury witness to refuse to respond to questions based on illegal interceptions. The Court noted, however, that it reserved the issue as to whether a witness could refuse to answer if the interceptions had been made pursuant to a court order issued under Title III. In that situation, the limitation of § 2518(10) might have a more substantial bearing.

Justice White, the crucial fifth vote for the *Gelbard* majority, wrote separately. He agreed that the witness could refuse to testify "at least where the United States has intercepted communications without a warrant in circumstances where court approval was required." However, "where the government produced a court order for the interception, and the witness nevertheless demands a full-blown suppression hearing to determine the legality of the order," there might be need for a "different accommodation between the dual functioning of the grand jury system and the federal wiretap statute." Allowance of a suppression hearing would result in "protracted interruption" of the grand jury proceedings. Moreover, the deterrent value of excluding the evidence where the prosecutor had relied in good faith on a court order would be "marginal at best."

Lower courts applying *Gelbard* have accepted Justice White's suggestion that a witness objecting to grand jury use of a court ordered interception should not be entitled to a full-blown suppression hearing, but have also sought to provide reasonable assurance that a witness is not required to respond to questions based upon an invalid court order. One line of cases has held that the proper accommodation requires no more than an in camera inspection of the surveillance documents to ensure that the court order is in compliance with the statute. Another line of decisions provides for witness access to the key documents unless the government can show that grand jury secrecy requires in camera review. The witness is still limited, however, to challenging defects found on the face of those documents.

Gelbard left to the lower courts the task of establishing procedures for determining whether grand jury questions were in fact based upon an electronic surveillance. Frequent *Gelbard* objections have produced a substantial number of lower courts opinions dealing in particular with two issues relating to those procedures: (1) the nature of the allegation that must be made by the witness to trigger a government obligation to make inquiry and respond as to the existence of wiretaps; and (2) the nature of the showing that must be made by the government in support of a response denying the existence of wiretaps. In determining the sufficiency of the witness' claim, courts recognize that the presence of wiretapping often is difficult to detect, and imposing a substantial burden on the witness would result in rewarding the use of more sophisticated equipment that leaves fewer traces of interception. On the other

5. 408 U.S. 41, 92 S.Ct. 2357, 33 L.Ed.2d 179 (1972).

6. See §§ 4.3–4.6.

hand, many courts also believe that recalcitrant grand jury witnesses, seeking delay, will not be reluctant to raise totally unfounded *Gelbard* objections. Balancing these concerns, some courts have concluded that the "mere assertion" of wiretapping is sufficient to require a response, but the prosecutor need not make an extensive investigation in responding to such a general claim. Other courts, however, have held that the prosecutor has no obligation to inquire and respond unless the witness makes some minimal showing, supported by specific factual averments. That showing may be based on the subject matter of the questions, the fact that the witness was required to furnish a voice exemplar, or unique telephone difficulties.

In determining whether a government denial of wiretapping is supported by sufficient investigation, the Court will consider the strength of the witness' showing that there may have been a wiretap, the likelihood that a particular unchecked source may have contributed to the investigation, and the range of the questions asked of the witness. The fact that law enforcement agents working directly on the case are unaware of a wiretap does not necessarily mean that one did not exist; the agents may be relying on information obtained from other agencies (perhaps more than once removed) that did come from a wiretap. However, prosecutors rarely are required to check with all seven of the federal agencies that customarily conduct electronic surveillance. Indeed, unless the witness' claim is supported by substantial indication of a probable wiretap, the courts are likely to permit a response that does not go beyond checking with the single agent in charge of the investigation.

§ 8.10 Grand Jury Testimony and the Privilege Against Self-Incrimination

(a) The Standard of Potential Incrimination. *Counselman v. Hitchcock,*[1] decided in 1892, put to rest any doubts as to whether the Fifth Amendment privilege against self-incrimination was available to a grand jury witness. The grand jury witness testifies pursuant to a subpoena so the requisite element of "compulsion" clearly is present. However, the Amendment states only that a person shall not be compelled to be a witness against himself "in a criminal case." But this language, the *Counselman* Court noted, refers to the eventual use of the testimony, not the nature of the proceeding in which testimony is compelled. The Fifth Amendment, it concluded, applies to a witness "in any proceeding" who is being compelled to give testimony that might be used against him in a subsequent criminal case.

Counselman furnished the subpoenaed party with what is undoubtedly his most significant safeguard in responding to a subpoena ad testificandum. Of course, the grand jury witness is not limited to the privilege against self-incrimination. He also may utilize any other testimonial privileges recognized in the particular jurisdiction. But it is the self-incrimination privilege that usually grants the witness his broadest range of privacy.

The Fifth Amendment privilege is available, of course, only where the compelled testimony causes a potential for incrimination. Although potential incrimination encompasses a great deal, it is not without limits. The threat of incrimination is limited only to criminal liability,[2] and that liability must relate to the witness himself, not others. Moreover, the threat must be "real and apprecia-

§ 8.10

1. 142 U.S. 547, 12 S.Ct. 195, 35 L.Ed. 1110 (1892).

2. Incrimination in what the Fifth Amendment describes as a "criminal case" extends to the determination of sentence as well as the assessment of guilt. See Estelle v. Smith, discussed in § 6.10(e). It also includes liability in a criminal forfeiture proceeding, see Boyd v. United States, discussed at §§ 8.7(a) and 8.12(a), or in a juvenile delinquency proceeding that is based on a criminal violation and permits potential institutional commitment, see In re Gault, discussed in § 6.10(e). It does not include the classification of an accused as a sexually dangerous person where that classification is made strictly for rehabilitative treatment purposes and thus is analogous to a traditional civil commitment though it looks in part to a propensity to commit a criminal act (e.g., sexual assault). See Allen v. Illinois, discussed at § 6.10(e). See also, Estelle v. Smith, supra (privilege does not encompass the determination of competency to stand trial); Baxter v. Palmigiano, discussed in § 6.10(e) (prison discipline not within protection of privilege).

ble," not "imaginary and unsubstantial." A witness' assertion of the privilege is not conclusive in this regard. As *Hoffman v. United States*[3] stressed, "it is for the court to say whether [the witness'] silence is justified, and to require him to answer 'if it clearly appears to the court that he is mistaken.'" *Hoffman* also indicated, however, that courts are to give the witness every benefit of the doubt in reviewing his assertion of the privilege. The Court there noted:

> This provision of the [Fifth] Amendment must be accorded liberal construction in favor of the right it was intended to secure. The privilege afforded not only extends to answers that would in themselves support a conviction * * * but likewise embraces those which would furnish a link in the chain of evidence needed to prosecute the claimant for a federal crime. * * * [T]his protection must be confined to instances where the witness has reasonable cause to apprehend danger from a direct answer. * * * However, if the witness, upon interposing his claim, were required to prove the hazard in the sense in which a claim is usually required to be established in court, he would be compelled to surrender the very protection which the privilege is designed to guarantee. To sustain the privilege, it need only be evident from the implications of the question, in the setting in which it is asked, that a responsive answer to the question or an explanation of why it cannot be answered might be dangerous because injurious disclosure could result.

Applying the *Hoffman* directive, it should be a rare case in which a claim of the privilege will be rejected by a court. Two leading decisions of the Supreme Court are illustrative. In *Hoffman* itself, the Court ruled that the district court had erred in holding the privilege inapplicable to questions concerning the witness' current occupation and his contacts with a person who was a fugitive witness. The lower court had held that there was "no real appreciable danger of incrimination," but the Supreme Court found that conclusion untenable. Since the lower court was aware that the grand jury was investigating racketeering, it should have recognized that questions concerning Hoffman's current occupation might require answers relating to violations of various gambling laws. It also should have recognized that the answers concerning Hoffman's contacts with the fugitive witness might relate to efforts to hide that witness. In *Malloy v. Hogan*,[4] the lower court was held to have erred in rejecting a self-incrimination claim by a witness who had pled guilty to a gambling charge and was now being asked about the circumstances surrounding his arrest and plea. The questions were obviously designed to determine the identity of his employer, and "if this person were still engaged in unlawful activity, disclosure of his identity might furnish a link in a chain of evidence sufficient to connect the [witness] with a more recent crime for which he still might be prosecuted."[5]

(b) Incrimination Under the Laws of Another Sovereign. For many years, American courts took the position that the privilege protected only against incrimination under the laws of the sovereign which was attempting to compel the incriminating testimony. Thus, if a witness appearing before a federal grand jury was granted immunity against federal prosecution, he could not refuse to testify on the ground that his answers might be incriminating under the laws of a state or a foreign nation. In *Murphy v. Waterfront Commission*,[6] the Supreme Court rejected this "separate sovereign" doctrine as applied to state and federal proceedings. Noting that the doctrine would allow a witness to

3. 341 U.S. 479, 71 S.Ct. 814, 95 L.Ed. 1118 (1951).

4. 378 U.S. 1, 84 S.Ct. 1489, 12 L.Ed.2d 653 (1964).

5. A different result would have followed if the questions were limited to the commission of the offense. Thus, Reina v. United States, 364 U.S. 507, 81 S.Ct. 260, 5 L.Ed.2d 249 (1960) notes: "The ordinary rule is that once a person is convicted of a crime, he no longer has the privilege against self-incrimination as he can no longer be incriminated by his testimony about the crime." However, if a person though convicted still has the opportunity for appellate review (and therefore a possible reversal and new trial), many courts hold that the privilege remains applicable as to questions concerning the offense. Where the individual has been pardoned or acquitted of the offense, the same standard applies as to a person whose conviction is final.

6. 378 U.S. 52, 84 S.Ct. 1594, 12 L.Ed.2d 678 (1964).

be "whipsawed into incriminating himself under both state and federal law," the Court concluded that the "policies and purposes" of the Fifth Amendment required that the privilege protect "a state witness against incrimination under federal as well as state law and a federal witness against incrimination under state as well as federal law."

Should *Murphy* be read as making the privilege available where testimony will be incriminating only in a foreign country? The *Murphy* opinion contains language suggesting that the separate sovereign doctrine has no stronger grounding as applied to prosecution by a different country than as applied to prosecution by a different jurisdiction within our federal system. On the other hand, *Murphy* was written within the context of the necessary reach of state and federal immunity grants. The federal government can grant immunity against state as well as federal prosecution, and state grants of immunity can be extended by federal courts to encompass federal prosecutions. Neither the federal government nor the states, however, have the authority to grant immunity against foreign prosecution.

In *Zicarelli v. New Jersey Investigation Commission,*[7] the Court suggested that it was an open issue as to whether a witness fully immunized under federal and state law could nevertheless plead the privilege because the state could not prevent "either prosecution or use of his testimony by a foreign sovereign." It also indicated that even if the privilege does apply to incrimination under foreign law, it may be used only when the witness would be in "real danger" of foreign prosecution, not simply relying upon a "remote and speculative possibility." Lower courts faced with self-incrimination claims based on potential foreign prosecution have commonly relied on this limitation to deny the claims without reaching the ultimate issue left open in *Zicarelli.* They have required the witness to make a substantial showing of likely foreign prosecution based upon both the applicability of foreign law and a demonstration of interest by foreign authorities in the enforcement of that law against a person in the witness' situation. Several courts have reasoned that the requirements of grand jury secrecy render the possibility that incriminating testimony will be "funneled to foreign officials" too "remote and speculative" to present the "real and substantial fear" required by *Zicarelli.*

(c) Compelling the Target to Appear. The self-incrimination privilege has long been held to prohibit the prosecution from forcing a defendant to appear as a witness at his own trial. Should the prosecutor similarly be prohibited from forcing the target of an investigation to appear before the grand jury, or is the Fifth Amendment satisfied by simply allowing the target-witness, like any other witness, to refuse to respond to individual questions where his answer might be incriminating? Several state courts have argued that the target of an investigation is, in effect, a "putative" or "de facto" defendant, and he therefore should be allowed to exercise his privilege in much the same manner as a "de jure defendant" at trial. They hold that, unless the target expressly waives his self-incrimination privilege, the prosecution cannot use the grand jury's subpoena authority to force him to appear. This protection presumably could be utilized by a subpoenaed target as a defense to a contempt charge for refusing to respond, but it most frequently comes into issue when the prosecution seeks to use against a defendant his earlier grand jury testimony that was given without an express waiver. The critical question for the court under this view of the privilege's protection therefore becomes whether the defendant was a mere witness or true target at the time he testified.[8]

7. 406 U.S. 472, 92 S.Ct. 1670, 32 L.Ed.2d 234 (1972).

8. In this setting, the issue posed is very much the same as that presented by prosecution use of the grand jury testimony of an "unwarned" witness in a jurisdiction that holds that the target may be compelled to appear (see discussion infra) but requires that the target be given appropriate warnings (see subsection (d) infra). Jurisdictions applying a prohibition against compelling the "putative defendant" to appear without an express waiver have experienced some difficulty in determining, in the context of a subsequent objection to the use of grand jury testimony, whether the witness fell within that category

Federal courts and most state courts have taken the position that the Fifth Amendment, as to all witnesses, presents only "an option of refusal and not a prohibition of inquiry." "The obligation to appear," the Supreme Court has noted, "is no different for a person who may himself be the subject of the grand jury inquiry." [9] The right of the defendant at trial to refrain from appearing as a witness is said to rest on considerations largely inapplicable to the grand jury. The defendant's right of silence grew out of the early common law rule on the incompetency of parties to testify, which had bearing only on the trial. It also rested in part on the fear that a defendant "forced in open court to refuse to answer questions" might be viewed by the jury as having something to hide. This concern has less significance in the grand jury setting; since that body looks only to the issue of probable cause, its proceedings need not be conducted "with the assiduous regard for the preservation of procedural safeguards which normally attends the ultimate trial of the issues."

Federal courts have also argued that the right to subpoena targets is inherent in the grand jury's combined investigative and shielding roles. Having an obligation to "run down every available clue," the grand jury cannot ignore the possibility that any one participant in a criminal enterprise may be willing to identify others. Having an obligation to "shield against arbitrary accusations," it has a right to be certain that the target's own testimony might not explain away the evidence against him. Some courts have also expressed concern that the establishment of a right not to appear based upon whether the prosecutor knew or should have known someone was a "target" would create a new source of tangential disputation.[10]

(d) Advice as to Rights. It generally is agreed that the Fifth Amendment does not demand that a non-target witness be advised of his privilege against self-incrimination. As to the target, however, there is a division of opinion. In the several jurisdictions in which the target cannot be compelled to appear without an express waiver, a notification of rights is an integral part of gaining such a waiver. In the vast majority of jurisdictions that do not recognize a target privilege not to appear, the courts have divided, with several of the more recent rulings holding that self-incrimination warnings are constitutionally

when he testified. It generally is agreed that a person already arrested on the charges under investigation falls within the category. Beyond that, some would prefer a subjectively oriented test (e.g., whether the prosecutor must have believed that an indictment would be sought against the witness), while others prefer a strictly objective test (e.g., whether the evidence known to the government established probable cause to believe the witness had committed a crime). New York, perhaps influenced by the difficulties posed in retrospective judicial identification of target witnesses, grants transactional immunity to all grand jury witnesses, subject only to the witness' right to waive that immunity. If the prosecution wishes to retain the possibility of bringing charges against a witness, it must obtain a written waiver from that witness (after giving complete warnings). See N.Y.—McKinney's Crim.P.Law §§ 190.40–190.45.

9. United States v. Dionisio, 410 U.S. 1, 93 S.Ct. 764, 35 L.Ed.2d 67 (1973). See also United States v. Washington, infra note 15.

10. See note 8 supra. Federal courts have indicated that the prosecution may not subpoena an indicted defendant for the purpose of asking him questions relating to the subject of the indictment. See United States v. Mandujano, infra note 11 (Brennan, J., concurring); United States v. Doss, 545 F.2d 548 (6th Cir.1976), on rehearing 563 F.2d 265 (1977). It is not clear, however, whether this prohibition is thought to rest on the Fifth Amendment or the rule against use of the grand jury for post-indictment discovery. See § 8.8(e).

Internal Justice Department guidelines provide that targets ordinarily should not be subpoenaed, but asked to appear voluntarily. Targets may be subpoenaed only with the approval of both the grand jury and federal prosecutor. In making that determination, consideration is to be given both to the importance of the target's anticipated testimony and the availability of other sources of information. If the subpoenaed target then gives advance notice of an intention to claim the privilege, he ordinarily should be excused from appearing. The grand jury and prosecutor can jointly insist upon appearance, however, where justified by consideration of the importance of the testimony and the possible inapplicability of the privilege. Also, while not constitutionally compelled to do so (see United States v. Washington, infra note 15), federal prosecutors are directed to advise witnesses who are known targets of their target status. A target is defined as "a person as to whom the prosecutor or grand jury has substantial evidence linking him to the commission of a crime, and who, in the judgment of the prosecutor is a putative defendant." United States Attorneys' Manual §§ 9–11.250, 9–11.254.

required. In *United States v. Mandujano,*[11] the Supreme Court left the issue open for future consideration. *Mandujano* held that even if warnings were required, the failure to give the warnings could not constitute a defense to a perjury charge based on the witness' false grand jury testimony.[12] Six justices, however, went on to speak to the need for warnings, with four suggesting that they were not required even as to the target.

Although the witness in *Mandujano* had been informed of both his privilege against self-incrimination and his right to consult with counsel, the district court had held that that warning was insufficient. It had reasoned that the witness was a "putative defendant" and therefore should have been given full *Miranda* warnings,[13] including notification of a right to appointed counsel. Chief Justice Burger's plurality opinion, speaking for four members of the Court, rejected the district court's reasoning. *Miranda,* he noted, applied only to "custodial interrogation," which clearly did not include questioning before the grand jury. The position of the subpoenaed witness could hardly be compared to that of the arrestee subjected to interrogation in the "hostile" and "isolated" setting of the police station. The appropriate analogy was to the questioning of a witness in an administrative or judicial hearing. As noted by Justice Frankfurter in *United States v. Monia,*[14] a witness in that setting "if * * * he desires the protection of the privilege, * * * must claim it or he will not be considered to have been 'compelled' within the meaning of the Amendment."

Chief Justice Burger added that, since Mandujano had been given self-incrimination warnings, there was no need to rule on whether such warnings were constitutionally required. Nevertheless, the Chief Justice's reliance on *Monia* would indicate that grand jury witnesses, whether targets or non-targets, are not entitled to any special notification of rights. Rather, they would seem to bear the obligation, like witnesses generally, to assert the privilege on their own initiative. Justice Brennan, joined by Justice Marshall, viewed the Chief Justice's reference to *Monia* in this way, and responded that the plurality had read the privilege too narrowly. The *Monia* principle, he argued, rests on the assumption that the government ordinarily had no grounds for assuming that its compulsory processes are eliciting incriminating information. However, where the prosecutor is questioning a target witness, he is "acutely aware of the potentially incriminating nature of the disclosures sought." This knowledge, Justice Brennan reasoned, carried with it an obligation to advise the witness of his rights so as to ensure that any waiver of the privilege was "intelligent and intentional."

Justice Brennan's opinion in *Mandujano* did not stop with requiring warnings as to the privilege alone. In his view, the Fifth Amendment also required the prosecution to inform the target-witness that "he was currently subject to possible criminal prosecution for the commission of a stated crime." In *United States v. Washington,*[15] the Court rejected (over Justice Brennan's dissent) any suggestion that the Fifth Amendment required some form of "target" warning. The witness there had been given full *Miranda*-type warnings, but had not been told that he might be indicted in connection with his possession of a stolen motorcycle. The Court initially noted that previous discussions with the police and prosecutor had given the witness ample notice that he was a suspect in the motorcycle theft, but it then added that such awareness was, in any event, "largely irrelevant." A failure to give a potential defendant

11. 425 U.S. 564, 96 S.Ct. 1768, 48 L.Ed.2d 212 (1976).

12. The Court followed a long line of cases holding that "the Fifth Amendment privilege against compulsory self-incrimination provides no protection for the commission of perjury." See Id. (Stewart, J., concurring). In United States v. Wong, 431 U.S. 174, 97 S.Ct. 1823, 52 L.Ed.2d 231 (1977), the same principle was applied to uphold a perjury conviction of a witness who claimed that, due to language difficulties, she had misunderstood the self-incrimination warnings and had therefore testified under compulsion.

13. See § 6.8.

14. 317 U.S. 424, 63 S.Ct. 409, 87 L.Ed. 376 (1943) (Frankfurter, J., dissenting).

15. 431 U.S. 181, 97 S.Ct. 1814, 52 L.Ed.2d 238 (1977).

a target warning simply did not put the witness at a "constitutional disadvantage." His status as a target "neither enlarg[ed] nor diminish[ed]" the scope of his constitutional protection. He "knew better than anyone else" whether his answers would be incriminating, and he also knew that anything he did say, after failing to exercise the privilege, could be used against him. The "constitutional guarantee," the Court noted, ensures "only that the witness be not *compelled* to give self-incriminating testimony."

Although the Court in *Washington* again left open the constitutional necessity of providing self-incrimination warnings to target witnesses,[16] the warnings are now used in almost all jurisdictions. In addition to the various states in which courts have held the warnings to be constitutionally required, roughly a dozen others have added statutory requirements. In most other jurisdictions, prosecutors give warnings to targets as a matter of local practice. Indeed, in a substantial number of jurisdictions, warnings are given to all witnesses, whether target or not. Several jurisdictions impose such a requirement as a matter of state law, while prosecutors in others simply find it easier to attach a notification of rights to all subpoenas than to attempt to distinguish between targets and non-targets. The Justice Department has been following such a practice for several years. Opponents of that practice express concern that: (1) "improvidently given warnings" may unduly frighten the non-target witness and deter him from testifying freely; (2) warnings may lead the non-target witness to obtain counsel, causing him an unnecessary expense; and (3) giving non-target witnesses warnings would be inconsistent with the treatment of trial witnesses, who are not given such warnings. In the end, administrative convenience and the favorable experience in the federal system is likely to outweigh these concerns.

(e) **Waiver.** Assuming the witness receives those warnings, if any, that are constitutionally required, the privilege may be relinquished by a witness without an express statement of waiver. When the witness answers the question, his waiver is automatically assumed. Indeed, a witness may by providing certain incriminating information relinquish his right to raise the privilege with respect to further incriminating information. *Rogers v. United States*[17] is the leading case on such "testimonial waiver." The witness there testified before a grand jury that, as treasurer of the Communist Party of Denver, she had been in possession of party records, but had subsequently delivered those records to another person. She refused, however, to identify the recipient of the records, asserting that would be incriminating. A divided Supreme Court affirmed her contempt conviction, holding the privilege inapplicable. The Court noted that Rogers had already incriminated herself by admitting her party membership and past possession of the records; disclosure of her "acquaintanceship with her successor present[ed] no more than a 'mere imaginary possibility' of increasing the danger of prosecution." A witness would not be allowed to disclose a basic incriminating fact and then claim the privilege as to "details." To uphold such a claim of the privilege would "open the way to distortion of facts by permitting a witness to select any stopping point in her testimony."

Although *Rogers* often is described as posing great danger for the witness who answers even seemingly "innocuous questions," the decision actually is fairly limited. Courts have held, for example, that where a witness' initial admission related to only one element of an offense, that did not constitute a waiver as to questions that might require him to admit other elements of the offense. The fact that the second question asks for further detail as to the same event does not in itself establish that the privilege is not available. Indeed,

16. See also Minnesota v. Murphy, discussed at § 6.6, note 16, where the Court, in holding *Miranda* inapplicable to the interrogation there, noted that it "subjected Murphy to less intimidating pressure than is imposed on grand jury witnesses, who are sworn to tell the truth and placed in a setting conducive to truthtelling," but "we have never held that [*Miranda* warnings] must be given to grand jury witnesses."

17. 340 U.S. 367, 71 S.Ct. 438, 95 L.Ed. 344 (1951).

most of the reported cases finding waiver have involved, as did *Rogers*, a refusal to "name others" in a setting in which it appeared likely that the witness was concerned about incriminating those persons rather than himself.

As with other constitutional rights, a waiver is acceptable only if voluntary. In the grand jury setting, as contrasted to in-custody police interrogation, the setting itself does not inherently exert pressures that might render the waiver involuntary. However, the waiver still may be rendered involuntary by unconstitutional burdens placed on the exercise of the privilege. Thus, in *Garrity v. New Jersey*,[18] where police officers were warned that they would be removed from office if they did not waive their privilege and testify as to the fixing of traffic tickets, the Court held that their waivers were coerced and their testimony could not be used against them in subsequent criminal proceedings.[19] If the grand jury witness should voluntarily waive the privilege, the generally accepted rule is that he may still exercise the privilege as an accused in a subsequent criminal prosecution.[20] If the witness should exercise the privilege before the grand jury and then decide to testify in his subsequent prosecution, *Grunewald v. United States*[21] holds that the earlier exercise of the privilege does not present such inconsistency with testifying at trial as to allow its use to impeach that testimony.[22]

§ 8.11 Immunity and Compelled Testimony

(a) Constitutionality. The use of immunity grants to preclude reliance upon the self-incrimination privilege predates the adoption of the Constitution. The English adopted an immunity procedure, known as providing "indemnity" against prosecution, soon after the privilege against compulsory self-incrimination became firmly established, and a similar practice was followed in the colonies. The first federal immunity act was not adopted until 1857, however, and the first Supreme Court ruling upholding immunity grants did not come until 1896, when *Brown v. Walker* was decided.[1] In that case, a sharply divided Court concluded that the immunity-grant procedure was consistent with the history and purpose of the Fifth Amendment privilege. The majority stressed that the Fifth Amendment could not be "construed literally as authorizing the witness to refuse to disclose any fact which might tend to incriminate, disgrace, or expose him to unfavorable comments." The history of the Amendment clearly indicated that its object was only to "secure the witness against criminal prosecution." Thus, the self-incrimination privilege had been held inapplicable where the witness' compelled testimony would relate only to an offense as to which he had been pardoned or as to which the statute of limitations had run. So too, the privilege had been held not to apply where the witness' response might tend to "disgrace him or bring him into disrepute" but would furnish no information relating to a criminal offense. Such rulings implicitly sustained the constitutionality of the immunity procedure. Since the immunity grant removed the only danger against which the privilege protected the witness, the witness

18. 385 U.S. 493, 87 S.Ct. 616, 17 L.Ed.2d 562 (1967).

19. So too, the Court has held that the state imposes an unconstitutional burden on the exercise of the privilege when it attaches administrative sanctions to a person's exercise or the privilege, even though that exercise precluded an inquiry into the appropriateness of otherwise imposing those sanctions. See e.g., Spevack v. Klein, 385 U.S. 511, 87 S.Ct. 625, 17 L.Ed.2d 574 (1967) (attorney could not be disbarred because he refused, in reliance on the privilege, to produce documents during an investigation into his alleged misconduct).

20. Waiver of the privilege applies only to the particular proceeding, and the dominant view is that the grand jury investigation and the criminal prosecution are separate proceedings (although all courts do not accept that position). The grand jury investigation is an ongoing proceeding, so waiver at one appearance bars exercise of the privilege in a later appearance.

21. 353 U.S. 391, 77 S.Ct. 963, 1 L.Ed.2d 931 (1957).

22. Although noting that this "evidentiary matter" had "grave constitutional overtones," the Court's ruling was based upon its supervisory power over the administration of federal criminal justice. Compare Doyle v. Ohio, § 9.6 at note 11 (barring impeachment use of the exercise of *Miranda* rights on constitutional grounds).

§ 8.11

1. 161 U.S. 591, 16 S.Ct. 644, 40 L.Ed. 819 (1896).

could no longer claim that he was being compelled to incriminate himself.

Subsequent Supreme Court decisions reaffirmed the *Brown* analysis, although the Court eventually accepted the contention of the *Brown* dissenters that an immunity grant must provide protection against both state and federal prosecution. Perhaps the most significant challenge to *Brown* came in *Ullman v. United States.*[2] Ullman, though granted immunity from prosecution, had refused to testify before a grand jury investigating alleged spying activities of certain members of the Communist Party. He contended that his case differed from *Brown* because of the wide range of disabilities that would be suffered by one who acknowledged membership in the Communist party, such as "loss of job, expulsion from labor unions, state registration and investigation statutes, passport eligibility, and general public opprobrium." A function of the privilege, he argued, was to protect political and religious deviants, and immunity from prosecution could not substitute for that protection. The Supreme Court, over the vigorous dissent of Justice Douglas (joined by Justice Black), rejected Ullman's constitutional claim. The majority reasoned that *Brown* had correctly defined the total purpose of the privilege, and that purpose was fully met by affording the witness immunity from prosecution. Indeed, since *Brown,* the practice of displacing the right to refuse to testify with an immunity grant had become "part of our constitutional fabric."

(b) Scope of the Immunity. In *Counselman v. Hitchcock,*[3] decided prior to *Brown,* the Court struck down a federal immunity statute that granted the witness protection only against receiving his immunized testimony in evidence in a subsequent prosecution. The Court stressed that there was no protection against derivative use of the witness' testimony. Thus, the statute "could not, and would not, prevent the use of his testimony to search out other testimony to be used in evidence against him." At the conclusion of its opinion, the Court spoke in terms of even broader protection than prohibiting derivative use. "To be valid," it noted, an immunity grant "must afford absolute immunity against future prosecution for the offense to which the question relates." This statement was taken as indicating that a valid immunity grant must absolutely bar prosecution for any transaction noted in the witness' testimony. Accordingly, Congress adopted a new immunity statute providing for such "transactional immunity." That statute provided that a witness directed to testify or produce documentary evidence pursuant to an immunity order could not be prosecuted "for or on account of any transaction, matter, or thing concerning which he may testify or produce evidence." The constitutionality of this provision was upheld in *Brown v. Walker,* and subsequent state and federal immunity statutes were largely patterned upon the *Brown* statute.

Later decisions—and the language of the later statutes—recognized two limitations in transactional immunity. The witness may still be prosecuted for perjury committed in his immunized testimony. Similarly, the immunity does not extend to a transaction noted in an answer totally unresponsive to the question asked. Thus, the witness cannot gain immunity from prosecution for all previous criminal acts by simply including a reference to those acts in his testimony without regard to the subject on which he was asked to testify.

In *Murphy v. Waterfront Commission,*[4] the Court first upheld immunity that was not as broad in scope as the traditional transactional immunity. *Murphy,* as previously discussed,[5] held that the self-incrimination privilege extended to possible incrimination under both federal and state law. Accordingly, to be constitutionally acceptable, the immunity granted to a witness had to provide adequate protection against both federal and state prosecutions. If that protection had to encompass transactional immunity, the state immunity

2. 350 U.S. 422, 76 S.Ct. 497, 100 L.Ed. 511 (1956).

3. 142 U.S. 547, 12 S.Ct. 195, 35 L.Ed. 1110 (1892).

4. 378 U.S. 52, 84 S.Ct. 1594, 12 L.Ed.2d 678 (1964).

5. See § 8.9(b).

provisions would necessarily fail. Congress could use its legislative authority to preempt state prosecutions, but the states lacked authority to prohibit federal prosecutions. The Court held, however, that the immunity grant need not absolutely bar prosecution in the other jurisdiction. It was sufficient that the witness was guaranteed that neither his testimony nor any fruits derived from that testimony would be used against him in any criminal prosecution. The Court, to accommodate "the interests of State and Federal Governments in investigating and prosecuting crime," would exercise its supervisory power to prohibit the federal government from using in federal courts state immunized testimony or the fruits thereof.

Following *Murphy,* Congress adopted a new immunity provision for federal witnesses, replacing transactional immunity with a prohibition against use and derivative use as to both federal and state prosecutions. The statute provided that "no testimony or other information compelled under the [immunity] order (or any information directly or indirectly derived from such testimony or other information) may be used against the witness in any criminal case, except a prosecution for perjury, giving a false statement, or otherwise failing to comply with the order."[6] In *Kastigar v. United States,*[7] a divided Court upheld the new federal provision. The "broad language in *Counselman,*" which suggested the need for transactional immunity, was discounted as inconsistent with the "conceptual basis" of the *Counselman* ruling. The crucial question, as *Counselman* noted, was whether the immunity granted was "coextensive with the scope of the privilege against self-incrimination." Both the immunity upheld in *Murphy* and the traditional Fifth Amendment remedy of excluding compelled statements and their fruits (as, for example, in the coerced confession cases) indicated that the privilege did not require an absolute bar against prosecution. A prohibition against use and derivative use satisfied the privilege by placing the witness "in substantially the same position as if * * * [he] had claimed his privilege."

The *Kastigar* majority rejected the argument, relied upon by the dissenters, that the bar against derivative use could not be enforced so effectively as to ensure that the witness really was placed in the same position as if he had not testified. The statute's "total prohibition on use," it noted, "provides a comprehensive safeguard, barring the use of compelled testimony as an 'investigatory lead,' and also barring the use of any evidence obtained by focusing investigation on a witness as a result of his compelled disclosures." Appropriate procedures for "taint hearings" would ensure that this prohibition was made effective. Once a defendant demonstrates that he previously testified under a grant of immunity, the prosecution must carry "the burden of showing that [its] evidence is not tainted by establishing that [it] had an independent, legitimate source for the disputed evidence." This requirement, the Court noted, would provide the immunized witness with "protection commensurate with that resulting from invoking the privilege itself."

In a companion case to *Kastigar, Zicarelli v. New Jersey,*[8] the Court upheld a state immunity statute providing for use/derivative-use immunity. Following *Zicarelli,* a substantial number of states moved from transactional to use/derivative-use immunity. However, various groups, including the American Bar Association and the Commissioners on Uniform State Laws, urged retention of transactional immunity, and a majority of the states continue to provide the broader immunity. The debate between the proponents of the two types of immunity has tended to focus on three issues—the adequacy of taint hearings in preventing derivative use of immunized testimony, the comparative effectiveness of the two types of immunity in achieving witness cooperation, and the practical significance of the prosecutor's ability to bring a subsequent prosecution under use/derivative-use immunity.

6. 18 U.S.C.A. § 6002.

7. 406 U.S. 441, 92 S.Ct. 1653, 32 L.Ed.2d 212 (1972).

8. 406 U.S. 472, 92 S.Ct. 1670, 32 L.Ed.2d 234 (1972).

With respect to taint hearings, proponents of transactional immunity contend that such hearings will not effectuate the goal of granting to the immunized witness the same protection against criminal prosecution that he would have had if allowed to refuse to testify on the basis of his self-incrimination privilege. They argue that the procedural safeguards required under *Kastigar* will not prevent: (1) a prosecutor acting in bad faith from "working backwards" from what he learns through immunized testimony to find a source that he will convincingly claim to be "independent"; (2) a prosecutor either purposefully or inadvertently relying on information derived from immunized testimony in determining trial strategy in a subsequent prosecution;[9] and (3) a prosecutor "playing off" one accomplice against the other by using the immunized testimony of each as an independent source against the other (sometimes described as the "ping-pong" use of immunity). Proponents of use/derivative-use immunity respond that: (1) the prosecutor's heavy burden of proof in establishing a truly independent source provides an adequate safeguard against prosecutors seeking to misrepresent their sources; (2) nonevidentiary use can be avoided by having any subsequent prosecution directed by a prosecutor who is not familiar with the immunized testimony;[10] and (3) the ping-pong use of immunity is no more than a "hypothetical possibility" since it would be almost impossible for the prosecutor to establish the accomplice's testimony as an independent source where the defendant gave overlapping immunized testimony himself.

With respect to the effectiveness of the immunity in gaining truthful and complete testimony from a recalcitrant witness, each side claims advantages for the type of immunity it favors. Proponents of transactional immunity claim that witnesses given use/derivative-use immunity lack confidence that the prosecutor will be prevented from making use of their testimony in any subsequent prosecution. Accordingly, it is argued, if a witness believes there is a significant possibility of subsequent prosecution, he may be willing to bear the sanctions for refusing to testify rather than run the risk of being subject to greater penalties as a result of a prosecution he aided. If the likelihood of subsequent prosecution appears slight, the witness still is likely to be cautious and therefore will offer the least amount of information that may be provided without incurring a contempt charge for evasive answers. Proponents of use/derivative-use immunity take quite a different view of the recalcitrant witness' likely response. Under transactional immunity, they argue, the witness is encouraged to give incomplete and shallow testimony. He will say no more than he has to since a single admission gains him full immunity from prosecution. On the other hand, they see use/derivative-use immunity as encouraging the witness to provide as much detail as possible. The

9. *Kastigar* did not specifically address the issue of whether use/derivative-use immunity prohibits prosecutorial consideration of immunized testimony in developing trial strategy unrelated to the production of evidence through that testimony. Immunized testimony might be used in this fashion in determining whether the prosecution's independently acquired evidence justifies an indictment in light of the target's immunized exculpatory statements, in determining the best direction to be taken in cross-examining the defendant based on independently acquired testimony, or in preparing prosecution witnesses against likely lines of defense cross-examination. Assuming that such uses are prohibited, the question then arises as to whether the prosecution must bear a burden of negating such use in much the same manner as it bears the burden of showing that its evidence is not tainted. Lower courts have expressed disagreement on both questions.

10. The easiest way for a prosecutor's office to ensure that no use is made of immunized testimony is through a "Chinese Wall" arrangement among the different prosecutors, as recommended in the United States Attorneys' Manual, § 1–11.400. The Justice Department Guidelines further provide that, if there is a likelihood that "the public interest may warrant a future prosecution of the witness on the basis of independent evidence, the attorney shall: (1) before the witness has testified or provided other information, prepare for the case file a signed and dated memorandum summarizing the evidence then known to exist concerning the witness, and designating its sources and date of receipt; (2) ensure that all testimony given, or information provided, by the witness be recorded verbatim and that the recording or reporter's notes, together with any transcript thereof, be maintained in a secure location and that access thereto be documented; and (3) maintain a record of the nature, source, and date of receipt of evidence concerning the witness's past criminal conduct that becomes available after he has testified or provided other information." United States Attorneys' Manual § 1–11.330.

witness will recognize, they argue, that complete testimony often makes it more difficult for the government to establish that no use was made of that testimony in any subsequent prosecution.

The final source of disagreement between supporters of the two types of immunity relates to the importance of the subsequent prosecutions that have been gained by granting use/derivative-use immunity rather than transactional immunity. Proponents of transactional immunity argue that "the small number" of successful prosecutions against witnesses previously granted use/derivative-use immunity indicates that the cost differential between transactional and use/derivative-use immunity is inconsequential. Proponents of use/derivative-use immunity acknowledge that the prosecutions of immunized witnesses can be characterized as rare occurrences in the federal system and at least as an infrequent occurrence in the states. They contend, however, that there are substantial reasons for such prosecutions, and the interests of justice would suffer if the witnesses involved, though small in number, were given the "gratuity of absolute immunity." There is no reason, they note, to run the "risk that a witness, who is subsequently and independently found to be more deserving of prosecution than originally thought, will be absolutely immune from a prosecution despite the existence of such independent evidence." Subsequent prosecution is also important, they argue, where the prosecutor from the outset has sufficient evidence to prosecute and would ordinarily prosecute, convict, and then grant immunity, but lacks the time to do so because the witness-defendant's testimony is needed immediately in investigating other participants. Finally, supporters of use/derivative-use immunity contend that the absence of an absolute protection against prosecution has value in making the immunized witness' testimony more credible to the jury.

(c) Immunity Procedures. In most jurisdictions, the prosecutor may not make a statutory grant of immunity on his own authority, but must obtain a court order. Ordinarily, however, the scope of judicial review of an immunity application is quite limited. Under the federal immunity statute, for example, the court is directed to issue the immunity order provided the prosecutor has followed specified procedural requirements. Those requirements are: (1) that the request for an immunity order be approved by specified higher-level Justice Department officials; and (2) that the U.S. Attorney making the request state that, "in his judgment," (i) the "testimony or other information * * * [sought from the witness] may be necessary to the public interest," and (ii) the witness "has refused or is likely to refuse to testify or provide other information on the basis of his privilege against self-incrimination." [11] If the U.S. Attorney has complied with these requirements, the court may not refuse to grant the order on the ground, for example, that it disagrees with the prosecutor's conclusion that the grant may be necessary to the public interest. While the witness is given an opportunity to be heard, only a challenge to the procedural regularity of the application will be considered.

Once the immunity order is granted, the witness must either testify or face contempt sanctions, unless he has some legal justification (e.g., the attorney-client privilege) for refusing to respond. The witness may not refuse to testify because his answers will subject him to substantial civil liability. Neither may he refuse to testify because he is fearful of physical or economic retaliation by associates or others.

(d) Informal Grants of Immunity. Where the witness is willing to testify in exchange for immunity, the prosecutor may prefer to provide immunity through an agreement (whereby the witness agrees to testify in exchange for a promise of non-prosecution) rather than an immunity grant. For the prosecutor, non-statutory immunity offers primarily two advantages. First, it bypasses the statutory procedure for obtaining an immunity order which may be cumbersome or pose a

11. 18 U.S.C.A. § 6003.

risk to grand jury secrecy. Second, it permits the prosecutor to tailor the scope of the immunity to the needs of the case. Thus, a prosecutor in a jurisdiction with a use/derivative-use statute may believe that an informal grant of transactional immunity will be more effective in gaining witness cooperation. In other situations, the immunity provided by statute may be more than the witness requires or the prosecutor is willing to give; an informal grant may be limited to barring prosecution only as to certain aspects of the transaction. For the witness, informal immunity has an advantage primarily where it will permit him to obtain broader protection than would otherwise be available.

Several courts have held that the prosecutor lacks authority to grant informal immunity, particularly where the informal grant bypasses legislative limitations. Where the witness has given testimony pursuant to an informal grant, these courts would not allow subsequent use of that testimony against him, as it is involuntary under traditional standards applied to confessions induced by promises, but some would deny the witness the benefit of any broader immunity promised by the prosecutor. Others have suggested, however, that even though the prosecutor may lack the authority to make the grant, a promise of non-prosecution will be enforced, upon principles of equity, where the witness fulfilled his promise to testify. Still other courts enforce the promise of non-prosecution as a lawful exercise of prosecutorial discretion, although they will not compel a recalcitrant witness to testify on the basis of such a promise. They note that the arrangement with the witness must be viewed simply as a lawful "promise not to prosecute," not as a form of "hip pocket immunity" that either replaces or bypasses statutory immunity.

§ 8.12 Self-Incrimination and The Subpoena Duces Tecum: Basic Principles

(a) *Boyd v. United States.* Although a subpoena duces tecum may be used to compel production of various types of physical evidence, it is most frequently used, at least in the grand jury setting, to require the production of documents. *Boyd v. United States,*[1] decided in 1886, was the first Supreme Court case to consider the applicability of the self-incrimination privilege to court ordered production of documents. Although *Boyd* involved a different form of court order,[2] the reasoning of the Court clearly encompassed the subpoena duces tecum. Under the analysis adopted in *Boyd,* a subpoena requiring the production of a document was subject to challenge under both the Fourth Amendment and self-incrimination clause of the Fifth Amendment. As noted in § 8.7(a), *Boyd*'s Fourth Amendment analysis was soon thereafter modified so as to limit the Fourth Amendment challenge to subpoenas that were overly broad in the documents requested. *Boyd*'s Fifth Amendment analysis survived for a considerably longer period and provided a far more significant barrier to the compelled production of documents. Indeed, *Boyd* formulated a theory of Fifth Amendment protection that, at one point, was thought to extend beyond documents to bar the forced production of other forms of property as well.

Under current precedent, very little, if anything, remains of *Boyd*'s Fifth Amendment analysis. Yet the *Boyd* analysis remains a universally accepted starting point for understanding the many strands of current Fifth Amendment doctrine applicable to the subpoena duces tecum. For much of the current doctrine was developed in the process of first limiting and then replacing the *Boyd* analysis. Moreover, there still remains a question, at least for some jurisdictions, as to whether some elements of the *Boyd* analysis might not have current vitality in limited situations.

Boyd upheld a self-incrimination challenge to a court order requiring an importing firm organized as a partnership to produce the invoice it had received for items allegedly imported illegally. Quoting from Lord Cam-

§ 8.12

1. 116 U.S. 616, 6 S.Ct. 524, 29 L.Ed. 746 (1886).

2. See the discussion of *Boyd* at § 8.7(a).

den's opinion in *Entick v. Carrington,*[3] the *Boyd* opinion noted that papers are an owner's "dearest property," respected by a well-established common law prohibition against forcing such evidence "out of the owner's custody by process." Allowing the state to compel production of private books and papers, even where necessary to convict for the most serious crime, would be "abhorrent to the instincts" of an American or Englishman and "contrary to the principles of a free government." Just as the Fifth Amendment prohibited "compulsory discovery by extorting the party's oath," it also prohibited discovery by "compelling the production of his private books and papers." The documentary production order was simply another form of "forcible and compulsory extortion of a man's own testimony."

Boyd relied on what has been described as a "property oriented" view of the Fourth and Fifth Amendments, built upon the owner's right of privacy in the control of his lawfully held possessions. It recognized a special Fifth Amendment interest in the privacy of documents, viewing the forced production of their contents as equivalent to requiring a subpoenaed party to reveal that content through his testimony. Although the Court spoke of "private books and papers," it obviously was not referring only to confidential documents relating to personal or private matters. The document at issue in *Boyd* was a business record that had not been prepared by the partners themselves but by the shipper of the item alleged to have been illegally imported.

Insofar as it relied upon the self-incrimination privilege, the *Boyd* ruling might well be read as limited to documents. As documents contain words, the compelled disclosure of their content could be seen as more closely analogous to the compelling of testimonial utterances than compelling the disclosure of other forms of property possessed by the subpoenaed party. Yet, the key to the Court's analysis appeared to be the invasion through forced production of the individual's privacy interest in his possession of property in which the public had no entitlement (such entitlement existing, the Court noted, only where a third-party had a superior right, as with stolen property, or the state had a superior interest, as with records required to be kept by law). Although the invasion might be more serious as to the individual's "dearest property" (i.e., his papers), the same principle would appear to forbid the forced production of any form of personally held property where there was no such public entitlement and the property could be used as incriminating evidence. Thus, the Supreme Court later spoke of the self-incrimination privilege as protecting the individual "from any disclosure, in the form of oral testimony, documents, or *chattels,* sought by legal process against him as a witness."[4]

Starting with *Hale v. Henkel,*[5] decided only two decades after *Boyd,* the Court gradually developed a series of doctrines that chipped away at the broad implications of *Boyd*'s property-rights/privacy analysis of Fifth Amendment protection. Finally, in *Fisher v. United States,*[6] decided close to a century after *Boyd,* the Court majority was forced to conclude that all that remained of *Boyd* was a "prohibition against forcing the production of private papers" that had "long been a rule searching for a rationale." The subsections that follow discuss the most significant of the doctrinal developments that restricted the privacy analysis of *Boyd,* and the quite different act-of-production analysis that was adopted in *Fisher.* Taken together, the rulings in those cases provided the basic legal principles currently governing the application of the privilege against self-incrimination to a subpoena duces tecum. The possibility that some remnant of the *Boyd* analysis remains is discussed in the last subsection. Because of its special significance and complexity, the act-of-production doctrine is given further at-

3. 19 Howell St.Tr. 1029 (1765) (awarding damages in trespass for a search and seizure of private papers).

4. United States v. White, infra note 11 (emphasis added).

5. Discussed infra at note 7.

6. Discussed infra in subsection (f).

tention in § 8.13, which discusses a variety of problems presented in applying that doctrine.

(b) The Entity Exception. *Hale v. Henkel*[7] not only reconstructed *Boyd*'s Fourth Amendment analysis,[8] but also added a major exception to the application of its Fifth Amendment analysis. *Hale* held that the self-incrimination privilege was not available to a corporation and therefore *Boyd* did not bar a grand jury subpoena duces tecum requiring production of corporate records. The Court's reasoning stressed the different status of the individual and the corporation. The individual, it noted, "owes no duty to the State * * * to divulge his business, or to open his doors to an investigation, so far as it may tend to incriminate him." The corporation, in contrast, "is a creature of the State," and exercises its franchise subject to the "reserved right" of the State to compel its assistance in ensuring that it has not "exceeded its powers." Although here a federal grand jury was investigating activities of a corporation created under state law, the federal government has the same right to ascertain that a corporation complied with its laws as the State would have with respect to the corporation's abuse of the privileges granted to it under state law.

The Court in *Hale* took special note of the enforcement needs of the government in compelling the production of corporate records; if such production were precluded by a self-incrimination claim, "it would result in a failure of a large number of cases where the illegal combination was determinable only upon such papers." In light of this concern, it was not surprising that, in *Wilson v. United States,*[9] the Court rejected the claim of a corporate officer possessing subpoenaed corporate records that he could refuse to produce those records because they would personally incriminate him. The State's "reserved power of visitation," the Court noted, "would seriously be embarrassed, if not wholly defeated in its effective exercise, if guilty officers could refuse inspection of the records and papers of the corporation." As the records were those of the corporation, not personal records, and were held "subject to the corporate duty," the official could "assert no personal right * * * against any demand of the government which the corporation was bound to recognize." The subpoena in *Wilson* was directed to the corporation, but *Drier v. United States*[10] held that the result was the same where the subpoena was directed to a specific individual in his capacity as corporate custodian.

In *United States v. White,*[11] the Court extended the *Hale* exception to other entities. *White* held that the president of an unincorporated labor union could not invoke his personal privilege to a subpoena demanding union records. Characterizing the Court's previous reliance on the State's visitorial power as "merely a convenient vehicle for justification of governmental investigation of corporate books and records," the *White* Court concluded that the exception recognized in *Hale* was derived from the inappropriateness of affording the privilege to an impersonal collective entity, whether or not that entity took the corporate form. The privilege against self-incrimination, the Court noted, "was essentially a personal [privilege], applying only to natural individuals," as evidenced by its underlying functions. The privilege grew out of "the high sentiment and regard of our jurisprudence for conducting criminal trials and investigatory proceedings upon a plane of dignity, humanity, and impartiality." It was "designed to prevent the use of legal process to force from the lips of the accused the evidence necessary to convict him or force him to produce and authenticate any personal documents that might incriminate him," and "thereby avoided * * * physical torture and other less violent but equally reprehensible modes of compelling the production of incriminating evidence." These concerns did not apply to the entity, which lacked the qualities of human personality and therefore could not

7. 201 U.S. 43, 26 S.Ct. 370, 50 L.Ed. 652 (1906).

8. See § 8.7(a).

9. 221 U.S. 361, 31 S.Ct. 538, 55 L.Ed. 771 (1911).

10. 221 U.S. 394, 31 S.Ct. 550, 55 L.Ed. 784 (1911).

11. 322 U.S. 694, 64 S.Ct. 1248, 88 L.Ed. 1542 (1944).

suffer the "immediate and potential evils of compulsory self-disclosure."

Just as *Hale* and *Wilson* noted how application of the privilege to corporate records would seriously undermine the State's exercise of its visitorial powers, the Court in *White* spoke to regulatory considerations "underlying the restriction of this constitutional privilege to natural individuals acting in their own private capacity." Justice Murphy's opinion noted:

> The scope and nature of the economic activities of incorporated and unincorporated organizations and their representatives demand that the constitutional power of the federal and state governments to regulate those activities be correspondingly effective. The greater portion of evidence of wrongdoing by an organization or its representatives is usually to be found in the official records and documents of that organization. Were the cloak of the privilege to be thrown around these impersonal records and documents, effective enforcement of many federal and state laws would be impossible. The framers of the constitutional guarantee against compulsory self-disclosure, who were interested primarily in protecting individual civil liberties, cannot be said to have intended the privilege to be available to protect economic or other interests of such organizations so as to nullify appropriate governmental regulations.

The *White* opinion characterized the labor union as an organization with "a character so impersonal in the scope of its membership and activities that it cannot be said to embody or represent the priority private or personal interests of its constituents, but rather to embody their common or group interests only." In *Bellis v. United States,*[12] however, the Court concluded that the entity exception remained applicable even though the entity embodied personal as well as group interests. The functional key was that the organization "be recognized as an independent entity apart from its individual members." Thus, a small law firm, organized as a partnership, was an entity for this purpose even though it "embodie[d] little more than the personal legal practice of the individual partners." The partnership was not an "informal association or a temporary arrangement for the undertaking of a few projects of short-lived duration," but a "formal institutional arrangement organized for the continuing conduct of the firm's legal practice." State law, through the Uniform Partnership Act, imposed a "certain organizational structure"; the firm maintained a bank account in the partnership name; it had employees who worked for the firm as such; and, the firm "held itself out to third parties as an entity with an independent institutional identity."[13]

The entity-exception cases did not directly question *Boyd,* apart from the recognition there of a self-incrimination claim as to a partnership document. As the Court later noted, "[i]t would appear that under [*Bellis*], the precise claim sustained in *Boyd* would now be rejected for reasons not there considered."[14] Yet, there were aspects of the Court's reasoning in establishing the entity exception that raised questions as to *Boyd* 's analysis of the privilege even as applied to the individual. The entity cases stressed the state's need to obtain documents in the exercise of its regulatory authority over business activities traditionally conducted by entities. Arguably, that concern was taken into account only because the historical starting point was a privilege that had been designed to protect the "natural individual." Yet, the state's regulatory interest was equally at stake when the privilege was utilized to bar a

12. 417 U.S. 85, 94 S.Ct. 2179, 40 L.Ed.2d 678 (1974).

13. *Bellis* noted that "this might be a different case if it involved a small family partnership, or * * * if there were some other pre-existing relationship of confidentiality among the partners." Lower courts have viewed any such exceptions as quite narrow. Indeed, even where there is no formal partnership agreement, a structured business organization may fall within the entity exception. Thus, the entity exception was held to apply to persons who owned commercial property as tenants in common, had a separate bank account for business activities relating that to that property, and utilized an assumed name in conducting such business. On the other hand, a husband-wife professional service firm, though organized as a partnership under the Uniform Partnership Act, was held not to constitute an entity where it had no employees and no office outside the couple's home. In re Grand Jury Subpoena, 605 F.Supp. 174 (E.D.N.Y.1985).

14. Fisher v. United States, infra note 24.

subpoena directing the production of business records of a sole proprietor. Businesses operated as sole proprietorships could be as extensive and impersonal as businesses typically operated as partnerships or corporations.

Also, much of the rationale advanced by the Court in restricting the privilege to the individual rested on functions of the privilege other than those stressed in *Boyd.* The emphasis in *White,* for example, was on the indignity imposed by compulsory self-condemnation. The entity, unlike a natural individual, did not have the moral autonomy that was offended by placing the witness in a position where he was compelled to either incriminate himself or be held in contempt (with the possible consequence of incarceration) for failing to comply with the court's order. *Boyd,* in contrast, presented a properly-oriented rationale that stressed the owner's right of privacy in his papers. *Hale,* while it held the privilege inapplicable to the entity, recognized that the entity had a Fourth Amendment privacy interest that allowed it to object to an unreasonable search and seizure (just as it could also protest a taking of its property without just compensation).

In *Bellis,* the Court did speak to a privacy grounding of the privilege, but its comments could be seen as casting doubt on the scope of *Boyd*'s view of the protected interest. The *Bellis* Court noted that the Fifth Amendment, serves to protect " 'a private inner sanctum of individual feeling and thought'—an inner sanctum which necessarily includes an individual's papers and effects to the extent that the privilege bars their compulsory production and authentication." It reasoned that the protection of such privacy was not at stake in the denial of the privilege to the entity. A "substantial claim of privacy or confidentiality," the Court noted, "cannot often be maintained with respect to financial records of an organized collective entity." Control of such records is typically regulated by the entity, with "access to the records * * * generally guaranteed to others in the organization." In *Boyd,* the subpoenaed invoice was also a financial record. Of course, with *Boyd*'s ruling limited after *Bellis* to the sole proprietorship, control over such financial records would lie in the hands of the subpoenaed proprietor, but here too, the practice of the proprietorship might well guarantee access to the records to various other participants in the enterprise.

(c) The Required Records Exception. Building upon dictum in *Wilson* to the effect that the privilege did not extend to corporate records because they were required by law to be kept for the public benefit, *Shapiro v. United States*[15] held that the same principle could apply to the records of individuals engaged in regulated businesses. *Shapiro* upheld against a self-incrimination object a subpoena directing production of records of commodity sales that the petitioner, a wholesale fresh produce dealer, was required to keep, and to make available for inspection by federal regulators, under the wartime Emergency Price Control Act. The Court acknowledged that "there are limits which the Government cannot constitutionally exceed in requiring the keeping of records which may be inspected by an administrative agency and may be used in prosecuting statutory violations committed by the record-keeper himself," but it concluded that there was no need in this case to define precisely where those limits might lie. For, the Court noted, "no serious misgivings that those bounds were overstepped would appear to be evoked where there is a sufficient relation between the activity sought to be regulated and the public concern so that the Government can constitutionally regulate or forbid the basic activity concerned." This broad description of the acceptable nexus between the records and regulating authority offered the possibility of a far reaching required records doctrine. Justice Frankfurter, dissenting in *Shapiro,* suggested that the Court had held that "all records which Congress may require individuals to keep in the conduct of their affairs, because they fall within some regulatory power of Government, become 'public records' and thereby, *ipso facto,* fall outside the protection of the Fifth

15. 335 U.S. 1, 68 S.Ct. 1375, 92 L.Ed. 1787 (1948).

Amendment." However, in the companion cases of *Marchetti v. United States*[16] and *Grosso v. United States,*[17] the Court later made clear that the required records doctrine could not be carried to that extreme.

Unlike *Shapiro, Marchetti* and *Grosso* did not present a government attempt to force production of existing records, but prosecutions for failure to comply with statutory schemes that included a reporting requirement. In both cases, self-incrimination challenges were presented to federal wagering tax statutes that required gamblers to identify themselves by registering with the government and by paying an occupational tax. Initially, the Court concluded that, in light of the comprehensive system of federal and state prohibitions against wagering activities, the required disclosure presented a "real and appreciable" hazard of self-incrimination. It then rejected the contention, suggested in earlier cases, that since the defendant had no constitutional right to gamble, the individual intending to engage in the wagering business could not complain because the government insists that he first inform it of his intended activities. Utilizing such a forced waiver or "antecedent choice" analysis, the Court noted, could abrogate the privilege's protection in numerous situations where it had historically been recognized. The privilege was designed to shelter "the guilty and imprudent as well as the innocent," and a state could not avoid its application by simply requiring that the potential criminal identify himself in advance. This left the government with the contention that the disclosure requirements were nonetheless constitutional because they fit within the rationale of the required records doctrine. The Court found that contention totally unpersuasive.

In rejecting the government's required records contention, the Court noted that it was unnecessary here to "pursue in detail the question left open in *Shapiro* of what limits the Government cannot constitutionally exceed in requiring the keeping of records." It was "enough that there [were] significant points of difference between the situations here and in *Shapiro.*" There were "three principle elements" of the required records doctrine, as it was "described in *Shapiro,*" and all three elements were missing in *Marchetti,* while at least two were missing in *Grosso.* As described in *Grosso,* those three elements, which furnished the "premises of the [required records] doctrine," were:

> "[F]irst, the purpose of the United States' inquiry must be essentially regulatory; second, information is to be obtained by requiring the preservation of records of a kind which the regulated party has customarily kept; and third, the records themselves must have assumed 'public aspects' which render them at least analogous to public documents."

With respect to the first of these elements, both the "characteristics of the activities about which information is sought" and the "composition of the groups to which inquiries are made" readily distinguished the wagering tax system at issue in *Marchetti* and *Grosso* from the price control regulations at issue in *Shapiro.* The wagering tax provisions were not dealing with "an essentially non-criminal and regulatory area," and their disclosure requirements were directed to a "selective group inherently suspect of criminal activities." As for the second requirement, at least in the *Marchetti* case, the contested disclosure requirements were not based on information contained in records that the person otherwise would have kept in the course of his occupation.

The Court also thought it obvious that the third element of the required records doctrine—that the records have assumed "public aspects" analogous to public records—had no bearing in the cases before it. Indeed, a contrary conclusion could be reached only by gutting the distinguishing character of such documents. In concluding that the record in question in *Shapiro* had "public aspects," the Court majority had noted that "the transaction which it recorded was one in which petitioner could lawfully engage solely by virtue of the license granted to him under the stat-

16. 390 U.S. 39, 88 S.Ct. 697, 19 L.Ed.2d 889 (1968).

17. 390 U.S. 62, 88 S.Ct. 709, 19 L.Ed.2d 906 (1968).

ute." An analogy had been drawn to state statutes requiring druggists to keep records of sales of intoxicating liquor. The *Shapiro* dissent had argued that even such qualities failed to make the records sufficiently analogous to public records. *Marchetti* concluded that "whatever public aspects there were to the records at issue in *Shapiro,* there are none to the information demanded [here]." The only basis for claiming that the information sought was public was the presence of a governmental demand "formalized * * * in the attire of a statute." If that were sufficient, "no room would remain for the application of the constitutional privilege."

Although decided in 1968, *Marchetti* and *Grosso* remain the Supreme Court's leading discussions of the required records doctrine. A later case, *California v. Byers,*[18] although not relying directly on the required records doctrine, did help to put that doctrine in perspective. In *Byers,* the Court upheld a "hit and run" statute which required a driver involved in an accident to stop at the scene and leave his name and address. The plurality noted that in judging the constitutionality of regulatory schemes requiring disclosures that might conceivably lead to criminal prosecutions, the Court had to "balanc[e] the public need on the one hand, and the individual claim to constitutional protections on the other."[19] That balancing approach presumably was at the core of the required records doctrine as well. Under such an approach, the critical factors in defining the limits of the required records doctrine, assuming a truly regulatory scheme, would be the significance of the government's regulatory interest, and the importance of the disclosure to making that interest effective. Such factors may readily be considered in determining whether the records can be characterized as having "public aspects." However, the importance of the second *Shapiro* element—that the records be of a type customarily kept—is problematic under such a balancing analysis. Arguably, the presence of that element may support the government's claim that its interest is truly regulatory, but there certainly may be instances, as suggested by *Byers,* in which a regulatory interest requires the keeping of records of activities that would not otherwise be recorded in the normal course of business. Of course, the starting assumption, as indicated in the first of the three elements, is that *Shapiro*'s government's interest truly be "regulatory," reflecting some interest other than facilitating the prosecution of crime.

Lower court rulings assessing the scope of the required records doctrine largely have been consistent with above analysis. A regulation that required automobile dealers to report altered serial numbers was held to extend beyond the limits of the doctrine: the regulation had no statutory purpose independent of a desire to "ferret out criminal activities." So too, check and deposit slips required by regulation to be kept as substantiation for a tax return were held not to have sufficient public aspects to constitute required records because the keeping of such records was not an ongoing condition of operating the taxpayer's business under a comprehensive regulatory scheme. On the other hand, found to be required records were records of a customhouse brokerage service kept pursuant to customs regulations, records relating to cattle purchases that licensed cattlemen were required to keep as part of a government program for controlling communicable diseases

18. 402 U.S. 424, 91 S.Ct. 1535, 29 L.Ed.2d 9 (1971).

19. The plurality opinion, upholding the statute in *Byers,* stressed that it was dealing with a regulatory measure "not intended to facilitate criminal convictions, but to promote the satisfaction of civil liabilities," that the measure's requirements applied to all persons who drove automobiles, and that the required disclosure was not to an inherently illegal activity as "most automobile accidents occur without creating criminal liability." The plurality also contended that compelled action was not "testimonial," a position rejected by Justice Harlan, who provided the fifth vote for the majority, as well as by the dissenters. Justice Harlan argued that though the risk of incrimination was sufficient to implicate the Fifth Amendment under traditional standards [see § 8.10(a)], the constitutionality of the statute should rest on a balancing of the "assertedly non-criminal governmental purpose in securing information, the necessity of self-reporting as a means of securing the information, and the nature of the disclosures required." He concluded that, given the strong governmental interest involved, the limited disclosures demanded were not sufficiently incriminating to violate the Fifth Amendment.

in domestic animals, and medical records as to patient treatment required for the purpose of reviewing professional competency. The thrust of these decisions is that a person who fears incrimination has no special exemption from record keeping duties imposed generally upon a regulated class that is not by its nature suspected of criminal activity.

The required records doctrine, although it restricted the potential scope of *Boyd*'s prohibition against compelling the production of incriminating documents, was seen from the outset as consistent with *Boyd*'s property-rights/privacy analysis of the Fifth Amendment. Thus, *Shapiro* noted that the *Boyd* Court had relied upon a "complex interpretation of the Fourth Amendment, taken as intertwined in its purpose and historical origins with the Fifth Amendment," and in the application of that interpretation, the *Boyd* Court had "carefully distinguished the 'unreasonable search and seizure' effected by the statute before it from the 'search and seizure' which Congress had provided for in revenue acts that required [distillers] to keep certain records, subject to inspection."

(d) The *Schmerber* Rule. Though it did not restrict the *Boyd* ruling as such, the limitation of the Fifth Amendment to "testimonial" compulsion, as held in *Schmerber v. California*,[20] did raise questions as to the scope of the *Boyd* analysis. As discussed in § 7.2(a), *Schmerber* held that the privilege did not prohibit the compelled extraction of a blood sample from an accused and subsequent admission of that sample as incriminatory evidence at his trial. The Court reasoned that the history of the privilege limited its application to compelled production of an accused's "communications" or "testimony." While this protection extended beyond statements compelled from "a person's own lips" and extended to "communications * * * in whatever form they may take," it did not encompass "compulsion which makes a suspect or accused the source of 'real or physical' evidence."[21] Citing *Boyd*, the *Schmerber* opinion distinguished the "compulsion of responses which are also communications, for example, compliance with a subpoena to produce one's papers." It did not explain, however, how such compliance could constitute a communication through the forced disclosure of contents of the subpoenaed document, as *Boyd* had suggested. Arguably, a document authored by the individual might be seen as "speaking" for him, as it contains his words. In *Boyd*, however, the required production was of a document written by another, an invoice sent to the *Boyd* partnership by a supplier.

Schmerber limited any "private inner sanctum" protected by the privilege to that of contents of the mind, which a compelled communication forces the individual to reveal. This limitation was later made evident in *Doe v. United States (Doe II)*.[22] The Court there held that a court order requiring an individual to sign a form directing any foreign bank to release the records of any account he might have at that bank did not compel "testimony." This was so since the government did not seek to use the consent form itself as a factual assertion of the individual, expressing the "contents of his mind." While the government did intend to use the contents of the document, if any, released by the bank, that document constituted statements not of the defendant, but of a third party. The same analysis arguably would apply to *Boyd* insofar as petitioner claimed that the content of the invoice to be produced there constituted an incriminating communication.

(e) Third-Party Production. *Couch v. United States*[23] and *Fisher v. United States*[24] both involved situations in which an individual had transferred records to an independent professional who was then served with an IRS

20. 384 U.S. 757, 86 S.Ct. 1826, 16 L.Ed.2d 908 (1966).

21. An attempt to distinguish *Schmerber* from compelled participation in identification procedures that require a "volitional act" was rejected in Wade v. United States. See § 7.1(b).

22. 487 U.S. 201, 108 S.Ct. 2341, 101 L.Ed.2d 184 (1988), further discussed in § 8.13 at note 3. This case is sometimes described as *Doe II* to distinguish it from United States v. Doe, discussed infra at note 26.

23. 409 U.S. 322, 93 S.Ct. 611, 34 L.Ed.2d 548 (1973).

24. 425 U.S. 391, 96 S.Ct. 1569, 48 L.Ed.2d 39 (1976).

summons requiring production of those records. In *Couch,* the sole proprietor of a restaurant had delivered various financial records to her accountant for the purpose of preparing her income tax returns. In *Fisher,* sole owners of separate businesses had delivered to their attorneys various workpapers that had been prepared by their accountants in the course of filing income tax returns. In both cases, the taxpayers relied upon *Boyd,* arguing that the government was seeking to obtain disclosure of papers of an even more confidential nature than the invoice involved in *Boyd.* The taxpayers acknowledged that the IRS summonses required their agents rather than the taxpayers themselves to produce the documents, but contended that factor was irrelevant since they had maintained a reasonable expectation of privacy in the documents even after delivered to their agents. They argued that *Boyd* had recognized a privacy interest in the contents of documents, arising out of the ownership of the documents, that was protected under the Fifth Amendment.

The Supreme Court rejected the taxpayers' position in both cases, noting that the taxpayers had read too much into *Boyd.* The Fifth Amendment applied only to personal compulsion and there was none here. Unlike the importers in *Boyd,* the taxpayers here were not themselves required "to do anything." The Court was not persuaded by the contention that its focus on personal compulsion was too formalistic to serve adequately the functions of the privilege. Responding in *Fisher,* it noted: "We cannot cut the Fifth Amendment completely loose from the moorings of its language and make it serve as a general protector of privacy—a word not mentioned in its text and a concept directly addressed in the Fourth Amendment." The Fifth Amendment, it continued, "protects against 'compelling testimony, not the disclosure of private information.' "[25]

(f) Testimonial Aspects of Production. Because the documents in *Fisher* had been transferred to an attorney, the Court found it necessary to decide whether the taxpayers there would have had a valid self-incrimination claim if they had been compelled themselves to produce the documents. Under the attorney-client privilege, the attorney could refuse to produce documents that "would have been privileged in the hands of the client by reason of the Fifth Amendment." The taxpayers argued that the documents here would have been privileged against self-production under the "*Boyd* rule" that "a person may not be forced to produce his private papers."

In separate concurring opinions, Justices Marshall and Brennan agreed with the taxpayers' statement of the *Boyd* rule, but held that rule inapplicable to the facts of this case. Ever since *Boyd,* they noted, the Fifth Amendment had protected a privacy interest that "extends not just to the individual's immediate declarations, oral or written, but also to his testimonial materials in the form of books and papers." That protection, however, read in light of the entity cases, was limited to the compelled production of papers that fell within the "zone of privacy recognized by the Amendment." Some business records of a sole proprietor could fall within the protected category of "personal" or private papers, but that was not true of the records subpoenaed here. "Given the prior access by the accountants" and the "wholly business rather than personal nature of the papers," the compelled production of the documents in question was not barred by the privilege.

25. Both *Fisher* and *Couch* acknowledged that "situations might exist where constructive possession is so clear or the relinquishment of possession is so temporary and insignificant as to leave the personal compulsions upon the accused substantially intact." Lower courts have suggested, however, that where documents have been delivered to an independent third party, this "constructive-possession exception" will be available only if the third party received the records strictly for custodial safekeeping and the owner retained ready access to the records. Constructive possession is more likely to be found where a sole proprietor seeks to raise the privilege in response to a subpoena directing an employee to produce company records kept by that employee. Even here, a constructive possession argument may be denied, and the employer barred from raising the privilege, where, for example, the employer was an absentee proprietor who had delegated exclusive responsibility for the records to the subpoenaed employee.

Justice White's opinion for the Court in *Fisher* also rejected the taxpayer's reliance upon *Boyd,* but on much broader grounds. Justice White noted that *Boyd* had relied on a combined Fourth and Fifth Amendment theory that had "not stood the test of time." Much of *Boyd*'s Fourth Amendment analysis had been flatly rejected and the rulings in cases like *Schmerber* and *Bellis* had adopted a different view of the Fifth Amendment. What was left was a "prohibition against forcing the production of private papers [that] has long been a rule searching for a rationale consistent with the proscriptions of the Fifth Amendment against compelling a person to give 'testimony' that incriminates him." In light of *Schmerber,* that prohibition could not rest on the incriminating content of the subpoenaed records. The court order of production of preexisting records does not require the subpoenaed party to author those records. Where the preparation of subpoenaed records was voluntary, those records "cannot be said to contain compelled testimonial evidence." The records may contain incriminating writing, but whether the writing of the subpoenaed party or another, that writing was not a communication compelled by the subpoena. Accordingly, the prosecution's acquisition of that writing by subpoena is no more compelling testimony than its acquisition of physical evidence with similar incriminating content.

Having found that application of the privilege could not rest on the declarations contained in the writings, the Court then turned to what it viewed as a more appropriate explanation of the *Boyd* rule. The act of producing subpoenaed documents, the Court noted, "has communicative aspects of its own, wholly aside from the contents of the papers produced." Compliance with a subpoena "tacitly concedes the existence of the papers demanded and their possession or control by the [subpoenaed party]." It also would indicate that party's "belief that the papers are those described in the subpoena," and in some instances this could constitute authentication of the papers. Indeed, post-*Boyd* decisions suggest that such "implicit authentication" is the "prevailing justification for the Fifth Amendment's application to documentary subpoenas." These three elements of production—acknowledgment of existence, acknowledgment of possession or control, and potential authentication by identification—are clearly compelled, but whether they also are "testimonial" and "incriminating" would depend upon the "facts and circumstances of particular cases or classes thereof." The resolution of that question, the Court reasoned, should determine whether a particular documentary production is subject to a Fifth Amendment challenge.

Upon examining the implications of the act of production in the case before it, the *Fisher* Court, for reasons explored in § 8.13, concluded that the taxpayer did not have a valid self-incrimination claim. "In light of the records now before us," the Court noted, "however incriminating the contents of the accountant's workpapers might be, the act of producing them—the only thing which the taxpayer is compelled to do—would not itself involve testimonial self-incrimination." The Court also added, however, a comment that might significantly limit its ruling. It noted: "whether the Fifth Amendment would shield the taxpayer from producing his own tax records in his possession is a question not involved here; for the papers demanded here are not 'private papers,' see *Boyd v. United States.*"

Following *Fisher,* some lower courts saw the act-of-production doctrine and *Boyd*'s content-based analysis as alternative grounds for sustaining a self-incrimination challenge to the compelled production of the business records of a sole proprietor. In *United States v. Doe (Doe I),*[26] the Court went out of its way to point out that this approach was mistaken. The rationale of *Fisher,* the Court concluded, implicitly rejected application of a content-based analysis of the privilege in such a situation.

Doe I involved a subpoena directing a sole proprietor to produce for grand jury use a broad range of business records, including

26. 465 U.S. 605, 104 S.Ct. 1237, 79 L.Ed.2d 252 (1984).

billings, ledgers, cancelled checks, telephone records, contracts and paid bills. The district court sustained the proprietor's claim of privilege. It concluded that compliance with the subpoena would require the proprietor to "admit that the records exist, that they are in his possession, and that they are authentic" and that each of these testimonial elements of production was potentially incriminatory. The Third Circuit agreed with this reasoning, but also added that the privilege applied because compelled disclosure of the contents of the documents violated the Fifth Amendment. Relying upon the privacy analysis of *Boyd,* it reasoned that the contents of personal records were privileged under the Fifth Amendment and that "business records of a sole proprietorship are no different from the individual's personal records."

Justice Powell's opinion for the Court in *Doe I* affirmed the rulings below insofar as they relied on the act-of-production doctrine. *Fisher* had recognized that the act of production could be testimonial and incriminatory under the facts of a particular case, and here two lower courts had so found. That finding would be accepted in accordance with the Court's traditional "reluctan[ce] to disturb findings of fact in which two courts below concurred." Three concurring Justices argued that, in light of the acceptance of this finding, there was no reason to speak to the alternative grounding of the Third Circuit's opinion, but the Court majority concluded that it was desirable to resolve the "apparent conflict" between that grounding and "the reasoning underlying this Court's holding in *Fisher.*" That resolution resulted in the majority's flat rejection of the Third Circuit's conclusion that the contents of the subpoenaed documents were protected by the privilege.

Justice Powell initially acknowledged that the Court in *Fisher* had "declined to reach the question whether the Fifth Amendment privilege protects the contents of an individual's tax records in his possession." The "rationale" underlying *Fisher*'s holding, however, was equally persuasive here. *Fisher* had emphasized that "the Fifth Amendment protects the person asserting the privilege only from *compelled* self-incrimination." That a record was prepared by a subpoenaed party and is in his possession is "irrelevant to the determination of whether its creation * * * was compelled." The business records here, like the accountant's workpapers in *Fisher,* had been prepared voluntarily, and therefore only their production, and not their creation, was compelled. The contention that the Fifth Amendment created a "zone of privacy" that protected the content of such papers had been rejected in *Fisher.*[27] The respondent could not avoid compliance with a subpoena "merely by asserting that the item of evidence which he is required to produce contains incriminating writing, whether his own or that of someone else."

(g) Possible Remnants of *Boyd.* While *Doe I* involved only business records, Justice O'Connor, in a concurring opinion, suggested that the *Doe–Fisher* rationale was more extensive. She noted:

> I write separately * * * to make explicit what is implicit in the analysis of [Justice Powell's] opinion: that the Fifth Amendment provides absolutely no protection for the contents of private papers of any kind. The notion that the Fifth Amendment protects the privacy of papers originated in *Boyd v. United States,* but our decision in *Fisher v. United States,* sounded the death-knell for *Boyd.*

27. The Court added that its conclusion that the contents of the documents were not privileged found support in the post-*Fisher* ruling of Andresen v. Maryland, 427 U.S. 463, 96 S.Ct. 2737, 49 L.Ed.2d 627 (1976), also discussed in § 3.2(i). In *Andresen,* the Court had rejected the claim that a search for business records violated the Fifth Amendment. The *Andresen* Court acknowledged that the defendant's contention found support in dicta in past precedents (e.g., *Boyd*) which suggested that "a search for and seizure of a person's private papers violated the privilege against self-incrimination," but noted that such broad statements had been "discredited by later opinions." The key here was that the "records seized contained statements that petitioner had voluntarily committed to writing" and their seizure did not require the defendant "to say or do anything." In dissent, Justice Brennan reiterated the "zone of privacy" analysis of the Fifth Amendment that he had set forth in his *Fisher* concurrence.

Justice O'Connor's opinion brought forth a strong response from Justice Marshall, joined by Justice Brennan. "This case," Justice Marshall noted, "presented nothing remotely close to the question that Justice O'Connor eagerly poses and answers." The documents in question here were business records, "which implicate a lesser degree of concern for privacy interests than, for example, personal diaries." It accordingly could not be said that the *Doe I* Court had "reconsidered the question of whether the Fifth Amendment provides protection for the content of 'private papers of any kind.'"

The Court subsequently has not had occasion to rule on the forced production of documents that are more likely than business records to reflect the private thoughts of the subpoenaed party. Since the act of producing such personal documents is highly likely to constitute in itself a testimonial and incriminating communication, a self-incrimination challenge ordinarily will be sustainable without need to consider whether any content-based protection remains. That issue is more likely to be posed in an assessment of the scope of the immunity that must be provided to compel production of such papers (i.e., whether the immunity may go simply to the act of production, see § 8.13(c), or must protect the contents as well).[28]

§ 8.13 Application of The Act-of-Production Doctrine

(a) Testimonial Character and the Foregone Conclusion Standard. The Court in *Fisher*[1] noted that the communicative aspects of the act-of-production might or might not constitute "testimony" for self-incrimination purposes, depending upon "the facts and circumstances of particular cases." In *Fisher* itself, the Court was concerned primarily with the testimonial significance of the implicit admission as to the existence and possession of accountant's workpapers through their production. Relying upon what came to be known as the "foregone conclusion" standard, the *Fisher* Court concluded:

> It is doubtful that implicitly admitting the existence and possession of the papers rises to the level of testimony within the protection of the Fifth Amendment. The papers belong to the accountant, were prepared by him, and are the kind usually prepared by an accountant working on the tax returns of his client. Surely the Government is in no way relying on the "truthtelling" of the taxpayer to prove the existence of or his access to the documents. The existence and location of the papers are a foregone conclusion and the taxpayer adds little or nothing to the sum total of the Government's information by conceding that he in fact has the papers. Under these circumstances by enforcement of the summons "no constitutional rights are touched. The question is not of testimony but of surrender."

Justice Brennan, in his concurring opinion, sharply criticized the Court's reliance on this "surrender only" rationale. He argued that the Court was holding, in effect, that an admission as to existence and possession is not testimonial "merely because the Government could otherwise have proved [those facts]." Such a position rested on the untenable proposition that "one's protection against incriminating himself * * * turn[s] on the strength of the Government's case against him." Undoubtedly, as Justice Brennan noted, in assessing whether compelled testimony falls within the privilege, courts have never deemed it significant that the government could otherwise establish the incriminating information that might be disclosed in the

28. As noted in § 8.13(a), the act of production will not present self-incrimination difficulties where possession, existence, and authentication can be established as a "foregone conclusion," but that is most unlikely in the case of a document so private as a diary. See Marshall, J., concurring in *Fisher* (noting "there would appear to be a precise inverse relationship between the private nature of the document and the permissibility of assuming its existence"). Indeed, as to such a document, even a grant of act-of-production immunity may not be a viable alternative since the extremely private nature of the document is likely to make it difficult for the government to establish the elements necessary for its use in evidence without referring to the act of production. See § 8.13(c).

§ 8.13

1. Fisher v. United States, 426 U.S. 391, 96 S.Ct. 1569, 48 L.Ed.2d 39 (1976), also discussed in § 8.12(f).

witness' testimony; the critical question is simply whether the witness "has reasonable cause to apprehend danger from * * * [his] answer." [2] However, the *Fisher* Court was not dealing with a traditional form of testimony, but with what it viewed as a quite different concern—whether the incidental communicative aspects of a physical act (production) should be deemed "testimonial." The Court cited by analogy its rulings holding the Fifth Amendment inapplicable to a court order requiring an accused to submit a handwriting sample. Incidental to the performance of that act, the Court noted, the accused necessarily "admits his ability to write and impliedly asserts that the exemplar is his writing." But the government obviously is not seeking this information—the "first would be a near truism and the latter self-evident"—, and therefore "nothing he has said or done is deemed to be sufficiently testimonial for purposes of the privilege." Where the existence and possession of the documents to be produced were a "foregone conclusion," the act of production was viewed by the *Fisher* Court as having the same non-testimonial character. The government in such a case obviously was not seeking the assertions of the subpoenaed party as to the facts of existence and possession, and his incidental communication as to those facts, inherent in the physical act that the government had the authority to compel, therefore would not rise to the level of compelled "testimony."

This special quality of governmental purpose, as it relates to the testimonial aspect of a required act, was recognized in a somewhat different context in *Doe II*.[3] The Court there held that requiring an individual to sign a form directing any foreign bank to release records did not rise to the level of compelling testimony under the Fifth Amendment. The government purpose was not to have the actor, through his act, "relate a factual assertion or disclose information." Indeed, the form was carefully drafted so that the signing party noted that he was acting under court order and did not acknowledge the existence of any account in any particular bank. It did not indicate whether the requested documents existed, and offered no assistance to the government in later establishing the authenticity of any records produced by the bank. Thus, while the signed form did constitute a communication, it did not constitute "testimony." The government was not relying on the "truth-telling" of the directive, but simply requiring the petitioner to engage in the act of producing that directive.[4] Similarly, where the communicative elements of the act of producing a preexisting document merely established what is already a foregone conclusion, that factor suggests that the government is compelling the act for what it will produce (the documents, with a content not itself compelled) rather than the communications inherent in the act. To allow the privilege to be claimed simply because the required act incidentally provided information, even though the government did not seek that information, would be to make every compelled act a testimonial communication, contrary to the *Schmerber* rule.[5]

The *Fisher* Court concluded that the existence and location of the accountant's workpapers were a foregone conclusion, but the Court never explained why that was so—apart from noting that the papers were of the kind usually prepared by an accountant. In *Doe I*,[6] in contrast to *Fisher*, the Court held the privilege applicable to an act of produc-

2. Hoffman v. United States, quoted at § 8.10(a).

3. Doe v. United States, 487 U.S. 201, 108 S.Ct. 2341, 101 L.Ed.2d 184 (1988), also discussed in § 8.12 at note 22.

4. The Court acknowledged that the directive could result in the production of evidence, but that was not because of any information that the petitioner Doe was required to provide. The directive did not point the government toward hidden accounts, but simply provided it with a document it could use, if the foreign banks were receptive, to obtain evidence located in such banks by the government's own efforts. While the dissent argued that requiring the petitioner to provide the directive was no different than compelling a person to reveal the combination to his safe, the majority characterized it as more like "requiring the individual to surrender a key to a strong box containing incriminatory documents."

5. See § 8.12(d).

6. United States v. Doe, 465 U.S. 605, 104 S.Ct. 1237, 79 L.Ed.2d 552 (1984), also discussed in § 8.12(f) at note 26.

tion, and noted that there the government had failed to "rebu[t] the respondent's claim" as it had not shown "that possession, existence, and authentication were a foregone conclusion." Unfortunately, because of its procedural setting, *Doe I* may be only slightly more helpful than *Fisher* in explaining the application of the foregone conclusion standard. In distinguishing *Fisher,* the *Doe I* Court relied basically on the presence here of the "explicit finding of the District Court that the act of producing the [subpoenaed] documents would involve testimonial self-incrimination." That finding rested essentially "on the determination of factual issues" and it had been affirmed by the Third Circuit. The Supreme Court had "traditionally been reluctant to disturb findings of fact in which two courts below have concurred" and there was no reason to do so here.

In light of the *Doe I* Court's emphasis on its limited role in reviewing the lower courts' findings, the significance of the lower courts' reasoning in reaching those findings is unclear. The Supreme Court did note that such a finding would be overturned if it had "no support" in the record, and it did set forth at length the reasoning of the lower courts. The district court had concluded that compliance with the subpoena would require respondent to "admit that the [subpoenaed] records exist, that they are in his possession, and that they are authentic," and that each of these elements was potentially incriminatory. The district court had added that while the government had argued that "existence, possession and authenticity * * * can be proved without [Doe's] testimonial communication," it was not satisfied "as to how that representation can be implemented." The Third Circuit had found "nothing in the record that would indicate that the United States knows, as a certainty, that each of the myriad documents demanded * * * in fact is in the appellee's possession or subject to his control." The "most plausible inference," it had noted, was that the government was "attempting to compensate for its lack of knowledge by requiring the appellee to become, in effect, the primary informant against himself."

Notwithstanding the Court's reliance on its limited role in reviewing factual findings, its discussion of the lower court rulings and its own comments on the government's failure to meet the foregone conclusion standard do add in several respects to *Fisher*'s explanation of that standard. Initially, *Doe* made clear that the foregone conclusion doctrine applies to the element of authentication as well as to existence and possession. *Fisher* had discussed the foregone conclusion concept only in connection with the latter two elements, but *Doe* noted that the government was "not foreclosed from rebutting respondent's claim by producing evidence that possession, existence, *and authentication* were a 'foregone conclusion' " (emphasis added). The application of the foregone conclusion concept to authentication logically follows from the nature of that concept. Just as with possession and existence, the government can readily have other sources through which it may establish authenticity, rendering any acknowledgment through production an unwanted, incidental byproduct of the act of production itself. Indeed, depending on the nature of the records subpoenaed, the ability to authenticate without relying on the act of production may be obvious. Some records will be self-authenticating or capable of being authenticated through other records in the government's possession. In some instances, the documents will be described in the subpoena with such specificity that the only acknowledgment made by the person producing those documents is that he has the capacity to identify that which would be obvious to anybody looking through the documents. (This stands in contrast to the usual situation, where the subpoena is so framed that the subpoenaed party must say something about the background or use of a document in identifying that document).

Doe I also may be read as implicitly rejecting a standard which assumes that the existence and possession of typical business records are a foregone conclusion. *Fisher* had been read by some lower courts as suggesting that possession and existence should be presumed to be a foregone conclusion whenever the material subpoenaed consisted of the type of records commonly used in business transactions (in *Fisher,* the preparation of tax returns). Under this view, a government showing as to foregone conclusion would be necessary only where the standard business records also were authored by the party subpoenaed (as then his act of production might also be viewed as attesting to their source or accuracy—elements not presumed to be a foregone conclusion). *Doe,* however, seemingly rejected any such constricted view as to when a specific government showing is needed to meet the foregone conclusion standard; the records there were typical business records and many presumably were not authored by Doe, but the government nonetheless had failed to "produce [the] evidence" necessary to meet the foregone conclusion standard. *Doe* might be viewed in this regard as one of those unusual cases in which some special showing was needed because it was not obvious that the subpoenaed party had any relationship to the businesses involved. More likely, however, its reasoning follows from a line of lower court cases holding that, even when the subpoenaed records are of a type commonly kept by businesses, the government does not establish existence and possession as a foregone conclusion unless it can establish the existence of these particular records, not just the general class of records. *Fisher* would be consistent with this approach since the attorneys there, in raising their clients' Fifth Amendment privilege via the attorney-client privilege, had to establish that they had received the accountant's workpapers from their clients.

(b) Potential Incrimination. To raise a successful self-incrimination claim based on the act of production doctrine, the subpoenaed party must establish not only that the communicative aspects of production rise to the level of testimony, but also that such testimony would meet the traditional standard of potential incrimination.[7] Thus, in *Fisher,* after indicating that act of production there would not be testimonial, the Court went on to conclude that the Fifth Amendment claim failed in any event because there had been no showing that the communicative aspects of production posed a "realistic threat of incrimination to the taxpayer." The Court there examined separately the potential incrimination stemming from implicit authentication and implicit acknowledgment of existence and possession. As to authentication, it noted that production would not provide the government with evidence that could be used to authenticate the subpoenaed workpapers since production by the taxpayer would "express nothing more than the taxpayer's belief that the papers are those described in the subpoena" and the taxpayer could not thereby authenticate as he "did not prepare the papers and could not vouch for their accuracy." As to existence and possession, "surely it was not illegal to seek accounting help in connection with one's tax returns or for the accountant to prepare workpapers and deliver them to the taxpayer." Accordingly, "at this juncture," the Court was "quite unprepared to hold that either the fact of the existence of the papers or their possession by the taxpayer" posed a sufficient threat to raise a legitimate self-incrimination claim.

Fisher's discussion of the incrimination possibilities, like its discussion of the testimony issue, was both brief and suggestive of broad implications. In its discussion of authentication, the Court appeared to suggest that the subpoenaed party's inability to establish the accuracy of papers he did not author rendered any testimonial communication irrelevant on this issue (and therefore not incriminatory). Yet the statement of the subpoenaed party as to his belief that documents in his possession were those prepared by another would appear to be admissible evidence in establishing authenticity, even if not sufficient to authenticate in itself. As to existence and possession, the Court appeared to be concerned only with the general nature of the records, ignoring the possibility that the admission of possession and existence might tie the party making production to the possible incriminatory content of the records. Admittedly, the records

7. See § 8.10(a).

at issue in *Fisher* were not of the type where acknowledging their existence or their possession in itself acknowledged illegality (as would be true where the records are described in the subpoena as evidencing an illegal transaction or constituting documents that a person should not legally have in his possession). However, acknowledging the existence and possession of the accountant's workpapers still could provide a link in the prosecution's chain of evidence if the contents of the records should prove incriminating, as those acknowledgments could readily indicate that the taxpayer was aware of what was in the documents.

In *Doe I,* the Court returned to the issue of incrimination in a footnote that seemingly rejected the broader implication of the discussion in *Fisher.* In that footnote, the *Doe I* Court responded to the government's contention that even if the act of production there were viewed as having sufficient "testimonial aspects," any incrimination would be "so trivial" that the Fifth Amendment would not be implicated. The Court agreed that the Fifth Amendment would only be implicated if the risk of incrimination were "substantial and real," not merely "trifling or imaginary." It rejected, however, the government's claim that the risk of incrimination here clearly did not meet that standard. Respondent Doe had never conceded that the records subpoenaed actually existed or were within his possession. As respondent also noted, "even if the government could obtain the documents from another source, by producing the documents, respondent would relieve the government of the need for authentication." The potential prosecution uses of respondent's production, the Court noted, "were sufficient to establish a valid claim of the privilege."

Doe I's comment on the incriminatory potential of production through authentication certainly put to rest any suggestion that such potential would not exist where the records were authored by another. Although the Court did not comment on the fact, many of the records subpoenaed (which included billings, ledgers, telephone records, and paid bills) obviously had not been authored by respondent Doe. Read in light of *Doe I,* the distinguishing feature in *Fisher* may have been the obvious availability there of the accountants as the most likely source of authentication testimony (although the availability of that independent source of authentication would more appropriately seem to relate to establishing authentication as a foregone conclusion rather than to establishing the absence of sufficient incriminatory potential in the possible use of the act of production in authentication).

Doe I's discussion of the incrimination element also made clear that the acknowledgment of the existence and possession of records legally possessed could have a sufficient incriminatory potential to give rise to a "valid claim of the privilege." The records described in the *Doe I* subpoena were as innocuous on their face as the accountant's workpapers subpoenaed in *Fisher.* The potential for incrimination existed in tying the subpoenaed party to the contents of those records through his acknowledgment that he was aware of their existence and possessed them—factors that were significant to the government's case as the respondent had never conceded that the records existed or were in his control. In *Fisher,* in contrast, those issues did not exist and the taxpayer had raised no more than a blanket claim of the privilege as it related to the records as a whole. In stating that it was unprepared "at this juncture" to find a realistic threat of incrimination, the Court may have been leaving the door open for the taxpayer to make a more particularized showing of possible incrimination. Thus, a valid self-incrimination claim arguably could have been presented in *Fisher* if the taxpayer had pointed to particular records that posed a real and appreciable threat of containing incriminatory information and had indicated that the government was seeking to link the taxpayer to those potentially incriminatory records through his act of production.

(c) Production Immunity. The *Doe I* Court also cast light on the reach of the act-of-production doctrine in responding to the government's alternative position, which accepted arguendo the lower court's finding of testimonial self-incrimination. The government maintained that the subpoena nevertheless should have been enforced by the district court, with that court granting respondent Doe immunity as to the act of production. The government contended that it had, in effect, requested such an order, since it "stated several times before the district court that it would not use the respondent's act of production against him in any way." Responding to this position, the Supreme Court conceded that the government "could have compelled respondent to produce the documents" by utilizing the federal immunity statute providing for use/derivative-use immunity.[8] Moreover, that immunity need not have covered the contents of the documents, but could have been limited to the act of production since "immunity need be only as broad as the privilege against self-incrimination." However, the government here had not used the immunity statute. Instead, it was asking the Court to adopt a doctrine of "constructive use immunity," whereby the federal courts would bypass the immunity statute and simply direct the government not to make use of the incriminatory aspects of production. This the federal courts could not do, since the decision to grant immunity involved a delicate balancing of interests that Congress had expressly delegated to appropriate Justice Department officials rather than the judiciary.

The critical aspect of this part of the *Doe I* ruling was the Court's acknowledgment that the necessary immunity need go only to the act of production itself, and not to the contents of the subpoenaed records. That such limited immunity was acceptable clearly followed from the mainspring of *Fisher*'s reassessment of the "*Boyd* rule." A significant question remains, however, as to what uses of the records will be seen as relying on information that was conveyed by the act of production. In particular, where the government was not aware of the existence of the record, does the record itself become the fruit of information garnered from the immunized act (i.e., the fact that the records exist); or does the act convey only information as to when, where, and how the records were produced in response to the subpoena, leaving the government with the same access to the records as it would have if the records mysteriously appeared on the prosecutor's desk? The few lower courts that have spoken to this issue appear to be divided. Of course, even where the records previously were known to exist, so the record (and its contents) need not be traced to any communication in the act of production, sources other than the act of production still must be found to meet the applicable evidentiary requirements (such as showing authenticity and relevancy) for admission at trial. Very often, however, the contents themselves and outside sources derived from the contents (e.g., additional witnesses) will easily enable the prosecution to meet those requirements.

(d) The Entity Agent. Because the entity had no self-incrimination privilege, and the entity agent was responding in a representative capacity in producing the documents of the entity, a series of cases dating back to the early 1900's had held that the agent could not invoke his personal privilege even though the content of the documents were clearly incriminating to him.[9] Prior to *Fisher,* the only major open issue as to production by an entity agent was where the agent's responsibility ended. The lower courts had held, with some suggestion of approval by the Supreme Court, that the agent could be required to testify for the purpose of identifying the documents. However, once this was done, the agent could exercise his personal privilege as to further questions relating to the records (e.g., how they were prepared). In an analogous situation, the Supreme Court held that an officer of a local union, having established that he no

8. See § 8.11.

9. See Wilson v. United States and Drier v. United States, discussed in § 8.12(b) at notes 9 and 10. Of course, this limitation applied only to records that were those of the entity, and not to personal documents that the agent might sometimes utilize in the course of his employment. Thus, a substantial body of lower court precedent was devoted to whether such items as employee desk and pocket calendars were personal or entity records under the circumstances of the particular case.

longer possessed the subpoenaed records, could then assert the privilege as to questions concerning their disposition.[10]

After *Fisher* introduced the act-of-production doctrine, several lower courts concluded that the entity agent should be allowed to claim the privilege as to his or her act of production, at least where the subpoena was directed to the particular entity official rather than to the entity itself. In *Braswell v. United States,*[11] the Supreme Court, by a 5–4 margin, rejected that position. The *Braswell* majority concluded that *Fisher*'s adoption of the act-of-production doctrine had not altered the unavailability of the privilege to the entity agent. The Court's pre-*Fisher* rulings on the responsibility of the agent had not ignored the testimonial aspects of the act of production, but had correctly considered any such testimonial elements to be properly attributed to the entity rather to the agent acting on its behalf. Even where the subpoena was directed by name to a particular entity official having control of the records, rather than simply to the entity itself, that official was not performing "a personal act, but rather an act of the [entity]" in complying with the subpoena. The dissent argued that this position was to allow the law "to be captive to its own fictions," but the majority responded that *Fisher* itself had accepted this distinction in the course of analyzing the act-of-production rationale. Thus, the majority noted, "whether one concludes—as did the Court [in *Fisher*]—that a custodian's production of corporate records is deemed not to constitute testimonial self-incrimination or instead that a custodian waives the right to exercise the privilege, the lesson of *Fisher* is clear: A custodian may not resist a subpoena for corporate records on Fifth Amendment grounds." To rule otherwise, as the Court had noted in its earlier rulings, would "substantially undermine the unchallenged rule that the organization itself is not entitled to claim any Fifth Amendment privilege, and largely frustrate legitimate government regulation of such organizations." [12]

Braswell, however, added an evidentiary limitation not mentioned in the earlier cases rejecting self-incrimination claims by entity agents. Since the agent's act of production is an act of the entity and not the individual, the government "may make no evidentiary use of the 'individual act' against the individual." Illustrating this point, the Court noted that "in a criminal prosecution against the custodian, the Government may not introduce into evidence before the jury the fact that the subpoena was served upon and the corporation's documents were delivered by one partic-

10. Curcio v. United States, 354 U.S. 118, 77 S.Ct. 1145, 1 L.Ed.2d 1225 (1957). The *Curcio* opinion, commenting upon the lower court rulings that had required identification testimony by the agent, indicated that such testimony may merely make explicit what was implicit in the act of production and thereby subject the agent "to little, if any, further danger." In United States v. Rylander, 460 U.S. 752, 103 S.Ct. 1548, 75 L.Ed.2d 521 (1983), the Court noted that *Curcio* did not relieve the agent of the obligation to establish that he no longer possessed the records, and he could not escape that burden by simply claiming the privilege.

11. 487 U.S. 99, 108 S.Ct. 2284, 101 L.Ed.2d 98 (1988).

12. The majority further noted in this regard that "recognizing a Fifth Amendment privilege on behalf of record custodians of collective entities would have a detrimental impact on the Government's efforts to prosecute 'white collar crime' * * * as the greater portion of evidence of wrongdoing by an organization or its representatives is usually found in the official records and documents of that organization." The majority rejected both of petitioner's suggestions as to how such concerns could be "minimized." As for the suggestion that the custodian simply be granted act-of-production immunity, that could impose serious obstacles in subsequent proceedings as the government would bear the "heavy burden" of establishing that its evidence came from other sources. Although the majority recognized, as discussed infra, a prohibition against evidentiary use of the custodian's act in a prosecution against him, that prohibition did not carry with it the burden of meeting the independent source requirement imposed in the immunity cases [see § 8.11(b)]. As for the suggestion that recognition of individual's privilege would not preclude a subpoena directed to the entity, with the entity then having the responsibility of finding some person to produce the records, the Court majority questioned how effective that would be if, as the petitioner urged, the individual official "could not be required to aid the appointed custodian in his search for the demanded records." Noted the majority: "If this [position] is correct, then petitioner's solution is a chimera."

The dissenters in *Braswell* viewed the grant of immunity as an appropriate response to the "majority's abiding concern" as to the "government's power to investigate * * * white collar crime." The dissenters also responded, however, that "the first, and most fundamental [answer], is that the text of the Fifth Amendment does not authorize exceptions premised on such rationales."

ular individual, the custodian." The government would be limited to showing that the entity had produced the document and to using that act of the entity in establishing that the records were authentic entity records that the entity had possessed and had produced. The Court added in a footnote to this discussion an important caveat: it was "leav[ing] open the question [of] whether the agency rationale supports compelling a custodian to produce corporate records when the custodian is able to establish, by showing for example that he is the sole employee and officer of the corporation, that the jury would inevitably conclude that he produced the records." [13]

(e) Non-documentary Subpoenas. The act-of-production doctrine is not limited in its potential application to documentary subpoenas. A subpoena requiring production of some item of physical evidence can also be challenged if the acknowledgment of existence and possession through the act of production is "testimonial" and "incriminating." Thus, a state court held the privilege to be applicable, under the act-of-production doctrine, to a court order requiring a defendant (charged with assault with a dangerous weapon) to produce a "Smith and Wesson 38 Caliber Revolver, Serial No. T-34354." [14]

The potential range of the act-of-production doctrine, and its relationship to other self-incrimination doctrines in this context, was illustrated in *Baltimore City Department of Social Services v. Bouknight.*[15] In that case, the Supreme Court rejected a self-incrimination objection to a subpoena directing respondent Bouknight to produce her infant son, who was a ward of the court. The Court noted that the respondent could not claim the privilege based upon "anything an examination of the [child] might reveal," as that would be a claim based upon "the contents or nature of the thing demanded." However, the mother could conceivably claim the privilege because "the act of production would amount to testimony regarding her control over and possession of [the child]." While the state could "readily introduce [other] evidence of Bouknight's continuing control over the child" (including the court order giving her limited custody and her previous statements), her "implicit communication of control over [the child] at the moment of production might aid the state in prosecuting Bouknight [for child abuse]." The Court had no need to decide, however, whether "this limited testimonial assertion is sufficiently incriminating and sufficiently testimonial for purposes of the privilege." In receiving conditional custody from the juvenile court, the mother had "assumed custodial duties related to production" (analogous to that of an entity agent) and had done so as part of noncriminal regulatory scheme which included a production component (analogous to regulations sustained under the required records doctrine). The Court added that it had no need in the case before it "to define the precise limitations that may exist upon the State's ability to use the testimonial aspects of Bouknight's act of production in subsequent criminal proceedings," but the "imposition of such limitations," as done in *Braswell,* was not "foreclosed."

§ 8.14 Judicial Decisions and the History and Policies of the Self-Incrimination Privilege

(a) Range of Self-Incrimination Issues. The Supreme Court has considered self-incrimination issues in a variety of different contexts, including police interrogation of sus-

13. The Court could respond to this situation with solutions that fall short of allowing the custodian to preclude the production of the records absent a grant to him of act-of-production immunity. One possibility is to preclude, in any subsequent prosecution of the custodian, a reference even to the corporation's act of production. Another would be to direct the subpoena to the corporation, require it to make production through some specially appointed custodian (e.g., counsel), and place upon the sole-employee/custodian the duty to provide the special appointee with sufficient assistance in locating and identifying the subpoenaed records (a duty the government could not exploit at trial by referring to the sole-employee as the source of the specially appointed custodian's capacity to comply with the subpoena).

14. Commonwealth v. Hughes, 380 Mass. 583, 404 N.E.2d 1239 (1980).

15. 493 U.S. 549, 110 S.Ct. 900, 107 L.Ed.2d 992 (1990).

pects, compelled arrestee participation in identification procedures, grand jury subpoenas, suppression procedures, court-ordered defense discovery to the prosecution, the defendant's exercise of the privilege (through silence) at his trial, sentencing procedures, claims in civil proceedings, claims in legislative investigations, and regulatory schemes requiring disclosures.[1] It has considered issues such as who is protected,[2] what constitutes "compulsion,"[3] what constitutes "incrimination,"[4] what kinds of compelled and incriminatory evidence may not be used against defendant,[5] how far does that prohibition against use extend,[6] what governmentally imposed burdens so impair the exercise of the privilege as to be unconstitutional,[7] and what should be required for waiver of the privilege.[8] The end result has been a variety of different doctrines, each shaped to fit both the particular issue and the particular context in which it is presented. Those doctrines are discussed at various points in the text as they arise in the chronological sequence of the criminal justice process.[9] Treated here is a common thread that runs through the Supreme Court opinions dealing with self-incrimination issues—the frequent reference to the history of the privilege and to the basic policies that underlie the privilege. While that common thread extends beyond the Supreme Court cases discussed in §§ 8.12–8.13, its consideration at this point is especially appropriate, as many of the most prominent discussions of the history and policies of the Fifth Amendment privilege are found in this group of opinions.

(b) History of the Privilege. The pre-1791 historical development of the privilege in England is clear in its major features but sometimes clouded in its grounding. In its initial formulation, the privilege reflected a rejection of the oath procedure used by the courts of High Commission and Star Chamber. A central feature of the opposition to those courts, which were active in the persecution of religious and political dissidents, was the objection to their use of the oath procedure to engage in roving inquiries. A person could be brought before the court without any substantiated charges filed against him, and there required to take an oath—the oath *ex officio* —to answer truthfully all questions that might be put to him. Although refusal to take the oath could result in serious consequences, there were those who refused to do so, citing the maxim *nemo teneture seipsum prodere* (no man is bound to produce himself). This maximum was in fact narrower than the quoted phrase. In full it stated that no man is bound to "produce himself" (i.e., accuse himself), but when accused by common repute, he would be held "to show, if he can, his innocence and purge himself."[10] Accordingly, when Parliament in 1641 abolished the courts of High Commission and Star Chamber and prohibited the administration of an *ex officio* oath requiring an answer to "things

§ 8.14

1. This text treats primarily those self-incrimination issues that arise in the course of the criminal justice process. See §§ 3.2(i), 3.4(a) (searches for documents); §§ 6.5–6.10 (police interrogation); § 7.2 (identification procedures); § 8.10 (grand jury testimony); § 8.11 (immunity grants); §§ 8.12–8.13 (documentary production); § 9.2 (suppression hearing testimony); §§ 9.5–9.6 (evidentiary uses of illegally obtained confessions); § 12.1(e) (bail hearing testimony); § 15.4 (indictments based on information obtained in violation of the privilege); § 20.4 (prosecution discovery); § 24.5 (defendant's right at trial); and § 26.4(c) (sentencing procedures). For a discussion of the self-incrimination privilege as it applies in a wider range of settings, see Cleary (ed.), McCormick on Evidence, Ch. 13 (3rd ed., 1984).

2. See § 8.12(b) (entity exception).

3. See § 6.5 (*Miranda*); § 9.2 (*Simmons*); § 8.12(e) (third party compulsion).

4. See § 8.10(a) (potential incrimination standard); § 8.10(b) (incrimination under laws of another sovereign); § 8.11 (immunity).

5. See §§ 7.2(a), 8.12(d) (*Schmerber* rule); § 8.12(c) (required records); §§ 8.12(f), 8.13 (act-of-production doctrine).

6. See § 8.11 (scope of immunity); § 9.5 (derivative use); § 9.6 (impeachment use).

7. See § 8.10 at note 19 (governmental sanctions); § 24.5 (comment and instruction on defendant's silence).

8. See § 6.9 (*Miranda* waiver standards); § 8.10(d) (witness waiver); § 23.4 (waiver by accused).

9. See notes 1–8 supra.

10. The full maxim was: Licet nemo tenetur seipsum prodere, tamen proditus per farman tenitur seipsum ostendere utrum possit suam innocentiam ostendere et seipsum purgare. Its precise interpretation is in dispute. See Silving, The Oath, 68 Yale L.J. 1329, 1527 (1959).

penal," the question remained as to whether a defendant could properly be put to oath after a proper presentment had been made against him. By the mid-1700's, however, that question had been clearly answered in the negative. Indeed, the privilege had been extended not only to the defendant in a criminal trial, but to mere witnesses as well.

Exactly why the English courts extended the privilege beyond the prohibition of the oath *ex officio* remains a subject of debate. Although some see in this development a response to the Star Chamber's use of torture, the practice of using judicially authorized torture to compel confessions apparently had been discarded even prior to the abolition of the oath *ex officio*. Others see the development as reflective of a growing judicial awareness that a person cannot be expected to contribute to his own potential conviction, but that view must be reconciled with the retention of the practice of magistrate interrogation of the accused at the preliminary examination (with any failure by the accused to respond noted by the magistrate in his testimony at trial). Of course, the examination by the magistrate was not under oath, and the *nemo teneture* maxim, when lifted out of its original context and applied to the charged defendant, might still have been seen as limited to compulsory oath taking. Still others suggest that the extension of the prohibition to the defendant and to witnesses reflected no major principle of justice, but simply the desire by the common law courts to avoid any form of procedure that remotely resembled that of the hated courts of High Commission and Star Chamber. This position must take account, however, of the possible influence of the forceful opponents of the oath *ex officio* who had broadly argued that the thrust of the *nemo teneture* maxim was to bar all judicial compulsion that forced a person to reveal what would subject him to penalty (with the only responsibility of the accused being to protest his innocence, if he could do so).

The privilege as developed in the English common law courts was carried over to the American colonies, at least as it applied to the accused, and it was included in the constitutions or bills of right of seven states prior to the adoption of the Fifth Amendment. Those state provisions referred to the right of an accused in a criminal prosecution not to be "compelled to give evidence against himself" or to the right of any person not to be "compelled to accuse or furnish evidence against himself." The phrasing of the privilege in the Fifth Amendment—as a prohibition against a person "being compelled in any criminal case to be a witness against himself"—was therefore quite distinctive, but its uniqueness at the time attracted no attention. Indeed, the privilege itself attracted little attention in the adoption of the Bill of Rights. There had been only a handful of references to the privilege in the earlier ratifying conventions that urged adoption of a federal bill of rights, and those were accompanied by no explanation of the privilege's scope apart from its general role as protection against employment of inquisitional practices. Subsequently, in presenting the privilege as part of the proposed Bill of Rights, Madison offered nothing except the language of the proposal.

What is to be made of this history? Initially, the Court has assumed that the key historical element is the privilege as developed in England, the constitutional framers being taken to have adopted the privilege as it then existed in English common law. As to the significance of that history, the treatment has varied with the setting. Justice Frankfurter once described the privilege as "a specific provision of which it is particularly true that 'a page of history is worth a volume of logic.'"[11] That statement was made, however, in a case presenting a self-incrimination issue on which the historical practice was quite clear—the use of immunity grants to displace the witness' right to claim the privilege. But such a square fit is rare. More often, the Court has been forced to look to the more general "lessons of history" as they point to the need for a "liberal construction" of the privilege. Moreover, when the historical confines of the privilege seem not to fit those

11. Ullman v. United States, § 8.11 at note 2.

general lessons of history, the Court has not hesitated to note, as it did in *Miranda,* that "a noble principle often transcends its origins." [12] Although the practice of magistrate questioning of the accused (not under oath) had continued for several decades following the adoption of the Constitution, the Court there concluded that the privilege could extend beyond the use of judicial process to compel testimony under oath where, as in the case of the "informal compulsion" of in-custody police interrogation, the policies underlying the privilege, as reflected by the basic themes of its "historical development," supported application of the privilege.

(c) Policies of the Privilege. While the Supreme Court's opinions have referred frequently to the history of the privilege, they even more commonly have cited the policy foundations of the privilege. That is to be expected, for where the history is entangled and the current context substantially changed, a broader, functional analysis is commonly seen as the more appropriate source for determining the modern day scope of a constitutional right. In the case of the self-incrimination privilege, however, the Court has recognized that such an analysis also has its limits.

The Court has viewed the policy foundations of the privilege quite broadly, arguably including not only the primary objectives of the privilege but also a variety of values which those objectives incidentally serve. The end result is a collection of values so extensive that, if each were followed to its logical end in defining the privilege, the practical consequences would not be tolerable—at least from the perspective of a Court majority. Consequently, the Court has been forced to note that, while it has said that the privilege should be construed "as broad[ly] as the mischief against which it seeks to guard," it also is true that "the privilege has never been given the full scope which the values it helps to protect suggests." Indeed, the Court has restricted the privilege through doctrinal limitations which, though they find support in certain values of the privilege, are acknowledged to leave the privilege short of fulfilling the full "complex of values [that] it helps to protect."

The classic listing of the "policies and purposes" underlying the privilege is that provided by Justice Goldberg in his opinion for the Court in *Murphy v. Waterfront Commission:*[13]

> [The privilege] reflects many of our fundamental values and most noble aspirations: [1] our unwillingness to subject those suspected of crime to the cruel trilemma of self-accusation, perjury or contempt; [2] our preferences for an accusatorial rather than an inquisitorial system of criminal justice; [3] our fear that self-incriminating statements will be elicited by inhumane treatment and abuses; [4] our sense of fair play which dictates "a fair state-individual balance by requiring the government in its contest with the individual to shoulder the entire load;" [5] our respect for the inviolability of the human personality and of the right of each individual "to a private enclave where he may lead a private life;" [6] our distrust of self-deprecatory statements; [7] and our realization that the privilege, while sometimes "a shelter to the guilty," is often "a protection to the innocent."

The policies cited by Justice Goldberg can usefully be divided, for analytical purposes, into two categories. First, there are those values that provide a "systemic rationale" for the privilege, viewing it as an instrumentalist guarantee designed to further procedural objectives that exist independent of the privilege. This category includes the second, fourth, sixth and seventh values listed by Justice Goldberg. Second, there are the values that recognize the privilege as an end in

12. *Miranda* is discussed in § 6.5. The reference was to a famous statement by Judge Frank in United States v. Grunewald, 233 F.2d 556 (2d Cir.1956), reversed 353 U.S. 391, 77 S.Ct. 963, 1 L.Ed.2d 931 (1957): "The critics of the Supreme Court, however, in their over-emphasis on the history of the Fifth Amendment privilege, overlook the fact that a noble privilege often transcends its origins, that creative misunderstandings account for some of our most cherished values and institutions; such a misunderstanding may be the mother of invention."

13. 378 U.S. 52, 84 S.Ct. 1594, 12 L.Ed.2d 678 (1964), also discussed in § 8.11 at note 4. In the quote that follows citations have been deleted and parenthetical numbering added.

itself, serving to recognize human dignity and individuality. The first, third, and fifth values in the *Murphy* listing fall in this category. The two subsections that follow consider the values within each of the two categories as they relate to Supreme Court rulings setting the scope of the privilege.

(d) Systemic Rationales. Justice Goldberg's sixth listed value sees the privilege as based in part on "our distrust of self-deprecatory statements." The basic assumption here is that such statements, at least where compelled, are less reliable as a class than other types of admissible evidence. While that assumption has been vigorously challenged by commentators, dating back at least to Bentham, it arguably finds some support in the common law prohibition against basing a conviction upon a confession that is not corroborated by other evidence.[14] Assuming the validity of the assumption, the question naturally arises as to why there is a need for the privilege in addition to the common law corroboration requirement. The usual response is the "lazy prosecutor" rationale for the privilege. This rationale sees the privilege as designed to serve a prophylactic function. Because it is much easier for the prosecution to build its case by forcing confessions from the suspect, the privilege bars the use of such statements and thereby forces the prosecution to establish its case through more reliable evidence. While the "lazy prosecutor" rationale is often seen as directed primarily against the compulsion of incriminatory statements in the investigative process, Wigmore saw it as justifying as well the application of the privilege to the accused at trial. Prosecutors anticipating a capacity to bolster their case by forcing the accused to testify at trial would lose the incentive to thoroughly investigate and would thereby risk the possibility both of missing exculpatory evidence that would prevent the conviction of the innocent accused and of failing to establish as conclusively as possible the guilt of the person rightfully convicted.

Accepting Wigmore's addendum to the lazy prosecutor argument, that argument would explain the application of the privilege in many contexts, but not all. The distinction drawn in *Schmerber* can be justified, for example, as recognizing the government's interest in acquiring evidence (e.g., blood samples) far more likely to be reliable than "self-deprecatory statements." On the other hand, this distinction would seem to extend as well to other areas in which the privilege is deemed applicable. Focusing on reliability, why should the privilege bar prosecutorial use of reliable physical evidence that is uncovered through use of a compelled statement of the accused?[15] Why too should the privilege be applicable to the act of producing documents or other physical evidence (and if some question as to reliability is seen in this context, why should the privilege be unavailable to a corporation—as surely the accuracy of verdicts is important in the prosecution of corporations as well as individuals)? Since the "lazy prosecutor" rationale is directed to the efforts of the government in gathering evidence, the availability of the privilege to a witness in a civil case not involving the government also may be questioned. Perhaps in part because of those questions, the Supreme Court has refused to characterize the privilege as a constitutional right aimed at discouraging the use of potentially unreliable evidence. The "privilege against self-incrimination," the Court has noted, "is not designed to enhance the reliability of the fact-finding determination: it stands in the constitution for entirely independent reasons."[16]

14. This prohibition was established after the recognition of the privilege against self-incrimination and therefore was directed primarily at confessions other than those made by the accused at trial. Jurisdictions varied as to the degree of corroboration required, with some insisting upon independent proof of the *corpus delecti* and others insisting only upon "substantial" independent evidence tending to establish the trustworthiness of the confession. A requirement of corroboration remains a part of the modern law of evidence, at least as to out-of-court confessions, with jurisdictions still divided as to the type of corroboration needed. See Cleary (ed.), McCormick on Evidence § 145 (3d ed., 1984).

15. See §§ 8.11, 9.5.

16. Allen v. Illinois, 478 U.S. 364, 106 S.Ct. 2988, 92 L.Ed.2d 296 (1986) (self-incrimination privilege was not a safeguard that had to be applied in a non-criminal pro-

Murphy's seventh value—protecting the innocent—is based in large part on the concern reflected in the sixth value as to the reliability of self-deprecatory statements. Commentators have suggested, however, that the privilege may also protect the innocent in another way. In some situations, an innocent accused, if forced to testify, would be likely to leave the jury with a false impression as to his guilt, even though he truthfully testified as to his innocence, because of his poor demeanor on the stand or an extensive criminal record used to impeach his credibility. But this grounding, even if thought to raise a situation of sufficient seriousness to justify a constitutional right, would explain only the defendant's right to refuse to testify. Neither it nor any other "innocence" rationale would justify many other aspects of the privilege (e.g., its availability to the witness and its application to the act of production). Moreover, here too, the Supreme Court has seemingly rejected such a rationale for the privilege. In those areas where the Court has been called upon to distinguish between constitutional rights designed to protect the innocent and other constitutional rights, the Court has placed the privilege in the latter category.[17]

Murhpy's fourth value—achieving a "fair state-individual balance" in the criminal justice process—actually has two components. The first, insisting that the government "leave the individual alone until good cause is shown," affords protection against investigative "fishing expeditions." The second, requiring the government "to shoulder the entire load" in its "contest with the individual," reflects the basic character of an accusatorial process. It thus coincides with *Murphy*'s second value—"our preference for an accusatorial rather than an inquisitorial system of justice." In an accusatorial system, the state must bear the responsibility for establishing guilt, as contrasted to a system in which the defendant is expected to come forward and establish his innocence.[18]

That the privilege should be seen as designed to protect the individual from being compelled to respond to a prosecutorial fishing expedition is hardly surprising. The opposition to the oath *ex officio* procedure used in the courts of High Commission and Star Chamber was directed at precisely such compulsion. However, the objective of providing such protection not only fails to justify the full breadth of the privilege, but actually raises questions as to the justification for at least one aspect of the *Schmerber* rule. The protection against prosecutorial fishing expeditions explains the availability of the privilege in the investigative process (and arguably in congressional investigations that often constitute a different form of roving inquiry), but not its availability at trial (the state by then having shown "good cause" for questioning the accused by virtue of its properly supported charge). Nor does it explain the availability of the privilege in a civil proceeding that is in no way connected with the investigative process. Moreover, if the individual truly has a broad right to be "let alone" absent a prosecutorial showing of "good cause," the privilege arguably should extend to compelled participation in identification procedures where the state has no greater grounding than a grand jury subpoena (which may issue without any showing of cause whatsoever). The restriction of the privilege to testimonial compulsion obviously looks to other values that are narrower than that right to be let alone.

The requirement that the state "bear the full responsibility for establishing guilt" also fails to fully explain the self-incrimination doctrine. While that requirement commonly is described as mandating that the prosecution establish its case through its "own independent labors," the Fourth Amendment makes clear that this does not preclude the

ceeding as part of the due process requirements designed to "guard against the risk of erroneous deprivation").

17. See Tehan v. United States ex rel. Shott, 382 U.S. 406, 86 S.Ct. 459, 15 L.Ed.2d 453 (1966) (under a doctrine focusing on this distinction in determining whether to apply retroactively new constitutional rulings, the Court refused retroactive application of an expanded self-incrimination ruling, noting that "the basic purposes that lie behind the privilege * * * do not relate to protecting the innocent from conviction").

18. See § 1.6(c).

use of defendant as a source of evidence. The questions therefore arise as to why compelling the defendant to disclose evidence is distinguished from "taking evidence" from the accused (through a search), and why even that direct compulsion is limited to testimonial evidence and thereby fails to encompass all compelled acts of the defendant that produce evidence for the prosecution (e.g., the acts compelled in *Doe II* and in identification procedures). The answers apparently lie in the special qualities of testimonial compulsion, but what gives those qualities particular significance is not the procedural structure produced by a preference for an accusatorial over an inquisitorial process, but values that exist independent of that structure. This was recognized in *Schmerber,* where the Court acknowledged that "the compulsion [through forced participation in an identification procedure] violates at least one meaning of the requirement that the State procure the evidence against an accused 'by its own independent labors.'" The *Schmerber* Court concluded, however, that the "independent-labors" concept, taken in light of other privilege values, was basically limited to precluding the state from producing evidence through "the cruel, simple expedient of compelling it through [defendant's] own mouth." So too, the entity cases implicitly recognize that the privilege rests on values that go beyond implementing an accusatorial process, since a corporation no less than an individual is entitled to the safeguards traditionally found in an accusatory process (e.g., the presumption of innocence).

(e) **Dignity Rationales.** The third value cited in *Murphy*—the "fear that self-incriminating statements will be elicited by inhumane treatment and abuses"—reflects a concern for human dignity that finds support in the earliest commentary on the privilege. While doubt exists as to whether the earlier use of torture in connection with Star Chamber proceedings played a significant role in gaining common law recognition of the privilege in the mid-seventeenth century, the *ex officio* oath procedure clearly was viewed by its opponents as an inhumane procedure. Indeed, it was characterized by some as a species of torture. Other abusive practices, such as the third degree and just plain browbeating or bullying, might be viewed as a similar mischief against which the privilege was to guard.[19] This would explain holding the privilege applicable to custodial interrogation or even grand jury questioning, but it would not explain its availability at trial, where the judge is available to prevent such tactics, or its application to the simple act of producing documents. Just as the privilege grew historically to bar more than the *ex officio* oath, so the rationale of the privilege must extend beyond precluding torture or similar abuses.

Just as the "torture rationale" is too narrow to explain the privilege, the "privacy rationale" suggested in *Murphy*'s fifth value is too broad. As the Court noted in *Fisher v. United States:* [20]

> It is true that the Court has often stated that one of the several purposes served by the constitutional privilege against compelled testimonial self-incrimination is that of protecting personal privacy. See, e.g., *Murphy v. Waterfront Comm'n.* But the Court has never suggested that every invasion of privacy violates the privilege. Within the limits imposed by the language of the Fifth Amendment, which we necessarily observe, the privilege truly serves privacy interests; but the Court has never on any ground, personal privacy included, applied the Fifth Amendment to prevent the otherwise proper acquisition or use of evidence which, in the Court's view, did

19. Of course abusive practices such as physical mistreatment would be contrary to the dignity of the individual even where not designed to elicit incriminating statements, and could be seen as a denial of liberty without due process where there was sufficient governmental involvement. See Screws v. United States, 325 U.S. 91, 65 S.Ct. 1031, 89 L.Ed. 1495 (1945). However, since such abusive practices would often be utilized to obtain incriminating statements and since the privilege would withdraw that incentive by barring prosecution use of such statements, the privilege could be seen as providing an additional remedial element that might be more effective in precluding such abuses. Cf. Rochin v. California, discussed at § 2.4(d).

20. 425 U.S. 391, 96 S.Ct. 1569, 48 L.Ed.2d 39 (1984), discussed at § 8.12(e), (f).

not involve compelled testimonial self-incrimination of some sort.

As *Fisher* suggests, the limitation of the privilege to testimonial disclosures narrows considerably the "private enclave" protected by the privilege. The focus is on the disclosure "of the contents of the mind," as the state seeks to secure a "communication * * * upon which reliance is to be placed as involving the accused's consciousness of the facts and the operation of his mind in expressing it." [21] Moreover, what *Murphy* described as "our respect for the inviolability of the human personality" does not preclude all efforts to obtain such information, but only that in which the individual is compelled to make the disclosure. Thus, as *Fisher* also noted in its rejection of a broad-scale privacy foundation for the privilege, *Katz v. United States* and its progeny clearly recognize the government's authority to electronically record and later use in evidence the private incriminating statements of the accused, though such statements also reflect his state of mind.[22] So too, as *Fisher* further noted, even where the individual is compelled to reveal the contents of his mind, the privilege is not violated unless the content poses a real and appreciable danger of incrimination. Thus, where immunity is granted consistent with *Kastigar,*[23] compelled disclosure does not violate the privilege no matter how personal and private the subject of the testimony.

With the elements of testimony, compulsion, and incrimination restricting the privacy protection of the privilege to a quite specific and narrow band of privacy, some explanation as to the special quality of that privacy is needed if the privilege is to be defined by reference to a privacy rationale. One suggestion, finding possible support in the Court's reference to the "inviolability of the human personality," is the special privacy of the individual's "conscience." Compelling a person to condemn himself out of his own mouth—and thereby to acknowledge his guilt—is said to deprive that person of his moral autonomy to come to grips with his conscience on his own terms. This view, however, fails to explain the application of the privilege to various instances of incriminating testimony, including that found in the act of production, which clearly fall far short of self-condemnation. Measured by reference to the preservation of moral autonomy, many of these forced disclosures are not readily distinguishable from being forced to provide an incriminating blood sample. Also, from this perspective, self-condemnation would seem to be measured by the content of the admission, not by whether the individual's statements can be used against him in a subsequent prosecution.

The cruel trilemma cited in *Murphy*'s first listed value arguably receives the strongest historical support as a grounding for the privilege. Although some commentators quarrel with the underlying moral judgment, almost all acknowledge that the privilege arose from a belief that it was uniquely cruel and inhumane to subject a person to the trilemma of "self-accusation, perjury, or contempt." That belief explains why the privilege was carried beyond the prohibition of the oath *ex officio* and made available to the accused at trial and to witnesses in all types of judicial proceedings. It also explains why the grant of immunity displaced the privilege, as the individual could then testify truthfully without fearing incrimination. The testimonial distinction, as drawn in *Schmerber,* also finds support in this rationale. For a critical element of the trilemma was the pressure imposed upon the individual to violate his oath by committing perjury, an act viewed as a cardinal sin for a religious person. Where the individual is not being required to communicate the content of his mind, as in his forced participation in identification procedures, he is not given the opportunity to lie. The act of production, in contrast, does present a perjury potential through the false disclaimer that the subpoenaed item does not exist or is not in the possession of the subpoenaed party. Of course, the same potential is present where

21. Doe v. United States, discussed at §§ 8.12(d), 8.13(a).

22. See § 3.2(a) and Chapter 4.

23. See § 8.11(a), (b).

one is required to produce "required records" or entity records, but here the special responsibility that the individual assumed for the records may be seen as a distinguishing factor.

The cruel trilemma does not, of course, explain the extension of the privilege to custodial interrogation. In that setting, the individual faces no threat of perjury. Nonetheless, the Court in *Miranda*[24] concluded that "all the principles embodied in the privilege apply to informal compulsion exerted by law-enforcement officers during in-custody questioning." The policies cited in *Murphy,* the Court noted, "point to one overriding thought"—that the government must respect "the dignity and integrity of its citizens." That respect was missing where the compulsion of custodial interrogation, which "may well be greater" than that imposed by judicial process, is used to force the individual to furnish incriminatory evidence "from his own mouth." Thus, the Court looked beyond the element of the oath, and focused on the need to respect the individual's instinct for self-preservation as it related to controlling whether he would reveal the contents of his mind. In effect, the "cruel trilemma" rationale was converted to a "cruel dilemma" rationale.

As evidenced by *Miranda,* the "complex of values" that underlie the privilege offer more than a little leeway in defining the "mischief against which the privilege seeks to guard." Those values do not necessarily explain in themselves why the privilege has the scope that it currently possesses. The Court has looked to a mixture of considerations—of which the values are only one—in setting the scope of the privilege. It has looked to the strength of historical patterns as they suggest the core elements of the privilege,[25] whether a particular interpretation flows logically from a value underlying that privilege,[26] the priority of the particular value where the values do not all combine to point in a particular direction (as is usually the case),[27] and the potential bearing of a particular interpretation upon the effectiveness of law enforcement.[28]

§ 8.15 The Witness' Right to Counsel

(a) Constitutional Requirements. Although the Supreme Court has not ruled directly on whether a grand jury witness has a constitutional right to the assistance of counsel, the justices have made major statements on that issue in two cases, *In re Groban,*[1] and *United States v. Mandujano.*[2] *Groban* did not involve a grand jury proceeding, but rather a special investigative proceeding of a state fire marshal at which the witness was not allowed to be accompanied by counsel. In finding that the exclusion of counsel did not violate due process, the Court majority drew an analogy to the grand jury proceeding. "A witness before a grand jury," the Court noted, "cannot insist, as a matter of constitutional right, on being represented by counsel." While it was possible that "the number of people present in a grand jury proceeding gives greater assurance that improper use will not be made of the witness' presence," the "presumption of fair and orderly conduct by state officials without coercion or distortion" was equally applicable to the proceeding before it, in absence of "facts to the contrary." Justice Black, in dissent, agreed that there was no constitutional right to counsel in the grand jury proceeding, but viewed the fire marshal's proceeding as not truly analogous. He stressed that the witness before the grand jury had the protection of "the presence of

24. See § 6.5.

25. See Schmerber v. California, discussed at § 8.12(d) and Brown v. Walker, discussed at § 8.11.

26. See Murphy v. Waterfront Commission, discussed at § 8.10(b) and Miranda v. Arizona, discussed supra.

27. See Fisher v. United States, discussed at § 8.12(e), and Doe v. United States, discussed at §§ 8.12(d), 8.13(a).

28. See United States v. White, discussed at § 8.12(b) and Braswell v. United States, discussed at § 8.13(d). Consider also Harlan, J., dissenting in Spevack v. Klein, 385 U.S. 511, 87 S.Ct. 625, 17 L.Ed.2d 574 (1967): "[T]he Court has chiefly derived its [self-incrimination] standards from consideration of two factors: the history and purposes of the privilege, and the character and urgency of other public interests involved."

§ 8.15

1. 352 U.S. 330, 77 S.Ct. 510, 1 L.Ed.2d 376 (1957).

2. 425 U.S. 564, 96 S.Ct. 1768, 48 L.Ed.2d 212 (1976).

jurors," which offered a "substantial safeguard" against abuse.

In *Mandujano,* a grand jury witness was told that "he could have a lawyer outside the room with whom he could consult," but he was not offered the assistance of an appointed attorney, although claiming to be indigent. The lower courts held that, as a "putative" or "virtual" defendant, he was in a position akin to an arrestee and should have been given complete *Miranda* warnings, including advice as to appointed counsel. As noted in § 8.10(d), the Court upheld Mandujano's perjury conviction without reaching the lower court's ruling on the *Miranda* warnings. Six members of the Court, however, did speak to that ruling. Four justices, through Chief Justice Burger's plurality opinion, concluded that the advice given Mandujano as to the availability of counsel was fully consistent with any constitutional requirements. Since "no criminal proceedings had been instituted," the "Sixth Amendment right to counsel had not come into play." The prerequisite of an "initiation of adversary judicial proceedings," as set forth in *Kirby v. Illinois,*[3] rendered the Sixth Amendment inapplicable. The *Miranda* right to counsel, "fashioned to secure the suspect's Fifth Amendment privilege," also did not apply. It was premised upon an "inherently coercive" interrogation setting, clearly distinguishable from grand jury questioning. Under "settled principles," as reflected in *Groban,* "the witness may not insist upon the presence of his attorney in the grand jury room."

Justice Brennan, joined by Justice Marshall, took a quite different view of the witness' right to counsel. Reliance upon cases like *Kirby* was inappropriate, Justice Brennan argued, because the questioning of a putative defendant "inextricably involve[s]" the privilege against self-incrimination, as well as the Sixth Amendment. "Given the inherent danger of subversion of the adversary system in the case of a putative defendant called to testify * * *, and the peculiarly critical role of the Fifth Amendment as the bulwark against such abuse, it is plainly obvious that some guidance by counsel is required." The defendant was at least entitled to be informed of the following:

> That he has a right to consult with an attorney prior to questioning, that if he cannot afford an attorney one will be appointed for him, that during the questioning he may have the attorney wait outside the grand jury room, and that he may at any and all times during questioning consult with the attorney prior to answering any question posed.

The dictum in *Groban,* Justice Brennan argued, must be reexamined in light of more recent decisions like *Miranda* and *Escobedo.*

Prior to *Mandujano,* the lower courts, relying on *Groban,* uniformly held that the grand jury witness had no constitutional right to counsel, and the 4–2 split in *Mandujano* has led them to largely reaffirm their earlier decisions. Their rulings, however, have tended to be quite limited. Since jurisdictions commonly allow the grand jury witness to consult with counsel located outside the grand jury room, the lower courts ordinarily have been required to deal only with the witness' right to have counsel present while he testifies. Lower court opinions have occasionally suggested that there is no constitutional right to even consult with counsel in the anteroom, but they have looked primarily to the Sixth Amendment in denying the existence of such a right. They have not considered the possibility that the self-incrimination privilege may carry with it a right of a witness to consult with counsel where the witness is uncertain as to the availability of the privilege.[4] The lower court cases also have not

3. See §§ 7.3(b); 11.2(b). Presumably a different result would apply if the witness had been formally charged, but a witness in that situation would not ordinarily be called before the grand jury. See § 8.10, note 10.

4. Some support for this position may be found in Maness v. Meyers, 419 U.S. 449, 95 S.Ct. 584, 42 L.Ed.2d 574 (1975). *Maness* held that the Fifth Amendment precluded holding a lawyer in contempt "for advising his client, during the trial of a civil case, to refuse to produce material demanded by a subpoena duces tecum when the lawyer believed in good faith the material might tend to incriminate his client." Noting the layman's need for legal advice in determining the "nuances and boundaries" of the Fifth Amendment privilege, the Court reasoned that the privilege would be "drained of its meaning

been required to rule upon the right of an indigent target-witness to the appointment of counsel for the purpose of anteroom consultations. Grand jury investigations deal largely with offenses committed by non-indigents, and in the occasional cases involving an indigent target-witness, appointed counsel has usually been made available as a matter of local practice. While only a small group of states have statutory provisions requiring the prosecutor to offer appointed counsel to an indigent target, judges in many other jurisdictions have adopted that practice in the exercise of their supervisory authority, especially where a public defender is available to represent such witnesses.

(b) Counsel Within the Grand Jury Room. Slightly more than a dozen states have statutes permitting at least certain witnesses to be assisted by counsel located within the grand jury room. Most of these provisions apply to all witnesses, but a few are limited to targets. The statutes commonly contain provisions limiting the role of counsel while before the grand jury. Several state that the lawyer may "advise the witness," but "may not otherwise take any part in the proceeding." One jurisdiction, however, also allows counsel to "interpose objections on behalf of the witness."

Most of the statutes noted above were adopted over the last two decades. During the same period, various other jurisdictions considered and rejected similar proposals. Allowing counsel within the grand jury room has proven to be one of the more controversial of the recent grand jury reform proposals. Supporters claim that only counsel within the grand jury room ensures adequate protection of the witness' legal rights. They argue that even the most liberal right to consult with counsel outside the grand jury room will prove unsatisfactory. They note that: (1) witnesses are reluctant to leave repeatedly for fear that the grand jury will believe they have "something to hide"; (2) because witnesses will not leave after every question, counsel often is forced to give advice based on speculation as to the probable phrasing of the next series of questions; (3) even where the witness is able to report each question to counsel before responding, it often is difficult for a lawyer who does not himself hear the question to judge the "flow of the questioning"; (4) since witnesses before the grand jury are under considerable stress, many have difficulty in following their counsel's directions; (5) since counsel does not hear the witness' precise testimony, he cannot assist the witness in correcting unintentional factual errors or misleading statements; and (6) the presence of the lawyer within the grand jury room, as opposed to the hallway, serves as a far superior deterrent to improper questioning and harassment of the witness.

Opponents of the new legislation acknowledge that the need to leave the grand jury room poses certain difficulties for the witness, but argue that those difficulties are not so great as to undermine the witness' ability to exercise his rights, particularly as to the privilege against self-incrimination. They see any additional protection of witness rights as clearly outweighed by the damaging effects that counsel's presence would have upon the grand jury's capacity to conduct effective investigations. They argue that, notwithstanding statutory prohibitions, counsel accompanying witnesses would find techniques, such as stage whispers and objections presented through the witness, for challenging the prosecutor's questions or conveying arguments to the jurors. With no judge present to put an immediate stop to such tactics, the end result would be disruption and delay of the investigation. They argue further, that with counsel at the witness' side, more witnesses will reply to questions by merely parroting responses formulated by counsel—responses that too often give away as little information as possible or are purposely ambiguous so as to avoid potential perjury charges. The crit-

if counsel, being lawfully present, * * * could be penalized for advising his client." The Court added, however, that it was not carrying its ruling as far as suggested by the concurring opinion of Justice Stewart, who argued that due process granted the witness in a civil case a general right to be advised by retained counsel. See § 11.1(b).

ics draw an analogy to the trial, where the defendant, once taking the stand, is not allowed to interrupt his testimony for further discussions with counsel. Finally, it is noted that, in some instances, the witness may not be entirely trustful of counsel and therefore prefer not to have counsel present. The witness may be forced to accept counsel provided by others (e.g., his employer) and fear retaliation if the full scope of his testimony is carried back to such persons. Once the law permits counsel to be present, the witness will be under pressure to allow counsel to accompany him, and will lose the capacity to be selective in the disclosure of his testimony to counsel.

(c) Counsel in the Anteroom. In those jurisdictions in which the witness must leave the grand jury room to consult with counsel, different approaches are taken as to the frequency of such consultations. Lawyers sometimes urge witnesses to consult after each question, which allows the lawyer to construct a complete record of the questions asked. Many federal courts permit such a practice, while others go almost that far, limiting witnesses to departures after every few questions. Other jurisdictions are more stringent. One court held that a grand jury could properly refuse a witness' request to leave where the witness was obviously seeking "strategic advice" rather than counseling as to the exercise of any legal rights. Another court concluded that rather than allow witnesses to leave for regular consultation, a witness should be advised that if he "should be doubtful as to whether he can properly refuse to answer a particular question, the witness can come before the court, accompanied by counsel, and obtain a ruling as to whether he should answer the question."

Jurisdictions that limit the witness' right to leave usually do so on two grounds—avoidance of "undue delay" and restricting counsel to his proper role. If witnesses are allowed to consult after each question, no matter what its nature, they may, it is argued, simply "wear the grand jury down." Moreover, if the attorney's advice properly is limited to counseling the witnesses on the exercise of testimonial privileges, there simply is no reason to allow consultation when the question clearly poses no such difficulty. Jurisdictions allowing more frequent consultations respond that: (1) it is too difficult to determine when a witness will or will not be seeking the advice of counsel relating to the exercise of a privilege—particularly in light of the possibility of "unintentionally waiving" the self-incrimination privilege; and (2) more delay will result from litigation relating to refusals to permit the witness to consult than will result from freely permitting consultation.

(d) Multiple Representation. In recent years, many state and federal prosecutors have adopted a policy of seeking disqualification of counsel who are simultaneously representing more than one witness or target (or combination thereof) in a particular grand jury investigation. The judicial response to such motions has been mixed. While the courts agree that multiple representation is subject to judicial control, they are divided as to general outlook and applicable standards.

Motions for disqualification have been based on two grounds. First, it has been argued that the courts have an obligation to preclude joint representation of clients with conflicting interests. This obligation stems from judicial authority to protect the interests of the client and to safeguard the integrity of the administration of justice. These same interests were recognized in *Wheat v. United States* [5] as giving the trial judge discretionary authority to preclude multiple representation at trial (notwithstanding the defendants' waiver of the right to conflict-free counsel) upon a showing of a "serious potential for conflict." Second, the government has maintained, often as a supplementary ground, that courts may bar multiple representation where it has been used to undermine "the right of the public to an effectively functioning grand jury investigation." As between these two grounds, the courts generally have been far more receptive to the former. Indeed, most of

5. See § 11.9(c).

the cases citing the second ground with approval have involved situations in which disqualification was basically justified by reference to the first ground.

Challenges to multiple representation based on the need to preclude a conflict of interest are viewed as presenting issues roughly analogous to those faced by a trial court when it is suggested that a potential conflict may exist between jointly represented co-defendants. There are, however, certain differences in the two settings that may lead a court to adopt a somewhat different approach for each. Initially, the criminal defendant's claim to the assistance of counsel rests squarely on the Sixth Amendment whereas the grand jury witness' claim arguably rests on a more flexible due process right to seek legal advice. On the other hand, the advantages of multiple representation may well be greater at the grand jury stage than at the post-indictment stage.[6] For example, representation by a single lawyer may give a group of witnesses far greater discovery as to the nature of the grand jury proceeding than they would obtain through separate representation; at the trial stage, joint representation is less likely to give co-defendants any substantial advantage in discovering the government's case.

Still another significant difference relates to the assessment by both court and client of the precise nature of any actual or potential conflict. Grand jury secrecy may preclude a full development in open court of all the facts that may have a bearing on the existence of a conflict. Very often, the presence of a conflict depends upon the government's view of the status of the jointly represented individuals (e.g., whether one is a target and another a prime candidate for immunity); however, disclosure of such information to those persons as a group would lose for the government a major advantage it hopes to gain through grand jury secrecy. The witness' ability to intelligently waive his right to conflict-free counsel is further hindered because even the subject under investigation may not be firm.

Taken together, the factors noted above would appear to justify, under the rationale of *Wheat,* granting the court somewhat greater latitude to bar multiple representation in the grand jury setting than in the trial setting. Still, unless one were to accept the view that a witness has no interest in counsel of his choice because he has no Sixth Amendment right to counsel, the *Wheat* rationale would not justify disqualification in all situations. Circumstances may clearly indicate that disqualification is not needed either to protect the client against an uninformed waiver, to avoid a whipsaw situation in which the client can later argue that he was adversely affected by an unknown conflict, or to ensure that legal proceedings are conducted within "the ethical standards of the profession." Such a case may be presented, for example, where all jointly represented witnesses are equally targets or non-targets, all participated in the same fashion in a clearly identified subject under inquiry, none have been offered immunity, and they have agreed on a joint strategy of exercising the privilege. Prosecutors have argued, however, that even in such a case disqualification may be ordered, basically to further the right of the public to an effectively functioning grand jury.

Though prosecutor motions for disqualification in joint "stonewalling" cases have been granted in several reported cases, those disqualifications cannot be said to clearly support the prosecutors' contention in this regard. Each case presented specific elements suggesting at least a serious potential for conflicting interests among the clients. Other courts, in denying disqualifications in "stonewalling" cases, have suggested that consideration should be given to "preserving the effectiveness of the grand jury investigation" only where the government also shows that the various witnesses in fact have directly conflicting interests. They note that "discomfort

6. It also is argued that, since counsel does not present a defense or otherwise play an active role in grand jury proceedings, conflicts of interest are likely to be less costly to jointly represented witnesses than to jointly represented co-defendants. On the other hand, at least equivalent damage can flow to one client from counsel's failure to seek immunity on behalf of that client in an effort to protect other clients.

to the grand jury process, without more, is not sufficient to vitiate an individual's important right to counsel of his own choosing."

On the other hand, the Colorado Supreme Court, stressing "society's interest in grand jury secrecy and effectiveness," upheld a statute that prohibited all multiple representation except with the permission of the grand jury.[7] That statute, however, had several unique elements. It also worked to the benefit of the grand jury witness by allowing counsel to be present in the grand jury room,[8] and it required both witness and lawyer to take an oath of secrecy which would be violated if counsel disclosed one client's testimony to another. These two elements, both tied to the structure of the state's grand jury process, arguably furnish a stronger grounding for barring multiple representation than the use of a stonewalling strategy, which very often is the strategy that would have been adopted (though perhaps with less ease) even if the witnesses had been represented separately.

7. People ex rel. Losavio v. J.L., 195 Colo. 494, 580 P.2d 23 (1978).

8. The court also held, however, that this provision precluded by implication the alternative of allowing a witness to choose joint representation and then freely leave the grand jury room to consult with counsel. The statutory provision was directed at "conservation of the time of the grand jury" as well as protecting the rights of the grand jury witness. A few of the other statutes authorizing counsel to accompany the witness before the grand jury also restrict or prohibit multiple representation.

Chapter 9

SCOPE OF THE EXCLUSIONARY RULES

Table of Sections

---

§ 9.1 Standing: The "Personal Rights" Approach

(a) "Personal Rights" as to Searches, Confessions and Identifications. When a motion to suppress evidence is made in a criminal case on the ground that the evidence was obtained in violation of the Constitution, there may be put in issue the question of whether the movant is a proper party to assert the claim of illegality and seek the remedy of exclusion. This question is ordinarily characterized as one of whether the party has "standing" to raise the contention.

One aspect of the standing requirement is that the party seeking relief must have an adversary interest in the outcome. As explained in *Baker v. Carr*,[1] requiring that this party establish "a personal stake in the outcome of the controversy" is intended "to assure that concrete adverseness which sharpens the presentation of issues upon which the court so largely depends for illumination of difficult constitutional questions." On this score, any defendant in a criminal case against whom evidence alleged to have been illegally seized is being offered surely qualifies. In most areas of constitutional law, however, it is also necessary that the adverse interest be based upon a violation of the rights of the individual raising the claim rather than the violation of the rights of some third party. This is generally true with respect to the various constitutional issues which might arise in the context of a suppression hearing.

For example, when a Fourth Amendment claim is involved it is not sufficient that the defendant "claims prejudice only through the use of evidence gathered as a consequence of a search or seizure directed at someone else"; rather, he "must have been a victim of a search or seizure." [2] "This standing rule," the Court explained on another occasion, "is premised on a recognition that the need for deterrence and hence the rationale for excluding the evidence are strongest where the Government's unlawful conduct would result in imposition of a criminal sanction on the victim of the search." [3] Just who should be deemed a "victim of the search" under this line of reasoning has proved over the years to be a difficult and provocative question. The current view of the Supreme Court, however, is that the fundamental inquiry to be made in ascertaining whether the defendant has Fourth Amendment standing is whether the conduct which the defendant wants to put in issue involved an intrusion into *his* reasonable expectation of privacy.[4] Because expectation-of-privacy analysis is also used in deciding whether any Fourth Amendment search has occurred, it has been concluded that there no longer exists a concept of standing "distinct from the merits" [5] of a Fourth Amendment claim. But this notion that the search and standing "inquiries merge into one" [6] is best avoided; the question traditionally labelled as standing (did the police intrude upon *this defendant's* justified expectation of privacy?) is not identical to the question of whether any Fourth Amendment search occurred (did the police intrude upon *anyone's* justified expectation of privacy?), and thus the former inquiry deserves separate attention no matter what label is put upon it.

Questions of standing seldom arise as to confessions because established evidentiary rules normally permit a confession to be admitted as substantive evidence only against the maker. But the issue comes to the fore when, for example, the confession reveals the location of physical evidence which is recovered and then offered as evidence in the trial of another person. Such was the situation in *People v. Varnum*,[7] where the confession had admittedly been obtained in violation of the *Escobedo–Miranda* rules and where the situation was further complicated by a well-established state rule that constitutional rights could be vicariously asserted. In holding the physical evidence admissible, the court reasoned no constitutional violation had occurred in that "the Fifth and Sixth Amendment rights protected by *Escobedo* * * * and *Mi-*

§ 9.1

1. 369 U.S. 186, 82 S.Ct. 691, 7 L.Ed.2d 663 (1962).

2. Jones v. United States, 362 U.S. 257, 80 S.Ct. 725, 4 L.Ed.2d 697 (1960).

3. United States v. Calandra, 414 U.S. 338, 94 S.Ct. 613, 38 L.Ed.2d 561 (1974).

4. Rawlings v. Kentucky, 448 U.S. 98, 100 S.Ct. 2556, 65 L.Ed.2d 633 (1980); Rakas v. Illinois, 439 U.S. 128, 99 S.Ct. 421, 58 L.Ed.2d 387 (1978); Mancusi v. DeForte, 392 U.S. 364, 88 S.Ct. 2120, 20 L.Ed.2d 1154 (1968).

5. Rakas v. Illinois, 439 U.S. 128, 99 S.Ct. 421, 58 L.Ed.2d 387 (1978).

6. Rawlings v. Kentucky, 448 U.S. 98, 100 S.Ct. 2556, 65 L.Ed.2d 633 (1980).

7. 66 Cal.2d 808, 59 Cal.Rptr. 108, 427 P.2d 772 (1967).

randa are violated only when evidence obtained without the required warnings and waiver is introduced against the person whose questioning produced the evidence." Although this reasoning has been questioned, the *Varnum* result would certainly be correct under a "personal rights" analysis, for any constitutional violation which occurred intruded only upon the rights of the person who made the confession. Thus, even if the defendant was himself subjected to an arrest or search based upon a confession obtained from another in violation of *Miranda,* he would lack standing to claim that what was obtained by the arrest or search should be suppressed as the fruits of the *Miranda* violation.

While the court in *Varnum* carefully distinguished the case from one in which the police obtained the confession by using "physically and psychologically coercive tactics condemned by due process," under the "personal rights" approach there would be no standing even as to such a confession. Thus, if the police beat *A* until he confesses his role as an accomplice in a murder and says that his gun (used by *B*) is in his house and the police then retrieve the gun from *A*'s house, defendant *B* is not entitled to have the gun suppressed as a fruit of *A*'s coerced confession. If *A* had said the gun was in *B*'s house and the police on that basis obtained a warrant to search *B*'s house and found the gun there, *B* would still lack standing to claim this was a fruit of the confession but would have standing to raise his own Fourth Amendment claim that the warrant was invalid because based upon information known to be unreliable. More problematical would be a case in which a coerced confession is itself offered, as might happen if *A* testifies at *B*'s trial on *B*'s behalf and the prosecution then wants to impeach that testimony with a confession coerced from *A*. Though *B* could not be impeached by a coerced or involuntary statement obtained from him,[8] it is unclear whether it follows from this that he would have standing as to *A*'s confession. It may well be that *B* is entitled to an assurance that "the trustworthiness of the evidence satisfies legal standards,"[9] but this is a narrower proposition, for *A*'s confession could be coerced or involuntary in a due process sense but yet be trustworthy.

Standing issues also arise infrequently with respect to unconstitutional identification procedures. But they can occur, as where in an accomplice's trial identification evidence is offered to show that his principal committed the crime charged. Where the nature of the constitutional violation was denial of the right to counsel at a lineup provided under *United States v. Wade,*[10] it has been held by analogy to Fourth Amendment standing rules that the defendant lacks standing to raise the other person's Sixth Amendment rights. Doubtless the cases noted above disallowing standing as to another's denial of counsel under *Miranda* might also be thought relevant here. But it may be seriously questioned whether either of these analogies is sound. *Wade,* after all, is grounded on the proposition that if a defendant's conviction rests on "a suspect pretrial identification which the accused is helpless to subject to effective scrutiny at trial, the accused is deprived of that right of cross-examination which is an essential safeguard to his right to confront the witnesses against him." In other words, the constitutional right at issue belongs to the person on trial rather than the person identified, and thus the defendant has standing, for otherwise there would be present a serious risk that the issue of his guilt or innocence might not be reliably determined. Whatever the result in such circumstances, surely a defendant has standing to object to an identification procedure conducted in violation of *Stovall v. Denno,*[11] for such a due process violation exists only when the procedure has been such as to create "a very substantial likelihood of irreparable misiden-

8. Mincey v. Arizona, 437 U.S. 385, 98 S.Ct. 2408, 57 L.Ed.2d 290 (1978).

9. Harris v. New York, 401 U.S. 222, 91 S.Ct. 643, 28 L.Ed.2d 1 (1971).

10. 388 U.S. 218, 87 S.Ct. 1926, 18 L.Ed.2d 1149 (1967).

11. 388 U.S. 293, 87 S.Ct. 1967, 18 L.Ed.2d 1199 (1967).

tification." [12] Such evidence is just as unreliable when it is directed toward the identity of an alleged coparticipant in a crime as when it relates to the identity of the defendant on trial.

A final word of caution concerning the "personal rights" approach: in determining in any particular case whether a defendant has standing, it is critical that the police conduct being objected to be properly identified, for this may turn out to be determinative on the standing issue. A very useful illustration of this point is provided by *Wong Sun v. United States.*[13] Federal narcotics agents made an illegal entry into the premises of Toy and then illegally arrested him, after which Toy in response to questioning said he had no narcotics but that Yee did. The agents then went to and entered Yee's premises and obtained narcotics from him, which Yee said he had obtained from Toy and Wong Sun. The narcotics were later admitted against both Toy and Wong Sun. The Court concluded that Wong Sun had no standing to seek their suppression, for their seizure "invaded no right of privacy of person or premises which would entitle Wong Sun to object." This would mean that Toy would likewise lack standing if he were also objecting merely to the agents' conduct at the Yee premises. However, Toy was held to have standing because he was objecting to the actions of the agents at his own premises which led to Yee and which thus made the narcotics obtained from Yee the "fruit of the poisonous tree" of the violation of his own Fourth Amendment rights.

(b) Residential Premises. It has long been true [14] and is still so under the modern expectation-of-privacy test [15] that an individual with a present possessory interest in the premises searched has standing to challenge that search even though he was not present when the search was made. This includes those who are tenants of a house or apartment or who are renting a room in a hotel, motel or rooming house, and also includes an owner-occupant but of course not an owner who has by lease given the full possessory right to another. Family members regularly residing upon the premises, such as a spouse or offspring, have standing of essentially the same dimensions. In *Bumper v. North Carolina,*[16] for example, the Supreme Court summarily concluded that there could "be no question of the petitioner's standing" to challenge a search of his grandmother's home during his absence in light of the fact that he regularly resided there as well.

Establishing such an interest in the premises searched itself suffices to establish standing, and thus the defendant need not also show an interest in the particular items which are seized by the police. As the Supreme Court explained in *Alderman v. United States:* [17]

> If the police make an unwarranted search of a house and seize tangible property belonging to third parties * * * the home owner may object to its use against him, not because he had any interest in the seized items as "effects" protected by the Fourth Amendment, but because they were the fruits of an unauthorized search of his house, which is itself expressly protected by the Fourth Amendment.

The majority in *Alderman* thus concluded that a person should have standing to object to illegal electronic eavesdropping which "overheard conversations of * * * himself or conversations occurring on his premises, whether or not he was present or participated in those conversations." A vigorous dissent contended this should not be so when the eavesdropping occurred without physical penetration of the premises, for then the house-

12. Simmons v. United States, 390 U.S. 377, 88 S.Ct. 967, 19 L.Ed.2d 1247 (1968).

13. 371 U.S. 471, 83 S.Ct. 407, 9 L.Ed.2d 441 (1963).

14. See Alderman v. United States, 394 U.S. 165, 89 S.Ct. 961, 22 L.Ed.2d 176 (1969), noting this to be the long-accepted rule.

15. In Rakas v. Illinois, 439 U.S. 128, 99 S.Ct. 421, 58 L.Ed.2d 387 (1978), the Court stated: "One of the main rights attaching to property is the right to exclude others, * * * and one who owns or lawfully possesses or controls property will in all likelihood have a legitimate expectation of privacy by virtue of this right to exclude."

16. 391 U.S. 543, 88 S.Ct. 1788, 20 L.Ed.2d 797 (1968).

17. 394 U.S. 165, 89 S.Ct. 961, 22 L.Ed.2d 176 (1969).

holder's property interest has not been intruded upon, and he can claim no privacy interest in conversations which he neither participated in nor heard.

If a defendant claims standing derived from his interest in the premises searched, he will not prevail if it appears that he had abandoned the premises prior to the time the search being objected to occurred.[18] But under the modern expectation-of-privacy approach the abandonment question must be examined in terms of reasonable expectations flowing from conduct rather than in a technical, property sense. In any event, abandonment must be distinguished from a mere disclaimer of a property interest made to the police prior to the search, which under the better view does not defeat standing.

It is sometimes important to ascertain the physical dimensions of defendant's property interest in the premises, as is reflected by the cases holding a lessee has no standing as to a portion of the premises not leased to him. But under the expectation-of-privacy approach it could be argued that at least sometimes one's justified expectations are somewhat broader than the area of exclusive possession. Consider *McDonald v. United States,*[19] where police illegally entered the house of defendant's landlady and then, by standing on a chair in a second-floor hallway, looked through the transom and saw illegal activity in defendant's room. Though a majority of the Court never responded specifically to the government's argument that McDonald could not complain of the police intrusion into his landlady's portion of the premises, Justice Jackson helpfully commented: "But it seems to me that each tenant of a building, while he has no right to exclude from the common hallways those who enter lawfully, does have a personal and constitutionally protected interest in the integrity and security of the entire building against unlawful breaking and entry." This is a very sensible approach, and seemingly has renewed vitality now that the Supreme Court has backed away[20] from its earlier position that one cannot have a legitimate expectation of privacy for standing purposes without having a "right to exclude other persons from access to" the place in question.[21]

Yet another way by which one could acquire standing as to residential premises was recognized in *Jones v. United States,*[22] where defendant was present in the apartment of another at the time of the search and he testified that the apartment belonged to a friend who had given him the use of it and a key with which he had admitted himself. The Court, after declaring that "[d]istinctions such as those between 'lessee,' 'licensee,' 'invitee' and 'guest,' often only of gossamer strength, ought not to be determinative in fashioning procedures ultimately referable to constitutional safeguards," held that "anyone legitimately on premises" at the time of the search had standing. Under *Jones,* courts held that a guest present at the search had standing, but that standing did not extend to a guest then absent or to one who was present but unlawfully so. In *Rakas v. Illinois,*[23] however, the Court rejected the "legitimately on premises" formulation on the view that "the holding in *Jones* can best be explained by the fact that Jones had a legitimate expectation of privacy in the premises he was using and therefore could claim the protection of the Fourth Amendment with respect to a governmental invasion of those premises, even though his 'interest' in those premises might not have been a recognized property interest at common law."

Rakas, it must be emphasized, did not question the *result* in *Jones;* the Court noted that Jones had been given a key and left alone in

18. Abel v. United States, 362 U.S. 217, 80 S.Ct. 683, 4 L.Ed.2d 668 (1960).

19. 335 U.S. 451, 69 S.Ct. 191, 93 L.Ed. 153 (1948).

20. In Minnesota v. Olson, 495 U.S. 91, 110 S.Ct. 1684, 109 L.Ed.2d 85 (1990), the Court concluded that guests "are entitled to a legitimate expectation of privacy despite the fact that they have no legal interest in the premises and do not have the legal authority to determine who may or may not enter the household."

21. Rawlings v. Kentucky, 448 U.S. 98, 100 S.Ct. 2556, 65 L.Ed.2d 633 (1980).

22. 362 U.S. 257, 80 S.Ct. 725, 4 L.Ed.2d 697 (1960).

23. 439 U.S. 128, 99 S.Ct. 421, 58 L.Ed.2d 387 (1978).

the apartment by the owner, so that, except with respect to the owner, "Jones had complete dominion and control over the apartment and could exclude others from it." But, the Court later held in *Minnesota v. Olson,*[24] this does not mark the outer limits of guest standing; "an overnight guest has a legitimate expectation of privacy in his host's home," even when the guest lacks such "complete dominion and control," as it is generally true "that hosts will more likely than not respect the privacy interests of their guests." This means that such a guest has standing to object to an illegal warrantless entry which leads to his own arrest in the host's premises, for that was the situation in *Olson.* It would also seem that such a guest has standing with respect to an illegal search of the guest's effects there. *Olson* describes the guest's privacy expectation in terms of "a place where he and his possessions will not be disturbed by anyone but his host and those his host allows inside," and in *Rakas* the Court emphasized it was *not* suggesting "that such visitors could not contest the lawfulness of the seizure of evidence or the search if their own property were seized during the search."

Does a guest have standing in other circumstances—that is, when the police illegality does not involve or culminate in either arrest of the guest or seizure of his effects? *Rakas* suggests the answer is no. By way of supporting the holding there that passengers in cars do not have standing simply by virtue of their lawful presence, the Court indicated by analogy that it would not "permit a casual visitor who has never seem, or been permitted to visit the basement of another's house to object to a search of the basement if the visitor happened to be in the kitchen of the house at the time of the search." But such a result is not inevitable under *Rakas,* for the four dissenters and two concurring justices all noted that the Fourth Amendment also protects security of the person and that this aspect of the Amendment was not at issue because the defendants there had not challenged the constitutionality of the police action in stopping the vehicle initially. In a premises context, this means that if the police, without required notice or without probable cause or without a required search warrant, burst into *B* 's home and disrupt a dinner party at which *A* is present as a guest, then certainly *A* should be deemed to have standing to object; he has had *his* freedom, privacy and solitude intruded upon by the police, and thus he has standing to object to that encroachment upon *his* right, even if it led to the discovery of evidence in *B* 's basement, a place *A* "has never seen, or been permitted to visit." On the other hand, it is fully consistent with the *Rakas* reasoning and result to say that if the intrusion itself was lawful, then *A* 's lawful presence would not alone give him standing as to any subsequent illegalities which did not increase appreciably the interference with *A* 's personal freedom. Unfortunately, some courts have not read *Rakas* carefully and thus have not recognized this critical distinction.

Still another type of case is that in which the defendant claims standing with respect to search of *his* personal property at a place which is not his and at a time when he was not present there. Standing has frequently been recognized in such circumstances, often by reliance upon *United States v. Jeffers.*[25] There, police entered defendant's two aunts' hotel room, for which he had a key and their permission to enter at will, and found his stash of drugs; the Supreme Court concluded with little by way of explanation that the government was in error in claiming "the search did not invade respondent's privacy." The Court expressly rejected the contention that defendant's interest in the seized property must be disregarded because it was illegal to possess such property,[26] but did not make it

24. 495 U.S. 91, 110 S.Ct. 1684, 109 L.Ed.2d 85 (1990).

25. 342 U.S. 48, 72 S.Ct. 93, 96 L.Ed. 59 (1951).

26. As for whether standing can be established under the *Jeffers* rule when the items in question are stolen property is unclear. Compare Combs v. United States, 408 U.S. 224, 92 S.Ct. 2284, 33 L.Ed.2d 308 (1972) (Court in remanding for standing determination as to stolen goods intimates one could have a privacy interest in stolen goods); with Brown v. United States, 411 U.S. 223, 93 S.Ct. 1565, 36 L.Ed.2d 208 (1973) (Court holds defendants without standing where they had sold the stolen goods to another, but then adds in footnote that in any event "their 'property interest' in the merchandise was

clear whether that interest alone conferred standing or whether his continuing access to the place was essential to the outcome. It has sometimes been held that absent such access there is not the expectation of privacy needed for standing, but it has been forcefully argued that a bailment arrangement without continued access confers standing because the bailor has sought to maintain the security and privacy of his possessions in a place he regarded as safe.

That analysis and even the *Jeffers* result has been put into doubt as a result of *Rawlings v. Kentucky,*[27] where police searched the purse of defendant's female companion and found therein the drugs she was carrying for him. The Supreme Court ruled that defendant had no standing to object to that search because he had no reasonable expectation of privacy as to the purse, but the several reasons given by the Court for this conclusion are less than convincing. Of particular interest here is the Court's assertion in *Rawlings* that it was extremely important the defendant did not "have any right to exclude other persons from access to Cox's purse." But while a "right to exclude" may be an easy way to establish the requisite legitimate expectation of privacy, it hardly follows that it is the only way; as the *Rawlings* dissenters note, "such a harsh threshold requirement was not imposed even in the heyday of a property rights oriented Fourth Amendment." A bailor's right to exclude others is important in Fourth Amendment law, but for another purpose: deciding the lawfulness of a search consented to by the bailee.[28] To now utilize the same approach for standing would produce the incredible result that whenever the police could conduct a lawful search with the bailee's consent, they may instead proceed to make that search without the bailee's consent because the bailor will lack standing. This is not only wrong, but is inconsistent with the Court's prior [29] and subsequent[30] pronouncements on the law of standing.

(c) Business Premises. Analysis similar to that in the preceding subsection is appropriate when the question concerns standing to challenge a search of business premises. In *Mancusi v. DeForte,*[31] for example, where state officials conducted a search and seized records belonging to a Teamsters Union local from an office defendant shared with several other union officials, the Court characterized the "crucial issue" as being "whether the area was one in which there was a reasonable expectation of freedom from governmental intrusion." The Court answered in the affirmative, reasoning that defendant would certainly have had standing if the search were of his private office and that the "situation was not fundamentally changed because DeForte shared an office with other union officers," for he "still could reasonably have expected that only those persons and their personal or business guests would enter the office, and that records would not be touched except with their permission or that of union higher-ups."

Consistent with *Mancusi,* courts have held that a corporate or individual defendant in possession of the business premises searched has standing, and that an officer or employee of the business enterprise has standing if there was a demonstrated nexus between the area searched and that individual's work space. Exclusive use would seem clearly to

totally illegitimate"). In expectation-of-privacy terms, it is difficult to see how it can be concluded that if *A* is permitted to leave certain effects on *B*'s property, his reasonable expectations as to the security of that place from police intrusion are somehow affected by the nature of those effects.

27. 448 U.S. 98, 100 S.Ct. 2556, 65 L.Ed.2d 633 (1980).

28. See § 3.10(e).

29. In Mancusi v. DeForte, 392 U.S. 364, 88 S.Ct. 2120, 20 L.Ed.2d 1154 (1968), for example, where the Court held an office worker had standing as to a search of records in an office used by him and his co-workers, it was properly said to be "irrelevant" that his employer and fellow employees "might validly have consented to a search of the area where the records were kept."

30. In Minnesota v. Olson, 495 U.S. 91, 110 S.Ct. 1684, 109 L.Ed.2d 85 (1990), the Court recognized that a guest has standing re his host's premises, a place where he expects that "he and his possessions will not be disturbed by anyone but his host and those his host allows inside," and expressly declared that the fact "the guest has a host who has ultimate control of the house is not inconsistent with the guest having a legitimate expectation of privacy."

31. 392 U.S. 364, 88 S.Ct. 2120, 20 L.Ed.2d 1154 (1968).

establish standing, but (as *Mancusi* teaches) there can be a justified expectation of privacy even absent exclusivity. As noted earlier, the "legitimately on the premises" basis of standing has now been rejected by the Supreme Court;[32] it was never a meaningful basis for analysis as to business premises of some size.

Sometimes the question is whether a person who was not present and who in addition was not related to the business premises, in the sense of being a participant in the business enterprise, might ever have standing as to those premises. If, as suggested above, standing may be based upon an expectation of privacy as to certain effects which are temporarily put into the custody of another (a matter put in doubt by *Rawlings v. Kentucky*[33]), the answer would be yes. Thus, if *A* leaves his jacket at *B*'s dry cleaning establishment to be cleaned and the police thereafter enter that establishment and search or seize that jacket, *A* would by virtue of his privacy interest in that item have standing to bring that police action into question. But if the customer does not have effects of his own on the premises, he is apparently out of luck. This is the thrust of *United States v. Miller,*[34] holding that the customer of a bank lacks standing to challenge subpoenas directed at the bank for records of his transactions which were "the business records of the banks." As the Court put it, "[t]he depositor takes the risk, in revealing his affairs to another, that the information will be conveyed by that person to the government," and consequently has no standing to challenge the subpoenas (or, as the Court concluded in a later case, to challenge acquisition of such records by burglary![35]). The reasoning and result in *Miller* are open to serious question. To resolve the standing issue on the basis that the person had assumed the risk of disclosure by someone else makes no sense, and simply cannot be squared with the Court's earlier standing decisions.[36]

(d) Vehicles. The holding in *Jones v. United States*[37] that standing could be founded upon being "legitimately on premises where a search occurs" prompted other courts to rule that a person driving a car with the owner's consent and a passenger who is present in the vehicle by permission have standing to object to a search of that vehicle. But then came *Rakas v. Illinois,*[38] where police stopped what they believed to be a robbery getaway car, ordered the occupants out of the car, and then searched the vehicle and found a rifle under the seat and shells in the glove compartment. The Court concluded that the passengers, who claimed no ownership of the seized objects, lacked standing because

> they made no showing that they had any legitimate expectation of privacy in the glove compartment or area under the seat of the car in which they were merely passengers. Like the trunk of an automobile, these are areas in which a passenger *qua* passenger simply would not normally have a legitimate expectation of privacy.

This should not be taken to mean that persons who are "merely passengers" will never have standing. It is important to note, as the *Rakas* concurring opinion emphasized, that the "petitioners do not challenge the constitutionality of the police action in stopping the automobile in which they were riding; nor do they complain of being made to get out of the vehicle," so that the question before the Court was "a narrow one: Did the search of their friend's automobile after they had left it violate any Fourth Amendment right of the petitioners?" This would indicate, as two-thirds of the Court recognized,[39] that a passenger *does* have standing to object

32. Rakas v. Illinois, 439 U.S. 128, 99 S.Ct. 421, 58 L.Ed.2d 387 (1978).

33. 448 U.S. 98, 100 S.Ct. 2556, 65 L.Ed.2d 633 (1980).

34. 425 U.S. 435, 96 S.Ct. 1619, 48 L.Ed.2d 71 (1976).

35. United States v. Payner, 447 U.S. 727, 100 S.Ct. 2439, 65 L.Ed.2d 468 (1980).

36. Such risks existed, for example, in Mancusi v. DeForte, 392 U.S. 364, 88 S.Ct. 2120, 20 L.Ed.2d 1154 (1968); Bumper v. North Carolina, 391 U.S. 543, 88 S.Ct. 1788, 20 L.Ed.2d 797 (1968); Jones v. United States, 362 U.S. 257, 80 S.Ct. 725, 4 L.Ed.2d 697 (1960).

37. 362 U.S. 257, 80 S.Ct. 725, 4 L.Ed.2d 697 (1960).

38. 439 U.S. 128, 99 S.Ct. 421, 58 L.Ed.2d 387 (1978).

39. Two concurring justices and four dissenters.

to police conduct which intrudes upon his Fourth Amendment protection against unreasonable seizure of his person. If either the stopping of the car or the passenger's removal from it are unreasonable in a Fourth Amendment sense, then surely the passenger has standing to object to those constitutional violations and to have suppressed any evidence found in the car which is their fruit.

It is very significant that the passengers in *Rakas* disclaimed ownership of the gun and shells. Even when there has been nothing unlawful about either the stopping of the vehicle or removal of the passengers from it, certainly a passenger has standing as to any search into *his* effects in the car. The Court's crabbed interpretation in *Rawlings v. Kentucky* [40] of what constitutes a justified expectation of privacy does not go so far as to bar such standing, though it may put in doubt whether standing can be gained by a nonpassenger whose effects in the car are searched.

Rakas deals only with passengers and thus does not place into question the notion that some persons with a stronger interest in the vehicle will have standing even as to vehicle searches in their absence. This is unquestionably so as to the owner of the car if he has not abandoned it or made a substantial bailment of it, the bailee of the vehicle, family members who share in the use of the car, and others who share use of the vehicle with the owner on a regular and recurring basis. This is not to suggest that such persons will have standing as to every kind of Fourth Amendment violation occurring in the vehicle; consistent with the earlier analysis, the owner-driver could not object if following the lawful stopping of his car a passenger's purse was opened.

The "wrongful presence" exception to the standing rule of the *Jones* case has its counterpart in the vehicle search cases: most courts agree that an occupant of a vehicle cannot be said to have standing by virtue of his presence if he is in possession of a stolen or otherwise illegally possessed or controlled vehicle. It has been argued that this should be so only if the police know they are dealing with a stolen car, but this is unsound, for a person's reasonable expectation of privacy hardly depends upon what someone else knows. While a thief driving a stolen car thus cannot gain standing as to the car by his wrongful possession of it, that possession does not deprive him of standing he otherwise has. This means that a thief is still entitled to challenge unlawful interferences with his person, and consequently it would be open to him to question a search of the car which was a fruit of his illegal arrest.

§ 9.2 Standing: Other Possible Bases

(a) "Automatic" Standing. In *Jones v. United States,*[1] the defendant charged with narcotics offenses was found by the court below to lack standing to object to the search of the apartment where the narcotics were found and where he was present as an invitee at the time of the search. The Supreme Court concluded otherwise and held that the "same element in this prosecution which has caused a dilemma, i.e., that possession both convicts and confers standing, eliminates any necessity for a preliminary showing of an interest in the premises searched or the property seized, which ordinarily is required when standing is challenged." The Court in *Jones* indicated it would be improper "to permit the Government to have the advantage of contradictory positions as a basis for conviction."

Some years later the Court took another look at the problem of a defendant who is confronted with the dilemma of having to give incriminating testimony to establish standing and came up with a different type of solution applicable to a broader range of cases. In *Simmons v. United States,*[2] defendant Garrett moved to suppress a suitcase and incriminating evidence found therein which the police had seized from another person. In an unsuccessful effort to establish standing, he testi-

40. 448 U.S. 98, 100 S.Ct. 2556, 65 L.Ed.2d 633 (1980).

§ 9.2

1. 362 U.S. 257, 80 S.Ct. 725, 4 L.Ed.2d 697 (1960).

2. 390 U.S. 377, 88 S.Ct. 967, 19 L.Ed.2d 1247 (1968).

fied that the suitcase was similar to one he had owned and that clothing therein was his, and this testimony was later admitted against him at trial. Noting that he could not benefit from the *Jones* rule because he was charged with bank robbery, a nonpossessory offense, and that testimony as to ownership was "the most natural way in which he could found standing," the Court reversed. As for the argument that such testimony was voluntary and thus not obtained in violation of the Fifth Amendment self-incrimination clause, the Court responded:

> However, the assumption which underlies this reasoning is that the defendant has a choice: he may refuse to testify and give up the benefit. When this assumption is applied to a situation in which the "benefit" to be gained is that afforded by another provision of the Bill of Rights, an undeniable tension is created. Thus, in this case Garrett was obliged either to give up what he believed, with advice of counsel, to be a valid Fourth Amendment claim or, in legal effect, to waive his Fifth Amendment privilege against self-incrimination. In these circumstances, we find it intolerable that one constitutional right should have to be surrendered in order to assert another. We therefore hold that when a defendant testifies in support of a motion to suppress evidence on Fourth Amendment grounds, his testimony may not thereafter be admitted against him at trial on the issue of guilt unless he makes no objection.

Simmons gave rise to the question of whether the *Jones* automatic standing rule had lost its vitality, which the Court finally answered affirmatively in *United States v. Salvucci.*[3] *Simmons,* the Court declared, provides protection "broader than that of *Jones*" because it "not only extends protection against this risk of self-incrimination in all of the cases covered by *Jones,* but also grants a form of 'use immunity' to those defendants charged with nonpossessory crimes." As for the vice of prosecutorial contradiction, the Court stated it need not decide if that "could alone support a rule countenancing the exclusion of probative evidence on the grounds that someone other than the defendant was denied a Fourth Amendment right," for at least after *Rakas v. Illinois*[4] it is clear "that a prosecutor may simultaneously maintain that a defendant criminally possessed the seized good, but was not subject to a Fourth Amendment deprivation, without legal contradiction," for a "person in legal possession of a good seized during an illegal search has not necessarily been subject to a Fourth Amendment deprivation."

The defendants in *Salvucci* claimed that there were reasons for the automatic standing rule "not articulated by the Court in *Jones,*" most significantly that *Simmons* "did not eliminate other risks to the defendant which attach to giving testimony on a motion to suppress," primarily that "the prosecutor may still be permitted to use the defendant's testimony to impeach him at trial." But the *Salvucci* majority chose to sidestep that argument with the curious and unconvincing comment that this issue "need not be and is not resolved here, for it is an issue which more aptly relates to the proper breadth of the *Simmons* privilege, and not to the need for retaining automatic standing." Moreover, the Court erroneously asserted that the "Court has held that 'the protection shield of *Simmons* is not to be converted into a license for false representations,' "[5] thus hinting how the issue would be resolved. But it is to be doubted that this would be a correct resolution. The best analogy here is not those cases holding that illegally obtained evidence can be admitted at trial for the limited purpose of impeachment,[6] but rather *New Jersey v. Portash,*[7] holding that testimony given before a grand jury following a grant of use immunity could not be used for impeachment purposes at the subsequent criminal trial. In *Portash* the Court reasoned that statements made af-

3. 448 U.S. 83, 100 S.Ct. 2547, 65 L.Ed.2d 619 (1980).

4. 439 U.S. 128, 99 S.Ct. 421, 58 L.Ed.2d 387 (1978).

5. Quoting from United States v. Kahan, 415 U.S. 239, 94 S.Ct. 1179, 39 L.Ed.2d 297 (1974). But *Kahan* involved use for impeachment purposes of false testimony given at a pretrial hearing to establish defendant's eligibility for appointed counsel, and the holding is somewhat different than is suggested by that selective quotation.

6. See § 9.6(a).

7. 440 U.S. 450, 99 S.Ct. 1292, 59 L.Ed.2d 501 (1979).

ter an immunity grant and thus under threat of contempt involved "the constitutional privilege against compulsory self-incrimination in its most pristine form," so that there was no occasion to balance the privilege against the interest in preventing perjury. It would seem that defendant's testimony at a suppression hearing is likewise "compelled" in the *Portash* sense, for, as *Simmons* teaches, the defendant is confronted with the choice "either to give up what he believed, with advice of counsel, to be a valid Fourth Amendment claim or, in legal effect, to waive his Fifth Amendment privilege against self-incrimination."

(b) "Target" Standing. Assume that *X* is arrested for armed robbery and that some time thereafter, acting with the specific intention of finding additional evidence which will incriminate *X* with respect to that crime, the police conduct a fruitful illegal search of *X*'s wife. Or, assume that the police are seeking robber *Y*, who was known to have taken refuge in a certain apartment building, and that they then conduct an apartment-by-apartment search until they find *Y* in the last apartment, as to which probable cause existed because of the other illegal searches. By virtue of their being the "target" of the searches, do *X* and *Y* have standing to object to those illegal searches? The Supreme Court finally confronted this issue directly in *Rakas v. Illinois* [8] and concluded that

> since the exclusionary rule is an attempt to effectuate the guarantees of the Fourth Amendment, * * * it is proper to permit only defendants whose Fourth Amendment rights have been violated to benefit from the rule's protections. * * * There is no reason to think that a party whose rights have been infringed will not, if evidence is used against him, have ample motivation to move to suppress it. * * * Even if such a person is not a defendant in the action, he may be able to recover damages for the violation of his Fourth Amendment rights * * * or seek redress under state law for invasion of privacy or trespass. * * *
>
> Conferring standing to raise vicarious Fourth Amendment claims would necessarily mean a more widespread invocation of the exclusionary rule during criminal trials. * * * Each time the exclusionary rule is applied it exacts a substantial social cost for the vindication of Fourth Amendment rights. Relevant and reliable evidence is kept from the trier of fact and the search for truth at trial is deflected. * * * Since our cases generally have held that one whose Fourth Amendment rights are violated may successfully suppress evidence obtained in the course of an illegal search and seizure, misgivings as to the benefit of enlarging the class of persons who may invoke that rule are properly considered when deciding whether to expand standing to assert Fourth Amendment violations.

A very forceful argument in favor of the concept of target standing can be put by merely reciting the facts of the remarkable case of *United States v. Payner.*[9] In 1965, the IRS launched an investigation into the financial activities of American citizens in the Bahamas. An IRS special agent, knowing that the vice president of a Bahamian bank would be in Miami, agreed to and participated in a scheme whereby that person's locked briefcase was stolen for a short period of time while the case was opened and 400 bank records photographed. This led to other information establishing that Payner had a bank account in that bank and that he had falsified his federal income tax return in that connection. This "briefcase caper," in fact a calculated and deliberate extreme violation of the banker's Fourth Amendment rights and also a criminal act, was undertaken with full understanding by the IRS agent that a person such as Payner—precisely the kind of violator they were seeking—would not have Fourth Amendment standing to object. It would seem that if ever a fact situation cried out for recognition of target standing, *Payner* was it. Nonetheless, the Supreme Court reaffirmed that there is no Fourth Amendment target standing, and even overturned the lower court's conferral of standing under the inherent supervisory power of the federal courts.

8. 439 U.S. 128, 99 S.Ct. 421, 58 L.Ed.2d 387 (1978).

9. 447 U.S. 727, 100 S.Ct. 2439, 65 L.Ed.2d 468 (1980).

As the *Payner* dissenters put it, that holding "effectively turns the standing rules created by this Court for assertion of Fourth Amendment violations into a sword to be used by the Government to permit it deliberately to invade one person's Fourth Amendment rights in order to obtain evidence against another person."

(c) "Derivative" Standing. In *McDonald v. United States,*[10] McDonald and Washington were together convicted of operating a lottery after McDonald's motion to suppress gambling paraphernalia was denied. The Supreme Court reversed and then, though assuming Washington was without personal standing, held he was also entitled to a new trial at which the seized items would not be admitted against him. The Court explained that denial of McDonald's motion "was error that was prejudicial to Washington as well" because if "the property had been returned to McDonald, it would not have been available for use at trial." But in *Wong Sun v. United States,*[11] the Court, without any mention of *McDonald,* held that defendant Wong Sun was not entitled to suppression of narcotics which were excluded as to co-defendant Toy, as the "seizure of this heroin invaded no right of privacy of person or premises which would entitle Wong Sun to object to its use at his trial." And in *Alderman v. United States*[12] the Court adhered to "the general rule that Fourth Amendment rights are personal rights" and thus concluded there was "no necessity to exclude evidence against one defendant in order to protect the rights of another."

McDonald might be thought to have survived *Wong Sun* and *Alderman* if it is viewed not as a rule of standing but rather as a rule to the effect that a person should not have admitted against him evidence which ought to have been returned to another person as a consequence of this other person's motion to suppress. But such a rule would make little sense. It ignores the fact that courts are empowered to retain suppressed evidence if it is of evidentiary value, and would make the outcome turn on the happenstance of whether the defendant without standing was tried after or contemporaneously with instead of before the defendant with standing. And the argument that *McDonald* produces necessary equality in results between co-defendants or co-conspirators is not convincing.

(d) Abolition of Standing. The California supreme court adopted a search and seizure exclusionary rule well before it was required to do so by *Mapp v. Ohio,*[13] and shortly thereafter held that a defendant would be recognized as having standing in all circumstances in that jurisdiction. This conclusion, the court reasoned in *People v. Martin,*[14] was a logical result of the fact that the exclusionary rule was based

> on the ground that "other remedies have completely failed to secure compliance with the constitutional provisions on the part of police officers with the attendant result that the courts under the old rule have been constantly required to participate in, and in effect condone, the lawless activity of law enforcement officers." * * * This result occurs whenever the government is allowed to profit by its own wrong by basing a conviction on illegally obtained evidence, and if law enforcement officers are allowed to evade the exclusionary rule by obtaining evidence in violation of the rights of third parties, its deterrent effect is to that extent nullified. Moreover, such a limitation virtually invites law enforcement officers to violate the rights of third parties and to trade the escape of a criminal whose rights are violated for the conviction of others by the use of the evidence illegally obtained against them.

Though the analysis in *Mapp* of the underpinnings of the exclusionary rule was very similar, the supreme court in *Alderman v. United States*[15] declined to adopt the *Martin* approach. Despite the fact that "the deterrent aim of the rule" might be advanced by aboli-

10. 335 U.S. 451, 69 S.Ct. 191, 93 L.Ed. 153 (1948).
11. 371 U.S. 471, 83 S.Ct. 407, 9 L.Ed.2d 441 (1963).
12. 394 U.S. 165, 89 S.Ct. 961, 22 L.Ed.2d 176 (1969).
13. 367 U.S. 643, 81 S.Ct. 1684, 6 L.Ed.2d 1081 (1961).
14. 45 Cal.2d 755, 290 P.2d 855 (1955).
15. 394 U.S. 165, 89 S.Ct. 961, 22 L.Ed.2d 176 (1969).

tion of the standing requirement, the Court was "not convinced that the additional benefits of extending the exclusionary rule to other defendants would justify further encroachment upon the public interest in prosecuting those accused of crime and having them acquitted or convicted on the basis of all the evidence which exposes the truth." [16]

Some argue that the *Alderman* approach to standing actually invites police illegality by telling them that they can direct a search at one person and use the evidence against another. But that problem, it has been countered, could be dealt with by recognition of "target" standing, which may be correct unless it is thought that defendants would be unable to establish their target status when it existed. In any event, total abolition of standing would seem to push the exclusionary rule on occasion to ridiculous results, such as that a criminal must go free because his crime was detected by conduct which only infringed upon the Fourth Amendment rights of his victim.

§ 9.3 "Fruit of the Poisonous Tree" Theories

(a) Generally. In the simplest of exclusionary rule cases, the challenged evidence is quite clearly "direct" or "primary" in its relationship to the prior arrest, search, interrogation, lineup or other identification procedure. Such is the case when that evidence is an identification occurring at the confrontation between suspect and victim or witness, a confession or admission made in response to questioning, or physical evidence obtained by search or arrest. Not infrequently, however, challenged evidence is "secondary" or "derivative" in character. This occurs when, for example, a confession is obtained after an illegal arrest, physical evidence is located after an illegally obtained confession, or an in-court identification is made following an illegally conducted pretrial identification. In these situations, it is necessary to determine whether the derivative evidence is "tainted" by the prior constitutional or other violation. To use the phrase coined by Justice Frankfurter, it must be decided whether that evidence is the "fruit of the poisonous tree." [1] As is apparent from the examples just given, the "poisonous tree" can be an illegal arrest or search, illegal interrogation procedures or illegal identification practices.[2]

The genesis of the "taint" doctrine was in *Silverthorne Lumber Co. v. United States,*[3] where federal officers unlawfully seized certain documents and, after a court ordered those documents returned, the prosecutor caused the grand jury to issue subpoenas to the defendants to produce the very same documents. In holding that the subpoenas were invalid, the Court declared:

> The essence of a provision forbidding the acquisition of evidence in a certain way is that not merely evidence so acquired shall not be used before the Court but that it shall not be used at all. Of course this does not mean that the facts thus obtained become sacred and inaccessible. If knowledge of them is gained from an independent source they may be proved like any others, but the knowledge gained by the Government's own wrong cannot be used by it in the way proposed.

In *Nardone v. United States,*[4] the Court refused to permit the prosecution to avoid an inquiry into its use of information gained by illegal wiretaps, observing that "[t]o forbid the direct use of methods * * * but to put no curb on their full indirect use would only invite the very methods deemed 'inconsistent

16. In light of *Alderman,* when California adopted a constitutional amendment requiring the admission of all relevant evidence except where suppression would be required by the federal constitution, the California Supreme Court held it would no longer follow the "vicarious standing" rule of *Martin.* See In re Lance W., 37 Cal.3d 873, 210 Cal.Rptr. 631, 694 P.2d 744 (1985).

§ 9.3

1. Nardone v. United States, 308 U.S. 338, 60 S.Ct. 266, 84 L.Ed. 307 (1939).

2. Because the fruits issues in this context are more closely connected with the development of doctrine concerning what identification practices are illegal, they are discussed in Chapter 7.

3. 251 U.S. 385, 40 S.Ct. 182, 64 L.Ed. 319 (1920).

4. 308 U.S. 338, 60 S.Ct. 266, 84 L.Ed. 307 (1939).

with ethical standards and destructive of personal liberty.' " This case established the doctrine of "attenuation" by authoritatively recognizing that the challenged evidence might sometimes be admissible even if it did not have an "independent source" because the "causal connection * * * may have become so attenuated as to dissipate the taint." Thus, in the later case of *Wong Sun v. United States,*[5] it was said that the question to be answered as to derivative evidence is "whether, granting establishment of the primary illegality, the evidence to which instant objection is made has been come at by exploitation of that illegality or instead by means sufficiently distinguishable to be purged of the primary taint." In more recent cases the Court has been concerned with what factors bear upon the determination of whether or not there has been attenuation.

(b) "But for" Rejected. In *Wong Sun,* the Court declined to "hold that all evidence is 'fruit of the poisonous tree' simply because it would not have come to light but for the illegal actions of the police." Thus the Court ruled that Wong Sun's confession was untainted by his illegal arrest because it was given after he had obtained his release and voluntarily returned to the station later, although there seemed to be no doubt that he would never have come in and confessed but for the prior arrest. But, it might quite appropriately be asked: Why not suppress the confession, for it was quite clearly caused by the arrest, and thus admission of the confession permits the government to profit from the Fourth Amendment violation?

Complete exclusion of all fruits would be excessive in light of the obvious competing considerations: that exclusion of evidence thwarts society's interest in convicting the guilty. The Court's rejection of the "but for" test, therefore, as Justice Powell pointed out, "recognizes that in some circumstances strict adherence to the Fourth Amendment exclusionary rule imposes greater cost on the legitimate demands of law enforcement than can be justified by the rule's deterrent purposes." [6]

(c) "Attenuated Connection." In neither *Nardone* nor *Wong Sun* did the Court elaborate upon the "attenuated connection" test, thus leaving it rather uncertain exactly what lower courts were expected to look for, to say nothing of what facts would be relevant to an "attenuation" determination. But here as well it is useful to view the question from the perspective of the exclusionary rule's deterrence function. "The notion of the 'dissipation of the taint' attempts to mark the point at which the detrimental consequences of illegal police action become so attenuated that the deterrent effect of the exclusionary rule no longer justifies its cost." [7] In short, the underlying purpose of the "attenuated connection" test is to mark the point of diminishing returns of the deterrence principle. When courts lose sight of that point the results can be most unfortunate, as is illustrated by the not uncommon holding prior to *Brown v. Illinois* [8] that the *Miranda* warnings alone supply the requisite attenuation between an illegal arrest and a confession. That is not attenuation in the deterrence function sense, for it is clear that "the effect of the exclusionary rule would be substantially diluted" [9] under such an approach. Of course, a court's judgment as to that point at which admission of the evidence will significantly dilute deterrence will be informed by the court's views on a variety of subsidiary questions, such as whether police are likely to view the court's ruling as providing a significant "incentive" to engage in illegal searches and whether judges ruling on suppression motions can and will readily identify those situations in which police act with the specific objective of exploiting the limitations of the fruits doctrine.[10] As evidenced by the majori-

5. 371 U.S. 471, 83 S.Ct. 407, 9 L.Ed.2d 441 (1963).

6. Concurring in Brown v. Illinois, 422 U.S. 590, 95 S.Ct. 2254, 45 L.Ed.2d 416 (1975).

7. Ibid.

8. 422 U.S. 590, 95 S.Ct. 2254, 45 L.Ed.2d 416 (1975).

9. Brown v. Illinois, 422 U.S. 590, 95 S.Ct. 2254, 45 L.Ed.2d 416 (1975).

10. This is true as well in determining the scope of the independent source and "inevitable discovery" doctrines that also limit the scope of the fruits doctrine. See

ty, concurring, and dissenting opinions in many of the leading Supreme Court opinions on the fruits doctrine, judges may bring widely different perspectives to these issues. However, at times, courts have appeared to be influenced as much by a desire to limit the scope of the exclusionary rule as by any judgment that a finding of attenuation would, indeed, not undermine the deterrence function of that rule.[11]

This is not to suggest that by focusing upon the underlying purpose of the "attenuated connection" test that it will always (or even usually) be apparent what amounts to sufficient attenuation. The "question of attenuation inevitably is largely a matter of degree,"[12] and thus application of the test is dependent upon the particular facts of each case. But while there may never be any litmus-paper test for determining when there is only an "attenuated connection" between a violation and certain derivative evidence, it is possible to point toward some relevant criteria. One thoughtful commentator has suggested these three:

(1) "Where the chain between the challenged evidence and the primary illegality is long or the linkage can be shown only by 'sophisticated argument,' exclusion would seem inappropriate. In such a case it is highly unlikely that the police officers foresaw the challenged evidence as a probable product of their illegality; thus it could not have been a motivating force behind it. It follows that the threat of exclusion could not possibly operate as a deterrent in that situation."

(2) The same may be said where evidence "is used for some relatively insignificant or highly unusual purpose. Under these circumstances it is not likely that, at the time the primary illegality was contemplated, the police foresaw or were motivated by the potential use of the evidence and the threat of exclusion would, therefore, effect no deterrence."

(3) "Since the purpose of the exclusionary rule is to deter undesirable police conduct, where that conduct is particularly offensive the deterrence ought to be greater and, therefore, the scope of exclusion broader."[13]

(d) "Independent Source." The Court in *Wong Sun* quoted from *Silverthorne* the proposition that "the exclusionary rule has no application" when "the Government learned of the evidence 'from an independent source.'" As ordinarily applied, this means that if not even the "but for" test can be met, then clearly the evidence is not a fruit of the prior violation. So stated, the "independent source" limitation upon the taint doctrine is unquestionably sound. It is one thing to say that officers shall gain no advantage from violating an individual's rights; it is quite another to declare that such a violation shall put that person beyond the law's reach even if his guilt can be proved by evidence lawfully obtained.

A useful illustration is provided by *State v. O'Bremski,*[14] where a 14-year old girl was found in an illegal search of defendant's apartment. The girl's testimony that defendant had carnal knowledge with her was held to be untainted because it had an independent source which even predated the search of the apartment. This was because in advance of the search the girl's parents had reported her missing and a police informant had already located her in defendant's apartment. *O'Bremski* is not a difficult case in light of this sequence of events. But when the independent source is found to exist or comes into existence after the initial illegality, then the situation must be much more carefully examined.

The problem, of course, is that there is no way to get the cat back into the bag, so that once illegally obtained evidence incriminating the defendant has been found it can always be asserted with some plausibility that any information acquired thereafter is attributable to

e.g., the discussions infra of Murray v. United States and Nix v. Williams.

11. See the discussion of the *Segura* case in § 9.4(b).

12. Powell, J., concurring in Brown v. Illinois, 422 U.S. 590, 95 S.Ct. 2254, 45 L.Ed.2d 416 (1975).

13. Comment, 115 U.Pa.L.Rev. 1136, 1148–51 (1967).

14. 70 Wash.2d 425, 423 P.2d 530 (1967).

the authorities being spurred on and their investigation focused by the earlier discovery. Thus the question of whether the "independent source" test sometimes can be met even though it may well be that "but for" the earlier violation the investigation which uncovered the tendered evidence would never have been commenced. An affirmative answer was given in *United States v. Bacall*,[15] where, after U.S. customs agents illegally seized inventory from the defendant, they contacted French officials and asked them to investigate a matter relating to him. In their investigation the French agents seized certain letters and checks which implicated defendant in certain crimes. In holding that evidence admissible the court declared:

> [W]e reiterate our assumption that illegal seizure *was* a "but for" cause of the foreign investigation. [But the] question to be answered is * * * whether anything seized or any leads gained from the seizure tended significantly to direct the foreign investigation toward those specific letters and checks—whether the Customs officers had after [the illegal] seizure a substantially greater reason to seek those specific items than they had before the seizure. We conclude that they did not and that the letter and checks were not tainted * * *.

This approach has been applauded on the ground that where unconstitutional action only leads the police to "focus" their investigation on a particular individual, this should not, in effect, grant him immunity from prosecution. Others object to the *Bacall* view, reasoning that if the police know that their initial illegality can be covered up later by legal police work, then there is nothing to stop them from committing the initial illegality. This objection is especially compelling under certain circumstances, as where the prior illegality has caused the authorities to "focus" upon the defendant as a likely tax violator.

Another troublesome independent source problem is presented where the police (i) have probable cause to obtain a search warrant, (ii) subsequently enter the premises without a warrant and discover that the contraband is indeed there, and (iii) then leave the premises, obtain a warrant based on the previously obtained probable cause (without any reference to the information obtained during the unlawful entry), and return with the warrant and seize the contraband in the execution of the warrant. In *Murray v. United States*,[16] the Court of Appeals assumed that it had such a situation before it and held that the independent source doctrine applied. The Supreme Court remanded the case for further findings of fact, but agreed that the independent source doctrine would apply if the agents' decision to seek the warrant had not been "prompted" by what had been seen during the earlier unlawful entry (i.e., if the lower court found that the agents "would have sought a warrant [even] if they had not earlier entered the [premises]"). The dissenters argued that this ruling would encourage police officers to enter premises illegally for the purpose of making certain that the contraband is actually there before they undertake the "inconvenient and time-consuming task" of obtaining a warrant. The majority responded:

> We see the incentives differently. An officer with probable cause sufficient to obtain a search warrant would be foolish to enter the premises first in an unlawful manner. By doing so, he would risk suppression of all evidence on the premises, both seen and unseen, since his action would add to the normal burden of convincing a magistrate that there is probable cause the much more onerous burden of convincing a trial court that no information gained from the illegal entry affected either the law enforcement officers' decision to seek a warrant or the magistrate's decision to grant it.[17]

15. 443 F.2d 1050 (9th Cir.1971).

16. 487 U.S. 533, 108 S.Ct. 2529, 101 L.Ed.2d 472 (1988).

17. In light of its view of the incentives, and its requirement that the district court "be satisfied that the warrant would have been sought without the illegal entry," the majority saw no adequate justification for adopting a "prophylactic rule" (as urged by the dissent) that would mandate per se inadmissibility absent a police demonstration by some "historically verifiable fact" (e.g., a prior initiation of the warrant process) that the "subsequent search pursuant to a warrant was wholly unaffected by the prior illegal search." The present case itself "provided no basis" for suggesting "a 'search first, war-

(e) "Inevitable Discovery." Yet another theory which has been utilized by many courts in dealing with "fruit of the poisonous tree" issues is the so-called "inevitable discovery" rule. This rule, which is recognized by the vast majority of lower courts and has been accepted by the Supreme Court,[18] is in a sense a variation upon the "independent source" theory. But it differs in that the question is not whether the police did in fact acquire certain evidence by reliance upon an untainted source but instead whether evidence found because of an earlier violation would inevitably have been discovered lawfully.[19] A useful illustration is provided by *Somer v. United States.*[20] There, federal agents made an illegal search of defendant's apartment and found a still in operation, and while there questioned his wife as to his whereabouts and learned from her that he was out delivering the "stuff" and "would be back shortly." The agents waited out on the street, and when defendant drove up about twenty minutes later he was arrested and when the odor of alcohol was then detected his car was searched and illicit liquor was found. On defendant's appeal, the court noted that the agents may well have had probable cause to search the car even before they searched the apartment, but added that

> even though the search might have been lawful if made upon that information alone, it was not so made. Somer's whereabouts was unknown to the officers; they might have waited his return in the apartment; they might have sought him elsewhere; or they might have gone to the street, and arrested him where in fact they did. If they had not done the last, they would not have caught him red-handed, or seized the evidence now in question.

Thus, the court concluded, the evidence must be suppressed *unless* on remand "further inquiry will show that, quite independently of what Somer's wife told them, the officers would have gone to the street, have waited for Somer and have arrested him, exactly as they did."

In the vast majority of the appellate cases in which the government has relied upon the "inevitable discovery" test, the court has accepted the test as a legitimate one and then proceeded to determine its applicability upon the facts presented. This is not, however, a unanimous position. Some object that the "inevitable discovery" rule is based on conjecture and can only encourage police shortcuts whenever evidence may be more readily obtained by illegal than by legal means.

These latter concerns, though unquestionably legitimate, are directed not so much to the rule itself as to its application in a loose and unthinking fashion. Courts must not lose sight of the fact that a mechanical application of the inevitable discovery doctrine will encourage unconstitutional shortcuts. Because one purpose of the exclusionary rule is to deter such shortcuts, it has been argued that the "inevitable discovery" rule should be applied only when it is clear the police did not act in bad faith to accelerate discovery of the evidence in question. The need for this limitation is particularly apparent when the shortcut was a bypassing of the Fourth Amendment warrant requirement, as is illustrated by *United States v. Griffin.*[21] There, after one agent had been dispatched to get a search warrant, others entered and made the search without a warrant, following which their colleague appeared on the scene with a warrant. Acceptance of the government's "inevitable discovery" argument in such cir-

rant later' [police] mentality." The district court had found that the agents had entered the premises in an effort to "apprehend any participants * * * and guard against the destruction of possibly critical evidence" rather than "merely to see if there was anything worth getting a warrant for."

18. Nix v. Williams, 467 U.S. 431, 104 S.Ct. 2501, 81 L.Ed.2d 377 (1984).

19. As the Supreme Court explained in Nix v. Williams, 467 U.S. 431, 104 S.Ct. 2501, 81 L.Ed.2d 337 (1984), the inevitable discovery doctrine is analytically similar to the independent source doctrine, in that both are intended to ensure that suppression does not outrun the deterrence objective: the prosecution is neither "put in a better position than it would have been in if no illegality had transpired" nor "put in a *worse* position simply because of some earlier police error or misconduct."

20. 138 F.2d 790 (2d Cir.1943).

21. 502 F.2d 959 (6th Cir.1974).

cumstances, the court correctly concluded, "would tend in actual practice to emasculate the search warrant requirement of the Fourth Amendment."

But in *Nix v. Williams*,[22] the Supreme Court rejected the court of appeals' limitation that the prosecution must prove the absence of bad faith, explaining that it "would place courts in the position of withholding from juries relevant and undoubted truth that would have been available to police absent any unlawful police activity" and "would put the police in a *worse* position than they would have been in if no unlawful conduct had transpired." The Court in *Williams,* which incidentally involved an unwitting violation of the subsequently-expanded *Massiah* doctrine,[23] went on to say that when the officer contemplates inevitable discovery "there will be little to gain from taking any dubious 'shortcuts' to obtain the evidence." But this simply is not so in a *Griffin*-type situation, where an illegal confirming search can determine whether obtaining a warrant is worth the bother. The answer here would seem to be applying a standard borrowed from the Supreme Court's independent-source ruling in *Murray v. United States*.[24] That case presented a *Griffin*-type situation except that the agents making the illegal entry there did not seize the evidence, but left and returned with a warrant (based on previously obtained probable cause) under which the seizure was then made.[25] The Court there noted that the independent source doctrine would not apply if the agents' decision to seek the warrant had been prompted by what they had discovered during the illegal entry. So too, in a *Griffin*-type situation, the government should be allowed to rely on inevitable discovery only where it can be shown that the warrant would have been obtained on independently based probable cause had there not been an illegal search (i.e., that the obtaining of a warrant was not dependent on whether the illegal search and seizure confirmed that the evidence was located on the premises).[26]

Looking in this direction, lower court decisions prior to *Murray* insisted on circumstances clearly indicating that the warrant would have been obtained even if there had not been an illegal search and seizure. One view was that the inevitable discovery doctrine would apply only if the police had obtained the warrant prior to the illegal search and seizure. Other courts did not go so far, but suggested that the process of obtaining the warrant should at least be in progress. Still others, however, required only that the police had possessed the leads making discovery inevitable at the time of the misconduct. Apparently all that was required was that the police have had independently based probable cause sufficient to obtain a warrant prior to the illegal search. While such a standard may be appropriate when the source of the inevitable discovery is a routine action such as an inventory search, it arguably is too loose as to the far-from-routine practice of obtaining a search warrant. Admittedly, in *Murray,* the warrant obtaining process was not in progress when the illegal entry was made, but there the police did in fact obtain a warrant based on previously acquired probable cause. In *Nix,* the ongoing independent investigation was well underway at the time of the illegal police conduct, and the Supreme Court had no need to speak to the necessary stage of development of the alleged source of

22. 467 U.S. 431, 104 S.Ct. 2501, 81 L.Ed.2d 377 (1984).

23. Brewer v. Williams, 430 U.S. 387, 97 S.Ct. 1232, 51 L.Ed.2d 424 (1977), discussed in § 6.4(d).

24. 487 U.S. 533, 108 S.Ct. 2529, 101 L.Ed.2d 472 (1988).

25. Because the evidence in *Murray* was not seized pursuant to the illegal entry, but pursuant to the later-acquired warrant, the independent source doctrine rather than the inevitable discovery doctrine was at issue; the government could argue that the evidence was "later obtained independently from * * * the initial illegality." In a *Griffin*-type situation, the evidence is "obtained" in the illegal search and the government therefore must argue that it inevitably would have been obtained by an "untainted" search pursuant to a warrant based on separately acquired probable cause.

26. The government presumably also would be required to show that the execution of the warrant would have been successful had the police not originally seized the evidence (i.e., that this was not a case where the illegal seizure precluded a likely removal of the evidence before the warrant could have been executed).

the inevitable discovery at the point that the police illegality occurred.

Nix did, however, provide a clear-cut answer as to the requisite showing of the likely success through the second, lawful process. Although both commentators and courts had noted prior to *Nix* that the inevitable discovery exception should not be based simply on speculation as to what might otherwise have occurred, some courts seemed to view it sufficient that the evidence "might" or "could" have been otherwise obtained. *Nix* held that the necessary probability must be measured in terms of what "would" have occurred, and the burden was on the government in this regard. The prosecution, the Court noted, must "establish by a preponderance of the evidence that the information ultimately or inevitably would have been discovered by lawful means."

§ 9.4 Fruits of Illegal Arrests and Searches

(a) Confessions. The question of whether a confession, otherwise admissible, must be suppressed as the fruit of an antecedent illegal arrest was first dealt with by the Supreme Court in *Wong Sun v. United States.*[1] Federal agents broke into Toy's laundry and pursued him into his living quarters, where his wife and child were sleeping, and there held him at gunpoint and handcuffed him, after which Toy made incriminating statements also implicating Yee. The agents then recovered drugs from Yee, who said he had obtained them from Toy and Wong Sun, both of whom were thereafter arrested and then released on their own recognizance after being charged. Later Wong Sun, on being questioned by an agent who advised him of his right to withhold incriminating information and that he was entitled to advice of counsel, made a confession. The Court concluded that Toy's admissions were the fruits of his unlawful arrest and, in response to the government's claim that the admissions resulted from "an intervening independent act of free will," noted the above facts and said that in "such circumstances it is unreasonable to infer that Toy's response was sufficiently an act of free will to purge the primary taint of the unlawful invasion." By contrast, the connection between Wong Sun's confession and his earlier arrest had "become so attenuated as to dissipate the taint" because of his release from custody and voluntary return to make a statement days later.

The more typical case was assayed in *Brown v. Illinois,*[2] where following his illegal arrest defendant was taken to the station and given the *Miranda* warnings, after which he gave incriminating statements within two hours of the arrest. The Supreme Court first rejected the per se rule of the Illinois court whereunder the *Miranda* warnings were deemed to break the causal chain between the arrest and confession. The Court explained that the mere fact a statement was voluntary under *Miranda* did not make it untainted, for if

> *Miranda* warnings, by themselves, were held to attenuate the taint of an unconstitutional arrest, regardless of how wanton and purposeful the Fourth Amendment violation, the effect of the exclusionary rule would be substantially diluted. * * * Any incentive to avoid Fourth Amendment violations would be eviscerated by making the warnings, in effect, a "cure-all," and the constitutional guarantee against unlawful searches and seizures could be said to be reduced to "a form of words."

The Court in *Brown* then declined to adopt a per se rule running the other direction, and instead concluded that such taint issues "must be answered on the facts of each case." It was explained that the "voluntariness of the statement is a threshold requirement"; this is obviously so, for absent voluntariness the statement could be suppressed without resort to any fruits analysis. Assuming voluntariness, various factors must be considered: (1) whether the *Miranda* warnings were given (though again, if they were not this would be a basis for suppression without reaching the fruits issue); (2) the "temporal

§ 9.4

1. 371 U.S. 471, 83 S.Ct. 407, 9 L.Ed.2d 441 (1963).

2. 422 U.S. 590, 95 S.Ct. 2254, 45 L.Ed.2d 416 (1975).

proximity of the arrest and the confession"; (3) "the presence of intervening circumstances"; and (4) "the purpose and flagrancy of the official misconduct." This meant the confession in the instant case was poisoned fruit, for it was obtained just two hours after the arrest without any intervening event of significance, and the arrest was obviously illegal and was undertaken "in the hope that something might turn up."

The Court's assumption in *Brown* that the mere passage of time between the arrest and the confession increases the likelihood of the confession being untainted is not sound, for illegal custody becomes more oppressive as it continues uninterrupted. It is fair to conclude, therefore, as the lower court cases indicate, that temporal proximity is the least important factor involved in the *Brown* formula. Though the short time lapse between arrest and confession is often relied upon in support of a holding that the confession is tainted, a lapse of time in itself cannot make a confession independent of an illegal arrest. Indeed, the passage of time without an appearance in court can bring about yet another Fourth Amendment violation under the rule of *Gerstein v. Pugh,*[3] and this will make the confession the fruit of yet another poisonous tree.

The "purpose and flagrancy" factor of *Brown* is certainly a legitimate consideration, for to maximize deterrence the Fourth Amendment exclusionary rule should be most strictly applied in cases where flagrantly unlawful police activity occurred. But, especially in light of the inherent difficulties in establishing an improper motive, this does not mean that an otherwise inadmissible confession should be admitted into evidence simply because a flagrant and purposeful Fourth Amendment violation has not been established. Lower courts have been especially willing to find taint if the arrest was made without any apparent justification, as part of a dragnet operation or upon a pretext, or where it appeared that the illegal arrest was for the purpose of obtaining a confession or was exploited for that purpose. On the other hand, suppression is less likely where the illegality is an arrest slightly short of probable cause after a lawful stopping for investigation, or an arrest on evidence which would be sufficient but for its acquisition during a stopping for investigation on grounds barely insufficient.

The Court in *Brown* did not elaborate what would qualify as an intervening circumstance, but significantly referred to *Johnson v. Louisiana,*[4] holding a lineup identification need not be excluded as the fruit of a prior Fourth Amendment violation where the detention at the time of the lineup was under the authority of the magistrate's commitment. The same would seem to be true where a confession is obtained after such commitment.[5] Termination of the illegal custody, as in *Wong Sun,* also qualifies as an intervening circumstance, as does consultation with counsel. Some courts have treated a volunteered statement, not made in response to police interrogation, as a significant intervening circumstance. That view is unobjectionable, but the same cannot be said for the conclusion that a statement given in response to interrogation following an illegal arrest is untainted because of the sense of remorse felt by the defendant or because the defendant was then confronted with his accomplice, who successfully urged him to confess. But such results may be more likely after *Rawlings v. Kentucky,*[6] where Rawlings and Ms. Cox were detained at a house while a search warrant was sought and when the warrant arrived Ms. Cox was compelled to empty her purse, after which she called upon Rawlings to claim what was his and he claimed the revealed controlled substances because he "wasn't going to try to pin that on her." The majority had

3. 420 U.S. 103, 95 S.Ct. 854, 43 L.Ed.2d 54 (1975), holding that the Fourth Amendment requires a judicial determination of probable cause as a prerequisite to an extended restraint on liberty following arrest without a warrant.

4. 406 U.S. 356, 92 S.Ct. 1620, 32 L.Ed.2d 152 (1972).

5. But *Johnson* does not mean that the mere issuance of an arrest warrant, an ex parte procedure which does not deliver defendant into the hands of the judiciary, is a significant intervening event. Taylor v. Alabama, 457 U.S. 687, 102 S.Ct. 2664, 73 L.Ed.2d 314 (1982).

6. 448 U.S. 98, 100 S.Ct. 2556, 65 L.Ed.2d 633 (1980).

"little doubt that this factor weighs heavily in favor of a finding that petitioner acted 'of free will unaffected by the initial illegality.'" The dissenters properly objected that Rawlings' statement was in response to Cox's demand, which was a product of the illegal search of her purse, which in turn was made possible by the illegal detention of the people at the house.

Given the nonutility of the "temporal proximity" factor, what ordinarily is required is a balancing of the last two *Brown* factors. The "clearest indication of attenuation," such as release from custody, is called for where the "official conduct was flagrantly abusive of Fourth Amendment rights."[7] Mere confrontation of defendant with untainted evidence, for example, clearly would not suffice. But when the police conduct is not flagrant, some lesser intervening circumstances (but more than mere *Miranda* warnings) will suffice.

The *Brown* approach, applied in that and other cases to situations in which the alleged poisonous tree was an arrest made without probable cause, was deemed inapplicable in *New York v. Harris*,[8] where the poisonous tree was an in-premises arrest on probable cause but without an arrest warrant as required by *Payton v. New York*.[9] The Court in *Harris* instead adopted, 5–4, a per se rule: "where the police have probable cause to arrest a suspect, the exclusionary rule does not bar the State's use of a statement made by the defendant outside of his home, even though the statement is taken after an arrest made in the home in violation of *Payton*." The majority reasoned (i) that once Harris had been removed from his home his continued custody was lawful, so that his statement given at the police station was not the product of unlawful custody; and (ii) that the statement was likewise not a fruit of the arrest occurring in the home instead of somewhere else, as the *Payton* warrant requirement "is imposed to protect the home" and thus is vindicated by suppression of "anything incriminating the police gathered from arresting Harris in his home, rather than elsewhere." The dissenters effectively challenged both points[10] and, in addition, cast serious doubt upon the majority's assumption that *Harris* would not create an incentive for police to violate the *Payton* rule for the express purpose of obtaining an incriminating statement.

Cases in which it is contended that a confession was the fruit of a prior illegal search are usually easier to resolve. In the typical case in which the defendant was present when incriminating evidence was found in an illegal search or in which the defendant was confronted by the police with evidence they had illegally seized, it is apparent that there has been an "exploitation of that illegality"[11] when the police subsequently question the defendant about that evidence or the crime to which it relates. Because the realization that the cat is out of the bag plays a significant role in encouraging the suspect to speak, the more fine-tuned assessment used in *Brown* is ordinarily unnecessary when the "poisonous tree" is an illegal search. Giving the *Miranda* warnings in such a case clearly will not break the causal chain, for these warnings do not advise the defendant whether the evidence he is confronted with is unlawfully obtained or whether it will be admissible at trial. If a magistrate or counsel did unequivocally and clearly advise the defendant that the evidence had been illegally seized and neither it nor its fruits could be used against him, this would dissipate the taint of the illegal search. Here again those cases which attribute defendant's confession to remorse or some similar feeling in holding that it is not a

7. Powell, J., concurring in *Brown*.

8. 475 U.S. 14, 110 S.Ct. 1640, 109 L.Ed.2d 13 (1990).

9. 445 U.S. 573, 100 S.Ct. 1371, 63 L.Ed.2d 639 (1980), discussed in § 3.6(a).

10. They responded (i) that *Brown* and the Court's other poisonous tree cases had never before required that the constitutional violation have been continuing at the very moment the challenged evidence was obtained; and (ii) that "violations of privacy in the home are especially invasive" and produce effects which "extend far beyond the moment the physical occupation of the home ends," meaning the *Brown* factors should be applied to determine "the point at which those effects are sufficiently dissipated that deterrence is not meaningfully advanced by suppression."

11. Wong Sun v. United States, 371 U.S. 471, 83 S.Ct. 407, 9 L.Ed.2d 441 (1963).

fruit of the earlier police illegality are unsound. More plausible, at least in some circumstances, is the claim that a confession was not the product of a prior illegal search because the defendant was equally influenced by other, lawfully obtained evidence already in the hands of the police.

(b) Searches. In the typical case in which an illegal arrest is followed by a search, no "fruits" problem of any magnitude is presented. Where the search of the person or the surrounding area has its only justification as being "incident to" the arrest under *Chimel v. California*,[12] then unquestionably the evidence found in the search must be suppressed if the antecedent arrest was unlawful. This is direct rather than derivative evidence, and there is no occasion to be concerned about the limits of the fruit of the poisonous tree doctrine.

On occasion, however, fruits issues do arise when the connection between the arrest and search is not that direct. One type of case is that in which there was an antecedent illegal arrest and the justification for the later search is that it is incident to arrest, but it is claimed a valid arrest intervened. Illustrative is *United States v. Walker*,[13] where defendant was illegally detained by officer Davis after which officer Shaull came to the scene and discovered evidence upon which to arrest defendant and did arrest him, after which evidence was found on defendant's person. Though the court held that "even assuming *arguendo* that Davis's arrest of Walker was illegal, it is obvious that the evidence seized by Shaull was not discovered through any exploitation of that initial arrest," this is at best a questionable result. It would seem to encourage the seizure of suspects on insufficient evidence while an investigation is conducted for the purpose of establishing probable cause.

A second type of situation is that in which the search is based upon a consent theory rather than a search-incident-to-arrest theory, as in *State v. Fortier*.[14] There, an officer made an illegal stop of a vehicle and then obtained defendant's consent to an opening of the trunk, and the court held the evidence thereby discovered admissible on the ground it was obtained by "an intervening act of free will" by defendant. But, the mere fact a consent to a search is "voluntary" within the meaning of *Schneckloth v. Bustamonte*[15] does not mean it is untainted. As noted earlier, in *Brown v. Illinois*[16] the Court rejected the notion that a confession is untainted merely because it is voluntary, and thus it follows that the voluntariness of a consent does not alone remove the taint. Rather, the factors from *Brown* discussed earlier should be applied to this situation.

Yet another situation is that in which the search is undertaken pursuant to a search warrant based upon lawfully acquired probable cause, but the police attempted to ensure that the warrant could be successfully executed by illegally holding the defendant until the warrant was obtained and served. On such facts, it has been held that the evidence obtained in execution of the warrant is a fruit of the illegal detention. This is a sound result, for to hold the evidence was not a fruit of a detention undertaken for the precise purpose of ensuring the later availability of that evidence, would unquestionably run contrary to the deterrence objective of the exclusionary rule. (This is not to suggest, however, that in any case in which execution of a search warrant has been preceded by an illegal arrest of the person who lives at the place searched, the evidence must be suppressed simply because that person, "but for" the arrest, might have disposed of the evidence. Certainly if the arrest was in no sense related to the pending application and execution of a warrant, then exclusion in the name of deterrence is not necessary.)

Somewhat related to the situation first discussed in the preceding paragraph, and per-

12. 395 U.S. 752, 89 S.Ct. 2034, 23 L.Ed.2d 685 (1969).

13. 535 F.2d 896 (5th Cir.1976).

14. 113 Ariz. 332, 553 P.2d 1206 (1976).

15. 412 U.S. 218, 93 S.Ct. 2041, 36 L.Ed.2d 854 (1973), on remand 479 F.2d 1047 (9th Cir.1973).

16. 422 U.S. 590, 95 S.Ct. 2254, 45 L.Ed.2d 416 (1975).

haps dictating a different result even there, is *Segura v. United States,*[17] where police entered premises without a warrant and arrested the occupants and then remained on the scene several hours until a search warrant was obtained and executed there. The claimed "poisonous tree" was "the initial illegal entry and occupation of the premises," which the Court held did not require suppression of the evidence later obtained in execution of the search warrant. This was because the warrant affidavit was based only on information acquired prior to the illegal entry, and because the possibility that absent the illegal entry the evidence would have been removed or destroyed "was pure speculation." "Even more important," the *Segura* majority added, "we decline to extend the exclusionary rule, which already exacts an enormous price from society and our system of justice, to further 'protect' criminal activity, as the dissent would have us do." The four dissenters forcefully argued that such a conclusion "provides an affirmative incentive for warrantless and plainly unreasonable and unnecessary intrusions into the home" because police now know that if they illegally impound premises for the very purpose of facilitating a later successful warrant execution, that illegality will have no effect upon the evidence first[18] discovered during the warrant execution.

Sometimes upon a motion to suppress evidence obtained in execution of a search warrant, a showing is made that some of the information in the affidavit presented to the magistrate was acquired in a prior illegal search. The question then becomes how this affects the status of the search warrant, which most courts have answered by saying that the warrant is nonetheless valid if it could have issued upon the untainted information in the affidavit. Illustrative is *James v. United States,*[19] where an officer lawfully looked through an open garage door and saw a partially stripped down car and then a few days later made same lawful observation and saw that the car was entirely stripped down, after which he illegally entered the garage and examined the license tag and owner's manual. He then determined that the car was listed as stolen, and on the basis of all these facts obtained a search warrant. Defendant argued that "any taint in the police conduct nullified the entire investigatory process so that no warrant can issue," but the court rejected this position as going "beyond the sound limits of the deterrence philosophy" and ruled: "If the lawfully obtained information amounts to probable cause and would have justified issuance of the warrant, apart from the tainted information, the evidence seized pursuant to the warrant is admitted."

The current status of the *James* rule is somewhat uncertain in light of the Supreme Court's decision in *United States v. Giordano.*[20] There the court first held that evidence obtained by certain court-ordered wiretaps

17. 468 U.S. 796, 104 S.Ct. 3380, 82 L.Ed.2d 599 (1984).

18. In *Segura,* the "only issue" was said to be whether items "not observed during the initial entry and first discovered by the agents the day after the entry, under an admittedly valid search warrant, should have been suppressed," and the Chief Justice argued that such illegal entries are deterred by officers' realization "that whatever evidence they discover as a direct result of the entry may be suppressed." But the Court did not hold that such suppression would be necessary, and the four dissenters understandably found the suggested distinction a curious one: "If the execution of a valid warrant takes the poison out of the hidden fruit, I should think that it would also remove the taint from the fruit in plain view."

In Murray v. United States, discussed in § 9.3(d), the Court concluded that the independent source doctrine could apply to evidence seen during an initial illegal entry but subsequently seized under a warrant based on previously acquired probable cause. However, the questioned relationship in *Murray* concerned the possible contribution of the initial discovery to the subsequent obtaining of the warrant, with the Court holding that the seizure under the warrant would constitute an independent source only if the initial discovery had not prompted the police to expend the effort to obtain the warrant. Since the police in *Murray* had left the premises after the illegal entry (although continuing to keep the premises under surveillance), the Court did not have before it the contention that the initially illegal entry had facilitated the subsequent seizure under the warrant by ensuring that contraband was not removed from the premises. In *Segura* too, although the actual entry into the premises was illegal, the Court stressed that the "impoundment" or "seizure" of the premises was not illegal—i.e., the police could lawfully have ensured against the removal by securing the premises from the outside and the entry did not further contribute to that capacity.

19. 418 F.2d 1150 (D.C.Cir.1969).

20. 416 U.S. 505, 94 S.Ct. 1820, 40 L.Ed.2d 341 (1974).

had to be suppressed, and then ruled that evidence obtained under two pen register extension orders and a wiretap extension order were derivatively tainted by the initial invalid interception. The Court explained that "the illegally monitored conversations should be considered a critical element in extending the pen register authority." Four members of the Court dissented; applying *James,* they concluded the pen register extension orders were valid because sufficiently supported by untainted information. Some have read *Giordano* as rejecting the *James* rule in favor of a "critical element" test, meaning an impressive or important element in relation to the totality of material put before the court, even though the rest independently establishes probable cause. Others have reasoned that the Court clearly meant the extension order could not have been granted absent the illegal evidence, and thus was merely applying the *James* rule.

Some courts have been a bit more demanding than *James,* and rightly so. If illegally-obtained information is merely stricken and the balance of the affidavit assessed as if the tainted information had never been included, then police are tempted to make illegal searches to bolster what would otherwise be borderline affidavits. If the illegality is never uncovered, then they have a warrant solidly based on probable cause where otherwise their warrant application might have been rejected. If, on the other hand, the illegality comes to light, then the police are no worse off than if they had not made the illegal search. At a minimum, a warrant should be held invalid where the tainted information was used to bolster what would otherwise have been a doubtful showing of probable cause. This involves nothing more than depriving such warrants of the special treatment they would otherwise receive under *United States v. Ventresca,*[21] where the Court declared that "in a doubtful or marginal case a search under a warrant may be sustainable where without one it would fall."

Sometimes a second search is undertaken to acquire precisely the same information which the authorities obtained under an earlier, illegal search. *Silverthorne Lumber Co. v. United States*[22] was such a case, for there federal officers unlawfully seized certain documents belonging to the Silverthornes and then, after a court ordered them returned, subpoenaed the same documents. The Court held the subpoenas invalid because based on knowledge obtained from illegally seized evidence, but cautioned that "this does not mean that the facts thus obtained become sacred and inaccessible. If knowledge of them is gained from an independent source they may be proved like any others." An independent source determination can be relatively easy where the information constituting the other source was obtained and used by officers who did not communicate with those who engaged in the initial illegality. But, as noted earlier,[23] that determination can raise troublesome questions of possible connection where there was such communication, especially where the alleged independent source came into existence after the initial illegality. However, as the discussion there of *Murray v. United States*[24] makes clear, an earlier illegal search can taint a later search warrant even if *no* information from the earlier search was included in the search warrant affidavit, for the taint can also arise from the fact that the illegal search otherwise "prompted" the seeking of a search warrant.

(c) Arrests. If police in an illegal search discover evidence which provides probable cause that a particular person has committed a crime, an arrest of that person based upon this information is unquestionably tainted, provided of course the arrestee had standing to object regarding the antecedent search. But the mere existence of such a prior illegal search does not inevitably taint a subsequent arrest, for it may be that the arrest will be found to have a sufficient factual basis apart from the illegal search. The reasoning of the

21. 380 U.S. 102, 85 S.Ct. 741, 13 L.Ed.2d 684 (1965).

22. 251 U.S. 385, 40 S.Ct. 182, 64 L.Ed. 319 (1920).

23. See § 9.3(d).

24. 487 U.S. 533, 108 S.Ct. 2529, 101 L.Ed.2d 472 (1988).

cases in the preceding subsection is applicable here as well, and thus, for example, an officer possessing legally obtained information constituting probable cause for arrest is not barred from making the arrest solely because he also has information which was unlawfully obtained. However, if the lawfully acquired evidence established probable cause but illegally obtained information influenced the making of the arrest at a particular time or place, which had a bearing on what was uncovered in the search incident to arrest, this would be yet another basis for concluding that the arrest was the fruit of the prior illegality.

(d) Identification of Person. Yet another issue is whether identification evidence (e.g., fingerprints, photographs, face-to-face confrontation) acquired following an illegal arrest is a tainted fruit of the arrest. Assume, for example, that defendant is illegally arrested on suspicion of armed robbery, after which he is placed in a lineup and identified by a victim of the robbery as the perpetrator of the crime. If the victim is later called to testify at trial, may he give evidence of his stationhouse identification or now identify the defendant in court?

As for the stationhouse identification, some decisions are to be found taking the position that this kind of evidence is not to be deemed the fruit of the prior illegal arrest. This result is explained upon reasons which will not withstand analysis, such as that somehow there would inevitably have been a confrontation between victim and defendant on some later occasion, that it was within the realm of possibility that defendant could have been identified without first being taken into custody, or that the arrest is not causally connected with the identification because the witness was merely applying his recollections from the time of the crime. But the correct view under ordinary circumstances is that because a stationhouse lineup is the direct result of the illegal arrest, that identification is unlawful fruit of the poisonous tree. This is not inevitably the case, however, for what is required here is analysis essentially like that used in *Brown v. Illinois* [25] in assaying the connection between an illegal arrest and a confession.

Brown enumerated three factors: "temporal proximity," "the presence of intervening circumstances," and "the purpose and flagrancy of the official misconduct." The "temporal proximity" factor is relatively unimportant, and thus it does not make much difference whether the identification occurs immediately after arrest or later. As for "purpose and flagrancy," the absence of a flagrantly illegal arrest for the purpose of obtaining an identification does not alone dissipate the taint, but merely means it will take something less than would otherwise be the case to constitute intervening circumstances. As for what intervening circumstances will dissipate the taint, such events as appearance before a magistrate [26] and a truly voluntary election by defendant to participate in a lineup will suffice in some circumstances at least.

Assuming now a case in which it may be concluded that the pretrial identification was a fruit of a prior illegal arrest and thus must be suppressed, what then of an at-trial identification by the same witness? The Supreme Court dealt with an analogous problem in *United States v. Wade*,[27] where the question was the admissibility of an in-court identification preceded by an at-the-station identification which was illegal for denial of counsel, and it was concluded the answer depended upon whether the in-court identification

> has been come at by exploitation of that illegality or instead by means sufficiently distinguishable to be purged of the primary taint. * * * Application of this test in the present context requires consideration of various factors; for example, the prior opportunity to observe the alleged criminal act, the existence of any discrepancy between any pre-lineup description and the defendant's actual description, any identification prior to lineup of another person, the identification by pic-

25. 422 U.S. 590, 95 S.Ct. 2254, 45 L.Ed.2d 416 (1975).

26. Johnson v. Louisiana, 406 U.S. 356, 92 S.Ct. 1620, 32 L.Ed.2d 152 (1972).

27. 388 U.S. 218, 87 S.Ct. 1926, 18 L.Ed.2d 1149 (1967).

ture of the defendant prior to the lineup, failure to identify the defendant on a prior occasion, and the lapse of time between the alleged act and the lineup identification. It is also relevant to consider those facts which, despite the absence of counsel, are disclosed concerning the conduct of the lineup.

Lower courts have used this same approach in determining whether an in-court identification is the fruit of a prior identification which was tainted because it occurred while defendant was being held in violation of the Fourth Amendment. The correctness of this was confirmed by the Supreme Court in *United States v. Crews*,[28] where the Court helpfully noted that a victim's in-court identification has "three different elements": (1) the victim is present at trial, (2) the victim possesses knowledge of and the ability to reconstruct the crime and to identify the defendant from observations at the time of the crime; and (3) the defendant is physically present. In then concluding that "none of these three elements 'has been come at by exploitation' of the violation of the defendant's Fourth Amendment rights," the Court readily determined, as to the first element, that the victim's identity and cooperation were not the product of any police misconduct; and, as to the third element, that because an "illegal arrest, without more, has never been viewed as a bar to subsequent prosecution, nor as a defense to a valid conviction," the defendant was "not himself a suppressible 'fruit.'" With respect to the second element, the Court declared:

> Nor did the illegal arrest infect the victim's ability to give accurate identification testimony. Based upon her observations at the time of the robbery, the victim constructed a mental image of her assailant. At trial, she retrieved this mnemonic representation, compared it to the figure of the defendant, and positively identified him as the robber. No part of this process was affected by respondent's illegal arrest. In the language of the "time-worn metaphor" of the poisonous tree, * * * the toxin in this case was injected only after the evidentiary bud had blossomed; the fruit served at trial was not poisoned.

In support of this conclusion, the Court in *Crews* applied several of the factors in the *Wade* "independent origins" test: "the victim viewed her assailant at close range for a period of 5–10 minutes under excellent lighting conditions and with no distractions * * *; respondent closely matched the description given by the victim immediately after the robbery * * *; the victim failed to identify anyone other than respondent * * *, but twice selected respondent without hesitation in nonsuggestive pretrial identification procedures * * *; and only a week had passed between the victim's initial observation of respondent and her first identification of him * * *."

It might well be argued, however, that facts which would suffice in a *Wade* context to show an in-court identification was reliable do not inevitably also show it was not obtained in exploitation of a prior Fourth Amendment violation, any more than showing a confession to be voluntary per se dissipates the taint. This reasoning appears to have been accepted by the Court in *Crews.* In a part of the opinion joined by all participating members of the Court, note was taken of defendant's contention that the *Wade* test "seeks only to determine whether the in-court identification is sufficiently reliable to satisfy due process, and is thus inapplicable in the context of this Fourth Amendment violation." The Court then agreed "that a satisfactory resolution of the reliability issue does not provide a complete answer to the considerations underlying *Wong Sun,*" but concluded "that in the present case both concerns are met."

It is far from clear exactly what the Court meant by this. In particular, it is uncertain whether a majority of the Court would agree with the conclusion of the court below,[29] which was that the "extreme sanction" of suppressing the in-court identification would have been necessary had there been "egregious misconduct" such as was present in *United States v. Edmons.*[30] In that case pre-

28. 445 U.S. 463, 100 S.Ct. 1244, 63 L.Ed.2d 537 (1980).

29. Crews v. United States, 369 A.2d 1063 (D.C.App. 1977).

30. 432 F.2d 577 (2d Cir.1970).

textual dragnet arrests were made on information falling far short of probable cause for the precise purpose of identifying persons who shortly before had interfered with the execution of an arrest warrant. The court concluded that "where flagrantly illegal arrests were made for the precise purpose of securing identifications that would not otherwise have been obtained, nothing less than barring any use of them can adequately serve the deterrent purpose of the exclusionary rule."

Only three members of the Court in *Crews* distinguished away an *Edmons*-type case by asserting it was unnecessary to "decide whether respondent's person should be considered evidence, and therefore a possible 'fruit' of police misconduct," because in the instant case "the record plainly discloses that prior to his illegal arrest, the police both knew respondent's identity and had some basis to suspect his involvement in the very crimes with which he was charged." Two members of the Court stated they "would reject explicitly * * * the claim that a defendant's face can be a suppressible fruit of an illegal arrest," while three others made essentially the same assertion and concluded with the "note that a majority of the Court agrees that the rationale of *Frisbie*[31] forecloses the claim that respondent's face can be suppressible as a fruit of the unlawful arrest." But that language should not be read as closing the door to an *Edmons* kind of argument, for the question is *not* (as those concurring opinions seem to assume) whether the Court should retreat from the *Frisbie* rule that an illegal arrest does not alone bar prosecution or conviction. Rather, what is involved is an application of the Court's own teaching in *Brown v. Illinois*[32] that sound fruit-of-the-poisonous-tree analysis necessitates very close attention to "the purpose and flagrancy of the official misconduct."

Turning now to the identification practice of viewing a photograph, one kind of case is that in which the illegal arrest and photographing was for the purpose of getting a picture which could be used in making such an identification, in which case the situation is indistinguishable from the face-to-face confrontation cases already discussed and must be resolved in the same way. But, because photographs are typically taken as matter of routine in the course of booking and then become a permanent part of the police files, it sometimes happens that a photograph routinely taken after an illegal arrest will on some future occasion serve to connect that person with some other crime totally unrelated to the reasons why the prephotographing illegal arrest was made. In these circumstances, courts are understandably inclined to find attenuation, although a contrary result is called for if the original arrest was so far lacking in probable cause as to justify the conclusion that it was made solely to acquire data regarding the defendant.

As for fingerprint identification, the Supreme Court dealt with it in *Davis v. Mississippi*,[33] where defendant's fingerprints, acquired when he was illegally arrested during a dragnet roundup conducted as part of a rape investigation, were matched with the prints at the crime scene. In holding the prints were the suppressible fruits of an illegal arrest, the Court rejected the state's claim that the taint concept should not be extended to fingerprints because of their inherent trustworthiness. (By like reasoning, it has been held that other trustworthy identification evidence, such as handwriting exemplars, may likewise be the fruit of an illegal arrest.) *Davis* must be distinguished from a case where the prints were taken as a matter of routine following an arrest which was illegal but not made for the express purpose of having the prints on file for later use, and then were used on a latter occasion to connect the defendant with some crime totally unrelated to the reasons underlying the illegal arrest. On such facts, a finding of attenuation is likely.

31. The reference is to Frisbie v. Collins, 342 U.S. 519, 72 S.Ct. 509, 96 L.Ed. 541 (1952), discussed in § 3.1(j).

32. 422 U.S. 590, 95 S.Ct. 2254, 45 L.Ed.2d 416 (1975).

33. 394 U.S. 721, 89 S.Ct. 1394, 22 L.Ed.2d 676 (1969).

(e) Testimony of Witness. In *United States v. Ceccolini*,[34] an officer in a flower shop on a social visit illegally picked up an envelope and found it to contain money and policy slips, and then learned from his friend, an employee there who did not notice his discovery, that the envelope belonged to defendant, who owned the shop. The information reached the FBI, and four months later an agent questioned the employee about defendant's activities without specific mention of the illegally discovered policy slips. She was most cooperative and later served as a witness against defendant at his trial for perjury based upon his grand jury testimony that he had not taken policy bets at the shop. The Court declined to accept the government's "*per se* rule that the testimony of a live witness should not be excluded at trial no matter how close and proximate the connection between it and a violation of the Fourth Amendment," but did renounce its earlier declaration in *Wong Sun v. United States*,[35] that "the policies underlying the exclusionary rule [do not] invite any logical distinction between physical and verbal evidence." The Court reasoned:

> [We] are first impelled to concluded that the degree of free will exercised by the witness is not irrelevant in determining the extent to which the basic purpose of the exclusionary rule will be advanced by its application. This is certainly true when the challenged statements are made by a putative defendant after arrest, * * * and *a fortiori* is true of testimony given by nondefendants.
>
> The greater the willingness of the witness to freely testify, the greater the likelihood that he or she will be discovered by legal means and, concomitantly, the smaller the incentive to conduct an illegal search to discover the witness. Witnesses are not like guns or documents which remain hidden from view until one turns over a sofa or opens a filing cabinet. Witnesses can, and often do, come forward and offer evidence entirely of their own volition. And evaluated properly, the degree of free will necessary to dissipate the taint will very likely be found more often in the case of live-witness testimony than other kinds of evidence. The time, place and manner of the initial questioning of the witness may be such that any statements are truly the product of detached reflection and a desire to be cooperative on the part of the witness. And the illegality which led to the discovery of the witness very often will not play any meaningful part in the witness's willingness to testify. * * *
>
> Another factor which is not only relevant in determining the usefulness of the exclusionary rule in a particular context, but also seems to us to differentiate the testimony of all live witnesses—even putative defendants—from the exclusion of the typical documentary evidence, is that such exclusion would perpetually disable a witness from testifying about relevant and material facts, regardless of how unrelated such testimony might be to the purpose of the originally illegal search or the evidence discovered thereby. * * * In short, since the cost of excluding live-witness testimony often will be greater, a closer, more direct link between the illegality and that kind of testimony is required.
>
> This is not to say, of course, that live-witness testimony is always or even usually more reliable or dependable than inanimate evidence. Indeed, just the opposite may be true. But a determination that the discovery of certain evidence is sufficiently unrelated to or independent of the constitutional violation to permit its introduction at trial is not a determination which rests on the comparative reliability of that evidence. Attenuation analysis, appropriately concerned with the differences between live-witness testimony and inanimate evidence, can consistently focus on the factors enumerated above with respect to the former, but on different factors with respect to the latter.

The two dissenters in *Ceccolini* quite correctly pointed out that the majority's approach involved "judicial 'double counting'" because it allowed a court to consider whether the witness in the particular case came forward and then, if defendant did not prevail, to consider the fact that generally (but not in

34. 435 U.S. 268, 98 S.Ct. 1054, 55 L.Ed.2d 268 (1978).

35. 371 U.S. 471, 83 S.Ct. 407, 9 L.Ed.2d 441 (1963).

this case) witnesses come forward. The dissenters made two other telling criticisms of the majority's logic: (1) the claim that the "greater the willingness of the witness to freely testify, * * * the smaller the incentive to conduct an illegal search to discover the witness" actually "reverses the normal sequence of events," for it is unlikely that "a witness' willingness to testify is known before he or she is discovered"; (2) the claim that exclusion would "perpetually disable" the witness ignores the fact that "at least as often the exclusion of physical evidence * * * will be as costly to the same societal interest."

The majority in *Ceccolini,* having concluded "that the exclusionary rule should be invoked with much greater reluctance where the claim is based on a causal relationship between a constitutional violation and the discovery of a live witness than when a similar claim is advanced to support suppression of an inanimate object," found that the taint had been dissipated in the instant case. The Court stressed the following factors, which have been utilized by lower courts in dealing with witness-as-a-fruit situations: (1) "the testimony given by the witness was an act of her own free will in no way coerced or even induced by official authority as a result of [the] discovery of the policy slips"; (2) the slips were not used in questioning the witness; (3) substantial time passed between the search and contact with the witness and between the contact and the testimony; (4) even before the search, "both the identity of [the witness] and her relationship with the respondent was well known to those investigating the case"; (5) there was "not the slightest evidence" that the officer made the search "with the intent of finding a willing and knowledgeable witness to testify against" defendant.

(f) New Crime. On occasion, when the police conduct an illegal arrest or an illegal search, this will prompt the person arrested or subjected to the search to react by committing some criminal offense. He might attack the officer, attempt to bribe him, or make some criminal misrepresentation in an effort to bring the incident to a close. In the bribery cases, the courts have consistently held that the evidence of the attempted bribe is admissible notwithstanding the prior illegal search or arrest. The most common explanation for this, that bribery attempts are sufficiently acts of free will to purge the taint, is not particularly satisfying, for it might be asked why the bribe offer is any more an act of free will than an incriminating admission or attempt to dispose of the evidence, neither of which is per se untainted. The answer may lie in the underlying deterrent purpose of the exclusionary rule, which is a prime consideration in marking the limits on fruit-of-the-poisonous-tree doctrine. Incriminating admissions and attempts to dispose of incriminating objects are common and predictable consequences of illegal arrests and searches, and thus to admit such evidence would encourage such Fourth Amendment violations in future cases. Bribery attempts, by comparison, are so infrequent and unpredictable that admission of evidence of such criminal activity in a particular case is not likely to encourage future illegal arrest and searches in order to accomplish the same result.

In cases where the response has been a physical attack upon the officer making the illegal arrest or search, courts have again held that the evidence of this new crime is admissible. Here as well the common explanation is that the attack was a free and independent action, but once more the better basis of distinction is that the rationale of the exclusionary rule does not justify its extension to this extreme. Of course, it is possible that the nature of a particular Fourth Amendment violation could be such that defensive action by the victim can fairly be characterized as having been brought about by exploitation, in which case a different result would be appropriate.

§ 9.5 Fruits of Illegally Obtained Confessions

(a) The Confession as a "Poisonous Tree." Under the early common law, the inadmissibility of a confession obtained from the defendant had no effect upon the admissibility of other evidence which was acquired as a consequence of that confession. The rationale of this position was that the defendant's statement was suppressed solely because of its untrustworthiness, and thus there was no reason to extend the exclusion to other evidence (e.g., the murder weapon disclosed by the confession) which itself did not suffer from that defect. The early Supreme Court cases suppressing confessions on due process grounds also focused upon their purported unreliability, and thus the reliable fruit of such constitutional violations was deemed admissible no matter how close the connection. But as this due process theory expanded to encompass other concerns, that rule was put into question. Some courts nonetheless adhered to the old view, but the better reasoned decisions reached a contrary conclusion on the ground that even indirect products of police misconduct violating our sense of fair play and decency must be suppressed. Although the Supreme Court has never had occasion expressly to adopt that position, it is unquestionably correct. This does not mean that an involuntary confession necessitates the rejection of all evidence which follows it, but merely requires application of the previously-discussed fruit-of-the-poisonous-tree doctrine to such confessions.

As for a confession merely obtained in violation of *Miranda,* the prophylactic exclusionary rule adopted in that case to ensure that the police follow certain interrogation procedures is in many respects like the Fourth Amendment exclusionary rule, and thus it might seem that the fruit-of-the-poisonous-tree doctrine (which developed in search and seizure cases) would also be applicable. But there has not been complete agreement on this score. One view is that if *Miranda* is read as meaning the Fifth Amendment violation occurs when defendant's statement is used against him in court rather than when it is obtained in violation of the *Miranda* procedures, then physical evidence discovered by the confession would be admissible. At the opposite extreme is the view that the need to suppress the by-product of a *Miranda*-tainted confession exists totally apart from the fruits doctrine, in that the Fifth Amendment's built-in exclusionary rule has long been interpreted to protect against such use of compelled testimony.

Although the lower courts were initially inclined to hold or assume that the fruit-of-the-poisonous-tree doctrine was applicable to cases involving confessions obtained in violation of *Miranda,* it is now clear that this is frequently (if not always) not so. The matter remains in some doubt, however, for the Supreme Court has not spoken to the issue unequivocally. The *Miranda* case itself states that unless the prosecution shows at trial that defendant waived his rights, "no evidence obtained as a result of interrogation can be used against him." But this would seem to be obiter dictum, for none of the several cases considered in *Miranda* involved the admissibility of evidence other than the confessions themselves. Equally puzzling is *Michigan v. Tucker,*[1] dealing with the admissibility of the testimony of a witness whose identity had been learned by questioning a defendant who was not given the full *Miranda* warnings. In holding the testimony was admissible even though defendant's confession was not, the Court viewed the *Miranda* warnings as "not themselves rights protected by the Constitution" but only "prophylactic standards" designed to "safeguard" or to "provide practical reinforcement" for the privilege against self-incrimination. Noting that the deviation from *Miranda* was slight because the police had merely failed to tell defendant that if he could not afford a lawyer one would be provided for him, the Court said this meant that "the police conduct here did not deprive respondent of his privilege against compulsory self-incrimination as such, but rather failed to make available to him the full measure of procedural safeguards associated with that right since *Miranda.*" Thus the *Wong Sun* fruits doctrine was dismissed, in effect, with the observation that there had been no constitutional violation, no "poisonous tree" for which the testimony of the witness could be a "fruit." Though *Tucker* thus might have been read as supporting the proposition that a

§ 9.5

1. 417 U.S. 433, 94 S.Ct. 2357, 41 L.Ed.2d 182 (1974).

confession obtained by violating *Miranda* cannot be a "poisonous tree," other aspects of the case made that a highly questionable interpretation. For one thing, though *Miranda* was technically applicable in *Tucker,*[2] the interrogation occurred prior to *Miranda* and thus at a time when the police could not have been aware of a responsibility to give the omitted warning. Suppression of the fruits in such circumstances would have been especially harsh. Secondly, the alleged fruit in *Tucker* was testimony of a witness, which the Supreme Court has since treated in a special way favoring admissibility even in a Fourth Amendment context.[3]

Nonetheless, in *Oregon v. Elstad,*[4] the Court rejected such a narrow reading of *Tucker* and held that *Tucker*'s reasoning applies with "equal force when the alleged 'fruit' of a noncoercive *Miranda* violation is neither a witness nor an article of evidence but the accused's own voluntary testimony." In *Elstad,* two officers initially questioned defendant at his home without first giving him *Miranda* warnings. When they expressed their belief that he had been involved in a burglary, he responded, "Yes, I was there." That this statement was excludable under *Miranda* was not contested. However, the defendant was questioned again at the stationhouse; there, after being given the *Miranda* warnings, and after waiving his rights, he made an extensive statement explaining his exact involvement in the burglary. Defendant argued that this statement should be excluded as the fruit of the poisonous tree, but the *Elstad* majority held the fruits doctrine was inapplicable.

The Court noted that the fruits doctrine had been developed in the context of the Fourth Amendment exclusionary rule, where the objective was to deter unreasonable searches no matter how probative their fruits. The objective of the Fifth Amendment, on the other hand, was to bar use of compelled statements. Moreover, *Miranda*'s exclusionary rule "sweeps more broadly" than the Fifth itself by establishing an irrebuttable presumption that unwarned statements obtained through custodial interrogation are compelled. The irrebuttable aspect of that presumption, however, is limited to the state's use of the unwarned statement in its case in chief. Just as *Miranda* did not bar use of such a statement, if in fact voluntary, for impeachment use,[5] so too it did not bar use of a subsequently obtained statement where there had been later compliance with *Miranda* and the initial unwarned statement was voluntary. Violation of the *Miranda* prophylactic rule did not in itself create a coercive atmosphere that rendered involuntary any subsequent, properly warned, statement. The relevant inquiry should be "whether, in fact, the second statement was also voluntarily made," considering the "surrounding circumstances and the entire course of police conduct with respect to the suspect.[6]

Yet another kind of illegally obtained confession is one obtained in violation of the *Massiah* right to counsel. In such a case, it is clear that the constitutional violation occurs at the time of the deprivation of counsel, and thus it may be concluded that such a confession can constitute the "poisonous tree" for purposes of a fruits analysis. The Supreme Court acknowledged as much when it indicated in *Brewer v. Williams* [7] that on retrial it would be necessary to determine whether evidence of the body's location and condition was a fruit of defendant's confession, obtained in violation of his right to counsel, revealing where the body could be located.

(b) Searches. Whether the confession was involuntary or was inadmissible for some other reason such as noncompliance with *Miranda,* physical evidence acquired as a result of the defendant's illegally obtained statements will be suppressed as a fruit when the

2. Because it was held applicable in all trials beginning after the *Miranda* decision. Johnson v. New Jersey, 384 U.S. 719, 86 S.Ct. 1772, 16 L.Ed.2d 882 (1966).

3. United States v. Ceccolini, 435 U.S. 268, 98 S.Ct. 1054, 55 L.Ed.2d 268 (1978).

4. 470 U.S. 298, 105 S.Ct. 1285, 84 L.Ed.2d 222 (1985).

5. See Harris v. New York, discussed in § 9.6(a).

6. See note 13 infra.

7. 430 U.S. 387, 97 S.Ct. 1232, 51 L.Ed.2d 424 (1977).

connection is rather close and direct. Such is the case when the confession supplies the probable cause for an evidence-producing arrest or search, when the defendant's statement indicates that the physical evidence is at a certain location and the police find it there as a consequence, or when the physical evidence was given to the police as part of the suspect's direct response to the illegal interrogation. Especially when the "poisonous tree" is a *Miranda* violation, which under *Tucker* perhaps does not require sweeping application of the fruit-of-the-poisonous-tree doctrine to all consequences of all violations, courts are inclined to find that the physical evidence has an independent source when the connection between the confession and physical evidence is lengthier but not nonexistent. Indeed, in light of *Elstad*'s reading of *Tucker,* it may be questioned whether the Supreme Court will uphold any application of the fruits doctrine to exclude physical evidence.[8] However, as Justice Brennan noted in his *Elstad* dissent, though the *Elstad* majority opinion stressed the prophylactic nature of the *Miranda* rule and the distinctive purposes of the Fourth and Fifth Amendments as they relate to the fruits doctrine, the opinion's additional emphasis upon the variety of factors that lead to a second confession and the insulating quality of the *Miranda* warnings given prior to that confession leaves open the possibility that the Court would require exclusion of physical evidence under a limited fruits doctrine. If so, exclusion would most likely be applied where the connection between the *Miranda* violation and the physical evidence is close and the purpose of the interrogation arguably was to locate that evidence.

In *Nix v. Williams,*[9] the Supreme Court held that the inevitable discovery doctrine could be applied in this context, and concluded the doctrine had been properly applied by the state court. That court ruled that the body discovered by police after defendant revealed its location under circumstances which deprived him of his right to counsel was not a suppressible fruit of that statement. Defendant led them to the body, which was found next to a culvert in a ditch beside a gravel road in Polk County, near the Jasper County line and about two miles from Interstate 80. However, before that occurred the police were already proceeding on the theory that the body was in that general area, based upon their knowledge of defendant's direction of flight and the discovery of some of the victim's clothing, and they had already commenced a search which involved checking all roads, ditches and culverts within 7 miles of Interstate 80. That search covered Jasper County and was about to move into Polk County, and thus the court was able to conclude that the body "would have been discovered by lawful means." Although the time that discovery would have occurred was uncertain, the court stressed the low temperatures prevailing at that time of year, which indicated that the "body would have been found in essentially the same condition it was in at the time of the actual discovery, so that all of the evidence which it actually yielded would have been available to the police." As the Supreme Court emphasized in *Nix,* the prosecution must "establish by a preponderance of the evidence that the information ultimately or inevitably would have been discovered by lawful means." Thus, *Nix* must be distinguished from those cases in which at best it is shown that the evidence might have been discovered, which is an insufficient basis upon which to hold the evidence admissible under the "inevitable discovery" test.

(c) Confessions. As for the admissibility of a confession obtained subsequent to an earlier one illegally obtained from the same party, one approach is reflected in *Lyons v. Oklahoma.*[10] There a confession was coerced from defendant, but 12 hours later in the presence of different persons and after having

8. In New York v. Quarles discussed in § 6.7(b), Justice O'Connor in her separate opinion, argued against application of the fruits doctrine to suppress "nontestimonial evidence derived from informal custodial interrogation" that violated *Miranda.* She maintained that defendant Quarles' statement concerning the location of the gun should have been excluded as obtained in violation of *Miranda,* but the gun itself should have been admitted.

9. 467 U.S. 431, 104 S.Ct. 2501, 81 L.Ed.2d 377 (1984).

10. 322 U.S. 596, 64 S.Ct. 1208, 88 L.Ed. 1481 (1944).

been transferred from a jail to a prison, defendant gave a second confession. The Court in *Lyons* first declared that the "admissibility of the later confession depends upon the same test—is it voluntary," and then ruled that while sometimes the "effect of earlier abuse may be so clear as to forbid any other inference than that it dominated the mind of the accused to such an extent that the later confession is involuntary," this was not such a case. The fruit-of-the-poisonous-tree doctrine was never mentioned and quite obviously was not being applied. The issue, as the Court saw it, was whether the events at the time of the first confession—not the confession itself—brought about the second confession, and the focus was on the continuing effect of the prior coercive practices. On other facts, the Court has held a second confession involuntary because the coercive circumstances of the first carried over to the second.[11]

In *United States v. Bayer*,[12] the lower court applied the fruit-of-the-poisonous-tree doctrine to exclude a second confession which, while preceded by a warning that it might be used against the defendant, was made after defendant had reread the first confession without being told it could not be used against him. But the Supreme Court reversed. The majority in *Bayer* first noted that though "after an accused has once let the cat out of the bag by confessing * * * [h]e can never get the cat back in the bag," this does not mean "that making a confession under circumstances which preclude its use, perpetually disables the confessor from making a usable one after those conditions have been removed."[13] That conclusion is unobjectionable, but some questioned whether the same could be said for the Court's next statement: that the lower court improperly used a fruits theory here because the Supreme Court's earlier cases in that line "did not deal with confessions but with evidence of a quite different category and do not control this question." The truth of the matter is that the question whether the fruits of an inadmissible confession are admissible should be analyzed in the same manner as whether the fruits of unreasonably seized evidence should be excluded. And when the alleged fruits are a second confession, what this means is that the defendant's second statement should be deemed tainted unless he was made aware of the inadmissibility of the initial confession or has consulted with counsel who has so advised him. Lower courts have utilized a fruits analysis in determining the admissibility of successive confessions even when the initial confession was suppressed for reasons other than involuntariness. *Elstad,* however, clearly rejects this position as to *Miranda* violations, and casts doubt upon its acceptability as to other non-Fourth Amendment violations rendering the initial confession inadmissible for reasons other than involuntariness.

Somewhat unusual circumstances concerning either the first or the second statement by the defendant may complicate the analysis. Where both are inculpatory in nature, then despite *Miranda* warnings intervening between the two confessions the accused will likely attach no importance to restatement of his guilt. But the situation is different when the first statement was exculpatory, and thus a finding that the taint is dissipated is more likely in such a case. When defendant's second statement is to a private party rather than a police officer, this also increases the possibility of such a finding. Situations of

11. Leyra v. Denno, 347 U.S. 556, 74 S.Ct. 716, 98 L.Ed. 948 (1954).

12. 331 U.S. 532, 67 S.Ct. 1394, 91 L.Ed. 1654 (1947).

13. Consider also Oregon v. Elstad, discussed supra at note 4. The Court there noted that it previously had refused to automatically exclude all second confessions under a "cat-out-of-the-bag" theory, and it was certainly not about to do so when the original confession was excludable only because of a *Miranda* violation. Any psychological compulsion that flowed from an unwarned but entirely voluntary statement was too speculative and attenuated, as it relates to official coercion, to justify exclusion of a second statement given after the administration of *Miranda* warning. While it was true that the defendant had not been told prior to his second statement that the first statement was excludable, the Court "has never embraced the theory that the defendant's ignorance of the full consequences of his decisions vitiates their voluntariness." The officers here had not attempted to "exploit the [earlier] unwarned admission to pressure [the suspect] into waiving his right to remain silent," and they should not be expected to give the suspect legal advice as to the inadmissibility of his earlier statement.

this kind are to be examined by use of the factors listed in *Brown v. Illinois*: [14] "temporal proximity"; "the presence of intervening circumstances"; and "the purpose and flagrancy of the official misconduct."

(d) Testimony of Witness. *Harrison v. United States* [15] involved these facts: after three confessions allegedly made by defendant were introduced at his trial, he took the stand and testified to his own version of the events, making damaging admissions in the process; his conviction was later reversed on the ground that the confessions had been obtained in violation of the *McNabb–Mallory* rule; upon retrial the prosecution introduced defendant's testimony at the first trial, and he was convicted once again. A 6–3 majority of the Court reversed, explaining:

> In his opening statement to the jury [at the first trial], defense counsel announced that the petitioner would not testify in his own behalf. Only after his confessions had been admitted in evidence did he take the stand. It thus appears that, but for the use of his confessions, the petitioner might not have testified at all. But even if the petitioner would have decided to testify whether or not his confessions had been used, it does not follow that he would have admitted being at the scene of the crime and holding the gun when the fatal shot was fired. On the contrary, the more natural inference is that no testimonial admission so damaging would have been made if the prosecutor had not already spread the petitioner's confession before the jury. That is an inference the Government has not dispelled.
>
> It has not been demonstrated, therefore, that the petitioner's testimony was obtained "by means sufficiently distinguishable" from the underlying illegality "to be purged of the primary taint."

The Court in *Harrison* cautioned that it was reserving for future decision the question of whether testimony by some other person could be a fruit. This question was later raised in *Michigan v. Tucker*,[16] where after incomplete *Miranda* warnings defendant gave a statement which identified a person the prosecution used as a witness at trial. The Court declined to treat that testimony as a suppressible fruit, but, for the reasons earlier stated [17] it is impossible to draw any general conclusions from *Tucker*. However, at least one court has concluded, even as to a post-*Miranda* interrogation, that the testimony of persons discovered thereby is not a fruit of the noncompliance with *Miranda*, but that a fruits inquiry is appropriate if the confession is either involuntary or obtained in violation of the Sixth Amendment right to counsel. Even as to the latter situations, however, it is well to remember the Supreme Court's recently stated "special" approach to claims that testimony is an inadmissible fruit, designed to limit the circumstances in which such evidence would be suppressed,[18] for it will doubtless be applied in this context as well. And in any event, the testimony of the discovered witness will be held admissible under the "inevitable discovery" rule if it appears to the court that sooner or later his identity would have been independently revealed by standard investigation procedures.

§ 9.6 Permissible Use of Illegally Seized Evidence at Trial

(a) Impeachment. Under the various exclusionary rules, if a constitutional violation has occurred then upon a timely objection by a defendant with standing the fruits of that illegality must be suppressed and consequently may not be introduced into evidence at the criminal trial of that defendant. There exist, however, a few exceptions to that statement, one of which concerns the use of that evidence for impeachment purposes. The dimensions of that particular exception have broadened over the years, which can best be seen by a brief chronological look at the Supreme Court's leading decisions in this area.

14. 422 U.S. 590, 95 S.Ct. 2254, 45 L.Ed.2d 416 (1975).

15. 392 U.S. 219, 88 S.Ct. 2008, 20 L.Ed.2d 1047 (1968).

16. 417 U.S. 433, 94 S.Ct. 2357, 41 L.Ed.2d 182 (1974).

17. See § 6.5(b).

18. United States v. Ceccolini, 435 U.S. 268, 98 S.Ct. 1054, 55 L.Ed.2d 268 (1978), discussed in § 9.4(e).

First in the series was *Agnello v. United States.*[1] Defendant, charged with conspiracy to sell cocaine, testified on direct examination that he received certain packages without knowing they contained cocaine, and on cross-examination said he had never seen narcotics, at which point the government was permitted to introduce in rebuttal a can of cocaine which had been illegally seized from his room and suppressed from the government's case in chief. A unanimous Court reversed, relying upon its earlier statement that the "essence of a provision forbidding the acquisition of evidence in a certain way is not merely that evidence so acquired shall not be used before the court but that it shall not be used at all." [2] About thirty years passed before a somewhat similar case, *Walder v. United States,*[3] reached the Court; there, defendant testified on direct and cross-examination that he had never purchased, sold or possessed any narcotics, which the government was allowed to impeach by questioning defendant concerning heroin illegally seized from his home two years earlier. The Court upheld this procedure, reasoning that the defendant could not use the exclusionary rule to "provide himself with a shield against contradiction of his untruths" where, as in *Walder,* he had been "free to deny all the elements of the case against him" without the impeached "sweeping claim that he had never dealt in or possessed any narcotics." *Walder* thus appeared to say that where a defendant (i) on direct examination (ii) did not merely deny the elements of the case against him but instead made sweeping claims putting his character in issue, then the government could introduce illegally obtained evidence (iii) for the limited purpose of impeachment (iv) if the evidence was obtained as a consequence of police misconduct unrelated to the instant case. So viewed, *Walder* seemed to strike a reasonable balance between the competing interests involved.

The third case is *Harris v. New York,*[4] where, after the defendant upon direct examination denied having made the charged sale of narcotics, the prosecutor was allowed to impeach the defendant's credibility by resort to a statement made by him to the police under circumstances which concededly made that statement inadmissible under *Miranda.* In a 5–4 decision, the Supreme Court affirmed, reasoning that though in *Walder* defendant "was impeached as to collateral matters" while here he "was impeached as to testimony bearing more directly on the crimes charged," this did not amount to a "difference in principle" between the two cases:

> The impeachment process here undoubtedly provided valuable aid to the jury in assessing petitioner's credibility, and the benefits of this process should not be lost, in our view, because of the speculative possibility that impermissible police conduct will be encouraged thereby. Assuming that the exclusionary rule has a deterrent effect on proscribed police conduct, sufficient deterrence flows when the evidence in question is made unavailable to the prosecution in its case in chief.
>
> Every criminal defendant is privileged to testify in his own defense, or to refuse to do so. But that privilege cannot be construed to include the right to commit perjury. * * * Having voluntarily taken the stand, petitioner was under an obligation to speak truthfully and accurately, and the prosecution here did no more than utilize the traditional truth-testing devices of the adversary process.

Harris was rightly criticized because it selectively quoted from *Walder,* carefully excising any reference to the broader principle that the defendant "must be free to deny all the elements of the case against him without thereby giving leave to the Government to introduce by way of rebuttal evidence illegally secured by it," and also because it claimed to be extending a general rule laid down in *Walder* when in truth *Walder* was a limited exception to the general rule established in

§ 9.6

1. 269 U.S. 20, 46 S.Ct. 4, 70 L.Ed. 145 (1925).

2. Quoting Silverthorne Lumber Co. v. United States, 251 U.S. 385, 40 S.Ct. 182, 64 L.Ed. 319 (1920).

3. 347 U.S. 62, 74 S.Ct. 354, 98 L.Ed. 503 (1954).

4. 401 U.S. 222, 91 S.Ct. 643, 28 L.Ed.2d 1 (1971).

Agnello, which thus was overruled without even being cited.

Next in the series was *United States v. Havens,*[5] where on direct examination defendant denied being involved with his codefendant in the transportation of cocaine, and on cross-examination denied being involved in sewing a pocket (in which drugs were found) into his codefendant's clothing or having in his own suitcase cloth from which the swatch was cut to make the pocket. That testimony was impeached by admitting the illegally seized cloth, but the appellate court reversed because the impeached testimony was not given on direct examination. But the Supreme Court, again in a 5–4 decision, ruled otherwise:

> In terms of impeaching a defendant's seemingly false statements with his prior inconsistent utterances or with other reliable evidence available to the government, we see no difference of constitutional magnitude between the defendant's statements on direct examination and his answers to questions put to him on cross-examination that are plainly within the scope of the defendant's direct examination.

What started out in *Walder* as a narrow and reasonable exception has thus taken on awesome proportions. Under *Havens,* statements elicited on cross-examination now may be impeached. This violates the waiver doctrine of *Walder,* and actually encourages constitutional violations for purposes of "boxing in" the defendant, for now "even the moderately talented prosecutor [can] 'work in * * * evidence on cross-examination * * * [as it would] in its case in chief * * *,' " and "a defendant will be compelled to forego testifying on his own behalf" to avoid this consequence.[6] Secondly, *Harris* (as the Court later put it in *Havens*) "made clear that the permitted impeachment by otherwise inadmissible evidence is not limited to collateral matters," but may relate directly to commission of the offense itself. Of course, the defendant's testimony must open the door to such impeachment, but neither *Harris* nor *Havens* indicated precisely how far the defendant had to go in his testimony relating to an element of the offense to permit impeachment as to that element. As a consequence, some courts allow impeachment when the defendant does no more than deny the elements of the crime, though many courts refuse to read *Harris* as bringing about such an unfair result. Thirdly, as *Havens* makes plain, a defendant may now be impeached by evidence bearing directly upon the crime charged. This departure from *Walder* is also most unfortunate, for the discarded limitation minimized the danger that a jury might view unconstitutionally obtained impeaching evidence as establishing guilt, even if instructed to consider it only for credibility purposes.

Yet another question which must be asked about the impeachment exception concerns what kinds of constitutional or other violations are encompassed within the exception. *Walder* and *Havens* make it clear that Fourth Amendment violations qualify. What then if instead the evidence was obtained in violation of Title III of the Omnibus Crime Control Act of 1968, which imposes limitations upon resort to eavesdropping and wiretapping? Though this legislation expressly provides that "no part" of the contents of an invalid interception and "no evidence derived therefrom may be received in evidence in any trial,"[7] the legislative history indicates that this and related provisions were not intended to press the scope of the suppression rule beyond present search and seizure law, and thus the result in such cases is no different.

The reasons which justify some sort of impeachment exception as to Fourth Amendment violations might well be thought not to carry over to violations of the Fifth Amendment privilege against self-incrimination. For one thing, illegally seized tangible evidence is inherently reliable, but the same cannot necessarily be said where there has been a *Miranda* violation. Moreover, the Fourth Amendment exclusionary rule is a court-created device intended to deter the police, and thus arguably ought not be applied

5. 446 U.S. 620, 100 S.Ct. 1912, 64 L.Ed.2d 559 (1980).

6. As noted by the *Havens* dissenters.

7. 18 U.S.C.A. § 2515.

when the objective of deterrence is outweighed by other considerations, while by contrast the Fifth Amendment on its face prohibits the government from using "compelled" statements "against" a defendant. But in *Harris,* where the defendant was not given the complete *Miranda* warnings and it was asserted he made "no claim that the statements made to the police were coerced or involuntary," the Court unhesitantly extended the impeachment exception to *Miranda* violations. The same result was reached in *Oregon v. Hass,*[8] although there the suspect was advised of his rights and then asked for counsel but was questioned without his request being honored. The majority saw the case as indistinguishable from *Harris* because "inadmissibility would pervert the constitutional right into a right to falsify," while the two dissenters argued that *Hass* was far worse because it provided police with an incentive for dishonoring such requests—they had nothing to lose and something significant to gain, "a statement which can be used for impeachment if the accused has the temerity to testify in his own defense."

In *New Jersey v. Portash,*[9] the Court emphasized that "central to the decisions" in *Harris* and *Hass* was the fact that the defendant made no claim the statements were coerced or involuntary. That served to distinguish the statements obtained in the instant case, defendant's testimony before a grand jury given in response to a grant of use immunity, which was "the essence of coerced testimony." Confronted with "the constitutional privilege against compulsory self-incrimination in its most pristine form," the Court concluded that the balancing of interests undertaken in *Harris* and *Hass* was "impermissible" in the present context. And in *Mincey v. Arizona*[10] the Court again distinguished *Harris* and *Hass* and declared that use of an "involuntary statement" even for impeachment purposes would constitute "a denial of due process of law." The Court did not comment on the fact that in a particular case a statement could be involuntary but yet very truthworthy.

In *Michigan v. Harvey,*[11] the Supreme Court overturned a state court ruling that because defendant's statement after arraignment and appointment of counsel was taken "in violation of defendant's Sixth Amendment right to counsel" it could not be used for impeachment purposes. The majority focused upon the state court's reliance upon *Michigan v. Jackson,*[12] which held that after a defendant requests assistance of counsel, any waiver of Sixth Amendment rights given in a discussion initiated by police is presumed invalid. Because it "simply superimposed the Fifth Amendment analysis" of *Edwards v. Arizona*[13] onto the Sixth Amendment right, the majority reasoned, *Jackson* did not mark the exact boundary of the Sixth Amendment right itself but rather constituted a "prophylactic rule * * * designed to ensure voluntary, knowing, and intelligent waivers of the Sixth Amendment right to counsel." From this, it was deemed to follow that the reasoning of such cases as *Hass* and *Havens* carried over to the instant case: once again, "the 'search for truth in a criminal case' outweighs the 'speculative possibility' that exclusion of evidence might deter future violations of rules not compelled directly by the Constitution in the first place."

It is important to note that the *Harvey* majority did *not* hold that the fruits of a violation of the Sixth Amendment right to counsel may be used for purposes of impeachment. Having characterized the case as it did, the Court did not have to "consider the admissibility for impeachment purposes of a voluntary statement obtained in the absence of a knowing and voluntary waiver of the right to counsel," that is, in a situation in which the prosecution even apart from the *Jackson* presumption could not carry its bur-

8. 420 U.S. 714, 95 S.Ct. 1215, 43 L.Ed.2d 570 (1975).

9. 440 U.S. 450, 99 S.Ct. 1292, 59 L.Ed.2d 501 (1979). For the argument that *Portash* may bar impeachment by use of defendant's testimony given at a suppression hearing, see § 10.5(c).

10. 437 U.S. 385, 98 S.Ct. 2408, 57 L.Ed.2d 290 (1978).

11. 494 U.S. 344, 110 S.Ct. 1176, 108 L.Ed.2d 293 (1990).

12. 475 U.S. 625, 106 S.Ct. 1404, 89 L.Ed.2d 631 (1986).

13. 451 U.S. 477, 101 S.Ct. 1880, 68 L.Ed.2d 378 (1981).

den of proving such a waiver. (The four dissenters cogently argued (1) that the Sixth Amendment right, unlike *Miranda,* extends "to all efforts to elicit information from the defendant whether for use as impeachment or rebuttal at trial or simply to formulate trial strategy"; (2) that "exclusion of statements made by a represented and indicted defendant outside the presence of counsel follows not as a remedy for a violation that has preceded trial but as a necessary incident of the constitutional right itself"; and (3) that under the majority's rule the police after formal charge "have everything to gain and nothing to lose by repeatedly visiting with defendant and seeking to elicit as many comments as possible about the pending trial.")

Sometimes the question is whether defendant's silence may be utilized for impeachment purposes. In *Doyle v. Ohio,*[14] the Court held that impeachment by defendant's post-arrest silence after he had received the *Miranda* warnings was impermissible. Not only is "every post-arrest silence * * * insoluably ambiguous" because it "may be nothing more than the arrestee's exercise of [his] *Miranda* rights," but use of the silence to impeach "would be fundamentally unfair" given the fact that the warnings carry the implicit "assurance that silence will carry no penalty." [15] *Doyle* has been distinguished in three later cases. In *Anderson v. Charles,*[16] impeachment by prior inconsistent statements given after *Miranda* warnings was permitted because "a defendant who voluntarily speaks after receiving *Miranda* warnings has not been induced to remain silent." In *Jenkins v. Anderson,*[17] where at his murder trial defendant claimed self defense, the Court ruled it was permissible to impeach that story by defendant's prearrest silence in not reporting the stabbing to the authorities for at least two weeks. This was not compelled self-incrimination, for, as the Court had concluded many years earlier,[18] the possibility of impeachment by prior silence is not an impermissible burden upon the exercise of Fifth Amendment rights. Nor was it a denial of fundamental fairness, for unlike *Doyle* "no government action induced petitioner to remain silent before arrest." The claim has been made that the silence in *Jenkins* was just as equivocal as that in *Doyle,* in that an individual's reluctance to hand himself over to the police and admit a stabbing, in self-defense or otherwise, is not probative of guilt. But in *Fletcher v. Weir* [19] the Court followed *Jenkins* and distinguished *Doyle* in allowing impeachment by post-arrest silence not preceded by *Miranda* warnings, explaining that this was not "a case where the government had induced silence by implicitly assuring the defendant that his silence would not be used against him."

An effort to extend the impeachment exception from the defendant's own testimony to the testimony of all defense witnesses was rejected in *James v. Illinois.*[20] The Court, 5–

14. 426 U.S. 610, 96 S.Ct. 2240, 49 L.Ed.2d 91 (1976).

15. *Doyle* was distinguished in South Dakota v. Neville, 459 U.S. 553, 103 S.Ct. 916, 74 L.Ed.2d 748 (1983), upholding a statute which permits a person suspected of driving while intoxicated to refuse to submit to a blood-alcohol test, but authorizing revocation of the driver's license of a person so refusing the test and permitting such refusal to be used against him at trial. Though the defendant in *Neville* had not been told of the latter possibility, he was warned he could lose his license by refusing, which "made it clear that refusing the test was not a 'safe harbor,' free of adverse consequences." Moreover, the failure to warn "was not the sort of implicit promise to forego use of evidence that would unfairly 'trick' [the defendant] if the evidence were later offered against him at trial."

In Greer v. Miller, 483 U.S. 756, 107 S.Ct. 3102, 97 L.Ed.2d 618 (1987), the Supreme Court held that a *Doyle* violation exists only where the post-arrest and post-warnings silence is actually used by the prosecution for impeachment purposes. The prosecution there asked the defendant on cross-examination why he hadn't "told this story to anybody when you got arrested", but the defense counsel immediately objected, the objection was sustained, and the jury was told to "disregard questions ... to which objections were sustained". The Court held that, under these facts, there was no *Doyle* violation. The prosecutor had not been " 'allowed to undertake impeachment on' or 'permit[ted] to call attention to' [defendant's] silence" and the fact of that silence "was not submitted to the jury as evidence from which it was allowed to draw any permissible inference".

16. 447 U.S. 404, 100 S.Ct. 2180, 65 L.Ed.2d 222 (1980).

17. 447 U.S. 231, 100 S.Ct. 2124, 65 L.Ed.2d 86 (1980).

18. Raffel v. United States, 271 U.S. 494, 46 S.Ct. 566, 70 L.Ed. 1054 (1926).

19. 455 U.S. 603, 102 S.Ct. 1309, 71 L.Ed.2d 490 (1982).

20. 493 U.S. 307, 110 S.Ct. 648, 107 L.Ed.2d 676 (1990).

4, concluded that such an expansion of *Walder* "would not promote the truth-seeking function to the same extent as did creation of the original exception, and yet it would significantly undermine the deterrent effect of the general exclusionary rule," thus serving to "frustrate rather than further the purposes underlying the exclusionary rule." The same beneficial effects would not be present, the Court reasoned, because (1) the threat of subsequent criminal prosecution is alone more likely to deter a defense witness than a defendant, already facing conviction for the underlying offense; and (2) such expansion "likely would chill some defendants from presenting their best defense—and sometimes any defense at all—through the testimony of others," as a variety of factors make it problematical whether a defense witness will testify as expected and thus avoid such impeachment. Moreover, there would be present under such expansion greater threat to "the exclusionary rule's deterrent effect on police misconduct"; the expansion would "vastly increase the number of occasions on which such evidence could be used" and would serve to deter not only perjury but also the calling of defense witnesses in the first place, from which "police officers and their superiors would recognize that obtaining evidence through illegal means stacks the deck heavily in the prosecution's favor."

(b) Defense Tactics Which "Open the Door." In the impeachment case of *Walder v. United States*,[21] the Court emphasized that it was the defendant who "opened the door" to the admissibility of the illegally seized evidence by his sweeping assertions upon direct examination. On rare occasion, defense tactics which likewise seek to gain extraordinary advantage from the fact of suppression of certain evidence may also be deemed to have "opened the door" to at least limited receipt of that evidence. As shown by *Commonwealth v. Wright*,[22] defense tactics are more likely to be found to have opened the door if they involved a calculated effort to create a high degree of confusion based upon knowledge that any adequate explanation would require some reference to evidence previously suppressed. In *Wright*, one packet of heroin taken from defendant was held admissible under the plain view doctrine, but nine others were suppressed. A chemist testified that the material turned over to him by the officer had been analyzed and found to be heroin, and he carefully avoided any reference to the number of packets involved so as to prevent the claim he had testified as to suppressed evidence. But defense counsel then conducted a cross-examination of the chemist which created considerable confusion about whether the packet received in evidence had been so analyzed, precisely because the witness could never make specific reference to the other packets. The court ruled that in these circumstances it was permissible to allow the chemist to state explicitly that he had examined all ten packets and found them all to contain heroin. "The references made to the nine bundles were clearly the result of the defendant's trial strategy. He cannot now complain of testimony which he produced."

This does not mean, however, that merely because the defendant intrudes an issue into the trial as to which illegally obtained evidence would be relevant, the door has thereby been opened to receipt of that evidence on the issue. In *United States v. Hinckley*,[23] the government asserted "that because insanity is an affirmative defense, and proof of sanity is therefore not part of the prosecution's case-in-chief," evidence obtained in violation of *Miranda* and the Fourth Amendment "can be used generally to rebut an insanity defense without jeopardizing constitutional principles." The court responded that such a drastic curtailment of the exclusionary rules "would provide little or no deterrence of constitutional violations against defendants whose sanity is the principal issue in the case."

21. 347 U.S. 62, 74 S.Ct. 354, 98 L.Ed. 503 (1954).

22. 234 Pa.Super. 83, 339 A.2d 103 (1975).

23. 672 F.2d 115 (D.C.Cir.1982). Accord: People v. Ricco, 56 N.Y.2d 320, 452 N.Y.S.2d 340, 437 N.E.2d 1097 (1982).

(c) Prosecution for Perjury of Other "New" Offense. In *Walder v. United States*[24] the Court saw no "justification for letting the defendant affirmatively resort to perjurious testimony in reliance on the Government's disability to challenge his credibility," and, as we have seen, this same view has been taken in the later impeachment cases. From this, it might be argued that illegally obtained evidence should be admissible in the prosecution's case in chief on a charge of perjury. This argument was accepted in *United States v. Raftery*,[25] where hashish found in defendant's house was suppressed in defendant's prosecution for possession of it because the warrant was improperly executed. Several months later defendant was summoned before a federal grand jury, given use immunity and questioned about his participation in marijuana smuggling and distribution activities. He was thereafter indicted for perjury as a result of his negative answer to the question of whether he had ever been on premises where hashish oil was manufactured, and the appellate court ruled that in the perjury prosecution the suppressed evidence would be admissible, stating: "The purpose of the rule would not be served by forbidding the Government from using the evidence to prove the entirely separate offense of perjury before a grand jury occurring after the illegal search and seizure and suppression of the evidence in the state court."

As stated in *United States v. Turk*,[26] such a result should be reached only when it is clear that "no significant additional deterrent effect could be realized" by suppression and that the benefits to be derived from admission are substantial. For one thing, this means the search must have preceded the perjured testimony, for otherwise there would be incentive to conduct such searches against individuals suspected of perjury. Likewise, actual awareness of the search by the defendant at the time his testimony was given is essential, as if that were not so there would be incentive to make undisclosed illegal searches and then subpoena the search victim. By contrast, certain other special facts noted in *Raftery*—that the search was by officers in a different jurisdiction, that the violation was a minor one, and that the perjury occurred after a grant of immunity—are less likely requirements. Finally, there is the question of whether the *Raftery* rule needs to be limited to perjury prosecutions. *Turk* suggests the answer is no, for it is said there that "no significant additional deterrent effect could be realized by suppressing the evidence at a trial of the search victim for a crime committed after the illegal search and with the knowledge that the illegal search occurred," and that to suppress "would in effect give the victim of an illegal search a license to commit any new crimes he cares to, free from the concern that the illegally seized evidence might be used against him in prosecution for these subsequent crimes." A few courts have so held.

24. 347 U.S. 62, 74 S.Ct. 354, 98 L.Ed. 503 (1954).

25. 534 F.2d 854 (9th Cir.1976).

26. 526 F.2d 654 (5th Cir.1976).

Chapter 10

ADMINISTRATION OF THE EXCLUSIONARY RULES

Table of Sections

§ 10.1 The Pretrial Motion to Suppress

(a) Contemporaneous Objection or Pretrial Motion. Some states continue to follow the "contemporaneous objection rule," which only requires that an objection be made at trial at the time the prosecution seeks to introduce evidence the defendant claims was illegally obtained. However, the great majority of jurisdictions have abandoned that rule in favor of a requirement that objections be raised before trial by way of a pretrial motion to suppress. This requirement usually applies to exclusion based on all grounds relating to the illegal acquisition of the evidence.

The minority of jurisdictions following the contemporaneous objection rule view it as a more efficient procedure. However, there are many valid reasons underlying the prevailing practice of requiring pretrial motions. The pretrial motion requirement eliminates from the trial disputes over police conduct not immediately relevant to the question of guilt, and avoids interruptions of a trial in progress with such auxiliary inquiries. It also prevents having to declare a mistrial because the jury has been exposed to unconstitutional evidence. Moreover, it is to the advantage of both the prosecution and defense to know in advance of the time set for trial whether certain items will or will not be admitted into evidence. If the pretrial motion is granted, this could result in abandonment of the prosecution, thus avoiding the waste of prosecutorial and judicial resources occasioned by preparation of a trial, or in the prosecution changing the theory of its case or developing untainted evidence. If the pretrial motion is denied, then the defendant is in a position at that time either to plead guilty and gain whatever concessions might be obtained by so pleading without causing the commencement of a trial, or to go to trial with a somewhat different defense strategy. Finally, in those jurisdictions where interlocutory appeal by the prosecution is permitted, the requirement of a pretrial motion to suppress protects that right of immediate appeal.

(b) Form of the Motion. The pretrial motion to suppress, which in many jurisdictions must be in writing, must identify the evidence which the defendant seeks to suppress and specify with particularity the grounds upon which the motion is based. This requirement is one of specificity in the statement of defendant's legal theory, which may be met, for example, by alleging that the evidence in question was obtained from the defendant incident to an arrest which was not made upon probable cause.

Many jurisdictions require a defendant making a pretrial suppression motion also to set out facts in support of the motion, and it may even be necessary that defendant's motion be accompanied by an affidavit on behalf of the defendant setting forth all facts within his knowledge upon which he intends to rely in support of the motion. This requirement has been held constitutional, which perhaps it is so long as the holding in *Simmons v. United States*[1]—that testimony given by the defendant at the hearing on his motion is not admissible against him at trial on the question of guilt or innocence—is extended to such affidavits.

(c) Pre-charge Motions Distinguished. The pretrial motion to suppress, made in the context of criminal proceedings, must be distinguished from the action which may be taken in many jurisdictions prior to the filing of criminal charges, in order to challenge continued government possession of objects acquired in an earlier search. Though this pre-charge motion is sometimes referred to as a motion to suppress, it is more correct to call it a motion for return of property or a motion to quash a search warrant, for even if the movant is successful it does not necessarily follow that this evidence will be suppressed if a criminal prosecution is later undertaken.

Such anomalous jurisdiction in the federal system is exercised with caution and restraint and subject to equitable principles. A foremost consideration is whether there is a clear and definite showing that constitutional rights have been violated. A second consideration is whether the plaintiff has an individual interest in and need for the material whose return he seeks, as where those goods are necessary to conduct a legitimate business. Yet a third consideration is whether the plaintiff would be irreparably injured by denial of the return of the property or whether he instead has an adequate remedy at law. But

§ 10.1

1. 390 U.S. 377, 88 S.Ct. 967, 19 L.Ed.2d 1247 (1968), discussed in § 10.5(c).

courts are disinclined to grant relief when a criminal prosecution is anticipated, for they usually take the view that in such circumstances intervention would impede prosecuting officers and interfere with the grand jury.

Pre-charge proceedings to quash search warrants or for the return of items seized in searches are also available in many states. They are commonly authorized by statutes governing the issuance of warrants, but in some jurisdictions are permitted by courts of equity without express statutory authority. Where such proceedings rest exclusively upon statute, they may be limited to searches made pursuant to a warrant or even to warrants for certain types of property (e.g., obscene materials).

§ 10.2 Waiver or Forfeiture of Objection

(a) Failure to Make Timely Objection. In those jurisdictions requiring a contemporaneous objection to the introduction of illegally obtained evidence, failure to make such an objection ordinarily bars consideration of any subsequent objection at trial or on appeal. Similarly, in states requiring that a pretrial motion to suppress be made by a specified time, a motion which is not made until trial or even until some later pretrial stage is not timely and thus ordinarily will not receive consideration. Noncompliance with these requirements is commonly characterized as a "waiver" of the constitutional objection, but because such a failure does not ordinarily involve an intentional relinquishment of a constitutional right it is better to view it as a "forfeiture."

In many jurisdictions a court may in its discretion entertain a suppression motion even when the motion could be barred as untimely. If the court entertains the motion and receives evidence going to the merits, under the prevailing view it may still decline to suppress on the ground that the motion was not timely. The minority position is that once the hearing has been held the timeliness of the motion becomes moot and can no longer be a proper ground for denial. In any event, if an untimely motion is denied on the merits, this denial may be appealed after conviction.

All jurisdictions grant relief from pretrial motion requirements when it is shown that the defendant lacked a reasonable opportunity to raise the objection by the required time. Statutes and court rules articulating this exception vary somewhat in their phrasing, and this may influence to some degree how courts construe its breadth. It is fair to say, however, that there is a general disinclination to find such lack of opportunity except under the most compelling circumstances. Ignorance of the legal grounds for having the evidence suppressed will not suffice, but ignorance by the defendant that the item in question had been seized will. If the defendant was personally aware of the police action which led to their acquisition of the evidence, he is responsible for informing counsel of those facts.[1]

In *Henry v. Mississippi*,[2] the Supreme Court, applying the "proposition that a litigant's procedural defaults in state proceedings do not prevent vindication of his federal rights unless the State's insistence on compliance with its procedural rule serves a legitimate state interest," concluded that the less demanding contemporaneous objection rule did serve such an interest. But the Court went on to say that the purpose of this rule was substantially served by the motion defendant had made at the close of the state's evidence, and thus suggested that noncompliance with the rule could not be deemed an independent state ground supporting defen-

§ 10.2

1. To avoid difficulties presented by defendant's unawareness of the need for a suppression motion, some states have mandatory disclosure provisions as to evidence subject to a suppression motion challenge. Some others have permissive provisions (as in Fed.R.Crim.P. 12(d)) which allow the prosecutor to preclude a claim of cause for an untimely suppression motion by making disclosure. Still other states have broad discovery provisions that allow the defense to determine through discovery whether the prosecution intends to use evidence in a manner that raises a possibility of a motion to suppress. See § 20.3.

2. 379 U.S. 443, 85 S.Ct. 564, 13 L.Ed.2d 408 (1965).

dant's conviction. A few states have read *Henry* as placing constitutional limits upon their power to treat failure to comply with a timely objection rule as a waiver of the constitutional objection. In the main, however, the courts have not read *Henry* as barring enforcement of either the contemporary objection rule or the pretrial motion rule, though *Henry* may have influenced some jurisdictions to be somewhat more ready to find the existence of good cause for failure to comply.

The Court in *Henry* found it unnecessary to resolve the independent state ground issue because the record suggested defendant's counsel had deliberately bypassed the opportunity to make a timely objection, which the Court concluded would constitute a forfeiture of the constitutional claim even "without prior consultation with an accused" by counsel. This branch of *Henry* has been relied upon by courts in holding that noncompliance with a timely objection rule, prompted by counsel's deliberate and strategic choice not to attempt to have the evidence in question suppressed, is binding upon the defendant even if that choice was made without the defendant's knowledge or participation.

(b) Failure to Renew Objection. In most jurisdictions a defendant will have preserved the suppression issue for appeal simply by having made the requisite pretrial motion which was denied. But some states require that the defendant renew his objection at the time the evidence is offered at trial. In support, it is argued that such a requirement ensures that the trial judge (as opposed to some lesser judicial officer) will have passed on the issue, serves to bar appeal where defendant later concludes as a matter of trial strategy that he would prefer to have the evidence admitted, also bars appeal where defense counsel later concludes the motion was without merit, and ensures reconsideration upon the added facts developed at trial. But requiring renewal robs the pretrial motion of its greatest benefit: the saving of much time during and immediately prior to trial.

Even where renewal of the motion is not generally required, special circumstances may make renewal essential. Such is the case where it appears at the pretrial hearing that the facts cannot be fully developed at that point, so that the judge defers ruling on the motion until trial or denies the motion "without prejudice" to renewal at trial. Even absent such circumstances, renewal is the safer course in a jurisdiction in which the pretrial order is not binding on the trial judge. If the motion is renewed and reconsidered by the trial court, then it is customary for the appellate court on review to consider all the evidence available to the trial judge up to that point.

Defense counsel must be alert to other traps for the unwary. For example, in some jurisdictions it is the law that even if the defendant made a timely pretrial motion to suppress and (if required) a contemporaneous objection at the time the evidence was offered against him, the issue is *still* not preserved for appellate review unless the objection is made yet another time in a motion for a new trial.

(c) Testimony by Defendant. A small number of jurisdictions adhere to the position that a defendant may not complain on appeal about the admission of illegally obtained evidence, notwithstanding timely objection at or before trial, if the defendant gave testimony at trial admitting possession of that evidence. A variety of reasons have been given for this result: that defendant's admission is a "waiver" of the constitutional objection; that it amounts to a judicial confession; and that it makes admission of the evidence harmless error. The rule has been applied when defendant's testimony was equivocal, remote in its relationship to the evidence, or given to explain away the evidence and make possession of it appear innocent. The rule serves no legitimate state interest, and places the defendant in the dilemma where he must either ignore the damaging evidence introduced against him or waive his right to appeal its erroneous introduction, and thus it is encouraging that some states have recently abandoned the rule.

Some courts have concluded that the rule is unconstitutional in light of *Harrison v. United States.*[3] In *Harrison,* after three confessions were introduced at defendant's trial he took the stand and testified as to his version of the events, making damaging admissions in the process; his conviction was reversed on the ground the confessions were illegally obtained, but on retrial defendant's testimony from the first trial was introduced and another conviction resulted. The Supreme Court reversed on the ground that the former testimony was a "fruit" of the illegally obtained confessions, as the "natural inference is that no testimonial admission so damaging would have been made if the prosecutor had not already spread the petitioner's confessions before the jury." Significantly, a dissent in *Harrison* objected that the majority, contrary to earlier "fruits" decisions,[4] had used a "broad 'but for' sense of causality" and had failed to consider whether such an extension of the exclusionary rule would serve its deterrence objective. Because the Supreme Court's more recent "fruits" cases have focused upon the issue of "exploitation" and upon the notion of deterrence, it is by no means clear that the minority rule under discussion here is unconstitutional.

(d) Plea of Guilty or Nolo Contendere. A plea of guilty is an admission of guilt and a waiver of all nonjurisdictional defects. It "represents a break in the chain of events which has preceded it in the criminal process," [5] and thus once a valid plea is received defendant may not appeal on the ground that his earlier suppression motion was erroneously denied. The same is true of a valid nolo contendere plea. As for a *Harrison*-type argument that the plea was a fruit of the prior illegality, this is "at most a claim that the admissibility of his confession was mistakenly assessed and that since he was erroneously advised * * * his plea was an unintelligent and voidable act." [6] And, the Supreme Court added in *McMann v. Richardson,*[7] this is not a claim which will prevail if the attorney's advice "was within the range of competence demanded of attorneys in criminal cases."

Some jurisdictions have by statute or court rule created an exception to the general rule, so that a "conditional" plea may be made which reserves the right to appeal an earlier denial of the suppression motion. Such pleas are discussed elsewhere herein.[8]

§ 10.3 Burden of Proof

(a) Generally. At a hearing on a motion to suppress, who has the burden of proof with respect to the matters at issue? To understand the full significance of this inquiry, it is first necessary to recall that the term "burden of proof" actually encompasses two separate burdens. One burden is that of producing evidence, sometimes called the "burden of evidence" or the "burden of going forward." If the party who has the burden of producing evidence does not meet that burden, the consequence is an adverse ruling on the matter at issue. The other burden is the burden of persuasion, which becomes crucial only if the parties have sustained their respective burdens of producing evidence and only when all the evidence has been introduced. It becomes significant if the trier of fact is in doubt; if he is, then the matter must be resolved against the party with the burden of persuasion.

It is not inevitably true that the burden of production and the burden of persuasion must both fall upon the same party, but the prevailing practice is to allocate the two burdens jointly to one party or another. Sometimes courts expressly state that this is what they are about, but more commonly it results as a consequence of a general ruling that the "burden of proof" on the motion to suppress rests upon either the defendant or the state.

Various principles are often advanced in the course of discussions of where, as a matter of sound policy, the burden of proof should lie

3. 392 U.S. 219, 88 S.Ct. 2008, 20 L.Ed.2d 1047 (1968).

4. See § 9.3(b).

5. Tollett v. Henderson, 411 U.S. 258, 93 S.Ct. 1602, 36 L.Ed.2d 235 (1973).

6. McMann v. Richardson, 397 U.S. 759, 90 S.Ct. 1441, 25 L.Ed.2d 763 (1970).

7. 397 U.S. 759, 90 S.Ct. 1441, 25 L.Ed.2d 763 (1970).

8. See § 21.6(b).

in various circumstances. In summary, they are: (1) that the burdens should be placed on the party who has the best access to the relevant facts; (2) that the burdens should be placed on the party desiring change; (3) that the burdens should be allocated so as to avoid providing an incentive for use of the objection primarily to gain general discovery of the other side's case, particularly where discovery is otherwise quite limited; (4) that the burdens should be allocated so as to have one party prove a limited ground rather than the other party disproving many grounds; (5) that the burdens should be allocated in accordance with the best judicial estimate of the probabilities of the particular event having occurred; and (6) that the burdens should be used to "handicap" disfavored contentions. These principles will sometimes be helpful in working out burden of proof issues, but they do not inevitably all point in the same direction and thus will not always show where as a matter of policy the burden would best be placed.

The practical significance of the allocation of the ultimate burden of proof at suppression hearings is a matter on which opinions differ, as is illustrated by *People v. Berrios*.[1] There the prosecutor joined the defendant in urging that the burden of persuasion be placed on the state in so-called "dropsy" cases—that is, where the police claim that a suspect dropped the seized item and thus created a situation in which a permissible plain view seizure could occur. The court declined to do so, and stated that such "a change in the burden of proof would be ineffective to combat the alleged evil" because the judge "would still be faced with the same credibility question" of whether the defendant or the officer was lying. But this is not so; the burden of persuasion is significant in those cases in which the trier of fact is actually in doubt. Thus, as stated in the *Berrios* dissent, if the burden was placed on the state the judge would "be permitted to suppress evidence in cases where, for instance, he finds the testimony of each side evenly balanced on the scales of credibility and is unable to make up his mind as to who is telling the truth."

But allocation of the burden of going forward may be of greater significance. A basic tactical objective of the defense is to avoid first disclosing its factual theories, lest the police conform their testimony to evade those theories. But if the defendant has the burden of going forward he must often take the stand first and tell his side of the story. Even if the officers, as prospective witnesses, may be excluded from the courtroom while that testimony is received, the defendant is still not in as good a position to rebut their testimony as he would be if he testified last. If the defense tries to satisfy its burden without defendant's testimony by calling the police officers as its own witnesses, this tactic may backfire; the court may be unwilling to treat the officers as "adverse" witnesses subject to impeachment.

(b) Search and Seizure. With respect to the issue which is usually central in a Fourth Amendment suppression hearing—the reasonableness of the challenged search or seizure—most states follow the rule which is utilized in the federal courts: if the search or seizure was pursuant to a warrant, the defendant has the burden of proof; but if the police acted without a warrant the burden of proof is on the prosecution. The warrant-no warrant dichotomy is typically explained on the ground that when the police have acted with a warrant an independent determination on the issue of probable cause has already been made by a magistrate, thereby giving rise to a presumption of legality, while when they have acted without a warrant the evidence comprising probable cause is particularly within the knowledge and control of the arresting agencies.

Some jurisdictions, however, do not draw a distinction between warrant and no warrant cases. A few uniformly place the burden of proof upon the prosecution on the ground that the state is the party which seeks to use the evidence and thus ought to bear the burden of

§ 10.3

1. 28 N.Y.2d 361, 321 N.Y.S.2d 884, 270 N.E.2d 709 (1971).

establishing that it was lawfully come by. Some states place the burden of proof uniformly upon the defendant. By way of explanation, it is commonly stated that the burden is so placed because (a) the burden should be upon the moving party, (b) there is a presumption of regularity attending the actions of law enforcement officials, (c) relevant evidence is generally admissible and thus exceptions must be justified by those claiming the exception, and (d) it will deter spurious allegations wasteful of court time.

Placing the burden upon the defendant even in the no warrant situation puts him in a most disadvantageous position. As one commentator has noted, "it would be impossible for a defendant to prove a lack of probable cause in the abstract," for he "cannot be expected to prove a lack of some item until he knows on what the government bases its claim of its existence."[2] However, the situation is not necessarily this bad in jurisdictions which purport to place the burden of proof upon the defendant, for they may in fact permit the defendant to shift the burden to the prosecution with a minimum of effort.

There are certain types of Fourth Amendment issues which customarily receive special treatment with respect to burden of proof. One of these is that of whether a so-called consent search occurred. In *Bumper v. North Carolina*,[3] the Supreme Court held: "When a prosecutor seeks to rely upon consent to justify the lawfulness of a search, he has the burden of proving that the consent was, in fact, freely and voluntarily given. This burden cannot be discharged by showing no more than acquiescence to a claim of lawful authority." *Bumper* so places the burden as a matter of constitutional law, meaning states may not adopt a contrary rule.

Another issue which has ordinarily been singled out for special treatment is that of whether the defendant has standing. In *Jones v. United States*,[4] the Court emphasized that the Fourth Amendment exclusionary rule keeps out evidence "otherwise competent" as "a means for making effective the protection of privacy," and thus concluded that it was "entirely proper to require of one who seeks to challenge the legality of a search as the basis for suppressing relevant evidence that he allege, and if the allegation be disputed that he establish, that he himself was the victim of an invasion of privacy." Most lower courts follow *Jones* and place the burden on the defendant to establish standing, though a few have gone the other way.

Yet another issue which usually receives special burden-of-proof treatment is that of whether any "search" in the Fourth Amendment sense has actually occurred. Thus, in *Nardone v. United States*,[5] where the defendant contended that the case against him was based upon evidence acquired as a consequence of an illegal wiretap, the Court ruled that the burden was on him to show that such a wiretap had occurred. The Court in *Nardone* expressed concern that if the rule were otherwise the defendant would obtain full pretrial discovery of the prosecution's case, but doubtless was influenced by the fact that unless the burden were on the defendant there would likely be a flood of frivolous claims of wiretapping. The lower courts have generally placed the burden on the defendant to prove the existence of a wiretap. Some courts also apply the *Nardone* rule to other occurrence-of-search issues, such as whether or not the object seized was in plain view, though some place the burden on the prosecution in such circumstances on the ground that plain view is a justification for not having a warrant and as such ought to be established by the party claiming the exception. The Supreme Court is divided on the question of whether the was-there-a-search burden should always fall on the defendant.[6]

2. Symposium, 25 Ohio St.L.J. 501, 528 (1964).

3. 391 U.S. 543, 88 S.Ct. 1788, 20 L.Ed.2d 797 (1968).

4. 362 U.S. 257, 80 S.Ct. 725, 4 L.Ed.2d 697 (1960).

5. 308 U.S. 338, 60 S.Ct. 266, 84 L.Ed. 307 (1939).

6. Florida v. Riley, 488 U.S. 445, 109 S.Ct. 693, 102 L.Ed.2d 835 (1989) (5 Justices say burden on defendant to show use of helicopters at 400 feet so rare as to produce reasonable expectation of privacy; 4 say burden on state to show nonrarity).

Nardone is also relevant with respect to yet another special situation, namely, that in which the issue is whether certain evidence is the fruit [7] of some prior Fourth Amendment violation. The Court said that once wiretapping was established the defendant would have an opportunity "to prove that a substantial portion of the case against him was a fruit of the poisonous tree," after which the government would have an opportunity "to convince the trial court that its proof had an independent origin." This language was cited with approval in *Alderman v. United States*,[8] holding that in such a situation the defendant "must go forward with specific evidence demonstrating taint," upon which the government "has the ultimate burden of persuasion to show that its evidence is untainted." This would mean, for example, that the government could prevail by showing an independent source for its evidence or the inevitability of its discovery by lawful means.[9] In the main, the lower courts have followed the *Nardone–Alderman* allocation of burdens in fruit-of-the-poisonous-tree situations.

The extent to which the states remain free to allocate the burden of proof in Fourth Amendment cases is a matter of considerable uncertainty. It appears clear the Court has held, albeit without any extended discussion of the issue, that the burden of proof *must* be on the prosecution when it is claimed the evidence was obtained in a search by consent.[10] However, the court has not spoken in such direct terms about the allocation of the burden in most other situations. True, the Court has frequently spoken of the burden being on those who claim an exemption from the Fourth Amendment warrant requirement,[11] but these assertions are subject to varying interpretations. They may be read as referring only to the state's burden in appellate argument of justifying any request that the Court recognize any new or expanded exception to the warrant requirement. Or, as some courts have concluded, they may be interpreted as signaling a requirement that the burden of proof be placed upon the state whenever the police have acted without a warrant. The latter interpretation seems closer to the mark. At least, it is more unlikely the Court would find it constitutionally permissible for a state to impose burdens of proof upon defendants to such a degree and extent as to foreclose "a reliable and clearcut determination" [12] of Fourth Amendment claims, as would be the case, for example, if a defendant had to bear the burden of production and persuasion on the issue of whether the police lacked probable cause for a warrantless arrest.[13]

(c) Confessions. When the issue at a suppression hearing is whether a confession obtained from the defendant was voluntary, most jurisdictions place upon the prosecution the burdens of production and persuasion. A few states, however, place the burden of proving involuntariness on the defendant. The Supreme Court's decision in *Lego v. Twomey* [14] raises serious doubts as to the constitutionali-

7. On the "fruit of the poisonous tree" doctrine, see § 9.3.

8. 394 U.S. 165, 89 S.Ct. 961, 22 L.Ed. 176 (1969).

9. See Nix v. Williams, 467 U.S. 431, 104 S.Ct. 2501, 81 L.Ed.2d 377 (1984), accepting the inevitable discovery doctrine (in a confessions context) but as a constitutional matter placing the burden of proof on the prosecution to show that inevitability by a preponderance of the evidence.

10. Bumper v. North Carolina, 391 U.S. 543, 88 S.Ct. 1788, 20 L.Ed.2d 797 (1968).

11. E.g., Coolidge v. New Hampshire, 403 U.S. 443, 91 S.Ct. 2022, 29 L.Ed.2d 564 (1971); United States v. Jeffers, 342 U.S. 48, 72 S.Ct. 93, 96 L.Ed. 59 (1951).

12. See Lego v. Twomey, 404 U.S. 477, 92 S.Ct. 619, 30 L.Ed.2d 618 (1972), reiterating that such a determination is constitutionally required as to the voluntariness of a confession, and seeming to make no distinction between Fourth and Fifth Amendment suppression hearings.

13. In Beck v. Ohio, 379 U.S. 89, 85 S.Ct. 223, 13 L.Ed.2d 142 (1964), where the Court ruled that the officer's testimony as to his knowledge of the defendant's physical appearance and criminal record and as to having received information about the defendant did not establish probable cause, it was said that "it was incumbent upon the prosecution to show with considerably more specificity than was shown in this case what the informer actually said, and why the officer thought the information was credible." It is virtually beyond belief that the Court would have reached a contrary conclusion if the state ruling had been expressly grounded upon the proposition that the burden was on the defendant to prove the absence of probable cause.

14. 404 U.S. 477, 92 S.Ct. 619, 30 L.Ed.2d 618 (1972).

ty of the latter position. Though the Court was concerned primarily with the applicable standard of proof, *Lego* indicated that it was the constitutional obligation of the prosecution to meet that standard of proof. The Court declared that "the prosecution must prove at least by a preponderance of the evidence that the confession was voluntary."

As for compliance with the requirements of the *Miranda* case, it is clear that as a constitutional matter the burden is on the prosecution. The Court in that case stated:

> If the interrogation continues without the presence of an attorney and a statement is taken, a heavy burden rests on the Government to demonstrate that the defendant knowingly and intelligently waived his privilege against self-incrimination and his right to retained or appointed counsel. This Court has always set high standards of proof for the waiver of constitutional rights, * * * and we re-assert these standards, as applied to in-custody interrogation. Since the State is responsible for establishing the isolated circumstances under which the interrogation takes place and has the only means of making available corroborated evidence of warnings given during incommunicado interrogation, the burden is rightly on its shoulders.

When a "fruits" issue arises with respect to a confession, either that the confession is the fruit of some earlier illegality or that some later-acquired evidence is the fruit of an illegal confession, it is customary to use the *Nardone* approach. This means that once the defendant has established a relationship between the unlawful police activity and the evidence to which objection is made, the burden is on the prosecution to show that the unlawful taint has been dissipated.[15]

(d) Identification. If a lineup or other identification procedure is conducted at a time and in a manner so that it is a "critical stage" for right to counsel purposes, then resort to such procedure without counsel imposes upon the prosecution the burdens of establishing that defendant intelligently waived his right to counsel.[16] If such a showing is not made, a per se rule of exclusion applies as to testimony about that identification,[17] while an at-trial identification by the witness who made the earlier identification is barred only if it is the fruit of the previous constitutional violation.[18] In *United States v. Wade,*[19] the Court held as a constitutional matter that the burden must be on the government to show "that the in-court identifications were based upon observations of the suspect other than the lineup identification."

An identification procedure may also be challenged on the ground that it was so unnecessarily suggestive as to violate due process. In such circumstances many courts have assumed, typically without extensive discussion, that the defendant has the burden of proving the due process violation because he is the moving party. But the prosecution should bear the burdens of production and persuasion whenever the identification procedure was conducted out of the presence of defendant's attorney, for in such a situation the defendant may not even be aware that witnesses were seeking to identify him (e.g., where a "showup" was conducted through a one-way mirror), and even if aware, he still may be unable to know what facts existed that might make the procedure unnecessarily suggestive. Beyond this, it would seem sensible to conclude that once a suggestive procedure is shown to have occurred, it is better to call upon the prosecutor to show it was necessary than to ask the defendant to negate all conceivable factors of necessity.

Under the due process approach, a later, at-trial identification must be excluded if there was an earlier identification which was "un-

15. See also Nix v. Williams, 467 U.S. 431, 104 S.Ct. 2501, 81 L.Ed.2d 377 (1984), holding the burden of proof is on the prosecution to show that the fruits of an illegally obtained confession would inevitably have been discovered by lawful means.

16. United States v. Wade, 388 U.S. 218, 87 S.Ct. 1926, 18 L.Ed.2d 1149 (1967).

17. Gilbert v. California, 388 U.S. 263, 87 S.Ct. 1951, 18 L.Ed.2d 1178 (1967).

18. United States v. Wade, 388 U.S. 218, 87 S.Ct. 1926, 18 L.Ed.2d 1149 (1967).

19. 388 U.S. 218, 87 S.Ct. 1926, 18 L.Ed.2d 1149 (1967).

necessarily suggestive" [20] to the degree that there was "a very substantial likelihood of irreparable misidentification." [21] In making the latter calculation, the factors to be considered [22] are essentially the same as those which are utilized in determining whether an at-trial identification is the fruit of a lineup held in violation of defendant's right to counsel. This being the case, it is not surprising that some courts have concluded that here as well the burden must be on the government to show that the in-court identification is not so tainted. However, in the due process cases the question whether the at-trial identification is unreliable in light of what occurred earlier is not a "fruits" issue at all, but is part and parcel of the basic question of whether any violation of the constitution has occurred.[23] Because this is so (and assuming that establishment of the due process violation is otherwise a burden which many be placed on the defendant), it may well be permissible to put on the defendant the burden of showing the unreliability of the at-trial identification.

§ 10.4 Standard of Proof

(a) Generally. Various standards of proof are used in the law. In the trial of criminal cases, as the Supreme Court held in *In re Winship*,[1] it is a requirement of due process that the defendant be proved guilty beyond a reasonable doubt. In civil cases, by contrast, the standard usually is a preponderance of evidence, commonly defined as proof which leads the jury to find that the existence of the contested fact is more probable than its non-existence. But in certain circumstances a standard somewhere between these two is utilized; it is usually called the clear and convincing evidence standard, and means that the factfinder must be persuaded that the truth of the contention is highly probable. Depending upon the jurisdiction and the matter at issue, any one of these three standards of proof may be used in the context of a suppression hearing. In large measure, the choice of the standard is a matter of local law, but at least in some circumstances the Constitution may compel use of something beyond the preponderance standard.

(b) Confessions. In *Lego v. Twomey*,[2] the Court rejected the contention that the voluntariness of a confession must be established beyond a reasonable doubt. The Court first concluded that *Winship* was not controlling:

> Since the purpose that a voluntariness hearing is designed to serve has nothing whatever to do with improving the reliability of jury verdicts, we cannot accept the charge that judging the admissibility of a confession by a preponderance of the evidence undermines the mandate of *In re Winship.* * * * A high standard of proof is necessary, we said, to ensure against unjust convictions by giving substance to the presumption of innocence. A guilty verdict is not rendered any less reliable or less consonant with *Winship* simply because the admissibility of a confession is determined by a less stringent standard.

Lego also rejected the contention that application of a reasonable doubt standard was necessary "to give adequate protection to those values that the exclusionary rules are designed to serve." The Court responded that it was

> unconvinced that merely emphasizing the importance of the values served by exclusionary rules is itself sufficient demonstration that the Constitution also requires admissibility to be proved beyond a reasonable doubt. Evidence obtained in violation of the Fourth Amendment has been excluded from federal criminal trials for many years. The same is true of coerced confessions offered in either federal or state trials. But, from our experience over this period of time no substantial

20. Stovall v. Denno, 388 U.S. 293, 87 S.Ct. 1967, 18 L.Ed.2d 1199 (1967).

21. Neil v. Biggers, 409 U.S. 188, 93 S.Ct. 375, 34 L.Ed.2d 401 (1972).

22. See Manson v. Brathwaite, 432 U.S. 98, 97 S.Ct. 2243, 53 L.Ed.2d 140 (1977).

23. Manson v. Brathwaite, 432 U.S. 98, 97 S.Ct. 2243, 53 L.Ed.2d 140 (1977).

§ 10.4

1. 397 U.S. 358, 90 S.Ct. 1068, 25 L.Ed.2d 368 (1970).

2. 404 U.S. 477, 92 S.Ct. 619, 30 L.Ed.2d 618 (1972).

evidence has accumulated that federal rights have suffered from determining admissibility by a preponderance of the evidence. * * * Sound reason for moving further in this direction has not been offered here nor do we discern any at the present time. This is particularly true since the exclusionary rules are very much aimed at deterring lawless conduct by police and prosecution and it is very doubtful that escalating the prosecution's burden of proof in Fourth and Fifth Amendment suppression hearings would be sufficiently productive in this respect to outweigh the public interest in placing probative evidence before juries for the purpose of arriving at truthful decisions about guilt or innocence.[3]

The three *Lego* dissenters[4] argued that while the preponderance standard was satisfactory in civil cases, where an error in favor of one party was no more serious than an error in favor of the other, its use on the voluntariness issue reflected acceptance of the mistaken view "that it is no more serious in general to admit involuntary confessions that it is to exclude voluntary confessions." It has been argued that a reasonable doubt standard was called for in *Lego* because the test of involuntariness (as opposed to other exclusionary rule standards) is designed to exclude unreliable evidence which, if admitted, would be given great weight by the jury.

Though the Supreme Court in *Lego* concluded that due process was satisfied by application of the preponderance standard and was not even persuaded "to impose the stricter standard of proof as an exercise of supervisory power" over federal courts, note was taken that the states were always "free, pursuant to their own law, to adopt a higher standard." Prior to *Lego,* several jurisdictions had utilized a reasonable doubt standard; some have shifted to a preponderance standard in light of *Lego,* while others have retained the reasonable doubt standard as a matter of local law. In addition, a few new states have joined the reasonable doubt grouping, but a substantial majority now follow the preponderance standard.

As for confessions challenged on *Miranda* grounds, the Supreme Court in that case declared that "a heavy burden rests on the Government to demonstrate that the defendant knowingly and intelligently waived his privilege against self-incrimination and his right to retained or appointed counsel."[5] But in *Colorado v. Connelly,*[6] the Court reaffirmed *Lego* and applied it in this context as well: "If, as we held in *Lego v. Twomey,* the voluntariness of a confession need be established only by a preponderance of the evidence, then a waiver of the auxiliary protections established in *Miranda* should require no higher burden of proof."

(c) Search and Seizure. That part of *Lego* rejecting the claim that *Winship* governs at the suppression stage of a criminal case is also applicable to Fourth Amendment suppression hearings. And the other branch of *Lego,* focusing upon the purpose of exclusionary rules, expressly encompasses Fourth Amendment suppression cases as well. Thus it is as a general matter constitutional to conclude, as the Supreme Court later put it in *United States v. Matlock,*[7] that "the controlling burden of proof at suppression hearings should impose no greater burden than proof by a preponderance of the evidence." Again, states are free to impose a higher standard, but state courts have generally held that the preponderance standard applies at a hearing where a search or seizure is challenged. Significantly, this position has been taken even in jurisdictions which apply a reasonable doubt standard when the voluntariness of a confession is at issue. This can be explained

3. Relying upon this analysis in *Lego,* the Court in Nix v. Williams, 467 U.S. 431, 104 S.Ct. 2501, 81 L.Ed.2d 377 (1984), held that the preponderance standard would suffice on the issue of whether certain fruits of an illegally obtained confession would have been inevitably discovered.

4. Brennan, J., joined by Douglas and Marshall, JJ. Powell and Rehnquist, JJ., did not participate in the decision. The dissenters also argued that the majority's position was inconsistent with "the rule that automatically reverses a conviction when an involuntary confession was admitted at trial."

5. Miranda v. Arizona, 384 U.S. 436, 86 S.Ct. 1602, 16 L.Ed.2d 694 (1966).

6. 479 U.S. 157, 107 S.Ct. 515, 93 L.Ed.2d 473 (1986).

7. 415 U.S. 164, 94 S.Ct. 988, 39 L.Ed.2d 242 (1974).

by the fact that an involuntary confession may be unreliable while illegally seized evidence is always reliable, and by the added fact that the police have a greater capacity to keep records and otherwise to prepare to meet a higher standard of proof in establishing the events surrounding a custodial interrogation as opposed to a typical warrantless search.

Some authority is to be found seeming to require more than a preponderance of evidence under certain circumstances. In particular, at least some courts have found the higher clear and convincing evidence standard appropriate when the prosecution's claim is that the search was consented to or that the evidence was obtained after a voluntary abandonment of it by the defendant. The policy judgment underlying these cases—that a higher standard is called for in situations where it would be particularly easy for the police to manipulate events or fabricate an interpretation of events which could not be effectively challenged by the defendant—does not conflict with the reasons given above as to why the preponderance standard should ordinarily suffice.

This is not to suggest that the states are constitutionally required to use this higher standard in those circumstances. True, the Supreme Court instructed in *Schneckloth v. Bustamonte* [8] that "[t]o approach [consent] searches without the most careful scrutiny would sanction the possibility of official coercion." But *Schneckloth* also teaches that the test to be applied in determining the validity of a consent is "voluntariness," the meaning of which "has been developed in those cases in which the Court has had to determine the 'voluntariness' of a defendant's confession." Because the Court in *Lego* was not prepared to require more than the preponderance standard where the question to be resolved was the voluntariness of a confession, there is no reason to believe that a higher standard will be imposed when the question is the voluntariness of a consent to a search.

(d) Identification. In *United States v. Wade,*[9] establishing a right to counsel at certain pretrial identification proceedings, the Court expressly stated that the burden was on the government "to establish by clear and convincing evidence that the in-court identifications were based upon observations of the suspect other than the lineup identification." [10] It is thus clear that the states are constitutionally compelled to utilize a standard at least this demanding. By contrast, in cases in which the defendant's claim is based upon the unnecessarily suggestive due process theory of *Stovall v. Denno,* the burden (which, as we have seen, is usually placed on the defendant) is merely that of the preponderance standard.

§ 10.5 The Suppression Hearing

(a) The Trier of Fact. Prior to the Supreme Court's decision in *Jackson v. Denno,*[1] at least three different factfinding allocations were used in determining whether a confession was voluntary. In states following the "orthodox rule," voluntariness was determined solely and finally by the judge. If the judge found the confession voluntary, it was admissible without any separate determination by the jury. Evidence relating to police methods in obtaining the confession might well be admitted to assist the jury in its assessment of the credibility of the confession, but the jury was not called upon to consider the voluntariness of the confession. By comparison, under the "Massachusetts rule" a determination that a confession was voluntary had to be made twice. Once again the

8. 412 U.S. 218, 93 S.Ct. 2041, 36 L.Ed.2d 854 (1973).

9. 388 U.S. 218, 87 S.Ct. 1926, 18 L.Ed. 1149 (1967).

10. *Wade* was distinguished in Nix v. Williams, 467 U.S. 431, 104 S.Ct. 2501, 81 L.Ed.2d 377 (1984), holding the preponderance standard sufficient on the issue of whether the fruits of defendant's illegally obtained confession would inevitably have been discovered. The Court stressed that while in a *Wade* situation there exists "the difficulty of determining whether an in-court identification was based on independent recollection unaided by the lineup identification," by contrast "inevitable discovery involves no speculative elements but focuses on demonstrated historical facts capable of ready verification or impeachment and does not require a departure from the usual burden of proof at suppression hearings."

§ 10.5

1. 378 U.S. 368, 84 S.Ct. 1774, 12 L.Ed.2d 908 (1964).

trial court initially ruled on the admissibility of the confession, and if the judge concluded the confession was involuntary his ruling excluding it was final. But if the judge found the confession voluntary, it was then admitted at trial subject to the jury's independent determination of voluntariness. The jury received evidence of the circumstances surrounding the confession, was charged as to the voluntariness standard, and was instructed that it could not consider the confession unless it first found it to be voluntary. Under the third alternative, the so-called "New York rule," the determination of voluntariness was left primarily to the jury. The judge would make an initial determination as to whether reasonable persons could differ on the issue of voluntariness, as where testimony was in conflict or different inferences could be drawn from undisputed facts. Unless there were "no circumstances" under which the confession could be voluntary, the voluntariness issue was passed along to the jury. The jury was instructed on the voluntariness standard and told to consider the confession only if it found it to be voluntary.

In the *Jackson* case, the Court divided 5–4 in holding the New York procedure unconstitutional. The crux of the majority's reasoning in *Jackson,* as later summarized in *Lego v. Twomey,*[2] was

> that the New York procedure was constitutionally defective because at no point along the way did a criminal defendant receive a clear-cut determination that the confession used against him was in fact voluntary. The trial judge was not entitled to exclude a confession merely because he himself would have found it involuntary, and, while we recognized that the jury was empowered to perform that function, we doubted it could do so reliably. Precisely because confessions of guilt, whether coerced or freely given, may be truthful and potent evidence, we did not believe a jury could be called upon to ignore the probative value of a truthful but coerced confession; it was also likely, we thought, that in judging voluntariness itself the jury would be influenced by the reliability of a confession it considered an accurate account of the facts.

As also noted in *Lego,* the Court in *Jackson* "cast no doubt upon the orthodox and Massachusetts procedures." As for the latter, the *Jackson* majority found it to be significantly different from the New York procedure because the judge "himself resolves evidentiary conflicts and gives his own answer to the coercion issue," so that the jury only considers those confessions the judges believes to be voluntary.[3] The orthodox rule is now followed in the federal courts and in most states, while a substantial minority use the Massachusetts rule. But even where the orthodox rule obtains, the defendant must be allowed to put before the jury testimony about the environment in which the police secured his confession so that he may thereby put its credibility into issue. Denial of that opportunity infringes upon the constitutional right to "a meaningful opportunity to present a complete defense," derived from the Fourteenth Amendment due process clause and the Sixth Amendment confrontation and compulsory process clauses.[4]

Only the orthodox rule is generally utilized outside the confession cases. The legality of a search is a matter of law to be determined by the court and not the jury, as is the admissibility of testimony claimed to be the fruit of unconstitutional identification procedures. Thereafter, the jury will determine the credibility of the identification by considering the conditions under which the observation was made, the physical ability of the witness to observe the defendant, and any possible problems which could distort the witness' observation powers and judgment. But if a hearing on the admissibility of identification testimony is held in the presence of the jury, this is

2. 404 U.S. 477, 92 S.Ct. 619, 30 L.Ed.2d 618 (1972).

3. The dissenters, on the other hand, responded that this acceptance of the Massachusetts rule revealed the "hollowness" of the Court's holding. They argued that the distinction between the New York and Massachusetts rule was more theoretical than real, and suggested that in "cases of doubt" a judge operating under the latter was likely to "resolve the doubt in favor of admissibility, relying on the final determination by the jury."

4. Crane v. Kentucky, 476 U.S. 683, 106 S.Ct. 2142, 90 L.Ed.2d 636 (1986).

not per se a violation of due process. In *Watkins v. Sowders*,[5] so holding, the Court distinguished *Jackson* on the theory that when identification evidence rather than a confession is at issue "no * * * special considerations justify a departure from the presumption that juries will follow instructions."

(b) Presence of Jury. If a defendant's objection is made initially at trial or the court has delayed a hearing on a pretrial motion to avoid inconvenience to witnesses, it would be possible for the hearing to be conducted in the presence of the jury. Courts have rather consistently ruled this should not be done as to search and seizure claims, reasoning that if suppression was ordered an admonition to the jury to disregard the evidence would hardly suffice. Such reasoning would seem to extend to other suppression hearings as well, and explains why the prevailing practice squares with the Supreme Court's teaching that the most prudent course of action is to hold hearings on the admissibility of confessions [6] and eyewitness identification [7] out of the presence of the jury.

The Supreme Court, dealing only with instances in which the suppression hearing before a jury did *not* result in exclusion of evidence, has declined to hold that there is a per se rule requiring all such hearings be held outside the jury's presence. In *Pinto v. Pierce*,[8] concerning a hearing on whether a confession should be suppressed as involuntary, the Court ruled the trial judge had not acted contrary to *Jackson v. Denno* [9] in holding the hearing in the jury's presence. But the Court placed considerable emphasis upon the fact that defendant through his counsel consented to that procedure, and Justice Fortas, concurring, reasoned the result should be otherwise absent such consent: "A telescoped hearing before judge and jury, in which the judge finds voluntariness for purposes of admissibility, in reality reduces the jury function to an echo. Hearing the evidence simultaneously with the judge, the jury is not apt to approach disagreement with him."

More recently, in *Watkins v. Sowders,*[10] the Court held there was no per se rule requiring all hearings into the constitutionality of witness identification procedures to be held outside the presence of the jury. Over a vigorous dissent, the majority reasoned that the notion a jury would not follow instructions to disregard certain evidence, perhaps acceptable in confession cases where a very reliable but coerced confession would be suppressed, had no application in the instant case because if identification evidence were suppressed it would be because of its unreliability. (Such reasoning suggests that in eyewitness identification cases the Court would reach the same result if, as was not the case in *Watkins,* the judge had suppressed the evidence.) As for the claim that the presence of the jury deterred defense counsel from vigorously and fully cross-examining the witnesses, the majority in *Watkins* found no specific instances in which counsel were so deterred and opined that defense counsel in this context runs only the usual risks in cross-examining an adverse witness.

(c) Testimony by Defendant. Often it will be necessary for the defendant to be a witness at a suppression hearing. The defendant may testify in a suppression hearing without waiving his right to decline to take the stand in his own defense at trial or any other rights stemming from his choice not to testify. If he testifies, he may be subjected to cross-examination, but he "does not, by testifying upon a preliminary matter, subject himself to cross-examination as to other issues in the cases." [11] Nonetheless, the cross-examination "may enable the prosecutor to elicit incriminating information beyond that offered on direct examination," and this "might be helpful to the prosecution in developing its

5. 449 U.S. 341, 101 S.Ct. 654, 66 L.Ed.2d 549 (1981).

6. Pinto v. Pierce, 389 U.S. 31, 88 S.Ct. 192, 19 L.Ed.2d 31 (1967).

7. Watkins v. Sowders, 449 U.S. 341, 101 S.Ct. 654, 66 L.Ed.2d 549 (1981).

8. 389 U.S. 31, 88 S.Ct. 192, 19 L.Ed.2d 31 (1967).

9. 378 U.S. 368, 84 S.Ct. 1774, 12 L.Ed.2d 908 (1964).

10. 449 U.S. 341, 101 S.Ct. 654, 66 L.Ed.2d 549 (1981).

11. Fed.R.Evid. 104(d).

case or deciding its trial strategy." [12]

In *Simmons v. United States*,[13] the Court held that the testimony given at the hearing by a defendant in order to establish his standing to object to illegally seized evidence may not be used against him at his trial on the question of guilt or innocence. The logic of *Simmons,* namely, that a defendant should not be "obliged either to give up what he believed, with advice of counsel, to be a valid Fourth Amendment claim or, in legal effect, to waive his Fifth Amendment privilege against self-incrimination," indicates that the same protection must be given to any testimony by the defendant at the suppression hearing.

Some courts have read *Simmons* with *Harris v. New York*,[14] holding that a confession obtained in violation of *Miranda* may be introduced at trial for impeachment purposes, so as to permit use of defendant's suppression hearing testimony for impeachment purposes at trial. It may be objected that this conclusion is incorrect in light of *New Jersey v. Portash*,[15] holding that testimony given after a grant of use immunity cannot be admitted even for impeachment purposes because such testimony "is the essence of coerced testimony" in that it was compelled under threat of contempt. So the argument goes, testimony by the defendant at a suppression hearing is likewise "compelled" in light of the Hobson's choice described in *Simmons.* But more recently in *United States v. Salvucci*,[16] a majority of the Supreme Court, while claiming the issue remained open, asserted that "the protective shield of *Simmons* is not to be converted into a license for false representations."

(d) Evidentiary Rules. As noted in *United States v. Matlock*,[17] the "rules of evidence normally applicable in criminal trials do not operate with full force at a hearing before the judge to determine the admissibility of evidence." Though it has long been clear that hearsay could be received on the issue of probable cause to search, *Matlock* held that hearsay statements could also be admitted on other issues as well. There, in an effort to show the search was consented to by defendant's roommate, the prosecution sought to put in evidence the roommate's out-of-court statements regarding her joint occupancy of the premises and representation that she was defendant's wife. The Supreme Court held that the trial judge erred in excluding those statements as hearsay, noting that a provision in the proposed (and since adopted) federal evidence rules specifically provided that on a preliminary question, such as the "admissibility of evidence," the trial court "is not bound by the rules of evidence except those with respect to privileges." [18] The Court added that there was "much to be said for the proposition that in proceedings where the judge himself is considering the admissibility of evidence, the exclusionary rules [such as the hearsay prohibition] should not be applicable, and the judge should receive the evidence and give it such weight as his judgment and experience counsel." Even if a trial court could not go that far, the court declared, it certainly should not exclude hearsay statements where, as here, "the court was quite satisfied that the statement had in fact been made" and "there is nothing in the record to raise serious doubts about the truthfulness of the statements themselves."

(e) Right of Confrontation. As indicated in *McCray v. Illinois*,[19] defendant's right of cross-examination at the suppression hearing may be substantially narrower than that available at trial. *McCray* held that neither due process nor the confrontation clause was violated when the suppression hearing judge refused to allow defense counsel to force the arresting officer, on cross-examination, to reveal the name and address of the informant alleged to have provided probable cause for

12. United States v. Salvucci, 448 U.S. 83, 100 S.Ct. 2547, 65 L.Ed.2d 619 (1980) (dissent).

13. 390 U.S. 377, 88 S.Ct. 967, 19 L.Ed.2d 1247 (1968).

14. 401 U.S. 222, 91 S.Ct. 643, 28 L.Ed.2d 1 (1971).

15. 440 U.S. 450, 99 S.Ct. 1292, 59 L.Ed.2d 501 (1979).

16. 448 U.S. 83, 100 S.Ct. 2547, 65 L.Ed.2d 619 (1980).

17. 415 U.S. 164, 94 S.Ct. 988, 39 L.Ed.2d 242 (1974).

18. Fed.R.Evid. 104(a).

19. 386 U.S. 300, 87 S.Ct. 1056, 18 L.Ed.2d 62 (1967).

defendant's arrest. Lower courts similarly have held that the combination of the limited function of the suppression hearing and valid security interests justify receiving certain prosecution evidence in camera (i.e., with the defendant excluded). Courts have stressed, however, that limitations on the opportunity for confrontation must be carefully circumscribed to fit the state's justification for restricted disclosure. And while the court may restrict cross-examination by defense counsel to avoid manipulation of the suppression hearing for discovery purposes, it may not cut off questioning that clearly is relevant to the defense challenge.

(f) Right of Compulsory Process. The constitutional right of compulsory process is essentially a trial right [20]; when the defendant's guilt or innocence is at issue, due process requires that the accused be able to present witnesses in his own defense "to the jury so it may decide where the truth lies." [21] But this right, albeit a "fundamental" one,[22] is not absolute, and thus it may yield to policy considerations such as the interest in the orderly conduct of trials.[23] Whatever lesser right of compulsory process exists at suppression hearings is likewise not absolute, and thus may be outweighed by various policy concerns. Thus, where there is other evidence of probable cause to arrest, the defendant may not call the undercover officer to testify about defendant's drug sale in his presence when such testimony might compromise the undercover officer's safety or the integrity of pending investigations. And similarly, at a suppression hearing which has not otherwise produced evidence raising "substantial issues as to the credibility of the lineup," the interest in protecting complainants against harassment has been deemed sufficient to bar the defendant from calling the complainant to inquire about any suggestive actions by the police.

§ 10.6 The Ruling and Its Effect

(a) Findings. In some jurisdictions the judge ruling on a motion to suppress is required to make specific findings of fact and law, while elsewhere formal findings are not required and it will suffice that a record is made supporting the ruling. In *Sims v. Georgia*,[1] the Supreme Court noted that the due process requirements of *Jackson v. Denno* [2] did not mandate that the judge "make formal findings of fact or write an opinion" though "his conclusion that the confession is voluntary must appear from the record with unmistakable clarity." Appellate courts, however, have urged trial judges to make findings because in their absence appellate review is often more difficult. Indeed, it has been said that findings are all but essential in multi-issue cases where the basis of the trial judge's decision would otherwise be in doubt.

(b) Recommendations. It is sometimes provided by law that a motion to suppress may be heard by a lesser judicial officer than the judge who has the ultimate responsibility for deciding the matter. Such is the case in the federal system, and in *United States v. Raddatz* [3] the Supreme Court had occasion to assess the respective responsibilities of the hearing magistrate and the district judge. Prior to trial, Raddatz moved to suppress his incriminating statements, and the judge referred the matter to a magistrate for an evidentiary hearing. This was done pursuant to the Federal Magistrates Act, which authorizes a district court to refer such a motion to a magistrate and thereafter to decide the motion based on the record developed before the magistrate, including the magistrate's proposed findings of fact and recommendations, and which also provides that the judge shall

20. Chambers v. Mississippi, 410 U.S. 284, 93 S.Ct. 1038, 35 L.Ed.2d 297 (1973); Webb v. Texas, 409 U.S. 95, 93 S.Ct. 351, 34 L.Ed.2d 330 (1972).

21. Washington v. Texas, 388 U.S. 14, 87 S.Ct. 1920, 18 L.Ed.2d 1019 (1967).

22. Chambers v. Mississippi, 410 U.S. 284, 93 S.Ct. 1038, 35 L.Ed.2d 297 (1973).

23. Taylor v. Illinois, 484 U.S. 400, 108 S.Ct. 646, 98 L.Ed.2d 798 (1988).

§ 10.6

1. 385 U.S. 538, 87 S.Ct. 639, 17 L.Ed.2d 593 (1967).

2. 378 U.S. 368, 84 S.Ct. 1774, 12 L.Ed.2d 908 (1964).

3. 447 U.S. 667, 100 S.Ct. 2406, 65 L.Ed.2d 424 (1980).

make a "de novo determination" of those portions of the magistrate's report, findings or recommendations to which objection is made, and that the judge may accept, reject or modify, in whole or in part, the magistrate's findings or recommendations and that alternatively the judge may receive further evidence or recommit the matter to the magistrate with instructions.[4] Based on his view of the credibility of the testimony, the magistrate found the statements voluntary and thus recommended the motion be denied. The district court accepted that recommendation over defendant's objection, but the court of appeals reversed on the ground Raddatz had been deprived of due process by the district court's failure personally to hear the controverted testimony.

After finding that the statute, by calling for a "de novo determination" rather than a de novo hearing, did not require the district court to rehear the testimony,[5] the Court concluded "that the statute strikes the proper balance between the demands of due process and the constraints of Art. III." As for the Article III question, the *Raddatz* Court concluded that because "the entire process takes place under the district court's total control and jurisdiction," the "delegation does not violate Art. III so long as the ultimate decision is made by the district court." On the due process issue, the Court, after noting that "the guarantees of due process call for a 'hearing appropriate to the nature of the case,'" concluded that "the nature of the issues presented and the interests implicated in a motion to suppress evidence" do not "require that the district court judge must actually hear the challenged testimony." This is because the interests underlying such a hearing "do not coincide with the criminal law objective of determining guilt or innocence."[6]

But there are limits on what the district judge may do with respect to the magistrate's findings and recommendations. It would be a rare case in which a district judge could resolve credibility choices contrary to the recommendations of the magistrate without himself having had an opportunity to see and hear the witnesses testify. And even if matters of credibility are not central to decision of the suppression motion, the district judge may not reject the recommendation of the magistrate without *at least* consulting the transcript of the hearing before the magistrate.

(c) Reconsideration at Trial. Except in those jurisdictions which actually require renewal of a suppression motion at trial, reconsideration at trial of a motion previously denied is a disfavored procedure. Such reconsideration, it is said, defeats the benefits of pretrial motion practice and unfairly imposes upon the prosecution the obligation of proving legality twice. Thus it is usually to be expected that the trial judge will rely upon the prior ruling as the law of the case.

A defendant is not likely to obtain reconsideration unless at trial new or additional evidence is produced bearing on the issue or substantially affecting the credibility of the evidence adduced at the pretrial hearing of the motion. The state cases in the main treat such a situation as one in which the court *may* reconsider, while federal cases commonly speak of a *duty* to reconsider where matters appearing at trial cast reasonable doubt on the pretrial ruling. But in light of the fact that a constitutional objection is deemed forfeited absent a showing of good cause for not complying with a pretrial motion rule, it would seem that a defendant is entitled to a redetermination of his claim at trial only if new evidence comes to light which was unavailable at the time of the original hearing on the motion through no fault of the movant.

4. 28 U.S.C.A. § 636(b)(1).

5. By comparison, in some jurisdictions a full de novo hearing may be provided, as where, following conviction by a lower court, the defendant is by law given a right to a trial de novo which is construed to include relitigation of the suppression issue. But a trial de novo system need not inevitably contain this feature.

6. There were four dissenters. Three of them concluded "that the statute itself required a hearing before the Judge in this case," while three were of the view that due process required a hearing "only in situations in which the case turns on issues of credibility that cannot be resolved on the basis of a record."

There is some authority that if defendant's pretrial suppression motion was granted, the prosecution may obtain a reconsideration of that ruling at trial under essentially the same circumstances in which reconsideration would be permitted in the defendant's behalf: where there is new relevant evidence available and good cause is shown as to why that evidence was not introduced at the pretrial hearing. But, while the doctrines of res judicata and collateral estoppel do not bar such reconsideration, the prosecution will not often be able to show cause for reconsideration because it is more able than the defendant to insure a full and fair resolution of any issue at a pretrial proceeding. In jurisdictions where the prosecutor may take an interlocutory appeal from the pretrial granting of a suppression motion, reconsideration at trial may well be barred as to matters which could have been raised by appeal.

(d) Effect of Ruling in Other Cases. If defendant's motion to suppress was granted but the prosecution later seeks to have the same evidence admitted against the defendant at a trial on a different charge, is relitigation of the admissibility issue barred? As a constitutional matter, an argument that the collateral estoppel doctrine of the double jeopardy clause bars relitigation cannot prevail if the charges were dropped in the first case, as then defendant was never placed in jeopardy. But it has been argued that in such circumstances the defendant might prevail because of collateral estoppel protections flowing from the due process clause. Whether the collateral estoppel doctrine has any application here remains in doubt, but if it does apply surely it is necessary that in the first case the state has had an opportunity for a full hearing on suppression and at least one appeal as of right.

Even if the Constitution, either as a general matter or in particular circumstances, does not require that the prosecution be bound by the granting of a suppression motion in another case, it is possible that the law of the jurisdiction will have this effect. This may occur, for example, where a statute declares that if a suppression motion is granted the evidence "shall not be admissible at any trial." In the absence of such law, the judge in the second case might nonetheless not reconsider the matter if he is convinced it was fully explored in the earlier case.

Assume now the reverse situation in which the motion was denied in an earlier case. The constitutional doctrine of collateral estoppel does not run both ways in criminal cases, and thus the defendant cannot be precluded upon such a theory even if the prosecutor would have been precluded. But, absent a showing of new evidence or some other basis for reconsideration, the judge in the second case may accept the admissibility ruling in the earlier case, provided of course that defendant was convicted at the first trial and thus had an opportunity to obtain appellate review of the ruling.

For a ruling on a motion to suppress in a prior case to have either conclusive or presumptive effect in a later case, there must be an identity of parties. Thus, notwithstanding prior suppression by a state court, a federal court may make an independent determination as to admissibility. And if the same evidence is offered in the separate trials of two defendants in the same jurisdiction, the ruling in the first of these cases is not binding in the second.

Part Three

THE COMMENCEMENT OF FORMAL PROCEEDINGS

Chapter 11

THE RIGHT TO COUNSEL

Table of Sections

---

§ 11.1 The Constitutional Rights to Retained and Appointed Counsel

(a) Sixth Amendment Rights. The Sixth Amendment provides that "in all criminal prosecutions, the accused shall enjoy the right * * * to have the assistance of counsel for his defense." That this provision guaranteed a right to representation by privately retained counsel was obvious from the outset; that it also included an obligation of the state to provide defense counsel for the indigent defendant (i.e., the defendant unable to afford a lawyer) was far less certain. Unlike the right to retained counsel, a right to appointed counsel lacked any substantial historical grounding. Nonetheless, the Court eventually came to interpret the Sixth Amendment as granting a right to representation by counsel to all defendants, with the state required to provide counsel where the defendant was indigent. Moreover, that Supreme Court precedent also indicated that the proceedings reached by the Sixth Amendment right to counsel were to be precisely the same whether the issue was allowing representation by retained counsel or requiring the state to appoint counsel for the indigent. In this respect, there appears to be but a single Sixth Amendment right to counsel.

The first major Supreme Court discussion of the constitutional right to counsel came in *Powell v. Alabama,*[1] a 1932 ruling that considered the rights of defendants both to utilized retained counsel and to be provided with court appointed counsel. *Powell* was not itself a Sixth Amendment case. It involved a state prosecution and was decided under the then prevailing "fundamental fairness" interpretation of Fourteenth Amendment due process.[2] Nonetheless, it has had continuing significance in the interpretation of the Sixth Amendment. When the Court later discarded the fundamental fairness interpretation in favor of a selective incorporation analysis that made the Sixth Amendment directly applicable to the states (through the Fourteenth Amendment), its interpretation of the Sixth Amendment rested heavily upon an analysis of the need for counsel first suggested by Justice Sutherland in his opinion for the Court in *Powell.*

The Supreme Court had before it in *Powell* a prosecution that was to become a cause celebre in the fight against racial injustice. Nine Negro youths had been charged with the rape of two white girls in the vicinity of Scottsboro, Alabama. Eight of the youths had been convicted, with the jury imposing the death sentence. On appeal, the defendants raised several constitutional claims, including two relating to their right to counsel. First, the trial court had failed to give them a sufficient opportunity to retain counsel. Second, assuming arguendo that they would have been unable to employ counsel even if they had been given that opportunity, the trial court would then have had an obligation to make an effective appointment of counsel. That obligation clearly had not been met, as the trial court had made appointments in such a haphazard way that counsel who even-

§ 11.1

1. 287 U.S. 45, 53 S.Ct. 55, 77 L.Ed. 158 (1932).

2. See § 2.4 at note 11.

tually represented the defendants were largely unprepared. The Supreme Court sustained both of defendants' claims, finding that each separately established a denial of due process.

The *Powell* opinion initially considered the trial court's failure to give defendants an adequate opportunity to retain counsel. Justice Sutherland here relied heavily upon the historical developments that had led to the adoption of the Sixth Amendment and similarly worded state constitutional provisions. The practice in England had been to allow the complete assistance of retained counsel in misdemeanor trials, but to deny defendants the right to utilize their counsel at felony trials, except for arguments on legal questions. This limitation had not been accepted in the American colonies, where defendants were allowed the full assistance of retained counsel in all criminal trials. At the time of the adoption of the Constitution, twelve of the thirteen states had rejected the English rule on felony cases, and the Sixth Amendment, not surprisingly, did the same. Justice Sutherland concluded that the right to utilize retained counsel, as reflected in these state and federal provisions, readily fit within the concept of due process. Due process guaranteed a right to a fair hearing, and such a hearing, "[h]istorically and in practice, in our country at least, has always included the right to the aid of counsel when desired and provided by the party asserting the right."

When the *Powell* opinion turned to the defendants' second claim, asserting an indigent's right to appointed counsel, it did not look to the history underlying the Sixth Amendment or to the early state provisions. This was understandable since the right of the indigent defendant to counsel provided by the state had a much narrower historical base. Where the original states had provided for the appointment of counsel, they usually had done so only in capital cases. Similarly, Congress, shortly before the ratification of the Sixth Amendment, had adopted a statutory provision requiring the appointment of counsel that was limited to capital crimes. Indeed, at the time of the *Powell* decision, almost half of the states apparently did not provide appointed counsel in most felony cases.

A constitutional right to appointed counsel could be derived, however, if not from historical traditions, from the due process right to a fair hearing. In concluding that the right to retained counsel was an essential element of due process, the first portion of the *Powell* opinion had stressed that the "right to be heard would be, in many cases, of little avail if it did not comprehend the right to be heard by counsel." The indigent defendant, Justice Sutherland noted, was as much entitled to a fair hearing as the more affluent defendant who could afford to retain a lawyer. The state accordingly had a due process obligation to provide the indigent defendant with a lawyer where counsel's assistance would be necessary to achieve a fair hearing. Language in the first portion of the opinion might have led the Court to conclude that an appointed lawyer would almost always be needed to guarantee the indigent such a hearing. Even the "intelligent and educated layman," Justice Sutherland had noted, needs the "guiding hand of counsel" to cope with the intricacies of the law. The Court's holding on appointed counsel, however, was carefully limited to the type of situation presented in the case before it. Justice Sutherland noted that the Court was deciding only that due process required appointed counsel "in a capital case, where the defendant is unable to employ counsel, and is incapable adequately of making his own defense because of ignorance, feeble-mindedness, illiteracy, or the like."

The *Powell* reasoning suggested that there were two distinct and separately grounded constitutional rights to counsel. As a result of the rejection of the English common law rule, the defendant had gained a right to be represented by counsel provided at his own expense. This right to retained counsel, reflected in the Sixth Amendment and similar state guarantees, recognized the defendant's freedom of choice in the use of his resources to obtain that form of representation that he deemed best suited for his defense. Representation by counsel would usually be of great value to the defendant, and the state had no justification for not permitting that option as an alternative to pro se representation. Whether or not a lawyer was needed in the particular case did not matter; the defendant had the right to make that assessment for himself since he was using his own funds.

The constitutional right to appointed counsel, on the other hand, arose out of the state's obligation to provide a fair hearing. That obligation carried with it an affirmative duty to provide counsel for the indigent defendant where a lawyer's assistance was needed to ensure a fair and accurate guilt-determining process. This right was narrower in scope than the right to retained counsel. Since public funds were being expended, the provision of counsel could be tied to cases where it was in fact needed. Thus, the *Powell* ruling on appointed counsel had been restricted to the special circumstances of that case, while its ruling on the right to use retained counsel had spoken of a general right applicable in all cases.

Six years after *Powell,* the Supreme Court, in *Johnson v. Zerbst,*[3] held that the right to appointed counsel, as well as the right to retained counsel, was to be found in the Sixth Amendment. Indeed, Justice Black's opinion for the Court drew no distinction between the two rights. *Johnson* involved a federal prosecution in which two apparently indigent defendants, charged with counterfeiting, had been refused appointed counsel because theirs was not a capital case. Justice Black held that their trial without counsel violated the Sixth Amendment, which applies by its terms to "all criminal prosecutions." The Sixth Amendment, he noted, "embodies a realistic recognition of the obvious truth that the average defendant does not have the professional legal skill to protect himself" in a criminal trial. It therefore "withholds from the federal courts, in all criminal proceedings, the power and authority to deprive an accused of his life or liberty unless he has or waives the assistance of counsel." This constitutional prerequisite for a valid conviction applied to all defendants, including those unable to afford counsel.

The *Johnson* opinion did not refer to the historical developments cited in *Powell v. Alabama.* It focused instead upon the language in *Powell* noting that the right to be heard often would be of little value without the assistance of counsel. That language was seen as supporting a reading of the Sixth Amendment that treated representation by counsel as a prescribed prerequisite for the criminal trial, no different than the elements of jury trial, notice, confrontation, and compulsory process. It was the trial court's obligation to ensure that these rights were available to defendant (although, at least as to the right to counsel, that did not preclude making the defendant bear the financial cost if he was able to do so). If the assistance of counsel otherwise would be unavailable because the defendant lacked funds to retain counsel, then the court had to make that assistance available by appointing counsel. The only exception was when the indigent knowingly and intelligently waived his Sixth Amendment right to counsel.

For a twenty-five year period following *Johnson,* the Supreme Court refused to extend that ruling to state cases. Although *Johnson* had held that the Sixth Amendment required appointed counsel in all cases encompassed by that Amendment, state cases were governed by the "less rigid and more fluid" requirement of the Fourteenth Amendment's due process clause. Relying upon a fundamental fairness analysis, the Court held in *Betts v. Brady*[4] that due process required the appointment of counsel only where the special circumstances of the particular case indicated that the indigent defendant needed a lawyer to obtain a fair trial. *Powell v. Alabama* and other capital cases presented one illustration of such special circumstances. The need for

3. 304 U.S. 458, 58 S.Ct. 1019, 82 L.Ed. 1461 (1938).

4. 316 U.S. 455, 62 S.Ct. 1252, 86 L.Ed. 1595 (1942). *Betts* found that such special circumstances were not present in that case and the state's refusal to appoint counsel to assist Betts in his robbery trial had not resulted in a denial of due process. The majority opinion concluded that the trial presented a "simple issue [of] the veracity" of prosecution and defense testimony on which Betts was well able to represent himself.

appointed counsel could also be established by the complicated nature of the offense or possible defenses thereto, events during trial that raised difficult legal questions, and personal characteristics of the defendant, such as youthfulness or mental incapacity. The special circumstances test of *Betts v. Brady* was sharply criticized by commentators, who argued that it was virtually impossible to render a retrospective judgment that a defendant forced to proceed pro se had not been prejudiced by the lack of counsel.

In 1963, in *Gideon v. Wainwright,*[5] the Court rejected the special circumstances rule of *Betts* and extended the right to appointed counsel in state cases to all indigent felony defendants. Unlike *Betts, Gideon* proceeded from the premise, consistent with the selective incorporation doctrine, that the Fourteenth Amendment rendered the Sixth Amendment right to counsel directly applicable to the states as a fundamental right. However, *Gideon* did not reject the *Betts* standard on the ground that the Sixth Amendment imposed a generalized mandate and therefore had a more extensive reach than the case-by-case approach of fundamental fairness. Justice Black, who had dissented in *Betts,* wrote for the Court in *Gideon,* and he stressed that *Betts* had erred in its fundamental fairness analysis by assuming that representation by counsel was not invariably "essential to a fair trial." Relying upon *Powell*'s discussion of the value of counsel, Justice Black noted that "reason and reflection require us to recognize that in our adversary system of criminal justice, any person hauled into court, who is too poor to hire a lawyer cannot be assured a fair trial unless counsel is provided for him." The "obvious truth," of this conclusion was evidenced by common experience: "Lawyers to prosecute are everywhere deemed essential * * * [and] there are few defendants * * * who fail to hire the best lawyers they can get to prepare and present their defenses." [6]

Both *Johnson* and *Gideon* viewed the Sixth Amendment as prescribing the basic elements of a fair trial and including the assistance of counsel among those elements. As previously noted, *Powell,* with its distinct treatment of the rights to retained and appointed counsel, could have been read to the contrary, with the state's obligation to provide counsel at its expense viewed as narrower than its obligation to allow representation by retained council. However, Justice Black, first in *Johnson* and then in *Gideon,* rejected any such reading of the Sixth Amendment. Under the *Johnson/Gideon* view of the Sixth Amendment, the Amendment imposes a single counsel requirement, designed to ensure a fair trial. Following from that premise, no Sixth Amendment distinction should exist between the indigent and affluent defendant as to the basic right to be represented by counsel.[7] Where a particular proceeding is deemed to be a part of the "criminal prosecution" for Sixth Amendment purposes, both will have an automatic right to representation by counsel (in the case of the indigent, at state expense). Where the proceeding is not

5. 372 U.S. 335, 83 S.Ct. 792, 9 L.Ed.2d 799 (1963).

6. In a concurring opinion, Justice Harlan justified the result reached by the Court under a fundamental fairness analysis and did so without accepting Justice Black's conclusion that *Betts* had erred in the application of that doctrine. Justice Harlan argued that decisions applying the *Betts* special circumstances rule had so frequently found such circumstances to be present that the rule in reality was meaningless; retention of a case-by-case analysis had only led the state courts astray, and it would be to their benefit to adopt a flat requirement that appointed counsel be made available for all "serious criminal charges." Adopting a similar view of the justification for *Gideon*'s automatic requirement for appointment of counsel, Justice Powell later described that requirement as prophylactic in nature. See § 2.8 at note 17. Several later cases, in characterizing the denial of counsel "as presumptively prejudicial," have suggested that *Gideon* rests not so much on the conclusion that defendants invariably need counsel to obtain an adjudication that is in fact fair, as on a reading of the Sixth Amendment as guaranteeing counsel's assistance as a general prerequisite of a fair trail. See §§ 2.8(d), 11.7(d), 27.6(d). The Sixth Amendment, under this view, imposes a flat requirement in recognition both that the denial of counsel's assistance has an "inherently indeterminate" impact and that there exists a substantial likelihood that a defendant would have needed counsel to gain a fair adjudication in an adversary process.

7. This is not to suggest that distinctions might not be drawn as to other aspects of the Sixth Amendment right. See § 11.4 discussing the defendant's constitutional right to counsel of choice.

so characterized, neither will have a Sixth Amendment right to counsel. The critical issue should be the characterization fully determine of the proceeding, and that should not be dependent upon whether the defendant's claim relates to retained or appointed counsel.

Support for such equivalency is found in a series of post-*Gideon* decisions (discussed in § 11.2) considering whether particular proceedings fell within the coverage of the Sixth Amendment. All involved the denial of appointed counsel for an indigent claimant, but the Court at no time suggested that a greater range of proceedings would be subject to the Sixth Amendment were the claim to relate to the assistance of retained counsel. Several of the cases held that the Sixth Amendment right to appointed counsel did not apply either because the overall proceeding was not a "criminal prosecution" or because the particular pretrial procedure did not present a "critical stage" of the criminal prosecution. So too, in a series of cases discussed in § 11.7(a), the Court did not distinguish between retained and appointed counsel in holding that a counsel's ineffective performance does not present a constitutional claim where the proceeding is one as to which an indigent defendant has no constitutional right to appointed counsel.

The end result, under this analysis, is that the state has no Sixth Amendment obligation to allow representation by retained counsel in a proceeding as to which it has no Sixth Amendment obligation to appoint counsel for the indigent. Thus, as the Court has held that the Sixth Amendment does not require the appointment of counsel for an indigent misdemeanor defendant who will be sentenced (if convicted) only to a fine,[8] the Sixth Amendment apparently also would not require the state to allow such a defendant to insist upon representation by retained counsel. Of course, no jurisdiction is likely to bar representation by retained counsel on a misdemeanor charge, even if punishable only by fine. Indeed, that current Sixth Amendment analysis would sustain such an unrealistic prohibition arguably raises doubts as to whether the Court truly is committed to the equivalency concept. Such a ruling could certainly be questioned in light of the historical background of the Sixth Amendment. For the right to retained counsel, as Justice Sutherland noted in *Powell,* had been recognized in misdemeanor cases even under the English practice that the framers deemed far too limited (although misdemeanors there were punished far more severely than by a fine alone). Then again, such a Sixth Amendment ruling would not fully determine a state's authority to bar retained counsel. As will be seen in the next subsection, due process can provide a constitutional grounding for assistance of counsel where the Sixth Amendment does not apply.

(b) Due Process Rights. *Powell v. Alabama* recognized due process rights to the assistance of appointed and retained counsel, and while *Powell* recognized those rights in a proceeding that today would be subject to the Sixth Amendment, the concept of a right to counsel grounded on due process has continuing significance for other proceedings. The two leading post-incorporation cases recognizing such a right in the context of the criminal justice process are *Gagnon v. Scarpelli*[9] and *Evitts v. Lucey.*[10] Both involved proceedings not part of the criminal prosecution itself and therefore not within the Sixth Amendment. *Gagnon* dealt with parole and probation revocation proceedings, and *Evitts* dealt with a first-level appeal granted as a matter of right. However, in contrast to *Gagnon* and *Evitts,* the Court, in a series of other cases (also discussed below), has rejected claims of a due process right to counsel at two other stages of

8. See Scott v. Illinois, § 11.2 at note 5.

9. 411 U.S. 778, 93 S.Ct. 1756, 36 L.Ed.2d 656 (1973).

10. 469 U.S. 387, 105 S.Ct. 830, 83 L.Ed.2d 821 (1985). Consider also In re Gault, 387 U.S. 1, 87 S.Ct. 1428, 18 L.Ed.2d 527 (1967). The Court there held that due process requiring the state to provide appointed counsel for indigent subjects in all juvenile delinquency proceedings "which may result in commitment to an institution in which the juvenile's freedom is impaired." The Court stressed the need for counsel in a proceeding which was "comparable in seriousness to a felony prosecution," raised similar legal issues, and dealt with individuals obviously not capable of representing themselves.

the criminal justice process not within the Sixth Amendment—the application for discretionary, second-tier appellate review and the application for collateral relief.

The starting point in the recognition of a due process right to counsel is the presence of a liberty interest, affected by the particular proceeding, of sufficient significance to merit due process protection. The Court has experienced no difficulty in concluding that such an interest is present when a convicted defendant seeks through the proceeding "to demonstrate that [his] conviction, with its consequent drastic loss of liberty, is unlawful." So too, *Gagnon* found that the loss of liberty resulting from parole or probation revocation also was a "serious deprivation" requiring the protection of due process. An interest sufficient to require due process protection, however, does not necessarily require a process that includes representation by counsel. In *Mathews v. Eldridge,*[11] a case involving an administrative proceeding, the Court set forth three factors that must be balanced in determining whether a particular procedural safeguard is part of the process due a litigant who presents an interest protected by due process:

> First, the private interest that will be affected by the official action; second, the risk of an erroneous deprivation of such interest through the procedures used, and the probable value, if any, of additional or substitute procedural safeguards; and finally, the Government's interest, including the function involved and the fiscal and administrative burdens that the additional or substitute procedural requirement would entail.

Since the interest typically presented in criminal justice proceedings, the loss of physical liberty, is of the highest order, the primary focus in determining whether a right to counsel is mandated has been upon the second and third of the *Mathews* factors.[12]

In *Gagnon,* a due process right to appointed counsel was thought to flow logically from hearing rights that had been mandated previously under the due process clause. Past precedent had established that parolee or probationer was entitled to substantial procedural safeguards in a revocation hearing, including the rights to present evidence and confront opposing witnesses. *Gagnon* concluded that due process also requires the state to provide appointed counsel where, under the facts of the particular case, counsel is needed to ensure the "effectiveness of the [hearing] rights guaranteed by [due process]." It refused to attempt to formulate "a precise and detailed set of guidelines" for determining when that need exists, but it did note that counsel ordinarily should be provided where there is a significant factual dispute or the individual relies upon contentions that a layman would have difficulty presenting.

The *Gagnon* opinion considered, but refused to impose, a flat requirement of counsel in all revocation cases. While such a requirement "had the appeal of simplicity, it would impose direct costs and serious collateral disadvantages without regard to the need or the likelihood in a particular case for a constructive contribution by counsel." In most revocation cases, the issue presented simply did not require the expertise of a lawyer. Quite often, "the probationer or parolee has been convicted of committing another crime [which automatically establishes grounds for revocation] or has admitted the charges against him." Although he may still contend that revocation would be too harsh in light of the nature of his violation, "mitigating evidence of this kind is often not susceptible of proof or is so simple as not to require either investigation or exposition by counsel." On the other side, "the introduction of counsel" would "alter significantly the nature of the [revocation] proceeding." The state would respond by re-

11. 424 U.S. 319, 96 S.Ct. 893, 47 L.Ed.2d 18 (1976).

12. Arguably, the claim would fail automatically if the only sanction at stake in the proceeding were a fine. In Lassiter v. Department of Social Services, 452 U.S. 18, 101 S.Ct. 2153, 68 L.Ed.2d 640 (1981) (holding that due process does not require the appointment of counsel in all parental status termination proceedings), the Court noted that the "pre-eminent generalization that emerges from this Court's precedents on an indigent's right to appointed counsel is that such a right has been recognized to exist only where the litigant may lose his physical liberty if he loses the litigation."

taining its own counsel and the role of the hearing body would become "more akin to that of a judge at trial, and less attuned to the rehabilitative needs of the individual probationer."

In contrast to *Gagnon,* which adopted a case-by-case approach similar to that of *Betts, Evitts* established a flat right to counsel, following under due process the approach taken in *Gideon.* At issue in *Evitts* was a due process right to representation by retained counsel,[13] but the Court's ruling extended to both retained and appointed counsel. Prior to *Evitts,* in *Douglas v. California,*[14] the Court had recognized an equal protection right of an indigent defendant to the assistance of appointed counsel on a first appeal granted by state law as a matter of right. *Evitts* held the *Douglas* ruling also had a constitutional grounding in due process and that grounding necessarily established as well a right to be represented by retained counsel. Moreover, this due process right, as indicated in *Douglas,* was not dependent upon the special circumstance of the case, but extended to all first appeals granted of right.

In *Evitts,* unlike *Gagnon,* the Court had not previously set forth a particular due process structure for the proceeding at issue. Indeed, the Court had held that the Constitution imposed no obligation upon a state to grant appeals of right in criminal cases. However, once the state had created such a procedure as " 'an integral part of [its] system for finally adjudicating the guilt or innocence of a defendant,' " it could not, consistent with due process, structure that procedure so that it was basically a "meaningless ritual" for a defendant without counsel and then fail to provide for the assistance of counsel. Drawing an analogy to *Gideon,* the Court noted that under a state's appellate procedure, as under its trial procedure, "the services of a lawyer will for virtually every layman be necessary" to effectively present his case. Here too, the defendant faced an "adversarial system of justice" in which "lawyers are 'necessities,' not luxuries." Accordingly, due process, as to the first appeal of right, mandated a right to counsel parallel to the trial-level right established in *Gideon* under the Sixth Amendment.

Although the *Evitts* opinion drew an analogy to *Gideon,* the Court in its earlier ruling in *Ross v. Moffitt*[15] had stressed that due process analysis places the convicted defendant seeking appellate review in a quite different position than the defendant who is an "accused" at trial. The defendant at trial has need for attorney "as a shield to protect him against being 'haled into court' by the State and stripped of his presumption of innocence." On appeal, in contrast, the attorney is to be utilized "as a sword to upset [a] prior determination of guilt." The defendant here is "seeking not to fend off the efforts of the State's prosecutor but rather to overturn a finding of guilt made by a judge or jury below." As one of the factors to be considered under a due process analysis is the "risk of an erroneous deprivation" of the protected liberty interest without the claimed procedural safeguard,[16] a defendant stands in a lesser position when he claims a right to appointed counsel following a conviction at trial. That lesser position, the Court noted in *Ross,* follows from the difference in the constitutional status of the trial and the appeal. "For, while no one would agree that the State may simply dispense with the trial stage of proceedings without a criminal defendant's consent, it is clear that the State need not provide any appeal at all."

As *Evitts* indicates, the defendant's lesser position in a proceeding that challenges a conviction does not necessarily preclude recognition of a due process right to counsel in that proceeding. Indeed, as in *Evitts,* such a due process right can exist without reference to the special needs of the particular defen-

13. That issue came into the case through respondent Lucey's claim that he had been denied the effective assistance of counsel when his retained counsel had failed to file the necessary papers to perfect his appeal. The Supreme Court had previously held that ineffective assistance constitutes a constitutional violation only where the litigant had a constitutional right to the assistance of counsel in the particular proceeding. See § 11.7(a).

14. Discussed at note 29 infra.

15. 417 U.S. 600, 94 S.Ct. 2437, 41 L.Ed.2d 341 (1974).

16. See Mathews v. Eldridge at note 11 supra.

dant. However, as *Ross* indicates, the Court will examine carefully the nature of the particular proceeding, considering both the role that counsel would play and the importance of the proceeding in protecting against an erroneous deprivation of the liberty interest at stake. Based on those factors, the Court has concluded that the due process right to counsel does not extend beyond the first appeal of right to the application for either subsequent appeals or collateral review of a conviction.[17]

At issue in *Ross* was the right to appointed counsel in preparing applications for discretionary appeals that followed defendants' first appeal as of right. Defendants had been represented by counsel on their initial appeal, but were denied appointed counsel to assist them in preparing petitions for discretionary review in the State Supreme Court and the United States Supreme Court. Finding that denial not to violate due process, the Court majority noted that defendants had already received a full review of their convictions and that the further assistance of counsel was not necessary to provide "meaningful access" to the higher appellate courts. In considering a defendant's petition for review, those higher courts would have before them the trial transcript, the intermediate court brief prepared by counsel, and in many instances, the opinion of the state's intermediate appellate court. Those materials, supplemented by any personal statement of the defendant, provided an "adequate basis" for determining whether to grant review. This was particularly true in light of the discretionary nature of the second-tier appellate review. The traditional standard utilized in determining whether to grant such discretionary review was whether the appeal presented issues worthy of high court consideration because of general legal significance, rather than whether there had been a "correct adjudication of guilt" in the individual. The *Ross* opinion did not comment on whether due process could require appointment of counsel if review were granted and the defendant then put to presenting a brief on the merits and oral argument. As a matter of practice, both the state high courts and the Supreme Court appoint counsel once review has been granted.

In *Pennsylvania v. Finley,*[18] the majority characterized the issue before it as whether due process required the state to appoint counsel to assist the respondent in preparing a collateral attack upon her conviction under a state postconviction relief procedure. The state there had appointed counsel, but counsel had then been allowed to withdraw after concluding that the collateral attack lacked arguable merit. The Court majority reasoned that the withdrawal procedure would present a constitutional issue only if respondent had an underlying constitutional right to the appointment of counsel (a position rejected by the dissenters). Turning to that question, the Court did not focus on the possible need for counsel. Arguably, a stronger case could be made here than in *Ross,* as collateral challenges in state proceedings commonly rest on issues that were not raised at trial or on appeal. The *Finley* Court stressed, instead, the place of the collateral attack within the totality of the proceedings for determining guilt. The majority stated:

> Postconviction relief is even further removed from the criminal trial than is discretionary direct review. It is not part of the criminal proceedings itself, and it is in fact considered to be civil in nature. It is a collateral attack that normally occurs only after the defendant has failed to secure relief through direct review of his conviction. States have no obligation to provide this avenue of relief, and when they do, the fundamental fairness man-

17. The Court was divided in *Ross, Evitts,* and the collateral review cases (*Finley* and *Murray,* discussed infra), and arguable inconsistencies in portions of the reasoning in *Evitts* (recognizing a due process right to counsel) and the other cases (rejecting such a right) may be attributed to shifts in the composition of the Court majority. Justice Brennan, who wrote for the Court in *Evitts,* had dissented in *Ross* and later dissented in *Finley* and *Murray.* Justice Rehnquist, who wrote for the Court majority in *Ross* and *Finley,* and for the plurality in *Murray,* dissented in *Evitts.* However, other justices joined the prevailing opinions in each of the cases, and a current majority accepts as correct the distinctions drawn in those cases.

18. 481 U.S. 551, 107 S.Ct. 1990, 95 L.Ed.2d 539 (1987).

dated by the Due Process Clause does not require that the State supply a lawyer as well.

In *Murray v. Giarratano,*[19] a later collateral relief case, the Court again rejected a due process claim to appointed counsel. *Murray,* however, was not simply a straightforward application of *Finley.* It raised a significant issue as to the level of generality at which a due process claim should be assessed, and produced a split within the Court that left that issue largely unresolved. At issue in *Murray* was the claim of Virginia's death row inmates that they were entitled to appointed counsel to assist them in preparing collateral attack challenges to their convictions and sentences. In upholding that claim, the Fourth Circuit had viewed the inmates' situation as presenting special circumstances that distinguished *Finley.* First, here, unlike *Finley,* the inmates had been sentenced to the death penalty. The Supreme Court had frequently noted that, the finality of the death penalty requires that its imposition be supported by a "greater degree of reliability," and to provide that assurance, it had insisted upon special procedural safeguards in death penalty cases. Second, the district court here had made special factual findings as to the inmates' need for counsel. That court had concluded "that death row inmates had a limited amount of time to prepare their petitions, that their cases were unusually complex, and that the shadow of impending execution would interfere with their ability to do legal work." While the state did assign "unit attorneys" to each penal institution, the district court had also found that those attorneys could not adequately assist the death row inmates because their role was limited to that of "legal advisor" rather than counsel for the inmate. Those district court findings were seen as providing a case-specific showing of the essentiality of counsel that had not been present in *Finley.*

Speaking for four justices, Chief Justice Rehnquist authored a plurality opinion that flatly rejected both of the distinctions cited by the lower court. While the special quality of the death penalty had been recognized, under both the Eighth Amendment and the due process clause, as requiring additional procedural safeguards, that concern had not been carried beyond the "trial stage of capital adjudication." On both appeal and collateral attack, the Court had refused in various cases to impose special standards for review of capital cases. The reasoning of such rulings "require[d] the conclusion that the rule of *Pennsylvania v. Finley* should apply no differently in capital cases than in noncapital cases." Justice Rehnquist also rejected any attempt to distinguish *Finley* on the basis of case-specific factual findings such as were made here by the district court. To rely upon such findings "would permit a different constitutional rule to apply in a different State if the district judge hearing that claim reached different conclusions." The Court's post-*Gideon* rulings on the right to counsel "ha[d] been categorical holdings as to what the Constitution requires with respect to a particular stage of a criminal proceeding in general." This "tact" had been adopted in light of past experience. As the dissenters acknowledged, it had been "the Court's dissatisfaction with the case-by-case approach in *Betts v. Brady* that led to the adoption of the categorical ruling * * * in *Gideon.*" There was nothing in the nature of the collateral proceeding that justified departure from the continued use of categorical holdings.

Also speaking for four justices, Justice Stevens' dissenting opinion argued that "particular circumstances" necessarily shape the scope of the due process right to counsel. The dissenters concluded that the circumstances cited by the lower court, as well as additional circumstances, clearly distinguished *Finley.* The "unique nature" of the death penalty had been recognized as shaping due process requirements as far back as *Powell,* which had established an automatic right to appointment of counsel in capital cases while a case-by-case approach was utilized for other felony defendants. The special needs of capital cases necessarily carried over to collateral relief in light of "significant evidence that in capital

19. 492 U.S. 1, 109 S.Ct. 2765, 106 L.Ed.2d 1 (1989).

cases what is ordinarily considered direct review does not sufficiently safeguard against miscarriages of justice." While "federal habeas courts granted relief in only 0.25% to 7% of noncapital cases in recent years," the "success rate in capital cases ranged from 60% to 70%." The district court's findings bolstered this conclusion by establishing the inability of death row inmates to prepare their own petitions. Further support was found in the character of collateral review as applied here: "In contrast to the collateral process discussed in *Finley,* Virginia law contemplate[d] that some claims ordinarily heard on direct review [e.g., incompetency of counsel] will be relegated to postconviction proceedings." Finally, insofar as due process analysis looks to the fiscal and administrative burdens imposed upon the State, here too the special circumstances applicable to the Virginia inmates strengthened their claim. Virginia already appointed counsel to assist death row inmates once their collateral attack petitions were found to assert at least one nonfrivolous claim. Accordingly, "the additional cost of providing [Virginia's] 32 death row inmates competent counsel to prepare such petitions should be minimal." That a state could readily bear such cost was evidenced by the fact that Virginia was one of no more than five capital-punishment states (out of a total of 37) that "ha[s] no system for appointing counsel for condemned prisoners before a postconviction petition is filed."

With eight justices evenly divided as to significance of the special circumstances presented by the Virginia inmates, the deciding vote in *Murray* was cast by Justice Kennedy. His very brief opinion appeared to give some weight to special circumstances, although Justice O'Connor found no inconsistency in the Kennedy and Rehnquist opinions and joined both. Justice Kennedy initially accepted Justice Stevens' analysis insofar as it established (1) that "collateral proceedings are a central part of the review process for prisoners condemned to death" and (2) that the "complexity of our jurisprudence in this area * * * makes it unlikely that capital defendants will be able to file successful petitions for collateral relief without the assistance of persons learned in the law." He noted, however, that the necessary assistance can be provided in "various ways" and there was no showing that Virginia's approach had been unsatisfactory. For "no prisoner on death row in Virginia ha[d] been unable to obtain counsel to represent him in postconviction proceedings, and Virginia's prison system is staffed with institutional lawyers to assist in preparing petitions for postconviction relief." Accordingly, Justice Kennedy concurred in the reversal of the lower court ruling based "on the facts and record of this case."

The division of the Court in *Murray* leaves open the extent to which the Court majority will give weight to the special elements of a procedural setting, as it relates to a particular type of litigant, in assessing a due process claim to appointed counsel. Arguably, the division among the justices may be limited to the capital case. Yet, *Gagnon v. Scarpelli,* which was not discussed in any of the *Murray* opinions, indicates that a special circumstances ruling remains a viable alternative as well for a noncapital case. Certainly the thrust of the Court's rulings is not so firmly settled as to impose a significant barrier to the adoption in future cases, especially by a Court of changed composition, of an approach that more strongly favors either categorical rulings, special-circumstances rulings, or a shifting from categorical to special-circumstances rulings depending upon the particular procedural setting.[20]

20. The Court's rulings leave open the right-to-counsel issue in several proceedings that may not be within the coverage of the Sixth Amendment, yet may affect the loss of liberty flowing from a criminal conviction. The Court has not, for example, directly considered whether due process requires appointed counsel where a discretionary appeal is the only appeal available to the defendant (unlike *Ross,* where the discretionary appeal followed a first appeal granted as a matter of right). So too, in Coleman v. Thompson, ___ U.S. ___, 111 S.Ct. 2546, 115 L.Ed.2d 640 (1991), the Court specifically left open the question of whether there exists an exception to *Finley* where state law provides that a claim of ineffective assistance of trial counsel cannot be raised on appeal but must be presented in a state collateral proceeding. In *Coleman,* the defendant had counsel on his state collat-

Still another due process issue left in limbo is whether the right to utilize retained counsel may have a broader scope than the right to appointed counsel. Pre–*Gideon* rulings had indicated that the right to representation by retained counsel had a broader due process grounding than the right to appointed counsel. Thus, during the same period in which the accused's right to appointed counsel in a noncapital felony case was controlled by the special circumstances rule of *Betts,* the right of such a defendant to representation by retained counsel was characterized as "unqualified." [21] Indeed, *Powell* had suggested in dicta that due process would be denied if a court, even in a civil case, "were arbitrarily to refuse to hear a party by counsel, employed by and appearing for him." [22] On the other hand, the later Sixth Amendment rulings have suggested that the rights to appointed and retained counsel are equivalent under that Amendment. Moreover, while one consideration weighed under a due process analysis is the burden placed upon the state in providing counsel at its expense, the due process rulings have tended to emphasize other factors in rejecting claims to appointed counsel. Those considerations could well be deemed equally controlling as to retained counsel—unless the Court recognizes an independent due process interest of the litigant not to be prevented from utilizing his own resources to present his case through counsel if he so chooses. The possibility that it would do so was raised in *Gagnon.* After holding that due process required appointment of counsel in revocation cases where the circumstances made counsel necessary to ensure the "effectiveness" of due process guaranteed hearing rights, the *Gagnon* Court cited several concerns in refusing to impose a flat requirement of appointed counsel in all revocation cases. Among these was the potentially adverse impact of automatic representation by counsel upon the special nature of the revocation proceeding (where the state typically did not use counsel and the focus often was upon a "predictive and discretionary" determination as to rehabilitative potential). That impact, of course, would flow from frequent representation by retained counsel as well as by appointed counsel. The Court added a warning, however, should a state decide to restrict the use of retained counsel. It stated in a footnote: "We have no occasion to decide in this case whether a probationer or parolee has a right to be represented at a revocation hearing by retained counsel in situations other than those where the State would be obliged to furnish counsel for an indigent." [23]

(c) Derivative Rights to Counsel. A constitutional right to the assistance of counsel also can be derived from other constitutional guarantees besides the due process right to a fair hearing. Thus, *Miranda v. Arizona* held that the right to consult with counsel was

eral challenge raising the ineffectiveness claim and the issue before the Court was the bearing of that counsel's ineffective performance in failing to properly pursue an appeal from the rejection of the collateral challenge. The Court noted that even if an exception existed and the collateral challenge itself was treated as the equivalent of the appeal in Evitts v. Lucey, the subsequent appeal from its rejection certainly would not fall within any such exception in light of Ross v. Moffitt and Pennsylvania v. Finley. Consider also the possibility of a due process right to counsel in the proceedings discussed in § 11.2 following notes 19 and 24.

21. Chandler v. Fretag, 348 U.S. 3, 75 S.Ct. 1, 99 L.Ed. 4 (1954).

22. See also Justice Stewart's concurring opinion in Manness v. Meyers, § 8.15 at note 4.

23. Consider, however, Wolff v. McDonnell, 418 U.S. 539, 94 S.Ct. 2963, 41 L.Ed.2d 935 (1974). After exploring various difficulties that would arise from the "insertion of counsel into the [prison] disciplinary process" and noting that the concerns cited in *Gagnon* were "even more pertinent here," the Court in *Wolff* concluded: "At this stage in the development of these procedures we are not prepared to hold that inmates have a right *to either retained* or appointed counsel in disciplinary proceedings" (emphasis added). *Wolff,* like *Gagnon,* stressed special proceeding attributes not likely to be found at those stages of the guilt-determining process that have been held not to require appointment of counsel—i.e., the trial of the misdemeanant punished only by fine, the petition for discretionary second-tier appellate review, and the petition for collateral relief. So too, while the Court has held that the defendant has no constitutional grounding for challenging the ineffectiveness of retained counsel in such proceedings, those rulings also can be distinguished. The recognition of a right not to have retained counsel precluded by the state need not carry with it a right to effective assistance of such counsel (in contrast to the due process right to counsel that extends

indispensible to the protection of the self-incrimination privilege of a person subjected to custodial interrogation.[24] The Court there required that the police inform such a person that "he has a right to consult with a lawyer and to have the lawyer with him during interrogation," and that "if he is indigent, a lawyer will be appointed to represent him." This requirement extends beyond the Sixth Amendment right to counsel since custodial interrogation often occurs before the individual is an "accused" in a "criminal prosecution." [25] The *Miranda* approach, requiring an opportunity to consult with counsel as a means of safeguarding another constitutional guarantee, has also been advanced in other situations not encompassed by the Sixth Amendment. In *Kirby v. Illinois,* this approach was urged by the dissenters in arguing that a suspect placed in a lineup should have a right to the presence of retained or appointed counsel, but it was rejected by the majority.[26] In *United States v. Mandujano,* two justices argued that the self-incrimination privilege of a target-witness before a grand jury carried with it a right to consult with a retained or appointed attorney prior to questioning. While the Court did not find it necessary to rule on that contention, four justices appeared to reject it.[27] Thus, the likely recognition of further derivative rights to counsel, beyond that established in *Miranda,* currently appears dim.

(d) Equal Protection and Appointed Counsel. Assume that a state allows a person to be represented by retained counsel in a proceeding as to which neither due process nor the Sixth Amendment requires the appointment of counsel. Does the equal protection guarantee then require the state to provide appointed counsel for indigent persons so as to ensure equal treatment? Supreme Court precedent suggests that the equal protection guarantee might possibly impose an independent obligation upon the state to provide appointed counsel, but that obligation probably is limited to situations in which either due process or the Sixth Amendment would come very close to requiring appointment of counsel. The key cases assessing the scope of the state's obligation under the equal protection clause are *Douglas v. California* and *Ross v. Moffitt.* An analysis of those rulings must begin, however, with an examination of the earlier case of *Griffin v. Illinois.*[28] Although *Griffin* did not involve the appointment of counsel, it is the seminal ruling on the state's general obligation to provide "equal justice" in the criminal justice process.

Griffin dealt with a state law that gave every defendant the right to appeal, but then conditioned appellate review on defendant's presentation of a trial record that often could not be prepared without a stenographic transcript. Defendant, who was indigent, asked the state to provide him with a free transcript so that he could prepare his appeal, but the state refused to do so. The Supreme Court held that this refusal resulted in a denial of due process and equal protection. Both Justice Black's plurality opinion and Justice Frankfurter's separate concurring opinion acknowledged that the state had no constitutional obligation to provide appellate review of criminal convictions. However, once the state had granted defendants a right to appeal, it could not condition the exercise of that right upon a prerequisite that discriminated against those defendants who were indigent. "In criminal trials," Justice Black noted, "a State can no more discriminate on account of poverty than on account of religion, race, or color" since "the ability to pay costs in advance bears no relationship to de-

to both retained and appointed counsel). See § 11.7(a), and § 28.4 at note 33.

24. See § 6.5.

25. See § 6.4. However, in Berkemer v. McCarty, 468 U.S. 420, 104 S.Ct. 3138, 82 L.Ed.2d 317 (1984), holding that *Miranda* warnings were required in the custodial interrogation of a person arrested for a traffic misdemeanor, the Court left open for future decision the question of "whether an indigent suspect has a right, under the Fifth Amendment, to have an attorney appointed to advise him regarding his responses to custodial interrogation when the alleged offense about which he is being questioned is sufficiently minor that he would not have a right, under the Sixth Amendment to the assistance of appointed counsel at trial."

26. See § 7.3.

27. See § 8.15(a).

28. 351 U.S. 12, 76 S.Ct. 585, 100 L.Ed. 891 (1956).

fendant's guilt or innocence." Commenting generally upon this country's dedication "to affording equal justice to all," Justice Black added, in an oft-quoted statement: "There can be no equal justice where the kind of trial a man gets depends on the amount of money he has."

Notwithstanding the sweeping language in Justice Black's opinion, it was far from certain that the *Griffin* ruling would be extended to the providing of appointed counsel. By requiring a transcript to perfect an appeal, the state had denied the indigent defendant access to an integral part of its process for ensuring against unjust convictions. In contrast, the indigent defendant denied appointed counsel still had his right to a hearing. Moreover, under the then prevailing due process analysis of the right to counsel, that defendant would be provided with a lawyer when the consequences of the hearing were significant and a lawyer's assistance was necessary to ensure that the hearing was fair. *Griffin,* it could be argued, surely did not impose upon the state the impossible burden of making available to the indigent all of the defense assistance a more affluent defendant might utilize. A reasoned stopping point arguably would be to limit the state's obligation to providing those services that were essential to obtaining a fair adjudication, and the due process guarantee already set the limits of that obligation as to appointed counsel.

In *Douglas v. California,*[29] the Court appeared to have rejected the above analysis in recognizing a *Griffin* -type right to appointed appellate counsel. *Douglas* held invalid on equal protection grounds an intermediate appellate court's practice of refusing to appoint counsel on appeal if that court, after reviewing the trial record, concluded that "such appointment would be of no value to either the defendant or the court." The majority opinion found this practice inconsistent with the "*Griffin* principle." Here too there was "discrimination against the indigent" with "the kind of appeal a man enjoys depend[ing] on the amount of money he has." Unlike the indigent, the more affluent defendant was not required to "run [the] gantlet of a preliminary showing of merit" to have his case presented by counsel. As the Court viewed the state's procedure, "the indigent, where the record was unclear or errors were hidden, had only the right to a meaningless ritual, while the rich man had a meaningful appeal."

The *Douglas* opinion stressed that it was not requiring "absolute equality" throughout the criminal justice process. What was at stake here was the first level of appeal, the "one and only appeal an indigent has as of right." The Court was not here concerned with review "beyond the stage in the appellate process at which the claims have once been presented by a lawyer and passed upon by an appellate court." Left open was the question whether the state would have to provide counsel for an indigent defendant seeking to obtain discretionary review from a second-level appellate court.

In stressing the importance of the first appeal, and in characterizing a defendant's presentation of his appeal without counsel as a "meaningless ritual," the *Douglas* opinion cited factors that would have been relevant in assessing a due process right to appointed appellate counsel. Accordingly, Justice Harlan, in his *Douglas* dissent, gave substantial attention to the possibility that due process there required appointed counsel on appeal. He concluded, however, that the state's preliminary review procedure for appointing counsel satisfied any such requirement. Traditional due process analysis would not recognize an absolute right to counsel, but would focus on the need for counsel to preserve meaningful appellate review in the individual case. Here, the state appellate court had provided such review. Thus, at least insofar as it imposed a flat requirement of appointed counsel, *Douglas,* from Justice Harlan's perspective, took the equal protection guarantee beyond the limits of the due process guarantee.

29. 372 U.S. 353, 83 S.Ct. 814, 9 L.Ed.2d 811 (1963).

In *Ross v. Moffitt,*[30] the Court refused to extend *Douglas* to indigent defendants seeking appointed counsel to prepare petitions for discretionary appellate review that came after the first appeal. The *Ross* majority opinion looked to both due process and equal protection in reaching that result. *Douglas* was described as receiving "some support" from both due process and equal protection clauses, with "neither clause by itself provid[ing] an entirely satisfactory basis for the result reached." Thus *Douglas* apparently was the product of the combined impact of the two clauses, although precisely how they interacted was left unclear. The Court did note that each clause "depend[s] on a different inquiry which emphasizes different factors." For due process the emphasis is on "fairness between the State and the individual dealing with the State, regardless of how other individuals in the same situation may be treated." "Equal protection, on the other hand, emphasizes disparity in treatment by a State between classes of individuals."

In refusing to extend *Douglas* to the petition for second-level discretionary review, the *Ross* majority examined separately the impact of the two clauses, and found that neither lent support to the defendant's claim. In discussing the due process element, the Court stressed the quite different relationship of the defendant and the state on an appeal as opposed to a trial. As discussed in subsection (b), the defendant's role as the person pressing the appeal and challenging a determination of guilt reduced the strength of his claim for procedural safeguards. The Court concluded that "unfairness" could result in such a proceeding only if indigents were "singled out" and denied "meaningful access * * * because of their poverty." That question, however, was "more profitably considered under an equal protection analysis."

In finding that there was no denial of meaningful access based on poverty, the *Ross* majority opinion discussed the ease with which an appellate court could determine whether to grant discretionary review even where the application had not been prepared by counsel. It acknowledged that "a skilled lawyer, particularly one trained in the somewhat arcane art of preparing petitions for discretionary review," could prove helpful to his client. However, the state had no "duty to duplicate the legal arsenal that may be privately retained by a criminal defendant in a continuing effort to reverse his conviction, but only to assure the indigent defendant an adequate opportunity to present his claims fairly in the context of the state appellate process." Here, unlike *Douglas,* that opportunity was available without counsel.

The *Ross* opinion left uncertain the significance of the equal protection component of *Douglas.* Arguably, *Douglas* presented a situation in which the procedural setting was not sufficient in itself to require counsel as a matter of due process (here too, the defendant was proceeding on appeal), but the value of the lawyer was so significant that the disparate treatment of the indigent resulted in an equal protection violation. However, any separate significance of the equal protection clause, at least in the *Douglas* setting, seemed to disappear with ruling in *Evitts v. Lucey.*[31] For the Court there clearly indicated that the right to counsel on the first appeal of right, even as a categorical guarantee as specified in *Douglas,* could also be grounded on due process alone. Consistent with traditional due process analysis, the Court there looked to defendant's need for counsel in the particular proceeding as one of the factors to be weighed in determining the demands of due process. The question presented previously under equal protection analysis—whether the lack of counsel rendered the appeal a "meaningless ritual"—was also an aspect of due process analysis.

Following *Evitts,* the equal protection clause would appear to add nothing to the right to counsel. Yet, in *Pennsylvania v. Finley,*[32] the Court returned to a separate analy-

30. See note 15 supra and the text following note 17 supra.

31. See note 10 supra and the text following note 13 supra.

32. See note 18 supra.

sis of the impact of the two clauses. Looking first to due process, the Court stressed collateral attack had the same characteristics as an appeal and was even farther removed from the criminal trial. Looking to equal protection, the Court stressed that meaningful access was available without counsel in light of the availability of other resources (the trial record and appellate briefs and opinions). This continued separate treatment of the two clauses suggests that there conceivably could be situations where equal protection would sustain a right to appointed counsel that would fail under due process. That, of course, would not be the case where the basic thrust of the due process ruling is that counsel would not be especially helpful in the particular setting. Where, for example, the circumstances of a particular revocation proceeding fail to establish a due process right to counsel under *Gagnon,* the indigent probationer or parolee could not successfully claim an equal protection right to counsel because the state allowed representation by retained counsel in such a revocation proceeding. On the other hand, due process could be found not to require appointed counsel, even though counsel might be essential to the litigant, simply because the proceeding is so far removed from the core of the criminal justice process (e.g., the presentation of argument on an appeal from the denial of postconviction relief). Here, should a state procedure be geared to representation by retained counsel, the equal protection guarantee of "meaningful access" might in itself require counsel for the indigent. Support for such an independent impact of equal protection is found in cases involving assistance other than counsel, where the court has required assistance under the equal protection clause that probably would not be demanded as a matter of due process.[33]

§ 11.2 Scope of the Indigent's Right to Counsel and Other Assistance

(a) Right to Appointed Counsel: Misdemeanor Prosecutions. Prior to the 1972 decision of *Argersinger v. Hamlin,*[1] the Court had not had occasion to rule on the applicability of the Sixth Amendment right to appointed counsel in misdemeanor prosecutions. *Johnson v. Zerbst, Gideon v. Wainwright,* and other Sixth Amendment cases had all involved felony prosecutions. Though the Sixth Amendment refers to "all criminal prosecutions," which would seem to encompass misdemeanor prosecutions, several lower courts had ruled that the Sixth Amendment right to appointed counsel, like the Sixth Amendment right to jury trial, did not apply to prosecutions for "petty offenses" (basically misdemeanors punishable by no more than six months imprisonment).[2] That position was presented to the Court in *Argersinger,* where it was unanimously rejected.

The Court in *Argersinger* could find no justification for extending the petty offense exception to the counsel clause of the Sixth Amendment. While there was "historical support" for the exception as applied to jury trials, "nothing in the history of the right to counsel" suggested "a retraction of the right in petty offenses, wherein the common law previously did require that counsel be provided." There also was no functional basis for drawing the line for the appointment of counsel at petty offenses. The "problems associated with * * * petty offenses," the Court noted, "often require the presence of counsel to insure the accused a fair trial." It could not be said that the legal questions involved in a misdemeanor trial were likely to be less complex because the jail sentence did not exceed

33. Consider, e.g., Mayer v. Chicago, 404 U.S. 189, 92 S.Ct. 410, 30 L.Ed.2d 372 (1971). The Court there held that an indigent defendant convicted of an ordinance violation punishable only by fine was entitled under *Griffin* to a free transcript that would permit him to challenge on appeal the sufficiency of the evidence supporting his conviction. Since the defendant was not threatened with the loss of liberty, the interest he advanced was substantially less than that recognized in the due process or Sixth Amendment cases involving the appointment of counsel. See note 12 supra and § 11.2(a). See also the filing fee cases cited at § 11.2, note 33.

§ 11.2

1. 407 U.S. 25, 92 S.Ct. 2006, 32 L.Ed.2d 530 (1972).

2. See § 22.1(b).

six months.[3] Nor was there less need for advice of counsel prior to entering a plea of guilty to a petty offense. Indeed, petty misdemeanors might well present a unique need for counsel because their great volume "may create an obsession for speedy dispositions, regardless of the fairness of the result."

Since the defendant in *Argersinger* had been sentenced to jail, the Court found it unnecessary to rule on the defendant's right to appointed counsel where "a loss of liberty was not involved." The opinion laid the foundation, however, for distinguishing between cases involving sentences of imprisonment and those in which only fines are imposed. Both *Johnson* and *Gideon* had referred to counsel's assistance as necessary to ensure "the fundamental human rights of life and liberty." There was a special significance in the loss of liberty, to both the accused and society, that could not be denied. "[T]he prospect of imprisonment for however short a time will seldom be viewed by the accused as a trivial or 'petty' matter and may well result in quite serious repercussions affecting his career and his reputation."

The *Argersinger* opinion also cited the practicability of applying an "actual imprisonment" standard. Responding to the contention that appointment of counsel for minor offenses was beyond the capacity of "the Nation's legal resources," it noted that an actual imprisonment standard would limit significantly the burden imposed upon the states. Although many jurisdictions classified traffic offenses as criminal, only a minute portion of all such offenses were likely to be "brought into the class where imprisonment actually occurs." Indeed, the opinion stated, "the run of misdemeanors will not be affected by today's ruling." [4]

In *Scott v. Illinois,*[5] the Court refused to carry the Sixth Amendment right to appointed counsel beyond the actual imprisonment standard suggested in *Argersinger.*[6] The petitioner there was an indigent defendant who had been convicted of shoplifting. Although that misdemeanor was punishable by a maximum sentence of one year in jail and a $500 fine, petitioner had been sentenced to only a fine of $50.00. Referring to both the Sixth Amendment and the Fourteenth Amendment's due process clause, the Supreme Court concluded that the "federal constitution does not require a state trial court to appoint counsel for a criminal defendant such as petitioner." [7] *Argersinger,* the Court stated, had rested on the "conclusion that incarceration was so severe a sanction that it should not be imposed * * * unless an indigent has been offered appointed counsel." It had thereby "delimit[ed] the constitutional right to appointed counsel in state criminal proceedings." The "central premise of *Argersinger*—that actual imprisonment is a penalty differ-

3. In North v. Russell, 427 U.S. 328, 96 S.Ct. 2709, 49 L.Ed.2d 534 (1976), the petitioner stressed this point in arguing that *Argersinger*'s recognition of a right to counsel, based on the defendant's need for legal expertise, necessarily implied a right also to a judge who is a lawyer rather than a layman. The Court held, however, that the state was not under a constitutional obligation to provide a lawyer-judge for a misdemeanor trial at the first level of a two-tier court system which guaranteed to defendant a trial de novo before a lawyer-judge at the next level. Cf. § 22.1(f) (noting analogous treatment of jury trial right in a two-tier system).

4. A major objection advanced against an actual imprisonment standard was that it would require the magistrate (who often would also be the trial judge) to "prejudge" the case in determining whether appointed counsel was necessary. The magistrate would have to determine prior to trial whether imprisonment might be imposed if the defendant were convicted. The Court, however, did not see any insurmountable difficulties in requiring the magistrate to make this "predictive evaluation of each case."

5. 440 U.S. 367, 99 S.Ct. 1158, 59 L.Ed.2d 383 (1979).

6. The *Argersinger* holding, repeated in *Scott,* was that, "absent a knowing and voluntary waiver, no person may be imprisoned for any offense, whether classified as petty, misdemeanor, or felony, unless he was represented by counsel at trial." The reference in this sentence to a felony resulting in imprisonment might be taken to suggest that a felony which would not result in imprisonment also would not require appointed counsel. However, while cases like *Johnson* and *Gideon* did involve felony sentences of imprisonment, numerous subsequent opinions described those cases as establishing an absolute right to appointed counsel in all felony cases, making no reference to the punishment imposed. See e.g., Mempa v. Rhay, infra note 21.

7. The Court did not discuss the possibility of an equal protection claim, but the tenor of the opinion suggests that the same result would be reached under the equal protection clause. See also note 8 infra.

ent in kind from fines or the mere threat of imprisonment"—was not altered by the fact that the misdemeanor involved here carried a potential punishment that took it beyond the petty offense category. The Court also noted that the actual imprisonment standard "had proved reasonably workable, whereas any extension would create confusion and impose unpredictable, but necessarily substantial, costs in 50 quite diverse states." [8]

Scott was a 5–4 decision, with Justice Powell noting that he had joined the majority opinion only to provide "clear guidance" to the lower courts. In *Argersinger,* he had concurred separately, arguing for an automatic right to appointed counsel for offenses carrying a constitutional right to jury trial, and for a flexible case-by-case adjudication of the need for appointed counsel in petty offense cases. Justice Powell had urged consideration of a series of factors in petty offense cases, including the complexity of the offense, the probable sentence, the competency of the individual to represent himself, and the "attitude of the community" toward the particular crime. Under this approach, a right to appointed counsel would not automatically exist (or not exist) in either imprisonment or non-imprisonment petty offense cases. The close division in *Scott,* combined with Justice Powell's reluctant concurrence, held open the possibility that the Court might require appointment of counsel, relying upon a due process analysis, in a particularly compelling non-imprisonment case. However, subsequent due process opinions referred to the loss of liberty as a key element in establishing a due process right to appointed counsel,[9] and later cases building upon *Argersinger* have focused solely upon the actual imprisonment standard.[10] Of course, states have the option of providing appointed counsel for all misdemeanor defendants and many states follow that policy (at least where the misdemeanors are not punishable only by fine).

(b) Right to Appointed Counsel: Stages of the Proceeding. The Sixth Amendment right to appointed counsel applies only to "critical stages" in the criminal prosecution. There is no need for the assistance of appointed counsel unless the "substantial rights of the accused may be affected" by counsel's absence. Since the trial obviously is a critical stage, the key issue under the critical stage test is the characterization of the various pretrial proceedings in a criminal prosecution. Applying that test, the Supreme Court has held that an "accused" has the right to the assistance of counsel at a preliminary hearing,[11] at some pretrial identification procedures (but not others),[12] and when subjected to police or prosecutor efforts to elicit inculpatory statements.[13] The first appearance before a magistrate and the arraignment before the trial judge have also been held to constitute a critical stage where the action or inaction of defendant at that proceeding could later be used against him. Thus, *Hamilton v. Alabama* [14] ruled that an indigent defendant was entitled to appointed counsel at an arraignment where state law viewed defenses not raised at that point as abandoned. Similarly, the Sixth Amendment right was held to apply where the defendant was asked to enter only

8. The petitioner in *Scott* had counsel on appeal and the Court therefore did not have to consider whether the actual imprisonment standard also governs a misdemeanor defendant's constitutional right to counsel on a first appeal of right. Both *Evitts* [§ 11.1(b)] and *Douglas* [§ 11.1(d)] involved felony defendants. See also note 7 supra.

9. See note 12 of § 11.1.

10. Consider e.g., Baldasar v. Illinois, 446 U.S. 222, 100 S.Ct. 1585, 64 L.Ed.2d 169 (1980), holding that an uncounseled misdemeanor conviction (valid under *Scott* because the sentence imposed had not included imprisonment) could not later be used under an enhanced penalty provision to obtain an additional term of imprisonment on a subsequent charge. In *Baldasar,* the four *Scott* dissenters noted their continued disagreement with that ruling, but looked only to the imprisonment consequence in assessing the constitutional right under *Scott.* Four dissenting justices, in an opinion by Justice Powell, looked to the same factor, but concluded that *Scott* should not bar use of the conviction because imprisonment under an enhancement provision was not truly imprisonment for the earlier offense.

11. See § 14.2(a). See also § 12.1(e) (discussing right at bail hearing).

12. See § 7.3(a) (right applies to lineup or show-up, occurring after the initiation of prosecution, but not at procedures more readily challenged at trial, such as the taking of a blood sample).

13. See § 6.4. See also § 21.3(a) (right to counsel during plea bargaining).

14. 368 U.S. 52, 82 S.Ct. 157, 7 L.Ed.2d 114 (1961).

a non-binding plea at the first appearance, but his non-binding plea of guilty, though later withdrawn, could still be used against him at trial.[15]

Of course, no matter how significant the particular proceeding, the Sixth Amendment right does not apply if the proceeding is not part of the "criminal prosecution." The starting point for the criminal prosecution is the initiation of "adversary judicial proceedings." It is at that point that the individual becomes an "accused" person entitled to the application of the Sixth Amendment guarantee. Precisely what constitutes the initiation of adversary judicial proceedings is an issue most frequently raised in connection with Sixth Amendment objections to pretrial investigative procedures in which defendant participated without being afforded counsel. Thus, the issue was discussed previously in this text in connection with lineups and police interrogation.[16] As those discussions indicate, the initiation of adversary judicial proceedings ordinarily requires a formal commitment of the government to prosecute, as evidenced by the filing of charges. This can occur prior to the filing of an indictment or information, as where the defendant is brought before the magistrate for an "arraignment" or "first appearance" on charges filed in the form of a complaint. In *United States v. Gouveia,*[17] the Court reaffirmed, however, that a person has not become an accused for Sixth Amendment purposes simply because he has been detained by the government with the intention of filing charges against him. This was so even though the detention there, in contrast to the typical arrest, was not of the type where the state would be required to take the detainee before a magistrate with reasonable promptness (and there either file charges or release him).[18]

Once started, the criminal prosecution continues through at least to the end of the basic trial stage, including sentencing. In the course of ruling upon due process and equal protection claims, *Douglas v. California, Ross v. Moffitt,* and *Evitts v. Lucey* clearly indicated that the "criminal prosecution" has ended where the defendant is pursuing an appeal from his conviction.[19] The status of post-trial proceedings before the trial judge that also challenge the conviction is less clear. The answer may depend, in part, upon the nature of issues presented. If the proceeding involves no more than an extension of a trial ruling, and occurs shortly after trial, as in a post-verdict motion for judgment of acquittal, it should be treated as subject to the Sixth Amendment. On the other hand, a motion for a new trial based on new evidence, which can occur months after the conviction, might be treated as closer to a collateral attack, which clearly is outside the criminal prosecution.[20]

While timing is a significant factor in assessing post-trial proceedings in the trial court, it is not necessarily conclusive. Thus, a probation revocation proceeding that occurred months after defendant's conviction was held to be a part of the criminal prosecution where that proceeding involved the setting of the defendant's basic prison term for the crime.

15. White v. Maryland, 373 U.S. 59, 83 S.Ct. 1050, 10 L.Ed.2d 193 (1963).

16. See §§ 6.4(c), 7.3(b).

17. 467 U.S. 180, 104 S.Ct. 2292, 81 L.Ed.2d 146 (1984).

18. The defendants in *Gouveia* were prison inmates who had been assigned to a special Administrative Detention Unit (ADU) on suspicion that they were responsible for the murder of a fellow inmate. A disciplinary hearing was held shortly thereafter, with the prison officials concluding that defendants had participated in the murder. The defendants remained in the ADU for a substantial period thereafter (19 months in one case) before they were indicted and counsel appointed. They claimed that the government's failure to honor their request for appointment of counsel during their confinement in the ADU constituted a violation of their Sixth Amendment right to counsel. The Court of Appeals sustained their claim. It reasoned that, in prison cases, there existed a substantial possibility that the government might delay the initiation of formal charges, resulting in the loss of evidence that could have been preserved through the preindictment investigation of appointed counsel. The Supreme Court acknowledged that the concern of the Court of Appeals was legitimate, but concluded that it was a concern met by other procedural protections (the statute of limitations and the due process protection against prejudicial delay in bringing charges, see § 18.5), rather than the Sixth Amendment right to counsel.

19. See § 11.1(c), (d).

20. See Pennsylvania v. Finley, § 11.1 at note 18.

In that case, *Mempa v. Rhay*,[21] the trial judge had placed the defendant on probation without fixing the term of imprisonment that would be imposed if probation were later revoked. The Court concluded that the subsequent determination and imposition of a prison sentence at the probation revocation proceeding was as much a part of the criminal prosecution as the sentencing of a defendant immediately after trial. In contrast to *Mempa, Gagnon v. Scarpelli*[22] held that a probation revocation hearing was not part of the criminal prosecution when a prison sentence had previously been imposed but then suspended in favor of probation. The only issue presented in such a hearing is whether to revoke probation, and that determination is based on defendant's subsequent conduct rather than the commission of the original offense.

Of course, even though a proceeding is not part of the criminal prosecution, there may still be a right to appointed counsel drawn from a constitutional provision other than the Sixth Amendment. Thus, *Douglas* and *Evitts* established an equal protection and due process right to appointed counsel on a first appeal provided as a matter of right, and *Gagnon* established a due process right to appointed counsel under special circumstances in a probation or parole revocation proceeding.[23] On the other hand, the Court has held that the state has no constitutional obligation to appoint counsel to assist a defendant in preparing an application for second-level discretionary review or a petition for postconviction relief through habeas corpus or other collateral proceeding.[24] It has not had occasion to consider whether those rulings apply as well to the defendant whose application for discretionary review has been granted or whose postconviction petition has sufficient merit to require a hearing. The universal practice is to appoint counsel at that point in the appellate or postconviction proceeding.

In many states, as a matter of local practice, appointed counsel also are provided in various settings where the indigent clearly does not have a constitutional right to appointed counsel. Numerous states furnish indigents with counsel in all probation and parole revocation hearings, without regard to the special circumstances test of *Gagnon.* States often expect counsel appointed for the first appeal to assist defendants in preparing timely applications for subsequent discretionary review within the state judicial system. The Supreme Court does not provide counsel for defendants preparing petitions for certiorari, but state and federal public defenders will carry through their representation to include the certiorari petition where warranted. Undoubtedly, the stage at which the state is least likely to provide counsel is in the preparation of postconviction relief petitions by noncapital defendants. Yet some states do provide attorneys to prepare such petitions, and various state correctional systems utilize attorneys who serve as legal advisors to prisoners in their preparation of pro se petitions. Many commentators have argued that providing counsel in all such settings serves in the end to conserve judicial and prosecutorial resources by promoting prompt resolution of all possible claims. Responding to such a contention in *Murray v. Giarratano*,[25] Chief Justice Rehnquist's plurality opinion noted that its correctness "as a matter of policy" was "by no means self-evident," and in any event, "this 'mother knows best' approach should play no part in traditional constitutional adjudication." The dissenters found persuasive, however, the fact that so many states had done with seemingly little inconvenience what the state of Virginia had failed to do.

(c) The *Anders* Rules. Representing the defendant at trial, the attorney violates no obligation of professional responsibility in forcing the state to prove its case, no matter how clear the defendant's guilt.[26] The defen-

21. 389 U.S. 128, 88 S.Ct. 254, 19 L.Ed.2d 336 (1967).

22. See § 11.1 at note 9.

23. See §§ 11.1(b), 11.1(d).

24. See Ross v. Moffitt, Pennsylvania v. Finley, and Murray v. Giarratano, discussed in § 11.1(b).

25. See § 11.1 at note 19.

26. See ABA Model Rules of Professional Conduct, Rule 3.1: "A lawyer shall not bring or defend a proceeding, or assert or controvert an issue therein, unless there is a basis for doing so that is not frivolous, which includes

dant has a right to require the state to prove guilt consistent with applicable legal standards and is entitled to the competent representation of counsel in this regard. On appeal, on the other hand, the defendant is presenting the challenge and the lawyer has an ethical obligation not to assert frivolous claims.[27] In *Anders v. California,*[28] the Supreme Court was required to resolve the potential tension between that professional obligation and the indigent defendant's constitutional right to appointed counsel on first appeal of right. At issue was a California procedure that allowed appointed counsel to withdraw, following counsel's review of the record and consultation with the defendant, upon "conscientiously concluding * * * that there are no meritorious grounds for appeal." Under that procedure, counsel sent a conclusory "no merit" letter to the appellate court, the court then reviewed the record and considered any contrary statement filed by the defendant, withdrawal was allowed upon the court's determination that counsel's conclusion was "correct," and the appeal then proceeded without appointment of other counsel (and without oral argument). The Supreme Court unanimously agreed that defendant's constitutional right to appointed counsel did not preclude withdrawal where (i) counsel, after "conscientious investigation," concludes that the appeal is "frivolous" and (ii) the appellate court "is satisfied that counsel has diligently investigated the possible grounds of appeal, and agrees with counsel's evaluation of the case." However, the *Anders* majority also found that the withdrawal procedure utilized in California failed to provide satisfactory safeguards against undermining the defendant's constitutional right to counsel. Not only was there confusion as to whether the appellate court's finding of "no merit" constituted a "finding of frivolity," but that finding had been made without the "full consideration" that is obtained when counsel is "acting in the role of an advocate."

To ensure that the withdrawal procedure is in accord with defendant's constitutional right, the *Anders* majority set forth what was later described as a "prophylactic framework" for allowing withdrawal.[29] That framework had four elements: (1) after a "conscientious examination" of the appeal, counsel must determine that it is "wholly frivolous" and "so advise the court and request permission to withdraw;" (2) "that request must be accompanied by a brief referring to anything in the record that might arguably support the appeal;" (3) "a copy of counsel's brief should be furnished the indigent [defendant] and time allowed him to raise any points that he chooses;" and (4) the appellate court, "after a full examination of all the proceedings," must find that "the case is wholly frivolous."

Several states, rather than adopt the *Anders* procedure, have simply barred withdrawals and required appointed counsel to file a brief on the merits, whether or not counsel views the appeal as frivolous.[30] Among the majority that continue to allow withdrawals, the courts have varied in their response to what has been described as the *Anders* dilemma—how does counsel, after concluding that the case is "unbriefable" (and that withdrawal is therefore required), then prepare a brief referring to anything in the record "that might arguably support the appeal"? Some courts have stated that counsel must present the possible defense contentions strictly as a

a good faith argument for an extension, modification or reversal of existing law. *A lawyer for the defendant in a criminal proceeding, or the respondent in a proceeding that could result in incarceration, may nevertheless so defend the proceeding as to require that every element of the case be established*". (Emphasis added).

27. See note 26 supra.

28. 386 U.S. 738, 87 S.Ct. 1396, 18 L.Ed.2d 493 (1967).

29. Pennsylvania v. Finley, § 11.1 at note 18 (also noting that this "prophylactic framework * * * is relevant when, and only when, a litigant has a previously established constitutional right to counsel," and therefore *Anders* did not govern the withdrawal by appointed counsel in a postconviction relief proceeding).

30. Courts supporting this position argue that: (1) a defendant is prejudiced by an improper motion to withdraw even if rejected by the appellate court; (2) an improper motion requires a substitution of new counsel, which is costly; (3) "as long as counsel must research and prepare an advocate's brief, he or she might as well submit it for the purposes of an ordinary appeal"; and (4) the avoidance of a double review in cases in which the appeal is not frivolous results in a savings of time and effort for the reviewing court.

positive advocate, "leaving it to us to determine whether and to what extent they have merit." Other courts have held that counsel should present, along with a statement of the strongest possible arguments for the contentions, a brief explanation of the contrary authority that led counsel to conclude that the contentions were frivolous. This procedure was held to be consistent with *Anders* in *McCoy v. Court of Appeals of Wisconsin.*[31] The Supreme Court reasoned that requiring counsel to cite contrary authority could further the interests underlying *Anders* by providing an additional safeguard against attorneys concluding that an appeal is frivolous without diligent research. The basic function of the *Anders* brief, it was noted, was not to serve as "a substitute for an advocate's brief," but to ensure "that counsel had been diligent in examining the record for meritorious issues and that the appeal is frivolous." Thus, just as *Anders* had concluded that "an attorney can advise the court of his or her conclusion that an appeal is frivolous without impairment of the client's fundamental rights," it should follow that "no constitutional deprivation occurs when the attorney explains the basis for that conclusion."

(d) Transcripts. *Griffin v. Illinois*[32] spawned a long line of Supreme Court and lower court cases dealing with the indigent defendant's right to a transcript provided at state expense. The courts have had no difficulty in extending *Griffin,* which dealt with a trial transcript to be used in presenting an appeal, to transcripts of other proceedings and to other uses of transcripts.[33] Thus, the Supreme Court has held that the "*Griffin* principle" applies to requests for a trial transcript to be used in a collateral attack upon a conviction, for a transcript of a habeas proceeding to be used on appeal from a denial of habeas relief, for a transcript of a habeas proceeding to be used in filing a second habeas petition, and for a transcript of a preliminary hearing to be used in preparing for trial. The Court has also noted, however, that the defendant is not entitled to a transcript simply because he is indigent and might have some use for a transcript. The need for the transcript must reach a level sufficient to impose an equal protection obligation upon the state, and the assessment of that level has frequently produced a division among the justices.

Transcripts for use on appeal have generally been required where a transcript was the usual and apparently preferable means of presenting a claim of the type urged by the indigent defendant. The Court has not been so willing to assume that a transcript is necessary, however, where it is desired simply for use in preparing for trial. Thus, in *Britt v. North Carolina,*[34] a divided Supreme Court upheld a state court's refusal to grant defendant a transcript of his first trial, which had ended in a mistrial, as there was available "an informal alternative which appears to be substantially equivalent." The Court noted that the same counsel had represented defendant at the first trial, only a month before, and that the court reporter would at any time have read back to counsel his notes of that trial.[35]

Assuming that a transcript is needed to present a particular claim, may a jurisdiction condition its obligation to provide that transcript on a preliminary judicial finding that the claim has possible merit? In *Eskridge v. Washington State Board,*[36] the Supreme Court struck down a state provision directing a trial

31. 486 U.S. 429, 108 S.Ct. 1895, 100 L.Ed.2d 440 (1988).

32. See § 11.1 at note 28.

33. *Griffin* has also been held to exempt indigent defendants from filing fees in proceedings challenging their convictions. See Burns v. Ohio, 360 U.S. 252, 79 S.Ct. 1164, 3 L.Ed.2d 1209 (1959) (fees for appeals); Smith v. Bennett, 365 U.S. 708, 81 S.Ct. 895, 6 L.Ed.2d 39 (1961) (fees for postconviction proceedings).

34. 404 U.S. 226, 92 S.Ct. 431, 30 L.Ed.2d 400 (1971).

35. The Court added that it was not suggesting that reliance on the memories of the defendant and defense counsel was itself an adequate alternative. See also Roberts v. LaVallee, 389 U.S. 40, 88 S.Ct. 194, 19 L.Ed.2d 41 (1967) (requiring a transcript of a preliminary hearing at which the major state witnesses had testified, though defendant and his counsel had both been present at the preliminary hearing and defendant had received a transcript of the grand jury testimony of those witnesses).

36. 357 U.S. 214, 78 S.Ct. 1061, 2 L.Ed.2d 1269 (1958).

judge to furnish a free transcript for use on appeal only upon finding that, "in his opinion, justice will thereby be promoted." The state then revised its procedure to condition the furnishing of the transcript on a finding of "non-frivolity," but a closely divided (5–4) Supreme Court held that this narrower standard still resulted in a denial of equal protection.[37] The majority noted that the indigent defendant was subjected to a "predictable finding of frivolity" by the same judge who had presided at his trial, which was followed by appellate review of that finding by a court that lacked a sufficiently complete record to accurately assess the trial court's brief description of the trial. However, in *United States v. MacCollom,*[38] a closely divided (5–4) Court upheld a federal statute allowing a free trial transcript to a prisoner challenging his conviction on collateral attack only upon a judicial certification that the prisoner's asserted claim is "not frivolous" and that the transcript is "needed to decide the issue." A plurality opinion for four justices stressed that the petitioner's equal protection claim must be judged in light of all of the avenues that had been made available to him. Under federal law, he would have had an unconditional right to a free transcript upon direct appeal, but he chose to forego that opportunity. The basic question was one of "access to procedures for review," and the statute's minimal requirements for furnishing transcripts in often long delayed collateral proceedings were consistent with the government's obligation to provide such access. The plurality opinion added that the prisoner had advanced only a "naked allegation of ineffective counsel," and suggested that his claim might well not have been deemed frivolous if it had been supported by some concrete factual allegations.[39]

(e) Assistance of Experts. Just a few years before its ruling in *Griffin,* the Supreme Court held in *United States ex rel. Smith v. Baldi* [40] that an indigent defendant had not been denied due process by a state court's failure to appoint a private psychiatrist to assist defense counsel in presenting an insanity defense. *Baldi* 's quite brief discussion of the appointed expert issue was, however, tied closely to the circumstances of that case; the trial court there had relied upon the testimony of an independent psychiatric expert, called as the court's own witness, and the defense had been able to call two other psychiatrists to testify as to its claim. In *Ake v. Oklahoma,*[41] the Supreme Court reassessed the psychiatric assistance issue, noting that in light of *Griffin* and *Gideon,* it was "not limited by [*Smith*] in considering whether fundamental fairness today requires a different result."

Ake held that, "when a defendant has made a preliminary showing that his sanity at the time of the offense is likely to be a significant factor at trial, due process requires that a State provide access to a psychiatrist's assistance on this issue, if the defendant cannot otherwise afford one." [42] The Court majority stressed that its ruling was limited to cases in which the defendant's mental condition was

37. Draper v. Washington, 372 U.S. 487, 83 S.Ct. 774, 9 L.Ed.2d 899 (1963).

38. 426 U.S. 317, 96 S.Ct. 2086, 48 L.Ed.2d 666 (1976).

39. Justice Blackmun, providing the fifth vote for affirmance, stressed the lack of any statement of "articulable facts" in the petitioner's claim that would suggest "that a transcript would assist him in his § 2255 proceeding." Since petitioner therefore apparently had a "*current* opportunity to present his claim fairly" without the transcript, there was "no need [to] consider the constitutional significance of what he might have done at the time a direct appeal from his conviction could have been taken." Of the four dissenting justices, only two relied on constitutional grounds. They argued that the opportunity available on appeal should have no bearing, as the indigent should not be denied a use of collateral attack that was available to nonindigents.

40. 344 U.S. 561, 73 S.Ct. 391, 97 L.Ed. 549 (1953).

41. 470 U.S. 68, 105 S.Ct. 1087, 84 L.Ed.2d 53 (1985).

42. The Court added that in this case psychiatric assistance was also mandated by due process because of defendant's need for such assistance in rebutting the psychiatric evidence presented by the state in the capital sentencing phase of the case. Chief Justice Burger, in a concurring opinion, argued that the "facts of the case" and the "question presented" (which he described as whether the state in a capital case may refuse an indigent defendant "any opportunity whatsoever" to obtain psychiatric assistance) confined the Court's "actual holding" to capital cases. However, the majority opinion did not tie the statement of its holding or its discussion of relevant considerations to capital cases.

"seriously in question." Moreover, the state's obligation did not go beyond providing the defense with the assistance of one competent psychiatrist, and it could provide that psychiatrist as it saw fit (i.e., the defendant's constitutional right did not include the authority "to choose a psychiatrist of his personal liking or to receive funds to hire his own"). The Court noted that it had never held that "a State must purchase for the indigent all the assistance that his wealthier counterpart might buy," but due process did require that the indigent defendant be given the "basic tools" needed to present his defense. Taking into consideration the defendant's interest "in the accuracy of the criminal proceeding," the limited financial burden that would be imposed upon the state under the proposed standard, and the probable value of psychiatric assistance in presenting an insanity defense, a court appointed psychiatrist clearly was such a "basic tool." [43]

Although the *Ake* opinion was limited to psychiatric assistance, earlier lower court opinions had employed a similar analysis to require the state to provide the indigent defendant with other types of expert assistance (e.g., ballistic experts) where needed to effectively present a defense. Contrary to the position generally taken with respect to transcripts, and consistent with *Ake*'s requirement that the defendant make a preliminary showing that his sanity would be a significant issue at trial, the lower courts have uniformly held that the constitutional right to the assistance of state-paid experts requires an initial defense showing of particularized need. Thus, in seeking the assistance of an expert in scientific analysis (e.g., ballistics), the defendant must show that "a substantial question exists over an issue requiring expert testimony for its resolution" and that the "defendant's position cannot be fully developed without professional assistance." Establishing sufficient need for a special investigator appears to be especially difficult, perhaps because it is assumed that investigation of the facts is ordinarily within the expertise of counsel.[44]

(f) The *Bounds* Right of Access. Although not limited to challenges to convictions or tied to indigency, the right of access recognized in *Bounds v. Smith* [45] provides a major avenue of assistance for indigent defendants. For those defendants who are incarcerated, the state under *Bounds* assumes a special obligation to facilitate at least their constitutional challenges to their convictions. That obligation had its seed in a line of cases which held unconstitutional state interference with prisoner efforts to present constitutional claims to the courts. *Ex parte Hull* [46] struck down a prison authority practice of advance screening of inmate federal habeas petitions so as to allow only those "properly drawn" petitions to be forwarded to the designated court. The necessary quality and content of habeas petitions, the Supreme Court noted, "are questions for [the habeas] court alone." *Johnson v. Avery* [47] later held unconstitutional a prison regulation that forbade prison inmates from seeking assistance from other inmates in preparing legal documents, including habeas corpus applications. The effect of the regulation, the Court noted, was to deny illiterate or poorly educated prisoners the opportunity to exercise their right to utilize the habeas writ. The state could adopt regulations to prohibit the abuses of "jail-

43. Although the Court did not refer specifically to the alternative of appointing an independent psychiatric expert, as was done in *Smith,* that procedure obviously would not meet the defense's legitimate needs as seen by the Court. In a field in which professional opinions "disagree widely," the defense had a need for its own psychiatric expert "to conduct a professional examination * * *, to help determine whether the insanity defense is viable, to present testimony, and to assist in preparing cross-examination of a state's psychiatric witness."

44. A substantial number of jurisdictions have adopted statutory provisions authorizing the appointment of a wide range of experts to assist appointed counsel. Many are modeled after 18 U.S.C.A. § 3006A(e)(1), which provides for "investigative, expert, or other services" upon a court finding that the particular service is "necessary for an adequate defense." Such provisions are frequently interpreted as requiring a less stringent showing of particularized need than might be required under a constitutional right to an expert's assistance.

45. 430 U.S. 817, 97 S.Ct. 1491, 52 L.Ed.2d 72 (1977).

46. 312 U.S. 546, 61 S.Ct. 640, 85 L.Ed. 1034 (1941).

47. 393 U.S. 483, 89 S.Ct. 747, 21 L.Ed.2d 718 (1969).

house lawyering" (e.g., demands for consideration), but it could not ban the practice altogether unless it provided some other source of assistance for those prisoners unable to proceed on their own. *Wolff v. McDonnell*[48] held that the non-interference principle announced in *Hull* and *Johnson v. Avery* applied as well to prisoners desiring to press claims under the federal Civil Rights Act. "The right of access," the Court noted, extends beyond the inmate's challenge to his confinement: it "assures that no person will be denied the opportunity to present to the judiciary allegations concerning violations of fundamental constitutional rights."

In *Bounds,* the issue presented was whether the state had a constitutional obligation to supply inmates with an adequate library or some alternative state-supported legal assistance program. The prison authorities contended that the previous access cases did no more than prohibit unreasonable restrictions interfering with "inmate communications on legal problems." The state, they argued, had "no further obligation to expend state funds to implement affirmatively the right of access."[49] Rejecting that contention, Justice Marshall's opinion for the *Bounds* majority noted that the "cost of protecting a constitutional right cannot justify its denial." The Court had not hesitated to impose economic burdens upon the states in cases such as *Griffin, Gideon,* and *Douglas.* So too, it was "undisputable that indigent inmates must be provided at state expense with paper and pen to draft legal documents, with notarial services to authenticate them, and with stamps to mail them." A right of access implicitly required "meaningful access," and therefore the critical issue was "whether law libraries or other forms of legal assistance are needed to give prisoners a reasonably adequate opportunity to present claimed violations of fundamental constitutional rights to the courts." Since lawyers could not prepare petitions without adequate libraries, the same would obviously be true for the prisoner proceeding pro se.

Justice Marshall stressed that the Court was leaving the states with considerable flexibility in meeting their constitutional obligation. It demanded only that prison authorities provide "adequate libraries or adequate assistance from persons trained in law." While libraries were "one constitutionally acceptable method to assure meaningful access," the state was not foreclosed from using "alternative means to achieve that goal." Numerous states were already providing "some degree of professional or quasi-professional legal assistance to prisoners" under programs that took "many imaginative forms." These included the training of inmates as paralegal assistants to work under lawyers' supervision, and the use of paraprofessionals and law students in clinical programs. Justice Marshall added that a "legal access program need not include any particular element we have discussed, and we encourage local experimentation." Any plan would be "evaluated as a whole to ascertain its compliance with constitutional standards."

Lower courts evaluating state inmate-assistance programs in light of *Bounds* soon learned of the limitations of even the most adequate law library. A substantial portion of the inmate population tends to be "functionally illiterate" and therefore unable to make even minimal use of library materials. Other prisoners, confined in segregated secur-

48. 418 U.S. 539, 94 S.Ct. 2963, 41 L.Ed.2d 935 (1974).

49. Justice Rehnquist's dissent basically agreed with this position, noting that the previous cases "depend on the principle that the State, having already incarcerated the convict and thereby virtually eliminated his contact with people outside the prison walls, may not further limit contacts which would otherwise be permitted simply because such contacts would aid the incarcerated prisoner in preparation of a petition seeking judicial relief from conditions or terms of his confinement." Chief Justice Burger, also in dissent, noted that the state may have an obligation to expend resources to support a constitutional right, as evidenced by its "Eighth Amendment obligation to provide its inmates with food, shelter, and medical care," but the right to pursue federal habeas and civil rights actions were clearly distinguishable as resting on no more than the federal statutes creating those remedies. The third dissenter, Justice Stewart, maintained that if the majority was correct in its assumption of a state duty to provide meaningful access, then that obligation could "seldom be realistically advanced by the device of making law libraries available to inmates untutored in their use."

ity units, must specially request specific books, which can then be used only in their cells. Some lower courts, looking to the *Bounds* characterization of the library as "one acceptable method" of meeting the state's obligation, have refused to order additional assistance. The Court in *Bounds* surely had not been unaware of the illiteracy and security problems when it spoke of the library and legal assistance programs as acceptable "alternatives." Other lower courts, stressing the *Bounds* requirement that access be "adequate, effective, and meaningful," have required the states to go beyond providing an adequate library. Several have directed that such additional assistance include a component of state-provided attorneys.

Part of the difficulty faced by the lower courts in applying *Bounds* has been the Court's failure to set forth clearly the constitutional underpinning of the State's obligation to facilitate meaningful access to the courts. The Court has most frequently described the right of access as a due process right, but it also has cited equal protection cases in its rulings and some justices have characterized the right as "an aspect of equal protection." From the perspective of a due process analysis, the Court has failed to specifically identify the elements weighed in assessing the state's obligation, apart from characterizing access to the courts as a protected liberty interest.[50] From an equal protection perspective, it has failed to identify the element that produces an unconstitutional classification in the state's failure to provide inmate-assistance. Undoubtedly, a critical feature under either analysis is the burden imposed upon the access right as a result of the individual's incarceration. For there was no suggestion in *Bounds* or any other access ruling that a similar level of assistance must be afforded the individual who is not incarcerated and desires to pursue a fundamental constitutional claim in the courts (e.g., a parolee who seeks through federal habeas corpus to challenge his conviction or through a civil rights action to present a constitutional claim against the parole agency). Incarceration undoubtedly takes from the individual various avenues for pursuing legal claims that are potentially available to the non-prisoner; the prison inmate is isolated from possible sources of free legal assistance, severely limited in his capacity to gain sufficient assets to hire a lawyer, and unable to travel freely and thereby take advantage of other possible resources (including libraries and personal fact-gathering). Whether *Bounds* required the state to offset all of these restrictions is unclear. The constitutional acceptability of incarceration carries with it the recognition that the prisoner will be in a disadvantaged position in exercising various constitutional rights, and correctional authorities have never been held to have an obligation to provide inmates with the resources that would place them on an even keel with non-prisoners even as to the exercise of those constitutionally protected liberties that are not inherently inconsistent with confinement. Moreover, even should the state have an obligation to produce substantial equivalency, that would not necessarily require it to offset the limitations of the individual (e.g., indigency and illiteracy) that presumably would restrict his capacity to exercise his right of access even if he were not incarcerated.

In the post-*Bounds* decisions of *Murray v. Giarratano* [51] the Court cast some light on the scope of *Bounds,* rendering a decision clearly inconsistent with the broader readings of *Bounds* adopted by some lower courts. The majority there rejected the contention that *Bounds* required the appointment of counsel

50. Even here, the exact scope of that interest is not without ambiguity. Earlier cases such as *Wolff,* supra note 48, spoke of a right of access to present constitutional claims. In *Bounds,* Justice Marshall repeatedly spoke simply of "the right of prisoners to access to the courts," although the issue there presented was described as whether libraries were needed to give prisoners a reasonable opportunity "to present claimed violations of fundamental constitutional rights to the courts." Justice Powell, explaining his concurrence in Justice Marshall's opinion for the Court, described the Court's "decision" as recognizing "that a prison inmate has a constitutional right of access to the courts to assert such procedural and substantive rights as may be available to him under state and federal law."

51. See § 11.1 at note 19.

to assist death row inmates in preparing habeas petitions challenging their capital convictions. The Court had earlier indicated in *Pennsylvania v. Finley* that neither due process nor equal protection requires the appointment of counsel to assist a prisoner in preparing a petition for postconviction relief.[52] The *Murray* Court was sharply divided as to whether the special circumstances presented by the death row inmates distinguished *Finley.* There was general agreement, however, as noted in Justice Stevens dissent, that "far from creating a discrete constitutional right, *Bounds* constitutes one part of a jurisprudence that encompasses 'right to counsel' as well as 'access to courts' cases." Thus, where the Court has held that an indigent defendant has no constitutional right to counsel, the "meaningful access" requirement of *Bounds* will not require that counsel be provided to the inmate defendant in the same procedural setting. The thrust of this position can readily be carried over also to reject other forms of legal assistance if the library is adequate—although the division of the Court in *Murray* might suggest an exception for the death row inmate.[53]

(g) Indigency Standards. Supreme Court opinions speak generally of the rights of an "indigent defendant" without offering any specific definition of "indigency." State and federal appellate courts have filled this vacuum by developing a series of guidelines for determining indigency, although studies suggest that magistrates and trial judges often tend to create their own individual standards without regard to those guidelines. The appellate courts agree that indigency is not a synonym for "destitute." A defendant may have income and assets yet still be unable to bear the cost of an adequate defense. Among the factors to be considered in evaluating the individual's financial capacity are: (1) income from employment and such governmental programs as social security and unemployment compensation; (2) real and personal property; (3) number of dependents; (4) outstanding debts; (5) seriousness of the charge (which suggests the likely fee of a retained attorney); and (6) other legal expenses (such as bail bond). While a defendant may be required to liquidate certain assets, he should not be asked to give up basic necessities, such as a comparatively inexpensive automobile needed for his employment.

Indigency is assessed by reference to the defendant's current status, not his earnings potential over some substantial future period. The state may seek to tap the defendant's future earnings, however, through the adoption of a recoupment program. Under such a program, an indigent defendant will be required to reimburse the state for counsel, transcript, and similar costs if his financial resources subsequently reach a level permitting reimbursement without undue hardship. Recoupment programs are directed primarily at defendants who are "temporarily indigent" (e.g., college students) or who just barely qualify as indigents. In *Fuller v. Oregon,*[54] the Supreme Court upheld a recoupment program that applied to those indigent defendants who were subsequently convicted. The Court concluded that the distinction drawn between convicted and acquitted defendants "reflect[ed] no more than an effort to achieve fundamental fairness" and therefore did not violate the equal protection guarantee.[55] The Court also rejected the contention that recoupment imposed a substantial burden on the indigent's right to appointed counsel and would therefore "chill" the exercise of that right. A defendant "who is just above the

52. See § 11.1 at note 18.

53. See the discussion of Justice Kennedy's limited concurrence in Murray v. Giarratano in § 11.1 following note 19.

54. 417 U.S. 40, 94 S.Ct. 2116, 40 L.Ed.2d 642 (1974).

55. Compare Rinaldi v. Yeager, 384 U.S. 305, 86 S.Ct. 1497, 16 L.Ed.2d 577 (1966) (holding unconstitutional a recoupment program requiring reimbursement only from those defendants sentenced to prison; distinguishing between imprisoned defendants and other convicted defendants sentenced only to probation or payment of a fine constitutes "invidious discrimination"); James v. Strange, 407 U.S. 128, 92 S.Ct. 2027, 32 L.Ed.2d 600 (1972) (equal protection denied by a recoupment statute that did not make available to indigent defendants restrictions on wage garnishment and other protective exemptions that were allowed to civil judgment debtors generally, including debtors subject to recoupment laws relating to other forms of public assistance).

line separating the indigent from the non-indigent," the Court noted, is also subjected to "considerable financial hardship in retaining a lawyer." The Constitution does not require that "those only slightly poorer must remain forever immune from any [similar] obligation to shoulder the expense of their legal defense."

§ 11.3 Waiver of the Right to Counsel

(a) General Requirements. Just as the doctrinal foundation of the right to counsel may change with the different stages of the criminal process, what is required for a valid waiver may also vary with the stage at which waiver occurs. Thus, the standards for a waiver of counsel in the course of a police investigation differ in certain respects from the standards governing a waiver in a judicial proceeding. A judge accepting a waiver at trial, for example, may be required to conduct a type of inquiry as to the defendant's state of mind that simply would not be feasible for a police officer accepting a waiver prior to custodial interrogation. The requisites for a valid waiver in the course of investigatory procedures have been discussed in previous chapters.[1] Our focus in this section is upon waivers in judicial proceedings, particularly at trial.

While the standards governing waiver vary with the nature of the proceeding, there are several general principles that apply to all waivers of the right to counsel. To be valid, a waiver of counsel must be made "knowingly and intelligently." There must be "an intentional relinquishment or abandonment of a known right or privilege." Moreover, the Supreme Court has many times warned the lower courts against "lightly assum[ing]" that the defendant has this state of mind. It has in fact directed those courts to "indulge in every reasonable presumption against waiver." Consistent with this approach, a waiver may not be presumed from a "silent record"; the evidence must show that the defendant was informed specifically of his right to the assistance of appointed or retained counsel and that he clearly rejected such assistance. "No amount of circumstantial evidence that the person may have been aware of his right will suffice to stand" in place of a specific notification of rights.

(b) Waiver at Trial: The *Von Moltke* Inquiry. Assume that a defendant, having been informed of his right to counsel, states unequivocally that he wishes to proceed without counsel. Is that sufficient to establish that his waiver was made "intelligently" as well as knowingly? While it may be enough for a waiver in the course of police investigatory procedures, an acceptable waiver before the trial court ordinarily requires considerably more. In *Von Moltke v. Gillies,*[2] Mr. Justice Black, in a four-justice plurality opinion, maintained that the trial court was constitutionally obligated to undertake a "thorough inquiry," ensuring that the accused has made an informed decision. Justice Black noted:

> This protecting duty imposes the serious and weighty responsibility upon the trial judge of determining whether there is an intelligent and competent waiver by the accused. To discharge this duty properly in light of the strong presumption against waiver * * *, a judge must investigate as long and as thoroughly as the circumstances of the case before him demand. * * * To be valid such waiver [of counsel] must be made with an apprehension of the nature of the charges, the statutory offenses included within them, the range of allowable punishments thereunder, possible defenses to the charges and circumstances in mitigation thereof,[3] and all other facts essen-

§ 11.3

1. See §§ 6.4(f), 6.9, 7.3(d).

2. 332 U.S. 708, 68 S.Ct. 316, 92 L.Ed. 309 (1948).

3. Precisely what Justice Black meant to include in this reference to possible defenses and mitigating circumstances is unclear. It seems unlikely that he meant to require a more substantial advisement than is traditionally given prior to acceptance of a guilty plea. *Von Moltke* itself involved a waiver of counsel prior to the entry of a guilty plea and Justice Black's opinion is sometime criticized as merging the requirements for waiving counsel with those for pleading guilty. Where defendant seeks to waive counsel and enter a guilty plea, the inquiry demanded in the acceptance of a plea also applies. See § 21.4. Where the defendant seeks to waive counsel and proceed to trial representing himself, the additional warnings required for pro se representation

tial to a broad understanding of the whole matter. A judge can make certain that an accused's professed waiver of counsel is understandingly and wisely made only from a penetrating and comprehensive examination of all the circumstances.

Perhaps because the *Von Moltke* opinion reflected only a plurality position, lower courts generally have rejected the view that a waiver, to be constitutionally valid, must emerge from a colloquy between trial judge and defendant covering every factor specified by Justice Black. They have perceived his list "as a catalog of concerns for trial court consideration," rather than "as a prescribed litany of questions and answers leading to mandatory reversal in the event that one or more is omitted." The lower courts have frequently noted that an "in-depth inquiry" covering all of the items specified in *Von Moltke* is to be "preferred," but they have also upheld waivers in cases involving very limited inquiries. The critical issue, it has been noted, "is what the defendant understood—not what the court said." Consideration must be given to all of the surrounding circumstances, including not only the statements of the trial judge and defendant, but also the defendant's age, mental condition, and prior experience with the criminal process, previous hearings in the case, and the general nature of the offense charged. Each factor will have a bearing on the other. Where "the background and experience of the defendant on legal matters [is] apparent from the record," the waiver may be sustained notwithstanding a trial judge's failure to explore several of the *Von Moltke* factors. On the other hand, where there is some question as to defendant's mental capacity, or where his statements before the court suggest that he is confused, anything short of a complete *Von Moltke* inquiry is likely to result in the waiver being held invalid.

(c) Forfeiture of the Right. Although commonly described as involving waivers, cases in which defendants have been forced to proceed pro se because they failed to obtain counsel prior to trial are more appropriately characterized as forfeiture cases.[4] In this group of cases, defendants were advised of their right to retain counsel, given ample time to obtain counsel prior to the scheduled trial date, and nevertheless appeared in court on that date without counsel and without a reasonable excuse for having failed to obtain counsel. The courts have characterized defendant's behavior as a waiver "shown by conduct of an unequivocal nature," but it is clear that in some instances the defendant had not intended to relinquish his right to counsel. Also, the trial court in some of these cases had dispensed with even the barest *Von Moltke* inquiry that would be needed for a true waiver. What these courts have held, in effect, is that the state's interest in maintaining an orderly trial schedule and the defendant's negligence, indifference, or possibly purposeful delaying tactic, combined to justify a forfeiture of defendant's right to counsel in much the same way that defendant's disruptive behavior or voluntary absence can result in the forfeiture of his right to be present at trial.[5]

§ 11.4 Choice of Counsel

(a) Judicial Discretion in Selecting Appointed Counsel. Courts generally hold that the initial selection of counsel to represent an indigent is a matter resting within the absolute discretion of the trial court (assuming, of

apply. See § 11.5(c). The discussion here, and presumably the focus in *Von Moltke,* is on the inquiry as to the waiver of counsel in itself, standing apart from those inquiries that attach to a decision (sometimes made contemporaneously and sometimes made later) either to enter a guilty plea or to proceed pro se to trial.

4. The term "forfeiture" is preferred to "waiver" because "waiver" in the context of the right to counsel is generally used to refer to an "intentional relinquishment of a known right," see § 11.3(a). However, courts often use different concepts of "waiver" in conjunction with different rights and different settings, and in other contexts, the term is commonly used to characterize actions comparable to those here described as forfeitures. See e.g., § 10.2(a). Indeed, "constitutional waiver" has been described as a doctrine "as protean in its manifestations as the number of constitutional rights which there are to be waived multiplied by the number of circumstances in which they may be waived." Miller v. Warden, 16 Md. App. 614, 299 A.2d 862 (1973).

5. See § 24.2(b).

course, that appointed counsel is competent).[1] The indigent has no right to counsel of his choice even though that attorney is available and his appointment would not be more costly to the state than the appointment of the attorney that the trial court would otherwise select. The trial court's authority to appoint any competent attorney it chooses, without regard to defendant's preference for another attorney, is said to rest on three grounds. First, judges assume that they can choose a more able attorney than the indigent because they know the abilities of the available local counsel. Second, there is concern that allowing defendant to choose his own attorney will disrupt the "even handed distribution of assignments." Accepting defendant's choice is likely to impose a substantial burden on the more experienced attorneys, as well as give an advantage to repeat offenders, who are most likely to know and select those attorneys. Third, since the Sixth Amendment guarantees the defendant a right only to representation that is competent, and not to that representation that he believes (correctly or not) to be the best, the trial court may value over the defendant's choice the administrative convenience of an appointment system that ignores defendant's preference. Such an appointment system saves time and effort, as the court need not determine the availability and competency of the attorney preferred by defendant, or offer an explanation when that attorney is not selected. Also, the government may reduce its costs by utilizing a public defender agency or contracting with private firms for regular representation of indigents.

(b) Replacement of Appointed Counsel. When an indigent defendant makes a timely and good faith motion requesting that appointed counsel be discharged and new counsel appointed, the trial court clearly has a responsibility to determine the reasons for defendant's dissatisfaction with his current counsel. If the defendant can establish "good cause, such as a conflict of interest, a complete breakdown of communication, or an irreconcilable conflict which [could] lead * * * to an apparently unjust verdict," the court must substitute new counsel.[2] However, the mere loss of confidence in his appointed counsel does not establish "good cause." Defendant must have some well founded reason for believing that the appointed attorney cannot or will not competently represent him. Thus the defendant is not entitled to new counsel simply because he doesn't like the appointed counsel's "attitude," his association with the prosecutor, or his approach on matters of strategy. While ideally a "relationship of trust and confidence" should exist between accused and his attorney, the Sixth Amendment, the Supreme Court has noted, guarantees only competent representation, not "a meaningful attorney-client relationship." [3]

(c) Choice of Retained Counsel. Where defendant has a Sixth Amendment or due

§ 11.4

1. A notable exception to this general rule, Harris v. Superior Court, 19 Cal.3d 786, 140 Cal.Rptr. 318, 567 P.2d 750 (1977), held that a trial court's refusal to appoint requested counsel, who was available and willing to take the appointment, was an abuse of discretion under the special circumstances of that case. Consider also People v. Chavez, 26 Cal.3d 334, 161 Cal.Rptr. 762, 605 P.2d 401 (1980) (noting that the trial court is obligated to explore the defendant's reasons for requesting appointment of a particular attorney, and not all of the special circumstances of *Harris* need be present to require serious consideration of the defendant's request).

2. McKee v. Harris, 649 F.2d 927 (2d Cir.1981). A defendant cannot force the appointment of new counsel, however, by simply refusing to cooperate with his attorney, notwithstanding the attorney's competence and willingness to assist. See United States v. Moore, 706 F.2d 538 (5th Cir.1983). In such a situation, if the attorney is forced to withdraw due to the defendant's non-cooperation, the defendant may be required to proceed pro se. Id.

3. Morris v. Slappy, 461 U.S. 1, 103 S.Ct. 1610, 75 L.Ed.2d 610 (1983). In *Slappy,* the public defender originally assigned to defendant's case was hospitalized for emergency surgery and a replacement was assigned. As the court of appeals read the record, defendant had "timely and in good faith moved for a delay" until the original defender could return to the case. The court of appeals concluded that the denial of this request had violated defendant's "right to a meaningful attorney-client relationship." The Supreme Court held that the court of appeals had (1) misread the record as to the timeliness and purpose of defendant's continuance motion, and (2) erred in concluding that "the Sixth Amendment guarantees an accused a meaningful attorney-client relationship." The majority opinion also stressed the "broad discretion that must be granted trial courts on matters of continuances."

process right to the assistance of counsel, that constitutional guarantee encompasses the "right to retained counsel of his choosing" as an aspect of his " 'right to spend his own money to obtain the advice and assistance * * * of counsel.' "[4] However, since the "essential aim of the [constitutional right to counsel] is to guarantee an effective advocate for each criminal defendant, rather than to ensure that a defendant will inexorably be represented by the lawyer whom he prefers," the right to counsel "of choice" can be circumscribed by a sufficient overriding interest of the judicial system.[5] Where that interest is directed at precluding representation by a particular individual or category of individuals, it usually will be related to preserving fundamental tenets of the adversary system—such as competent representation by counsel, adherence of counsel to the ethical standards of the legal profession, or preserving an appearance of fairness. Common illustrations of instances in which defendant's right to retain counsel of choice is overridden on such grounds include the denial of defendant's choice to be represented by a person who is not a member of the bar, by an attorney who is not licensed in the particular state,[6] and by a former prosecutor who was involved previously in the prosecution of the same or related charges.[7]

In some instances, categorical prohibitions can be utilized by a court to bar defense representation by a particular person. The court need not assess whether representation by that person in this particular instance would be inconsistent in fact with the requirements of the adversary system. Thus, as the Supreme Court has noted, a court may automatically reject representation by a person not a current member of the bar, "regardless of his persuasive powers."[8] In other instances, as illustrated by *Wheat v. United States,*[9] the court must engage in a case-by-case evaluation of the interests at stake. In *Wheat,* as discussed in § 11.9(c), the Supreme Court sustained the trial court's discretion to preclude representation by an attorney who was also representing codefendants, even though the defendant was willing to waive his right to conflict-free counsel. That discretion was subjected to restrictions, however, that required consideration of a variety of factors as they related to the particular case.

The defendant's capacity to retain counsel of choice may also be restricted by judicial action that is not directed at precluding representation by a particular attorney, but nonetheless has that impact. The classic illustration is the scheduling of the trial at a time when defendant's preferred counsel would be unavailable (usually due to a schedule-conflict). While the judicial interest here is not as significant as the interest in preserving fundamental elements of the adversary system, it nonetheless need not give way entirely to the defendant's preference for particular counsel. The right to counsel of one's choice, appellate courts have frequently noted, may not be insisted upon at the expense of the trial court's power to ensure that there is an "orderly disposition of its docket." At the

4. Caplin & Drysdale, Chartered v. United States, 491 U.S. 617, 109 S.Ct. 2646, 105 L.Ed.2d 528 (1989).

5. Wheat v. United States, 486 U.S. 153, 108 S.Ct. 1692, 100 L.Ed.2d 140 (1988).

6. In Leis v. Flynt, 439 U.S. 438, 99 S.Ct. 698, 58 L.Ed.2d 717 (1979), the Court rejected the claim of out-of-state attorneys that a state court's refusal to permit them to represent the defendant violated their constitutional rights. The Court held that the interest of the attorney in being allowed to appear *pro hac vice* did not rise to the level of a "cognizable property or liberty interest within the terms of the Fourteenth Amendment." The Court noted, however, that it was not ruling on whether the constitutional rights of the defendant might be violated by disallowing *pro hac vice* representation, as that claim was not before it. Three dissenting judges rejected "the notion that a state trial judge has arbitrary and unlimited power" to deny such representation, noting that "the client's interest in representation by out-of-state counsel [surely] is entitled to some protection."

7. See ABA Model Rules of Professional Conduct, Rule 1.9(a) (a lawyer who has "formerly represented a client in a matter shall not thereafter * * * represent another person on the same or substantially related matter in which the person's interests are materially adverse to the interests of the former client unless the former client consents after consultation"). The defendant has a corresponding right to disqualify a prosecutor who previously represented the defendant on "the same or a substantially related matter."

8. Wheat v. United States, supra note 5.

9. Supra note 5. See also § 11.9 at note 19.

same time, the appellate courts have also recognized that, under some circumstances, the failure of a trial court to alter its preferred schedule so as to allow defendant to be represented by counsel of choice will result in a constitutional violation.

When will a trial court be required constitutionally to schedule a trial so as to allow representation by defendant's counsel of choice? Perhaps because scheduling accommodations are more readily made in the initial setting of the trial date, appellate decisions considering that issue have in large part dealt with trial court refusals to grant continuances requested by defendants to allow them to retain new counsel. As noted in subsection (b), where an indigent defendant with appointed counsel seeks to have that counsel replaced, even without asking for a continuance, defendant much establish "good cause," such as a conflict of interest or complete breakdown of communications with counsel. Of course, if the defendant with retained counsel can likewise show that current counsel is likely not to present competent representation, then the continuance to allow replacement of that counsel will be necessary to protect defendant's constitutional right to the "effective assistance" of counsel. However, unlike the situation with respect to appointed counsel, defendant's interest in being represented by retained counsel of choice may require granting a continuance to allow substitution of counsel on far less than a "good cause" showing. The trial court in each case must balance the defendant's interest in counsel of choice against the "public's interest in prompt and efficient administration of justice." As the Supreme Court has noted: "There are no mechanical tests for deciding when a denial of a continuance is so arbitrary as to violate [defendant's constitutional rights]. The answer must be found in the circumstances present in every case." [10]

Appellate rulings have identified the following factors as among those to be considered in determining whether a continuance should be granted include: (1) whether the request came at a point sufficiently in advance of trial to permit the trial court to readily adjust its calendar; (2) the length of the continuance requested; (3) whether the continuance would carry the trial date beyond the period specified in the state speedy trial act; (4) whether the court had granted previous continuances at defendant's request; (5) whether the continuance would seriously inconvenience the witnesses; (6) whether the continuance request was made promptly after the defendant first became aware of the grounds advanced for discharging his counsel; (7) whether the defendant's own negligence placed him in a situation where he needed a continuance to obtain new counsel; (8) whether the defendant had some legitimate cause for dissatisfaction with counsel, even though it fell short of likely incompetent representation; (9) whether there is a "rational basis" for believing that defendant is seeking to change counsel "primarily for the purpose of delay"; (10) whether the current counsel is prepared to go to trial; and (11) whether denial of the motion is likely to result in "identifiable prejudice to the defendant's case of a material or substantial nature." [11] While appellate courts note that they will give considerable leeway to the trial court in its determination not to grant a continuance, a substantial body of cases have found abuses of discretion resulting in a denial of defendant's constitutional rights.

Restrictions upon the defendant's right to counsel generally flow, as in the continuance

10. Ungar v. Sarafite, 376 U.S. 575, 84 S.Ct. 841, 11 L.Ed.2d 921 (1964). In *Ungar,* the Court rejected a constitutional challenge to a denial of a continuance which led to the withdrawal of defense counsel and self-representation by the defendant (who was a lawyer). The Court cited a variety of factors, including defendant's delay in bringing the motion, ample time given for preparation in light of the readily available evidence and clearly identified issues, and the need to give deference to the trial judge's judgment.

11. Although appellate courts commonly look to possible trial prejudice as one factor to be considered, they do not insist upon a finding of prejudice as a prerequisite for concluding that defendant's Sixth Amendment rights were violated. Moreover, once a denial of defendant's constitutional right to counsel of his choice is found, that violation traditionally has been treated as a per se reversible error. Consider also Flanagan v. United States, discussed at § 27.2, note 22.

cases, from a countervailing governmental interest relating to judicial administration. The impact of the restriction generally is to limit the defendant's choice, but not to eliminate it altogether by forcing the defendant to accept counsel selected by the court. Also, such restrictions are not directed at particular offenses, so their impact ordinarily does not fall disproportionately upon a certain class of defendants. In *Caplin & Drysdale, Chartered v. United States,*[12] the Supreme Court upheld a restriction on defendant's ability to retain counsel of choice that had none of these characteristics. At issue there was the asset forfeiture provisions of the Continuing Criminal Enterprise statute, which applies to specified drug violations, and encompasses all properties "constituting or derived from" the "proceeds" of those offenses.[13] With the forfeiture provisions allowing for both a government recapture of all such properties transferred to third parties (including lawyers [14]) and a pretrial freeze on their transfer, the Court assumed that their impact in particular cases would be to render defendant unable to hire any counsel, forcing him to accept court appointed counsel.[15] It held that the provisions nonetheless did not impermissibly burden a defendant's Sixth Amendment right to counsel of choice.

Justice White's opinion for the Court majority initially cited the well established principle that a "defendant has no Sixth Amendment right to spend another person's money for services rendered by an attorney, even if those funds are the only way that defendant will be able to retain the counsel of his choice." Petitioner had conceded as much, but had argued that the property here was not truly that of another, as would be the case with stolen property. Petitioner maintained that a defendant's use of assets in which others have "a pre-existing property right" should be distinguished from the "fictive property law concept" that underlies the government's claim to the proceeds of criminal transactions. While the four dissenters found this distinction persuasive, the majority

12. Supra note 4.

13. 21 U.S.C.A. § 853. These forfeiture provisions are not limited to CCE violations, but extend to all felony drug offenses. Similar forfeiture provisions are found in the Racketeer Influenced and Corrupt Organization Act, 18 U.S.C.A. § 1963.

14. The recapture or "relation-back" provision allows the government to recapture forfeited property that has been transferred to a third party prior to the conviction and entry of the special verdict of forfeiture—unless the third party was both a bona fide recipient and a person "reasonably without cause to believe" that the property was subject to forfeiture at the time of receipt. The freeze provision allows the government, upon a proper showing, to obtain a restraining order before, at the time of, or after indictment. In United States v. Monsanto, 491 U.S. 600, 109 S.Ct. 2657, 105 L.Ed.2d 512 (1989), the Court rejected the contention that the statute should be read as exempting from the forfeiture provisions moneys used to retain an attorney. In enacting the forfeiture provision, the majority noted, "Congress decided to give force to the old adage that 'crime does not pay' " and there was no indication in the "plain and unambiguous" language of the statute or its legislative history that "Congress intended to modify the nostrum to read 'crime does not pay' except for attorney's fees."

15. The petitioner in *Caplin & Drysdale* was a law firm that had received funds from a defendant after he had been charged in an indictment seeking forfeiture and after a restraining order had been issued freezing his assets. It argued that both the relation-back and the freeze provisions burdened a defendant's Sixth Amendment rights. A pretrial restraining order would deprive defendant of assets that could otherwise be used to retain counsel of choice. The relation-back provision also would restrict defendant's ability to hire counsel since a prospective defense attorney would be reluctant to accept the assignment knowing that the retainer paid by defendant could be subject to recapture if defendant were convicted. The Supreme Court initially noted that the provisions would not invariably keep a defendant from retaining counsel of choice. Defendant might be able to pay counsel with funds clearly not subject to forfeiture. Defense counsel might receive payment at an early enough point so as to be categorized as a bona fide recipient reasonably without cause to believe that the retainer was subject to forfeiture (although the petitioner maintained that attorneys would by nature of their position typically have reasonable cause and the Court did not challenge that assumption). Also, defense counsel might be willing to represent a defendant "hoping that their fees will be paid in the event of an acquittal, or via some other means that a defendant might come by in the future." (The suggestion that this would create, in effect, a "contingency fee" system was rejected by the Court; the payment of the fee would simply "turn on the outcome of the trial," which may "often be the case in criminal defense work"). In light of such possibilities for retaining counsel notwithstanding the forfeiture provisions, the Court characterized the burden those provisions placed on defendants as a "limited one." Nonetheless, the Sixth Amendment challenge was rejected on the assumption that "there will be cases where a defendant will be unable to retain the attorney of his choice," and some in which defendant will be required to rely on appointed counsel.

did not. Justice White responded that petitioner's argument failed to recognize the "substantial" property rights of the government under the forfeiture statute. Under the well accepted "taint theory," long recognized in forfeiture law generally, the defendant never had "good title" to the property, as the government obtained a "vested property interest" in the proceeds at the point at which the illegal transaction occurred. Moreover, the government's interest was not limited to simply "separating a criminal from his ill-gotten gains," although Congress obviously has a legitimate interest in "lessen[ing] the economic power of organized crime and drug enterprises" by stripping them of their "undeserved economic power" (including "the ability to command high priced legal talent"). The assets forfeited pursuant to the statute were to be deposited in a fund used to support law-enforcement efforts in various ways, and where the assets came from rightful owners, defrauded of their property, those owners could seek restitution. Finally, to sustain petitioner's argument here was to cast doubt on such accepted practices as the use of jeopardy assessments in criminal tax cases, and to open the door to forfeiture exemptions for defendants desiring to exercise any constitutionally protected freedom that may require the expenditure of funds.

The petitioner in *Caplin & Drysdale* also contended that the forfeiture statute "upset the balance of forces between the accused and accuser" by allowing the prosecution, through its discretion as to the utilization of the forfeiture remedy and the pretrial restraining order, to exercise what the dissenters described as "an intolerable degree of power over any private attorney." The majority saw this claim as analogous to that rejected in *Wheat v. United States,* where government motions to disqualify defense counsel on conflict-of-interest grounds had been challenged as likely to be used by prosecutors to eliminate effective adversaries.[16] Here too, an otherwise permissible procedure would not be struck down because of the potential for abuse. "Cases involving particular abuses," Justice White noted, "can be dealt with by the lower courts, when (and if) any such cases arise."

(d) The Pro Se Alternative. When a court denies a defense request for appointment of new counsel or for a continuance to permit the defendant to hire new counsel, it commonly will inform the defendant that he either must proceed with his current counsel or represent himself. Very often the defendant will choose the latter alternative, noting that he does so only because it is the lesser of two evils. If an appellate court concludes on appeal that the trial judge erred in failing to appoint new counsel or in denying the continuance, defendant's choice of proceeding pro se will be viewed as "involuntary" and his conviction reversed. However, if trial court's decision is upheld, the defendant cannot complain about being "forced into" proceeding pro se. It is not inconsistent with the concept of a voluntary waiver to require a choice between waiver and another option, provided that other option is itself consistent with the protection of his constitutional rights.

§ 11.5 The Constitutional Right to Self-Representation

(a) The *Faretta* Right. In *Faretta v. California,*[1] the defendant requested, well before trial, that he be allowed to represent himself. After holding a hearing on defendant's ability to conduct his own defense, which raised questions as to defendant's knowledge of such matters as the hearsay rule, the trial court refused defendant's request and appointed counsel to represent him. On appeal from defendant's conviction, the state appellate court found no error, noting that defendant had no constitutional right to proceed pro se. A divided Supreme Court rejected that con-

16. The petitioner presented the abuse contention as a due process rather than a Sixth Amendment claim, but the Court saw the issue as essentially the same as that presented in a Sixth Amendment form in *Wheat.* It noted further that here, unlike *Wheat,* the "case does not involve a situation where the government has asked a court to prevent a defendant's chosen counsel from representing him."

§ 11.5

1. 422 U.S. 806, 95 S.Ct. 2525, 45 L.Ed.2d 562 (1975).

tention and held that defendant had been denied a right guaranteed by the Sixth Amendment.

Justice Stewart's opinion for the *Faretta* majority relied heavily on the "structure of the Sixth Amendment" and the "English and colonial jurisprudence from which [the Sixth Amendment] emerged." Although the colonial practice had deviated from the English common law in permitting representation by counsel in felony cases, such representation always was at the choice of the defendant. Indeed, the right of self-representation was specifically noted in various state constitutional provisions that established a right to counsel. While the Sixth Amendment did not refer explicitly to self-representation, that right was "necessarily implied by the structure of the Amendment." The Amendment speaks of confrontation, compulsory process, and notice as rights of "the accused." The implication of this wording, Justice Stewart noted, was that those rights were not merely made available to the defense, but were rights of the accused personally, that he could exercise himself in presenting his own defense. The counsel provision "supplemented this design" by referring to the defendant's right to the "assistance" of counsel. The clear purpose of the Amendment, Justice Stewart concluded, was to make "counsel, like the other defense tools guaranteed, * * * an aid to a willing defendant—not an organ of the State interposed between an unwilling defendant and his right to defend himself personally."

The *Faretta* majority acknowledged that a constitutional right to proceed pro se "seems to cut against the grain" of decisions, like *Powell v. Alabama* and *Gideon v. Wainwright,* that are based on the premise that "the help of a lawyer is essential to assure a fair trial." The majority rejected, however, the dissenters' contention that the state's interest in providing a fair trial permitted it to insist upon representation by counsel. The framers of the Sixth Amendment were well aware of the value of counsel in obtaining a fair trial, but placed on a higher plane the "inestimable worth of free choice." Notwithstanding the lawyer's expertise, "it is not inconceivable that in some rare instances, the defendant may in fact present his case more effectively by conducting his own defense." Since "the defendant, and not his lawyer or the State, will bear the personal consequences of the conviction," he should be free to decide whether his is such a case. Although his decision may not be wise, his "choice must be honored out of that respect for the individual which is the lifeblood of the law."

Having established a constitutional right to self-representation, the Court then turned to the question of whether the defendant Faretta had been denied that right. The defendant who proceeds pro se, it noted, must act "knowingly and intelligently" in giving up those "traditional benefits associated with the right to counsel." He should "be made aware of the dangers and disadvantages of self-representation, so that the record will establish that he 'knows what he is doing and his choice is made with eyes open.'" The defendant need not, however, "have the skill and experience of a lawyer in order competently and intelligently to choose self-representation." Here the record showed that the defendant was "literate, competent, and understanding, and that he was voluntarily exercising his informed free will." That he may not have mastered the intricacies of the hearsay rule, or that he lacked other "technical legal knowledge," was "not relevant to an assessment of his knowing exercise of the right to defend himself." Accordingly, the lower court had erred in forcing him to accept appointed counsel.

The Court in *Faretta,* once it found trial error in failing to allow defendant to proceed pro se, reversed defendant's conviction. This disposition suggested that the denial of the right to proceed pro se was not subject to a harmless error analysis, but Justice Blackmun, in dissent, cited as an issue left open by the Court's opinion the possible application of the harmless error rule of *Chapman v. California.*[2] Any doubts raised by Justice Black-

2. See § 27.6(c).

mun's dissent were put to rest, however, by a footnote in the later case of *McKaskle v. Wiggins.*[3] The Court there noted:

> Since the right of self-representation is a right that when exercised usually increases the likelihood of a trial outcome unfavorable to the defendant, its denial is not amenable to "harmless error" analysis. The right is either respected or denied; its deprivation cannot be harmless.

McKaskle also clarified a possible ambiguity in *Faretta*'s discussion of the role of standby counsel. Justice Stewart had noted in *Faretta* that "a state may—even over objection by the accused—appoint a 'standby counsel' to aid the accused if and when the accused requests help, and to be available to represent the accused in the event that termination of the defendant's self-representation is necessary." This statement was viewed by the lower court in *McKaskle* as restricting the role of standby counsel, in the absence of a defendant's request for assistance, to "being seen but not heard." Counsel's failure to restrict his participation to that limited role was held by the lower court to have violated defendant's *Faretta* right, thereby requiring a new trial. A divided Supreme Court disagreed, holding that the seen-but-not-heard standard was entirely too narrow.

The *McKaskle* majority noted initially that the trial court had the authority, notwithstanding defendant's objection, to both appoint standby counsel and direct that counsel to "steer [the] defendant through the basic procedures of the trial." It was appropriate for the trial court "to relieve [itself] of the need to explain and enforce the basic rules of court room protocol or to assist the defendant in overcoming routine [procedural] obstacles that stand in the way of defendant's achievement of his own clearly indicated goals." Unsolicited participation by standby counsel did present a difficulty, however, when it went beyond this limited role and involved more than "routine clerical or procedural matters." Even here, however, all such participation did not per se constitute a violation of defendant's right of self-representation.[4] In determining whether such participation undermined defendant's *Faretta* right, the Court would apply a two-pronged test. First, did "standby counsel's participation over defendant's objection effectively allow counsel to make or substantially interfere with any significant tactical decisions, or to control the questioning of witnesses, or to speak *instead* of the defendant on any matter of importance"? Such action necessarily undermines the defendant's right of self-representation since it deprives him of the "actual control over the case he chooses to present to the jury." Second, even if the defendant was able to present his case in his own way, did the additional unsolicited participation of counsel "destroy the jury's perception that the defendant is representing himself"? Such action also eviscerates defendant's *Faretta* right since the "defendant's appearance in the status of one conducting his own defense" is an important aspect of the "dignity and autonomy" of the individual protected in *Faretta.* Moreover, "from the jury's perspective, the message conveyed by the defense may depend as much on the messenger as the message itself." [5]

3. 465 U.S. 168, 104 S.Ct. 944, 79 L.Ed.2d 122 (1984).

4. The Court did not suggest that such unsolicited participation was appropriate, or that it should not be controlled by the trial judge, but only that it did not necessarily produce a constitutional violation. In contrast, participation by counsel "to steer a defendant through the basic procedures of trial," even where not desired by defendant, was appropriate and would be upheld "even in the unlikely event that it somewhat undermines the pro se defendant's appearance of control over his own defense."

5. Applying these two tests, the Court concluded in *McKaskle* that the facts there did not establish a constitutional violation through standby counsel's unsolicited participation. Counsel's unsolicited comments made in front of the jury "were infrequent and for the most part innocuous." The more troublesome unsolicited comments occurred when the jury was not present. Though counsel and defendant conflicted on various occasions, resulting in several "regrettable incidents," all of the conflicts were resolved in the defendant's favor. Moreover, in many respects, the difficulties were occasioned by defendant's frequent shifts in his attitude toward counsel's assistance. It was often difficult "to determine how much of counsel's participation was in fact contrary to [defendant's] desires of the moment." Where, as here (see note 9 infra), a "defendant is given the opportunity and elects to have counsel appear before the court or jury, his complaints concerning subsequent unsolicited participation lose much of their force."

(b) Notification. Dissenting in *Faretta,* Justice Blackmun raised the question of whether "every defendant [must] be advised of his right to proceed pro se"? The Court has held that notification of the right to counsel is essential; might not a similar requirement apply to the "other side" of defendant's Sixth Amendment right? Lower courts have uniformly assumed that there is no constitutional obligation to inform the defendant of his constitutional right to proceed pro se in the absence of a clear indication on his part that he desires to consider that option. This position is based in part on concern that notification of the right to proceed pro se might undermine the "overriding constitutional policy" favoring the provision of counsel. Thus, one court has noted:

> Inasmuch as the defendant represented by counsel cannot claim that by having counsel he has been denied a fair trial * * *, the right to proceed pro se lacks the force and urgency of the right of counsel and there is no necessity to inform every defendant of his right to conduct his own defense.[6]

(c) Requisite Judicial Inquiry. In the course of exercising his constitutional right to proceed pro se, the defendant must necessarily waive his Sixth Amendment right to counsel. Accordingly, *Faretta* stressed that trial courts, before permitting a defendant to represent himself, must determine that he is knowingly and intelligently relinquishing the benefits of representation by counsel. Courts are agreed as to the preferred procedure in making that determination. Initially, the trial court should ascertain that the defendant is aware of the various matters noted in Justice Black's *Von Moltke* opinion.[7] Then, because the defendant here desires to represent himself at trial (rather than to simply plead guilty without a lawyer), the trial court should take special care to advise the defendant of the pitfalls of self-representation. Appellate opinions have suggested that the defendant should be informed at least of the following matters: (1) that "presenting a defense is not a simple matter of telling one's story," but requires adherence to various "technical rules" governing the conduct of a trial; (2) that a lawyer has substantial experience and training in trial procedure and that the prosecution will be represented by an experienced attorney; (3) that a person unfamiliar with legal procedures may allow the prosecutor an advantage by failing to make objections to inadmissible evidence, may not make effective use of such rights as the voir dire of jurors, and may make tactical decisions that produce unintended consequences; (4) that a defendant proceeding pro se will not be allowed to complain on appeal about the competency of his representation; and (5) "that the effectiveness of his defense may well be diminished by his dual role as attorney and accused."

If the defendant persists in his request to proceed pro se, notwithstanding the court's warning as to the possible disadvantages of self-representation, then the preferred procedure directs the court to ascertain that the defendant understands and appreciates those disadvantages and their possible consequences. This requires, appellate courts note, a "penetrating and comprehensive inquiry," including an interchange with the defendant that produces more than passive "yes" and "no" responses. The trial court should explore the primary factors that might have a bearing on defendant's ability to comprehend, including age, education, social background, mental health history, prior experience or familiarity with criminal trials, and prior consultation with counsel in deciding to proceed pro se. This process of explanation and inquiry will not only assist the trial court in making an accurate assessment of defendant's waiver, but provide the appellate court with "an objective basis for review" upon the almost inevitable challenge to the waiver by the defendant who proceeds pro se and is subsequently convicted.

As discussed in § 11.3(b), while it is preferred that the trial court inform the defendant (and inquire into his understanding) as

6. People v. McIntyre, 36 N.Y.2d 10, 364 N.Y.S.2d 837, 324 N.E.2d 322 (1974).

7. See § 11.3(b).

to each of the *Von Moltke* factors, that procedure is not viewed as a constitutional necessity for the waiver of counsel. Arguably, *Faretta* suggests otherwise as to informing the defendant of the pitfalls of self-representation at trial. The *Faretta* opinion noted that the defendant "should be made aware of the dangers and disadvantages of self-representation, so that the record will establish that 'he knows what he is doing and his choice is made with his eyes open.'" Relying upon this statement, several courts have suggested that a waiver is not constitutionally acceptable unless the trial judge specifically warns the defendant of the dangers of self-representation and then engages in a colloquy that establishes defendant's understanding. Other courts take the position that *Faretta* requires only that the defendant have been aware of the disadvantages of proceeding pro se, and that that awareness can be established without regard to any admonitions or colloquies. They argue that a waiver is constitutionally acceptable where such factors as defendant's involvement in previous criminal trials, his representation by counsel before trial, and his explanation of his reasons for proceeding pro se indicate that he was fully aware of the difficulties of self-representation. For at least some of these courts, however, such factors can serve the same function as an extensive colloquy only when they provide "a compelling case of circumstantial evidence that the pro se defendant knew what he or she was doing."

(d) Grounds for Denial. The defendant in *Faretta* made a clear and unequivocal request to proceed pro se, and courts insist upon such a request as a prerequisite for the exercise of the *Faretta* right. Once such a request is made, *Faretta* suggests only three possible grounds for refusing to allow pro se representation. First, *Faretta* stressed that the request in that case was made "well before the date of trial." This suggested that, at some point, a request might be so disruptive of the orderly schedule of proceedings as to justify rejection on that ground alone. Second, *Faretta* noted that "the trial judge may terminate self-representation by a defendant who engages in serious and obstructionist misconduct." Ordinarily, this authority would be exercised only after the defendant has begun to represent himself. However, in exceptional situations, the defendant's behavior in the course of seeking to obtain self-representation may in itself be disruptive and thereby justify denying his pro se motion.

Third, by requiring a valid waiver of counsel as a prerequisite for self-representation, *Faretta* recognized the authority of a trial court to refuse to permit self-representation when, despite its efforts to explain the consequences of waiver, defendant is unable to reach the level of appreciation needed for a knowing and intelligent waiver. *Faretta* also makes clear, however, that a defendant does not need legal expertise nor unusual intelligence to meet its standard of awareness of the dangers and disadvantages of self-representation. Accordingly, lower courts have read *Faretta* as indicating that, with a proper explanation by the trial judge, a defendant "who is sui juris and mentally competent" should almost always be able to make a knowing and intelligent waiver. The waiver also must be voluntary, but as noted in § 11.4(d), the most common source of "pressure"—dissatisfaction with counsel—does not render the choice to proceed pro se involuntary unless the trial court erred constitutionally in failing to provide or allow for new counsel.

(e) Subsequent Challenge to Ineffective Representation. Commenting upon the limitations of self-representation, the *Faretta* opinion noted:

> Neither is * * * [the right of self-representation] a license not to comply with relevant rules of procedural and substantive law. Thus, whatever else may or may not be open to him on appeal, a defendant who elects to represent himself cannot thereafter complain that the quality of his own defense amounted to a denial of "effective assistance of counsel."

Relying upon this statement lower courts have consistently rejected claims of defendants that their pro se representation was so inadequate as to result in a denial of a fair trial.[8]

Lower court rulings generally have also adhered to the principle that pro se defendants are to be treated on appeal no differently than defendants with counsel as to objections that were not properly preserved at trial. This position is viewed as logically dictated by *Faretta's* comment that pro se defendants are not thereby granted a "license not to comply with relevant rules of procedural and substantive law." Appellate courts also sustain, as within the trial court's discretion, the refusal to bend rules governing presentation of evidence, especially when those rules serve the important function of ensuring fairness to the opposing party. While the pro se defendant who is incarcerated may have a right of access to legal materials (within limits), he will not be heard to complain on appeal that his ignorance of various procedural requirements should be excused because the prison's law library was inadequate (particularly where standby counsel was available).

(f) Hybrid Representation. Under a hybrid form of representation, defendant and counsel act, in effect, as co-counsel, with each speaking for the defense during different phases of the trial. Defendants have claimed that *Faretta's* recognition of self-representation and representation by counsel as "independent constitutional rights" logically establishes a constitutional grounding for hybrid representation. Such representation, they argue, simply is the product of partially waiving each of these rights, no different than the partial waiver allowed with respect to other rights (e.g., the partial waiver of confrontation when the defense cross-examines some witnesses and not others). They note that the Sixth Amendment guarantee speaks of the "assistance" of counsel, a term that readily suggests active participation by both counsel and the defendant himself. Although raised in a substantial number of cases, this contention has failed to persuade either federal or state courts. They have uniformly held that there is no Sixth Amendment right to hybrid representation.[9] The constitutional rights to self-representation and representation by counsel are viewed as mutually exclusive, though the trial court may permit hybrid representation, in its discretion, as "a matter of grace."

Lower court opinions rejecting defense assertions of a right to hybrid representation have relied on several grounds. Most often cited is the need to grant the trial judge sufficient authority to maintain the "dignity and decorum" of the courtroom and to ensure an orderly and expeditious trial. Another judicial concern is the impact that a right to hybrid representation would have upon the role of counsel as the "manager of the lawsuit." Traditionally, tactical decisions may be made by counsel without even consulting his client. Recognition of a constitutional right to hybrid representation arguably would allow the defendant to force at least appointed counsel to relinquish that authority and accept an "inferior position" as to those portions of the trial in which defendant would proceed pro se. Finally, there is suspicion that hybrid representation would often be used by the defense primarily to permit defendant to present an unsworn statement to the jury. Counsel would carry most of the load, but the defendant would present an opening or closing argument to the jury that would allow him, in effect, to "testify" without being subjected to cross-examination. Although a defendant acting as his own counsel can be

8. Opinions denying ineffectiveness claims of pro se defendants not infrequently note that the defendant's failure to utilize even the ordinary skills of laymen may in itself be a strategic ploy of a defendant hoping to create grounds for an appellate reversal of an almost certain conviction. They also commonly cite the efforts of the trial judge to assist the defendant (though noting that such efforts are not constitutionally mandated) or the availability of consultation with standby counsel.

9. Although the issue was not before the Court in McKaskle v. Wiggins, supra note 3, dictum in the majority opinion there supports this view. The defendant Wiggins objected to the unsolicited participation of standby counsel, but he also had expressly agreed to counsel's questioning of a witness on voir dire and presentation of a closing statement. The Court noted that "*Faretta* does not require a trial judge to permit 'hybrid' representation of the type Wiggins was actually allowed," but once "a defendant is given the opportunity and elects to have counsel appear before the court or jury, his complaints concerning counsel's subsequent unsolicited participation lose much of their force." See also note 4 supra.

restricted to the traditional limits applicable to opening or closing statements, it might be difficult to impose those limitations in a rigid fashion, particularly where he claims a constitutional right to assume this portion of his representation.

§ 11.6 Counsel's Control Over Defense Strategy

(a) "Strategic" vs. "Personal" Decisions. Prior to *Faretta,* a long line of cases had held that defense counsel had the authority to make various defense decisions on his own initiative. These defense decisions, commonly characterized as relating to matters of "strategy" or "tactics," were said to be within the "exclusive province" of the lawyer. Counsel had no obligation to consult with the defendant,[1] and if he did consult, had no obligation to follow the defendant's wishes.[2] Other defense decisions, however, were said to rest in the ultimate authority of the defendant. As to those decisions, commonly said to require the "personal choice" of the defendant, counsel had to advise the client and abide by his directions.[3]

The Supreme Court's decision in *Faretta* was thought by some to have altered this basic division between strategic and personal decisions. The *Faretta* opinion had referred to the "law and tradition" that granted counsel ultimate authority to make "binding decisions of trial strategy in many areas." Indeed it had cited that law and tradition as a factor pointing towards the recognition of an alternative of self-representation where defendant wanted to control his own destiny. The argument was advanced, however, that the overall perspective of the *Faretta* opinion also required that the attorney's ultimate authority be limited, perhaps only to "on-the-spot" decisions where timing considerations precluded consultation with the defendant. *Faretta,* it was argued, was "predicated on the view that the function of counsel under the Sixth Amendment is to protect the dignity and autonomy of a person on trial by *assisting* him in making choices that are his to make, not to make choices for him, although counsel may be better able to decide what tactics will be most effective." [4]

In *Jones v. Barnes,*[5] a divided Supreme Court rejected this view of *Faretta. Jones* held that appellate counsel did not have to present a nonfrivolous claim that his client wished to press if counsel believed that the better strategy was to limit his argument and

§ 11.6

1. Our discussion deals only with those obligations of counsel that may require reversal of a conviction when violated. Thus, though it is said in this regard that the lawyer has no obligation to consult with his client as to those decisions over which counsel has exclusive control, he may nevertheless have such an obligation to consult under standards of professional responsibility. See ABA Model Rules of Professional Conduct, Rule 1.4. Consider also 21.3(b) as to the special obligations attending counsel's advice in the entry of a plea.

2. See Jones v. Barnes, infra note 5, and note 7 infra. Of course, a defendant with a retained attorney theoretically can discharge his attorney and look for another who will abide by his wishes. The indigent defendant has no right to a substitute counsel where the disagreement with counsel relates to a matter within the exclusive province of the lawyer. See § 11.4(b). Thus his choice commonly is either to keep the counsel or proceed pro se. See § 11.4(d). The courts have not viewed such a distinction in the ability of the non-indigent and indigent defendant to "control counsel" as presenting a significant equal protection problem. In practice, the situations of the two types of defendants may be quite similar. Many non-indigents are not in a position to "shop around" for a lawyer more willing to accept the defendant's judgment on matters of strategy. If the disagreement between counsel and client arises at a point where substitution of new counsel can be achieved only with a continuance, the non-indigent, like the indigent, may face the choice of proceeding pro se or retaining his current counsel and accepting counsel's decisions. See § 11.4(c), (d). Moreover, just as equal protection has never been thought to guarantee to the indigent a lawyer as experienced or skillful as the best that a non-indigent might obtain, neither does it require a lawyer as compliant in his relationship with his client as the most submissive attorney a non-indigent may retain. See generally, State v. Superior Court, 2 Ariz.App. 458, 409 P.2d 742 (1966).

3. The attorney who disagrees with his client's decision on those matters may be allowed to withdraw, depending upon the timing, if the withdrawal will not work to the prejudice of his client. See ABA Model Rules of Professional Conduct, Rule 1.16(b), (c), and Commentary. However, if withdrawal is not allowed, the attorney must implement the client's directions on a matter of personal decision, assuming that implementation does not require the attorney to violate standards of professional responsibility.

4. Brennan, J., dissenting in Jones v. Barnes, infra note 5 (emphasis in original).

5. 463 U.S. 745, 103 S.Ct. 3308, 77 L.Ed.2d 987 (1983).

brief to other issues. Counsel was free to follow the time tested advice of countless advocates that inclusion of "every colorable claim" will "dilute and weaken a good case and will not save a bad one." It was for counsel to decide which claims were strong enough to be presented consistent with this strategy. *Faretta* gave the defendant an opportunity to control the presentation of his case by proceeding pro se. Neither it nor decisions defining the obligation of appointed appellate counsel had altered counsel's right to act upon his best professional judgment as to matters of strategy.[6]

The issue of client control was raised in *Jones* through a claim of ineffective assistance of counsel. While that is probably the most common avenue for presenting that issue, questions of client control also may be raised in other procedural settings. An indigent defendant may claim that he has a right to appointment of new counsel because his current attorney refuses to accept his directions on an issue that should be within defendant's control. A defendant may seek a continuance for the purpose of replacing retained counsel on the same ground. Many of the leading rulings on client control have involved habeas petitions in which prisoners raised constitutional claims that their counsel failed to present at trial. Although not necessarily controlling, a significant issue here is whether the decision not to raise the particular claim was within counsel's strategic control. At least where that is the case, the failure to raise the issue ordinarily will constitute a procedural default barring habeas review.[7] *Taylor v. Illinois*[8] presented an analogous procedural context. Defendant there claimed that the trial court had violated his Sixth Amendment rights by refusing to allow the testimony of a defense witness, a sanction imposed because defense counsel had failed to give the prosecution advance notice of the witness as required by state discovery rules. In rejecting defendant's claim, the Supreme Court viewed as especially significant the defense attorney's authority to adopt without consulting his client the tactic of attempting a surprise presentation of a witness in violation of discovery requirements.

Although the difference in procedural setting could conceivably influence a court's analysis of the client-control issue, the courts have tended to treat the issue as basically the same whether presented in one procedural context or another. Rulings recognizing attorney or client control with respect to a particular defense decision will be carried over from one procedural context to another. Thus, judicial discussions relating to decision-making authority can appropriately be pieced together, notwithstanding differences in procedural context, in providing a listing of those defense decisions that have been categorized as within either defendant's personal choice or defense counsel's strategic control.

The Supreme Court has stated, in dictum or holding, that it is for the defendant to decide whether to take each of the following steps:[9] plead guilty or take action tantamount to entering a guilty plea[10]; waive the right to

6. Defendant had relied on Anders v. California, described at § 11.2(c), as well as *Faretta*. The two dissenters (per Brennan, J.) argued that the thrust of both opinions demanded that defendant have the "ultimate authority" over what nonfrivolous issues would be presented in his appeal.

7. See e.g., the cases cited in § 28.4(e)–(f). In those cases, defense counsel apparently had not consulted with the defendant, and unlike *Jones*, there was no specific request by defendant that counsel present the claim. Opinions concluding that a defense counsel's decision not to raise a claim is binding upon defendant have frequently indicated, however, that the outcome would not be different if the client had discussed the matter with his attorney and had disagreed with counsel's strategic decision. To rule otherwise, courts have noted, would discourage consultation and give greater authority to the defendant who knew enough about the law to direct his attorney on his own initiative. Nelson v. California, 346 F.2d 73 (9th Cir.1965). As to procedural defaults on steps within the client's control, see § 28.4 at notes 27–28.

8. 484 U.S. 400, 108 S.Ct. 646, 98 L.Ed.2d 798 (1988), also discussed at note 14 infra and at § 20.6(c).

9. See Jones v. Barnes, supra note 5; Taylor v. Illinois, supra note 8.

10. See also Brookhart v. Janis, 384 U.S. 1, 86 S.Ct. 1245, 16 L.Ed.2d 314 (1966). *Brookhart* held that defense counsel could not enter an agreement, without defendant's informed consent, "that all the state had to prove was a prima facie case, that he would not contest it, and that there would be no cross-examination of witnesses." The Court noted that the defendant had desired to plead not guilty, but the counsel had accepted a procedure largely inconsistent with such a plea. That procedure

jury trial; waive the right to be present at trial; testify on his own behalf; or forego an appeal. Lower court rulings have added to this group: the waiver of the right to attend a deposition; the waiver of the constitutional right to a speedy trial; the refusal (by a competent defendant) to enter an insanity plea; and the decision to withhold defendant's sole defense at the guilt/special circumstances phase of a capital case and use it solely in the penalty phase. On the other side, the Supreme Court has indicated, in dictum or holding, that counsel has the ultimate authority in deciding whether or not to advance the following defense rights: barring prosecution use of unconstitutionally obtained evidence; obtaining dismissal of an indictment on the ground of racial discrimination in the selection of the grand jury; wearing civilian clothes, rather than prison garb, during the trial; striking an improper jury instruction cross-examining a prosecution witness; presenting the testimony of a potential witness (other than the defendant himself); refusing to provide discovery of potential defense evidence to the prosecution (and thereby risking the possible sanction of exclusion of that evidence from trial); and including a particular nonfrivolous claim among the issues briefed and argued on appeal. Lower court rulings have added to this list a variety of other determinations, including the following: whether to request, or object to, the exclusion of the public from the trial; whether to seek a change of venue, continuance, or other relief due to prejudicial pretrial publicity; whether to seek a continuance and thereby relinquish a statutory right to trial within a specified period; and whether to enter an evidentiary stipulation even as to the entire transcript of a prior trial.

Taken together, the judicial discussions of the division of authority between counsel and client produce a line of demarcation that is clear at many points but uncertain at others. Although many of the Supreme Court's categorizations were not actual holdings, they have been treated as firmly settling the issue as to the particular defense decisions discussed by the Court. As to defense decisions considered only by lower courts, there has been substantial agreement on most, but division on some. Also, there remain many defense decisions on which the courts simply have not spoken. The resulting ambiguity is illustrated by Justice Brennan's suggestion in *Jones v. Barnes* that a defendant would have the right to insist that his counsel forego other strategies more likely to produce a dismissal or a reduction of punishment in favor of relying exclusively on a claim of innocence. Though Justice Brennan was speaking to a defense decision of critical importance in the division of responsibility between lawyer and client, it was one not readily categorized under available precedent and certainly open to argument on both sides.[11] Of course, one cannot expect a ruling on each and every decision on which lawyer and client are likely to disagree. The problems of uncertainty are exacerbated, however, by the absence of any well reasoned guidelines for distinguishing between those decisions requiring defendant's personal choice and those subject to counsel's control over strategy.

(b) Balancing of Interests. The Supreme Court's explanations of why particular deci-

was characterized by Justice Harlan, in his concurring opinion, as having "amounted almost to a plea of guilty or nolo contendere."

11. Justice Brennan's position finds possible support as to certain defenses. Thus, the California Supreme Court has held that, in light of statutory prerequisites, a plea of insanity cannot be entered over defendant's objection. People v. Gauze, 15 Cal.3d 709, 125 Cal.Rptr. 773, 542 P.2d 1365 (1975). So too, the commentary to 1 ABA Standards for Criminal Justice § 4–5.2 argues that "because this decision is so important as well as similar to the defendant's decision about the charges to which to plead, the defendant should be the one to decide whether to seek submission to the jury of lesser included offenses." If Justice Brennan had in mind a more substantial group of strategies (including, for example, a decision to refuse to raise a speedy trial objection and rely solely on a claim of innocence), then his suggestion would appear to be inconsistent with the basic thrust of the views expressly taken by the Supreme Court in cases in which he has dissented. See note 4 supra and notes 12 and 15 infra. Although Supreme Court and lower court decisions have almost always dealt with defense counsel's decision not to pursue a particular legal objection or line of defense, opinions commonly have described counsel's authority as extending as well to the affirmative decision to make use of that particular objection or defense.

sions are for counsel or client have been brief and conclusionary. Decisions within the client's control are simply described as involving "fundamental rights," while those within the lawyer's control are said to involve matters requiring the "superior ability of trained counsel" in assessing "strategy." While the rights subject to defendant's "personal choice" clearly are "fundamental," the Court has not explained why various rights subject to counsel's authority are not equally fundamental. Arguably, the decision to plead guilty has a special quality because it involves the relinquishment of so many basic rights. But it is more difficult to distinguish the right to be tried before a jury, for example, from the right to present a particular witness or to cross-examine an opposing witness. If the fundamental nature of a right is measured by its importance, its historic tradition, or its current status in constitutional or state law, those rights would appear to be on the same plane.

The Court's emphasis upon the strategic element in those decisions subject to counsel's control also fails to fully explain the distinctions that have been drawn. Certainly the decisions to waive a jury or not have the defendant testify also involve substantial strategic considerations. It may be argued that the elements of strategy involved in such decisions are more readily understood by the layman because they do not as frequently rest on technical concerns as many of the tactical decisions made by counsel. But they are hardly distinguishable in this regard from still other decisions made by counsel. For example, counsel's decision not to have a particular witness testify often rests on considerations of the same kind that would lead counsel, if he had such control, to keep the defendant from testifying. Similarly, much the same type of judgment is involved in deciding that a jury should be waived because the trial judge is likely to be the more sympathetic factfinder as in deciding that an unconstitutionally composed jury should not be challenged because discriminatory jury selection has produced a more sympathetic group of jurors. In sum, just as the fundamental rights characterization could be applied to many of the rights subject to counsel's control, so could the characterization of a decision as strategic and requiring counsel's expertise be applied to certain basic determinations subject to defendant's control.

As various lower courts have noted, the determination that particular decisions do or do not require defendant's personal choice has obviously rested on a balancing of several factors. The fundamental nature of the right involved and the significance of strategic considerations obviously are two important considerations. Other factors given substantial weight appear to be the objective of avoiding the disruption of the litigation process, the "inherently personal character" of the particular decision, and the need to maintain a strong defense bar.

The court's concern with the possible disruption of the litigation process is manifested most clearly in opinions stressing the timing of the particular decision. The exercise of defendant's personal choice requires an opportunity for meaningful consultation that often is not consistent with the exigencies of litigation. Thus, Justice Brennan, who would grant defendant far more control than the Supreme Court majority, nevertheless acknowledges that defense counsel must be given "decisive authority * * * with regard to the hundreds of decisions that must be made quickly in the course of a trial." [12] Still another concern of judicial administration is that the trial judge be able to establish on the record, without a lengthy disruptive procedure, that the decisions subject to defendant's control were actually made by the defendant. Many of the rights within the control of the

12. See Jones v. Barnes, supra note 5 (Brennan, J., concurring). Justice Brennan has argued against "a constitutional rule that encourages lawyers to disregard their clients' wishes without compelling need." It is not clear what factors other than the exigencies of litigation would establish such "compelling need." The Court majority clearly has rejected such a stringent standard. It has held subject to counsel's control many decisions made at points in the proceeding where there is ample time for consultation with counsel. See the text following note 10 supra.

defendant require the "publicly acknowledged consent of the client" for their waiver,[13] but that can hardly be demanded for all of the rights that might fit within the general characterization of being "fundamental."

Such administrative concerns were noted by the Supreme Court in *Taylor v. Illinois*[14] in the course of rejecting defendant's challenge to the trial court's imposition of an exclusion sanction where the prosecution had not been given the required advance notice of a potential defense witness. The decision to violate discovery rules and seek to present a surprise witness had been made by counsel without consulting defendant, and the defendant argued that he should not be bound by a decision of counsel that amounted to purposeful misconduct even if done on his behalf and not falling below the standard of effective assistance. The Court responded that defendant's argument "strikes at the heart of the attorney-client relationship." The "adversary process could not function effectively if every tactical decision required client approval." Moreover, "given the protections afforded by the attorney-client privilege and the fact that extreme cases may involve unscrupulous conduct by both the client and the lawyer, it would be highly impracticable to require an investigation into their relative responsibilities before applying the sanction of preclusion." Apart from "the exceptional case" in which the lawyer is ineffective, "the client must accept the consequences of the lawyer's decision to forego cross-examination, to decide not to put certain witnesses on the stand, or to decide not to disclose the identity of certain witnesses in advance of trial." As part of the adversary system it must be recognized that "[w]henever a lawyer makes use of the sword provided by the Compulsory Process Clause, there is some risk that he may wound his client."[15]

Still another factor that has apparently influenced the balancing process, though it tends to be cited more frequently by commentators than courts, is the probability that defendant's interest in the particular decision extends beyond simply presenting a successful defense. The client, it is often said, must be able to control the "end," while the lawyer determines the "means" for reaching that end. Where, as is usually the case, the client's primary objective is to gain an acquittal, the lawyer is only controlling the means to that end when he decides whether or not to advance certain claims or raise particular objections. However, as to the exercise of a few rights, the client may often have a different or additional objective in mind. For example, a defendant may have an interest in testifying himself even though he recognizes that doing so may hurt his chances for acquittal (perhaps because cross-examination will reveal his prior convictions). He may view as more important his opportunity to "tell his story to the public." Similarly, a defendant may want a prompt trial, to relieve his anxiety, even though he recognizes that delay might weaken the prosecution's evidence. Decisions of this type are said to more appropriately rest with the defendant because they have an "inherently personal" quality, reflecting defendant's interest in controlling objectives rather than simply tactics. Of course, a wide variety of decisions may have this quality under the circumstances of an individual case. The courts have indicated, however, that they will judge the decision in terms of the general nature of the interests protected by the particular right. None have suggested, for example, that counsel will lose his control over whether a suppression motion

13. See Taylor v. Illinois, supra note 8 (offering as illustrations the relinquishment of trial rights through a guilty plea, the waiver of the right to trial by jury, and the waiver of the right to be present at trial). This is not to say, of course, that a decision will be held to be within the control of counsel rather than client simply because a record of defendant's personal participation in the waiver is not easily established. Whether to appeal is a decision for the defendant to make, though the failure of counsel to file an appeal hardly indicates in itself (or readily permits a court to establish on the record) that defendant participated in that decision.

14. Supra note 8.

15. Justice Brennan's dissent argued that the "rationale for binding defendants to attorneys routine tactical errors do not apply to attorney misconduct," as much misconduct was "amenable to direct punitive sanctions against attorneys."

should be made when the particular defendant's political beliefs make it so important to him that police illegality be revealed that he insists on the motion even though it might work against the possibility of an acquittal.

Finally, the line drawn between "personal" and "strategic" decisions probably also reflects some concern that lawyers not be placed in a position so inhibiting or embarrassing, as it relates to their professional expertise, that they are discouraged from engaging in criminal defense work. A lawyer is not placed in a professionally embarrassing position when he is reluctantly required to try his case to a jury rather than a judge. Neither should he be embarrassed because he is required to go to trial in a weak case, since that decision is clearly attributed to his client. The situation would be somewhat different, however, were a lawyer required to raise a "colorable" procedural objection simply because his client insisted that he do so. An objection may be "nonfrivolous" yet so unlikely to succeed that the lawyer who raises it will be viewed as wasting the time of the court. If the lawyer were forced to raise such a claim because of his client's insistence, he could hardly inform the court that he was presenting the claim only because he was required to do so. So too, if forced to present the testimony of an exceptionally weak witness, the lawyer could hardly inform the jury that the witness was called at his client's direction. In the end, this concern that the lawyer not be forced to sacrifice his professional reputation while providing no true assistance to his client may explain, as well as any other factor, the narrow range of decisions assigned to the control of the client.

§ 11.7 The Right to Effective Assistance of Counsel: Guiding Principles

(a) The Prerequisite of a Constitutional Right to Counsel. The Supreme Court first recognized a constitutional right to the effective assistance of counsel in *Powell v. Alabama.*[1] *Powell* noted that where due process requires the state to provide counsel for an indigent defendant, "that duty is not discharged by an assignment at such a time or under such circumstances as to preclude the giving of effective aid in the preparation and trial of the case." Ten years later, in *Glasser v. United States,*[2] the Court held in a federal case that the Sixth Amendment was violated by judicial action that denied defendant his "right to have the effective assistance of [his] counsel." Following its recognition of an equal protection right to appointed counsel on first appeal, the Court held that a defendant taking such an appeal also had a constitutional right to the effective assistance of his appellate counsel.[3] In *Evitts v. Lucey,*[4] after concluding that the constitutional right to counsel on a first appeal of right also had a due process grounding and therefore applies as well to retained counsel, the Court found that defendant was entitled *a fortiori* to effective representation by retained counsel on that appeal. For "a party whose counsel is unable to provide effective representation is in no better position than one who has no counsel at all." [5]

§ 11.7

1. 287 U.S. 45, 53 S.Ct. 55, 77 L.Ed. 158 (1932). See § 11.1(a).

2. 315 U.S. 60, 62 S.Ct. 457, 86 L.Ed. 680 (1942). In *Glasser,* the trial court appointed defendant's retained counsel to also represent a codefendant and thereby placed counsel in a position where his effectiveness was limited by a conflict of interest. See § 11.9(b).

3. Anders v. California, 386 U.S. 738, 87 S.Ct. 1396, 18 L.Ed.2d 493 (1967); Jones v. Barnes, 463 U.S. 745, 103 S.Ct. 3308, 77 L.Ed.2d 987 (1983).

4. 469 U.S. 387, 105 S.Ct. 830, 83 L.Ed.2d 821 (1985).

5. In *Evitts,* the retained counsel had failed to comply with a state requirement that counsel serve on the appellate court both the record on appeal and a statement of appeal, and that failure to perfect the appeal led to its dismissal. The state conceded that counsel's failure constituted ineffective assistance, but contended both that there was no underlying due process right to counsel (see § 11.1 following note 13) and that any such right did not encompass a requirement of effective assistance of counsel. In rejecting the latter argument, the Court characterized as "exaggerated" the state's argument that recognition of an effective assistance requirement would disable state courts from enforcing a wide range of requirements for perfecting appeals (the state contending that counsel henceforth could disobey such rules with impunity, being assured that the state courts would nevertheless have to grant review upon defendant's claim that counsel's omission resulted in ineffective assistance of counsel). The Court noted the longstanding recognition of a right to effective assistance at trial had not rendered ineffective the more complex procedural rules governing

Taken together, the above cases establish that a constitutional requirement of effective assistance extends to counsel's performance in any proceeding as to which there would be both a constitutional right to appointed counsel for the indigent and to retained counsel for the non-indigent. In other words, a necessary corollary of a constitutional right to counsel that is based on the fair-hearing grounding of the Sixth Amendment or due process, or the concept of equal protection, is that counsel actually serve the role that led to the constitutional recognition of the right to counsel. Where, however, there is no such constitutional right to the assistance of counsel, *Wainwright v. Torna* [6] and *Pennsylvania v. Finley* [7] establish that the same constitutional requirement of effective assistance of counsel does not apply.

In *Wainwright v. Torna,* defendant argued that he had been denied the effective assistance of counsel when his retained attorney failed to file a timely application for discretionary review at the state's second-level appeal. Noting that "*Ross v. Moffitt* [had] held that a criminal defendant does not have a constitutional right to counsel to pursue [such] discretionary state appeals," the per curiam majority opinion concluded that the lawyer's negligence therefore did not violate any constitutional right of the defendant. The Court reasoned: "Since respondent had no constitutional right to counsel, he could not be deprived of the effective assistance of counsel by his retained counsel's failure to file the application timely."

In § 11.1, it was suggested that in proceedings as to which there is no right to appointed counsel (such as that involved in *Torna*), the defendant nonetheless may have a constitutionally protected interest in being represented by retained counsel and the state therefore cannot preclude such representation absent a compelling justification.[8] *Wainwright v. Torna* indicates that, even if such a right to utilize retained counsel were to be recognized as to a particular proceeding, it would not carry with it the guarantee of effective assistance that is a part of the traditional right to counsel. Since a right to retained counsel in those additional proceedings would rest only on the "state's duty to refrain from unreasonable interference with the individual's desire to defend himself in whatever manner he deems best," rather than on the need for counsel to ensure a fair proceeding, it would not carry with it a state obligation to ensure that counsel was effective. The defendant alone would bear the consequences of his unwise choice of counsel, as he did in *Torna.* Thus, the Court there found unpersuasive the defendant's claim that he had been "denied due process * * * [when] counsel deprived him of his right to petition the Florida Supreme Court for review." The majority responded: "Such deprivation—even if implicating a due process interest—was caused by his counsel and not by the State. Certainly, the actions of the Florida Supreme Court in dismissing the application for review that was not filed timely did not deprive respondent of due process of law." [9]

trials nor had the dire consequences predicted by the state materialized in those jurisdictions that previously recognized a right to effective assistance on appeal. There remained open to the state several courses of action (e.g., imposing sanctions on the attorney) that could ensure enforcement of its procedural rules without intruding upon the due process rights of the attorney's client.

6. 455 U.S. 586, 102 S.Ct. 1300, 71 L.Ed.2d 475 (1982).

7. See note 10 infra.

8. See § 11.1 following note 20.

9. See also Coleman v. Thompson, ___ U.S. ___, 111 S.Ct. 2546, 115 L.Ed.2d 640, (1991) (where the defendant had no constitutional right to counsel in the particular proceeding, he is "bound by the acts of his lawyer-agent" even though such performance is clearly deficient; but where there is such a right, the consequence of counsel's ineffective performance can be "imputed to the State").

Following essentially the reasoning advanced by the Court in *Torna,* a series of lower court rulings have rejected constitutional claims based on the allegedly incompetent performance of retained counsel in advising defendant during conversations with police or prosecutor that occurred prior to the initiation of adversary judicial proceedings (which marks the start of the Sixth Amendment right to counsel). See e.g., People v. Claudio, 59 N.Y.2d 556, 466 N.Y.S.2d 271, 453 N.E.2d 500 (1983) (where defendant confessed to police "in a noncustodial setting," following his retained counsel's advice, at a time when the police acknowledged that they lacked sufficient evidence to "book" him, that confession would not be suppressed even though counsel's performance had been "woefully inadequate").

Would the result in *Torna* have been different if the counsel there had been appointed a counsel? Although the state would not have had constitutional obligation to provide counsel on the application for discretionary second-tier review, having done so, would it then bear greater responsibility for counsel's performance? That issue was posed in *Pennsylvania v. Finley,*[10] where the Court's narrow ruling suggested only a partial answer. *Finley* involved counsel appointed to represent an indigent prisoner in challenging her conviction through a state postconviction procedure. The appointed counsel advised the habeas court that the prisoner's claim was totally without merit, which resulted in the court-approved withdrawal of counsel and the dismissal of the petition for postconviction relief. The prisoner then challenged that dismissal, arguing that her counsel's action had constituted ineffective assistance because it was inconsistent with the withdrawal safeguards that the Supreme Court had prescribed in *Anders v. California.*[11] *Anders* had involved appointed appellate counsel on a first appeal of right and it had prescribed those safeguards to ensure that the constitutional right to counsel established in *Douglas v. California* was not subverted by no-merit withdrawals. The Court in *Finley* held that the *Anders* safeguards were not constitutionally required in a postconviction proceeding because the state had no constitutional obligation to appoint counsel in such proceeding. The Court did not go so far as to say that a defendant had no constitutional grounding for complaining about an appointed counsel's ineffective representation where, as in *Finley,* the state provided appointed counsel under state practice rather than a constitutional mandate. Rather, the Court simply noted that *Anders* established "a prophylactic framework that is relevant when, and only when, a litigant has a previously established constitutional right to counsel," and that "the procedures followed by respondent's habeas counsel fully comported with 'fundamental fairness.' "

Both *Torna* and *Finley* involved proceedings that the state had no constitutional obligation to provide. Where the state has a constitutional obligation to provide a particular process, but that obligation does not include a duty to appoint counsel, the ineffective performance of counsel (either retained or appointed pursuant to local practice) might be successfully challenged by reference to the adequacy of that process. Such a possibility would be presented, for example, by the ineffective assistance of retained counsel at a misdemeanor trial which resulted in the imposition only of a fine (and therefore was not a proceeding at which the Sixth Amendment would guarantee a right to appointed counsel).[12] The defendant could argue here that ineffectiveness of counsel resulted in a proceeding in which defendant was so deprived of his ability to make use of the procedural rights constitutionally guaranteed to him in such a trial that the proceeding itself did not comport with due process. The state might respond that its due process obligation was only to make those hearing rights available to the defendant, and the failure of the defendant to take advantage of those rights due to counsel's incompetency is not the state's responsibility, just as the loss of the appeal was not the state's responsibility in *Torna.* Here, however, what is at stake is the state's basic authority to impose a sanction, which is conditioned constitutionally on a fair determination of liability. In light of that constitutional prerequisite, the state might not so readily be allowed to ignore the actions of counsel, though it had no duty to provide or allow for counsel, where counsel's actions rendered meaningless the rights afforded the defendant to ensure that fair determination of liability.

(b) Retained vs. Appointed Counsel. Prior to the Supreme Court's 1980 decision in *Cuyler v. Sullivan,*[13] many lower courts utilized different standards for reviewing ineffective assistance claims depending upon whether counsel was appointed or privately re-

10. 481 U.S. 551, 107 S.Ct. 1990, 95 L.Ed.2d 539 (1987). See also § 11.1 following note 18.

11. See § 11.2(c).

12. See § 11.2(a).

13. 446 U.S. 335, 100 S.Ct. 1708, 64 L.Ed.2d 333 (1980).

tained. Those courts found a basis in the state-action requirement of the Fourteenth Amendment for applying a less stringent standard of review to the alleged incompetency of retained counsel. A constitutional violation, it was argued, required state participation of a sufficient level to render the state responsible for counsel's inadequacies. That responsibility was seen as arising automatically from the trial court's selection of appointed counsel. As for retained counsel, the state bore responsibility for counsel's inadequacies only where they were so obvious that they should have been apparent to the trial court. Other lower courts rejected this distinction. They argued that the necessary element of state action was provided by the trial of the defendant without competent counsel, and that involvement did not hinge on counsel's status as court-appointed or privately retained.

Cuyler put to rest this division among the lower courts. The ineffective assistance claim in *Cuyler* was based upon a retained attorney's multiple representation of codefendants with possibly conflicting interests. Although arguing that counsel was not ineffective, the prosecution also claimed that, in any event, "the alleged failings of * * * retained counsel cannot provide a basis for a * * * [constitutional violation] because the conduct of retained counsel does not involve state action." Rejecting that contention, the Supreme Court noted:

> A proper respect for the Sixth Amendment disarms [the prosecution's] contention that defendants who retain their own counsel are entitled to less protection than defendants for whom the State appoints counsel. * * * The vital guarantee of the Sixth Amendment would stand for little if the often uninformed decision to retain a particular lawyer could reduce or forfeit the defendant's entitlement to constitutional protection. Since the State's conduct of a criminal trial itself implicates the State in the defendant's conviction, we see no basis for drawing a distinction between retained and appointed counsel that would deny equal justice to defendants who must choose their own lawyers.

Adhering to the obvious thrust of this statement, lower courts have refused to limit the Court's analysis to the multiple representation situation presented in *Cuyler.* Since *Cuyler,* they have uniformly held that the standard of review applied to all types of ineffectiveness claims will not vary with the status of counsel as retained or court-appointed.

(c) The Nature of Effective Assistance. Prior to the 1984 rulings in *United States v. Cronic* [14] and *Strickland v. Washington,*[15] the Supreme Court had not attempted to deal with concept of effective assistance of counsel in a general fashion. Previous rulings had not gone beyond offering standards tied to particular settings likely to result in a lack of effective assistance. Responding to divisions among the lower courts, the opinions for the Court in *Cronic* and *Strickland,* which were announced on the same day, sought to provide a general framework for analysis of ineffective assistance claims. The critical element, both opinions noted, was to evaluate the performance of counsel in light of the underlying purpose of the constitutional right to counsel. Since both cases involved challenges to the performance of counsel at the trial level, the opinions focused on the purpose of the Sixth Amendment right to counsel. However, since the Court indicated that the role of counsel under that Amendment flowed from the adversary nature of the trial process, and that the same principles would apply to other stages of the criminal justice process that were "like a trial in its adversarial format and in the existence of the standards for decision," the analysis of *Cronic* and *Strickland* has apparent applicability as well to those stages of the process in which due process or equal protection establish a constitutional right to counsel.[16]

14. 466 U.S. 648, 104 S.Ct. 2039, 80 L.Ed.2d 657 (1984).

15. 466 U.S. 668, 104 S.Ct. 2052, 80 L.Ed.2d 674 (1984).

16. The defendant's challenge in *Strickland* was to the performance of counsel in a capital sentencing proceeding. After discussing the role of counsel in the adversary adjudication of guilt, the Court noted that the same principles applied to a capital sentencing proceeding as it was "sufficiently like a trial in its adversarial

The Sixth Amendment right to counsel, the Court noted in *Strickland,* was aimed, like other Sixth Amendment rights, at providing the "basic elements of a fair trial." A key component of that fair trial was an adversarial system of litigation. The Sixth Amendment included a guarantee of assistance of counsel because "it envision[ed] counsel playing a role that is critical to the ability of the adversarial system to produce just results." The " 'very premise of our adversary system * * * is that partisan advocacy on both sides of a case will best promote the ultimate objective that the guilty be convicted and the innocent go free,' " and it was this " 'very premise' that underlies and gives meaning to the Sixth Amendment." Effective assistance therefore must be measured by reference to the functioning of the adversary process in the particular case. "The right to effective assistance," the *Cronic* opinion noted, is "the right of the accused to require the prosecution's case to survive the crucible of meaningful adversary testing. When a true adversarial criminal trial has been conducted—even if defense counsel may have made demonstrable errors—the kind of testing envisioned by the Sixth Amendment has occurred." The critical question therefore is whether counsel's performance was so deficient that the process "lost its character as a confrontation between adversaries," producing an "actual breakdown of the adversary process." Emphasizing this same point of reference, the Court stated in *Strickland*: "The benchmark for judging any claim of ineffectiveness must be whether counsel's conduct so undermined the proper functioning of the adversarial process that the trial cannot be relied on as having produced a just result."

In tieing the concept of effective assistance to the functioning of the adversary process, the Court clearly rejected a measurement based solely on a comparison of counsel with his or her peers. The key was not how close counsel came to gaining for defendant the best possible result that an attorney might have realistically achieved. Neither was it the grade counsel might receive as measured against some model for attorney performance, whether theoretical or reflective of empirical data. Rather the focus was on the presence of the requisite adversarial testing. The most obvious case of ineffectiveness would be that in which counsel simply did not act as an advocate, either because he was prevented from doing so or simply did not make the effort. Where counsel sought to perform as advocate, the question would then be whether his effort provided a "meaningful adversary testing." What was "meaningful" for this purpose would be measured by reference to the basic objective of the adversary process, to ensure the reliability of any conviction. Thus, as the *Cronic* opinion noted, a failing to provide adversarial testing as to a single issue, when that issue is critical to a finding of guilt, may in itself produce a breakdown in the adversarial process. On the other hand, as *Strickland* further noted, meaning adversarial testing hardly requires that challenges be made and investigations directed at all points without regard to their likely insignificance in testing the reliability of the prosecution's case.

(d) Per Se vs. Actual Ineffectiveness. The concept of effective assistance advanced in *Cronic* and *Strickland* appeared to call for a determination of "actual ineffectiveness" under the facts of the particular case. A constitutional challenge could be found only upon a determination both that counsel had actually failed in some respect to discharge the duties of an advocate in an adversarial system and that the failure so affected the adversary process as to undermine confidence in the outcome of the proceeding. This required a fact-sensitized judgment that evaluated the nature and impact of counsel's representation under the circumstances of the individual case. Not all of the Court's past rul-

format and in the existence of standards for decision." In Smith v. Murray, 477 U.S. 527, 106 S.Ct. 2661, 91 L.Ed.2d 434 (1986), the Court later applied the "test of Strickland v. Washington" to the alleged incompetency of appellate counsel. See also § 11.10 at note 4. However, the *Strickland* opinion did note that "the role of counsel in an ordinary sentencing proceeding, which may involve informal proceedings and standardless discretion on the sentencer, * * * may require a different approach to the definition of constitutionally effective assistance."

ings, however, had adopted such a "judgmental" approach. Some had seemingly relied upon categorical or per se standards of ineffective assistance. Here, constitutional violations were established primarily by reference to the setting which affected counsel's performance. In some instances, the Court had not pointed to particular failings of counsel. In others, particular failings were automatically presumed to have had a prejudicial impact undermining confidence in the reliability of defendant's conviction.

Numerous commentators and several jurists had applauded this per se approach, and several lower courts had sought to extend it to other settings. They saw the per se approach as a necessary tool in obtaining quality representation by counsel, particular for the poor. There was a need, they argued, for prophylactic measures. The courts had to respond to severe institutional restraints impeding effective representation, such as caseload pressures, cut-rate fees for court appointments, and inexperienced defenders. To require a fact-specific finding of actual ineffectiveness was to allow too many cases of incompetency to survive judicial review, as counsel's inadequacies are often hidden in investigative failure and prejudice to the defendant takes forms that are often imperceptible.

In *Cronic,* the Court was presented with a case in which the lower court had extended the per se approach in determining ineffectiveness. The Supreme Court used the occasion to firmly establish that a determination of actual effectiveness is the usual prerequisite for sustaining an ineffective assistance claim. The use of a per se or "inferential approach" was limited to special circumstances not present in the case before it. In *Strickland,* as discussed in § 11.10, the Court built upon the analysis of *Cronic* to reject the use of performance guidelines in assessing counsel's contribution to the adversary process. The "purpose of the effective assistance guarantee," the Court noted, "is not to improve the quality of legal representation, although that is a goal of considerable importance to the legal system." Rather, the guarantee serves "simply to ensure that criminal defendants receive a fair trial."

The lower court in *Cronic* had sustained defendant's ineffectiveness claim without referring to any specific error or inadequacy in counsel's performance. Instead, it had inferred that "counsel was unable to discharge his duties" based upon the circumstances relating to five factors: "(1) the time afforded for investigation and preparation; (2) the experience of counsel; (3) the gravity of the charge; (4) the complexity of possible defenses; and (5) the accessibility of witnesses to counsel." Justice Stevens' opinion for eight members of the Court concluded that the lower court's adoption of this "inferential approach" lacked support in the Court's prior precedent and was inconsistent with the function of the effective assistance requirement.

Justice Stevens' opinion initially stressed that a judicial evaluation of an ineffectiveness claim must "begin by recognizing that the right to the effective assistance of counsel is recognized not for its own sake, but because of the effect it has on the ability of the accused to receive a fair trial." Accordingly, establishment of an ineffectiveness claim ordinarily requires some showing of an adverse effect on the reliability of the trial process. Moreover, because "we presume that the lawyer is competent," the burden ordinarily rests on the accused to make that showing. "There are, however, circumstances that are so likely to prejudice the accused that the cost of litigating their effect in a particular case is unjustified." In such situations, constitutional effectiveness, amounting to a "breakdown of the adversarial process," could be presumed.

Justice Stevens then turned to the Court's past decisions and found only two settings in which such a presumptive approach was justified. First, there was the situation in which "counsel was either totally absent or prevented from assisting the accused during a critical stage of the proceeding." Falling in this category were cases in which the trial court had unconstitutionally refused to appoint counsel or had restricted counsel's assistance.[17] Another instance would be that in which counsel was present in fact but absent in performance—where counsel "entirely fails to subject the prosecution's case to meaningful adversarial testing." Second, there were "occasions when, although counsel is available to assist the accused during trial, the likelihood that any lawyer, even a fully competent one, could provide effective assistance is so small that a presumption of prejudice is appropriate without inquiry into the actual conduct of the trial." *Powell v. Alabama* was such a case.[18] The trial court there had utilized such a haphazard process of appointment—ordering admittedly unprepared outstate counsel to proceed with whatever help the local bar, appointed en masse, might provide—that ineffective assistance was properly presumed without further inquiry.

The circumstances presented in *Powell* and in the absent or restricted counsel cases were viewed as exceptional. "Apart from circumstances of that magnitude," the *Cronic* opinion noted, "there is generally no basis for finding a Sixth Amendment violation unless the accused can show specific errors undermining the reliability of the finding of guilt." A footnote cited the conflict-of-interest cases as another setting in which prejudice would be presumed, but there it must be shown either that an actual conflict of interest adversely affected counsel's performance or that the trial court failed to respond as constitutionally required to an apparent conflict.[19] In the case before the Court in *Cronic,* the lower court had not cited any "actual conduct of the trial" indicating "a breakdown in the adversarial process that would justify a presumption that respondent's conviction was insufficiently reliable to satisfy the Constitution." It simply had relied on the surrounding circumstances to "justify a presumption of ineffectiveness * * * without inquiry into counsel's performance at trial." The five circumstances cited to justify that presumption hardly presented a setting "so likely to prejudice" as to be analogous to *Powell* or the cases in which a defendant was denied the assistance of counsel at a critical stage. While all five were "relevant to an evaluation of a lawyer's ineffectiveness in a particular case, * * * neither separately nor in combination [did] they provide a basis for concluding that competent counsel was not able to provide * * * the guiding hand that the Constitution guarantees." [20]

§ 11.8 Ineffective Assistance Claims Based Upon State Interference

(a) Restrictions Upon Counsel's Assistance. The "right to the assistance of counsel," the Supreme Court noted in *Herring v. New York,*[1] "has been understood to mean that there can be no restrictions upon the function of counsel in defending a criminal prosecution in accord with the traditions of the adversary factfinding process." Accordingly, state action, whether by statute or trial court ruling, that prohibits counsel from making full use of traditional trial procedures may be viewed as denying defendant the effective assistance of counsel. In considering the constitutionality of such "state interference," courts are directed to look to whether

17. See §§ 11.2(b), 11.8(a). These errors are characterized as requiring "automatic reversal" of a conviction, and thereby constituting exceptions to the constitutional harmless error doctrine of Chapman v. California. See § 27.6(d).

18. Supra note 1.

19. See § 11.9(b), (d).

20. The Court noted in this regard that: (1) even though counsel had far less time to prepare his case than the government spent in its investigation, it could not be said that the time he did have (25 days) was necessarily insufficient; (2) the character of a lawyer's experience may shed light on an evaluation of his actual performance, but the fact that counsel was young and conducting his first jury trial "would not justify a presumption on ineffectiveness in the absence of such an evaluation"; (3) "the three other criteria—the gravity of the charge, the complexity of the case, and the accessibility of witnesses—* * * [also failed to] identif[y] circumstances that in themselves make it unlikely that respondent received the effective assistance of counsel." The Court stressed that it was not holding that counsel's representation met Sixth Amendment standards, but only that the determination of that issue must rest on an examination of his actual performance in light of the circumstances of the case.

§ 11.8

1. 422 U.S. 853, 95 S.Ct. 2550, 45 L.Ed.2d 593 (1975).

the interference denied counsel "the opportunity to participate fully and fairly in the adversary factfinding process." If the interference had that effect, then the overall performance of counsel apart from the interference and the lack of any showing of actual prejudice are both irrelevant. For as the Court noted in *Cronic,* [2] where defendant is "denied counsel at a critical stage of his trial," the "presumption that counsel's assistance is essential requires * * * [the] conclu[sion] that a trial is unfair."

Four Supreme Court cases illustrate the type of state imposed restriction upon counsel's performance that will be held to violate the Sixth Amendment. In *Geders v. United States,*[3] the trial court ordered the defendant not to consult with his attorney during an overnight recess which separated the direct-examination and the cross-examination of the defendant. The court of appeals affirmed the conviction because the defendant made no claim of prejudice from the order. The Supreme Court reversed, holding the 17 hour denial of counsel, regardless of demonstrated prejudice, constituted a deprivation of the effective assistance of counsel. While a trial court could require that the defendant, like any other witness, not be allowed to consult with counsel during the course of giving testimony, the extensive prohibition here could well have precluded discussion on a variety of defense concerns unrelated to the content of the defendant's testimony.[4] In *Herring v. New York,*[5] the Court held that defendant's Sixth Amendment right to counsel was violated by a statute under which the trial court could refuse to permit a closing argument in a bench trial. The Court reasoned that a final summation by counsel was as basic an element of the adversary process in a bench trial as it was in a jury trial. In *Brooks v. Tennessee,*[6] a statute requiring the defendant to testify as the first defense witness or not at all was held to deny due process by depriving the defendant of the " 'guiding hand of counsel' in the timing of this critical element of the defense." In *Ferguson v. Georgia,*[7] a pre-*Gideon* decision, a statute which allowed the defendant to make an unsworn statement but denied direct examination by his counsel was held to violate due process.

In each of the cases described above, the Court arguably might also have held the particular restriction unconstitutional on the ground that it imposed an undue burden on the exercise of a constitutionally protected trial right.[8] Whether such a ruling would have required a conviction reversal is uncertain, however, because most constitutional violations are subject to the harmless error standard of *Chapman v. California.*[9] The unconstitutional state imposed interference with counsel, in contrast, is presumed prejudicial and therefore requires automatic reversal. In explaining why this presumption is drawn, the Court has cited the similar treatment of Sixth Amendment violations arising from the failure to appoint counsel and counsel ineffectiveness based on a conflict of interest.[10] The fit of both analogies, however, is less than perfect.

2. See § 11.7(d).

3. 425 U.S. 80, 96 S.Ct. 1330, 47 L.Ed.2d 592 (1976).

4. Thus, the Court later distinguished (and upheld) an order prohibiting defendant's consultation with counsel over a 15 minute recess declared during the course of defendant's testimony. See Perry v. Leeke, § 24.5, note 15.

5. Supra note 1.

6. 406 U.S. 605, 92 S.Ct. 1891, 32 L.Ed.2d 358 (1972).

7. 365 U.S. 570, 81 S.Ct. 756, 5 L.Ed.2d 783 (1961).

8. *Brooks* also held that the state ruling requiring defendant to testify first, or lose his right to testify, imposed an unconstitutional burden upon defendant's free exercise of his Fifth Amendment right not to testify. See § 24.5 at note 4. In *Ferguson,* two justices, in a concurring opinion, argued that the underlying state statute prohibiting the defendant from testifying on his own behalf was unconstitutional. *Geders* might similarly have been viewed as imposing an excessive burden (considering the extent of the prohibition) upon a defendant's right to testify. Cf. Perry v. Leeke, supra note 4. See also § 24.5(d). *Herring* might have rested on a due process right to a summation as a necessary element of a fair factfinding process. But see Rehnquist, J., dissenting in *Herring.*

9. See § 27.6(d).

10. See United States v. Cronic, § 11.7(d); Perry v. Leeke, supra note 4 (rejecting the contention that the ruling in *Strickland,* infra note 13, insisting upon a showing of actual prejudice in lawyer incompetency cases, required reexamination of the position that actual prejudice need not be shown in state-interference cases).

As for the failure to appoint counsel, the analogy here rests on the long accepted rule that a violation of *Gideon v. Wainwright* (i.e., a total failure to provide the assistance of counsel) constitutes automatic grounds for reversal. The *Chapman* opinion itself reaffirmed that rule in noting that *Gideon* violations were not appropriately subjected to a harmless error analysis. That position, however, has been explained as following from the inherently indeterminate impact of the lack of counsel's assistance for the entire criminal prosecution. Where the Sixth Amendment violation is based on the failure to appoint counsel only for a particular critical stage of the prosecution, that violation has required automatic reversal as to some stages and has been subjected to the *Chapman* standard as to others.[11] While the precise factors that have led to distinguishing between different critical stages for this purpose have not always been clearly identified, one undoubtedly is the ability to isolate the likely impact of the absence of counsel at the particular stage. Thus the harmless error standard has been applied to the denial of counsel at the preliminary hearing because an appellate court can identify those benefits that could have been gained through counsel's assistance and assess whether they could have had a bearing upon the outcome of the subsequent trial.[12] That the same task could be accomplished in the state-interference cases is suggested by the standard that would be applied in assessing an ineffectiveness claim where counsel, rather than being prevented by the state procedure from rendering the particular assistance, had simply failed to render such assistance due to ineptitude. Consider, for example, a case where counsel failed to present a final summation (as in *Herring*) or required defendant to make an early decision as to testifying (as in *Brooks*) because of a mistaken view of the law. There the standard announced in *Strickland* would apply, and the defendant would have to establish the likelihood of actual prejudice.[13] Under the *Strickland* standard, it is readily conceivable that a court could find that such ineffectiveness by counsel had a discrete impact so minimal as not to meet the prejudice prong of the *Strickland* standard.

The above analysis suggests that the critical factor leading to the presumption of prejudice in the state-interference cases does not flow from an inability to assess the impact of the violation, or a likelihood of prejudicial impact so great as to make the cost of litigating that impact unjustified, but rather the role played by the state in restricting counsel's representation. Support for this view may be found in the analogy drawn to the presumption of prejudice applied in the conflict-of-interest cases. Initially, that analogy too might be distinguished, as the presumption drawn in conflict cases commonly is seen as a product of the potentially indeterminate impact of representation corrupted by an actual conflict acted upon by counsel.[14] However, that presumption also has been justified on the ground that the trial court bears some responsibility for the presence of a conflict problem that it could avoid through a pretrial inquiry and appropriate precautionary action.[15] Indeed, that special responsibility has led the Court to recognize a constitutional violation in some circumstances simply on the trial court's failure to conduct an inquiry.[16] In the interference cases as well, the presumption of prejudice may be described as a prophylactic measure designed to discourage state action that may well preclude effective representation.

(b) Late Appointment of Counsel. Although the late appointment of counsel may also constitute a "direct state interference" with counsel's performance, late appointments do not necessarily have that impact. Thus, they are distinguishable from the state impediments condemned in cases like *Herring* and *Geders,* which clearly prevented counsel

11. See § 27.6 at notes 18, 26–29.

12. See Coleman v. Alabama, discussed at § 14.4(d) and § 27.6 at note 27.

13. See § 11.10(a), (d).

14. See § 11.9 at note 9.

15. See note 13, § 11.9.

16. See § 11.9(b).

from fully utilizing important procedural rights. A counsel appointed only shortly before trial, depending upon the circumstances of the case, may be as able to proceed as fully and effectively as he might have had he been appointed several weeks earlier. Accordingly, it is not surprising that the Supreme Court, in *Chambers v. Maroney,*[17] declined to "fashion a per se rule requiring reversal of every conviction following tardy appointment of counsel." The facts of that case reflect the difficulties that would be presented in shaping any hard and fast rules as to the time needed to ensure that counsel is adequately prepared. Indeed, it was not even clear in *Chambers* exactly when counsel had assumed responsibility for representing the defendant.

The defendant in *Chambers* had been represented at his first trial by a Legal Aid Society attorney who had ample time to prepare. That trial ended in a mistrial, and defendant was retried three weeks later. Another Legal Aid attorney represented the defendant at the second trial, and he did not consult with defendant until a few minutes before the trial. Defendant argued that "counsel['s] appearance * * * was so belated that he could not have furnished effective legal assistance at the second trial." The district court rejected defendant's claim without holding an evidentiary hearing to determine what counsel actually had done to prepare for the trial. It noted that counsel had access to the case file prepared by the original attorney, who apparently had consulted with the defendant. The Third Circuit affirmed. It concluded that counsel's initial appearance on the morning of the trial constituted a "tardy appointment" and an evidentiary hearing therefore would have been advisable. However, on review of the record, it found "adequate affirmative evidence of lack of prejudice." Defendant's primary complaint was that counsel failed to make certain pretrial suppression motions, but those motions clearly would have failed. The Supreme Court, in its affirmance, noted that it was "not inclined to disturb the judgment of the court of appeals as to what the record shows." That court had carefully examined the record and found "ample grounds for holding that the appearance of a different attorney at the second trial had not resulted in prejudice to petitioner." The Supreme Court added that it was not prepared to hold that a tardy appointment automatically required a reversal of a conviction or even an evidentiary hearing.

While the *Chambers* ruling indicates that a tardy appointment will not require reversal if it clearly did not prejudice the defendant, the Court there did not discuss the allocation of the burden on the matter of prejudice. The Third Circuit in *Chambers* had held that a tardy appointment establishes a presumption of prejudice which must be overcome "either by evidence produced by the state in an evidentiary hearing * * * or by adequate affirmative proof otherwise appearing in the record demonstrating that the appellant was not prejudiced." *Chambers* failure to comment upon this approach suggested that it might be deemed acceptable. However, the Court's later discussion in *Cronic* of the general need for proof of actual ineffectiveness, and its treatment there of the claim of inadequate preparation time, clearly suggests otherwise.[18]

The *Cronic* opinion warned against using any rule of thumb—such as the time spent by the government in its preparation—in determining how much time was needed for defense preparation.[19] It also stressed that only the most exceptional situations would relieve the accused of the burden of showing specific ineffectiveness in the actual conduct of the trial. These comments appear to at least favor, if not directly support, the position

17. 399 U.S. 42, 90 S.Ct. 1975, 26 L.Ed.2d 419 (1970).

18. See § 11.7(d).

19. See § 11.7, note 20. See also, Morris v. Slappy, 461 U.S. 1, 103 S.Ct. 1610, 75 L.Ed.2d 610 (1983). The Court here held that a trial court had not committed constitutional error in denying defendant's request for a delay to permit his recently appointed counsel to conduct further investigations. Although counsel had been appointed only six days before the scheduled trial, he was replacing another attorney in the same office who had supervised an extensive investigation. Counsel had informed the trial court that, on the basis of his study of that investigation and his conferences with his predecessor, he was convinced that a further delay would not be helpful.

taken by those lower courts that have refused to shift the burden in tardy appointment cases. Those courts have reasoned that the time needed for preparation varies too greatly from one case to another to designate a particular time period as creating even a rebuttable presumption of prejudice. The lateness of an appointment is viewed as simply another factor to be considered, under the totality of the circumstances, in determining whether counsel failed to provide effective assistance. However, though the defendant continues to bear the burden of showing counsel's inadequacy, a "belated appointment" is treated as "strong evidence in a defendant's behalf," requiring close scrutiny of counsel's performance.

(c) State Invasions of the Lawyer–Client Relationship. State invasions of the lawyer-client relationship are similar to late appointments, and unlike the direct impediments involved in cases like *Geders* and *Herring,* in that they do not necessarily restrict the lawyer's performance. Indeed, the circumstances surrounding the invasion may often negate any realistic likelihood that the invasion had any adverse impact upon counsel's performance. In *Weatherford v. Bursey,*[20] the Supreme Court refused to find an automatic Sixth Amendment violation in one such setting. In that case, Bursey, a convicted defendant, brought a civil rights action against Weatherford, a former undercover agent, alleging that Weatherford's actions had denied Bursey the effective assistance of counsel at his criminal trial. In order to maintain Weatherford's undercover status, police had arrested him, along with Bursey, for an offense in which both had participated. Weatherford subsequently attended, at Bursey's request, two pretrial meetings with Bursey and his lawyer. Weatherford did not disclose to his superiors any information derived from those discussions that related to defense plans for the trial. Similarly, when Weatherford was unexpectedly called as a prosecution witness at that trial, he carefully limited his testimony so as not to touch upon anything he might have learned through the lawyer-client meetings.

The basic issue presented in *Weatherford v. Bursey* was whether the Supreme Court would adopt what it described as a "per se" or "prophylactic rule." The lower court had adopted such a rule. Relying on Supreme Court precedent, it had held that "whenever the prosecution knowingly arranges or permits intrusions into the attorney-client relationship the right to counsel is sufficiently endangered to require reversal and a new trial." A divided Supreme Court held that the lower court had misread the relevant precedent and had adopted a rule that failed to give sufficient weight to the "unfortunate necessity of undercover work and the value it often [has] to effective law enforcement." Admittedly, in *Hoffa v. United States,*[21] another case in which an undercover agent had been present during attorney-client conversations, the Court had assumed, without deciding, that a conviction would be overturned if the informer had reported the substance of those conversations to the authorities. Here, however, as in *Hoffa,* the undercover agent had not reported the substance of the lawyer-client conversations and his trial testimony had not related to those conversations. The Court noted that "Bursey would have a much stronger case" if either (1) Weatherford had testified at trial as to those conversations, (2) the "State's evidence [had] originated from those conversations," (3) the "overheard conversations had been used in any other way to the substantial detriment of Bursey," or (4) "even had the prosecution learned from Weatherford * * * the details of the * * * conversations about trial preparations." But "none of these elements [were] * * * present here," and without "at least a realistic possibility of injury to Bursey or benefit to the state, there [could] be no Sixth Amendment violation." The protection of defendant's Sixth Amendment rights did not require adoption of a per se rule simply to give clients and lawyers the assurance that third parties

20. 429 U.S. 545, 97 S.Ct. 837, 51 L.Ed.2d 30 (1977).

21. 385 U.S. 293, 87 S.Ct. 408, 17 L.Ed.2d 374 (1966). See § 3.10(c).

invited to their meetings are not undercover agents, especially when the cost of such a rule may be, "for all practical purposes," to "unmask" the agent.

Weatherford's conclusion that a state invasion of the lawyer-client relationship does not violate the Sixth Amendment unless there is at least a realistic likelihood of a governmental advantage arguably was limited to cases in which there was a significant justification for the invasion. In *United States v. Morrison*,[22] the Court dealt with an invasion that lacked any such justification. In that case, D.E.A. agents, although aware that the defendant had been indicted and had retained counsel, met with her without defense counsel's knowledge or permission, and while seeking her cooperation, disparaged her retained attorney. The Third Circuit held that defendant's right to counsel was violated irrespective of allegation or proof of prejudice to her case, and that the only appropriate remedy was a dismissal of the prosecution with prejudice. The Supreme Court unanimously reversed. The Court found it unnecessary to rule on the government's contention that a Sixth Amendment violation could not be established here without "some [defense] showing of prejudice." Even if it were assumed that there had been a Sixth Amendment violation, the remedy imposed by the lower court was incorrect because it was not "tailored to the injury suffered." Since "[r]espondent has demonstrated no prejudice of any kind, either transitory or permanent, to the ability of her counsel to provide adequate representation in these criminal proceedings," there was no justification for such "drastic relief" as a dismissal with prejudice.

In declining to reach the government's contention that a showing of prejudice would be needed to establish a Sixth Amendment violation, the *Morrison* opinion left open the possibility that the Court might adopt a per se standard for those state invasions of the lawyer-client relationship that are not supported by any legitimate state motivation. However, even if that position is eventually adopted, the *Morrison* ruling would reintroduce the prejudice element in the assessment of the appropriate remedy for that constitutional violation. Arguably, the requisite showing need not rise to the level of establishing that counsel was restricted in his ability to take specific action at trial (e.g., to introduce particular evidence). A significant potential for an indirect adverse impact upon the defense (e.g., through a general impediment of lawyer-client interaction) might be viewed as sufficient for a less severe remedy than that involved in *Morrison* (e.g., granting a new trial), given a totally unjustified interference with the lawyer-client relationship.

§ 11.9 Ineffective Assistance Claims Based Upon Attorney Conflicts of Interest

(a) The Range of Possible Conflicts of Interest. The courts have long recognized that the constitutional right to effective assistance of counsel entitles the defendant to the "undivided loyalty" of his counsel. The defendant does not receive the full benefit of the adversary process when his attorney's decisions are influenced by obligations owed to persons other than the defendant. Such a division of loyalty can arise in a variety of settings. Without doubt, however, the situation that most frequently produces conflict claims is the representation of more than one codefendant by the same attorney.

The potential for conflict in the representation of codefendants is so grave that many attorneys simply will not undertake joint representation. Although the codefendants may start out with identical concerns, a divergence of interests may develop at almost every point in the progress of the litigation. In the plea bargaining process, the prosecutor may offer a reduced charge or dismissal to one defendant in exchange for testimony against the other. If the case goes to trial, that will usually increase the potential for conflict, especially if the codefendants are jointly tried. The codefendants may raise conflicting defenses, with each implicating the other, or they may adopt a joint defense but offer contradictory expla-

22. 449 U.S. 361, 101 S.Ct. 665, 66 L.Ed.2d 564 (1981).

nations of relevant factual events. Even where their testimony would be entirely consistent, a conflict may arise because the advantages and disadvantages of taking the stand may be quite different for each codefendant. A decision to have both codefendants testify or not testify might work to the disadvantage of one or the other, while a decision to have only one testify would undoubtedly highlight the lack of testimony from the other. In presenting closing argument, the attorney may again find that the interests of his clients diverge. If the prosecution's evidence is much weaker against one client, that defendant's interest suggests that the comparison be brought to the jury's attention, but the other's interest argues against that tactic. A similar conflict may arise at the sentencing stage when the codefendants' roles in the planning and commission of the crime or their backgrounds and prior criminal records vary substantially.

A lawyer also may be placed in a conflict situation when he or she has a professional relationship with both the defendant and a third party who has some interest in the case. Consider, for example, the situation in which defense counsel has previously represented, or is currently representing, in another matter, either the victim of the crime or a prosecution witness. Defense counsel here might hesitate to proceed as vigorously as possible because of his interest in retaining that client's business or his fear that he will be using against that client information obtained from their confidential relationship. A somewhat analogous potential for conflict arises when a third party with some interest in the case pays the legal fees of defense counsel. This situation typically involves an employer paying counsel to represent employees prosecuted for their participation in allegedly illegal acts of the employer's business enterprise. As the Supreme Court has noted, "one risk [presented by this fee arrangement] is that the lawyer will prevent his client from obtaining leniency by preventing the client from offering testimony or from taking other actions contrary to the employer's interest." [1] Still another is that the lawyer may fail to raise certain arguments favorable to the employee in order to force a court ruling on an issue on which the employer has a long-range interest.

Conflicts of interest extend beyond those created by the duties owed by counsel to codefendants or third parties. At times a conflict may exist because the defense counsel has personal interests that affect his professional judgment in representing the client. Thus, a substantial conflict of interest claim is presented where a lawyer representing the defendant at trial is himself under investigation for an offense relating to that being tried. So too, where counsel has been forced by subpoena to present testimony or furnish other evidence used by the prosecution, that participation may restrict counsel's capacity and inclination to challenge such evidence. Certain fee arrangements also can create a conflict between the interests of the defendant and his counsel. Consider, for example, a compensation agreement under which counsel has an interest in the royalties to be received from a movie or book that will portray the trial or related events. Agreements of this kind, the courts have noted, "tempt lawyers, consciously or subconsciously and adversely to the client's interests, to tilt the defense for commercial reasons." Finally, divided loyalties may be present when counsel has a familial or other especially close relationship with a critical prosecution witness or the prosecuting attorney.

While all of the above situations create a potential for inhibiting counsel's actions on behalf of his client, none do so inevitably. Indeed, few situations creating potential conflicts are viewed as so fraught with the danger of dividing counsel's loyalties as to produce an absolute prohibition of representation under prevailing standards of professional responsibility. Of course, the profession's willingness to tolerate representation in settings

§ 11.9

1. Wood v. Georgia, 450 U.S. 261, 101 S.Ct. 1097, 67 L.Ed.2d 220 (1981).

that create a potential for divided loyalty is not based simply upon the fact that there is no certainty that the lawyer actually will face a conflict. If nothing positive could be said for allowing representation in those settings, there would be no reason to risk the possibility of conflict. Skeptics of professional self-regulation suggest that the primary positive value in allowing representation in potential conflict situations is preserving the revenue of the chosen counsel, but supporters of the prevailing standards of professional responsibility contend that the primary consideration in allowing such representation is facilitating the adversary process. They note that arrangements that create a conflict but have no positive value, such as compensation agreements giving the attorney publication rights, have been flatly prohibited. Those arrangements that remain, they argue, were accepted because they may, in many situations, provide a positive benefit to the client.[2] Initially, such arrangements may permit the client to obtain the services of the one lawyer that he wants to represent him. Some defendants put their trust in a particular lawyer and would want that lawyer even though he may have previously represented one of the prosecution's witnesses or even the victim. Some would prefer a privately retained lawyer and can afford one only if their employer, a codefendant, or some other interested person will pay that lawyer. Joint representation of codefendants, in particular, may have strategic advantages. Thus the Supreme Court has noted: "Joint representation is a means of ensuring against reciprocal recrimination. A common defense often gives strength against a common attack." [3]

As one might anticipate, the courts have not been willing to find in the Constitution a prophylactic bar against representation in potential conflict settings when the profession itself has been unwilling to ban absolutely such representation. On the other hand, the courts have been willing to view representation in many of those settings as suspect. They have recognized also that it is often impossible to reconstruct the precise impact of a divided loyalty upon counsel's performance. In particular, a conflict of interest may have as much bearing on matters that are not reflected in the appellate record (e.g., the failure to interview witnesses or seek a plea bargain) as it does on those acts or omissions at trial that are a part of the record. Very often the only person who knows exactly what the conflict's full ramification might have been is the defense lawyer himself, and courts are naturally wary of his disclaimers of influence (or even his acknowledgement of influence, which may be seen as a "last ditch" effort to help his client). One response to these difficulties inherent in a postconviction attempt to trace the impact of a possible conflict has been the development of a trial court obligation to make a pretrial inquiry into possible conflicts.

(b) The Trial Court Duty to Inquire. The two leading cases on the trial court's constitutional duty to inquire into possible conflicts of interest, *Holloway v. Arkansas* [4] and *Cuyler v. Sullivan,*[5] both involved multiple representation situations. In *Holloway,* a public defender had been appointed to represent three codefendants who were to be jointly tried on charges of robbery and rape. Three weeks before trial, defense counsel requested the appointment of separate counsel for each of the defendants, noting that defendants' statements to him indicated "a possibility of a conflict of interest." The trial court rejected the request and defense counsel continued his joint representation. On the day of the trial, before the jury was empaneled, defense counsel renewed his request. He informed the court that one or two of the defen-

2. See ABA Model Rules of Professional Conduct, Rule 1.7 (1983) (representation allowed where it will be limited by responsibilities owed to another client, if the lawyer reasonably believes the representation will not be adversely affected and the clients affected consent after consultation). Compare Id. at Rule 1.8(d) (prohibiting agreements giving counsel "literary or media rights to a portrayal or account based in substantial part on information relating to the representation").

3. Holloway v. Arkansas, infra note 4 (quoting Frankfurter, J., in an earlier opinion).

4. 435 U.S. 475, 98 S.Ct. 1173, 55 L.Ed.2d 426 (1978).

5. Infra note 10.

dants might testify, and if they did, he would not be able to cross-examine them on behalf of the other defendants since he had received "confidential information" from each of the defendants. The trial court again denied counsel's request. It directed him to simply "put them on the stand * * * and tell the man to go ahead and relate what he wants to." Each of the defendants subsequently testified, giving unguided narrative testimony without cross-examination by defense counsel. All three alleged that they were not at the scene of the crime. The defendants' ineffective assistance claims were subsequently rejected by the state appellate court on the ground that neither an actual conflict of interest nor prejudice had been demonstrated. The Supreme Court, by a 6–3 majority, reversed the convictions of all three codefendants.

Chief Justice Burger's opinion for the Court initially noted that, as had been previously recognized, "joint representation is not per se violative of constitutional guarantees of effective assistance." Such representation could, under some circumstances, be in the best interest of all of the codefendants. On the other hand, each defendant was entitled to representation free of an actual conflict of interest. Here, however, there was no need to determine whether a conflict in fact existed. The trial judge's failure to properly respond to the possibility of defendants' "different interests," after that possibility was "brought home to the court" by counsel's requests for separate representation, was sufficient ground in itself for reversal. In *Glasser v. United States,*[6] the Court had held that defendant was denied his Sixth Amendment right to the effective assistance of counsel when the trial court placed his retained attorney in a conflict situation by appointing that attorney to also represent a codefendant. The *Glasser* Court had noted that the trial judge has a duty not to insist that counsel "undertake to concurrently represent interests which might diverge." The trial judge here violated that duty. The defense counsel's request was timely and obviously not made for "dilatory purposes." The trial court should have responded with more than a cursory dismissal of that request. Its failure "either to appoint separate counsel or take adequate steps to ascertain whether the risk [of a conflict] was too remote to warrant separate counsel" violated the defendants' Sixth Amendment rights.

Having concluded that the trial court committed constitutional error, the *Holloway* opinion turned to the state's claim that reversal of the defendants' convictions still was not required as there had been no showing of specific prejudice. *Glasser,* the Court noted, was to the contrary. Although the language of *Glasser* was not without ambiguity, the *Glasser* opinion was properly read as "holding that whenever a trial court improperly requires joint representation over timely objection reversal is automatic." As *Glasser* had noted, determining the "precise degree of prejudice" in a conflict situation was highly speculative, and the right to counsel was "too fundamental and absolute to allow courts to indulge in [such] nice calculations." Subsequent to *Glasser,* the Supreme Court had recognized in *Chapman v. California*[7] that certain constitutional violations could constitute harmless error. However, *Chapman* and other cases had also recognized that the denial of the right to counsel is "so basic to a fair trial that * * * [it] can never be treated as harmless error."[8] The reasoning of *Glasser,* the *Holloway* opinion concluded, placed in the same category the Sixth Amendment violation presented there. In "the normal case where [*Chapman's*] harmless-error rule is applied, * * * the reviewing court can undertake with some confidence its relatively narrow task of assessing the likelihood that the error materially affected the deliberations of the jury." But as *Glasser* had suggested, in the case of joint representation of conflicting interests, "the evil * * * is in what the advocate finds himself compelled to *refrain* from doing." While "it may be possible in some

6. 315 U.S. 60, 62 S.Ct. 457, 86 L.Ed. 680 (1942).

7. See § 27.6(d).

8. See § 27.6 at notes 18, 25–26.

cases to identify from the record the prejudice resulting from an attorney's failure to undertake certain trial tasks," to "judge intelligently the impact of a conflict on the attorney's [total] representation of a client," including such matters as potential plea negotiations, "would be virtually impossible." An "inquiry into a claim of harmless error here would require, unlike most cases, unguided speculation." [9]

After *Holloway,* what was a trial court to do when counsel sought to withdraw from multiple representation on conflict grounds? The *Holloway* opinion emphasized that its ruling was not "transferring to the defense counsel the authority of the trial judge to rule on the existence or the risk of a conflict." Although "most courts" had held that "an attorney's request for appointment of separate counsel, based on his representation as an officer of the court * * *, should be granted," automatic acceptance of the attorney's request was not constitutionally mandated. The trial court had the alternative of conducting its own inquiry to determine "the adequacy of the basis of defense counsel's representations regarding a conflict of interests." Commentators analyzing *Holloway* suggested, however, that this option might prove largely illusory. The *Holloway* opinion had also noted that the trial court, in making its inquiry, was limited in the extent to which it could inquire into confidential communications between lawyer and client. As a result, if a defense lawyer moving for separate counsel asserted that either the attorney-client privilege or his clients' privilege against self-incrimination precluded a detailed disclosure of the basis for the conflict of interest claim, the trial court's only practical alternative under *Holloway* would be to appoint separate counsel. Lower court rulings since *Holloway* suggest that the commentators correctly perceived the impact of *Holloway* in this regard. Those rulings indicate that a trial court that fails to appoint separate counsel, notwithstanding defense counsel's request, takes a substantial risk of reversal unless the request is clearly dilatory.

Also left open in *Holloway* was the full range of the situations in which the trial court constitutionally was required to at least conduct an inquiry into the risk of a conflict. The fact situation presented in *Holloway* was especially suited for requiring trial court action. As the lower courts later noted, the "imposition upon the state * * * is not heavy" when the trial court has before it a timely objection by counsel, and an appropriate response at that point will avoid the need subsequently for a difficult post-hoc determination as to whether counsel was inhibited by an actual conflict. A more troublesome issue, it was noted, was what "affirmative duty" should be placed upon the trial court to inquire into the propriety of multiple representation when defense counsel fails to request separate representation. That issue came before the Supreme Court in *Cuyler v. Sullivan.*[10] The defendant Sullivan had been represented by two attorneys, retained by his two codefendants and paid in part by friends of the group. Each defendant had a separate trial, and Sullivan was the only one of the three convicted. Neither defense counsel nor Sullivan had objected to the multiple representation, but Sullivan later challenged his conviction on the ground that counsel had operated under a conflict of interest. Rejecting that claim, the Supreme Court held that the trial court's failure to conduct an inquiry into the propriety of the multiple representation did not in itself constitute a Sixth Amendment violation, and a claim based on counsel's actual performance required a showing of more than a mere possibility of conflict (see subsection (c) infra).

In ruling that the trial court had no constitutional obligation to inquire into the propriety of counsels' multiple representation, the *Sullivan* majority found *Holloway* clearly distinguishable. Justice Powell's opinion for the Court reasoned:

9. See also note 13 infra, and § 27.6 at note 24, suggesting other factors that may also contribute to the Court's refusal to apply a harmless error standard in this line of cases.

10. 446 U.S. 335, 100 S.Ct. 1708, 64 L.Ed.2d 333 (1980).

Holloway requires state trial courts to investigate timely objections to multiple representation. But nothing in our precedents suggests that the Sixth Amendment requires state courts themselves to initiate inquiries into the propriety of multiple representation in every case. Defense counsel have an ethical obligation to avoid conflicting representations and to advise the court promptly when a conflict of interest arises during the course of trial. Absent special circumstances, therefore, trial courts may assume either that multiple representation entails no conflict or that the lawyer and his clients knowingly accept such risk of conflict as may exist. Indeed, as the Court noted in *Holloway,* trial courts necessarily rely in large measure upon the good faith and good judgment of defense counsel. "An attorney representing two defendants in a criminal matter is in the best position professionally and ethically to determine when a conflict of interest exists or will probably develop in the course of a trial." Unless the trial court knows or reasonably should know that a particular conflict exists, the court need not initiate an inquiry.

The two dissenters in *Sullivan* (Justices Brennan and Marshall) argued that the dangers of multiple representation were so grave that in every case in which two or more defendants were jointly charged or had been joined for trial, the trial court should be under an obligation "to inquire whether there is multiple representation, to warn the defendants of the possible risk of such representation, and to ascertain that the representation is the result of the defendant's informed choice." The majority acknowledged that such a procedure would be desirable. Indeed, under proposed (and subsequently adopted) Federal Rule 44(c), a similar obligation was about to be imposed upon federal trial courts. However, to so substantially extend the essentially prophylactic rule of *Holloway* as a constitutional mandate was another matter. The inquiry that the dissenters would require was not without costs. It would impose a burden on both the trial court and the lawyer-client relationship. Indeed, Chief Justice Burger in *Holloway* had warned that a trial court's attempt to explore the nature of the relationship between jointly represented codefendants, including their potential defenses, could present "significant risks of unfair prejudice" to the defense. It therefore should not be unconstitutional for the state court to seek to limit such costs by relying in general on the professional obligation of counsel to advise the court when an actual conflict arises. Where counsel has not taken that step, the trial court should have a constitutional obligation to act on its own initiative only where it has good cause to believe that counsel may have erred in assuming that there was no actual conflict. Accordingly, the controlling Sixth Amendment standard, the *Sullivan* majority concluded, would be that, in the absence of objection by counsel, an inquiry was not mandated "[u]nless the trial court knows or reasonably should know that a particular conflict exists."

The *Sullivan* opinion did not explain precisely what information would place a trial judge in a position where he or she "knows or reasonably should know" that a conflict exists. The Court did explain, however, why the *Sullivan* case did not present such a situation. Relevant factors cited were the separate trials of the codefendants, an opening statement that outlined a defense compatible with the view that none of the defendants were involved in the offense, and a suggestion in that statement that counsel were willing to call all relevant witnesses. While the defense later rested without presenting those witnesses, that decision "on its face" appeared to be "a reasonable tactical response" to the weakness of the prosecution's case. *Sullivan*'s discussion of the relatively innocuous appearance of the joint representation in that case holds open the possibility that a trial judge would be required constitutionally to conduct an inquiry in situations presenting the more common signs of conflict. Arguably, a judge reasonably should know that a conflict exists when, for example, jointly represented defendants are tried together and the judge learns that one defendant's testimony will inculpate another or finds that a substantial variation exists in the alleged culpability of different defendants.[11]

(c) Postconviction Review. Most conflict of interest claims are presented through postconviction challenges in cases in which the possibility of a conflict had not been an issue for the trial court. These are cases in which neither the defense counsel nor the prosecution suggested to the court that a conflict problem existed, there was no trial court obligation to conduct an inquiry (and none was undertaken), and there was no waiver by defendant of the right to conflict-free counsel. The prevailing standard of review for such postconviction conflict claims was established in the second branch of the *Cuyler v. Sullivan* ruling.[12] The Court there initially rejected the lower court's ruling that a possible conflict of interest was sufficient to establish an ineffectiveness claim. The lower court had adopted that standard from *Holloway*'s finding that the trial court there should have inquired into the "risk of conflict." The issue here, the Supreme Court noted, was substantially different from that presented in *Holloway:*

> [A] defendant who objects to multiple representation must have the opportunity to show that potential conflicts impermissibly imperil his right to a fair trial. But unless the trial court fails to afford such an opportunity, a reviewing court cannot presume that the possibility of a conflict has resulted in ineffective assistance of counsel. Such a presumption would preclude multiple representation even in cases where "a common defense * * * gives strength against a common attack." * * * In order to establish a violation of the Sixth Amendment, a defendant must demonstrate an actual conflict of interest adversely affected his lawyer's performance.

The *Sullivan* opinion then added that its rejection of a potential conflict standard should not be taken to suggest that the defendant must establish prejudice. As the Court has noted first in *Glasser* and again in *Holloway,* "unconstitutional multiple representation is never harmless error." Thus, once a defendant "shows that a conflict of interest actually affected the adequacy of his representation," he is automatically entitled to relief; there is no need to establish that the Sixth Amendment violation might have adversely affected the outcome of the case.

The *Sullivan* opinion requires that the defendant presenting a postconviction challenge "demonstrate [that] an actual conflict of interest adversely affected the lawyer's performance." This requires a showing both that counsel was placed in a situation where conflicting loyalties pointed in opposite directions (an "actual conflict") and that counsel proceeded to act against the defendant's interests ("adversely affect[ing] his performance"). Because of the Court's adoption of an automatic reversal standard, and the majority opinion's reference at another point simply to counsel having "actively represented conflicting interests," Justice Marshall, in dissent, questioned whether the Court meant to insist on the second prong of this standard. If the impact of an actual conflict upon the outcome of the case required an unduly speculative judgment, was not, he asked, the same true of its impact upon counsel's performance? The thrust of the Court's opinion, however, clearly was that these were two separate determinations of a quite different character. It would not be sufficient for reversal to show only that counsel had faced a situation in which action

11. Federal Rule 44(c) imposes a far more extensive obligation upon the trial court. It provides for an inquiry whenever defendants have been jointly charged under Rule 8(b) or have been joined for trial under Rule 13 and are represented "by the same retained or assigned counsel who are associated in the practice of law." The trial court is directed to "inquire with respect to such representation" and to "personally advise each defendant of his right to the effective assistance of counsel, including separate representation." To avoid providing discovery to the prosecution, the court may conduct the inquiry in chambers. Once the inquiry is completed, Rule 44(c) directs the court, unless there is "good cause to believe no conflict of interest is likely to arise," to take "such measures as may be appropriate to protect each defendant's right to counsel." Lower courts have held that the failure to comply with the inquiry requirement of Rule 44(c) does not in itself require reversal of a conviction. As to the scope of the trial court's authority in taking "appropriate measures," see subsection (d) infra. States generally leave the holding of an inquiry to the discretion of the trial court.

12. Supra note 10.

or inaction that might benefit his client would work to the detriment of another interest that divided counsel's loyalty. There would be no harm to the defendant if counsel actually pursued the route favoring his client, disregarding the conflicting interest. Moreover, even where counsel did not pursue that route, counsel's action or inaction may have been influenced solely by a reasonable determination that the route not taken was inferior to an alternative route that was even more beneficial to his client, putting aside any concern for the conflicting interest. Having identified an actual conflict of interest, defendant should be able to establish as well precisely how counsel acted in response to that conflict. However, once it is shown that counsel was actually influenced by the conflict in one aspect of his performance, it would be inappropriate to measure the impact of that conflict solely by reference to that action or inaction. A court could not assume that counsel so motivated had not also been influenced by the conflict in various other aspects of his representation. For this reason, and others, here, as in *Holloway,* outcome prejudice would be presumed and automatic reversal required.[13]

The *Sullivan* requirement of adversely affected counsel performance found support in two earlier cases discussed in *Sullivan* and it was subsequently reaffirmed in *Burger v. Kemp.*[14] *Sullivan* did not decide whether the defendant there had made a sufficient showing of adversely affected performance, but it offered as illustrations of sufficient and insufficient showings those presented in *Glasser v. United States*[15] and *Dukes v. Warden.*[16] In *Glasser,* the record showed that counsel had failed to cross-examine a key witness and had failed also to object to "arguably inadmissible evidence." Both omissions were held to have resulted from counsel's desire to diminish the jury's perception of the guilt of a codefendant also represented by counsel. Thus, the Court noted in *Sullivan,* an "actual conflict of interest [had] impaired Glasser's defense." In contrast to *Glasser, Dukes v. Warden* had rejected an "actual conflict" claim. Defendant there had relied solely on a showing that the lawyer who advised him to plead guilty had later sought leniency for his codefendants by arguing that their cooperation with the police had induced defendant's plea. Unlike Glasser, Dukes could not "identify an actual lapse in representation" and "nothing in the record * * * indicated that the alleged conflict resulted in ineffective assistance."

In *Burger v. Kemp,* in a twist upon the usual order of analyzing a postconviction challenge under *Sullivan,* the Court turned first to the question of adversely affected performance, and finding none, concluded that there also had not been an actual conflict. Counsel in *Burger* had prepared the appellate brief for both his trial client (the habeas petitioner in *Burger*) and the client's separately tried accomplice (who had been represented by counsel's partner). The petitioner claimed that this dual responsibility presented an actual conflict of interest for counsel, who was forced to choose between using and discarding a "lesser culpability" argument that would help petitioner but hurt the accomplice. Such an argument had been presented at petitioner's separate trial, but counsel had not

13. Dissenting in *Burger v. Kemp,* infra note 14, Justice Blackmun noted several considerations that "warranted" adoption of this "presumption of prejudice in cases presenting a conflict of interest that adversely affected counsel's performance." Justice Blackmun noted: (i) "the duty of loyalty to a client is 'perhaps the most basic' responsibility of counsel"; (ii) it is "'difficult to measure the precise effect on the defense of representation corrupted by conflicting interest' * * * due in part to the fact that the conflict may affect almost any aspect of the lawyer's preparation and presentation * * * [and] because the conflict primarily compels the lawyer not to pursue certain arguments or take certain actions"; (iii) "lawyers are charged with knowledge that they are obliged to avoid such a conflict"; and (iv) "a judge can avoid the problem by questioning the defendant, at an early stage of the criminal process, in any case presenting a situation that may give rise to conflict, in order to determine whether the defendant is aware of the possible conflict and whether he has waived his right to conflict free representation."

14. 483 U.S. 776, 107 S.Ct. 3114, 97 L.Ed.2d 638 (1987).

15. Supra note 6. Although *Glasser* involved a situation in which the trial court was responsible for the creation of a potential conflict, see text at note 6 supra, the Supreme Court there also concluded that, as the trial developed, an actual conflict materialized and defendant was deprived of the effective assistance of counsel.

16. 406 U.S. 250, 92 S.Ct. 1551, 32 L.Ed.2d 45 (1972).

raised it on appeal, where both parties were before the court. In holding that there was no conflict, the Court majority stressed the federal habeas court's complete acceptance of counsel's testimony before that court. Counsel had explained his tactics, noting that he had "in no way tailored his strategy toward protecting [the accomplice]," and the habeas court had rejected any "attribution of [counsel's] motivation to the fact that his partner was [the accomplice's] lawyer or to the further fact that he assisted his partner in that representation." Noting that this finding had been twice sustained by the Eleventh Circuit, the Court concluded that both "respect for the bar and deference to the shared conclusion of two reviewing courts" precluded substitution of "speculation" for the lower courts' "heavily fact-based rulings." Thus, the question of whether a conflict in fact existed was controlled by the factual finding that counsel's actions had been influenced only by his client's interest.[17]

Lower courts applying the *Sullivan* standard have most readily found it met in cases that could well have required a trial court inquiry under the first branch of the *Sullivan* ruling. Typically, those cases presented situations in which jointly tried codefendants were represented by a single counsel and "the factual circumstances require[d] counsel to offer evidence which assist[ed] one codefendant but adversely affect[ed] the other." [18] Thus, one defendant may have attempted to exonerate himself by pointing the finger of guilt at his codefendant or the two defendants may have presented truly antagonistic defenses (as opposed to defenses that merely varied in detail or were different but not inconsistent). In the latter instance, the counsel's performance clearly has been adversely affected as to both defendants. In the former, the prosecution may argue that there was no adverse influence as to the defendant who gave the testimony inculpating his codefendant, but that defendant may respond that the actual conflict prevented counsel from emphasizing that portion of the defendant's testimony. Moreover, as such a situation presumably would impose a duty of inquiry upon the trial court (as the court "reasonably should have known" of the conflict), the defendant also may have an option of establishing a constitutional violation based on the trial court's failure to take such action, which will avoid the necessity of showing an adverse impact as to him.

In contrast to the above situations, most applications of the *Sullivan* standard will require consideration of circumstances that are not reflected in the trial record. That usually will be the case, for example, where a defendant claims that an entirely different type of defense would have been presented on his behalf if he had not been tried with his jointly represented codefendant. While the trial record will indicate if counsel might have stressed different degrees of culpability, it is not likely to be helpful where defendant claims counsel could have presented some special affirmative defense (e.g., duress) on his behalf but instead relied on a tactic that would encompass all of the defendants (e.g., presenting no defense testimony and simply challenging the strength of the prosecution's evidence). In such cases, the court will often be unable to resolve the claim without holding an evidentiary hearing that includes the testimony of counsel, as in *Burger*. An evidentiary hearing is also likely to be needed

17. The *Burger* dissent responded that counsel's "joint representation" of petitioner and his accomplice on appeal precluded counsel "as a matter of professional responsibility" from pursuing the lesser culpability argument (which would have worked to the accomplice's disadvantage) and therefore compelled on the record a finding of a direct conflict that worked to the prejudice of petitioner.

18. The presence of a joint trial is often a critical feature in meeting the *Sullivan* standard in such case. As the Court noted in Burger v. Kemp, supra note 14, where codefendants are represented by the same counsel but tried separately, counsel is less likely to face an actual conflict. In *Burger*, where the accomplices arguably had different degrees of culpability but were tried separately, the Court noted that trial counsel "would have had no particular reason for concern about the possible impact of the tactics employed in [the lesser-culpable defendant's] trial on the outcome of the [accomplice's] trial." While multiple representation could still present a conflict by deterring counsel from seeking a plea bargain favoring the lesser-culpable accomplice, the record here showed that counsel did seek such a plea arrangement but the prosecutor was unreceptive.

where the alleged conflict relates to counsel's former representation of a prosecution witness. Here the court is likely to find it necessary to ascertain (i) whether the lawyer's relationship with the former client was such that his interest in possible future business might have induced him to avoid challenging the veracity of the witness, and (ii) whether counsel had previously obtained relevant privileged information from the witness and therefore would have been inhibited in his cross-examination by a fear of misusing that information. On occasion, however, such an inquiry may be unnecessary since the trial record will reveal a cross-examination so rigorous that it is apparent that counsel was not subject to such restraining influences.

Defendants are likely to have the greatest difficulty in demonstrating that an actual conflict adversely affected counsel's performance where that conflict arose from counsel's personal stake in the litigation. Consider, for example, the claim that counsel was influenced by the anticipation that his fee would come from royalties paid to a defendant after the publication of his "life story." Here, the question to be asked—whether counsel took some action that might have promoted the commercial value of the forthcoming publication at the expense of the accused's presentation—is likely to require a far more comprehensive and speculative examination of counsel's representation than how he treated a particular defense or cross-examined a former client. Even greater difficulty is presented where the conflict does not focus on a specific tactic or outcome, as where counsel himself is the subject of an ongoing investigation or has some other special relationship with the prosecution that might lead counsel to place that relationship above the best interests of his client. Here some lower courts have turned to a standard of per se ineffectiveness, discarding the second prong of the *Cuyler v. Sullivan* test.

(d) Disqualification of Counsel. Where counsel seeks to withdraw on the basis of a conflict (as in *Holloway*), the trial court may readily avoid the difficulties of a likely post-conviction challenge by granting that request. Where there is no such motion, the trial court may nonetheless conduct an inquiry in its discretion, and under a Rule 44(c)-type provision or the constitutional standard of *Sullivan,* it may actually be required to conduct an inquiry. That inquiry, however, will not necessarily resolve all difficulties. The court may determine that there clearly will be no conflicts or defendant, after being advised of the dangers of a conflict, may request a different lawyer. In many instances, however, the court may conclude that there is an actual or potential conflict, and the defendant may nonetheless state that he wants to retain the same attorney and is willing to waive his right to conflict-free counsel.

At this point, as the Supreme Court noted in *Wheat v. United States,*[19] trial courts "face the prospect of being 'whipsawed' by assertions of error no matter which way they rule." If the trial court refuses to accept the defendant's counsel, the defendant will raise a claim (as did defendant in *Wheat*) that he was denied his Sixth Amendment right to counsel of choice. On the other hand, "if the trial court agrees to the multiple representation, and the advocacy of counsel is thereafter impaired as a result, the defendant may well claim that he did not receive effective assistance of counsel." Although some lower courts had suggested that the defendant's waiver bars such a claim (assuming the waiver was "knowing and intelligent"), the Court in *Wheat* "note[d], without passing judgment on, the apparent willingness of Courts of Appeals to entertain ineffective assistance claims from defendants who have specifically waived the right to conflict-free counsel." In *Wheat,* the Court sought to reduce this "whipsaw" potential by setting forth the standards under which a trial court constitutionally could refuse to allow multiple representation notwithstanding defendant's waiver.

The *Wheat* majority initially rejected the defendant's contention that "the provision of waivers by all affected defendants cures any problems created by the multiple representa-

19. 486 U.S. 153, 108 S.Ct. 1692, 100 L.Ed.2d 140 (1988).

tion." "No such flat rule," the Court noted, "can be deduced from the Sixth Amendment presumption in favor of counsel of choice." The Sixth Amendment right to choose one's counsel is not absolute; because of countervailing considerations, a defendant cannot insist upon counsel who is not a member of the bar nor can he insist upon representation by an attorney "who has a previous or ongoing relationship with an opposing party, even when the opposing party is the Government."[20] In the conflict situation also, a countervailing consideration is present. The courts "have an independent interest in ensuring that criminal trials are conducted within the ethical standards of the profession and that legal proceedings appear fair to all who observe them." In light of this interest, "where a court justifiably finds an actual conflict of interest, there can be no doubt that it may decline a proffer of waiver and insist that defendants be separately represented."

The *Wheat* majority recognized, however, that the critical situation, as a practical matter, was that in which the trial court found multiple representation to present a "potential" rather than an "actual" conflict. Only in the "rare" case would the trial court be able to determine before trial that an actual conflict existed; more commonly, the most that will be demonstrated at this point in the proceedings is that "a potential for conflict exists which may or may not burgeon into actual conflict." Because the likely materialization and dimensions of such potential conflicts are "notoriously hard to predict" in the "murkier pretrial context when relationships between parties are seen through a glass darkly," the Court concluded that a trial court can properly find, upon a showing of "a serious potential for conflict," that the presumption favoring defendant's choice of counsel should be overridden.

Wheat further noted that the trial court, in deciding whether to override that presumption, could take into consideration the fact that potential conflicts often reflect "imponderables" that "are difficult enough for a lawyer to assess, and even more difficult to convey by way of explanation to a criminal defendant untutored in the niceties of legal ethics." So too, it need not ignore the reality "that the willingness of an attorney to obtain such waivers from his clients may bear an inverse relation to the care with which he conveys all the necessary information to them." On the other hand, the trial court should also be aware of the possibility that the "government may seek to 'manufacture' a conflict to prevent the defendant from having a particular able counsel at his side." In the end, the trial court, in its evaluation of these and other relevant considerations, must be "allowed substantial latitude in refusing waivers" in cases of potential conflict as well as in cases of actual conflict.

Turning to the case before it, the *Wheat* majority found that the trial court had acted within its discretion in refusing defendant's request to substitute counsel who had been representing two separately charged accomplices of the defendant. The trial court had been "confronted not simply with an attorney who wished to represent two coequal defendants in a straightforward criminal prosecution: rather, [counsel] proposed to defend three coconspirators of varying stature in a complex drug distribution scheme." Moreover, one of the codefendants had pleaded to a lesser count as part of a plea agreement, and the government intended to call him as a prosecution witness at defendant's trial. The other codefendant, although previously acquitted on the drug charges, remained open to a trial on tax evasion and other charges relating to the conspiracy (his offer to plead to those charges had not yet been accepted by the district court and could still be withdrawn), with a distinct likelihood that defendant would be called as a government witness at that trial. Thus, counsel in two different situations could have been placed in a setting where he would be cross-examining a former client. Ruling on a motion made "close to the time of trial," the trial court had relied on "instinct and judgment based on experience" in evaluating these factors, and it could not

20. See § 11.4 at note 7.

be said to have "exceeded the broad latitude which must be accorded it in making this decision." [21]

In its discussion of the "broad latitude" that must be accorded the trial court, the *Wheat* Court emphasized that this latitude worked both ways—that it also applied to a trial court's determination to allow multiple representation with appropriate waivers. While sustaining the decision of the trial court below to deny multiple representation, the Court noted that other trial courts might have reached an opposite conclusion "with equal justification," and that it was not suggesting one conclusion was "right" and the other "wrong." Moreover, this discussion of the trial court's two-way discretion referred generally to both "potential" and "actual" conflicts.

The Court did not state that the trial court allowing counsel to continue must obtain a waiver from the defendant, but its discussion appeared to assume that there would be such a waiver. Indeed, where the trial court finds an actual conflict or a "serious risk" of actual conflict, the failure to obtain a waiver could be viewed as a violation of the trial court's constitutional obligations under *Holloway.* However, ensuring that the waiver is in fact knowingly and intelligently made is no easy task. For reasons noted in *Wheat,* due to the pretrial setting, the conflicting interests of counsel in advising his client, and the subtleties of many conflicts, the court cannot readily assume that the defendant is both adequately informed and making a voluntary decision. Several appellate courts have set forth fairly detailed directions for trial courts in advising defendants and determining whether their waivers are acceptable. Although no court insists that defendant first consult with independent outside counsel, it is certainly advisable to at least inform each defendant that he might consider doing so.[22]

§ 11.10 Ineffective Assistance Claims Based Upon Lawyer Incompetence

(a) Guiding Considerations. Prior to the Supreme Court's ruling in *Stickland v. Washington,*[1] lower courts had been divided on several issues bearing on those ineffective assistance claims that were grounded on the allegedly incompetent performance of counsel.[2] One of those issues was the appropriateness of using specific guidelines in gauging counsel's performance. Several courts had adopted such guidelines, based in large part on American Bar Association's Standards relating to the Defense Function.[3] To establish incompetency, a defendant simply need point to a substantial departure from a particular guide-

21. Two dissenters criticized the majority for giving "unwarranted deference to a trial court's decision respecting a constitutional right." That deference was seen as basically incorporating an "abuse of discretion" standard for appellate review, which "accords neither with the nature of the trial court's decision nor with the importance of the interest at stake." Two other dissenters noted their agreement with "the Court's premise that district judges must be afforded wide latitude in passing on motions of this kind," but found it "abundantly clear" that the district judge here "abused his discretion."

22. Where the potential conflict relates to obligations owed to a person other than a codefendant (e.g., a former client), the court may insist upon waiver from that person also, absent a defense waiver of rights that serves to protect that other person. Moreover, a waiver, even though complete, may not be responsive to prejudice to the prosecution that can flow from some conflicts. See e.g., note 7 of § 11.4 on the disqualification of counsel who formerly worked on the case as a prosecutor. That element may explain, in part, the automatic disqualification of defense counsel who will appear as a witness even by those courts that, prior to *Wheat,* otherwise recognized a defendant's right to insist upon conflict-burdened counsel with an appropriate waiver. The prosecution is thought to be at a disadvantage where defense counsel is allowed to both participate as an advocate and give testimony as a defense witness. So too, the prosecution may contend that where it has a legitimate interest in calling defense counsel as a prosecution witness, it loses part of the persuasiveness of that testimony (and risks the appearance of having acted unfairly) when that witness is allowed also to appear before the jury as defense counsel.

§ 11.10

1. 466 U.S. 668, 104 S.Ct. 2052, 80 L.Ed.2d 674 (1984).

2. To distinguish these claims from ineffective claims based on state inference, see § 11.8, the Court in *Strickland* characterized the incompetency claims as "actual ineffectiveness claims." The Court viewed the conflict-of-interest cases as presenting a special type of actual ineffectiveness claim.

3. See 1 ABA Standards for Criminal Justice Ch. 4 (2d ed. 1980).

line. Most lower courts, however, rejected any such concept of "per se incompetency." They turned instead to a fact-sensitive analysis that sought to measure the quality of counsel's representation under all of the circumstances of the case. They rejected a guidelines approach as far too rigid for a task "so rich in variables" and as too likely to invite trial court intervention (to ensure guideline compliance) that would both reorder the adversary process and interfere with the lawyer-client relationship. Supporters of guidelines argued in response that categorical standards, mandating specific responsibilities for each aspect of counsel's representation, were needed to ensure that the inadequacies of counsel were not "papered over" by a reviewing court's evaluation of the totality of the circumstances. They argued that attorneys had been granted so much leeway under traditional standards that incompetent performance was all too common, with the costs usually borne by those indigent and near-indigent defendants who were without any realistic choice in selecting or controlling their attorneys.

Among those courts that focused on the totality of the circumstances, there was a division, in turn, as to the appropriate standard for measuring counsel's performance. Courts traditionally had used the "farce and mockery" standard; counsel's incompetency reached the level of a constitutional error only when it rendered the particular proceeding a "farce" or "mockery of justice." That test had been criticized as far too subjective, and many courts had moved to a standard that focused on whether counsel's performance fell within the range commonly found among "reasonably competent" attorneys. This standard was thought to require a somewhat higher level of attorney diligence, although it too was challenged as vague and susceptible to varying subjective impressions of typical counsel performance.

Lower courts also were divided as to the appropriate role of the element of prejudicial impact upon the outcome of the proceeding. They generally rejected the concept of "prophylactic reversals," arguing that defendant should not receive a windfall benefit from incompetency that clearly had no bearing on his conviction. Some courts, however, contended that a showing of incompetency should shift to the government the burden of establishing beyond a reasonable doubt that counsel's failures did not affect the outcome. Others argued that this standard was too harsh when neither the prosecution nor trial court had been at fault. They placed on the defendant the obligation of showing some substantial degree of likelihood that the outcome would have been different but for counsel's incompetency.

In *Strickland,* the Court responded to all of these divisions among the lower courts. Moreover, while it focused primarily upon alleged incompetency at trial, the Court clearly indicated that the standards announced there would be applicable to alleged incompetency in any adversary stage of the criminal justice process. Thus, the *Strickland* case itself applied those standards to the performance of counsel at a capital sentencing proceeding, and later cases held those standards applicable both to guilty plea challenges based on counsel's incompetency and to alleged incompetency by appellate counsel.[4]

Building upon the role of the effective assistance guarantee as discussed in *United States v. Cronic,*[5] the *Strickland* Court held that: (1) to establish ineffective assistance requiring reversal of a conviction, a defendant must show both (i) that "counsel made errors so serious that counsel was not functioning as 'counsel' guaranteed * * * by the Sixth Amendment," and (ii) that the "deficient performance prejudiced the defense"; (2) the "proper standard for [measuring] attorney performance is that of reasonably effective assistance," as guided by "prevailing professional norms" and consideration of "all the circumstances" relevant to counsel's performance; (3) more specific guidelines in applying that standard are "not appropriate"; and (4)

4. See note 16 of § 11.7; Hill v. Lockhart, § 21.6 at note 13.

5. See § 11.7(c).

the proper standard for measuring prejudice is whether there is a "reasonable probability that, but for counsel's unprofessional errors, the result of the proceedings would be different." Of a significance arguably equal to these rulings, Justice O'Connor's opinion for the Court also discussed at length the basic considerations that should guide a court's judgment on an incompetency claim.

Justice O'Connor noted initially that a court's judgment as to the constitutional inadequacy of counsel's performance was not usefully guided by particularized standards:

> When a convicted defendant complains of the ineffectiveness of counsel's assistance, the defendant must show that counsel's representation fell below an objective standard of reasonableness. * * * More specific guidelines are not appropriate. The Sixth Amendment refers simply to "counsel," not specifying particular requirements of effective assistance. It relies instead on the legal profession's maintenance of standards sufficient to justify the law's presumption that counsel will fulfill the role in the adversary process that the Amendment envisions. The proper measure of attorney performance remains simply reasonableness under prevailing professional norms.

Justice O'Connor acknowledged that competent representation "entails certain basic duties." Counsel had an obligation to "avoid conflicts of interest," to "advocate the defendant's cause," to "consult with the defendant on important decisions and * * * keep [him] informed of important developments," and to "bring to bear such skill and knowledge as will render the trial a reliable adversarial testing process." However, the use of these duties or others as a simple "checklist" for determining competency was inappropriate, for several reasons:

> [T]he performance inquiry must be whether counsel's assistance was reasonable considering all the circumstances. Prevailing norms of practice as reflected in American Bar Association standards and the like * * * are guides to determining what is reasonable, but they are only guides. No particular set of detailed rules for counsel's conduct can satisfactorily take account of the variety of circumstances faced by defense counsel or the range of legitimate decisions regarding how best to represent a criminal defendant. Any such set of rules would interfere with the constitutionally protected independence of counsel and restrict the wide latitude counsel must have in making tactical decisions. * * * Indeed, the existence of detailed guidelines for representation could distract counsel from the overriding mission of vigorous advocacy of the defendant's cause. Moreover, the purpose of the effective assistance guarantee of the Sixth Amendment is not to improve the quality of legal representation, although that is a goal of considerable importance to the legal system. The purpose is simply to ensure that criminal defendants receive a fair trial. * * *
>
> The availability of intrusive post-trial inquiry into attorney performance or of detailed guidelines for its evaluation would encourage the proliferation of ineffectiveness challenges. Criminal trials resolved unfavorably to the defendant would increasingly come to be followed by a second trial, this one of counsel's unsuccessful defense. Counsel's performance and even willingness to serve could be adversely affected. Intensive scrutiny of counsel and rigid requirements for acceptable assistance could dampen the ardor and impair the independence of defense counsel, discourage the acceptance of assigned cases, and undermine the trust between attorney and client.

In evaluating an attorney's performance, Justice O'Connor concluded, the best approach was to keep in mind the basic Sixth Amendment standard: "Whether, in light of all the circumstances, the identified acts or omissions [of counsel] were outside the range of professionally competent assistance." The lower court had set forth a series of general guidelines for judging the particular deficiency here alleged by defendant—counsel's failure to conduct a full factual investigation. However, the basic standard of professional competency required "no special amplification in order to define counsel's duty to investigate." It was sufficient to say that "counsel has a duty to make reasonable investigations or to make a reasonable decision that makes particular investigation unnecessary." What decisions were reasonable would depend on the total setting, including, in particular, the information the attorney received from his client.

Having established the need for a fact-sensitized judgment, Justice O'Connor looked to much the same concerns in describing the principles that should guide the making of that judgment. Justice O'Connor noted:

> Judicial scrutiny of counsel's performance must be highly deferential. It is all too tempting for a defendant to second-guess counsel's assistance after conviction or adverse sentence, and it is all too easy for a court, examining counsel's defense after it has proved unsuccessful, to conclude that a particular act or omission of counsel was unreasonable. A fair assessment of attorney performance requires that every effort be made to eliminate the distorting effects of hindsight, to reconstruct the circumstances of counsel's challenged conduct, and to evaluate the conduct from counsel's perspective at the time. Because of the difficulties inherent in making the evaluation, a court must indulge a strong presumption that counsel's conduct falls within the wide range of reasonable professional assistance; that is, the defendant must overcome the presumption that, under the circumstances, the challenged action "might be considered sound trial strategy." There are countless ways to provide effective assistance in any given case. Even the best criminal defense attorneys would not defend a particular client in the same way.

Although stressing the need for deference, Justice O'Connor warned that, here too, general principles could not be converted into "mechanical rules." The "ultimate focus must be the fundamental fairness of the proceeding." In every case, the court must retain its concern as to "whether, despite the strong presumption of reliability, the result of the particular proceeding is unreliable because of a breakdown in the adversarial process."

The focus on fundamental fairness, Justice O'Connor noted, logically also required that defendant make a showing of prejudice to gain relief. Since the purpose of the Sixth Amendment guarantee is "to ensure that a defendant has the assistance necessary to justify reliance on the outcome of the proceeding," any deficiency in counsel's performance "must be prejudicial to the defense in order to constitute ineffective assistance under the Constitution." Here, unlike other Sixth Amendment contexts, prejudice could not be presumed: "Attorney errors come in an infinite variety and are as likely to be utterly harmless in a particular case as they are to be prejudicial. They cannot be classified according to likelihood of causing prejudice."

(b) The Competency Standard. The *Strickland* opinion, in its initial discussion of the deficient performance component of an incompetency claim, characterized that component as requiring "counsel * * * errors so serious that counsel was not functioning as the 'counsel' guaranteed the defendant by the Sixth Amendment." Since prejudicial impact was a separate component of the claim, the "seriousness" of counsel error apparently was to be measured by reference to the role of counsel in providing what *Cronic* had described as "the kind of [adversarial] testing envisioned by the Sixth Amendment."[6] As

6. See § 11.7(c). The distinction between the "seriousness" of the error in determining incompetency and its "seriousness" in measuring impact was made clear in Kimmelman v. Morrison, 477 U.S. 365, 106 S.Ct. 2574, 91 L.Ed.2d 305 (1986). During defendant's trial for rape, the prosecution had introduced a sheet seized from his bed and expert testimony concerning stains and hair found on the sheet. Defendant based his Sixth Amendment claim solely upon counsel's error in failing to timely present a Fourth Amendment objection to the seizure of that evidence, which had resulted in the forfeiture of his claim under state law. The Supreme Court concluded that counsel's error brought his performance below the reasonably effective assistance standard, but there remained the question (to be considered by the lower court on remand) as to whether the prejudice prong of *Strickland* was met. In finding counsel's representation to be "constitutionally deficient," the Court found unpersuasive the state's attempt to "minimize the seriousness of counsel's errors by asserting that [its] case turned far more on the credibility of witnesses than on the bedsheet and related testimony." Counsel's forfeiture of the suppression issue stemmed from his "total failure to conduct pretrial discovery," for which he had no possible justification (see text following note 14 infra). That glaring omission would not be measured by a "hindsight" evaluation of the "relative importance of various components of the State's case"; at the time he failed to seek discovery, counsel "did not * * * know what the State's case would be." While "the relative importance of witness credibility vis-a-vis the bedsheet and related expert testimony [would be] pertinent to the determination of prejudice," it

Cronic also had noted, the level of performance required to fulfill that role does not preclude the presence of "demonstrable errors" by counsel. The critical question is whether, in the context of the particular case, counsel's failing (whether in a single error or a series of errors and whether in commission or omission) kept him or her from meeting the necessary responsibilities of an advocate. To assist lower courts in making that determination, the Court in *Strickland* set forth a "standard" for assessing attorney performance in light of that role. It adopted for this purpose the "reasonably effective assistance" standard that had been advanced by the federal Courts of Appeals. This same standard, it noted, had been "indirectly recognized" as the relevant measure of attorney competency in the Court's opinion in *McMann v. Richardson.*[7] The Court had there stated that a guilty plea could not be challenged "as based on inadequate legal advice unless counsel was not a 'reasonably competent attorney' and the advice was not 'within the range of competence demanded of attorneys in criminal cases.'" This provided an "objective standard of reasonableness" below which counsel's representation must fall to meet the inadequate performance component of a successful Sixth Amendment claim.

Prior to *Strickland,* several commentators had suggested that the standard used to describe the expected level of counsel performance was far less significant than the attitude and concerns that a court brought to its assessment of counsel's failures. Indeed, the variations among the state and federal courts in formulating that standard, including both the older "farce and mockery" standard and several versions of the newer "reasonably competent attorney" standard, had been characterized as presenting a "semantic merry-go-round." No such standard, it was noted, can be "self-answering"; all must rely, as *McMann* had noted, on the "good sense and discretion of the trial courts." The Court's opinion in *Strickland* lent support to this view. Far more discussion was devoted to the concerns that should guide a court in applying the standard (e.g., the variation in circumstances that render inappropriate a guidelines approach, the need for "deferential" scrutiny that avoids second-guessing, and the importance of considering the totality of the circumstances) than to explaining the standard itself. The Court also refused to attach to the standard such significance as to render suspect lower court rulings that had relied on somewhat differently worded standards. Even cases that had rejected incompetency claims under the farce and mockery standard did not necessarily require reconsideration. If the "guiding inquiry" in the lower court correctly had been whether counsel's failures produced in fact a "breakdown in the adversary process," the difference in the articulation of the standard applied was unimportant.

Justice Marshall, dissenting in *Strickland,* argued that the majority's reasonableness test was subject to "debilitating ambiguity." The Court had failed to address such important issues as whether reasonableness was to be judged by reference to "the adequately paid retained attorney" or to the appointed attorney who had less time and resources to devote to the case. Nor had the Court indicated whether the reference was to the standard of competence of the local bar or of defense lawyers generally. These concerns, however, appear to be irrelevant under the approach that majority took to its "reasonably effective assistance" standard. There was no suggestion that reasonableness was to be judged by reference to any empirical survey of attorney practices. The majority did characterize the applicable standard as one of "reasonableness under prevailing professional norms," but it also made clear that "prevailing norms of practice" are no more than "guides" to determining what is reasonable. The ultimate point of reference is that action by counsel needed, under the circumstances of the case, to ensure "the proper functioning of the adversarial process." That level of performance provides the "objective standard of reasonableness" and defines what is "within the

"shed no light on the reasonableness of counsel's decision not to request discovery."

7. 397 U.S. 759, 90 S.Ct. 1441, 25 L.Ed.2d 763 (1970), also discussed in § 21.6(a).

range of competence demanded of attorneys in criminal cases." As the Court later noted in *Nix v. Whiteside,*[8] an attorney's performance could conceivably meet that standard even where the attorney breached an "ethical standard of professional responsibility."[9] Indeed, although the Court majority in *Whiteside* appeared to conclude that action taken pursuant to a widely recognized ethical standard necessarily constituted adequate performance under the Sixth Amendment, four justices were not willing to accept such a sweeping conclusion.[10] Thus, the content of reasonably effective assistance basically must be gleaned, not from the practice patterns of the bar, but from the pattern of court decisions applying that standard, as discussed in the next subsection.

(c) **Applying the Reasonableness Standard.** As one commentator has noted, the range of claims of allegedly incompetent representation "has been limited only by the ingenuity of convicts and their post-trial counsel. Defense counsel's actions from the earliest stages of criminal proceedings to the bitter end have been assailed." Trial counsel have been attacked for their failure to investigate, their failure to consult sufficiently with the defendant, their failure to challenge the indictment on various grounds, their representation in plea bargaining, their failure to challenge the makeup of the jury, their failure to move to suppress illegally obtained evidence, their failure to either raise or properly present various defenses, their failure to object to improper argument by the prosecution, their waiver of opening or closing arguments, and their failure to present various postconviction motions.[11] Space limitations preclude a thorough review of the hundreds of

8. 475 U.S. 157, 106 S.Ct. 988, 89 L.Ed.2d 123 (1986).

9. The *Whiteside* majority noted: "Under the *Strickland* standard, breach of an ethical standard does not necessarily make out a denial of the Sixth Amendment guarantee of assistance of counsel. When examining attorney conduct, a court must be careful not to narrow the wide range of conduct acceptable under the Sixth Amendment so restrictively as to constitutionalize particular standards of professional conduct and thereby intrude into the State's proper authority to define and apply the standards of professional conduct applicable to those it admits to practice in its courts. In some future case challenging attorney conduct * * *, we may need to define with greater precision the weight to be given to recognized canons of ethics, the standards established by the State in statutes or professional codes, and the Sixth Amendment, in defining the proper scope and limits on that conduct. Here we need not face that question, since virtually all of the sources speak with one voice."

10. Defendant Whiteside's counsel, upon learning that Whiteside intended to commit perjury, had warned Whiteside that such action would (1) lead counsel to seek to withdraw, (2) require counsel to advise the trial court of the perjury, and (3) "probably" result in counsel then being "allowed to attempt to impeach that testimony." As a result of those warnings, Whiteside testified without perjuring himself. The Eighth Circuit, in reversing a denial of habeas relief, concluded that counsel's warning breached the "obligations of confidentiality and zealous advocacy" imposed on defense counsel by the Sixth Amendment. Rejecting that conclusion, Chief Justice Burger's opinion for the Court found counsel's assumption of an obligation to report known client perjury to be "wholly consistent with the Iowa standards of professional conduct and law, with the overwhelming majority of courts, and with codes of professional ethics [i.e., the Model Code of Professional Responsibility and the Model Rules of Professional Conduct]." It then concluded: "Since there has been no breach of any recognized professional duty, it follows that there can be no deprivation of the right to assistance of counsel under the *Strickland* standard."

Four Justices concurred only in the judgment, relying solely on defendant's failure to meet the prejudice prong of the *Strickland* standards (see note 18 infra). Speaking for the four, Justice Blackmun expressed concern as to the Court's "implicit adoption of a set of standards of professional responsibility for attorneys in state criminal proceedings" through its reliance upon counsel's adherence to the codes of professional responsibility. Justice Blackmun warned that "whether an attorney's response to what he sees as a client's plan to commit perjury" constitutes ineffective assistance depends upon a variety of factors (e.g., certainty that the client's testimony will be false, stage of the proceedings, means of dissuading the client), which therefore "makes inappropriate a blanket rule that defense attorneys must reveal, or threaten to reveal, a client's anticipated perjury to the [trial] court."

11. Where counsel has failed to raise a constitutional claim, that claim may still be cognizable under special circumstances in a federal habeas challenge to the conviction. See § 28.4(g) (noting the "fundamentally unjust incarceration" exception to the foreclosure of claims not properly raised in state proceedings). In general, however, unless counsel's failure constituted ineffective assistance under the *Strickland* standard, the failure to raise the claim will bar habeas relief. See § 28.4. Since a Sixth Amendment violation is itself cognizable on habeas review, where counsel's failure resulted in such a violation, the challenge will ordinarily be presented on that ground. See § 28.4(f). *Strickland* held that because an ineffectiveness standard focuses on "fundamental unfairness," which is the "central concern" of the habeas remedy, there was no need, notwithstanding finality concerns, to apply a different standard of ineffectiveness on habeas review. Because of the difficulties encountered in raising an incompetency claim on appeal (appellate coun-

rulings dealing with these and other alleged inadequacies. As might be expected, the rulings are hardly consistent in their treatment of even roughly similar fact situations. Nevertheless, they do suggest some general patterns, at least as to those claims most likely and least likely to be successful.

In general, the defendant is most likely to establish incompetency where counsel's alleged errors of omission or commission are attributable to a lack of diligence rather than an exercise of judgment. Courts will far more readily find incompetency where there has been "an abdication—not an exercise—of professional judgment." The crucial question therefore often becomes, how far will the particular reviewing court go in assuming, in accordance with the general presumption of attorney competence, that counsel's actions were strategic?

A leading case illustrating the Supreme Court's willingness to assume that counsel's actions were molded by strategy is *Tollett v. Henderson.*[12] In that case, counsel had allowed defendant to plead guilty without even exploring the possibility that blacks had been systematically excluded from the indicting grand jury. Although the defendant was himself black and the basis for a successful equal protection challenge was fairly clear, the Court held that those factors hardly suggested in themselves that counsel had failed to exercise reasonable diligence. Counsel's course of action may have been dictated by strategic considerations consistent with the "range of competence demanded of attorneys in criminal cases." The Court reasoned:

> Counsel's concern is the faithful representation of the interest of his client, and such representation frequently involves highly practical considerations as well as specialized knowledge of the law. Often the interests of the accused are not advanced by challenges that would only delay the inevitable date of prosecution, or by contesting all guilt. A prospect of plea bargaining, the expectation or hope of a lesser sentence, or the convincing nature of the evidence against the accused are considerations that might well suggest the advisability of a guilty plea without elaborate consideration of whether pleas in abatement, such as unconstitutional grand jury selection procedures, might be factually supported.

The defendant in *Tollett v. Henderson* unsuccessfully sought to convince the Court that counsel had, in fact, acted on the basis of ignorance rather than professional judgment. Where a possible tactical basis is apparent, that task is exceedingly difficult, but not impossible. In exceptional situations, contrary evidence may lead a court to reject the usual assumption that counsel's actions were strategically motivated. For example, one glaring, obviously non-tactical error may cast doubt on whether counsel's decisions in other matters truly reflected a tactical choice. Similarly, though counsel's failure to exercise any one of several defense rights might be viewed as tactical, taken together his several omissions may clearly indicate that he simply had abdicated his responsibilities. Finally, where a decision apparently was made on the basis of a tactical judgment, but that judgment had no reasonable justification (as where counsel relinquished at trial an objection that was essential to gaining an acquittal), even the good faith exercise of professional judgment may not preclude a finding of incompetency.

Courts reviewing competency claims frequently stress that, even apart from tactical judgments, they do not demand that counsel's performance be flawless. It must be anticipated that the lawyer will occasionally fail to recognize that a certain course of action may be available to his client. Accordingly, an incompetency claim is most likely to be successful when the defendant can point to a long series of questionable omissions by counsel. This suggests that the lawyer's errors were not simply the product of human fallibility, but the result of a lack of conscientious effort. Very often, however, a single error

sel will often have been the trial counsel, and the trial record will often provide an unsatisfactory source in itself for assessing performance), many jurisdictions allow that claim to be raised only in collateral proceedings.

12. 411 U.S. 258, 93 S.Ct. 1602, 36 L.Ed.2d 235 (1973), also discussed in § 21.6(a).

which was both glaring and potentially prejudicial has been held sufficient to establish incompetency. Although the court must look to the level of counsel's overall performance, clearly negligent treatment of a crucial deficiency in the prosecution's case or an obvious strength of the defense will outweigh the adequate handling of a series of minor matters.[13]

Perhaps the clearest fact pattern establishing incompetency in a single error is that in which the record reveals that counsel failed to object to a critical prosecution evidence solely because he was unfamiliar with clearly settled legal principles. The Supreme Court found incompetency in such a situation in *Kimmelman v. Morrison.*[14] Counsel there failed to assert a timely objection to illegally seized evidence because of a "startling ignorance of the law," assuming that it was the state's legal obligation to inform him, even without a discovery request, of the evidence it intended to produce at trial. Courts also have little difficulty when trial counsel's testimony at an evidentiary hearing establishes that his failure to act on an important matter was a product of inattention rather than strategic choice. A failure to raise an apparently meritorious legal objection often is placed in the same category, even without specific evidence of legal ignorance or inattention, when a ruling sustaining that objection would have produced a complete victory for the defense. Strategy may explain why counsel would not raise an objection that would only result in a new indictment (as in *Tollett*). It may also explain why counsel might not seek to exclude inadmissible evidence when such evidence is not critical to the prosecution's case nor necessarily inconsistent with his client's defense. A possible strategic justification is more difficult to hypothesize, however, where counsel failed to raise a claim of apparent merit which would have resulted in dismissal of the charges with prejudice—such as double jeopardy, the denial of a speedy trial, or the statute of limitations.

Illustrative of incompetency claims that courts often find more difficult to evaluate are those based on counsel's failure to interview possible defense witnesses or otherwise pursue possible sources of helpful information. On the one hand, numerous studies have characterized the lack of pretrial preparation as "the preeminent cause of poor legal performance." On the other, courts also recognize that "the amount of pretrial investigation that is reasonable defies precise measurement." What is satisfactory to meet minimum standards of competency "will necessarily depend on a variety of factors, including the number of issues in the case, the relative complexity of those issues, the strength of the government's case, and the overall strategy of counsel." The Supreme Court in *Strickland* advised that special attention be given in this regard to the "information supplied [to counsel] by the defendant." Counsel has no need to pursue a particular line of investigation when "defendant has given counsel reason to believe that pursuing * * * [that line] would be fruitless or even harmful." So, too, the Court noted, "when the facts that support a certain potential line of defense are generally known to counsel because of what the defendant has said, the need for further investigation may be considerably diminished or eliminated altogether." A court is most likely to find counsel's investigation unreasonable when the information available suggested a single line of defense and counsel either failed to make any investigation or conducted only a minimal investigation. Cases finding incompetency on this ground have tended to involve defenses such as alibi and insanity. The measurement of competency becomes more complex where counsel did conduct a substantial investigation into one line of defense, but failed to inquire into others also suggested by information received from his client or other sources. Here, the primary concern is that counsel have had some reasonable basis for focusing on only one avenue of investigation

13. The significance that should have attracted counsel's attention will be measured, for this purpose, by the state of the case at the time of counsel's failing. See Kimmelman v. Morrison, note 6 supra.

14. Supra note 6.

in light of the information and resources available to him, and that his decision not have been based on a desire to prepare for trial with as little effort as possible.

The difficulties presented in judging the adequacy of counsel's factual investigation are reflected in the quite different perspectives of the majority and dissenting justices in *Burger v. Kemp.*[15] In that case, petitioner's habeas counsel established that there was considerable mitigating evidence, relating to petitioner's background, that could have been presented at the capital sentencing hearing. Petitioner's trial counsel had obtained some of that evidence in the course of interviewing petitioner, his mother, and a family friend. Counsel had concluded, however, based on what he had learned from them and from a psychologist's testimony at a suppression hearing, that presenting such evidence would open the door to cross-examination that would reveal petitioner's juvenile record and certain damaging aspects of his personality. Accordingly, trial counsel did not pursue a further investigation that would have produced the other mitigating evidence developed by habeas counsel.

The Court majority in *Burger* noted that petitioner's trial counsel "could well have made a more thorough investigation." Nonetheless, having made "a reasonable professional judgment" in light of information obtained from "all potential witnesses who had been called to his attention," counsel's failure to mount "an all-out investigation into petitioner's background" did not constitute incompetency. As *Strickland* itself had noted, "strategic choices made after less than complete investigation are reasonable precisely to the extent that reasonable professional judgments support the limitations on investigation," and in determining the reasonableness of counsel's decision not to further investigate, a reviewing court should provide "a heavy measure of deference to counsel's judgments."

The four dissenters in *Burger* saw counsel's performance quite differently. In a capital sentencing proceeding, where petitioner's psychological problems and troubled background were obviously of great significance, counsel's failure to obtain a complete psychological examination of petitioner could not be excused by his lack of confidence in the local mental hospital, nor could counsel's failure to more fully explore petitioner's background be justified by the petitioner's failure to suggest additional witnesses when asked "whether he could produce evidence of 'anything good about him.'" The dissent saw *Burger* as a case where "further investigation was compelled" under the *Strickland* standard "because there was inadequate information on which the reasonable professional judgment to limit the investigation could have been made."

Courts are least likely to find incompetency where the record suggests that counsel was fully prepared and the defendant's ineffectiveness claim is based largely on his counsel's decision not to pursue a particular line of attack. Thus, when an attorney fully investigates several defenses and decides to advance only one at trial, that choice is "virtually unchallengeable." Similarly, where the alleged incompetency lies in counsel's failure to call a witness who had offered to give favorable testimony, courts respond that the judgment of counsel as to the value of that witness' testimony "will not be second-guessed by hindsight." In general, the same view is taken of counsel's decision to relinquish a particular defense right where he had exercised various other rights. Thus, if counsel's performance otherwise appears to be adequate, a court is most unlikely to find that incompetency was shown by the failure to refer to a prior criminal record in impeaching a prosecution witness, the failure to refer to a particular item of favorable evidence in closing argument, or even the waiver of closing or opening arguments. Such decisions are too likely to reflect a tactical judgment or a "minor slip" to justify in themselves a finding of ineffective assistance. So too, where counsel raises and develops a legal objection, he will

15. 483 U.S. 776, 107 S.Ct. 3114, 97 L.Ed.2d 638 (1987).

not be found to be incompetent simply because he failed to advance additional supporting arguments or to specifically rebut the prosecution's counter-arguments.

Consistent with the above cases, the Supreme Court in *Smith v. Murray*[16] easily dispatched an incompetency claim based on counsel's failure to raise on appeal a claim that he had researched and rejected in favor of other claims that he viewed as having greater merit. Defendant Smith's counsel had challenged at a capital sentencing proceeding a court appointed psychiatrists' testimony describing a prior criminal episode revealed by defendant during a psychiatric examination. Counsel failed to pursue that objection on appeal, however, having concluded that it lacked support under then prevailing state law. On habeas review, defendant claimed that had counsel "investigated the claim more fully, it [was] inconceivable that he would have concluded that the claim was without merit." Thus, it was noted, amicus curiae had raised precisely that claim on the same appeal (with the state appellate court refusing to rule upon it since the claim had not been presented by the defendant himself). Rejecting defendant's incompetency contention, the Supreme Court noted that: (1) counsel had conducted a vigorous defense at both the guilt and capital sentencing phases of the trial; (2) counsel had researched a wide range of claims prior to filing an appeal and had included thirteen other claims; (3) the process of 'winnowing out weaker arguments on appeal' and 'focusing on those more likely to prevail' * * * is the hallmark of effective appellate advocacy"; (4) "often * * * even the most informed counsel will fail to anticipate a state appellate court's willingness to reconsider a prior holding or will underestimate the likelihood that a federal habeas court will repudiate an established state rule"; and (5) a " 'fair assessment of attorney performance requires every effort be made to eliminate the distorting effects of hindsight' " (quoting *Strickland*).

(d) The Prejudice Element. Prior to the ruling in *Strickland,* lower courts had adopted a confusing array of standards governing the prejudice component of an incompetency claim. *Strickland* replaced those standards with a single test—whether "there is a reasonable probability that, but for counsel's unprofessional errors, the result of the proceeding would have been different." In the course of adopting this test, the Court discussed and rejected various other possibilities. It noted initially that the burden rested with the defendant to establish the prejudice element. Thus, contrary to the suggestion of certain lower courts, it was inappropriate to presume prejudice and shift the burden to the government to establish that counsel's incompetency was harmless error. It would be equally inappropriate to adopt a prejudice standard so lenient as to have a similar effect. Thus, to require that defendant show only that counsel's errors "had some conceivable effect on the outcome" was meaningless; "virtually every act or omission of counsel would meet that test."

On the other side, it would require too much to insist that defendant show that counsel's conduct "more likely than not" altered the outcome in the particular case. While such an outcome-determinative test was traditionally applied to motions for new trial based on newly discovered evidence, the situation here was distinguishable. The high standard for newly discovered evidence presupposed an "accurate and fair proceeding," but an "ineffective assistance claim asserts the absence of one of the crucial assurances that the result of the proceeding is reliable." In the *Brady* line of prosecutorial nondisclosure cases, the Court had also rejected a new-trial standard in assessing the materiality of nondisclosed exculpatory evidence. It had adopted instead a "reasonable probability" standard, which was equally suited to this setting.[17] A "reasonable probability" was a "probability sufficient to undermine confidence in the outcome."[18]

16. 477 U.S. 527, 106 S.Ct. 2661, 91 L.Ed.2d 434 (1986).

17. See § 20.7(b).

18. The Court added that this judgment should be based on the assumption that a decisionmaker is "reasonably, conscientiously, and impartially" applying the ap-

The Court also noted in *Strickland* that the question of the adequacy of counsel's performance need not be considered before examining the issue of prejudice, and lower courts clearly have been influenced by that suggestion. Indeed, in case after case alleging that counsel's factual investigation was inadequate, the standard response is that there has been no showing of prejudice because defendant has failed to establish exactly what further evidence existed for counsel to discover if he had investigated more thoroughly. Of course, in many of these cases, the absence of such evidence suggests circumstances that would have supported counsel's decision not to investigate further. But there also will be situations in which the information known to counsel before trial clearly would have indicated that further inquiry was needed. The no-prejudice rulings avoid the need to consider whether that was the situation in defendant's case, because defendant is now unable to establish a reasonable probability that what counsel allegedly should have been looking for would in fact have been found. The difficulty for the defendant, of course, is that he usually will be an incarcerated habeas petitioner, lacking the assistance of counsel at this point, and thus forced to rely primarily upon his own allegations as to what counsel would have found.

Broad language in *Strickland* concerning the scope and purpose of the "reasonable probability" standard—such as the references to "confidence in the outcome" and the avoidance of "unjust convictions"—led Justice Powell, concurring in *Kimmelman v. Morrison,*[19] to offer a rather startling interpretation of that standard. It should not be too readily assumed, he argued, that *Strickland* 's prejudice prong would be satisfied simply because, but for counsel's incompetence, the outcome might have been different. That might not be the case where counsel's incompetence led to the admission of constitutionally excludable evidence, there was a reasonable probability that the state's use of that evidence affected the jury's verdict, but that evidence was entirely reliable. The improper admission of evidence that harmed the defendant only in allowing the factfinder to render a more well-informed determination of guilt might not be the type of injury that establishes prejudice under *Strickland.* Notwithstanding the language cited by Justice Powell, such an interpretation of *Strickland*'s prejudice component would appear to be inconsistent with much of the discussion of that component in *Strickland.* Moreover, it would be difficult to square with Justice Brennan's opinion for the Court in *Kimmelman v. Morrison,* which carefully distinguished between a habeas petitioner's Sixth Amendment rights and his Fourth Amendment claim in concluding that the former was cognizable on habeas review even though the latter was not.[20] To hold that a Sixth Amendment claim based on counsel's failure to exclude illegally seized evidence invariably fails to meet the prejudice component would place that habeas claim in essentially the same position as the non-cognizable Fourth Amendment claim. Still, as Justice Powell noted, the Court did not rule on the prejudice issue in *Kimmelman v. Morrison,* and its other ineffective assistance cases have involved actions of counsel that could not be narrowed in impact to the admission of specific items of excludable evidence.

Finally, it should be noted that the *Strickland* discussion of prejudice must be read in light of *Cronic* 's recognition that in extreme

plicable legal standards. It could not rest on the "unusual propensities" of a particular decisionmaker toward harshness or leniency. Consistent with this position, the Court in Nix v. Whiteside, supra note 8, held that prejudice could not be founded on the likelihood that a different result would have been reached if counsel had not prevented defendant from offering perjured testimony. Defendant had no right to a jury verdict based on a perjured testimony, just as he had no right to the "luck of a lawless decisionmaker" (Blackmun, J., concurring).

19. Supra note 6.

20. See § 28.3 at note 24.

situations, as presented in *Powell v. Alabama,* prejudice will be presumed. However, to take advantage of that exception, defendant must show such a total lack of performance by counsel as to constitute, in effect, "a constructive denial of counsel." [21]

21. See § 11.7(d).

Chapter 12

PRETRIAL RELEASE

Table of Sections

---

§ 12.1 Pretrial Release Procedures

(a) The Federal Bail Reform Act. The federal Bail Reform Act of 1966, which governed bail and release practices in the federal courts for several years, has also served as an important model for reform legislation in the states. Its central theme is that personal recognizance is the preferred method of pretrial release in lieu of the traditional reliance upon money bail as a prerequisite to release. The Act had an immediate impact in terms of the pretrial release rate of federal defendants and the extent of reliance upon personal recognizance as the mode of release. But that Act has now been repealed and replaced by the Bail Reform Act of 1984. The 1984 legislation is in several respects similar to the earlier Act, but it also has many new features. The most significant of them, provisions authorizing preventive detention, are discussed later[1] rather than at this point.

The 1984 Bail Reform Act provides that when a person charged with a crime appears before a judicial officer, the judicial officer "shall order the pretrial release of the person on personal recognizance, or upon execution of an unsecured appearance bond in an amount specified by the court * * * unless the judicial officer determines that such release will not reasonably assure the appearance of the person as required or will endanger the safety of any other person or the community."[2] In the event of such a determination, the judicial officer is then to "order the pretrial release of the person * * * subject to the least restrictive further condition, or combination of conditions, that such judicial officer determines will reasonably assure the appearance of the person as required and the safety of any other person and the community which may include the condition that the person":

(i) remain in the custody of a designated person, who agrees to supervise him and to report any violation of a release condition to the court, if the designated person is able reasonably to assure the judicial officer that the person will appear as required and will not pose a danger to the safety of any other person or the community;

(ii) maintain employment, or, if unemployed, actively seek employment;

(iii) maintain or commence an educational program;

(iv) abide by specified restrictions on personal associations, place of abode, or travel;

(v) avoid all contact with an alleged victim of the crime and with a potential witness who may testify concerning the offense;

(vi) report on a regular basis to a designated law enforcement agency, pretrial services agency, or other agency;

(vii) comply with a specified curfew;

(viii) refrain from possessing a firearm, destructive device, or other dangerous weapon;

(ix) refrain from excessive use of alcohol, or any use of a narcotic drug or other controlled substance * * * without a prescription by a licensed medical practitioner;

(x) undergo available medical or psychiatric treatment, including treatment for drug or alcohol dependency, and remain in a specified institution if required for that purpose;

(xi) execute an agreement to forfeit upon failing to appear as required, such designated property, including money, as is reasonably necessary to assure the appearance of the person as required, and post with the court such indicia of ownership of the property or such percentage of the money as the judicial officer may specify;

(xii) execute a bail bond with solvent sureties in such amount as is reasonably necessary to assure the appearance of the person as required;

(xiii) return to custody for specified hours following release for employment, schooling, or other limited purposes; and

(xiv) satisfy any other condition that is reasonably necessary to assure the appearance of the person as required and to assure the safety of any other person and the community.[3]

But it is expressly stated that the "judicial officer may not impose a financial condition that results in the pretrial detention of the person."[4]

The 1984 Act also specifies the factors which, on the basis of "the available information," are to be taken into account in determining which conditions will suffice, namely:

(1) the nature and circumstances of the offense charged, including whether the offense is a crime of violence or involves a narcotic drug;

(2) the weight of the evidence against the person;

(3) the history and characteristics of the person, including—

§ 12.1

1. See § 12.3.
2. 18 U.S.C.A. § 3142(b).
3. 18 U.S.C.A. § 3142(c).
4. Id.

(A) the person's character, physical and mental condition, family ties, employment, financial resources, length of residence in the community, community ties, past conduct, history relating to drug or alcohol abuse, criminal history, and record concerning appearance at court proceedings; and

(B) whether, at the time of the current offense or arrest, the person was on probation, on parole, or on other release pending trial, sentencing, appeal or completion of sentence for an offense under Federal, State, or local law; and

(4) the nature and seriousness of the danger to any person or the community that would be posed by the person's release.[5]

A release order must include a written "clear and specific" statement of all conditions imposed and advise the person released of the penalties for and other consequences of violating those conditions.[6] The judicial officer may at any time amend the order to impose additional or different conditions.[7] On motion of either the defendant or the government, the release conditions may be reviewed by the court with jurisdiction over the offense charged, and a release order may be appealed to the court of appeals.[8] Violation of a condition of release is punishable by contempt [9] and, in addition, can result in revocation of the release upon a judicial finding that the person is unlikely to abide by any condition of release or that there is no combination of conditions which will assure his appearance or nondanger.[10]

The 1984 Act also provides penalties for failure to appear. A person who "knowingly * * * fails to appear [11] before a court as required by the conditions of release" [12] is to incur a forfeiture of "any property" designated in his bond or forfeiture agreement [13] and, in addition, may be subjected to fine and imprisonment.[14]

(b) State Practice Generally. It is not possible to describe state procedure with the same particularity, for there are significant variations in law and practice among the fifty jurisdictions. The typical state statute declares that the objective of bail is to secure the defendant's attendance at the proceedings against him and to prevent his punishment before conviction. Some of these statutes provide no guidance on what factors may be taken into account, while others provide a detailed list of factors in the manner of the federal Act.

Typically, an arrested defendant is taken to the nearest stationhouse and then transported to the city jail within 24 hours. For defendants charged with a minor offense listed in a fixed bail schedule, the first opportunity for release comes at that time. Those defendants unable to obtain their release at the station must await their appearance before a judicial officer, often the following morning, at which time the judge will set the terms of release. Defendants who obtained their release earlier, if their cases are not immediately disposed of at their subsequent court appearance, may have the amount of their bail revised upward or downward.

Judges are inclined to give primary consideration to the seriousness of the offense charged, most likely because it is a factor which is clear-cut and easy to apply. The strength of the case against the defendant, as communicated by the prosecutor or police, is also an important yardstick in practice. A

5. 18 U.S.C.A. § 3142(g).

6. 18 U.S.C.A. § 3142(h).

7. 18 U.S.C.A. § 3142(c).

8. 18 U.S.C.A. § 3145(a), (c).

9. 18 U.S.C.A. § 3148(c).

10. 18 U.S.C.A. § 3148(b).

11. Under 18 U.S.C.A. § 3146(c) it is an affirmative defense "that uncontrollable circumstances prevented the person from appearing or surrendering, and that the person did not contribute to the creation of such circumstances in reckless disregard of the requirement to appear or surrender, and that the person appeared or surrendered as soon as such circumstances ceased to exist."

12. 18 U.S.C.A. § 3146(a).

13. 18 U.S.C.A. § 3146(d).

14. The maximum penalties depend upon the crime charged: 10 years and/or a fine for an offense punishable by death, life imprisonment or a term of 15 years or more; 5 years and/or a fine for an offense punishable by 5 years or more; 2 years and/or a fine for any other felony; 1 year and/or a fine for a misdemeanor. 18 U.S.C.A. § 3146(b).

third factor considered very relevant is the defendant's prior criminal record. In many localities it is unusual for the judge to determine or consider other facts about the defendant's background and character, such as whether he is employed and how long he has resided in the community. The common explanations for this are that the judges believe they are overworked and do not have time to inquire into such matters and that they doubt defendants can be trusted to supply truthful answers to such inquiries. Bail projects, now in operation in many major cities, obtain this information and supply it to the court.

As for the methods by which a defendant may obtain pretrial release in the state courts, one frequently used procedure is cash bail. The defendant may raise the full amount of the bond through personal savings or money supplied by friends and family, in which case the entire amount is usually returned to him if he shows up as required. But if, as is often the case, the defendant must rely upon the services of a bail bondsmen, then he will have to pay a fee usually not less than 10 percent of the bond amount, a payment which is not recoverable by the defendant. Another method by which pretrial release may be obtained in many locales is via the 10 percent plan. The defendant pays 10 percent of the bond directly to the court and then recovers most or all of that amount if he appears in court as scheduled. Yet another possibility is that a defendant may obtain his release on a property bond, which means he offers property as bail in lieu of cash. Still another possibility is personal bond, sometimes referred to as personal surety or release on recognizance (r.o.r.), which is used when the judge concludes the defendant is sufficiently motivated to show up that he can be released on his own signature without bail. In addition to or in lieu of these methods, some localities utilize daytime release, release to the custody of an approved individual or organization, or release on conditions.

(c) Counsel at Bail Hearing. If the defendant is represented by counsel at his bail hearing, this greatly improves his chances for either bail set in a modest amount or release on his own recognizance. One reason that the participation of a defense attorney makes such a difference is that he can bring relevant facts about his client's background to the judge's attention. Bail reform in the fashion of the federal Act has, if anything, made participation by defense counsel more significant than ever before. Because modern bail laws permit a variety of alternatives to money bail, defense counsel are rightly expected to present reasonable alternative plans for release and invoke available community resources for this purpose.

Because counsel for the defendant can make such an impact at the bail hearing, there is much to be said for the contention that the Sixth Amendment right to counsel applies at that time. Such a conclusion is certainly consistent with the general notion, as the Supreme Court has put it, that this right comes into play upon "the initiation of adversary judicial criminal proceedings," at which time the "defendant finds himself faced with the prosecutorial forces of organized society, and immersed in the intricacies of substantive and procedural criminal law."[15] Moreover, it finds strong support in *Coleman v. Alabama*,[16] where the holding that a preliminary hearing is a "critical stage" for right to counsel purposes was based in part on the fact that "counsel can also be influential * * * in making effective arguments for the accused on such matters as * * * bail." But even after *Coleman* some authority is to be found that there is no constitutional right to counsel at a bail hearing.

(d) Proof at Bail Hearing. Information received at a bail hearing need not conform to the rules pertaining to the admissibility of evidence at a trial. However, this should not be taken to mean that information must be accepted by the court without regard to its reliability. Thus, whether hearsay is admissible in a bail hearing must ultimately be determined on a case by case basis by asking

15. Kirby v. Illinois, 406 U.S. 682, 92 S.Ct. 1877, 32 L.Ed.2d 411 (1972).

16. 399 U.S. 1, 90 S.Ct. 1999, 26 L.Ed.2d 387 (1970).

whether in the particular circumstances it is the kind of evidence on which responsible persons are accustomed to rely in serious affairs.

Questions concerning the burdens of production and persuasion in a bail hearing seldom reach the appellate courts. As a matter of general practice, it is customary for the prosecution to supply such facts as defendant's prior bad record in order to show that this defendant's bail should be higher or the conditions of his release more strict than would typically be true for a person so charged, and for the defense to supply favorable facts about defendant's ties to the community to show the contrary. Thus, each side supplies that information to which it has both ready access and an interest in producing. To some extent at least, the approach of the applicable bail statute may have some influence on who feels compelled to show what; a scheme based on a presumption that personal recognizance is appropriate until the contrary is shown would seem to put the prosecution in a more difficult position.

(e) Defendant's Statements. Sometimes the question has arisen whether defendant's incriminating statements made at the bail hearing are admissible against him at trial. An enlightened view of this matter was taken in *State v. Williams,*[17] where the court concluded:

> Defendant's own testimony regarding the crime may be critical to a court's determination whether he should be set free pending trial. Since the "law favors the release of defendants pending determination of guilt or innocence," a defendant should be encouraged to testify at a hearing on a motion to set bail without the fear that what he says may later be used to incriminate him. * * * Both the purposes of the bail hearing to insure defendant's appearance and the strong policy of our law to avoid unnecessary deprivations of liberty require that the defendant's testimony at the bail hearing in this case be excluded from evidence at his later trial.

That reasoning also supports the conclusion that if the defendant makes incriminating statements to a bail agency interviewer charged with the responsibility of gathering facts from the defendant and other sources relevant to the bail decision, they should likewise be inadmissible.

Whether the *Williams* result is mandated by the Constitution is a more difficult matter. A negative answer was given in *United States v. Dohm,*[18] though the court held on the circumstances there presented that defendant's statements at his bail hearing were inadmissible at trial because "the magistrate failed to accurately advise Dohm of his *Miranda* rights." The defendant's broader claim that in any event "he was compelled to forfeit his fifth amendment right to remain silent, in order to safeguard his eighth amendment right to reasonable bail," was based largely upon the Supreme Court's decision in *Simmons v. United States.*[19] The court rejected the *Simmons* analogy because in that case the Court emphasized that "at one time, a defendant who wished to assert a fourth amendment objection was required to show that he was the owner or possessor of the seized property or that he had a possessory interest in the searched premises," while by contrast "a defendant at a bail bond hearing need not divulge the facts in his case in order to receive the benefits of the eighth amendment right to bail." But there is much to be said for the view that *Dohm* confronts the defendant at the bail hearing with an impermissible compelled election. As the dissent noted, the applicable constitutional guarantee is "not just the right to bail, but the right to non-excessive bail," and in the instant case "the defendant not unreasonably concluded that the recommended amount of bail would be determined to be appropriate for him unless he rebutted the government testimony portraying him as a big-time drug dealer."

§ 12.2 Constitutionality of Limits on Pretrial Freedom

(a) Amount of Money Bail. The Eighth Amendment to the United States Constitu-

17. 115 N.H. 437, 343 A.2d 29 (1975).

18. 618 F.2d 1169 (5th Cir.1980).

19. 390 U.S. 377, 88 S.Ct. 967, 19 L.Ed.2d 1247 (1968), discussed in § 10.5(c).

tion, which is also applicable to the states through the Fourteenth Amendment due process clause,[1] provides in part: "Excessive bail shall not be required." The traditional question which has been raised under this provision is that of what amount of money bail may constitutionally be required of a defendant. The leading case is *Stack v. Boyle,*[2] involving twelve petitioners who had been charged with conspiring to violate the Smith Act, which made it a crime to advocate the overthrow of the government by force or violence. Bail was fixed in the district court in the uniform amount of $50,000 for each petitioner. The petitioners then moved to reduce bail on the ground it was excessive under the Eighth Amendment, and in support submitted statements as to their financial resources, family relationships, health, prior criminal records, and other information. Though the only response of the government was a certified record showing that four other persons previously convicted under the Smith Act had forfeited bail, the district court denied the motion and thereafter denied writs of habeas corpus for the petitioners. The court of appeals affirmed, but the Supreme Court ruled that bail had "not been fixed by proper methods," and then concluded that "petitioners' remedy is by [a renewed] motion to reduce bail" in the district court.

One respect in which the *Stack* decision is important is in its specification of the purposes underlying bail which may be legitimately taken into account in setting the amount. The Court declared:

> The right to release before trial is conditioned upon the accused's giving adequate assurance that he will stand trial and submit to sentence if found guilty. * * * Like the ancient practice of securing the oaths of responsible persons to stand as sureties for the accused, the modern practice of requiring a bail bond or the deposit of a sum of money subject to forfeiture serves as additional assurance of the presence of an accused. Bail set at a figure higher than an amount reasonably calculated to fulfill this purpose is "excessive" under the Eighth Amendment.[3]

In addition, *Stack* stresses that setting an amount of bail which properly serves this single purpose requires an assessment of the facts of the particular case. The Court declared that "standards relevant to the purpose of assuring the presence of that defendant" must "be applied in each case to each defendant." The "traditional standards" recognized by the Court in *Stack* were "the nature and circumstances of the offense charged, the weight of the evidence against him, the financial ability of the defendant to give bail and the character of the defendant." It was relatively easy to find noncompliance with the Eighth Amendment in *Stack,* for (as the Court noted) "bail for each petitioner has been fixed in the sum much higher than that usually imposed for offenses with like penalties and yet there has been no factual showing to justify such action in this case."

As this last comment reflects, the nature of the offense and in particular the "risk" the defendant is running in terms of the potential punishment is an important factor in the Eighth Amendment equation. But *Stack* teaches that it is by no means the only factor. This would indicate that use of a bail schedule, wherein amounts are set solely on the basis of the offense charged, violates the Eighth Amendment except when resorted to as a temporary measure pending prompt judicial appearance for a particularized bail setting. Indeed, such use of a master bond schedule may be constitutionally objectionable on other grounds as well, including that procedural due process requires a hearing before depriving a person of his liberty, and that the procedure violates the equal protection clause because based upon the irrational view

§ 12.2

1. In Schilb v. Kuebel, 404 U.S. 357, 92 S.Ct. 479, 30 L.Ed.2d 502 (1971), the Court observed in passing that "the Eighth Amendment's proscription of excessive bail has been assumed to have application to the States through the Fourteenth Amendment."

2. 342 U.S. 1, 72 S.Ct. 1, 96 L.Ed. 3 (1951).

3. This language was later narrowly construed as not barring preventive detention. See § 12.3(b).

that a poor person should post precisely the same amount of bail as a rich person.

One question which might be raised under the *Stack* formulation is whether it is possible for there to be circumstances where no amount of bail will suffice to ensure the defendant's appearance at the proceedings against him. This issue has not often been litigated, most likely because a court confronted with a high risk defendant will in all probability proceed to set the bail in an unreachable amount rather than deny bail altogether. But with some defendants, especially those alleged to be major drug dealers, in a position to post bail in amounts up to a million dollars, the question is taking on increasing importance. In *United States v. Abrahams,*[4] the court characterized this issue as "one of first impression" because it had not found a case "that holds directly that a defendant has an absolute right to bail pending trial regardless of the circumstances," and then concluded the instant case was "the rare case of extreme and unusual circumstances that justifies pretrial detention without bail." The defendant in *Abrahams,* charged with fraud (punishable by up to five years imprisonment and a $10,000 fine), had three previous convictions, was an escaped prisoner from New Jersey, had given false information at the previous bail hearing, had failed to appear on the previous bail of $100,000, had failed to appear in a California case and was a fugitive from that state, had used several aliases in the past, and in the last two years had transferred one and a half million dollars to Bermuda. These facts, the court concluded, supported the district court's findings that "none of the five conditions spelled out in" the federal Act, "or any combination thereof, will reasonably assure the appearance of defendant for trial if admitted to bail."

An issue which has been debated more frequently is whether the amount of bail which would suffice to ensure the defendant's appearance in a particular case is constitutionally objectionable because the defendant is indigent and thus cannot come up with bail even in a modest amount. It has been argued that an indigent defendant suffers several constitutional violations under our bail system:

1. He is being denied the fundamental fairness guaranteed by the due process of law because, although he alleges he is innocent, he is being punished by imprisonment before he has been tried.

2. He is being denied procedural due process because detention adversely affects the disposition of his case and thereby deprives him of a fair trial.

3. He is denied equal protection of the law because, solely on account of his poverty, he is being denied pretrial liberty.

4. His right to bail under the eighth and fourteenth amendments is being violated because the proscription against "excessive" bail must be construed in such a way as not automatically to foreclose for indigents the fundamental right to freedom pending trial.[5]

As for the first of these, it cannot be said that there is a constitutional "presumption of innocence" which entitles all defendants to pretrial release.[6] The other contentions, however, are worthy of closer attention.

(b) Poverty and Pretrial Release. As for the relevance of the defendant's indigency upon the Eighth Amendment bail question, *Stack v. Boyle*[7] is itself instructive, for it expressly states that "the financial ability of the defendant to give bail" is one of the factors which must be taken into consideration. This is certainly sensible, for an impe-

4. 575 F.2d 3 (1st Cir.1978).

5. Foote, The Coming Constitutional Crisis in Bail, 113 U.Pa.L.Rev. 959, 1125, 1135 (1965).

6. In Bell v. Wolfish, 441 U.S. 520, 99 S.Ct. 1861, 60 L.Ed.2d 447 (1979), the Court concluded as to a related point:

"The presumption of innocence is a doctrine that allocates the burden of proof in criminal trials; it also may serve as an admonishment to the jury to judge an accused's guilt or innocence solely on the evidence adduced at trial and not on the basis of suspicions that may arise from the fact of his arrest, indictment or custody or from other matters not introduced as proof at trial. * * * But it has no application to a determination of the rights of a pretrial detainee during confinement before his trial has even begun."

7. 342 U.S. 1, 72 S.Ct. 1, 96 L.Ed. 3 (1951).

cunious person who pledges a small amount of collateral constituting all or almost all of his property is likely to have a stake at least as great as that of a wealthy person who pledges a large amount constituting a modest part of his property. But it is a substantial jump from that truism to the proposition that an amount of bail which a defendant cannot meet because of his poverty is thereby "excessive" under the Eighth Amendment. Courts have refused to take that leap; they instead continue to adhere to the proposition that bail is not excessive merely because the defendant is unable to pay it.

As for an equal protection claim, note must be taken of the oft-quoted comments of Justice Douglas in *Bandy v. United States.*[8] Observing that the Court had held in *Griffin v. Illinois*[9] "that an indigent defendant is denied equal protection of the law if he is denied an appeal on equal terms with other defendants, solely because of his indigence," Justice Douglas opined that it must be similarly unconstitutional for "an indigent [to] be denied freedom, where a wealthy man would not, because he does not happen to have enough property to pledge for his freedom." Some have argued that this position has been bolstered by such cases as *Williams v. Illinois*[10] and *Tate v. Short,*[11] deemed to provide a close analogy because they held that equal protection bars subjecting indigent defendants to sentences of imprisonment beyond that which other defendants could receive. However, *Williams* and *Tate* did not bar imprisonment for indigents merely because a wealthier defendant would likely escape such a consequence by being fined instead, and *Griffin* has since been given a rather narrow interpretation by the Supreme Court.[12] Thus, the courts have not been inclined to accept the equal protection argument that bail is unconstitutional when set in an amount a particular indigent defendant cannot meet. But several courts, relying upon *Williams* and *Tate,* have held that failure to grant credit against a maximum sentence for presentence incarceration imposed because of the defendant's inability to post bail violates the equal protection clause.

Because of bail reform efforts in recent years, the dimensions of the debate concerning the indigent defendant have changed somewhat. Under laws based upon the federal Bail Reform Act of 1966, money bail is but one of several alternative forms of release, and thus the issue is now often cast in terms of the purported "right" of indigent defendants to one of the non-financial forms of pretrial release. Where, as was true under the 1966 Act, those nonfinancial alternatives must be considered by the judge, the argument has been made that in the case of an indigent defendant the judge is obligated to select one of those alternatives. But that argument has not prevailed in the courts as a constitutional imperative. It is noteworthy, however, that the successor federal Bail Reform Act of 1984 expressly provides: "The judicial officer may not impose a financial condition that results in the pretrial detention of the person."[13]

A more compelling argument, and one of particular importance in those jurisdictions which have not adopted bail reforms in the manner of the federal Act, is that money bail may no longer be constitutionally viewed as the sole means of pretrial release or even as the preferred means of gaining pretrial freedom. Important here is *Pugh v. Rainwater,*[14] involving a challenge to the Florida bail system, which was construed as making available the same alternatives as the 1966 federal statute but as being different from the federal system in two important respects: (1) there

8. 81 S.Ct. 197, 5 L.Ed.2d 218 (1960).

9. 351 U.S. 12, 76 S.Ct. 585, 100 L.Ed. 891 (1956).

10. 399 U.S. 235, 90 S.Ct. 2018, 26 L.Ed.2d 586 (1970) (defendant unable to pay fine could not be incarcerated beyond maximum term of imprisonment fixed by statute; equal protection requires that "statutory ceiling placed on imprisonment * * * be same for all defendants irrespective of their economic status").

11. 401 U.S. 395, 91 S.Ct. 668, 28 L.Ed.2d 130 (1971) (indigent convicted of offenses punishable by fine only cannot be incarcerated a sufficient time to satisfy fines).

12. See Ross v. Moffitt, 417 U.S. 600, 94 S.Ct. 2437, 41 L.Ed.2d 341 (1974).

13. See § 12.1(a).

14. 557 F.2d 1189 (5th Cir.1977).

was no presumption in favor of release on recognizance; and (2) the nonfinancial alternatives were not given priority. The court concluded:

> Because it gives the judge essentially unreviewable discretion to impose money bail, the rule retains the discriminatory vice of the former system: When a judge decides to set money bail, the indigent will be forced to remain in jail. We hold that equal protection standards are not satisfied unless the judge is required to consider less financially onerous forms of release before he imposes money bail. Requiring a presumption in favor of non-money bail accommodates the State's interest in assuring the defendant's appearance at trial as well as the defendant's right to be free pending trial, regardless of his financial status.

This would mean, as the court later put it,[15] "that in the case of an indigent, whose appearance at trial could reasonably be assured by one of the alternative forms of release, pretrial confinement for inability to post money bail would constitute imposition of an excessive restraint."

As bail reform efforts result in alternative methods of release being provided, other equal protection issues can arise, as is illustrated by *Schilb v. Kuebel.*[16] At issue there was a state statute which provided, as to a defendant not released on his own recognizance, that he could either deposit cash equal to 10% of the bond, in which case 10% of the amount deposited (i.e., 1% of the amount of the bond) would be retained by the state as "bail bond costs" even if defendant appeared as required, or else he could deposit the full amount of the bail, in which event there would be no charge or retention if the defendant appeared as required. Though the defendant claimed this meant a charge was imposed only on the nonaffluent and thus constituted a denial of equal protection, the Court concluded otherwise, finding the distinction drawn by the statute was not "invidious and without rational basis." The defendant's assumption that the affluent would always opt for the full deposit alternative and thus escape the charge was itself doubted by the Court, which noted that "in these days of high interest rates" it would make more sense for an affluent person to post only 10% and earn interest on the balance.

(c) Opportunity to Prepare a Defense. There is little reason to doubt the proposition that pretrial detention has a significant adverse impact upon the ability of a defendant to vindicate himself at trial or secure leniency in sentencing: He cannot contribute either money or labor to pretrial investigation. In particular he is unable to help locate witnesses or evidence which might be more accessible to him than to an outsider. His contacts with counsel may be impeded, so that he must plan a defense in cramped jail facilities within the limited hours set aside for visitors. The pretrial prison experience may adversely affect his demeanor in court and on the witness stand. Finally, a defendant who has lost his job and been removed from his family will stand a far poorer chance for probation than the one who has been employed and maintained strong family ties. Nonetheless, courts have not been particularly receptive to post-conviction claims by defendants that they were entitled to relief because their pretrial incarceration in some way interfered with preparation of their defense.

However, a particularized claim made during the time of pretrial detention will sometimes produce limited relief, as is illustrated by *Kinney v. Lenon.*[17] There the juvenile defendant, in custody awaiting trial on charges arising out of a schoolyard fight, alleged in support of his claim for pretrial release "that there were many potential witnesses to the fight, that he cannot identify them by name but would recognize them by sight, that appellant's attorneys are white though he and the potential witnesses are black, that his attorneys would consequently have great practical difficulty in interviewing and lining up the witnesses, and that appellant is the sole per-

15. Upon rehearing en banc, 572 F.2d 1053 (5th Cir. 1978).

16. 404 U.S. 357, 92 S.Ct. 479, 30 L.Ed.2d 502 (1971).

17. 425 F.2d 209 (9th Cir.1970).

son who can do so." Convinced that there had been "a strong showing that the appellant is the only person who can effectively prepare his own defense," the court concluded that defendant's detention was infringing upon his constitutional right to compulsory process to obtain witnesses in his behalf, which "as a practical matter would be of little value without an opportunity to contact and screen potential witnesses before trial." The court thus held that release of the defendant into the custody of his parents was necessary to protect "his due-process right to a fair trial." In cases of this general type, it would be most appropriate for the court to consider release for limited periods of time and in the custody of some person, such as defendant's lawyer or a law enforcement officer.[18]

(d) Nature of Pretrial Custody. There is yet another sense in which it may be said that constitutional objections may be raised regarding limits on pretrial freedom, and that is when persons unable to obtain their release challenge the circumstances of their pretrial custody. There has been extended litigation in recent years challenging various facets of pretrial detention, which is none too surprising in light of the fact that unconvicted defendants typically receive worse treatment prior to trial than convicted defendants receive after trial. A brief look at this problem is appropriate, for it adds a perspective to the custody vs. no custody issues addressed in this Chapter.

The Supreme Court first had an opportunity to assess conditions of pretrial incarceration in *Bell v. Wolfish,*[19] a class action brought by detainees in a federally operated short-term custodial facility in New York City. The Court of Appeals, reasoning from the "premise that an individual is to be treated as innocent until proven guilty," concluded that pretrial detainees retain the "rights afforded unincarcerated individuals" and that consequently they could be "subjected to only those 'restrictions and privations' which 'inhere in their confinement itself or which are justified by compelling necessities of jail administration.'" The *Bell* majority disagreed. As for the presumption of innocence, it is "a doctrine that allocates the burden of proof in criminal trials" and thus "has no application to a determination of the rights of a pretrial detainee during confinement before his trial has even begun." And while clearly "the Due Process Clause protects a detainee from certain conditions and restrictions of pretrial detainment," the question under that provision (that is, where an aspect of the detention "is not alleged to violate any express guarantee of the Constitution") is "whether those conditions amount to punishment of the detainee." The mere fact "that such detention interferes with the detainee's understandable desire to live as comfortably as possible and with as little restraint as possible during confinement" does not itself make the conditions of that confinement "punishment" for due process purposes. Rather, the question is "whether the disability is imposed for the purpose of punishment or whether it is but an incident of some other legitimate governmental purpose." The *Bell* majority also emphasized that while ensuring the detainees' appearance at trial might be the only legitimate purpose of keeping them in custody, it did not follow that this "is the *only* objective that may justify restraints and conditions once the decision is lawfully made to confine a person." Once an individual is lawfully confined, "the effective management of the detention facility" (i.e., maintaining security and order and ensuring that no weapons or illicit drugs reach detainees) is also a permissible objective.

As for the specific complaints, the Court in *Bell* first held that double-bunking did not violate due process where detainees were free to move to a common area, and that the prohibition on receipt of packages of food or

18. The federal Bail Reform Act of 1984 provides, as to a person ordered detained, that the "judicial officer may, by subsequent order, permit the temporary release of the person, in the custody of a United States marshal or another appropriate person, to the extent that the judicial officer determines such release to be necessary for preparation of the person's defense or for another compelling reason." 18 U.S.C.A. § 3142(i).

19. 441 U.S. 520, 99 S.Ct. 1861, 60 L.Ed.2d 447 (1979).

personal property did not violate due process even though there might be lesser restrictions which would be "a reasonable way of coping with the problems of security, order, and sanitation." The court then acknowledged that the First and Fourth Amendment rights of the detainees were not lost by virtue of their pretrial detentions but concluded that "maintaining institutional security and preserving internal order and discipline are essential goals that may require limitation or retraction of the retained constitutional rights." The prohibition against receipt of hardback books unless mailed directly from publishers, book clubs or bookstores was upheld against First Amendment objections because it is "a rational response by prison officials to an obvious security problem," namely, "that hardback books are especially serviceable for smuggling contraband into an institution." Because a detainee's "reasonable expectation of privacy" in his living area under the Fourth Amendment is, at best, "of a diminished scope" in light of "the realities of institutional confinement," the Court held that Amendment was not violated by a practice of irregular "shakedowns" of cells in the inmates' absence. As for the practice of conducting visual body cavity searches as part of strip searches conducted after contact visits with any person from outside the institution, the Court balanced "the significant and legitimate security interests of the institution against the privacy interests of the inmates" and concluded such searches were reasonable.

§ 12.3 Constitutionality of Mandating Pretrial Detention

(a) Preventive Detention. As noted earlier, the *Stack v. Boyle* [1] interpretation of the Eighth Amendment prohibition on "excessive" bail was that in setting pretrial release conditions there is but one legitimate consideration: what is necessary to provide a reasonable assurance that the particular defendant will subsequently appear at the proceedings against him? There is no question, however, but that this legal theory is not always respected in practice and that bail determinations are sometimes influenced by such considerations as the accused's assumed danger to the community. Especially in earlier days, when there was almost exclusive reliance upon money bail and little opportunity for a defendant to obtain review of his bail setting, this could quite easily occur. Because of the sub rosa character of such action, the concept of "preventive detention" (pretrial custody of a defendant for the purpose of protecting some other person or the community at large) did not receive close scrutiny.

In recent years, by comparison, the subject of preventive detention has been much debated. This is largely attributable to bail reform activities, for from the very beginning of those efforts one of the most serious impediments to bail reform has been the fear that a greater number of pretrial releases would mean a greater amount of serious crime. As alternatives to money bail were implemented and as judicial review of the conditions set for defendants as yet unable to obtain their relief was mandated, it became increasingly likely that those defendants perceived by some as "dangerous" would obtain their freedom pending trial. This concern has produced some legislative activity.

The District of Columbia preventive detention law, which took effect in 1971, authorizes pretrial detention of a defendant for up to 60 days, after which he is eligible for release if his expedited trial has not yet commenced.[2] Such detention is permitted only upon a showing that "there is no condition or combination of conditions of release which will reasonably assure the safety of any other person or the community," [3] and only of a defendant who falls into one of the following categories: (1) a person charged with a "dangerous

§ 12.3

1. 342 U.S. 1, 72 S.Ct. 1, 96 L.Ed. 3 (1951).

2. D.C.Code § 23–1322(d). However, for "good cause shown" the detention may be continued "for the additional time required to prepare for the expedited trial," not to exceed 30 more days.

3. D.C.Code § 23–1322(b)(2)(B).

crime"[4] (e.g., robbery, burglary, rape, arson, sale of narcotics[5]), upon a finding there is a "substantial probability" he committed the charged crime[6]; (2) a person charged with a "crime of violence" (e.g., murder, rape, robbery, burglary, arson, serious assault[7]), upon a like finding, if in addition that person is an addict,[8] or has been convicted of such a crime within the past 10 years, or allegedly committed the charged crime while on bail, probation or parole regarding such a crime[9]; or (3) a person charged with any offense who, "for the purpose of obstructing or attempting to obstruct justice, threatens, injures, intimidates, or attempts to threaten, injure or intimidate any prospective witness or juror."[10]

A preventive detention scheme is also an important part of the federal Bail Reform Act of 1984. A detention hearing is to be held, upon motion of the attorney for the government, where the case involves a crime of violence, an offense for which the maximum penalty is death or life imprisonment, certain serious drug offenses, or any felony by one with two or more convictions of the aforementioned type offenses. Also, such a hearing is to be held on motion of either the attorney for the government or the judicial officer that the case involves a serious risk that the person will flee or will obstruct or attempt to obstruct justice or interfere with a prospective witness or juror.[11] If at the hearing the judicial officer "finds that no condition or combination of conditions will reasonably assure the appearance of the person as required and the safety of any other person and the community," then detention is to be ordered.[12] A rebuttable presumption in support of such a finding exists in certain circumstances.[13] The Act also makes nonviolation of any federal, state or local crime a condition of any release under the Act,[14] and upon violation of that condition revocation of the release is required upon a finding of probable cause that such a crime was committed while on release, and also a finding that the person is unlikely to abide by any conditions of release or that there is no combination of release conditions that will assure the person will not flee or pose a danger.[15] A person ordered detained may obtain review of the order from the court with original jurisdiction over the offense charged,[16] and may appeal from the detention order.[17]

No state has yet seen fit to adopt such a full-scale preventive detention scheme, but there nonetheless has been some activity at the state level. Nearly half of the states presently permit some consideration of defendant dangerousness in the pretrial release determination. In addition, many states by statute, court rule or court decision permit revocation of release because of commission of a crime or other misconduct. Moreover, preventive detention objectives are also served by state laws which permit the denial of bail to defendants charged with certain serious noncapital offenses. This includes provisions which actually specify certain noncapital crimes as not bailable and those which have been construed to allow denial of bail for certain crimes which would be capital but for constitutionally defective sentencing procedures.

(b) The Eighth Amendment Ambiguity. Whether the Eighth Amendment posed a con-

4. D.C.Code § 23–1322(a)(1).

5. D.C.Code § 23–1331(3).

6. D.C.Code § 23–1322(b)(2)(C).

7. D.C.Code § 23–1331(4).

8. D.C.Code § 23–1323.

9. D.C.Code § 23–1322(a)(2).

10. D.C.Code § 23–1322(a)(3).

11. 18 U.S.C.A. § 3142(f). The Act states that this detention hearing, except upon a grant of a continuance, "shall be held immediately upon the person's first appearance before the judicial officer." "Nothing in § 3142(f) indicates that compliance with the first appearance requirement is a precondition to holding the hearing or that failure to comply with the requirement renders such a hearing a nullity," and thus "a failure to comply with the first appearance requirement does not defeat the Government's authority to seek detention of the person charged." United States v. Montalvo–Murillo, ___ U.S. ___, 110 S.Ct. 2072, 109 L.Ed.2d 720 (1990).

12. 18 U.S.C.A. § 3142(e).

13. Id.

14. 18 U.S.C.A. § 3142(b), (c).

15. 18 U.S.C.A. § 3148(b).

16. 18 U.S.C.A. § 3145(b).

17. 18 U.S.C.A. § 3145(c).

stitutional barrier to such preventive detention schemes remained unclear until the Supreme Court addressed the issue in *United States v. Salerno.*[18] True, a literal reading of the relevant language of the Amendment, "Excessive bail shall not be required," suggested the answer was no. But because the pre-*Salerno* utterances of the Court contained language helpful to those on both sides of the debate, lower courts were divided on the issue.

Those holding to the view that the Eighth Amendment does *not* encompass a right to bail found it useful to trace the excessive bail provision back to a comparable provision in the English Bill of Rights of 1689. The latter provision, it was noted, was not prompted by the well established statutory provisions which carefully enumerated which offenses were bailable and which were not, but rather by judicial circumvention of the protections of the Habeas Corpus Act by setting prohibitively high bail for bailable offenses. The English excessive bail clause, therefore, was developed as a specific remedy for judicial abuse of the bail procedure as otherwise established by law and did not, in and of itself, imply any right to bail. This distinction, it was argued, was recognized in the colonies and early states, as reflected by three significant developments: (1) several states dealt with the right to bail by statute, thus indicating an understanding that the subject was open to legislative limitation; (2) several states adopted constitutional provisions which were explicitly directed to limiting the power of the judiciary; and (3) several states adopted constitutional provisions which granted a right to bail and also an excessive bail clause, manifesting a recognition that the latter did not encompass the former.

The view that the Eighth Amendment does not confer a right to bail was also claimed to be consistent with the contemporary understanding when the Amendment was considered and adopted. It was pointed out that some of the states proposing an excessive bail clause for the federal Constitution had such a clause and a right to bail provision in their state constitutions, and thus would have proposed both had they desired a constitutional right to bail against the federal government. Also noteworthy is the fact that in the same session in which Congress considered and approved the Bill of Rights, it drafted and enacted the Judiciary Act of 1789, which established a statutory right to bail in noncapital cases. This view of history, it was argued, has been accepted by the Supreme Court, for in *Carlson v. Landon*[19] the Court stated:

> The bail clause was lifted with slight changes from the English Bill of Rights Act. In England that clause has never been thought to accord a right to bail in all cases, but merely to provide that bail shall not be excessive in those cases where it is proper to grant bail. When this clause was carried over into our Bill of Rights, nothing was said that indicated any different concept.

This argument for a narrow reading of the Eighth Amendment concluded with the contention that such an interpretation is consistent with the general constitutional scheme. In response to the objection that it would make little sense to prohibit judicial imposition of excessive bail but not forbid the legislative denial of bail altogether, it was said that such a construction squares with the fact that the chief concern of the Bill of Rights generally is the conduct of the judicial branch of government.

As for those holding to the view that the Eighth Amendment *does* include a constitutional right to bail, they took a somewhat different view as to the significance of the Amendment's English antecedents. They agreed that English law denied bail for some offenses, but found no evidence that such a denial was ever permitted for the purpose of protecting the community. Rather, they suggested, the underlying assumption was that certain classes of offenders, particularly those whose lives were at stake, ought to be detained simply to assure their presence at trial. In any event, so the argument proceeded, the English history is not controlling here be-

18. 481 U.S. 739, 107 S.Ct. 2095, 95 L.Ed.2d 697 (1987).

19. 342 U.S. 524, 72 S.Ct. 525, 96 L.Ed. 547 (1952).

cause from the very beginning the American concept of bail differed significantly from that of the English. This is reflected by the fact that most states put in their state constitutions a provision that "all persons shall be bailable." And while these state constitutional provisions contain an exception for capital cases, this hardly reflects acceptance of the concept of preventive detention. Rather, these provisions were enacted in this form because it had been thought that most defendants facing a possible death penalty would likely flee regardless of what bail was set.

Those favoring a broader reading of the Eighth Amendment to include a right to bail contended that this is the only logical construction of the bail provision. So the argument proceeded, to read the Amendment as barring judicial setting of excessive bail but not legislative denial of bail would make it virtually meaningless. After all, the interests at stake are identical whether a legislature or a court has made the basic decision resulting in pretrial imprisonment. Moreover, an interpretation of the bail clause as limited to judicial abuse is inconsistent with the general approach taken in the Bill of Rights, which is concerned primarily with curtailing the powers of Congress. This is evident within the Eighth Amendment itself, for the prohibitions on cruel and unusual punishments and excessive fines have traditionally been viewed as limitations on legislative abuse.

As for the *Carlson* case, it was noted that the language quoted above was dictum set out in the context of a civil rather than a criminal case, in which the actual holding was that bail could be denied to prevent sabotage by alien Communists pending their deportation. More relevant, so the argument proceeded, is the Court's declaration in *Stack v. Boyle*[20] that the

> right to freedom before conviction permits the unhampered preparation of a defense, and serves to prevent the infliction of punishment prior to conviction. * * * Unless this right to bail before trial is preserved, the presumption of innocence, secured only after centuries of struggle, would lose its meaning.

Then came *United States v. Salerno*,[21] involving a facial challenge to the Bail Reform Act of 1984 (meaning, the Court emphasized, that "the challenger must establish that no set of circumstances exists under which the Act would be valid"). The Supreme Court found the *Stack* language "far too slender a reed on which to rest" the argument that the Eighth Amendment grants "a right to bail calculated solely upon consideration of flight," especially when "*Stack* is illuminated by the Court's holding just four months later in *Carlson.*" But the Court's brief discussion of the subject concluded with the caution that

> we need not decide today whether the Excessive Bail Clause speaks at all to Congress' power to define the classes of criminal arrestees who shall be admitted to bail. * * * Nothing in the text of the Bail Clause limits permissible government considerations solely to questions of flight. The only arguable substantive limitation of the Bail Clause is that the government's proposed conditions of release or detention not be "excessive" in light of the perceived evil. Of course, to determine whether the government's response is excessive, we must compare that response against the interest the government seeks to protect by means of that response. Thus, when the government has admitted that its only interest is in preventing flight, bail must be set by a court at a sum designed to ensure that goal, and no more. * * * We believe that when Congress has mandated detention on the basis of a compelling interest other than prevention of flight, as it has here, the Eighth Amendment does not require release on bail.

Thus, there exists in *Salerno* at least the suggestion that under the Eighth Amendment the risk of future crimes by certain types of arrestees could be so insubstantial as to make preventive detention of such persons excessive.

(c) Other Constitutional Objections. The language from *Strack* quoted above has understandably prompted the argument that preventive detention schemes are unconstitu-

20. 342 U.S. 1, 72 S.Ct. 1, 96 L.Ed. 3 (1951).

21. 481 U.S. 739, 107 S.Ct. 2095, 95 L.Ed.2d 697 (1987).

tional simply because they run afoul of the presumption of innocence. But while it is now generally accepted that the presumption of innocence has constitutional stature, as currently viewed by the Supreme Court it appears to have no bearing upon the preventive detention issue. The Court in *Bell v. Wolfish* [22] concluded that the presumption "is a doctrine that allocates the burden of proof in criminal trials" and requires the factfinder "to judge an accused's guilt or innocence solely on the evidence adduced at trial and not on the basis of suspicions that may arise from the fact of his arrest, indictment, or custody or from other matters not introduced as proof at trial," and that it has "no application * * * before his trial has even begun."

Presumption of innocence aside, it is nonetheless possible that a particular preventive detention scheme would be vulnerable to an attack on due process grounds on the theory that it amounts to an impermissible imposition of punishment. As the Supreme Court recognized in *Bell v. Wolfish,* the Constitution "includes freedom from punishment within the liberty of which no person may be deprived without due process of law," so that generally "punishment can only follow a determination of guilt after trial or plea." But the Court in *Bell* deemed it beyond dispute that pretrial incarceration is not inevitably "punishment" within the meaning of this doctrine. As for how to draw the "distinction between punitive measures that may not constitutionally be imposed prior to a determination of guilt and regulatory restraints that may," the Court identified a series of three factors: (1) "whether the disability is imposed for the purpose of punishment or whether it is but an incident of some other legitimate governmental purpose"; (2) absent an intent to punish, whether "an alternative purpose to which [the restriction] may rationally be connected is assignable for it"; and (3) if there is such a purpose, a "legitimate governmental objective," whether the disability "appears excessive in relation to the alternative purpose assigned [to it]."

Applying these factors, the Supreme Court in *United States v. Salerno,*[23] in response to a facial challenge to the Bail Reform Act of 1984,[24] concluded the Act did not violate substantive due process. The legislative history "clearly indicates that Congress did not formulate the pretrial detention provisions as punishment for dangerous individuals"; rather, they serve a legitimate function, as "there is no doubt that preventing danger to the community is a legitimate regulatory goal." As for the third *Bell* factor, the Court concluded that "the incidents of pretrial detention" were not excessive because the Act "carefully limits the circumstances under which detention may be sought to the most serious crimes," the arrestee "is entitled to a prompt detention hearing" at which "the government must convince a neutral decisionmaker by clear and convincing evidence that no conditions of release can reasonably assure the safety of the community or any person," "the maximum length of pretrial detention is limited by the stringent time limitations of the Speedy Trial Act," and the conditions of confinement reflect the regulatory purpose because detainees are, to the extent possible, to be housed separately from convicted defendants. The Court's emphasis upon these characteristics of the Act, together with the assertion that what is involved here is a balancing of the "particularized government interest" against "the individual's strong interest in liberty," suggests that a more expansive type of preventive detention law would be vulnerable under the *Bell* test.

Next, there is the possibility that a preventive detention scheme could be questioned on equal protection grounds. The traditional standard of review under the equal protection clause requires only that the law be shown to bear some rational relationship to legitimate state purposes,[25] though there are special in-

22. 441 U.S. 520, 99 S.Ct. 1861, 60 L.Ed.2d 447 (1979).

23. 481 U.S. 739, 107 S.Ct. 2095, 95 L.Ed.2d 697 (1987).

24. Meaning, the Court noted, that "the challenger must establish that no set of circumstances exists under which the Act would be valid."

25. San Antonio School District v. Rodriguez, 411 U.S.

stances in which a more demanding "strict scrutiny" approach is required. Even assuming the latter test is not applicable here, a matter on which there is not complete agreement, it might be argued that a preventive detention scheme which selects only from those charged with crimes is arbitrary. The reasoning is that there certainly are persons not charged with any crime who give every indication of being at least as dangerous as anyone awaiting trial on a pending charge, and that this being so it is arbitrary to imprison the man who is about to be tried for a past offense while imposing no restraint on the man who is not facing trial. Obviously relevant to this line of reasoning is *Jackson v. Indiana,*[26] holding that "pending criminal charges" provide no justification for incarcerating incompetents under less demanding standards than apply to mentally ill persons not so charged. *Jackson,* it has been argued, is directly relevant to the preventive detention question. Yet, authority is to be found supporting the conclusion that it is rational for a legislative body to conclude that those charged with a particular type of offense are likely to repeat their crimes and thus to authorize preventive detention as to persons so charged.

Finally, it is well to note that even if a particular preventive detention scheme suffers from none of the previously discussed constitutional defects, it is nonetheless necessary that the procedures whereby it is determined which individuals will actually be confined be fair in a procedural due process sense. Even in a situation in which it is conceded that the defendant has no absolute right to bail, a fair adjudicatory procedure must be followed. Just what constitutes fair procedure for due process purposes depends to some extent upon the circumstances and matter at issue. Thus, in *Gerstein v. Pugh,*[27] concerning the judicial determination of probable cause after a warrantless arrest, the Court held that "the full panoply of adversary safeguards—counsel, confrontation, cross-examination, and compulsory process for witnesses," is not constitutionally required, while in *Morrissey v. Brewer,*[28] concerning parole revocation, the Court ruled the parolee was entitled to notice, an opportunity to present evidence, and a right to confront and cross-examine adverse witnesses. In *United States v. Edwards,*[29] upholding the District of Columbia preventive detention statute, the majority ruled that *Gerstein* rather than *Morrissey* governed because it concerned a hearing with a similar issue: "whether the accused may be detained pending trial." That reasoning is unconvincing. As one of the *Edwards* dissenters noted, it affords "less constitutional protection to an accused at a pretrial detention hearing than the Supreme Court has granted convicted felons facing possible revocation of probation or parole." Moreover, he correctly added, *Gerstein* is hardly analogous because it involves only a probable cause determination, which (1) is not a basis for further detention per se but only for requiring bail; and (2) is much less complicated than the "far more complex, inherently speculative prediction that the accused is likely to be dangerous in the future."

In *United States v. Salerno,*[30] the Court briefly discussed the procedural due process question in upholding the facial constitutionality of the Bail Reform Act of 1984. Seemingly consistent with the discussion above, the Court stressed the procedures mandated by the Act: "a right to counsel at the detention hearing," and a right to "testify in their own behalf, present information by proffer or otherwise, and cross-examine witnesses who appear at the hearing." The Court declared "these extensive safeguards suffice to repel a facial challenge,"[31] but may or may not have intended *Gerstein* as the benchmark in stating enigmatically that these procedures "far

1, 93 S.Ct. 1278, 36 L.Ed.2d 16 (1973).

26. 406 U.S. 715, 92 S.Ct. 1845, 32 L.Ed.2d 435 (1972).

27. 420 U.S. 103, 95 S.Ct. 854, 43 L.Ed.2d 54 (1975).

28. 408 U.S. 471, 92 S.Ct. 2593, 33 L.Ed.2d 484 (1972).

29. 430 A.2d 1321 (D.C.App.1981).

30. 481 U.S. 739, 107 S.Ct. 2095, 95 L.Ed.2d 697 (1987).

31. As the Court emphasized, on a facial challenge "the challenger must establish that no set of circumstances exists under which the Act would be valid."

exceed what we found necessary to affect limited postarrest detention" in that case.

(d) Detention Where Serious Offense Charged. One variety of preventive detention scheme is that which withholds the right to pretrial release for defendants charged with a certain type of serious offense. Illustrative is the state constitutional provision held unconstitutional in *Hunt v. Roth;*[32] it excepted cases of "sexual offenses involving penetration by force or against the will of the victim * * * where the proof is evident or the presumption great." The court in *Hunt* held that this provision violated the Eighth Amendment, construed to bar an "unreasonable and arbitrary denial of bail," but the court's reasoning would also be relevant were the provision instead subjected to a due process or equal protection analysis:

> We do not hold and need not decide that there is a constitutional right in every case to release on bail. As we have discussed, there exists a strong argument that bail may be properly denied without encroaching on constitutional concerns where a judicial officer weighs all the appropriate factors and makes a reasoned judgment that the defendant's past record demonstrates that bail will not reasonably assure his or her appearance or, arguendo, that he or she, because of the overall record and circumstances, poses a threat to the community. The fatal flaw in the Nebraska constitutional amendment is that the state has created an irrebuttable presumption that every individual charged with this particular offense is incapable of assuring his appearance by conditioning it upon reasonable bail or is too dangerous to be granted release. * * * The state may be free to consider the nature of the charge and the degree of proof in granting or denying bail but it cannot give these factors conclusive force.

Because *Salerno,* discussed above, placed great emphasis on the need for proof that the particular "arrestee presents an identified and articulable threat to an individual or the community," it does not put the *Hunt* analysis in doubt.

(e) Detention Upon Individual Finding of Dangerousness. Even if a preventive detention law requires a case-by-case determination of the defendant's dangerousness, as do both the D.C. and federal statutes, it can be argued that there is a fundamental constitutional defect. Whether the question is viewed in terms of an Eighth Amendment right against "unreasonable and arbitrary denial of bail," a due process right under *Bell* to a disability which is not "excessive" in relation to its purpose, or an equal protection right against irrational distinctions, the asserted defect is that there appears to be no simple, reliable technique for predicting which defendants are likely to be dangerous. Various studies show that only 5 percent of the defendants eligible for detention under the District of Columbia preventive detention statute would, if released, be rearrested for dangerous or violent crimes. Moreover, it has also been shown that persons charged with some very serious crimes like homicide, persons arrested while on pretrial release, and persons with prior arrest records all pose no greater release risks than does the average defendant. Still another study concluded that it was not possible to develop a reliable set of predictors that could accurately identify the relatively small proportion of released defendants who would be rearrested while on bail. However, the Supreme Court's decision in *Schall v. Martin,*[33] upholding a preventive detention statute for juvenile proceedings, suggests a challenge based upon this uncertainty is unlikely to prevail. The Court there declared "that from a legal point of view there is nothing inherently unattainable about a prediction of future criminal conduct," which "forms an important element in many decisions" regarding sentencing and parole and probation release and revocation.[34] That language was relied upon in *Salerno,* discussed above, upholding

32. 648 F.2d 1148 (8th Cir.1981).

33. 467 U.S. 253, 104 S.Ct. 2403, 81 L.Ed.2d 207 (1984).

34. The Court also concluded that the governing statute need not specify the factors to be taken into account in making this judgment, as "a prediction of future criminal conduct is 'an experienced prediction based on a host of variables' which cannot be readily codified."

the facial constitutionality of the Bail Reform Act of 1984.

(f) Detention for Misconduct During Release. The one form of preventive detention which is most likely to pass constitutional muster is that allowing revocation of pretrial release and detention until trial upon a showing that the defendant engaged in misconduct during that release. This is most obviously the case where the defendant has unlawfully tried to thwart his prosecution or conviction by such conduct as threatening, injuring or intimidating a prospective witness, juror, prosecutor, or court officer. Notwithstanding any constitutional or statutory right to bail, a court has the inherent power to confine the defendant in such circumstances in the interest of safeguarding the integrity of its own process.

As for the broader proposition that a defendant may have his bail revoked for any serious criminal conduct, one court has reached the remarkable result that a defendant charged with possessing sawed-off shotguns could not have his bail rescinded after he mailed a live bomb to the police station where he had been booked. The reasoning was that the state constitutional provision granting a right to bail prohibited denial of bail solely because of a defendant's dangerous propensities. But the prevailing view is to the contrary. Thus, a statute declaring that a felony defendant released on bail may have his bail revoked upon a showing he has committed another felony has been upheld. Indeed, it has been held that it is within the inherent power of a court to impose a release condition that the defendant not engage in further serious criminal conduct, and that revocation for violation of the condition is thus permissible even absent such a statutory provision. Such a system does not contain the defects of outright pretrial detention, where one of the main failings is the fact that the judge has no reliable indicator available by which to determine which defendants will commit further crimes. It is necessary, of course, that the revocation hearing be conducted in conformance with the requirements of procedural due process, but this does not mean that the new crime must be proved beyond a reasonable doubt.

More extensive use of this revocation procedure, with expedited trials for those so detained, might well make considerable inroads upon the crime problem cited by preventive detention advocates. Individual cases have surfaced in which a person has been charged over and over with serious crimes while on pretrial release without any effort to terminate that release. Moreover, one study concluded that of those defendants rearrested while on release, about a third were rearrested more than once, frequently without any change in their release status.

§ 12.4 Special Situations

(a) Capital Cases. In 1818 the State of Connecticut adopted a constitutional provision reading: "All prisoners shall, before conviction, be bailable by sufficient sureties, except for capital offenses, where the proof is evident, or the presumption great." Since that time, forty states have adopted substantially the same clause. Although, as we have seen, there has been considerable uncertainty as to whether the Eighth Amendment creates a right to bail and, if so, to what extent, it has always been generally assumed that the exception in these state constitutional provisions does not offend the federal Constitution. On the federal level, the Supreme Court declared in *Carlson v. Landon.*[1] "The Eighth Amendment has not prevented Congress from defining the classes of cases in which bail shall be allowed in this country. Thus in criminal cases it is not compulsory where the punishment may be death."

In states with these provisions, legislative abolition of the death penalty has been consistently held to mean that persons charged with offenses formerly subject to capital punishment are in all cases bailable. This conclusion has been reached even when the abolition was accompanied by legislation declaring that persons charged with the offenses so af-

§ 12.4

1. 342 U.S. 524, 72 S.Ct. 525, 96 L.Ed. 547 (1952).

fected were not bailable if the proof was evident or the presumption great. But there has not been agreement as to how these constitutional provisions should be applied when the legislature has provided for the death penalty but has done so in such a way that imposition of the penalty is constitutionally barred. The courts are split, depending upon whether they adopt the penalty theory or the classification theory. The former is that these constitutional provisions are based upon the strong flight urge because of the possibility of an accused forfeiting his life, and thus are inapplicable once that possibility is removed by either the legislature or the courts. The classification theory, on the other hand, is that the underlying gravity of those offenses endures and the determination of their gravity for the purpose of bail continues unaffected by the decision that the death penalty provision is unconstitutional. Which of these two views is correct depends, of course, on the rationale underlying these constitutional provisions. If, as is sometimes assumed, they were adopted to permit pretrial detention because of danger to the community, then the classification theory is correct. But if, as seems more likely, the underlying assumption was that certain classes of offenders, particularly those whose lives were at stake, ought to be detained simply to assure their presence at trial, then the penalty theory is the correct one.

Because these constitutional provisions prohibit bail only in those capital cases where "the proof is evident or the presumption great," a defendant is not barred from obtaining his release on bail merely because he has been charged in such a way that he could receive the death penalty. Rather, these provisions contemplate that bail should be denied when the circumstances disclosed indicate a fair likelihood that the defendant will be convicted of an offense punishable by death, for only if such likelihood exists is his life in jeopardy and the well recognized urge to abscond present. Under the traditional grading of criminal homicide whereby the death penalty can be returned only upon a finding of guilty of murder in the first degree, this means a fair likelihood of such a verdict. But under the Supreme Court's decisions holding unconstitutional a mandatory death penalty for first degree murder [2] but upholding the imposition of a sentence of death where the jury or judge is required to weigh statutory aggravating and mitigating circumstances,[3] it would seem that this fair likelihood exists only if it appears likely one of the requisite aggravating circumstances is present.

Where does the burden of proof lie? One line of cases takes the view that since the defendant is entitled to bail only on application and when he so applies is trying to change the status quo, the burden is rightly on him to show that the proof is not evident or that the presumption is not great. The other and better view is that these constitutional provisions confer a right to bail except under the limited circumstances specified and that the burden should rest on the party relying on the exception, that is, the prosecution. Assuming the latter approach, the next question is what probative force the indictment has with respect to this burden. The decisions on this issue fall into three categories: (1) the burden is on the state to adduce some facts in addition to the indictment in order to satisfy the court that the case against the accused meets the constitutional requirement; (2) the indictment is *prima facie* evidence of a capital offense within the constitutional exception; and (3) the indictment is conclusive against the allowance of bail. Courts have been more receptive to viewing the indictment as prima facie evidence where the grand jury must specify whether the crime charged is murder in the first or second degree. But in light of the Supreme Court's death penalty decisions alluded to above, even such an indictment would not as a matter of logic seem to constitute prima facie evidence, for the grand jury would not have made a judgment about whether any of the requisite aggravating circumstances were present in the particular case. In any event, another

2. Woodson v. North Carolina, 428 U.S. 280, 96 S.Ct. 2978, 49 L.Ed.2d 944 (1976).

3. Gregg v. Georgia, 428 U.S. 153, 96 S.Ct. 2909, 49 L.Ed.2d 859 (1976).

reason for not giving the indictment even prima facie effect is that proceedings of the grand jury are secret and wholly *ex parte.*

A somewhat similar question is whether, in those jurisdictions which permit the institution of even capital offense prosecutions by information rather than indictment, it can be said that the filing of the information raises such a presumption of defendant's guilt as to constitute a prima facie showing. Although some courts have answered this question in the affirmative, that conclusion is open to even greater criticism than reliance upon a grand jury indictment. Such a result is inconsistent with the reasoning in *Gerstein v. Pugh,*[4] where the Supreme Court held an information (as distinguished from an indictment) would not suffice to justify continued custody of a defendant arrested without a warrant.

Assuming the prosecution is obligated to put in proof on the issue at the bail hearing, the question then is how this may be done. Mere representations by the prosecutor that he has and will introduce at trial certain evidence which he specifies with particularity is not sufficient. The hearing may well be conducted somewhat informally, as upon affidavits, if the defendant agrees, but affidavits and copies of grand jury testimony may not be received if the defendant objects, as he has a right of cross-examination in this context. Hearsay is not totally barred; the admissibility of such evidence must be determined on a case by case basis, and receipt of hearsay is proper if it is the kind of evidence on which responsible persons are accustomed to rely in serious affairs. Quite obviously, it is necessary that the nature of the hearsay be such as to indicate that admissible evidence of the same variety will be available at trial (as where a detective indicates what witnesses have told him), for otherwise it does not contribute to the requisite fair likelihood determination. By like reasoning it has been held that evidence subject to suppression, such as a confession obtained in violation of *Miranda,* may not be received on this issue, though concern about unduly complicating pretrial proceedings has prompted at least one court to conclude that the state need only make a prima facie showing of compliance with *Miranda.*

(b) Juvenile Cases. Because state courts have typically relied upon juvenile code safeguards in dealing with pretrial release issues in juvenile cases, there has for some time existed considerable uncertainty as to what extent a constitutional right to bail exists in this context. But under the general "fundamental fairness" approach which the Supreme Court has utilized in determining what rights of adult defendants also apply in juvenile proceedings,[5] it may be concluded that there is no unqualified constitutional right to bail for a juvenile. This is clearly reflected in the fact that the Supreme Court in *Schall v. Martin*[6] upheld a preventive detention statute applicable to juvenile court cases.

For one thing, certain problems peculiar to these proceedings make a blanket application of the right to pre-adjudication release upon adequate assurance of future court appearance unworkable and undesirable. Thus an exception to the bail rights an adult would have must be recognized when the child would be endangered by release, as where his parents are not willing to care for the child or harm will come to the child in his present home situation. More controversial is whether the concept of preventive detention has a place in the juvenile court process, as presently contemplated by the laws of all states. In *Schall* the Supreme Court upheld a statutory provision authorizing pretrial detention of an accused juvenile delinquent based on a finding that there is a "serious risk" that the child "may before the return date commit an act which if committed by an adult would constitute a crime." The Court, in holding this provision conformed to the "fundamental fairness" demanded by the due process clause, first concluded that the statute served a legit-

4. 420 U.S. 103, 95 S.Ct. 854, 43 L.Ed.2d 54 (1975).

5. McKeiver v. Pennsylvania, 403 U.S. 528, 91 S.Ct. 1976, 29 L.Ed.2d 647 (1971).

6. 467 U.S. 253, 104 S.Ct. 2403, 81 L.Ed.2d 207 (1984).

imate state objective, "protecting the community from crime," deemed to be more weighty than the juvenile's countervailing interest in freedom from restraint, which "must be qualified by the recognition that juveniles, unlike adults, are always in some form of custody." As for the added constitutional requirement that the pretrial detention not constitute punishment, the Court concluded there was "no indication in the statute itself that preventive detention is used or intended as a punishment." The Court emphasized in this connection that the challenged provision required a prompt probable cause hearing, an expedited fact-finding hearing for detained juveniles, and nonpunitive conditions of confinement.

Due process also requires adequate procedural safeguards, and thus the Supreme Court in *Schall* also declared that as a constitutional matter it was necessary that the procedures afforded juveniles "provide sufficient protection against erroneous and unnecessary deprivation of liberty." Such procedures were deemed present there, as the juvenile was entitled to a prompt adversarial determination of probable cause of a delinquent act and that the serious risk of a criminal act in the immediate future existed. Because the statute required a finding of facts and statement of reasons supporting preventive detention, the Court concluded the statute need not enumerate the specific factors upon which the juvenile court judge might rely. The Court in *Schall* also emphasized "that from a legal point of view there is nothing inherently unattainable about a prediction of future criminal conduct."

(c) During Trial. Once the defendant's trial has commenced, he is in a somewhat different posture regarding his right to be at large on bail or other form of release. As the Supreme Court recognized in *Bitter v. United States:* [7]

> A trial judge indisputably has broad powers to ensure the orderly and expeditious progress of a trial. For this purpose, he has the power to revoke bail and to remit the defendant to custody. But this power must be exercised with circumspection. It may be invoked only when and to the extent justified by danger which the defendant's conduct presents or by danger of significant interference with the progress or order of the trial.

Thus, bail may be revoked during trial where a defendant has made threats to government witnesses, or where he has engaged in obstructive misconduct during the course of the trial. But in *Bitter,* where the revocation was apparently based upon nothing more than "a single, brief incident of tardiness," there was no basis for committing the defendant to custody. Except when the conduct which serves as the basis of the revocation occurred within the observation of the judge, a hearing must be held to determine whether the conduct did take place.

(d) Pending Appeal. Once the defendant's trial is completed and he has been convicted, his situation with respect to his release, even if he plans to take an appeal, changes significantly. The typical state constitutional provision guaranteeing a right to bail is limited to the time "before conviction," and this distinction is ordinarily observed in state statutes just as it is in the Federal Bail Reform Act of 1984. But the federal Act is especially strict. On appeal by a person who has been convicted and sentenced to imprisonment, he is to be ordered detained unless the judicial officer finds by clear and convincing evidence that the person is not likely to flee or pose a danger and also that the appeal is not for the purpose of delay and raises a substantial question of law or fact likely to result in reversal.[8] Few defendants are likely to obtain their release under that provision.

The United States Supreme Court held as early as 1894 that there is no constitutional right to bail pending appeal from a conviction.[9] Sometimes this result is explained on the ground that since there is no constitutional right to appeal, there is no constitutional right to be free pending an appeal, which perhaps by itself is not entirely convincing.

7. 389 U.S. 15, 88 S.Ct. 6, 19 L.Ed.2d 15 (1967).

8. 18 U.S.C.A. § 3143(b).

9. McKane v. Durston, 153 U.S. 684, 14 S.Ct. 913, 38 L.Ed. 867 (1894).

But the situation is different after conviction in other respects. A defendant who has been convicted and has little hope for reversal might be strongly tempted to flee, and one with greater hope for reversal might be tempted to tamper with witnesses who had been especially useful to the prosecutor so as to minimize the chances of conviction after remand. Another reason given is that the presumption of innocence and the right to participate in the preparation of a defense to ensure a fair trial are not present where the defendant has already been tried and convicted.

Individual members of the Supreme Court when passing upon applications for bail pending disposition of an appeal have sometimes asserted that the "command of the Eighth Amendment that 'Excessive bail shall not be required * * *' *at the very least* obligates judges passing upon the right to bail to deny such relief only for the strongest of reasons." [10] Yet, courts have held that it is permissible for the legislature to exclude certain types of cases from judicial consideration on the question of post-conviction bail, which is consistent with the generally accepted proposition that there is no federal constitutional right to bail pending appeal after conviction in a state court. But that proposition has in turn not foreclosed the holding that once a state makes provision for such bail, the Eighth and Fourteenth Amendments require that it not be denied arbitrarily or unreasonably. There is a split of authority as to who must show what on this latter issue. Some courts hold to the view that denial of bail pending appeal without a statement of reasons is arbitrary per se, while others have taken the position that a presumption of regularity attaches to a state court's denial of bail and that the defendant bears the burden of showing that there is no rational basis in the record to support such denial.

(e) Probation or Parole Revocation. Even assuming a constitutional right to have bail set in other circumstances, it does not follow that a defendant held pending a revocation hearing for an alleged violation of probation has a right to bail. As explained in *In re Whitney:* [11]

> The probationer has been convicted of a crime, subjected to the sanctions prescribed by law, and has been granted conditional release in order to serve the interests of society. The interests which the government may protect at this stage of the process are properly much broader than before trial. Since a conviction has been obtained, for example, it is hardly unreasonable to use incarceration pending the revocation hearing to protect society against the possible commission of additional crimes by the probationer. There is no presumption of innocence in the probation revocation process, at least not in the sense in which the phrase is used with reference to the criminal process. Hence, when a probationer is incarcerated pending a hearing, the balance of interests is not the same as that involved in confining an accused who has not been found guilty.

The same is true of a person who is awaiting parole revocation proceedings.

(f) Material Witnesses. The federal Bail Reform Act provides that if the testimony of a person is material in a criminal proceeding and it is shown "that it may become impracticable to secure the presence of the person by subpoena," then the release conditions otherwise provided for in that Act shall be utilized. Detention of a material witness for inability to comply with the conditions set is not allowed "if the testimony of such witness can adequately be secured by deposition, and if further detention is not necessary to prevent a failure of justice," and in such case release may be delayed "for a reasonable period of time until the deposition of the witness can be taken." [12]

Nearly all states have enacted provisions dealing with the pretrial confinement of material witnesses. Typically these statutes provide that a prospective witness in a case in-

10. Harris v. United States, 404 U.S. 1232, 92 S.Ct. 10, 30 L.Ed.2d 25 (1971) (Douglas, J.); Sellers v. United States, 89 S.Ct. 36, 21 L.Ed.2d 64 (1968) (Black, J.).

11. 421 F.2d 337 (1st Cir.1970).

12. 18 U.S.C.A. § 3144.

volving a felony or major crime can be brought before a judge on application of counsel, generally the prosecutor. The magistrate determines the importance of the witness to the case and gives the witness the option of posting some form of bail or recognizance, either personal or with sureties. If the witness must post bail but refuses or fails to do so, he can be confined until he has given his testimony or the case is dismissed. Several states authorize the taking of depositions for preserving testimony so that the witness may be released when the deposition is obtained. Some jurisdictions have adopted alternatives to incarceration, such as placing the witness in the custody of a designated person or organization, placing restrictions on his travel, association, or place of abode during the period of release, requiring the witness to return to custody after daylight hours, and requiring the execution of an appearance bond.

§ 12.5 Alternatives to Arrest

(a) Summons in Lieu of Arrest Warrant. Another avenue of reform in the efforts to prevent unnecessary pretrial detention, especially in minor cases, is invocation of the criminal process against a person without even taking custody in the first place. One way in which this may be done is by a judicial officer issuing a summons instead of an arrest warrant, as is now authorized by the law in most jurisdictions. Some of these laws permit the magistrate to issue a summons instead of an arrest warrant only if the prosecutor so requests, while many others merely indicate that the magistrate has the option of utilizing either a warrant or a summons. Some provisions express a preference for the summons alternative by providing that it is to be utilized, at least as to lesser offenses, except when a specified reason appears for not doing so. Some others, however, appear to express a preference for warrants by stating that a warrant shall issue unless a specified reason for not resorting to that alternative appears.

This legislation has had little impact in decreasing the number of arrests. For one thing, arrest warrants are seldom required and are seldom sought, so that the occasion for choosing between a warrant and summons rarely arises. For another, it is generally the practice (even when not required) for the magistrate to rely upon the prosecutor or police officer to ask for a summons, and such requests are seldom made. Moreover, it is unlikely that information relevant to a judicial determination of the likelihood of the person's appearance in response to a summons will be tendered to the court. This suggests that summons statutes and rules should be drafted so as to make it clear that the magistrate is responsible for making an intelligent choice between the two modes of proceeding, and that in minor cases the summons is presumed to be the preferred alternative.

Such a proposal fails to take note of the fact that on occasion an arrest warrant might be sought primarily because the contemplated arrest will provide a means of making a constitutionally permissible search of the person. This suggests the magistrate should be directed by statute to issue a warrant instead of a summons when it is desirable to conduct a search. More revolutionary would be an effort to authorize search of persons when there are grounds for their arrest without actually requiring that an arrest be made, so that the independent and orderly development of a law of arrest and a law of search could occur.

(b) Citation in Lieu of Arrest Without Warrant. Despite the success of the longstanding practice of having the police issue citations for all but the most serious traffic violations, for years there was very little movement toward extending those procedures to more ordinary criminal cases. As recently as 1960 only four states had adopted police citation statutes which extended beyond traffic offense cases, though more recently the number has increased dramatically. These provisions, however, do not ordinarily require the police to utilize the citation alternative in certain circumstances or for specified nontraffic offenses. And thus, while police citations are used extensively in some localities, nationwide there has been virtually no implementation of this reform measure.

Again, the proposal has been made that what is needed is mandatory resort to the noncustody alternative in lesser cases absent unusual circumstances. But in this context as well, the situation is complicated by the fact that a warrantless arrest may and often does provide an opportunity for the officer to make a lawful search of the defendant and the surrounding area. In *United States v. Robinson,*[1] the Supreme Court held that a search of the person could be conducted incident to "a lawful custodial arrest," which the Court distinguished from a more temporary detention "where the officer would simply issue a notice of violation and allow the offender to proceed." Thus, here as well it would seem that unless the right to search is somehow disentangled from the right to arrest, the need (or, in some cases, just the opportunity) to conduct a search will discourage resort to the citation alternative.

§ 12.5

1. 414 U.S. 218, 94 S.Ct. 467, 38 L.Ed.2d 427 (1973).

Chapter 13

THE DECISION WHETHER TO PROSECUTE

Table of Sections

§ 13.1 Nature of the Decision

(a) In General. The charging decision, involving a determination of whether a person should be formally accused of a crime and thus subjected to trial if he does not first plead guilty, is a vitally important stage in the criminal process with serious implications for the individual involved. A decision to charge will result in the defendant's loss of freedom pending and during trial or at best release only upon financial or other conditions, and will confront him with the economic and social costs of a trial. Whatever the outcome at trial, the charge itself can be and often is damaging to reputation and imposes upon the defendant the considerable expense of preparing a defense. Charging decisions, viewed collectively, are also of obvious importance to the community. Among other things, the manner in which these decisions are made permits adjustment of the criminal justice process to local conditions. In this way, it is possible to take account of the marked variations in the crime problem and in the community resources available to combat it which often exist from area to area.

Although the charging decision is not inevitably so complex, it frequently involves several of the following potentially difficult determinations: (1) whether there is sufficient evidence to support a prosecution; (2) if so, whether there are nonetheless reasons for not subjecting the defendant to the criminal process; (3) if so, whether nonprosecution should be conditioned upon the defendant's participation in a diversion program; and (4) if prosecution is to be undertaken, with what offense or offenses the defendant should be charged.

In minor cases, most notably those involving lesser traffic offenses, this decision is commonly made exclusively by police. The "ticket" given the violator serves as the charge, and the case goes directly to court for trial or plea without prosecutorial review. In other cases, however, it is usually the prosecutor who plays the central role, although this is not inevitably so. Even when the prosecutor does play the central role, other actors may play a significant part. The police, for example, nonetheless exercise considerable influence in both a negative and positive sense. The overwhelming majority of cases that reach the prosecutor are brought to his attention by police after they have made an arrest, a decision as to which they exercise vast and largely uncontrolled discretion. Thus, if in a particular instance an officer decides not to arrest, doubting whether the evidence is sufficient or whether any good purpose would be served by invoking the criminal process, he has in effect virtually assured that there will be no prosecution. As for positive influence, police sometimes accomplish this by an especially solid presentation of their evidence or by articulation of some law enforcement interest that presumably would be served by prosecution.

Another actor who may play an important part is the victim. In many locales certain crimes such as nonsupport and the passing of bad checks are unlikely to come to official attention unless reported directly to the prosecutor's office by a concerned citizen. Here again, a decision not to bring the matter before the prosecutor virtually assures no charge. As for positive influence, in these kinds of cases (and, to a lesser extent, in cases first handled by the police) the complainant may prompt a charge by expressing strong interest in, or promising full cooperation in, the prosecution. Except where the concept of a screening conference has been adopted, participation in the charging decision by defendant and his counsel does not ordinarily occur.

(b) Evidence Sufficiency. It is not possible to state categorically how much evidence is required before the prosecutor is justified in charging a suspect with a crime, as the law does not expressly provide a distinct probability of guilt standard for the charging decision. Although the prosecutor's decision to charge is often reflected in the post-arrest issuance of an arrest warrant, and though it is clear that such a warrant may issue only upon "probable cause," that phrase has been interpreted by courts only in cases where the warrant was challenged as a basis for arrest rather than as a basis for the decision to charge. An arrest, the Supreme Court declared in *Brinegar v. United States,*[1] may be based upon "the factual and practical considerations of everyday life on which reasonable and prudent men, not legal technicians, act." But it does not necessarily follow that charging would be proper on the same quantum of evidence, if for no other reason than that the proecutor, as a legal technician, will have to consider whether his decision to charge will withstand review at the preliminary hearing and before the grand jury.

As a practical matter, the prosecutor is likely to require admissible evidence showing a high probability of guilt, that is, sufficient evidence to justify confidence in obtaining a conviction. This, however, may vary from case to case, based upon the prosecutor's experience with juries in that locale. For example, one former federal prosecutor has reported that in his office it was the practice to require a higher quantum of proof in receipt of stolen goods cases, where the prosecution witnesses were usually admitted thieves and the defendant would usually come from the middle class and not have a prior criminal record, than in narcotics cases, where jury acquittals were rare and defendants were usually persons of lower class. Even in the latter category of cases, however, it was the practice to insist upon a high quantum of evidence in order to continue the 100% conviction record for these offenses and thereby induce pleas of guilty.

(c) Screening Out Cases. Even when it is clear that there exists evidence which is more than sufficient to show guilt beyond a reasonable doubt, the prosecutor might nonetheless decide not to charge a particular individual with a criminal offense. Such discretionary enforcement of the criminal law has traditionally been an important part of the American prosecutor's function. Whether this exercise of discretion at the charging stage is a vice or a virtue is a matter on which there is not complete agreement. It does seem fair to say, however, that something less than full enforcement of the law by the prosecutor is an absolute necessity. As one judge once noted, if every prosecutor "performed his * * * responsibility in strict accordance with rules of law, precisely and narrowly laid down, the criminal law would be ordered but intolerable."[2] But this is not to suggest that there does not reside in the prosecutorial screening function considerable potential for abuse. The danger, of course, is that the screening process is so informal and invisible and so lacking in adequate information and policy guidance or rules that it may neither operate fairly upon those individuals subjected to the process nor accurately identify those who should be prosecuted.

(d) Diversion. The choices for the prosecutor when making the charging decision are not merely those of prosecution or no action at all. An intermediate course, commonly referred to as deferred prosecution or pretrial diversion, may be available. Typically, the effect of diversion is to "stop the clock" on criminal prosecution while the defendant is offered counselling, career development, education and supportive treatment services. If he participates and responds as required for a specified period of time, then the charges are dismissed without trial. But if the defendant does not meet his obligations then he may be subjected to prosecution on the deferred charge.

§ 13.1

1. 338 U.S. 160, 69 S.Ct. 1302, 93 L.Ed. 1879 (1949).

2. Breitel, Controls in Criminal Law Enforcement, 27 U.Chi.L.Rev. 427 (1960).

The extent to which diversion exists as a meaningful alternative depends upon a number of factors. In many communities the resources for dealing with offenders and their problems are totally inadequate, and even if these resources exist, there may be little liaison between the prosecutor and community agencies which could assist an offender. Even with sufficient liaison, there may be pressures to divert only defendants who will represent the lowest risk to the community, in which case that diversion will bring many people into the criminal process who either would not have been processed at all or would have been screened out at an early stage.

(e) Selection of the Charge. If the prosecutor has decided upon prosecution, there often remains the question of what the charge should be. Sometimes it is simply a matter of whether the charge should be of a greater or lesser crime—for example, felony burglary versus misdemeanor breaking and entering. This involves judgments about both evidence sufficiency (whether the greater crime can be proved at trial) and enforcement policy (whether prosecution for the greater crime would be unduly harmful to this defendant). However, sometimes the prosecutor will initially charge a defendant with a higher offense than can be proved or than would be "just," hoping to use that charge as leverage to obtain a guilty plea to a lesser crime.

Sometimes the defendant's conduct will appear to violate more than one criminal statute, in which case the prosecutor will need to decide whether the defendant is to be charged with more than one offense. This occurs (1) when it appears the defendant has committed a series of acts, such as a number of burglaries, over a period of time; or (2) when it appears the defendant violated more than one statute during a single course of conduct, as where a burglary is followed by theft of property. Resort to multiple charges is most common when undertaken to encourage a plea of guilty to one of the crimes or when deemed necessary to provide the judge with a sufficient range of sentencing options.

§ 13.2 Discretionary Enforcement

(a) The Prosecutor's Discretion. The notion that the prosecuting attorney is vested with a broad range of discretion in deciding when to prosecute and when not to is firmly entrenched in American law. Prosecutors in this country have long exercised this discretionary authority, but it would be in error to assume that discretionary enforcement by prosecutors is essentially the same in all locales. The extent of and reasons for nonenforcement vary considerably from place to place, often because of factors over which the individual prosecutor has no control. It is nonetheless possible to identify the most common explanations:

(1) Because of legislative "overcriminalization." As one commentator has said, "The criminal code of any jurisdiction tends to make a crime of everything that people are against, without regard to enforceability, changing social concepts, etc. The result is that the criminal code becomes society's trash bin." [1] Examination of the typical state code of criminal law supports this judgment. Included therein are likely to be crimes which are over-defined for administrative convenience (e.g., the gambling statute which bars *all* forms of gambling so as "to confront the professional gambler with a statutory facade that is wholly devoid of loopholes" [2]); crimes which merely constitute "state-declared ideals" [3] (e.g., the crime of adultery, which is "unenforced because we want to continue our conduct, and unrepealed because we want to preserve our morals" [4]); and now-outdated crimes which found their way into the law because of "the mood that dominated a tribunal or a legislature at strategic moments in

§ 13.2

1. Statement by a representative of the FBI, quoted in President's Comm'n on Law Enforcement and Administration of Justice, Task Force Report: The Courts 107 (1967).

2. 2 ABA Comm'n on Organized Crime, Organized Crime and Law Enforcement 75 (1952).

3. R. Pound, Criminal Justice in America 67 (1930).

4. T. Arnold, The Symbols of Government 160 (1935).

the past, a flurry of public excitement on some single matter." [5]

(2) Because of limitations in available enforcement resources. No prosecutor has sufficient resources available to prosecute all of the offenses which come to his attention. To deny the authority to exercise discretion under these circumstances, it is said, is "like directing a general to attack the enemy on all fronts at once." [6] Thus, so the argument goes, the prosecutor must remain free to exercise his judgment in determining what prosecutions will best serve the public interest.

(3) Because of a need to individualize justice. A criminal code can only deal in general categories of conduct. "No lawmaker has been able to foresee more than the broad outlines of the clash of interests or more than the main lines of the courses of conduct to which the law even of his own time must be applied. Moreover, a legal system which seeks to cover everything by a special provision becomes cumbrous and unworkable." [7] Individualized treatment of offenders, based upon the circumstances of the particular case, has long been recognized in sentencing, and it is argued that such individualized treatment is equally appropriate at the charging stage so as to relieve deserving defendants of even the stigma of prosecution.

Decisions not to prosecute, when not motivated by doubts as to the sufficiency of the evidence, usually fall within one of these three broad categories. A closer look at the practice makes it possible to particularize further those situations in which prosecutors most commonly decline to prosecute. They are:

(i) When the victim has expressed a desire that the offender not be prosecuted. Particularly in assault cases involving a dispute between spouses or prior acquaintances, the victim's disinterest in prosecution usually is determinative. The assumption apparently is that uncoerced forgiveness reflects a lack of importance attached to the incident by the victim (and, perhaps, by the aggressor), so that nonprosecution is not contrary to the statutory policy of discouraging the settlement of disputes by force.

(ii) When the costs of prosecution would be excessive, considering the nature of the violation. Most significant here are those cases which would involve unusual costs, as where the offender is now known to be in a distant state and could be extradited and returned only at considerable expense. Prosecution of certain offenders who would be prosecuted if they were in custody within the jurisdiction (e.g., professional bad check passers), is abandoned under these circumstances.

(iii) When the mere fact of prosecution would, in the prosecutor's judgment, cause undue harm to the offender. For example, when it was learned that a married woman had filed a false report of rape with the police and that she had done so to conceal her indiscretion from her husband, it was decided that prosecution for filing a false crime report would be unwise because it would jeopardize her marriage.

(iv) When the offender, if not prosecuted, will likely aid in achieving other enforcement goals. Nonprosecution is used as an inducement to make informants out of offenders, and also as an inducement for present informers to take on additional duties. This occurs most frequently when the individual is in a position to aid in vice enforcement, particularly against the sale of narcotics.

(v) When the "harm" done by the offender can be corrected without prosecution. The best example is the frequent decision not to prosecute persons who have committed minor property crimes, such as writing bad checks, if full restitution to the victim is made.

A full appreciation of the extent of the prosecutor's power, however, requires consideration of the fact that his discretion may be exercised in the other direction. A particular individual may be selected out for prosecution notwithstanding the fact that the case is one

5. Wechsler, The Challenge of a Model Penal Code, 65 Harv.L.Rev. 1097, 1101 (1952).

6. T. Arnold, supra note 4, at 153.

7. R. Pound, supra note 3, at 40–41.

which ordinarily would not result in an affirmative charging decision. Such selection may occur in response to press and public pressure for "law and order," to rid society of certain "bad actors" who are thought to have committed more serious crimes, and for similar reasons.

(b) Police Discretion. Although the principal concern here is with the exercise of discretion by the prosecutor, note must also be taken of discretionary enforcement by the police, for it is clear beyond question that discretion is regularly exercised by the police in deciding when to arrest and that such decisions have a profound effect upon prosecution policy. This is so for the simple reason that for the most part the police determine what cases come to the attention of the prosecutor.

As a general matter, it may be said that the exercise of discretion by the police at the arrest stage occurs for much the same reasons as the charging discretion of the prosecutor described above. This police discretion is in a practical sense even less restricted than the prosecutor's discretion, for it is exercised at an earlier and generally less visible stage of the criminal process. But in the eyes of the law, discretion by the prosecutor is considered proper while discretion by the police is with rare exception viewed with disfavor. Arrest statutes are commonly drafted in mandatory terms, and on the infrequent occasions when courts are called upon to speak to the question they typically assert that the police lack authority not to invoke the criminal process when the evidence is sufficient to arrest.

One reason for police nonenforcement, as with prosecutor nonenforcement, is legislative "overcriminalization." A second is because of limitations in available enforcement resources, while a third reason involves the judgment that sometimes even arrest would be unduly harmful to the offender. There is every reason to believe that police discretion is absolutely essential and will remain with us. That conclusion, however, is entirely consistent with two other important propositions—that excessive or unnecessary police discretion can and should be eliminated, and that necessary discretion should be properly controlled.

(c) Jury and Judge Discretion. The prosecutor does not function in a vacuum, and thus a decision not to prosecute is often based upon the expectation that the judge or jury would refuse to convict notwithstanding proof of guilt beyond a reasonable doubt. A full understanding of the prosecutor's discretion, therefore, necessitates an awareness of the discretion which may be exercised at the trial stage by judge or jury.

The jury in a criminal case has uncontrolled discretion to acquit the guilty.[8] Juries acquit the guilty because: (1) they sympathize with the defendant as a person; (2) they apply personal attitudes as to when self-defense should be recognized; (3) they take into account the contributory fault of the victim; (4) they believe the offense is de minimis; (5) they take into account the fact that the statute violated is an unpopular law; (6) they feel the defendant has already been punished enough; (7) they feel the defendant was subjected to improper police or prosecution practices; (8) they refuse to apply strict liability statutes to inadvertent conduct; (9) they apply their own standards as to when mental illness or intoxication should be a defense; and (10) they believe the offense is accepted conduct in the subculture of the defendant and victim.

Because there is not agreement on whether such discretionary action by a jury is a desirable safety valve in the criminal justice system or an unavoidable evil, it is a debatable point whether it is proper for the trial judge to act in a similar fashion when a case is tried before him without a jury. Although express conferral of such authority on the trial judge has been proposed, the law generally seems to take the view that it is not the business of a judge trying a case without a jury to act "like" the jury could be expected to act. Yet judges do acquit guilty defendants for the same reasons as juries.

8. See § 22.1(g).

(d) The "Problem" of Discretion. It is tempting to view discretionary enforcement in general and charging discretion by the prosecutor in particular as practices which need not be a matter of concern. After all, what harm can there be in the benign act of not invoking the criminal process against one who has violated an obsolete or over-broad law, one whose conduct is not serious enough to warrant the expenditure of scarce enforcement resources, or one who has committed a crime under strongly mitigating circumstances? But this vast and largely uncontrolled discretion cannot be dismissed on the notion that only acts of leniency are involved. Absent procedures which ensure that the "right" decisions are being reached regarding who should receive leniency and when, society at large and also the individuals dealt with by the criminal justice system are jeopardized.

As for society at large, the fundamental point is that what is characterized as the bestowal of leniency can sometimes work contrary to the public interest in effective law enforcement. As for the individuals involved, the basic point is that the discretionary power to be lenient is an impossibility without a concomitant discretionary power not to be lenient. If provable cases against *A, B, C,* and *D* cross the prosecutor's desk and he elects not to prosecute *D,* it cannot be said that the rationality of that decision is of no moment because *A, B,* and *C* are guilty and thus deserving of conviction. Rather, if we strive for equal justice it is important that this discretion have been exercised reasonably, that *D* has escaped prosecution for a legitimate reason which is not also applicable to *A, B,* or *C.* Sometimes the process is viewed more in terms of a selection of those who *will* be prosecuted. It is said, for example, that the substantive criminal law amounts to "an arsenal of weapons to be used against such persons as the police or prosecutor may deem to be a menace to public safety." [9] From this perspective, the potential for arbitrary and discriminatory enforcement stands out more starkly.

While it is thus fair to say that discretionary enforcement in the charging process is a significant problem in current criminal justice administration, clearly the answer does not lie in depriving the prosecutor of any discretion whatsoever. Full enforcement is neither possible nor tolerable. The issue is not discretion versus no discretion, but rather how discretion should be confined, structured, and checked.

(e) Confining the Prosecutor's Discretion. Because a major source of excess prosecutorial power is the loose drafting and overly casual definition of conduct as criminal that characterize the nation's penal codes, adequate reform of the substantive criminal law would eliminate many cases now screened out only at the option of the prosecutor. Clearly, some significant portion of the prosecutor's discretion could be rendered unnecessary if obsolete or largely unenforceable statutes were repealed. In addition, some statutes could be more narrowly drawn, again eliminating certain cases which are now screened out only at the will of the prosecuting attorney, and some statutes could be subdivided so as to reflect degrees of severity, thus providing a clear basis upon which the prosecutor could determine whether a greater or lesser charge is called for.

But there are limits on what can be achieved in this way, and thus no one would seriously contend that the prosecutor's discretion could be entirely eliminated by penal law reform. Framing statutes that identify and prescribe for every nuance of human behavior is impossible, and even to the extent that the numerous operative factors *could* be expressed in a substantive criminal statute, there may be reasons for not doing so. There is a need to confront those at whom the law is aimed "with a statutory facade that is wholly devoid of loop-holes," [10] and in any event a need to avoid unduly complicating criminal statutes.

(f) Structuring the Prosecutor's Discretion. Three basic needs must be met before

9. Arnold, Law Enforcement—An Attempt at Social Dissection, 42 Yale L.J. 1, 17 (1932).

10. 2 ABA Comm'n on Organized Crime, Organized Crime and Law Enforcement 74 (1952).

the prosecutor's charging discretion can become more structured and thus more rational. They are:

(i) The need for more information. More detailed background information about the offender is needed so that it may be determined whether he is a dangerous or only marginal offender. (In the absence of any information, or only the limited information provided by a brief police report, the temptation is great to resort to rule-of-thumb policies based only upon the nature of the crime.) In addition, most prosecutors lack sufficient information about alternative treatment facilities and programs in the community to be able to make a rational determination of whether there exists some better course than prosecution.

(ii) The need for established standards. What is needed is for each prosecutor's office to develop a statement of general policies to guide the exercise of prosecutorial discretion, particularizing such matters as the circumstances that properly can be considered mitigating or aggravating, or the kinds of offenses that should be most vigorously prosecuted in view of the community's law enforcement needs. Such rulemaking can aid in the training of new assistant prosecutors and in the internal review of all prosecution decisions, so that office policy is consistently and efficiently carried out. Such an administrative law approach, to be helpful, requires standards which are fairly specific, though certainly the exactitude to be expected in a criminal statute would be neither necessary nor always possible in this rulemaking context. Some prosecutors' offices have undertaken the drafting of such rules and have found it feasible to express enforcement policy in this way.

Whether these standards should generally be available to the public presents a most difficult issue. On the one hand, it is said they should be because defendants and complainants and the public at large are entitled to know and be able to question such rules and whether they have been complied with. However, reasons have sometimes been advanced for not making them available to the public, including the following: (1) that publication will reduce the legitimate moralizing and deterrent effects of the criminal law; (2) that publication will inevitably result in more frequent attempts to invoke judicial review of prosecution policy and decisions, thereby further clogging an already overburdened court system; (3) that if prosecutors knew their policy would be published, they would be reluctant to formulate it; and (4) that if potential defendants in minor cases knew in advance they would not be prosecuted they would not cooperate with law enforcement agents in the investigation and prosecution of more serious offenders.

(iii) The need for established procedures. These procedures might include a "precharge conference" at which the prosecutor and defense counsel could discuss the appropriateness of a noncriminal disposition. Such a practice would make it less likely that favored defense counsel or clients will have the sole opportunity to discuss their cases with the prosecutor and receive the benefits of such exchanges, and would also provide a natural occasion for an exchange of information that might be useful to each side in deciding whether to agree on a disposition. In addition, it might be well if a decision not to prosecute was supported by a written statement of the underlying reasons. Such a procedure has been found to facilitate internal review and to produce fairly consistent results.

(g) Checking the Prosecutor's Discretion. Although the American criminal justice system has reasonably effective controls to ensure that the prosecutor does not abuse his power by prosecuting upon less than sufficient evidence, there are—as a practical matter—no comparable checks upon his discretionary judgment of whether or not to prosecute one against whom sufficient evidence exists. The prosecution function has traditionally been decentralized, so that state attorneys-general exercise no effective control over local prosecutors. Actions such as impeachment and quo warranto have only served to reach extreme cases of continued and flagrant abuse. If a specific instance of nonenforcement is challenged in the courts by way of mandamus action, the usual response is that the matter rests with the executive rather than the judicial branch of government. Or, if a specific instance of enforcement is called into question as an arbitrary deviation from a general pattern of nonenforcement, the complaining prospective defendant can seldom overcome the several hurdles to establishing his denial-of-equal-protection claim. And while the local prosecutor is in theory responsible to the electorate, the public can hardly assess prosecution policies which are kept secret.

While it may be apparent that this is an unfortunate state of affairs, it is not so apparent how the situation might be best remedied. One leading authority on discretionary enforcement has suggested close administrative review, modeled after what is said to be the practice in West Germany: "A German prosecutor can never simply forget about the case as his American counterpart may do. The file cannot be closed without a statement of written reasons, which in important cases must be approved by the prosecutor's superior * * *. Every prosecutor is supervised by a superior in a hierarchial system headed by the Minister of Justice." [11] But such administrative review would require a hierarchial arrangement quite different from the present structure of most state governments. Whether such a significant change in structure would be an improvement is not readily apparent. Moreover, some have questioned the conclusion that the West German experience shows such administrative controls work.

Another possibility is judicial review of the prosecutor's discretionary enforcement decisions. One proposal is that decisions by a prosecutor not to prosecute be subjected to regular review by a judicial officer, who would determine whether the prosecutor's decision conformed to his pre-existing written standards. In support of such judicial screening, it is argued that it would ensure uniformity of treatment and would enhance the various benefits to be derived from giving the prosecutor's enforcement policies greater publicity. Others have suggested that judges would be unable to review prosecution policies because of the practical difficulties of evaluating the allocation of scarce prosecution resources, and would be unable to achieve meaningful review of prosecution decisions because the court would be unable to go behind the record to determine that there was an insufficient factual basis for the reasons the prosecutor has provided. The Supreme Court has expressed the latter view.[12]

A more limited form of judicial review would focus upon the prosecutor's decisions *in favor of* prosecution by permitting defendants in a pretrial setting to question whether their selection squares with existing prosecution policies. The policies themselves would be subjected only to limited scrutiny to see if they drew arbitrary or capricious distinctions or were too vague to enable review of specific cases, and the decision in the particular case would be examined to see if it amounted to a significant deviation from these policies for which the prosecutor is unable to give a permissible reason. Quite obviously, meaningful review even in this context would be possible only if the reforms discussed earlier, written prosecution policies and written reasons for prosecution decisions, were first adopted. Finally, it is well to note that the written policies and written decisions reforms, if those documents are given publicity, might be said to provide another kind of check upon the prosecutor in the sense of making political accountability a reality.

11. K. Davis, Discretionary Justice 194–195 (1969).

12. In Wayte v. United States, 470 U.S. 598, 105 S.Ct. 1524, 84 L.Ed.2d 547 (1985), the Court asserted "that the decision to prosecute is particularly ill-suited to judicial review. Such factors as the strength of the case, the prosecution's general deterrence value, the Government's enforcement priorities, and the case's relationship to the Government's overall enforcement plan are not readily susceptible to the kind of analysis the courts are competent to undertake. Judicial supervision in this area, moreover, entails systematic costs of particular concern. Examining the basis of a prosecution delays the criminal proceeding, threatens to chill law enforcement by subjecting the prosecutor's motives and decisionmaking to outside inquiry, and may undermine prosecutorial effectiveness by revealing the Government's enforcement policy. All these are substantial concerns that make the courts properly hesitant to examine the decision whether to prosecute."

(h) Mandating the Prosecutor's Discretion. Given the well established principle that a prosecutor possesses vast discretion in the enforcement of the criminal law, does it follow that he is obligated to exercise it? At least one court has answered in the affirmative. In *State v. Pettitt,*[13] the defendant, after his conviction for taking a motor vehicle without permission, was charged under the habitual criminal statute pursuant to the prosecutor's "mandatory policy of filing habitual criminal complaints against all defendants with three or more prior felonies." The defendant, who had prior convictions for taking a motor vehicle without permission, second degree burglary, and unauthorized use of a vehicle, argued that "a policy which prevents the prosecutor from considering mitigating factors is a failure to exercise discretion, which may, as in this case, result in an unfair and arbitrary result." The court agreed:

> In the present case, the prosecutor (now former prosecutor) admitted that he relied on the record alone in deciding to file the habitual criminal information. He testified that he did not consider any mitigating circumstances in reaching his decision, and that he could imagine no situation which would provide for an exception to the mandatory policy.
>
> In our view, this fixed formula which requires a particular action *in every case* upon the happening of a specific series of events constitutes an abuse of the discretionary power lodged in the prosecuting attorney.

Given the draconian nature of full enforcement of habitual criminal laws, the result in *Pettitt* is an appealing one. But it does not necessarily follow that full enforcement of any particular criminal statute is inevitably an abuse of discretion. There may well be statutes which are so narrowly drawn and which encompass conduct so serious that a prosecutor would be justified in fully enforcing them.

§ 13.3 Challenges to and Checks Upon the Decision Not to Prosecute

(a) Mandamus. It sometimes happens that one or several private citizens will attempt to force a reluctant prosecutor to initiate a criminal prosecution by asking a court to issue a writ of mandamus—an order directing the prosecutor to take affirmative action with respect to a particular case. It is unlikely that this effort will succeed, as mandamus is available only to compel performance of a duty owed to the plaintiff and not to direct or influence the exercise of discretion in the making of a decision. This means, of course, that because of the long-standing acceptance of the notion that a prosecutor does have discretion in deciding when to prosecute, mandamus is deemed an inappropriate remedy in this context. The force of this principle is highlighted by the fact it applies even when a serious question has been raised in the complaint as to the fair administration of the criminal justice system, and also when a statute declared that prosecutors were "required * * * to institute prosecutions against all persons" violating the criminal statutes in question.

Other reasons commonly given for this result are that it is compelled by the separation of powers doctrine, that is, the notion that courts are not to interfere with exercise of discretion by the executive branch of government, and that judicial review of prosecutorial action is simply impractical. But some commentators have criticized this "hands off" approach and the reasons given for it. Most vulnerable is the separation of powers argument, for many Supreme Court decisions state that it is the function of the judiciary to review the exercise of executive discretion. As for the practical problems, they mght be largely overcome if prosecutors moved to a system of written prosecution guidelines and written reasons for non-prosecution decisions.

(b) Private Prosecution; Qui Tam Actions. It has sometimes been argued that private criminal prosecution when the public prosecutor fails to act is desirable and ought to be recognized by more jurisdictions. But the generally accepted view is that the prosecution function should be performed by a pub-

13. 93 Wash.2d 288, 609 P.2d 1364 (1980).

lic prosecutor because prosecution by a private party without authorization or approval of the prosecutor presents a serious danger of the vindictive use of the criminal process. Thus, even in the face of apparent authority in the law permitting private prosecution, it has been refused on the ground that it is desirable to seek uniformity of prosecutorial policy. Indeed, one court has gone so far as to rule that it is unconstitutional to permit an individual to institute criminal proceedings without the prosecutor's approval.

A criminal prosecution brought by a private individual must be distinguished from a *qui tam* legal action, so called because the plaintiff in this civil action states that he sues *as well* for the state as for himself. It is an action which may be brought only when specifically authorized by a statute providing a penalty for the commission or omission of a certain act and further providing that this penalty may be recovered in a civil action, with part of it to go to the person bringing such action and the remainder to the state. *Qui tam* statutes were once an important part of the law enforcement scheme, but this was before the time of organized police forces and effective conventional law enforcement procedures. They have been abolished in England, and are seldom to be found in this country. The virtual demise of the *qui tam* action is certainly understandable. The legislature may well prefer to have no citizen enforcement at all rather than a complete *qui tam* enforcement scheme that is susceptible to abuse. Similarly, courts are disinclined to construe statutes providing for informer fees as allowing *qui tam* suits, reasoning that prosecutors must be immune from interference by private citizens in exercising discretion whether to prosecute.

(c) Judicial Approval of Nolle Prosequi. An initial decision not to prosecute may be reached by the prosecutor without his being required as a matter of course to explain his decision to or obtain the approval of a judicial officer. The situation may change, however, after some initial steps toward prosecution have been taken. The common law view was that a prosecutor was free to nol pros (from the Latin phrase *nolle prosequi*—an entry on the record by the prosecutor declaring that he will not prosecute) even after a formal charge was embodied in an indictment or information lodged against the defendant. Concern over this unbridled discretion in the prosecutor resulted in legislation or rules of court in many jurisdictions intended to restrain the nol pros power of the prosecutor. These provisions, at a minimum, forced the prosecutor to explain his reasons for doing so in writing, thus assuring greater visibility of the manner in which the prosecutor acted; at a maximum they required that he receive judicial approval to make his decision effective. Most jurisdictions have imposed such restraints only after formal accusation by indictment or information, but some others apply them to all cases which have passed the preliminary hearing stage. Doubtless the effect of these restrictions varies from place to place, depending upon established custom, but at least in some locales they are of little significance. A requirement of a statement of reasons may result in boilerplate "in the interests of justice" explanations, and where required judicial approval may be given perfunctorily.

Where the law requires judicial approval of a nolle prosequi, the next question is what standard the judge is to apply in passing upon the prosecutor's request. Although this question can be answered with precision only by carefully examining the applicable statute or court rule and cases in the particular jurisdiction where the issue arises, the law on the federal level is fairly representative. A United States Attorney may file a dismissal of an indictment, information or complaint only "by leave of court." [1] As the Supreme Court has noted, the "principal object" of this "requirement is apparently to protect a defendant against prosecutorial harassment, e.g., charging, dismissing and recharging, when the Government moves to dismiss an indictment over the defendant's objection." [2] But

§ 13.3

1. Fed.R.Crim.P. 48(a).

2. Rinaldi v. United States, 434 U.S. 22, 98 S.Ct. 81, 54 L.Ed.2d 207 (1977).

this does not mean that the court must concur whenever the defendant does not object to the proposed dismissal, for this requirement of court approval is "intended to clothe the federal courts with a discretion broad enough to protect the public interest in the fair administration of criminal justice."[3] This means that the executive branch's "exercise of its discretion with respect to the termination of pending prosecutions should not be judicially disturbed unless clearly contrary to manifest public interest."[4]

(d) Grand Jury. Most jurisdictions permit the grand jury to initiate prosecution by indictment even though the prosecutor opposes prosecution. Some require only that the foreman, acting on behalf of the grand jury, sign the indictment, while others require the prosecutor's signature but view that requirement as mandating only a "clerical act" by the prosecutor. However, it takes a most unusual case for a grand jury to act as a "runaway" and indict notwithstanding the prosecutor's opposition. It is fair to conclude, therefore, that the grand jury is not a meaningful check upon the prosecutor's decisions not to prosecute.

Especially noteworthy because of the variety of views expressed therein is *United States v. Cox*,[5] where the court reviewed a district judge's action in holding a U.S. Attorney in contempt for refusing, upon instructions from the Acting Attorney General, to prepare or sign indictments charging with perjury two blacks who had testified in a civil rights action against a voting registrar. Three members of the court concluded the U.S. Attorney was not obligated to either prepare or sign the indictments because the "role of the grand jury is restricted to a finding as to whether or not there is probable cause" and does not extend to matters of enforcement policy. Three others concluded he was required to prepare and sign the indictments, after which he could refuse to go forward "in open court and not in the secret confines of the grand jury room," at least upon "a showing of good faith, and a statement of some rational basis for dismissal." The seventh member of the court concluded the U.S. Attorney must prepare (but need not sign) the indictments so as to "reveal the difference of view as between the Grand Jury and the prosecuting attorney."

(e) Attorney General. In most jurisdictions the state Attorney General may initiate local prosecutions in at least some circumstances. This authority ranges from power concurrent with that of the local prosecutor to power to initiate prosecution under certain circumstances, such as at the request of certain officials or in order to enforce specified statutes. In addition, most states allow the Attorney General to intervene in a local prosecution. About half the states give the Attorney General broad authority to intervene on his own initiative, while some others allow intervention only at the direction or request of another official. In theory the power of the Attorney General to initiate a local prosecution is a check upon the local prosecutor's exercise of discretion in deciding not to undertake a prosecution. In practice, however, initiation of prosecution by Attorneys General only rarely occurs. Moreover, the great majority of interventions come at the request of the local prosecutor, though occasionally the Attorney General will prosecute where it appears the local prosecutor has failed to act because of a conflict of interest.

(f) Removal; Special Prosecutor. Various mechanisms are available in the several states by which a local prosecutor might be removed from office. Impeachment is the most common method of removal, but some states have provided for removal by the governor, removal by a court, removal on recommendation of the Attorney General, impeachment by the legislature, or recall by the electorate. The grounds for removal vary among the states and include such causes as "malfeasance, misfeasance, nonfeasance, or nonadministration in office," "incompetency, neglect of duty or misuse of office when such

3. United States v. Cowan, 524 F.2d 504 (5th Cir.1975).

4. Ibid.

5. 342 F.2d 167 (5th Cir.1965).

incompetency, neglect of duty or misuse of office has a material adverse effect upon the conduct of such office," and "incompetency, corruption, malfeasance or delinquency in office, or other sufficient cause." Disbarment and conviction of a serious crime are other common grounds for removal. Removal proceedings are seldom utilized, and the same may be said for criminal prosecution of a prosecutor for nonfeasance, misfeasance, or malfeasance in office. The risk of such sanctions, it is fair to say, has only a limited effect upon the making of decisions not to prosecute. But they may influence charging patterns by motivating a prosecutor to, at a minimum, exercise his discretion based on criteria that are not clearly illegal.

Another possibility is that a prosecutor will be replaced with respect to a particular case by a special prosecutor. Considerable authority is to be found in support of the validity of an appointment of a special prosecutor under some circumstances. The need for the services of a special prosecutor may arise because the prosecuting attorney is legally precluded from proceeding due to a conflict of interest, because he is faced with a difficult case beyond his investigative and legal abilities, or because public confidence requires an "uninvolved" outsider to investigate and prosecute local corruption within the judicial/governmental system. It does not appear, however, that the special prosecutor mechanism constitutes a meaningful check upon the decision not to prosecute.

A federal statute which requires the Attorney General to conduct a preliminary investigation of allegations that enumerated high-ranking federal officials have committed a crime and, unless the allegations prove insubstantial, to ask a special three-judge panel to appoint an "independent counsel" to complete the investigation and conduct any prosecutions, was upheld in *Morrison v. Olson.*[6] The provision in the law restricting the Attorney General's power to remove the independent counsel to instances in which he can show "good cause" does not violate the constitutional principle of separation of powers, as the President's need to control the exercise of discretion by that counsel is not "so central to the functioning of the executive branch as to require as a matter of constitutional law that the counsel be terminable at will by the President." Moreover, while the Act as a whole "reduces the amount of control or supervision" that the President through the Attorney General "exercises over the investigation and prosecution of a certain class of alleged criminal activity," this does not violate the separation of powers doctrine either, for the Act gives the Attorney General "several means of supervising or controlling the prosecutorial powers that may be wielded by an independent counsel." [7]

6. 487 U.S. 654, 108 S.Ct. 2597, 101 L.Ed.2d 569 (1988).

7. Scalia, J., dissenting, noted that various independent counsel were collectively spending an equivalent of 10% of the Criminal Division's budget, and complained that the Act permits investigations and prosecutions even when the executive branch might conclude they are not "worth the cost in money and in possible damage to other governmental interests."

§ 13.4 Challenging the Decision to Prosecute: Equal Protection

(a) Discriminatory Prosecution. The Fourteenth Amendment to the United States Constitution prohibits any state from taking action which would "deny to any person within its jurisdiction the equal protection of the laws." Though there is no comparable language in the Constitution applicable to the federal government, it has been held that the Fifth Amendment due process clause imposes a similar restraint upon actions by the national government.[1] This guarantee, which of course applies with respect to the enactment of laws by the legislative branches,[2] also extends to the conduct of the executive branches in the enforcement of these laws.[3]

§ 13.4

1. Bolling v. Sharpe, 347 U.S. 497, 74 S.Ct. 693, 98 L.Ed. 884 (1954).

2. Skinner v. State of Oklahoma ex rel. Williamson, 316 U.S. 535, 62 S.Ct. 1110, 86 L.Ed. 1655 (1942).

3. Yick Wo v. Hopkins, 118 U.S. 356, 6 S.Ct. 1064, 30 L.Ed. 220 (1886).

Although the United States Supreme Court has never had occasion to hold that a prosecutor's charging decision was in violation of the equal protection clause, the Court has in several instances indicated that a charging decision could suffer such a defect.[4] In *Oyler v. Boles*,[5] for example, though the Court found the defendant had not established that the state habitual criminal statute had been discriminatorily enforced against him, a distinction was drawn between the permissible "conscious exercise of some selectivity in enforcement" and an impermissible selection "deliberately based upon an unjustifiable standard such as race, religion, or other arbitrary classification." In recent years, therefore, a host of federal and state courts have entertained claims of discriminatory prosecution. These claimants have seldom prevailed because of their heavy burden to overcome the presumption of legal regularity in enforcement of the penal law by proving the three essential elements of a discriminatory prosecution claim: (1) that other violators similarly situated are generally not prosecuted; (2) that the selection of the claimant was "intentional or purposeful"; and (3) that the selection was pursuant to an "arbitrary classification."

Although some authority is to be found that a discriminatory prosecution claim is a "defense" which is to be raised during the course of the trial and sent to the jury as part of the case just as with, say, a defense of self-defense, this is not a sound procedure. Because the question of discriminatory prosecution relates not to the guilt or innocence but rather to an alleged constitutional defect in the institution of the prosecution, the claim should be treated as an application for dismissal of the prosecution to be decided by the court. As for the remedy of injunction, it is of limited utility because of the common restrictions that it is available only if there is a threat of immediate and irreparable injury to property and only if the party suing has clean hands. In any event, an attempt to obtain injunctive relief is likely to be met with the response that resolution of the matter would be premature and is unnecessary because the person can raise the issue in the context of the criminal prosecution if and when it is actually brought.[6]

(b) Problems of Proof. The defendant bears the initial burden of demonstrating selective enforcement, and this burden is described in various ways: "a clear preponderance of the proof"; "a reasonable inference of impermissible discrimination"; a "prima facie case"; or "convincing evidence." This burden exists as to all three elements of a discriminatory prosecution claim.

The defendant's more immediate hurdle, however, is to make a sufficient showing to require that an evidentiary hearing be held. There is little agreement among the courts as to what constitutes a threshold showing; the defendant may be required to allege facts sufficient to raise a reasonable doubt about the prosecutor's purpose, to establish a colorable basis for his claim, or even to constitute a prima facie case. If the defendant meets that hurdle, he then has the burden of going forward with the evidence at the evidentiary hearing. Some of the cases speak of the burden shifting to the government at some point, which has prompted some uncertainty as to when this ought to occur and exactly what kind of burden is then on the government.[7]

One such case is *United States v. Crowthers*,[8] where the defendants were convicted of disturbing the peace by their conduct in holding several "masses for peace" in the Penta-

4. United States v. Batchelder, 442 U.S. 114, 99 S.Ct. 2198, 60 L.Ed.2d 755 (1979); Oyler v. Boles, 368 U.S. 448, 82 S.Ct. 501, 7 L.Ed.2d 446 (1962); Two Guys from Harrison–Allentown, Inc. v. McGinley, 366 U.S. 582, 81 S.Ct. 1135, 6 L.Ed.2d 551 (1961).

5. 368 U.S. 448, 82 S.Ct. 501, 7 L.Ed.2d 446 (1962).

6. Two Guys from Harrison–Allentown, Inc. v. McGinley, 366 U.S. 582, 81 S.Ct. 1135, 6 L.Ed.2d 551 (1961).

7. In Wayte v. United States, 470 U.S. 598, 105 S.Ct. 1524, 84 L.Ed.2d 547 (1985), the district court dismissed the indictment on the ground that the defendant had made out a prima facie case of selective prosecution entitling him to discovery of government documents and testimony of government officials, which the prosecution refused to supply. The Supreme Court decided the case without dealing with these problems of proof, much to the chagrin of the two dissenters.

8. 456 F.2d 1074 (4th Cir.1972).

gon public concourse. It was shown that in the months immediately preceding the masses the area had been used 16 times for various religious, recreational and award assemblies, including band recitals and a speech by the Vice President. The court concluded that

> when the record strongly suggests invidious discrimination and selective application of a regulation to inhibit the expression of an unpopular viewpoint, and where it appears that the government is in ready possession of the facts, and the defendants are not, it is not unreasonable to reverse the burden of proof and to require the government to come forward with evidence as to what extent loud and unusual noise and obstruction of the concourse may have occurred on other approved occasions. It is neither novel nor unfair to require the party in possession of the facts to disclose them.

This language is especially significant when it is considered that the record also showed that the defendants had "created loud and unusual noise," for this left it quite unclear whether the defendants' conduct had been singled out from the 16 previous events on the legitimate basis that it had been noisier or on the improper basis of the defendants' opposition to government policy. Despite this defect in the defendant's showing of discriminatory prosecution, the court deemed it appropriate to call upon the government for clarification because the government had unique access to the relevant facts. Some other cases have taken this approach, though it is fair to say that *Crowthers* is not typical of how courts have treated discriminatory prosecution claims.

If the problem is that the critical facts are often in the hands of the prosecutor rather than the defendant, an alternative approach to it is to afford the defendant more ready access to those facts. One longstanding difficulty, of course, is that prosecution policies are not reduced to writing and made available to the public. In lieu of or in addition to that information, it would be helpful to the defendant if he could require the prosecutor to give testimony concerning the reasons underlying his inaction in other cases or his affirmative action in the instant case, but courts are understandably reluctant to require prosecutors to so testify even when this might be the only way the defendant could establish his claim. Similarly, government documents about the particular case which might reveal motivation may also be very helpful, but courts are likewise reluctant to order such discovery. Here again, the result may be that the discovery will be denied even when it would be the only way the defendant could be expected to establish his claim.

Statistical evidence can be of some assistance to a defendant who is trying to establish a discriminatory enforcement defense. Illustrative is *United States v. Ojala*,[9] where the defendant made what the court characterized as "a strong showing" of his selection for enforcement within a general pattern of nonenforcement. This was done by statistical evidence showing that in a two year period there were about 51,000 tax delinquency investigations in the state, that about 4,000 of them were referred to the IRS Intelligence Division, and that only nine criminal prosecutions for failure to file were recommended. But most courts have found statistical evidence insufficient to establish a prima facie case of intentional discrimination. For example, evidence comparing the percentage of blacks in the population with the percentage of prosecutions for certain kinds of offenses involving black defendants has been held insufficient because it reveals nothing about the number of minority and majority group members who in fact have committed the particular crimes or about how many violations by each group are known to law enforcement authorities.

(c) "Arbitrary Classification." In *Oyler v. Boles*,[10] the Supreme Court emphasized that "the conscious exercise of some selectivity in enforcement is not in itself a federal constitutional violation," and that to prevail on an equal protection claim a defendant would have to show that he was selected pursuant to an "arbitrary classification" such as "race" or

9. 544 F.2d 940 (8th Cir.1976).

10. 368 U.S. 448, 82 S.Ct. 501, 7 L.Ed.2d 446 (1962).

"religion." Notwithstanding the number of appellate cases in which a discriminatory enforcement claim has been raised (usually without success), it is far from clear just what constitutes an "arbitrary classification" in this context. The lower court cases indicate that a rather limited number of classifications have been rather readily held or assumed to be "arbitrary." Included are those instances in which the selection for prosecution was based upon race, national origin, sex, political activity or membership in a political party, union activity or membership in a labor union, or more generally the exercise of First Amendment rights.

But while at least as to some of these categories it may be highly unlikely if not impossible that there could ever be a sufficient explanation for an enforcement policy so limited, it must be stressed that the classification in question cannot be looked at only in the abstract. Rather, it must be examined as it relates to legitimate law enforcement objectives. Under traditional equal protection analysis, the question which *usually* must be asked is whether there is a "rational relationship" between the classification and those objectives. (A few classifications, such as those based on race or national origin or those which restrict the exercise of fundamental constitutional rights, are subjected to a more demanding strict scrutiny-compelling interest test, while a few others, such as those based on gender, are subjected to an intermediate level of scrutiny.)

Consider, for example, a classification which is or appears to be based upon the sex of the offender, sometimes challenged with respect to enforcement of the prostitution laws. With rare exception, courts have not been receptive to equal protection claims directed to enforcement practices which bring about the prosecution of female prostitutes but not their male customers. The prostitute-customer distinction, which could be made by the legislature, has been deemed appropriate in light of legitimate law enforcement interests. The use of male "decoys" to catch prostitutes without equivalent use of female "decoys" to catch persons seeking prostitutes has been upheld as a rational way to maximize the deterrent effect of the law and to utilize resources in a way which are most likely to lead to convictions. By comparison, if the policy was to enforce the prostitution laws against female prostitutes but not against male prostitutes, then it seems much more likely a court would conclude there was a denial of equal protection.

The broader point is that a prosecutor's enforcement classification is "arbitrary" only if people have been classified according to criteria which are clearly irrelevant to law enforcement purposes. There is certainly nothing wrong, for example, with a decision to employ a statute against only the certain kinds of conduct that present a threat to the central interests intended to be protected by the law. Illustrative of enforcement policies deemed to fit this description are the following: enforcement of gambling laws against bookmakers but not those placing bets with them, prosecuting draft evaders but not those who abet them, prosecuting those who violate the law against selling securities without a license only if they have sold 10 or more securities, and enforcement of the law prohibiting public officials from accepting money only against those receiving over $100. By comparison, in *United States v. Robinson*[11] a policy to enforce the statutes prohibiting wiretapping against private detectives but not government officials was deemed arbitrary, for such a distinction could not serve a legitimate enforcement purpose. There was simply no basis upon which it could be rationally argued that illegal intrusions into privacy are less serious when done by those working for the government. Similarly, in *People v. Acme Markets, Inc.*,[12] a denial of equal protection was found where the Sunday closing laws were enforced only upon complaint and the complaints in question were motivated by a dispute between a union and certain businesses. The court in *Acme* stressed that in these

11. 311 F.Supp. 1063 (W.D.Mo.1969).

12. 37 N.Y.2d 326, 372 N.Y.S.2d 590, 334 N.E.2d 555 (1975).

circumstances the motives of the private complainants must be taken to be the motives of the state for purposes of applying the "rational relation" test.

Some cases are a bit more difficult, as where it is arguable that the persons selected for enforcement were chosen because of their personal characteristics rather than the nature of their conduct. It has been held, however, that selective enforcement may be justified when a striking example or a few examples are sought in order to deter other violators, and on this basis it has been deemed permissible to proceed against the most notorious violators or the most prominent persons who are violating a particular law. Sometimes the notoriety of the person selected for prosecution is largely attributable to his public stands on issues, in which case the matter must be scrutinized more closely. As stated in *United States v. Steele*[13]: "An enforcement procedure that focuses upon the vocal offender is inherently suspect, since it is vulnerable to the charge that those chosen for prosecution are being punished for their expression of ideas, a constitutionally protected right." The defendant in *Steele* prevailed when he showed that he was one of only four persons in the state prosecuted for refusing to answer questions on the census form and that all four had publicly participated in the census resistance movement. But in *Steele* the government denied it had exercised any selectivity at all; the court might have come out differently if the government had instead argued that its selection standard was to prosecute only those offenses that were likely to have a strong deterrent effect on potential offenders and that offenses by vocal census resistors would have a broader impact than would offenses by ordinary citizens.

One way of looking at the issue of what constitutes an "arbitrary classification" for discriminatory enforcement purposes is to inquire whether that question is different than when it is asked whether a criminal statute employs a classification which violates the equal protection clause. Courts have sometimes upheld an enforcement classification on the ground that it would have been permissible for the legislature to draft a statute which matches the actual enforcement practice, yet some decisions have held invalid enforcement policies identical to those which have been permitted when expressed in criminal statutes. Except perhaps as to highly sensitive issues which are better left to the political-legislative process, the former is the better view. Surely if the legislature encompasses more conduct than can be reasonably reached by available enforcement resources, then those responsible for making enforcement policy must be allowed to focus on those aspects of the problem which are most serious, just as the legislature could have done initially.

Another issue, essentially the reverse of that put above, is whether an enforcement scheme employed by a prosecutor is inevitably "arbitrary" whenever the applicable criminal statute could not have been lawfully drawn in a fashion which would square precisely with the enforcement practice. The answer is no. One reason that discretionary enforcement is necessary is because the inherent limitations upon the effective use of language in criminal statutes make it impossible to state exactly and completely all that is to be included and excluded. This being so, an enforcement policy is not constitutionally invalid merely because it could not have been expressed in the criminal statute without running afoul of equal protection or void for vagueness limitations. The most obvious example is the policy discussed earlier of maximizing deterrence by enforcing certain laws against notorious or prominent violators.

Yet another important issue regarding the meaning of the "rational relationship" test in this context concerns the subject matter against which the classification must appear to be rational. Is it sufficient that the classification bears a rational relationship to *some* permissible governmental purpose, or must the classification be rationally related to the purposes of the criminal law under which the defendant is charged? The answer may de-

13. 461 F.2d 1148 (9th Cir.1972).

pend on the circumstances. Consider, for example, *United States v. Sacco*,[14] where the defendant objected that he was singled out, "based on his suspected role in organized crime," for investigation and prosecution under the alien registration laws. That this was the basis of selection was not disputed, yet the court unhesitantly held that it "cannot be said that that standard for selection is not rationally related to the purposes of * * * the alien registration laws." In other words, it is quite rational, considering the purposes underlying the alien registration statute, to focus upon those aliens suspected not to be law-abiding. One might well doubt whether the result would be the same were Sacco singled out on the same basis for prosecution under a generally nonenforced criminal adultery statute; there is nothing relating to the policies underlying *that* law which would explain a focus upon those suspected of organized crime. Yet, authority is to be found which would seemingly produce the same result on those facts.

(d) "Intentional or Purposeful." In *Oyler v. Boles*,[15] the Supreme Court declared that there is no equal protection violation unless "the selection was *deliberately* based upon an unjustifiable standard." [16] In support, the Court cited *Snowden v. Hughes*,[17] wherein it stated: "The unlawful administration by state officers of a state statute fair on its face, resulting in its unequal application to those who are entitled to be treated alike, is not a denial of equal protection unless there is shown to be present in it an element of intentional or purposeful discrimination." It is not immediately apparent, however, precisely what that language means.

In *Snowden*, the words were used in a way that implied bad faith, or awareness of the unjustifiability of the standard of selection. Given the context in which the matter arose in that case, this is not surprising. *Snowden* involved a civil suit to recover damages for infringement of civil rights, and it is understandable that the Court might not have wished to have an administrative official held personally liable in damages for a good faith mistake on his part. But this sensible notion that a nonmalicious official should not be required to pay out damages clearly has no application when a defendant in a criminal prosecution is seeking dismissal of the charges against him because of the basis upon which he was selected for prosecution. In such a case, the question ought to be whether the classification used by the prosecutor is *in fact* arbitrary, not whether the prosecutor was personally aware that it was arbitrary. This principle is unquestionably sound, but it cannot be said with assurance that it is always grasped by the courts or applied by them.

But if malice ought not be required when a discriminatory prosecution defense is interposed, then in what sense can it be said that there must be "intentional or purposeful discrimination"? The answer, which is fully consistent with the more generalized development of equal protection doctrine, is that it is not enough that a particular enforcement policy has the *effect* of singling out those who happen to be in an impermissible class; there must have been an *intent* to single out that class.[18] A decision to prosecute black gam-

14. 428 F.2d 264 (9th Cir.1970).

15. 368 U.S. 448, 82 S.Ct. 501, 7 L.Ed.2d 446 (1962).

16. Emphasis added.

17. 321 U.S. 1, 64 S.Ct. 397, 88 L.Ed. 497 (1944).

18. Illustrative is Wayte v. United States, 470 U.S. 598, 105 S.Ct. 1524, 84 L.Ed.2d 547 (1985), involving a challenge of the government's passive enforcement policy as to nonregistration for the draft, under which it would investigate and prosecute only those who had advised Selective Service that they had failed to register or who were reported by others as having failed to register. The Court concluded the government had not thereby subjected "vocal nonregistrants to any special burden," but then added:

"Even if the passive policy had a discriminatory effect, petitioner has not shown that the Government intended such a result. The evidence he presented demonstrated only that the Government was aware that the passive enforcement policy would result in prosecution of vocal objectors and that they would probably make selective prosecution claims. As we have noted, however, ' "[d]iscriminatory purpose" ... implies more than ... intent as awareness of consequences. It implies that the decision-maker ... selected or reaffirmed a particular course of action at least in part "because of," not merely "in spite of," its adverse effects upon an identifiable group.' * * * In the present case, petitioner has not shown that the Government prosecuted him *because of* his protest activi-

blers but not white gamblers would clearly be impermissible, but this is not also true of a decision to focus upon the numbers racket rather than poker in private clubs because of the former's ties to organized crime. Nor does this latter policy become arbitrary merely because it has the effect that most of the defendants prosecuted for gambling are black. By the same token, the mere fact that the latter policy would be legitimate does not mean that enforcement intended to discriminate against blacks can be "papered over" by this other reason. This highlights the significance of the earlier discussion of burden of proof, and in particular the important question of whether a defendant who has succeeded in showing a discriminatory effect should be deemed to have shifted the burden to the prosecution to establish that this effect was not deliberate but instead was an incidental consequence of a legitimate enforcement policy.

(e) Nonprosecution of Others. Many cases reflect the view that a defendant cannot prevail on a discriminatory prosecution claim unless he shows, inter alia, that the law in question is generally not enforced against others similarly situated. Whether this is a sensible limitation is a matter on which there is a difference of opinion. Consider, for example, the situation alleged in *People v. Walker*,[19] namely, that closely following her exposure of corrupt practices in the Department of Buildings, defendant was charged with violating several building code provisions which were generally enforced. One view is that once

> it is recognized that the equal protection clause requires each state to enact and enforce its laws in an impartial manner, it follows that Miss Walker should be given the opportunity to prove that even though there was general or random enforcement of the statute in question she would not have been prosecuted but for the purposeful discrimination on the part of the borough superintendent. For example, assume that the superintendent has a list of 1,000 known violators and reasonably exercises his discretion to enforce the law selectively by prosecuting every other person on the list, namely, even numbers. If Miss Walker's name is 149th on the list and the superintendent admits deviating from his selective enforcement formula in order to vent his personal prejudice against her, she has been deprived of equal protection of the laws and should be permitted to quash the prosecution.[20]

Although, at least in abstract terms, that is a most appealing position, it has frequently been challenged on practical grounds. It is argued that general nonenforcement must remain an essential prerequisite of a discriminatory prosecution defense so that it cannot be too readily invoked. "Were the law otherwise all enforcement proceedings could be turned into subjective expeditions into motive without the stabilizing, objectively verifiable, element of an unequal pattern of enforcement." [21] Moreover, so the argument proceeds, a prosecutor ought not to be obligated to forego prosecuting a violator he believes to be guilty merely because of some personal antagonism he has toward that violator. And then there is the possibility that the personal animus did not actually make a difference, given the general pattern of enforcement. The point is that even if it can be proved that the prosecution might have been improperly motivated, it will be exceedingly difficult to prove that the defendant would not have been selected for prosecution in the normal course of events.

§ 13.5 Other Challenges to the Decision to Prosecute

(a) Vindictive Prosecution. In *Blackledge v. Perry*,[1] where defendant was convicted of misdemeanor assault, exercised his right to trial de novo, and then was charged with felony assault based upon the same conduct,

ties. Absent such a showing, his claim of selective prosecution fails."

19. 14 N.Y.2d 901, 252 N.Y.S.2d 96, 200 N.E.2d 779 (1964).

20. Recent Case, 78 Harv.L.Rev. 884, 885–86 (1965).

21. Burke, J., dissenting in *Walker*.

§ 13.5

1. 417 U.S. 21, 94 S.Ct. 2098, 40 L.Ed.2d 628 (1974).

the Court held that a person "is entitled to pursue his statutory right to a trial *de novo,* without apprehension that the State will retaliate by substituting a more serious charge for the original one." The felony charge was barred on due process grounds. *Blackledge* emphasized that this result was necessary even absent "evidence that the prosecutor in this case acted in bad faith or maliciously," because it was the appearance of vindictiveness which would chill the right to appeal. But in *United States v. Goodwin,*[2] the Court declined "to apply a presumption of vindictiveness" in a pretrial setting because a realistic likelihood of vindictiveness was deemed not to exist at that stage. The Court added, however, that it did not "foreclose the possibility that a defendant in an appropriate case might prove objectively that the prosecutor's charging decision was motivated by a desire to punish him for doing something that the law plainly allowed him to do."

That an initial decision to prosecute might be undertaken to chill the exercise of rights cannot be denied, as is illustrated by *Dixon v. District of Columbia.*[3] Dixon, a black retired detective sergeant, was stopped by two white police officers for alleged traffic violations. He filed a complaint with the police department concerning the conduct of the officers, after which the prosecutor entered into a tacit agreement with Dixon that if he proceeded no further with his complaint the government would not prosecute the traffic charges. Dixon later filed a complaint with the Council on Human Relations, and he was then charged and convicted for the traffic offenses.

Though the court in *Dixon* relied upon its supervisory power to grant relief because of government misconduct, it was recognized that constitutional considerations were lurking very close to the surface:

> Of course prosecutors have broad discretion to press or drop charges. But there are limits. If, for example, the Government had legitimately determined not to prosecute appellant and had then reversed its position solely because he filed a complaint, this would clearly violate the first amendment. The Government may not prosecute for the purpose of deterring people from exercising their right to protest official misconduct and petition for redress of grievances.

The court then noted that the instant case was "more complicated" because the government's initial decision not to prosecute was improper because based upon Dixon's tentative agreement to drop his complaint; "if the Government should have prosecuted Dixon in the first place, there is arguably no reason why it should be barred from prosecuting him now." But the court concluded there was a countervailing consideration of greater importance, namely, the need not to "suppress complaints against police misconduct which should be thoroughly aired in a free society."

If this is so, then it well might be asked whether it is essential that there first have been a decision not to charge. Should not a defendant prevail simply by showing that he was selected for charging by a vindictive prosecutor who was annoyed by the defendant's exercise of his first amendment rights in complaining about government policy or the conduct of government officials? Where this has occurred with respect to a statutory provision not generally enforced as to those similarly situated, a prerequisite to an equal protection claim, defendants making such a showing have prevailed on a discriminatory prosecution theory. But it has been suggested that these cases truly are not so much equal protection cases as they are cases in which the defendants have been deemed entitled to relief because prosecutors have retaliated against the exercise of First Amendment rights by defendants. If this is so, then presumably a defendant should likewise prevail upon a showing that the authorities focused upon him because of his exercise of First Amendment rights *even when* the law under which he is charged is generally enforced against others, a result certainly not favored by the Supreme Court.[4]

2. 457 U.S. 368, 102 S.Ct. 2485, 73 L.Ed.2d 74 (1982).

3. 394 F.2d 966 (D.C.Cir.1968).

4. In Wayte v. United States, 470 U.S. 598, 105 S.Ct. 1524, 84 L.Ed.2d 547 (1985), the defendant challenged the government's passive enforcement policy re the draft

Whether a vindictive prosecution defense this broad will ever be generally accepted by the courts is not entirely clear. There will likely be considerable resistance to such a development, primarily because of a perceived need to impose some limits on the number of criminal prosecutions in which a defendant would be entitled to put the prosecutor's motivations and intentions into issue. In the equal protection area, that objective is largely served by the requirement that the defendant show the law in question is not being enforced against others similarly situated. In the *Blackledge–Goodwin–Dixon* line of vindictive prosecution cases, so the argument goes, this stabilizing, objectively verifiable, element is provided by the necessity that the defendant establish an exercise of a right by him which was both preceded by a favorable charging decision and followed by an unfavorable one.

Another issue which can arise in a *Dixon* type of case is whether all charging decisions intended to foreclose or discourage a complaint by the defendant are improper. In *MacDonald v. Musick*,[5] for example, the prosecutor moved to dismiss a drunken driving charge against the defendant but then, when defendant declined to stipulate that there was probable cause for his arrest, the prosecutor not only withdrew that motion but amended the charge by adding a resisting arrest count, on which defendant was convicted. The prosecutor explained his actions by saying that one of his duties was "to protect the police officers" and that he thus had properly sought the stipulation "so that the defendant cannot sue the police department." But the federal court disagreed, stating it "is no part of the proper duty of a prosecutor to use a criminal prosecution to forestall a civil proceeding by the defendant against policemen, even where the civil case arises from the events that are also the basis for the criminal charge." At least one court has reached a contrary result. In *Hoines v. Barney's Club, Inc.*,[6] the court enforced the plaintiff's agreement with the prosecutor that the charge against him for disturbing the peace would be dropped in exchange for his release from any civil liability of the private persons who arrested him. In concluding that such an agreement did not contravene public policy, the court likened what had occurred in the instant case to legitimate plea bargaining. But as the *Hoines* dissenters noted, this analogy is faulty. The agreement in the instant case did "not achieve any legitimate function of the criminal process," while proper plea bargaining does, as there "the state benefits by saving the expense of trial and expediting the disposition of the criminal case."

In *Town of Newton v. Rumery*,[7] the issue was whether "a court properly may enforce an agreement in which a criminal defendant releases his right to file a § 1983 action in return for a prosecutor's dismissal of pending criminal charges." The Court concluded that waiver of a right to sue under a federal statute was itself a matter of federal law, as to which the "relevant principle is well-established: a promise is unenforceable if the interest in its enforcement is outweighed in the circumstances by a public policy harmed by enforcement of the agreement." The waiver

registration laws on the ground that it infringed upon his First Amendment right to protest registration. In rejecting that claim, the Court noted:

"We think it important to note as a final matter how far the implications of petitioner's First Amendment argument would extend. Strictly speaking, his argument does not concern passive enforcement but self-reporting. The concerns he identifies would apply to all nonregistrants who report themselves even if the Selective Service engaged only in active enforcement. For example, a nonregistrant who wrote a letter informing Selective Service of his failure to register could, when prosecuted under an active system, claim that the Selective Service was prosecuting him only because of his 'protest.' Just as in this case, he could have some justification for believing that his letter had focused inquiry upon him. Prosecution in either context would equally 'burden' his exercise of First Amendment rights. Under the petitioner's view, then, the Government could not constitutionally prosecute a self-reporter—even in an active enforcement system—unless perhaps it could prove that it would have prosecuted him without his letter. On principle, such a view would allow any criminal to obtain immunity from prosecution simply by reporting himself and claiming that he did so in order to 'protest' the law. The First Amendment confers no such immunity from prosecution."

5. 425 F.2d 373 (9th Cir.1970).

6. 28 Cal.3d 603, 170 Cal.Rptr. 42, 620 P.2d 628 (1980).

7. 480 U.S. 386, 107 S.Ct. 1187, 94 L.Ed.2d 405 (1987).

in the instant case, by a sophisticated businessman represented by an experienced lawyer, was voluntary, and "the possibility of coercion in the making of similar agreements" was deemed "insufficient by itself to justify a *per se* rule against release-dismissal bargains." Moreover, all such agreements do not offend public policy, for they "protect public officials from the burdens of defending * * * unjust claims." The prosecutor had acted properly in the instant case, the Court concluded, for he "had an independent, legitimate reason to make this agreement directly related to his prosecutorial responsibilities," namely, sparing a sexual assault victim the "public scrutiny and embarrassment she would have endured if she had to testify in either" the criminal or § 1983 trial. O'Connor, J., who supplied the necessary fifth vote,[8] wrote separately "to emphasize that it is the burden of those relying upon such covenants to establish that the agreement is neither involuntary nor the product of an abuse of the criminal process."

(b) **Reneging on a Promise.** In *United States v. Bethea,*[9] the United States attorney agreed with defendant that he would not be prosecuted for his failure to report for induction if defendant now submitted himself for induction, the defendant did so but the Army refused to induct him on moral grounds, after which defendant was prosecuted for his earlier failure to report. The defendant relied upon *Santobello v. New York,*[10] holding a plea bargain enforceable against the government, but the court ruled it was not controlling here:

> The concern of *Santobello* was to protect a defendant who by pleading guilty has surrendered valuable constitutional rights in exchange for the prosecution's assurances. That concern has no application to the facts of this case. Appellant's submission for induction surrendered none of the rights protected by *Santobello.* In the context of this case, Bethea's conduct was at most only a factor to be considered by the prosecutor in deciding whether or not to prosecute, a decision not reviewable here.

Bethea, which requires that the unkept promise have produced a waiver of constitutional rights, means a defendant would prevail only in limited circumstances, such as those in which the agreement is that the charges will be dropped if defendant passes a lie detector test but that otherwise defendant will plead guilty or otherwise the results of the test will be admissible against defendant at trial.

The soundness of the *Bethea* rule is to be doubted, and has been rejected by those courts which have enforced prosecution agreements that the charges would be dropped if the defendant passed a polygraph examination or aided a criminal investigation in some way. Sometimes this has been achieved by utilizing contract principles and focusing upon the "consideration" the defendant has supplied, and sometimes this has resulted from application of the even broader principle that a "pledge of public faith" is enforceable in any event.[11] The result might be otherwise, of course, if the prosecutor is misled by force of defendant's connivance into a disadvantageous agreement or where facts not within the fair contemplation of agreement have come to light.

(c) **Desuetude and Lack of Fair Notice.** Virtually every jurisdiction has some criminal statutes which, as a practical matter, have become ineffective without any legislative or judicial action invalidating or repealing them. These statutes have been long unenforced, and are totally ignored by those charged with enforcing the law and by the public at large. But it sometimes happens that these old laws

8. The four dissenters objected that the fact a criminal defendant "made a knowing and voluntary choice to sign a settlement agreement should not be determinative," for a prosecutor's offer to drop charges in this context "is inherently coercive," "exacts a price unrelated to the character of the defendant's conduct" (unlike plea bargaining), and conflicts with the public entitlement that the decision whether to prosecute be made independently of "concerns about the potential damages liability of the police department." They concluded the "strong presumption against the enforceability of such agreements" had not been overcome in the instant case.

9. 483 F.2d 1024 (4th Cir.1973).

10. 404 U.S. 257, 92 S.Ct. 495, 30 L.Ed.2d 427 (1971).

11. Workman v. Commonwealth, 580 S.W.2d 206 (Ky. 1979).

are resurrected and enforced by a prosecutor, in which case the question may arise as to whether the defendant so proceeded against can object. One possibility is a discriminatory prosecution defense grounded in the equal protection clause, but such a defense is seldom successful, and will not necessarily prevail merely because of the prior period of nonenforcement.

There is a doctrine which exists in the civil law, called desuetude, whereunder a statute is abrogated by reason of its long and continued nonuse. But no such rule exists in English law, and it is commonly assumed that the concept of desuetude has no place in American law. Such was the conclusion of the Supreme Court in *District of Columbia v. John R. Thompson Co.*[12] The lower court, though holding a criminal statute on refusal to serve blacks unenforceable on other grounds, asserted that "the enactments having lain unenforced for 78 years, in the face of a custom of race disassociation in the District, the decision of the municipal authorities to enforce them now, by the prosecution of the instant case, was, in effect, a decision legislative in character." The Supreme Court responded:

> The repeal of laws is as much a legislative function as their enactment. * * *
>
> Cases of hardship are put where criminal laws so long in disuse as to be no longer known to exist are enforced against innocent parties. But that condition does not bear on the continuing validity of the law; it is only an ameliorating factor in enforcement.

This analysis has not escaped criticism. For one thing, it has been questioned whether the prosecutor's conduct in now enforcing the long dormant law can fairly be said to be nothing more than a carrying out of the wishes of the legislative branch of government. More significant, however, for present purposes, is the argument that these "innocent parties" will sometimes have available a lack-of-fair-notice defense under the due process clause. The notion is that a penal enactment which is linguistically clear, but has been notoriously ignored by both its administrators and the community for an unduly extended period, imparts no more fair notice of its proscriptions than a statute which is phrased in vague terms. From this, it has been argued that a person should have a valid defense when he believed his conduct was not criminal and acted in reasonable reliance upon a clear practice of nonenforcement of the statute or other enactment defining the offense by the body charged by law with responsibility for enforcement, unless notice of intent to enforce the statute or other enactment is reasonably made available prior to the conduct alleged. No case expressly recognizing such a defense has been found, although courts have occasionally suggested that given the right set of circumstances the due process lack of notice defense would prevail here. Apparently it would be necessary that there have been a long period of nonenforcement and also that defendant's conduct have acquired the status of customary usage.

(d) Federal Relief From State Prosecution: Removal. In limited circumstances, pretrial relief in federal court is available to defendants who establish a possibility or probability of certain sorts of impropriety in the commencement of a state prosecution. One possibility is removal of the criminal case from the state court to the federal court for trial there. A federal officer or a person acting under him[13] or a member of the armed forces,[14] if charged in a state court for acts done under color of office, is entitled to such removal. The constitutional basis for such legislation "rests on the right and power of the United States to secure the efficient execution of its laws and to prevent interference therewith, due to possible local prejudice, by state prosecutions instituted against federal officers in enforcing such laws, by removal of the prosecutions to a federal court to avoid the effect of such prejudice."[15] A person petitioning for removal under these statutes need

12. 346 U.S. 100, 73 S.Ct. 1007, 97 L.Ed. 1480 (1953).

13. 28 U.S.C.A. § 1442.

14. 28 U.S.C.A. § 1442a.

15. Maryland v. Soper, 270 U.S. 9, 46 S.Ct. 185, 70 L.Ed. 449 (1926).

not admit the acts charged or establish his innocence,[16] but must be "candid, specific and positive in explaining his relation to the transaction growing out of which he has been indicted, and in showing that his relation to it was confined to his acts as an officer." [17] But the "color of office" requirement means "that federal officer removal must be predicated on the allegation of a colorable federal defense," and thus removal is unavailable where federal employees are charged "with traffic violations and other crimes for which they would have no federal defense in immunity or otherwise." [18]

Yet another statute permits removal to federal court of a state criminal prosecution brought against "any person who is denied or cannot enforce in the courts of such State a right under any law providing for the equal civil rights of citizens of the United States, or of all persons within the jurisdiction thereof." [19] The circumstances which will support removal under this provision are quite limited. Thus, removal was denied in *City of Greenwood v. Peacock*,[20] where the petitioners alleged that they were arrested and charged with various state offenses because they were blacks or were helping blacks assert their rights, that they were innocent of the charges, and that they would be unable to obtain a fair trial in state court. The Court reasoned:

> It is *not* enough to support removal * * * to allege or show that the defendant's federal equal civil rights have been illegally and corruptly denied by state administrative officials in advance of trial, that the charges against the defendant are false, or that the defendant is unable to obtain a fair trial in a particular state court. The motives of the officers bringing the charges may be corrupt, but that does not show that the state trial court will find the defendant guilty if he is innocent, or that in any other manner the defendant will be "denied or cannot enforce in the courts" of the State any right under a federal law providing for equal civil rights. The civil rights removal statute does not require and does not permit the judges of the federal courts to put their brethren of the state judiciary on trial. * * * [T]he vindication of the defendant's federal rights is left to the state courts except in the rare situations where it can be clearly predicted by reason of the operation of a pervasive and explicit state or federal law that those rights will inevitably be denied by the very act of bringing the defendant to trial in the state court.

Illustrative of that rare situation is the companion case of *Georgia v. Rachel*,[21] where removal was permitted because the relevant federal civil rights statute "specifically and uniquely" barred "any prosecution" and thereby granted immunity from the institution of a state prosecution based upon petitioners' sit-in activities.

(e) Federal Relief From State Prosecution: Injunction and Declaratory Judgment. In *Dombrowski v. Pfister*,[22] a divided Court held that the district court erred in dismissing on abstention grounds a complaint seeking to enjoin state officials in Louisiana from prosecuting or threatening to prosecute petitioners for alleged violations of the state Subversive Activities and Communist Control Law and the Communist Propaganda Control Law. The Court noted, inter alia, that there was no readily apparent construction that would render the statute constitutional, and that the complaint alleged bad faith of the prosecutor in threatening further prosecutions, holding public hearings on petitioner's activities, and the like. But in *Younger v. Harris*,[23] the *Dombrowski* case was given a narrow interpretation. The Court in *Younger* stressed the concept of "Our Federalism," which represents "a system in which there is sensitivity to the legitimate interests of both State and National Government, and in which

16. Willingham v. Morgan, 395 U.S. 402, 89 S.Ct. 1813, 23 L.Ed.2d 396 (1969).

17. Maryland v. Soper, 270 U.S. 9, 46 S.Ct. 185, 70 L.Ed. 449 (1926).

18. Mesa v. California, 489 U.S. 121, 109 S.Ct. 959, 103 L.Ed.2d 99 (1989).

19. 28 U.S.C.A. § 1443.

20. 384 U.S. 808, 86 S.Ct. 1800, 16 L.Ed.2d 944 (1966).

21. 384 U.S. 780, 86 S.Ct. 1783, 16 L.Ed.2d 925 (1966).

22. 380 U.S. 479, 85 S.Ct. 1116, 14 L.Ed.2d 22 (1965).

23. 401 U.S. 37, 91 S.Ct. 746, 27 L.Ed.2d 669 (1971).

the National Government, anxious though it may be to vindicate and protect federal rights and federal interests, always endeavors to do so in ways that will not unduly interfere with the legitimate activities of the States." Thus, "a federal court should not enjoin a state criminal prosecution begun prior to the institution of the federal suit except in very unusual situations, where necessary to prevent immediate irreparable injury," [24] that is, only on a "showing of bad faith, harassment, or any other unusual circumstance that would call for equitable relief." The possibility of a "chilling effect" on First Amendment rights is not enough to justify federal intervention, and the testing of the constitutionality of a statute "on its face" is "fundamentally at odds with the function of the federal courts in our constitutional plan," as it requires detailed analysis of statutes without the focus of their application to specific facts previously established in a criminal trial. There are thus only "narrow exceptions" [25] to the *Younger* bar to federal injunctive relief, and litigants have rarely been successful in trying to bring themselves within them.

Younger emphasized that the barriers it erected governed whenever there was a prosecution pending in the state courts, for that pendency meant that federal action would interfere with this state activity and also that the individual would soon have an opportunity to raise his objections in the context of the state criminal trial.[26] Not surprisingly, the Court also held that in such circumstances relief by way of a declaratory judgment is also barred.[27] But a unanimous Court in *Steffel v. Thompson* [28] concluded that "regardless of whether injunctive relief may be appropriate, federal declaratory relief is not precluded when no state prosecution is pending and a federal plaintiff demonstrates a genuine threat of enforcement of a disputed state criminal statute, whether an attack is made on the constitutionality of the statute on its face or as applied." This was not at all inconsistent with *Younger;* a person against whom state criminal charges are pending may be able to vindicate his rights in defense of a single criminal action, but the person against whom no charges are pending has no remedy except that provided by *Steffel.* From this it follows, as the Court shortly thereafter concluded, that *Steffel* rather than *Younger* governs where federal action for injunctive relief was sought prior to the commencement of state criminal proceedings.[29]

But then came *Hicks v. Miranda,*[30] involving federal action for declaratory and injunctive relief, where the Court recognized two exceptions to *Steffel.* The first is that the federal plaintiff against whom state proceedings are *not* pending is nonetheless bound by the *Younger* limitations if his interests "were intertwined" with those of others against whom state criminal proceedings have been commenced.[31] The second and more controversial is "that where state criminal proceedings are begun against the federal plaintiffs after the federal complaint is filed but before any proceedings of substance on the merits have taken place in the federal court, the principles of *Younger v. Harris* should apply in full force." The four dissenters in *Hicks* objected that the majority "virtually instructs state officials to answer federal complaints with state indictments," and noted, which is still the case, that it was quite unclear what

24. As the court characterized the *Younger* holding in the companion case of Samuels v. Mackell, 401 U.S. 66, 91 S.Ct. 764, 27 L.Ed.2d 688 (1971).

25. Huffman v. Pursue, Ltd., 420 U.S. 592, 95 S.Ct. 1200, 43 L.Ed.2d 482 (1975).

26. And thus, notwithstanding *Younger,* state criminal procedures can be challenged in federal court if the relief sought is not directed to the prosecution as such and if the federal claim is one which cannot be raised in defense of the state prosecution. See, e.g., Gerstein v. Pugh, 420 U.S. 103, 95 S.Ct. 854, 43 L.Ed.2d 54 (1975).

27. Samuels v. Mackell, 401 U.S. 66, 91 S.Ct. 764, 27 L.Ed.2d 688 (1971).

28. 415 U.S. 452, 94 S.Ct. 1209, 39 L.Ed.2d 505 (1974).

29. Village of Belle Terre v. Boraas, 416 U.S. 1, 94 S.Ct. 1536, 39 L.Ed.2d 797 (1974).

30. 422 U.S. 332, 95 S.Ct. 2281, 45 L.Ed.2d 223 (1975).

31. Such was the case in *Hicks,* for the federal plaintiffs were a theater owner and his corporate alter ego, but state charges were pending against two employees of the theater following police seizure of allegedly obscene films there.

constitutes "proceedings of substance on the merits."

(f) Federal Relief From State Prosecution: Habeas Corpus. By statute, federal habeas corpus is provided for a prisoner "in custody in violation of the Constitution or laws or treaties of the United States." [32] Another provision says that an application for such a writ "in behalf of a person in custody pursuant to the judgment of a State court shall not be granted unless it appears that the applicant has exhausted the remedies available in the courts of the State, or that there is either an absence of available State corrective process or the existence of circumstances rendering such process ineffective to protect the rights of the prisoner." [33] Despite the "in custody pursuant to the judgment of a State court" language, the requirements of this latter statute also govern instances of pretrial applications for habeas relief. This means that constitutional objections to pending state prosecutions can sometimes be heard and decided in federal court via habeas corpus,[34] though often this will not be the case because of the petitioner's inability to satisfy the "custody" and "exhaustion" requirements, which are discussed elsewhere herein.[35]

(g) Civil Action Against Prosecutor. In the event that a defendant in a criminal case later brings a tort action for malicious prosecution against the prosecutor on the ground that the latter's decision to prosecute was improper, the action will be dismissed on the ground that the prosecutor is absolutely immune. This is the clear majority view in the state courts, and is also the rule adopted by the Supreme Court for application when such a suit is brought against a federal prosecutor.[36] This common-law immunity of a prosecutor is grounded in "concern that harassment by unfounded litigation would cause a deflection of the prosecutor's energies from his public duties, and the possibility that he would shade his decisions instead of exercising the independence of judgment required by his public trust." [37]

In *Imbler v. Pachtman,*[38] the Supreme Court relied upon this concern in holding that such absolute immunity also exists when a federal civil rights action is brought against a state prosecutor in federal court. The Court stressed that this did "not leave the public powerless to deter misconduct or to punish that which occurs," for the prosecutor could be criminally prosecuted for willful denial of constitutional rights and could be subjected to professional discipline. The holding in *Imbler* was confined to circumstances in which the prosecutor's activities "were intimately associated with the judicial phase of the criminal process," which apparently covers the prosecutor's decision to charge. The Court added it was not deciding whether like immunity existed "for those aspects of the prosecutor's responsibility that cast him in the role of an administrator or investigative officer rather than that of advocate." Even assuming that the prosecutor in these latter two roles has only qualified immunity, thus making the distinction between them and the prosecutor's other duties of some importance, it seems unlikely that decisions regarding who to prosecute for what will be deemed to be either administrative or investigative.

§ 13.6 Challenges to the Decision to Forego or Terminate Diversion

(a) The Diversion Process. For years, individual prosecutors have in a very informal and often haphazard way permitted pretrial diversion in some circumstances, agreeing not to proceed with prosecution of a defendant if he in return makes restitution to the victim or does some other act. Of primary concern here, however, is the kind of diversion which is now becoming quite common: a formalized procedure authorized by legislation or court

32. 28 U.S.C.A. § 2241(c)(3).

33. 28 U.S.C.A. § 2254(b).

34. Braden v. 30th Judicial Circuit Court, 410 U.S. 484, 93 S.Ct. 1123, 35 L.Ed.2d 443 (1973).

35. See §§ 28.7(a), 28.8(a).

36. Yaselli v. Goff, 275 U.S. 503, 48 S.Ct. 155, 72 L.Ed. 395 (1927).

37. Imbler v. Pachtman, 424 U.S. 409, 96 S.Ct. 984, 47 L.Ed.2d 128 (1976).

38. 424 U.S. 409, 96 S.Ct. 984, 47 L.Ed.2d 128 (1976).

rule whereby persons who are accused of certain criminal offenses and meet preestablished criteria have their prosecution suspended for a three month to one year period and are placed in a community-based rehabilitation program, after which the case is dismissed if the conditions of the diversion referral are satisfied. In the earlier and informal days of pretrial diversion, it was perceived as just another aspect of the prosecutor's discretion, meaning that the prosecutor's decisions on when to divert and when to terminate a diversion were largely uncontrolled. That is still the case in some jurisdictions, although there is a noticeable trend toward limiting the prosecutor's discretion in these respects as diversion programs become more formalized.

(b) Statutory Standards for Diversion. One consequence of the greater attention which has been given to the pretrial diversion alternative is that efforts have been made to identify criteria by which to select those defendants who are the most likely candidates for diversion. Sometimes these criteria are set out in statutes or rules of court. It has sometimes been claimed that such provisions are unconstitutional attempts to limit the prosecutor's discretion, barred by the separation of powers doctrine, but such challenges have been rejected where the legislation does not destroy or unreasonably restrict the prosecutor's discretion. If the statute provides that the courts are to administer the program or if the program was adopted by rule of court, then it is clear that the setting of standards does not encroach upon the executive power because then a judicial function is involved.

If a particular defendant were made ineligible for a pretrial diversion program by virtue of certain criteria in a statute or rule of court, a defendant might attack those criteria on equal protection grounds. Except in extraordinary circumstances, however, it is unlikely that such a challenge will prevail. In *Marshall v. United States*,[1] for example, the Supreme Court held there was no equal protection denial in the statutory exclusion from the treatment alternative under the Narcotic Addict Rehabilitation Act of those persons with two prior felony convictions. The Court reasoned that it was not "unreasonable or irrational for Congress to act on the predicate * * * that a person with two or more prior felonies would be less likely to adjust and adhere to the disciplines and rigors of the treatment program and hence is a less promising prospect for treatment than those with lesser criminal records." Various other classifications would appear to be legally defensible, even if seemingly unwise or not fully supported by empirical evidence, such as those denying eligibility to felons, perpetrators of violent crimes, recidivists, juveniles, youthful offenders, addicts or alcoholics.

(c) Decision Not to Divert. A decision by the prosecutor not to divert a particular defendant and instead to proceed with prosecution on the pre-existing charge is, in essence, a decision to prosecute, and thus at a minimum is subject to challenge in the same way as any other decision to prosecute. One possibility, therefore, is that a nondiversion decision will be contested as a discriminatory decision to prosecute which violates the equal protection clause. As we have already seen, defendants seldom are successful in bringing such a challenge. If it is brought within the context of a formalized diversion program, the defendant's chances may be somewhat better in the sense that he may find it easier to carry his "heavy burden" of proof. Because of the established criteria in a statute, rule of court or a prosecutor's policy statement, the defendant may be able to establish more readily that others similarly situated are not being prosecuted and that he was singled out on an arbitrary basis.

Another possible basis upon which to challenge a decision to charge is that the prosecution is vindictive or has the appearance of vindictiveness. As already noted, the *Blackledge v. Perry*[2] presumption-of-vindictiveness was held inapplicable in a pretrial setting in

§ 13.6

1. 414 U.S. 417, 94 S.Ct. 700, 38 L.Ed.2d 618 (1974).

2. 417 U.S. 21, 94 S.Ct. 2098, 40 L.Ed.2d 628 (1974).

United States v. Goodwin.[3] Although this means that in such circumstances the defendant cannot prevail without proving the existence of a vindictive motive, the chances of a defendant carrying that burden would seem somewhat greater when the prosecution does not square with established diversion criteria. Illustrative is *State v. Eash,*[4] where the prosecutor exercised his statutory veto of defendant's diversion application because of dissatisfaction with the breadth of defendant's waiver of speedy trial. Upon application of the defendant, the court then ruled that defendant's waiver was sufficient under the diversion statute, which contemplated waiver only "for the period of his diversion." The prosecutor persisted in his refusal to consent to diversion, and "admitted that the sole basis for refusing to accept such a waiver was that such a ruling conflicted with [his] 'total waiver' policy with regard to speedy trial waivers in pretrial intervention situations." The *Eash* court ruled that refusal on this basis was constitutionally impermissible: "Such conduct on the part of the state is tantamount to coercion and has a chilling effect upon the exercise of the right to a vigorous defense."

Seemingly inconsistent with *Eash* is *United States v. Smith,*[5] where defendant moved to dismiss a marijuana possession charge on cruel and unusual punishment grounds and the motion was granted but that ruling was reversed on appeal, after which the prosecutor refused to divert the defendant because it was his policy to deny such treatment to defendants who had chosen to litigate any issues in their case. The lower court found this objectionable and dismissed the charge, but the appellate court disagreed. The court asserted "that a policy intended to deter defendants from exercising their legal rights cannot be tolerated in the name of prosecutorial discretion," but that this was not such a case because "if a defendant applies for, is accepted into the program, and successfully completes the requisite activities, charges are dropped without his having to go to court, and no conviction or criminal record results." Thus, the court concluded, the "beneficiary of such a disposition of charges against him can scarcely be said to be deterred from exercising his right to defend himself, for, by dismissing such charges, the government has done away with any reason for him to do so."

Whether the *Smith* result is constitutionally objectionable is not entirely clear. *Smith* certainly is not as serious a matter as *Eash,* for the defendant in the latter case was confronted with the necessity of making a total and permanent waiver of Sixth Amendment speedy trial rights with respect to that charge, while Smith apparently could have opted for diversion initially and then, if his diversionary status was later terminated, moved to dismiss the charge on whatever theory he had previously entertained. There is also the argument that the prosecutor's policy in *Smith* should be upheld because it is totally consistent with one of the two objectives of diversion programs, namely, reducing the litigation burden in the courts. This is apparently what the *Smith* court had in mind when it asserted that if "it is permissible, in plea bargaining, to induce a defendant to plead guilty and waive his right to trial, *a fortiori* no substantial constitutional question is presented when a prosecutor offers to drop all charges provided the accused conforms to certain conditions, including, *inter alia,* forgoing the filing of any motions or pleas in defense." But it is this analogy which suggests that *Smith* may be somewhat vulnerable, for there is authority that even in a plea bargaining context there are limits upon what conditions the prosecutor may impose in terms of surrender of rights.[6]

Though it has been argued that the decision by the prosecutor not to divert a particular defendant should not be subject to judicial review, and though it seems clear that such a decision does not implicate rights which entitle the defendant to a hearing as a matter of course, as a general matter it is fair to say

3. 457 U.S. 368, 102 S.Ct. 2485, 73 L.Ed.2d 74 (1982).

4. 367 So.2d 661 (Fla.App.1979), disapproved in Cleveland v. State, 417 So.2d 653 (Fla.1982).

5. 354 A.2d 510 (D.C.App.1976).

6. See § 21.3(c).

that such decisions, at least when they occur within the context of a formalized diversion program, are likely to be subject to somewhat greater judicial scrutiny than the usual decision to charge. The extent to which this is so, however, will depend upon the exact nature of the diversion program. A program created by court rule is likely to be construed to include judicial power to interpret and enforce the rule. Under such a scheme an "abuse of discretion" standard is likely to be used upon review, which prompts somewhat closer scrutiny than under the equal protection arbitrariness test. Greater court control is also likely if a diversion program is interpreted to be an aspect of the court's sentencing function or if the applicable statute expressly assigns responsibility for the program to the courts. Also, if the statute puts the program in the hands of the prosecutor but says that he "shall consider" certain enumerated factors, a defendant might prevail upon a showing of a substantial departure from them.

(d) Decision to Terminate by Prosecution. If a defendant is accepted into a diversion program, the operating assumption is that if he carries out his responsibilities under the program the charges against him will be dropped. But this gives rise to the question of how free the prosecutor is, on his own, to decide that the "deal is off" or to conclude that the defendant has defaulted in some respect. In *United States v. Bethea,*[7] which might be viewed as an unusual type of diversion case, the prosecutor promised that he would drop the charges against defendant for failure to report for induction in the Army if defendant submitted himself for induction. The defendant complied, but the Army rejected him on moral grounds, after which the prosecutor proceeded with the prosecution. Relying upon the plea bargaining case of *Santobello v. New York,*[8] defendant tried to enforce the agreement in court, but the court ruled the prosecutor's decision was "not reviewable here" because, unlike the situation in *Santobello,* the defendant had not "surrendered valuable constitutional rights in exchange for the prosecution's assurances." But there is much to be said for the proposition, which has been accepted in a related context,[9] that such contract law analysis is inappropriate here and that the government should be required to keep its word without regard to whether the defendant has supplied "consideration." And even if the premise underlying *Bethea* is sound, it would seem not to govern the more typical diversion case. As held in *United States v. Garcia,*[10] *Santobello* is controlling where, "by entering into the deferred prosecution agreement, [the defendant] waived his valuable right to a speedy trial."

Even assuming that the prosecutor cannot simply renege on the agreement, obviously the defendant cannot complain about now being subjected to prosecution if he fails to carry out his part of the bargain. But whether there has been such a failure in a particular case may not be entirely clear. This being so, the question naturally arises as to how the prosecutor is to make that determination and whether it is subject to review. One view is that the prosecutor should have the discretionary authority to determine whether the offender is performing his duties adequately under the agreement and, if he determines that the offender is not, to reinstate the prosecution. But there is much to be said for the procedural scheme advocated in the Model Code of Pre–Arraignment Procedure, by which the defendant is entitled to "a hearing before the prosecutor to determine" whether defendant "violated a material term of the agreement or * * * made a misrepresentation materially affecting the agreement" and, "if so, whether the prosecution should be reinstated or the agreement modified." [11] If the prosecutor decides to reinstate the prosecution, the defendant may move in court for continuation of the diversion "on the ground that the record does not support the prosecutor's determination or that the prosecutor has

7. 483 F.2d 1024 (4th Cir.1973).

8. 404 U.S. 257, 92 S.Ct. 495, 30 L.Ed.2d 427 (1971) discussed in § 20.2(d).

9. See § 13.5(b).

10. 519 F.2d 1343 (9th Cir.1975).

11. ALI Model Code of Pre–Arraignment Procedure § 320.9(1) (1975).

not complied with the provisions" governing the aforementioned hearing.[12]

Indeed, it would seem that some sort of hearing is ordinarily required in this context as a matter of procedural due process. Revoking a person's diversion status is quite similar to parole revocation and probation revocation, and this has prompted some courts to conclude that the procedures mandated in *Morrissey v. Brewer* [13] and *Gagnon v. Scarpelli* [14] with respect to the latter revocations are equally necessary here. Those procedures are: (1) written notice of the claimed violation; (2) disclosure to the defendant of the evidence against him; (3) an opportunity to be heard in person and to present witnesses and documentary evidence; (4) the right to confront and cross-examine adverse witnesses, unless good cause is found for not allowing such confrontation; (5) a "neutral and detached" hearing body; and (6) a written statement by the factfinders as to the reasons for revocation. Whether this is so as to every type of diversion program is hard to say. In *Meachum v. Fano*,[15] holding no hearing was needed regarding transfer of a convict for alleged misconduct from a medium to a maximum security prison, the Court reasoned (1) that the prisoner's fundamental interest in liberty had been protected by his prior criminal trial, and (2) that state law had not conferred upon the prisoner any right to remain in the prison where he was assigned. From this, it may be argued that the once-diverted defendant's liberty interest will be protected by his forthcoming criminal trial and that therefore a hearing regarding the termination of diversion status is constitutionally required only if diversion is a statutorily created entitlement. This in turn depends upon whether the statutory language creates an expectancy in the defendant that diversion will continue until the fact of violation of the agreement's explicit conditions has been found.

12. Id. at § 320.9(2).

13. 408 U.S. 471, 92 S.Ct. 2593, 33 L.Ed.2d 484 (1972).

14. 411 U.S. 778, 93 S.Ct. 1756, 36 L.Ed.2d 656 (1973).

15. 427 U.S. 215, 96 S.Ct. 2532, 49 L.Ed.2d 451 (1976).

§ 13.7 Challenges to the Charge Selection

(a) Duplicative and Overlapping Statutes. Sometimes a defendant's challenge to a prosecutor's charge selection in a particular case is directed to the statutory scheme under which the prosecutor acted. This occurs when the defendant claims that the legislature has bestowed unnecessary discretion upon the prosecutor by defining the same criminal conduct in two different statutes carrying different penalties. Such a challenge reached the Supreme Court but was rejected by a unanimous Court in *United States v. Batchelder*.[1]

The defendant in *Batchelder* was convicted under a statute making it a crime for various persons, including one who "has been convicted in any court of a crime punishable by imprisonment for a term exceeding one year," to "receive any firearm * * * which has been shipped or transported in interstate or foreign commerce." He objected to his five year prison term, the maximum under this provision, because another statute carrying a two year maximum covers any person, among others, who "has been convicted by a court of the United States or of a State or any political subdivision thereof of a felony * * * and who receives, possesses, or transports in commerce or affecting commerce * * * any firearm." The Court of Appeals ruled he could receive no more than the two year maximum because of doubts as to whether Congress had intended the two penalty provisions to coexist, and added that without such a construction the statute might (1) be void for vagueness, (2) implicate "due process and equal protection interest[s] in avoiding excessive prosecutorial discretion and in obtaining equal justice," and (3) constitute an impermissible delegation of congressional authority. But the Supreme Court construed the statute otherwise and, in the process, found "no constitutional infirmities" in such a statutory scheme.

§ 13.7

1. 442 U.S. 114, 99 S.Ct. 2198, 60 L.Ed.2d 755 (1979).

As for the vagueness issue, the Court acknowledged that lack of fair notice as to the potential punishment might well violate due process, but concluded that the provisions at issue were not deficient because, though they created "uncertainty as to which crime may be charged and therefore what penalties may be imposed, they do so to no greater extent than would a single statute authorizing various alternative punishments." As for the Court of Appeals' concern that the legislative redundancy left the prosecutor with "unfettered" discretion, the Court responded that

> there is no appreciable difference between the discretion a prosecutor exercises when deciding whether to charge under one of two statutes with different elements and the discretion he exercises when choosing one of two statutes with identical elements. In the former situation, once he determines that the proof will support conviction under either statute, his decision is indistinguishable from the one he faces in the latter context. The prosecutor may be influenced by the penalties available upon conviction, but this fact standing alone does not give rise to a violation of the Equal Protection or Due Process Clauses.

On the delegation point, the *Batchelder* Court concluded that because the provisions at issue "plainly demarcate the range of penalties that prosecutors and judges may seek and impose," this meant "the power that Congress has delegated to those officials is no broader than the authority they routinely exercise in enforcing the criminal laws."

In assaying the *Batchelder* reasoning, it is useful to think about three types of situations in which a defendant's conduct may fall within two statutes. They are: (1) where one statute defines a lesser included offense of the other and they carry different penalties (e.g., whoever carries a concealed weapon is guilty of a misdemeanor; a convicted felon who carries a concealed weapon is guilty of a felony); (2) where the statutes overlap and carry different penalties (e.g., possession of a gun by a convicted felon, illegal alien or dishonorably discharged serviceman is a misdemeanor; possession of a gun by a convicted felon, fugitive from justice, or unlawful user of narcotics is a felony); (3) where the statutes are identical (e.g., possession of a gun by a convicted felon is a misdemeanor; possession of a gun by a convicted felon is a felony). The Court in *Batchelder* had before it a situation falling into the second category, but seems to have concluded that the three statutory schemes are indistinguishable for purposes of constitutional analysis. But in terms of either the difficulties which are confronted at the legislative level in drafting statutes or in the guidance which is given to a prosecutor by the legislation, the three schemes are markedly different.

The first of the three is certainly unobjectionable. Such provisions are quite common (robbery-armed robbery; battery-aggravated battery; joyriding-theft; housebreaking-burglary), and usually are a consequence of a deliberate attempt by the legislature to identify one or more aggravating characteristics which in the judgment of the legislature should ordinarily be viewed as making the lesser crime more serious. They afford guidance to the prosecutor, but—as noted in *Batchelder*—do not foreclose the prosecutor from deciding in a particular case that, notwithstanding the presence of one of the aggravating facts, the defendant will still be prosecuted for the lesser offense.

By contrast, the third of the three is highly objectionable. It is likely to be a consequence of legislative carelessness, and even if it is not such a scheme serves no legitimate purpose. There is nothing at all rational about this kind of statutory scheme, as it provides for different penalties without any effort whatsoever to explain a basis for the difference. It confers discretion which is totally unfettered and which is totally unnecessary. And thus the Court in *Batchelder* is less than convincing in reasoning that this third category is unobjectionable simply because in other instances, falling into the first category, the need for discretionary judgments by the prosecutor has not been and cannot be totally eliminated.

The second of the three categories presents a harder case. Here as well, the dilemma is likely to have been created by legislative carelessness, though this is not inevitably so. In the illustration given above, where the possession of a gun by a felon is listed in both misdemeanor and felony statutes which otherwise cover distinct circumstances, carelessness in the legislative process seems the most likely explanation. However, overlapping statutes are very common at both the federal and state level, and it can hardly be said that in every instance they are a consequence of poor research or inept drafting. Drafting a clear criminal statute and still ensuring that in *no* instance could it cover conduct embraced within any existing criminal statute in that jurisdiction can be a formidable task. (This fact alone may make courts somewhat reluctant to find overlap per se unconstitutional, although the consequence of such a finding, limiting punishment to that under the lesser of the two statutes until such time as the legislature decides what to do about the now-identified overlap, is hardly a cause for alarm.) Moreover, in the overlap scheme the two statutes will at least *sometimes* assist the prosecutor in deciding how to exercise his charging discretion. To the extent of the overlap, however, the conduct is the same, and thus the guidance afforded here falls considerably short of that in the first of the three categories.

Just how broad the *Batchelder* holding is in other respects remains to be seen. Of particular importance is the question of whether more dramatic or more certain disparities between the sentences allowed or required under the two statutes at issue makes a difference. In response to the Court of Appeals' objection that the prosecutor was given unfettered discretion in "selection of which of two penalties to apply," the Supreme Court answered that the government had not been allowed "to predetermine ultimate criminal sanctions" but instead had simply enabled "the sentencing judge to impose a longer prison sentence." That is, the prosecutor's choice of the statute which allowed imprisonment "not more than five years" rather than the one providing for imprisonment "not more than two years" had simply added to the judge's sentencing discretion. But what if, for example, one statute permitted imprisonment up to ten years and the other made ten years the mandatory minimum? In such a case, where the prosecutor actually makes a sentencing decision without either sentencing information or expertise in sentencing there is more force to the equal protection argument.

Prior to *Batchelder* some states held unconstitutional statutes which provided different punishment for exactly the same conduct. Some of the decisions went so far as to also cover criminal statutes which merely overlapped with one another. Though the reasoning in these cases was often similar to that found wanting in *Batchelder,* meaning that decision has created some chance that the courts so holding will retreat from their earlier position, a state might well reject *Batchelder* as a matter of state constitutional law. And of course there remains open the possibility that a court will be able to avoid the problem entirely by utilizing canons of statutory construction, such as that a later statute should prevail over the earlier one with which it would otherwise overlap, or that the more specific statute should prevail over the more general one with which it would otherwise overlap.

(b) Discriminatory Charge Selection. Even if the statutory scheme whereunder the prosecutor selected the charge is not objectionable, the defendant might nonetheless claim that the seriousness of the charge or number of charges lodged against him are the result of discriminatory enforcement. In *United States v. Batchelder,*[2] the Court expressly noted that the prosecutor's conduct in selecting the charge is "subject to constitutional constraints," in particular the equal protection clause's prohibition upon "selective enforcement 'based upon a unjustifiable standard such as race, religion, or other arbitrary classification.' " As for exactly what must be shown to make out an equal protection claim, what was said on this matter earlier regard-

2. 442 U.S. 114, 99 S.Ct. 2198, 60 L.Ed.2d 755 (1979).

ing the decision to charge[3] is generally applicable in this context as well. Here, as there, it is extremely difficult to make out a successful equal protection claim.

(c) Vindictive Charge Selection. A defendant who cannot make out an equal protection claim might nonetheless, given the right sequence of events, prevail on a due process vindictiveness theory under *Blackledge v. Perry*.[4] There, defendant was convicted in district court of misdemeanor assault, exercised his right to trial de novo in the superior court, and was then charged with the felony of assault with a deadly weapon with intent to kill. Relying upon *North Carolina v. Pearce*,[5] holding that due process prohibits a judge from imposing a more severe sentence upon retrial for the purpose of discouraging defendants from exercising their statutory right to appeal, defendant claimed the felony charge deprived him of due process. The Supreme Court agreed:

> There is, of course, no evidence that the prosecutor in this case acted in bad faith or maliciously in seeking a felony indictment against Perry. The rationale of our judgment in the *Pearce* case, however, was not grounded upon the proposition that actual retaliatory motivation must inevitably exist. Rather, we emphasized that "since the fear of such vindictiveness may unconstitutionally deter a defendant's exercise of the right to appeal or collaterally attack his first conviction, due process also requires that a defendant be freed of apprehension of such a retaliatory motivation on the part of the sentencing judge." We think it clear that the same considerations apply here. * * * A person convicted of an offense is entitled to pursue his statutory right to a trial *de novo,* without apprehension that the State will retaliate by substituting a more serious charge for the original one, thus subjecting him to a significantly increased potential period of incarceration.

Because the Court in *Blackledge* did not require proof of "actual retaliatory motive," the defendant there prevailed merely by showing that he exercised a "right" and that this was followed by "a more serious charge" by the same prosecutor.[6] The right in *Blackledge* was the right to appeal and the more serious charge was lodged after he had been once tried and convicted, but lower courts often took the same approach when the defendant's exercise of the right and the prosecutor's escalation of the charge all occurred in a pretrial setting. However, the Supreme Court rejected such an extension of *Blackledge* in *United States v. Goodwin*.[7] There, defendant was charged with several misdemeanor and petty offenses which were scheduled for trial before a federal magistrate until defendant exercised his right to have them tried by jury in district court. The case was accordingly transferred to another prosecutor, who upon review of it obtained a felony indictment. The defendant's subsequent felony conviction was overturned on appeal on the theory that the more serious charge was barred under *Blackledge* even absent proof of actual vindictiveness. The Supreme Court disagreed and reversed.

The *Goodwin* majority, characterizing *Blackledge* as a case in which the Court "found it necessary to 'presume' an improper

3. See § 13.4.

4. 417 U.S. 21, 94 S.Ct. 2098, 40 L.Ed.2d 628 (1974).

5. 395 U.S. 711, 89 S.Ct. 2072, 23 L.Ed.2d 656 (1969), discussed in § 27.1(c).

6. In Thigpen v. Roberts, 468 U.S. 27, 104 S.Ct. 2916, 82 L.Ed.2d 23 (1984), where the relevant facts were essentially identical to those in *Blackledge* except that in the instant case the first trial was the responsibility of the county prosecutor while the indictment and trial on the felony was the responsibility of the district attorney, the Court noted: "It might be argued that if two different prosecutors are involved, a presumption of vindictiveness, which arises in part from assumptions about the individual's personal stake in the proceedings, is inappropriate. * * * On the other hand, to the extent the presumption reflects 'institutional pressure that * * * might * * * subconsciously motivate a vindictive prosecutorial * * * response to a defendant's exercise of his right to obtain a retrial of a decided question,' * * * it does not hinge on the continued involvement of a particular individual. A district attorney burdened with the retrial of an already-convicted defendant might be no less vindictive because he did not bring the initial prosecution." But the Court then found it unnecessary to "determine the correct rule when two independent prosecutors are involved," for here the county prosecutor participated fully in the later proceedings, as was his statutory duty, and thus "the addition of the district attorney to the prosecutorial team changes little."

7. 457 U.S. 368, 102 S.Ct. 2485, 73 L.Ed.2d 74 (1982).

vindictive motive," concluded that such a presumption was "not warranted in this case" because actual vindictiveness was so unlikely on these facts. One major consideration, the Court explained, was "the timing of the prosecutor's action in this case":

> There is good reason to be cautious before adopting an inflexible presumption of prosecutorial vindictiveness in a pretrial setting. In the course of preparing a case for trial, the prosecutor may uncover additional information that suggests a basis for further prosecution or he simply may come to realize that information possessed by the State has a broader significance. At this stage of the proceedings, the prosecutor's assessment of the proper extent of prosecution may not have crystallized. In contrast, once a trial begins—and certainly by the time a conviction has been obtained—it is much more likely that the State has discovered and assessed all of the information against an accused and has made a determination, on the basis of that information, of the extent to which he should be prosecuted. Thus, a change in the charging decision made after an initial trial is completed is much more likely to be improperly motivated than is a pretrial decision.

A second consideration which the *Goodwin* Court deemed relevant in determining the reach of the *Blackledge* rule was the "nature of the right asserted" by the defendant:

> As compared to the complete trial *de novo* at issue in *Blackledge,* a jury trial—as opposed to a bench trial—does not require duplicative expenditures of prosecutorial resources before a final judgment may be obtained. Moreover, unlike the trial judge in *Pearce,* no party is asked "to do over what it thought it had already done correctly." A prosecutor has no "personal stake" in a bench trial and thus no reason to engage in "self-vindication" upon a defendant's request for a jury trial. Perhaps most importantly, the institutional bias against the retrial of a decided question that supported the decisions in *Pearce* and *Blackledge* simply has no counterpart in this case.

It thus appears unlikely that the *Blackledge* prophylactic rule has any application whatsoever in a pretrial setting. (There is some dispute as to whether the *Blackledge* prophylactic rule applies beyond the pretrial setting when there was not a conviction and appeal.)

In a case falling within *Blackledge,* where again the defendant is not obligated to prove actual vindictiveness, should the prosecutor be allowed to make some showing that there was a valid reason for his "adjustment" of the charges against the defendant? In *Pearce,* on which *Blackledge* is grounded, the Court held a judge could impose a higher sentence on retrial only if based upon "identifiable conduct on the part of the defendant occurring after the time of the original sentencing proceeding." This very strict rule, not even allowing a higher sentence on retrial based upon very relevant preexisting facts simply not brought to the attention of the judge at the first trial (e.g., an earlier conviction of the defendant for some other crime), was deemed necessary "to assure the absence of" an improper motivation. If that approach were carried over to all *Blackledge*-type cases, where the concern is with prosecutorial rather than judicial vindictiveness, then there would likewise be only one situation in which a higher charge would be permitted. Significantly, it is the one situation specifically mentioned by the Court in *Blackledge:* where the prosecutor has "shown that it was impossible to proceed on the more serious charge at the outset," as where the defendant was originally tried for assault and battery but was later tried for murder after the victim died.

The courts have not held the line there, however, which is none too surprising in light of intervening events. The Supreme Court has now taken a broader view of *Pearce* [8] and

8. In Wasman v. United States, 468 U.S. 559, 104 S.Ct. 3217, 82 L.Ed.2d 424 (1984), concerning the *Pearce* rule and thus discussed more fully in § 26.1(c), a four-Justice plurality asserted that both *Pearce* and *Blackledge* involve only a presumption of vindictiveness and that "where the presumption applies, the sentencing authority or the prosecutor must rebut the presumption that an increased sentence or charge resulted from vindictiveness." Five members of the Court declined to join that part of the opinion because, as Justice Powell put it, the *Pearce–Blackledge* presumption "is not simply concerned with actual vindictiveness, but also was intended to protect against reasonable apprehension of vindictiveness that could deter a defendant" from exercising his rights.

has also asserted somewhat ambiguously that "the *Blackledge* presumption is rebuttable" [9] and "could be overcome by objective evidence justifying the prosecutor's action." [10] But there is not complete agreement as to what other showings by the prosecutor will suffice. One approach, apparently limited to where the prosecutor has added charges, is merely to require the prosecutor to present a nonvindictive reason. This approach is objectionable because it makes it too easy to conceal actual vindictiveness and creates an atmosphere in which other defendants will be most reluctant to exercise their rights. Under another approach it is necessary that the prosecutor dispel any appearance of prosecutorial vindictiveness. At least if taken literally, this seems a too demanding test, for an appearance of vindictiveness arises every time a defendant asserts a right and a prosecutor subsequently takes a position contrary to the defendant's interests. An attractive middle ground is provided by *United States v. Andrews*,[11] which holds that in the case of added counts the question is "whether a reasonable person would think there existed a realistic likelihood of vindictiveness," so that the prosecutor must come up with an "objective explanation" for his actions (e.g., governmental discovery of previously unknown evidence). This approach (1) takes account of the due process value stressed in *Blackledge* that defendants be "freed of apprehension of such a retaliatory motivation" by the prosecutor; (2) is a realistic way to police vindictiveness, for a determination of actual motivation (as the Court said in *Pearce*) would "be extremely difficult to prove in any individual case"; and (3) allows the judge to avoid the necessity of either allowing the extra charge or making an explicit finding of prosecutorial bad faith.

In any event, the situation is quite different in a case which is governed by *Goodwin* rather than *Blackledge,* for the Court in the former case said that when the "presumption of vindictiveness" is not applicable it is then necessary for the defendant to "prove objectively that the prosecutor's charging decision was motivated by a desire to punish him for doing something that the law plainly allowed him to do." The Court made it quite clear that it would be most difficult for the defendant to meet this burden.

As for the "more serious charge" element of *Blackledge,* in that case it was a shift from misdemeanor assault to felony assault which, the Court noted, subjected defendant "to a significantly increased potential period of incarceration." The charge is "more serious" for *Blackledge* purposes even when the change is only to a higher minimum sentence, when the prosecutor has increased the number of charges, and when the new charge entails more serious collateral consequences. But, where the charges are not more severe in the above senses, it is not objectionable that the later charge is different in a way which enhances the probability of conviction.

But in Texas v. McCullough, 475 U.S. 134, 106 S.Ct. 976, 89 L.Ed.2d 104 (1986), also discussed more fully in § 26.-1(c), a majority of the Court made it clear that "even if the *Pearce* presumption were to apply here" it could be overcome "by objective information * * * justifying the increased sentence."

9. Thigpen v. Roberts, 468 U.S. 27, 104 S.Ct. 2916, 82 L.Ed.2d 23 (1984) (a footnote observation which, however, cites back to the footnote in *Blackledge* referring to the situation where it was impossible to proceed on the more serious charge originally).

10. United States v. Goodwin, 457 U.S. 368, 102 S.Ct. 2485, 73 L.Ed.2d 74 (1982) (a footnote observation which, however, is followed by quotation of the footnote in *Blackledge* referring to the situation where it was impossible to proceed on the more serious charge originally). In Wasman v. United States, 468 U.S. 559, 104 S.Ct. 3217, 82 L.Ed.2d 424 (1984), concerning the *Pearce* rule and thus discussed more fully in § 27.1(c), a four-Justice plurality asserted that both *Pearce* and *Blackledge* involve only a presumption of vindictiveness and that "where the presumption applies, the sentencing authority or the prosecutor must rebut the presumption that an increased sentence or charge resulted from vindictiveness." Five members of the Court declined to join that part of the opinion because, as Justice Powell put it, the *Pearce–Blackledge* presumption "is not simply concerned with actual vindictiveness, but also was intended to protect against reasonable apprehension of vindictiveness that could deter a defendant" from exercising his rights.

11. 633 F.2d 449 (6th Cir.1980).

Chapter 14

THE PRELIMINARY HEARING

Table of Sections

§ 14.1 Functions of the Preliminary Hearing

(a) Screening. The preliminary hearing, also known as the "preliminary examination" or the "probable cause" or "bindover" hearing, is a judicial proceeding, commonly conducted by a magistrate and available only in felony prosecutions. At that proceeding, the prosecution in an open and adversary hearing must establish that there is sufficient evidence supporting its charge to "bind the case over" to the next stage in the process (either review by the grand jury or the filing of an information in the trial court). In determining whether the prosecution has made such a showing, the magistrate provides an independent screening of the prosecution's decision to charge. Indeed, most courts view this screening objective as the sole legally cognizable purpose of the preliminary hearing. The importance of this screening in the overall functioning of the criminal justice process has frequently been noted by appellate courts. Preliminary hearing screening is said to serve to prevent hasty, malicious, improvident, and oppressive prosecutions, to protect the person charged from open and public accusations of crime, to avoid both for the defendant and the public the expense of a public trial, and to save the defendant from the humiliation and anxiety involved in public prosecution, and to discover whether or not there are substantial grounds upon which a prosecution may be based.[1]

The actual effectiveness of the preliminary hearing screening in achieving these ends is a matter of some dispute. Commentators and courts have offered arguments and statistics on both sides. Fruitful evaluation of their conclusions is made especially difficult, however, by substantial variations in the hearing's structure and operation from one jurisdiction to another (and sometimes, in its operation from one court to another in the same jurisdiction). Studies of the preliminary hearing in different jurisdictions have produced, for example, quite disparate statistics on preliminary hearing dispositions. The percentage of dismissals to the total number of hearings ranged from 2% to more than 30%.[2] Equally significant differences were found for the percentage of cases in which the magistrate's bindover was restricted to a lesser offense than that originally charged.

A variety of differences among jurisdictions have been cited as having a possible bearing on the disparate rates of dismissals and reductions. Those differences relate not only to the legal standards governing the preliminary hearing, but also to the institutional structure and local traditions that influence the participants in the hearing. Among the differences mentioned are the following: (1) whether prosecutorial screening before the case reaches the preliminary hearing stage is extensive (as in jurisdictions where 30–50% of the cases presented by the police do not result in the filing of charges) or is superficial or not even utilized for all but exceptional cases; (2) whether prosecutors are assigned horizontally to cases (with different prosecutors responsible for initial screening, preliminary hearing presentation, and trial) or vertically (with the same prosecutor responsible for the case from initial presentation to final disposition); (3) where the prosecutor may bypass the preliminary hearing by taking the case directly to the grand jury [see § 14.2(b)–(d)], whether the prosecutor regularly uses the bypass alternative (so that preliminary hearings are used in only a small group of cases) or regularly utilizes the preliminary hearing; (4) whether the use of the bypass procedure is tied to the strength of the particular case or to unrelated, administrative concerns; (5) whether the magistrates conducting the hearings are lay persons or lawyer/judges; (6) whether the magistrates operate under heavy or light caseloads; (7) whether the caseload at the trial level necessarily precludes trial of all cases which could justifiably be boundover (thereby encouraging the magistrate to reduce charges in cases more appropriately disposed of at the misdemeanor level); (8) whether cases are settled by plea bargains prior to the

§ 14.1

1. Thies v. State, 178 Wis. 98, 189 N.W. 539 (1922). Two related functions of preliminary hearing screening are also mentioned: (1) ensuring that the defendant who has been unjustifiably charged will be promptly released from custody or, if he made bail, from the conditions of that bail; and (2) requiring reduction of excessive charges and thereby serving as a check against the prosecutorial practice of "overcharging" in anticipation of plea negotiations.

2. Perhaps a better statistical measure of the success of the preliminary hearing in weeding out groundless prosecutions would be the ultimate disposition of cases that are boundover at the preliminary hearing. Here, however, the statistics are clouded by alternative hypotheses. In many jurisdictions, a substantial percentage of such cases are dismissed on the motion of the prosecutor, but the precise grounds for such dismissals ordinarily need not be stated by the prosecutor, see § 13.3(c), and they may be attributed to various factors other than a weakness in the prosecution's case (which itself may have developed after the bindover), see § 13.2(c). Most jurisdictions do not keep statistics on the percentage of cases dismissed by the trial judge as failing to present sufficient evidence to reach the jury, and the standard of evidentiary sufficiency applied here tends, in any event, to be higher than that applied at the grand jury, see § 14.3(a). Where the jurisdiction has a very high percentage of convictions for all boundover cases, that statistic may suggest effective screening, but it also has limitations. Many of these convictions may be by negotiated guilty pleas to lesser offenses, and those reductions may or may not have been influenced by weaknesses in the prosecution's evidence that would have produced a lesser charge in the first instance with more effective preliminary hearing screening.

preliminary hearing stage or plea bargaining begins and cases are settled largely after the case is boundover to the trial level; (9) whether defense counsel regularly insist upon a preliminary hearing even in open and shut cases (largely to obtain discovery) or usually waive the hearing in such cases; (10) whether the evidentiary standard governing the magistrate's decision to bindover is essentially the same probable cause standard applied on the issuance of an arrest warrant or a standard comparable to that imposed by a trial judge in determining whether there is sufficient evidence to send a case to the jury [see § 14.3(a)]; (11) whether the prosecutor must meet the bindover standard through evidence that would be admissible at trial or may rely instead on hearsay and other evidence generally inadmissible at trial [see § 14.4(b)]; (12) whether the prosecution, even though not required to do so in order to satisfy the bindover standard, follows the practice of presenting all of its key witnesses, or instead seeks to limit defense discovery and reduce the burden on its witnesses by introducing just enough evidence to meet the bindover standard; (13) whether the magistrate has the same leeway as a trial court factfinder in judging credibility or can only reject inherently incredible testimony [see § 14.3(b)]; (14) whether the scope of permissible defense presentations is comparable to that at trial or restricted through limitations on such matters as the presentation of affirmative defenses or the range of cross-examinations [see § 14.4(c)(d)]; (15) whether the practical impact of a magistrate's order of dismissal is to end the case unless new evidence is uncovered, or the prosecutor frequently reinitiates prosecution without additional evidence by either taking the case to the grand jury or refiling when another judge is sitting as preliminary hearing magistrate [see § 14.3(c)].

Assuming that substantially different dismissal and reduction rates for two jurisdictions are explained in large part by one or more of the differences noted above, depending upon the nature of the influential factor, the lesson suggested will be quite different. As for some differences, such as differences in the extent of pre-hearing prosecutorial screening, their impact might suggest that the disparate rates do not reflect significant differences in the effectiveness of preliminary hearing screening, but rather differences in the types of cases that reach the preliminary hearing. As for others, such as caseload or institutional factors that promote efforts to sharply reduce the number of cases that reach the felony trial courts, their impact might suggest that rate differentials are attributable to one jurisdiction adopting a screening determination that goes substantially beyond assessment of the technical sufficiency of the evidence. Here, magistrates, with the prosecutor's acquiescence, may be looking as well to other factors that reflect upon the "prosecutorial worth" of the offense (e.g., the likelihood of jury sympathy that could produce an acquittal, the comparative seriousness of the crime, and the need for criminal sanctions), even though legally the only issue for the court is evidentiary sufficiency. Finally, as to those factors that relate to the character of the evaluation of evidentiary strength (such as the requirement of admissible evidence), a correlation between more rigorous standards and higher rates here would suggest that the disparate rates do reflect significant differences in the effectiveness of the preliminary hearing in serving its basic screening function.

(b) Discovery. In meeting the evidentiary standard for a bindover, the prosecutor will necessarily provide the defense with some discovery of the prosecution's case. The defendant may obtain even more discovery by cross-examining the prosecution's witnesses at the hearing and by subpoenaing other potential trial witnesses to testify as defense witnesses at the hearing. The extent of the discovery obtained in this manner will depend upon several factors, including: (1) whether the prosecution can rely entirely on hearsay reports and thereby sharply limit the number of witnesses it presents [see § 14.4(b)]; (2) whether, even assuming hearsay cannot be used, the bindover standard may be satisfied by the presentation of a minimal amount of testimony on each element of the offense [see

§ 14.3(a)]; (3) whether, notwithstanding the ease with which the standard is met, the prosecution still follows a general practice of presenting most of its case; (4) whether the defendant is limited, both in cross-examination and in the calling of witnesses, to direct rebuttal of material presented by the prosecution [see § 14.4(c), (d)]; (5) whether the defendant is willing to bear the tactical costs that may be incurred in utilizing his subpoena and cross-examination authority for discovery purposes.[3]

In many jurisdictions, these factors combine to provide preliminary hearing discovery that is of quite limited use. The importance of such limited discovery to the defendant will depend in part on the alternatives available for obtaining the same or even broader discovery and the comparative costs of those alternatives. Where the identity of prosecution witnesses and the content of their prior statements to the police are automatically available under state discovery rules, along with all material physical evidence, the discovery available through the preliminary hearing tends to be costly and of little significance. On the other hand, where discovery rules give the defense discovery of only limited aspects of the prosecution's case, and the defense counsel can otherwise learn of likely prosecution testimony only by finding and interviewing (if they are willing) prospective prosecution witnesses, the preliminary hearing may be so important a discovery tool as to easily justify going through a hearing notwithstanding the certainty of a bindover. Moreover, even where state law provides extensive discovery, if that discovery is not available until after the critical time for plea settlements has passed, the preliminary hearing may still serve as the primary discovery vehicle for the substantial percentage of cases resolved by guilty pleas.

For all but a few jurisdictions, the defense discovery available through the hearing is treated as an incidental byproduct rather than a basic function of the hearing. Indeed, if the defense's use of cross-examination or subpoena authority seems aimed basically at discovery, rather than at challenging the sufficiency of the prosecution's evidence, the magistrate may prohibit such use.[4] So too, where a magistrate's error is found to have had no bearing on defendant's right to a fair finding on evidentiary sufficiency, a defense showing that the error cost it the opportunity for discovery will not justify relief.[5] Both legislatures and courts have been unreceptive to the suggestion that discovery should be recognized as a basic function of the preliminary hearing and its procedures shaped accordingly. The preliminary hearing, it is noted, imposes significant burdens on witnesses and is a costly use of the time of prosecutor, defense counsel, and magistrate. It makes no sense to expand its use to serve a function that can be fulfilled more expeditiously and with more appropriate timing through traditional discovery procedures.

(c) Future Impeachment. Extensive cross-examination of prosecution witnesses at the preliminary hearing may be of value to the defense even though there is little likelihood of successfully challenging the prosecution's showing of evidentiary sufficiency and little to be gained by way of discovery. This is because, as the Supreme Court has noted, "the skilled interrogation of witnesses [at the preliminary examination] by an experienced lawyer can fashion a vital impeachment tool for use in cross-examination of the State's witnesses at the trial." [6] In many instances, witnesses are more likely to make damaging admissions or contradictory statements at the preliminary hearing because they are less thoroughly briefed for that proceeding than

3. Among those costs are the preservation of damaging testimony that might not otherwise be available at trial (see subsection d infra), the "strengthening" of the memories of prosecution witnesses as to details that might have been forgotten by the time of trial, and the possibility of "educating" the prosecution as to gaps in its case. The defense counsel also may find that efforts to obtain discovery through an amiable and far-ranging cross-examination work at cross-purposes with efforts to prepare for future impeachment (see subsection (c) infra).

4. See § 14.4(c).

5. See § 14.4(e).

6. Coleman v. Alabama, 399 U.S. 1, 90 S.Ct. 1999, 26 L.Ed.2d 387 (1970).

they are for trial. Also, with respect to some witnesses, the more they say before trial, the more likely that there will be some inconsistency between their trial testimony and their previous statements. Arguably, the jury may view such inconsistencies as more damaging to the witness' credibility when the inconsistency is with preliminary hearing testimony, as opposed to prior statements given to the police, since the preliminary hearing testimony was given under oath in a judicial setting. Moreover, in some jurisdictions, the use of the inconsistent statement is not limited to impeachment; it may be used as well as substantive evidence.[7]

Cross-examination designed to lay the foundation for future impeachment carries with it certain dangers for the defense. If the cross-examination focuses too much on potential weaknesses in the witness' testimony, it may educate the witness as to these weaknesses. The witness may rehabilitate himself for the trial and state that at the hearing he was confused, but that everything is now clear in his mind. If the witness is one who otherwise might "soften" his view of the facts as time passes and his emotional involvement lessens, extensive cross-examination at the preliminary hearing may only harden his position and make him less able to retreat to a more friendly position.

(d) The Perpetuation of Testimony. Preliminary hearing testimony traditionally has been admitted at trial as substantive evidence, under the "prior testimony" exception to the hearsay rule, where the witness is not available to testify at trial. Thus, the hearing perpetuates the testimony of witnesses, ensuring that it may be used even if the witness should die, disappear, or otherwise become unavailable to testify.[8] While the Supreme Court has stated that a major advantage of the hearing for the defense is its availability to "preserve testimony favorable to the accused of a witness who does not appear at the trial,"[9] the hearing is not commonly used by the defense for this purpose. For reasons discussed in § 14.4(d), the defense rarely will have its own witnesses testify at the preliminary hearing. Accordingly, the perpetuation of testimony is of practical significance primarily as it relates to prosecution witnesses, and the possibility of perpetuation tends to be viewed by the defense as a negative feature of the hearing.

The admission of the preliminary hearing testimony of a prosecution witness who is unavailable at trial (and therefore is not subject to trial cross-examination) must be reconciled with the defendant's Sixth Amendment right of confrontation. *California v. Green*[10] established the basic guidelines for admitting such testimony consistent with defendant's Sixth Amendment right. The Court there upheld the constitutionality of admitting preliminary hearing testimony over a defense objection that it should not be admissible where the prosecution witness was "unavail-

7. See California v. Green discussed infra following note 10 (upholding the constitutionality of such use where the witness testified at trial, as well as where the witness is unavailable); E. Cleary (ed.), McCormick on Evidence, § 251 (3d ed. 1984).

8. Fed.R.Evid. 804(a) sets forth the traditional grounds of unavailability: " 'Unavailability as a witness' includes situations in which the declarant: (1) is exempted by ruling of the court on the ground of privilege from testifying concerning the subject matter of his statement; or (2) persists in refusing to testify concerning the subject matter of his statement despite an order of the court to do so; or (3) testifies to a lack of memory of the subject matter of his statement; or (4) is unable to be present or to testify at the hearing because of death or then existing physical or mental illness or infirmity; or (5) is absent from the hearing and the proponent of his statement has been unable to procure his attendance * * * by process or other reasonable means. * * *" It should be noted in connection with this 5th ground that persons located outside the trial jurisdiction will not for that reason alone be "unavailable." If his whereabouts are known, a witness located in another state ordinarily may be subjected to compulsory process under the Uniform Act to Secure The Attendance of Witnesses from Without A State In Criminal Proceedings, 11 U.L.A. 2 (1974).

9. Coleman v. Alabama, supra note 6 discussed in § 14.4(a). A pretrial deposition also may be used to preserve the witness' testimony, but most jurisdictions allow its use for that purpose only on a showing of good cause to believe the witness will be unavailable. See § 20.2(e). The preliminary hearing offers the advantage of perpetuating the testimony of witnesses who unexpectedly become unavailable, as well as eliminating the burden of establishing likely unavailability that ordinarily must be met to obtain judicial authorization for use of the deposition.

10. 399 U.S. 149, 90 S.Ct. 1930, 26 L.Ed.2d 489 (1970).

able" solely because of a claimed loss of memory. The defendant in *Green* had been charged with furnishing marijuana to a minor, Porter. When Porter was called to testify, he was evasive and uncooperative on the stand, claiming a lapse of memory. The prosecution then introduced two prior statements of Porter, including his preliminary hearing testimony, "to prove the truth of the matter asserted in the statements." The state court held that admission of these statements as substantive evidence violated defendant's right to confrontation, but the Supreme Court reversed.

The Court in *Green* initially held that if Porter was subject to cross-examination as to the statements at the trial, then the confrontation clause was not violated by admission of the statements as substantive evidence. The Court added, however, that there was a question as to whether Porter was subject to effective cross-examination at trial in light of his lapse of memory. It accordingly went on to consider the admissibility of the preliminary hearing testimony on the assumption that Porter was an "unavailable" witness at trial:

> * * * [P]orter's statement at the preliminary hearing had already been given under circumstances closely approximating those that surround the typical trial. Porter was under oath; respondent was represented by counsel—the same counsel in fact who later represented him at the trial; respondent had every opportunity to cross-examine Porter as to his statement; and the proceedings were conducted before a judicial tribunal, equipped to provide a judicial record of the hearings. * * * In the present case respondent's counsel does not appear to have been significantly limited in any way in the scope or nature of his cross-examination of the witness Porter at the preliminary hearing. If Porter had died or was otherwise unavailable, the Confrontation Clause would not have been violated by admitting his testimony given at the preliminary hearing—the right of cross-examination then afforded provides substantial compliance with the purposes behind the confrontation requirement, as long as the declarant's inability to give live testimony is in no way the fault of the State. * * * As in the case where the witness is physically unproducible, the State here has made every effort to introduce its evidence through the live testimony of the witness; it produced Porter at trial, swore him as a witness, and tendered him for cross-examination. Whether Porter * * * claimed a loss of memory, claimed his privilege against compulsory self-incrimination or simply refused to answer, nothing in the Confrontation Clause prohibited the State from also relying on his prior testimony to prove its case against Green.

As various lower courts have noted, *Green* requires "an opportunity to effectively cross-examine and merely providing an opportunity to cross-examine at the preliminary hearing is not per se adequate opportunity." Ordinarily, however, unless the defense counsel was limited by "unusual circumstances," the opportunity for cross-examination provided in the typical preliminary hearing will be deemed sufficient. In his *Green* dissent, Justice Brennan cited a series of factors that might inhibit cross-examination at the typical preliminary hearing. Since the issue presented there is one of probable cause, counsel may view cross-examination to be of little value. Counsel may also be concerned that cross-examination will give the prosecutor discovery, that the magistrate will not look kindly on extending the length of the hearing, and that the short time available for preparation makes cross-examination too risky at this point. The Court majority did not find persuasive Justice Brennan's reliance on these potential restraints, noting that Justice Brennan nonetheless acknowledged that the preliminary hearing testimony could be used where the witness was unavailable for reasons (e.g., death) that prevented his appearance.

In *Ohio v. Roberts,*[11] however, the Court raised the possibility that *Green* would be limited to cases in which the opportunity to cross-examine had been extensively utilized. The Court there held that *Green* permitted admission of the preliminary hearing testimo-

11. 448 U.S. 56, 100 S.Ct. 2531, 65 L.Ed.2d 597 (1980).

ny of an unavailable prosecution witness who had been called by the defense at the preliminary hearing, but had been examined, in effect, as a hostile witness. The Court noted that counsel, in his "direct examination," had challenged the witness' perception of events and her veracity, and had not been limited "in any way" in this line of questioning. The end result was, as in *Green,* a "substantial compliance with the purposes behind the confrontation requirement." The Court added that, in light of the facts before it, there was no need to determine whether *Green* applied where a defense counsel had not actually cross-examined the witness or had engaged in only "de minimus questioning." It acknowledged that passages in *Green* "suggest that the opportunity to cross-examine at the preliminary hearing—even absent actual cross-examination—satisfies the Confrontation Clause." Yet, the Court there also recognized that "defense counsel in fact had cross-examined Porter." As defense counsel here had acted similarly, it would leave for another day the question of whether "the mere opportunity to cross-examine render[s] the prior testimony admissible."

(e) **Other Functions.** In a particular jurisdiction the preliminary hearing may be utilized to serve other incidental functions, such as to gain reduction of bail or other terms of pretrial release. This is particularly true where bail is set at the initial appearance largely on the basis of a schedule tied to the offense charged, and the preliminary hearing provides the magistrate with his first extensive examination of the facts of the individual case.

The preliminary hearing also may serve as an integral part of the plea bargaining process, particularly where negotiations have been undertaken prior to the hearing. The hearing may then operate as a valuable "educational process" for the defendant who is not persuaded by his counsel's opinion that the prosecution has such a strong case that a negotiated plea is in the defendant's best interest. In other jurisdictions, the preliminary hearing may serve as an occasion for the initiation of plea bargaining. As discussed in § 14.4(b), the hearing in some jurisdictions offers the initial point at which the constitutional validity of police acquisition of evidence may be challenged, and under some circumstances, it may offer sufficient advantages over the pretrial motion to suppress that defense counsel will insist upon a preliminary examination for this purpose alone. The preliminary hearing also may be utilized to establish mitigating circumstances that can then be presented at sentencing through the preliminary hearing transcript.

§ 14.2 Defendant's Right to a Preliminary Hearing

(a) **The Federal Constitution.** In *Hurtado v. California,*[1] the Court held that the Fifth Amendment guarantee of prosecution by grand jury indictment was not a fundamental right applicable to the states through the due process clause of the Fourteenth Amendment. The procedure challenged in that case provided for charging by prosecutor's information rather than by indictment, but it also required a magistrate's determination of probable cause at a preliminary hearing. In *Lem Woon v. Oregon,*[2] however, the Court was faced with a procedure permitting direct filing of an information without "any examination or commitment by a magistrate * * * or any verification other than [the] prosecutor's official oath." A unanimous Supreme Court held that the lack of a preliminary hearing caused no due process difficulties. Having held earlier in *Hurtado* that a grand jury indictment was not required, the Court was "unable to see upon what theory it can be held that an examination or the opportunity for one, prior to the formal accusation by the district attorney, is obligatory upon the States." The Court has continued to adhere to the *Lem Woon* holding, and in *Gerstein v. Pugh,*[3] rejected the contention that a preliminary hearing was required by the Fourth

§ 14.2

1. 110 U.S. 516, 4 S.Ct. 111, 28 L.Ed. 232 (1884).
2. 229 U.S. 586, 33 S.Ct. 783, 57 L.Ed. 1340 (1913).
3. 420 U.S. 103, 95 S.Ct. 854, 43 L.Ed.2d 54 (1975). See also § 3.5 at note 6.

Amendment. Though the Court in *Gerstein* did hold that a reasonably prompt "judicial determination of probable cause [is] a prerequisite to extended restraint on liberty following [a warrantless] arrest," it concluded this could be done in a nonadversary proceeding. (Though a state could use its preliminary hearing procedure as a means of meeting this Fourth Amendment requirement, most have not done so, for a preliminary hearing often cannot be scheduled promptly enough to meet the *Gerstein* mandate.)

While holding that the "prosecutor's assessment of probable cause is not sufficient alone to justify restraint on liberty following arrest" (and therefore at least an ex parte judicial determination was necessary), the *Gerstein* Court added: "[W]e do not imply that the accused is entitled to judicial oversight or review of the decision to prosecute. Instead, we adhere to the Court's prior holding that a judicial hearing is not prerequisite to prosecution by information. * * * *Lem Woon v. Oregon.*" Although the *Lem Woon* precedent is well established, such a brusque rejection of a possible constitutional requirement of judicial screening for a serious charge which has not otherwise been screened by a neutral body (e.g., the grand jury) may seem surprising in light of the growth in due process since *Lem Woon* was decided. As the *Gerstein* Court itself noted, in civil cases, a series of modern due process rulings have required some form of judicial screening in connection with the imposition of various pretrial restraints.[4] In light of the burdens of accusation and litigation imposed upon a criminal defendant,[5] could not due process similarly require screening by some neutral body—court or grand jury—to ensure that there at least be some minimal evidence supporting the charge? Of course, through its Fourth Amendment ruling, *Gerstein* ensured that there would be at least the neutral screening that comes with a magistrate's ex parte determination of probable cause in all cases in which the defendants are subjected to a "significant restraint" on their liberty.[6] That protection, however, would not extend to cases in which the defendants are charged by summons or arrested without a warrant and promptly released on their own recognizance. Here, *Gerstein* indicates that the constitution does not preclude forcing a defendant to trial without any type of neutral body determination that there is some basis for the charge against him.[7]

While the constitution does not require that the defendant be afforded a preliminary hearing, once a jurisdiction provides for a preliminary hearing, it may not then restrict the defendant's right to that hearing in a manner that would violate constitutional protections. Thus, *Coleman v. Alabama* [8] held that a state cannot grant defendants a right to a preliminary hearing and then refuse to appoint counsel to represent an indigent defendant who exercises that right. For reasons discussed at § 14.4(a), *Coleman* held that the preliminary hearing, though not itself constitutionally required, is a "critical stage" in the criminal prosecution rendering applicable a defendant's Sixth Amendment right to counsel. So

4. See e.g., North Georgia Finishing, Inc. v. Di–Chem., Inc., 419 U.S. 601, 95 S.Ct. 719, 42 L.Ed.2d 751 (1975) (garnishment of bank account); Mitchell v. W.T. Grant Co., 416 U.S. 600, 94 S.Ct. 1895, 40 L.Ed.2d 406 (1974) (sequestration of personal property).

5. See § 1.6(e).

6. The *Gerstein* ruling does not require a post-arrest determination of probable cause where the defendant had been arrested pursuant to a warrant, but the defendant then would have received a prior judicial determination of probable cause in the issuance of the arrest warrant. The *Gerstein* Court also noted that warrants could be issued by a magistrate simply on the basis of the return of an indictment, but the charge there would have been screened by the grand jury. The Court reasoned that the historical role of the grand jury in "protecting individuals from unjust prosecution" allowed the "grand jury's judgment [to] substitute for that of a neutral and detached magistrate."

7. Under state law as it exists today, this tends to occur as a regular matter only on a misdemeanor charge. As discussed in subsections (c) and (d) infra, for felony charges, all but a handful of jurisdictions require screening either by a grand jury or by a magistrate at a preliminary hearing, and the handful that allow direct filing without those screening procedures impose alternative screening safeguards that allow for a form of judicial screening. For misdemeanors, however, the only form of screening ordinarily required is the ex parte determination of probable cause for an arrest where *Gerstein* applies.

8. See § 14.4(a) at note 1.

too, by analogy to cases dealing with other rights that have only a state law grounding, due process would prohibit prosecutorial vindictiveness in charging or judicial vindictiveness in sentencing that was directed against a defendant who exercised his right to a preliminary hearing under state law.[9] A state also could not engage in discrimination that would violate the equal protection clause in determining which groups of defendants will be entitled to a preliminary hearing. Thus, where the prosecutor has authority under state law to bypass a preliminary hearing by taking a case directly to the grand jury,[10] a defendant may challenge that bypass tactic on equal protection grounds by showing intentional discrimination based on an arbitrary classification, analogous to the showing required on a discriminatory prosecution claim.[11]

(b) The Federal Practice. In the federal system, the Fifth Amendment requires grand jury screening (unless waived) in all felony cases. Nonetheless, federal law has for many years granted to the felony defendant a right to a preliminary hearing. That right was established because, in many parts of the country, charges were not presented before the grand jury until weeks after a defendant's arrest. An earlier review procedure was needed to ensure that a person was not held in custody, or subjected to the continued burdens associated with release on bail, without a fairly prompt prosecutorial showing of probable cause. While the magistrate made a probable cause determination where a warrant was issued, the *Gerstein* requirement of a similar determination for warrantless arrests had not yet been imposed, and the warrant determination was, in any event, based solely on affidavits.

The preliminary hearing screening, however, remained subordinate to the eventual screening by the grand jury. Thus, where a grand jury indictment was issued prior to the time set for the preliminary hearing, the defendant's right to a hearing was "mooted." As one court noted:

> "The return of an indictment, which establishes probable cause, eliminates the need for a preliminary examination. * * * A post-indictment preliminary examination would be an empty ritual, as the government's burden of showing probable cause would be met merely by offering the indictment. Even if the [magistrate] disagreed with the grand jury, he could not undermine the authority of its finding." [12]

This position was later incorporated in the federal statutory and court rules provisions governing the preliminary hearing.[13]

Current federal law grants to the defendant a right to preliminary hearing when charged with any offense, other than a petty offense, which is to be tried by a judge of the district court. The defendant is informed of that right at his initial appearance before the magistrate, and if the defendant does not waive that right, the magistrate is directed to schedule a preliminary hearing. The hearing date must be set in accordance with the requirement that the hearing be held within a "reasonable time but in any event not later than 10 days following the initial appearance if the defendant is in custody and no later than 20 days if the defendant is not in custody." A proviso adds, however, that the "preliminary examination shall not be held if the defen-

9. See § 13.5(a), § 26.9.

10. See subsections (b), (c), and (d) infra.

11. See § 13.4. Applying their state equal protection guarantees, the California Supreme Court held that the preliminary hearing afforded the defendant so much greater screening protection than the grand jury that the bypass tactic inherently produced an equal protection violation, Hawkins v. Superior Court, 22 Cal.3d 584, 150 Cal.Rptr. 435, 586 P.2d 916 (1978), and the Oregon Supreme Court held that "a constitutional claim for equal treatment is made out when the accused shows that preliminary hearings are offered or denied to individual defendants, or to social, geographic, or other classes of defendants * * * purely haphazardly or otherwise in terms that have no satisfactory explanation," State v. Freeland, 295 Or. 367, 667 P.2d 509 (1983). However, the dominant view is that selectivity in the exercise of the bypass tactic only violates equal protection where the defendant can make the type of showing required under the Supreme Court's leading selective enforcement rulings, such as Wayte v. United States and Oyler v. Boles (discussed in § 13.4).

12. Sciortino v. Zampano, 385 F.2d 132 (2d Cir.1967).

13. 18 U.S.C.A. § 3060; Fed.R.Crim.P. 5(c), 5.1.

dant is indicted or if an information against the defendant is filed in the district court before the date set for the preliminary examination." Since a felony information can be filed only with the defendant's waiver of his Fifth Amendment right to prosecution by indictment, the key to the prosecutor's ability to "bypass" or "moot" the preliminary hearing without a defense waiver is the obtaining of grand jury indictment prior to the scheduled hearing.

In many federal districts, the impact of the bypass alternative has been to eliminate virtually all preliminary hearings. Where a grand jury sits daily and can promptly dispose of submitted cases, the U.S. Attorney may regularly moot scheduled preliminary hearings by obtaining prior indictments. Various U.S. Attorneys have been able to perfect this practice to the point where there are no more than one or two preliminary hearings for every hundred felonies processed. In other districts, it is more difficult to obtain indictments within the prescribed time limits and preliminary hearings are mooted somewhat less frequently. At one time it was common practice in some districts for magistrates to regularly grant extensions allowing the prosecutor to first obtain an indictment. The current federal law, however, prohibits extensions of time, without the consent of the defense, except "upon a showing that extraordinary circumstances exist and that delay is indispensable to the interests of justice."

(c) Indictment States. Nineteen states, as in the federal system, require prosecution by indictment (unless waived) for all felonies.[14] All of these "indictment states" also have statutes or court rules granting the defendant a right to a preliminary hearing within a specified period after his arrest. Although a few of these states prohibit or sharply restrict the prosecutor's authority to moot that right by obtaining a prior indictment, the common pattern is to allow bypassing without restriction. In most, the state preliminary hearing provision contains a proviso, identical to that in federal law, stating that the hearing shall not be held if an indictment is returned prior to the scheduled hearing. In others, that result has been reached by judicial ruling.

Though indictment states commonly grant prosecutors the same legal authority to bypass as is granted to federal prosecutors, state prosecutors tend to utilize that tactic far less frequently. In many state judicial districts, regular mooting would not be feasible since the grand jury's caseload is too heavy to permit prompt consideration of charges prior to the scheduled preliminary hearings. In districts where grand jury review readily can be obtained shortly after arrest, there tends to be more frequent mooting, but the practice varies. In some districts, prosecutors regularly bypass but recognize exceptions for certain types of cases. Like federal prosecutors, they see no reason to provide dual screening procedures, but unlike federal prosecutors, they regularly create exceptions when special circumstances would make a showing of proof in an open proceeding desirable from the prosecutor's perspective.[15] In other districts, the prosecutors take the opposite tact. Here, the general rule is to have a preliminary hearing first and then take the case to the grand jury, although bypassing will be used for a limited group of cases. This approach is sometimes the product of a tradition established when prompt grand jury review was not as readily available. It may also reflect the prosecutor's conclusion that the extra expenditure of effort will be offset in the long run by advantages

14. See § 15.1, note 8.

15. Those special circumstances can include: (1) perpetuating testimony of a witness who might well be unavailable at trial; (2) some special reason for putting a prosecution witness to the test of testifying in public; (3) promoting the victim's interest in pursuing the matter by presenting it in a public forum; (4) learning of the defense perspective as to the events involved where there is some uncertainty as to what actually happened and the defense has indicated a willingness to present its side of the story at the preliminary hearing; (5) gaining a further identification of the suspect by having the witness make that identification at the hearing; (6) promoting public confidence in a sensitive prosecutorial decision by having the evidence presented in a public forum and the decision to proceed ratified by a magistrate (or if the case is likely to be dismissed, by inviting dismissal in an open proceeding rather than a grand jury proceeding, where the prosecutor might be accused of having "dumped" the case due to political pressures).

gained from the preliminary hearing (e.g., the better preparation for trial of witnesses and prosecutors, and the facilitation of plea bargaining by impressing upon defendants the strength of the prosecutor's case).

Where the common practice is to go forward with the preliminary hearing, approaches vary in identifying those exceptional cases in which mooting will be utilized. Uniformly, the indictment will come first (with the preliminary hearing thereby precluded) on those charges that are developed through a grand jury investigation. Indeed, the indictments in such cases are often issued even before the defendant is arrested. The indictment will also come before arrest where the defendant is a fugitive or outside the jurisdiction. Beyond this, prosecutors differ as to the need for further exceptions. Some will bypass in particular cases or particular types of cases in which they find special justification for limiting the number of instances in which the victim will be forced to testify in public. Thus, a prosecutor's office may regularly bypass in all sex offense prosecutions. Some prosecutors will bypass where the preliminary hearing process would be protracted due to the number of exhibits or witnesses or the number of separate hearings that would have to be held for separate defendants. Thus, where a single agent is the key witness on a number of separate drug buys, the prosecutor may go directly to the grand jury (where the agent can testify as to all of the drug buys in a single presentation) rather than have the agent be forced to testify at each of the separate preliminary hearings that the individual defendants would demand. Finally, many prosecutors will bypass where they judge the discovery inherent in a preliminary examination to be too costly. Some will limit that judgment to the most pressing case for avoiding discovery, as where a key witness is an informer whose identity must be shielded until the last possible moment. Others also will bypass in particular types of cases likely to present an especially broad range of discovery (e.g., homicide prosecutions based on extensive circumstantial and forensic evidence), especially where that discovery would not be available under pretrial discovery procedures or would be available only if the defense granted reciprocal discovery to the prosecution. Critics of the bypass tactic, viewing the grand jury as by far the easier screening procedure, suggest that prosecutors are most likely to bypass where the prosecution's case is weak, but available studies do not support that contention.

(d) Information States. Almost two-thirds of the states permit felony prosecutions to be brought by either information or indictment (although several in this group allow only for indictments for capital or life-sentence felonies).[16] These states are commonly described as "information states" (although technically they are "option" states) because the overwhelming choice of prosecutors is to use the information alternative. All but a few of these states also provide for a preliminary hearing. Even among the information states, however, only a few give the defense an absolute right to a preliminary hearing by prohibiting bypassing. In those few states, if an indictment is first obtained (as where the charge arose out of a grand jury investigation), the indictment must be followed by a preliminary hearing at which the magistrate makes an independent determination of probable cause. In all of the remaining information states with a preliminary hearing, bypassing is allowable, although the routes may differ.

In most information states allowing a bypass, a preliminary hearing bindover (or defense waiver) is a prerequisite for prosecution by information. Thus, the only means of bypassing (without defense consent) is through prosecution by an indictment obtained prior to the scheduled preliminary hearing. In general, prosecutors in information states make infrequent use of the grand jury alternative. In some districts, the preliminary hearing is never mooted and in others the percentage of cases taken to the grand jury rarely exceeds 5%. There are some districts in certain information states, however, where

16. See § 15.1, notes 6 and 7.

the prosecutor will prefer the indictment to the information and preliminary hearings will be mooted in the vast majority of felony prosecutions. Where prosecutors engage in only occasional mooting, they usually use this route for many of the same reasons as the prosecutors in indictment states who bypass as the exception rather than the general rule. However, because the grand jury tends to be less readily available (not being a necessary part of the process), the prosecutors here generally will not recognize as broad a group of exceptional cases calling for bypassing.[17] In contrast, in those districts where prosecutors prefer the indictment, the tendency is to allow the preliminary hearing only where special circumstances make desirable an open presentation of the prosecution's evidence before trial.

A handful of information jurisdictions accept direct filing of an information without a preliminary hearing bindover. Some of these states provide for a preliminary hearing but allow a prosecutor to bypass by a direct filing prior to the scheduled hearing. Special safeguards are added to ensure that the information so filed has adequate evidentiary support. The direct filing procedure may require, for example, that the trial court approve the filing and that the information be accompanied by affidavits establishing probable cause. Another approach is to allow the defendant, after obtaining complete discovery, to move for dismissal on the ground that the evidence available to the prosecution, even if taken as undisputed, fails to establish a prima facie case. Other direct filing states have abolished the preliminary hearing and rely entirely upon the availability to defense of such a post-discovery motion to dismiss for insufficient evidence. That motion is utilized to screen in a fashion roughly analogous to the motion for summary judgment in civil cases.

(e) Waiver and Demand. Although a few jurisdictions condition the defendant's right to a preliminary hearing upon a timely demand for the hearing, the prevailing view is that the right can be lost only by a waiver reflecting a voluntary and knowledgeable choice by the defendant. To obtain a knowledgeable waiver, the magistrate ordinarily must explain the purpose of the hearing, the rights available at the hearing, and the nature of the charges on which the hearing would be held. Most states will not accept a waiver until the defendant either has waived his right to counsel or has been given the opportunity to consult with counsel, a position arguably mandated by the Constitution in light of *Coleman v. Alabama.*[18]

Practice manuals generally urge defense counsel not to waive a preliminary hearing unless circumstances suggest that the hearing would pose a substantial danger to the defense that outweighs its value. Such circumstances include: (1) an essential prosecution witness is able to testify at the preliminary hearing but may well be unavailable at trial; (2) a complainant appears likely to "mellow" with time if he is not required at this point to put his testimony "on the record;" (3) the preliminary hearing may add to adverse publicity that will make it difficult to obtain a fair trial;[19] (4) the preliminary hearing will call the prosecutor's attention to a curable defect in the prosecution's case that otherwise would not be noticed until trial, when it would be too late to correct it; and (5) the preliminary hearing will alert the prosecutor to the fact that the defendant is undercharged.

The potential value of the preliminary hearing to the defense might suggest that waiver of the hearing would be rare. In fact, waivers by the defense sometimes exceed fifty percent even in jurisdictions which provide quite extensive preliminary hearings. A variety of factors may influence the waiver rate in a particular jurisdiction, including: (1) the availability of alternative discovery devices; (2) the inadequacy of the payment schedule of appointed counsel for representation at a pre-

17. Prosecutors may also bypass where they see special value in prosecuting by indictment rather than information. See § 15.1(c).

18. See § 14.4 at note 1.

19. As to the possibility of closing the hearing, see § 23.1(d), (e).

liminary hearing; (3) a prosecution practice of offering significant concessions to defendants who waive their preliminary hearings; and (4) the conventional wisdom of the local defense bar that the preliminary hearing is (i) unnecessary where the prosecution has a strong case and defendant intends to plead guilty, or (ii) an inherently risky process because the disadvantages noted above often cannot be foreseen until after the hearing is underway.

In most jurisdictions, the prosecutor has a right to insist upon the preliminary hearing even though the defendant desires to waive the hearing. The prosecutor's right is based on the premise that the state has an interest, independent of the defendant, in determining whether or not there is sufficient cause to proceed. Usually, the prosecutor will only insist upon a hearing where it offers a special advantage akin to that which may lead a prosecutor not to bypass in a district in which bypassing is the general rule.

(f) Time of Hearing. Assuming that the defendant has a right to a hearing and that right is not mooted by a prior indictment, the timing of that hearing is likely to vary from a few days to a few weeks following defendant's first appearance. Most states have statutory provisions or court rules governing timing. Many require that the hearing be held within a specified number of days, often with a shorter period for the person held in custody and a longer period for the person released on bail. Other states use more general standards (e.g., "within a reasonable time"). Continuances ordinarily may be granted only on a showing of "good cause" or consent of the parties. Appellate courts generally have sustained continuances granted to the prosecution due to temporary absences of prosecution witnesses or similar prosecution difficulties in presenting known evidence.

(g) Remedies. Because a preliminary hearing bindover is a prerequisite to the defendant's continued detention beyond the statutory time limit for the hearing, a defendant held in custody beyond that time without a preliminary hearing may obtain his release through a writ of habeas corpus. The defendant also should be able to obtain dismissal of the complaint, although that will not preclude the prosecution from refiling when it becomes able to provide the hearing. The defendant may be without any remedy, however, where the prescribed time period elapses without a hearing but an indictment is obtained before the magistrate's failure to hold a hearing can be challenged before the trial court. The defendant is now being held on the basis of the indictment, and consequently is not entitled either to his release or to dismissal of the prosecution. The courts recognize that the defendant may have lost certain incidental advantages (e.g., discovery) through the denial of the hearing, but have rejected the contention that the defendant therefore should be given a post-indictment hearing at which he could obtain those advantages.

What if the defendant is denied a hearing within the prescribed time period but a hearing is held after that period has elapsed and the magistrate binds the case over for prosecution? Most courts have held that violation of a timing requirement is only an "irregularity," not "jurisdictional," and therefore requires dismissal only if prejudice can be shown. The assumption apparently is that recognizing a challenge based on delay alone would constitute an "empty" remedy because the prosecutor could simply file a new complaint if the statute of limitations has not run.

§ 14.3 The Bindover Determination

(a) The Applicable Standard. The standard to be applied by the magistrate in determining whether the defendant will be boundover typically is set forth in the statute or court ruling that establishes the right to the hearing. The most common description of the standard requires "probable cause to believe that an offense has been committed and that the defendant committed it." [1] Exactly what

§ 14.3

1. Provisions in some jurisdictions use the phrase "sufficient cause" or "reasonable cause," but those terms are interpreted as having the same content as "probable cause." On the other hand, a somewhat different stan-

"probable cause" means in this context is left to judicial interpretation. Appellate courts often have found no need to further define the probable cause standard. Opinions will merely note that the evidence before the magistrate supports a finding of probable cause and that the magistrate was not required to be convinced of guilt beyond a reasonable doubt. Where opinions have set forth a further definition, they usually have used language taken from cases applying the Fourth Amendment probable cause standard to arrests. Thus, probable cause will be said to be present where "a man of ordinary caution or prudence would be led to believe and conscientiously entertain a strong suspicion of the guilt of the accused."

The use of the Fourth Amendment arrest standard in describing probable cause at a preliminary hearing indicates only the requisite degree of probability. It does not mean that the magistrate's ruling will merely duplicate the decision made in the same case (often by the same magistrate) in the issuance of an arrest warrant or in the ex parte post-arrest finding of probable cause made pursuant to the *Gerstein* requirement.[2] The difference in context will necessarily lend a different shading to the preliminary hearing determination. Here, the assessment of probable cause will be made at an adversary rather than an ex parte proceeding. Although some use of hearsay may be permitted,[3] the magistrate at the preliminary hearing ordinarily will be considering evidence presented through the testimony of witnesses rather than a showing based entirely on affidavits. The arrest standard, directed primarily at police, is expressed in terms of "the factual and practical distinctions of everyday life in which reasonable and prudent men, not legal technicians act,"[4] while the charging decision being reviewed at the preliminary hearing is, by its nature, the responsibility of "legal technicians," the attorneys in the prosecutor's office. Under the arrest standard, considerable uncertainty must be tolerated on occasion because of the need to allow the police to take affirmative action in ambiguous circumstances, but no comparable exigencies are presented as the charging decision is made. Thus, a police officer may make an arrest where the circumstances suggest that the property possessed by the suspect may have been stolen, but the prosecutor ordinarily has no justification for proceeding to charge without first determining that a theft actually did occur.[5]

The differences between the preliminary hearing setting and the arrest setting have led some courts to warn against incorporating the Fourth Amendment standard even as to the degree of probability required for a bindover. Thus, it has been stated both that the probable cause required for a bindover is "greater" than that required for an arrest and that it imposes a different standard of proof. Such statements seem to refer not only to the requisite degree of probability, but also to a forward-looking aspect of the bindover determination. Consider, for example, the classic hypothetical in which the evidence known to the police establishes beyond a reasonable doubt that one of two independent actors committed a crime, but does not distinguish between the two. The usual view of Fourth Amendment probable cause would allow an arrest of both actors,[6] but the same could not be said for a preliminary hearing bindover, assuming no further evidence was there produced. One explanation of a rejec-

dard may be suggested where the provision requires a bindover "if it appears that an offense has been committed and that there is probable cause to believe that the defendant is guilty thereof." See note 5 infra.

2. See § 14.2 at note 3.

3. See § 14.4(b).

4. Brinegar v. United States, 338 U.S. 160, 69 S.Ct. 1302, 93 L.Ed. 1879 (1949).

5. This difference may explain the standard in several states, see note 1, which requires a finding that the offense "was committed," and that there is "probable cause" that it was committed by the accused. The reference to probable cause only as to the second element of this finding might suggest that a higher degree of probability is required as to the proof of the commission of the crime itself.

6. See § 3.3 following note 38.

tion of a bindover in this situation would be the application of a higher degree of probability than is applied to an arrest. At the preliminary hearing, it could be argued, the probable cause standard requires proof meeting a more-probable-than-not test. Another explanation is that the arrest standard looks only to the probability that the person committed the crime as established at the time of the arrest, while the preliminary hearing looks both to that probability at the time of the preliminary hearing *and* to the probability that the government will be able to establish guilt at trial. If the police were unable to develop further evidence pointing to the guilt of one of the actors, and there is not a reasonable likelihood that such evidence will be forthcoming, it would be contrary to the screening function of the preliminary hearing to bindover either actor. This view of probable cause as encompassing consideration of the prosecution's likely future development of the case finds support in occasional language in preliminary hearing provisions and may explain certain otherwise irreconcilable applications of the bindover standard.

Building upon this forward-looking aspect of the bindover determination, some commentators have argued that the more appropriate analogy for the preliminary hearing bindover standard is the prima facie evidence standard applied by the trial judge in deciding whether the prosecution's case is strong enough to send to the jury. In support of this standard, which has been adopted in a few jurisdictions, the authors of a leading article on the preliminary hearing note:

> [I]f the evidence is such that a jury would not be permitted to convict, then it is difficult to justify not disposing of the case at the preliminary hearing stage. The assumption might be that the prosecution is entitled to hold the defendant on a lesser standard while it hunts for additional evidence. This rule may have been supportable in the middle of the last century when the police were not as sophisticated as they are today and when it may have been easier to flee to avoid prosecution. Today, however, unless the statute of limitations is about to run, it is difficult to defend binding over the defendant while the police search for evidence that will support a conviction. As a practical matter, in most cases police investigation ceases once the complaint has been issued. The prosecutor wants to have the defendant held, not so that the police have time to find more evidence of guilt, but in order that incarceration, the costs of defense, the risk of conviction and other pressures will lead the defendant to plead guilty.[7]

The factual assumptions advanced by the authors make a persuasive case for a screening standard more rigorous than the usual view of the probable cause standard. Several jurisdictions accept those assumptions, although they do not necessarily depart from the probable cause terminology. Their basic approach is to increase the rigor of the screening by employing what is described as a "mini-trial" type of preliminary hearing. The prosecution is limited to use of evidence that would be admissible at trial, and the defense is allowed full scope in cross-examination and the presentation of defense evidence. The assumption is that, as a practical matter, the preliminary hearing provides the one and only instance of a true adjudication of guilt for the vast majority of cases. It is not simply a minor step preliminary to a trial, as the overwhelming majority of defendants, if boundover at the preliminary hearing, will then enter a plea of guilty in response to incentives offered by the prosecution.

From the perspective associated with a mini-trial preliminary hearing, the bindover standard should be aimed at requiring an evidentiary showing sufficient to offer a realistic likelihood of conviction if the case would actually be tried. A jurisdiction accepting that perspective may nonetheless refuse to characterize that standard as one of prima facie evidence, as the directed verdict analogy does not precisely fit the context of the preliminary hearing. A prima facie evidence

7. Graham and Letwin, The Preliminary Hearing in Los Angeles: Some Field Findings and Legal Policy Observations, 18 U.C.L.A. 635, 691–92 (1971).

standard looks solely to the prosecutor's evidence, and asks whether that evidence, if unexplained and uncontradicted, could lead a jury reasonably to find guilt beyond a reasonable doubt. In the preliminary hearing setting, the prosecution's case may be contradicted or given an innocent explanation, as the defense has the opportunity to present its case. Thus, what is sought in the preliminary context under the mini-trial approach is a screening generally "analogous in function" to the prima facie evidence standard. It is a standard that looks to the totality of the evidence presented and asks whether, recognizing the leeway which must be granted the jury in making its own evaluation of the evidence on both sides, there is a fair probability that a reasonable jury could sustain the charge. While this function may be performed more readily under a standard characterized as roughly comparable to the prima facie evidence determination, it also may fit, with a little stretching, within the concept of a forward-looking probable cause determination that goes substantially beyond the arrest standard.

A substantial majority of the states reject the mini-trial type of preliminary hearing. Such a view of the preliminary hearing is deemed inconsistent with various provisions of the typical statute or court rule establishing the preliminary hearing. The bindover standard is described in terms of "probable cause" that the defendant committed the offense, language that does not suggest reference to prima facie evidence (a standard used in many grand jury indictment provisions), to the function of a trial judge in considering a motion for a directed verdict, or to the probability of a conviction at trial. The timing requirements are stringent and do not suggest affording the prosecution adequate time to bring together its full case in the form of admissible evidence. Indeed, the basic thrust of reform in preliminary hearing procedure has been to shorten time periods and preclude continuances so as to ensure that no person is being held in custody or otherwise subjected to significant restraints on his liberty where the prosecution does not have some reasonable grounding for its charge. Consistent with this purpose, and contrary to the mini-trial concept, these states do not limit the prosecutor to admissible evidence and often allow extensive use of hearsay. So too, in accordance with this perspective, a standard analogous to the prima facie evidence test is rejected. Although the appropriate standard may be somewhat more rigorous in its proof demands than Fourth Amendment probable cause, it still is tied to a concept of probable cause that requires only the same general level of probability as the Fourth Amendment standard.

(b) Assessment of Credibility. Closely related to the definition of the applicable bindover standard is the extent of the magistrate's authority to pass judgment on the credibility of witnesses in applying that standard. It is uniformly agreed that the magistrate has authority to judge credibility. If that were not so, there would be no reason for allowing the defense to cross-examine prosecution witnesses and present contradicting evidence of its own. The critical issue is how much leeway is granted to the magistrate in judging credibility. In particular, does the magistrate have the same authority as would a judge in a bench trial? That position finds support in the language of several opinions, most notably from jurisdictions utilizing a mini-trial type of hearing.

Considering the magistrate as a basic factfinder in assessing credibility goes beyond the application even of a screening standard analogous to that applied on a motion for a directed verdict. Consider, for example, a case in which the prosecution's proof of a particular element rests primarily on the testimony of a single witness. Assume also that the magistrate concludes that reasonable persons might disagree as to whether the witness is telling the truth, but the magistrate's own judgment is that the witness is probably lying. If the magistrate is to make a credibility judgment as would a factfinder, the magistrate should discount that witness' testimony and conclude that there is insufficient evidence on the one element to support a bindover. Yet, at the same time, the magistrate would have to acknowledge that if he were reviewing a jury conviction based on the same evidence, that conviction would not be viewed as lacking sufficient evidentiary support.

In *Hunter v. District Court*,[8] in a jurisdiction that the court pointedly characterized as not utilizing a mini-trial type hearing, an attempt was made to reconcile the magistrate's authority to judge credibility and the use of a traditional probable cause standard for bindovers. The court concluded that a "judge in a preliminary hearing has jurisdiction to consider the credibility of witnesses only when, as a matter of law, the testimony is implausible or incredible. When there is a mere conflict in testimony, a question of fact exists for the jury, and the judge must draw the inference favorable to the prosecution." A slightly broader standard, also noted in *Hunter*, would allow the magistrate to resolve conflicts in testimony, "but only 'where the evidence in overwhelming.'" Available studies suggest that magistrates in practice hesitate to judge credibility except in such glaring cases.

(c) Consequences of a Dismissal. In several jurisdictions, a dismissal at the preliminary hearing may be appealed to the next highest court, which will be the felony trial court. Most state provisions authorizing prosecution appeals, however, do not encompass preliminary hearing dismissals; they provide for appeals from orders dismissing indictments or informations, but not complaints. In these jurisdictions, appellate review of a dismissal might be obtained by application for a writ of mandamus (also made to the felony trial court), but that remedy ordinarily is available only if the magistrate's refusal to bind over constitutes a "gross abuse" of discretion.

In most jurisdictions, whether or not appellate review is available, a prosecutor will look to alternative procedures to obtain a "reversal" of a dismissal. The dismissal occurs before jeopardy has attached, and the Fifth Amendment does not bar initiation of a new prosecution for the same offense.[9] Where prosecutions commonly are brought by indictment, the prosecutor most often will take the same charge directly to the grand jury. The grand jury may indict notwithstanding the magistrate's refusal to bindover and the defendant may be rearrested on the indictment. Where grand jury indictments are not used or are used only in connection with grand jury investigations, the prosecutor often will refile the complaint and attempt to obtain a bindover at a subsequent preliminary hearing (possibly before a different magistrate).

Several state courts have maintained that refiling undermines the magistrate's authority and should not be permitted unless the prosecution offers substantial new evidence. The majority, however, reject that position and permit refiling on the same evidence, absent proof that the prosecutor's purpose is to harass the defendant. Limits upon refiling are more likely where the avenue of appeal is open to the prosecutor, as courts refusing to impose such limits often stress that review of an improper dismissal might otherwise not be available because the prosecutor has no right of direct appeal. Also, in many jurisdictions, support for unlimited refiling is found in preliminary hearing provisions which specifically state that a dismissal "shall not preclude the state from instituting a subsequent prosecution for the same offense."

Where state law allows refiling only with "new evidence," the question arises as to what will satisfy that requirement. One view is that "new evidence" is limited to evidence which was not known to the state at the time of the first preliminary hearing or which could not easily have been acquired at that time. In support of this approach, it has been argued that the preliminary hearing is a public procedure subjecting the defendant to the usual hazards of public accusation of crime and that the prosecution therefore should be fully prepared and should bear the consequences of its misjudgment in failing to present all available evidence, just as it would

8. 190 Colo. 48, 543 P.2d 1265 (1975).

9. See § 25.1(d); United States ex rel. Rutz v. Levy, 268 U.S. 390, 45 S.Ct. 516, 69 L.Ed. 1010 (1925).

at trial. But because of the well established doctrine that the prosecution is not required to present all of its evidence at a preliminary hearing and the natural reluctance of prosecutors to disclose all of their evidence at that time, courts are more inclined to accept the proposition that the prosecutor's misjudgment as to the evidence needed should not immunize the defendant from further prosecution. "New evidence" is held to include any additional evidence, whether or not previously available.

(d) Consequences of a Bindover. In all but a few jurisdictions, the grand jury is in no way limited by a bindover. It may refuse to indict despite the bindover or may indict for a lesser or higher offense, depending upon the evidence presented to it. Once the grand jury indicts, the indictment serves as the basis for defendant's continued detention and the bindover itself is no longer subject to challenge. Where prosecution is by information, on the other hand, the bindover will largely control the subsequent charges. Most information states limit the information to offenses included in the bindover order.

If the magistrate binds over on a lesser charge than that requested, and grand jury indictment is not available, the prosecution ordinarily has two avenues of relief. It may seek appellate review, which will be by extraordinary writ in most jurisdictions and will require a showing that the magistrate abused his discretion. As an alternative, it may seek to have the complaint dismissed without prejudice, which will permit it to refile on the higher charge and obtain a "second chance" at a new preliminary hearing. In several states the prosecutor may ignore a bindover on a lesser charge because its information is not strictly limited by the bindover order. These states require only that the defendant be charged with the offense for which he is held to answer or any other offense established by the evidence at the preliminary hearing. This means the prosecution may charge the higher offense and place the burden on the defendant to challenge the information as not supported by the evidence presented at the preliminary hearing.

Pending the filing of an information or indictment, the defendant may be able to challenge the bindover decision by writ of habeas corpus. When the bindover is followed by an information, the appropriate challenge usually is by a motion to dismiss or quash the information, which often must be presented prior to pleading to the information. Courts reviewing a bindover decision often stress that they may not substitute their judgment for that of the magistrate who saw and heard the testimony. Indeed, it is sometimes stated that the magistrate's decision will only be overturned when there has been a clear abuse of discretion. Accordingly, the magistrate's decision (ordinarily not supported by opinion or findings of fact) is most likely to be reversed when a misinterpretation of substantive law (or perhaps oversight) resulted in a total absence of proof on a particular element of the offense. On occasion, however, bindover decisions also are rejected on the ground that, without attempting to reconcile conflicts or judge the credibility of witnesses, the inferences drawn from the evidence simply are not sufficient to support a probable cause finding.

Assume now that a magistrate binds over on a record that clearly fails to establish probable cause, after which the prosecutor files an information based on that bindover. If a timely challenge in the trial court is rejected, as to which interlocutory appeal is unavailable, and the defendant is then convicted at trial, may he raise again the improper bindover issue on his appeal? In some jurisdictions, a proper bindover is viewed as a jurisdictional prerequisite to the filing of an information, and where that is the law a new trial is required if it is shown on appeal that the bindover was not supported by sufficient evidence. Others hold that the magistrate's error in binding over and the trial court's error in failing to quash the information are cured where sufficient evidence to convict is adduced at trial.[10]

10. See also § 14.4(e). Cf. United States v. Mechanik, discussed in § 15.6(e).

§ 14.4 Preliminary Hearing Procedures

(a) Right to Counsel. *Coleman v. Alabama*[1] holds that the Sixth Amendment right to counsel extends to the preliminary hearing and therefore grants to the indigent defendant a right to the appointment of counsel to represent him at that hearing. The *Coleman* Court concluded that the preliminary hearing is a "critical stage" in the criminal prosecution,[2] as the assistance of counsel at the preliminary hearing is "necessary to preserve the defendant's basic right to a fair trial as affected by his right meaningfully to cross-examine the witnesses against him and to have effective assistance of counsel at the trial itself." The Court majority was not persuaded by the argument of the state (and the dissenters) that counsel was not needed because state law protected the unrepresented accused by prohibiting the prosecution's use at trial of "anything that occurred" at the preliminary hearing. The majority responded by reciting the various significant steps which counsel could take at the preliminary hearing:

> First, the lawyer's skilled examination and cross-examination of witnesses may expose fatal weaknesses in the State's case that may lead the magistrate to refuse to bind the accused over. Second, in any event, the skilled interrogation of witnesses by an experienced lawyer can fashion a vital impeachment tool for use in cross-examination of the State's witnesses at the trial, or preserve testimony favorable to the accused of a witness who does not appear at the trial. Third, trained counsel can more effectively discover the case the State has against his client and make possible the preparation of a proper defense to meet that case at the trial. Fourth, counsel can also be influential at the preliminary hearing in making effective arguments for the accused on such matters as the necessity for an early psychiatric examination or bail.

Coleman, it should be noted, was written with reference to a state in which the ultimate prosecution was by indictment, and the first of the possible benefits cited by the Court (precluding a bindover) would arguably be less significant than in an information state. Moreover, that benefit would be available even in a preliminary hearing that authorized procedures (e.g., prosecution reliance on hearsay) which might preclude or minimize the other benefits. Accordingly, *Coleman* has uniformly been read as requiring the appointment of counsel in all types of preliminary hearings in both indictment and information jurisdictions.

(b) Application of the Rules of Evidence. While all jurisdictions require magistrates to recognize testimonial privileges at the preliminary hearing, from that point on they vary considerably in their treatment of the applicability of the rules of evidence. With a modest degree of overgeneralization, the various positions can be divided into three basic approaches: (i) full applicability; (ii) inapplicability with varying magistrate discretion to exclude evidence that would not be admissible at trial; and (iii) general applicability with exceptions for certain types of evidence not admissible at trial.

Only a handful of states require full application of the rules of evidence, restricting the preliminary hearing evidence to that which would also be admissible at trial. These jurisdictions will not reject a bindover, however, simply because the magistrate erroneously admitted incompetent evidence. If the reviewing court concludes that there was sufficient admissible evidence before the magistrate to meet the bindover standard, the bindover will be upheld. The magistrate's error in admitting the incompetent evidence will be treated, in effect, as per se harmless error. Contrary to the usual application of harmless error analysis, however, the trial court does not ask whether the evidence was such as to possibly have influenced the magistrate notwithstanding the sufficiency of the remaining evidence.[3] Instead, it substitutes its own judgment of the

§ 14.4

1. 399 U.S. 1, 90 S.Ct. 1999, 26 L.Ed.2d 387 (1970).

2. See § 11.2(b), discussing the "critical stage" concept.

3. Compare § 27.6(b). Consider also the somewhat different standard applied in those jurisdictions that allow challenges to the competency of the evidence before the indicting grand jury. See § 15.5(c).

weight of the remaining evidence and sustains the bindover if deemed correct in light of that evidence.

A somewhat larger group of jurisdictions start from the premise that the rules of evidence do not apply, leaving the magistrate with discretion to accept evidence that would be inadmissible at trial. In the federal system, which falls within this group, the applicable court rule simply states that evidentiary rules, "other than with respect to privileges, do not apply in * * * preliminary examinations in criminal cases."[4] In other jurisdictions, the controlling provision stresses the magistrate's discretion, as where it is noted that the magistrate "may temper the rules of evidence in the exercise of sound discretion" or "may receive evidence that would be inadmissible at trial." In some of those jurisdictions, the other side of the magistrate's discretion—the authority to insist that evidence meet standards of trial admissibility—is restricted as to particular evidence. Thus, the provision may note, as under Federal Rule 5.1, that the "finding of probable cause may be based on hearsay in whole or in part" (thereby suggesting that the prosecution has a right to rely on hearsay), or that "objections to evidence on the ground that it was acquired by unlawful means are not properly made at the preliminary hearing."[5] Where the magistrate's discretion is limited in this fashion, the most common categories of evidence placed within the limitation are the two noted in Federal Rule 5.1—hearsay and evidence that would be excluded at trial as illegally obtained. Where the magistrate has unrestricted discretion to accept or reject evidence inadmissible at trial, the inadmissible evidence most commonly allowed also is that which falls in those two categories. However, in such jurisdictions, considerable variation can exist even as to such evidence from one magistrate to another. Thus, some magistrates may accept any type of inadmissible hearsay and some may accept such hearsay only under very limited circumstances (e.g., reports of scientific testing where not challenged as to accuracy by the defense). So too, some magistrates may never give consideration to the possible illegality of the acquisition of evidence, while others may allow exclusionary rule objections where a constitutional violation in acquiring the evidence is readily apparent. Other evidentiary rules that magistrates might well refuse to apply include authentication and best evidence requirements for writings and foundation requirements (e.g., chain of custody showing) for certain types of demonstrative evidence.

A third group of jurisdictions, probably reflecting the majority position, hold the rules of evidence to be generally applicable, but create exceptions for certain categories of evidence that would be inadmissible at trial. The two most common exceptions again relate to hearsay and to evidence obtained by police methods that could lead to suppression at trial, although other exceptions also are specified in particular states (e.g., to the best evidence rule). The exceptions commonly are set forth in statute or court rule and suggested by their wording that magistrates do not have discretion to exclude evidence that falls within the exception. In some instances, it is not clear whether a jurisdiction falls in this grouping or in the second grouping of states that hold the rules of evidence inapplicable and provide further that certain evidentiary standards cannot be applied even at the magistrate's discretion. A state's statute or court rule may simply identify certain non-cognizable objections and fail to directly address the question of whether evidentiary rules otherwise apply. However, the statutory recognition of exceptions, where it stands alone (i.e., without a further provision stating that the evidentiary rules do not apply), would ordinarily suggest by implication that the other evidentiary rules do apply.

Where, as in most jurisdictions, a specific provision holds hearsay admissible, that provision can range from a limited acceptance of specific types of hearsay to a broad accept-

4. Fed.R.Evid. 1101(d)(3).

5. Fed.R.Crim.P. 5.1. Fed.R.Crim.P. 12, governing the motion to suppress, requires that the motion be presented before the trial court.

ance of all hearsay under all circumstances. The narrowest provisions require admissibility only of reports of experts, with some covering only certain forensic testing and others all "written reports of expert witnesses." Other limited provisions also encompass written statements of persons attesting to their ownership of property that was stolen, damaged, or broken into, to their lack of consent to the taking of property, and to the authenticity of their signature on a written instrument. Somewhat broader provisions apply to any type of hearsay statement, but impose certain prerequisites before the statement may be admitted. Thus, the prosecutor may be required to establish initially that there are "reasonable grounds to believe that the declarant will be personally available at trial," that "it is demonstrably inconvenient to summon witnesses able to testify to facts from personal knowledge," or that "there is a substantial basis for believing the source of the hearsay is credible and for believing that there is a factual basis for the information furnished." Finally, the broadest provisions simply state, as under Federal Rule 5.1, that the bindover "may be based on hearsay evidence in whole or in part." Of course, even under such a provision, before basing a bindover on hearsay, the magistrate must determine that it is sufficiently likely to be reliable to meet the probable cause standard, but that conclusion can be reached without finding all of the prerequisites commonly imposed under the restricted provisions.[6]

The various positions taken on the allowance of hearsay obviously reflect differences of opinion both as to the likely reliability of hearsay and the character of preliminary hearing screening, but they may also reflect differences in judgments relating to other factors as well. The variety of the arguments advanced for and against admission of hearsay is illustrated by the debate over the treatment of that issue in what eventually became Federal Rule 5.1. Those supporting the Rule 5.1 provision argued: (1) that hearsay will often provide a reliable basis for decision; (2) federal magistrates did not have to be lawyers, and laymen simply were not equipped to cope with the hearsay rule and the various exceptions thereto; (3) many witnesses would be even more reluctant to assist police if they were required to make two court appearances, first at the preliminary examination and then at trial; (4) in many instances, the witness' testimony would relate to a matter not really in dispute that could be summarized quite briefly by an investigating officer (e.g., where the owner of the stolen vehicle usually can furnish testimony only as to the fact that his car disappeared); (5) the federal grand jury, which will make the final charging decision, can indict solely on the basis of hearsay; (6) requiring a more strict evidentiary standard for preliminary hearings would only encourage prosecutors to bypass the preliminary hearing by taking cases directly to the grand jury; (7) a magistrate can issue a warrant based on hearsay attributed to a reliable informant, and the probable cause standard at a preliminary hearing should approximate that for issuance of an arrest warrant; and (8) narrower exceptions that allowed hearsay only under certain conditions would only prove cumbersome.[7]

Those arguing against the Rule 5.1 provision maintained that a bindover must be based on admissible evidence if the accused is to be protected against the unwarranted ordeal of a trial where the prosecution lacks the evidence needed to obtain a conviction. They rejected the contention that inadmissible hearsay provides a sufficient basis to make a reliable assessment of the likely strength of the prosecution's case at trial. Such an assumption, they argued, was inconsistent with the recognized right of the defense to challenge the prosecution's case at the prelimi-

6. The approach here is similar to that applied in the issuance of arrest and search warrants. See § 3.3(c), (d).

7. Another argument sometimes advanced in favor of allowing prosecution use of hearsay is that the defense will have the option of itself subpoenaing the declarant, having him declared a hostile witness, and then cross-examining him. That tactic, however, could well be precluded by the magistrate as a use of the defense's subpoena authority more to gain discovery than to challenge the prosecution's case or as inappropriate in light of the strength of the prosecution's case. See subsection (d) infra.

nary hearing through cross-examination. Moreover, since both sides would be represented by counsel, and most magistrates were lawyers, application of the hearsay rule should present no greater difficulty than application of other rules of evidence. The burden placed on witnesses would not be excessive, especially since they need not appear before the grand jury. Indeed, the acceptability of hearsay at that screening proceeding made it especially important that inadmissible hearsay not be allowed at the preliminary hearing.

Even more common than the provisions accepting hearsay are the prohibitions against a preliminary hearing objection to the admissibility of evidence as having been obtained through unlawful means. Several states, however, take a contrary position. They either specifically require or permit magistrates to exclude illegally obtained evidence. Unlike the pretrial suppression motion, which is made in anticipation of the prosecution's use of illegally acquired evidence, the preliminary hearing objection is tied to the prosecutor's attempt to actually use that evidence at the hearing. Thus, if the prosecution has sufficient evidence to support a bindover without using the fruits of an arguably unconditional police activity, it can avoid an exclusionary rule challenge by limiting the evidence it uses at the hearing.

Where objections to illegally obtained evidence are allowed, the magistrate's ruling on the objection, like all evidentiary rulings at the preliminary hearing, will not be binding at any subsequent trial. The preliminary hearing ruling can nonetheless have a significant bearing in several ways on the subsequent proceedings. If the magistrate should exclude the evidence and find insufficient remaining evidence to bindover, the prosecution will be required to either refile or gain an appellate reversal of the magistrate's ruling. As discussed in § 14.3(c), either alternative may present significant obstacles. In particular, should the prosecutor gain appellate review by the felony trial court, either through an extraordinary writ or a statutory right of appeal, that court will ordinarily accept the magistrate's factual findings as to the acquisition of the evidence and reinstate the complaint only if the magistrate erred in applying the applicable law to those factual findings. Basically the same standard will apply, here to the disadvantage of the defendant, where the magistrate rejects the objection, finds the evidence sufficient to bindover, and the defendant then challenges the bindover by motion to quash the information. Indeed, even if the magistrate might have erred, the defendant will not necessarily gain review of the exclusionary rule issue as the trial court will have no need to consider it where the bindover is supported by sufficient additional evidence (as will be true also where the magistrate sustains the objection but grants the bindover on other evidence). Assuming a bindover is made and any challenge thereto fails, the magistrate's ruling technically is no longer before the trial court. The defendant must file a pretrial motion to suppress which will be considered de novo by the trial court. However, the challenge at the preliminary hearing still may contribute to the trial court's determination. The transcript of the testimony offered in connection with the preliminary hearing objection will often serve as the primary evidentiary foundation for the ruling on the suppression motion, although each side will have the opportunity to present new testimony as well.

The basic rationale advanced in favor of allowing exclusionary rule objections at the preliminary hearing is largely that advanced in support of applying evidentiary rules generally—that reliance upon evidence inadmissible at trial undercuts the screening function of the preliminary hearing. In that respect, allowing the prosecutor to utilize illegally obtained evidence is viewed as more pernicious than allowing use of hearsay. In many instances, the hearsay used at the preliminary hearing will be replaced at trial by admissible testimony, as the declarant will himself testify at trial. The character of illegally obtained evidence, on the other hand, cannot be altered, and it will necessarily be inadmissible at trial. Moreover, where the prosecution relies on such evidence at the preliminary hearing, the evidence is likely to be a critical part of the prosecution's proof, and not simply cumulative in impact.

The majority position refusing to allow exclusionary rule objections finds support both in the general arguments advanced against requiring adherence to evidentiary rules and in special procedural considerations raised by exclusionary rule objections. The key to the procedural considerations is the availability of the pretrial motion to suppress. Thus, it is noted that a preliminary hearing bindover based on illegally obtained evidence, unlike a bindover based on other inadmissible evidence, will not force the defendant to trial on incompetent evidence. The suppression motion can still be utilized to gain a pretrial ruling that will exclude the evidence and thereby preclude a trial. If the defendant is successful on that motion, and the excluded evidence is potentially critical to the prosecution's case, the prosecution cannot risk proceeding with the trial, but must either dismiss (and hope to obtain additional untainted evidence) or gain interlocutory appellate review of the suppression ruling.[8] Accordingly, allowing the defendant also to raise the suppression issue before the magistrate is seen as providing an unnecessary advantage of "two bites at the apple" and as imposing on the judicial system a wasteful duplication of review. It is thought to open the door, moreover, to various tactical games at the preliminary hearing. With its second opportunity before the trial judge guaranteed, the defense can consider not objecting where concerned about the magistrate's disposition in shaping the record and ruling on the suppression issue, or even using the preliminary hearing objection as a "dry run" for its later pretrial objection. The prosecution can seek, in turn, to avoid the issue by presenting its case without the evidence subject to challenge or by simply bypassing the hearing with a prior indictment. In jurisdictions where the hearing is held with exceptional promptness, another argument advanced is that there often will not be adequate time for the two sides to investigate and prepare for exclusionary rule objections.

(c) The Defendant's Right of Cross-Examination. All jurisdictions grant the defense a right to cross-examine those witnesses presented by the prosecution at the preliminary hearing. This right is based on local law (usually a statute or court rule); the Supreme Court has long held that cross-examination at a preliminary hearing is not required by the confrontation clause of the Sixth Amendment.[9] The relevant provisions typically describe the right in general terms, leaving to the judiciary the formulation of applicable limitations. As would be expected, the courts uniformly agree that cross-examination at the preliminary hearing should at least be subject to those restrictions that the particular jurisdiction imposes on trial cross-examination. A few jurisdictions would stop there, but most recognize one or more additional limitations that would not be applicable in the trial setting. These additional restrictions almost always can be attributed either to the limited screening function of the preliminary hearing or the early stage in the process at which the hearing occurs.

A common restriction that stems in large part from the pretrial stage of the hearing is the prohibition against discovery-oriented cross-examination. Almost all jurisdictions recognize the magistrate's authority to cut-off examination that seems to be aimed more at obtaining pretrial discovery than at challenging the witness' testimony. The possible use of cross-examination for discovery purposes is not a significant concern at trial, where the defense has already obtained discovery and presumably has its case fully prepared. In contrast, magistrates are well aware that defense counsel may utilize the preliminary hearing primarily for discovery purposes. The response to that possibility varies with the individual magistrate. Some will make no effort to single out questions that could be aimed primarily at discovery, and will regularly allow such questions, even over a prose-

8. See § 27.3(b).

9. Goldsby v. United States, 160 U.S. 70, 16 S.Ct. 216, 40 L.Ed. 343 (1895).

cution objection, so long as the cross-examination is fairly brief. Others, however, will uphold prosecutorial objections whenever the questions seem aimed at discovery, or will at least require the defense to show why that is not the purpose of the particular question.[10] Questions most likely to be challenged on this score are those asking about other sources of evidence (e.g., the names of known eyewitnesses) or exploring the range of investigative procedures that were utilized by the police. Also, where a jurisdiction holds that a particular defense is not cognizable at a preliminary hearing, as discussed in subsection (d) infra, cross-examination apparently designed to bring forth information relating to such a defense will be prohibited either as an attempt at discovery or as failing to relate to an issue properly before the magistrate.

Since the issue for determination at the preliminary hearing is only that of probable cause, a magistrate may also have authority to bar cross-examination that clearly challenges the prosecution's case but is deemed not to carry sufficient force to upset the prosecution's showing of probable cause. Thus, courts sometimes state that while cross-examination must be permitted to challenge the witness's credibility as to the events described in his or her testimony, the magistrate may bar cross-examination aimed at challenging only the witness' "general trustworthiness." So too, where the magistrate takes the position that credibility judgments at the preliminary hearing should be limited only to apparent falsehoods,[11] and the initial questioning indicates that witness will not retreat from his or her testimony, a magistrate may cut-off all further questioning as unlikely to alter the magistrate's judgment on probable cause. Critics of this practice argue that the statutory grant of a right to cross-examination is thereby rendered meaningless, and the preliminary hearing reduced to no more than a bare-bones inquiry into the presence of testimony supporting each element of the crime. They note further that even if the magistrate assumes a most limited authority to judge credibility, there always exists the possibility that a defense counsel allowed to conduct a probing cross-examination could eventually force the witness to retreat or produce inconsistencies so significant as to totally undermine the witness' credibility.

As noted in § 14.1(d), the preliminary hearing testimony of a witness who later becomes unavailable at trial may be admitted there as substantive evidence, provided the defendant was given an adequate opportunity to cross-examine the witness at the preliminary hearing. Restriction of cross-examination by the magistrate always runs the risk of later being deemed to have denied the defense that adequate opportunity. While a bar against questions apparently aimed at discovery is not likely to cause difficulties, the preclusion of questions referring to defenses not cognizable at the preliminary hearing conceivably could be viewed otherwise. Restrictions on questions relating to the witness' credibility are most likely to be seen as having a bearing on the adequacy issue as they go directly to the function of cross-examination. Thus, the magistrate must decide, even where the authority to restrict cross-examination is clear, whether the imposition of that restriction is justified if its cost may be to preclude possible trial use of the witness' testimony. The critical factor here may be whether the prosecution requests that the magistrate restrict the cross-examination. If the prosecutor is will-

10. Differing views as to the need to bar cross-examination aimed at discovery are also reflected in the defendant's ability to gain disclosure of the prior recorded statements of a preliminary hearing witness for possible use in cross-examining the witness. While some jurisdictions make such statements available to the defense, just as they do at trial [under provisions similar to the federal Jencks Act, see § 24.4(c)], others require disclosure only in subsequent proceedings as provided under pretrial discovery provisions or trial disclosure requirements. Consider, however, State v. Mitchell, 200 Conn. 323, 512 A.2d 140 (1986) (in light of the significance of the preliminary hearing under state law, the prosecution's due process obligation to disclose material exculpatory evidence within its control, as developed in the *Brady* line of cases [see § 20.7], was applicable to the preliminary hearing; accordingly, a state provision prohibiting discovery motions at the preliminary hearing did not govern where the prosecutor had in its possession impeachment material that constituted material exculpatory evidence under the *Brady* doctrine).

11. See § 14.3(b).

ing to risk the possible inability to use the testimony at trial, the magistrate's obligation arguably is to impose the restriction; but where the prosecution would prefer to allow the cross-examination, a magistrate should be hesitant to insist upon the restriction. While the magistrate has an independent interest in properly confining cross-examination so as to avoid a hearing more lengthy than it need be, the prosecution may be seen as having an equally weighty interest in being able to perpetuate the testimony of its witnesses. This is especially true where the jurisdiction's deposition procedure is limited in availability on the assumption that the preliminary hearing ordinarily will be used to perpetuate testimony.

(d) The Right to Present Defense Witnesses. Several jurisdictions allow the defense to call its own witnesses at the preliminary hearing only with the permission of the court. Ordinarily, the defendant must set forth the substance of the anticipated testimony, and the magistrate will then allow the witnesses to be called only after determining that such testimony, if accepted as credible, would be sufficient to rebut the prosecution's probable cause showing. Most jurisdictions have provisions granting the defendant a general right to call defense witnesses, not contingent on advance approval by the court. However, as with the defendant's right of cross-examination, that general right is assumed to be subject to limitations as developed by the courts. Ordinarily, those limitations give to the magistrate the authority to cut-off the testimony of defense witnesses on grounds similar to those justifying curtailment of cross-examination. Thus, the magistrate may refuse to allow further testimony where the defense counsel appears to be seeking primarily to obtain discovery from the witness (e.g., where the witness appears to be a person who would be called by the prosecution at trial). A magistrate also may cut short the witness' testimony where the magistrate concludes that the witness' testimony will simply present a credibility issue not sufficient to offset the prosecution's showing of probable cause.

Even where magistrates are not prone to disallow or cut short defense testimony, the use of defense witnesses to challenge the prosecution's probable cause showing is highly unusual. Most often, the defense anticipates a bindover and is focusing upon discovery. If counsel should conclude that opportunity exists to shake the prosecution's showing, that will usually be attempted through vigorous cross-examination of the prosecution's witnesses. Conventional wisdom holds that producing defense testimony contradicting the prosecution's case carries costs that ordinarily far outweighs its benefits. Unless the credibility of prosecution witnesses has been shaken substantially on cross-examination, the contrary testimony of defense witnesses is likely to be viewed by the magistrate as simply presenting the kind of credibility conflict that should be resolved by the factfinder at trial. On the other hand, by presenting the defense witness at the preliminary hearing, the defendant runs the risk of making that witness' testimony less effective at trial. Just as the defense may use its cross-examination of prosecution witnesses to gain discovery and to prepare for future impeachment, the prosecution may use its cross-examination of the defense witnesses to achieve the same goals.

Much the same analysis argues against presenting witnesses whose testimony will not directly challenge the prosecution's showing as to the elements of the offense, but will point to additional factors that would excuse or justify the actor's behavior. Here, however, an additional concern is whether such as "affirmative defense" (i.e., a defense that does not negate a basic element of the crime) is even cognizable at the preliminary hearing. Because presenting such a defense at the preliminary hearing is contrary to conventional wisdom, case law on the subject is sparse. Not surprisingly, the leading cases deal with attempts to present a defense of entrapment. Under the majority view that treats entrapment as an issue of substantive law to be resolved by the jury, rather than an issue of police impropriety to be resolved by the court, the presentation of that defense at trial is a highly risky venture.[12] As a result, counsel might readily conclude that the entrapment defense should be presented at the preliminary hearing with an eye towards not repeating it as a trial defense should it not persuade or come close to persuading the magistrate. Entrapment also has special qualities that might make the defense more appealing to a magistrate of a certain disposition than to the typical jury. Insanity is still another defense that arguably might fall in the same category under certain circumstances.

In California, which generally takes a minitrial approach to the preliminary hearing, the California Supreme Court has held that the defendant could not be barred from raising an entrapment defense at the preliminary hearing.[13] The function of "weed[ing] out groundless changes" necessitates that the defendant be allowed to "introduce evidence tending to overcome the prosecution's case *or* establish an affirmative defense." Taking a contrary position, the Arizona Supreme Court ruled that an entrapment defense went beyond the limited facets of the case to be decided by the magistrate—whether "a public offense has been committed and whether there is sufficient cause to believe the accused committed it."[14] Entrapment was characterized as an "affirmative defense to be resolved at trial" as an element of the determination of actual guilt. Whether that court would have taken the same position as to an affirmative defense viewed as less tangential to the criminal behavior, such as self-defense, is unclear. Arguably one concern as to the more tangential defenses is that they would not necessarily have been investigated by the prosecution and the prosecution would be unprepared to respond to the defense testimony. However, this might also be true of some defenses that directly rebut the prosecution's case, such as alibi (which ordinarily requires advance notice to be raised at trial[15]). A standard geared to restrictions on prosecutorial preparation is more appropriately tied directly to that factor than to whether the particular defense happens to rebut a basic element of the offense.

A special concern raised by the presentation of affirmative defenses at the preliminary hearing is the standard of proof to be applied. Application of the traditional probable cause standard would suggest that once the defense has established some evidentiary basis for the defense, such as would make it an issue at trial, the prosecution must make a probable cause showing that the elements of the defense are not present. In making that determination, the magistrate would handle credibility issues no differently than with the basic elements of the crime. This approach proceeds from the assumption, however, that the prosecutor at trial would have the burden of negating the affirmative defense by proof beyond a reasonable doubt. In many jurisdictions, the defense will carry the burden of proof as to at least some affirmative defenses. As to such defenses, the prosecution might argue that there is no need for it to make an affirmative probable cause showing. Even where the prosecution has not produced substantial contradictory evidence, a jury could always find for the prosecution on the ground that the defense witnesses were not sufficiently credible to carry the defense's burden of proof. Acceptance of that conclusion might lead a court simply to bar the consideration of an affirmative defense by the magistrate. In rejecting the cognizability of the entrapment defense, the Arizona Supreme Court relied upon a similar ruling that had stressed that the defendant carried the burden of proof on that defense.

(e) Challenging Procedural Rulings. If a magistrate makes an improper procedural ruling at a preliminary hearing and subsequently binds over, and the defendant then moves to dismiss the ensuing information be-

12. See §§ 5.2, 5.3(a).

13. Jennings v. Superior Court, 66 Cal.2d 867, 59 Cal.Rptr. 440, 428 P.2d 304 (1967).

14. State v. Altman, 107 Ariz. 93, 482 P.2d 460 (1971).

15. See § 20.5(b). The defense of insanity similarly requires advance notice, see § 20.5(c). As to that defense, however, even if the prosecution were given notice of a defendant's intent to raise the claim prior to the preliminary hearing, the timing requirements for the hearing rarely would allow the prosecution (or the defense) adequate time for the development of its evidence prior to the hearing.

cause of the magistrate's procedural error, what weight should be given to the strength of the prosecution's case in determining whether that error requires rejection of the bindover. Three different approaches may be taken here. As noted previously in subsection (c), in jurisdictions holding the rules of evidence applicable to the preliminary hearing, a magistrate error in admitting incompetent evidence will be viewed as harmless if there was sufficient competent evidence to support the bindover. A similar analysis can also be applied to other errors, such as the improper curtailment of cross-examination or the refusal to allow a defense witness. Here, however, since the defense was not allowed to proceed, the court may be required to give the defense the benefit of the doubt as to what would have been shown if the magistrate had not erred. It can nonetheless find that the prosecution's evidence would have been sufficient even with that showing and therefore sustain the bindover notwithstanding the magistrate's error.

A variation of the above approach would look to a standard for reversal similar to that applied by the Supreme Court in evaluating the impact of the unconstitutional restriction of the right of confrontation at trial. There, *Delaware v. Van Arsdall* holds that a reversal will not be required if the appellate court concludes that, beyond a reasonable doubt, the jury would have reached the same result even if the cross-examination had not been restricted and had been totally successful in achieving its objective.[16] In the context of the preliminary hearing, the trial court would ask whether the magistrate clearly would have reached the same result if the defense had made the showing that was precluded by the magistrate's error. The strength of the prosecution's case would remain significant, but the question would not be whether it merely would be sufficient for a bindover notwithstanding the added defense showing, but whether it would be so overwhelming that the magistrate's bindover clearly would not have been influenced by that additional showing.

A third approach is suggested by *Jennings v. Superior Court.*[17] *Jennings* held that automatic reversal of a bindover is required where the magistrate's erroneous ruling deprived the defendant of a "substantial right," such as his right to cross-examine or to present witnesses. Finding reversible error in the denial of cross-examination relating to a possible entrapment defense, the court rejected the prosecution's contention that the error was not prejudicial because the prosecution's evidence still would have been sufficient to support a bindover. The crucial issue, the court noted, was whether the defendant was denied a "fair hearing." If so, he was entitled to relief "without further showing." While every improper curtailment of cross-examination would not deny a fair hearing, the restriction here clearly did so as it concerned a key witness and deprived the defendant of cross-examination that went "directly to the matter at issue." The court's willingness to adopt a standard for reversal apparently more rigorous than the *Van Arsdall* harmless error standard might be explained by the fact that redoing a preliminary hearing imposes substantially less of a burden on the judicial system than redoing a trial.

Assume that a magistrate improperly curtails cross-examination or denies a request to present a defense witness, but an indictment is issued before the magistrate's ruling can be challenged in the trial court. Has the defendant lost his right to relief even though the magistrate's ruling clearly resulted in an erroneous bindover? The tradition rule is that all "defects" in the preliminary hearing are "cured by the subsequent indictment." The rationale here is similar to that underlying the practice of mooting the defendant's right to a preliminary hearing by obtaining a prior indictment.[18] Once an indictment has been issued, the preliminary hearing proceedings are no longer subject to either direct or collateral attack because the defendant has been afforded an independent determination that probable cause exists, which overrides any

16. See note 18, § 27.6.

17. Supra note 13.

18. See § 14.2(b), (d), (d).

decision that the magistrate might render at a new preliminary hearing.

Assume next that the magistrate erroneously restricts defendant's right to cross-examination or to present evidence at a preliminary hearing, the magistrate subsequently binds over, and an information is filed. The defense challenges the information as based on a defective preliminary hearing, but the trial court erroneously finds that the magistrate's rulings were proper. Interlocutory review is not available, so defendant next raises the issue on appeal following conviction. At this point, the information jurisdictions are divided. Most take the view that the conviction should be treated as having rendered harmless the magistrate's error—at least in the absence of a showing by defense counsel of actual prejudice at trial flowing from the preliminary hearing error.[19] Others, viewing a proper bindover as a jurisdictional prerequisite to the filing of an information, will require a new trial without regard to whether the preliminary hearing had a prejudicial impact upon the outcome of the trial. *Mascarenas v. State* [20] is illustrative. The court there concluded that an improper restriction of cross-examination amounted, in effect, to a "denial of a preliminary examination"; accordingly, since state law required a preliminary hearing as a prerequisite to "holding any person on an information," the trial court was "without jurisdiction" and the subsequent conviction was invalid.

In *Coleman v. Alabama*,[21] the Supreme Court spoke to the impact of a subsequent conviction upon a constitutional violation at the preliminary hearing. After the defendants there had been denied unconstitutionally the assistance of appointed counsel at the preliminary hearing, they had been indicted by a grand jury and convicted at a trial in which they were represented by counsel. The state contended that the subsequent conviction at trial rendered harmless per se the failure to appoint counsel at the preliminary hearing. The defendants, in response, argued that denial of the Sixth Amendment right to counsel required an automatic reversal of any subsequent conviction, as the Court had held where counsel was denied at trial.[22] The Supreme Court took a middle position, remanding the case for consideration as to whether the denial of counsel at the preliminary hearing had been a harmless error under the standard of *Chapman v. California*.[23] The Court noted in this regard that while the "trial transcript indicates that the prohibition against use by the State at trial of anything that occurred at the preliminary hearing was scrupulously observed," the record before it did not reflect "whether or not petitioners were otherwise prejudiced by the absence of counsel at the preliminary hearing." Justice Harlan, in a separate opinion, sought to add specificity to the remand order, which he viewed as "too broad and amorphous." Reversal should not follow, he argued, "unless petitioners are able to show on remand that they have been prejudiced in their defense at trial, in that favorable testimony that might otherwise have been preserved was irretrievably lost by virtue of not having counsel to help present an affirmative case at the preliminary hearing." Similarly, Justice White asserted that because "petitioners had been tried and found guilty by a jury," the denial of counsel at the preliminary hearing "was harmless beyond a reasonable doubt" (the *Chapman* standard) unless "important testimony of witnesses unavailable at the trial could have been preserved had counsel been present to cross-examine opposing witnesses or to examine witnesses for the defense." It would be inappropriate, he noted, for a lower court to hold that the constitutional error had not been harmless on the speculative assumptions either "(1) that the State's witnesses at the trial testified inconsistently with what their testimony would have been if petitioner had counsel to cross-examine them at the preliminary hearing, or (2) that counsel, had he been present at the hearing, would have

19. Cf. Mechanik v. United States, § 15.6(e).

20. 80 N.M. 537, 458 P.2d 789 (1969).

21. Supra note 1.

22. See § 27.6(d).

23. See § 27.6 at note 21.

known so much more about the State's case than he actually did when he went to trial that the result of the trial might have been different."

Although the failure of the *Coleman* majority opinion to respond to the concurring opinions creates some ambiguity as to the exact nature of the required harmless error inquiry, all of the opinions clearly indicated that the inquiry was to take account of at least some incidental benefits that the hearing could have provided the defense. Most lower courts, in looking to the impact of violations of preliminary hearing rights guaranteed under state law, have focused on the single preliminary hearing function of eliminating prosecutions not supported by probable cause. *Coleman* 's broader inquiry is treated as a product of the Sixth Amendment right involved there, which looked to the preliminary hearing as a critical stage because of the impact that the lack of counsel could have upon the subsequent trial. The defendant's rights under local law to cross-examine prosecution witnesses and present defense witnesses are viewed, in contrast, as aimed solely at facilitating the screening function of the preliminary hearing. Tactical advantages in gaining discovery, laying the ground work for future impeachment, or perpetuating testimony are seen as incidental byproducts of a hearing, with their loss not being sufficient in itself to justify overturning an indictment or a subsequent conviction.

In *Coleman v. Burnett,*[24] however, the Court of Appeals adopted a much broader interpretation of *Coleman v. Alabama,* which encompassed the denial of procedural rights afforded at the preliminary hearing under local law. There, the preliminary hearing magistrate had denied defense counsel's request for a subpoena requiring the attendance of an unnamed undercover agent, who apparently was the sole available eyewitness to the marijuana transactions with which defendant was charged. The magistrate found probable cause on the basis of the hearsay testimony of the undercover agent's supervisor, and the defendant was indicted shortly thereafter. Prior to the indictment, the defendant had unsuccessfully sought a declaratory judgment that the preliminary hearing was defective, a writ of mandamus reopening the hearing, and an injunction prohibiting prosecution presentation to the grand jury. On subsequent review prior to trial, the Court of Appeals concluded that the provision in the federal rules permitting the accused to "introduce evidence on his own behalf" had been violated by the magistrate's refusal to compel attendance of a witness "whose testimony promise[d] appreciable assistance on the issue of probable cause." Moreover, the right violated was one "reinforced by the holding in *Coleman v. Alabama* " because the right to counsel established there "would amount to no more than a pious overture unless it is a right to counsel able to function efficaciously in his client's behalf." Turning to the question of how the magistrate's mistake should be corrected, the appellate court noted that the indictment "itself establishes probable cause," that a long line of cases had held that a defendant "is not entitled to a preliminary hearing where he is indicted before a hearing is held," and that this line of decisions was now incorporated in federal statutory law governing preliminary hearings.[25] However, the harm flowing from the magistrate's error could be remedied without requiring a new preliminary hearing. Thus, the district court might make the undercover agent's grand jury testimony available to defense counsel, have the agent produced for a voluntary interview of "appropriate bounds" as set by the judge, or allow a deposition by written interrogatories to the agent. These suggestions were not meant to "exhaust the possibilities," and the case would be remanded to the trial court to fashion "suitable relief."

Coleman v. Burnett appeared to adopt a "bootstrap analysis" under which the denial of procedural rights afforded under state law result in a denial of the Sixth Amendment right to counsel. Under this analysis, the state is constitutionally required to provide

24. 477 F.2d 1187 (D.C.Cir.1973).

25. See § 14.2 at notes 12–13.

some remedy, akin to that suggested in *Coleman v. Burnett,* where the error is brought to the trial court's attention before trial, notwithstanding the intervening indictment. The focus of the remedy is to ensure that defendant is not harmed by the loss of those incidental benefits of the preliminary hearing that could have a bearing on the defense presentation at trial. So too, if the trial court erroneously concludes that magistrate's ruling was correct and a trial and conviction follow, an appellate court would be required to apply a *Chapman* harmless error review, as prescribed in *Coleman v. Alabama,* as to the possible impact upon the trial of the magistrate's procedural error at the preliminary hearing. The ramifications of the *Coleman v. Burnett* analysis could be carried even further, perhaps, to challenge the practice of mooting itself, as a state action that deprives defense counsel of a valuable tool in preparing for trial. Such a result, of course, could be seen as creating a direct conflict with *Lem Woon* and its reaffirmance in cases like *Gerstein,*[26] and it is perhaps for that reason that the *Coleman v. Burnett* analysis has been largely disregarded in preliminary hearing jurisprudence.

26. See § 14.2(a).

Chapter 15

GRAND JURY REVIEW

Table of Sections

---

§ 15.1 Defendant's Right to Prosecution by Indictment

(a) Federal Constitutional Requirements. As noted in Chapter 8, the English grand jury was originally instituted to assist the Crown in investigating crimes, but it later came to be valued as the primary shield against the arbitrary initiation of prosecution by the Crown.[1] This shielding function was held in especially high esteem by the American colonists, in large part because of colonial grand juries that had refused to indict various persons opposed to Royalist power. It was hardly surprising therefore that grand jury screening was mandated in the Bill of Rights. The Fifth Amendment provides that, except for certain military cases, "no person shall be held to answer for a capital, or otherwise infamous crime, unless on a presentment or indictment of a Grand Jury." Under this guarantee, the federal government, in bringing a prosecution for an infamous crime, must first gain the approval of the grand jury as expressed in its issuance of an indictment.[2] *Ex parte Wilson* [3] gave the indictment requirement broad scope by defining an "infamous crime" as one "punishable by imprisonment at hard labor in a * * * penitentiary." This definition renders the indictment guarantee applicable to all federal felony offenses. The phrase "hard labor" is read as including the standard conditions of imprisonment, and federal sentencing law provides for possible imprisonment in a penitentiary for all felonies.

At the time of the adoption of the Fifth Amendment, all of the states also required that felony prosecutions be brought by indictment. Michigan in 1859 became the first state to authorize prosecutors to bring felony prosecutions on an information. Several states followed Michigan's lead, and in 1884, the constitutionality of this shift from indictment to information reached the Supreme Court in *Hurtado v. California*.[4] Since it had long been held that the Bill of Rights applied only to the federal government, the issue posed in *Hurtado* was whether the due process clause of the Fourteenth Amendment imposed an indictment requirement similar to that contained in the Fifth Amendment. The Court held that it did not. Due process, it noted, required only those procedures essential to preserving "fundamental principles of liberty and justice." Grand jury screening was not essential to ensuring adequate protection against unwarranted prosecutions. The substitute procedure adopted in California, which required a magistrate's finding of probable cause following a preliminary examination, served to similarly safeguard the "substantial interests" of the accused. In the years since *Hurtado*, the Supreme Court, by holding or dictum, has incorporated within due process all of the other criminal procedure guarantees found in the Bill of Rights.[5] At the same time, however, the Court has frequently reaffirmed its *Hurtado* ruling. Prosecution by indictment continues to be viewed as a procedure not essential to due process and therefore not required of the states.

(b) State Requirements. Over the years, the number of states rejecting an indictment

§ 15.1

1. See § 8.2. Although this chapter focuses on the "shielding" or "screening" function of the grand jury, that function cannot be entirely separated from the grand jury's investigative function. Accordingly, this chapter builds upon the material previously considered in Chapter 8, particularly the discussions of the grand jury's history and structure in §§ 8.2–8.5.

2. Although the Fifth Amendment also refers to prosecution by presentment (a formal charge brought by the grand jury on its own initiative), Federal Rule 7 allows only the use of an indictment, which requires approval of the prosecutor. See § 13.3(d).

3. 114 U.S. 417, 5 S.Ct. 935, 29 L.Ed. 89 (1885).

4. 110 U.S. 516, 4 S.Ct. 111, 28 L.Ed. 232 (1884), also discussed in §§ 2.4, 14.2(a).

5. See § 2.6(a).

requirement and allowing felony prosecutions to be brought by information has grown steadily. Twenty-seven states now allow for prosecution by information for all felony charges,[6] and four additional states allow for prosecution by information for all felonies except capital and life imprisonment offenses.[7] These states are commonly known as "information states." While they typically grant the prosecutor the option of proceeding by indictment or information, the overwhelming choice in favor of the information has made it the standard charging instrument in all of the states allowing that alternative. The remaining 19 states, commonly described as "indictment states," require prosecution by indictment for all felonies.[8] In all but a few indictment states, misdemeanors may be prosecuted by information (or complaint) at the prosecutor's option.

(c) Use of Indictments in Information States. In some information states, prosecution by indictment is never used. In most, however, at least occasional use is made of the indictment alternative. Ordinarily that use will not exceed 5% of all felony prosecutions, although prosecutors in atypical districts may go so far as to make the indictment the primary mode of charging. Where prosecutors make only occasional use of the indictment, they usually turn to the indictment alternative only when the grand jury process offers a special advantage under the circumstances of the particular case. In many information jurisdictions, the primary use of indictments is in cases that were brought before the grand jury because its investigative authority was needed to develop sufficient evidence to prosecute. While the prosecutor could conceivably ask the grand jury to do no more than investigate, once a case is before the grand jury, it ordinarily will stay there; after the investigation is completed, the grand jury will review the evidence and decide whether to indict.

Prosecutors in information states also present to the grand jury, though less frequently, fully investigated cases that are ready for possible indictment. The prosecutor's decision to utilize the grand jury in such cases most often has very little to do with the grand jury's screening expertise. For example, the prosecution may take the case before the grand jury simply because it wants to avoid a preliminary hearing.[9] So too, where the defendant is a fugitive or outside the jurisdiction, and there is an immediate need to file charges in the trial court, the indictment may be the only available route as an information would require a preliminary hearing at which the defendant must be present.

In rare instances, the prosecution in an information state will seek an indictment in order to gain the element of "peer review" provided by the grand jury. Thus, the prosecutor may look to the grand jury in politically sensitive situations as a buffer against adverse public reaction. Recognizing that the decision to prosecute or not prosecute will give rise to substantial controversy, the prosecutor may seek to share the responsibility for that decision with the grand jury. Similarly, where the case presents a close question under a legal standard that looks to the community's judgment, the prosecutor may prefer not to proceed without an expression of that judgment as reflected in the grand jury's decision to indict. A prosecutor who has difficulty with the credibility of a key witness may likewise prefer to proceed only after a grand jury judges that witness to be truthful. Such considerations are more likely to lead a prosecutor to the grand jury where the magistrate at the preliminary hearing will make only a

6. Those states are: Arkansas, Arizona, California, Colorado, Connecticut, Hawaii, Idaho, Illinois, Indiana, Iowa, Kansas, Maryland, Michigan, Missouri, Montana, Nebraska, Nevada, New Mexico, North Dakota, Oklahoma, Oregon, South Dakota, Utah, Vermont, Washington, Wisconsin, and Wyoming.

7. Those states are: Florida, Louisiana, Minnesota, and Rhode Island.

8. Those states are: Alabama, Alaska, Delaware, Georgia, Kentucky, Maine, Massachusetts, Mississippi, New Hampshire, New Jersey, New York, North Carolina, Ohio, Pennsylvania (with local option to adopt a plan for prosecution by information), South Carolina, Tennessee, Texas, Virginia, and West Virginia.

9. See § 14.2(d).

very limited credibility judgment, or the jurisdiction is one of the few that does not provide for a preliminary hearing.

(d) Waiver in Indictment Jurisdictions. In the indictment jurisdiction, the key to the frequency of prosecution by indictments is the use of waiver. While the Fifth Amendment and similarly worded state constitutional provisions do not specifically state that the requirement of prosecution by indictment can be waived, courts have almost uniformly held that these provisions do not preclude a knowing and voluntary defense waiver. Many of the same courts have suggested, however, that since waiver of an indictment was not permitted at common law, it should be allowed only if authorized by statute. Most indictment jurisdictions have statutes or court rules allowing knowing and voluntary waivers, with the effect of the waiver being to permit the prosecution to proceed by information. A few permit waiver in all cases; several, like Federal Rule 6(b), permit waiver in all but capital cases; and a few deny waiver as well in certain types of non-capital cases.

Waivers are most frequently made where the prospective defendant intends to plead guilty to the charges that the prosecution would otherwise present to the grand jury. Very often, such waivers are part of a plea bargaining agreement with the prosecutor. Where the prospective defendant anticipates contesting the proposed charge, defense counsel often advise against waiver, although not because they have high hopes that the grand jury will refuse to indict. Prosecution by indictment may offer the defense a potential procedural advantage since pleading defects in an indictment cannot be cured as readily by amendment as similar defects in an information.[10] Also, if the jurisdiction precludes the use of hearsay before the grand jury, key witnesses will have to testify before the grand jury and that testimony ordinarily will be available for impeachment use at trial. On the other hand, there are situations in which a waiver will be to the advantage of the defense even though it intends to contest the charge. In some instances, the defense may be concerned that the prosecutor will gain valuable preparation for trial in presenting witnesses before the grand jury. Defendant also has an incentive to waive if he is in jail or would otherwise be inconvenienced by delay and his case cannot promptly be presented to the grand jury. Some defense counsel also prefer that charges be presented by information because they believe that trial jurors, contrary to the court's instructions, do give weight to the fact that another group of lay persons reviewed the case and issued an indictment.

§ 15.2 The Structure of Grand Jury Screening

(a) Prosecutor Control Over Proof. As discussed in § 8.4(b), the prosecution, through its ex parte presentation of the case against the prospective defendant, exercises primary control over the proof that will be presented to the grand jurors. That control, however, is subject to limitations stemming from the independence of the jurors, the supervisory authority of the court, and the general responsibilities of the prosecutor to seek justice rather than simply victory. Initially, most jurisdictions, in keeping with historical tradition, allow the grand jurors to go beyond the prosecution's presentation and consider any information the grand jurors personally have obtained regarding the events in question. Of course, that authority has little practical significance in the larger communities of today, apart from the unusual case in which the alleged offense occurred before the grand jury (e.g., perjury in grand jury testimony).

An independent authority of the jurors with a slightly greater potential for application is the right of the jurors to insist upon the presentation of evidence beyond that initially offered by the prosecutor. That right stems from the grand jury's well established authority to set the scope of its investigation and therefore to obtain all relevant evidence. Indeed, in several jurisdictions, when the grand jury "has reason to believe that other evi-

10. See § 19.5.

dence within its reach will explain away the charge," it has a statutory obligation "to order the evidence to be produced." Jurors rarely call for additional evidence, however. Most often, they will not be aware of those persons who might provide additional relevant evidence, particularly exculpatory evidence. Moreover, even where the grand jury learns from the evidence before it that a certain individual might possess exculpatory information, the jurors ordinarily will accept the prosecutor's explanation as to why that witness should not be called to testify.

The prosecutor's control over the proof presented may also be overridden by the supervisory authority of court. The supervising judge (usually the judge who impaneled the grand jury) generally is recognized to have the authority to insist that the grand jury consider particular evidence where that is necessary to prevent a "miscarriage of justice." The supervising judge, however, is even less likely to be aware of such evidence than the grand jury. Absent a communication from the prosecutor, jurors, or prospective defendant, the judge ordinarily will have no knowledge of what evidence is being presented to the grand jury.

A much more likely restraint upon the prosecutor's control over the proof presented comes from the prosecutorial obligation to produce known exculpatory evidence. As noted in § 15.7(e), not all jurisdictions recognize such an obligation and its scope varies in those jurisdictions in which it is recognized. In general, it requires presentation of evidence known to the prosecutor that could readily be viewed by the grand jury as negating the guilt of the prospective defendant. Jurisdictions recognizing the obligation commonly give it teeth by allowing a defense challenge to any subsequent indictment based upon the prosecutor's failure to inform the grand jury of such exculpatory evidence. Yet, even with such a deterrent, the obligation is likely to have limited significance, as the prosecutor often will not be aware of the existence of exculpatory evidence. Here, as with the judicial control noted above, the key is the intervention of the prospective defendant. Thus, the critical factor will be whether the prospective defendant is able and willing to call potentially exculpatory evidence to the attention of the prosecutor and request its presentation before the grand jurors. Not all prospective defendants are aware in advance that the prosecution will be seeking an indictment, and others are aware but do not yet have the assistance of counsel. Even where the timing poses no difficulties, counsel for a prospective defendant may not be willing to reveal to the prosecution exculpatory evidence, knowing that such evidence must convince the grand jury without the support of counsel's argument and without counsel being able to challenge the prosecution's response to that evidence.

(b) The Prospective Defendant's Testimony. In most jurisdictions, the testimony of the prospective defendant legally is treated no differently than any other evidence that the prospective defendant may request to be presented before the grand jury. Indeed, here the prosecutor and the grand jury are most likely to have absolute discretionary authority in responding to the request, for the self-serving nature of a prospective defendant's testimony makes it highly unlikely that such testimony would be characterized as critical exculpatory evidence. Nonetheless, as a matter of practice, prosecutors are most likely to accede to a prospective defendant's request to give testimony himself—if for no other reason than that the prosecutor's cross-examination of the prospective defendant will provide an excellent opportunity to lay the ground work for impeachment at trial and may even produce incriminating statements. Those prosecutorial advantages are not lost on defense counsel, however. Few will advise the prospective defendant to run the risks presented in submitting to the cross-examination of the prosecutor in a setting in which neither the defense counsel (in most jurisdictions) nor the judge (in all jurisdictions) will be present.[1]

§ 15.2

1. As to the presence of counsel for the witness (which will include a testifying prospective defendant), see § 8.15(b).

Several jurisdictions ensure that the prospective defendant who wants to gamble on the persuasiveness of his own testimony will be able to do so. Those jurisdictions have established a statutory right of the target to testify. Statutory provisions recognizing that right require that the prosecutor give the target advance notice of his right, at least where the individual already has been arrested on the charges to be presented, and the failure to give that notice can result in the dismissal of any subsequent indictment. Where the particular jurisdiction automatically immunizes witnesses before the grand jury, the prospective defendant will not be allowed to exercise his right to testify without first waiving that immunity. The statutory right will guarantee to the prospective defendant the opportunity initially to present without interruption his version of the facts, but he then must respond to fair cross-examination by the prosecutor and any relevant questions of the grand jurors.

(c) Evidentiary Rules. Although all jurisdictions require that testimonial privileges be recognized in grand jury proceedings, they vary substantially as to the applicability of the remaining rules of evidence. Several states make the rules of evidence fully applicable to the grand jury, but these jurisdictions are almost all information states in which the grand jury indictment is rarely used. Another grouping of several states, including some indictment states, hold the rules of evidence generally applicable, recognizing only a few narrow exceptions (e.g., allowing written sworn statements as to ownership or value of property or written reports of non-testifying experts).[2] Another handful of states have provisions that preclude prosecutorial reliance upon the recorded statements of witnesses by limiting admissible evidence to physical evidence, documentary evidence, and the testimony of witnesses produced before the grand jury. Finally, the majority of jurisdictions hold the rules of evidence not to be applicable (apart from testimonial privileges).

The contentions advanced for and against the various state positions on the use of inadmissible evidence are much the same as the contentions presented in the debate over the applicability of the rules of evidence to the preliminary hearing.[3] Those favoring application of the rules contend that the grand jury must be given admissible evidence if it is to serve the task of preventing unwarranted prosecutions. The grand jury can hardly assess the strength of the prosecution's case where it is allowed to rely upon evidence that cannot be used at trial. Even where the inadmissible evidence might be replaced by admissible evidence at trial, as in the case of hearsay, the grand jury is being deprived of the opportunity to fully evaluate the evidence as it will be seen by a trial jury. While an investigating officer's neatly capsulized summary of the anticipated testimony of various eyewitnesses might suggest a case with few weaknesses, a grand jury which actually hears the "often halting, inconsistent and incomplete testimony of [those] honest observers" might well reach a different conclusion. So too, the grand jury's authority to ask its own questions is of little value where the only witness to be questioned can do no more than restate what others have told him. Though exemptions from the evidentiary rules may be appropriate as to issues likely to be uncontested, thereby allowing the laboratory report to be presented without the accompanying testimony of the technician, heavy reliance on inadmissible evidence, it is argued, readily will serve to mask deficiencies in the prosecution's case.

Those opposing application of the rules of evidence maintain that insistence upon admissible evidence is not necessary for, and indeed is inconsistent with, the grand jury's fulfillment of its various functions. They note that: (1) grand jurors who may have doubts about witness summaries provided by the prosecution can always request that the actual witnesses be presented before them; (2)

2. Such exceptions often parallel those recognized in the context of the preliminary hearing. See § 14.4(b).

3. See § 14.4(b).

to perform its varied functions—which include both investigation and possible consideration of grounds for nullifying notwithstanding sufficient evidence—the grand jury must be able to ask for, and receive, material that would not be admissible at trial; and (3) busy prosecutors are not interested in building a case based on incompetent evidence that cannot be replaced at trial with admissible evidence, as their concern is with gaining a conviction rather than gaining an indictment that has no chance of success at trial. Also advanced against applying the evidentiary rules are a series of administrative difficulties, including (1) the increased length of the grand jury proceeding and inconvenience to witnesses, (2) the absence of opposing counsel, who at trial would make the prosecution aware of potential evidentiary objections and thereby facilitate the prosecution's substitution of other evidence that would not be objectionable, and (3) the unavailability of a judicial officer to provide a prompt ruling on admissibility where the prosecutor is aware of evidentiary uncertainty.

(d) Legal Advice. The prosecutor serves not only as the state's advocate in presenting its case to the grand jury, but also as the primary legal advisor to the grand jury. The tension produced by these seemingly conflicting roles tends to be moderated, however, by other aspects of the process. The two most significant portions of prosecutorial legal advice tend to be the prosecutor's explanations of the authority of the grand jury and the elements of the particular crimes under consideration. As to the former, the grand jury also is given extensive direction by the supervising court in its charge to the jury upon its impanelment. That charge commonly will speak to such matters as the grand jury's obligation to act as an independent body in screening charges, juror recognition that the prosecutors present evidence as "advocates for the government," the authority of the grand jury to have appropriate questions put to witnesses and to request the production of additional witnesses, the need for the jurors to make their own judgment of the credibility of witnesses, the possible limitations of hearsay evidence (where such evidence is allowed), and the level of proof needed to indict. In the course of offering further legal advice on the grand jury's authority, the prosecutor must maintain a consistency with the court's charge. Indeed, in some jurisdictions, the jurors are informed in that charge that they may return to the court for additional instructions if they should find an inconsistency, or otherwise lack confidence, in the further legal advice provided by the prosecutor.

While the court's charge ordinarily will not touch upon the elements of particular offenses, prosecutorial leeway here commonly is limited by the practice of utilizing the same jury instructions that would be presented by a trial judge in charging a jury. Very often, these will be standard jury instructions or instructions otherwise well established under state law. Role conflicts are likely to be felt only where the prosecutor must decide whether the instructions should go beyond the offense itself to encompass excuses or justifications or where the prosecutor is asked by jurors to expand upon the instructions. As discussed in § 15.7(f), where the prosecutor errs in his or her judgment on these matters, the result can be the quashing of the indictment issued by the grand jury.

Many jurisdictions also allow the prosecutor to present to the grand jury his or her opinion as to the sufficiency of the evidence to establish possible charges. As noted in § 15.-7(b), some jurisdictions view this authority as resting on the prosecutor's role as legal advisor to the grand jury, while others view it as an aspect of the prosecutor's role as the state's advocate. Under either view, the authority will be subject to various limitations, also discussed in § 15.7(b).

(e) Quantum of Proof. There is a sharp division among the states as to the quantum of proof needed to indict. Approximately a third of the states allow for indictment upon a finding of "probable cause" to believe that the accused has committed the crime charged. A slightly larger group of states utilize a "prima facie evidence standard," authorizing indictment only "when all the evidence taken together, if unexplained or uncontradicted, would warrant a conviction of the defendant." Another group of states, consisting largely of information states, have no clear precedent as to the applicable standard. In the federal courts, the governing standard apparently is the probable cause standard, but some judges use a prima facie instruction. Since the trial jury may convict only if convinced of the accused's guilt beyond a reasonable doubt, it generally is assumed that the prima facie evidence standard is a substantially more rigorous test than the traditional probable cause standard.[4] However, where the supervising judge follows the common charging practice of simply quoting the prima facie standard, without explaining the degree of proof needed to "warrant a conviction," that greater rigor will be lost. The distinction ordinarily has no bearing beyond the grand jurors' own weighing of the evidence since, as noted in § 15.5, the vast majority of jurisdictions do not allow for judicial review of the sufficiency of the evidence before the grand jury.

Of course, even if the necessary standard of proof is met, the grand jury need not indict. The authority of the grand jury to nullify was, perhaps, the most important attribute of the grand jury review from the perspective of those who insisted that it be included in the Bill of Rights. That authority and its historical grounding have frequently been noted in appellate opinions discussing the screening function of the grand jury. Contrary to the dominant position taken with respect to the petit jury, many judges will inform the grand jurors of their authority to nullify in the course of the charge to the jury upon its impanelment. This probably reflects a minority position, however, and is nowhere statutorily required.

(f) Resubmission. As noted in § 8.4(a), jurisdictions vary as to the proportion of the jurors who must vote in favor to have an indictment, although all require at least a majority and none require unanimity. Where the number of jurors favoring indictment is sufficient, the proposed indictment put before the grand jury by the prosecutor will be approved as a "true bill." Where the number is insufficient the grand jury will return a finding of *ignoramus* ("we ignore it") or "no bill." At this point, jurisdictions vary with respect to the prosecutor's authority to resubmit the charge to a new grand jury. Since jeopardy has not attached, there is no constitutional limitation against resubmission, and the issue is one to be resolved by local law. The division here, as in the case of resubmission following a preliminary hearing dismissal,[5] clearly favors unrestricted resubmission, but a significant minority group of jurisdictions do impose limitations.

The longstanding federal rule is that resubmissions are permissible, without court approval, even when the prosecutor presents no additional evidence to the second grand jury. The rationale underlying this rule was set forth by the Supreme Court in *United States v. Thompson:*[6] "[T]he power and duty of the grand jury to investigate * * * is continuous and is therefore not exhausted or limited by adverse action [previously] taken by a grand jury or by its failure to act." The federal rule clearly constitutes the majority position today, although it was not always so. During the early part of this century, roughly half of the states had statutory provisions requiring judicial approval for resubmissions. Such provisions are now found in only about one-fourth of the states. While these provisions generally do not prescribe standards as to when the court should allow resubmission, they have been construed as ordinarily requiring a showing of substantial additional evidence not submitted to the first grand jury. A few jurisdictions have added a prohibition against more than a single resubmission.

§ 15.3 The Effectiveness of Grand Jury Screening

(a) The Ongoing Debate. The value of grand jury review has been a subject of ongoing debate in this country ever since American law reformers, following the lead of Bent-

4. See § 14.3(a).

5. See § 14.3(c).

6. 251 U.S. 407, 40 S.Ct. 289, 64 L.Ed. 333 (1920).

ham in England, launched the first major attack upon prosecution by indictment in the mid–1800's. During this century, periods of heated debate were sparked by reports of National Commissions, issued in the 1930's and the 1970's, urging elimination of statutory and constitutional provisions requiring prosecution by indictment. In recent years, almost all of the commentary in legal periodicals has been critical of grand jury screening. The critics tend to fall into two categories. The first group would abolish grand jury screening, although not the grand jury itself. The role of the grand jury would be limited to investigations. While the grand jury would retain the authority to issue indictments in cases it investigated, those indictments would be given no greater weight than a complaint; they would be followed by the preliminary hearing or other screening procedure used in issuing an information in the particular jurisdiction. The second group of critics urge a more limited reform—eliminating compulsory prosecution by indictment. They urge indictment jurisdictions to become information jurisdictions, granting the prosecutor the option to proceed either by indictment or information, with the information preferred for all but exceptional cases.

Critics in the first group see grand jury review as essentially worthless. Grand juries, they argue, are no more than a "rubber stamp" for the prosecutor. They cite statements of former prosecutors who note that a prosecutor, if he so desires, "can indict anybody, at any time, for almost anything before a grand jury." Statistics on refusals to indict are also said to show an almost complete lack of grand jury independence. Grand juries issue "no-bills" in only a very small percentage of the cases presented to them (less than 5% in many indictment jurisdictions), and even that small percentage does not necessarily reflect disagreement with the prosecutor. Critics suggest that many of the "no-bills" may have come in cases in which the prosecutor preferred not to charge but wanted the grand jury to bear the burden of that decision.

The second group of critics view grand jury review as having some value, but not enough to require it in every case. They argue that grand jury screening, even if minimally adequate, is less effective and less efficient than the preliminary hearing. Since they reject use of both screening devices as unnecessary duplication, these critics would reserve grand jury review for exceptional situations, as determined by the prosecution in its discretion. Those exceptional situations would consist largely of cases in which the prosecution has need for the grand jury's investigative authority or the special qualities that lay judgment can bring to the charging decision. In all other cases, the preliminary hearing would be the exclusive screening device and the prosecution would charge by information.

Critics in this second category maintain that the preliminary hearing, because it is an adversary proceeding, generally provides a better safeguard against unwarranted prosecutions, even if one assumes that grand jurors exercise independent judgment. These critics also stress the preliminary hearing's value as an open screening procedure, as opposed to the secret grand jury proceeding. This feature is particularly important today, they say, when so many cases are resolved by guilty plea rather than by trial. Finally, they argue, the preliminary hearing is preferable simply because it is more efficient. Impaneling and servicing a grand jury is costly in terms of space, manpower, and money. The grand jury also adds to the delay in processing cases since grand juries, particularly in rural areas, are not as readily available as magistrates. The critics also point to the "intricacies and complexities" of grand jury law, claiming that they spawn "uncertainty and additional litigation" and increase the likelihood of successful challenges based on "reasons unrelated to innocence." "In short," this second group of critics note, "any benefits to be derived from a requirement that all offenses be charged by grand jury indictment are * * * outweighed by the probability that the indictment process will be ineffective as a screening device, by the cost of the proceeding, and by the procedural intricacies involved."

Supporters of grand jury review reject the contentions of both groups of critics. Initially, they maintain that the grand jury is a highly effective screening agency. They cite prosecutors who have characterized the grand jury as a valuable sounding board with a mind of its own. The typical low rate of no-bills, they argue, is not inconsistent with this assessment. One should not expect a high percentage of refusals to indict if prosecutors carefully screen their cases in anticipation of mandatory grand jury review. Moreover, the rate of no-bills is not universally low. In New York, grand juries have refused to indict in approximately 10% of their cases and have reduced charges in an almost equal percentage of their cases, notwithstanding that their review often was preceded by a preliminary hearing bindover. Supporters also suggest that the crucial statistic is not the percentage of no-bills, but the percentage of indictments that were not supported at trial with sufficient evidence to get the case to the jury. In most grand jury jurisdictions, they argue, that percentage is quite low, indicating that the grand jury rarely errs in its conclusion that the evidence supports an indictment.[1]

Supporters of grand jury review also reject the contention that the preliminary hearing is a superior screening agency. The strength of grand jury review, they note, lies exactly where independent screening is most needed—in those cases in which special factors, e.g., the involvement of politics or racial animosity, are likely to result in unjust accusations. Such cases require a screening agency that can carefully judge credibility and can give consideration to community notions of fairness and justice. The preliminary hearing magistrate often is restricted in his judgment of credibility, whereas the grand jury can weigh credibility in much the same fashion as a trial jury. Unlike the magistrate, the grand jury also has a recognized authority to disregard legally sufficient evidence and indict for a lesser offense or refuse to indict altogether. As a group selected from the community, it can and will act to leaven the rigidity of the law.

Supporters of the grand jury contend that its screening advantages justify any additional costs associated with grand jury review, but many also argue that the grand jury actually is less costly than the preliminary hearing. The modern preliminary hearing, they note, has developed into a time consuming mini-trial. The major cost factor in the grand jury process, the use of jurors, is more than offset by the extra costs of the preliminary hearing—the participation of the defense counsel and the magistrate, and the investment of far more time by the prosecutor and witnesses. Similarly, with defense counsel frequently seeking continuances, the preliminary hearing is likely to produce greater delay in processing a charge than grand jury screening. Difficulties in scheduling prompt grand jury review are said to be a problem only in rural areas, and appropriate provisions for waiver and bail can largely alleviate the consequences of delays even in those areas. Supporters also argue that minor reforms could eliminate the legal intricacies that sometimes result in successful challenges to indictments on technical grounds. Moreover, they note, with the preliminary hearing procedure growing more complex, there is at least equal potential for a successful technical challenge to a bindover.

Finally, supporters contend that grand jury review clearly comes out ahead when the symbolic impact of the information and indictment processes are compared. What the grand jury loses through a non-adversary, secret proceeding is more than offset by its inclusion of community representatives in the screening process. Participation of laymen contributes to public confidence in the criminal justice system and thereby justifies grand

§ 15.3

1. Critics respond that this low rate is deceptive since a substantially higher percentage of cases often are dismissed on the prosecutor's nolle prosequi motion, see § 1.4(f), and many cases are resolved by guilty pleas to reduced charges, which may reflect overcharging that passed through the grand jury. They also cite the number of successful challenges to indictments (although still relatively small) in those jurisdictions that allow pretrial challenges to the sufficiency of the evidence before the grand jury [see § 15.5(c)].

jury review even in cases that are "open and shut." Supporters note that, in a system where most cases do not go to trial, it is especially important that "private citizens" are given an "active role" in the "front lines" of the criminal justice process.

(b) Screening Variations. Both supporters and critics commonly characterize grand jury screening as if the grand jury's processes were largely uniform throughout the country. There are, however, numerous variations that relate to both grand jury independence and standards for indictment. These include variations in: (1) the method used in selecting the grand jury venire (i.e., whether a random selection system utilizing a general representative list or a "key-man" selection system) [see § 8.4(a)]; (2) the length of the grand jury term, which may lead in a jurisdiction with a longer term (e.g., 12 or 18 months) to more frequent excusals on hardship grounds and a different mix of jurors [see § 8.4(a)]; (3) the recognition of bias challenges to jurors [see § 15.4(e)]; (4) the size of the jury and the proportion of the jurors that must vote in favor of indictment [see § 8.4(a)]; (5) the authority of the prosecutor to present and examine witnesses over grand juror objection [see § 8.4(b)]; (6) the recognition of an obligation of the prosecutor to present known exculpatory evidence or the grand jury to call for such evidence [see § 15.2(a)]; (7) the recognition of a right of a prospective defendant to testify [see § 15.2(b)]; (8) the extent of the application of the rules of evidence to grand jury proceedings [§ 15.2(c)]; (9) the scope of the court's initial charge upon impaneling the grand jury and use of standard instructions in the prosecutor's charge on the legal elements of the offenses considered [see § 15.2(d)]; (10) the use of a "probable cause" or "prima facie case" standard as to the quantum of proof required for indictment [see § 15.2(e)]; (11) the scope of the prosecutor's authority to resubmit following a grand jury refusal to indict [see § 15.2(f)]; (12) the availability of trial court review of the sufficiency of the evidence before the grand jury to support its indictment [see § 15.5]; (13) the scope of the trial court's review of alleged prosecutorial misconduct before the grand jury [§ 15.6]; and (14) the scope of judicial review of alleged errors in grand jury proceeding where there has been an intervening conviction on the indictment [§§ 15.4(h), 15.5(c), 15.6(e)].

Not surprisingly, critics and supporters of grand jury screening disagree as to the significance of these differences in the grand jury structure and screening process. Some supporters argue that, with the right structural and procedural components, the grand jury can be an effective screening process. Others argue that the lay composition of the grand jury is the critical element which ensures its basic effectiveness and other features are largely peripheral. Critics maintain that the deficiencies inherent in grand jury screening are too significant to be offset by procedural and structural features designed to "improve" grand jury screening.

(c) Judicial Responses. While the debate over the effectiveness of grand jury review has been aimed primarily at legislative reform, it has not gone unnoticed by the courts. Several courts have suggested that the critics probably are correct in concluding that grand jury review almost always is a rubber stamp operation. Their response has been to downplay in various respects the significance of the indictment process. Thus, the California Supreme Court has held that grand jury screening is so inferior to preliminary hearing screening that its state's equal protection guarantee bars granting some defendants only grand jury review while others receive a preliminary hearing.[2] So too, courts have suggested that the safeguards required to ensure against inadvertent "waivers" of other constitutional rights need not be applied to waivers of the right to indictment since that right is rarely of importance to the defense.

2. Hawkins v. Superior Court, 22 Cal.3d 584, 150 Cal.Rptr. 435, 586 P.2d 916 (1978), also discussed in § 14.2 at note 11. See also Commonwealth v. Webster, 462 Pa. 125, 337 A.2d 914 (1975) (equal protection is not denied by a local option to proceed by information because "no aspect of the operation and procedures of an indicting grand jury works to the advantage and protection of an accused").

Other courts have expressed concern as to the possible "rubber stamp" quality of grand jury review, but have cited that concern as a basis for insisting upon procedural safeguards designed to offset prosecutorial dominance. They apparently share the view of many supporters of the grand jury that any weaknesses in its screening are not inherent in the grand jury structure, but simply require the development of new safeguards to protect against possible prosecutorial abuses. Finally, still other courts largely reject the criticism of grand jury screening. They view grand jury review as continuing to function effectively, although that judgment may rest upon a view of the process as designed to provide screening less finely tuned than that envisaged by many of those most critical of the process.

These differences in judgment as to the potential value of grand jury screening are reflected in the judicial treatment of almost all of the various grounds urged for challenging an indictment. While some opinions treating such challenges openly discuss the merits of grand jury review, most do not speak to the issue directly. Very often the court's underlying policy perspective will be obvious from the result it reaches. At times, however, the same ruling might be supported by either of two quite different judgments as to the value of grand jury review. Thus, a court rejecting a challenge to an indictment that was based in part on illegally obtained evidence may be taking the position that: (1) even if use of such evidence were prohibited, the grand jury still would almost always indict upon the prosecutor's request, so adding a prohibition against such use would simply cause delay without significant gain for an inherently weak screening process; or (2) the grand jury is functioning well as a rough screening body guided by a community sense of justice and the addition of prohibitions against the use of illegally obtained evidence is not needed for effective performance of its assigned role.

§ 15.4 Indictment Challenges Based Upon Grand Jury Composition

(a) Grand Jury Selection Procedures. As will be seen in the subsections that follow, the law governing the composition of the grand jury differs in several respects from that governing the composition of the petit jury. Those differences are influenced primarily by the different roles of the grand jury and the petit jury, but they also reflect differences in the procedures utilized in selecting the two juries. As noted in § 8.4(a), the first step in the jury selection process—the summoning of prospective jurors (commonly described as the "calling of the array" or the "selection of the venire")—ordinarily is the same for both the grand jury and the petit jury. The jurisdiction will use either random selection from a general representative list (such as a voter registration list), random selection from a list of persons nominated by key-man selectors, or discretionary selection by the key-man selectors. The same basic qualifications for jury service (e.g., residency, age, and citizenship) will be applicable to both juries, and the unqualified jurors will be eliminated by the court or jury commissioners either before the list is used or after the prospective jurors are summoned. Those persons statutorily exempted from jury service will be eliminated in a similar fashion.

Once the venire of qualified and non-exempt prospective jurors is established, the selection procedures for grand juries and petit juries begin to vary. Initially, because the grand jury sits for a longer term, a larger group of prospective jurors is likely to be excused on hardship grounds. Following the excusals, in the selection of the petit jury, the next steps will be the voir dire and the exercise of peremptory challenges and challenges for cause by both the prosecution and the defense. In the grand jury process, in contrast, there is no voir dire or peremptory challenge, and while challenges for cause are available, the defense challenges ordinarily are presented in a quite different fashion and only after the jury has been impaneled and has taken action against the defendant.

Various factors explain the lack of a voir dire in the grand jury process. Initially, the voir dire comes before the jury is empaneled, and at that point in the grand jury process, there ordinarily is no defendant who could participate in a two-sided voir dire. Indeed, some of the offenses that will be considered by the grand jury over the course of its term have not yet been committed, and as to others, the offender will not yet have been arrested. Also, the basic function of voir dire, facilitating challenges, is of limited significance as to the grand jury. There are no peremptory challenges, which also could not be made two-sided. Challenges for cause are available, but they tend to be limited to much narrower grounds than petit jury challenges, and therefore create much less of a need for voir dire to obtain relevant information.

Though the grand jury process does not utilize a voir dire, the supervising judge may on occasion ask the jurors about their background as it relates to a particular type of case (e.g., drug offenses) or a particular case. That is most likely to be done where the judge is aware that the grand jury will be utilized to conduct an investigation of particular events or a particular type of criminal activity. Where the juror's background suggests that he or she might have some involvement with the activities or persons to be investigated, or might be an inappropriate juror for the particular investigation for other reasons, the court may excuse the juror on its own initiative.

Ordinarily, the judge does not question the prospective jurors, apart from a possible secondary check to ensure that all the members are qualified, and the next step in the selection process is the exercise of any challenges to the venire or challenges for cause to particular jurors. Challenges at this point are rare. The only persons who may present such challenges are the prosecutor and defendants who have been "held to answer" (i.e., the complaint filed against the defendant was sustained by the magistrate, at the first appearance or preliminary hearing, and sent forward for grand jury review). Moreover, in many jurisdictions, the challenge to an individual juror is limited to a lack of "legal qualifications." Thus, in all but the most unusual case, pre-impanelment challenges are not made, and after excusing persons making satisfactory hardship claims, the court simply calls forth in numerical order the necessary number of venire members and impanels them as a grand jury.

In the petit jury process, once the jurors are impaneled, the jurors select one of their members as the foreperson. In the grand jury process, however, the judge commonly appoints one of the jurors to be foreperson. The use of judicial appointment probably relates back to the period when the grand jury acted with less reliance upon the prosecutor and the foreperson played a critical role in directing the grand jury investigation. Indeed, a few jurisdictions allow the court to appoint a foreperson from outside the jury panel, and that authority, where still used, is commonly employed with respect to investigative grand juries. In the federal system and most states, the foreperson today performs basically ministerial functions (e.g., administering oaths and signing indictments) and presides during deliberations.

Once the petit jury is impaneled, the composition of the jury is set, apart from the dismissal of any alternate jurors prior to deliberations. The composition of the grand jury, on the other hand, can readily shift over the term of the jury. Particularly in those jurisdictions in which grand juries sit for a long term, one or more jurors are likely to be excused over the course of the term. Ordinarily, jurors are excused because of changed circumstances that make continued service a hardship or render the juror ineligible for service (e.g., a change in residence). Less commonly, a juror will respond affirmatively to the prosecutor's standard query as to whether any reason exists for a juror not to participate in the matter about to be presented, with the supervising judge then excusing that juror on request of the prosecutor. Occasionally, the court, on recommendation of the prosecutor, will dismiss a juror for "cause shown," which can include both actual misconduct and an extreme lack of diligence (e.g., excessive absences or frequent dozing during proceedings). Where the number of remaining jurors is still sufficient to meet the statutory minimum, the excused juror may not be replaced. Very often, however, the court will find it necessary or desirable to add replacements. Those persons will then be selected following the same procedure used in selecting the original jurors.

(b) Timing of the Defense Objection. A defense objection to the composition of the petit jury ordinarily must be made before the jury is impaneled. A challenge to the array must be made prior to voir dire, and a challenge for cause to an individual juror must be made immediately following voir dire, except for the unusual situation in which the grounds for objection could not then have been discovered by the exercise of due diligence. In the grand jury setting, in contrast, defense objections cannot be expected prior to impanelment except where the particular defendant had been held to answer and had a reasonable period prior to impanelment in which to object. Since few defendants fall in that category, all jurisdictions provide an alternative route for defense objections.

Most jurisdictions allow to all defendants a post-indictment challenge through a motion to dismiss the indictment. Ordinarily, a challenge to an indictment based upon a defect in the grand jury process simply must be made before trial, but a more stringent timing requirement often is applied to a motion to dismiss based upon a defect in the composition of the grand jury. Thus, the Federal Jury Selection Act and the Uniform Jury Selection Act both provide that a motion to dismiss based upon a failure to comply with the requirements of those statutes must be brought "within seven days after the defendant discovered or could have discovered, by the exercise of diligence, the grounds therefor." [1] Assuming that the defendant is represented by counsel, this provision will ordinarily mandate that the motion be brought within seven days after the issuance of the indictment. The short time period is imposed as a reasonable counterpart to the requirement in petit jury selection that the objection ordinarily be raised prior to the impanelment of the jury. While requiring an objection before the grand jury initiates its proceedings is deemed impracticable, the objection should at least come promptly after the grand jury has taken action against the accused. Since the grand jury is likely still to be sitting, requiring a prompt challenge increases the potential for damage control through the discharge of an irregularly selected grand jury before it has completed its term and issued more defective indictments.

A small group of jurisdictions require an even more prompt objection by insisting that a defendant held to answer present his challenge prior to indictment where he reasonably could do so. Unlike the federal system, these jurisdictions generally do not limit preindictment challenges to those brought before the grand jury is impaneled, but allow the defendant also to object after impanelment and before indictment. Thus, whenever a defendant is held to answer and has several days before the grand jury will consider his case, he will have the opportunity to file his challenge prior to the issuance of an indictment. These jurisdictions also allow a challenge to be made through a prompt post-indictment motion to dismiss, but that route is not available to the defendant who had a reasonable opportunity to raise a preindictment challenge. Accordingly, a motion to dismiss ordinarily can be used to challenge the composition of the grand jury only where defendant was not held to answer because the indictment preceded his arrest, the indictment was issued shortly after the defendant was held to answer, or the defendant held to answer had good cause for not raising the objection within the several-day period prior to his indictment. "Good cause" for this purpose may include such factors as the failure to the trial court to promptly appoint counsel for an indigent accused or the inability to discover the grounds for the objection notwithstanding counsel's due diligence.

§ 15.4

1. 28 U.S.C.A. § 1867(a); Uniform Jury Selection Act § 12 (Approved Draft 1972). This limit apparently applies only to statutory violations. In many jurisdictions, time limits requiring objections within a specific number of days after indictment apply to both constitutional and statutory violations.

Exceptionally restrictive state timing requirements may be challenged as imposing an undue burden on a defendant's right to contest selection procedures that violate the federal constitution. The Supreme Court has held that stringent timing requirements are constitutionally acceptable, provided that, as applied, they do not deny the defendant a reasonable opportunity to raise his constitutional claim.[2] Looking to that standard, the Court held valid "on its face" a state rule requiring that objections be raised within 3 days after the end of the grand jury term (or before trial, if it came earlier). Although defendants indicted on the last day of the grand jury term would have only three days within which to raise the claim, that period was not per se unreasonable. The Court also upheld the same state's refusal to consider claims made outside the three day limit where one defendant had been a fugitive from justice over the period and another had received appointed counsel on the day the term ended but had not filed an objection until several days thereafter. On the other hand, it held unconstitutional a different state's requirement that a challenge be made prior to indictment as applied to an indigent defendant who was not provided with counsel until a day after he was indicted.

(c) Equal Protection Claims. Not long after the adoption of the Fourteenth Amendment, its equal protection clause was held to prohibit racial discrimination by the state in the selection of grand juries as well as petit juries.[3] Though a defendant in a state prosecution has no federal constitutional right to grand jury review, he does have "a right to equal protection of the laws [which is] denied when he is indicted by a grand jury from which members of a racial group purposefully have been excluded." Provided a timely objection is made, an indictment issued by such a grand jury cannot stand, without regard to the sufficiency of the evidence before the grand jury, since the racial discrimination "strikes at the fundamental values of our judicial system and our society as a whole." Under the Fifth Amendment's due process clause, the same prohibition applies to racial discrimination in selection of grand juries in federal cases.

An alleged equal protection violation in grand jury selection will be analyzed under the same standards regarding suspect classifications and proof of purposeful discrimination as are applied to equal protection challenges to petit jury selection.[4] Since most jurisdictions utilize the same selection procedures in drawing the grand jury and the petit jury array, an equal protection violation found in grand jury selection is also likely to be present in petit jury selection. Indeed, many of the leading Supreme Court rulings have treated claims going to both juries and have applied to each the same constitutional analysis.

One aspect of the grand jury selection process does require a separate equal protection analysis and that is the selection of the foreperson. In most jurisdictions the foreperson is appointed by the court rather than elected by the jurors. Since the judge makes the appointment fully aware of the juror's race, the selection procedure is naturally suspect where the number of minority forepersons has been substantially disproportionate to the representation of minorities on the grand jury panels. Such a showing can establish a prima facie case of illegal discrimination, shifting to the prosecution the obligation of showing that there was not intentional discrimination.[5] Assuming that there has been an adequate showing of discrimination, however, the question remains as to whether the appropriate remedy is dismissal of the indictment. That

2. See Michel v. Louisiana, 350 U.S. 91, 76 S.Ct. 158, 100 L.Ed. 83 (1955); Reece v. Georgia, 350 U.S. 85, 76 S.Ct. 167, 100 L.Ed. 77 (1955), both discussed below.

3. Ex parte Virginia, 100 U.S. (10 Otto) 339, 25 L.Ed. 676 (1880).

4. See § 22.2(c); Castaneda v. Partida, 430 U.S. 482, 97 S.Ct. 1272, 51 L.Ed.2d 498 (1977).

5. See § 21.2(c). The prosecution might seek to carry its burden by showing through the testimony of the appointing judge that any disparity was simply the product of the judge's practice of selecting forepersons primarily on the basis of such factors as leadership and managerial experience. See e.g., United States v. Perez–Hernandez, 672 F.2d 1380 (11th Cir.1982).

issue was first put to the Supreme Court in *Rose v. Mitchell.*[6] The Court there found no need to reach the issue because the defendant had failed to make out a prima facie case of discrimination. It apparently concluded that the remedy issue was sufficiently troublesome to reserve judgment on that issue and move to the easier ground of lack of proof. Indeed, while it considered other questions that need not have been decided in light of the lack of proof, it noted as to the remedy issue only that it would "assume without deciding that discrimination with regard to the selection of only the foreman requires that an indictment be set aside, just as if the discrimination proved had tainted the selection of the entire grand jury venire."

In *Hobby v. United States,*[7] the issue was again raised, but the context was different and the Court's response was limited so as to avoid answering the precise question reserved in *Rose.* The defendant in *Hobby* had unsuccessfully moved for dismissal of the federal indictment against him on the ground that discrimination against blacks and women had entered into the selection of the grand jury's foreman. Since the defendant, a white male, was not a member of the classes discriminated against, he did not base his claim on equal protection grounds. Instead, he looked to the due process analysis of *Peters v. Kiff,*[8] a case involving a white defendant's successful challenge to racial discrimination in the selection of grand and petit juries. There, three justices, in an opinion by Justice Marshall, had concluded that due process was violated where a state selected it juries in an "arbitrary and discriminatory manner" by excluding from jury service "a substantial and identifiable class of citizens." The defendant in *Hobby* argued that the due process analysis of *Peters* also required dismissal of the indictment when the discrimination was limited to the appointment of the foreperson.

The Court in *Hobby* was unanimous in its conclusion that "purposeful discrimination against Negroes or women in the selection of federal grand jury foreman is forbidden by the Fifth Amendment." It was split, however, as to whether such a constitutional violation invariably required dismissal of an ensuing indictment. The dissenters argued that the "injury caused by race and sex discrimination * * * is measured not only in terms of actual prejudice caused to individual defendants but also in terms of the injury done to public confidence in the judicial process," and it therefore required the deterrent impact of automatic dismissal of the indictment. The majority responded that dismissal was appropriate only if the discrimination adversely affected the defendant's personal due process interests as set forth in Justice Marshall's opinion in *Peters.* Absent such an injury to defendant, "less draconian measures" would suffice to ensure that "no citizen is excluded from consideration for service [as foreperson] * * * on account of race, color, religion, sex, national origin or economic status."

The *Hobby* majority concluded that dismissal there was not required, as the defendant's due process interests could not have been violated by intentional discrimination that was limited to the appointment of the foreperson. *Peters* had recognized "representational due process values" that granted to the defendant a right not to be indicted by a grand jury unfairly selected through the exclusion of any "large and identifiable segment of the community." Here, however, no such exclusion had been applied to "the grand jury *as a whole,*" but simply to the grand jury member performing the additional duties of the foreperson. Unlike the situation presented in *Rose,* the foreperson here was a member of the randomly selected panel, so all of the persons voting on the indictment had been fairly selected. Neither could the discrimination have "impugn[ed] the fundamental fairness of the [grand jury] process itself," as one foreperson could make no appreciable difference from another. Again in contrast to *Rose,* the foreperson on a federal grand jury performed basically ministerial duties that

6. 443 U.S. 545, 99 S.Ct. 2993, 61 L.Ed.2d 739 (1979).

7. 468 U.S. 339, 104 S.Ct. 3093, 82 L.Ed.2d 260 (1984).

8. Infra note 13.

would have no bearing upon the substantive decisions of the grand jury.

The *Hobby* majority distinguished *Rose* on three grounds: (1) the foreman in *Rose* had been appointed from outside the randomly selected panel; (2) the foreman in *Rose* had substantial powers that might be used to influence the substance of the indictment (e.g., the authority to issue subpoenas for witnesses); and (3) *Rose* did not present a due process objection, but "a claim brought by two Negro defendants under the Equal Protection Clause." If the key to resolving the issue left open in *Rose* is the first two grounds, then any future ruling by the Court requiring dismissal of an indictment based upon an equal protection violation in the appointment of the foreperson would be limited in impact to a small number of states. Only a few states allow the foreperson to be appointed from outside the regularly selected grand jury panel. A somewhat larger group give to the foreperson more extensive powers than the federal system, but few grant powers that reach the level found in *Rose.*

The third ground of distinction, on the other hand, could lead to a ruling having a much broader impact, extending to all jurisdictions without regard to whether the foreperson has significant powers or is appointed from outside the original panel. Speaking to the distinct nature of the racial discrimination claim raised in *Rose,* the *Hobby* majority noted: "As members of the class allegedly excluded from service as the grand jury foreman, the *Rose* defendants had suffered the injuries of stigmatization and prejudice associated with racial discrimination." The majority did not seek to explain the bearing of such injuries upon the remedy of dismissal. One possible explanation is that the defendant thereby has a closer relationship to those persons excluded from service as foreperson and therefore can more appropriately be allowed to vindicate their rights through the deterrent impact of dismissal of the indictment. That explanation would be consistent with equal protection doctrine as it apparently stood at the time of the *Hobby* and *Rose* decisions. The Court had previously indicated that only a member of the class discriminated against had standing to raise an equal protection claim, which explained why the defendant in *Hobby* relied on a fair cross-section claim (available, under *Peters,* to any defendant). However, in the subsequent decision of *Powers v. Ohio,*[9] the Court held that a criminal defendant, whether or not a member of the class discriminated against, had standing to present an equal protection objection to racial discrimination in the selection of a jury. Thus, if the Court should decide that the key factor distinguishing *Rose* and *Hobby* is the different constitutional groundings for the claims presented in those two cases, then any future holding that equal protection requires dismissal as a remedy for racial discrimination in the selection of the grand jury foreperson should extend to all defendants, and not merely to those who were members of the class discriminated against.

On the other hand, the analysis of *Powers* makes more problematic the recognition of such a broad equal protection claim with respect to the selection of the grand jury foreperson. *Powers* rejected the contention that the defendant's equal protection claim arose out of any special injury suffered by a defendant, even where of the same race as that discriminated against. It found the defendant's equal protection claim to be based on a concept of third-party standing that allowed the defendant to vindicate the rights of the "excluded venire persons." *Hobby,* in contrast, specifically rejected such a premise as to discrimination in the selection of the foreperson. The Court majority there insisted that, in light of other means of eliminating such discrimination, relief should be available only if the "distinctive interests of the defendant" had been affected. Thus, to recognize an equal protection claim, apart from the special type of foreperson and selection process involved in *Rose,* the Court would have to either reject the *Hobby* reasoning or distinguish the equal protection grounding as one that, in contrast to a cross-section grounding, more appropriately allows the defendant to

9. See § 22.2 at note 4.

vindicate the interests of the jurors excluded from the foreperson position.

(d) The "Fair Cross-Section Requirement." The Sixth Amendment right to jury trial requires that a petit jury be drawn from a "fair cross-section of the community."[10] This requirement overlaps to a substantial extent with equal protection restrictions upon jury selection, but the two guarantees are distinct. In particular, the cross-section requirement apparently applies to a broader range of cognizable groups than the equal protection guarantee, and it does not require a showing of intentional discrimination against the group. Rather, it requires a showing only of systemic exclusion that results in a venire that is not "reasonably representative." Insofar as the cross-section requirement applies to the grand jury venire, it apparently imposes the same basic standards as would apply to the venire for the petit jury. The critical question here is whether the due process clause imposes upon the states a cross-section requirement for grand jury venires, or whether the cross-section requirement is strictly a Sixth Amendment concept applicable only to petit jury venires.

Prior to the decision in *Peters v. Kiff,* the primary Supreme Court support for a constitutional cross-section requirement for the grand jury venire was found in various statements in equal protection cases noting that the " 'very idea of a jury,' whether it be a grand or petit jury, is 'a body truly representative of the community.' " It was far from certain, however, that such statements, offered in the special context of racial discrimination (characterized by the Court as "at war with our basic concepts of a democratic society") and defendants themselves members of the excluded racial group, would be carried over to grant all defendants a right to insist that the grand jury be selected from a fair cross-section of the community. The equal protection guarantee and the cross-section guarantee had substantially different groundings that could readily lead to only the former being applied to the grand jury setting.

In the context of jury selection, the equal protection guarantee had been applied only to discrimination against historically disadvantaged groups that constituted a "suspect class" and the focus had been on the state's denial of equal treatment as a harm in itself. Thus, the Court had held unconstitutional racial discrimination in the selection of both grand and petit juries at a time when due process clearly did not require that the state provide the defendant with either. The fair cross-section requirement, on the other hand, had been tied to the functions of the jury. Thus, it had not been held applicable to the state petit jury until the Court had first held that the Sixth Amendment was applicable to the states under the Fourteenth Amendment. At that point, the fair cross-section requirement had been judged a necessary element of the Sixth Amendment right to trial by jury. It served, the Court noted, to promote impartiality, to "make available the common sense judgment of the community," and to allow for "community participation in the administration of the criminal law."[11] The Court had never held, however, that the state has the obligation to provide these basic functions of peer review in the screening of the decision to charge. Under *Hurtado,*[12] a state has no obligation to provide grand jury screening. Indeed, a state has no obligation to provide any type of screening. That would appear to give it leeway to fashion a screening system that utilizes only the "blue ribbon" elements of the community, as was the common practice in many jurisdictions (particularly as to investigative grand juries) prior to the jury selection reforms of the 1960's. The only clear limitation on a blue ribbon grand jury would be the equal protection prohibition of discriminatory treatment of historically disadvantaged groups.

In *Peters v. Kiff,*[13] Justice Marshall's opinion for three justices did not address directly the above analysis, but nonetheless seemed to

10. See § 22.2(d).

11. Taylor v. Louisiana, § 22.2 at note 22.

12. See § 15.1 at note 4.

13. 407 U.S. 493, 92 S.Ct. 2163, 33 L.Ed.2d 83 (1972).

reject it by implication. At issue there was a white defendant's challenge to a state jury selection system that had excluded blacks both from the grand jury that had indicted him and the petit jury that had convicted him. Justice Marshall's opinion treated both challenges under the due process clause rather than the equal protection clause. Moreover, the challenges to the grand jury and the petit jury were viewed as subject to the same due process principles, as the trial in *Peters* had occurred prior to the Court's holding of the Sixth Amendment applicable to the states under the Fourteenth Amendment. Justice Marshall's opinion noted initially that the state's exclusion of blacks from jury service was clearly unconstitutional under a long line of equal protection cases. Accordingly, the question here was "whether a state may subject a defendant to indictment and trial by grand and petit juries that are plainly illegal in their composition, and leave the defendant without recourse on the ground that he had in any event no right to a grand or petit jury at all." The answer was that the state could not because its discrimination violates basic due process interests of the defendant that became applicable once the state decides to use a petit or grand jury. "Due process," Justice Marshall noted, "is denied by circumstances that create the likelihood or appearance of bias" on the part of the decisionmaker. This principle "compel[s] the conclusion that a state cannot * * * subject a defendant to indictment or trial by a jury that has been selection in an arbitrary and discriminatory manner, in violation of the Constitution." The arbitrary exclusion of a "substantial and identifiable class of citizens" creates a "risk of bias" that extends to all defendants, and not just to "issues involving race." For "when any large and identifiable segment of the community is excluded from jury service, the effect is to remove from the jury room qualities of human nature and varieties of human experience the range of which is unknown," and such exclusion therefore "may have unsuspected importance in any case that may be presented."

In *Hobby v. United States,*[14] without substantial discussion, the Court appeared to lend majority support to Justice Marshall's due process analysis in *Peters.* In the course of measuring the impact of racial and gender discrimination in the selection of the grand jury foreperson, the Court characterized the issue presented as whether that discrimination violated the "representational due process values expressed in *Peters.*" Although a footnote explained that those values had been set forth originally in an opinion for three justices, there was no suggestion that the Court majority was merely assuming arguendo that they applied to grand jury selection. Moreover, the representational due process values were described as requiring that "no large and identifiable segment of the community be excluded from jury service," which suggested their applicability to any group that would be cognizable under the fair cross-section guarantee. However, the *Hobby* opinion did not actually refer to the fair cross-section cases (although it did cite the cross-section mandate of the Federal Jury Selection Act), and it characterized the *Peters* opinion as dealing with the "appearance of institutional bias" created by "unconstitutionally discriminatory jury selection." *Hobby,* like *Peters,* dealt with discrimination directed at groups that would be cognizable under the equal protection cases. The Court has yet to consider the application to the grand jury of a cross-section analysis that is as encompassing as that applied to the petit jury venire.

(e) Statutory Violations. Most jurisdictions hold that certain violations of statutory selection procedures will require dismissal of an indictment though falling short of constitutional error. Ordinarily those violations must be so "substantial" as to violate a fundamental policy of the statutory procedure. Perhaps the most common violation is the selection of a juror who does not meet the statutory qualifications for service, such as residency or citizenship. Dismissal will be granted in such cases only if, after deducting the number of jurors not legally qualified, the

14. Supra note 7.

number of votes supporting the indictment does not meet the statutory prerequisite.

(f) Juror Bias. Grand jurors are commonly advised, at the time of their impanelment, that they should ask to be excused from any case in which their vote is likely to be influenced by "friendship or hatred or some other similar motivation." If the prosecutor has reason to believe that a particular juror may be biased due to a special relationship to the victim or target, he also may ask the court to excuse that juror. Less than a dozen states, however, have statutory provisions authorizing a motion to dismiss an indictment based on the alleged bias of one or more grand jurors. Several of these provisions are limited to challenges based upon juror qualification statutes that disqualify complainants or persons related to complainants. Others are broader, permitting a challenge to any juror whose "state of mind prevent[s] him from acting impartially." In practice, however, such provisions may allow successful challenges only where the juror had some personal relationship to a witness or victim. Without such a showing, courts are unlikely to allow the defendant to question the juror as to his state of mind, notwithstanding the bias provision. They clearly will not allow a general post-indictment voir dire since it threatens the "traditional secrecy" of grand jury deliberations.

Why is it that the vast majority of jurisdictions do not permit any challenge to an indictment based on the alleged bias of a particular grand juror? Although some express concern that bias objections would inevitably lead to a post-indictment voir dire of the grand jurors, they more frequently argue that such an objection is inconsistent with the function of the grand jury. The classic statement of this position was set forth by Judge Holtzhoff in *United States v. Knowles:* [15]

> The basic theory of the functions of a grand jury, does not require that grand jurors should be impartial and unbiased. In this respect, their position is entirely different from that of petit jurors. The Sixth Amendment to the Constitution of the United States expressly provides that the trial jury in a criminal case must be "impartial." No such requirement in respect to grand juries is found in the Fifth Amendment, which contains the guaranty against prosecutions for infamous crimes unless on a presentment or indictment. * * * A grand jury does not pass on the guilt or innocence of the defendant, but merely determines whether he should be brought to trial. It is purely an accusatory body. This view can be demonstrated by the fact that a grand jury may undertake an investigation on its own initiative, or at the behest of one of its members. In such event, the grand juror, who instigated the proceeding that may result in an indictment, obviously can hardly be deemed to be impartial, but he is not disqualified for that reason.

In recent years, several courts that formerly adhered to the *Knowles* position have suggested that they would give serious consideration to dismissing an indictment if the defendant could establish a clear case of actual juror bias. The analysis of *Knowles* is said to be "rooted more in history than in justice." Grand jurors are no longer expected to act upon personal knowledge, and should, no less than trial jurors, "be free from any taint of discriminatory purpose." Indeed, the failure of a supervising court to discharge a grand juror known to be biased (or the failure of a prosecutor to call a juror's bias to the attention of the court) is seen as a potential violation of due process in light of Supreme Court rulings.

In the leading Supreme Court case speaking directly to the issue of grand juror bias, *Beck v. Washington,*[16] the Court noted that "[i]t may be that the Due Process Clause of the Fourteenth Amendment requires the State, having once resorted to a grand jury procedure, to furnish an unbiased grand jury." The *Beck* plurality found it unnecessary to reach that issue, but Justice Douglas, in dissent, argued that the state clearly did have such an obligation. The requirement that a grand jury be unbiased, he argued, followed

15. 147 F.Supp. 19 (D.D.C.1957).

16. 369 U.S. 541, 82 S.Ct. 955, 8 L.Ed.2d 98 (1962).

from the language and reasoning of various prior decisions, particularly the equal protection decisions regulating the grand jury selection process. The "systematic exclusion of Negroes from grand jury service" was barred because it "infects the accusatory process * * * [with an] unfairness" akin to that resulting from juror bias. To refuse to acknowledge a bias objection, Justice Douglas argued, would lead to the inconceivable result of sustaining an indictment even "where the grand jury that brought the charge was composed of the accused's political enemies."

While the Court has not returned to the bias issue, subsequent opinions may be seen as bolstering Justice Douglas' position. Justice Douglas' reliance upon equal protection rulings barring racial discrimination in grand jury selection was criticized as missing the focus of those cases. The key to those rulings, the critics noted, was the denial of equal treatment, both to the defendant and the excluded jurors, rather than the assumption that the white jurors actually seated were likely to be prejudiced against the black defendant. While that position finds support in various opinions for the Court,[17] Justice Marshall's opinion for three justices in *Peters v. Kiff* and his opinion for the Court in *Vasquez v. Hillary*[18] viewed racial exclusions as also related to the likely bias of the grand jury. Insofar as *Hobby* imposed a form of cross-section requirement, it may also be seen as a ruling that seeks to provide greater assurance of grand jury impartiality. Reading such cases as seeking not only to eliminate the appearance of institutional bias, but to preclude a potential for actual juror bias, the command of due process would seem equally to require the discharge of a specific juror who is known to be biased.

If the issue left open in *Beck* is eventually resolved with a ruling rejecting the analysis of *Knowles,* the Court will then have to decide what steps a state must take to ensure that a grand jury is not biased. The alleged bias in *Beck* stemmed from extensive preindictment publicity, and the issue that divided the Court there was whether the judge empaneling the jury had gone far enough in determining "whether any prospective [grand] juror had been influenced by the adverse publicity." The plurality found that he had done so when he asked the prospective jurors whether they were conscious of any prejudice and excused three who acknowledged possible bias. *Beck* involved an unusual situation in which the judge was aware of the potential source of bias prior to empaneling the grand jury. Ordinarily, the issue of bias will not be called to the court's attention until after an indictment has been issued. At that point, an inquiry that goes beyond considering bias inherent in a juror's special relationship to the parties (as where the juror is a relative of the complainant) runs the risk of invading the secrecy of the juror's deliberations in casting his vote. This danger, combined with the limited inquiry found acceptable in *Beck,* suggests that an extensive investigation of the juror's state of mind (through, for example, a post-indictment voir dire) is not likely to be required by due process even if the *Knowles* rationale eventually is rejected by the Supreme Court.

(g) Preindictment Publicity. Another question that would arise with the rejection of the *Knowles* rationale is whether a showing of extensive prejudicial pretrial publicity would be sufficient to establish the degree of bias necessary to require dismissal of an indictment. So far, lower courts accepting the premise of a defense right to an unbiased grand jury have nevertheless uniformly rejected motions to dismiss based on preindictment publicity. These decisions have rested in large part on the conclusion that the right to an unbiased grand jury would not mandate application of the concept of inherently prejudicial publicity, which is often utilized at the trial stage to presume juror bias.[19] In the grand jury setting, the courts insist upon a specific showing of actual bias on the part of the seated jurors. Since defendant has no right to voir dire the grand jurors and access

17. See e.g., Powers v. Ohio, supra note 9; Rose v. Mitchell, supra note 6.

18. Supra note 13 and infra note 21.

19. See § 23.2(d).

to the grand jury transcript is both difficult to obtain and not very likely to reveal juror bias, this required showing has been aptly characterized as rendering preindictment publicity claims almost "inevitably doomed as a matter of law."

The imposition of such a substantial burden on defendants raising preindictment publicity claims is justified on several grounds. First, the "role of the grand jury historically has differed from that of a petit jury" in a way that does not require that it have "the same freedom from outside influences." The grand jury, as an investigative body, is allowed to look to "rumor, tips, and hearsay," which would include much of the material found in preindictment publicity. Second, "if preindictment publicity could cause the dismissal of an indictment, many persons, either prominent or notorious, could readily avoid indictment, a result detrimental to the system of justice." The impact of pretrial publicity upon the petit jury can be eliminated or alleviated by a change of venue, but an indictment can be returned only by a grand jury of the judicial district in which the offense occurred. Finally, courts note that the prospective defendant has other safeguards. In cases of extensive preindictment publicity, the prospective defendant is likely to be aware that the case against him will go to the grand jury, and he can always request that the supervising judge conduct a brief inquiry into the open-mindedness of the prospective jurors, as was done in *Beck*. Also, there remains the far deeper inquiry that will precede any trial. Thus it is noted that the "taint" of any preindictment publicity that may have been "inherently prejudicial" will "be purged by the deliberations of an untainted petit jury."

(h) Postconviction Review. Assume that a defendant makes a timely objection to the composition of the grand jury, but that objection is denied by the trial judge. Assume also that the defendant is subsequently convicted by a properly selected petit jury. On appeal from a subsequent conviction, should the illegality of the grand jury's composition be treated as harmless error? In *Rose v. Mitchell,*[20] Justice Stewart, dissenting, argued that "any possible prejudice" to a defendant from racial discrimination in the selection of the grand jury "disappears when a constitutionally valid trial jury later finds him guilty beyond a reasonable doubt." The majority rejected this contention, noting that it was inconsistent with a long line of cases and failed to give adequate consideration to the varied interests at stake in prohibiting racial discrimination in the selection of the grand jury. "[B]ecause discrimination on the basis of race * * * strikes at the fundamental values of our judicial system and our society as a whole," it was entirely appropriate to "revers[e] the conviction * * * in such cases without inquiry into whether the defendant was prejudiced in fact by the discrimination at the grand jury stage." While there were "costs associated with this approach," those costs (basically the reindictment and retrial of the defendant) were "out-weighed by the strong policy the Court consistently has recognized of combatting racial discrimination in the administration of justice."

In *Vasquez v. Hillery,*[21] the Court reaffirmed the *Rose* ruling and added another ground for failing to treat the conviction before a fairly selected petit jury as "curing" the racial discrimination in the selection of the grand jury. The grand jury, the Court noted, "does not determine only that probable cause exists," but also "has the power to charge * * * a lesser offense" than the evidence might support. "Thus even if a grand jury's determination of probable cause is confirmed in hindsight by a conviction on the indicted offense, that confirmation in no way suggests that the discrimination did not impermissibly infect the framing of the indictment and consequently, the nature or existence of the proceedings to come."

Although the *Vasquez* and *Rose* rulings were characterized in *Mechanik v. United States* as based upon "considerations that have little force outside the context of racial

20. Supra note 6.

21. 474 U.S. 254, 106 S.Ct. 617, 88 L.Ed.2d 598 (1986).

discrimination,"[22] the reasoning of *Vasquez* would appear to apply to any constitutional violation that relates to the composition of the grand jury. Thus, in discussing *Rose* and *Vasquez,* the Court in *Bank of Nova Scotia v. United States*[23] noted that it had appropriately "reached a like conclusion in *Ballard v. United States,*[24] when women had been excluded from the grand jury." The key in such cases, the Court noted, was that "the nature of the violation allowed a presumption that the defendant was prejudiced, and any inquiry into harmless error would have required unguided speculation."

Of course, even if the reasoning of *Rose* and *Vasquez* do not require appellate court consideration of a claimed constitutional error in grand jury selection notwithstanding a subsequent conviction by a fairly selected petit jury, a state court always remains free to treat the issue as open to consideration under state law. Many state courts have done that with a wide range of challenges to the composition of the grand jury, including some that arguably would not present federal constitutional violations. Their position apparently rests in part on the rationale that an illegally composed grand jury is itself a nullity and therefore its indictment fails to provide a jurisdictional grounding for the subsequent conviction. The courts also may be concerned that treating the subsequent trial as having purged the illegality in grand jury composition would effectively preclude appellate review of such errors, at least in jurisdictions that bar or sharply restrict interlocutory appeals.[25]

§ 15.5 Indictment Challenges Based Upon Evidentiary Grounds

(a) The Federal Standard: The *Costello* Rule. *Costello v. United States*[1] is the seminal Supreme Court ruling on defense challenges to a federal grand jury indictment based on the alleged incompetency or insufficiency of the evidence before the grand jury. *Costello* involved a tax-evasion prosecution in which the government sought to establish defendant's underreporting of income through proof of substantial increases in his net worth. Prior to trial, defendant moved for inspection of the grand jury minutes and dismissal of the indictment, alleging that there could not have been before the grand jury any competent evidence supporting its indictment. Both motions were denied and the case went to trial. The government initially called 144 witnesses who testified to various financial transactions of the defendant, and then followed with three government agents who summarized the earlier testimony and analyzed the transactions within the context of a net worth case. Although the agents' testimony describing the transactions would have been inadmissible hearsay standing alone, it was acceptable at trial in light of the foundation established by the 144 earlier witnesses. Cross-examination of the various witnesses established, however, that only the three agents had testified before the grand jury. Defendant then renewed his motion to dismiss, claiming that the indictment was invalid since the grand jury obviously had before it only inadmissible hearsay testimony. The trial court again denied the motion, and the defendant was subsequently convicted. On review before the Supreme Court, defendant argued that an indictment founded "solely on hearsay" should be held invalid under the Fifth Amendment's indictment clause, or, in the alternative, under the Court's exercise of its supervisory power over federal courts. Justice Black's opinion for the Court not only rejected defendant's argument as to indictments based upon hearsay, but spoke generally of the unavailability of any indictment challenge grounded upon the "competency

22. *Mechanik* is discussed at § 15.6(d). The Court there referred to the racial discrimination cases in distinguishing its ruling that a subsequent conviction after a fairly conducted trial rendered moot a violation of statutory requirements governing the presentation of witnesses before the indicting grand jury.

23. See § 15.6(d).

24. 329 U.S. 187, 67 S.Ct. 261, 91 L.Ed. 181 (1946).

25. See § 27.2(e).

§ 15.5

1. 350 U.S. 359, 76 S.Ct. 406, 100 L.Ed. 397 (1956).

and adequacy of the evidence before the grand jury."

The *Costello* opinion placed considerable stress upon the "history" and "traditions" of the grand jury. The Fifth Amendment's grand jury provision assumed a grand jury that "operates substantially like its English progenitor." The independence of the English grand jury provided freedom from the control of the judges as well as the Crown. Grand jurors were not "hampered by rigid procedural or evidentiary rules," but could act on "such information as they deemed satisfactory," including "their own knowledge." This tradition of a "body of laymen, free from technical rules," was carried over to this country. Consistent with it, early decisions had established that a court could not "revis[e] the judgment of the grand jury upon the evidence, * * * whether or not [the grand jury's] finding was founded upon sufficient proof."

Justice Black's rejection of Costello's Fifth Amendment claim appeared to be based primarily upon its inconsistency with "the whole history of the grand jury institution." However, Justice Black also noted, partially in response to defendant's suggestion that the Court look to its supervisory authority, that adoption of defendant's position would impose unacceptable administrative costs. "If indictments were to be held open to challenge on the ground that there was inadequate or incompetent evidence before the grand jury, the resulting delay would be great indeed." Such a rule would allow defendants in every case to "insist on a kind of preliminary trial to determine the competency and adequacy of the evidence before the grand jury." Defendants would obtain at trial "a strict observance of all the rules designed to bring about a fair verdict." There was no need to adopt "a rule which would result in interminable delay, but add nothing to the assurance of a fair trial."

The reasoning and language of *Costello* went far beyond the particular evidentiary challenge presented there. The challenge in *Costello* was to hearsay, and the lower court had stressed the special characteristics of hearsay evidence. It had noted that hearsay often is quite reliable, and that the primary reason for its exclusion, the inability to cross-examine the declarant, had no bearing in the ex parte process of the grand jury. Moreover, hearsay had been used in *Costello* under unusual circumstances. Though hearsay, the agents' summaries could be converted into admissible evidence with the laying of a proper foundation, and there was considerable administrative justification for not establishing that foundation before the grand jury. To have done so would have imposed a considerable burden upon numerous witnesses who would be testifying only to financial transactions largely established by documents. Justice Black's opinion, however, relied upon none of these limiting features. Indeed, it spoke of the grand jury's freedom to rely on incompetent evidence in general, and not simply to the use of hearsay.

The *Costello* opinion, moreover, rejected challenges not only to the competency of the evidence, but also of its sufficiency. The two issues might well have been separated. A court might allow use of evidence that would be inadmissible at trial, but then insist that such evidence have sufficient probative weight to establish probable cause. Justice Black's opinion, however, viewed the challenges to sufficiency and competency as equally inconsistent with the historical role of the grand jury. Indeed, his opinion was written so broadly as to suggest that federal courts would be powerless to dismiss an indictment even in the extreme case in which the grand jury had received absolutely no evidence that was probative. Thus, Justice Black noted that the judicial response to an indictment should be governed by a single, overriding principle: "An indictment returned by a legally constituted and unbiased grand jury, like an information drawn by the prosecutor, if valid on its face, is enough to call for a trial of the charge on the merits." Responding to the implications of that principle, Justice Burton concurred separately in an attempt to hold open some possibility for judicial review of the grand jury evidence. Noting that the Court apparently "would not preclude an examination of grand jury action to ascertain the existence of bias or prejudice in an indictment," Justice Burton contended that an indictment likewise should be quashed "if it is shown that the grand jury had before it no substantial or rationally persuasive evidence."

Subsequent Supreme Court cases have not put before the Court the situation hypothesized by Justice Burton, but they have produced general reaffirmations of the breadth of the *Costello* principle. Thus, a series of rulings have stated that an indictment will not be subject to challenge in the federal courts even when based on unconstitutionally obtained evidence. In the latest of these rulings, *United States v. Calandra,*[2] the Court relied upon the *Costello* principle in refusing to fashion a remedy that would preclude grand jury consideration of evidence obtained through an unconstitutional search and seizure.[3] Citing *Costello* and the broad reading of *Costello* in *Lawn v. United States,*[4] it noted:

> The grand jury's sources of information are widely drawn and the validity of an indictment is not affected by the character of the evidence considered. Thus, an indictment valid on its face is not subject to challenge on the ground that the grand jury acted on the basis of inadequate or incompetent evidence; or even on the basis of information obtained in violation of a defendant's Fifth Amendment privilege against self-incrimination.

As might be expected in an opinion authored by Justice Black, *Costello* did not acknowledge that the Court was engaged in a balancing process, that it was weighing the administrative costs of judicial review of the grand jury's evidence against the value of such review in eliminating unwarranted prosecutions. Yet, at least with respect to the exercise of its supervisory power, where historical traditions arguably have less bearing, it was open to the Court to conclude, as have several states, that the modern grand jury should no longer be treated as a lay body responsible in its judgments only to the citizenry from which it is selected. With the prosecutor playing such a dominant role in determining what evidence comes before the grand jury, the grand jury process certainly has the capacity to distinguish between admissible and inadmissible evidence, notwithstanding the grand jury's lay composition. A prosecutor readily could be called upon to ensure that the indictment is supported by sufficient admissible evidence, with that obligation enforced through judicial review of the evidence before the grand jury. To impose such a requirement, however, a court would have to conclude that it benefited the screening process (i.e., made the grand jury more effective as a screening body) and that any such benefit outweighed the resulting administrative costs. That the Court viewed those administrative costs as substantial is clear from Justice Black's opinion. Why it deemed the value of requiring admissible evidence and providing judicial review as not worthy of those substantial costs is less clear. Justice Black simply noted that "no persuasive reasons" had been advanced for "permitting defendants to challenge indictments on the ground that they are not supported by adequate or competent evidence." Commentators have seen in this judgment a series of different assumptions relating to the grand jury screening process.

Some commentators, noting Justice Black's comment that there was no need to impose upon the grand jury process new requirements that would "add nothing to the assurance of a fair trial," have argued that the Court simply concluded that an effective screening process was not an important objective, as the final adjudication adequately safeguarded the innocent. Support for this contention is found in the fact that the Supreme Court had held that the Fourteenth Amendment does not require the states to use the grand jury or any similar screening process (although Justice Black himself would have ruled otherwise). It is also noted that *Costello* said very little about the importance of

2. 414 U.S. 338, 94 S.Ct. 613, 38 L.Ed.2d 561 (1974).

3. *Calandra* did not involve a challenge to an indictment, but a grand jury witness' objection to questions based on information derived from an unconstitutional search. See § 8.9(a).

4. 355 U.S. 339, 78 S.Ct. 311, 2 L.Ed.2d 321 (1958).

avoiding unfounded indictments. Lower courts have noted that a wrongful indictment inflicts a "blot on a man's escutcheon * * * seldom wiped out by a subsequent judgment of not guilty," and have stressed the need to protect the innocent defendant against "the heavy burden of expending time, energy and capital in the defense of his case." *Costello* contained no such message. Yet, other Supreme Court cases decided during the same period as *Costello* spoke almost reverently of the grand jury's screening function. These statements plus *Costello's* discussion of the historic tradition of the grand jury suggest that the Court in *Costello* may not have downgraded the grand jury's screening function, but simply concluded that allowing challenges to the grand jury's evidence was not necessary to ensure effective screening. It may have assumed that grand jurors ordinarily have sufficient common sense to recognize the weakness in a case based entirely on hearsay of suspect reliability (which certainly was not the situation presented in *Costello* itself).

Arguably, the *Costello* Court simply concluded that a "hands-off" judicial stance served, in the end, to strengthen the grand jury in the exercise of all of its functions. It was better to trust the grand jurors' common sense in dealing with the evidence presented by the prosecution than to open the door to judicial intervention. Historically, the threat to grand jury independence, particularly in the grand jury's exercise of its power to nullify, had come from the judiciary as well as the Crown. Indeed, the requirement of secrecy had been developed in part to preclude judicial coercion of the grand jury. The exercise of supervisory judicial authority to review the evidence before the grand jury necessarily weakened that cloak of secrecy. Even though a defense challenge would be available only where the grand jury indicted, the evidence revealed could often relate as well to the grand jury's decision not to indict others involved in the same transaction. Also, recognition of judicial authority to bar indictments based on incompetent evidence could readily lead to judicial intervention during an ongoing grand jury investigation to preclude the presentation of such evidence before the grand jury. Such intervention would undercut, however, the long recognized authority of the investigative grand jury to consider even "tips and rumors" (and thus to receive hearsay of suspect reliability). Thus, the *Calandra* Court saw in the hands-off stance of *Costello* a contribution to the independent investigative authority of the grand jury. Rejecting a witness' objection to the prosecution's alleged use of illegally seized evidence before the grand jury, the Court there noted that allowing judicial intervention would "saddle a grand jury with minitrials and preliminary showings [that] would assuredly impede its investigation and frustrate the public's interest in the fair and expeditious administration of the criminal laws." [5]

(b) The Federal Standard: The "Misconduct Exception" to *Costello*. Many lower federal courts were not entirely comfortable with the breadth of the *Costello* ruling. They expressed appreciation for "Mr. Justice Black's fear of minitrials for indictments," but noted that there also was a need to respond to the "growing use of the grand jury as a pawn or 'mere tool' of the prosecutor." These courts sought to establish a half-way station between full review of the competency and adequacy of evidence and a refusal to consider evidentiary challenges under any circumstances. That half-way station was founded on the doctrine of supervisory control over prosecutorial misconduct. *Costello,* it was argued, did not take from the lower federal courts their traditional authority to "preserve the integrity of the judicial process" by dismissing indictments that were the product of "flagrantly abusive prosecutorial conduct" before the grand jury. Indeed, support for exercising that authority was found in *Costello*'s caveat that an indictment must be returned by "an unbiased grand jury" in order

5. Witness objections to the use of inadmissible evidence in the course of their examination can be rejected under the rationale of Blair v. United States, see § 8.8(a), without regard to the availability of a defense challenge to a resulting indictment that was based on such evidence. While *Calandra* relied on that rationale, it also cited *Costello* and *Lawn* as additional support for its position. See the text following note 3 supra.

to be enough in itself "to call for trial." Abusive prosecutorial practices, such as insults and insinuations directed against the target, traditionally had been held inconsistent with this requirement since they served no purpose other than to have the grand jury indict out of bias. The same could be true of prosecutorial misconduct in inappropriately presenting certain types of evidence to the grand jury.

The assumption of the lower courts that *Costello* did not bar dismissals based on prosecutorial misconduct was open to question. A strong case could be made against such authority on the basis of various statements in *Costello.* While *Costello* had spoken of an indictment "valid on its face" as being "enough to call for trial" only where issued by a "legally constituted and unbiased grand jury," the reference to a lack of bias arguably extended only to the composition of the grand jury. The reference was followed by a footnote citing a ruling barring racial discrimination in the selection of the grand jury, and the thrust of the Court's reasoning separated the judicial role in reviewing grand jury composition and grand jury proceedings. Justice Black stressed the historical status of the grand jury as the independent representative of the community, free to act as it wished on behalf of the community. That position would leave the courts with authority only to ensure that the grand jury was properly selected as the representative of the community. Thus, Justice Black noted that the judiciary traditionally lacked authority to impose "procedural or evidentiary rules" upon the grand jury process. Restrictions imposed upon prosecutorial actions before the grand jury would constitute, in effect, judicially imposed "procedural rules" for the process. Very often such a rule would simply restate in another fashion an evidentiary rule. A Court could say that an indictment must be supported by some substantive evidence (as Justice Burton argued) or that a prosecutor engaged in misconduct by seeking an indictment without any substantive evidence. Judicial intervention to enforce either rule would involve "revising the judgments of the grand jury upon the evidence." Moreover, allowing challenges to indictments to enforce judicially imposed rules governing prosecutorial conduct before the grand jury would open the door to the delays and disruptions in the process that *Costello* viewed as intolerable.

Those lower court opinions that looked beyond *Costello*'s reference to an unbiased grand jury suggested various responses to the above arguments. *Costello* was read as limited only to judicial review of the soundness of the judgment of the grand jury in deciding to indict. Dismissal based on prosecutorial misconduct judged the behavior of the prosecutor, an officer of the court, and not the grand jury itself. Federal courts traditionally had exercised their supervisory authority to prevent prosecutorial misconduct in the judicial process, and the prosecutor was utilizing an element of that process, the subpoena power of the court, in the grand jury proceeding. Also, the concern expressed in *Costello* as to the substantial administrative costs of allowing evidentiary challenges had less bearing as applied to challenges to prosecutorial misconduct. An objection based on prosecutorial misconduct would not automatically be available to any defendant. Neither would it require the automatic disclosure of the grand jury minutes to the defendant. Federal Rule 6(e) permits disclosure incident to a challenge to an indictment only upon a substantial preliminary showing that grounds for the challenge may exist. To require such a showing in connection with a pretrial challenge alleging that the grand jury relied largely on incompetent evidence would procedurally eviscerate that challenge since the defendant ordinarily has no way of determining the full range of the grand jury's evidence without examining the grand jury transcript. On the other hand, evidence of misconduct could come from other sources (e.g., the witness who was harassed by the prosecutor), and a misconduct objection therefore could be recognized and implemented without cutting back upon the preliminary showing requirement of

Rule 6(e).[6]

Although the federal lower courts almost uniformly recognized a "misconduct exception" to *Costello,* they varied considerably as to what they deemed misconduct in the prosecutor's presentation of evidence before the grand jury. Some treated as misconduct only actions that amounted, in effect, to the intentional deception of the grand jury in the presentation of evidence (e.g., the knowing presentation of perjured testimony). Others, however, included any significant action (or inaction) by the prosecutor that prevented the grand jury from fully assessing the credibility of the evidence. Thus, dismissal was held appropriate where the government introduced false testimony and was patently negligent in failing to recognize its inaccuracy. So too, the use of hearsay evidence was held to constitute grounds for dismissal where there was a "high probability that with eyewitness rather than hearsay testimony the grand jury would not have indicted." Indeed, several district courts warned that dismissals would be forthcoming if prosecutors should make extensive use of hearsay where "first-hand evidence is readily and conveniently available." Accordingly, where the prosecution had to seek a new indictment as a result of some flaw in the original charge, it could not simply summarize the evidence presented before the first grand jury or present the transcripts of that grand jury proceeding, as the appropriate procedure was to have the witnesses testify again before the new grand jury. As the Federal Rules Advisory Committee noted, while "*Costello* continue[d] to be followed by the federal courts generally," various federal courts had utilized the misconduct rationale to make substantial "inroads" upon the "broad rule" of *Costello.*

The development of the misconduct doctrine was left to the lower federal courts for roughly thirty years after *Costello.* At that point, in the mid–1980's, the Supreme Court, in two major rulings, rejected a good part of what at least the more adventurous lower courts had done. Many of the leading lower court rulings on the scope of the misconduct doctrine had been Court of Appeals rulings that had been issued on review of a conviction. In *United States v. Mechanik,*[7] the Supreme Court held that a challenge to an indictment based upon prosecutor misconduct was, in effect, rendered moot by the defendant's subsequent conviction at a fairly conducted trial. The challenge presented in *Mechanik* was based upon the violation of Federal Rule 6(d) in allowing two witnesses to appear simultaneously before the grand jury and testify in tandem. As discussed in § 15.6(e), some question remains as to whether the *Mechanik* ruling covers all types of misconduct, but it would appear to extend to most types of misconduct that could arise from the presentation of evidence. Accordingly, where such a misconduct challenge is rejected before trial, that usually will end the matter. Since interlocutory review is not available under the traditional standards governing defense appeals in the federal courts, the defendant will not be able to reach the appellate court until after a conviction that will have rendered harmless the alleged misconduct. Indeed, under the rationale of *Mechanik,* the Court in *Costello* should never have reached the issue it decided there as the alleged deficiency in the grand jury evidence had come before the Court following defendant's conviction.

The government in *Mechanik* had argued that a violation of Rule 6(d) in presenting evidence to the grand jury could not constitute grounds for an indictment dismissal in light of the reasoning of *Costello.* Indeed, it questioned the whole line of lower court rulings recognizing defense challenges based on alleged prosecutorial misconduct in presenting evidence, contending that such objections sought, in the end, judicial review of the strength of the evidence before the grand jury. The Supreme Court responded that it "need not reach this argument" in light of its

6. See § 15.6(f), discussing the operation of Rule 6(e) in limiting the instances in which defendants can present successfully a prosecutorial misconduct claim.

7. 475 U.S. 66, 106 S.Ct. 938, 89 L.Ed.2d 50 (1986). See also § 15.6(e).

"narrower" ruling that the trial conviction had "rendered harmless any conceivable error in the charging decision." Shortly thereafter, however, in *Bank of Nova Scotia v. United States,*[8] the Court did have occasion to consider the relationship of the misconduct rationale to *Costello.* The end result was a ruling that recognized district court authority to dismiss an indictment based on prosecutorial misconduct, but sharply limited that authority through a much narrower definition of misconduct, at least as applied to the presentation of evidence, than had been adopted by many of the lower courts.

Bank of Nova Scotia involved a pretrial challenge to an indictment, alleging various acts of prosecutorial misconduct before the grand jury, that had been granted by the trial court. The primary issue before the Court, as discussed in § 15.6(c), was whether a dismissal could be granted without a showing that the alleged misconduct had likely prejudiced the defendants. In the course of holding that such a showing was necessary, and that it had not been made in the case before it, the Court briefly referred to *Costello* and *Calandra.* Those rulings were characterized as prohibiting a challenge "to the reliability or competence of the evidence presented before the grand jury." They would not govern here if the defendant could show true government misconduct in the presentation of evidence (as well as the likelihood of resulting prejudice). The Court did not explain why the presence of misconduct was a distinguishing factor that allowed the exercise of supervisory authority to dismiss an indictment. Apparently the long line of lower court rulings recognizing a misconduct exception to *Costello* made such an explanation unnecessary. Justice Scalia, in a concurring opinion, noted his assumption that the Court's ruling was based on the principle that "every United States court has an inherent authority over the proceedings conducted before it, which assuredly includes the power to decline to proceed on the basis of an indictment obtained in violation of law."

In its discussion of the nature of the requisite prosecutorial misconduct, the *Bank of Nova Scotia* opinion did not refer to the lower court rulings which had broadly construed that concept as it related to the presentation of evidence. However, the Court clearly adopted a much narrower construction of such misconduct, that was hinged to an element of prosecutorial scienter. That narrower concept was illustrated in the Court's discussion of two alleged instances of misconduct that related to the nature of the evidence presented to the grand jury. The first concerned the trial court's finding that, to the prejudice of the defendants, testifying IRS agents had given to the grand jury "misleading and inaccurate" summaries of the evidence previously presented. The Court concluded that the presentation of the summaries, even if they were false and misleading, did not constitute an appropriate ground for dismissal of the indictment since "the record [did] not reveal any prosecutorial misconduct with respect to these summaries." The trial court's finding, the Court noted, "boiled down to a challenge to the reliability or competence of the evidence before the grand jury," and the Court had previously held "that an indictment valid on its face is not subject to such a challenge" (citing *Calandra* and *Costello*). There was no support in the record for a finding "that the prosecutors knew the evidence to be false or misleading, or that the Government caused the agents to testify falsely." Although "the Government may have had doubts about the accuracy of certain aspects of the summaries," that did not establish misconduct.

That misconduct in presenting evidence would require improper prosecutorial purpose (and that the focus was on the misconduct and not merely the possible unreliability of the evidence presented) was made evident also by the Court's treatment of a second defense claim relating to the reliability of the evidence presented. The defendant contended that the government had threatened to withdraw immunity from a witness in order to manipulate his testimony. The Court responded that, assuming that had been done, it

8. 487 U.S. 250, 108 S.Ct. 2369, 101 L.Ed.2d 228 (1988). See also § 15.6(e).

"might have given rise to a finding of prejudice" that would justify dismissal of the indictment, but the prosecution in fact had not made such a threat. While the prosecuting attorney did say to the witness' attorney that "all bets were off" if the witness testified for the target, as the witness' attorney himself ultimately concluded, the prosecutor had not meant to imply that immunity would be withdrawn, but only that the witness would be "validly subject to a perjury prosecution." Although the witness allegedly misinterpreted the prosecutor's statement and believed that the immunity would be withdrawn, his "subjective fear" could not "be ascribed to governmental misconduct and was, at most a consideration bearing on the reliability of his testimony."

As discussed in § 15.7, *Bank of Nova Scotia* hardly provides a complete exploration of what will constitute prosecutor misconduct in the presentation of evidence before the grand jury. There remain significant questions as to the precise nature of the requisite prosecutorial scienter as well as to the scope of the prosecutor's obligation to respond to known unreliability in its evidence. These issues are best examined in light of the principals applied in defining prosecutorial misconduct in general, as set forth in § 15.6. In its discussion of both the nature of misconduct and the required showing of prejudice, the *Bank of Nova Scotia* opinion did not place prosecutorial actions relating to the presentation of evidence in a separate category, different from other prosecutorial actions (e.g., the berating of witnesses) that could have a bearing on the grand jury's decision to indict.

(c) State Standards. A substantial majority of the states, including all but a few of the indictment states, follow the basic philosophy of *Costello.* These jurisdictions will not allow challenges to the evidence underlying an indictment. Some reach this result based on statutory provisions that limit challenges to indictments to enumerated grounds and do not include the insufficiency or incompetency of the evidence among those grounds. In others, courts have adopted the reasoning of *Costello* as a judicially imposed limitation. A few of these jurisdictions hold open the possibility of dismissing an indictment where the grand jury received no evidence whatsoever or no sworn testimony. They will not, however, dismiss an indictment because it was based on hearsay evidence or unconstitutionally obtained evidence. Like the lower federal courts, state courts following *Costello* do allow for dismissal of indictments based upon prosecutor misconduct in presenting evidence. At least some of these state courts, however, restrict the misconduct exception to misconduct so fundamentally contrary to grand jury independence as to violate due process.

Approximately a dozen states flatly reject the position taken in *Costello.* Most of these states are information jurisdictions, but a few are indictment states. Jurisdictions rejecting Costello allow challenges both to the sufficiency and competency of the evidence underlying an indictment. Several do so by statutory command, but others have reached this position through judicial decision. The broad rule of Costello, these courts argue, can be justified only "if the institution of the grand jury is viewed as an anachronism." If the grand jury is to "protect * * * the innocent against oppression and unjust prosecution," a defendant "with substantial grounds for having an indictment dismissed should not be compelled to go to trial to prove the insufficiency."

Jurisdictions rejecting *Costello* uniformly insist that the trial court act with caution in reviewing the sufficiency of the evidence before the grand jury. They stress that "every legitimate inference that may be drawn from the evidence must be drawn in favor of the indictment," and note that "probable cause * * * may be based on 'slight' or even marginal evidence." As a result, most of the successful sufficiency challenges arise from the prosecution's failure to offer any evidence on a particular element of the crime charged.

There tends to be greater variation among non–*Costello* states in the treatment of challenges to the competency of the grand jury's evidence. Some of these jurisdictions direct the grand jury to consider only evidence that would be admissible at trial. Others generally apply the rules of evidence, but permit consideration of limited types of hearsay (such as scientific reports). A few permit a broader hearsay exception, tied to the burden that would be imposed in presenting the primary source of the evidence. In all non–*Costello* jurisdictions, however, the presentation of inadmissible evidence is not necessarily a fatal error. The indictment ordinarily will be sustained if, after excluding the inadmissible evidence, there remains sufficient admissible evidence to support the charge. However, where the inadmissible evidence was so prejudicial as to necessarily have influenced the grand jury, the indictment will be dismissed notwithstanding otherwise sufficient legal evidence. This result can also be supported under a misconduct rationale where the prosecution sought to manipulate the grand jury through the knowing use of inadmissible evidence.

To assist the defendant in presenting an evidentiary challenge, jurisdictions rejecting *Costello* commonly grant defendant an automatic right to inspect the grand jury transcript. New York, however, provides initially for an in camera inspection by the trial court, with the court having authority to deny defense inspection if it "determines there is not reasonable cause to believe that the evidence before the grand jury may have been legally insufficient."[9] This authority is viewed as necessary to preclude use of the evidentiary challenge as a delaying tactic or as a means of obtaining pretrial discovery. Courts in other jurisdictions have argued, however, that an automatic right of inspection "is essential to give meaning to the defendant's right to challenge the indictment." Requiring a prior showing is condemned as unlikely to reach numerous deficiencies that will not be detectable on the face of the proceedings. In camera inspection has been rejected on the grounds that the court needs the "assistance of counsel for both sides if it is to judge wisely."

Where evidentiary challenges are allowed, the trial court's failure to dismiss in response to such a challenge ordinarily can be raised on appeal following a conviction. If the appellate court concludes that the trial court erred in failing to dismiss the indictment, the conviction will be reversed and the indictment dismissed. A contrary position, as taken in *Mechanik,* is seen as giving the trial court the capacity to render the "right to indictment * * * a nullity"; it could simply reject evidentiary challenges at will and be fairly assured that there would be no opportunity for appellate reversal since review prior to conviction would ordinarily not be available. However, here again, New York departs from the general position of the non-*Costello* states. In New York, an order denying a motion to dismiss or to inspect the grand jury transcript is "not reviewable upon appeal from an ensuring judgment of conviction based on legally sufficient trial evidence."[10]

§ 15.6 Misconduct Challenges: General Principles

(a) Prosecutorial Misconduct. Precedent can be found in almost all jurisdictions that regularly use grand jury indictments which recognizes judicial authority to dismiss an indictment, under at least some circumstances, based upon prosecutorial "misconduct" in the grand jury proceedings. In jurisdictions that allow challenges to the sufficiency and competency of the grand jury's evidence, it follows naturally to also allow prosecutorial misconduct challenges since prosecutorial misconduct can just as readily lead to an unwarranted indictment as evidentiary deficiencies. Justifying misconduct dismissals is not as easy, however, where the jurisdiction otherwise adheres to the *Costello* principle that an indictment valid on its face should be enough to "call for trial" where issued by a "legally constituted and unbiased grand jury." Here, the authority to dismiss an indictment based on prosecutorial misconduct may be quite limited.

9. N.Y.Crim.P.Law § 210.30(4).

10. N.Y.Crim.P.Law § 210.30(6).

In some *Costello* jurisdictions, adherence to the *Costello* position follows from a statutory provision, read to be exclusive, that allows challenges to indictments on a list of enumerated grounds that does not include evidentiary deficiencies. Where those statutes also fail to include prosecutorial misconduct among the enumerated grounds, they are read to bar misconduct challenges that fall short of alleging a due process violation. Since the legislature cannot immunize constitutional violations, an indictment still may be dismissed where the process that led to its issuance violated the defendant's right to due process. In other *Costello* jurisdictions, courts are not legislatively restricted, and misconduct dismissals often will encompass nonconstitutional prosecutorial errors in the grand jury proceedings. Such misconduct dismissals will be based on the supervisory authority of the trial court, as in federal courts, or on the common law authority of the judiciary to insist upon prosecutor recognition of the independence of the grand jury. As noted in § 15.5(b), several distinctions may be offered to explain why dismissals based on such authority are not inconsistent with the jurisdiction's adherence to *Costello* as to evidentiary challenges. Misconduct challenges may be seen as implementing *Costello's* assumption that the grand jury is not biased, as focusing upon the actions of the prosecutor rather than the judgment of the grand jurors, and as involving lesser administrative costs than challenges to the sufficiency and competency of the evidence before the grand jury.

Where misconduct challenges are limited to due process violations, prosecutorial actions are measured by the traditional fundamental fairness standard of due process.[1] The defendant's indictment may not be the product of "conduct * * * contrary to 'those fundamental principles of liberty and justice' which lie at the base of all our civil and political institutions." While those principles do not require that the defendant be proceeded against by a grand jury indictment, they do prohibit the state from electing to utilize that process and then basically depriving the defendant of the independent screening procedure it has supposedly given him. Basic unfairness exists where the prosecutor has so manipulated the grand jury process as to render the process no more than a sham. Ordinarily, this requires that the prosecutor have coerced, deceived, or inflamed the grand jury through actions that would, at the least, be deemed a due process violation at trial if done to manipulate the jury there. Thus, due process violations have been found on the basis of flagrant improprieties in argument before the grand jury and on the purposeful presentation of critical perjured testimony to the grand jury.[2] So too, under a "totality of the circumstances" analysis, a series of actions aimed at undermining the independence of the grand jury may result in a due process violation.

Where the misconduct challenges are not limited to constitutional violations, misconduct also is defined by reference to a variety of specific standards governing the prosecutor's interaction with the grand jury. Thus, misconduct may be found where there is: (1) a violation of a statutory standard governing grand jury proceedings, such as a provision requiring the transcription of testimony presented to the grand jury; (2) the failure to fulfill prosecutorial obligations in assisting the grand jury, such as the obligation to give proper legal advice; (3) the use of the grand jury process for an improper purpose, such as compulsion of statements from the target in violation of his or her privilege against self-incrimination; (4) actions that interfere with the grand jury's exercise of its independent authority, such as withdrawing a case from a grand jury that requested additional evidence and submitting it to another grand jury sitting concurrently; and (5) actions that go beyond the traditional limitations upon prosecutorial advocacy as developed largely in the trial context, such as berating witnesses or

§ 15.6

1. See § 2.6(d)(e).

2. See § 24.5(h) and § 24.3(c) as to such due process violations at trial. See §§ 15.7(b), (c) as to those violations in the grand jury proceeding.

injecting into the case issues broader than the accused's liability for the particular offense.

The range of prosecutorial behavior that may be challenged by reference to the above guideposts is extremely broad. Those claims most frequently raised by defendants will be considered in greater detail in § 15.7. While each has its own analytical shading, three overriding considerations provide a common structure for the claims discussed there and all other misconduct claims. First, as discussed in subsection (e), the defendant bears the burden of establishing the existence of the misconduct within the restrictions imposed by grand jury secrecy requirements. Second, as discussed in subsections (b) and (c), prosecutorial misconduct ordinarily will not justify a dismissal absent some showing of likely prejudice. Third, as discussed below, to establish misconduct, the defendant often will be required to show that the prosecutor acted with some measure of scienter.

While the term "misconduct" might suggest an element of prosecutorial culpability, a mental element commonly associated with wrongdoing is not necessarily required to establish prosecutorial misconduct. For example, prosecutorial misconduct exists in the erroneous charging of the grand jury as to the elements of an offense even though the prosecutor adopted an interpretation of the offense that was reasonably arguable, but later held to be erroneous by the trial court. For most acts of misconduct, however, scienter is an essential element. Thus, as discussed in § 15.5(b), *Bank of Nova Scotia* indicated that the introduction of false testimony does not rise to the level of misconduct unless the prosecutor has "knowledge of its falsity." So too, in discussing the prosecutor's alleged threat to withdraw immunity from a witness, which affected the witness' testimony, the Court indicated that misconduct would exist only if the prosecutor had acted for the purpose of manipulating the witness' testimony. An improper purpose also enters into the definition of various other aspects of misconduct. Thus, as discussed in § 15.7(b), the presentation of irrelevant and highly prejudicial information to the grand jury may not constitute misconduct where the prosecutor was not attempting to influence the grand jury's decision to indict. Similarly, as discussed in § 8.8(e), alleged misuse of the grand jury process to gain discovery as to a pending criminal charge requires a showing that such discovery was the primary purpose of the prosecutor. In some instances, statutory standards may incorporate an element of scienter. Thus, Federal Rule 6(e) provides that an "unintentional failure of any [transcription] to reproduce all or any portion of a proceeding shall not affect the validity of the prosecution."

(b) The Requirement of Prejudice. Assuming misconduct is established, must there be some showing of prejudicial impact upon the grand jury's decision to indict in order to justify a dismissal? Prior to the Supreme Court's ruling in *Bank of Nova Scotia v. United States,*[3] several lower federal courts had suggested that, in the exercise of their supervisory powers, trial courts could dismiss an indictment even where the defendant clearly had suffered no prejudice. The judiciary had authority, they argued, to dismiss an indictment simply as a "prophylactic tool" designed to deter prosecutorial misconduct, at least where that misconduct was "flagrant and entrenched." The *Bank of Nova Scotia* ruling, as discussed in the next subsection, rejected the use of the supervisory authority in this fashion. Although the propriety of prophylactic dismissals has not been widely considered in the state courts, a similar result presumably would be reached in the vast majority (if not all) of the states. In some states, the rejection of prophylactic dismissals would seem to follow *a fortiori* from their reading of the state statute governing dismissals as barring supervisory dismissals of indictments on misconduct grounds. As noted in subsection (a), jurisdictions so construing their statutes

3. See note 7 infra.

allow dismissals only for misconduct that reaches the level of a constitutional violation. Such violations commonly are characterized as either inherently prejudicial or as requiring some likelihood of specific prejudicial impact to establish the constitutional violation. In other states, statutory provisions specifically authorize dismissals based upon misconduct in the grand jury process, but include a requirement of likely prejudicial impact. Here again, a prophylactic dismissal would be barred by the directly applicable statute. Finally, in *Bank of Nova Scotia,* the Court concluded that prophylactic supervisory dismissals, because they operated without regard to prejudice, were inconsistent with the general statutory command of Federal Rule 52(a), which bars reversal of an adjudication based on an error that was "harmless" in its impact. All states have similar harmless error statutes or rules. Of course, Justice Marshall, dissenting in *Bank of Nova Scotia,* argued against the application of a traditional harmless-error analysis to prosecutorial violations of the Federal Rule 6 requirements governing grand jury proceedings. A particular state court could find his reasoning more persuasive than that of Court majority and therefore read its harmless error rule as not precluding prophylactic dismissals. That seems unlikely since state courts in other contexts generally have not been receptive to a broad exercise of supervisory sanctions without regard to the implications of the harmless error rule.

Assuming dismissals will be tied to an element of prejudice, that does not necessarily require a case-by-case showing of likely prejudice. A presumption-of-prejudice rationale may be utilized to treat particular types of misconduct as per se prejudicial. This rationale ordinarily rests on the premise that the impact of the particular type of misconduct is too difficult to ascertain and the defendant therefore must be given the benefit of the doubt, with the court conclusively assuming that defendant was prejudiced. The automatic dismissal of indictments issued by unconstitutionally composed grand juries has been justified under this rationale.[4] Thus, *Bank of Nova Scotia* noted that in such cases "the nature of the violation allow[s] a presumption that the defendant was prejudiced, and any inquiry into harmless error would * * * require unguided speculation." Most state courts appear willing to apply this line of reasoning to at least some instances of misconduct. In particular, where juror misconduct at the petit jury level would automatically require reversal of a conviction, the same type of misconduct by grand jurors (e.g., taking bribes) will require automatic dismissal of an indictment. So too, as discussed in § 15.-7(g), many courts hold that prosecutorial presence during the deliberations of the grand jury is inherently prejudicial and therefore requires automatic reversal. Indeed, some courts find inherent prejudice in all unauthorized presence situations. Where the misconduct is characterized as so fundamental as to violate due process, that characterization, as used by some courts, also carries with it a presumption of inherent prejudice. Here, however, the presumption seems to flow not so much from the difficulty in ascertaining prejudice as the high likelihood that errors of this type will in almost all cases be prejudicial.

Assuming that the misconduct will not be deemed inherently prejudicial, some showing of prejudice will be needed to justify a dismissal. The setting of the level of that showing raises a series of issues that can lead to diverse approaches. Initially, the court must determine whether prejudice is to be measured by reference to the actual impact of the misconduct upon the grand jury in deciding to indict or upon the correctness of the decision to indict. The latter approach asks whether the evidence properly before the grand jury clearly would have supported the issuance of an indictment. If the evidence meets that standard, then the defendant is deemed not to have been prejudiced by the misconduct on the assumption that another grand jury, not exposed to the misconduct, would reach the same result. Courts generally have rejected

4. See § 15.4(h).

such a correct-judgment analysis in measuring the prejudicial impact of trial errors, concluding that it inappropriately converts the reviewing court into the trier of fact and allows guilty verdicts to stand notwithstanding basic unfairness in the underlying proceeding.[5] Nonetheless, that standard finds some support in the grand jury setting. This position apparently reflects the view that a less stringent standard of review is appropriate where the adjudicator determines only whether there is sufficient evidence to establish probable cause.

Most courts will measure prejudice by reference to the impact of the misconduct upon the grand jury's judgment. Here, the weight of the evidence before the grand jury remains significant, but not the primary focus of the court's inquiry. The presence of exceptionally strong evidence of guilt may indicate that the grand jurors probably looked to such evidence and were not influenced by the misconduct in their ultimate conclusion, but that will depend on the nature of the misconduct. Even with the strongest evidence, the misconduct may have been so inflammatory that it most likely would have played a role in the grand jury's decision to indict.

A critical question presented in assessing prejudice by reference to possible influence upon the grand jury's judgment is what degree of likelihood must exist that the misconduct actually had that influence. From a defense perspective, the most favorable standard is the harmless error standard that *Chapman v. California* holds applicable to various constitutional errors at trial.[6] Under that standard, a dismissal would be required unless the prosecution can convince the court beyond a reasonable doubt that the misconduct had no bearing on the grand jury's judgment. This standard, if used at all, will be applied only to misconduct reaching the level of a constitutional error. A few courts, however, appear willing to apply a standard that comes close to *Chapman* for certain nonconstitutional errors.

More frequently, courts place the burden on the defense to show some likely impact of the prosecutor's misconduct on the grand jury's decision to indict. The degree of likelihood that must be shown has been variously described. Thus, state courts have spoken of a showing that the grand jury "otherwise might not have returned an indictment," that the misconduct "probably made a difference" and that "a reasonable likelihood * * * exists that [the misconduct] may induce action other than that which the grand jurors in their uninfluenced action would take." Still other courts speak of a showing that the misconduct substantially infringed upon the "integrity" of the grand jury process. While this standard might be read to require a showing that the grand jury actually was influenced, it commonly is used in a context that focuses upon the flagrancy of the prosecutor's misuse of the grand jury process and assumes prejudice where the prosecution obviously sought improperly to influence the grand jury. In particular, it has been cited to justify dismissal where the prosecutor engaged in a series of improprieties and the "totality of the circumstances" were said to have produced a cumulative impact requiring dismissal of the indictment.

(c) The Prejudice Standard of *Bank of Nova Scotia*. As noted in § 15.5(b), in *Bank of Nova Scotia v. United States,*[7] the Supreme Court, for the first time, recognized the authority of federal courts to dismiss indictments prior to trial on the basis of prosecutorial misconduct in the grand jury proceedings. The primary focus of the opinion there was on what role the element of prejudicial impact should play in the exercise of that authority. The Court initially concluded that indictment dismissals were inappropriate in the absence of a likely prejudicial impact, and it then set forth a standard for assessing whether that element of prejudice is present. While Justice Kennedy's opinion for the Court was not without ambiguities, the combination of its general discussion of the prejudice question,

5. See § 27.6(b).

6. See § 27.6(c).

7. 487 U.S. 250, 108 S.Ct. 2369, 101 L.Ed.2d 228 (1988).

its formulation of a general standard for assessing prejudice, and its application of that standard in the case before it provided substantial direction to lower federal courts that had previously splintered on the prejudice issue. Indeed, Justice Kennedy's opinion contains one of the most extensive judicial discussions of the prejudice issue, and though binding only on lower federal courts, that discussion, because of its preeminence, could readily produce greater uniformity among state courts as well.

The prejudice issue came before the Court in *Bank of Nova Scotia* as a result of a trial court's pretrial dismissal of an indictment, and a prosecutor's decision to appeal that ruling rather than seek a new indictment from another grand jury. The trial court's ruling had been based on its finding of several violations of the Rule 6 provisions governing grand jury proceedings, and its additional finding that the "totality of the circumstances," as reflected in various additional acts of misconduct, had resulted in a prosecutorial undermining of the integrity of the grand jury process. The cited violations of Rule 6 included disclosing grand jury materials to Internal Revenue Agents for use in civil cases, disclosing to potential witnesses the names of the targets of the grand jury inquiry, misinforming grand jury witnesses that they could not reveal to others the substance of their testimony or the fact that they had testified before the grand jury, and allowing the joint appearance of IRS agents to present testimony in tandem. The additional instances of misconduct contributing to the totality of the circumstances included the use of "pocket" immunity grants, the berating of an expert witness during a recess (which was witnessed by some jurors), the misdescription of IRS agents as "agents of the grand jury," the use of erroneous summaries of testimony given in prior proceedings, and the alleged threat to withdraw immunity in an effort to manipulate a witness' testimony. The Court of Appeals found that some of the alleged acts of misconduct had been mischaracterized and those that remained did not justify a dismissal since they had not "significantly infring[ed] on the grand jury's ability to exercise independent judgment." A dissenting judge argued, however, that the trial court had supervisory authority to dismiss without any such showing of "prejudice" where there was, as here, "egregious prosecutorial misconduct." Such misconduct, the dissent argued, justified the use of dismissal as a prophylactic measure to "safeguard the integrity of the judicial process."

The Supreme Court initially considered and rejected the use of a prophylactic dismissal. The Court had previously ruled that a federal court's supervisory power may not be used in conflict with either constitutional or statutory command. Among the statutory commands held to limit the use of the supervisory power was that of Federal Rule 52(a). That rule requires federal courts to disregard any error or irregularity that "does not affect [the] substantial rights" of the accused. The "harmless error" standard of Rule 52(a) had been held to preclude the prophylactic reversal of a conviction even where the prosecutorial misconduct at trial was systemic and involved constitutional error. The same limitation, the Court reasoned, surely should also govern a nonconstitutional error in the grand jury setting. As applied to the grand jury, the harmless error standard required that the alleged prosecutorial misconduct present a sufficient potential for having harmed the defendant in the grand jury's decision to indict. In the absence of a finding of such potential prejudice, the misconduct must be deemed "harmless" and dismissal therefore barred by Rule 52(a).[8]

8. Justice Marshall, in dissent, argued that defense discovery of prosecutorial misconduct before the grand jury was already made difficult by grand jury secrecy requirements and "to afford the occasional revelation of prosecutorial misconduct the additional insulation of harmless error analysis leaves Rule 6 toothless." The majority noted, however, that where misconduct did not have a prejudicial effect on the grand jury's decision to change, there remained other means of deterrence, more narrowly tailored than dismissal. It cited in this regard the use of the contempt power to punish knowing violation of Rule 6, the "chastis[ing]" of the prosecutor in a published opinion, and the disciplinary process of the bar and the Justice Department. "Such remedies," the Court

Turning to the standard to be utilized in applying Rule 52(a), the Court adopted, the following measure for the necessary showing of prejudice: "Dismissal of the indictment is appropriate only 'if it established that the violation substantially influenced the grand jury's decision to indict,' or if there is 'grave doubt' that the decision to indict was free from the substantial influence of such violations." This standard was derived from the traditional federal harmless error standard governing the reversal of a conviction based on a nonconstitutional error, as set forth in *Kotteakos v. United States.*[9] The Court there had held that a conviction could not be overturned unless a reviewing court concludes "after examining the record as a whole, * * * that an error may have had 'substantial influence' on the outcome of the proceeding."

By looking to *Kotteakos,* the Court gave content to at least the "substantial influence" element of its standard. The *Kotteakos* opinion made clear that influence of the error was to be measured by its impact on the decision of the adjudicator, regardless of the correctness of the result reached by the adjudicator. Thus, the presence of sufficient evidence to convict would not necessarily render the error harmless; the question to be asked was whether "even so, * * * the error itself had substantial influence." The particular error may have been so influential as to have played an important role in the jury's decision to convict even though it was most likely that the same result would have been reached by another jury not exposed to the error. In the grand jury setting, the federal court similarly must go beyond the question of whether the grand jury had before it substantial evidence of guilt. Misconduct may be so influential as to make it likely that the grand jury gave it great weight in deciding to indict notwithstanding that the untainted remainder of the prosecution's presentation would have been sufficient to support indictment.

The Court's reliance on *Kotteakos* offered less direction as to the second element of the *Bank of Nova Scotia* standard—the requisite degree of likelihood that the misconduct had a substantial influence. *Kotteakos* stated that the critical issue is "what effect the error had or reasonably may be taken to have had upon the jury's decision." *Bank of Nova Scotia* reformulated that standard to require that it either be "established that the violation substantially influenced the grand jury's decision to indict" or that there exist in the mind of the court a " 'grave doubt' " that the indictment decision was "free from the substantial influence of [the] violations." The second prong of this standard obviously is the easier for the defense to meet. Indeed, the first prong presumably is included in the second. Where the defense has "established" that the error substantially influenced the grand jury's decision, the court obviously goes well beyond merely having a "grave doubt" as to whether that decision was free from substantial influence; since the misconduct's actual influence has been "established," the court presumably is convinced that it is more likely than not that the decision was not free from such influence. Thus, the critical issue under the Court's standard will be what degree of likelihood of substantial influence creates a "grave doubt," and on that issue, neither *Kotteakos* nor *Bank of Nova Scotia* provides a precise answer.

Kotteakos spoke of a court being able to say with "fair assurance" that the jury was not "substantially swayed by the error." Lower courts have disagreed as to the precise degree of likelihood suggested by this "fair assurance" language. They do agree, however, that a fair assurance can be present notwithstanding the minimal contrary indicators that would establish a "reasonable doubt" as to prejudicial impact. A reasonable doubt is all that is necessary to preclude a finding of harmless error for constitutional violations under the standard of *Chapman v. California,* but *Kotteakos* is seen as requiring a greater likelihood of prejudice to preclude such a finding for nonconstitutional trial errors. The

noted, "allow the Court to focus on the culpable individual rather than granting a windfall to the unprejudiced defendant".

9. See § 27.6(b).

"grave doubt" language of *Bank of Nova Scotia* similarly suggests a doubt with a more substantial basis than that necessary merely to create a reasonable doubt. Beyond this, the only additional direction offered in Justice Kennedy's opinion came from a single comment to the effect that a grave doubt required more than simply raising a "substantial question" as to likely impact in the mind of the reviewing court.

The Court in *Bank of Nova Scotia* applied the prejudice standard announced there to the misconduct alleged in that case, but that application was so obvious as to say very little about either the "grave doubt" or "substantial influence" elements of the standard. Some of the alleged prosecutorial violations did not directly relate to the persuasiveness of the presentation before the grand jury (e.g., the alleged misuse of the subpoena authority for civil discovery) and they therefore could have had no influence on the grand jury's decision to indict. Others clearly had no influence under the facts of the case (e.g., while two IRS agents testified in tandem, they gave no personal testimony, but simply read from transcripts). The prosecutor had acted improperly in having IRS agents sworn in as "agents" of the grand jury and later referring to them as "your guys," but "nothing in the record * * * indicat[ed] that their reliability or credibility was [thereby] elevated," so the "effect, if any, on the grand jury's decision" was "negligible." Another alleged violation, which the Court described as one that "might have given rise to prejudice" (an alleged governmental threat "to withdraw immunity from a witness in order to manipulate that witness' testimony"), did not in fact occur. Also, as the Court noted, the various incidents of misconduct were "isolated episodes in the course of a 20 month investigation * * * involving dozens of witnesses and thousands of documents."

Although applying its reformulation of the *Kotteakos* standard to the full range of prosecutorial misconduct in the case before it, the *Bank of Nova Scotia* opinion also contained language suggesting that this prejudice standard might not govern in all situations. At the outset of his opinion, Justice Kennedy stated that the Court was holding that, "*as a general matter,* a district court may not dismiss an indictment for errors in grand jury proceedings unless such errors prejudiced the defendants" (emphasis added). In the course of his subsequent discussion of the prejudice element, Justice Kennedy noted that the Court did not have before it a case in which either (1) "constitutional error occurred during the grand jury proceedings," (2) the "grand jury's independence was infringed," or (3) there was a history of systemic prosecutorial misconduct spanning several cases and raising a "serious question" of "fundamental fairness." The applicability of the reformulated *Kotteakos* standard to these three situations accordingly may be treated as an open question, although the context of the discussion of the latter two situations arguably indicates that they are subject to the standard and distinctive only in providing inferences in its application.

As for constitutional violations, the Court initially noted that a case-specific showing of prejudice had not been held necessary where indictment dismissals were based on certain "fundamental" errors of a constitutional nature. It pointed in this regard to cases involving both racial and gender discrimination in the selection of the grand jury. There, "the structural protections of the grand jury have been so compromised as to render the proceedings fundamentally unfair," and the Court accordingly adopts a "presumption of prejudice." Indeed, "any inquiry into harmless error" in such cases would require "ungrounded speculation." Having identified the special considerations underlying the composition cases, which were described as "isolated exceptions to the harmless error rule," the Court then added that "such considerations are not presented here." The Court later noted also that none of the acts of prosecutorial misconduct before it presented a "constitutional error," and it could be argued that this absence of a constitutional violation was critical in distinguishing the composition cases. However, the special considerations said to govern the composition-case "exception" appear to relate to the nature of the violations there rather than simply the constitutional grounding of those violations. Prosecutorial misconduct in the grand jury proceedings, even if it reached the level of a constitutional violation, ordinarily would not go to the "structure" of the grand jury nor would its impact be incapable of measurement.

The Court did consider one claim of constitutional error in *Bank of Nova Scotia,* and while that claim was rejected, the Court's analysis of the claim made evident the characteristics that would distinguish a constitutional misconduct claim from a composition claim and make inappropriate a requirement of dismissal without a case-specific finding of possible prejudice. The defendant alleged that the prosecutor violated the Fifth Amendment by "calling seven witnesses to testify despite an avowed intention to invoke their Fifth Amendment privilege." That claim, the Court concluded, lacked a factual foundation. The "Government was not required to take at face value the unsworn assertions made by the witnesses," and once witnesses did in fact invoke the privilege, they were promptly dismissed. Moreover, "throughout the proceedings, the prosecution warned the grand jury against drawing any adverse inference from a witness' invocation of the Fifth Amendment." While the Court had no need to decide whether the prosecutor would have committed constitutional error if he had sought to have the grand jury draw an adverse inference from the invocation of the Fifth Amendment, its very frame of reference for analyzing the claim indicates that such a constitutional violation would be subject to a harmless error analysis. *Chapman v. California* holds that the analogous violation of the Fifth Amendment at trial—the prosecutor's comment upon a defendant's failure to testify—does not give rise to an automatic presumption of prejudice, but instead requires application of a case-specific harmless error analysis in determining whether a new trial is needed. The standard applied there, however, is not the *Kotteakos* standard, but a "beyond a reasonable doubt" standard.[10]

The *Bank of Nova Scotia* Court also noted that it was not necessary in the case before it to "inquire whether the grand jury's independence was infringed." The Court of Appeals had concluded that there had been no significant infringement upon "the grand jury's ability to exercise independent judgment," and the Supreme Court had not granted certiorari to review that conclusion. "Such an infringement," the Court added, "may result in grave doubt as to a violation's effect on the grand jury's decision to indict." This characterization left somewhat uncertain both the significance and content of an infringement upon the grand jury's independence. The court below had referred to such infringement as the standard to be utilized in determining whether misconduct warranted dismissal of an indictment. While the Supreme Court accepted the lower court's finding that there had been no infringement, it apparently did not view infringement as constituting a per se basis for dismissing the indictment. The Court stated only that an infringement "may result" in a "grave doubt" under the *Kotteakos* standard. The court below also had viewed an infringement of grand jury independence as potentially encompassing a flagrant abuse of the grand jury process that extended beyond the presentation of evidence before the grand jury (e.g., the misuse of the process to obtain discovery for civil litigation). Here too, the Supreme Court's brief discussion suggests a narrower view, as evidenced by its earlier discussion of the need for a showing of prejudice as to the issuance of the indictment. Precisely what the Court had in mind, however, is unclear. Perhaps its most likely point of reference was that misconduct, relating to the presentation of evidence, which had the special quality of keeping the grand jury from making its own evaluation of the case (e.g., a prosecutorial refusal to present exculpatory evidence requested by the grand jury).

Finally, the Court also noted, with no further comment, that the case before it did not present "a history of prosecutorial misconduct, spanning several cases, that is so sys-

10. See § 27.6 at note 11.

temic and pervasive as to raise a substantial and serious question about the fundamental fairness of the process which resulted in the indictment." Some lower courts and commentators view this statement as indicating that such a history of misconduct could justify automatic dismissal of an indictment. However, since the Court renounced in its harmless error analysis the use of supervisory power as a prophylactic tool, that suggestion does not appear to be well taken. It seems more likely that the Court was suggesting that a persistent pattern of misconduct evidences an overall prosecutorial disregard for the fairness of the grand jury process that would be relevant to a finding of prejudice. Even where the identified misconduct is not so significant as to raise by itself the necessary "grave doubt," a court might well assume the presence of an overall atmosphere of disrespect for grand jury fairness (suggesting the possible presence also of undetected misconduct) combines with the identified misconduct to meet that standard.

(d) Postconviction Review. In *Bank of Nova Scotia,* the misconduct challenge was presented before trial and was considered in a preconviction context by both the trial and the appellate courts. It is not unusual, however, for a misconduct challenge to be considered by the trial or appellate court only after the defendant has gone to trial and been convicted. Ordinarily, the defense must raise the objection before trial or risk its forfeiture, but the defense will be excused in making a late objection where it could not reasonably discover the misconduct at an earlier point. Such excused late objections commonly will come during trial, often as a result of information learned at trial, but the trial court is likely at this point to postpone considering the objection until after the trial is completed and the jury has rendered its verdict. Thus, where the objection is not made before trial, even if it is presented prior to the completion of the trial, rulings by both the trial and appellate court ordinarily are made only after the defendant has been convicted. Indeed, even where the objection is made before trial, only the trial court is certain to rule on it prior to the conviction. If that court rejects the challenge, a preconviction appellate review of that ruling is most unlikely. In most jurisdictions, defendant will not be able to gain interlocutory review of a pretrial ruling against his motion to dismiss, so appellate review will be available only in connection with the appeal from the conviction.

Where a misconduct challenge is reviewed following a conviction, the court must consider whether the element of prejudice should be analyzed in light of that conviction. State courts are divided on this issue. Most hold that misconduct which had sufficient impact to justify a dismissal prior to trial will also require dismissal of the indictment upon review following a conviction. Under this view, the indictment must be dismissed because the grand jury process was inadequate and the conviction reversed because it was based upon an invalid indictment. Thus, even though the prosecution may have proven the offense in a fair trial, it must start over again with the issuance of a new indictment and a retrial of the charge. A contrary position holds that the defendant's conviction at a fairly conducted trial renders "moot" or "harmless" any misconduct in the indictment process. Since the grand jury's task was to determine whether there was sufficient evidence to meet the standard for indictment, and since the trial jury has now found the evidence sufficient to meet the higher standard of proving guilt beyond a reasonable doubt, any misconduct that influenced the grand jury can no longer be said to have had a substantial bearing on the outcome of the case. Unlike a constitutional violation in the selection of the grand jury, prosecution misconduct does not nonetheless justify a conviction reversal under a theory tied either to potential grand juror nullification or to third-party standing to vindicate the rights of others.

In *United States v. Mechanik,*[11] the Supreme Court held the latter approach to govern in federal cases. Whether that holding extends to all types of misconduct or only certain kinds of misconduct remains an open

11. 475 U.S. 66, 106 S.Ct. 938, 89 L.Ed.2d 50 (1986).

issue. *Mechanik* presented an alleged violation of the Federal Rule 6(d) provision that allows only specified persons, including "the witness under examination," to be present before the grand jury. The prosecutor had presented before the grand jury two government witnesses who appeared together and testified in tandem. The defendants' motion to dismiss was presented midway through the trial, but there was good cause for the late objection (the defendants had been unable to discover that the two witnesses appeared simultaneously until the defense gained impeachment discovery of the witnesses' grand jury testimony at trial). The district judge delayed ruling on the defendants' motion until after the trial was completed and the defendants had been convicted. The district judge then found that there had been a Rule 6(d) violation, but also concluded that dismissal was inappropriate since the particular circumstances of the case suggested that the violation had not affected the grand jury's indictment decision. The Fourth Circuit, on appeal from the conviction, agreed that Rule 6(d) had been violated, but concluded that the violation did require reversal of the conviction and dismissal of the indictment. The Supreme Court reversed that ruling.

The *Mechanik* majority "assumed arguendo" that there had been a Rule 6(d) violation, and that the trial court "would have been justified in dismissing * * * the indictment on that basis had there been actual prejudice and had the matter been called to its attention before the commencement of the trial." However, since the violation was ruled upon after the defendants had been convicted on the indictment at a fair trial, it should have been treated by the lower courts as a per se harmless error. The Court (per Rehnquist, J.) explained:

> Both [courts below] observed that Rule 6(d) was designed in part, "to ensure that grand jurors, sitting without the direct supervision of a judge, are not subject to undue influence that may come with the presence of an unauthorized person." The Rule protects against the danger that a defendant will be required to defend against a charge for which there is no probable cause to believe him guilty. * * * But the petit jury's subsequent guilty verdict not only means that there was probable cause to believe that the defendants were guilty as charged, but that they are in fact guilty as charged beyond a reasonable doubt. Measured by the petit jury's verdict, then, any error in the grand jury proceedings connected with the charging decision was harmless beyond a reasonable doubt.
>
> It might be argued in some literal sense that because the Rule was designed to protect against an erroneous charging decision by the grand jury, the indictment should not be compared to the evidence produced by the Government at trial, but to the evidence produced before the grand jury.[12] But even if this argument were accepted, there is no simple way after the verdict to restore the defendant to the position in which he would have been had the indictment been dismissed before trial. He will already have suffered whatever inconvenience, expense, and opprobrium that a proper indictment may have spared him. In courtroom proceedings as elsewhere, "the moving finger writes, and having writ moves on."

The key to the above analysis, as the Court recognized, lies in the conclusive significance attached to the jury's finding of guilt. The Court assumes that the misconduct could not have influenced the outcome of the case because the defendant in any event would have been convicted of the offense. Even if the original grand jury would not have indicted but for the misconduct, another grand jury, presented with the same evidence that led the petit jury to convict, surely would have indicted. As it relates to the grand jury's decision to indict, the Court analysis focuses on a correct-result evaluation rather than the ef-

12. Three justices, concurring in the judgment, so argued. They contended that the Rule 52(a) harmless error rule and Rule 6(d) could appropriately be read in conjunction only by holding that "the focus of the prejudice inquiry [for harmless error] should be on the effect of the alleged error on the grand jury's decision to indict" even in the setting of a postconviction review. Justice Marshall, in dissent, similarly contended that the Rule 6(d) violation should be viewed solely in terms of its probable impact upon the indictment decision, but contended that such an error should be treated as per se prejudicial.

fect-on-the-judgment evaluation suggested by the *Kotteakos*-derived standard of *Bank of Nova Scotia.* That is considered appropriate because the reviewing court is not substituting its own evaluation of the strength of the prosecution's case, but that of the petit jury. The *Mechanik* majority acknowledged that a quite different approach had been adopted in considering claims of racial discrimination in the selection of the grand jury.[13] There, even though the indictment had been followed by the defendant's conviction by a fairly selected petit jury, the Court had applied a rule of automatic reversal of the conviction and dismissal of the indictment. That position was explained as based on grounds that had no bearing in the situation presented in *Mechanik.* The "remedy of automatic reversal was necessary as a prophylactic means of deterring grand jury discrimination in the future" and "one could presume that a discriminatorily selected grand jury would treat defendants of excluded races unfairly." Such considerations had "little force outside the context of racial discrimination in the composition of the grand jury." Here, in contrast, a prophylactic sanction could not be imposed consistent with the harmless error standard of Rule 52(a), and it was appropriate to conclude that "reversal of a conviction after a trial free from reversible error cannot restore to the defendant whatever benefit might have accrued to him from a trial on an indictment returned in conformity with Rule 6(d)."

Read broadly, the *Mechanik* reasoning would characterize as per se harmless almost all forms of prosecutorial misconduct before the grand jury where there has been an intervening conviction. The only possible exception would be the unusual situation in which one could say with fair assurance that a grand jury might not have indicted, or might have indicted on a lesser charge, even if it had before it the evidence presented at trial. Only there could it be said that reversal of the conviction and dismissal of the indictment could possibly restore to the defendant a benefit that he might have received except for the misconduct before the grand jury. The *Mechanik* reasoning otherwise would apply even to prosecutorial misconduct that reaches the level of a constitutional violation. Assuming that misconduct reached that level only where it was parallel to the misconduct that constituted a constitutional violation at trial, analogous precedent clearly indicates that the misconduct should not be grounds for automatic reversal of the intervening conviction. Even at trial, such misconduct is subject to the harmless error standard of *Chapman v. California* (in contrast, for example, to the inherently prejudicial violation of unconstitutional selection of the petit jury). Applying that standard, *Mechanik's* reasoning would suggest that any unconstitutional misconduct before the grand jury (e.g., adverse comment upon the target's refusal to appear and testify) would be rendered per se harmless by a conviction at a trial in which that misconduct was not repeated.

Lower courts have disagreed, however, as to whether *Mechanik* can be extended even to most instances of prosecutorial misconduct that do not present constitutional difficulties. Those that would restrict *Mechanik* to a limited class of errors argue that the "*Mechanik* [ruling] was carefully crafted along very narrow lines" and involved misconduct that "at worst, was technical, and at most, would have affected only the grand jury's determination of probable cause." Postconviction review should be available, they argue, where it is alleged that the government "attempted to unfairly sway the grand jury or to otherwise affect the accusatory process." This standard presumably would leave open to review many of the usual misconduct claims, including those alleging prosecutorial argument before the grand jury calculated to arouse prejudice, the intentional prosecutorial reliance upon false testimony, and the typical "totality of the circumstances" claim alleging a series of improper prosecutorial actions. Several circuits have rejected such a position. They note that the rationale of *Mechanik* did not depend on the "technical * * * nature of the rule at hand; [for] the Court assumed that the

13. See § 15.4(h).

violation was sufficiently substantial to permit the dismissal of the indictment." *Mechanik,* it is said, "proceeds by identifying the purpose of the rule (to protect the innocent from being indicted) and then says that a rule with this purpose should not be enforced by reversing a conviction after trial—because we know, as surely as courts 'know' anything, that the convicted defendant is not a member of the class of the beneficiaries of the rule."

One argument advanced for a narrow reading of *Mechanik* is that appellate reversals must be available to deter flagrant and persistent prosecutorial misconduct that can result in fundamental unfairness. This argument must overcome, however, the contrary force of the Court's rejection of prophylactic pretrial dismissals in *Bank of Nova Scotia* and the Court's reliance in both *Mechanik* and *Bank of Nova Scotia* upon the Supreme Court's ruling in *United States v. Hasting.*[14] The Court in *Hasting* held that a federal appellate court could not utilize its supervisory authority to mandate automatic reversals (without regard to the possible lack of prejudicial impact) for constitutionally improper prosecutorial action at trial even where the appellate court contended that automatic reversal was needed because such conduct was occurring "with disturbing frequency * * * throughout the circuit." The Court insisted upon harmless error analysis even where the prosecution was persistently engaging in constitutional violations at trial (there, adverse comment on the defendant's failure to testify). It would seem to follow that the harmless error analysis advanced in *Mechanik* likewise could not be discarded or narrowed in reach simply for the sake of using postconviction dismissals to deter persistent acts of prosecutorial misconduct before the grand jury.

Of course, one factor distinguishing the *Hasting* situation is that an appellate court will have the opportunity to identify and condemn trial misconduct through conviction reversals where such misconduct was not harmless in impact. In the federal grand jury setting, with interlocutory appellate review generally unavailable,[15] rejected pretrial claims of prosecutorial misconduct will not reach the appellate court until after conviction, and at that point, a broad reading of *Mechanik* would render fruitless any appeal as the alleged misconduct would automatically be deemed harmless error. However, Justice Marshall's dissent in *Mechanik* dissent clearly pointed out that the majority's ruling thus would leave enforcement of Rule 6(d) to the "unreviewable largesse of the district court," and the majority there obviously did not view that consequence as a sufficient reason to change its position. It noted simply that the "societal costs of retrial after a jury verdict of guilty are far too substantial to justify setting aside a verdict simply because of an error in the earlier grand jury proceedings."

(e) Establishing Misconduct. Except for the most unusual case, prosecutorial misconduct in the grand jury process will not have occurred in the presence of the defendant. Thus, the defense's ability to raise a misconduct challenge will be heavily dependent upon the availability of measures that will enable it to learn of possible misconduct. In most jurisdictions, however, those measures tend to be so restricted that many instances of misconduct are likely to go undiscovered.

The best source for determining what happened before the grand jury ordinarily would be the transcript of the grand jury proceedings. Some jurisdictions, however, do not require that grand jury proceedings be transcribed. Others require transcription only of the testimony presented to the grand jury, leaving off the record all discussions between the prosecutor and the jurors. Moreover, whether complete or partial, the transcript is

14. 461 U.S. 499, 103 S.Ct. 1974, 76 L.Ed.2d 96 (1983).

15. As to interlocutory review, see § 27.2 at note 14. As noted there, *Midland Asphalt Corp. v. United States* held that interlocutory review would not be available in federal courts even if the particular act of misconduct would automatically constitute harmless error in a postconviction setting under the reasoning of *Mechanik.* Appellate review would be available, of course, where the trial court sustained the objection, dismissing the indictment, and the government then appealed.

not likely to be readily available to the defense. As noted in § 15.5(c), automatic access to the grand jury transcript generally is provided only in that small group of states that reject *Costello,* where automatic disclosure is deemed necessary to implement defendant's right to challenge the sufficiency of the grand jury evidence. In the many jurisdictions that follow *Costello,* which includes most of the indictment jurisdictions, the principle of grand jury secrecy sharply restricts defense access to the transcript. Federal Rule 6(e) is typical. It allows for court-ordered discovery in connection with "a motion to dismiss an indictment because of matters occurring before the grand jury," but such discovery does not follow automatically with the filing of such a motion. The defense must overcome a presumption of regularity in the grand jury process by making a preliminary showing of likely misconduct. That showing, for most courts, must be substantial.

In applying provisions like Rule 6(e), courts take into consideration the distinct possibility that a defense motion may be made simply for the purpose of delay or as an attempt to gain valuable defense discovery unrelated to any misconduct. They recognize also that, to allow the defense to make a showing of likely prejudicial impact of any misconduct, it might be necessary to disclose the entire grand jury transcript. Disclosure thus could include matters that will not come out at trial and seriously breach the promise of secrecy that encourages "free and untrammeled" disclosure by witnesses. Accordingly, a typical standard for court-ordered disclosure is that the defense establish preliminarily "a substantial likelihood of gross procedural irregularities." To meet that standard, the defense often must present either the affidavit of a person who was present when the misconduct occurred or a portion of the transcript otherwise released to the defense (e.g., for discovery purposes) that contains a strong suggestion of impropriety.

§ 15.7 Common Prosecutorial Misconduct Claims

(a) The Range of Objections. Speaking of misconduct objections, Professor Wright has noted: "Almost every case of this kind presents a novel set of facts, since the range of prosecutorial misconduct capable of inspiring allegations of unfairness appears unlimited." [1] Any attempt to categorize misconduct objections necessarily looses sight of a substantial number of objections that fail to fit any common mold. Nonetheless, the objections discussed in the reported cases seem to cluster around certain basic categories of misconduct. The sections that follow discuss these general types of misconduct.

Not considered in the discussion below are various types of misconduct that ordinarily would not have an impact upon the grand jury's evaluation of the case presented by the prosecution. Included in this category are such actions as the purposeful leaking of grand jury material and the misuse of the grand jury process to develop civil suits or gain discovery relevant to a pending criminal prosecution. In *Bank of Nova Scotia,* the Court found that several such acts of misconduct could not justify a dismissal because they could not, by their nature, have influenced the grand jury's decision to indict. They automatically constituted harmless error in the context of a challenge to an indictment.[2] Most jurisdictions apparently adhere to this viewpoint, although some courts might take such actions into consideration in determining whether the totality of the circumstances reflect a prosecutorial undermining of the integrity of the grand jury.

(b) Impermissible Comments. The American Bar Association standards provide that the prosecutor, in his appearances before the grand jury, "should not make statements or efforts to influence grand jury action in a manner which would be impermissible at trial

§ 15.7

1. C. Wright, Federal Practice and Procedure—Criminal § 111.1 (2d ed. 1982).

2. There are, however, other procedures for objecting to such misconduct, as discussed in §§ 8.5(a), 8.8(d), and 8.8(e).

before a petit jury."[3] This standard applies both to impermissible prosecution arguments and impermissible references in the examination of witnesses and the introduction of evidence. Although courts frequently have cited the A.B.A. standard with approval, their rulings suggest that its incorporation of the standards applicable to trial presentations will be subject to some modification. The prosecutor in the grand jury setting wears several hats that are not worn by the trial prosecutor, and these additional roles must be taken into consideration in evaluating alleged misconduct. The grand jury prosecutor serves as the legal advisor to the grand jury and his performance in that role may give him leeway to make comments that would not be permitted of a trial attorney, who acts strictly as an advocate and leaves the legal advice to the trial judge. So too, the prosecutor occupies a leadership role in the exercise of the grand jury's investigative authority and that role may require a reference to matters that could not be put before the petit jury by a trial prosecutor.

One trial limitation that clearly applies to the prosecutor in the grand jury setting is the prohibition of arguments or references that are calculated to inflame the passions or prejudices of the grand jury or to inject broader issues than the guilt of the particular defendant under the controlling law. Thus, courts have characterized as misconduct such actions as the following: (1) asking a witness who is a prospective defendant questions about irrelevant personal matters in an effort to "discredit and impugn her in the eyes of the jurors,"; (2) informing the grand jurors that the target is suspected of other serious crimes that are not before them; (3) referring to the target's criminal record where it is irrelevant to the offense; (4) inviting the jurors, through unfounded references in questions put to witnesses, to "associate the defendants with a disfavored criminal class [Cosa Nostra leaders]"; (5) informing the grand jurors that the target had sought to plea bargain; and (6) appealing to the grand jurors' personal pride in their office.

On the other hand, as the legal advisor to the grand jury, the prosecutor may be allowed statements of personal opinion that would not be appropriate at trial, where the prosecutor generally may not express his personal opinion as to the guilt of the defendant. Thus the ABA Standards note that the prosecutor may "express an opinion on the legal significance of the evidence," though adding that such expression "should give due deference to [the grand jury's] status as an independent legal body." Indeed, the ABA Standards require the prosecutor to recommend to the grand jury that it not indict where "he believes the evidence presented does not warrant an indictment under governing law."[4] While the latter principle is well accepted, not all courts would read as broadly the prosecutor's authority to express a personal opinion adverse to the defendant. Some courts will not allow the prosecutor to go beyond presenting the same type of general argument for the sufficiency of the evidence as would be allowed at trial. Statements as to the overall strength of the evidence are permissible, but not in the form of a personal conclusion or a personal recommendation to indict. This position apparently rests on the premise that the prosecutor's role of legal advisor simply places him in the same position as the charging judge, who would not be allowed to express such personal opinions. Courts rejecting this position, and allowing an expression of personal opinion, view the giving of legal "advice" as extending to the applicability of the law to the facts presented. They also see little harm in the expression of an opinion on that issue, particularly where the prosecutor reminds the grand jury that it is not bound by his opinion and should exercise its own independent judgment in weighing the evidence. Since grand jurors realize that the case is being presented precisely because the prosecutor believes the grand jury should indict, a statement of opinion on the sufficiency of the evidence does no more than openly convey what otherwise is implicit. Similarly, in

3. 1 ABA Standards for Criminal Justice, §§ 3–3.5 (2d ed. 1980).

4. Id. at § 3–3.6.

many jurisdictions, the presentation of a proposed indictment already signed by the prosecutor is not itself viewed as misconduct.

The prosecutor's broader role before the grand jury also may justify informing the grand jury of otherwise irrelevant and prejudicial information or even expressing a personal opinion as to a witness' credibility. Thus, in responding to grand juror questions, the prosecutor may have to explain that there had been a previous indictment which had been dismissed on particular grounds or that the charges were part of a particular prosecutorial strategy. Similarly, in the course of examining a recalcitrant witness, in order to encourage the witness to reveal the truth, the prosecutor may find it necessary to warn the witness that the prosecutor knows that he is perjuring himself. A critical factor in such cases is whether the prosecutor's comments appear to be aimed primarily at having the grand jury give weight to the prejudicial information in deciding whether to indict. Telling the witness that he has just committed perjury will be acceptable where the prosecutor's obvious purpose was to facilitate the inquiry by having the witness testify truthfully, but not where the prosecutor's objective was to ensure that the grand jurors disbelieve the witness or to encourage their indictment of the witness for perjury. Along the same lines, courts recognize that a broad ranging grand jury investigation will almost inevitably produce certain potentially prejudicial information that will not be relevant to the particular charge eventually put forth for indictment. Accordingly, the critical factor is not the presentation of that evidence per se, but whether the prosecutor relied on that irrelevant and prejudicial material in arguing for indictment. In this connection, the prosecutor often will be presumed to have acted in good faith absent specific evidence to the contrary. Thus, where the prosecutor admonishes the jurors not to consider particular irrelevant evidence, that admonishment will not be viewed skeptically as a strategic tactic designed to remind the grand jury of that evidence.

Very often, courts will conclude that there is no need to determine whether the prosecutor's comments were impermissible as those comments did not, in any event, present a sufficient likelihood of prejudicial impact to justify dismissal of the indictment. Even in those jurisdictions that treat certain misconduct as inherently prejudicial, that treatment generally will not be accorded to improper references to inflammatory and irrelevant material. A case-specific finding of a likely prejudicial impact upon the decision to indict will be required no matter how inappropriate the prosecutor's comments. Such a finding is least likely where the prosecutor's misstatement can be characterized as an isolated incident in a lengthy proceeding. It is most likely where the prosecution's evidence was not especially strong and the comments were highly inflammatory and frequently repeated.

(c) Violations of the Privilege Against Self–Incrimination. In jurisdictions that adhere to the *Costello* principle, a grand jury indictment is not subject to challenge because the prosecutor introduced before the grand jury statements obtained from the defendant in violation of his privilege against self-incrimination. Nonetheless, several lower courts have argued that where the grand jury process itself was used to violate the defendant's privilege against self-incrimination, the ensuing indictment may be challenged on misconduct grounds. This exception to *Costello* has been applied both where the prospective defendant was compelled to testify before the grand jury in violation of his self-incrimination privilege and where the prosecution used before the grand jury prior testimony of the prospective defendant that had been given under a grant of immunity. Courts allowing challenges in such cases have distinguished *Costello* on the ground that "there is no historical basis for grand juries to be permitted to violate the rights of witnesses who testify before them." They also note that the potential delay occasioned by such indictment challenges pose far less of a problem than the basic evidentiary challenges considered in *Costello,* as prosecutors "only rarely" will utilize the grand jury process itself to violate a prospective defendant's privilege. In the case of the use of immunized testimony, further support is found in the statutory prohibition against prosecutorial use of such testimony in any "criminal case." [5]

A quite distinct self-incrimination claim is presented where the prosecution makes an adverse comment on the prospective defendant's exercise of the privilege in past proceedings or his failure to testify before the grand jury. Here the challenge to the indictment can more readily be characterized as a misconduct challenge since the basic complaint is to the irrelevant and inflammatory nature of the prosecutor's comments rather than to the obtaining of evidence in violation of the self-incrimination privilege. In *Bank of Nova Scotia,* the defendant presented a variation of such a claim, contending that the prosecutor had sought to turn the jury against the prospective defendant by subpoenaing associates for the purpose of calling to the jury's attention their claim of the self-incrimination privilege. While the Supreme Court rejected that misconduct claim as factually unsupportable, it did not suggest, as it had with defendant's objection to erroneous summaries, that the defense was raising, in effect, an evidentiary challenge barred by *Costello.*

(d) Deception in Presenting Evidence. The Supreme Court has held that prosecution at trial has a due process obligation to correct any material false evidence presented by its witnesses when the prosecution knows that the evidence is false.[6] While the courts generally have agreed that the basic components of this obligation also apply to the grand jury setting, its exact grounding and scope are matters of some dispute. Initially, there is disagreement as to whether the obligation to correct known false evidence here can be grounded on the due process clause. Some courts prefer to treat the prosecution's knowing reliance upon false testimony as action clearly inconsistent with the prosecutor's roles both as advocate and legal advisor and therefore subject to the general judicial authority to dismiss indictments based upon prejudicial prosecutorial misconduct. They express doubt as to whether the Supreme Court's due process rulings governing the use of false testimony at trial, where that testimony relates to the issue of conviction, can readily be carried over to the grand jury's decision to indict. They note the limited function of the indictment and the continued availability of the trial "to correct errors before the grand jury." That grounding for distinguishing the grand jury and trial processes, however, would be equally applicable to any claim of a constitutional violation in the grand jury process that builds upon rulings holding unconstitutional analogous trial actions by prosecutors. If a constitutional violation is to be found in prosecutorial comments pressuring the grand jurors to indict and in the prosecution's adverse comment upon the defendant's exercise of his self-incrimination privilege, then such a violation seemingly should be found as well where the prosecutor intentionally uses false testimony to gain an indictment.

Courts also disagree as to the precise element of scienter needed for prosecutorial misconduct in the use of false testimony. As discussed in § 15.5(b), the Supreme Court in *Bank of Nova Scotia* limited such misconduct claims to situations in which the prosecution knowingly allowed or caused its witnesses to present false testimony. The presence of "some doubts" about the accuracy of the witness' testimony was held not sufficient, as that is "quite different from having knowledge of falsity." In its due process ruling at the trial stage, the Court has held that "knowledge" is judged by reference to the prosecution's office as a whole and takes into consideration information given to that office that would establish the falsity of the witness' testimony.[7] The Court in *Bank of Nova Scotia* arguably meant to incorporate a similar concept of knowledge as it spoke to the knowledge of "the Government." Even with this broader concept of knowledge, however, the

5. 18 U.S.C.A. § 6002. See § 18.11(b).

6. See § 24.3(c).

7. See § 24.3 at note 25.

Court would not be extending the prosecutor's responsibility as far as certain state courts. The *Bank of Nova Scotia* view of misconduct appears to be somewhat narrower, for example, than that of the state court holding misconduct to exist where the prosecutor acted with "reckless disregard of the truth" in presenting "false or deceptive evidence." It most certainly would not encompass lower court rulings that a prosecutor engages in misconduct, even where he first learns of the falsity of the evidence after the indictment is issued, if he does not then return the case to the grand jury for reconsideration. Under *Bank of Nova Scotia,* there having been no deception and therefore no misconduct, a challenge to the indictment in such a case would rest on the falsity of the evidence alone and therefore be barred by *Costello.*

Another point of diversion among the courts is the measure of the "materiality" of false testimony. The critical factor here is the likely impact of the false testimony upon the grand jury's decision to indict. The Supreme Court's due process rulings at the trial stage hold that the false testimony is material if the reviewing court cannot conclude beyond a reasonable doubt that the same verdict would have been reached without the false testimony. Assuming that the knowing use of false testimony before the grand jury is not a due process violation *Bank of Nova Scotia* would find the likelihood of prejudice sufficient only where the reviewing court concludes that there is at least a "grave doubt that the decision to indict was free from the substantial influence" of the false testimony. A somewhat similar state standard requires that the "presentation of the false or deceptive evidence probably influenced the grand jury's determination to hand up an indictment." A quite different standard holds that dismissal is not appropriate unless the reviewing court concludes that evidence before the grand jury would have been insufficient to support an indictment without the false testimony.

(e) Failure to Present Known Exculpatory Evidence. In 1975, the California Supreme Court, in *Johnson v. Superior Court,*[8] dismissed an indictment based upon the prosecutor's failure to present before the grand jury known evidence "reasonably tending to negate guilt." The *Johnson* opinion relied upon a California statute requiring the grand jury to consider "evidence within its reach which will explain away the charge." It reasoned that this requirement imposed a corresponding duty on the prosecutor to inform the grand jury of known exculpatory evidence. In the years since *Johnson,* roughly a dozen states have followed *Johnson* to the extent of stating that, under some circumstances, the prosecutor's failure to present known exculpatory evidence will constitute ground for dismissal. Another group of several states has disagreed, holding that the prosecutor has no obligation to inform the grand jurors of known exculpatory evidence. Still other states, primarily information jurisdictions, have not had occasion to reach the issue. The federal lower courts generally have spoken to the issue, but are divided in their rulings. Of course, even where courts have held that the prosecution has no duty to produce exculpatory evidence on its own initiative, the failure to respond to a specific request of the grand jury to produce particular exculpatory evidence may be viewed as an infringement upon grand jury independence and thereby provide a basis for challenging the indictment.

Courts recognizing a prosecutorial duty to disclose have cited several different groundings for that duty. Some have relied upon statutory provisions that either require the grand jury to order the production of known exculpatory evidence or specifically direct the prosecutor to present known evidence that "directly negates the guilt of the accused." A few find support in Supreme Court rulings holding that the failure to disclose at trial known exculpatory evidence of sufficient materiality violates due process.[9] They argue that a similar obligation of fairness applies to basic pretrial procedures, including the grand

8. 15 Cal.3d 248, 124 Cal.Rptr. 32, 539 P.2d 792 (1975).

9. See § 20.7.

jury presentation by the prosecutor. Moreover, apart from any constitutional grounding, such an obligation follows from the prosecutor's basic ethical responsibilities. Several courts have suggested that the prosecutor's failure to present known exculpatory evidence constitutes a form of deception analogous to the use of perjured testimony.

Courts rejecting any prosecutorial obligation to present known exculpatory evidence rely upon the non-adversary nature of the grand jury proceeding. The function of the grand jury, they note, is to determine whether the evidence supporting guilt is sufficient to meet the standard for indictment. The prospective defendant has no right to present conflicting evidence and the prosecutor cannot appropriately be placed in a position of assisting the defense in the exercise of a right it does not have. At trial, in contrast, the jury is expected to weigh conflicting evidence and the prosecutor accordingly is required to either call known exculpatory evidence to the attention of the defense or present it directly to the jury. Though a case might be made for strengthening the grand jury screening process by ensuring that the jurors be informed of known weaknesses in the prosecution's case, adoption of such a major restructuring of the process is seen as a function for the legislature, not the courts in the exercise of their supervisory power. While the courts may prohibit prosecutorial deception through the intentional use of false testimony, exculpatory evidence at its strongest simply "explains away" prosecution evidence that is not false, but merely appears more convincing in the absence of conflicting evidence. Thus, it is argued, an indictment challenge based upon the prosecutor's failure to present exculpatory evidence constitutes, in effect, a challenge to the sufficiency of the evidence before the grand jury, which is barred from review under the *Costello* principle.

State and federal courts recognizing a prosecutorial obligation to present to the grand jury known exculpatory evidence have varied in their description of the scope of that obligation. In general, they have construed that obligation more narrowly than the language of *Johnson* might suggest. *Johnson* spoke of the prosecutor's duty to present known evidence "reasonably tending to negate guilt." That standard is generally thought to be similar to the standard of a "reasonable probability" of negating a conviction that is applied under the prosecution's due process obligation to disclose exculpatory evidence at trial.[10] Most courts considering the question have rejected that analogy as imposing too heavy a burden on the prosecution in the grand jury setting. Four considerations are said to require a narrower definition of the known exculpatory evidence that must be presented to the grand jury. First, the prosecutor at this stage of the proceedings ordinarily does not have the advantage of defense motions identifying those items that the defense views as potentially exculpatory. It would impose an intolerable burden on the government to require it to "sift through all the evidence to find statements or documents that might be exculpatory." Second, at this preliminary stage of the proceeding, where both the possible charges and defenses may be uncertain, the prosecutor is likely to have greater difficulty in determining what evidence is exculpatory. Third, consideration must be given to the "unique role of * * * grand jury [review] as a flexible and non-adversarial process." It is a basic premise of grand jury screening that the "prosecutor does not have a duty to present defendant's version of the facts." Finally, taking a page from *Costello,* courts stress the need to avoid "convert[ing] a grand jury proceeding from an investigative one into a mini-trial of the merits." Such a step, they note, "would be unnecessarily burdensome and wasteful, since, even if an indictment should be filed, the defendant can be found guilty only after a guilty plea or criminal jury trial in which guilt is established beyond a reasonable doubt."

10. The obligation there is stated in terms of an after-the-fact evaluation of the consequence of nondisclosure—whether there is a "reasonable probability" that the jury would not have convicted if the evidence had been disclosed. See § 20.7(b).

Decisions rejecting a *Johnson*-type standard have offered various formulations of narrower disclosure requirement. Many courts have spoken of an obligation to present only exculpatory evidence which "clearly negates the target's guilt." Others have stated that dismissal will be appropriate only where the prosecutor fails to disclose "exculpatory evidence" which "would have materially affected the grand jury determination," or would have "preclud[ed] indictment." Still other courts state the appropriate standard as whether the non-disclosure "impaired the integrity of the grand jury" or resulted in "fundamental unfairness."[11] Notwithstanding these variations in phrasing, the cases are fairly consistent in the illustrations they offer as to categories of evidence which need be and need not be disclosed. This suggests that the varying standards are not viewed as terms of art, but rather as indicators of a general policy limiting the duty to disclosure to exceptional cases.

Initially, these courts agree that the prosecutor need not disclose evidence that simply challenges the credibility of the government's witnesses (although some might rule otherwise as to evidence substantially impeaching an especially critical witness). They also agree that the prosecutor need not introduce evidence which might suggest that it is less likely that the defendant committed the crime, but would not necessarily contradict his guilt. The prosecutor's disclosure obligation basically is limited to evidence which, if believed, would establish in itself that he had not committed the crime—such as a confession by another to the crime or evidence that "the accused was nowhere near the scene of the crime when it occurred." Even then, consideration will be given to the likely reliability of the non-disclosed evidence. In particular, self-serving statements of the defendant, where contradicted by the prosecution's evidence, need not be presented even though they directly negate guilt.

Apart from the weight of the evidence itself, courts also look to factors suggesting that the prosecutor acted in good faith in failing to disclose exculpatory evidence. Of course, since the obligation is limited to "known" exculpatory evidence, the prosecution will not be faulted for non-disclosure when it was not aware of the evidence. Even where the non-disclosed evidence was known, however, the prosecution may point to its affirmative efforts to meet its obligation. Thus, where the prosecutor presented various items of exculpatory evidence, but did not produce other items that the defendant viewed as more persuasive, the defense objection is likely to be met by the statement that "there is no requirement that the prosecutor disclose allegedly exculpatory evidence in the manner preferred by the defendant." So too, courts give weight to the fact that the defendant was invited to testify and present his own version of the facts, but refused that opportunity. On the other hand, evidence of bad faith will clearly tip the scales in favor of dismissal.

(f) Erroneous Legal Advice. As legal advisor to the grand jury, the prosecutor has an obligation to give the grand jury sufficient information concerning the applicable law "to enable it intelligently to decide whether a crime has been committed." The handful of courts that have commented extensively upon that obligation have stressed that the prosecutor need not give legal instructions even roughly approximating the comprehensiveness of the trial judge's charge to the petit jury. Nevertheless, an instruction may be "so misleading," due to mistakes or omissions, that the ensuing indictment "will not be permitted to stand even though it is supported by legally sufficient evidence." Prosecutors are most likely to run into difficulties when they go beyond the statutory language or standard jury instructions and offer their own erroneous interpretation of the law, especially where the erroneous interpretation is tied directly to the facts of the case. Courts often are somewhat more reluctant to grant dismis-

11. Many courts, as the above standards suggest, describe the prosecution's obligation by reference to whether the failure to disclose creates a sufficient likelihood of prejudicial impact to justify a dismissal. Thus, there is no need for a separate determination of the element of prejudice [see § 15.6(b)], as that element is necessarily encompassed in deciding that the failure to disclose will be characterized as misconduct.

sals on the basis of omissions in the instructions. A trial judge can rely upon defense counsel to call to his attention the need for references to those elements of the offense, special proof requirements, or defenses on which the prosecution's case is likely to falter. In contrast, the prosecutor instructing a grand jury on the applicable law must rely entirely on his own view of the case. Still, an indictment will be dismissed if the prosecutor fails to take even the minimal step of reading the relevant statute to the jury. So also, where the evidence before the grand jury "clearly establishes" a defense to the charge, failure to inform the grand jury of the legal requirements for that defense will require dismissal. Informing the jurors of the legal elements of a defense is not mandatory, however, if the evidence no more than simply makes the defense "viable and arguable."

(g) Presence of Unauthorized Persons. Grand jury secrecy provisions commonly provide that no person other than the grand jurors may be present during deliberations and voting, while only the jurors, prosecutors, supporting personnel (e.g., stenographers) and the witness under examination may be present during any other portion of the proceedings. It is uniformly accepted that a violation of these provisions on presence may justify a pretrial dismissal of an indictment, but a division exists as to whether dismissal here should be conditioned on the usual requirement of a case-specific showing of likely prejudice. Courts requiring such a showing see no basis for distinguishing the presence of an unauthorized person from other irregularities in grand jury proceedings (e.g., improper comments by the prosecutor). In determining whether an unauthorized presence presents a sufficient likelihood of prejudicial impact, these courts look to such factors as: (1) the relationship of the person improperly present to the alleged offense (e.g., whether that person was complainant, whose very presence might impose pressure on the jurors, or merely a clerk); (2) the stage at which that person was improperly present (i.e., during deliberations and voting, or simply during the presentation of evidence or argument); (3) where a person was improperly present during the presentation of testimony, whether that person had a relationship to the witness that could have influenced the witness' testimony; (4) the length of the unauthorized presence; and (5) whether the individual made any overt attempt to influence the grand jurors or a witness. Thus, dismissal was granted where the prosecutor was present during deliberations and urged the grand jury to indict, but not where a police officer who had testified previously happened to remain in the grand jury room during the testimony of the complaining witness.

A substantial number of state courts treat unauthorized presence as a per se ground for dismissal, requiring no specific showing of likely prejudice. A per se approach is required, these courts argue, because dismissal only upon a showing of likely prejudice would offer "too great a possibility for the exercise of undue influence to be condoned." A prejudicial impact is so difficult to determine that it often would be missed. In most cases, the precise influence of the unauthorized presence would not be apparent on the face of the grand jury transcript. "A change in expression, a pressure on the hand or a warning glance would not be shown upon the minutes, but might well influence, suppress, or alter testimony to the prejudice of the defendant." A court could attempt to assess the influence that the presence of a particular person is likely to have had upon the witness or jurors, but such a determination would be too speculative to afford the defendant proper protection. How could one be certain, for example, that the unauthorized presence of custodial officers might not have influenced the testimony of the prisoner-witness the officers were guarding? Where two witnesses appeared simultaneously before the grand jury, isn't there always the possibility that each was hesitant to repudiate what was said by the other in the presence of that person? The appropriate approach, these courts argue, is to hold that even "the slightest intrusion of an unauthorized person into a grand jury proceeding voids the indictment."

While the determination of likely prejudice stemming from an unauthorized presence obviously entails some difficulty, it is doubtful whether that determination is substantially more speculative than the determination of prejudice made by courts considering whether other types of irregularities require dismissal of indictments. The adoption of a per se approach may be explained, however, by additional factors that more readily distinguish the unauthorized presence violation. The federal courts adopted a per se approach when transcripts were unavailable and unauthorized presence therefore was one of the few grand jury irregularities that could readily be established by the defendant. There was no need at that time to square their per se approach with the rulings on numerous other types of misconduct. Courts also have noted that an unauthorized presence should be a rare occurrence if the prosecutor exercises proper control over access to the grand jury chambers. The rules governing presence are clear and most violations are the product of the prosecutor's failure to adopt proper safeguards to ensure compliance. Assuming that unauthorized presence could readily be avoided, a per se approach has been justified on the ground that "a standard of actual or even potential prejudice would impose upon the court a difficult burden that would outweigh the benefits to be derived."

The various arguments for a per se approach were strongly advanced by Justice Marshall's dissent in *United States v. Mechanik,*[12] but he could find no support from the other justices. Since the *Mechanik* majority concluded that an unauthorized presence violating Federal Rule 6(d) was rendered harmless by a subsequent conviction at trial, there was no need for the Court to rule on whether such a violation should be treated as a per se ground for dismissal when considered prior to conviction. Nevertheless, Justice Rehnquist's opinion for the Court strongly suggested that the majority would not accept a per se approach and Justice O'Connor's concurring opinion flatly rejected that approach. Subsequently, in *Bank of Nova Scotia,*[13] the Court majority, without extensive discussion of the issue, proceeded to treat a Rule 6(d) violation in the same manner as the other irregularities presented there. Such a violation would justify dismissal of the indictment, the Court held, only where its likely impact upon the grand jury's decision to indict rendered it a prejudicial error under the *Kotteakos*-derived harmless error standard that is applicable to grand jury proceedings. Since the violation in *Bank of Nova Scotia* clearly was the responsibility of the prosecutor, the Court obviously did not leave the door open to separate treatment of unauthorized presence based on that factor. Neither did its discussion even remotely hint at the possibility of applying a presumption of inherent prejudice in the situation sometimes thought to pose a stronger justification for automatic dismissal—the unauthorized presence of the prosecutor during grand jury's deliberations.

12. See § 15.6(d).

13. See § 15.6(c).

Chapter 16

THE LOCATION OF THE PROSECUTION

Table of Sections

§ 16.1 Venue: General Principles

(a) Distinguishing Jurisdiction. The term "venue" refers to the locality of the prosecution, as venue sets the particular judicial district in which a criminal charge is to be tried. Venue is to be distinguished from "jurisdiction," which refers to the authority or power of the court to take action on a particular charge. The concept of jurisdiction encompasses several different types of limitation upon judicial authority, but only two of those jurisdictional limits have aspects likely to overlap in any significant degree with venue.

The jurisdiction of a court necessarily is constrained by limitations upon the reach of the legislative enactments that the court enforces. If a political entity lacks the legislative authority to govern behavior outside a certain geographical area, its judiciary will be said to lack "jurisdiction" to apply its criminal laws to such behavior. This is not to suggest that the reach of a political entity's legislative authority necessarily must be limited to the geographical boundaries of the entity. As evidenced by certain federal statutes applicable to conduct committed abroad, an entity can extend its authority beyond its territory based on its power to regulate the conduct of, and to provide protection for, its citizens. At the state level, however, the common law established, and states continue to adhere to, a territorial principle as the jurisdictional foundation for the reach of state law. Under that principle, states have power to make conduct a crime only if that conduct takes place, or its results occur, within the state's territorial borders. For two types of offenses, application of this territorial limitation often will raise issues quite similar to those presented in determining venue under the "crime-committed formula," which is discussed in subsections (c) and (d) below and in § 16.2.

At common law, the territorial principle was governed in its application by an assumption that all but a small group of crimes had a single situs. In general, that situs was the place where the act (or omission) occurred if the crime was defined only in those terms, and place of the result if the definition of the crime hinged on that result. Thus, a murder occurred in the state where the fatal force struck the victim, even though that force may have been initiated in another state. The common law did recognize an exception, however, for crimes that were "continuing" (e.g., kidnapping). Those crimes could be committed in more than one place and prosecuted in more than one state. In determining whether an offense is a continuing crime, so that more than one state has jurisdiction, a court makes a determination analogous to that made in establishing venue. There too, as discussed in subsection (d), a crime may be deemed "continuing," so that venue lies in more than one district under the crime-committed formula.

Even as to crimes that do not traditionally fall in the continuing category, many states today have legislation that recognizes more than one situs for the crime. The territorial principle does not demand a single situs; it recognizes the state's authority to reach criminal conduct performed partly within and partly without the state, conduct performed within the state that results in harm outside the state, and conduct performed outside the state that produced harm within. Where states have sought to carry the territorial principle to its full reach through such "territorial scope" legislation, the issues presented again tend to be analogous to those presented in establishing venue. There too, as discussed in subsection (d), the crime-committed formula allows for multi-venue as to an offense "begun in one district and completed in another." Thus, where the defendant ships poisoned candy from State A, the victim receives the candy in State B, eats it in State C, and dies in State D, and all the states involved have broad territorial scope provisions, the issue as to whether each has jurisdiction closely resembles that which would be presented if everything occurred within four different judicial districts in a single state and the issue was whether the prosecution could be brought in any of the four districts.[1]

Where states have a tradition of a court system that was not unified, one aspect of "subject matter" jurisdiction also will present issues similar to those involved in the application of the crime-committed formula to venue. Magistrate courts in judicial systems that were not unified had their subject matter jurisdiction defined both by the level of offense (e.g., trial authority only as to misdemeanors) and by the territory of the judicial district (e.g., as to a municipal court, crimes committed within the municipality). In most states today, such a territorial limitation has been abandoned as a jurisdictional concept and the appropriate location of the criminal proceeding is left entirely to provisions governing venue. Some states, however, continue to have provisions that utilize locality in defining the subject matter jurisdiction of local courts. The application of that jurisdictional limitation, as with the territorial limitation upon the reach of the state's legislative authority, also presents issues analogous to those raised in determining where a crime was "committed" for venue purposes.

(b) Distinguishing Vicinage.[2] Venue also should be distinguished from "vicinage." Both venue and vicinage refer to locality as defined by a particular geographical district, but they identify that locality for different purposes. Whereas venue refers to the locali-

§ 16.1

1. Though the issues presented are similar, important distinctions exist, including: (1) the governing language of such territorial scope provisions is not the same as that in the typical multi-venue provision (see note 3 infra); (2) the interests at stake in determining which state may prosecute are quite different from those at stake in determining where the trial will be held within that state, as evidenced by the fact that there is no provision for transfer from a state with jurisdiction to a state without jurisdiction [in contrast to venue transfer provisions, as discussed in subsection (g)]; and (3) whereas venue limitations are subject to voluntary waiver or to forfeiture by failure to raise a timely objection [see subsection (f)], jurisdictional limitations are not subject to waiver and can be raised at any point in the proceeding.

2. See also § 22.2(e).

ty in which charges will be brought and adjudicated, vicinage refers to the locality from which jurors will be drawn. Also, while the concept of venue does not inherently point to a particular district, but rather requires simply that a district be designated in a venue provision (constitutional or statutory), the concept of vicinage in itself identifies a particular district and arguably delimits the geographical boundaries of that district. The vicinage concept requires that the jurors be selected from a geographical district that includes the locality of the commission of the crime, and it traditionally also mandates that such district not extend too far beyond the general vicinity of that locality. Thus, while a venue provision must specify how the appropriate district for trial is to be determined (or even identify that district by name), a vicinage provision can merely state (as many do) that the defendant has a right to a jury "of the vicinage."

In some instances, vicinage and venue are treated together in the same statute, but even when that is not the case, the provisions governing the two subjects are likely to interrelate. Though a provision may speak only to vicinage or only to venue, it usually will have a bearing on the other subject as well, as the locality requirements of venue and vicinage ordinarily go hand in hand. A provision giving to the defendant a right to a jury selected from a judicial district constituting the vicinage commonly will also grant, by implication, a parallel right to be tried in that judicial district; for unless the legislature specifically provides otherwise, the prevailing assumption is that the trial should be held in the district from which the jury is selected. So too, since venue provisions commonly provide for trial in the local judicial district in which the alleged offense was committed, which will often coincide with the vicinage, venue provisions frequently operate by implication to require that jurors be selected from the vicinage; for it is assumed also that the jury will be drawn from the judicial district in which the trial takes place.

The overlap of venue and vicinage, however, is not inevitable. There remains the possibility of prescribing different districts under the two concepts. This can be done by providing for a jury selected from the district of the crime, as required by the concept of vicinage, while setting the venue for the trial elsewhere. Moreover, even where, as is almost always the case, the venue provision refers to the district in which the crime was committed, and therefore encompasses the vicinage, the vicinage concept can impose a narrower geographical limit that will not be required by the venue provision alone. Traditionally, the vicinage concept demands that the geographical boundaries of the district of jury selection not extend substantially beyond the general vicinity of the place of the crime. Tieing a venue provision to the district of the crime, on the other hand, says nothing about the boundaries of the district except that the district include the locality of the crime. The potential for utilizing the venue and vicinage concepts to refer to different geographical districts is reflected in the adoption of separate jury selection and venue provisions in the federal constitution and in the initial legislation adopted by Congress to implement those constitutional provisions.

While the framers of the Constitution initially saw no need to safeguard by constitutional provision the basic rights of the individual (a position later altered with the agreement to add the Bill of Rights), they nonetheless did include in the body of the Constitution certain requirements of criminal procedure that would guarantee a few basic rights of the accused. Not surprisingly, one of those few safeguarded rights was the right of the accused not to be forced to trial outside of the state in which the charges against him arose. Appropriate venue had been a matter of great concern to the colonists. They had fiercely opposed Acts of Parliament that allowed the Crown to take colonists to England or to another colony for trial on various capital offenses. Article III, Section 2, of the Constitution prohibited the federal government from engaging in a similar practice. It provided: "The Trial of all Crimes, except in Cases of Impeachment, shall be by Jury, and such Trial shall be held in the State where said

Crimes shall have been committed; but when not committed within any State, the Trial shall be at such Place or Places as the Congress may by Law have directed."

Article III, Section 2, did not guarantee that an accused would be tried in the most convenient forum. An accused charged with committing a crime in one part of a state could be tried in any other part of the state, notwithstanding its distance from the place of the crime. Still, the constitutional guarantee would not allow the bringing of the defendant to trial in what was basically the alien setting of another state. Even though some of the states were quite large, where the prosecutor and jurors were of the state in which the crime was committed, they were likely to have some familiarity with the environment in which the offense occurred. So too, while the logistical burdens imposed on the defense could still be substantial, particularly in the larger states, the prosecution would not be able to force a defendant to move his witnesses, counsel and others he might want at his trial (such as his family) from one end of the country to another.

When the Constitution came before the states for ratification, Article III was strongly criticized for failing to guarantee to the accused a jury drawn from the vicinage. It provided for a right to jury trial, but said nothing about the selection of the jury. Supporters of the Constitution noted that Article III's venue provision guaranteed a trial in the state in which the alleged crime was committed, so the defendant, by implication, would also have a jury of that state. That assurance did not satisfy proponents of a vicinage requirement, for they deemed the state as a whole to be a far too large district. Consequently, the First Congress had before it a proposal to amend Article III by including a requirement of trial by an "impartial jury of freeholders of the vicinage." That proposal was defeated, however, by opponents who argued, in part, that the vicinage requirement simply was not practicable. At the time, only a few states required that the jury venire be selected from the county in which the crime occurred (a fairly common geographical boundary for the vicinage), and the practical obstacles to imposing such a requirement would be even greater for the newly created federal trial courts, whose judges were to sit only at a few centrally located sites in each state. Continued debate produced a compromise in the jury trial provision eventually included in the Sixth Amendment of the Bill of Rights. That provision granted to the accused a right to trial "by an impartial jury of the State and district wherein the crime shall have been committed, which district shall have been previously ascertained by law."

Unlike Article III, Section 2, the Sixth Amendment specifically recognized a right to have the jury selected from a particular district. That right was no longer left to the implication of a venue provision. However, the geographical boundaries of the particular district were not defined in the Constitution, nor were they left to a judicial determination that might look to the county or some other local district commonly associated with the vicinage concept. Rather the appropriate district for jury selection was to be "previously ascertained" by Congress, which could choose either a district as large as the state itself or a smaller district more in keeping with the traditional view of the vicinage. In the First Judiciary Act, Congress took both approaches, distinguishing between capital and non-capital offenses.

The Judiciary Act initially established federal judicial districts that coincided with the boundaries of the individual states, except for two states which were subdivided into two districts each. As to non-capital cases, it was required only that jurors be summoned from somewhere in the district. The federal judges were given guidance, however, in their exercise of discretion. The Judiciary Act provided that the jurors be summoned "from such parts of the district from time to time as the court shall direct, so as shall be most favourable to an impartial trial, and so as not to incur an unnecessary expense, or unduly to burthen the citizens of any part of the district with such services." For capital offenses, there was a requirement that at least 12 prospective jurors be summoned from the county in which that offense was allegedly committed. Ordinarily, the trial was to be held in that county, so that the entire venire was likely to be selected from that county of the offense. Where "great inconvenience" was found, the capital case could be tried in another county within the judicial district, but at least 12 prospective jurors from the county of commission had to be summoned and moved to the place of trial. Thus, as to capital offenses, Congress clearly separated the concept of vicinage and venue and recognized that they could refer to geographical units with different boundaries. This stood in contrast to the usual approach of either utilizing the same district for both or having the narrower vicinage district prevail over the broader venue district (by leaving stand the implication that the jurors will sit in the community from which they are selected).

(c) **The "Crime-Committed" Formula.** The standard formula for setting venue is to divide the jurisdiction into geographical districts and then select as the appropriate venue that district in which the crime was committed. This formula is found in both constitutional and statutory venue provisions. The most common geographical districts are legislatively defined judicial districts, as illustrated by the federal judicial districts, or political entities, such as counties or parishes. While the type of geographical district varies from one jurisdiction to another, the standard for selecting the particular district for trial—that in which the "crime shall have been committed"—is common to all general venue provisions. As discussed in subsection (e), special venue provisions may otherwise identify the district of venue for particular crimes, but for most offenses, the general venue provision will govern and thereby set venue according to the crime-committed formula. Federal Rule 18 is typical of such a general provision. It provides: "Except as otherwise permitted by statute or by these rules, the prosecution shall be had in a district in which the offense was committed."

Although not always followed by the English, the crime-committed formula was well established prior to the adoption of the Constitution. Indeed, it probably dates back to the earliest stages of trial by jury, when the jury's functions included both accusation based on personal knowledge and adjudication of guilt. After those functions were distinguished, with the separation of the petit and grand juries, trials continued to be held in the place where the crime was committed. The charge was brought by a grand jury of the place the crime, and it might be thought to follow naturally that the trial should be in the same district. The function of the petit jury had certain common elements with the function of the grand jury that arguably were best served by selecting the petit jurors from the general vicinity of the crime. Local residents could call on their community background in judging the evidence and were more likely to apply the criminal law in accordance with the customs and values of the local community. It was the concept of the vicinage, however, that looked primarily to the function of the jury; the concept of venue looked to the convenience of the forum. Thus, though it was important that the crime-committed formula often facilitated use of jury of the vicinage, presumably its development in English common law also reflected its independent value in providing a forum convenient to the accused in presenting his defense.

The crime-committed formula offered several elements of convenience for the defense. Relevant evidence would most readily be accessible at the place where the incident constituting the alleged offense had occurred. Any witnesses to the incident were most likely to live in the vicinity and any relevant tangible evidence was most likely to be found there. Trial in a distant place would impose upon the defendant the often serious hardship of arranging for the transportation of such witnesses and tangible evidence. Of course, the trial could still be in a distant place if the district of the offense were large and the trial could take place anywhere in the district, but venue provisions commonly employed counties as the relevant judicial district. In the United States, there was some departure from the use of the county as the crucial district, but only the federal government had judicial districts as large as an entire state.

At the time of the adoption of the Constitution, mobility of individuals still was quite limited, and the place of the commission of the crime was most likely also to be at or near the accused's place of residence. This added to the convenience of trial in the district of the offense. It was in the place of his residence that the accused was most likely to find witnesses willing to vouch for his character, and a trial there avoided the need to arrange for the transportation of those witnesses to some other location. An accused tried in the vicinity of his residence also would have the benefit of friends and relatives being close at hand. Those persons could not only provide moral support, but they also could assist in preparing for trial. They could, for example, both help in investigation and provide insights that might be useful in challenging jurors, who would ordinarily come from the same community. So too, an accused tried at his place of residence was more likely to know the local attorneys and thereby have greater confidence in his selection of counsel.

Of course, there would be instances in which the accused would have traveled to another district and be accused there of having committed a crime. In that situation, the crime-committed formula would deprive him of the convenience of being tried in his home district. The choice nonetheless was made for the place where the critical events had occurred. That choice may have reflected a belief that greater convenience to the accused was in a trial where the witnesses to the events were located rather than the place of his residence. It may also have been based, however, on other considerations related less to his convenience and more to the assurance of a fair trial. The crime-committed formula facilitated selection of a jury of the vicinage and such a jury presumably was better able to judge evidence that related to the local scene. It certainly added the element of participation by the community most directly affected by the crime. These benefits, of course, looked to the interests of society as well as the defendant. If only the defendant's interests had been at stake, the defense could have been given a choice of having venue placed either in the district of the offense or the district of the defendant's residence. Still another factor possibly influencing the preference for the crime-committed formula was convenience to the prosecution. Its primary witnesses (including the complainant) were likely to be located in the place where the crime occurred and therefore could more easily be presented at a trial in that district. Also, the defendant most frequently would have been arrested at the place of the offense, and a trial in the same district would avoid the necessity of transporting him a long distance.

(d) Multi–Venue Offenses. When the framers of the Constitution included the crime-committed formula in both Article III, Section 2, and the Sixth Amendment, they referred in the singular to the "state" and "district" in which the crime "shall have been committed." This reflected the assumption that a crime ordinarily would be committed in a single place. At a time when travel was difficult and slow, and communications systems were rudimentary, all of the action constituting an offense and all of the immediate harm flowing from that action commonly occurred within a limited geographic area. Even at that time, however, there were certain federal offenses that could occur in more than one place and those two or more places would occasionally be in two different states. At the state level, where the judicial districts typically were counties, it was even more likely that some offenses would be committed in more than one judicial district.

The offenses most likely to be multi-venue offenses were those commonly described as "continuing offenses." These were offenses having basic elements that continued (or, some would say, "repeated themselves") over a period of time as part of a single crime. A prime illustration is kidnapping, which starts when the victim is taken into custody and continues until the victim is no longer under the control of the kidnappers. If the kidnapped victim was moved from one district to another in the course of the kidnapping, the offense was committed in each of those districts. At common law, larceny was placed in the same category as the continued possession of the stolen property by the thief was viewed as a continuation of the trespassory taking.

A crime could also occur in more than one place when it had two or more distinct parts. Such offenses created a multi-venue potential when they required two separate elements that could occur at separate places. A criminal statute, for example, might define the offense as requiring first the doing of a prohibited act and then the causing of a certain victim response, with the act and response capable of occurring in two different localities. In other situations, the offense was one that could be committed by two separate actions as to the same subject matter, with venue lying in the district of either action. Thus, embezzlement in many jurisdictions could be charged either in the district where the agent converted the property to his personal use or in the district where he had a duty to account for the property and failed to do so.

Multi-venue also was possible where the offense could be committed by a single act that could start in one place and finish in another. Thus, the "making" of a false claim might start with the placing of that claim in motion and end with its actual presentation. So too, the attempted evasion of tax liability might start with the arrangement of a false transaction and end with the filing of a false return utilizing that transaction. While these offenses are distinguishable from those in which the act is repetitive, such as kidnapping, they are sometimes also characterized as capable of "continuation" in the sense that the activity prohibited, as it involves a multipart path of action, may start at one place and finish elsewhere.

The possibility of a multi-venue commission of an offense was recognized as early as the sixteenth century, when Parliament adopted a provision governing homicides committed through actions in one county that resulted in death in another. Crimes committed in more than one district were rare, however, and they were limited to a small group of offenses. When case law presented difficulties, as where courts concluded that such offenses were not committed in any one district and therefore no proper venue existed, the legislature could respond with a statutory provision tied to the particular type of offense. That legislation could either allow for venue in either district or provide for venue in the district where a certain element of the offense occurred. By the mid-nineteenth century, with significant advances made in transportation and communications, crimes committed in more than one judicial district became much more common. This was particularly true for the federal system, which dealt with many crimes relating to commerce. In 1867, Congress adopted a general provision governing offenses committed in more than one district. That provision, in a slightly modified form, is now contained in Section 3237 of the federal criminal code. It provides:

> Except as otherwise expressly provided by enactment of Congress, any offense against the United States begun in one district and completed in another, or committed in more than one district, may be inquired of and prosecuted in any district in which such offense was begun, continued, or completed.[3]

Most states have adopted similar provisions. They apply to all offenses committed in more than one district, whether that is the product of repetitive action or harm, two distinct elements of establishing the offense, or a single action that has more than one part. The only exception is where the legislature has enacted a special provision limiting venue for a particular offense to the district in which a particular aspect of the offense occurred even though the offense as a whole was committed in more than one district.

As will be seen in § 16.2, courts often have experienced difficulties in determining whether an offense was committed in more than one place. The legislature, however, can readily shape the offense so that it clearly will fall in the multi-venue category. For example,

3. 18 U.S.C.A. § 3237.

though the crime of "sending" an item to another state might be limited to the place at which the item was placed in the stream of transportation, the crime of "transporting" would occur in any district through which the item is carried. While many criminal transactions continue to be centered in a single place, numerous others involve actions and ramifications that extend over time and space. Legislatures have often responded to such transactions by shaping offenses so that they clearly can be committed in more than one place. That is especially the case for those federal crimes which are enacted under Congressional authority to regulate interstate commerce. Article III and the Sixth Amendment hardly impose a significant limitation on Congress' capacity to allow for a substantial choice of venues for such offenses. By defining the offenses so that they can be committed in more than one place, Congress can provide for extremely flexible venue consistent with the federal constitution. Indeed, as to certain types of commercial activities affecting products distributed throughout the United States, Congress may, if it so chooses, provide for what is, in effect, nationwide venue. As discussed in § 16.2(e), precisely that strategy has been employed for certain federal offenses.

The increased likelihood that criminal transactions will involve events and have ramifications in more than one place has led to criticism of the crime-committed formula as an often inappropriate measure of the functions of venue. Thus, Professor Abrams, after an extensive review of the multi-venue possibilities in the prosecution of federal crime, offered the following analysis:

> The crime committed test, as amply illustrated by the foregoing study, is basically a formalistic approach which focuses on the elements constituting the offense, the acts done, how they relate to the offense and where they had impact. Whether interpreted loosely or restrictively, it has no necessary connection to the location of the victim, witnesses, documents or other similar factors. It does not take account of the residence of the accused or his whereabouts at the time of arrest nor even sometimes at the time of the offense. It is not directly concerned with the possibilities for joint trial of parties or joint prosecution of offenses. In short, it does not deal directly and necessarily with most of the practical factors which should be relevant in determining the place of trial. The best defense that can be made of the committed approach is that "as a general rule, the * * * [place] where the offense was committed would be the most convenient place for [trial] * * *." The suggestion is that the formula is a good rule of thumb or mechanical test for determining the convenient forum. It may be that at some time past as applied to traditional crimes this was generally true. As applied today, however, to the complex variety of modern federal offenses often involving numerous participants scattered throughout the country who may move freely about in connection with their criminal operations and communicate long distances by letter, telegram or telephone, the formula is very often a poor index of the convenient place of trial. Interpreted restrictively it often impedes trial in such a forum. Interpreted very loosely it becomes practically meaningless; trial might as well be permitted anywhere.[4]

One response to the above criticism is the use of special legislation that seeks to offset the possible flaws in the crime-committed formula as applied to specific situations. Such legislation, as well as other offense-specific venue legislation, is discussed in the subsection that follows.

(e) Special Legislation. Almost all jurisdictions have special legislation dealing with specific difficulties presented by application of the crime-committed formula. One such difficulty is posed by the crime committed within the territorial reach of the government but not within the territorial boundaries of any judicial district. The federal constitution recognized that difficulty when it provided in Article III that Congress could designate the

4. Abrams, Conspiracy and Multi-Venue in Federal Criminal Prosecutions: The Crime Committed Formula, 9 U.C.L.A.L.Rev. 751 (1962).

"place or places" of trial when the crime "was not committed within any State." In its exercise of that authority, Congress has adopted a special provision governing the trial of offenses committed upon the high seas "or elsewhere outside the jurisdiction of any particular state or district." [5] States have responded to a similar difficulty where they border bodies of water that separate neighboring states or mark national boundaries. Thus, a Great Lakes state will have a provision placing venue in the counties bordering on the shore of its boundary lake for offenses committed on that lake.

Another troubling situation under the crime-committed formula is that in which it is extremely difficult or impossible to establish exactly where the events in question occurred. Several different legislative approaches are used to meet such situations. Recognizing that the exact location of a particular event is often difficult to prove, states have adopted "either county legislation" for offenses alleged to have been committed within a specified distance (e.g., one mile) of the boundary between two counties. The difficulty of proving the exact location of a homicide has led to statutes allowing trial in the place where the body of the victim is found, although the person might well have been killed elsewhere and his body then moved to that location. Other provisions are tied specifically to the inability to establish the location of the offense. Thus, a statute will provide that where an offense was committed within a moving vehicle and it cannot be determined in exactly which county it occurred, venue will be in any county through which the vehicle passed on the trip in question. Even broader legislation provides that where an attorney general concludes that an offense was committed somewhere within the state, but "it is impossible to determine in which county it occurred, the offense may be alleged in the indictment to have been committed and may be prosecuted * * * in such county as the attorney general may designate."

In some instances, legislatures apparently have found troubling the breadth of the multi-venue consequences of applying the crime-committed formula and have responded with legislation limiting venue to the district in which a particular aspect of the crime was committed. Thus, Congress has provided that the prosecution of a fugitive felon for flight in interstate commerce may be brought only in the district "in which the original crime was alleged to have been committed, or in which the person was held in custody or confinement, or in which an avoidance of service of process or a contempt [for disobedience of process] * * * is alleged to have been committed." [6] Without that provision, the flight, as a continuing offense, might provide venue in any district through which the felon traveled. So too, to preclude an interpretation of homicide as having occurred both in the district where the fatal blow was struck and the district in which the victim died, many jurisdictions provide that venue will be only in the district of the fatal blow.

More frequently, special legislation is geared to ensuring that offenses will be viewed as allowing for venue in more than one district. Thus, embezzlement statutes often provide for venue in any district into which the embezzled property is brought. So too, an embezzlement state may provide for venue in the place where the property was received even though it was not there converted to the embezzler's use. A federal statute similarly provides that a prosecution for illegal entry into the county may be prosecuted in the district in which the accused was apprehended even though that was not the district in which he illegally crossed the border. In most instances of special legislation providing for multi-venue, the legislation can be seen as merely recognizing as to a particular offense that its elements can occur in more than one district. There are exceptions, however, as illustrated by a provision allowing an

5. 18 U.S.C.A. § 3238, providing basically for venue in the district where the offender is "arrested" or "first brought" following arrest outside the country.

6. 18 U.S.C.A. § 1073.

escaped convict to be tried in the county in which the prison is located for both the escape and offenses committed in other places while the convict was at large.

Where a state has either a constitutional venue guarantee of a right to trial in the county in which the offense was committed or a constitutional guarantee of a jury of the vicinage, special venue legislation can pose constitutional difficulties insofar as it can be seen as going beyond the implementation of the crime-committed formula. Of course, the crime-committed formula was not designed to impose a requirement so rigid as to preclude trial anywhere within the state. Thus, courts have no difficulty in squaring with such constitutional guarantees special legislation governing offenses committed in border waters or governing offenses committed in the course of transportation where the precise location is incapable of determination. Some courts have questioned, however, the constitutionality of provisions allowing for prosecution in an adjacent county where the offense simply was committed close to the boundary of that county, although others have suggested that such provisions should be viewed merely as establishing districts of commission that slightly overlap, consistent with the leeway to which the legislature is entitled in setting boundaries under the constitutional venue or vicinage provisions.

Clearly, the most constitutionally suspect special legislation is that which adds an alternative venue to facilitate prosecutorial convenience as to an offense defined so as to have occurred only in one place (as illustrated by the previously noted prison escapee statute). Such legislation, however, is most likely to be found in jurisdictions that have not given the crime-committed formula a constitutional status. Of course, the Sixth Amendment has been held applicable to the states under the Fourteenth Amendment, and courts frequently have assumed that this includes the provision requiring that the jury be selected from the district in which the crime was committed. However, as discussed in § 22.2(e), these courts generally also read that provision as requiring only that the state jury be selected from within the federal judicial district in which the crime was committed. For most states, this interpretation allows the state considerable leeway in placing venue outside the county in which the offense was committed, as the federal judicial district will encompass a large number of counties.

(f) Proof of Venue. Unlike other prerequisites for a proper prosecution (e.g., a valid preliminary hearing bindover), venue is not automatically assumed to be present in the absence of a defense showing to the contrary. Venue instead is treated as a fact that must be proven by the prosecution at trial. The court has the responsibility for determining whether, as a matter of law, the events alleged to have occurred in the judicial district are sufficient to say that the crime was committed there, but it is then the province of the jury (or the judge in a bench trial) to determine whether those events actually occurred and whether the locality was actually within the district. In establishing the place of the crime, the prosecution may rely on inferences drawn from circumstantial evidence as well as direct evidence, and the trial court may ease the prosecution's task by taking judicial notice of the geographical locations within the district. Thus, the judge may charge the jury that Manhattan is within the Southern District of New York, leaving to it only the issue as to whether the events in question did occur in Manhattan.

Jurisdictions are divided as to the required level of persuasiveness of the prosecution's proof of venue. The federal courts and a substantial number of state courts hold that the facts supporting venue only need be established by a preponderance of the evidence. They contend that venue is not a material element of the crime (which elements constitutionally must be established by proof beyond a reasonable doubt), noting that it does not relate even remotely to the issues of guilt or innocence or the level of culpability. Other states disagree with this analysis, and require proof beyond a reasonable doubt. They characterize venue as a "jurisdictional fact," a necessary element of the prosecution's case, and an "element of the offense." The distinction between the two proof standards may lose much of its practical significance, however, where the state holds the prosecution to the reasonable doubt standard but then notes that "slight evidence" will be sufficient to meet that standard where the defense offers no conflicting evidence.

It is universally recognized that if the defendant fails to raise a timely objection to the prosecution's failure properly to establish venue, the defendant's venue claim is thereby "waived" or "forfeited." The requisite timing of the objection will vary with nature of the objection. When the complaint is that the court failed to submit the issue to the jury, the objection must be presented along with other objections to the jury charge. Where the claim is that the prosecution's evidence fails to establish venue, most courts will require that the objection at least be raised prior to the issuance of the jury verdict. An objection after that point is deemed untimely since the failure to establish venue will often be the result of inadvertence, and had the objection been made while the jury was still sitting, the trial court might have been willing to allow the prosecution to reopen its case to establish venue. Some courts have suggested that the venue objection must come at the first reasonably opportune point at which it could be raised. Thus, it has been stated that when the government concludes its case and the defendant "specifies grounds for acquittal but is silent as to venue," that silence should foreclose a later objection. So too, where the lack of venue is apparent from the face of the indictment, a pretrial objection may be required.

(g) Change of Venue. As noted earlier, the crime-committed formula will not always produce the most convenient forum from the defendant's perspective, especially where the offense is committed in more than one place and the prosecution has a choice of districts. One response to that possibility is to grant the trial court the authority to order a change of venue upon request of the defense. All jurisdictions currently grant the trial judge such authority, but the allowable grounds for ordering the change of venue vary. The applicable statutory provisions all allow for a venue change where necessary to escape local prejudice so great that the defendant cannot obtain an unbiased jury. This ground commonly is utilized where there has been extensive prejudicial pretrial publicity, and it will be discussed in § 23.2, which deals with various measures that may be taken to ensure that the jurors are not influenced by such publicity.

Venue-change provisions typically also allow for a change based on at least some considerations relating to the defense's ability to present its case. Some statutes sharply limit those considerations by requiring a finding that the defense would be so restricted as to be unable to obtain a fair trial. That standard commonly goes only slightly beyond the biased jury situation, taking into consideration also such possibilities as physical disruption of the proceedings or likely intimidation of witnesses. Other provisions are far more flexible, and allow consideration of general convenience. Federal Rule 21(b) is typical of such a provision. It provides that, "for the convenience of parties and witnesses, and in the interest of justice, the court upon motion of the defendant may transfer the proceeding as to that defendant or any one or more of the counts thereof to another district." [7]

Under provisions like Rule 21(b), trial courts have broad discretion in ruling upon transfer motions, and they may consider a variety of factors in deciding whether a change is justified. In the leading Supreme Court ruling on a Rule 21(b) motion, the Court cited nine specific factors that had been considered by the district court, and while the court's ruling related to another point, it did add that both the parties and the appellate

7. The reference is to transfer for trial. Fed. R.Crim.P. 20 establishes separate standards for a defendant who desires to enter a guilty plea. A defendant "arrested, held, or present" in a district other than that in which a charge is pending against him may waive trial where the charge is pending and, "subject to the approval of the United States attorney for each district," enter a plea of guilty or nolo contendere and be sentenced in the district where he is.

court had agreed that the consideration of those nine factors was "appropriate." [8] The nine factors, frequently relied upon in subsequent lower court decisions, were: "(1) location of the corporate defendant [which was the apparent counterpart of the location of one's residence for an individual]; (2) location of possible witnesses; (3) location of events likely to be in issue; (4) location of documents and records likely to be involved; (5) disruption of defendant's business unless the case is transferred; (6) expense to the parties; (7) location of counsel; (8) relative accessibility of place of trial; and (9) docket condition of each district or division involved."

In weighing general factors of convenience, courts consider the burdens imposed upon both the prosecution and the defense, but in some settings, the burden imposed upon the prosecution may be downgraded in light of the government's greater resources. Thus, in the federal system, with U.S. Attorneys' offices spread across the country, the government's burden in moving lawyers to another district (or even shifting lawyers) may be considered less significant than imposing a similar burden upon the defense. One factor not considered under Rule 21(b) is the potentially greater sympathy of the jury to one side or another in the district of possible transfer. The defendant cannot gain a transfer because the jury in that district would be more sympathetic to the defense, and a transfer justified on grounds of convenience cannot be denied because the prosecution believes that the jury in that district would be less sympathetic to its position. Indeed, federal courts have held that it is inappropriate for a district court to deny a transfer because it believes the prosecution might not be able to obtain a fair and impartial jury in the district of transfer. On the other hand, where the offense requires the jury to apply community standards, the prosecution may properly emphasize the importance of having a jury selected from the community in which the offense occurred.

Federal Rule 21 and most state provisions authorize the ordering of a change of venue only upon request of the defense. Over a dozen state provisions, however, allow for a change upon request of the prosecution, notwithstanding defense objection. Such provisions often tend to be quite limited. They allow for a change only where necessary to preserve a fair trial, which basically limits prosecution-requested changes to instances in which the prosecution can establish that a local jury will be biased against the government. Changes based on that ground will be considered in § 23.2, since they are commonly analogized to changes granted on defense motion due to adverse pretrial publicity. Only a handful of states have provisions applying to both prosecution and defense that utilize a broader standard (e.g., "good cause") which might allow a venue change to provide a less burdensome forum for the prosecution and its witnesses. Moreover, even in those states, the reported decisions on approved prosecution-requested changes have dealt almost exclusively with claims of jury bias.

The failure of more states to provide for a prosecutorial-requested change of venue on convenience grounds, and the absence of reported decisions granting changes on such grounds in those states with sufficiently broad statutes, is probably attributable to two factors—constitutional difficulties and a lack of need. A change granted to facilitate prosecutorial convenience would present serious constitutional difficulties in a substantial number of states. Where the state has a constitutional provision guaranteeing venue in the district of the crime, that provision clearly would bar transfer to any other district without a waiver by the defendant. While the more common constitutional provisions guaranteeing a jury selected from the district of commission would not constitute an absolute bar, they would require a transfer of the jury to the chosen venue. Courts are divided as to whether vicinage provisions invariably grant to the defendant a right to a

8. Platt v. Minnesota Mining & Mfg. Co., 376 U.S. 240, 84 S.Ct. 769, 11 L.Ed.2d 674 (1964). While *Platt* involved a transfer request by a corporate defendant, the factors cited by the Court generally are considered equally relevant to a request of an individual defendant.

jury selected from the district of the offense. Some have recognized an exception, based on common law practice, where local community bias would prevent the state from obtaining a fair adjudication in that district. However, as noted in § 23.2, that exception is quite narrow, and it presumably would not extend to a change based on prosecutorial inconvenience even where the burdens of presenting proof in the district of commission are quite substantial. Of course, some states do not face these constitutional difficulties, as they have neither constitutional venue nor vicinage provisions. Even there, however, decisions holding the Sixth Amendment fully applicable to the states might prove troublesome, as the Sixth Amendment guarantee of the right to a jury of the district of commission has been held by some lower courts to permit no exceptions. Since those lower court rulings also suggest that the Sixth Amendment right is measured by federal judicial districts, the Sixth Amendment would not bar prosecutor-requested changes to state judicial districts within the boundaries of the same federal judicial district.

The lack of a significant need for transfers to further prosecutorial convenience stems in large part from the general effectiveness of the crime-committed formula in identifying the district most convenient from a prosecutorial perspective. The district of the defendant's actions usually is the district in which the prosecution's evidence is located, and where that is not the case, the offense is likely to have a multi-venue potential that includes the district providing the prosecution's evidence. Perhaps the most telling case for a venue change to promote prosecutorial convenience would be that in which the change would allow joinder of offenses that were committed in different districts and therefore otherwise would have to be tried separately. Consider, for example, the case in which the defendant is charged with separate burglaries in different counties and the primary evidence against him is that found through a search of his residence in one of those counties and his subsequent confession given there to the local police. Considerable savings might be obtained if the trial of the burglaries committed in the other counties could be transferred to the county of defendant's residence, where the charges could be consolidated for a single trial relying heavily on evidence obtained there. But in most states, those burglaries would have been committed within the bailiwicks of separate prosecutors, each being an official of a separate county and having an immediate interest only in the prosecution of the burglary of that county. Thus, even if a state statute were to allow for a change of venue in such a case, the division of prosecutorial authority might make its use politically unfeasible. In the federal system, where there is a single prosecutorial authority and greater interest in consolidating prosecutions, the availability of offenses framed so as to allow overlapping venue for transactions occurring in different places substantially reduces the need for a venue transfer to achieve a single trial in such cases.[9]

§ 16.2 Applying the Crime–Committed Formula

(a) Recurring Questions. When all the acts of the defendant and all the consequences of those acts occur in the same district, application of the crime-committed formula is straight forward and simple. Complexities began to arise, however, where the acts occur in one district and the consequences in another. They increase where the acts as well as consequences are spread over several districts. In applying the crime-committed formula to such cases, courts must determine initially whether the offense is one that can be committed only in a single place or an offense that can be committed in more than one place. If the answer is that the offense can be committed only in one place, the court must then identify the act or consequence that

9. If the crimes were the product of the use of the mails or interstate transportation and that use included a single overlapping district (e.g., the same starting point in travelling to the separate site of each crime), federal offenses tied to such use (e.g., the Travel Act) may allow prosecution to reach all of those criminal activities through substantive charges that could be brought in that district. See § 16.2(e).

marks that place. If the answer is that the offense can be committed in more than one place, then the court must determine the point at which the offense starts and the point at which it finishes. These are recurring questions that arise in the context of both traditional common law offenses and newly created statutory offenses.

The offenses and situations presenting these recurring questions are too diverse to be placed in a few basic groupings or otherwise categorized. A few illustrations will have to suffice in suggesting their range. Consider first a comparatively simple case. Defendant makes a false pretense to the victim in district A and the victim responds by transferring funds to the defendant in district B. On a charge of false pretenses, does venue lie only in district A, only in district B, or in both districts A and B? The possibilities are more numerous in a classic homicide hypothetical. Defendant manufactures a bomb in district A, places it in the victim's car in district B, the bomb explodes and injures the victim while he is driving in district C, and the victim dies in the hospital to which he is taken in district D. Is the homicide offense one that starts with the manufacture of the bomb and finishes with the death of the victim, so that it is committed in all four districts? Does it start with the placing of the bomb in the car, so that district A is excluded, or only with the infliction of the injury, so that districts A and B are both excluded? Is homicide a crime that cannot start at one place and finish at another, so that venue lies in only one district? If so, is the single place of the crime that where the injury occurs or that where the victim dies? Courts have struggled with such cases for years. As to false pretenses, there is a general agreement that the offense has multiple parts and occurs both where the misrepresentation is made and funds obtained. As to homicide, there is less uniformity. Some courts have viewed the offense as committed only where the fatal injury was inflicted, while others have viewed it as an offense committed in more than one district, so that the places of the death and the starting point of the act inflicting injury are also proper venues. As to the appropriate starting point, some courts would start with significant preliminary acts such as manufacture of the bomb, while others would start only where defendant has actually set in motion the agency of death, as in the placing of the bomb in the car.

Although there may not be agreement among the various jurisdictions, the basic venue questions should be firmly settled in any particular jurisdiction as to a traditional offense. However, as to each new offense, these questions must be considered again (assuming the legislature does not add a provision specifically identifying the district of venue for that offense). Very often, analogies can be drawn to similar common law offenses, but these can be deceiving as the very purpose of the new offense may be to change the nature of the traditional offense in a way that may be critical for venue purposes. On occasion, the new offense will have no counterpart among the common law offenses. Indeed, the basic structure of the offense may be substantially different from that of common law offenses in general. Especially for such offenses, there is likely to be a substantial period of uncertainty until the courts finally provide definite answers to each of the relevant questions for the particular offense.

Courts have adopted a variety of not always distinct approaches in responding to the recurring questions presented in the application of the crime-committed formula. Perhaps the three most common approaches are (1) looking to a technical analysis of the language of the statute, (2) looking to some overriding venue "policy," and (3) looking to a series of different interests. Each of these approaches is discussed below. Because federal crimes more often implicate more than one place, and because they more frequently present offenses lacking precise counterparts in traditional common law crimes, primary attention will be given to federal rulings. The same divergence in approach can also be found, however, among state rulings, at least as between different jurisdictions.

(b) Literalism. In an article written in the mid–1920's, Judge Dobie set forth an analysis that captures the crux of the literalist approach to the application of the crime-committed formula:

> All federal crimes are statutory, and these crimes are often defined, hidden away amid pompous verbosity, in terms of a single verb. That essential verb usually contains the key to the solution of the question: In what district was the crime committed? [1]

While all would agree that the "essential verb" often characterizes the offense and thereby helps to set venue, the critical question is whether that verb should invariably be viewed as providing an answer in itself. The Supreme Court's ruling in *United States v. Lombardo* [2] came close to responding in the affirmative, although the *Lombardo* opinion also contained additional reasoning suggesting that policy concerns were not totally ignored.

The defendant in *Lombardo,* the operator of a house of prostitution is Seattle, was charged in the Western District of Washington with failing to comply with a federal statute requiring any person who harbored an alien for the purpose of prostitution to report that alien's identity to the Commissioner General of Immigration. The district court sustained a demurrer to the indictment on the ground that the offense was not committed in Seattle, but in the District of Columbia, where the offices of the Commissioner General were located. Affirming that ruling, the Supreme Court initially quoted with approval from the district court's analysis of the critical statutory verb:

> "The word 'file' was not defined by Congress. No definition having been given, the etymology of the word must be considered and ordinary meaning applied. The word 'file' is derived from the Latin word '*filum,*' and relates to the ancient practice of placing papers on a thread or wire for safe-keeping and ready reference. Filing, it must be observed, is not complete until the document is delivered and received. 'Shall file' means to deliver to the office and not send through the United States mails. A paper is filed when it is delivered to the proper official and by him received and filed."

The Court then rejected the government's response that this was an unduly narrow reading of the term "shall file." The government contended that a filing could begin in the place where the document was sent and therefore the defendant's failure to send the document from Seattle marked the beginning of the crime. The Court's answer to this contention was that it "was constrained by the meanings of the words of the statute." The requirement of a filing demanded delivery in a specific place; it had never been deemed satisfied by "a deposit in a post office at some distant place." The statute thus was quite distinct from one that imposed a "general duty" upon a person, such as the "duty of the father to support his children," which could be enforced both "where the 'actor' is and where the 'subject' is." Here, in contrast, there was a specific duty that required an action at a single place.

While the *Lombardo* opinion stressed what it viewed as the clear meaning of the verb "file," it also offered several administrative justifications for the interpretation it adopted. These included difficulties relating to proof of the mailing (or the lack thereof) and to setting the "instant of time" for compliance if a mailing was to be taken as compliance in itself. In *Travis v. United States,* [3] the Supreme Court relied upon *Lombardo* but offered no reasons other than the structure of the statute to support its reading of the offense involved there as capable of being committed only in one place. Justice Douglas' opinion for the *Travis* majority reasoned that the statutory language controlled, notwithstanding that a contrary view would allow for a trial in the district of greater convenience to the defense and more ready access to relevant evidence by both parties.

The defendant in *Travis,* a union official in Colorado, was charged under a statute appli-

§ 16.2

1. Dobie, Venue in Criminal Cases in the United States District Court, 12 Va.L.Rev. 287 (1926).

2. 241 U.S. 73, 36 S.Ct. 508, 60 L.Ed. 897 (1916).

3. 364 U.S. 631, 81 S.Ct. 358, 5 L.Ed.2d 340 (1961).

cable to any person who, "in a matter within the jurisdiction of any department or agency of the United States," knowingly "makes" any false statement. The false statements at issue were non-Communist affidavits executed and mailed in Colorado to the offices of the N.L.R.B. in Washington, D.C. The defendant contended, and the Court majority agreed, that the government had erred in bringing the prosecution in Colorado as the offense only could be committed in the District of Columbia. Justice Douglas' opinion's stressed that the offense required that the false statement be "within the jurisdiction" of the N.L.R.B. Section 9(h) of the National Labor Relations Act did not require union officers to file non-Communist affidavits, but provided for their voluntary filing as a prerequisite to invoking the Board's authority in the investigation and issuance of complaints against employers. Accordingly, Justice Douglas reasoned, "filing [of the affidavit] must be completed before there is a 'matter within the jurisdiction' of the Board." *Lombardo* had held that "when a place is explicitly designated where a paper must be filed, a prosecution for failure to file lies only at that place." The same was true for an actual filing. Accordingly, the charge could be brought only in the District of Columbia, where the affidavit was filed.

The *Travis* majority acknowledged that "Colorado, the residence of the [defendant] might offer conveniences and advantages to him which a trial in the District of Columbia might lack." It did not disagree with Justice Harlan's contention in dissent that "the witnesses and relevant circumstances surrounding the contested issues in such cases more probably will be found in the district of the execution of the affidavit than at the place of filing." Its response was that the "constitutional requirement is as to the locality of the offense, and not the personal presence of the offender," and here the nature of the offense set that locality in only one place. To argue, as the government did, that the offense started in Colorado because the defendant there "irrevocably set in motion and placed beyond his control the train of events which would normally result (and here did result) in the consummation of the offense" was to ignore that Congress here "has so carefully indicated the locus of the crime." That was done in the "explicit provision of 9(h)," which combined with the "agency jurisdiction" requirement of the false statement statute to render the crime incapable of commission until the affidavit was delivered to the N.L.R.B.

Dissenting in *Travis,* Justice Harlan found no such clear designation in the statutory language. At the least, the statutory language was just as readily read as creating an offense that could be started in one place and finished in another. The prohibited act was the "making" of a false statement to the government, which certainly could "begin at the place where the false affidavit is actually made, sworn, and subscribed." At that point, the process that constituted the crime was started, and it was with the bringing of the statement within the jurisdiction of the N.L.R.B., through its filing, that the other necessary element was added and the crime completed. Unlike the offense presented in *Lombardo,* this offense could be seen as either having more than one part or involving a continuing path of action. *Lombardo* involved a "failure to file," where "it is difficult to see how the defendant does anything at all except at the place where he files." The appropriate venue, Justice Harlan continued, should be determined by reference to the "nature of the crime alleged" and the "location of the act or acts constituting it." From that perspective, it would be difficult to distinguish the case in which the affidavit was within the N.L.R.B.'s jurisdiction at the time of execution because the official had an obligation to file and the situation presented in *Travis.* Yet Justice Douglas had noted that if § 9(h) had required the filing of the non-Communist affidavits, "the whole process of filing, including the use of the mails, might logically be construed to constitute the offense."

While Justice Harlan's *Travis* dissent did not ignore Judge Dobie's advice to look to the "essential verb," it stressed the need to interpret that verb in light of the "unfairness and hardship involved when an accused is prosecuted in a remote place." The "place where the union offices are located," Justice Harlan noted, was the place of trial most likely "to respect the basic policy of the Sixth Amendment" and the statute should not be construed to foreclose its use. Commentators have agreed with Justice Harlan's analysis, arguing that the *Travis* majority placed formalism over function. They note that there is only so much weight that language can carry in deciding a question that the legislature most likely did not have in mind in its choice of language. Should it be determinative, for example, whether a statute states that it is a crime to "obtain" property through a false pretense or states that the crime consists of the "making" of a false pretense and thereby "obtaining" the transfer of property? Very often, it is argued, differences in phrasing are the product of drafting goals that have little to do with clearly indicating the gist of the crime. That is especially the case for older statutes that are the product of a style of draftsmanship that sought to include all means of commission, all conditions, and all exceptions in something close to a single sentence. The end product of such drafting, as Judge Dobie noted, often was to produce statutes with several of what he characterized as "essential verbs," and to require, as he put it, the necessity for "scrupulous, even meticulous, nicety in exact quotation" so as to "prevent these statutes * * * from proving a snare and delusion to the unwary." Such niceties, it is argued, should not provide the sole grounding for determining an issue as important as venue. Where the legislature has in mind a specific venue, it can append an explicit venue provision to the substantive criminal provision. Absent that, where the language does not clearly indicate otherwise, the statute should be interpreted consistently with what is characterized as "constitutional venue policy."

As discussed in the next subsection, the Supreme Court frequently has professed its adherence to an approach similar to that suggested by these commentators. Indeed, no statement on venue determination is more frequently cited than the Supreme Court's admonition in *United States v. Johnson*[4] that "questions of venue in criminal cases" should not be viewed as presenting "merely matters of formal legal procedure," but as "rais[ing] deep issues of public policy in light of which legislation must be construed." However, as both commentators and lower courts have noted, the Court has been unable to achieve a consistent consensus on the precise content of those policies.

(c) Constitutional Policy. Although the Court had referred occasionally to policy consideration in earlier opinions, Justice Frankfurter's opinion for the majority in *United States v. Johnson*[5] clearly constitutes the seminal Supreme Court opinion on the guidance provided by "constitutional venue policy" in applying the crime-committed formula. Prosecution there was brought under a statute prohibiting the "use of the mails * * * for the purpose of sending or bringing into" any state a denture the cast of which was taken by a person not licensed to practice dentistry in that state. The defendant, the sender of the dentures, objected to his prosecution in the state of delivery, arguing that the offense was committed only where the dentures were deposited in the mail. The government countered that the statute prohibited the use of the mails and the offense therefore was committed "in every state through which the dentures were carried" by the mails, including the state of delivery. Responding to that argument, Justice Frankfurter noted for a 5–4 majority:

> An accused is so triable, if a fair reading of the Act requires it. But if the enactment reasonably permits the trial of the sender of outlawed dentures to be confined to the district of sending, and that of the importer to the district into which they are brought, such construction should be placed upon the Act. Such construction, while not required by the compulsions of Article III, § 2 of the Constitution and of the Sixth Amendment, is more consonant with the considerations of historic

4. Infra note 5.

5. 323 U.S. 273, 65 S.Ct. 249, 89 L.Ed. 236 (1944).

experience and policy which underlie those safeguards in the Constitution regarding the trial of crimes. Aware of the unfairness and hardship to which trial in an environment alien to the accused exposes him, the Framers wrote into the Constitution * * * [Article III, § 2 and the Sixth Amendment provision on jury selection]. * * * By utilizing the doctrine of a continuing offense, Congress may, to be sure, provide that the locality of a crime shall extend over the whole area through which force propelled by an offender operates. Thus, an illegal use of the mails or of other instruments of commerce may subject the user to prosecution in the district where he sent the goods, or in the district of their arrival, or in any intervening district. Plainly enough, such leeway not only opens the door to needless hardship to an accused by prosecution remote from home and from appropriate facilities for defense. It also leads to the appearance of abuses, if not to abuses, in the selection of what may be deemed a tribunal favorable to the prosecution.

These are matters that touch closely the fair administration of criminal justice and public confidence in it, on which it ultimately rests. * * * They have been adverted to, from time to time, by eminent judges; and Congress has not been unmindful of them. * * * If an enactment of Congress equally permits the underlying spirit of the constitutional concern for trial in the vicinage to be respected rather than to be disrespected, construction should go in the direction of constitutional policy even though not commanded by it.

The *Johnson* majority concluded that the statute presented there did not demand a reading that would allow venue in any district in which the mails were used. When Congress in the past had desired to give the government such a broad choice of venue, it had done so by a specific venue provision. There was no such provision here. Moreover, the statutory language did not make it a crime to "transport" the unlawful dentures, but instead referred to use of the mails for sending or importing the dentures. A "strained construction" was not needed to hold that the "crime of the sender is complete when he uses the mails in Chicago, and the crime of the unlicensed dentist in California or Florida or Delaware, who orders the denture from Chicago, is committed in the State into which he brings the dentures." Not only was such an interpretation favored by constitutional venue policy, but "no considerations of expediency" required otherwise. Allowing prosecution of the sender in the State of delivery was not needed to safeguard against the possible reluctance of a local prosecutor in the sending district to press charges on an offense that had no local victim. All United States Attorneys were subject to the "general supervision of the Attorney General," which ensured a broader perspective. "While it might facilitate the Government's prosecution in a case like this to have its witnesses near the place of trial," there should be "balanced against * * * [that interest] the serious hardship of defending prosecutions in places remote from home (including the accused's difficulties, financial and otherwise, of marshalling witnesses) as well as the temptation to abuses" of possible prosecutorial forum-shipping. Four dissenters in *Johnson* found unpersuasive Justice Frankfurter's policy arguments. They responded that "the Court misapprehends the purpose of constitutional provisions. We understand them to assure a trial in the place where the crime is committed and not to be concerned with domicile of the defendant nor with his familiarity with the environment of the place of trial."

In the years since *Johnson,* the Court has continued to be divided over whether it should apply a preference for a reading of the crime-committed formula that would allow prosecution in the district where the defendant was physically present, which most often will be the district of his residence. In *Johnston v. United States,*[6] the Court majority held that persons charged with the failure to report to hospitals for civilian work as ordered by their local draft boards could be prosecuted only in the districts where the hospitals were located and not in the districts where they lived and their draft boards were located.

6. 351 U.S. 215, 76 S.Ct. 739, 100 L.Ed. 1097 (1956).

Speaking for the majority, Justice Reed, a dissenter in *Johnson,* stated that the case was governed by the "general rule that where the crime charged is a failure to do a legally required act, the place fixed for its performance is the situs of the crime." Justice Reed added: "This requirement of venue states the public policy that fixes the situs of the trial in the vicinage of the crime rather than the resident of the accused." Here, it was the dissenters who responded that they would have preferred "to read the statute with an eye to history and try the offenders at home where our forefathers thought that normally men would receive their fairest trial."

Only two years later, in *United States v. Cores,*[7] the Court majority, in construing an immigration law violation to be continuing in nature, noted that an advantage of that construction was to produce a result "in keeping with the policy of relieving the accused, where possible, of the inconvenience incident to prosecution in a district far removed from his residence." *Cores* involved the prosecution of an alien seaman for "willfully remain[ing]" in the United States beyond the time permitted under his landing permit. If the prosecution were limited to the district in which the seaman was located at the moment the permit expired, that often would not be the district in which he eventually took up residence. While construing the offense to be continuing in nature did not ensure that the government would bring the prosecution in his place of residence, it did ensure that the defendant could move for a change of venue to that district at a time when Rule 21(b) allowed transfers only to a district in which the offense was committed.[8] *Cores,* however, was followed by a contrary construction of the false statements statute in *Travis v. United States,* discussed in the previous subsection. The Court majority there refused to adopt an application of the crime-committed formula that would have allowed the government to bring the prosecution in district of the execution of the false affidavit, which ordinarily would be the district of the affiant's residence. *Travis* also was decided at a time when Rule 21(b) allowed transfer only to a district where the crime was committed, and by holding that the offense occurred only in the District of Columbia, it precluded a defendant prosecuted there from obtaining transfer to his home district where he had executed and mailed the false affidavit.

In *Johnson,* Justice Frankfurter argued in favor of an application of the crime-committed formula that would both establish venue in the place of the accused's residence and avoid granting the government a broad choice of venues that would "lead to the appearance of abuses, if not to abuses," in its decision to prosecute in one district rather than another. In that case, those two values would be served by the same reading of the Federal Denture Act, as the limitation of venue to the single district of the mailing typically also would produce the district of the sender's residence. In other instances, as in *Cores* and *Travis,* the two goals suggested opposite readings. If the offense were held to be committed in only one district, that district would not be the most likely site of the accused's residence. The district of residence could only be made an allowable venue by holding that the crime was committed in more than one district and thereby granting to the prosecution an opportunity to choose between districts according to its own interests. The outcomes in *Travis* and *Cores*—with the former limiting the prosecution to a single district and the latter deciding in favor of multi-venue that would include the district of residence—indicate no clear choice in balancing the two goals. Indeed, it is unclear whether those cases were seen by the Court majority as involving a choice between those goals. Only the *Travis* opinion mentioned the value of restricting the prosecution's choice, and it did so in a brief review of considerations possibly relevant to venue determinations in general. The *Travis* opinion did not suggest that it was refusing to grant the prosecution a choice between the district of the defendant's residence and

7. 356 U.S. 405, 78 S.Ct. 875, 2 L.Ed.2d 873 (1958).

8. This limitation was later deleted. See § 16.1 at note 7.

Washington, D.C. because such flexibility might be used by the prosecution to select the district in which it would find the more favorable tribunal. Indeed, it seems unlikely that allowing the government to choose the district of the defendant's residence over Washington, D.C. would give to it a substantial advantage in selecting a forum.

In general, courts discussing venue policy have given far less attention to the possibility of narrowing venue so as to restrict the prosecutor's choice than to the possibility of including the district most likely to be that of defendant's residence. At the state level, the lack of concern for limiting prosecutorial options may be explained by the typical division of prosecutorial authority. Each judicial district is likely to have a different prosecutor, so the scenario of a coordinated prosecutorial decision to bring charges in a district most likely to present a "favorable tribunal" does not seem realistic. If more than one prosecutor has an interest in the case, the primary concern is an unseemly race to file charges rather than a plot to select the most favorable venue.

At the federal level, the lack of lower court discussion of a possible preference for narrowing the government's choice of venues probably stems from the Supreme Court's infrequent references to that policy. Still another possibility is the availability to the defendant of transfer under current Rule 21(b). Admittedly, *Johnson* was decided prior to the adoption of Rule 21(b), when statutory provisions allowing for transfer were exceptionally narrow. Nonetheless, the broad scope of current Rule 21(b) provides less than a complete explanation. If Rule 21(b) is deemed an adequate response to the dangers of prosecutorial venue-shopping, it also should be a response to the more frequently pressed preference for a reading that includes the defendant's likely district of residence. In fact, as applied, Rule 21(b) hardly renders moot either policy. Rule 21(b) transfers are not available simply by showing that the prosecution has selected that venue most likely to produce a jury sympathetic to its cause or that the defendant would find more convenient a trial in the district of his residence. Indeed, it was in the context of a Rule 21(b) motion that the Court unanimously rejected the notion "that criminal defendants have a constitutionally based right to a trial in their home districts." [9]

(d) Multiple Interests. In *United States v. Reed*,[10] the Second Circuit crystallized an approach to determining venue that finds considerable support in the rulings of the lower federal courts. Judge Winter's opinion in *Reed* initially noted that venue analysis should not proceed from the premise that the "constitutional venue requirement," as expressed in the crime-committed formula, will fix a "single proper situs for trial." Where the "acts constituting the crime and the nature of the crime charged implicate more than one location," those factors can readily produce multiple venue, provided that conclusion is not "contrary to an explicit policy underlying venue law." While the Supreme Court had noted in *Johnson* that venue questions " 'raise deep issues of public policy in light of which legislation must be construed,' " the "precise policies be furthered by venue law" had not been "clearly defined" by the Court. Though reference had been made to protecting defendants against the unfairness of prosecution in places remote from their homes, that obviously could not be the "sole grounds for determining venue because the most convenient venue for [defendants] may often have little, if any, connection with the crimes charged." Obviously relevant as well was what Justice Harlan had described as the "basic policy of the Sixth Amendment"—holding trial where the " 'witnesses and relevant circumstances surrounding the contested issues' could be gathered." As Justice Harlan had further noted, where "competing jurisdictions have those attributes, venue in either [should] not offend the Constitution." Accordingly, Judge Winter noted, there could be

9. See Platt v. Minnesota Mining Co., discussed in § 16.1 at note 8.

10. 773 F.2d 477 (2d Cir.1985).

no single defined policy or mechanical test to determine constitutional venue. Rather, the test is best described as a substantial contacts rule that takes into account a number of factors—the site of the defendant's acts, the elements and nature of the crime, the locus of the effect of the criminal conduct, and the suitability of each district for accurate factfinding.

Turning to an examination of each of the four listed factors, Judge Winter stated that the first—the site of the defendant's acts—should always fix one place of permissible venue. The presence of the "alleged criminal acts" in itself "provide[s] substantial contact with the district" and ensures that the district "is usually as suitable for factfinding as any other." Also, "this site may seem fair to defendants at least in the perverse sense of having been freely chosen by them as the place at which the acts were committed." Of course, there may be situations in which the defendant's acts were spread over several districts. In that setting, the federal courts commonly have distinguished between preparatory acts and acts that are "part of the offense," with only the latter setting a place of permissible venue.

With the acts of the defendant having set one place of venue, a court applying the "substantial contacts" approach will then turn to the other factors noted by Judge Winter to determine whether venue is also proper elsewhere. The second factor—the elements and nature of the crime—will often clearly implicate another district by requiring a specific occurrence there, as "where interstate transportation is a jurisdictional prerequisite." Very often, the elements of the offense will require a specific harm in another district and thus overlap with the third factor—the locus of the effect of the criminal conduct. Judge Winter offered as an illustration of multiple venue arising from such specific harm the venue applicable when a criminal contempt occurs through action in one district that violates a court order issued in another. "Federal courts," he noted, "have never required that criminal contempt proceedings be brought only where the acts occurred, even where the contumacious conduct is committed by one who is not a party to the underlying action." Venue is also proper in the district where the order was issued as the courts issuing the violated orders have a special interest in their enforcement. With the "integrity" of their proceedings at stake, those tribunals "should not be left to the generosity of prosecutors or judges in other districts to defend their powers."

As to the fourth factor, the "suitability of the district for accurate factfinding," that was a factor to be considered in addition to the other factors, rather than as a *sine qua non* for establishing venue. Thus, in the contempt situation, venue was proper in the district of the court order even though the evidence of the contempt was more likely to be found in the district in which defendant's acts occurred. So also, in a prosecution under the federal extortion statute, venue was proper in the district where interstate commerce was affected (an element of the crime), even though district in which the defendant acted (also a proper venue) was the likely source of most of the evidence relating to the offense. In determining whether the element of factfinding suitability contributed to the designation of the district as an appropriate venue, the appropriate point of reference, Judge Winter added, should not be to the particular case, but to the likely location of evidence as measured by the general nature of the offense. Where "factors peculiar to a particular case" pointed to an additional district as most appropriate for factfinding, a transfer of venue could be ordered under Federal Rule 21.

While the multiple-interests analysis of *Reed* would be difficult to square with a ruling such as *Travis,* it finds support in numerous federal rulings that have held venue to be appropriate in more than one district. These have included prosecutions under the same false statements provision involved in *Travis,* other false statement provisions, fraud provisions, and the prohibition against bail jumping.

(e) Transportation Offenses. At common law, multi-venue possibilities were most often presented where the proscribed criminal conduct included the movement of an item or person (e.g., kidnapping). Because the offense continued with the movement, venue was available in all of the different districts in which the movement took place. With rare exceptions, those were districts in which the defendant was physically present as the item or person moved would have been within his personal control. Modern counterparts of those offenses include crimes such as driving while intoxicated where the basic wrongdoing lies in the transportation itself. However, the same principle has been utilized to create broad venue by making transportation an element of the offense where the basic wrongdoing relates more to events occurring before or after the transportation than the transportation itself. This is especially true of federal legislation, where Congress has often looked to its authority over the interstate facilities and the United States mails as a touchstone for extending federal criminal jurisdiction.

The Supreme Court sustained the constitutionality of one of the earliest of these broad venue provisions in *Armour Packing Co. v. United States.*[11] At issue there was a statute prohibiting the transportation of goods at rates below those set in the carrier's published tariff and the accompanying venue provision, which stated that prosecution could be brought in any federal district "through which the transportation may have been conducted." The defendant contended that allowance for such venue violated the crime-committed formula as constitutionalized in both Article III, Section 2, and the Sixth Amendment. Rejecting that contention, the Court reasoned: "[T]he transportation being the essence of the offense, when it takes place, whether in one district or another, whether at the beginning, at the end, or in the middle of the journey, it is equally and at all times committed." As for the defendant's policy arguments, they were directed to the wrong authority: "To say that this construction may work serious hardship in permitting prosecutions in places distant from the home and remote from the vicinage of the accused is to state an objection to the policy of the law, not to the power of Congress to pass it."

In later years, the Court expressed a reluctance to interpret federal offenses as prohibiting the act of transportation itself, and thereby allowing for venue in all districts through which goods passed, absent a clear Congressional indication that it intended to provide such broad venue. Congress responded by adopting various offense-specific venue provisions modeled after that involved in *Armour Packing.* Finally, in 1948, Congress adopted a general provision designed to make unnecessary the inclusion of special venue provisions for each offense involving an element of transportation. Added to the basic multi-venue provision of § 3237 of the criminal code was a second paragraph, which now reads:

> Any offense involving the use of the mails, transportation in interstate or foreign commerce, or the importation of an object or person to the United States is a continuing offense and, except as otherwise expressly provided by enactment of Congress, may be inquired of and prosecuted in any district from, through, or into which such commerce, mail matter, or imported object or person moves.[12]

This paragraph was added partially in response to the Court's reliance in *Johnson* on the absence of any special provision in the Denture Act specifically providing for venue in any district through which the illegally shipped dentures passed. With the amendment of § 3237, the courts were now to be directed by a single provision applicable to all "mailing" and "transportation" offenses. The judicial response, however, often has been to continue to treat as controlling (as did *Johnson*) the presence of a verb in the basic statute which refers to a specific aspect of the

11. 209 U.S. 56, 28 S.Ct. 428, 52 L.Ed. 681 (1908).

12. 18 U.S.C.A. § 3237. The basic multi-venue provision of § 3237 is quoted in § 16.1 at note 4. Congress later added to § 3237, in subsection (b), a limitation of prosecutorial venue choice applicable to specified internal revenue offenses and instances in which venue for an internal revenue offense "is based solely on a mailing to the Internal Revenue Service." Subsection (b) grants the defendant in such cases a right, upon timely demand, to be tried in the district in which he was residing at the time of the alleged offense.

mailing or transportation. Thus, the offense of "depositing" proscribed obscene materials "for mailing or delivery" was held not to be subject to the continuing offense provision of § 3237. To make that provision applicable, Congress subsequently amended the obscenity provision to reach any person who "knowingly uses the mails for the mailing, carriage in the mails, or delivery" of the obscene matter. Courts have also held that the § 3237 reference to offenses "involving the use of the mails" does not apply to the situation in which the offender happens to use the mails but such use is not a specified element of the crime. Thus, § 3237 was not applicable in the false statements prosecution in *Travis* although the defendant there mailed the false affidavits to the N.L.R.B. offices.

(f) **Multiple Participants.** Where multiple parties participate in a criminal transaction, venue often can be extended through the special venue rules applicable to accomplice liability and the offense of conspiracy. As to accomplices, the acts of the accomplice constituting the aiding and abetting may have occurred in a different district than the commission of the crime. In such a case, the prosecutor can choose between those districts in the prosecution of the accomplice. As to conspiracy, the formation of the conspiratorial agreement may have occurred in one district and overt acts in furtherance of the conspiracy may have occurred in other districts. Here, the prosecution has the option of proceeding against all the conspirators in the district of formation or in any district in which an overt act occurred.

The option granted as to accomplices finds its grounding in three somewhat distinct legislative developments. At English common law, an accomplice could be prosecuted only in the district of his accessorial acts. This rule often precluded joinder of the accomplice and principle in a single trial at the place of the commission of the crime. Various states responded by adopting statutes that permitted venue over the accomplice also to lie in the place of the commission of the crime. When the states adopted general provisions abolishing the common law distinctions between principles and accessories, courts commonly read such statutes also as having the effect of abolishing the venue limitation of the English common law rule. The accomplice now could be treated simply as an accomplice and prosecuted in the place of his accessorial acts or treated as a principal and prosecuted in the place of the commission of the substantive offense. Modern statutes establishing complicity liability furnish a refinement of this rationale. They often refer to the accomplice as having legal accountability based upon two distinct elements—his acts constituting an aiding and abetting and the conduct of the person he sought to assist. If the accomplice is seen as committing the offense through these combined elements, it follows that the prosecution, as with any other multi-part offense, may be brought in the district of the existence of either element.

In certain respects, the rule governing conspiracy venue provides a prosecutorial option even broader than that applicable to accomplices. That rule is limited to the conspiracy charge itself, and does not encompass any substantive offense committed pursuant to the conspiracy. All conspirators may be charged with the conspiracy offense either where the conspiracy was formed (i.e., the district of agreement) or in any other district in which an overt act to effect the object of the conspiracy was perpetuated. This venue standard is sometimes described as the *Hyde* rule, based on the 1912 Supreme Court ruling that first established the standard in the federal courts. The majority opinion in *Hyde v. United States*[13] concluded that conspiracy was a continuing crime committed wherever an overt act furthering the conspiracy was performed. The Court noted that the federal conspiracy offense required as its elements both the conspiratorial agreement and at least one overt act by a conspirator in furtherance of the conspiratorial objective. Accordingly, each such overt act constitutes a partial execution of the offense, allowing the prosecution of the conspiracy at that place under the

13. 225 U.S. 347, 32 S.Ct. 793, 56 L.Ed. 1114 (1912).

crime-committed formula. While the remaining conspirators may not be physically present in the district when their associate commits that act, they have a "constructive presence" there based on the vicarious liability of conspirators.

Although the *Hyde* opinion stressed the overt act element of the federal conspiracy offense, it cited various common law rulings that had reached a similar result under a conspiracy offense that did not require an overt act in addition to the conspiratorial agreement. The reasoning of those rulings was that the overt act, although not an element of the offense, constituted a "renewal" or "continuation" of the agreement and thus carried its commission into the district of that act. In later years, the *Hyde* reasoning came to be viewed as incorporating both rationales, and the *Hyde* rule was applied, on both state and federal levels, to conspiracy offenses that did not require an overt act. This suggests that perhaps the key to the *Hyde* opinion was the pragmatic justification offered by the Court for the standard adopted there. The dissenters in *Hyde* had argued that venue should be limited to that place "where the conspiracy exists in fact"—i.e., the place where the agreement was formed or where the conspirators continued its operation by acting together. The Court majority responded that this approach might make it impossible to establish venue. With conspirators often meeting in secret, it would impose too great a burden on the government to require it to establish precisely where and when the conspirators reached an agreement. Often the primary evidence of the conspiracy was the coordinated action by individuals indicating the obvious presence of an agreement. Moreover, it was not "an oppression in the law to accept the place where an unlawful purpose is attempted to be executed as the place of its punishment, and rather conspirators be taken from their homes than the witnesses and victims of the conspiracy be taken from theirs."

Although the *Hyde* case itself involved substantial overt acts, the *Hyde* rule has been held to impose only a few basic limitations upon the overt acts that will suffice to establish venue. The act must occur subsequent to the formation of the conspiracy agreement and prior to or in completion of the conspiratorial objective. It also must have been done in furtherance of the accomplishment of that objective, but that requirement is readily satisfied. No distinctions are drawn based on the importance of the act to the accomplishment of the objective or on the legality of the act. A simple and commonplace legal activity may be sufficient, even though the action may be one that would have been taken in any event even had there been no illegal purpose. The critical question is whether the act can be seen as designed to contribute even in minimal way to the accomplishment of that purpose. The act can be that of a single conspirator or even an innocent agent who is acting at his direction. The other conspirators need not have counseled the commission of the act nor even have been aware that it was to be done.

Chapter 17

THE SCOPE OF THE PROSECUTION: JOINDER AND SEVERANCE

Table of Sections

---

§ 17.1 Joinder and Severance of Offenses

(a) Joinder: Related Offenses. It is commonly provided that offenses which were committed at the same time and place or are otherwise related to one another may be joined together so that the defendant may be prosecuted for all of them in a single trial. In the federal system, for example, offenses may be so joined if they are "based on the same act or transaction or on two or more acts or transactions connected together or constituting parts of a common scheme or plan." [1] A number of states follow the federal approach, some others specify the kinds of offenses which can be joined when committed together, and yet others more generally allow join-

§ 17.1

1. Fed.R.Crim.P. 8(a).

der of offenses connected together in their commission.

A brief look at the manner in which the federal provision has been interpreted provides some insight into what are likely to be viewed as related offenses for joinder purposes. Under the "same transaction" test, it is proper to join a conspiracy charge with a substantive offense committed in furtherance of the conspiracy, or to join offenses which are closely related in that they were interrelated parts of a particular criminal episode. But under the general notion that the offenses must arise out of the same sequence of events, it is sufficient that they were occurring simultaneously but yet not part of a common scheme. As for the "common scheme or plan" part of the federal provision, it will permit joinder of offenses which may not be close together in a time-space sense but which may be viewed as facets of a general criminal undertaking. The "connected together" part of the test, by contrast, focuses more upon the time-space relationship between the crimes and does not require that the crimes be connected in terms of their motivation.

The provisions permitting joinder of related offenses have generally been viewed with favor, for such joinder may have substantial advantages for both the prosecution and the defendant. The state can avoid the duplication of evidence required by separate trials, reduce the inconvenience to victims and witnesses, and minimize the time required to dispose of the offenses. The defendant can avoid the harassment, trauma, expense, and prolonged publicity of multiple trials, obtain faster disposition of all cases, and increase the possibility of concurrent sentences in the event of conviction.

(b) Joinder: Offenses of Similar Character. In the federal system, it is also permissible to join offenses for disposition in a single trial of the defendant if those offenses are "of the same or similar character." [2] Approximately one-third of the states have adopted comparable provisions, and generally they have been interpreted in the same fashion as the federal rule. Under such a provision, it is permissible to join together several instances of the same crime, such as bank robbery, though they were committed by the defendant at distinct times and places and not as part of a single scheme. But the mere fact that the crimes carry different labels is not determinative of the joinder issue, as if they have a general likeness they are still of "similar character."

Joinder of offenses of the same or similar character has its advantages. For one thing, it also helps save judicial and prosecutorial resources. The defendant may prefer the disadvantages of joinder to the delay and expense of multiple prosecutions, especially because disposal of all of the charges in a single prosecution may facilitate concurrent sentencing and will avoid the possibility of a detainer being filed against him for later offenses not tried. But some have strongly criticized this form of joinder. It is said that the savings to the government are substantially reduced because unrelated offenses normally involve different times, separate locations, and distinct sets of witnesses and victims. Moreover, the joint trial of offenses creates a significant risk that the jury will convict the defendant upon the weight of the accusations or upon the accumulated effect of the evidence.

(c) Severance: Separate Defenses. In the federal system, offenses which have been joined for trial will be severed, so that they will be tried separately, if "it appears that a defendant or the government is prejudiced by a joinder of offenses." [3] State laws also provide for severance of offenses where otherwise a party would be prejudiced or where it would be in the interests of justice and for good cause shown. With respect to prejudice of the defendant, it is likely to fall into one of three categories: (1) he may become embarrassed or confounded in presenting separate defenses; (2) the jury may use the evidence of one of the crimes charged to infer a criminal disposition on the part of the defendant and thereby find

2. Fed.R.Crim.P. 8(a).

3. Fed.R.Crim.P. 14.

him guilty of the other crime or crimes charged; or (3) the jury may cumulate the evidence of the various crimes charged and find guilt when, if they were considered separately, it would not so find.

As for the first of these, one type of case is that discussed in *Cross v. United States*[4]:

> Prejudice may develop when an accused wishes to testify on one but not the other of two joined offenses which are clearly distinct in time, place and evidence. His decision whether to testify will reflect a balancing of several factors with respect to each count: the evidence against him, the availability of defense evidence other than his testimony, the plausibility and substantiality of his testimony, the possible effects of demeanor, impeachment, and cross-examination. But if the two charges are joined for trial, it is not possible for him to weigh these factors separately as to each count. If he testifies on one count, he runs the risk that any adverse effects will influence the jury's consideration of the other count. Thus he bears the risk on both counts, although he may benefit on only one. Moreover, a defendant's silence on one count would be damaging in the face of his express denial of the other. Thus, he may be coerced into testifying on the count upon which he wished to remain silent.

In *Cross,* the court was satisfied that the defendant was "embarrassed or confounded," for his alibi testimony as to one robbery charge led to his acquittal, but "to avoid the damaging implication of testifying on only one of the two joined counts" he had given "dubious testimony" concerning the other robbery count and had been convicted of that charge. However, *Cross* has not been interpreted as requiring the granting of a severance whenever a defendant asserts a desire to testify on one count and not another. Absent prejudice, it is not a violation of the Fifth Amendment privilege against self-incrimination to require a defendant to elect to testify as to both charges or to none at all. And the burden is on the defendant to show that a joint trial would be prejudicial, so that no need for a severance exists until the defendant makes a convincing showing that he has both important testimony to give concerning one count and a strong need to refrain from testifying on the other.

(d) Severance: Evidence of Other Crimes. As a general matter, the prosecution may not admit at the trial of a defendant on one charge evidence that this defendant has on another occasion committed some other crime. This established rule of evidence[5] rests upon two very legitimate concerns: (1) that the jury might convict on the notion that the defendant is a "bad man" who deserves to be punished because of his other misdeeds; and (2) that the jury might infer from defendant's other crimes that he probably committed the crime charged as well. Because the same dangers exist when two crimes are joined for trial, courts have had to confront the question of whether a defendant must be granted a severance so that the jury trying the defendant on each of the crimes charged does not have available to it evidence of these other offenses. A leading case on this issue is *Drew v. United States,*[6] concluding that the answer depends upon (i) whether evidence of the other crimes would be admissible even if a severance was granted; and (ii) if not, whether the evidence of each crime is simple and distinct.

As for the first of these, the essential point is that there are several limited exceptions to the other-crimes-as-evidence prohibition, and that if one of the exceptions applies to the case in question then (as the court put it in *Drew*) "the prejudice that might result from the jury's hearing the evidence of the other crime in a joint trial would be no different from that possible in separate trials." These exceptions are where the evidence of the other crime is offered as proof of motive, opportunity, intent, preparation, plan, knowledge, identity, or absence of mistake or accident, in which instances the evidence is admissible unless its probative value is substantially outweighed by the risk that its admission will

4. 335 F.2d 987 (D.C.Cir.1964).

5. Fed.R.Evid. 404(b).

6. 331 F.2d 85 (D.C.Cir.1964).

result in unfair prejudice to the accused. In *Drew,* therefore, where the two charges were of robbery and attempted robbery, respectively, of two High's neighborhood stores a few weeks apart, the first task of the court was to determine whether any of the aforementioned exceptions applied. The court concluded that the facts did "not show such a close similarity in the manner of committing the crimes as would make them admissible in separate trials," and thus further inquiry into defendant's prejudice claim was necessary. Had it been determined that evidence of the joined offenses would be received in any event under an exception to the "other crimes" rule, that would be the end of the inquiry.

As for the "simple and distinct" part of the inquiry, the court in *Drew* explained that it rested "upon the assumption that, with a proper charge, the jury can easily keep such evidence separate in their deliberations and, therefore, the danger of the jury's cumulating the evidence is substantially reduced." But because the record in the instant case reflected repeated confusion as to which of the two crimes was being referred to, the court concluded defendant had been prejudiced by the joinder. By contrast, in other cases where the crimes charged were sufficiently distinct in nature that such confusion did not occur, no prejudice has been found.

(e) Severance: Cumulation of Evidence. Although the possibility that the joinder may have prejudiced the defendant by causing the jury to cumulate the evidence against him has been recognized in *Drew* and other cases, relief is seldom obtained on this basis. If the trial judge is not moved to grant a severance on this basis, it is especially unlikely that appellate relief will be forthcoming; weighing the danger of confusion and undue cumulative inference is generally a matter for the trial judge within his sound discretion. The defendant's chances may be somewhat better if in addition it is shown that he was convicted on a count as to which the evidence was relatively weak. Absent that, appellate courts are inclined to accept unquestionably the notion that an instruction to the jury not to cumulate the evidence will avoid any prejudice.

(f) Severance as of Right. Defendants generally have not fared very well under rules and statutes which permit them to obtain a severance of offenses only upon proof of prejudice. For one thing, it is very difficult for the trial judge to make a finding on the prejudice issue before trial, for it involves speculation about many things which may or may not occur. Also, judges are understandably reluctant to make a finding of prejudice during trial, after the prosecution has put in most or all of its proof. And if the trial judge denies defendant's severance motion on the ground that a showing of prejudice has not been made, experience has shown that it is virtually impossible for the defendant to prevail on appeal. This has given rise to the proposal, reflected in recent law reform efforts, that severance of offenses should exist as a matter of right in many instances.

§ 17.2 Joinder and Severance of Defendants

(a) Joinder of Defendants. Statutes and rules of court commonly provide for the joinder of defendants, whereby two or more persons may together be prosecuted in a single trial. For example, in the federal courts "[t]wo or more defendants may be charged in the same indictment or information if they are alleged to have participated in the same act or transaction or in the same series of acts or transactions constituting an offense or offenses. Such defendants may be charged in one or more counts together or separately and all of the defendants need not be charged in each count." [1] Some states have identical provisions, while others utilize similar language. These rules and statutes are designed to promote economy and efficiency and to avoid a multiplicity of trials.

A brief look at the way in which the federal provision quoted above has been construed will provide some insight into the kind of joinder of defendants which is likely to be

§ 17.2

1. Fed.R.Crim.P. 8(b).

permitted. At the outset, it is important to understand that the previously discussed joinder-of-offenses provision cannot somehow be read into the just-quoted joinder-of-defendants provision so as to produce the result that all offenses which could be joined as to a single defendant may likewise be joined as to multiple defendants. This means, the courts have held, that though defendant *X* could be jointly charged with crimes *A* and *B* because they are of the same or similar character, defendant *X* and *Y* may not together be jointly charged with crimes *A* and *B*. Assuming one accepts the principle of similar offense joinder, it is difficult to see why it is unobjectionable only when a single defendant is charged.

One fairly common situation which falls within the federal joinder-of-defendants provision is that in which the several defendants are connected by virtue of a charged conspiratorial relationship. Thus, where the joined defendants are all charged in the conspiracy count and they or some of them are also charged with various substantive offenses alleged to have been committed in furtherance of the conspiracy, joinder is proper. But it would not be proper also to join offenses alleged to have been committed outside the conspiracy period or by defendants not parties to the conspiracy. Joinder where there are multiple conspiracies is improper where nothing is shown except for a slight membership overlap between the conspiracies. But even a single common conspirator will suffice where in addition it appears that the two conspiracies are a series of acts or transactions, as where they both related to the common conspirator's gambling operations. In support of permitting joinder of several conspiracies involving different parties when they are so related that they constitute different aspects of a scheme of organized criminal conduct, it is argued that in the case of complex and far-flung networks of crime, such a presentation may be essential to an understanding of the entire operation and the role played by each participant.

Even absent a conspiracy count, defendants may be joined together when their acts were part of a common plan, as where the offenses charged to less than all of the joined defendants were tied in with an underlying joint crime. This point can best be made by comparing the cases of *United States v. Roselli*[2] and *United States v. Granello*,[3] both involving the joinder of separate counts of income tax evasion against multiple defendants. The joinder was upheld in *Roselli* because the unreported income was derived from the defendants' joint gambling and racketeering activities. But in *Granello*, where each of the two defendants individually failed to report income from their lawful joint business venture, joinder was improper because the individual instances of nonreporting could not be said to be part of the "same series of acts or transactions."

Yet another basis for joining defendants is where their crimes are so closely connected in respect to time, place and occasion, that it would be difficult, if not impossible, to separate the proof of one charge from the proof of the other. This close connection is deemed a basis for joinder even absent proof of a common scheme—indeed, even when it is apparent that no such scheme exists. Thus, where the driver of a bus and the driver of an automobile have both been charged with the negligent homicide of a motorist whose car was struck by the other vehicles, these charges are properly joined. This is not to suggest, however, that joinder is proper whenever two defendants have separately committed similar crimes at about the same time and place. Thus, two defendants who happen to live in the same apartment building and who separately sold cocaine to the same individual may not be jointly charged.

(b) Severance: Codefendant's Confession Incriminates. Assume a case in which defendants *A* and *B* have been lawfully joined for trial, but at that trial the prosecution intends to offer against *A* a confession by him which says, in effect, that he and *B* committed the crime. Although this confession is

2. 432 F.2d 879 (9th Cir.1970).

3. 365 F.2d 990 (2d Cir.1966).

admissible only against *A* and not against *B*, a point on which the jury will be instructed, is *B* entitled to a severance or some other relief? In *Delli Paoli v. United States,*[4] the Supreme Court answered this in the negative, reasoning that the jury could be trusted to follow those instructions. But *Delli Paoli* was later overruled in *Bruton v. United States.*[5] The Court in *Bruton* first noted it was dealing with the constitutional right of cross-examination, which it had previously held "is included in the right of an accused in a criminal case to confront the witnesses against him"[6] secured by the Sixth Amendment. That right would be violated if *A*, by his confession, was a witness against *B* but could not be cross-examined. Whether *A* was, in effect, such a witness depended upon the correctness of the assumption in *Delli Paoli,* which the Court now concluded was in error. As the Court explained,

> there are some contexts in which the risk that the jury will not, or cannot, follow instructions is so great, and the consequences of failure so vital to the defendant, that the practical and human limitations of the jury system cannot be ignored. * * * Such a context is presented here, where the powerfully incriminating extra-judicial statements of a codefendant, who stands accused side-by-side with the defendant, are deliberately spread before the jury in a joint trial. Not only are the incriminations devastating to the defendant but their credibility is inevitably suspect, a fact recognized when accomplices do take the stand and the jury is instructed to weigh their testimony carefully given the recognized motivation to shift blame onto others. The unreliability of such evidence is intolerably compounded when the alleged accomplice, as here, does not testify and cannot be tested by cross-examination. It was against such threats to a fair trial that the Confrontation Clause was directed.

A significant limitation upon the *Bruton* rule was later recognized by a plurality of the Court in *Parker v. Randolph,*[7] a case involving what the court below had called "interlocking inculpatory confessions." Each of the three respondents had given confessions implicating the others, and all of these confessions had been admitted at the trial, which the plurality concluded made cross-examination something less than a constitutional imperative. The plurality reasoned that because "one can scarcely imagine evidence more damaging to his defense than his own admission of guilt," "the incriminating statements of a codefendant will seldom, if ever, be of the 'devastating' character referred to in *Bruton.*" But the Court held otherwise in the 5—4 decision of *Cruz v. New York,*[8] reasoning:

> In fact, it seems to us that "interlocking" bears a positively inverse relationship to devastation. A codefendant's confession will be relatively harmless if the incriminating story it tells is different from that which the defendant himself is alleged to have told, but enormously damaging if it confirms, in all essential respects, the defendant's alleged confession. It might be otherwise if the defendant were *standing by* his confession, in which case it could be said that the codefendant's confession does no more than support the defendant's very own case. But in the real world of criminal litigation, the defendant is seeking to *avoid* his confession—on the ground that it was not accurately reported, or that it was not really true when made. * * Quite obviously, what the "interlocking" nature of the codefendant's confession pertains to is not its *harmfulness* but rather its *reliability*: If it confirms essentially the same facts as the defendant's own confession it is more likely to be true. Its reliability, however, may be relevant to whether the confession should (despite the lack of opportunity for cross-examination) be *admitted as evidence* against the defendant, but cannot conceivably be relevant to whether, assuming it cannot be admitted, the jury is likely to obey the instruction to disregard it, or the jury's failure to obey is likely to be inconsequential.

4. 352 U.S. 232, 77 S.Ct. 294, 1 L.Ed.2d 278 (1957).

5. 391 U.S. 123, 88 S.Ct. 1620, 20 L.Ed.2d 476 (1968).

6. Pointer v. Texas, 380 U.S. 400, 85 S.Ct. 1065, 13 L.Ed.2d 923 (1965).

7. 442 U.S. 62, 99 S.Ct. 2132, 60 L.Ed.2d 713 (1979).

8. 481 U.S. 186, 107 S.Ct. 1714, 95 L.Ed.2d 162 (1987).

The Court in *Bruton* emphasized the fact that "the hearsay statement inculpating petitioner was clearly inadmissible against him under traditional rules of evidence," and thus lower courts have concluded *Bruton* has no application when a statement by defendant's partner in crime is received under some exception to the hearsay rule. Illustrative are cases where the evidence was admissible because the statement was made by a co-conspirator during the course of and in furtherance of the conspiracy or fell within the spontaneous exclamation or business record exception to the hearsay rule. These decisions seem correct in light of *Dutton v. Evans,*[9] where the Supreme Court upheld the use of hearsay evidence in the form of a statement by a co-conspirator not on trial made during the concealment phase of the conspiracy.[10] Distinguishing *Bruton* because the instant case did not involve evidence which was "devastating" or "a confession made in the coercive atmosphere of official interrogation," the Court in *Dutton* held the admitted statement was "sufficiently clothed with 'indicia' of reliability" that it was properly "placed before the jury though there is no confrontation with the declarant." In short, the "right of confrontation * * * is not absolute."

Because *Bruton* is grounded upon denial of the constitutional right of confrontation, it governs only in those instances in which "effective confrontation" was not possible. Such was the case in *Bruton,* for the codefendant who made the confession did not take the stand. Though language in that case suggested that a sufficient confrontation opportunity would exist only if the codefendant took the stand *and* "affirmed the statement as his," that position was later rejected in *Nelson v. O'Neil.*[11] There, the codefendant took the stand, denied making the confession, and asserted that the substance of it was false, and the Court reasoned that this placed defendant in a "more favorable" situation than if the codefendant had affirmed the statement as his. The Court in *Nelson* thus held "that where a codefendant takes the stand in his own defense, denies making an alleged out-of-court statement implicating the defendant, and proceeds to testify favorably to the defendant concerning the underlying facts, the defendant has been denied no rights protected by the Sixth and Fourteenth Amendments." But whether the codefendant admits or denies having made the statement, it has been questioned whether the opportunity for cross-examination sufficiently deals with the incriminated defendant's dilemma. So the argument goes, severance would be a much better remedy, for otherwise the fact remains that the jury will be considering as to that defendant evidence not admissible against him which has actually been highlighted by the cross-examination. Indeed, the cross-examination of one defendant by another may sometimes involve such conflict and antagonism between them that a severance will thereby be necessary.

Though the lesson of *Nelson* is that ordinarily any *Bruton* problem is avoided if the maker of the confession testifies at trial, this is not inevitably the case. For example, if the two defendants are represented by the same attorney, he can hardly engage in effective cross-examination on behalf of one client without discrediting the other, and thus his decision not to cross-examine or to do so only pro forma would constitute a violation of the *Bruton* rule. Notwithstanding *Nelson,* it has been held that a sufficient opportunity for cross-examination may have been afforded even if the maker of the confession does not testify at the criminal trial. Specifically, such opportunity has been held to be present where the confessing codefendant testified at an earlier proceeding, such as a hearing on his motion to suppress the confession, and could have been cross-examined about the

9. 400 U.S. 74, 91 S.Ct. 210, 27 L.Ed.2d 213 (1970).

10. On the other hand, the statement of a co-conspirator not on trial is not admissible where given in response to police interrogation upon being told he had been implicated by another, as "a reality of the criminal process [is] that once partners in a crime recognize that the 'jig is up,' they tend to lose any identity of interest and immediately became antagonists, rather than accomplices." Lee v. Illinois, 476 U.S. 530, 106 S.Ct. 2056, 90 L.Ed.2d 514 (1986).

11. 402 U.S. 622, 91 S.Ct. 1723, 29 L.Ed.2d 222 (1971).

confession at that time. This result is supported by *California v. Green,*[12] where the Supreme Court held that a witness' "preliminary hearing testimony was admissible as far as the Constitution is concerned wholly apart from the question of whether respondent had an effective opportunity for confrontation at the subsequent trial," in that his "statement at the preliminary hearing had already been given under circumstances closely approximating those that surround the typical trial." Though there is language in *Green* supporting the dubious proposition that an earlier "opportunity to cross-examine" would suffice, the Court has more recently cautioned that it has not yet decided what the result should be where in fact there was no questioning or only de minimus questioning.[13] And in *Lee v. Illinois,*[14] the state's argument that it was sufficient that defendant could have examined the maker of the confession at the suppression hearing was rejected; because the "function of a suppression hearing is to determine the voluntariness * * * of a confession," as to which the "truth or falsity of the statement is not relevant," there really "was no opportunity to cross-examine [the maker] with respect to the reliability of that statement."

Because the *Bruton* rule was stated in terms of "a codefendant's confession inculpating the defendant," sometimes the question is whether that has occurred. The courts are generally rather demanding in that regard, insisting that the challenged statements must be clearly inculpatory. It is not enough, the Court concluded in *Richardson v. Marsh,*[15] that the codefendant's confession provides "evidentiary linkage," that is, information which by itself does not incriminate the other defendant but which does have some tendency to link him to the crime when considered together with other evidence admitted at the trial (there, that an intent-to-kill statement was uttered by an accomplice on the way to the crime while the implicated defendant was, by his own testimony, in the car with the others). In refusing to extend *Bruton* to such a situation, the majority reasoned (i) that jury instructions, deemed insufficient in a true *Bruton* situation, would suffice as to the risk of mere "inferential incrimination"; (ii) that the pretrial redaction solution would not work in an "evidentiary linkage" case because the linkage would be apparent only at the conclusion of the case; and (iii) that the solution of severance in all cases of potential "evidentiary linkage" "would impair both the efficiency and the fairness of the criminal justice system."

Assuming now that a case falling within *Bruton* is identified in a pretrial setting, the question remaining is what alternative remedies exist.[16] One, of course, is severance of the implicated defendant. Another is a joint trial at which the prosecution elects to make no use of the confession. Yet another possibility is a joint trial at which the confession is admitted after it has been "redacted," that is, edited so as to delete any reference to the other defendant. But this solution will often

12. 399 U.S. 149, 90 S.Ct. 1930, 26 L.Ed.2d 489 (1970).

13. Ohio v. Roberts, 448 U.S. 56, 100 S.Ct. 2531, 65 L.Ed.2d 597 (1980).

14. 476 U.S. 530, 106 S.Ct. 2056, 90 L.Ed.2d 514 (1986).

15. 481 U.S. 200, 107 S.Ct. 1702, 95 L.Ed.2d 176 (1987).

16. In slightly different circumstances there may be no remedy other than jury instructions. Illustrative is Tennessee v. Street, 471 U.S. 409, 105 S.Ct. 2078, 85 L.Ed.2d 425 (1985), where Street testified at trial that his confession to murder and burglary had been coerced by the sheriff reading to him the prior confession of severed co-defendant Peele and then directing Street to say the same thing. Peele's confession was then admitted in rebuttal to show the several differences in the two confessions. The Court, after concluding that use of Peele's confession for this "legitimate, nonhearsay purpose" itself "raises no Confrontation Clause concerns," noted that the "only similarity to *Bruton* is that Peele's statement, like the codefendant's confession in *Bruton,* could have been misused by the jury." However, the Court concluded that in the present context the trial court's limiting instruction—that Peele's confession was to be considered "for the purpose of rebuttal only"—constituted an "appropriate way to limit the jury's use of that evidence in a manner consistent with the Confrontation Clause." This was because here, "unlike the situation in *Bruton,* there were no alternatives that would have both assured the integrity of the trial's truthseeking function and eliminated the risk of the jury's improper use of evidence." The already-granted severance did not solve the problem, and redaction of Peele's confession "would have made it more difficult for the jury to evaluate" Street's claim that his confession was a coerced imitation of Peele's.

not be feasible. For one thing, the maker of the confession is entitled to object if it is edited in such a way as to change its sense to his detriment, as where the deletion would leave out his claim of a valid defense. For another, the deletion must be effective in terms of removing a reference which will be perceived by the jury as referring to the codefendant. Though some courts unfortunately continue to uphold trial decisions to admit a *Bruton* confession with what amounts to a sham deletion, the better view is that it will not suffice to simply replace the defendant's name with an X, a blank, or the phrase "another person." Other alternatives have been used on occasion but have not been viewed with enthusiasm by appellate courts. One is a bifurcated joint trial at which the confession is withheld until the jury returns a verdict as to the implicated codefendant, and another is a joint trial utilizing a separate jury for each defendant which is allowed to be present only when evidence admissible against that defendant is received.

(c) Severance: Codefendant's Testimony Would Exculpate. A situation which is in some respects the reverse of that just discussed involves a request by one defendant for the severance of another defendant so that the latter can be called as a defense witness in the trial of the former. Even assuming such testimony is needed, the granting of a severance may be the only way by which it can be obtained. One defendant may not compel another defendant to testify in a joint trial. Moreover, the other individual is unlikely to want to give favorable testimony for his codefendant in a joint trial, for there are many tactical reasons why a defendant would wisely elect not to take the stand.

The seminal case on this subject is *United States v. Echeles,*[17] which provides a useful illustration. An attorney and his client were jointly charged with suborning perjury and perjury, respectively. In earlier proceedings involving the client, he had said that the attorney had not advised him to commit perjury. Consequently, the attorney asked for a severance so that the client could so testify at his trial, but the government opposed the motion and argued that there was no assurance the client would give such testimony even if the severance were granted. The appellate court held it was error to deny the attorney's severance motion, stating that "a fair trial for Echeles necessitated providing him the *opportunity* of getting the [client's] evidence before the jury, regardless of how we might regard the credibility of that witness or the weight of his testimony."

Although some other courts have viewed such severance requests sympathetically, in the main courts have viewed such tactics as an alibi-swapping device which is not to be encouraged. As a consequence, most courts place a much heavier burden upon the requesting defendant, typically requiring him to show that he would call the codefendant at a severed trial, that the codefendant would in fact testify, and that the testimony would be favorable to the moving defendant. This often is not an easy burden to meet. For one thing, the severance would not likely produce the testimony unless the defendant who is to give the testimony has already been tried, for if he has not yet been tried his testimony could be used against him at his later trial even if he does not then take the stand. By the simple device of declaring that a defendant seeking a severance has no right to dictate the order in which the two cases would be tried if severed, courts have been able to conclude that the requesting defendant has not carried his burden. Moreover, even if the testifying defendant *is* tried first, this alone will not inevitably wipe out any basis for his later claiming reliance upon the privilege against self-incrimination, and it does not seem that this defendant can somehow be forced to waive his privilege and promise to testify as a condition of the severance being granted. Based upon such considerations, courts often deny these severance motions because it has not been shown that the severed defendant would in fact testify when called upon to do so. Secondly, the moving defendant may be unable even to show that

17. 352 F.2d 892 (7th Cir.1965).

the testimony sought would be favorable. *Echeles* was a unique case because the codefendant's exoneration of his attorney was already a matter of record. Absent that, the moving defendant will have to do more than file conclusory affidavits that exculpatory testimony would be forthcoming, but may be confounded by the other defendant's reluctance to reveal the nature of his testimony. Finally, the moving defendant may be unable to establish that the testimony is sufficiently important, which is especially likely when courts reach the highly questionable conclusion that it is not enough that the testimony would corroborate other defense evidence.

(d) Severance: Conflicting Defenses and Strategies. The joint trial of defendants who truly have antagonistic defenses is most unfair, and thus the remedy of severance is needed to prevent the kind of trial described by one appellate court: "The trial was in many respects more of a contest between the defendants than between the people and the defendants. It produced a spectacle where the people frequently stood by and witnessed a combat in which the defendants attempted to destroy each other." [18] This is not to suggest, however, that a severance will necessarily be granted even when there is a rather significant difference between the defensive posture of the several defendants. It is common doctrine that a severance is necessary only if the defenses are mutually exclusive (i.e., belief of one compels disbelief of the other), and that the mere fact that there is hostility between defendants or that one may try to save himself at the expense of another is in itself alone not sufficient grounds to require separate trials. Similarly, it has been asserted that the fact the defendants have conflicting versions of what took place or the extent of their participation is a reason for rather than against a joint trial because it is easier for the truth to be determined if they all are tried together. Though courts in some jurisdictions are more sympathetic to antagonistic defense claims, often a failure to grant a severance motion will not be deemed error unless the defendants were directly accusing one another. The mere fact that the joined defendants have conflicting strategies is unlikely to be viewed as mandating an affirmative ruling on a severance motion.

Another kind of conflict situation is represented by *De Luna v. United States.*[19] There, de Luna and Gomez, after denial of a severance motion, were jointly tried on a narcotics charge. They were the occupants of a moving car from which police had seen Gomez throw a package of narcotics. Gomez testified that he was innocent, explaining that de Luna had thrown the package to him and told him to throw it out the window when the police approached. De Luna did not testify, but his lawyer argued that Gomez had the package at all times. Gomez's attorney commented on de Luna's failure to take the stand, and Gomez was acquitted but de Luna was convicted. On appeal his conviction was reversed because of the violation of his privilege against self-incrimination. But two members of the court went on to say that under these circumstances the proper result below would have been to permit the comment and grant a severance. This was because Gomez's "attorneys should be free to draw all rational inferences from the failure of a co-defendant to testify, just as an attorney is free to comment on the effect of any interested party's failure to produce material evidence in his possession or to call witnesses who have knowledge of pertinent facts."

But *De Luna* has had a limited impact. For one thing, it has been deemed not to require a severance when the defense attorney for the other defendant has merely called attention to the fact that his client had taken the stand, for in such instance it is thought to be a sufficient remedy that the defendant who elected not to testify could have a jury instruction in support of his exercise of the privilege. For another, some courts have held that *De Luna* applies only when it is counsel's *duty* to make a comment and that such duty arises only when the defenses are clearly antagonistic. Still others have rejected *De Luna*

18. People v. Braune, 363 Ill. 551, 2 N.E.2d 839 (1936).

19. 308 F.2d 140 (5th Cir.1962).

on the ground that its reasoning is defective. So the argument goes, there are no "rational inferences" to be drawn from a codefendant's silence, for, as the Supreme Court instructed in *Griffin v. California,*[20] even one "entirely innocent of the charge against him" might have a good reason [21] for staying off the stand. Moreover, a similar tactic could not have been utilized had there been a severance at the outset, for it is improper to call a witness it is known will claim his privilege against self-incrimination and then require him to make that claim in the presence of the jury.

(e) Severance: Guilt by Association. One of the inherent risks attending the joint trial of criminal defendants is that some defendants might be convicted only because of their association with others who were proved guilty at that trial. As Justice Jackson stated in his oft-quoted opinion in *Krulewitch v. United States* [22]: "There generally will be evidence of wrongdoing by somebody. It is difficult for the individual to make his own case stand on its own merits in the minds of jurors who are ready to believe that birds of a feather are flocked together." This is obviously so, but it is equally obvious that a defendant who shows no more than this common risk will not have established the prejudice which would entitle him to a severance. The harm from being so tainted would seem to be greatest as to relatively minor participants, but, while they may occasionally be held entitled to relief, there is certainly no general willingness to free minor figures from the risks and burdens of standing trial with more culpable associates.

A guilt-by-association claim takes on somewhat more substance when it is shown that highly prejudicial evidence admissible only against a co-defendant was or will be admitted at the joint trial. One situation is where a defendant is joined with another defendant whose substantial criminal record was admitted or will be admitted at trial. A few jurisdictions mandate severance in such circumstances, but most states approach the problem on an ad hoc basis and require the defendant to show actual prejudice before compelling severance. A *Bruton*-type analysis [23] would seem appropriate here, though it is well to note that unlike a *Bruton* confession, prior act evidence is not so inevitably prejudicial to co-defendants that the worth of limiting instructions can be totally discounted.

(f) Severance: Confusion of Evidence. Yet another basis upon which a severance of defendants might be sought is to avoid confusion by the factfinder. If the case is so confusing that the trier of fact cannot be expected to keep straight the evidence relating to the various defendants and counts, then surely a severance should be granted. But in face of the almost certain lack of evidence that the jury was actually confused, a defendant's complaint on appeal is likely to be dismissed as in *Opper v. United States* [24]: "To say that the jury might have been confused amounts to nothing more than an unfounded speculation that the jurors disregarded clear instructions of the court in arriving at their verdict." A claim of confusion may receive somewhat readier acceptance as the other disadvantages of joinder, such as guilt by association, also become apparent.

(g) Severance as of Right. At one time nearly half of the jurisdictions granted criminal defendants a severance as a matter of right, but now only a very few statutes so provide. Some have argued, however, that the uncertain benefits of joint trials and the mischief they so frequently work justify a statute or rule of court giving defendants a right to separate trials. Underlying the assumption that joint trials are more economical and minimize the burden of witnesses, prosecutors, and courts is the expectation that if defendants had a right of severance then

20. 380 U.S. 609, 85 S.Ct. 1229, 14 L.Ed.2d 106 (1965).

21. "Excessive timidity, nervousness when facing others and attempting to explain transactions of a suspicious character, and offenses charged against him, will often confuse and embarrass him to such a degree as to increase rather than remove prejudices against him." Wilson v. United States, 149 U.S. 60, 13 S.Ct. 765, 37 L.Ed. 650 (1893), quoted in *Griffin.*

22. 336 U.S. 440, 69 S.Ct. 716, 93 L.Ed. 790 (1949).

23. See § 17.2(b).

24. 348 U.S. 84, 75 S.Ct. 158, 99 L.Ed. 101 (1954).

each defendant would undergo a separate trial. But experience in at least one jurisdiction is to the contrary; what has ordinarily happened there is that upon conviction of one defendant at the first trial the severed defendants are induced to negotiate a guilty plea. Another consideration is that defendants generally have not fared well under rules requiring proof of prejudice: it is difficult to ascertain the degree of prejudice in advance of trial; once the trial is under way there is great reluctance to grant a severance and allow some defendants a fresh start; and on appeal there is even greater reluctance to find the trial judge's denial of the motion erroneous.

§ 17.3 Joinder and Severance: Procedural Considerations

(a) Court's Authority to Consolidate and Sever. Whether offenses or defendants are initially joined together for trial is a matter determined by the prosecuting attorney (or, in the case of an indictment, the prosecutor and the grand jury). If a defendant believes that the prosecutor has joined together offenses or defendants beyond that permitted by law, he may by motion challenge the prosecutor's action as misjoinder. Or, as we have seen, if a defendant believes the lawful joinder would be prejudicial to him in some way, he may seek a severance of offenses or of defendants. On occasion, the prosecutor may move for severance of offenses or defendants he had originally joined. Although it has occasionally been held that a prosecutor should not be granted a severance for lack of evidence, that position has been strongly criticized as running contrary to speedy trial interests.

Though the court must of course rule upon motions made by the prosecutor and defendant, the court also has authority of its own in determining what the scope of a pending trial will be. For one thing, the court will likely be empowered to consolidate existing charges. In the federal system, for example, the court "may order two or more indictments or informations or both to be tried together if the offenses, and the defendants if there is more than one, could have been joined in a single indictment or information." [1] Some states have comparable provisions, while elsewhere case law recognizes this authority as within the inherent power of the court. Under the better view, the court also had the power to order a severance, even when such action has not been specifically requested by either the prosecution or a defendant, because of the court's responsibility for the orderly progress of the trial.

(b) Misjoinder. The term "misjoinder" refers to the inclusion within a single charge of offenses or defendants which the law does not permit to be joined together. An apt illustration under the law of virtually all jurisdictions would be an instance in which a single indictment includes two offenses which are neither similar in character nor part of a single scheme or otherwise connected together in their commission. Misjoinder must be distinguished from certain other charging defects. It is different from "duplicity," the joining in a single count of two or more distinct and separate offenses, and from "multiplicity," the charging of a single offense in several counts. As to these latter two defects, the defendant is entitled upon timely demand to require the prosecution to elect which offense or which count, respectively, will be relied upon. By contrast, in the case of misjoinder the remedy is a separate trial of the misjoined offenses or defendants. What these three defects have in common is that neither duplicity, multiplicity, nor misjoinder constitutes grounds for dismissal of the charge.

Where a misjoinder has been shown to exist, in contrast to the case in which the joinder was initially proper but a severance is sought on grounds of prejudice, the trial judge has no discretion to deny a motion for severance. But there is not complete agreement on the question of whether a failure to grant the motion should inevitably require reversal on appeal. There was for years a split in the federal courts, but this conflict was resolved

§ 17.3

1. Fed.R.Crim.P. 13.

in *United States v. Lane,*[2] holding that "misjoinder under rule 8 of the Federal Rules of Criminal Procedure is subject to the harmless-error rule." The Court stressed that the argument for harmless error, applicable to most constitutional violations,[3] "is even stronger [here] because the specific joinder standards of Rule 8 are not themselves of constitutional magnitude"; and rather questionably opined that *Schaffer* (discussed below) applied here because in that case, once the court found the evidence to be insufficient on the count supporting joinder, there was "at that point in the trial * * * a clear error of misjoinder."

(c) Failure to Prove Joinder Basis. The misjoinder situation discussed above must be distinguished from that in which the charge is not defective on its face but at trial there is a failure to prove some fact on which the joinder rested. This might be the case, for example, where the conspiracy charge fails completely or as to a particular defendant, the conspiracy charged turns out to be several unrelated conspiracies, or two offenses alleged to be related turn out to be independent of one another. In such circumstances, it must be asked whether an affected defendant is entitled to relief equivalent to that in the misjoinder situation, to consideration for relief under some less demanding standard, or to no relief at all.

This question split the Supreme Court 5–4 in *Schaffer v. United States.*[4] The four-count indictment in that case charged: (1) that petitioners and the Stracuzzas transported stolen goods; (2) that Marco and the Stracuzzas transported other stolen goods; (3) that Karp and the Stracuzzas transported still other stolen goods; and (4) that all of them were joined in a single conspiracy to commit such offenses. At the close of the government's case the court dismissed the conspiracy count, but permitted the trial to proceed on the other counts. In affirming the petitioners' conviction, the *Schaffer* majority asserted that the validity of the joinder was to be determined solely by the allegations in the indictment and that consequently the issue was not one of misjoinder but rather whether a severance should have been ordered on grounds of prejudice. Because "the proof was carefully compartmentalized as to each petitioner," the Court concluded that the trial judge properly concluded no prejudice was present. While cautioning that in such circumstances "a trial judge should be particularly sensitive to the possibility of such prejudice," the majority in *Schaffer* declined to adopt "a hard-and-fast formula that, when a conspiracy count fails, joinder is error as a matter of law." The four dissenters, on the other hand, while stressing the potential for prejudice in such circumstances, challenged the majority's major premise. For them, an allegation in the charge is a sufficient basis for judging the validity of joinder only "at the preliminary stages," as "once it becomes apparent during the trial that the defendants have not participated 'in the same series' of transactions, it would make a mockery of Rule 8(b) to hold that the allegation alone, now known to be false, is enough to continue the joint trial."

One view of the *Schaffer* rule is that it may have the effect of encouraging an unscrupulous prosecutor to frame a baseless conspiracy count in order that several defendants, accused of similar but unrelated offenses, may be tried together. This is a legitimate concern, also reflected in the post-*Schaffer* authority that reversal would be required if bringing the conspiracy charge constituted bad faith on the part of the prosecutor in the sense that he lacked a reasonable expectation that sufficient proof of the charge would be forthcoming at trial. It is not easy for a defendant to show such bad faith.

The other view is that the *Schaffer* minority's position is unsound, because such a rigid sanction would require the prosecutor to undertake new trials even when there had been no prejudice. Moreover, the dissent's argument, in practice, might militate against the very result it seeks to achieve, as a trial judge

2. 474 U.S. 438, 106 S.Ct. 725, 88 L.Ed.2d 814 (1986).

3. See § 27.6(c).

4. 362 U.S. 511, 80 S.Ct. 945, 4 L.Ed.2d 921 (1960).

facing such a rigid rule might be extremely reluctant to dismiss the charge upon which joinder is founded.

The *Schaffer* situation must be distinguished from that in which the evidence *was* sufficient to go to the jury, but the jury then acquitted on the count which was the basis upon which the other counts were joined. In such circumstances, it is clear that the acquittal does not affect the propriety of joinder. As was conceded by the *Schaffer* dissenters, in such a case there "is then no escape from the quandary in which defendants find themselves. Once the conspiracy is supported by evidence, it presents issues for the jury to decide. What may motivate a particular jury in returning a verdict of not guilty on the conspiracy count may never be known."

(d) Waiver or Forfeiture. A defendant can lose his rights under joinder and severance law by failing to assert them in a timely fashion. This is true even in the instances of misjoinder; a defendant is thus well advised to raise that issue by pretrial motion, though a motion at trial would suffice at least when the circumstances establishing the misjoinder only then emerged. Misjoinder claims raised for the first time on appeal will not ordinarily be considered, though an exception may be made when the record reveals some circumstances explaining why the issue was not raised earlier.

Likewise, a claim that a severance should have been granted to avoid prejudice may be lost for failure to assert it in a timely fashion. Certainly a motion for severance is appropriate in advance of trial. However, in a pretrial setting the motion often can be assessed only in terms of the potential for prejudice, while events later occurring at trial may provide something more concrete in terms of actual prejudice. Thus, the fact a pretrial motion has been denied is no reason for not renewing the motion during the course of the trial. Indeed, failure to do so may operate to the defendant's detriment in one of several ways. While the Supreme Court in *Schaffer v. United States*[5] spoke of the trial judge's "continuing duty at all stages of the trial to grant a severance if prejudice does appear," this does not mean that a pretrial severance motion previously ruled upon somehow remains open for reconsideration without further efforts by the defendant. Failure to renew the motion at trial may be treated as a waiver of any severance claim, or at a minimum is likely to limit appellate review to the question of whether the judge properly decided the pretrial motion on the facts then available to him.

(e) Appellate Review of Prejudice Claim. On appeal, the defendant has the burden of showing that he was prejudiced by the joinder, and a reversal will ordinarily be forthcoming only if it appears there was a clear abuse of discretion by the trial judge. Appellate courts have traditionally relied on four doctrines to support a finding of absence of prejudice through joinder and to justify denial of relief. One is that the judge's instructions sufficed to confine the evidence to one offense or one defendant. But the Supreme Court has rejected it in one setting,[6] and it is dubious in other joinder contexts as well. It is not generally realistic to expect jurors to ignore relevant data once they have heard it, and limiting instructions are likely to do more harm by emphasizing the challenged evidence than good by erasing it. A second doctrine is that if the jury convicted as to some counts or defendants but not as to others, this shows that the jury carefully examined each count as to each defendant and rendered its verdict accordingly. But this ignores the possibility that absent the prejudicial joinder the jury might have acquitted on more counts or on all counts, and the same may be said for the third doctrine that any prejudice has been cured by concurrent sentencing. The fourth doctrine is that any prejudice is deemed harmless if, putting the prejudicial information to one side, defendant *could* still have been convicted on the balance of the evidence. But this involves considera-

5. 362 U.S. 511, 80 S.Ct. 945, 4 L.Ed.2d 921 (1960).

6. Bruton v. United States, 391 U.S. 123, 88 S.Ct. 1620, 20 L.Ed.2d 476 (1968).

ble speculation as to what the jury would have done under other circumstances.

§ 17.4 Failure to Join Related Offenses

(a) Collateral Estoppel. Usually the prosecutor will be in favor of as much joinder of offenses and defendants as he can get, while the defendant will want as much severance as can be obtained. But sometimes the prosecutor will want to maintain the opportunity to proceed with multiple trials, while the defendant prefers a prompt and unified disposition of all charges—or, if such a disposition is not undertaken, a bar to any subsequent related prosecutions. One possibility, discussed in the following subsections, is that on constitutional or other grounds a prosecution will be barred because of the failure of the prosecutor to join that charge with one earlier prosecuted. Another, of concern here, is that a verdict or finding of guilty in the second prosecution will be barred because it would be inconsistent with the result reached in the first prosecution.

This last notion, which goes by the name of "collateral estoppel," was given constitutional status in *Ashe v. Swenson.*[1] There, four armed men broke into the basement of a house and robbed six poker players and then fled in the car belonging to one of the victims. Ashe and three others were arrested shortly thereafter, and he and the others were charged with seven separate offenses—robbery of each of the poker players and theft of the car. Ashe was put on trial for robbery of victim Knight. The proof that the robbery had occurred was unassailable, but the evidence that Ashe was one of the robbers was weak. The defense never questioned the testimony about the occurrence of the robbery, but concentrated on exposing weaknesses in the identification of Ashe. The case went to the jury with instructions that if Ashe was in the group participating in this scheme he would be guilty whether or not he personally took the money from this particular victim; the jury returned a verdict of not guilty. Over his objection, Ashe was then tried for robbery of victim Roberts. The witnesses, essentially the same as in the prior trial, were now more certain of Ashe's identity, and Ashe was convicted. The Supreme Court reversed, reasoning:

> "Collateral estoppel" is an awkward phrase, but it stands for an extremely important principle in our adversary system of justice. It means simply that when an issue of ultimate fact has once been determined by a valid and full judgment, that issue cannot again be litigated between the same parties in any future lawsuit. Although first developed in civil litigation, collateral estoppel has been an established rule of federal criminal law [for] more than 50 years. * * *.
>
> Straightforward application of the federal rule to the present case can lead to but one conclusion. For the record is utterly devoid of any indication that the first jury could rationally have found that an armed robbery had not occurred, or that Knight had not been a victim of that robbery. The single rationally conceivable issue in dispute before the jury was whether the petitioner had been one of the robbers. And the jury by its verdict found that he had not. The federal rule of law, therefore, would make a second prosecution for the robbery of Roberts wholly impermissible.
>
> The ultimate question to be determined, then, * * * is whether this established rule of federal law is embodied in the Fifth Amendment guarantee against double jeopardy. We do not hesitate to hold that it is. For whatever else that constitutional guarantee may embrace, * * * it surely protects a man who has been acquitted from having to "run the gauntlet" a second time.

Although *Ashe* represents an important principle, it must be recognized at the outset that this collateral estoppel defense will not often be available to a criminal defendant, for it is seldom possible to determine how the judge or jury has decided any particular issue. For example, in the not atypical criminal case in which the crime consists of elements *A, B, C* and *D* and the defendant interposes defenses *X* and *Y*, and the case goes to the jury on

§ 17.4

1. 397 U.S. 436, 90 S.Ct. 1189, 25 L.Ed.2d 469 (1970).

instructions to convict only if it is found that facts *A, B, C* and *D* all exist and that neither *X* nor *Y* exist, the jury's verdict of "not guilty" will not itself reveal what the jury decided as to *A, B, C, D, X* or *Y*. In such a situation, the Court in *Ashe* instructed, it will be necessary to "examine the record of a prior proceeding, taking into account the pleadings, evidence, charge, and other relevant matter, and conclude whether a rational jury could have grounded its verdict upon an issue other than that which the defendant seeks to foreclose from consideration." But unless this inquiry shows that *all* the issues in the first trial are also present in the second one or, as in *Ashe,* that there was but one "rationally conceivable issue in dispute" at the first trial, that will be the end of the collateral estoppel claim.

If a defendant at the first trial wishes to act in a fashion which will maximize his chance of being able to make a collateral estoppel defense later, he is placed in a dilemma. He must either put only a few of his defenses in issue, thus assuring a collateral-estoppel effect in any future proceedings but at the same time increasing the risk of a conviction in this trial, or he must put all the defenses he has before the jury, thereby better shielding himself against a conviction but destroying the possibility of any future collateral-estoppel effect on the issues raised. It has been suggested that the solution is to utilize special verdicts in criminal cases, but this procedure is generally not available and is disadvantageous to a criminal defendant in other respects. In some jurisdictions a defendant tried by the court may upon request have the judge find the facts specially, which is another way the defendant can overcome this problem—at the price of surrendering his right to jury trial.

In trying to determine whether a particular factual matter has been determined adversely to the prosecution, it is especially important to consider the legal theory underlying the prior trial. Illustrative is *Turner v. Arkansas,*[2] where, some time after petitioner, his brother, Yates and a fourth person played poker, Yates was robbed and murdered. Turner was charged with murder on a felony-murder theory and acquitted, after which he was charged with the robbery. The state's theory was that this second prosecution was not foreclosed by the earlier acquittal, for it might have occurred because the jury concluded that both Turner and his brother robbed Yates but that only the brother actually committed the murder. But the Court responded that if the jury had "found petitioner present at the crime scene, it would have been obligated to return a verdict of guilty of murder" even in those circumstances, as revealed by the judge's instructions that any party to the felony would be guilty of felony murder. Of course, even if it is correct to say that the jury was "obligated" to convict on such facts,[3] it is possible that the jury in the first trial disregarded those instructions and acquitted because it believed Turner should not be convicted of murder merely because of his participation in a robbery where his brother actually did the killing. Thus *Turner* indicates, in effect, that such possibilities are not to be taken into account in applying the *Ashe* rule. By like token, *Ashe* has been applied even where the first trial involved only an implicit acquittal, that is, where the jury returned no verdict on the offense charged but did return a guilty verdict on a lesser included offense.

In *Ashe,* the Court made note of the fact that the prosecutor there "frankly conceded" that "it treated the first trial as no more than a dry run for the second prosecution." But this does not mean that *Ashe* is inapplicable just because the prosecution's conduct can be viewed somewhat more sympathetically. The Court so held in *Harris v. Washington,*[4] in which the state court had declined to apply *Ashe* where the issue of identity had not been "fully litigated" at the first trial because the trial judge had excluded evidence on grounds having "no bearing on the quality of the evidence." The Court reversed, holding that

2. 407 U.S. 366, 92 S.Ct. 2096, 32 L.Ed.2d 798 (1972).

3. On jury nullification, see § 22.1(g).

4. 404 U.S. 55, 92 S.Ct. 183, 30 L.Ed.2d 212 (1971).

"the constitutional guarantee applied, irrespective of whether the jury considered all relevant evidence, and irrespective of the good faith of the State in bringing successive prosecutions." But this last observation should not be taken to mean that a defendant who himself is responsible for the separate disposition of the several charges against him may invoke the *Ashe* rule. In *Ohio v. Johnson,*[5] where defendant, charged with both murder and manslaughter based on the same killing and robbery and theft based on the same taking, entered a guilty plea over the state's objection to manslaughter and theft, the Supreme Court held that he could not rely on *Ashe* even if those offenses were mutually exclusive of the murder and robbery charges still pending. The Court explained that "in a case such as this, where the State has made no effort to prosecute the charges seriatim, the considerations of double jeopardy protection implicit in the application of collateral estoppel are inapplicable."

Because the Court in *Ashe* said that once "an issue of ultimate fact has once been determined * * * that issue cannot again be litigated," it is of course necessary to consider whether the issue in the second proceedings is actually the same as the issue decided in the earlier criminal trial. This requires, for one thing, consideration of the burden and standard of proof applicable in the two proceedings, as is indicated by *One Lot Emerald Cut Stones v. United States.*[6] One Klementova had been acquitted on charges of smuggling certain goods into the United States, after which the government instituted a civil forfeiture action with respect to those goods. In holding that he had no valid *Ashe* defense to this action, the Court reasoned that

> the difference in the burden of proof in criminal and civil cases precluded application of the doctrine of collateral estoppel. The acquittal of the criminal charges may have only represented " 'an adjudication that the proof was not sufficient to overcome all reasonable doubt of the guilt of the accused.' " * * * As to the issue raised, it does not constitute an adjudication on the preponderance-of-the-evidence burden application in civil proceedings.[7]

Thus, the acquittal only is a bar to a later determination that there is *not* a reasonable doubt on the same fact issue. This is why most jurisdictions which have passed on the issue have held that an acquittal in a criminal proceeding does not bar revocation of parole or probation on the underlying charge. The failure to prove guilt beyond a reasonable doubt does not foreclose proof of the same crime by a preponderance of the evidence at the later revocation proceedings. (From this it might be thought that if the revocation proceedings come first and not even the preponderance standard is met then the government is barred by *Ashe* from trying to show the same crime beyond a reasonable doubt in a criminal prosecution, but this is not so for the reason that no jeopardy attached at the revocation proceeding.) Special circumstances may produce different results; thus, where at the prior criminal trial the defendant successfully defended on grounds of entrapment, as to which he had the burden of proof by a preponderance of the evidence, this is a bar to a later determination in a revocation hearing that he did commit the crime. On similar reasoning, the Court held in *Dowling v. United States*[8] that notwithstanding a defendant's prior acquittal of a certain crime, evidence of that crime may be received in a later prosecution under some exception to the "other crimes" rule (e.g., that it helps show identity or motive in the instant case). In such a situation, proof of the prior crime is an "evidentiary fact" rather than an "ultimate fact" in the second prosecution, and as such it is not a matter the prosecution must now prove beyond a reasonable doubt but rather is a matter which, if proved by a preponderance of the evidence, can contribute to a conviction

5. 467 U.S. 493, 104 S.Ct. 2536, 81 L.Ed.2d 425 (1984).

6. 409 U.S. 232, 93 S.Ct. 489, 34 L.Ed.2d 438 (1972).

7. To the same effect is United States v. One Assortment of 89 Firearms, 465 U.S. 354, 104 S.Ct. 1099, 79 L.Ed.2d 361 (1984).

8. 493 U.S. 342, 110 S.Ct. 668, 107 L.Ed.2d 708 (1990). The Court also rejected the contention that introduction of that evidence failed the due process test of "fundamental fairness."

beyond a reasonable doubt for the second crime.

Burden of proof issues aside, it still must be determined whether there is an identity of issues in the two proceedings, for only if there is can *Ashe* be used as a defense. The *One Lot Emerald Cut Stones* case also provides a useful illustration of this point. At the earlier criminal trial for smuggling, the government had to prove both the physical act of unlawful importation and the mental state of intent to defraud, and in the trial to the court the judge expressly found that the government had failed to establish intent. That being so, the acquittal could in no event bar the later forfeiture proceedings at which there was no need to prove such intent. Ascertaining whether the issues in the two cases are identical is not always that easy, as is illustrated by those decisions on whether two killings were sufficiently proximate that a finding of not guilty by reason of insanity in the first murder trial foreclosed conviction in the second murder trial. The same may be said of those decisions on whether an acquitted defendant may be prosecuted for perjury based upon his exonerating testimony given at the earlier trial, where the exact nature and breadth of the testimony is likely to be determinative.

Some other limitations upon the *Ashe* collateral estoppel rule remain to be briefly noted. For one thing, there must have been a valid final judgment in the earlier case, which means, for example, that no estoppel can be based upon an informal probation-like disposition which involved neither verdict nor judgment or upon a judge's dismissal on the merits which was beyond his power because done in the absence of a waiver of jury trial. But the judgment need not be one of acquittal as in *Ashe,* and thus a defendant may not be prosecuted for an assault which occurred during a robbery after he was convicted of receiving the fruits of that robbery from another party. Perhaps the result is otherwise if the conviction is on a guilty plea, for in the *Johnson* case[9] the Court in rebuffing defendant's collateral estoppel claim asserted that "the taking of a guilty plea is not the same as an adjudication on the merits after full trial, such as took place in *Ashe.*" As for the "issue of ultimate fact" requirement, this means that a defendant cannot use *Ashe* to foreclose a ruling on an issue of law contrary to that made in the earlier case, or to prevent a factual determination contrary to one which was not of the "ultimate" kind in the first trial (e.g., that a certain witness was not credible). And the "same parties" requirement means that under *Ashe* one defendant cannot take advantage of another defendant's prior acquittal, just as one sovereign cannot be barred from prosecuting because of a factual determination concerning the same defendant in a trial by another sovereign.

Can collateral estoppel operate against the defendant, so that if defendant Ashe had been convicted at his first trial he would have been barred from making a mistaken identity defense at the second trial? The prevailing view is no, and the Supreme Court has assumed that the result in such circumstances is so apparent as not to require extended discussion. In *Simpson v. Florida,*[10] where two men entered a store and robbed the manager and a customer, Simpson was convicted of robbing the manager, when that conviction was overturned for a defect in jury instructions he was acquitted of robbing the manager, and then he was prosecuted for robbing the customer. The state court characterized the two prior trials as presenting a "double collateral estoppel" which presumably left both sides free to dispute whether or not Simpson was one of the robbers. In rejecting that line of reasoning as "plainly not tenable," the Court noted that "had the second trial never occurred, the prosecutor could not, while trying the case under review, have laid the first jury verdict before the trial judge and demanded an instruction to the jury that, as a matter of law, petitioner was one of the armed robbers in the store that night."

9. See text at note 5 supra.

10. 403 U.S. 384, 91 S.Ct. 1801, 29 L.Ed.2d 549 (1971).

Finally, it must be emphasized that the foregoing comments are directed only at the *Ashe* collateral estoppel doctrine, grounded in the Fifth Amendment guarantee against double jeopardy. Issue preclusion in a criminal law context may occur for other reasons. For one thing, it has been suggested that there may be another constitutionally-based collateral estoppel rule, this time derived from the due process clause, upon which a defendant could rely even as to pretrial rulings not governed by *Ashe* because jeopardy had not attached. And then of course there is the real possibility that the jurisdiction in question may have developed a good deal of law on collateral estoppel which is not grounded in the Constitution at all but which nonetheless could be utilized to advantage by a criminal defendant. This largely explains why collateral estoppel decisions going beyond those heretofore discussed are to be found. Illustrative are decisions finding collateral estoppel even though the sovereign or defendant was not the same in the two cases or even though the second proceeding involved a lower burden of proof on the government than the earlier criminal prosecution. It also explains why, at least as to matters not going to guilt or innocence, principles of collateral estoppel are sometimes applied both against and in favor of criminal defendants.

(b) Double Jeopardy: Same Offense. A second way in which the Constitution prohibits a prosecution because of a failure to join the charge in an earlier trial is illustrated by *Brown v. Ohio.*[11] On November 29 Brown stole a car from a parking lot in one Ohio county and on December 8 was apprehended while driving the car in another Ohio county. Charged there with joyriding on that date, Brown pled guilty, after which he was indicted in the first county for auto theft and joyriding on November 29, and his conviction for the latter crimes was affirmed by the state court despite his double jeopardy objection. The Supreme Court first set out to interpret the double jeopardy clause of the Fifth Amendment, which states that no person shall "be subject for the same offence to be twice put in jeopardy of life or limb," and concluded that offenses could be the "same" for jeopardy purposes without being "identical." The Court then took note of the long-standing *Blockburger* test,[12] which originated as a device for determining congressional intent as to cumulative sentencing: "The applicable rule is that where the same act or transaction constitutes a violation of two distinct statutory provisions, the test to be applied to determine whether there are two offenses or only one, is whether each provision requires proof of an additional fact which the other does not." And the Court in *Brown* then held:

> If two offenses are the same under this test for purposes of barring consecutive sentences at a single trial, they necessarily will be the same for purposes of barring successive prosecutions. * * * Where the judge is forbidden to impose cumulative punishment for two crimes at the end of a single proceeding, the prosecutor is forbidden to strive for the same result in successive proceedings.

The Court deemed it unnecessary to explain or justify this parallelism, and it was accepted even by the dissenters in *Brown,* though the proposition is by no means an obvious one. Certainly it might be argued that when one offense is contained entirely within the other, so that one is the greater and the other the lesser included, then punishment only for one (certainly the greater) should be the limit, but that the happenstance of an earlier prosecution for the lesser should not bar a later prosecution for the greater, after which again the defendant could be required to serve only one sentence (that for the greater crime, with a deduction for time already served for the lesser).[13] Indeed, the notion accepted in

11. 432 U.S. 161, 97 S.Ct. 2221, 53 L.Ed.2d 187 (1977).

12. Blockburger v. United States, 284 U.S. 299, 52 S.Ct. 180, 76 L.Ed. 306 (1932).

13. Cf. Ohio v. Johnson, 467 U.S. 493, 104 S.Ct. 2536, 81 L.Ed.2d 425 (1984), where defendant, charged with murder and manslaughter based on the same killing and robbery and theft based on the same taking, entered a guilty plea to the two lesser offenses over the state's objection. Defendant's claim that under *Brown* he could not be tried for the murder and robbery was rejected because defendant was solely responsible for the separate disposition; see note 20 infra. But defendant also raised

Brown that the successive prosecution and cumulative punishment issues are governed by the same test appears now to have been rejected by a majority of the Court. In *Albernaz v. United States,*[14] concerning the question of cumulative punishment, the Court treated *Blockburger* as only a method for ascertaining legislative intent when nothing more concrete was available. It was said that "the question of what punishments are constitutionally permissible is not different from the question of what punishment the Legislative Branch intended to be imposed." Thus, as the Court later put it in *Missouri v. Hunter,*[15] where "a legislature specifically authorizes cumulative punishment under two statutes, regardless of whether those two statutes proscribe the 'same' conduct under *Blockburger,* a court's task of statutory construction is at an end and the prosecutor may seek and the trial court or jury may impose cumulative punishment under such statutes in a single trial."

Having adopted the *Blockburger* test, the Court in *Brown* then proceeded to apply it to the facts of the particular case. Looking to the definitions of joyriding and auto theft under Ohio law, the Court determined that the former consists of taking or operating a vehicle without the owner's consent and the latter of joyriding plus intent permanently to deprive the owner of possession. That is, the relationship of the two offenses was that of concentric circles rather than overlapping circles, and thus they were the "same" under *Blockburger* unless the time factor dictated a different result. Though the state court had concluded that the two prosecutions were distinct because based upon separate acts nine days apart, the Supreme Court responded that as a matter of Ohio law only a single continuing offense was involved. This somewhat dubious characterization of Ohio law, seemingly critical to the outcome in view of the Court's apparent concession that the result would be otherwise if Ohio law made each day of joyriding a separate offense, may have been made in order to avoid other difficult issues.

The Court in *Brown* commented at one point that "the sequence is immaterial," and this proved to be true in the subsequent case of *Harris v. Oklahoma.*[16] There Harris was convicted of felony murder on proof that his companion shot and killed a clerk during a robbery of a store by two men. Though proof of the underlying felony of robbery with firearms was necessary for the felony murder conviction, Harris was thereafter tried and convicted of that felony. The Supreme Court reversed, holding that "the Double Jeopardy Clause bars prosecution for the lesser crime after conviction of the greater one."

With respect to the *Blockburger* test, the Court in *Brown* asserted the critical question is "whether each provision requires proof of an additional fact which the other does not." In *Brown* itself, this involved nothing more than a comparison of the statutory elements of the two crimes; as noted earlier, auto theft was simply joyriding with the additional element of intent to permanently deprive. But, does this mean that if two statutory provisions are such that violation of one does not inevitably involve a violation of the other that the offenses are not the "same" under *Brown?* No, the Court answered in *Illinois v. Vitale,*[17] citing the *Harris* decision as an illustration. In *Harris,* as the Court now explained it, the

a cumulative punishment type of double jeopardy claim, grounded in "the Ohio Supreme Court's determination that the Ohio legislature did not intend cumulative punishment for the two pairs of crimes involved here." The court responded: "While the Double Jeopardy Clause may protect a defendant against cumulative punishments for convictions on the same offense, the Clause does not prohibit the State from prosecuting respondent for such multiple offenses in a single prosecution." Reference was also made to the *Pearce* concept of credit for time previously served, see § 24.4(d), suggesting that the Court deemed it possible notwithstanding the Ohio sentencing scheme to, e.g., sentence for the murder despite the earlier sentence for manslaughter, provided only the higher sentence was served and provided also that credit was given for any time served on the manslaughter conviction.

14. 450 U.S. 333, 101 S.Ct. 1137, 67 L.Ed.2d 275 (1981).

15. 459 U.S. 359, 103 S.Ct. 673, 74 L.Ed.2d 535 (1983). See also Garrett v. United States, 471 U.S. 773, 105 S.Ct. 2407, 85 L.Ed.2d 764 (1985).

16. 433 U.S. 682, 97 S.Ct. 2912, 53 L.Ed.2d 1054 (1977).

17. 447 U.S. 410, 100 S.Ct. 2260, 65 L.Ed.2d 228 (1980).

"felony murder statute on its face did not require proof of a robbery to establish felony murder, other felonies could underlie a felony-murder prosecution," but yet the Court held the subsequent robbery prosecution barred because of the earlier felony-murder prosecution where that same robbery was used as the necessary felony. In essence, *Harris* indicated that in comparing "each provision" as *Brown* required, some attention to the theory of the prosecutions was also necessary: once it appeared that the robbery was the felony relied upon in the earlier felony-murder prosecution, that felony became a lesser included "same" offense under *Brown–Blockburger.*

But then came *Grady v. Corbin,*[18] in which the Court asserted that *Blockburger* itself involved only "a technical comparison of the elements of the two offenses" and that *Harris* in fact illustrated that the Court had "not relied exclusively on the *Blockburger* test to vindicate the Double Jeopardy Clause's protection against multiple prosecutions." The Court in *Corbin* thus held that "the Double Jeopardy Clause bars any subsequent prosecution in which the government, to establish an essential element of an offense charged in that prosecution, will prove conduct that constitutes an offense for which the defendant has already been prosecuted."[19] To distinguish *Dowling v. United States,*[20] the Court stressed that the "critical inquiry is what conduct the State will prove, not the evidence the State will use to prove that conduct." This expanded version of the double jeopardy protection, the *Corbin* majority explained, was necessary to protect criminal defendants from the ordeal of multiple prosecutions which would give "the State an opportunity to rehearse its presentation of proof, thus increasing the risk of an erroneous conviction for one or more of the offenses charged."

Corbin illustrates application of the new rule to a clearly non-*Blockburger* situation. The defendant was involved in an automobile accident in which one person was killed and another injured. He received traffic tickets for driving while intoxicated and crossing the median, pleaded guilty to those offenses a few weeks later, and then raised a double jeopardy objection when he was later indicted for, inter alia, criminally negligent homicide and reckless assault. The prosecution's bill of particulars specified the negligent and reckless acts as (1) driving under the influence, (2) crossing the median, and (3) driving too fast for conditions. The Court ruled that because the state had thus "admitted that it will prove the entirety of the conduct for which Corbin was convicted [earlier] to establish essential elements of the homicide and assault offenses," the double jeopardy clause barred the prosecution. But, the Court added, this prosecution would not be barred if the state were to amend its bill of particulars to rely "solely on Corbin's driving too fast."

The extent to which this concession really is true is not entirely clear, for the parameters of the new *Corbin* rule are themselves less than certain. Even if the prosecution's recklessness-negligence theory is limited to the defendant's speed, presumably the testimony about the accident in the homicide-assault trial would include evidence that the defendant's speeding car crossed the median and struck the car in which the deceased and injured parties were riding. Is that enough to bring *Corbin* into play? True, *Corbin* says the proof must have been "to establish an essential element of an offense," but is this not (as the *Corbin* dissenters claim) "a meaningless limitation" because *all* the prosecution's evidence has that tendency? And in any event, may it not be contended that in the scenario now under discussion the crossing of the median *is* being offered "to establish an essential element," namely, that the speeding recklessness-negligence was the cause of the harm?

18. ___ U.S. ___, 110 S.Ct. 2084, 109 L.Ed.2d 548 (1990).

19. When, as in *Harris,* the greater offense is prosecuted first, the proposition must be stated somewhat differently. As *Corbin* put it: "if in the course of securing a conviction for one offense the State necessarily has proved the conduct comprising all of the elements of another offense not yet prosecuted * * *, the Double Jeopardy Clause would bar subsequent prosecution of the component offense."

20. 493 U.S. 342, 110 S.Ct. 668, 107 L.Ed.2d 708 (1990), summarized at note—supra.

The "proves conduct" part of *Corbin* may also prove a source of difficulty; as the dissenters ask with respect to the present scenario, does this even include evidence defendant's car was weaving or that it ended up on the wrong side of the road after the accident? And, if the testimony of weaving is not enough, what if defense counsel seeks the clarification by which the witness then indicates defendant crossed the median? These questions suggest that if the *Corbin* rule is to be at all workable, it will need to be rather narrowly construed.

The *Brown* rule, barring the prosecution in separate trials of several crimes which are the "same" for double jeopardy purposes, is not absolute. As noted in *Brown,* an exception "may exist where the State is unable to proceed on the more serious charge at the outset because the additional facts necessary to sustain that charge have not occurred or have not been discovered despite the exercise of due diligence." The Court cited *Diaz v. United States,*[21] which is an apt illustration, for there the victim died after the defendant was convicted of assault and battery. Despite the tentative nature of the language used in *Brown,* such an exception is sound, for in such circumstances the inconvenience to the defendant is clearly outweighed by the public's interest in assuring that the defendant does not fortuitously escape responsibility for his crimes.

But a plurality of the Supreme Court has now indicated its willingness to extend this exception beyond instances of actual necessity. In *Garrett v. United States,*[22] the defendant, two months after pleading guilty to importing marijuana, was charged with engaging in a continuing criminal enterprise, which requires proof of three or more successive violations of a certain type within a set period of time. At trial, the government's proof in that respect included the earlier importation offense, which the plurality deemed permissible under *Brown* simply because "the continuing criminal enterprise charged against Garrett in Florida had not been completed at the time that he was indicted" on the importing charge. While the dissenters[23] objected the exception was not applicable because all the facts needed to prove a continuing criminal enterprise of shorter duration existed prior to that indictment, the plurality deemed it irrelevant "whether the Government could [at the time of the importing charge] have successfully indicted and prosecuted Garrett for a different continuing criminal enterprise" of less expansive temporal dimensions. For them, the exception in *Brown* is not limited to instances in which the government absolutely could not have charged the offenses together, but rather is based also on the notion that "one who at the time the first indictment is returned is continuing to engage in other conduct found criminal" cannot complain about multiple prosecutions. *Garrett* thus lends no support to the claim that mere prosecutorial oversight falls within the *Diaz* exception. Consequently, in the previously-discussed *Corbin* case the Court deemed it of no significance that the assistant prosecutor who was handling the traffic charges to which defendant pleaded guilty was unaware there had been a fatality, then under investigation by another assistant prosecutor.[24]

The Court also cautioned in *Brown* that the case did not "raise the double jeopardy questions that may arise * * * after a conviction is reversed on appeal." Stressing that in *Brown* the defendant did not overturn the first conviction but rather served the sentence assessed for that crime, the Court held in *Montana v. Hall*[25] that if a defendant does obtain a reversal of the first conviction, then

21. 223 U.S. 442, 32 S.Ct. 250, 56 L.Ed. 500 (1912).

22. 471 U.S. 773, 105 S.Ct. 2407, 85 L.Ed.2d 764 (1985).

23. Stevens, J., joined by Brennan and Marshall, JJ. O'Connor, J., concurring, found "merit to this position" of the dissenters, but reached "a different conclusion upon balancing the interests protected by the Double Jeopardy Clause," including the desirability of allowing the government to decide prosecution is warranted whenever "the defendant continues unlawful conduct after the time the Government prosecutes him for a predicate offense." Powell, J., took no part in the decision.

24. The Court stated: "With adequate preparation and foresight, the State could have prosecuted Corbin for the offenses charged in the traffic tickets and the subsequent indictment in a single proceeding."

25. 481 U.S. 400, 107 S.Ct. 1825, 95 L.Ed.2d 354 (1987).

he may thereafter be prosecuted for another crime which is the "same" offense for double jeopardy purposes.[26] Such a case, the Court reasoned, "falls squarely within the rule that retrial is permissible after a conviction is reversed on appeal." [27]

Because of the separate sovereigns exception to the double jeopardy clause,[28] clearly no *Brown* issue is presented when the crime involved in the earlier prosecution, no matter how similar in its elements to the present one, was an offense against another sovereign. What remains unclear, however, is whether when the sovereign is the same the failure to join the "same" offenses in the first prosecution may be excused because the court in which the first prosecution was commenced could not have tried the other offense. On the subject of exceptions, *Brown* cites to a footnote in Justice Brennan's concurring opinion in *Ashe v. Swenson* [29] which recognized the *Diaz* type of exception and then said: "Another exception would be necessary if no single court had jurisdiction of all the alleged crimes." It is unfortunate that the issue went unrecognized in *Brown,* for the facts of that case reveal the nature of the problem. Though never mentioned by the Court, the first prosecution was in a different county than the second one, and it would appear that while the county of the first prosecution could as it did prosecute there for the continuing crime of joyriding, it probably could not prosecute for the crime of theft in the other county. Presuming that to be so, it might be asked whether the defendant should be entitled to complain about the impossible failure to join the theft charge in the first trial.

One way to look at that problem, especially if a change of venue to the county in which both offenses occurred was a possibility, is by asking whether the lack of joinder should be placed at the feet of the prosecutor or the defendant. That this is a relevant inquiry was recognized by the Court in *Jeffers v. United States.*[30] There, defendant was charged in two separate indictments with conspiracy to distribute drugs and conducting a continuing criminal enterprise to violate the drug laws, respectively. The government moved to join the charges for trial, but defendant objected on the ground that much of the evidence admissible on the conspiracy count would not be admissible on the other charge, and thus the court denied the motion. In upholding defendant's subsequent separate convictions for these two offenses, the Court stated: "If the defendant expressly asks for separate trials on the greater and the lesser offenses, or, in connection with his opposition to trial together, fails to raise the issue that one offense might be a lesser included offense of the other, [an] exception to the *Brown* rule emerges." Because "he was solely responsible for the successive prosecutions," his "action deprived him of any right that he might have had against consecutive trials." The exact scope of the *Jeffers* rule is uncertain.[31] For one

26. At the first trial, defendant was convicted of incest, but that conviction was reversed on appeal because at the time of defendant's conduct the incest statute was not applicable to sexual assaults upon stepchildren. Relying upon *Brown,* the state supreme court ruled that retrial on a charge of sexual assault, grounded in the very same conduct, was barred.

27. See § 25.4(a).

28. See § 25.5.

29. 397 U.S. 436, 90 S.Ct. 1189, 25 L.Ed.2d 469 (1970).

30. 432 U.S. 137, 97 S.Ct. 2207, 53 L.Ed.2d 168 (1977).

31. The Court has more recently decided a case which did not clarify matters because it involved a situation the Court rightly declared was "an even clearer case than *Jeffers.*" In Ohio v. Johnson, 467 U.S. 493, 104 S.Ct. 2536, 81 L.Ed.2d 425 (1984), where defendant was charged in a single indictment with both murder and manslaughter for the same killing and robbery and theft for the same taking, and defendant entered a guilty plea to the two lesser offenses and thus "offered only to resolve part of the charges against him, while the State objected to disposing of any of the counts against respondent without a trial," the Court held *Brown* inapplicable because "respondent's efforts were directed to separate disposition of counts in the same indictment where no more than one trial of the offenses charged was ever contemplated."

In light of *Johnson,* what then if the defendant pleaded guilty to a minor offense before the state got around to charging (and possibly joining) a greater offense? In Grady v. Corbin, ___ U.S. ___, 110 S.Ct. 2084, 109 L.Ed.2d 548 (1990), the defendant pleaded guilty to traffic offenses without revealing that the accident had resulted in a fatality (unknown to the assistant prosecutor handling the traffic charges, but then under investigation by another assistant prosecutor). The Court accepted the state court's "characterization of the proceedings," namely, that defendant and his counsel "should not be expected to *volunteer* information that is likely to be highly damaging," but cautioned it "need not decide whether our

thing, the Court by footnote said that the "considerations relating to the propriety of a second trial obviously would be much different if any action by the Government contributed to the separate prosecutions." This indicates, at a minimum, that where defendant is not "solely responsible," as where the government obtains separate indictments and defendant merely fails to seek their joinder for trial, *Jeffers* is not controlling. Secondly, the Court notes that in the instant case "trial together of the [two] charges could have taken place without undue prejudice to petitioner's Sixth Amendment right to a fair trial," thus indicating that the result would be different if defendant's waiver of his rights under *Brown* was necessitated by the need to protect some other constitutional right.

(c) "Same Transaction" Joinder. In *Ashe v. Swenson,*[32] Justice Brennan, joined by two other members of the Court, indicated he would resolve the issue at hand (whether a defendant acquitted of one robbery on mistaken identity grounds could be tried for another robbery occurring at the same time and place and obviously committed by the same person) by redefining the "same offence" part of the double jeopardy clause to mean "same transaction" rather than "same evidence." The latter, traditional definition, he objected,

> does not enforce but virtually annuls the constitutional guarantee. For example, where a single criminal episode involves several victims, under the "same evidence" test a separate prosecution may be brought as to each. * * * The "same evidence" test permits multiple prosecutions where a single transaction is divisible into chronologically discrete crimes. * * * Even a single criminal act may lead to multiple prosecutions if it is viewed from the perspective of different statutes. * * * Given the tendency of modern criminal legislation to divide the phases of a criminal transaction into numerous separate crimes, the opportunities for multiple prosecutions for an essentially unitary criminal episode are frightening. And given our tradition of virtually unreviewable prosecutorial discretion concerning the initiation and scope of a criminal prosecution, the potentialities for abuse inherent in the "same evidence" test are simply intolerable. * * *
>
> In my view, the Double Jeopardy Clause requires the prosecution, except in most limited circumstances, to join at one trial all the charges against a defendant which grow out of a single criminal act, occurrence, episode, or transaction. This "same transaction" test of "same offence" not only enforces the ancient prohibition against vexatious multiple prosecutions embodied in the Double Jeopardy Clause, but responds as well to the increasingly widespread recognition that the consolidation in one lawsuit of all issues arising out of a single transaction or occurrence best promotes justice, economy, and convenience.

Although a majority of the Court has refused to accept the "same transaction" test as a constitutional imperative,[33] several states have adopted that standard as matter of local law. By statute, rule of court or judicial decision, a number of jurisdictions now provide that the prosecutor must join (or, that on motion of the defendant, there must be joined) all offenses arising out of the same transaction. But some have criticized this trend:

> The absurdity of the "same transaction" standard can be easily illustrated. Assume that one breaks and enters a building to commit larceny of an automobile, does thereafter in fact steal the automobile and drive away, killing the night watchman in the process, and two blocks away runs a red light which brings about his arrest by the municipal police. Could it be said with any logic that a plea of guilty to breaking and entering would bar a subsequent prosecution for murder? If so, presumably a plea of guilty to the traffic of-

double jeopardy analysis would be any different if affirmative misrepresentations of fact by a defendant or his counsel were to mislead a court into accepting a guilty plea it would not otherwise accept."

32. 397 U.S. 436, 90 S.Ct. 1189, 25 L.Ed.2d 469 (1970).

33. Brown v. Ohio, 432 U.S. 161, 97 S.Ct. 2221, 53 L.Ed.2d 187 (1977). In Grady v. Corbin, text at note 18 supra, the Court noted that *if* the "same transaction" test were the law it "would bar the homicide and assault prosecutions even if the State were able to establish the essential elements of those crimes without proving the conduct for which Corbin previously was convicted." The dissenters objected that the *Corbin* rule would in practice "come down to" a same transaction test.

fense would likewise, since all arise out of the "same transaction." [34]

However, this problem and others which might arise from an unqualified application of the "same transaction" standard can be overcome by various limitations upon its use, such as: that the offenses must be within the jurisdiction of a single court; that the offenses must have been known by the prosecutor at the time he commenced the first prosecution; that as to offenses charged the burden is on the defendant to move for joinder; or that entry of a plea of guilty or nolo contendere does not bar later prosecution for other offenses which are part of the same transaction.

34. State v. Conrad, 243 So.2d 174 (Fla.App.1971).

Chapter 18

SPEEDY TRIAL AND OTHER PROMPT DISPOSITION

Table of Sections

---

§ 18.1 The Constitutional Right to Speedy Trial

(a) Generally. The Sixth Amendment to the Constitution provides that "[i]n all criminal prosecutions, the accused shall enjoy the right to a speedy * * * trial." This right, the Supreme Court has noted, "is as fundamental as any of the rights secured by the Sixth Amendment."[1] For one thing, the right to speedy trial "has its roots at the very foundation of our English law heritage."[2] Recogni-

§ 18.1

1. Klopfer v. North Carolina, 386 U.S. 213, 87 S.Ct. 988, 18 L.Ed.2d 1 (1967).

2. Ibid. Even if the proceeding is not within the "criminal prosecutions" category of the Sixth Amendment, its nature may be such that as a matter of due process comparable protection is provided by the Constitution. See United States v. Eight Thousand Eight Hundred and Fifty Dollars, 461 U.S. 555, 103 S.Ct. 2005, 76 L.Ed.2d 143 (1983) (in forfeiture action under 31 U.S.C.

tion of a right to speedy justice has been traced back to the twelfth century, and it was articulated in Magna Carta. The importance of this right was acknowledged in the earliest days of this nation, and today virtually all state constitutions also expressly guarantee the right. It is not surprising, therefore, that the Sixth Amendment right applies not only to prosecutions in the federal courts,[3] but also to state prosecutions through the Fourteenth Amendment due process clause.[4]

(b) Interests Involved. As the Supreme Court explained in *Smith v. Hooey,*[5] the constitutional right to speedy trial protects "at least three basic demands of criminal justice in the Anglo–American system: '[1] to prevent undue and oppressive incarceration prior to trial, [2] to minimize anxiety and concern accompanying public accusation and [3] to limit the possibilities that long delay will impair the ability of an accused to defend himself.' " As for the first of these, clearly the disadvantages for the accused who cannot obtain his pretrial release are most serious. The time spent in jail awaiting trial often means loss of a job; it disrupts family life; and it enforces idleness. Moreover, if a defendant is locked up, he is hindered in his ability to gather evidence, contact witnesses, or otherwise prepare his defense. The second interest on the list concerns even the defendant who has been able to secure his release on bail. While the criminal charges are outstanding, he may be subjected to public scorn, deprived of employment, and chilled in the exercise of his First Amendment rights of speech and association. But of the three interests, "the most serious is the last, because the inability of a defendant adequately to prepare his case skews the fairness of the entire system. If witnesses die or disappear during a delay, the prejudice is obvious. There is also prejudice when defense witnesses are unable to recall accurately events of the distant past." [6]

In *Barker v. Wingo,*[7] the Court declared that the right to a speedy trial "is generically different from any of the other rights enshrined in the Constitution for the protection of the accused" because

> there is a societal interest in providing a speedy trial which exists separate from, and at times in opposition to, the interests of the accused. The inability of courts to provide a prompt trial has contributed to a large backlog of cases in urban courts which, among other things, enables defendants to negotiate more effectively for pleas of guilty to lesser offenses and otherwise manipulate the system. In addition, persons released on bond for lengthy periods awaiting trial have an opportunity to commit other crimes. * * * Moreover, the longer an accused is free awaiting trial, the more tempting becomes his opportunity to jump bail and escape. Finally, delay between arrest and punishment may have a detrimental effect on rehabilitation.
>
> If an accused cannot make bail, he is generally confined * * * in a local jail. This contributes to the overcrowding and generally deplorable state of those institutions. Lengthy exposure to these conditions "has a destructive effect on human character and makes the rehabilitation of the individual offender much more difficult." At times the result may even be violent rioting. Finally, lengthy pretrial detention is costly. * * * In addition, society loses wages which might have been earned, and it must often support families of incarcerated breadwinners.

But, while this is a useful explanation of why society should be interested in the prompt disposition of criminal cases, it is rather misleading to say, as it is put in *Barker,* that this "societal interest" is somehow part of the right. The fact of the matter is that the Bill

§ 1102(a), whether post-seizure delay violates due process is not to be determined by the *Lovasco* rule for pre-arrest/charge delay in criminal cases, discussed in § 18.5(b), as the "more apt analogy is to a defendant's right to a speedy trial," and thus the *Barker* balancing test, discussed in § 18.2 governs).

3. Beavers v. Haubert, 198 U.S. 77, 25 S.Ct. 573, 49 L.Ed. 950 (1905).

4. Klopfer v. North Carolina, 386 U.S. 213, 87 S.Ct. 988, 18 L.Ed.2d 1 (1967).

5. 393 U.S. 374, 89 S.Ct. 575, 21 L.Ed.2d 607 (1969).

6. Barker v. Wingo, 407 U.S. 514, 92 S.Ct. 2182, 33 L.Ed.2d 101 (1972).

7. 407 U.S. 514, 92 S.Ct. 2182, 33 L.Ed.2d 101 (1972).

of Rights does not speak of the rights and interests of the government. Moreover, to assert that this "societal interest" might well be disserved if the defendant was to surrender his right (or, indeed, even to insist that it not be honored) is not to point out anything which makes the speedy trial right different from other Sixth Amendment rights.

(c) When Right Attaches. In *United States v. Marion*[8] the Court was called upon to determine when the speedy trial right attaches. The government appealed the dismissal of a business fraud indictment two months following its return based upon defendants' claim that the 38–month delay between the end of the scheme charged and the indictment violated their speedy trial right. The Supreme Court reversed. It was first noted that the Sixth Amendment on its face applies "only when a criminal prosecution has begun and extends only to those persons who have been 'accused' in the course of that prosecution," and thus "would seem to afford no protection to those not yet accused, nor would [it] seem to require the Government to discover, investigate, and accuse any person within any particular period of time." Most important, however, was the fact that the defendant's position did not square with the previously noted purposes of the speedy trial guarantee:

> Arrest is a public act that may seriously interfere with the defendant's liberty, whether he is free on bail or not, and that may disrupt his employment, drain his financial resources, curtail his associations, subject him to public obloquy, and create anxiety in him, his family and his friends. * * * So viewed, it is readily understandable that it is either a formal indictment or information or else the actual restraints imposed by arrest and holding to answer a criminal charge that engage the particular protections of the speedy trial provisions of the Sixth Amendment.
>
> Invocation of the speedy trial provision thus need not await indictment, information, or other formal charge. But we decline to extend the reach of the amendment to the period prior to arrest. Until this event occurs, a citizen suffers no restraints on his liberty and is not the subject of public accusation: his situation does not compare with that of a defendant who has been arrested and held to answer. Passage of time, whether before or after arrest, may impair memories, cause evidence to be lost, deprive the defendant of witnesses, and otherwise interfere with his ability to defend himself. But this possibility of prejudice at trial is not itself sufficient reason to wrench the Sixth Amendment from its proper context. Possible prejudice is inherent in any delay, however short; it may also weaken the Government's case.[9]

Because in *Marion* "the indictment was the first official act designating appellees as accused individuals," the speedy trial right attached at the time of indictment. But, as the language quoted above makes apparent, had an arrest preceded the formal charge the right would have attached at the time of that arrest.[10]

The general rule that the speedy trial right attaches at the time of arrest or formal charge, whichever comes first, is easy to apply in most cases, but on occasion it may be unclear exactly what point in time governs. If the first critical event is indictment but the indictment is sealed until some later time, the Sixth Amendment right attaches on the date of unsealing, as there has been neither oppressive incarceration nor public accusation until then. The assumption seems to be that the possibility of prejudice to the defense from such delay is standing alone not enough to invoke the speedy trial right. A charging document short of an indictment, such as a complaint, will suffice if it alone gives the court jurisdiction to proceed to trial. Problems can arise where after the initial charge some other charge is filed against the same defendant. It is difficult to generalize about this situation, except to say that the date of

8. 404 U.S. 307, 92 S.Ct. 455, 30 L.Ed.2d 468 (1971).

9. But, as the Court later said in United States v. Lovasco, 431 U.S. 783, 97 S.Ct. 2044, 52 L.Ed.2d 752 (1977), in such circumstances "the Due Process Clause has a limited role to play in protecting against oppressive delay." On just how limited it is, see § 18.5(b).

10. Dillingham v. United States, 423 U.S. 64, 96 S.Ct. 303, 46 L.Ed.2d 205 (1975).

the first charge is more likely to be deemed controlling if the second charge is a refinement of the first rather than a charge of different crimes arising out of the same incident. In any event, continuous custody of the defendant between the two charges when there is some relationship between them makes it more likely the earlier date will be deemed controlling.

When the first event is arrest, the question may be whether in a nature-of-the-offense sense that arrest is sufficiently related to the later formal charge to be viewed as part of the same criminal prosecution for speedy trial purposes. Though it would be absurd if an arrest on one charge triggered the Sixth Amendment's speedy trial protection as to any other chargeable offenses, the result may well be otherwise if the crimes ultimately prosecuted really only gild the charge underlying the initial arrest. A variation of the problem arises when the arrest is made by a jurisdiction other than that which later returns the charge, as where state officers apprehend a person for a violation of local law but that individual is later turned over to federal authorities for prosecution based upon the same or related conduct. Where the initial arrest is solely for violation of state law, then it is generally accepted that this arrest does not mark the commencement of the speedy trial right as to a subsequent federal charge even if based on the same activity, a result which is consistent with the dual sovereignty limitation upon the double jeopardy guarantee.[11] But where there is close state-federal cooperation in the investigation preceding the arrest or significant federal involvement promptly after the arrest, a contrary result may be justified.

(d) Waiver or Forfeiture of the Right. A defendant's claim that his Sixth Amendment right to speedy trial was violated must be brought before the trial court by a timely motion to dismiss the charges. If the defendant fails to so move and instead enters a guilty plea or submits to trial, he may not raise the issue for the first time on appeal. The right is that of the defendant rather than his attorney, and thus counsel cannot waive this constitutional right over his client's objection. Failure of defense counsel to raise a speedy trial objection could in some circumstances constitute ineffective assistance of counsel, which perhaps explains why appellate courts not infrequently assess speedy trial claims even when there was no timely motion for dismissal below. If a defendant made a timely motion for dismissal on speedy trial grounds but it was denied, and the defendant thereafter entered a plea of guilty or nolo contendere, then under the traditional view he may not ordinarily obtain appellate review of the speedy trial claim. This rule has been criticized on the ground that a defendant who has interposed what he believes to be a valid speedy trial objection should not have to surrender it in order to obtain whatever benefits are to be derived from pleading guilty, and has been put into serious question by the Supreme Court's decisions on what rights are forfeited by a guilty or nolo plea.[12]

(e) Remedy for Violation. In *United States v. Strunk,*[13] where defendant's denial of a speedy federal trial occurred while he was serving a state prison sentence, the court concluded:

> The remedy for a violation of this constitutional right has traditionally been the dismissal of the indictment or the vacation of the sentence. Perhaps the severity of that remedy has caused courts to be extremely hesitant in finding a failure to afford a speedy trial. Be that as it may, we know of no reason why less drastic relief may not be granted in appropriate cases. Here no question is raised about the sufficiency of evidence showing defendant's guilt, and, as we have said, he makes no claim of having been prejudiced in presenting his defense. In these circumstances, the vacation of the sentence and a dismissal of the indictment would seem inappropriate.

The court thus ordered that defendant receive credit on his sentence for the period of imper-

11. See § 25.5.

12. See § 21.6(a).

13. 467 F.2d 969 (7th Cir.1972).

missible delay, reasoning that this would compensate him for the lost opportunity to serve part of the federal sentence concurrently with the state sentence. But a unanimous Supreme Court reversed, noting that delay even in a situation such as this "may subject the accused to an emotional stress" and that as a result "the prospect of rehabilitation may also be affected." The Court thus concluded: "In light of the policies which underlie the right to a speedy trial, dismissal must remain * * * 'the only possible remedy.'"[14] One commentator, doubtless sharing the lower court's view that the availability of lesser sanctions would make courts more willing to find that a violation had occurred, has argued that dismissal with prejudice should be reserved for those cases in which there was a possible impairment of defendant's ability to defend himself or in which such a powerful sanction "is needed to compel prosecutorial obedience to norms of speedy trial which judges cannot otherwise enforce."[15]

§ 18.2 The Constitutional Balancing Test

(a) The *Barker* Case. Manning and Barker were arrested in July of 1958 for killing an elderly couple and were indicted in September. The prosecution believed it had a stronger case against Manning and that Barker could not be convicted unless Manning testified against him, so Manning was prosecuted first, but it took six trials until finally, in December of 1962, he had been convicted of the two murders. In the meantime, a series of continuances were granted as to Barker, who after 10 months in jail obtained his release on bond. Barker raised no objection until the twelfth continuance was sought in February 1962 and he failed to object to some later continuances, though he did object to continuances granted in March and June of 1963 because of the unavailability of a prosecution witness. He was tried over objection in October 1963 and convicted, and his speedy trial contention was later rejected by the state and lower federal courts. The Supreme Court affirmed in *Barker v. Wingo,*[1] but in the process "attempted to set out the criteria by which the speedy trial right is to be judged."

Noting first the "amorphous quality of the right," the Court examined "two rigid approaches" urged "as ways of eliminating some of the uncertainty." One, the proposal that the Court "hold that the Constitution requires a criminal defendant to be offered a trial within a specified time period," was rightly rejected on the ground that it "would require this Court to engage in legislative or rulemaking activity." The other proposal was that the Court adopt "the demand-waiver doctrine," which "provides that a defendant waives any consideration of his right to speedy trial for any period prior to which he has not demanded a trial." This was rejected as "inconsistent with this Court's pronouncements on waiver of constitutional rights," whereunder the test is whether there has been "an intentional relinquishment or abandonment of a known right or privilege."[2] Mere lack of demand does not evidence such a waiver, especially because defense counsel is often "in an awkward position" in deciding whether and when to make such a demand. Moreover, nonapplication of the waiver doctrine to this particular constitutional right on the ground "that delay usually works for the benefit of the accused" would be improper, as "it is not necessarily true that delay benefits the defendant."

The Court in *Barker* thus proceeded to adopt "a balancing test, in which the conduct of both the prosecution and the defendant are weighed," and to "identify some of the factors which courts should assess in determining whether a particular defendant has been deprived of his right." They are: (1) the length of the delay; (2) the reason for the delay; (3) whether and when the defendant asserted his speedy trial right; and (4) whether defendant

14. Strunk v. United States, 412 U.S. 434, 92 S.Ct. 2260, 37 L.Ed.2d 56 (1973).

15. Amsterdam, Speedy Criminal Trial: Rights and Remedies, 27 Stan.L.Rev. 525, 535 (1975).

§ 18.2

1. 407 U.S. 514, 92 S.Ct. 2182, 33 L.Ed.2d 101 (1972).

2. Johnson v. Zerbst, 304 U.S. 458, 58 S.Ct. 1019, 82 L.Ed. 1461 (1938).

was prejudiced by the delay. In finding no constitutional denial in the instant case, the Court utilized these factors as follows: (1) the delay, well over five years, "was extraordinary"; (2) there was good reason for 7 months of delay while a witness was unavailable, and some delay so that Manning could be tried first was proper, but a 4–year delay for the latter reason was too long given the state's failure or inability to try Manning promptly; (3) for a long time defendant did not assert his right, and this was a calculated tactical decision based on the hope that Manning would be acquitted and the case against him dropped; (4) the prejudice "was minimal" as, though he lived "for over four years under a cloud of suspicion and anxiety," most of this time he was free on bail, and there was no showing his defense at trial was prejudiced.

(b) The Length of the Delay. With respect to this first factor, the Court in *Barker* declared that "length of the delay is to some extent a triggering mechanism," so that "[u]ntil there is some delay which is presumptively prejudicial, there is no necessity for inquiry into the other factors that go into the balance." The reference to "delay which is presumptively prejudicial" is somewhat confusing, but viewing the case in its entirety it seems fair to say that this phrase does *not* mean a period of time so long that it may actually be presumed the defense at trial would be impaired. Nor does it mean that once a sufficient time has been shown the prosecution has the burden of establishing that in fact there was no prejudice. The Court apparently meant that a claim of denial of speedy trial may be heard after the passage of a period of time which is, prima facie, unreasonable in the circumstances.

The Court in *Barker* says that this length of time is "dependent upon the peculiar circumstances of the case," and by way of example it is added that "the delay that can be tolerated for an ordinary street crime is considerably less than for a serious, complex conspiracy charge." What this illustration is intended to reveal about the kind of "peculiar circumstances" deserving of notice is far from clear. Perhaps it is meant to show that it takes more time to trigger further inquiry when the nature of the case is more complex and thus in need of more trial preparation. But if that is the point, then it may be criticized on two counts: the example really does not reflect such a distinction; and to the extent the prosecutor by reason of the nature of the charge or otherwise is hampered by special difficulties, this could best be taken into account under the reason-for-delay factor. The lower courts have been inclined to apply this first *Barker* factor without any extensive assessment of the unique facts of the particular case. Rather, the courts have usually tried to settle upon some time period after which, as a general matter, it makes sense to inquire further into why the defendant has not been tried more promptly. Generally, any delay of eight months or longer is deemed "presumptively prejudicial," any delay of less than five months is not, while there is judicial disagreement as to the six to seven month range.

In determining whether the requisite period of time has passed, it is necessary of course to know how the counting is to be done. In the usual case, this is simply a matter of calculating the time which has elapsed from when the Sixth Amendment right attached[3] until trial (or, until the pre-trial motion to dismiss on this ground is determined). But when the situation is out of the ordinary it may be necessary, as to certain portions of this intervening period, to determine whether the circumstances then prevailing were such that the interests protected by the Sixth Amendment right were implicated. Such was the approach taken in *Klopfer v. North Carolina*,[4] where defendant was indicted in February 1964 for criminal trespass but the prosecutor in August 1965 obtained a "*nolle prosequi* with leave," which served to toll the statute of limitations but left the prosecutor free to reinstate the prosecution on that indictment at some future date. Though the state court ruled that the subsequent delay was not relevant to defendant's speedy trial claim, the

3. See § 18.1(c).

4. 386 U.S. 213, 87 S.Ct. 988, 18 L.Ed.2d 1 (1967).

Supreme Court disagreed, noting that even though the defendant was free without recognizance he was nonetheless subject to "anxiety and concern" because of the continuing pendency of the indictment.

But in *United States v. MacDonald,*[5] the Court held that the time between dismissal of military charges and the subsequent indictment on civilian charges may not be considered in determining whether the delay in bringing the defendant to trial violated his Sixth Amendment right to speedy trial. The majority reasoned that once charges are dismissed the person is no longer a subject of public accusation and has no restraints on his liberty, a situation analogous to that in *United States v. Marion,*[6] holding the Sixth Amendment protection inapplicable in a pre-arrest, pre-indictment situation. *Klopfer* was distinguished as a case in which the charges were suspended rather than dismissed.

MacDonald rather than *Klopfer* was deemed controlling in *United States v. Loud Hawk,*[7] holding that the time during which the government appealed the district court's dismissal of the indictment, while the defendants were not incarcerated and not subject to bail (and could not have been subjected to any actual restraints without further judicial proceedings), was not to be counted. This was because there was neither public accusation nor restraint of liberty during that period; mere "public suspicion" flowing from the fact that "the Government's desire to prosecute them was a matter of public record" was not deemed sufficient to trigger Sixth Amendment protections.

(c) Reason for Delay. As for the second *Barker* factor, "the reason the government assigns to justify the delay," the Court cautioned that "different weights should be assigned to different reasons." Three categories of reasons were then listed: (1) a "deliberate attempt to delay the trial in order to hamper the defense," which "should be weighed heavily against the government"; (2) a "more neutral reason such as negligence or overcrowded courts," which "should be weighed less heavily but nevertheless should be considered since the ultimate responsibility for such circumstances must rest with the government"; and (3) "a valid reason, such as a missing witness," which "should serve to justify appropriate delay."

The initial question which must be asked is where the burden lies to supply the reasons in a particular case. The reference to "the reason the government assigns" indicates that the burden is on the government. As a practical matter, however, this is likely to mean that the prosecution is afforded an opportunity to show a reason which falls in the "valid" category, failing which the case will be treated as if there was a "more neutral reason." This is because a reason which is to be heavily weighed against the government will rarely be admitted or otherwise apparent from the record. And when the government simply offers no explanation at all, it has been held that the court can presume neither a deliberate attempt to hamper the defense nor a valid reason for the delay.

Although the first of the three categories put in *Barker* might be objected to on the ground that the balancing procedure should not continue once an inexcusable breach of the state's acknowledged duty appears, the lower courts, in compliance with *Barker,* proceed with the balancing even when it is determined that there is present in the case a reason for delay which is to be weighed heavily against the government. With respect to the second category, the illustration of "negligence" has sometimes been questioned on the ground that it seems more logically joined to the invalid reason than to the unavoidable condition of docket crowding. But it is well to remember that this second category, involving such reasons as negligence, court congestion, and an understaffed prosecutor's office, should not be described (as sometimes is the case) as the "neutral reason" category; after all, "the duty of the charging authority is to

5. 456 U.S. 1, 102 S.Ct. 1497, 71 L.Ed.2d 696 (1982).

6. 404 U.S. 307, 92 S.Ct. 455, 30 L.Ed.2d 468 (1971).

7. 474 U.S. 302, 106 S.Ct. 648, 88 L.Ed.2d 640 (1986).

provide a prompt trial,"[8] and thus such reasons weigh against the government albeit "less heavily than intentional delay."[9]

It must be stressed, as to the Court's third category, that while it is called "a valid reason" this does not mean that existence of a reason falling within this grouping will necessarily compel the conclusion that defendant's speedy trial rights were not violated. This is but one of the four factors in the balancing test and, as is highlighted by the Court's statement that such a reason will "justify appropriate delay," even a valid reason does not necessarily permit delay indefinitely. And certainly a close look at the circumstances of the particular case is in order. To take, for example, the Court's hypothesis of a missing witness, it is appropriate to determine how important the witness is, why he is missing, and how hard the government has looked to find him. Courts have recognized several other situations which fall within the "valid reason" category, such as incompetency of the defendant, the unavailability of the defendant, the unavailability of a codefendant in a joint trial situation, interlocutory appeal by the prosecution, and the necessity to rule on defendant's pretrial motions.

The reason-for-delay factor was assessed with respect to interlocutory appeals "when the defendant is subject to indictment or restraint"[10] in *United States v. Loud Hawk.*[11] As for the rare case in which such an appeal may be and is taken by a defendant, the Court stated that where the defendant's claim is clearly without merit he cannot complain about appellate delay, and that even if it was "meritorious" he would have a "heavy burden of showing an unreasonable delay," for a defendant "normally" cannot complain about the very process he invoked. As for government appeal, the Court said it "ordinarily is a valid reason that justifies delay" (i.e., in *Barker* category (3)), but seemed to acknowledge that a particular case could fall into category (2) because of crowded appellate courts or into category (1) if the prosecution misused the appellate process. Thus, courts must consider "the strength of the Government's position on the appealed issue, the importance of the issue in the posture of the case, and—in some cases—the seriousness of the crime."

(d) Defendant's Responsibility to Assert the Right. Although *Barker* rejected the notion that failure to demand a speedy trial constitutes a waiver of that right, the Court hastened to add that this "does not mean, however, that the defendant has no responsibility to assert his right." The Court thus held that "the defendant's assertion of or failure to assert his right to a speedy trial is one of the factors to be considered." Assertion of the right, the Court said, "is entitled to strong evidentiary weight," but yet it was cautioned that not all demands need to be assessed in the same way; the "frequency and force of the objections" should be taken into account. Thus, a mere pro forma demand will not count for much, and even a more substantial demand is weakened where the defendant subsequently engaged in delaying tactics or indicated a desire not to be tried promptly.

The Court in *Barker* deemed it important to "emphasize that failure to assert the right will make it difficult for a defendant to prove that he was denied a speedy trial." Consequently, lower courts rather readily assume that a lack of demand indicates that the defendant really did not want a prompt trial. It is important, however, to examine carefully the circumstances of the particular case. As the Court cautioned in *Barker,* a case in which the defendant knowingly fails to object to ongoing delay is quite different from "a situation in which his attorney acquiesces in long delay without adequately informing his client, or from a situation in which no counsel is appointed." Moreover, failure to make a demand can hardly be counted against the defendant during those periods when he was

8. Dickey v. Florida, 398 U.S. 30, 90 S.Ct. 1564, 26 L.Ed.2d 26 (1970).

9. Strunk v. United States, 412 U.S. 434, 93 S.Ct. 2260, 37 L.Ed.2d 56 (1973).

10. On this limitation, see the discussion of *Loud Hawk* in § 18.2(b).

11. 474 U.S. 302, 106 S.Ct. 648, 88 L.Ed.2d 640 (1986).

unaware that charges had been lodged against him or when he was incompetent.

(e) Prejudice. As for the final factor of prejudice, *Barker* teaches that it must "be assessed in the light of the interests of defendants which the speedy trial right was designed to protect": (i) to prevent oppressive pretrial incarceration; (ii) to minimize anxiety and concern of the accused; and (iii) to limit the possibility that the defense will be impaired. As with the previous three factors, *Barker* treats prejudice as neither "a necessary or sufficient condition to the finding of a deprivation of the right of speedy trial," and thus, as the Court later held, it is a "fundamental error" to say that a defendant cannot prevail unless he makes an affirmative showing of prejudice.[12] Just when a defendant will succeed without such a showing is a matter on which the courts are not in complete agreement. It is sometimes said that defendant must have shown bad motives by the prosecutor, sometimes that the other three factors must be in defendant's favor, and sometimes that they must weigh heavily in his favor.

As for prejudice of the first type, it is noteworthy that in *Barker* the defendant's incarceration for 10 months was not deemed sufficiently oppressive to call for a ruling in his favor. Lower courts have reached the same conclusion as to substantially longer periods of imprisonment. As for the second type of prejudice, it is always present to some extent, and thus absent some unusual showing is not likely to be determinative in defendant's favor. The third type of prejudice, as the Court stressed in *Barker,* is "the most serious." One kind of situation described by the Court is where witnesses die or disappear. As to this, some substantiation is required; generally, it may be said that the defendant must show that the witness truly is now unavailable, that he would have been available for a timely trial, and that his testimony would have been of help to the defendant. Another variation of the third type of prejudice noted in *Barker* is where "defense witnesses are unable to recall accurately events of the distant past." As to this, special note must be taken of the Court's caution that loss of memory "is not always reflected in the record because what has been forgotten can rarely be shown." This suggests, at a minimum, that courts should not be overly demanding with respect to proof of such prejudice. And to some it suggests that in instances of lengthy delay the burden should be on the prosecution to show an absence of prejudice.

12. Moore v. Arizona, 414 U.S. 25, 94 S.Ct. 188, 38 L.Ed.2d 183 (1973).

§ 18.3 Statutes and Court Rules on Speedy Trial

(a) The Need. It is apparent that the *Barker* speedy trial doctrine is not standing alone adequate to deal with the matter of prompt disposition of criminal cases. For one thing, *Barker* and related cases "have * * * tended to convert the right of every criminal defendant to have a speedy trial into a very different sort of right: the right of a few defendants, most egregiously denied a speedy trial, to have the criminal charges against them dismissed on that account."[1] Quite obviously, criminal defendants as a class need some additional basis upon which to compel the government to try them promptly. Secondly, the *Barker* balancing test, as the Court fully recognized, of necessity has an "amorphous quality" to it, for unlike what can be done via "legislative or rulemaking activity," there is "no constitutional basis for holding that the speedy trial right can be quantified into a specified number of days or months." Finally, notwithstanding the articulation in *Barker* of the "societal interest" in speedy trial, it is clear from the manner in which the Court proceeds to describe the factors to be placed in the balance (especially "the defendant's responsibility to assert his right") that this societal interest will not be sufficiently protected by the Sixth Amendment alone.

All of this points up the need for and significance of other law dealing with the subject of

§ 18.3

1. Amsterdam, Speedy Criminal Trial: Rights and Remedies, 27 Stan.L.Rev. 525 (1975).

speedy trial. Such other law exists in all jurisdictions. On the federal level, there is the Speedy Trial Act of 1974; as for the states, rules of court or statutes impose prompt trial requirements. These rules and statutes are sometimes rather complex, as is true of the federal legislation, and elsewhere contain little detail, in which case a process of "fleshing-out" by court decision has typically occurred.

(b) Federal Speedy Trial Act of 1974. The Speedy Trial Act of 1974 [2] imposes time requirements for the trial of criminal cases in the federal courts. Because this Act worked a rather dramatic change in federal law in this respect, a five-year transition period was provided for; the final time limits and sanctions became effective only at the end of that time. This transition period allowed the federal courts to engage in research and planning which would facilitate compliance with the statutory requirements and provide a basis for recommending changes in the Act.

As for the time limits provided under the Act, an indictment or information is to "be filed within thirty days from the date on which such individual was arrested or served with a summons in connection with such charges," except that if in a felony case no grand jury was in session during that time the period "shall be extended an additional thirty days." As for trial, it is to "commence within seventy days from the filing date (and making public) of the information or indictment, or from the date the defendant has appeared before a judicial officer of the court in which such charge is pending, whichever date last occurs." The Act also protects the defendant from undue haste, for absent defendant's consent "the trial shall not commence less than thirty days from the date on which the defendant first appears through counsel or expressly waives counsel and elects to proceed pro se." [3]

The Act specifies the point at which the counting of the time to charge and to trial is to be commenced in certain special circumstances. If the charge was dismissed on motion of the defendant but he is later charged "with the same offense or an offense based on the same conduct or arising from the same criminal episode," then the time is to be calculated "with respect to such subsequent complaint, indictment, or information, as the case may be." If a charge was dismissed but reinstated following an appeal, then trial must ordinarily commence "within seventy days from the date the action occasioning the retrial becomes final." As for a second trial occasioned by a mistrial, order for new trial, appeal or collateral attack, again the retrial must ordinarily begin "within seventy days from the date the action occasioning the retrial becomes final."

As for the "periods of delay" which "shall be excluded in computing the time" for charge or trial, the Act specifies the following:

(1) any "period of delay resulting from other proceedings concerning the defendant," such as examinations and other proceedings to determine competency to stand trial, trial of other charges, interlocutory appeal, transfer to another district, consideration of a proposed plea agreement, "delay resulting from any pretrial motion, from the filing of the motion through the conclusion of the hearing on, or other prompt disposition of, such motion," and delay up to 30 days "during which any proceeding concerning the defendant is actually under advisement by the court." [4]

2. 18 U.S.C.A. §§ 3161–3174. The Act was amended in 1979. The discussion which follows is of the Act as amended and without reference to provisions which are of no effect after the transitional period.

3. In United States v. Rojas–Contreras, 474 U.S. 231, 106 S.Ct. 555, 88 L.Ed.2d 537 (1985), the Court held that this 30–day period does not begin to run anew upon the filing of a superseding indictment; that the authority of the court under 3161(h)(8) to grant an "ends of justice" continuance "should take care of any case in which the Government seeks a superseding indictment which operates to prejudice a defendant"; and that there was no prejudice in the instant case because the superseding indictment merely corrected the date of a prior conviction.

4. The statute excludes "all time between the filing of a [pretrial] motion and the conclusion of the hearing on that motion, whether or not a delay in holding that hearing is 'reasonably necessary,'" and also "time after a hearing has been held where a district court awaits additional filings from the parties that are needed for proper disposition of the motion." Henderson v. United States, 476 U.S. 321, 106 S.Ct. 1871, 90 L.Ed.2d 299 (1986).

(2) any "period of delay during which prosecution is deferred" by agreement of the prosecutor, defendant and court.

(3) any "period of delay resulting from the absence or unavailability of the defendant [5] or an essential witness." A person is absent "when his whereabouts are unknown and, in addition, he is attempting to avoid apprehension or prosecution or his whereabouts cannot be determined by due diligence," and is unavailable "whenever his whereabouts are known but his presence for trial cannot be obtained by due diligence or he resists appearing at or being returned for trial."

(4) any "period of delay resulting from the fact that the defendant is mentally incompetent or physically unable to stand trial."

(5) any "period of delay resulting from the treatment of the defendant" under the Narcotics Addict Rehabilitation Act.

(6) "any period of delay from the date the charge was dismissed to the date the time limitation would commence to run as to the subsequent charge had there been no previous charge," provided the dismissal was on motion of the prosecutor.

(7) a "reasonable period of delay when the defendant is joined for trial with a codefendant as to whom the time for trial has not run and no motion for severance has been granted."

(8) a "period of delay resulting from a continuance granted by any judge on his own motion or at the request of the defendant or his counsel or at the request of the attorney for the Government," provided the judge makes findings for the record as to why "the ends of justice served by the granting of such continuance outweigh the best interests of the public and the defendant in a speedy trial." The judge is to consider whether failure to grant the continuance would likely "make a continuation of such proceeding impossible, or result in a miscarriage of justice"; whether the case is so complex "that it is unreasonable to expect adequate preparation for pretrial proceedings or for the trial itself within the time limits"; whether, as to preindictment delay, it is "because the facts upon which the grand jury must base its determination are unusual or complex"; and whether failure to grant the continuance would deny defense counsel or prosecutor "the reasonable time necessary for effective preparation, taking into account the exercise of due diligence." In addition, the statute expressly forbids the granting of a continuance "because of general congestion of the court's calendar, or lack of diligent preparation or failure to obtain available witnesses on the part of the attorney for the Government." This provision on continuances, virtually unprecedented in prior speedy trial statutes and rules, is the heart of this statutory scheme.

(9) a "period of delay, not to exceed one year, ordered by a district court upon an application of a party and a finding by a preponderance of the evidence that an official request * * * has been made for evidence of any such offense and that it reasonably appears, or reasonably appeared at the time the request was made, that such evidence is, or was, in such foreign country."

As for sanctions, the Act provides that if the charge is not filed within the 30 day limit extended by any excluded periods or if defendant has moved for dismissal because trial did not commence within the 70 day limit extended by any excluded periods, then the case or charge shall be dismissed. "In determining whether to dismiss the case with or without prejudice, the court shall consider, among others, each of the following factors: the seriousness of the offense; the facts and circumstances of the case which led to the dismissal; and the impact of a reprosecution on the administration of this chapter and on the administration of justice." This "with or without prejudice" provision, the result of an

5. Pursuant to a 1988 amendment to the Act, if a defendant is absent on the date set for trial and later appears before the court not more than 21 days later, the time limit as otherwise extended is extended by 21 days. If the defendant's appearance is more than 21 days later, the date of that appearance is to be treated as defendant's first appearance before a judicial officer for purposes of calculating that defendant's statutory speedy trial right.

amendment on the floor of the House, is not only anticlimatic but also very unclear. The legislative history indicates, however, that dismissal with prejudice is permitted under circumstances which would not require dismissal under the sixth amendment, and that the extent of prejudice to the defendant, government "fault," and defense "fault" are other factors which weigh in the balance. But, "Congress did not intend any particular type of dismissal to serve as the presumptive remedy for a Speedy Trial Act violation." [6] A "district court must carefully consider [the aforementioned] factors as applied to the particular case and, whatever its decision, clearly articulate their effect in order to permit meaningful appellate review," during which the appellate court can "ascertain whether a district court has ignored or slighted a factor that Congress has deemed pertinent to the choice of remedy." [7]

Finally, it must be noted that the federal Act expressly provides for punishment of any prosecutor or defense attorney who "(1) knowingly allows the case to be set for trial without disclosing the fact that a necessary witness would be unavailable for trial; (2) files a motion solely for the purpose of delay which he knows is totally frivolous and without merit; (3) makes a statement for the purpose of obtaining a continuance which he knows to be false and which is material to the granting of a continuance; or (4) otherwise willfully fails to proceed to trial without justification." The punishment may be a fine up to $250 on the prosecutor or up to 25% of the compensation due appointed or retained defense counsel, denial of the right to practice before that court for up to 90 days, or filing of a report with the appropriate disciplinary committee.

(c) State Provisions. Virtually all states have provisions in their own constitutions safeguarding the right to speedy trial. Usually the language is identical to that in the Sixth Amendment, and thus the tendency of state courts is to use the balancing test of *Barker v. Wingo* [8] in construing those provisions. In addition, all but a few states have adopted statutes or rules of court on the subject of speedy trial. These provisions usually provide protection beyond that of the state constitutional guarantee, and thus to understand fully the speedy trial situation in any particular jurisdiction, it is necessary to examine the applicable court rule or statute and the case law which has developed from it. The objective here is the more modest one of providing a general description of those provisions collectively.

Most of the state provisions declare that trial must commence within a specified period of time from a specified event. These time limits range from 75 days to 6 months. As for the event which will start the speedy trial clock running, these provisions usually state that where defendant was indicted prior to arrest, or, where indictment is not required, a complaint, affidavit, or information was filed before arrest, the time runs from the date the charge was filed; otherwise, the time begins to run when the defendant is held to answer or committed (when defendant first appears before a judicial officer). If there is to be a retrial following a mistrial, order for a new trial, appeal or collateral attack, then the counting begins on the date of mistrial, order or remand. No clearcut pattern is discernible in state law regarding trial on a charge once dismissed; some count anew from the time of the second charge and some count from the time of the initial charge, though the latter result is more likely if the time had already run by the time the first charge was dismissed or if dismissal was not at the instance of the defendant.

A growing number of states have adopted provisions in the style of the federal Act, specifically listing all of the periods which are to be excluded in determining whether the time for trial has run. Many jurisdictions, however, merely provide for additional time

6. United States v. Taylor, 487 U.S. 326, 108 S.Ct. 2413, 101 L.Ed.2d 297 (1988).

7. United States v. Taylor, 487 U.S. 326, 108 S.Ct. 2413, 101 L.Ed.2d 297 (1988).

8. 407 U.S. 514, 92 S.Ct. 2182, 33 L.Ed.2d 101 (1972).

upon a showing of "good cause" or some other exceptional circumstances. A number of other states have taken a middle course; the statute or rule identifies only some of the more common permissible reasons for delay, such as "on application of the defendant," because of the absence of material evidence, or because of other judicial proceedings involving the defendant. In jurisdictions of the latter two types it is necessary for the courts to articulate further the lawful grounds for delay.

In dealing with court congestion, these state rules and statutes come down on both sides of the issue, some effectively excluding such delay from consideration in measuring expiration of time-precise periods, while others do not. As for continuances, these provisions often do no more than state that a continuance may be granted in the "interests of justice," for "cause" or "sufficient cause" or "good cause," or (less common) only upon a showing of extraordinary or exceptional circumstances. As a practical matter, in most jurisdictions if a represented defendant has moved for or acquiesced in a continuance, then the interim period is not counted if he later claims the trial time set by statute or court rule has run. As a result, it is common practice for continuances to be routinely granted, and this is a major reason for the very substantial trial delays to be found in many locales.

As for the applicable sanction when a defendant by timely motion has shown that the time specified by a statute or court rule has run, the prevailing view is dismissal with prejudice. Some states, however, provide only for dismissal without prejudice, limit dismissal with prejudice to lesser offenses, or put the choice of the form of dismissal in the hands of the judge. In certain jurisdictions there are shorter time limits for defendants in custody, and failure to begin trial within that time may also be a basis for whatever remedy is otherwise available—dismissal with or without prejudice. The sounder position, however, is that the running of this shorter time should merely require discharge from custody.

§ 18.4 The Imprisoned Defendant

(a) Constitutional Rights. Despite numerous prior lower court decisions to the contrary, the Supreme Court in *Smith v. Hooey,*[1] held that prisoners also have Sixth Amendment speedy trial rights and that consequently upon demand by the prisoner the charging jurisdiction "had a constitutional duty to make a diligent, good-faith effort to bring him before the * * * court for trial." This result was assured once the Court in *Smith* concluded that the interests protected by the constitutional right are especially threatened "in the case of an accused who is imprisoned by another jurisdiction." As for the interest in preventing undue and oppressive incarceration prior to trial, delay as to an imprisoned defendant may "result in as much oppression as is suffered by one who is jailed without bail upon an untried charge":

> First, the possibility that the defendant already in prison might receive a sentence at least partially concurrent with the one he is serving may be forever lost if trial of the pending charge is postponed. Secondly, under procedures now widely practiced, the duration of his present imprisonment may be increased, and the conditions under which he must serve his sentence greatly worsened, by the pendency of another criminal charge against him.

The reference is to the fact that the filing of a detainer[2] on a prisoner may have adverse

§ 18.4

1. 393 U.S. 374, 89 S.Ct. 575, 21 L.Ed.2d 607 (1969).

2. A detainer, or hold order, may be filed by a prosecutor, court, police chief or any other official empowered to take persons into custody, and it need not be supported by an indictment or information. A detainer notifies the incarcerating authorities that the prisoner is wanted, and requests that the authorities desiring custody be forewarned of the prisoner's release date so that they can arrange to pick him up at the institution. Filing a detainer is an informal process; it does not bind the requesting authority to act (and roughly half are never acted upon), nor does it bind the incarcerating authorities to hold the prisoner, although this is usually done as a matter of comity between sovereigns.

effects upon the prisoner's situation.[3] As for the interest in minimizing the anxiety and concern accompanying public accusation of crime, the Court in *Smith* noted that delay could be particularly harmful to a prisoner in this respect, for it would tend to thwart efforts at rehabilitation. Likewise, the interest in preventing impairment of the ability to defend is especially strong as to a prisoner, for he "is powerless to exert his own investigative efforts to mitigate [the] erosive efforts to the passage of time."

A year later, in *Dickey v. Florida,*[4] the Court had occasion to apply *Smith* and actually hold that a particular prisoner's speedy trial right had been violated. Although Dickey preceded the Court's announcement of the four-pronged balancing test in *Barker v. Wingo,*[5] the holding in *Dickey* can easily be placed into the *Barker* framework. In holding that the defendant's Sixth Amendment right to a speedy trial had been violated, the Court emphasized: (1) the length of the delay, here a "seven-year period"; (2) the reason for the delay, here that "no tenable reason" was ever offered for not seeking to obtain custody of defendant from a federal prison; (3) that over this period defendant made "diligent and repeated efforts * * * to secure a prompt trial"; and (4) prejudice was apparent, for in the interval "two witnesses died and another potential witness is alleged to have become unavailable," and "[p]olice records of possible relevance have been lost or destroyed."

More recently and quite correctly, lower courts have applied the *Barker* formula to prisoner cases in much the same way as in other cases. What this means, with respect to the reason for the delay, is that the government has the burden of showing that the reason is something other than a failure (as stated in *Smith*) to "make a diligent, good-faith effort to bring him before the * * * court for trial." If the government makes no such showing, this counts against the government, but not as heavily as it would if an actual intent to hamper the defense were shown. And *Smith,* which stresses the "increased cooperation between the States themselves and between the States and the Federal Government," makes it perfectly clear that the fact the charging jurisdiction lacks the power to compel the defendant's return is not a valid reason for failing to make the effort. But there is no need to make this effort when the other jurisdiction is holding the defendant pending or during trial and sentencing, for return during such period would not occur. And there is some tendency not to be as demanding when the defendant is being held in a foreign country, in which case presumably the chances of cooperation may at least sometimes be diminished.

Although, as in other situations governed by *Barker,* a defendant who fails to demand a prompt trial is ordinarily unlikely to prevail, note must be taken of two special circumstances which may be present in the prisoner case. On occasion, especially where the charging authorities have not filed a detainer against the prisoner, the prisoner may be unaware of the outstanding charge, in which case his lack of demand can hardly be counted against him. And when he is aware, as is more commonly the case, the imprisoned defendant is unlikely to have the assistance of counsel, which has influenced courts to be fairly generous in deciding exactly what constitutes a demand. Finally, it should be noted that the presence of a demand may also have an important bearing on the reason-for-delay factor, as it will deprive the charging jurisdiction of the excuse which otherwise might be valid: that the defendant's whereabouts were unknown.

3. The existence of a detainer may have several adverse effects upon the prisoner. He may, for that reason, be held under maximum security or be denied opportunities open to other prisoners, such as transfer to a minimum security area, the privilege of being a trusty, or assignment to a job involving a degree of trust. The detainer makes the prisoner's future uncertain, and thus renders more difficult the formulation of an effective rehabilitation program. Many parole boards will not consider parole for a prisoner who has a detainer lodged against him, although some jurisdictions are now using the parole-to-detainer device, which allows release of the detainee while he serves another sentence or answers other charges.

4. 398 U.S. 30, 90 S.Ct. 1564, 26 L.Ed.2d 26 (1970).

5. 407 U.S. 514, 92 S.Ct. 2182, 33 L.Ed.2d 101 (1972).

As for the prejudice factor, it is unlikely to weigh heavily in the prisoner's favor unless he makes the kind of showing accepted by the Court in *Dickey.* Something more than mere speculation is ordinarily required to establish impairment of the defense. As for the anxiety factor, it will count substantially in defendant's favor only if it is shown that there was a rather special situation giving rise to an inordinate amount of anxiety. Similarly, courts often do not take favorably to speculative assertions of loss of concurrent sentencing.

If a person serving a prison term in state *A* has a detainer filed against him by state *B* because of an outstanding charge there, but state *B* has failed to act upon that person's demand for a prompt trial, the prisoner may seek relief via federal habeas corpus. In such circumstances, the prisoner is in a unique situation whereby he has a choice of the federal court in which to file his habeas petition. It may be filed in *either* the federal district where he is presently incarcerated *or* the federal district of the outstanding charge, though either district could transfer the case to the other if it proved to be a more convenient forum.[6]

(b) Federal Speedy Trial Act of 1974. This Act deals specially with the situation in which the prosecutor knows that a person charged with a federal offense is serving a term of imprisonment in any penal institution. In such a case, the prosecutor has the option of doing either of two things: (1) he may undertake to obtain the prisoner's presence for trial; or (2) he may cause a detainer to be filed with the person having custody of the prisoner and request him to so advise the prisoner and to advise him of his right to demand trial. If, in the latter instance, the prisoner informs the person having custody that he does demand trial, this person is to cause that notice to be sent promptly to the prosecutor who caused the detainer to be filed. Upon receipt of that notice, the prosecutor must "promptly seek to obtain the presence of the prisoner for trial." [7]

Because under the Act generally it does not take a demand by the defendant to start the speedy trial clock running, it might be asked why an exception has been made in this particular case. A part of the explanation is that the public interest in speedy trial is not as intense in the situation just discussed; there is no additional cost associated with such correctional custody, nor any of the risks associated with pretrial release. But more important is the fact that this exception opens up an important tactical choice for the prisoner. Absent a desire by the prosecutor to go to trial, the prisoner retains the option of demanding trial in order to overcome whatever disadvantages may flow from the fact that a detainer has been lodged against him or of not making the demand in the hope that the charges will be dropped before or at the time he completes his sentence.

(c) Interstate Agreement on Detainers. Under the Uniform Criminal Extradition Act,[8] which has been adopted in the overwhelming majority of the states, procedures are set out whereby a person imprisoned in another state may be extradited for purposes of criminal prosecution.[9] However, the necessity for extradition often can be avoided by proceeding under the Interstate Agreement on Detainers,[10] a Compact which has been adopted by the federal government and virtually all the states. The IAD provides that a prisoner against whom a detainer has been filed must be promptly notified of that fact and of his right to demand trial, and if he demands trial then trial must be had within 180 days thereafter; the request is a waiver of extradition by the prisoner, and the state by adopting the Compact has agreed to surren-

6. Braden v. 30th Judicial Circuit Court, 410 U.S. 484, 93 S.Ct. 1123, 35 L.Ed.2d 443 (1973).

7. 18 U.S.C.A. § 3161(j).

8. 11 U.L.A. 59 (1974).

9. Article III of the IAD, which by its terms applies to detainers based on an "indictment," "information," or "complaint," refers to documents charging a person with a criminal offense, and thus is not applicable to a detainer based on probation violation charges. Carchman v. Nash, 473 U.S. 716, 105 S.Ct. 3401, 87 L.Ed.2d 516 (1985).

10. 11 U.L.A. 323 (1974).

der the prisoner under such circumstances; if trial is not had within 180 days and good cause for delay is not shown, the charges are dismissed with prejudice.

The prosecutor is an appropriate officer to file the detainer, though in practice the filing might be by a court clerk or police official. Failure of the custodian to notify the prisoner of the detainer is a serious matter, but the IAD has no sanction for failure to notify timely an inmate about a detainer. As for the inmate's demand for trial, some courts are quite particular and thus have held that a motion for speedy trial is insufficient or that a request not sent through channels is inadequate compliance with the Compact, while others are less demanding. It has been held that if the inmate makes his request of the custodial officials but they fail promptly to forward the request to the officer who filed the detainer, this failure is not to be charged to the inmate. Though one might ask why the prosecuting officials and indirectly the public of the charging state should bear the brunt of another jurisdiction's failure to comply with the IAD, the answer given is that between the prosecutor and the inmate the former is better situated to see that the requirements of law are met. Except when there has been such a failure, the prevailing view is that the 180 days begin running from the time the request and accompanying documents are received by the prosecutor and court. The 180 days can be tolled in some circumstances, as where the prisoner is standing trial in another state, and can be extended by continuances for good cause, as where a witness is unavailable. If trial of the charge is not commenced on time, then the court is to "enter an order dismissing the same with prejudice, and any detainer based thereon shall cease to be of any force or effect." Also, if the inmate is returned to his original place of imprisonment without trial, the charge "shall not be of any further force or effect."

(d) Uniform Mandatory Disposition of Detainers Act. Eight states have adopted this Act,[11] and several others have enacted similar legislation. The UMDDA provides that the inmate's custodian must promptly inform him of any charges against him by that jurisdiction of which the custodian has knowledge or notice and of his right to request disposition of such charges. If a detainer has been filed against the inmate, failure of the custodian to advise the inmate of the detainer within a year of the filing entitles the inmate to dismissal of the charge with prejudice. An inmate can request disposition of any outstanding charge, and this request is to be forwarded by the custodian to the appropriate court and prosecutor. Failure of the custodian to perform that responsibility entitles the prisoner to relief. Trial is to commence within 90 days of the time the court and prosecution receive the request, though additional time can be granted for good cause. The defendant has no further burden to seek a timely trial, and if the prosecutor does not ensure that the trial starts on time the defendant is entitled to dismissal with prejudice.

§ 18.5 The Right to Other Speedy Disposition

(a) Statutes of Limitations. In *United States v. Marion,*[1] in the course of holding that the Sixth Amendment right to speedy trial had no application to delay which preceded both arrest and charge, the Court noted that statutes of limitations provide "the primary guarantee against bringing overly stale criminal charges." As the Court earlier noted in *Toussie v. United States:*[2]

> The purpose of a statute of limitations is to limit exposure to criminal prosecution to a certain fixed period of time following the occurrence of those acts the legislature had decided to punish by criminal sanctions. Such a limitation is designed to protect individuals from having to defend themselves against charges when the basic facts may have be-

11. 11 U.L.A. 328 (1974).

§ 18.5

1. 404 U.S. 307, 92 S.Ct. 455, 30 L.Ed.2d 468 (1971).

2. 397 U.S. 112, 90 S.Ct. 858, 25 L.Ed.2d 156 (1970).

come obscured by the passage of time and to minimize the danger of official punishment because of acts in the far-distant past. Such a time limit may also have the salutary effect of encouraging law enforcement officials promptly to investigate suspected criminal activity.

Other objectives are served by these statutes. They prevent prosecution of those who have been law abiding for some years, avoid prosecution when the community's retributive impulse has ceased, and lessen the possibility of blackmail. But foremost is the desirability of requiring that prosecutions be based upon reasonably fresh evidence so as to lessen the possibility of an erroneous conviction. Thus, these statutes share an important common purpose with speedy trial protections, and to that end are liberally construed in favor of criminal defendants.

All jurisdictions make a distinction between serious and minor offenses, permitting longer lapses of time for prosecution of the former. For felonies the times usually range between three and six years; for misdemeanors they are ordinarily somewhere between one and three years. The assumption appears to be that a longer time is justified for serious crimes because in such instances there is a greater need for deterrence, a greater likelihood the perpetrator is a continuing danger to society, and a lesser likelihood that the perpetrator would reform on his own. It is commonly provided that a few of the most serious offenses, usually murder and treason, have no statute of limitations.

Virtually all jurisdictions provide that the period of limitation begins to run with the commission of the crime, that is, when every element in the statutory definition of the offense has occurred. Certain crimes are properly characterized as continuing offenses, and as to them the time begins to run only when the course of conduct or defendant's complicity therein terminates. Illustrative of continuing offenses are possession-of-contraband crimes, falsification schemes which continue to produce fruits, and of course conspiracy (where the counting begins with the last overt act or, with respect to a particular conspirator, his effective withdrawal from the enterprise).

It is common to deal with certain special situations by provisions which allow either for tolling of the time or for the time to commence at some time later than commission of the offense. The assumption underlying the rules which usually apply is that most offenses are known at least to the victim at the time of or soon after its commission, or that the offense can be discovered by adequate investigation by enforcement officials. But this is not likely to be true of cases involving fraud or breach of fiduciary obligation or those involving misconduct by a public officer or employee, and thus some statutes provide that the times for such offenses run from the date of discovery or departure from office, respectively. Many statutes more generally provide that the time does not run when commission of the crime has been concealed; these provisions are narrowly construed, for efforts at concealment are so common that literal application of such provisions would deprive the statute of limitations of most of its effect. Limitations statutes also usually provide for tolling during the period of nonavailability of the defendant.

Though the purpose of these statutes is to ensure a timely commencement of prosecution, there is not agreement on what act will suffice to show such commencement. Some legislation expressly requires that an indictment be found or an information filed, but where this is not the case it is generally held sufficient that an arrest warrant has issued or that a complaint has been filed. Assuming diligence in arresting the defendant or notifying him of the complaint, these latter interpretations square with the basic purpose of a statute of limitations—insuring that the accused is informed of the decision to prosecute and the general nature of the charge with sufficient promptness to allow him to prepare his defense before evidence of his innocence becomes weakened with age. So as not to foreclose recharging after proceedings terminated prior to final adjudication, it is commonly provided that the statute is tolled during the time a prosecution was pending for the same offense or, as it is put in some jurisdictions, for an offense arising out of the same transaction. If the original charge, timely brought, resulted in conviction for a lesser offense as to which the time had run before the original charge was brought, this conviction is barred by the statute of limitations (unless that defense is waived by the defendant [3]) for the reason that otherwise the prosecutor might overcharge to avoid the limitation period on the lesser offense.

Two different views are to be found as to the effect of the running of the applicable statute of limitations in a criminal case. One is that this is a matter of affirmative defense, meaning that the requirements of timely objection and the like which ordinarily apply to the raising of such a defense must be complied with. The other is that once the time has run the court is without jurisdiction to try the offense, which means, for example, that a defendant would be entitled to relief even if he had previously entered an otherwise valid plea of guilty.

(b) Unconstitutional Pre-accusation Delays. In *United States v. Marion,*[4] the Court cautioned that "the statute of limitations does not fully define the appellees' rights with respect to the events occurring prior to indictment," and noted that the government conceded that the due process clause "would require dismissal of the indictment if it were shown at trial that the preindictment delay in this case caused substantial prejudice to appellees' rights to a fair trial and that the delay was an intentional device to gain tactical advantage over the accused." Because the posture of the case was such that defendants' due process claims were "speculative and premature," the Court did not elaborate on this due process test.

The contours of the test were elucidated to some extent in the later case of *United States v. Lovasco,*[5] overturning the lower court's ruling that defendant's rights were violated where he established actual prejudice (loss of the testimony of a significant witness) and the government's explanation for the 17–month delay was the desire for further investigation notwithstanding the presence of sufficient evidence to support a charge. The Court first rejected unequivocally the contention that a due process violation exists whenever precharge delay actually prejudices the defendant. Prejudice, the court concluded, "is generally a necessary but not sufficient element of a due process claim," and its existence merely "makes a due process claim concrete and ripe for adjudication." What remains to be assessed in such circumstances are "the reasons for the delay," and so the Court in *Lovasco* turned to that question and concluded that no due process violation exists in the case of "investigative delay." As for just what is encompassed within that term, the

3. A variation of this problem reached the Supreme Court in Spaziano v. Florida, 468 U.S. 447, 104 S.Ct. 3154, 82 L.Ed.2d 340 (1984), where at defendant's trial for the capital offense of first-degree murder the trial judge refused to instruct on the lesser included offenses of attempted first-degree murder, second-degree murder, third-degree murder, and manslaughter because defendant refused to waive the statute of limitations, which had already run on those offenses. Defendant claimed this violated the Supreme Court's ruling in Beck v. Alabama, 447 U.S. 625, 100 S.Ct. 2382, 65 L.Ed.2d 392 (1980), that in a capital trial a lesser included offense instruction is a necessary element of a constitutionally fair trial, but the Supreme Court disagreed. *Beck,* the Court explained, was intended "to eliminate the distortion of the fact-finding process that is created when the jury is forced into an all-or-nothing choice between capital murder and innocence," but requiring "that the jury be instructed on lesser included offenses for which the defendant may not be convicted * * * would simply introduce another type of distortion into the fact-finding process." The Court concluded a proper compromise of the defendant's and prosecution's interests would be to give the defendant "a choice between having the benefit of the lesser included offense instruction or asserting the statute of limitations on the lesser included offenses."

4. 404 U.S. 307, 92 S.Ct. 455, 30 L.Ed.2d 468 (1971).

5. 431 U.S. 783, 97 S.Ct. 2044, 52 L.Ed.2d 752 (1977). In United States v. Eight Thousand Eight Hundred and Fifty Dollars, 461 U.S. 555, 103 S.Ct. 2005, 76 L.Ed.2d 143 (1983), the government argued *Lovasco* provided the standard by which to test post-seizure delay in a forfeiture proceeding under 31 U.S.C.A. § 1102(a), but the Court concluded that a "more apt analogy is to a defendant's right to a speedy trial," and thus applied the *Barker* balancing test discussed in § 18.2.

Applying *$8,850,* the Court held in United States v. Von Neumann, 474 U.S. 242, 106 S.Ct. 610, 88 L.Ed.2d 587 (1986), that the owner of a car seized at the border for failure to declare it had no constitutional right to a speedy disposition of his remission petition without awaiting a forfeiture proceeding.

Court explained: (1) that it unquestionably covers the case where probable cause was lacking, because "it is unprofessional conduct for a prosecutor to recommend an indictment on less than probable cause"; (2) that it also covers the case where probable cause existed, for "prosecutors are under no duty to file charges * * * before they are satisfied they will be able to establish the suspect's guilt beyond a reasonable doubt," as such charging would "increase the likelihood of unwarranted charges being filed," cause "potentially fruitful sources of information to evaporate," and "cause scarce resources to be consumed on cases that prove to be insubstantial"; and (3) that it even covers the case where there is "evidence sufficient to establish guilt," for to compel immediate charging upon such evidence "would preclude the Government from giving full consideration to the desirability of not prosecuting in particular cases."

With respect to what reasons for delay are "bad," in the sense that their coexistence with actual prejudice would entitle the defendant to prevail on his due process claim, the *Lovasco* Court declined to deal with that question "in the abstract." The Court did note that the government had renewed its concession in *Marion* that dismissal would be required if the delay was undertaken solely "to gain tactical advantage over the accused," and then in a footnote observed that the government had now broadened its concession by stating: "A due process violation might also be made out upon a showing of prosecutorial delay incurred in reckless disregard of circumstances, known to the prosecution, suggesting that there existed an appreciable risk that delay would impair the ability to mount an effective defense."

Under the two-pronged test of *Lovasco,* as interpreted by the lower courts, it will be extremely difficult for a defendant to prevail on his due process claim.[6] As for the prejudice prong, though *Lovasco* contains the somewhat qualified statement that "proof of prejudice is generally a necessary * * * element," the lower courts take the view that prejudice must always be shown. The burden of proof is on the defendant to show prejudice by a preponderance of the evidence; actual prejudice must be established, for courts are disinclined to presume prejudice no matter what the reason for delay, and some courts also insist that the prejudice must be substantial in degree. As for what it takes to meet this burden, it is not enough that the defendant is unable to recall or reconstruct the events in question, for he must show an actual loss of a witness or physical evidence. And it must be established that this loss was prejudicial. This means, for example, that in the case of a lost witness it must be shown that the witness would have been available at an earlier time, would have testified for the defendant, and would have aided the defense.

As for the reason-for-delay prong, it is unclear where *Lovasco* places this burden. The government gave no explanation for the delay in the district court, and the Supreme Court proceeded as had the Court of Appeals to accept the government's representations as to the motivation for the delay which had been set out in the government's appellate brief. Some lower courts have read *Lovasco* to mean that once the defendant proves prejudice, then "the burden shifts" to the prosecution to show a valid reason for the delay. This is a sensible allocation of the burden, for the reasons underlying the delay are peculiarly within the knowledge of the prosecution. Nonetheless, the prevailing view is that the defendant must shoulder this burden as well. It is not an easy burden to meet, especially because there is no discernible inclination of the lower courts to treat anything except an in-

6. In an apparent effort to avoid such difficulties, the defendants in United States v. Gouveia, 467 U.S. 180, 104 S.Ct. 2292, 81 L.Ed.2d 146 (1984), argued without success that the Sixth Amendment required appointment of counsel prior to the initiation of adversary judicial proceedings against indigent inmates who are confined in administrative detention for lengthy periods while being investigated for crimes committed in prison, for the reason that counsel could minimize the risks which attend a delay in the bringing of charges. The Court concluded that though these concerns were "certainly legitimate," the protections of the statute of limitations and the *Lovasco* due process rule were sufficient that it was not necessary "to depart from our traditional interpretation of the Sixth Amendment right to counsel in order to provide additional protections."

tent to hamper the defense as an improper reason.

It can certainly be argued that the *Lovasco* rule is too demanding. "Loss of memory," the Supreme Court noted in *Barker v. Wingo*,[7] "is not always reflected in the record because what has been forgotten can rarely be shown." That being so, it would not be inappropriate to require the prosecution to establish that no such harm has occurred when it has acted for the purpose of hampering the defense. Indeed, it has been argued that the *Lovasco* test should be restated in a disjunctive fashion, so that constitutional guarantees of due process of law would mandate dismissal if the delay were perpetrated by the state to gain a tactical advantage over the accused, or if the accused demonstrated that he had suffered actual, substantial and irremediable prejudice.

(c) **Post-Trial Delays.** Even if the criminal trial has commenced on time, the defendant might object to delays occurring thereafter. If the case was tried without a jury, the objection, as in *Campodonico v. United States*,[8] might be that the trial judge unduly delayed his findings as to defendant's guilt or innocence. In that case, where the criminal trial lasted only 14 hours but defendant was adjudged guilty more than a year after commencement of that trial, he claimed this delay violated his Sixth Amendment right to a speedy trial. The court, though not questioning the applicability of the constitutional right to a speedy trial in this context, ruled against the defendant on the theory that he could not now complain in light of his failure "to press the trial court for a quick decision." Both that result and the assumption that the Sixth Amendment right was applicable are consistent with the later analysis in *Barker v. Wingo*.[9]

As for delays in sentencing, the Supreme Court in *Pollard v. United States*[10] assumed that the Sixth Amendment right to speedy trial was applicable to such delays. This is also consistent with the later analysis in *Barker*, where the Court stressed that delay in punishment "may have a detrimental effect on rehabilitation" and thus be harmful to the particular defendant and to society at large. Other courts have rather consistently held that the Sixth Amendment right applies to sentencing delay, but then have typically ruled against the defendant because of his failure at any time during the interval between conviction and sentence to request prompt sentencing.

Because appeals are not a part of the "criminal prosecutions" to which Sixth Amendment rights attach,[11] it seems clear that a speedy trial claim may not be made with respect to delays in the appellate process.[12] But, while the Constitution apparently does not require the states to afford a right to appellate review of a criminal conviction,[13] when a state does provide the right it must do so in a manner which meets the requirements of due process and equal protection.[14] As concluded in *Rheuark v. Shaw*,[15] "due process can be denied by any substantial retardation of the appellate process, including an excessive delay in the furnishing of a transcription of testimony necessary for completion of an appellate record." Though this might suggest that the *Lovasco* decision concerning pre-charge delays in violation of due process would provide the best analogy for purposes of analysis, the court in *Rheuark* concluded this was not the case. Noting that "the reasons for constraining appellate delay are analogous to the motives underpinning the Sixth Amendment right to a speedy trial," the court decided that application of the four factors in *Barker* was the best

7. 407 U.S. 514, 92 S.Ct. 2182, 33 L.Ed.2d 101 (1972).

8. 222 F.2d 310 (9th Cir.1955).

9. 407 U.S. 514, 92 S.Ct. 2182, 33 L.Ed.2d 101 (1972).

10. 352 U.S. 354, 77 S.Ct. 481, 1 L.Ed.2d 393 (1957).

11. Douglas v. California, 372 U.S. 353, 83 S.Ct. 814, 9 L.Ed.2d 811 (1963).

12. Except in the case of interlocutory appeal "when the defendant is subject to indictment or restraint." See discussion of the *Loud Hawk* case in § 18.2(c).

13. Ross v. Moffitt, 417 U.S. 600, 94 S.Ct. 2437, 41 L.Ed.2d 341 (1974).

14. Douglas v. California, 372 U.S. 353, 83 S.Ct. 814, 9 L.Ed.2d 811 (1963).

15. 628 F.2d 297 (5th Cir.1980).

way "to determine whether a denial of due process has been occasioned in any given case."

Proceedings to revoke probation or parole, while likewise not a part of the "criminal prosecutions" covered by the Sixth Amendment,[16] are subject to due process limits. In *Morrissey v. Brewer,*[17] dealing exclusively with the due process protections which attend the parole revocation process, the Court concluded a parolee is entitled to two hearings, a preliminary hearing and a final revocation hearing, and that both must be conducted in a timely fashion. Because the latter might occur after "a substantial time lag" and at a place distant from where the alleged violation of parole occurred, the Court concluded that "due process would seem to require that some minimal inquiry be conducted at or reasonably near the place of the alleged parole violation or arrest and as promptly as convenient after arrest while information is fresh and sources are available." As for the final hearing, the Court in *Morrissey* declared that it "must be tendered within a reasonable time after the parolee is taken into custody," but added that a "lapse of two months * * * would not appear to be unreasonable." Later in *Gagnon v. Scarpelli,*[18] the Court held that a probationer "is entitled to a preliminary and final revocation hearing, under the conditions specified in *Morrissey,*" and thus a probationer also has a due process right to timely hearings.

An exception was recognized in the later case of *Moody v. Daggett,*[19] holding that a federal parolee was not constitutionally entitled to a prompt parole revocation hearing under the facts of that case. The parolee killed two people while he was on parole, for which he was convicted and sentenced to two concurrent 10–year terms. A parole violator warrant was then issued and lodged with prison officials as a detainer, which thus was to be executed only at the end of the new sentences, and the parolee then unsuccessfully sought dismissal of the warrant on the ground he had been denied a prompt hearing. The Court affirmed, ruling that *Morrissey* was not controlling because the parolee was not presently in custody as a parole violator; not even his opportunity for parole on the intervening sentences was affected by the outstanding warrant, and the question of whether the new sentences should run concurrently with the balance of the old one could be addressed whenever revocation was undertaken. Moreover, the Court was strongly influenced by the fact that in this particular situation there was a "practical aspect" making delay of the revocation issue a preferable course of action. Because the parolee had been convicted of new crimes which obviously amounted to a violation of his parole, "the only remaining inquiry is whether continued release is justified notwithstanding the violation." Given "the predictive nature" of such a determination, as to which "a parolee's institutional record can be perhaps one of the most significant factors," it "is appropriate that such hearing be held at the time at which prediction is both most relevant and most accurate—at the expiration of the parolee's intervening sentence."

16. Except when sentencing has been deferred to the time of probation revocation. Mempa v. Rhay, 389 U.S. 128, 88 S.Ct. 254, 19 L.Ed.2d 336 (1967).

17. 408 U.S. 471, 92 S.Ct. 2593, 33 L.Ed.2d 484 (1972).

18. 411 U.S. 778, 93 S.Ct. 1756, 36 L.Ed.2d 656 (1973).

19. 429 U.S. 78, 97 S.Ct. 274, 50 L.Ed.2d 236 (1976).

Part Four

THE ADVERSARY SYSTEM AND THE DETERMINATION OF GUILT AND INNOCENCE

Chapter 19

THE ACCUSATORY PLEADING

Table of Sections

---

§ 19.1 The Liberalization of Pleading Requirements

(a) Common Law Technicalities. As first developed, the accusatory pleading was a simple document. In the early fourteenth century, it was sufficient to allege in an indictment that "*A* stole an ox, *B* burgled a house, or *C* slew a man." Over the next few centuries, however, as the criminal law grew more complex and defendants were allowed to use counsel to challenge indictments, courts came to demand that the pleading contain a full statement of the facts and legal theory underlying the charge. Pleading requirements for particular crimes often paralleled in their complexity and formalism the special civil pleadings required for the different forms of action. Indictments were lengthy, highly detailed, and filled with technical jargon. Thus, an indictment charging forcible entry had to include the words "with strong hand" and an indictment alleging murder had to describe not only the means used but also the nature and extent of the wound inflicted.

For many years, American courts demanded strict adherence to the technical niceties of common law pleading rules. Indictments were not infrequently quashed for the most picayune errors in form. Moreover, defects in an indictment were not waived by defendant's failure to object before trial; most defects could also be challenged after conviction by a motion in arrest of judgment. As a result, courts were striking down convictions fully supported by the evidence simply because indictments were inartfully drawn or awkwardly worded. Pleading requirements also were largely responsible for numerous convictions reversed because the evidence at trial varied from the detailed allegation of facts in the indictment. Here too, the courts generally were strict. Thus, an early Delaware decision reversed a conviction under an indictment alleging the theft of a "pair of shoes" because the evidence established that both of the shoes stolen were for the right foot and therefore did not constitute a pair.

While the formalism and detail mandated by the common law pleading rules were designed in part to provide notice to the accused, they clearly went beyond what was needed to provide notice alone. Indeed, commentators contended that the common law indictment was often a "lengthy and tortuous document, which * * * served more to mystify than to inform the defendant." Sir James Stephen contended that the common law demanded "strictness and technicality" in pleadings as a safeguard against "looseness in the legal definitions of crimes." At a time when "the concepts and definitions of offenses took form largely through the experience of administration and without the aid of definitive statutes," the requirement that the offense be stated according to a particular formula, specifying in detail each element of the crime, was seen as providing assurance both that the grand jury understood what was necessary to establish an offense and that the courts did not engage in unanticipated extensions of the substance of the offense. Courts in later years suggested that perhaps an equally significant function of the complex common law requirements was to supply the judiciary with readily available grounds for reversing convictions in "hard cases." As one court put it: "When stealing a handkerchief worth £1 was punished by death, and there were nearly 200 different capital offenses, it was to the credit of humanity that technicalities could be invoked in order to prevent the cruelty of a strict and literal enforcement of the law."

(b) Initial Attempts at Reform. By the mid–1800's, with the increasing codification of the substantive criminal law and the reduction in the number of capital offenses, many courts no longer insisted upon strict adherence to the technical rules of pleading. The judiciary, they noted, would "no longer permit the guilty man to escape punishment by averring that he cannot comprehend * * * what is palpable and evident to the common sense of everybody else." Numerous other courts, however, continued to adhere to the technical rules of common law pleading and extended those rules to informations in those jurisdictions that allowed felony prosecutions to be brought by information rather than indictment. This judicial refusal to liberalize pleading requirements led to legislative reform enactments carrying such titles as the "Common Sense in Indictments Act." In general, the new legislation was directed at relaxing specific common law requirements. Thus, it was provided that a murder charge need not allege the manner or means of causing death, that there was no need to specify the denomination or species of money taken in a theft, and that the absence of specified phrases, such as "with force and arms," did not render an indictment invalid. More general provisions stated that variances would not be fatal unless they were "material," and that indictments should not "be deemed insufficient * * * by reason of any defect or imperfection in form only, which shall not tend to the prejudice of the defendant."

The judicial response to the new legislation was mixed. Although most jurisdictions had adopted some form of pleading reform by the start of the twentieth century, courts in many states continued to insist that offenses be charged with technical accuracy and nicety of language. Illustrative are two notorious rulings of the early 1900's. One reversed a conviction on appeal because the indictment charged that the offense was against the "peace and dignity of State," having left out the necessary word "the" before "State." The other set aside a larceny conviction because the indictment stated that the property was stolen from the "American Express Company, an association" and thereby failed to aver "ownership in any person, firm, corporation, or other entity that * * * [could] be the owner of property." The legislative response to these and similar decisions was the enactment of broader pleading reform legislation.

(c) The Short–Form Pleading Movement. One legislative avenue to the liberalization of pleading requirements was the authorization of "short-form" pleadings. The authorizing statute would specify the particular language to be used in alleging the most common criminal offenses. That language would present an extremely truncated description of the criminal conduct. A murder pleading, for example, would allege only that "*A.B.* murdered *C.D.*" If the defendant wanted more information, he was entitled to a "bill of particulars setting up specifically the nature of the offense charged." The theory underlying the short-form pleading was that the pleading would be immune from attack (assuming the specified language was followed) and the defendant would receive the basic elements of notice through the bill of particulars. The only postconviction challenge available to the defendant would be based on the sufficiency of that notice, and such a challenge would be lost if the defendant had not specifically indicated before trial exactly what additional information was needed.

At one time, more than a dozen states authorized some form of short-form pleading, but prosecutors in many of those jurisdictions were hesitant to use the short-forms. One concern was the constitutionality of the short-form process. Courts generally rejected challenges based on state counterparts of the Sixth Amendment guarantee of notice, as ample notice was given by the bill of particulars even if the pleading itself failed to meet the constitutional guarantee. In indictment jurisdictions, however, the additional claim was raised that the short-form process failed to preserve the role of the grand jury since the bill of particulars came from the prosecutor and did not necessarily reflect the thinking of the grand jury. Prosecutors apparently also had misgivings raised by the uncertainty as to precisely what had to be included in the mandatory bill of particulars. If they should be required to furnish as much detail as formerly included in the common law pleadings (or even more), that would create a substantial risk of fatal variance between the trial proof and the bill. The end result was that the short-form legislation was eventually discarded in several of the states that had first authorized such pleadings. But short-form pleadings are still authorized and used today in a handful of states.

(d) The Successful Reforms. The legislative effort that eventually did succeed in liberalizing pleading requirements centered upon the enactment of three interrelated reforms: a single simplified pleading standard; official forms for the most commonly prosecuted crimes; and an expanded waiver rule. These reforms, which had been instituted at an earlier point in many states, were incorporated in the Federal Rules of Criminal Procedure, which became effective in 1946. Today, they are found in almost all jurisdictions, with many states having pleading provisions that are almost a verbatim copy of the Federal Rules provisions.

Federal Rule 7(c) sets forth the most common formulation of a simplified pleading standard: "The indictment or information shall be a plain, concise, and definite written statement of the essential facts constituting the offense charged." This standard offered several advantages over the provisions adopted in the first wave of pleading reforms. Many of those provisions dealt either with a specific common law pleading requirement or the pleadings for a particular crime. Rule 7(c), on the other hand, established a single standard, applicable to the pleading of all crimes and all elements of the pleading. Moreover, the language describing that standard was quite similar to that which reformers had employed in obtaining simplified pleadings in civil cases. Although the parallel between the civil complaint and the criminal pleading was far from perfect, the new standard clearly incorporated the basic thrust of simplification already achieved in civil pleadings. Finally, apart from any analogy to the reform of civil pleadings, the language of the Rule 7(c) standard, combined with other provisions speaking to specific parts of the pleading, clearly evidenced a rejection of the formalism and verbosity of common law pleadings.

While the Rule 7(c) requirement of a "concise" statement of the "essential" facts allowed for far less detail than required under traditional common law pleading, it did not go so far as to allow the truncated short-form pleading of "*A* murdered *B*." The essential facts included more than the identification of the offense and the victim. Exactly how much more factual allegation was needed would vary with the offense, but most jurisdictions adopted official forms, which provided both specific and general guidance. The Federal Rules included only 11 forms (which were later deleted as unnecessary after the thrust of Rules' reform took hold), but many states adopted (and retained) forms for a much larger group of offenses. In addition to providing the prosecutor with a safe path for pleading each of those offenses, the forms served to "illustrate the simplicity of statement which the Rules are designed to achieve." Thus, Federal Rule Form 1, for the offense of murder in the first degree of a federal officer, simply stated:

> On or about the * * * day of * * *, in the * * * District of * * *, John Doe with premeditation and by means of shooting murdered John Roe, who was then an officer of the Federal Bureau of Investigation of the Department of Justice engaged in the performance of his official duties.

The third element of the pleading reform provisions was an expansive waiver doctrine that forced most pleading objections to be raised before trial. Thus, Federal Rule 12 provides that five specified defense claims must be raised before trial, with the failure to do so constituting a "waiver thereof."[1] Subsection (b) of Rule 12 includes among these claims:

> Defenses and objections based on defects in the indictment or information (other than it fails to show jurisdiction in the court or to charge an offense which objections shall be noticed by the court at any time during the pendency of the proceedings).

This provision sharply restricts the defense tactic of "sandbagging" that was available in many jurisdictions under common law pleading. Recognizing that there was a defect in the pleading, counsel would often forego raising that defect before trial, when a successful objection would merely result in an amendment of the pleading. If the trial ended in a conviction, counsel could then raise the defect on a motion in arrest of judgment and obtain a new trial. Federal Rule 12 eliminated this tactic as to all objections except the failure to show jurisdiction or to charge an offense. While those objections can be raised for the first time at any point in the proceeding (including on appeal), any lesser objection to the pleadings is lost if not raised before trial.

Of course, the requirement that the objection be raised before trial does not preclude the possibility that a conviction will be reversed on appeal due to a lesser pleading error, such as lack of specificity. The trial

§ 19.1

1. Fed.R.Crim.P. 12(b), (f). However, the trial court "for cause shown, may grant relief from the waiver."

court may reject the defendant's pretrial objection and an appellate court may later hold that that ruling was erroneous. However, if the prosecutor has any doubt as to the validity of the pleading, he or she can always avoid the possibility of a subsequent reversal on appeal by substituting before trial a new pleading that meets the objection raised in defendant's pretrial objection. In the case of an indictment, this would usually require a return to the grand jury since amendments are not permitted. However, the delay involved in obtaining a new indictment might be well worth the preclusion of a possible reversal on appeal.

While the requirement of a pretrial objection hopefully would reduce the number of convictions that were reversed due to pleading defects, it did not respond to the problem of convictions reversed due to minor variances between the allegations contained in a proper pleading and the proof introduced at trial. Many states sought to meet this problem through provisions permitting the pleading to be amended at trial to conform to the proof (thereby "curing" the variance), provided the defendant was not prejudiced by the amendment. The Federal Rules did not include such a provision as to indictments, although it did allow liberal amendment of an information. This omission was not as significant as it might be in other jurisdictions, since federal courts had traditionally applied a functional standard to variances that allowed for proof variations which did not take the defense by surprise or undercut the charging role of the grand jury.[2]

The effectiveness of the pleading reforms of the type incorporated in the Federal Rules varied with the receptiveness of the particular jurisdiction's courts. The reform provisions were not so precise as to preclude a court from retaining much of the common law approach to pleadings, at least where the official forms were not applicable. The federal courts generally were quite receptive to the spirit of the reform movement. The Supreme Court noted that "the Rules * * * were designed to eliminate technicalities in criminal pleading and are to be construed to secure simplicity in procedure." Lower courts stressed that the sufficiency of the pleading would be determined by reference to functional rather than technical considerations. While good draftsmanship was still desirable, indictments and informations would not be dismissed because of errors in grammar or sentence structure that were not misleading; a "common sense construction" would be applied.

Most state courts responded to the pleading reforms in much the same way as the federal courts. Other state courts were slightly less receptive to the liberalization of pleading requirements. They adhered as a general matter to a functional analysis of pleading requirements, but insisted upon somewhat greater preciseness in meeting those functions. In still other states, the initial response was hostile to the relaxation of at least certain aspects of common law pleading requirements. Courts here usually were willing to forego the common law's insistence upon perfection in the formalistic elements of the pleading (e.g., caption and conclusion) and they allowed for somewhat less detail in describing certain acts and consequences. They insisted, however, that the basic elements of the crime be spelled out with literal correctness and as to some elements, a substantial degree of specificity. They also found fatal all but the most minor variances between proof and pleading. While their approach was hardly as rigid as that reflected in the most technical of the common law rulings, they did stress compliance with the pleading "rules of the game" rather than a functional analysis that looked to the purpose of the particular pleading requirement and the case-specific operation of the pleading. The number of courts adopting this largely mechanical approach to pleading rules gradually decreased, and today few courts, if any, can be said generally to adhere to such a position. Still, there remain a small group of states in which defendants sometimes find success in challenging pleadings, pleading amendments,

2. See § 19.6.

or variances on grounds that would quickly be rejected as without functional justification in more reform-minded jurisdictions.

§ 19.2 Pleading Functions

(a) Functional Analysis. Courts frequently note that under modern pleading philosophy, the accusatory instrument must be tested by the basic objectives that a pleading should achieve rather than by technical pleading requirements. The reforms incorporated in the Federal Rules and similar state provisions were designed to allow simplified pleadings, but they were not intended to modify the fundamental functions of the written charge. Accordingly, it is noted, the sufficiency of an indictment or information should ultimately depend on whether it fulfills those functions. The Supreme Court has consistently adhered to this "functional approach," which it utilized even before the Federal Rules were adopted. In *Hamling v. United States*,[1] it set forth the following standard for testing pleading sufficiency, based on a long line of cases applying a functional analysis:

> Our prior cases indicate that an indictment is sufficient if it, first, contains the elements of the offense charged and fairly informs a defendant of the charge against which he must defend, and, second, enables him to plead an acquittal or conviction in bar of future prosecutions for the same offense.

Although sometimes described as a two-pronged test, the *Hamling* standard includes three requirements: (1) inclusion of the elements of the offense; (2) providing adequate notice as to the charge; and (3) providing protection against double jeopardy. These three requirements have been cited repeatedly by both federal and state courts. They are widely treated as providing the basic analytical framework for determining whether a particular pleading sets forth a "plain, concise, and definite * * * statement of the essential facts constituting the offense charged," as required by Federal Rule 7(c) and similar state provisions.

The second and third requirements of *Hamling* clearly identify basic functions of the accusatory pleading. The need for notice and protection against double jeopardy are commonly accepted as pleading goals and regularly are looked to in evaluating alleged pleading deficiencies. The first requirement of *Hamling*—that the pleading set forth the presence of each of the essential elements of the offense—is less helpful in identifying the basic functions to be served by an adequate pleading. That requirement clearly identifies what must be included in the pleading, but does not explain why that content is needed. Courts quite often refer to the "essential elements" requirement as a pleading objective in itself, without seeking to explore what lies beneath that requirement. Yet, it is in the application of the essential elements requirement that the functions of the pleading are most fully developed. For that requirement, as *Hamling* implicitly suggests, may find its grounding in functions that exist apart from providing notice and protection against double jeopardy.

The discussion of pleading functions that follows focuses primarily upon the relationship of those functions to the essential elements requirement. This should not be taken to suggest that a functional analysis is less helpful in determining the scope of other pleading requirements. Courts utilize a functional analysis in applying all four of the basic pleading standards discussed in § 19.3—the essential elements requirement, the requirement of sufficient factual specificity, the prohibition against duplicity (i.e., charging separate offenses in a single count), and the prohibition against multiplicity (i.e., charging a single offense in more than one count). Indeed, the functions underlying the latter three standards are more readily identified and therefore more frequently lead to a functional analysis in the application of those standards.

(b) Double Jeopardy Protection. Protecting the defendant against multiple jeopardy for the same offense was a pleading func-

§ 19.2

1. 418 U.S. 87, 94 S.Ct. 2887, 41 L.Ed.2d 590 (1974).

tion given considerable attention at common law. Since offenses are distinguished for double jeopardy purposes by reference to their different elements, that pleading function may explain in part the requirement that all of the essential elements of the alleged crime be specified in the charging instrument. Where a first and second charge are based on the same event, they could readily be charging separate offenses or the same offense. By insisting that each charge contain all the elements of the crime and looking to the degree of overlap in the elements specified in the two charges, a court can ensure that the charges are actually for two different offenses. Of course, even a complete overlap of the elements does not mean the offenses in the two charges are the same, as each charge may refer to separate actions involving separate victims. Accordingly, to allow the court to distinguish between the same and separate offenses, the pleading also has to contain sufficient factual specificity to separate one series of actions from another.

The double jeopardy function thus explains a considerable portion of both the essential elements requirement and the requirement of sufficient factual specificity. It does not, however, explain the full scope of either requirement. The identification of the offense by name or statutory citation and the identification of the event by reference to date, place, and victim would usually be sufficient to separate one offense from another. As will be seen in § 19.3, considerably more is required to satisfy the essential elements and factual specificity requirements. Thus, even at a time when the charging instrument was the primary record of the trial, it is questionable whether the double jeopardy function gave to those pleading requirements any special content above and beyond that demanded by other pleading functions.

More significantly, the determination of double jeopardy—especially with the introduction of doctrine of collateral estoppel and the broadened definition of the same offense [2]—is no longer a matter that courts expect to resolve on the basis of matching charging instruments in the first and second prosecutions. Transcriptions of trial proceedings are available to determine exactly what was put before the jury in the first case and the prosecution can be expected, in response to a defense objection, to explain how the anticipated proof in the second case will differ. Thus, commentators and a few courts have questioned whether the double jeopardy function of pleadings has any modern relevancy, as related either to the essential elements requirement or the sufficient specificity requirement.[3] Many courts continue, however, to cite the double jeopardy function in discussing both of those pleading requirements, although it rarely is cited as an independent grounding for finding that a pleading fails to satisfy either requirement.

(c) **Providing Notice.** Discussions of pleading functions almost invariably start by noting that the pleading must "fairly inform" the accused of charges against him. Indeed, the notice function has been characterized by the Supreme Court as constitutionally mandated by the defendant's Sixth Amendment right "to be informed of the nature and cause of the accusation." The major issue presented by the notice function is not whether it should exist, but rather what scope it should have. Disagreements exist as to both the subjects for which notice is needed, and the degree of particularization that should be required in providing notice as to those subjects.

The notice function clearly requires that the pleading identify the conduct of the defendant alleged to have constituted a crime. The primary disagreement here, as discussed in § 19.3(b), concerns the amount of factual detail that must be included in describing that conduct. Whether the notice function also underlies the essential elements pleading requirement is not so clear. Some argue that

2. See § 17.4.

3. The function of implementing the double jeopardy bar is recognized as retaining relevance, however, in the application of the multiplicity and duplicity prohibitions. Multiplicity is barred largely because it can lead to multiple sentences for a single offense, while duplicity is prohibited in part because it may expose the defendant to double jeopardy. See § 19.3(c).

the notice function requires notification of the prosecution's legal theory and that this objective, in turn, mandates that the pleading set forth the presence of each of the essential elements. Others disagree, arguing that the notice function requires no more than the identification of the crime charged by reference to its name or statutory citation. They view the essential elements pleading requirement as resting primarily upon other pleading functions to be discussed below. The issue is not simply of theoretical significance. Where a pleading requirement is viewed as tied to the notice function, courts are more likely to treat an objection based on the pleading's alleged failure to meet that requirement as "forfeited" or "waived" by the defendant's failure to raise that objection before trial (that failure supposedly suggesting that the defendant did not see the need for further notice in preparing for trial). Moreover, where notice is the key to a pleading requirement, courts are more likely to look to the availability of other means of obtaining notice, such as the bill of particulars, in determining the degree of particularity that satisfies that requirement. Finally, on post-trial review, a pleading defect based on the failure to provide notice is more likely to be treated as harmless since the trial record will often suggest that defendant was not surprised or otherwise prejudiced by his lack of notice.

Courts have undoubtedly looked to the notice function in formulating certain dictates of the requirement that the pleading allege the essential elements of the offense. Thus, in *United States v. Cruikshank*,[4] the Supreme Court stressed the absence of fair notice in holding invalid an indictment which charged defendants, in the language of the applicable criminal provision, with having intentionally hindered certain citizens in their "free exercise and enjoyment * * * of the several rights and privileges granted and secured to them by the constitution." This pleading was defective because the defendants had not received adequate notice of which of the many constitutional rights of citizens had been taken from the alleged victims. The Court noted that when the definition of an offense "includes generic terms," such as "rights and privileges granted and secured by the constitution," the indictment may not simply repeat those terms; "it must state the species,—it must descend to particulars."

In *Cruikshank,* the defendants might well have been uncertain as to the content of that element of the crime that was held not to be adequately stated. Other cases, however, have overturned indictments for failing to allege a particular element of a crime where there was no suggestion of defense uncertainty as to the element's content or legal significance. Thus, indictments have been held invalid for failing to allege the element of intent even though the statute was cited and that element was either included in the statute or apparent from decisions interpreting the statute. Similarly, courts have overturned convictions for an indictment's failure to allege a particular element even though the defendant did not claim to be surprised when the jury was charged on that element and, indeed, first raised the pleading defect after his conviction. That the courts are concerned here with a function other than providing notice is also reflected in cases holding indictments invalid even though the missing element was alleged in a bill of particulars.

(d) Facilitating Judicial Review. Commentators have argued, with considerable force, that the essential elements requirement is based primarily upon a separate pleading function that they characterize as a "judicial review" function. This function was described in *Cruikshank* as requiring that the pleading "inform the [trial] court of the facts alleged, so that it may decide whether they are sufficient in law to support a conviction, if one should be had." Although the judicial review function is mentioned by courts far less frequently than the "notice" and "double jeopardy" functions, it remains a cornerstone of both federal and state pleading require-

4. 92 U.S. (2 Otto) 542, 23 L.Ed. 588 (1876). Although an older case, the *Cruikshank* ruling is repeatedly cited and followed by cases applying the Federal Rules. See e.g., Russell v. United States, 369 U.S. 749, 82 S.Ct. 1038, 8 L.Ed.2d 240 (1962).

ments. It probably explains more reversals of convictions based upon pleading defects than either of the other pleading functions.

One objective of the judicial review function is to permit the trial court to rule before trial on the sufficiency of the prosecution's theory of the statutory elements. Consider, for example, a situation in which the statute does not include a particular mens rea element, and there is some question as to the level of mens rea required. The pleading's inclusion of a specific mens rea allegation could be helpful in settling that issue in advance of trial and possibly even in avoiding an unnecessary trial. Thus, if the trial court were to decide, on a motion to dismiss, that the offense requires actual intent rather than some lower level of mens rea alleged in the pleading, the prosecution might conclude that its evidence would be insufficient and not even seek to return with a new pleading alleging the required intent. This aspect of the review function also explains why courts sometimes have insisted upon more factual specificity in allegations as to the elements of a particular offense most likely to raise difficult legal questions.[5] It does not explain, however, why courts have so often dismissed indictments for failing to allege elements of the offense that were clear under the prevailing law and proven at trial without any objection by the defense. These rulings suggest that there is more to the judicial review function than simply facilitating pretrial clarification of the substance of the law. That additional component arguably is to ensure that there is a jurisdictional grounding for the issuance of the court's judgment. Such judicial review builds on the concept that an adequate pleading serves a further function—to provide a formal basis for the exercise of court authority.

(e) Providing a Jurisdictional Grounding. The common law viewed the accusatory instrument as "providing a formal basis for the judgment, so that the indictment or information * * * [had to] set forth everything necessary for a complete case on paper." This function of the pleading has been challenged as unnecessary now that complete trial records are available. That record, whether defendant enters a guilty plea or is convicted after a trial, should establish the presence of all elements necessary to support the trial court's authority to have entered judgment against the defendant. Of course, prior to trial, the evidentiary grounding for jurisdiction has not yet been put before the court, but there is nothing inherently offensive to the concept of jurisdiction in proceeding to the adjudication stage simply on an initial allegation that the defendant has committed a crime that is within the jurisdiction of the court. Such a general allegation could be presented, of course, without also setting forth the presence of each of the essential elements of the crime. Thus, it is argued that, with the availability of the trial record, the demands upon the pleading to provide jurisdictional grounding have diminished to the point where a pleading that simply identifies the offense and its place should be sufficient.

Although perhaps having some influence in certain jurisdictions, the above argument has failed to produce a significant shift in the view of the pleading as a formal document. Adequate pleading specificity, at least as to the essential elements of the offense, continues to be treated as a prerequisite for the exercise of judicial authority. Thus, courts frequently describe an indictment or information that fails to allege "each and every ele-

5. Russell v. United States, supra note 4, is illustrative. The Supreme Court there held insufficient an indictment charging a violation of 2 U.S.C.A. § 192, which makes it a misdemeanor for a witness to refuse to answer before a Congressional Committee "any question pertinent to the * * * [subject] under inquiry." The indictment was held defective because it failed to specifically identify the subject of the Committee's inquiry, which had to be known to determine whether the questions asked (which were set forth in the indictment) met the statutory requirement of pertinency. The Court noted that the pertinency element had been the subject of frequent litigation, with the lower courts often beset with "difficulties and doubts" in identifying the inquiry subject. Since this "critical and difficult question * * * could be obviated by a simple averment," the prosecution would not be allowed to simply describe the question asked as "pertinent," but had to also identify the particular subject under inquiry to which the question was allegedly pertinent.

ment of the offense" as importing a "jurisdictional defect" that renders "void ab initio" any subsequent conviction, notwithstanding the adequacy of the evidence produced at trial. The trial record may undercut a jurisdictional grounding that was alleged satisfactorily in the pleading, but it cannot likewise cure the failure of the pleading to provide that grounding initially. Some courts, apparently recognizing the diminished need to rely on the charging instrument in providing a formal basis for the judgement, have demanded less from that instrument where the procedural context of the objection focuses basically on that function of pleading. This is the case, for example, where the defense challenges an accusatory pleading of "failing to charge an offense" and that objection is not raised until after the trial is completed (thereby largely eliminating concern as to providing notice or facilitating judicial review). The difference among courts in their willingness to broadly construe the charge so as to negate such a "jurisdictional" contention is probably explained in part by different perspectives on the importance of the pleading in providing a formal basis for the judgment. All courts, however, will continue to uphold such a contention, and reverse the conviction, where the pleading clearly fails to include an essential element of the offense, notwithstanding adequate proof and presentation of that element at trial.

(f) Safeguarding Defendant's Right to Prosecution by Indictment. In recent years, courts have cited yet another pleading function, relevant only to the indictment, that may also contribute to the categorization of certain pleading defects as jurisdictional in nature. As the Supreme Court has long noted, the indictment is the product of the grand jurors and the defendant is entitled to be tried only on the offense that the jurors desired to charge. To allow a defendant "to be convicted on the basis of facts not found by, and perhaps not even presented to, the grand jury which indicted him" is to deprive him "of a basic protection which the guaranty of the intervention of the grand jury was designed to secure." [6] This concern is said to be reflected in "the prohibition against the amendment of indictments except by resubmission to the grand jury, and the bar against the 'curing' of defective indictments by issuance of a bill of particulars."

Some courts have suggested that the preservation of the defendant's right to be tried only upon a charge properly found by the grand jury also underlies basic pleading requirements. The essential elements requirement is said to serve this function in two respects. First, the inclusion of each of the essential elements in the indictment tends to structure the grand jury's charging decision, focusing its attention on the specific requirements for criminal liability rather than a general sense of the accused's wrongdoing. Second, insofar as the essential elements requirements demands a reference to the factual basis for each of these elements, it prevents the prosecution from shifting to basic factual groundings other than those upon which the grand jury relied. Other pleading requirements also serve to implement that safeguard. The requirement that the pleading include sufficient factual specificity to provide adequate notice furnishes additional protection against departure from the grand jury's factual charging theory. The prohibition against duplicity ensures that the grand jury recognized the distinction in the necessary elements of separate crimes and found sufficient evidence to indict on each.

At a time when grand jury proceedings were not transcribed, the indictment furnished the only evidence of what was before the grand jury and what it had decided. Today, however, such transcriptions are readily available and can be used to ensure both that

6. Russell v. United States, supra note 4. As Justice Harlan noted in his *Russell* dissent, such statements do not mean to suggest that the prosecution may never use at trial any fact that was not before the grand jury. The basic concern here simply is that the prosecutor not shift to a different factual theory of the offense than was before the grand jury—i.e., that the prosecution's facts be consistent with "what was in the minds of the grand jury as to essential elements of the specific offenses charged." United States v. Rizzo, 373 F.Supp. 204 (S.D.N.Y.1973), affirmed 493 F.2d 1399 (2d Cir.1974).

the grand jury was made aware of each of the distinct elements of the crime and that the prosecution is not seeking at trial to establish the offense by reference to events different than those presented to the grand jury. With that record available, the continued use of pleading requirements as an indirect means of safeguarding the defendant's right to grand jury screening has been questioned. Of course, in most jurisdictions, following the Supreme Court's rulings in *Costello* and *Bank of Nova Scotia,* courts will not look to the grand jury transcript absent a strong indication of prosecutorial misconduct.[7] The defendant's interest in obtaining judicial review to ensure correct grand jury screening is thought not to outweigh the delay and other costs presented in allowing challenges that would entail review of the grand jury transcript. Although the costs are reduced somewhat where the court need not look beyond the pleading, arguably similar considerations should carry over to pleading challenges designed only to safeguard that same defense interest in correct grand jury screening. Thus, commentators have questioned whether challenges should be sustained where the indictment otherwise satisfies basic pleading functions such as providing notice and allowing for pretrial judicial review. Use of the pleading challenge to safeguard the grand jury's screening process is thought to be especially vulnerable where defendant first objected to the alleged pleading deficiency after conviction. In many jurisdictions, most flaws relating to grand jury screening are treated as mooted by a conviction following a fair trial, even where the alleged flaw was called to the attention of the trial court prior to trial.[8]

Notwithstanding the above analysis, many courts continue to refer to the safeguarding of the defendant's right to grand jury screening as an independent function of pleading requirements as applied to indictments. Moreover, they treat that function as imposing pleading prerequisites that are jurisdictional in nature. Thus, where the indictment was so uncertain that the prosecution could readily have based its case on factual elements that were not before the grand jury, courts have characterized the indictment as "failing to charge an offense" and struck down convictions even though the pleading defect was first raised on appeal. In some instances, all elements of the offense were described in general terms and it was questionable whether the lack of specificity would have required a reversal if judged by reference only to other pleading functions. Indeed, a lack of specificity has been held to require a reversal as to a felony which had to be alleged by an indictment even though the same pleading would have been satisfactory for an included misdemeanor charge that could be brought by information.

§ 19.3 Basic Pleading Defects

(a) Failure to Allege Essential Elements. No pleading defect has resulted in more dismissals of indictments and informations than the failure to allege all of the essential elements of the offense. The essential elements requirement demands that the pleading allege the presence of each of the basic elements required for the commission of the offense—in general, the elements of mental state, criminal conduct, and resulting harm. It does not demand, however, that the pleading negate exemptions, excuses, or justifications that relieve one of liability notwithstanding the presence of the basic elements.

To avoid omitting a crucial element of the offense, prosecutors frequently draft pleadings that track the language of the criminal statute, adding appropriate factual references (e.g., the victim's name) along the way. Reliance upon the statutory language will be acceptable, however, only if "the words of [the statute] themselves fully, directly, and expressly, without any uncertainty or ambiguity, set forth all the elements necessary to constitute the offence." If the statute fails to refer to an essential element, such as mens rea, then that element must be added to the tracked statutory language in framing the

7. See §§ 15.5, 15.6.

8. See § 15.6(e).

pleading. Similarly, if courts have added a significant refinement in the interpretation of a particular statutory element, that element often must be pleaded as interpreted rather than as stated in the statutory language, especially if the judicial interpretation substantially limits the scope of the statutory language. Thus, where a manslaughter statute spoke of unlawful killings resulting from actions taken "without due caution and circumspection" and that phrase had been interpreted as requiring a "wanton or reckless disregard for human life" based on "actual knowledge of the threat imposed," the indictment could not allege the mens rea element by simply using the statutory "due caution and circumspection" language.[1] The majority rejected the contention of the dissenting judge that the judicial interpretation had merely added a "judicial gloss" to the meaning of the "due caution and circumspection" element, so that the statutory language had become a "term of art" that incorporated the judicial phrasing of the element. The statutory language, the majority noted, did not have a meaning "sufficiently precise" to convey its legal content in the statute charged. In particular, it had "not been consistently defined by judicial decision" in other contexts to include the "knowledge requirement" that the past decisions had incorporated in the special context of the manslaughter statute.

Most failures to allege essential elements are found in pleadings which do not track the statutory language (either because that language is not sufficient in itself or because the prosecutor prefers to set forth the substance of the statute in other terms). Here, the critical issue often is whether a particular element, though not set forth explicitly, is nevertheless included by implication. Courts tend to be more willing to find certain elements alleged by implication than others. Thus, indictments for murder need not state that the victim was a human being; the courts have long held that the very nature of the charge of "murder" suggests the presence of that element. On the other hand, the element of mens rea ordinarily will require a more explicit allegation. For example, in a typical ruling, one court held that an allegation that defendant "unlawfully sold" a pornographic magazine was insufficient to allege that defendant acted with scienter.[2] If the activity would have been one that inherently encompassed the mens rea (as in the case of "assaulting" another, which implies an intent to do bodily harm), the description of the act might have been sufficient in itself to allege the necessary mental element. But here the act lacked that quality, and describing it as "unlawful" was not a satisfactory alternative to setting forth explicitly the necessary knowledge and intent.

Although a pleading must contain the "essential facts" constituting the offense, the need for factual detail generally stems from the factual specificity pleading requirement rather than the essential elements requirement. An element of a crime very often can be pleaded without providing any specific factual reference. Thus, a defendant can be alleged to have acted with "depraved indifference" without further alleging an awareness of specific circumstances that produced that level of mens rea. So too, if the aggravated assault statute requires the infliction of "serious bodily injury" or the use of a "deadly instrument," the presence of these elements can be alleged in the very terms of the statute. If the pleading should require an identification of the particular injury or particular instrument, that additional detail flows from the factual specificity requirement rather than the essential elements requirement.

Many courts do view as an essential elements defect the description of an essential element without sufficient specificity to distinguish between alternative legal components of the element. As the Supreme Court noted in *Cruikshank,*[3] where the statute uses "generic terms," the accusatory instrument must go beyond those terms and "descend to

§ 19.3

1. United States v. Keith, 605 F.2d 462 (9th Cir.1979).

2. Fitzsimmons v. State, 48 Md.App. 193, 426 A.2d 4 (1981).

3. See § 19.2 at note 4.

particulars." The primary illustration of this principle is found in offenses that prohibited certain action when tied to the commission or attempted commission of another crime. The charge here ordinarily may not simply allege in a generic form that a relationship existed to other criminality (e.g., in burglary, alleging that the illegal entry was with an "intent to commit a felony"); it must specify the particular ulterior offense that fulfills the relationship in this case (e.g., by alleging an entry with "an intent to commit theft"). So too, in *Cruikshank,* the prosecution could not allege that the defendant hindered the victim's exercise of constitutional rights without specifying the particular constitutional right involved. Often also, where a statute specifies several different ways in which the crime can be committed, the pleading must refer to the particular alternative presented in the individual case. Simply using a verb that encompasses all of the statutorily proscribed methods of commission may be deemed too conclusory even where the statute itself uses that verb in describing the crime and sets forth the different methods in its definition section.[4] Rulings barring conclusory pleading of elements may not differ functionally from those requiring greater factual specificity, but they commonly are characterized as essential elements rulings because they look not so much to factual detail as to a further refinement in legal theory. As noted in subsection (d), the characterization of the defect as a failure to plead the essential elements rather than as a lack of sufficient specificity can have critical significance where the defense objection was not timely made.

(b) Insufficient Factual Specificity. As courts repeatedly note, "an indictment [or information] must not only contain all the elements of the offense charged, but must also provide the accused with a sufficient description of the acts he is alleged to have committed to enable him to defend himself adequately." The charging instrument must include a satisfactory response to the questions of "who * * *, what, where, and how." Precisely how much factual specificity is needed to make that response satisfactory will necessarily vary from one case to another. Relevant factors include the nature of the offense, the likely significance of particular factual variations in determining liability, the ability of the prosecution to identify a particular circumstance without a lengthy and basically evidentiary allegation, and the availability of alternative procedures for obtaining the particular information. It generally is agreed that the issue is not whether the alleged offense could be described with more certainty, but whether there is "sufficient particularity" to enable the accused to "prepare a proper defense."

In assessing the factual specificity of a charging instrument, courts start from the assumption that the defendant is innocent and consequently "has no knowledge of the facts charged against him." But even from the perspective of the innocent person, comparatively little information is needed to prepare a defense for some crimes. A charge of assault, for example, provides enough information if it identifies who was assaulted and when and where the assault occurred. There is no need to inform the defendant of how the assault occurred (at least where the charge is simple assault and not assault with a deadly weapon). If the defendant wasn't there, the manner of assault will be irrelevant to his defense, and if he was present, he will be aware of the circumstances. Greater specificity will be required, however, where the crime encompasses more factual variations. Thus, if the defendant is charged with fraud arising from a series of statements made to the victim, he ordinarily must be informed as to which of his representations is alleged to be false. On the other hand, he need not also be

4. The charging instrument need not, however, allege a single method. Disjunctive pleadings of different methods is commonly allowed where more than one method may have been used. In those jurisdictions not allowing disjunctive pleadings, conjunctive pleadings are allowed, even as to inherently inconsistent means, and the prosecution at trial is required to prove either, rather than both, notwithstanding the use of the conjunctive. Cf. United States v. Miller, § 19.5 at note 4. The same is true also of different mental elements and even different harms.

furnished with a factual explanation as to why those statements were both false and material to the transaction. To insist that the charge include such matter would be tantamount to requiring that the supporting evidence be alleged and could often require a lengthy and highly detailed allegation.

In general, courts are more likely to require specificity as to facts establishing an element of the offense than as to facts which merely identify the event, particularly where other identifying elements are already included. Thus, in the case of a theft, the court is more likely to insist upon a specification of the property taken than the name of the owner, provided the place from which the property was taken is identified. Traditionally, time and place have been viewed as not requiring considerable specificity because they ordinarily do not involve proof of an element of crime. Thus, the time allegation can refer to the event as having occurred "on or about" a certain date and, within reasonable limits, proof of a date before or after that specified will be sufficient, provided it is within the statute of limitations. Similarly, the allegation of place may state only that the event occurred within the jurisdiction of the court (e.g., within a particular county).

(c) Duplicity and Multiplicity. Duplicity is the charging of separate offenses in a single count. This practice is unacceptable because it prevents the jury from deciding guilt or innocence on each offense separately and may make it difficult to determine whether the conviction rested on only one of the offenses or both. Duplicity can result in prejudice to the defendant in the shaping of evidentiary rulings, in producing a conviction on less than a unanimous verdict as to each separate offense, in determining the sentence, and in limiting review on appeal. A valid duplicity objection raised before trial will force the government to elect the offense upon which it will proceed, but will not require the dismissal of the indictment. If a pretrial objection is not made, but the defect is noted before the case is submitted to the jury, the trial court can still cure the error by making a corrective instruction. Where the objection is first raised after verdict, however, the duplicity defect is viewed as waived.

A multiplicitous indictment charges a single offense in several counts. It often is the product of a prosecutor's mistaken assumption that a particular statute creates several separate offenses rather than a single crime that can be accomplished through multiple means. A multiplicity issue is also presented when a series of repeated acts are charged as separate crimes but the defendant claims they are part of a continuous transaction and therefore a single crime. The principle danger in multiplicity is that the defendant will receive multiple sentences for a single offense, although courts have noted that multiple counts may also work against defendant by leading the jury to believe that defendant's conduct is especially serious because it constitutes more than one crime. Multiplicity does not require dismissal of the indictment. The court may respond to a successful objection by requiring the prosecutor to elect one count, consolidating the various counts, or simply advising the jury that only one offense is charged. If the objection is first raised after conviction, the defendant will be entitled to relief from an improperly imposed multiple sentence, but he cannot object to the possible impact of the multiplicity upon the jury's assessment of his guilt.

(d) Late Objections. As noted in § 19.1(d), a critical element of the modern pleading reform was to provide for a "waiver" or "forfeiture" of pleading objections that were not raised before trial. That reform was not carried over, however, to what Federal Rule 12(b) and similar state provisions describe as the "failure to charge an offense," which "shall be noticed * * * at any time during the pendency of the proceedings." The "failure to charge an offense" generally is read as including only the failure to meet the essential elements requirement. Why is that pleading requirement singled out and basically exempted from the timely-objection rule? The answer appears to lie in the non-notice functions of the essential elements requirement, with special emphasis on the concept that the pleading serve as the formal basis of the judgment of conviction. Thus, it is commonly paired with the "fail[ure] to show jurisdiction," which may also be "noticed * * * at any time during the pendency of the proceedings" under Rule 12(b)(2).

The jurisdictional nature of the essential elements requirement allows such an objection to be raised for the first time after conviction, even though previously known to the defense, and thereby provides an incentive to the defense to delay making the objection. Where made before trial, a successful objection is likely to result only in the production of a new indictment or information which cures the defect by correctly alleging all of the elements. While the delay resulting from the process of forcing the prosecution to start over again may be of value to the defense under certain circumstances, that advantage hardly compares to the value of overturning a conviction. Here too, the prosecution is likely to return with a new indictment or information that now alleges all of the elements, but the defense has gained a second opportunity to avoid a conviction (and sometimes a somewhat stronger plea-bargaining position where the prosecution prefers not to force upon the complainant and other witnesses the inconvenience of another trial).

In considering essential elements objections first raised after conviction, appellate courts are fully aware of the defense incentive to sandbag and they often react accordingly. Noting that the failure of the defense to raise the objection at an earlier point suggests that it was not misled by any defect in the charging instrument, the courts repeatedly state that the charging instrument not previously challenged "should be construed liberally in favor of its sufficiency." Indeed, it is said that the pleading will be held sufficient unless it is "so defective that it does not by any reasonable construction" charge the necessary elements. Nonetheless, there is considerable variation to be found from one appellate court to another in its willingness to stretch the language of the pleading to find that an allegedly missing element was sufficiently set forth "by implication." One will find satisfactory, against a late objection, a pleading that simply alleged "the commission of a battery," without referring to any of the elements of the crime. Another will hold invalid a murder indictment that alleged that the defendant "unlawfully, willfully, deliberately and with premeditation" killed a particular person, reasoning that such language could not reasonably be construed as alleging the necessary element of "malice aforethought." Some will lend weight to a statutory citation where the statute clearly set forth the element in question, while others will deem the citation to add nothing (a standard position where the challenge is presented before trial).

Appellate courts frequently note that the lack of factual specificity does not in itself result in a "failure to charge an offense" and therefore a deficiency in specificity is lost by the defense's failure to raise the objection before trial. Thus, in *United States v. Varkonyi*,[5] the Court of Appeals carefully distinguished between two alleged defects, raised for the first time on appeal, in an indictment charging the defendant with the crime of interfering with a federal official. The defendant could raise the indictment's failure to allege that the victim of defendant's assault was a federal official; because that went to the pleading of an element of the crime. The defendant could not raise, however, the failure of the allegation of "forcible interference" to spell out how defendant had interfered with the official's performance of his governmental duties as that merely related to providing notice through factual specificity. Appellate courts, however, do not always find the distinction between an essential elements defect and a factual specificity defect so easy to apply. Thus, disagreements may be found on precisely the same pleading defect—as where one court holds that the failure to identify the ulterior offense in charging burglary (i.e., charging only entry with "an intent to commit a crime") is an elements defect requiring reversal even where first raised on appeal, and another holds that it is a specifici-

5. 645 F.2d 453 (5th Cir.1981).

ty defect lost because it was not raised before trial.

§ 19.4 Bill of Particulars

(a) Nature of the Bill. The motion for a bill of particulars requests that the prosecution be directed to furnish further information (i.e., "particulars") concerning the offense charged in the information or indictment. The motion ordinarily lists a series of questions concerning the events cited in the charge that the defense would have the prosecution answer. Thus, if an indictment charging the obstruction of a public official has simply tracked the language of the statute, the motion might ask for the answers to such questions as what official duties were obstructed and how did the obstruction occur. Assuming that the motion is granted, the status of the prosecution's response falls somewhere between a pleading and a discovery response. The factual allegations contained in the bill of particulars will limit the government's case at trial in the same manner as factual allegations in an original charging instrument. Thus, the rules governing variance between proof and pleading apply to the bill of particulars just as they do to an indictment or information. The allegations of the bill of particulars are not treated as equivalent to those in the original charging instrument, however, when it comes to meeting basic pleading requirements. If an indictment or information does not state all of the essential elements, it cannot be cured by a bill of particulars that alleges facts establishing the missing element. The bill arguably may offset a lack of factual specificity, but it clearly will not save a pleading that fails completely to charge an offense. On the other hand, in providing factual allegations beyond those contained in the original pleading, the bill can undermine the pleading. If it reveals that the facts underlying the pleading do not establish a crime, the result will be the dismissal of a charge that would otherwise have been upheld on its face.

(b) Standards for Issuance. Aside from its use in connection with short-form pleading, the issuance of a bill of particulars lies in the discretion of the trial court. Moreover, appellate courts give considerable leeway to the trial court when reviewing its exercise of that discretion (in part, perhaps, because the trial judge's ruling ordinarily is challenged on appeal following a conviction). Appellate courts do, however, offer various guidelines to trial courts as to where the bill should or should not be granted. The difficulty here is that those guidelines tend to be overgeneralizations that provide limited assistance in individual cases.

The basic standard for passing on a motion for a bill of particulars is "whether it is necessary that defendant have the particulars sought in order to prepare his defense and in order that prejudicial surprise will be avoided." Taken literally, this standard might require that defendant gain disclosure of everything in the prosecution's files, because only such broad discovery can assure that defendant will not be subjected to "prejudicial surprise." But the bill relates to the pleading, and the concern therefore should be with surprise only as to the particular acts or events that underlie the pleading, not with the manner in which they will be established at trial. Its function is only to give the defendant somewhat more factual detail, if needed, as to what will constitute the elements of the offense. Yet, at the same time, in recognizing defendant's need for particulars to "prepare his defense," trial courts often allow the bill to go somewhat beyond what would be obtained in even the most detailed pleading of the charges. Indeed, some courts have been willing to include an extremely broad range of circumstances among the required particulars as to the acts that constituted the crime (e.g., the names of non-participant eyewitnesses to the acts), but most have resisted efforts to expand the bill beyond the basics of who, what, where, and how.

In light of the bill's relationship to the pleading, it is not surprising that the courts repeatedly state that "a bill of particulars may not call for evidentiary matter." The discovery of the prosecution's evidence is a task for the procedures of pretrial discovery, which often require a certain degree of reciprocal disclosure from the defense. Yet, in many instances, a request for more information relating to the factual elements of the charge necessarily also provides information about the government's evidence. Moreover, as courts place more emphasis upon the defense's use of the bill to facilitate its own investigation of the underlying events, the overlap becomes greater. In the end, the issue may not be whether granting the motion will disclose the government's evidence, but whether the formulation of the defendant's request fits the basic function of the bill. Thus, a court may be willing to grant a motion asking that the government identify those persons who participated in the conduct it seeks to establish, but not a motion asking for a list of the government's witnesses.[1]

In ruling upon a defense motion for a bill of particulars, a trial court must also take into consideration the scope of the pretrial discovery that will be available to the defense. The government will often cite discovery opportunities as providing the defense with ample protection against prejudicial surprise at trial and with adequate leads for preparing a meaningful defense. It will note also that discovery procedures, in contrast to the bill of particulars, will often require reciprocal disclosure from the defense. The defense, on the other hand, is likely to argue that even the most complete discovery, if combined with a broadly stated accusatory instrument, is likely to be of limited use because it may suggest several different directions in which the prosecution may proceed. Only the bill of particulars, the defense will argue, serves to limit the shape of the case, and thereby allow the defense to properly focus its limited investigatory resources. To this contention the prosecution will respond that it should not be required before trial to virtually set its case in stone so that the differences that almost invariably occur between pretrial investigation and trial testimony can become the source of a constant stream of defense challenges to variances between the trial proof and the particulars. The evaluation of these arguments will require consideration of several factors, including the nature of the offense involved, the nature of the events that serve as the basis for the charge, and the breadth of the pleading. Consideration must be given, in particular, to the complexity of the offense, the range of activities it encompasses, and the time span it covers. Massive indictments, sprawling over many years and implicating a large number of defendants, obviously present a stronger case for a bill of particulars.

Application of the principles discussed above necessarily varies with both the circumstances of the case and the approach of the individual judge. As a result, as both courts and commentators have noted, rulings on motions for bills of particulars tend to reflect highly particularized judgments. In almost any jurisdiction, and particularly in the federal system, "precedent can be found for every ruling from one extreme to another."

§ 19.5 Amendments of the Pleading

(a) Varied Uses. Various circumstances may lead the prosecution to propose an amendment to a charging instrument. The prosecution may find a technical irregularity in the indictment or information (e.g., an improper statutory citation) and utilize an amendment to make a correction even though the error would not render the pleading fatally defective. The prosecution may conclude on its own initiative (or in response to a defense motion to dismiss) that the charge fails to include a necessary element or lacks needed specificity and seek to cure that fatal defect with an amendment. Either before or during trial the prosecution may discover that its evidence will vary from the allegations in the pleading and seek to avoid that variance by an amendment that renders the pleading

§ 19.4

1. Matching the prohibition against disclosure of evidentiary matter—and raising similar problems in application—is the prohibition against disclosure of the government's legal theory. Here again, an absolute prohibition must fail if the bill is to serve its purpose. A bill that provides the detail behind a very general factual allegation will often suggest a legal theory not apparent from the original allegation. See e.g., United States v. Cooney, 217 F.Supp. 417 (D.Colo.1963) (requiring prosecution to state in what respects defendants charged with civil rights violations, had acted "under color of law").

consistent with such evidence. The prosecution may also move to amend following the completion of its case. Evidence may have been introduced at variance with the pleading without a defense objection, and the prosecution may move to amend to conform the pleading to the proof. So too, some aspect of the pleading may not have been supported by the prosecution's evidence, and the prosecution may move to delete that portion of the charge and have only the remainder presented to the jury. Whether amendments will be allowed to achieve these different objectives will depend upon the character of the proposed amendment and the standard governing amendments that is applied in the particular jurisdiction.

(b) The Prejudice/Different–Offense Standard. The dominant standard governing amendments is the two-pronged standard that permits an amendment provided it does not either (i) result in prejudice to the accused or (ii) charge a different crime. This standard is set forth in Federal Rule 7(e), which provides:

> The court may permit an information to be amended at any time before verdict or finding if no additional or different offense is charged and if substantial rights of the defendant are not prejudiced.

Although Federal Rule 7(e) is limited to amendments of the information, most states apply the two-pronged standard to both indictments and informations. The federal practice of utilizing different standards for amendments of the information and the indictment, while not unique, reflects a minority position.

Of the two prongs of the dominant standard, the prejudice prong clearly has produced the greater consistency in approach among the various state and federal courts. General agreement exists that the concept of "prejudice" to the "substantial rights" of the accused requires an inquiry that focuses on the element of surprise. Ordinarily, the defense, in opposing an amendment, must make some showing that the proposed change introduces an element of surprise that will interfere with the defense's ability to defend against the charges. Since such prejudice may be avoided before trial by granting an appropriate continuance, the defense usually must combine with its prejudice showing substantial grounds for opposing a continuance. On appeal, an amendment allowed before trial is unlikely to be held to have injured the substantial rights of the defendant where a continuance was granted or none was requested. Since continuances during trial (particularly a jury trial) are less likely to be granted, the prosecution faces a much more difficult task in overcoming a defense claim of surprise as to an amendment offered during trial. Such amendments are most likely to be accepted where the prosecution can show that the amendment does not change substantially the factual basis of the offense as set forth in the original pleading, the bill of particulars, or the discovery made available to the defense. Where the amendment seeks to conform the pleading to prosecution proof that varied from the pleading and the defense failed to object to that variance, the prosecution often may successfully utilize that failure as evidence of a lack of prejudicial surprise. So too, since a charge on a higher offense necessarily encompasses all lesser included offenses, the defense cannot readily argue prejudicial surprise where the prosecution, even during trial, seeks to discard the higher offense and amend the charge to retain only the elements of the lesser included offense.

The prohibition against amendments that charge a different offense has produced somewhat greater divergence in its interpretation. There is general agreement that this prohibition stands without regard to the absence of prejudicial surprise. The precise content of the "different offense" standard, however, has been the source of disagreement at its edges. A different offense clearly is presented where the indictment alleges an offense under a different statutory provision and that offense is not a lesser included offense under the original charge. A charge even under the same statute generally is recognized as producing a new offense if the underlying "identity" of the original charge is changed by relying on an entirely different series of events as the basis for the violation. Division arises when the statute remains the same, the basic incident remains the same, but the statute lists alternative means of commission, harms, or subjects, and the shift is from one alternative to another. Many courts would view such a shift as not changing the offense charged. They treat the amendment as merely shifting the facts that will be relied upon to establish the same basic element of the crime. From this perspective, to disallow the amendment would be to draw a functionally unpersuasive distinction between basically similar amendments depending upon whether the statute describes an element generally (e.g., simply uses the term "narcotics") or specifies various alternatives that will satisfy that element (e.g., by listing different types of narcotics). If a shift from one alternative to another does not change the element of the offense (and therefore does not allege a new offense) under the first type of statute, neither should it do so under the second type of statute.

Carrying this single-element analysis to its logical extreme, one court allowed a shift in a first degree murder charge from premeditated killing to a killing in the course of a felony since all that was altered was means of establishing the mens rea element for a single statutory offense.[1] Other courts would not accept such an amendment, as they would define the elements of the offense far more narrowly. The most confining position in this regard treats each statutory alternative as establishing a separate element (and therefore a separate offense) if it requires proof that the other alternative does not. A less restrictive position would find a new offense only where the newly pleaded alternative related to a distinction that was central to the nature of the offense or that resulted in an increase in the severity of the potential penalty.

Divergence in the judicial interpretation of the prohibition against amendments alleging a different offense may be the product of quite different perspectives on the purpose of that prohibition. One characterization of the prohibition is that of a flat rule safeguarding against prejudicial surprise.[2] If the concept of a different offense is limited to different underlying criminal events or different statutory prohibitions, then it can readily be assumed that a shift to a different offense, even before trial, ordinarily will create a substantial possibility of such surprise. Of course, prejudicial surprise is not inevitable, particularly where the basic incident remains the same, but the potential may be so great as to justify an automatic bar where the defense objects to the amendment. On the other hand, the different-offense prohibition may be seen as an attempt to protect the role of the agency that screened the charge, whether the grand jury in the case of an indictment or the magistrate in the case of an information. From this perspective, the confines of an offense arguably should be narrower. While one might not demand that the precise evidentiary basis presented to the screening agency be the grounding for the charge presented by amendment, the basic factual theory of the offense arguably should remain the same or the defendant has not truly had the particular charge against him screened by that agency.

The desire to protect the role of the screening agency also may be reflected in the treatment of amendments that seek to cure a defective charging instrument by adding an element of the statutory offense that was not originally pleaded. Arguably the underlying assumption of the prohibition against charg-

§ 19.5

1. State v. Foy, 227 Kan. 405, 607 P.2d 481 (1980). The court added that there was no possibility of prejudice as the previously issued bill of particulars had "set forth the evidence the State intended to rely on to prove felony murder."

2. Although the separate offense concept is also critical in the application of the double jeopardy clause, the prohibition against amendments alleging a new offense appears to have no relationship to the pleading function of protecting against multiple jeopardy. An amendment shifting to a new offense prior to the attachment of jeopardy would pose no threat to the double jeopardy bar, and even if the amendment were allowed during trial, the original charge would still stand as evidence that the defendant had been placed in jeopardy on the offense charged there as well as that charged in the amendment. See also § 19.2(b).

ing an "additional or different offense" is that the original charge did, indeed, successfully charge an offense. Under this view, if the original charge was fatally defective because it omitted an essential element, an amendment to cure that error necessarily alleges a "new offense." A contrary reading, however, is not clearly forbidden by the language of the typical different-offense prohibition. That prohibition also could be read as barring only a change in the offense from that which the original charge sought to allege, whether successfully or not. Such a reading would, however, remove the teeth from the jurisdictional quality of the essential elements pleading requirement. A challenge to the charge as failing to allege an element of the offense, whether made before, during, or after trial, could be met by an amendment to add the missing element (assuming no prejudicial surprise). Courts therefore refuse to consider the possibility of an amendment in such cases. While they do so basically in recognition of the jurisdictional grounding of the pleading (the failure of the pleading to charge an offense leaving the court with no basis for proceeding further), they also note that allowing such an amendment would undercut the role of the essential elements requirement in ensuring that all elements were found by the relevant screening agency (i.e., the grand jury in an indictment jurisdiction and the preliminary hearing magistrate in an information jurisdiction).

(c) The Form/Substance Distinction. A substantial group of states adhere to the formulation that permits amendment as to "form," but not as to "substance." Although some of these states apply this distinction to allow roughly the same type of amendments that would be permitted under the prejudice/different-offense standard, others apply it to allow only a considerably narrower range of amendments. Here, even though there is no indication of prejudice, an amendment that falls short of changing the basic offense can nonetheless be prohibited as an alteration of substance. Amendments are said to fall into that category if they change or supply "essential facts that must be proved to make the act complained of a crime." Thus, a jurisdiction adopting a restrictive interpretation of the form/substance distinction is likely to bar automatically an amendment that substantially changes the pleading's description of the criminal act, the mens rea accompanying that act, or the consequences of that act. Such rulings have prohibited amendments that changed the original allegation that defendant defrauded an automobile dealer of a dollar amount to defrauding the dealer of an automobile selling for that amount, that changed the name of the owner of a stolen vehicle, and that changed the action involved in shoplifting from altering the price tag to removing the price tag.

(d) The *Bain* Rule. In the federal courts, the permissible scope of the amendment of an indictment is controlled by the *Bain* rule, which is based on the Supreme Court's ruling in *Ex parte Bain.*[3] The *Bain* ruling relied on common law principles that treated the indictment as the sole product of the grand jury, subject to alteration only by that body. As originally announced, the *Bain* rule imposed a prohibition against amending indictments that arguably was more restrictive than even the most stringent interpretation of the form/substance distinction. A few states that continue to look to the same common law principles (and thus are described as "*Bain* jurisdictions") have only slightly relaxed that original standard. In the federal courts, however, the *Bain* rule is now held to allow a somewhat broader range of amendments to the indictment, although not so broad as the Rule 7(e) standard applicable to informations.

Bain was decided in 1887, at a time when several states had started to depart from the early common law rule that "indictments could not be amended." The Supreme Court noted, however, that its ruling was "not left to the requirements of the common law," but was controlled by the "positive and restrictive language" of the Fifth Amendment guarantee of indictment by grand jury. That guarantee, the Court noted, entitles the defendant to be

3. 121 U.S. 1, 7 S.Ct. 781, 30 L.Ed. 849 (1887).

tried on the indictment as issued by the grand jury, not as amended by the prosecutor with permission of the trial court. A trial court could not allow alteration even as to matter that it deemed "surplusage" and therefore not critical to the grand jury's decision to indict. That prohibition followed, the Court reasoned, from its constitutional obligation to preserve the Fifth Amendment right to grand jury review:

> If it lies within the province of the court to change the charging part of an indictment to suit its own notions of what it ought to have been, or what the grand jury would probably have made if their attention had been called to suggested changes, the great importance that the common law attaches to an indictment by a grand jury * * * without which the Constitution says "no person shall be held to answer," may be frittered away until its value is almost destroyed.

Read broadly, Justice Miller's opinion in *Bain* would have barred any amendment to what he described as the "body of the indictment." His discussion of common law authority included cases that refused to permit amendments to correct a misnomer or even amendments offered with the consent of the defendant. Modern federal cases have refused to read the *Bain* prohibition against amendment as so absolute. Consent to an amendment generally makes the prohibition inapplicable, at least in those cases where the right to an indictment could be waived altogether. Federal courts also have allowed amendments that deal with matters of "form" rather than substance. This includes corrections of misnomers or typographical errors. *Bain* itself continues to be cited, however, as an illustration of the type of change, relating to the substance of the crime, that cannot be permitted even though there is no suggestion that the change will affect the preparedness of the defendant.

The indictment in *Bain* charged the defendant with having made a false statement "with intent to deceive the Comptroller of the Currency and the agent appointed to examine the affairs of said association." The trial court sustained a demurrer to the indictment, apparently on the ground that the statute applied only to deception of the person who actually examined the records, and therefore did not prohibit the derivative deception of the Comptroller. Under the pleading rule then prevailing, an offense was not charged if any of the alternative actions cited in the indictment did not constitute a crime. Responding to the trial court's ruling, the government, with the permission of the trial court, then "corrected" the indictment by deleting the reference to the Comptroller of the Currency. The Supreme Court held that this amendment was impermissible and the defendant's subsequent conviction on that amended indictment therefore had to be reversed. The Court rejected the view that the reference to the Comptroller was merely "surplusage" that had no bearing on the grand jury's view of the case. There may well have been at least one juror "who was satisfied that the report was made to deceive the Comptroller, but was not convinced that it was made to deceive anybody else." Accordingly, it could not be said that, "with those words stricken out, * * * [the amended indictment] is the indictment which was found by the grand jury."

In its most recent interpretation of *Bain, United States v. Miller,*[4] the Supreme Court stated that *Bain* today stands only for "the proposition that a conviction cannot stand if based on an offense that is different from that alleged in the grand jury indictment." In *Miller,* the indictment had alleged that the defendant defrauded an insurance company by both arranging for a burglary at his place of business and by lying to the insurer as to the value of the loss, but the evidence at trial established only the lying. Although there was no element of surprise involved, the trial court denied the government's motion to strike from the indictment the allegation of the defendant's prior knowledge of the burglary. After the case was submitted to the jury on the full indictment, and the defendant was convicted, the defense challenged the convic-

4. 471 U.S. 130, 105 S.Ct. 1811, 85 L.Ed.2d 99 (1985).

tion on the ground that the government's proof had fatally varied from the scheme alleged in the indictment by failing to cover both aspects of that scheme. In the course of rejecting that contention, the Supreme Court noted that the government's amendment, which would have limited the indictment to the proof presented, would have been permissible under a proper reading of *Bain.* The Court acknowledged that the language in *Bain* quoted above could "support the proposition that the striking out of part of an indictment invalidates the whole of the indictment, for a court cannot speculate as to whether the grand jury had meant for any remaining offense to stand independently, even if that remaining offense clearly was included in the original text." However, later cases had implicitly rejected that proposition by holding that, "as long as the crime and elements of the offense that sustain the conviction are fully and clearly set out in the indictment, the right to a grand jury is not normally violated by the fact that the indictment alleges more crimes or other means of committing the same crime." In light of these rulings, *Miller* noted, where an indictment alleges two separate offenses or two separate means of committing the same offense, *Bain* should not be read to prohibit dropping from the indictment those allegations concerning the one offense or one means that was not supported by the evidence at trial.

As it relates to the deletion of allegations, the *Miller* reading of *Bain* presents a principle fairly easily applied. Indeed, perhaps the only complexity is how that principle can be squared with *Bain*'s holding on the facts presented there. The answer here may be that the *Miller* analysis would call for a different ruling on the *Bain* facts today, but it was nonetheless consistent with the *Bain* ruling in light of the pleading rules applied in 1887. The trial court in *Bain* had viewed the indictment as fatally defective under the then-prevailing view of the essential elements requirement. Under that view, an indictment was fatally flawed if it alleged one method of committing the offense (deceiving the Comptroller) that did not violate the statute. With the indictment therefore failing to charge an offense in the first instance, any amendment was, as the Court noted in *Miller,* setting forth a "different offense." Today, the *Bain* indictment could be viewed, in the terms of *Miller,* as alleging "two separate means of committing the offense," with one being defective. Under the analysis of *Miller,* which treats the grand jury as having made an independent judgment as to each, there should be no difficulty in dropping that means held to be deficient and relying on the other, which clearly did set forth criminal conduct. In this regard, *Miller* specifically noted:

> To the extent *Bain* stands for the proposition that it constitutes an unconstitutional amendment to drop from an indictment those allegations that are unnecessary to an offense that is clearly contained within it, that case has simply not survived. To avoid further confusion, we now explicitly reject that proposition.

Miller had no need to discuss the application of the *Bain* rule to amendments that would add new material to the indictment. It noted only that *Bain* continues to stand for the proposition "that a conviction cannot stand if based on an offense that is different from that alleged in the grand jury's indictment." The Court had no reason to explore the question of what new matter results in alleging an offense "different" from that originally charged. It described as "the most important reaffirmation" of this aspect of *Bain* the Court's ruling in *Stirone v. United States.*[5] In that case, as discussed in § 19.6(c), the Court found that the trial court's admission of evidence establishing a factual theory of liability at variance with that alleged in the indictment resulted in a prohibited constructive amendment of the indictment. The indictment there alleged that the element of interference with interstate commerce had been produced through one consequence of defendant's extortion activities while the trial evidence and jury instruction allowed for the

5. 361 U.S. 212, 80 S.Ct. 270, 4 L.Ed.2d 252 (1960).

finding of interference based on a different consequence. In a jurisdiction that applied the dominant two-pronged standard discussed in subsection (b), that new factual theory probably would not be viewed as alleging a different offense (although a contrary conclusion might be reached in a state that takes a more confining view of that standard).[6] The *Miller* opinion also cited language in other rulings suggesting that changes that would fall short of producing a new offense under the dominant two-pronged standard could readily be considered under the *Bain* rule to have produced an offense "different" from that originally charged. Thus reference was made to allowing changes only as to "matters of form" and to the impermissible broadening of grand jury's determination of the "means" of committing the crime. Lower federal courts applying the *Bain* rule accordingly have distinguished between acceptable amendments that merely explain or expand upon factual elements originally alleged (e.g., by more specifically identifying an altered commercial draft) and impermissible amendments that add new factual theories (e.g., by citing a different property interest obtained by fraud from the same victim). The end result is an approach that approximates in many respects the middle-range state applications of the form/substance standard.

For the federal prosecutor who wishes to avoid repeated trips to the grand jury, the *Bain* rule, as modified by *Miller,* offers two obvious lessons. First, all possible factual theories of liability should be included in the initial indictment.[7] If post-indictment investigation should reveal that a theory is not worthy of carrying forward at trial, it may always be deleted; on the other hand, if a factual theory originally is omitted on the ground that it is not as strong as other theories, and post-indictment investigation reveals its strength was underestimated, the addition of that theory will require a new indictment under the *Bain* rule. Second, there is an advantage in utilizing less specificity so that allegations can cover more factual variations that might arise as a result of post-indictment investigation. In case after case, federal prosecutors have avoided *Bain* difficulties as a result of broad initial descriptions of essential elements. Of course, the prosecution often walks a fine line in adopting this tact, as the lack of factual specificity, as discussed in § 19.3(b), may provide a basis for a successful defense challenge to the sufficiency of the pleading.

§ 19.6 Variances

(a) Challenging Variances. A variance arises when the proof offered at trial departs from the allegations in the indictment or information. A defense objection to a variance may be made initially at the point that the prosecution introduces its proof, with the defense arguing that the prosecutor's evidence is irrelevant to the charges. Very often that objection may have escaped the defense's notice, or the evidence may have had relevance to a similar happening or transaction, and the defense objection will first be raised in opposition to the prosection's request for a jury instruction resting liability on a theory supported only by that proof which departs from the pleading. The defendant objecting at this

6. The original charge relied upon disruption of the victimized company's own operations in interstate commerce while the new material relied upon the disruption of the interstate potential of a customer of the victimized company. Thus, the basic act of extortion remained the same, with a new allegation added as to how the harm to interstate commerce had occurred. In a jurisdiction that rejects the single-element analysis described at note 1 supra, the difference in the two harms conceivably could be seen as sufficiently altering the character of the element of interference as to allege a different offense. In general, however, since the different consequences are not specified in the statute as distinct modes of interference, a shift from one to the other would be acceptable under the dominant two-pronged standard in the absence of prejudice to the defense in preparing its case. A jurisdiction following a form/substance standard, on the other hand, would be far more likely to characterize the different consequences as an improper subject for amendment.

7. See note 4 of § 19.3 as to the permissible uses of disjunctive and conjunctive pleadings.

point states, in effect: "The state may have introduced evidence sufficient to establish a crime, but it is not the crime alleged in its accusatory pleading and I therefore am entitled to an acquittal." If the state has introduced evidence covering the allegations in its pleading and the variance relates to evidence establishing an additional theory of liability, then the defense objection is to allowing the jury to find liability based on this additional theory. Frequently, the prosecution, recognizing the existence of a variance, will seek to amend the pleading to conform to the evidence. If this is permitted, and the defendant is convicted, then the issue raised on appeal will be whether the amendment was properly allowed. If the trial judge does not allow the amendment (or no request for amendment is made), and the case is sent to the jury over the defendant's variance objection, then the defendant, if convicted, will contend on appeal that allowance of the variance constitutes reversible error.

(b) The *Berger* Standard. Without doubt, the most frequently cited analysis of the law governing variances is that of Justice Sutherland in *Berger v. United States:* [1]

> The true inquiry, * * * is not whether there has been a variance in proof, but whether there has been such a variance as to "affect the substantial rights" of the accused. The general rule that allegations and proof must correspond is based upon the obvious requirements (1) that the accused shall be definitely informed as to the charges against him, so that he may be enabled to present his defense and not be taken by surprise by the evidence offered at the trial; and (2) that he may be protected against another prosecution for the same offense.

Justice Sutherland's analysis has been adopted by various state courts as the sole measure for testing the acceptability of a variance. Under what is described as the "*Berger* standard," a variance requires reversal of a conviction only when it deprives the defendant of his right to fair notice or leaves him open to a risk of double jeopardy.

In applying the notice element of the *Berger* standard, courts look to the record to determine whether it suggests "a possibility that the defendant may have been misled or embarrassed in the preparation or presentation of his defense." A failure to object to the variance at trial generally is viewed as a waiver of a claim of prejudice, and an eleventh hour objection is taken as strong evidence belying any such claim. If the defendant was previously aware of the prosecution's proof as a result of pretrial discovery or a preliminary hearing, that factor also will weigh against a finding of prejudice. The court also will look to the relationship of the variance to the defense presented by the defendant. Thus, variances as to factors that ordinarily are not part of the material elements of the crime (e.g., time and place) are viewed as unlikely to prejudice a defendant whose defense centered on challenging the government's proof as to one of those material elements.

The possibility of actual prejudice at trial is put aside when courts test a variance against the risk of exposing the defendant to double jeopardy. The only element considered here is the extent to which the variance alters the scope of the charge. Indeed, a challenge based on this ground may be raised by a defendant who failed to object to the variance at trial. The concern of *Berger* apparently was that if defendant were tried on the proof presented in the variance and the jury concluded that such proof did not establish the offense charged, the record would be such that a reprosecution on the theory of the variance would not necessarily be barred. The original pleading would establish the scope of the jeopardy that attached at the first trial and it would not bar a second trial on the theory of the variance if that theory established a different offense. Today, however, the pleading alone would not control the scope of the jeopardy that attached at the original proceeding, as the trial record would

§ 19.6

1. 295 U.S. 78, 55 S.Ct. 629, 79 L.Ed. 1314 (1935).

be available to show that the defendant had been placed in jeopardy on the theory of the variance. Since the defendant went to trial on the original pleading, a reprosecution on that charge alone would also be barred. Thus, the concept that variances establishing a new offense must be struck to protect the defendant against double jeopardy may be questioned.

Assuming, however, that the focus on the pleading as a protection against multiple jeopardy remains viable, then the double jeopardy prong of *Berger* still should not bar a variance unless it constitutes a separate offense for double jeopardy purposes. Yet, courts have barred, presumably under *Berger*'s double jeopardy prong, variances that changed the offense only by alleging a different means of commission as part of the same incident or a different ultimate victim of a property offense. In many such cases, the distinction between what was alleged in the initial charge and what was established through the variance clearly would not produce different offenses under the currently prevailing double jeopardy standard of *Blockburger* and *Grady v. Corbin.*[2] Such rulings, may reflect an outdated view of separate offenses for double jeopardy purposes, but they seem more likely to reflect the state's conversion of the second prong of *Berger* into a constructive amendment limitation as discussed in the next subsection.

(c) The Constructive Amendment Limitation. The Supreme Court, in its treatment of variances, has looked to both the *Berger* standard and the limitations that apply to amendments of the charge, particularly as to indictments. The Court accordingly has drawn a distinction between trial court allowance of departure in the proof from the indictment so great as to be regarded as a "constructive amendment," which constitutes a reversible error in itself, and a "mere variance," which is reversible error only if it is likely to have caused surprise or otherwise been prejudicial to the defense. The analysis underlying this distinction was described by Circuit Judge Gibbons as follows:[3]

> It is, of course, elementary that neither the prosecutor nor the trial court may constitutionally amend a federal indictment. *Ex parte Bain.* The Supreme Court has recognized, however, that if there is no amendment of the indictment, but only a variance between the facts alleged in the indictment and the evidence offered at trial, the problem is not one of usurping the constitutionally guaranteed role of the grand jury, but one of promoting the fairness of the trial and ensuring the defendant notice and an opportunity to be heard. See e.g., *Kotteakos v. United States;*[4] *Berger v. United States.*[5] The variance rule, to the extent that it is constitutionally required, is more of a due process rule than is the flat fifth amendment prohibition against being tried on an indictment which a grand jury never returned. In *Stirone v. United States,*[6] however, the Supreme Court recognized that even though a trial court did not formally amend an indictment, it could accomplish the practical result of trying a defendant on a charge for which he was not indicted by a grand jury if it permitted proof of facts on an essential element of an offense which were different than those charged in the indictment. The trial court would not be permitted, in the guise of a variance, to accomplish a constructive amendment so as to modify the facts which the grand jury charged as an essential element of the substantive offense. * * * The consequence of a constructive amendment is that the admission of the challenged evidence is per se reversible error, requiring no analysis of additional prejudice to the defendant.

The three Supreme Court rulings cited by Judge Gibbons offer the best illustration of the distinction between "mere variance" and a variance that amounts to a "constructive amendment." Both *Berger* and *Kotteakos* involved situations in which one large conspiracy was charged but proof at trial established

2. See § 17.4(b).

3. United States v. Crocker, 568 F.2d 1049 (3d Cir. 1977).

4. 328 U.S. 750, 66 S.Ct. 1239, 90 L.Ed. 1557 (1946).

5. See supra note 1.

6. 361 U.S. 212, 80 S.Ct. 270, 4 L.Ed.2d 252 (1960).

a series of separate conspiracies. The Court in each case applied the *Berger* standard. Since the variances did not create double jeopardy difficulties, the focus was on whether the distinction in proof resulted in prejudice, with the Court finding that it had in one case but not in another.[7] Neither opinion spoke to whether an amendment to charge separate conspiracies would have violated the *Bain* rule, but the Court in *Miller* later suggested that *Berger* and *Kotteakos* rulings were consistent with the amendment principle announced there.[8] The more confined conspiracies of which the defendants were convicted were described in *Miller* as "technically included" within the broader conspiracy originally alleged. Thus, if the variances had been viewed as amendments, they would have been acceptable under *Miller* (and *Bain* as interpreted in *Miller*) because they simply reduced the scope of the charge. They did not add new material, as in the case of the variance in *Stirone.*

In *Stirone,* the indictment charged a violation of the Hobbs Act through extortion that obstructed interstate commerce by preventing the victim (Rider) from importing sand that was shipped from another state. At trial, over the defendant's objection, the court admitted evidence (and charged the jury) on obstruction of interstate commerce that resulted from Rider's inability to supply concrete for the construction of a local steel plant which had intended to ship its product in interstate commerce. The lower court found that this variance had not been fatal since defense counsel had been prepared for the introduction of that evidence. Without disturbing this finding of no prejudice, the Supreme Court reversed. Justice Black, speaking for a unanimous Court, noted:

> The grand jury which found this indictment was satisfied to charge that Stirone's conduct interfered with interstate importation of sand. But neither this nor any other court can know that the grand jury would have been willing to charge that Stirone's conduct would interfere with interstate exportation of steel from a mill later to be built with Rider's concrete. * * * Although the trial court did not permit a formal amendment of the indictment, the effect of what it did was the same.

The variance in *Stirone* would not have created a "new offense" for double jeopardy purposes. The act of extortion was the same under both theories, with the variation extending only to the consequences establishing the element of harm (i.e., the obstruction of interstate commerce). However, as noted in § 19.5, many jurisdictions apply a much more restrictive view of what constitutes a different offense in the context of limiting amendments. The federal system, under the *Bain* rule, certainly falls within this group. Under that rule, an amendment adding the theory of harm advanced by the *Stirone* variance clearly would not have been permitted. The variance altered a substantial element of the crime, providing an entirely different theory of impact upon interstate commerce. In contrast to *Berger* and *Kotteakos,* it added a new factual element rather than simply rearranging the elements alleged in the original indictment. Moreover, it was a new factual element substantially different from that previously presented; the possible interference with prospective steel shipments had a much more remote and speculative impact upon interstate commerce than the interference with the importation of sand. Under these circumstances, as various lower courts have noted, there was a "substantial likelihood that a defendant may have been convicted of an offense other than the one the grand jury had in mind."

7. Berger v. United States, supra note 1, held that the variance was not prejudicial when it established two conspiracies involving contemporaneous transactions rather than a single conspiracy. *Kotteakos,* supra note 4, held otherwise as to a situation "in which one conspiracy only is charged and at least eight having separate though similar objects are made out * * * and in which the more numerous participants in the different schemes were, on the whole, except for one, persons who did not know or have anything to do with one another." There, thirteen parties were jointly tried, and as to all but one defendant, the variance resulted in the jury having before it evidence of additional conspiracies which had no bearing on individual defendant's liability.

8. *Miller* is discussed in § 19.5 at note 4.

Stirone appeared to draw an absolute parallel between the *Bain* prohibition of amendments and the prohibition of variances as constructive amendments. A strict application of the *Bain* prohibition could certainly bar variances far less extreme than that in *Stirone.* Some federal lower courts, however, have looked to *Stirone* as the prototype of the variance that will be barred automatically, without application of the *Berger* standard. They have suggested that the variance must change the basic character of an element of the offense, producing a modification that could possibly have affected the grand jury's assessment of the charges. Others have taken a position arguably more consistent with *Bain* and construed as a constructive amendment any variance that basically alters the prosecution's factual theory as to any element. In states that adhere to a restrictive form/substance limitation on amendments, the constructive amendment doctrine has barred even the most minor variances. Thus, one court rejected a variance where the indictment charged armed robbery with a pistol and evidence was that defendant had used a rifle.[9]

9. State v. Brooks, 224 Tenn. 712, 462 S.W.2d 491 (1970). See also Wilson v. State, 200 Tenn. 309, 292 S.W.2d 188 (1956) (proof of theft of bronze rollers constituted a material variance from indictment charging theft of brass rollers).

Chapter 20

DISCOVERY AND DISCLOSURE

Table of Sections

---

§ 20.1 The Expansion of Discovery

(a) The Break From the Common Law. Although the English common law may not have been quite so absolute, American courts, relying on the English precedent, adopted a common law rule holding that the judiciary lacked any inherent authority to order pretrial discovery in criminal cases. Absent specific legislative authorization, a trial court could not order the prosecution to make a pretrial disclosure of its evidence to defense or the defense to make a pretrial disclosure of its evidence to the prosecution. Well into the early 1900's, in all but the few states that had legislatively authorized pretrial discovery, the only pretrial discovery available to the parties was that which was obtained informally through the mutual exchange of information or incidentally in the course of such pretrial proceedings as the preliminary hearing. By the late 1930's, however, formal pretrial discovery had come onto the scene in a substantial number of jurisdictions, and that number grew to include a majority of the states over the next decade.

The initial development of pretrial discovery had several components. A small group of states adopted legislation allowing the accused to move for pretrial disclosure of specific types of evidence under limited circumstances. A somewhat larger group of states adopted statutes requiring the accused to give the prosecution advance notice of his intention to present an alibi defense and to provide specific information relating to that alibi defense (the defendant's alleged location at the time of the crime and the names of the defense witnesses who would support the alibi claim). An even larger number of states had come to accept Professor Wigmore's position that the common law prohibition was a rule "of policy, not of power." They recognized a discretionary authority of the trial court, in the exercise of its inherent authority to control the trial process, to require the prosecution to make a pretrial disclosure of specified evidence to the defense. Such authority could be exercised, however, only upon a defense showing that pretrial disclosure was essential to its capacity to meet the prosecution evidence in question (as where the defense needed the advice of a scientific expert to evaluate the prosecution's forensic evidence). The end result was that, by the mid-century mark, a substantial majority of the states allowed or required pretrial discovery, but such discovery was treated primarily as an exceptional practice for a limited group of situations rather than as a standard element of pretrial procedure.

The expansion of pretrial discovery in civil cases moved at a much more rapid pace. During the 1930's and 1940's, through court rules and legislation, the vast majority of jurisdictions adopted procedures designed to promote full and open pretrial discovery in civil cases. By providing for depositions, interrogatories, production of documents, inspection of intangible items, and physical and mental examinations, civil discovery provisions sought to give each side pretrial access to almost all relevant information within the knowledge of the other side. The success of this liberalization of civil discovery naturally led courts and legislatures to consider whether a similar expansion of discovery should be attempted in criminal cases. The proposals for expansion in the criminal area did not utilize precise counterparts to the civil vehicles for discovery, but sought to achieve the same basic end—avoidance of "trial by surprise"—through somewhat different procedures. The primary distinctions were in the focus on discovery only as to one side, the defense, and the use of different forms of disclosure.

Since prosecution discovery from the defense was thought to be largely prohibited by the defendant's privilege against self-incrimination, and since many states already had alibi-discovery provisions (arguably meeting the prosecution's greatest need for disclosure), the proposals for expansion looked primarily to granting to the defense broader discovery from the prosecution. For reasons noted in § 20.2(d), the deposition of possible witnesses for the opposition, a primary tool of discovery in civil cases, was thought ill-suited for the criminal arena (or at least not appropriately a part of the initial stages of liberalization of defense discovery). Since the prosecution, unlike the plaintiff in the civil case, was not a participant in any of the events involved, an interrogatory procedure (commonly used to probe the opposing party's knowledge) also was deemed inappropriate. Instead, the proposals for expansion focused on requiring the prosecutor to make available for defense inspection the critical information in its files that related to the case it intended to present at trial. Thus, the prosecution would be required to disclose statements it had obtained from the defendant, his codefendants, and any witnesses it intended to present. It would also be required to make available to the defense, as in civil discovery, relevant documents and tangible items. Finally, it would be required to inform the defense of certain information (e.g., the names and addresses of potential prosecution witnesses) that ordinarily was obtained in civil cases through interrogatories.

Though the proposed vehicles for disclosure and the one-sided focus differed from the expansion that had occurred on the civil side, expanding discovery in criminal cases was thought, at least by its proponents, to raise basically the same policy concerns as had been encountered in the dramatic expansion of civil discovery. Critics disagreed, and there occurred during the 1950's and 1960's one of the classic debates in the field of criminal procedure.

(b) The Debate. An extensive exploration of the numerous arguments and counter-arguments presented in the discovery debate would occupy far more space than the purposes of this treatise allow. What follows is a brief review of the major contentions advanced by proponents and opponents. It is limited primarily to those policy considerations that have been stressed in judicial opinions commenting upon the discovery question.

The need to eliminate "trial by surprise." Proponents of liberal defense discovery emphasized the need to make the trial "less a game of blind man's bluff and more a fair contest with the basic issues and facts disclosed to the fullest practicable extent." As noted by Justice Brennan, a leading advocate of expansive defense discovery, the trial must emphasize the "quest for the truth" rather than a "sporting theory of justice." [1] The recent experience with discovery reforms in the field of civil discovery, proponents maintained, clearly had established that this objective was best achieved by providing broad pretrial discovery. The end result there had been the fuller marshalling of all available evidence and trials that were far more effective in revealing the truth.

§ 20.1

1. Brennan, The Criminal Prosecution: Sporting Event or Quest for Truth?, 1963 Wash.U.L.Q. 279 (1963). See also Brennan, infra note 7.

Opponents of expansive defense discovery did not deny that a trial should be a quest for truth rather than a "sporting event." Neither did they quarrel with the premise (though it may be debatable) that expansive discovery in civil cases had reduced surprise and thereby permitted a more complete presentation of all relevant evidence. They argued, however, that three factors distinguished criminal discovery from civil discovery and made expansive criminal discovery far less desirable. Those factors were: (1) the criminal defendant's privilege against self-incrimination, which would not permit the fully reciprocal discovery found in civil practice; (2) the greater likelihood that defense discovery in criminal cases would be used to facilitate successful perjury; and (3) the greater likelihood that criminal defense discovery would lead to the intimidation of witnesses. Opponents of expansive criminal discovery argued that when these three factors were taken into account, along with the availability of alternative procedures that served to combat unfair surprise, the costs of expansive defense discovery would clearly outweigh its benefits. Proponents of expansive discovery responded that such costs either did not exist or were exaggerated and that alternative procedures for combatting surprise were ineffective.

The "reciprocity argument." Critics of liberal defense discovery warned that the defendant's constitutional rights—particularly his privilege against self-incrimination—would limit the legislature's ability to provide for extensive prosecution discovery from the defense. This limitation, they argued, should not be ignored in determining the proper scope of defense discovery. In an adversary system, it would be unfair to give one side discovery rights that could not also be made available to the other side. Indeed, apart from considerations of equity, discovery simply would not be an effective tool in developing the truth unless it was a "two-way street," as in civil discovery. Anticipating the contention that a lack of reciprocity should be acceptable because the greater concern is to avoid convicting the innocent (rather than to ensure conviction of the guilty), the critics further argued that the overall "balance of advantage" already was sufficiently stacked in favor of the defense to protect the innocent. The requirement of prosecution proof beyond a reasonable doubt and the defendant's various procedural rights, including the right not to be forced to testify, afforded the defendant ample protection against unjust conviction. To grant the defendant another advantage, in non-reciprocal discovery rights, would make the prosecutor's task "almost insurmountable."

Supporters of liberal defense discovery argued against each prong of the "equity" or reciprocity argument. Some maintained that the barrier to prosecution discovery imposed by the self-incrimination privilege was quite limited, and there was not greater prosecution discovery simply because, outside of the alibi area, the prosecution had no need for such discovery. Most, however, assumed that prosecution discovery constitutionally had to be sharply restricted, and argued that this did not detract from the case for expansive defense discovery. They maintained that expansive defense discovery would be a useful tool in the truth-seeking process even though similar discovery was not available to the prosecution. If the privilege against self-incrimination created a discovery imbalance in favor of the defense, that imbalance would be consistent with the intent of the framers; the defendant should not be denied a procedure essential to the establishment of the truth in an attempt to offset a protection granted by the Constitution.

Proponents of expansion also rejected the contention that discovery can appropriately be denied the defendant because he has other "advantages" in the criminal justice process. This position, they argued, looks at the process as a sporting contest and ignores the need to take every precaution to ensure that the innocent are not convicted. In any event, as they viewed the "realities of administration," the alleged advantage of the defendant was largely a myth. They noted, for example, that even at trial, where the defendant supposedly possesses his greatest advantage, many of his rights, such as the right not to testify, are of limited practical significance. Of more relevance, they argued, was the defendant's decided disadvantage in the preparation of his case. Here, the state will have all of the advantages. Its investigators will be first at the scene of the crime, and they will have greater resources, including search and subpoena authority and a capacity to obtain voluntary cooperation of witnesses that the defense rarely can match. Indeed, the proponents of discovery argued, the typical defense counsel operates at such an investigative disadvantage that the adversary system is substantially undermined without the partial equalization provided by liberal defense discovery. The critics of expansive discovery responded that the investigative advantage varies with the nature of the crime and the resources of the particular defendant, and that it was not, in any event, truly relevant. They noted that in the field of civil proceeding, it has never been suggested that the better financed side should therefore be barred from equal discovery.

The perjury argument. Opponents of liberal discovery also contended that pretrial disclosure of the prosecution's evidence would greatly facilitate a defendant's use of perjury. They acknowledged that most defendants who desire to fabricate a defense will do so whether or not they are given discovery, but they saw discovery as granting such defendants the means through which they could make their perjury more believable. If a defendant learned in advance of the state's evidence, he could carefully tailor his testimony, both to minimize conflict with the prosecution's evidence and to take advantage of the weakest point in the prosecution's evidence. For example, if a dishonest defendant learns through pretrial discovery that the prosecution can place him at the scene of the crime, he can respond by switching his fabricated defense from alibi to a defense consistent with his presence at the scene. So too, if he learns that the prosecution's witnesses saw him flee from the scene, he now knows better than to testify that he was just taking a leisurely stroll. Of course, since the defendant does not testify until after the state has presented its case-in-chief, he will obtain some advance notice even without pretrial discovery. But pretrial defense discovery gives him far more time to skillfully plan his fabrication and thereby makes it more likely that the fabrication will be successful.

Proponents of expansive defense discovery viewed the claimed facilitation of perjury as an "old hobgoblin" based on "untested folklore." They argued that civil discovery had proven successful notwithstanding similar objections. They saw the experience there as indicating either that civil discovery had produced no appreciable increase in successful perjury or that any such increase had been more than offset by the overall benefits of discovery to the truth-seeking process. They asked: "Why should discovery in criminal cases be different"? In responding, opponents of liberal defense discovery generally accepted the alleged success of civil discovery, but argued that criminal cases offer a far greater risk of successful perjury. They contended that a greater potential for perjury exists in criminal cases because the criminal defendant has more at stake. Some also suggested that more criminal defendants are likely to be basically dishonest (and therefore potential perjurers) than the parties in civil cases. Finally, they noted that a party in a civil case may depose the opposing party and thereby "freeze" his opponent's "story" before his opponent can use the discovery to fabricate. That possibility is not available in criminal cases, they maintained, since the prosecution cannot depose the defendant.

Proponents of expansive defense discovery disputed the contention that criminal litigation poses a greater danger of perjury than civil litigation. They rejected the assumption that there necessarily is a greater incentive for perjury, noting that civil cases too often involve substantial stakes. To assume that criminal defendants are more likely to be dishonest is to ignore, they argued, the presumption that the defendant is innocent. They also stressed that the prosecution, though it cannot depose the defendant, uses various other devices (e.g., police interrogation) to "pin down" the defendant. In any event, they noted, "we must remember that society's interest is equally that the innocent shall not suffer and not alone that the guilty shall not escape." The proper safeguard against perjury, they argued, "is not to refuse to permit any inquiry at all, for that will eliminate the true as well as the false, but the inquiry should be conducted so as to separate and distinguish the one from the other."

The intimidation argument. The arguments relating to possible intimidation of witnesses followed much the same lines as the arguments relating to perjury. Opponents of liberal discovery contended that a defendant armed with knowledge of the prosecution's case could take steps to bribe or frighten witnesses into giving perjured testimony or into absenting themselves so that they are unavailable to testify. Admittedly, not all defendants would use such tactics, but enough would do so, it was argued, to make many witnesses reluctant to come forward to assist the police. Witnesses, it was argued, were already under considerable pressure, and even aggressive discovery efforts by defense counsel were likely to prove frightening.

In response to the intimidation argument, supporters of liberal discovery again noted that a similar contention had been rejected in the expansion of civil discovery. They again denied that criminal cases were likely to present a greater problem than civil cases. Insofar as the concern here relates to actual intimidation, the appropriate response, they argued, was to allow discovery generally, but grant the trial court authority to limit that discovery where the prosecution can establish a realistic threat of physical or economic intimidation. Opponents of liberal discovery responded that such a protective order procedure would place an impracticable burden on the prosecution by requiring it to establish a defendant's intent to intimidate, but proponents responded that it should not be assumed a defendant will act improperly without such a substantial showing. Proponents of discovery also rejected arguments based on a general concern for accommodating witnesses. The search for truth should not be made more difficult, they argued, simply because witnesses have unfounded fears or don't want to be "bothered" by the investigative efforts of defense counsel.

Other means of discovery. In evaluating the need for liberal rules of discovery, opponents and proponents frequently disagreed as to the value of other means of discovery available to the defendant. The preliminary hearing and the bill of particulars were the two alternative procedures most frequently mentioned, but the bail hearing, motions challenging the grand jury process, the motion to suppress, and the pretrial conference were also cited as possible sources of discovery. Of course, not all of these procedures are available in every case. Also, each has distinct limits as a discovery device. Opponents of liberal defense discovery nonetheless claimed that, even with such restrictions, these alternative procedures provided more than enough discovery to avoid unfair surprise. Proponents of discovery disagreed, but they also argued that, in any event, the law should not encourage defense manipulation of these procedures to achieve a discovery objective they were not designed to fulfill.[2]

(c) The Outcome. The debate over the merits of expanding defense discovery produced a reassessment of discovery law in every jurisdiction. Overall, the proponents of extensive defense discovery had far more success than their opponents. As far back as

2. In many jurisdictions, prosecutors, as a matter of "grace," commonly provide defense counsel with pretrial discovery beyond that required under the discovery rules. Where such "informal discovery" is widely available, it adds an extra dimension to the debate over whether there should be further expansion of formal discovery. Opponents of expansion commonly argue that informal discovery practices serve all legitimate needs of the defense while avoiding the time-consuming motions and hearings that may accompany formal discovery. Defense counsel who are beneficiaries of informal discovery sometimes also prefer it because such discovery does not carry with it the element of reciprocal defense disclosure that may be a politically necessary quid pro quo for any expansion of defense discovery. Proponents of expansive discovery requirements respond that discovery is too significant to be left to the discretion of the prosecutor, which will often produce arbitrary distinctions among defense counsel.

1966, the Supreme Court spoke of "the growing realization that disclosure, rather than suppression, of relevant materials ordinarily promotes the proper administration of criminal justice," and referred to "the expanding body of materials, judicial and otherwise, favoring disclosure in criminal cases analogous to the civil practice." [3] That there is to be defense discovery in criminal cases is now taken as a matter of course. The issues that divide the various jurisdictions today relate only to exactly how far that discovery should be carried. Moreover, the trend has been in the direction of consistently broadening the reach of defense discovery, as illustrated by the changes over the years in Federal Rule 16. As originally adopted in 1946, Rule 16 simply allowed the defendant access, on a showing of materiality, to documents obtained by the government. In 1966, Rule 16 was completely revised to grant the trial court discretion to order discovery of a broad range of items (basically written or recorded statements of the defendant, reports of physical and medical examinations, and relevant documents and "other tangible objects"). In 1975, there was still another revision of Rule 16 which produced essentially the current provision. That revision further broadened the range of discoverable statements (including, for example, the substance of oral statements of the defendant) and made prosecutorial disclosure mandatory (rather than leaving it to the discretion of the trial court). The original draft of the 1975 revision, as approved by the Supreme Court, would also have required disclosure of the names, addresses, and felony conviction records of all prosecution witnesses, but Congress struck that provision from the Rule as it was eventually adopted.

In contrast to Congress, many states have been willing to take defense discovery several steps beyond current Rule 16. The American Bar Association, in 1970,[4] recommended adoption of discovery provisions extending substantially beyond even the broadest federal proposal, and a large number of states revised their discovery provisions in accordance with the ABA's proposed standards. They provided for defense discovery of a wide range of items, including not only the names of prospective prosecution witnesses, but also any statements they had given to the police. The ABA later expanded upon even those standards and proposed "open file" discovery. The prosecutor's disclosure obligation, under that later standard, extended to "all the material and information within the prosecutor's possession or control." [5] So far, however, not even the most liberal discovery jurisdiction has been willing to adopt such an open-ended provision.

While clearly the "winners," at least as measured by the direction that the law has taken, proponents of liberal defense discovery hardly claim "total victory." The focus even under the broadest state provisions has been primarily upon disclosure of the evidence that the prosecution intends to introduce at trial. A considerably narrower scope is applied to the discovery of possible sources of information that the prosecution does not intend to use, but that the defense might find helpful in the preparation of its case. Proponents argue that defense discovery should be broadened in this regard to more closely resemble civil discovery. They favor discovery depositions (currently available in a small group of states) and allowing a form of interrogatory that would require the prosecution to reveal all possible sources of relevant information known to it (currently not required in any jurisdiction).

(d) The "Two-Way Street" Movement. The expansion of defense discovery led prosecutors, not unexpectedly, to insist that the government be given equally broad discovery from the defense. The avoidance of trial by surprise, they argued, necessarily required that both parties be aware of the evidence to be introduced by its adversary. Discovery, as

3. Dennis v. United States, 384 U.S. 855, 86 S.Ct. 1840, 16 L.Ed.2d 973 (1966).

4. ABA Minimal Standards on Discovery and Procedure Before Trial, Part II (1970).

5. 2 ABA Standards for Criminal Justice § 11–2.1 (2d ed. 1980).

evidenced by the form it took in civil cases, was designed to be a two-way street. This concept of requiring the defense to show its case to the prosecution was not new. Alibi-notice provisions (requiring the defense to give pretrial notice regarding its use of an alibi defense) had been in place in numerous states before the discovery debate even started. Some had thought, however, that such provisions had a very special character that provided a stronger foundation for meeting defense challenges based on the self-incrimination privilege than would broader forms of compulsory defense disclosure to the prosecution. However, in 1970, the Supreme Court in *Williams v. Florida*[6] upheld the constitutionality of an alibi-notice provision under a rationale that could readily be seen as extending to a much broader range of prosecutorial discovery. That decision, in effect, removed the primary obstacle to the long-standing prosecutorial effort to make discovery a two-way street.

Reading the *Williams* case broadly, the ABA, in its first set of discovery standards, proposed prosecution discovery rights that would go substantially beyond alibi-notice. Indeed, a major argument advanced in support of broad discovery granted to the defense under those 1970 ABA Standards was that the ABA drafters also had been innovative in extending discovery to the prosecution. Post-*Williams* amendments to the Federal Rules extended preexisting prosecution discovery provisions and allowed for discovery only slightly narrower than the ABA proposal. Neither the ABA proposal nor the Federal Rules, however, sought to provide full-fledged reciprocal discovery, although the Federal Rules came somewhat closer to full reciprocity because of their narrower provisions on defense discovery.

The response of the states to the ABA proposal and the Federal Rules amendments was quite positive. The vast majority adopted provisions that went at least as far as the Federal Rules. Many expanded upon the ABA and Federal Rules models to make prosecution discovery more fully equivalent to defense discovery. Only a small group adopted narrower versions of the ABA proposal (as did the ABA itself in the subsequent revision of its standards). The end result was that the number of states with some form of prosecutorial discovery provision had increased dramatically (from only 16 pre-*Williams* to all but a few in 1990). Still, the majority of those states have provisions much narrower in scope than their defense-discovery provisions. To some extent that narrower scope may flow from lingering doubts as to the constitutionality and policy justifications for certain types of prosecution discovery. However, since prosecution discovery, apart from alibi-notice provisions, is a much more recent innovation than defense discovery, the narrower prosecution-discovery provisions may simply reflect the same type of caution in first round efforts as dominated the development of defense discovery.

§ 20.2 The Structure of Discovery Law

(a) "Common Law" Jurisdictions. In a handful of states, pretrial discovery by the defense is governed almost completely by judicially developed standards. Although these jurisdictions may have an occasional statute providing for a single aspect of discovery, they treat discovery basically as a "common law" subject. None, however, adhere to the early common law rulings which held that the judiciary lacked the power to order discovery in the absence of legislative authorization. All recognize a trial court's inherent authority to require pretrial discovery as an element of its control over the trial process. The "common law jurisdictions" vary, however, in the leeway that they grant to the trial court in the exercise of that authority. As to defense discovery, that variation includes: (i) the use of a strong presumption in favor of a broad discovery, placing upon the trial court a duty to order disclosure of a broad range of items unless the prosecution makes a particularized showing of a "paramount interest in nondisclosure"; (ii) the use of such a presumption as to a much narrower range of items, with the

6. See § 20.4 at note 1.

burden placed on the defense to show special need as to other items; and (iii) an approach that largely leaves discovery to the trial court's discretion, with appellate courts generally refusing to find an abuse of that discretion irrespective of whether the trial judge grants or denies discovery. As to prosecution discovery, the variation ranges from a jurisdiction that encourages trial judges to provide reciprocal discovery as broad as constitutionally permissible to a jurisdiction holding that trial courts may not order the defense to make any disclosure to the prosecution in the absence of legislation specifically granting the prosecution a right to such disclosure.

(b) Court Rules and Statutes. In the federal system and in the vast majority of the states, discovery is governed by statutes or court rules which are comprehensive in their coverage. In many states, there is a single court rule or statute governing all aspects of discovery by both sides. Other jurisdictions, following the pattern of the Federal Rules, utilize both a basic provision governing discovery in general and separate provisions setting forth the obligations of pretrial disclosure where defense seeks to advance a claim of alibi or an insanity defense.[1] Although the basic discovery provisions vary in content, they tend to be similar in structure. Typically, the basic statute or court rule performs the following major tasks: (1) it establishes a procedure by which the defense and the prosecution can put into effect the other side's obligation to make pretrial disclosure; (2) it designates those items which shall or may (upon court order) be disclosed by the prosecution to the defense; (3) it designates those items that shall or may (upon court order) be disclosed by the defense to the prosecution; (4) it establishes certain exemptions from disclosure based upon content (e.g., work product) or, in some instances, based on the nature of the item (e.g., witness' statements); (5) it authorizes the trial court to issue under special circumstances a protective order that will bar or limit disclosures that would otherwise be required; (6) it imposes a continuing duty to disclose discoverable items so that the process automatically encompasses items acquired after the initial disclosure; and (7) it provides a procedure for judicial administration and enforcement of the discovery provisions, including the imposition of sanctions.

While the discovery provisions of the different jurisdictions are roughly similar in structure, there is substantial variation in the discovery they allow. Items listed as discoverable as a matter of right in one jurisdiction may be discoverable only by judicial discretion in a second jurisdiction or even be barred from discovery in a third jurisdiction. The provisions dealing with protective orders tend to be worded similarly, but they are phrased so broadly as to offer considerable room for considerable diversity in application. The provisions on remedies and sanctions ordinarily do no more than list alternatives, leaving it to the state appellate court to develop general guidelines.

Still another source of variation lies in the interaction of inherent judicial authority and the court rule or statute. In some jurisdictions, the basic discovery provisions clearly are designed to preempt the field. In others, the court rule or statute, though extensive in coverage, is held not to set forth the full range of the trial court's authority to order discovery. Where a discovery provision neither authorizes nor prohibits discovery of a particular item, the jurisdiction recognizes an inherent discretionary authority of the trial court to grant discovery of that item. However, because of the controversial nature of prosecution discovery (including some unanswered questions regarding what can be done constitutionally), provisions on prosecution discovery tend to be viewed as not containing any gaps, but implicitly rejecting discovery whenever not specifically authorized.

§ 20.2

1. See Fed.R.Crim.P. 16 (general provision) and Fed.R.Crim.P. 12.1 (alibi) and Fed.R.Crim.P. 12.2 (insanity and expert testimony on mental condition). The Federal Rules also include a special provision (R.12.3) governing disclosure obligations where the defense intends to raise a claim of actual or believed exercise of public authority on behalf of a law enforcement or federal intelligence agency.

Notwithstanding the variations among state provisions, they can be loosely categorized by reference to three basic coverage patterns as to first defense and then prosecution discovery. Allowable defense discovery can be helpfully categorized by comparison to the Federal Rules and the 1970 ABA Standards.[2] The narrowest state provisions roughly provide the same discovery as the Federal Rules, with some slightly narrower due to a failure to incorporate the 1975 expansion of Federal Rule 16. Slightly over a dozen states fall within this category. A group of a similar size follows fairly closely the ABA model, which provides the broadest discovery. The remaining states with comprehensive discovery provisions fall somewhere in between these two models. Several are similar to Federal Rule 16 except that they include the 1975 proposed amendments to the Federal Rules that Congress rejected.

The Federal Rules model also provides the standard for the narrowest range of prosecution disclosure (although a few states have even narrower provisions). The original ABA Standards were roughly similar to the Federal Rules as to prosecution discovery, so it is not surprising that almost half of the states with comprehensive discovery provisions can be placed in this category. The broadest prosecution discovery standards come largely from states that utilize the ABA Standards for defense discovery and seek to provide prosecution discovery roughly equivalent in breadth as to the evidence that the defense intends to use at trial. Perhaps a dozen states can be placed in this group. A slightly larger group go beyond the Federal Rules and the original ABA Standards but fall short of seeking discovery that reciprocates ABA defense discovery.

(c) The Operation of Discovery Provisions. Discovery statutes and court rules commonly apply only to proceedings before the court of general jurisdiction. This means that the basic discovery provisions will govern only felonies and such high level misdemeanors as fall within the jurisdiction of the general trial court. Discovery in misdemeanor cases tried before the magistrate's court typically rests in the discretion of the magistrate, although a small group of jurisdictions make their basic discovery provisions applicable to all criminal cases in all courts. Ordinarily, discovery provisions do not take effect prior to the filing of charges in the court of general jurisdiction. Thus, those provisions are not available during the course of the preliminary proceedings in the magistrate's court, such as the preliminary hearing and the bail hearing. They also are not available to an accused or prospective accused who seeks some precharge remedy in the court of general jurisdiction.

Once the discovery provision takes effect, that discovery which is granted as a matter of right, in all but a few jurisdictions, should be provided without resort to judicial action. A motion for a court order directing a party to provide discovery is required only where there is a dispute as to what must be disclosed as a matter of right or the particular item is discoverable only at the discretion of the court. Under many state discovery provisions, the prosecution has an automatic obligation to disclose the items discoverable as of right within a specified number of days following the filing of the indictment or information. Under other discovery provisions, the defense must make a request of the prosecutor. That request, however, need contain no more than a listing of those categories of items specified in the discovery provision as to which disclosure is desired. The primary function of the request is to relieve the prosecutor of the burden of collecting and disclosing items listed in the provision that may not

2. See § 20.1(c).

be needed in the particular case. Where the prosecution's right to discovery is conditioned on the defense having received similar discovery, the request also serves to trigger the prosecution's authority to seek parallel discovery. In other jurisdictions, the prosecution's right is not so conditioned, and the defense, like the prosecution, has an automatic obligation to provide disclosure within a specified period following the filing of the indictment or information.

(d) Depositions. In civil cases, the deposition is a major discovery device. Both parties may subject to a deposition any person thought to have relevant information, including the opposing party. The deposition may be taken without court order, on notice to the other party. A party simply obtains a subpoena from the clerk of the court and serves it on the deposition witness, directing him to appear at a certain place for that purpose. At the deposition, the witness is placed under oath, and subjected to questioning by the party taking the deposition, with the opportunity given to the adversary to cross-examine and object to improper questions. The deposition is stenographically transcribed and in many jurisdictions may also be videotaped.

In criminal cases, the form of the deposition is quite similar, but the availability of the deposition is much more restricted. Only about 10 states allow for the use of depositions as a basic discovery procedure. In the vast majority of the states and in the federal system, the deposition is available in criminal cases primarily for the purpose of preserving the testimony of a witness likely to be unavailable at trial.[3] To utilize the deposition procedure, the side seeking to take the deposition must obtain a court order upon a showing that the proposed deponent would be a material witness at trial but is unlikely to be available to testify there due to illness or other difficulty. In many jurisdictions, the language of the deposition provision is not limited to cases of physical unavailability, but speaks more broadly as to the general grounds for preserving testimony. Thus, Federal Rule 15(a) allows for the deposition to be ordered "whenever due to the exceptional circumstances of the case it is in the interest of justice that testimony of a prospective witness of a party be taken and preserved for use at trial." Such language apparently gives the trial courts somewhat greater leeway to order depositions where the factors that might preclude the witness' testimony at trial are less than clear (e.g., where the witness might shift his stance and rely upon his self-incrimination privilege to refuse to testify). However, the focus is still on preserving testimony rather than using the deposition for other purposes, such as discovery.

Considerable variation exists as to the availability of depositions in that small group of states that treat the deposition as a vehicle for discovery as well as a means for preserving testimony. In some, the discovery deposition is available only to the defense, while others allow for prosecution discovery depositions as well. Consistent with the focus on discovery, and in contrast to the deposition limited to preserving testimony, a party may depose persons expected to be a trial witness for the other side. The one exception, of course, is that the prosecution may not depose the defendant, unless the defendant consents and waives his privilege against self-incrimination (a highly unlikely event). In some of these jurisdictions, the utilization of a discovery deposition requires court approval upon a special showing of need. In others, discovery depositions are automatically available as to witnesses in general, but require court approval for certain classes of witnesses (e.g., persons under 16, or a person designated by the prosecution as performing only a "ministerial function with respect to the case"). At least where the defendant is in custody,

3. Where a deposed person is unavailable to testify at trial, his deposition, having been taken under oath and subject to cross-examination, is admissible as substantive evidence at trial under the "prior testimony" exception to the hearing rule, discussed in § 14.1(d). In many jurisdictions, evidentiary provisions like Fed.R.Evid. 801(d)(1) also allow the deposition to be used as substantive evidence if the witness is available but gives testimony at trial inconsistent with his deposition. Of course, the deposition, like any prior recorded statement, may also be used to impeach the witness. See Fed.R.Crim.P. 15(e).

the standard procedure may be to conduct the deposition without the defendant being present.

Several factors help to explain why the discovery deposition, a mainstay of civil discovery, is unavailable in criminal cases in the vast majority of jurisdictions. Initially, discovery depositions are utilized in civil cases in conjunction with interrogatories that allow each party to discover from the other the names of persons with relevant knowledge. This facilitates the economical and effective use of the depositions by identifying the potential trial witnesses. In criminal discovery, the many jurisdictions with provisions modeled after the Federal Rules do not provide any similar discovery. Of course, depositions could be used without witness-list discovery, as the defense in particular ordinarily is aware of at least some of the other side's potential witnesses. However, the ability to depose those known witnesses (who otherwise could simply refuse to be interviewed) could lead the defense to the identification of the other witnesses and thereby circumvent the prosecution's refusal to identify the witness.

Still another factor that distinguishes criminal discovery is the availability of the prior recorded statements of potential witnesses. In civil pretrial discovery, those statements are not available except under special circumstances, as it is expected that each party will depose the other's potential witnesses, rather than rely upon statements the other side obtained in the course of its trial preparation. In criminal discovery, jurisdictions with ABA-type provisions all provide the defense with pretrial discovery of statements obtained by the prosecution from its witnesses and many of those jurisdictions also provide the prosecution with discovery of statements obtained by the defense. Of course, such statements are far from a perfect substitute for a deposition, as they provide only the witness' responses to an interview conducted by the opposite side. Nonetheless, the availability of the witness' prior statement contributes to the argument that there is less need for discovery depositions in the criminal justice process and therefore the value of such further disclosure is more readily out-weighed by the burden imposed upon the deposed witness (particularly the victim who is placed in the sometimes awkward position of testifying in the presence of the alleged offender). This contention is also made where the jurisdiction utilizes the preliminary hearing as a screening device. The defense, it is noted, will have had an opportunity to "depose" the witness at that hearing (calling the witness itself if the prosecution failed to do so), and there is no reason to require the witness to testify in still another pretrial proceeding. Of course, the defense may have been unaware of the witness at the time of the hearing, but it is assumed that all of the critical witnesses ordinarily will be known to the defense at that point. Among the jurisdictions allowing for discovery depositions, several do not make regular use of the preliminary hearing and one provides for a prosecution objection to the deposition of a witness who was "adequately examined at the preliminary hearing."

The potential cost of the discovery deposition is still another concern that may have contributed in many states to the decision to limit depositions to the exceptional case requiring the preservation of testimony. The Commentary to the 1970 ABA Standards expressed that concern, noting as to defense depositions: "There is no inherent limitation of cost on the conduct of unnecessary depositions, because in many cases the cost of the defense must be borne by the state * * * [and] if stated as a right, the need to take depositions might be construed as part of the adequacy of representation required by the constitutional right to counsel." It is obviously true that in civil discovery the deposition is one of the most costly and time-consuming elements of pretrial proceedings.

§ 20.3 Defense Discovery

(a) Prosecution Possession or Control. An element bearing on almost all portions of a typical defense discovery provision is the scope of the prosecution's obligation to obtain and make available for discovery items that are not within its immediate possession. As to each item designated as subject to discovery, apart from those obviously within the prosecution's possession (e.g., items to be used at trial), the discovery provision will attach a clause describing the necessary connection of the prosecution to the particular item. States with ABA-type discovery provisions commonly describe the prosecutor's discovery obligation as extending to specified "material and information" that is "within the possession or control of the prosecuting attorney." As to items which are "in the possession or control of other government personnel," some ABA jurisdictions add a provision imposing on the prosecution an obligation to "use diligent good faith efforts to cause such material to be made available to defense counsel" (supplemented by judicial subpoena when such other "government personnel" are subject to the court's jurisdiction). Federal Rule 16 applies its basic discovery provisions to items "within the possession, custody, or control of the government," but then adds the limitation that the "existence of [the item] be known, or by the exercise of due diligence may become known to the attorney for the government." [1] Where the point of reference for possession, custody, or control is to the government as a whole and not simply to the prosecutor's office, some limitation tied to the prosecution's actual or potential awareness of the item is thought to be necessary because of the wide range of potentially discoverable material that may have been acquired by "the government" in connection with matters not directly related to the criminal investigation. Relevant written statements of the defendant, for example, could include various reports submitted by a defendant (especially a corporate defendant) to many different agencies in connection with regulatory, tax, and other governmental activities.

Courts interpreting typical "scope" clauses uniformly have held that the basic obligation to disclose extends to items within the files of those investigative agencies of the same government that have participated in the development of the particular prosecution. Their files are deemed within the "control" of the prosecutor under an ABA-type provision or matter "within the possession" of the government that should be known to the prosecutor under a federal-type provision. Under the broad language of Federal Rule 16, material which is possessed by any agency of the "government," whether or not investigatory, should be discoverable if it is identified by reference to its likely location in the defense request (and thereby made "known" to the "attorney for the government"). However, "government" for this purpose arguably does not extend to agencies outside of the executive branch (e.g., a probation department). Whether "control" extends to investigative agencies of other governments with which the prosecution has a working relationship is a matter on which courts have divided, with the majority holding that it does not.

(b) Written or Recorded Statements. Another issue that has a bearing on several parts of a typical defense discovery provision is the reach of the phrase "written or recorded statement." All discovery provisions provide for discovery of written or recorded statements of the defendant, and many allow for discovery of written or recorded statements of codefendants and prosecution witnesses as well. Neither the ABA Standards nor the Federal Rules sought to define the phrase "written or recorded statement." The drafting committees in both instances recognized the possible incorporation of the definition of "statement" used in the Jencks Act.[2] That Act, which applies to federal courts, gives the defendant a right to inspect the prior statements of a prosecution witness, following that witness' testimony, for the purpose of possible impeachment of the witness. The Jencks Act defines "statement" for this purpose as (1) "a written statement made by said witness and signed or otherwise adopted by him," (2) "a

§ 20.3

1. This limitation is not used with respect to defense requests for inspection of documents and tangible objects under Rule 16(a)(1)(C), which refers simply to such items "which are in the possession, custody, or control of the government" and are either "material" to defense preparation, intended to be used in evidence, or were obtained from or belong to the defendant.

2. See § 24.3 at note 20.

stenographic, mechanical, electrical or other recording, or a transcription thereof, which is a substantially verbatim recital of an oral statement made by said witness and recorded contemporaneously with the making of such oral statement," and (3) grand jury testimony. The drafters of both the ABA Standards and Federal Rule 16 agreed that the "written or recorded statement" phrase in their respective discovery provisions should include all statements that fell within the Jencks Act definition of "statement." The unresolved issue was whether the discovery provisions should have a broader scope, and that centered upon possibly rejecting the Jencks Act limitations as to a "recording" of an oral statement—i.e., not insisting that the recordation be substantially verbatim and be made contemporaneously with the making of the oral statement.[3]

The majority of ABA's Advisory Committee argued that the Jencks Act was too narrow, as it was directed at a recordation usable for impeachment purposes, and discovery had broader objectives. A minority favored the Jencks Act definition. They argued that persons who furnished information to investigators should not be forced to explain or account for the agent's written recollection of those statements that were not substantially in the speaker's own words or specifically approved by the speaker. The end result of this Committee division was to leave the issue unresolved. The Advisory Committee on the 1975 amendment to Federal Rule 16 took a similar approach.

Unlike the ABA Standards and the Federal Rules, a handful of states have included a general definition of "written or recorded statements" in their discovery provisions. These state definitions include, in addition to those that simply incorporate the Jencks Act definition, a definition that encompasses any statement "recorded or summarized in any writing or recording," and a definition that encompasses any "written statements or notes which are in substance recitals of an oral statement." Courts lacking the guidance of a statutory definition occasionally have also strayed from the Jencks Act definition, including written "summaries of oral statements" that are neither substantially verbatim recitals nor contemporaneously made. Most, however, have looked basically to the Jencks Act definition. They have required that the recordation of an oral statement be both substantially verbatim and contemporaneously made, although enough leeway has been allowed to include a relatively contemporaneous recordation. The recorded statement provision of Federal Rule 16 has been held not to encompass investigative reports or notes of undercover agents which summarized their conversations with defendants or overheard statements of defendants. So too, the federal provision has been held not to apply where defendant made an oral statement to a third person who later repeated that conversation in his own written or recorded statement given to investigators. An additional difficulty presented in such cases is that the Federal Rules would not allow discovery of the personal statement of the third party if that third party were to be a government witness, and his personal comments would often be intertwined with even an attempted verbatim recount of what the defendant had said to him. Third party witnesses can be the source of the defendant's written or recorded statement, however, as where the third party secretly tape-records the oral statements of the defendant or receives a letter from the defendant that he later submits to government agents. The same is true of the undercover agent who secretly tapes a conversation or makes a substantially verbatim record of

3. A separate issue was presented with respect to grand jury transcripts. Transcribed grand jury testimony clearly met the requirements for recordation, so the primary concern here was whether the interest in preserving grand jury secrecy should create an exception for such recorded statements. While such an exception was once widely recognized, today grand jury testimony commonly is afforded no special treatment in the context of defense discovery. Where the defendant is entitled to receive his written or recorded statement, he also can receive his recorded testimony before the grand jury. So too where the defendant may discover the written or recorded statements of codefendants or government witnesses, he may also discover their recorded grand jury testimony. See § 8.5(f).

the conversation with reasonable promptness after its completion.

(c) **Defendant's Statements.** Perhaps no item is more readily discoverable by the defense than the defendant's own written or recorded statement. In the federal system and all but a handful of the states, such discovery is granted as a matter of right. The remaining states allow discovery of the defendant's written or recorded statements at the trial judge's discretion. In many of these jurisdictions, however, the disclosure of such statements is almost automatic. Disclosure generally is granted without any showing of need beyond defendant's allegation that inspection is "necessary to refresh his recollection" of the statement.

Providing discovery of a defendant's written or recorded statement has been supported on the grounds that: (1) the precise wording of defendant's statement is especially helpful to defense counsel in preparing for trial or in determining whether a guilty plea is advisable; (2) disclosure does not pose a substantial threat of successful perjury since the defendant may be impeached effectively by reference to his statement; (3) disclosure of defendant's statement does not create a reciprocity problem since the state obviously gained discovery from the defendant in obtaining the statement from him originally; and (4) if disclosure is not granted directly, the defense simply will use the motion to suppress as an indirect discovery device.

The ABA Standards impose no prerequisite that the defendant's prior recorded statement relate to the subject of the criminal prosecution. The apparent assumption here is that the statements will almost always be relevant; if they are within the possession or the control of the prosecutor, they are most likely to have some potential value to the defense even if the prosecutor does not intend to use them in evidence. In any event, to occasionally require disclosure of some unrelated material is deemed a lesser cost than to open the door to potentially burdensome litigation over what is relevant and what is not.

Federal Rule 16(a)(1)(A), on the other hand, does impose a requirement of "relevancy," and a similar restriction is found in state provisions modeled after Rule 16. Most courts have taken a broad view of "relevancy" for this purpose, basically assuming that any statement made by the defendant during the course of the investigation was relevant. The presumption should be in favor of disclosures, they note, for while the government can easily assess relevance to its own case, it can only guess as to what would be relevant from the defense viewpoint. This position is consistent with the assumption that the relevancy requirement exists primarily as a safeguard against imposing upon the prosecution the obligation of collecting and disclosing the countless forms and other written statements that a defendant may have submitted to different governmental units; where the disclosure obligation extends to items within the possession of "the government" that could reasonably become known to the prosecutor, many of the standard documents filed by a defendant could be viewed as discoverable if not for the relevancy limitation. Some courts, however, see the relevancy requirement as playing a much more significant role and would exclude as well certain statements obtained during the course of the investigation. They suggest that the prosecutor can properly judge relevancy by reference to its case-in-chief, and therefore need not disclose those written and recorded statements of the defendant that have no possible bearing upon that case. Thus, the prosecution's failure to disclose a recorded statement later used to impeach the defendant has been justified on the ground that Rule 16 does not require the government to anticipate every possible explanation a defendant might assert in his testimony and then furnish him with "otherwise irrelevant material" that might conflict with that testimony.

All of the state discovery provisions modeled after the ABA Standards and most of those modeled after Federal Rule 16 also require disclosure of the substance of certain oral statements of defendant known to the prosecution. Where these provisions apply, they eliminate dispute over whether a particular documentation of an oral statement is sufficient in content and manner of recording to fall within the recorded statement provision; the government must disclose the substance of the comments in any event. However, the oral statement provisions often are much narrower in scope than the recorded statement provisions. Some of the ABA-type provisions do apply to all oral statements within the prosecution's possession or control. Many other states, however, will require disclosure only as to oral statements that the prosecution "intends to offer in evidence at the trial." This limitation stems from the concern that the range of unrecorded statements between the defendant and investigators and between defendant and various persons interviewed by the police is too broad to impose an obligation of disclosure without regard to the possible use of those statements at trial.

A 1991 amendment of Federal Rule 16 discarded the prerequisite of prosecution use as to a written record containing the substance of oral statements (although prosecution use remains a prerequisite for disclosure of the substance of an oral statement that is not summarized in a written record). Rule 16 and several states do impose, however, a further limitation—the defendant's oral statement must have been made "in response to interrogation" to a "person then known to the defendant to be a government agent." This limitation allows the prosecution to keep from the defense the fact that undercover agents or non-agent witnesses will be testifying as to oral statements made by the defendant. It is seen as flowing from concerns relating to the defendant's misuse of that information which are similar to those concerns—discussed in subsections (h) and (i)—that have led these same jurisdictions not to provide for witness-disclosure and to bar pretrial disclosure of witness statements.

(d) Codefendant's Statements. Required disclosure of codefendants' statements has been urged on the grounds that such statements: "(1) are potentially important to defense counsel in preparing to meet the government's case and developing evidence on defendant's behalf; (2) aid defense counsel in deciding whether to make a severance motion and in assisting the judicial determination of such a motion; and (3) mitigate the well-known proclivities of some criminal defendants not to give their own lawyers a truthful account of their actions." These grounds have not proven as convincing to the drafters of discovery provisions as the grounds supporting the required disclosure of the defendant's own statements. Here, there is substantially greater division as to whether and under what conditions disclosure should be required.

Only slightly over one-third of the states have provisions requiring disclosure of a codefendant's statement, and those provisions vary substantially in coverage. Several states provide for the disclosure of recorded or oral statements of codefendants without limitation. Others, following the original ABA model, restrict required disclosure to cases in which the codefendants will be jointly tried. The focus here is basically on the second ground noted above—giving the defense that information which will be critical in its determination as to whether to seek a severance. Of course, if the codefendant is a coconspirator and his statement was made in the course of the conspiracy, that statement will be admissible against the defendant, and it therefore will be discoverable whether the two are to tried together or not in those jurisdictions that grant disclosure of the statements of prosecution witnesses.

Federal Rule 16 does not include a provision requiring disclosure of a codefendant's statements, but federal courts have held that they have discretion to order such disclosure. However, that discretion is limited by the prohibition against disclosure of the statements of prospective government witnesses. That prohibition has been held to encompass the coconspirator's statement made in the course of the conspiracy. Although its admissibility is based in part on the theory that each coconspirator speaks for the other, federal courts have rejected the contention that the coconspirator's statement should be treated as another form of statement of the defendant himself rather than as a statement of a prosecution witness. Of course, nothing prevents each codefendant from obtaining discovery of his own statement and sharing that information with the others.

(e) Criminal Records. Federal Rule 16 and a substantial majority of the state discovery provisions grant the defendant a right to discovery of his criminal record. The theory underlying this requirement is aptly summarized in the Commentary to the ABA Standards:

> Disclosure of prior records in no way disadvantages the prosecution while the contents of the records are important to the defense in such issues as whether or not the defendant should plead guilty, should testify at trial, or should move to restrict the use of prior convictions for impeachment purposes. The prior record will also show whether the defendant faces treatment under enhanced sentencing provisions.[4]

Although the defendant's criminal record is helpful in assessing the likely sentence if convicted upon plea or trial, pretrial discovery otherwise provides a very limited vehicle for making a sentencing assessment. Much of the material that would be considered relevant under sentencing guidelines will be unrelated to the proof of the crime charged and therefore not be discoverable pretrial under even the broadest discovery provisions.

(f) Scientific Reports. Federal Rule 16 and almost all state discovery provisions provide for the disclosure of various reports of medical and physical examinations, scientific tests, and experiments. Most jurisdictions encompass all such reports that are "made in connection with the particular case." A few require that the reports be intended for use by the government at trial, while several follow the federal formula of requiring that they are either "material to the preparation of the defense or * * * intended for use by the government as evidence in chief at the trial." Among the reports commonly sought under these provisions are those relating to the physical examination of the victim (e.g., autopsy reports) or the analysis of evidence found at the scene of the crime (e.g., fingerprint comparisons and tests on seized drugs).

A substantial majority of jurisdictions make mandatory the disclosure of scientific reports, but a small group of states continue to make such disclosure discretionary. Appellate courts in these jurisdictions suggest, however, that disclosure of scientific reports should ordinarily be granted without any special showing of need. This position is justified on several grounds. Once the report is prepared, the scientific expert's position is not readily influenced, and therefore disclosure presents little danger of prompting perjury or intimidation. Disclosure is also justified on the ground that "it lessens the imbalance which may result from the State's early and complete investigation in contrast to [defendant's] * * * late and limited investigation." It is further noted that "this sort of evidence is practically impossible for the adversary to test or rebut at trial without an adversary opportunity to examine it closely."

(g) Documents and Tangible Objects. Jurisdictions that require mandatory disclosure of scientific tests ordinarily also have mandatory disclosure provisions governing documents and tangible objects. The remaining jurisdictions allow for disclosure at the discretion of the trial court. Provisions governing disclosure of documents and tangible objects generally encompass those items "which the prosecution will use at trial or which were obtained from or purportedly belong to the defendant." The justification for requiring disclosure of the items to be used at trial is similar to that for disclosure of scientific reports. Here too, there is no substantial threat of perjury and an inspection in advance of the trial often will be necessary to challenge the evidence. In many instances, the defense may have need to have its own experts examine documents or tangible items. The justification for requiring disclosure of items obtained from or belonging to the defendant lies largely in recognizing the defense's right to sources of information that it origi-

4. II ABA Standards for Criminal Justice (2d ed., 1980), Commentary to § 11–2.1(a)(vi). The ABA Standards also provide for disclosures of a codefendant's prior criminal record.

nally possessed. Even if the prosecution does not intend to use the particular items at trial, they may be helpful to the defense, and they presumably are relevant by virtue of their very acquisition by the government through methods such as subpoena or seizure. Some illegally seized items may be used only for impeachment (and therefore would otherwise not be discoverable where the concept of intended "use at trial" is limited to the prosecution's case-in-chief); thus, this category of disclosure can be especially helpful to the defense in anticipating a possible source of impeachment.

The Federal Rules and state provisions modeled after the Federal Rules include a third category of discoverable documents and objects—those "which are material to the preparation of the defendant's defense." Here the burden is on the defendant to demonstrate the requisite materiality. Moreover, the use of the term "material" suggests that more than a showing of potential relevancy is demanded. The defense must also show that the item has special significance in light of the limitations of the discovery provided by the other evidence available to it. The trial court may, if it so chooses, examine the requested item in camera to determine whether it has that potential significance. Of course, the court must be wary of underestimating the possible bearing of the evidence as it relates to a defense posture still to be developed (and not yet fully disclosed), but it can determine whether the item deals with the particular subject matter or otherwise has the type of content on which the defense bases it claim of materiality.

(h) Witness Lists. State provisions patterned after the ABA Standards generally require the prosecution to provide the defense with "the names and addresses of persons whom the State intends to call as witnesses." A few states with ABA-type provisions have a broader standard requiring the prosecutor to list the names and addresses of all persons "known by the government to have knowledge of relevant facts" without regard to whether they will be called as witnesses. Although the Federal Rules do not include a witness disclosure provision, various states which started with provisions similar to the Federal Rules added witness-list disclosure in accordance with the proposed amendment to the Federal Rules that Congress rejected in 1975.[5] A few additional jurisdictions have pleading provisions requiring that the names of witnesses be endorsed upon the information or indictment. With those jurisdictions included, almost half of the states can be said to provide for some form of mandatory pretrial disclosure of the names of the prosecution's witnesses.

In most of the jurisdictions with mandatory disclosure requirements, the prosecution must list only those witnesses that it expects to present in building its case-in-chief. If the prosecution expects that the defendant will raise a certain contention that might call for rebuttal witnesses, it need not list those witnesses even if fairly certain as to who they will be. In other jurisdictions, the prosecution must also list rebuttal witnesses when it can anticipate who they will be. Of course, as with other disclosure obligations, the duty is continuing, so the prosecution must add to the list as it discovers new witnesses.

The states that do not mandate pretrial disclosure of witness lists generally allow the trial court to order such disclosure at its discretion. In some jurisdictions, discovery provisions specifically recognize this discretionary authority, while other jurisdictions rely upon the inherent power of the trial court to order that disclosure needed to "aid the ends of justice." Disclosure of witness lists in the federal courts, aside from capital cases (where a statute requires such disclosure), rests on the latter authority. Since the Federal Rules do not contain any reference to witness lists, and since Congress in 1975 rejected only a proposed amendment that would have made such disclosure mandatory, federal courts have held that Rule 16 does not preclude the exercise of their inherent authority to require pretrial disclosure of witness identities where

5. See § 21.1(c).

such disclosure is justified by the circumstances of the particular case.

Where disclosure of witness lists lies in the discretion of the trial court, the defendant usually must make some showing of need to obtain disclosure. In many of these jurisdictions, including the federal system, the burden placed on the defendant is especially heavy, with the courts starting from the presumption that witness-list disclosure generally is not available. Factors that courts have considered in determining whether the defense should gain witness identification include: (1) whether the crime charged is one of violence; (2) whether the defendant has a past history of violence; (3) whether the evidence in the case consists largely of material that cannot readily be altered (e.g., documents); (4) whether a realistic possibility exists that the government witnesses might not appear or might be unwilling to testify at trial; (5) whether the offense charged covers a long time span, making more difficult the defendant's recollection of all potential witnesses; and (6) whether the defense has limited resources available for investigation and trial preparation.

The primary objection to presumptive or mandatory disclosure of witness lists is the potential for intimidation of witnesses. In opposing the proposed 1975 amendment to the Federal Rules, the Department of Justice offered a study listing more than 700 instances of witness intimidation ranging from assault to assassination. Concern has also been expressed that even in cases far removed from violence, such as white collar cases, there remains a potential for the use of economic coercion against witnesses. The basic response of the proponents of broad discovery is that a realistic potential of such intimidation or coercion exists in only a relatively small portion of all cases and the proper response therefore is the "'scalpel' of the protective order," which would allow disclosure in the vast majority of cases, rather than a policy that allows disclosure only in the most exceptional cases. Opponents of the regular disclosure of witness lists reply that the protective order is not a sufficient answer. They note that the protective order procedure puts the government in the position of having to make a special showing, which itself creates difficulties in protecting witnesses, and that the judicial emphasis upon protective measures short of denying disclosure often produces an insufficient safeguard. This response does not fully explain, however, why jurisdictions allowing for discretionary disclosure typically follow a practice of regularly denying discovery, absent a strong defense showing of need, notwithstanding the prosecution's failure to even hint at a possible intimidation difficulty. The concern here apparently is that allowing disclosure as a regular matter, even with a broad exception for cases presenting any threat of intimidation, would inevitably reinforce the natural reluctance of many persons to willingly come forward and testify in criminal cases. The prosecution, it is argued, should be able regularly to assure reluctant or fearful witnesses that their identity will not be revealed until trial (and, indeed, may not ever be revealed if the defendant pleads guilty).

(i) Witness Statements. American jurisdictions can be divided into three groups in their treatment of pretrial disclosure of the written or recorded statements of prosecution witnesses. One group requires the prosecution to disclose all such statements within its possession or control; another allows the trial court to order such disclosure at its discretion; and a third specifically prohibits such orders. While these groups are of roughly equal size, most of the jurisdictions recognizing a discretionary authority tend to frown upon the exercise of that authority, and pretrial discovery of witness statements therefore is readily available in no more than twenty states.

Jurisdictions barring pretrial discovery of witness statements ordinarily include in their discovery rules a specific prohibition similar to that found in Federal Rule 16(a)(2). That provision states that Rule 16 "does not authorize the discovery or inspection of * * * statements made by government witnesses or prospective government witnesses except as provided in 18 U.S.C.A. § 3500." The cited exception is to the Jencks Act (18 U.S.C.A. § 3500), which was designed to ensure that prior recorded statements of witnesses are available for impeachment use, but not subject to pretrial discovery.[6] The Jencks Act provides that after a government witness testifies on direct examination, the government shall make available his prior recorded statement insofar as that statement relates to the subject matter of the defendant's testimony, but it also adds:

> [N]o statement * * * in the possession of the United States which was made by a Government witness or prospective Government witness (other than the defendant) shall be the subject of subpoena, discovery, or inspection until said witness has testified on direct examination in the trial of the case.

Discovery of witness statements is left to the discretion of the trial judge not only in common law jurisdictions that generally rely upon discretion, but also in several jurisdictions with provisions that are otherwise modeled after the ABA Standards or the Federal Rules. In some of the latter jurisdictions, the basic discovery provision explicitly makes witness statements a subject of discretionary discovery, while in others, the provision makes no mention of such statements and thereby leaves disclosure subject to the court's inherent power to require discovery. Most of the jurisdictions relying upon the trial judge's discretionary authority assume that disclosure of witness statements should not ordinarily be available, so a trial court's refusal to order discovery will rarely be deemed an abuse of discretion. General requests for the disclosure of the written or recorded statements of all prospective prosecution witnesses are commonly condemned as "fishing expeditions" or attempts to require the prosecutor to "open his files to the attorney for the accused." To be successful, the defense ordinarily must show a special need for the statement of a particular witness and convince the trial court that the later disclosure of that statement at trial (for use in cross-examination) is not a satisfactory alternative.

Jurisdictions with provisions patterned after the ABA Standards generally include witness statements among the required items of disclosure. In most of these jurisdictions, disclosure is limited to "relevant written or recorded statements." A few states go beyond the witness category and require pretrial disclosure of the written or recorded statements of all persons known to have knowledge of relevant facts.

The division among the states in their treatment of witness statements follows in part from their division on the disclosure of witness lists. A jurisdiction that does not grant witness lists as a matter of right will not make witness statements available as a matter of right. However, there are jurisdictions that grant discovery of witness lists as a matter of right but do not do the same for witness statements, and jurisdictions that allow a court in its discretion to order the disclosure of a witness list but not witness statements. One factor said to support a narrower position on witness statements is the potential misuse of the statement to facilitate defense perjury. Providing the defendant with witness statements is seen as more likely to facilitate his use of perjury than providing any other item of discovery. Very often, however, the advocates of a complete bar on discovery of witness statements rely on other justifications as well. They argue that: (1) defendant has an ample opportunity to challenge the testimony of prosecution witnesses at trial since the witness' prior recorded statement may be obtained at that point under state provisions similar to the Jencks Act or common law rules on witness impeachment; (2) where witness lists are available or the defense is otherwise aware of likely prosecution witnesses, defense counsel has ample opportunity for pretrial preparation by interviewing those witnesses, and it will be in the best interests of defendant to encourage defense counsel to conduct his own investigation through such interviews rather than rely on the prosecution's investigative efforts; and (3) recorded statements of witnesses ordinarily are within the work product privilege since they are obtained by the prosecutor or his agents "in anticipation of litigation."

6. See § 24.3 at note 20.

As might be expected, proponents of the ABA–type provisions find none of the above arguments persuasive. Disclosure at trial pursuant to a Jencks-type provision is viewed as an unsatisfactory alternative. It is said that, "for adequate preparation and to minimize surprise," disclosures must be made prior to trial. The opportunity to interview a witness is also considered an inadequate substitute for pretrial discovery of witness statements. Witnesses frequently either refuse to talk to defense counsel or insist upon very limited interviews.[7] Moreover, even if the witness is willing to cooperate fully (or the defense has the right to depose the witness under state law), the interview will not come nearly as promptly after the event as the initial police investigation. The witness is likely to have forgotten details that were included in his initial statement, and those details might provide helpful leads for further defense investigation. For similar reasons, it is argued, counsel who obtains a witness' statement is not likely to "ride the coattails" of the prosecution's investigative efforts. Since there may be more to be learned than is contained in the statement, counsel will still want to interview the witness if he is willing to cooperate. Reliance upon the work product doctrine to bar discovery of a witness' statements is also challenged. As discussed in the next subsection, the work product doctrine generally is not viewed as so broad as to automatically encompass all prior recorded witness statements in whatever form they might take.

(j) The Work Product Exemption. States with provisions requiring the prosecution's mandatory pretrial disclosure of a prospective witness' recorded statement commonly also include a specific exemption for "work product." Where courts have discretionary authority to order disclosure, a common law work product exemption restricts the exercise of that discretion. As developed in civil discovery, the work product doctrine seeks to preserve against discovery materials developed in the course of preparing for litigation. The underlying purpose of the doctrine, as set forth in the leading case of *Hickman v. Taylor,*[8] is to preclude "unwarranted inquiries [through discovery] into the files and mental impressions of an attorney." *Hickman* did not absolutely bar civil discovery of "written materials obtained or prepared by an adversary's counsel with an eye toward litigation," but it did recognize a "general policy" against discovery of such "work product" of counsel. As incorporated in the Federal Rules of Civil Procedure, Rule 26(b)(3), the *Hickman* work product doctrine (1) encompasses documents and tangible things prepared in anticipation of litigation, (2) allows discovery of such items only upon a showing of "substantial need" and inability without "undue hardship" to obtain equivalent materials, but (3) also requires the court ordering such discovery to "protect against disclosure of the mental impressions, conclusions, opinions, or legal theories of an attorney or other representative of a party concerning the litigation."[9]

Application of the work product doctrine to the criminal justice process raises a series of issues. First, there is the question of whether the interests protected by the doctrine are sufficiently strong that they should even be recognized in the context of criminal procedure. The doctrine's basic objective is to protect the adversary system by affording counsel free rein in the development of litigation materials and the analysis that material reflects. This is to be done by providing assurance that those materials will not automatically be available to counsel's adversary and that counsel's mental processes (i.e., "mental impressions, conclusions, opinions or legal

7. Courts have consistently held that prosecutors cannot encourage witnesses in this regard by advising or directing them not to cooperate with defense counsel. But they have also stated that since "the witness is free to decide whether to grant or refuse an interview * * * it is not improper for the government to inform the witness of that right." United States v. White, 454 F.2d 435 (7th Cir.1971).

8. 329 U.S. 495, 67 S.Ct. 385, 91 L.Ed. 451 (1947).

9. The Rule does not require a special showing for a party to obtain a copy of his own statement, and thus, where extended to criminal cases, would have no bearing on the defendant's right to inspect his own recorded statement.

theories") will be given close to absolute protection from discovery by an adversary. Some commentators have argued that a work product exception is inappropriate as to the trial preparation material of the prosecutor. The prosecutor, they note, is not simply an adversary, but a representative of the people who bears a duty to "promote justice," which points toward full discovery and avoidance of trial by surprise. Both courts and legislatures, however, have consistently rejected the view that the prosecutor's broader role renders the work product privilege irrelevant. Thus, the Supreme Court, in *United States v. Nobles,*[10] expressed no qualms in holding the work product doctrine applicable in federal criminal cases as a basic common law doctrine. Indeed, the Court noted that the work product doctrine was "even more vital" in the criminal justice system than in civil litigation for "the interests of society and the accused in obtaining a fair and accurate resolution of the question of guilt or innocence demand that adequate safeguards assure the thorough preparation and presentation of each side of the case."

A second issue is whether, as in civil cases, the doctrine will operate to require a showing of special need for what is commonly described as "fact" work product—i.e., the content of a trial preparation document apart from that which reflects counsel's mental processes. In the civil setting, fact work product is given less protection than mental process work product (often called "opinion" work product), but disclosure of fact work product does require a showing of need and unavailable alternatives. As to a recorded statement of a witness, the party seeking discovery must show, at the least, that the deposition process is unavailable or otherwise unsatisfactory. In the criminal justice process, of course, the deposition process ordinarily is not available as a discovery tool, but there remain other alternatives, such as interviewing the witness. In jurisdictions that place discovery of a prosecution witness' statement in the discretion of the trial court, the showing required often will parallel if not surpass that mandated in civil cases. Jurisdictions with ABA-type provisions, however, view the witness' statement as so important to defense preparation that they simply dispatch with a showing of need and automatically make it available insofar as it contains no more than "fact" work product.

All jurisdictions allowing disclosure of witness statements do protect, however, "opinion" work product. The primary issue here is whether what is to be protected is solely the mental impressions of the prosecution's legal staff, or also the mental impressions of their investigators—the police. In civil cases, as the Supreme Court noted in *Nobles,* the doctrine has developed "as an intensely practical one, grounded on the realities of litigation," and one of those realities is that "attorneys often must rely on assistance of their investigators." *Nobles* concluded that the federal work product rule in criminal cases should also extend to statements taken by investigators. Many states do likewise, often with specific reference made to "police officers," but others follow the ABA model, which is limited to opinions, theories, or conclusions of the "prosecuting attorneys or members of his legal staff." This difference in coverage is unlikely to have great practical significance as applied to prior recorded statements of witnesses. Statements obtained by police officers will ordinarily not reflect a significant amount of "opinion" work product. Very often, the statement will consist of little more than the witness' narrative of events in response to an open-ended question. On occasion, the interrogator's questions may reflect some legal theory or factual judgment, but such material often can be deleted without detracting from the flow of the witness' statement.

(k) Police Reports. Police investigative reports may fall in one or more of several categories of discoverable material. Where the report contains a recital of the comments of a defendant, codefendant or witness sufficiently complete to constitute a recorded statement of that person, that portion of the

10. 422 U.S. 225, 95 S.Ct. 2160, 45 L.Ed.2d 141 (1975).

report may be subject to discovery under the appropriate provision for recorded statements. So too, an abridged description of a statement may be subject to discovery when state law requires disclosure of summaries of oral statements of defendants or codefendants. Most often, the police reports will contain considerable additional information that would not fall under the provisions governing either recorded or oral statements. This would include the officer's own observations and comments and references to conversations with persons whose statements are not subject to disclosure. In many jurisdictions, one or more avenues of discovery may be available to obtain even that portion of the report. These include: (1) provisions for discovery of documents "which are material to the preparation of the defense"; (2) provisions requiring disclosure of statements of persons having knowledge of relevant facts; (3) provisions requiring disclosure of statements of prosecution witnesses where the officer himself will testify at trial; and (4) provisions authorizing discretionary disclosure of "relevant material and information" not otherwise listed in the discovery rule.

The Federal Rules and a substantial number of states specifically exempt police reports and similar documents from discovery under most of the provisions noted above. Federal Rule 16(a)(2) provides that except as authorized under provisions for disclosure of defendant's statements, criminal records, and scientific reports, Rule 16 "does not authorize the discovery or inspection of reports, memoranda, or other internal government documents made by the attorney for the government or other internal government agents in connection with the investigation or prosecution of the case." States without specific exemptions for police reports vary in their treatment of such reports. Some effectively bar disclosure through rulings that hold such reports to automatically constitute work product. Others, however, take a narrower view of work product that either does not apply to the police at all or is limited to "opinion" work product that will rarely appear in a police report. Here, if the police report otherwise fits within one of the categories of discoverable material, it receives basically no special protection and is discoverable.

(*l*) Protective Orders. All jurisdictions with an extensive statute or court rule governing discovery include a provision authorizing the issuance of a protective order. In common law jurisdictions, the trial court's discretionary authority similarly permits it to defer or deny discovery for protective purposes. Federal Rule 16(d) and various state protective-order provisions authorize the trial court to direct that discovery otherwise available be "denied, restricted, or deferred." Other states, however, limit protective orders to restricting or deferring discovery and add the requirement that "all material and information to which a party is entitled must be disclosed in time to make beneficial use thereof." A denial of discovery, as authorized under Federal Rule 16, ordinarily will only keep material from defendant until it is introduced at trial. However, insofar as the Federal Rule or a similar state provision encompasses discoverable material that would not be introduced at trial, the denial will keep the defendant from ever inspecting that material.

What constitutes appropriate grounds for the issuance of a protective order? Federal Rule 16(d) simply notes that the order shall be issued "upon sufficient showing." Several state provisions list various interests that may be weighed against the value of disclosure to the defendant. Thus, the New Jersey Rule notes that the trial court may consider the following interests:

> Protection of witnesses and others from physical harm, threats of harm, bribes, economic reprisals and other intimidation; maintenance of such secrecy regarding informants as is required for effective investigation of criminal activity; protection of confidential relationships and privileges recognized by law; any other relevant consideration.[11]

In the end, as one court rule notes, the judge must determine "that the disclosure would

11. N.J.R.Crim.P. 3:13–3(d)(1).

result in a risk or harm outweighing any usefulness of the disclosure." [12]

The burden of establishing a need for a protective order rests, of course, on the government as the party seeking that order. The trial court may allow the government to make its showing in camera so as to avoid disclosing to the defense that information which the government seeks to protect under the order. This procedure often places the defense in the difficult position of having to respond to the motion without fully knowing what facts have been presented by the other side. Of course, if the court enters the order, the record of the government's showing will be sealed and made available for review on appeal. At that point, however, the defense is again in a difficult position. In light of the broad discretion granted the trial judge and the fact that appellate review ordinarily is not available prior to an appeal from a conviction, the protective order is likely to either be sustained on appeal as within the trial judge's discretion or held to constitute harmless error even if its issuance was an abuse of discretion. In particular, where disclosure is simply deferred until trial and the defendant is then granted an opportunity to examine the material before proceeding, it is especially difficult to establish a sufficient likelihood of prejudice to gain a reversal.

(m) Constitutional Overtones. The major portion of defense discovery focuses on avoiding "trial by surprise" by giving the defense advance notice of the evidence that the prosecution intends to use at trial. This aspect of defense discovery has been viewed as a matter to be determined by local legislative or judicial policy, with the Constitution imposing no significant requirements as to what must be disclosed before trial. The Supreme Court has noted, for example, that while it may be the "better practice" to grant the defendant pretrial discovery of his confession where the prosecution intends to use it at trial, the failure to follow that practice does not violate due process.[13] So too, in a case in which the prosecution failed to inform defendant that his associate and codefendant had become an informant and would testify for the police, the Court, in rejecting defendant's constitutional objection, noted: "There is no general constitutional right to discovery in a criminal case." [14] Still, exceptional cases do arise, and state courts have occasionally found due process violated where the prosecution's failure to disclose certain critical portions of its evidence before trial deprived the defendant of an adequate opportunity to prepare to meet the prosecution's case (as where that evidence was a scientific report that would have required consultation with an expert).

Insofar as discovery seeks to provide the defense with material and information that might be used to negate the prosecution's case (as in the Federal Rule 16's application to documents "material to the preparation of the defense"), the Constitution may play a significant role. As discussed in § 20.7, the Supreme Court, in a series of cases starting with *Brady v. Maryland,* has established a constitutional obligation of the prosecution to disclose exculpatory evidence within its possession when that evidence might be material to the outcome of the case. Although the *Brady* doctrine does not necessarily require disclosure prior to trial, insofar as *Brady* disclosure must be made before trial to allow the defense to take advantage of that exculpatory evidence, it creates a defense right to pretrial discovery that necessarily overrides any limitations imposed by a particular jurisdiction's discovery rules. While some states have added special "*Brady* provisions" to their discovery rules (requiring the prosecution to disclose pretrial "all material or information which tends to mitigate or negate the defendant's guilt"), most have simply assumed that,

12. Ariz.R.Crim.P. 15.5(a) (also requiring a finding that the risk cannot be eliminated by a less substantial restriction on discovery rights).

13. Cicenia v. La Gay, 357 U.S. 504, 78 S.Ct. 1297, 2 L.Ed.2d 1523 (1958).

14. Weatherford v. Bursey, 429 U.S. 545, 97 S.Ct. 837, 51 L.Ed.2d 30 (1977). See also Moore v. Illinois, 408 U.S. 786, 92 S.Ct. 2562, 33 L.Ed.2d 706 (1972) (no constitutional right to pretrial discovery of witness' prior recorded statement).

insofar as *Brady* requires pretrial discovery, that discovery will be available apart from what is otherwise required under state discovery provisions. *Brady* is most likely to require pretrial disclosure apart from a discovery provision where the prosecution is aware of persons (e.g., other eyewitness) who would give testimony flatly contradicting the critical testimony of it witness.[15]

§ 20.4 Constitutional Limitations Upon Pretrial Discovery for the Prosecution

(a) Due Process. The constitutionality of pretrial discovery for the prosecution was first considered by the Supreme Court in *Williams v. Florida.*[1] That case considered a challenge to an alibi-notice provision that was typical of most such provisions. It required the defendant, on written demand of the prosecutor, to give notice in advance of any claim of alibi, to specify the place where he claims to have been at the time of the crime, and to provide the names and addresses of alibi witnesses. The prosecution was required, in return, to notify the defense of any witnesses it proposed to offer in rebuttal of the alibi. The possible sanction for violation of disclosure obligations by the prosecution or defense was the exclusion of its alibi witnesses (except for the defense's use of the defendant's own testimony). The defendant in *Williams* had complied with the alibi-notice requirement, providing the prosecution with the name and address of his alibi witness. The prosecution then deposed that witness, and when she testified at trial, used that deposition to challenge her alibi testimony. The prosecution also introduced the testimony of an investigator who stated that the witness herself had been at still a different place during the time when she claimed to have been with the defendant.

The defense challenge to the alibi-notice rule in *Williams* rested on three grounds: violation of due process by altering the balance of the adversarial process, violation of the Fifth Amendment privilege against self-incrimination by forcing the defendant to furnish the state with information (the name and address of his alibi witness) that was useful to the state in convicting him, and violation of the Sixth Amendment by providing for a sanction of exclusion under which the defendant could be denied the right to present alibi witnesses if he failed to provide pretrial notice as required by the alibi rule. The Supreme Court found it unnecessary to consider the Sixth Amendment issue since the defendant had complied with the alibi-notice requirement and the exclusion sanction had not been applied in his case. The Constitutionality of that sanction was later upheld in *Taylor v. Illinois* (discussed in § 20.6) as applied to the circumstances there presented. The Court considered and rejected the defendant's due process and self-incrimination arguments. The *Williams* opinion, by Justice White, treated the self-incrimination issue (discussed in subsection (c) infra) as the "petitioner's major contention." The due process issue was treated as not very troublesome and disposed of in a paragraph.

The Court saw nothing in the Florida alibi-notice rule that unfairly affected the adversarial process. Given "the ease with which an alibi can be fabricated," the government's interest in "protecting itself against an eleventh hour defense" was characterized as "both obvious and legitimate." The adversary system was not "a poker game in which players enjoy an absolute right always to conceal their cards until played." There was "ample room in that system" for a notice requirement "designed to enhance the search for truth * * * by insuring both the defendant and the State ample opportunity to investigate certain facts crucial to the determination of guilt or innocence." The Florida rule, the Court stressed, was fairly constructed to meet that end. Florida law generally provided liberal discovery to the defendant and the alibi rule was "carefully hedged with reciprocal duties requiring state disclosure to the defendant."

15. See § 20.7(g).

§ 20.4

1. 399 U.S. 78, 90 S.Ct. 1893, 26 L.Ed.2d 446 (1970).

The critical nature of the reciprocal disclosure provided by the Florida alibi rule was subsequently brought home in *Wardius v. Oregon.*[2] Distinguishing *Williams,* the Court there held that an alibi rule which failed to provide reciprocal discovery by the prosecution of its rebuttal alibi witnesses violated due process. The Court noted: "The State may not insist that trials be run as a 'search for the truth' so far as the defense witnesses are concerned, while maintaining 'poker game secrecy' for its own witnesses." "Due process," it added, has "little to say regarding the amount of discovery which the parties must be afforded, [but] it does speak to the balance of force between the accused and his accuser." It was "fundamentally unfair" for the state to "require a defendant to divulge the details of his own case while at the same time subjecting him to the hazard of surprise concerning refutation of the very pieces of evidence which he disclosed to the State."

The reciprocity required by *Wardius* is now commonly found in all aspects of prosecution discovery. Moreover, the range of items that the prosecution must disclose is always broader than the range of items the prosecutor must disclose. Of course, this does not necessarily mean that the defense disclosure will always be matched in type by prosecution disclosure, as the prosecutor may not have in its possession the same type of evidence as the defense.

(b) Self-Incrimination: Non-Testimonial Disclosures. Consistent with standard self-incrimination doctrine, as discussed in § 8.12, a compelled disclosure will not violate the defendant's privilege against self-incrimination unless it requires a testimonial disclosure by the defendant. Although the Supreme Court's ruling in *United States v. Nobles*[3] did not involve pretrial discovery, its reasoning clearly establishes that most types of prosecution discovery do not present self-incrimination difficulties because they do not demand a testimonial communication by the defendant. *Nobles* upheld the required defense disclosure at trial of the prior recorded statement of a defense witness. When the defense there called its investigator to testify to his conversations with two prosecution witnesses, the trial court granted the prosecutor's request to inspect that portion of the investigator's written report that had recorded the essence of those conversations. The Supreme Court, in an unanimous ruling, held that the inspection order had not violated the defendant's privilege against self-incrimination. The Court reasoned:

> In this instance disclosure of the relevant portions of the defense investigator's report would not impinge on the fundamental values protected by the Fifth Amendment. The court's order was limited to statements allegedly made by third parties who were available as witnesses to both the prosecution and the defense. Respondent did not prepare the report, and there is no suggestion that the portions subject to the disclosure order reflected any information that he conveyed to the investigator. The fact that these statements of third parties were elicited by a defense investigator on respondent's behalf does not convert them into respondent's personal communications. Requiring their production from the investigator therefore would not in any sense compel respondent to be a witness against himself or extort communications from him.

Nobles holds that the recorded statement of another person, though obtained on defendant's behalf, remains the communication of that person and not the communication of the defendant. Accordingly, there can be no self-incrimination violation even though the statement produced is used against the defendant by the prosecution. One year after *Nobles* was decided, in *Fisher v. United States,*[4] the Court recognized that the act of production of a document authored by another could constitute a testimonial communication of the person producing the document insofar as that act acknowledged the existence and possession of the document and provides evidence

2. 412 U.S. 470, 93 S.Ct. 2208, 37 L.Ed.2d 82 (1973).

3. 422 U.S. 225, 95 S.Ct. 2160, 45 L.Ed.2d 141 (1975).

4. See § 8.12(f).

that could be used in its authentication. *Fisher,* however, does not alter the result reached in *Nobles.*

Initially, in *Nobles,* it was the lawyer rather than the client who was being compelled to produce the investigator's report. *Fisher* did recognize that a lawyer, relying on the attorney-client privilege, could object to compelled production of a document received from a client where the client could successfully have challenged on self-incrimination grounds a court order directing the client to produce that document. The investigator's report, however, was never in the possession of the client. Unlike *Fisher,* the lawyer in *Nobles* was not being compelled to produce a document that a client had given to him for the purpose of seeking legal advice. Secondly, even if the investigator's report had been placed in the possession of the client, and it was the client who then was ordered to produce the report, a self-incrimination claim would not have been successful. The client could not establish the elements critical to sustaining such a claim under *Fisher's* act-of-production doctrine when, as in *Nobles,* the government merely sought the known recorded statement of a known defense witness. Since the government is aware of the witness' identity and knows that the witness has given a statement to the defense, the existence of that statement and its possession by the defendant constitute foregone conclusions and thereby negate the potential testimonial character of those aspects of production.[5] So too, the witness himself (or if his statement was recorded by another, that person as well) can serve as the source of authentication, rendering irrelevant the production by the defendant who was not even present when the statement was prepared.

While the forced production in *Nobles* occurred at trial, the Court's basic rationale—that there was no testimonial communication of the defendant—should apply without regard to the point at which production was compelled. This is evidenced by the ruling in *Fisher,* which presented a compelled precharge production by the target of a grand jury investigation. Thus, lower courts have regularly rejected, on the basis of *Nobles,* self-incrimination challenges to prosecutorial discovery provisions that require the defense to disclose the recorded statements of both experts and ordinary witnesses. While these provisions have dealt basically with persons the defense intended to use as witnesses, from the perspective of the Fifth Amendment, it should not matter whether the recorded statements were made by persons who will testify for the defense or persons the defense has decided not to call. That distinction may have significance as to constitutional challenges based upon the Sixth Amendment (as discussed infra), but it has no bearing on the character of the statements as not those of the defendant.

The above analysis assumes that the prosecution can identify those persons whose written or recorded statements it seeks (as it could identify the investigator in *Nobles*). Where the prosecution cannot identify those persons, there may be a testimonial communication inherent in the act-of-production that does present self-incrimination difficulties. In producing the written or recorded statements of persons described in the discovery request simply by a generic category (e.g., all experts consulted or all persons at the scene of the crime), the defense is being asked to identify specific persons as falling within those categories. At this point, there is a testimonial communication in the act-of-production and the initial issue posed is similar to that discussed in subsection (c) infra—determining whether the communication can be attributed to the defendant or simply to the defense counsel. Where the communication can be said to be that of the defendant, as where it requires the defense to identify certain persons by reference to defendant's personal knowledge, the production of their recorded statement should be governed by the same principles that apply to other instances

5. The "foregone conclusion" doctrine, which *Fisher* recognized as negating the potential testimonial character of the act-of-production, is discussed at § 8.13(a).

of a defendant's testimonial disclosures through discovery, such as the identification of alibi witnesses (also discussed infra).

The *Nobles* opinion, as quoted above, distinguished the case in which the statement to be disclosed "reflected * * * information that he [the defendant] conveyed to the investigator." While the presence of such information may have a bearing on Sixth Amendment and attorney-client privilege objections to the compelled disclosure, its bearing on the self-incrimination issue is dubious. The *Fisher* line of cases hold that where a person voluntarily records his or her thoughts in a document (or speaks to another who records them), the self-incrimination difficulties lie not in the content of the document, as its creation was not compelled. Rather, the key is the testimonial content of the compelled act of producing the document. Thus, just as self-incrimination objections are rejected where a person is required to produce a self-authored document as to which existence, possession and authentication are foregone conclusions, such objections should not prevail against required disclosure of a known written statement of an investigator even when that statement reveals information voluntarily conveyed by the defendant as well as others that were interviewed.

While *Nobles* and *Fisher* have been applied by lower courts primarily in connection with prosecutorial discovery of the recorded statements of third parties, the *Fisher* ruling in particular also has a bearing on provisions relating to prosecution discovery from the defense of relevant tangible objects. Since this disclosure obligation commonly is imposed upon the defense counsel, the initial issue under the *Fisher* analysis is whether the object was obtained by counsel from the defendant in a context that makes the attorney-client privilege applicable. Assuming that was so, *Fisher* then allows a defense objection where compelled production from the client would have produced a self-incrimination violation due to an implicit communication relating to the existence, possession, and authentication of the item to be disclosed.[6] In the most likely setting, that in which the defense has already announced its intention to introduce the item at trial and the prosecution seeks pretrial inspection, the communication inherent in the act-of-production presumably would not be sufficient under *Fisher* to be protected under the self-incrimination privilege. The defense's notification of anticipated use would constitute an acknowledgment of existence, possession, and authenticity that renders irrelevant any further communication through the act-of-production itself.

(c) Self–Incrimination: The Testimonial Disclosure. In *Williams v. Florida,*[7] the Court treated the Florida alibi-notice provision before it as requiring a testimonial disclosure of the defendant. That provision imposed an obligation upon "a defendant" who intended to offer a defense of alibi to give pretrial notice of (1) "his intention to claim such alibi," (2) "specific information as to the place at which the defendant claims to have been" and (3) "the names and addresses of the witnesses by whom he proposes to establish such alibi." Justice White did comment in a footnote that "it might be argued that the 'testimonial disclosures' protected by the Fifth Amendment include only the statements relating to the historical facts of the crime, not statements relating solely to what a defendant proposes to do at trial." There was no need to further explore this possibility because the Court found no element of compulsion, as discussed in the next subsection. Moreover, the defendant clearly is being asked to cite an historical fact in identifying the place at which he claims to have been at the time of the crime. The identification of the alibi witnesses also incorporates an historical fact, in addition to describing defendant's intended future behavior, as it states that these are persons who were in that same place at the same time. The disclosure of an intent to raise an alibi is most likely to be viewed as non-testimonial under the distinction suggested in the *Williams* footnote, but that characterization obviously would be altered if the notice of alibi is treated like any

6. See § 8.13(e).

7. See note 1 supra.

other statement of a party and is available to the prosecution to be used to impeach the defendant should he shift to another defense in his testimony at trial. Where that use is not allowed, as is true in many states,[8] whether the notice is characterized as testimonial or not may be unimportant, since the information conveyed is so limited that it is likely not to be sufficiently incriminating to implicate the Fifth Amendment. Ordinarily, the notice of alibi standing by itself would not provide the prosecution with a true link in the development of a chain of incriminating evidence.

The alibi-notice provision in *Williams* required disclosure by the defendant, but many discovery provisions place the obligation of disclosure on the defense counsel. Of course, if the defense counsel can respond based on his or her own knowledge obtained in the course of the investigation, then the response may be subject to challenge on other grounds (e.g., as demanding work-product), but it would not require the testimony of the defendant. On the other hand, if the disclosure can be made by counsel only by obtaining the information from the defendant, the formal structure of the disclosure obligation should not alter the treatment of the disclosure as a testimonial communication of the defendant. Indeed, in jurisdictions that treat a defendant's discovery response as a party admission, a response will be treated as such whether made by the defendant personally or by counsel who is merely echoing information received from the client.

Thus, it ordinarily would not matter whether counsel or the defendant is required to identify the place of the alibi or the alibi witness, as such information would obviously come from the defendant and thereby present a self-incrimination issue. The same would commonly be true of the notification of defenses or the listing of witnesses who might support certain defenses. As to the identification of many other witnesses, however, the information is more likely or just as likely to come from counsel. Thus, where the defense must list experts consulted to conduct scientific tests, the listing would ordinarily be that of the defense counsel, not the defendant speaking through the defense counsel. Where the required disclosure does not indicate by its nature that the defendant is the almost inevitable source of the required response, the burden should be on the defendant, as the party claiming the privilege, to allege that the requested answer would require the defendant to provide testimony through the response by counsel to the prosecution's discovery request.

(d) Self–Incrimination: The Acceleration Doctrine. Although the disclosure under the alibi-notice rule challenged in *Williams v. Florida* clearly required a testimonial communication by the defendant, the Court there rejected defendant's self-incrimination claim. It concluded that the alibi-notice rule did not meet an additional prerequisite for a successful self-incrimination claim. The pressure imposed to disclose was not the kind of "compulsion" against which a person is protected by the Fifth Amendment privilege.

Speaking for the *Williams* majority, Justice White reasoned that the alibi-notice provision imposed no greater compulsion than would be present at trial when the defendant eventually had to decide whether or not to raise the alibi defense. At that point, if the defendant decided to present his alibi witnesses, he would be forced to "reveal their identity and submit them to cross-examination which in itself may prove incriminating or which may furnish the State with leads to incriminating rebuttal evidence." In deciding whether to take this risk, the defendant might be subject to "severe pressures" generated by the strength of the government's evidence, but such pressures had never been viewed as prohibited by the Fifth Amendment. The alibi-notice requirement simply imposed "very similar constraints" upon the defendant. It did no more than "accelerate the timing of his disclosure, forcing him to divulge at an earlier date information which * * * [he] planned to divulge at trial." Moreover, it was only the

8. See § 20.5(a).

disclosure rather than the final choice that was accelerated. The defendant could give an alibi notice before trial, but then decide not to raise the defense at trial. Nothing in the Florida procedure prevented him "from abandoning the defense" in his "unfettered discretion."

The defendant in *Williams* argued that the accelerated disclosure in itself violated the privilege because it forced him to make his decision before the state had presented its case-in-chief. Justice Black, in dissent, found that argument persuasive. The dissent noted: "When a defendant is required to indicate whether he might plead alibi in advance of trial, he faces a vastly different decision than that faced by one who can wait until the state has presented the case against him before making up his mind." The majority responded, however, that the defendant had no constitutional right to insist that his decision to disclose be delayed until trial. The Court stated:

> Nothing in the Fifth Amendment privilege entitles a defendant as a matter of constitutional right to await the end of the State's case before announcing the nature of his defense, any more than it entitles him to await the jury's verdict on the State's case-in-chief before deciding whether or not to take the stand himself. * * * Petitioner concedes that absent the notice-of-alibi rule the Constitution would raise no bar to the court's granting the State a continuance at trial on the grounds of surprise as soon as the alibi witness is called. Nor would there be self-incrimination problems if, during that continuance, the State was permitted to do precisely what it did here prior to trial: to depose the witness and find rebuttal evidence. But if so utilizing a continuance is permissible under the Fifth and Fourteenth Amendments, then surely the same result may be accomplished through pretrial discovery as it was here, avoiding the necessity of a disrupted trial.

The key to the *Williams* ruling clearly was this conclusion that accelerated disclosure did not violate the Fifth Amendment. How far that ruling extends has been a subject of considerable debate among commentators and, to a lesser extent, among lower courts.

The commentators agree that accelerated disclosure provides to the prosecution several potential benefits over disclosure at trial. Initially, by indicating the direction that the defense is likely to take, accelerated disclosure permits the prosecution to husband its resources and focus on the primary areas of dispute. The commentators agree that *Williams* obviously did not view that advantage as one the state could not receive consistent with defendant's self-incrimination privilege. Another advantage placed in the same category was the primary focus of the Court's opinion. The information furnished in the defense disclosure, such as the names of defense witnesses, could be used, as it was in *Williams,* to develop grounds for impeaching that evidence and otherwise rebutting defendant's alibi defense. It often would be much more difficult for the prosecution to attempt to investigate the alibi defense when that defense first is revealed at trial, even when it could obtain a continuance for that purpose. *Williams* clearly concluded that defendant had no constitutionally protected right to a "surprise element" that would restrict the prosecution's investigative capacity in this regard.

The status of a third potential advantage of accelerated disclosure—that of using the disclosure to prepare an affirmative case rather than simply to rebut a defense—is the primary source of division among the commentators. Accelerated disclosure, they agree, is not always the same as the disclosure that would be made at trial. *Williams* clearly found that difference inconsequential insofar as the uncertainty at the pretrial stage might produce a different defense disclosure than would be made after the defense actually saw the prosecution's evidence. There also exists, however, the possibility of a more extreme differential—forcing the defense pretrial to make a choice that it would never even face at trial. That could occur where the prosecution would otherwise not be able to establish a prima facie case in its case-in-chief (resulting in a directed acquittal and no need for the defendant to present any defense), but the pretrial disclosure by the defense gives the prosecution leads that allow it to sufficiently bolster its case-in-chief to avoid a directed acquittal. Here, it is argued, the defendant is not simply being asked to accelerate a decision that otherwise must be assessed at trial, but to risk assisting the state in fulfilling its basic obligation of establishing a prima facie case. The disclosure requirement is not being used simply to avoid the element of surprise that might make it more difficult for the prosecution to rebut the defendant's defense, but to allow the state to shore up a weak prosecution case on the basic elements of the offense. Some would place in the same category the situation in which the defendant's disclosure may be used to connect the defendant with other crimes.

Does the accelerated disclosure doctrine of *Williams* take into account the potential for such disclosure being utilized by the prosecution to obtain evidence of the formative elements of the crime that would not have been obtained if disclosure was required only after the prosecution established a prima facie case? Commentators taking a narrow view of *Williams* argue that it does not and that the Court would distinguish *Williams* if fairly faced with such a case. *Williams,* they note, simply did not present a situation in which pretrial disclosure would "accelerate" a choice that would otherwise never have to be made because the prosecution, without leads provided by the disclosure, would not have established a prima facie case in its case-in-chief. Indeed, they argue, the facts there clearly negated such a possibility. In describing the prosecution's use of the alibi disclosure, the Court noted that the prosecution had responded by laying the groundwork for impeaching the alibi witness and establishing by independent evidence the falseness of her testimony. Although Justice Black in dissent raised the possibility that an accelerated disclosure might be used directly or derivatively to enhance the strength of the prosecution's case-in-chief, there was no suggestion in the facts presented by the majority that such had been the case and, indeed, no such claim had been made by the defendant. Moreover, the very nature of an alibi defense, the commentators note, made such use largely unlikely. Alibi witnesses, as persons who were elsewhere, are not likely to be helpful sources to the prosecution in proving the elements of the offense. While they conceivably could have some relevant information on that score in unusual cases, that possibility as a general matter falls far below the requirement of a "real and appreciable danger"—the standard commonly used in determining whether the likelihood of incrimination is sufficient to raise a legitimate self-incrimination claim. The likelihood would be far greater, the commentators note, as to other types of defense witnesses, particularly those who would be present at the scene (as in the case of witnesses supporting a claim of self-defense). Where a pretrial discovery rule would require disclosure of the identity of such witnesses, the Court might be far less willing to accept the disclosure requirement by drawing an analogy between the pretrial and the trial choice to disclosure. At the least, it is argued, the Court might hold that pretrial discovery could not be ordered where the defense can establish in camera that there exists a real and appreciable danger that the disclosure could be used by the prosecution in developing its case-in-chief. Arguably disclosure also would not be required where the defense could make a showing in camera that the disclosure would be incriminating with respect to some unrelated offense. Here too, the defense would not be required to decide whether the disclosure is worth the risk until it is clear that the prosecution can meet its burden of establishing its case-in-chief.

Other commentators contend that there is no limitation to the Court's acceptance of the accelerated disclosure concept in *Williams.* The *Williams* ruling demands at most that the defense be given broad discovery of the prosecution's case, as was true in Florida, so it can make a reasoned tactical judgment as it would at trial. *Williams* then allows the state leeway in structuring the timing of that judgment, provided its timing requirement is justified by a reasonable state interest that satisfies due process. The choice may be somewhat more difficult at an earlier stage, but that does not so alter the character of the pressure exerted as to justify characterizing as Fifth Amendment "compulsion" at the pretrial stage the same type of pressure, produced by the strength of the prosecution's case, as has long been accepted at the trial stage. As *Williams* noted, were the state to have a Fifth Amendment obligation to minimize such pressure, there would be no ending point; the defendant could claim that the state must provide a jury verdict on the prosecutor's case-in-chief so that defendant would not be required to present a defense until he was certain that the jury would otherwise convict.

Commentators taking the above view find nowhere in *Williams* the suggestion of a possible distinction based on whether the accelerated disclosure might assist the prosecution in building its case-in-chief or prove incriminating as to other offenses. Such a distinction focuses on the likelihood and type of incrimination flowing from the disclosure. *Williams,* however, held that there was no compulsion, and that is a separate prerequisite for a self-incrimination claim that does not vary with the incriminating quality of the testimonial communication. Moreover, the development of rebuttal evidence, a use *Williams* clearly acknowledged, is also an incriminating use, and the Court has not otherwise drawn a distinction in self-incrimination doctrine between adverse evidence relating to different parts of the state's case. If there were compulsion, a defendant could no more be compelled to produce evidence to be used to impeach defense witnesses or rebut the defendant's case than evidence to be used in bolstering the state's case-in-chief.

In assessing the scope of *Williams'* accelerated disclosure doctrine, commentators sometimes look to *Brooks v. Tennessee,*[9] a case decided after *Williams.* The Court there held unconstitutional, as imposing an impermissible burden on defendant's right not to testify, a state rule that defendant could testify on his own behalf only if he testified before any other defense witnesses gave testimony. Commentators favoring a narrower reading of *Williams* see *Brooks* as acknowledging that the mandated timing of a decision to present evidence can trigger the compulsion element of self-incrimination. The impermissible compulsion in *Brooks* resulted from the defendant being forced to make a choice as to whether to testify before he could evaluate the strength of his defense by actually presenting the testimony of his defense witnesses. The dissenters in *Brooks* would have sustained the state rule on the basis of *Williams,* but the majority there did not even refer to *Williams.* They obviously recognized, it is argued, that the accelerated disclosure doctrine did not extend beyond the special situation presented in the alibi-notice context of *Williams.* Commentators on the other side see *Brooks* as presenting a situation quite distinct from any discovery requirement. What was involved in *Brooks,* they note, was not compulsion that forced the defendant to disclose a possible source of incriminatory evidence, but a restriction on defendant's unfettered choice in deciding whether to exercise his personal right to testify.[10] Moreover, the defendant there was not asked to make an initial decision from which he could withdraw (as in the discovery cases), but an accelerated final decision on whether to testify.

While lower court readings of *Williams* are not quite as diverse as that of the commentators, they also reflect some disagreement on the reach of the accelerated disclosure doctrine. Some lower courts view that doctrine as extending to disclosure of a wide range of evidence that defendant intends to introduce at trial, including all witnesses, experts' reports, documents, and tangible items. Indeed, though the *Williams* Court noted that the Florida rule sustained there allowed the defendant an "unfettered choice" to abandon the alibi defense, courts have held that the accelerated disclosure doctrine sustains the constitutionality of a state practice that allows the prosecution to use the notice of alibi in cross-examining the defendant who

9. See § 24.4 at note 4.

10. In this respect, the case is seen as coming closer to Rock v. Arkansas, discussed at § 24.4(d).

presents a different defense at trial. Other courts view the accelerated disclosure doctrine as extending somewhat beyond the alibi-notice rule presented in *Williams,* but as also being subject to significant limitations. Thus, they hold that the abandonment of an alibi defense cannot be used to impeach the defendant (although a shift at trial in the substance of the alibi might be called to the jury's attention as a response to defendant's abuse of the alibi-notice requirement). So too, while the accelerated disclosure doctrine is held to sustain the validity of a broad witness disclosure requirement on its face, the court will add that the defendant should be exempted from making disclosure where the prosecution "seeks information that might serve as an unconstitutional link in a chain of evidence tending to establish the accused's guilt." The California Supreme Court, which originally developed the accelerated disclosure doctrine in a context that presented no realistic possibility of using the defendant's disclosure in the prosecution's case-in-chief, has adopted the most limited view of the doctrine. It has held that the doctrine cannot sustain even the facial validity of reciprocal defense disclosure of its complete witness list, as it requires "no great effort or imagination to conceive of a variety of situations wherein the disclosure of the * * * [witnesses] names and addresses could easily provide an essential link in the chain of evidence underlying the prosecution's case-in-chief." [11] However, the California court also expressed doubt as to whether this limitation of the accelerated disclosure doctrine was consistent with the general direction taken in *Williams,* and therefore rested its ruling on state constitutional grounds.

(e) Self-Incrimination: The Special Case of the Insanity Defense. Even under the broadest reading of *Williams, Nobles,* and *Fisher,* self-incrimination doctrine still should preclude a discovery provision that requires the defendant himself to make a testimonial disclosure where that disclosure creates a realistic danger of providing a link in the chain of evidence that will be used against him and does not merely accelerate revealing information that would be forthcoming at trial in the presentation of the defense's evidence. Thus, where a defendant indicated pretrial that he would contend that an earlier injury rendered him physically incapable of committing the crime charged, the accelerated disclosure doctrine was held to justify requiring the defendant to list pretrial those doctors who would testify on his behalf, but the self-incrimination clause precluded requiring him to list other treating physicians that he did not intend to call.[12] In one area, however, the defendant commonly is required personally to make a statement for possible prosecution use that he otherwise would not make. Where a defendant intends to rely upon a defense of insanity or to introduce expert testimony on another mental-condition defense (e.g., diminished responsibility), he commonly is required not only to make accelerated disclosure of that defense, but also to submit to a psychiatric examination by a psychiatrist designated by the court.[13] Statements made by the defendant during that psychiatric examination may not be used for other purposes, but the psychiatrist, relying on those statements, can testify that the defendant was sane or had sufficient mental capacity to meet the prescribed mens rea and thereby convince the jury to reject the defendant's insanity or mental-condition defense. Thus, a defendant required to submit to a court-ordered psychiatric exam clearly is participating in the development of evidence that may be used against him (albeit on a single issue) by offering infor-

11. See Prudhomme v. Superior Court, 2 Cal.2d 320, 85 Cal.Rptr. 129, 466 P.2d 673 (1970). The California decision initially setting forth the accelerated disclosure doctrine involved a defendant who had been charged with rape and had indicated his intent to introduce medical reports showing that he was impotent. The California court sustained a pretrial disclosure order insofar as it required disclosure of the names of the medical witnesses and the expert's reports that he intended to produce on his impotency claim, but rejected that order on self-incrimination grounds insofar as it required defendant to identify any treating physician he did not intend to call. Jones v. Superior Court, 58 Cal.2d 56, 22 Cal.Rptr. 879, 372 P.2d 919 (1962).

12. See Jones v. Superior Court, note 11 supra.

13. See § 20.5(b).

mation in response to the psychiatrist's questions that he otherwise would not offer at trial.

Lower courts have uniformly upheld the required participation of the defendant in a psychiatric exam, although they have varied somewhat in their reasoning. At one time, it had been suggested that the defendant's statements during the examination were not testimonial, but that contention is contrary to the Supreme Court's analysis in *Estelle v. Smith,*[14] which considered in another context the allowable use of psychiatric testimony that was the fruit of a compelled examination. The Court there reasoned that the defendant's responses during the psychiatric examination were testimonial where the doctor was relying not on his observation of the defendant's behavior but on the substance of defendant's responses. Some courts have stressed that the defendant's responses, though testimonial, will be used only on the issue of insanity, which is characterized as an "objective" medical issue that relates to the appropriateness of a special type of verdict rather than the basic issue of whether the defendant committed the crime. However, as other courts have noted, this makes the examination offered by the prosecution in establishing defendant's sanity no less incriminating than evidence rejecting any other defense, for the defendant's statements are still being used against him to avoid an acquittal (albeit of a special character) and to produce a conviction. Moreover, there is nothing in the nature of an insanity claim, or the other mental-capacity claims also requiring an examination, that would render testimony on such claims any less subject to the self-incrimination clause than testimony on other scientifically based issues such as physical causation of death.

Perhaps the most widely accepted rationale as to why a court-ordered psychiatric examination does not violate the Fifth Amendment is that of waiver. Of course, the waiver here is not the traditional waiver by entirely voluntary action, but waiver that is produced by conditions that the state attaches to the defendant's use of experts on the psychiatric issue. The state may duly be concerned about allowing the use of fully informed expert testimony on one side only, and therefore may insist that each side's expert have access to the subject of the examination (here the defendant) just as they might insist that a defendant who offers expert testimony on the physical characteristics of a tangible object within the defendant's possession also make that object available for examination by the prosecution's experts. The defendant, in choosing to use his own expert testimony, is taken as agreeing to submit the subject of that testimony to the other side for the same use as has been made by his experts.

The critical factor in this waiver rationale appears to be the special character of psychiatric testimony on mental capacity. There are many defenses on which defendant is likely to be the critical eyewitness, but the state cannot condition defendant's use of such a defense either on an obligation of defendant to testify himself or an obligation to reveal pretrial the substance of his testimony if he intends to testify. Indeed, the discovery provisions on mental capacity defenses illustrate that point. The prescribed sanction for the defendant's failure to submit to a court ordered examination is the exclusion of the testimony of the defense experts. The defendant is not barred from presenting the defense without relying on expert testimony. Indeed, it has been argued that the insanity provisions should be read not to authorize any sanction where defendant refuses to submit to the examination, but then seeks to utilize only experts who testify without the benefit of their own psychiatric exam of the defendant. By introducing psychiatric testimony based upon a psychiatric examination of the defendant, the defense is seen as "constructively put[ting] the defendant himself on the stand" and thereby rendering the defendant "subject to psychiatric examination by the State in the same manner." Where the defense experts

14. See § 6.7 at note 12. Estelle v. Smith involved a court ordered examination in a case where the defense had not interposed an insanity defense. See also Buchanan v. Kentucky, § 6.4 at note 13.

do not utilize a psychiatric examination, but rely upon other adequate sources for judging insanity, the defendant arguably has not been placed in that position.

(f) Sixth Amendment Limitations. Sixth Amendment challenges to prosecution discovery have been raised primarily where (i) the defense is required to disclose information it does not intend to offer at trial, (ii) that information was developed by defense counsel or defense investigative agents but is not exempted from discovery under the particular jurisdiction's work-product exemption, and (iii) the information does not reveal lawyer/client communications and therefore is not protected against discovery by the attorney-client privilege. Statutes and court rules governing prosecution discovery typically are not so broad as to authorize discovery of such materials, but there are exceptions. Several states, for example, include catch-all provisions that allow court-ordered disclosure of materials beyond those listed in the discovery statute upon a showing of materiality and prosecution inability to obtain the material by other means. In jurisdictions that rely on the inherent authority of trial courts to order discovery, that authority also has been used occasionally to order disclosures of the type that will be challenged under the Sixth Amendment.

The discovery orders that most often have caused courts to give serious consideration to Sixth Amendment challenges have been those directing the defense to produce for prosecution inspection items such as the following: the reports of non-testifying experts who were consulted on a scientific issue that the defense intends to raise at trial through different experts; the recorded statements of prosecution witnesses that were given to defense investigators in the course of interviewing those witnesses; and physical evidence relating to the crime that was either given to counsel or was discovered in the course of counsel's investigation, often apart from any communication by the client.[15] The basic rationale of the objection is that pretrial disclosure of such information has a chilling effect upon the investigative efforts of counsel and therefore undermines the defendant's right to the effective assistance of counsel. Defense counsel, it is argued, must be afforded the "maximum freedom" to pursue various avenues of inquiry, including consultation with experts, interviews of prosecution witnesses, and the collection of physical evidence, without fearing that any unfavorable material thereby obtained will be used against the defendant. If the attorney cannot be ensured of the absolute confidentiality of the fruits of such efforts, then he or she may very well refuse to pursue such avenues and miss the opportunity to uncover exculpatory evidence.

Judicial responses to such a Sixth Amendment contention have varied with the court

15. As to some of these orders, some jurisdictions would find work-product or attorney-client protection, but many other jurisdictions would not. Work-product is limited in many jurisdictions to material that expresses the opinions, theory, or conclusions of legal personnel. It would not include statements of experts, transcripts of witness statements (particularly if taken by investigators), or physical objects. The attorney-client privilege in many jurisdictions is limited to the communications to the attorney and therefore would not include reports of experts, without regard to the nature of the communications relied upon by the expert. Other jurisdictions will extend the privilege to the expert's report only if the client made statements to the expert or defense counsel reveals to the expert private data. Here, the privilege will apply to the reports of non-testifying psychiatric experts, but not to such experts as handwriting and ballistics experts. Still other states will hold the privilege applicable to any type of expert simply on a showing that the attorney transmitted information to the expert relating to the case. Under this view, the reports of experts in general are discoverable only where the defense intends to use the expert at trial, which waives the attorney-client privilege. The privilege would not pose an obstacle, under even its broadest interpretation, to the required disclosure of statements of prosecution witnesses that are obtained by investigators or of physical objects acquired independent of the client's communication. Where the item is discovered through client communications given in the course of seeking legal advice, that communication is privileged, but not the attorney's continued possession of the item.

Self-incrimination objections to discovery orders of the type noted above fail for two reasons. First, the production tends not to be testimonial, as the existence, possession, and authentication of the items to be produced are often foregone conclusions. Second, even if the production is testimonial, it does not call for a testimonial communication of the defendant. The attorney is commonly asked to disclose information (e.g., consulted experts) that he obtained from sources independent of any confidential communication with his client. See subsection (c) supra.

and the type of disclosure demanded. Lower courts are divided on the constitutionality of requiring defense disclosures of the reports of non-testifying experts. Courts sustaining a Sixth Amendment challenge have argued that the "confidentiality and loyalty of expert consultants traditionally enjoyed by defendants and defense counsel is a crucial element in the effective legal representation of the defendant." Courts on the opposite side have responded with rationales similar to those advanced to support the constitutionality of requiring an insanity defense defendant to submit to a psychiatric exam. They note that the defendant has put into issue the scientific claim on which the non-testifying expert reported and will introduce other expert testimony on that claim. The state, in the interest of having objective scientific evidence freely available to all sides, may insist that the defense, once it raises the issue, make all of its experts available, just as it allows the defense discovery of the reports of all experts consulted by the prosecution, including those that the prosecution may later decide not to use at trial. This rationale, which is commonly described as resting on a "waiver" by the defense, would not extend to the situation in which the defense has decided (perhaps as a result of the expert's negative report) not to challenge on a certain issue, but the prosecution still wants disclosure because it must prove each element of crime, whether or not challenged by the defense, and the defense expert's report might be helpful in that regard.

Sixth Amendment challenges have been considerably less persuasive outside of the context of disclosure of non-testifying defense experts. The tendency here is to look to the work-product exemption and the attorney-client privilege as providing sufficient protection of defense counsel's role and not to impose further limitations upon otherwise prescribed disclosures through the Sixth Amendment. Thus, where counsel discovers and takes possession of physical evidence of a crime even as a result of a confidential communication with his client, disclosure will be required. The communication will be protected, perhaps even by prohibiting any reference to counsel as the source of the evidence, but the tangible item itself will be treated no differently than if it were in the hands of some third party. The adversary role of counsel, the courts note, may not turn counsel's office into a sanctuary for evidence that the government could otherwise have obtained from its original location by seizure or subpoena.

So too, where a recorded statement obtained by defense from a prosecution witness is not work-product, the Sixth Amendment will not prohibit its discovery by the prosecution. Pretrial interviewing of opposing witnesses has been characterized as such a fundamental technique of trial preparation that counsel is unlikely to be chilled in pursuing that activity by the prospect that the witness may reveal some information damaging to the defendant that he cannot later recall and that the prosecution may be able to obtain from defense counsel a record of that statement. At the most, it is suggested, counsel simply may make records of such interviews that are not sufficiently complete to be discoverable as recorded statements.

(g) Conditional Discovery. In the federal system and in roughly half of the states, prosecution discovery, apart from that on insanity and alibi, is "conditional"—i.e., dependent upon the defendant's exercise of a right to discovery rather than existing as an independent right of the prosecutor. Unlike the defense, the prosecutor cannot simply institute a demand for disclosure of the items specified in the applicable discovery provision. The prosecutor may only insist upon disclosure if the defendant has demanded and received disclosure of material within the possession or control of the prosecution. Federal Rule 16(b)(1)(B), for example, permits the prosecution to seek from the defense scientific reports made in connection with the case only after the defendant has used the corresponding provision in 16(a)(1)(D) to obtain scientific reports from the government.

Supporters of conditional discovery contend that, by giving the defendant the capacity to foreclose prosecution discovery, conditional discovery minimizes the risk that prosecution discovery will be held to violate defendant's constitutional rights. They argue that defendant's decision to seek discovery from the prosecution may be treated as a waiver of his privilege against self-incrimination or of any other constitutional objection to reciprocal discovery. Defense has no constitutional right to discovery of the prosecution's evidence, and the state can appropriately condition the grant of such discovery to the defense on a defense obligation to make reciprocal discovery.

Although a substantial number of jurisdictions utilize conditional discovery, the courts have said very little about the impact of the conditional element on the analysis of constitutional objections to mandating defense disclosure to the prosecution. The Supreme Court certainly has upheld state inducements to the waiver of constitutional rights in the context of plea bargaining, and conditioning discovery on reciprocity is sometimes analogized to that situation. However, the plea bargaining decisions find support in both the tradition and necessity of that process and the utilization of a plea acceptance procedure that is designed to insure that the defendant's relinquishment of rights is made knowingly and voluntarily. The discovery "bargain" arguably is distinguishable as to each of these elements.

§ 20.5 Prosecution Discovery Provisions

(a) Variations in Approach. Few courts or legislatures would disagree with the general policy that, consistent with restraints imposed by constitutional limitations, discovery should be a "two way street" that accords neither party an "unfair advantage" and seeks to promote the determination of the truth. The difficulty arises in determining precisely what this policy should produce in the way of prosecution discovery from the defense. As suggested in the preceding section, there may readily be disagreement over the extent to which the defendant's constitutional rights preclude granting the prosecution full reciprocity in discovery. Disagreements are even more likely to arise as to how much reciprocity is needed to provide an adversarial balance that does not give an unfair advantage to the prosecution. Some argue that, even where the defense receives exceptionally broad discovery, the prosecution need be given very little discovery since it already has an "advantage over the accused through its use of the subpoena power, the grand jury, and the right to make reasonable searches and seizures for discovery purposes and through the use of the police as an investigative resource to obtain statements." Others disagree both with this conclusion and with the suggestion that an unfair advantage exists unless each party can precisely match the other in its investigative authority. They note that the government, even with all of its investigative resources, cannot be expected to uncover everything relevant that the defendant might learn from his special resources, so the prosecution is placed at a disadvantage where the defense gains discovery of everything relevant learned by the prosecution. Moreover, they argue, even if the prosecution ordinarily can learn a great deal on its own, it does not thereby follow that there is no need for discovery as a safety net for those cases in which the prosecution has failed through its own resources to identify the evidence the defense is likely to use. The aim is to determine the truth—not to test the skills of the two sides in the use of their investigatory resources—and this can be achieved only by complete disclosure to both sides that will avoid a battle by surprise.

As might be expected, the division on these issues has led to considerable variation in the treatment of prosecution discovery, sparked initially by judicial decisions but also reflected in the court rules and statutes governing discovery. Perhaps the greatest diversity in the treatment of prosecution discovery is found among those jurisdictions that do not have discovery legislation, but rely solely on the common law authority of the courts to regulate discovery. In one such jurisdiction, California, the state Supreme Court has gone so far as to rule that, because of the complexity of the constitutional issues presented, trial courts may not order reciprocal defense disclosure to prosecutors in the absence of enabling legislation.[1] Other common law jurisdictions, in contrast, hold that trial courts have discretionary authority to allow prosecution discovery roughly as broad as that granted to the defense.

Jurisdictions with discovery statutes or court rules uniformly provide for some degree of prosecution discovery, but they vary substantially in their treatment of the comparative scope of prosecution and defense discovery. While one court rule or statute will allow the prosecution discovery that roughly parallels defense discovery, at least as to the evidence that the defense intends to use at trial, another will provide the prosecution with far less disclosure than is granted the defense. Moreover, these differences in coverage most often will not be subject to modification by the trial judge's inherent authority to grant discovery beyond that specifically authorized in the discovery provision. In the area of prosecution discovery, in contrast to defense discovery, statutory provisions commonly are viewed as preemptive in purpose. The failure of the state's discovery provisions to specifically authorize a particular type of disclosure is taken as indicating the draftsmen did not intend to allow the prosecution such discovery.

Another element of variation in prosecution discovery provisions arises from the separate treatment of the insanity and alibi defenses. Even before the states had adopted general discovery provisions, many had legislation allowing prosecution discovery as to these two defenses. In many jurisdictions, the two are still governed by a separate statute or court rule. Other aspects of prosecution discovery are covered in the general discovery provision that also governs defense discovery. Those general provisions often differ in several aspects of their structure from the alibi and insanity provisions. While alibi and insanity disclosure obligations tend to be automatic, the general discovery provision may be conditional, allowing for prosecution discovery only where the defense has first requested discovery. The separate alibi and insanity provisions also tend to have somewhat differently worded remedy provisions as well as different timing provisions.

(b) Alibi Defense Provisions. Unlike the practice in civil pleadings, the criminal law traditionally has not required the defendant to plead specifically his defense. A plea of not guilty ordinarily brings into issue all possible defenses to the substantive charge. However, the federal system and more than forty states require the defendant to give advance notice of his intent to raise an alibi defense. Several characteristics of the alibi defense are said to make a more pressing case for advance notice of alibi than for most other defenses. These include: (1) alibi is a "hip pocket" defense, easily prepared for introduction in the final hours of trial and therefore more likely to catch the prosecutor by surprise; (2) a false alibi defense will be based on perjured testimony of third parties, which can be readily discouraged by affording the prosecution an opportunity to prepare for their testimony; (3) alibi requires an independent investigation by the prosecutor, and the failure to facilitate that investigation before trial will often necessitate a continuance during trial; (4) alibi is the type of defense which will lead the prosecution to dismiss the charges if it determines from its pretrial investigation that the alibi witnesses are not lying.

Most alibi provisions are similar in procedure and scope of Federal Rule 12.1. Initially, the government must issue a demand for notification, stating therein the time, date, and place of the alleged offense. If the defendant intends to raise the defense, he is required to respond within a specified number of days. His response must state the specific place or places where he claims to have been at the time of the alleged offense and the names and addresses of the witnesses upon whom he intends to rely to establish his alibi.

§ 20.5

1. People v. Collie, 30 Cal.3d 43, 177 Cal.Rptr. 458, 634 P.2d 534 (1981).

The prosecution is then required, within a specified period, to list those witnesses that will be used to establish the defendant's presence at the scene of the crime and any other witnesses that will be used to rebut the alibi defense. As with other discovery obligations, there is a continuing duty to disclose on both sides; if either side finds an additional witness that it intends to use, that person must be added to its list. For good cause shown, the trial court may grant an exception or modification to any of the above requirements. Good cause exceptions most often are requested by the prosecution on grounds similar to those that would justify a protective order under the general discovery provisions.

Federal Rule 12.1 also provides that "evidence of an intention to rely upon an alibi defense, later withdrawn, or of statements made in connection with such intention is not * * * admissible against the person who gave notice of the intention." This provision prohibits the prosecution from commenting upon the defendant's failure to call a listed witness in presenting the alibi defense at trial. More significantly, it also bars an attempt to impeach the defendant by reference to his shift in position should he advance an entirely different defense in his trial testimony. Many states do not afford the defendant the same protection. They allow adverse use of the notice of intention under varying circumstances. In some jurisdictions, the notice (often signed by the defendant) is treated like any other evidentiary admission, and can be used by the prosecution as to any position of the defendant that is inconsistent, including the adoption of a different defense. In other states, impeachment use is allowed only where the defendant offers a different version of his alibi defense. This position is thought to more likely fit the rationale of *Williams v. Florida,* where the Court took note of the fact that the defendant there had unfettered discretion to withdraw his alibi defense.[2] The defendant is viewed not as having withdrawn the defense but as having violated the disclosure obligation by providing inaccurate details as to his alibi. Rather than exclude the alibi testimony that is at a variance with the alibi notice, impeachment as to that variance may be utilized as a less severe penalty.

(c) Insanity and Related Defenses. The federal system and almost all of the states have provisions requiring the defendant to give advance notice if he intends to rely upon the defense of insanity. That requirement typically is found in a special discovery provision on insanity, but it also may be a part of a general disclosure obligation of the defendant as to all basic defenses or a provision dealing generally with the adjudication of issues of insanity and incompetency. Once the defense has filed notice, the trial court may or must (under specified circumstances) order that the defendant be examined by one or more psychiatrists designated by the court. In some jurisdictions, the court-ordered examination is conducted at the prosecution's request by the prosecution's expert, while other jurisdictions allow only for an examination conducted by independent experts. Of course, the defendant can voluntarily submit to an examination by his own expert, and under the Supreme Court's ruling in *Ake v. Oklahoma,*[3] the indigent defendant is entitled to court appointment of a defense expert upon a showing that insanity is likely to be a significant issue in the case. The provision authorizing the court-ordered examination commonly will add that, if the defendant should refuse to submit to the examination, the appropriate sanction is the exclusion of the defense experts on the issue. This conclusion also has been reached by judicial decision.

In many states, as under Federal Rule 12.2, the obligation of notice and the authority to require a mental examination is extended beyond insanity to encompass the introduction of expert testimony "relating to mental disease or defect or any other mental condition of the defendant bearing upon the issue of guilt." Such provisions have been held to apply to the use of psychiatric experts to support defense claims of diminished responsibility, "brainwashing," and the innate lack

2. See § 20.4(d).

3. See § 11.2(e).

of aggressiveness needed to purposely place another in fear. Indeed, it seems unlikely that any psychiatric testimony would escape its reach except that which is utilized only as to sentencing.

Where the defendant enters a notice of insanity or other mental condition defense, he remains free to change his mind and proceed at trial with another defense. The responses given in any court-ordered psychiatric exam can be introduced only on the mental condition issues raised by the defense. Neither the defendant's statements during the examination, nor the fruits of those statements, can be used by the prosecutor in any other fashion. That safeguard is usually specified in the discovery provision, and it is held to follow, in any event, from the rationale underlying the acceptance of the court-ordered examination as consistent with the defendant's self-incrimination privilege. As for the notice of intention itself, that is specifically barred from use where it is later withdrawn under Federal Rule 12.2 and similar state provisions. Although as to alibi, various jurisdictions reject such a bar and allow the withdrawn notice to be used to impeach a defendant, the same issue has not arisen under the insanity notice. The notice of an intent to raise an insanity defense reflects a legal judgment as to the defendant's mental condition which may be subject to reconsideration in light of additional psychiatric information. The notice of alibi, in contrast, sets forth a statement of fact within the specific knowledge of the defendant.

(d) Identification of Defenses. Approximately a dozen states require the defendant to give notice in advance of trial of various defenses beyond alibi and insanity that defendant intends to raise at trial. These provisions sometimes are designed to encompass all defenses and sometimes are limited to a series of enumerated offenses. Even when all defenses are included, the statutory provision may include an illustrative listing of the types of defenses which a defendant is expected to identify. Typical examples cited are a claim of authority (such as ownership of the property involved), the justifiable use of force, entrapment, duress, intoxication, and the lack of the requisite mens rea. The defense-notice provisions are interpreted as encompassing only those defense claims on which testimony will be offered. The defendant need not include matters on which he will challenge the state's case as simply insufficient on its face. The function of the defense-notice requirement is to make the prosecution aware of those areas as to which the defense is likely to introduce evidence and the prosecution therefore might neeed to look for rebuttal evidence.

Many of the jurisdictions requiring notification of defenses also mandate disclosure of witness lists. The two discovery requirements are designed to supplement each other. Defense witnesses will not necessarily be willing to speak to the prosecution. The notice of defense ensures that the prosecution will nonetheless have a general idea as to the subject of their testimony. Some jurisdictions provide even better notice in this regard by requiring disclosure of the recorded statements of defense witnesses or allowing discovery depositions of those witnesses. Several of these jurisdictions have found it unnecessary to also require a notice of defenses.

The selection of defenses generally is within the province of counsel and depends on strategic factors that may vary even though the information known to counsel does not change. Courts therefore may be reluctant to impose sanctions where the defense at trial seeks to shift to a defense not originally listed. There are, however, certain defenses that rest on events within the personal knowledge of the defendant himself and where a defendant lists one such defense in his initial notice and then shifts to a factually inconsistent defense, the circumstances may well suggest a willful violation of the discovery requirement. In such a situation, the treatment of the shift raises issues similar to those presented in the withdrawal of an alibi notice and the presentation of an inconsistent defense.

(e) Witness Lists. Roughly half the states authorize court-ordered defense disclosure of the names and addresses of the witnesses that the defendant intends to introduce at trial. In many of these jurisdictions, the prosecution has an independent right to such discovery. In some, discovery is conditional upon the defense having first sought discovery, and in still others, the trial court has discretion as to whether to order witness-list disclosure. In all of these jurisdictions, the defendant is entitled to a listing of the witnesses that the prosecution intends to call.

The primarily legal question presented by the witness-list provisions, apart from their constitutionality, is what degree of likely use imposes upon the defense an obligation to list a witness? The defense, it has been noted, has no obligation to list every person who has come to defense counsel's attention as a "possible witness," especially where counsel has not interviewed or otherwise confirmed that the person has helpful information. Indeed, to provide such a listing would often undercut the function of the notice requirement by forcing the prosecution to sift through a long list of potential witnesses. On the other hand, if the defense counsel knows that a person's testimony will support a point that the defense desires to make in challenging a prosecution witness, and it is "reasonably predictable" that the prosecution witness will deny that point, the defense cannot omit that person from its list because the prosecution witness might admit the point and the witness therefore would be unnecessary. The witness must be listed not only where the defense feels certain that the witness will be called, but also where there is a distinct likelihood that the witness will be called.

(f) Witness Statements. More than a dozen states have provisions requiring defense disclosure of the recorded statements of the witnesses included in its witness list. In general, a "recorded" statement for this purpose follows the Jencks Act definition, but some states utilize broader definitions that encompass written summaries of the witness' oral statement. In all jurisdictions requiring disclosure of witness statements, the defendant has a right to receive from the prosecution the recorded statements, similarly defined, of the prosecution's witnesses.

As noted in § 20.4(b), the Supreme Court in *United States v. Nobles*[4] rejected a self-incrimination objection to court-ordered disclosure at trial of a defense witness' recorded statement. At the same time, however, the Court laid the ground work for what has proven to be the major limitation upon the required pretrial disclosure of the recorded statements of defense witnesses. The defendant in *Nobles* also objected to the court order there on the basis of the work product doctrine, and while the Court rejected that claim, its analysis generally has been viewed as favorable to those opposing pretrial disclosure of a defense witness' recorded statement. The *Nobles* Court noted initially that defendant was correct in assuming that the work product doctrine would be applied in the federal courts to criminal as well as civil cases. The Court also indicated that the defendant was correct in assuming that the doctrine was not simply limited to reports prepared by counsel, but could also apply to a report written by a defense investigator. The "realities of litigation in our adversary system," it noted, make it "necessary that the doctrine protect material prepared by agents for the attorney as well as those prepared by the attorney himself." Defendant's work product claim ultimately failed, however, because of waiver. The protection of the doctrine had been waived as to that portion of the investigator's report covered by his testimony when the defense elected to have the investigator testify.

Relying upon *Nobles*, several state courts have held that the work product doctrine bars pretrial disclosure of a defense witness' statement that was prepared by either counsel or an investigator working under the direction of counsel. While *Nobles* sustained disclosure based on the waiver that occurs once the witness testifies, the waiver doctrine cannot operate pretrial on the anticipation that the witness will testify. The primary function of the work product rule, it is noted, is basically to protect against pretrial disclosure; it is

4. See § 20.4 at note 3.

such disclosure which permits the opposing attorney to build upon his opponent's efforts.

Other jurisdictions, including most of those with discovery provisions specifically requiring defense disclosure of its witnesses' statements, take a contrary position. Though acknowledging the need to preclude pretrial disclosure of the defense's work product, they view the *Nobles* concept of work product as overly broad. Since that concept was not constitutionally based, the states are free to reject it. Consistent with the position they have taken as to recorded statements of prosecution witnesses,[5] these jurisdictions hold that a lawyer's or investigator's largely verbatim summary of a witness' oral statement does not constitute work product. Only those portions of the recordation reflecting the "opinions, theories and conclusions" of the person recording the statement will be exempt, and even then, in some jurisdictions, only where that person was part of defense counsel's legal staff. This narrower definition is justified in part by the fact that the subject matter in question is the statements of witnesses who will be testifying at trial. Thus, disclosure here merely accelerates a work product waiver that would be made at trial when the witness testified for the defense. However, the work product exemption also is held not to apply to the defense's recordation of interviews with *prosecution* witnesses in the few jurisdictions that require the defense to disclose the recorded statements in its possession of *all* persons who will testify at trial.

(g) Documents and Tangible Objects. Almost all of the jurisdictions with general discovery provisions authorize prosecution discovery of documents and tangible objects which the defense intends to introduce in evidence. In some jurisdictions, the prosecution has an independent right to such discovery, while in others, discovery is conditioned on the defendant first requesting discovery from the prosecution. The types of items encompassed are the same as under similar provisions authorizing defense discovery of documents and tangible objects. The primary difference between the defense and prosecution provisions is that the prosecution's obligation to disclose goes beyond items the prosecution intends to use as evidence.

The nature of the items subject to disclosure under these provisions makes it unlikely that they will contain work product. Several jurisdictions, however, to ensure that the statutory reference to "papers" and "documents" is not read to encompass work product, specifically exempt "reports, memoranda, or other internal documents made by the defendant, or his attorneys or agents in connection with the investigation or defense of the case." This provision also assures that the reference to "documents" will not be read to encompass the recorded statements of witnesses in those jurisdictions that do not provide for such discovery.

(h) Scientific Reports. Almost all jurisdictions with general discovery provisions allow for prosecution discovery of reports and results of medical and physical examinations, scientific tests, and experiments made in connection with the particular case. Most of these provisions, like Federal Rule 16(b)(1)(B), apply to scientific reports "which the defendant intends to introduce as evidence in chief at the trial or which were prepared by a witness whom the defendant intends to call at trial when the results or reports relate to his testimony." The materials subject to discovery under such provisions ordinarily would not fall within even the broadest definitions of work product utilized in criminal discovery; those provisions, even where they go beyond the attorney's mental impressions and legal theories, do not extend beyond the reports of investigators working under the defense counsel's direction. In some jurisdictions, part or all of an expert's report might be protected by the attorney-client privilege, but that will be waived by the introduction of the report at trial.

Defense discovery of scientific reports in the possession of the prosecution typically extends beyond that material the prosecution

5. See § 20.3(j).

will use at trial. It commonly encompasses all reports and results on scientific tests and examinations made in connection with the case, whether or not they will be used at trial. Similar prosecution discovery from the defense may be available under occasional provisions that are broader than Federal Rule 16(b)(1)(B) or under catch-all provisions allowing the trial court to order additional discovery as to items that are material and not otherwise available to the prosecution. As discussed in § 20.4(f), such orders have been successfully challenged on Sixth Amendment grounds. Where the item sought is the interpretative report of an expert, rather than simply a test result, the attorney-client privilege may also come into play, depending upon the content of the report, the communications of the attorney or client to the expert, and the view of the privilege taken in the particular jurisdiction.[6]

§ 20.6 Sanctions

(a) **Range.** Federal Rule 16(d)(2) provides that a trial court, upon learning "that a party has failed to comply with this rule, * * * may order such party to permit the discovery or inspection, grant a continuance, or prohibit the party from introducing evidence not disclosed, or it may enter such order as it deems just under the circumstances." State statutes or court rules authorizing discovery contain similar provisions, and common law jurisdictions recognize that appropriate sanctions or remedies may be imposed as part of the trial court's inherent authority to order discovery. The measures noted in Rule 16(d)(2)—ordering immediate disclosure, granting a continuance, and excluding evidence—are the three most commonly imposed remedies. However, judicial opinions and statutory provisions also recognize several other sanctions or remedies, including (1) a charge directing the jury to assume certain facts that might have been established through the nondisclosed material, (2) granting a mistrial, (3) holding in contempt the party responsible for the nondisclosure, and (4) dismissal of the prosecution.

Alibi-notice and insanity-notice statutes usually have their own sanction provisions, which sometimes appear to be more narrowly confined than the general discovery provisions. In several states, the alibi statute states that the trial court shall exclude the testimony of any unlisted witness "except for good cause shown." This language might arguably give the trial court less leeway in the selection of a sanction than the typical general discovery provision, which will merely note that the court "may enter such * * * order as it deems just under the circumstances." However, the "good cause" language tends to be interpreted to provide essentially the same flexibility as is found in the general provisions. On the other hand, alibi-notice and insanity-notice provisions may contain explicit restrictions that bar the use of certain sanctions. Thus, alibi-notice provisions commonly provide that the exclusion sanction as to undisclosed alibi witnesses "shall not limit the right of the defendant to testify on his own behalf," and insanity-notice provisions allow for exclusion only of expert witnesses.

(b) **Prosecution Violations.** Perhaps no defense claim relating to discovery is more frequently raised on appeal than the claim that the trial court failed to utilize the proper remedy when the defendant discovered shortly before or during trial that the prosecution had breached a discovery order. The claim usually relates to the prosecution's presentation of a witness who was not endorsed on its witness list or its introduction into evidence of a previously undisclosed statement of the defendant or a scientific report. On occasion, it will be based upon the late disclosure of discoverable material that was not used as prosecution evidence, but which might have been helpful to the defense, if disclosed earlier, in developing its own case or in impeaching a prosecution witness. The usual defense complaint is that the trial court should have excluded the evidence or declared a mistrial as opposed to granting some lesser remedy, such as simply ordering immediate disclosure, or combining such disclosure with a brief continuance. Appellate courts frequently note

6. See note 15 of § 20.4

that trial court must be given "broad latitude" in its selection of an appropriate remedy. Nevertheless, they also have advanced certain guidelines for the exercise of that discretion, and reversals for the failure to follow those guidelines are not infrequent.

Once the trial court learns of the prosecution's non-compliance, it is expected initially to determine why disclosure had not been made previously and whether the defendant has been prejudiced by the nondisclosure. In some jurisdictions, the trial court's failure to conduct an appropriate inquiry (e.g., by not offering the defense counsel an opportunity to show possible prejudice) will constitute a sufficient ground in itself for reversal. Thus, if the trial court simply orders immediate disclosure without conducting an inquiry to assess whether other sanctions also are needed, the appellate court will automatically reverse a subsequent conviction, without attempting any post hoc determinations as to whether other sanctions should have been ordered or whether the failure to utilize those sanctions might have had a bearing on the outcome of the trial.

In conducting an inquiry to determine the appropriate sanction, the trial court must assess the potential prejudice to the defense that could result from the prosecution's failure to have made timely disclosure. In general the concept of "prejudice" for this purpose is limited to an adverse impact upon the defense's ability to prepare and present its case. Some courts, moreover, will not give weight to all types of adverse impact. In particular, they will not consider harm to the defendant's presentation that flows from a defense choice of a strategy designed to mislead the jury. The function of discovery, these courts note, is to permit the defense to marshal its evidence so as to challenge the possible falsity of the prosecution's evidence. Prejudice, they argue, therefore should be limited to restrictions on the defense's capacity to present such a challenge, and should not encompass self-inflicted wounds resulting from the defendant's unsuccessful attempt to use a fabricated defense. Thus, where the prosecution negligently failed to disclose that it possessed a document written by defendant, and the defendant then gave apparently false testimony that was clearly contradicted by that document, the defense was not allowed to look to the harm it obviously suffered when the prosecution subsequently used the document to impeach the defendant. The court reasoned that, just as the unconstitutional seizure of evidence does not bar use of that evidence to impeach the defendant, a discovery violation should not bar impeachment use of defendant's own written statement simply because it was not disclosed in a timely fashion; the defendant knew fully well that the written statement existed and that it refuted his testimony, and he should not be allowed to claim harm based on his supposition that the prosecution was not aware of the statement and that he therefore could contradict it with impunity.[1]

Decisions holding that the prejudice element will not encompass the prosecution's contradiction of a fabricated defense through evidence that should have been disclosed pretrial have not dealt with instances of purposeful prosecutorial "sandbagging." The discovery violations involved could be characterized as resulting from negligence or good faith misreadings of discovery obligations. Arguably a different result would be reached where the defendant was lured into "ensnaring himself in his self-made trap" by a purposeful prosecutorial nondisclosure. Indeed, other courts have indicated that the defense should be viewed as prejudiced and entitled to relief whenever a position taken by the defense is contradicted by prosecution evidence that was not properly disclosed during pretrial discovery, even though the defendant was fully aware that reliable evidence contradicted that position and proceeded because he assumed that the prosecution was unaware of

§ 20.6

1. People v. Taylor, 159 Mich.App. 468, 406 N.W.2d 859 (1987). The court relied on the Supreme Court rulings discussed in § 9.6(a).

that evidence. These courts note that while defendant has no right to fabricate a defense, the purpose of discovery is to avoid "trial by surprise," and to simply allow the trial to proceed, with the defense suffering from a presentation it would not have made with proper discovery, is to undercut that objective. While it would be inappropriate to bar impeachment use of the previously nondisclosed evidence and thus allow what appears to be false testimony to stand, the court may utilize a remedy that would restore the parties to where they would have been if timely disclosure had been made as required by the discovery rules—declaring a mistrial and disallowing prosecution use at the second trial of the defendant's inconsistent testimony of the first trial.

Very often, the discovery violation is called to the attention of the trial court during the prosecution's case-in-chief. Commonly, the prosecution will attempt to introduce a document or a witness that was not noted in pretrial discovery, with either the prosecutor acknowledging a discovery violation or the court determining that disclosure should have been given under the general discovery provision or the court's specific discovery directive. At other times, the defense will learn in cross-examining the witness that there exists some relevant evidence that should have been made available to it under the applicable discovery standard. The likely prejudice here ordinarily flows from the defense lacking sufficient time to digest and prepare either to meet or to use the previously undisclosed evidence. Many courts therefore view the continuance as playing a critical role in assessing the potential for prejudice. The continuance is seen as the vehicle that commonly will eliminate the prejudice of surprise by placing the defense in a position similar to that in which it would have stood if timely disclosure had been made. Accordingly, where the defense is truly surprised, it will be expected to demand a continuance or at least accept a court offer of a continuance. The lack of demand, or the rejection of the trial court's offer, is taken as strong evidence that the discovery violation has not been prejudicial. Where a demand for a continuance is made, that tends to support the defense claim of likely prejudice, but it is not conclusive. Courts recognize that continuances are not always needed, and defendants may seek a continuance for purposes unrelated to true surprise (including imposing pressure on the trial court to look to the alternative of a mistrial where the continuance would not be convenient). Accordingly, a trial court is not forced to grant a continuance request, but it must have a sound basis for concluding that the defense will be able to present its case as effectively notwithstanding the lack of earlier notice of the previously undisclosed evidence.

Courts also recognize that there are occasions in which a continuance will not eliminate potential prejudice even though the previously undisclosed evidence comes to light during the prosecution's case-in-chief. The defense may already have committed itself—in opening statement or in cross-examination—to a line of attack that it would not have utilized if aware of the undisclosed testimony. Such a defense predicament is not limited to the situations discussed above in which the defendant sought to fabricate a defense later shown to be false by evidence that should have been disclosed pretrial. It can also arise when the prosecution is now coming forward with previously undisclosed evidence filling gaps in its case that had been the focus of the defense's initial challenge to the prosecution's proof. While the defense here is not placed in the embarrassing position of having the defendant's testimony revealed to be false, it still suffers from the impression that it simply is fishing for a line of attack, shifting its challenge from one unfounded ground to another. Where the circumstances clearly could convey that impression to the jury, the court may be forced to recognize that the continuance will be a less than complete remedy, and that the potential prejudice to the defense can be eliminated only by a mistrial or by precluding the use of the new evidence. The defense, however, cannot readily characterize a discovery violation as presenting such irreversible prejudice merely by offering speculative theories as to how its challenge might have differed if it had learned earlier of all information that is only now being disclosed.

Consistent with their advice to trial courts to first look to the continuance as a remedy, appellate courts frequently warn against the unnecessary use of the preclusion sanction. The trial court, it is noted, "should seek to apply sanctions that affect the evidence at trial and the merits of the case as little as possible." Sanctions generally should not have "adverse effects on the rights of the parties rather than the offending attorneys themselves," and preclusion necessarily has such an adverse effect on the interests of the community, the party represented by the prosecutor. Accordingly, some courts treat preclusion as a remedy that should be available only where there was actual prejudice and where no other remedy will respond adequately to that prejudice. It is a "remedy of last resort," to be used only where absolutely needed. Other jurisdictions, while viewing preclusion as a remedy to be used sparingly, will not place the trial court in a position where it can exclude previously undisclosed evidence only upon finding that lesser sanctions could not eliminate the prejudice to the defense. Here, the trial court is given considerably greater leeway. It may, for example, choose preclusion over a continuance where a continuance would be disruptive or would not provide the same degree of assurance that the prejudice would be eliminated.

The jurisdictions also are divided as to the possible use of preclusion simply as a deterrent, without regard to the presence of prejudice. Some courts would allow such use where the trial court finds that the discovery violation was intentional or reflects a recurring disregard for discovery obligations. These courts view exclusion as offering the same prophylactic impact in the enforcement of discovery rules as the exclusion of illegally seized evidence offers in the enforcement of the Fourth Amendment. Indeed, a few courts have gone beyond that position and approved the use of a dismissal with prejudice to respond to glaring prosecutorial discovery violations that suggest either gross negligence or purposeful misconduct. Other jurisdictions would allow exclusion to be used only where needed to respond to prejudice. Similarly, dismissal would be allowed only where the prosecution is ordered to provide discovery as to a certain item and prefers dismissal to complying with the court's order. Where the trial court believes that there is need for a deterrent measure, it is directed to make use of contempt orders directed against the offending prosecutor. A sanction, they note, should "not be regarded as a bonus awarded without regard to its need in the furtherance of fair trial rights."

(c) Defense Violations. In many jurisdictions, the judicial treatment of sanctions is quite similar for discovery violations by both the defense and the prosecution. The one major distinction is the bearing of the Sixth Amendment upon the sanction of precluding defense use of the evidence that it should have disclosed pretrial under its discovery obligations. The Supreme Court in *Williams v. Florida* had no need to determine whether the alibi-notice statute at issue there constitutionally could be enforced by excluding a witness who had not been listed during pretrial disclosure as required by the discovery rules.[2] The Court did answer that question, however, in *Taylor v. Illinois.*[3] Although *Taylor* rejected the contention that the preclusion sanction constituted a per se violation of the defendant's Sixth Amendment right to compulsory process and upheld the sanction as applied in the circumstances of that case, it also indicated that the preclusion sanction might not be used against the defendant quite as freely as some courts have allowed it to be used against the prosecution.

Taylor involved the exclusion of the testimony of a defense witness after defendant had failed to list that witness in responding to a prosecution discovery request (the discovery rule authorizing the request itself not being challenged). The Supreme Court initially re-

2. See § 20.4(a).

3. 484 U.S. 400, 108 S.Ct. 646, 98 L.Ed.2d 798 (1988).

jected the claim of the defendant that the compulsory process clause established an "absolute bar" to the exclusion of a witness. While it was true that that clause embraced the right to have the witness' testimony heard (and not simply the right to compel the witness' attendance by subpoena), that right was not without limits (as evidenced by the fact "the accused does not have an unfettered right to offer testimony that is incompetent, privileged, or otherwise inadmissible under standard rules of evidence"). Indeed, in *Nobles,*[4] the Court had upheld the exclusion of the testimony of a defense witness where the defense refused to comply with an order to disclose the witness' prior recorded statement. *Nobles* had reasoned that exclusion was an appropriate sanction since the defense's refusal had restricted the prosecution's opportunity for effective cross-examination of the witness. The petitioner Taylor argued that the exclusion of an unlisted witness was different, since "a less drastic sanction" would always be available where a disclosure is made, though late: prejudice to the prosecution "can be minimized by granting a continuance or mistrial * * * [and] further violations can be deterred by disciplinary sanctions against the defendant or defense counsel." The Court responded that, while "it may well be true that alternative sanctions are adequate and appropriate in most cases * * *, it is equally clear that they would be less effective than the preclusion sanction" and would sometimes "perpetuate rather than limit the prejudice to the State." A primary purpose of discovery rules, the Court reasoned, is to "minimize the risk that fabricated testimony will be believed." Quite often, it is "reasonable to presume that there is something suspect about a defense witness who is not identified until after the eleventh hour has passed." Where "a pattern of discovery violations is explicable only on the assumption that the violations were designed to conceal a plan to present fabricated testimony,[5] it would be entirely appropriate to exclude the tainted evidence regardless of whether other sanctions [e.g., contempt] would also be merited."

To reject petitioner's claim "that preclusion is *never* a permissible sanction," the Court noted, it was "neither necessary nor appropriate * * * to attempt to draft a comprehensive set of standards to guide the exercise of discretion" as to the permissible use of that sanction. It was sufficient to recognize that, while "a trial court may not ignore the fundamental character" of the defendant's right to present evidence, the "mere invocation of that right cannot automatically and invariably outweigh countervailing public interests." Also to be "weigh[ed] in the balance" were: "the integrity of the adversary process, which depends both on the presentation of reliable evidence and the rejection of unreliable evidence; the interest in the fair and efficient administration of justice; and the potential prejudice to the truth-determining function of the trial process." Thus, where the defense failed to comply with a discovery requirement and "that omission was willful and motivated by a desire to obtain a tactical advantage that would minimize the effectiveness of cross-examination and the ability to adduce rebuttal testimony, it would be entirely consistent with the purposes of the Confrontation Clause simply to exclude the witness' testimony." Also "relevant" in this regard was the "simplicity of compliance with the discovery rule," as the burden of compliance "adds little" to the routine demands of trial preparation that naturally fall upon defense counsel.

Turning to the case before it, the Court also found unpersuasive the defendant's claim that preclusion was unnecessarily harsh since the trial court, prior to applying the sanction, had conducted a voir dire examination of the unlisted witness which "adequately protected the prosecution from any possible prejudice resulting from surprise." "More is at stake," the Court noted, "than possible prejudice to

4. See § 20.4 at note 3.

5. The reference here was to violations by the defense in the particular case. The trial court had mentioned, in justifying the sanction it imposed, the desire to put an end to what it viewed as widespread discovery violations within its district. The Supreme Court noted, however, that such "unrelated violations * * * would not normally provide a proper basis for curtailing the defendant's constitutional right to present a complete defense."

the prosecution." Also of concern was "the impact of this conduct on the integrity of the judicial process itself." Here, the judge found that the defense counsel's failure to list the witness was "both willful and blatant." The defense counsel had interviewed the witness previously, had added the witness only after the weak testimony of others, and had misinformed the judge as to counsel's previous knowledge of the witness and the probable character of his testimony. Thus, "regardless of whether prejudice to the prosecution could have been avoided * * *, it [was] plain that the case fits into the category of willful misconduct in which the severest sanction is appropriate." [6]

The *Taylor* opinion arguably raises as many questions as it answers. At the least, it lacks the kind of clear directive that is necessary to shape a lower court consensus on the bounds of the constitutionally permissible use of the preclusion sanction. Lower courts have had the least difficulty with cases that fit the *Taylor* description of a "willful [violation] * * * motivated by a desire to obtain a tactical advantage." Such willful misconduct is seen as sufficient in itself to justify the preclusion sanction. It calls upon the combined judicial interests of deterring willful violations of discovery rules and avoiding a possible affront to the integrity of the trial process through the offering of probably perjurious testimony.

Some courts suggest that the tactically motivated willful violation may be the only situation in which preclusion is constitutionally acceptable. Others, noting the broad range of interests cited by *Taylor* as relevant to the constitutional balancing process, have looked to several additional factors that may justify imposing the preclusion sanction. They would consider the degree of fault in the violation that was not intentional (asking, for example, whether the discovery requirement was clear and whether compliance was relatively simple), the degree of prejudice suffered by the prosecution, the impact of preclusion upon the total evidentiary showing (including consideration of factors suggesting that the precluded evidence is unreliable), and the degree of effectiveness of less severe sanctions. Arguably also, at least in certain contexts, the extent of the defendant's personal responsibility for the omission also would be considered. The balance struck by reference to these factors could conceivably justify preclusion in a case that did not involve a willful violation designed to gain a tactical advantage. Nonetheless, post-*Taylor* rulings upholding preclusion under such a balancing standard have involved, in large part, violations that readily could be characterized as fitting the willful and tactical mold even when they were not so described.

Of course, a state may impose restrictions upon the use of the preclusion sanction that extend beyond those imposed by the Sixth Amendment. Some courts have done exactly that. They view judicial adoption of a "conscious mandatory distortion of the fact-finding process" as especially inappropriate where the risk taken (by excluding evidence that defendant claims to be exculpatory) is the possible conviction of the innocent rather than the risk (through exclusion of prosecution evidence) of the possible conviction of the guilty. Accordingly, they would allow use of the preclusion sanction only where the prosecution was prejudiced by the defense's discovery violation. Moreover, the prosecution will be required to establish actual prejudice by showing exactly what it would have done differently if earlier notice would have been received in conformity with discovery requirements. Even then, the court may also insist

6. The Court also rejected the contention that exclusion was inappropriate because defendant had not participated in the failure to list and the "sins of the lawyer" should not be visited on his client. The Court responded that the right involved here was not one of those which could be waived only with the consent of the client and given the "protections afforded by the attorney-client privilege * * *, it would be highly impracticable to require an investigation into the * * * relative responsibilities [of attorney and client] before applying the sanction of preclusion." The three dissenting justices stressed the absence of defendant's personal participation and concluded that, "absent evidence of a defendant's personal involvement in a discovery violation, the Compulsory Process Clause *per se* bars discovery sanctions that exclude criminal defense evidence." See also § 11.6 at note 8.

that exclusion be the sanction of "last resort," used only where no other remedy would cure the prejudice.

One limitation commonly found in state law is the prohibition against excluding the defendant's own alibi testimony even where there has been a purposeful violation of the requirement of advance notification as to alibi witnesses. This limitation has been justified on various grounds. Allowing the defendant himself to testify as to the alibi, even though the prosecution did not receive advance notice and therefore is limited to on-the-spot cross-examination, is seen as having a limited prejudicial impact upon the prosecution. Initially, the surprise element is not the same as when the defense presents some other witness previously unknown to the prosecution. The prosecution is aware that the defendant might testify and should be prepared to challenge his credibility. Moreover, the defense must overcome a significant credibility hurdle in presenting an otherwise unsupported alibi. As one court put it: "The optimistic defendant who hopes to convince the jury through his own unsupported testimony that he was not in the vicinity of the crime has sufficient credibility problems to offset any disadvantage to the state from surprise." Another grounding is that the defendant's right to testify requires greater protection than his right to present the testimony of others, as it has significance beyond the content of his testimony. It is also argued that the exclusion of the defendant's own testimony has greater impact with respect to the alibi defense itself. Where only other witnesses are excluded, the defendant is not barred entirely from presenting the defense, as he can testify himself. If the preclusion sanction is extended to the defendant as well, then the defense simply cannot be presented.

§ 20.7 The Prosecutor's Constitutional Duty to Disclose

(a) The *Brady* Rule. In *Mooney v. Holohan,*[1] decided in 1935, the Supreme Court first held that a prosecutor's use of false testimony could constitute a violation of due process. The defendant there alleged that the prosecutor had fabricated the case against him by procuring and introducing at trial perjured testimony. The Supreme Court had little difficulty in finding that defendant's claim had constitutional dimensions. A per curiam opinion noted:

> [Due process] is a requirement that cannot be deemed to be satisfied by mere notice and hearing if a state has contrived a conviction through the pretense of a trial which in truth is but used as a means of depriving a defendant of liberty through a deliberate deception of court and jury by the presentation of testimony known to be perjured. Such a contrivance by a state to procure the conviction and imprisonment of a defendant is as inconsistent with the rudimentary demands of justice as is the obtaining of a like result by intimidation.

As discussed in § 24.3(c), a series of later rulings extended the "*Mooney* principle" to prosecutorial uses of false testimony not nearly as flagrant as the planned use of perjured testimony in *Mooney.* Taken together, *Mooney* and its progeny came to establish a constitutional obligation of the prosecution not to knowingly deceive the jury or allow it to be deceived by prosecution witnesses. This obligation required that the prosecution not suborn perjury, not purposely use evidence known to be false, and not allow the known false testimony of its witnesses to stand uncorrected. Where the government failed to fulfill that obligation, it mattered not whether its failure was attributable to negligence or to willful misconduct. The state in either event bore the responsibility for possibly denying the defendant a fair trial. The question therefore was not the state's "good faith" or "bad faith," but whether the state's treatment of false testimony had denied the defendant a fair trial. That determination, in turn, required that consideration be given to the impact of the prosecutor's action (or inaction)

§ 20.7

1. 294 U.S. 103, 55 S.Ct. 340, 79 L.Ed. 791 (1935). See also § 24.4(c).

upon the outcome of the trial. Even the most reprehensible conduct by the prosecutor would not deny the defendant due process if it had no bearing upon the outcome of the proceeding. The requisite likelihood of a prejudicial impact was placed at a far lower threshold, however, than would ordinarily be applicable if the government bore no responsibility for the false testimony. Thus, if the defendant discovered after trial that there had been perjury by a prosecution witness, but that perjury was not known to the government (and therefore not within *Mooney*), most jurisdictions would grant a new trial only if the defendant could show that the jury's awareness of that perjury "probably would have resulted in an acquittal." [2] Under the *Mooney* principle, in contrast, where the prosecutor has a constitutional responsibility for the false testimony, due process was violated and a new trial required simply if there was "any reasonable likelihood" that the false evidence could have affected the judgment of the jury. Thus, the defendant's conviction would be reversed if the reviewing court found any reasonable likelihood that the jury, if it had not heard that false testimony or had heard it but been informed that it was false, would have reached a judgment other than conviction, including an inability to decide as a result of disagreement (i.e., a hung jury) as well as an acquittal.

In *Brady v. Maryland,*[3] the Supreme Court extended the *Mooney* principle to the prosecution's failure to disclose to the defense exculpatory evidence within its possession. In that case, the defendant Brady and a companion, Boblit, were found guilty of felony murder and sentenced to death. Prior to defendant's separate trial, defense counsel had asked the prosecutor to allow him to examine all of the statements that Boblit had given to the police. Counsel was shown several of Boblit's statements, but for some unexplained reason failed to receive one statement in which Boblit admitted that he had done the actual killing. At trial, defendant admitted his participation in the crime, but claimed that he had not himself killed the victim. Defense counsel stressed this claim in his closing argument, asking the jury to show leniency and not impose the death penalty. Following defendant's conviction, defense counsel learned of the undisclosed statement and sought a new trial based on this newly discovered evidence. The state court granted a new trial as to the issue of punishment alone. It reasoned that whether or not defendant himself killed the victim had no bearing on his liability for the homicide, and Boblit's statement therefore would not have been admissible in evidence on that issue. On the other hand, the statement could have been used to support defendant's plea for leniency as to punishment, and the prosecution's failure to disclose the statement had deprived the defendant of a fair hearing on that issue.

The Supreme Court affirmed the state court's ruling, holding that the prosecutor's nondisclosure of Boblit's statement had resulted in a denial of due process on the punishment issue. The Court noted that the state court had not erred in holding that the *Mooney* principle was applicable to the "suppression of evidence favorable to the accused" as well as the presentation of false testimony. The prosecution bears responsibility for what is equally a deception of the jury and trial court when it "withholds evidence on demand of an accused which, if made available, would tend to exculpate him or reduce the penalty." The Court also agreed with the lower court's conclusion that the prosecutor bore that responsibility even though his failure to disclose "was not the result of guile." The "principle of *Mooney v. Holohan,*" the Court noted, "is not punishment of society for misdeeds of a prosecutor but avoidance of an unfair trial to the accused."

The *Brady* opinion summarized the constitutional rule established in that case in a single sentence:

> [T]he suppression by the prosecution of evidence favorable to an accused upon request

2. This is the standard traditionally applied to newly discovered evidence. See the *Agurs* discussion of Fed. R.Crim.P. 33, in subsection (b) infra.

3. 373 U.S. 83, 83 S.Ct. 1194, 10 L.Ed.2d 215 (1963).

violates due process where the evidence is material either to guilt or to punishment, irrespective of the good faith or bad faith of the prosecution.

Unfortunately, the Court's application of that rule to the facts of the case before it said very little about the content of the rule's critical terms. The nondisclosed evidence here clearly was favorable, clearly was requested, and clearly was within the prosecution's possession and therefore "suppressed" by it, with its underlying motivation irrelevant. All that was left to be determined was whether the nondisclosed evidence had been "material" to the issue of guilt or punishment.

The use of term "material" suggested that more than relevancy was required of the suppressed evidence. Indeed, relevancy was assumed in characterizing the evidence as "favorable" to the accused. Materiality suggested that the evidence must also have had some significant potential for actually influencing the outcome under the facts of the case. Thus, under the *Mooney* line of cases, the false testimony, to be "material," had to present some "reasonable likelihood" of affecting the jury's verdict. The *Brady* opinion, however, had no reason to carve out any specific standard of materiality for suppressed exculpatory evidence. The state had acknowledged that Boblit's statement was critical to the issue of punishment, and the Court's discussion therefore focused on whether the statement was material as to guilt. The Court found that issue easily resolved; a statement would not be viewed as material when the jury could have considered it only by disregarding a judge's instruction that it was relevant only as to another issue. Accordingly, the suppression of Boblit's statement had resulted in a due process violation as to the capital punishment determination, but not as to the conviction itself.

The "*Brady* rule" left the lower courts with a series of questions to resolve. The Court spoke of "suppression by the prosecutor"; did this limit the government's responsibility to evidence which was in the immediate possession of the prosecutor? Did the concept of "suppression" suggest an element of keeping evidence from the accused, so that the *Brady* rule would not apply where the defense could otherwise have obtained the evidence with due diligence? The *Brady* rule applied to "favorable evidence," which was also described as "exculpatory evidence." Did this require that the evidence affirmatively point to the defendant's innocence and that it always constitute evidence that would itself be admissible in the relevant proceeding? The *Brady* rule was stated in terms of the failure to disclose exculpatory evidence in response to a defense request. There was no explanation in the opinion, however, as to why the request was important and whether it was always required. Finally, there remained the question of precisely what degree of likely influence of the suppressed evidence fulfilled the element of materiality.

Following *Brady,* lower courts struggled for over a decade, with little direction from the Supreme Court, with questions such as those posed above. Finally, in *United States v. Agurs,*[4] the Court sought to provide some definitive answers. However, those answers apparently did not settle matters within the Court, for less than ten years later, in *United States v. Bagley,*[5] a sharply divided Court produced somewhat different answers on some of the same questions.

(b) The *Agurs–Bagley* Materiality Standard. *Agurs* presented a case in which the defendant, charged with murder, had argued that self-defense was apparent from the prosecution's own evidence as to the incident that had resulted in her killing the deceased (Sewell). That evidence indicated that the defendant had screamed for help, that Sewell was on top of her when the help arrived, and that Sewell possessed two knives, which indicated that he was a violence-prone person. In rejecting the self-defense claim, the jury apparently concluded that it was inconsistent with other factors suggesting that defendant initiated the attack and then sought help only

4. 427 U.S. 97, 96 S.Ct. 2392, 49 L.Ed.2d 342 (1976).

5. See note 7 infra.

when Sewell resisted. Three months after the conviction, defense counsel sought a new trial, alleging that he had recently discovered that Sewell had a prior criminal record, with convictions for assault and the possession of a deadly weapon. That record would have been admissible at trial to show that Sewell was violence-prone, and defense counsel claimed that the prosecution's failure to bring it to the attention of the defense constituted a *Brady* violation. The trial court rejected the claim on the ground that (1) Sewell's criminal record would shed no light on his character that was not already apparent from the uncontradicted evidence (particularly his possession of two knives) and (2) the jury had ample justification for rejecting the self-defense claim. A divided Supreme Court affirmed the trial court's ruling. It held that, in light of the trial judge's ruling, the undisclosed evidence did not meet the applicable standard of materiality.

Justice Stevens' opinion for the Court in *Agurs* initially divided the nondisclosure cases into three groups. First, there were the cases, typified by *Mooney,* in which "the undisclosed evidence demonstrates that the prosecution's case includes perjured testimony and that the prosecution knew, or should have known of the perjury." Here a conviction would be overturned if "there is any reasonable likelihood that the false testimony could have affected the judgment of the jury." This "strict standard of materiality" was appropriate, Justice Stevens noted, "not just because [such cases] * * * involve prosecutorial misconduct, but more importantly because they involve a corruption of the truth seeking function of the trial process." Since there was "no reason to question the veracity of any of the prosecution witnesses" in *Agurs,* the "test of materiality followed in the *Mooney* line of cases" was not applicable here.[6]

The second group of cases, Justice Stevens stated, was illustrated by *Brady.* There, unlike *Agurs,* defense counsel had made a request for disclosure of particular evidence. Such a specific request puts the prosecutor on notice as to the defense belief that certain evidence will be helpful to it, and that notice raises the level of the prosecution's obligation of disclosure. That obligation was described by Justice Stevens as follows:

> Although there is, of course, no duty to provide defense counsel with unlimited discovery of everything known by the prosecutor, if the subject matter of such a request is material, or indeed if a substantial basis for claiming materiality exists, it is reasonable to require the prosecutor to respond either by furnishing the information or by submitting the problem to the trial judge. When the prosecutor receives a specific and relevant request, the failure to make any response is seldom, if ever, excusable.

Since the *Agurs* case did not involve a defense request, Justice Stevens had no reason to describe the standard that would be used in determining whether requested evidence is "material" under the *Brady* standard. Justice Stevens had noted in an earlier part of his opinion that a "fair analysis of the holding in *Brady* indicates that implicit in the requirement of materiality is a concern that the suppressed evidence might have affected the outcome of the trial." There was no clear statement, however, that "might have affected" was to be the materiality standard in request cases. Neither was there any suggestion as to how such a standard would compare to the "any-reasonable-likelihood" standard of the *Mooney* line of cases. The one point that Justice Stevens appeared to firmly establish was that the situation involving a specific defense request was quite distinct from that in which no request was made (as in *Agurs* itself).

Though Justice Stevens' opinion attached considerable significance to the presence of a

6. In *Brady, Agurs,* and the other exculpatory evidence cases, the nondisclosed evidence might detract from the strength of the government's evidence and indeed, contradict the incriminating inferences flowing from the prosecution's evidence, but it never directly established the falsity of that evidence. Where that was the case, as where the government indicated that the shorts worn by the defendant had bloodstains and the nondisclosed scientific analysis showed that the stains came from paint, the Court has treated the case as falling under the false testimony line of cases. See Miller v. Pate, 386 U.S. 1, 87 S.Ct. 785, 17 L.Ed.2d 690 (1967).

specific defense request, it did not go so far as to limit the prosecution's duty to disclose to cases involving such requests. Justice Stevens noted that in this third class of cases, nondisclosure could also result in a due process violation, though not so readily. Encompassed here were instances of both "no request at all" and only a "general request." (A general request, as where the defendant asks for "all *Brady* material," was characterized as giving the prosecutor "no better notice than if no request is made" and therefore appropriately placed in the same category as the case without a request). In this non-request situation, the prosecutor's obligation to disclose must be based upon the notice provided by the character of the evidence itself. If the evidence is "so clearly supportive of a claim of innocence" that "elementary fairness" suggests it should be disclosed, the prosecutor's duty exists even if no specific request has been made. Of course, the level of materiality of exculpatory evidence in this category must be higher than the level imposed in request-cases. If it were not, the Court noted, the due process obligation in a non-request case would almost mandate that the prosecutor "allow complete discovery of his files." On the other hand, the Court also noted, it would be inappropriate to impose a standard of materiality as high as that imposed under the Federal Rule 33 motion for a new trial:

> If the standard applied to the usual motion for a new trial based on newly discovered evidence were the same when the evidence was in the State's possession as when it was found in a neutral source, there would be no special significance to the prosecutor's obligation to serve the cause of justice.

What was required was a materiality standard that fell between the "lower-threshold" or "strict" standard (from the prosecution's perspective) of request-cases and the "high" threshold standard of Rule 33.

As the *Agurs* Court noted, the Rule 33 standard ordinarily requires a showing that the "newly discovered evidence probably would have resulted in an acquittal." Applying this standard, the trial court must conclude that all of the jurors probably would have switched their votes from conviction to acquittal. At the other extreme, under the "any reasonable likelihood" standard applied in the false testimony cases, the Court need find only a reasonable likelihood that one juror would have switched his vote, thereby producing a different jury judgment. In the case involving no request, or only a general request, the *Agurs* Court opted for a standard that looked to a likely shift from guilt to acquittal as measured by the trial court's own evaluation of the evidence. That standard was described in *Agurs* as whether "the omitted evidence creates a reasonable doubt that did not otherwise exist." As noted in the *Agurs* dissent, this test does not ask the judge to assess whether one or all of the jurors would be swayed by the nondisclosed material, but to make a personal judgment based upon his view of the total evidentiary picture. If the judge concludes that, "in the context of the entire record," the omitted evidence creates a reasonable doubt in his mind, then a new trial must be ordered. A judge may reach this result even though he or she believes it probable that not all of the jurors would have reached the same conclusion.

The Court in *Agurs* illustrated this personal aspect of the judge's review in its discussion of the trial court's ruling in that case. The trial judge in *Agurs,* it noted, had applied the standard now prescribed by the Court. Evaluating the omitted arrest record in light of his first-hand appraisal of the record, the trial judge had "remained convinced of respondent's guilt beyond a reasonable doubt." Accordingly, the lower court had correctly held that the prosecutor's failure to tender the arrest record to the defense had not violated due process.

In addition to distinguishing the three different types of nondisclosure situations, the *Agurs* opinion offered some general observations directed primarily at the prosecutor's constitutional obligation to disclose exculpatory evidence. That obligation, the Court noted, is not measured by the "moral culpability, or the willfulness of the prosecutor." The applicable standards of materiality look to the "character of the evidence, not the character of the prosecutor." The Court's "overriding concern" in fashioning those standards was "with the justice of the finding of guilt." Because the "significance of an item of evidence can seldom be predicted accurately until the record is complete," the "prudent prosecutor" was advised to "resolve doubtful questions in favor of disclosure." However, in the end, the prosecutor "will not have violated his constitutional duty" unless a court subsequently determines that the nondisclosed evidence was in fact material under the applicable standard.

Nine years later, in *United States v. Bagley,*[7] the Court reaffirmed much of the underlying analysis of *Agurs,* but at the same time modified substantially the *Agurs* materiality standard and extended it to all cases of nondisclosure of exculpatory evidence. *Bagley,* unlike *Agurs,* involved a specific request. Before trial, defense requested notification of "any deals, promises, or inducements made to [government] witnesses in exchange for their testimony." The government produced signed affidavits of its two principal witnesses, private security officers, which detailed their undercover activities and concluded with the statement that the affidavits were given without any promises of reward. Following defendant's trial and conviction, it was discovered that both witnesses had signed contracts with the federal investigating agency stating that they would be paid "a sum commensurate with services and information rendered." The prosecuting attorney testified that he would have furnished the contracts if he had known of their existence, and the trial judge agreed that this should have been done. The trial judge refused to order a new trial, however, reasoning that the impeachment evidence would not have affected the outcome of defendant's bench trial. The Ninth Circuit reversed. It viewed the government's disclosure as impairing defendant's right of confrontation, and concluded that the violation therefore required automatic reversal. The Supreme Court rejected that conclusion and remanded for reconsideration. The eight participating Justices were in agreement that any constitutional violation here was to be judged under the due process standard of *Brady,* rather than the confrontation clause,[8] and therefore automatic reversal was not appropriate. Four separate opinions were written, however, on the standard to be applied in determining whether a new trial was required under *Brady.*

Justice Marshall's dissenting opinion in *Bagley* (joined by Brennan, J.) expanded upon a position he had advanced earlier in dissenting in *Agurs*—that in all cases (request and non-request), the prosecutor has a constitutional duty "to turn over to the defendant all information known to the government that might reasonably be considered favorable to the defendant's case," with the violation of that duty requiring a new trial unless the prosecution could establish that the error was harmless beyond a reasonable doubt. Once again, however, that standard failed to gain the support of the other Justices. Such an approach had been rejected in *Agurs* as one that would force the prosecutor, to assure compliance, basically to "allow complete discovery of his files as a matter of routine." The Court had repeatedly stated that the prosecution has no obligation to inform the defendant of all it had learned about the case and its witnesses, no matter how "preliminary, challenged, or speculative" the information. Justice Marshall's proposed standard was seen as imposing exactly that type of obligation, for the prosecution could hardly say with certainty that even a trivial piece of evidence might not influence a jury or give some help to the defense.

Also in dissent in *Bagley,* Justice Stevens, following the implications of his opinion for the Court in *Agurs,* stressed that this case, unlike *Agurs,* involved a specific request. He argued that due process should demand more of the prosecutor in such cases—and therefore impose a lesser showing as to the likelihood of prejudice. Accordingly, he would hold that

7. 473 U.S. 667, 105 S.Ct. 3375, 87 L.Ed.2d 481 (1985).

8. The Sixth Amendment issue is discussed in § 24.-3(a).

the prosecutor has an obligation to disclose requested evidence whenever it is "favorable," "admissible," and "relevant to the dispositive issues of guilt" and apply to that obligation the same standard as to likely prejudice as was applied in the false testimony case—that there simply be "any reasonable likelihood that it [the non-disclosure] could have affected the outcome of the trial." Only as to such requested evidence would he adopt a position similar to that of Justice Marshall. This position too was rejected by the Court majority, as reflected by the separate opinions of Justice Blackmun (joined by O'Connor, J.) and Justice White (joined by Burger, C.J., and Rehnquist, J.).

Of the two *Bagley* opinions that combined to present the majority viewpoint, that of Justice Blackmun contained the far more extensive discussion of the applicable due process standard. Justice Blackmun noted initially that the false testimony cases had adopted, in effect, the traditional constitutional harmless error standard, although that standard might also be stated as a materiality test "under which the fact that testimony is perjured is considered material unless failure to disclose it would be harmless beyond a reasonable doubt." The traditional materiality phrasing—finding sufficient "any reasonable likelihood" of affecting the jury verdict—was developed prior to the establishment of the constitutional harmless error standard and merely stated the same concept by expressing what would preclude a finding of harmlessness beyond a reasonable doubt. For reasons stated in *Agurs,* this standard, however expressed, did not apply to nondisclosures where there had been no specific request. The materiality standard applied there was "stricter than the harmless-error standard but more lenient to the defense than the newly discovered evidence standard." In two post-*Agurs* decisions, both "arising outside the *Brady* context," the Court had "relied on and reformulated" the *Agurs* materiality standard. In determining whether the deportation of witnesses had resulted in a denial of due process, the Court in *Valenzuela–Bernal* had asked whether there was a "reasonable likelihood" that unavailability of their testimony "could have affected the judgment of the trier of fact." [9] And in *Strickland v. Washington,* in defining the prejudice element of an incompetency claim, the Court had required that there be "a reasonable probability that, but for counsel's unprofessional errors, the result of the proceedings would have been different." [10] This reformulation, Justice Blackmun noted, pointed to a single materiality standard that could be applied to all nondisclosure cases:

> We find the *Strickland* formulation of the Agurs test for materiality sufficiently flexible to cover the "no request," "general request," and "specific request" cases of prosecutorial failure to disclose evidence favorable to the accused: The evidence is material only if there is a reasonable probability that, had the evidence been disclosed to the defense, the result of the proceeding would have been different. A "reasonable probability" is a probability sufficient to undermine confidence in the outcome.

Although adopting a single standard for all nondisclosure cases, Justice Blackmun noted that specific request cases presented special considerations in applying the "reasonable probability" standard. A nondisclosure in a specific request case might have an influence on the outcome that extended beyond the weight of the nondisclosed evidence itself. "[A]n incomplete response to a specific request not only deprives the defense of certain evidence, but has the effect of representing to the defense that the evidence does not exist." Relying on "this misleading representation, the defense might abandon lines of independent investigation, defenses, or trial strategies that it otherwise would have pursued." However, the *Strickland* formulation was sufficiently flexible to take into consideration the possible impact of the nondisclosure on the "preparation or presentation of the defendant's case." Under that standard, "[t]he reviewing court should assess the possibility

9. See § 24.3 at note 34.

10. See § 11.10(d).

that such effect might have occurred in light of the totality of the circumstances and with an awareness of the difficulty of reconstructing in a post-trial proceeding the course that the defense and the trial would have taken had the defense not been misled by the prosecutor's incomplete response."

Justice White's concurring opinion gave majority support to a considerable part of Justice Blackmun's opinion. Justice White agreed that nondisclosed evidence " 'is material only if there is a reasonable probability that, had the evidence been disclosed to the defense, the result of the proceeding would have been different.' " He also agreed that this standard "is 'sufficiently flexible' to cover all instances of prosecutorial failure to disclose evidence favorable to the accused." However, "given the flexibility of the standard and the inherently fact-bound nature of the cases to which it will be applied," he saw "no reason to attempt to elaborate on the relevance to the inquiry of the specificity of the defense's request for disclosure."

Taken together, the Blackmun and White opinions establish a majority position on several aspects of the due process standard governing the prosecution's failure to disclose favorable evidence. Initially, they reaffirm that a nondisclosure does not entitle a defendant to reversal of his conviction unless the nondisclosed evidence is "material." Second, they establish a single test of materiality applicable to all nondisclosure cases, including specific request, general request, and no request cases. That test requires "a reasonable probability" that, had disclosure been made, the "result of the proceeding would have been different." Whether this standard is more or less favorable to the defendant than the standard announced in *Agurs* (that the nondisclosed evidence creates "a reasonable doubt that otherwise did not exist") is not entirely clear. Justice Stevens, in his *Bagley* dissent, viewed the reasonable probability standard as similar to that which he set forth in *Agurs* for no request/general request cases. Some lower courts also have viewed the *Bagley* and *Agurs* standards as essentially the same and continue to apply the *Agurs* standard (sometimes interchangeably with the *Bagley* standard). Most, however, have moved strictly to the *Bagley* formulation. Unlike the *Agurs* test, the *Bagley* formulation is not framed so as to be tied exclusively to the judge's own evaluation of the evidentiary picture, and that difference could have a bearing on the application of the test. Certainly, a judge who believes that the nondisclosed evidence creates a reasonable doubt is likely to conclude that there is a reasonable probability that the outcome would have been different. Yet, where the case obviously troubled the jury, a judge arguably should also find a reasonable probability even though a reasonable doubt is not created in his own mind. The test of "reasonable probability" focuses on the likelihood that the trial would have produced a different verdict (either an acquittal or a hung jury) if the evidence in question had been disclosed to the defense. That focus obviously requires consideration of how the jury responded to the evidence that was before it, especially where that response indicates that the jury, even without the nondisclosed evidence, considered the case to be a close one.

Of course, the *Bagley* standard of "reasonable probability" is far from precise, as the Court acknowledged in its original formulation of the standard in *Strickland*. The *Agurs* test of reasonable doubt might be more helpful to the judge in this regard as it looks to a standard that judges frequently apply as triers of fact in bench trials. Justice Blackmun's opinion offers only limited direction as to the degree of probability that constitutes a reasonable probability. It is a probability "sufficient to undermine confidence in the outcome," higher than the "any reasonable likelihood" that had been applied in the *Mooney* line of cases, and less than the "more-likely-than-not standard" applied in the Rule 33 new evidence cases. However, as Justice Blackmun indicated, its use in other areas of constitutional litigation—particularly the frequently litigated Sixth Amendment claim of ineffective assistance of counsel—should eventually provide trial courts with as good a sense of its content as they have of the reasonable doubt standard. Moreover, the *Bagley* standard more readily lends itself to appellate court review than a trial judge's conclusion under *Agurs* that the nondisclosed evidence creates a reasonable doubt that did not previously exist.

(c) **The Specific Request Element.** While the combination of the Blackmun and White opinions in *Bagley* produce a single standard for all nondisclosure cases, those opinions also accepted, at least to some degree, the distinction drawn in *Agurs* between specific request cases and no request/general request cases. Both the Blackmun and White opinions stated that the reasonable probability standard was sufficiently flexible to take into consideration any relevant differences between the two types of cases. Of course, there was no consensus on the precise relevance of the specific request to the due process inquiry. Unlike the *Agurs* opinion, where Justice Stevens distinguished the specific request primarily on the presence of a greater level of prosecutorial responsibility for the nondisclosure, Justice Blackmun emphasized the potentially greater prejudicial impact of a failure to respond to a specific request because such a failure might have misled counsel. This difference in emphasis might have little practical significance, however, if the Court majority also should adhere to Justice Blackmun's comments concerning the difficulty of reconstructing the course that counsel would have taken if he had not been misled. Indeed, Justice Blackmun's *Bagley* opinion quoted, without apparent concern, the warning in *Agurs* that nondisclosures in specific request cases will "seldom, if ever, [be] excusable." In addition, the Stevens and Marshall opinions in *Bagley* certainly suggest that Justices not satisfied with *Bagley's* single standard will seek to use the flexibility of that standard to afford greater due process protection to the defendant who places the prosecution on notice with a specific request. In sum, as the Fifth Circuit put it: "Viewing the [*Bagley*] opinions as a whole, it is fair to say that all the participating Justices agreed on one thing at least: that reversal for suppression of evidence by the government is most likely where the request for it was specific." [11]

Where a case involves a specific request, lower courts have continued to take note of that factor, although not always identifying its precise significance. Both before *Bagley* and afterwards, however, there has been some disagreement as to what should be seen as a "specific request" as opposed to a "general request." The focus in the pre-*Bagley* rulings was on the nature of the notice given to the prosecution by the request. That focus followed from the reasoning offered in *Agurs* for treating separately specific request cases. Although Justice Blackmun in *Bagley* offered a different analysis of the relevancy of notice, the same focus continues to be applied. To some extent, the degree of notice and the likelihood of detrimental reliance on the prosecution's failure to respond go hand in hand. Where the request is narrow and precise, giving the prosecutor considerable direction as to what is wanted, the defense counsel is more likely to treat the prosecutor's failure to disclose as an indication that the evidence does not exist. Where the request does not have those qualities, the defense counsel must also account for the possibility that no disclosure was made or that the disclosure made was not complete because the prosecution adopted a somewhat different interpretation of what was included in the request or could not readily put together all that was encompassed by the request.

In dealing with recorded statements of possible witnesses, lower courts have generally included in the specific-request category any request for a specific statement of a particular person. The statement need not be identified by content; it is sufficient simply to request,

11. Lindsey v. King, 769 F.2d 1034 (5th Cir.1985). Moreover, some state courts, relying upon their state constitutions, continue to use a separate materiality standard, characterized as easier to meet than the reasonable probability standard, in specific request cases. See People v. Vilardi, 76 N.Y.2d 67, 556 N.Y.S.2d 518, 555 N.E.2d 915 (1990) ("reasonable possibility"); Commonwealth v. Gallarelli, 399 Mass. 17, 502 N.E.2d 516 (1987) (where there is a "substantial basis" for claiming that the specifically requested evidence was "material," reversal required unless the trial court is "sure that the error did not influence the jury, or had but very slight effect").

for example, any statement that the person gave to the police. Courts have also treated as specific a request that asked for all recorded statements of a particular witness without identifying to whom the statements were made. However, where the government had thousands of pages relating to a particular witness, it was held that a specific request would require identification of the particular documents sought. Similarly, a request for any material "bearing adversely on the credibility, character, and reputation" of a particular witness was held not to be specific.

Even though a particular person is not identified, a request may be viewed as specific if it identifies a particular type of evidence. Thus, requests have been held specific where they sought the statements of any eyewitnesses who were unable to identify the defendant. Similarly, a court deemed specific a request for "all internal affairs records, files and reports relating to complaints filed against * * * [particular government agents] for use of excessive force or other aggressive behavior." The lower courts generally have refused to treat as specific those requests that simply identify a potentially large category of items without narrowing the requested items by reference to content. Thus, a request for the recorded statements of all persons interviewed by the police in connection with the case will be deemed a general request (although occasional rulings have held otherwise). While all such statements might be readily identified by the prosecutor, there is nothing in the request that distinguishes those statements believed by the defense to have exculpatory value. A failure of the prosecutor to respond or a limited response would suggest nothing more than the judgment of an adversary that the statements do not contain exculpatory material.

(d) The Character of Favorable Evidence. The nondisclosed material in *Brady* was not relevant to the issue of guilt and the Court relied on that factor in holding that the element of materiality was not satisfied as to that issue. Some courts and commentators have accordingly assumed that the prosecution's duty to disclose is limited to matter that would be admissible in evidence, as only such matter could be relevant to the jury's decision. Others view admissibility as a critical end-product, but note that the duty to disclose could encompass inadmissible material where that material appears likely to lead the defense to the discovery of admissible evidence. A few courts have suggested that admissibility is an irrelevant factor. They apparently would hold that *Brady* requires disclosure of material not itself admissible and not likely to produce admissible evidence provided the information contained therein could have some other use (e.g., in developing trial strategy). At least the latter position seems inconsistent with the thrust of the explanation of the prosecutor's duty to disclose in *Agurs*. The emphasis there clearly was on the substantive, exculpatory nature of the nondisclosed material itself and the prosecutor's likely awareness of its significance. Indeed, the *Agurs* Court specifically rejected the view that the standard for judging materiality "should focus on the impact of the undisclosed evidence on the defendant's ability to prepare for trial, rather than the materiality of the evidence to the issue of guilt or innocence." [12] This point was reaffirmed in *Weatherford v. Bursey.*[13] The Court there rejected the contention that the government had violated *Brady* when it used as a prosecution witness an informant who had previously assured defendant that he would not testify against him. *Brady,* the Court noted, relates only to concealing evidence favorable to the accused, not to providing the defense with notice that will

12. See *Agurs,* supra note 4, at n. 20. The Court noted two reasons for rejecting an approach that looked primarily to trial preparation benefit. First, that approach would "necessarily encompass incriminating as well as exculpatory evidence," since the knowledge of the prosecution's "entire case" would be "useful to the defense" under a standard looking to trial preparation. Second, such an approach would stress "the adequacy of the notice given to the defendant by the State," and the due process requirement of notice has traditionally been limited to notice of the charge contained in the accusatory pleading rather than notice of the government's "evidentiary support for the charge."

13. 429 U.S. 545, 97 S.Ct. 837, 51 L.Ed.2d 30 (1977). See also § 11.8, at note 20.

improve its preparation for meeting the government's evidence.

Courts sometimes have been troubled by the question of whether evidence that does not point directly to the defendant's innocence nevertheless is "favorable to the accused." Most agree that evidence can be favorable even though it does no more than demonstrate that "a number of factors which could link the defendant to the crime do not." Thus, where the circumstances of the crime suggested that the offender's clothes might have been stained, and defendant's clothes were found not to have been stained, the laboratory report on the examination of his clothes was treated as "favorable" rather than "neutral" evidence. Under some circumstances, however, the rejected links may be so unlikely that the nondisclosed evidence is truly neutral. Thus, where robbers wore loosefitting coveralls and their faces were masked, the inability of the eyewitnesses to positively identify the defendants was viewed as not really helpful to the defense and therefore not subject to *Brady.* Of course, where the question is close as to whether the evidence is "favorable" or "neutral," the nondisclosure most likely will not meet the *Bagley* test for materiality even if it is determined that the evidence is favorable.

Because both *Brady* and *Agurs* involved affirmative exculpatory evidence, some lower courts questioned whether the same standards for judging materiality should apply to nondisclosed material that could be used only to challenge the credibility of a prosecution witness. Their concern was that impeachment evidence usually is specifically requested and that *Agurs* suggested a materiality standard for requested material that would put the prosecutor who failed to disclose at risk in all but unusual cases. The end result, they warned, would be to require prosecutors to regularly disclose impeachment material, thereby "entail[ing] the risk that government witnesses will be less open with the prosecutor." *Bagley,* however, refused to adopt a special standard of materiality for nondisclosure of impeachment material, just as the *Mooney* line of cases had refused to draw such a distinction in dealing with the prosecutor's failure to respond to false responses of its witnesses to defense cross-examination designed to show their bias or general lack of credibility. Justice Blackmun's opinion in *Bagley* did not discuss the concern previously noted by the lower courts, but that was not surprising in light of the materiality standard adopted there for all nondisclosure cases, including those involving a specific request. The "reasonable probability" test hardly goes so far as to require disclosure of all possible impeachment evidence, even as to principal witnesses. In particular, since witnesses are not likely to acknowledge serious flaws in their credibility in the information they give to the prosecutor, any impeachment material they furnish to the prosecution only rarely would have the great bearing on credibility needed to meet the *Bagley* standard. The nondisclosure cases finding materiality in impeachment material generally have dealt with obviously significant impeachment material otherwise known to the prosecutor (such as the promise to compensate involved in *Bagley*), not statements furnished by the witnesses themselves.

(e) Prosecution Control Over the Evidence. In *Brady* and *Agurs,* the items not disclosed were within the prosecutor's files, and it is well established that the *Brady* obligations of the prosecutor's office are institutional and do not depend upon the knowledge of the individual prosecutor who is conducting the trial. In *Bagley,* the nondisclosed contracts apparently were in the files of the investigative agency that had been assisted by the security guards, but the Court saw no reason to even comment on that factor in discussing the prosecution's responsibility. Lower courts have regularly held that the prosecution's obligation under *Bagley* extends to the files of those police agencies that were responsible for the primary investigation in the case. They commonly include also material available to other members of the "prosecution team" in the particular case, including even case workers from social service agencies. On the other hand, the prosecution's obligation has been held not to extend to independent agencies not involved in the investigation of the case, such as a probation department. Courts have suggested, however, that the prosecution, on a specific request for potentially exculpatory material not available to the defense, may have a *Brady* obligation to attempt to obtain such material even from an independent agency (such as a law enforcement agency of another jurisdiction). One court has cited four factors that must be weighed in determining whether the prosecution has such an obligation: "the potential unfairness to defendant; the defendant's lack of access to the evidence; the burden on the prosecutor of obtaining the evidence; and the degree of cooperation between authorities [of the two jurisdictions], both in general and in the particular case." [14]

(f) Defense Diligence. In *Agurs,* the Court described the "*Brady* rule" as applicable to situations "involv[ing] the discovery, after trial, of information which had been known to the prosecution but unknown to the defense." Looking to this language, various courts have held that the prosecutor's constitutional obligation was not violated, notwithstanding the nondisclosure of apparently exculpatory evidence, where that evidence was known to the defense and no request for disclosure was made. The defense must be held responsible for its failure to request known items, leaving the prosecution to assume that the defense has no interest in the item despite its potentially exculpatory character.

Courts holding the defense responsible for its lack of diligence have insisted that the defense be aware of the potentially exculpatory nature of the evidence as well as its existence. Of critical significance here is whether the knowledge of the defense is to be measured by reference to counsel and client individually or taken together. There are instances in which the client is aware that the prosecution has certain evidence but does not appreciate its potentially exculpatory nature and does not inform counsel, who would be aware of its exculpatory significance. Some courts have held, in effect, that the requirement of due defense diligence should not assume that defense counsel will obtain from his client every bit of relevant information. Thus, where the prosecutor has material of exculpatory value that is known to the defendant (e.g., because it was obtained from him), but its potential significance is likely to be missed by most laypersons, or by this defendant in particular, the prosecution cannot assume that the defense counsel necessarily is aware of that evidence. Arguably a different result would be reached should it be discovered that defense counsel actually had the foresight to ask the client about such evidence but the client lied (perhaps because he viewed the evidence as incriminating).

Still another troublesome issue under the due diligence concept is how far the defense must go to obtain the material. If the defense makes a request and the prosecutor fails to furnish the item, does the defense have the further obligation to obtain the item by subpoena (assuming that process is available), or can it proceed without the item and raise a *Brady* claim after conviction? Several decisions suggest that the defense must exhaust all efforts to obtain the item where it knows of its existence. This includes obtaining the item from an alternative source where it would be available as well from that source (e.g., as to a matter of public record).

(g) The Timing of the Disclosure. Though *Brady* itself involved a request for pretrial disclosure, lower courts agree that the *Brady* rule does not impose a general requirement of pretrial disclosure of exculpatory evidence that is material to the issue of guilt. Due process, it is said, requires only that disclosure of exculpatory evidence be made in sufficient time to permit defendant to make effective use of that evidence. Depending upon the nature of the evidence, this standard may sometimes require pretrial disclosure. Thus, where the prosecution has the statement of a witness who could present exculpatory testimony and does not intend itself to call that witness, disclosure before trial would be necessary to ensure that the defense has an opportunity to subpoena that witness.

14. Commonwealth v. Donahue, 396 Mass. 590, 487 N.E.2d 1351 (1986).

Insofar as such disclosure exceeds what is permitted under local pretrial discovery provisions, the constitutional obligation will, of course, prevail over those provisions.

For most exculpatory evidence, the prosecutor should be able to satisfy his constitutional obligation by disclosure at trial. Where the disclosure is made at that point, the burden rests with the defendant to establish that the "lateness of that disclosure so prejudiced [defendant's] preparation or presentation of his defense that he was prevented from receiving his constitutionally guaranteed fair trial." Moreover, if the defendant failed to request a continuance when disclosure was first made at trial, that failure often will be viewed as automatically negating any claim of actual prejudice.

While pretrial disclosure may not be required, prosecutor's commonly respond to pretrial requests for specific exculpatory evidence with pretrial disclosure. Indeed, in many jurisdictions, pretrial "*Brady* discovery" is a regular part of discovery practice. For example, prosecutors are asked for, and commonly disclose pretrial, standard impeachment items such as promises to witnesses. In some jurisdictions, discovery statutes or court rules contain a "*Brady* provision," which brings such disclosure within the formal discovery apparatus. In others, prosecutors simply furnish pretrial *Brady* disclosures apart from the discovery procedures and without court orders. This practice is consistent with the recommendation of numerous courts that "the prosecutor disclose *Brady* material as soon as possible, preferably pretrial."

If the prosecutor refuses to respond to a specific pretrial request, stating that the material need not be disclosed under *Brady,* the defense may ask the trial court to examine the requested material in camera and order disclosure if it should find it to be exculpatory and material. Courts have varied considerably in their approach to such requests. Many have been extremely reluctant to undertake a pretrial review of a *Brady* request. In support of this position, it is noted: (1) "the judge is ordinarily less oriented to the facts of the case and possible defenses than is the prosecuting attorney"; (2) "requiring the judge to review prosecution files for information useful to the defendant casts the judge in a defense advocate's role"; and (3) in camera inspection can become a "ponderous, time-consuming task if utilized in every case merely on demand." Courts expressing such concerns ordinarily will not provide in camera inspection unless the request is limited to no more than a few items of evidence and the defendant can show some strong basis for believing that the material may be favorable to the defense. Other courts would not impose such a burden on the defense, noting that it "realistically * * * cannot know" if requested evidence would fall within *Brady.* They generally will provide in camera review if the request is fairly specific (i.e., does not reflect a "fishing expedition") and the material requested is "obviously relevant, competent, and not privileged." Some prosecutors do not oppose such review, preferring to have the court order disclosure before trial rather than find a *Brady* violation following a conviction.

(h) Postconviction Challenges. The division among the courts in their approach to pretrial consideration of *Brady* issues carries over to postconviction *Brady* challenges. Here, more courts tend to be reluctant to undertake an inquiry without some significant defense showing that there exists a specific item of exculpatory evidence that was not disclosed. The courts will not undertake a postconviction hearing into an alleged *Brady* violation based upon bare allegations that such evidence exists. The defense ordinarily is expected to have discovered that the evidence exists and to have a substantial basis for believing that it might be exculpatory.

Even in a postconviction hearing, the trial court may conduct a review of the specified item in camera under appropriate circumstances. The Supreme Court held that it had such a case before it in *Pennsylvania v. Ritchie.*[15] In that case, involving a postconviction challenge to a trial court's refusal to

15. 480 U.S. 39, 107 S.Ct. 989, 94 L.Ed.2d 40 (1987).

order pretrial disclosure of potentially exculpatory material in the confidential records of a state protective agency, the Court initially held that the *Brady* rule set the appropriate standard for determining whether the lack of disclosure resulted in a constitutional violation. It then considered the state appellate court's decision on the appropriate procedure for making that determination in the context of confidential state records. The state court "apparently had concluded that whenever defendant alleges that protected evidence might be material, the appropriate method of assessing this claim is to grant full access to the disputed information, regardless of the state's interest in confidentiality." Rejecting that conclusion, the Supreme Court noted that it had never held—even in the absence of a confidentiality statute—that a defense counsel has a "right to conduct his own search of the state's files to argue relevance." Indeed, under "settled practice," where a defendant makes only a general request, the prosecution decides what it must disclose under *Brady* and that decision is "final" unless the defense counsel brings to the trial court's attention the existence of particular nondisclosed exculpatory evidence. Thus, the Court continued, the trial court here could appropriately conclude, upon balancing the state's interest in the confidentiality of the record against the "benefits of an 'advocate's eye' " in aiding its materiality ruling, that its ruling should be based on an in camera review.[16]

16. The Court added that, within this general framework, a "trial court's discretion is not unbounded. If a defendant is aware of specific information contained in the file (e.g., the medical report [of a complainant alleged to have been sexually assaulted]), he is free to request it directly from the court, and argue in favor of materiality."

Chapter 21

PLEAS OF GUILTY

Table of Sections

§ 21.1 The Plea Negotiation System

(a) Forms of Plea Bargaining. In the United States, the great majority of criminal cases are disposed of by a plea of guilty. Sometimes this plea is the result of nothing more than implicit plea bargaining in that the defendant enters his plea merely because it is generally known that this is the route to a lesser sentence. But more common is explicit bargaining in which the defendant enters a plea of guilty only after a commitment has been made that concessions will be granted (or at least sought) in his particular case.

One common form of plea negotiation consists of an arrangement whereby the defendant and prosecutor agree that the defendant should be permitted to plead guilty to a charge less serious than is supported by the evidence. There are several reasons why this kind of "deal" may seem advantageous to the defendant. For one, the less serious offense is likely to carry a lower statutory maximum penalty than the offense actually committed, so that the defendant has an assurance at the time of his plea that the judge's sentencing discretion will be limited. Or, the plea to the lesser offense may instead maximize the judge's sentencing discretion; by his plea, the defendant may avoid a high statutory minimum sentence or a statutory bar to probation. A third reason why defendants bargain as to the charge is to avoid a record of conviction on the offense actually committed. Sometimes the desire is to avoid a repugnant conviction label, as where a defendant charged with a sex offense is permitted to plead to the nondescript charge of disorderly conduct. On other occasions, the purpose is to avoid conviction on a felony charge, which would carry with it certain undesirable collateral consequences (e.g., loss of certain civil rights, loss of eligibility for certain types of employment).

A second form of plea bargaining involves an agreement whereby the defendant pleads "on the nose," that is, to the original charge, in exchange for some kind of promise from the prosecutor concerning the sentence to be imposed. The prosecutor may agree in a general way to seek leniency, or he may promise to ask for some specific disposition, such as probation. On occasion the prosecutor may do no more than promise that he will refrain from making any recommendation to the judge, or that he will not oppose a request for leniency put to the judge by the defendant. Or, the prosecutor may be so bold as to promise a certain sentence upon a guilty plea, a promise he may know he can fulfill because of the trial judge's practice of following the prosecutor's recommendations. Sentence bargaining carries with it a somewhat greater risk than charge bargaining, as there remains some possibility (slight in most locales) that in this case the trial judge will not follow the prosecutor's recommendations.

One final form of plea negotiation deserves mention: the on-the-nose plea of guilty to one charge in exchange for the prosecutor's promise to drop or not to file other charges. Multiple charges, either actual or potential, against a single defendant are not uncommon; a single criminal episode may involve violation of several separate provisions of the applicable criminal code, or investigation of the defendant may show that he was responsible for several unrelated crimes (e.g., several burglaries committed in the course of many months). This kind of bargain is most likely to be illusory, in that multiple charges are seldom brought against the defendant who does not plead guilty, and, if brought, often result in concurrent sentencing.

(b) Development of Plea Bargaining. The practice of plea bargaining, though not limited exclusively to the United States, is doubtless more firmly established here than in any other country. It began to appear during the early or mid-nineteenth century, and became institutionalized as a standard feature of American urban criminal courts in the last third of the nineteenth century. One common explanation is that plea bargaining came about and exists because of crowded court dockets. But this is certainly not the only reason, for plea negotiation practices have developed at times and places where there was no serious court congestion problem.

Other important reasons why the plea negotiation system has reached its present proportions in this country are: (1) the rise of professional police and prosecutors who developed and selected their cases more carefully, so that there are relatively few genuine disputes over guilt or innocence left to be resolved by juries; (2) the rise of specialization and professionalism on the defense side and broadening of the right to counsel, meaning that many more defendants had counsel and that those attorneys appreciated they could be of assistance to their clients at the pretrial stage; (3) changes in the jury trial process from a relatively simple proceeding to one so cumbersome and expensive that our society refuses to provide it; (4) the due process revolution, which made additional demands on the prosecutor's office in pretrial and post-conviction proceedings and gave the defendant additional rights which strengthened his bargaining position; (5) the expansion of the substantive criminal law, and in particular new criminal legislation which did not always have the full weight of the community behind it; and (6) the desire of prosecutors and judges to reach a sentence that, in their view, would be more appropriate for the needs of the individual offender than that otherwise permissible under rigid sentencing statutes. Some years ago there was a widely held view that prosecutors never bargain, but in recent times the practice has become highly visible, and the United States Supreme Court has now upheld the practice as necessary and proper.[1]

(c) Administrative Convenience. The most commonly asserted justification of plea bargaining is its utility in disposing of large numbers of cases in a quick and simple way. The assumption is that the system can function only if a high percentage of cases are disposed of by guilty plea and that this will happen only if concessions are granted to induce pleas. So the argument goes, our present criminal justice system is "based on the premise that approximately 90 per cent of all defendants will plead guilty, leaving only 10 per cent, more or less, to be tried," meaning that even a small reduction in the percentage of pleas received would have a tremendous impact. "A reduction from 90 per cent to 80 per cent in guilty pleas requires the assignment of twice the judicial manpower and facilities—judges, court reporters, bailiffs, clerks, jurors and courtrooms."[2]

One view is that society should and can pay the price for whatever increase in the number of trials would be brought about by ending plea bargaining. But it has sometimes been questioned whether an increase in funding and staffing for this purpose would, in the broad view of things, be beneficial. Even if the money were readily available, it is unclear that we could call upon sufficient numbers of competent personnel. Moreover, funds and personnel might be diverted from other segments of the criminal process where they are more needed.

The issue is further complicated by the fact that it is unclear whether bringing plea negotiations to an end would significantly increase the burdens on the criminal justice system. Some argue that eliminating plea bargaining would eliminate the incentive for prosecutors to overcharge or otherwise inappropriately charge, meaning defendants would plead guilty in the many cases in which they and their attorneys conclude that the prosecutor's charge reflects the likely result at trial. It has also been contended that barring plea bargaining would lift those burdens which are attributable to bargaining: defense strategies whose only utility lies in the threat they pose to the court's and the prosecutor's time.

(d) Accurate and Fair Results. Another concern which has been expressed about the plea negotiation system is that, by its nature,

§ 21.1

1. E.g., Bordenkircher v. Hayes, 434 U.S. 357, 98 S.Ct. 663, 54 L.Ed.2d 604 (1978); Santobello v. New York, 404 U.S. 257, 92 S.Ct. 495, 30 L.Ed.2d 427 (1971).

2. Address of Chief Justice Burger at ABA Annual Convention, N.Y. Times, Aug. 11, 1970, p. 24, col. 4.

it is likely to produce results which are unfair or inaccurate. The objection is that the disposition of cases is influenced by factors irrelevant to the correctional needs of the defendant or the requirements of law enforcement, such as court and prosecutor workload or the aggressiveness of the lawyers, so that either of two undesirable consequences may occur: (1) a serious offender may escape with undeserved leniency; or (2) an innocent person may be convicted.

It would seem that the possibility of the first of these consequences is somewhat greater in those urban centers where the pressures to move the docket are most intense. Criticism of plea bargaining on this ground is sometimes made by the police, but it is often difficult to ascertain whether excessive leniency actually exists in a particular jurisdiction. As for the second of these consequences, the fear is that even an innocent person might be tempted to plead guilty and receive the tendered concessions rather than risk conviction at trial and a more severe penalty. But we do not know how common such a situation is, nor do we know how often innocent persons are convicted at trial. The latter possibility must also be taken into account here if the matter is to be kept in proper perspective, for the significant question is whether there is a likelihood that innocent people who would be (or have a fair chance of being) acquitted at trial might be induced to plead guilty.

Indeed, it has been argued that in some instances plea negotiation leads to more intelligent results than could be obtained at trial. The premise is that the categories of guilt and innocence are not always simple and clear-cut, that instead of a black-or-white dichotomy there are many gray areas at the boundaries of criminal culpability. This being so, the reasoning proceeds, in a case in which the defendant's conduct falls into one of these gray areas it is preferable to achieve an intermediate judgment via plea bargaining than to undertake a trial at which only an all or nothing result is possible. Thus, because the line between responsibility and irresponsibility due to insanity is not as sharp as the alternatives posed to a jury would suggest, some view it not at all irrational that a negotiated compromise might be reached in a case in which the defendant, charged with murder, has raised an insanity defense which might or might not succeed at trial. Others find it inconceivable that what is at stake in the insanity defense (criminal versus custodial disposition) should be left to defendants and prosecutors to negotiate away.

The notion that a bargained plea may produce a fairer result is grounded in the supposition that the flexibility of plea bargaining as a dispositional device has substantial advantages over the formal rigidities of the jury trial. Opponents of plea bargaining offer two responses to this. One is that unjustifiably harsh provisions in the substantive law can be avoided without plea bargaining by the simple expedient of more careful and considerate initial charge selection. The other, doubtless unappealing to the defendants who would be sacrificed, is that unjustifiably harsh and otherwise unavoidable provisions of the substantive criminal law should be applied strictly in order to influence changes in the formal law producing greater flexibility.

(e) The Problem of Disparity. Because the plea negotiation system is grounded in the granting of concessions in exchange for guilty pleas, it raises the fundamental question of whether the fact that the defendant has pleaded guilty should have any legitimate bearing on the punishment he receives. The issue is exposed by the case of *People v. Snow,*[3] where the defendant, tried and convicted of prison escape by a jury, received a sentence of 2 to 5 years. On appeal he showed that of 234 prison escape cases in the county over a 26–month period, 207 pled guilty and (except in 5 cases where aggravated circumstances were present) received minimum sentences of one and a half years or less, while 13 were tried by a jury and (except in one case in which the defendant entered a guilty plea during trial) received sentences of two years

3. 386 Mich. 586, 194 N.W.2d 314 (1972).

or more. The court concluded that because "in the usual escape case a minimum sentence of 1½ years has been deemed appropriate by the sentencing judge" and "examination of the record in this case fails to reveal a single fact that would place this defendant in a different category," the case should be remanded for resentencing. But, while *Snow* thus seems to view sentencing concessions for pleas to be improper, the courts generally do not take this view, and certainly the Supreme Court's excursions into the plea bargaining area lend little support to the *Snow* position.[4]

One view is that dispositional disparity between guilty plea and trial defendants, arising out of and essential to a plea negotiation system, is proper so long as it is achieved without being unduly harsh to the latter category of defendants. Thus it is argued that it is proper for guilty plea defendants to receive concessions so long as a court does not impose any sentence in excess of that which would be justified by any of the protective, deterrent, or other purposes of the criminal law upon a defendant who has chosen to require the prosecution to prove guilt at trial rather than to enter a guilty plea. Others object that the normal sentence is the average sentence for all defendants, so that if we are lenient toward those who plead guilty we are by precisely the same token more severe toward those who do not.

The disparity in treatment of guilty plea and trial defendants has sometimes been explained on the ground that the circumstances of a trial are often such as to justify a more severe sanction than would have been imposed had the defendant entered a guilty plea. Thus, a defendant who goes to trial may be punished more severely because the brutal circumstances of the crime are more vividly portrayed if there is a trial. Others argue that this is not a valid reason because if these circumstances are relevant to sentencing they should be revealed in the presentence report of a pleading defendant. A second reason why a defendant who goes to trial may receive a higher sentence is because the judge is convinced he committed perjury in the course of his defense. In *United States v. Grayson*[5] the Supreme Court held that perjury by the defendant has a proper bearing on the sentence to be imposed and that consideration of it by the judge does not infringe upon the defendant's right to testify on his own behalf. More troublesome is a third reason given, that a higher sentence is justified when the defendant has presented a frivolous defense. Some object that a defendant whose punishment has been increased for demanding what the court considers a useless trial is in effect being penalized for asserting his constitutional rights.

Still another approach is to explain the disparity in terms of factors which are likely to call for leniency when a guilty plea is entered. There is considerable disagreement, however, as to the legitimacy of various factors which have been put forward, as may be best seen by examining the list of six factors in the original ABA Standards:[6]

"(i) that the defendant by his plea has aided in ensuring the prompt and certain application of correctional measures to him." Although this factor is fully consistent with the longstanding principle that punishment need not be as severe if it is certain and prompt in application, it has been criticized because of its universal applicability to all guilty pleas. It was omitted from the reformulated Standards on the ground that standing alone this factor is not sufficient to justify lesser punishment.

"(ii) that the defendant has acknowledged his guilt and shown a willingness to assume responsibility for his conduct." This factor is consistent with accepted sentencing criteria, which emphasize the relevance of the attitudes of the defendant and his willingness to assume responsibility for his actions. But its use has been criticized on the ground that because of plea bargaining guilty pleas are often tendered for reasons other than repent-

4. See cases discussed in § 21.2.

5. 438 U.S. 41, 98 S.Ct. 2610, 57 L.Ed.2d 582 (1978).

6. ABA Standards Relating to Pleas of Guilty § 1.8(a)(i) (Approved Draft, 1968).

ance and that it is not feasible to distinguish the truly repentant from those merely bargaining in the marketplace.

"(iii) that the concessions will make possible alternative correctional measures which are better adapted to achieving rehabilitative, protective, deterrent or other purposes of correctional treatment, or will prevent undue harm to the defendant from the form of conviction." Some support this notion that plea bargaining can provide needed flexibility, especially when the judge's sentencing discretion is unduly limited. It has been objected, however, that whatever concessions are appropriate in this respect could be achieved without exacting the plea in exchange for the concession. But sometimes the concession is possible only if there is a plea because it would be unavailable if at a trial the true legal nature of defendant's conduct were established.

"(iv) that the defendant has made public trial unnecessary when there are good reasons for not having the case dealt with in a public trial." Illustrative are cases in which the defendant by his plea has made unnecessary a rape or indecent liberties trial at which the victim would have to testify or an espionage trial at which secret information would have to be disclosed. But there is some authority that this is not a legitimate sentencing consideration.

"(v) that the defendant has given or offered cooperation when such cooperation has resulted or may result in the successful prosecution of other offenders engaged in equally serious or more serious criminal conduct." The notion here is that if complete immunity can be granted in exchange for testimony, as is sometimes essential as a Fifth Amendment matter, then surely "partial immunity" by sentencing concessions is appropriate. It has sometimes been asserted that this is not a factor which can properly be taken into account at sentencing, but the Supreme Court has decided otherwise.[7]

"(vi) that the defendant by his plea has aided in avoiding delay (including delay due to crowded dockets) in the disposition of other cases and thereby has increased the probability of prompt and certain application of correctional measures to other offenders." This factor reflects the view that in localities with a significant court congestion problem, guilty plea defendants as a class make a meaningful contribution toward the attainment of the objectives of the criminal justice system, and thus are entitled to concessions because they have increased both the proximity and probability of punishment for other defendants. But this provision is omitted from the reformulated Standards on the ground that the solution for crowded criminal dockets is the availability of sufficient personnel and other resources.

It has been forcefully argued that plea bargaining is legitimate and noncoercive if and only if it is responsive to a "substantial uncertainty concerning the likely outcome of a trial." As Judge Bazelon explained in *Scott v. United States:*[8]

> Superficially it may seem that even in such a case the defendant who insists upon a trial and is found guilty pays a price for the exercise of his right when he receives a longer sentence than his less venturesome counterpart who pleads guilty. In a sense he has. But the critical distinction is that the price he has paid is not one imposed by the state to discourage others from a similar exercise of their rights, but rather one encountered by those who gamble and lose. After the fact, the defendant who pleads innocent and is convicted receives a heavier sentence. But, by the same token, the defendant who pleads innocent and is acquitted receives no sen-

7. Roberts v. United States, 445 U.S. 552, 100 S.Ct. 1358, 63 L.Ed.2d 622 (1980), where the Court held that the district court properly considered, as one factor in imposing consecutive sentences on a petitioner who had pleaded guilty to two counts of using a telephone to facilitate the distribution of heroin, petitioner's refusal to cooperate with government officials investigating a related criminal conspiracy to distribute heroin in which he was a confessed participant. Citing this provision in the ABA Standards, the majority expressed "doubt that a principled distinction may be drawn between 'enhancing' the punishment imposed upon the petitioner and denying him the 'leniency' he claims would be appropriate if he had cooperated."

8. 419 F.2d 264 (D.C.Cir.1969).

tence. To the extent that the bargain struck reflects only the uncertainty of conviction before trial, the "expected sentence before trial"—length of sentence discounted by probability of conviction—is the same for those who decide to plead guilty and those who hope for acquittal but risk conviction by going to trial.

Whether one accepts or rejects this line of reasoning is likely to depend upon how one views some rather fundamental questions about the plea negotiation process. One such question is that of what kinds of cases are best disposed of by plea and what kinds by trial. Some see plea bargaining as a device to screen out those cases where there is no real dispute, but under the *Scott* approach bargaining would be limited to cases in which "there is a substantial uncertainty concerning the likely outcome of a trial." Under the latter approach, it is objected, trials would tend to be limited to open-and-shut cases. Moreover, if the *Scott* theory is otherwise valid, there is the troublesome question of whether it should make any difference why there is a "substantial uncertainty concerning the likely outcome of a trial"? For example, when the uncertainty is whether the prosecutor has enough evidence to convict, should the tendering of concessions be limited to instances in which guilt is fairly certain but unprovable (e.g., where defendant's accomplice, having made a full, substantiated confession implicating the defendant, cannot now be found) or may it be legitimately extended to cases in which guilt is in real doubt (e.g., where there has been a shaky eyewitness identification of the defendant)?

(f) Other Attributes and Consequences. Even if the plea negotiation process is seen as having certain positive attributes, such as facilitating the processing of criminal cases and permitting needed flexibility in sentencing, there remains the difficult question of whether those attributes are outweighed by certain undesirable consequences of plea bargaining. One of these consequences, it is claimed, is an unhealthy relationship between the prosecutor and defense counsel, especially when the latter is the public defender. A related concern is the effect which plea bargaining has on the criminal defense bar. Some have concluded that the plea negotiation system subjects defense attorneys to serious temptations to disregard their clients' interests. Finally and consequently, there is the fact that plea bargaining often gives the defendant an image of corruption in the system, or at least an image of a system lacking meaningful purpose and subject to manipulation by those who are wise to the right tricks.

(g) Prohibiting Plea Bargaining. In the eyes of some, the practice of plea bargaining as it has developed in this country is undesirable and ought to be abolished entirely. What is not known is whether, assuming the plea negotiation process could be and was entirely eliminated, we would end up with a criminal justice system which is better or worse than we have now. For one thing, it is unclear whether abolition would produce intolerable congestion in the courts and unsatiable demands upon available resources. For another, it is not known whether without any form of plea bargaining to mitigate mandatory or excessive sentencing laws, the dispositions as to some types of criminal defendants would be unduly harsh.

There is a considerable body of thought that it is unnecessary to ponder such matters for the simple reason that it is not possible to abolish plea bargaining. Some believe that though it might be possible to proscribe explicit negotiation between prosecutor, defense attorney, and judge, it would be impossible to proscribe implicit plea bargaining—agreement among all court actors that most guilty defendants should plead guilty and be rewarded for their plea. Some foretell a somewhat different accommodation in a system where plea bargaining is prohibited, such as that there would result increased pre-indictment plea adjustments. The notion is that eliminating discretion at one stage of the process fosters it at others, so that efforts to eliminate plea bargaining will be counterproductive by serving to shift the discretion to some other, less visible stage. Some empirical studies lend support to this thesis.

Some plea bargaining abolitionists believe abolition will work if the system is structured so as to encourage a large volume of jury trial waivers. They see jury waiver bargaining as preferable to plea bargaining because the defendant retains most of his adversary trial rights. For this to be a viable alternative, it must be concluded that the Sixth Amendment right to jury trial is not absolute and thus can be lawfully discouraged by tendering concessions for its surrender. This conclusion finds support in the fact that the present system of plea bargaining has withstood attack even though it involves waiver of jury trial with other rights.

§ 21.2 Kept, Broken, Rejected and Non-existent Bargains

(a) Statutory Inducements to Plead Guilty. One troublesome aspect of the plea negotiation system is the disparity which can result between the sentences imposed upon defendants who plead guilty and those given to defendants who choose to go to trial. But the problem is by no means limited to situations in which bargaining on a case-by-case basis occurs, for it is possible that the disparity will be facilitated or mandated by sentencing laws. This occurs when a sentencing provision requires or allows a certain kind or degree of sentence to be imposed upon a defendant who stands trial, but does not require or allow that same punishment to be inflicted upon another defendant, charged with the same offense, who enters a trial-avoiding plea. Under such a statutory scheme, it may legitimately be asked: (1) whether a defendant who elects to go to trial is being punished to an unconstitutional extent or in an unconstitutional manner; and (2) whether a defendant who elects to forego trial has, by virtue of the statute, entered a coerced and thus involuntary plea.

The first of these issues reached the Supreme Court in *United States v. Jackson,*[1] where a defendant who had not opted to plead guilty challenged the Federal Kidnapping Act because of its provision that the punishment of death could be imposed only "if the verdict of the jury shall so recommend." This meant, the Court noted, that "the defendant who abandons the right to contest his guilt before a jury is assured that he cannot be executed; the defendant ingenuous enough to seek a jury acquittal stands forewarned that, if the jury finds him guilty and does not wish to spare his life, he will die." Because the legitimate goal of this statute, "limiting the death penalty to cases in which a jury recommends it," could be accomplished in other ways, and because the "inevitable effect" of the provision was "to discourage assertion of the Fifth Amendment right not to plead guilty and to deter exercise of the Sixth Amendment right to demand a jury trial," the Court in *Jackson* concluded that the death penalty provision in the statute "needlessly penalizes" the assertion of those constitutional rights and thus was unconstitutional. The Court continued:

> It is no answer to urge, as does the Government, that federal trial judges may be relied upon to reject coerced pleas of guilty and involuntary waivers of jury trial. For the evil in the federal statute is not that it necessarily *coerces* guilty pleas and jury waivers but simply that it needlessly *encourages* them. A procedure need not be inherently coercive in order that it be held to impose an impermissible burden upon the assertion of a constitutional right. Thus the fact that the Federal Kidnaping Act tends to discourage defendants from insisting upon their innocence and demanding trial by jury hardly implies that every defendant who enters a guilty plea to a charge under the Act does so involuntarily. The power to reject coerced guilty pleas and involuntary jury waivers might alleviate, but it cannot totally eliminate, the constitutional infirmity in the capital punishment provision of the Federal Kidnaping Act.

This language suggested, as the Supreme Court subsequently held, that a defendant who challenged a guilty plea entered under such a sentencing scheme would not necessarily prevail. In *Brady v. United States,*[2] a defendant who had entered a guilty plea under this same Act prior to the *Jackson* deci-

§ 21.2

1. 390 U.S. 570, 88 S.Ct. 1209, 20 L.Ed.2d 138 (1968).

2. 397 U.S. 742, 90 S.Ct. 1463, 25 L.Ed.2d 747 (1970).

sion and who had been sentenced to a 30 year term unsuccessfully claimed that his plea was invalid. Declaring that *Jackson* "neither fashioned a new standard for judging the validity of guilty pleas nor mandated a new application of the test theretofore fashioned by courts and since reiterated that guilty pleas are valid if both 'voluntary' and 'intelligent,'" the Court concluded (a) that a guilty plea is not rendered unintelligent merely "because later judicial decision indicate that the plea rested on a faulty premise"; and (b) that a guilty plea is not rendered involuntary "merely because entered to avoid the possibility of a death penalty."

Although *Brady* did not involve a bargained plea in the true sense of that term, it appears that the Court was influenced to some degree by a perceived need to reach a result which would not cast doubts upon the plea negotiation process. The same may be said of the later case of *Corbitt v. New Jersey,*[3] which unlike *Brady* and like *Jackson* involved a defendant who had elected to stand trial. Defendant was tried and convicted of first degree murder and sentenced to the mandatory punishment of life imprisonment. Had he entered a plea of non vult or nolo contendere,[4] then by state law the punishment would have been "either imprisonment for life or the same as that imposed upon a conviction of murder in the second degree," i.e., a term of not more than 30 years. The defendant thus claimed that this scheme was unconstitutional under *Jackson,* but the Court responded that the more recent case of *Bordenkircher v. Hayes*[5] provided the better analogy. For one thing, there were deemed to be "substantial differences between this case and *Jackson*" in that the instant case (a) did not involve the death penalty and (b) did not involve a scheme whereby the maximum penalty was reserved exclusively for those who insisted on a jury trial. For another, the *Corbitt* majority saw "no difference of constitutional significance" between the instant case and *Bordenkircher,* approving a prosecutor's conduct in having defendant charged and convicted as a habitual criminal and subjected to the mandatory sentence of life imprisonment because the defendant refused to plead guilty to the original forgery charge punishable by 2–10 years.[6] Here, as there, the defendant was free to choose either "to go to trial and face the risk of life imprisonment" or to enter a plea which would make possible a lesser penalty.

Lying at the heart of the *Corbitt* decision, it appears, is the debatable assumption that no constitutional distinction can be drawn between the tendering of concessions for pleas as a result of negotiations on a case-by-case basis and the wholesale tendering of concessions by statute. The majority saw both as serving a legitimate function, "the encouragement of guilty defendants not to contest their guilt," and declared that the Court could not permit bargaining by a prosecutor "and yet hold that the legislature may not openly provide for the possibility of leniency in return for a plea." To this, the author of *Bordenkircher*—Justice Stewart—objected that "there is a vast difference between the settlement of litigation through negotiation between counsel for the parties, and a state statute such as is involved in the present case," for the prosecutor "necessarily must be able to settle an adversary criminal lawsuit through plea bargaining with his adversary," while "a state legislature has a quite different function to perform." That is, while it cannot be said that authorizing plea bargaining "needlessly penalizes" the assertion of constitutional rights under the *Jackson* test, it hardly follows, as the *Corbitt* majority assumed, that this statutory scheme "is at the very heart of an effective plea negotiation program." Moreover, as the three *Corbitt* dissenters noted: "In the bargaining process, individual factors relevant to the particular case may be considered by the prosecutor in charging and by the trial judge in sentencing, regardless of the defendant's plea; the process

3. 439 U.S. 212, 99 S.Ct. 492, 58 L.Ed.2d 466 (1978).

4. On the difference between such a plea and a plea of guilty, see § 21.4(a).

5. 434 U.S. 357, 98 S.Ct. 663, 54 L.Ed.2d 604 (1978).

6. For further discussion of this case, see § 21.2(b).

does not mandate a different standard of punishment depending solely on whether or not a plea is entered."

Just how far *Corbitt* undercuts *Jackson* is unclear. The majority cautioned it was not suggesting "that every conceivable statutory sentencing structure" would be constitutional, and upheld the challenged statute because it was "unconvinced" that it "exerts such a powerful influence to coerce inaccurate guilty pleas that it should be deemed constitutionally suspect." Certainly there is such a "powerful influence" when it is the risk of the death penalty, "unique in its severity and irrevocability,"[7] that is involved, but the Court in *Corbitt* denied it was holding "that the *Jackson* rationale is limited to those cases where a plea avoids any possibility of the death penalty being imposed." Lower courts continue to apply *Jackson* even where the death penalty has not been involved.

Corbitt also distinguished *Jackson* because there "any risk of suffering the maximum penalty could be avoided by pleading guilty," but it is debatable whether this ought to be determinative. It is far from apparent that a may/cannot system (i.e., defendant *may* get the maximum if he goes to trial, but *cannot* if he pleads guilty) is more coercive than a must/may system (i.e., defendant *must* get the maximum if he goes to trial, and *may* if he pleads guilty). This is especially true when, as was the case under the New Jersey statute challenged in *Corbitt,* the statutory scheme is accompanied by an established practice of not giving the maximum to a pleading defendant. Moreover, there is a sense in which the must/may system is more pernicious, for under it the price for exercising constitutional rights is the total loss of any chance of sentencing leniency.

The *Corbitt* decision may actually reflect a broader point, namely, that statutory inducements to plead guilty are to be assessed in terms of the extent to which they make the choice between plea and trial determinative and remove discretion from the prosecutor and court.[8] This would mean that Justice Stewart was correct in asserting it would be "clearly unconstitutional" for a state legislature to provide "that the penalty for every criminal offense to which a defendant pleads guilty is to be one-half the penalty to be imposed upon a defendant convicted of the same offense after a not guilty plea."

(b) Inducements by the Prosecutor. The plea bargaining system as it has developed in this country depends not upon such statutory inducements but rather upon inducements frequently put forward by prosecutors in individual cases, a practice not assayed by the Surpeme Court until recently. In *Brady v. United States,*[9] upholding as voluntary and intelligent a guilty plea entered under the statutory scheme found unconstitutional in *Jackson,* the Court cast its decision in terms which appeared calculated to lend support to some forms of plea bargaining:

> We decline to hold, however, that a guilty plea is compelled and invalid under the Fifth Amendment whenever motivated by the defendant's desire to accept the certainty or probability of a lesser penalty rather than face a wider range of possibilities extending from acquittal to conviction and a higher penalty authorized by law for the crime charged.
>
> The issue we deal with is inherent in the criminal law and its administration because guilty pleas are not constitutionally forbidden, because the criminal law characteristically extends to judge or jury a range of choice in setting the sentence in individual cases, and because both the State and the defendant often find it advantageous to preclude the possibility of the maximum penalty authorized by law. For a defendant who sees slight possibility of acquittal, the advantages of pleading guilty and limiting the probable penalty are obvious—his exposure is reduced, the correc-

7. Gregg v. Georgia, 428 U.S. 153, 96 S.Ct. 2909, 49 L.Ed.2d 859 (1976).

8. The *Corbitt* majority emphasized that the statute "leaves much to the judge and to the prosecutor," in that "pleas may be rejected even if tendered" and when accepted "there is discretion to impose life imprisonment," and that as for the defendant who does go to trial it is "true that under normal circumstances, juries in New Jersey may find a defendant guilty of second-degree murder rather than first."

9. 397 U.S. 742, 90 S.Ct. 1463, 25 L.Ed.2d 747 (1970).

tional processes can begin immediately, and the practical burdens of a trial are eliminated. For the State there are also advantages—the more promptly imposed punishment after an admission of guilt may more effectively attain the objectives of punishment; and with the avoidance of trial, scarce judicial and prosecutorial resources are conserved for those cases in which there is a substantial issue of the defendant's guilt or in which there is substantial doubt that the State can sustain its burden of proof. It is this mutuality of advantage which perhaps explains the fact that at present well over three-fourths of the criminal convictions in this country rest on pleas of guilty, a great many of them no doubt motivated at least in part by the hope or assurance of a lesser penalty than might be imposed if there were a guilty verdict after a trial to judge or jury.

Of course, that the prevalence of guilty pleas is explainable does not necessarily validate those pleas or the system which produces them. But we cannot hold that it is unconstitutional for the State to extend a benefit to a defendant who in turn extends a substantial benefit to the State and who demonstrates by his plea that he is ready and willing to admit his crime and to enter the correctional system in a frame of mind which affords hope for success in rehabilitation over a shorter period of time than might otherwise be necessary.

That theme was sounded by the Court on other occasions, but again in circumstances where the prosecutor's bargaining tactics were not directly at issue.[10] Moreover, the Court gave no indication it was extending wholesale approval to all forms of prosecutorial inducements. In *Brady,* for example, the Court spoke approvingly only of the prosecutor allowing the defendant "to plead guilty to a lesser offense included in the offense charged" or "with the understanding that other charges will be dropped," but indicated a guilty plea could not stand if "induced by threats (or promises to discontinue improper harassment), misrepresentation (including unfulfilled or unfulfillable promises), or perhaps by promises that are by their nature improper as having no proper relationship to the prosecutor's business (e.g., bribes)."

But this left unsettled exactly where the line should be drawn between the permissible tender of concessions and impermissible "threats." What if the prosecutor confronted the defendant with dramatically different punishment consequences depending upon whether or not he entered a guilty plea? What if the prosecutor indicated that failure of the defendant to plead guilty would result in the filing of more serious charges against the defendant? Such were the issues in *Bordenkircher v. Hayes,*[11] for there the prosecutor carried out his threat that if the defendant did not plead guilty to the existing charge of uttering a forged instrument, punishable by two to 10 years, he would be indicted under the Habitual Criminal Act, which would subject defendant to a mandatory sentence of life imprisonment by reason of his two prior felony convictions. On federal habeas corpus, the court of appeals had held that defendant's prosecution and conviction under that Act violated the principles of *Blackledge v. Perry,*[12] where a prosecutor's escalation of charges against a defendant who had exercised his right to appeal was held to violate due process because there was a "realistic likelihood of 'vindictiveness' " in such circumstances.[13]

The Supreme Court, in a 5—4 decision, reversed the court of appeals. The majority reasoned that while in *Blackledge* and related cases "the Court was dealing with the State's unilateral imposition of a penalty upon a defendant who had chosen to exercise a legal right to attack his original conviction," that situation was "very different from the give-and-take negotiation common in plea bargaining between the prosecution and the defense, which arguably possess relatively equal bargaining power." In the latter circumstances, the Court asserted, "there is no such element

10. E.g., Blackledge v. Allison, 431 U.S. 63, 97 S.Ct. 1621, 52 L.Ed.2d 136 (1977); Santobello v. New York, 404 U.S. 257, 92 S.Ct. 495, 30 L.Ed.2d 427 (1971).

11. 434 U.S. 357, 98 S.Ct. 663, 54 L.Ed.2d 604 (1978).

12. 417 U.S. 21, 94 S.Ct. 2098, 40 L.Ed.2d 628 (1974).

13. For further discussion of this principle, see § 13.-5(a).

of punishment or retaliation so long as the accused is free to accept or reject the prosecution's offer." And consequently, the Court concluded, "the course of conduct engaged in by the prosecutor in this case, which no more than openly presented the defendant with the unpleasant alternatives of foregoing trial or facing charges on which he was plainly subject to prosecution, did not violate the Due Process Clause of the Fourteenth Amendment." The majority treated this result as a foregone conclusion in light of the Court's earlier favorable words concerning the institution of plea bargaining. Because "acceptance of the basic legitimacy of plea bargaining necessarily implies rejection of any notion that a guilty plea is involuntary in a constitutional sense simply because it is the end result of the bargaining process," it was said by way of explanation, it "follows that, by tolerating and encouraging the negotiation of pleas, this Court has necessarily accepted as constitutionally legitimate the simple reality that the prosecutor's interest at the bargaining table is to persuade the defendant to forego his right to plead not guilty."

Given the fact that this left the defendant with the life sentence he had received for failing to plead guilty to a charge carrying a 10 year maximum, the Court's decision in *Bordenkircher* is, at best, unsettling. The tensions which contributed to this troublesome result can best be seen by considering the alternative courses which the Court might have taken. One, that taken by the court below and urged by three of the dissenting Justices, is that the original charge should be presumed to reflect the prosecutor's judgment of what would be an appropriate disposition in the case, so that in the event of a subsequent enhancement of the charge the prosecutor would have to justify his action on some basis other than discouraging the defendant from exercising his constitutional rights. But as the dissenters acknowledged, such a ruling "merely would prompt the aggressive prosecutor to bring the greater charge initially in every case, and only thereafter to bargain." They went on to note that the "consequences to the accused would still be adverse, for then he would bargain against a greater charge, face the likelihood of increased bail, and run the risk that the court would be less inclined to accept a bargained plea."

Judicial scrutiny of the motives underlying even initial charging decisions, particularly with a view to determining whether the charges brought were filed to gain bargaining leverage, is not feasible either. "Normally," the *Bordenkircher* dissenters observed, "it is impossible to show that this is what the prosecutor is doing, and the courts necessarily have deferred to the prosecutor's exercise of discretion in initial charging decisions." Moreover, if, as the dissenters seem to suggest, "a prosecutor ought not to bring charges more serious than he thinks 'appropriate for the ultimate disposition of a case' without any consideration of plea bargaining leverage," then there would be little meaningful bargaining, for the only way to induce a plea would be for the prosecutor to accept a plea at a level *below* what the prosecutor thinks appropriate for the ultimate disposition of the case.

A third approach to the *Bordenkircher* situation would focus upon sentences which technically lie within the legal range of sentence options but violate our sense of fairness. Perhaps the most disturbing part of the case is the extreme severity of the sentence under the circumstances. As Justice Powell noted in his separate dissent: "Although respondent's prior convictions brought him within the terms of the Habitual Criminal Act, the offenses themselves did not result in imprisonment; yet the addition of a conviction on a charge involving $88.30 subjected respondent to a mandatory sentence of imprisonment for life. Persons convicted of rape and murder often are not punished so severely." But for the Court to take on this issue would involve the judiciary in the sensitive and difficult task of making judgments about the constitutionality of legislative action in setting the permissible range of imprisonment for a variety of offenses. The Court is understandably reluctant to go this route, as is illustrated by the more recent decision in *Rummel v. Es-*

telle.[14]

Still a fourth approach would be to view the prosecutor's conduct in *Bordenkircher* as outside the boundaries of permissible plea bargaining tactics because of the degree of leverage utilized by him. This is where Justice Powell came out; he was prepared to intrude upon the prosecutor's bargaining discretion only "in the most exceptional case," and he found the instant case to fall within this limited exception because the prosecutor proceeded "to penalize with unique severity [the defendant's] exercise of constitutional rights." The Court's reluctance to take on this issue is also understandable, for it would have been almost impossible for the Court to articulate how great a sentence differential was too great. A holding that the difference in *Bordenkircher* was excessive thus might have plunged the Court into a review of innumerable other sentences that defendants had received after rejecting prosecutorial offers of lenient treatment in exchange for pleas of guilty.

Understandably, the *Bordenkircher* case has been treated as encompassing all of the typical charge bargain situations, where the prosecutor offers to allow the defendant to plead guilty to a lesser offense or a lesser number of offenses than originally charged or to plead guilty to the original charge and thus escape charges for other crimes or a charge of a higher degree of offense than originally charged. Presumably *Bordenkircher* also extends to the prosecutor's involvement in sentence bargaining, though it is well to note that in *Brady* the Court expressly declined to give approval to a situation in which the defendant is "threatened * * * with a harsher sentence if convicted after trial in order to induce him to plead guilty."[15] But, as a practical matter, that was the effect of what the prosecutor was allowed to do in *Bordenkircher.*

Bordenkircher should not be read as declaring that a defendant who refuses to plead guilty and then is convicted on added charges is never entitled to relief. The Court emphasized that it did not have before it a case "where the prosecutor without notice brought an additional and more serious charge after plea negotiations relating only to the original indictment had ended with the defendant's insistence on pleading not guilty," and the holding in the case was stated in terms of the prosecutor having "openly presented the defendant with the unpleasant alternatives" he faced. This suggests that if the prosecutor fails to tell the defendant that there is a price attached to his refusal to plead guilty or only makes an unspecified threat of increased criminal liability, so that defendant has no means by which to weigh the potential liabilities of that refusal, the prosecutor might be barred from thereafter upping the ante because the defendant refuses to plead guilty.

Another way to look at *Bordenkircher* is to ask what significance the case has, if any, in a situation where the defendant *does* plead guilty. That is, what if the defendant in that case, upon being confronted with the prospect of life imprisonment from an added charge under the Habitual Criminal Act, had entered a guilty plea to the forgery charge and then later challenged that plea as coerced? Strictly speaking, *Bordenkircher* should not be viewed as foreclosing a finding of involuntariness, for the Court was only addressing the vindictive prosecution issue raised by a defendant who did not give in to the pressure. Yet, a reading of *Bordenkircher* with *Brady* indicates the defendant is not likely to prevail. The former case establishes that the prosecu-

14. 445 U.S. 263, 100 S.Ct. 1133, 63 L.Ed.2d 382 (1980), reversing 568 F.2d 1193 (5th Cir.1978), striking down, as imposing cruel and unusual punishment, a Texas habitual criminal statute which required the trial court to sentence a defendant to life imprisonment upon a third conviction for any felony. The court of appeals pointed out that each of the offenses committed by the defendant was solely a property crime and the amounts taken were not substantial, that no legislative judgment that Texas could achieve its penalogical objectives only by imposing a life sentence on such a defendant was discernible, and that life imprisonment was too harsh a punishment compared with the statutory punishments for violent felonies, for which Texas does not bind the court's hands in granting leniency.

15. However, this reference was to a threat by "the trial judge," which might be viewed differently. See § 21.2(c).

tor's conduct does not involve an improper threat or promise, and the latter seems to say that in such circumstances the plea is voluntary if the defendant was aware of "the actual value of any commitments made to him." But that phrase, together with the strong emphasis in *Bordenkircher* upon the prosecutor having charging discretion "so long as the prosecutor has probable cause," indicates the defendant's attack would be strengthened if the threatened charge in fact could not have been brought.

Bordenkircher should not be read as manifesting approval of any type of threat or promise made by the prosecutor in a plea bargaining context. In a footnote the Court cautioned that the case did not "involve the constitutional implications of a prosecutor's offer during plea bargaining of adverse or lenient treatment for some person *other* than the accused, which might pose a greater danger of inducing a false guilty plea by skewing the assessment of the risks a defendant must consider." It has been forcefully argued that such inducements present a special risk that an innocent defendant will plead guilty and that a guilty defendant will receive treatment that does not meet his correctional needs, but the courts have rather consistently held that there is no intrinsic infirmity in broadening plea negotiations to permit third party beneficiaries. However, guilty pleas made in consideration of lenient treatment to third persons pose a greater danger of coercion than purely bilateral plea bargaining and thus deserve close scrutiny.

A prosecutor's bargaining tactics may come under attack because of commitments exacted from the defendant in addition to the guilty plea. Illustrative is a plea bargain which included a promise by defendant to leave the state for ten years, a commitment held unenforceable because contrary to public policy; or one which included a promise by defendant not to testify in favor of a codefendant, unenforceable because a violation of the codefendant's right to compulsory process. Courts are not in agreement concerning a prosecutor-induced commitment by the defendant not to take an appeal. One view is that such a bargain is a proper method of making a plea agreement enforceable, while another treats the right to appeal as non-negotiable because otherwise plea bargains could be insulated from appellate review. A middle view is that such a waiver is neither inherently coercive nor fully enforceable, so that a defendant remains free to file a timely appeal, which relieves the state of its part of the bargain.

(c) Inducements by the Judge. As discussed later,[16] there exists a considerable difference of opinion as to how the plea negotiation process should be structured in terms of judicial involvement, and in particular with whether it is better that the judge participate directly in negotiation sessions or remain completely aloof from them. Some jurisdictions have adopted the latter position; the federal rule is that the "court shall not participate in any such discussions,"[17] and several states are in accord. If in one of those jurisdictions a defendant brings his guilty plea into question by showing that it was preceded by some inducements from the judge, the case might well be disposed of in the defendant's favor without any determination of whether the judge's involvement in the particular case was so extreme as to make the plea involuntary. That is, it might well be concluded that this absolute prohibition upon judicial involvement can best be enforced by permitting a defendant to withdraw his plea without first showing that actual prejudice resulted from the judge's participation.

In a jurisdiction not taking that view, the question then to be considered is whether the nature and circumstances of the judge's participation was such that the defendant's plea was coerced and thus invalid. The generally accepted view is that such participation, in and of itself, does not require setting a guilty plea aside as a constitutional matter. Rather, there must be a more particularized assessment of the individual case, during which the

16. See § 21.3(d).

17. Fed.R.Crim.P. 11(e)(1).

trial judge's participation in the plea bargaining process must be carefully scrutinized.

There remains considerable uncertainty, however, as to exactly what kind of involvement by the judge will make the defendant's plea involuntary. The Supreme Court has not had occasion to address the issue directly, though in *Brady v. United States,*[18] indicating approval of prosecutor bargaining, the Court in a cautionary footnote observed that those remarks were not intended to encompass a case "where the prosecutor or judge, or both, deliberately employ their charging and sentencing powers to induce a particular defendant to tender a plea of guilty." Of course, the Court has since approved such action by the prosecutor,[19] but it is unclear whether that has any significance as to judicial involvement. One view is that judicial participation has a substantially different effect than negotiations between the parties because of the unequal positions of the judge and the accused and the judge's awesome power to impose a substantially longer or even maximum sentence if the defendant rejects the court's proposal. In response, it may be argued that this assertion is inconsistent with the Supreme Court's teachings as to what is a voluntary plea,[20] and also with the fact that because the prosecutor has many means not available to the judge of putting pressure upon the defendant, this disparity of positions may be even greater between prosecutor and defendant.

Examination of the decisions assessing the voluntariness of a plea entered subsequent to some judicial involvement in the negotiation process sheds some light on the factors which may influence a determination that the plea is or is not valid. Certainly the defendant's plea cannot be upheld where the judge significantly overstated the defendant's predicament were he to stand trial, as where the judge erroneously indicated that in such circumstances he would have no choice but to sentence defendant to prison. Also, a plea is likely to be held involuntary where the judge was the moving force in pressing for a guilty plea after defendant had manifested a desire not to so plead or where the judge indicated conviction at trial was a foregone conclusion. On the other hand, the judge's involvement is not likely to be deemed coercive where the bargaining was not initiated by the judge, where the judge merely said he would abide by the agreement previously reached by the parties, or where the judge only suggested a compromise position between the different sentencing proposals of the defendant and prosecutor.

Assume now a different scenario, one in which again there has been judicial involvement in the bargaining process (e.g., a promise of a 5-year sentence if defendant pleads guilty) but the defendant elected to stand trial, was convicted, and then received a more severe sentence (e.g., a 7-year sentence). Even if we are prepared to say that this defendant's plea would have been voluntary had he accepted the judge's proposal, it does not necessarily follow that the defendant in the above scenario lacks a valid constitutional claim, for the Supreme Court in a related context has made it unmistakably clear that the two situations are different and necessitate different analysis.[21] In the above scenario (or, indeed, even when the judge was not involved at all in the bargaining but at sentencing so explained his harsh sentence [22]), the defendant's argument will be that these events amount to a violation of due process because of the vindictiveness—or, at least, the appearance of vindictiveness—against the defendant for his exercise of his constitutional right to stand trial. So the argument goes, if, as the Supreme Court held in *North Carolina*

18. 397 U.S. 742, 90 S.Ct. 1463, 25 L.Ed.2d 747 (1970).

19. Bordenkircher v. Hayes, 434 U.S. 357, 98 S.Ct. 663, 54 L.Ed.2d 604 (1978).

20. Brady v. United States, 397 U.S. 742, 90 S.Ct. 1463, 25 L.Ed.2d 747 (1970), asserting that a plea of guilty is generally to be deemed voluntary if "entered by one fully aware of the direct consequences, including the actual value of any commitments made to him by the court."

21. See the discussion of the *Jackson* and *Brady* cases in § 21.2(a).

22. In re Lewallen, 23 Cal.3d 274, 152 Cal.Rptr. 528, 590 P.2d 383 (1979).

v. Pearce,[23] due process "requires that vindictiveness against a defendant for having successfully attacked his first conviction must play no part in the sentence he receives after a new trial," then surely the same is true as to a defendant's exercise of a constitutional right.

That argument, of course, bears a distinct similarity to that made with respect to prosecutorial inducements and rejected by the Supreme Court in *Bordenkircher v. Hayes.*[24] The defendant's position there was that if, as the Court had previously held,[25] the prosecutor could not ordinarily escalate the charges after defendant had exercised his right to appeal, then he likewise could not do so after defendant had rejected the prosecutor's plea inducements and exercised his constitutional right to trial. But, as we have seen,[26] the Court declined to apply the vindictiveness concept to plea negotiations, reasoning that "in the 'give-and-take' of plea bargaining, there is no such element of punishment or retaliation so long as the accused is free to accept or reject the prosecution's offer."

Whether that analysis carries over to cases of judicial involvement is a matter on which there is a difference of opinion, as is revealed by the en banc decision in *Frank v. Blackburn.*[27] Prior to and during defendant's state trial the trial judge conducted plea bargaining sessions in his chambers at which he stated the sentence would be 20 years if defendant were to plead guilty, but defendant rejected those offers and was convicted of armed robbery, after which the judge sentenced him to a term of 33 years. On federal habeas corpus, a majority of the court of appeals read *Bordenkircher* as making "it clear that a state is free to encourage guilty pleas by offering substantial benefits to a defendant, or by threatening an accused with more severe punishment should a negotiated plea be refused," necessitating the finding that "the rule of *North Carolina v. Pearce* [is] completely inapplicable to post-plea bargain sentencing proceedings." But the dissenters in *Frank* reasoned that *Bordenkircher* had merely declined to apply the vindictiveness doctrine to plea bargaining between the parties because a contrary result would have, in effect, foreclosed what the Court had repeatedly said was a necessary aspect of the criminal process. Judicial participation, they reasoned, had no such credentials and thus was not equally deserving of exemption from the *Pearce* rule. The dissenters also noted that the opinion in *Bordenkircher* had been carefully crafted to make it unmistakably clear that it did not extend to judicial involvement. Specifically, the Supreme Court emphasized that the *Pearce* rule had been applied in situations "very different from the give-and-take negotiations common in plea bargaining between the prosecution and the defense, which arguably possess relatively equal bargaining power." It is not surprising, therefore, that there exists post-*Bordenkircher* authority applying the *Pearce* rule to judicial sentencing activity having the appearance of vindictiveness in relation to defendant's exercise of his constitutional right to trial.

Even assuming the majority is correct in *Frank,* there remains here (as with prosecutorial inducements) the troublesome question of whether certain inducements are improper simply because of the substantial disparity in the contemplated disposition depending upon whether the defendant opts to plead guilty or go to trial. In the *Frank* case, for example, one might well ask what legitimate objective of the plea bargaining system is served by a sentencing differential of 13 years. An even more dramatic illustration is provided by *People v. Dennis,*[28] where the judge offered defendant a term of either 2–4 or 2–6 years if he would plead guilty, the defendant elected to stand trial and was convicted, and that judge then sentenced him to a term of 40–80 years. The appellate court, noting that the judge at sentencing had before him no relevant facts of

23. 395 U.S. 711, 89 S.Ct. 2072, 23 L.Ed.2d 656 (1969).

24. 434 U.S. 357, 98 S.Ct. 663, 54 L.Ed.2d 604 (1978).

25. Blackledge v. Perry, 417 U.S. 21, 94 S.Ct. 2098, 40 L.Ed.2d 628 (1974).

26. See § 21.2(b).

27. 646 F.2d 873 (5th Cir.1980).

28. 28 Ill.App.3d 74, 328 N.E.2d 135 (1975).

which he had been unaware at the time of his plea offer, reduced defendant's sentence to 6–18 years. As one critic asked, does this mean "that a defendant may be penalized for exercising his right to trial by a sentence three times more severe than that he could have secured by pleading guilty, but not by a sentence twenty times more severe"? [29] Certainly this is an important question, central to the entire plea negotiation process, but it is one that courts are understandably reluctant to address.

(d) The Broken Bargain. In *Santobello v. New York,*[30] the Supreme Court ruled that it was constitutionally impermissible to hold a defendant to his negotiated plea when the promises upon which it was based were not performed. The defendant in that case entered a guilty plea to a lesser included offense upon the prosecutor's promise to make no recommendation as to sentence, but at the sentencing hearing some months later that prosecutor's successor recommended the maximum sentence, which the judge imposed. After speaking approvingly of the plea negotiation system, the Court concluded:

> This phase of the process of criminal justice, and the adjudicative element inherent in accepting a plea of guilty, must be attended by safeguards to insure the defendant what is reasonably due in the circumstances. Those circumstances will vary, but a constant factor is that when a plea rests in any significant degree on a promise or agreement of the prosecutor, so that it can be said to be part of the inducement or consideration, such promise must be fulfilled.

The Court in *Santobello* thus remanded the case to the state court for a determination of whether the defendant should be given the relief he sought, withdrawal of his plea, or whether instead he should be granted specific performance by resentencing before another judge.

The first step in applying the *Santobello* rule is to determine if promises were made and, if so, precisely what they were. If the plea agreement is ambiguous, then courts are inclined to apply the law of contracts to resolve the ambiguity. However, because the defendant's "contract" right is constitutionally based, the prosecution is held to a greater degree of responsibility than the defendant for ambiguities, especially when the prosecutor has proffered the terms or prepared a written agreement.

One kind of promise is a commitment by the prosecutor that he will recommend or at least not oppose a particular sentence sought by the defendant. If the prosecutor does recommend or not oppose that sentence but the judge imposes a more severe sentence, the defendant is not entitled to relief under *Santobello,* for the promise to seek or not oppose the lesser sentence has been kept. However, some jurisdictions as a matter of state law have adopted the contrary position, apparently on the assumption that there is an element of unfairness in holding the defendant to his plea when there was such uncertainty as to the actual result.

If as a part of the plea agreement the prosecutor has promised to recommend a particular disposition, then certainly there has been a broken bargain if the prosecutor fails to make that recommendation or makes a contrary recommendation. Some lower courts had held that such agreements include an implied promise of effective advocacy of the recommendation which, should it not occur, would also entitle the defendant to relief. But in *United States v. Benchimol,*[31] where the prosecutor engaged in no advocacy of and gave no reason for his promised probation recommendation, the Supreme Court rejected the court of appeals' conclusion that there had been a breach. It "was error," said the Court, "for the Court of Appeals to imply as a matter of law a term which the parties themselves did not agree upon." The Court in *Benchimol* emphasized that the instant case was not one in which the government had made an express commitment either to make the recommendation enthusiastically or to

29. Alschuler, The Trial Judge's Role in Plea Bargaining, Part I, 76 Colum.L.Rev. 1059, 1134 (1976).

30. 404 U.S. 257, 92 S.Ct. 495, 30 L.Ed.2d 427 (1971).

31. 471 U.S. 453, 105 S.Ct. 2103, 85 L.Ed.2d 462 (1985).

state reasons for it, and distinguished those lower court cases in which "the Government attorney appearing personally in court at the time of the plea bargain expressed personal reservations about the agreement to which the Government had committed itself."

If, on the other hand, the plea bargain was that the prosecutor would not recommend a sentence or would not oppose defendant's recommendations, it may be claimed that the prosecutor did too much. Certainly if the prosecutor promised to make no recommendation, there is a breach of the agreement when the prosecutor later recommends that the defendant be given the maximum possible sentence. By contrast, it is generally accepted that a promise of this limited nature is not broken merely by the prosecutor's conduct in supplying relevant facts at the sentencing hearing. But if the prosecutor has entered into a broader commitment, stated in terms of remaining silent or taking no position whatsoever with regard to the sentence, this may be construed as meaning that the prosecutor is barred from volunteering any information detrimental to the defendant. However, there is a disinclination to interpret such promises as commitments to remain silent under all circumstances, and thus it has been held that the prosecutor is free to speak for the purpose of correcting misstatements by the defense or in response to a question from the court, and that he is likewise free to follow his customary practice of responding to requests from the probation office for information on defendant's background and character to be included in the presentence report.

If the prosecutor has made a promise to recommend or not oppose a certain sentence, the question may arise whether that commitment extends beyond the sentencing hearing and imposition of sentence. For example, if the prosecutor kept that promise at the sentencing hearing but nonetheless the judge imposed a higher sentence than was sought by the defendant, is the prosecutor bound to maintain the same posture if the defendant thereafter moves for a reduction in sentence? This depends upon what the parties to the plea bargain reasonably understood to be the terms of the agreement. A promise not to oppose a certain lenient sentence might well be construed as creating in the defendant's mind a reasonable expectation that the benefits of that promise would be available throughout the proceedings, including the hearing on defendant's motion to reduce the sentence. But the same might not be true where the prosecutor's promise was to make no recommendation or to make a particular recommendation.

In the case of charge bargaining, where the defendant enters a guilty plea to a lesser charge or fewer charges than originally brought, the more obvious type of broken bargain situation rarely occurs because typically the more serious or additional charges are dismissed at the very time of defendant's plea. But defendants sometimes claim a violation of the *Santobello* rule when either the court or parole agency takes into account an aspect of defendant's conduct encompassed within a charge dropped pursuant to a plea bargain. Illustrative is a case in which the negotiated plea was to robbery in lieu of the original charge of armed robbery, but at sentencing the judge considered the fact that the defendant had been armed. In these and like circumstances, courts have consistently held that there has been no breaking of the plea bargain. It is emphasized that these facts have obvious and direct relevance to the matters to be decided, so that it would be detrimental to the sentencing and parole release processes if it were necessary to disregard them totally. Moreover, permitting their use is deemed not inconsistent with the terms of the agreement, as a bargain which involves dropping charges is attractive to a defendant primarily because the total length of time to which he can be sentenced is reduced.

Some authority is to be found to the effect that a defendant may be disentitled from prevailing on a broken bargain claim because of his own misconduct. One type of situation is that in which the defendant was able to obtain a promise of concessions by misrepresenting the material facts. Thus, it has been held that where a defendant claiming to have no prior convictions was promised probation but it was later determined he had an out-of-state felony conviction, making him ineligible for probation as a matter of state law, a sentence of imprisonment was properly imposed on the basis of the guilty plea. (If the defendant enters a plea to a lesser offense before his misrepresentation is discovered, some courts treat this as a "misplea," a guilty plea equivalent of a "mistrial" which permits the plea to be rescinded and the higher charge reinstated.) A second situation is that in which additional criminal conduct by the defendant occurs prior to the time of sentencing, which has been held to be a sufficient change in circumstances to justify the State in retreating from the promised recommendation. Certainly the defendant should not be entitled to enforce the bargain in this latter situation, but it is less apparent that permitting withdrawal of the plea would be inappropriate.

Yet another variation of the changed circumstances problem is that in *State v. Thomas,*[32] where the defendant was initially charged with atrocious assault and battery, assault with intent to rob, and robbery of one Murray. A negotiated plea was entered to the first count in exchange for the prosecutor's promise to dismiss the remaining counts, and they were subsequently dropped, but after Thomas died the defendant was charged with murder. On defendant's motion to dismiss, the court ruled that under the collateral estoppel rule of *Ashe v. Swenson*[33] the defendant could not be prosecuted on a felony-murder theory. The court reasoned that the "dismissal of the two counts must be treated as a general verdict of acquittal" and that "two issues can be deemed already litigated and decided—defendant did not assault Fannie Murray with intent to rob her nor did he rob her." But this analysis is faulty. Collateral estoppel, as defined in *Ashe,* "means simply that when an issue of ultimate fact has once been determined by a valid and final judgment, that issue cannot again be litigated between the same parties in any future lawsuit," but the dynamics of plea bargaining are such that the dropping of the two counts can hardly be said to rest upon a factual determination that the defendant did not commit the robbery or assault with intent to rob. Moreover, even the concurring Justices in *Ashe,* who preferred a considerably broader rule, acknowledged that any double jeopardy requirement that related crimes be disposed of together did not apply "where a crime is not completed or not discovered, despite diligence on the part of the police, until after the commencement of a prosecution for other crimes arising from the same transaction."

Finally, mention must be made of the case in which the government is relieved of the obligation to carry out its promise because the defendant failed to carry out some obligation under the plea agreement beyond entering the plea. Illustrative is *United States v. Simmons,*[34] where part of the agreement was that the government would recommend a sentence of 15 years "in exchange for the defendants' full, complete, and truthful cooperation regarding this bank robbery." The court held that "in a plea bargain the government's obligation to make a recommendation arises only if defendant performs his obligation (in this instance, full disclosure)," but then added the important caveat that under *Santobello* "the question whether defendant did in fact fail to perform the condition precedent is an issue not to be finally determined unilaterally by the government, but only on the basis of adequate evidence by the Court."

The defendant may not escape the consequences of his nonperformance merely because the quid pro quo was a concession already given up by the prosecution, such as allowing the defendant to enter a plea to a lesser offense. In *Ricketts v. Adamson,*[35] where defendant, charged with first degree murder, was allowed to plead guilty to second degree murder in exchange for his promise to testify against his confederates, and the agreement specified that if defendant refused to testify "this entire agreement is null and void and the original charge will be automati-

32. 114 N.J.Super. 360, 276 A.2d 391 (1971).

33. 397 U.S. 436, 90 S.Ct. 1189, 25 L.Ed.2d 469 (1970).

34. 537 F.2d 1260 (4th Cir.1976).

35. 483 U.S. 1, 107 S.Ct. 2680, 97 L.Ed.2d 1 (1987).

cally reinstated" and the parties "returned to the positions they were in before this agreement," the Court held there was no double jeopardy barrier to vacating the second degree murder conviction and prosecuting defendant for first degree murder. This is because "the Double Jeopardy Clause * * * does not relieve a defendant from the consequences of his voluntary choice."[36] Though that conclusion is not objectionable, the manner in which the Court applied it in *Ricketts* is troublesome. The defendant *did* testify against his confederates and they were convicted, but after their convictions were reversed he refused to testify a second time on the not totally implausible contention that he had already fulfilled completely his part of the bargain.[37] Once the state supreme court ruled defendant's construction of the agreement was in error, defendant offered to testify in the pending retrial of his confederates, but the prosecution rejected that offer in favor of prosecuting defendant for first degree murder. As the four dissenters cogently reasoned, the "logic of the plea bargaining system requires acknowledgment and protection of the defendant's right to advance against the State a reasonable interpretation of the plea agreement." Thus, if the defendant and state disagree as to how the agreement is to be interpreted, the state should not be allowed to treat this as a breach by the defendant permitting the state to revoke the agreement; rather, at that point "either party may seek to have the agreement construed by the court in which the plea was entered." In light of *Ricketts,* defense counsel would be well advised to insist that plea agreements of this type include an express provision mandating judicial construction of it in the event of a disagreement.

(e) Remedy for Broken Bargain. Assuming now a broken bargain which is not excused because of the defendant's misconduct or subsequent events, the next question concerns the relief to which the defendant is entitled. This is a matter of some uncertainty, for while the Supreme Court was unequivocal in ruling in *Santobello v. New York*[38] that there was a constitutional right to relief, that decision is less explicit on the constitutional source of that right and on what remedy is required under what circumstances. The opinion of the Court, joined in by three Justices, makes reference to the requirement that guilty pleas be "knowing and voluntary" and says defendant was entitled to relief in the "interests of justice." The choice of remedy was left to the state court in the first instance, but there is an unexplained intimation that either specific performance or plea withdrawal might be "required" by the "circumstances of the case." Justice Douglas, concurring, indicated that the choice of remedy was itself a constitutional matter, and he asserted that the defendant's preference should be given "considerable, if not controlling, weight." The three remaining members of the Court[39] were no more certain as to the source of the right. They claimed that a breaking of the bargain constitutes "ample justification for rescinding the plea" if the defendant wishes and that if he prefers "it may be appropriate to permit the defendant to enforce the plea bargain."

As for the source of the right, most certainly it is not the requirement that guilty pleas be voluntary, for without regard to subsequent events a plea is either voluntary or involuntary at the time it is made. Perhaps the source is the constitutional requirement that guilty pleas be intelligent, for that requirement reflects the notion that the defendant has a constitutional interest in making an informed choice and that the state cannot mislead the defendant into making a disadvantageous choice. But if this is all there is

36. Quoting from and analogizing to United States v. Scott, discussed in § 25.3(a).

37. As the dissenters noted, that was not an unreasonable interpretation of the agreement because it referred to defendant being sentenced "at the conclusion of his testimony" and remaining in the sheriff's custody "until the conclusion of his testimony," but by the time the state demanded defendant's testimony on retrial the defendant had been sentenced and was no longer in the sheriff's custody.

38. 404 U.S. 257, 92 S.Ct. 495, 30 L.Ed.2d 427 (1971).

39. The Supreme Court had only seven members sitting at the time of the decision.

to *Santobello,* then the intimation therein that a particular remedy might be required in certain unspecified circumstances cannot be taken seriously. By affording the defendant an opportunity to choose again on the basis of accurate information, the court fully protects the defendant's opportunity to make a meaningful choice, while the remedy of specific performance gives the defendant the full benefit of his original choice and thus suffices to vindicate his constitutional interest in deciding what course is best. This suggests another interpretation of the case: that it extends constitutional protection to the personal expectations created in defendants by plea agreements, on the notion that it is fundamentally unfair for the state to create and then destroy a defendant's expectations.

Although federal courts finding a *Santobello* violation on habeas corpus by a state prisoner must ordinarily give the state court the opportunity to decide which remedy is more appropriate, federal courts ruling on claims by federal prisoners and state courts ruling on claims of state defendants rather regularly opt for the remedy of specific performance. This may be taken as some support for the protection-of-expectations theory noted above, which would generally call for such a remedy, or it may only reflect that these courts have perceived that as a policy matter specific performance is usually the most appropriate remedy, one which serves the state's interest in the continued vitality of the process of plea negotiation. Whichever is the case, clearly specific performance is usually the remedy to be preferred, which may be seen by a closer look at two situations: that in which the defendant's preference for vacatur of the plea is contested; and that in which his preference for specific performance is challenged.

Assume first a case in which the plea bargain was not kept and consequently the defendant asks that he be allowed to withdraw his plea, but the prosecution counters that withdrawal should not be permitted because it is prepared to carry out the remedy of specific performance. Four members of the Court in *Santobello* appeared to conclude that in such circumstances withdrawal of the plea and trial on the original charges[40] should be ordered, but their explanations for this conclusion are less than compelling. Justice Douglas offered only the non sequitur that because it is the defendant's rights which were violated it must be the defendant's choice of remedy which is given preference, while the three dissenters asserted that the breaking of the bargain "undercuts the basis for the waiver of constitutional rights implicit in the plea" and thus allows those rights to be reclaimed by the defendant. But whether the constitutional basis for *Santobello* is to protect defendants from entering guilty pleas that are not intelligent or to enforce their state-created expectations, the defendant need not be given an option to rescind if the state agrees to give him the benefit of the original bargain. Both the intelligent-plea interest and the protection-of-expectations interest can be satisfied by specific performance because it gives the defendant everything on which he relied in entering the plea.

Although some authority is to be found supporting the proposition that the defendant is entitled to elect the remedy of recision, these cases do not indicate that the prosecutor had any objection. It has also been held that there is no right to the remedy of plea withdrawal, and on remand in *Santobello* the court ruled such a remedy was inappropriate where the prosecution objected because due process and the interest of justice would be fully served by specific performance of the prosecutor's promise. The court emphasized that the facts of the case did not produce an "outraged sense of fairness," perhaps a reference to the inadvertence of the prosecution's noncompliance. From this, it might be argued that in the case of a deliberate breaking of the plea agreement by the prosecutor it would be justifiable to "punish" the prosecutor by allowing the defendant to withdraw the plea if he wishes, for a belated specific per-

40. On the question of whether, after plea withdrawal, trial on the previously dismissed charges is permissible, see § 21.5(e).

formance only requires the prosecutor to do what he had agreed to do in the first place. But because in most cases the state's breach is either inadvertent or arguably justified by some change in circumstances, this punishment theory would be useful in a relatively few cases and might not be worth the added burden of a specific determination regarding the character of the prosecutor's conduct.

Assume now the reverse situation, where again the plea bargain was not kept but the defendant wants specific performance while the prosecution takes the position that only withdrawal of the plea should be permitted. When the breach was a failure by the prosecutor to carry out a promise which was fulfillable, then certainly the defendant's request for specific performance should be honored. This is most certainly the case when the defendant has relied on the promise to his detriment, as where a prosecutor failed to keep his promise as to what sentence recommendation he would make if the defendant first were to plead guilty and spend 60 days at a correctional center for evaluation. Though it has occasionally been held that withdrawal is the preferred remedy in the absence of such irrevocable prejudice, that position is unsound. Even absent a showing of prejudice, there is no reason why a prosecutor who has failed to keep his fulfillable plea bargain promise should be allowed to force the defendant into a withdrawal of the plea and thus, presumably, a permanent breach of the bargain.

Much more difficult are those cases in which the promise which was made by the prosecutor or some other agent of the state is "unfulfillable" in the sense that it is a commitment to produce a result not authorized by law or beyond the power of the promisor to produce. Illustrative of the latter are where the prosecutor makes commitments as to the sentence actually to be imposed, the time of release on parole, nonprosecution outside his county or district or even in another jurisdiction, nonextradition to another country, or favorable action by an administrative agency. In such circumstances the court faces an unpleasant choice: order specific enforcement and thus bind officials who took no part in the plea negotiations, or merely allow plea withdrawal of the guilty plea and thereby ignore defendant's reliance on the bargain. But when that reliance is nothing more than an expectation that the promise would be kept and withdrawing the plea will approximate the *status quo ante,* there is good reason to deny the defendant his desired remedy of specific performance. Otherwise there would be unnecessary encroachment upon established doctrine on the allocation of authority, such as that the prosecutor cannot bind the judge as to the sentence and cannot bind a prosecutor in another jurisdiction as to charging.

When the defendant's reliance is more substantial, then a more delicate balancing process is required. One factor which must be considered is the precise nature and extent of the detrimental reliance. If the defendant has served a period of imprisonment under the plea, has provided information to the authorities as part of the plea agreement, or has been jeopardized as to his defense by the turn of events, a court may be more willing to turn to specific enforcement even though the necessary consequence is to limit the discretion of persons who were not even parties to the plea agreement. A second factor which appears to enter into the resolution of these cases is the extent to which it is important to preserve the independence of the other agency which would be required to act in a certain way if specific performance were ordered. One would expect, therefore, that in the case of significant detrimental reliance a court would be more ready to grant specific performance which estopped charges by another prosecutor serving a different county or district of the same jurisdiction than such a remedy which barred charges in a different jurisdiction. Such analysis is also useful as to the so-called illegal promise. For example, if the prosecutor has promised a sentence which the law does not allow under the circumstances, it is not unthinkable that some manipulation of the defendant's sentence to produce a comparable benefit might occur.

(f) The Withdrawn Offer. The thrust of the preceding discussion is that once the defendant enters his negotiated plea the prosecutor may not now withdraw his offer, even if he does so prior to sentencing, the time when the prosecutor was to deliver on his promises. This is not to suggest, however, that withdrawal prior to the defendant's plea is inevitably permissible. The prevailing doctrine is that the state may withdraw from a plea bargain agreement at any time prior to, but not after, the entry of the guilty plea by the defendant or other action by him constituting detrimental reliance upon the agreement (e.g., giving a self-incriminating deposition).

Going well beyond that position is *Cooper v. United States,*[41] holding that unless the prosecutor's plea proposal is properly conditioned it is enforceable by a defendant who, prior to the prosecutor's withdrawal of the offer, had neither entered a guilty plea nor relied to his detriment on the bargain. Counsel for Cooper, charged with two counts each of bribery of a witness and obstruction of justice, was told by an assistant U.S. Attorney that if his client would plead guilty to one count, remain in jail and testify in upcoming narcotics trials, then the government would dismiss the other charges and bring Cooper's cooperation to the attention of the sentencing judge. Counsel immediately communicated this proposal to Cooper, who accepted, but when counsel finally was able to reach the prosecutor by phone a few hours later he was told that the offer was withdrawn. Cooper was thereafter convicted on all counts, but on appeal it was held "that the defendant's constitutional rights were here violated by the government's failure to honor its plea proposal." The court declared that there were "two distinct sources" for that ruling: (1) the Sixth Amendment right to effective assistance of counsel, involved here because to "the extent that the government attempts through defendant's counsel to change or retract positions earlier communicated, a defendant's confidence in his counsel's capability and professional responsibility * * * are necessarily jeopardized and the effectiveness of counsel's assistance easily compromised"; and (2) a due process right to enforcement of the plea proposal "on the basis alone of expectations reasonably formed in reliance upon the honor of the government in making and abiding by its proposals" where, as here, the offer was unambiguous and not unreasonable and was promptly assented to by the defendant and no "extenuating circumstances affecting the propriety of the proposal" intervened.

A unanimous Supreme Court rejected the *Cooper* approach in *Mabry v. Johnson.*[42] As for the right to counsel argument, the Court stated it failed "to see how an accused could reasonably attribute the prosecutor's change of heart to his counsel any more than he could have blamed counsel had the trial judge chosen to reject the agreed-upon recommendation, or, for that matter, had he gone to trial and been convicted." Moreover, there was no guilty plea obtained in violation of due process. When his agreement to accept the prosecution's offer of a 21-year concurrent sentence for a murder plea resulted in that offer being withdrawn as "a mistake" and replaced by an offer of a 21-year consecutive sentence, the defendant accepted the second offer after the trial began. Noting that this plea "was in no sense induced by the prosecutor's withdrawn offer," the Court concluded that defendant's "inability to enforce the prosecutor's offer is without constitutional significance" because that offer "did not impair the voluntariness or intelligence of his guilty plea." (Because there was neither a guilty plea *nor* any other form of detrimental reliance in *Mabry*, that decision does not address the question whether reliance short of a plea or other waiver of constitutional rights would be the basis for a due process objection.) As for the prosecutor's possible negligence or culpability in making and withdrawing the first offer, the Court deemed that irrelevant because the due process clause "is not a code of ethics for prosecutors" but is concerned "with the manner in which persons are deprived of their liberty."

A variation of the withdrawn offer issue arises when a defendant declines to accept a

41. 594 F.2d 12 (4th Cir.1979).

42. 467 U.S. 504, 104 S.Ct. 2543, 81 L.Ed.2d 437 (1984).

plea bargain tendered by the prosecutor before trial and then, some time after the trial is under way or even after conviction and at the time of sentencing, the defendant asserts a right to receive the concessions earlier tendered. A defendant is even less likely to prevail in such circumstances, for if the concessions offered earlier had to remain available there would be little point in a defendant not going to trial and taking his chances on acquittal. Once a trial begins, a prosecutor has less reason to negotiate a plea bargain than prior to trial, and thus a decision by a prosecutor to cut off plea bargaining at the time trial begins follows logically from one reason for engaging in plea bargaining: judicial economy through the avoidance of trials.

(g) The Unrealized Expectation. As a general matter, it may be said that a guilty plea defendant is not entitled to relief merely because the sentence which he received is greater than he had hoped or anticipated would be imposed in his case. And this is so even if the defendant's hope or anticipation was attributable to comments made by his attorney. For example, where defense counsel told the defendant that he believed a two-year sentence would be imposed but this was related to the defendant in equivocal terms of what "could" or "perhaps" happen, but the defendant was thereafter sentenced to eight years, the guilty plea is valid. The rule in *Santobello v. New York*[43] to the effect that the Constitution compels relief in the case of a broken plea bargain has no application here. However, if the defense attorney's "prediction" is stated in more definite terms and, as it turns out, is significantly inaccurate, there is the possibility that the defendant will be able to mount a successful attack upon his plea on the ground that he lacked the effective assistance of counsel.

Such cases must be distinguished from those in which the defendant is led to believe, most likely because of comments made by defense counsel, that a plea agreement has actually been reached with the prosecutor or the judge, but in fact there is no such agreement and the defendant does not thereafter receive the concessions contemplated under the nonexistent plea agreement. In such circumstances the courts have rather consistently held that the plea is involuntary, although it is more precise to say that the guilty plea is constitutionally defective because not "intelligent" due to the defendant's misunderstanding of what the consequences of his plea were to be. But the fundamental point is that in such a case the defendant was entitled to credit his attorney's representation as to the fact of such an agreement and to rely on it, so that he is entitled to relief if his guilty plea was induced by such a representation.

That situation must likewise be distinguished from yet another, where the defendant had a belief that there existed a plea bargain which included certain concessions he did not thereafter receive, but that belief was erroneous and was based upon comments by the defense attorney or others which did not specifically state that a plea agreement with those concessions had been reached. Purely as a matter of logic, this case would seem to be no different than the preceding one. As explained in *United States ex rel. Thurmond v. Mancusi:*[44]

> If, at the time he pled guilty, the defendant believed that a coercive promise or threat had been made by either the court or the prosecutor, though in fact no such promise or threat had been made, and his plea was induced by this belief, it is an involuntary and void plea. This conclusion necessarily follows from the fact that voluntariness connotes a state of mind of an actor. If the actor—i.e., the defendant—believes that a promise has been made, the effect on his state of mind is exactly the same as if such a promise had in fact been made. Thus, any test of whether a person acts voluntarily is necessarily "subjective."

But that is not the prevailing view. Rather, state and federal courts have taken the position that the defendant must in addition show that his belief was a reasonable one under the circumstances. This burden of showing a reasonable belief has been imposed

43. 404 U.S. 257, 92 S.Ct. 495, 30 L.Ed.2d 427 (1971).

44. 275 F.Supp. 508 (E.D.N.Y.1967).

because of a fear that otherwise the granting of a motion for plea withdrawal would be automatic upon the movant's assertion that his guilty plea resulted from a subjectively mistaken belief, for it could not be established whether in fact this misunderstanding was actual or feigned. Some argue, however, that those fears are unwarranted and do not justify abandonment of the subjective test which, on principle, is correct. They believe that issues of fact such as a person's state of mind can be accurately decided on the basis of reasonable inferences drawn from the known surrounding facts and circumstances.

In any event, a valid unrealized expectation claim should be rare under the reforms which have been adopted regarding receipt of guilty pleas. The practice of having any plea bargain placed on the record and of making specific inquiry of the defendant regarding his expectations and understandings[45] will make it highly unlikely, albeit not impossible, that under either a subjective or reasonableness test a defendant can make out a plausible mistaken belief claim thereafter. If such a claim is made out, it must be remembered that this is not a broken bargain under the *Santobello* case and that consequently the defendant is not entitled to demand specific performance of a promise which in fact was never made; the remedy is withdrawal of the plea. However, if the prosecution is able to alter the disposition so that it conforms to the defendant's expectations and elects to do so, then the defendant will obtain all he says he was promised and can then have no right to withdraw his plea.

(h) Admission of Statements Made During Bargaining. The modern trend to hold inadmissible the defendant's offer to plead guilty, the plea agreement or statements made in the course of plea negotiations when no guilty plea is subsequently entered or if entered is withdrawn, makes obvious sense. A contrary rule would discourage plea negotiations and agreements, for defendants would have to be constantly concerned whether, in light of their plea negotiation activities, they could successfully defend on the merits if a plea ultimately was not entered.

There has been some dispute as to how broad this rule ought to be, and in particular whether it should ever extend to admissions by the defendant to someone other than the prosecutor. The current federal rule covers only statements made by the defendant in court when a plea is tendered or during plea discussions with the prosecutor.[46] The theory is that such a rule fully protects the plea discussion process authorized by federal law without attempting to deal with confrontations between suspects and law enforcement agents, which involve problems of quite different dimensions best resolved by that body of law dealing with police interrogations. Some have criticized this position on the ground that it fails to provide protection for defendants who plea bargain under the reasonable belief that the agent has bargaining authority, as where representations by the law enforcement officer or other circumstances lead the defendant to conclude that the officer is the proper person with whom to negotiate. At least some states follow the broader view.

The rule regarding statements made during plea negotiations must be distinguished from that concerning statements made subsequent to a plea which is later withdrawn. The Supreme Court dealt with such a situation in *Hutto v. Ross,*[47] reversing the holding below that defendant's confession, given subsequent to a negotiated plea agreement from which the defendant later withdrew, was involuntary because it would not have been made "but for the plea bargaining." Noting that "causation in that sense has never been the test of voluntariness," the Court concluded:

> The existence of the bargain may well have entered into respondent's decision to give a statement, but counsel made it clear to respondent that he could enforce the terms of the plea bargain whether or not he confessed. The confession thus does not appear to have been the result of "any direct or implied

45. See § 21.4(b).

46. Fed.R.Crim.P. 11(e)(6).

47. 429 U.S. 28, 97 S.Ct. 202, 50 L.Ed.2d 194 (1976).

promises" or any coercion on the part of the prosecution, and was not involuntary.

A different result has been reached with respect to post-plea statements made by the defendant in compliance with a commitment made in the plea bargain or on the representation of defense counsel that they were necessary to comply with the plea agreement.

Assuming now a statement made during plea discussions under circumstances which would as a general matter make it inadmissible against the defendant, a question may arise as to whether the rule of inadmissibility is absolute. What, for example, if the statement is offered for the limited purpose of impeachment? Although it has been argued by analogy to *Harris v. New York,*[48] holding admissible for impeachment purposes a voluntary statement obtained in violation of *Miranda,* that the answer should be yes, the courts have quite properly rejected that argument. *Harris* has no application in a plea bargaining context in which a waiver of the privilege against self-incrimination is an aspect of the plea obtained by active participation of the prosecution. A better analogy is *New Jersey v. Portash,*[49] holding that testimony obtained by a grant of immunity involves "the constitutional privilege against compulsory self-incrimination in its most pristine form" and does not permit a balancing which takes into account the need to prevent perjury. A contrary rule in the plea bargaining context, even if constitutionally permissible, would be unwise, for it would have a strong chilling effect on plea negotiations.

§ 21.3 Plea Negotiation Responsibilities of the Attorneys and Judge

(a) Right to Counsel During Plea Bargaining. The Sixth Amendment right to counsel in criminal cases applies not only at the criminal trial, but also at various other "critical stages" of the criminal process. For one thing, this means that this right extends to the arraignment, the time when the defendant is called upon to enter his plea.[1] For another, it means that there is a constitutional right to counsel at extrajudicial proceedings occurring after "the initiation of adversary judicial criminal proceedings" whenever "a defendant finds himself faced with the prosecutorial forces of organized society, and immersed in the intricacies of substantive and procedural criminal law." [2]

Applying this test, it is clear that there is a Sixth Amendment right to the assistance of counsel at a plea negotiation session with the prosecutor or his agents. For a prosecuting attorney to talk with the defendant in the absence of his counsel and attempt to have him change a plea of not guilty to a plea of guilty is to deprive the defendant of the effective assistance of counsel at a time when it was needed. And if such a violation of the defendant's Sixth Amendment right to counsel occurs, it cannot be dismissed on the supposition that the defendant effectively represented himself at the bargaining session.

What is less clear is how the situation is to be handled when defense counsel reenters the case at some later point. What if, for example, the prosecutor improperly meets with defendant in the absence of defense counsel and engages in plea bargaining with him but the plea of guilty subsequently entered by the defendant is pursuant to a bargain which defendant's counsel was aware of and had discussed with defendant prior to the entry of his plea? One view is that pursuant to *McMann v. Richardson* [3] the defendant's constitutional claim comes down to whether counsel's advice "was within the range of competence demanded of attorneys in criminal cases." But it is more precise to say that in such circumstances there exists *both* the question of the effectiveness of counsel's representation and of the voluntariness of the

48. 401 U.S. 222, 91 S.Ct. 643, 28 L.Ed.2d 1 (1971).

49. 440 U.S. 450, 99 S.Ct. 1292, 59 L.Ed.2d 501 (1979).

§ 21.3

1. Cf. White v. Maryland, 373 U.S. 59, 83 S.Ct. 1050, 10 L.Ed.2d 193 (1963).

2. Kirby v. Illinois, 406 U.S. 682, 92 S.Ct. 1877, 32 L.Ed.2d 411 (1972).

3. 397 U.S. 759, 90 S.Ct. 1441, 25 L.Ed.2d 763 (1970).

plea; the uncounseled bargaining session may not be divorced from any effect it had on the adequacy of defense counsel's subsequent performance *or* defendant's subsequent volition.

As for waiver of the constitutional right to counsel in the plea bargaining context, it has been argued that such waiver should not be permitted because (unlike the possible tactical advantage at trial) there is nothing for a defendant to gain by being unrepresented in the guilty plea context. This may explain why a few jurisdictions, at least in the past, have taken the position that felony defendants may not plead guilty without counsel. But in light of the Supreme Court's recognition in *Faretta v. California*[4] of a constitutional right to proceed pro se, which presumably is applicable in the guilty plea context as well, it appears that waiver must be permitted.

Waiver of counsel, to be effective, must be "intelligent and competent."[5] Certainly a defendant who is contemplating waiver of his constitutional right to counsel "should be made aware of the dangers and disadvantages of self-representation,"[6] and surely this requires an especially careful procedure in a guilty plea context because of defendant's likely ignorance of what assistance counsel can provide even if there will be no trial. Yet some courts have reached the remarkable conclusion that when the defendant was informed of the charge against him and of his right to appointed counsel and responded that he desired to plead guilty, this was an implicit waiver of counsel. Equally troubling is the occasional ruling that the right to counsel at a plea bargaining session was waived because it was the defendant, rather than the prosecutor or his agents, who initiated the meeting at which defense counsel was absent.

(b) Effective Assistance by Defense Counsel. The Sixth Amendment right of a guilty plea defendant is to the *effective* assistance of counsel, which is to be determined not by a hindsight assessment of whether the attorney's actions and conduct were right or wrong, but rather by an inquiry into whether they fell "within the range of competence demanded of attorneys in criminal cases."[7] There is greater uncertainty as to what this means in a guilty plea context as compared to a trial context, perhaps because until recent years courts were disinclined to acknowledge either the existence or the legitimacy of plea negotiations. In any event, there is an additional requirement that the defendant have been prejudiced by the ineffective assistance,[8] and what this means in a guilty plea context is that the defendant must show "a reasonable probability that, but for counsel's errors, he would not have pleaded guilty and would have insisted on going to trial."[9]

For example, there is not complete agreement by the courts as to the defense attorney's responsibility to conduct an investigation of the relevant facts when his client has indicated a disposition toward a plea of guilty. One view is that an extensive, independent investigation would be superfluous in such circumstances, but this overlooks the fact that in an adversary system it is not the role of counsel merely to acquiesce in a guilty plea decision made independently by his client. Thus it is the responsibility of the defense attorney in that setting to conduct a prompt investigation of the circumstances of the case and to explore all avenues leading to facts relevant to the merits of the case and the penalty in the event of conviction. Courts in recent years have been more inclined to find that a defense attorney's failure to interview

4. 422 U.S. 806, 95 S.Ct. 2525, 45 L.Ed.2d 562 (1975).

5. Johnson v. Zerbst, 304 U.S. 458, 58 S.Ct. 1019, 82 L.Ed. 1461 (1938).

6. Faretta v. California, 422 U.S. 806, 95 S.Ct. 2525, 45 L.Ed.2d 562 (1975).

7. McMann v. Richardson, 397 U.S. 759, 90 S.Ct. 1441, 25 L.Ed.2d 763 (1970).

8. Strickland v. Washington, 466 U.S. 668, 104 S.Ct. 2052, 80 L.Ed.2d 674 (1984), discussed in § 11.10.

9. Hill v. Lockhart, 474 U.S. 52, 106 S.Ct. 366, 88 L.Ed.2d 203 (1985). For example, the Court elaborated, if the error was a failure to discover potentially exculpatory evidence, the question is whether "discovery of the evidence would have led counsel to change his recommendation as to the plea," which in turn depends on "whether the evidence likely would have changed the outcome of a trial."

witnesses or otherwise investigate the case falls short of effective assistance, and that the defendant's guilty plea cannot stand where it appears such investigation would have uncovered facts significantly strengthening the defense case or where the absence of such investigation prejudiced the defendant's ability to make an intelligent and voluntary plea of guilty.

This responsibility to investigate is related to defense counsel's broader obligation to confer with his client and to give him advice. It is essential that the attorney advise the defendant of the available options and possible consequences, though there is not complete agreement on the extent of a defense attorney's responsibilities in this regard. For example, there is a split of authority on the question of when, if ever, a defense attorney is responsible for alerting an alien defendant of the fact conviction could result in deportation. The view that if deportation is a "collateral consequence" about which the judge receiving the plea need not warn, then it follows defense counsel is not rendering ineffective assistance in failing to so admonish the defendant, is certainly open to question. It is not apparent why defense counsel's obligations should be deemed to be no more extensive than those of the judge. It is also quite necessary and proper for the attorney to express a view on the appropriate course of action, including whether a particular plea appears to be desirable. But it is for the client to decide what plea should be entered. Courts have held that defense counsel coerced defendant's plea where he threatened to withdraw from the case if a guilty plea was not entered and where the lawyer's advice was so strongly worded as to constitute a threat.

Sometimes the question is whether the particular recommendation of defense counsel constitutes ineffective assistance under the circumstances of the case. For example, what of a recommendation to accept a plea bargain made to a defendant who has asserted his innocence? One view is that it is unreasonable for counsel to recommend a guilty plea to a defendant without first cautioning him that, no matter what, he should not plead guilty unless he believed himself guilty, for our judicial system has so many safeguards that it may not be assumed that an innocent person will be convicted. The contrary view is that if a fair assessment of the prosecution's case indicates a substantial likelihood of conviction and severe sanctions, then defense counsel should not be barred from recommending the negotiated plea route merely because the defendant might in fact be innocent or because the defendant cannot bring himself to acknowledge his guilt. The latter position draws support from *North Carolina v. Alford,*[10] where the Supreme Court ruled it was constitutionally permissible to accept a guilty plea from a defendant who claimed to be innocent if there was a "strong factual basis for the plea." Even more troublesome is somewhat the reverse situation, where an apparently guilty defendant has entered a guilty plea on advice of counsel notwithstanding the likelihood that defendant would not have been convicted if he had gone to trial. The fundamental dilemma is whether defense counsel's duty to his client should be viewed solely in terms of obtaining for him as lenient a disposition as possible, or whether instead the attorney should advise his client in terms of what appears to be an appropriate correctional disposition.

A defendant has no right to be present at a plea negotiation conference between his attorney and the prosecutor, and typically he will not be present. As a result, problems can arise concerning communication or lack thereof to the defendant of any plea bargain offer put forward by the prosecutor. One difficulty, discussed earlier,[11] is that the defense attorney may intentionally or inadvertently cause the defendant to believe the prosecutor (or, if he is involved in the negotiation process, the judge) has agreed to certain concessions in exchange for defendant's plea when in fact that has not occurred. Another, in a sense the opposite of this, is that the

10. 400 U.S. 25, 91 S.Ct. 160, 27 L.Ed.2d 162 (1970), discussed in § 21.4(f).

11. See § 21.2(g).

defense attorney may fail to communicate to the defendant a plea offer. It has been held that just as a defendant has the right to make a decision to plead not guilty, he also has the right to make the decision to plead guilty, which has been denied if his attorney has not informed him of the concessions offered. A more difficult case would be that in which defense counsel did not convey the offer because he feared that the defendant, who theretofore had asserted his innocence, would unwisely accept it, but even there it would seem that the better course is for counsel to communicate the offer and then give his professional opinion as to whether it should be accepted.

Another question is whether in the absence of such overtures by the prosecutor it is always or sometimes an obligation of defense counsel to sound out the prosecutor as to what concessions would be granted in exchange for a plea of guilty by his client. One view is that at least when the lawyer concludes, on the basis of full investigation and study, that under controlling law and the evidence, a conviction is probable, he should so advise the accused and seek his consent to engage in plea discussions with the prosecutor. Indeed, it has been asserted that such plea discussions should be considered the norm, and that failure to seek them is excusable only when defense counsel concludes that sound reasons exist for not doing so. But just when a failure of defense counsel to take the initiative in this way constitutes ineffective assistance is not entirely clear, as the issue has seldom reached the courts. It has been held, however, that defendant's guilt is not by itself an excuse for not exploring plea bargaining opportunities, and that the failure to initiate plea bargain negotiations is inexcusable when there is a fairly apparent weakness in the prosecution's case.

If plea negotiations are undertaken, there are ethical and tactical questions which can arise concerning defense counsel's dealings with the prosecutor or the judge. Unquestionably it is unethical for the defense attorney to circumvent the prosecutor and in a secret ex parte proceeding attempt to extract a promise of concessions from the judge. As for his dealings with the prosecutor, certainly some degree of "bluffing" is engaged in by both the prosecutor and the defense attorney. Excesses in this regard by the prosecutor can amount to a denial of due process, but as a matter of professional ethics it is improper for defense counsel knowingly to make false statements concerning the evidence in the course of plea discussions with the prosecutor. Such action is also counterproductive, for it severely handicaps counsel's usefulness to the accused and to future clients. But the defense attorney is not obligated to reveal evidence to the prosecution; counsel must preserve the client's confidences unless granted consent to make disclosures for this purpose. Informal discovery in the plea bargaining context is often treated by defense attorneys as a two-way street, on the ground that they thereby establish with the prosecutor a good working relationship from which ultimately will flow substantial benefits to the defendant.

Yet another aspect of the Sixth Amendment right to the effective assistance of counsel is that defendant is entitled to be represented by an attorney who is not hampered by a conflict of interest. The mere existence of a conflict does not inevitably mean that a particular defendant has received less than adequate representation, but the problem is that it is extremely difficult to ascertain whether the conflict had any impact upon the attorney's representations. Indeed, as the Supreme Court has noted, "to assess the impact of a conflict of interests on the attorney's options, tactics and decisions in plea negotiations would be virtually impossible." [12] Joint representation is not per se a violation of the constitutional guarantee of effective assistance by counsel,[13] but conflicts most frequently arise out of such arrangements. Illustrative are these situations: (1) where there was a "package deal" in which defense counsel could obtain a favorable disposition for one

12. Holloway v. Arkansas, 435 U.S. 475, 98 S.Ct. 1173, 55 L.Ed.2d 426 (1978).

13. Holloway v. Arkansas, 435 U.S. 475, 98 S.Ct. 1173, 55 L.Ed.2d 426 (1978).

client only if the other defendants in the case, also represented by him, also plead guilty; (2) where defense counsel was representing one client who implicated others in the hope of favorable treatment, and also one of those implicated, whose plea of guilty as recommended by counsel served to build a record of cooperation by the first client; (3) where defense counsel, representing two persons charged with joint possession of marijuana, stressed the relatively minor role of one defendant and consequently made the other appear more culpable; and (4) where defense counsel advised against a plea bargain which contemplated that the defendant would then testify at the trial of another defendant, also represented by this attorney. Conflicts may arise for other reasons as well, as where counsel might advise against a negotiated plea because his fee is collectible only if the defendant is acquitted.

Once the defendant establishes that "a conflict of interest actually affected the adequacy of his representation," he is entitled to relief without also establishing the proof of prejudice required in other circumstances.[14] In the guilty plea context this means, for example, that if an attorney's multiple representation caused him to forego plea negotiations for one defendant, that defendant is entitled to relief without any showing separate counsel would have brought about a more advantageous disposition of the case.

(c) The Prosecutor's Bargaining Tactics. In considering the prosecutor's role in the plea negotiation process, a logical first inquiry is whether there is some obligation upon the prosecutor to engage in bargaining with defendants. The courts have rather consistently answered in the negative. As the Supreme Court declared in *Weatherford v. Bursey,*[15] "there is no constitutional right to plea bargain; the prosecutor need not do so if he prefers to go to trial. It is a novel argument that constitutional rights are infringed by trying the defendant rather than accepting his plea of guilty." This is because plea bargaining is an aspect of the prosecutor's broad charging discretion whereunder he is permitted to decide when and whether to institute criminal proceedings, or what precise charge shall be made, or whether to dismiss a proceeding once brought.

But it would not be correct to say that a court should in no circumstances become involved in assessing the prosecutor's refusal to bargain. For example, if a prosecutor were to adopt a practice of refusing to bargain with any defendants represented by certain attorneys, disciplining of the prosecutor would certainly be appropriate. Moreover, just as is true of the prosecutor's charging decision,[16] a court is entitled to grant relief to a defendant when he shows that the prosecutor's conduct is so arbitrary as to constitute a denial of equal protection of the laws under the Fourteenth Amendment. But as we have already seen with respect to the charging decision, a defendant is likely to prevail on an equal protection claim only rarely and in extraordinary circumstances. Constitutional inequality is not demonstrated by the mere fact that two or more individuals are charged with the same or similar offenses and a plea-offer was not extended to all of them.

This notion that plea bargaining is simply an aspect of the prosecutor's charging discretion and thus subject to no greater judicial supervision has sometimes been questioned. So the argument goes, prosecutors may usually be trusted when they exercise unilateral discretion in deciding whether and what to charge, but there is greater reason for mistrust when it comes to plea negotiations because then prosecutors gain something of value for deciding that a certain punishment is adequate. But whether there is judicial supervision or not, prosecutors should affirmatively act to ensure that their plea bargaining practices are rational. Certainly similarly situated defendants should be afforded equal plea agreement opportunities, though a more common problem may be that equal bargaining opportunities and concessions will be

14. Holloway v. Arkansas, 435 U.S. 475, 98 S.Ct. 1173, 55 L.Ed.2d 426 (1978).

15. 429 U.S. 545, 97 S.Ct. 837, 51 L.Ed.2d 30 (1977).

16. See § 13.4.

made available to defendants whose situations are only superficially similar. A plea negotiation process which is fair, which is perceived to be fair, and which permits the attainment of desirable correctional goals can therefore be achieved only if the prosecutor establishes policy guidelines and procedures for bargaining and ensures that facts relevant to determining the appropriate disposition are at hand at the time the bargaining occurs.

If a prosecutor were to bring a greater charge against the defendant than is supported by the evidence in order to increase his plea bargaining leverage, this would unquestionably be improper. More controversial, however, is the not uncommon practice of "overcharging" in another sense, as where the prosecutor files a felony charge which is supported by the evidence in the hope of inducing a plea to a misdemeanor when, as a matter of general prosecutive policy, the case would actually be tried only on a misdemeanor charge. Although the Supreme Court held in *Bordenkircher v. Hayes* [17] that such conduct was not unconstitutional, there is a division of opinion as to whether this charging practice is ethical and proper.

Yet another practice which a prosecutor may engage in during plea negotiations is some degree of "bluffing" concerning the strength of his case against the defendant at the present time. The range of possibilities here is substantial, all the way from withholding exculpatory evidence to not volunteering the immediate unavailability of a certain witness, though most prosecutors feel obligated to produce evidence indicating factual innocence. The Supreme Court, albeit dealing with cases which had gone to trial, has held that it is a violation of due process for a prosecutor to withhold favorable evidence whenever there exists "a reasonable probability" that, had disclosure been made, the "result of the proceeding would have been different." [18] The prosecutor's obligation in a guilty plea context is no less. This means, for example, that a prosecutor should reveal to a defendant contemplating a plea to possessing an incendiary device that prior to the time of the possession the dynamite had been replaced with sawdust. By contrast, it is constitutionally permissible for a prosecutor to negotiate a robbery plea without revealing that the victim had since died and thus could not testify, for the prosecutor is not obliged to share his appraisal of the weaknesses of his own case (as opposed to specific exculpatory evidence) with defense counsel.

A most interesting question, yet to be fully explored by the courts, is whether as a constitutional matter or at least as a policy matter the prosecutor has a greater disclosure responsibility in the guilty plea context than he does in the trial context. The issue is suggested by the fact that a violation of the due process disclosure requirements, when occurring in a guilty plea context, has sometimes been characterized in terms of a guilty plea which is constitutionally defective because not intelligently made. Especially if, as the Supreme Court once intimated, for a guilty plea to be valid the defense must be aware of "the actual value of any commitments made," [19] which is not possible if there exists a significant misperception of the likelihood that the prosecution could succeed at trial, then it may be that the prosecutor is obligated to make disclosures during plea bargaining beyond those otherwise mandated in order to satisfy the intelligent plea requirement. To put the matter somewhat differently, if (as seems to be indicated from the Supreme

17. 434 U.S. 357, 98 S.Ct. 663, 54 L.Ed.2d 604 (1978).

18. United States v. Bagley, 473 U.S. 667, 105 S.Ct. 3375, 87 L.Ed.2d 481 (1985). Brady v. Maryland, 373 U.S. 83, 83 S.Ct. 1194, 10 L.Ed.2d 215 (1963), dealt only with requested evidence, and the Court thereafter developed a different test where there was no request or only a generalized request, United States v. Agurs, 427 U.S. 97, 96 S.Ct. 2392, 49 L.Ed.2d 342 (1976), but *Bagley* merged *Brady* and *Agurs* and the knowing-use-of-perjured-testimony cases into a single test.

The phrase "the proceeding" in *Bagley* clearly refers to a criminal trial, and thus *Bagley* cannot be readily converted, in a guilty plea context, to cover any information which, if known by defendant, would have changed his guilty plea decision. This is highlighted by the *Bagley* Court's repeated and consistent characterization of the withheld information as "evidence."

19. Brady v. United States, 397 U.S. 742, 90 S.Ct. 1463, 25 L.Ed.2d 747 (1970), quoting Shelton v. United States, 246 F.2d 571 (5th Cir.1957).

Court's decisions[20]) the legitimacy of the negotiated plea process rests upon the consent of defendants to surrender their chance of acquittal at trial in exchange for concessions, then it is essential that the defendant have had a meaningful opportunity to make a rational prediction of what the outcome at trial would be. From this would derive a broad pre-plea duty to disclose to the defendant all information bearing on the likelihood of trial conviction. In any event, there is much to be said for more openness in plea negotiations; it would permit the defendant to play a more meaningful role in the negotiation process, produce fairer bargains, and minimize the risk of duress and mistake.

(d) Judicial Involvement in Negotiations. Some years ago there was a general consensus that trial judges should not participate in the pretrial negotiations which influence a great many defendants to plead guilty. But as a matter of current practice, considerable variation is to be found. Four different kinds of plea bargaining systems have been identified: (1) no judicial involvement of any kind, (2) involvement through unannounced but known sentencing breaks to those who plead guilty, (3) involvement by the judge in sentencing discussions in an occasional, vague, and inconsistent manner, and (4) direct participation in which the judge makes a sentence commitment before the defendant pleads. In some localities the judicial involvement has become formalized to the extent that as a routine matter the parties often meet with the judge at a pretrial settlement conference. Elsewhere, by contrast, there is no established routine, but at least some judges on occasion will become involved in the negotiation process beyond merely being advised of the agreement at arraignment when the defendant's negotiated plea is tendered.

There is also considerable variation among jurisdictions as to the legal position on judicial involvement in plea negotiations. Some jurisdictions have by statute or court rule absolutely prohibited such involvement, and it is claimed that these provisions have in fact substantially deterred judicial involvement. These provisions mean the sentencing judge is to take no part whatever in any discussion or communication regarding the sentence to be imposed prior to the entry of a plea of guilty or conviction, or at least the submission to him of a plea agreement. The law in some states gives express approval to at least limited involvement by the judge in plea negotiations, and further movement in this direction can be expected. This reflects growing acceptance of the view that the "evils" of judicial participation are not as substantial as had once been commonly assumed and that they are, in any event, outweighed by certain benefits which can be achieved by having the judge more actively involved in the negotiation process.

One reason often given for keeping the judge out of the negotiation process is that his participation would have a coercive effect upon the defendant. As stated in *United States ex rel. Elksnis v. Gilligan*[21]:

> The unequal positions of the judge and the accused, one with the power to commit to prison and the other deeply concerned to avoid prison, at once raise a question of fundamental fairness. When a judge becomes a participant in plea bargaining he brings to bear the full force and majesty of his office. His awesome power to impose a substantially longer or even maximum sentence in excess of that proposed is present whether referred to or not. A defendant needs no reminder that if he rejects the proposal, stands upon his right to trial and is convicted, he faces a significantly longer sentence.

So the argument goes, the situation is quite different when only the prosecutor is involved, as the prosecutor's threat is highly diluted because he lacks power to sentence. But this line of reasoning has not gone unchallenged; in response it is contended that because the prosecutor has many means not available to the judge of putting pressure upon the defendant, the disparity of positions

20. See, e.g., Santobello v. New York, 404 U.S. 257, 92 S.Ct. 495, 30 L.Ed.2d 427 (1970); North Carolina v. Alford, 400 U.S. 25, 91 S.Ct. 160, 27 L.Ed.2d 162 (1970).

21. 256 F.Supp. 244 (S.D.N.Y.1966).

may be even greater between prosecutor and defendant than between judge and defendant. Specifically, it has been noted that prosecutorial sentence recommendations are so universally followed that their effect is virtually indistinguishable from that of judicial promises of specific sentences.

A second concern underlying the traditional position is that if a judge was involved in the bargaining but the negotiations did not result in a guilty plea, then it would be difficult for that judge to conduct a fair trial thereafter. But the case law has generally rejected the notion that unfairness is inherent in such circumstances. It is reasoned that if the case goes to jury trial the judge will have little opportunity to influence the outcome, and that if there is a bench trial the judge will likely understand that the fact the defendant engaged in plea bargaining says nothing at all about his guilt. Any actual or perceived risk of unfairness could be overcome by having the judge who participated in the bargaining recuse himself from the trial, but this practice would have to be carefully controlled to ensure against judge-shopping in cases plainly headed for trial and also offer-shopping in guilty plea cases.

A third objection to judicial participation in plea negotiations is that such activity is inconsistent with the judge's responsibilities at the arraignment. As stated in *Elksnis,*

> a bargain agreement between a judge and a defendant * * * impairs the judge's objectivity in passing upon the voluntariness of the plea when offered. As a party to the arrangement upon which the plea is based, he is hardly in a position to discharge his function of deciding the validity of the plea—a function not satisfied by routine inquiry, but only, as the Supreme Court has stressed, by "a penetrating and comprehensive examination of all the circumstances under which such a plea is tendered."

In response, it is argued that the inquiry could be by another judge if this is a problem and that the judge's presence at the negotiations rather than his after-the-fact inquiry into them provides greater assurance of voluntariness.

Still another objection is that judicial participation to the extent of promising a certain sentence is inconsistent with the theory behind the use of the presentence investigation report. A possible solution lies in ordering the preparation of a presentence report prior to the initiation of plea bargaining, as is the practice in some jurisdictions. But this procedure poses some dangers, as an interview with the defendant is typically part of a presentence investigation. Absent rigorous safeguards to ensure against even indirect use of defendant's statements at trial, it would violate the privilege against self-incrimination to require him to answer questions about his alleged crime at this early stage.

Finally, there is the concern over the unseemliness of judicial plea bargaining—that the procedure leads defendants to think of the judge as just one more official to be bought off. In response it is said that it is better for judges to administer our system of justice—however indecorous that system is—than for them to leave the task to prosecutors, especially since a regime of prosecutorial plea bargaining cannot be successful unless judges substantially abdicate their power.

Because the reasons which have been given for nonparticipation in plea negotiations by the judiciary are not entirely without merit and substance, another important consideration is that of what is to be gained by greater judicial involvement. These benefits have been identified: (1) it would restore the sentencing function to the judiciary, in contrast to the prevailing practice which causes some judges to ratify agreements they would not have formulated had they participated in the negotiations; (2) it would facilitate the flow of information relevant to sentencing to the judge; (3) it would remove the cloak of uncertainty whereby the defendant is required to plead in the dark in the sense of not knowing whether the judge will grant the concessions the prosecutor has promised to seek; (4) it would cause the prosecutor to open his file and to freely discuss the strength of his case; (5) it would ensure that the various sentencing provisions applicable are discussed and understood; and (6) it would permit the judge to perform as an effective check on prosecutorial power, police behavior, and defense counsel effectiveness, and thus equalize the opportunity of all defendants to negotiate.

It has been proposed that all plea negotiations occur at an on-the-record pretrial conference held on motion of the defendant. In attendance would be the defendant and his attorney, the prosecutor and the judge. A limited presentence investigation, not including an interview with the defendant, would be conducted in advance of the conference and a presentence report would be available. The judge should permit the defense and prosecution to discuss the circumstances of the case, present one or more proposals for disposition, and argue in support of them, after which the judge would indicate the sentence he would impose if the defendant enters a plea of guilty and, when necessary to that result, how the charges would be reduced. If the defendant decided to plead guilty, that judge would conduct the arraignment; otherwise the matter would be assigned to another judge. Such a system contemplates a much more central role for the judge in the plea negotiation process than presently is permitted in many jurisdictions. It stands in especially sharp contrast to the view that the defendant should be able to bargain only for a sentence recommendation, and to the even more extreme view that judicial sentencing should occur even without knowledge of what the plea bargain contemplates. But it is also quite different from the more common current view that the judge has no business tendering sentence concessions or granting charge concessions without the prosecutor's approval.

(e) Judicial Evaluation of Contemplated Concessions. Even if the judge does not become involved in the plea negotiation process, he will usually have a critical role to play whenever the defendant tenders a plea as a consequence of the negotiations. If the plea agreement contemplates the granting of sentence concessions to the defendant, then quite obviously the judge will play an essential part, for sentencing is the responsibility of the judge. In those many jurisdictions where charges which have been filed may be dropped only with the consent of the court, the judge will likewise perform a necessary part whenever the plea agreement contemplates the reduction of the charge or the dropping of some counts. In all of these circumstances, quite clearly the judge is under no obligation to grant the contemplated concessions merely because the parties are agreeable. Nor, under the better but not prevailing view, is the judge free to refuse to give any consideration to the agreement which has been reached by the parties. Rather, the judge should give the agreement due consideration, but notwithstanding its existence reach an independent decision on whether to grant charge or sentence concessions.

Just how much "consideration" should be given to the disposition agreed to by the prosecutor and just how "independent" the judge should be in these circumstances is a most difficult issue, seldom addressed in the cases. Rather unique is *United States v. Ammidown,*[22] where defendant appealed his first degree murder conviction, based upon proof that he hired the man who killed his wife, because the trial was necessitated by the judge's rejection of a plea bargain which contemplated defendant entering a plea to second degree murder and testifying against the killer. In reversing and remanding for acceptance of a plea to second degree murder, the court seemed to view the judge as having a rather limited function to perform with respect to charge reduction bargains. The court declared that

> the trial judge must provide a reasoned exercise of discretion in order to justify a departure from the course agreed on by the prosecution and defense. This is not a matter of absolute judicial prerogative. The authority has been granted to the judge to assure protection of the public interest, and this in turn involves one or more of the following components: (a) fairness to the defense, such as protection against harassment; (b) fairness to the prosecution interest, as in avoiding a dis-

22. 497 F.2d 615 (D.C.Cir.1973).

position that does not serve due and legitimate prosecutorial interest; (c) protection of the sentencing authority reserved to the judge.

Noting that the first of these, concerning "protecting a defendant from harassment through a prosecutor's charging, dismissing without having placed a defendant in jeopardy, and commencing another prosecution at a different time or place deemed more favorable to the prosecution," was not involved in the instant case, the court elaborated on the second component:

> As to fairness to the prosecution interest, here we have a matter in which the primary responsibility, obviously, is that of the prosecuting attorney. The District Court cannot disapprove of his action on the ground of incompatibility with prosecutive responsibility unless the judge is in effect ruling that the prosecutor has abused his discretion. The requirement of judicial approval entitles the judge to obtain and evaluate the prosecutor's reasons. * * * The judge may withold approval if he finds that the prosecutor has failed to give consideration to factors that must be given consideration in the public interest, factors such as the deterrent aspects of the criminal law. However, trial judges are not free to withhold approval of guilty pleas on this basis merely because their conception of the public interest differs from that of the prosecuting attorney. The question is not what the judge would do if he were the prosecuting attorney, but whether he can say that the action of the prosecuting attorney is such a departure from sound prosecutorial principle as to mark it an abuse of prosecutorial discretion.

The court in *Ammidown* then went on to assert, with respect to the third component, "that the judge is free to condemn the prosecutor's agreement as a trespass on judicial authority only in a blatant and extreme case," and explained:

> When we come to the possible ground of intrusion on the sentencing function of the trial judge, we have a consideration that is interdependent of the other. That is to say, a dropping of an offense that might be taken as an intrusion on the judicial function if it were not shown to be related to a prosecutorial purpose takes on an entirely different coloration if it is explained to the judge that there was a prosecutorial purpose, an insufficiency of evidence, a doubt as to the admissibility of certain evidence under exclusionary rules, a need for evidence to bring another felon to justice, or other similar consideration.

Under the *Ammidown* approach, then, the trial judge is clothed with a discretion to determine whether the dismissal of these charges was clearly contrary to the public interest, but this is a limited discretion which is subjected to rather strict appellate review. By contrast, if the plea bargain agreed to by the prosecution and the defendant were to deal directly with sentence concessions, rather than charge concessions as in *Ammidown*, then the ultimate determination of an appropriate sentence is to be made by the court.

The *Ammidown* approach has not escaped criticism. It is argued that there is insufficient screening and supervision within the executive branch to ensure that the interests of the public and the defendant have been properly balanced, and that under *Ammidown* many highly imprudent plea agreements would survive judicial scrutiny if the impropriety were not sufficiently blatant to support a finding of abuse of prosecutorial discretion. Moreover, it has been pointed out that to distinguish between charge bargains and sentence bargains in determining the range of the judge's discretion in deciding whether the contemplated concessions should be granted assumes a difference which does not exist, as the primary significance of the charge-reduction process plainly lies in its effect on the sentence the defendant will receive. This being so, the anti-*Ammidown* argument proceeds, that decision is in error because it, in effect, amounts to a formal recognition of the prosecutor's authority over sentencing. Decisions are to be found on both the state and federal level accepting this latter view and thus recognizing broader discretion in the judge to determine whether a charge bargain with sentencing consequences should be approved.

§ 21.4 Receiving the Defendant's Plea

(a) Arraignment; Pleading Alternatives. The word "arraignment" is sometimes used to refer to the defendant's first appearance in court before a magistrate. The defendant will not normally be called upon to plead at that time unless the offense charged is a minor one. The more common use of the word "arraignment" is to refer to a later appearance in the court of trial jurisdiction, when the defendant is advised of the formal charge and called upon to enter a plea. Typically this will occur weeks or even months after the initial appearance, and thus the defendant will have had adequate time to consult with counsel and to reflect on what his plea should be. On occasion, however, a defendant is brought into court after arrest, where he waives all rights and procedures which would delay the proceedings (right to counsel, preliminary hearing, grand jury indictment) and then immediately enters a guilty plea. Some courts have upheld this practice, while others have criticized it. Certainly the better view is that even a defendant who has waived his other rights should not be called upon to decide on his plea so promptly.

When the defendant is called upon to enter his plea at arraignment, he may enter a plea of (1) not guilty, (2) guilty, (3) not guilty by reason of insanity (in a few jurisdictions where such a plea is a prerequisite to the presentation of an insanity defense at trial); or (4) nolo contendere (in the federal system and about half of the states). A plea of nolo contendere—sometimes referred to as a plea of non vult contendere or of non vult—is simply a device by which the defendant may assert that he does not want to contest the issue of guilt or innocence. Such a plea may not be entered as a matter of right, but only with the consent of the court. Although the prevailing view is that the consent of the prosecutor is not also required, it is common practice for the court to determine the views of the prosecutor and to give them considerable weight in deciding whether to accept the nolo plea.

Although some minor variations are to be found from jurisdiction to jurisdiction, a plea of nolo contendere usually has the following significance: (1) Unlike a plea of guilty or a conviction following a plea of not guilty, a plea of nolo contendere may not be put into evidence in a subsequent civil action as proof of the fact that the defendant committed the offense to which he entered the plea. (2) Judgment following entry of a nolo contendere plea is a conviction, and may be admitted as such in other proceedings where the fact of conviction has legal significance (e.g., to apply multiple offender penalty provisions, to deny or revoke a license because of conviction, or to claim double jeopardy in a subsequent prosecution). (3) When a nolo contendere plea is accepted, it has essentially the same effect in that case as a guilty plea. The procedures for receiving the plea are essentially the same, the defendant may receive the same sentence, and the nolo plea is like a guilty plea in terms of its finality, its effect as a waiver of claims unrelated to the plea, and the circumstances in which withdrawal of the plea would be permitted.

Opinions differ as to whether it is desirable to have the nolo contendere pleading alternative. Some say there should not be such an "in between" plea, for if a defendant is innocent he should go to trial and if he is guilty he should be required to acknowledge that guilt if he is not prepared to stand trial. The assumption is that existence of the nolo plea as an alternative will have two undesirable effects: (i) some innocent persons will so plead just to avoid the expense and notoriety of trial; and (ii) some guilty persons will be allowed to so plead and thereby receive the unwarranted benefit of freedom in subsequent civil proceedings to deny the facts regarding their crimes. The contrary view is that the nolo plea serves an important function in certain circumstances, such as where the charge is a criminal antitrust violation, in that otherwise the defendant would impose upon the system the need for a costly and lengthy trial solely in an effort to avoid the collateral civil consequences of a guilty plea.

It is in the discretion of the court to reject or accept a nolo plea, but no criteria have been established to guide the exercise of this discretion. Some courts operate under the assumption that the plea should be accepted in the absence of some compelling reason to the contrary, while others take the directly opposite view. The question of whether to accept a nolo plea, it would seem, is similar to that of whether a defendant should be given concessions in a plea bargaining context. Of particular relevance is whether the nature of the case is such that having the defendant admit guilt or be convicted at trial is desirable in order to maximize the deterrent or rehabilitative effects of the prosecution, and whether enhancing the likelihood of the defendant being held liable in damages in collateral civil proceedings would further the goals of the criminal prosecution.

In the material which follows, the concern is with what procedures are appropriate at the arraignment if the defendant enters a plea of guilty or nolo contendere. Statutes or rules of court often prescribe a set of procedures for such a situation. At least some of those procedures are constitutionally required, though it remains unclear in many respects just how much of the usual plea-receiving process is constitutionally mandated.

(b) Determining Voluntariness of Plea and Competency of Defendant to Plead. When a defendant tenders a plea of guilty or nolo contendere in court at arraignment, one important responsibility of the court is to determine whether the plea is voluntary. Consistent with the Supreme Court's standard as to what constitutes a voluntary plea,[1] this means the court will inquire whether the tendered plea was the result of any threats or promises. At an earlier time, when the legitimacy of plea bargaining was in doubt, the general practice was not to reveal in court that a bargain had been struck, but today the prevailing practice is for the voluntariness inquiry to include a determination of whether a plea agreement has been reached and, if so, what it is. Depending upon the nature of the agreement, the judge will then advise the defendant of the effect of the agreement.

Although it is the responsibility of the judge presiding at the arraignment to reject a guilty or nolo plea which is not voluntary, it is well to note that a judge who is unduly demanding with respect to the voluntariness determination may harm a defendant rather than protect him. Illustrative is *United States v. Martinez,*[2] where defendant was indicted for conspiracy to import marijuana, importation of marijuana, possession of marijuana with intent to distribute it, and assault upon a federal officer. Martinez tendered a plea to the second count as a result of an agreement with the prosecution that the other charges would then be dismissed. Upon inquiry into the voluntariness of the plea, the judge learned that Martinez' waiver of his *Miranda* rights had been obtained by a promise that nothing would happen to him, and thus declined the plea as involuntary notwithstanding counsel's efforts to persuade him that the government possessed sufficient evidence to convict independent of Martinez' statement. Martinez was then tried and convicted of all four counts, but on appeal all but the second count was vacated. The appellate court viewed the action of the district court as improper in that he rejected a guilty plea which was not involuntary merely "because of the possibility of later collateral attack on the judgment to be entered upon the plea." It thus appears that a judge must proceed with special care when rejecting defendant's plea

§ 21.4

1. In Brady v. United States, 397 U.S. 742, 90 S.Ct. 1463, 25 L.Ed.2d 747 (1970), the Court accepted the standard first set out in Shelton v. United States, 246 F.2d 571 (5th Cir.1957), reversed on other grounds, 356 U.S. 26, 78 S.Ct. 563, 2 L.Ed.2d 579 (1958): "[A] plea of guilty entered by one fully aware of the direct consequences, including the actual value of any commitments made to him by the court, prosecutor, or his own counsel, must stand unless induced by threats (or promises to discontinue improper harassment), misrepresentation (including unfulfilled or unfulfillable promises), or perhaps by promises that are by their nature improper as having no proper relationship to the prosecutor's business (e.g. bribes)."

2. 486 F.2d 15 (5th Cir.1973).

if, as a consequence, the defendant would be deprived of bargained-for concessions.

The voluntariness determination does not include, as a matter of course, an inquiry into the defendant's competency to plead. However, in much the same way that a trial judge has a constitutional responsibility to act upon circumstances suggesting a defendant is not competent to stand trial,[3] a judge must defer acceptance of defendant's guilty or nolo plea whenever he has a reasonable ground to doubt the defendant's competence. Then he must put into motion the process whereby the defendant's mental condition may be inquired into and determined. Whether the standard for competence to stand trial, that the defendant "has sufficient present ability to consult with his lawyer with a reasonable degree of rational understanding—and * * * has a rational as well as factual understanding of the proceedings against him,"[4] also applies in this context is a matter as to which courts are not in complete agreement. One view is that a more stringent standard applies in the pleading context: whether mental illness has substantially impaired his ability to make a reasoned choice among the alternatives presented to him and to understand the nature of the consequences of his plea. But the prevailing view is that the degree of competence required to plead guilty is the same as that required to stand trial, for otherwise there would exist the anomalous situation of a class of defendants adjudged competent to stand trial but incompetent to take advantage of the leniency in punishment accorded by plea bargaining agreements.

(c) Determining Understanding of Charge. Yet another responsibility of the judge at an arraignment at which a guilty or nolo plea is tendered is to determine that the defendant understands the charge to which he is pleading. In federal court, "the court must address the defendant personally in open court and inform him of, and determine that he understands, * * * the nature of the charge to which the plea is offered."[5] Similar requirements are to be found in state procedure. As the Supreme Court explained in *Henderson v. Morgan,*[6] a plea of guilty

> cannot support a judgment of guilt unless it was voluntary in a constitutional sense. And clearly the plea could not be voluntary in the sense that it constituted an intelligent admission that he committed the offense unless the defendant received "real notice of the true nature of the charge against him, the first and most universally recognized requirement of due process."

The better practice is for the judge to inform the defendant of the nature and elements of the offense to which the plea is offered, that is, the acts and mental state and attendant circumstances which the prosecution would have to prove in order to establish guilt at trial. However, the *Henderson* case indicates that the constitutional requirement does not in all instances go this far. The defendant there was indicted for first degree murder. His attorneys unsuccessfully sought to have the charge reduced to manslaughter, but were able to obtain a bargained plea to second degree murder. The attorneys did not tell defendant that the new charge had a required element of intent to kill, and no reference was made to this element at the time of the defendant's plea. The opinion of the Court[7] concluded that this oversight constituted a violation of due process where, as in the instant case, there was no indication that the defendant was otherwise aware that the offense to which he was pleading had an intent-to-kill element. But the Court then dropped this cautionary footnote:

> There is no need in this case to decide whether notice of the true nature, or substance, of a charge always requires a description of every element of the offense; we assume it does not. Nevertheless, intent is such a critical element of the offense of second-

3. Pate v. Robinson, 383 U.S. 375, 86 S.Ct. 836, 15 L.Ed.2d 815 (1966).

4. Dusky v. United States, 362 U.S. 402, 80 S.Ct. 788, 4 L.Ed.2d 824 (1960).

5. Fed.R.Crim.P. 11(c).

6. 426 U.S. 637, 96 S.Ct. 2253, 49 L.Ed.2d 108 (1976).

7. By Stevens, J., which did not command the unqualified support of a majority of the Court. Two Justices dissented, and four others joined in a concurring opinion.

degree murder that notice of that element is required.

Just what makes an element "critical" within the meaning of *Henderson* is far from clear, though it appears that the Court in that case deemed the "design to effect the death of the person killed" critical because it was the element which differentiated the offense of second degree murder from that of manslaughter. Lower courts, in declaring a certain element to be critical in the *Henderson* sense, have often rested this conclusion upon the fact that the omitted or unexplained element was one which elevated the degree and seriousness of the crime to which the plea was offered above some other offense. Courts have also taken into account whether or not the charge is a self-explanatory legal term or so simple in meaning that it can be expected or assumed that a lay person understands it. On this basis it has been held that the elements of a conspiracy charge should be explained but that an element-by-element parsing of such offenses as escape and altering a check is unnecessary. With regard to possible affirmative defenses, the judge is not obligated to mention or explain them unless made aware of facts that would constitute such a defense.

Due process is denied only if the defendant was actually unaware of the nature of the charge. Thus, essential to the result in *Henderson* was the fact that defendant's attorneys did not tell him that intent to kill was required for second degree murder or "explain to him that his plea would be an admission of that fact." In *Henderson* it is noted that the record in a guilty plea case will normally contain "either an explanation of the charge by the trial judge, or at least a representation by defense counsel that the nature of the offense has been explained to the accused," thereby suggesting that either will suffice. More troublesome, however, is the Court's added comment that "even without such an express representation, it may be appropriate to presume that in most cases defense counsel routinely explain the nature of the offense in sufficient detail to give the accused notice of what he is being asked to admit." Though lower courts have sometimes entertained such a presumption in order to defeat a defendant's *Henderson* claim, this is a highly questionable result. Of course, when the defendant was not represented by counsel it cannot be presumed that any part of this function of informing defendant of the charge was performed by the defense attorney, and thus the court should make a more exacting inquiry to assure a defendant's understanding of the charge in such a case.

Yet another troublesome aspect of the Court's opinion in *Henderson* is the assumption that if a defendant admits facts amounting to an element of the offense to which he entered his plea, then he cannot complain about not being told that the offense contained that element. The Court asserted that proof at trial that defendant had "repeatedly stabbed" the victim would not inevitably have led the jury to infer intent to kill, and that consequently "an admission by respondent that he killed Mrs. Francisco does not necessarily also admit that he was guilty of second-degree murder." This was followed with the conclusion that the unadvised defendant's plea could not be deemed voluntary "in these circumstances," namely, where "he made no factual statement or admission necessarily implying that he had such intent." From this, lower courts have understandably concluded that factual statements or admissions by the defendant necessarily implying the existence of unexplained elements of the crime are sufficient.

To the extent that the due process requirement of notice of the charge is grounded upon a need, absent some other showing of guilt, for defendant to admit that he committed the crime, this is an understandable result. That is, if having the judge tell the defendant that second degree murder requires an intent to kill is important so that when the defendant says "I plead guilty" this may be taken to mean "I admit that I killed while acting with an intent to kill," then the presence of such a specific admission is a suitable substitute for the advice from the judge. But it would seem that the notice requirement serves another important function, one of particular significance in a system which authorizes plea bargaining: it ensures that the defendant understands that if he pleads not guilty the state will be required to prove certain facts, thus permitting the defendant to make an intelligent judgment as to whether he would be better off accepting the tendered concessions or chancing acquittal if the prosecution cannot prove those facts beyond a reasonable doubt. If that is so—which would seem to be what the Supreme Court meant when it said in *McCarthy v. United States*[8] that a guilty plea cannot be voluntary "unless the defendant possesses an understanding of the law in relation to the facts"—then admissions by the defendant are not an adequate substitute for advice from the court as to the elements of the offense.

(d) Determining Understanding of Possible Consequences. If the defendant offers a plea of guilty or nolo contendere at arraignment, yet another responsibility of the judge is to advise the defendant of certain consequences which could follow if the plea is accepted. The conventional wisdom is that this obligation extends to those consequences which are "direct" but not to those which are only "collateral" in nature. There is not complete agreement, however, as to the manner in which it should be determined whether a particular consequence is of the direct or collateral type. The distinction between these two categories, it is sometimes said, turns on whether the result represents a definite, immediate and largely automatic effect on the range of the defendant's punishment. That is a useful albeit not fool-proof test, and considerable variation is to be found in both federal and state cases on the direct-collateral dichotomy.

Matters concerning the nature of the sentence that could be imposed are most likely to be viewed as direct consequences. Traditionally, the emphasis in the case law has been upon the requirement that the judge inform the defendant of the maximum possible punishment. But the current requirement in federal practice is that the judge advise the defendant not only of "the maximum possible penalty provided by law" but also "the mandatory minimum penalty provided by law, if any,"[9] and several states have adopted comparable requirements. This is a welcome change, for advising the defendant in this way gives him a more realistic picture of what might happen with regard to sentencing. The same may be said of the current federal requirement that the defendant be warned, when such is the case, that a part of the sentence may be a requirement that defendant make restitution to the victim. It has also been suggested that the defendant should be expressly warned in multiple charge situations of the possibility of consecutive sentences, but the cases reflect a split of authority on this point. The courts are even less demanding with respect to possible elaboration of how low the sentence might be; it has been held that the defendant need not be told that some of the multiple charges might be merged for sentencing purposes or that there is an included offense carrying a lesser penalty of which he might be convicted were he to stand trial.

The better view is that the maximum possible sentence about which the defendant should be warned includes punishment possible by virtue either of the sentence provisions of the statute under which the charge is brought or of other statutes that authorize added penalties because of special circumstances in the case, as where a statute provides for added punishment of persons who commit crimes while armed. Equally desirable is a warning to the defendant of the fact, where the law so provides, that the sentencing provisions of the statute under which he is charged or a more general multiple offender statute provides for specified higher penalties if the instant offense puts the defendant into the repeater category. With respect to parole and probation, there is no need specifically to advise the defendant that if he achieves such conditional release status then any violation of a condition of the release could result in revocation. But because the

8. 394 U.S. 459, 89 S.Ct. 1166, 22 L.Ed.2d 418 (1969).

9. Fed.R.Crim.P. 11(c)(1).

availability of parole is assumed by the average defendant, the better view is that the defendant should be so advised if the offense to which he is pleading may not lead to parole.

As for the collateral consequences of which the defendant need not be warned, they include such matters as the diminished reputation or other adverse social consequences which may follow conviction, loss of the right to vote, loss of a passport and the opportunity to travel abroad, and loss of a business license or driver's license. The majority view is that deportation is a collateral consequence and that consequently an alien defendant is not entitled to be advised by the judge of that consequence. It has been argued rather unconvincingly that this is so even when deportation is automatic upon conviction of the charged offense. Some courts view deportation as such a serious consequence that the alien defendant is entitled to be aware of it before entering his plea. In cases involving the question of whether various consequences deserve to be characterized as direct or collateral, two considerations, though seldom articulated, seem to influence the courts. One is that it is simply impracticable for a trial judge to advise the defendant of all possible consequences, especially because often the judge will not be aware at the time of the plea of the special circumstances which would make some of those consequences possible. Another is that defense counsel should be expected to discuss with his client the range of risks attendant his plea.

If a judge fails to advise the defendant of certain direct consequences of his plea and thus violates the obligation imposed upon him by statute, court rule, or court decision, does it follow that this failure amounts to a violation of due process? Although some courts have answered in the affirmative, the prevailing view is to the contrary, which accords with the Supreme Court's position on the matter.[10] Thus, while due process might be violated because of the failure of the judge taking the plea to tell defendant of the maximum sentence or any mandatory minimum sentence, the constitutional issue can be resolved only by considering other matters. Certainly there is no due process violation if the defendant was otherwise aware of the sentencing possibilities. If he was not aware, then the question is whether the defendant was prejudiced by the lack of information or by misinformation, which usually comes down to whether having the accurate information would have made any difference in his decision to enter the plea. (Where the government is responsible for defendant's lack of the correct sentencing information at the time of his plea, then it is quite appropriate to place upon the government the burden of showing that having the accurate information would not have made any difference.) If the defendant received a sentence longer than he knew could be imposed, then surely the judge's failure does amount to a due process violation. On the other hand, a defendant is not likely to prevail on his constitutional claim if he knew he could receive the sentence he did receive but lacked correct or certain knowledge of what maximum above that was possible. In the latter situation, however, it would seem that a significant overstatement of the maximum possible punishment would be objectionable whenever it skewed defendant's understanding of the value of his plea bargain.

(e) Determining Understanding of Rights Waived. *Boykin v. Alabama*[11] concerned a defendant who had pleaded guilty in state court to five armed robbery indictments and thereafter received the death penalty. At arraignment, "so far as the record shows, the judge asked no questions of petitioner concerning his plea, and petitioner did not address the court." The Supreme Court reversed, concluding that it "was error, plain on the face of the record, for the trial judge to accept petitioner's guilty plea without an affirmative showing that it was intelligent and voluntary." Noting that it had earlier established in another context the "requirement

10. United States v. Timmreck, 441 U.S. 780, 99 S.Ct. 2085, 60 L.Ed.2d 634 (1979), discussed in § 21.5(c).

11. 395 U.S. 238, 89 S.Ct. 1709, 23 L.Ed.2d 274 (1969).

that the prosecution spread on the record the prerequisites of a valid waiver," the Court in *Boykin* asserted:

> We think that the same standard must be applied to determining whether a guilty plea is voluntarily made. For, as we have said, a plea of guilty is more than an admission of conduct; it is a conviction. Ignorance, incomprehension, coercion, terror, inducements, subtle or blatant threats might be a perfect coverup of unconstitutionality. The question of an effective waiver of a federal constitutional right in a proceeding is of course governed by federal standards. * * *
>
> Several federal constitutional rights are involved in a waiver that takes place when a plea of guilty is entered in a state criminal trial. First is the privilege against compulsory self-incrimination guaranteed by the Fifth Amendment and applicable to the States by reason of the Fourteenth. * * * Second is the right to trial by jury. * * * Third, is the right to confront one's accusers. * * * We cannot presume a waiver of these three important federal rights from a silent record.

In the wake of *Boykin,* most jurisdictions revised their procedures for taking pleas so that defendants were specifically warned of the constitutional rights lost by entry of a plea other than not guilty. Although this is a desirable procedure, does *Boykin* mean that a guilty plea is constitutionally defective whenever the judge failed to articulate specifically the constitutional rights listed in the *Boykin* case? Some courts have answered in the affirmative, reasoning that there cannot be a knowledgeable waiver of those rights unless the defendant was so informed of them. But most courts, often stressing the uniqueness of *Boykin* in that the defendant had been sentenced to death and his plea had apparently been accepted without any admonishments or inquiry whatsoever, have reached the contrary conclusion. The latter view is supported by Supreme Court decisions subsequent to *Boykin: Brady v. United States,*[12] citing *Boykin* but upholding a guilty plea even though defendant had not been specifically advised of the three rights discussed in *Boykin;* and *North Carolina v. Alford,*[13] stating that in determining the validity of guilty pleas the "standard was and remains whether the plea represents a voluntary and intelligent choice among the alternative courses of action open to the defendant."

(f) Determining Factual Basis of Plea. In recent years, many jurisdictions have imposed an added obligation upon the judge receiving a plea of guilty, which is to make a determination regarding the accuracy of the plea. In federal procedure, for example, the judge is not to "enter a judgment upon such a plea without making such inquiry as shall satisfy [him] that there is a factual basis for the plea."[14] Many states have adopted a comparable provision. Generally, these provisions leave the judge free to decide in the particular case how this determination can best be made; the factual basis is most commonly established by inquiry of the defendant, inquiry of the prosecutor, examination of the presentence report, or a combination of those methods. Nor do they attempt to establish a precise quantum of evidence which must be met.

This inquiry into the factual basis serves a number of worthwhile functions. Most importantly, it should protect a defendant who is in the position of pleading voluntarily with an understanding of the nature of the charge but without realizing that his conduct does not actually fall within the charge. As the cases indicate, this does happen on occasion. In addition, the inquiry into the factual basis of the plea provides the court with a better assessment of defendant's competency and willingness to plead guilty and his understanding of the charges, increases the visibility of charge reduction practices, provides a more adequate record and thus minimizes the likelihood of the plea being successfully challenged later, and aids correctional agencies in the performance of their functions.

Difficulties with regard to establishing a factual basis matching the offense to which

12. 397 U.S. 742, 90 S.Ct. 1463, 25 L.Ed.2d 747 (1970).

13. 400 U.S. 25, 91 S.Ct. 160, 27 L.Ed.2d 162 (1970).

14. Fed.R.Crim.P. 11(f).

the plea is entered occasionally arise when the plea is the result of charge bargaining. Sometimes a defendant apparently guilty of a greater offense will be permitted to plead guilty to a logical included offense, in which case presumably the factual basis for the latter can be easily established by disclosing so much of the full occurrence which would constitute the lesser offense. But sometimes the offense to which the plea is made is not a logical included offense of the crime committed. For example, in a jurisdiction with an offense of breaking and entering in the nighttime (a nonprobationable offense with a 15–year maximum) and an offense of breaking and entering in the daytime (a probationable offense with a 5–year minimum), a bargained plea to the latter offense might be tendered although the facts show that the crime occurred at midnight. Or, the plea might be to a hypothetical crime which produces the range of sentencing possibilities the parties are agreeable to, as where a defendant charged with manslaughter is allowed to plead guilty to attempted manslaughter. Even in the hypothetical crime situation, an appellate court which is called upon to overturn the plea is not likely to do so, reasoning that the anomalous situation was sought by the defendant as part of a bargain struck for his benefit. But an appellate court which applies the factual basis requirement literally might overturn a plea even in the face of a clear factual basis for the more serious charge which was dropped as a part of the plea bargain.

Although as a general matter the determination of a factual basis for the plea is not constitutionally required, the situation is otherwise in one special set of circumstances as a result of *North Carolina v. Alford*.[15] Alford, indicted for first degree murder, pleaded guilty to second degree murder but then took the stand and declared he had not committed the murder and was pleading guilty to avoid the risk of the death penalty. Because he persisted in his plea and because a summary of the state's case indicated Alford had taken a gun from his house with the stated intention of killing the victim and had later returned with the declaration that he had carried out the killing, the judge accepted the plea. The Supreme Court upheld the plea, reasoning that

> while most pleas of guilty consist of both a waiver of trial and an express admission of guilt, the latter element is not a constitutional requisite to the imposition of criminal penalty. An individual accused of crime may voluntarily, knowingly, and understandingly consent to the imposition of a prison sentence even if he is unwilling or unable to admit his participation in the acts constituting the crime.
>
> * * * Confronted with the choice between a trial for first-degree murder, on the one hand, and a plea of guilty to second-degree murder, on the other, Alford quite reasonably chose the latter and thereby limited the maximum penalty to a 30–year term. When his plea is viewed in light of the evidence against him, which substantially negated his claim of innocence and which further provided a means by which the judge could test whether the plea was being intelligently entered, its validity cannot be seriously questioned. In view of the strong factual basis for the plea demonstrated by the State and Alford's clearly expressed desire to enter it despite his professed belief in his innocence, we hold that the trial judge did not commit constitutional error in accepting it.

The Court did not state just how strong this factual basis must be, but it would appear that when a pleading defendant denies the crime the factual basis must be significantly more certain than will suffice in other circumstances.

The Court in *Alford* observed that some courts require trial judges to reject pleas in such circumstances, and then in an oft-quoted footnote indicated no intention to foreclose such a result:

> Our holding does not mean that a trial judge must accept every constitutionally valid guilty plea merely because a defendant wishes to so plead. A criminal defendant does not have an

15. 400 U.S. 25, 91 S.Ct. 160, 27 L.Ed.2d 162 (1970).

absolute right under the Constitution to have his guilty plea accepted by the court, although the States may by statute or otherwise confer such a right. Likewise, the States may bar their courts from accepting guilty pleas from any defendants who assert their innocence.

This language has been cogently criticized on the ground that it would permit a trial judge for no good reason to deny a defendant such as Alford the opportunity to obtain concessions via plea bargaining unless he misrepresents his own perception of the circumstances. This same footnote in *Alford* goes on to say that the Court "need not now delineate" the scope of a federal judge's discretion in this regard, but since that time at least one court has held that when there is strong factual evidence implicating the defendant it is an abuse of discretion to refuse a guilty plea solely because the defendant does not admit the alleged facts of the crime.

(g) Acting on the Plea Bargain. In any case in which the tendered plea of guilty or nolo contendere is the result of a plea bargain, the judge receiving the plea will have added responsibilities. In some circumstances, at least, he will have to advise the defendant of the legal effect of the bargain, and he will of course have to decide whether or not to approve the terms of the bargain to which the parties have agreed.

In federal procedure, for example, there are three recognized types of plea bargains. The parties may agree

> that upon the entering of a plea of guilty or nolo contendere to a charged offense or to a lesser or related offense, the attorney for the government will do any of the following:
>
> (A) move for dismissal of other charges; or
>
> (B) make a recommendation, or agree not to oppose the defendant's request, for a particular sentence, with the understanding that such recommendation or request shall not be binding upon the court; or
>
> (C) agree that a specific sentence is the appropriate disposition of the case.[16]

A critical distinction, which determines the nature of the judge's responsibilities in a particular case, is that an agreement of the (B) type involves only a promise by the prosecution to seek or not oppose a certain result, while an agreement of either of the other two types involves a promise actually to bring about a certain result. This means that when the judge learns that an agreement of the (B) type has been made, he must tell the defendant of his precarious position; "the court shall advise the defendant that if the court does not accept the recommendation or request the defendant nevertheless has no right to withdraw his plea." [17] No such caution is required as to the other two types of agreements, for they do not carry this risk. Rather, as to them the court may simply proceed to "accept or reject the agreement, or may defer its decision as to the acceptance or rejection until there has been an opportunity to consider the presentence report." [18] But if the court ultimately rejects a type (A) or type (C) agreement, it must so advise the parties, "afford the defendant the opportunity to then withdraw his plea, and advise the defendant that if he persists in his guilty plea or plea of nolo contendere the disposition of the case may be less favorable to the defendant than that contemplated by the plea agreement." [19]

Somewhat similar procedures are required by state law, though there is some variation to be found as to when the defendant is to be informed that if he persists in his plea he has no assurance of the anticipated concessions and when he is to be told that he retains the right to withdraw his plea if those concessions are not granted. In large measure, the disparity is attributable to the fact that the states are not in agreement on how to deal with what in federal practice is known as a type (B) agreement. In some states that type of agreement is recognized as a situation in which the defendant assumes the risk that the prosecutor's recommendation will not be followed, which means that the judge is obligated to advise the defendant of the risk he is

16. Fed.R.Crim.P. 11(e)(1).

17. Fed.R.Crim.P. 11(e)(2).

18. Fed.R.Crim.P. 11(e)(2).

19. Fed.R.Crim.P. 11(e)(4).

taking. In some other states, however, that type of agreement is not viewed as calling for different treatment. In those jurisdictions no advance warning is required; if the judge ultimately decides not to accept the prosecutor's recommendation, the defendant must then be so advised and be given an opportunity to withdraw his plea. Which of these two systems is preferable is understandably a matter as to which there is disagreement. In favor of the first approach, it is argued that there is nothing inherently unfair in permitting a defendant to bargain for nothing more than a calculated risk that the punishment might be less severe than he would receive upon a trial. In support of the second approach, it is argued that the first one allows for at least the taint of false inducement even when the trial court is not bound by the prosecutor's dispositional recommendation.

Under either system, of course, the judge has an independent responsibility to pass upon the merits of all plea bargains which contemplate certain consequences which can be achieved only by the judge or with his approval. If the bargain goes to the sentence to be imposed, quite obviously this is a matter ultimately to be decided by the judge. If the bargain necessitates the dropping of other charges where, as is common, this can be accomplished only with the judge's approval, there is at least a limited role for the judge to perform here as well.[20]

§ 21.5 Challenge of Guilty Plea by Defendant

(a) Withdrawal of Plea. A defendant who enters a plea of guilty is not foreclosed from subsequently challenging that plea or his disposition pursuant thereto. Procedurally, one means commonly employed in an effort to "undo" a plea of guilty is a motion to withdraw the plea. Contrary to earlier practice, such a motion may now be made in the federal system only before sentencing, when withdrawal is permitted for "any fair and just reason." [1]

There is considerable variation on the state level. In some jurisdictions plea withdrawal is allowed only before sentence or only before "judgment" (which may refer to the time of sentencing or some earlier time). Many states follow the former federal approach and thus recognize that withdrawal of a plea is possible both before and after sentence and judgment. In these latter jurisdictions, there has been a distinct trend in the direction of utilizing the terminology which had been used in the federal cases. Where the defendant seeks to withdraw his guilty plea before sentence, he is generally accorded that right if he can show any fair and just reason, but where the guilty plea is sought to be withdrawn after sentence, it may be granted only to avoid manifest injustice. The prevailing approach of utilizing a more demanding standard after imposition of sentence is based upon (i) the fact that after sentence the defendant is more likely to view the plea bargain as a tactical mistake and therefore wish to have it set aside; (ii) the fact that at the time of sentencing, other portions of the plea bargain agreement will often be performed by the prosecutor (e.g., dismissal of additional charges), which might be difficult to undo if the defendant later attacked his plea; and (iii) the policy of giving finality to criminal sentences which result from a voluntary guilty plea.

As for the presentence "fair and just" reason test, the courts disagree as to how it should be applied. Some courts proceed as if any desire to withdraw the plea before sentence is "fair and just" so long as the prosecution fails to establish that it would be prejudiced by the withdrawal. The other view is that there is no occasion to inquire into the matter of prejudice unless the defendant first shows a good reason for being allowed to withdraw his plea. The latter position is the sounder and prevailing view. Given the great care with which guilty pleas are now taken—including placing the plea agreement on the

20. See United States v. Ammidown, 497 F.2d 615 (D.C.Cir.1973), and further discussion of the judge's responsibility in this regard in § 21.3(e).

§ 21.5

1. Fed.R.Crim.P. 32(d).

record, making full inquiry into the voluntariness of the plea, advising the defendant in detail concerning his rights and the consequences of his plea, determining that the defendant understands these matters, and determining that the plea is accurate—there is no reason to view pleas so taken as merely "tentative," subject to withdrawal before sentence whenever the government cannot establish prejudice. A few states once gave defendants an absolute right of presentence plea withdrawal, but they have been inclined to abandon that position in more recent years.

Under the "fair and just" test, whether the movant has asserted his innocence is an important factor to be weighed, as is the explanation for why the reason now asserted was not put forward at the time of the original pleading. The amount of time which has passed between the plea and the motion must also be taken into account. Illustrative of a reason which would meet this test but not the post-sentence "manifest injustice" standard is where the defendant now wants to pursue a certain defense which he for good reason did not put forward earlier. If the defendant establishes such a reason, its strength must be balanced against any prejudice which would be suffered by the government if the plea were withdrawn.

The "manifest injustice" test is not self-defining, and doubtless does not mean precisely the same thing in every jurisdiction. But it may generally be said that withdrawal is necessary to correct a manifest injustice if

(A) the defendant was denied the effective assistance of counsel guaranteed by constitution, statute, or rule;

(B) the plea was not entered or ratified by the defendant or a person authorized to so act in the defendant's behalf;

(C) the plea was involuntary, or was entered without knowledge of the charge or knowledge that the sentence actually imposed could be imposed;

(D) the defendant did not receive the charge or sentence concessions contemplated by the plea agreement and the prosecuting attorney failed to seek or not to oppose these concessions as promised in the plea agreement;

(E) the defendant did not receive the charge or sentence concessions contemplated by the plea agreement, which was either tentatively or fully concurred in by the court, and the defendant did not affirm the plea after being advised that the court no longer concurred and after being called upon to either affirm or withdraw the plea; or

(F) the guilty plea was entered upon the express condition, approved by the judge, that the plea could be withdrawn if the charge or sentence concessions were subsequently rejected by the court.[2]

The courts commonly treat the "manifest injustice" test as being no broader than the available grounds for relief upon collateral attack. If the defendant shows a manifest injustice, under the better view it is unnecessary that he also assert his innocence. The defendant has the burden of satisfying the trial judge that there are valid grounds for withdrawal. Courts rarely articulate the extent of this burden; it is sometimes said to be a showing of a basis of relief "by clear and convincing evidence," and sometimes a showing by a "preponderance of the evidence."

(b) Other Challenges to Plea. A defendant who has entered a plea of guilty might also challenge that plea by resorting to certain procedures likewise utilized by defendants convicted at trial, such as appeal, habeas corpus or a statutory post-conviction hearing. These procedures are discussed in more detail later,[3] and thus it will suffice here to make brief note of the limits on their use by defendants who have previously pled guilty.

In federal procedure, a defendant may take a direct appeal from a guilty plea conviction.[4] Direct appeal offers the plea-convicted defendant a significant advantage over collateral attack, as the appeal is reviewed by a three-judge panel of the court of appeals which can

2. 3 ABA Standards for Criminal Justice § 14–2.1(b)(ii), (2d ed. 1980).

3. See chs. 27 and 28.

4. McCarthy v. United States, 394 U.S. 459, 89 S.Ct. 1166, 22 L.Ed.2d 418 (1969).

overturn the plea conviction on a finding of error less than constitutional, jurisdictional, or fundamental magnitude. The states also generally allow an appeal to be taken from a guilty plea, where again there is this advantage. But the appeal alternative is more limited in that the appeal must be taken promptly after the plea, and the only matters which can be raised are those which can be resolved on the basis of the record in the case—mainly the transcript of the proceedings at which the defendant's plea of guilty was received.

A state guilty plea defendant will also have available state habeas corpus or a statutory post-conviction hearing procedure in lieu thereof. These avenues, in contrast to direct appeal, provide an opportunity for a hearing at which additional facts supporting defendant's claim may be adduced. However, relief is unlikely to be available unless any defect shown is of constitutional magnitude. As for the federal defendant, he may resort to the post-conviction procedures provided for in 28 U.S.C.A. § 2255. If he does so, he will prevail only by showing "a fundamental defect which inherently results in a complete miscarriage of justice" or "an omission inconsistent with the rudimentary demands of fair procedure." [5] Finally, mention must be made of the fact that the state defendant may ultimately end up in federal court raising constitutional objections via federal habeas corpus.

(c) Significance of Noncompliance With Plea-Receiving Procedures. One issue which arises with some frequency when a defendant moves to withdraw or otherwise challenges his guilty plea is whether a failure to comply fully with the established procedures for receiving the plea is inevitably a basis for relief. The answer may turn to some extent upon the procedural context in which that issue is raised.

If, for example, that question is asked regarding a federal defendant's attack upon his guilty plea in a § 2255 proceeding, the answer given by the Supreme Court in *United States v. Timmreck* [6] is no. In *Timmreck,* the judge at the rule 11 hearing told defendant that he could receive a sentence of 15 years imprisonment but failed to add that there was a mandatory special parole term of at least 3 years. He then accepted defendant's guilty plea and thereafter sentenced him to 10 years imprisonment plus a special parole term of 5 years. The district court concluded the rule 11 violation did not entitle defendant to § 2255 relief because he had not suffered any prejudice, as his sentence fell within that described to him when the plea was accepted, but the court of appeals disagreed and concluded that "a Rule 11 violation is per se prejudicial." A unanimous Supreme Court rejected the latter view. Noting that relief under § 2255 is available only when "the error resulted in a 'complete miscarriage of justice' or in a proceeding 'inconsistent with the rudimentary demands of fair procedure,'" the Court concluded this could hardly be the case when there has been merely "a technical violation of the rule" rather than one which "occurred in the context of other aggravating circumstances." The Court added that this result made good sense, given the fact that "the concern with finality served by the limitation on collateral attack has special force with respect to convictions based on guilty pleas."

The Court in *Timmreck* intimated that the result might have been otherwise had the defendant raised the claim on direct appeal, and cited *McCarthy v. United States* [7] in support. In *McCarthy,* the trial judge failed to address the defendant personally and determine that his plea was made voluntarily and with an understanding of the nature of the charge, as required by rule 11, and defendant raised that omission on appeal. In rejecting the government's contention that in such circumstances the government should still be allowed to prove that defendant in fact pleaded voluntarily and with an understanding of the charge, the Court concluded

> that prejudice inheres in a failure to comply with Rule 11, for noncompliance deprives the defendant of the Rule's procedural safeguards,

5. Hill v. United States, 368 U.S. 424, 82 S.Ct. 468, 7 L.Ed.2d 417 (1962).

6. 441 U.S. 780, 99 S.Ct. 2085, 60 L.Ed.2d 634 (1979).

7. 394 U.S. 459, 89 S.Ct. 1166, 22 L.Ed.2d 418 (1969).

which are designed to facilitate a more accurate determination of the voluntariness of his plea. Our holding that a defendant whose plea has been accepted in violation of Rule 11 should be afforded the opportunity to plead anew not only will insure that every accused is afforded those procedural safeguards, but also will help reduce the great waste of judicial resources required to process the frivolous attacks on guilty plea convictions that are encouraged, and are more difficult to dispose of, when the original record is inadequate.

Read narrowly, *McCarthy* says that a defendant's violation–of–rule–11 complaint on appeal cannot be defeated by the government's claim that *if* it could produce more facts by an evidentiary hearing it could show the violation was insignificant. But the above language was given a broader reading by some courts, which held that on direct appeal a defendant's conviction *must* be reversed whenever there was not full adherence to the procedure provided for in rule 11. In support of this automatic reversal standard, it was asserted that it better protects the defendant's rights and conserves judicial resources. Other federal courts took the harmless error approach on direct appeal where it appeared that the nature and extent of the deviation from rule 11 was such that it could not have had any impact on the defendant's decision to plead or the fairness in now holding him to his plea. On the notion that it exalts form over substance to ignore what has been established to be a truly harmless error, this latter position has now been incorporated into the federal rules.[8]

States are not obligated to grant relief whenever a failure to follow plea-receiving procedures has been established. True, in *Boykin v. Alabama*[9] the Court noted that "so far as the record shows, the judge asked no questions of petitioner concerning his plea, and petitioner did not address the court," and then concluded that it "was error, plain on the face of the record, for the trial judge to accept petitioner's guilty plea without an affirmative showing that it was intelligent and voluntary." But in *North Carolina v. Alford*[10] the Court explained that it would suffice if at a hearing on a post-conviction petition it was established that defendant's plea was in fact knowing and voluntary. It of course follows that this is the case if a state defendant challenges his plea by federal habeas corpus.

(d) Significance of Compliance With Plea–Receiving Procedures. An issue which is in a sense the converse of that just discussed is whether full compliance with all the established procedures for taking a plea of guilty should foreclose any subsequent attack upon the plea which would necessitate a factual determination contrary to that made when the plea was taken. The Supreme Court has confronted this question on two occasions, first in *Fontaine v. United States.*[11] The Court there held that upon a federal defendant's § 2255 motion to vacate his sentence on the ground that his plea of guilty had been induced by a combination of fear, coercive police tactics, and illness (including mental illness), a hearing was required "on this record" notwithstanding full compliance with rule 11, as § 2255 calls for a hearing unless "the motion and the files and records of the case conclusively show that the prisoner is entitled to no relief." The Court, in concluding such was not the case, noted that the objective of rule 11 "is to flush out and resolve all such issues, but like any procedural mechanism, its exercise is neither always perfect nor uniformly invulnerable to subsequent challenge calling for an opportunity to prove the allegations." But because one of the defendant's allegations in *Fontaine* concerned whether he had been mentally ill, a matter not routinely explored in a rule 11 proceeding, the case does not settle whether a hearing would be required if defendant's factual allegations were in all respects contrary to what had been determined at the time the plea was received.

8. Fed.R.Crim.P. 11(h).

9. 395 U.S. 238, 89 S.Ct. 1709, 23 L.Ed.2d 274 (1969).

10. 400 U.S. 25, 91 S.Ct. 160, 27 L.Ed.2d 162 (1970).

11. 411 U.S. 213, 93 S.Ct. 1461, 36 L.Ed.2d 169 (1973).

In the second case, *Blackledge v. Allison*,[12] Allison had pled guilty to attempted safe robbery in North Carolina, answered that he understood the judge's advice that he could receive 10 years to life, and responded in the negative when asked by the judge if anyone "made any promises or threats to you to influence you to plead guilty in this case." The only record of the proceedings was the executed form from which the judge had read those and other questions. Allison, later sentenced to 17–21 years, sought relief via federal habeas corpus; he claimed that his lawyer had told him that the prosecutor and judge had agreed to a sentence of 10 years but that he should nonetheless answer the questions at the arraignment as he did. The district court denied the petition on the ground that the form "conclusively shows" no constitutional violation and thus met the *Fontaine* standard, but the court of appeals' reversal was upheld by the Supreme Court. The Court declared: "In the light of the nature of the record of the proceeding at which the guilty plea was accepted, and of the ambiguous status of the process of plea bargaining at the time the guilty plea was made, we conclude that Allison's petition should not have been summarily dismissed."

The Court in *Allison* clearly signaled that if the plea had been received at another time with a more complete record, the result would be otherwise. It was emphasized that the plea here was entered in 1971, at a time when there were "lingering doubts about the legitimacy of the practice" of plea bargaining and thus reason not to disclose bargains in court, and that the only record was the printed form, which did not disclose whether the judge "deviated from or supplemented the text of the form" or what others at the hearing had said regarding promised sentence concessions. Most significantly, the Court observed:

> North Carolina has recently undertaken major revisions of its plea bargaining procedures in part to prevent the very kind of problem now before us. Plea bargaining is expressly legitimate. * * * The judge is directed to advise the defendant that courts have approved plea bargaining and he may thus admit to any promises without fear of jeopardizing an advantageous agreement or prejudicing himself in the judge's eye. Specific inquiry about whether a plea bargain has been struck is then made not only of the defendant, but also of his counsel and the prosecutor. * * * Finally, the entire proceeding is to be transcribed verbatim. * * *
>
> Had these commendable procedures been followed in the present case, Allison's petition would have been cast in a very different light. The careful explication of the legitimacy of plea bargaining, the questioning of both lawyers, and the verbatim record of their answers at the guilty plea proceedings would almost surely have shown whether any bargain did exist and, if so, insured that it was not ignored.

Although lower courts before *Allison* were inclined to give little credence to the record made when the guilty plea was received, this is much less true today. Of course, there are still some circumstances in which a court must conduct an evidentiary hearing to resolve a challenge to a guilty plea even when the earlier proceedings were flawless. This is certainly true when the allegation goes to a matter, such as incompetence in representation by defense counsel, which is not likely to be disproved by the record made when the plea is received, or to unusual or extreme pressures which could be expected to "carry over" to the plea proceedings and influence the defendant to give false or incomplete responses. But in the more common situations in which the defendant asserts a prior misperception of the possible consequences of his plea, of whether there was a bargain, or of the terms of the bargain, and the record of the plea proceedings clearly indicate otherwise, courts are now inclined to hold that relief can be denied without an evidentiary hearing.

(e) Effect of Withdrawn or Overturned Plea. If a defendant entered a plea of guilty in exchange for certain concessions (for example, reduction of the charge from murder to

12. 431 U.S. 63, 97 S.Ct. 1621, 52 L.Ed.2d 136 (1977).

manslaughter) but thereafter managed to withdraw or overturn that guilty plea, so that the matter will now go to trial, is the prosecutor somehow "bound" by the concessions which were given earlier? Although the Supreme Court in *Santobello v. New York* [13] assumed that the answer was no, some lower courts have found this issue to be a very difficult one. Two conflicting points of view have been expressed. One is that by his earlier action in giving the defendant concessions the prosecutor vouched that the ends of justice would be served by such a disposition, so that he is now foreclosed from asserting the contrary. The other and prevailing view is that holding the prosecutor to his end of the bargain while allowing the defendant to extricate himself from his plea, so that the defendant takes nothing more than a "heads-I-win-tails-you-lose" gamble, would restrain prosecutors from entering into plea bargains, and judges from exercising their discretion in favor of permitting withdrawal of a guilty plea.

One question is whether the latter position conflicts with the protections of the double jeopardy clause. Defendants have argued that it does, relying upon *Green v. United States*,[14] holding a defendant may not be prosecuted again for first degree murder following reversal of his conviction upon a jury verdict of guilty of second degree murder, returned at the conclusion of an earlier prosecution for first degree murder. The Court ruled that for double jeopardy purposes that jury verdict constituted "an implied acquittal on the charge of first degree murder," barring further prosecution for that offense. It has occasionally been held that when in a guilty plea context a judge finds a factual basis for the lesser offense to which the defendant is pleading and dismisses the higher charge at the state's request, this provides defendant with the same double jeopardy protection as the jury verdict in *Green.* But the great weight of authority is to the contrary, and rightly so. The other view ignores the importance of the plea milieu and the fact that acceptance of the guilty plea does not constitute an inferential finding of not guilty of the higher charge, in that no trier of fact was presented with a choice between the greater and lesser charge.

Yet another line of attack is to assert that trial on the greater charge after the guilty plea is withdrawn or overturned amounts to a violation of due process under *Blackledge v. Perry.*[15] In that case, where defendant was prosecuted on a felony assault charge after he exercised his right to trial de novo on a misdemeanor assault charge based upon the same incident, the Court held it was constitutionally impermissible for the state to respond to defendant's invocation of his statutory right to appeal in that way. Without regard to whether the prosecutor was acting in bad faith, due process "requires that a defendant be freed of apprehension of such a retaliatory motivation." But surely *Blackledge* has no application when all that the prosecutor has done is to return to the original charge, for there is no appearance of retaliation when a defendant is placed in the same position as he was before he accepted the plea bargain. It may be, however, that this "same position" must include a continuing opportunity for the defendant to enter a guilty plea to the same reduced charge as before.

But what if the prosecutor really does "up the ante" after defendant withdraws or overturns his guilty plea, now filing more charges or a more serious charge than had been brought originally? Here, courts are more likely to find that *Blackledge* applies and that due process has been violated, in that the charge enhancement has the appearance of vindictiveness in response to defendant's successful challenge of his guilty plea. As discussed elsewhere herein,[16] there exists considerable uncertainty as to what kind of showing by the prosecutor will suffice to justify the escalation of charges. But, even assuming some such limits otherwise govern, it is unclear whether they are applicable in a plea

13. 404 U.S. 257, 92 S.Ct. 495, 30 L.Ed.2d 427 (1971).

14. 355 U.S. 184, 78 S.Ct. 221, 2 L.Ed.2d 199 (1957), discussed in § 25.4(c).

15. 417 U.S. 21, 94 S.Ct. 2098, 40 L.Ed.2d 628 (1974).

16. See § 13.7(c).

bargaining context. In *Bordenkircher v. Hayes*,[17] where the prosecutor carried out his threat to prosecute defendant as a habitual offender because of his unwillingness to plead guilty to a forgery charge, the Court concluded that this conduct was not barred by *Blackledge* because the vindictiveness rationale of that case had no application to "the 'give-and-take' of plea bargaining." If that is so, then it would seem to follow that if the defendant had instead entered a guilty plea on the original forgery count but then later overturned that plea, the prosecutor would again be free to threaten prosecution under the habitual offender law and to carry out the threat if defendant did not again plead guilty to forgery.

In some cases, the due process objection may be stated somewhat differently and be grounded in *North Carolina v. Pearce*.[18] In that case, two defendants who had successfully challenged their original convictions were reprosecuted and convicted of the same offense but received higher sentences the second time around. The Court held that due process bars vindictive sentencing in response to exercise of the statutory right to appeal and also necessitates that defendants be free of "the fear of such vindictiveness," and thus concluded that a higher sentence could be imposed only if "based upon objective information concerning identifiable conduct on the part of the defendant occurring after the time of the original sentencing proceeding." In the guilty plea context, *Pearce* has not been read as barring a higher sentence where the prosecutor properly filed a higher charge after vacation of the guilty plea. As for when the sequence was plea of guilty, a setting aside of that plea, prosecution and conviction on the same charge to which the plea was entered, and imposition of a higher sentence, there was a split of authority until the Supreme Court's decision in *Alabama v. Smith*.[19] The Court held that the *Pearce* presumption, limited to circumstances presenting a " 'reasonable likelihood' that the increase in sentence is the product of actual vindictiveness," did not apply in this situation for two reasons: (i) because plea bargaining may "be pursued * * * by providing for a more lenient sentence if the defendant pleads guilty"; and (ii) because of "the greater amount of sentencing information that a trial generally affords as compared to a guilty plea." By contrast, the *Pearce* presumption *is* applicable if the defendant also pleads guilty the second time around but receives a higher sentence than he received after the first plea.

(f) Admissibility of Withdrawn or Overturned Plea and Related Statements. In the past, some courts have held that if a defendant's plea of guilty is subsequently withdrawn or otherwise vacated, the fact of that plea may nonetheless be admitted into evidence against the defendant at his later trial because it constitutes conduct inconsistent with innocence and is comparable to an extrajudicial confession to the crime. The federal rule has long been otherwise,[20] and the more recent state decisions have consistently held that such a plea is not admissible. This is as it should be, as the privilege extended to withdrawing the plea would be an empty one if the withdrawn plea could be used against the defendant on his trial.

It is not uncommon for a defendant to make incriminating statements in connection with the entry of a guilty plea, especially when he is called upon to supply information which establishes a factual basis for the plea. If that plea has been vacated, then those statements are not admissible in evidence against the defendant either. When the nature of the statements is such as to make it evident that a guilty plea was entered, then this result is an inevitable consequence of the rule that the vacated plea is itself inadmissible. But the result is just as compelling when the statements are incriminating but do not disclose that they were given in connection with a

17. 434 U.S. 357, 98 S.Ct. 663, 54 L.Ed.2d 604 (1978).

18. 395 U.S. 711, 89 S.Ct. 2072, 23 L.Ed.2d 656 (1969).

19. 490 U.S. 794, 109 S.Ct. 2201, 104 L.Ed.2d 865 (1989).

20. Kercheval v. United States, 274 U.S. 220, 47 S.Ct. 582, 71 L.Ed. 1009 (1927).

plea of guilty. A contrary rule would discourage the giving of information needed by the court in the plea receiving and sentencing process. Moreover, the compelling of such information from the defendant is justified by the fact that the plea constitutes a waiver of the privilege against self-incrimination as to the offense to which the plea was entered, a justification which no longer exists when the plea has been overturned. Sometimes limited exceptions have been recognized or urged to this rule on the nonadmissibility of statements given in connection with a since vacated plea. One is that such statements may be admitted against a defendant in a criminal proceeding for perjury or false statement if the statements were made by the defendant under oath, on the record, and in the presence of counsel; and another is that the statements may be used for impeachment purposes.

§ 21.6 Effect of Guilty Plea

(a) Rights Waived or Forfeited by Plea. A valid plea of guilty generally bars the defendant from subsequently raising objections which might well be a basis for overturning his conviction had he gone to trial. Why this should be so and the extent to which it is so was first addressed by the Supreme Court in *McMann v. Richardson* [1] and two companion cases. In *McMann,* a federal court of appeals ordered evidentiary hearings for three petitioners who had entered pleas of guilty some years earlier in New York but now asserted their pleas had been motivated by confessions coerced from them. Although those pleas had been received prior to the Court's decision in *Jackson v. Denno,*[2] holding unconstitutional the New York procedure requiring submission of the admissibility-of-a-confession issue to the jury, and though *Jackson* had been applied retroactively to the benefit of defendants who had gone to trial, the Court nonetheless concluded these petitioners were not entitled to relief:

> A conviction after trial in which a coerced confession is introduced rests in part on the coerced confession, a constitutionally unacceptable basis for conviction. * * * The defendant who pleads guilty is in a different posture. He is convicted on his counseled admission in open court that he committed the crime charged against him. The prior confession is not the basis for the judgment, has never been offered in evidence at a trial, and may never be offered in evidence.

The Court added that a contrary rule "would be an improvident invasion of the State's interest in maintaining the finality of guilty plea convictions which were valid under constitutional standards applicable at the time," and concluded: "It is no denigration of the right to trial to hold that when the defendant waives his state court remedies and admits his guilt, he does so under the law then existing; further, he assumes the risk of ordinary error in either his or his attorney's assessment of the law and facts."

In the companion case of *Brady v. United States,*[3] defendant had entered a guilty plea to violating the Federal Kidnapping Act, later held to contain an unconstitutional penalty provision whereby only those exercising their constitutional right to jury trial could receive the death penalty. Although assuming "that Brady would not have pleaded guilty except for the death penalty provision," the Court ruled he was not entitled "to withdraw his plea merely because he discovers long after the plea had been accepted that his calculus misapprehended the quality of the State's case or the likely penalties attached to alternative courses of action." In the third case in the trilogy, *Parker v. North Carolina,*[4] both the death penalty and coerced confession issues were held to be foreclosed by defendant's guilty plea. Similarly, just a few years later the Court in *Tollett v. Henderson* [5] held that a defendant who had pled guilty to murder could not subsequently challenge the racial composition of the grand jury that had indict-

§ 21.6

1. 397 U.S. 759, 90 S.Ct. 1441, 25 L.Ed.2d 763 (1970).
2. 378 U.S. 368, 84 S.Ct. 1774, 12 L.Ed.2d 908 (1964).
3. 397 U.S. 742, 90 S.Ct. 1463, 25 L.Ed.2d 747 (1970).
4. 397 U.S. 790, 90 S.Ct. 1458, 25 L.Ed.2d 785 (1970).
5. 411 U.S. 258, 93 S.Ct. 1602, 36 L.Ed.2d 235 (1973).

ed him, as "a guilty plea represents a break in the chain of events which has preceded it in the criminal process. When a criminal defendant has solemnly admitted in open court that he is in fact guilty of the offense with which he is charged, he may not thereafter raise independent claims relating to the deprivation of constitutional rights that occurred prior to the entry of the guilty plea."

Any thought that this was an absolute rule, extending to *all* constitutional rights, was soon dispelled. In *Blackledge v. Perry*,[6] holding that escalation of the charge against defendant from misdemeanor to felony following defendant's assertion of his right to trial de novo violated due process, the Court explained why defendant's guilty plea to the felony was no bar:

> Although the underlying claims presented in *Tollett* and the *Brady* trilogy were of constitutional dimension, none went to the very power of the State to bring the defendant into court to answer the charge brought against him. * * * Unlike the defendant in *Tollett*, Perry is not complaining of 'antecedent constitutional violations' or of a 'deprivation of constitutional rights that occurred prior to the entry of the guilty plea.' Rather, the right that he asserts and that we today accept is the right not to be hailed into court at all upon the felony charge.

Thereafter, in *Menna v. New York*,[7] defendant's previously asserted claim that his indictment should be dismissed on double jeopardy grounds was held not to be "waived" by his guilty plea. The Court explained in a footnote

> that a counseled plea of guilty is an admission of factual guilt so reliable that, where voluntary and intelligent, it *quite validly* removes the issue of factual guilt from the case. In most cases, factual guilt is a sufficient basis for the State's imposition of punishment. A guilty plea, therefore, simply renders irrelevant those constitutional violations not logically inconsistent with the valid establishment of factual guilt and which do not stand in the way of conviction if factual guilt is validly established.

The dissenters in the *Brady* trilogy and in *Tollett* objected that those decisions cannot be squared with established doctrine on the waiver of constitutional rights, whereunder there is no effective waiver absent an "intentional relinquishment or abandonment of a known right or privilege." [8] But as a unanimous Court later pointed out, "these decisions did not rest on any principle of waiver," [9] but instead reflect the fact that constitutional rights can be "forfeited" by entering a plea of guilty just as they can be forfeited by a failure to raise them in a timely fashion.

The Supreme Court has not been particularly helpful on the question of what constitutional rights can be lost in this fashion. The *Blackledge* "power of the State" test cannot mean that a guilty plea defendant may later challenge his conviction on any constitutional ground that, if asserted before trial and left uncorrected, would have left the state with no power to obtain a valid conviction against him at trial, for if that were the rule the defense in *Tollett* would have survived. Nor can it mean that a defendant who has been convicted on a plea of guilty may challenge his conviction on any constitutional ground that would preclude the state from obtaining a valid conviction without regard to whether the defendant asserts it as a defense, as such a rule would not cover the defense in *Blackledge.* As for the "factual guilt" theory of *Menna*, it cannot be squared with *Tollett*, where the defendant was barred even though he was asserting a claim independent of his factual guilt. Nor can the matter be resolved by saying that whether constitutional claims survive a guilty plea depends on whether they are "jurisdictional," for this simply begs the question.

6. 417 U.S. 21, 94 S.Ct. 2098, 40 L.Ed.2d 628 (1974).

7. 423 U.S. 61, 96 S.Ct. 241, 46 L.Ed.2d 195 (1975).

8. Johnson v. Zerbst, 304 U.S. 458, 58 S.Ct. 1019, 82 L.Ed. 1461 (1938).

9. Haring v. Prosise, 462 U.S. 306, 103 S.Ct. 2368, 76 L.Ed.2d 595 (1983), holding that consequently the respondent's damages action under 42 U.S.C.A. § 1983 against police who allegedly subjected him to an illegal search was not barred by his earlier plea of guilty to the offense discovered by that search.

One commentator has articulated the *Blackledge–Menna* exception as follows: "a defendant who has been convicted on a plea of guilty may challenge his conviction on any constitutional ground that, if asserted before trial, would forever preclude the state from obtaining a valid conviction against him, regardless of how much the state might endeavor to correct the defect. In other words, a plea of guilty may operate as a forfeiture of all defenses except those that, once raised, cannot be 'cured.' "[10] Where an error can be cured, the entry of the plea itself may have impaired the state's ability thereafter to prove the defendant guilty at trial. And it is not unfair to assume that the state relied on the plea to its detriment, particularly because entry of the plea has made the issue so difficult to resolve later. But when the constitutional error is incurable the state is in precisely the same position after the entry of the guilty plea as it occupied beforehand with respect to its ability to prove the defendant guilty at trial: the error would always have prevented it from obtaining a valid conviction at trial. This reasoning conforms to the results in the Supreme Court's decisions. In *Tollett* the alleged defect could have been cured by reconstituting the grand jury and obtaining a proper indictment, but the due process claim in *Blackledge* and the double jeopardy claim in *Menna* involved errors which could not be cured. Other constitutional defenses of this character, which likewise should not be deemed forfeited by a guilty plea, include the Sixth Amendment right to speedy trial and the right not to be convicted of conduct which cannot constitutionally be made criminal.

This is not to suggest, however, that a constitutional defense of that special character will in all instances survive a guilty plea, for *United States v. Broce*[11] holds to the contrary. The defendants pleaded guilty to two conspiracy indictments charging the rigging of bids on two highway projects but later, relying on a ruling re other defendants who had *not* pleaded guilty, interposed the double jeopardy claim that only one conspiracy was involved. The Court ruled that "a defendant who pleads guilty to two counts with facial allegations of distinct offenses concede[s] that he has committed two separate crimes," and thereby has relinquished any "opportunity to receive a factual hearing on a double jeopardy claim." The *Broce* Court distinguished *Blackledge* and *Menna* as cases which "could be (and ultimately were) resolved without any need to venture beyond [the] record," while in the instant case the defendants "cannot prove their claim by relying on [the] indictments and the existing record" or, indeed, "without contradicting those indictments, and that opportunity is foreclosed by the admissions inherent in their guilty pleas."[12]

Even if the constitutional violation has produced an incurable defect so that the right is not automatically forfeited by a plea of guilty, there still might occur an enforceable waiver of that same right in a particular case. For example, what if a defendant is charged with count one (as to which he has a colorable speedy trial defense) and with count two (as to which he has no apparent defense), but as a result of negotiations with the prosecutor he agrees to plead guilty to count one, which carries a lower sentence, in exchange for dismissal of count two? Because the state has given up something of value, in that its prosecutorial position on count two has deteriorated because of its reasonable assumption that it would never have to go to trial on that charge, the state's interest in preserving its opportunity to prosecute the defendant justifies foreclosing him from asserting his constitutional claim. This conclusion conforms to the Supreme Court's declaration in *Menna* that it was not holding "that a double jeopardy claim may never be waived."

10. Westen, Away From Waiver: A Rationale for the Forfeiture of Constitutional Rights in Criminal Procedure, 75 Mich.L.Rev. 1214, 1226 (1977).

11. 488 U.S. 563, 109 S.Ct. 757, 102 L.Ed.2d 927 (1989).

12. The three dissenters argued that "nothing in *Blackledge* or *Menna* indicates that the general constitutional rule announced in those cases was dependent on the fortuity that the defendants' double jeopardy claims were apparent from the records below without resort to an evidentiary hearing."

If the right in question is one which *is* subject to forfeiture under the line of Supreme Court cases discussed above, this does not inevitably mean that the defendant's attack upon his guilty plea will be unsuccessful. As the Court emphasized in *McMann,* it means that to prevail the defendant must "allege and prove serious derelictions on the part of counsel sufficient to show that his plea was not, after all, a knowing and intelligent act." The Court then said this depends "not on whether a court would retrospectively consider counsel's advice to be right or wrong, but on whether that advice was within the range of competence demanded of attorneys in criminal cases." But the advice by counsel in *McMann* was deemed to be within that range, for the New York procedure which was not challenged had theretofore been upheld by the Supreme Court. In *Tollett,* by contrast, it appears that defense counsel had not even investigated the facts upon which a claim of unconstitutional selection of the grand jury could have been grounded, yet the Court also declined to treat that as beyond the range of competence required. The Court emphasized, however, that had counsel done otherwise he could at best "only delay the inevitable date of prosecution," which suggests a more rigorous standard might be applied if counsel failed to explore possible constitutional objections more likely to affect the outcome of the case.

As the Court later concluded in *Hill v. Lockhart,*[13] the two-part ineffective assistance of counsel test of *Strickland v. Washington*[14] applies in a guilty plea context. The first half of that test is "nothing more than a restatement of the standard of attorney competence" stated in *Tollett* and *McMann* and discussed above, while the second or "prejudice" part "focuses on whether counsel's constitutionally ineffective performance affected the outcome of the plea process." What the defendant must show is "a reasonable probability that, but for counsel's errors, he would not have pleaded guilty and would have insisted on going to trial." This means, the Court elaborated, that if the error was a failure to discover potentially exculpatory evidence, the question is whether "discovery of the evidence would have led counsel to change his recommendation as to the plea," which in turn depends on "whether the evidence likely would have changed the outcome of a trial." Similarly, if the error was failure to advise defendant of an affirmative defense it must be asked "whether the affirmative defense would likely have succeeded at trial." In *Hill,* where the error was a failure by counsel to advise defendant correctly on his parole eligibility under the plea bargain, prejudice was not shown because it did not appear defendant "placed particular emphasis on his parole eligibility in deciding whether or not to plead guilty."

Finally, it must be emphasized that the forfeiture rule discussed above has no application to defects which go directly to the guilty plea itself. This includes not only defects concerning advice of counsel, as just noted, but also defects in the procedure by which the plea was received or circumstances which make the plea other than voluntary, knowing and intelligent. As the Court noted in *McMann,* it is beyond dispute that "a guilty plea is properly open to challenge" if, for instance, "the circumstances that coerced the confession have abiding impact and also taint the plea." Moreover, a defendant after his plea of guilty remains free to raise objections regarding the sentence subsequently imposed, at least when the sentence now objected to was not itself a part of the plea agreement.

(b) Conditional Pleas. There are many defenses and objections which a defendant must ordinarily raise by pretrial motion, and if that motion is denied interlocutory appeal of the ruling by the defendant is seldom permitted. As noted above, a plea of guilty is with rare exception treated as a waiver or forfeiture of such claims. This is also true of a plea of nolo contendere, which means that in most jurisdictions a defendant who wishes to preserve his pretrial objections for appeal

13. 474 U.S. 52, 106 S.Ct. 366, 88 L.Ed.2d 203 (1985).

14. 466 U.S. 668, 104 S.Ct. 2052, 80 L.Ed.2d 674 (1984), discussed in § 11.10.

must go to trial. A few jurisdictions have provided for a contrary result by statutory provisions to the effect that certain pretrial motions, such as suppression motions, may be reviewed upon appeal from an ensuing conviction notwithstanding the fact that such judgment is based upon the defendant's plea rather than a finding of guilty after trial.

These statutes serve to avoid the necessity for trials undertaken for the sole purpose of preserving pretrial objections. As the Supreme Court put it in *Lefkowitz v. Newsome,*[15] holding that such a provision has the effect of preserving the claim for federal habeas corpus review as well, it constitutes a "commendable effort to relieve the problem of congested trial calendars in a manner that does not diminish the opportunity for the assertion of rights guaranteed by the Constitution." The four major arguments which have been made against such conditional pleas, that the procedure encourages a flood of appellate litigation, militates against achieving finality in the criminal process, reduces effectiveness of appellate review due to the lack of a full trial record, and forces decision on constitutional questions that could otherwise be avoided by invoking the harmless error doctrine, are less than compelling.

In the great majority of jurisdictions which have not enacted such statutes, the parties in a particular case may be able to create a situation whereby the defendant's plea of guilty or nolo contendere does not foreclose appeal of the denial of a pretrial motion. In recent years there has developed a practice whereby a defendant will enter such a plea but expressly reserve his right to appeal a specified pretrial ruling. Some appellate courts, either because they view this plea-with-reservation procedure to be a desirable alternative to an otherwise unnecessary trial or because they feel bound to honor the plea agreement made below, proceed to decide the reserved issue. Others, most often because they believe conditional pleas are undesirable and should be discouraged, refuse to decide the reserved question and remand so that the defendant may be permitted to withdraw his plea.

(c) **Trial on Stipulated Facts.** Yet another device which is sometimes utilized to avoid both the necessity for a full trial and the waiver-forfeiture consequences which attend a nolo or guilty plea is a trial on stipulated facts. Under this procedure, the defendant enters a plea of not guilty, after which the case is submitted to the judge for decision upon the preliminary hearing transcript or other statement of facts agreed to by the parties. If the judge finds the defendant guilty, the defendant will have retained his usual right to appeal. But the conditional plea is a better procedure: it saves time by avoiding the need for even a short trial; it is more likely to be understood by the defendant; and there is a risk that in some circumstances the stipulation procedure will be viewed by an appellate court as foreclosing the very issue the defendant sought to preserve.

15. 420 U.S. 283, 95 S.Ct. 886, 43 L.Ed.2d 196 (1975).

Chapter 22

TRIAL BY JURY AND IMPARTIAL JUDGE

Table of Sections

---

§ 22.1 The Right to Jury Trial

(a) Generally; Applicable to the States. Royal interference with jury trial in the colonies was deeply resented, and thus it is not surprising that the constitutions of the original states (and every state entering the Union thereafter) guaranteed jury trial, and that the United States Constitution commanded from the outset: "The Trial of all Crimes, except in Cases of Impeachment, shall be by Jury; and such Trial shall be held in the State where the said Crimes shall have been committed." [1] That language was criticized as inadequate, and thus the Bill of Rights specifically provid-

§ 22.1

1. U.S. Const. Art. III, § 2.

ed for jury trial in civil cases,[2] grand jury indictment in criminal cases,[3] and in the Sixth Amendment that in "all criminal prosecutions" the defendant was entitled to trial "by an impartial jury of the State and district wherein the crime shall have been committed."

The Supreme Court on several occasions indicated that this Sixth Amendment right was not applicable to the states via the Fourteenth Amendment due process clause.[4] When the incorporation issue was resolved by asking whether "a fair and enlightened system of justice would be impossible without" the right in question,[5] that conclusion seemed beyond dispute, for then (as now) jury trial was not utilized in most countries. But when, as the Court put it in *Duncan v. Louisiana*,[6] it was deemed more appropriate to settle the incorporation question by asking whether the right "is necessary to an Anglo–American regime of ordered liberty," then it was apparent that the Sixth Amendment right to jury trial was also applicable to the states. As the Court explained in *Duncan,* "[p]roviding an accused with the right to be tried by a jury of his peers [gives] him an inestimable safeguard against the corrupt or overzealous prosecutor and against the compliant, biased, or eccentric judge." The *Duncan* majority conceded that jury trial has "its weaknesses and the potential for misuse," but concluded it was well established that in criminal cases "juries do understand the evidence and come to sound conclusions in most of the cases presented to them."

The right recognized in *Duncan* is to have a jury pass on the ultimate question of guilt or innocence and to ascertain the facts[7] relevant to that determination; it does not include the matter of sentencing. As stated in *Spaziano v. Florida*,[8] the Sixth Amendment "never has been thought to guarantee a right to jury determination" of "the appropriate punishment to be imposed on an individual." The Court there held that this was so even as to the death penalty, and that consequently there was no constitutional prohibition upon a sentencing scheme which permitted a trial judge to override a jury's recommendation of a life sentence instead of the death penalty. In response to the claim that because "the jury serves as the voice of the community, the jury is in the best position to decide whether a particular crime is so heinous that the community's response must be death," the Court declared that the "community's voice is heard at least as clearly in the legislature when the death penalty is authorized and the particular circumstances in which death is appropriate are defined."[9]

(b) Petty Offenses. The Court in *Duncan* noted in passing that "there is a category of petty crimes or offenses which is not subject to the Sixth Amendment jury trial provisions and should not be subject to the Fourteenth Amendment jury trial requirement here applied to the States." Shortly thereafter, in

2. "In Suits at common law, where the value in controversy shall exceed twenty dollars, the right of jury trial shall be preserved, and no fact tried by jury, shall be otherwise re-examined in any Court of the United States, than according to the rules of the common law." U.S. Const. Amend. 7.

3. "No person shall be held to answer for a capital or otherwise infamous crime, unless on a presentment or indictment of a Grand Jury." U.S. Const. Amend. 5.

4. Palko v. Connecticut, 302 U.S. 319, 58 S.Ct. 149, 82 L.Ed. 288 (1937); Snyder v. Massachusetts, 291 U.S. 97, 54 S.Ct. 330, 78 L.Ed. 674 (1934); Maxwell v. Dow, 176 U.S. 581, 20 S.Ct. 448, 44 L.Ed.2d 597 (1900).

5. Palko v. Connecticut, 302 U.S. 319, 58 S.Ct. 149, 82 L.Ed. 288 (1937).

6. 391 U.S. 145, 88 S.Ct. 1444, 20 L.Ed.2d 491 (1968).

7. Difficult questions as to what is an issue of fact for the jury and what is an issue of law for the judge sometimes arise. See, e.g., United States v. Johnson, 718 F.2d 1317 (5th Cir.1983).

8. 468 U.S. 447, 104 S.Ct. 3154, 82 L.Ed.2d 340 (1984).

9. Stevens, J., joined by Brennan and Marshall, JJ., dissenting in part, concluded: "The same consideration that supports a constitutional entitlement to a trial by a jury rather than a judge at the guilt or innocence stage—the right to have an authentic representative of the community apply its lay perspective to the determination that must precede a deprivation of liberty—applies with special force to the determination that must precede a deprivation of life. In many respects capital sentencing resembles a trial on the question of guilt, involving as it does a prescribed burden of proof of given elements through the adversarial process. But more important than its procedural aspects, the life-or-death decision in capital cases depends upon its link to community values for its moral and constitutional legitimacy."

Baldwin v. New York,[10] where appellant had been denied a jury trial when convicted of a misdemeanor punishable by imprisonment up to one year, a 5–3 majority held that "no offense can be deemed 'petty' for purposes of the right to trial by jury where imprisonment for more than six months is authorized." Justice White's opinion stressed that in the federal system petty offenses had long been "defined as those punishable by no more than six months in prison and a $500 fine," that "crimes triable without a jury in the American States since the late 18th century were also generally punishable by no more than a six-month prison term," and that after *Duncan* "New York City alone denies an accused the right to interpose between himself and a possible prison term of over six months, the common sense judgment of a jury of his peers." He concluded: "This near-uniform judgment of the Nation furnishes us with the only objective criterion by which a line could ever be drawn—on the basis of the possible penalty alone—between offenses which are and which are not regarded as 'serious' for purposes of trial by jury."

Two points must be emphasized regarding the *Baldwin* test. For one thing, it should be noted that the Court used the word "punishable," so that the right to jury trial (unlike the right to counsel [11]) is to be determined on the basis of the punishment which *could* be imposed rather than that which it turns out is actually imposed in the particular case. This is because the maximum penalty authorized by the legislature is a truer indicator of society's judgment as to the seriousness of the crime charged. But where the legislature has not set any maximum penalty, as is typically the case as to criminal contempt, the "petty offense" distinction must be made on the basis of the penalty actually imposed.[12] In that connection, the Court ruled in *Frank v. United States* [13] that where petitioner was convicted of criminal contempt without a jury and received a suspended sentence and probation for three years, and the government conceded that he could receive not more than six months imprisonment if he violated the terms of probation, the contempt was a petty offense for jury trial purposes. The Court in *Frank* stressed that conditional release is a much lesser imposition than incarceration, and noted that in "noncontempt cases, Congress has not viewed the possibility of five years' probation as onerous enough to make an otherwise petty offense 'serious.' "

Secondly, it is important to note that *Baldwin* describes a particular situation (i.e., offense punishable by more than six months' imprisonment) in which the offense is not petty, but did not hold that all other situations qualify as petty offenses. Thus, it was then open to contention that some such situations did *not* qualify, because of either (a) the very nature of the offense charged, or (b) the magnitude of other punishment (e.g., a fine) authorized by statute.

Well before the *Baldwin* decision, the Supreme Court had refused to view the maximum potential sentence as the sole criterion for determining whether or not an offense was petty for jury trial purposes. Rather, the Court looked to the nature of the offense, considering such factors as whether it was indictable at common law,[14] whether it was morally offensive,[15] and whether it was malum in se rather than malum prohibitum.[16] But that approach was abandoned by a unanimous Court in *Blanton v. City of North Las*

10. 399 U.S. 66, 90 S.Ct. 1886, 26 L.Ed.2d 437 (1970).

11. See § 11.2(a).

12. Dyke v. Taylor Implement Mfg. Co., 391 U.S. 216, 88 S.Ct. 1472, 20 L.Ed.2d 538 (1968) (jury trial not required where maximum sentence authorized by statute is 10 days in jail and a $50 fine); Bloom v. Illinois, 391 U.S. 194, 88 S.Ct. 1477, 20 L.Ed.2d 522 (1968) (no statutory limits; denial of requested jury trial to defendant sentenced to imprisonment for 24 months constitutional error).

13. 395 U.S. 147, 89 S.Ct. 1503, 23 L.Ed.2d 162 (1969).

14. District of Columbia v. Clawans, 300 U.S. 617, 57 S.Ct. 660, 81 L.Ed. 843 (1937).

15. Schick v. United States, 195 U.S. 65, 24 S.Ct. 826, 49 L.Ed. 99 (1904).

16. District of Columbia v. Colts, 282 U.S. 63, 51 S.Ct. 52, 75 L.Ed. 177 (1930).

Vegas.[17] Noting that the earlier "common law approach has been undermined by the substantial number of statutory offenses lacking common law antecedents," the Court in *Blanton* declared: "The judiciary should not substitute its judgment as to seriousness for that of a legislature, which is 'far better equipped to perform the task, and [is] likewise more responsive to changes in attitude and more amenable to the recognition and correction of their misperceptions in this respect.' "

The focus, therefore, is upon the various penalties which the legislature has attached to the offense in question. As a unanimous Court explained in *Blanton:*

> Although we did not hold in *Baldwin* that an offense carrying a maximum prison term of six months or less automatically qualifies as a "petty" offense, and decline to do so today, we do find it appropriate to presume for purposes of the Sixth Amendment that society views such an offense as "petty." A defendant is entitled to jury trial in such circumstances only if he can demonstrate that any additional statutory penalties, viewed in conjunction with the maximum authorized period of incarceration, are so severe that they clearly reflect a legislative determination that the offense in question is a "serious" one. This standard, albeit somewhat imprecise, should ensure the availability of a jury trial in the rare situation where a legislature packs an offense it deems "serious" with onerous penalties that nonetheless "do not puncture the 6–month incarceration line."

The Court then applied those principles to the instant case, involving defendants charged with driving under the influence, and concluded they were not entitled to jury trial, as (1) the maximum authorized prison sentence did not exceed six months; (2) the 20–day mandatory minimum is "immaterial," as in drawing the constitutional line the Court has "assumed that a defendant convicted of the offense in question would receive the *maximum* authorized prison sentence"; (3) the mandatory 90–day license suspension "will be irrelevant if it runs concurrently with the prison sentence, which we assume for present purposes to be the maximum of six months"; (4) the alternative sentence of 48 hours community service while dressed in clothing identifying the defendant as a DUI offender "is less embarrassing and less onerous than six months in jail"; and (5) as for the possible additional penalty of a $1,000 fine, "it is well below the $5,000 level set by Congress in its most recent definition of a 'petty' offense," [18] and is not "out of step with state practice for offenses carrying prison sentences of six months or less."

Special problems are presented in cases involving defendants other than individuals, as in *Muniz v. Hoffman*,[19] where a labor union contended it was entitled to a jury trial in a criminal contempt proceeding for violating temporary injunctions, which resulted in the imposition of a fine of $10,000 on the union. The Court, after finding no statutory right to jury trial in such circumstances, went on to consider the constitutional right and in that connection declined to

> accept the proposition that a contempt must be considered a serious crime under all circumstances where the punishment is a fine of more than $500, unaccompanied by imprisonment. * * * From the standpoint of determining the seriousness of the risk and the extent of the possible deprivation faced by a contemnor, imprisonment and fines are intrinsically different. It is not difficult to grasp the proposition that six months in jail is a serious matter for any individual, but it is not tenable to argue that the possibility of a $501 fine would be considered a serious risk to a large corporation or a labor union. Indeed, * * * we cannot say that the fine of $10,000 imposed on Local 70 in this case was a deprivation of such magnitude that a jury should have been interposed to guard against bias or mistake. This union, the Government suggests, collects dues from some 13,000 persons; and although the fine is not insubstantial, it is not of such magnitude that the union was

17. 489 U.S. 538, 109 S.Ct. 1289, 103 L.Ed.2d 550 (1989).

18. 18 U.S.C.A. § 1.

19. 422 U.S. 454, 95 S.Ct. 2178, 45 L.Ed.2d 319 (1975).

deprived of whatever right to jury trial it might have under the Sixth Amendment.

Assuming that in some circumstances there is a right to jury trial when a fine for criminal contempt is imposed upon a labor union or corporation, a matter the Court in *Muniz* declined to reach, certainly the result in that case is unobjectionable, for the fine came to less than a dollar per member. Other courts, expressing doubts as to whether there was a right to jury trial in any event in such circumstances, have also looked at the impact per member in holding, for example, that it is not objectionable that the fine on a union amounted to $50 per member or to no more than a member's weekly union dues for each day of the contempt. Similar uncertainty exists as to corporate defendants. Fines of $1,000 have been upheld almost routinely, and fines well in excess of that have been allowed when the corporation's illicit activity produced much revenue.

Finally, there is the question of whether in the joint trial of several petty offenses there is a right to jury trial if the cumulative penalty which could be imposed exceeds the petty offense limits. One aspect of this problem reached the Supreme Court in *Codispoti v. Pennsylvania.*[20] The Court there held that in the case of post-verdict adjudications of various acts of contempt committed during trial, the Sixth Amendment requires a jury trial if the sentences imposed [21] aggregate more than six months, even though no sentence for more than six months was imposed for any one act of contempt, as "the salient fact [is] that the contempts arose from a single trial, were charged by a single judge and were tried in a single proceeding." Some lower courts have reached the same conclusion as to joint charges outside the contempt area, while some others have reached the contrary conclusion on the seemingly erroneous assumption that in all joint charge situations the jury trial right is to be determined on the basis of the penalty actually imposed.

(c) Noncriminal Trials. Although the Sixth Amendment right to jury trial by its own terms extends only to "criminal prosecutions," it has been argued from time to time that the right extends also to other proceedings which bear some similarity to criminal trials. Courts have generally not been receptive to this contention. It has been held, for example, that this right does not extend to suits by the government to collect civil penalties, sexual psychopath proceedings, or paternity actions. In *McKeiver v. Pennsylvania,*[22] the Supreme Court held that "trial by jury in the juvenile court's adjudicative stage is not a constitutional requirement," reasoning that compelling jury trial might make the proceeding fully adversary and deprive it of its informal and protective character.

(d) Size of Jury. Although the Supreme Court had originally ruled that the right guaranteed by the Sixth Amendment was a trial by the traditional jury of 12 persons,[23] in *Williams v. Florida* [24] the Court held that the Sixth Amendment was not violated by use of 6–person juries. Justice White explained:

> The purpose of the jury trial, as we noted in *Duncan,* is to prevent oppression by the Government. * * * Given this purpose, the essential feature of a jury obviously lies in the interposition between the accused and his accuser of the commonsense judgment of a group of laymen, and in the community participation and shared responsibility which results from that group's determination of guilt or innocence. The performance of this role is not a function of the particular number of the body which makes up the jury. To be sure, the number should probably be large enough to promote group deliberation, free from outside attempts at intimidation, and to provide a fair possibility for obtaining a representative cross section of the community. But we find

20. 418 U.S. 506, 94 S.Ct. 2687, 41 L.Ed.2d 912 (1979).

21. Again, the sentence actually imposed governs when there is no legislative maximum. This means that in a criminal contempt case several contempts which are individually petty because of the sentence imposed for each do not become serious when tried together if the sentences are directed to run concurrently. Taylor v. Hayes, 418 U.S. 488, 94 S.Ct. 2697, 41 L.Ed.2d 897 (1974).

22. 403 U.S. 528, 91 S.Ct. 1976, 29 L.Ed.2d 647 (1971).

23. Thompson v. Utah, 170 U.S. 343, 18 S.Ct. 620, 42 L.Ed. 1061 (1898).

24. 399 U.S. 78, 90 S.Ct. 1893, 26 L.Ed.2d 446 (1970).

> little reason to think that these goals are in any meaningful sense less likely to be achieved when the jury numbers six, than when it numbers 12—particularly if the requirement of unanimity is retained. And, certainly the reliability of the jury as a factfinder hardly seems likely to be a function of its size.[25]

He went on to assert that a 12-person jury was not "necessarily more advantageous to the defendant" in that a smaller group reduced the chances of a holdout juror on either side, and that the cross section objective would not be "significantly diminished" by a 6-person jury if arbitrary exclusions from the jury rolls were forbidden.

The analysis in *Williams* has frequently been criticized. It is argued that 6-person juries are significantly less reliable than 12-person juries, and support for this conclusion is drawn from studies showing that civil juries of six are more erratic in their awarding of damages. There are also studies indicating that use of smaller juries does not result in significant savings of time, although it is true that smaller juries "hang," necessitating retrial, less often. That might be viewed as a mark of efficiency by some, but not those who see the hung jury as representing the legal system's respect for the minority viewpoint. It has also been shown that as a statistical matter a 6-person jury is much less likely to represent diverse groups in the community. Some of these studies were relied upon by the Court in *Ballew v. Georgia,*[26] where it was unanimously held that petitioner's trial before a 5-member jury deprived him of his constitutional right to jury trial. Although the Court did "not pretend to discern a clear line between six members and five," this data was deemed to justify the conclusion that "any further reduction" in jury size "attains constitutional significance," especially in light of the fact that there is "no significant state advantage in reducing the number of jurors from six to five."

(e) Unanimity. In *Apodaca v. Oregon,*[27] where petitioners had been convicted of felonies by 11-1 and 10-2 votes, the Supreme Court overruled earlier decisions and held that the Sixth Amendment does not require jury unanimity. As in *Williams,* the Court began the analysis with the assertion that "the essential feature of a jury obviously lies in the interposition between the accused and his accuser of the commonsense judgment of a group of laymen," and then concluded:

> A requirement of unanimity, however, does not materially contribute to the exercise of this commonsense judgment. * * * In terms of this function we perceive no difference between juries required to act unanimously and those permitted to convict or acquit by votes of 10 to two or 11 to one. Requiring unanimity would obviously produce hung juries in some situations where nonunanimous juries will convict or acquit. But in either case, the interest of the defendant in having the judgment of his peers interposed between himself and the officers of the State who prosecute and judge him is equally well served.

The plurality opinion in *Apodaca* also rejected the contention, raised without success in the companion case of *Johnson v. Louisiana,*[28] that unanimity was required to effectuate the constitutional requirement that the defendant be proved guilty beyond a reasonable doubt. It was noted that the reasonable doubt standard developed separately from the jury trial right and that, in any event, lack of unanimity was not the equivalent of a reasonable doubt. As for the claim that unanimity was a necessary precondition for effective application of the requirement that jury panels

25. Harlan, Stewart, Black and Douglas, JJ., concurred in the result. Blackmun, J., took no part in the case. Marshall, J., dissenting, adhered "to the decision of the Court in Thompson v. Utah that the jury guaranteed by the Sixth Amendment consists 'of twelve persons, neither more nor less.' "

26. 435 U.S. 223, 98 S.Ct. 1029, 55 L.Ed.2d 234 (1978).

27. 406 U.S. 404, 92 S.Ct. 1628, 32 L.Ed.2d 184 (1972).

28. 406 U.S. 356, 92 S.Ct. 1620, 32 L.Ed.2d 152 (1972), involving a 9-3 verdict. There, the case had been tried before *Duncan,* so appellant conceded that the Sixth Amendment was not applicable and instead argued he must prevail in order to give substance to the proof beyond a reasonable doubt standard. *Apodaca* involved the slightly different contention that the Sixth Amendment right to jury trial should be read as requiring unanimity so as to give support to the reasonable doubt standard.

reflect a cross section of the community, the *Apodaca* plurality opinion rejected the assumption that "minority groups, even when they are represented on a jury, will not adequately represent the viewpoint of those groups simply because they may be outvoted in the final result." The Court did not say in *Apodaca* and *Johnson* how great a departure from unanimity would be tolerated, but in a brief concurring opinion Justice Blackmun, noting the assertion in *Johnson* that "a substantial majority of the jury" are to be convinced, declared that "a 7–5 standard, rather than a 9–3 or 75% minimum, would afford me great difficulty." Justice Powell, who supplied the critical fifth vote in *Apodaca*, explained in his concurrence that he based it upon his conclusion that unanimity was a part of the jury trial right which was not incorporated by the due process clause. This meant that *Apodaca* had no significance for federal trials.

With *Williams* having declared that there is no right to a jury of 12 and *Apodaca* that there is no right to unanimity, it was perhaps inevitable that the Court would ultimately have to consider the extent to which both variations from the traditional jury could be simultaneously permitted. *Burch v. Louisiana* [29] presented such a question, for at issue there was a provision that misdemeanors punishable by more than 6 months "shall be tried before a jury of six persons, five of whom must concur to render a verdict." A unanimous Court struck down that provision. Noting "that lines must be drawn somewhere if the substance of the jury trial right is to be preserved," the Court concluded that the "near-uniform judgment of the Nation," reflected by the fact that only two states allowed nonunanimous verdicts by 6–person juries, "provides a useful guide in delimiting the line between those jury practices that are constitutionally permissible and those that are not."

(f) Trial De Novo. In *Callan v. Wilson*,[30] the Supreme Court held that the Sixth Amendment right to jury trial barred procedures whereby a trial was held in the first instance without a jury but at the first appellate stage a de novo trial by jury was provided. But in *Ludwig v. Massachusetts*,[31] involving a two-tier system of trial courts in which there was a right to jury trial only at the second tier, available after a conviction upon a trial without a jury at the first tier, the Court in upholding that particular system placed considerable emphasis upon the fact that the right to jury trial was not burdened by the cost of an additional trial. This was because under the Massachusetts system a defendant may reach the second tier by "admitting sufficient findings of fact," meaning he "need not pursue, in any real sense, a defense at the lower tier." It was thus different than the District of Columbia system found wanting in *Callan*, where it was necessary for the defendant to be "fully tried" in the first tier.

The Court in *Ludwig* also concluded that the right to jury trial was not unconstitutionally burdened by the danger of a harsher sentence at the second tier. This was because the Court's prior decisions [32] effectively guarded against that possibility. Finally, the Court declared that it had not been established that the right to jury trial was unconstitutionally burdened by the psychological and physical hardships of the two trials, as appellant "has not presented any evidence to show that there is a greater delay in obtaining a jury in Massachusetts than there would be if the Commonwealth abandoned its two-tier system." But this did not require reconsideration of *Callan*, the Court cautioned, for that decision also rested upon Article III, § 2, clause 3 of the Constitution, which is not applicable to the states.

(g) Jury Nullification. Except in a few states where a constitutional provision provides that in criminal cases the jury shall be entitled to determine both the law and the facts, the function of the jury is commonly

29. 441 U.S. 130, 99 S.Ct. 1623, 60 L.Ed.2d 96 (1979).

30. 127 U.S. 540, 8 S.Ct. 1301, 32 L.Ed. 223 (1888).

31. 427 U.S. 618, 96 S.Ct. 2781, 49 L.Ed.2d 732 (1976).

32. See § 27.1(d).

said to be that of ascertaining the facts and then applying the law, as stated by the judge, to those facts. Indeed, it is not at all unusual for a jury in a criminal case to be instructed that it has the "duty" to proceed in such a fashion. But it is nonetheless true that a jury in a criminal case has the power to acquit even when its findings as to the facts, if literally applied to the law as stated by the judge, would have resulted in a conviction. This is because a jury verdict of not guilty is not subject to reversal or to review in any manner whatsoever. On occasion, juries exercise this power by acquitting defendants who are charged with violating an unpopular law and defendants otherwise viewed sympathetically.

This practice, usually referred to as jury nullification, would seem to be a part of the right to jury trial guaranteed by the Sixth Amendment. At least, the language which the Supreme Court has used to describe that right appears to encompass the nullification process. In *Duncan v. Louisiana*,[33] holding that right applicable to the states, the Court declared that in the view of the framers "[i]f the defendant preferred the common-sense judgment of a jury to the more tutored but perhaps less sympathetic reaction of the single judge, he was to have it." Similarly, in emphasizing the need for juries drawn from a cross-section of the community the Court later asserted: "The purpose of a jury is to guard against the exercise of arbitrary power—to make available the commonsense judgment of the community as a hedge against the overzealous or mistaken prosecutor and in preference to the professional or perhaps overconditioned or biased response of a judge." [34] And in ruling a defendant is entitled to a fairly selected jury sufficiently open-minded on the death penalty issue, the Court explained that "one of the most important functions any jury can perform * * * is to maintain a link between contemporary community values and the penal system." [35]

But, should the jury be told specifically that it has this power? The prevailing view today—that it should not be so informed—is often attributed to *Sparf and Hansen v. United States*,[36] upholding a jury instruction that "a jury is expected to be governed by law, and the law it should receive from the court." But *Sparf* did not settle the jury nullification issue, for the Court did not address the specific question whether jurors should be told they can refuse to enforce the law's harshness when justice so requires. But lower courts have rather consistently ruled that no such instruction should be given. The leading case is *United States v. Dougherty*,[37] where the court concluded that the "jury system has worked out reasonably well overall" without resort to a nullification instruction, "with the jury acting as a 'safety valve' for exceptional cases, without being a wildcat or runaway institution." This is because, the court explained, the jury "gets its understanding as to the arrangements in the legal system" not only from the judge's instructions but also through "the informal communication from the total culture," and the "totality of input generally convey adequately enough the idea of prerogative, of freedom in an occasional case to depart from what the judge says." The court expressed the fear that a nullification instruction would upset the existing balance and produce many more hung juries. Finally, the court in *Dougherty* declared that such an instruction would deprive the individual juror of an important protection which he now enjoys and to which he is entitled: that "when he takes action that he knows is right, but also knows is unpopular, either in the community at large or in his own particular grouping, that he can fairly put it to friends and neighbors that he was merely following the instructions of the court."

33. 391 U.S. 145, 88 S.Ct. 1444, 20 L.Ed.2d 491 (1968).

34. Taylor v. Louisiana, 419 U.S. 522, 95 S.Ct. 692, 42 L.Ed.2d 690 (1975).

35. Witherspoon v. Illinois, 391 U.S. 510, 88 S.Ct. 1770, 20 L.Ed.2d 776 (1968).

36. 156 U.S. 51, 15 S.Ct. 273, 39 L.Ed. 343 (1895).

37. 473 F.2d 1113 (D.C.Cir.1972).

There is considerable commentary supporting the *Dougherty* position, although the contrary position has also been vigorously argued. In opposition, it is contended that there is no reason to assume that juries will act in a different and less desirable way if informed about their nullification power, that there are political advantages to be gained by not lying to the jury, and that a nullification instruction would serve to discourage acquittals based on prejudice instead of encouraging them because it sets justice and conscience as the standards for acquittal rather than leaving the jurors to use their own biases as standards.

(h) Waiver of Jury Trial. Contrary to earlier practice, waiver of jury trial is now generally permitted except when expressly prohibited by a constitutional or statutory provision, as is the case in a few jurisdictions with respect to capital cases. A major influence in bringing about this shift was *Patton v. United States*,[38] settling that waiver of jury trial was permissible in a federal criminal trial. In support of this conclusion, the Court in *Patton* pointed out that: (1) constitutional provisions as to jury trials are primarily for the protection of the accused, and thus waiver by the party sought to be benefited should be possible; (2) absence of a jury does not affect the jurisdiction of the court; (3) the argument that public policy requires jury trials is fallacious, as a defendant may plead guilty and thus dispense with trial altogether; and (4) the common law rule not permitting waiver was justified by conditions which no longer exist.

The Court in *Patton* emphasized that for a waiver of jury trial to be effective there must be "the express and intelligent consent of the defendant." Waiver cannot be presumed from a silent record, and thus the better practice is for the defendant to be specifically advised by the court of his right to jury trial and for the waiver to be by the defendant personally either in writing or for the record in open court. Whether to be tried by a jury is an important matter to be decided by the defendant personally; it is not merely a tactical decision which may be left to defense counsel. In the federal courts and in several states waiver of jury trial must be in writing. Jury waiver tends to vary depending upon the offense category, and the pattern is similar to that for guilty pleas, suggesting that the motivations are similar: the expectation of a lesser sentence.

However, only a minority of states give the defendant an unconditional right to trial without a jury; elsewhere the defendant must also obtain the consent of the court, the consent of the prosecution, or both. In the federal system the defendant must have "the approval of the court and the consent of the government."[39] In support of requiring the consent of the prosecutor, it is argued that the state and defendant should have an equal voice as to the method of trial, that the prosecutor should be allowed to prevent trial before a biased judge, that the prosecutor should be entitled to prevent a defendant from waiving his rights when it is against his best interests, and that the prosecutor is also entitled to protect the public interest in maintaining the role of the jury in the criminal process. In favor of requiring the court's consent, it is asserted that the judge should be so involved so that he can protect the defendant, protect himself from criticism regarding the outcome of the case, obtain valuable input on matters of witness credibility and community standards, and ensure that juries continue to have a role in criminal proceedings. On the other hand, in favor of an unconditional right to waive jury trial it has been contended that such waiver should suffice because jury trial is solely for the protection of the accused, that waiver of a jury may sometimes be important to ensure a fair and impartial trial, that either the prosecutor or the court might refuse consent for unjustified reasons, that prosecutor and court consent can impede the public interest in more efficient and less expensive trials, and that jury trial is like other constitutional safeguards which can be waived by the defendant alone.

38. 281 U.S. 276, 50 S.Ct. 253, 74 L.Ed. 854 (1930).

39. Fed.R.Crim.P. 23(a).

In *Singer v. United States,*[40] the Court found "no constitutional impediment to conditioning a waiver of this right on the consent of the prosecuting attorney and the trial judge when, if either refuses to consent, the result is simply that the defendant is subject to an impartial trial by jury—the very thing that the Constitution guarantees him." The Court emphasized that there was no common law right to trial by the court, that generally the "ability to waive a constitutional right does not ordinarily carry with it the right to insist upon the opposite of that right," and that jury trial is the "normal and * * * preferable mode of dispensing of issues of fact in criminal cases." But the Court concluded with this cautionary note:

> We need not determine in this case whether there might be some circumstances where a defendant's reasons for wanting to be tried by a judge alone are so compelling that the Government's insistence on trial by jury would result in the denial to a defendant of an impartial trial. Petitioner argues that there might arise situations where "passion, prejudice * * * public feeling" or some other factor may render impossible or unlikely an impartial trial by jury. However, since petitioner gave no reason for wanting to forgo jury trial other than to save time, this is not such a case, and petitioner does not claim that it is.

Experience has shown that defendants relying upon this passage have generally been unable to convince the court that their reasons for wanting a trial by the court alone are sufficiently "compelling" that defendant's waiver motion must be granted despite the prosecution's opposition.

Finally, note should be taken of the possibility of a "partial" waiver of the right to jury trial. The *Patton* case actually involved such a situation, for the waiver upheld there concerned only the requirement that the jury consist of 12 persons. Some states expressly provide for pretrial election by the defendant to be tried by a smaller jury. Waiver of the number of jurors also occurs when the defendant agrees in advance or at the time of the event that the trial may continue with some lesser number of jurors when otherwise a mistrial would be necessitated by the excusal of some jurors during the trial or deliberations. In contrast to the situation in *Patton,* courts are generally not inclined to permit waiver by a defendant of his right to a unanimous verdict.

40. 380 U.S. 24, 85 S.Ct. 783, 13 L.Ed.2d 630 (1965).

§ 22.2 Selection of Prospective Jurors

(a) Federal Jury Selection Procedures. Jury selection in the federal courts is governed by the Federal Jury Selection and Service Act of 1968.[1] The purpose of this Act is to ensure that juries are "selected at random from a fair cross section of the community in the district or division wherein the court convenes" and that "[n]o citizen shall be excluded from service as a grand or petit juror in the district courts of the United States on account of race, color, religion, sex, national origin, or economic status." Each district court is required to devise and implement a jury selection plan designed to achieve those objectives.

Each plan must: (1) either establish a jury commission (consisting of one citizen and the clerk of the court) or authorize the clerk to manage the jury selection process; (2) specify whether the names of prospective jurors are to be selected from voter registration lists or the lists of actual voters of the political subdivisions within the district or division, and prescribe other sources when necessary to achieve the objectives stated above; (3) specify procedures for selecting names from those sources designed to ensure that each political subdivision is substantially proportionally represented in the master jury wheel; (4) provide for a master jury wheel into which the names of at least one-half of 1 per cent of the names on the source lists are placed; (5) specify those groups of persons or occupational classes whose members shall on individual request be excused from jury service because such service would entail undue hardship or extreme inconvenience; (6) specify that active members of the armed forces, members of fire

§ 22.2

1. 28 U.S.C.A. §§ 1861–1869.

or police departments, and members of the executive, legislative or judicial branches of government who are actively engaged in the performance of official duties are barred from jury service on the ground that they are exempt; (7) fix the distance beyond which jurors shall on individual request be excused from jury service on the ground of undue hardship in traveling to where court is held; (8) fix the time when the names drawn from the jury wheel shall be disclosed to the parties and to the public; and (9) specify the procedure for assigning persons whose names have been drawn from the jury wheel to jury panels.

From time to time as directed by the district court, the clerk or a district judge is publicly to draw at random from the jury wheel the names of as many persons as may be required for jury service. A juror qualification form is to be sent to each person drawn. A district judge is to determine whether a person is unqualified for, or exempt, or to be excused from jury service. A person is deemed qualified unless he "(1) is not a citizen of the United States eighteen years old who has resided for a period of one year within the judicial district; (2) is unable to read, write, and understand the English language with a degree of proficiency sufficient to fill out satisfactorily the juror qualification form; (3) is unable to speak the English language; (4) is incapable, by reason of mental or physical infirmity, to render satisfactory jury service; or (5) has a charge pending against him for the commission of, or has been convicted in a State or Federal court of record of, a crime punishable by imprisonment for more than one year and his civil rights have not been restored."

The names of all persons drawn from the master jury wheel who are determined to be qualified as jurors and not exempt or excused are to be placed in a qualified jury wheel, from which the names of persons to be assigned to jury panels are to be publicly drawn from time to time. Summonses for those persons are then to be issued. A person drawn is not to be disqualified, excluded, excused or exempted from service except as indicated above, provided that a person summoned may be "(1) excused by the court, upon a showing of undue hardship or extreme inconvenience, for such period as the court deems necessary * * *, or (2) excluded by the court on the ground that such person may be unable to render impartial jury service or that his service as a juror would be likely to disrupt the proceedings, or (3) excluded upon peremptory challenge as provided by law, or (4) excluded pursuant to the procedure specified by law upon a challenge by any party for good cause shown, or (5) excluded upon determination by the court that his service as a juror would be likely to threaten the secrecy of the proceedings, or otherwise adversely affect the integrity of jury deliberations."

Before the voir dire examination begins, or within seven days after the grounds therefor were discovered or could have been discovered by the exercise of diligence, the defendant or Attorney General may move to stay the proceedings for failure to comply with the above procedures in selecting the jury. If the motion contains a sworn statement of facts which, if true, would constitute a substantial failure to comply with the provisions of the Act, the movant is entitled to submit supporting proof. If the court determines that there has been such substantial failure, the court is to stay the proceedings pending proper jury selection.

(b) State Jury Selection Procedures. Largely as a result of changes adopted in recent years, most states now follow procedures similar to those described above in an effort to select jurors at random from some standard list. Lists of voters are most commonly used, although some states instead or in addition utilize other lists, such as a local census, the tax rolls, city directories, telephone books, and drivers' license lists. But about a third of the states, all located in New England and the South, still authorize the key-man system in one form or another. Under this system, political and civic leaders (the "key men") are asked for suggestions of prospective jurors. They are likely to recommend persons they know, and as a result the list of prospective jurors is not likely to be representative of the community at large.

A high percentage of those persons whose names are drawn for state jury service seek to be excused, and in many states excuses are rather readily granted. The courts have generally found it easier, administratively and financially, to excuse unwilling people from service on juries than to try to ensure that all qualified jurors are able to serve. Especially in those states which require jurors to serve for a considerable period of time at low pay, excuses for economic hardship are quite common. Others are excused because of poor health, advanced age, a need to care for small children, or the distance they live from the courthouse. In addition, state jury selection statutes typically list those persons who are disqualified from serving as jurors (e.g., persons not of voting age, persons who have not resided in the jurisdiction some minimum time, persons unable to read and write English, and persons with a felony conviction) and those who are exempted from jury service because of their occupations (e.g., doctors, pharmacists, teachers, clergy, and certain public employees).

(c) Denial of Equal Protection. Long before the Sixth Amendment right to jury trial was applied to the states, state jury selection procedures were subjected to constitutional challenge on the ground that they violated the equal protection clause of the Fourteenth Amendment. Just a few years after the Amendment was adopted, the Supreme Court held in *Strauder v. West Virginia* [2] that it was a denial of equal protection for a state to try a black defendant before a jury from which all members of his race had been excluded pursuant to a statute limiting jury service to "white male persons." A year later, in *Neal v. Delaware*,[3] the principle was extended to the discriminatory administration of ostensibly fair jury selection laws to achieve the same result. Under the *Strauder–Neal* equal protection approach, it was long accepted that the constitutional challenge could be made only by a defendant who was a member of the excluded class. But in *Powers v. Ohio* [4] the Court held that the defendant in a criminal case has standing to raise the equal protection rights of excluded jurors, who would themselves confront "considerable practical barriers" to challenging their exclusion.

An equal protection challenge can succeed only upon a sufficient showing of intentional or deliberate discrimination. For many years, defendants seldom succeeded in making the requisite showing; the state action was presumed constitutional and the lower court findings were presumed to be true unless the defendant proved the contrary.[5] But then came the important decision in *Norris v. Alabama*,[6] where the Supreme Court held that a defendant in a criminal case could make out a prima facie case of discriminatory jury selection by showing (i) the existence of a substantial number of blacks in the community, and (ii) their total or virtual exclusion from jury service. Once such a prima facie case is established, the burden then shifts to the state to prove that the exclusion did not flow from intentional discrimination,[7] which is not met merely by testimony from a jury commissioner that he did not intend to discriminate or that he did not know any qualified blacks.[8]

Much of the litigation that followed *Norris* concerned the question of what constitutes a "prima facie case" and what the government must do to rebut such a case. The Supreme Court's initial approach to this question was troublesome at best. *Swain v. Alabama*,[9] for example, was rightly criticized because of the Court's willingness to accept statements by the jury commissioners of a nondiscriminatory intent at face value and because of the Court's primitive statistical analysis. The post-*Swain* decisions of the Court reflect more

2. 100 U.S. (10 Otto) 303, 25 L.Ed. 664 (1880).

3. 103 U.S. (13 Otto) 370, 26 L.Ed. 567 (1881).

4. ___ U.S. ___, 111 S.Ct. 1364, 113 L.Ed.2d 411 (1991).

5. See, e.g., Thomas v. Texas, 212 U.S. 278, 29 S.Ct. 393, 53 L.Ed. 512 (1909).

6. 294 U.S. 587, 55 S.Ct. 579, 79 L.Ed. 1074 (1935).

7. Avery v. Georgia, 345 U.S. 559, 73 S.Ct. 891, 97 L.Ed. 1244 (1953).

8. Eubanks v. Louisiana, 356 U.S. 584, 78 S.Ct. 970, 2 L.Ed.2d 991 (1958); Hill v. Texas, 316 U.S. 400, 62 S.Ct. 1159, 86 L.Ed. 1559 (1942), respectively.

9. 380 U.S. 202, 85 S.Ct. 824, 13 L.Ed.2d 759 (1965).

careful and sophisticated analysis. While the Court has declined to hold that a statute is unconstitutional merely because it requires jury commissioners to apply rather subjective criteria which provide some opportunity for discrimination,[10] that opportunity plus a significant statistical disparity will constitute a prima facie case. Thus in *Turner v. Fouche,*[11] a prima facie case was made out by showing that 60% of the county population was black, that only 37% of those on the jury list were black, and that 171 of the 178 persons disqualified for lack of "intelligence" or "uprightness" were black, so that "the disparity originated, at least in part, at the one point in the selection process where the jury commissioners invoked their subjective judgment rather than objective criteria." Similarly, in *Alexander v. Louisiana,*[12] where 21% of the population was black, and jury questionnaires with a racial designation on them were returned by 7,000 persons 14% of whom were black, and the pool was then reduced to 400, of which 7% were black, this was deemed to constitute a prima facie case which was not rebutted by testimony of one commissioner that race was no consideration in reducing the pool. More recently, in *Castaneda v. Partida,*[13] the Court held that a showing the population was 79% Mexican–American but that over an 11–year period only 39% of the persons summoned for jury service were Mexican–American established a prima facie case, which was unrebutted absent evidence that racially neutral qualifications produced the disparity.

The Court in *Castaneda* emphasized that "an official act is not unconstitutional *solely* because it has a racially disproportionate impact." Discriminatory intent must be shown, but a prima facie case of such intent may be shown by "substantial underrepresentation," for when "a disparity is sufficiently large, then it is unlikely that it is due solely to chance or accident, and, in the absence of evidence to the contrary, one must conclude that racial or other class-related factors entered into the selection process." Because, as the Court also noted, "a selection procedure that is susceptible of abuse or is not racially neutral supports the presumption of discrimination raised by the statistical showing," it would seem that a somewhat smaller disparity will suffice when it occurs within a selection process containing subjective selection criteria.

(d) The "Fair Cross Section" Requirement. In *Glasser v. United States,*[14] the defendant claimed but did not prove that all the names of women placed in the box from which the federal jury panel was drawn were taken from a list of the members of the Illinois League of Women Voters. The Court indicated that if the allegations had been proved all the petitioners would be entitled to a new trial. Because "the proper functioning of the jury system, and, indeed, our democracy itself, requires that the jury be a 'body truly representative of the community', and not the organ of any special group or class," the Court declared that jury officials "must not allow the desire for competent jurors to lead them into selections which do not comport with the concept of the jury as a cross-section of the community." In other cases also involving federal juries, the Court held it improper to exclude women [15] or day laborers.[16]

By contrast, efforts during that era to upset state juries on grounds other than racial exclusion did not meet with success. The Court early on held that states could exempt certain occupational groups from jury service,[17] and later in *Fay v. New York* [18] and *Moore v. New York* [19] held that the mere fact of dispropor-

10. Carter v. Jury Commission of Greene County, 396 U.S. 320, 90 S.Ct. 518, 24 L.Ed.2d 549 (1970).

11. 396 U.S. 346, 90 S.Ct. 532, 24 L.Ed.2d 567 (1970).

12. 405 U.S. 625, 92 S.Ct. 1221, 31 L.Ed.2d 536 (1972).

13. 430 U.S. 482, 97 S.Ct. 1272, 51 L.Ed.2d 498 (1977).

14. 315 U.S. 60, 62 S.Ct. 457, 86 L.Ed. 680 (1942).

15. Ballard v. United States, 329 U.S. 187, 67 S.Ct. 261, 91 L.Ed. 181 (1946).

16. Thiel v. Southern Pacific Co., 328 U.S. 217, 66 S.Ct. 984, 90 L.Ed. 1181 (1946).

17. Rawlins v. Georgia, 201 U.S. 638, 26 S.Ct. 560, 50 L.Ed. 899 (1906).

18. 332 U.S. 261, 67 S.Ct. 1613, 91 L.Ed. 2043 (1947).

19. 333 U.S. 565, 68 S.Ct. 705, 92 L.Ed. 881 (1948).

tionate economic representation, resulting from character, literacy, and property requirements for jurors, did not violate the due process or equal protection clauses, even when this was accomplished by the use of special "blue-ribbon" juries for some cases. The majority in these cases emphasized that the Sixth Amendment right to jury trial was not applicable to the states and that *Glasser* and other cases concerned with federal juries were based upon the Court's supervisory power over federal courts.

When the Supreme Court thereafter, in *Duncan v. Louisiana*,[20] held that the Sixth Amendment right to "an impartial jury" was applicable to the states through the Fourteenth Amendment due process clause, it appeared very likely that this meant the cross-section requirement was now applicable to the states as a part of that right. A majority of the Court so indicated a few years later,[21] and a square holding to that effect came in *Taylor v. Louisiana*.[22] The Court in *Taylor* declared that the purpose of a jury, "to guard against the exercise of arbitrary power," is not served "if the jury pool is made up of only segments of the populace or if large, distinctive groups are excluded from the pool."

Several points must be emphasized concerning the fair cross section requirement adopted in *Taylor*. For one thing, the requirement is simply that juries "must be drawn from a source fairly representative of the community"; the earlier rule that defendants are not entitled to a jury of any particular composition [23] still obtains.[24] Secondly, this fair cross section requirement is a right of *all* defendants.[25] Thus, in *Taylor* a male defendant prevailed though the constitutional violation was the exclusion of women, just as in *Peters v. Kiff* [26] a white man was entitled to claim that blacks had been systematically excluded. Thirdly, and also a departure from the limitations which exist when there is an equal protection challenge, a defendant raising a cross section objection can prevail without showing purposeful discrimination; he "need only show that the jury selection procedure 'systematically exclude[s] distinctive groups in the community and thereby fail[s] to be reasonably representative thereof.' " [27] But the "systematic exclusion" requirement, repeatedly stressed in *Taylor,* would seem to mean that a constitutional violation is not made out by a showing that on a particular occasion a member of a distinct group happened to be mistakenly excused. On the other hand, as the Court made clear in *Duren v. Missouri*,[28] a cross section violation can occur without there being total exclusion of a distinct group.

Next, it would appear that exclusion of only certain kinds of groups conflicts with the cross section objective. However, the Court in *Taylor,* while concluding that women were such a class, did not establish with clarity just what the nature of the excluded group must be. Reference is made to "large, distinctive groups" and "identifiable segments playing major roles in the community," and the Court asserts that "women are sufficiently numerous [53% of the citizens eligible for jury ser-

20. 391 U.S. 145, 88 S.Ct. 1444, 20 L.Ed.2d 491 (1968).

21. See Apodaca v. Oregon, 406 U.S. 404, 92 S.Ct. 1628, 32 L.Ed.2d 184 (1972).

22. 419 U.S. 522, 95 S.Ct. 692, 42 L.Ed.2d 690 (1975).

23. Fay v. New York, 332 U.S. 261, 67 S.Ct. 1613, 91 L.Ed. 2043 (1947).

24. Thus in Lockhart v. McCree, discussed in § 22.3(c), the Court reasoned the *Taylor* cross-section requirement could not be violated by the manner in which peremptory challenges were exercised, noting the Supreme Court had "never invoked the fair cross-section principle * * * to require petit juries, as opposed to jury panels or venires, to reflect the composition of the community at large." The point was reaffirmed in Holland v. Illinois, 493 U.S. 474 110 S.Ct. 803, 107 L.Ed.2d 905 (1990), asserting that the Sixth Amendment goal of "jury impartiality with respect to both contestants * * * would positively be obstructed by a petit jury cross-section requirement which * * * would cripple the device of peremptory challenges."

25. Holland v. Illinois, 493 U.S. 474, 110 S.Ct. 803, 107 L.Ed.2d 905 (1990) ("the Sixth Amendment entitles every defendant to object to a venire that is not designed to represent a fair cross section of the community, whether or not the systematically excluded groups are groups to which he himself belongs").

26. 407 U.S. 493, 92 S.Ct. 2163, 33 L.Ed.2d 83 (1972).

27. Castaneda v. Partida, 430 U.S. 482, 97 S.Ct. 1272, 51 L.Ed.2d 498 (1977) (emphasized by dissent to distinguish instant case, involving state grand jury, where defendant would have to rely upon equal protection clause and thus prove "discriminatory intent").

28. 439 U.S. 357, 99 S.Ct. 664, 58 L.Ed.2d 579 (1979).

vice] and distinct from men that if they are systematically eliminated from jury panels, the Sixth Amendment's fair cross section requirement cannot be satisfied." This suggests that some groups may be so small as to not come within *Taylor* and that some groups may be insufficiently "distinct" to fall within the cross section requirement. As for the nature of the required distinctness, the Court in *Taylor* indicated that it is not necessary that the members of the group "act or tend to act as a class," but only that by their absence "a flavor, a distinct quality is lost." The Court has since declined "to precisely define the term 'distinctive group,'" but has declared that exclusion of a particular group was unobjectionable where it did not contravene the three purposes of the cross-section requirement: avoiding "the possibility that the composition of juries would be arbitrarily skewed in such a way as to deny criminal defendants the benefit of the common-sense judgment of the community," avoiding an "appearance of unfairness," and ensuring against deprivation of "often historically disadvantaged groups of their right as citizens to serve on juries in criminal cases." [29] Lower courts have in the main managed to avoid application of this amorphous standard by instead resolving cross section objections by finding a justification for the challenged exclusion, though decisions are now to be found holding such groups as "young adults" not distinctive under *Taylor.*

This logically leads to the final point, which is that even if there is a systematic exclusion of a distinct group, this is not a constitutional violation if the exclusion is no broader than is necessary to serve a valid governmental interest. In *Taylor,* where the defective procedure was that women were not selected for jury service except when they filed a written declaration of a desire to so serve, the Court rightly concluded that this practice could not be justified on the ground that many women would find jury service unduly burdensome. Similarly, in *Duren v. Missouri,*[30] where any woman could decline jury service by so indicating on the jury-selection questionnaire, by returning the jury duty summons or simply by not showing up, the Court concluded that "exempting all women because of the preclusive domestic responsibilities of some women is insufficient justification for their disproportionate exclusion on jury venires." The Court added that "a State may have an important interest in assuring that those members of the family responsible for the care of children are available to do so," and suggested that an exemption "appropriately tailored to this interest would * * * survive a fair-cross-section challenge." In cases decided before and after *Taylor,* the lower courts have upheld as rationally based statutory provisions or excusal procedures which result in exclusion or underrepresentation of young people, old people, persons not registered to vote, persons in the professions, aliens, persons lacking proficiency in English, and convicted felons.

(e) Vicinage. The concept of "vicinage" is frequently confused with that of "venue." The former refers to the place from which the jurors must be selected, while the latter makes reference to the place at which the trial must be held. The right to have juries drawn from the vicinage is guaranteed by that part of the Sixth Amendment which assures a jury "of the State and district wherein the crime shall have been committed, which district shall have been previously ascertained by law." Vicinage provisions are also found in state constitutions, commonly declaring a right to a jury "of the county in which the offense is alleged to have been committed."

29. Lockhart v. McCree, 476 U.S. 162, 106 S.Ct. 1758, 90 L.Ed.2d 137 (1986), concerning exclusion of "*Witherspoon*-excludables"; see § 22.3(c).

Members of the Court are not in agreement as to how many such groups there might be. See Holland v. Illinois, 493 U.S. 474, 110 S.Ct. 803, 107 L.Ed.2d 905 (1990) (majority says if cross-section requirement were extended to the use of peremptories "there is every reason to believe that many commonly exercised bases for peremptory challenges would be rendered unavailable," while Marshall, J., dissenting, objects to the "majority's exaggerated claim that 'postmen, or lawyers, or clergymen' are distinctive groups within the meaning of our fair cross-section cases").

30. 439 U.S. 357, 99 S.Ct. 664, 58 L.Ed.2d 579 (1979).

Courts have had few occasions to construe the vicinage requirement in the Sixth Amendment. As for its application in federal trials, the Supreme Court has decided that there is no constitutional right to have jurors drawn from the entire district in which the crime occurred.[31] Lower courts have extended this proposition a bit farther by holding that the Sixth Amendment confers no right to have a jury drawn in whole or in part from that portion of the district encompassing the location of the crime. This means, for example, that a trial could be had and jurors selected in a division of the district other than the division in which the crime occurred. It is noteworthy, however, that some of these decisions cautiously noted that the attitudes of jurors in the excluded area appeared to be reflected in the population of the part of the district from which the jurors were selected.

As for application of the Sixth Amendment vicinage requirement to state prosecutions, the courts have generally assumed that it is applicable for the most part. But there is not complete agreement as to what the vicinage requirement of the Sixth Amendment means in a state trial context. One view is that it merely requires that the petit jurors be drawn from within the state and federal judicial district in which the crime was committed, so that it would be permissible for a state to draw a jury and try the defendant in a county other than that in which the crime occurred so long as the two counties were in the same federal district. *People v. Jones,*[32] on the other hand, reflects a quite different position. That court concluded that while "a jury drawn either from an entire county wherein the crime was committed or from that portion of a county wherein the crime was committed will satisfy the constitutional requirement" concerning vicinage, "a jury drawn from only a portion of a county, exclusive of the place of the commission of the crime, will not satisfy the requirement." Although the rule announced in *Jones* does not appear to depend upon demography, the court may have been influenced by the facts of the particular case. Jones resided in a precinct, where the crime occurred, which was 75% black, but he was not tried in the district containing that precinct, which was 31% black, but in another only 7% black. In any event, *Jones* was later overruled; in *Hernandez v. Municipal Court,*[33] the court held that "the boundaries of the vicinage are coterminous with the boundaries of the county" and that consequently it is sufficient that the jurors are selected from the county—they need not be from the particular judicial district where the crime occurred. It was noted that other states had declined to go as far as *Jones* and that the federal decisions (discussed above) likewise could not be squared with *Jones.*

This suggests the question of whether upon such or similar facts the defendant has a valid objection based upon the cross section requirement. *Jones* rests in part on the cross section rationale, but residents of a particular county are not per se a distinct group for cross section analysis. Thus other courts have declined to invalidate trials by jurors drawn from a county other than that in which the crime was committed where there was no significant disparity in the racial, ethnic or sexual composition of the population of the two counties.

(f) Challenge to the Array. A challenge to the array, sometimes referred to as a motion to quash the venire or panel (all jurors eligible to be called in that case), is the procedural device which is utilized to raise objections concerning the manner in which the entire panel was summoned. The objections may be constitutional in dimension, or may simply be grounded in the statutes of that jurisdiction concerning the manner in which jury panels are to be selected. As for the latter, the better view is that a defendant is entitled to relief only if there has been a "material departure" from or "substantial failure" to comply with jury selection legisla-

31. Ruthenberg v. United States, 245 U.S. 480, 38 S.Ct. 168, 62 L.Ed. 414 (1918).

32. 9 Cal.3d 546, 108 Cal.Rptr. 345, 510 P.2d 705 (1973).

33. 49 Cal.3d 713, 203 Cal.Rptr. 513, 781 P.2d 547 (1989).

tion. Often the matter is put in terms of whether the particular statutory provision at issue is directory or mandatory, with the latter characterization being appropriate if its essential purpose is to insure that jurors be indifferently rather than arbitrarily selected. This does not mean that the defendant must show he has suffered prejudice because of the deviation; under the better but not unanimous view no showing of prejudice is necessary upon a challenge to the array. This is as it should be, for in this context proof of actual harm is virtually impossible to adduce. It is typically provided that absent a showing of good cause for later filing, the challenge must be made before trial or before commencement of the voir dire examination.

§ 22.3 Voir Dire; Challenges

(a) Nature of Voir Dire. If the defendant has not waived jury trial, then it is necessary to select from the panel of prospective jurors those individuals who will actually serve as jurors in his case. The examination of prospective jurors for this purpose is commonly referred to as the voir dire, an ancient phrase which literally means "to speak the truth." This process, by which both the defense and the prosecution try to eliminate certain prospective jurors, is a very important part of trial procedure. Prospective jurors can be challenged in two ways during the voir dire: by a challenge for cause, which requires the challenging party to satisfy the judge that there is a sufficient likelihood that the prospective juror is biased in some way, or by a peremptory challenge, which may be exercised in specified numbers without giving any reason and without control by the court. The latter is used to eliminate those prospective jurors suspected of being biased or believed, by virtue of their backgrounds and experience, to be more likely to favor the trial opponent.

One important function of the voir dire examination of prospective jurors is to elicit information which would establish a basis for challenges for cause. A second is to facilitate the intelligent use of peremptory challenges. A third function of the voir dire, albeit one which many would not view as legitimate, is that of indoctrinating the potential jurors on the merits of the case and developing rapport. The trial judge has considerable discretion in deciding what questions may be asked of the prospective jurors. He must be free to exclude those questions which are intended solely to accomplish such improper purpose or which are not phrased in neutral, non-argumentative form, to restrict the examination of jurors within reasonable bounds so as to expedite the trial, and on occasion to restrict questioning in order to give some protection to the privacy of prospective jurors.

An appellate court is unlikely to reverse a trial judge's decision not to permit certain questions unless it seems likely that as a result of the limited voir dire the jury was prejudiced. Illustrative is *Rosales–Lopez v. United States,*[1] where the four-Justice plurality opinion concluded

> it is usually best to allow the defendant to resolve this conflict by making the determination of whether or not he would prefer to have the inquiry into racial or ethnic prejudice pursued. Failure to honor his request, however, will only be reversible error where the circumstances of the case indicate that there is a reasonable possibility that racial or ethnic prejudice might have influenced the jury.

That opinion goes on to say "that federal courts must make such an inquiry when requested by a defendant accused of a violent crime and where the defendant and the victim are members of different racial or ethnic groups" because such a situation falls within the "reasonable possibility" standard. The Court then concluded no such inquiry was necessary in the instant case, where defendant, of Mexican descent, was charged with aiding members of his own ethnic group gain illegal entry into the United States.

A defendant is even less likely to prevail if he makes a constitutional challenge to the limited scope of the voir dire. Such a challenge will sometimes prevail, as is shown by

§ 22.3

1. 451 U.S. 182, 101 S.Ct. 1629, 68 L.Ed.2d 22 (1981).

Ham v. South Carolina.[2] That case concerned a black civil rights worker convicted of possession of marijuana. During his voir dire examination of prospective jurors, the trial judge asked general questions as to bias, prejudice or partiality,[3] but declined to ask more specific questions tendered by defense counsel which sought to elicit any possible prejudice against the defendant because of his race.[4] The Court concluded:

> Since one of the purposes of the Due Process Clause of the Fourteenth Amendment is to insure [the] "essential demands of fairness," and since a principal purpose of the adoption of the Fourteenth Amendment was to prohibit the States from invidiously discriminating on the basis of race, we think that the Fourteenth Amendment required the judge in this case to interrogate the jurors upon the subject of racial prejudice. * * * [T]he trial judge was not required to put the question in any particular form, or to ask any particular number of questions on the subject, simply because requested to do so by petitioner. * * * In this context either of the brief, general questions urged by petitioner would appear sufficient to focus the attention of prospective jurors to any racial prejudice they might entertain.

Ham has had a rather limited impact. For one thing, the Court has as yet declined to extend the doctrine to matters other than racial prejudice. In the *Ham* case itself, the Court rejected petitioner's claim that the trial judge should have also inquired about possible prejudice against defendant because of his beard, in light of "the traditionally broad discretion accorded to the trial judge in conducting voir dire, and our inability to constitutionally distinguish possible prejudice against beards from a host of other possible similar prejudices." Similarly, the Court later held that where "the trial judge made a general inquiry into the jurors' general views concerning obscenity," *Ham* does not mean that the court in an obscenity case is required upon request "to ask questions as to whether the jurors' educational, political, and religious beliefs might affect their views on the question of obscenity."[5]

More significant is the fact that the Supreme Court and lower courts have applied *Ham* narrowly even on the question of racial prejudice. In *Ristaino v. Ross,*[6] the Court declined to find that "the need to question veniremen specifically about racial prejudice also rose to constitutional dimensions in this case," reasoning that the "mere fact that the victim of the crimes alleged[7] was a white man and the defendants were Negroes was less likely to distort the trial than were the special factors involved in *Ham.*" Similarly, in *Dukes v. Waitkevitch*[8] the court held that where a black man was accused of participation in a gang rape of several white women, the trial court did not commit constitutional error in refusing to inquire into racial prejudice on voir dire. The incredible assumption is that a black civil rights worker charged with possession of marijuana is more likely to have prejudice distort his trial than a black defendant charged with participation in a gang rape of white women.

In *Turner v. Murray,*[9] the *Ham–Ristaino* line of authority was applied to capital cases in a special way. The Court held "that a capital defendant accused of an interracial crime is entitled to have prospective jurors informed of the race of the victim and questioned on the issue of racial bias." But only four members of the Court (not counting the Chief Justice, who concurred in the judgment without opinion) joined in the assertion that

2. 409 U.S. 524, 93 S.Ct. 848, 35 L.Ed.2d 46 (1973).

3. The three questions asked were, in substance, the following: "1. Have you formed or expressed any opinion as to the guilt or innocence of the defendant, Gene Ham? 2. Are you conscious of any bias or prejudice for or against him? 3. Can you give the State and the defendant a fair and impartial trial?"

4. They were: "1. Would you fairly try this case on the basis of the evidence and disregarding the defendant's race? 2. You have no prejudice against negroes? Against black people? You would not be influenced by the use of the term 'black'?"

5. Hamling v. United States, 418 U.S. 87, 94 S.Ct. 2887, 41 L.Ed.2d 590 (1974).

6. 424 U.S. 589, 96 S.Ct. 1017, 47 L.Ed.2d 258 (1976).

7. Armed robbery, assault with a dangerous weapon, and assault with intent to murder.

8. 536 F.2d 469 (1st Cir.1976).

9. 476 U.S. 28, 106 S.Ct. 1683, 90 L.Ed.2d 27 (1986).

only the death sentence—not the guilty verdict—need be vacated. The first conclusion was attributed to "the broad discretion given the jury at the death penalty hearing, and the special seriousness of the risk of improper sentencing in a capital case"; the second to the fact that in the guilt phase of the trial "the jury had no greater discretion" than in a noncapital case, meaning that part of the case was "indistinguishable from *Ristaino.*" One other member of the Court found that distinction unconvincing because "the opportunity for bias to poison decisionmaking operates at a guilt trial in the same way as it does at a sentencing hearing." Two others attacked the distinction from the other direction, arguing that "many procedural and substantive safeguards" (e.g., the state must prove statutorily-defined aggravating factors beyond a reasonable doubt, the jury must consider any relevant mitigating evidence offered by defendant) "circumscribe the capital jury's sentencing decision," so that even the death penalty should stand.

As for the manner in which the voir dire should be conducted, in the federal system the "court may permit the defendant or his attorney and the attorney for the government to conduct the examination of prospective jurors or may itself conduct the examination." But in the latter event "the court shall permit the defendant or his attorney and the attorney for the government to supplement the examination by such further inquiry as it deems proper or shall itself submit to the prospective jurors such additional questions by the parties or their attorneys as it deems proper." [10] One study showed that over half of the federal judges questioned the jurors by themselves, about a third allowed the attorneys to ask supplemental questions, and the rest allowed the attorneys to ask all of the questions. There is also considerable variation in the permitted practice at the state level.

There is not agreement as to whether the judge or the attorney should have the predominant role in questioning prospective jurors. Proponents of attorney-conducted voir dire maintain that personal contact and selection of questions relevant to the particular trial are necessary for informed challenges, and that only the attorney knows what prejudices are important to explore. Proponents of judge-conducted voir dire argue that lawyer-conducted questioning takes excessive amounts of time and that lawyers abuse their privilege by asking inappropriate questions and indoctrinating the jurors. A suggested compromise of these conflicting positions is that the questioning should be conducted initially and primarily by the judge, after which counsel for each side should have the opportunity, subject to reasonable time limits, to question jurors directly.

(b) Prosecution and Defense Access to Information. Most states have adopted statutes providing for defendants in criminal cases to receive in advance of trial a list of prospective jurors. Some of these enactments confer this right upon all defendants, while some are limited to felony cases or capital cases. Even in the absence of such legislation, it has sometimes been held that the defendant upon timely motion is entitled to obtain that list in advance of trial. On the federal level, a statute declares that one "charged with treason or other capital offense shall at least three entire days before commencement of trial be furnished with * * * a list of the veniremen, * * * stating the place of abode of each venireman," which has been interpreted to mean that there is no such right in other cases.[11] However, it is provided in the Federal Jury Selection and Service Act that a defendant "shall be allowed to inspect, reproduce, and copy" those "records or papers used by the jury commission or clerk in connection with the jury selection process" at "all reasonable times during the preparation and pendency" of a motion to stay the proceedings because of noncompliance with the Act.[12]

10. Fed.R.Crim.P. 24(a).

11. Hamer v. United States, 259 F.2d 274 (9th Cir. 1958), construing 18 U.S.C.A. § 3432.

12. 28 U.S.C.A. § 1867(f).

This latter provision has been characterized by the Supreme Court as giving the defendant "essentially an unqualified right to inspect jury lists," [13] but it is important to note that this statute is limited to instances in which a challenge to the entire panel is being made and thus is inapplicable where the list is desired only for purposes relating to conducting the voir dire. It thus is different from the other statutes previously mentioned, which have as their purpose assisting the defendant in acquiring information upon which to ground challenges for cause and to exercise peremptory challenges. Some have argued that this function would be better served and time at the voir dire saved if the parties were also provided in advance of trial with additional information about each of the prospective jurors. (In limited circumstances in which there is good reason to believe the jury needs protection, the names of the jurors and their addresses and places of employment may be withheld in advance of trial and even during the jury selection.)

When the identity of the prospective jurors is known, the prosecution or the defense or both may undertake a pretrial investigation of them. As a general matter, the prosecution is in a better position to conduct such a pretrial investigation. Because members of the prosecution staff may have conducted earlier trials involving members of the same panel, the prosecution may be able to compile information on the voting habits of particular jurors. The prosecution will likewise have more ready access to the arrest and conviction records and other government records relating to the prospective jurors. Moreover, the prosecution may utilize the investigative services of local police or the FBI in acquiring background information. Wealthy defendants and those in so-called political cases often have pretrial investigation conducted on their behalf.

One question raised by these practices is that of whether some investigative procedures are improper. As for the mere use of law enforcement agents to conduct investigations of prospective jurors, it has been held that it does not result in juries biased against the defendant, but merely eliminates bias against the government, and that the assertion such investigations will discourage citizens from serving as jurors is far fetched. But there are limits beyond which neither the prosecution nor defense is permitted to go; a lawyer may not seek to influence a prospective juror by means prohibited by law, or communicate ex parte with such a person except as permitted by law.[14]

Another question raised by pretrial investigation of jurors is whether the fruits of such investigations should be subject to discovery by the other party. The traditional view is that discovery of juror information by either the prosecution or defense is not allowed. Illustrative is *Hamer v. United States,*[15] where the court dismissed defendant's claim that he should have had access to the prosecutor's jury book, describing the conduct and votes of jurors in prior cases. The court asserted that otherwise the "ultimate and ridiculous conclusion" would be that "no defendant could be prosecuted by a government attorney who had more information about how jurors on that panel had voted, in other cases, than his own counsel had." However, a few courts have viewed sympathetically the proposition that the jury selection process is harmed when the parties have dramatically disparate amounts of information about the prospective jurors. It has been recognized that trial courts must have the discretion to permit a defendant, who lacks funds to investigate prospective jurors, to inspect prosecution jury records and investigations. On the notion that avenues of investigation available to the prosecution cannot be completely closed to the defense, it has been held that once a police department makes its records of convictions of prospective jurors available to the prosecutor, they must be equally available to

13. Test v. United States, 420 U.S. 28, 95 S.Ct. 749, 42 L.Ed.2d 786 (1975).

14. ABA Model Rules of Professional Conduct, rule 3.5.

15. 259 F.2d 274 (9th Cir.1958).

defense counsel. Defendants permitted to obtain disclosure of the prosecutor's dossier may not preserve the secrecy of their own investigative reports. When there has been a governmental impetus affecting a juror's prior service (e.g., scolding by the judge for an acquittal), and it is of a nature likely to escape the attention even of reasonably diligent defense counsel, the prosecutor has an affirmative obligation to make disclosure to the defense even absent a request.

In some recent trials, social science techniques have been employed in jury selection. The first step is to survey randomly as large a sample as possible of the population from which the jury will be selected. The researchers attempt to discern attitudes relevant to the issues in the particular forthcoming trial. Data from the survey is fed into a computer with socioeconomic background characteristics (e.g., religion, age, sex, occupation) in order to identify a favorable and unfavorable juror. The questions asked on voir dire are geared to ascertaining those characteristics found to be associated with favorable or unfavorable attitudes. Instead or in addition, the jury panel may be observed in court and rated by psychologists or psychiatrists on authoritarianism scales or by kinesiologists in terms of body language. This development is certainly a cause for concern. If the outcome of a trial can be manipulated simply by impaneling jurors designated acceptable by social scientists, then trial by jury may cease to function satisfactorily. Even if these techniques are not as useful as they are made out to be, there is the matter of the public perception of the criminal justice system. Perhaps the proper response to the increasing use of such juror information at voir dire is to allow its discovery by both the prosecution and the defense.

(c) Challenges for Cause. Both the defense and the prosecution may challenge an unlimited number of jurors for cause, but no juror can be removed on this ground unless the judge agrees that one of the bases for such a challenge is present. The grounds for a challenge for cause are commonly set out by statute, and are typically stated in terms of a series of specific situations: that the person lacks the legal qualifications for jury service; that he has previously served as a juror on some related matter, such as on the grand jury which indicted the defendant, on the petit jury which formerly tried defendant on this charge, or on a jury which tried another person charged with the same offense; that he has served or will serve as a witness regarding the subject matter of the pending trial; or that he is related in some degree to the defendant or others directly involved in this case. In addition, a more general ground for challenge is typically stated in terms such as the following:

> That the juror has a state of mind in reference to the cause or to the defendant or to the person alleged to have been injured by the offense charged, or to the person on whose complaint the prosecution was instituted, which will prevent him from acting with impartiality; but the formation of an opinion or impression regarding the guilt or innocence of the defendant shall not of itself be sufficient ground of challenge to a juror, if he declares, and the court is satisfied, that he can render an impartial verdict according to the evidence.

If the prospective juror is found to have the "state of mind" described above, then this is a case of actual bias requiring that the challenge for cause be granted.[16] But, as the

16. This is not to suggest that any single statement by a prospective juror, standing in isolation, compels granting the challenge. In Patton v. Yount, 467 U.S. 1025, 104 S.Ct. 2885, 81 L.Ed.2d 847 (1984), one juror said he had an opinion of defendant's guilt based on pretrial publicity but that it was not "fixed" and that he would be able to change his mind "if the facts were so presented," but the court declined to accept the habeas petitioner's claim that this juror had adopted a presumption of guilt and thus should not have been seated over his challenge for cause. The Court stated that the issue of the partiality of an individual juror was "plainly one of historical fact: did a juror swear that he could set aside any opinion he might hold and decide the case on the evidence, and should the juror's protestation of impartiality have been believed," and that consequently the state court's finding was entitled to a presumption of correctness on habeas corpus. But the Court added that "the trial court's resolution of such questions is entitled, even on direct appeal, to 'special deference,'" as "the determination is essentially one of credibility, and therefore largely one of demeanor." As for the individual expression seeming to indicate partiality, the "trial judge properly may choose to believe

language quoted above indicates, this is not to suggest that a prospective juror must be excused merely because he knows something of the case to be tried or has formed some opinions regarding it. It was long ago recognized that

> to say that any man who had formed an opinion on any fact conducive to the final decision of the case would therefore be considered as disqualified from serving on the jury, would exclude intelligent and observing men, whose minds were really in a situation to decide upon the whole case according to the testimony, and would perhaps be applying the letter of the rule requiring an impartial jury with a strictness which is not necessary for the preservation of the rule itself.[17]

This actual bias is not limited to specific bias, that is, a bias grounded in personal knowledge or a personal relationship. Virtually all courts authorize the questioning of jurors in areas of nonspecific bias, such as actual prejudice grounded in the prospective juror's feelings regarding the race, religion, and ethnic or other group to which the defendant belongs.

If during the voir dire a certain prospective juror actually admits to such a "state of mind," he will of course be challenged and excused. It is unlikely that a prejudiced juror would recognize his own personal prejudice or admit it, and thus such admissions are not frequently made. This raises the important question of whether, at least in some circumstances, bias should be implied and the prospective juror excused notwithstanding his claim of impartiality. One way in which this issue arises is when there has been extensive pretrial publicity. In *Irvin v. Dowd,*[18] for example, there had been extensive publicity announcing that defendant had confessed to six murders and 24 burglaries and that he had offered to plead guilty. On voir dire, 8 of the 12 jurors selected expressed the opinion that defendant was guilty, but all said they would render an impartial verdict. In overturning the defendant's conviction, the Supreme Court concluded that "such a statement of impartiality can be given little weight" where, as here, the voir dire reflected a "pattern of deep and bitter prejudice" in the community. But in *Murphy v. Florida,*[19] the Court rejected the contention that *Irvin* or the Court's other prior decisions [20] stood "for the proposition that juror exposure to information about a state defendant's prior convictions or to new accounts of the crime with which he is charged alone presumptively deprives the defendant of due process," so that bias should be implied in such circumstances notwithstanding the juror's claim of impartiality.

The implied bias issue has also been raised when prospective jurors are employees of the governmental unit undertaking the prosecution. But in *Dennis v. United States,*[21] the Court held that in a case where the federal government is a party, its employees are not challengeable for cause solely by reason of their employment. The Court also rejected the argument that the failure to sustain the challenge denied petitioner an "impartial

those statements that were the most fully articulated or that appeared to have been least influenced by leading."

17. As stated by John Marshall at the trial of Aaron Burr. See United States v. Burr, 25 F.Cas. 49 (D.Va. 1807). The same point was made by the Supreme Court in Irvin v. Dowd, 366 U.S. 717, 81 S.Ct. 1639, 6 L.Ed.2d 751 (1961): "It is not required, however, that the jurors be totally ignorant of the facts and issues involved. In these days of swift, widespread and diverse methods of communication, an important case can be expected to arouse the interest of the public in the vicinity, and scarcely any of those best qualified to serve as jurors will not have formed some impression or opinion as to the merits of the case. This is particularly true in criminal cases. To hold that the mere existence of any preconceived notion as to the guilt or innocence of an accused, without more, is sufficient to rebut the presumption of a prospective juror's impartiality would be to establish an impossible standard. It is sufficient if the juror can lay aside his impression or opinion and render a verdict based on the evidence presented in court."

18. 366 U.S. 717, 81 S.Ct. 1639, 6 L.Ed.2d 751 (1961).

19. 421 U.S. 794, 95 S.Ct. 2031, 44 L.Ed.2d 589 (1975).

20. The defendant specifically relied upon Marshall v. United States, 360 U.S. 310, 79 S.Ct. 1171, 3 L.Ed.2d 1250 (1959), reversing because of "the exposure of jurors to information of a character which the trial judge ruled was so prejudicial it could not be directly offered as evidence." The Court rejected this reliance, pointing out that the decision there rested on the Court's supervisory power over federal courts rather than on due process grounds.

21. 339 U.S. 162, 70 S.Ct. 519, 94 L.Ed. 734 (1950).

jury" under the "special circumstances of this case"—a prosecution of a Communist for contempt of the House Un–American Activities Committee, where the government's interest was said to be "the vindication of a direct affront, as distinguished from its role in an ordinary prosecution," and where, because of an alleged "aura of surveillance and intimidation" said to exist because of a "Loyalty Order," government employees "would be hesitant to vote for acquittal because such action might be interpreted as 'sympathetic association' with Communism." The ruling of the Court, that a "holding of implied bias to disqualify jurors because of their relationship with the Government is no longer permissible," continues to be followed. Lower courts are not in agreement as to whether bias may be implied because the prospective juror is employed by the victim of the crime, but are generally disinclined to imply bias because of a prospective juror's membership in some special interest organization.

The implied bias issue can arise in a constitutional context and outside the voir dire, as is reflected by *Smith v. Phillips.*[22] The defendant, convicted in state court, sought to overturn his conviction because he later learned that during the trial one of the jurors submitted an application for employment as an investigator in the district attorney's office. On federal habeas corpus, the district court found insufficient evidence of actual bias by the juror, but nonetheless imputed bias to him because "the average man in Smith's position would believe that the verdict of the jury would directly affect the evaluation of his job application." But the Supreme Court, in concluding that defendant had not been denied due process by the juror's conduct, rejected the district court's approach. Disagreeing with the defendant's claim that because of "the human propensity for self-justification" a trial court "cannot possibly ascertain the impartiality of a juror by relying solely upon the testimony of the juror in question," the Supreme Court reaffirmed the position that "the remedy for allegations of juror partiality is a hearing in which the defendant has the opportunity to prove actual bias." *Smith* may influence lower courts, even when the issue is not cast in constitutional terms, to be even more reluctant to resort to the implied bias theory.

Sometimes, as in *Witherspoon v. Illinois,*[23] a defendant will object that the trial court was too generous in granting challenges for cause made by the prosecution. In selecting jurors for a murder trial at which the jury would have the responsibility for deciding on the death penalty if a guilty verdict was returned, nearly half of the panel was eliminated pursuant to a statute declaring it a cause for challenge that a prospective juror states "that he has conscientious scruples against capital punishment." The Court concluded:

> If the State had excluded only those prospective jurors who stated in advance of trial that they would not even consider returning a verdict of death, it could argue that the resulting jury was simply "neutral" with respect to penalty. But when it swept from the jury all who expressed conscientious or religious scruples against capital punishment or all who opposed it in principle, the State crossed the line of neutrality. In its quest for a jury capable of imposing the death penalty, the State produced a jury uncommonly willing to condemn a man to die. * * *
>
> [W]e hold that a sentence of death cannot be carried out if the jury that imposed or recommended it was chosen by excluding veniremen for cause simply because they voiced general objections to the death penalty or expressed conscientious or religious scruples against its infliction. No defendant can constitutionally be put to death at the hands of a tribunal so selected.

More recently, the Court has held this rule equally applicable where the jury was only permitted to answer certain questions about the presence of statutorily-defined aggravated circumstances which, if present, mandate a sentence of death by the judge.[24]

22. 455 U.S. 209, 102 S.Ct. 940, 71 L.Ed.2d 78 (1982).

23. 391 U.S. 510, 88 S.Ct. 1770, 20 L.Ed.2d 776 (1968).

24. Adams v. Texas, 448 U.S. 38, 100 S.Ct. 2521, 65 L.Ed.2d 581 (1980), habeas corpus granted 768 S.W.2d 281 (Tex.Crim.App.1989). The Court stressed that jurors

Although several lower courts, relying upon language in *Witherspoon,* concluded that veniremen could be constitutionally excluded only if it was "unmistakably clear" they would "automatically" vote against the death penalty, in *Wainwright v. Witt*[25] the Court opted for a less demanding standard: "whether the juror's views would 'prevent or substantially impair the performance of his duties as a juror in accordance with his instructions and his oath.'" Requiring unmistakable clarity, the Court observed, is unrealistic, for "many veniremen simply cannot be asked enough questions to reach the point where their bias has been made 'unmistakably clear.'" And the "automatically" language was now inappropriate because it could not "be squared with the duties of present-day capital sentencing juries," who now are typically asked to respond to factual inquiries bearing on whether death is the appropriate penalty.

In *Gray v. Mississippi,*[26] the Court rejected a variety of contentions made in support of the proposition that a single deviation from the *Witherspoon–Witt* standard would not inevitably nullify the sentence of death. As for the claim that the granting of an invalid *Witherspoon* motion was somehow cancelled out by the erroneous denial of an earlier valid *Witherspoon* motion, the Court reasoned that a violation of the prosecutor's statutory right to exclusion of a juror could not be equated with a violation of the defendant's Sixth Amendment rights. As for the claim that "a *Witherspoon* violation constitutes harmless error when the prosecution has an unexercised peremptory challenge that he states he would have used to excuse the juror," the Court rejected it because adoption of such an argument would "insulate jury-selection error from meaningful appellate review," as prosecutors would routinely make such an assertion. As for the claim that the single *Witherspoon* error was harmless "because it did not have any prejudicial effect," the Court deemed this "*Chapman* harmless-error analysis"[27] inapplicable here, where the right at issue "goes to the very integrity of the legal system." The Court added that a single *Witherspoon* violation really is not "an isolated incident" when, as here, the prosecutor also used his peremptories to remove prospective jurors who expressed any degree of hesitation against the death penalty.[28]

In *Ross v. Oklahoma,*[29] the trial judge erred in denying a *Witherspoon* motion from the *defense* against a juror unwilling to consider any penalty short of death, so the defendant used one of his nine peremptories to strike that juror. Four members of the Court concluded that the "defense's loss of a peremptory challenge thus resulted in a 'tribunal organized to return a verdict of death' in exactly the fashion we rejected so recently in *Gray,*" but the majority disagreed. The defendant had not been denied an impartial jury, as that juror "was thereby removed from the jury as effectively as if the trial court had excused him for cause," and the loss of a peremptory was likewise no such denial because "peremptory challenges are not of constitutional dimension." As for the defendant's claim it constituted a violation of due process to deprive him, in effect, of a full complement of peremptories as provided by statute, the Court in *Ross* answered that "peremptory challenges are a creature of statute," meaning the state may "define their purpose and manner of exercise." Here, by state law the grant of nine peremptories in capital cases "is qualified by the requirement that the defendant must use those challenges to cure erroneous refusal by the trial court to excuse jurors for cause."

Alluding to what he described as "competent scientific evidence that death-qualified

"will characteristically know that affirmative answers to the questions will result in the automatic imposition of the death penalty" and will "unavoidably exercise a range of judgment and discretion while remaining true to their instructions and their oaths."

25. 469 U.S. 412, 105 S.Ct. 844, 83 L.Ed.2d 841 (1985).

26. 481 U.S. 648, 107 S.Ct. 2045, 95 L.Ed.2d 622 (1987).

27. See § 27.6(c).

28. Powell, J., concurring, and also the four *Gray* dissenters, objected to the intimation that such use of his peremptories by the prosecutor was in any sense improper or unconstitutional.

29. 487 U.S. 81, 108 S.Ct. 2273, 101 L.Ed.2d 80 (1988).

jurors are partial to the prosecution on the issue of guilt or innocence," the defendant in *Witherspoon* contended that his conviction (not just the death penalty) should be set aside. But the Court found that data "too tentative and fragmentary to establish that jurors not opposed to the death penalty tend to favor the prosecution in the determination of guilt." The continued vitality of this branch of *Witherspoon* is unclear. For one thing, there is now available more empirical support for the conclusion that a death-qualified jury is more likely to convict than a non-death-qualified one. This data might produce a different result unless perceived as another improper effort to obtain dismissal of prospective jurors on an implied bias theory. Secondly, it might be argued that the Douglas dissent in *Witherspoon,* concluding there is no requirement of "a showing of specific prejudice when a defendant has been deprived of his right to a jury representing a cross-section of the community," has taken on added force in light of subsequent developments concerning the constitutional right to trial by jury. There is, for example, the holding in *Taylor v. Louisiana*[30] that exclusion of women from jury panels is unconstitutional even if, in the particular case, the exclusion made not "an iota of difference." *Taylor,* of course, held only that there is a Sixth Amendment right to "the presence of a fair cross section of the community on venires, panels or lists from which petit juries are drawn." This right, the Supreme Court later concluded is not violated by subsequent challenges to individuals on a fairly selected panel.[31]

In *Lockhart v. McCree,*[32] involving a somewhat different albeit related issue, the Court held that the Constitution does not "prohibit the removal for cause, prior to the guilt phase of a bifurcated capital trial, of prospective jurors whose opposition to the death penalty is so strong that it would prevent or substantially impair the performance of their duties as jurors at the sentencing phase of the trial." (The Court emphasized this was so even if it were shown, which the studies relied upon by defendant did not establish, that juries so selected are "somewhat more 'conviction-prone.' ") There was no violation of the *Taylor* cross-section requirement here, the Court concluded, as it had not theretofore been invoked by the Court "to invalidate the use of either for-cause or peremptory challenges * * * or to require petit juries, as opposed to jury panels or venires, to reflect the composition of the community at large," and in any event that requirement has to do only with a "distinctive" group in the community (e.g., "blacks, women, or Mexican–Americans") and not "groups defined solely in terms of shared attitudes that would prevent or substantially impair members of the group from performing or substantially performing one of their duties as jurors." As for defendant's claim he had been denied his constitutional right to an impartial jury, the Court responded this was not so because the exclusion complained of "serves the State's entirely proper interest in obtaining a single jury that could impartially decide all of the issues in McCree's case." The three dissenters found most unconvincing the majority's two reasons for why that interest was substantial: (i) "the possibility that, in some capital cases, the defendant might benefit at the sentencing phase of the trial from the jury's 'residual doubts' about the evidence presented at the guilt phase"; and (ii) "much of the evidence adduced at the guilt phase of the trial will also have a bearing on the penalty phase," so that two juries would require presentation of much testimony twice.

McCree was deemed controlling in *Buchanan v. Kentucky,*[33] holding defendant was not deprived of his Sixth Amendment rights when the prosecution was permitted to "death-qualify" the jury at his joint trial where the death penalty was sought against his codefendant. Defendant's reliance on the cross-section requirement was again unavailing because it "applies only to venires," and his impartial jury argument was rejected on the ground

30. 419 U.S. 522, 95 S.Ct. 692, 42 L.Ed.2d 690 (1975).

31. Lockhart v. McCree, discussed in text immediately following.

32. 476 U.S. 162, 106 S.Ct. 1758, 90 L.Ed.2d 137 (1986).

33. 483 U.S. 402, 107 S.Ct. 2906, 97 L.Ed.2d 336 (1987).

that "a balancing of jurors with different predilections" is not required. The majority stressed that joint trials are beneficial to defendants and serve to promote "the reliability and consistency of the judicial process," while the three dissenters responded that the defendant should be allowed "the option of waiving this perceived benefit" and that any interest in reliability and consistency could be served by trying the defendants jointly before a non-death-qualified jury and then having the other defendant sentenced by a death-qualified jury.

(d) Peremptory Challenges. "The essential nature of the peremptory challenge," the Supreme Court declared in *Swain v. Alabama,*[34] "is that it is one exercised without a reason stated, without inquiry and without being subject to the court's control." The peremptory challenge serves important functions: it (i) "teaches the litigant, and through him the community, that the jury is a good and proper mode for deciding matters and that its decision should be followed because in a real sense the jury belongs to the litigant" because "he chooses it"; (ii) "avoids trafficking in the core of truth in most common stereotypes" by making unnecessary the grounding of challenges for cause in claims of group bias, thus allowing "the covert expression of what we dare not say but know is true more often than not"; and (iii) serves "as a shield for the exercise of the challenge for cause," in that questioning to determine "the appropriateness of a cause challenge may have so alienated a potential juror that, although the lawyer has not established any basis for removal, the process itself has made it necessary to strike the juror peremptorily."[35] It is understandable, therefore, as the Court put it in *Swain,* that though " '[t]here is nothing in the Constitution of the United States which requires the Congress [or the States] to grant peremptory challenges,' * * * nonetheless the challenge is one of the most important of the rights secured to the accused."[36]

In the federal system, each side has 20 peremptories in a capital case and each has 3 in a misdemeanor case, while for a felony trial the defendant has 10 and the prosecution 6.[37] Similar provisions are found in the states, where the prosecution usually has the same number of peremptories as the defendant. There is considerable variation in the practice where more than one defendant is being tried, all the way from giving each defendant the usual number of peremptories to be exercised individually to requiring all defendants collectively to exercise the number of peremptories a single defendant would have. In some jurisdictions, the parties are required to exercise their peremptories as to each juror as he is individually selected, which deprives them of the opportunity intelligently to compare several veniremen before exercising any challenges. The prevailing practice is for the prosecutor to call and examine 12 veniremen, exercise his challenges for cause and such peremptory challenges as he then wishes to use, replace those excused with others, and then tender a group of 12 to the defendant. The defendant then follows a similar procedure with this group and tenders a jury of 12 back to the prosecutor, and they continue on in this manner until both parties have exhausted their challenges or indicated their satisfaction with the jury. By contrast, under the so-called struck jury system jurors are first examined and challenged for cause by both sides, excused jurors are replaced on the panel, and the examination of replacements continues until a panel of qualified jurors is presented. The size of the panel at this time is 12 plus the number of peremptory strikes allowed all parties. The parties then proceed to exercise their peremptories in some order which will result in all exhausting their strikes at approximately the same time. This latter system, while perhaps more time consuming because in every case it is neces-

34. 380 U.S. 202, 85 S.Ct. 824, 13 L.Ed.2d 759 (1965).

35. Babcock, Voir Dire: Preserving "Its Wonderful Power," 27 Stan.L.Rev. 545, 552–55 (1975).

36. Quoting Stilson v. United States, 250 U.S. 583, 40 S.Ct. 28, 63 L.Ed. 1154 (1919).

37. Fed.R.Crim.P. 24(b).

sary to examine and qualify a large group of jurors, allows more intelligent exercise of peremptories because each party, at the time he exercises each peremptory challenge, is confronted with the total number of persons from whom the final jury will be formed, and thus is always in a position to exclude the person most objectionable to him.

In *Swain v. Alabama,*[38] the defendant claimed that the prosecutor's conduct in using his peremptory challenges to remove all six blacks from the jury constituted a denial of equal protection. But the Supreme Court, after noting the credentials and purposes of peremptories and the longstanding practice of exercising peremptories on the basis of group affiliations, disagreed. The Court in *Swain* observed that to subject the prosecutor's challenges to the traditional standards of the equal protection clause would mean that the prosecutor's reasons for making a particular challenge would have to be subjected to scrutiny, which "would entail a radical change in the nature and operation of the challenge," and then concluded:

> In the light of the purpose of the peremptory system and the function it serves in a pluralistic society in connection with the institution of jury trial, we cannot hold that the Constitution requires an examination of the prosecutor's reasons for the exercise of his challenges in any given case. The presumption in any particular case must be that the prosecutor is using the State's challenges to obtain a fair and impartial jury to try the case before the court. The presumption is not overcome and the prosecutor therefore subjected to examination by allegations that in the case at hand all Negroes were removed from the jury or that they were removed because they were Negroes. Any other result, we think, would establish a rule wholly at odds with the peremptory challenge system as we know it.

The defendant in *Swain* then went on to make another claim, namely, that in the county where he was tried prosecutors consistently exercised their peremptories to prevent any blacks from serving on juries. The Court agreed "that this claim raises a different issue and it may well require a different answer." This is because if the prosecutor always challenges blacks, without regard to the nature of the crime or the defendant or the victim, then "it would appear that the purpose of the peremptory challenges is being perverted" and thus "the presumption protecting the prosecutor may well be overcome." But the Court in *Swain* then concluded that the record did not support this claim. While apparently no black had served on a jury in that county for at least 15 years, the record did not, "with any acceptable degree of clarity, show when, how often, and under what circumstances the prosecutor alone has been responsible for striking those Negroes who have appeared on petit jury panels." Although courts were inclined to say that the defendant's burden of showing such systematic exclusion by the prosecutor is not insurmountable, experience clearly indicated the virtual impossibility of doing so. A great many cases held the defendant did not meet this burden, but almost none are to be found ruling that the defendant had established such systematic exclusion by the prosecutor's use of his peremptory challenges.

In *Batson v. Kentucky,*[39] the Court finally rejected the *Swain* approach. Although the defendant presented his claim in terms of the *Taylor* fair cross-section right,[40] the Court did not decide the case on that basis, doubtless because (as the Court immediately thereafter held) that principle cannot be invoked "to invalidate the use of either for-cause or peremptory challenges to prospective jurors, or to require petit juries as opposed to jury panels or venires, to reflect the composition of the community at large." [41] Rather, *Batson* is an

38. 380 U.S. 202, 85 S.Ct. 824, 13 L.Ed.2d 759 (1965).

39. 476 U.S. 79, 106 S.Ct. 1712, 90 L.Ed.2d 69 (1986). *Batson* is not retroactively applicable to cases which became final before *Batson* was decided. Teague v. Lane, 489 U.S. 288, 109 S.Ct. 1060, 103 L.Ed.2d 334 (1989).

40. See § 21.2(d).

41. Lockhart v. McCree, 476 U.S. 162, 106 S.Ct. 1758, 90 L.Ed.2d 137 (1986). *Lockhart* was a challenge for cause case, but the same conclusion was later reached as to peremptory challenges in Holland v. Illinois, 493 U.S. 474, 110 S.Ct. 803, 107 L.Ed.2d 905 (1990) (asserting that the Sixth Amendment goal of "jury impartiality with

equal protection case and rests on the conclusions that "*Swain* has placed on defendants a crippling burden of proof" and does so unnecessarily in light of intervening decisions of the Court recognizing "that a defendant may make a prima facie showing of purposeful racial discrimination in selection of the venire by relying solely on the facts concerning its selection *in his case.*" *Batson* thus holds "that a defendant may establish a prima facie case of purposeful discrimination in selection of the petit jury solely on evidence concerning the prosecutor's exercise of peremptory challenges at the defendant's trial."

Under *Batson,* the defendant upon timely objection [42] was required to show "that he is a member of a cognizable racial group" and "that the prosecutor has exercised peremptory challenges to remove from the venire members of the defendant's race." Most courts took this to mean that a white defendant could not object to the exclusion of blacks from his jury by the prosecutor's use of peremptories. But in the later case of *Powers v. Ohio,*[43] the Supreme Court rejected such a limitation. The court first reasoned, as to the substantive guarantees of the equal protection clause, that under *Batson* the harm to be avoided is not merely trial of a defendant by a jury from which members of his own race have been excluded, but also the harm to the community at large and to excluded jurors by excluding persons from jury service "solely by reason of their race, a practice that forecloses a significant opportunity to participate in civic life." Moreover, the Court concluded in *Powers,* the defendant in a criminal case has standing to raise the equal protection rights of excluded jurors, who would themselves confront "considerable practical barriers" to challenge their exclusion. As for the emphasis in *Batson* on racial identity between the defendant and the excused jurors, the Court noted such racial identity simply "may provide one of the easier cases to establish both a prima facie case and a conclusive showing that wrongful discrimination has occurred."[44]

A defendant making a *Batson* challenge, who may rely on the fact that peremptory challenges provide an opportunity for discrimination, "must show that these facts and other relevant circumstances raise an inference that the prosecutor used that practice to exclude veniremen from the petit jury on account of their races," which is an "inference of purposeful discrimination." It is then for the trial court, considering "all relevant circumstances," such as a pattern of exercising strikes from the venire on the basis of race and the nature of the prosecutor's questions and statements on voir dire, to decide if the showing "creates a prima facie case of discrimination." If it does,[45] then "the burden shifts to the State to come forward with a neutral explanation [46] for challenging black

respect to both contestants * * * would positively be obstructed by a petit jury cross-section requirement which * * * would cripple the device of peremptory challenges").

42. "The requirement that any *Batson* claim be raised not only before trial, but in the period between the selection of the jurors and the administration of their oaths, is a sensible rule." Ford v. Georgia, ___ U.S. ___, 111 S.Ct. 850, 112 L.Ed.2d 935 (1991) (but is no bar to federal review in this case, as it was not "firmly established and regularly followed" at time applied).

43. ___ U.S. ___, 111 S.Ct. 1364, 113 L.Ed.2d 411 (1991).

44. In the earlier case of Holland v. Illinois, 493 U.S. 474, 110 S.Ct. 803, 107 L.Ed.2d 905 (1990), foretelling *Powers,* the author of the later case, Kennedy, J., commented that "where this obvious ground for suspicion is absent," i.e., where the defendant is not of the same race as the excluded jurors, "different methods of proof may be appropriate."

45. In Hernandez v. New York, ___ U.S. ___, 111 S.Ct. 1859, 114 L.Ed.2d 395 (1991), the prosecutor defended his peremptory strikes without a prior ruling that the defendant had made out a prima facie case. The Court's plurality opinion states: "Once a prosecutor has offered a race-neutral explanation for the peremptory challenges and the trial court has ruled on the ultimate question of intentional discrimination, the preliminary issue of whether the defendant had made a prima facie showing becomes moot."

46. In Hernandez v. New York, ___ U.S. ___, 111 S.Ct. 1859, 114 L.Ed.2d 395 (1991), the plurality concluded that a "neutral explanation * * * means an explanation based on something other than the race of the juror," and that the issue is whether "a discriminatory intent" was present, not whether there resulted "a racially disproportionate impact," though if the prosecutor "articulates a basis for a peremptory challenge that results in the disproportionate exclusion of members of a certain race, the trial judge may consider that fact as evidence that the prosecutor's stated reason constitutes a pretext for racial discrimination." The Court decided the record supported the conclusion that the prosecutor's peremptory challenges in the instant case "rested neither on the

jurors," which requires more than a denial of a discriminatory motive or the explanation "that he challenged jurors of the defendant's race on the assumption—or his intuitive judgment—that they would be partial to the defendant because of their shared race." The Court declined to say whether, upon a finding of discrimination, it is better to start jury selection over with a new venire or simply to reinstate improperly challenged jurors onto the present venire. Nor did the Court express any views "on whether the Constitution imposes any limit on the exercise of peremptory challenges by defense counsel," though it is to be noted that some lower court decisions hold that the right to challenge the manner in which peremptories are used runs both ways, and that the two *Batson* dissenters argued that now a black defendant would have to supply a neutral explanation for his pattern of striking white jurors. That conclusion finds some support in the Court's later application of *Batson* to the exercise of peremptory challenges by private litigants in civil cases.[47] Finally, it must be emphasized again that the analysis and holding in *Batson* is confined to the special problem of "racial discrimination in selection of jurors";[48] the dissenters objected that "if conventional equal protection principles apply, then presumably defendants could object to exclusion on the basis of not only race, but also sex, age, religion or political affiliation," and a host of other characteristics.

(e) Alternate Jurors. The rule at common law was that if there was some reason for discharging a juror during trial, then it was necessary to discharge the entire jury and begin the trial anew. To avoid this undesirable result, statutes and court rules have been adopted providing for the selection of alternate or additional jurors during protracted trials. Two different systems are to be found. The most common is the alternate juror or substituted juror type, under which one or more persons specifically identified at the outset as alternates are chosen in advance of trial. If a regular juror is discharged prior to the time the jury retires (or, in a few jurisdictions, prior to the time of verdict), an alternate juror is then designated to take his place. By contrast, under the additional juror or eliminated juror system, more than 12 jurors are selected in advance of trial. If a juror must be discharged during the trial, this is done without any further action at that time. Should more than 12 jurors remain at the time the jury is to retire, the 12 who are to participate in the deliberations are selected by lot. A preference for the latter approach

intention to exclude Latino or bilingual jurors, nor on stereotypical assumptions about Latinos or bilinguals," but rather on an intent to exclude only those who "might have difficulty in accepting the translator's rendition of Spanish-language testimony."

47. Edmonson v. Leesville Concrete Co., ___ U.S. ___, 111 S.Ct. 2077, 114 L.Ed.2d 660 (1991). Much of the Court's analysis in finding the requisite state action in that case would seem to apply to exercise of peremptories in criminal cases by the defense. The Court asserted state action was present under the applicable two-pronged test: (1) "the claimed constitutional deprivation resulted from the exercise of a right or privilege having its source in state authority," as peremptory challenges are permitted only when "the government, by statute or decision law," permits them; and (2) "the private party charged with the deprivation could be described in fairness as a state actor," as (a) "without the overt, significant participation of the government, the peremptory challenge system, as well as the jury trial system of which it is a part, simply could not exist," (b) the "peremptory challenge is used in selecting an entity that is a quintessential governmental body, having no attributes of a private actor," and (c) "the injury caused by the discrimination is made more severe because the government permits it to occur within the courthouse itself." The majority distinguished Polk County v. Dodson, 454 U.S. 312, 102 S.Ct. 445, 70 L.Ed.2d 509 (1981), holding a public defender is not a state actor in his general representation of a criminal defendant, on the curious ground that the relationship between the government and public defender "is adversarial in nature," while in civil litigation "the government and private litigants work for the same end." One of the *Edmonson* dissenters responded: "The effect of today's decision * * * logically must apply to criminal prosecutions" so that "the minority defendant can no longer seek to prevent an all-white jury, or to seat as many jurors of his own race as possible."

48. In Hernandez v. New York, ___ U.S. ___, 111 S.Ct. 1859, 114 L.Ed.2d 395 (1991), the plurality noted it had no occasion to "resolve the more difficult question of the breadth with which the concept of race should be defined for equal protection purposes. We would face a quite different case if the prosecutor had justified his peremptory challenges with the explanation that he did not want Spanish-speaking jurors. It may well be, for certain ethnic groups and in some communities, that proficiency in a particular language, like skin color, should be treated as a surrogate for race under an equal protection analysis."

has sometimes been stated on the ground that it is undesirable to give a juror who might turn out to be involved in deciding the case a second-class status during some or all of the trial.

In the federal system as many as six alternates may be selected,[49] while in the states the number is typically one or two. Whether to select alternate or additional jurors pursuant to these statutes and rules and what number to select within the number authorized is generally a matter left to the discretion of the trial judge. As for the judge's decision that the circumstances are such that a juror must be excused and replaced by an alternate or additional juror, the judge has considerable discretion here as well, and the judge's action in excusing a juror will be upheld if the record shows some legitimate basis for his decision. This is because the defendant has still been tried by 12 persons selected by him.

In the federal system, alternates may replace regular jurors only "prior to the time the jury retires to consider its verdict," [50] and this is likewise true in most but not all states. This position has been criticized because of the problem presented if one of the jurors in a protracted trial becomes unavailable during the deliberations. There is a growing body of authority that substitution of an alternate at that time is constitutionally permissible, at least if the substituted juror had not theretofore been relieved of the obligations of a juror or otherwise become tainted and if in addition the jury was carefully instructed to begin its deliberations anew when its composition changed. But a contrary line of authority holds to the view that such substitution is unconstitutional, for if deliberations had progressed to a stage where the original eleven were in substantial agreement, they were in a position to present a formidable obstacle to the alternate juror's attempts to persuade and convince them. Whether or not this objection has Sixth Amendment status, it casts serious doubt upon the wisdom of the substitution approach. As for sending each alternate juror into the jury room at the very beginning of deliberations with instructions not to participate until such time, should it occur, that he is substituted for some other juror, the view most often taken is that such a procedure is unsound because the alternate jurors' very presence in the jury room may inhibit certain jurors from participating freely in the deliberations. Another possible solution, now authorized in federal practice,[51] simply proceeding with a jury of 11 should it become necessary to excuse one of the jurors during the course of the deliberations, would seem constitutionally permissible under *Williams v. Florida* [52] but might be opposed on the ground that the availability of any alternative to a mistrial will result in judges being too willing to excuse a juror in the minority who wishes to "bail out."

§ 22.4 Challenging the Judge

(a) Right to Impartial Judge. Just as the defendant's right to jury trial is to an "impartial" jury, he also has a constitutional right to an impartial judge. As the Supreme Court held in *Tumey v. Ohio,*[1] "it certainly violates the Fourteenth Amendment and deprives a defendant in a criminal case of due process of law to subject his liberty or property to the judgment of a court, the judge of which has a direct, personal, substantial pecuniary interest in reaching a conclusion against him in his case." The Court concluded that such was the case in *Tumey,* where the mayor, authorized to try certain offenses, in addition to his regular salary, received the fees and costs levied by him against violators. This was so, the Court reasoned, because the mayor's situation was one "which would offer a possible temptation to the average man as a judge to forget the burden of proof required to convict the defendant, or which might lead him not to

49. Fed.R.Crim.P. 24(c).

50. Fed.R.Crim.P. 24(c).

51. Fed.R.Crim.P. 23(b).

52. 399 U.S. 78, 90 S.Ct. 1893, 26 L.Ed.2d 446 (1970).

§ 22.4

1. 273 U.S. 510, 47 S.Ct. 437, 71 L.Ed. 749 (1927).

hold the balance nice, clear, and true between the state and the accused."

In *Ward v. Monroeville,*[2] the Court held that the pecuniary interest does not necessarily have to be personal in order for *Tumey* to apply. The situation in *Ward* was that the mayor before whom defendant was compelled to stand trial for traffic offenses was responsible for village finances, and the mayor's court through fines, forfeitures, costs and fees provided a substantial portion of the village funds. The Court ruled that the "possible temptation" under the *Tumey* rule exists when "the mayor's executive responsibilities for village finances may make him partisan to maintain the high level of contribution from the mayor's court." *Dugan v. Ohio*[3] was distinguished because there the mayor had limited executive authority as one of five members of a city commission, so that his relation to the finances and financial policy of the city was too remote to warrant a presumption of bias. The Supreme Court in *Ward* also decided that a defendant "is entitled to a neutral and detached judge in the first instance," so that it made no difference that defendant had a right to trial de novo in another court.

Impartiality in the constitutional sense may also be lacking because the judge is involved in a very personal way in the matter at issue, as is reflected in the contempt cases. In *Mayberry v. Pennsylvania,*[4] for example, where a criminal defendant repeatedly insulted and vilified the trial judge during trial and at the conclusion of the trial was pronounced guilty of 11 contempts and sentenced to 11–22 years, the Court vacated the judgment of contempt. The Court first noted that as the separate acts or outbursts occurred, the trial judge "could with propriety, have instantly acted, holding [defendant] in contempt, or excluding him from the courtroom." But when the judge waits until the end of the trial, due process requires that "another judge, not bearing the sting of these slanderous remarks, and having the impersonal authority of the law," sit in judgment on defendant's conduct. Similarly, in *Taylor v. Hayes*[5] the Court held that another judge should have been substituted for the purpose of finally disposing of contempt charges against a defense attorney where the record showed that "marked personal feelings were present on both sides" and that marks of "unseemly conduct [had] left personal stings." And in *Johnson v. Mississippi*[6] the Court ruled that an end-of-trial contempt proceeding should have been conducted by another judge because the trial judge "immediately prior to the adjudication of contempt was a defendant in one of petitioner's civil rights suits and a losing party at that."

This is not to suggest that it is objectionable that the trial judge was involved in some prior proceedings in that case and thus might be aware of facts which have no direct bearing on guilt and which could not be put in the hands of a juror trying the case. As the Supreme Court explained in *Withrow v. Larkin*[7].

> Judges repeatedly issue arrest warrants on the basis that there is probable cause to believe that a crime has been committed and that the person named in the warrant has committed it. Judges also preside at preliminary hearings where they must decide whether the evidence is sufficient to hold a defendant for trial. Neither of these pretrial involvements has been thought to raise any constitutional barrier against the judge presiding over the criminal trial and, if the trial is without a jury, against making the necessary determination of guilt or innocence.

(b) Challenge for Cause. Trial judges, like jurors, are subject to challenge for cause. Grounds for challenge usually are set forth in a statute or rule of court. These provisions sometimes include specific situations, such as where there is a family relationship between the judge and the defendant, counsel, or the victim of the crime, but in any event refer more generally to situations of bias. Under

2. 409 U.S. 57, 93 S.Ct. 80, 34 L.Ed.2d 267 (1972).
3. 277 U.S. 61, 48 S.Ct. 439, 72 L.Ed.2d 784 (1928).
4. 400 U.S. 455, 91 S.Ct. 499, 27 L.Ed.2d 532 (1971).
5. 418 U.S. 488, 94 S.Ct. 2697, 41 L.Ed.2d 897 (1974).
6. 403 U.S. 212, 91 S.Ct. 1778, 29 L.Ed.2d 423 (1971).
7. 421 U.S. 35, 95 S.Ct. 1456, 43 L.Ed.2d 712 (1975).

some statutes it is enough that the party seeking a substitution of a judge has filed an affidavit which sufficiently states the facts and the reasons for the belief that bias or prejudice exists, while in other jurisdictions a hearing must be held on the matter and the facts showing prejudice judicially determined. Under the latter circumstances, the better practice is for the matter to be heard by a judge other than the one challenged.

(c) **Recusal by Judge.** It is not sufficient for a judge to proceed on the assumption that he may serve in any trial except when a party has successfully alleged or proved, as may be required, that he is actually biased. As a matter of judicial ethics, the judge has a responsibility to recuse himself under certain circumstances, including whenever the judge believes his or her impartiality can reasonably be questioned. Because one concern here is with the appearance of impropriety, this ethical obligation of the judge clearly extends beyond instances of actual bias. Especially where this recusal responsibility is accepted as part of the law of the jurisdiction and is recognized as not merely a self-enforcing duty on the judge but as a matter which may be asserted also by a party to the action, the obvious result is a broader basis upon which to bring into question whether a particular judge may try a particular case.

(d) **Peremptory Challenge.** In 17 states there are provisions which allow a party to challenge an assigned judge without alleging or proving the precise facts which lead him to believe he cannot get a fair trial. In some states, this peremptory challenge of the judge may be exercised merely by filing a notice or motion requesting that the matter be transferred to another judge. Elsewhere an affidavit of prejudice, alleging that a fair trial cannot be had before the judge and that the motion is made in good faith and not for delay, will suffice. But unlike the type of provision discussed earlier, specific facts need not be alleged, and thus the provision is properly characterized as permitting a peremptory challenge. When peremptories are allowed in criminal cases, they are almost always available to both the defendant and the prosecution. Some available statistics indicate that where peremptory challenge of a judge is permitted, the right is exercised sparingly.

The arguments for a procedure of this kind are that it is a necessary means for dealing with actual but unprovable bias, and that a party will more readily accept the outcome of the trial if he perceives that the judge was fair. In opposition to allowing peremptory challenge of a judge, it is said that to allow litigants to remove judges because of their substantive views, could penalize judicial independence and creativity, encourage "judge shopping," and impose burdens on judges who are not the subject of removal motions. At a minimum, these arguments justify rather strict limits on any right to peremptorily challenge a judge.

(e) **Substitution of Judge.** The provisions discussed above must be distinguished from those permitting substitution of a judge because of death, sickness or other disability of the judge before whom the trial commenced. In the federal courts, such substitution is permissible if the case is being tried by a jury and if the substituted judge certifies "that he has familiarized himself with the record of the trial." [8] Similar provisions are to be found in some states, while some other jurisdictions allow substitution even when the case is being tried without a jury. The better view, however, is that if a judge is also the trier of the facts, the same judge should hear all the witnesses, unless the parties consent to substitution. It is sometimes contended that such consent should be required even if the case is being tried by a jury, a view that may rest in part on the notion that the right to jury trial includes the right to have the same judge present throughout the trial.

8. Fed.R.Crim.P. 25(a). In addition, Fed.R.Crim.P. 25(b) allows substitution "after a verdict or finding of guilt."

Chapter 23

FAIR TRIAL AND FREE PRESS

Table of Sections

§ 23.1 Preventing Prejudicial Publicity

(a) The Problem of Prejudicial Publicity. News media reporting on the operation of the criminal justice process, like other types of news reporting, is protected by the First Amendment.[1] As in the case of other reporting, criminal news reporting commonly provides many benefits both to the public generally and to those persons involved in the events that are the subject of the news report. Yet, at the same time, criminal news reporting may also produce severe adverse consequences. It may, for example, thwart investigations and expose to danger some persons, such as undercover agents or crime victims then within the control of the criminals. It may repeat false, unsubstantiated accusations or invade the privacy of those who have been victimized. It may also bear adversely upon the fairness of the criminal trial, and that is the sole focus of our concern here.

The potential adverse impact of the criminal news reporting upon trial fairness relates basically to three concerns. One is that a public outcry for a conviction, fanned or ignited by the news media, will prompt action by some public official—a policeman, a prosecutor, or a judge—that is other than impartial and objective. Another concern is that extensive news coverage will result in a jury that is not impartial and does not base its verdict solely on the evidence presented at trial. Excluding from the jury all persons who have been exposed to news coverage is often im-

§ 23.1

1. Nebraska Press Ass'n v. Stuart, 427 U.S. 539, 96 S.Ct. 2791, 49 L.Ed.2d 683 (1976).

practicable, and even where that can be done, it may result in a skewed sampling of the community. Seating jurors who have been exposed to the news coverage, even with extensive voir dire to screen out "biased" jurors and judicial admonitions on impartiality, always run the risk that some of those seated jurors nonetheless will approach the case with preconceived opinions or will be unable to exclude from their consideration facts or allegations that were reported in the news coverage but never presented at trial. Third and finally, even if all participants act impartially, their very exposure to the news coverage, particularly where it is inflammatory, may create an appearance of likely prejudice that brings the judicial process into disrepute.

The possible adverse impact of news coverage on the fairness of the criminal trial can be met in various ways. One is through procedural safeguards designed to offset the potentially pernicious influence of the coverage. Section 23.2 discusses the most prominent of those safeguards, which focus on the selection of the jury and timing and place of the trial. Another approach is to seek to reduce or eliminate that news coverage most likely to have a prejudicial influence. The subsections that follow discuss the major procedural devices aimed at that objective.

(b) Restricting Public Statements. In *Sheppard v. Maxwell*,[2] the Supreme Court held that defendant was deprived of his due process right to a fair trial "because of the trial judge's failure to protect Sheppard sufficiently from the massive, pervasive and prejudicial publicity that attended his prosecution." In discussing the various ways by which the trial judge could have exercised his "power to control the publicity about the trial," the Court asserted that

> the court should have made some effort to control the release of leads, information, and gossip to the press by police officers, witnesses, and the counsel for both sides. * * * The fact that many of the prejudicial news items can be traced to the prosecution, as well as the defense, aggravates the judge's failure to take any action. * * * Effective control of these sources—concededly within the court's power—might well have prevented the divulgence of inaccurate information, rumors, and accusations that made up much of the inflammatory publicity, at least after Sheppard's indictment. * * * More specifically, the trial court might well have proscribed extra-judicial statements by any lawyer, party, witness, or court official which divulged prejudicial matters * * *. Being advised of the great public interest in the case, the mass coverage of the press, and the potential prejudicial impact of publicity, the court could also have requested the appropriate city and county officials to promulgate a regulation with respect to dissemination of information about the case by their employees.

Despite this strong language, there continues to be considerable uncertainty as to the extent to which it is proper, both as a policy and constitutional matter, for a trial judge to restrict public statements. As for statements by counsel, standards of professional responsibility, contained in both the ABA Model Code and the ABA Model Rules, bar a lawyer connected with the investigation of a criminal matter from making other than general comments about the investigation,[3] and bar both the prosecutor and defense attorney from making "an extrajudicial statement that a reasonable person would expect to be disseminated by means of public communication" and which the lawyer should know "will have a substantial likelihood of materially prejudicing" the trial.[4] Declared "likely to have such effect" are statements relating to the following topics: (1) the character, credibility, reputation, or criminal record of a party or witness, or the identity of a witness or the expected testimony of a party or witness; (2) the possibility of a plea of guilty, or the existence or contents of any confession, admission,

2. 384 U.S. 333, 86 S.Ct. 1507, 16 L.Ed.2d 600 (1966).

3. ABA Model Code of Professional Responsibility, DR 7–107(A); ABA Model Rules of Professional Conduct, Rule 3.6(c). See § 1.5 at note 4.

4. While the Model Rules use the above quoted language in Rule 3.6(a), the Model Code uses "reasonably likely to interfere with a fair trial" in describing the requisite potential for interference as measured by a reasonable person. See DR 7–107(D).

or statement given by the defendant or his refusal or failure to make a statement; (3) the performance or results of any examination or test or the refusal or failure of a person to submit to examination or test, or the identity or nature of physical evidence; (4) any opinion as to the guilt or innocence of the defendant; (5) information likely to be inadmissible but prejudicial; and (6) the fact defendant has been charged, unless accompanied by a statement that the charge is only an accusation and that defendant is presumed innocent.[5]

In *Gentile v. State Bar of Nevada,*[6] the Supreme Court had before it the application of a state professional responsibility rule (Nevada Rule 177) that followed largely verbatim the ABA Model Rules' provisions described above. The petitioner there, a defense attorney, had been disciplined for statements made at a press conference held shortly after his client's indictment (and six months before the anticipated trial). The client had been charged, following a highly publicized investigation, with the theft of cocaine and travelers' checks from a safety deposit box, rented from the client's vault company, that had been used in a police undercover operation. At the press conference, the petitioner made statements to the effect that: (1) his client was innocent and was "being used as a scapegoat"; (2) the evidence pointed to a named police undercover officer as the true thief; (3) the defense had a video tape which showed the officer in a condition described implicitly as suggesting cocaine use; and (4) the other vault customers claiming safety deposit thefts were not credible, as most were drug dealers or money launderers who had accused the defendant in response to police pressure when they tried to "work themselves out of something." In concluding that petitioner had violated Nevada Rule 177, the state disciplinary board found that: (1) the petitioner expected both the named police officer and the other vault customers to be prosecution witnesses; (2) the petitioner's admitted purpose for calling the press conference was to influence public sentiment and the possible venire by offsetting information that had been released by the prosecutor and police (relating, in particular, to the lack of culpability of the police officer); (3) although the subsequent trial revealed there was no actual prejudice, the content, purpose, and timing of petitioner's statements (when public interest was "at its peak") established that petitioner either knew or should have known that there was a substantial likelihood that his remarks would materially prejudice the anticipated trial; and (4) petitioner's comment went beyond the "safe harbor" provision of Rule 177(3), which allowed defense counsel to "state without elaboration the general nature of the * * * [client's] defense." Before the Supreme Court, the petitioner claimed that the disciplinary board's sanction (a private reprimand) should be overturned because: (1) Nevada Rule 177 on its face violated the First Amendment; (2) the application of the Rule 177 prohibition to the facts of his case violated the First Amendment; and (3) Rule 177 was "void for vagueness" as interpreted by the Nevada authorities in their application of the Rule to his case. A Supreme Court majority (per Rehnquist, C.J.) rejected the first claim, and a differently composed majority (per Kennedy, J.) sustained the third claim. The Court was evenly divided (4–4) on petitioner's second claim of a First Amendment violation in the application of Rule 177. In a brief concurring opinion, Justice O'Connor joined the Rehnquist opinion on First Amendment facial validity and the Kennedy opinion on vagueness, but did not speak to that second claim.

Petitioner's First Amendment challenge to the facial validity of Rule 177 centered on the Rule's use of a "substantial likelihood of material prejudice" standard. Petitioner claimed that the First Amendment allowed the state to impose disciplinary sanctions only upon a showing of "a 'clear and present dan-

5. ABA Model Rules, Rule 3.6(b). See also ABA Model Code, DR 7–107(B). Specifically allowed is the disclosure of basic factual information such as the identity of the victim, information that will aid in the apprehension of the accused where he has not yet been apprehended, the date and place of arrest, and the "general nature of the claim or defense."

6. ___ U.S. ___, 111 S.Ct. 2720, 115 L.Ed.2d 888 (1991).

ger' of 'actual prejudice or imminent threat.' " Chief Justice Rehnquist's opinion for the majority on the facial validity issue flatly rejected that contention. The opinion acknowledged that the First Amendment had been held, in cases such as *Nebraska Press* (discussed in subsection (c) below), "to require a showing of 'clear and present danger' that a malfunction in the criminal justice system will be caused before a State may prohibit media speech or publication about a particular pending trial." Accordingly, the issue presented by petitioner's claim was "whether a lawyer who represents a defendant involved with the criminal justice system may insist on the same standard before he is disciplined for public pronouncements about the case, or whether the State instead may penalize that sort of speech upon a lesser showing." Following a review of statements in earlier cases, including *Sheppard,* the opinion concluded that those cases had "rather plainly indicat[ed] that the speech of lawyers representing clients in pending cases may be regulated under a less demanding standard than that established for regulation of the press." In support of this position, Chief Justice Rehnquist noted:

> Lawyers representing clients in pending cases are key participants in the criminal justice system, and the State may demand some adherence to the precepts of that system in regulating their speech as well as their conduct. As noted by Justice Brennan in his concurring opinion in *Nebraska Press,* * * * "[a]s officers of the court, court personnel and attorneys have a fiduciary responsibility not to engage in public debate that will redound to the detriment of the accused or that will obstruct the fair administration of justice." Because lawyers have special access to information through discovery and client communications, their extrajudicial statements pose a threat to the fairness of a pending proceeding since lawyers' statements are likely to be received as especially authoritative.

Chief Justice Rehnquist's opinion also concluded that the Model Rules' standard on potential prejudice, incorporated in Nevada Rule 177, fully satisfied that "less demanding" First Amendment restriction upon state regulation of lawyer speech. The opinion stated in this regard:

> We agree with the majority of the States that the "substantial likelihood of material prejudice" standard constitutes a constitutionally permissible balance between the First Amendment rights of attorneys in pending cases and the state's interest in fair trials. * * * The "substantial likelihood" test is designed to protect the integrity and fairness of a state's judicial system, and it imposes only narrow and necessary limitations on lawyers' speech. The limitations are aimed at two principal evils: (1) comments that are likely to influence the actual outcome of the trial, and (2) comments that are likely to prejudice the jury venire, even if an untainted panel can ultimately be found. Few, if any, interests under the Constitution are more fundamental than the right to a fair trial by "impartial" jurors, and an outcome affected by extrajudicial statements would violate that fundamental right. Even if a fair trial can ultimately be ensured through voir dire, change of venue, or some other device, these measures entail serious costs to the system. * * * The State has a substantial interest in presenting officers of the court, such as lawyers, from imposing such costs on the judicial system and on the litigants.
>
> The [Model Rules'] restraint on speech is narrowly tailored to achieve those objectives. The regulation of attorneys' speech is limited—it applies only to speech that is substantially likely to have a materially prejudicial effect; it is neutral as to points of view, applying equally to all attorneys participating in a pending case; and it merely postpones the attorney's comments until after the trial. While supported by the substantial state interest in preventing prejudice to an adjudicative proceeding by those who have a duty to protect its integrity, the rule is limited on its face to preventing only speech having a substantial likelihood of materially prejudicing that proceeding.

Four justices, in an opinion by Justice Kennedy, spoke against the application of what they described as a "standard more deferential than is usual where speech is concerned." They acknowledged "that an attorney's speech about pending cases may present dangers that could not arise from statements of a nonparticipant, and that an attorney's duty to cooperate in the judicial process may prevent him or her from taking actions with an intent to frustrate that process." They suggested that this should not alter the basic standard as to the likelihood of harm, but should enter only into the proper "weighing of dangers," which could include "the harm that occurs when speech about ongoing proceedings forces the court to take burdensome steps such as sequestration, continuance, or change of venue." They found no need, however, to "defin[e] with precision the outer limits under the Constitution of a court's ability to regulate an attorney's statements about ongoing adjudicative statements." Here, those limits had been exceeded by imposing disciplinary sanctions where the lawyer's speech clearly did not pose a danger "of the necessary gravity, imminence, or likelihood." The disciplinary sanction here also was invalid, Justice Kennedy noted, because it rested in an interpretation of Nevada Rule 177 which rendered that rule void for vagueness as applied. With Justice O'Connor joining this portion of the Kennedy opinion, the Court, by a 5–4 majority, reversed the disciplining of the petitioner.

The majority's holding as to vagueness centered on the "safe harbor" provision of Nevada Rule 177(3). That provision, also taken from the ABA Model Rules (see note 5 supra), created an exception to both the Rule's general prohibition of public communications that met the "substantial likelihood" standard and the Rule's subsequent listing of specific types of content that "ordinarily are likely" to present such a potential for prejudice. The safe harbor provision states that, "notwithstanding" those provisions, a lawyer involved in the litigation "may state without elaboration, * * * the general nature of the claim or defense." Prior to holding the press conference, the petitioner in *Gentile* had studied Rule 177 and what he considered to be applicable case law. Relying on both constitutional cases governing the seating of jurors exposed to pretrial publicity and the safe harbor provision, he had concluded that a limited press conference would not violate Rule 177. At the press conference, while making the statements described above, he also told reporters that there were certain areas he could not further explore "because ethics prohibits me from doing so." Justice Kennedy's opinion for the Court on the vagueness issue relied on both petitioner's actions and the special concerns presented by a statute that used such general terms in regulating speech. The opinion noted:

> As interpreted by the Nevada Supreme Court, the Rule is void for vagueness, * * * for its safe harbor provision, Rule 177(3), misled petitioner into thinking that he could give his press conference without fear of discipline. * * * A lawyer seeking to avail himself of Rule 177(3)'s protection must guess at its contours. The right to explain the "general" nature of the defense without "elaboration" provides insufficient guidance because "general" and "elaboration" are both classic terms of degree. In the context before us, these terms have no settled usage or tradition of interpretation in law. The lawyer has no principle for determining when his remarks pass from the safe harbor of the general to the forbidden sea of the elaborated.
>
> Petitioner testified he thought his statements were protected by Rule 177(3). A review of the press conference supports that claim. He gave only a brief opening statement, and on numerous occasions declined to answer reporters' questions seeking more detailed comments. * * * Nevertheless, the disciplinary board said only that petitioner's comments "went beyond the scope of the statements permitted by [Rule] 177(3)," and the Nevada Supreme Court's rejection of petitioner's defense based on Rule 177(3) was just as terse * * *. The fact Gentile was found in violation of the Rules after studying them and making a conscious effort at compliance demonstrates that Rule 177 creates a trap for the wary as well as the unwary.
>
> The prohibition against vague regulations of speech is based in part on the need to eliminate the impermissible risk of discriminatory enforcement, * * * for history shows that speech is suppressed when either the speaker

or the message is critical of those who enforce the law. The question is not whether discriminatory enforcement occurred here, and we assume it did not, but whether the Rule is so imprecise that discriminatory enforcement is a real possibility. The inquiry is of particular relevance when one of the classes most affected by the regulation is the criminal defense bar, which has the professional mission to challenge actions of the State. * * *

The several factors cited by Justice Kennedy raise a series of questions as to how far the Court's vagueness ruling will be carried. Initially, the references to the counsel's criticisms of the actions of the State might suggest that Rule 177(3) would not be unduly vague as applied to a prosecutor's whose comments on the charge were held to be more than a statement "without elaboration [of] the general nature of the charge." Indeed, the same might be true of a defense counsel's statement that did not accuse the state of misusing the process (e.g., by describing specific exculpatory evidence not known to the prosecution). Secondly, the question arises as to whether the Court's vagueness ruling would benefit an attorney who, in contrast to the petitioner in *Gentile,* made absolutely no effort to fit his discussion of the defense or charge within the confines of the safe harbor provision. At least where such an attorney's statement went into far more detail than the statement in *Gentile,* as where the attorney discussed at length each item of evidence that might be presented, it might be argued that the non-elaboration limit of the safe harbor provision surely did not operate as a "trap for the * * * wary." Third, and most significantly, the question arises as to what type of state elaboration upon the meaning of the safe harbor provision would provide sufficient guidance to attorneys to overcome future vagueness objection. That some degree of elaboration would serve this purpose seems to follow from the Court's reference both to the lack of any "settled usage or tradition of interpretation" and to the lack of explication by the disciplinary board and the Nevada Supreme Court in rejecting petitioner's reliance on the safe harbor defense. Arguably, an official interpretation holding that the *Gentile* statement exceeded the safe harbor provision when the attorney referred to specific evidence (in particular, the video tapes) would have provided sufficient guidance for an attorney who issued such a statement in the future. Of course, even without further elaboration as to the meaning of the safe harbor provision, the Model Rule should not present vagueness difficulties as to statements that deal with content specified in the rule that has no relation to the safe harbor provision (e.g., a prosecutor's reference to the accused's failure to make a statement or the accused's willingness to enter into plea negotiations).

Where the vagueness issue is eliminated, a court still must determine whether the statement in question meets the substantial likelihood standard. In *Gentile,* the Court was evenly divided on that issue. In portions of those opinions not joined by Justice O'Connor, the Kennedy opinion concluded that the record "reveal[ed] no basis for the Nevada Court's conclusion that the speech presented a substantial likelihood of material prejudice," and the Rehnquist opinion concluded that the finding below had enough support in the record so that it could not be deemed "mistaken." The Kennedy opinion stressed that in this First Amendment area, the Supreme Court was called upon to make its own independent review of the record. It found various factors in the record that made unsupportable a "substantial likelihood" finding, if that term was to be given "any meaningful content." The Kennedy opinion noted that: (1) the press conference was held six months before the trial; (2) the community from which the venire would eventually be drawn exceeded 600,000 in population; (3) petitioner's statement lacked "any of the more obvious bases for a finding of prejudice" (such as mention of confessions); (4) petitioner held the press conference to respond to information that had been released in the press by the police and prosecutor (including repeated press reports that the police had "complete trust" in their undercover officers and that those officers had been officially cleared after passing lie detector tests); (5) petitioner had acted with the primary motivation of merely "counter[ing] publicity already deemed prejudicial"; and (6) when the case came to trial, the jury was empaneled with no apparent difficulty, all material information disseminated at petitioner's press conference was admitted in evidence, and the jury acquitted petitioner's client.

The Rehnquist opinion agreed that "we must review the record for ourselves," but also noted that "respectful attention" should be given to the findings below because Nevada's disciplinary board and Supreme Court were "in a far better position than we are to appreciate the likely effect of petitioner's statements * * * in a highly publicized case like this." Petitioner's strongest points were "that the statement was made well in advance of trial, and that the statements did not in fact taint the jury panel," but the Nevada Supreme Court had responded adequately to both. It had noted that the timing of the statement, "when public interest * * * was at its height," and the highly inflammatory portrayal of prospective government witnesses presented a substantial likelihood of prejudicing the prospective jury, even though that did not in fact happen. The Chief Justice noted that "there was evidence pro and con" on this point, and he found it "persuasive" that the petitioner, by his own admission, called the press conference "for the express purpose of influencing the venire." The Chief Justice rejected in this regard the suggestion of the Kennedy opinion that this purpose was irrelevant because it was aimed only at combatting adverse publicity on the other side. Such an approach would place upon a court the difficult test of trying to distinguish between publicity that would influence by neutralizing and that which would create an affirmative bias. But "more fundamentally, it misconceives the constitutional test for an impartial juror," for a "juror who may have been initially swayed from open mindedness by publicity favorable to the prosecution is not rendered fit for service by being bombarded by publicity favorable to the defense." The proper defense remedy for adverse publicity was voir dire, change of venue, jury instructions, and discipline of the prosecutor, but "not * * * self-help in the form of similarly prejudicial comments by defense counsel."

The Kennedy and Rehnquist opinions reflect a series of disagreements not only as to the interpretation of the record in *Gentile,* but as to general approach in assessing whether the substantial likelihood test is met. At issue here is the degree of deference to be given to the judgment of courts and agencies more familiar with the local scene, and the weight to be given to such factors as the attorney's purpose in making the statement, previous publicity favoring the other side, and the eventual outcome of the jury selection process. Yet, the focus of the Kennedy opinion on the special role of the defense counsel, particularly in counsel's criticism of governmental action, suggests that the currently composed Court might more readily be in agreement where the attorney being sanctioned is the prosecutor and the information disseminated is that which falls within one of the "more obvious bases for a finding of prejudice" (e.g., the incriminating result of a scientific test). Here the justices who joined the Kennedy opinion could well join with those who joined the Rehnquist opinion in sustaining a lower court finding of a substantial likelihood notwithstanding a significant period of time between the statement and the trial and the lack of apparent difficulties in the later selection of the jury.

Also uncertain is whether the Court would allow a state to apply the substantial likelihood standard to prohibitions against statements by other participants in the criminal justice process. *Sheppard* stated that the trial court there might well have proscribed extrajudicial statements by "any lawyer, party, witness, or court official which divulged prejudicial matter." The Court there also referred to statements made by law enforcement authorities, but here it was less clear as to what was contemplated. The *Sheppard* opinion noted that the trial court should have made "some effort" to control the release of prejudicial information by the police and that "neither prosecutors * * * nor enforcement officers coming under the jurisdiction of the court should be permitted to frustrate its function." Yet, it also stated the judge might have "requested" that city and county officials control the statements "of their employees," the most obvious of whom would be the police. While some trial courts have issued orders directing "all participants," including the police, to refrain from making statements that would violate standards of the ABA Model Rules, those orders generally have not reached the appellate courts. The legal grounding for extending the standards of the ABA Model Rules to persons other than attorneys and court personnel was doubted by the drafters of the original ABA proposal on pretrial publicity. The trial court was thought to have no special authority over the statements of witnesses and parties that were not made as part of the judicial process or statements of the police who are independent of prosecutorial control (as is true of most police departments). The Kennedy opinion in *Gentile* clearly suggests that the First Amendment standard applied to statements by such persons should be the same as that applied to any private citizen. The majority's position, as expressed in Chief Justice Rehnquist's discussion of the facial validity of the Nevada Rule 177, leaves open the possibility of a different conclusion. The Rehnquist opinion spoke at length on the special obligations of the attorney, but it also referred at one point to the judiciary's special interest in regulating the speech "of those participating before the courts." It then added the following footnote:

> The Nevada Supreme Court has consistently read all parts of Rule 177 as applying only to lawyers in pending cases, and not to other lawyers or nonlawyers. We express no opinion on the constitutionality of a rule regulating the statements of a lawyer who is not participating in the pending case about which the statements are made. We note that of all the cases petitioner cites as supporting the use of the clear and present danger standard, the only one that even arguably involved a non-third party was *Wood v. Georgia*,[7] where a county sheriff was held in contempt for publicly criticizing instructions given by a judge to a grand jury. Although the sheriff was technically an "officer of the court" by virtue of his position, the Court determined that his statements were made in his capacity as a private citizen, with no connection to his official duties.

(c) Restricting the Media. The teaching of *Nebraska Press Association v. Stuart*[8] is that a prohibition upon the media publishing certain information which might be prejudicial to a criminal defendant will seldom, if ever, be a permissible means for preventing prejudicial publicity from occurring. At issue in that case were orders, entered prior to the trial of a mass murder, which barred the publication of "any testimony given or evidence adduced" in court and which also barred the reporting of any confessions or incriminating statements made by the defendant to the police or to anyone else other than the press or of other facts "strongly implicative" of the defendant. The Supreme Court (per Burger, C.J.) first and unequivocally concluded that the bar on reporting what happened "at the open preliminary hearing * * * plainly violated settled principles," namely, that "once a public hearing had been held, what transpired there could not be subject to prior restraint."

As for the prohibition upon publication of information from other sources, the Chief Justice concluded that the state had not met the heavy burden imposed as a condition to securing a prior restraint. Noting a "common thread" running through the prior cases, "that prior restraints on speech and publication are the most serious and the least tolerable infringement on First Amendment rights," the Chief Justice proceeded to examine the facts of the case to determine whether the danger was great enough to justify such an invasion of free speech. "To do so," he noted, requires examination of "the evidence before the trial judge when the order was entered to determine (a) the nature and extent of pretrial news coverage; (b) whether other measures would be likely to mitigate the effects of unrestrained pretrial publicity;

7. 370 U.S. 375, 82 S.Ct. 1364, 8 L.Ed.2d 569 (1962).

8. 427 U.S. 539, 96 S.Ct. 2791, 49 L.Ed.2d 683 (1976).

(c) how effectively a restraining order would operate to prevent the threatened danger."

With respect to the first of these, it was noted that the trial judge "found only 'a clear and present danger that pretrial publicity *could* impinge upon the defendant's right to a fair trial,'" and that his "conclusion as to the impact of such publicity on prospective jurors was of necessity speculative, dealing as he was with factors unknown and unknowable." As to the second, the Court observed that the record did not reflect careful consideration of "the alternatives to prior restraint * * * discussed with obvious approval in *Sheppard v. Maxwell,*" that is, change of venue, continuance, voir dire, and admonitions to the jurors. And as to the third point, it was noted that the trial took place in a very small community where "it is reasonable to assume" that rumors "could well be more damaging than reasonably accurate news accounts."

Although the Chief Justice declined to "rule out the possibility of showing the kind of threat to fair trial rights that would possess the requisite degree of certainty to justify" a prior restraint of the press, the other opinions in the case suggest that this possibility is a highly unlikely one. Justice Brennan, joined by two other members of the Court, would hold that prior restraint "is a constitutionally impermissible method for enforcing" the right to a fair trial. Justice Stevens agreed as to "information in the public domain," and indicated he might reach the same conclusion in other circumstances as well. Justice White expressed "grave doubt" that a prior restraint "would ever be justifiable," while Justice Powell emphasized the "unique burden" resting on one who would justify a prior restraint. Moreover, the Supreme Court has in somewhat related contexts held impermissible under the First Amendment prior restraints upon the dissemination of information in the public domain.[9]

In *Nebraska Press* a prior restraint was characterized as involving "an immediate and irreversible sanction," in contrast to a "criminal penalty or a judgment in a defamation case [which] is subject to the whole panoply of protections afforded by deferring the impact of the judgment until all avenues of appellate review have been exhausted." This might suggest that it would be constitutionally permissible for a state to adopt criminal statutes prohibiting certain identifiable prejudicial reporting, such as of a defendant's prior criminal record or of his confession not yet ruled admissible. But the Court's other recent cases indicate that criminal sanctions are not permissible except to "further a state interest of the highest order" [10] which cannot be adequately protected by less stringent measures.[11]

(d) Closed Proceedings: The First Amendment Right of Access. If, as the cases discussed above indicate, it is generally impermissible to restrain the press from reporting what occurs at an open hearing, then it must be asked whether the risk of prejudicial information being disclosed at that hearing may be avoided by closing the hearing or a portion thereof to the press and the public. This depends upon whether there is a press/public constitutional right of access to such proceedings and, if so, whether a weighing of that right against the defendant's right of a fair trial permits closure under some circumstances.

9. Oklahoma Publishing Co. v. District Court, 430 U.S. 308, 97 S.Ct. 1045, 51 L.Ed.2d 355 (1977) (freedom of press violated by pretrial order enjoining publication of name or picture of minor charged with juvenile delinquency, where without objection "members of the press were in fact present at the hearing with the full knowledge of the presiding judge, the prosecutor, and the defense counsel"); Cox Broadcasting Corp. v. Cohn, 420 U.S. 469, 95 S.Ct. 1029, 43 L.Ed.2d 328 (1975) (holding unconstitutional a civil action against a television station for breach of privacy based entirely on dissemination of information that was already in the public domain).

10. Smith v. Daily Mail Pub. Co., 443 U.S. 97, 99 S.Ct. 2667, 61 L.Ed.2d 399 (1979) (striking down a state statute making it a misdemeanor for a newspaper to publish, without written order of the juvenile court, the name of any youth charged as a juvenile offender, as "a penal sanction for publishing lawfully obtained truthful information * * * requires the highest form of state interest to sustain its validity," which was lacking here).

11. Landmark Communications, Inc. v. Virginia, 435 U.S. 829, 98 S.Ct. 1535, 56 L.Ed.2d 1 (1978) (holding unconstitutional as applied a state statute making it a crime to divulge information regarding proceedings before a state judicial tenure commission, and noting any risk that premature disclosure would endanger a judge's reputation could largely be eliminated through careful internal procedures by the commission).

As for the contention that a right of access is to be derived from the Sixth Amendment "public trial" provision, it was rejected by the Court in *Gannett Co. v. DePasquale.*[12] The Court concluded that history "fails to demonstrate that the Framers of the Sixth Amendment intended to create a constitutional right in strangers to attend a pretrial proceeding, when all that they actually did was to confer upon the accused an explicit right to demand a public trial." The issue of whether there exists a First Amendment right of access to criminal proceedings, was addressed shortly thereafter in *Richmond Newspapers v. Virginia.*[13] Although there was no opinion of the Court in that case, seven Justices recognized that this right of access is embodied in the First Amendment and is applicable to the states through the Fourteenth Amendment. As a majority later explained in *Globe Newspaper Co. v. Superior Court,*[14] the First Amendment is

> broad enough to encompass those rights that, while not unambiguously enumerated in the very terms of the Amendment, are nonetheless necessary to the enjoyment of other First Amendment rights. * * * Underlying the First Amendment right of access to criminal trials is the common understanding that "a major purpose of that Amendment was to protect the free discussion of governmental affairs" * * *. By offering such protection, the First Amendment serves to ensure that the individual citizen can effectively participate in and contribute to our republican system of self-government. * * * Thus to the extent that the First Amendment embraces a right of access to criminal trials, it is to ensure that this constitutionally protected "discussion of governmental affairs" is an informed one.

The Court in *Globe Newspaper* added that there were two features of the criminal justice system which "together serve to explain why a right of access to *criminal trials* in particular is properly afforded protection by the First Amendment": (1) such trials have historically been open to the press and public; and (2) the right of access plays a particularly significant role in the functioning of the judicial process, for public access not only enhances "the quality and safeguards the integrity of the factfinding process, with benefits to both the defendant and to society as a whole," but also "fosters an appearance of fairness, thereby heightening public respect for the judicial process."

While *Richmond Newspapers* and *Globe Newspaper* firmly established a First Amendment right of access to the trial itself, there remained the question of whether such a right also applied to pretrial hearings. In *Press–Enterprise I,*[15] the Court suggested that possibility in holding that the First Amendment right was applicable to the voir dire examination. The Court's opinion there stressed the two factors cited in *Globe*—an historical tradition of openness and the functional value of openness for the particular proceeding—rather than any characterization of the jury selection process as a part of the trial itself. In *Press–Enterprise II,*[16] the Court again relied upon those two factors, but this time held that a public right of access extended to a proceeding that clearly was not part of the trial—the preliminary hearing.[17] Turning to whether there existed as to preliminary hearings a "tradition of accessibility" (which would imply the "favorable judgment of experience"), the Court adopted a focus quite different from that suggested in *Gannett.* In

12. 443 U.S. 368, 99 S.Ct. 2898, 61 L.Ed.2d 608 (1979).

13. 448 U.S. 555, 100 S.Ct. 2814, 65 L.Ed.2d 973 (1980).

14. 457 U.S. 596, 102 S.Ct. 2613, 73 L.Ed.2d 248 (1982).

15. Press–Enterprise Co. v. Superior Court, 464 U.S. 501, 104 S.Ct. 819, 78 L.Ed.2d 629 (1984).

16. Press–Enterprise Co. v. Superior Court, 478 U.S. 1, 106 S.Ct. 2735, 92 L.Ed.2d 1 (1986).

17. The precise issue before the Court was the petitioner newspaper's right to have the transcript of a completed preliminary hearing released, but the opinion spoke in terms of a general First Amendment right of access to the preliminary hearing. So too, while the Court framed its ruling as applicable to "preliminary hearings as conducted in California," the basic features of the California hearing that were stressed in the Court's opinion tend to be found in preliminary hearings generally. The Court did mention certain aspects of the California preliminary hearing that are not common (e.g., the exclusion of illegally seized evidence, and the defendant's right to a preliminary hearing even after being indicted), but the general thrust of its reasoning would certainly be applicable as well to hearings that lacked those features.

discussing the possibility of a Sixth Amendment right of the public to attend a suppression hearing, the *Gannett* majority had concluded that "there exists no persuasive evidence that at common law members of the public had any right to attend pretrial proceedings; indeed there is substantial evidence to the contrary." The *Press–Enterprise II* opinion looked more to the common practice (which was to have open preliminary hearings) than to the existence of some specifically recognized legal right of access. The Court acknowledged that the code which dominated when the preliminary hearing came into prominence in the mid–1800's (the Field Code of New York) allowed the preliminary hearing to be closed on motion of the accused, but it discounted the significance of that provision. Even in the several states that still retained the Field Code provision, the Court noted, preliminary hearings are "presumptively open to the public and are closed only for good cause shown." As for the functional value of openness, its advantages in this trial-type proceeding were much the same as in the trial itself. Admittedly, the preliminary hearing, unlike a trial, cannot result in a conviction; but with so many cases being resolved without a trial, the preliminary hearing would often be the most significant stage at which the public could observe the criminal justice process.

Although *Press–Enterprise II* dealt only with the preliminary hearing, the Court's reasoning appears applicable to a wide range of pretrial hearings, including bail hearings, suppression hearings, and the evidentiary hearings held on various motions (e.g., change of venue). The only proceedings that would clearly be excluded are those of the grand jury. As the *Press–Enterprise II* Court noted in contrasting the preliminary hearing, the grand jury has a long history of secrecy. Also, although the dissenters in *Press–Enterprise II* argued that much of the Court's functional analysis would apply as readily to the grand jury, the traditional secrecy of grand jury proceedings has been viewed as serving the grand jury's screening and investigatory functions, not simply the concern for ensuring the accused's fair trial that had occasionally led to the closing of preliminary hearings.

(e) Closed Proceedings: Restricting the First Amendment Right. Assuming now a trial or other proceeding to which the First Amendment right of access applies, the next question is whether that right must sometimes give way to other competing interests, such as the defendant's right to a fair trial. The answer is yes. The Court declared in *Globe Newspaper* that the right of access "is not absolute," but cautioned that the circumstances when it can be withheld "are limited"; "it must be shown that the denial is necessitated by a compelling governmental interest, and is narrowly tailored to serve that interest." That case, while not involving a competing fair trial interest, illustrates the two ways in which the necessary showing can be lacking. At issue there was a statute requiring judges at rape and other sex-offense trials involving an alleged victim under 18 to exclude the press and general public during the testimony of that victim. As for the state's asserted interest in encouraging minor victims of sex crimes to come forward and provide accurate information, the Court concluded there was no showing whatsoever that closure would further that interest. As for the interest in protecting minor victims of sex crimes from further trauma and embarrassment, the Court found it to be "a compelling one" which would allow a trial judge to "determine on a case-by-case basis whether closure is necessary to protect the welfare of a minor victim" but which did not justify the mandatory closure necessitated by the challenged statute.

Another illustration of the need to narrowly tailor any closure to meet an offsetting privacy interest is provided by *Press–Enterprise I.* The Court there acknowledged that a prospective juror's privacy interests regarding personal matters inquired into on voir dire could outweigh public trial interests, but concluded that the court below had erred in not considering alternatives to closure and, in any event, in closing virtually all of a six week voir dire. The proper procedure, as outlined in *Press–Enterprise,* would have been for the trial judge to inform prospective jurors of their opportunity to raise with the judge in camera (but on the record and with counsel present) concerns about embarrassing questions, after which the judge would decide if "there is in fact a valid basis for a belief that disclosure infringes a significant interest in privacy." If such a finding was made, then the judge could either excuse that juror or order limited closure.

Where the interest asserted to justify closure is the accused's right to a fair trial, just how likely must it be that the publicity resulting from an open proceeding will prejudice that right? Some suggested that the Court should apply here the same clear and present danger standard held applicable to attempts to restrain reporting by the media. Others saw in *Gannett* implicit approval of the standard used by the lower court in that case: whether "an open proceeding would pose a 'reasonable probability of prejudice' to those defendants." In *Press–Enterprise II,* the Supreme Court adopted a standard that fell between the above alternatives. Rejecting the "reasonable likelihood" standard imposed by the lower courts there, the *Press–Enterprise II* majority set forth the following standard:

> If the interest asserted is the right of the accused to a fair trial, the preliminary hearing shall be closed only if specific findings are made that first, there is a substantial probability that the defendant's right to a fair trial will be prejudiced by publicity that closure would prevent and second, reasonable alternatives to closure cannot adequately protect the defendant's free trial rights.

Although this standard was stated in the context of the preliminary hearing, it should be equally applicable to other proceedings. Indeed, it is essentially the standard first proposed by the four dissenters in *Gannett,* a case involving a suppression hearing.

Perhaps the most critical aspect of the Court's "substantial probability" standard will be the weighing of alternatives. In *Press–Enterprise II,* for example, the Court noted that the lower court there should have taken into account the possibility that "voir dire, cumbersome as it is in some circumstances," would permit a trial court to identify and exclude any prospective jurors who might have become biased upon learning of prejudicial information disclosed in an open preliminary hearing. The Court did not clearly indicate, however, whether it meant also to suggest that voir dire almost always should be deemed a satisfactory alternative. The Court in *Richmond Newspapers* made specific mention of "sequestration of the jurors" as an alternative, and it might have been thought that, in light of that alternative, closing the trial would never be necessary to avoid the risk of jurors learning through outside sources of something that occurred in the courtroom while they were excused. Yet *Richmond Newspapers* did not set forth any such absolute prohibition against closure, and lower courts accordingly have held that the trial judge need not inevitably opt for sequestration. Accepting this conclusion, it would follow that a judge should have even more leeway in rejecting voir dire as an alternative remedy where highly prejudicial publicity is almost certain to flow from an open pretrial hearing. Not only is the voir dire as to prospective jurors a less effective remedy than sequestration as to sitting jurors, but it may also produce a side effect of a less representative jury when the voir dire can be expected to result in the exclusion of a substantial portion of the array. Similarly, the change of venue is a less than ideal alternative where it will force the defense to give up one right (venue in the district of commission) to obtain another (an unbiased jury).

A common theme running throughout the Court's discussions of potential justifications for closure is the need for a careful consideration of the facts of the particular case. A closure order, to be upheld, must be supported by specific findings both as to the compelling interest served and the alternatives considered and found deficient to serve that interest.[18] Moreover, even if the closure is justi-

18. In addition to the interests recognized in the Supreme Court's rulings, several other interests have been cited by lower courts as possibly justifying closure orders as to pretrial proceedings or papers filed in connection

fied, it appears that a transcript of the portion of the proceedings closed must be made available at the earliest time that is consistent with the overriding interest that required the closure. That procedure, followed in *Gannett* and cited with approval by many members of the Court, is essential to preserve a major function of the First Amendment right. For "public confidence cannot long be maintained where important judicial decisions are made behind closed doors and then simply announced in conclusive terms without ever revealing their factual basis to the public."

The *Gannett* majority stressed that before the suppression hearing there had been closed, the petitioning newspaper had been given "an opportunity to be heard." An independent right of the media to be heard would be firmly grounded today in the Court's subsequent recognition of a separate First Amendment right of access in the press and public, for that independent interest would not necessarily be protected either by the defense or prosecution. However, a majority of the Court has as yet advanced such a right only as to those media representatives present and objecting when closure is sought. The four dissenters in *Gannett* stated:

> This opportunity need not take the form of an evidentiary hearing; it need not encompass extended legal argument that results in delay; and the public need not be given prior notice that a closure order will be considered at a given time and place. But where a member of the public contemporaneously objects, the court should provide a reasonable opportunity to that person to state his objection.

Similarly, Justice Powell noted that "this opportunity extends no farther than the persons actually present at the time the motion for closure is made, for the alternative would require substantial delays in trial and pretrial proceedings while notice was given to the public." Representatives of the news media find this approach unduly strict, for it means that usually the media will be without legal representation at an unscheduled closure hearing. Some lower courts have ruled, however, that closure motions must be docketed sufficiently in advance of any hearing the closure motion to afford interested members of the public an opportunity to intervene and present their views to the court. None have suggested that the court must wave a red flag and attract media attention to a previously unnoticed case by informing the local press of the possibility of closure.

§ 23.2 Overcoming Prejudicial Publicity

(a) Change of Venue. If prejudicial publicity has already occurred or if it seems likely that such publicity later cannot be effectively prevented, then it is necessary for the trial court to consider other means of ensuring that the defendant is not denied a fair trial. One possibility is a change of venue, that is, a removal of the case to another locality where hopefully such publicity has not reached and will not occur. Indeed, it is constitutionally impermissible to make this remedy totally unavailable. In *Groppi v. Wisconsin,*[1] striking down a law barring change of venue in misdemeanor cases, the Court ruled that "under the Constitution a defendant must be given an opportunity to show that a change of venue is required in his case."

In some cases, change of venue will not be a realistic solution. But when the prejudicial publicity is rooted in a particular community or particular part of the state, removal of the case to another judicial district may be a most effective remedy. This may be true even

with those proceedings. These include: privacy interests of both defendants and "innocent third parties," as recognized in Title III provisions authorizing sealing of wiretaps and related documents, the chilling effect that disclosure of pretrial motion papers may have on the filing of such motions; the reputation of those listed in a bill of particulars as persons "who could conceivably be considered unindicted coconspirators"; and the need to protect informants and to preserve the integrity of an ongoing investigation, with respect to disclosure of arrest warrant affidavits. See also Fed.R.Crim.P. 6(e)(5): "Subject to any right to an open hearing in contempt proceedings, the court shall order a hearing on matters affecting a grand jury proceeding to be closed to the extent necessary to prevent disclosure of matters occurring before a grand jury."

§ 23.2

1. 400 U.S. 505, 91 S.Ct. 490, 27 L.Ed.2d 571 (1971).

where the publicity is widely disseminated, as very often public interest is much greater and public sentiment much stronger in the community in which the events occurred and the prosecution was originally brought.

At least under some circumstances, a denial of a requested change of venue will constitute a violation of the defendant's constitutional rights. Such was the conclusion reached in *Rideau v. Louisiana,*[2] where two months prior to trial a local TV station broadcast three different times a 20–minute film of defendant admitting in detail the commission of the various offenses with which he was charged. The parish had a population of about 150,000 and the estimated audiences for these broadcasts were 24,000, 53,000 and 29,000, respectively. Defendant's change of venue motion was denied, and he was convicted and sentenced to death. The Supreme Court held

> that it was a denial of due process of law to refuse the request for a change of venue, after the people of [the] Parish had been exposed repeatedly and in depth to the spectacle of Rideau personally confessing in detail to the crimes with which he was later to be charged. For anyone who has ever watched television the conclusion cannot be avoided that this spectacle, to the tens of thousands of people who saw and heard it, in a very real sense *was* Rideau's trial—at which he pleaded guilty to murder. Any subsequent court proceedings in a community so pervasively exposed to such a spectacle could be but a hollow formality.

In *Rideau,* the record indicated that three members of the jury had seen the TV broadcast but, at voir dire, had testified that they "could lay aside any opinion, give the defendant the presumption of innocence as provided by law, base their decision solely upon the evidence, and apply the law as given by the court." But the Supreme Court declared that it did "not hesitate to hold, without pausing to examine a particularized transcript of the *voir dire* examination of the members of the jury, that due process of law in this case required a trial before a jury drawn from a community of people who had not seen and heard Rideau's 'interview.' " This language and that quoted above, if taken literally, would seem to mean that the defendant would likewise prevail even if none of the jurors had seen or heard about the television interview. It is far from clear, however, what the theoretical basis of such a decision would be. One might be that reversal is necessary as a sanction against the police for permitting one in their custody to be unnecessarily put on display before others in circumstances very likely to be prejudicial, but the Court in a somewhat similar context has declined to go that route where there was no actual prejudice carrying over to the trial.[3] Another possibility is that such pervasive publicity requires reversal because it would necessitate the excusal of so many prospective jurors as to run afoul of the cross-section requirement, but this does not square with the fact that this requirement has been treated by the Court as applying to the panel from which the jury is selected and not the jury itself.[4]

Though this may mean that *Rideau* should not be read quite as broadly as its language suggests, it nonetheless is clear that the case stands for the proposition that there exist some situations in which a change of venue is constitutionally mandated even though the voir dire of a jury seated without changing venue does not contain sufficient signs of likely prejudice to establish a "presumption of partiality" under the due process standard of *Irvin v. Dowd* (discussed in subsection (d) infra). *Rideau* recognizes that prejudicial publicity may be so inflammatory and so pervasive that the voir dire simply cannot be trusted to fully reveal the likely prejudice among prospective jurors. Publicity may so affect the community that jurors will not be able to openly recognize the community pressures thrust upon them and may well be less than candid in their responses. Of course, the *Irvin v. Dowd* standard does not look solely to

2. 373 U.S. 723, 83 S.Ct. 1417, 10 L.Ed.2d 663 (1963).

3. Manson v. Brathwaite, 432 U.S. 98, 97 S.Ct. 2243, 53 L.Ed.2d 140 (1977), holding a reliable identification need not be suppressed merely because the police engaged in an unnecessarily suggestive identification procedure.

4. See § 22.2(d).

juror responses, and a presumption of partiality is most likely to be established in such a case. *Rideau,* however, sees certain cases as so exceptional that the risk of error under the *Irvin v. Dowd* standard, which does give considerable weight to juror responses, should not be tolerated.

Rideau itself presented a most compelling fact situation for concluding that there was no need to look to the voir dire to conclude that an impartial jury almost certainly could not have been produced without a change of venue. That fact situation included the following: the information conveyed was as inflammatory and prejudicial as might be conceived—what the Court characterized as the equivalent of a guilty plea combined with a detailed description of the crimes involved; the medium of a 20-minute television program, with the defendant himself speaking in camera, was the most likely to make a lasting impression on all who saw it; there was a saturation of the community, with such a large portion of the populace viewing the film (even taking account of possible repeat viewers) that those who did not view it were almost certain to have heard about it; and the nature of the case (involving robbery, kidnapping, and murder) and the size of the community obviously made the trial an event of major importance. Lower courts have stressed these special qualities and have found only the most extreme cases to fall within the "presumed prejudice doctrine" of *Rideau.* Some courts are willing to apply a more encompassing standard under state law, but as a constitutionally prescribed standard, *Rideau* has been held not to reach even the most highly publicized cases that are covered step-by-step and scoop-by-scoop in evening newscasts and front page stories. One factor that may have contributed to the judicial reluctance to carry *Rideau* beyond its extreme facts is the limited value of a venue change in many of the smaller states. If publicity is held to be of such a nature as to require a presumption of prejudice, a court in a small state simply may have nowhere to move the case as the same level of publicity often is found throughout the state.

With *Rideau* limited to the most exceptional cases, the common practice of trial judges is to postpone ruling on a change of venue until after an attempt to seat an impartial jury is made. If that attempt appears successful, at least in the sense that the court feels confident as to exclusion of all prospective jurors whose participation might give rise to a substantial due process claim under *Irvin v. Dowd,* the trial court will then deny the motion. Rarely will a trial court grant a change of venue out of a combination of caution and a desire to avoid an extensive voir dire. This may be due to the inconvenience associated with the change to another location, the concern that the citizens of the community should not be lightly treated as incapable of giving the defendant a fair trial, and the feeling that the community most directly concerned with the crime should be the place of the trial (although a few jurisdictions have experimented with a compromise designed to serve that interest while also responding to the prejudicial publicity—importing a jury from another venue and not changing the locale of the trial itself). Moreover, on an appeal following a conviction, a reviewing court is likely to be quite differential to the trial judge's decision not to order a change of venue, provided the jury selection process produced a jury that would be deemed acceptable under the standards of *Irvin v. Dowd.*

(b) Continuance. Doubtless there are a number of cases in which the granting of a continuance is not the solution to prejudicial pretrial publicity, as where the publicity has aroused antagonism so intense that there is no reason to suppose that it would subside by any delay which would not put off the trial indefinitely. But a continuance is a useful technique when this hostility can be expected to fade within a reasonable time, as where the problem has arisen because of some event or disclosure occurring on the eve of the time set for trial. Another kind of situation is that noted by the Court in *Sheppard v. Maxwell,*[5]

5. See § 23.1 at note 2.

where the trial began two weeks before a hotly contested election at which both the judge and chief prosecutor were candidates for judgeships. The Court noted that "a short continuance would have alleviated any problem with regard to the judicial elections."

Continuances are infrequently allowed on the grounds of prejudicial publicity, and generally only when there are extraordinary circumstances. Here, as with change of venue motions, judges are inclined to adopt a wait-and-see attitude by reserving the ruling on the continuance request until after some effort is made to select a jury. They recognize that, even if the defendant is willing to waive his right to a speedy trial, there is also a societal interest in a prompt trial. Whether the presumed prejudice doctrine of *Rideau* should be carried over to the continuance is an unresolved issue. Arguably the type of prejudicial publicity that is so inflammatory and so pervasive as to preclude reliance on voir dire is not the type that could be cured by a continuance.

(c) Severance. In a multidefendant trial, publicity about one particular defendant might prove detrimental to other defendants joined with him for trial. By analogy to those decisions permitting a severance when the disparity in the weight of evidence against one or more defendants is such that it would tend to prejudice the defense of another defendant involved in a relatively unimportant part of the case, it would appear that the granting of a severance would be an appropriate remedy under such circumstances.

(d) Jury Selection. Yet another way to overcome the prejudicial impact of pretrial publicity is by a voir dire that identifies those prospective jurors influenced by the publicity and a challenge procedure that eliminates all persons in that group who actually have been biased by the publicity. The theory here is that the voir dire examination of prospective jurors will reveal which of them have actually been exposed to the pretrial publicity and what effect that exposure has had upon them. If the voir dire reveals that a prospective juror is biased, then he may be challenged for cause.[6] Even if it does not establish bias to the satisfaction of the judge, the defense counsel who nonetheless believes that the pretrial publicity might have affected the prospective juror can still eliminate that juror if the defense has remaining peremptory challenges.[7] Primary reliance is placed on the voir dire and the challenge for cause, but the peremptory challenge serves as a safety net.

As noted above, courts refusing to adopt measures designed to avoid prejudicial publicity (e.g., closed proceedings) or alternative approaches to overcoming such publicity (e.g., change of venue) commonly assume that the combination of voir dire and challenges will provide an effective remedy. That assumption, however, is questionable. It rests in large part on the effectiveness of voir dire in uncovering prejudice in potential jurors, and there is reason to doubt whether voir dire always has that capacity. Thus, the ABA Commentary to the Criminal Justice Standards on *Fair Trial* and *Free Press* notes:

> Wigmore's faith in voir dire now seems excessive: Voir dire, in his view, was "beyond doubt the greatest legal engine ever invented for the discovery of truth." Today, judges, legal commentators, and social scientists are considerably more guarded about its effectiveness. This caution is attributable to at least three distinct but closely related factors: (1) inadequate understanding of the way pretrial publicity influences the thought process of prospective jurors; (2) the tendency among a significant number of prospective jurors to underplay the importance of exposure to prejudicial publicity and to exaggerate their ability to be impartial; and (3) persistent concern about the ability of attorneys and trial judges to discern bias, particularly at the subconscious level, even when the prospective juror is being completely candid.[8]

6. See § 22.3(c).

7. See § 22.3(d).

8. 2 ABA Standards for Criminal Justice § 8–3.5 (2d ed. 1980). Additional concerns are raised by the tactical costs which may lead counsel to make less than full use of voir dire. Voir dire questioning of juror fairness in light of publicity may antagonize jurors by suggesting that they are not open minded, that they could not take a position that might upset their neighbors, and that they

In light of these limitations, it might be thought that, as a matter of caution, the defense should be allowed to exclude automatically all jurors who are aware of adverse pretrial publicity. But that quite obviously is not feasible. As the Supreme Court long ago noted: "In these days of newspaper enterprise and universal education, every case of public interest is almost, as a matter of necessity, brought to the attention of all the intelligent people in the vicinity, and scarcely any one can be found among those best fitted for jurors who has not read or heard of it, and who has not some impression or some opinion in respect to its merits." [9] Another, more promising approach is to presume prejudice under some circumstances, that is, to excuse prospective jurors for cause without regard to their assertions of impartiality if they had been exposed to information of a certain type. Such an approach is proposed in the ABA Standards and apparently was adopted by the Supreme Court in *Marshall v. United States,*[10] holding that "persons who have learned from news sources of a defendant's prior record are presumed to be prejudiced." But in *Murphy v. Florida,*[11] the Court rejected the defendant's reliance upon *Marshall* in a state case, pointing out that the decision there rested on the Court's exercise of its supervisory authority over federal courts rather than on constitutional grounds.

Irvin v. Dowd,[12] decided in 1961, sets forth the basic constitutional framework for determining whether the jury selection process was inadequate to combat the prejudicial impact of adverse pretrial publicity and thereby deprived the defendant of his due process right to a fair tribunal. *Irvin* was the first of the state cases reaching the Court that focused exclusively on prejudicial pretrial publicity, and it therefore required the Court to determine how much of what had been said about jury selection and pretrial publicity in its earlier federal rulings was constitutionally grounded. The Court noted initially that, consistent with the position taken in those federal cases, the quest for juror impartiality under the Constitution certainly did not require the automatic exclusion of all prospective jurors who were aware of adverse pretrial publicity. Indeed, it also did not necessarily require the exclusion of persons who had a "preconceived notion" based on that publicity, but at that point, the Constitution did require a careful examination of the totality of the circumstances. Justice Clark's opinion for a unanimous Court reasoned:

> "The theory of the law is that a juror who has formed an opinion cannot be impartial." * * * [But] to hold that the mere existence of any preconceived notion as to the guilt or innocence of an accused, without more, is sufficient to rebut the presumption of a prospective juror's impartiality would be to establish an impossible standard. It is sufficient if the juror can lay aside his impression or opinion and render a verdict based on the evidence presented in court. * * * The adoption of such a rule, however, "cannot foreclose inquiry as to whether, in a given case, the application of that rule works a deprivation of * * * due process." [T]he test is "whether the nature and strength of the opinion formed are such as in law necessarily * * * raise the presumption of partiality."

The issue thus posed under *Irvin* is whether the adverse pretrial publicity and the circumstances surrounding its dissemination created "such a presumption of prejudice * * * that the jurors' claims that they can be impartial should not be believed." That issue, the Court noted, was not simply one of historical

come from a community that is not capable of providing a fair trial. While this "backfiring" potential may be minimized by skilled counsel, critics of heavy reliance upon voir dire argue that counsel often will be unable to fully utilize that skill because of judges who either insist upon conducting voir dire themselves or pressure counsel to keep the voir dire brief. So too, where jurors are questioned as a group, the voir dire may bring to the attention of some jurors adverse publicity of which they were previously unaware, and jurisdictions vary as to whether counsel can avoid such "contamination" by insisting upon questioning each juror out of the presence of the others. See also the discussion of Mu'Min v. Virginia at note 15 infra.

9. Reynolds v. United States, 98 U.S. (8 Otto) 145, 25 L.Ed. 244 (1878).

10. 360 U.S. 310, 79 S.Ct. 1171, 3 L.Ed.2d 1250 (1959).

11. 421 U.S. 794, 95 S.Ct. 2031, 44 L.Ed.2d 589 (1975).

12. 366 U.S. 717, 81 S.Ct. 1639, 6 L.Ed.2d 751 (1961).

fact, but of "mixed law and fact." The answer therefore could not lie entirely in the trial judge's acceptance of the truthfulness of a juror's response that, notwithstanding the publicity and any preconceived notions, he or she could render an impartial verdict. As Chief Justice Hughes had earlier noted, "impartiality" was not a "technical conception" but a "mental attitude of appropriate indifference," and for its ascertainment, "the Constitution lays down no particular tests and procedure is not chained to any ancient and artificial formula." On the other hand, the finding of impartiality by the trial judge who witnessed the jurors on voir dire was not to be lightly set aside; the circumstances should make "manifest" the inability of the jurors, notwithstanding their claims of impartiality, to decide the case solely upon the evidence presented at trial.

The *Irvin* Court found before it a case in which the circumstances clearly required it to impose a presumption of partiality and override the trial court's finding of jury impartiality. The media reports, described by the Court as a "barrage of newspaper headlines, articles, cartoons and pictures," had contained prejudicial and inflammatory information, including defendant's confession to six homicides, his past criminal record, and his alleged willingness to enter a guilty plea in return for a life sentence. These reports had been widely disseminated, creating a "pattern of deep and bitter prejudice" in the community. As a result, over half of the 430 venire members were excused on challenges for cause because they admitted to fixed opinions, almost 90% of those examined on the point entertained some opinion as to defendant's guilt, and eight of the twelve jurors seated had said they thought defendant was guilty. Though those jurors also said they could put aside that opinion and judge the case impartially, "where so many, so many times, admitted prejudice, such a statement of impartiality * * * [could] be given little weight." The Court concluded that "with his life at stake, it is not requiring too much that petitioner be tried in an atmosphere undisturbed by so huge a wave of public passion and by a jury other than one in which two-thirds of the members admit, before hearing any testimony, to possessing a belief in his guilt."

In two later cases, *Murphy v. Florida* [13] and *Patton v. Yount,*[14] the Court distinguished *Irvin* and held that the surrounding circumstances there did not warrant presuming partiality and thereby overriding a trial judge's assessment that the selection process had resulted in the seating of an impartial jury. The Court in *Murphy* found insufficient the defendant's notoriety (due to previous, highly publicized criminal activities) and the fact that 20 of 78 persons questioned were excused because they indicated an opinion as to his guilt. The Court noted that the news articles about defendant's prior crimes had appeared seven months before jury selection and were "largely factual in nature." The voir dire, moreover, evidenced no hostility towards petitioner by the jurors who were seated. There was only one "colorable claim of partiality" relating to one juror's concession that his prior impression of the defendant would "dispose him to convict." Moreover, the Court could not attach "great significance to this statement * * * in light of the leading nature of counsel's questions and the juror's other testimony indicating that he had no deep impression of petitioner at all."

Patton v. Yount appeared to come closer to *Irvin* than *Murphy.* It presented, like *Irvin,* a notorious murder case tried in a small community. Here too, the reports had made reference to damaging inadmissible information, including a prior conviction for the same crime, a prior confession, and a prior plea of temporary insanity. Also, the percentage of persons in the jury panel who acknowledged having some opinion was high (77%) and eight of the fourteen seated jurors (including the two alternates) admitted that at some time they had formed an opinion as to guilt. The Court noted, however, that the "extensive adverse publicity and the community sense of

13. See note 11 supra.

14. 467 U.S. 1025, 104 S.Ct. 2885, 81 L.Ed.2d 847 (1984).

outrage" were "at their height" prior to defendant's first trial. The jury selection at the second trial, which was all that was before it, came four years later, at a time when "prejudicial publicity was greatly diminished and community sentiment had softened." While "a number of jurors and veniremen" had made reference to opinions earlier held, "for many, time had weakened or eliminated any conviction they had had." In the end, it could not be said that the trial judge was manifestly incorrect in concluding that the jury was impartial, as the voir dire suggested that the jurors with prior opinions who had been selected were those "who had forgotten or would need to be persuaded again."

Although the Court stressed in *Murphy* and *Patton* that each case rested on the totality of its circumstances, the primary factors that appeared to distinguish *Murphy* and *Patton* from *Irvin* were: (i) the strength of the voir dire responses of the jurors with reference to their previously developed opinions, (ii) the nature of the pretrial publicity (far less inflammatory in *Murphy* and *Patton*), and (iii) the time elapsed between the height of the publicity and the trial (especially significant in *Patton*).

In *Mu'Min v. Virginia,*[15] the Court considered the bearing of the *Irvin* line of rulings on the scope of voir dire in pretrial publicity cases. The end result was a 5–4 decision, with the majority's ruling apparently limited to the special circumstances presented there. In *Mu'Min,* 16 out of 26 prospective jurors (including 8 of the actual panel) answered affirmatively when asked if they had acquired any information about the case from the news media or any other source. The defense had asked that each of the prospective jurors be questioned out of the presence of the other jurors and be asked to respond to 64 proposed questions, but the trial court concluded that it was satisfactory to question the prospective jurors in groups of four and to put to them only some of the proposed questions. The judge did ask the prospective jurors whether any information acquired from outside sources would affect their impartiality and whether they had formed an opinion in the case. None of the persons eventually seated were among those who stated that they had an opinion or were no longer impartial or who otherwise indicated possible prejudice in their answers. The defense contended that this was not constitutionally sufficient because the judge had refused to ask of those jurors who had acquired outside information additional questions concerning the content of that information.

Writing for the majoring in *Mu'Min,* Chief Justice Rehnquist acknowledged a content inquiry might well "be helpful in assessing whether a juror is impartial." The issue before the Court, however, was whether the failure to conduct such an inquiry "must render the defendant's trial fundamentally unfair." Traditionally, trial judges had been given "great latitude" in voir dire questioning, and while some jurisdictions had restricted that discretion by requiring content-based questions as to pretrial publicity, others had not. One difficulty posed by such questions is that they basically required the questioning of each prospective juror in isolation so that others will not be exposed to content that had not previously come to their attention. In any event, the Chief Justice noted, whether or not the judge decides to put content questions to potential jurors, the ultimate issue remains the same—whether there is a sufficient basis for the judge's assessment that the juror is credible in stating that he or she has not formed an opinion and would be impartial. In making that assessment, the judge would have to evaluate the "depth and extent of news stories that might influence a juror," and where that publicity engendered a "wave of public passion," as in *Irvin v. Dowd,* it "might well * * * requir[e] more extensive examination of potential jurors than under[taken] here." However, the publicity in this case, though "substantial," was "not of the same kind and extent as that found to exist in *Irvin.*" In such a case, a judge could constitutionally make a finding of juror im-

15. ___ U.S. ___, 111 S.Ct. 1899, 114 L.Ed.2d 493 (1991).

partiality in light of the responses given, without further questioning.

In her separate concurring opinion in *Mu'Min,* Justice O'Connor, who supplied the critical fifth vote for affirmance, further developed the significance of the content of the adverse publicity and the responses of the jurors actually seated. While it was true that the trial judge "did not know precisely what each juror had read," he was aware "of the full range of the information that had been reported." With this information in mind, and with each juror having indicated that no opinion had been formed, the trial judge could not be said to have violated the Sixth Amendment in accepting the jurors' assurances of impartiality. Justice O'Connor, as did Chief Justice Rehnquist, found support for this conclusion in *Patton v. Yount.* The Court there had drawn a distinction between two types of issues presented in prejudicial publicity cases. One was the basically legal question as to whether the adverse publicity had reached a point where a presumption of prejudice required the trial court to reject assurances of impartiality by jurors exposed to that publicity. Where that presumption was not applicable, the trial judge's determination as to credibility was basically a factual judgment, and such credibility determinations were "entitled to 'special deference,'" allowing for reversal "only for 'manifest error.'" That was the kind of determination that was presented in this case, and while a content inquiry would have been helpful in making such an assessment, the judge's determination cannot be viewed as manifest error because the judge decided "to evaluate a juror's credibility instead by reference to the full range of potentially prejudicial information that had been reported." [16]

(e) Admonishment or Sequestration of Jury. Even if by a process of careful jury selection it has been possible to nullify the effects of prejudicial pretrial publicity, there remains the risk of prejudicial publicity during the trial. Once the trial is under way, the media may report initially or again preexisting prejudicial information about the defendant, such as his prior record or evidence of his guilt not admissible at trial, or may report prejudicial events occurring at trial while the jury has been excused. One way to try to deal with this is by an admonition to the jury not to read, listen to, or watch news about the case which may appear in the newspapers or on radio or television. There persists a considerable difference of opinion about the effectiveness of this instruction. The concern, of course, is that such an admonition may actually whet the jurors' appetites to discover via the media information about the case which they feel is being kept from them. There is no doubt but that the instruction is not inevitably effective, as is shown by those cases in which the admonition was disregarded by some of the jurors.

This being the case, it might be thought that sequestration of the jury during the trial and until a verdict is reached or the jury is discharged, so as to prevent the jurors from having access to the media during that time, is the solution. It would appear to be an effective way to prevent the jury from being influenced by the notoriety of the case, except insofar as community sentiment is reflected by the atmosphere in the courtroom. But it is a safeguard with considerable costs, including the expense to the state and the inconvenience to the jurors themselves in a trial of any length. Moreover, even if the trial judge sequestering a jury is careful not to inform the jurors which party requested the sequestra-

16. One of the four dissenters in *Mu'Min,* Justice Kennedy, agreed that the publicity in *Mu'Min* presented only a factual credibility judgment of the type noted in Patton v. Yount, and that "any need for content questioning disappears if the trial judge evaluating jury impartiality assumes a worst-case hypothesis that the jurors have read or seen all of the pretrial publicity." He concluded, however, that the voir dire here was deficient in that the questions were phrased so as to allow the jurors to remain silent as an implied indication of lack of bias. Speaking for the remaining dissenters, Justice Marshall argued that, in light of the "profoundly prejudicial" nature of the publicity, any "juror exposed to the bulk of it certainly would have been disqualified as a matter of law," and content questioning therefore was essential to determine whether a juror should be so disqualified. He added, however, that even where the publicity is not per se disqualifying, "content questioning is still essential to give legal depth to the trial court's finding of impartiality."

tion, there is the possibility that the sequestration might produce resentment by the jury which would ultimately work to the disadvantage of one of the parties in the case. Thus, while the Supreme Court has recognized sequestration as one remedy which must be considered by the trial judge,[17] it is not a solution inevitably so superior to others that it must be selected by the judge. In particular, sequestration need not always be selected even over closure of a portion of the trial.

(f) Excusal of Jurors. Finally, if material published during the trial raises the question of possible prejudice, the trial judge may inquire of the jurors concerning their possible exposure to that material. The jurors should be questioned individually out of the presence of the others, and the inquiry should be sufficiently probing to elicit a candid answer from each of the jurors regarding exposure to such material. The juror should be excused and replaced by an alternate if the circumstances now existing are such that the juror would have been challengeable for cause at the voir dire. Indeed, when a juror has been exposed to highly prejudicial information during (rather than before) the trial, there may be reason to be less willing to accept a juror's assertion that he remains able to act impartially. That is particularly true where the juror purposely violated the court's admonition not to read, listen to, or watch media coverage of the case.

§ 23.3 Conduct of the Trial

(a) Newsmen in the Courtroom. As we have seen, there is "embodied in the First Amendment, and applied to the States through the Fourteenth Amendment," a right in the press "of access to criminal trials."[1] That right of access, however, does not mean that media representatives cannot be restrained in their conduct while they are in and near the courtroom. Indeed, the failure of the judge to take such steps may under some circumstances deprive the defendant of his due process right to a fair trial.

The problem is well illustrated by the case of *Sheppard v. Maxwell,*[2] involving a murder trial which was subjected to massive media coverage from the very outset. During the entire nine weeks of trial, the courtroom was crowded to capacity with representatives of the news media, and their movements in and out of the courtroom "often caused so much confusion that, despite the loud speaker system installed in the courtroom, it was difficult for the witnesses and counsel to be heard." Reporters were seated inside the bar, which "made confidential talk among Sheppard and his counsel almost impossible during the proceedings." During recesses pictures were taken in the courtroom, and newsmen even handled and photographed trial exhibits laying on the counsel table. The corridors were crowded with photographers and TV cameramen, who took pictures of the defendant, counsel, witnesses and jurors as they entered and left the courtroom. Broadcasting facilities were set up in a room adjacent to the jury room.

Viewing the "totality of circumstances in this case," including the above recited events and exposure of the jurors to prejudicial information not admitted into evidence, the Supreme Court concluded the defendant had been denied a fair trial. The Court made it absolutely clear that the trial judge had no excuse as there were many steps which could have been taken to ensure courtroom decorum:

> The carnival atmosphere at trial could easily have been avoided since the courtroom and courthouse premises are subject to the control of the court. * * * [T]he presence of the press at judicial proceedings must be limited when it is apparent that the accused might otherwise be prejudiced or disadvantaged. Bearing in mind the massive pretrial publicity, the judge should have adopted strict rules govern-

17. Sheppard v. Maxwell, 384 U.S. 333, 86 S.Ct. 1507, 16 L.Ed.2d 600 (1966).

§ 23.3

1. Globe Newspaper Co. v. Superior Court, 457 U.S. 596, 102 S.Ct. 2613, 73 L.Ed.2d 248 (1982). See § 23.1(d).

2. 384 U.S. 333, 86 S.Ct. 1507, 16 L.Ed.2d 600 (1966).

ing the use of the courtroom by newsmen * * *. The number of reporters in the courtroom itself could have been limited at the first sign that their presence would disrupt the trial. * * * Furthermore, the judge should have more closely regulated the conduct of newsmen in the courtroom.

(b) Electronic and Photographic Coverage. In the year 1937 the American Bar Association adopted Judicial Canon 35, which declared that all photographic and broadcast coverage of courtroom proceedings should be prohibited. In 1952 that provision was amended to proscribe television coverage as well. This proscription became the law in the federal courts and in most state courts as well. But in more recent years the ban on trial coverage by electronic or photographic means has undergone considerable reassessment, and as a result a number of states now permit such coverage under closely controlled circumstances, an approach today endorsed by the American Bar Association.

The televising of criminal trials has been before the Supreme Court on two occasions. In the first case, *Estes v. Texas,*[3] pretrial hearings were televised and were seen by some of the persons selected as jurors, and much of the trial was also televised. In a 5–4 decision, the Court reversed the conviction on the ground that the "procedure employed by the State involves such a probability that prejudice will result that it is deemed inherently lacking in due process." The Court added that "there are numerous situations in which it might cause actual unfairness—some so subtle as to defy detection by the accused or control by the judge," and then proceeded to enumerate some reasons why televising a trial could cause unfairness: (1) it could have an impact upon the jurors by distracting them and making the case appear a cause celebre; (2) it could have an impact upon witnesses and decrease the quality of testimony received; (3) it could have an impact upon the judge by adding to his responsibilities and by subjecting him to greater political pressure; and (4) it could have an impact upon the defendant because it would be distracting to him and might reduce the effectiveness of his attorney's representation.

It was unclear, at best, whether *Estes* announced a constitutional rule barring still photographic, radio and television coverage in all cases and under all circumstances, for the fifth vote of the majority was by Justice Harlan, who in a separate opinion concluded only that televised trials were banned "in cases like this one." The Court's subsequent references to *Estes* arguably indicated that it was not viewed as having announced a per se rule, and the Supreme Court so held in *Chandler v. Florida.*[4] Chandler upheld a regulated state practice that allowed electronic media and still photography coverage of public criminal proceedings over the objection of the accused. The unanimous Court emphasized that "no one has been able to present empirical data sufficient to establish that the mere presence of the broadcast media inherently has an adverse impact on that process," and stressed that in the instant case the televising was done pursuant to carefully crafted guidelines designed to ensure that the excesses found in the *Estes* case were avoided. Thus, the guidelines included restrictions on the type and manner of equipment used, designed to keep the recording unobtrusive, and a prohibition against the filming of the jury itself. Moreover, they "placed on [the] trial judges positive obligations to be on guard to protect the fundamental right of the accused to a fair trial." It is still open to a particular defendant, the Court added, "to show that the media's coverage of his case * * * compromised the ability of the jury to judge him fairly" or to "show that broadcast coverage of his particular case had an adverse impact on the trial participants sufficient to constitute a denial of due process." But such prejudice is not established by merely showing "juror awareness that the trial is such as to attract the attention of broadcasters."

The Court in *Chandler* appeared to go out of its way to call attention to the fact that the state court had "pointedly rejected any state

3. 381 U.S. 532, 85 S.Ct. 1628, 14 L.Ed.2d 543 (1964).

4. 449 U.S. 560, 101 S.Ct. 802, 66 L.Ed.2d 740 (1981).

or federal constitutional right of access on the part of photographers or the broadcast media to televise or electronically record and thereafter disseminate court proceedings." Moreover, the Court noted that this assertion was grounded in the Supreme Court's decision in *Nixon v. Warner Communications, Inc.*,[5] declaring that the press has "no right to information about a trial superior to that of the general public." But now that a First Amendment right of the media to have access to the courtroom has been clearly recognized,[6] the continued vitality of that proposition may be questioned. It has been argued that, given the *Chandler* decision that television does not inherently violate due process, there are no longer any grounds on which television can be denied the same rights of access that *Richmond Newspapers* upholds for the public and the print press. Indeed, it has been argued that *Chandler* itself is difficult to accept absent recognition of such a First Amendment right, for one would think that only interests at least similar to those protected by the First Amendment would justify running the risks of prejudice to the defendant that the Court acknowledged are created whenever trials are televised. This reasoning has not persuaded the courts, however. Cameras continue to be excluded where print reporters are allowed (including arguments before the Supreme Court) and challenges by television and radio broadcasters to such restrictions have been rejected. Television and broadcasting continue to be more obtrusive than the reporter scribbling notes and it remains within the discretion of the jurisdiction as to whether it desires to expend the resources necessary to allow and regulate the use of cameras.

5. 435 U.S. 589, 98 S.Ct. 1306, 55 L.Ed.2d 570 (1978), holding the First Amendment does not require a court to release subpoenaed tapes to the media for copying.

6. Globe Newspaper Co. v. Superior Court, 457 U.S. 596, 102 S.Ct. 2613, 73 L.Ed.2d 248 (1982).

Chapter 24

THE CRIMINAL TRIAL

Table of Sections

---

§ 24.1 The Right to a Public Trial

(a) Nature of the Right. The Sixth Amendment provides that "In all criminal prosecutions, the accused shall enjoy the right to a * * * public trial." This very fundamental right was one of the first Sixth Amendment rights held by the Supreme Court to be an essential element of due process and therefore applicable in state proceedings under the Fourteenth Amendment.[1] The Sixth Amendment right to a public trial belongs to the defendant rather than the public; a separate First Amendment right governs the interests of the public and the press in attending a trial.[2] The Sixth Amendment guarantee extends to all criminal trials, including criminal contempt trials,[3] and it covers the entire trial, including the impaneling of the jury, the opening statements, the presentation of evidence, the arguments of counsel, the instructions to the jury, and the return of the verdict. It also has been held to extend to certain pretrial proceedings, such as a suppression hearing, which bear a resemblance to a trial.[4]

There are several ways in which a defendant can benefit from having a public trial. Most importantly, it is "a safeguard against any attempt to employ our courts as instruments of persecution. The knowledge that every criminal trial is subject to contemporaneous review in the forum of public opinion is an effective restraint on possible abuse of judicial power." [5] In addition, a public trial makes the proceedings known to possible material witnesses who might otherwise be unknown to the parties and also tends to assure testimonial trustworthiness by inducing a fear that any false testimony would be detected. In resolving issues relating to the scope of the Sixth Amendment right, courts often turn to the relevance of these functions. Thus, *Waller v. Georgia*,[6] in holding the right applicable to a suppression hearing, reasoned that the usual public trial interests of ensuring that the judge and prosecutor carry out their duties responsibly, encouraging witnesses to come forward, and discouraging perjury "are no less pressing in a hearing to suppress wrongfully seized evidence."

The defendant's right to a public trial is adequately protected so long as there is freedom of access by the public to the trial, and it is not necessary that everyone who wants to attend be accommodated. But the trial must be held at a place where there are not significant inhibitions upon public attendance. To show a violation of this right, it is not necessary for the defendant to establish that he was prejudiced in any specific way by the exclusion. An improper exclusion of the public from the trial establishes grounds in itself for a new trial.[7] Of course, the exclusion is not improper, at least from the perspective of the Sixth Amendment, if the defendant waived his right. However, the fact that defendant can waive his right does not mean that there is any right in the defendant to compel a private trial.[8]

§ 24.1

1. In re Oliver, 333 U.S. 257, 68 S.Ct. 499, 92 L.Ed. 682 (1948).

2. See § 23.1(d); Gannett Co. v. DePasquale, 443 U.S. 368, 99 S.Ct. 2898, 61 L.Ed.2d 608 (1979).

3. In re Oliver, 333 U.S. 257, 68 S.Ct. 499, 92 L.Ed. 682 (1948).

4. Waller v. Georgia, 467 U.S. 39, 104 S.Ct. 2210, 81 L.Ed.2d 31 (1984).

5. In re Oliver, supra note 3.

6. Supra note 4.

7. See Waller v. Georgia, supra note 4, agreeing with that position as to the trial, but concluding that where it was a pretrial suppression hearing which was improperly closed, defendant was entitled only to a new suppression hearing and not a new trial unless the new hearing resulted in suppression of evidence admitted at the first trial.

8. Gannett Co. v. DePasquale, 443 U.S. 368, 99 S.Ct. 2898, 61 L.Ed.2d 608 (1979). Of central concern in opposition to waiver is the First Amendment right of the public to have access to criminal trials, discussed in § 23.1(d). However, the prosecution may also advance a separate interest in a public trial.

(b) Competing Interests. The defendant's right to a public trial is not absolute; it must be balanced against other interests which might justify closing the trial. But in striking a fair balance the trial judge must proceed with caution; the court's discretion to order exclusion must be sparingly exercised and limited to those situations where such action is deemed necessary to further the administration of justice. Generally, the better course of action is for the trial judge to hold an evidentiary hearing on the issue of closure whenever it arises, though in some circumstances the judge will be able to take judicial notice of the essential facts. As the Supreme Court put it in *Waller v. Georgia,*[9] "the party seeking to close the hearing must advance an overriding interest that is likely to be prejudiced, the closure must be no broader than necessary to protect that interest, the trial court must consider reasonable alternatives to closing the proceeding, and it must make findings adequate to support the closure." Thus, the task facing a trial judge in ruling upon a possible restriction of the defendant's right to a public trial is very like that facing a trial judge in considering a restriction of the public right of access.[10] Indeed, the ruling in *Waller* was similar to rulings that have rejected restrictions upon the First Amendment right because the closure order was not narrowly tailored to meet an offsetting privacy interest.[11] *Waller* concluded that the lower court clearly erred in closing an entire 7–day suppression hearing in the interest of protecting the privacy of persons named in tapes played for two and one-half hours.

Trials have occasionally been closed to protect the public morals. Earlier cases took the view that in the trial of sex offenses the general public could be excluded from the courtroom for this purpose, but today the judge would at most be allowed to exclude youthful spectators. That situation must be distinguished from those in which a portion of the trial of a sex offense has been closed for the protection of the victim. As noted in *United States ex rel. Latimore v. Sielaff,*[12]

> exclusion of spectators during the testimony of an alleged rape victim "is a frequent and accepted practice when the lurid details of such a crime must be related by a young lady." * * * Primary justification for this practice lies in protection of the personal dignity of the complaining witness. The Supreme Court has recognized that, short of homicide, rape is the "ultimate violation of self." * * * Rape constitutes an intrusion upon areas of the victim's life, both physical and psychological, to which our society attaches the deepest sense of privacy. Shame and loss of dignity, however unjustified from a moral standpoint, are natural byproducts of an attempt to recount details of a rape before a curious and disinterested audience. The ordeal of describing an unwanted sexual encounter before persons with no more than a prurient interest in it aggravates the original injury. Mitigation of the ordeal is a justifiable concern of the public and of the trial court.

It does not follow from this, however, that it would be proper to adopt a standing policy of automatic closure during the testimony of the victim at any rape trial. Rather, as the Supreme Court held in dealing with a First Amendment challenge to a closure order, the trial court should "determine on a case-by-case basis whether closure is necessary" to protect the welfare of the victim, taking into account "the minor victim's age, psychological maturity, and understanding, the nature of the crime, the desires of the victim, and the interests of parents and relatives."[13]

Limited exclusion of spectators is also permissible when there is a demonstrated need to protect a witness from threatened harassment or physical harm. Such action has been upheld where the witness had been subjected to pretrial threats and also where actions by

9. Supra note 4.

10. See § 23.1(e).

11. See e.g., *Globe Newspaper* and *Press Enterprise I,* discussed in § 23.1(e).

12. 561 F.2d 691 (7th Cir.1977).

13. Globe Newspaper Co. v. Superior Court, 457 U.S. 596, 102 S.Ct. 2613, 73 L.Ed.2d 248 (1982), discussed in §§ 23.1(d), (e).

spectators at the trial were understandably perceived by the witness as threatening. Similarly, exclusion during the testimony of an undercover agent engaged in ongoing investigations is proper when it appears that exposure in a public courtroom would not only imperil the agent but would render him useless for any further investigative activities. This latter consideration reflects yet another competing interest—the confidentiality of certain information.[14] Also illustrative of that category are cases permitting limited closure to protect the confidentiality of trade secrets and the government's hijacker detection profile. Finally, exclusion of spectators is also permissible when necessary to preserve order in the courtroom. But the reason most often relied upon to justify a closure against the First Amendment interest of the public and media, to avoid prejudicing the jury against the defendant, is relatively unimportant in the Sixth Amendment context, for it "is largely absent when a defendant makes an informed decision to object to the closing of the proceeding." [15]

§ 24.2 Presence of the Defendant

(a) Scope of Right to Be Present. The defendant's constitutional right to be present has been described by the Supreme Court as extending to "every stage of the trial." [1] While that right is "rooted to a large extent in the confrontation clause of the Sixth Amendment," it also has a due process component. Accordingly, it is not restricted to situations where the defendant is "actually confronting witnesses or evidence against him," but encompasses all trial-related proceedings at which defendant's presence " 'has a relation, reasonably substantial, to the fullness of his opportunity to defend against the charge.' " [2]

The right has been held to extend to jury selection and to communications between the judge and jury, including the giving of jury instructions initially, re-instruction later, the replaying of taped testimony in the courtroom in connection with jury deliberations, and an in-chamber conversation with a single juror that is substantive in nature. It has also been held to apply to sentencing. On the other hand, the right has been held not to extend to in-chamber pretrial conferences, to post-trial motions for a new trial, to brief bench conferences with attorneys conducted outside the defendant's hearing, and to various other conferences characterized as relating only to the resolution of questions of law. In determining whether the privilege extends to a particular proceeding apart from the trial itself, the Supreme Court has looked to the function of the right as it relates to the content of the particular proceeding in the individual case. This approach is illustrated by the rulings in *Kentucky v. Stincer* [3] and *United States v. Gagnon.*[4]

In *Stincer,* the defendant (but not his counsel) was excluded from an in-chambers hearing at which the trial court made a preliminary determination as to whether the two children who were the victims of the charged sex offense had sufficient understanding of their obligation to tell the truth and sufficient intellectual capacity to be competent to testify. The Supreme Court initially noted that even though a particular hearing might be characterized as a "pretrial proceeding," it could still be a "stage of the trial" for confrontation clause purposes. That was true of the competency hearing since it "determines whether a key witness will testify." Under the circumstances of this case, however, the defendant's exclusion from the hearing did not interfere with his opportunity for cross-examination. The questions asked at the competency hearing did not relate to the crime itself (but only to each child's general

14. In Waller v. Georgia, supra note 4, the Court acknowledged that the "interest in protecting the privacy of persons not before the court," under certain circumstances, "may well justify closing portions of a suppression hearing to the public."

15. Waller v. Georgia, supra note 4.

§ 24.2

1. Illinois v. Allen, infra note 9.

2. United States v. Gagnon, infra note 4.

3. 482 U.S. 730, 107 S.Ct. 2658, 96 L.Ed.2d 631 (1987).

4. 470 U.S. 522, 105 S.Ct. 1482, 84 L.Ed.2d 486 (1985).

capacity to recall facts and distinguish between truth and falsehood), many of the background questions asked at the hearing were repeated at trial, the children were subject to "full and complete" cross-examination at trial, and the judge's preliminary ruling at the in-chambers hearing was subject to reconsideration in light of the witnesses' trial testimony. Finally, the due process component of defendant's right of presence was not violated since, in light of the limited scope of the hearing, defendant's personal participation would not have borne "a substantial relationship to [the] defendant's opportunity better to defend himself at trial."

In *Gagnon,* after a juror expressed concern that one of the defendants was sketching portraits of the jurors, the judge directed the defendant to desist and, at the request of defendant's counsel, announced that he would conduct a brief in camera inquiry (with that counsel present) to ensure that the sketching had not prejudiced the juror. Counsel for the defendant did not request that his client be present and counsel for the remaining defendants did not request that they or their clients be present. Proceeding to his chambers, the judge there explained to the juror that the sketching was innocuous (the defendant simply was an artist) and received assurance from the juror that he was willing to proceed as an impartial juror. The Court majority concluded that due process "does not require that all the parties be present when the judge inquires into such a minor occurrence." [5] It noted that the four defendants "could have done nothing had they been present nor would they have gained anything by attending."

Where the particular proceeding is one at which defendant had a clear right to be present (as at trial), but defendant was absent for only a brief period, that absence will not invalidate the conviction if the error is harmless beyond a reasonable doubt. If a verbatim record was made and it shows that defendant's attorney was present during that brief interval and that no legal error was committed in defendant's absence, then it is likely that the error will be found to be harmless. So too, where application of the right in the particular proceeding is debatable, but the defendant's absence clearly had no impact, a court may readily turn to harmless error doctrine to dispose of the defendant's claim rather than rule upon whether the right of presence was applicable. The key in both of these situations is the clear lack of prejudice, not the willingness of counsel to proceed without the defendant being present. For, as the Supreme Court has noted, the defendant's constitutional right to be present is one of those "basic rights that the attorney cannot waive without the fully informed and publicly acknowledged consent of the defendant." [6]

(b) The Disorderly Defendant. In *Illinois v. Allen,*[7] the Supreme Court held that the defendant's constitutional right to be present was subject to forfeiture by the defendant's disruptive behavior. In concluding that the trial judge acted lawfully in excluding Allen from the courtroom following his repeated outbursts, the Court declared that "there are at least three constitutionally permissible ways for a trial judge to handle an obstreperous defendant like Allen: (1) bind and gag him, thereby keeping him present; (2) cite him for contempt; (3) take him out of

5. Statutes or court rules may well grant a right of presence that extends beyond the constitutional right. The *Gagnon* opinion raised the possibility that Federal Rule 43 (referring to presence "at every stage of the trial") might do exactly that, but found it unnecessary to determine whether Federal Rule 43 extended to the proceeding in question because any such statutory right had been waived when no defendant objected to the trial judge's announcement that he was about to hold the conference in camera with the single defendant's counsel present.

The Court in *Gagnon* spoke only to the claim of the defendants to be present themselves during the in camera inquiry. It did not refer to their right to have counsel present, the counsel for the one defendant having been present and the counsel for the others having made no request to participate. Although the Sixth Amendment right to counsel arguably could have a broader reach in the juror-communication context than the defendant's constitutional right to be present, requiring counsel's presence even where defendant need not be present, the lower courts tend not to have treated it as such.

6. Taylor v. Illinois, 484 U.S. 400, 108 S.Ct. 646, 98 L.Ed.2d 798 (1988). See § 11.6.

7. 397 U.S. 337, 90 S.Ct. 1057, 25 L.Ed.2d 353 (1970).

the courtroom until he promises to conduct himself properly." Since the first two responses were properly rejected by the trial court, the defendant could not complain when his own behavior had cost him his right to be present at his trial.

Although the Court in *Allen* stated there could be situations in which "binding and gagging might possibly be the fairest and most reasonable way to handle a defendant who acts as Allen did here," it is not apparent what circumstances would justify such a conclusion. Indeed, the view that removal is preferable to gagging or shackling finds support in language in *Allen* to the effect that

> even to contemplate such a technique, much less see it, arouses a feeling that no person should be tried while shackled and gagged except as a last resort. Not only is it possible that the sight of shackles and gags might have a significant effect on the jury's feelings about the defendant, but the use of this technique is itself something of an affront to the very dignity and decorum of judicial proceedings that the judge is seeking to uphold. Moreover, one of the defendant's primary advantages of being present at the trial, his ability to communicate with his counsel, is greatly reduced when the defendant is in a condition of total physical restraint.

The Court in *Allen* also noted the limitations of the contempt alternative. It would hardly be effective against a defendant who is determined to prevent any trial or who is already facing very serious sanctions. Thus, in the case of the persistently disruptive defendant, as here, removal was the only realistic alternative.

Although the *Allen* ruling has been criticized on the ground that it cannot be squared with longstanding doctrine as to what is required for a knowing and intelligent waiver of a constitutional right, the decision can best be explained as involving a "forfeiture" (rather than a "waiver") of a constitutional right.[8] Thus, whether or not the defendant actually made a "knowing and intelligent" decision to relinquish his right is not critical. However, to be justified as a reasonable forfeiture rule, two other factors, present in *Allen,* may be essential to the exclusion: (1) Allen was "repeatedly warned by the trial judge that he would be removed from the courtroom if he persisted in his unruly conduct"; and (2) he was "constantly informed that he could return to the trial when he would agree to conduct himself in an orderly manner." Moreover, as Justice Brennan noted in his *Allen* concurrence, if a defendant is excluded "the court should make reasonable efforts to enable him to communicate with his attorney and, if possible, to keep apprised of the progress of his trial."

(c) The Absent Defendant. In *Taylor v. United States,*[9] the Court held that the defendant can also lose his right to be present by absenting himself during the trial. In rejecting the defendant's contention that "his mere voluntary absence from his trial cannot be construed as an effective waiver * * * unless it is demonstrated that he knew or had been expressly warned by the trial court not only that he had a right to be present but also that the trial would continue in his absence," the Court noted:

> It is wholly incredible to suggest that petitioner, who was at liberty on bail, had attended the opening session of his trial, and had a duty to be present at the trial, * * * entertained any doubts about his right to be present at every stage of his trial. It seems equally incredible to us * * * "that a defendant who flees from a courtroom in the midst of a trial—where judge, jury, witnesses and lawyers are present and ready to continue—would not know that as a consequence the trial could continue in his absence."

That analysis is also difficult to square with traditional waiver-of-rights theory, and thus here again it would seem preferable to view the matter in terms of forfeiture of a right by misconduct.

The Court in *Taylor* relied upon the old case of *Diaz v. United States,*[10] which declared "that if, after the trial has begun in his pres-

8. See § 27.5, note 5.

9. 414 U.S. 17, 94 S.Ct. 194, 38 L.Ed.2d 174 (1973).

10. 223 U.S. 442, 32 S.Ct. 250, 56 L.Ed. 500 (1912).

ence, [the defendant] voluntarily absents himself, this does not nullify what has been done or prevent the completion of the trial." That language gave birth to the notion that a defendant who took flight *before* trial could not be tried in absentia. One grounding for such a distinction is that the judicial system has a greater interest in continuing what has been started due to the disruptive impact, than in proceeding with a trial that was never underway. That grounding was rejected as an absolute standard in *United States v. Tortora.*[11] The Court of Appeals there upheld the initiation of a trial in absentia where one of five defendants failed to appear and the trial had been postponed previously because of conflicting schedules of defense attorneys and the absence of other defendants. The *Tortora* opinion stressed, however, that greater care is necessary in proceeding where a defendant who has failed to appear before the trial has commenced. For one thing, it should be clearly established that the defendant was aware when the proceedings were to commence. For another, the trial should begin without an absent defendant "only when the public interest clearly outweighs that of the voluntarily absent defendant." The *Tortora* court added that it was "difficult for us to conceive of any case where the exercise of this discretion would be appropriate other than a multiple-defendant case."

In the *Taylor* case, the Court noted that "no issue of the voluntariness of his disappearance was ever raised." When a defendant does not appear before or during trial, it is unlikely to be certain that his absence was voluntary, and thus it must be open to the defendant to set aside his conviction following a trial in absentia by showing his absence was not voluntary.

(d) Prejudicial Circumstances of Presence. The right to a fair trial is a fundamental liberty secured by the Fourteenth Amendment, and a "basic component" of that right is the presumption of innocence. Because that presumption is likely to be impaired if the defendant is required to stand trial in prison or jail clothing, the courts have rather consistently held that such a procedure is improper. The Supreme Court reached that conclusion in *Estelle v. Williams,*[12] where it was emphasized (1) "that the constant reminder of the accused's condition implicit in such distinctive, identifiable attire may affect a juror's judgment," (2) that "compelling an accused to wear jail clothing furthers no essential state policy," and (3) "that compelling the accused to stand trial in jail garb operates usually against only those who cannot post bail prior to trial." But because the record in *Estelle* was "clear that no objection was made to the trial judge concerning the jail attire either before or at any time during the trial," the Court declined to reverse the conviction, for it could not be concluded "that respondent was compelled to stand trial in jail garb or that there was sufficient reason to excuse the failure to raise the issue before trial."

As a general rule, a defendant in a criminal case has the right to appear before the jury free from shackles or other physical restraints. This right also springs from the fundamental notion that a person accused of crime is presumed innocent until his guilt has been established beyond a reasonable doubt. The defendant also has a right to have his witnesses appear without physical restraints. Though shackling witnesses does not directly affect the presumption of innocence, it nonetheless may harm his defense by detracting from the credibility of his witnesses. Although the defense's right here is not absolute, where a defense objection has been raised, a showing of extreme need is required to justify the use of physical restraints at trial, and this showing ordinarily must be made on the record after a hearing so that an appellate court can more readily determine whether there was an abuse of discretion. Shackles may be used on witnesses who are inmates of maximum security prisons and whose records reflect a propensity for violence or escape, but a policy of shackling all prison inmates does not meet the "extreme need" standard.

11. 464 F.2d 1202 (2d Cir.1972).

12. 425 U.S. 501, 96 S.Ct. 1691, 48 L.Ed.2d 126 (1976).

The conspicuous use of identifiable security officers is treated somewhat differently. In *Holbrook v. Flynn*,[13] the Supreme Court acknowledged that the courtroom presence of a substantial number of uniformed officers could present constitutional difficulties in an extreme case, but concluded that the state generally did not have to make a specific showing of a special security need to sustain the constitutionality of deploying several such officers. Since the deployment of uniformed officers "need not be interpreted as a sign that [defendant] is particularly dangerous," but may just as readily be viewed as a measure intended to "guard against disruptions emanating from outside the court room," or as "mere elements of an impressive drama," it was not "the sort of inherently prejudicial practice that, like shackling, should be permitted only where justified by an essential state interest specific to each trial." The Court also concluded that, since the deployment of the security guards was "intimately related to the State's legitimate interest in maintaining custody during the proceeding," it "did not offend the Equal Protection Clause by arbitrarily discriminating against those unable to post bond or to whom bail has been denied."

Questions sometimes arise concerning the location of the defendant in the courtroom during the trial. Routine placement of the defendant in a separate docket has been proposed as a security measure that should not be viewed as stigmatizing under the analysis of *Holbrook*, but even if that is so, past cases indicated that it would still be unconstitutional because it places the defendant in a position where he cannot freely communicate with counsel. So too, it is necessary that the defendant be situated where he can see and hear the witnesses and they can see him. In *Coy v. Iowa*,[14] the Supreme Court held that the right of confrontation extends beyond cross-examination and encompasses also the right to a "face to face meeting with the witnesses appearing before the trier of fact." *Coy* held that the defendant's confrontation right was infringed when a state trial court, seeking to protect two juvenile victims of alleged sex abuse from the emotional trauma of viewing the defendant when giving their testimony, placed between the witnesses and the defendant a screen which blocked the defendant from their sight but did allow defendant to dimly perceive them as well as hear them. In *Coy*, the trial court had acted upon a generalized legislative presumption of witness trauma without making any individualized findings. Subsequently, in *Maryland v. Craig*,[15] the Court upheld on its face a state procedure that allowed the use of one-way closed circuit television to present the testimony of a child witness/victim in a sex abuse case. The Court stressed that here, unlike *Coy*, the statute required a case-specific finding that the child would suffer from such extreme emotional trauma, due to the presence of the defendant, that he or she could not "reasonably communicate." Another distinguishing factor was that the method of separation used in *Craig*—having the victim testify from another room, with the defendant, jury, and judge remaining in the courtroom—would probably be viewed by the jury as suggesting that the witness was fearful of testifying in the courtroom setting rather than fearful of testifying while looking at the defendant. The Court majority in *Coy* had no reason to reach defendant's additional contention there that the screen was an "inherently prejudicial" method of separating the witness, although the two dissenters discounted that claim on the ground that the screen, unlike prison garb, was not the "sort of trapping that generally is associated with those who have been convicted."

§ 24.3 The Defendant's Right of Access to Evidence

(a) Constitutional Grounding. Various statutes, common law rules, and constitutional commands combine to shape the capacity of

13. 475 U.S. 560, 106 S.Ct. 1340, 89 L.Ed.2d 525 (1986).

14. 487 U.S. 1012, 108 S.Ct. 2798, 101 L.Ed.2d 857 (1988).

15. ___ U.S. ___, 110 S.Ct. 3157, 111 L.Ed.2d 666 (1990).

the defense to gain access to evidence it might use at trial. The subsections that follow describe the basic components of this defense "right of access," with those components categorized by reference to the type of process or protection provided rather than to the different legal groundings involved. This subsection, in contrast, focuses on one of those groundings, the federal constitution, and provides an overview of the different constitutional strands that contribute to various components of the right of access. The constitutional grounding for the right of access, both because of its primacy and its doctrinal diversity, deserves separate consideration.

The Supreme Court has characterized various constitutional standards as combining to create "what might loosely be called the area of constitutionally-guaranteed access to evidence." [1] Although the Court has not provided a comprehensive listing of the constitutional directives that shape this "area of constitutionally-guaranteed access to evidence," the following constitutional obligations and prohibitions would certainly be on any such list: (1) the prosecution's duty to disclose evidence within its possession or control that is exculpatory and material; (2) the prohibition against the government's bad faith destruction of such evidence; (3) the state's duty to provide the defense with the power through subpoena to gain the production of witnesses and physical items at trial; (4) the state's duty to provide certain types of assistance or information to the defense that will allow it to use that subpoena power to gain evidence; and (5) the prohibition against certain governmental actions that interfere with the defense's utilization of its subpoena power.

The constitutional directives listed above have been grounded on either or both of two basic constitutional guarantees—the Fifth and Fourteenth Amendment due process guarantee and the Sixth Amendment's command that the accused "shall have compulsory process for obtaining witnesses in his favor." That the compulsory process clause should contribute to a constitutional right of access to evidence is hardly surprising. Indeed, what is surprising is how rarely the Court has relied upon that provision. As the Supreme Court noted in *Pennsylvania v. Ritchie*,[2] it "has had little occasion to discuss the contours of the Compulsory Process Clause." This paucity of compulsory process rulings is attributable largely to two factors. First, the state and the federal judicial systems all make the trial court's subpoena authority readily available to the defense. The primary difficulties facing the defense with respect to compulsory process lie in identifying and locating those persons who should be served as defense witnesses. As discussed in subsection (b), the Court has not yet decided whether the compulsory process clause speaks to those concerns. Second, while the compulsory process clause could readily be applied to governmental actions that interfere with the defense's use of subpoenas, the initial cases dealing with claims of improper interference relied on the due process clause and subsequent rulings have built upon those cases (though acknowledging that the compulsory process clause could serve as an alternative grounding for prohibiting such interference).

The reliance upon due process to establish elements of a defense right of access also is not surprising. In an adversary system, fundamental fairness requires that the defense be given the tools with which it can obtain any existing evidence that challenges the prosecution case, either by tending to establish affirmatively the defendant's innocence or by simply casting doubt upon the persuasiveness of the prosecution's evidence. The touchstone of fundamental fairness, however, lends special qualities to the assessment of what tools are needed and what actions the state must take to either facilitate their use or avoid interfering with their use. As discussed in Chapter 2, traditional due process methodology tends to be case-specific, focusing on the totality of the circumstances and

§ 24.3

1. Arizona v. Youngblood, 488 U.S. 51, 109 S.Ct. 333, 102 L.Ed.2d 281 (1988).

2. 480 U.S. 39, 107 S.Ct. 989, 94 L.Ed.2d 40 (1987).

weighing such factors as administrative justifications and burdens and the likelihood of prejudicial impact on the outcome of the particular case.[3] As will be seen, the due process rulings that contribute to the "area of constitutionally-guaranteed access to evidence" have been largely consistent with that tradition.

Commentators and occasional judicial opinions have looked to the confrontation clause of the Sixth Amendment as an additional source of a constitutional right of access and one that would provide a structure to that right considerably different than that provided by due process. The premise here is that the right of confrontation includes not only a right to cross-examination but a right of access to material that could serve as a basis for cross-examination. Moreover, the state's failure to provide or facilitate access to that material would be treated in the same fashion as the denial or restriction of cross-examination itself. There, the Supreme Court has held that no showing of actual prejudice or likely prejudice is necessary to establish the violation. Indeed, the substantial restriction of cross-examination constitutes a "constitutional error of the first magnitude and no amount of showing of want of prejudice will cure it."[4] The state can avoid reversal of the conviction only by establishing that the constitutional error was harmless beyond a reasonable doubt (i.e., that the witness' testimony was so insignificant that the jury undoubtedly would have reached the same result even if the defense had achieved all that it could possibly expect from cross-examination).[5] As applied to the denial of access, traditional confrontation clause analysis would eliminate the need for a defense showing of likely prejudice, as required for due process violation; the constitutional violation would automatically exist if the material sought could be used on cross-examination.

In *United States v. Bagley*,[6] the lower court had relied on such a Sixth Amendment analysis in reversing a conviction. The defense there had requested notification of any promises made to government witnesses and the prosecution, unaware that the government's investigative agency had entered into a compensation arrangement with two key witnesses, failed to disclose that arrangement. The lower court reasoned that the compensation agreement could have been used on cross-examination, that the failure to disclose it therefore violated the confrontation clause, and that an automatic reversal therefore was required. The Supreme Court, however, rejected that line of analysis. The failure to disclose exculpatory material, including impeachment material, traditionally had been tested by reference to the due process standards of the *Brady* rule,[7] which required a showing of a reasonable probability that the nondisclosure had altered the outcome of the case. To treat impeachment material differently than other exculpatory evidence, because of its relationship to the confrontation clause, would be both contrary to past precedent and illogical as measured by the function of the prosecutor's duty to disclose.

In *Pennsylvania v. Ritchie*,[8] four justices were prepared to move a step beyond *Bagley* in confining the scope of the confrontation clause as it relates to the obtaining of evidence. The issue posed there was whether a state court violated defendant's constitutional rights in holding that, because of their confidential status, various records of a state protective service agency relating to defendant's minor daughter would not be open to defense inspection in preparing for trial. The defendant had been charged with sexually assaulting his daughter, and the state's intermediate appellate court had held that he should have been allowed through a pretrial subpoena to obtain from the agency that portion of its

3. See §§ 2.4, 2.6(d), (e).

4. Davis v. Alaska, 415 U.S. 308, 94 S.Ct. 1105, 39 L.Ed.2d 347 (1974). Thus, the government will not be able to respond to the violation by contending that, if the cross-examination had been allowed, the witness' answers would not have hurt his credibility.

5. See § 27.6, note 18.

6. 473 U.S. 667, 105 S.Ct. 3375, 87 L.Ed.2d 481 (1985), also discussed in § 20.7(b).

7. See § 20.7(d).

8. Supra note 2.

records containing verbatim recorded statements that the daughter had made to a youth counselor in reporting the alleged sexual assault. The state high court had gone a step beyond that ruling, holding that the Sixth Amendment required that the entire file of the state agency be made available to defense counsel for the purpose of determining whether any other items were also relevant to the case. Reliance had been placed on the Supreme Court's ruling in *Davis v. Alaska*,[9] which found a confrontation clause violation in a state court's refusal to allow the cross-examination of a key witness by reference to his juvenile record. The Court there reasoned that the statutory privilege of confidentiality that attached to the juvenile record was overridden by the essentiality of the cross-examination and the state high court had concluded in *Ritchie* that the same principle applied to the confidentiality of the records of the state protective service agency.

In the Supreme Court, the plurality opinion concluded that defendant's constitutional claim should be judged solely under the *Brady* due process standard requiring the government "to turn over evidence in its possession that is both favorable to the accused and material to guilt or punishment." The Sixth Amendment confrontation clause had no bearing since the "ability to question adverse witnesses * * * does not include the power to require the pretrial disclosure of any and all information that might be useful to contradicting unfavorable testimony." The right of confrontation is a "trial right" and it came into play in *Davis* because the trial judge there prohibited cross-examination at trial with a presumptively confidential juvenile record that the defense already had available to it. *Davis* could not be read "to mean that a statutory privilege cannot be maintained when a defendant asserts a need, prior to trial, for the protected information that might be used at trial to impeach or otherwise undermine a witness' testimony," because such a reading would, in effect, "transform the Confrontation Clause into a constitutionally-compelled rule of pretrial discovery." Thus, the plurality apparently was willing to extend *Bagley's* holding that the confrontation clause did not apply to a defense discovery request for disclosure of potential impeachment material within the prosecutor's control. They would have held the confrontation clause also inapplicable to a defendant's utilization of a subpoena, directed to any person, to obtain potential impeachment material.

Whether the position taken by the *Ritchie* plurality will gain majority support remains to be seen. Three justices disagreed with the plurality's reading of the confrontation clause and two others did not reach the issue. Of course, even if the plurality's position prevails, that does not leave the defense without any constitutional grounding for access. Application of due process standards still resulted in the *Ritchie* Court requiring the state to disclose such information within the files of the protective service agency as was exculpatory and material. Indeed, *Ritchie* required an in camera review of the files by the trial judge to determine whether the state had violated this obligation.[10] In making that determination, the lower court would build upon *Davis* in assessing whether the nondisclosed material would be admissible for impeachment purposes. Thus, under the facts of the *Ritchie* case, the rejection of the defense's confrontation clause argument only served, as did a similar rejection in *Bagley,* to define the defendant's right of access by reference to a due process requirement of materiality (considering both relevancy and impact on the outcome), rather than by reference simply to possible relevancy for confrontation purposes. Arguably, it also substituted an in camera review by the trial judge for review by the defense itself, but Justice Blackmun who expressed disagreement with the plurality's characterization of the confrontation clause as strictly a trial right, agreed that the in camera review was "adequate to address any confrontation problem" under the facts of the *Ritchie* case. Of course, the due process disclosure obligation of *Brady* applies only to

9. Supra note 4.

10. See § 20.7 at note 15.

material within the possession or control of the prosecution,[11] whereas the confrontation clause would extend to material in the possession of a third party. However, *Ritchie* left open the possibility that the compulsory process clause has a reach in this regard parallel to the due process clause,[12] and that clause also applies to information in possession of a third party.

(b) Defense Use of Subpoenas. All jurisdictions have statutes or court rules authorizing the defense to use the trial court's subpoena power to compel persons to whom subpoenas are directed to appear as witnesses at trial or to produce at trial designated documents or other objects. Availability of such subpoenas commonly is automatic. Thus, Federal Rule 17 directs the clerk to issue a subpoena "signed and sealed but otherwise in blank" upon request of the defense. Where the defendant is financially unable to pay the witness fee, the state will bear that cost and here the issuance might require more than a mere request. Federal Rule 17 requires an ex parte application that makes a "satisfactory showing" both that the defendant is financially able to pay and "that the presence of the witness is necessary to an adequate defense." In light of defendant's "Sixth Amendment right to compulsory process" and his "Fifth Amendment [i.e., equality of treatment] right not to be subject to disabilities * * * because of financial status," the word "necessary" has been construed to mean only "relevant, material, and useful to an adequate defense." Even under this liberal construction, however, courts have denied numerous defense requests, usually on the ground that the witness would only be cumulative or would not have personal knowledge that would allow him to give relevant testimony. Some states impose upon the indigent defendant a more substantial burden in establishing need and also make that showing a matter of public record, so that the defense request often becomes an avenue of discovery for the prosecution. Others seek to avoid the issue of need by granting to the indigent defendant the automatic authority to subpoena a certain number of witnesses at state expense (although a showing of need is required if the defense goes beyond that number). Where a defendant in a state case seeks to direct a subpoena to a person in another state, then the applicable Uniform Act will require all defendants (and the prosecution as well when it is using the Act) to show that the designated witness is "material and necessary."[13]

A primary limitation on a subpoena is that it must be for "evidence." That limitation will rarely be called into question on a subpoena directing a person to testify. The individual may be able to claim a privilege or immunity that will excuse him from testifying, but ordinarily the witness must appear and make that claim rather than seek to quash the subpoena. Still a challenge may occasionally be allowed by motion to quash when the party subpoenaed claims an absolute and clearly evident immunity from being required to testify. More frequently, the question of privilege is raised in a motion to quash directed at a subpoena duces tecum. Whether dealing with a subpoena ad testificandum or a subpoena duces tecum, a court assessing the evidentiary character of subpoenaed testimony, documents, or other items must look beyond the local law defining witness competency, privileges, and other evidentiary limitations or immunities. For as the leading compulsory process case shows, the Constitution can override the state law and declare admissible and subject to subpoena that which would otherwise not be evidentiary. In that case, *Washington v. Texas*,[14] the Court held unconstitutional a local rule that made accomplices incompetent to testify for one another, although allowing them to testify for the state.[15]

11. The Court in *Ritchie* did not discuss how the relationship between the state agency and the prosecution fit this requirement [discussed in § 20.7(e)], but it perhaps viewed that as irrelevant where a subpoena had been used as allowed by state law.

12. See subsection (b) infra following note 16.

13. Uniform Act to Secure the Attendance of Witnesses From Without A State in Criminal Proceedings, § 2, 11 U.L.A. 2 (1974).

14. 388 U.S. 14, 87 S.Ct. 1920, 18 L.Ed.2d 1019 (1967).

Even though what is subpoenaed would be admissible, a subpoena may be challenged where the circumstances indicate that the defense's use is directed at a purpose other than a "good faith" effort to obtain evidence. Since the primary non-evidentiary use of the subpoena is discovery, this objection is presented largely in situations in which the defense seeks by subpoena duces tecum to gain production of the documents or other items for inspection prior to trial (as is allowed on court order in many jurisdictions). The contention here is that the defense is not merely seeking to examine the items before trial in order to facilitate their use at trial, but instead is conducting a fishing expedition in which it will determine whether there is anything in the documents worth using at trial and possibly gain additional information for trial preparation. The critical factor in determining the defense's purpose here is often the scope of the subpoena. Where the subpoena seeks a specific document that clearly is relevant, it almost always will be concluded that the subpoena is intended for use at trial. Of course, the defense may decide, after inspecting the document, not to use it at trial, but the same could happen to any evidentiary subpoena, as where the defense decides not to call a subpoenaed witness after speaking further with the witness or viewing the state's case. Where the subpoena seeks a broad range of documents described generically (e.g., all documents relating to a particular transaction or a particular person), it is much more likely to be characterized as other than a good faith effort to produce evidence for use in trial. That conclusion will be significant even in a jurisdiction that has extremely broad pretrial discovery for the defense. Discovery obligations are limited to documents and other items within the possession or control of the prosecution, while subpoenas can be directed to third persons.

Pennsylvania v. Ritchie[16] left unresolved the exact bearing of the compulsory process clause upon the use of the subpoena to obtain a pretrial inspection of documents that could constitute trial evidence. The trial court there had quashed a pretrial subpoena that would have directed a protective service agency to allow the defense to inspect all of its records that related to the events that produced the current charges against the defendant for sexually abusing his daughter as well as certain records compiled in connection with an earlier incident of alleged abuse. On review following defendant's conviction, the Supreme Court held that the appropriate relief was an in camera review of the records to ensure that there had been no violation of the government's due process obligation to disclose evidence that fit the *Brady* standard of being both exculpatory and material. The state supreme court, in requiring full disclosure of the records, had "apparently concluded that the right of compulsory process includes the right to have the state's assistance in uncovering arguably useful information." Defendant argued further that this right went beyond *Brady* material and allowed him to "learn * * * the names of 'witnesses in his favor' as well as other evidence that might be contained in the file." Responding to this position, Justice Powell noted (in a portion of his opinion receiving majority support):

> This Court has never squarely held that the Compulsory Process Clause guarantees the right to discover the *identity* of witnesses, or to require the Government to produce exculpatory evidence. * * * Instead, the Court traditionally has evaluated claims such as those

15. *Washington* rejected the contention that the compulsory process clause dealt only with the production of the witnesses and not with the admissibility of their testimony. In Taylor v. Illinois, discussed in § 20.6 at note 3, the Court reexamined this issue and reached the same conclusion. The Court there acknowledged that the position it had rejected in *Washington* was "supported by the plain language of the Clause, by the historical evidence that it was intended to provide defendants with subpoena power they lacked at common law, by some scholarly comment, and by a brief excerpt from the legislative history of the Clause." Nonetheless, the broader reading of the Clause developed in *Washington* found support in state constitutional provisions that influenced the adoption of the Sixth Amendment and the basic aim of the Amendment to promote an adversary system of adjudication.

16. 480 U.S. 39, 107 S.Ct. 989, 94 L.Ed.2d 40 (1987) also discussed in § 24.3(a) at note 8.

raised by Ritchie under the broader protections of the Due Process Clause of the Fourteenth Amendment. See *United States v. Bagley*. Because the applicability of the Sixth Amendment to this type of case is unsettled, and because our Fourteenth Amendment precedents addressing the fundamental fairness of trials establish a clear framework for review, we adopt a due process analysis for purposes of this case. Although we conclude that compulsory process provides no *greater* protections in this area than those afforded by due process, we need not decide today whether and how the guarantees of the Compulsory Process Clause differ from those of the Fourteenth Amendment.

Since the due process obligation of the prosecution extends only to evidence within its control, the Court presumably will have to decide the issue left open in *Ritchie* where a subpoena is directed to a private party or an unrelated governmental agency. Lower courts, in dealing with records similar to those involved in *Ritchie,* have ordered the same type of in camera review as required there without regard to whether the records were subpoenaed from a related state agency or a private hospital.

(c) Prosecution Disclosure of Evidence Within Its Control. To issue a subpoena for evidence, the defense must be aware that such evidence exists and know enough about it to describe the items sought with the specificity required for a subpoena.[17] Under some circumstances, as to certain potential defense evidence within the prosecution's control, the prosecution will have an obligation to disclose even though defendant makes no more than a general request for disclosure or, in some circumstances, no request at all. The three major sources of the defense's access to such evidence are the due process duty of disclosure under *Brady,*[18] discovery requirements under state law,[19] and the disclosure of prior statements of witnesses for impeachment use as required under the Jencks Act and similar state provisions. Also relevant here, although it goes beyond merely providing defense access to evidence, is the prosecution's constitutional duty to correct testimony of its witnesses known to be false.

The *Brady* duty to disclose, as discussed in § 20.7, may be operative without a request as well as with a request. It is limited by the requirement of materiality, but ensures that the defense will not miss a critical piece of exculpatory evidence possessed by the prosecution because it was unaware of that evidence (and therefore failed to subpoena it). Under the *Brady* line of cases, the prosecutor's failure to disclose to the defense such exculpatory evidence will constitute a due process violation if there is a "reasonable probability" that disclosure would have resulted in the jury's failure to convict.

The disclosure required by discovery rules tends to be broader than *Brady* in some respects and narrower in others. Even under the narrowest discovery rules, defense discovery will extend to some evidence beyond that which the prosecution intends to use at trial. It will here include items that could be helpful to the defense but might very well not meet the reasonable probability standard of *Brady.* The Federal Rules, for example, provide for discovery of documents and scientific test results and reports that are "material to the preparation of the defendant's defense." On the other hand, discovery requirements commonly are limited to certain categories of evidence and therefore can miss items that must be disclosed under *Brady,* which is not so limited. As in the case of *Brady,* the disclosure obligation under discovery rules may not be dependent upon a request, and even where a request is required, it may simply ask for all evidence within a general category of discoverable material.

Where the prosecution has within its control the prior recorded statements of its witnesses, the defense will desire to obtain those statements for use in impeaching the prosecution witnesses. Under limited circumstances,

17. The test here is one of "reasonable particularity," providing sufficient direction so that the person served can readily identify what must be produced. See § 8.7(c).

18. See § 20.7.

19. See § 20.3.

Brady may require that the prosecution make such statements available to the defense. *Brady* does encompass impeachment material, but the failure to disclose will only constitute a due process violation where the lost opportunity for impeachment is so critical that there is a reasonable probability that a different result would have been reached if the statement had been made available for that purpose. Another possibility is obtaining the prior recorded statement under discovery rules. Some jurisdictions make prior recorded statements of witnesses automatically discoverable, but most either prohibit pretrial disclosure or allow disclosure at the discretion of the trial court. Thus, for most jurisdictions, the only avenue providing assurance that the defense will receive the prior recorded statements of prosecution witnesses is a statute, court rule, or common law ruling modeled upon the federal Jencks Act, which provides for disclosure after the witness has testified at trial.

The Jencks Act was adopted by Congress in 1957 in response to the Supreme Court's ruling earlier that year in *Jencks v. United States.*[20] The Court in *Jencks* had held, in the exercise of its supervisory power, that the trial court erred in denying a defense request to inspect the prior recorded statements of two government witnesses who were F.B.I. undercover agents. The agents had acknowledged that the statements referred to the subject of their testimony, and the defense had requested the statements for use in cross-examining the witnesses. The government contended, however, that the trial court properly denied the defense request because the defense had failed to make any showing of likely inconsistency between the prior statements and the witnesses' current testimony. The Supreme Court flatly rejected that argument, noting that the defense could not be expected to know of inconsistencies until after it viewed the reports. The Court also rejected the contention that the judge could, through in camera inspection, properly determine if the statements were appropriate for use by the defense in cross-examination. The defense, the Court stated, should be given the statements so it could make its own determination as to whether they might provide a basis for cross-examination.

Controversy sparked by a vigorous dissent in *Jencks* (which accused the Court of affording defendants "a Roman holiday for rummaging through confidential information") led Congress to take immediate legislative action. The statute it produced incorporated the basic thrust of the *Jencks* decision but also introduced some procedural modifications. Like the *Jencks* decision, the Jencks Act establishes a right of access that is not conditioned on a showing of likely inconsistency between the witness' testimony and his prior recorded statement. Following the testimony of a government witness (and not before), the trial court, on application of the defense, must direct the government to disclose any "statement" of the witness "in the possession of the United States" that "relates to the subject matter as to which the witness testified." For this purpose, a "statement" is limited to: (1) a "written statement made by the witness that is signed or otherwise adopted or approved by the witness"; (2) "a substantially verbatim recital of an oral statement made by the witness that is recorded contemporaneously * * * in a stenographic, mechanical, electrical or other recording"; and (3) "a statement, however taken or recorded * * *, made by the witness to a grand jury." If the government contends that the entire statement or any portion of it does not relate to the subject matter of the witness' testimony, it submits the statement to the trial court for in camera review. The court then excises such material as it finds not to relate to the witness' testimony, orders disclosure of the remainder, and preserves the excised material so that its decision to excise can be reviewed on appeal if the case should result in a conviction. If the government elects not to make the statement available as ordered by the court, the testimony of the witness is stricken, with a mistrial declared where the court views that as appropriate.

20. See 353 U.S. 657, 77 S.Ct. 1007, 1 L.Ed.2d 1103 (1957); 18 U.S.C.A. § 3500.

Over the years since *Jencks,* a large group of states have either adopted statutes or court rules patterned after the Jencks Act or fashioned their common law rulings to incorporate the Jencks Act practice.[21]

The *Brady* duty to disclose applies only where its "reasonable probability" standard is met, and Jencks Act disclosure, though largely automatic, is limited to written or recorded statements of the witness. Where discovery rules provide for pretrial disclosure of a witness' earlier statement, they also are limited to written or recorded statements. If a prosecution witness should testify falsely, however, the disclosure obligation imposed upon the prosecutor sheds such limitations. Here, the prosecution has a constitutional obligation to disclose to the trier of fact that it has been deceived by the testimony of the witness. This must be done without regard to whether the defense has requested access to the evidence that establishes that falsehood or whether such evidence takes the form of a written or recorded statement.

The prosecutor's due process obligation with respect to false evidence builds upon the Supreme Court's seminal ruling in *Mooney v. Holohan.* [22] In that 1935 ruling, the Court found that the prosecutor's knowing procurement and use of perjured testimony rendered defendant's trial no more than a "pretense" in which the government utilized a "deliberate deception of judge and jury" to obtain a conviction—a result no more consistent with the "rudimentary commands of justice * * * [than] obtaining a like result by intimidation." *Mooney* involved a knowing and intentional use of perjured testimony that related directly to the defendant's commission of the offense charged, but a series of subsequent Supreme Court rulings carried the "*Mooney* principle" far beyond that fact situation. Those rulings established that *Mooney* was not limited to perjury suborned by the prosecutor, but also encompassed the prosecution's failure to correct testimony known to be perjured that the witness had advanced on his initiative. Thus, where the witness denied that he had kissed the deceased shortly before she was killed by her husband, and claimed that they had been no more than casual friends, the prosecutor violated due process by letting that testimony stand where the prosecutor knew, from previous conversations with the witness, that he and the deceased had an ongoing sexual relationship.[23] Neither was *Mooney* limited to perjured statements that dealt with a substantive element of the prosecution's case. It could encompass, for example, perjury related to the witness' motivation for testifying. Thus, where a key witness denied having received any promise of lenient treatment, the prosecutor's failure to correct that testimony, which he knew to be false, resulted in a denial of due process.[24] Most significantly, the knowledge element of the *Mooney* principle was held to be the collective knowledge of the prosecution, not the knowledge of the individual prosecutor. Thus, where a critical prosecution witness testified falsely that he had not received a promise that he would not be indicted, the state was not excused from correcting that statement by virtue of the trial attorney's belief that the

21. In 1975, a new dimension was added to Jencks-type disclosure with the Supreme Court's ruling in United States v. Nobles. In that case, as discussed in § 20.4(b), the Court upheld a trial court order that directed the defense to produce, for prosecution use on cross-examination, a written statement of one of the defense's witnesses. Such "reverse-Jencks" disclosure was then incorporated in Federal Rule 26.2. That rule largely tracks the Jencks Act procedure, but makes it applicable to disclosure by both sides of the statement of its witness, excepting only the defense witness who is also the defendant. Many states with Jencks provisions have similarly made their provisions applicable to both sides, but others have not.

22. 294 U.S. 103, 55 S.Ct. 340, 79 L.Ed. 791 (1935). See also § 20.7(a).

23. Alcorta v. Texas, 355 U.S. 28, 78 S.Ct. 103, 2 L.Ed.2d 9 (1957). The defendant claimed that he killed his wife in the heat of passion after discovering her kissing the witness. The prosecutor had told the witness not to volunteer the information that he and the wife had sexual relations on several occasions, but to answer truthfully if asked about it. The Court stressed that the witness' testimony created a "false impression" as to a material fact that could have had a bearing on the jury's rejection of defendant's provocation claim and that the prosecutor was fully aware that this was so.

24. Napue v. Illinois, 360 U.S. 264, 79 S.Ct. 1173, 3 L.Ed.2d 1217 (1959).

witness was telling the truth. A promise of immunity had been made by another prosecutor who handled the case at an earlier stage, that promise was attributable "to the Government," and the due process obligation of *Mooney* was that of the prosecutor's office as a whole, for it operated as an entity in serving as "the spokesman for the Government." [25]

Taken together, *Mooney* and its progeny establish a constitutional obligation of the prosecution as an entity not to deceive the jury or allow it to be deceived by prosecution witnesses. This obligation requires that it not suborn perjury, not use evidence known to be false, and not allow known false testimony of its witnesses to stand uncorrected. Where the government fails to fulfill that obligation, it matters not whether its failure is attributable to negligence or an intent to deceive. The state in either event bears a responsibility for possibly denying the defendant a fair trial. Similarly, as lower courts have noted, it matters not whether the witness giving false testimony is mistaken or intentionally lying. If the prosecution knows that the witness' statement is untrue, it has a duty to correct it.

Because the *Mooney* principle is based upon the defendant's right to a fair trial, the Court has refused to go so far as to hold that the knowing failure to correct false testimony produces a due process violation without regard to whether the false testimony was likely to have had an impact upon the outcome of the trial. The cases note that the false testimony must have been "material," but the standard of materiality imposed here has a lower threshold than the "reasonable probability" requirement of *Brady*. It is sufficient that there is a "reasonable possibility" that a different result would have been reached if the prosecutor had revealed that the testimony was false. Indeed, the Court has come to look upon this standard as no more than a reformulation of the *Chapman v. California* standard for determining whether a constitutional violation constitutes harmless error.[26] As was explained in Justice Blackmun's plurality opinion in *United States v. Bagley,* [27] the materiality element of the false testimony cases was defined prior to the *Chapman* ruling. Whereas the *Mooney* line of cases spoke of requiring the reversal of a conviction if there "was any reasonable likelihood that the false testimony could have affected the judgment of the jury," *Chapman* spoke of a constitutional violation requiring the reversal of convictions unless that error was "harmless beyond a reasonable doubt." The *Chapman* Court had noted, however, that "there was little if any difference between a rule formulated as in [the *Mooney* line of cases] in terms of 'whether there is a reasonable possibility that the evidence complained of might have contributed to the conviction' and a 'rule requiring the beneficiary of a constitutional error to prove beyond a reasonable doubt that the error complained of did not contribute to the verdict obtained.'" "It is therefore clear," the *Bagley* plurality concluded, that the two standards of review should now be viewed as "equivalent."

(d) The Government's Obligation to Preserve Evidence. In *California v. Trombetta,*[28] the defendants, relying on "the *Brady* principle," argued that the state had a due process obligation to preserve potentially exculpatory material that came into its possession during the course of an investigation. The police there, after having the defendants submit to an Intoxilyzer (breath-analysis) test, followed their standard practice of purging

25. Giglio v. United States, 405 U.S. 150, 92 S.Ct. 763, 31 L.Ed.2d 104 (1972). Relying on *Giglio,* lower courts often speak of the *Mooney* principle as applicable when the prosecution knew or "should have known" that the testimony was false. The Supreme Court itself has used similar language. It has never suggested, however, that the government has an obligation to check a witness' statement against information that might be provided by others who have not been contacted but might be in a position to contradict the witness. It seems likely that the phrase "should have known" was meant to encompass only the situation, as in *Giglio,* where positive information already in the possession of the prosecution as an entity established that the testimony was false. As lower courts have noted, this concept may take into consideration information known not only to the prosecution staff, but also to the policy agency involved in the investigation. Cf. § 20.7(e).

26. See § 27.6(c).

27. See § 20.7(b), preceding note 9.

28. 467 U.S. 479, 104 S.Ct. 2528, 81 L.Ed.2d 413 (1984).

the Intoxilyzer chambers with clean air, thereby destroying the breath samples. Noting that it would have been technically feasible to preserve the breath samples, and that the samples could then have been used to challenge the Intoxilyzer test results, the defendants argued that those results therefore should be suppressed. The California Court of Appeals agreed, holding that due process required the state "to establish and follow rigorous and systematic procedures to preserve the captured evidence." A unanimous Supreme Court, per Marshall, J., reversed that ruling.

Justice Marshall's *Trombetta* opinion initially noted that the question of the "government's duty to take affirmative steps to preserve evidence" was only roughly analogous to the question presented in "nondisclosure cases" such as *Brady* and *Mooney*. Special difficulties were presented "in developing rules to deal with evidence destroyed through prosecutorial neglect or oversight":

> Whenever potentially exculpatory evidence is permanently lost, courts face the treacherous task of divining the import of materials whose contents is unknown and, very often, disputed. Cf. *United States v. Valenzuela-Bernal.*[29] Moreover, fashioning remedies for the illegal destruction of evidence can pose troubling choices. In nondisclosure cases, a court can grant the defendant a new trial at which the previously suppressed evidence may be introduced. But, when evidence has been destroyed in violation of the Constitution, the court must choose between barring further prosecution or suppressing—as the California Court of Appeal did in this case—the State's most probative evidence.

The Court did see a close analogy, however, in an earlier case in which it had rejected a due process objection to a government agent's destruction of his preliminary interview notes after he had prepared his final report. Here, as in that case, the police had acted in good faith, destroying material they had obtained only for the "limited purpose of providing raw data to the Intoxilyzer." There was "no allegation of official animus toward [defendants] or of a conscious effort to suppress exculpatory evidence."

Although stressing that the officers had acted "in good faith and in accord with normal practices," the *Trombetta* opinion did not rest its ruling on that factor alone. Justice Marshall also added:

> More importantly, California's policy of not preserving breath samples is without constitutional defect. Whatever duty the Constitution imposes on the States to preserve evidence, that duty must be limited to evidence that might be expected to play a significant role in the suspect's defense. To meet this standard of constitutional materiality, see *United States v. Agurs,*[30] evidence must both possess an exculpatory value that was apparent before the evidence was destroyed, and also be of such a nature that the defendant would be unable to obtain comparable evidence by other reasonably available means.

In the case before it, the Court noted, neither of these conditions were met. The established accuracy of the Intoxilyzer test indicated that "in all but a tiny fraction of cases, preserved samples would simply confirm the Intoxilyzer's results." Moreover, even if it were assumed that the test results in this case were inaccurate, that inaccuracy could be attributed only to a limited number of possible malfunctions, and all of those possibilities could be raised at trial without resort to the preserved breath samples.

In *Arizona v. Youngblood,*[31] the Court built upon the *Trombetta* reference to "good faith" in analyzing the due process implications of the loss of evidence where, unlike *Trombetta,* the defendant could not obtain "comparable evidence by other reasonably available means." In that case, the defendant, convicted of the sexual molestation and kidnapping of a 10–year–old boy, had protested the state's failure to properly preserve evidence so as to permit testing for blood group identification. A hospital physician had obtained semen samples from the victim's rectum and the police

29. Infra note 34.

30. See § 20.7(b).

31. 488 U.S. 51, 109 S.Ct. 333, 102 L.Ed.2d 281 (1988).

had collected the victim's clothing, but due to the inadvertent failure of police criminologists to promptly perform tests on the samples and to refrigerate the clothing, it later proved impossible to perform blood group testing that could have been matched against defendant's blood. The lower court had held that since the main issue at trial was that of identity and since the government was responsible for the destruction of evidence that could have conclusively eliminated the defendant as the perpetrator, a conviction was precluded by due process. Rejecting that reasoning, the Supreme Court majority held that "unless a criminal defendant can show bad faith on the part of the police, failure to preserve potentially useful evidence does not constitute a denial of due process of law."

In explaining why the due process standard governing the failure to preserve evidentiary material imposed a prerequisite showing of bad faith, though "good or bad faith" was admittedly "irrelevant" under the due process standard of *Brady,* the Court focused on two factors. First, as had been noted in *Trombetta,* "whenever potentially exculpatory evidence is permanently lost, courts face the treacherous task of divining the import of materials whose contents are unknown, and, very often, disputed." Second, the Court was "unwilling ... to read the fundamental 'fairness requirement' of the Due Process Clause as imposing on the police an undifferentiated and absolute duty to retain and to preserve all material that might be of conceivable evidentiary significance in a particular prosecution." "Requiring a defendant to show bad faith on the part of the police," the Court noted, would appropriately restrict the constitutional "obligation [of police] to preserve evidence to ... that class of cases where the interests of justice most clearly require it, i.e., those cases in which the police themselves by their conduct indicate that the evidence would form a basis for exonerating the defendant." The significance of this limitation, the Court added, was evidenced by the facts presented in *Youngblood.* The police there had collected the rectal swab and the clothing on the night of the crime, a full six weeks before the defendant was taken into custody. Moreover, one of the tests the state criminologist later found he could not utilize (because the clothing had not been refrigerated) was a protein molecule test that the police department had only recently started to use. The suggestion of the lower court that the state had some due process obligation to employ a particular investigatory tool was mistaken: "The situation here is no different than a prosecution for drunk driving that rests on police observation alone; the defendant is free to argue to the finder of fact that a breathalizer test might have been exculpatory, but the police do not have a constitutional duty to perform any particular tests." [32]

Of course, *Youngblood* and *Trombetta* set forth only the baseline, constitutionally compelled obligation of the state with respect to the preservation of potential defense evidence. A greater obligation may flow from the state law governing discovery and judicial authority to fashion remedies for discovery violations. Lower courts frequently have noted that the prosecution's obligation to provide discovery, as set forth in court rule or statute, carries with it a commensurate duty to preserve that material within its control that is discoverable. Although that duty is commonly stated as absolute, when measured by reference to the availability of a remedy for a failure to preserve, it sharply diminishes in scope. In most jurisdictions, the inadvertent failure to preserve discoverable material rarely will lead to a judicial remedy, especially where the prosecution has otherwise recognized its obligation and made a good faith effort to comply (e.g., by adopting systematic procedures for preservation).

In determining whether the government's failure to preserve discoverable materials re-

32. Justice Stevens, in a concurring opinion, stressed that defense counsel had impressed upon the jury the state's failure to preserve the evidence, and that the trial judge had given the jury a "permissive inference" charge ("If you find that the State has ... allowed to be destroyed or lost any evidence whose content or quality are in issue, you may infer that the true fact is against the State's interest"). Three dissenters disagreed with the majority's focus on "good faith."

quires some form of relief benefitting the defense, lower courts have tended to adopt what one court described as a "pragmatic balancing approach." The "appropriateness or extent of sanctions * * * depends upon a case-by-case assessment of the government's culpability for the loss, together with a realistic appraisal of its significance when viewed in light of its nature, its bearing upon critical issues in the case, and the strength of the government's untainted proof." Under this approach, extreme culpability or a highly likely impact upon outcome may justify relief in itself. If the evidence was destroyed for the very purpose of hindering the defense, such conscious impropriety may be enough without any further showing as to the likely impact of the destroyed evidence. The prosecution's motivation in destroying the evidence carries with it a sufficient inference of prejudice to justify relief. On the other hand, even where the loss clearly was inadvertent, some relief will be required if the evidence clearly had an exculpatory character and a potentially significant impact on the outcome of the case. Of course, with the evidence not available, it will be extremely difficult to make a clear showing of exculpatory character and even where that showing can be made, the relief may be limited to simply informing the jury that the evidence was lost and should be assumed to have had the exculpatory characteristics claimed by the defense.

(e) Government Interference With Defense Access. The teaching of *Webb v. Texas* [33] is that due process also comes into play when the court or prosecution takes steps that undermine the defense's ability to utilize the subpoena authority to gain testimony at trial. In that case, the trial judge on his own initiative warned defendant's sole witness, who had an extensive criminal record and currently was serving a prison sentence, against committing perjury. The judge said if he lied he could "get into real trouble," that any lies would be "personally" brought to the attention of the grand jury by the judge, and that a perjury conviction was "probably going to mean several years," and "will be held against you * * * when you're up for parole." After hearing those remarks and the judge's comment to defense counsel that the witness could "decline to testify," the witness refused to give any testimony. Although quoting extensively from a leading compulsory process case, the Court in *Webb* reversed defendant's conviction on due process grounds. "In the circumstances of this case," said the Court, the judge's remarks violated defendant's right to a fair trial because they had been cast in "unnecessarily strong terms" and "effectively drove that witness off the stand."

Although *Webb* involved judicial action, the same principle is applied to prosecutorial efforts to discourage prospective witnesses from testifying for the defense. Such prosecutorial action as threatening the prospective witness with prosecution (either for perjury or for some other offense) if he should testify or isolating the prospective witness by taking him into police custody can result in a due process violation. As with the application of the *Brady* doctrine, and in contrast to *Youngblood's* standard for the failure to preserve evidence, an element of bad faith is not essential to establishing a constitutional violation. Rather, the critical questions are whether (i) the witness was important to the defense, and (ii) as a result of the prosecutor's action, the defendant was denied the witness' testimony or the witness changed his testimony so as to be less favorable to the defense. As in *Webb*, due process violations have been found in cases in which the prosecution acted in the honest belief that its action was necessary to ensure against witness perjury.

Though some lower courts concluded that the *Webb* principle produced a per se due process violation when the government charged a defendant with smuggling aliens into the country and then deported many of those aliens before defendant even had an opportunity to interview them, the Supreme Court in *United States v. Valenzuela–Bernal* [34] declined to go that far. Stressing that the

33. 409 U.S. 95, 93 S.Ct. 351, 34 L.Ed.2d 330 (1972).

34. 458 U.S. 858, 102 S.Ct. 3440, 73 L.Ed.2d 1193 (1982).

government was responsible both for enforcing the criminal law and faithfully executing the congressional policy favoring prompt deportation of illegal aliens, the Court concluded it was proper for the government to undertake "the prompt deportation of illegal-alien witnesses upon the Executive's good-faith determination that they possess no evidence favorable to the defendant in a criminal prosecution." Accordingly, the mere act of deportation would not in itself constitute a violation of either the due process or compulsory process clauses. To establish a violation of those constitutional guarantees, which were treated as imposing basically the same constitutional standard, the defense would have to show "that the evidence lost would be both material and favorable to the defense." But, because the prompt deportation deprived defense of an opportunity to interview the witnesses to determine precisely what favorable evidence they possessed, the defense would not be expected to render "a detailed description of their lost testimony." It would be satisfactory to make "a plausible showing that the testimony of the deported witness would have been material and favorable to the defense in ways not merely cumulative to the testimony of available witnesses." Materiality here would require a "reasonable likelihood that the testimony could have affected the judgment of the trier of fact," although courts in making that assessment would have to "afford some leeway for the fact that the defendant necessarily proffers a description of the material evidence rather than the evidence itself."

(f) Assisting the Defense in Obtaining Evidence. In some situations, the prosecution may have a duty to assist defense efforts to obtain evidence. Perhaps the most common illustration is the prosecution duty, imposed under discovery rules in various jurisdictions, to make the prosecution's physical evidence available to the defense so that it may conduct its own scientific tests on that evidence. Several courts, relying on *Brady,* have held that the defense has a constitutional right to such assistance where it can establish a reasonable basis for believing that the test results may be both "favorable" and "material." A contrary position argues the due process is satisfied by providing the defense with full opportunity to challenge the testimony of the prosecution's expert with respect to the physical evidence. Similarly, although various courts have stated that the defendant has "no constitutional right to a lineup," several courts have held that due process requires the prosecution to honor a lineup request under special circumstances. Ordinarily, the defense must establish that eyewitness identification will be a material issue in the case and that "there exists a reasonable likelihood of a mistaken identification which a lineup would resolve."

In some circumstances, the prosecution may have an obligation to assist the defendant in finding potential defense witnesses, as is reflected by *Roviaro v. United States.*[35] Defendant there, charged with (i) an illegal sale of heroin to "John Doe," and (ii) illegal transportation of that heroin, sought before and during trial to ascertain Doe's identity. Those efforts were rejected on the ground that Doe was a government informer and his identity was protected by the "informer's privilege." Defendant was convicted on both counts on the basis of testimony by two police officers. One testified that, while keeping Doe under surveillance, he observed Doe drive defendant to a location where defendant retrieved a package (later found to contain narcotics) from under a tree, transferred that package to Doe, and then departed. The second officer testified that he had been hiding in the trunk of Doe's car and had heard defendant discuss with Doe the proposed transfer of the package. Before the Supreme Court, the government conceded that the nondisclosure of Doe's identity was improper as to the illegal sale charge, for as to it Doe had been an "active participant," but contended that the transportation charge was distinct and did not require disclosure. The Supreme Court disagreed. Writing for the majority, Justice Burton first sought to place in proper perspective the so-

35. 353 U.S. 53, 77 S.Ct. 623, 1 L.Ed.2d 639 (1957).

called "informer's privilege." [36] What was at stake was "in reality the Government's privilege to withhold from disclosure the identity of persons who furnish information of violations of the law." While that privilege furthered "the public interest in effective law enforcement," it was limited in scope by "fundamental requirements of fairness." Thus, "where the disclosure of an informant's identity * * * is relevant and helpful to the defense of an accused, or is essential to a fair determination of a cause, the privilege must give way" and the government must choose between disclosing the informant's identity or dismissing its prosecution. There was, however, "no fixed rule" as to when disclosure was required to make that choice. "The problem is one that calls for balancing" of the interests involved on a case-by-case basis, "taking into consideration the crime charged, the possible defenses, the possible significance of the informant's testimony, and other relevant factors."

On the facts of the *Roviaro* case, the Court held that the balancing process tipped in favor of requiring disclosure of the informer's identity. The defendant here was placed in the position of explaining or justifying his alleged possession of narcotics. Unless he waived his constitutional right not to take the stand on his own defense, Doe was "his one material witness." Doe's testimony "might have disclosed an entrapment" or "might have thrown doubt upon petitioner's identity or the identity of the package." He was "the only witness who might have testified to petitioner's possible lack of knowledge of the contents of the package." Doe was, in sum, "the only witness in a position to amplify or contradict the testimony of the government witnesses" and the "unfairness" of denying defendant access to Doe was "emphasized" by the government's use itself of testimony regarding an alleged conversation between defendant and Doe.

Although *Roviaro* was based on the Court's supervisory authority over the federal courts, both lower courts and commentators have viewed the Supreme Court's "reasoning and language" as "suggest[ing] that the decision was constitutionally compelled." Lower courts also have applied *Roviaro* in somewhat different circumstances, such as where police undercover agents were additional eyewitnesses to the alleged crime and thus were in essentially the same position vis-a-vis the offense as the informant. On the other hand, the lower courts have quite consistently held that disclosure is not required where the informant merely provided information concerning the offense, such as by telling the police of the location of contraband. However, if the informant arranged for the illegal transaction but was not present when it occurred, it would seem that disclosure would be called for if the defendant should claim entrapment.

Some authority is to be found holding that whenever under *Roviaro* the prosecution must disclose the informer's identity, it must also "undertake reasonable efforts" to obtain the information needed in order for defendant to find the informant. Even where the government has no responsibility for the witness, it may have an obligation to disclose information available to it that will assist the defense in finding the witness. Thus, where the prosecution knew that the defense was having trouble locating a material witness and also knew that the witness was currently incarcerated under a different name, it could not simply remain silent while the defense found itself unable to produce the witness.

(g) Defense Witness Immunity. *Roviaro* required the government to sacrifice a governmental interest relating to effective law enforcement in order to assist the defense in gaining access to a potentially critical witness. Defendants frequently have argued that the same principle should mandate that the government make available to the defense the testimony of critical defense witnesses who refuse to testify based on their Fifth Amendment privilege against self-incrimination. This situation is argued to be distinguishable from other instances in which a

36. See also § 3.3 at note 55.

witness' exercise of a privilege stymies the defense in obtaining testimony. Here, the defense notes, the interest of the witness underlying the privilege can be preserved and the testimony made available by a government grant of use/derivative use immunity (which replaces the privilege [37]).

Lower courts have been unanimous in holding that there is no general constitutional right of a criminal defendant to have immunity granted to witnesses so that they can testify on the defendant's behalf. No such right has been found in the Sixth Amendment's compulsory process clause, for the subpoena is made fully available by the trial court and the compulsory process clause has been held not to override the exercise by witnesses of privileges as significant as the self-incrimination privilege. So too, "while the prosecutor may not prevent or discourage a defense witness from testifying, * * * it is difficult to see how the [compulsory process clause] of its own force places upon either the prosecutor or the court an affirmative obligation * * * of replacing the protection of the self-incrimination privilege with a grant of use immunity." Finally, the due process obligation of *Brady* is held not to apply, for that deals only with the disclosure of evidence in the government's possession, not with the extraction of evidence from others.

Lower courts have suggested, however, that a "more plausible basis for defense witness immunity" exists under a "fundamental fairness" analysis that looks, as in *Roviaro,* to the circumstances of the particular case, and considers, in particular, whether the government is gaining any evidentiary advantage through its failure to grant immunity to defense witnesses. Perhaps the easiest case for requiring the state to grant immunity under this approach is that in which the government has used an undercover agent to instigate the criminal transaction and then allowed that agent to plead the privilege when the defense attempts to call him as a defense witness. More difficult is the situation in which the government builds its case on the testimony of prosecution witnesses who have been granted immunity, while refusing to grant immunity to similar persons whom the defense would call as witnesses. Several courts have suggested that in such a situation, the prosecution should have a responsibility, as a matter of fundamental fairness, to also grant immunity to the prospective defense witness. In response, it has been argued that "in the context of criminal investigation and criminal trials, where accuser and accused have inherently different roles, with entirely different powers and rights, equalization is not a sound principle on which to extend any particular procedural device."

Apart from the case in which the government's opposition to granting immunity reflects a "deliberate intention of distorting the fact finding process," can a court appropriately direct the government to either grant immunity or dismiss the prosecution based on a balancing process that looks to the needs of the defendant for the witness' testimony and the risk to the public interest in conferring immunity upon the particular witness? While occasional judicial opinions suggest that such authority exists, many more reject it on grounds that relate both to judicial competency and public policy. Such opinions note that absent a due process violation that comes from deliberate government distortion of the factfinding process, the judiciary is bound by the legislation governing the granting of immunity, which entrusts solely to the executive branch the discussion as to whether to grant immunity.[38] They argue that courts should not be propelled into "unchartered waters" where they are required to weigh "public interests" that are not always apparent from the record or readily measured. They reject the concept that the prosecution's loss often will be limited because the prosecution remains free to prosecute the immunized witness based on evidence either previously or later acquired from other sources. They note that (i) the prosecution carries a "heavy burden" in establishing any such independent source and (ii) "awareness of the obstacles to

37. See § 8.11.

38. See § 8.11(c).

successful prosecution of an immunized witness may force [it] to curtail its cross-examination of the witness in the case on trial to narrow the scope of the testimony that the defendant will later claim tainted his subsequent prosecution." The opinions also warn that "[d]efense witness immunity could create opportunities for undermining the administration of justice by inviting cooperative perjury among law violators. Codefendants could secure use immunity for each other, and each immunized witness could exonerate his codefendant at a separate trial by falsely accepting sole responsibility for the crime, secure in the knowledge that his admission could not be used at his own trial for the substantive offense." In the end, what is said to be at stake are policy considerations "normally better assessed by prosecutors than by judges."

§ 24.4 Defendant's Rights to Remain Silent and to Testify

(a) Right Not to Take the Stand. The self-incrimination clause of the Fifth Amendment, applicable to the states through the Fourteenth Amendment due process clause, states that no person "shall be compelled in any criminal case to be a witness against himself." But the constitutional privilege against self-incrimination is much broader than those words would suggest. As discussed earlier, assertion of the privilege is not limited to defendants nor is it limited to criminal trials.[1] However, the privilege does have special meaning in a criminal trial as it relates to the defendant. The privilege entitles the witness not to answer specific questions posed in a criminal trial or in any other proceeding where he is under compulsion if his answers to those questions furnish a "link in the chain of evidence" needed to prosecute. The privilege entitles the defendant, in contrast, not to even appear as a witness. Basically, the right of the defendant is not only to avoid giving incriminating responses to particular inquiries, but not to even be placed in a position where the inquiries can be put to him. There is good reason for applying the privilege so broadly in this particular context. As the Supreme Court explained in *Wilson v. United States*[2]:

> It is not every one who can safely venture on the witness stand though entirely innocent of the charge against him. Excessive timidity, nervousness when facing others and attempting to explain transactions of a suspicious character, and offences charged against him, will often confuse and embarrass him to such a degree as to increase rather than remove prejudices against him. It is not every one, however honest, who would, therefore, willingly be placed on the witness stand.

The rule regarding waiver of the privilege by a defendant at a criminal trial is also different. The Supreme Court in *Brown v. United States*[3] rejected the contention that a defendant should, like an ordinary witness, be held to have waived the privilege only when incriminating testimony was given. The Court explained that the defendant

> has the choice, after weighing the advantage of the privilege against self-incrimination against the advantage of putting forward his version of the facts and his reliability as a witness, not to testify at all. He cannot reasonably claim that the Fifth Amendment gives him not only this choice but, if he elects to testify, an immunity from cross examination on the matters he has himself put in dispute. It would make of the Fifth Amendment not only a humane safeguard against judicially coerced self-disclosure but a positive invitation to mutilate the truth a party offers to tell.

Courts have generally held that once a defendant testifies he becomes liable to cross-examination under whatever rules would be applicable to any other witness, and thus by testifying has waived his privilege to that extent. At a minimum, this means that he may be

§ 24.4

1. See §§ 8.10, 8.11, 6.5.

2. 149 U.S. 60, 13 S.Ct. 765, 37 L.Ed. 650 (1893), discussing a statutory provision. The Court later said this language reflects "the spirit of the Self-incrimination Clause." Griffin v. California, 380 U.S. 609, 85 S.Ct. 1229, 14 L.Ed.2d 106 (1965).

3. 356 U.S. 148, 78 S.Ct. 622, 2 L.Ed.2d 589 (1958).

questioned concerning all facts relevant to the matters he has testified to on direct examination, but in some jurisdictions the rule is that he is subject to cross-examination on all phases of the case. In any event, he is subject to searching cross-examination for impeachment purposes.

In *Brooks v. Tennessee,*[4] the petitioner questioned the constitutionality of a statute requiring that a defendant "desiring to testify shall do so before any other testimony for the defense is heard," a rule related to the ancient practice of sequestering prospective witnesses in order to prevent them from being influenced by other testimony in the case. The Court majority held that the statute "violates an accused's constitutional right to remain silent," as a defendant "cannot be absolutely certain that his witnesses will testify as expected or that they will be effective on the stand" and thus "may not know at the close of the State's case whether his own testimony will be necessary or even helpful to his cause." This statute, the Court added, "may compel even a wholly truthful defendant, who might otherwise decline to testify for legitimate reasons, to subject himself to impeachment and cross-examination at a time when the strength of his other evidence is not yet clear." The Court then went on to rule that the statute also constituted "an infringement on the defendant's right of due process," as "by requiring the accused and his lawyer to make [the choice of whether to testify] without an opportunity to evaluate the actual worth of their evidence," it deprives the accused "of the 'guiding hand of counsel' in the timing of this critical element of his defense."

Brooks did not suggest that the state is deprived of all authority to adopt procedures, otherwise supported by the legitimate ends of procedural efficacy, where those procedures might operate to make more difficult the defendant's exercise of his choice between testifying and remaining silent. If that were the case, the state would not be allowed to force the defendant to make his choice as to whether to testify before he has a jury evaluation of the strength of the prosecution's case-in-chief. The Court will weigh, in the individual case, the nature of the state's interest and the character of the burden placed upon the defendant in making his choice, especially as it compares to burdens traditionally faced by the defense. The resulting balancing process tends to be circumstance specific and dependent upon the value structure brought to the issue by the individual justice. Thus, only a year before *Brooks,* in *Cramton v. Ohio,*[5] a somewhat differently composed Court (again divided) had rejected in a different procedural setting an "undue-burden" argument very much like that which won the day in *Brooks.* The defendant in *Cramton* contended that Ohio's law providing for the jury determination of the death penalty option in the proceeding in which it determined guilt created "an intolerable tension" between his constitutional right not to be compelled to be a witness against himself on the issue of guilt and his constitutional right to be heard on the issue of punishment. He argued further that the tension readily could have been avoided by the state's adoption of the bifurcated trial procedure used by other states, whereby the jury decides the issue of guilt before presentation and argument on the issue of punishment. In finding no constitutional need for a bifurcated trial, the Court concluded that "the policies of the privilege against compelled self-incrimination are not offended when a defendant in a capital case yields to the pressure to testify on the issue of punishment at the risk of damaging his case on guilt" and that a state is "not required to provide an opportunity for [a defendant] to speak to the jury [on the issue of punishment] free from any adverse consequences on the issue of guilt." The Court acknowledged that it might well be that "bifurcated trials * * * are superior means of dealing with capital cases," but from "a constitutional standpoint," it could not "conclude that * * * the compassionate purposes of jury sentencing in capital cases are better served by having the issues of guilt

4. 406 U.S. 605, 92 S.Ct. 1891, 32 L.Ed.2d 358 (1972), also discussed in § 20.4(d).

5. One of the cases decided in McGautha v. California, 402 U.S. 183, 91 S.Ct. 1454, 28 L.Ed.2d 711 (1971).

and punishment determined in a single trial than by focusing the jury's attention solely on punishment after the issue of guilt has been determined."

(b) Comment on Defendant's Silence. Prior to *Griffin v. California,*[6] a small number of states permitted comment by the court or the prosecutor or both regarding the defendant's failure to take the stand, but the Court in *Griffin* concluded such comment was constitutionally impermissible. The Court characterized comment on defendant's silence as "a penalty imposed by courts for exercising a constitutional privilege" in that it "cuts down on the privilege by making its assertion costly." As for the state's claim that "the inference of guilt for failure to testify as to facts peculiarly within the accused's knowledge is in any event natural and irresistible," the Court responded that this is not inevitably the case, as where a defendant declines to testify merely because his prior convictions would then be admissible for impeachment purposes.

The *Griffin* ruling has spawned an immense body of case law addressed to the question of when a statement that does not refer directly to a defendant's failure to take stand is nonetheless a comment on that failure. Courts agree on the general standard for resolving that issue—"whether the language used was manifestly intended or was of such character that the jury would naturally and necessarily take it to be a comment on the accused's failure to testify." The variation arises in their evaluation of roughly similar remarks in roughly similar settings. Thus, the prosecutor's comment that defendant "failed to exhibit shamefulness" may be viewed by one court as a comment on defendant's failure to testify and by another as a reference to his behavior. Among the frequently challenged comments producing such a variation are those that refer to the prosecution's case as "unrefuted" or "uncontradicted." Most challenges to such comments fail, although appellate courts often avoid the need to decide whether the statement was a *Griffin*-prohibited comment by holding that any constitutional error was harmless beyond a reasonable doubt.[7] The challenge is most likely to be successful where the statement was repeated several times, included a specific reference to the defendant, or was made in a case in which the prosecution's evidence was such that only the defendant himself could have contradicted it. The Supreme Court added still another element to the analysis in *Lockett v. Ohio,*[8] where the prosecution repeatedly referred to the state's case as "unrefuted" and "uncontradicted." The Court there stated that those comments did not "violate constitutional prohibitions [as] Lockett's own counsel had clearly focused the jury's attention on her silence, first by outlining her contemplated defense in his opening statement and, second, by stating * * * near the close of the case that Lockett would be the next witness." So too, where defense counsel had noted at several points that the government had never allowed the defendant to explain his side of the story, the Supreme Court held that *Griffin* did not bar the prosecutor's response that the defendant "could have taken the stand and explained it to you."[9] Applying the "*Lockett* principle that the prosecutorial comment must be examined in context," the Court concluded that "the prosecutorial comment did not treat the defendant's silence as substantive evidence of guilt," but, in a "fair response" to defense counsel's claim, cited one of "several opportunities" for explanation that had been available to defendant.

(c) Instruction on Defendant's Silence. The Court in *Griffin* reserved decision on whether a defendant can require that the jury be instructed that his silence must be disregarded. The matter was settled in *Carter v. Kentucky:*[10]

6. 380 U.S. 609, 85 S.Ct. 1229, 14 L.Ed.2d 106 (1965).

7. See Chapman v. California, discussed in § 27.6 at note 11.

8. 438 U.S. 586, 98 S.Ct. 2954, 57 L.Ed.2d 973 (1978).

9. United States v. Robinson, 485 U.S. 25, 108 S.Ct. 864, 99 L.Ed.2d 23 (1988).

10. 450 U.S. 288, 101 S.Ct. 1112, 67 L.Ed.2d 241 (1981).

A trial judge has a powerful tool at his disposal to protect the constitutional privilege—the jury instruction—and he has an affirmative constitutional obligation to use that tool when a defendant seeks its employment. No judge can prevent jurors from speculating about why a defendant stands mute in the face of a criminal accusation, but a judge can, and must, if requested to do so, use the unique power of the jury instruction to reduce that speculation to a minimum.[11]

Somewhat the reverse problem reached the Court in *Lakeside v. Oregon,*[12] where petitioner argued "that this protective instruction becomes constitutionally impermissible when given over the defendant's objection" because it "is like 'waving a red flag in front of the jury.'" The Court rejected that argument because it "would require indulgence in two very doubtful assumptions," namely, "that the jurors have not noticed that the defendant did not testify and will not, therefore, draw adverse inferences on their own," and "that the jurors will totally disregard the instruction, and affirmatively give weight to what they have been told not to consider at all." Petitioner's reliance upon the right to counsel was equally unavailing, for to "hold otherwise would mean that the constitutional right to counsel would be implicated in almost every wholly permissible ruling of a trial judge, if it is made over the objection of the defendant's lawyer."

(d) The Defendant's Right to Testify. Although at an earlier time it was recognized that a criminal defendant could plead his cause in person and therefore as a practical matter—though not in theory—could furnish evidence in his own behalf, in 18th century England there took hold the rule that a defendant was incompetent to give testimony. This rule was based on the fear that a person so directly interested in the case was likely to testify falsely. The English rule was inherited by American jurisprudence as a part of the common law but was rejected thereafter. On the federal level, for example, the Supreme Court first abrogated the general rule of incompetency based on interest and then specifically acknowledged the right of a federal defendant to testify. There were similar developments at the state level so that, by the end of the 19th century, all but one state (which later changed its practice) granted criminal defendants a right to testify. As a result of the recognition of that right under local law, the Supreme Court did not find it necessary to squarely rule on the defendant's constitutional right to testify until the mid-1980s.

In *Rock v. Arkansas,*[13] the Court, after citing dicta to that effect in previous opinions, held that there was, indeed, a constitutional right "to testify on one's own behalf at a criminal trial." That right was said to stem from three sources: (1) the guarantee of due process (which ensures a "fair adversary process," including a "right to be heard and to offer testimony"); (2) the Sixth Amendment's compulsory process clause (which "logically include[s]" defendant's "right to testify himself"); and (3) the Fifth Amendment's guarantee against compulsory self-incrimination (a "necessary corollary" of which is the defendant's right to testify "in the unfettered exercise of his own will").

While the defendant's right to testify is constitutionally based, that right, like the right of defendant to present other witnesses in his own behalf, is not without limitation. It may be restricted to accommodate other "legitimate interests in the criminal trial process,"[14] but those restrictions, as *Rock* noted,

11. In James v. Kentucky, 466 U.S. 341, 104 S.Ct. 1830, 80 L.Ed.2d 346 (1984), the Court held that, notwithstanding an ambiguous distinction in state law between "admonitions" and "instructions," defense counsel's request for an admonition to the jury on defendant's right to remain silent was sufficient to invoke the protections of *Carter.* In declining to characterize counsel's action as a request for an oral rather than a written statement to the jury, the Court stated, with respect to both the *Carter* and *Lakeside* (note 12 infra), that the Constitution "does not afford the defendant the right to dictate, inconsistent with state practice, *how* the jury is to be told."

12. 435 U.S. 333, 98 S.Ct. 1091, 55 L.Ed.2d 319 (1978).

13. 483 U.S. 44, 107 S.Ct. 2704, 97 L.Ed.2d 37 (1987).

14. See e.g., Perry v. Leeke, 488 U.S. 272, 109 S.Ct. 594, 102 L.Ed.2d 624 (1989) (a testifying defendant, like any other witness, may be precluded from discussing his testimony with counsel during the course of giving that

"may not be arbitrary or disproportionate to the purposes they are designed to serve." Thus, *Rock* held that, though the state has a legitimate interest in imposing evidentiary restrictions designed to exclude unreliable evidence, that interest could not justify a per se exclusion of a defendant's hypnotically refreshed testimony. Such a rule was excessive because it operated without regard either to procedural safeguards employed in the particular hypnosis process to reduce inaccuracies or to the availability of corroborating evidence and other traditional means of assessing the accuracy of the particular testimony.

§ 24.5 The Arguments of Counsel

(a) Opening Statements. Prior to the presentation of evidence, both sides may present opening statements. It is the rule in all jurisdictions that the prosecutor presents the initial opening statement. As for the statement by defense counsel, there is a variation in the practice; in some states the defense must present its opening statement immediately following the prosecutor's statement, while elsewhere the defense may reserve its opening statement until after the close of the prosecutor's case. Strategies differ on whether and when the defense should present an opening statement.

Because the purpose of the opening statement is a narrow one, counsel are limited to a brief statement of the issues and an outline of what it is believed can be supported with competent and admissible evidence. Indeed, it is unprofessional conduct for the prosecutor or defense attorney "to allude to any evidence unless there is a good faith and reasonable basis for believing that such evidence will be tendered and admitted in evidence."[1] The prohibitions applicable to the closing argument, as discussed in subsection (e), are certainly binding upon the opening statements as well. If anything, those prohibitions should be applied with greater strictness to opening statements, for unlike the closing arguments, these statements are not supposed to be argumentative. Yet, as is also true of prosecutorial misconduct during closing arguments, courts are inclined to find that the prosecutor's excessive remarks during his opening statement have been "cured" by a judge's admonition to the jury to disregard. There are instances, however, in which the prosecutor's remarks have been so inflammatory, or the judge's response so inadequate, that the appellate court has reversed defendant's conviction.

The most common appellate challenge to a prosecutor's opening statement is that it referred to evidence that subsequently was not admitted at trial. In this situation as well, appellate courts are inclined to conclude from assessment of the other circumstances in the case that this does not amount to reversible error. Courts taking that approach typically rely upon the fact that the prosecutor later disavowed the erroneous opening statement or that the jury had been given the standard instruction that it "must not regard any statements made by counsel * * * concerning the facts * * * as evidence."

(b) Closing Argument. The special significance of closing argument was recognized in *Herring v. New York.*[2] Although the trial there was to the bench rather than a jury, the Supreme Court held that there had been an unconstitutional interference with defendant's right to counsel when the trial court reached its decision without giving defense counsel the opportunity to present final argument. Justice Stewart noted that even when other aspects of fair procedure, such as compulsory process and confrontation, were in their infancy, the English criminal trial recognized the need for argument between the adversaries. The further development of those other rights, moreover, did not result in a dilution of the system's commitment to ar-

testimony, including a short recess declared in the midst of his testimony).

§ 24.5

1. 1 ABA Standards for Criminal Justice §§ 3–5.5, 4–7.4 (2d ed. 1980).

2. 422 U.S. 853, 95 S.Ct. 2550, 45 L.Ed.2d 593 (1975).

gument, but simply resulted in "shifting the primary function of argument to summation of the evidence at the close of trial, in contrast to the 'fragmented' factual argument that had been typical of the earlier common law." The result was to give such argument a central role in the adversary system:

> It can hardly be questioned that closing argument serves to sharpen and clarify the issues for resolution by the trier of fact in a criminal case. [I]t is only after all the evidence is in that counsel for the parties are in a position to present their respective versions of the case as a whole. Only then can they argue the inferences to be drawn from all the testimony, and point out the weaknesses of their adversaries' positions. * * * The very premise of our adversary system of criminal justice is that partisan advocacy on both sides of a case will best promote the ultimate objective that the guilty be convicted and the innocent go free. In a criminal trial, which is in the end basically a factfinding process, no aspect of such advocacy could be more important than the opportunity finally to marshal the evidence for each side before submission of the case to judgment.

While recognizing the special importance of closing argument to the adversary process, *Herring* also noted that, as with other aspects of the adversary process, there was room as well for some degree of judicial control. The trial judge should be given "great latitude in controlling the duration and limiting the scope of closing summaries." The judge must have authority, for example, to "terminate argument when continuation would be repetitive or redundant." So too, the judge "may ensure that argument does not stray unduly from the mark, or otherwise impede the fair and orderly conduct of the trial." Balanced against this authority, however, is the recognition that persuasion is a matter of style as well as content, and counsel must be given considerable leeway to shape his or her own style in presenting argument. The closing argument traditionally has been the one place in the trial where counsel is given greatest leeway in manner of expression even as the courts strive also to bar the excesses of the overzealous advocate.

(c) Order of Closing Argument. The prevailing view with respect to the order of closing arguments is that followed in the federal system: the prosecution opens the argument, the defendant is then permitted to reply, and the prosecution then is allowed to reply in rebuttal. This structure is grounded in the notion that the fair administration of justice is best served if the defendant knows the arguments actually made by the prosecution in behalf of conviction before being faced with the decision whether to reply and what to reply. Although it has occasionally been contended that it is unfair to allow the prosecution to make both the first and the last arguments in the case, this is not so in view of the fact that the prosecution carries the burden of proving guilt beyond a reasonable doubt. Statutes prescribing this order of argument have been upheld against both due process and right to counsel challenges. Of course, if the prosecutor improperly interjects a new argument at the time of his rebuttal, then the trial judge might well allow defense counsel to respond to that point.

(d) The Roles of the Prosecutor and Defense Counsel. Although closing arguments are quite clearly a time for advocacy, the prosecutor is often said to be under special restraints because of his unique role in the criminal process. In the oft-quoted language of *Berger v. United States* [3]:

> The United States Attorney is the representative not of an ordinary party to a controversy, but of a sovereignty whose obligation to govern impartially is as compelling as its obligation to govern at all; and whose interest, therefore, in a criminal prosecution is not that it shall win a case, but that justice shall be done. As such, he is in a peculiar and very definite sense the servant of the law, the twofold aim of which is that guilt shall not escape or innocence suffer. He may prosecute with earnestness and vigor—indeed, he should do so. But, while he may strike hard blows, he is not at liberty to strike foul ones. It is as much his duty to refrain from improper meth-

3. 295 U.S. 78, 55 S.Ct. 629, 79 L.Ed. 1314 (1935).

ods calculated to produce a wrongful conviction as it is to use every legitimate means to bring about a just one. * * * It is fair to say that the average jury, in a greater or lesser degree has confidence that these obligations, which so plainly rest upon the prosecuting attorney, will be faithfully observed. Consequently, improper suggestions, insinuations, and, especially, assertions of personal knowledge are apt to carry much weight against the accused when they should properly carry none.

Pointing to special responsibilities of the prosecutor and the special weight likely to be given to his argument, some commentators have suggested that defense counsel should be given somewhat more leeway in the defense's closing argument. That position is thought to follow from the need to provide every assurance that the innocent are not convicted. An acquittal based on an emotional appeal of defense counsel is said to be of far less concern, even where clearly against the weight of the evidence, than a conviction achieved through the emotional appeal of the prosecutor that is equally against the weight of the evidence. This position finds no support, however in the traditional statements of the standards of professional responsibility. They either contain a single listing, applicable to both sides, of the prohibitions governing final argument, or offer separate lists of mirror image content for the defense and the prosecution.[4] Of course, equality in theory and equality in practice may be two different matters. Some have argued that defense counsel have greater incentives to engage in improper argument because if they are successful and the defendant is acquitted, the prosecution has no remedy, whereas an improper prosecution argument that produces a conviction is subject to being reversed on appeal. They therefore conclude that, especially before trial courts who are prone to allow counsel considerable leeway in argument, defense counsel are much more likely to go over the edge. There is some suggestion that appellate courts often view this as the state of the practice. Apart from their recognition of the invited response doctrine discussed in subsection (f), those courts sometimes suggest that there is need to allow leeway to the prosecution as a general matter to compensate for such a defense-oriented state of the practice.

Appellate courts infrequently have the opportunity to consider the propriety of defense counsel's argument, and when they do, commonly operate from a procedural context that requires consideration of more than just that issue. As an acquittal cannot be challenged by prosecution appeal, the propriety of defense counsel's argument can come before the appellate court only in a case in which the defendant himself is appealing. That issue is unlikely to be presented on such an appeal, except in connection with one of three quite distinct defense objections. First, where the defense challenges the prosecution's closing argument, the propriety of the defense's closing argument may be raised by the prosecution under the "invited response" doctrine discussed in subsection (f). Second, where the trial court viewed the defense argument as so egregious as to require a mistrial, the defendant may challenge his subsequent retrial as violating the double jeopardy prohibition. As with the invited response doctrine, the applicable standard of review here, although giving consideration to the propriety of defense counsel's argument, also requires consideration of other factors.[5] Finally, where the trial judge cut off defense argument as inappropriate, the defense may claim that such action constituted reversible error. Courts here tend to stress the broad discretion of the trial court, noting that the critical issue is not whether the appellate court agrees that counsel's argument overstepped the bounds of propriety, but whether "there has been a clear abuse of discretion resulting in some prejudice to the accused."

(e) Prohibited Argument. The traditional formulations of prohibited categories of argument often utilize broad generalities which

4. See 1 ABA Standards for Criminal Justice §§ 3–5.8, 4–7.8; ABA Model Rules of Professional Conduct, Rule 3.4.

5. See Arizona v. Washington, discussed in § 25.2(e).

require further definitional content through case-specific rulings if they are to provide any significant degree of guidance. In many areas, those rulings do provide considerable guidance, but they also have their limitations. For one, the rulings focus almost entirely on challenges to arguments by the prosecution since, as noted above, appellate courts rarely are placed in a procedural context where they must rule directly on the propriety of a defense counsel's argument. Second, appellate opinions that reject challenges to alleged forensic misconduct by prosecutors are sometimes less than clear as to the grounding of their rulings. It may be difficult at time to determine whether the court is stating that argument of the prosecutor was (i) appropriate without regard to the argument of defense counsel, (ii) appropriate only in light of defense counsel having opened the door, or (iii) not prejudicial and therefore not requiring reversal even if inappropriate. Finally, the immense body of appellate opinions deals with such a variety of prosecutorial comments, both upheld and rejected, that a complete description of what has been held to fall within and without a particular prohibition risks drowning the reader in a flood of endless detail. The description that follows therefore provides a far less than exhaustive review of the different categories of arguments, is limited to prosecution arguments, and seeks to exclude rulings that did not clearly reach a conclusion on the propriety of the particular comment apart from the issue of prejudice.

Going beyond the record. It is commonly stated that the prosecutor may not refer to or build an argument upon evidence that is not within the record. To do so not only violates accepted trial norms, but also deprives the defendant of the right to cross-examine a person (the prosecutor) who is, in effect, testifying against him. The question often is presented, however, as to what is argued as evidence beyond the record, what is argued as inference from record evidence, and what is argued as common knowledge. Prosecutors are not prohibited from drawing inferences from the record, and although it is often said these factual inferences must be "reasonably" based on the record evidence, "the latitude is so broad that even deductions which might otherwise seem to be absurd are not necessarily matters for rebuke by the trial court." The key here is that the inference be identified as such rather than represented to be a fact actually in the record. The prosecutor also is not prohibited from referring to matters of common public knowledge or basic human experience. References to common sayings about behavior, classic illustrations, and commonplace behavior escapes the "non record facts" prohibition. As with inferences, there are points at which what the prosecutor sees as a general illustration of human behavior the defense counsel sees as a factual reference to defendant's specific situation that was not established by the record evidence.

Misrepresentation of the law. As with misrepresentations of the evidence, misrepresentations of the law also constitute improper argument. Counsel may anticipate jury instructions and tie the facts of the case to the elements of the law that will be set forth in those instructions. Indeed, that usually is a major component of closing argument. Because the jury is informed that the law comes from the court, and not from the attorneys, this commonly causes no significant difficulties even if an attorney should misstate somewhat the law as presented in the instruction. Occasionally, however, where the prosecutor's argument was tied in substantial part to a basic misstatement in the law (e.g., the allocation of proof), that misstatement will prove fatal. More frequently, successful challenges to prosecutorial argument have involved references (often accurate) to aspects of the law that are beyond the elements considered in the judge's charge. Indeed, those references usually are to matters on which a judge would refuse to charge a jury (if requested) because they detract from its responsibility to decide the issue before it. Thus, the jury would not be told that the judge had to find the evidence reasonably sufficient to convict in order for the case to reach the jury, that the defendant could appeal a jury's mistake in convicting (but the prosecution could not appeal a mistake in acquitting), or that the defendant would be eligible under sentencing guidelines for possible probation. Here, whether or not the statement of the law is correct, it deals with an aspect of the process not to be considered by the jury and therefore no more to be brought to its attention by counsel than by the court.

Personal beliefs and opinions. Courts have repeatedly noted that it is improper for a prosecutor to inform the jury of his or her personal belief in the accused's guilt or in the truth or falsity of a witness' testimony. This practice is pernicious not only because the jury may view the prosecutor's opinion as "carry[ing] with it the imprimatur of the Government," but also because such comments often convey to the jury "the impression that [there exists] evidence not presented to the jury, but known to the prosecutor." Of course, the prosecutor is not prohibited from explaining to the jury why it should conclude the defendant was guilty or accept or reject a particular witness' testimony. Where the prosecutor avoids a direct reference to phrases like "I think," "I believe," and "I know," it is often difficult to draw the line between a characterization based on the evidence and an expression of personal belief. Thus, one court will say that the prosecutor was vouching for the witness when he stated that the two complainants in a rape case "were good and fine girls and not the type the defendant and his witnesses alleged they were," while another will characterize as no more than advocacy the prosecutor's reference to "the 'reputable officers' and 'very sweet' complaining witness who testified for the government."

Comments on privileges. As discussed in § 24.4(b), prosecutorial comment on the defendant's failure to testify constitutes constitutional error in itself. Adverse references to the exercise of privileges by others ordinarily also are inappropriate, as will be the reference to the defense's failure to call a particular witness where that witness was known to be unavailable due to his exercise of the privilege. Here, however, the consequence of the improper comment is determined, as with other inappropriate comments, by reference to its impact on the outcome of the trial (as discussed in subsection (i) infra), rather than as a constitutional error requiring a conviction reversal absent a prosecutorial showing that the error was harmless beyond a reasonable doubt.

Appeals to emotion and prejudice. Closing arguments traditionally have included appeals to emotion. It is said to be the "time honored privilege" of counsel to "drown the stage in tears." Such appeals, however, are subject to limits. Most of those limits are brought together under the general prohibition against "arguments calculated to inflame the passions or prejudices of the jury." Illustrative of prohibited appeals to the prejudices of the jury are references to race and religion in characterizing the qualities of the defendant or the reliability of a witness. An illustration of a prohibited appeal to passion is the "Golden Rule" argument that asks the jury to step into the shoes of the victim. Still another is the dramatic and abusive characterization of the defendant (e.g., as a "cheap, slimy, scaly crook") or defense counsel (e.g., a "flat liar"). Yet, here too, distinctions will be drawn and courts will vary in their assessment of what goes "too far." The prosecutor may appropriately call the jury's attention to the plight of the victim and the seriousness of the crime, provided he does not take the "extra step" of asking the jurors to put themselves in the victim's position. So too, the prosecutor may characterize the defendant with disparagement that is reasonably deduced from the evidence in the case. Thus, while one court will hold improper the characterization of the defendant as a "Judas Iscariot," another will consider as fair comment (with some dramatic license) the description of the defendant as a "trafficker in human misery."

Injecting broader issues. The limitation that most frequently lends itself to the drawing of fine lines is that barring the injecting of issues "broader than the guilt or innocence of the accused." Courts ordinarily will allow the prosecutor "to dwell upon the end results of the crime and to urge a fearless administration of the criminal law." They also have accepted arguments that a conviction would deter others from committing similar crimes, but this tends to come close to the impermissible. The impermissible is reached where the prosecutor asserts that a guilty verdict would relieve community fears or would serve as a good example for the young people in the community. Courts have also condemned appeals to jurors as the taxpayers who pay for the costs of law enforcement and as the parents of children who could someday themselves be victimized.

(f) The Invited Response. Arguments by the prosecution that would otherwise be improper are sometimes deemed appropriate (or at least "excusable") because defense "opened the door" with its own improper argument and the prosecution merely "replied in kind." In *United States v. Young,*[6] the defendant challenged this "invited response" doctrine as bottomed on the false premise that "two wrongs make a right." The Supreme Court agreed that two wrongs did not make a right, but it also found justification for the doctrine where properly applied. The Court acknowledged that it was inappropriate for the prosecution to respond to the defense's improper argument with forensic misconduct of its own. The proper response, the Court stressed, is a prosecution objection, accompanied by a "request that the [trial] court give a timely warning [to defense counsel] and curative instructions to the jury." However, because a "criminal conviction is not to be lightly overturned on the basis of a prosecutor's comments alone," even though the prosecutor did not respond in the correct manner, the reviewing court cannot avoid evaluating the prosecutor's improper, responsive comments in light of the "opening salvo" of defense counsel. Recognition of this factor, the Court noted, should not be seen as giving a "license to make otherwise improper arguments," but simply as fulfilling the task of a reviewing court, which is to determine whether the prosecutor's comments, "taken in context, unfairly prejudiced the defendant." The Court added that the invited response doctrine was limited to situations in which the prosecutor's remarks were relevant to the earlier defense comments and designed to "right the scale." This was in apparent response to Justice Brennan's complaint that too many appellate courts, "rather than apply the [invited response] doctrine as a limited corrective," treated it as "a rule of unclean hands that altogether prevents a defendant from successfully challenging * * * [even] virtually unchecked prosecutorial appeals going far beyond a fair response to defense counsel's arguments."

(g) Objections. In some localities, immediate objections to improper closing arguments are expected, while others consider it a matter of common courtesy, verging on obligation, for opposing counsel not to interrupt one another's closing arguments by objections. While appellate courts recognize that the latter custom may result in a delayed objection, they do expect an objection. Though a failure to object is not necessarily fatal to the defense's appellate challenge, it does require a more egregious error by the prosecutor and a clearer showing of prejudice to obtain a reversal. Without objection, the improper argument must reach the level required for a reversal under the plain error doctrine,[7] which was described in *Young* as demanding an error so grave as to "undermine the fundamental fairness of the trial and contribute to a miscarriage of justice."

Judicial insistence upon an objection has been challenged on the ground that objections may be counter-productive. The jury, it is argued, may resent repeated objections. Moreover, the defense attorney's objection, if sustained, may have exactly the opposite effect from that intended as the trial judge's condemnation of the argument may simply call attention to the prosecutor's improper remarks and reemphasize them in the jurors' minds. To meet the first of these concerns, the appellate courts do not necessarily require that the objection be made in the presence of the jury. As for the second, the response is that the defense should at least indicate its concern and give the trial judge the opportunity to consider the appropriate remedy,

6. 470 U.S. 1, 105 S.Ct. 1038, 84 L.Ed.2d 1 (1985).

7. See § 27.5(d).

whether that be a curative instruction, a mistrial, or even granting the defense an additional opportunity to argue in response.

(h) Due Process. In *Donnelly v. DeChristoforo,*[8] the Supreme Court held that improper prosecutorial argument could reach the level of a federal constitutional violation. That would occur, however, only if the argument "so infected the trial with unfairness as to make the resulting conviction a denial of due process." In finding that this standard had not been violated in *Donnelly,* the Court noted that the alleged improper remark constituted but "one moment in an extended trial," that the remark was highly ambiguous and might not have been interpreted by the jury as the defendant interpreted it (as suggesting that the defendant had been willing to plead to a lesser offense), and that the trial judge had clearly admonished the jury to disregard the remark. In *Darden v. Wainwright,*[9] the Court had before it, in contrast, a closing argument in a capital case that contained numerous patently improper remarks, reflecting the prosecutor's highly emotional reaction to both the defendant and the gruesome homicide with which he was charged. Nonetheless, a majority held that there had been no constitutional violation under the appropriate standard of review—" 'the narrow one of due process and not the broad exercise of supervisory power.' " No matter how glaring the prosecutor's misconduct (the Court characterized the prosecutor's closing argument as "fully deserving the condemnation it received from every court to review it"), due process did not mandate a new trial unless that misconduct had such an impact as to deprive the defendant of a fair trial. Various aspects of the trial, taken together, supported the lower court's conclusion that the trial " 'was not perfect—few are—but neither was it fundamentally unfair.' " These included the following: the prosecutor's improper comments did not misstate or manipulate the evidence; the comments also did not implicate other specific rights of the accused; much of their objectionable content was responsive to the opening summation of the defense; the defense was able to use its final rebuttal argument (available under state rule) to portray the prosecution's argument "in a light that was more likely to engender strong disapproval than result in enflamed passions"; the trial judge instructed the jurors "several times" that their decision was to be based only on the evidence and that arguments of counsel were not evidence; and the "weight of the evidence against petitioner was heavy." Taking a quite different view of the trial as a whole, the four dissenters in *Darden* characterized the majority opinion as relying upon "an entirely unpersuasive one-page laundry list of reasons for ignoring this blatant misconduct."

(i) Standard of Review. Jurisdictions vary in their approach under local law to the prerequisites for reversing a conviction based upon improper prosecutorial argument. Some apply what is basically the due process standard of *Donnelly* and *Darden.* Others determine initially whether the prosecution's argument was improper, and if it was, then proceed to apply the same harmless error standard that is otherwise utilized in the jurisdiction for nonconstitutional errors.[10] Still others utilize some separate standard of potential prejudice for this particular type of error, with that standard allowing more readily for reversal than the due process standard of *Donnelly.* All, however, start from the premise that there must be shown some likelihood of prejudice, perhaps reflecting the view set forth by the Supreme Court in one of its earliest rulings on improper closing argument:

> There is no doubt that, in the heat of argument, counsel do occasionally make remarks that are not justified by the testimony, and which are, or may be, prejudicial to the accused. * * * If every remark made by counsel outside of the testimony were grounds for a reversal, comparatively few verdicts would stand, since in the ardor of advocacy, and in the excitement of trial, even the most experi-

8. 416 U.S. 637, 94 S.Ct. 1868, 40 L.Ed.2d 431 (1974).

9. 477 U.S. 168, 106 S.Ct. 2464, 91 L.Ed.2d 144 (1986).

10. See § 27.6(b).

enced counsel are occasionally carried away by this temptation.[11]

In determining whether the improper remarks were likely to have had sufficient impact to require reversal, appellate courts look to a variety of factors, including the following: (1) whether the improper remarks were particularly egregious; (2) whether the improper remarks were only isolated or brief episodes in an otherwise proper argument; (3) whether the improper remarks were balanced by the comments of the defense (either themselves improper or turning the improper remarks against the prosecution); (4) whether defense counsel made a timely and strong objection to the prosecutor's improper remarks, thereby indicating fear of prejudice; (5) whether the trial judge took appropriate corrective action, such as instructing the jury to disregard the improper remarks; (6) whether the improper remarks were combined with other trial errors; and (7) whether there was overwhelming evidence of guilt. The end result will be dependent upon a consideration of all of these factors taken together; no single factor will necessarily control in itself. Thus, where the prosecutor's comments were repeated and particularly inflammatory, a reversal might be required notwithstanding the presence of other factors that would ordinarily weigh heavily in the other direction (e.g., the presence of substantial evidence of guilt).

Appellate courts, while commonly finding a lack of prejudice flowing from improper summation by the prosecutor, have with mounting frustration expressed concern over the frequency with which such prosecutorial improprieties occur. Sometimes courts have even suggested that they might well be required to reverse convictions without a showing of prejudice in order to deter such prosecutorial misconduct, but this has been done only rarely. Some commentators have expressed the view that prosecutors would be effectively deterred if courts more readily reversed for misconduct in closing arguments, but others contend that this is not the case and defendants would simply receive windfall reversals. Those of the latter view are more inclined to favor judicial reprimand, contempt penalties for flagrant misconduct, and disciplinary proceedings for repeated misconduct, remedies which heretofore have been infrequently utilized.

§ 24.6 Jury Procedures

(a) Sequestering the Jury. Sequestration of the jury in a criminal case, that is, keeping the jury in seclusion, is a step which may be undertaken during the course of the trial because of the risk of unfair publicity in the media, and is discussed in that context in § 23.2(e). Sequestration of the jury also can be used during deliberations. At common law, such confinement of the jury was undertaken in all cases as a matter of course in order to prevent contamination of the jury by extraneous communications and improper influences, and also to coerce a verdict by withholding from the jurors their accustomed comforts and conveniences. The current rule in the federal courts and a number of state courts is that the trial judge may permit a deliberating jury to separate, and to constitute reversible error there must be an objection supported by specific reasons against separation and a showing that the defendant was actually prejudiced by the separation. State decisions reaching a contrary result are often grounded in statutes which appear to require that a jury be kept together while deliberating its verdict, but some of the state cases hold that this statutory right is sufficiently insubstantial that it may be lost merely by failure to make a timely objection to the dispersal of the jury. The ancient common law doctrine prohibiting jury separation is not such an integral part of the right to a jury trial that sequestration has constitutional status.

(b) Jury Note Taking and Questions. Are jurors required to simply sit and listen to testimony? That depends in large part on the discretion of the trial judge. Whether or not jurors have some type of right to ask questions of witnesses, any such right clearly is subject to the trial court's authority to screen

11. Dunlop v. United States, 165 U.S. 486, 17 S.Ct. 375, 41 L.Ed. 799 (1897).

any questions and exclude those it deems inappropriate. Ordinarily, this authority is implemented by directing the jurors to write out any questions they may have after the witness has finished testifying and to submit those questions to the judge. If the judge finds the question to be appropriate, then the judge may ask the question and counsel and the witness may treat the question as if it came from the judge himself. If the judge concludes that the question relates to inadmissible or irrelevant matter, as often might be expected, the judge can simply note that the question will not be asked. If the judge did not screen and jurors were allowed to ask their questions directly, counsel would be placed in the delicate position of objecting to the juror's action in the presence of the juror.

It is clear that jurors do not have a right to take notes. They may do so only with the permission of the trial judge, and the predominating view at one time was that judges should rarely grant that permission. Note taking was thought to be an unwise practice because: (1) the best note taker would come to dominate the jury; (2) jurors, not having an overview of the case, are likely to include in their notes interesting sidelights and ignore important (but boring) facts; (3) a dishonest juror may falsify notes; (4) the act of taking notes will draw the juror's attention away from the demeanor of the witness and may leave the juror writing rather than listening; and (5) the notes will receive undue attention during deliberations. Courts today tend to treat some of these objections (e.g., the dishonest juror scenario) as "far-fetched" and "imaginary" and others simply as "overstated." The problems presented by note taking are seen as surmountable in large part with appropriate instructions. Thus, jurors are warned that if they take notes, they should take care not to let note taking distract them from hearing the full testimony of the witness, they should not discuss their notes with fellow jurors until deliberations begin, they should rely on their notes as memory aids and not as a substitute for independent recollection, and a juror not taking notes should not be overly influenced by another's notes, as notes are "not entitled to any greater weight than the recollection or impression of each juror."

(c) Items Taken to the Jury Room. When the jury begins its deliberations, it ordinarily may have with it the charging instrument and written jury instructions where they are used. In most jurisdictions, the trial judge has discretion to allow the jurors to take with them other materials, such as pertinent exhibits, which have been received in evidence. Where that practice is followed, an exception ordinarily is made for any depositions that have been read into the record, as they are simply another form of testimony and should not be given any greater attention than other testimony.

At one time, it simply was not feasible to give the jury a transcript in all but the exceptional cases where counsel was able to order daily transcripts (at their expense), and transcripts simply were not made available in any case. Today, however, where courts use a tape recording back-up to the stenographic transcript, that tape recording probably could be made available in every case. Nonetheless, the practice of not providing transcripts or transcript-substitutes continues. This suggests that the concern is not so much cost as bogging down the deliberations with a rerun of the trial. That same concern may influence the judge to allow very little into the jury room, particularly in cases where much of the evidence consists of documents.

It sometimes happens that the jury after retiring will submit to the trial judge a request to review certain testimony or evidence. About a third of the states have statutes or court rules which appear to require the judge to honor such a request, but the courts are not in agreement as to whether these provisions are mandatory or discretionary. Elsewhere the judge has some discretion as to whether to act favorably upon the jury's request.

(d) The Deadlocked Jury. After the jury has been deliberating for some time, it may report to the judge that it has been unable to reach a decision. Except in a few states where statutes limit the number of times a judge may order a jury to renew deliberations, the rule is that the judge may send the jury back for further deliberations once, twice or several times. However, the court may not require or threaten to require the jury to deliberate for an unreasonable length of time. The reasonableness of the deliberation period depends on such factors as the length of the trial, the nature or complexity of the case, the volume and nature of the evidence, the presence of multiple counts or multiple defendants, and the jurors' statements to the court concerning the probability of agreement. The judge is given considerable discretion in this regard, but there are limits, and if the judge declares a mistrial without making an adequate effort to ensure the jury is incapable of reaching a verdict, the mistrial may not be justified by "manifest necessity," and double jeopardy may bar a retrial.[1]

What if the judge, in an effort to determine whether further deliberations by the jury are likely to be fruitful, inquires into the numerical division of the jury, that is, whether it is divided 6–6 or 11–1 or whatever? Many years ago the Supreme Court criticized the practice even when the response did not reveal which votes were for and which against conviction,[2] and the Court later condemned the practice in no uncertain terms:

> We deem it essential to the fair and impartial conduct of the trial, that the inquiry itself should be regarded as ground for reversal. Such procedure serves no useful purpose that cannot be attained by questions not requiring the jury to reveal the nature or extent of its division. Its effect upon a divided jury will often depend upon circumstances which cannot properly be known to the trial judge or to the appellate courts and may vary widely in different situations, but in general its tendency is coercive. It can rarely be resorted to without bringing to bear in some degree, serious, although not measurable, an improper influence upon the jury, from whose deliberations every consideration other than that of the evidence and the law as expounded in a proper charge, should be excluded. Such a practice, which is never useful and is generally harmful, is not to be sanctioned.[3]

Although it has frequently been held that this decision by the Supreme Court was grounded in the Court's supervisory power over the federal courts and thus is not a constitutional rule binding upon the states, some have argued that such a result ought to be required as an aspect of the Sixth Amendment right to trial by an impartial jury. At the state level, some jurisdictions nonetheless have concluded that inquiry into numerical division is proper so long as the judge does not ask whether the majority is for or against conviction or so long as the inquiry is not accompanied by other coercive conduct.

Another troublesome issue is what the judge may permissibly do to "encourage" agreement by a deadlocked jury. In *Allen v. United States,*[4] the Supreme Court held that the trial judge had not committed error in giving the jury a supplemental instruction, when it returned during its deliberations, that

> in a large proportion of cases absolute certainty could not be expected; that, although the verdict must be the verdict of each individual juror, and not a mere acquiescence in the conclusion of his fellows, yet they should examine the question submitted with candor, and with a proper regard and deference to the opinions of each other; that it was their duty to decide the case if they could conscientiously do so; that they should listen, with a disposition to be convinced, to each other's arguments; that, if much the larger number were for conviction, a dissenting juror should consider whether his doubt was a reasonable one which made no impression upon the minds of so many men, equally honest, equally intelligent with himself. If, upon the other hand, the majority were for acquittal, the minority ought to ask themselves whether they might not reasonably doubt the correctness of a judg-

§ 24.6

1. See § 25.2(e).

2. Burton v. United States, 196 U.S. 283, 25 S.Ct. 243, 49 L.Ed. 482 (1905).

3. Brasfield v. United States, 272 U.S. 448, 47 S.Ct. 135, 71 L.Ed. 345 (1926).

4. Allen v. United States, 164 U.S. 492, 17 S.Ct. 154, 41 L.Ed. 528 (1896).

ment which was not concurred in by the majority.

This kind of instruction, commonly referred to as the "*Allen* charge" or "dynamite charge," was used for many years in state and federal courts. But in recent years both state and federal courts have been inclined to require use of more guarded language.

In *Lowenfield v. Phelps,*[5] the Supreme Court upheld against constitutional challenge in a capital case a charge that did not go as far as *Allen* but arguably had more of a "coercive" quality than many lower courts would recommend. The charge there directed the jurors to "discuss the evidence with the objective of reaching a just verdict if you can do so without violence to [your] individual judgment," but it did not include an *Allen*-charge direction to minority jurors to consider the views of majority and to ask themselves whether their position was reasonably founded in light of that taken by the majority. Rather, the charge told the jurors not to "hesitate to reexamine your own views and to change your opinion if you are convinced you are wrong," while adding a warning against "surrendering your honest belief * * * solely because of the opinion of your fellow jurors or for the mere purpose of returning a verdict." In rejecting the defense's claim that the charge had combined with other circumstances to create an unacceptable potential for coercion in a capital case, the Court majority noted that the general observations in *Allen* concerning the value of jurors being open to the views of others and "securing unanimity by a comparison of views" had "continuing validity."

(e) Polling the Jury. Once the jury reaches a verdict and that verdict is announced in court, the defendant (assuming a guilty verdict) may wish to poll the jury. Polling is a procedure under which each juror is separately asked whether he or she concurs in the verdict. Its purpose is to determine whether the verdict announced actually reflects the conscience of each of the jurors. In the great majority of jurisdictions, the jury must be polled upon the request of a party, while elsewhere the matter is left to the sound discretion of the trial judge. The right to a poll is waived if not requested before the jury has dispersed, and it is not required that the defendant be specifically advised of his right to poll the jury.

The poll is conducted by the judge or the clerk of court. A common practice is to ask: "Was this then and is this now your verdict?" If a juror indicates some hesitancy or ambivalence in his answer, then it is the trial judge's duty to ascertain the juror's present intent by affording the juror the opportunity to make an unambiguous reply as to his present state of mind. If the poll reveals that there are not a sufficient number of votes for a valid verdict, then under the better view the court has the discretion either to direct the jury to retire for further deliberations or to discharge the jury.

(f) Misconduct. The term "jury misconduct" is often used to describe both action by jurors that is contrary to their responsibilities and conduct by others (often improper) which contaminates the jury process with extraneous influence. Courts are in basic agreement as to what constitutes such "misconduct" in the jury process. The troublesome issue often dividing them is what to do once it is determined that there has been misconduct.

A large part of the content of jury misconduct is readily derived from the prohibitions noted in the typical preliminary instructions to jurors. There jurors are told not to talk to each other about the case until deliberations begin, not to talk to anyone else about the case or about anything or anyone related to the case until the trial is ended, not to converse on any matter with the attorneys, witnesses, or defendant, not to read, view, or listen to any media reporting on the case or on anyone or anything related to it, and not to do any research or investigation on their own. Those instructions naturally lead to characterizing as misconduct a large range of conduct that is inconsistent with such admonitions—such as a juror discussing the merits

5. 484 U.S. 231, 108 S.Ct. 546, 98 L.Ed.2d 568 (1988).

of the case with a bailiff, inspecting the scene of the crime, writing a love letter to an assistant prosecutor, reading a newspaper article about the defendant and his family, or using a legal dictionary to define some term mentioned by the judge. Indeed the only violations of those admonitions not characterized as misconduct are those hypertechnical in nature and obviously having no potential prejudicial impact, such as brief exchange of greetings between the juror and an attorney or a comment to a fellow juror about the boring nature of the case.

Other aspects of misconduct in the jury process follow equally logically from the role of the jury. Efforts to intimidate, bribe, or otherwise pressure the jurors are clearly inconsistent with juror independence. Presenting or trying to present information to the juror outside the trial process obviously interferes with jury's responsibility to rule only on the basis of the evidence before it. The juror who is intoxicated as he listens to testimony clearly fails to fulfill his obligation to listen attentively to the evidence. The prospective juror who lies on voir dire questioning undermines the selection process. In the end, whether motivated by good faith or bad, any action by a juror himself, a participant in the process, or an outsider that has the potential for interfering with juror decisionmaking in accordance with the juror's responsibilities constitutes misconduct and calls for some response from the court.

Courts are in general agreement that the critical element in shaping that response is the court's assessment of the likely prejudicial impact of the misconduct. In *Remmer v. United States,*[6] a case involving an alleged attempt to bribe a juror and a subsequent FBI investigation of that attempt, the Supreme Court described the extraneous influence upon the juror as "presumptively prejudicial." State and federal courts have since come to use that designation in characterizing a good many instances of misconduct. Those courts do not always indicate, however, the precise significance of the designation. *Remmer* held only that the trial judge there had erred in concluding that the juror had not been influenced without holding a hearing. That the presumption of prejudice requires an inquiry, with appropriate witnesses called, is well accepted. So too, courts agree that the burden of proof rests on the party seeking to show that the juror was not influenced (invariably the prosecutor where the misconduct is called to the court's attention in a postconviction challenge, but either prosecutor or defense where the misconduct is noted during trial, depending on the direction that the influence was likely to take). The precise weight of the burden, however, often is murky. Many courts suggest that the hearing must eliminate all "reasonable possibility" of prejudicial impact—a standard also expressed as requiring proof beyond a reasonable doubt that the misconduct did not influence the juror. Others suggest only that the presumption must be "overcome" and that it must be "adequately demonstrated" that there was no prejudicial impact. Courts also speak of the trial court having before it a "reasonable basis" for concluding that there had been no prejudicial impact.

In conducting an investigation into the likelihood of prejudice, the juror or jurors who may have been affected are often the key witnesses. However, for reasons discussed in subsection (e), rules of evidence may sharply restrict the permissible range of their testimony. Courts also face the problem, particularly when the hearing is held after the verdict has been rendered, that the juror may not be candid in recognizing the prejudicial impact, but will profess that he was not affected and thereby justify his action in casting a vote to convict. Thus, in many instances, the critical question may be whether, under the particular circumstances, a reasonable person would have been influenced. If the judge arrives at that conclusion, a juror's assurance to the contrary may mean very little.

Not all acts of misconduct are presumptively prejudicial and therefore automatically requiring an inquiry on prejudice. Some appar-

6. 347 U.S. 227, 74 S.Ct. 450, 98 L.Ed. 654 (1954).

ently require no inquiry unless the party raising the challenge can make some special showing of actual prejudice. The misconduct so treated is difficult to categorize, but it commonly involves actions that on their face appear innocuous, suggesting that in fact a forbidden contact did not occur or was so casual as to be meaningless. On the other side, some acts of misconduct apparently are per se prejudicial, requiring the trial court to take action without regard to what any hearing might suggest. The reading of a newspaper containing highly prejudicial matter apparently falls in this per se category, at least in some jurisdictions.[7]

In two cases decided during the mid–1960's, the Supreme Court held that misconduct in the jury proceedings reached the level of a constitutional violation. *Turner v. Louisiana*[8] found that a defendant's right to an impartial jury was violated when two deputy sheriffs, who were key prosecution witnesses, were placed in charge of the jury and fraternized with the jurors throughout the proceedings. In *Parker v. Gladden,*[9] a bailiff said of defendant to a juror: "Oh, that wicked fellow, he is guilty." The Court found that comment violated not only defendant's right to an impartial jury, but also his right to confront witnesses against him, since the bailiff was seen as presenting evidence outside the trial process. At one time, it was thought that these two constitutional rulings raised to the level of per se prejudicial any type of misconduct that would come within their reach. However, *Taylor* presented a situation, characterized there as producing inherent prejudice, which simply did not allow for isolating the precise impact of the relationship in question, and the Court in *Parker* pointed to specific evidence of prejudice (including the testimony of one juror). Moreover, in its subsequent rulings, the Court has held that violations of the confrontation clause do not invariably require a reversal of a conviction, but are subject to the harmless error rule applied to constitutional error.[10] That rule requires a showing that the error was harmless beyond a reasonable doubt, which is the standard many courts utilize under a presumptive prejudice approach to misconduct.

The prejudice inquiry ordinarily centers on whether the misconduct in question might have influenced the juror in his evaluation of case. Some courts have suggested that a somewhat different focus is appropriate when the misconduct consists of a juror's failure to respond accurately to a question posed on voir dire. They would find prejudice, and require a new trial on a post-verdict challenge, where the false answer could have deceived the defense "into foregoing a peremptory challenge." They have suggested, moreover, that this standard should apply regardless of whether the false answer reflects intentional lying. A quite different approach was taken in the leading federal case on such misconduct, the Supreme Court's ruling in *McDonough Power Equipment v. Greenwood.*[11] Although a civil case, *McDonough* has been applied by the federal lower courts to criminal as well as civil cases. A juror there failed to disclose that his son had been injured by an apparently defective product and the defense claimed that this falsehood had deprived it of an opportunity intelligently to exercise its peremptory challenges. The Supreme Court held, however, that a quite different standard governed the right to a new trial in a false voir dire case. A party raising such a claim

> must first demonstrate that a juror failed to answer honestly a material question on voir dire, and then further show that a correct response would have provided a valid basis for a challenge for cause.

Not only does this standard look solely to the possible loss of a challenge for cause, but it also applies only where the juror answered dishonestly. A false answer produced by a juror's misunderstanding of the question

7. See Marshall v. United States, § 23.2 at note 10, where the Court held that the trial judge should have discharged the jurors notwithstanding their assurances of continued impartiality. See also § 23.2(e).

8. 379 U.S. 466, 85 S.Ct. 546, 13 L.Ed.2d 424 (1965).

9. 385 U.S. 363, 87 S.Ct. 468, 17 L.Ed.2d 420 (1966).

10. See § 27.6(d).

11. 464 U.S. 548, 104 S.Ct. 845, 78 L.Ed.2d 663 (1984).

would not be significant. So too, there would be no basis for a misconduct challenge where the juror answered according to what he thought was the right at the time (e.g., that he did not know a certain party), realized he was mistaken during trial, and then came forward and reported the matter to the court.

Some federal lower courts have suggested that *McDonough* is not as restricted as it might first appear. Where the juror purposely lied so as to avoid a peremptory challenge, that motivation is seen as providing a foundation for establishing actual bias. This is said to furnish an independent grounding for challenge, with the *McDonough* standard treated as aimed only at the question of whether the impact of the false answer in itself requires a new trial. All knowingly false answers, however, would not necessarily establish bias under this position. The juror may have lied without a purpose of avoiding a challenge and gaining a seat on the jury.

Where the misconduct challenge is raised in a post-verdict setting, and the applicable prejudice standard is met, the single available remedy is the granting of a new trial. This is true even if the misconduct affected a single juror and that juror's vote was not needed (i.e., the jurisdiction accepted less than unanimous verdicts), as the juror participated in the deliberations and may have influenced others. Where the misconduct challenge is established during trial and before the jury begins its deliberations, the trial court may often have several options. Where the misconduct affected only a few jurors and there exists an equal number of alternatives or extra jurors, the jurors affected by the misconduct can be replaced. Indeed, courts have been held to have discretion to replace jurors even though the showing as to prejudice does not meet what would be needed to order a new trial. If the jurors cannot be replaced with alternates or extras, the parties may be willing to proceed with less than the full number of jurors and that will also allow the affected jurors to be discharged without declaring a mistrial.

(g) Juror Testimony on Misconduct. The rule at early common law was that the testimony or affidavits of jurors could be received on a motion for a new trial based on misconduct in the jury room, and this practice was accepted and followed in this country. But then came the landmark English case of *Vaise v. Delaval,*[12] where Lord Mansfield refused to consider affidavits showing a verdict by lot on the ground that "a witness shall not be heard to allege his own turpitude." As a consequence, it became generally accepted in this country that a juror was incompetent to testify concerning the verdict under any circumstances. But there later arose discontent over the occasional harshness and injustice of this strict rule, and thus a number of jurisdictions began to develop exceptions to it. In several states, it was held that evidence was barred only as to matters that "inhere in the verdict." Other approaches included the aliunde rule, which allows a verdict to be impeached by a member of the jury only if a foundation is first laid by competent evidence from another source, a rule permitting impeachment when the misconduct is that of a third party rather than a juror, and a rule allowing impeachment if the misconduct occurred outside the jury room.

All of these approaches start from the premise that there are very sound reasons for limiting after-the-fact inquiry into jury verdicts. As the Supreme Court explained in *McDonald v. Pless,*[13] if verdicts were subject to being attacked and set aside on the testimony of those who participated in them, then

> all verdicts could be, and many would be, followed by an inquiry in the hope of discovering something which might invalidate the finding. Jurors would be harassed and beset by the defeated party in an effort to secure from them evidence of facts which might establish misconduct sufficient to set aside a verdict. If evidence thus secured could be thus used, the result would be to make what was intended to be a private deliberation, the constant subject of public investigation; to the

12. 99 Eng.Rep. 944 (KB 1785).

13. 238 U.S. 264, 35 S.Ct. 783, 59 L.Ed. 1300 (1915).

destruction of all frankness and freedom of discussion and conference.

Perhaps the prevailing standard today is that set forth in Rule 606(b) of the Federal Rules of Evidence. That Rule notes initially that, upon an inquiry into the validity of a verdict, "a juror may not testify as to any matter or statement occurring during the course of the jury's deliberations or the effect of anything upon his or any other juror's mind or emotions as influencing him to assent to or dissent from the verdict or * * * concerning his mental processes in connection therewith." This is a universally accepted prohibition, although a minority of states recognize a limited exception, namely, that evidence may be received to show the verdict was reached by lot; in defense thereof it has been said that "judicial economy is a weak justification for a completely arbitrary disposition of parties' rights."

A second provision of the Federal Rule acknowledges certain circumstances in which impeaching testimony by a juror may be received: "a juror may testify on the question whether extraneous prejudicial information was improperly brought to the jury's attention or whether any outside influence was improperly brought to bear upon any juror." An increasing number of state courts are following essentially this approach, although not always stated in those terms. As noted in the previous subsection, the Supreme Court in *Parker v. Gladden* held that extraneous prejudicial information improperly brought to a juror's attention could violate the defendant's Sixth Amendment rights both to confrontation of witnesses and impartiality of jury. The *Parker* ruling has led states to recognize a limited avenue of juror impeachment of a verdict by reference to such extraneous information (although, as with the Federal Rule, the juror may be prohibited from testifying as to whether that information was mentioned during deliberations or actually influenced his or her vote). As one state court put it, "where the Supreme Court holds that a particular series of events, when proven, violates a defendant's constitutional rights, implicit in that determination is the right of the defendant to prove facts substantiating his claim."

It should be emphasized, however, that both *Parker* and the Federal Rule refer only to external influences. The Supreme Court noted in *Tanner v. United States* [14] that no constitutional difficulties were presented in a jurisdiction prohibiting impeaching testimony by a juror with reference to "internal" influences, particularly where those influences are equally capable of outside proof. *Tanner* held that juror use of drugs and alcohol during trial was not an "external influence" within the Federal Rule 606(b) exception and therefore juror testimony about such use was barred under that Rule. Juror intoxication was to be treated no differently than mental incompetence or inattentiveness, matters that had long been viewed as "internal" influences. Rejecting the petitioners' contention that this exclusion of juror testimony infringed upon their right to a jury both "impartial and mentally competent," the Court noted that the Sixth Amendment right to "an unimpaired jury" was adequately protected by "several aspects of the trial process." It cited in this regard the availability of voir dire to examine the suitability of a prospective juror, the ability of counsel and the court to observe juror behavior during the trial, the ability of jurors to report misconduct to the trial judge during the trial, and the defense's ability to impeach a verdict by use of nonjuror evidence of misconduct.

"The right to use juror evidence," courts have noted, "necessarily implies a method to gather that evidence," and thus the growing recognition of the limited possibility of verdict impeachment by a juror naturally prompts the question of whether it is permissible for counsel to interview the jurors after verdict in an effort to discover grounds for challenging the verdict. As a matter of legal ethics, there is no absolute bar to such contacts: "After discharge of the jury from further consideration of a case with which the lawyer was connected, the lawyer shall not ask questions of or make comments to a member of that

14. 483 U.S. 107, 107 S.Ct. 2739, 97 L.Ed.2d 90 (1987).

jury that are calculated to harass or embarrass the juror or to influence his actions in future jury service." [15] But in some jurisdictions it is required that such contacts be first authorized by the trial judge, who can either conduct the questioning himself or pass upon the questions which may be asked by counsel. The notion is that "the jury system is best protected by a rule requiring that any post-verdict interviews of jurors by counsel, litigants, or their agents take place under the supervision and direction of the judge."

§ 24.7 Jury Verdicts

(a) Special Verdicts. The use of special verdicts, whereby the jury is required to respond to a series of fact questions in connection with the return of its verdict, is a common practice in civil but not criminal cases. The reason why special verdicts in criminal cases are not favored was pointed out in *United States v. Spock,*[1] where the jury was called upon, if it reached a general verdict of guilty on the charge that the defendants conspired to counsel, aid and abet registrants to resist the draft, to answer a series of questions called "special findings" about the defendants' conduct. In reversing the convictions, the court expressed concern

> with the subtle, and perhaps open, direct effect that answering special questions may have upon the jury's ultimate conclusion. There is no easier way to reach, and perhaps force, a verdict of guilty than to approach it step by step. A juror, wishing to acquit, may be formally catechized. By a progression of questions each of which seems to require an answer unfavorable to the defendant, a reluctant juror may be led to vote for a conviction which, in the large, he would have resisted. * * * It may be said that since the law should be logical and consistent, if the questions were proper in substance this would be a desirable rather than an undesirable result. [But in criminal cases there are other considerations, especially] the principle that the jury, as the conscience of the community, must be permitted to look at more than logic. * * * The constitutional guarantees of due process and trial by jury require that a criminal defendant be afforded the full protection of a jury unfettered, directly or indirectly.

Although the *Spock* decision was grounded in the court's supervisory power, the above language makes it apparent that the issue is of constitutional dimensions. If, as concluded earlier,[2] an aspect of the Sixth Amendment right to jury trial is what is commonly referred to as jury nullification, then certainly the use of special questions and verdicts in any criminal proceeding is suspect as a matter of due process. But there is no constitutional violation if the questions put to the jury lacked any capacity to catechize, color or coerce the jury's decision making.

If defendants ask for special findings, a trial court should not be concerned about those drawbacks of the process that relate to rights guaranteed to the defense. The defense should have it within its power to accept the risk that the special findings will reduce the potential for nullification or make more likely a compromise verdict by a jury that otherwise would have hung (by fragmenting the offense into various means of commission and therefore affording a divided jury a vehicle for compromise by saying no to some means and yes to others).

(b) Inconsistent Verdicts or Findings. In the federal courts, it is not necessary that the verdict returned by a jury be logically consistent in all respects. One type of situation is that in which there is inconsistency regarding separate counts against a single defendant, as in *Dunn v. United States.*[3] In affirming, the Court declared that the "most that can be said in such cases is that the verdict shows that either in the acquittal or the conviction the jury did not speak their real conclusions, but that does not show that they were not convinced of the defendant's

15. ABA Model Rules of Professional Conduct, Rule 4.4.

§ 24.7

1. 416 F.2d 165 (1st Cir.1969).

2. See § 22.1(g).

3. 284 U.S. 390, 52 S.Ct. 189, 76 L.Ed. 356 (1932).

guilt." The point was elaborated in *United States v. Dotterweich,*[4] affirming notwithstanding an inconsistency with respect to jointly tried defendants. In rejecting the defendant's contention that he was entitled to relief because the jury had convicted him, the corporation president, but not the corporation which was responsible for his conduct, the Court explained: "Whether the jury's verdict was the result of carelessness or compromise or a belief that the responsible individual should suffer the penalty instead of merely increasing, as it were, the cost of running the business of the corporation, is immaterial. Juries may indulge in precisely such motives or vagaries."

Although most state courts have followed the same approach, a substantial minority have taken the position that such inconsistency is reversible error. But it is better to have such inconsistency than to try to forbid it, for the rationale behind the rule permitting inconsistent verdicts in a single trial is that a jury may convict on some counts but not on others because of compassion or compromise. The exercise of such leniency, which is an aspect of the right to jury trial, is preferable to a system in which jurors, whenever they believed the defendant guilty, would be strong-armed into rendering an all-or-nothing verdict. By this reasoning, it has been held that the collateral estoppel rule of *Ashe v. Swenson*[5] has not undercut the *Dunn* line of authority.

In *United States v. Powell,*[6] the Supreme Court rejected the contention that the *Dunn* rule should be open to challenge in the particular case on a showing by the defense that the inconsistency in the verdict in that case was not in fact a product of lenity. The defendant there argued that lenity did not explain the verdict in his case, where the jury found him guilty of using the telephone to facilitate the commission of certain felonies, but acquitted on the counts charging the commission of those felonies. Where a jury was told that it must find the defendant guilty of the predicate offense to convict on the compound offense, and the jury then acquitted on the former and convicted on the latter, the logical explanation for the inconsistency, defendant noted, was a jury mistake adverse to the defendant. The *Powell* Court acknowledged that the *Dunn* rule rested in part on the fact that "it is unclear whose ox had been gored" by an inconsistent verdict. That uncertainty, presenting the distinct possibility that the inconsistency favored the defendant, coupled with the government's inability to challenge any harm to it by appeal of an acquittal, had led the Court to conclude that "inconsistent verdicts should not be reviewable." While a different conclusion might follow if it could positively be shown that the inconsistency was a product of an error that worked against the defendant, that simply could not be done. Any attempt at an "individualized assessment of the reason for the inconsistency would be based either on pure speculation or would require inquiries into the jury's deliberations that courts generally will not make." Defendant retains the protection of challenging the sufficiency of the evidence to support the verdict. But where the evidence was sufficient to sustain the conviction on the compound offense, it can hardly be said that this conviction was a "mistake" and acquittal on the predicate offense was "the one the jury 'really meant.'" Since the defendant was "given the benefit of her acquittal on the counts in which she was acquitted, * * * it is neither irrational nor illogical to require her to accept the burden of conviction on the counts in which the jury convicted."

What if the inconsistency appears in the findings of a judge who has tried the case without a jury? It has sometimes been held

4. 320 U.S. 277, 64 S.Ct. 134, 88 L.Ed. 48 (1943).

5. *Dunn* was written before Ashe v. Swenson held collateral estoppel to be a basic element of the double jeopardy protection of the Fifth Amendment, see § 17.-4(a), and the *Dunn* opinion therefore noted that the same inconsistent verdicts would have been allowed if the different charges had been tried separately—a result that would not hold true today, under collateral estoppel, if the acquittal came first. However, in United States v. Powell, infra note 6, the Court concluded that the *Dunn* rule remain supported by "a sound rationale that is independent of the theories of res judicata."

6. 469 U.S. 57, 105 S.Ct. 471, 83 L.Ed.2d 461 (1984).

that *Dunn* has no application in this context because it would not enhance respect for law or for the courts to recognize that a judge has the same power in the disposition of criminal charges that, for historic reasons, has been granted the jury. But in *Harris v. Rivera,*[7] the Supreme Court declined to reach that result as a constitutional matter, explaining that it was "not persuaded that an apparent inconsistency in a trial judge's verdict gives rise to an inference of irregularity in his finding of guilt that is sufficiently strong to overcome the well-established presumption that the judge adhered to basic rules of procedure." The Court added that there were various constitutionally acceptable explanations for the apparent inconsistency between the finding of defendant guilty and his accomplice not guilty: (1) that the judge had "a lingering doubt" about the guilt of the accomplice which he "might not be able to articulate in a convincing manner," in which case the law should not influence him "to convict all * * * rather than to try to articulate the basis for his doubt"; (2) that the judge made an error of law concerning the acquitted defendant, which as a constitutional matter certainly need not "redound to the benefit" of the convicted defendant; and (3) that "the acquittal is the product of a lenity that judges are free to exercise at the time of sentencing but generally are forbidden to exercise when ruling on guilt or innocence," which also would not amount to a constitutional violation, for there is "nothing in the Federal Constitution that would prevent a State from empowering its judges to render verdicts of acquittal whenever they are convinced that no sentence should be imposed for reasons that are unrelated to guilt or innocence."

(c) **Multi-Theory Verdicts.** Must a jury be instructed in such a way as to require that the jurors be in agreement on the theoretical basis of the defendant's guilt? In *Schad v. Arizona,*[8] the Supreme Court examined the constitutional aspects of this issue. The defendant there was convicted of first degree murder, defined by state law as murder that is "wilful, deliberate or premeditated * * * or which is committed * * * in the perpetration of, or attempt to perpetrate * * * robbery." The case was submitted to the jury under instructions that did not require unanimity on either of the available theories of premeditated murder and felony murder. In an opinion joined by three other members of the Court, Justice Souter declared that the due process clause places "limits on a State's capacity to define different courses of conduct, or states of mind, as merely alternative means of committing a single offense, thereby permitting a defendant's conviction without jury agreement as to which course or state actually occurred." It was, of course, well established that "an indictment need not specify which overt act, among several named, was the means by which a crime was committed" and that juries could return "general verdicts" in such cases without agreeing upon a "single means of commission." However, due process has long been held to impose a requisite degree of specificity, so that no person is punished "save upon proof of some specific illegal conduct." That requisite degree of specificity would be compromised if the state were allowed to join separate offenses with the jury not being directed to return separate verdicts on each, and the same would be true if a state were allowed to obtain a conviction under a single statutory offense "so generic" in coverage as to permit any combination of separate crimes to suffice for conviction. Thus, the critical issue was to ascertain "the point at which differences between means become so important that they may not reasonably be viewed as alternatives to a common end, but must be treated as differentiating what the Constitution requires to be treated as separate offenses."

Justice Souter initially rejected two possible standards for drawing the line required by due process. One, suggested in lower court rulings, was to ask whether the different alternatives fell into "distinct conceptual groupings," but this was unsatisfactory because "conceptual groupings may be identified at

7. 454 U.S. 339, 102 S.Ct. 460, 70 L.Ed.2d 530 (1981).

8. ___ U.S. ___, 111 S.Ct. 2491, 115 L.Ed.2d 555 (1991).

various levels of generality, and we have no *a priori* standard to determine what level of generality is appropriate." Another, suggested by the *Schad* dissenters, would rest on the characterization of the alternatives as independent elements of the offense, but having the Court render its own judgment in this regard "runs afoul of the fundamental principle that we are not free to substitute our own interpretations of state statutes for those of a State's courts." In the end, no "single criterion" could control. Ultimately, the Court's "sense of appropriate specificity" must be a "distillate of the concept of due process with its demands for fundamental fairness." In translating this demand for fairness into "concrete judgments," the Court would look initially to both "history and widespread practice as guides to fundamental values." At the same time, it would proceed from a "threshold presumption of legislative competence to determine the appropriate relationship between means and ends in defining the elements of the crime."

Applying this general approach, Justice Souter found that the Arizona statute provided sufficient specificity in treating premeditation and felony murder as alternative modes of establishing the "blameworthy state of mind required to prove a single offense of first-degree murder." Here "substantial historical and contemporary echoes" supported that characterization. At common law, "the intent to kill and the intent to commit a felony were alternative aspects of the single concept of 'malice aforethought.' " American jurisdictions, though modifying the common law by legislation classifying murder by degrees, had "in most cases retained premeditated murder and some form of felony murder * * * as alternative means of satisfying the mental state that first degree murder presupposes." A series of state decisions interpreting these first degree murder statutes reflected "widespread acceptance" of the concept that they simply established alternative means of satisfying the mens rea element of a single crime and therefore required unanimity only as to that ultimate element of mens rea and not as to the means themselves.

Cautioning that it cannot be said "that either history or current practice is dispositive," Justice Souter also emphasized the lack of "moral disparity" in the two alternative mental states. "Whether or not everyone would agree that the mental state that precipitates death in the course of robbery is the moral equivalent of premeditation, it is clear that such equivalence could reasonably be found, which is enough to rule out the argument that this moral disparity bars treating them as alternative means to satisfy the mental element of a single offense." By contrast, Justice Scalia, providing the fifth vote for affirmance, relied solely upon the fact that the challenged practice was "as old as the common law and still in existence in the vast majority of States." He was critical of the plurality's "moral equivalence" test, and noted that if it were not for the historical and current acceptance of a general verdict in first degree murder cases, he "might well be with the dissenters in this case." The four dissenters (per White, J.) argued that the statute here, "under a single heading, criminalizes several alternative patterns of conduct." The jury charge therefore rested on a due process violation, since "a State [cannot] invoke more than one statutory alternative, each with different specified elements, without requiring that the jury indicate on which of the alternatives it has based the defendant's guilt." The issue was not one of appropriate specificity, the dissent argued, but a due process requirement the jury find proof beyond a reasonable doubt of each of the elements required for criminal liability as specified by the state.

The different viewpoints expressed in *Schad* would seem to coalesce where modern statutes lump together in a single offense what was recognized at common law as separate offenses (e.g., including in a single theft state the obtaining of property by such diverse methods as larceny and false pretenses). Here, there would not exist historical support for treating those different means as what Justice Souter would characterize as "alternatives to a common end," reflecting "an immaterial difference as to mere means" rather than "separate theories of crime to be treated as separate offenses." While one could argue that "moral equivalence" existed as to culpability, that apparently would not be sufficient standing alone. As for the *Schad* dissenters, such a statute clearly would prohibit "alternative patterns of conduct," each "with different specified elements."

The more difficult case will be that of a crime that has no common law analogy. Here, however, there is not likely to be widespread acceptance of a generic verdict for a crime that specifies different means of commission unless those means reflect no more than different modes of establishing the same basic conduct (e.g., establishing driving while intoxicated under a statute that refers both to driving under the influence and driving with a specified blood-alcohol content). Where statutes prohibit distinct acts (as where a single code section prohibits a series of different acts of unlawful driving, such as speeding, illegal turns, and following too closely), state courts commonly require separate verdicts on each line of action alleged. A contrary position, in light of the combination of opinions in *Schad,* would be of doubtful constitutionality.

(d) Partial Verdicts. The term "partial verdict" refers to the situation in which the jury after some deliberation returns a verdict as to only some of the counts or some of the defendants because it has as yet been unable to decide the remaining matters before it. The return and receipt of a partial verdict as to less than all defendants or less than all counts is permitted in the state and federal courts. Depending upon the circumstances, it is permissible for the court to accept the partial verdict and then discharge the jury because of its inability to agree regarding the remaining matters, or to accept the partial verdict and then require the jury to resume deliberations concerning the matters still to be decided.

Chapter 25

RETRIALS AND DOUBLE JEOPARDY

Table of Sections

---

§ 25.1 Dimensions of the Guarantee

(a) Introduction. The double jeopardy clause of the Fifth Amendment states: "[N]or shall any person be subject for the same offence to be twice put in jeopardy of life or limb." Although this language might seem to have a bearing only in the single procedural context of retrying a person for the same crime, its applicability and influence extend far beyond that context. As a result, discussions of the double jeopardy limitation are scattered throughout this treatise.[1] The most significant and direct impact of the double jeopardy clause, however, is in the area of retrials and that is the aspect of double jeopardy law considered in this chapter. Sections two, three, and four consider retrials by the same sovereign on the same charges as were brought in an earlier trial. Section five deals with a second prosecution by a different sovereign on counterpart charges. Combined with the discussion in § 17.4(b) of second prosecutions by the same sovereign for separate statutory offenses that may be part of the "same offence" for double jeopardy purposes, this material presents the core of the double jeopardy prohibition.

Because of the central role of the limitations discussed in this chapter, an overview of the general features of the double jeopardy guarantee is most appropriately placed here. The overview seeks to bring together those structural principles that shape the overall scope of the double jeopardy bar.

(b) Policies and History. The most complete discussion by the Supreme Court of the policies underlying the double jeopardy clause is found in *United States v. DiFrancesco*.[2] As Justice Blackmun noted there, the preservation of the "finality of judgments" is commonly said to be "the," "the primary" or at least "a" purpose of the double jeopardy bar. This is not to suggest, however, that the double jeopardy clause is "simply res judicata dressed in prison grey." Finality here looks less to concerns of avoiding the costs of redundant litigation and relieving crowded dockets and more to the concerns of protecting the defendant against prosecution oppression. Thus, Justice Blackmun noted also that the "general design" of the double jeopardy bar was that set forth in an oft-quoted passage from Justice Black's opinion in *Green v. United States*:[3]

> The constitutional prohibition against "double jeopardy" was designed to protect an individual from being subjected to the hazards of trial and possible conviction more than once for an alleged offense. * * * The underlying idea, one that is deeply ingrained in at least the Anglo–American system of jurisprudence, is that the State with all its resources and power should not be allowed to make repeated attempts to convict an individual for an alleged offense, thereby subjecting him to embarrassment, expense and ordeal and compelling him to live in a continuing state of anxiety and insecurity, as well as enhancing the possibility that even though innocent he may be found guilty.

As *DiFrancesco* further explained, the adverse consequences of the governmental oppression described in *Green* are checked in several different ways by a double jeopardy clause aimed at preserving the "finality" or "integrity" of final judgments.

Initially, the protection of the innocent is served by what Justice Blackmun characterized as the "special weight" accorded to an "acquittal." The "public interest in the finality criminal judgments" here is recognized to be "so strong that an acquitted defendant may not be retried even though 'the acquittal was based on an egregious erroneous foundation.'" This "absolute finality" is "justified on the ground that, however mistaken the individual acquittal may have been, there would be an unacceptably high risk" to the innocent in allowing the government to override such a judgment and proceed anew. Where the verdict is that of the jury, there is always the possibility that the acquittal reflects the "jury's prerogative to acquit against the evidence." Moreover, to allow an acquittal to be less than absolutely final is to accept the possibility that a progression of juries could acquit, with each verdict losing its finality due to some flaw in the proceedings, until,

§ 25.1

1. See e.g., § 17.4(b) (joinder); §§ 21.2(d), 21.5(e) (plea withdrawal); § 26.7 (sentencing); § 27.3 (prosecution appeals).

2. 449 U.S. 117, 101 S.Ct. 426, 66 L.Ed.2d 328 (1980). Justice Blackmun noted that the Court had decided over 20 double jeopardy cases over the previous decade, and while application of the clause had proven "not * * * to be facile or routine," as evidence by various shifts and overrulings during that relatively short period, there had emerged a group of "general principles" that could be regarded as "essentially settled."

3. 355 U.S. 184, 78 S.Ct. 221, 2 L.Ed.2d 199 (1957).

sooner or later, some jury finally convicted. The danger of an "erroneous conviction from [such] repeated trials" is too great to acknowledge any exception to the absolute finality of the acquittal. Where "the innocence of the accused has been confirmed by a final judgment, the Constitution conclusively presume [through the double jeopardy clause] that a second trial would be unfair."

The threat of governmental oppression cited in *Green* poses a concern, however, that clearly goes beyond the threat to the innocent. There is also the unfairness of using the criminal prosecution to inflict additional burdens upon the individual, guilty or innocent, by subjecting him to "the embarrassment, expense, and ordeal" of repeated trials. The finality of judgments protects against such unfairness by according finality to judgments of conviction as well as acquittal. A defendant who is convicted and wishes to end the matter there can do so by simply accepting that judgment. This also serves to avoid the "continual state of anxiety and insecurity" mentioned in *Green,* for one consequence of allowing the prosecution to reprosecute after a conviction would be to allow it to seek a new and higher sentence for the same conviction. Indeed, speaking to the defendant's entitlement to a sense of repose following his acceptance of his conviction, the Supreme Court has noted that "it is the punishment that would legally follow the second conviction [if retrial were permitted] which is the real danger guarded against by the Constitution." [4] Accordingly, as *DiFrancesco* noted, the guarantee against double jeopardy has been said

> to consist of three separate constitutional protections. It protects against a second prosecution for the same offense after acquittal. It protects against a second prosecution for the same offense after conviction. And it protects against multiple punishments for the same offense.[5]

One might have thought, with the double jeopardy clause's central concern for preserving the finality of judgments, that the clause would apply only where the trial had reached a verdict. That position would follow from the common law grounding of the double jeopardy bar in the pleas of *autrefois acquit, autrefois convict,* and pardon. However, the Supreme Court recognized at an early point that the protection of verdict finality could be subverted by actions that terminated a trial prior to verdict and thereby took away from the defendant his opportunity to gain an acquittal. If such actions invariably allowed the prosecution to retry the defendant, the finality of a likely acquittal could be avoided and the prosecution could be given the opportunity to regroup and try again by simply not allowing the trial to proceed to a final verdict. Accordingly, the Court recognized as an aspect of jeopardy bar the protection of "the defendant's 'valued right' to have his trial completed by a particular tribunal." [6] Implicit in this protection is the recognition not only that there must be a barrier to prosecution manipulation of a trial termination to give it another chance, but also that the termination of the trial without verdict may hurt the defendant even without such manipulation. Every jury has its own character and the jury lost may be more favorably disposed to the defendant than the next jury. Also, apart from any difference in the trier of fact, "if the Government may reprosecute, it gains an advantage from what it learns at the first trial about the strengths of the defense case and the weakness of its own." [7] On the other hand, since the protection being afforded here was designed basically as a supplement to the core interest in preserving the integrity of judgments, the Court has concluded that these potential harms may be offset by other

4. Ex parte Lange, 85 U.S. 163 (18 Wall.) 163, 21 L.Ed. 872 (1873).

5. Quoting North Carolina v. Pearce, 395 U.S. 711, 89 S.Ct. 2072, 23 L.Ed.2d 656 (1969). As discussed in § 26.7, the latter prohibition is considerably less absolute than the language in *Pearce* might suggest and largely is aimed at multiple punishments that exceed the allowable punishment for the offense or that fail to give credit for the fulfillment of a previously imposed punishment for the same offense.

6. Wade v. Hunter, 336 U.S. 684, 69 S.Ct. 834, 93 L.Ed. 974 (1949).

7. United States v. DiFrancesco, supra note 1.

interests. This produces a case-by-case balancing approach, as compared to the absolutist standards often imposed in protecting verdict finality.

The double jeopardy clause has been described by commentators both as constitutional guarantee serving multiple purposes and as a guarantee serving a single purpose—"verdict finality"—that has several strands. From either perspective, one must deal with related but somewhat different values that move in the same direction but not necessarily with the same force. Thus even if those values alone shaped double jeopardy law, that law would produce somewhat different standards for different procedural contexts. But double jeopardy doctrine is also shaped by history. Indeed, the Court has stated that this is an area in which "Justice Holmes' aphorism that 'a page of history is worth a volume of logic' sensibly applies," as it involves a guarantee that "is rooted in history and is not an evolving concept like * * * due process." [8] Application of a truly functional approach would often take the doctrine beyond its historical content. On occasion, the Court has been willing to move in that direction. In dealing with the "same offence" limitation, for example, the Court has been willing to adopt positions that could not have been utilized nearly as readily at common law because of the lack of complete trial record available today. *Grady v. Corbin* went beyond an abstract matching of elements to find separate statutory offenses to be the "same offence" based on an analysis of the conduct utilized in establishing the two violations.[9] *Ashe v. Swensen* held that collateral estoppel was an element of double jeopardy based on the close functional relationship between that doctrine and the traditional acquittal rule in protecting a final adjudication favorable to the defense.[10] On the other hand, although one could argue that it constitutes oppression akin to that described in *Green* for a prosecutor to bring four separate prosecutions against a person who allegedly robbed the same bank by the same method on four consecutive days, the Court clearly is not willing to require that those prosecutions be brought together under a double jeopardy provision that speaks only to "the same offence." [11] Here, as in various other areas, well established historical distinctions override any concerns as to the functional validity of those distinctions.

The combination of several related but somewhat distinct values underlying the double jeopardy clause and an uneven response to history has produced a body of double jeopardy doctrine that various commentators have criticized as inconsistent, confusing, outmoded in a modern day procedural system, unduly technical, and too readily subject to manipulation by prosecutor and trial judge. On occasion, the Court itself has acknowledged that at least some of these criticisms are not that far off the mark. Indeed, it has described its double jeopardy decisions as "a veritable Sargasso Sea which would not fail to challenge the most interpreted judicial navigator." [12] It thus is not surprising that the Court has been led on more than one occasion to "rethink" and revise seemingly settled aspects of its double jeopardy jurisprudence,[13] and it would not be surprising if that process of rethinking and revision were continued in the future.

(c) Proceedings to Which Applicable. Read literally, the Fifth Amendment prohibition against a person being "twice put in jeopardy of life or limb" for "the same offence" would seem to be applicable only to criminal prosecutions and, indeed, only to

8. Richardson v. United States, 468 U.S. 317, 104 S.Ct. 3081, 82 L.Ed.2d 242 (1984); Gore v. United States, 357 U.S. 386, 78 S.Ct. 1280, 2 L.Ed.2d 1405 (1958).

9. See § 17.4(b).

10. See § 17.4(a).

11. See § 17.4(c), noting the Court's unwillingness to mandate even a "same transaction" standard that presumably would not extend so far as to include the four robberies noted above.

12. Albernaz v. United States, 450 U.S. 333, 101 S.Ct. 1137, 67 L.Ed.2d 275 (1981).

13. See e.g., United States v. Scott, 437 U.S. 82, 98 S.Ct. 2187, 57 L.Ed.2d 65 (1978), where Justice Rehnquist wrote for a majority reversing in part a majority opinion he had written only three years before. Justice Rehnquist there acknowledged "the force of the doctrine of *stare decisis,*" but concluded that the Court has "pressed too far" in his earlier opinion. See also note 2 supra.

those risking capital or corporal punishment. But the guarantee has been given a somewhat broader construction. For one thing, as the Court held in *Ex parte Lange*,[14] the double jeopardy clause extends to all "crimes." The Court in *Lange* reasoned that because the double jeopardy bar was based on the common law pleas of *autrefois acquit* and *autrefois convict*, which subsequently were held to apply to "felonies, minor crimes, and misdemeanors alike," the double jeopardy provision should follow this common law extension.

It may generally be said that the prohibition has no application in noncriminal cases. As the Supreme Court put it in *Helvering v. Mitchell*[15]: "Congress may impose both a criminal and a civil sanction in respect to the same act or omission; for the double jeopardy clause prohibits merely punishing twice, or attempting a second time to punish criminally, for the same offense." But this is not to suggest that merely labelling a proceeding as civil is the end of the matter. In *Breed v. Jones*,[16] holding that defendant could not be criminally tried for the same offense which was the basis of his prior juvenile court adjudicatory hearing, the Court rejected the contention that the double jeopardy clause was inapplicable by virtue of "the 'civil' label-of-convenience which has been attached to juvenile proceedings." Rather, the Court in *Breed* stressed that "in terms of potential consequences, there is little to distinguish an adjudicatory hearing such as was held in this case from a traditional criminal prosecution." This is because the adjudicatory hearing's "potential consequences include both the stigma inherent in * * * a determination [that defendant had violated the criminal law] and the deprivation of liberty for many years," so that the psychological, physical and financial burdens attending such a proceeding are comparable to those incident to a criminal prosecution.

Although *Breed*'s reference to comparable physical, psychological and financial burdens readily could be extended to place certain civil litigation or administrative hearings within the reach of the double jeopardy prohibition, *Breed* generally is viewed as having singled out only juvenile court hearings, as a part of the general "constitutionalization" of the juvenile court process. In other contexts, lower courts are more inclined to look to the Supreme Court's earlier precedent in *One Lot Emerald Cut Stones v. United States*,[17] holding the clause inapplicable to a proceeding to forfeit undeclared imports. The Court there posed as the critical question whether the purposes of the proceeding in question "characterize remedial rather than punitive sanctions." Thus, the double jeopardy guarantee has been held inapplicable to such actions as commitment proceedings for mental illness or sexual psychopathy, disciplinary proceedings against prisoners affecting their release date, civil contempt proceedings, civil paternity actions, civil lawsuits recovering treble damages or punitive damages, and proceedings to suspend or terminate government employment, a government contract, or a license to engage in a profession or business.

There always remains the possibility, however, as the Supreme Court found in *United States v. Halper*,[18] that even the application in a civil suit of a sanction normally deemed remedial can be so clearly unrelated to any purpose other than punishment, under the circumstances of the particular case, as to bring that sanction within the reach of the double jeopardy prohibition. In *Halper*, that was held to be the case where a defendant, initially convicted under the criminal false-claims act, was later sued under the civil false-claims act for "civil penalties" for the same violations, with the government seeking $130,000 for 65 false claims that totaled $585. *One Lot Emerald Cut* had recognized that the calculation of remedial justice could be "rough," allowing for "imprecise formulas" such as "a fixed sum plus double damages."

14. Supra note 4.

15. 303 U.S. 391, 58 S.Ct. 630, 82 L.Ed. 917 (1938).

16. 421 U.S. 519, 95 S.Ct. 1779, 44 L.Ed.2d 346 (1975).

17. 409 U.S. 232, 93 S.Ct. 489, 34 L.Ed.2d 438 (1972).

18. 490 U.S. 435, 109 S.Ct. 1892, 104 L.Ed.2d 487 (1989).

Halper, however, was one of those "rare cases" where application of such a formula produced a result so completely unrelated to the remedial goal "of making the government whole" that it could be explained only as serving the "retributive or deterrent purposes" associated with "punishment."

(d) When Jeopardy Attaches. Termination of a proceeding before jeopardy has attached, even if clearly harmful to the defendant in some way, does not entitle him to relief under the double jeopardy clause, while termination thereafter brings into play the various rules of double jeopardy, most of which operate automatically on a presumption of harm. In a case to be tried by a jury, jeopardy attaches when the jury is empaneled and sworn, that is, when the entire jury has been selected and has taken the oath required for service at trial. The effect of this rule is illustrated by *Downum v. United States* [19] and *Serfass v. United States.*[20] In *Downum* a mistrial was declared without sufficient reason just after the jury had been sworn but before any testimony had been taken, and thus retrial was impermissible. But in *Serfass* a dismissal by the trial judge which was arguably viewed as an acquittal did not bar a later trial because the defendant had sought a jury trial and the jury had not yet been selected when the judge entered the dismissal.

Crist v. Bretz[21] holds that the double jeopardy clause does not allow a stae sufficient flexibility to utilize a slightly later point of attachment of jeopardy in jury cases. In that case a mistrial was granted without sufficient reason after the jury was sworn but before the first witness was called, which the lower court held did not prevent retrial because of a state rule that jeopardy attaches in both jury and non-jury cases only after the first witness is sworn. The state contended that the sworn-jury standard, traditionally applied in federal courts, was "no more than an arbitrarily chosen rule of convenience, similar in its lack of constitutional status to the federal requirement of unanimous verdict of 12 jurors." Rejecting that contention, the Court majority stressed the historical development of the double jeopardy bar. Though the Fifth Amendment guarantee was once viewed as protecting only the finality of judgment and thus came into play only after entry of a judgment of conviction or acquittal, over the years the defendant's "valued right to have his trial completed before a particular tribunal" had become an essential element of the constitutional guarantee. This meant that the federal rule had become a part of that guarantee, as it

> reflects and protects the defendant's interest in retaining a chosen jury. We cannot hold that this rule, so grounded, is only at the periphery of double jeopardy concerns. Those concerns—the finality of judgments, the minimization of harassing exposure to the harrowing experience of a criminal trial, and the valued right to continue with the chosen jury—have combined to produce the federal law that in a jury trial jeopardy attached when the jury is empaneled and sworn.

In a case which is to be tried by a judge without a jury, jeopardy attaches only after the first witness has been sworn. As for those cases in which a guilty plea disposes of the case without trial, jeopardy attaches when the court accepts the defendant's plea unconditionally and enters the conviction thereon.

Under eighteenth century English common law, exceptions to the pleas of prior conviction or acquittal existed where the trial court was said to lack jurisdiction, the theory being that defendant therefore was not placed in jeopardy. The Supreme Court in *United States v. Ball* [22] refused to follow an important aspect of that English rule. *Ball* rejected the contention that a defendant had not been placed in jeopardy because he had been tried under a defective indictment. It also rejected the additional "jurisdictional" contention that jeopardy did not terminate because the order discharging the jury was improperly issued on a

19. 372 U.S. 734, 83 S.Ct. 1033, 10 L.Ed.2d 100 (1963), discussed in § 25.2 at note 9.

20. 420 U.S. 377, 95 S.Ct. 1055, 43 L.Ed.2d 265 (1975), discussed at note 24 infra.

21. 437 U.S. 28, 98 S.Ct. 2156, 57 L.Ed.2d 24 (1978).

22. 163 U.S. 662, 16 S.Ct. 1192, 41 L.Ed. 300 (1896).

Sunday, when the trial court had no authority to act. In the later case of *Kepner v. United States*,[23] the Court's lengthy discussion of the double jeopardy clause referred at several points to the finality of a verdict issued by a trial court "having jurisdiction." The Court also spoke of application of the double jeopardy clause where one has been tried before a "tribunal properly organized and competent to try him." Its point of reference, however, was to the extension of the double jeopardy clause to the trial verdicts of judges, as well as juries. The cited limitation apparently was not to "jurisdiction" in its usual sense, for *Ball* seemingly had rejected such a prerequisite, but to the authority of the court rendering the judgment to exercise trial authority. A court could not take a case that simply was in any way before it and render a verdict that would be entitled to the finality that attached under the double jeopardy clause. This quite narrow concept of a judicial "competency" or "jurisdiction" acting as a prerequisite for double jeopardy protection is illustrated by *Serfass v. United States*,[24] where the Court quoted from *Kepner* in holding that the double jeopardy clause did not come into play because the judgment in question there was entered by a judge who did not have "jurisdiction to try the question of the guilt or innocence of the accused."

The trial court in *Serfass* made factual as well as legal determinations in granting a motion to dismiss prior to the scheduled trial date. If that ruling were viewed simply as pretrial dismissal, then jeopardy obviously had not attached. The defense argued, however, that the ruling should be viewed as the equivalent of a bench trial acquittal, for the judge had ruled that evidence available to him through the disclosure of a government file established an automatic defense to the charge. That argument failed on several grounds, including the analysis of *Kepner*. If the ruling were to be taken as an acquittal, as the defense urged, then the judge clearly lacked authority to enter such an order at that point in the proceeding. No jury had been selected (nor any evidence presented to it), and the presentation of the file to the judge could not be viewed as a form of bench trial, since the parties had not waived their right to a jury and agreed to a bench trial. A similar lack of authority defeated an attempt to portray a dismissal as an acquittal in *United States v. Sanford*,[25] although jeopardy there clearly had attached and the issue was whether jeopardy had been terminated by a dismissal on the evidence. In that case, a hung jury in the original trial resulted in the scheduling of a retrial. Four months later, prior to the second trial, the trial judge dismissed the indictment on the basis of his view of the evidence at the first trial. Defendant claimed that the judge's ruling had been an acquittal, and therefore was entitled to finality. The Supreme Court rejected that claim because the judge was not a "competent tribunal," at that point, for entering an acquittal; if the judge had entered his order within seven days after the ending of the first trial, which was the period allowed for a post-trial judgment of acquittal, then that order would have been treated as an acquittal and would have precluded further proceedings.[26] As it stood, however, the ruling was no different than that in *Serfass*.

A roughly analogous ruling, based on a different rationale, is found in *Ohio v. Johnson*.[27] There a state trial judge, over the prosecutor's objection, accepted a plea to a lesser-included offense, and sought to treat that plea as final conviction barring prosecution on the offense charged, since it was for the "same offence" for double jeopardy purposes. Holding that double jeopardy did not bar prosecution on the original charge, the Court reasoned that the defendant had no authority to subdivide the indictment, enter a plea to only one part, and then maintain that

23. 195 U.S. 100, 24 S.Ct. 797, 49 L.Ed. 114 (1904).

24. Supra note 20.

25. 429 U.S. 14, 97 S.Ct. 20, 50 L.Ed.2d 17 (1976).

26. See United States v. Martin Linen Supply, 430 U.S. 564, 97 S.Ct. 1349, 51 L.Ed.2d 642 (1977), finding an order entered within the 7 day period to be an acquittal. Consider also Fong Foo v. United States, § 25.3 at note 9.

27. 467 U.S. 493, 104 S.Ct. 2536, 81 L.Ed.2d 425 (1984).

the plea ended the case. The state not having agreed and the court lacking the capacity to deny the prosecution the opportunity to prove its charge, the guilty plea could not be taken as a final judgment disposing of that charge. Unlike other cases where guilty pleas barred subsequent charges, the state here had not sought to present the lesser-included and higher charges in separate proceedings,[28] and the defense could not force separate treatment and then "use the double jeopardy clause as a sword to prevent the State from completing its prosecution on the remaining charges." Just as the trial court could not have created a double jeopardy bar on the higher charge by dismissing that charge prior to the swearing of the jury, neither could it do so by accepting a plea to the lesser charge.

(e) Termination of Jeopardy. In *Kepner v. United States*,[29] Justice Holmes, in a dissenting opinion, formulated a concept of "continuing jeopardy" which was rejected in the context in which he presented it, but which continues to survive in other settings. Holmes argued that once jeopardy attached, it continued on through the proceedings that flowed from that original charge. "Logically, and rationally," Holmes argued, "a man cannot be said to be more than once in jeopardy on the same cause, however often he may be tried. The jeopardy is one continuing jeopardy from its beginning to the end of the cause." Under this view, there would be no prohibition against a government appeal from an acquittal, a reversal by the appellate court, and a retrial on the original charge. The majority in *Kepner* rejected that position, as it concluded that the acquittal terminated the initial jeopardy so that a second trial would place the defendant twice in jeopardy. The same position has also been taken with respect to a judgment of conviction, although the defendant who elects to challenge the conviction opens the door to removing its finality.

In *Justices of Boston Municipal Court v. Lydon*,[30] the Court did rely on a continuing jeopardy rationale in the context of a trial de novo system of appeal. In that case, the defendant, after being convicted in the magistrate's court, sought to raise, on appeal to the general trial court, the alleged insufficiency of the evidence underlying that conviction. The general trial court ruled that such a challenge was not allowed, as the only remedy available was a trial de novo. Defendant then responded that if the prosecution's case before the magistrate court was insufficient to sustain a conviction, he should have been acquitted and the trial de novo would now place him twice in jeopardy. The Supreme Court majority, in rejecting that argument, viewed the trial in the magistrate's court and the trial de novo as a two-stage continuous proceeding rather than as two separate trials. Thus, the defendant's claim was no different than that of the defendant who loses a motion for directed acquittal at the end of the prosecution's case-in-chief and then is forced to continue to the end of the trial. If the evidence is sufficient at the end of the trial, he may be convicted, and he cannot claim to have been twice exposed to jeopardy because he should have been acquitted at the end of the case-in-chief.

The trial that is terminated without a verdict on defendant's guilt or innocence, as when a mistrial is declared, also presents a case in which jeopardy is continuing. Thus, in *Richardson v. United States*,[31] the Court reached a result that paralleled that in *Justices of Boston Municipal Court* in a mistrial case. Defendant there claimed that he should not be forced to a second trial following a jury deadlock that resulted in a mistrial since the trial judge had erred in failing to grant defendant's motion for a judgment of acquittal based on the insufficiency of the evidence at that first trial. The Court rejected that contention as improperly viewing the first and second trials as separate subjections to jeopardy. "The failure of the jury to reach a verdict," the Court reasoned, "is not an event which terminates jeopardy," and the mistrial

28. See e.g., Grady v. Corbin, discussed in § 17.4(b).

29. Supra note 22.

30. 466 U.S. 294, 104 S.Ct. 1805, 80 L.Ed.2d 311 (1984).

31. 468 U.S. 317, 104 S.Ct. 3081, 82 L.Ed.2d 242 (1984).

ordered by the judge in response to the jury deadlock had been entered consistent with double jeopardy principles. Accordingly, the government remained "entitled to resolution of the case by verdict from the jury," and the situation presented was essentially that of a completed first stage in an ongoing proceeding.

The lack of a termination of jeopardy where there has been no verdict relates back to the double jeopardy's primary concern with the protection of verdict finality. However, the Court has also recognized a need to guard against subversion of that protection through governmental action that denies the defendant the opportunity to see the trial through to a verdict. It therefore finds in the double jeopardy clause, as discussed in § 25.2, certain restrictions upon judicial authority to grant a mistrial. Where those restrictions are violated, the retrial of the defendant amounts, in effect, to a second jeopardy. Thus, while a mistrial declared consistent with double jeopardy principles does not terminate jeopardy, as recognized in *Richardson,* a mistrial that violates those principles will be viewed otherwise.

(f) The "Same Offence." Offenses for double jeopardy purposes are not defined by reference to separate titles or separate statutory sections. Two offenses may have different titles and be prohibited by different statutory sections yet constitute the "same offence" for double jeopardy purposes. As discussed in § 17.4(b), whether separate statutory or common law offenses are the same for double jeopardy purposes requires an inquiry into both the elements of the two crimes and the conduct used in the individual case to satisfy the elements of the two charges. However, as discussed in § 17.4(a), even if the two offenses are not the same, an acquittal in the first prosecution may bar prosecution in the second under the doctrine of collateral estoppel, which is also an aspect of the double jeopardy bar.

Although two offenses would otherwise be the same when tested by reference to their statutory elements and the conduct establishing those elements, separate prosecutions will not be prohibited when different sovereigns (state and federal or different states) are involved. Under the doctrine of dual sovereignty, discussed in § 25.5, prosecutions by different sovereigns for precisely the same conduct under even identical statutes are not barred by the double jeopardy prohibition.

(g) Reprosecutions: An Overview. The balance of this chapter is concerned with the double jeopardy implications, in various procedural settings, of a second prosecution that rests on much the same criminal conduct as an earlier prosecution. Even as to such reprosecutions, however, that discussion provides less than a complete picture as material in other chapters also deals with certain aspects of such multiple prosecutions. The overview that follows, at the risk of oversimplification, seeks to bring together the essence of the double jeopardy principles relevant to reprosecutions that are discussed both in this chapter and in several others. Those principles are:

(1) Multiple initiation of a prosecution that never reaches the point of bringing jeopardy into play, as where the prosecution repetitively files complaints that are subsequently rejected in judicial or grand jury screening, does not create a double jeopardy difficulty. See § 25.1(c).

(2) Multiple prosecutions that produce multiple trials are not prohibited if they are for different offenses—unless collateral estoppel applies because the first trial resulted in an acquittal based on a failure of proof as to an element also required for the offense presented in the second trial. See § 17.4(a), (b).

(3) Separate prosecutions producing separate trials on statutory offenses that are the same offense are not prohibited where the defendant, by his request or otherwise, is solely responsible for the separate trials. See § 17.4(b).

(4) Multiple trials on a single charge are not prohibited if the first trial resulted in a mistrial that was justified under the manifest necessity doctrine or was requested or consented to by the defense (absent prosecutorial

overreaching that is aimed at forcing the mistrial). See § 25.2.

(5) If there has been a dismissal of the prosecution after jeopardy attached, and that dismissal is based on some preliminary error that does not permanently terminate the prosecution, but allows the prosecution to reprosecute after curing that error (as where the dismissal was based on a defective pleading), that dismissal is treated in much the same fashion as a mistrial. Where the principles governing mistrials would allow the prosecution to cure the error and return for a retrial, the prosecution may also, consistent with double jeopardy, seek appellate review of the dismissal and renew the prosecution if the appellate court holds that the dismissal was erroneous. See § 25.2(f).

(6) If there has been a dismissal of the prosecution after jeopardy attached, that dismissal was on a ground permanently terminating the prosecution (e.g., denial of a speedy trial), and the defendant moved for the dismissal, double jeopardy does not prohibit a prosecution appeal and a subsequent retrial if the dismissal is held to be erroneous. See § 25.3(a).

(7) If the jury reaches a verdict of acquittal or the judge grants a judgment of acquittal prior to jury verdict, double jeopardy bars a new trial even if it appears that the acquittal was based on an erroneous interpretation of the law. Included in the concept of an acquittal is the implied acquittal that comes when a jury returns a verdict of guilty on a lesser-included offense and fails to indicate its disposition of the higher charge. The one exception to the concept that an acquittal ends all further proceeding arises in the special setting in which the trial judge grants a judgment of acquittal after the jury returned a guilty verdict. Here, if the appellate court should find that the judge erred in entering the acquittal, the jury verdict of conviction can be restored. See §§ 25.3, 25.4(d).

(8) If there is a jury verdict of conviction, defendant may rest on the conviction, and it will bar any reprosecution on the same offense in much the same manner as an acquittal. If the defendant appeals the conviction and it is reversed, then the defendant ordinarily may be proceeded against by reprosecution without running afoul of the double jeopardy bar. The one exception is where the appellate court set aside the conviction on the ground that the evidence was insufficient for a reasonable person to find guilt beyond a reasonable doubt. See § 25.4.

(9) If the court enters a conviction based upon a plea of guilty accepted without condition, the defendant may rest upon that conviction and double jeopardy will bar a new prosecution for the same offense. However, where the defendant enters a plea only to a lesser aspect of the charge, the entry of a conviction on that plea does not present a double jeopardy bar to the continuation of the same prosecution to verdict on the higher aspect of the charge, though it is a part of the same offense. See § 25.1(d). Also, if a plea and conviction are entered with a condition that the defendant take certain action, and the prosecution reserves the right to reinstitute the prosecution if the defendant violates that condition, double jeopardy will not bar the reinstitution of the charge as provided in the plea agreement. See § 21.2(d). Finally, where the defendant chooses not to rest on the conviction, and has it overturned by challenging or gaining withdrawal of the underlying plea, double jeopardy does not bar a subsequent trial for the same offense. See §§ 21.5(e), 25.4.

(10) If a second trial is allowed after an overturned conviction, the court is not barred by double jeopardy from imposing a greater sentence on a reconviction for the same offense than had been imposed on the original conviction. The resentenced defendant must, however, receive credit for any time served on the first sentence. Moreover, double jeopardy will not bar an appropriate statute providing for a government appeal of a sentence as legally incorrect. See § 26.7.

(11) Multiple prosecutions that would otherwise be barred under the principles noted above are not prohibited where the prosecutions are brought by separate sovereigns

(state and federal or different states). See § 25.5.

§ 25.2 Reprosecution Following Mistrial

(a) With Defendant's Consent. The mistrial situation which is usually the easiest to deal with in terms of the double jeopardy guarantee is that which is brought about by the request of or with the acquiescence of the defendant. The leading case is *United States v. Dinitz,*[1] where the trial judge excluded defense counsel from the case for misconduct and then gave the defendant the choice of a recess while the court of appeals passed upon the exclusion, a mistrial, or continuation of the trial with the assistant defense counsel. The defendant opted for a mistrial, but the court of appeals held he could not be retried because there was no manifest necessity for the mistrial and defendant's action had not constituted a valid waiver of his double jeopardy claim. The Supreme Court disagreed, noting that there is a significant distinction between a mistrial declared by the court sua sponte, where the "manifest necessity" test applies, and one granted at defendant's request, where "a motion by the defendant for mistrial is ordinarily assumed to remove any barrier to reprosecution, even if the defendant's motion is necessitated by prosecutorial or judicial error." That rule, the Court explained in *Dinitz,* is fully consistent with the purposes underlying the double jeopardy protection:

> The defendant may reasonably conclude that a continuation of the tainted proceeding would result in a conviction followed by a lengthy appeal and, if a reversal is secured, by a second prosecution. In such circumstances, a defendant's mistrial request has objectives not unlike the interests served by the Double Jeopardy Clause—the avoidance of the anxiety, expense, and delay occasioned by multiple prosecutions.

As for the court of appeals' contention that Dinitz had not voluntarily waived his double jeopardy protection because of the "Hobson's choice" he was confronted with, the Court responded that "traditional waiver concepts have little relevance" in this context. Rather, the "important consideration * * * is that the defendant retains primary control over the course to be followed in the event of such error." The approach of the court of appeals, the Supreme Court added, would often deprive the defendant of the type of relief which would be most desirable to him. "In the event of severely prejudicial error a defendant might well consider an immediate new trial a preferable alternative to the prospect of a probable conviction followed by an appeal, a reversal of the conviction, and a later retrial."

Although in *Dinitz* the defendant actually requested a mistrial, the "consent doctrine" of that case also applies in those instances in which the defendant did not move for a mistrial but expressed agreement with the judge's announced intention to grant one. Some courts have gone so far as to suggest that silence constitutes tacit consent even where defense counsel was not asked for his views on the mistrial, but this position has been rightly criticized. The better view is that mere silence is not enough, especially when the proceedings were fast paced, the termination of the proceedings abrupt, or the announced basis one which hardly would be affected by defense opposition. Similarly, the mere fact that a codefendant has moved for a mistrial does not mean that a defendant joined with him for trial is bound by that consent.

(b) The "Goaded" Mistrial Motion. For some years prior to *Oregon v. Kennedy,*[2] the Supreme Court had recognized that even if a mistrial was brought about with the consent of the defendant, in some limited circumstances there would still exist a double jeopardy bar to reprosecution. To use the language employed by the Court in *United States v. Jorn,*[3] this was where the circumstances prompting the mistrial were "attributable to prosecutorial or judicial overreaching." As

§ 25.2

1. 424 U.S. 600, 96 S.Ct. 1075, 47 L.Ed.2d 267 (1976).

2. 456 U.S. 667, 102 S.Ct. 2083, 72 L.Ed.2d 416 (1982).

3. 400 U.S. 470, 91 S.Ct. 547, 27 L.Ed.2d 543 (1971).

the Court explained in *Kennedy:* "In such a case, the defendant's valued right to complete his trial before the first jury would be a hollow shell if the inevitable motion for mistrial were held to prevent a later invocation of the bar of double jeopardy in all circumstances." Exactly what it would take to constitute such overreaching remained in doubt, as the Court's dictum on this point utilized seemingly conflicting language. In *United States v. Dinitz,* for example, the Court at one point articulated the exception in terms of "government actions intended to provoke mistrial requests," but at another point stated it as covering "bad faith conduct" or "harassment" by the judge or prosecutor. In *Kennedy,* a sharply divided Court resolved this issue. The majority there held that "[o]nly where the governmental conduct in question is intended to 'goad' the defendant into moving for a mistrial may a defendant raise the bar of Double Jeopardy to a second trial after having succeeded in aborting the first on his own motion."

The Court in *Kennedy* reasoned that an "intent" test was necessary in order to have "a manageable standard to apply" in mistrial cases. The intent standard, the Court explained, "merely calls for the [trial] court to make a finding of fact," using the "familiar process in our criminal justice system" of "[i]nferring the existence or nonexistence of intent from objective facts and circumstances." By contrast, a broader bad faith or harassment standard would be difficult to apply and would be at issue in virtually every case, as "[e]very act on the part of a rational prosecutor during a trial is designed to 'prejudice' the defendant by placing before the judge or jury evidence leading to a finding of his guilt." A second consideration was that a broader test would be counterproductive because it would influence the denial of mistrial requests: "Knowing that the granting of the defendant's motion for mistrial would all but inevitably bring with it an attempt to bar a second trial on grounds of double jeopardy, the judge presiding over the first trial might well be more loath to grant a defendant's motion for mistrial."

Four justices dissented from the Court's standard, although joining in its judgment on the facts of the case. They maintained that it should be "sufficient that the court is persuaded that egregious prosecutorial misconduct has rendered unmeaningful the defendant's choice to continue or to abort the proceeding." Where the prosecution's intentional misconduct had forced the defense to seek a mistrial, the double jeopardy clause should protect the defense against a retrial without regard to whether the prosecutor had intended either to force the mistrial motion, to harass and embarrass the defendant, or to ensure a conviction. Responding to the majority's concern that such a standard would lead defense counsel to seek to turn every act of prosecutorial error into an overreaching that forced a mistrial motion and thereby barred retrial, the dissenters argued that their proposed requirement of a two-pronged ruling of (i) "deliberate misconduct" and (ii) resulting prejudice "that * * * at least substantially reduced the probability of an acquittal" would limit successful overreaching claims to the "rare and compelling case." Several state courts, relying on their state constitutions, have adopted overreaching standards similar to that advanced by the *Kennedy* minority.

The *Kennedy* dissenters also argued that it would be virtually impossible for a defendant ever to prevail under the Court's intent standard: "It is almost inconceivable that a defendant would prove that the prosecutor's deliberate misconduct was motivated by an intent to provoke a mistrial instead of an intent simply to prejudice the defendant." The dissenters argued that even when the prosecution's case was weak and seemed destined for jury rejection, one could just as readily assume that intentional prejudice introduced by the prosecutor was designed to turn the jury around rather than to face a mistrial. Justice Powell, who concurred in the majority's opinion, also wrote separately to underscore the majority's apparent response to this contention. While the intention of the prosecutor was the key, " 'subjective' intent often may be unknowable," and therefore a trial court would "rely primarily upon the objective facts and circumstances of the particular case" in determining intent. The strength of the evidence would seem to be one of the most telling of those circumstances, along with the timing of the misconduct, the immediate event that provoked the misconduct, and whether it was an instance of repetitive misconduct that came after a trial court warning that continued misconduct could lead to a mistrial. Looking to these factors, at least in the scenario posed by the minority of a last ditch introduction of prejudice in a weak case, a trial court could quite readily conclude that the prosecutor met the intent test of the *Kennedy* majority.

(c) The "Manifest Necessity" Standard. As for the declaration of a mistrial by the trial judge sua sponte or over the defendant's objection, the "fountainhead decision" is *United States v. Perez.*[4] In that case, in which a unanimous Court held that the failure of the jury to agree on a verdict of either acquittal or conviction did not bar retrial of the defendant, the Court reasoned:

> We think, that in all cases of this nature, the law has invested Courts of justice with the authority to discharge a jury from giving any verdict, whenever, in their opinion, taking all the circumstances into consideration, there is a manifest necessity for the act, or the ends of public justice would otherwise be defeated. They are to exercise a sound discretion on the subject; and it is impossible to define all the circumstances, which would render it proper to interfere. To be sure, the power ought to be used with the greatest of caution, under urgent circumstances * * *.

The Court in *Perez* spoke of either a "manifest necessity" or the "ends of public justice" requiring the mistrial. Later opinions collapsed these alternatives into a single standard, described as a "manifest necessity" standard that means less than what the words might suggest on their face. As the Court stated in *Arizona v. Washington*[5]:

> "The words 'manifest necessity' appropriately characterize the magnitude of the prosecutor's burden. * * * [But] it is manifest that the key word 'necessity' cannot be interpreted literally; instead, contrary to the teaching of Webster, we assume that there are degrees of necessity and we require a 'high degree' before concluding that the mistrial is appropriate."

In the end, the manifest necessity standard requires a balancing process. On the one side, the court considers the defendant's interest in having the trial completed in a single proceeding, and thereby preserving the possibility of obtaining an acquittal before that "particular tribunal." On the other side is the strength of the justification for turning to a mistrial rather than attempting to carry the trial through to a verdict, if possible. Of course, lurking in the background is the recognition that an appellate court ruling which finds that the trial judge improperly balanced these factors in ordering a mistrial operates to deprive the state of a full opportunity to establish the guilt of a person who well may be guilty. On top of these considerations, *Kennedy*[6] indicates that manifest necessity will not provide the complete answer as to whether a retrial is permissible. Even if the mistrial was compelled by necessity so great as to be almost absolute, where the condition that prevented the trial from continuing was purposely created by the prosecution in order to compel a mistrial, the rationale of *Kennedy* suggests that double jeopardy would bar a retrial. A prosecution can no more be allowed to "goad" a judge into declaring a mistrial than to goad a defendant into requesting a mistrial.

The Supreme Court has emphasized that each manifest necessity ruling is bottomed on its own facts. The manifest necessity standard "abjures the application of any mechanical formula by which to judge the propriety of declaring a mistrial in the varying and often unique situations arising during the course of a criminal trial." At the same time, some general guidelines can be distilled from past cases. The two subsections that follow examine the most significant of those guidelines.

4. 22 U.S. (9 Wheat.) 579, 6 L.Ed. 165 (1824).

5. 434 U.S. 497, 98 S.Ct. 824, 54 L.Ed.2d 717 (1978).

6. Supra note 2.

(d) Manifest Necessity and Alternatives to a Mistrial. Much of the case law applying the manifest necessity doctrine revolves upon the proper evaluation of alternatives to a mistrial. The Supreme Court has insisted that the trial judge give consideration to such alternatives and the failure to do so may, in itself, lead to a finding of a lack of manifest necessity. Illustrative is *United States v. Jorn.*[7] The trial judge, upon concluding that the government's witnesses did not understand the extent to which they might incriminate themselves, ordered a mistrial so as to allow the witnesses to consult with attorneys before deciding whether to testify. In finding a lack of manifest necessity, the plurality stressed that the trial judge gave absolutely "no consideration" to the alternative of a trial continuance, and "indeed, * * * acted so abruptly in discharging the jury" that the parties were given no opportunity to suggest the alternative of a continuance or to object in advance to the jury discharge. The plurality concluded that where, as here, a trial judge simply "made no effort to exercise sound discretion to assure that * * * there was a manifest necessity for the * * * sua sponte declaration of a mistrial," a "reprosecution would violate the double jeopardy provision of the Fifth Amendment." In the later case of *Arizona v. Washington,*[8] the Court rejected the contention that the *Jorn* analysis mandated that the trial judge make explicit findings as to the need for a mistrial in light of alternatives, but it did insist that there be apparent from the trial record a "sufficient justification" for the mistrial ruling that reflected consideration of those alternatives.

At times, the issue arises as to whether the alternatives that must be considered would include those requiring a relinquishment of rights or an alteration of the usual trial process. Consider, for example, the case in which there does not remain the requisite number of jurors because a juror has been disqualified, discharged, or excused because of illness. If the jurisdiction is one in which the trial may continue with eleven jurors on agreement of the judge and the parties, must the eleven person jury be adopted as alternative to the mistrial if the defense, desiring to continue through to verdict, agrees to the smaller jury? Some authority suggests that a mistrial is inappropriate where the state blocks the eleven juror alternative and gives no compelling reason for insisting upon a twelve person jury that can be obtained only through a new trial. Elsewhere it has been held that the prosecution is never obligated to waive its right to a twelve person jury. A similar issue arises where defendant becomes ill but is willing to proceed with the trial without being present.

In some instances, the defect that has occasioned the request for a mistrial does not prevent the case from being fairly tried to a verdict, but will render any conviction inherently defective. The argument has been advanced that defense should have the right in such cases to insist that the trial continue through to verdict, especially where the defect was the fault of the prosecution. That position, however, was rejected in *Illinois v. Somerville.*[9] The trial court there had declared a mistrial, upon request of the prosecution and over the defendant's objection, when the prosecution discovered on the first day of trial that its theft indictment was fatally defective. The indictment had failed to allege the necessary mens rea element of an intent to permanently deprive, and under Illinois law, that defect was jurisdictional in nature, being neither waivable by the defense nor curable by amendment. Under that circumstance, the trial court considered continuation of the trial to be impracticable and inconsistent with the ends of justice since any conviction the trial might produce would automatically be set aside by the defense. The Supreme Court majority held that this conclusion was allowable under the manifest necessity standard. Attesting to the continuing validity of the doctrine of *Wade v. Hunter*[10] that "a defendant's valued right to have his trial completed

7. Supra note 3.

8. Supra note 5.

9. 410 U.S. 458, 93 S.Ct. 1066, 35 L.Ed.2d 425 (1973).

10. 336 U.S. 684, 69 S.Ct. 834, 93 L.Ed. 974 (1949).

by a particular tribunal must in some instances be subordinated to the public's interest in fair trials designed to end in just judgments," the Court concluded that this public interest justified the mistrial in this case:

> A trial judge properly exercises his discretion to declare a mistrial if an impartial verdict cannot be reached, or if a verdict of conviction could be reached but would have to be reversed on appeal due to an obvious procedural error in the trial. If an error would make reversal on appeal a certainty, it would not serve "the ends of public justice" to require that the Government proceed with its proof, when, if it succeeded before the jury, it would automatically be stripped of that success by an appellate court.

As illustrations of other instances in which a mistrial was constitutionally permissible because the prosecution was in a similar no-win situation attributable to a fatal defect in the proceedings, the Court in *Somerville* referred to *Thompson v. United States,*[11] upholding a mistrial declared after the trial judge learned one of the jurors was disqualified because he had served on the indicting grand jury, and *Lovato v. New Mexico,*[12] where the trial judge properly directed the case moved back to the pleading stage because after jeopardy had attached it was discovered that the defendant had not pleaded to the indictment.

While such cases as *Somerville, Thompson* and *Lovato* support the notion that ordinarily there is a "manifest necessity" when it develops at trial that the prosecution is in a no-win posture because of a legal defect by which the defendant, though not now seeking a mistrial, could prevail in a post-trial setting, this is not inevitably so. The *Somerville* Court cautioned that "the declaration of a mistrial on the basis of a rule or a defective procedure that lent itself to prosecutorial manipulation would involve an entirely difficult question," but added that such a situation was not before it. Although the defect there was the responsibility of the prosecutor's office, which drafted the indictment, a prosecutor was not likely to include an inherent defect in a charging instrument for the purpose of seeking a mistrial if his case did not progress well. The Court distinguished in this regard its ruling in *Downum v. United States,*[13] where it saw at least a "suggestion" that the state policy calling for the mistrial "could be manipulated so as to prejudice the defendant."

While the Court in *Somerville* spoke primarily of prosecutorial manipulation in distinguishing *Downum,* the critical distinction between *Somerville* and *Downum* apparently reaches back to the different types of no-win situations facing the prosecutor in those two cases. The prosecutor in *Downum* had recognized on the morning of the scheduled trial that a key witness had not been subpoenaed and had not been found. Relying on the promise of the witness' spouse to let the marshal know when she found him, and apparently assuming that he would be found before the trial began that afternoon, the prosecutor went ahead with the jury selection. When the witness failed to appear in the afternoon, the prosecution moved for mistrial on the ground that the witness was critical to obtaining a conviction on two of the six counts. That motion then was granted over the objection of the defense (which asked that the two counts be dismissed for nonprosecution and the trial continue on the other four). The Supreme Court, in holding that the mistrial was not justified by manifest necessity, did not distinguish between the two counts on which the witness' testimony was critical and the remaining four counts. While the facts in *Downum* indicated that the prosecutor there had not manipulated the justification for the mistrial so as to save a case in which he misjudged the strength of the state's evidence, the mistrial was sought to save a case that appeared to be headed toward an acquittal because of an event the prosecutor could have anticipated. In *Somerville,* in contrast, the prosecution was not motivated in any sense by concern that it could not prove its case. The *Somerville* majority distinguished *Downum* in this regard, noting that the mistrial

11. 155 U.S. 271, 15 S.Ct. 73, 39 L.Ed. 146 (1894).

12. 242 U.S. 199, 37 S.Ct. 107, 61 L.Ed. 244 (1916).

13. 372 U.S. 734, 83 S.Ct. 1033, 10 L.Ed.2d 100 (1963).

there had "operated as a post-jeopardy continuance to allow the prosecution an opportunity to strengthen its case." It recognized also the obvious incentive and potential for manipulation when that is the prosecutor's purpose. So too, *Arizona v. Washington* [14] noted that the "strictest scrutiny is appropriate when the basis for the mistrial is the unavailability of critical prosecution evidence." Of course, there may be situations where the prosecution can survive that scrutiny by showing that the critical evidence suddenly becomes unavailable through circumstances beyond the prosecution's control and reasonable anticipation (e.g., a witness' sudden illness). Here, where there clearly is no effort to avoid the consequences of an earlier miscalculation as to the strength of the prosecution's case and no prosecutorial negligence that contributed to the situation, lower courts have distinguished *Downum* and sustained mistrials as consistent with the manifest necessity standard.

(e) Manifest Necessity and Trial Court Discretion. In various instances, a particular circumstance clearly would justify a mistrial, and the critical issue is how much deference will be given to the trial judge's determination that the circumstance was in fact present. One common case in this category is that in which the jury is apparently deadlocked. As the Supreme Court noted in *Arizona v. Washington,*[15] a hopelessly deadlocked jury presents the "classic basis" for a proper mistrial as there is no sense in proceeding if a verdict cannot be reached. The apparent deadlock, the Court added, also presents a situation in which the trial judge must be given broad discretion: "If retrial of the defendant were barred whenever an appellate court views the 'necessity' for a mistrial differently from the trial judge, there would be a danger that the latter, cognizant of the serious societal consequences of an erroneous ruling, would employ coercive means to break the apparent deadlock." Consistent with this analysis, lower court decisions have accorded great deference to trial court rulings in hung jury cases, extending even to cases where, for example, the trial judge relied on the foreman's statement of deadlock without polling the other jurors, or the judge failed to assure that the deadlock applied to all counts. The decisions tend to be based on an evaluation of a wide range of circumstances, however, and the lack of manifest necessity will be found when several different circumstances point to a trial judge's failure to take account of the defendant's interest in obtaining a verdict in his first trial. Among the factors considered in this regard are: (1) whether the defense argued that the jury not be discharged; (2) the length of the deliberations; (3) the complexity of the issues; and (4) the nature of the communications between judge and jury.

Arizona v. Washington itself presented still another situation in which the trial judge will be given considerable leeway in evaluating the justification. The trial court there had granted a mistrial after defense counsel in opening argument made an improper and prejudicial reference to the prosecution having withheld exculpatory evidence in an earlier trial. The Supreme Court acknowledged that "some trial judges might have proceeded with the trial after giving the jury appropriate cautionary instructions." However, it added, in making certain types of mistrial determinations, trial judges must be given "broad discretion" in deciding "whether or not 'manifest necessity' justifies a discharge of the jury." The classic illustration was the trial judge's decision as to whether to discharge or require further deliberations from a hung jury. "[A]long the spectrum of trial problems which may warrant a mistrial and which vary in their amenability to appellate scrutiny, the difficulty which lead to the mistrial in this case also [fell] in an area where the trial judge's determination is entitled to special respect." Two reasons supported this conclusion: (1) the trial judge had heard the argument and observed the reaction of the jury, had seen and heard the jurors during voir dire, and was most familiar with the evidence and the background of the case, and

14. Supra note 5.

15. Supra note 5.

thus was "far more 'conversant with the factors relevant to the determination' than any reviewing court can possibly be"; and (2) because alternative remedies would "not necessarily remove the risk of bias," a contrary result would mean that "unscrupulous defense counsel are to be allowed an unfair advantage." Where the record revealed that the "trial court acted responsibly and deliberately, after according careful consideration to respondent's interest in having the trial concluded in a single proceeding," the judge's ruling in an area of such broad discretion should not be overturned.

Commentators have questioned whether the great deference *Washington* extended to the trial judge's evaluation of the need for a mistrial in responding to prejudicial misconduct during a trial should extend to situations in which the prejudicial impact would be borne by the defendant rather than the prosecution. They argue that the judge here should give deference to the defense, and if the defense prefers to proceed to verdict and rely on an instruction to the jury to attempt to cure the prejudice, then the manifest necessity standard should not approve the mistrial. Support for this position is found in the Supreme Court's comment in *United States v. Dinitz* [16] that the "important consideration, for purposes of the Double Jeopardy Clause, is that the defendant retains primary control over the course to be followed in the event of such error." Several lower courts have suggested, however, that trial judges must be given considerable leeway here, just as in *Washington,* because the judge may also give weight to the need to preserve the "appearance of impartiality." They conclude that this interest may justify a mistrial notwithstanding the defense's willingness to accept the risk that the jury may have been prejudiced against it. Still another concern is that the defense opposition to a mistrial may not amount to the acceptance of a jury instruction to disregard as a satisfactory cure for the prejudice, so that any subsequent conviction, as in *Somerville,* will be subject to reversal.

The Supreme Court's ruling in *Gori v. United States* [17] arguably suggests that the trial judge should be given even greater deference when he acts to protect the defendant, but the continuing force of that ruling is subject to question. In that case, the trial judge "on his own motion and with neither approval nor objection by counsel," declared a mistrial during the government's direct examination of its fourth witness. The trial judge apparently had believed that the prosecutor's questioning "presaged inquiry calculated to inform the jury of other crimes by the accused" and had declared the mistrial "to forestall" that prejudice. Unlike the situation presented in the later case of *Arizona v. Washington,* the trial judge in *Gori* acted without any significant deliberation or consideration of the views of counsel. Nonetheless, a closely divided Supreme Court held that reprosecution was not barred by double jeopardy. The majority viewed the mistrial order as "neither apparently justified nor clearly erroneous" and emphasized the need for granting the trial court leeway in the exercise of its discretion. The majority concluded: "We are unwilling, where it clearly appears that a mistrial has been granted in the sole interest of the defendant, to hold that its necessary consequence is to bar all retrial."

In *United States v. Jorn,* [18] where the Court stressed the judge's failure to consider alternatives, the government had sought to rely on *Gori.* The judge there had directed that the prosecution's witnesses not testify until they discussed their waiver of the self-incrimination privilege with counsel, and the net effect of those discussions, if the witnesses did not testify, would have been to benefit the defense. Looking to *Gori,* the government argued that even a mistrial order that constitutes an "abuse of discretion" should not preclude a retrial when the mistrial ruling "benefited" the defendant. The Supreme Court plurality rejected that contention, noting that: (i) if "benefit" was to be measured by reference to the person whom the judge was

16. Supra note 1.

17. 367 U.S. 364, 81 S.Ct. 1523, 6 L.Ed.2d 901 (1961).

18. Discussed supra at note 7.

seeking to prevent from being prejudiced, then that person was the witness rather than the defendant, and (2) if "benefit" was to turn on "a post hoc assessment as to which party would in fact have been aided" in the "hypothetical event" that the judge had ruled differently, then that concept unacceptably rested "on an exercise in pure speculation." The plurality concluded that *Jorn* therefore was clearly distinguishable from "a case of mistrial made 'in the sole interest of the defendant' " as presented in *Gori.* It added, however:

> Further, we think that a limitation on the abuse-of-discretion principle based on an appellate court's assessment of which side benefited from the mistrial ruling does not adequately satisfy the policies underpinning the double jeopardy provision. Reprosecution after a mistrial has unnecessarily been declared by the trial court obviously subjects the defendant to the same personal strain and insecurity regardless of the motivation underlying the trial judge's action.

The dissenters in *Jorn* contended that the decision there was "flatly inconsistent" with *Gori.* Of course, even if that is the case, and no special weight is to be given to the fact that the trial judge acted to protect the defendant from prejudice, the *Washington* ruling may restore considerable deference to the trial court in the situation presented in *Gori*—provided the judge acts after deliberate consideration of alternatives as was done in *Washington.*

(f) Dismissals Equivalent to Mistrials. In some instances, as discussed in § 25.3(a), a dismissal may be imposed as a permanent ending to all prosecution, but in other instances, a dismissal is granted in apparent contemplation of the renewal of the prosecution. Such is the case, for example, if the dismissal is based on some curable error in the course of the preliminary proceedings or an error in the charging instrument. Most often, such dismissals are issued before trial, but occasionally they will occur after jeopardy has attached. The leading case on such dismissals, *Lee v. United States,*[19] indicates that they will be treated as the functional equivalents of mistrials, and governed by the same double jeopardy principles.

The Court in *Lee* was confronted with a situation in which the defendant had moved to dismiss the information after the prosecutor's opening statement in a bench trial, the trial court tentatively denied the motion subject to further study, and then at the close of the two hour trial the court took a brief recess and granted the motion to dismiss. In holding that the defendant could be tried again, the Court rejected the contention that he should not have had to undergo the first trial because the court was made aware of the defective information before jeopardy attached. The Court concluded that the defendant "had only himself to blame" for the events as they developed, for by "the last-minute timing of his motion to dismiss, he virtually assured the attachment of jeopardy." Justice Brennan, concurring, emphasized that "an entirely different case would be presented if the petitioner had afforded the trial judge ample opportunity to rule on his motion prior to trial, and the court, in failing to take advantage of this opportunity [had] permitted the attachment of jeopardy before ordering dismissal of the information."

The Court in *Lee* then concluded that the dismissal came within the *Dinitz* rule,[20] as "by failing to withdraw the motion after jeopardy had attached," the defendant "virtually invited the court to interrupt the proceedings before formalizing a finding on the merits." Of particular significance was the fact that the court's initial remarks "left little doubt that the denial was subject to further consideration at an available opportunity in the proceedings—a fact of which the court reminded counsel after the close of the prosecution's evidence," following which defense counsel "made no effort to withdraw the motion." By contrast, in cases where the defendant has moved for a mistrial but has withdrawn that motion prior to the judge's ruling, lower courts have held that the *Dinitz* rule

19. 432 U.S. 23, 97 S.Ct. 2141, 53 L.Ed.2d 80 (1977).

20. Discussed supra at note 1.

does not apply. Of course, if the pleading defect is not waivable, the withdrawal of the motion should not be critical. Under *Somerville,* the dismissal on the judge's own motion, or on request of the prosecution, would be supported by manifest necessity.

§ 25.3 Reprosecution Following Acquittal or Dismissal

(a) Dismissals vs. Acquittals. In contrast to either a mistrial or a dismissal of the type presented in *Lee,* there are dismissals that "contemplate that the proceedings will terminate then and there in favor of the defendant," with no reprosecution possible because the grounds for the dismissal (e.g., denial of speedy trial) constitute a permanent bar to the prosecution of the charge. In *United States v. Jenkins,*[1] decided in 1975, the Court assumed that the double jeopardy clause granted to the defendant the right to rely on such a "final judgment" in much the same manner as an acquittal or conviction where it came after jeopardy had attached. Accordingly, a government appeal from such any post-jeopardy "judgment discharging the defendant" was barred whenever "further proceedings of some sort, devoted to the resolution of factual issues going to the elements of the offense charged, would have been required upon reversal and remand."[2] However, three years after *Jenkins,* in *United States v. Scott,*[3] the Court retreated from the *Jenkins* ruling insofar as it treated similarly all final judgments.

Scott presented the question of the permissibility of a government appeal following the trial judge's midtrial dismissal of the prosecution on the ground of prejudicial pretrial delay. In overruling *Jenkins,* which had relied upon the principle "that the State with all its resources and power should not be allowed to make repeated attempts to convict an individual for an alleged offense," the Court in *Scott* affirmed the soundness of that proposition as to an acquitted defendant, but distinguished the defendant who was the beneficiary of a defense-requested dismissal. Justice Rehnquist (who had also written for the Court in *Jenkins*) offered the following analysis:

> It is quite true that the Government with all its resources and power should not be allowed to make repeated attempts to convict an individual for an alleged offense. This truth is expressed in the three common law pleas of *autrefois acquit, autrefois convict,* and pardon which lie at the core of the area protected by the Double Jeopardy Clause. As we have recognized in [numerous] cases, * * * a defendant once acquitted may not be again subjected to trial without violating the Double Jeopardy Clause. * * * But that situation is obviously a far cry from the present case, where the Government was quite willing to continue with its production of evidence to show the defendant guilty before the jury first empaneled to try him, but the defendant elected to seek termination of the trial on grounds unrelated to guilt or innocence. * * *
>
> [A] defendant is acquitted only when "the ruling of the judge, whatever its label, actually represents a resolution in defendant's favor, correct or not, of some or all of the factual elements of the offense charged. * * * We think that in a case such as this the defendant, by deliberately choosing to seek termination of the proceedings against him on a basis unrelated to factual guilt or innocence of the offense of which he is accused, suffers no injury cognizable under the Double Jeopardy Clause if the Government is permitted to appeal from such a ruling of the trial court in favor of the defendant [and to reprosecute if successful on appeal].

The Court in *Scott* added that it was not thereby adopting the view that defendant had "waived" his double jeopardy protection, but rather was only concluding that the scope of the double jeopardy clause was not such as to "relieve a defendant from the consequences of his voluntary choice." Because the defendant in *Scott* had moved for dismissal, this was an accurate characterization of the situation there. But that will not always be the case.

§ 25.3

1. 420 U.S. 358, 95 S.Ct. 1006, 43 L.Ed.2d 250 (1975).

2. As to the separate significance of this "further proceedings" limitation, see subsection (e) infra.

3. 437 U.S. 82, 98 S.Ct. 2187, 57 L.Ed.2d 65 (1978).

If the trial judge was the instigator and the primary mover of the events that led to the dismissal of the indictment and took complete control of the proceedings and set off on a course over which the defendant had not control, then the "voluntary choice" which was an essential ingredient of *Scott* is not present. The issue then presented is whether the dismissal that is intended as a permanent bar against reprosecution should be treated as a mistrial so that a reversal on appeal and a reprosecution would be permitted if the judge's sua sponte action was justified by manifest necessity. Although the *Scott* majority rejected the dissent's contention that the double jeopardy clause should allow the defendant the same sense of repose as to any type of final judgment favorable to the defendant, it did not go quite so far as to state that the defendant had no greater right of reliance upon a dismissal intended as a permanent bar than upon a dismissal of the type involved in *Lee.* Segments of the Court's rationale, however, could readily lead to that conclusion. Historically, the acquittal and the conviction stood apart from any other type of disposition of the case. Moreover, as with *Lee*-type dismissals, the dismissal that imposes a permanent bar to reprosecution ordinarily would be granted prior to the attachment of jeopardy. Indeed, the circumstances that lead to that disposition mid-trial rather than before trial is often judicial uncertainty. Motions to dismiss on such grounds as unconstitutional delay in bringing a prosecution ordinarily must be raised before trial, but rather than rule on the motion at that time, a trial court may put off ruling until the evidence presented at trial furnishes it with a better basis for determining whether the defendant was prejudiced. That shift in timing would not appear to be a sufficient basis for denying the prosecution the opportunity to challenge the court's ruling unless the court, in shifting the timing of its ruling and thereby depriving the defense of the completion of the first trial, acted without a justification sufficient to meet the manifest necessity standard.

The Court in *Scott* stressed that, in distinguishing between a dismissal and an acquittal, the "trial judge's characterization of his own action cannot control the classification of the action." The critical question was whether the grounding of the trial court's ruling established an acquittal (i.e., whether it went to a "failure of proof" in establishing the elements of the offense or in rebutting a defense to the crime). The dissent argued that this distinction would not be easily applied. It questioned, in particular, how the majority could hold that delay in prosecution was a defense that did not produce an "acquittal" while offering as illustrations of defenses that did both insanity and entrapment. The majority responded that both of those defenses went to the basic substantive element of individual "culpability,"[4] while "the dismissal for preindictment delay represents a legal judgment that a defendant, although criminally culpable, may not be punished because of a supposed constitutional violation." Lower courts, relying on this culpability touchstone, generally have had little difficulty in applying the distinction between acquittals and dismissal. Thus, a trial court's ruling that the prosecution's case-in-chief failed to establish venue, though framed as a judgment of acquittal, has been held to be a dismissal because venue is an element "more procedural than substantive" that does not go to culpability.

(b) The Jury Acquittal. The Supreme Court has long held that when a jury in a criminal case has returned a verdict of not guilty, the double jeopardy prohibition bars further prosecution of the defendant for the same offense. That standard was first laid down in *Ball v. United States,*[5] and it has been accepted ever since as the cornerstone of double jeopardy jurisprudence. The Court has noted that this absolute bar finds support in the common law plea of *autrefois acquit* as well as the policy underlying the double jeop-

4. The Court's reference was to the subjective standard for entrapment utilized in the federal courts. See § 5.2(a).

5. 163 U.S. 662, 16 S.Ct. 1192, 41 L.Ed. 300 (1896).

ardy clause. As to the latter, the most frequently cited policy justification is that set forth in *Scott:* "To permit a second trial after an acquittal, however mistaken the acquittal may have been, would present an unacceptably high risk that the Government with its vast superior resources, might wear down the defendant so that 'even though innocent, he may be found guilty.' "

Some commentators questioned the *Scott* explanation by comparison of the risk allowed to the innocent when the trial results in a conviction influenced by trial error. In such a case, as will be seen in § 25.4, the defendant may obtain a reversal of his conviction, but he then may be retried even though it is quite possible that the jury would have acquitted if not for the trial error that required the reversal. On the other side, the critics note, when a trial results in an acquittal, that verdict is final even though a court believes it almost certain that the jury would have convicted if not for a trial error that favored the defense. They therefore ask, if the defendant must bear the risk of being retried when the state introduced an error into the trial which now requires reversal of his conviction, why should he not likewise bear the risk of being retried when error in his favor was introduced in a trial which resulted in his acquittal. In each instance, it is argued, one cannot be certain what the jury would have done if not for the error, so there is no reason to assign to one defendant more than the other the risk of being an innocent who could be convicted on retrial.

One answer to the above line of criticism is that the acquittal could be based on the jury's right to nullify, a prerogative that the jury obviously did not exercise favorably to defendant where it convicted. The protection of the innocent includes the protection of one who may have been the beneficiary of the jury's leniency. Another answer is that, while estimating the impact of a trial error always presents uncertainties, whether the result is a conviction or an acquittal, only in the latter situation is there concrete evidence, in the form of the not guilty verdict, that the jury may have resolved factual issues in favor of the defendant's innocence. That concrete evidence entitles the defendant to the benefit of the doubt that conclusively presumes his innocence, while a conviction, even where probably influenced by trial error, offers no such starting point for assuming the jurors would have found defendant not guilty except for the error. Still another answer to the critics is that the fundamental policy concern here lies not so much in protection of the innocent as in granting a sense of repose to the defendant who went through a trial that produced a final decision on his guilt or innocence. The defendant who challenges a conviction is willing to put aside the finality of that verdict, but the defendant who is acquitted obviously does not desire to put aside his sense of repose.

(c) Acquittal by the Judge. The Supreme Court has long treated as parallel the directed acquittal entered by the judge and the jury verdict of not guilty. Here again, some commentators have questioned the court's position. They note that the protection of the jury's right of nullification is not at stake in the judicial acquittal, and that the protection of a factual resolution favorable to the defendant also is not necessarily at stake. While some directed acquittals are based on a judicial evaluation of the persuasiveness of the evidence, others are based solely on the trial court's view of the substantive law. Where that view is erroneous, the commentators note, there is no basis for arguing that the acquittal must be given finality in order to protect the innocent. A practical response to this line of argument is that the end result of drawing such a distinction would be to discourage defense requests for directed verdicts. If such a distinction were drawn, where the judge had a view of the substantive law that would render the prosecution's case clearly insufficient, the defense, instead of asking for a directed verdict, simply would allow the case to go to the jury under the judge's view of the law so that the jury would then acquit. It is unclear whether this practical consideration, or some other consideration, has convinced the Supreme Court to treat all directed acquittals alike, and to treat all as parallel to a jury acquittal. The Court simply has noted, without extensive explanation, that the double jeopardy clause "nowhere distinguishes" between bench and jury acquittals. Thus, double jeopardy bars reprosecution following judicial termination of a trial by directed acquittal, without regard to whether the judicial determination as to the insufficiency of the evidence is based on its total lack of its persuasiveness or its failure "as a matter of law" due to the substantive content of the offense in question.

The leading case on judicial acquittals is *Sanabria v. United States.*[6] The trial judge in that case granted a judgment of acquittal that flowed from two alleged errors. First, the court excluded certain evidence as being legally irrelevant under its view that the indictment had failed to set forth a particular grounding for liability. Second, in reviewing the evidence that remained, the trial court applied an erroneous reading of the substantive law by limiting liability for participation in illegal enterprises to persons actually engaged in the illegal activities. The Supreme Court viewed the critical issue before it as whether the trial judge's ruling was actually an acquittal. Although the judge had looked to the indictment in striking certain evidence, it has not dismissed the indictment for failure to plead an offense, but had taken the indictment as stating an offense under a limited theory of liability, excluded evidence not consistent with that theory, and then held the remaining evidence insufficient under that theory. The Court therefore concluded:

> [W]e believe the ruling below is properly to be characterized as an erroneous evidentiary ruling, which led to an acquittal for insufficient evidence. That judgment of acquittal, however erroneous, bars further prosecution on any aspect of the count and hence bars appellate review of the trial court's error.

Sanabria, it has been noted, will often place the trial court in a position "to control the double jeopardy consequences of its rulings by choosing the form employed." In some instances, the charging instrument will fail to allege all of the elements of the crime, and the trial judge may be able to choose between a dismissal of the indictment or information as in *Lee,*[7] or an acquittal for the failure to establish all of the elements of the crime (the prosecution not having offered evidence on what it did not plead). The presence of such discretion, in turn, raises the question as to whether the defense properly can place the trial court in a position where it lacks that discretion by failing to object to the charging instrument before trial and then, at trial, objecting only to the lack of proof rather than the deficiency of the pleading. *Sanabria* allowed a roughly similar tactic but did so in a manner that left open the possibility of a different response to the precise tactic posed above. Because the acquittal in *Sanabria* was intertwined with the trial judge's ruling that certain evidence was not admissible, a matter which the defendant could have raised before trial, the government argued that the delay by the defendant constituted a "waiver" of his subsequent double jeopardy objection. Although a similar consideration entered into permitting retrial following the midtrial dismissal in *Lee,*[8] the *Sanabria* Court deemed that case unrelated to the instant problem because double jeopardy principles applicable to mistrials "have no bearing" on acquittal cases. The Court also noted that the issue of evidence admissibility was unlike such issues as whether an indictment states an offense or whether a statute is unconstitutional, in that a ruling in defendant's favor would not have barred conviction on the existing charge. That being the case, defendant there could not be faulted for not having raised the issue prior to the time that jeopardy attached. This rationale seemingly holds open the possibility that a "forfeiture" or "waiver" might be found where the defense could have obtained a pretrial ruling on the interpretation of the crime that later led to a directed acquittal, but chose not to do so because the prosecution could have appealed that pretrial ruling if it favored the defense.

6. 437 U.S. 54, 98 S.Ct. 2170, 57 L.Ed.2d 43 (1978).

7. See § 25.2 at note 19.

8. See § 25.2 following note 19.

(d) Pre-jeopardy "Acquittals." Even when the judge's ruling unquestionably is grounded solely on a determination that there is insufficient evidence for conviction, it does not inevitably follow that the ruling will be treated as an acquittal under *Sanabria* and *Scott.* The ruling cannot be placed in that category if it is issued in a pretrial setting, as that is before jeopardy has attached. As discussed in § 25.1(d), verdict finality will not attach where the trial court had no authority to sit as a tribunal judging the weight of the government's evidence, and it has none at that point. On the other hand, once the trial has started, an acquittal will be treated as such even though it was not granted in accord with proper procedures. Thus, in *Fong Foo v. United States,*[9] a judge's entry of an acquittal because he viewed the government's initial witnesses as inherently incredible constituted a bar to further proceedings even though the judge went beyond the relevant Federal Rules provision by directing the acquittal before the prosecution had completed its case-in-chief.

(e) Postconviction Judgments of Acquittal. In *United States v. Wilson,*[10] after the jury returned a verdict of guilty, the trial court reconsidered an earlier motion and dismissed the indictment on the ground that the government's preindictment delay had resulted in a denial of due process. *Wilson* was decided before *Scott* and the question was open at the time as to whether such a ruling should be treated as the equivalent of an acquittal for double jeopardy purposes. The Court had no need to consider that issue, however, as it concluded that double jeopardy would not bar an appeal from the trial court's ruling in any event. The key to double jeopardy, the Court reasoned, was exposing the defendant to multiple trials. Although "review of any ruling of law discharging a defendant obviously enhances the likelihood of conviction and subjects him to continuing expense and anxiety, a defendant has no legitimate claim to benefit from an error of law when that error could be corrected without subjecting him to a second trial before a second trier of fact." That was exactly the case here. If the trial judge's ruling was reversed, the appellate court would merely reinstate the jury's verdict and defendant would not be tried again.

Wilson did not in fact involve an acquittal, but in *United States v. Jenkins,*[11] the Court relied upon *Wilson* in noting: "[W]here the jury returns a verdict of guilt, but the trial court thereafter enters a judgment of acquittal, an appeal is permitted." *Scott,* in turn, adhered to this aspect of the *Jenkins* opinion, as it noted that a judgment of acquittal bars an appeal only "when a second trial would be necessitated by a reversal." The Court added that this principle, as announced in *Jenkins,* had not been repudiated by "the Court's heavy emphasis on the finality of an acquittal" in more recent cases.

The end result of the position established in the above opinions, albeit without a direct ruling on point, is to give to trial judges a means for preserving the government's opportunity to appeal where the judge sides with the defense on a legal issue that will control as to the sufficiency of the evidence. Assume for example, that an issue first arises at trial concerning the admissibility of evidence, that the evidence is crucial to the prosecution's case, and that the judge believes that it is inadmissible, but considers this position debatable and most appropriately decided finally by an appellate court. In such a situation, to preserve the prosecution's right of appeal and grant the defense the acquittal that the judge believes it deserves, the judge may take the following approach: allow the evidence to go before the jury, and if the jury should convict, then grant a post-verdict judgment of acquittal on the ground that the evidence is inadmissible and without it, the prosecution's proof is insufficient. Similarly, if there is disagreement as whether the prosecution must prove a certain element to establish a crime, the judge can send the case to the jury on instructions that do not require the finding of that element and then, if the jury convicts,

9. 369 U.S. 141, 82 S.Ct. 671, 7 L.Ed.2d 629 (1962).

10. 420 U.S. 332, 95 S.Ct. 1013, 43 L.Ed.2d 232 (1975).

11. Supra note 1.

grant a post-verdict judgment of acquittal on the ground that proof of the element is wanting. In a bench trial, the process is even easier, as the judge can make findings of facts and indicate that he would hold the defendant guilty except for his adoption of a certain legal interpretation that produces an acquittal. That ruling can then readily be reviewed by the appellate court and if it disagrees as to the legal interpretation, remanded for entry of the judgment of guilt, which can be done without further factfinding. However, as *Jenkins* indicates, if the trial judge fails to make adequate findings, so that further factual determinations will be needed, that will be treated as subjecting the defendant to a multiple trial even though the same judge would be finding the facts on the basis of evidence previously admitted.[12]

§ 25.4 Reprosecution Following Conviction

(a) The General Rule. In the seminal double jeopardy decision of *Ball v. United States,*[1] the Supreme Court recognized an exception to the general constitutional prohibition against reprosecuting a person for an offense of which he has already been convicted. That exception, as it now stands, is that the double jeopardy clause does not bar reprosecution where the convicted defendant has managed through appeal or some other procedure to set aside his conviction on grounds other than evidence insufficiency. Some uncertainty existed for some time as to the doctrinal basis for this rule, but today the Supreme Court considers the "most reasonable" justification for the *Ball* rule to be that advanced by Justice Harlan in *United States v. Tateo*[2]:

> While different theories have been advanced to support the permissibility of retrial, of greater importance than the conceptual abstractions employed to explain the *Ball* principle are the implications of that principle for the sound administration of justice. Corresponding to the right of an accused to be given a fair trial is the societal interest in punishing one whose guilt is clear after he has obtained such a trial. It would be a high price indeed for society to pay were every accused granted immunity from punishment because of any defect sufficient to constitute reversible error in the proceedings leading to conviction. From the standpoint of a defendant, it is at least doubtful that appellate courts would be as zealous as they now are in protecting against the effects of improprieties at the trial or pre-trial stage if they knew that reversal of a conviction would put the accused irrevocably beyond the reach of further prosecution. In reality, therefore, the practice of retrial serves defendants' rights as well as society's interest.

As discussed earlier,[3] under the standard applicable to mistrials a prosecution error causing a mistrial may, depending upon the circumstances, bar further prosecution. Under the *Ball* rule, on the other hand, if a mistrial is not declared and the same error results in a conviction reversed on appeal, reprosecution apparently will never be prohibited. The explanation traditionally given for the different consequences is that in the latter situation "the defendant has not been deprived of his option to go to the first jury and, perhaps, end the dispute then and there with an acquittal." The notion is that there is a substantial constitutional difference between receiving "a jury trial, albeit not the error-free jury trial to which by law the defendant is entitled" and being deprived entirely of the "valued right to have the original jury consider [the] case."

(b) The Evidence Insufficiency Exception. It was not until the case of *Burks v. United States*[4] that the Supreme Court held that the *Ball* rule did not apply where the

12. See also Finch v. United States, 433 U.S. 676, 97 S.Ct. 2909, 53 L.Ed.2d 1048 (1977), acquittal bar applies notwithstanding dissenters' objection that a retrial would be based on a factual stipulation entered by the parties and therefore would not produce the same ordeal, embarrassment, and expense as a factually contested retrial.

§ 25.4

1. 163 U.S. 662, 16 S.Ct. 1192, 41 L.Ed. 300 (1896).
2. 377 U.S. 463, 84 S.Ct. 1587, 12 L.Ed.2d 448 (1964).
3. See § 25.2(c).
4. 437 U.S. 1, 98 S.Ct. 2141, 57 L.Ed.2d 1 (1978).

appellate reversal was based on the insufficiency of the evidence at trial to sustain a guilty verdict. In holding a remand in such circumstances inconsistent with the double jeopardy prohibition, a unanimous Court emphasized that if the trial court had done what the reviewing court said should have been done "a judgment of acquittal would have been entered and, of course, petitioner could not be retried for the same offense," and that "it should make no difference that the *reviewing* court, rather than the trial court, determined the evidence to be insufficient."

The *Burks* opinion rejected several earlier decisions that had misconstrued *Ball* as allowing a retrial in a case such as the instant one. In concluding that *Ball* was limited to the separate problem of a reversal based upon trial error, the *Burks* opinion reasoned that

> reversal for trial error, as distinguished from evidentiary insufficiency, does not constitute a decision to the effect that the government has failed to prove its case. As such, it implies nothing with respect to the guilt or innocence of the defendant. Rather, it is a determination that a defendant has been convicted through a judicial process which is defective in some fundamental respect, e.g., incorrect receipt or rejection of evidence, incorrect instructions, or prosecutorial misconduct. When this occurs, the accused has a strong interest in obtaining a fair readjudication of his guilt free from error, just as society maintains a valid concern for insuring that the guilty are punished.
>
> The same cannot be said when a defendant's conviction has been overturned due to a failure of proof at trial, in which case the prosecution cannot complain of prejudice, for it has been given one fair opportunity to offer whatever proof it could assemble. Moreover, such an appellate reversal means that the Government's case was so lacking that it should not have even been *submitted* to the jury. Since we necessarily afford absolute finality to a jury's *verdict* of acquittal—no matter how erroneous its decision—it is difficult to conceive how society has any greater interest in retrying a defendant when, on review, it is decided as a matter of law that the jury could not properly have returned a verdict of guilty.

The analogy *Burks* drew between the trial court's entry of a judgment of acquittal and an appellate court ruling on evidence insufficiency arguably provides answers to several questions raised in the aftermath of *Burks.*[5] One of those questions is the consequence of an appellate ruling that the evidence is insufficient where that ruling comes from the intermediate appellate court and the prosecution then seeks review by the highest appellate court. Because it is generally accepted that appeal is permissible from a trial court's granting of a motion for acquittal after a jury verdict of guilty,[6] an appeal similarly will be available from what is the equivalent of an appellate court's entry of an acquittal after conviction. Here too, if the government prevails, the defendant is not subject to a new trial, but to reinstatement of the trial court judgment.

State and federal appellate courts have long exercised the power to reverse a conviction on grounds of evidence insufficiency while at the same time ordering the entry of judgment on a lesser-included offense. Since *Burks,* the question has arisen as to whether appellate courts are still free to take this step. The Supreme Court in *Sanabria v. United States*[7] took note of this issue but found no need to reach it. Appellate courts generally assume that they still have this power. The explanation is that in a situation like *Burks,* where the evidence is completely insufficient, reversal without remand is the only permissible action because that produces the result which would have been reached had the trial judge decided defendant's acquittal motion properly. On the other hand, where the evidence is found insufficient on appeal only as to the greater offense, then it is clear both that, had the trial judge acted properly, the lesser offense would have gone to the jury, and it would have resulted in conviction, as is reflected by the fact that the jury's actual ver-

5. See also § 25.2(e) as to the applications of *Burks* to two-stage proceedings involving continuing jeopardy.

6. See § 25.3(e).

7. 437 U.S. 54, 98 S.Ct. 2170, 57 L.Ed.2d 43 (1978).

dict shows that it found the existence of every element of the lesser-included offense. In a similar vein, when an appellate court finds a trial error that goes only to the higher offense (as with an improper jury instruction on that offense), it may remand for entry of judgment on the lesser offense and a retrial (if the government desires) on the higher offense.

Trial court rulings on the strength of the prosecution's evidence fall into two quite distinct types of rulings. The directed acquittal holds that the evidence is insufficient for any reasonable juror to find guilt. The granting of a new trial on the ground that the verdict is against the weight of the evidence, on the other hand, recognizes that the jurors could rationally reach the result that they reached, but grants the defendant another chance because the trial court has concerns, based on that judge's own evaluation of the evidence, that an injustice may have been done. This distinction has been carried over in many state courts to appellate review of the evidence and the question therefore arises as to its bearing on the application of *Burks*.

In *Hudson v. Louisiana*,[8] the trial court had granted a new trial following conviction on the ground that there "certainly [was] not evidence beyond a reasonable doubt, to sustain the verdict," and the defendant argued that this made the trial court's ruling one on the sufficiency of the evidence and barred a new trial. Relying on *Burks*, the Supreme Court agreed. It rejected the contention that *Burks* was inapplicable because the trial court had found that there was some evidence of guilt. The reasoning of *Burks*, the Court concluded, was not limited to insufficiency rulings based on a total lack of evidence. In *Tibbs v. Florida*,[9] in contrast, it was clear the appellate court was acting only as a "thirteenth juror," rendering a "weight of the evidence" reversal. Here, a closely divided Supreme Court held that *Burks* did not apply. The majority stressed that such a reversal does not rest on the premise that an acquittal was the only proper verdict the jury could have reached, but simply expresses the appellate court's disagreement with the jury's resolution of the conflicting testimony. The *Tibbs* majority reasoned that just as a deadlocked jury does not result in an acquittal barring retrial, an appellate court's disagreement, as the "thirteenth juror," with the trial jurors' weighing of the evidence also does not require the special deference accorded verdicts of acquittal. A thirteenth-juror reversal, the Court stressed, is designed primarily to "give the defendant a second chance" in "the interests of justice." It was not true, as the dissent argued, that the appellate court in practical effect was stating that the conviction would not stand without additional evidence. Precisely the same evidence could lead to an appellate court affirmance of any ensuing conviction, for while "reversal of a first conviction based on sharply conflicting testimony may serve the interests of justice, reversal of a second conviction based on the same evidence may not."

Finally, it should be noted that the *Burks* doctrine is limited to a finding of an insufficiency of the evidence under the offense charged rather than an error in charging under an offense barred by law from applying to the particular event. A reversal on the latter ground is treated as resting on a defect in the charging instrument and permits a retrial under the correct charge (albeit for the "same offence") in accordance with the *Ball* rule.[10]

(c) The Determination of Sufficiency. The Court in *Hudson* stressed that the appellate court has an obligation to determine the sufficiency of the evidence under the standard of proof beyond a reasonable doubt, which is required by due process. It could not consider a thirteenth-juror reversal without first deter-

8. 450 U.S. 40, 101 S.Ct. 970, 67 L.Ed.2d 30 (1981).

9. 457 U.S. 31, 102 S.Ct. 2211, 72 L.Ed.2d 652 (1982).

10. See Montana v. Hall, 481 U.S. 400, 107 S.Ct. 1825, 95 L.Ed.2d 354 (1987), also discussed in § 17.4 at note 25. Since the appellate court there reversed defendant's conviction for incest solely on the ground that the legislature's amendment of the incest statute to include sexual assaults on stepchildren had not come into effect until after this particular assault on a stepchild, the Court held that defendant, consistent with *Ball*, could be tried for the offense of sexual assault, which did apply to an assault upon a stepchild at the time.

mining that the evidence was sufficient for a reasonable trier of fact to find guilt beyond a reasonable doubt. So too, where the appellate court finds reversible error, it cannot stop with that determination but must consider the sufficiency of the evidence if the defendant raised that issue.

Lockhart v. Nelson [11] raised the question of what evidence an appellate court should consider in reviewing the sufficiency issue after it has first held that the conviction must be overturned because of the erroneous admission of evidence. The Court there held that *Burks* does not bar a retrial where the appellate court concludes that the evidence would be insufficient only if it does not include the evidence that the appellate court has now held to be inadmissible. *Burks,* the Court noted, had carefully distinguished between reversals based solely on evidentiary insufficiency and reversals based on "such ordinary trial errors" as the "incorrect receipt or rejection of evidence," with the latter remaining subject to the *Ball* rule. Where the evidentiary insufficiency exists only because of the appellate court's initial conclusion that there was error in admitting prosecution evidence, the reversal, under the logic of *Burks,* should be characterized simply as one based upon a "trial error." The "basis for the *Burks* exception to the general rule is that a reversal for insufficiency of the evidence should be treated no differently than a trial court's granting a judgment of acquittal at the close of all the evidence." Since a "trial court in passing on such a motion considers all of the evidence it has admitted," to "make the analogy complete, it must be the same quantum of evidence which is considered by the reviewing court" in determining whether double jeopardy bars a retrial. Thus *Burks* should bar a retrial only if the evidence was insufficient even with the erroneously admitted evidence. Where that is not the case, allowing a retrial following reversal is consistent with giving the prosecution "one fair opportunity to offer whatever proof it could assemble." Had the trial court excluded the inadmissible evidence, the prosecution would have been given the opportunity to introduce other evidence on the same point, and allowing a retrial where the proof is deemed insufficient on appeal only because of that inadmissible evidence merely recreates the situation that would have existed if not for the trial court's error.[12]

In describing the appellate court's ruling on the insufficiency of the evidence, the Supreme Court in *Burks* noted "there is no claim in this case that the trial court committed error by excluding prosecution evidence which, if received would have rebutted any claim of evidentiary insufficiency." This statement has been taken as suggesting that a reprosecution would not be barred if the insufficiency of the government's evidence would have been "cured" by evidence erroneously excluded by the trial court. Such a view of the matter is certainly consistent with another observation in *Burks,* namely, that the prosecution there had been given "one fair opportunity offer whatever proof it could assemble." It is arguably inconsistent, however, with the *Lockhart* premise that the appellate court should, in effect, stand in the shoes of the trial court and consider the evidence that was before it.

(d) Conviction as Implied Acquittal. The teaching of *Green v. United States* [13] is that under some circumstances a conviction of one crime must, for double jeopardy purposes, be taken as an acquittal of another crime. In that case the defendant Green was charged with first degree murder, and the jury was informed that they could find him guilty either of that crime or the lesser included offense of second degree murder. The jury returned a verdict of guilty on the latter charge but said nothing as to the first degree murder charge. Green's conviction was reversed on

11. 488 U.S. 33, 109 S.Ct. 285, 102 L.Ed.2d 265 (1988).

12. *Lockhart* involved a recidivist prosecution in which the prosecution erroneously relied on a prior conviction as to which defendant had received a pardon. The Court noted that there was "no indication that the prosecutor * * * was attempting to deceive the [trial] court" in using that conviction, and it therefore "had no occasion to consider what the result would be if the case were otherwise." On retrial, the prosecution had substituted another prior conviction of the defendant.

13. 355 U.S. 184, 78 S.Ct. 221, 2 L.Ed.2d 199 (1957).

appeal for trial error, and he was then retried on the original first degree murder charge and convicted of that offense. In holding that the double jeopardy clause barred conviction on that charge, the Supreme Court explained:

> Green was in direct peril of being convicted and punished for first degree murder at his first trial. He was forced to run the gantlet once on that charge and the jury refused to convict him. When given the choice between finding him guilty of either first or second degree murder it chose the latter. In this situation the great majority of cases in this country have regarded the jury's verdict as an implicit acquittal on the charge of first degree murder. But the result in this case need not rest alone on the assumption, which we believe legitimate, that the jury for one reason or another acquitted Green of murder in the first degree. For here, the jury was dismissed without returning any express verdict on that charge and without Green's consent. Yet it was given a full opportunity to return a verdict and no extraordinary circumstances appeared which prevented it from doing so. Therefore it seems clear, under established principles of former jeopardy, that Green's jeopardy for first degree murder came to an end when the jury was discharged so that he could not be retried for that offense. * * * In brief, we believe this case can be treated no differently, for purposes of former jeopardy, than if the jury had returned a verdict which expressly read: "We find the defendant not guilty of murder in the first degree but guilty of murder in the second degree."

The defendant in *Green* would have prevailed even if the jury at the second trial had found him guilty of second degree murder, the same result as at the first trial, upon reprosecution for first degree murder. As the Court explained in *Price v. Georgia,*[14] "to be subjected to a second trial for first-degree murder is an ordeal not to be viewed lightly" and it might even have affected the outcome in that it was possible "the murder charge against petitioner induced the jury to find him guilty of the less serious offense rather than to continue to debate his innocence." Accordingly, *Price* reversed the defendant's conviction at the second trial for second degree murder and remanded the case for a new trial limited to that offense. However, as *Morris v. Mathews*[15] later noted, the appropriate remedy for the double jeopardy violation that occurs when a defendant is tried on a jeopardy-barred offense (along with a non-barred offense) is not always to order a new trial. If the jury on the second trial convicted on the jeopardy-barred count, an adequate remedy was simply to reduce that conviction to the lesser-included offense that was not jeopardy-barred. In *Price,* the Court was concerned that the jury had reached a compromise verdict (i.e., some jurors may have preferred conviction on the jeopardy-barred higher charge, others may have preferred acquittal, and they may have compromised as to murder-two). In *Morris,* in contrast, with the jury having convicted on the higher, jeopardy-barred count, it necessarily found, without any compromise, that the defendant's conduct also satisfied the elements of the lesser-included, non-barred offense. It would be "incongruous," said the Court, to remedy the double jeopardy violation that occurred in trying the defendant again for the higher offense by "ordering yet another trial" when the jury, uninfluenced by that violation, had found defendant guilty of the lesser-included offense that was not jeopardy-barred.

Application of *Green* depends, of course, on a verdict setting that indicates an implied acquittal. That is not present, for example, where the jury has been told that it should look first at a single charge and then not bother with the other charges if it finds guilt on that charge. There, saying nothing as to the other charges indicates only that they were not reached. Assuming that they were not lesser-included in the sense that conviction on the higher necessarily includes conviction on the lesser, the issue then becomes whether the jury charge which, in effect, kept defendant from receiving a verdict on the other charges is justified under the standards applied to mistrials.

14. 398 U.S. 323, 90 S.Ct. 1757, 26 L.Ed.2d 300 (1970).

15. 475 U.S. 237, 106 S.Ct. 1032, 89 L.Ed.2d 187 (1986).

So too, an acquittal is not present where the defendant entered a guilty plea to a lesser charge in return for a dismissal of the higher charge. If the plea later is successfully challenged, double jeopardy does not preclude a trial on the higher charge. The acceptance of the guilty plea and even the determination that there is a factual basis for it does not constitute an inferential finding of not guilty of the higher charge. Moreover, the defendant has not really been in jeopardy as to the higher charge, as unlike the jury in *Green,* the judge receiving the plea could not have convicted the defendant of the higher charge.

§ 25.5 Reprosecution by a Different Sovereign

(a) Federal Prosecution After State. In the case of *United States v. Lanza* [1] the Supreme Court promulgated what is customarily referred to as the "dual sovereignty" doctrine: "an act denounced as a crime by both national and state sovereignties is an offense against the peace and dignity of both and may be punished by each." That the dual sovereignty doctrine allows a federal prosecution notwithstanding a prior state prosecution for the same conduct was thereafter affirmed in *Abbate v. United States.*[2] There, defendants who allegedly had conspired to dynamite telephone company facilities pleaded guilty to a state charge of conspiring to injure the property of another and received a three-month sentence, after which they were prosecuted in federal court for conspiring to injure those facilities that were part of a communications system "operated and controlled by the United States." The Court held that the federal conviction was not prohibited by the double jeopardy clause.

In declining to depart from the *Lanza* rule, the majority in *Abbate* reiterated the fears voiced in earlier cases that

> if the States are free to prosecute criminal acts violating their laws, and the resultant state prosecutions bar federal prosecutions based on the same acts, federal law enforcement must necessarily be hindered. For example, the petitioners in this case insist that their Illinois convictions resulting in three months' prison sentences should bar this federal prosecution which could result in a sentence of up to five years. Such a disparity will very often arise when, as in this case, the defendants' acts impinge more seriously on a federal interest than on a state interest.

When the Supreme Court later held that the double jeopardy clause of the Fifth Amendment was also applicable to the states through the Fourteenth Amendment and rejected efforts to limit other constitutional rights with "dual sovereignty" reasoning similar to that in *Abbate,*[3] some suggested that the Court might be inclined to overrule *Abbate.* But this did not come to pass; indeed, the dual sovereignty doctrine now seems to be more firmly entrenched than ever before. Thus in *United States v. Wheeler* [4] a unanimous Court, explaining that *Abbate* rests "on the basic structure of our federal system," held that a federal prosecution of an Indian was not barred by his earlier conviction in a tribal court because Indian tribes had retained their "sovereign power to punish tribal offenders" and thus were comparable to states in that respect.

Critics of *Abbate* claimed that the ruling there was overbroad. They argued that in most instances the basic policies underlying the double jeopardy bar against reprosecution are equally applicable to prosecutions by different sovereigns. Insofar as there is a need

§ 25.5

1. 260 U.S. 377, 43 S.Ct. 141, 67 L.Ed. 314 (1922).

2. 359 U.S. 187, 79 S.Ct. 666, 3 L.Ed.2d 729 (1959).

3. Murphy v. Waterfront Com'n, 378 U.S. 52, 84 S.Ct. 1594, 12 L.Ed.2d 678 (1964), ("dual sovereignty" doctrine does not limit scope of privilege against self-incrimination); Elkins v. United States, 364 U.S. 206, 80 S.Ct. 1437, 4 L.Ed.2d 1669 (1960) (pre-*Mapp* case rejecting "silver platter" doctrine which allowed state police to turn over fruits of unconstitutional search for use in federal prosecution).

4. 435 U.S. 313, 98 S.Ct. 1079, 55 L.Ed.2d 303 (1978).

to offset those policies in order to preserve the separate interests of the state and federal governments, that could be done, the critics argued, by adoption of a "separate interests" approach. Under that approach, a federal prosecution following the state conviction or aquittal would only be allowed if the federal statute invoked was intended to protect an interest distinct from that underlying the state statute. In a separate opinion in *Abbate,* Justice Brennan rejected incorporating a "separate interests" concept within the Fifth Amendment double jeopardy prohibition on the ground that it would then have to be equally applicable to reprosecutions by a single sovereign under separate statutes and such a redefinition of the "same offence" concept would result in repetitive harassment of the defendant. Subsequently, in *Heath v. Alabama,*[5] the Court rejected a similar attempt to reshape the dual sovereignty doctrine that would have been restricted to that doctrine alone. The defendant there contended that the doctrine should be restricted "to cases in which two government entities, having concurrent jurisdiction and pursuing quite different interests, can demonstrate that allowing only one entity to exercise jurisdiction over the defendant will interfere with the unvindicated interests of the second entity." Such a "balancing of interests approach," the Court responded, "cannot be reconciled with the dual sovereignty principle"; for that principle holds that "two identical offenses" simply "are not the 'same offense' within the meaning of the Double Jeopardy Clause if they are prosecuted by different sovereigns."

Shortly after the *Abbate* decision, the Attorney General issued a memorandum to all United States Attorneys noting the need for cooperation "with state and local authorities to the end that the trial occur in the jurisdiction, whether it be state or federal, where the public interest is best served," and barring a federal trial "when there has already been a state prosecution for substantially the same act or acts" except with the approval of an Assistant Attorney General. This policy was noted by the Supreme Court in *Petite v. United States*[6] and has since been referred to as the *Petite* policy. It has served as the basis for dismissing indictments and vacating convictions, on the government's motion, in numerous cases in which federal prosecutions were inadvertently initiated after state prosecutions. Indeed, in *Rinaldi v. United States*[7] it was held that it is an abuse of discretion for a district court to refuse to vacate a conviction where such action was requested by the government on the ground that it had violated its *Petite* policy. But the defendant may not obtain a dismissal of an indictment, over the objection of the government, simply because the United States Attorney failed to obtain prior approval of an Assistant Attorney General as required by that policy. The policy is an internal guideline, and if the government now concludes that the separate prosecution is appropriate under the criteria it has specified, the defendant cannot complain either that those guidelines were incorrectly interpreted in his case or that the internal process requirements were not met.[8]

(b) State Prosecution After Federal. The reverse of the *Abbate* situation was presented in the companion case of *Bartkus v.*

5. 474 U.S. 82, 106 S.Ct. 433, 88 L.Ed.2d 387 (1985).

6. 361 U.S. 529, 80 S.Ct. 450, 4 L.Ed.2d 490 (1960).

7. 434 U.S. 22, 98 S.Ct. 81, 54 L.Ed.2d 207 (1977).

8. Now set forth in the United States Attorneys' Manual § 9–2.142, these guidelines "preclude the initiation or continuation of a federal prosecution following a state prosecution * * * based on substantially the same act, acts or transaction unless there is a compelling federal interest supporting the dual * * * prosecution." Assessment of whether the state prosecution left "substantial federal interests demonstrably unvidicated" depends upon a case-by-case analysis. The guidelines note in this regard that a federal prosecution may be warranted "where there is a substantial basis for believing that the choice by either the prosecutor or grand jury of the state charges * * * or the state determination regarding guilt or severity of sentence was * * * affected by * * * the following factons: infection of the proceeding by incompetence, corruption, intimidation, or undue influence; court or jury nullification involving an important federal interest, in blatant disregard of the evidence; the failure of the state to prove an element of the state offense which is not an element of the federal offense; or the unavailability of significant evidence in the state proceeding either because it was not timely discovered or because it was suppressed on state law grounds or on an erroneous view of the federal law."

Illinois,[9] where after defendant's acquittal in federal court for robbery of a federally insured bank he was convicted in state court for the same bank robbery. The Court again applied the dual sovereignty doctrine and upheld the state conviction. Once more the concern was that the action of one sovereign should not cut off the enforcement of a superior interest by the other. Putting the illustration of *Screws v. United States,*[10] a federal civil rights prosecution where the permissible punishment was but a few years while at the state level defendant's conduct was a capital offense, the Court declared that were

> the federal prosecution of a comparatively minor offense to prevent state prosecution of so grave an infraction of state law, the result would be a shocking and untoward deprivation of the historic right and obligation of the States to maintain peace and order within their confines. It would be in derogation of our federal system to displace the reserved power of States over state offenses by reason of prosecution of minor federal offenses by federal authorities beyond the control of the States.

A good many states have followed *Bartkus* in interpreting their state constitutional provisions on the subject of double jeopardy, although some have held that their constitutional provisions bar a state prosecution in the *Bartkus* situation. A majority of the states have adopted statutes prohibiting state prosecution for offenses that relate to a previous federal prosecution, but these statutes vary considerably as to the extent of the prohibition. Some do not allow a state prosecution based on the same "act or omission" as the federal prosecution, some do not permit a state prosecution unless it and the federal prosecution each require proof of a fact not required in the other, and a few bar a state prosecution whenever based upon the "same transaction" as the prior federal prosecution.

(c) State–State and State–Municipal. Prosecution by two different states for basically the same conduct is quite unusual as state jurisdictional authority tends to be tied to a territorial principle. However, certain criminal transactions may have a sufficient bearing on two states (usually adjoining) as to produce criminal liability in both for basically the same harm and conduct. Where such successive prosecutions are brought, as held in *Heath v. Alabama,*[11] the double jeopardy bar does not apply because each state is a separate sovereign. In *Heath,* where two states prosecuted the defendant for the same murder (which occurred in Georgia in the course of a kidnapping that started in Alabama and provided the grounding for a felony-murder charge in that state), Justice Marshall argued in dissent that fundamental fairness standard of due process was violated in light of the cooperative effort of the two states aimed at securing a death sentence in the second state after defendant had entered a guilty plea to avoid the death penalty in the first. The majority, however, did not consider that issue to be before it and ruled only on the double jeopardy claim, which failed under the dual sovereignty doctrine.

The *Heath* situation must be distinguished from one involving successive municipal and state prosecutions, as in *Waller v. Florida.*[12] Petitioner had removed a canvas mural which was affixed to a wall in city hall and had carried it through the streets until, after a scuffle with police, it was recovered in damaged condition. Following his conviction for violating two city ordinances (destruction of city property and disorderly breach of the peace), he was convicted of the felony of grand larceny in violation of state law. On the basis of the state court's assumptions that the felony charge was based on the "same acts" as the city ordinance violations and "that the ordinance violations were included offenses of the felony charge," the Supreme Court unanimously held that the second trial violated the double jeopardy prohibition. As the Court had concluded on a prior occasion, cities are not sovereign entities but rather "have been traditionally regarded as subordinate govern-

9. 359 U.S. 121, 79 S.Ct. 676, 3 L.Ed.2d 684 (1959).

10. 325 U.S. 91, 65 S.Ct. 1031, 89 L.Ed. 1495 (1945).

11. Supra note 5.

12. 397 U.S. 387, 90 S.Ct. 1184, 25 L.Ed.2d 435 (1970).

mental instrumentalities created by the State to assist in the carrying out of state governmental functions." This meant, the Court concluded in *Waller,* that "the judicial power to try petitioner * * * in municipal court springs from the same organic law that created the state court of general jurisdiction," and thus the "dual sovereignty" doctrine has no application here.

Lower courts have recognized some deserving exceptions to the *Waller* rule. One is that prosecution for the state crime is not barred when that offense was not fully consummated when the ordinance prosecution was brought, as where the victim dies after an ordinance prosecution for assault. This is consistent with the standard applied to prosecutions under separate state statutes.[13] Another exception is the "collusion exception," applicable to situations in which the ordinance conviction was procured by collusion between the offender and city officials for the purpose of protecting the offender against more serious state charges.

13. See Diaz v. United States, discussed at note 16 of § 17.4. In general, lower courts have assumed that the standard for assessing what constitutes the "same offence" should be the same for separate state statutes and ordinances and statutes. See § 17.4.

Chapter 26

SENTENCING PROCEDURES

Table of Sections

§ 26.1 Legislative Structuring of Sentencing: Sanctions

(a) Structure and Procedure. Although this chapter is concerned with sentencing procedure, we start with a fairly detailed description of the basic structure of sentencing authority. To a considerable extent, sentencing procedure follows from that structure and varies with structural differences. The sentencing structure is set largely by the legislature. Its basic components are: (1) the authorization of specific types of punishments and the placing of limitations on their use and range; (2) the allocation of responsibility for individualized sentencing decisions; and (3) the choice as to the degree of guidance that will be provided to the primary sentencer, the trial court, in the exercise of its discretion. The first of these components is discussed in this section and the second and third are discussed in the two sections that follow. While the focus here is on the structure itself, attention also will be given to any "special" procedures—i.e., procedures that differ from the primary procedures discussed in §§ 26.5–26.6—that are associated with a particular sentencing structure.

(b) Capital Punishment. All but roughly a dozen states have capital punishment provisions. Consistent with the Supreme Court's holdings, those capital punishment provisions can be applied only in homicide cases and only to those participants who actually killed or at least contemplated the killing. The permissible use of capital punishment also is restricted by a line of Supreme Court decisions insisting that the sentencer be given guidance in determining whether capital punishment is appropriate in the particular case. Among the requirements imposed by those decisions are the listing of aggravating circumstances, at least one of which must be present to justify imposing capital punishment, the required consideration of mitigating factors that may outweigh those aggravating circumstances, and appellate review of the sentencer's decision to impose capital punishment.

Because of these special requirements and the close regulation of the death penalty under the Eighth Amendment, the procedural requirements governing capital sentencing, and its appellate review, are both extensive and complex. Space limitations preclude more than a brief summary of their range. Capital sentencing hearings are subject to burden of proof requirements similar to those imposed for the offense itself, to various restrictions regarding the type of evidence that can be introduced with respect to mitigating and aggravating factors, to special restrictions relating to the prosecution's argument to the jury and to the judge's charge to the jury regarding its sentencing function, to limitations on the process utilized where the judge has the authority to impose a sentence of death notwithstanding a jury recommendation of a life sentence, and to special requirements for appellate review of the death sentence. The end result is a sentencing procedure which is quite distinct from the typical sentencing procedure and which much more closely resembles the trial on the issue of guilt.

(c) Incarceration. Typically, the sanction of incarceration, either in a prison (for longer terms, usually one year or more) or in a jail (for shorter terms), is a legislatively authorized punishment for all offenses except a limited class of misdemeanors. This, however, is only the start of the legislature's shaping of the sentence of incarceration. The legislation authorizing incarceration also determines whether the incarceration sentence will be determinate or indeterminate in structure. In either case, it further sets the range of the allowable incarceration for each offense. Very often, the legislature will add to that range by providing for alternative or extended terms of incarceration under special offender or enhancement provisions.

Indeterminate sentences. The indeterminate sentence sets a maximum and minimum term of incarceration and leaves to the parole board the task of determining the precise point between the minimum and maximum at which the release will actually occur. Introduced on a large scale basis in the late nineteenth century, the indeterminate sentence became the standard form of incarceration sentence for felony cases during the early twentieth century. Today, a substantial number of states and the federal system have discarded indeterminate sentencing and moved to determinate sentences. Over half of the states, however, continue to utilize indeterminate sentences for felony cases.

Legislation providing for indeterminate sentencing always sets an upper-limit on the maximum term for each offense. Beyond this, there are three different structures governing judicial options in setting indeterminate sentences. In some states, the court is required to use the legislatively set upper-limit as the maximum term, which means that it has discretion only in setting the minimum term. In setting that minimum, the court commonly is limited by a statutory requirement that the minimum be no higher than a certain percentage of the statutorily prescribed maximum (e.g., 50%). It has discretion, however, to set a lower minimum, usually as low as one year, unless the legislature has specified a higher mandatory minimum for the particular offense. Under a second structure, the judge sets only the maximum term (at or under the legislative upper-limit) and the minimum is automatically set by law as a percentage of that maximum term. Here again, the legislature may set a mandatory minimum for a particular offense that will override the automatic minimum otherwise prescribed. Other states use still a third structure under which the judge has discretion in setting both the maximum and minimum terms. The maximum may not be higher than the upper-limit set by the legislature. Unless the legislature has set a mandatory minimum, the minimum can be as low as one year, but it cannot be higher than a certain percentage of the maximum set by the judge. Under all three structures, even most life sentences will be indeterminate, as state legislation typically provides for parole eligibility on all but a limited class of life sentences after the defendant has served a specified number of years.

Sections 26.5 and 26.6 describe the sentencing process typically used in the setting of the basic sentence of incarceration in felony cases. As applied to indeterminate sentences, that procedure is utilized only with respect to that portion of the sentence—maximum, minimum, or both maximum and minimum—as to which the judge has discretion. The description above assumes that, insofar as the judge has discretion, that discretion is completely unguided. As discussed in § 26.3, indeterminate sentencing can be accompanied by guidance of the exercise of discretion, particularly through sentencing guidelines. To some extent, as noted in §§ 26.5–26.6, the sentencing process will vary depending upon whether the indeterminate sentencing structure includes that additional element.

Determinate sentences. The determinate sentence sets a definite term of incarceration, and that is the term the offender must serve. Such sentences have always been the norm for misdemeanor terms (one year or less) and are now being used in a substantial number of states for felony offenses as well. With the determinate sentence, there is no parole board release prior to the end of the term set by the court. Once the defendant serves that determinate term, he is entitled to be released, but that does not necessarily free him of all restraints. For most felonies, jurisdictions using determinate sentences impose an automatic additional period of supervised release that operates in much the same way as parole supervision.

The determinate sentence always must be set within the statutory upper-limit for incarceration for the particular offense. For misdemeanor sentences, the legislature ordinarily imposes no further controls. As for felonies, however, there is considerable variation in the use of additional controls. In some jurisdictions, the only additional limit will be a mandatory minimum level for the determinate sentence, which is used for the most serious offenses. Where such a minimum does not apply, the sentence ordinarily may be set anywhere within a broad range (e.g., one to 15 years). Where a minimum is applicable, the sentence must meet at least that threshold, but that may still allow considerable range between the minimum and the legislative maximum (e.g., anywhere between 5 and 30 years). As discussed further in § 26.3, most jurisdictions using determinate sentences seek also to restrict judicial discretion in setting that sentence. The sentence process used in setting a determinate sentence typically is that described in §§ 26.5–26.6.

Alternative terms. Almost all jurisdictions have legislation providing for certain alternative terms. The alternative term provisions fall into two categories. One substitutes a particular type of sentence based on the need for certain rehabilitative programs. Prime examples are special sentences for drug-dependent offenders, sexually disturbed offenders, and youthful offenders. These terms tend to be indeterminate and tied to successful rehabilitation. Another type of alternative sentence provision substitutes a life sentence (or some other exceptionally long determinate term) where the offender's past criminal conduct places him in the category of a "habitual offender" (based on a record of prior convictions) or a "dangerous offender" (based on a pattern of a particular type of criminal conduct).

The procedure utilized in determining whether an alternative sentence applies often differs substantially from that described in §§ 26.5–26.6. Initially, the prosecution will give advance notice of an intent to invoke the statute providing for an alternative term. Indeed, in the context of recidivist statutes, the Supreme Court has held that such notice is constitutionally required.[1] A substantial number of jurisdictions further require that the applicability of a repeat offender provision be determined by the trial factfinder. This determination usually is made in a bifurcated trial. Following the finding of guilt, in a second portion of the trial, the state must establish that the defendant is a recidivist by proof beyond a reasonable doubt. Other jurisdictions treat the applicability of recidivist provisions as basically a sentencing issue to be decided by the judge, but they too commonly require a trial-type hearing, with the burden of proof, procedural rights, and evidentiary requirements often similar to those imposed at trial. As for dangerous offender provisions, the common sentencing procedure, consistent with the Supreme Court's ruling in *Specht v. Colorado,*[2] also is a trial-type hearing held after the finding of guilt, with the judge making the determination as to whether the dangerous offender provision applies. As with other trial-type hearings, defendants have the right to compulsory process and to cross-examine prosecution witnesses, but here the evidentiary standards are likely to be relaxed somewhat and the prosecution's burden of proof commonly is by a preponderance of the evidence rather than by proof beyond a reasonable doubt.

Extended terms. Extended term or "enhancement" provisions may be used with both determinate and indeterminate sentencing. In a determinate sentencing structure, they require (or allow) the addition of a specified term of years to the sentence the judge would otherwise impose for the offense. With an indeterminate sentencing structure, they will add to the maximum term where that is set by law, or extend either the maximum or minimum terms when the judge generally has discretion in setting those terms. Enhancements commonly are tied to a record of past convictions or to aggravating circumstances in the commission of the offense (e.g., use of a weapon or an especially vulnerable victim, such as a handicapped or elderly person). Where jurisdictions provide by statute for lengthy maximum sentences, they may prefer not to use extended terms and simply take such factors into account in guiding judicial discretion in setting the sentence within those maximums.

§ 26.1

1. Oyler v. Boles, 368 U.S. 448, 82 S.Ct. 501, 7 L.Ed.2d 446 (1962).

2. See § 26.4(g).

Under a typical enhancement statute, notice of the prosecution's reliance on the enhancement provision will be given after conviction and prior to sentencing, and the determination as to the enhancement's application will be made by the sentencing judge. The evidentiary standards commonly are the quite flexible standards that apply to sentencing generally. Special proof requirements may be imposed, however, where past convictions are the critical enhancement factor and the enhancement provision operates, in effect, like a recidivist statute. The defense may, in any event, challenge the reliability of the evidence cited as establishing the enhancement factor and may offer additional evidence of its own. The judge's determination that the enhancement applies must be supported by a preponderance of the evidence.

(d) Community Release. Sentences of community release take various forms. Not all can fit within the traditional definition of probation which assumes release pursuant to one or more conditions and some degree of supervision to ensure adherence to those conditions. In particular, courts have authority for some offenses to simply "suspend" the sentence, which releases the defendant into the community without supervision and subject only to the condition of non-violation of the law over the term of the sentence. Also, some forms of community release go beyond traditional probation by imposing some measure of confinement. Thus, many jurisdictions now utilize electronically monitored home confinement programs (which require the offender to remain at home during curfew hours) or "intensive supervision" programs that require the offender to reside in a group home under daily supervision and subject to curfews.

Judicial authority to utilize community-release sentences is dependent upon legislative authorization. All jurisdictions have provisions authorizing the use of probation for certain offenses, but none allow it for all offenses. Statutory prohibitions against allowing probation are commonly contained in the general probation statute, but they also are established, by implication, in statutes imposing mandatory minimum sentences of incarceration. In many states, the relevant legislation simply identifies those offenses that are probationable and does not seek to provide any guidance to the court in deciding between probation and incarceration. In other jurisdictions, however, the tradition has been to provide some general guidance by reference to the criteria that should be used in determining the appropriateness of probation. These provisions commonly create a presumption in favor of probation, noting that it shall be imposed for probationable offenses unless the sentencing judge is of the opinion that imprisonment is necessary because of such factors as the risk that defendant will commit another crime, defendant's need for correctional treatment, or concern that a sentence of probation "will depreciate the seriousness of the defendant's crime." An additional source of guidance may be found in sentencing guidelines, as described in § 26.3.

Where the judge has an option to utilize a sentence of community release, the sentencing process applicable to the exercise of that option ordinarily is that described in §§ 26.5–26.6—i.e., the same as that applied to the discretionary elements of setting a term of incarceration. The determination to revoke probation, based upon the violation of a condition of probation, presents a different situation. Here, due process requires for a probation violation determination, as it does for a parole violation determination, that the process meet the following "minimal requirements":

> "(a) written notice of the claimed violations of [probation or] parole; (b) disclosure to the [probationer or] parolee of evidence against him; (c) opportunity to be heard in person and to present witnesses and documentary evidence; (d) the right to confront and cross-examine adverse witnesses (unless the hearing officer specifically finds good cause for not allowing confrontation); (e) a 'neutral and detached' hearing body such as a traditional parole board, members of which need not be judicial officers or lawyers; and (f) a written statement by the factfinders as to the evi-

dence relied on and reasons for revoking [probation or] parole." [3]

The process that the states use in meeting these requirements is a trial-type hearing, conducted by the court, but not restricted to the evidence that would be admissible in a criminal trial and not requiring proof so convincing as to establish a violation beyond a reasonable doubt.

(e) Financial Sanctions. All jurisdictions provide for the use of fines in misdemeanor cases, and commonly allow the fine to be the only sanction for such offenses. All jurisdictions also authorize the use of fines for at least some felonies. Here, however, fines often are not authorized for certain felonies (e.g., murder) and the use of the fine as the only sanction (except as to corporate defendants) commonly is prohibited. Where the fine is an authorized sanction, the legislature sets an upper-limit and commonly allows the court complete discretion to set the fine at any point up to that maximum. The procedure utilized in determining whether a fine would be appropriate, and if so, at what level, is the same as that applied to the exercise of judicial discretion with respect to the term of incarceration or the use of community release.

While the required payment of restitution is not commonly viewed as a "punishment," it often is a part of the "financial restrictions" that will flow from a sentence. Required payment of restitution has long been imposed as a condition of probation without a specific statutory directive, but as a result of the victims' rights movement, recently enacted statutes have given restitution requirements a new prominence. These statutes often require the court to determine the appropriateness of ordering restitution either in every case or in every case in which such an order is requested. A directive to pay restitution need no longer be imposed as a condition of probation, but can be included as a separate order where probation is not utilized. Because the ordering of restitution commonly requires a series of factual determinations related to the permissible scope of restitution, the process applied here may be somewhat different from that applied to sentencing generally, including the imposition of fines. Many jurisdictions, however, find the general sentencing process, as described in §§ 26.5–26.6, adequate for a fair determination of those factual issues that must be resolved in ordering restitution.

Another financial directive that has gained prominence in recent years is the forfeiture order. Criminal forfeiture statutes have most commonly been enacted in connection with drug offenses and criminal enterprise offenses (e.g., the federal RICO provision). They allow forfeiture that reaches beyond property used in the commission of criminal activity itself. In general, criminal forfeiture proceedings are treated as a separate element of the criminal trial. They require pretrial notice of an intent to demand forfeiture, prosecution proof beyond a reasonable doubt that the assets are forfeitable, and a special verdict on that issue by the trier of fact. Ordinarily, a bifurcated trial is used, with the forfeiture issue tried separately after the trier of fact finds the defendant guilty of the crime charged.

§ 26.2 Legislative Structure: The Allocation of Sentencing Authority

(a) Judicial Sentencing. The legislature determines not only what sanctions will be allowed and what the parameters of those sanctions will be, but also which actor will be responsible for deciding within those legislatively prescribed limits, what sentence should be imposed in the individual case. The legislature's primary choice here is the trial judge. Indeed, the judge is so commonly the sentencer that sentencing often is viewed as exclusively a judicial function. As discussed in the subsections that follow, however, such exclu-

3. Gagnon v. Scarpelli, 411 U.S. 778, 95 S.Ct. 1756, 36 L.Ed.2d 656 (1973), quoting from Morrissey v. Brewer, note 4 of § 26.2. As to right to counsel in this proceeding, see the discussion of *Gagnon* at § 11.2(b).

sivity is rarely the case. In almost every jurisdiction, the jury will have a sentencing role with respect to at least one kind of sanction and an executive agency will have a role in determining the length of the sanction of incarceration. Still, the judge remains so dominant in the sentencing arena that, apart from the three subsections that follow, the discussion of sentencing procedures in this chapter concentrate entirely on judicial sentencing.

(b) Jury Sentencing. Jury sentencing is most common in capital cases where it is the norm. Indeed, even in those jurisdictions that give the judge final authority in determining whether a capital sentence will be imposed, the jury makes an initial recommendation based upon its evaluation of aggravating and mitigating factors. A substantial number of jurisdictions also make at least limited use of jury sentencing in noncapital cases. Most of these jurisdictions use jury sentencing only for "special offender" sentencing (e.g., recidivist) or for special sanctions (e.g., criminal forfeitures). A handful of states, however, make much more general use of jury sentencing. These jurisdictions provide for jury sentencing in all felony cases. At one time, the number of states in this group was considerably larger, but jury sentencing today tends to be looked upon as an "historical anachronism" in the context of traditional discretionary sentencing.[1]

Even though a state provides for jury sentencing in all felony cases, the jury is likely not to be the most frequent sentencer. Although the jury sentencing provisions vary, the jury's authority to sentence commonly is limited to cases in which the defendant goes to trial before a jury. In most jury sentencing states, a defendant will be sentenced by the court where he pleads guilty or waives his right to a jury trial (although such waiver may require prosecutorial acquiescence). Also, even in a case tried to the jury, the jurisdiction may allow a defense waiver of the right to jury sentencing.

In general, the jury's function in a jury sentencing system is to set the maximum term of an indeterminate sentence of incarceration, staying within the upper-limit for the offense set by the legislature. The minimum term then is set by law, as a certain percentage of the maximum. Where probation is an allowable alternative sentence for the particular offense, the choice of that alternative will not necessarily be within the jury's authority. The jurisdiction may reserve the probation determination to the judge, who thereby is given the power to set aside the jury's sentence and substitute the alternative of probation or even a suspended sentence.

Jurisdictions with jury sentencing may use either a unitary or bifurcated trial. The Supreme Court upheld the constitutionality of a unitary trial in *Spencer v. Texas,*[2] although the unitary trial places the defense at a substantial disadvantage. In general, jury sentencing tends to focus on the circumstances of the crime rather than the background of the offender. The crime is the focus of the trial on guilt, and there are limitations in what can be introduced even with a separate sentencing stage. Although the jury may receive evidence regarding the defendant's past record and reputation in the community, much of the information that ordinarily is included in a presentence report will be inadmissible.

§ 26.2

1. In Hildwin v. Florida, 490 U.S. 638, 109 S.Ct. 2055, 104 L.Ed.2d 728 (1989), a capital case, the Court noted that there is no Sixth Amendment right to jury sentencing even when the sentence turns on specific findings of fact. The key is that the relevant factor, there an aggravating circumstance in the commission of the crime, is "not an element of the offense, but instead 'a sentencing factor' that comes into play only after the defendant has been found guilty."

2. 385 U.S. 554, 87 S.Ct. 648, 17 L.Ed.2d 606 (1967). See also § 26.4 at note 17.

(c) Administrative Agency Decisions. In jurisdictions that utilize indeterminate sentences of incarceration, the parole board plays an important role in determining the actual term of imprisonment. Whether and at what point the defendant will be released on parole, during the period between the minimum and maximum sentence, depends on the decision of that agency. Jurisdictions vary in the guidance given to parole boards in making this determination. Some provide no direction by legislation. The predictive determination made by the parole board is thought not to be readily reduced to specific criteria established by the legislature. The preferred approach is to allow the parole board to fashion its own standards. In several jurisdictions parole boards have done this through comprehensive guidelines, similar to the sentencing guidelines discussed in § 26.3. Other states have adopted legislation setting forth general criteria for release on parole. In large part, these criteria seek to ensure that dangerous offenders will not receive early parole. They provide, for example, that the board only may release an offender who has served his minimum sentence if it "is satisfied * * * [that] the inmate will be paroled * * * without danger to society." The criteria also may refer to other factors that a parole board is likely to consider (e.g., suitable employment), but make those factors absolute prerequisites rather than discretionary concerns. Occasionally, a statute will be worded so that the inmate is entitled to be released if certain criteria are met. The Supreme Court dealt with such a statute in *Greenholtz v. Inmates of Nebraska Penal & Correctional Complex,*[3] and the result of that statutory structure was to vest in the inmate a due process right to limited procedural protections.

The *Greenholtz* Court had before it two issues: (1) whether the inmate's interest in parole release was a protectable interest under the due process clause, and (2) if so, whether the procedures followed by the Nebraska parole board satisfied due process requirements. Speaking to the first issue, Chief Justice Burger's opinion for the Court reasoned that the inmate's interest in parole release, in general, did not establish a protectable right. The Chief Justice noted that "there is no constitutional or inherent right of a convicted person to be released before expiration of a valid sentence." Moreover, a state's decision to establish a parole system did not in itself give the inmate "a legitimate claim of entitlement," as the state was free to give the parole board absolute control over "the sensitive choices presented by the * * * decision to grant parole release." It could recognize "that there is no prescribed or defined combination of acts" which should "mandate release," and that "the choice involves a synthesis of record facts and personal observation, filtered through the experience of the decisionmaker and leading to a predictive judgment as to what is best both for the individual inmate and for the community." The end result is then "an 'equity' type judgment" that cannot be said to give the inmate more than "a mere hope that the benefit will be obtained."

Having determined that "the presence of a parole system by itself does not give rise to a constitutionally protected liberty interest in parole release," the Court then turned to the Nebraska statutory language and found that it did create "a protectable expectation of parole." That statute stated that the parole board "shall order [the inmate's] release unless it is of the opinion" that any of four conditions existed. While those conditions involved judgments that were necessarily "subjective in part and predictive in part," the mandatory structure of the provision nonetheless served to "bind" the parole board and

3. 442 U.S. 1, 99 S.Ct. 2100, 60 L.Ed.2d 668 (1979).

thereby created an "expectancy of release * * * provided to some measure of constitutional protection." However, the presence of an interest protected by due process did not demand the formal hearing that the lower court had prescribed as an absolute requirement. Due process had long been held to have a "flexible" content that "calls for such procedural protections as the particular situation demands." Here, consideration had to be given to the predictive and subjective aspects of the release determination, the need to allow "experimentation involving analysis of psychological factors combined with fact evaluation guided by * * * practical experience," the danger of creating a "continuing state of adversary relations between society and the inmate," and the concern that the imposition of procedures viewed as "burdensome and unwarranted" would lead states to "abandon or curtail parole." The Nebraska Board did not grant a formal hearing where, after examining the inmate's file and holding a personal interview, it concluded that the inmate was not a good risk for release. To require that it go beyond this inquiry, and hold a formal hearing, would "provide at best a negligible decrease in the risk of error," especially since the inmate was allowed to present letters and statements on his behalf at the interview. So too it was not necessary to always provide the inmate with a summary of the evidence on which the Board relied. Here, there had been no challenge by inmates regarding their access to their prison files, and the factual information governing the parole decision ordinarily came from the files. To require a final Board summary of the evidence "would tend to convert the process into an adversary proceeding and to equate the Board's parole-release determination with a guilt determination." It was sufficient that the "Nebraska procedure affords an opportunity to be heard, and when parole is denied it informs the inmate in what respects he falls short of qualifying for parole."

Whether or not the state statute creates a protected expectation interest, states commonly provide those procedures that were held in *Greenholtz* to be adequate to meet due process demands. At one time, the practice in many states was to simply review the file, but informal hearings or "interviews" conducted by a hearing officer or a board member are now the norm. The prisoner usually will be informed of the general nature of the information in his file, or have access to that file, and will be given the opportunity to offer corrections or otherwise state his case for parole. In this connection, he may offer the statements of other persons in the form of letters or affidavits. In many jurisdictions, all or some inmates will be entitled to a more formal hearing. Here, the inmate may be represented by counsel (usually only if he can retain counsel on his own), may present his own witnesses, and will be present during the testimony of persons opposing his release (although cross-examination ordinarily is not permitted). Where release is denied, the inmate commonly is informed of the basis for that decision, although the statement of grounds may be quite general.

Parole boards also are assigned the responsibility of determining whether parole should be revoked due to a violation of a parole condition. Here, *Morrissey v. Brewer*[4] set forth a series of due process prerequisites, which basically are the same as the requirements applicable to probation revocation. These start with a prompt preliminary hearing following the parolee's arrest to determine whether there is probable cause to believe he has violated the parole condition (unless that is established per se by his conviction on a criminal charge). That hearing is later followed by an adversary, trial-type hearing, with counsel appointed under some circumstances. Explaining why due process re-

4. 408 U.S. 471, 92 S.Ct. 2593, 33 L.Ed.2d 484 (1972). See also § 26.1 at note 3.

quired so much more in a parole revocation proceeding, the *Greenholtz* Court noted:

> [P]arole *release* and parole *revocation* are quite different. There is a crucial distinction between being deprived of a liberty one has, as in parole, and being denied a conditional liberty that one desires. The parolees in *Morrissey* were at liberty and as such could "be gainfully employed and [were] free to be with family and friends and to form the other enduring attachments of normal life." The inmates here, on the other hand, are confined and thus subject to all of the necessary restraints that inhere in a prison. * * * A second important difference between discretionary parole *release* from confinement and *termination* of parole lies in the nature of the decision that must be made in each case. As we recognized in *Morrissey,* the parole-revocation determination actually requires two decisions: whether the parolee in fact acted in violation of one or more conditions of parole and whether the parolee should be recommitted either for his or society's benefit. "The first step in a revocation decision thus involves a wholly retrospective factual question." The parole-release decision, however, is more subtle and depends on an amalgam of elements, some of which are factual but many of which are purely subjective appraisals by the Board members. * * * Unlike the revocation decision, there is no set of facts which, if shown, mandate a decision favorable to the individual.

Under both determinate and indeterminate sentences, the length of the incarceration often is automatically reduced through provisions for "good time" credits. The executive department in charge of prisons usually has the responsibility for calculating the good time credit, which involves both applying a statutory formula and determining whether the inmate's behavior qualifies him for such credit. Good time commonly is lost by a violation of prison rules. Major misconduct can result in the loss of more than a year and thus can be the equivalent of a felony conviction in terms of impact upon actual incarceration. *Wolff v. McDonnell,*[5] held that such a sanction brought into play due process, although not the full range of procedural requirements demanded in the parole revocation setting. The due process requirements for a major-conduct disciplinary determination were: advance written notice of the disciplinary charges; a hearing at which the inmate can call witnesses and present documentary evidence, except where those rights will jeopardize institutional safety or correctional goals; and "a written statement by the factfinders as to evidence relied upon and the reasons" for taking disciplinary action.

§ 26.3 The Guidance of Judicial Discretion

(a) Unguided Discretion. Judicial discretion in sentencing has always been subject to the limitations imposed by the statutory framework of sentencing. As discussed in § 26.1, those limitations have varied with the sanction. In the case of fines, the primary statutory limits are the unavailability of that sanction for certain crimes and the upper-limit on the amount of the fine. As for probation, the statutory limits include prohibitions against use of that sentence for certain crimes, and the statutory framing of the length of the probation term and the range of conditions that can be imposed. With incarceration, the traditional statutory limitations are the upper-limit for the term, the required use of that upper-limit as the maximum term in some indeterminate sentencing jurisdictions, the requirement that the minimum for an indeterminate sentence be no more than a certain fraction of the maximum, and mandatory minimum terms for certain offenses. Insofar as the sentencing judge is given discretion within these limitations (and the others discussed in § 26.1), that discretion traditionally was granted without legislative guidance as to its use. The one major exception was found in probation statutes that referred to factors that the judge should weigh and that sometimes created a presumption in favor of probation.

Over the last few decades, a movement to restrict such broad discretion has gained considerable support. Several approaches have

5. 418 U.S. 539, 94 S.Ct. 2963, 41 L.Ed.2d 935 (1974).

been used to achieve this end. One, the extensive use of mandatory sentences of incarceration, has had little bearing on sentencing procedure. It simply limits the range of options that are available to the judge. Three others—presumptive sentencing, sentencing guidelines, and substantive appellate review of sentences—have had considerable influence in reshaping the sentencing process. Indeed the providing of appellate review is itself often characterized as a procedural as well as a structural reform.

(b) Presumptive Sentencing. Presumptive sentencing structures generally apply only to the sentence of incarceration, where they are used in conjunction with determinate sentences. The court retains whatever discretion was otherwise available as to use of sentences of community release and financial sanctions. Under presumptive sentencing, the legislature initially sets a "presumptive" term of incarceration for each offense, which falls within the statutory maximum for that offense. That presumptive term typically is stated as a term within a range of at least a few years (e.g., 3–5) and, in some instances, within a much broader range of years (e.g., 5–20). The judge must set the incarceration term at a specific number of years within that range unless mitigating or aggravating factors justify a downward or upward departure. The permissible range for departures also is set by the legislature, and in some jurisdictions, the relevant aggravating and mitigating circumstances are specified by the legislature. Those circumstances relate either to the offense or the character of the actor. Circumstances of aggravation relating to the offense include such factors as the use of a weapon, the vulnerability of the victim, and, in a transaction involving contraband, the quantity of the contraband. Mitigating circumstances relating to the offense include passive participation and the presence of substantial provocation. Aggravating circumstances relating to character deal with such factors as prior criminal record, while mitigating circumstances include factors such as a voluntary acknowledgment of wrongdoing.

The presumptive sentencing structure, in requiring the judge to justify departures from the presumptive sentence by reference to aggravating and mitigating circumstances, substantially narrows judicial discretion to make a predictive judgment. Although those circumstances relating to the character of the offender often have a certain evaluative component, aggravating and mitigating circumstances in large part rest on historical fact. Also, in contrast to the practice under traditional discretionary sentencing, which requires no explanation of the reasons for the sentence, the judge here must set forth findings that justify any upward or downward departure. These changes necessarily have a bearing on the sentencing process. They require a process that allows each side to present information relating to mitigating and aggravating factors and that facilitates judicial determination of disputes over historical facts. As discussed in §§ 26.5–26.6, such needs have produced various changes in the sentencing process in presumptive sentencing jurisdictions. By requiring findings as to departures, presumptive sentencing also facilitates appellate review of that portion of the sentencing decision.

(c) Sentencing Guidelines. Sentencing guidelines are set by a commission or by the highest court, rather than by the legislature. In many jurisdictions, they deal with fines and community-release sentences as well as terms of incarceration. Where the guideline system is used in conjunction with determinate sentences, it guides discretion in setting that single term of the incarceration sentence. Where used in conjunction with indeterminate sentences, it guides discretion as to that portion of the term which is not automatically set by legislation.

Like presumptive sentencing, a guidelines system also uses a presumed sentence, but it incorporates substantially greater refinement in setting that sentence and a limited judicial discretion to depart from the presumed sentence. The presumed sentence is determined through the use of a sentencing table that has two axes. Together they produce a grid that sets the presumed sentence for the particular case. One of the axes ranks the criminal history of the offender by reference to past convictions. The other ranks the severity of the crime by reference to such factors as the harm caused, the range of the criminal activity, and the role of the offender. The severity scale utilizes a point system that starts with a certain number based on the general character of the offense and then adds and subtracts points by reference to specified factors. This total then provides a presumptive range that moves to an upward grid as the criminal history increases in level. The grid ranges tend to be fairly narrow. For example, if the severity scale places a crime in the middle range, the presumed sanction may be 20–24 months for a person in the first criminal history category (no prior convictions) and 90–104 months for the person in the highest criminal history category. Presumed ranges at a certain level will treat probation as an alternative.

The presumed range is not binding upon the court. It must set forth its reasons for departure, however, and these grounds may be quite limited. Appellate review will be available both as to departures and as to the judicial determination of the proper score under the severity range and the proper placement in the criminal history category. Plea bargained reductions on charge may affect the sentence, but their impact is more limited. The severity scale is likely to be such that the point total under a lesser offense often can come close to what it would be under the higher offense.

The application of a sentencing guidelines system can best be illustrated by following a particular offense through a particular system, and for that purpose we use the Federal Sentencing Guidelines System.[1] The federal guidelines initially place each crime in one of nineteen offense category designations. This permits the grouping of various offenses of a similar character. "Offenses against the person," for example, includes homicide, kidnapping, assault and other threatening behavior. A base level is set for each offense, and added to this are points for offense characteristics. The base level for kidnapping, for example, is 24. The specific offense characteristics include (1) a ransom demand (6 level increase), (2) victim injury (2–6 levels based on its nature), (3) use of a dangerous weapon (2 levels), (4) the release of the victim (a deduction of 1 level to an increase of 2 levels, depending upon whether the kidnapping lasted less than 24 hours or more than 30 days), and (5) connection to another offense (4 level increase). After the level is set by reference to the offense characteristics, adjustments are made. The guidelines include five major categories of adjustments: (1) victim related adjustments, (2) adjustments for the defendant's role in the offense, (3) adjustments for obstructing the administration of justice, (4) adjustments for multiple count convictions, and (5) adjustments for a defendant's acceptance of responsibility. Thus, the severity level will be increased if the kidnap victim was especially vulnerable due to age (2 levels) or was a public official (3 levels) or if the defendant was the leader of the criminal activity (4 levels). It will be reduced if the defendant had a "mitigating role" (4 levels) or if the defendant "clearly demonstrated a recognition and affirmative acceptance of responsibility" (2 levels). With these adjustments, the total offense level will be set.

The next step is determining the defendant's criminal history category. A new composite number is constructed much like that for the offense level, but totally separate. The criminal-history category is determined by the sum of the points given for each prior sentence. The number of points per sentence varies dependent on whether the sentence was to imprisonment and the length of the imprisonment. Both federal and state sentences are included. If the defendant should fall in the category of a "career offender" or

§ 26.3

1. 28 U.S.C.A. § 994 establishes the statutory framework for the system. The guidelines are set forth in the United States Sentencing Commission Manual, with a new edition issued each year.

"criminal livelihood offender," then the offense level itself can be affected.

Once the offense level and the criminal history category are set, the presumed sentence is determined by using those two axes to find the appropriate sentencing grid in the guideline's sentencing table. For a kidnapping defendant with an offense level of 30 and a criminal history category of II, the table produces, for example, a sentence of 108–135 months. If the table produced a presumed sentence of 0–6, probation would be an alternative under the presumed sentence. If it produced a sentence not higher than 6–12 months, a community release program involving intermittent confinement or community confinement would be within the presumed sentence.

The district court is not bound to sentence within the guidelines, but may depart when it finds "an aggravating or mitigating circumstance * * * that was not adequately taken into consideration" by the Commission's relevant guideline. In some instances, the guidelines themselves provide specific guidance for possible departures, such as an interpolation between two adjacent guideline rules or a government motion for departure based upon the defendant having provided substantial assistance in the investigation or prosecution of another person. Whether the departure is based upon a ground suggested by the guidelines or upon other grounds, the specific reason for departure must be set forth in the record. Indeed, even where a sentence within the presumed range is imposed, the court still must set forth "its reasons for its imposition of the particular sentence" (i.e., explain its application of the guidelines), and where the guideline range exceeds 24 months, must give the reason for imposing a sentence at a particular point within the range. These determinations are then subject to appellate review.

Unlike a presumptive sentencing structure, which requires findings as to certain circumstances only where there is a departure from the presumed sentence, the sentencing guidelines require that a series of findings be made in every case in the course of fixing the presumed sentence. Under the federal guidelines system, for example, a worksheet is prepared assigning points in the development of the total for the offense level and the criminal history category. The guidelines system accordingly requires a sentencing process that affords each side an opportunity both to submit its own information relating to the guideline factors and to challenge information before the court that is contrary to its position. The process must also provide for a fair resolution by the sentencing judge of disputes as to the presence or proper interpretation of those factors. In addition, it must provide a record sufficient for appellate review as to factual and legal determinations made both in setting the presumed sentence and in any departure from that sentence. As will be seen in §§ 26.5–26.6, these functions of the process have led guideline jurisdictions to alter their sentence process from that traditionally employed in sentencing dominated by unguided judicial discretion.

(d) Appellate Review. In virtually all common law jurisdictions except the United States, appellate review of sentences has been the principal method used to develop principles for, and achieve consistency in, individual sentences. The traditional position in this country, however, as stated by the Supreme Court in *Dorszynski v. United States,*[2] has been that "once it is determined that a sentence is within the limits set forth in the statute under which it is imposed, appellate review is at an end." This position of no substantive review of sentences was said to follow from the nature of traditional indeterminate sentencing. Sentencing was not subject to established criteria, except for the statutory framework that set its outer limits, and the appellate court therefore had no standards it could invoke to determine whether a particular sentence was excessive in length or otherwise inappropriate. Of course, this analysis did not apply to sentencing procedure and thus a violation of statutory or con-

2. 418 U.S. 424, 94 S.Ct. 3042, 41 L.Ed.2d 855 (1974).

stitutional requirements in the sentencing process could always be challenged by the defendant. So too, an appellate challenge was available where the judge was alleged to have exceeded his sentencing "authority" as defined by statute and the constitution. Thus, an appellate court could reject a sentence where it constituted cruel and unusual punishment, where a probation condition was inconsistent with applicable statutory standards, where the judge relied upon impermissible criteria, such as race, and where the judge failed to fulfill his statutory obligation to exercise discretion by using a "fixed and mechanical" sentencing policy. On occasion, even in a jurisdiction professing no substantive review, an appellate court might take a step beyond review as to basic authority and strike down a sentence within the statutory limits because it was so excessive as to "shock" the court.

The traditional position on appellate review has long been rejected in a substantial number of states. These states did not limit appellate review to whether the proper process was followed and whether the substance of the sentence was statutorily or constitutionally prohibited. They looked openly to the sentencing judge's exercise of discretion and held that such discretion should not protect a sentence where there was a "clear abuse" or the sentencing judge "was clearly mistaken." The case for at least such review was set forth in *People v. Coles.*[3] The court there noted that: (1) unchecked discretion leads to the imposition of sentences "which may be excessively severe, excessively lenient, or excessively disparate in relation to similarly situated defendants who have committed similar crimes and which thereby create a feeling of betrayal on the part of the defendant and the public, with confidence in the criminal justice system correspondingly diminished"; (2) while the "interplay between society and crime" conceivably could justify come degree of disparity based on "different priorities of the community," it certainly did not justify "disparity in sentences which results from considerations such as the race or economic status of a defendant or the personal bias and attitude of an individual sentencing judge"; (3) the claimed increased burden on appellate courts in providing sentence review was exaggerated because "[m]any defendants now appeal their convictions simply because of their dissatisfaction with the severity of their sentences, [with their] * * * appeals based upon the subterfuge of attacking their convictions rather than directly attacking what concerns them most, the appropriateness of their sentences"; (4) such defendants sometimes win because the appellate judges agree that their sentences are inappropriate and "strain the law to reach the desired relief," and therefore "a wider scope of sentence review [should] will promote honesty and clarity in criminal appeals"; and (5) even if the "number of sentences * * * which would warrant relief are few, any injustice committed is still deserving a remedy" and the failure to provide such relief undermines "public confidence in the courts."

In *Coles,* the court held that, to facilitate appellate review, the trial court would be required to "articulate on the record its reasons for the sentence given." Such a requirement traditionally has not been applied to unguided discretionary sentencing, and that may explain in part why in many jurisdictions allowing for limited appellate review under an abuse standard, such review has had only a limited impact. Thus, one study of appellate review in such jurisdictions found that the rate of sentence review was moderate in about half of them, seldom in a quarter, and almost nil in the remaining quarter. The key appeared to be that meaningful review was often impossible to achieve absent a statement of grounds by the sentencing judge and the development of standards against which those grounds could be assessed.

With the advent of presumptive sentencing and guideline sentencing, the landscape of appellate sentencing review in this country has been altered dramatically. Both sentencing schemes provide for appellate review as an integral part of the sentencing structure.

3. 417 Mich. 523, 339 N.W.2d 440 (1983).

In the case of presumptive sentencing, that review is likely to be focused on departures, because here the court will have a statement of grounds justifying the sentence. Under guideline sentencing, the criteria and the statement of reasons will exist for sentences within the guidelines as well as for departures. Here meaningful review should be available in all cases.

The primary appellate-review issue under a guidelines system is what range of issues should be considered on review. In the federal system, review extends to all errors in the application of guidelines (as well, of course, to violations of statutory and constitutional standards). This reaches beyond the correctness of the sentencing court's interpretation of the guidelines and also includes its factual assessments. As to the latter, however, a "clearly erroneous standard" will apply, as with other trial-court factual findings. Moreover, as to departures, the federal courts have held that "essentially plenary" review will be utilized in determining whether the case is sufficiently unusual to warrant a departure, and if a departure is appropriate, a standard of "reasonableness" (giving weight to the "trier's superior 'feel' for the case") will apply in reviewing the "direction and degree of the departure."

Where jurisdictions had only limited "abuse" review of traditional sentencing, allowance of prosecution appeal of a sentence was highly controversial. However, with presumptive and guideline sentencing now presenting clear issues of legal interpretation, and the Supreme Court having upheld the constitutionality of appellate review of such issues,[4] prosecution appeals are now widely accepted. Under the federal system, the prosecutor may appeal on the ground that the sentence: "(a) was imposed in violation of law; (b) was imposed from the use of an inapplicable guideline range; (c) was less than the sentence specified in the applicable guideline range to the extent it is below the minimum [specified] * * * in the guideline range or includes a less limiting condition of probation * * * (d) was imposed for a crime for which no guideline was applicable [i.e., a departure] and was plainly unreasonable."[5] The availability of prosecution review renders moot the troublesome question of whether a court, on an appeal by the defense, can not only reject the defendant's claim, but also conclude that the sentence should have been higher. With prosecution appeals available, the prosecution can ensure that the court has that range of review by filing a cross-appeal.

4. See § 26.7(b).

5. 18 U.S.C.A. § 3742(b). This provision is largely the counterpart of § 3742(a) governing defense appeals. Provision is also made for appeals of sentences alleged to be in violation of plea agreements.

§ 26.4 Due Process Requirements

(a) *Williams v. New York.* Although decided over a half-century ago, *Williams v. New York*[1] remains the leading ruling on the content of due process as it applies to procedures in traditional discretionary sentencing. Over the years commentators continuously have predicted that the "revolution" in constitutional criminal procedure is on the verge of reaching such sentencing and that this development will mark the demise of at least the basic thrust of *Williams,* if not its precise holding. So far, such predictions have turned out to be no more than "wishful thinking" of academicians. The Court continues to cite *Williams* with approval and to rely upon the reasoning of Justice Black's opinion for the Court in *Williams.* While there has been considerable change in the procedures applied in traditional discretionary sentencing, as discussed in §§ 26.5 and 26.6, those changes are largely the product of legislation or of judicial rulings based on the appellate court's supervisory power, rather than of new content given to the concept of due process.

Williams itself was a capital sentencing case decided at a time when capital sentencing was subject in large part to the usual procedures of traditional discretionary sentencing. Defendant Williams had been sen-

§ 26.4

1. 337 U.S. 241, 69 S.Ct. 1079, 93 L.Ed. 1337 (1949).

tenced to death by the trial judge, notwithstanding the jury's recommendation of a life sentence. Justice Black initially noted that the "narrow contention" presented here "makes it unnecessary to set out the facts at length." He then briefly described the basic elements of the sentencing process employed in Williams' case. Following the conviction, a presentence investigation report had been compiled by the probation department and presented to the judge, apparently without disclosure to the defense. The judge had then held a brief sentencing hearing at which first the defendant and then his counsel had been allowed to address the issue of whether the judge should follow the jury's recommendation. The judge then explained why he felt the death sentence should be imposed. He pointed to both the "shocking details of the crime as shown by the trial evidence" and information contained in the presentence report. The judge noted that the presentence investigation "had revealed many material facts concerning the appellant's background which though relevant to the question of punishment could not properly have been brought to the attention of the jury." He then referred specifically to the defendant's involvement in 30 other burglaries in the vicinity, and noted that while defendant had not been convicted of those crimes, "the judge had information that [defendant] had confessed to some and had been identified as the perpetrator of others." The judge also referred to "certain activities * * * as shown by the probation report" indicating that defendant possessed a "morbid sexuality" and was a "menace to society." Justice Black, following his description of these remarks by the judge, added: "The accuracy of the statements made by the judge as to appellant's background and past practices were not challenged by appellant or his counsel, nor was the judge asked to disregard any of them or afford appellant a chance to refute or otherwise discredit any of them by cross-examination or otherwise."

Justice Black described the question before the Court as relating "to the rules of evidence applicable to the manner in which a judge may obtain information to guide him in the imposition of sentence." The defendant had raised a "broad constitutional challenge" to the "New York procedural policy [that] encourages [the judge] to consider information about the convicted person's past life, health, habits, conduct and mental and moral propensities." The defendant had challenged that policy as contrary to basic due process fundamentals ensuring that an accused be given "reasonable notice" and be afforded "an opportunity to examine adverse witnesses." Rejecting this broad challenge, Justice Black referred to both the history and function of sentencing.

As to history, Justice Black noted that, "both before and since the American colonies became a nation, courts in this country and in England practiced a policy under which the sentencing judge could exercise a wide discretion in the sources and types of evidence used to assist him in determining the kind and extent of punishment to be imposed within the limits fixed by law." As to function, Justice Black stressed the distinction between the roles of the factfinder at trial and the sentencing judge. The trial was concerned "solely with the issue of guilt of a particular offense" and utilized rules of evidence designed to "narrowly confine" the factfinder to material "strictly relevant" to that issue. A sentencing judge was not so confined. Highly relevant to his task was the possession of "the fullest information possible concerning the defendant's life and characteristics." This was especially true under the "modern philosophy of penology that the punishment should fit the offender and not merely the crime."

Having established the need for a range of information far broader than that considered at trial, Justice Black then turned to the form in which such relevant information was presented. He noted in this regard:

> Under the practice of individualizing punishments, investigational techniques have been given an important role. Probation workers making reports of their investigations have not been trained to prosecute but to aid offenders. Their reports have been given a high value by conscientious judges who want to sentence persons on the best available infor-

mation rather than on guess-work and inadequate information. To deprive sentencing judges of this kind of information would undermine modern penological procedural policies. * * * We must recognize that most of the information now relied upon by judges to guide them in the intelligent imposition of sentences would be unavailable if information were restricted to that given in open court by witnesses subject to cross-examination. And the modern probation report draws on information concerning every aspect of a defendant's life. The type and extent of this information make totally impractical if not impossible open court testimony with cross-examination. Such a procedure could endlessly delay criminal administration in a retrial of collateral issues.

Such "sound practical reasons," Justice Black noted, were highly relevant under the concept of due process, which was flexible and not frozen in all settings to the "mold of the trial."

Justice Black concluded by noting that there was no justification for creating a "rigid constitutional barrier" even as to capital sentencing. While "leaving a judge free to avail himself of out-of-court information does secure to him a discretionary power [that is] susceptible to abuse," the same kind of broad judgmental authority is available to the judge in evaluating such factors as the defendant's demeanor at trial. The Court could not say that "due process renders a sentence void because a judge gets additional out-of-court information" when "no constitutional objection would have been possible if the judge had sentenced appellant to death because appellant's trial manner impressed the judge that appellant was a bad risk for society, or if the judge had sentenced him to death for no reason at all."

Williams is viewed as the hallmark due process ruling on four basic elements of sentencing procedure—(i) the range of the factors that a judge may consider in imposing a sentence, (ii) the kinds of evidence relating to those factors that may be relied upon in the sentencing determination, (iii) the right of the defendant to be informed of both the factors being considered by the judge and the evidence being advanced in support of those factors, and (iv) the opportunity given to the defendant to challenge both the relevancy of those factors and the proof of their existence. The bearing of Williams upon each of those elements is considered in the subsections that follow, along with the modifications or reenforcement provided by post-*Williams* rulings. In the case of the first element, the discussion is divided into two subsections to afford separate treatment of a special line of post-*Williams* rulings.

(b) The Range of Relevant Information. *Williams* obviously opens to the sentencing court's consideration a wide range of factors that may be deemed relevant to the function of discretionary sentencing as described in *Williams.* In particular, *Williams* clearly upholds what is now described as "real offense" sentencing—that is, sentencing that looks beyond the statutory elements of the charged offense and considers the gravity of defendant's actual conduct (although the maximum sentence must be within the legislatively allowed limit for the charged offense). Indeed, *Williams* obviously considers as relevant conduct extending beyond the transaction that gave rise to the charged offense. Thus, courts do not violate due process when they consider unrelated criminal conduct, even if it did not result in a criminal conviction (as in the case of the burglaries cited by the judge in *Williams*). *Williams* also treats as relevant aspects of the defendant's life that go beyond antisocial conduct. The Court noted the need for the sentencing judge, in evaluating the "lives and personalities of convicted offenders," to draw on information concerning "every aspect of a defendant's life." Indeed, the Court cited in this connection the federal form for presentence reports that directed the probation officer to gather information concerning such factors as "family history," "home and neighborhood," "education," "religion," "interests and activities," "employment," and "health (physical and mental)."

In light of *Williams* sweeping description of relevant information, it could be argued that there is no aspect of a defendant's life that may not be weighed in assessing the appropriate sentence under a discretionary sentencing scheme. Post–*Williams* rulings, however, have held that due process does either limit or absolutely bar consideration of a small group of factors. The post-*Williams* Supreme Court rulings have dealt primarily with the consideration of the defendant's exercise of procedural rights within the criminal justice process. Those rulings, as discussed in subsection (c), have held that certain aspects of the exercise (or non-exercise) of those rights may be considered as positive or negative factors in sentencing, but that giving adverse weight to other aspects of the exercise of those rights is forbidden by due process.

McCleskey v. Kemp,[2] another post-*Williams* ruling, indicates that the race is an element that simply may not be considered, negatively or positively, in sentencing. Although a capital case and looking in part to the Eighth Amendment, *McCleskey* noted that "purposeful discrimination" in sentencing based upon race would be unconstitutional under traditional equal protection analysis. While the sentencing jury in a capital case had been held to have the authority to "consider *any* factor relevant to the defendant's background, character, and the offense," that authority did not extend so far as to allow the more harsh treatment of a particular defendant because of his or her race (or because of the race of the victim). The *McCleskey* Court added, however, that the defendant carried the burden "of proving" the existence of such purposeful discrimination by "the decisionmakers in *his* case," and this burden could not be met by simply showing a statistical disparity across capital sentencing decisions throughout the state. In refusing to accept the statistical disparity as sufficient even to create a rebuttable presumption of discriminatory purpose, the Court distinguished its willingness to draw an inference based on statistical proof in other settings (e.g., jury and grand jury venire-selection).[3] There, the statistics related to "fewer entities" and "fewer variables [were] relevant to the challenged decisions."

Lower courts have suggested that another factor that may not be considered in sentencing is the defendant's exercise of First Amendment freedoms. Although usually finding that the facts did not support such a claim in the case before it, courts have stated that a sentence would be invalid if the judge imposed a heavier sentence because of the defendant's political belief, political speech, or political association. While *Williams* referred to the defendant's "religion" as one factor commonly covered in presentence reports, the reasoning of these courts also suggests that a sentencing court could not weigh against the defendant his religious beliefs or his atheism or agnosticism. Here, however, unlike the situation with respect to race, associations, activities, and beliefs protected by the First Amendment may cast light on personality traits that bear on the risk that defendant will commit further crimes. Indeed, the defendant's active participation in a particular religious or political association may be one of the factors that contributed to his decision to engage in certain criminal activity. Although it could be argued that consideration of such protected activity would "clearly be impermissible in determining defendant's sentence because it would impair the rights of the defendant under the First Amendment,"[4] limiting that consideration to the impact of such associations upon the defendant's motivation and likely future behavior might be viewed as acceptable since it would not reflect a judicial purpose of punishing the defendant based on dislike for those associations. While the drawing of such a distinction may be viewed as placing form over substance, the Supreme Court arguably has taken exactly that tact in its rulings on the consideration in sentencing of the defendant's exercise of procedural rights.

(c) Consideration of the Defendant's Exercise of Procedural Rights. The Supreme Court has held in several different contexts

2. 481 U.S. 279, 107 S.Ct. 1756, 95 L.Ed.2d 262 (1987).

3. See § 23.2(c).

4. United States v. Lemon, 723 F.2d 922 (D.C.Cir. 1983).

that due process is violated where the sentencing court "punishes" the defendant for his exercise of a procedural right in the criminal justice process, whether or not that right is constitutionally required. Thus, in *North Carolina v. Pearce,*[5] the Court unanimously agreed that the sentencing judge could not impose a higher sentence upon a defendant in retaliation for his having successfully appealed his original conviction. The Court acknowledged that *Williams* allowed the sentencing court on reconviction to take into consideration conduct of the defendant subsequent to his first conviction "that may throw new light upon defendant * * * 'moral propensities,'" but that did not authorize "punish[ing] a person because he has done what the law plainly allows him to do" in pursuing an appeal. To allow such "vindictiveness" to play a part in his sentence would be to allow the sentencing court "to put a price on an appeal" and thereby inhibit the "free and unfettered" exercise of that right as granted under state law. In *Pearce* the Court conceded that the "existence of a retalitory motivation would * * * be extremely difficult to prove in any individual case," and concluded that further steps were needed to free the defendant "of the apprehension" of masked retaliation. It therefore established a presumption of vindictiveness under the special circumstances presented there, involving an increased sentence imposed upon reconviction for the same offense that had lead to the conviction overturned on appeal. However, apart from that special situation, as discussed in § 26.8, the defendant does not have the benefit of such a presumption. To establish a due process violation, he must show by reference to the sentencing record that the judge in fact sentenced vindictively, seeking to punish defendant for his exercise of some procedural right.

Though holding that due process prohibits punishment of a defendant's exercise of a trial right, the Supreme Court has allowed the sentencing court to give consideration to certain elements of defendant's behavior related to those rights that are seen as relevant to the sentencing functions recognized in *Williams.* Thus, as discussed in § 21.2, the Court has repeatedly noted in its guilty plea cases that, while the sentencing court may not punish with an increased sentence the defendant who goes to trial, it may reward with a reduced sentence the defendant who pleads guilty. The reward is justified because the entry of a guilty plea produces conditions that justify leniency in accordance with the traditional functions of sentencing. The defendant in pleading guilty proffers to the state various administrative advantages, allows for the more effective attainment of the objectives of punishment through its more prompt imposition, and acknowledges his responsibility for the offense. Consideration of such factors through a reduction of sentence is consistent with objective of individualizing punishment as noted in *Williams.* Of course, the granting of leniency to the defendant who pleads guilty may have the same practical impact in discouraging the exercise of the right to go to trial as a vindictive sentence aimed at the exercise of that right. The Court refuses, however, to therefore preclude constitutionally the granting of leniency in guilty plea cases. It will not disallow consideration of a factor (the entry of a guilty plea) that is otherwise appropriately considered under *Williams* simply because the incidental impact of that practice may be to discourage the exercise of right to trial. Thus, under the guilty plea cases, the key to the due process prohibition against punishing the exercise of procedural rights is the improper purpose of the sentencing judge, rather than merely the presence of a chilling impact upon the exercise of those procedural rights.

In *United States v. Grayson,*[6] the Court adopted a similar analysis in holding that the trial judge could weigh against the defendant a misuse of a trial right that reflected badly upon his character. In that case, the defendant's testimony on his own behalf at trial had been contradicted in several crucial respects by the government's rebuttal evidence, and the trial judge explained at sentencing

5. See § 26.8 at note 1.

6. 438 U.S. 41, 98 S.Ct. 2610, 57 L.Ed.2d 582 (1978).

that he was taking into account "the fact that your defense was a complete fabrication without the slightest merit whatsoever." The defendant had not argued that the sentencing court thereby considered a factor irrelevant to the function of sentence. As the Supreme Court noted, lower courts, relying on *Williams,* had almost without exception concluded that "a defendant's truthfulness or mendacity while testifying on his own behalf * * * [is] probative of his attitudes toward society and prospects for rehabilitation and hence relevant to sentencing." Neither had defendant argued that the judge had acted with the intent of punishing his alleged act of perjury. "Rather, he argue[d] that [the] Court, in order to preserve due process rights, not only must prohibit the impermissible sentencing practice of incarcerating for the purpose of saving the Government the burden of bringing a separate and subsequent perjury prosecution but also must prohibit the otherwise *permissible* practice of considering a defendant's untruthfulness for the purpose of illuminating his need for rehabilitation and society's need for protection." In support of this claim, the defendant had presented "two interrelated reasons: [i] The effect of both permissible and impermissible sentencing practices may be the same: additional time in prison; and [ii] [I]t is virtually impossible * * * to identify and establish the impermissible practice." The Supreme Court found both reasons unpersuasive.

The *Grayson* Court cited three factors that led it to reject the due process standard urged by defendant. First, the judge's function in a discretionary sentencing scheme, as set forth in *Williams,* "demonstrates that it is proper—indeed, even necessary for the rational exercise of discretion—to consider the defendant's whole person and personality, as manifested by his conduct at trial and his testimony under oath, for whatever light those might shed in the sentencing decision." The " 'parlous' effort to appraise 'character'," the Court noted, "degenerates into a game of chance to the extent that a sentencing judge is deprived of relevant information." Second, the risk of improper use here was no different than that presented in *Williams,* where the Court permitted the sentencing judge to consider burglaries for which the defendant had not been convicted despite the risk that the judge might use his knowledge of those prior offenses "for an improper purpose." Third, the efficacy of the "exclusionary rule" suggested by defendant was open to serious doubt, as "no rule of law, even one garbed in constitutional terms, can prevent improper use of firsthand observations of perjury." The "integrity of the [sentencing] judges" necessarily provided "the only, and in our view, adequate assurance" against improper use of such information. Finally, the Court also rejected the defendant's claim that the sentencing judge's action impermissibly "chilled" his constitutional right to testify in his own behalf, noting that this right "is narrowly the right to testify truthfully in accordance with the oath" and that there "is no protected right to commit perjury."

In *Roberts v. United States,*[7] the Court did not find it necessary to consider whether the reasoning of *Grayson* could be extended to allow a sentencing judge to hold against a convicted defendant his subsequent refusal on self-incrimination grounds to assist in the investigation of his former associates. Such a situation may be distinguished from *Grayson* because the defendant is not abusing the right involved (assuming the information sought could be incriminating as to other offenses). Also, unlike the situation presented in the guilty plea cases, the issue here is not whether the court can grant leniency to the defendant who does cooperate, but rather whether it can draw an inference that the defendant was a poor candidate for rehabilitation because he refused to cooperate, albeit on self-incrimination grounds. The *Roberts* Court found that, in the case before it, there was insufficient indication that the refusal to cooperate was actually based upon the privilege, which the defendant had never invoked or called to the attention of the sentencing court. The Court did note, however, that the defen-

7. 445 U.S. 552, 100 S.Ct. 1358, 63 L.Ed.2d 622 (1980).

dant's claimed justification for failure to cooperate "would have merited serious consideration" if it had been properly presented to the sentencing judge. Also, in commenting upon the relevancy of a refusal to cooperate as a rejection of a "deeply rooted social obligation" of the citizen, it noted that this obligation carries over to criminal defendant "unless his silence is protected by the privilege against self-incrimination."

(d) Evidentiary Reliability. Commentators urging a narrow reading of *Williams* have argued that *Williams* stands only for the following proposition: "In the absence of a specific request to do so, due process does not require confrontation and cross-examination of persons who have supplied out-of-court information used in the determination of sentence." This reading of *Williams* suggests that the sentencing court can receive information in a form that would render it inadmissible at trial, but only if the defendant does not contest that evidence. Although it is true that the defendant in *Williams* had not challenged the information cited by the judge in explaining his sentence, the Supreme Court's discussion of the judge's need to obtain a broad range of information presented in various forms was not in any way limited to the lack of objection by the defense. The Court stated flatly that due process did not require that a "sentencing judge * * * be denied an opportunity to obtain pertinent information by a requirement of rigid adherence to restrictive rules of evidence properly applicable to the trial." In light of this statement, courts have not questioned the constitutional validity of state and federal statutes providing that the rules of evidence, apart from those dealing with privilege, simply do not apply to the sentencing process.[8] Lower courts frequently have noted, however, that due process still demands that any information relied upon by the sentencing judge carry a "sufficient indicia of reliability to support its probable accuracy." This requirement is said to follow from a due process right "not to be sentenced on the basis of materially untrue information." Support for such a "constitutional right to accuracy" is usually found in *Townsend v. Burke,*[9] a case decided a year before *Williams.*

In *Townsend,* the defendant, unassisted by counsel, entered a plea of guilty, which was followed by a brief sentencing hearing. A police officer recited the details of the crime and the judge then proceeded to ask the defendant a series of questions that focused on the defendant's prior criminal record. The judge referred to several convictions and asked about the circumstances of one. When defendant stated that the offense was committed by his brother, and that he had been tried for the offense but was "not guilty," the court responded by moving on to ask about other offenses. In the course of that questioning, certain facetious remarks by the judge indicated that he obviously thought the defendant had committed all of the offenses. As was later established, the charge on one of those additional offenses had been dismissed and defendant had indeed been found not guilty on the charge he attributed to his brother, as well as another charge. The Supreme Court concluded that "this uncounseled defendant was either overreached by the prosecutor's submission of information to the court or was prejudiced by the court's own misreading of the record." It noted that "counsel, if any had been present," surely would have been "under a duty to prevent the court from proceeding on such false assumptions." With the defendant having been so disadvantaged by the lack of counsel, and the sentencing court having sentenced based on "assumptions concerning his criminal record which were materially untrue," the "result, whether caused by carelessness or design," was a lack of due process. The Court added that it did not mean to say that "mere error in resolving a question of fact on a plea of guilty by an uncounseled defendant in a non-capital case would necessarily indicate a want of due process of law." For "fair prosecutors and conscientious judges, sometimes are misinformed * * *, and even an erroneous judgment, based

8. See § 26.5(a).

9. 334 U.S. 736, 68 S.Ct. 1252, 92 L.Ed. 1690 (1948).

on scrupulous and diligent search for the truth, may be due process of law." Here, however, counsel clearly would have "taken steps to see that the sentence was not predicated on misinformation or misreading of court records."

Townsend could be read as merely supporting a right to counsel at sentencing where counsel's representation could have made a difference. However, lower courts often have read *Townsend* as establishing the broader principle that the sentencing court must utilize procedures reasonably designed to avoid reliance upon critical information that is "materially untrue." *Townsend* itself may suggest only that the sentencing court take steps to ensure the accuracy of information presented to it where that information is challenged by the defense. The presence of this element of a defense challenge would distinguish *Williams,* where the Court noted that the defense had never challenged the accuracy of judge's statements as to the defendant's background. However, later Supreme Court cases arguably have given a broader reading to *Townsend.*

In *United States v. Tucker,*[10] the Court relied upon *Townsend* in holding that the defendant's sentence could not stand where the judge had relied upon defendant's prior felony convictions without knowledge that those convictions were constitutionally infirm because defendant had been denied his constitutional right to appointed counsel in the proceedings that produced the convictions. The defendant in *Tucker,* who was represented by counsel, had not objected when the sentencing court had noted that it was taking into consideration three prior convictions that the defendant had acknowledged while being cross-examined at trial. Nonetheless, the Court noted that a new sentencing proceeding was necessary because the

> "sentence [was] founded at least in part upon misinformation of constitutional magnitude. As in *Townsend v. Burke,* 'this prisoner was sentenced on the basis of assumptions concerning his criminal record which were materially untrue.'"

This portion of the *Tucker* opinion might suggest that the due process violation exists simply because the sentence judge relied heavily on information that was not true. However, *Townsend* had noted that a misinformed sentencing decision did not necessarily violate due process, as errors were possible even where there had been a "scrupulous and diligent search for the truth." Thus, the flaw in *Tucker* more likely rested on the sentencing court's failure to make some effort to ensure that the convictions in question were not uncounseled convictions. The convictions in question had been obtained in state courts a good many years before *Gideon v. Wainwright* imposed an absolute right of the indigent to counsel in felony cases, and two had come from the very state that was involved in *Gideon.* The Court has noted in its Sixth Amendment rulings that uncounseled convictions are not sufficiently reliable to support the sanction of imprisonment,[11] and the possibility that defendant's convictions might fall in that category of inherently unreliable evidence apparently was sufficient to require some further inquiry by the sentencing court on its own initiative. Not having pursued such an inquiry, the reliance on "materially untrue" information could not be said to nonetheless have been consistent with due process, as the sentencing court had not engaged in a "diligent and scrupulous search for the truth."

(e) Notice. Does the *Williams* opinion indicate that due process allows a defendant to be sentenced without the sentencing court informing the defense of the grounding for its exercise of discretion? The *Williams* case certainly did not present such a situation in absolute terms. The judge had told the defendant that he was taking into consideration both the defendant's participation in various burglaries and certain other activities noted in the presentence report, that evidenced defendant's "morbid sexuality" and classified him as a "menace to society." This explanation, however, hardly provided full notice of

10. 404 U.S. 443, 92 S.Ct. 589, 30 L.Ed.2d 592 (1972).

11. See Argersinger v. Hamlin and Baldasar v. Illinois, discussed in § 11.2(a) at notes 1 and 10.

the grounding for the sentencing judge's conclusions relating to the defendant's past behavior. As to the burglaries, the judge noted that defendant had confessed as to "some" and had been identified as the perpetrator as to "others," but did not state which of the burglaries fell in each category, how he knew that defendant had confessed (or precisely what defendant was supposed to have said), or who had identified the defendant as the perpetrator. As to the other activities, the judge did not identify the precise nature of those activities or what the presentence report offered in support of the conclusion that he had engaged in those activities. In arguing that the sentencing court should have before it the sworn testimony of relevant witnesses, the defendant had noted that this was necessary to give him "reasonable notice." The Court, in rejecting that contention and holding that the sentencing judge could rely on "out-of-court information," suggested that the provision of such notice might well undercut the sentencing judge's ability to use such information. It noted that most of that information would be "unavailable" if the sources had to appear and give testimony in open court. Indeed, in exploring why the sentencing judge's willingness to identify some of the factors relied upon should not operate to give the defendant additional rights, the Court stated that "no federal constitutional objection would have been possible * * * if the judge had sentenced [defendant] to death giving no reason at all."

In light of these aspects of *Williams,* it is not surprising that an Advisory Committee Note on the Federal Rules stated: "It is not a denial of due process of law for a court in sentencing to rely on a report of pre-sentence investigation without disclosing such report to the defendant or giving him an opportunity to rebut it." Commentators have challenged this reading, however, as ignoring *Williams* continued acceptance of *Townsend v. Burke.* The assumption of *Townsend* was that counsel could have assisted the defendant in avoiding a sentence based on factual error. That assumption was reaffirmed in *Mempa v. Rhay,*[12] where the Court held that the defendant has a Sixth Amendment right to counsel at sentencing. How could counsel play an important role in ensuring the accuracy of the information put before the sentencing judge, it is asked, if that information is inaccessible to the defense? One answer is that counsel is needed (1) to offer affirmative evidence on behalf of the defense, and (2) to respond to adverse information if such information is disclosed by the sentencing court in its discretion (as it was in *Townsend*). At the time that *Mempa* was decided, federal courts were not required to state the grounds for their sentencing decisions and disclosure of the presentence report rested in the discretion of the sentencing court. While the Supreme Court had not had occasion to rule on a constitutional challenge to this rule of discretion, it had transmitted to Congress the Federal Rule that incorporated that standard. Moreover, it had done so over the objection of Justice Douglas, who had maintained that the "rule for the federal courts ought not to be one which permits a judge to impose sentence on the basis of information of which the defendant may be unaware and to which he has not been afforded an opportunity to reply." [13]

Whatever the correct reading of *Williams* as to notice, today that issue must be analyzed in light of the Supreme Court's ruling in *Gardner v. Florida.*[14] The trial judge in *Gardner* had sentenced the defendant to death without stating on the record the substance of any information in the confidential portion of the presentence report that he might have considered material to his decision. This was held to be unconstitutional, but there was no opinion for the Court on that issue. Two justices concluded that the procedure was contrary to the Court's previous ruling on an Eighth Amendment challenge to the statute in question, one concluded that the state judicial system's cavalier approach to the death

12. 389 U.S. 128, 88 S.Ct. 254, 19 L.Ed.2d 336 (1967).

13. 383 U.S. 1089, 1092–93, 86 S.Ct. 236, 238, 15 L.Ed.2d xcvii, xcix (1966).

14. 430 U.S. 349, 97 S.Ct. 1197, 51 L.Ed.2d 393 (1977).

penalty issue required reassessment of the constitutionality of the underlying statute, and another concurred in the reversal without opinion. However, three justices, in a plurality opinion by Justice Stevens, concluded that there had been a violation of due process, and another expressed general agreement with the analysis of that opinion.

The state in *Gardner* had placed primary reliance upon *Williams,* but the plurality opinion viewed *Williams* as readily distinguishable. For one thing, in *Williams,* relevant information had been disclosed but went unchallenged; in the instant case, there was "no similar opportunity for petitioner's counsel to challenge the accuracy or materiality of any such information." For another, since *Williams* had been decided, two important constitutional developments had occurred: (i) a majority of the Court now recognized that death is a different kind of punishment requiring closer scrutiny; and (ii) "it is now clear that the sentencing process, as well as the trial itself, must satisfy the requirements of the Due Process Clause." Decisions like *Mempa v. Rhay* and *Specht v. Patterson* [15] had firmly established that "the defendant has a legitimate interest in the character of the procedure which leads to the imposition of sentence even if he may have no right to object to a particular result of the sentencing process." Accordingly, the plurality concluded, the Constitution today demanded application of the traditional due process balancing approach that weighed the interests in nondisclosure asserted by the state against the interests of the defendant in a procedure that ensured a rationally imposed death sentence.

The state in *Gardner* sought to justify its practice of non-disclosure by reference to several interests. It maintained (i) that an assurance of confidentiality was "essential to enable investigators to obtain relevant but sensitive disclosures from persons unwilling to comment publicly about a defendant's character," (ii) that judges could be trusted to rely only on reliable information, and (iii) that disclosure of the presentence report would cause delay. The plurality found each of those justifications to be flawed. While assurances of secrecy were "conducive to the transmission of confidences," those confidences might "bear no closer relationship to fact than the average rumor or gossip." The "risk that some of the information accepted in confidence may be erroneous or may be misinterpreted, by the investigator or by the sentencing judge, [was] manifest." The assumption that trial judges could be relied upon to exercise their discretion in a responsible manner, even though relying on "secret information," was contrary to the Court's Eighth Amendment rulings and rested on the "erroneous premise that the participation of counsel is superfluous to the process of evaluating the relevance and significance of aggravating and mitigating factors." Finally, the likelihood of significant delay clearly was "overstated" if, as the Court would presume, the "reports prepared by professional probation officers * * * are generally reliable." Moreover, if critical matter should be disputed, then "the time invested in ascertaining the truth would surely be well spent if it makes the difference between life or death." Thus, the defendant's interest in a reliable process clearly prevailed, and a defendant was denied due process "when the death sentence was imposed, at least in part, on the basis of information which he had no opportunity to deny or explain."

As discussed in § 26.5(b), presentence reports commonly are made available to defendant today, even in noncapital cases. Still, that practice is not universal, and application of *Gardner* to noncapital cases therefore remains a live issue. Even as to the *Gardner* plurality, however, the exact significance of the death penalty there is debatable. The plurality eschewed reliance on the Eighth Amendment and used a more general due process analysis. Most of the state justifications that it rejected, and most of the concerns that it expressed regarding the subversion of reliable factfinding, apply equally to nondisclosure in non-capital sentencing. On the other hand, the presence of a death sen-

15. See note 20 infra.

tence quite clearly was viewed as increasing the significance of the interests of the defendant and society that were balanced against the state justifications for nondisclosure. Also, while the factors considered in capital sentencing are not as clearly distinct from the offense as the special proceedings discussed in subsection (g), where disclosure also is required, neither does capital sentencing present the traditional open-ended and unguided discretionary determination that was involved in *Williams.*

(f) Defense Opportunity to Be Heard. Even if defendant lacks a due process right to be informed of the general nature of the factors relied upon by the judge in sentencing, it hardly follows that due process does not guarantee to the defense an opportunity to be heard. Nonetheless, courts occasionally have suggested that no such right exists. Surprisingly, one such statement is found in a Supreme Court ruling in which the Court distinguished *Williams* and imposed broad due process requirements. In *Specht v. Patterson,*[16] Justice Douglas opened his opinion for the Court with the comment: "We held in *Williams v. New York,* that the Due Process Clause of the Fourteenth Amendment did not require a judge to have [sentencing] hearings and to give the convicted person an opportunity to participate in those hearings when he came to determine the sentence to be imposed." Other aspects of the *Specht* opinion suggest that Justice Douglas was referring only to a trial-type hearing, and that certainly is the more appropriate reading of *Williams.* The Court in *Williams* obviously did not have before it the question of whether the defense could be denied the opportunity to present its own evidence relevant to the sentencing function. Moreover, the reasoning of the Court would certainly work against such an absolute denial of a defense right to be heard. Justice Black's opinion stressed that "modern concepts have made it all the more necessary that a sentencing judge not be denied an opportunity to obtain pertinent information." Accordingly, due process would not erect a constitutional barrier to receipt of out-of-court information from the wide range of sources available to the probation officer in preparing a presentence report. A state could hardly argue that such information is relevant, yet deny to the defense any opportunity to present its information to the court. Indeed, defendants traditionally have been afforded that opportunity, although courts may impose limits on the mode and length of that defense presentation.

In *McGautha v. California,*[17] one of petitioners claimed that because the sentencing in his capital case was left to the jury and because the state had refused to utilize a bifurcated trial, he had lost his right to present evidence on the issue of sentence when he exercised his self-incrimination privilege not to testify at trial. Rejecting that claim, the Court noted:

> This Court has not directly determined whether or to what extent the concept of due process of law requires that a criminal defendant wishing to present evidence or argument presumably relevant to the issues involved in sentencing should be permitted to do so. Assuming, without deciding, that the Constitution does require such an opportunity, there was no denial of such a right in Crampton's case. The Ohio Constitution guarantees defendants the right to have their counsel argue in summation for mercy as well as for acquittal. * * * [Also], the record in Crampton's case does not reveal that any evidence offered on the part of the defendant was excluded on the ground that it was relevant solely to the issue of punishment.

The *McGautha* opinion, in a footnote to the first sentence quoted above, cited Justice Douglas' description of *Williams* in *Specht v. Patterson,* which it characterized as reading *Williams* "broadly." The *McGautha* Court itself described *Williams* only as a case holding that "due process did not require a State to choose between prohibiting the use of [presentence] reports and holding an adversary hearing at which the defendant could cross-examine the sources of information contained therein."

16. See note 20 infra.

17. 402 U.S. 183, 91 S.Ct. 1454, 28 L.Ed.2d 711 (1971). See also § 24.5 at note 5.

The *McGautha* Court also cited in the same footnote *Mempa v. Rhay.*[18] *Mempa* had held that the Sixth Amendment right to counsel extended "to sentencing" and thus included sentencing that was deferred to a probation revocation hearing. The argument has been advanced that *Mempa* implicitly establishes a defense right to be heard on sentence because without such a right the assistance of counsel would not be constitutionally required. However, the state in *Mempa* did provide a right to be heard, and the Supreme Court has held in other Sixth Amendment rulings that the state can provide a hearing that is not constitutionally required (e.g., a preliminary hearing) and thereby establish a "critical stage" of the prosecution to which the Sixth Amendment applies.[19]

(g) Special Factor Sentencing. In *Specht v. Patterson,*[20] the Court had before it a constitutional challenge to the Colorado Sex Offenders Act. The Act gave the trial court the authority to impose an indeterminate sentence of one day to life upon a person convicted of any of a group of specified sex offenses. Initially, the trial court had to be "of the opinion that [the] person, if at large, constitutes a threat of bodily harm to members of the public, or is an habitual offender and mentally ill." The trial court then had to order "a complete psychiatric exam" and the report of that exam, including the psychiatrist's recommendation as to disposition, was to be considered by it in deciding whether to apply the Act. The defendant in *Specht* had been sentenced to an indeterminate life sentence under the Act following his conviction for indecent liberties, an offense carrying a maximum sentence of ten years. He challenged the application of the Act as denying him due process because the court's finding was made "(1) without a hearing at which * * * [he] could confront and cross-examine adverse witnesses and present evidence of his own by use of compulsory process * * * and (2) on the basis of hearsay evidence to which * * * [he was] not allowed access." In sustaining the defendant's challenge, the Court distinguished *Williams.* It "adher[ed] to *Williams,*" but would "decline the invitation to extend it to this radically different situation."

The Colorado Act, the *Specht* Court noted, did "not make the commission of a specified crime the basis for sentencing." Rather "it ma[de] one conviction the basis for commencing another proceeding under another Act to * * * [to make] a new finding of fact that was not an ingredient of the offense charged." As a lower court had noted in speaking of a similar statute: " 'It is a separate criminal proceeding which may be invoked after conviction of one of the specified crimes. Petitioner therefore was entitled to a full judicial hearing before the magnified sentence was imposed.' " Turning to the particular rights required for that "full judicial hearing," the Court stated: "Due process requires that [defendant] be present with counsel, have an opportunity to be heard, be confronted with witnesses against him, have the right to cross-examine, and to offer evidence of his own. And there must be findings adequate to make meaningful any appeal that is allowed."

In *Morrissey v. Brewer*[21] and *Gagnon v. Scarpelli,*[22] the Court held that due process also demanded a variety of procedural requirements in probation and parole revocation proceedings.[23] Those proceedings were viewed as so clearly distinguishable from the traditional sentencing proceeding that the Court found no need to discuss *Williams* or *Specht* in either opinion. The revocation hearing obviously presented a proceeding distinct from the original sentencing hearing. Moreover, it was directed to determining whether subsequent conduct of the defendant constituted a "violation" in itself, rather than to determining the appropriate sanction for the offense for which defendant had already been sentenced. Both lower courts and commentators have found the distinction between *Specht* and *Williams* not nearly so evident as

18. Supra note 12.

19. See §§ 11.2(b); 14.4(a).

20. 386 U.S. 605, 87 S.Ct. 1209, 18 L.Ed.2d 326 (1967).

21. 408 U.S. 471, 92 S.Ct. 2593, 33 L.Ed.2d 484 (1972).

22. 411 U.S. 778, 93 S.Ct. 1756, 36 L.Ed.2d 656 (1973).

23. See § 26.11.

the distinction between sentencing and revocation proceedings. One distinction drawn by the Court in *Specht,* the presence of a separate proceeding under a separate statute, seems too mechanical. Another, the critical new finding as to conduct or tendencies that were not an element of the underlying crime seems to reach too deeply into traditional sentencing, which also often looks to behavior apart from the offense (as did the sentencing judge in *Williams*). The critical aspect of *Specht* may be the Court's conclusion that the nature and length of the sentence imposed bore no relationship to the offense committed; the sentence was for life, although the indecent liberties offense had only a ten year maximum, and the sentence was completely indeterminate so that release was geared to a psychiatric determination of defendant's current dangerousness rather than to the severity of the underlying offense. This would suggest that the Court viewed the Act as providing, in effect, for an independent commitment proceeding that used the offense as a triggering device but looked basically to separate qualities justifying commitment.

The various possible readings of *Specht* open a range of possibilities as to its application to a variety of special sentences. The most likely candidates are the various special offender provisions, such as recidivist and dangerous offender statutes, that impose extended terms of imprisonment upon a finding of previous convictions or a pattern of "professional" criminal activity. Such statutes commonly require procedures that meet the due process standards of *Specht,* but that is not always the case.[24] Support for the applicability of *Specht* is found in the comment by the *Specht* court that the case before it was "not unlike those under recidivist statutes where an habitual criminal issue is a distinct issue on which a defendant must 'receive reasonable notice and an opportunity to be heard.' " However, the Court has also stated with respect to recidivist statutes that they do not constitute separate criminal charges, but merely aggravate penalties for the defendant's most recent offense. Under this rationale, the evidence of past crimes is considered simply to demonstrate the added seriousness of the offender's commission of the single crime for which he is current punished.

In *McMillan v. Pennsylvania,*[25] the Court distinguished *Specht* in dealing with an offense-enhancement provision. That provision imposed a mandatory minimum term of five years where the defendant "visibly possessed a firearm" during the commission of the offense. The due process issue before the Court was whether proof of the enhancement factor constitutionally required a higher degree of persuasion than that of a "preponderance of the evidence." Although *Specht* had not dealt with the burden of proof issue, the defense argued that *Specht* had been decided prior to the Court's holding that due process required a reasonable doubt standard of proof for a criminal offense, and that *Specht* today would also require that standard for distinct post-trial findings. Responding to that contention, the Court noted:

> [E]ven if we accept petitioners' hypothesis, we do not think it avails them here. The Court in *Specht* observed that following trial the Colorado defendant was confronted with "a radically different situation" from the usual sentencing proceeding. The same simply is not true under the Pennsylvania statute. The finding of visible possession of a firearm of course "ups the ante" for a defendant, or it would not be challenged here; but it does so only in the way that we have previously mentioned, by raising the minimum sentence that may be imposed by the trial court.

The distinction noted by the Court raises the question as to whether the Court would have viewed as closer to *Specht* the more common enhancement factor that "ups the ante" by applying an extended term.[26] Such an enhancement provision might still be distinguished from the special offender provision, for it will look to a characteristic of the underlying offense rather than unrelated behavior, but it still would require a specific finding

24. See § 26.1(c).

25. 477 U.S. 79, 106 S.Ct. 2411, 91 L.Ed.2d 67 (1986).

26. See § 26.1(c).

as to an historical fact that is not itself an element of the substantive crime.

The *McMillan* analysis would appear to clearly distinguish from *Specht* guideline factors that refer to historical facts. Here too, the factor is considered only with reference to setting the sentence within the maximum range allowed for the substantive offense.[27] Commentators have suggested, however, that due process might require more procedural protections with respect to those findings than is demanded by *Williams* and the other cases discussed in subsections (a) to (f), though not necessarily all the protections that *Specht* demanded. *Williams,* it is noted, was grounded on the importance of procedural flexibility within a system of indeterminate sentencing that looked to all the diverse facts of the offender's personality. Guideline provisions are said to weaken this justification for procedural flexibility by narrowing the judge's discretion and looking away from the rehabilitative concerns underlying the traditional indeterminate sentence. This position acknowledges that guideline sentencing allows for some degree of discretion and looks to a wide range of factors, and that due process therefore may not require the broad range of trial-type rights imposed in cases like *Specht, Morrissey,* and *Gagnon.* It maintains, however, that due process should nonetheless demand more than suggested by *Williams* with respect to notice, opportunity to be heard, and the capacity to cross-examine witnesses on any disputed factual issue that is critical to a guideline factor. Courts operating under guidelines have clearly displayed a tendency to move in this direction, although not necessarily on a due process analysis. As a constitutional matter, this produces a rather ironic result: allowable informality in sentencing procedure is lost as the legislature imposes guidelines designed to eliminate the arbitrary disparities that flow from a system in which that informality is constitutionally acceptable. Still "our conceptions of fair process often do imply a need for more rigorous procedural standards when more definite substantive standard are introduced." [28]

§ 26.5 Sentencing Information

(a) Evidentiary Standards. The traditional policy regarding the range and nature of the information that may be received by a sentencing judge is succinctly stated in 18 U.S.C.A. § 3661:

> No limitation shall be placed on the information concerning the background, character, and conduct of a person convicted of an offense which a court of the United States may receive and consider for the purpose of imposing an appropriate sentence.

This policy is reflected also in the statements of state courts, where it has been noted that "the latitude allowed the sentencing judge * * * is almost with limitation." It finds support as well in the Supreme Court's reasoning in *Williams v. New York,*[1] and its comment there that "modern concepts individualizing punishment have made it all the more necessary that a sentencing judge not be denied an opportunity to obtain pertinent information by a requirement of rigid adherence to restrictive rules of evidence properly applicable to the trial."

The Federal Rules of Evidence incorporate this traditional position in Rule 1101(d), which provides that "the rules (other than with respect to privileges) do not apply in * * * sentencing." Similar provisions are found in the many states that have statutes or court rules governing the rules of evidence, and states utilizing common law evidentiary rulings tend to reach the same general conclusion. Inapplicability of the rules of evidence means, for one thing, that affidavits may be received at sentencing even though the defendant has no opportunity to confront or cross-examine the affiant. So too, the sentencing court can consider hearsay, whether contained in the presentence report or offered by the prosecution or defense. Sentencing

27. See § 26.3(c).

28. Schulhofer, Due Process of Sentencing, 128 U.Pa. L.Rev. 733 (1980). See also § 26.1 following note 3.

§ 26.5

1. See § 26.4(a).

courts also can consider testimony given at a trial, even though the defendant was not a participant in that trial. Even though evidence was unconstitutionally obtained and barred from trial use under an exclusionary rule, that ordinarily will not prevent its use in the sentencing proceeding[2]; a defendant may preclude evidence only where its very use constitutes a constitutional violation (e.g., violating defendant's self-incrimination privilege). In sum, with the possible exception of privileged material, the basic approach, as stated in the official commentary to the Federal Sentencing Guidelines, is that "any information may be considered, so long as it has 'sufficient indicia of reliability to support its probable accuracy.' "

Notwithstanding the above policy, courts have noted the need for caution in utilizing two categories of evidence. One is hearsay from an unnamed informant. Several courts here have suggested that such hearsay should not be included in a presentence report unless there is "good cause" for the nondisclosure of the informant's identity or there is "sufficient corroboration by other means." A contrary position argues that such hearsay, when not supported by some indicia of reliability, can simply be given no weight if and when it is disputed by the defense. Without a defense challenge, however, it should not be assumed to be unreliable.

The second troublesome area involves the treatment of various criminal justice records. Law enforcement compilations of prior criminal records require some degree of caution for several reasons. First, there is a tendency to accept such records as inherently reliable, without seeking any type of corroboration. In fact, "rap sheets" have proven to be incorrect with alarming frequency. Second, informal methods of communication sometimes utilized may result in even correct records being mistakenly reported. Finally there is a need to identify prior convictions which fall within *United States v. Tucker,*[3] which held that a defendant's sentencing could not stand when imposed by a judge who considered a prior conviction without knowing that the conviction was unconstitutionally obtained because defendant had been denied counsel.

By analogy to *Tucker,* it sometimes has been argued that the sentencing judge may not take into account an offense of which the defendant has been acquitted, but this is not the governing rule. Notwithstanding the acquittal, there is nothing improper in the judge "looking at all the evidence implicating defendant, including evidence which was used in the unsuccessful prosecution." Such evidence is still reliable, as it "was given under oath and was subject to cross-examination." Where the trial was before the same judge, he or she would have had the opportunity for personal observation of the witness. In some instances, the acquittal may relate to a defense that negates criminal liability but hardly excuses misbehavior. Finally, the proof standard at sentencing being substantially less than proof beyond a reasonable doubt, the presence of a reasonable doubt does not in itself negate the significance of the proof even as to the criminal misconduct, as evidenced by both the indictment and the trial court's refusal to grant a directed acquittal (if that was the case).

A more persuasive case can be made for excluding arrest records. Such records are often inaccurate or incomplete, and the lack of a subsequent charge suggests that the arrest may very well not have been supported by probable cause. Nonetheless, courts are divided on the propriety of including such information in presentence reports. Here again, it is sometimes assumed that the proper response is to discount the information if it is challenged by the defense. One difficulty, however, is that defendants may not be able to recollect the events in question, and defense counsel too often fail to pursue an extensive presentence investigation.

2. Rulings here have related primarily to Fourth Amendment violations. See § 3.1(f). Courts have occasionally noted, however, that exclusion might be required, as a deterrent measure, where the evidence was sought for the express purpose of use in sentencing. See e.g., State v. Habbena, 372 N.W.2d 450 (S.D.1985).

3. See § 26.4 at note 10.

(b) The Presentence Report. Presentence reports are prepared by probation officers and represent the product of their presentence investigation. The report is intended to provide information bearing upon the choice between probation and imprisonment, upon what probation conditions should be imposed if the former alternative is chosen, and upon how long the prison term should be if the latter alternative is selected. In addition, the report is usually the major information source on other significant decisions: if the defendant is placed on probation, the probation officer's determination of the appropriate level of supervision; and if the defendant is incarcerated, decisions regarding the institution at which he will be held, his classification within the institution, and his release on, and supervision during, parole.

The probation officer's preparation of a presentence report typically involves, in the first instance, an in-depth interview with the defendant in order to obtain his version of the offense and other information about his background and circumstances. The probation officer then contacts the prosecutor and law enforcement agents connected with the case in order to get their version of the offense and other information they may have about defendant's activities. Next, by using the FBI "rap sheet" or similar records, the probation officer ascertains the defendant's prior criminal record. He then will contact various individuals and agencies who might provide additional information about the defendant, such as members of his family, present and past employers, the victim of the crime, and medical, educational, financial and military institutions with whom the defendant has had dealings. Often a second interview with the defendant occurs at this point for the purpose of obtaining a more complete statement from him and resolving any discrepancies in the information previously collected. The report is then prepared by following a standard format.

Under a presumptive sentencing system, the presentence report will respond to each of the elements identified in the statutory listing of aggravating or mitigating factors, and under a guidelines system, it will consider all of the factors contributing to the offense level and the criminal-history category. The inclusion of a detailed description of the crime is especially important where the defendant pleads guilty, as the court will not have the trial evidence to look to in applying the various distinctions relevant to characterizing the offense. Under the federal guidelines system, the probation officer also is required to inform the court of: (1) the guideline categories that the officer believes apply to the particular case; (2) the kinds of sentences and the sentencing range believed to apply; (3) any factors that may indicate that a sentence of a different kind or type would be more appropriate; (4) pertinent policy statements issued by the Sentencing Commission; and (5) the nature and extent of non-prison programs available to the defendant.

In the federal system and in some states the presentence report may be prepared prior to the defendant's guilty plea or conviction. There are several reasons for delaying preparation of the presentence report until after the determination of guilt, most importantly the danger that otherwise the contents of the report might come to the attention of the court, the prosecution, or the jury prior to conviction. The Supreme Court has intimated that disclosure of the report before conviction may prejudice the judge and constitute reversible error.[4] It may often be wise, however, for the defense to give its consent to having the judge inspect the report earlier, so that the judge will have a basis for determining whether he will concur in a plea agreement which has been reached by the parties.

Jurisdictions vary as to the use of the presentence report. Many jurisdictions make it mandatory for all felony cases. Others make it mandatory unless the judge makes a specific finding that the evidence on the record is

4. Gregg v. United States, 394 U.S. 489, 89 S.Ct. 1134, 22 L.Ed.2d 442 (1969) (finding no evidence that the judge saw the report before the jury verdict was returned).

sufficient to stand alone. Many states make it discretionary, although some then require it for certain dispositions (e.g., probation). In still other jurisdictions, there is no statutory provision governing the use of presentence reports. Where the report is mandatory, the failure to utilize a report is not a defect of constitutional magnitude and therefore must be raised on direct review.

(c) Disclosure of the Presentence Report. At one time, presentence reports were considered "confidential" documents, and there was a presumption against disclosure to the defense. The primary argument against disclosure was that it would impair the collection of vital information from persons afraid of reprisal or public notoriety. Opponents of disclosure also contended that disclosure would damage the defendant's rehabilitation by adversely affecting his relationships with family and friends and with the probation officer who might supervise his community release. Those arguments were found wanting in light of the experience of courts that experimented with regular disclosure of presentence reports. At the same time, decisions such as *Gardner*[5] cast doubt upon the constitutionality of failing to give the defense any notice of the contents of the report, although the general thrust of the lower court rulings continued to be that disclosure was not constitutionally required. The end result was the gradual emergence of a consensus that disclosure should be the norm, if not invariably required. Today the vast majority of jurisdictions have adopted, by statute, court rule, or judicial decision, a mandatory requirement for disclosure of at least a portion of the presentence report. In the remaining jurisdictions, disclosure is either specifically stated to be discretionary or there is no rule on disclosure. No jurisdiction has a rule prohibiting disclosure. Where disclosure is made to the defense, the applicable standard ordinarily provides that the same disclosure will be made to the prosecution.

Among those jurisdictions mandating disclosure, the majority have provisions that either specifically refer to the disclosure of the entire report or have been interpreted by courts as not allowing exclusion. In those jurisdictions authorizing exclusions, they tend to be fairly limited. Federal Rule 32(c) is typical. It generally requires disclosure of the full report, except for "any recommendation as to sentence," but then directs the court to make exclusions where it is of "the opinion" that disclosure would (i) reveal "diagnostic opinion which might seriously disrupt a program of rehabilitation," (2) compromise "sources of information obtained upon a promise of confidentiality," or (3) "result in harm, physical or otherwise, to the defendant or other persons." Where an exclusion is made, the court is then required to provide "a summary of the factual information contained therein to be relied on in determining sentence."

(d) Victim Impact Statement. In recent years, the victims' rights movement has resulted in the adoption in many jurisdictions of statutes that authorize or require consideration of victim impact statements during the sentencing stage. In other jurisdictions, such statements have been included in presentence reports as a matter of practice. A victim for this purpose typically is defined as including any individual who suffers direct or threatened physical, emotional, or financial harm as a result of the crime. In the case of a victim who is a minor or is incapacitated, any immediate family member may author the statement. The function of the statement is to provide information about the financial, emotional, and physical effects of the crime on the victim and the victim's family. It may also include information regarding the circumstances surrounding the crime and the manner in which it was perpetrated. Unlike the presentence report, which would only summarize the probation officer's interview of the victim, the victim impact statement is written in the victim's own words. Where there are numerous victims and obtaining a statement from each would not be feasible, one or more representative statements may be used. The statute may also grant to the victim the alter-

5. See § 26.4 at note 14.

native of making an oral statement to the court at the sentencing hearing. Of course, the victim is not required to make an impact statement.

(e) Defense and Prosecutions Submissions. Federal Rule 32(c) provides that the "court shall afford the defendant and defendant's counsel an opportunity to comment on the [presentence] report and, in the discretion of court, to introduce testimony or other information relating to any alleged factual inaccuracy contained in it." This constitutes standard practice where the presentence report is disclosed, and, indeed, may well be a constitutionally required element of a defense opportunity to be heard. The defense opportunity to present relevant information, moreover, is not limited to challenging the accuracy of the presentence report, but also extends to the supplementation of that report by presenting other information that will give the court a complete picture of all factors relevant to sentencing. As the Supreme Court stated in concluding there was a Sixth Amendment right to counsel at sentencing, "the necessity for the aid of counsel in marshaling the facts, introducing evidence of mitigating circumstances and in general aiding and assisting the defendant to present his case as to sentence is apparent." [6] Of course, as many courts have noted, this does not necessarily grant to the defense a right to present the live testimony of witnesses, but the defense at least will be allowed to submit a written report, including affidavits, that is parallel to the presentence report.

As for the role of the prosecutor at sentencing, there is considerable variation in current practice. Some prosecutor's offices play virtually no role in sentencing, but the prevailing approach is for the prosecutor to make a specific sentence recommendation or to make argument concerning the nature and severity of the crime and the criminal history of the defendant or to do both. If relevant information is omitted from the presentence report, the prosecutor can also call such information to the attention of the court. Under the federal sentencing guidelines, any reduction for assisting the government in an investigation or prosecution is dependent upon a motion by the government.

(f) Right of Allocution. Distinct from the right to be represented by counsel at sentencing is the personal right of the defendant, recognized in the federal courts and the courts of most states, to make a statement on his own behalf relative to sentencing. This right has its origins in the long-established common law right of a defendant to "allocution," a formal statement by the defendant of any legal reason why he could not be sentence. Because the right of allocution arose at a time when many crimes were punishable by death and when the defendant had no right to be represented by counsel or even to testify on his own behalf, it has sometimes been suggested that it is of little importance in modern times. But a right in the defendant to make a personal statement has both symbolic and practical significance. It has value in terms of maximizing the perceived equity of the process. Moreover, as the Supreme Court noted in *Green v. United States,*[7] there are times when a plea in mitigation can best be presented by the defendant: "The most persuasive counsel may not be able to speak for a defendant as the defendant might, with halting eloquence, speak for himself."

Though it has been held that the failure to accord allocution to a defendant represented by counsel is not an error of constitutional dimensions, the Supreme Court has not yet decided whether silencing a defendant who wished to speak would be constitutionally impermissible. However, the Court has concluded that, in the absence of any aggravating circumstances, the mere failure of the judge to ask the defendant whether he wished to say anything before imposition of sentence "is not a fundamental defect which inherently results in a complete miscarriage of justice." [8]

6. Mempa v. Rhay, 389 U.S. 128, 88 S.Ct. 254, 19 L.Ed.2d 336 (1967).

7. 365 U.S. 301, 81 S.Ct. 653, 5 L.Ed.2d 670 (1961).

8. Hill v. United States, 368 U.S. 424, 82 S.Ct. 468, 7 L.Ed.2d 417 (1962) (therefore holding that relief was not available on collateral attack).

§ 26.6 Sentencing Factfinding

(a) Defense Right to Challenge. While the defense through its submissions is given the right to challenge information contained in the presentence report (or at least that portion which is disclosed) and any additional information presented by the prosecution, the exercise of that right may carry with it certain responsibilities beyond a timely objection. Information that the prosecution is seeking to present may most readily be placed in dispute, often simply by a denial of its accuracy. As to the presentence report, however, considerably more usually will be required. Initially, the defendant must identify the specific factual inaccuracies, rather than rely on a general characterization of the report as erroneous. Beyond that, it is said to be the "general rule throughout this country that when matters contained in a report are contested by the defendant, the defendant has, in effect, an affirmative duty to present evidence showing the inaccuracies contained in the report."[1] Placing this burden on the defendant follows from the treatment of the presentence report as "a theoretically neutral document" which may be "accepted as true" unless the defendant produces evidence to the contrary.

Exactly what type of evidence must defendant produce, or offer to produce, in order to place in dispute information contained in a presentence report? Courts commonly state only that the defense must be able to come forward with "rebuttal evidence." Certainly, as with the presentence report itself, the rebuttal evidence need not be admissible under the rules of evidence. As to the substantiality of that evidence, perhaps the best analogy is the "some evidence" rule applied at trial as to defenses on which the defendant bears the burden of production. However, even that standard may ask too much of the defense. As illustrated by *United States v. Weston,*[2] there may be situations in which the defense cannot reasonably be expected to come forward with more than a denial of an alleged fact.

In *Weston,* the trial court imposed the maximum sentence for the offense of transporting narcotics because of a statement in the presentence report that federal agents believed defendant to be a major drug dealer. The sentencing court noted that it would take more than defendant's "vehement denial" to challenge the "factual information" presented by the agents relating to defendant's drug-dealing activities. The court invited the defense to conduct its own investigation and produce contrary evidence, but defense counsel responded that he was at a loss to determine how to respond as the defense did not know the basis for the agents' statements. The court later inquired in camera into that basis, and expressed concern because the agents' statements apparently did no more than repeat information received from an informant (claimed to have been reliable in the past). Nonetheless, in the absence of contrary evidence from the defense, it refused to alter its sentence. On appeal, the Ninth Circuit vacated the sentence, finding unpersuasive the government's claim that the defendant should have presented evidence showing that she had not made the trips to Mexico cited by the agents and did not have assets reflecting the substantial profits from narcotics-dealings that were attributed to her. The appellate court reasoned that it would be "a great miscarriage of justice" to place on the defendant the burden and expense of proving an "elusive negative," and it directed the sentencing court not to rely upon the disputed allegation "unless it is amplified by information such as to be persuasive of the charge

§ 26.6

1. State v. Radi, 85 Mont. 38, 604 P.2d 318 (1979). Fed.R.Crim.P. 32(c)(3)(D) would not appear to call for anything more than a specific challenge to the accuracy of the presentence report. It states that "if the comments of the defendant and the defense counsel or testimony or other evidence introduced by them allege any factual inaccuracy in the presentence report," then the trial court has an obligation to resolve the dispute as to "each matter controverted" that will be considered in the sentencing. Several federal courts have suggested, however, that more than a simple denial is needed to controvert a factual statement in the presentence report.

2. 448 F.2d 626 (9th Cir.1971).

here made." While the *Weston* ruling could be restricted to uncorroborated information supplied by an informant whose identity was kept from the defense, other courts have more broadly expressed the proposition that a defendant need only deny to place in dispute at least those presentence report statements that cannot be rebutted by proof readily available to the defense. As one court noted, while "there is a burden of going forward in the defendant to show that that a genuine controversy exists," defendants should "not be required to prove negative propositions, and thus this burden ought to be slight." [3]

(b) Resolving Disputed Facts. If the defendant does not object to the presentence report or fails to meet any evidentiary threshold for supporting such an objection, the court may adopt the information set forth in the presentence report without further inquiry, provided it has some minimal factual basis. Where that information is properly contested, however, the court must either (i) rule that the disputed fact will not be taken into account in sentencing, or (ii) conduct a further inquiry for the purpose of making a finding as to that fact. The former alternative tends to be more readily available under a traditional sentencing structure that does not guide or restrict the judge's discretion apart from statutory limits on the minimum and maximum terms for an indeterminate sentence of incarceration. Here, what is included in the presentence report typically is determined by local practice, and the court has no obligation to give consideration to all of the elements spoken to in the report. The court has broad discretion which may lead it to refuse to consider contested factual allegations for a variety of reasons (e.g., that the same sentencing result would be reached in any event, or that the resolution of the factual dispute would be too time-consuming). That option is far less likely to be available, however, with guideline sentencing. Under a guidelines system, certain factors must be considered by the court; the presentence report must speak to each of those factors; and the court must make a factual determination as to each factor possibly applicable. A disputed fact in the presentence report is only likely to be one the court can put aside when uncontested facts otherwise establish the same guideline factor or resolution of the disputed fact would affect only overlapping sentencing grids and the court has determined that it would impose the same sentence under either grid. Under a presumptive sentencing structure, the court similarly has an obligation to resolve factual disputes relating to aggravating and mitigating circumstances.

Where the court is called upon to resolve a disputed fact, it ordinarily has considerable discretion in shaping its inquiry regarding that fact. A variety of options are available, including use of written submissions, affidavits, previously recorded testimony taken at a deposition or trial, the testimony of the probation officer who prepared the presentence report, and a full blown evidentiary hearing. In the federal courts, sentencing judges are directed to look to the due process balancing test of *Mathews v. Eldridge* [4] in choosing among those options, and particularly, in deciding whether an evidentiary hearing is needed. The court is to balance: (1) "the nature of the individual interest" (highest where the disputed fact could have a significant bearing on the length of a sentence of incarceration); (2) "the risk of error associated with the present procedures" (relating especially to the likely reliability of the evidence set forth in the presentence report); (3) "the value of additional procedural safeguards" (relating, as to the evidentiary hearing, to the potential value of hearing live testimony, with witnesses subject to cross-examination); and (4) the "government's inter-

3. United States v. Restrepo, 832 F.2d 146 (11th Cir. 1987). The above analysis arguably is tied to the placing of the burden of persuasion on the prosecution. As discussed in subsection (c) infra, some jurisdictions may place that burden on the defense. Here, the defendant's obligation to produce rebuttal evidence would be much more substantial, but even then, the *Weston* ruling might be upheld on the ground that the information provided in the presentence report there was too conclusory to be accepted as a basis for sentencing where it had been denied.

4. 424 U.S. 319, 96 S.Ct. 893, 47 L.Ed.2d 18 (1976).

est in avoiding undue fiscal or administrative burdens" (of special significance where the evidentiary hearing is likely to be lengthy and involve the testimony of numerous agents). In the era of unguided discretionary sentencing, evidentiary hearings in the federal courts (often called "*Fatico* hearings"[5]) were most commonly used where the prosecution sought to have the court take into consideration the defendant's alleged participation in non-prosecuted criminal acts. Some courts have suggested, however, that the use of such hearings will be "even greater under the guidelines * * * because of the substantial restrictions placed on the sentencing judge's discretion." While the *Sentencing Commission Manual* § 6A1.3 states only that the "parties shall be given an adequate opportunity to present information" as to any factor "reasonably in dispute," the commentary adds that an "evidentiary hearing may sometimes be the only reliable way to resolve disputed issues."

After utilizing a procedure that affords the parties an adequate opportunity to present evidence, the sentencing court must come to a resolution on the disputed fact (or if it has the discretion to do so, determine that it will simply disregard that fact). In the federal system, Rule 32 requires that the court append to the presentence report a written record of its finding. A required announcement on the record of the finding on a disputed fact is common under guideline and presumptive sentencing structures, but it is also found in some jurisdictions with traditional unguided discretionary sentencing. While it is commonly said that courts in such jurisdictions need not state the reasons for their decisions, requiring a court to announce its resolution of a disputed fact imposes far less burden on the sentencing court and does not detract from the judge's capacity to weigh the various factors according to his or her sense of what will produce "justice" in the particular case.

(c) Burden of Proof. Of obvious relevance to the court's resolution of a disputed fact is the placement of the burden of proof. In many jurisdictions, whether that burden falls on the prosecution or the defense is far from clear. Courts speaking to the defendant's obligation to present rebuttal evidence often have used language suggesting that the burden lies on the defense, but usually have not squarely stated that the presentence report is entitled to such a strong presumption of accuracy that the defense must carry the ultimate burden of persuasion as well as the burden of production. Indeed, courts for many years seemed to studiously avoid discussing the burden of proof issue, reflecting a concern that such discussion would characterize sentencing as an "evidentiary proof" proceeding and thereby "tend to formalize the sentencing procedure, narrow its traditional open format, and impinge on the broad discretion of the sentencing judge." In recent years, however, numerous courts have come forth with direct holdings on the burden of proof. Looking to the balance of interests involved, they generally have concluded that burden of persuasion on disputed facts should lie with the prosecution. Most of these rulings have dealt only with information relating to factors calling for a more severe punishment (e.g., other criminal behavior). Under a guidelines system, the presentence report also must speak to factors that would work to reduce punishment. The same is true of mitigating factors under a presumptive sentencing structure. Where the defense challenges the presentence reports on facts relating only to those factors (e.g., whether defendant has made restitution), some federal courts have held that the burden should lie with the defense.

Where the prosecution bears the burden of persuasion, the courts generally have deemed the preponderance of the evidence standard to be the necessary level of proof. However, a few federal courts have suggested that a lesser standard might also be acceptable. Thus, one court noted that it might be satisfactory

5. The name comes from the prominent use of such a hearing in United States v. Fatico, 458 F.Supp. 388 (E.D.N.Y.1978), affirmed 603 F.2d 1053 (2d Cir.1979).

to simply require that the government establish the disputed fact by "some reliable evidence," permitting the presentence report to be "accepted as true even in situations where the sentencing judge might find there is a balance of probabilities."[6] In *McMillan v. Pennsylvania,*[7] the Supreme Court found constitutionally acceptable the preponderance of the evidence standard, but had no reason to consider whether a lesser standard would also be acceptable. At issue there was the application of a statute under which the visible possession of a weapon during the commission of an offense required a mandatory minimum sentence. The statute directed the sentencing judge to make a determination as to the presence of that element, under a preponderance of the evidence standard, based upon the evidence introduced at trial and any additional evidence offered at a sentencing hearing. The Court initially rejected defendant's reliance upon cases requiring proof beyond a reasonable doubt in criminal cases, as that standard had been held to be a due process requirement only as to the elements defining the crime.[8] It then rejected the contention that at least a clear and convincing evidence standard should be required where, as here, the sentencing factor in question had a mandatory consequence. Defendant had no grounding for such a claim, said the Court, in light of the fact that the preponderance standard has been found constitutionally acceptable at trial for proof of defenses and mitigating factors that do not negate elements of the crime.[9] The Court also took brief note of sentencing tradition, commenting that "sentencing courts have traditionally heard evidence and found facts without any prescribed burden at all." It remains to be seen whether this history would support a sentencing procedure, at least as to discretionary sentencing, that simply gives the sentence court freedom to rely on such factual allegations as it desires, without imposing a preponderance level of persuasion, provided there exists some minimal indicia of reliability as to the particular fact.

§ 26.7 Resentencing: Double Jeopardy

(a) Resentencing Following a Reconviction. Where a defendant is convicted of a crime, that conviction is overturned on appeal under circumstances permitting reprosecution, and the second prosecution results in a valid conviction, the question arises as what weight must be given to the original sentence under the double jeopardy clause. One aspect of that question, addressed by the Supreme Court in *North Carolina v. Pearce,*[1] is "whether, in computing the new sentence, the Constitution requires that credit must be given for that part of the original sentence already served." Emphasizing that one of the protections of the double jeopardy clause is "against multiple punishments for the same offense,"[2] a unanimous Court answered that question in the affirmative, reasoning:

> Suppose, for example, in a jurisdiction where the maximum allowable sentence for larceny is 10 years' imprisonment, a man succeeds in getting his larceny conviction set aside after serving three years in prison. If, upon reconviction, he is given a 10–year sentence, then, quite clearly, he will have received multiple punishments for the same offense. For he will have been compelled to

6. United States v. Restrepo, supra note 3. See also United States v. Fernandez–Vidana, 857 F.2d 673 (9th Cir.1988).

7. 477 U.S. 79, 106 S.Ct. 2411, 91 L.Ed.2d 67 (1986). See also § 26.4 at note 25.

8. Thus, the Court had previously held that the reasonable doubt requirement did not apply to factors relating to the level of the crime where those factors were not elements of the legislative definition of the crime. See e.g., Patterson v. New York, 432 U.S. 197, 97 S.Ct. 2319, 53 L.Ed.2d 281 (1977) (where mitigating factor of provocation did not negate the required mental element for murder and therefore was not an element of that offense or the lesser offense of manslaughter, the state could shift the burden of proof as to provocation to the defense, under a preponderance standard, rather than require the prosecution to prove beyond a reasonable doubt that provocation did not exist).

9. Indeed, in those cases, the Court had allowed the burden to be shifted to the defense. See Patterson v. New York, supra note 8. Consider also Lego v. Twomey, discussed in § 10.4, accepting a preponderance standard on suppression motions.

§ 26.7

1. 395 U.S. 711, 89 S.Ct. 2072, 23 L.Ed.2d 656 (1969).

2. See § 25.1 at note 5.

serve separate prison terms of three years and 10 years, although the maximum single punishment for the offense is 10 years' imprisonment. Though not so dramatically evident, the same principle obviously holds true whenever punishment already endured is not fully subtracted from any new sentence imposed.

A second issue presented in *Pearce* was whether, assuming proper credit is given for time already served, the trial court may impose a longer sentence on reconviction than was imposed following the original conviction. The defendants challenged their longer sentences as violating three distinct constitutional guarantees: double jeopardy, equal protection, and due process. The Court rejected the equal protection claim, ruled that the due process clause barred a longer sentence in some circumstances,[3] and then decided against the double jeopardy claim as well. In doing so, the Court declined to depart from the longstanding rule "that a corollary of the power to retry a defendant is the power, upon the defendant's reconviction, to impose whatever sentence may be legally authorized, whether or not it is greater than the sentence imposed after the first conviction." This was a sensible rule, the *Pearce* majority asserted, for "it rests ultimately upon the premise that the original conviction has, at the defendant's behest, been wholly nullified and the slate wiped clean."

Pearce was distinguished in *Bullington v. Missouri,*[4] where a divided Court held that a state could not seek the death penalty on a retrial where the original jury had decided against imposing capital punishment following a trial-type sentencing procedure. The majority noted that under Missouri law the jury determination as to capital punishment involved application of specific factual standards, relating to the presence of aggravating and mitigating factors, following an extensive trial-type hearing in which the prosecution bore the burden of proof beyond a reasonable doubt. The original jury's determination not to impose capital punishment was therefore comparable to a trial acquittal as to the issue of the death penalty, rather than to the traditional sentencing determination.

The special character of *Bullington* was reflected in the distinctions drawn there between capital sentencing and the resentencing that had been upheld in *United States v. DiFrancesco.*[5] In *DiFrancesco,* which is discussed in subsection (b), the Court had rejected a double jeopardy challenge to a provision that allowed the prosecutor to appeal a sentencing judge's alleged error in the application of a dangerous offender sentencing provision, with the defendant to be resentenced if the appellate court found that there had been error. While *DiFrancesco* also involved a special factfinding determination by the sentencer, appellate review there was "on the record of the sentencing court" and did not involve giving the government "the opportunity to convince a second factfinder of its view of the facts." Moreover, the choice presented to the federal judge in *DiFrancesco* was far broader than that given to the jury here, which had "only two choices, death or life imprisonment." Finally, the government's burden of proof in *DiFrancesco* as to special offender status was only by a preponderance of the evidence, rather than the reasonable doubt standard applicable under capital sentencing. With all of these factors distinguishing the capital sentencing process, the longstanding rule that the defendant may receive any legally authorized sentence upon retrial, even if it is greater than the sentence imposed the first time, would not be extended to "this very different situation."

The analogy drawn by the *Bullington* Court between a trial acquittal and a sentencing determination made by the trier of fact under guidelines that refer to specific factors so far has been applied by the Supreme Court only to capital sentencing, and even there has been limited to situations in which there was a clear ruling that the prosecution had failed to make its case. In *Lockhart v. Nelson,*[6] the

3. See § 26.8(a).

4. 451 U.S. 430, 101 S.Ct. 1852, 68 L.Ed.2d 270 (1981).

5. See note 7 infra.

6. 488 U.S. 33, 109 S.Ct. 285, 102 L.Ed.2d 265 (1988). See § 25.4 at note 11.

Court noted that it had no need to decide whether "the rule that the Double Jeopardy Clause limits the State's power to subject a defendant to successive capital sentencing proceedings, see *Bullington,* carries over to noncapital sentencing proceedings." At issue there was a recidivist sentencing determination. As noted in § 26.1(c), some jurisdictions treat the recidivist issue as a matter for determination by the trier of fact and apply a reasonable doubt standard as to proof. In this respect, the analogy to *Bullington* would be close. On the other hand, the recidivist determination does not deal with the circumstances of the principal offense, and it need not constitutionally be established by the same proof standard that is applicable to the elements of the offense. Also, if double jeopardy were to be held applicable to a recidivist charge basically because it involves a trial type hearing and a specific factual finding, the same analysis arguably would extend to enhancements and even determinations as to aggravating and mitigating factors in presumptive sentencing and guideline factors in guideline sentencing. At this point, *Pearce,* which is seen as the general rule applicable to sentencing, would be reduced to the rule only for traditional unguided discretionary sentencing.

(b) Resentencing and Sentencing Appeals. In jurisdictions that allow for substantive appellate review of a sentence, two provisions may produce a higher resentence as a result of the appeal. First, where defendant's appeal is viewed as opening the door to appellate court assessment of all aspects of the sentence, the appellate court may decide not only that the defendant's complaint is not well taken, but that the sentence is too low and should be raised. Second, where the prosecution is allowed to appeal a sentence, the appellate court may sustain the prosecution's challenge and impose a higher sentence or remand for consideration of a higher sentence. The leading double jeopardy decision, *United States v. DiFrancesco,*[7] involved the latter type of provision.

The Federal Organized Crime Control Act authorized the imposition of an increased sentence upon a convicted "dangerous offender" and granted the government the right, under specified conditions, to gain appellate review of that sentence. In *DiFrancesco,* the trial judge had concluded that the defendant fell within the Act's dangerous offender definition and imposed an additional sentence, but ordered that the sentence run concurrently with the sentence for the underlying offense. The government appealed, arguing that the use of a concurrent dangerous offender sentence constituted an abuse of sentencing discretion since it added only one year to the length of the defendant's incarceration. The Supreme Court upheld the constitutionality of the appellate review provision and agreed with the prosecution as to the sentencing judge's error.

The Court noted initially that its "decisions in the sentencing area clearly establish that a sentence does not have the qualities of constitutional finality that attend an acquittal." That principle was reflected in *Pearce.* For "while *Pearce* dealt with the imposition of a new sentence after retrial rather than, as here, after appeal, that difference [was] no more than a 'conceptual nicety.'" Functionally, the Court stressed, resentencing here would be quite different from a retrial on guilt:

> "The basic design of the double jeopardy provision, * * * is, as a bar against repeated attempts to convict, with consequent subjection of the defendant to embarrassment, expense, anxiety, and insecurity, and the possibility that he may be found guilty even though innocent. These considerations, however, have no significant application to the prosecution's statutorily granted right to review a sentence. This limited appeal does not involve a retrial or approximate the ordeal of a trial on the basic issue of guilt or innocence. Under [the Federal Act], the appeal is to be taken promptly and is essentially on the record of the sentencing court.[8] The defen-

7. 449 U.S. 117, 101 S.Ct. 426, 66 L.Ed.2d 328 (1980).

8. At a later point in its opinion, the Court noted: "The federal statute specifies that the [appellate court]

dant, of course, is charged with knowledge of the statute and its appeal provisions, and has no expectation of finality in his sentence until the appeal is concluded or the time to appeal has expired."

(c) Resentencing by the Trial Judge. Yet another group of double jeopardy issues are presented where the trial judge, in a system utilizing traditional judicial sentencing, initially imposes a particular sentence and then, learning of some deficiency in that original sentence, alters the sentence to the prejudice of the defendant. Here *Pearce* is distinguishable because there has been no reversal of the underlying conviction; *DiFrancesco* is distinguishable because reconsideration is not part of a specifically authorized review procedure analogous to appellate review of the sentence; and the capital sentencing cases are distinguishable because the initial sentence is not based on a trial-type factual finding. *Ex parte Lange,*[9] an 1870's Supreme Court ruling, contained language so broad as to arguably suggest that all such resentencing was constitutionally prohibited, but later cases have limited that precedent to the "specific context" there presented.

In *Lange,* the applicable penal statute authorized a sentence of a fine *or* imprisonment, but the trial court erroneously imposed a sentence consisting of both the maximum term of imprisonment (1 year) and the maximum fine ($200). After having paid the fine and having served five days in prison, the defendant petitioned the trial court for relief, demanding his immediate release on the ground that the imprisonment portion of the sentence could not be imposed along with the fine. Recognizing its error in imposing both a fine and imprisonment, the trial court vacated the original sentence and imposed a new sentence limited to imprisonment for the maximum term of one year. The Supreme Court held that the new sentence violated the double jeopardy prohibition against imposing "multiple punishments" for the same offense, and the defendant therefore was entitled to his release, as he had fully satisfied one of the two allowable alternative sentences by paying the fine. The *Lange* opinion spoke at points of the "finality" of a "judgment" once it is "carried into execution," rendering the trial powerless to substitute a new sentence. But it also stressed that the end result of the resentencing before it was to impose upon the defendant punishment beyond that authorized by statute. The fine having been paid and passed into the Treasury (where it was beyond the reach of judiciary), the defendant would have suffered both a fine *and* imprisonment, and even the imprisonment would be for five days more than the one-year maximum allowed by law. The Supreme Court eventually came to read this element of imposing "excessive" punishment, as measured by the legislatively authorized sanction for the offense, to be the key to the double jeopardy violation in the resentencing in *Lange.*

In its first major analysis of the *Lange* opinion, *United States v. Benz,*[10] the Court held that *Lange* 's discussion of the "finality" of the initially imposed sentence did not mean that the trial court lacked authority to reconsider and reduce a sentence during the same term of court in which it was initially imposed. Since such resentencing was in defendant's favor, the Court's reasoning did not foreclose the possibility that the double jeopardy prohibition barred an increased sentence following the initial imposition of a sentence. Subsequently, in *Bozza v. United States,*[11] the Court upheld the action of a trial court in increasing a previously announced sentence to meet the mandatory minimum required by statute. In that case, however, the trial court had corrected its error within hours of the announcement of its original sentence and before the defendant was transported to the

may increase the sentence only if the trial court has abused its discretion or employed unlawful procedures or made clearly erroneous findings. The appellate court thus is empowered to correct only a legal error." Provisions on appellate sentencing review generally are so limited. They tend to prohibit de novo sentencing by the appellate court, although factual determinations by the sentencing court may be subject to review under a "clearly erroneous" standard. See § 26.3(d).

9. 85 U.S. (18 Wall.) 163, 21 L.Ed. 872 (1873).

10. 282 U.S. 304, 51 S.Ct. 113, 75 L.Ed. 354 (1931).

11. 330 U.S. 160, 67 S.Ct. 645, 91 L.Ed. 818 (1947).

penitentiary to serve his prison term. Thus, the case could be viewed as one in which the initially announced sentence had not yet been "imposed," although the Court's opinion focused on the fact that the trial judge had modified the originally announced sentence simply to correct his error and provide the sentence required by law. "The Constitution," the Court noted, "does not require that sentencing should be a game in which a wrong move by the judge means immunity for the prisoner."

In re Bradley,[12] like *Lange* and in contrast to *Bozza,* presented a situation in which resentencing occurred after the defendant had fulfilled part of the initial sentence. Indeed, as in *Lange,* the first of two sanctions imposed under an impermissible cumulative sentence had been fully satisfied before the trial court sought to resentence the defendant. The sentencing statute applicable in *Bradley* provided for punishment of a fine *or* imprisonment, but the trial court had erroneously imposed an initial sentence of both fine and imprisonment. Two days later, after defendant had paid the fine, the trial court realized its mistake, amended its sentencing order to vacate the fine, and directed that the moneys paid be returned to the defendant. Although, with the return of the fine, the trial court's order would have produced an ultimate sentence not in excess of that allowed by statute, the Supreme Court held that *Lange* barred the resentencing and defendant therefore was entitled to his immediate release. The Court reasoned that since the defendant had fully satisfied "one valid alternative provision of the original sentence," which constituted the limit of the punishment allowed under the penal statute, the trial court had lost authority to impose any further punishment. The subsequent amendment of the sentence to return the fine, it noted, "could not avoid the satisfaction of the judgment," and *Lange* therefore controlled.

Bradley, with little discussion of the issue, had indicated that *Lange* 's prohibition against multiple punishments was tied to the dual execution of the sentence, rather than the quantum of the punishment eventually imposed. However, the Supreme Court's later decision in *DiFrancesco,* and its rulings in cases involving legislatively authorized cumulative punishments imposed in a single proceeding for a course of conduct constituting a single offense,[13] suggested otherwise. Although not involving resentencing, those opinions characterized the multiple punishment prohibition of *Lange* as directed basically against imposing punishment beyond that authorized by the legislature. Building upon those comments, a divided court in *Jones v. Thomas* [14] held that the multiple punishment prohibition did not bar resentencing that fell within the statutory limits where defendant received full credit for the time served under the original sentence. *Bradley* was restricted to the special structure of the resentencing there presented.

In *Jones,* the defendant (Thomas) had been convicted of felony murder and the underlying felony of attempted robbery, both charges being tried in the same proceeding as they presented the same offense for double jeopardy purposes.[15] The trial court originally had sentenced defendant to consecutive terms of 15 years for the attempted robbery and life imprisonment for the felony murder. After the initial sentence for the attempted robbery had been satisfied (due to several years incarceration and a subsequent commutation), the state's highest court held that the felony murder statute did not authorize separate punishments for the felony murder and the underlying felony. The trial court then vacated the attempted robbery sentence, leaving only the

12. 318 U.S. 50, 63 S.Ct. 470, 87 L.Ed. 608 (1943).

13. See Missouri v. Hunter, 459 U.S. 359, 103 S.Ct. 673, 74 L.Ed.2d 535 (1983) (upholding multiple sentences imposed on a defendant convicted in the same trial of both armed robbery and armed criminal action, where the latter mandated a separate and additional punishment for any person committing a felony with a weapon; the double jeopardy limitation on multiple punishments does not prohibit the legislature from providing for more severe punishment through dual statutory punishment of the same conduct).

14. 491 U.S. 376, 109 S.Ct. 2522, 105 L.Ed.2d 322 (1989).

15. See § 17.4.

felony murder sentence, and gave the defendant credit for the entire time of his incarceration under the vacated sentence as against the remaining life sentence for felony murder. Defendant claimed that the credit was not sufficient, that he had fully satisfied one of two sentences allowable under state law, and that imposition of further imprisonment pursuant to the trial court's modification of the sentence would constitute multiple punishment contrary to *Lange* and *Bradley.* Rejecting defendant's reliance upon *Lange,* the Supreme Court majority noted that here, unlike *Lange,* the consequence of upholding the modified sentence was not to impose punishment in excess of that authorized by statute. The multiple punishment prohibition of *Lange,* as applied in *Lange* itself and as interpreted in *DiFrancesco* and the cumulative punishment cases, therefore was not violated.

The *Jones* majority acknowledged, however, that *Bradley* provided a "closer analogy" to the resentencing before it, for just as the judge here provided credit for the time served in order to keep the sentence within that authorized by the legislature, the judge there sought to return the fine. However, the *Bradley* precedent, as seen by the *Jones* majority, was limited by two factors that distinguished the resentencing in *Bradley* from that in *Jones.* First, *Bradley* involved alternative punishments, each intended by the legislature to be sufficient in itself for the single offense on which the defendant stood convicted; *Jones,* in contrast, presented "separate sentences imposed for what the sentencing court thought to be separately punishable offenses, one far more serious than the other." While the legislature would have viewed each of the allowable punishments as appropriate for the particular offense in a "true alternative sentences case" (such as *Bradley*), it hardly could be deemed here to have viewed a punishment for attempted robbery as sufficient for felony murder. Second, the alternative sentences in *Bradley* "were of a different type, fine and imprisonment," whereas the two sentences in *Jones* were of the same type (imprisonment). It "would not have been possible to 'credit' a fine against time in prison," but the crediting of time served under one sentence against the term of another "has long been an accepted practice." Moreover, where both sentences are for terms of imprisonment, the application of *Bradley,* grounded as it would be upon the completion of the shorter sentence, would produce "anomalous results" based on fortuitous circumstances. A defendant previously incarcerated for the full period of the shorter sentence would be able to advance a double jeopardy claim if he had been sentenced to the shorter imprisonment term as the first of the two consecutive sentences, but a defendant sentenced to the longer term as the first consecutive sentence would have no such claim, as he would not have completed either branch of his sentence, even though incarcerated for the same length of time prior to the resentencing.

Although *Jones* held that the *Lange* prohibition against multiple sentences was limited to excessive punishment and narrowly construed *Bradley,* it acknowledged that another interest protected by the double jeopardy prohibition—a defendant's "legitimate expectation of finality" in an imposed sentence—could also stand as a bar to resentencing. The *Jones* majority did not disagree with the dissent's contention that "the Double Jeopardy Clause protects not only against punishment in excess of legislative intent, but also against additions to a sentence in a subsequent proceeding that upset a legitimate expectation of finality." Neither did it disagree with the dissent's illustration of an unconstitutional resentencing notwithstanding an ultimate sentence less than the authorized maximum—a case "where a judge imposes only a 15 year sentence under a statute that permitted 15 years to life, has second thoughts after the defendant serves the sentence, and calls him back to impose another 10 years." The majority concluded that the case before it simply did not present the concerns raised by such a case as the defendant here "plainly had no expectation of serving only an attempted robbery sentence" when the sentencing court announced its initial sentence, which included the life term as part of the cumulative sentence. In *DiFrancesco,* the

Court similarly had taken note of defendant's legitimate expectation of finality, but had concluded that the sentencing procedure there gave rise to no such expectation. *DiFrancesco* reasoned that the double jeopardy protection of such an interest did not preclude the use of an appeal procedure, known to defendant at the outset, as that procedure forewarned the defendant that the final determination of his sentence would not come until after that appeal and the defendant had no constitutional right to the initial setting of a final sentence (as evidenced by the well accepted practice of setting the imprisonment term in probation revocation cases only after probation is revoked).

While neither *Jones* nor *DiFrancesco* found in the case before it a violation of defendant's legitimate expectation of finality in a sentence, both opinions indicate that double jeopardy would protect such an interest and therefore could bar resentencing even where the new sentence did not either impose punishment beyond the statutory maximum or override defendant's prior fulfillment of a true alternative sentence. Such a case might be presented where the modification of a sentence after its original imposition results in punishment beyond that originally announced (in contrast to *Jones*) and is not made pursuant to an initially announced procedure for review and subsequent modification (in contrast to *DiFrancesco*). Exactly what time span is needed between the initial imposition of the sentence and the modification to create a protected expectation of finality is unclear. It seems likely, however, that the modification could present constitutional difficulties even though the time span is not as extreme as that in the hypothetical offered by the *Jones* dissenters (where the modification came after defendant had completed the initially announced 10 year sentence). The *DiFrancesco* majority took note of the early common law rule which held that the trial court could not add to a previously announced and executed prison sentence if that addition was made after the same term of court. It also noted the more stringent "established practice in federal courts" that permitted a sentencing judge to "recall a defendant and increase his sentence" only if the defendant "had not yet begun to serve the sentence"—although the Court added that it would "venture no comment as to this limitation."

Of course, a defendant may not have a "legitimate" expectation of finality in a previously imposed sentence apart from the factors that precluded such an expectation in *Jones* and *DiFrancesco.* The dissenters in *Jones* described *Bozza* as such a case, noting that "the defendant [there] could not argue that his *legitimate* expectation of finality in the original sentence had been violated, because he was charged with knowledge that the court lacked statutory authority to impose the subminimum sentence in the first instance." Lower courts have suggested that a defendant could not rely on a legitimate expectation of finality where the subsequent upward modification responded to defendant's intentional deception in the original sentencing proceeding. So too, by analogy to *Pearce,* some lower courts have rejected defendant's reliance on an expectation of finality where the sentence being revised upward is part of a "sentencing plan" for a multi-count conviction challenged by defendant on appeal. Thus, where defendant was sentenced to imprisonment on the first of several counts and probation on the others, and an appeal from the multi-count conviction resulted in the reversal of only that first count, those courts find no double jeopardy bar against allowing modification of the sentences on the affirmed counts to produce a sentencing package of imprisonment and probation equivalent to that originally imposed. The defendant is seen here as challenging through the appeal the combined sentence on the total conviction, thereby opening the door to resentencing on the affirmed counts where the "sentencing package" has been altered by the reversal of part of the conviction.

§ 26.8 Resentencing: The Prohibition Against Vindictiveness

(a) Presumed Vindictiveness: The *Pearce* Ruling. In *North Carolina v.*

Pearce,[1] the petitioners successfully overturned their original convictions in postconviction proceedings, were retried and convicted on the same charges, and then were sentenced to imprisonment terms that were longer than those imposed on the original convictions. The petitioners claimed that the trial courts had imposed heavier sentences in order to punish them for having challenged their original convictions. The Supreme Court was unanimous in concluding that such a sentencing purpose would violate due process. Justice Stewart's opinion for the Court noted that "a court is 'without right to put a price on an appeal'" and that "vindictiveness against a defendant for having successfully attacked his first conviction" could "play no part" in the sentencing on retrial.[2]

While agreeing that vindictive sentencing was constitutionally barred, the Court in *Pearce* was divided as to how it should approach the claim that the sentences before it had actually been based on such a "retaliatory motive." On that issue, a majority concluded that it was unnecessary to determine whether the trial judges had in fact acted vindictively. Due process also required that a "defendant be freed of apprehension of such a retaliatory motivation on the part of the sentencing judge," since that apprehension could itself "deter a defendant's exercise of the right to appeal or collaterally attack his first conviction." Accordingly, the majority reasoned, where a higher sentence was imposed following a successful defense challenge to a conviction (and subsequent reconviction and resentencing), it would presume vindictiveness and impose upon the resentencing judge the burden of rebutting that presumption. This would be done through what was later described as the "prophylactic limitation" of *Pearce*. The *Pearce* majority described that limitation as follows:

> In order to assure the absence of such a motivation, we have concluded that whenever a judge imposes a more severe sentence upon a defendant after a new trial, the reasons for his doing so must affirmatively appear. Those reasons must be based upon objective information concerning identifiable conduct on the part of the defendant occurring after the time of the original sentence proceeding. And the factual data upon which the increased sentence is based must be made part of the record, so that the constitutional legitimacy of the increased sentence may be fully reviewed on appeal.

Justice White in a concurring opinion agreed that a presumption of vindictiveness was appropriate and that rebuttal of that presumption required that the trial court set forth legitimate reasons for the increased sentence. He disagreed, however, with the Court's limitation of those reasons. An "increased sentence on retrial" should be allowed, he noted, "on any objective, identifiable factual data not known to the trial judge at the time of the original sentencing." Justice Black would not go even that far. While due process prohibited vindictiveness in sentencing, "nothing in the Due Process Clause grants [to] the Court" the authority "to prescribe particular devices 'in order to assure the absence of such a motivation.'" The danger of improper motivation was always present. A judge might in any case "impose a specially severe penalty solely because of a defendant's race, religion, or political views" or because "defendant exercised his right to counsel or insisted on a trial by jury." But "it ha[d] never previously been suggested * * * [that the] Court could, as a matter of constitutional law, direct all trial judges to spell out in detail their reasons for setting a particular sentence." The resentencing setting, Justice Black argued, gave the Court no greater authority. The Court, from his perspective, was engaging in "pure legislation."

As discussed in the subsections that follow, later decisions have retreated from the implications of *Pearce* in light of the objections raised by Justices White and Black. The Court, consistent with Justice White's objection, refused to restrict the rebuttal of the *Pearce* presumption of vindictiveness to "iden-

§ 26.8

1. 395 U.S. 711, 89 S.Ct. 2072, 23 L.Ed.2d 656 (1969).

2. See § 26.4(c) following note 5 as to the prohibition against vindictiveness.

tifiable conduct of the defendant occurring after the time of the original proceeding." Responding to Justice Black's objection, it also restricted the applicability of the presumption of vindictiveness to the particular resentencing setting presented in defendant Pearce's case (and, indeed, held the presumption inapplicable to the setting presented in a companion case also decided under the *Pearce* majority opinion). The focus was not on the potential chilling impact of a higher resentence upon the defendant's exercise of his right to challenge his conviction, but on the presence of specific circumstances presenting a reasonable likelihood that vindictiveness had played a role in the imposition of the higher second sentence.

(b) Rebutting the *Pearce* Presumption. Since the trial judges in the cases considered in *Pearce* had not set forth any reasons for increasing the petitioners' sentences, the Court found it unnecessary to explore in any detail the type of conduct that might justify a higher sentence under its prophylactic rule. That issue was not reached until roughly 15 years later, when the Court decided *Wasman v. United States.*[3] In the interim, the lower courts generally had adopted a rigorous interpretation of the *Pearce* limitation. They focused on both *Pearce*'s explicit reference to "identifiable conduct on the part of the defendant occurring after the time of original sentence" and on the function that they saw as underlying that restriction—the need to preclude trial court reliance upon factors that could be used to mask vindictiveness. Accordingly, the lower courts held that a sentencing judge on a retrial could not justify an increased sentence by reference to new information indicating that defendant played a larger role in the offense, had a worse preexisting criminal record, or had caused greater harm than originally supposed at the first sentencing proceeding. Such information did not refer to conduct of the defendant occurring after the original sentence. Moreover, new information relating to the seriousness of the crime or the extent of defendant's participation was too readily to be found in almost every retrial, thereby opening the door to widespread masked vindictiveness. Indeed, the potential for ready evasion of *Pearce* had even caused some lower courts to limit the trial judge's authority to impose an increased sentence based upon the alleged perjury of the defendant at the second trial. The perjury clearly would constitute conduct of the defendant occurring after the first sentence and the Supreme Court had held in *United States v. Grayson*[4] that a defendant's perjury at trial could be considered against him in sentencing. However, where a defendant had testified at both his first and second trials, a vindictive judge could readily find that testimony which was almost unbelievable at the first trial had become totally unbelievable at the second and therefore should be treated as perjury, justifying a higher sentence than earlier imposed. Accordingly, it was suggested that the alleged perjury would have to consist of substantial false testimony of the defendant at the second trial that had not been presented at the first trial.

The rigorous view of *Pearce* adopted by most lower courts was subsequently rejected, however, by two Supreme Court rulings. In the first case, *Wasman v. United States,*[5] the Supreme Court rejected a reading of *Pearce* that focused exclusively on *Pearce*'s reference to post-sentence conduct of the defendant. The trial court there, in imposing its original sentence, noted that no consideration would be given to those criminal charges then pending against the defendant; it was that court's policy to consider only the prior convictions of a defendant. Following a successful appeal, retrial, and reconviction, the same judge imposed a second sentence higher than the first. The greater sentence was justified by reference to a conviction (on a previously pending charge) that had occurred during the interim between the first and second sentence. Defendant maintained that *Pearce* did not allow

3. 468 U.S. 559, 104 S.Ct. 3217, 82 L.Ed.2d 424 (1984).

4. See United States v. Grayson, discussed in § 26.4(c) at note 6.

5. Supra note 3.

the higher sentence to be based on the intervening conviction since that conviction, though occurring after the time of the original sentence, was not itself "conduct of the defendant." A unanimous Supreme Court rejected that claim, noting that *Pearce*'s prophylactic rule must be given a common sense interpretation consistent with the function of that rule. There was no suggestion of actual vindictiveness, and allowing consideration of an intervening conviction did not open the door to likely manipulation to mask vindictive sentencing. Indeed, *Pearce* itself had suggested the appropriateness of giving weight to that factor. Although referring to the post-sentence conduct of the defendant, *Pearce* had also noted that a "trial judge is not constitutionally precluded * * * [from imposing a higher sentence] in light of events subsequent to the first trial that may have thrown new light upon defendant's life, health, habits, conduct, and mental and moral propensities." As this statement suggested, there was "no logical support for [drawing] a distinction between 'events' and 'conduct' of the defendant occurring after the initial sentencing insofar as the kind of information that may be relied upon to show a nonvindictive motive is concerned."

While *Wasman* opened the *Pearce* prophylactic rule to intervening events extending beyond defendant's own conduct, its thrust could be squared with most of the rigorous interpretations of *Pearce* that had been adopted by the lower courts. The same could not be said, however, of the Supreme Court's next ruling, in *Texas v. McCullough.*[6] A divided Court there basically restructured *Pearce*'s prophylactic rule to allow an increased sentence to be based on any new information logically relevant to sentencing. Although initially holding that the *Pearce*'s prophylactic rule did not apply to the setting of the case before it,[7] the *McCullough* majority then went on to consider whether the justifications for the higher sentence there offered by the trial judge would have been sufficient "even if the *Pearce* presumption were to apply here." Chief Justice Burger's opinion for the Court noted initially that the *Pearce* opinion had not "intended to describe exhaustively all of the possible circumstances in which a sentence increase could be justified." In particular, "restricting justifications for a sentence increase to *only* 'events that occurred subsequent to the original sentencing proceedings' could in some circumstances lead to absurd results." Such a restriction would, for example, prohibit an increased sentence where the initial sentence was based on the assumption that the defendant had no prior criminal record, but it was later learned in the second sentencing investigation that defendant had been using an alias and in fact had a long criminal record of serious offenses. Prohibiting a higher sentence in such a case was a "bizarre" result that *Pearce* obviously had not intended. Accordingly, *Pearce* should be read, as the Court had suggested in *United States v. Goodwin,*[8] as establishing " 'a presumption of vindictiveness, which may be overcome only by objective information ... justifying the increased sentence.' " Admittedly, "a defendant may be reluctant to appeal if there is a risk that new, probative evidence supporting a longer sentence may be revealed on retrial," but *Pearce* itself, in allowing justified higher sentences, had refused to accept such a " 'chilling effect' as sufficient reason to create a constitutional prohibition against considering relevant information" in sentencing following a retrial.

Having found that *Pearce*'s prophylactic rule could be satisfied by "objective information" not considered in the initial sentencing, the *McCullough* Court had no difficulty with the "careful explanation of the trial judge" in the case before it. The trial judge had cited "the testimony of two new witnesses which she concluded 'had a direct effect upon the strength of the State's case at both the guilt and punishment phases of the trial.' " She had "also found that McCullough had been released from confinement only four months before the murder, another obviously relevant

6. 475 U.S. 134, 106 S.Ct. 976, 89 L.Ed.2d 104 (1986).

7. See the text following note 12 infra.

8. See § 13.5 at note 2. *Goodwin* had held that a presumption of vindictiveness did not apply to the pre-

fact not before the sentencing jury in the first trial." This "new objective information also amply justified McCullough's increased sentence."

(c) Applying the *Pearce* Presumption in Other Resentencing Sentencing Settings. Prior to the ruling in *McCullough*, the vindictiveness presumption of *Pearce* had been held not to apply to all settings presenting a resentencing following a reversed conviction and subsequent reconviction. Distinguished in this regard had been jury sentencing and sentences imposed by a higher court following a trial *de novo*. In *Colten v. Kentucky*,[9] the Supreme Court held that a Kentucky trial court, when sentencing a defendant following a trial *de novo* "appeal" of a misdemeanor conviction, did not have to set forth reasons justifying a sentence higher than that which had been imposed by the magistrate. A divided Court concluded that the Kentucky "two-tier system of administering criminal justice" did not contain the same potential for vindictive sentencing as was found in *Pearce*. Accordingly, there was no basis for assuming that "defendants convicted in Kentucky's inferior courts would be deterred from seeking a second trial out of fear of judicial vindictiveness." Three factors, in particular, were stressed: (1) the court which conducted the trial *de novo* and imposed the second sentence was not the same court as had tried the case initially; unlike *Pearce*, this was not a case of a court being "asked to do over what it had thought it had already done correctly"; (2) the *de novo* court was not being asked to "find error in another court's work," but simply to provide the defendant with the same trial that would have been provided if his case had begun in that court; and (3) the attitude of the Kentucky courts was that the inferior courts were not "designed or equipped to conduct error-free trials," but were "courts of convenience," so there was no suggestion that a defendant "ought to be satisfied" with the informal proceeding provided by an inferior court.

Chaffin v. Stynchcombe[10] held that the prophylactic rule of *Pearce* also did not apply to jury sentencing. A closely divided Court concluded that, unlike the situation in *Pearce*, the potential for vindictive sentencing by a jury was "*de minimus* in a properly controlled retrial." Two factors were stressed. First, the jury sitting in the second trial would not know of the earlier sentence. While it probably would be aware that there had been an earlier trial, it would not know whether that trial was on the same charge or whether it resulted in a conviction or a mistrial. Second, as was true in *Colten*, "the second sentence is not meted out by the same judicial authority" that had its earlier proceeding reversed on appeal. The jury has no personal stake in the earlier proceeding, and it "is unlikely to be sensitive to the institutional interests that might occasion higher sentences by a judge desirous of discouraging what he regards as meritless appeals." Responding to the dissent, the *Chaffin* majority also rejected the contention that the application of *Pearce* to judge sentencing, but not jury sentencing, placed an unconstitutional burden on the defendant's right to jury trial. It was true that the defendant who chose trial by jury (and thereby jury sentencing) opened the door to a more severe second sentence, a result that *Pearce* ordinarily would bar if he chose a bench trial. But this distinction in the possible consequence of selecting a jury over a bench trial did not impose the kind of "needless burden" held invalid in other cases.[11] Here, the distinction flowed from a legitimate state policy that favored unfettered jury sentencing, with each jury allowed to make its own determination based on its personal assessment of the evidence before it.

One factor emphasized in both *Colten* and *Chaffin* was the presence of different sentencers at the first and second proceedings. This factor was generally assumed by lower courts to be irrelevant, however, when the different sentencers were both trial judges of the same court. Although the second trial judge would

trial prosecutorial charging setting presented there, but had also discussed the significance of the presumption in general.

9. 407 U.S. 104, 92 S.Ct. 1953, 32 L.Ed.2d 584 (1972).

10. 412 U.S. 17, 93 S.Ct. 1977, 36 L.Ed.2d 714 (1973).

11. See United States v. Jackson, discussed in § 21.2 at note 1.

have no "personal stake" in the earlier proceedings, that judge arguably would still have an "institutional interest" in discouraging appeals from the trial court's rulings. In *Texas v. McCullough,*[12] the Supreme Court strongly suggested, if it did not so hold, that such an "institutional interest" was too speculative a basis for imposing the *Pearce* presumption of vindictiveness (and thereby requiring a higher sentence to be justified in accordance with *Pearce* 's prophylactic rule).

McCullough did not itself involve one trial judge imposing a higher sentence on a reconviction than another trial judge of the same court had assessed after the initial conviction. Defendant McCullough had originally been sentenced by a jury, but then sought a new trial based on alleged prosecutorial misconduct. That motion was granted by the trial judge who subsequently presided also at McCullough's second trial. After McCullough was again convicted, he requested that he be sentenced by the trial judge rather than the jury. The judge then imposed a substantially higher sentence than the twenty year sentence assessed by the jury at the first trial. In doing so, she "candidly stated" that, had she fixed the first sentence, she would have imposed more than twenty years.

Although the judge in *McCullough* also justified the higher sentence on the basis of new information that had not been presented to the jury in the earlier trial, the Supreme Court initially held that the higher sentence did not need that justification as the *Pearce* presumption of vindictiveness was inapplicable under the circumstances of this case. The Court reasoned:

> In contrast to *Pearce,* McCullough's second trial came about because the trial judge herself concluded that the prosecutor's misconduct required it. * * * "[U]nlike the judge who has been reversed," the trial judge here had "no motivation to engage in self-vindication" [quoting *Chaffin*]. In such circumstances, there is also no justifiable concern about "institutional interests that might occasion higher sentences by a judge desirous of discouraging what he regards as meritless appeals" [quoting *Chaffin*]. In granting McCullough's new trial motion, Judge Horney went on record as agreeing that his "claims" had merit.

The *McCullough* majority also rejected the dissent's suggestion that a judge might well grant a defense motion for a new trial yet be vindictive either because she was forced to "publicly concede" that the trial had been flawed (or face appellate reversal) or because the prosecutorial error requiring a new trial did not really cast doubt upon defendant's guilt and she therefore would be required to "sit through a trial whose result was a foregone conclusion." Such assumptions, the Court noted were far too "speculative" to support application of the *Pearce* presumption. The Court would not "adopt the view that the judicial temperament of our Nation's trial judge will suddenly change upon the filing of a successful trial motion." Indeed, its fallacy was suggested in this very case when the defendant chose to be resentenced by the judge who had granted the new trial motion rather than the jury.

Having relied upon the special circumstances of the case before it, the *McCullough* Court then went on to speak more broadly of the general relevance of two different sentencers. In this segment of its opinion,[13] the Court noted:

> The [Pearce] presumption is also inapplicable because different sentencers assessed the varying sentences that McCullough received. In such circumstances, a sentence "increase" cannot truly be said to have taken place. In *Colten v. Kentucky,* which bears directly on this case, we recognized that when different sentencers are involved "[i]t may often be that the [second sentencer] will impose a punishment more severe than that received from the [first]. But it no more follows that such a sentence is a vindictive penalty for seeking a

12. 475 U.S. 134, 106 S.Ct. 976, 89 L.Ed.2d 104 (1986).

13. A footnote accompanying the Court's discussion of what it described as the "two-sentencer issue" clearly indicated that the Court was referring to "different sentencing judges" as well as the situation presented in *McCullough* itself, with first a jury and then a judge sentencing.

[new] trial than that the [first sentencer] imposed a lenient penalty." Here, the second sentencer provides an on-the-record, wholly logical, nonvindictive reason for the sentence. We read *Pearce* to require no more, particularly since trial judges must be accorded broad discretion in sentencing, see *Wasman.*

In this case, the trial judge stated candidly her belief that the 20-year sentence respondent received initially was unduly lenient in light of significant evidence not before the sentencing jury in the first trial. On this record, that appraisal cannot be faulted. In any event, nothing in the Constitution prohibits a state from permitting such discretion to play a role in sentencing.[14]

McCullough led to a further reshaping of the *Pearce* doctrine in *Alabama v. Smith.*[15] With only Justice Marshall dissenting, the Court there overturned an aspect of the *Pearce* ruling—its application of the presumption in a companion case of *Simpson v. Rice*—that had long troubled lower courts. Unlike defendant Pearce's case, which presented differing sentences imposed after two trials, defendant Rice's case involved a vacated guilty plea and a higher sentence imposed after a subsequent trial and reconviction. The *Pearce* Court had applied the presumption of vindictiveness to both situations, but *Smith* concluded that the application of the presumption to the situation presented in *Rice* could not be sustained in light of post-*Pearce* rulings such as *Colten, Chaffin,* and *McCullough.* Those cases had held that the presumption of vindictiveness properly applied only in circumstances presenting "a 'reasonable likelihood' that the increase in sentence is the product of actual vindictiveness on the part of the sentencing authority," and had provided direction in determining whether a particular situation fell within that standard. "The same reasoning," the *Smith* Court noted, "leads to the conclusion that when a greater penalty is imposed after trial than was imposed after a prior guilty plea," the presumption should not apply, "for the increase in sentence is not more likely than not attributable to the vindictiveness on the part of the sentencing judge."

Stressing the distinctions between guilty pleas and trials (as developed in part in post-*Pearce* rulings on the plea negotiation process), the *Smith* Court found that "even when the same judge imposes both sentences," there exist "enough justifications for a heavier second sentence" following a subsequent trial as to undercut any grounding for applying the presumption. Because the information considered by the judge in accepting a guilty plea "will usually be far less than that brought out in a full trial on the merits" the judge imposing a second sentence after that trial is likely to have had "a fuller appreciation of the nature and extent of the crime charged." So too, the defendant's conduct during trial may have given the judge "insights into his moral character and suitability for rehabilitation," as suggested by *United States v. Grayson* (a case described by the Court as authorizing the sentencing authority to take into consideration its "perception of the truthfulness of a defendant testifying on his own behalf").[16] Still another relevant distinction is that, "after trial, the factors that may indicate leniency as consideration for the guilty plea are no longer present." The Court also noted that since the trial court had originally accepted a guilty plea and then conducted a trial after that plea was vacated, it would not be in a position of "simply 'doing over what it thought it had already done correctly.' "

14. The scope of the above discussion is not without ambiguity. While the Court initially seems to be saying that the *Pearce* presumption simply does not apply to cases involving different sentencers, its subsequent reference to the judge's statement in *McCullough* may indicate that the presumption applies unless the second judge sets forth a non-vindictive reason for imposing a higher sentence than the first judge. If some such reason is needed, it apparently need not be an explanation that would justify a higher sentence if *Pearce's* prophylactic rule were applicable. For the Court treated as a separate issue, relevant only if the *Pearce* presumption were to apply here," the question of whether the judge had relied upon new objective information that would rebut that presumption. See the discussion of *McCullough* in subsection (b) supra.

15. 490 U.S. 794, 109 S.Ct. 2201, 104 L.Ed.2d 865 (1989).

16. See note 3 supra.

Part Five

POST-CONVICTION REVIEW; APPEALS AND COLLATERAL REMEDIES

Chapter 27

APPEALS

Table of Sections

---

§ 27.1 Constitutional Protection of the Defendant's Right to Appeal

(a) No Constitutional Right. *McKane v. Durston,*[1] an 1894 case, involved a constitutional challenge to a state practice that denied defendants bail pending their appeal within the state judicial system. In the course of rejecting that claim, the Court responded to the suggestion that the state had a constitutional obligation to provide appellate review of a criminal conviction. It stated:

§ 27.1

1. 153 U.S. 684, 14 S.Ct. 913, 38 L.Ed. 867 (1894).

> An appeal from a judgment of conviction is not a matter of absolute right, independently of [state] constitutional or statutory provisions allowing such appeal. A review by an appellate court of the final judgment in a criminal case, however grave the offense of which the accused is convicted, was not at common-law and is not now a necessary element of due process of law. It is wholly within the discretion of the State to allow or not to allow such a review.

This statement in *McKane* came against a background of a federal judicial structure that had not granted circuit courts the authority to review federal criminal convictions until 1879 and had not given the Supreme Court jurisdiction to entertain writs of error in federal criminal cases until 1889. Commentators have suggested that the significance of appellate review in the contemporary criminal justice system would lead to a different constitutional conclusion today, and in *Jones v. Barnes,*[2] both a concurring and a dissenting opinion lent support to that suggestion.[3] However, the majority opinion in *Jones,* along with several other contemporary opinions dealing with the appellate process,[4] accepted in dictum the *McKane* dictum. As the Court put it in *Jones:* "There is, of course, no constitutional right to an appeal."

While noting that there is no constitutional right to appellate review, the Supreme Court has also acknowledged that appellate review is an important element of the criminal justice process throughout the United States. Every state and the federal system provides some means of appellate review for defendants in criminal cases. In the federal system and in most states, defendants in all felony cases have a right to appellate review. In several of the states that do not have an intermediate appellate court, review for most felony cases remains at the discretion of the state's highest court, but unlike the common law position noted in *McKane,* the defendant has at least the opportunity to gain appellate review. In misdemeanor cases, defendants commonly have a right of review in the general trial court (in some states, by trial de novo), with subsequent appellate review discretionary.

(b) Constitutional Protection of the Statutory Right of Appeal. Various strands of constitutional doctrine protect the defendant's access to that appellate review which is provided under state law. Perhaps the most significant and certainly the most extensive line of cases in this regard are the equal protection decisions safeguarding the indigent's access to appellate review. As noted in Chapter 11, *Griffin v. Illinois* holds that once a state grants defendants a right of appeal, it cannot condition that right in a manner that violates the constitutional guarantee of equal protection.[5] The *Griffin* principle has been utilized primarily to ensure that the indigent defendant has equal access to the appellate process. Thus, the state is precluded from conditioning appellate review on an appellate transcript and then failing to provide a free transcript for an indigent appellant.[6] Similarly, *Douglas v. California*[7] held that, to ensure the indigent defendant "meaningful access" to the appellate process, the state had to provide defendant with appointed counsel for his first appeal. *Anders v. California*[8] added to this protection by ensuring that appointed counsel did not withdraw from that obligation by mere assertion that the appeal would be frivolous.

The constitutional guarantee of effective assistance of counsel on the first appeal granted of right under state law is not limited to the appointed counsel. The Supreme Court has held that the constitution guarantees to all defendants under due process a right to be represented by counsel on such an appeal and to effective assistance by such counsel.[9] How-

2. 463 U.S. 745, 103 S.Ct. 3308, 77 L.Ed.2d 987 (1983).

3. See the concurring opinion of Justice Blackmun and the dissent of Justices Brennan and Marshall.

4. See e.g., Ross v. Moffitt and Douglas v. California, discussed in § 11.1(d).

5. See § 11.1(d).

6. See § 11.2(e).

7. See § 11.1(d).

8. See § 11.2(c).

9. See Evitts v. Lucey, discussed in §§ 11.1(b), 11.7(a).

ever, beyond that point, as on application for discretionary review, the defendant with retained or appointed counsel has no such guarantee.[10]

The prohibition against sentencing vindictiveness also serves to safeguard the defendant's right of appeal under state law. Indeed, in *North Carolina v. Pearce,* as discussed in § 26.8, the Court established a presumption of vindictiveness for cases in which a defendant, retried and reconvicted after a successful appeal, received a sentence higher than that imposed following his original trial. While the scope of that presumption has been narrowed, the Court remains firmly committed to the prohibition against actual vindictiveness announced in *Pearce.* The Court in *Pearce* was unanimous in holding that due process was violated where a sentencing judge sought to punish a defendant for having taken an appeal by imposing a more severe sentence following reconviction. Justice Stewart's opinion for the Court noted that "a court is 'without right to put a price on an appeal.' " As in *Griffin,* though a state had no duty to establish avenues of appellate review, it could not subject those avenues, once established, to "unreasoned distinctions" that would deter a defendant's "free and unfettered" exercise of his right to challenge his conviction.

§ 27.2 Defense Appeals and the Final Judgment Rule

(a) The Statutory Requirement of a Final Judgment. Statutory provisions governing defense appeals uniformly reflect the view, carried over from the law governing civil appeals, that piecemeal appellate review of a litigation is generally inappropriate and therefore appeals ordinarily should be allowed only from a final judgment. The implementation of this policy in the context of prosecution appeals is discussed in § 27.3. In this section, we will consider the final judgment rule as it applies to appeals by defendants and, to some extent, potential defendants (e.g., grand jury targets) and third parties (e.g., witnesses).

Because of special double jeopardy concerns, appeals by the prosecution are governed in each jurisdiction by a separate provision dealing with that subject alone. In many jurisdictions, all other appeals in criminal cases are governed by the same statute that applies to civil appeals. The federal provision, 28 U.S.C.A. § 1291, is typical. Its predecessor provided for appeals from "final decrees and judgments," but the change to the current "final decisions" was viewed as producing no substantive difference. Counterpart state statutes often refer to appeals from "final orders." In those states with separate statutes governing defense appeals in criminal cases, the statutes commonly refer to a "final judgment of conviction." Notwithstanding such references to "convictions" or "adverse verdicts of guilt," the prevailing view is that an appealable final judgment does not come with conviction alone, but requires the imposition of a sentence on that conviction.

(b) Underlying Policies and Statutory Exceptions. The final judgment rule, as applied to both civil and criminal cases, reflects a determination that, on balance, postponing appeal until a final judgment is reached both protects the interests of the litigants in a fair and accessible process and conserves judicial resources. Standing against the final judgment rule is the possibility that not allowing an interlocutory appeal from a potentially erroneous pretrial ruling may result in a final judgment reversed on appeal, causing the litigants to repeat the entire trial. If that happens, there is not only additional expense and anxiety, and the waste of judicial resources, but possibly a final determination that is considerably different from what it might have been if the error could have been caught before the case was first tried. The added delay in final adjudication may result in memory lapses, counsel on one side or another may have gained from the strategies revealed in the first trial, and witnesses may be

10. See § 11.7(a).

less (or more) susceptible to impeachment. On the other side, however, the costs of permitting interlocutory appeals are thought to be greater.

Initially, awaiting a final judgment is seen as benefitting the interests of litigants as a group even if it does occasionally require a particular litigant to undergo a wasted trial. Permitting either or both parties to postpone the trial with interlocutory appeals is likely overall to result in even greater delay in the final adjudications than allowing appeals only from final judgments. Most such interlocutory appeals, rather than correcting some trial court error, would affirm the trial judge's ruling. The end result would be a greater injustice to litigants generally than is occasioned by that small portion of cases in which trials must be repeated because appellate review was delayed until after final judgment was reached. That injustice would be particularly likely when the adversaries had unequal resources and interests in securing or avoiding a prompt disposition of the case. The party interested in a prompt adjudication would be at the mercy of an opponent willing and able to delay litigation by appealing every adverse pretrial ruling.

The advantages of the final judgment rule in securing efficient judicial administration are even more apparent. The rule provides savings for both trial and appellate courts. A major responsibility of the trial court is self-correction, and the delay of appellate review until final judgment permits the trial court to reassess its decisions in light of later trial developments. From the perspective of the appellate court, rulings also are better judged in light of the completed proceeding. At that point, the impact of the error upon the outcome is better measured (as through application of the harmless error rule). Moreover, even reversible errors are judged more efficiently since a single appeal may consider more than one error. Most significantly, the final judgment rule avoids appeals that become unnecessary as the case develops. Thus, pretrial rulings often become moot when the party adversely affected by the erroneous ruling ultimately gains a favorable jury verdict.

While all of the above considerations have relevance to both civil and criminal cases, the delay that would accompany interlocutory appeals has been characterized as especially pernicious in the criminal justice process, where the constitutional right to a speedy trial is said to reflect a "societal interest * * * which exists separate from * * * the interests of the accused." [1] In his frequently quoted opinion in *Cobbledick v. United States,*[2] Justice Frankfurter concentrated primarily on the element of delay in urging strict adherence to the final judgment rule in criminal cases. He noted:

> These considerations of policy are especially compelling in the administration of criminal justice. * * * An accused is entitled to scrupulous observance of constitutional safeguards. But encouragement of delay is fatal to the vindication of the criminal law. Bearing the discomfiture and cost of a prosecution for crime even by an innocent person is one of the painful obligations of citizenship. The correctness of a trial court's rejection even of a constitutional claim made by the accused in the process of prosecution must await his conviction before its reconsideration by an appellate tribunal.

The viewpoint expressed in *Cobbledick* has clearly dominated the federal statutory scheme for defense appeals in criminal cases. Congress has adopted several statutory provisions allowing interlocutory appeals that are limited to civil cases. The most significant is 18 U.S.C.A. § 1292(b), which grants the courts of appeals discretionary jurisdiction to hear an interlocutory appeal on certification of the trial judge that the challenged order "involves a controlling question of law as to which there is a substantial ground for difference of opinion" and that an "immediate appeal from the order may materially advance

§ 27.2

1. See Barker v. Wingo, discussed at § 18.1(b), note 7. See also DiBella v. United States, 369 U.S. 121, 82 S.Ct. 654, 7 L.Ed.2d 614 (1962).

2. 309 U.S. 323, 60 S.Ct. 540, 84 L.Ed. 783 (1940).

the ultimate termination of the litigation." In contrast to this provision, the only federal statute authorizing interlocutory appeals in criminal cases is quite narrow and carefully limited to prosecution appeals.[3]

Contrary to the federal position, a substantial number of states have broad provisions permitting discretionary interlocutory appeals by defendants in criminal cases. Several have adopted provisions similar to 28 U.S.C.A. § 1291(b) that apply to criminal as well as civil cases. Others simply provide for interlocutory appeal by leave of the appellate court, without requiring certification by the trial judge. Such provisions often identify a series of factors to be considered by the appellate court in determining whether to grant review, such as whether immediate review will "clarify an issue of general importance in the administration of justice" or "protect the petitioner from substantial or irreparable injury." In general, these discretionary appeal provisions will be available only for review of orders issued substantially in advance of the scheduled trial, unless the trial judge is willing to grant a stay pending disposition of the application for leave to appeal. The jurisdictions with such provisions have not rejected Justice Frankfurter's conclusion that defendants may be required, as one of the "painful obligations of citizenship," to "bear the discomfiture and cost" of an unnecessary trial. They have concluded, however, that the final judgment rule should be subject to exception where the circumstances of the individual case convince the appellate court that the protection of the defendant's substantive rights or the conservation of judicial resources would be better served by interlocutory review.

(c) Collateral Orders. Although the major federal statutes authorizing interlocutory appeals have been limited to civil cases, one of the major judicially recognized "exceptions" to the final judgment rule—the collateral order doctrine—has been carried over by federal courts to criminal cases. The collateral order doctrine was first clearly articulated in the civil case of *Cohen v. Beneficial Industrial Loan Corp.*[4] In that case, the defendant in a stockholder's derivative suit sought to appeal a district court ruling refusing to direct the plaintiffs to post a security bond as would be required if state law governed that procedure. The Supreme Court held that the ruling was appealable under 28 U.S.C.A. § 1291. A final decision, the Court noted, did not necessarily have to terminate an action. Given a "practical rather than technical construction," the final judgment concept also encompassed certain orders collateral to the basic litigation. These were described as

> that small class [of orders] which finally determine claims of right separable from, and collateral to, rights asserted in the action, too important to be denied review and too independent of the cause itself to require that appellate consideration be deferred until the whole case is adjudicated.

The *Cohen* discussion of these collateral orders suggested several general characteristics that allowed them to be characterized as final decisions. Over the years, these were condensed into a three-pronged test, most prominently set forth in *Coopers & Lybrand v. Livesay.*[5]

> To come within the "small class" of decisions excepted from the final-judgment rule by *Cohen,* the order must conclusively determine the disputed question, resolve an important issue completely separate from the merits of the action, and be effectively unreviewable on appeal from a final judgment.

The first of these three prerequisites demands that the ruling not be "tentative, informal, or incomplete," but constitute a firm and final denial of the challenge sought to be appealed. If there is a reasonable prospect that the trial court might alter its ruling as the litigation further develops, an immediate

3. See 18 U.S.C.A. § 3731, discussed in § 27.3(b), (c). While 18 U.S.C.A. § 3154(c) provides for both defense and prosecution appeal from a pretrial release or pretrial detention order [see § 12.1(a)], that appeal provides only limited legislative expansion of review that would be allowed under the final judgment rule through the collateral order doctrine. See Stack v. Boyle, infra note 6.

4. 337 U.S. 541, 69 S.Ct. 1221, 93 L.Ed. 1528 (1949).

5. 437 U.S. 463, 98 S.Ct. 2454, 57 L.Ed.2d 351 (1978).

appellate intrusion clearly is not appropriate. As to the second prerequisite, it demands that the challenge ruled upon not "affect, or * * * be affected by" any subsequent decision on the merits of the case. If the trial court ruling is not "independent of the cause" itself, determining rights "separable from and collateral to [those] rights asserted in the action," then review prior to the ultimate disposition constitutes a wasteful use of appellate resources. Depending upon the disposition of the case, it will produce either an unnecessary review or a review that will only be repeated, possibly in a new light that would require the appellate court to withdraw from any earlier ruling. The second prerequisite also requires that the issue resolved by the trial court, apart from its independent bearing, be "important." Thus, the *Cohen* Court noted that the collateral order there might not have been appealable if the only issue presented was one of the proper exercise of the trial court's discretion. Finally, the third prerequisite insists that review on appeal following the final disposition not provide a satisfactory remedy for the right being asserted. Thus, the *Cohen* Court noted that the claim presented there, the petitioner's right to security for its costs, would be lost, "probably irreparably," if review came only after the petitioner had won the case on the merits.

The Supreme Court first applied the collateral order doctrine to a criminal case in *Stack v. Boyle.*[6] The defendants there, unable to make bail, brought habeas corpus proceedings to challenge the trial court's denial of their motion to reduce the level of their bail. The Supreme Court concluded that the use of the habeas remedy was inappropriate since the defendants had an unexhausted remedy available in a direct appeal from the trial court's order. The Court said very little about why the bail ruling met the prerequisites of *Cohen.* It noted only that here, as in *Cohen,* the rejected motion "did not merely invoke the discretion of the district court" as it "challenged the bail as violating statutory and constitutional standards." In a concurring opinion, Justice Jackson, the author of *Cohen,* added a brief additional explanation. "An order fixing bail," he noted, "can be reviewed without halting the main trial—its issues are entirely independent of the issues to be tried—and unless it can be reviewed before sentence, it can never be reviewed at all."

Six years later, in *Carroll v. United States,*[7] the Court in a much more extensive discussion of the final judgment rule, warned against too ready extension of the *Cohen* rule to criminal cases and characterized those orders in criminal cases that fit within *Cohen* as "very few." For a substantial period thereafter, lower court and Supreme Court rulings, consistent with the *Carroll* discussion, treated *Stack* as an almost one-of-a-kind ruling. A broad range of pretrial rulings in criminal cases were held not to fall within the collateral order doctrine. Thus, defense appeals were not allowed as to orders denying motions to suppress evidence, orders granting or denying discovery, orders denying or granting a transfer or change of venue and the denial of motions challenging indictments on various grounds. Aside from the order presented in *Stack,* the only ruling recognized to be appealable was an order holding the defendant incompetent to stand trial. That order had a consequence similar to the denial of bail reduction in *Stack* since the defendant held incompetent was automatically detained in a mental institution.

In *Abney v. United States,*[8] the Supreme Court added only one additional ruling to this group of two, but its opinion seemed to many to open the door to substantial further extensions of the *Cohen* doctrine. The Court there held appealable the denial of a pretrial defense motion seeking dismissal of an indictment on double jeopardy grounds. Chief Justice Burger's opinion for the Court concluded that the trial court's order met all the prerequisites for fitting within " 'the small class of cases' that *Cohen* has placed beyond the con-

6. 342 U.S. 1, 72 S.Ct. 1, 96 L.Ed. 3 (1951).

7. 354 U.S. 394, 77 S.Ct. 1332, 1 L.Ed.2d 1442 (1957).

8. 431 U.S. 651, 97 S.Ct. 2034, 52 L.Ed.2d 651 (1977).

fines of the final-judgment rule." Initially, there had been a "fully consummated decision" of the trial court. The denial of the motion to dismiss had constituted a "complete, formal and * * * final rejection" of the defendant's double jeopardy claim. Secondly, the double jeopardy issue was "collateral to, and separable from, the principal issue at the accused's impending criminal trial, i.e., whether or not the accused is guilty of the offense charged." The defendant's challenge did not go to the "merits of the charge against him" nor did it relate to the evidence the government might use in proving its case. Finally, "the rights conferred upon the criminal accused by the Double Jeopardy Clause would be significantly undermined if appellate review of double jeopardy claims were postponed until after conviction and sentence." The function of the double jeopardy clause, the Court stressed, was not simply to insulate the defendant against being subjected to double punishment, but also to protect the defendant against being forced "to endure the personal strain, public embarrassment, and expense of a criminal trial more than once for the same offense." Reversal on appeal from a conviction following a second trial was too late to afford protection against "being twice put to *trial* for the same offense." Admittedly, allowing review prior to trial might "encourage some defendants to engage in dilatory appeals," but that was a necessary cost of protecting the double jeopardy right. Moreover, that problem, the Court noted, could be "obviated [by] * * * summary procedures and calendars [designed] to weed out frivolous claims of former jeopardy."

Abney, unlike *Stack,* dealt with a claim that was not mooted on review following a conviction, but was held for other reasons not to be adequately protected by a reversal at that point. Arguably, various other claims could fall in the same category. Relying on *Abney,* lower courts thereafter held immediately appealable the denial of motions to dismiss that claimed a violation of the Speech or Debate Clause, a violation of the constitutional right to a speedy trial, and vindictive prosecution contrary to due process. On review of these rulings, the Supreme Court held that the *Cohen* principle encompassed a pretrial rejection of the first claim, but not the other two. *Helstoski v. Meanor,*[9] found appealable an order denying a former Congressman's claim that the indictment against him violated the Speech or Debate Clause (which provides that "for any speech or debate," a Congressman "shall not be questioned in any Place"). But *United States v. MacDonald*[10] and *United States v. Hollywood Motor Car Company*[11] concluded that orders denying speedy trial and vindictive prosecution claims did not have the special qualities needed to fall under the "collateral order exception," which was to be construed "with the utmost strictness in criminal cases."

A critical factor distinguishing *Abney* and *Helstoski* on the one hand, and *MacDonald* and *Hollywood Motor Car* on the other, was the Court's characterization of the nature of the claim presented by defendant's pretrial motion. *Helstoski* held that the constitutional right of a Congressman not to "be questioned" encompassed a protection against trial as well as conviction and therefore was analogous to the double jeopardy claim presented in *Abney. Hollywood Motor Car* and *MacDonald* concluded that the claims presented there did not include a right not to be tried. The dissenters in *Hollywood Motor Car* argued that the constitutional prohibition against vindictive prosecution was designed to avoid prosecutorial punishment of the exercise of rights and that should encompass protection against the burdens of trial, but the majority viewed the scope of the right quite differently. While earlier vindictive prosecution cases had spoken of a defendant's right "not to be haled into court" by a prosecutor who raised a criminal charge to punish the defendant for his earlier exercise of a procedural right,[12] those cases had also recognized

9. 442 U.S. 500, 99 S.Ct. 2445, 61 L.Ed.2d 30 (1979).

10. 435 U.S. 850, 98 S.Ct. 1547, 56 L.Ed.2d 18 (1978).

11. 458 U.S. 263, 102 S.Ct. 3081, 73 L.Ed.2d 754 (1982).

12. See e.g., Blackledge v. Perry, discussed at § 13.-5(a).

that the appropriate relief was simply the dismissal of the additional charge. The defendant was never thought to be free of retrial on the original charge that was not tainted by vindictiveness. Hence, the petitioner's claim could not be characterized as presenting "a right not to be tried," but only as "a right whose remedy requires the dismissal of charges." As in the case of other challenges to the validity of a charge, such as a challenge to the constitutionality of the statute on which a charge is based, dismissal on an appeal following a conviction constituted an adequate remedy. Thus, what was at stake here was not "an asserted legal right, the legal and practical value of which would be destroyed if it were not vindicated before trial."

In *MacDonald,* a unanimous Court similarly characterized a defendant's speedy trial claim as not encompassing a "right not to be tried." Here, it was "the delay before trial, not the trial itself that offends the constitutional guarantee." Indeed, to present an appeal prior to trial would threaten many of the interests protected by the speedy trial clause. *MacDonald* also distinguished *Abney* on other grounds. The determination as to whether there had been a denial of a speedy trial was often dependent upon an assessment of the prejudice caused by the delay, which could best be considered "only after the relevant facts had been developed at trial." Hence, the pretrial denial of the defendant's motion could not be considered a "complete, formal, and final rejection" of that claim, and the prejudice element of the claim could not be viewed as separable from the trial on the merits. Also, unlike the double jeopardy claim presented in *Abney,* which required an initial showing of prior jeopardy, there was "nothing about * * * a speedy trial claim which inherently limits the availability of the claim." If a right to immediate appeal were recognized, "any defendant" could raise such a claim in anticipation of a dilatory pretrial appeal. When these two grounds are added to the Court's insistence that the claim present a right "not to be tried," any door to immediate appeals left open in *Abney* would seem to have been fairly tightly shut. Indeed, the dismissal motions presented in *Abney* and *Helstoski* may well be the only motions to dismiss that can result in orders immediately appealable under *Abney,* as it has subsequently been interpreted.

Another attempt to expand the "very few" instances in which pretrial rulings come within *Cohen* was rejected in two cases in which it was argued that pretrial rulings adverse to the defendant were "effectively unreviewable on appeal for a conviction." *Flanagan v. United States*[13] presented an order disqualifying defense counsel on conflict grounds under Federal Rule 44(c). In an earlier ruling involving a disqualification motion in a civil case, the Court had concluded that even if such a motion raised an "issue completely separate from the merits of the action," it still did not meet the *Cohen* test because denial of immediate review would not lead to "irreparable harm" in light of relief that could be granted (through a new trial) on review of the final disposition of the case. The petitioners in *Flanagan* argued that the situation was different in a criminal case because even though there had been improper disqualification of defense counsel, relief on appeal from a conviction would be available only upon a showing that the loss of preferred counsel resulted in some "specifically demonstrated prejudice to the defense." That would require an impossibly speculative judgment, assuming that the replacement counsel had been competent. Responding to this contention, the Supreme Court noted that providing fully effective review would present no difficulty if the asserted right to counsel of one's choice were treated like the Sixth Amendment right to represent oneself, with a denial of the right requiring automatic reversal. However, that question need not be decided because, even if a showing of prejudice were required, as petitioner contended, the second condition of *Cohen*—"that the order be truly collateral"—was not satisfied. Assuming that a constitutional violation was tied to a finding

13. 465 U.S. 259, 104 S.Ct. 1051, 79 L.Ed.2d 288 (1984).

of prejudice, a disqualification order could hardly be said to be "independent of the issues to be tried." The "effect of the disqualification on the defense, and hence whether the asserted right had been violated, cannot be fairly assessed until the substance of the prosecution's and defendant's case is known." In this respect, the petitioner's claim was analogous to the speedy trial presented in *MacDonald*.

In *Midland Asphalt Corp. v. United States,*[14] the defendant had a stronger grounding for arguing that his constitutional claim would be "effectively unreviewable on appeal from a conviction," but the Court held that the ruling below still failed to fall with the *Cohen* exception because the very quality that made it unreviewable on appeal also established that it was not truly collateral to a decision on the merits of the case. The lower court there had assumed that an erroneous denial of the defendant's motion to dismiss the indictment based on an alleged violation of Rule 6(e) would be treated as a per se harmless error on an appeal following a conviction, under the reasoning of *Mechanik v. United States.*[15] The Supreme Court held that if the *Mechanik* ruling did indeed apply to Rule 6(e) violations, that would follow only because the purpose of Rule 6(e) was to protect against the indictment of a defendant where there was insufficient evidence of guilt to indict (with *Mechanik* finding such an error to be per se harmless because of the subsequent petit jury finding of guilt beyond a reasonable doubt). Accordingly, denial of a pretrial dismissal motion alleging a Rule 6(e) violation obviously did not "resolve an important issue completely separate from the merits of the action," but instead "involve[d] considerations 'enmeshed in the merits of the dispute' and would ... 'be *affected by*' the decision on the merits."

The collateral order of doctrine of *Cohen* is applied in many states, and several others apply doctrines that are roughly similar but utilize somewhat differently worded standards. These jurisdictions generally reach the same results as the federal courts, and often follow closely the leading Supreme Court rulings. Another group of states, however, do not recognize even the narrow "exception" to the final judgment concept recognized in *Cohen.* In most of these jurisdictions, alternative routes are available for obtaining immediate review of the few orders that the federal courts would describe as collateral. Thus, some provide review through a discretionary interlocutory appeal. Defendants commonly do not have, however, the assurance of review that they would have with a right to immediate appeal under the collateral order doctrine. Lower courts have questioned whether such an arrangement, insofar as it fails to grant a right to immediate appeal from a denial of a double jeopardy claim, is constitutionally acceptable. *Abney,* they note, stated that the protection afforded by the double jeopardy clause "would be significantly undermined if appellate review of double jeopardy claims were postponed until after conviction." These courts therefore suggest that the state, as part of its constitutional obligation to effectively enforce the double jeopardy bar, must provide for an immediate appeal from the trial court's denial of a nonfrivolous double jeopardy objection.

(d) Independent Proceedings. The collateral order doctrine permits an immediate appeal from orders that clearly are a part of the ongoing litigation. Certain proceedings, though related to an ongoing or contemplated litigation, may be viewed as sufficiently separate from that litigation so that an order terminating that proceeding is itself a final judgment and therefore appealable. The crucial question here, the Supreme Court has noted, is whether the proceeding is "independent * * * or merely a step in the trial of the criminal case."[16] Perhaps the clearest illustration of an independent proceeding is the third party challenge to an order issued in a criminal case. Consider, for example, an objection to a closure order. Where the chal-

14. 489 U.S. 794, 109 S.Ct. 1494, 103 L.Ed.2d 879 (1989).

15. See § 15.6(e).

16. Cogen v. United States, 278 U.S. 221, 49 S.Ct. 118, 73 L.Ed. 275 (1929).

lenge is raised by the defendant, the order rejecting that challenge is part of the criminal case and its immediate appeal subject to the limitations of the *Cohen* doctrine. On the other hand, if a third party (e.g., the press) brings an action to vindicate its alleged right to be present at the proceedings, that action is deemed independent and the denial of its challenge is appealable as a final judgment without applying the *Cohen* standards. Similarly, while the denial of a defense motion to strike surplusage in an indictment would not be appealable, an unindicted co-conspirator may appeal from rejection of his action to have his name stricken from the indictment.

Where the party seeking to appeal is a defendant or a potential defendant who has sought relief that would have a direct bearing on the criminal trial, both federal and state courts are much less likely to find that his action, though filed separately, is actually an independent proceeding. The leading case on the application of the independent proceeding doctrine in this context is *DiBella v. United States.*[17] A unanimous Supreme Court there held nonappealable the denial of a motion to suppress that had been filed by the petitioner before he was indicted but after he had been arrested. The Court, per Frankfurter, J., reasoned that the factors that led to the characterization of a post-indictment suppression ruling as an interlocutory order were equally applicable to a pre-indictment ruling. The ruling was not "fairly severable from the context of a larger litigious process" since the disposition of the motion, whether made before or after indictment, would "necessarily determine the conduct of the [eventual] trial." Similarly, whether the suppression motion was filed before or after indictment, the same "practical reasons" existed for not granting immediate review. First, treating "such a disjointed ruling on the admissibility of a potential item of evidence as an independent proceeding, with full panoply of appeal and attendant stay, [would] entail serious disruption of the conduct of a criminal trial." Second, appellate intervention prior to trial would result in a "truncated presentation of the issue of admissibility because the legality of the search too often cannot truly be determined until the evidence at the trial has brought all circumstances to light."

Although holding that pre-indictment and post-indictment suppression motions would be treated alike for the purpose of appellate review, Justice Frankfurter held open the possibility that a pre-charge motion challenging an illegal search could, under some circumstances, be immediately appealable. After noting that a suppression motion must be viewed "as a step in the criminal case preliminary to the trial thereof" when the criminal process has reached the stage of an arrest or a filing of a complaint, he added: "Only if the motion is solely for return of property and is in no way tied to a criminal prosecution *in esse* against the movant can the proceedings be regarded as independent." Lower courts have subsequently held that such a motion is an independent proceeding, but they have disagreed as to exactly what constitutes a motion "solely for the return of property," and exactly when a criminal prosecution is "*in esse.*" As to the first issue, the primary difficulty arises from the 1972 amendment of Federal Rule 41(e), which governs the motion for return of property unlawfully seized. Under that amendment, a successful Rule 41(e) motion automatically results not only in the return of the property but also in a preclusion of its use at trial. Lower courts agree that this amendment should not automatically bar a Rule 41(e) motion from being treated as a motion "solely for return of property" under the *DiBella* dictum, and that the key should be whether the primary objective of motion is to gain return of the property. They disagree, however, as to how that determination should be made, with some courts looking to such factors as whether the Rule 41(e) motion alleges that irreparable harm will be suffered if the property is not returned immediately and others assuming that the primary objective is return of the property so long as the movant has a lawful right to the possession of the item in question. As to when the prosecu-

17. 369 U.S. 121, 82 S.Ct. 654, 7 L.Ed.2d 614 (1962).

tion is "*in esse*" (i.e., "in being"), the primary division here hinges on the significance of the initiation of a grand jury investigation. Noting that the *DiBella* opinion characterized a presentation before a grand jury as a "part of the federal prosecution," some courts hold that the prosecution is "*in esse*" when the movant is the target of a grand jury investigation, but others maintain that it is the prosecution itself that must be in being and this requires more than mere investigation.

(e) Grand Jury Proceedings. Application of both the independent proceeding and collateral order doctrines often has proven especially troublesome in the analysis of court orders growing out of grand jury proceedings. Courts have generally rejected the contention that, because "a grand jury proceeding is 'party-less,' " each challenge of a witness or other person to a separate grand jury order should be viewed as an independent proceeding producing a final judgment. In *Cobbledick v. United States,*[18] the Supreme Court refuted such an argument in holding that the denial of a motion to quash a grand jury subpoena was not appealable. The Court distinguished the proceeding to enforce an administrative subpoena which is commonly regarded as an independent action for agency discovery, thereby rendering orders granting or quashing an agency subpoena final and appealable. The ongoing grand jury proceeding, *Cobbledick* noted, was instead comparable to the ongoing post-indictment prosecution:

> The proceeding before a grand jury constitutes "a judicial inquiry" * * * of the most ancient lineage. The duration of its life, frequently short, is limited by statute. It is no less important to safeguard against undue interruption the inquiry instituted by a grand jury than to protect from delay the progress of the trial after an indictment has been found. * * * That a grand jury proceeding has no defined litigants and that none may emerge from it is irrelevant to the issue.

In the context of a trial, the Supreme Court had held that the rejection of a witness' objection to a subpoena was not a final order. To gain appellate review, the witness had to refuse to comply and be held in contempt, which did produce a final order. The same requirement, *Cobbledick* held, was applicable to the grand jury witness. If the witness "chooses to disobey and is held in contempt," an immediate appeal will be allowed. That appeal "may involve an interruption of * * * the investigation," but allowing it is essential to preserve the witness' rights. "[N]ot to allow this interruption," the Court reasoned, "would forever preclude review of the witness' claim, for his alternatives are to abandon the claim or languish in jail." Accordingly, once held in contempt, the "witness' situation becomes so severed from the main proceeding as to permit an appeal." [19]

18. 309 U.S. 323, 60 S.Ct. 540, 84 L.Ed. 783 (1940).

19. Under the ruling of Perlman v. United States, 247 U.S. 7, 38 S.Ct. 417, 62 L.Ed. 950 (1918), an exception to the contempt prerequisite exists when a subpoena duces tecum is directed at a person other than the appellant and the appellant cannot expect that person to risk contempt for the purpose of protecting the appellant's interest in the property subpoenaed. In *Perlman,* the clerk of a federal court was directed to produce before a grand jury documents that Perlman had deposited with the clerk in connection with a patent infringement suit. Claiming a continuing right to those documents, Perlman challenged the order directed to the clerk and subsequently appealed from the denial of that challenge. As later explained in United States v. Ryan, 402 U.S. 530, 91 S.Ct. 1580, 29 L.Ed.2d 85 (1971), that appeal was allowed without the witness (the clerk) meeting the contempt prerequisite of *Cobbledick* because the witness did not share the interest of the intervenor (Perlman) in challenging the order. Without immediate review, Perlman would have been "powerless to avert the mischief of the [challenged] order," yet the witness had no interest in risking contempt to gain such review. The lower courts have not restricted the *Perlman* exception to situations in which the intervenor and witness are total strangers, but have also applied that exception to a bank depositor's appeal of a motion to quash a grand jury subpoena issued to his bank, to an employer's appeal of its motion to quash a grand jury subpoena issued to its employee, and to a client's appeal of its motion to quash a subpoena issued to its attorney. The latter two situations, however, have produced a division among the lower courts, with some holding that *Perlman* ordinarily should not apply because the interests presented in the employee-employer and client-lawyer relationships are such that the witness can be expected to run the risk of contempt in order to gain an appeal. In United States v. Ryan, supra, the Court stressed that *Perlman* created only a narrow exception to a sound policy that, in the interest of limiting appeals that would disrupt "expedition in the administration of the criminal law," puts the objecting witness to the inhibiting cost of standing in contempt.

Where the challenge to ongoing grand jury proceedings does not relate to the appearance of a witness, the contempt alternative of *Cobbledick* is not available. In such cases, courts focus on whether the petitioner (who is usually the target of the investigation) will have a subsequently available appellate remedy if an immediate appeal from his denied request for relief is not available. Thus, if the target is objecting to the alleged use of the grand jury to develop evidence for a civil case, a court is likely to hold that an immediate appeal is not permissible since a later objection (and appeal) is available if the government should seek to transfer any such evidence to a potential civil litigant or to use it in a civil proceeding. Similarly, if the target claims that the grand jury proceeding is being tainted by misconduct, a court may hold that such an objection can be advanced when (and if) an indictment is issued and an appeal can then be taken when (and if) the target is convicted. Some courts are less willing than others, however, to view such subsequent avenues of appeal as adequate. Thus, appeals have been allowed from rulings denying target-petitioner motions to terminate a grand jury proceeding on the ground that favorable evidence was being withheld, to preclude grand-jury gathering of evidence to be used in prosecuting a pending indictment, and to conduct an evidentiary hearing into the alleged resumption of prosecutorial misconduct that had led to the dismissal of a prior indictment.

Once the grand jury investigation has ended, a petitioner seeking relief unrelated to an ongoing prosecution can more readily claim that his request involves an independent proceeding. Thus, an appeal can be taken from the grant or denial of a Rule 6(e) motion for disclosure of grand jury minutes for use in an unrelated proceeding. So too, an appeal was allowed from a district court order providing for the transfer of the grand jury transcripts to a court in another district.

§ 27.3 Prosecution Appeals

(a) The Need for Specific Statutory Authorization. It is a basic premise of American jurisprudence that absent specific statutory authorization, the prosecution lacks the right to appeal an adverse ruling in a criminal case. The policy underlying that position was set forth by the Supreme Court's ruling in *United States v. Sanges*[1]:

> the defendant, having been once put upon his trial and discharged by the court, is not to be again vexed for the same cause, unless the legislature, acting within its constitutional authority, has made express provision for a review of the judgment at the instance of the government.

This policy also guides judicial interpretation of statutory provisions authorizing prosecution appeals. Thus, after Congress adopted in 1907 a statute allowing government appeals under specified circumstances, the Supreme Court, consistent with *Sanges,* strictly limited such appeals to the letter of that provision. When the government sought to expand those limits utilizing the general appeals statute, 18 U.S.C.A. § 1291 (allowing for appeals from final decisions), the Supreme Court rejected that position in *Carroll v. United States,*[2] where it noted:

> [A]ppeals by the Government in criminal cases are something unusual, exceptional, not favored. The history shows resistance of the Court to the opening of an appellate route for the Government until it was plainly provided by the Congress, and after that a close restriction of its uses to those authorized by the statute.

The philosophy expressed in *Sanges* and *Carroll* is repeated frequently in state as well as federal decisions. With one exception, all of the states now have provisions allowing prosecution appeals from at least a limited class of orders in criminal cases. Some, like the Federal Criminal Appeals Act of 1970 (18 U.S.C.A. § 3731), reflect the policy of allowing prosecution appeals from all final orders except where "the double jeopardy clause * * *

§ 27.3

1. 144 U.S. 310, 12 S.Ct. 609, 36 L.Ed. 445 (1892).

2. 354 U.S. 394, 77 S.Ct. 1332, 1 L.Ed.2d 1442 (1957).

prohibits further prosecution."[3] However, unless the statutory language clearly evidences such intent, the courts will not turn first to double jeopardy concerns in determining whether the appeal should be allowed. Where the statutory language refers to appeals from specific types of orders (e.g., an "order arresting judgment"), the court must find initially that the ruling in question squarely fits within the specified category. The provision will not automatically be expansively interpreted so as to bring the government's right to appeal to the outer limits of the double jeopardy prohibition.[4]

(b) Pretrial Rulings. While state provisions commonly authorize prosecution appeals from at least some pretrial rulings that would fall in the final judgment category, they vary substantially in scope. Some apply to all such rulings. They refer either to appeals from all "final judgments," or (as in the federal provision) from all "dismissals of an indictment or information * * * as to one or more counts." These provisions encompass dismissals based upon such grounds as the insufficiency of the accusatory pleading, prior jeopardy, denial of a speedy trial, lack of sufficient evidence to support a bindover, and prosecutorial misconduct. Other jurisdictions, with provisions utilizing somewhat narrower language (e.g., allowing appeals from a successful "motion to quash") have insisted that the lower court ruling be based on a deficiency in the pleading itself rather than some matter "dehors the record" (such as double jeopardy or denial or a speedy trial).

The states also vary in their treatment of prosecution appeals from interlocutory pretrial rulings. As noted in § 27.2, a defendant has no right to appeal an adverse interlocutory order, though some states do allow discretionary appeals from interlocutory orders issued before trial. Of course, if the defendant is convicted, he can gain review of the adverse pretrial ruling on the appeal from his conviction. The prosecution, however, is in a quite different position. If it is not allowed an immediate appeal from an adverse interlocutory ruling, there will be no opportunity for later appellate review. An erroneous interlocutory ruling may result in the prosecution losing its case at trial, but the acquittal of the defendant will end the matter since the double jeopardy prohibition then bars further prosecution. For most jurisdictions, this circumstance justifies providing the prosecution with an opportunity to appeal one or more classes of adverse pretrial interlocutory orders. For others, the defendant's interest in the "swift resolution of his case" is a more important consideration. Since a prosecution appeal from an adverse interlocutory ruling necessarily delays the trial (in contrast to a pretrial ruling constituting a final judgment,

3. 18 U.S.C.A. § 3731 provides:

In a criminal case an appeal by the United States shall lie to a court of appeals from a decision, judgment, or order of a district court dismissing an indictment or information or granting a new trial after verdict or judgment as to any one or more counts, except that no appeal shall lie where the double jeopardy clause of the United States Constitution prohibits further prosecution.

This provision has been read as intending "to remove all statutory barriers to Government appeals and to allow appeals whenever the Constitution would permit." United States v. Wilson, 420 U.S. 332, 95 S.Ct. 1013, 43 L.Ed.2d 232 (1975). Section 3731 also contains a separate provision governing appeals from suppression orders (discussed infra), and a separate provision allowing an appeal from a district court order "granting the release of a person charged with or convicted of an offense, or denying a motion for revocation of, or modification of the conditions of, a decision or order granting release" (see note 7 infra).

4. As to double jeopardy limitations, see § 25.3. While it is sometimes said that double jeopardy itself "bars an appeal by the prosecution following a jury verdict of acquittal," see Arizona v. Manypenny, 451 U.S. 232, 101 S.Ct. 1657, 68 L.Ed.2d 58 (1981), that analysis is subject to question. 18 U.S.C.A. § 3731, like the Supreme Court opinions discussed in § 25.3, asks whether reprosecution following a successful appeal would be barred. See § 25.3(e). If the government's victory on appeal would not permit a reprosecution (due to the double jeopardy prohibition), then the appeal presents "basically a moot issue" and will not be allowed for that reason. In several jurisdictions in which justiciability is not limited by a "case or controversy" restriction, "moot appeals" from acquittals have been accepted as consistent with the double jeopardy prohibition. In a moot appeal, the prosecution raises issues solely for the purpose of determining the law for future cases, with the appellate court lacking authority to upset the judgment of acquittal. To ensure that the prosecution's appeal is contested, defense counsel is commonly paid by the state to argue the defense side. The discussion that follows excludes such moot appeals.

which will only have that effect if that judgment is reversed on appeal), and since such a ruling still leaves the prosecution with the opportunity to go to trial, these jurisdictions will not grant to the prosecution a right of appeal from any such non-final orders.

Most jurisdictions do allow a prosecution appeal from one pretrial interlocutory order—the granting of a pretrial motion to suppress evidence. A suppression order is generally held not to fall within a provision authorizing appeals from a "final judgment" or a "dismissal of an indictment" since it does not formally terminate the proceeding. Even where the prosecution has no additional evidence, the termination comes only with a subsequent *nolle prosequi* motion. Accordingly, suppression orders will be appealable in all but a few jurisdictions only if authorized by a provision referring specifically to such orders. The federal government and approximately half of the states have adopted such provisions, with most providing for review as a matter of right. Two grounds are advanced in support of allowing a prosecution appeal from a pretrial suppression order. First, it is noted that the practical effect of the granting of a suppression motion often is comparable to the dismissal of an indictment since the suppression order frequently will eliminate the heart of the prosecution's case. Consistent with this justification for review, many jurisdictions limit prosecution appeals from suppression orders to cases in which the suppressed evidence is shown to be critical to the prosecution's case. Several condition appeal on a prosecution certification that the suppression order will eliminate any "reasonable possibility" of a successful prosecution. The federal statute [18 U.S.C.A. § 3731] and several state provisions require certification that "the appeal is not taken for the purpose of delay and that the [suppressed] evidence is a substantial proof of a fact material in the proceeding." In other jurisdictions, certification is not required, but the prosecution must otherwise establish that the trial court's ruling will have a substantial impact upon the outcome of the prosecution.

Those jurisdictions that grant a right to appeal but do not require certification or other special showing may simply assume that prosecutors will rarely seek review of a suppression order unless the excluded evidence is critical to the individual case or the legal issue raised by the suppression determination has broader ramifications. The latter possibility relates to the second justification advanced for granting the prosecution review of pretrial suppression orders—the special need for appellate court rulings in the fields covered by suppression motions. The rules relating to searches and seizures and interrogation, it is argued, are often uncertain. Accordingly, law enforcement officers are not likely to be satisfied with the varying judgments of individual trial judges. If appellate review is not readily available, the police will seek to obtain a higher court ruling by persisting in the challenged practice until they obtain a favorable decision from another trial judge, which will then be taken to the appellate court by the defendant on appeal from a conviction. The better practice, it is argued, is to give the prosecution the opportunity to gain immediate review of those trial court rulings that it considers questionable.

This second justification for permitting prosecution appeals has relevance primarily to suppression orders based upon police illegalities in acquiring evidence. Several of the statutory provisions authorizing prosecution appeal of suppression orders are limited to such orders. Others, like 18 U.S.C.A. § 3731, speak generally of orders "suppressing or excluding" evidence. These provisions, which usually also include a certification requirement, have been held applicable to a broad range of pretrial suppression orders. Thus, the state was allowed under such a provision to appeal a court order directing it to disclose psychiatric reports pertaining to its witnesses where the sanction for failing to disclose was the exclusion of the testimony of those witnesses. So too, *United States v. Helstoski*[5] suggests that the prosecution, by gaining a pretrial determination of evidentiary

5. 442 U.S. 477, 99 S.Ct. 2432, 61 L.Ed.2d 12 (1979).

issues, can utilize the provision to obtain appellate review of adverse evidentiary rulings that otherwise would be made at trial with no appeal possible. There, after the trial court indicated in its rejection of a motion to dismiss that the Speech or Debate Clause would bar prosecution reference to the legislative activities of the defendant (a former Congressman), the government sought a pretrial ruling on the admissibility of 23 categories of evidence. When the district court responded with an adverse ruling, the government obtained appellate review since that ruling was treated as one "excluding evidence" and the prosecution was able to file the necessary certification under 18 U.S.C.A. § 3731 based on the significance of the evidence.

Since the provisions authorizing appeal from a suppression order apply only to pretrial suppression rulings, the defendant arguably can cut off appellate review if it presents its objection so as to obtain a ruling only after jeopardy has attached. In the case of the typical suppression motion claiming the unconstitutional acquisition of evidence, state law ordinarily makes it difficult, if not impossible, to employ such a strategy. All but a few jurisdictions require that such a motion be presented before trial. However, most jurisdictions also allow the trial court at least limited discretion to entertain a defense motion to suppress made during trial. Obviously one factor to be considered in determining whether to exercise that discretion is the impact of the timing of the motion on the state's right to appeal, but there are cases in which the surrounding circumstances nevertheless justify allowing an otherwise untimely motion (e.g., where defendant lacked a reasonable opportunity to present the motion before trial). At least one jurisdiction has adopted as a response to that situation the treatment of the successful mid-trial suppression motion as also constituting a defense acquiescence to the granting of a mistrial (thereby arguably overcoming a double jeopardy objection to a reprosecution[6]), with the prosecution then allowed to file what becomes a pretrial appeal.

Most jurisdictions allowing prosecution appeals from interlocutory pretrial orders do not extend that authority beyond suppression orders. Several jurisdictions, however, also authorize appeals from one or more additional rulings as specified by statute. Thus, the 1984 federal revision of the Bail Reform Act allows a prosecution appeal from a district court's pretrial release order.[7] State provisions make appealable such rulings as the granting or denying of a change of venue, and the denial of a protective order for the nondisclosure of witnesses. In several other states, provisions allowing state appeals from pretrial interlocutory orders are not limited to rulings on particular issues. A few states permit discretionary review of interlocutory rulings subject to the same standards that apply to defense requests for interlocutory review. A few grant a right to appeal if the interlocutory ruling will have a "reasonable likelihood of causing either serious impairment to or a termination of the prosecution." [8]

(c) Post–Jeopardy Rulings. With only a few exceptions, statutory provisions authorizing prosecution appeals include one or more provisions applicable to rulings issued after jeopardy has attached. Most allow a prosecution appeal from "an order arresting judgment." These provisions have not met significant opposition because: (1) the order arresting judgment clearly constitutes a final judgment; (2) since the defendant has been found guilty prior to the issuance of the order, reversal on appeal does not require a new trial but simply reinstituting the original verdict;

6. See § 25.2(a). As to possibly characterizing the mistrial as justified by manifest necessity, if not consent, see § 25.2(c).

7. 18 U.S.C.A. § 3145(c) (cross referencing to § 3731, discussed in note 4 supra). See also §§ 12.1, 12.3 (discussing the federal pretrial release provisions).

8. In authorizing the pretrial appeal, the state also must adopt measures to ensure that delay in the appellate process does not result in a denial of the defendant's right to a speedy trial. However, the leading ruling on such a claim, United States v. Lowd Hawk, discussed in § 18.2 at note 7, seemingly allows the jurisdiction considerable leeway, at least where the charges against the defendant are dismissed and he therefore is not subject to any form of restraint.

(3) the order arresting judgment commonly must be based on grounds that are unrelated to the factual innocence of the defendant (e.g., lack of jurisdiction).

While only the second factor cited above applies to the grant of a new trial following a conviction, the federal system and a substantial number of states allow a prosecution appeal from a new trial order. Such an appeal permits the prosecution to challenge underlying rulings that could not have been appealed if they had been made before or during trial. The new trial order might be based, for example, on a trial court's post-verdict determination that the trial had been marred by allowing improper joinder or by an erroneous charge to the jury. If the trial court had originally ruled in favor of the defendant on the same points, the end result would have been a mistrial (on the joinder issue) or perhaps an acquittal (depending upon the influence of the jury charge) and the prosecution would not have had the opportunity to appeal either ruling.

Statutory provisions allowing prosecution appeals from the dismissal of an indictment or information also provide a basis for a post-jeopardy appeal. Although some of these provisions refer specifically to dismissals prior to trial, most do not contain that limitation. Where the dismissal occurred after jeopardy attached, but before a verdict was reached, reprosecution will be barred by the double jeopardy prohibition if the "dismissal" was in fact an "acquittal" or constituted the equivalent of a mistrial not justified by "manifest necessity" or a defense request.[9] Section 3731 and several state provisions specifically prohibit an appeal from a post-jeopardy "dismissal" where reprosecution would be barred. In other jurisdictions, the provisions are read in light of that prohibition, and held not to allow an appeal where reprosecution is prohibited.

Where a guilty verdict has been returned, but the judge rejects that verdict and enters an acquittal, double jeopardy again does not bar appellate review.[10] Appeal from such an order is not clearly authorized, however, by the usual provisions governing prosecution appeals. An acquittal, based as it is on the insufficiency of the evidence, does not fall within the permissible grounds for an arrest of judgment. The federal courts treat the postconviction acquittal order as an order "dismissing an indictment," but that interpretation has been questioned. Accordingly, several states have adopted provisions specifically allowing appeals from acquittals entered by the trial court following a guilty verdict.

§ 27.4 Review by Writ

(a) Habeas Corpus. Where a trial court's order is not appealable, the defense or prosecution may seek higher court review through an application for one of those writs commonly described as the "extraordinary" or "prerogative" writs. Of these writs, habeas corpus probably has the most limited utility for this purpose.[1] Since it serves to challenge illegal custody, the habeas writ will be helpful only to the defendant. Moreover, its focus on custody limits defendant to challenges to orders that either have placed him in custody or are continuing his custody. This limitation is sufficiently flexible, however, to encompass several fairly common pretrial rulings that relate to a defendant's pretrial detention. Thus, numerous states allow the writ to be used to challenge a bail order, the grant of extradition, a preliminary hearing bindover, or a contempt adjudication—provided those rulings are not directly appealable in the particular jurisdiction.

(b) Prohibition and Mandamus: Traditional Limits. In most jurisdictions, the writs of mandamus and prohibition—or a lo-

9. See § 25.3(a).

10. See § 25.3(e).

§ 27.4

1. The habeas route to appellate court review ordinarily is indirect, as the application for the writ initially must be presented to the court of general jurisdiction in the district of detention. Jurisdictions are divided as to whether that court's ruling is then appealable, with those allowing the appeal treating the habeas proceeding as an independent proceeding subject to appellate review.

cal law replacement for those writs [2]—provide an avenue for both prosecution and defense to obtain review of a broad range of rulings that are not appealable. Both sides may utilize the writs to gain review of pretrial orders not otherwise subject to immediate review because they are interlocutory. Since the defense has a right to appeal from all final judgments, it has no need to look to the writs to obtain review of final orders. The prosecution, however, may be forced to turn to the writs where particular final orders, though they could be appealed consistent with double jeopardy, are not within the authorization of the state's appeals statute.

Though the writs may reach a broad range of orders, the type of objections that may be presented through writ applications is often quite limited. In all jurisdictions, the writs are generally available to raise certain types of objections (e.g., lack of subject matter jurisdiction) and almost certainly unavailable to raise others (e.g., error in a factual determination). There is a substantial group of objections, however, as to which there will be significant variation from one jurisdiction to another. Whether the writs are more or less likely to encompass a wide range of objections will depend in large part on the particular jurisdiction's position on four issues: (1) whether it adheres closely to the traditional limitations on the availability of the writ; (2) whether assuming it has otherwise discarded those limitations, it nevertheless returns to them for writs sought in criminal cases; (3) whether it treats the defendant's right of appeal from a final judgment of conviction as a satisfactory alternative that should bar defense use of the writ for all except the most narrow range of objections; and (4) whether the failure of the state to authorize a prosecution appeal from a particular type of order should be taken as an almost irrebuttable presumption against allowing review of such orders through the use of a writ. The first of these issues is discussed in this subsection, and the other three are discussed in the subsections that follow.

The writs of prohibition and mandamus traditionally were available only to control jurisdictional excesses. Prohibition was used to confine a lower court to a lawful exercise of its prescribed jurisdiction and mandamus was used to compel it to exercise that jurisdiction. Some argued that the writs were concerned only with the lower court's jurisdiction over the person and the subject matter, although many decisions dealt also with the court's authority to take particular action in a case properly before it. Under the latter view, mandamus could be used to require a lower court to take action that it had no discretion to avoid (action commonly described as "ministerial" in nature), and prohibition could be used to bar an order that the court lacked authority to issue under any set of circumstances. Some jurisdictions continue to adhere largely to this position. A majority, however, have moved substantially beyond the traditional limits.

In several jurisdictions, appellate courts, though continuing to speak of jurisdictional defects, readily hold that the trial court's discretion was so limited by the case's particular circumstances as to produce an unauthorized exercise of jurisdiction. In other jurisdictions, courts simply note that the writs are now available to correct a ruling "so arbitrary and capricious as to amount to an abuse of discretion." Many courts have recognized also that the writ may be used in an "exceptional case" to correct a ruling characterized as a "mere legal error, rather than an act in excess of * * * jurisdiction." Such an exceptional case is said to be presented where the appellate court must exercise its supervisory jurisdiction to ensure that there will be a prompt resolution of "important questions" which "are of a recurring nature." In those jurisdictions taking this most expansive view of the writs, which includes the federal system, there is almost no error (except, possibly,

2. In some jurisdictions, the separate writs of prohibition and mandamus have been replaced by a single writ of superintending control. The common law writ of certiorari, although restricted in many jurisdictions to obtaining discretionary review of final judgments, is still used in some jurisdictions as a means of obtaining immediate review of pretrial orders on grounds essentially similar to the writs of mandamus and prohibition.

for an erroneous factual determination) that is beyond their reach. As the commentators have noted, "the question becomes whether the court in its discretion should issue the writ."

Even in those jurisdictions that treat the broadest range of issues under the writs, courts stress that the writs should be sparingly allowed. It is often said in this regard that a writ "is not to be used as a substitute for appeal." This does not mean, however, that the writ will not be available as long as the issue could later be reviewed on appeal from a final judgment. It means only that a court should weigh that factor against the use of the writ. Similarly, while it also is said that a writ will issue only when the petitioner relies on a "clear and indisputable right," courts have acknowledged that in exceptional cases the writ may be used "to decide disputed and difficult questions of law." Thus, statements that the writs are not to be used as a mode of appeal or to resolve close questions are useful primarily in emphasizing a "principle of parsimony" in the employment of the writs. They reflect the concern of the courts that the writs not be used so frequently as to imperil the policies that limit the right of appeal, particularly the final judgment rule. They also reflect the concern that the writs not be converted into a judicially created form of open-ended discretionary review procedure for orders not appealable as of right.

Without doubt, the writs are most commonly used to gain higher court review of apparently meritorious challenges that raise issues that are clearly jurisdictional. Here it can be argued that the writs serve to protect the "interests of the judicial system as a whole" by correcting action or inaction contrary to the structural limits (i.e., the limits of jurisdiction) that control the system. Beyond this point, the appellate courts will look to a series of factors in determining whether the writs should apply. Obviously, the availability of an alternative means of obtaining relief (e.g., a subsequent appeal) will be given great weight. Yet, if the harm to the petitioner is likely to be irreparable on later review, the issue presented is of great significance, or there is a need to preclude a recurring error, the appellate court may conclude that the advantages of immediate disposition outweigh the policies of finality.

(c) Restriction of the Writs in Criminal Cases. A jurisdiction may ordinarily treat the writs as flexible devices allowing review of a wide range of nonappealable orders, but sharply restrict that flexibility in the context of criminal cases. The Supreme Court appeared to look in this direction in *Will v. United States.*[3] The Court there noted that the "general policy against piecemeal appeals takes on added weight in criminal cases, where the defendant is entitled to a speedy resolution of the charges against him." However, the ultimate ruling in *Will* was quite limited. The government there attempted to use the writ of mandamus to compel a district judge to vacate an order requiring the government to furnish a bill of particulars that encompassed items not then covered by the discovery rules. In holding the writ to be unavailable, the Court found that the very skimpy record before it did not support the grounds that the government had advanced for its issuance—an allegation that the lower court's ruling reflected "a pattern of manifest noncompliance" with the Federal Rules.

Lower federal courts have given *Will* quite diverse readings. Some maintain, in light of the caution expressed in *Will,* that use of the writs in criminal cases must be carefully limited by the distinction between a lack of " 'jurisdiction' and 'power' on the one hand," and the mere presence of " 'error,' however substantial, on the other." Other courts find no bar in *Will* to recognition of the "vital corrective and didactive function of the writs." They would allow their use to overturn a pretrial interlocutory order whenever the

3. 389 U.S. 90, 88 S.Ct. 269, 19 L.Ed.2d 305 (1967).

"district court's finding of fact and conclusions of law [are] in error" and could readily have an "immediate and continuing detrimental impact on the administration of criminal justice in the district." Still other courts see *Will* as looking to concerns that largely limit use of the writs where it is the government that petitions. They recognize considerably more leeway to exercise through the writs the appellate court's "expository and supervisory functions" where it is the defendant who seeks relief. This division among federal appellate courts in their interpretation of *Will* roughly parallels the division among state appellate courts in their treatment of the writs in criminal cases.

(d) Defense Petitions. Even in those jurisdictions that exercise the greatest caution in the use of the writs in criminal cases, certain types of defense claims will be readily subject to review by writ. These claims are thought to raise interests so urgently demanding immediate relief that the judicial system cannot rely upon the ordinarily adequate avenue of correction, the defense appeal available following a conviction. Immediate review is deemed necessary to prevent a harm that goes beyond the ordinarily acceptable hardship of a possibly needless or flawed trial. Claims establishing that the lower court lacked jurisdiction over the proceeding fall within this category because of their impact upon the validity of the overall judicial process. Thus, review by writ has been available where the grand jury or prosecutor lacked authority to initiate prosecution of a particular crime or the lower court lacked authority to try the particular offense. Similarly, many courts have held that the writ is available where the trial court may not proceed because of a clear violation of a statutory or constitutional right to a speedy trial. In other situations, the writ is held available because the defendant seeks to prevent infringement of a significant interest that cannot be protected by a reversal following a conviction. Thus, the writs are commonly used to obtain immediate review of a trial court's denial of a potentially meritorious double jeopardy claim in those jurisdictions that do not treat the denial of a double jeopardy claim as automatically appealable under the collateral order doctrine.

In a small group of jurisdictions, defense use of the writs goes far beyond any of the above limitations. Appellate courts will consider on a writ application a broad range of challenges that may be directed at almost any pretrial ruling, provided the legal issue presented has some general significance. Among these jurisdictions, California probably makes the most extensive use of the writs. California courts have reviewed through defense writ applications pretrial orders denying defense motions to obtain broader pretrial discovery, to authorize a hypnotic examination of the defendant, to change venue to a community less saturated by publicity, to dismiss an indictment where the prosecutor failed to present exculpatory evidence to the grand jury, to appoint a requested attorney as defense counsel, to place defendant in a statutorily prescribed diversion program, and to exclude from consideration in a pending prosecution a prior conviction obtained without an effective waiver of counsel. The "common thread" woven through these cases, the California Supreme Court has noted, is "the responsiveness of appellate tribunals when initiative is required to protect a defendant's right to a fair trial," recognizing that "the burden, expense and delay involved in a trial" may often render "an appeal from an eventual judgment an inadequate remedy." [4]

(e) Prosecution Applications. Prosecutors have sought to use the extraordinary writs to gain appellate review of a wide variety of orders issued at various stages of the criminal process. Prior to the issuance of charges, the prosecution may attempt through the writ to gain review of orders issued in connection with a grand jury investigation or similar investigative proceeding. Once a charge is brought, the prosecution may seek through the writs to obtain review of significant pretrial interlocutory orders. Apart from a suppression ruling, such orders will not be appealable in most jurisdictions.

4. Maine v. Superior Court, 68 Cal.2d 375, 66 Cal. Rptr. 724, 438 P.2d 372 (1968).

Where appeals of final judgments are limited to a particular class of orders (e.g., the granting of a motion to quash), the prosecutor may also look to the writs to gain review of a pretrial dismissal that does not fit within the appeals statute. Finally, the writs may be used to gain review of unappealable rulings entered after a jury returns a guilty verdict. Thus, where the appeals statute refers only to appeals from post conviction orders arresting a judgment or dismissing an indictment, challenges to the grant of a new trial or the entry of a judgment n.o.v. may be pursued through a writ application.

Appellate courts have varied in their approach to prosecution writ applications. Some have held that the writ will be available only when the lower court "acted in excess of its jurisdiction"—i.e., where it issued an order that it had no authority to issue under any circumstances or failed to issue an order that it had no discretion under any circumstances not to issue—and even then, only if the "need for review [by writ] outweighs the risk of harassment of the accused." Other courts have held that where a significant prosecution interest is at stake, the writ will issue to correct a gross abuse of discretion. Still other courts hold that the prosecution may utilize the writ to gain review of a ruling that raises a legal question of general significance, even though the lower court's error consisted of no more than an arguably incorrect reading of a statute or case law.

In part, whether the scope of review is broad or narrow will depend upon the appellate court's view of the appropriate role of the writs in general, without regard to fact that the applicant is the prosecutor. There are two concerns, however, that may lead a court to apply more stringent standards to prosecution petitions than are applied to either civil cases or defense petitions in criminal cases. Citing the *Will* case, courts frequently note the need to approach the prosecution's use of the writs with "an awareness * * * that a man is entitled to a speedy trial." Courts also express concern that the writs not be used so as to undermine the limitations that the legislature has placed on the prosecution's right to appeal. The significance of each of these concerns may vary, however, with the nature of the lower court ruling challenged by the prosecutor.

As many appellate courts have noted, there are various settings in which a prosecutor's writ application will not threaten the defendant's speedy trial interest. When the prosecution's challenge is directed at an order issued in connection with a precharge investigatory proceeding (such as a grand jury proceeding), granting review will delay the determination as to whether to charge, but the person affected is hardly in the same position as a defendant awaiting trial. Similarly, if the government challenges an order issued after the defendant was tried and found guilty, there is delay in the final disposition, but usually not in the presentation of evidence. Delay generally causes far less judicial concern where the only consequence of the delay is, for example, a continued period of uncertainty as to what sentence will be imposed. Thus, in jurisdictions that do not provide for appellate review of sentences, the writs are regularly used by the prosecution to obtain review of sentences that are allegedly outside the trial court's sentencing authority under the facts of the case.

Distinctions also are drawn in applying the principle that the writs not be used "to give the People the very appeal which the legislature had denied them." Where the government contends that the lower court clearly exceeded its jurisdiction, courts have little difficulty in squaring use of the writs with the absence of legislative authorization of a prosecution appeal from the challenged order. The use of the writs for this purpose was recognized long before the government was given a right to appeal, and was never thought to be inconsistent with limitations contained in statutory provisions governing appeals in either criminal or civil cases. Some would argue that the same approach should apply to the use of the writs to correct judicial action that constitutes a gross abuse of discretion or fails to recognize clearly established limits on the use of a particular judicial authority. In limiting the government's right to appeal, it is argued, the legislature "has made clear that the government cannot complain of ordinary trial errors," but it "cannot have intended that the Government be obliged to submit to arbitrary judges who refuse to behave as judges." This contention will not justify, however, the use of the writs to review rulings that are merely erroneous, but present issues of great importance in the administration of justice. Those appellate courts allowing prosecution use of the writs in such cases, notwithstanding the lack of authorization for prosecution appeal, must rely on a characterization that distinguishes the function of the writ. Thus, it is argued that review by writ "serves the interest of the judicial system," rather than "litigant interests" as in the case of appeal. Occasionally, the statutory authorization of prosecution appeal, though not encompassing the particular lower court ruling in question, will be seen as favoring use of the writ. Thus, where the statutory authorization reflects the view that a government appeal from a final judgment does not impose an undue burden on the defendant, but limits the statutory right to appeal to a particular class of final judgments (e.g., the "quashing of an indictment"), a court may be less hesitant to allow prosecution use of the writ to challenge a final judgment that falls outside that class, provided the issue raised has some exceptional quality.

§ 27.5 The Scope of Appellate Review

(a) Mootness. An appellate court will not review a lower court decision, in either a civil or criminal case, where post-trial events have rendered the case moot. In criminal cases, an appeal traditionally was viewed as having become moot when the sentence imposed by the trial court was fully satisfied—i.e., when the defendant had paid his fine and served the full period of imprisonment or probation. While some jurisdictions still adhere to this view, most have departed from it to at least a limited extent. Several jurisdictions have gone so far as to hold that a defense appeal from a conviction is never moot since the defendant retains an interest in removing "the stigma of guilt" even after his sentence has been served. Most, however, have been satisfied with the adoption of one or more "exceptions" to the fully-satisfied-sentence standard.

The most significant exception to the traditional rule is the collateral consequences exception. Indeed, broadly construed, it is an exception that basically overrides the fully-satisfied-sentence standard in virtually all of its possible applications. The collateral consequences exception holds that a case is not moot, notwithstanding full satisfaction of the sentence, if the defendant is still subject to a collateral legal disability as a result of his conviction. Courts taking a narrow view of this exception require the defendant to show that a particular adverse collateral consequence is likely to be applied to him (e.g., that he is in a licensed profession and the conviction will result in loss of his license). Merely pointing to the "hypothetical effects" of a conviction are insufficient. Moreover, if the defendant has been previously convicted, he must establish that the collateral disability flowing from the conviction being appealed differs from that which would result from his prior conviction. In *Sibron v. New York,*[1] the Supreme Court rejected both of these positions, and adopted for the federal courts a liberal view of the collateral consequences exception that also has been followed by many state courts.

The Supreme Court in *Sibron* construed its earlier mootness opinions as having "abandoned all inquiry into the actual existence of specific collateral consequences and in effect presumed that they existed." The "mere possibility" that there would be "adverse collateral legal consequences" was sufficient to keep a case "from ending 'ignominously in the limbo of mootness.'" The Court added that, "without pausing to canvass the possibilities in detail," it was clear that Sibron's case met that "mere possibility" standard. New York statutes would allow Sibron's conviction to be used to impeach him if he should become a defendant in a future trial, and they

§ 27.5

1. 392 U.S. 40, 88 S.Ct. 1889, 20 L.Ed.2d 917 (1968).

required that the conviction be considered in sentencing should he be convicted of a future offense. Moreover, the fact that Sibron was already a multiple offender was not critical. Sentencing judges and trial juries might be willing to discount a certain number of prior transgressions. It was "impossible * * * to say at what point the number of convictions on a man's record renders his reputation irredeemable." So too, the Court could not "foretell what opportunities might present themselves in the future for the removal of [the] other convictions."

In holding that the mere possibility of collateral legal consequences forestalled a finding of mootness, the *Sibron* opinion stressed the need to face the reality of the broad range of legal disabilities that traditionally attach to a criminal conviction in this country. The Court also stressed the importance of adopting a mootness standard that was consistent with both the policies underlying "the constitutional rule against entertaining moot controversies" and the need for an efficient system of adjudication. There was nothing "abstract or feigned" about the appeal before it, and neither the defendant nor the prosecution had been "wanting in diligence or fervor in the litigation." Moreover, "the question of the validity of [Sibron's] criminal conviction" could arise in "many [future] contexts," and it was "always preferable to litigate a matter when it is directly and principally in dispute, rather than in a proceeding where it is collateral to the central controversy." Reviewing the conviction on direct appeal would ensure that the dispute would be fully litigated when it was "fresh," and when additional facts could be gathered, if necessary, "without a substantial risk that witnesses will die or memories fade."[2]

Some lower courts, building upon the rationale of *Sibron,* have taken the position that the possibility of adverse collateral consequences will be " 'presumed' as an 'obvious fact of life.' " Other lower courts do not face directly the presumption issue. In finding that an appeal is not moot, they simply refer to some specific disability found under a state or federal law that would apply to the particular conviction, thereby suggesting a case-by-case analysis. Other courts clearly do apply a case-by-case approach, requiring the defendant to cite a provision that might make a particular disability applicable to him in a future circumstance. This approach is only likely to cause the defendant difficulties where his conviction is for a low-level misdemeanor, and even then a careful search of state law is likely to prove fruitful.

(b) The Concurrent Sentence Doctrine. Under the concurrent sentence doctrine, where defendant received concurrent sentences on each of several counts of an indictment and the appellate court finds no error in the conviction on any one count carrying a sentence at least equal to the others, the validity of the convictions on the remaining counts will not be reviewed. Prior to the Supreme Court's decision in *Sibron,* this doctrine was often described as an application of traditional mootness principles. There was thought to be no "live controversy" as to the remaining counts since, once a count carrying an equal concurrent sentence was affirmed, reversal of the remaining counts would not reduce the length of the defendant's confinement. In *Benton v. Maryland,*[3] the Supreme Court held that, in light of its *Sibron* ruling, the concurrent sentence doctrine could no longer be justified on mootness grounds. The defendant had an obvious interest in challenging all of the counts on which he was convicted because separate collateral consequences could flow from each. It was possible, for example, that petitioner might find himself in a jurisdiction in which each of the counts was treated separately under a recidivist statute. Although "this possibility might well be a remote one, it is enough," the *Benton* opinion

2. These policies may be limited to a direct appeal that challenges a conviction. Lane v. Williams, 455 U.S. 624, 102 S.Ct. 1322, 71 L.Ed.2d 508 (1982), indicates that a defendant must present a much more substantial showing of collateral consequences to avoid a mootness ruling where he is proceeding by collateral attack to challenge only a sentence (there, a parole term) that he has already served.

3. 395 U.S. 784, 89 S.Ct. 2056, 23 L.Ed.2d 707 (1969).

noted, "to give this case an adversary cast and make it justiciable."

While rejecting mootness as a grounding for the concurrent sentence doctrine, the *Benton* opinion left open the possibility that the doctrine might be justified as a "rule of judicial convenience," to be applied at the discretion of the appellate court. The Court's comments upon the doctrine suggested, however, that even if still viable, it should be used with caution. Several state courts, reassessing the concurrent doctrine in light of *Benton,* have rejected its use even as a rule of judicial convenience. Most federal circuits and several state appellate courts, however, accept the discretionary application of the concurrent sentence doctrine, stressing its value in preserving scarce judicial resources and in avoiding the unnecessary decision of potentially difficult legal questions. The Supreme Court lent implicit support to this position in a post-*Benton* ruling in which it applied the doctrine. Without discussing *Benton*'s refusal to rule on the continuing use of the doctrine in federal courts as a rule of judicial convenience, the Court there noted that while the remaining counts were not moot, it would "decline as a discretionary matter" to rule on their validity.[4]

(c) Issues Not Raised at Trial. Perhaps no standard governing the scope of appellate review is more frequently applied than the rule that "an error not raised and preserved at trial will not be considered on appeal." The values underlying this rule were aptly summarized by the Oregon Court of Appeals:

> There are many rationales for the raise-or-waive rule [5]: that it is a necessary corollary of our adversary system in which issues are framed by the litigants and presented to a court; that fairness to all parties requires a litigant to advance his contentions at a time when there is an opportunity to respond to them factually, if his opponent chooses to; that the rule promotes efficient trial proceedings; that reversing for error not preserved permits the losing side to second-guess its tactical decisions after they do not produce the desired result; and that there is something unseemly about telling a lower court it was wrong when it never was presented with the opportunity to be right. The principal rationale, however, is judicial economy. There are two components to judicial economy: (1) if the losing side can obtain an appellate reversal because of error not objected to, the parties and public are put to the expense of retrial that could have been avoided had an objection been made; and (2) if an issue had been raised in the trial court, it could have been resolved there, and the parties and public would be spared the expense of an appeal.[6]

There is, of course, nothing in these rationales that requires that the "raise-or-waive" rule be absolute, and all jurisdictions recognize one or more situations in which issues not raised below will be considered on appeal. The plain error rule, discussed in the next subsection, is clearly the most important of these "exceptions" to the raise-or-waive rule. Several other exceptions, discussed below, either do not cover as broad a range of objections, or are not as widely accepted, but they nevertheless have a fairly significant impact upon the scope of review in many jurisdictions.

It is, of course, a basic premise of the raise-or-waive rule that the defense will have ample opportunity to present its objection before the trial court in compliance with the jurisdiction's procedural rules. Where that opportunity was not present, or was not likely to be exercised for some legitimate reason, the defendant's failure to raise his objection below is likely to be excused. The clearest case for considering an issue not raised in accordance with a particular procedural requirement oc-

4. Barnes v. United States, 412 U.S. 837, 93 S.Ct. 2357, 37 L.Ed.2d 380 (1973). See also Andresen v. Maryland, 427 U.S. 463, 96 S.Ct. 2737, 49 L.Ed.2d 627 (1976), at n. 4; Pinkus v. United States, 436 U.S. 293, 98 S.Ct. 1808, 56 L.Ed.2d 293 (1978), at n. 7.

5. The description of the rule as one of "waiver," rather than "forfeiture" has been sharply criticized. "Waiver," it is argued, suggests an "intentional relinquishment of a known right", while forfeiture may occur either inadvertently or intentionally. See §§ 10.2(a); 11.3(a), (c); 21.6(a); 24.2(b); 28.4(e). Most courts nevertheless speak of "waiver", although some refer to the rule as one of "forfeiture" or "default."

6. State v. Applegate, 39 Or.App. 17, 591 P.2d 371 (1979).

curs when that requirement fails to allow the defense a reasonable time within which to raise the issue. Indeed, the refusal to consider a claim where the procedural rule arbitrarily imposes an impossible time limit on the defense may in itself constitute a violation of due process.[7] In other situations the general timing requirements may be fair, but the defendant may be in a special situation where the failure to comply was excusable. Thus, appellate court's may also consider objections not raised at trial where an intervening ruling established the grounds for the objection and counsel's failure to raise the issue was understandable in light of the controlling precedent at the time of trial.

Since a lack of jurisdiction traditionally may be raised at any point in the proceedings, such an objection also is treated as an exception to the raise-or-waive rule. However, courts tend to utilize a narrower and somewhat more traditional definition of a jurisdictional defect for this purpose than in other areas in which jurisdictional claims are given separate treatment.[8] A challenge to subject matter jurisdiction clearly may be raised for the first time on appeal, and many courts will also consider on a similar basis an allegation that the offense occurred outside the territorial jurisdiction of the state. Courts generally are reluctant, however, to include within the jurisdictional category objections to other elements of the proceedings. Thus, defects in the indictment process generally cannot be presented for the first time on appeal. While several appellate courts allow a first-time challenge to the constitutionality of the statute on which the prosecution is based, most hold that such an objection also is not jurisdictional and therefore cannot be raised unless it fits within some other exception to the raise-or-waive rule. Similarly, although some jurisdictions treat a double jeopardy claim as a "quasi-jurisdictional" defect that can be raised for the first time on appeal, most deny it that status. On the other hand, the failure of the information or indictment to state an offense can be raised initially on appeal in almost all jurisdictions, either by virtue of its characterization as a jurisdictional defect, or by reliance upon a specific provision, such as Federal Rule 12(b), requiring that it "be noticed * * * at any time."[9]

Appellate courts in numerous states have noted their discretion to consider an issue on appeal, notwithstanding the lack of objection below, when appellate review of that issue would serve the "interest of judicial economy." Thus, a court may consider an issue raised for the first time on appeal where there is a "strong possibility of reoccurrence" or the "issue is one of public policy or of broad * * * concern." Several courts have held that where federal habeas corpus would be available to present a constitutional claim even though not presented at trial, an appellate court should ordinarily consider that constitutional issue on appeal, provided the record is sufficient to permit a determination of the issue. Ordinarily, however, as discussed in § 28.5, failure to comply with the raise-or-waive rule also will block habeas review.

(d) Plain Error. All but a few jurisdictions recognize the authority of an appellate court to reverse on the basis of a plain error even though that error was not properly raised and preserved at the trial level. The plain error exception is recognized in Federal Rule 52(b) and in similar provisions in most states. In others, it has been adopted as a common law exception to the raise-or-waive rule, based upon the appellate court's inherent authority to prevent a "miscarriage of justice." In most jurisdictions, the doctrine extends to all types of errors provided they are "plain errors or defects affecting substantial rights." In some jurisdictions, however, the doctrine is restricted by statute or judicial interpretation to a limited class of "plain errors." Thus, one state limits it to errors that are discoverable "by a mere inspection of the

7. See e.g., Reece v. Georgia, 350 U.S. 85, 76 S.Ct. 167, 100 L.Ed. 77 (1955), discussed at § 15.4, note 2.

8. See e.g., the discussions of "jurisdictional" defects at §§ 27.4(b), 28.3(a), 21.6(a).

9. See § 19.3(e).

pleadings and proceedings * * * without inspection of the evidence." Another includes only errors that could not have been cured by the trial judge if an objection had been made at trial. Several apply it only to the most flagrant constitutional violations. As for those jurisdictions without such limitations, the essence of the application of the doctrine has been admirably captured by Professor Wright in his description of the federal court rulings:

> [W]hether an appellate court should take notice of an error not raised below must be made on the facts of the particular case, and there are no "hard and fast classifications in either the application of the principle or the use of a descriptive title." Indeed the cases give the distinct impression that "plain error" is a concept appellate courts find impossible to define, save that they know it when they see it.[10]

Consistent with Professor Wright's analysis, opinions frequently stress that "no talismanic method exists for determining plain error," and each case must be examined on its own facts. There are, however, certain factors which clearly have a positive influence on an appellate court's willingness to find plain error. The more closely balanced the evidence, for example, the greater the likelihood that an error otherwise not viewed as sufficiently patent or fundamental will meet the standard. Courts also acknowledge that errors of constitutional magnitude will be noticed more freely under the plain error doctrine than violations of most statutes or common law standards. Various rulings also suggest that the doctrine is more likely to be applied where there might be a good reason for the lack of objection below, or where the error could not have been remedied by the trial judge even if called to his attention. On the other side, the doctrine is less likely to be applied where the error could have been readily corrected by an objection at trial, or where such an objection may have led the government to introduce additional evidence on the issue.

10. 3A C. Wright, Federal Practice and Procedure—Criminal, 336–37 (2d ed. 1982) (footnotes omitted).

§ 27.6 Harmless Error

(a) English Heritage and American Modification. During the mid–1800's the English courts adopted a rule of appellate review that became known as the Exchequer Rule. Under that rule, a trial error as to the admission of evidence was presumed to have caused prejudice and therefore almost automatically required a new trial. The presumption of prejudice was designed to ensure that the appellate court did not encroach upon the jury's fact-finding function by discounting the improperly admitted evidence and sustaining the verdict on its belief that the remaining evidence established guilt. The presumption of prejudice was stringently applied to even the most insignificant items of evidence, and a similar policy was extended to errors in jury instruction. As a result, retrials became so commonplace that English litigation "seemed to survive until the parties expired." Parliament responded with harmless error legislation, which was included in the Judicature Act of 1873. That Act stated that the Court of Appeal was not to order a new trial on the basis of "the improper admission or rejection of evidence" or a "misdirection" of the jury "unless in the opinion of the Court of Appeal some substantial wrong or miscarriage has thereby been occasioned." Exactly what constituted a "substantial wrong" or "miscarriage of justice" was left for judicial definition, but the courts clearly were directed to look to the actual impact of the error upon the outcome of the proceeding, and not simply to assume that every error in the admission of evidence or the charging of the jury was per se prejudicial.

While the American courts had adopted the Exchequer Rule, they generally were not influenced by its subsequent rejection in England. They extended the philosophy of the Exchequer Rule to a wide range of trial errors, requiring new trials no matter how technical or seemingly insignificant the error. As the retrials mounted, the appellate courts were criticized as "impregnable citadels of technicality," and reformers urged adoption of harmless error legislation. Their efforts began to bear fruit during the early 1900's when a substantial number of states adopted such legislation. Today, as the Supreme Court noted in *Chapman v. California,*[1] "all 50 states have harmless error statutes or rules."

Unlike the English legislation, the American harmless error provisions were not limited to specific types of errors. The American criticism of "reversals on technicality" had focused as much on rulings based upon technical pleading errors as rulings concerned with incorrect admission of insignificant evidence. The federal statute, adopted in 1919, provided the model for much of the state legislation. It required a federal appellate court to "give judgment after an examination of the entire record before the court, without regard to technical errors, defects, or exceptions which do not affect the substantial rights of the parties." [2]

American appellate courts recognized that the newly adopted harmless error legislation, though phrased in terms of an adverse impact upon a substantial right, had a different frame of reference as to different types of rights. In particular, as to errors of the type covered by the English Judicature Act, the legislation remained concerned with whether the error had a bearing that resulted in a "miscarriage of justice." In judging the impact of an error on a matter such as jury selection, it was appropriate to focus on whether the error was technical in nature or deprived the defendant of the substance of what that right was designed to provide. However, where the error related to the admission or evaluation of evidence, the issue presented was not whether the defendant had been denied the basic benefit of the evidentiary rule, but whether the error had produced a miscarriage of justice as measured by its likely impact upon the outcome of the proceeding. For example, if a trial judge erroneously admitted hearsay, the issue was not simply whether the particular violation of the hearsay rule was largely "technical" (e.g., where the court admitted a single hearsay statement that would have fit within a hearsay exception but for some minor detail); even if a substantial quantity of patently inadmissible hearsay evidence had been introduced, the court still had to decide whether that evidence had a sufficient bearing upon the total evidentiary picture to require a reversal. So too, where a judge mischarged a jury as to some element of the crime, the court had to look to the findings of the jury as to other elements of the charge and determine whether, in light of those findings, the mischarge could have played a role in the jury's decision to convict. As to these errors that related to the consideration of specific evidence, where impact could more readily be measured, the concern of the harmless error provision "was not merely with putting technical error in its place, but also with precluding reversal when the denial or impairment of a substantial right had caused no injury."

That the American legislation intended to incorporate this "outcome-impact" approach was suggested by the statutory directive that the appellate court base its decision upon an "examination of the entire record." As applied to an issue like the proper drawing of the jury venire, an examination of the full record was not needed to determine whether a "substantial right" was adversely affected. If the defendant had been denied a basic ingredient of the jury trial right (e.g., the jurors came from outside the vicinage), there was no suggestion that the strength of the government's evidence could lead to a conclusion that the error was harmless. It was in the tradition of testing an evidentiary error against the remaining evidence that an examination of the full record was most likely to be needed.

Accepting the need to draw distinctions based on the type of right violated, the American courts developed two modes of analysis for applying the harmless error statutes. For

§ 27.6

1. See note 15 infra.

2. Act of Feb. 26, 1919, ch. 48, 40 Stat. 1181. See also 28 U.S.C.A. § 2111, and Fed.R.Crim.P. 52(a), both based on this provision.

those rights that might loosely be described as concerned with the structure of the proceeding, the question becomes one of whether the error was merely a technical violation or took from the defendant the substantive protection of the right. Here, no evaluation of the bearing of the error on the jury's verdict is necessary. A violation of the substance of the right automatically requires a new trial, and the strength of the evidence supporting the conviction is therefore irrelevant. This mode of analysis is applied to errors relating to such matters as jury selection, pleadings, and venue. As to such issues, there is no single standard for determining whether the error requires reversal of the conviction; each error has to be analyzed in terms of its relationship to the substance of the particular right. Accordingly, this mode of harmless error analysis is best considered in the course of a discussion of the substantive right rather than in a general discussion of harmless error doctrine. Indeed, the question of whether a reversal is required often is not even described by the courts as a harmless error issue, but rather as a question of defining the scope of the right.

The second line of analysis is applied primarily to errors that relate to evidentiary issues. It is here that courts utilize the more traditional harmless error standards, looking to such factors as the weight of the evidence and the likely impact of the error upon a juror's determination of guilt. This line of analysis is applied to trial errors that determine what evidence is presented to the jury, such as rulings on admissibility, cross-examination, and joinder. It also is applied to erroneous pretrial rulings that have an impact upon the presentation of evidence, such as rulings on discovery, or the restriction of cross-examination at a preliminary hearing. Finally, it is applied to actions of the judge and prosecutor that may have influenced the jury in its evaluation of the evidence, such as erroneous jury instructions, an improper comment by the judge, or trial misconduct by the prosecutor.

In general, appellate courts have had little difficulty in distinguishing between structural errors and errors bearing on evidentiary issues. Disagreements do arise, however, as illustrated by the split in the Supreme Court in *Young v. United States ex rel Vuitton et Fils S.A.*[3] The defendant there challenged the district court's appointment as special prosecutor in his criminal contempt case the attorney for the party that had obtained the court order that defendant was convicted of having violated. Seven justices viewed that appointment as exceeding the district court's inherent authority to initiate contempt proceedings because the attorney appointed was not "disinterested." Of those seven, four argued that the violation was "fundamental and pervasive" and not subject to a traditional harmless error analysis that looked to the impact of the error upon the outcome of the proceedings. They maintained that automatic reversal was required because: (i) "appointment of an interested prosecutor creates an appearance of impropriety that diminishes faith in the fairness of the criminal justice system" and the "narrow focus of harmless error analysis is not * * * sensitive to this concern"; and (ii) "determining the effect of * * * [such an] appointment would be extremely difficult" since "a prosecution contains a myriad of occasions for the exercise of discretion, each of which goes to shape the record in a case, but few of which are part of the record." Three justices, arguing that a traditional harmless error analysis should apply, reasoned that the trial structure had not been affected as defendant had been tried before an impartial jury and had been represented by competent counsel. They also suggested that the impact of the error was readily capable of judicial assessment, as they noted that the lower court had found " 'no reason to believe' that the private prosecutor in this case acted unethically" and that there had been "ample" evidence to support the conviction.[4]

3. 481 U.S. 787, 107 S.Ct. 2124, 95 L.Ed.2d 740 (1987).

4. A similar division is found in United States v. Lane, 474 U.S. 438, 106 S.Ct. 725, 88 L.Ed.2d 814 (1986), also discussed in § 17.3 at note 2. There, Justice Stevens in dissent argued that a misjoinder of parties in violation of Federal Rule 8(b) should not be subject to harmless

Once the appellate court concludes that the error being reviewed properly is subject to a harmless error standard that looks to the impact of the error on the outcome of the proceeding, it then must identify the proper standard for measuring that impact. This issue, which has produced numerous divisions among the appellate courts, is discussed in the subsection that follows.

(b) Standards for Non-Constitutional Errors. Few areas of doctrinal development have been marked by greater twisting and turning than the development of standards for applying the harmless error rule to evidence related errors. Its history has been described as one "of innovation and regression, of instability and uncertainty," that cannot be explained in terms of any "evolving progression of jurisprudential theories." For this reason alone, one cannot discard consideration of what may be described as the "correct result" test of harmless error, although perhaps no court today continues to adhere to that standard. That test asks whether, in light of all of the admissible evidence (including any defense evidence improperly excluded), the jury's finding of guilt is clearly correct. The test rests on the premise that the defendant has not been harmed by the error if he clearly should have been convicted in any event. Critics of the test contend that it converts the appellate court into the trier of fact and fails to recognize that the defendant has a right to a fair trial even when he is clearly guilty. The Supreme Court looked to both of those factors in rejecting a "correct result" standard in *Kotteakos v. United States.*[5] In the course of an extensive discussion of the harmless error guidelines to be applied by federal courts, Justice Rutledge noted:

> Some aids to right judgment may be stated more safely in negative than in affirmative form. Thus, it is not the appellate court's function to determine guilt or innocence. Nor is it to speculate upon probable reconviction and decide according to how the speculation comes out. Appellate judges cannot escape such impressions. But they may not make them sole criteria for reversal or affirmance. Those judgments are exclusively for the jury * * *. But this does not mean that the appellate court can escape altogether taking account of the outcome. To weigh the error's effect against the entire setting of the record without relation to the verdict or judgment would be almost to work in a vacuum. In criminal causes that outcome is conviction. This is different, or may be, from guilt in fact. It is guilt in law, established by the judgment of laymen. And the question is, not were they right in their judgment, regardless of the error or its effect upon the verdict. It is rather what effect the error had or reasonably may be taken to have had upon the jury's decision. The crucial thing is the impact of the thing done wrong in the minds of other men, not on one's own, in the total setting.

Today, it is generally agreed that the harmless error test for evidentiary related errors must be an "effect on the judgment test," as suggested by Justice Rutledge. As to non-constitutional errors, however, there certainly is not agreement as to the standard to be applied in determining when the error's impact is so slight as to be viewed as harmless. *Kotteakos* itself offered the following standard:

> If, when all is said and done, the conviction is sure that the error did not influence the jury, or had but very slight effect, the verdict and the judgment should stand, except perhaps where the departure is from a constitutional norm or a specific command of Con-

error analysis because (i) Rule 8(b) implicates an "independent value besides reliability of outcome," namely "our deep abhorrence of the motion of 'guilt by association,' " and (ii) the impact of the error upon the outcome "cannot be measured with precision." The majority, holding the traditional harmless error standard to be applicable, saw the Rule 8(b) restriction as directed at ensuring reliability by setting the scope of relevancy in the admission of evidence and saw the impact of its violation as no more difficult to measure than other evidentiary errors. Responding to Justice Steven's independent-value argument, Justice Brennan, in a concurring opinion, noted that limitations upon joinder "are based on recognition that the multiplication of charges or defendants may confuse the jury and lead to inferences of habitual criminality or guilt by association," and that those were concerns that related directly to the quality of the evidence before the jury.

5. 328 U.S. 750, 66 S.Ct. 1239, 90 L.Ed. 1557 (1946).

gress.[6] But if one cannot say, with fair assurance, after pondering all that happened without stripping the erroneous action from the whole, that the judgment was not substantially swayed by the error, it is impossible to conclude that substantial rights were not affected.

Though most federal courts have adhered closely to the language of *Kotteakos,* several have offered somewhat different descriptions of the federal harmless error test. At the state level also, courts have used a variety of different phrases in describing the requisite likelihood that the error did not contribute to the jury verdict. Thus, courts have spoken of the need for a "fair assurance" that the judgment of the jury was not "substantially swayed" by the error, the lack of any "reasonable possibility" that the error "might have contributed to the conviction," a "high probability" that the error did not contribute to the judgment, and even whether it was "more probable than not that the error did not materially affect the verdict." [7]

Commentators generally have favored still another standard, which has been adopted by the Pennsylvania Supreme Court. Pennsylvania applies to non-constitutional errors basically the same standard that the United States Supreme Court has required for constitutional errors—the appellate court must be convinced "beyond a reasonable doubt" that there is no "reasonable possibility" that the error contributed to the verdict.[8] This standard is viewed as more stringent than *Kotteakos* (or variations on *Kotteakos*), and it is supported as providing the greatest protection against a "lenient" application of the harmless error rule that would effectively undercut the force of the procedural requirements that are being violated. The Pennsylvania Supreme Court has also concluded that any lesser standard would be inconsistent with the constitutional requirement that guilt be determined under a reasonable doubt standard. Most state courts, however, view the trial-proof standard as a false analogy, no more applicable in testing the harmlessness of an error than in making the initial assessment as to whether the error occurred.

As various courts have acknowledged, the principle that the error should be judged by its likely impact on the jury's judgment, whatever the standard as to requisite probability of impact, only "sets the stage for the harmless error inquiry." The courts have also sought, with varying success, to identify the process for determining whether a particular error is so unlikely to have influenced the jury's judgment that it meets the applicable probability standard. Considerable attention has been given, for example, to the allocation of the burden of showing potential prejudice. Many contend that the burden naturally falls upon the defendant. This allocation naturally follows, it is argued, from the rejection of the Exchequer Rule's presumption of prejudice. Others disagree, noting that primary flaw of the Exchequer Rule was the conclusiveness of its presumption. These courts hold that once an error is established, the burden lies with the beneficiary of the error, the prosecution, to establish the requisite probability that it did not influence the jury's decision. In *Kotteakos,* the Supreme Court rejected the idea of uniformly placing the burden on either party. Warning "against attempting to generalize broadly, by presump-

6. The error in *Kotteakos* was a violation of a common law right, but federal courts generally have found no reason to apply a different standard to violations of federal statutes or the Federal Rules. As for constitutional violations, see § 27.6(c) infra.

7. While these tests refer to the likely impact of the error upon the jury's deliberations, some state courts prefer to phrase the test in terms of the likelihood that the jury would have reached a different result without the error. To avoid converting such a standard into a "correct result" test, these jurisdictions commonly stress that the appellate court's answer to the question of what would have happened without the error should not be based on the court's own satisfaction with the verdict or on whether the evidence was sufficient for the jury to have reached the same verdict. The issue, they note, is what the jury actually would have done without the error. Courts using this type of formulation have said that an error will not be harmless if there is a "reasonable likelihood" that the result would have been different, a "significant probability" (rather than only a "rational probability") that the jury would have acquitted, or a showing that the result "might probably have been more favorable."

8. Commonwealth v. Story, 476 Pa. 391, 383 A.2d 155 (1978).

tion or otherwise," *Kotteakos* stressed the need for a case-by-case inquiry. Any presumptions of prejudice, shifting the burden to one side or the other, should "aris[e] from the nature of the error and its 'natural effect' for or against prejudice in the particular setting." Chief Justice Traynor of the California Supreme Court suggested that the entire issue of presumptions and burdens was largely meaningless in the harmless error context.[9] In evaluating what effect, if any, an error had on the jury's verdict, the appellate court may look only to the record before it. The function of a party carrying the burden is simply to suggest, in light of that record, how prejudice may or may not have occurred. At that point, the court makes its own assessment as to what degree of likelihood exists as to that prejudicial or non-prejudicial impact and then applies to that assessment the likelihood-standard of the particular jurisdiction.

One issue that clearly does have practical significance, but has not been fully explored by most courts, is what weight should be assigned to overwhelming evidence of guilt in determining the impact of a trial error. Several possibilities have been suggested. One approach, certainly not accepted by most courts, is to look to the error almost in isolation. The critical question under this approach is whether the error is of a type likely to have influenced a reasonable juror. Where evidence was erroneously admitted, the court would focus on the extent to which that evidence was incriminating. Thus, evidence that improperly brought out a prior offense would be judged according to the damaging quality of that information. If the offense revealed was serious and roughly similar to that charged, the error clearly would not be harmless (in contrast, for example, to the revelation of an unrelated traffic offense). It would not matter that the evidence overwhelmingly established guilt or even that another prior offense, similar in nature, had been properly placed before the jury.

Proponents of an approach that looks only to the quality of the error argue that it affords protection against appellate court usurption of the jury's function, precludes extensive reliance on the harmless error doctrine (and the resulting dilution of defendant's procedural rights), and serves to deter intentional misconduct by prosecutors who might otherwise rely on the strength of the evidence to shield their misconduct on appellate review. Appellate courts generally have not been receptive to these arguments, in part because they are viewed as imposing an artificial restriction on the task before the court, assessing the impact of the error. As various courts have noted, one can hardly evaluate the impact of an error upon a juror's decision without considering the totality of the case before the juror. The courts may also be troubled by the inconsistency of adopting an approach that refuses to give consideration to overwhelming government evidence while retaining the traditional view that virtually precludes a finding of harmlessness when the overall proof is finely balanced. Courts have long noted their reluctance to judge harmless any but the most technical errors where the government's case is barely sufficient. In such "weak cases," reversals have been ordered on the basis of errors that would hardly be characterized as having significant prejudice potential if viewed in the abstract.

Once it is agreed that the impact of an error must be measured in light of all of the evidence before the jury, it does not follow that an overwhelming prosecution case will inevitably render the error harmless. Courts have stated that they will not allow the overwhelming evidence to automatically render the error harmless, since to do so comes too close to returning to a "correct result" standard. They stress the need to consider what impact the error had upon the jury. One method of measuring that impact, and ensuring that the weight of the state's evidence does not become definitive, is to match the potential element of prejudice against the state's evidence. For example, to render harmless the erroneous admission of potentially prejudicial evidence, it would have to be shown that the government had properly in-

9. R. Traynor, The Riddle of Harmless Error, 25–26 (1970).

troduced other, more persuasive evidence on the same point. Most courts, however, view a requirement that the prosecution's evidence independently establish the same fact as the inadmissible evidence as unduly restrictive. Even without a "perfect match," strong prosecution evidence may indicate that a particular error was most unlikely to have contributed to the jury's verdict. For example, erroneously admitted evidence may have been the only evidence casting doubt upon defendant's reputation for honesty, but it may nevertheless have been inconsequential in light of strong eyewitness testimony clearly establishing that the defendant had committed the crime.

Many courts apply what may be described as a comparative analysis of the likely impact of the error and the overwhelming evidence. The question to be answered, they note, is "whether the properly admitted evidence of guilt is so overwhelming and the prejudicial effect of the error is so insignificant by comparison," that the court can say, with the requisite degree of certainty, that the error could not have contributed to the verdict. As for some types of error, such as the erroneous admission or exclusion of evidence, overwhelming evidence of guilt will ordinarily lead to the conclusion that the error was harmless. It would take evidence of an extraordinary quality to conclude that its erroneous admission or exclusion may have contributed to the verdict where the government had before the jury other evidence that would clearly and positively establish guilt. On the other hand, certain types of jury charging errors ordinarily should not be viewed as harmless if the true test is influence on the judgment actually rendered rather than what the jury would have decided without the error. When, for example, a judge erroneously tells the jury that proof of a certain element is not needed to establish an offense, it must be assumed that the jury relied upon that direction. This should preclude a finding of harmlessness even though, if it had been properly charged, the jury most likely would have found that element to be present. Even as to such an error, however, special circumstances may make it possible to conclude that the erroneous charge did not influence the jury, as where it found the same element in reaching a guilty verdict on a different count involving the same facts.

(c) Application to Constitutional Violations. Prior to the 1960's, it was generally assumed that constitutional violations could never be regarded as harmless error. Aside from one ambiguous ruling at the turn of the century, a Supreme Court finding of constitutional error had always resulted in a reversal of the defendant's conviction. Since the Court's opinions had never sought to analyze those reversals under a harmless error rule, both commentators and lower courts concluded that the rule simply did not apply to constitutional violations. This assumption was called into question in the 1963 case of *Fahy v. Connecticut.*[10] The state court there had held harmless a violation of the *Mapp v. Ohio* requirement that evidence obtained through an unconstitutional search not be admitted into evidence at trial. The Supreme Court majority found it unnecessary to decide whether the harmless error rule applied to *Mapp* violations. If it was assumed arguendo that the rule applied, the state court had still erred in its analysis of the alleged harmlessness of the *Mapp* violation in this particular case. The four dissenters in *Fahy* did reach the issue reserved by the majority. They could "see no reason" why the harmless error rule should not apply, as there was "no necessary connection between the fact that evidence was unconstitutionally seized and the degree of harm caused by its admission."

Four years later, in *Chapman v. California*[11] the Court majority resolved the issue left open in *Fahy. Chapman* involved a clear violation of the Court's recent decision in *Griffin v. California* prohibiting comment on the defendant's failure to testify at trial.[12] The California Supreme Court, stressing the overwhelming evidence of guilt, had held the

10. 375 U.S. 85, 84 S.Ct. 229, 11 L.Ed.2d 171 (1963).
11. 386 U.S. 18, 87 S.Ct. 824, 17 L.Ed.2d 705 (1967).
12. See § 24.4(b).

Griffin violation harmless under the California harmless error rule. Before the Supreme Court, the defendant contended that no constitutional error could be harmless, while the prosecution claimed that the state court could appropriately apply to a constitutional violation the same harmless error standard it applied to non-constitutional errors. The Court majority rejected both arguments.

The *Chapman* majority held initially that federal rather than state law determined whether the harmless error rule applied to constitutional violations, and if so, whether a particular constitutional violation was harmless. "Whether a conviction for a crime should stand when a state had failed to accord federally constitutionally guaranteed rights" was as much a matter of constitutional law as the definition of the constitutional right itself. The Court then turned to the question of whether the constitution required automatic reversal as to all constitutional errors. It was true, the Court noted, that a rule of automatic reversal had been applied to certain constitutional errors in the past, but that did not mean constitutional errors could never be treated as harmless. A proper harmless error standard could appropriately be applied to some constitutional violations, including a violation of the *Griffin* ruling. However, that standard was not the harmless error rule applied by the California court, but rather a standard that required the appellate court to be convinced "beyond a reasonable doubt that the error complained of did not contribute to the verdict obtained."

The *Chapman* opinion presents a two-step analysis for an appellate court dealing with a constitutional error. First, the court must determine whether the error falls in that category of violations subject to the harmless error rule or that category requiring automatic reversal. Second, if the harmless error rule is applicable, the court must determine the impact of the error in the case before it under the federal standard laid down in *Chapman*. These two determinations are analyzed in the subsections that follow.

(d) Harmless Error vs. Automatic Reversal. The *Chapman* opinion focused primarily on responding to the contention that the harmless error rule should never apply to constitutional error. Its reasoning in this regard was very much like that offered by the dissenters in *Fahy*. The Court found no basis in theory or past precedent for granting constitutional errors a blanket exemption from this traditional rule of appellate review. It noted that the harmless error statutes, including the federal provision, did not on their face distinguish between federal constitutional errors and non-constitutional errors. These statutes, the Court noted, served "a very useful purpose insofar as they block setting aside convictions for small errors or defects that have little, if any, likelihood of having changed the result of the trial." The Court was not prepared to conclude that there could not be "some constitutional errors which in the setting of a particular case are so unimportant and insignificant that they may, consistent with the Federal Constitution, be deemed harmless."

The *Chapman* opinion acknowledged, that prior cases had indicated "that there are some constitutional rights so basic to a fair trial that their infraction can never be treated as harmless error." A footnote to this statement cited and described three illustrative cases:

> *Payne v. Arkansas* (coerced confessions)[13]; *Gideon v. Wainwright* (right to counsel)[14]; [and] *Tumey v. Ohio* (impartial judge)[15].

The Court made no attempt to identify the characteristics that distinguished these constitutional errors from the *Griffin* violation before it. An improper comment on defendant's silence was the type of "trial error" as to which a harmless error analysis traditionally had been applied, and the Court apparently concluded that once it was decided that "some constitutional errors" could be deemed

13. 356 U.S. 560, 78 S.Ct. 844, 2 L.Ed.2d 975 (1958). See § 6.2.

14. 372 U.S. 335, 83 S.Ct. 792, 9 L.Ed.2d 799 (1963). See § 11.1(a).

15. 273 U.S. 510, 47 S.Ct. 437, 71 L.Ed. 749 (1927). See § 21.4(a).

harmless, the *Griffin* violation clearly fell within that group. Only Justice Stewart disagreed with that conclusion. He suggested that recognition of a harmless constitutional error should be limited narrowly to constitutional requirements, like the exclusionary rule, that involved a balancing of a deterrence objective against the exclusion of "relevant and reliable evidence."

The *Chapman* opinion was criticized for providing "little guidance on the matter of determining when an error automatically requires reversal and when it does not." Obviously, the Court majority favored a harmless error concept that extended beyond the limited class of constitutional violations identified by Justice Stewart. However, it was also obvious that Court's citation to three constitutional errors requiring automatic reversal was only by example and did not serve to exhaust the list of constitutional violations so treated. As Justice Stewart noted, past precedent had clearly indicated that certain other violations would also be placed in the automatic-reversal category. The *Chapman* opinion said only that "some constitutional errors," including a *Griffin* violation, could be deemed harmless. It did not clearly indicated whether "some" would be "most," "many," or only a "few." That determination awaited further development, but the logic of *Chapman* did exclude from the outset two very different types of constitutional violations.

The very nature of the harmless error inquiry made harmless error analysis irrelevant to one major group of constitutional violations. A harmless error inquiry only applies where the appropriate remedy for the constitutional violation would be a new trial. The basic issue raised by the *Chapman* standard is whether it is sufficiently unlikely that the constitutional error had an impact upon the jury's decision as to relieve the state of undertaking a new trial that would be free of that error. Where the constitutional error is one that would require a remedy of barring reprosecution, the *Chapman* standard has no bearing and reversal is automatic upon concluding that there was such a violation. That is the case, for example, where defendant establishes a violation of his right to a speedy trial or the bar against double jeopardy.

An additional group of violations were destined not to be analyzed under the *Chapman's* harmless error test because they were, in effect, per se harmful errors, inherently incapable of meeting the rigorous *Chapman* prerequisite for finding an error to be harmless. *Chapman* insisted upon a judicial finding of lack of prejudicial impact "beyond a reasonable doubt." As a result, it would be wasted effort to look to *Chapman* where the constitutional violation is one of those that requires as an element of the violation a finding of likely prejudicial impact. Typically, those violations do not exist unless the challenged behavior presented a "reasonable probability" of having affected the outcome of the proceeding. Where a court has made such a finding in concluding that there was a constitutional violation (as where it concludes that counsel's representation was ineffective under the *Strickland* standard,[16] or that nondisclosed exculpatory evidence was material under the *Bagley* standard [17]), then there is no reason to superimpose the *Chapman* standard to determine whether a new trial is necessary; the presence of the requisite "reasonable probability" necessarily establishes the reasonable doubt required for a new trial under *Chapman.* Indeed, one issue that has frequently divided the Court in recent years is whether particular conduct should be viewed as a constitutional violation in itself, with that violation then subject to the *Chapman* standard, or instead should be viewed as a violation only if the defendant can establish a reasonable probability of that conduct having a prejudicial impact upon the outcome of the proceeding.[18]

16. See § 11.10(d).

17. See § 20.7(b).

18. Consider in this regard United States v. Bagley, discussed in § 20.7(b), and Delaware v. Van Arsdall, 475 U.S. 673, 106 S.Ct. 1431, 89 L.Ed.2d 674 (1986). In *Bagley*, the Court majority held that an element of the due process violation was a showing of "materiality," established by a reasonable probability that disclosure of the exculpatory evidence would have produced a different result. Justice Marshall, in dissent, argued that once it

Leaving aside those constitutional violations that bar reprosecution and those that require a finding of probable impact upon outcome, the *Chapman* harmless error analysis still offered the potential of applying to a broad range of constitutional errors. In the years after *Chapman,* that potential was fully realized. *Chapman's* harmless error standard has now been held by Supreme Court ruling to apply to each of the following constitutional violations: improper comment on the defendant's failure to testify; admission of evidence obtained in violation of the Fourth Amendment; admission of a confession obtained in violation of an accused's right to counsel; admission of an out-of-court statement of a non-testifying codefendant in violation of the Sixth Amendment; admission of identification evidence obtained in violation of the Sixth Amendment's counsel clause; admission of evidence at the sentencing stage of a capital case in violation of the Sixth Amendment's counsel clause; a restriction on a defendant's right to cross-examine in violation of the Sixth Amendment's confrontation clause; denial of defendant's right to be present during a trial proceeding; denial of an indigent's right to appointed counsel at a preliminary hearing; the exclusion of defendant's testimony at trial regarding the circumstances that produced his confession; a statutory restriction that unconstitutionally precluded the giving of a charge on a lesser-included offense in a capital case; the failure to instruct the jury on the presumption of innocence; a jury instruction containing an unconstitutional rebuttable presumption; a jury instruction containing an unconstitutional conclusive presumption; a jury instruction committing constitutional error in defining an offense; an unconstitutionally overbroad jury instruction in a capital case; and finally, in *Arizona v. Fulminante,*[19] overruling one of *Chapman's* three illustrations of automatic-reversal errors, the *Chapman* standard was held applicable to the admission of a coerced confession. This long string of rulings is supplemented by lower court rulings holding *Chapman* applicable to many analogous violations, such as the admission of a statement obtained in violation of *Miranda.*

In *Rose v. Clark,*[20] the Supreme Court, looking to the wide range of constitutional errors held subject to the *Chapman* standard, offered the following synopsis of the Court's rulings:

> [W]hile there are some errors to which *Chapman* does not apply, they are the exception and not the rule. Accordingly, if the defendant had counsel and was tried by an impartial adjudicator, there is a strong presumption that any other errors that may have occurred are subject to harmless error analysis.

In a separate opinion in *Rose,* Justice Stevens questioned whether the Court's prior decisions truly supported a "broad presumption in favor of harmless error." As he noted, the "exceptions" to the "general rule" of applying *Chapman* are more than a few and they reach beyond those violations that deprive the defendant of counsel or an impartial adjudicator. Protection of those two guarantees was involved in two of the automatic-reversal illustrations cited in *Chapman*—the *Gideon* violation of failing to provide trial counsel for an indigent defendant and the *Tumey* violation of allowing the judge to have a financial interest in the outcome of the case. Following *Chapman,* the rule of automatic-reversal also was held to apply to numerous other violations, including several that arguably were far removed from the *Gideon* and *Tumey* violations. Placed in the automatic-reversal category were: the denial of defendant's constitutional right to self-representation; discrimination in the selection of the petit jury;

had been shown that the prosecutor failed to disclose favorable evidence, a constitutional violation was established and the prosecutor then bore the burden of showing that the error was harmless under the *Chapman* standard. In *Van Arsdall,* the majority held that defendant's constitutional right of confrontation was violated by a state ruling prohibiting inquiry into a prosecution witness' bias, and a new trial was required unless the prosecution could establish that error to be harmless under the *Chapman* standard. Justice White, concurring in the judgment, argued that "it makes more sense to hold that no violation of the Confrontation Clause has occurred unless there is some likelihood that the outcome of the trial was affected."

19. ___ U.S. ___, 111 S.Ct. 1246, 113 L.Ed.2d 302 (1991).

20. 478 U.S. 570, 106 S.Ct. 3101, 92 L.Ed.2d 460 (1986).

the improper exclusion of a juror because of his views on capital punishment; racial discrimination in the selection of the grand jury; the violation of the *Anders* standards governing the withdrawal of appointed appellate counsel; the denial of consultation between defendant and his counsel during an overnight trial recess; the denial of a defendant's right to a public trial; representation by counsel acting under an actual conflict of interest that adversely affect his performance; and the failure of the trial court to make an appropriate inquiry into a possible conflict of interest under those special circumstances that constitutionally mandate such an inquiry. While several of the above errors relate to the provision of counsel, other aspects of the right to counsel, including the failure to provide counsel at a preliminary hearing, have been held subject to harmless error analysis. So too, those errors not relating to counsel do not necessarily go to the impartiality of the adjudicator. Indeed, even the jury selection violations commonly are not founded on the premise that jury actually selected was less than impartial. Thus, the presumption noted in *Rose* may be a starting point, but additional analytical tools are needed to separate the automatic-reversal errors from those subject to the *Chapman* standard.

In *Fulminante,* the majority characterized those errors placed within the automatic-reversal category as involving "structural defect[s] affecting the framework within which the trial proceeds." Their nature was quite distinct, the Court noted, from those errors held subject to the *Chapman* harmless error standard. The latter group of violations were tied together by the "common thread" of "involv[ing] 'trial error'—error which occurred during the presentation of the case to the jury and which may therefore be quantitatively assessed in the context of other evidence presented in order to determine whether its admission was harmless beyond a reasonable doubt." Although Justice White criticized this distinction as "drawing a meaningless dichotomy," it very much resembles the traditional distinction drawn in harmless error analysis outside of the area of constitutional violations, where harmlessness is limited to the technical nature of the error as to some violations but also includes a lack of impact upon the outcome of the proceeding as to others. Perhaps the two most significant factors governing the distinction among violations drawn there is the capacity of the appellate court to measure the error's impact on the outcome of the trial and the relationship of the right violated to interests that stand apart from ensuring that the trial verdict is not improperly influenced. Supreme Court opinions have cited basically the same factors in distinguishing between those violations that are subject to the *Chapman* harmless error analysis and those that call for automatic-reversal.

Undoubtedly the characteristic of "structural" defects most frequently mentioned in Supreme Court opinions is their "inherently indeterminate" impact upon the outcome of the trial. Unlike trial errors, they do not relate to the introduction or evaluation of particular items of evidence. Of course, certain violations held subject to the *Chapman* standard, such as the failure to charge on the presumption of innocence, could also be said to have a pervasive effect. But the impact of that omission can be measured by reference to the other charges given (including the one on proving guilt beyond a reasonable doubt). Very often, the impact of violations in the structural category could not be measured by reference to the evidence produced because the violation might well have had a bearing on the failure to produce other evidence, or to take other actions, that would have been influential.

The Court's treatment of the various constitutional violations relating to the right to counsel reflect this focus on the indeterminate impact of the error. The absence of counsel at trial obviously has an inherently indeterminate impact. The same can be said of a counsel operating under an actual conflict of interest that adversely affected his performance. While it might be possible to evaluate the impact of the particular action that reveals the conflict, there is no assurance that the conflict may not also have affected other aspects of counsel's performance. So too, when counsel is kept from consulting with his client, only speculation can answer the question of what would have been done differently and how that would have influenced the remainder of the trial. On the other hand, in other settings, particularly pretrial procedures, the function of counsel is more limited and the impact of denial more readily measured. In some instances, such as post-accusation interrogation, the right to counsel is aimed entirely at preserving other rights of the accused as they relate to the prosecution's acquisition of evidence. Here the impact of the denial can be measured in terms of the impact of the admission of that evidence at trial. Here also, the denial of counsel can hardly be viewed as related to "the basic trial machinery." Thus, the court readily found the harmless error rule applicable to the admission of statements and lineup identifications obtained in violation of defendant's right to counsel. *Coleman v. Alabama,*[21] presented an arguably more difficult issue, whether the denial of counsel at a preliminary hearing could be harmless error. The function of counsel at a preliminary hearing relates to several aspects of trial preparation, and one might have thought it would be difficult indeed to trace the impact of that denial. The *Coleman* majority, however, held that the denial of counsel at a preliminary hearing was subject to the harmless error rule. It apparently viewed the violation as not dissimilar to a denial of discovery, a nonconstitutional matter as to which an outcome-impact harmless error rule traditionally had been applied.

The treatment of the counsel violations also suggests that, at times, a critical factor is the bearing of harmless error analysis upon the function that the violated aspect of the right is designed to achieve. Consider, for example, the withdrawal of appellate counsel without fulfilling the procedures specified by *Anders.*[22] Here, a subsequent analysis could determine that the appeal truly was frivolous and that defendant was not hurt since counsel would have been allowed to withdraw after filing an *Anders* brief. But as the court noted in *Penson v. Ohio,*[23] applying *Chapman* to an *Anders* violation would leave the defendant without the very protection that *Anders* sought to provide when it barred withdrawal on counsel's bare assertion that the appeal was frivolous. In applying a harmless error analysis, *Penson* noted, the appellate court would be required to assess the potential merits of the defendant's appeal, finding the error harmless or not harmless according to its view as to whether a reversal on the merits would be required. To allow such an analysis would thereby "render * * * meaningless the protections afforded * * * *Anders.*" A similar consideration may underlay the decision in *Holloway v. Arkansas*[24] to hold per se prejudicial (and thus not subject to harmless error analysis) a trial court's failure to inquire into a possible conflict of interest when the circumstances strongly suggest such a conflict exists. It might be possible in a postconviction hearing to determine that, notwithstanding those circumstances, there was in fact no actual conflict and thus the lack of a hearing was not prejudicial. But the very premise of the constitutionally mandated inquiry was that a postconviction inquiry (the usual situation on conflict claims) was not adequate protection where such special circumstances existed. Though allowing a postconviction harmless error inquiry would not go so far as to "render meaningless" *Holloway's* inquiry requirement, it would certainly undermine a basic premise of that requirement.

In some instances, constitutional violations have fallen in the automatic-reversal category because an impact upon outcome, or a lack thereof, simply is irrelevant to the function of the right violated. The refusal to apply *Chapman* to a denial of defendant's right to proceed pro se was so explained in *McKaskle v. Wiggins.*[25] That right, the Court noted, is designed to permit the defendant to control

21. See § 14.4(a), (e).

22. See § 11.2(c).

23. 488 U.S. 75, 109 S.Ct. 346, 102 L.Ed.2d 300 (1988).

24. See § 11.9(e).

25. See § 11.5 at note 3.

his own destiny, even though its exercise "usually increases the likelihood of a trial outcome unfavorable to the defendant"; accordingly, "its denial is not amenable to 'harmless-error' analysis." The broader function of the right involved may also explain, in part, the Court's refusal to apply a harmless-error analysis in the jury selection cases. The Court has required automatic reversal even where a single juror was excluded unconstitutionally and there was no suggestion of bias on the part of the jurors actually selected.[26] This position may follow from those functions of the jury trial guarantee (e.g., community participation) that extend beyond simply ensuring that the factfinding process is reliable.

Of course, the presence of a function that extends beyond factfinding reliability does not in itself place a constitutional violation beyond the reach of *Chapman.* The self-incrimination privilege serves a variety of functions beyond the protection of the innocent, yet *Chapman* itself applied the harmless error standard to an infringement of that right. Admittedly, those additional functions might be thought less significant in the context of the *Griffin* prohibition against adverse prosecutorial comment, but they certainly are at the core of prohibition against the admission of coerced confessions, which has also been held subject to the *Chapman* rule. The key here is that the self-incrimination privilege, despite the breadth of its concerns, operates solely as a prohibition against the use of evidence. So too, while the Fourth Amendment serves privacy interests unrelated to factfinding reliability, in applying *Chapman* to *Mapp* violations, the Court was concerned only with a bar against evidentiary use that serves basically a prophylactic function and does not itself preclude a violation of privacy. Not surprisingly in light of the other limitations imposed upon the *Mapp* exclusionary rule,[27] the Court concluded that a requirement of automatic reversal was not needed to satisfy that prophylactic function.

While function does not always determine whether or not a particular violation will fall in the automatic-reversal category, there are times when the function of the right involved outweighs all other considerations, including an almost certain lack of impact upon the outcome of the proceedings. Thus, the Court has noted that where the violation casts a shadow upon the integrity of the judicial process, that may be a sufficient reason in itself to require automatic-reversal. This "judicial integrity" rationale has been cited as an explanation for the requirements of automatic-reversal in both the improper exclusion of jurors because of their views on capital punishment and the trial of a case by a judge with a pecuniary interest in the outcome. Although the refusal to apply *Chapman* in these cases can as readily be justified on other grounds, the judicial integrity rationale clearly is the central justification for the automatic-reversal rule in *Rose v. Mitchell.*[28] The Court there held that racial discrimination in the selection of the grand jury requires an automatic reversal of a subsequent conviction notwithstanding that the petit jury rendering that conviction was fairly selected. *Rose* "reasoned that racial discrimination in the selection of the grand jury is so pernicious and other remedies so impracticable, that the remedy of automatic reversal was necessary as a prophylactic means of deterring grand jury discrimination in the future." [29]

(e) Applying the Reasonable Doubt Standard for Constitutional Errors. Although *Fahy v. Connecticut* left open the application of the harmless error standard to

26. See Gray v. Mississippi, discussed in § 22.3 at note 26.

27. See §§ 3.1, 9.1, 9.3, 9.4.

28. See § 15.4(h).

29. United States v. Mechanik, 475 U.S. 66, 106 S.Ct. 938, 89 L.Ed.2d 50 (1986). But consider Vasquez v. Hillary, discussed at note 21 of § 15.4, suggesting the possible prejudicial impact of such discrimination through the loss of possible grand jury nullification. Of course, if that were the primary concern here, the remedy might be to require the prosecutor to seek a new indictment, and if that was achieved, consider that evidence of the harmless nature of the earlier discrimination in grand jury selection and allow the conviction to stand.

constitutional errors,[30] it provided the foundation for the harmless error standard later adopted in *Chapman.* In holding that the lower court had improperly applied its harmless error standard, the *Fahy* majority noted that it was "not concerned here with whether there was sufficient evidence on which the petitioner could have been convicted without the evidence complained of." The crucial question, the Court stated, was "whether there is a reasonable possibility that the evidence complained of might have contributed to the conviction." When the *Chapman* opinion reached the point where it was ready to fashion a federal harmless error standard for constitutional errors, it looked to the analysis adopted in *Fahy.* In a passage that is generally viewed as the key to *Chapman* ruling, the Court reasoned:

> The California * * * [harmless error] rule emphasizes "a miscarriage of justice," but the California courts have neutralized this to some extent by emphasis, and perhaps overemphasis, upon the court's view of "overwhelming evidence." We prefer the approach of this Court in deciding what was harmless error in our recent case of *Fahy v. Connecticut.* There we said: "The question is whether there is a reasonable possibility that the evidence complained of might have contributed to the conviction." * * * An error in admitting plainly relevant evidence which possibly influenced the jury adversely to a litigant cannot, under *Fahy,* be conceived of as harmless. Certainly error, constitutional error, in illegally admitting highly prejudicial evidence or comments, casts on someone other than the person prejudiced by it a burden to show that it was harmless. It is for that reason that the original common-law harmless error rule put the burden on the beneficiary of the error either to prove that there was no injury or to suffer a reversal of his erroneously obtained judgment.[31] There is little, if any, difference between our statement in *Fahy v. Connecticut* about "whether there is a reasonable possibility that the evidence complained of might have contributed to the conviction" and requiring the beneficiary of a constitutional error to prove beyond a reasonable doubt that the error complained of did not contribute to the verdict obtained. We, therefore, do no more than adhere to the meaning of our *Fahy* case when we hold, as we now do, that before a federal constitutional error can be held harmless, the court must be able to declare a belief that it was harmless beyond a reasonable doubt.

The *Fahy–Chapman* standard clearly rejected a "correct result" test, especially if the correct result was to be measured simply by sufficient evidence to sustain a conviction. The standard looked not to whether the jury could have convicted without regard to the error, or whether the appellate court itself would have convicted without the error, but to whether the error had influenced the jury in reaching its verdict. It required that the appellate court be convinced "beyond a reasonable doubt" that there was no "reasonable possibility" that the error contributed to the jury's verdict. The *Chapman* opinion did not clearly indicate, however, precisely what weight was to be given to the presence of overwhelming untainted evidence in making that judgment. The government's case in *Chapman* clearly was not overwhelming, and the Court had no reason to deal directly with the issue.

Harrington v. California [32] brought into sharper focus the question of the appropriate treatment of the government's untainted evidence in applying the *Chapman* standard. The constitutional error in question was a *Bruton* violation,[33] the introduction of the confessions of two codefendants who did not take the stand. The confessions placed the defendant at the scene of the crime, but so did the defendant's own statements and several eyewitnesses. Moreover, the third codefendant, who did take the stand, placed him at the scene with a gun in his hand. Justice Douglas, speaking for the majority, concluded that

30. See text following note 10 supra.

31. As to the significance of this allocation of the burden of establishing harmlessness, see text following note 9 supra.

32. 395 U.S. 250, 89 S.Ct. 1726, 23 L.Ed.2d 284 (1969).

33. See § 17.2(b).

the error was harmless in light of the remaining evidence. Justice Douglas stressed that the improperly admitted confessions of the codefendant was merely "cumulative" evidence. Justice Douglas also noted that the untainted evidence against the defendant was "so overwhelming" that if this *Bruton* violation were not deemed harmless, the Court would, in effect, be placing *Bruton* violations in the category of errors subject to the automatic-reversal rule.

Justice Brennan's dissent in *Harrington* claimed that the court had departed from *Chapman* (which the majority flatly denied). As Justice Brennan read the majority opinion, the Court had "shifted the inquiry from whether the constitutional error contributed to the conviction to whether the untainted evidence provided 'overwhelming' support for the conviction." Justice Brennan apparently read *Chapman* as looking only to the potentially prejudicial quality of the constitutional error without regard to the strength of the remaining evidence. If this is what *Chapman* meant, then *Harrington* clearly had shifted the inquiry. There was no indication, however, that the inquiry had been shifted away from the contribution of the constitutional error to the jury's verdict. The *Harrington* opinion can be read narrowly as reasoning that the codefendants' statements did not influence the jury because it had before it stronger, similar evidence on the same point. It can be read broadly as concluding that, in light of the overwhelming evidence against the defendant, the jury would not have given any significant weight to the codefendants' statements. Under either reading, the Court was still focusing on the impact of the error, and not suggesting that the presence of overwhelming evidence would per se render an error harmless no matter how inflammatory the error or how much emphasis was placed upon it by the prosecution.

Milton v. Wainwright,[34] decided three years after *Harrington*, indicated that consideration of the untainted evidence would not be limited to precisely matching cumulative evidence, as a narrow reading of *Harrington* might suggest. *Milton* held harmless the admission of defendant's confession, assuming arguendo that it had been obtained in violation of the Sixth Amendment. The Court majority relied heavily on the presence of "overwhelming evidence of guilt," including three recorded confessions of the defendant and "other evidence, highly damaging to petitioner in its totality." Although the challenged confession was described as containing "incriminating statements * * * essentially the same as those given in the prior confessions," the majority opinion did not stress that factor. It emphasized instead the strength of all of the remaining evidence and did not bother to characterize the challenged confession as merely cumulative. The four dissenters did not quarrel with the majority's consideration of the other confessions, but raised questions as to their voluntariness, suggesting that the jury therefore would not have given them significant weight.

Both *Milton* and *Schneble v. Florida*[35] do raise some doubt as to whether the overwhelming weight of the evidence will continue to be considered only as it relates to the influence that the constitutional error had upon the jury. Neither opinion can be said, however, to have rejected that clear directive of *Chapman,* which *Harrington* professed to follow. At points the *Milton* opinion suggests that the jury obviously gave the challenged confession little weight in light of the remaining evidence available to it. Yet the opinion also contained language suggesting that the error was harmless because the jury would have reached the same result in a trial from which the challenged confession was excluded. Similarly, in *Schneble,* a case holding harmless a *Bruton* violation, the opinion appeared to rely on both points of reference. The Court spoke of the need to determine the "probable impact" of the inadmissible confession "on the minds of an average jury," yet it also noted that it was certain that the jury "would not have found the State's case significantly less persuasive had the testimony as to

34. 407 U.S. 371, 92 S.Ct. 2174, 33 L.Ed.2d 1 (1972).

35. 405 U.S. 427, 92 S.Ct. 1056, 31 L.Ed.2d 340 (1972).

[the codefendant's] admissions been excluded." For all but the truly exceptional case, the difference in these two formulations would have no practical significance. The acid test will arise when the Court faces a case in which the untainted evidence of guilt is overwhelming, but the information presented through the constitutional error was emphasized to the point that the jury obviously could have thought it highly significant (as where the prosecutor made repeated references to the defendant's failure to testify). If the Court remains faithful to the *Chapman* formulation, the error should not be held harmless notwithstanding evidence so strong that the court is certain the jury would have reached the same result in a trial that did not include the error.[36]

36. Consider also Yates v. Evatt, ___ U.S. ___, 111 S.Ct. 1884, 114 L.Ed.2d 432 (1991). In considering the application of the *Chapman* standard to a jury charge containing an unconstitutional presumption, the Court there noted: "To say that an error did not 'contribute' to the ensuing verdict is not, of course, to say that the jury was totally unaware of that feature of the trial later held to have been erroneous. When, for example, a trial court has instructed a jury to apply an unconstitutional presumption, a reviewing court can hardly infer that the jurors failed to consider it, a conclusion that would be factually untenable in most cases, and would run counter to a sound presumption of appellate practice, that jurors are reasonable and generally follow the instructions they are given. * * * To say that an error did not contribute to the verdict is, rather, to find that error unimportant in relation to everything else the jury considered on the issue in question, as revealed in the record. Thus, to say that an instruction to apply an unconstitutional presumption did not contribute to the verdict is to make a judgment about the significance of the presumption to reasonable jurors, when measured against the other evidence considered by those jurors independently of the presumption."

Chapter 28

COLLATERAL REVIEW: THE FEDERAL HABEAS WRIT

Table of Sections

§ 28.1 Current Collateral Remedies and Historical Antecedents

(a) The Nature of Collateral Remedies.[1] What avenues, if any, are available to a convicted defendant for challenging his conviction after all opportunities for appellate review have been exhausted? The answer to that question could readily occupy a volume in itself. Every jurisdiction has one or more procedures through which defendants can present post-appeal challenges to their convictions on at least limited grounds. In addition, through the federal writ of habeas corpus, a state defendant may challenge his state conviction on federal constitutional grounds in the federal courts.

The various state and federal procedures for presenting post-appeal challenges are commonly described as "collateral remedies," although that description may often be attributed more to their heritage than their current form. The current collateral remedies are derived in large part from the common law writs of habeas corpus and coram nobis. The common law habeas proceeding presented a truly collateral attack upon the conviction. It was a separate civil action in which a defendant-petitioner challenged his continued detention and, through that custody challenge, attacked the conviction on which his detention was based. Because the relief sought was the release from custody, the habeas petition was filed in that court having jurisdiction over the official holding the petitioner in custody (e.g., the prison warden), rather than the court of conviction. The writ of coram nobis directly attacked the conviction and was sought in the court of conviction, but it also was commonly viewed as an independent civil action. Today, jurisdictions commonly rely on statutory collateral remedies which, even where they refer to habeas corpus or coram nobis, almost invariably have modified the common law remedy. While some of these statutory proceedings are viewed as independent civil actions, many are considered part of the original criminal case, paralleling a post-appeal motion for a new trial. Thus, the designation of a post-appeal remedy as "collateral" tends today to mean simply that the remedy "provide[s] an avenue for upsetting judgments [of conviction] that have become otherwise final." [2]

The modern collateral remedies vary considerably in their scope. While some are available only to defendants who are held in custody, others permit a challenge by any convicted defendant whose litigation has not become moot. The narrowest allow challenges only to jurisdictional defects, while the broadest extend to jurisdictional defects, constitutional violations, and various nonconstitutional claims. Under some collateral remedies, the defendant cannot advance a claim that was previously presented unless there has been a significant change in the governing law with retroactive application. Under others, the concept of res judicata has been abandoned, and previously considered claims can be advanced at least one more time. Some remedies bar consideration of claims that were not raised at trial and on appeal if the defendant had a reasonable opportunity to present the claim in those proceedings. Others allow consideration of claims that the defendant failed to raise previously, notwithstanding adequate opportunity, provided those claims were not knowingly and voluntarily relinquished in the original proceedings.

No matter how broad or narrow the particular remedy, its relationship to the common law writs of habeas corpus and coram nobis remains significant. A common judicial starting point for analyzing the scope of a modern statutory remedy is to ask to what extent the legislature sought to incorporate or expand upon one or the other of the common law's collateral remedies. The history of the common law writ of habeas corpus has played an especially important role in the Supreme Court's interpretation of the federal habeas remedy, which traditionally has looked to the

§ 28.1

1. Modern collateral remedies are the subject of several extensive treatises. See J. Liebman, Federal Habeas Corpus Practice and Procedure (1988); O. Wilkes, Federal and State Postconviction Remedies and Relief (1983); L. Yackle, Postconviction Remedies (1981).

2. Mackey v. United States, 401 U.S. 667, 91 S.Ct. 1160, 28 L.Ed.2d 404 (1971).

common law for its scope. The Court's use of history in this context in itself establishes the importance of the common law antecedents of the modern writs, since federal habeas corpus clearly is the most significant of today's collateral remedies.

Except for the brief review in this section of the common law writs of habeas corpus and coram nobis, the discussion in this chapter focuses on the federal writ of habeas corpus. Federal habeas is the one common collateral remedy available to all state prisoners. It also provides the doctrinal framework for the primary statutory collateral remedy for challenging federal convictions (the 28 U.S.C.A. § 2255 motion to vacate a sentence). Many states similarly have used the federal writ as their primary model in fashioning their collateral remedies.

(b) The Common Law Writ of Habeas Corpus. The common law writ of habeas corpus, simply defined, is a judicial order directing a person to have the body of another brought before a tribunal at a certain time and place. The writ apparently takes its name from its directive, originally stated in Latin, that the court would "have the body." As initially developed sometime before the thirteenth century, the writ was a form of mesne process by which courts compelled the attendance of parties whose presence would facilitate their proceedings. It was not until the mid-fourteenth century that it came to be used as an independent proceeding designed to challenge illegal detention. The subsequent characterization of habeas corpus as the Great Writ of Liberty—the alleged procedural underpinning of the guarantees of the Magna Charta—stemmed primarily from battles fought in establishing its effectiveness against imprisonment by the Crown without judicial authorization.

The use of the writ to enforce the Magna Charta's guarantee of adherence to the "law of the land" (later described as "due process") was forcefully advocated by leading counsel in *Darnel's Case,*[3] a 1627 litigation in which the writ was sought to gain release of five knights imprisoned for refusing to comply with the King's "forced loan" program. The King's Bench apparently accepted counsels' contention that the writ could be used to enforce the Magna Charta's guarantee, but responded that it could not look beyond the Crown's return, which stated on its face that the detention was lawfully authorized. Dissatisfaction with this ruling eventually led to a 1641 Act that removed the power of the Crown to arrest without probable cause and granted to any arrested person immediate access by writ of habeas corpus to a judicial determination of the legality of his detention. When procedural difficulties undermined the effectiveness of that Act, the Parliament responded with the celebrated Habeas Corpus Act of 1679. The 1679 Act reinforced judicial authority to utilize the writ to release persons illegally detained by the Crown, but specifically excluded from its coverage persons confined as a result of criminal conviction.

Although it could be argued that the exclusion in the 1679 Act eliminated the authority of English courts to issue the writ on behalf of convicted persons, it seems unlikely that Parliament intended to bar use of the writ in such cases, at least where the court of conviction lacked jurisdiction. In *Bushell's Case,*[4] decided in 1670, the writ had been used to order the release of a juror who had been held in contempt for refusing to return a guilty verdict as directed by the trial court. The ruling in *Bushell's Case* had attracted widespread attention (partly because the case arose out of jury's refusal to convict William Penn and other Quakers charged with an allegedly unlawful assembly), and it is doubtful that a Parliament intent upon strengthening the writ would have deprived the courts of that precedent. However, assuming that the writ remained available to convicted persons, how far *Bushell's Case* extended the scope of habeas review as to convicted persons remains a matter of disagreement. Justice Brennan concluded in *Fay v. Noia* that *Bushell's Case* established that the writ was

3. 3 How.St.Tr. 1 (1627) (also known as the *Case of the Five Knights*).

4. 124 Eng.Rep. 1006 (C.P.1670); 6 State Trials 999 (1670).

available at common law to challenge imprisonment based on a conviction obtained in violation of due process.[5] However, Justice Powell later suggested, based on the historical analysis of Professor Oaks, that Justice Brennan's reading of *Bushell's Case* was far too broad.[6] Professor Oaks maintained that *Bushell's Case* did not expand the reach of the writ, but left convicted persons only with the traditional challenge to the jurisdiction of the convicting court. In both England and the colonies, he argued, the writ had "won its place as the most important safeguard of personal liberty," not as applied to convicted persons, but "when employed against the crown and its officers * * * to elicit the cause for an individual's imprisonment and to ensure that he was released, admitted to bail, or promptly tried." As a remedy for persons detained upon a conviction, the writ historically had very limited utility and was infrequently successful.

(c) The Common Law Writ of Coram Nobis. The writ of coram nobis can be traced back to the sixteenth century, but it was viewed at common law as a writ not nearly as important as habeas corpus. At the time of its development, a trial court was not authorized to correct its own errors, and a higher court on writ of error could consider only alleged mistakes of law. Accordingly, there was no means available for correcting errors of fact. The writs of error *quae coram nobis resident* and *quae coram vobis resident* were developed to fill this gap. The former was issued to challenge a judgment of the King's Bench while the latter applied to judgments of the Court of Common Pleas. Both forms of the writ extended to civil as well as criminal cases. The writ provided for review by the trial court. Its objective was "to bring to light errors of fact that the trial court could not have avoided—mistakes that, if known at the time of the trial, would have prevented entry of the judgment." Thus, it allowed presentation of facts not apparent on the face of the record, such as the death or infancy of a party or an error of the clerk in recording the judgment. The writ could be used only where no other remedy was available and the defendant was "without negligence" in failing to alert the trial judge to the crucial fact.

Although the common law writ of coram nobis was noted primarily for its use in civil cases, it came to have some significance in criminal cases in this country during the 1800s. Thus, coram nobis was used to challenge a conviction on the ground that the defendant was an escaped slave (and therefore could not be confined against the wishes of his master), that defendant was insane at the time of trial, and that defendant had entered a guilty plea out of fear of mob violence. However, with the development of the motion for a new trial based on newly discovered evidence, and the expansion of the writ of habeas corpus, the availability of alternative remedies commonly precluded use of the writ of coram nobis. Moreover, with defendants more frequently represented by counsel, it became more difficult to contend that the defense's failure to bring the factual error to the attention of the trial court was excusable. Accordingly, the common law writ tended to fall into disuse. It continues to be influential, however, as modern statutory collateral remedies tend to bring together concepts borrowed from both habeas corpus and coram nobis.

§ 28.2 The Statutory Structure

(a) Constitutional Right or Legislative Grace? The habeas clause in Article I of the federal constitution states: "[T]he Privilege of the Writ of Habeas Corpus shall not be suspended, unless when in Cases of Rebellion or Invasion the public Safety may require it." [1] On its face, this provision might suggest an inherent authority of federal courts to issue the writ in the absence of a valid suspension.

5. 372 U.S. 391, 83 S.Ct. 822, 9 L.Ed.2d 837 (1963). The reasoning and result in *Bushell's Case*, the Court argued, showed that the writ was available to respond to "judicial as well as executive restraints" that were "contrary to fundamental law." See § 28.3 at note 14.

6. Schneckloth v. Bustamonte, § 28.2 at note 14, citing with approval Oaks, Legal History in the High Court—Habeas Corpus, 64 Mich.L.Rev. 401, 461–68 (1966).

§ 28.2

1. U.S. Const. Art. I, § 9, cl. 2.

Such a reading would establish, in effect, a constitutional right to habeas relief, at least to the extent such relief was available at common law,[2] for persons held in custody by officials subject to the jurisdiction of the federal courts. However, as Professor Duker, has noted, "the debates in the federal and state conventions, the location of the habeas clause [among restrictions upon congressional power], and the contemporary commentary" suggest that the habeas clause was designed only "to restrict congressional power to suspend *state* habeas for federal prisoners." [3] Insofar as issuance of the writ by federal courts was concerned, that apparently was a matter to be determined by Congress if it should create inferior federal courts. Additional support for this view is found in the fact that the first Congress, in the Judiciary Act of 1789, specifically authorized the issuance of the writ by the newly created federal courts, thereby suggesting that it did not believe that those courts had any inherent power under the habeas clause to issue the writ.

Since congressional authorization of the issuance of the writs has existed since 1789, the Supreme Court has never found it necessary to rule on whether the habeas clause itself guarantees that the federal courts have that authority. Chief Justice Marshall's opinion in *Ex parte Bollman,*[4] the first major ruling on the 1789 habeas provision, employed arguably contradictory language in describing the bearing of the habeas clause on the availability of the writ for federal prisoners. In large part, however, the *Bollman* opinion suggested that a congressional refusal to authorize federal habeas corpus relief would be inconsistent with the assumption of the Framers, but would nevertheless be constitutionally acceptable, leaving the federal judiciary without authority to issue the writ. Moreover, even if occasional language in *Bollman* is read as recognizing a constitutionally protected privilege of federal habeas corpus, that reading cannot readily be extended to persons other than those held in federal custody. The Judiciary Act of 1789, after authorizing federal courts to issue the writ, added the proviso that the writ "shall in no case extend to prisoners in goal, unless where they are in custody under or by colour of the authority of the United States or are committed for trial before some court of the same, or are necessary to be brought into court to testify." Although this proviso arguably could have been read otherwise, Chief Justice Marshall described it in *Bollman* as barring issuance of the federal writ on behalf of a state prisoner, a result treated as entirely consistent with any "obligation" that the Constitution's habeas clause imposed upon Congress. In *Ex parte Dorr,*[5] the Court faced the issue squarely in a case actually involving a state prisoner, and it held that the proviso barred issuance of the writ. In 1833, the federal habeas statute was extended by Congress to a limited class of persons held in state custody, but it was not until 1867 that the statute was made applicable to state prisoners generally. Throughout this period, there was no suggestion by the Court that this "gap" in the availability of the federal coverage posed any constitutional difficulties.

Notwithstanding the language in *Bollman* and the ruling in *Dorr,* the Supreme Court, in later years, occasionally suggested that the 1867 provision making the writ available to state prisoners might have constitutional

2. As suggested by Chief Justice Burger, concurring in Swain v. Pressley, 430 U.S. 372, 97 S.Ct. 1224, 51 L.Ed.2d 411 (1977), the habeas clause, even assuming that it guarantees a federal writ of habeas corpus, may provide a right to the writ only as it existed when the Constitution was drafted. On the other hand, it has been argued that a constitutional guarantee would be capable of expansion in accord with the fundamental objectives of the writ, just as the common law writ was capable of expansion.

3. W. Duker, A Constitutional History of Habeas Corpus 126 (1980). At the time of the Constitution's adoption, the habeas remedy was widely available in the state courts. It was assumed, moreover, that the state courts could use the writ on behalf of federal prisoners, particularly if there were no federal courts. Indeed, even after inferior federal courts were created, the state courts commonly issued the writ on behalf of federal prisoners. It was not until 1859 that the Supreme Court held that practice to constitute an unauthorized infringement upon federal authority. See Ableman v. Booth, 62 U.S. (21 How.) 506, 16 L.Ed. 169 (1859).

4. 8 U.S. (4 Cranch) 75, 2 L.Ed. 554 (1807).

5. 44 U.S. (3 How.) 103, 11 L.Ed. 514 (1845).

roots. Thus, in *Fay v. Noia,*[6] a case concluding that the 1867 Act allowed for judicial application consistent with the common law tradition (and therefore encompassed all constitutional claims presented by state prisoners [7]), the Court noted that it "need not pause to consider whether it was the Framers' understanding that congressional refusal to permit the federal courts to accord the writ its full common-law scope as we have described it might constitute an unconstitutional suspension of the privilege of the writ." In still another state prisoner case, the Court described the current habeas corpus statutes, apparently with reference to their application to both state and federal prisoners, as "implement[ing] the constitutional command that the writ of habeas corpus be available." [8] On the other hand, in the one instance in which Congress amended the statutory provisions governing state prisoner claims to arguably give the writ a narrower interpretation than the Court's previous ruling, the Court did not suggest that the amendment posed any constitutional difficulties.[9]

(b) The Habeas Corpus Act of 1867. The Habeas Corpus Act of 1867 provides the basic statutory framework for federal habeas relief on behalf of state prisoners. The Act clearly expanded the scope of the federal habeas remedy in providing that

> the several courts of the United States ... within their respective jurisdictions, in addition to the authority already conferred by law, shall have power to grant writs of habeas corpus in all cases where any person may be restrained of his or her liberty in violation of the constitution, or of any treaty or law of the United States. * * *.[10]

This language was far more sweeping than the language of the 1789 provision. It applied to any person "restrained of his or her liberty," thereby clearly including state prisoners, who had been excluded under the proviso of the 1789 Act. It is for this reason, perhaps, that while the 1789 Act simply authorized issuance of the writ without reference to available grounds for relief, the 1867 Act referred to relief only from restraints imposed in violation of the constitution, treaties, and statutes of the United States. A federal court, in applying the writ to a person held in state custody, was not to examine the legality of the detention without limitation, since that would require it to apply state as well as federal law.

The 1867 Act also made a major change in habeas procedure by providing that petitioners could "deny any of the material facts set forth in the return" or allege any additional fact. Thus, "the habeas court was now empowered to conduct an inquiry into the facts underlying the detention and was no longer limited to bare legal review." The Act did not indicate, however, how extensive that inquiry would be or whether it would encompass facts contrary to the state record.

What was the objective of the thirty-ninth Congress in adopting the Habeas Corpus Act of 1867? The sparse legislative history has produced considerable division among commentators. Of the several views advanced, two in particular have attracted the attention of the courts. The narrower of the two interpretations argues that the language of the 1867 Act must be read in light of earlier cases that had applied the 1789 Act to federal prisoners. Those cases had limited habeas review of petitions by convicted persons to a determination of whether the convicting court had jurisdiction over the person and the subject matter. It is argued that Congress clearly would not have intended to go beyond that limitation and thereby provide the federal courts, through the vehicle of the writ, the

6. 372 U.S. 391, 83 S.Ct. 822, 9 L.Ed.2d 837 (1963).

7. The Court later departed from such a broad reading of the common law tradition. See note 22 infra and § 28.3(b).

8. Jones v. Cunningham, 371 U.S. 236, 83 S.Ct. 373, 9 L.Ed.2d 285 (1963).

9. See § 28.7(b), (c), discussing the 1966 legislative response to the decision in Townsend v. Sain, and the cases interpreting that legislation. Of course, the *Townsend* ruling arguably was not based on what Fay v. Noia would have described as the "common-law scope of the writ" and the 1966 legislation came sufficiently close to the Court's ruling in any event to be described by many as a "codification" of that ruling. See § 28.7(c).

10. 14 Stat. 385 (1867).

authority to review all state convictions for possible federal law violations in any aspect of the state proceeding. Such an objective, it is maintained, would "tear habeas corpus entirely out of the context of its historical meaning and scope and convert it into an ordinary writ of error with respect to all federal questions in all criminal cases." Indeed, allowing habeas review of all federal law violations would even be inconsistent with the 1867 Act's application to convicted federal prisoners (who could as readily fit within the description of persons restrained in violation of federal law as state prisoners). Such a broad range of review, it is argued, would have undercut the then existing limitations on appellate review of federal convictions. At the time, the federal prisoner did not have a right to direct appellate review of his conviction by the Supreme Court (although Supreme Court review was available to state defendants as to federal questions); habeas challenges, on the other hand, were subject to Supreme Court review, and an expansive habeas challenge therefore would give the federal prisoner indirectly the appellate review denied him directly, without the previously accepted reconciliation based on the special quality of jurisdictional defects.[11]

The broader view of the 1867 Act's purpose stresses both the language of the provision and the Reconstruction–era context in which it was adopted. The thirty-ninth Congress, it is argued, distrusted the courts of the southern states, and expected that they would be totally unreceptive to the Reconstruction legislation. The object of the Act was to give the federal courts superintending control so as to ensure that there would be full recognition of the federal rights already established in the 1866 Civil Rights Act and about to be established in the Fourteenth Amendment. This was a Congress that "was not overly wary of interfering with state criminal prosecutions," as evidenced by the removal provisions it had included in the Civil Rights Act.[12] That the impact of the expanded writ was also to broaden the scope of the relief available to federal prisoners was inconsequential. Even if the earlier federal prisoner cases had been limited to jurisdictional defects, it had always been recognized that the writ was capable of growth to meet "changed conceptions of the kind of criminal proceedings so fundamentally defective as to make imprisonment pursuant to them constitutionally intolerable."

Although they did not discuss the purposes of the Act at length, Supreme Court rulings applying the Act for its first several decades appeared to favor the narrower of the two interpretations outlined above. However, in *Fay v. Noia,* decided in 1963, the Court majority quite clearly adopted the broader interpretation of the Act's purpose.[13] Several years later, in *Schneckloth v. Bustamonte,*[14] Justice Powell, speaking for four members of the Court, characterized "*Fay v. Noia's* version of the writ's historic function" as resting upon a "revisionist view of history." This was followed by the 1976 ruling of *Stone v. Powell,*[15] where Justice Powell, now speaking for a majority, appeared again to reject the broader *Noia* interpretation, although that interpretation was not specifically disowned.

Stone and subsequent opinions suggest that the Court today views the narrower interpretation of the 1867 Act as the more accurate reflection of how Congress anticipated that the Act would be applied to persons detained pursuant to a conviction. The Court also recognizes, however, that even though Congress may have anticipated a narrower inter-

11. Commentators reading the Act as limited to the jurisdictional challenges recognized in the earlier federal prisoner cases contend that this reading fully satisfies the major concern of Congress in adopting the 1867 Act. That concern, it is argued, was that the states not be allowed to keep the newly freed slaves from exercising their rights by applying to them broadly phrased state laws that were contrary to the recently enacted Thirteenth Amendment and Civil Rights Act. Detention pursuant to such state statutes could be challenged under the writ, consistent with the earlier habeas rulings, because the unconstitutionality of the statute under which it proceeded deprived the state court of its jurisdiction. See § 28.3, at note 5.

12. See § 13.5(d).

13. Supra note 6. See § 28.3, at note 14.

14. 412 U.S. 218, 93 S.Ct. 2041, 36 L.Ed.2d 854 (1973).

15. 428 U.S. 465, 96 S.Ct. 3037, 49 L.Ed.2d 1067 (1976). See also § 28.3, at note 19.

pretation, Supreme Court precedent has carried the writ's application substantially beyond review of convictions for jurisdictional defects. This extension is not necessarily considered to be inconsistent with the general philosophy of the Act. While Congress may have anticipated the writ's immediate use in a manner consistent with the earlier federal prisoner cases, it undoubtedly also recognized that the writ was capable of expansion to encompass other actions of state trial courts that were clearly without authority and in violation of a defendant's basic rights. This would not necessarily encompass all constitutional violations under all circumstances, but would be determined by reference to the equities justifying use of what was an extraordinary remedy, particularly as applied to a person convicted by a court competent to render that judgment. Thus, the 1867 Act (including the subsequent statutory revisions repeating its critical language) is read by the current Court majority as vesting in the habeas court considerable discretion to determine the precise scope of habeas review, within the limitation that such review be restricted to violations of federal law.

(c) Current Statutes. Over the years, as the Court has shifted back and forth in its interpretation of the 1867 Act and its subsequent codifications, Congress has offered little further direction. While it has added various provisions to the federal habeas statutes, those additions have rarely sought to modify what might be described as the core of the statutory authorization set forth in the Habeas Act of 1867. The current version of the Habeas Act is found in 28 U.S.C.A. §§ 2241–2255.[16] Section 2241 contains the basic authorization of the federal courts to issue the writ, with its subsection (c) setting forth the conditions under which the writ may "extend to a prisoner." Subsection (c)(3), with only a slight alteration of the language of the 1867 Act, provides that the writ may issue when the prisoner "is in custody in violation of the Constitution or laws or treaties of the United States." Section 2254, dealing specifically with applications "on behalf of a person in custody pursuant to the judgment of a state court," repeats that language. In 1948, Congress established a separate procedure—described as a motion to vacate a sentence—to replace the habeas writ for federal prisoners. That procedure, codified in § 2255, similarly refers to "violation[s] of the Constitution or laws of the United States" (treaty violations falling within the latter category), although it also encompasses challenges to illegal sentences and to sentences issued by a court "without jurisdiction to impose such sentence."

Other provisions that have a bearing upon the scope given the writ are found in §§ 2243, 2244, and 2254. Section 2243, although it deals primarily with matters of procedure (e.g., the use of show cause orders and the timing of the hearings), ends by noting that the habeas court, after concluding its hearing, shall "dispose of the matter as law and justice require." This provision has been cited by the Supreme Court as evidencing the "equitable nature" of the habeas court's jurisdiction. Section 2244 deals with successive petitions and sets forth circumstances under which a judge may refuse to consider a petition on the basis of the disposition of an earlier petition. Section 2254(d) sets forth circumstances under which a state court's findings of fact will be "presumed to be correct." Section 2254(b)–(c) imposes the requirement that the petitioner exhaust the remedies available in state courts before presenting his petition. The remaining provisions in §§ 2241–45 deal basically with matters of pleading and procedure.

(d) Open Issues. The language of the current statutes leaves open a variety of issues. Space limitations limit our discussion to those issues that go to the heart of the ongoing controversy as to the proper scope of the habeas remedy. Before those issues are reached, however, a habeas petition must overcome two initial hurdles, which are briefly discussed below: the petitioner must be in

16. Most of these provisions were adopted as part of the 1948 revision of the Judicial Code, but others were added by later amendments, primarily in 1966. See 62 Stat. 964–68 (1948); 80 Stat. 811, 1105–06 (1966).

"custody" and he must have complied with the requirement of "exhaustion of state remedies."

The custody requirement is found in both § 2241 and § 2254. The former makes the writ available only to the person who is "in custody in violation of the Constitution or laws or treaties of the United States" and the latter refers to the application by a person "in custody pursuant to a judgment of a State court." Historically the writ was available to the defendant who was seeking release from actual physical confinement, but today the concept of "custody" has a much broader reach. The writ now is available to any person currently under some form of restraint pursuant to a challenged conviction and even to some others as well. Custody encompasses persons on probation, on parole, and even persons released on their own recognizance pending execution of a sentence.[17] It includes a person who was incarcerated at the time the writ was filed, even though unconditionally discharged prior to the point that the habeas court ruled on his petition.[18] The custody requirement also is met by a prisoner incarcerated under an unchallenged conviction who is challenging a second conviction that provides the future portion of his consecutive sentence or a separately imposed future sentence of another jurisdiction which has filed a detainer with the jurisdiction where he currently is incarcerated.[19]

The exhaustion requirement, though currently set forth in § 2254, was initially developed by the Court in the exercise of its discretionary authority over "the time and mode in which it will exert the powers conferred" under the 1867 Act.[20] Based on considerations of comity, the exhaustion requirement insists that the state prisoner give the state courts an adequate opportunity to first rule on his claim. Once the state courts have been given one such opportunity, the state remedies have been exhausted and the claim can be presented to a federal court on a habeas petition. Even where the state courts were not given such an opportunity, if the state procedural avenues for obtaining state review are no longer available, then the exhaustion requirement is met—as it applies only to exhausting remedies still open to the habeas petitioner.[21] Thus, exhaustion is a requirement that may delay habeas review, but it does not pose a permanent bar to such review.

Assuming that the habeas petitioner meets the custody and exhaustion requirement, the question arises as to whether the claim is one that is cognizable on habeas review. This issue is considered in § 28.3 as it relates to constitutional claims. Although the habeas statutes speak to persons held in custody in violation of the "laws and treaties of the United States," as well as the Constitution, the convictions of state prisoners are unlikely to be affected by federal statutes or treaties, apart from federal law that preempts the state substantive law and thereby raise a constitutional claim under the Constitution's supremacy clause. Even if the nature of the constitutional claim would otherwise render it cognizable, a further issue of cognizability arises where that claim would be procedurally barred under state law by a failure to present the issue properly before state courts. This question of when a habeas claim will be foreclosed by a state procedural default is considered in § 28.4. Section 28.5 considers the analogous issue as to when review is foreclosed by the consideration or lack of presentation of a claim in an earlier habeas petition. Once the claim is found to be cognizable and not procedurally barred, the question arises as to the standard of review to be applied by the federal habeas court. Section 28.6 consid-

17. Jones v. Cunningham, 371 U.S. 236, 83 S.Ct. 373, 9 L.Ed.2d 285 (1963); Hensley v. Municipal Court, 411 U.S. 345, 93 S.Ct. 1571, 36 L.Ed.2d 294 (1973).

18. Carafas v. LaVallee, 391 U.S. 234, 88 S.Ct. 1556, 20 L.Ed.2d 554 (1968).

19. Peyton v. Rowe, 391 U.S. 54, 88 S.Ct. 1549, 20 L.Ed.2d 426 (1968); Braden v. 30th Judicial Circuit Court, 410 U.S. 484, 93 S.Ct. 1123, 35 L.Ed.2d 443 (1973).

20. Ex parte Royall, 117 U.S. 241, 6 S.Ct. 734, 29 L.Ed. 868 (1886).

21. Brown v. Allen, 344 U.S. 443, 73 S.Ct. 397, 97 L.Ed. 469 (1953); Rose v. Lundy, 455 U.S. 509, 102 S.Ct. 1198, 71 L.Ed.2d 379 (1982).

ers that standard as it applies to the interpretation of the Constitution, and § 28.7 considers it with reference to issues of fact.

To some extent, each of the issues posed in §§ 28.3–28.7 raises distinct concerns. Nonetheless, the resolution of all of these issues has been guided to a considerable extent by the Court's overall perspective on the role of the writ. While shifts in that perspective are noted in the discussions of individual issues, that narrower focus does not lend itself to developing for the reader an overview of the underlying divisions that have produced those shifts. That task is delegated to the two subsections that follow.

(e) Balancing Within the Statutory Framework. As noted by Justice Rehnquist, the Supreme Court's habeas decisions have illustrated an "historic willingness to overturn or modify its earlier views on the scope of the writ, even where the statutory language authorizing judicial action has remained unchanged."[22] Except where the language of the federal habeas statute is quite specific (as in the provision relating to state court findings of fact), the Court usually has not found much guidance in the language or legislative history of the habeas provisions. In deciding a wide range of matters—including the types of claims cognizable on habeas review, the consequence of a procedural default in state proceedings, and the standard of review as to constitutional interpretation—the Court has viewed its task as achieving an appropriate balance between the value of expansive habeas review and the costs of providing such review.

The benefits of expansive collateral review for both state and federal prisoners have been advocated most forcefully in the opinions of Justice Brennan. Plenary review of constitutional claims on collateral attack, Justice Brennan maintains, is essential to fulfilling the historic function of habeas corpus—providing relief against the detention of persons in violation of their fundamental liberties. Even as applied to federal convictions, where the defendant has had the advantage of a federal forum, "adequate protection of constitutional rights * * * requires the continuing availability of a mechanism for relief." That open-ended mechanism is needed, in particular, to consider claims that were not presented, often through no fault of the defendant himself, in the original proceeding that led to conviction. But even if the habeas court considers a claim raised in the original proceeding, in this field, Justice Brennan argues, there is a justification for redundancy. "Conventional notions of finality of litigation," including concepts of res judicata, should "have no place where life or liberty is at stake and infringement of constitutional rights is alleged."

While critics of Justice Brennan's viewpoint tend to focus on the costs of providing a broad "continuing mechanism for relief," they also question whether plenary habeas review will actually provide a substantial safeguard of constitutional rights. There is no reason to assume, they note, that a second review will be more accurate than the first.[23] Responding to this criticism, proponents of broad habeas review offer two arguments. First, they maintain that review of a constitutional claim by a habeas court is more likely to produce a "correct result" because that court's review is not so closely tied to the "inquiry into guilt or innocence." The "momentum of the trial process and the trial judge's focus upon the central issue of the accused's guilt or innocence," it is argued, "tend to divert attention from ancillary questions relating to constitutional guarantees." Collateral review, in contrast, provides a "dispassionate second look focused exclusively on adjudication of constitutional issues." The second response accepts the con-

22. Wainwright v. Sykes, 433 U.S. 72, 97 S.Ct. 2497, 53 L.Ed.2d 594 (1977).

23. Justice Jackson, objecting to habeas review of issues considered in the original proceeding, expressed such skepticism with reference even to review by the Supreme Court itself. He noted: "[R]eversal by a higher court is not proof that justice is thereby better done. There is no doubt that if there were a super-Supreme Court, a substantial proportion of our reversals of state courts would also be reversed. We are not final because we are infallible, but we are infallible only because we are final." Brown v. Allen, 344 U.S. 443, 73 S.Ct. 397, 97 L.Ed. 469 (1953) (concurring opinion).

tention that the habeas review may be no more likely to achieve a "correct result" than the original proceeding. It maintains, however, that if an error is to be made, then it should be made on the side of finding violations that may not in fact exist, rather than on the side of not finding violations that do exist. Constitutional rights are sufficiently important that, if the first proceeding finds there was no violation and the habeas court disagrees, that establishes a sufficient likelihood that a constitutional violation in fact occurred to grant relief on that assumption.

In the case of constitutional claims presented by state prisoners, an additional factor is cited in favor of providing expansive habeas review. The institutional and political premises underlying the Fourteenth Amendment, as well as the 1867 Habeas Act, are said to require that "federal courts have the 'last say' with respect to questions of federal law." Federal habeas corpus rests, it is said, on "the proposition that persons convicted of crimes in state courts are entitled to at least one opportunity to litigate their federal claims in a federal forum." Since the Supreme Court obviously lacks the resources necessary to review all but a small portion of the state cases in which direct review is sought, the federal habeas court must serve as its functional surrogate in providing federal review. Moreover, it is argued, only the federal habeas court can provide the evidentiary hearings often needed to provide a complete federal review of the constitutional claims of state prisoners.

The demand for a federal forum, Justice Brennan has noted, is not based on any doubts as to the personal integrity of state judges but simply recognition of the institutional limitations under which state judges operate:

> State judges popularly elected may have difficulty resisting popular pressures not experienced by federal judges given lifetime tenure designed to immunize them from such influences, and the federal habeas statutes reflect the congressional judgment that such detached federal review is a salutary safeguard * * *.[24]

Other Supreme Court justices, however, have questioned the assumption that institutional factors render state judges less receptive to federal constitutional claims than federal judges. Justice O'Connor has noted, for example, that many states utilize merit selection systems (e.g., the Missouri Plan) that gives state judges security against "majoritorian pressures" comparable to that provided by the life tenure afforded federal judges.[25] In any event, it is argued, the Court should not downgrade, on the basis of largely speculative impressions, the obligation of state judges to uphold federal law. The appropriate assumption, it is argued, is that adopted by the Supreme Court in *Stone v. Powell.* The Court there noted:

> Despite differences in institutional environment and the unsympathetic attitude to federal constitutional claims of some state judges in years past, we are unwilling to assume that there now exists a general lack of appropriate sensitivity to constitutional rights in the trial and appellate courts of the several States. * * * [T]here is "no intrinsic reason why the fact that a man is a federal judge should make him more competent, or conscientious, or learned with respect to the [consideration of Fourth Amendment claims] than his neighbor in the state courthouse.[26]

The costs of expansive federal habeas review, especially as to state cases, have been discussed at length in the opinions of various justices, but most of these discussions build on

24. Stone v. Powell, supra note 15 (dissenting opinion). Commentators point to various other factors that allegedly make state judges less disposed to enforce constitutional claims. These include the state judge's "proximity to the state's enforcement of its criminal law" and differing "psychological attitudinal characteristics" (e.g., that federal courts tend to reflect a "utopian perspective" while state courts tend to reflect a "pragmatic perspective").

25. O'Connor, Trends in the Relationship Between the Federal and State Courts From the Perspective of a State Court Judge, 22 Wm. & Mary L.Rev. 801, 812–15 (1981) (written prior to her appointment to the Supreme Court, but reflecting a viewpoint reiterated in her opinions, see e.g., Engle v. Isaac, infra note 27).

26. Stone v. Powell, supra note 15, at n. 35, quoting Bator, Finality in Criminal Law and Federal Habeas Corpus for State Prisoners, 76 Harv.L.Rev. 441 (1963).

arguments advanced initially by Justice Powell.[27] He stressed primarily three cost-factors. First, broad habeas review is said to result in an unwise expenditure of scarce judicial resources. Second, systematic habeas review of state decisions is said to be inconsistent with the "constitutional balance upon which the doctrine of federalism is founded." Finally, plenary habeas review is said to work against the important objective of achieving a rational point of finality in the criminal justice process.

Over the past decade the federal courts have borne the burden of ruling each year upon roughly 9,000–10,000 habeas petitions file by state prisoners. These petitions constitute roughly 5% of the total civil docket of federal trial courts and almost 10% of the total docket of the courts of appeals. Moreover, with the prison population rapidly expanding, that share of the caseload is seen as likely to increase in the future. Justice Powell argued that such a significant expenditure of the finite resources of the federal judiciary would be more wisely devoted to other portions of the federal docket. In requiring federal courts to perform a task that "has or should have been done before," habeas review necessarily detracts from their ability to promptly and carefully respond to the "call on federal courts both in civil actions * * * which affect intimately the lives of greater numbers of people and in original criminal trials and appeals." Indeed it has been argued that the failure to restrict the scope of habeas works against even that small class of state prisoners for whom habeas review may be necessary to ensure a full and fair opportunity for litigation of their constitutional claim. Thus, Justice Jackson, commenting upon a "progressive trivialization of the writ" that could "inundate the dockets of the lower courts," warned that "he who must search a haystack for a needle is likely to end up with the attitude that the needle is not worth the search."[28] Habeas relief, it is noted, typically has been granted in less than 4% of all petitions filed and an even smaller percentage of petitioners gain release from custody.[29]

Proponents of broad review argue that the burden imposed upon the federal courts is exaggerated. They note that evidentiary hearings are held on less than 2% of the petitions filed, as compared to a higher trial rate for civil cases in general. Moreover, they argue, the burden imposed is justified by the importance of the quest. Thus, Justice Schaeffer of Illinois, responding to Justice Jackson's comment, noted: "It is not a needle we are looking for in these stacks of papers, but the rights of a human being." [30]

Justice Powell has further characterized expansive federal habeas review as "tend[ing] to undermine the values inherent in our federal system of government." State appellate courts naturally resent the review of their decisions by federal district judges (who may, in turn, rely heavily on the factfinding of a United States magistrate). But the harm is said to extend beyond the promotion of friction between the state and federal judiciaries. There is concern that the state courts will become "so frustrated with the extent of federal court intervention that they [will] simply abdicate in favor of the federal jurisdiction." Yet, with only a small percentage of all state defendants likely to seek federal habeas corpus review, the primary protection of constitutional rights must come from a state judiciary that has a strong sense of responsibility for performing that function.

Proponents of broad habeas review argue that the "federalism costs" of habeas review have largely dissipated as state courts have become accustomed to such review. Moreover, they see no sound basis for state court resentment insofar as it still exists. Resentful state courts, they argue, have simply failed to appreciate the realities of federal

27. See Schneckloth v. Bustamonte, supra note 14 (concurring opinion); Stone v. Powell, supra note 15; Rose v. Mitchell, 443 U.S. 545, 99 S.Ct. 2993, 61 L.Ed.2d 739 (1979) (concurring opinion). See also Engle v. Isaac, 456 U.S. 107, 102 S.Ct. 1558, 71 L.Ed.2d 783 (1972).

28. Brown v. Allen, supra note 23.

29. The percentage is much higher, however, in capital cases. See § 11.1 following note 19.

30. Schaefer, Federalism and State Criminal Procedure, 70 Harv.L.Rev. 1, 25 (1956).

habeas practice. The proponents note that "district court reversal of the considered and thoughtful decisions of the state's highest courts rarely occurs in actual practice." Even then, the responsibility for the reversal ordinarily lies not only with the single district judge, but also with the federal appellate court that has affirmed the district court's ruling on appeal. Indeed, it is even argued that federal habeas review has had a positive impact on federal-state relations. It is said to have encouraged a useful dialogue between federal and state courts, with each learning from the other. Finally, the proponents note, even if friction is inevitable, an unjustly incarcerated prisoner should not have his liberty sacrificed on the altar of improving federal-state relations.

Justice Powell also cites among the costs of broad habeas review its detrimental impact upon those interests underlying the achievement in the criminal justice process of a definite point of finality. Deterrence depends upon the expectation that one violating the law will swiftly and certainly be subject to punishment, but the reopening of convictions through habeas corpus is said to cast doubt upon the judicial system's ability to achieve that objective. Society can rightfully question, it is argued, whether broad habeas review does not invite defendants to postpone presentation of their claims to that point at which a successful petition cannot feasibly be followed by reprosecution. Justice Powell notes further that broad habeas review undercuts the need "at some point [for] the law * * * to convey to those in custody that a wrong has been committed, that consequent punishment has been imposed, that one should no longer look back with the view to resurrecting every imaginable basis for further litigation but rather should look forward to rehabilitation and to becoming a constructive citizen." Expansive habeas review is also said to undercut society's need to reach a point of repose, where it can say that the system has gone far enough and one can now safely assume that "justice has been done."

Proponents of expansive habeas review do not quarrel with the basic objectives of finality, but claim that the adverse impact of habeas review upon those objectives is grossly exaggerated. While there is delay in final disposition, the length of that delay is substantially less than might be suggested by occasional cases in which relief is granted many years after the initial conviction. Rehabilitation is an objective about which we know far too little to warrant firm judgments as to the impact of offering the prisoner a further opportunity for litigation. Broad habeas review is praised as serving an interest that is more important than a too readily achieved sense of repose—providing the "appearance of just imposition of punishment" that is an essential "component of public confidence and respect for the criminal justice system."

(f) Competing Models of Habeas Review. How should the Court balance the costs and benefits of habeas review that are discussed above? Over the years, majority, dissenting, and concurring opinions have offered a variety of answers. Ordinarily, those opinions have dealt only with a single aspect of habeas review, but the combined opinions of any particular justice usually has put forth a consistent overall theory or model of habeas review. To some extent, each of those models has varied with the particular justice, but they also have tended to reflect, in general, one or another of a small group of distinct (but not always conflicting) theories regarding the appropriate role of habeas review. The basic contours of those theories are set forth below.

Ensuring responsible state court adjudication of constitutional rights. Perhaps the narrowest of the models of habeas review still exerting considerable influence is that which views habeas jurisdiction as a backstop measure designed to ensure that state judges "toe the constitutional mark." Under this view, the primary function of habeas review is to ensure that the state judicial systems fulfill their obligation to apply in a responsible manner the prevailing constitutional doctrine. Such a model, supplemented by the traditional review of jurisdictional defects, furnished the foundation for the standards that governed habeas review for a good part of the first half of this century. Utilizing what was later described as a "due process" approach to habeas review, those standards looked basically to whether the state process had afforded the habeas petitioner an adequate opportunity to gain a fair determination of his constitutional claim.

By the 1960's, however, federal habeas review clearly had moved beyond such a due process model. A state court could provide meaningful review of a defendant's constitutional claim only to have the conviction it affirmed overturned by a federal habeas court that took a different view of a Supreme Court precedent. A state could provide an adequate procedure for review of a constitutional claim, the defendant could fail to use that procedure, and a habeas court might still be required, or at least have discretion, to consider that claim.[31] This almost complete rejection of the due process model did not last very long, however. Today, that model exerts considerable influence. The Court gives greater deference to state procedural rules[32]; it refuses altogether to consider Fourth Amendment claims if the state procedure granted a defendant a "full and fair opportunity for litigating the claim"[33]; and for most constitutional claims, it allows the federal habeas court to reject a state court's constitutional interpretation only if that interpretation is not reasonably debatable.[34] Thus, the state's provision of an adequate process for gaining a fair determination of a constitutional claim has returned as an important factor in limiting habeas review, although it generally is not the single controlling factor that it would be under a strict due process model.

Vindicating federal constitutional rights in a federal forum. Certainly the broadest model of habeas review was that espoused by Justice Brennan. In his view, the function of the writ, simply put, was to provide a "prompt and efficacious remedy" for the denial of constitutional rights. This required the "fullest opportunity for plenary federal review." The foundation for providing that opportunity included (i) an expansive notion of custody that would make the writ available to defendants not incarcerated; (ii) a writ that took cognizance of all constitutional errors; (iii) the complete rejection of "conventional notions of finality"; and (iv) a tolerance for procedural irregularity, provided that the defendant's failure in this regard was not a product of purposeful abuse of the judicial process. Justice Brennan recognized certain grounds that would justify denying habeas review, but they were few and not jurisdictional in nature. The basic philosophy, in sum, was that set forth by Court of Appeals Judge Lay:

> We would not send two astronauts to the moon without providing them with at least three or four back-up systems. Should we send literally thousands of men to prison with even less reserves? * * * [W]ith knowledge of our fallibility and a realization of past errors, we can hardly insure our confidence by creating an irrevocable end to the guilt determining process.[35]

The model espoused by Justice Brennan is basically a model of the past, although it retains some current influence. A series of majority opinions in the 1960's, mostly authored by Justice Brennan, laid the foundation for this "rights vindication/federal forum" model. However, first Congress imposed a partial barrier to full implementation of the model in its 1966 amendment to the Habeas Act[36] and then a Supreme Court of changed composition began in the 1970's to either withdraw from, or substantially modify most of those cornerstone rulings of the 1960's.[37]

Surrogate Supreme Courts. Another model of federal habeas review sees the federal habeas courts as exercising primarily a quasi-appellate review function and thereby serving

31. See e.g., Brown v. Allen and Fay v. Noia, discussed in §§ 28.3(b), 28.4(d) and 28.6(a).

32. See § 28.4(e), (f).

33. See Stone v. Powell, discussed in § 28.3(b), (d).

34. See Teague v. Lane, discussed in § 28.6.

35. Lay, Modern Administrative Proposals for Federal Habeas Corpus, 21 DePaul L.Rev. 701, 709–10 (1972).

36. See § 28.7.

37. See §§ 28.4(d); 28.5(c); 28.6. The broad custody rulings, however, remain intact. See notes 17–19 supra.

as a replacement for a Supreme Court that can review only a small fraction of all petitions for certiorari presented to it. This model too sees the Habeas Act as designed to provide a federal forum for the final determination of federal constitutional rights, but the focus is not so much on ensuring that there is a vindication of those rights in each and every case as it is upon federal court development and interpretation of federal constitutional guarantees. Thus, in common with the Supreme Court and its exercise of appellate review, federal habeas courts, under this model, will give considerable attention to the concerns of comity and procedural efficiency. The habeas court must recognize that what it is reviewing is a state court judgment, and where that judgment rests adequately on a determination of state law (such as a procedural forfeiture of the claim under state law), the habeas court, like the Supreme Court on direct review, will not reach behind that state ruling to consider the merits of the constitutional claim.

The "surrogate model" finds its strongest support in *Brown v. Allen,* and *Daniels v. Allen,* companion decisions of the 1950's.[38] It was pushed aside by the opinions of the 1960's, but certain limitations reflected in the model made a reappearance in the 1970's in an altered form. Supreme Court review of a state conviction will come fairly promptly after the conviction, but that will not necessarily be the case with federal habeas review. One concern reflected in the Court's post-1960's decisions is the consequence of habeas review of "stale" defense claims. As Justice O'Connor noted for the Court in *Engle v. Isaac*[39]:

> [W]rits of habeas corpus frequently cost society the right to punish admitted offenders. Passage of time, erosion of memory, and dispersion of witnesses may render retrial difficult, even impossible. While a habeas writ may, in theory, entitle the defendant only to retrial, in practice it may reward the accused with complete freedom from prosecution.

Partially meeting this concern, current habeas standards often operator to foreclose consideration of a claim because of unjustified defense delay in raising that claim, although those standards hardly require the promptness in presentation that might follow from a strict adherence to a surrogate model. Supreme Court review of a state conviction, in its refusal to consider the merits of a claim rejected by the state courts on the basis of an adequate state ground, also reflects respect for state procedural rules governing the raising of claims. To the extent that current habeas standards frown upon review of claims that state courts have held to be procedurally forfeited they may again be viewed as strongly influenced by values drawn from a surrogate model.[40]

The "fundamental fairness" model. Justice Stevens, in a series of separate opinions in the key habeas cases of the 1980's,[41] advanced what has come to be known as the "fundamental fairness" model of habeas review. Although that model has never received majority support, it advanced two important concepts that are a part of current habeas doctrine. Justice Stevens position was that "constitutional errors are not fungible," at least with respect to remedies. Just as there are some errors that call for reversal on appeal only if deemed not to have been harmless and some that call for automatic reversal, there are some errors "important enough" to require reversal on direct appeal but not to require the overturning of a conviction collat-

38. See § 28.3 at note 13, discussing *Brown,* and § 28.4 at note 7, discussing *Daniels.*

39. Supra note 27.

40. Other aspects of current habeas law, however, are flatly inconsistent with the surrogate model. See e.g., § 28.6 (discussing the habeas standard of review applied to the state court's interpretation of constitutional requirements) and § 28.3(b) (discussing the Stone v. Powell limitation on cognizable claims). Moreover, even as to those aspects arguably influenced by the model, the fit is far from perfect. Thus, recognition of state procedural forfeitures is subject to limitations that would not apply on direct review by the Supreme Court. On habeas review, certain claims are exempted from procedural forfeitures, see § 28.4(g), and the standard governing the excuse of forfeitures extends beyond the standard for judging the adequacy of a state ground on direct review, see § 28.4(c), (e). See also § 28.7(c) as to the treatment of state findings of fact

41. See e.g., Justice Stevens' opinions in Rose v. Lunday, 455 U.S. 509, 102 S.Ct. 1198, 71 L.Ed.2d 379 (1982); Wainwright v. Sykes, supra note 22; Engle v. Isaac, supra note 27; Teague v. Lane, supra note 34.

erally and some errors so significant that they should be recognized on habeas review under almost any circumstance. In this latter category, Justice Stevens placed "errors so fundamental that they infect the validity of the underlying judgment itself, or the integrity by which that judgment was obtained." Justice Stevens acknowledged that this category of error could not be "precisely defined," but pointed to the "classic" due process or "fundamental fairness" grounds for issuance of the writ, such as a trial dominated by mob violence, the prosecutor's knowing use of perjured testimony, and the admission of a confession "extorted from the defendant by brutal methods."

A key component of the fundamental fairness model is its willingness to draw distinctions between different types of constitutional claims. The Court majority has accepted this premise in its treatment of procedural forfeitures, the retroactive application of rulings that impose "new" constitutional restraints, and the basic range of issues cognizable on habeas review—although it has refused in each area to use the fundamental fairness yardstick urged by Justice Stevens.[42] While the federal habeas statute does not by its terms distinguish between different constitutional violations, such a distinction is seen as consistent with the historical use of the habeas remedy. Indeed, support for the particular distinction urged by Justice Stevens is found in the fact that the Congress that adopted the 1867 Act, and even the Congress that incorporated the substance of that Act in the 1948 revision of the habeas statutes, did so within a then prevailing constitutional law framework that made "fundamental fairness" the touchstone for determining whether a state had violated a defendant's constitutional rights.[43] But of even more significance, at least from the perspective of current habeas law, is that aspect of Justice Stevens' rationale that grounded the distinction among constitutional errors in the law of remedies rather than in a general hierarchical ranking of constitutional guarantees. As Justice Stevens put the issue, the process of distinguishing between rights on habeas review no more classifies certain constitutional rights as second class than does the process of drawing distinctions between constitutional rights in harmless error analysis or in fashioning various other aspects of remedial law (e.g., impeachment use of the fruits of a violation).[44] It is this reasoning that largely underlies the drawing of distinctions among constitutional errors by the current Supreme Court majority.

For Justice Stevens, the nature of the constitutional error would override almost all of the various procedural restrictions that attach to federal habeas law. Thus, while Justice Stevens accepted the general validity of extreme caution in considering claims that were not raised at trial (in part on the premise that the tardiness in their presentation suggests in itself their likely irrelevance), he was willing to push aside even weighty state interests in procedural regularity when a clear denial of fundamental fairness was presented. Here too, although the Court majority has not accepted Justice Stevens' fundamental fairness doctrine, it has adopted the basic premise that procedural bars are not absolute. Certain claims will prevail over limits that would otherwise bar habeas review, although those claims are largely defined by another model of habeas review, which looks to the protection of the innocent.

Protection of the "innocent". In 1969, Justice Black, in a brief dissent from a majority ruling granting collateral relief based on a Fourth Amendment violation, noted: "I would always require that the convicted defendant raise the kind of constitutional claim that casts some shadow of a doubt on his guilt."[45] This comment was expanded upon in a highly influential article by Judge Henry Friendly, with the provocative title *"Is Inno-*

42. See e.g., the rejection of this standard in Teague v. Lane, as discussed in § 28.6(c).

43. See §§ 2.4, 2.5.

44. See §§ 27.6(d), 9.6.

45. Kaufman v. United States, 394 U.S. 217, 89 S.Ct. 1068, 22 L.Ed.2d 227 (1969) (Black, J., dissenting).

cence Irrelevant?".[46] Judge Friendly argued that "with a few important exceptions," [47] "convictions should be subject to collateral attack only when the prisoner supplements his constitutional plea with a colorable claim of innocence." There were distinctions in the manner in which Judge Friendly and Justice Black would have used habeas review as a safety net for the innocent. Justice Black apparently would have focused on the general nature of the constitutional claim, asking whether its basic function is to protect the innocent by safeguarding the reliability of the guilt determining process. Judge Friendly, on the other hand, would have focused on actual factual innocence. The defendant would have to show a possible factual innocence that may have gone unrecognized due to constitutional violation that affected the determination of guilt. In 1973, in a highly influential concurring opinion for four justices, Justice Powell lent support to both the Black and Friendly positions in arguing against granting habeas relief based on Fourth Amendment violations.[48]

The model of habeas review as a safety net for the innocent has now been incorporated into various aspects of habeas law. It has not, however, become the exclusive theme of habeas review. Relief can be obtained on various constitutional claims that do not cast any doubt on the factual accuracy of the verdict, and habeas review remains focused on the question of whether a constitutional right was violated, not whether the defendant was in fact innocent. Even a convicted defendant who now has conclusive proof of his innocence cannot gain habeas relief in the absence of some constitutional violation in the state proceedings. On the other hand, that a claim goes to factfinding reliability is critical in determining whether a habeas court can adopt a "new" constitutional ruling; [49] a claim of actual factual innocence will allow for habeas review notwithstanding a procedural forfeiture or abuse of the habeas writ that would otherwise bar review; [50] and certain aspects of innocence are likely to have a bearing on whether the "ends of justice" justify reconsideration of a constitutional claim that was raised in a prior habeas petition.[51] So too, the Court's holding in *Stone v. Powell* that Fourth Amendment claims ordinarily are not cognizable on habeas review relates in part to the fact that Fourth Amendment violations have no bearing on the reliability of a guilt determination.[52]

The mixing of models. Current law, as the above discussion indicates, does not exclusively follow any of the models described above. Rather, it contains elements, sometimes inconsistent, taken from several different models. In part, this is a product of stare decisis. Although the Court has been especially open to shifts in position in this area of the law, and that has produced considerable twisting and turning in doctrinal development, there remains some reluctance to wipe the slate clean and start all over again. Thus, the tendency has been to withdraw the cornerstones of a particular model while somehow preserving some aspects of its structure. The tendency also is to hold sacrosanct a traditional element of the writ (e.g., the special treatment of jurisdictional defects) even though that element may not readily fit within any of the currently dominant models of habeas review. The "mixed" content of current habeas law may also be a product of a failure of any single model to capture the full support of a majority of the Court over at least the past two decades. With the members of the Court likely to approach any particular habeas issue

46. Friendly, Is Innocence Irrelevant? Collateral Attack or Criminal Judgments, 38 U.Chi.L.Rev. 142 (1970).

47. Those exceptions were: (1) the claim went to the jurisdiction of the convicting court, establishing that it lacked authority to proceed (a traditional ground for habeas review); (2) the claim was based on facts "dehors the record" which were "not open to consideration and review on appeal"; or (3) the state failed to provide a proper procedure for advancing the claim in the state proceeding. See Friendly, supra note 46.

48. Schneckloth v. Bustamonte, 412 U.S. 218, 93 S.Ct. 2041, 36 L.Ed.2d 854 (1973). See § 28.3(b).

49. See § 28.6(c).

50. See §§ 28.4(g); 28.5(b).

51. See § 28.5(a).

52. See § 28.3(b).

from several different perspectives, the result often may be determined by the convergence, as they apply to the particular situation, of somewhat inconsistent philosophies favored by different justices. This leads, in turn, to majority opinions that are likely to be interpreted quite differently in future cases even by those justices who joined the opinion, and to shifts in the alignment of the justices to produce a differently composed majority and a different position of convergence in a slightly different situation.

§ 28.3 Cognizable Claims

(a) Constitutional–Jurisdictional Defects. For over a century, first under the 1789 Act and later under the 1867 Act, Supreme Court rulings limited federal habeas review for convicted prisoners to those constitutional claims that challenged the jurisdiction of the court of conviction. While federal habeas review is no longer so limited, the Court's development of the concept of a constitutional-jurisdictional defect during that period remains important. In some states, the common law writ is still tied to jurisdictional defects, and state courts may look to the early Supreme Court decisions in determining the scope of that limitation. More significantly, the inclusion of jurisdictional defects remains the common starting point in the current interpretation of the scope of the federal writ. Whatever the changes in the writ's scope that may be made in the future, the inclusion of jurisdictional defects appears to be a "given" (although the definition of a jurisdictional defect does not). In addition, as noted at the end of this subsection, at least certain types of jurisdictional defects continue to receive special treatment in certain aspects of habeas law.

That the earliest Supreme Court rulings looked only to jurisdictional defects is not surprising in light of the history of the English common law writ. As described in § 28.-1(b), the common law writ was aimed basically at illegal pretrial custody; its use generally was thought to be barred by a judgment of conviction, since that judgment, on its face, established the legality of continuing custody. Accordingly, to make the writ available in a postconviction setting, it had to be established that there could be no true judgment of a court and therefore no bar to habeas review. This required reliance on the principle that any judgment was "void," and not truly a judgment at all, where issued by a court that lacked jurisdiction over either the subject matter or the person. Consistent with this very limited principal, the Supreme Court initially took a narrow view of what constituted a jurisdictional defect. In *Ex parte Watkins,*[1] the Court refused to review on habeas a federal prisoner's claim that his conviction was obtained on an indictment that failed to state a crime. Chief Justice Marshall's opinion for the Court noted: "A judgment * * * concludes the subject on which it is rendered" and "puts an end to inquiry" unless "that judgment be an absolute nullity," but "it is not a nullity if the [trial] court has general jurisdiction of the subject, although it should be erroneous." As long as the petitioner's conviction was rendered by a court of competent jurisdiction, his detention was not "illegal" for purposes of habeas corpus.

In 1873, in *Ex parte Lange,*[2] the Court initiated what has been described as "a long process of expansion of the concept of a lack of jurisdiction." Lange contended that he had been twice sentenced for the same offense, in violation of the Fifth Amendment's double jeopardy clause, when he had been resentenced to a term of imprisonment after having paid the fine originally imposed. Carefully disclaiming the use of habeas as a writ of error, the Supreme Court ordered Lange released from imprisonment because the lower court's jurisdiction terminated upon the satisfaction of the original sentence. The *Lange* ruling was extended in *Ex parte Wilson*[3] to a defendant who challenged his sentence on the ground it imposed punishment for an "infamous" crime even though he had not been

§ 28.3

1. 28 U.S. (3 Pet.) 193, 7 L.Ed. 650 (1830).

2. 85 U.S. (18 Wall.) 163, 21 L.Ed. 872 (1873).

3. 114 U.S. 417, 5 S.Ct. 935, 29 L.Ed. 89 (1885).

indicted by a grand jury as the Fifth Amendment required for all infamous offenses. Both *Lange* and *Wilson* stressed the trial court's lack of power to impose a sentence beyond its jurisdictional authority, rather than the constitutional character of the petitioners' claims. Accordingly, during the same period, when a federal prisoner sought habeas relief on the ground that he had been retried in violation of the double jeopardy clause, the Court held his claim was not cognizable on a habeas challenge since a trial court obviously had jurisdiction to determine whether a retrial was permissible.[4]

Ex parte Siebold,[5] decided in 1879, produced another doctrinal expansion of the concept of a jurisdictional defect. The Court held there that a prisoner could properly raise on habeas corpus the claim that the statute under which he was convicted violated the federal constitution. If the petitioner was correct in his claim, the Court noted, then "the foundation of the whole proceeding" would be affected. Since "an unconstitutional law is void and is as no law," a "conviction obtained under it is not merely erroneous, but is illegal and void." The trial court's authority to try the petitioners "arose solely upon these laws," so if the "laws were unconstitutional and void," the trial court "acquired no jurisdiction of the causes." The Court did not explain why a trial court had jurisdiction when double jeopardy barred a retrial or an indictment failed to state an offense, but lacked jurisdiction when it erroneously concluded that the statute underlying the indictment was constitutional. The unconstitutional statute could more readily be seen, perhaps, as affecting "the foundation" of the proceeding under the prevailing legal analysis of the times.

Frank v. Mangum[6] and *Moore v. Dempsey,*[7] decided in 1915 and 1923, have occasionally been viewed as cases that departed from the jurisdictional limitation, but they also can be read as having simply extended the analysis of *Siebold.* Both cases involved claims of a mob-dominated trial, and the majority opinions in both suggested that such a claim went to the "jurisdiction" of the trial court. The Court in *Frank* noted that the writ would only lie "where the judgment under which the prisoner is detained is shown to be absolutely void for want of jurisdiction in the court that pronounced it, either because such jurisdiction was absent at the beginning or because it was lost in the course of the proceedings." It also accepted, however, petitioner's contention that his claim would fall within the loss-of-jurisdiction category since mob domination would "in effect wrought a dissolution of the [trial] court, so that the proceedings were *coram non judice.*" In *Moore,* the Court similarly noted that, where the "proceeding is a mask," with the "counsel, jury, and judge * * * swept to the fatal end by an irresistible wave of public passion," the trial becomes "absolutely void."

In *Johnson v. Zerbst,*[8] Justice Black's opinion for the Court expanded upon the "loss-of-jurisdiction" analysis of *Frank* and *Moore.* The petitioner in *Johnson,* a federal prisoner, claimed that his conviction had been obtained in violation of the Sixth Amendment because the trial judge had failed to provide him with appointed counsel. Justice Black concluded that such a defect was cognizable on habeas review. He reasoned:

> Since the Sixth Amendment constitutionally entitles one charged with crime to the assistance of counsel, compliance with this constitutional mandate is an essential jurisdictional prerequisite to a federal court's authority to deprive an accused of his life or liberty. * * * A court's jurisdiction at the beginning of trial may be lost "in the course of the proceedings" [quoting *Frank*] due to failure to complete the court—as the Sixth Amendment requires—by providing counsel for an accused. * * * If this requirement of the Sixth Amendment is

4. In re Bigelow, 113 U.S. 328, 5 S.Ct. 542, 28 L.Ed. 1005 (1885).

5. 100 U.S. (10 Otto) 371, 25 L.Ed. 717 (1879).

6. 237 U.S. 309, 35 S.Ct. 582, 59 L.Ed. 969 (1915). See also the discussion following note 12 infra.

7. 261 U.S. 86, 43 S.Ct. 265, 67 L.Ed. 543 (1923).

8. 304 U.S. 458, 58 S.Ct. 1019, 82 L.Ed. 1461 (1938). See § 11.1, at note 3.

not complied with, the court no longer has jurisdiction to proceed.

Four years after *Johnson v. Zerbst,* the Court faced on habeas review a constitutional claim that it could not so readily characterize as undermining the structure of the proceeding and therefore causing the trial court to "lose jurisdiction." In *Waley v. Johnston,*[9] the petitioner claimed that his guilty plea had been coerced by an F.B.I. agent. In a per curiam opinion, the Court concluded that petitioner's claim was subject to habeas review:

> The facts relied on are dehors the record and their effect on the judgment was not open to consideration and review on appeal. In such circumstances the use of the writ in the federal courts to test the constitutional validity of a conviction for crime is not restricted to those cases where the judgment of conviction is void for want of jurisdiction of the trial court to render it. It extends also to those exceptional cases where the conviction has been in disregard of the constitutional rights of the accused, and where the writ is the only effective means of preserving his rights.

As various commentators have noted, *Waley* "finally dispensed with" the touchstone of jurisdiction that had been carried to "fictional extremes" in cases such as *Frank, Moore,* and *Johnson.*

Subsequent Supreme Court rulings dealing with the scope of habeas review have not looked to whether the claimed defect deprived the trial court of its authority to proceed. However, in a series of recent cases determining what claims may be raised on habeas following a valid plea of guilty, the Court has utilized a concept that incorporates a major feature of the jurisdictional defect principle as it existed prior to *Frank, Moore,* and *Johnson.* The cognizable claims in this context have been limited to "incurable" defects that deprived the trial court of its authority to proceed notwithstanding the valid guilty plea (such as a double jeopardy violation that barred the prosecution under which the plea was taken).[10] So too, in deciding whether a habeas court can adopt a "new ruling" expanding a constitutional protection, the Court looks to the nature of the constitutional defect recognized in the ruling and one of the two allowable categories encompasses at least one strand of what traditionally were viewed as jurisdictional defects.[11]

(b) Constitutional Claims in General: From *Brown v. Allen* to *Stone v. Powell.* While *Waley* put to rest the jurisdictional-defect limitation, it did not go so far as to hold that all constitutional claims were subject to habeas review. The Court had stressed that petitioner's claim rested on facts dehors the record. It was not the type of claim that petitioner could readily have raised in the original proceeding that produced his conviction or on appeal. On the other hand, where the claim could have been raised and fully litigated in the original state proceedings, allowing for possible direct review by the Supreme Court, there remained a possible standard derived from different treatments of the same type of claim in *Frank v. Mangum* and *Moore v. Dempsey.*[12] *Frank* had denied relief on defendant's claim of a mob-dominated trial since that claim had been fully presented in the state court system and had there been held to be groundless. This state review procedure, the *Frank* majority had noted, gave the defendant all the process he was due and the federal habeas court should not interfere. *Moore,* on the other hand, had ordered the habeas court to conduct a hearing on petitioner's claim of a mob-dominated trial. The defendant Moore had not received the same extensive review of his claim in the state courts that had been obtained by Frank, but it was not clear from the *Moore* opinion whether its ruling was to be tied to this factor or whether *Frank* was to be viewed as a largely abandoned precedent. Thus, it was still possible to argue after *Waley* that a detention was not subject to habeas review if based upon the judgment of a competent state court which had afforded a full corrective process for the litigation of petitioner's consti-

9. 316 U.S. 101, 62 S.Ct. 964, 86 L.Ed. 1302 (1942).

10. See § 21.6(a).

11. See § 28.6(c).

12. See notes 6 and 7 supra.

tutional claim. It was not until 1953, in *Brown v. Allen,*[13] that the Court flatly rejected that position.

At issue in *Brown* was whether a federal habeas court could review two constitutional claims—jury discrimination and admission of a coerced confession—that had been fully litigated and decided against the petitioner in the state courts. There were two separate opinions for the Court because of a division on the weight to be given to the Supreme Court's denial of certiorari in the earlier proceedings (with the majority stating that the habeas court should give it no weight). Except for Justice Jackson, the Court was in agreement that the habeas court should consider and render its own independent judgment on the merits of petitioner's claims, notwithstanding the state adjudication. While the state court rulings were entitled to the same respect ordinarily given to opinions of a court of another jurisdiction, they did not preclude federal review of those claims on a habeas application. The habeas court could rely on the state court's findings of fact (unless there was a vital flaw in the latter's factfinding procedures), but it was required to "exercise its own independent judgment" as to the legal consequences of those facts. This mandate, Justice Frankfurter argued in one of the lead opinions, followed from the purposes of the 1867 Act. Simply put, that Act gave to federal courts the "final say" on federal claims. Congress had "seen fit" to "give to the lower federal courts power to inquire into federal claims, by way of habeas corpus," and it therefore would be "inadmissible to deny the use of the writ merely because a State court had passed on a federal constitutional issue." The habeas writ guaranteed federal review of the petitioner's federal claim, not simply a fair state consideration of the claim, for such consideration "may have misconceived a federal constitutional right."

In *Fay v. Noia,*[14] the Supreme Court reaffirmed and defended its *Brown* decision. Responding to criticism that *Brown* had constituted a departure from past precedent, Justice Brennan's majority opinion traced the history of the writ from the common law through earlier Supreme Court decisions. The majority concluded that the writ had always been available "to remedy any kind of governmental restraint contrary to fundamental law" (as evidenced, in particular, by *Bushell's Case*[15]), and that objective logically encompassed detention imposed pursuant to a conviction that had been obtained in violation of the defendant's constitutional rights. *Brown* accordingly had been consistent with the "historic office of The Great Writ," as well as the language of the federal habeas provisions, in holding that all constitutional claims were cognizable under the writ, without regard to their relationship to the trial court's jurisdiction or the full litigation of the claim in the state proceedings.

Since *Noia,* like *Brown,* involved a constitutional claim presented by a state prisoner, the question remained as to whether the collateral remedy for federal prisoners (28 U.S.C.A. § 2255) would also encompass the full range of constitutional claims. The language of § 2255 was similar to that of § 2254, and the purpose of § 2255 was simply to provide federal prisoners with a procedurally more convenient counterpart to the habeas writ, but there had been considerable discussion in *Brown* about the congressional objective of giving the "final say" on federal claims to federal courts. The federal prisoner, of course, had the opportunity to have his claim reviewed initially by federal courts. If the key to the *Brown* opinion was the need for a federal review of the state ruling, then there was no need to allow federal prisoners to raise claims that were considered (or could have been considered) in their original federal proceedings. On the other hand, if the focus was on the historic function of the writ as described in *Fay v. Noia*—the need to always keep open to review the possibility that a person was being detained in violation of his fundamental rights—then § 2255, like § 2254, would extend to all constitutional

13. 344 U.S. 443, 73 S.Ct. 397, 97 L.Ed. 469 (1953).

14. 372 U.S. 391, 83 S.Ct. 822, 9 L.Ed.2d 837 (1963).

15. See § 28.1, at note 4.

claims. In *Kaufman v. United States,*[16] the Court adopted the latter view of the purpose of the federal collateral remedies. Justice Brennan, speaking for the Court, reasoned that § 2255, like the habeas writ for state prisoners, "rests * * * fundamentally upon a recognition that adequate protection of constitutional rights relating to the criminal trial process requires the continuing availability of a mechanism for relief."

Dissenting in *Kaufman,* Justice Black did not quarrel with the majority's conclusion that the scope of collateral attack under § 2255 should be "substantially the same [as] in federal habeas corpus cases." He maintained that the majority had erred, however, in extending habeas review to the constitutional claim presented in that case, the admission at trial of evidence allegedly obtained through an unconstitutional search and seizure. *Brown* and *Noia,* Justice Black argued, should not be read as "lay[ing] down an inflexible rule compelling the courts to release every prisoner who alleges in collateral proceedings some constitutional flaw, regardless of its nature, regardless of his guilt or innocence, and regardless of the circumstances of the case." Since the "great historic role of the writ * * * has been to ensure that reliability of the guilt-determining process," it was appropriate to give weight to the relationship of the constitutional error to "the element of probable or possible innocence."

Four years later, in *Schneckloth v. Bustamonte,*[17] four concurring justices expressed agreement with the general thrust of Justice Black's *Kaufman* dissent. In a widely noted opinion, Justice Powell argued that a "nonguilt-related claim," such as the admission at trial of unconstitutionally seized evidence, should not be considered on collateral attack, provided "the petitioner was provided a fair opportunity to raise and have adjudicated the question in state courts." Justice Powell contended that this conclusion was supported by the underlying function of the Fourth Amendment exclusionary rule, recognition of the historically narrow scope of the writ as applied to persons detained pursuant to a conviction, and an appropriate balancing of the benefits and costs of habeas review.[18]

Shortly thereafter, in *Stone v. Powell,*[19] Justice Powell had his majority. By a 6–3 vote, with Justice Powell writing for the Court, *Stone* held that

> where the State has provided an opportunity for full and fair litigation of a Fourth Amendment claim, the Constitution does not require that a state prisoner be granted federal habeas corpus relief on the ground that the evidence obtained in an unconstitutional search and seizure was introduced at his trial.

Although the *Stone* opinion reached the result Justice Powell had urged in *Schneckloth,* its analysis was not as far-reaching as the *Schneckloth* concurrence. The *Stone* opinion placed greater emphasis upon the function of the exclusionary rule as opposed to the general role of federal habeas review. The Court's ruling was said to be based on a "weighing [of] the utility of the exclusionary rule against the costs of extending it to collateral review of Fourth Amendment claims." The exclusionary rule, Justice Powell noted, was not a "personal constitutional right," but a "judicially created means of effectuating rights secured by the Fourth Amendment," which had a "primary function" of deterring police illegality. Accordingly, it "has never been interpreted to proscribe the introduction of illegally seized evidence in all proceedings against all persons." Thus, the Court had previously concluded, through the application of a "balancing process," that the exclusionary rule would not "prevent the use of illegally seized evidence in grand jury proceedings" or "exclude such evidence from use for impeachment of a defendant." Applying the same "balancing process" here, it was clear that "the additional contribution, if any, of the consideration of search-and-seizure claims of state prisoners in collateral review is small in relation to the costs."

16. 394 U.S. 217, 89 S.Ct. 1068, 22 L.Ed.2d 227 (1969).

17. 412 U.S. 218, 93 S.Ct. 2041, 36 L.Ed.2d 854 (1973).

18. See § 28.2, at notes 14 and 27, and § 28.1 at note 6.

19. 428 U.S. 465, 96 S.Ct. 3037, 49 L.Ed.2d 1067 (1976).

In reaching this cost/benefit conclusion, Justice Powell proceeded from the premise that the deterrent function of the exclusionary rule was adequately served by exclusion at trial and on direct appeal. Petitioners argued that habeas review was essential because state courts might not enforce the Fourth Amendment as rigorously as federal courts, and the effectiveness of the exclusionary remedy as a deterrent therefore depended upon police awareness that "federal habeas might reveal flaws in a search or seizure that went undetected" in the state proceedings. For reasons noted previously,[20] the *Stone* opinion refused to accept such "a basic mistrust of state courts as fair and competent forums for adjudication of constitutional rights."

Turning to the other side of its cost/benefit ledger, the *Stone* opinion first noted the "costs of applying the exclusionary rule even at trial." Application of the rule necessarily "deflects the truthfinding process and often frees the guilty." While such costs were justified by the deterrence gained from applying the rule in the original proceedings, they could not be sustained by the marginal increase in deterrence that might be provided by the rule's application in a collateral proceeding. Moreover, "resort to habeas corpus, especially for purposes other than to assure that no innocent person suffers an unconstitutional loss of liberties," entailed in itself additional costs. These costs included the consumption of scarce federal judicial resources, the delayed finality of criminal proceedings, and the frustration of good-faith state court efforts to fulfill their responsibilities to honor federal constitutional rights.

Although the *Stone* majority stated that "[o]ur decision today is *not* concerned with the scope of the habeas statute as authority for litigating constitutional claims generally," [21] Justice Brennan's dissent expressed concern that the Court was laying the groundwork "for a drastic withdrawal of federal habeas jurisdiction." Many commentators shared Justice Brennan's view. *Stone* was seen as carrying the potential for at least three possible "cutbacks" in the scope of habeas review. Some commentators argued that the Court might go so far as to hold not cognizable on habeas review any claim (except possibly a jurisdictional defect) as to which the state had provided an opportunity for full and fair litigation. Other commentators, along with Justice Brennan, foresaw the possibility of excluding from habeas review, under a standard similar to that applied in *Stone,* all constitutional claims that might not be "guilt related." Finally, it was suggested that the *Stone* approach might be extended to other exclusionary requirements that are characterized as "prophylactic rules." Post–*Stone* rulings clearly rejected the first two possibilities. The third remains open.

(c) The Post–*Stone* Rulings. The Supreme Court's post-*Stone* rulings that have a bearing on the range of constitutional claims cognizable under federal habeas review can be placed into three categories. First, there are a series of cases in which the Court reached the merits of particular claims without any suggestion in the majority or dissenting opinions that the claim might not be cognizable under an extension of *Stone.* Second, in three major rulings, the Court considered and rejected contentions that particular claims should not be cognizable. Finally, in other cases, one or more opinions questioned whether a particular claim should be cognizable, but the majority found it unnecessary to reach that issue.

20. See § 28.2, at note 26.

21. In his *Stone* dissent, Justice Brennan accused the majority of somehow transforming what was a constitutional violation at trial into a non-violation on habeas review. Only such an analysis, he argued, could explain how the majority concluded that the petitioners were outside the scope of the habeas statute as persons not being held in custody in violation of their constitutional rights. The majority, however, specifically noted that it was not contending that "federal [habeas] courts lack jurisdiction over" the Fourth Amendment claims that were being excluded from review. The Court had "long recognized" that a federal habeas court, out of concern for the extraordinary nature of collateral relief, could "forego the exercise of its habeas corpus power." Section 2243 of the habeas provisions, directing the habeas court to "dispose of the matter as law and justice require," was cited as further evidence of the "equitable nature of the writ." See also § 28.2(c).

Post–*Stone* habeas decisions in which the Court considered constitutional claims on the merits, without any mention of *Stone,* cover a wide range of constitutional claims. Included are claims related to double jeopardy, defendant's presence at trial proceedings, restriction of voir dire, the improper exclusion of prospective jurors in a death penalty case, interference with defendant's right to proceed pro se, the denial of defendant's choice of counsel, improper closing argument by the prosecutor, and the use of trial testimony that arguably violated defendant's Fifth and Sixth Amendment rights. Since the question of cognizability apparently was not raised in the above cases, the assumption that the claims presented there were cognizable may be subject to reconsideration at some later point. However, with individual justices showing no hesitancy to at least note that a cognizability question existed in other cases in which the state had not raised that issue, the lack of any mention of the issue in these rulings is not without significance.

Of the three cases that dealt explicitly with the possible extension of *Stone, Jackson v. Virginia,*[22] appeared to pose the easiest issue. The question presented there was whether a federal habeas court, on a due process challenge to the sufficiency of the evidence before the state trier of fact, had to look to the *In re Winship* standard of proof beyond a reasonable doubt [23] or could utilize a lesser standard, taken from a pre-*Winship* ruling, that would hold due process violated only when the record was "wholly devoid of any relevant evidence of a crucial element of the offense charged." Since the *Winship* standard was clearly related to the reliability of the guilt-determining process, it might have been thought that there would be no doubt as to its application on habeas review. However, three dissenting justices, in an opinion by Justice Stevens, argued against its application. Justice Stevens contended that the evidentiary standard formulated by the majority was not logically compelled by *Winship* even on direct review, but he also argued that applying it on habeas review would both have an especially burdensome impact and provide little benefit to the defendant, thus presenting a situation similar to that considered in *Stone.* Responding to this contention, the majority, per Stewart, J., noted that the constitutional issue presented here was "far different" from that presented in *Stone:* "The question whether a defendant has been convicted upon inadequate evidence is central to the basic question of guilt or innocence." Habeas review would not be denied because of the alleged burden that review of the constitutional sufficiency of the evidence would place on federal habeas courts or because of concerns that such review would "increase friction between the federal and state judiciaries." Justice Stewart's analysis strongly suggested that, as applied to guilt-related claims, a showing that habeas review will carry significant costs, along the lines outlined by Justice Powell in *Schneckloth* and *Stone,* will be irrelevant.

In *Kimmelman v. Morrison,*[24] the state contended that the reasoning of *Stone* barred habeas review of a Sixth Amendment claim of ineffective assistance of counsel where counsel's incompetency lay solely in failing at trial to properly present a Fourth Amendment exclusionary rule objection to damaging evidence that had been illegally seized. Rejecting that argument, the Court held that an ineffective assistance claim is based on a separate constitutional right and therefore is cognizable even though the alleged ineffective assistance consisted of counsel's mishandling of a Fourth Amendment objection. Habeas review of such a claim, the Court reasoned, was entirely consistent with *Stone.* Such review served to vindicate the defendant's right to a fair trial within the structure of an adversary system rather than the exclusionary rule objection that counsel mishandled through his incompetency. The Court added, however, that such review imposed upon the

22. 443 U.S. 307, 99 S.Ct. 2781, 61 L.Ed.2d 560 (1979).

23. 397 U.S. 358, 90 S.Ct. 1068, 25 L.Ed.2d 368 (1970). See § 2.6 at note 40.

24. 477 U.S. 365, 106 S.Ct. 2574, 91 L.Ed.2d 305 (1986).

petitioner more demanding elements of proof than would habeas review of the Fourth Amendment claim itself. Although a "meritorious Fourth Amendment claim [would] be necessary to the success of the Sixth Amendment claim," habeas petitioners also must establish under the standard of *Strickland v. Washington* that "they have been denied a fair trial by the gross incompetence of their attorneys." [25]

The precise significance of the *Kimmelman* Court's refusal to extend *Stone* to the claim presented there was clouded by the Court's failure to explore exactly what that Sixth Amendment claim would reach. As discussed in § 11.10(d), Justice Powell's concurring opinion in *Kimmelman* suggested that the prejudice component of *Strickland* 's Sixth Amendment standard could not be satisfied where counsel's incompetency consisted only of failing to exclude reliable evidence that was adverse to his client.[26] While that analysis seemed inconsistent with much of the discussion in Justice Brennan's opinion for the Court, the majority did not speak directly to Justice Powell's analysis and issued no ruling on the prejudice issue. Thus, *Kimmelman* may be seen as a case that refused to extend *Stone* in the limited context of a constitutional claim that could not be based on the failure to keep reliable evidence from the jury. This would leave open the possibility of extending *Stone* to a large group of constitutional prohibitions that may be seen as deflecting the search for the truth.

Rose v. Mitchell,[27] in contrast, was clear in its refusal to extend *Stone* to a constitutional claim that was recognized to have no bearing on the reliability of the truth-finding process at trial. The habeas petitioner in *Mitchell* claimed that the foreman of the indicting grand jury had been selected on the basis of racial discrimination in violation of the equal protection clause of the Fourteenth Amendment. Relying largely on the analysis advanced in his concurring opinion in *Schneckloth,* Justice Powell, in dissent, argued that this claim should not be cognizable on habeas review. The defendant had been found guilty by a fairly drawn petit jury, following a fair trial, so the claim clearly did not involve the "protect[ion] of the innocent from incarceration." The historical function of the writ, Justice Powell contended, did not justify its use solely for the purpose of "furthering the general societal goal of grand jury integrity." A five-justice majority, however, disagreed.

Justice Blackmun's opinion for the *Mitchell* majority offered several reasons for not extending *Stone* to bar habeas review of grand jury discrimination claims. Initially, the Court noted that while *Stone* assumed that state courts were as capable as federal courts in dealing with Fourth Amendment claims, the same could not be said of a grand jury discrimination claim. That claim required the state bench to review its own procedures rather than the actions of police. In most cases, the trial court that initially rules on the claim will be the same court that has responsibility for the grand jury selection process. These differences, the Court noted, led it "to doubt that claims of * * * [grand jury discrimination] in general will receive the type of full and fair hearings deemed essential to the holding of *Stone.*" For similar reasons, it could not be said here, as it was said in *Stone,* that federal habeas review would have no significant "educative and deterrent effect." There was "strong reason to believe that federal review would indeed reveal flaws not appreciated by state judges perhaps too close to the day-to-day operation of the system." While *Stone* doubted that habeas rulings would have a substantial additional deterrent or educative impact with respect to the police, the responsible state offi-

25. See § 11.10(a).

26. See § 11.10 at note 19. Justice Powell's narrow reading of prejudice was not tied to use of the habeas writ to raise the claim. Indeed, *Strickland* had held that the Sixth Amendment incompetency claim was governed by the same standards whether raised on appeal or collateral attack. See note 11 at § 11.10. In both contexts, courts have recognized *Strickland* claims based on counsel's failure to raise other objections that are not guilt-related (e.g., a double jeopardy claim). See § 11.10(c), (d).

27. 443 U.S. 545, 99 S.Ct. 2993, 61 L.Ed.2d 739 (1979).

cials here, the courts and their employees, were very likely to take note of the federal decisions and respond accordingly.

Justice Blackmun also stressed the differences in the nature of the rights involved. *Stone* had characterized the exclusionary rule as a "judicially created remedy" rather than a "personal constitutional right." The same was not true here. Indeed, unlike the exclusionary rule, the prohibition against racial discrimination in the criminal justice process had been applied to the states "for nearly a century." Moreover, the "costs associated with quashing an indictment returned by an improperly constituted grand jury" were "significantly less than those associated with suppressing evidence." A prisoner who "is guilty in fact" is "less likely to go free" since the prosecution, after a reindictment, can retry the defendant on the same evidence. Finally, the "constitutional interests" that are vindicated in rectifying grand jury discrimination were characterized as "substantially more compelling than those at issue in *Stone.*" Racial discrimination "strikes at the core concerns of the Fourteenth Amendment and at fundamental values of our society and our legal system." The "harm is not only to the accused," but "to society as a whole."

The various distinctions cited in *Mitchell* render problematic the impact of that ruling upon the possible extension of *Stone* to other claims not guilt-related. It is difficult to predict what the Court would do with a claim that had some, but not all of the characteristics attributed to the grand jury claim. Consider, for example, a claim that the prosecutor was vindictive in his charging decision because of the defendant's unrelated exercise of First Amendment rights. On the one hand, the trial court would not have any special responsibility for that violation. On the other, the presence of First Amendment interests might lead the Court to conclude that, as with racial discrimination, "larger concerns" than harm to the accused are presented. In light of *Mitchell's* reference to the comparative "costs" of quashing an indictment that may be reinstituted and suppressing evidence, the incurable nature of a vindictiveness violation might work in favor of applying *Stone.* Yet, that same quality might also work in the opposite direction by leading the Court to characterize the claim as analogous to the jurisdictional defects traditionally cognizable on habeas review.

Certainly, if one seeks to identify those non-guilt-related claims that have none of the features that *Mitchell* attributed to the claim of grand jury discrimination, the most likely candidates are the prophylactic rules utilized to exclude reliable evidence because of the actions of the police. Two pairs of cases in which the Supreme Court majority did not reach the question of cognizability suggest that the extension of *Stone* to such claims is a live possibility. In two cases involving the same defendant, the procedural setting did not render appropriate consideration of the question of whether *Stone* should be extended to Sixth Amendment claims based on the prosecution's use first of a confession obtained in violation of defendant's right to counsel and then of the physical fruits of that confession. Opinions in both cases clearly indicated, however, that this was considered to be an open issue.[28] In two cases involving *Miranda* claims, the Court noted that it left open the question of "whether a bare allegation of a *Miranda* violation, without accompanying assertions going to the actual voluntariness or reliability of the confession, is a proper subject for consideration on federal habeas review, where there has been a full and fair opportunity to raise the argument in the state proceeding." [29] In the second of the two cases, four justices did speak to the issue and divided evenly. Justice O'Connor, joined by Scalia, J., maintained that "the weighing process applied in *Stone* leads ineluctably to the conclusion that the suppression remedy should not be available on federal habeas where the state courts have accorded a petitioner a full and

28. Brewer v. Williams, 430 U.S. 387, 97 S.Ct. 1232, 51 L.Ed.2d 424 (1977); Nix v. Williams, 467 U.S. 431, 104 S.Ct. 2501, 81 L.Ed.2d 377 (1984).

29. Wainwright v. Sykes, 433 U.S. 72, 97 S.Ct. 2497, 53 L.Ed.2d 594 (1977); Duckworth v. Eagan, 492 U.S. 195, 109 S.Ct. 2875, 106 L.Ed.2d 166 (1989).

fair opportunity to litigate a claim that *Miranda* warnings were not given or were somehow deficient." Indeed, she argued, the scales here "tip further toward finality and repose" than in *Stone*. *Miranda* was a "prophylactic rule * * * [that] 'overprotects the [Fifth Amendment] values at stake" and the "awarding of habeas relief years after conviction will often strike like lightening," rendering it "absurd to think that this added possibility of exclusion * * * will have any appreciable effect on police training or behavior." Justice Marshall, joined by Justice Brennan, started from the premise that "*Stone* was wrong when it was decided," but also found *Stone* distinguishable. Here, he argued, the *Miranda* violation should be taken as rendering the defendant's statement "presumptively unreliable," in contrast to the obviously reliable evidence considered in *Stone*. Moreover, since "many habeas petitioners will have coupled their *Miranda* claims with traditional involuntariness claims," which clearly are cognizable on habeas review, the "purported 'costs' of collateral review * * *, such as preventing finality and overburdening the federal courts, * * * will still exist." Since the arguments cited by Justice O'Connor relating to the nature of the *Miranda* rule are similar to those that have been advanced by the Court majority in limiting other remedial aspects of *Miranda*,[30] and since *Stone* relied on exactly that type of analogy with respect to the Fourth Amendment, an extension of *Stone* to *Miranda* violations seems likely. Violations of the Sixth Amendment's *Massiah* doctrine, on the other hand, have not been subjected to quite the same limitations in those other remedial contexts.[31]

(d) The Opportunity for Full and Fair Litigation. Consistent with the *Stone* ruling's underlying assumption that state courts would conscientiously enforce Fourth Amendment rights, the *Stone* Court held also that federal habeas review would be available if the state had not provided the petitioner an "opportunity for full and fair litigation." This "exception" arguably is broader than what would be needed simply to serve *Stone*'s view of the deterrent function of the exclusionary rule. Certainly, if a state regularly fails to provide an adequate litigation opportunity, its enforcement of the exclusionary rule would not provide a substantial deterrent and habeas review would then provide more than a marginal increment in deterrence. The *Stone* exception, however, focuses on the individual case, encompassing even an occasional lapse in state procedures. Thus, the *Stone* majority apparently concluded that even though the exclusionary rule is a "judicially created" remedy rather than a "personal constitutional right," the defendant is entitled to at least one opportunity for a "full and fair consideration" of his claim.

The *Stone* opinion offered little by way of definition of its full and fair opportunity standard. Several formulations of the standard were used, with the Court referring at different points to "a fair and full opportunity to raise and have adjudicated the question," an opportunity for "full and fair consideration" of the claim, and an opportunity for "full and fair litigation * * * at trial and on direct review." Lower courts applying the *Stone* standard have generally agreed that it requires a two step inquiry: (1) whether the state procedural mechanism is satisfactory in the abstract, and (2) whether there was a failure of the mechanism in the individual case.[32] Since the typical state procedure for raising Fourth Amendment claims is very much like the federal procedure, a finding of inadequacy is most likely to come under the second inquiry. Thus, it was held that petitioner did not receive a full and fair opportunity when his counsel was appointed one day before the expiration of the time period for presenting a suppression motion and the trial court applied an unwritten local rule mandat-

30. E.g., treatment of *Miranda* violations as to the exclusion of fruits and use for impeachment. See §§ 9.5(a), 9.6(a).

31. See Michigan v. Harvey, discussed in § 9.6 at note 11.

32. The failure must be in the mechanism, not in counsel. However, a failure of counsel can be challenged on habeas review as a Sixth Amendment violation. See Kimmelman v. Morrison, supra note 24.

ing a written application in denying counsel's oral request for an extension. Similarly, the petitioner was denied an adequate opportunity to present his claim where a state appellate court rejected his motion to suppress on the ground that a recent decision had eliminated the concept of automatic standing, but then failed to remand the case so as to allow a surprised petitioner (the standing issue had not been raised by the state) to establish his standing under the newly adopted decision.

The lower courts generally also have agreed that an erroneous application of the Fourth Amendment, without more, does not constitute a denial of an opportunity for full and fair litigation. It is said to be "of no consequence whether the state courts employed an incorrect legal standard, misapplied the correct standard, or erred in finding the underlying facts." Support for this position is found in the fact that the state appellate court in one of the cases before the Court in *Stone* apparently applied an incorrect legal standard. Lower courts have also noted that if the *Stone* exception could be based on the misapplication of Fourth Amendment standards, "*Stone*'s bar would become a nullity, since petitioners would routinely allege the necessary error." However, the Tenth Circuit has held that a state court's "willful refusal to apply the appropriate constitutional standard" fell within the *Stone* exception.

§ 28.4 Claims Foreclosed by State Procedural Defaults

(a) State Procedural Defaults. No habeas corpus issue has engendered more commentary and debate than the question of what impact a state procedural default should have upon habeas review of an otherwise cognizable constitutional claim. The procedural default question arises when a petitioner failed to present his claim in the state proceedings in accordance with applicable state procedural requirements and the state court has held (or would so hold where the claim was never presented to it) that this lapse bars consideration of the claim on the merits. The issue then presented to the habeas court is under what conditions, if any, should that state procedural default also bar federal habeas review. Resolution of that issue has required balancing on the one hand, the state's interest in preserving both procedural regularity and the finality of judgments, and on the other, the prisoner's interest in having his constitutional claim heard at least once. The difficulties presented in the balancing of these interests are reflected in a wavering course of Supreme Court decisions, almost always of a divided Court. In large part, the justices have divided over what weight should be given to these basic interests, but they also have divided over the desirability of drawing distinctions among different types of defaults and claims according to their impact upon those interests.

One concern frequently noted by those justices placing a heaving emphasis on finality is that habeas review of a claim that was not properly presented in the state proceedings will require initial factfinding by the habeas court long after the critical event has passed. The strength of this concern arguably may be tied to distinctions relating to the nature of both the procedural default and the habeas petitioner's claim. For example, when a claim was heard and decided at the trial level, and the default occurred through a failure to appeal, the federal habeas court can rely upon the state factfinding just as it could if the claim had been considered by the state appellate court. Also, certain types of claims, such as a double jeopardy objection, may be readily resolved on the basis of the state court record even if they were not pressed at trial. While there may be reasons for barring review based on such procedural defaults, the problem of delayed factfinding is not one of them.

The Supreme Court has also expressed concern that the habeas review not reward what has been described as "sandbagging" tactics by defense counsel. If habeas review is available, there are situations in which counsel may prefer not to raise an issue at trial, holding it in reserve as a means of obtaining a new trial through the writ if the trial should result in a conviction. Here again, a distinction might be drawn as to the nature of the defense objection. Assuming that such sandbagging will bar habeas review, counsel arguably is more likely to run the risk of a forfeiture on that ground as to certain types of claims. Where a successful objection will not constitute a permanent bar to prosecution, or result in the exclusion of incriminating evidence, there is an obvious incentive to sandbag even if there is only a remote possibility of habeas review. Consider, for example, an objection to grand jury composition in a case in which the grand jury would almost certainly have indicted even if fairly composed. Raising the issue before trial will "only delay the inevitable date of prosecution," [1] but holding the issue in reserve opens up the possibility of gaining a second trial through habeas review if the first results in a conviction. On the other hand, if a successful objection would absolutely bar prosecution (as in the case of a double jeopardy or speedy trial claim), then there would be absolutely no incentive for sandbagging. Here, it is almost certain that the failure to present a potentially meritorious objection would be the product simply of counsel's failure to recognize the strength of the claim.

Still another concern relates to forfeitures that are the product of counsel's error. It is undoubtedly true that many procedural defaults are the product of the ignorance or negligence of counsel rather than a tactical decision. When that is the case, the Court must consider whether the client should bear the cost of his counsel's error. Justice Brennan has argued that "closing the federal courthouse doors" on the basis of counsel's ignorance or inadvertence imposes an "unnecessary and misdirected sanction." [2] Such a sanction is unnecessary because even if one assumes that a default sanction would "induce greater care and caution on the part of trial lawyers, thereby forestalling the negligent conduct or error, the potential loss of all valuable state remedies would be sufficient." The sanction also is misdirected because the defendant, who often is without any "realistic choice" in determining who represents him, is not the person responsible for the default. One possible response to this concern is to draw a distinction based on the level of counsel's performance. Thus, it has been argued that sufficient protection against counsel's errors is provided by the Sixth Amendment right to the effective assistance of counsel. Under this view, the habeas petitioner may gain relief only where counsel's negligence in procedurally forfeiting a claim is so great as to constitute a Sixth Amendment violation under the standards of *Strickland.*[3] That the client otherwise must bear the imperfections of counsel is not unique in legal process in general or in the criminal justice process in particular. That process, this position argues, should not open the door to a continuous reevaluation and second guessing of counsel's performance, apart from a Sixth Amendment violation.

Another concern noted by the Court is the potential for habeas review resulting in the loss to "society [of] the right to punish admitted offenders" as "passage of time, erosion of memory, and dispersion of witnesses * * * render retrial difficult, even impossible." [4] Some justices argue that this cost is overborne by the need to ensure that the conviction, even of an obviously guilty defendant, was not infected by constitutional error. Others, however, would hold that the defense's failure to properly object to that constitutional error should be overriding, and the state's interest in finality therefore should prevail, unless that constitutional error may have resulted in the conviction of a defendant who is in fact innocent of the charges. They thus would draw a distinction based upon the possible impact of the error in producing an unreliable verdict of guilt under the facts of the particular case.

The distinctions noted above have had a mixed reception. As noted in the subsections

§ 28.4

1. Tollett v. Henderson, 411 U.S. 258, 93 S.Ct. 1602, 36 L.Ed.2d 235 (1973), discussed in § 11.10, at note 12.

2. Brennan, J., dissenting in Wainwright v. Sykes, infra note 22.

3. See § 11.10.

4. Engle v. Isaac, infra note 23.

that follow, some are currently drawn by the Court majority, some have been accepted in the past but are now rejected, and others have never received majority support. All have been advanced at one time or another, however, and with the frequent shifts in the law governing procedural forfeitures, and the tendency of dissenters to stay with their original positions, all remain subjects of current debate.

(b) State Excused Defaults. In one aspect of its treatment of a procedural default, the Court's position has remained steady. Where the state courts ignore the procedural default and reach the merits of the petitioner's claim, federal habeas review will not be precluded by that default. As the Supreme Court has stated, the different standards adopted over the years in barring consideration of habeas claims because of procedural defaults in the state courts have all hinged upon a recognition of the need to "accord respect to the sovereignty of the states," but if state courts themselves are willing to ignore a procedural default, a federal court "implies no disrespect" in doing the same.

In *Harris v. Reed,*[5] the Court added to the reach of this "state excused default" doctrine by holding that the "plain statement rule"—a rule originally adopted in the exercise of the Court's direct appellate review of state court decisions—will also apply to federal habeas proceedings. That rule basically states that the state court must plainly base its decision upholding the conviction on the adequate state ground of procedural default (which forecloses direct Supreme Court review) or the Supreme Court will assume that the state court has not relied on that ground. As it is applied to habeas proceedings, where a habeas petitioner failed to raise a claim in accordance with state procedures, but did present that claim before state courts, it will be assumed that the state court rulings rejecting that claim were based on the merits of the claim (excusing the procedural default) where "the decision of the last state court to which the petitioner presented his federal claims * * * fairly appear[s] to rest primarily on federal law or to be interwoven with federal law."[6] Thus, if the "necessary predicate" of ambiguity is found in the state decision, the *Harris* presumption will assume a state excused default. That ambiguity often will not to be present, however, where the relevant state appellate court ruling is unexplained (as on a denial of discretionary review) or contains only a brief statement of grounds. Thus, the *Harris* presumption was held not to apply where the prosecution on appeal advanced a procedural forfeiture argument and the state court then issued a summary order dismissing the appeal, noting that it did so "upon consideration" of the prosecution's motion and the briefs filed by the parties (even though those briefs dealt with the merits as well as the procedural forfeiture).[7]

The excusal of a default is possible, of course, only when the state courts actually have been presented with the claim that the habeas petitioner now raises. Where that was not done, the exhaustion requirement noted in § 28.2(d) may require that the claim be presented to state courts through the state's procedure for collateral attack. That is not required, however, where that procedural forfeiture would clearly bar relief under that procedure. In both that situation and the situation in which the state court was presented with the issue and relied on the procedural forfeiture, the issue then becomes whether the procedural forfeiture should also bar federal habeas review. The major shifts in the Court's response to that issue are presented in the next three subsections, with

5. 489 U.S. 255, 109 S.Ct. 1038, 103 L.Ed.2d 308 (1989).

6. Coleman v. Thompson, ___ U.S. ___, 111 S.Ct. 2546, 115 L.Ed.2d 640 (1991).

7. Coleman v. Thompson, supra note 6. See also Ylst v. Nunnemaker, ___ U.S. ___, 111 S.Ct. 2590, 115 L.Ed.2d 706 (1991) (where there has been "one reasoned state judgment rejecting a federal claim, later unexplained orders upholding that judgment * * * [will be assumed to] rest upon the same ground," so the *Harris* predicate was not present where the "last reasoned opinon" imposed a procedural default and was then followed by formulary order that, unlike the order in *Coleman,* referred to a "denial" rather than a "dismissal" of defendant's petition for state collateral relief).

subsections (f) and (g) further exploring the Court's current position.

(c) The "Adequate State Ground" Standard. Prior to the 1963 decision of *Fay v. Noia,* federal habeas courts applied to state procedural defaults the same standard that would have been applied if the case had come to the Supreme Court on direct review from the state courts. The Court had long held that on direct review it would not reach the merits of an appellant's constitutional claim if the court below had relied upon an "adequate state ground." If the state court ruling had been based on a state ground, independent from the merits of the federal constitutional claim, then that ground would necessarily control the outcome of the case. Even if the Court were to find that there had been a constitutional violation, it lacked authority to review the question of state law and the state court's ruling would therefore have to be affirmed. Although this analysis was developed initially in connection with state rulings based on substantive grounds, it was soon held applicable as well to rulings involving procedural grounds. Application of the same principle on habeas review was viewed as consistent with the role of the habeas court as a functional surrogate of the Supreme Court in providing a federal forum for federal claims. If a procedural default constituted an independent and adequate state ground, thereby barring direct review by the Supreme Court, it would also bar federal habeas review. Thus, a default not excused by the state court could only be excused by the habeas court if the state procedural ruling did not constitute an adequate state ground.

The standard for determining whether a state procedural ruling constitutes an adequate state ground, as developed in direct review cases, looks primarily to the evenhandedness of the state in applying its ordinary rules of criminal procedure. The state may not manipulate its rules to evade federal rights or exercise its procedural discretion to discriminate against the presentation of such rights. However, the Court has also indicated that evenhanded application of a procedural rule will not be enough when either the state procedural requirement or its forfeiture sanction fails to serve a "legitimate state interest."[8] In general, state procedural rulings have been deemed inadequate under this standard only when applied in such an arbitrary manner as to "force resort to arid ritual of meaningless form."[9] Undoubtedly the most harsh application of the adequate state ground standard on habeas review occurred in *Daniels v. Allen,*[10] a companion case to *Brown v. Allen.*[11] Like the defendants in *Brown,* Daniels had raised at trial constitutional challenges to the composition of the jury and to the use of an allegedly coerced confession. Daniels' counsel, however, had failed to file a timely appeal. The trial court had granted the defense 60 days in which to prepare and serve its statement of the case on appeal, but that statement was not delivered until the 61st day. The state appellate court refused to hear the appeal even though, if the papers had been mailed on the 60th day, as permitted under court rules, they would not have arrived any earlier. A divided Supreme Court held that the procedural default barred federal habeas review of the petitioner's claims. In dissent, Justice Black characterized the majority's ruling as having adopted a philosophy which, when combined with *Brown,* "prompts this Court to grant a second review where the state has granted one but to deny any review at all where the state has granted none."

In *Fay v. Noia,*[12] the Court was faced with another "hard case," but responded quite differently. The petitioner there was one of three codefendants who had been convicted primarily on the basis of their signed confessions. All three had contended at trial that the confessions were coerced. Noia's two codefendants took unsuccessful appeals, but

8. Henry v. Mississippi, 379 U.S. 443, 85 S.Ct. 564, 13 L.Ed.2d 408 (1965).

9. Staub v. City of Baxley, 355 U.S. 313, 78 S.Ct. 277, 2 L.Ed.2d 302 (1958).

10. 344 U.S. 443, 73 S.Ct. 397, 97 L.Ed. 469 (1953).

11. See § 28.3 at note 13.

12. 372 U.S. 391, 83 S.Ct. 822, 9 L.Ed.2d 837 (1963).

subsequent legal proceedings resulted in their release on findings that the confessions had been obtained in violation of the Fourteenth Amendment. Noia had failed to appeal following his conviction, but responding to the release of his codefendants, sought to utilize the state remedy of coram nobis. That relief was denied on the ground that his failure to appeal precluded collateral inquiry into the voluntariness of his confession. The Supreme Court, in an opinion by Justice Brennan, held that Noia's claim was nevertheless open to federal habeas corpus review.

Justice Brennan's opinion assumed, without deciding, that the state court's ruling on Noia's failure to appeal would have constituted an adequate state ground precluding direct review of Noia's conviction. The Court ruled, however, that the adequate state ground doctrine should not "limit the power granted the federal courts under the habeas corpus statute." That doctrine, it stated, is only appropriate on direct review, where the Court is reviewing the judgment of the state court. Habeas corpus presented a different situation. The "jurisdictional prerequisite" for issuance of the writ, Justice Brennan noted, "is not the judgment of the state court, but detention *simpliciter.*"

Dissenting in *Noia,* Justice Harlan, accused the majority of relying on a formalistic distinction. The important point, he noted, is that "if the [habeas] applicant is detained *pursuant* to a judgment, termination of the detention necessarily nullifies the judgment." It was to ignore reality to attempt to "divorce the writ from the judgment of conviction if that judgment is the basis of the detention." If the adequate state ground standard was appropriate on direct review, it was also appropriate on habeas review.

Perhaps recognizing the weakness in the distinction it had drawn, the *Noia* opinion acknowledged that the focus of the writ on the legality of the detention "may not be the entire answer to the contention that the adequate state-ground principle should apply * * * in habeas corpus." There were, however, other distinctions that also should be considered. The adequate state ground doctrine had stronger support when the state ruling was based on an independent substantive ground rather than, as here, a procedural ground. The state's interest in an "airtight system of [procedural] forfeitures" was of a "different order" than the "autonomy of state law" within "the proper sphere of its substantive regulation." The Court had long held that state procedural rulings would be rejected when they "made burdensome the vindication of federal rights." While there was reason to respect the states' "substantial interest in exacting compliance with their procedural rules," sufficient deference was provided by denial of direct review, which placed a burden upon the noncomplying defendant to seek habeas review.

As discussed in subsection (d), the *Noia* ruling replaced the adequate state ground standard with a standard that excused procedural defaults unless they were a product of a "deliberate bypassing" of "the orderly procedure of the state courts." However, as discussed in subsection (e), the deliberate bypass standard was replaced, in turn, by a "cause and prejudice" standard developed in the 1970's. In *Wainwright v. Sykes,*[13] the case that largely closed the door on the deliberate bypass standard, the Court described the issue before it as determining when "an adequate and independent state ground [will] bar consideration of otherwise cognizable federal issues in federal habeas corpus." The Court, however, appeared to use this language only with reference to a particular adequate state ground—one that recognized an excuse from the default consistent with its "cause and prejudice" standard. There was no suggestion that a state rule that was less flexible and did not allow for a cause and prejudice excuse could also serve to bar habeas review. In *Harris v. Reed,*[14] the Court arguably muddied the waters somewhat when it noted that "the procedural default ruling of *Wainwright v. Sykes* has its historical and theoretical basis

13. Infra note 22.

14. Supra note 5.

in the 'adequate and independent state ground' doctrine" and that "*Wainwright v. Sykes* made clear that the adequate state ground doctrine applies in federal habeas." As Justice Kennedy pointed out in his *Harris* dissent, there were important distinctions between the *Sykes* standard and the adequate state ground standard. The adequate state ground standard as applied by the Supreme Court on direct review is seen as a jurisdictional limit, whereas the cause and prejudice standard of *Sykes,* consistent with the analysis advanced in *Noia,* was imposed in the interest of "comity and federalism" and not as a jurisdictional limitation that flowed from "some mechanical application of the law governing [the Supreme Court's] appellate jurisdiction." Also, the cause and prejudice standard provided a more expansive excuse of state procedural defaults than would be accepted under an adequate state ground analysis. For example, it recognizes in "cause" the novelty of the claim raised, a factor that had not been a part of traditional adequate state ground doctrine. So too, there exists an unjust incarceration exception to the *Sykes* standard that finds no counterpart in adequate state ground doctrine.

The later case of *Coleman v. Thompson*[15] appeared to recognize the basic distinction noted by Justice Kennedy. The Court there stated that while the adequate state ground doctrine had a bearing on both direct review and habeas review, the basis for its application was "somewhat different" in the habeas setting, where its recognition was not "jurisdictional" but based on "concerns of comity and federalism." In light of *Coleman's* analysis, the appropriate treatment of the adequate state ground doctrine on habeas review appears to be that advanced in *Dugger v. Adams.*[16] *Dugger* noted that the procedural default presented there would not bar habeas review if either (i) the state procedural rule had been applied so unevenly as not to constitute an adequate state ground or (ii) the default was excused under the cause and prejudice standard. Thus, the adequate state ground doctrine applies to habeas review in the sense that the default must at a minimum be justified by a procedural rule that would constitute an adequate state ground on direct review, but even if it meets that test, the default will not preclude review if it is excused under the *Sykes* standard or falls within the unjust incarceration exception.

(d) The Development of the "Deliberate Bypass" Standard. Having held that adequate state ground standard was not applicable to habeas corpus proceedings, the *Noia* opinion did not fall back on the habeas statute's broad reference to detention "in violation of the Constitution" and contend that review therefore was required whenever the petitioner's conviction was constitutionally flawed, without regard to the state procedural default. The Court noted that while "the jurisdiction of the federal courts on habeas corpus is not affected by procedural defaults incurred * * * during the state proceedings," there was a "limited discretion in the federal judge to deny relief under certain circumstances." Such discretion was implicit in the "equitable principles" that traditionally governed the exercise of habeas jurisdiction, as recognized in the § 2243 direction to "dispose of the matter as law and justice required." However, consistent with those principles, the discretion was appropriately limited to situations in which "the suitor's conduct in relation to the matter at hand may disentitle him to relief." As applied to procedural defaults, such conduct consisted of a "deliberate bypassing" of "the orderly procedure of the state courts."

The *Noia* opinion did not explore at length what would constitute a deliberate bypass. It did, however, offer some guidance to the lower courts:

15. Supra note 6. The procedural bar there consisted of the filing of a notice of appeal three days beyond the 30 day limit imposed by state rule. Cf. Daniels v. Allen, supra note 10. Since the certiorari petition in *Coleman* had not raised the question of whether the state's procedural ground was "adequate," the Court accepted the Fourth Circuit's conclusion that it was. It then went on, however, to consider whether habeas review nonetheless was justified under *Skyes'* "cause and prejudice" standard.

16. 489 U.S. 401, 109 S.Ct. 1211, 103 L.Ed.2d 435 (1989).

> * * * [T]his grant of discretion is not to be interpreted as a permission to introduce legal fictions into federal habeas corpus. The classic definition of waiver enunciated in *Johnson v. Zerbst*[17]—"an intentional relinquishment or abandonment of a known right or privilege"—furnishes the controlling standard. If a habeas applicant, after consultation with competent counsel or otherwise, understandingly and knowingly forewent the privilege of seeking to vindicate his federal claims in the State courts, whether for strategic, tactical, or any other reasons that can fairly be described as the deliberate bypassing of state procedures, then it is open to the federal court on habeas to deny him all relief if the state courts refused to entertain his federal claims on the merits—though of course only after the federal court has satisfied itself, by holding a hearing or by some other means, of the facts bearing upon the applicant's default. * * * At all events we wish it clearly understood that the standard here put forth depends on the considered choice of the petitioner. * * * A choice made by counsel not participated in by the petitioner does not automatically bar relief. Nor does a state court's finding of waiver bar independent determination of the question by the federal courts on habeas, for waiver affecting federal rights is a federal question.

Although *Fay v. Noia* was widely recognized as one of the "landmark decisions" of the Warren Court, it took the Court only two years to begin to withdraw from the full breadth of its language. *Noia* had stated that a deliberate bypass required "the considered choice of the petitioner," but *Henry v. Mississippi,*[18] in an opinion by Justice Brennan, indicated that the defendant's personal participation was not always needed. The Court there noted that waiver of certain constitutional objections could be controlled by counsel alone, and as to those claims, a tactical decision by counsel to forego the objection would constitute a deliberate bypass. *Murch v. Mottram*[19] added that a deliberate bypass by counsel did not require knowledge that a tactical maneuver would result in a procedural default under state law, provided counsel had "reasonable warning" that he ran that risk.

While *Henry* and *Mottram* expanded somewhat the concept of a deliberate bypass, the federal lower courts often went far beyond those rulings in applying the deliberate bypass standard. Indeed, their rulings sometimes appeared to make a deliberate bypass the customary rather than the extraordinary explanation of a procedural default. If the record carried no indication that counsel was unaware of the claim or simply negligent, many lower courts were willing to find a deliberate bypass if any strategic reason could be hypothesized for failing to object. This position was viewed as following logically from *Noia*'s citation of *Johnson v. Zerbst* as providing the analogue to the deliberate bypass. *Johnson* had stated that in collateral proceedings, it was the petitioner who should bear the burden of proving that his waiver was not made "competently and intelligently." The same position, it was argued, should be taken with respect to the deliberate bypass. Here, however, unlike the situation as to the waiver of counsel, a silent record was often taken to carry a presumption of a tactical decision shifting the burden to the petitioner to show otherwise. At the same time, the lower courts often declined to hold (or at least to give great weight to) an evidentiary hearing at which counsel would testify "as to why he did what he did, or failed to do what he did not do." Such a procedure, one court noted, "places counsel in the unenviable position where, if he can recall his reasons and they are good, he is hurting his former client, and if he can't recall his reasons or they are bad, or even not very good, he is impugning his professional competence." The end result was a series of default rulings that often extended far beyond the exceptional case envisaged in *Noia,* and that may have suggested to the Supreme Court a need to reexamine the *Noia* standard.

17. 304 U.S. 458, 58 S.Ct. 1019, 82 L.Ed. 1461 (1938). Johnson v. Zerbst dealt with the waiver of the assistance of counsel. See § 11.3(a). Compare § 3.10(a).

18. Supra note 8. See also § 11.6, at note 11.

19. 409 U.S. 41, 93 S.Ct. 71, 34 L.Ed.2d 194 (1972).

(e) The Substitution of the "Cause and Prejudice" Standard. In 1973, in *Davis v. United States,*[20] the Court started down a path that eventually led to the replacement of the deliberate bypass standard with a "cause and prejudice standard." Interestingly, that standard was derived not from prior decisions relating to comity or constitutional adjudication, but from an interpretation of a provision in the Federal Rules of Criminal Procedure. *Davis* involved a § 2255 motion of a federal prisoner, filed three years after his trial, in which he claimed that there had been racial discrimination in the selection of the grand jury. Davis argued that his failure to raise that claim at trial should be judged under the deliberate bypass standard, which had been held after *Noia* to apply to § 2255 proceedings as well as § 2254 proceedings. Treating the issue as a matter of statutory interpretation, the Supreme Court rejected that contention. The Court noted that if Davis' case had come before it on direct review, it would have been decided under Federal Rule 12(b). That Rule provided that the failure to raise before trial a defect in the institution of the prosecution, such as grand jury discrimination, would "constitute a waiver, but the court for cause shown may grant relief from the waiver." The Court found it "inconceivable" that Congress, having foreclosed such a claim from review in the initial proceeding, meant to nonetheless allow it to be presented on collateral attack. Accordingly, the Rule 12(b) standard was held to apply under § 2255 as well as in the original proceeding. This meant that the petitioner could have his claim considered only if his failure to object was justified by "cause shown." Here the district court specifically had held that "cause" was not shown. In making that determination the lower court had correctly looked to both the defendant's lack of explanation for failing to comply with Rule 12(b) and the lack of any showing of actual prejudice. Although racial discrimination in the selection of the grand jury was presumed to be prejudicial where a timely objection was made, a petitioner attempting to fall within the "cause shown" exception had to establish actual prejudice.

Francis v. Henderson,[21] presented to the Court a case almost identical to *Davis* except that the petitioner was a state prisoner seeking federal habeas review. A state statute required objections to the grand jury's composition to be raised before trial and the petitioner had failed to object, resulting in a procedural default. Without mentioning the deliberate bypass standard, the Court held that the standard announced in *Davis*—now described as requiring a showing of "cause" and "actual prejudice"—was applicable. The state requirement of a pretrial objection, the Court noted, served essentially the same salutary purposes as Rule 12(b). "Surely," the Court concluded, "considerations of comity and federalism require that * * * [habeas courts] give no less effect to the same clear interests when asked to overturn state convictions." Dissenting in *Francis,* Justice Brennan foresaw the eventual demise of the deliberate bypass standard, but that remained an open question. The *Francis* opinion was tied sufficiently to the special attributes of the grand jury discrimination claim—an objection as to which there was a decided tactical advantage in postponing the challenge if it were later available—that it could not be said that the cause and prejudice standard was bound to replace the deliberate bypass standard for other claims as well.

Unlike *Francis, Wainwright v. Sykes*[22] challenged the deliberate bypass standard head on. The petitioner Sykes had sought habeas relief on the ground that his conviction had been based on a confession obtained without his full understanding of the *Miranda* warnings. Although the state's rules required at least a contemporaneous objection to the admission of illegally obtained evidence, there had been no objection before or during the trial. Justice Rehnquist's opinion for the Court noted initially that the ruling in *Francis* had rejected the view that "the dicta of *Fay v. Noia*" established an "all-inclusive rule

20. 411 U.S. 233, 93 S.Ct. 1577, 36 L.Ed.2d 216 (1973).

21. 425 U.S. 536, 96 S.Ct. 1708, 48 L.Ed.2d 149 (1976).

22. 433 U.S. 72, 97 S.Ct. 2497, 53 L.Ed.2d 594 (1977).

rendering state timely objection rules ineffective * * * in federal habeas proceedings * * * [absent] a deliberate bypass." The issue here, it was noted, was "whether the rule of *Francis v. Henderson,* barring federal habeas review absent a showing of 'cause' and 'prejudice' attendant to a state procedural waiver [should] be applied to a waived objection to the admission of a confession at trial." For reasons discussed below, the Court answered that question in the affirmative. It noted that there was no need to determine in this case "the precise definition of the 'cause' and 'prejudice' standard" except to note "that it is narrower than the standard set forth in dicta in *Fay v. Noia,* which would make federal habeas review generally available * * * absent a knowing and deliberate waiver of the federal constitutional contention." As for *Noia* itself, the Court noted that it had "no occasion today to consider the *Fay* rule as applied to the facts there confronting the Court." It was only "the sweeping language of *Fay v. Noia,* going far beyond the facts of the case eliciting it, which we today reject."

The *Sykes* opinion offered basically three reasons for preferring the *Francis* test over *Noia* 's deliberate bypass standard. First, the "contemporaneous-objection" rule applied in the state court deserved "greater respect" then the deliberate bypass standard would give it, both because "it is employed by a coordinate jurisdiction within the federal system" and because of the many valid interests it served. Application of a contemporaneous-objection rule, it was noted, ensures development of a factual record when "the recollections of witnesses are freshest" (rather than "years later in a federal habeas proceeding"), allows the judge "who observed the demeanor of the witnesses [at trial] to make the factual determinations," offers the opportunity for exclusion at a point where doing so will make "a major contribution to finality in a criminal litigation," and forces the prosecution at a propitious time "to take a hard look at its hole card" (which might lead it to decide not to rely upon the challenged evidence).

Second, the Court expressed the view that the "rule of *Fay v. Noia,* broadly stated, may encourage 'sandbagging' on the part of defense lawyers, who may take their chances on a verdict of not guilty in a state trial court with the intent to raise their constitutional claims in a federal habeas court if their initial gamble does not pay off." Justice Brennan, in dissent, argued that the deliberate bypass standard barred exactly that tactical maneuver, but the majority apparently concluded that the potential looseness of that standard in application (and perhaps *Noia* 's recognition of district court discretion to ignore a bypass) offered a continuing incentive to sandbag. This possibility, the majority noted, also interfered with the state's ability to set its own level of enforcement of its procedural rules. Faced with a choice of tolerating violations of its rules or having the same cases heard in a federal court, it might accept enforcement "less stringent" than it would otherwise desire.

Finally the *Sykes* majority criticized the deliberate bypass rule for detracting from the appropriate role of the trial. The "failure of the federal habeas courts generally to require compliance with a contemporaneous-objection rule [would] tend to detract from the perception of the trial in a criminal case * * * as a decisive and portentous event." The "adoption of the *Francis* rule," on the other hand, would have "the salutary effect of making the trial on the merits the 'main event,' so to speak, rather than a 'tryout on the road' for what will later be the determinative federal habeas hearing." Responding to Justice Brennan's dissent, the majority also stressed that the *Francis* test would still serve the basic function of habeas review:

> The "cause"-and-"prejudice" exception of the *Francis* rule will afford an adequate guarantee, we think, that the rule will not prevent a federal habeas court from adjudicating for the first time the federal constitutional claim of a defendant who in the absence of such an adjudication will be the victim of a miscarriage of justice.

There were several separate opinions in *Sykes,* but only Justice Brennan's dissent, which characterized the Court's ruling as instituting an "air tight system of forfeitures," accused the Court of making a dramatic departure from *Noia.* Justice Stevens, in a separate concurring opinion, suggested that denying Sykes relief was consistent with lower court decisions applying *Noia.* Justice White, concurring in the judgment, noted that the Court's ultimate ruling as to the lack of "prejudice" was "tantamount to a finding of harmless error." Chief Justice Burger, who joined the majority opinion, wrote separately to emphasize a single point: "[T]he 'deliberate bypass' standard enunciated in *Fay v. Noia* was never designed for, and is inapplicable to, errors—even of constitutional magnitude—alleged to have been committed during trial." *Noia,* he stressed, "applied the 'deliberate bypass' standard to a case where the critical procedural decision—whether to take a criminal appeal—was entrusted to a convicted defendant." Where the defendant's personal participation was involved, it made sense to apply the *Johnson v. Zerbst* standard of a "knowing and intelligent decision by the defendant himself." However, where the decision involved was one "entrusted to the accused's attorney," that standard was "simply inapplicable."

Perhaps because of the influence of *Stone v. Powell,* some observers speculated that the cause and prejudice test (now commonly described as the "*Sykes*" test or the "*Francis–Sykes*" test) might not apply to the failure to raise at trial a constitutional objection that related to the reliability of the guilt-determining process. That possibility was put to rest in the Court's companion rulings in *Engle v. Isaac*[23] and *United States v. Frady.*[24] *Isaac* was a § 2254 case in which the state prisoner claimed that he had been denied due process by a jury charge that required the defense to carry the burden of proving self-defense by a preponderance of the evidence. *Frady* presented a § 2255 challenge by a federal prisoner to a jury charge that allegedly required the jury to presume malice and thereby relieved the government of its obligation to prove a major element of the offense. In both cases the petitioner's counsel had not objected to the jury charge at trial, and petitioner explained that failure by reference to counsel's ignorance, contending that the invalidity of the instruction was not apparent under the then prevailing precedent. Petitioners accordingly claimed that there had not been a deliberate bypass. Moreover, they argued, if some other standard were to be applied, it should be the "plain error" standard traditionally utilized by appellate courts to review claims not raised at trial.[25] Writing for the majority in both cases, Justice O'Connor rejected petitioners' contentions, held that the defaults were subject to the *Sykes* standard, and concluded that neither petitioner had established cause and prejudice.

Justice O'Connor's opinion in *Isaac* initially reviewed the historic function of the habeas writ (characterized as a "bulwark against convictions that violate 'fundamental fairness' "), outlined the costs of "liberal allowance" of habeas review (stressing the degradation of the "prominence of the trial," the difficulties of retrials long after the event, and the impact upon the interests of the state), and explained that there was an escalation of those costs "when a trial default has barred a prisoner from obtaining adjudication of his constitutional claim in the state courts." All of those considerations, it was noted, argued against "limit[ing] *Sykes* to cases in which the constitutional error did not affect the truth-finding function of the trial." While the *Miranda* claim raised in *Sykes* did not go to that function, the principles announced in *Sykes* had a broader reach. Justice O'Connor concluded:

> The costs outlined above do not depend upon the type of claim raised by the prisoner. While the nature of a constitutional claim may affect the calculation of cause and actual prejudice, it does not alter the need to make that threshold showing. We reaffirm, therefore, that any prisoner bringing a constitutional claim to the federal courthouse after a state procedural default must demonstrate

23. 456 U.S. 107, 102 S.Ct. 1558, 71 L.Ed.2d 783 (1982).

24. 456 U.S. 152, 102 S.Ct. 1584, 71 L.Ed.2d 816 (1982).

25. See § 27.5(d).

cause and actual prejudice before obtaining relief.

The possibility of substituting a "plain error" standard for the *Sykes* standard was considered in both *Isaac* and *Frady,* but the primary discussion was in the latter case. Relying on Federal Rule 52(b), which states that plain errors may be noticed by a court even if not brought to its attention by counsel, Frady argued that, as in *Davis,* the Federal Rule provision should be held applicable to collateral review. The Court responded that Rule 52(b) obviously was aimed at the court's role on direct review. Application of the same standard was "out of place when a prisoner launches a collateral attack against a criminal conviction after society's legitimate interest in the finality of the judgment has been perfected by the expiration of the time allowed for direct review or by the affirmance of the conviction on appeal." The petitioner here, for example, was seeking habeas "nineteen years after his crime." To adopt the same standard for collateral attack that was used on direct appeal would "accord no significance whatever to the existence of a final judgment perfected by appeal." It would be inconsistent with the "long and consistently affirmed [principle] that a collateral challenge may not do service for an appeal."

Isaac, Frady, and *Sykes* left no doubt that the cause and prejudice had become the dominant standard for assessing procedural defaults. The question remained, however, as to what, if anything, was left of *Noia*'s deliberate bypass standard. *Sykes* limited its rejection of *Noia* to the "sweeping language" of *Noia,* as opposed to the holding under the facts of *Noia,* and specifically left open the possibility that the deliberate bypass standard might still be applied to the procedural default of *Noia*—the failure to appeal. Two grounds might justify applying a standard more lenient than cause and prejudice to such a default. Chief Justice Burger had suggested one when he argued in his *Sykes* concurrence that deliberate bypass was a standard geared to a procedural decision over which the defendant himself exercised exclusive control and that the decision to appeal was such a "personal decision." Another ground was that a default on appeal does not present all of the costs associated with a default at trial, as it "does not detract from the significance of the trial," is far less likely to be a product of "sandbagging," and does not require fresh factfinding (as the state trial court will have ruled on the merits of the claim).

The second ground noted above was rejected in *Murray v. Carrier.*[26] The Court there applied the cause and prejudice standard to a procedural default resulting from counsel's failure to include a particular claim among the issues raised on appeal. The Court majority found "unpersuasive" the contention that the concerns underlying *Sykes* have less force as to a default on appeal and therefore such a default should be governed by a separate standard, or at least a more lenient view of "cause." Here too, the Court noted, there were significant state interests in requiring the defendant to raise his claim (e.g., permitting an appellate resolution of the claim "shortly after trial, while evidence is still available both to assess the defendant's claim and to retry the defendant effectively if he prevails on appeal"), and the cause and prejudice standard was needed to ensure proper respect for those interests. The Court added, however, that it was expressing "no opinion" as to whether *Fay v. Noia*'s deliberate bypass standard might not be more appropriate where the default stems from "counsel's decision not to take an appeal at all."

It was not until 1991, almost thirty years after the *Noia* decision, that the Court was forced to rule directly on that issue. In *Coleman v. Thompson,*[27] *Fay v. Noia* was finally laid to rest even as to failure to take an appeal. Justice O'Connor noted that while this aspect of the *Fay v. Noia* ruling had been left open in *Sykes* and *Carrier,* those rulings and others had "taken a markedly different view [from *Noia*] of the important interests served by state procedural rules." Statements in those opinions "hint[ed] strongly

26. 477 U.S. 478, 106 S.Ct. 2639, 91 L.Ed.2d 397 (1986).

27. Supra note 6.

that *Fay* had been superseded" and the time had come to turn that hint into a holding:

> "We now make it explicit: In all cases in which a state prisoner has defaulted his federal claims in state court pursuant to an independent and adequate state procedural rule, federal habeas review of the claim is barred unless the prisoner can demonstrate cause for the default and actual prejudice as a result of the alleged violation of federal law, or demonstrates that failure to consider the claims will result in a fundamental miscarriage of justice."

Justice O'Connor's opinion did not speak directly to the distinction drawn by Chief Justice Burger in *Sykes* as to procedural decisions that require the defendant's personal approval. However, the *Coleman* opinion, as discussed in subsection (f), recognized that "cause" would be present where the procedural forfeiture was a product of action by counsel that itself constituted constitutionally ineffective assistance of counsel. Where the defendant has a constitutional right to counsel, and counsel makes a decision that relinquishes a right over which the defendant has personal control without first obtaining defendant's acquiescence, such action traditionally has been viewed as constitutionally ineffective assistance of counsel.[28]

(f) The Meaning of Cause and Prejudice. Prior to the decisions in *Isaac* and *Frady*, the Supreme Court had said very little about the precise content of the cause and prejudice standard. It had established that the burden was on the petitioner to show that his default fell within this "exception," that both "cause" and "actual prejudice" had to be established, that the standard was "narrower" than the deliberate bypass test of *Noia*, and that it was sufficiently broad to allow review when necessary to prevent a "miscarriage of justice." Aside from these principles, however, the content of the standard was left to development in "later cases." That development was provided first in *Isaac* and *Frady* and then in *Reed v. Ross*, *Murray v. Carrier*, and *Coleman v. Thompson*.

The petitioners in *Isaac* [29] offered two justifications for their failure to object to a jury instruction that required the defense to carry the burden of proving self-defense. First, they contended that, in light of the clarity and consistency of Ohio law at the time, it would have been futile to object to the jury instructions at trial. Justice O'Connor responded that "the futility of presenting an objection to state courts cannot alone constitute cause for a failure to object at trial." A defendant who "perceives a constitutional claim and believes it may find favor in the federal courts" cannot "bypass the state courts simply because he thinks they will be unsympathetic to the claim."

The petitioners' second justification for their failure to object was their alleged legitimate unawareness of the constitutional difficulty posed by the Ohio self-defense instruction. Justice O'Connor responded that perhaps the "novelty" of a constitutional issue could constitute "cause" for failure to object, but defendants' claims here "were far from unknown at the time of their trials." Their basic contention flowed from language in the *Winship* case decided over four years prior to their trial.[30] "Dozens of defendants" had relied on the same language to make similar claims, even where those claims too "countered well-established principles of [state] law." Moreover, numerous courts had overturned such state law proof requirements in

28. See § 11.6(a). *Noia* itself did not involve such a situation. The decision not to appeal there had been made with defendant's approval. It was held not to constitute a deliberate bypass because it was not a "voluntary relinquishment" of that right, having been motivated by a comment of the trial judge (relating to the judge's charity in imposing a life sentence) that led defendant to "fear that, if successful [on appeal], he might get the death sentence if convicted on retrial." *Noia* was decided several years before North Carolina v. Pearce, § 26.8(a). Of course, if counsel's decision without defendant's approval comes at a point in the appellate process where defendant lacks a constitutional right to counsel (as on a second-level appeal), then there can be no claim of constitutionally ineffective assistance. See note 33 infra.

29. Supra note 23.

30. In re Winship, 397 U.S. 358, 90 S.Ct. 1068, 25 L.Ed.2d 368 (1970). See § 2.6 at note 40.

reliance upon *Winship.* Justice O'Connor concluded:

> We do not suggest that every astute counsel would have relied upon *Winship* to assert the unconstitutionality of a rule saddling criminal defendants with the burden of proving an affirmative defense. Every trial presents a myriad of possible claims. Counsel might have overlooked or chosen to omit respondents' due process argument while pursuing other avenues of defense. We have long recognized, however, that the Constitution guarantees criminal defendants only a fair trial and a competent attorney. It does not insure that defense counsel will recognize and raise every conceivable constitutional claim. Where the basis of a constitutional claim is available, and other defense counsel have perceived and litigated that claim, the demands of comity and finality counsel against labelling alleged unawareness of the objection as cause for a procedural default.

The thrust of *Isaac,* as evidenced by the above statement, was that defendant must bear the cost of counsel's error, provided that error does not establish a valid Sixth Amendment incompetency claim. Accordingly, it was not surprising that the Court in *Murray v. Carrier* [31] rejected any attempt to limit "cause" to instances of tactical defaults. The lower court there had held that "cause" was present when the procedural default was the product of "defense counsel's ignorance or oversight" rather than a "deliberate withholding" for "tactical reasons." This reading of "cause," the *Carrier* majority noted, was "plainly inconsistent" with *Isaac.* That decision had stressed the high costs of a federal habeas review that disregarded a state procedural default, and those costs "do not disappear when the default stems from counsel's ignorance or inadvertence rather than from a deliberate decision, for whatever reason, to withhold a claim." Therefore, the "mere fact that counsel failed to recognize the factual or legal basis for a claim, or failed to raise the claim despite recognizing it, does not constitute cause for a procedural default." "So long as defendant is represented by counsel whose performance is not constitutionally ineffective," the Court concluded, "we discern no inequity in requiring him to bear the risk of attorney error that results in a procedural default."

Engle v. Isaac and *Murray v. Carrier* both acknowledged that counsel's negligence or error would amount to "cause" where counsel's performance denied the defendant the effective assistance of counsel. However, in such cases, petitioners ordinarily will have little incentive for pursuing the underlying constitutional claim under the *Sykes* test, rather than simply seeking relief on the basis of the Sixth Amendment violation. Competency of counsel for Sixth Amendment purposes generally looks to the overall performance of counsel. This will work to defendant's advantage where counsel's failures extend beyond the default on the cognizable constitutional claim. Moreover, it should not work to the defendant's disadvantage where counsel's only error related to the default; as the Court noted in *Carrier,* "the right to effective assistance of counsel * * * may in a particular case be violated by even an isolated error of counsel if that error is sufficiently egregious and prejudicial." Of course, to establish a Sixth Amendment violation, the defendant ordinarily must show a "reasonable probability" of prejudice, but that requirement certainly does not demand more than the "actual prejudice" prong of the *Sykes* test.

Coleman v. Thompson [32] presented a case in which petitioner lacked a constitutional claim of ineffective assistance, but sought to establish cause by reference to attorney incompetence equivalent to that required under the *Strickland* standard. The alleged incompetence was the failure of counsel to file a timely notice of appeal from a denial of a state habeas corpus petition. Since the defendant had no constitutional right to the assistance of counsel in such a collateral proceeding, the incompetency of his attorney could not give rise to a constitutional claim of inef-

31. Supra note 26.

32. Supra notes 6, 27.

fective assistance.[33] The Court concluded that without the linchpin of a constitutional claim, incompetency could not constitute cause. Justice O'Connor reasoned for the majority:

> Attorney ignorance or inadvertence is not "cause" because the attorney is the petitioner's agent when acting, or failing to act, in furtherance of the litigation, and the petitioner must "bear the risk of attorney error." *Carrier.* * * * Attorney error that constitutes ineffective assistance of counsel is cause, however. This is not because, as Coleman contends, the error is so bad that "the lawyer ceases to be an agent of the petitioner." * * * Rather, as *Carrier* explains, "if the procedural default is the result of ineffective assistance of counsel, the Sixth Amendment itself requires that responsibility for the default be imputed to the State." In other words, it is not the gravity of the attorney's error that matters, but that it constitutes a violation of petitioner's right to counsel, so that the error must be seen as an external factor, i.e., "imputed to the State." * * * Where a petitioner defaults a claim as a result of the denial of the right to effective assistance of counsel, the State, which is responsible for the denial as a constitutional matter, must bear the cost of any resulting default and the harm to state interests that federal habeas review entails. A different allocation of costs is appropriate in those circumstances where the State has no responsibility to ensure that the petitioner was represented by competent counsel. As between the State and the petitioner, it is the petitioner who must bear the burden of a failure to follow state procedural rules.

Should a habeas petitioner also be foreclosed by counsel's failure to raise a claim when that claim was not reasonably foreseeable by diligent counsel, or does that special circumstance constitute cause? This issue, left open in *Isaac,* was later answered in *Reed v. Ross.*[34] A divided Court there held the failure to raise a claim "so novel that its legal basis [was] not reasonably available" did not "seriously implicate any of the concerns that might otherwise require deference to a state's procedural bar" and therefore should not preclude habeas review. Justice Brennan's opinion for the Court reasoned:

> Just as it is reasonable to assume that a competent lawyer will fail to perceive the possibility of raising such a claim, it is also reasonable to assume that a court will similarly fail to appreciate the claim. * * * Despite the fact that a constitutional concept may ultimately enjoy general acceptance, * * * when the concept is in its embryonic stage, it will, by hypothesis, be rejected by most courts. Consequently, a rule requiring a defendant to raise a truly novel issue is not likely to serve any functional purpose. * * * In addition, if we were to hold that the novelty of a constitutional question does not give rise to cause for counsel's failure to raise it, we might actually disrupt state-court proceedings by encouraging defense counsel to include any and all remotely plausible constitutional claims that could, some day, gain recognition.

Four dissenters in *Reed* questioned how a claim so novel as to meet the *Reed* test was also the kind of fundamental claim that should be cognizable on habeas review. Subsequently, in *Teague v. Lane,*[35] the Court generally limited habeas review to the law as it stood when the defendant's conviction became final. Since a claim so novel as to fit within *Reed* obviously is also a "new ruling" under *Teague,* the practical impact of *Reed* is only to allow habeas review when the novel claim fits within one of the two exceptions recognized in *Teague.*

The *Carrier* majority suggested still another circumstance in which cause would be present because one could not reasonably expect counsel to raise the constitutional claim in the state proceedings. The Court there noted that, absent ineffective assistance of counsel, the "existence of cause for a procedural default must ordinarily turn on whether the prisoner can show that some objective factor external to the defense impeded counsel's efforts to comply with the state's procedural rule." Quoting and citing *Brown v. Allen,* it

33. See § 11.7(a).

34. 468 U.S. 1, 104 S.Ct. 2901, 82 L.Ed.2d 1 (1984).

35. See § 28.6.

stated that "cause" would be established by a showing of "'some interference by officials' that made compliance impracticable." The cited discussion in *Brown v. Allen,* referred to a case in which a warden had suppressed the prisoner's timely appeal papers.[36] So too, in *Amadeo v. Zant,*[37] the Court had before it a district court finding that a memorandum of the local prosecutor, evidencing a direction to the jury commissioners to underrepresent blacks and women without giving rise to prima facie case of discrimination, had been concealed by local officials and therefore was "not reasonably discoverable" by petitioner's trial counsel (who had failed to object to the composition of the jury). The primary issue before the Supreme Court was whether this finding was subject to review under a "clearly erroneous" standard (the Court held that it was), but the Court also characterized the district court's finding as fitting "squarely" within the concept of "cause" as set forth in *Ross* and *Carrier.*[38] Lower courts have refused, however, to extend this "objective external factor" analysis to encompass the contention that counsel lacked financial resources to fully develop the facts needed to support a claim, noting that counsel should at least call such a matter to the attention of the trial court. So too, courts have rejected the contention that cause exists simply by virtue of the fact that defendant was acting pro se, even though the proceeding was one at which the petitioner was not constitutionally entitled to appointed counsel.

Assuming that cause is established, what type of showing will establish the "actual prejudice" also required under the *Sykes* standard? Here again, *Sykes* left the "precise content" of the term to be filled out on a case-by-case basis. However, the Court's rulings in *Davis v. United States*[39] had already provided some indication of what the Court had in mind. *Davis* rejected the contention that the petitioner could rely upon a presumption of prejudice provided by the substantive law governing the claim. Thus, where the substantive law does not require a showing of a likely adverse impact to establish a constitutional violation (as it does not for racial discrimination in the selection of grand jury), the petitioner is nevertheless required to make such a showing to meet the actual prejudice standard of *Sykes.* Unfortunately, *Davis* did not indicate how that prejudice was to be measured, but the assumption seemed to be that a likely difference in outcome was necessary. In *Sykes,* the Court clearly indicated that, at least as to claims relating to the admission of evidence (there, a *Miranda* objection), actual prejudice would be measured by reference to the likely impact of the constitutional error on the outcome of the case. No precise gauge of the requisite probability was given, but the Court did note that the remaining evidence there "was substantial to a degree that would negate any possibility of actual prejudice."

Justice White, in his separate opinion in *Sykes,* suggested that the Court's application of the actual prejudice test had been "tanta-

36. Dowd v. United States ex rel. Cook, 340 U.S. 206, 71 S.Ct. 262, 95 L.Ed. 215 (1951).

37. 486 U.S. 214, 108 S.Ct. 1771, 100 L.Ed.2d 249 (1988).

38. Consider, however, McCleskey v. Zant, ___ U.S. ___, 111 S.Ct. 1454, 113 L.Ed.2d 517 (1991), where the Court majority held that the prosecution's failure to disclose a recorded statement of an informant prior to a second habeas petition did not constitute "cause" and therefore did not relieve the petitioner of the forfeiture that occurred when counsel failed to include in the first petition a Sixth Amendment challenge to the use of the informant's statement at trial. See § 28.5(b). The Court concluded that the recorded statement was not "critical" to the substance of petitioner's Sixth Amendment challenge (which had been raised in an earlier state habeas proceeding), that there had been no intentional government concealment of the evidence that would fall within the analysis of "cause" in Amadeo v. Zant, and that petitioner had sufficient information to raise the claim in his first petition in any event. The Court described the question before it in this regard as "whether petitioner possessed, or by reasonable means could have obtained, a sufficient basis to allege a claim in the first petition and pursue the matter through the habeas process, see 28 U.S.C.A. § 2254 Rule 6 (Discovery); Rule 7 (Expansion of Record); Rule 8 (Evidentiary Hearing)." It noted further that a petitioner's inability to obtain relevant evidence "fails to establish cause if other known or discoverable evidence could have supported the claim," and that the failure to assert the claim "will not be excused merely because evidence discovered later might also have supported or strengthened the claim."

39. Supra note 20.

mount to a finding of harmless error" under the traditional "harmless beyond a reasonable doubt" standard applied to constitutional errors. While the constitutional claim in *Sykes* may have fallen within the traditional harmless error category, there was no suggestion in the majority opinion that a test so favorable to the defendant would ordinarily apply. The Court had clearly indicated that the burden of showing prejudice was on the petitioner, whereas the state on direct review bears the burden of establishing the harmlessness of a constitutional error. Subsequently, the Court's reasoning in *Frady*,[40] where it refused to apply the plain error rule on habeas review, indicated that a more substantial showing of harm will be required on collateral attack than on direct appeal. Lower courts, recognizing this weakness in a harmless-error analogy, have been unwilling to find prejudice simply because a reasonable doubt exists as to whether the claimed constitutional error may have affected the jury decision to convict. They have insisted that petitioner make a showing of some significant probability that the outcome would have been different if not for the constitutional error. Support for such a standard is found in the Court's treatment of the constitutional error alleged in *Frady*.

The constitutional claim considered in *Frady* was that the trial judge's charge had improperly equated intent with malice, thereby allowing the jury to convict petitioner on a higher charge without proof beyond a reasonable doubt. The Supreme Court held that petitioner's failure to object to the charge at trial barred habeas review upon application of the *Sykes* standard. It was not necessary to consider the matter of "cause," since the Court was "confident" that Frady has "suffered no actual prejudice of a degree sufficient to justify collateral relief nineteen years after the crime." Justice O'Connor's opinion noted that its analysis of likely prejudice was informed by the constitutional test applied in determining whether a jury charge violated due process. The Court had held that as to charges to which there was no trial objection, due process was violated only when the charge "infected the entire trial." The same standard would be applied in determining whether there was "actual prejudice" in this case. There had been strong "uncontradicted evidence of malice in the record." Moreover, an analysis of the full charge and the jury's verdict showed "no substantial likelihood that the same jury that found Frady guilty of first-degree murder would have concluded, if only the malice instructions had been better framed, that his crime was only manslaughter."

The *Frady* analysis, including its reference to due process standards, suggests an analogy to those constitutional violations that require a showing of prejudicial impact on the outcome to establish the constitutional violation. In recent years, the standard most commonly applied in these cases requires a defense showing of a "reasonable probability" that the outcome would have been different except for the alleged constitutional violation.[41] A "reasonable probability" is described as "a probability sufficient to undermine confidence in the outcome." While the Court has not expressly adopted this test for the prejudice prong of *Sykes*, as both commentators and lower courts have noted, opinions like *Frady* suggest something quite similar. This would produce a consistent approach where the defendant sought to convert the procedural default into a Sixth Amendment claim of ineffective assistance of counsel, because the reasonable probability standard is also used to measure the prejudice prong of such Sixth Amendment claims.

(g) The "Fundamental Miscarriage of Justice" Exception. Justice O'Connor's opinion in *Engle v. Isaac* stressed that "cause" and "prejudice" were not rigid concepts, but were based upon general principles of "comity and finality." "In appropriate cases," Justice O'Connor noted, "those principles must yield to the imperative of fundamentally unjust incarceration." This was not a new concept

40. Supra note 21.

41. See the cases cited at note 18 of § 27.6. See also the discussion of the *Strickland* and *Bagley* cases at § 11.10(d) and § 20.7(b).

as *Sykes* had noted that the standard developed there would not bar habeas relief for a victim of a "miscarriage of justice." Subsequent discussions have used interchangeably the phrases of "fundamental miscarriage of justice" and "fundamentally unjust incarceration" to describe this additional element of the current default standard.

The initial discussions of this element did not make clear whether the presence of a fundamental miscarriage of justice required a more lenient definition of cause or created an exception to the cause and prejudice standard, allowing relief where the cause standard is not met. So too, while it was clear that the fundamental miscarriage element covered a narrower range of prejudice than the prejudice prong of the *Sykes* standard, its precise scope was uncertain. The primary discussions of both of these issues came in *Murray v. Carrier*[42] and *Smith v. Murray.*[43]

The Court in *Carrier* first made clear that the cause and prejudice standard was not one of a series of considerations to be balanced in determining whether habeas review was appropriate. That position was advocated by Justice Stevens, who argued that each case required the habeas court to weigh the "fundamental importance" of the asserted constitutional right, the "nature and strength of the [petitioner's] constitutional claim," and the "nature and strength of the state procedural rule that has not been observed." The majority rejected such a "reworking of the cause and prejudice test" as basically dispensing with the "cause" requirement in favor of an amorphous inquiry into the element of prejudice. The *Sykes* standard required that both prongs be met; a showing of "actual prejudice" without also establishing "cause" was insufficient. However, while "victims of a fundamental miscarriage" ordinarily should be able to meet both prongs of the *Sykes* standard, there remained an additional safeguard: "[I]n an extraordinary case, where a constitutional violation has probably resulted in the conviction of one who is actually innocent, a federal habeas court may grant the writ even in the absence of a showing of cause for the procedural default." With this exception recognized, as well as the availability of the Sixth Amendment ineffective counsel claim, the "cause and prejudice test" established a "sound and workable means of channeling the discretion of federal habeas courts" in treating procedural defaults at the state level.

Speaking further to the fundamental miscarriage exception in *Smith,* the Court noted that the exception's focus was on "actual" as distinct from "legal innocence." The petitioner there claimed that the state court had violated his self-incrimination privilege when it allowed into evidence at his capital sentencing hearing a psychiatrist's testimony recounting a damaging statement defendant had made during a psychiatric examination without being warned as to its possible use against him. The Court majority refused to ask whether the erroneous introduction of that evidence might have had a bearing on the jury's death-sentence recommendation. Such an impact-upon-outcome inquiry would have been appropriate in applying the "actual prejudice" prong of the *Sykes* test, but that prong was not relevant since the Court had determined that the procedural default here (failing to raise the evidentiary challenge on appeal) was not justified by "cause."[44] For the purpose of determining whether there was an unjust incarceration, the key was whether admission of the defendant's statement to the psychiatrist had "pervert[ed] the jury's deliberations concerning the ultimate question whether *in fact* petitioner constituted a continuing threat to society." Since there was no suggestion that his statement was "false or in any way misleading," it obviously had not adversely influenced the factual correctness of the jurors' verdict even though that verdict might have been otherwise if the

42. Supra note 26.

43. 477 U.S. 527, 106 S.Ct. 2661, 91 L.Ed.2d 434 (1986).

44. Counsel's failure to raise the self-incrimination objection on appeal was held not to constitute constitutionally ineffective assistance. See § 11.10 at note 16.

statement had been excluded as constitutionally inadmissible.[45]

§ 28.5 Claims Foreclosed by Successive or Delayed Applications

(a) Grounds Advanced in Prior Applications. At common law the doctrine of res judicata did not apply to the rulings of the habeas court. Denied relief by one judge, a prisoner could simply turn to another, seeking the same relief on the same grounds. Although numerous explanations have been offered, the common law's refusal to limit habeas applications through the doctrine of res judicata was most frequently attributed to the lack of direct appellate review of a denial of the writ.[1] Accordingly, in *Salinger v. Loisel,*[2] a 1924 ruling, the Supreme Court concluded that, with appellate review long available in the federal system, continued application of the common law position, giving no weight whatsoever to the rejection of a prior application, was ripe for reconsideration. The federal habeas statutes directed the habeas court "to dispose of the party as law and justice may require." "[A] prior refusal to discharge a like application" clearly was among the matters that should be "considered, and even given controlling weight," in applying that standard. The doctrine of res judicata should not itself be applicable, but the habeas court could give the rejection of a previous application such weight as it deemed appropriate in light of factors such as the "fullness of the consideration" given to the prior application. When the habeas statutes were revised in 1948, section 2244 arguably codified or even expanded upon the principle announced in *Salinger.* Section 2244 stated that no federal habeas court was "required to entertain an application" by a federal or state prisoner if "the legality of the [the applicant's] detention has been determined * * * on a prior application for a writ of habeas corpus and the petition presents no new ground not theretofore presented and determined, and the judge * * * is satisfied that the ends of justice will not be served by such inquiry."

The benchmark interpretation of the 1948 revision came in *Sanders v. United States,*[3] one of three major rulings during the 1962 term that adopted expansive interpretations of the federal writ.[4] *Sanders* involved a successive application by a federal prisoner under § 2255, but the Supreme Court held that the somewhat differently worded § 2255 provision had the same content as the § 2244 provision. *Sanders* concluded as to both provisions that it clearly had not been the purpose of Congress to incorporate the doctrine of res judicata. To have done so, it was noted, would be inconsistent with the basic function of the writ. The *Salinger* ruling, in rejecting application of res judicata, implicitly recognized that the common law position did not lose all of its support with the adoption of appellate review. Much more was at stake: "If 'government ... [is] always [to] be accountable to the judiciary for a man's imprisonment,' *Fay v. Noia,* access to the courts on habeas must not be thus impeded."

With res judicata rejected, the *Sanders* Court turned to a two pronged question: What weight, if any, should then be given to a prior disposition where the habeas petition presents (1) the same ground advanced in the

45. See also Dugger v. Adams, supra note 15, rejecting the contention that "a fundamental miscarriage of justice results whenever * * * 'the very essence' of [the constitutional claim] * * * is that the accuracy of the sentencing determination is undermined." The *Dugger* majority noted: "Demonstrating that an error is by its nature the kind of error that might have affected the accuracy of a death sentence is far from demonstrating that a defendant probably is 'actually innocent' of the sentence he or she received." So too, the mere fact that the trial judge found an equal number of aggravating and mitigating circumstances established at petitioner's capital sentencing proceeding "was not sufficient to show that an alleged error in instructing the jury [conveying the false impression that sentencing responsibility rested elsewhere] * * * resulted in a fundamental miscarriage of justice."

§ 28.5

1. See § 27.4, at note 1. The federal system, in contrast to other jurisdictions, provided for appellate review as far back as the 1800's. See § 28.2, text preceding note 11.

2. 265 U.S. 224, 44 S.Ct. 519, 68 L.Ed. 989 (1924).

3. 373 U.S. 1, 83 S.Ct. 1068, 10 L.Ed.2d 148 (1963).

4. The other rulings were Fay v. Noia, discussed in §§ 28.3(b), 28.4(c), (d), and Townsend v. Sain, discussed in § 28.7(a).

prior application or (2) a ground not previously advanced? The Court's answer to the second prong of this question is discussed in the next subsection. As to the first, it set forth the following standard:

> Controlling weight may be given to denial of a prior application for federal habeas corpus or § 2255 relief only if (1) the same ground presented in the subsequent application was determined adversely to the applicant on the prior application, (2) the prior determination was on the merits, and (3) the ends of justice would not be served by reaching the merits of the subsequent application.

The Court stressed that this standard determined only when a habeas court had discretion to give controlling weight to the prior adjudication. Even if the standard was met, the habeas court retained "the power" to give full consideration to a claim without regard to the prior habeas adjudication.

The key to the first condition of the *Sanders* standard was the determination as to whether the ground advanced in the current application was the "same ground" presented in the prior application. "By ground," the Court noted, "we mean simply a sufficient legal basis for granting the relief sought by the applicant." A single ground could be supported by "different factual allegations." Thus, there would not be a new ground if the petitioner, in challenging the state's use of an allegedly involuntary confession, initially claimed "physical coercion" and then subsequently alleged "psychological coercion." Similarly, "identical grounds may often be supported by different legal arguments, or be couched in different language, or vary in immaterial respects." The Court warned, however, that doubts about whether a new ground has been presented "should be resolved in favor of the applicant."

If the habeas court determined that the petition did in fact raise the same ground as the prior petition, the *Sanders* guideline then required it to determine if the previous ruling on that ground had been on the "merits." Where a factual issue was raised, this meant that the earlier habeas court had either held an evidentiary hearing or denied relief "on the basis that the files and records conclusively resolved those issues." Finally, even if the petition raised a ground previously decided on the merits, the habeas court could not give controlling weight to that determination if "the ends of justice would be served by permitting the redetermination of the ground." The burden was on the applicant, the Court noted, to establish that he fell within this exception. Two illustrations of satisfactory showings were offered. If factual issues were involved, the applicant would be "entitled to a new hearing upon showing that the evidentiary hearing on the prior application was not full and fair." If a "purely legal question" were involved, the applicant might be entitled to a new hearing "upon showing an intervening change in law or some other justification for having failed to raise a crucial point or argument in the prior application." The Court stressed that its two illustrations were "not intended to be exhaustive." Moreover, as previously noted, the habeas court always had the authority to reach the merits at its discretion; the "ends of justice" standard only prescribed when it had "the duty" to do so.

In 1966, Congress amended § 2244, and added a new subsection (b), specifically addressed to successive petitions brought by state prisoners. The language of § 2244(b) varies somewhat from the earlier provision considered in *Sanders.* Section 2244(b) provides that a successive application "need not be entertained" unless the application alleges a "factual or other ground not adjudicated in the hearing of the earlier application." Thus, unlike the earlier provision, it does not refer to the "ends of justice." In 1976, Rule 9(b) of the Federal Rules Governing Section 2254 Cases was adopted. It also contained a provision on successive petitions, stating that such a petition "may be dismissed if it fails to allege new or different grounds for relief and the prior determination was on the merits." Here again the language varies somewhat from the provision interpreted in *Sanders,* particularly in its failure to refer to the "ends of justice" exception.

In *Kuhlmann v. Wilson,*[5] the seven justices who spoke to the successive petition question agreed that neither the 1966 amendment nor Rule 9(b) mandated a departure from the general guidelines set forth in *Sanders.* While it was true that Congress in those provisions "intended for district courts, as the general rule, to give preclusive effect to a judgment denying on the merits a habeas petition alleging grounds identical in substance to those raised in the subsequent petition," its use of "permissive language" evidenced an intent to retain the district court's "discretion to entertain successive petitions under some circumstances." The "ends of justice" standard could still serve as an appropriate point of reference for determining when that discretion should be exercised to consider a claim previously decided on its merits. So too, *Sanders* could be looked to for guidance as to what constituted an "other" or "new or different" ground and what constituted a prior "adjudication" or "determination on the merits."

Although there was agreement in *Kuhlmann* that federal habeas courts still "must consider the 'ends of justice' before dismissing a successive petition," there was disagreement as to the content of that standard and the significance of *Sanders'* illustrations of its content. The habeas petitioner in *Kuhlmann* challenged the admissibility under the Sixth Amendment of statements that he had made to a fellow jailhouse inmate who turned out to be an informant.[6] Petitioner argued that the ends of justice demanded reconsideration of this claim, which had been rejected in an earlier habeas proceeding, because a Supreme Court ruling issued between the first and second habeas petitions had strengthened his claim by extending the scope of the Sixth Amendment as it applied to the elicitation of incriminatory statements from an accused. An "intervening change in the law" was one of *Sanders'* two illustrations of circumstances in which the ends of justice would be served by a reconsideration of a previously rejected claim. Justice Brennan, joined by Justice Marshall, agreed that *Sanders* was controlling. He argued that, to give " 'fair effect' to the intent of Congress," the Court should "construe the ends of justice as *Sanders* did," as legislative history clearly indicated Congress' "express endorsement" of *Sanders.* Justice Stevens, in a brief opinion, did not cite *Sanders* in concluding that the situation before the habeas court was one which neither demanded nor precluded a reconsideration of the habeas petitioner's claim. He saw the intervening Supreme Court decision as providing a justification adequate for the habeas court to exercise its discretion to entertain the claim, but not so compelling that a refusal to entertain the claim would constitute an abuse of discretion. Justice Powell, writing for a four-justice plurality, took an entirely different approach and concluded that the lower court "erred in concluding that the 'ends of justice' would be served by consideration of [the] successive petition."

Justice Powell's plurality opinion looked to the legislative history of the 1966 Amendment and Rule 9(b), rather than to the *Sanders'* illustrations, in defining the content of the ends of justice standard. The legislative history of the 1966 amendments "demonstrate[d] that Congress intended * * * to introduce 'a greater degree of finality of judgments in habeas corpus proceedings.' " So too, the Advisory Committee Note to Rule 9(b) stated that "federal courts should entertain successive petitions only in 'rare instances.' " Accordingly, the Court's task was "to provide a definition of the 'ends of justice' that will accommodate Congress' intent to give finality to federal habeas judgments with the historic function of habeas corpus to provide relief from unjust incarceration." This required limiting the circumstances in which the prisoner's interest in relitigation outweighed the "countervailing interests served by * * * finality" to those situations in which the prisoner retains the most "powerful and legitimate interest in obtaining release from custody." Such an interest, he noted, exists only

5. 477 U.S. 436, 106 S.Ct. 2616, 91 L.Ed.2d 364 (1986).

6. See § 6.4 at note 53, discussing this aspect of *Kuhlmann.*

where the prisoner "is innocent of the charge for which he is incarcerated," and therefore obviously is not present where the prisoner's guilt "is conceded or plain." Accordingly, "the 'ends of justice' [should] require federal courts to entertain [successive] petitions only where the petitioner supplements his constitutional claim with a colorable showing of factual innocence." That "evidentiary showing" would be required "even though—as argued in this case—the evidence of guilt may have been unlawfully admitted," since the constitutional challenge to the evidence may not relate to its reliability and therefore may "not itself raise any question as to * * * guilt or innocence."

In *McCleskey v. Zant,*[7] in dealing with the ends of justice standard in a somewhat different context, the Court majority lent strong support to the approach adopted by the *Kuhlmann* plurality. At issue there was the content of the second grounding for rejecting a successive petition, the abuse of writ through failure to have raised in the earlier petition the claim now presented in the successive petition. As discussed in subsection (b), the *McCleskey* majority held that the abuse of writ concept should be governed by the "cause and prejudice" standard that had been developed in determining when a procedural default in state proceeding precludes habeas consideration of the defaulted claim.[8] One aspect of that standard is the exception for cases of "unjust incarceration." That exception provides for habeas review, notwithstanding the habeas petitioner's failure to establish cause and prejudice with respect to the procedural default, where "the constitutional violation has probably resulted in the conviction of one who is actually innocent." [9] The Court in *McCleskey* noted that "this exception to cause for fundamental miscarriages of justice gives meaningful content to the otherwise unexplained 'ends of justice' inquiry mandated by *Sanders.*" In support of this conclusion, it noted that a "plurality of the Court in *Kuhlmann* [had] held that this inquiry * * * required federal courts to entertain successive petitions when a petitioner supplements a constitutional claim with a 'colorable showing of factual innocence.' " Applying the unjust incarceration in the case before it, the *McCleskey* majority duplicated the analysis of the *Kuhlmann* plurality. As in *Kuhlmann,* the petitioner in *McCleskey* presented a claim challenging the admission of incriminatory statements allegedly elicited in violation of petitioner's Sixth Amendment right to counsel, and as in *Kuhlmann,* the Court noted that such a claim did not establish a possible unjust incarceration since the alleged constitutional violation at most "resulted in the admission at trial of truthful inculpatory evidence which did not affect the reliability of the guilt determination."

As a practical matter, the *Kuhlmann–McCleskey* requirement of a showing of a "colorable claim of innocence" is likely to have little significance in those cases, like *Kuhlmann,* in which the habeas petitioner looks to an intervening change in the law as the justification for reconsidering a claim previously rejected. Any such intervening change will come after the petitioner's conviction is final, and *Teague v. Lane* holds that a new ruling will not be applied retroactively to a final conviction except under two circumstances.[10] Under the first, retroactive application is given to a new ruling holding that the state cannot constitutionally punish the conduct in which the defendant engaged. Such a ruling in itself establishes that the habeas petitioner is innocent, so no further showing would be necessary to meet the ends of justice standard. The second *Teague* exception applies to the new ruling establishing a constitutional guarantee "central to an accurate determination of innocence or guilt." *Teague* noted that it was unlikely that many such components of basic due process are still likely to emerge, but should a new ruling establish such a guarantee, its very nature will ordinarily suggest a "colorable showing of

7. ___ U.S. ___, 111 S.Ct. 1454, 113 L.Ed.2d 517 (1991), also discussed infra at note 19.

8. See § 28.4(e).

9. See § 28.4(g).

10. See § 28.6.

factual innocence."[11] Thus, the *Kuhlmann–McCleskey* requirement is most likely to make a difference only where the justification advanced for reconsideration relates to the factual grounding of the previously adjudicated claim—as where the initial hearing was not full and fair or the habeas petitioner has newly discovered evidence that was not previously available.

(b) New Grounds. The original version of § 2244, which was before the Court in *Sanders,* stated that the habeas court need not consider a successive petition that "present[ed] no new ground not therefore presented and determined." One possible reading of this language was that § 2244 did not authorize dismissal of a successive petition that presented a new ground. In *Sanders* the government responded to this reading by arguing that the § 2244 reference to "new grounds" included only a ground "that had not previously been asserted and had not previously been known." The *Sanders* majority rejected this contention, holding that the § 2244 reference to a "new ground" should be read literally to encompass all "grounds not previously heard and decided." However, that did not mean that all new grounds had to be entertained by the habeas court. Congress in adopting § 2244 had not intended to foreclose the continued application of the "abuse-of-writ" doctrine that had been developed in a series of earlier decisions, including *Wong Doo v. United States,*[12] and *Price v. Johnston.*[13] Those cases, the *Sanders* opinion noted, had recognized that "the prisoner who on prior motion * * * has deliberately withheld a ground for relief need not be heard if he asserts that ground on a successive motion; his action is inequitable—an abuse of the remedy—and the court may in its discretion deny him a hearing." Section 2244, was addressed only to judicial discretion in treating the previously adjudicated claim and left to judicial development those principles that might justify not entertaining a claim that had not been raised and decided in previous petitions.

Having held that the abuse-of-writ doctrine existed apart from § 2244, *Sanders* then set forth a "formulation of basic rules to guide the lower federal courts" in applying the abuse-of-writ doctrine. As established in the earlier cases, the government had the responsibility of pleading the alleged abuse of the writ, with the habeas petitioner then required to respond to a well pleaded allegation. In evaluating that response, the habeas court would be guided by the "equitable principles" traditionally governing habeas review, "among them * * * the principle that a suitor's conduct in relation to the matter at hand may disentitle him to the relief he seeks." The Court furnished two illustrations of defense tactics that would constitute an abuse of writ. The first was the prisoner who "withholds one of two grounds for federal collateral relief at the time of filing his first application in the hope of being granted two hearings rather than one." The second, as illustrated by *Wong Doo,* was the situation in which "the prisoner deliberately abandons one of his grounds at the first hearing." The Court also cited *Fay v. Noia*[14] and *Townsend v. Sain*[15]

11. While *Kuhlmann-McCleskey* looks to a likelihood of factual innocence under the facts of the particular case, *Teague*'s second exception, though differently stated, often will do the same. Traditional due process analysis looks not only to the potential impact of the alleged violation upon factfinding reliability in general, but also to the impact upon the outcome of the particular case. See e.g., §§ 2.6(e); 18.5(b); 20.7(d); 24.3(a); 24.5(h). However, due process violations have also been found in certain structural flaws based on potential impact or the appearance of unfairness (e.g., Tumey v. Ohio, § 2.4 at note 8). Here the due process violation would not necessarily provide a grounding for the requisite *Kuhlmann-McCleskey* showing, as the evidence of guilt may be so strong as to suggest the correctness of the verdict notwithstanding that flaw. Indeed, due process violations though the improper use of presumptions in jury charges have been held in some settings to present an insufficient likelihood of prejudice to satisfy more lenient standards for obtaining relief—i.e., the reasonable doubt harmless error standard of *Chapman,* see § 27.6(d), and the prejudice prong under *Sykes,* see § 28.4 at note 40 (discussing United States v. Frady). See also Dugger v. Adams, note 45 of § 26.4, where a constitutionally invalid jury charge was held not to automatically satisfy the fundamental miscarriage standard, which is similar to *Kuhlmann-McCleskey* in requiring a showing of factual innocence.

12. 265 U.S. 239, 44 S.Ct. 524, 68 L.Ed. 999 (1924).

13. 334 U.S. 266, 68 S.Ct. 1049, 92 L.Ed. 1356 (1948).

14. See § 28.4(d).

15. See § 28.7(b).

for further guidance. Finally, *Sanders* added as a "final qualification" that the federal habeas court always had "the duty" to "reach the merits" when the "ends of justice" so demand.

When Congress reframed the successive application provision in 1966, it included in § 2244(b) a reference to the abuse-of-writ doctrine. In noting that the habeas court need not entertain a successive application unless it alleges a new ground, the section added the proviso that the court be "satisfied that the applicant has not in the earlier application deliberately withheld the newly asserted ground or otherwise abused the writ." Rule 9(b) of the § 2254 Rules also referred to the doctrine. It states that the habeas court may dismiss the application if it finds "the failure of the petitioner to assert those grounds [referring to "new and different grounds"] in a prior petition constituted an abuse of writ."

The two provisions clearly allowed for the continued application of the abuse-of-writ doctrine. The primary issue raised by their reference to that doctrine was whether they incorporated the specific guidelines set forth in *Sanders* or continued to leave the content of the doctrine to judicial development. The *Sanders* ruling had relied heavily on the deliberate bypass standard of *Fay v. Noia,* but the Supreme Court had later rejected that standard as to procedural defaults. It had substituted the more demanding standard of *Wainwright v. Sykes,*[16] which required cause and prejudice except for those rare cases falling within the fundamental miscarriage exception. If the *Sanders–Noia* guidelines had not been codified by § 2244(b) and Rule 9(b), it seemed likely that the Court would similarly modify the content of the abuse-of-writ doctrine.

In *McCleskey v. Zant,*[17] a divided Court reviewed these developments and concluded that the abuse of writ doctrine should now be read as incorporating the *Sykes'* standard. Justice Marshall, in dissent, argued that § 2244(b) and Rule 9(b) had codified *Sanders* and thereby restricted the abuse-of-writ doctrine to cases in which there was a "form of bad faith," akin to a deliberate bypass, in the petitioner's failure to have raised the new ground in a previous habeas petition. The majority, per Kennedy, J., responded that § 2244(b) and Rule 9(b) did no more than "incorporat[e] the judge made principle governing the abuse-of-writ set forth in *Sanders.*" Congress had not sought to "state the limits on the district court's discretion to entertain abusive petitions," nor had it "defin[ed] the term 'abuse of writ.'" "[T]he doctrine of abuse of writ," Justice Kennedy noted, "refers to a complex and evolving body of equitable principles informed and controlled by historical usage, statutory developments, and judicial decisions." *Sanders* had mentioned "deliberate abandonment as but one example of conduct that disentitled a petitioner to relief." Indeed, it had cited a passage in *Townsend* that had referred to the concept of "inexcusable neglect," which subsequent lower court and Supreme Court rulings had held to bar the raising of new claims that could have been raised in earlier petitions "regardless of whether [that] failure * * * stemmed from a deliberate choice."

The *McCleskey* opinion acknowledged that the concept of inexcusable neglect, though not limited to instances of deliberate abandonment, had not been given the "content necessary to guide district courts." To provide a guideline familiar to those courts, the "determination of inexcusable neglect in the abuse of writ context" would now be assessed by reference to the "same standard used to determine whether to excuse procedural defaults." That standard was appropriate because "[t]he doctrines of procedural default and abuse of writ implicate nearly identical concerns flowing from the significant costs of federal habeas review."[18] Accordingly, an abuse of writ

16. See § 28.4(e)–(g).

17. Supra note 7.

18. The Court noted in this regard: "Our procedural default jurisprudence and abuse of the writ jurisprudence [both] help define this dimension of procedural regularity. Both doctrines impose on petitioners a burden of reasonable compliance with procedures designed to discourage

would be present unless the failure of the petitioner to have raised the new claim in an earlier petition was justified under the "cause and prejudice" standard that excuses the failure to have raised a claim in the original state proceedings in accordance with state procedures. In addition, consistent with the "ends of justice" standard of *Sanders,* a new claim would be considered, notwithstanding the absence of excuse under the cause and prejudice standard, where necessary to "correct a miscarriage of justice." [19] This would require a "colorable showing of factual innocence," as set forth in *Kuhlmann* [20] and such state-default cases as *Murray v. Carrier,*[21] and thereby would provide " 'an additional safeguard against compelling an innocent man to suffer an unconstitutional loss of liberty.' "

The *McCleskey* Court provided further guidance to lower courts by prescribing the procedure through which the "cause and prejudice analysis" should be applied to "an abuse of writ inquiry." The Court noted:

> When a prisoner files a second or subsequent application, the government bears the burden of pleading abuse of the writ. The government satisfies this burden if, with clarity and particularity, it notes petitioner's prior writ history, identifies the claims that appear for the first time, and alleges that petitioner has abused the writ. The burden to disprove abuse then becomes petitioner's. To excuse his failure to raise the claim earlier, he must show cause for failing to raise it and prejudice therefrom as those concepts have been defined in our procedural default decisions. The petitioner's opportunity to meet the burden of cause and prejudice will not include an evidentiary hearing if the district court determines as a matter of law that petitioner cannot satisfy the standard. If petitioner cannot show cause, the failure to raise the claim in an earlier petition may nonetheless be excused if he or she can show that a fundamental miscarriage of justice would result from a failure to entertain the claim.

(c) Laches. As noted by Professor Yackle, "Supreme Court decisions regarding federal [collateral] remedies have routinely insisted that they are available 'without time limit' and that, accordingly, the equitable defense of laches is inapposite in postconviction litigation on constitutional issues." [22] That position apparently was altered, however, by the Court's adoption of Rule 9(a) of the § 2254 Rules and the similarly worded Rule 9(a) of

baseless claims and to keep the system open for valid ones; both recognize the law's interest in finality; and both invoke equitable principles to define the court's discretion to excuse pleading and procedural requirements for petitioners who could not comply with them in the exercise of reasonable care and diligence. It is true that a habeas court's concern to honor state procedural default rules rests in part on respect for the integrity of procedures 'employed by a coordinate jurisdiction within the federal system,' Wainwright v. Sykes, and that such respect is not implicated when a petitioner defaults a claim by failing to raise it in the first round of federal habeas review. Nonetheless, the doctrines of procedural default and abuse of the writ are both designed to lessen the injury to a State that results through reexamination of a state conviction on a ground that the State did not have the opportunity to address at a prior, appropriate time; and both doctrines seek to vindicate the State's interest in the finality of its criminal judgments."

Challenging the above analysis, Justice Marshall argued that the "strictness of the cause-and-prejudice test had been justified on the ground that the defendant's procedural default is akin to an independent and adequate state-law ground for the judgment of conviction," but here similar concerns of comity were not present. The dissent also argued that there was no need for a cause-and-prejudice test because "a habeas petitioner's own interest in liberty furnishes a powerful incentive to assert on his first petition all claims that the petitioner (or his counsel) believes have a reasonable prospect for success." However, the majority had noted, in its general discussion of the costs of habeas review, that "habeas corpus review may give litigants incentives to withhold claims for manipulative purposes and may establish disincentives to present claims when evidence is fresh." *McCleskey* was a capital case, and several justices in earlier cases had expressed concern about "a pattern that seems to be developing in capital cases of multiple review in which claims that could have been presented years ago are brought forward—often in a piecemeal fashion—only after the execution date is set or becomes imminent." Woodard v. Hutchins, 464 U.S. 377, 104 S.Ct. 752, 78 L.Ed.2d 541 (1984) (Powell, J., concurring).

19. See the discussion of this portion of the Court's ruling following note 7 supra.

20. Supra note 5.

21. See § 28.4 at note 42.

22. L. Yackle, Postconviction Remedies § 114 (1981). Professor Yackle also notes, however, that some lower courts, prior to the adoption Rule 9(a), discussed infra, had "demanded that petitioners pursuing stale claims assume a heavier burden of proof," and others had "simply taken account of the passage of time in determining the credibility of the applicant's evidence."

the § 2255 Rules. The § 2254 Rule provides that

> [a] petition may be dismissed if it appears that the state * * * has been prejudiced in its ability to respond to the petition by delay in its filing unless the petitioner shows that it is based on grounds of which he could not have had knowledge by the exercise of reasonable diligence before the circumstances prejudicial to the state occurred.

The Advisory Committee Note states that Rule 9 was based "on the equitable doctrine of laches" and created a "flexible rule analogous to laches." As drafted, the Rule also provided that if a petition was filed more than five years after the imposition of sentence, prejudice to the state would be presumed. While that provision was eliminated by Congress, this action did not alter the overall objective of granting the habeas court discretion to dismiss the writ in accordance with the principle that one party should not be allowed to unreasonably delay enforcement of his rights so as to undercut the adversary position of the other party.[23]

In *Vasquez v. Hillery,*[24] the Court emphasized that the laches doctrine rested on the habeas petitioner's unreasonable delay in filing his petition, not simply the passage of time that would make reprosecution of the petitioner more difficult. The petitioner there had not reached the federal habeas court until 16 years after his conviction, but that delay was due to his persistent pursuit of appeals and collateral relief in the state courts. Rejecting the suggestion that habeas courts "condition the grant of relief upon the passage of time between a conviction and the filing of a habeas petition, depending upon the ability of a State to obtain a second conviction," the Court noted that Congress "ha[d] not seen fit" in adopting Rule 9(a) to provide the state with such an "additional defense to habeas corpus petitions."

§ 28.6 Constitutional Interpretation on Habeas Review

(a) *Teague*'s "Law-at-the-Time" Principle. *Brown v. Allen*[1] directed federal habeas courts to "independently apply the correct constitutional standards" to a petitioner's claim, "no matter how fair and completely the claim had been litigated in state courts." Both of the separate opinions for the *Brown* Court[2] flatly rejected the contention that the state court's interpretation of the Constitution should be binding on the federal habeas court. Such a position would be inconsistent with the function of the 1867 Habeas Act, characterized by Justice Frankfurter as giving to federal courts the "final say" on the merits of a state prisoner's federal constitutional claim. In exercising de novo review of constitutional questions, the federal habeas court was to give the state court's adjudication no more "weight" than what "federal practice [commonly] gives to the conclusion of a court last resort of another jurisdiction on federal constitutional issues." Almost forty years after *Brown, Teague v. Lane*[3] substantially altered the nature of that "final say" given to the federal habeas courts.[4] The net

23. The Advisory Committee suggested that the primary candidate for application of this principle might be the stale claim of incompetency of counsel. Where the habeas challenge is brought long after the original state proceeding, the original defense attorney often has "little or no recollection as to what took place" and many of the other participants may be dead or their whereabouts unknown. Especially where the case was decided on a guilty plea, the trial record, even where still available, "may not satisfactorily reveal the extent of the defense attorney's efforts on behalf of the petitioner."

24. 474 U.S. 254, 106 S.Ct. 617, 88 L.Ed.2d 598 (1986), also discussed in § 15.3.

§ 28.6

1. 344 U.S. 443, 73 S.Ct. 397, 97 L.Ed. 469 (1953).

2. See § 28.3 following note 13.

3. 489 U.S. 288, 109 S.Ct. 1060, 103 L.Ed.2d 334 (1989).

4. The Court in *Teague* apparently did not view its ruling as inconsistent with *Brown.* There was no discussion of *Brown* in any of the *Teague* opinions, as all of the justices focused on the retroactivity cases discussed infra. Unlike *Teague, Brown* had not involved an issue of retroactively applying a new Supreme Court precedent, but neither had it suggested that the habeas court was in anyway prohibited from adopting a more expansive interpretation of preexisting precedent than the state court had adopted. Dissenting in Butler v. McKellar, infra note 15, Justice Brennan argued that the *Teague* prohibition against "new" rulings on habeas review had been read so broadly as to undercut the principle of "*de novo* review" that had been recognized in *Brown.*

result of *Teague* and its progeny is that, for most constitutional claims, the task of the federal habeas court is not to ask how it would interpret the Constitution, but to ask whether the state court's interpretation was a reasonably debatable reading of the Supreme Court precedent prevailing at that point in time when the opportunity for direct review of the prisoner's conviction ended.

The habeas petitioner in *Teague* raised a constitutional objection to the prosecutor's use of peremptory challenges to exclude blacks from his jury. While his habeas petition was working its way through the federal appellate process, the Supreme Court rendered its decision in *Batson v. Kentucky,*[5] which overruled an early precedent and established a more stringent equal protection safeguard against racial discrimination in the use of peremptory challenges. The petitioner argued that *Batson* sustained his constitutional claim. He further argued that even if *Batson* had come too late for him to take advantage of the *Batson* ruling itself, a similar prohibition should be incorporated in the Sixth Amendment right to a jury venire selected from a fair cross-section of the community, as that cross-section right had been recognized several years prior to his conviction in *Taylor v. Louisiana.*[6]

The initial issue posed in *Teague* was whether a habeas petitioner could gain the benefit of a Supreme Court ruling that had come after the exhaustion of the direct appellate review of his conviction and had clearly expanded constitutional protection beyond what previous precedent had required. As discussed in § 2.9(a)–(c), the Court during the 1960's had developed the *Linkletter–Stovall* tripartite standard for determining whether there should be retroactive application of a "new ruling" that came after the defendant's conviction. Application of that standard was not tied to the procedural posture of a defendant's challenge to his conviction; the same test applied whether the timing of the intervening ruling allowed it to be raised on direct appellate review of a conviction or only on collateral review. However, as discussed in § 2.9(d), the Court, in a series of cases decided in the early 1980's, reversed itself as to limiting retroactivity on direct appellate review. Those cases held that all new rulings would be applied retroactively to convictions that were not final—i.e., a conviction that had not yet reached the point in the appellate process where the Supreme Court had denied certiorari or the time period for petitioning for certiorari had elapsed. Once the Court adopted this position as to convictions not yet final on the date of the new ruling, it turned the issue of retroactivity into a question of the appropriate scope of the habeas remedy. Where a defendant's conviction was finalized prior to the issuance of a new ruling, it was only through the writ that he might present a challenge based upon that intervening ruling.

The primary intervening ruling relied upon by the petitioner in *Teague, Batson v. Kentucky,* had already been held not to apply retroactively on collateral review in a decision applying the *Linkletter–Stovall* standard. Nonetheless, through other aspects of the petitioner's claim, the Court was presented with the question of whether the *Linkletter–Stovall* standard should continue to govern the use of new rulings on habeas review. Justices Brennan and Marshall found no need to reach that issue, but the seven remaining justices disagreed. While they produced four separate opinions, with none gaining majority support, they found common ground in rejecting the *Linkletter–Stovall* approach and replacing it with a new standard based on the function of habeas review.

The crux of *Teague* 's new standard is that, subject to certain exceptions, a habeas petitioner's conviction should be reviewed by reference to the "law prevailing at the time [his] conviction became final." Justice O'Connor's plurality opinion, joined by three other justices, provided the leading discussion of this "law-at-the-time" principle. Justice Stevens, joined by Justice Blackmun, expressed agreement both with that principle and the basic

5. See § 22.3 at note 39.

6. See § 22.2 at note 21.

thrust of the plurality's reasoning supporting it. Justice White expressed regret as to the Court's earlier departure from the application of *Linkletter–Stovall* on direct review, but that having been done, he found "acceptable" the application of this different standard in collateral proceedings.

Justice O'Connor's plurality opinion in large part derived the "law-at-the-time" principle from what was described as the "deterrence function" of the habeas writ. A central function of federal habeas review, it was argued, is ensuring that the state courts faithfully apply the prevailing "constitutional principles" as announced by the Supreme Court. The Supreme Court's docket limitations obviously would preclude its review of all but a small number of state court departures from prevailing constitutional principles. The role of habeas review was to deter state courts from taking advantage of the likelihood that their departures from prevailing precedents would escape Supreme Court review. Federal habeas review was to provide a broad avenue for correcting any such departures and thereby "serve as a necessary incentive for trial and appellate judges * * * to conduct their proceedings in a manner consistent with established constitutional principles." Such a "deterrence function" requires no more than that the conviction be reviewed by reference to the law prevailing at the time of its final review in the state system. The state courts can hardly be required to have applied constitutional principles that did not exist at the point that the petitioner's conviction was "finalized." [7] Hence, a federal habeas court, as a general principle, should not invalidate a conviction based upon a "new ruling" of constitutional law issued after that point.

The *Teague* plurality opinion recognized two exceptions to the "law-at-the-time" principle, which are discussed in subsection (c). While *Teague* did not produce a majority viewpoint on the scope of those exceptions, all seven justices agreed that the "law-at-the-time" principle otherwise imposes two primary limitations.[8] Initially, unless the exceptions apply, a habeas petitioner may not obtain the benefit of a "new" Supreme Court ruling decided after his conviction became final.[9] Secondly, and of far greater practical significance, the habeas court may not read the preexisting precedent (i.e., the Supreme Court rulings prevailing at the time the conviction became final) so as to convert that precedent into a "new ruling" that expands constitutional protection. The state court, in applying the law as it stood at the time, can no more be held to a subsequent habeas court's interpretation of preexisting precedent that amounts to a new ruling than it can to the retroactive application of a subsequent Supreme Court decision amounting to a new ruling. Thus, the *Teague* Court, on the basis of the "law-at-the-time" principle, concluded that a habeas court could neither apply retroactively the *Batson* decision, which came after the defendant's conviction had become final, nor itself establish a new ruling by reading a similar prohibition into a series of Sixth Amendment cases which came before the defendant's conviction became final. So too, in

7. The point of conviction finalization adopted by the Court is not entirely consistent with this rationale as it encompasses not only final review by the state's highest court (or exhaustion of the opportunity for such review), but also denial of certiorari by the Supreme Court (or exhaustion of the time for seeking certiorari). The assumption may be that if certiorari were sought, the Court would remand the case to the state court for reconsideration in light of its new rule, so that the state appellate court would have the opportunity to apply any new ruling handed down between the time of its decision and the Supreme Court's disposal of a petition for certiorari. Of course, such a remand would not occur where the defense failed to seek certiorari, but even then, the defendant is likely to have had the opportunity to petition the state court for a rehearing prior to the exhaustion of the time period for filing for certiorari.

8. As to the division on whether the principle required consideration of those limitations prior to reaching the merits of the petitioner's claim, see § 2.9 at note 28.

9. The "law-at-the-time" principle presumably does not operate as a two-way barrier. Thus, if the habeas court should find that the petitioner clearly should have prevailed on his claim on the basis of the law of the time, but the Supreme Court has subsequently adopted a new ruling that narrows constitutional protection and defeats that claim, relief will be denied on the ground that the petitioner is not now being held in custody in violation of the Constitution.

Penry v. Lynaugh,[10] the Court rested its reversal on a ruling rendered long before the habeas petitioner's conviction became final, but before applying that ruling had to determine that its current interpretation did not so extend that earlier precedent as to constitute a new ruling.

(b) The "New Ruling" Concept. Under *Teague,* in all habeas cases, whether looking to precedent that came before or after petitioner's conviction became final, the habeas court has to ask whether the particular constitutional interpretation that the petitioner would have it adopt (and thereby reject the state court's interpretation) would constitute a "new ruling" by reference to the law prevailing when the petitioner's conviction became final. If that would be so, and if the *Teague* exceptions do not apply, then the habeas court's hands are tied. Of course, the strength of this limitation depends in large part on the scope of the "new ruling" concept. Seeking to salvage broad de novo review by the habeas court, Justice Brennan argued that the habeas court must be allowed to expand upon the basic premises of preexisting precedent and resolve even novel questions clearly not controlled by that precedent. In earlier decisions applying the *Linkletter–Stovall* standard to assess the retroactive application of intervening Supreme Court decisions, the Court had held that considerably less expansion of earlier precedent rendered those decisions new rulings. An intervening ruling deciding a true case of first impression in the Supreme Court was likely to be deemed a new ruling, even where it relied on concepts developed in earlier precedent. This was especially so if a former decision specifically had left open the issue decided in the intervening ruling, or if the intervening ruling overturned a widely accepted practice. On the other hand, there was not a new ruling when the intervening Supreme Court decisions had "simply applied a well-established constitutional principle to govern a case which [was] closely analogous to those which had been previously covered in the prior case law." [11] *Teague* not only rejected the position urged by Justice Brennan, but it also laid the groundwork for a more inclusive concept of a new ruling than had been adopted in these earlier decisions. The *Teague* plurality advanced a broad definition of a new ruling that was later extended to include applications of prior precedent that would not have been classified as new rulings under the Supreme Court's previous retroactivity decisions.

Justice O'Connor in *Teague* acknowledged that it was "often difficult to determine when a case announces a new rule," and declined to "attempt to define the spectrum of what may or may not constitute a new rule for retroactivity purposes. She added, however, that

> [I]n general * * *, a case announces a new rule when it breaks new ground or imposes a new obligation on the States or the Federal Government. See e.g., *Rock v. Arkansas,*[12] (per se rule excluding all hypnotically refreshed testimony infringes impermissibly on a criminal defendant's right to testify on his behalf); *Ford v. Wainwright,*[13] (Eighth Amendment prohibits the execution of prisoners who are insane). To put it differently, a case announces a new rule if the result was not *dictated* by precedent existing at the time the defendant's conviction became final.

Because *Rock* and *Ford* were quite expansive interpretations of past precedents, and because the Sixth Amendment ruling petitioner sought to gain in *Teague* would have required rejection of "strong language" in past precedent, it was far from clear as to how literally lower courts should read Justice O'Connor's reference to a result "not dictated" by precedent. *Penry v. Lynaugh*[14] suggested that what was "dictated" would not be read too narrowly, that it would include the application of the logic of the earlier precedent to an analogous situation. Justice O'Connor, speaking for the majority there, concluded that upholding petitioner's challenge did not demand a new rule

10. 492 U.S. 302, 109 S.Ct. 2934, 106 L.Ed.2d 256 (1989).

11. Desist v. United States, 394 U.S. 244, 89 S.Ct. 1030, 22 L.Ed.2d 248 (1969) (Harlan, J., dissenting).

12. See § 24.4 at note 13.

13. 477 U.S. 399, 106 S.Ct. 2595, 91 L.Ed.2d 335 (1986).

14. Supra note 10.

as it "merely asked the State to fulfill the assurances upon which [the Court's prior precedent] was based" by applying a general prohibition that was "clear" under earlier rulings. In dissent on this point, Justice Scalia argued that "a 'new rule,' for purposes of *Teague,* must include not only a new rule that replaces an old one, but a new rule that replaces palpable uncertainty as to what the rule may be." He saw this case as one in which it was "utterly impossible to say that a judge acting in good faith and with care would have known [that] the rule announced today" had been established by prior precedents. Later cases indicated that Justice Scalia had correctly captured the majority's sense of a "new rule," if not its reading of the particular precedent applied in *Penry.*

In three subsequent applications of *Teague,* the Court set forth in greater detail the general principles governing the determination as to whether a particular interpretation of preexisting Supreme Court precedent constitutes a new ruling. The Court there stressed that the basic object of the *Teague* ruling, consistent with the deterrent function of habeas review that it sought to implement, was to "validate reasonable good faith interpretations of existing precedents made by state courts." Accordingly, where "it would not have been an illogical or even a grudging application of a Supreme Court precedent" to utilize the interpretation applied by the state courts, the federal habeas court may not impose a more expansive interpretation that it views as more in keeping with the flavor, spirit, or logic of that Supreme Court precedent. The key is whether the interpretation adopted by the state court, as measured by the earlier precedent, "was susceptible to debate among reasonable minds." If so, the habeas court can only impose a contrary standard if its "new ruling" would fit within one of the *Teague* exceptions.

Applying this general approach, the Court majority in *Butler v. McKellar* [15] rejected the defendant's claim that the standard in question did not constitute a new rule because it fell within the "logical compass" of an earlier precedent. There had been a significant difference among the lower courts as to whether that standard followed from that precedent, and that division in itself evidenced that the state court had adopted a position "susceptible to debate among reasonable minds." The Court did not seek to respond to the obvious question of why the division within the Supreme Court itself in *Penry* as to the meaning of the Court's earlier precedent did not similarly establish that the state court's interpretation there was "susceptible to debate among reasonable minds." The answer apparently lies in the same type of analysis which allows a court majority to hold that an error is so obvious as to constitute plain error while a dissenter holds there was no error at all, and which similarly permits a majority to hold that there was a clear abuse of discretion while a dissenter argues that the trial judge acted correctly. A division within the appellate court is treated as going only to the interpretation of the standard of appellate review, which is distinguished from a division among different courts in their interpretation of the content of a particular procedural guarantee.

Saffle v. Parks [16] and *Sawyer v. Smith* [17] similarly concluded that a ruling is not "dictated" by prior precedent where it calls for the fashioning of a rule that is logically distinguishable from that of the earlier precedent, though it follows from general premise adopted in that precedent. Thus *Saffle* held that the defendant sought to establish a new rule by converting an earlier precedent as to "what mitigating evidence the jury must be permitted to consider" into a rule as to "how it must consider the mitigating evidence." So too, in *Sawyer,* the Court held that a new rule had been created when the Court converted a general due process prohibition against fundamental unfairness in closing arguments into a

15. 494 U.S. 407, 110 S.Ct. 1212, 108 L.Ed.2d 347 (1990).

16. 494 U.S. 484, 110 S.Ct. 1257, 108 L.Ed.2d 415 (1990).

17. ___ U.S. ___, 110 S.Ct. 2822, 111 L.Ed.2d 193 (1990).

per se prohibition of a specific closing argument.

Speaking for four dissenters in *Butler*, Justice Brennan suggested that the end result of the majority's reading of *Teague* was to "limit [the] federal courts' habeas corpus function to reviewing state courts' legal analysis under the equivalent of a 'clearly erroneous' standard of review." This characterization comes close to the mark, and is consistent with the view that a primary function of habeas review is to ensure that state courts meaningfully attempt to apply controlling constitutional precedent. It reflects a philosophy that tracks back to the due process model of federal habeas review,[18] although it obviously goes beyond that model in recognizing the two *Teague* exceptions and in directing the habeas court to look to more than whether the defense had a meaningful opportunity to present its constitutional claim.[19] The habeas court must look also to the substance of the state court ruling. Its role here, however, is quite limited. It must ensure that the state courts did not subvert Supreme Court precedent by drawing hypertechnical distinctions and that they did not ignore the obvious reading of that precedent. However, it may not operate as Supreme Court surrogate by making independent contributions to the development of the law, even if that means no more than choosing between two arguable interpretations of Supreme Court precedent. It may perform the same role as the Supreme Court in "correcting" state court interpretations of constitutional guarantees only insofar as it finds, in effect, that the state court ruling is so obviously erroneous that it probably would produce a summary reversal by the Supreme Court on direct review.

One question not considered in *Teague* and its progeny is what will constitute a new ruling when the state court has not reached the merits of the habeas petitioner's claim. This may occur where the state court relied upon a procedural default, but that default is not based on an adequate state ground or is excused under the *Sykes* standard.[20] As to Fourth Amendment claims, a state's failure to give the petitioner a full and fair opportunity to present the claim may result in no state ruling on the merits or a ruling that does not consider the full claim.[21] The rulings in the *Teague* line of cases started with state court interpretations of the preexisting precedent and then ask whether the contrary interpretation urged by the petitioner constitutes a new ruling. If the state court's interpretation was a reasonably debatable interpretation of that precedent, then a broader ruling could not be said to be dictated by that precedent. If the state courts never reached the merits, however, there is no assurance that they would have taken the narrowest of the reasonably debatable interpretations. Quite often the state itself will be responsible for improperly precluding review on the merits, as where its actions provided "cause" under *Sykes* or it failed to provide the full and fair opportunity required by *Stone*. At least here, the habeas court should not be limited to the narrowest of reasonable alternative interpretations, but should be allowed instead to adopt a broader interpretation. The state has, in a sense, "forfeited" its opportunity to argue for acceptance of a state's good faith and reasonable effort to protect constitutional rights. Of course, the state may not bear responsibility for the lack of a decision on the merits, as where the procedural default is excused under *Sykes* only because it presents a case of a fundamental miscarriage of justice. Such cases, however, ordinarily should fit under the *Teague* exceptions.

(c) The *Teague* Exceptions. Exceptions to the prohibition against adopting new rulings were recognized in *Teague* in both Justice O'Connor's plurality opinion and Justice Stevens' concurring opinion. Both opinions relied upon Justice Harlan's earlier criticism of the use of the *Linkletter–Stovall* standard

18. See § 28.2(f).

19. In applying the Stone v. Powell prerequisite of an opportunity for full and fair litigation, lower courts generally have held that a state court's misapplication of Supreme Court precedent does not deprive a defendant of that opportunity. See § 28.3(d).

20. See § 28.4(c), (e)–(f).

21. See § 28.3(d).

to allow retroactive application on habeas review of new rulings rendered by the Supreme Court after the habeas petitioner's conviction had become final. Justice Harlan had argued that such retroactive application should be permissible only as to two types of new rulings. The first was a new ruling that "place[s] certain kinds of primary, private individual conduct beyond the power of the criminal law-making authority." [22] Such a ruling had been recognized in earlier cases as requiring an automatic retroactive application without regard to the *Linkletter–Stovall* standard. Thus, where the Court held that the substantive law creating an offense violated the self-incrimination privilege, all defendants previously convicted of that offense were entitled to the benefit of that new ruling.[23] In *Teague,* Justice O'Connor's plurality opinion and Justice Stevens' concurring opinion expressly approved this exception as described by Justice Harlan. They did not speak, however, to the possibility that the exception was somewhat broader than Justice Harlan had indicated—extending to any new ruling that held, in effect, that the state had no authority to try and convict a defendant (as in the case of a double jeopardy ruling). The earlier retroactivity decisions had given such a ruling automatic retroactive application without regard to the *Linkletter–Stovall* standard—a position consistent with the historical recognition of jurisdictional defects on habeas review.[24]

Justice Harlan's second exception was for the new ruling that requires observance of procedures "implicit in the concept of ordered liberty." The reference here was to the basic "fundamental fairness" standard applied to define due process prior to the adoption of the selective incorporation doctrine.[25] Justices Stevens and Blackmun stated in *Teague* that they would retain this exception as described by Justice Harlan. The *Teague* plurality, however, looking to Justice Harlan's objective of limiting the second exception to "watershed rule of criminal procedure," suggested that it be modified. Justice O'Connor argued that the second exception should be limited to new rulings that implicate "fundamental fairness" by mandating procedures "central to an accurate determination of innocence or guilt." This was consistent with a basic function of the habeas writ as stated by Justice Harlan—"to assure that no man has been incarcerated under a procedure which creates an impermissibly large risk that the innocent will be convicted."[26] The plurality opinion added that it seemed "unlikely that many such components of basic due process have yet to emerge." The Court's later opinions have framed this exception as Justice O'Connor did in *Teague.*[27]

Although rejecting Justice Stevens' broader view of fundamental fairness, Justice O'Connor in *Teague* did look to an earlier opinion of Justice Stevens in defining the scope of this second exception. She stated that procedures "central to an accurate determination of innocence or guilt" were best illustrated by what Justice Stevens had once described as the "classic" grounds for habeas review—the mob-dominated trial, the knowing use of perjured testimony, and conviction based on a confession "extorted from defendant by brutal methods."[28] The new ruling advanced by the petitioner in *Teague* did not rest on such an absolute prerequisite for accurate factfinding. The petitioner asked for an innovative Sixth Amendment cross-section reading that would provide a *Batson*-like prohibition against racially discriminatory prosecutorial use of peremptory challenges. While the Sixth Amend-

22. Mackey v. United States, 401 U.S. 667, 91 S.Ct. 1160, 28 L.Ed.2d 404 (1971).

23. See United States v. United States Coin and Currency, 401 U.S. 715, 91 S.Ct. 1041, 28 L.Ed.2d 434 (1971) (retroactive application of Fifth Amendment rulings that invalidated a forfeiture proceeding for money possessed by one who failed to comply with the wagering tax law).

24. See Robinson v. Neil, 409 U.S. 505, 93 S.Ct. 876, 35 L.Ed.2d 29 (1973) (applying retroactively the double jeopardy ruling in Waller v. Florida, which prohibited the state from prosecuting the defendant for the same acts that had served as the basis for a previous municipal ordinance prosecution).

25. See § 2.4.

26. See Desist v. United States, supra note 11.

27. See the cases cited in notes 15–17 supra.

28. See § 28.2 following note 41.

ment's cross-section guarantee is supported by a variety of significant values, it "does not rest on the premise that every criminal trial, or any particular trial, is necessarily unfair because it is not conducted in accordance with what we determine to be the requirements of the Sixth Amendment." Though a *Batson*-type rule might promote accuracy in a systemic sense, it did not necessarily affect accuracy in any particular case, and it therefore fell outside of *Teague*'s second exception.

In *Sawyer v. Smith,*[29] the Court again stressed the narrowness of *Teague*'s second exception. The "new rule" in question there—prohibiting a prosecutorial closing argument which suggested that the ultimate responsibility for determining the appropriateness of the death penalty rested on the appellate court and thereby reduced the jury's responsibility—certainly was "aimed at improving the accuracy of the trial." It was not, however, a "watershed ruling" in this regard; it did not "alter our understanding of the *bedrock procedural elements* essential to the fairness of the proceeding." Rather it was a per se prohibition of a particular type of argument that served basically to supplement the traditional due process prohibition against closing arguments that "so infected the trial with unfairness" as to violate due process, and the lower court here had held that the prosecutor's argument had not violated that more basic standard.

§ 28.7 Independent Factfinding and Evidentiary Hearings

(a) The Special Status of State Factfinding. *Brown v. Allen*[1] held that the federal habeas court could not accept as binding the state court's interpretation of constitutional requirements, but must make its own independent judgment as to the application of the "correct constitutional standard" to the habeas petitioner's claim.[2] The two majority opinions in *Brown* took a quite different approach, however, as to the state court's findings of fact relevant to that claim. They both concluded that the federal habeas court could, in most circumstances, rely upon the state court's findings of historical fact rather than conduct its own independent factfinding. Thus, Justice Reed noted that, while the habeas court had the power to retry the facts, "where there is material conflict of fact in the [state] transcripts of evidence as to deprivation of constitutional rights, the [habeas court] may properly depend upon the state's resolution" in the absence of "unusual circumstances calling for a hearing." Similarly, Justice Frankfurter stated that the habeas court could rely upon the state court's determination of adjudicated factual issues "unless a vital flaw be found in the [state's] process of ascertaining such facts."

Neither majority opinion in *Brown* explained exactly why the "final say" given the federal habeas court permitted it to accept the state court's determination of historic facts, in contrast to the independent judgment required as to the legal consequences of those facts. There was nothing in § 2243, the provision on evidentiary hearings, that suggested such a distinction between factual and legal determinations, and one might have argued that the protection of a federal claim in a federal forum required independent assessment of the facts as well as the law. The distinction has been justified, however, on several grounds. It has been argued that there is less need for independent federal factfinding because the trial court's "guilt determining momentum" and "judicial loyalty to state institutional interests" are not as likely to influence the accuracy of its factfindings as they are to impair application of constitutional standards. Arguably also, any value that federal procedures and federal judges would bring to the accuracy of the factfinding process is more than offset by the timing advantage of the state court hearing, as compared to a federal habeas hearing typically held long after the events in question occurred. As Justice Frankfurter noted in *Brown,* basic

29. Supra note 17.

§ 28.7

1. 344 U.S. 443, 73 S.Ct. 397, 97 L.Ed. 469 (1953).

2. See § 28.6 following note 2.

principles of factfinding support the "soundness of giving great weight to testimony earlier heard." Finally, it is generally agreed that independent federal factfinding exacerbates many of the costs of habeas review, extending substantially the call on scarce judicial resources and increasing the friction between state and federal courts.

Today, the distinction between the habeas court's review of the state court's factual and legal determinations is hardly as stark as it was in *Brown.* A combination of Supreme Court rulings and congressional legislation have imposed more precise guidance as to when a court *must* (the issue no longer is one of discretion) accept the state court's factual findings. At the same time, *Teague v. Lane,*[3] has given a somewhat narrower scope to what it means for a habeas court to have the "final say" in applying independently the "correct constitutional standard." Under *Teague,* the habeas court is directed to assess only whether the state court's interpretation of constitutional safeguards falls within the range of "reasonable good faith interpretations of existing [constitutional] precedents as of the time the conviction became final." The habeas court must accept a state court interpretation "susceptible to debate among reasonable minds" even though its independent judgment would lead it to a more expansive reading of the constitutional guarantee. The habeas court's role in reviewing the state court's finding of fact today is in many ways similar. Under § 2254(d), as discussed in subsection (c) infra, that finding is entitled to a presumption of correctness unless some flaw exists in the process that led to the finding or the finding simply is not "fairly supported by the record." That presumption then controls unless the petitioner can establish by clear and convincing evidence that the state finding was "erroneous." The practical impact of § 2254(d) and the Supreme Court rulings interpreting that provision is to direct the habeas court to accept a "reasonable good faith" factual finding that was the product of a fair and complete adjudication process, just as it must accept a "reasonable good faith" constitutional interpretation that is the product of a fair consideration of the preexisting constitutional precedents.

(b) Evidentiary Hearings and the *Townsend* Guidelines. *Brown* held that a federal habeas court always could hold an evidentiary hearing at its discretion, but that it must hold such a hearing where there was a "vital flaw" in the state's factfinding process (per Frankfurter, J.) or "unusual circumstances" called for such a hearing (per Reed, J.). In *Townsend v. Sain,*[4] one of the three decisions of the 1962 term that reshaped habeas law,[5] the Court went substantially beyond *Brown* in identifying those situations that demanded an evidentiary hearing. *Townsend* reaffirmed *Brown* insofar as that case recognized that the habeas court always had discretion to hold a hearing, but the *Townsend* majority also concluded that the "vital flaw" and "unusual circumstances" standards were too general to provide adequate guidance as to when the habeas court had an obligation to "receive evidence and try the facts anew."

Townsend substituted for the *Brown* tests a "full and fair hearing" standard: "Where the facts are in dispute, the federal court in habeas corpus must hold an evidentiary hearing if the habeas applicant did not receive a full and fair evidentiary hearing in a state court, either at the time of trial or in a collateral proceeding." Recognizing a need for greater particularization of this standard, the Court also listed the specific circumstances under which an evidentiary hearing was mandatory. A hearing was required if:

> (1) the merits of the factual dispute were not resolved in the state hearing; (2) the state factual determination is not fairly supported by the record as a whole; (3) the fact-finding procedure employed by the state court was not adequate to afford a full and fair hearing; (4) there is a substantial allegation of newly discovered evidence; (5) the material facts were not adequately developed at the state court

3. 489 U.S. 288, 109 S.Ct. 1060, 103 L.Ed.2d 334 (1989). See § 28.6.

4. 372 U.S. 293, 83 S.Ct. 745, 9 L.Ed.2d 770 (1963).

5. See § 28.5 at note 4.

hearing; or (6) for any reason it appears that the state trier of fact did not afford the habeas applicant a full and fair hearing.

The *Townsend* opinion, by Chief Justice Warren, explored at length the content of each of these six circumstances.

Speaking to the first circumstance, the Chief Justice stated that a state court decision on the merits required not only a resolution of petitioner's claim, but also some indication of the state court's factual findings. Where there were no express findings, the habeas court often could reconstruct those findings. The state trial court's ultimate ruling, measured against the evidence before it, would often indicate that court's factual conclusions. Reconstruction was possible, however, only if the trial court had applied the correct constitutional standards. In the "ordinary case," the habeas court could assume that the trial court had done so, even if the state court had failed to articulate the standards which it applied.

The second circumstance, the Court noted, demanded that the habeas court carefully examine the state court's factual determinations in light of the evidence before the state court, just as the Supreme Court itself often had done on direct review of state court cases (with the Court's coerced confession cases cited as an illustration). As an example of a state proceedings that fell within the third circumstance, the Court cited the situation in which the "state trial judge has made serious procedural errors (respecting the claim pressed in federal habeas) in such things as the burden of proof." It was not necessary, it added, that the defect itself constitute a constitutional violation. A federal hearing was required if the state proceeding "appears to be seriously inadequate for the ascertainment of the truth."

The fourth and fifth circumstances, the Court noted, were tied together. The conventional notion of that newly discovered evidence which will permit the reopening of a judgment was "too limited" for habeas purposes. Accordingly, while the fourth guideline incorporated the traditional standard, the fifth also required an evidentiary hearing whenever "evidence crucial to an adequate consideration was not developed at the state hearing." That the evidence may have been previously available was not controlling, providing there had not been "inexcusable neglect of the petitioner," with that standard defined by *Fay v. Noia*. The sixth category was left "intentionally open-ended," recognizing that it was impossible to anticipate "all the situations where a hearing is demanded."

The Supreme Court subsequently described *Townsend* as a decision that "substantially increased the availability of evidentiary hearings in habeas corpus proceedings and made mandatory much of what had previously been within the broad discretion of the District Court." [6] In fact, the huge increase in evidentiary hearings anticipated by commentators and lower court judges did not materialize. There was a sharp increase in evidentiary hearings in the immediate wake of *Townsend*, reaching a high of 11% of all habeas petitions, but that percentage dropped dramatically over the next several years and leveled off below the 3% rate that existed shortly after *Brown* was decided. A critical factor in this return to the pre-*Townsend* rate appears to have been the adoption of § 2254(d) in 1966 and the Supreme Court's expansive interpretation of that provision.

(c) The § 2254(d) Presumption. In 1966, Congress responded to *Townsend* by adding subsections (d)–(f) to 28 U.S.C.A. § 2254. Subsection (e) authorized the habeas court to require production of the state trial records (without cost to the applicant if indigent), and to exercise its best judgment if the records should no longer be available. Subsection (f) provided for the admissibility of those records in the federal court proceeding. The key provision was the lengthy and complex subsection (d). That provision can be broken down into three segments. The first segment describes the type of state finding to which the provision applies—"a determination after a hearing on the merits of a factual dispute

6. Smith v. Yeager, 393 U.S. 122, 89 S.Ct. 277, 21 L.Ed.2d 246 (1968).

made by a state court of competent jurisdiction * * *, evidenced by a written finding, written opinion, or other reliable and adequate written indicia." The second segment provides that the finding "shall be presumed to be correct," unless the habeas court finds that one of eight conditions are present. Those conditions are:

> (1) that the merits of the factual dispute were not resolved in the State court hearing; (2) that the factfinding procedure employed by the State court was not adequate to afford a full and fair hearing; (3) that the material facts were not adequately developed at the State court hearing; (4) that the State court lacked jurisdiction of the subject matter or over the person of the applicant in the State court proceeding; (5) that the applicant was an indigent and the State court, in deprivation of his constitutional right, failed to appoint counsel to represent him in the State court proceeding; (6) that the applicant did not receive a full, fair, and adequate hearing in the State court proceeding; or (7) that the applicant was otherwise denied due process of law in the State court proceeding; (8) or unless that part of the record of the State court proceeding in which the determination of such factual issue was made, pertinent to a determination of the sufficiency of the evidence to support such factual determination, is produced as provided for hereinafter, and the Federal court on a consideration of such part of the record as a whole concludes that such factual determination is not fairly supported by the record.

The third segment of subsection (d) indicates the consequence of the presumption of correctness. It provides that in an evidentiary hearing, upon "due proof" of a state factfinding subject to subsection (d) and not exempted by any of the conditions (1)–(8), the "burden shall rest upon the applicant to establish by convincing evidence that the factual determination by the State court was erroneous."

Although § 2254(d) has been described by lower courts as "in the main codifying *Townsend,*" it actually rejects certain assumptions implicit in *Townsend,* though incorporating other aspects of that ruling. The immediate focus of *Townsend* was on those circumstances that required an evidentiary hearing. Section 2254(d), on the other hand, does not speak directly to when a hearing must be held; its focus is on the burden of proof applicable at that hearing. However, by implication, it would suggest that a hearing be held where there is a factual dispute and the state court findings are not entitled to the presumption of correctness under one of the eight exceptions noted in the statute. In this regard, it would seem to reinforce, if not codify, *Townsend*'s six circumstances.[7] On the other hand, its bearing on the discretionary holding of hearings would appear to be contrary to *Townsend.* The Court there held that the habeas court had discretion to hold an evidentiary hearing even where the six *Townsend* guidelines did not mandate a hearing. While section 2254(d) does not directly affect that authority, it was the apparent assumption of *Townsend* that the habeas court, at a discretionary hearing, could make a completely independent determination of the historical facts. Section 2254, however, raises a substantial barrier to such a finding through its "presumption of correctness." A habeas corpus might naturally hesitate to hold a discretionary hearing under such circumstances, recognizing that the heavy burden that then falls on the petitioner makes it unlikely that the petitioner will be able to prevail on the factual issue.

The impact of § 2254(d)'s presumption upon the discretionary evidentiary hearing is illustrated by the Supreme Court and lower court rulings in *La Vallee v. Delle Rose.*[8] The peti-

7. The eight exceptions specified in § 2254(d) are not identical to those six circumstances, but the differences are not particularly significant. Items (4), (5), and (7) in the statute—lack of jurisdiction, failure to appoint counsel, and denial of due process—were not specified in the *Townsend* list, but they surely would fit within its third or sixth circumstance. Indeed, their inclusion in the statute is questionable, since they ordinarily would constitute in themselves an independent basis for relief. The fourth circumstance cited in *Townsend*—a substantial allegation of newly discovered evidence—is not specified in the statute, but it could be readily subsumed in the third exception (that the "material facts were not adequately developed").

8. 410 U.S. 690, 93 S.Ct. 1203, 35 L.Ed.2d 637 (1973). The Court of Appeals' ruling is discussed in Delle Rose v.

tioner there sought habeas relief on the ground that involuntary confessions had been admitted at his trial. The state court had found the confessions admissible, but had failed to indicate to what extent it had considered petitioner's testimony, which alleged various elements of coercion. The habeas court concluded that this omission resulted in the lack of "adequate indicia" of the state court's determination of fact and § 2254(d) therefore did not control. The habeas court then held an evidentiary hearing, made its own findings of fact, and concluded that the confessions were involuntary. A divided Supreme Court reversed. Looking to *Townsend* 's discussion of the first of its six circumstances, the Court concluded that the state court's factual findings could readily be reconstructed. The state court's opinion had indicated that it applied the correct legal standard, which would have required a finding of coercion if one accepted the allegations of the petitioner. Since the trial judge had held the confession voluntary, it was reasonably certain that he had rejected the petitioner's testimony. Accordingly, the habeas court had before it a state ruling that provided sufficient evidence of actual factual findings to bring the § 2254(d) presumption into play.

As Justice Marshall noted in his *Delle Rose* dissent, the Court there "[did] not hold that the District Court erred in holding a *de novo* evidentiary hearing." It held only that the district court had erred in independently assessing the facts without affording the presumption of correctness to the state court's findings. Thus, the Court did not order the dismissal of the habeas petition, but remanded for reconsideration by the district court upon its application of the § 2254(d) presumption of correctness. It was still possible for the habeas court to find historical facts contrary to the state court's factual determination, but only if that contrary finding was supported by clear and convincing evidence. This was a substantially higher standard than the preponderance of the evidence standard that had been applied by most habeas courts prior to the adoption of § 2254(d). On remand in *Delle Rose,* the Court of Appeals apparently concluded that a petitioner simply could not meet the § 2254(d) standard where, as here, he had offered no significant evidence that had not been before the state court. Even if the habeas court itself believed petitioner's testimony, it could not reject the state court's contrary determination. Accordingly, the appellate court itself ordered the petition dismissed. While the district court had retained discretion under *Townsend* to hold an evidentiary hearing, the § 2254(d) presumption had largely determined the outcome of that hearing.

The Court of Appeals' assessment of the impact of § 2254(d) standard in *Delle Rose* finds support in the Supreme Court's later rulings in *Maggio v. Fulford* [9] and *Marshall v. Lonberger.* [10] In *Fulford,* the federal habeas court had relied heavily on the trial testimony of a psychiatrist who suggested that the petitioner "had paranoid delusions" and therefore was not competent to stand trial. The state court had rejected this testimony in concluding, based on its own observations of the defendant, that he was "cognizant of everything around him" and that his eleventh-hour motion for a competency commission was simply a "subterfuge." The Supreme Court majority concluded that the habeas court's ruling could not be sustained under the § 2254(d) standard of proof. It noted that the federal court "erroneously substituted its own judgment as to the credibility of witnesses for that of the Louisiana courts—a prerogative which 28 U.S.C.A. § 2254 does not allow." The habeas court had sought to escape from the confines of § 2254(d) by relying upon the eighth exception contained in that provision (that the record in the state court did not "fairly support" its factual determination), but the Supreme Court rejected that conclusion in light of the trial court's observation of defendant and various other

LaVallee, 414 U.S. 1014, 94 S.Ct. 380, 38 L.Ed.2d 251 (1973) (Marshall, J., dissenting from a denial of certiorari).

9. 462 U.S. 111, 103 S.Ct. 2261, 76 L.Ed.2d 794 (1983).

10. 459 U.S. 422, 103 S.Ct. 843, 74 L.Ed.2d 646 (1983).

aspects of the proceeding. *Marshall v. Lonberger* involved a similar ruling. The issue here was whether petitioner had been aware that his guilty plea was to an attempted murder charge. The federal court had relied heavily on petitioner's own testimony, noting that the state had not introduced contrary evidence. The state court, however, had rejected that testimony. In light of that court's familiarity with the surrounding circumstances, including its conclusion that the defendant was "an intelligent individual, well experienced in the criminal law, and well represented by counsel," who had been informed previously of the charges, the federal habeas court was required under § 2254(d)'s presumption to accept the state court's factual findings.[11]

In *Sumner v. Mata,*[12] the Supreme Court gave further reinforcement to § 2254(d)'s presumption of correctness. The Court held initially that § 2254(d)'s presumption applies to a factual determination by a state appellate court just as it does to a factual determination by a state trial court. Moreover, when a federal habeas court makes a contrary finding of fact, it would not be assumed without explanation that the federal court had properly applied § 2254(d). "In order to ensure that this mandate of Congress is followed," a federal habeas court would be required to "include in its opinion granting the writ the reasoning which led it to conclude that any of the first seven factors were present, or the reasoning which led it to conclude that the state finding was 'not fairly supported by the record.'" This responsibility, the Court added, would not be fulfilled by mere "'boiler plate language,'" but required a specific listing of findings similar to that required of a judge in a bench trial under Rule 52 of the Civil Rules.

(d) Mixed Determinations of Law and Fact. The Supreme Court has noted on several occasions that § 2254(d) applies only to a determination of "historic fact" as opposed to "a mixed determination of law and fact that requires the application of legal principles to the historical facts." Thus, in *Cuyler v. Sullivan,*[13] there was unanimous agreement that the determination of the state court that counsel had not undertaken multiple "representation" of three codefendants was outside the reach of § 2254(d). The state court's findings as to the role counsel played in the defense of petitioner and his codefendants related to historic fact, but the holding that this did not constitute multiple representation involved a legal conclusion, "open to review on collateral attack in a federal court."[14] The Court has not always found the distinction between a "factual" and a "mixed determination" so easy to apply, however. Its rulings in the *Sumner v. Mata* litigation are illustrative.

In the *Mata* litigation, the Court was sharply divided over whether state court findings concerning a due process challenge to the admission of a pretrial photo-identification were limited to historic fact. The state court had held there was no showing that the witnesses had been "influenced" by the investigating officer, that the witnesses had an "adequate opportunity" to view the crime, and that their initial descriptions of the assailant were "accurate." The habeas court, holding the photo-identification impermissibly suggestive, concluded that the circumstances surrounding the witnesses' observation of the

11. Consider also Patton v. Yount, 467 U.S. 1025, 104 S.Ct. 2885, 81 L.Ed.2d 847 (1984), where the Court held that the testimony of a prospective juror on voir dire provided "fair support" for the state court's factual determination that the juror would be impartial. While the juror's testimony was "ambiguous and at times contradictory," and the "cold record arouses some concern," deference had to be given to the trial judge as the judge best situated to evaluate that testimony. He could properly have relied upon those statements of the juror suggesting impartiality in the belief that they were the "most fully articulated" or the "least influenced by [the] leading" of defense counsel.

12. 449 U.S. 539, 101 S.Ct. 764, 66 L.Ed.2d 722 (1981).

13. 446 U.S. 335, 100 S.Ct. 1708, 64 L.Ed.2d 333 (1980).

14. In Strickland v. Washington, 466 U.S. 668, 104 S.Ct. 2052, 80 L.Ed.2d 674 (1984) (discussed at § 11.10), the Court similarly held that a state court's conclusion that counsel's performance constituted effective assistance "is not a finding of fact binding on the federal court to the extent stated by 28 U.S.C.A. § 2254(d)." Although "state court findings of fact made in the course of deciding an ineffectiveness claim are subject to the deference requirement of § 2254(d) * * *, both the performance and prejudice components of the ineffectiveness inquiry are mixed questions of law and fact."

crime were suspect, the witnesses had failed to give sufficiently detailed initial descriptions, and "considerable pressure" had been brought to bear on them. After the Supreme Court initially remanded the case to the habeas court for an explanation as to why it had not applied § 2254(d),[15] the habeas court responded that the section did not apply since its rulings dealt with a mixed question of fact and law. Justice Brennan had dissented from the Supreme Court's original remand order on exactly that ground. He had argued that whether a "person's opportunity to view a crime is 'adequate' for constitutional purposes" was a legal question. Legal issues were also involved in evaluating the action of the state officials who sought to obtain the identification and in characterizing the witnesses' initial description as not sufficiently detailed to dispel doubts about the photographic procedure.

Reviewing the case again, the Supreme Court held in *Mata II*[16] that the lower court had erred in concluding that § 2254(d) was inapplicable. The Court reasoned:

> We agree with the * * * [lower court] that the ultimate question as to the constitutionality of the pretrial identification procedures used in this case is a mixed question of law and fact that is not governed by § 2254. In deciding this question, the federal court may give different weight to the facts as found by the state court and may reach a different conclusion in light of the legal standard. But the questions of fact that underlie this ultimate conclusion are governed by the statutory presumption as our earlier opinion made clear. Thus, whether the witnesses in this case had an opportunity to observe the crime or were too distracted; whether the witnesses gave a detailed, accurate description; and whether the witnesses were under pressure from prison officials or others are all questions of fact as to which the statutory presumption applies.

The Court's description of the "factual issues," it should be noted, differs somewhat from Justice Brennan's earlier description of the "mixed issues." Thus, the Court refers to the question of whether the witness had an opportunity to view the crime rather than whether that opportunity was legally "adequate." The habeas court had concluded that the witnesses "quite likely" were distracted while observing the crime, thus apparently disagreeing with the state court's finding as to their behavior under the circumstances. If the habeas court had reasoned that, even accepting the state court's conclusion as to the witness' capacity to observe, the opportunity to observe was insufficient to offset the suggestive quality of the photo-display, that finding might well have been categorized as involving an application of legal analysis to historic fact. So too, whether the witnesses were under pressure may be an historic fact, but whether the pressure was so great as to render their identification suspect would be a mixed issue.

A series of Supreme Court rulings after *Mata*, each considering the appropriate treatment of state trial court rulings relating to juror prejudice, lend support to the above analysis. They suggest that the crucial factor in that context is whether the question before the state court is viewed as (1) what was the juror's actual state of mind, as determined in light of his response to voir dire questions; or (2) do the surrounding circumstances justify adopting a presumption of prejudice, not to be ordinarily overcome by juror voir dire response alone. Section 2254(d), these cases indicate, applies to the resolution of the former issue, but not the latter. It applies to a determination based on the state of mind of a particular individual, but not to a generalized determination based on the inappropriateness of particular governmental action or the impermissible impact of a particular factual setting. Thus, § 2254(d) does not encompass a state court's finding as to whether prejudicial publicity had made a fair trial impossible, but it does apply to a trial judge's finding, based on the juror's responses on voir dire, that the individual juror was not biased.[17] So too

15. See Sumner v. Mata, supra note 12.

16. Sumner v. Mata, 455 U.S. 591, 102 S.Ct. 1303, 71 L.Ed.2d 480 (1982).

17. Patton v. Yount, supra note 11.

Rushen v. Spain[18] held § 2254(d) applicable to a finding that a juror's ex parte communication with the judge had no bearing on the juror's impartiality, and *Wainwright v. Witt*[19] held § 2254(d) applicable to a finding that a prospective juror's opposition to capital punishment would substantially impair her ability to comply with the trial court's instructions. In *Rushen,* the Court rejected the dissent's contention that a conclusive presumption of bias should follow from certain aspects of an ex parte communication, and in *Witt,* it rejected the dissent's contention that a special standard of proof applied to an exclusion based on the juror's opposition to capital punishment. Arguably, if the Court had accepted those contentions, the findings would have been so intertwined with the application of legal principles as to produce a mixed determination of fact and law.

Recognizing the sharp division within the Court in most of its § 2254(d) rulings (including the juror prejudice cases noted above), Justice O'Connor, in *Miller v. Fenton,*[20] sought to explain why the "appropriate methodology for distinguishing questions of fact from questions of law has been, to say the least, elusive." She there noted that,

> perhaps much of the difficulty * * * stems from the practical truth that the decision to label an issue a "question of law," a "question of fact" or a "mixed question of law and fact" is sometimes as much a matter of allocation as it is of analysis. * * * At least in those instances in which Congress has not spoken and in which the issue falls somewhere between a pristine legal standard and a simple historical fact, the fact/law distinction at times has turned on a determination that, as a matter of the sound administration of justice, one judicial actor is better positioned than another to decide the issue in question.

Illustrating the application of this allocation determination, Justice O'Connor, citing earlier cases that had held the "voluntariness" of a confession to be "a legal question requiring independent federal determination, noted that "on rare occasions in years past the Court has justified independent federal or appellate review as a means of compensating for 'perceived shortcomings of the trier of fact by ways of bias or some other factor.' "[21] As an example of a setting in which allocation considerations led to the opposite conclusion, Justice O'Connor cited the prejudiced juror cases. Where, as in those cases, "the issue involves the credibility of witnesses and therefore turns largely on an evaluation of demeanor," the process of "applying law to fact" was appropriately left to the trial court, "according its determinations presumptive weight."

The ruling in *Miller v. Fenton* itself reflected the broad range of factors that may enter into the characterization of a particular issue as one within or without the § 2254(d) presumption. The Court there held that the voluntariness of a confession was a "legal inquiry requiring plenary federal review." "Subsidiary factual questions," such as whether a drug had certain properties or whether the police used certain interrogation tactics, are governed by the § 2254(d) presumption, but not the "ultimate question whether, under the totality of the circumstances, the challenged confession was obtained in a manner compatible with the requirements of the Constitution." In reaching this conclusion, the Court noted that: (1) a long line of cases had held that the voluntariness of a confession was an issue for independent federal determination, and the weight of *stare decisis* was not lightly to be cast aside; (2) Congress, in its adoption of § 2254(d), relied heavily upon the *Townsend* ruling, and *Townsend* had specifically noted that voluntariness of a confession was a "mixed question of fact and law"; (3) although sometimes framed as "an issue of 'psychological fact,' " the "dispositive question of * * * voluntariness has always had a uniquely legal dimension," turning "as much on whether the [in-

18. 464 U.S. 114, 104 S.Ct. 453, 78 L.Ed.2d 267 (1983).

19. 469 U.S. 412, 105 S.Ct. 844, 83 L.Ed.2d 841 (1985).

20. 474 U.S. 104, 106 S.Ct. 445, 88 L.Ed.2d 405 (1985).

21. The early confession rulings had not been limited to habeas review, but also included cases sustaining the Supreme Court's independent determination of voluntariness on direct review of state court decisions. See § 6.2(b).

terrogation] techniques * * * are compatible with a system that presumes innocence and assures that a conviction will not be secured by inquisitorial means as on whether the defendant's will was in fact overborne"; and (4) the "practical considerations" that led the Court to find other issues within the scope of the § 2254(d) presumption were not applicable here. (As to those practical considerations, the Court noted that, unlike the impartiality of a given juror, assessments of credibility and demeanor are not crucial in resolving the ultimate issue of voluntariness; and unlike the allocution on a guilty plea (*Fulford*) or the determination of competency to stand trial (*Lonberger*), the critical events here were likely to have taken place in a "secret and inherently coercive atmosphere," thereby "escalat[ing] the risk" of an erroneous resolution). In sum, voluntariness was held in *Miller* to be an issue beyond the § 2254(d) presumption due to the combined influence of *stare decisis,* congressional intent, the analytical content of the determination, and allocation considerations that favored "independent federal review" as a needed additional means of "protecting the rights at stake."

Appendix

CRIMINAL PROCEDURE RESEARCH ON WESTLAW

Analysis

Sec.

Section 1. Introduction

The discussion of the law of criminal procedure in this text provides a strong base for analyzing even the most complex criminal procedure problem. Whether your research requires examination of case law, statutes, rules, regulations or commentary, West books and WESTLAW are excellent sources of research materials.

In the area of criminal procedure, WESTLAW expands your library by giving you access to documents issued by federal and state courts and legislatures. To assist you in keeping up-to-date with the activities of these government bodies, WESTLAW provides a topical highlights database for criminal justice issues, as well as information from publications such as the *American Criminal Law Review*, the *Criminal Justice Periodical Index*, and *Federal Sentencing Law and Practice*.

You can retrieve documents on WESTLAW by accessing a database and entering a query; by using Find, a one-step document retrieval service; or by using such services as Insta–Cite®,

Shepard's®, Shepard's PreView™ and Quick*Cite*™. You can also use West's menu-driven research system, EZ ACCESS™, for additional help.

Additional Resources

If you have not used WESTLAW or have questions not addressed in this appendix, see the *WESTLAW Reference Manual* or contact the West Reference Attorneys at 1–800–688–6363.

Section 2. Criminal Procedure Databases

Each database is assigned an identifier, which you use to access the database. You can find identifiers for all WESTLAW databases in the WESTLAW Directory and in the *WESTLAW Database List.* When you need to know more detailed information about a database, use the Scope command. Scope displays unique commands and related databases for each WESTLAW database and service.

Because new information is continually being added to WESTLAW, you should check the WESTLAW Directory for any new database information.

Description	Database Identifier	Coverage
FEDERAL DATABASES		
Case Law		
Federal Criminal Justice—Federal Cases	FCJ–CS	From 1945*
Federal Criminal Justice—Supreme Court Cases	FCJ–SCT	From 1945*
Federal Criminal Justice—Courts of Appeals Cases	FCJ–CTA	From 1945*
Federal Criminal Justice—District Courts Cases	FCJ–DCT	From 1945*
Statutes and Regulations		
Federal Criminal Justice—U.S. Code Annotated	FCJ–USCA	Current
United States Public Laws	US–PL	Current
Federal Criminal Justice—Rules	FCJ–RULES	Current
Federal Orders	US–ORDERS	Current
Federal Criminal Justice—Federal Register	FCJ–FR	From July 1980
Federal Criminal Justice—Code of Federal Regulations	FCJ–CFR	Current
Federal Criminal Justice—Federal Sentencing Guidelines	FCJ–FSG	Current
Federal Criminal Justice—Federal Sentencing Guidelines—Old	FCJ–FSG–OLD	Prior versions
STATE DATABASES		
Case Law		
Multistate Criminal Justice Cases	MCJ–CS	Varies by state

Description	Database Identifier	Coverage
Individual State Criminal Justice Cases	XXCJ–CS**	Varies by state
Statutes and Rules		
Individual State Statutes—Annotated	XX–ST–ANN**	See Scope for the specific state
Individual State Statutes Unannotated	XX–ST**	See Scope for the specific state
Individual State Legislative Service	XX–LEGIS**	See Scope for the specific state
Individual State Court Rules	XX–RULES**	See Scope for the specific state
Individual State Court Orders	XX–ORDERS**	See Scope for the specific state
SPECIALIZED DATABASES		
ABA Standards for Criminal Justice	CJ–SCJ	1980–present
Criminal Justice Abstracts	CJ–CJA	October 1968–present
From the State Capitals: Justice Policies	FTSC–JP	October 1988–present
WESTLAW Topical Highlights—Criminal Justice	WTH–CJ	Current data
DIALOG® Databases		
Criminal Justice Periodical Index	CJ–PI	1975–present
National Criminal Justice Reference Service	NCJRS	1972–present
TEXTS & PERIODICALS		
Criminal Justice—Law Reviews, Texts & Journals	CJ–TP	Varies by publication
American Criminal Law Review	AMCRLR	1982 (vol. 19)
American Journal of Criminal Law	AMJCRL	1984 (vol. 13)
Criminal Justice	CRIMJUST	1986 (vol. 1)
Federal Sentencing Law & Practice	FSLP	1989 edition
Federal Sentencing Reporter	FCJ–FSR	1988 (vol. 1)
Journal of Criminal Law and Criminology	JCRLC	1983 (vol. 74)

* Cases dated before 1945 are contained in databases whose identifiers end with the suffix –OLD, e.g., the identifier for the Federal Criminal Justice—Supreme Court Cases—Before 1945 database is FCJ–SCT–OLD.

** XX is a state's two-letter postal abbreviation.

Section 3. EZ ACCESS™

EZ ACCESS is West Publishing Company's menu-driven research system. It is ideal for new or infrequent WESTLAW users because it requires no experience or training on WESTLAW.

EZ ACCESS assists you in performing the following research tasks on WESTLAW:

1. Retrieving a document using its citation or title
2. Retrieving cases using a West topic or key number
3. Retrieving documents using significant words
4. Retrieving references to a document using Insta-Cite, Shepard's Citations, Shepard's PreView and WESTLAW as a citator

To access EZ ACCESS, type **ez.** Whenever you are unsure of the next step, or if the choice you want is not listed, simply type **ez**; additional choices will be displayed. Once you retrieve documents with EZ ACCESS, use standard WESTLAW commands to browse your documents. For more information on browsing documents, see the browsing commands listed later in this appendix or the *WESTLAW Reference Manual.*

Section 4. Find

Overview. Find is a WESTLAW service that allows you to retrieve a document by entering its citation. Find allows you to retrieve documents from anywhere in WESTLAW without accessing or changing databases or losing your search result. Find is available for many documents including federal court rules, case law (federal and state), state statutes, *United States Code Annotated®*, *Code of Federal Regulations* and *Federal Register* materials, and state and federal public laws.

☐ To use Find, type **fi** followed by the document citation.

☐ When you are finished using Find, you have several options. You can access other services, such as Insta-Cite, Shepard's Citations, Shepard's PreView or Quick*Cite.* You can also return to the last database or service accessed before using Find by typing **gb** or **map**.

To Find This Document	Type
Arizona v. Fulminante, 111 S.Ct. 1246 (1991)	fi 111 sct 1246
Florida Statutes Annotated § 905.34	fi fl st s 905.34
18 U.S.C.A. § 3237	fi 18 usca 3237
U.S. Const. amend. VIII	fi const amend 8
Fed.R.Crim.P. 12.1	fi frcrp rule 12.1
Standards for Criminal Justice § 18-1.1 (1986)	fi scj 18-1.1

Section 5. Query Formulation

Overview. A query is a request you make to WESTLAW specifying the information you wish to retrieve. The terms in a query are words or numbers that you include in your request so that WESTLAW will retrieve documents containing those words or numbers. These terms are linked together by connectors, which specify the relationship in which the terms must appear.

5.1 Terms

Plurals and Possessives. Plurals are automatically retrieved when you enter the singular form of a term. This is true for both regular and irregular plurals (e.g., **child** retrieves *children*). If you do not want to retrieve the plural form, you can turn off the automatic pluralizer by typing the # symbol in front of the singular form. If you enter the plural form of a term, you will not retrieve the singular form.

If you enter the non-possessive form of a term, WESTLAW automatically retrieves the possessive form as well. However, if you enter the possessive form, only the possessive form is retrieved.

Automatic Equivalencies. Some terms have alternative forms or equivalencies; for example, *5* and *five* are equivalent terms. WESTLAW automatically retrieves equivalent terms. The *WESTLAW Reference Manual* contains a list of equivalent terms.

Compound Words and Acronyms. When a compound word is one of your search terms, use a hyphen to retrieve all forms of the word. For example, the term **cross-examination** retrieves *cross-examination, cross examination* and *crossexamination.*

When using an acronym as a search term, place a period after each of the letters in the acronym to retrieve any of its forms. For example, the term **a.b.a.** retrieves *aba, a.b.a., a b a* and *a. b. a.*

Root Expander and Universal Character. Placing a root expander (!) at the end of a root term generates ALL other terms with that root. For example, adding the ! symbol to the root *confess* in the query

confess! /s miranda

instructs WESTLAW to retrieve such words as *confess, confesses, confessed, confessing, confession* and *confessions.*

The universal character (*) stands for one character and can be inserted in the middle or at the end of a term. For example, the term

withdr*w

will retrieve *withdraw* and *withdrew.* More than one universal character can be used in a term. Adding two asterisks to the root *jur* in the query

jur**

instructs WESTLAW to retrieve all forms of the root with up to two additional characters. Terms like *jury* or *juror* are retrieved by this query. However, terms with more than two letters following the root, such as *jurisdiction,* are not retrieved. Plurals are always retrieved, even if more than two letters follow the root.

Phrase Searching. To search for a phrase on WESTLAW, place it within quotation marks. For example, to search for references to probable cause, type **"probable cause"**. You should use phrase searching only when you are certain that the phrase will not appear in any other form.

5.2 Alternative Terms

After selecting the terms for your query, consider which alternative terms are necessary. For example, if you are searching for the term *custody,* you might also want to search for the terms *detain!* and *detention.* You should consider both synonyms and antonyms as alternative terms.

5.3 Connectors

After selecting terms and alternative terms for your query, use connectors to specify the relationship that should exist between search terms in your retrieved documents. The connectors you can use are described below:

Connector	Meaning	Example
or (space)	Retrieves documents containing either term or both terms.	**murder homicide**
& (and)	Retrieves documents containing both terms.	**miranda & waiver**
/p	Retrieves documents containing both terms in the same paragraph.	**warrant! /p search!**
/s	Retrieves documents containing both terms in the same sentence.	**death /s penalty**
+s	Retrieves documents in which the first term precedes the second within the same sentence.	**peremptory +s challenge**
/n	Retrieves documents in which terms are within a specified number of terms of each other.	**search /3 seizure**
+n	Retrieves documents in which the first term precedes the second by no more than the specified number of terms.	**plea +2 bargain!**
% (but not)	Excludes all documents containing the term(s) following the % symbol.	**jur** /s select! % to(193)**

5.4 Restricting Your Search by Field

Overview. Documents in each WESTLAW database consist of several segments, or fields. One field may contain the citation, another the title, another the synopsis, and so forth. A query can be formulated to retrieve only those documents that contain search terms in a specified field. Not all databases contain the same fields. Also, depending on the database, fields of the same name may contain different types of information.

To view the fields and field content for a specific database, type **f** while in the database. Note that in some databases, not every field is available for every document. To restrict your search to a specific field, type the field name or two-letter abbreviation followed by search terms enclosed in parentheses. For example, to retrieve a case entitled *Florida v. Bostick,* restrict your search to the title field:

ti(florida & bostick)

The following fields are available in some WESTLAW databases you might use for researching the law of criminal procedure:

Digest and Synopsis Fields. The digest and synopsis fields, provided in case law databases by West Publishing Company's editors, summarize the main points of a case. A search in these fields is useful because it retrieves only cases in which a search term was significant enough to be included in a summary.

Consider restricting your search to one or both of these fields if

- ☐ you are searching for common terms or terms with more than one meaning, and you need to narrow your search; or
- ☐ you cannot narrow your search by moving to a smaller database.

For example, suppose you wish to retrieve Supreme Court cases that discuss the entrapment defense. Access the Federal Criminal Justice—Supreme Court Cases database (FCJ–SCT) and type a query like the following:

sy,di(entrap!)

Headnote Field. You can also restrict your search to the headnote field. The headnote field, which is part of the digest field, does not include the topic number, the key number, the citation or the title. The headnote field contains only the one-sentence summary of the point of law and any supporting statutory citations given by the author of the opinion. A headnote field search is useful when you are searching for references to specific code sections or rule numbers.

For example, to retrieve federal courts of appeals cases that discuss Rule 12.1 of the Federal Rules of Criminal Procedure, access the Federal Criminal Justice—Courts of Appeals Cases database (FCJ–CTA) and type the following query:

he(12.1)

Topic Field. The topic field includes the West digest topic number, the topic name, the key number and the text of the key line for each key number. You should restrict your search to the topic field in a case law database if

- ☐ a digest field search retrieves too many documents; or
- ☐ you want to retrieve cases with digest paragraphs classified under more than one topic.

For example, the topic number for Criminal Law is 110. To retrieve California state court cases that discuss sanctions for failure to comply with discovery requests, access the California Criminal Justice Cases database (CACJ–CS) and type a query like the following:

to(110) /p discover! /p sanction

To retrieve West headnotes classified under more than one topic number, search for the topic name in the topic field. For example, to retrieve other headnotes discussing sanctions for the failure to comply with discovery requests, modify the above query as follows:

to(criminal) /p discover! /p sanction

Be aware that cases from slip opinions and looseleaf services do not contain the digest, synopsis, headnote or topic fields.

Prelim and Caption Fields. Restrict your search to the prelim and caption fields in a database containing statutes, rules or regulations to retrieve documents where your terms are important enough to appear in the heading or name of a statute or rule. For example, to retrieve sections of the *United States Code Annotated* governing pretrial detention, access the Federal Criminal Justice—United States Code Annotated database (FCJ–USCA) and type

pr,ca(pre-trial trial & detention detain!)

5.5 Restricting Your Search by Date

You can instruct WESTLAW to retrieve documents *decided or issued* before, after, or on a specified date, as well as within a range of dates. The following are examples of queries that contain date restrictions:

da(bef 1991 & aft 1986) & "plain view" /p warrant!

da(1990) & "plain view" /p warrant!

da(4/26/90) & "plain view" /p warrant!

You can also instruct WESTLAW to retrieve documents *added to a database* on or after a specified date, as well as within a range of dates. The following are examples of queries that contain added date restrictions:

ad(aft 1-1-91) & "plain view" /p warrant!

ad(aft 2-1-91 & bef 3-1-91) & "plain view" /p warrant!

Section 6. Insta-Cite®

Overview. Insta-Cite is West Publishing Company's case history and citation verification service. It is the most current case history service available. Insta-Cite provides the following types of information about a citation:

Direct History. In addition to reversals and affirmances, Insta-Cite gives you the complete reported history of a litigated matter. Insta-Cite provides federal direct history of a case from 1754 and state direct history from 1879. Direct history includes related references, which are other cases related to the litigation. Insta-Cite provides related references from 1983 to date.

Negative Indirect History. Insta-Cite lists subsequent cases that have a substantial negative impact on your case, including cases overruling your case or calling it into question. Cases affected by decisions from 1972 to date will be displayed on Insta-Cite. To retrieve negative indirect history prior to 1972, use Shepard's Citations (discussed in Section 7).

Secondary Source References. Insta-Cite also provides references to secondary sources that cite your case, such as *Corpus Juris Secondum®*.

Parallel Citations. Insta-Cite provides parallel citations for cases including citations to *U.S. Law Week* and many other looseleaf reporters.

Citation Verification. Insta-Cite confirms that you have the correct volume and page number for a case. Citation verification information is available from 1754 for federal cases and from 1879 for state cases.

Commands

The following commands can be used in Insta-Cite:

ic xxx or **ic**	Retrieves an Insta-Cite result when followed by a case citation (where xxx is the citation), or when entered from a displayed case, Shepard's result or Shepard's PreView result.
pubs	Displays a list of publications and publication abbreviations available in Insta-Cite.
sc	Displays the scope of Insta-Cite coverage.
expand	Displays the Insta-Cite result including cases that affect precedential history cases. (Locate is not available in an expanded Insta-Cite result.)
Loc xxx	Restricts an Insta-Cite result to direct or indirect history or to secondary source references when followed by the appropriate code. For example, **Loc dir** restricts the Insta-Cite result to the direct history of your case.
xLoc	Cancels your Locate request.
Loc auto xxx	Automatically restricts subsequent Insta-Cite results according to your Locate request (where xxx is a Locate request).
xLoc auto	Cancels your Locate Auto request.
gb or **map2**	Returns you to your previous service or search result, if one exists.

Section 7. Shepard's® Citations

Overview. Shepard's provides a comprehensive list of cases and publications that have cited a particular case. Shepard's also includes explanatory analysis to indicate how the citing cases have treated the case, e.g., "followed," "explained."

In addition to citations from federal, state and regional citators, Shepard's on WESTLAW includes citations from specialized citators, such as *Federal Law Citations in Selected Law Reviews.* This citator contains citing references from selected law reviews, including the *Harvard Law Review, Stanford Law Review* and *Yale Law Journal.*

Commands

The following commands can be used in Shepard's:

sh xxx or **sh**	Retrieves a Shepard's result when followed by a case citation (where **xxx** is the citation), or when entered from a displayed case, Insta-Cite result or Shepard's PreView result.
pubs	Displays a list of publications that can be Shepardized® and their publication abbreviations.
sc xxx	Displays the scope of coverage for a specific publication in Shepard's, where **xxx** is the publication abbreviation (e.g., **sc f.r.d.**).
cmds	Displays a list of Shepard's commands.
Loc	Restricts a Shepard's result to a specific category when followed by the analysis code, headnote number, or state/circuit or publication abbreviation to which you want the display restricted. For example, **Loc 5** restricts the Shepard's result to cases discussing the point of law contained in headnote number five of the cited case. Type **xLoc** to cancel Locate.
gb or **map2**	Leaves Shepard's and returns you to your previous service or search result, if one exists.

Section 8. Shepard's PreView™

Overview. Shepard's PreView gives you a preview of citing references from West's® National Reporter System® that will appear in Shepard's Citations. Depending on the citation, Shepard's PreView provides citing information days, weeks or even months before the same information appears in Shepard's online. Use Shepard's PreView to update your Shepard's results.

Commands

The following commands can be used in Shepard's PreView:

sp xxx or **sp**	Retrieves a Shepard's PreView result when followed by a case citation (where **xxx** is the citation), or when entered from a displayed case, Insta-Cite result or Shepard's result.
pubs	Displays a list of publications and publication abbreviations that are available in Shepard's PreView.

sc xxx	Displays the scope of citing references.
cmds	Displays a list of Shepard's PreView commands.
Loc xxx	Restricts a Shepard's PreView result to a specific publication, where xxx is the publication abbreviation.
gb or **map2**	Leaves Shepard's PreView and returns you to your previous service or search result, if one exists.

Section 9. Quick*Cite*™

Overview. Quick*Cite* is West Publishing Company's citator service that enables you to automatically update Shepard's PreView with more recent citing cases.

There is a four to six-week gap between citing cases listed in Shepard's PreView and citing cases available on WESTLAW. This gap occurs because cases go through an editorial process at West before they are added to Shepard's PreView. To retrieve the most recent citing cases, therefore, you need to search case law databases on WESTLAW for references to your case; this search technique is known as using WESTLAW as a citator. Quick*Cite* makes using WESTLAW as a citator automatic.

After you've checked your case in the other citator services on WESTLAW, type qc to display the Quick*Cite* screen. From this screen, you can press **ENTER** to retrieve the most recent citing cases on WESTLAW, including slip opinions. You can also type qc and the citation to display the Quick*Cite* screen, e.g., **qc 83 sct 407.**

Quick*Cite* formulates a query using the title, the case citation(s), and an added date restriction. Quick*Cite* then accesses the appropriate database, either ALLSTATES or ALLFEDS, and runs the query for you.

Quick*Cite* also allows you to choose a different date range and database for your query so you can tailor it to your specific research needs.

Commands

The following commands can be used in Quick*Cite:*

qc xxx or **qc**	Retrieves a Quick*Cite* result when followed by a case citation (where xxx is the citation), or when entered from a displayed case, Insta–Cite result, Shepard's result or Shepard's PreView result.
db	Leaves your Quick*Cite* result and returns you to the WESTLAW Directory.

Quick*Cite* is designed to retrieve documents that cite cases. To retrieve citing references to other documents, such as statutes and law review articles, use WESTLAW as a citator.

Section 10. WESTLAW as a Citator

Using WESTLAW as a citator, you can search for documents citing a specific statute, regulation, rule or law review article. To retrieve documents citing 18 U.S.C.A. § 3142(b), for example, access the Federal Criminal Justice—Federal Cases database (FCJ–CS) and search for the citation:

18 +5 3142(b)

If the citation is not a unique term, add descriptive terms. For example, to retrieve cases citing Fed.R.Crim.P. 7(b) governing waiver of indictment, access the Federal Criminal Justice—Federal Cases database (FCJ–CS) and type a query like the following:

7(b) /p waive* /s indictment

Section 11. Research Examples

11.1 Retrieving Legal Articles

In Chapter 28, "Collateral Review," the author cites an article by Professor Ira P. Robbins, "Whether (or Wither) Habeas Corpus," 111 F.R.D. 265 (1986). You would like to read the entire article. How can you retrieve the article on WESTLAW?

Solution

☐ Access the Federal Rules Decisions (Articles from the West Reporter) database (FEDRDTP). Restricting your search to the citation field, type the following query:

ci(111 +5 265)

11.2 Retrieving Federal Rules

You want to obtain oral statements your client made to F.B.I. agents prior to his arrest. Before making your discovery request, you decide to review the applicable federal rules of criminal procedure. Use WESTLAW to retrieve the rules.

Solution

☐ Access the Federal Criminal Justice—Rules database (FCJ–RULES). To restrict your search to the Federal Rules of Criminal Procedure, include a citation field restriction in your query. Type

ci(cr) & discovery /p defendant /s oral /2 statement

☐ To see if the rule has been amended or repealed, use the Update service. Simply type **update** while viewing the rule to display any court order that amends or repeals the rule.

Update does not retrieve material that has been so substantially changed it is considered completely new. It also does not contain new rules that had no prior counterpart in existing law. To ensure that you retrieve all relevant documents, run a descriptive word search in the Federal Orders database (US–ORDERS).

11.3 Retrieving Federal Statutes

Your client is being detained prior to trial under provisions of the Bail Reform Act of 1984, 18 U.S.C.A. § 3142(e). You want to read subsection (e).

Solution

☐ Use Find to retrieve 18 U.S.C.A. § 3142. Type

fi 18 usca 3142

☐ Use Locate to go to subsection (e). Type **Loc e.**

☐ To look at surrounding sections of the Bail Reform Act, use the Documents in Sequence command. To retrieve the section immediately preceding § 3142, type **d–**. To retrieve the section immediately following § 3142, type **d.**

☐ To see if the statute has been amended or repealed, use the Update service. Simply type **update** while viewing the statute to display any public law that amends or repeals the statute.

Update does not retrieve material that has been so substantially changed it is considered completely new. It also does not contain slip laws or new legislation that had no prior counterpart in existing law. To ensure that you retrieve all relevant documents, run a descriptive word search in the United States Public Laws database (US-PL).

11.4 Retrieving Supreme Court Cases

Your client has been charged with possession with intent to distribute cocaine. The police stopped him as he was driving away from a known crack house and found the drugs in a suitcase on the floor of the car. The police searched the suitcase without first obtaining a warrant. Although the police had probable cause to believe the suitcase contained drugs, they did not have probable cause to believe the car contained drugs. You believe the warrantless search of the suitcase violated the Fourth Amendment, and you want to move to suppress the evidence obtained from the search. Use WESTLAW to retrieve Supreme Court cases discussing this issue.

Solution

☐ Access the Federal Criminal Justice—Supreme Court database (FCJ-SCT). Restricting your search to the synopsis and digest fields, type the following query:

sy,di(automobile auto car vehicle /p container bag luggage suitcase /p warrant!)

Your client is convicted of possession with intent to distribute. The members of the jury that convicted him were all white. You believe that the prosecutor used his peremptory challenges to exclude prospective black jurors because of their race. Although your client is white, you want to challenge your client's conviction arguing that the exclusion of prospective black jurors based on their race violated the equal protection clause of the Fourteenth Amendment. Does your client have standing to raise this issue?

Solution

☐ Type **s** to display the Enter Query screen. Then type the following query:

defendant /p rac* /p jur** /p peremptory /p "equal protection" (fourteen ** /5 amendment const.amend)**

One of the cases retrieved by the above query is *Powers v. Ohio,* 111 S.Ct. 1364 (1991). While reading the headnotes in this case, you decide that you want to read other Supreme Court cases containing similar points of law. Use the West topic number 230, Jury, and key number 33(5.1), Peremptory challenges, to retrieve similarly classified cases.

☐ Type **s** to display the Enter Query screen. Then type the following query:

230k33(5.1)

11.5 Finding and Verifying Supreme Court Cases

In *Booth v. Maryland,* 107 S.Ct. 2529 (1987), the Supreme Court held that the introduction of a victim impact statement during the sentencing phase of a capital trial violated the Eighth Amendment. Use WESTLAW to retrieve this case.

Solution

☐ Use Find to retrieve a case when you know its citation. Type

fi 107 sct 2529

☐ Use Insta-Cite to retrieve the direct and negative indirect history of *Booth.* Type **ic.**

☐ You want to Shepardize *Booth.* Type **sh.**

Limit your Shepard's result to decisions that have followed Booth. Type **Loc f.**

☐ Check Shepard's PreView for more current cases citing *Booth*. Type **sp.**

☐ Check Quick*Cite* for the most current cases citing *Booth*. Type **qc** and follow the online instructions.

11.6 Researching State Court Rules

According to the author of this treatise, the majority of states now allow for the prosecution of all felonies by information rather than indictment. One of these states is Iowa. Use WESTLAW to retrieve the rules governing prosecution by information in Iowa.

Solution

☐ Access the Iowa Court Rules database (IA–RULES) by typing **db ia-rules.** Restricting your search to the prelim and caption fields, type the following query:

pr,ca(criminal & procedure & information)

One of the documents retrieved by your query is Rule 5 of the Iowa Rules of Criminal Procedure (Iowa Code Annotated § 813.2, Rule 5). Retrieve Iowa cases construing Rule 5.

Solution

☐ While viewing Rule 5, display the annotations field, which contains Notes of Decisions or annotations discussing specific point of law. Type **f an.**

A Notes of Decisions index appears at the beginning of the annotations field. To view cases under a particular index heading, type the page number listed in the index.

☐ One of the cases listed in the Notes of Decisions is *State v. Epps,* 322 N.W.2d 288 (Iowa 1982). Use Find to retrieve it.

fi 322 nw2d 288

☐ Use Locate to quickly scan this case for references to Rule 5. Type

Loc rule +s 5

Section 12. WESTLAW Commands

General Commands

ez	Accesses the EZ ACCESS system; when entered from EZ ACCESS, displays additional choices.
help	Displays explanatory messages.
scope	Displays a database description when followed by a database identifier or when entered from a database; displays the scope of coverage when entered from a service, such as Insta–Cite.
time	Displays the amount of chargeable time used in your research session.
off	Signs off WESTLAW.
pr	Displays the Offline Printing and Downloading Menu.
opd	Displays the Offline Print Directory.
client	Allows you to change your client identifier.
options	Displays the WESTLAW Options Directory.

Search Commands

s	New search—displays the Enter Query screen.

Search Commands

q	Edit query—displays the last query for editing.
x	Cancels a search in progress.
db	Returns to the WESTLAW Directory from a database; accesses a database when followed by a database identifier: **db fcj-sct.**
sdb xxx	Runs the same query in a different database, where xxx is the database identifier: **sdb fcj-cs.**
qdb xxx	Displays the query for editing in a different database, where xxx is the database identifier: **qdb mcj-cs.**
read	In selected databases, retrieves the most recent documents when entered at the Enter Query screen.
List	In selected databases, retrieves a list of the most recent documents when entered at the Enter Query screen.

Browsing Commands

t	Term mode—displays the next page containing the terms in the requested relationship; **t-** displays the previous page containing the terms in the requested relationship.
p	Page mode—displays the next page of a document; **p-** displays the previous page of a document. To display a specific page, type **p** followed by the page number: **p5.**
Loc	Locate—locates selected terms in retrieved documents; also restricts a Shepard's display to selected categories, such as history and treatment codes, headnote numbers and citing publications.
LLoc	Retrieves a citations list of Locate documents.
xLoc	Cancels a Locate command.
r	Displays the next ranked document; displays a specific document when followed by the document's rank number: **r3.**
L	Displays a citations list.
Lr#	Displays a citations list beginning with a specific rank number: **Lr8.**
g	Search summary—displays the query and the number of documents retrieved by it.
h+	Advances one half page in a document.
h−	Moves back one half page in a document.
d	Documents in Sequence—displays sections preceding or following the retrieved statutory document: **d+#, d−#.**
xd	Cancels Documents in Sequence and displays the document you were viewing when you entered the Documents in Sequence command.
f	Displays a list of fields in a database; restricts your display to a selected field or fields when followed by the field name: **f opinion.**
xf	Cancels your command to restrict your display by field.

Service Commands

fi	Find—retrieves a document when followed by its citation: **fi 86 sct 1602.**
ic	Retrieves an Insta–Cite result when followed by the case citation, **ic 86 sct 1602,** or when entered from a displayed case, Shepard's result or Shepard's PreView result.
sh	Retrieves a Shepard's result when followed by the case citation, **sh 86 sct 1602,** or when entered from a displayed case, Insta–Cite result or Shepard's PreView result.
sp	Retrieves a Shepard's PreView result when followed by the case citation, **86 sct 1602,** or when entered from a displayed case, Insta–Cite result or Shepard's result.
qc	Retrieves a Quick*Cite* result when followed by the case citation, **qc 86 sct 1602,** or when entered from a displayed case, Insta–Cite result, Shepard's result or Shepard's PreView result.
pdq	Personal Directory of Queries—displays a list of saved queries for selection and update.
di	Enters the Black's Law Dictionary® service or displays a definition when followed by the word or phrase: **di venue.**
update	Displays any document amending or repealing the statute, rule or regulation you are viewing.
rm	Displays the Related Materials Directory for a statute, legislative service document, rule or order.
gm	Displays General Materials, which are references and tables applicable to the entire title, chapter and subchapter containing the displayed statute.
annos	Displays annotations (Notes of Decisions) for the displayed statute.
refs	Displays references to the unannotated statutory document you are viewing.
st-ann	Displays the annotated statute(s) amended or repealed by the displayed document.
stat	Displays the unannotated statute(s) amended or repealed by the displayed document.
rules	Displays the court rule(s) affected by the displayed court order.
gb	Go Back—returns to a previous location in WESTLAW from a service, e.g., Insta–Cite, Shepard's, Find.
map	Displays a list containing the most recent database and services accessed and allows you to return to them.
map1	Returns to the WESTLAW Directory.
map2	Returns to your search result, if one exists.

*

Table of Cases

A

B

D

Dunaway v. New York, 442 U.S. 200, 99 S.Ct. 2248, 60 L.Ed.2d 824 (1979)—**§ 3.3; § 3.3, n. 23; § 3.8; § 3.8, n. 4, 10, 57; § 6.6; § 6.6, n. 13.**
Duncan v. Louisiana, 391 U.S. 145, 88 S.Ct. 1444, 20 L.Ed.2d 491, 45 O.O.2d 198 (1968)—**§ 2.3, n. 2; § 2.4, n. 1, 21; § 2.5, n. 2, 9; § 2.6; § 2.6, n. 7, 11, 12, 14; § 22.1; § 22.1, n. 6, 28, 33; § 22.2; § 22.2, n. 20.**
Dunlop v. United States, 165 U.S. 486, 17 S.Ct. 375, 41 L.Ed. 799 (1897)—**§ 24.5, n. 11.**
Dunn, United States v., 480 U.S. 294, 107 S.Ct. 1134, 94 L.Ed.2d 326 (1987)—**§ 3.2; § 3.2, n. 31, 35, 44, 45.**
Dunn v. United States, 284 U.S. 390, 52 S.Ct. 189, 76 L.Ed. 356 (1932)—**§ 24.7; § 24.7, n. 3, 5.**
Duren v. Missouri, 439 U.S. 357, 99 S.Ct. 664, 58 L.Ed.2d 579 (1979)—**§ 22.2; § 22.2, n. 28, 30.**
Dusky v. United States, 362 U.S. 402, 80 S.Ct. 788, 4 L.Ed.2d 824 (1960)—**§ 21.4, n. 4.**
Dutton v. Evans, 400 U.S. 74, 91 S.Ct. 210, 27 L.Ed.2d 213 (1970)—**§ 3.3, n. 51; § 17.2; § 17.2, n. 9.**
Dyke v. Taylor Implement Mfg. Co., 391 U.S. 216, 88 S.Ct. 1472, 20 L.Ed.2d 538 (1968)—**§ 3.7; § 3.7, n. 25, 28; § 22.1, n. 12.**

E

Eash, State v., 367 So.2d 661 (Fla.App. 2 Dist.1979)—**§ 13.6; § 13.6, n. 4.**
Echeles, United States v., 352 F.2d 892 (7th Cir.1965)—**§ 17.2; § 17.2, n. 17.**
Edmons, United States v., 432 F.2d 577 (2nd Cir.1970)—**§ 9.4; § 9.4, n. 30.**
Edmonson v. Leesville Concrete Co., Inc., ___ U.S. ___, 111 S.Ct. 2077, 114 L.Ed.2d 660 (1991)—**§ 22.3, n. 47.**
Edwards v. Arizona, 451 U.S. 477, 101 S.Ct. 1880, 68 L.Ed.2d 378 (1981)—**§ 2.7, n. 11; § 2.9; § 6.4, n. 30, 32; § 6.9; § 6.9, n. 23, 25, 26; § 9.6; § 9.6, n. 13.**
Edwards, United States v., 430 A.2d 1321 (D.C.App. 1981)—**§ 12.3; § 12.3, n. 29.**
Edwards, United States v., 415 U.S. 800, 94 S.Ct. 1234, 39 L.Ed.2d 771 (1974)—**§ 3.5; § 3.5, n. 24, 26, 34; § 3.7; § 3.7, n. 47.**
Eight Thousand Eight Hundred and Fifty Dollars ($8,850) in U.S. Currency, United States v., 461 U.S. 555, 103 S.Ct. 2005, 76 L.Ed.2d 143 (1983)—**§ 18.1, n. 2; § 18.5, n. 5.**
Elkins v. United States, 364 U.S. 206, 80 S.Ct. 1437, 4 L.Ed.2d 1669 (1960)—**§ 3.1; § 3.1, n. 11, 20, 42; § 4.1; § 4.1, n. 12; § 25.5, n. 3.**
Elksnis, United States ex rel. v. Gilligan, 256 F.Supp. 244 (D.C.N.Y.1966)—**§ 21.3; § 21.3, n. 21.**
Elrod, United States v., 441 F.2d 353 (5th Cir.1971)—**§ 3.10; § 3.10, n. 3.**
Engle v. Isaac, 456 U.S. 107, 102 S.Ct. 1558, 71 L.Ed.2d 783 (1982)—**§ 28.2; § 28.2, n. 27, 41; § 28.4; § 28.4, n. 4, 23.**
Entick v. Carrington, 19 Howell St.Tr. 1029 (1765)—**§ 8.12; § 8.12, n. 3.**
Escobedo v. Illinois, 378 U.S. 478, 84 S.Ct. 1758, 12 L.Ed.2d 977, 32 O.O.2d 31 (1964)—**§ 3.10, n. 2; § 6.1; § 6.1, n. 3, 5; § 6.4; § 6.4, n. 11, 13; § 6.5; § 6.5, n. 4, 7; § 6.6; § 6.6, n. 1; § 8.15; § 9.1.**
Eskridge v. Washington State Bd. of Prison Terms and Paroles, 357 U.S. 214, 78 S.Ct. 1061, 2 L.Ed.2d 1269 (1958)—**§ 11.2; § 11.2, n. 36.**
Estelle v. Smith, 451 U.S. 454, 101 S.Ct. 1866, 68 L.Ed.2d 359 (1981)—**§ 6.4, n. 43; § 6.7; § 6.7, n. 19; § 6.10; § 6.10, n. 4, 6, 7; § 8.10, n. 2; § 20.4; § 20.4, n. 14.**
Estelle v. Williams, 425 U.S. 501, 96 S.Ct. 1691, 48 L.Ed.2d 126 (1976)—**§ 24.2; § 24.2, n. 12.**
Estes v. Texas, 381 U.S. 532, 85 S.Ct. 1628, 14 L.Ed.2d 543 (1965)—**§ 23.3; § 23.3, n. 3.**
Eubanks v. Louisiana, 356 U.S. 584, 78 S.Ct. 970, 2 L.Ed.2d 991 (1958)—**§ 22.2, n. 8.**
Euge, United States v., 444 U.S. 707, 100 S.Ct. 874, 63 L.Ed.2d 141 (1980)—**§ 7.2; § 7.2, n. 9.**
Evans v. Superior Court of Contra Costa County, 114 Cal.Rptr. 121, 522 P.2d 681 (Cal.1974)—**§ 7.4; § 7.4, n. 19.**
Evitts v. Lucey, 469 U.S. 387, 105 S.Ct. 830, 83 L.Ed.2d 821 (1985)—**§ 11.1; § 11.1, n. 10, 17; § 11.2; § 11.7; § 11.7, n. 4, 5; § 27.1, n. 9.**
Ex parte (see name of party)

F

Fahy v. Connecticut, 375 U.S. 85, 84 S.Ct. 229, 11 L.Ed.2d 171 (1963)—**§ 27.6; § 27.6, n. 10.**
Fare v. Michael C., 442 U.S. 707, 99 S.Ct. 2560, 61 L.Ed.2d 197 (1979)—**§ 6.9; § 6.9, n. 5, 7, 16; § 6.10, n. 5.**
Faretta v. California, 422 U.S. 806, 95 S.Ct. 2525, 45 L.Ed.2d 562 (1975)—**§ 2.7, n. 10; § 11.5; § 11.5, n. 1; § 11.6; § 11.6, n. 6; § 21.3; § 21.3, n. 4, 6.**
Fatico, United States v., 458 F.Supp. 388 (D.C.N.Y.1978)—**§ 26.6, n. 5.**
Fay v. New York, 332 U.S. 261, 67 S.Ct. 1613, 91 L.Ed. 2043 (1947)—**§ 22.2; § 22.2, n. 18, 23.**
Fay v. Noia, 372 U.S. 391, 83 S.Ct. 822, 9 L.Ed.2d 837, 24 O.O.2d 12 (1963)—**§ 28.1; § 28.1, n. 5; § 28.2; § 28.2, n. 6, 31; § 28.3; § 28.3, n. 14; § 28.4; § 28.4, n. 12; § 28.5; § 28.5, n. 4; § 28.7; § 28.7, n. 1.**
Ferguson v. Georgia, 365 U.S. 570, 81 S.Ct. 756, 5 L.Ed.2d 783 (1961)—**§ 11.8; § 11.8, n. 7, 8.**
Fernandez-Vidana, United States v., 857 F.2d 673 (9th Cir.1988)—**§ 26.6, n. 6.**
Finch v. United States, 433 U.S. 676, 97 S.Ct. 2909, 53 L.Ed.2d 1048 (1977)—**§ 25.3, n. 12.**
Fisher v. United States, 425 U.S. 391, 96 S.Ct. 1569, 48 L.Ed.2d 39 (1976)—**§ 8.12; § 8.12, n. 14, 24, 25, 27, 28; § 8.13; § 8.13, n. 1; § 8.14; § 8.14, n. 20, 27; § 20.4.**
Fitzsimmons v. State, 48 Md.App. 193, 426 A.2d 4 (Md. App.1981)—**§ 19.3, n. 2.**
Flanagan v. United States, 465 U.S. 259, 104 S.Ct. 1051, 79 L.Ed.2d 288 (1984)—**§ 11.4, n. 11; § 27.2; § 27.2, n. 13.**
Fletcher v. Weir, 455 U.S. 603, 102 S.Ct. 1309, 71 L.Ed.2d 490 (1982)—**§ 9.6; § 9.6, n. 19.**
Florida v. Bostick, ___ U.S. ___, 111 S.Ct. 2382, 115 L.Ed.2d 389 (1991)—**§ 3.8; § 3.8, n. 14, 15, 16, 17, 20; § 3.10, n. 12.**
Florida v. Casal, 462 U.S. 637, 103 S.Ct. 3100, 77 L.Ed.2d 277 (1983)—**§ 2.10, n. 12.**
Florida v. Jimeno, ___ U.S. ___, 111 S.Ct. 1801, 114 L.Ed.2d 297 (1991)—**§ 3.10, n. 36, 37, 38.**
Florida v. Meyers, 466 U.S. 380, 104 S.Ct. 1852, 80 L.Ed.2d 381 (1984)—**§ 3.7, n. 8.**
Florida v. Riley, 488 U.S. 445, 109 S.Ct. 693, 102 L.Ed.2d 835 (1989)—**§ 3.2; § 3.2, n. 15, 37; § 10.3, n. 6.**
Florida v. Rodriguez, 469 U.S. 1, 105 S.Ct. 308, 83 L.Ed.2d 165 (1984)—**§ 3.8, n. 32.**
Florida v. Royer, 460 U.S. 491, 103 S.Ct. 1319, 75 L.Ed.2d 229 (1983)—**§ 3.8; § 3.8, n. 11, 19.**
Florida v. Wells, 495 U.S. 1, 110 S.Ct. 1632, 109 L.Ed.2d 1 (1990)—**§ 3.7; § 3.7, n. 38.**

G

Gouled v. United States, 255 U.S. 298, 41 S.Ct. 261, 65 L.Ed. 647 (1921)—§ **3.2**; § **3.2, n. 61**; § **3.4, n. 1.**
Gouveia, United States v., 467 U.S. 180, 104 S.Ct. 2292, 81 L.Ed.2d 146 (1984)—§ **7.3, n. 7**; § **11.2**; § **11.2, n. 17, 18**; § **18.5, n. 6.**
Grady v. Corbin, 495 U.S. 508, 110 S.Ct. 2084, 109 L.Ed.2d 548 (1990)—§ **17.4**; § **17.4, n. 18, 19, 31, 33**; § **19.6**; § **25.1.**
Graham v. Connor, 490 U.S. 386, 109 S.Ct. 1865, 104 L.Ed.2d 443 (1989)—§ **3.5, n. 17.**
Grand Jury Matters, In re, 751 F.2d 13 (1st Cir.1984)—§ **8.8, n. 13.**
Grand Jury Proceedings, In re, 486 F.2d 85 (3rd Cir. 1973)—§ **8.2, n. 5**; § **8.8**; § **8.8, n. 6.**
Grand Jury Subpoena Duces Tecum Addressed to Provision Salesmen and Distributors Union, Local 627, AFL–CIO, In re, 203 F.Supp. 575 (D.C.N.Y.1961)—§ **8.7, n. 13.**
Grand Jury Subpoena Duces Tecum (Doe), In re, 605 F.Supp. 174 (D.C.N.Y.1985)—§ **8.12, n. 13.**
Grand Jury Subpoena Served Upon Doe, In re, 781 F.2d 238 (2nd Cir.1985)—§ **8.8, n. 12.**
Granello, United States v., 365 F.2d 990 (2nd Cir.1966)—§ **17.2**; § **17.2, n. 3.**
Grau v. United States, 287 U.S. 124, 53 S.Ct. 38, 77 L.Ed. 212 (1932)—§ **3.3, n. 31.**
Gray v. Mississippi, 481 U.S. 648, 107 S.Ct. 2045, 95 L.Ed.2d 622 (1987)—§ **22.3**; § **22.3, n. 26**; § **27.6, n. 26.**
Grayson, United States v., 438 U.S. 41, 98 S.Ct. 2610, 57 L.Ed.2d 582 (1978)—§ **21.1**; § **21.1, n. 5**; § **26.4**; § **26.4, n. 6**; § **26.8**; § **26.8, n. 4.**
Green v. United States, 365 U.S. 301, 81 S.Ct. 653, 5 L.Ed.2d 670 (1961)—§ **26.5**; § **26.5, n. 7.**
Green v. United States, 356 U.S. 165, 78 S.Ct. 632, 2 L.Ed.2d 672 (1958)—§ **2.8, n. 5, 6.**
Green v. United States, 355 U.S. 184, 78 S.Ct. 221, 2 L.Ed.2d 199 (1957)—§ **21.5**; § **21.5, n. 14**; § **25.1**; § **25.1, n. 3**; § **25.4**; § **25.4, n. 13.**
Greenholtz v. Inmates of Nebraska Penal and Correctional Complex, 442 U.S. 1, 99 S.Ct. 2100, 60 L.Ed.2d 668 (1979)—§ **26.2**; § **26.2, n. 3.**
Greenwood, Mississippi, City of v. Peacock, 384 U.S. 808, 86 S.Ct. 1800, 16 L.Ed.2d 944 (1966)—§ **13.5**; § **13.5, n. 20.**
Greer v. Miller, 483 U.S. 756, 107 S.Ct. 3102, 97 L.Ed.2d 618 (1987)—§ **9.6, n. 15.**
Gregg v. Georgia, 428 U.S. 153, 96 S.Ct. 2909, 49 L.Ed.2d 859 (1976)—§ **12.4, n. 3**; § **21.2, n. 7.**
Gregg v. United States, 394 U.S. 489, 89 S.Ct. 1134, 22 L.Ed.2d 442 (1969)—§ **26.5, n. 4.**
Griffin v. California, 380 U.S. 609, 85 S.Ct. 1229, 14 L.Ed.2d 106, 32 O.O.2d 437 (1965)—§ **17.2**; § **17.2, n. 20, 21**; § **24.4**; § **24.4, n. 2, 6**; § **27.6.**
Griffin v. Illinois, 351 U.S. 12, 76 S.Ct. 585, 100 L.Ed. 891 (1956)—§ **11.1**; § **11.1, n. 28, 33**; § **11.2**; § **11.2, n. 33**; § **12.2**; § **12.2, n. 9**; § **27.1.**
Griffin, United States v., 502 F.2d 959 (6th Cir.1974)—§ **9.3**; § **9.3, n. 21, 25.**
Griffin v. Wisconsin, 483 U.S. 868, 107 S.Ct. 3164, 97 L.Ed.2d 709 (1987)—§ **3.9**; § **3.9, n. 48, 49, 50.**
Griffith v. Kentucky, 479 U.S. 314, 107 S.Ct. 708, 93 L.Ed.2d 649 (1987)—§ **2.9**; § **2.9, n. 17, 23.**
Grimes, United States v., 438 F.2d 391 (6th Cir.1971)—§ **5.4**; § **5.4, n. 2.**
Groban's Petition, In re, 352 U.S. 330, 77 S.Ct. 510, 1 L.Ed.2d 376, 3 O.O.2d 127 (1957)—§ **8.6, n. 3**; § **8.15**; § **8.15, n. 1.**
Groppi v. Wisconsin, 400 U.S. 505, 91 S.Ct. 490, 27 L.Ed.2d 571 (1971)—§ **23.2**; § **23.2, n. 1.**
Grosso v. United States, 390 U.S. 62, 88 S.Ct. 709, 19 L.Ed.2d 906, 43 O.O.2d 226 (1968)—§ **8.12**; § **8.12, n. 17.**
Grunewald v. United States, 353 U.S. 391, 77 S.Ct. 963, 1 L.Ed.2d 931 (1957)—§ **8.10**; § **8.10, n. 21.**
Grunewald, United States v., 233 F.2d 556 (2nd Cir. 1956)—§ **8.14, n. 12.**
Gurule, United States v., 437 F.2d 239 (10th Cir.1970)—§ **8.7, n. 13.**
Gustafson v. Florida, 414 U.S. 260, 94 S.Ct. 488, 38 L.Ed.2d 456, 66 O.O.2d 275 (1973)—§ **3.5**; § **3.5, n. 20.**

H

Habbena, State v., 372 N.W.2d 450 (S.D.1985)—§ **26.5, n. 2.**
Hale v. Henkel, 201 U.S. 43, 26 S.Ct. 370, 50 L.Ed. 652 (1906)—§ **8.7**; § **8.7, n. 2, 4, 14**; § **8.12**; § **8.12, n. 7.**
Haley v. Ohio, 332 U.S. 596, 68 S.Ct. 302, 92 L.Ed. 224, 36 O.O. 530 (1948)—§ **6.4, n. 1.**
Hall, United States v., 421 F.2d 540 (2nd Cir.1969)—§ **6.6**; § **6.6, n. 8.**
Halper, United States v., 490 U.S. 435, 109 S.Ct. 1892, 104 L.Ed.2d 487 (1989)—§ **25.1**; § **25.1, n. 18.**
Ham v. South Carolina, 409 U.S. 524, 93 S.Ct. 848, 35 L.Ed.2d 46 (1973)—§ **22.3**; § **22.3, n. 2.**
Hamer v. United States, 259 F.2d 274 (9th Cir.1958)—§ **22.3**; § **22.3, n. 11, 15.**
Hamilton v. Alabama, 368 U.S. 52, 82 S.Ct. 157, 7 L.Ed.2d 114 (1961)—§ **11.2**; § **11.2, n. 14.**
Hamling v. United States, 418 U.S. 87, 94 S.Ct. 2887, 41 L.Ed.2d 590 (1974)—§ **19.2**; § **19.2, n. 1**; § **22.3, n. 5.**
Hampton v. United States, 425 U.S. 484, 96 S.Ct. 1646, 48 L.Ed.2d 113 (1976)—§ **5.4**; § **5.4, n. 11.**
Haring v. Prosise, 462 U.S. 306, 103 S.Ct. 2368, 76 L.Ed.2d 595 (1983)—§ **21.6, n. 9.**
Harlow v. Fitzgerald, 457 U.S. 800, 102 S.Ct. 2727, 73 L.Ed.2d 396 (1982)—§ **3.1, n. 76.**
Harrington v. California, 395 U.S. 250, 89 S.Ct. 1726, 23 L.Ed.2d 284 (1969)—§ **27.6**; § **27.6, n. 32.**
Harris v. New York, 401 U.S. 222, 91 S.Ct. 643, 28 L.Ed.2d 1 (1971)—§ **9.1, n. 9**; § **9.5, n. 5**; § **9.6**; § **9.6, n. 4**; § **10.5**; § **10.5, n. 14**; § **21.2**; § **21.2, n. 48.**
Harris v. Oklahoma, 433 U.S. 682, 97 S.Ct. 2912, 53 L.Ed.2d 1054 (1977)—§ **17.4**; § **17.4, n. 16.**
Harris v. Reed, 489 U.S. 255, 109 S.Ct. 1038, 103 L.Ed.2d 308 (1989)—§ **28.4**; § **28.4, n. 5, 7.**
Harris v. Rivera, 454 U.S. 339, 102 S.Ct. 460, 70 L.Ed.2d 530 (1981)—§ **24.7**; § **24.7, n. 7.**
Harris v. South Carolina, 338 U.S. 68, 69 S.Ct. 1354, 93 L.Ed. 1815 (1949)—§ **6.4, n. 1.**
Harris v. Superior Court of Alameda County, 140 Cal. Rptr. 318, 567 P.2d 750 (Cal.1977)—§ **11.4, n. 1.**
Harris v. United States, 404 U.S. 1232, 92 S.Ct. 10, 30 L.Ed.2d 25 (1971)—§ **12.4, n. 10.**
Harris, United States v., 403 U.S. 573, 91 S.Ct. 2075, 29 L.Ed.2d 723 (1971)—§ **3.3**; § **3.3, n. 2, 50.**
Harris v. United States, 390 U.S. 234, 88 S.Ct. 992, 19 L.Ed.2d 1067 (1968)—§ **3.7, n. 28.**
Harris v. United States, 382 U.S. 162, 86 S.Ct. 352, 15 L.Ed.2d 240 (1965)—§ **8.3, n. 2.**
Harris v. United States, 331 U.S. 145, 67 S.Ct. 1098, 91 L.Ed. 1399 (1947)—§ **2.7, n. 15**; § **3.4, n. 40.**
Harris v. Washington, 404 U.S. 55, 92 S.Ct. 183, 30 L.Ed.2d 212 (1971)—§ **17.4**; § **17.4, n. 4, 19.**

Harrison v. United States, 392 U.S. 219, 88 S.Ct. 2008, 20 L.Ed.2d 1047 (1968)—**§ 9.5; § 9.5, n. 15; § 10.2; § 10.2, n. 3.**
Hasting, United States v., 461 U.S. 499, 103 S.Ct. 1974, 76 L.Ed.2d 96 (1983)—**§ 1.5, n. 3; § 15.6; § 15.6, n. 14.**
Havens, United States v., 446 U.S. 620, 100 S.Ct. 1912, 64 L.Ed.2d 559 (1980)—**§ 9.6; § 9.6, n. 5, 6.**
Hawkins v. Superior Court of City and County of San Francisco, 150 Cal.Rptr. 435, 586 P.2d 916 (Cal.1978)—**§ 14.2, n. 11; § 15.3, n. 2.**
Hayes v. Florida, 470 U.S. 811, 105 S.Ct. 1643, 84 L.Ed.2d 705 (1985)—**§ 3.8, n. 10, 58.**
Haynes v. Washington, 373 U.S. 503, 83 S.Ct. 1336, 10 L.Ed.2d 513 (1963)—**§ 6.2, n. 14; § 6.4; § 6.4, n. 7.**
Heath v. Alabama, 474 U.S. 82, 106 S.Ct. 433, 88 L.Ed.2d 387 (1985)—**§ 25.5; § 25.5, n. 5.**
Heller v. New York, 413 U.S. 483, 93 S.Ct. 2789, 37 L.Ed.2d 745 (1973)—**§ 3.4, n. 5.**
Helstoski v. Meanor, 442 U.S. 500, 99 S.Ct. 2445, 61 L.Ed.2d 30 (1979)—**§ 27.2; § 27.2, n. 9.**
Helstoski, United States v., 442 U.S. 477, 99 S.Ct. 2432, 61 L.Ed.2d 12 (1979)—**§ 27.3; § 27.3, n. 5.**
Helvering v. ______ (see opposing party)
Henderson v. Morgan, 426 U.S. 637, 96 S.Ct. 2253, 49 L.Ed.2d 108 (1976)—**§ 21.4; § 21.4, n. 6.**
Henderson v. United States, 476 U.S. 321, 106 S.Ct. 1871, 90 L.Ed.2d 299 (1986)—**§ 18.3, n. 4.**
Henry v. Mississippi, 379 U.S. 443, 85 S.Ct. 564, 13 L.Ed.2d 408 (1965)—**§ 10.2; § 10.2, n. 2; § 28.4; § 28.4, n. 8.**
Henry, United States v., 447 U.S. 264, 100 S.Ct. 2183, 65 L.Ed.2d 115 (1980)—**§ 6.4; § 6.4, n. 32, 44, 53, 54; § 6.7, n. 26.**
Henry v. United States, 361 U.S. 98, 80 S.Ct. 168, 4 L.Ed.2d 134 (1959)—**§ 3.3, n. 1, 4.**
Hensley v. Municipal Court, San Jose Milpitas Judicial Dist., Santa Clara County, California, 411 U.S. 345, 93 S.Ct. 1571, 36 L.Ed.2d 294 (1973)—**§ 28.2, n. 17.**
Hensley, United States v., 469 U.S. 221, 105 S.Ct. 675, 83 L.Ed.2d 604 (1985)—**§ 3.8; § 3.8, n. 5, 7, 21, 39, 48.**
Hernandez v. Municipal Court for Los Angeles Judicial Dist. of Los Angeles County (People), 263 Cal.Rptr. 513, 781 P.2d 547 (Cal.1989)—**§ 22.2; § 22.2, n. 33.**
Hernandez v. New York, ___ U.S. ___, 111 S.Ct. 1859, 114 L.Ed.2d 395 (1991)—**§ 22.3, n. 45, 46, 48.**
Hernandez, United States v., 486 F.2d 614 (7th Cir. 1973)—**§ 3.8; § 3.8, n. 37.**
Herring v. New York, 422 U.S. 853, 95 S.Ct. 2550, 45 L.Ed.2d 593 (1975)—**§ 11.8; § 11.8, n. 1; § 24.5; § 24.5, n. 2.**
Hester v. United States, 265 U.S. 57, 44 S.Ct. 445, 68 L.Ed. 898 (1924)—**§ 3.2; § 3.2, n. 40, 55.**
Hickman v. Taylor, 329 U.S. 495, 67 S.Ct. 385, 91 L.Ed. 451 (1947)—**§ 20.3; § 20.3, n. 8.**
Hicks v. Miranda, 422 U.S. 332, 95 S.Ct. 2281, 45 L.Ed.2d 223 (1975)—**§ 13.5; § 13.5, n. 30, 31.**
Higgins v. United States, 209 F.2d 819, 93 U.S.App.D.C. 340 (D.C.Cir.1954)—**§ 3.10; § 3.10, n. 11.**
Hildwin v. Florida, 490 U.S. 638, 109 S.Ct. 2055, 104 L.Ed.2d 728 (1989)—**§ 26.2, n. 1.**
Hill v. Lockhart, 474 U.S. 52, 106 S.Ct. 366, 88 L.Ed.2d 203 (1985)—**§ 21.3, n. 9; § 21.6; § 21.6, n. 13.**
Hill v. Texas, 316 U.S. 400, 62 S.Ct. 1159, 86 L.Ed. 1559 (1942)—**§ 22.2, n. 8.**
Hill v. United States, 368 U.S. 424, 82 S.Ct. 468, 7 L.Ed.2d 417 (1962)—**§ 21.5, n. 5; § 26.5, n. 8.**
Hinckley, United States v., 672 F.2d 115, 217 U.S.App. D.C. 262 (D.C.Cir.1982)—**§ 9.6; § 9.6, n. 23.**
Hobby v. United States, 468 U.S. 339, 104 S.Ct. 3093, 82 L.Ed.2d 260 (1984)—**§ 15.4; § 15.4, n. 7.**
Hoffa v. United States, 385 U.S. 293, 87 S.Ct. 408, 17 L.Ed.2d 374 (1966)—**§ 3.2; § 3.2, n. 68; § 3.4, n. 50; § 3.10; § 3.10, n. 18; § 6.4; § 6.4, n. 27; § 6.6; § 6.6, n. 2; § 6.7; § 6.7, n. 25; § 11.8; § 11.8, n. 21.**
Hoffman v. United States, 341 U.S. 479, 71 S.Ct. 814, 95 L.Ed. 1118 (1951)—**§ 8.10; § 8.10, n. 3.**
Hoines v. Barney's Club, Inc., 170 Cal.Rptr. 42, 620 P.2d 628 (Cal.1980)—**§ 13.5; § 13.5, n. 6.**
Holbrook v. Flynn, 475 U.S. 560, 106 S.Ct. 1340, 89 L.Ed.2d 525 (1986)—**§ 24.2; § 24.2, n. 13.**
Holland v. Illinois, 493 U.S. 474, 110 S.Ct. 803, 107 L.Ed.2d 905 (1990)—**§ 22.2, n. 24, 25, 30; § 22.3, n. 41, 44.**
Holloway v. Arkansas, 435 U.S. 475, 98 S.Ct. 1173, 55 L.Ed.2d 426 (1978)—**§ 11.9; § 11.9, n. 3, 4; § 21.3, n. 12, 13, 14; § 27.6.**
Hollywood Motor Car Co., Inc., United States v., 458 U.S. 263, 102 S.Ct. 3081, 73 L.Ed.2d 754 (1982)—**§ 27.2; § 27.2, n. 11.**
Holt v. United States, 218 U.S. 245, 31 S.Ct. 2, 54 L.Ed. 1021 (1910)—**§ 7.2; § 7.2, n. 3.**
Hopt v. People, 110 U.S. 574, 4 S.Ct. 202, 28 L.Ed. 262 (1884)—**§ 6.2, n. 1.**
Horowitz, In re, 482 F.2d 72 (2nd Cir.1973)—**§ 8.7, n. 5.**
Horton v. California, ___ U.S. ___, 110 S.Ct. 2301, 110 L.Ed.2d 112 (1990)—**§ 3.1, n. 34; § 3.2, n. 22, 23; § 3.4; § 3.4, n. 46, 51; § 3.6; § 3.6, n. 37, 41, 42; § 3.7; § 3.7, n. 22, 49.**
Hudson v. Louisiana, 450 U.S. 40, 101 S.Ct. 970, 67 L.Ed.2d 30 (1981)—**§ 25.4; § 25.4, n. 8.**
Hudson v. Palmer, 468 U.S. 517, 104 S.Ct. 3194, 82 L.Ed.2d 393 (1984)—**§ 3.9; § 3.9, n. 38.**
Huffman v. Pursue, Ltd., 420 U.S. 592, 95 S.Ct. 1200, 43 L.Ed.2d 482 (1975)—**§ 13.5, n. 25.**
Hughes, Commonwealth v., 380 Mass. 583, 404 N.E.2d 1239 (Mass.1980)—**§ 8.13, n. 14.**
Hull, Ex parte, 312 U.S. 546, 61 S.Ct. 640, 85 L.Ed. 1034 (1941)—**§ 11.2; § 11.2, n. 46.**
Hunt v. Roth, 648 F.2d 1148 (8th Cir.1981)—**§ 12.3; § 12.3, n. 32.**
Hunt, State v., 91 N.J. 338, 450 A.2d 952 (N.J.1982)—**§ 2.10; § 2.10, n. 14.**
Hunter v. District Court In and For Twentieth Judicial Dist., 190 Colo. 48, 543 P.2d 1265 (Colo.1975)—**§ 14.3; § 14.3, n. 8.**
Hurtado v. California, 110 U.S. 516, 4 S.Ct. 111, 28 L.Ed. 232 (1884)—**§ 2.4; § 2.4, n. 2; § 8.2; § 8.2, n. 1; § 14.2; § 14.2, n. 1; § 15.1; § 15.1, n. 4; § 15.4.**
Hutto v. Ross, 429 U.S. 28, 97 S.Ct. 202, 50 L.Ed.2d 194 (1976)—**§ 21.2; § 21.2, n. 47.**
Hyde v. United States, 225 U.S. 347, 32 S.Ct. 793, 56 L.Ed. 1114 (1912)—**§ 16.2; § 16.2, n. 13.**

I

Illinois v. Allen, 397 U.S. 337, 90 S.Ct. 1057, 25 L.Ed.2d 353, 51 O.O.2d 163 (1970)—**§ 24.2; § 24.2, n. 1, 7.**
Illinois v. Andreas, 463 U.S. 765, 103 S.Ct. 3319, 77 L.Ed.2d 1003 (1983)—**§ 3.2, n. 23, 27; § 3.5; § 3.5, n. 47.**
Illinois v. Gates, 462 U.S. 213, 103 S.Ct. 2317, 76 L.Ed.2d 527 (1983)—**§ 3.1; § 3.1, n. 31; § 3.3; § 3.3, n. 14, 43, 58; § 3.8; § 3.8, n. 36.**
Illinois v. Krull, 480 U.S. 340, 107 S.Ct. 1160, 94 L.Ed.2d 364 (1987)—**§ 3.1; § 3.1, n. 25; § 3.3, n. 40.**

J

K

Kahan, United States v., 415 U.S. 239, 94 S.Ct. 1179, 39 L.Ed.2d 297 (1974)—**§ 9.2, n. 5.**

Kahn, United States v., 415 U.S. 143, 94 S.Ct. 977, 39 L.Ed.2d 225 (1974)—**§ 4.4; § 4.4, n. 10, 14.**

Karo, United States v., 468 U.S. 705, 104 S.Ct. 3296, 82 L.Ed.2d 530 (1984)—**§ 3.2; § 3.2, n. 71.**

Kastigar v. United States, 406 U.S. 441, 92 S.Ct. 1653, 32 L.Ed.2d 212 (1972)—**§ 8.6, n. 1; § 8.11; § 8.11, n. 7; § 8.14.**

Katz v. United States, 389 U.S. 347, 88 S.Ct. 507, 19 L.Ed.2d 576 (1967)—**§ 2.7, n. 8; § 2.9, n. 8; § 3.2; § 3.2, n. 12; § 4.1; § 4.1, n. 22; § 4.2; § 4.2, n. 7, 11, 18, 23; § 4.3; § 4.3, n. 5; § 8.15.**

Katzenbach v. Morgan, 384 U.S. 641, 86 S.Ct. 1717, 16 L.Ed.2d 828 (1966)—**§ 6.5; § 6.5, n. 14.**

Kaufman v. United States, 394 U.S. 217, 89 S.Ct. 1068, 22 L.Ed.2d 227 (1969)—**§ 28.2, n. 45; § 28.3; § 28.3, n. 16.**

Keith, United States v., 605 F.2d 462 (9th Cir.1979)—**§ 19.3, n. 1.**

Kelley v. State, 184 Tenn. 143, 197 S.W.2d 545 (Tenn. 1946)—**§ 3.10; § 3.10, n. 27.**

Kemmler, In re, 136 U.S. 436, 10 S.Ct. 930, 34 L.Ed. 519 (1890)—**§ 2.3, n. 7.**

Kentucky v. Dennison, 65 U.S. 66, 16 L.Ed. 717 (1860)—**§ 3.1, n. 73.**

Kentucky v. Stincer, 482 U.S. 730, 107 S.Ct. 2658, 96 L.Ed.2d 631 (1987)—**§ 24.2; § 24.2, n. 3.**

Kepner v. United States, 195 U.S. 100, 24 S.Ct. 797, 49 L.Ed. 114 (1904)—**§ 25.1; § 25.1, n. 23.**

Ker v. California, 374 U.S. 23, 83 S.Ct. 1623, 10 L.Ed.2d 726, 24 O.O.2d 201 (1963)—**§ 2.6; § 2.6, n. 1; § 3.1; § 3.1, n. 40; § 3.3, n. 63; § 3.4, n. 29; § 3.6; § 3.6, n. 10; § 4.2; § 4.2, n. 9.**

Ker v. Illinois, 119 U.S. 436, 7 S.Ct. 225, 30 L.Ed. 421 (1886)—**§ 3.1; § 3.1, n. 66, 67, 68.**

Kercheval v. United States, 274 U.S. 220, 47 S.Ct. 582, 71 L.Ed. 1009 (1927)—**§ 21.5, n. 20.**

Kimmelman v. Morrison, 477 U.S. 365, 106 S.Ct. 2574, 91 L.Ed.2d 305 (1986)—**§ 11.10; § 11.10, n. 6, 13; § 28.3; § 28.3, n. 24, 32.**

Kinney v. Lenon, 425 F.2d 209 (9th Cir.1970)—**§ 12.2; § 12.2, n. 17.**

Kirby v. Illinois, 406 U.S. 682, 92 S.Ct. 1877, 32 L.Ed.2d 411 (1972)—**§ 3.10, n. 15; § 6.4; § 6.4, n. 17, 23, 26, 28, 34; § 7.3; § 7.3, n. 6, 7; § 8.15; § 11.1; § 12.1, n. 15; § 21.3, n. 2.**

Klopfer v. North Carolina, 386 U.S. 213, 87 S.Ct. 988, 18 L.Ed.2d 1, 41 O.O.2d 168 (1967)—**§ 2.6, n. 6; § 18.1, n. 1, 2, 4; § 18.2; § 18.2, n. 4.**

Knoll Associates, Inc. v. F. T. C., 397 F.2d 530 (7th Cir.1968)—**§ 3.1; § 3.1, n. 59.**

Knotts, United States v., 460 U.S. 276, 103 S.Ct. 1081, 75 L.Ed.2d 55 (1983)—**§ 3.2; § 3.2, n. 72.**

Knowles, United States v., 147 F.Supp. 19 (D.C.D.C.1957)—**§ 15.4; § 15.4, n. 15.**

Kolender v. Lawson, 461 U.S. 352, 103 S.Ct. 1855, 75 L.Ed.2d 903 (1983)—**§ 3.3, n. 68.**

Kotteakos v. United States, 328 U.S. 750, 66 S.Ct. 1239, 90 L.Ed. 1557 (1946)—**§ 15.6; § 19.6; § 19.6, n. 7; § 27.6; § 27.6, n. 5, 6.**

Krulewitch v. United States, 336 U.S. 440, 69 S.Ct. 716, 93 L.Ed. 790 (1949)—**§ 17.2; § 17.2, n. 22.**

Kuhlmann v. Wilson, 477 U.S. 436, 106 S.Ct. 2616, 91 L.Ed.2d 364 (1986)—**§ 6.4; § 6.4, n. 55; § 28.5; § 28.5, n. 5, 6, 11.**

L

Lakeside v. Oregon, 435 U.S. 333, 98 S.Ct. 1091, 55 L.Ed.2d 319 (1978)—**§ 24.4; § 24.4, n. 11, 12.**

Lamb, United States v., 575 F.2d 1310 (10th Cir.1978)—**§ 7.2; § 7.2, n. 17.**

Lance W., In re, 210 Cal.Rptr. 631, 694 P.2d 744 (Cal. 1985)—**§ 9.2, n. 16.**

Landmark Communications, Inc. v. Virginia, 435 U.S. 829, 98 S.Ct. 1535, 56 L.Ed.2d 1 (1978)—**§ 23.1, n. 11.**

Lane, United States v., 474 U.S. 438, 106 S.Ct. 725, 88 L.Ed.2d 814 (1986)—**§ 17.3; § 17.3, n. 2; § 27.6, n. 4.**

Lane v. Williams, 455 U.S. 624, 102 S.Ct. 1322, 71 L.Ed.2d 508 (1982)—**§ 27.5, n. 2.**

Lange, Ex parte, 85 U.S. 163, 21 L.Ed. 872 (1873)—**§ 25.1; § 25.1, n. 4; § 26.7; § 26.7, n. 9; § 28.3; § 28.3, n. 2.**

Lanza, United States v., 260 U.S. 377, 43 S.Ct. 141, 67 L.Ed. 314 (1922)—**§ 25.5; § 25.5, n. 1.**

Lassiter v. Department of Social Services of Durham County, North Carolina, 452 U.S. 18, 101 S.Ct. 2153, 68 L.Ed.2d 640 (1981)—**§ 11.1, n. 12.**

Latimore, United States ex rel. v. Sielaff, 561 F.2d 691 (7th Cir.1977)—**§ 24.2, n. 12.**

Latshaw, Commonwealth v., 481 Pa. 298, 392 A.2d 1301 (Pa.1978)—**§ 3.10; § 3.10, n. 33.**

LaValle v. Delle Rose, 410 U.S. 690, 93 S.Ct. 1203, 35 L.Ed.2d 637 (1973)—**§ 28.7; § 28.7, n. 8.**

Lawn v. United States, 355 U.S. 339, 78 S.Ct. 311, 2 L.Ed.2d 321 (1958)—**§ 3.1, n. 46; § 15.5; § 15.5, n. 4, 5.**

Lee v. Florida, 392 U.S. 378, 88 S.Ct. 2096, 20 L.Ed.2d 1166 (1968)—**§ 4.1; § 4.1, n. 14.**

Lee v. Illinois, 476 U.S. 530, 106 S.Ct. 2056, 90 L.Ed.2d 514 (1986)—**§ 17.2; § 17.2, n. 10, 14.**

Lee v. United States, 432 U.S. 23, 97 S.Ct. 2141, 53 L.Ed.2d 80 (1977)—**§ 25.2; § 25.2, n. 19.**

Lee, United States v., 274 U.S. 559, 47 S.Ct. 746, 71 L.Ed. 1202 (1927)—**§ 3.2; § 3.2, n. 30, 31.**

Lefkowitz v. Newsome, 420 U.S. 283, 95 S.Ct. 886, 43 L.Ed.2d 196 (1975)—**§ 21.6; § 21.6, n. 15.**

Lefkowitz, United States v., 285 U.S. 452, 52 S.Ct. 420, 76 L.Ed. 877 (1932)—**§ 3.2, n. 7, 62.**

Lego v. Twomey, 404 U.S. 477, 92 S.Ct. 619, 30 L.Ed.2d 618 (1972)—**§ 3.4, n. 18; § 10.3; § 10.3, n. 12, 14; § 10.4; § 10.4, n. 2; § 10.5; § 10.5, n. 2; § 26.6, n. 9.**

Leis v. Flynt, 439 U.S. 438, 99 S.Ct. 698, 58 L.Ed.2d 717, 11 O.O.3d 302 (1979)—**§ 11.4, n. 6.**

Lemon, United States v., 723 F.2d 922, 232 U.S.App.D.C. 396 (D.C.Cir.1983)—**§ 26.4, n. 4.**

Lem Woon v. Oregon, 229 U.S. 586, 33 S.Ct. 783, 57 L.Ed. 1340 (1913)—**§ 14.2; § 14.2, n. 2; § 14.4.**

Leon, United States v., 468 U.S. 897, 104 S.Ct. 3405, 82 L.Ed.2d 677 (1984)—**§ 3.1; § 3.1, n. 24, 30; § 3.3; § 3.3, n. 17.**

Levy, United States ex rel. Rutz v., 268 U.S. 390, 45 S.Ct. 516, 69 L.Ed. 1010 (1925)—**§ 14.3, n. 9.**

Lewallen, In re, 152 Cal.Rptr. 528, 590 P.2d 383 (Cal. 1979)—**§ 21.2, n. 22.**

Lewis v. United States, 385 U.S. 206, 87 S.Ct. 424, 17 L.Ed.2d 312 (1966)—**§ 3.10; § 3.10, n. 19.**

Leyra v. Denno, 347 U.S. 556, 74 S.Ct. 716, 98 L.Ed. 948 (1954)—**§ 6.2; § 6.2, n. 21; § 9.5, n. 11.**

Lindsey v. King, 769 F.2d 1034 (5th Cir.1985)—**§ 20.7, n. 11.**

Linkletter v. Walker, 381 U.S. 618, 85 S.Ct. 1731, 14 L.Ed.2d 601, 33 O.O.2d 118 (1965)—**§ 2.9; § 2.9, n. 1, 5, 15, 22, 28; § 3.1; § 3.1, n. 14; § 28.6.**

Lockett v. Ohio, 438 U.S. 586, 98 S.Ct. 2954, 57 L.Ed.2d 973, 9 O.O.3d 26 (1978)—**§ 24.4; § 24.4, n. 8.**
Lockhart v. McCree, 476 U.S. 162, 106 S.Ct. 1758, 90 L.Ed.2d 137 (1986)—**§ 22.2, n. 24, 29; § 22.3; § 22.3, n. 32, 41.**
Lockhart v. Nelson, 488 U.S. 33, 109 S.Ct. 285, 102 L.Ed.2d 265 (1988)—**§ 25.4; § 25.4, n. 11, 12; § 26.7; § 26.7, n. 6.**
Lo–Ji Sales, Inc. v. New York, 442 U.S. 319, 99 S.Ct. 2319, 60 L.Ed.2d 920 (1979)—**§ 3.1, n. 28; § 3.4; § 3.4, n. 15.**
Lombardo, United States v., 241 U.S. 73, 36 S.Ct. 508, 60 L.Ed. 897 (1916)—**§ 16.2; § 16.2, n. 2.**
Lopez v. United States, 373 U.S. 427, 83 S.Ct. 1381, 10 L.Ed.2d 462 (1963)—**§ 3.2; § 3.2, n. 69; § 3.10, n. 20; § 4.2; § 4.2, n. 22; § 4.3; § 4.3, n. 16.**
Los Angeles, City of v. Heller, 475 U.S. 796, 106 S.Ct. 1571, 89 L.Ed.2d 806 (1986)—**§ 3.1, n. 81.**
Losavio, People ex rel. v. J. L., 195 Colo. 494, 580 P.2d 23 (Colo.1978)—**§ 8.15, n. 7.**
Loud Hawk, United States v., 474 U.S. 302, 106 S.Ct. 648, 88 L.Ed.2d 640 (1986)—**§ 18.2; § 18.2, n. 7, 10, 11; § 18.5, n. 12; § 27.3, n. 8.**
Lovasco, United States v., 431 U.S. 783, 97 S.Ct. 2044, 52 L.Ed.2d 752 (1977)—**§ 18.1, n. 2, 9; § 18.5; § 18.5, n. 5.**
Lovato v. New Mexico, 242 U.S. 199, 37 S.Ct. 107, 61 L.Ed. 244 (1916)—**§ 25.2; § 25.2, n. 12.**
Lowenfield v. Phelps, 484 U.S. 231, 108 S.Ct. 546, 98 L.Ed.2d 568 (1988)—**§ 24.6; § 24.6, n. 5.**
Luckett v. State, 259 Ind. 174, 284 N.E.2d 738 (Ind. 1972)—**§ 3.8; § 3.8, n. 29.**
Ludwig v. Massachusetts, 427 U.S. 618, 96 S.Ct. 2781, 49 L.Ed.2d 732 (1976)—**§ 22.1; § 22.1, n. 31.**
Lustig v. United States, 338 U.S. 74, 69 S.Ct. 1372, 93 L.Ed. 1819 (1949)—**§ 3.1, n. 62.**
Lynumn v. Illinois, 372 U.S. 528, 83 S.Ct. 917, 9 L.Ed.2d 922 (1963)—**§ 6.2; § 6.2, n. 18.**
Lyons v. Oklahoma, 322 U.S. 596, 64 S.Ct. 1208, 88 L.Ed. 1481 (1944)—**§ 9.5; § 9.5, n. 10.**

M

Mabry v. Johnson, 467 U.S. 504, 104 S.Ct. 2543, 81 L.Ed.2d 437 (1984)—**§ 21.2; § 21.2, n. 42.**
MacCollom, United States v., 426 U.S. 317, 96 S.Ct. 2086, 48 L.Ed.2d 666 (1976)—**§ 11.2; § 11.2, n. 38.**
MacDonald v. Musick, 425 F.2d 373 (9th Cir.1970)—**§ 13.5; § 13.5, n. 5.**
MacDonald, United States v., 456 U.S. 1, 102 S.Ct. 1497, 71 L.Ed.2d 696 (1982)—**§ 18.2; § 18.2, n. 5.**
MacDonald, United States v., 435 U.S. 850, 98 S.Ct. 1547, 56 L.Ed.2d 18 (1978)—**§ 27.2; § 27.2, n. 10.**
Mackey v. United States, 401 U.S. 667, 91 S.Ct. 1160, 28 L.Ed.2d 404 (1971)—**§ 2.9, n. 15; § 28.1, n. 2; § 28.6, n. 22.**
Maggio v. Fulford, 462 U.S. 111, 103 S.Ct. 2261, 76 L.Ed.2d 794 (1983)—**§ 28.7; § 28.7, n. 9.**
Maine v. Moulton, 474 U.S. 159, 106 S.Ct. 477, 88 L.Ed.2d 481 (1985)—**§ 6.4; § 6.4, n. 36, 52.**
Maine v. Superior Court of Mendocino County, 68 Cal.2d 375, 66 Cal.Rptr. 724, 438 P.2d 372 (Cal.1968)—**§ 27.4, n. 4.**
Malinski v. New York, 324 U.S. 401, 65 S.Ct. 781, 89 L.Ed. 1029 (1945)—**§ 6.4, n. 1.**
Malley v. Briggs, 475 U.S. 335, 106 S.Ct. 1092, 89 L.Ed.2d 271 (1986)—**§ 3.1, n. 32, 76.**
Mallory v. United States, 354 U.S. 449, 77 S.Ct. 1356, 1 L.Ed.2d 1479 (1957)—**§ 1.5, n. 3; § 3.3, n. 38; § 6.3; § 6.3, n. 3.**
Malloy v. Hogan, 378 U.S. 1, 84 S.Ct. 1489, 12 L.Ed.2d 653 (1964)—**§ 2.5, n. 7; § 2.6; § 2.6, n. 5; § 6.2, n. 6; § 6.5; § 6.5, n. 3; § 8.10; § 8.10, n. 4.**
Mancusi v. DeForte, 392 U.S. 364, 88 S.Ct. 2120, 20 L.Ed.2d 1154 (1968)—**§ 3.2, n. 45; § 9.1; § 9.1, n. 4, 29, 31, 36.**
Mancusi, United States ex rel. Thurmond v., 275 F.Supp. 508 (D.C.N.Y.1967)—**§ 21.2; § 21.2, n. 44.**
Mandujano, United States v., 425 U.S. 564, 96 S.Ct. 1768, 48 L.Ed.2d 212 (1976)—**§ 6.6; § 6.6, n. 4; § 8.10; § 8.10, n. 11; § 8.15; § 8.15, n. 2; § 11.1.**
Maness v. Meyers, 419 U.S. 449, 95 S.Ct. 584, 42 L.Ed.2d 574 (1975)—**§ 8.15, n. 4; § 11.1, n. 22.**
Manson v. Brathwaite, 432 U.S. 98, 97 S.Ct. 2243, 53 L.Ed.2d 140 (1977)—**§ 7.4; § 7.4, n. 11; § 10.3, n. 22, 23; § 23.2, n. 3.**
Mapp v. Ohio, 367 U.S. 643, 81 S.Ct. 1684, 6 L.Ed.2d 1081, 16 O.O.2d 384 (1961)—**§ 2.4, n. 19; § 2.6; § 2.6, n. 1; § 2.9; § 3; § 3.1; § 3.1, n. 13, 39; § 4.1; § 4.1, n. 13; § 9.2; § 9.2, n. 13; § 25.5, n. 3; § 27.6.**
Mara, United States v., 410 U.S. 19, 93 S.Ct. 774, 35 L.Ed.2d 99 (1973)—**§ 3.2; § 3.2, n. 52; § 7.2, n. 9; § 8.6, n. 2; § 8.7; § 8.7, n. 9; § 8.8.**
Marchetti v. United States, 390 U.S. 39, 88 S.Ct. 697, 19 L.Ed.2d 889, 43 O.O.2d 215 (1968)—**§ 8.12; § 8.12, n. 16.**
Marion, United States v., 404 U.S. 307, 92 S.Ct. 455, 30 L.Ed.2d 468 (1971)—**§ 18.1; § 18.1, n. 8; § 18.2; § 18.2, n. 6; § 18.5; § 18.5, n. 1, 4.**
Marron v. United States, 275 U.S. 192, 48 S.Ct. 74, 72 L.Ed. 231 (1927)—**§ 2.7, n. 6; § 3.4; § 3.4, n. 22, 42.**
Marsh v. Alabama, 326 U.S. 501, 66 S.Ct. 276, 90 L.Ed. 265 (1946)—**§ 3.1; § 3.1, n. 57.**
Marshall v. Barlow's, Inc., 436 U.S. 307, 98 S.Ct. 1816, 56 L.Ed.2d 305 (1978)—**§ 2.8, n. 23; § 3.9; § 3.9, n. 9.**
Marshall v. Lonberger, 459 U.S. 422, 103 S.Ct. 843, 74 L.Ed.2d 646 (1983)—**§ 28.7; § 28.7, n. 10.**
Marshall v. United States, 414 U.S. 417, 94 S.Ct. 700, 38 L.Ed.2d 618 (1974)—**§ 13.6; § 13.6, n. 1.**
Marshall v. United States, 360 U.S. 310, 79 S.Ct. 1171, 3 L.Ed.2d 1250 (1959)—**§ 22.3, n. 20; § 23.2; § 23.2, n. 10; § 24.6, n. 7.**
Martin, People v., 45 Cal.2d 755, 290 P.2d 855 (Cal. 1955)—**§ 9.2; § 9.2, n. 14.**
Martinez, United States v., 486 F.2d 15 (5th Cir.1973)—**§ 21.4; § 21.4, n. 2.**
Martinez–Fuerte, United States v., 428 U.S. 543, 96 S.Ct. 3074, 49 L.Ed.2d 1116 (1976)—**§ 3.8; § 3.8, n. 42, 45; § 3.9; § 3.9, n. 29, 33.**
Martin Linen Supply Co., United States v., 430 U.S. 564, 97 S.Ct. 1349, 51 L.Ed.2d 642 (1977)—**§ 25.1, n. 26.**
Maryland v. Buie, 494 U.S. 325, 110 S.Ct. 1093, 108 L.Ed.2d 276 (1990)—**§ 3.6; § 3.6, n. 16, 17.**
Maryland v. Craig, ___ U.S. ___, 110 S.Ct. 3157, 111 L.Ed.2d 666 (1990)—**§ 24.2; § 24.2, n. 15.**
Maryland v. Garrison, 480 U.S. 79, 107 S.Ct. 1013, 94 L.Ed.2d 72 (1987)—**§ 3.4; § 3.4, n. 20, 21.**
Maryland v. Macon, 472 U.S. 463, 105 S.Ct. 2778, 86 L.Ed.2d 370 (1985)—**§ 3.2, n. 46.**
Maryland, State of v. Soper, 270 U.S. 9, 46 S.Ct. 185, 70 L.Ed. 449 (1926)—**§ 13.5, n. 15, 17.**
Mascarenas v. State, 80 N.M. 537, 458 P.2d 789 (N.M.1969)—**§ 14.4; § 14.4, n. 20.**
Masciale v. United States, 356 U.S. 386, 78 S.Ct. 827, 2 L.Ed.2d 859 (1958)—**§ 5.2; § 5.2, n. 8.**

N

O

P

Q

R

S

T

U

V

W

Y

Z

*

Index

References are to Sections

References are to Sections

References are to Sections

References are to Sections

References are to Sections

References are to Sections

†